Official 1994
National Football League

Record
& Fact Book

A National Football League Book.
Workman Publishing Co., New York.

NATIONAL FOOTBALL LEAGUE, 1994

410 Park Avenue, New York, N.Y. 10022 (212) 758-1500

Commissioner: Paul Tagliabue
President: Neil Austrian

LEAGUE OFFICE
Executive Vice President and League Counsel: Jay Moyer
Vice President-Communications & Government Affairs:
Joe Browne
Vice President-Business Development: Roger Goodell
Vice President-Broadcasting & Productions:
Val Pinchbeck, Jr.
Chief Financial Officer: Tom Spock
Executive Director of Special Events: Jim Steeg
Vice President-Internal Audit: Tom Sullivan

COMMUNICATIONS
Director of Communications: Greg Aiello
Director of International Public Relations: Pete Abitante
Director of Information, AFC: Leslie Hammond
Director of Information, NFC: Reggie Roberts

BROADCASTING
Director of Broadcasting Services: Dick Maxwell
Director of Broadcasting Research: Joe Ferreira
Assistant Director of Broadcasting/Productions: Nancy Behar

OPERATIONS
Director of Club Relations/Stadium Operations: Joe Ellis
Director of Game Operations/League Secretary: Jan Van Duser
Director of Football Development: Gene Washington
Assistant Director of Game Operations: Tim Davey

OFFICIATING
Director of Officiating: Jerry Seeman
Assistant Director of Officiating: Jack Reader
Supervisor of Officials: Leo Miles
Supervisor of Officials: Ron DeSouza

ADMINISTRATION
Director of Administration: John Buzzeo
Comptroller: Joe Siclare

SECURITY
Director of Security: Warren Welsh
Assistant Director of Security: Charles Jackson, Jr.

NFL ENTERPRISES
President: Ron Bernard
Vice President-Marketing & Sales: Tola Murphy-Baran
Vice President-Worldwide Distribution: Bill Moses

NFL FILMS
President: Steve Sabol
Vice President-Television Sponsorships: John Collins
Vice President-In Charge of Production: Jay Gerber
Vice President-Video Operations: Jeff Howard
Vice President-Editor-in-Chief: Bob Ryan
Vice President-Special Projects: Phil Tuckett
Vice President-Finance and Administration: Barry Wolper

NFL MANAGEMENT COUNCIL
Executive Vice President-Labor Relations/Chairman NFLMC:
Harold Henderson
Vice President-General Counsel: Dennis Curran
Vice President-Operations & Compliance: Peter Ruocco
Director of Player Programs: Lem Burnham
Director of Player Personnel/Football Operations: Joel Bussert
Director of Compliance: William Duffy
Director of Labor Operations: Peter Hadhazy

NFL PROPERTIES
Vice President-Worldwide Retail Licensing: Jim Connelly
Vice President-Business Development/Special Events:
Don Garber
Vice President-Marketing/Sales: Jim Schwebel
Vice President-Creative Services: John Wiebusch

Vice President-Sales: Roger Atkin
Vice President-Creative Director: Bruce Burke
Vice President-Legal/Business Affairs and General Counsel:
Gary Gertzog
Vice President and Chief Financial Officer: Ken Hall
Vice President-Player Relations and Retail/Club Marketing:
Mark Holtzman

Cover Photograph by James D. Smith.

Copyright © 1994 by the National Football League. All rights reserved. The information in this publication has been compiled for use by the news media to aid in reporting of the games and teams of the National Football League. No part of this book may be reproduced or transmitted in any form or by any means, electronic or mechanical, including photocopying, recording, or by any information storage and retrieval system, without permission in writing from the National Football League.

Printed in the United States of America.

A National Football League Book.
Compiled by the NFL Communications Department and Seymour Siwoff, Elias Sports Bureau.

Edited by Chris Hardart, NFL Communications Department and Chuck Garrity, Jr., NFLP Creative Services.
Statistics by Elias Sports Bureau.
Produced by NFL Properties, Inc., Creative Services Division.

Workman Publishing Co.
708 Broadway, New York, N.Y. 10003
Manufactured in the United States of America.
First printing, July 1994.
10 9 8 7 6 5 4 3 2 1

1994 SCHEDULE AND NOTE CALENDAR

(All times local except Barcelona, Berlin, Mexico City, and Tokyo which are EDT.)
Nationally televised games in parentheses.

PRESEASON/FIRST WEEK

Saturday, July 30 — Pro Football Hall of Fame Game at Canton, Ohio

Atlanta _____ vs. San Diego _____	(ABC)	12:00
Miami _____ at New York Giants _____		8:00

Sunday, July 31 — American Bowl at Barcelona

Denver _____ vs. Los Angeles Raiders _____	(NBC)	1:00 *
Houston _____ at Kansas City _____		8:00
Minnesota _____ at Dallas _____		8:00

Friday, August 5

New Orleans _____ at New England _____	8:00
New York Jets _____ at Detroit _____	7:30
Philadelphia _____ at Chicago _____	7:00
San Francisco _____ at Arizona _____	6:30
Seattle _____ at Indianapolis _____	7:30

Saturday, August 6 — American Bowl at Tokyo (August 7)

Kansas City _____ vs. Minnesota _____	(ESPN)	10:00 **
Atlanta _____ at Denver _____		7:00
Cincinnati _____ at Tampa Bay _____		7:30
Cleveland _____ at New York Giants _____		8:00
Houston _____ vs. San Diego _____ at San Antonio, Tex.		7:00
Los Angeles Rams _____ vs. Green Bay _____ at Madison, Wis.		12:00
Pittsburgh _____ at Miami _____		8:00

Sunday, August 7 — Los Angeles Raiders_____ at Dallas _____ — 8:00

Monday, August 8 — Washington _____ at Buffalo _____ — (ABC) 8:00

* Barcelona game actual kickoff 7:00 P.M., July 31.
** Tokyo game actual kickoff 11:00 A.M., August 7.

PRESEASON/SECOND WEEK

Friday, August 12

Denver _____ at San Francisco _____	(FOX)	5:00
Buffalo _____ at Atlanta _____		7:00
Kansas City _____ at Washington _____		8:00

Saturday, August 13 — American Bowl at Berlin

New York Giants _____ vs. San Diego _____	(NBC)	1:30 †
Chicago _____ at Arizona _____		6:00
Detroit _____ at Cleveland _____		7:30
Indianapolis _____ at Cincinnati _____		7:30
Los Angeles Raiders _____ at Pittsburgh _____		6:00
Miami _____vs. Green Bay _____ at Milwaukee		7:00
New England _____ at Los Angeles Rams _____		7:00
New Orleans _____ at Minnesota _____		7:00
New York Jets _____ at Philadelphia _____		7:30
Tampa Bay _____ at Seattle _____		6:00

Monday, August 15 — American Bowl at Mexico City

Dallas _____ vs. Houston _____	(ABC)	9:00 ††

† Berlin game actual kickoff 7:30 P.M., August 13.
†† Mexico City game actual kickoff 7:00 P.M., August 15.

PRESEASON/THIRD WEEK

Thursday, August 18

San Francisco _____ at San Diego _____	(TNT)	5:00
Washington _____ at New England _____		7:00

Friday, August 19

Arizona _____ at Detroit _____		7:30
Atlanta _____ at Cleveland _____		7:30
Green Bay _____ at New Orleans _____	(FOX)	7:00

Saturday, August 20

Buffalo _____ vs. Houston _____ at San Antonio, Tex.	(ESPN)	7:00
Cincinnati _____ at Philadelphia _____		7:30
Indianapolis _____ at Pittsburgh _____		6:00
Los Angeles Raiders _____ at Los Angeles Rams _____		7:00
Minnesota _____ at Seattle _____		7:00
New York Giants _____ at New York Jets _____		8:00
Tampa Bay _____ at Miami _____		8:00

Sunday, August 21 — Denver _____ at Dallas _____ — (TNT) 7:00

Monday, August 22 — Chicago _____ at Kansas City _____ — (ABC) 7:00

PRESEASON/FOURTH WEEK	**Thursday, August 25**	Arizona _____ at Denver _____	7:00
		Cleveland _____ at Indianapolis _____	7:30
		Dallas _____ at New Orleans _____	(ESPN) 7:00
		Los Angeles Rams _____ at San Diego _____	7:00
	Friday, August 26	Detroit _____ at Cincinnati _____	7:30
		Kansas City _____ at Buffalo _____	(TNT) 8:00
		Miami _____ at Minnesota _____	7:00
		New England _____ at Green Bay _____	7:00
		New York Jets _____ at Tampa Bay _____	7:30
		Philadelphia _____ at Atlanta _____	7:00
		Pittsburgh _____ at Washington _____	8:00
		Seattle _____ at San Francisco _____	6:00
	Saturday, August 27	Los Angeles Raiders _____ at Houston _____	(NBC) 1:00
		New York Giants _____ at Chicago _____	(FOX) 7:00
FIRST WEEK	**Sunday, September 4**	Arizona _____ at Los Angeles Rams _____	1:00
	(FOX-TV National Weekend)	Atlanta _____ at Detroit _____	1:00
		Cleveland _____ at Cincinnati _____	1:00
		Dallas _____ at Pittsburgh _____	4:00
		Houston _____ at Indianapolis _____	12:00
		Kansas City _____ at New Orleans _____	12:00
		Minnesota _____ at Green Bay _____	12:00
		New England _____ at Miami _____	4:00
		New York Jets _____ at Buffalo _____	4:00
		Philadelphia _____ at New York Giants _____	1:00
		Seattle _____ at Washington _____	1:00
		Tampa Bay _____ at Chicago _____	12:00
	Sunday Night	San Diego _____ at Denver _____	(TNT) 6:00
	Monday, September 5	Los Angeles Raiders _____ at San Francisco _____	(ABC) 6:00
SECOND WEEK	**Sunday, September 11**	Buffalo _____ at New England _____	1:00
	(NBC-TV National Weekend)	Cincinnati _____ at San Diego _____	1:00
		Denver _____ at New York Jets _____	4:00
		Detroit _____ at Minnesota _____	12:00
		Houston _____ at Dallas _____	3:00
		Indianapolis _____ at Tampa Bay _____	1:00
		Los Angeles Rams _____ at Atlanta _____	1:00
		Miami _____ vs. Green Bay _____ at Milwaukee	12:00
		Pittsburgh _____ at Cleveland _____	1:00
		San Francisco _____ at Kansas City _____	12:00
		Seattle _____ at Los Angeles Raiders _____	1:00
		Washington _____ at New Orleans _____	3:00
	Sunday Night	New York Giants _____ at Arizona _____	(TNT) 5:00
	Monday, September 12	Chicago _____ at Philadelphia _____	(ABC) 9:00
THIRD WEEK	**Sunday, September 18**	Arizona _____ at Cleveland _____	1:00
	(FOX-TV National Weekend)	Buffalo _____ at Houston _____	12:00
		Green Bay _____ at Philadelphia _____	1:00
		Indianapolis _____ at Pittsburgh _____	1:00
		Los Angeles Raiders _____ at Denver _____	2:00
		Minnesota _____ at Chicago _____	12:00
		New England _____ at Cincinnati _____	1:00
		New Orleans _____ at Tampa Bay _____	1:00
		New York Jets _____ at Miami _____	1:00
		San Diego _____ at Seattle _____	1:00
		San Francisco _____ at Los Angeles Rams _____	1:00
		Washington _____ at New York Giants _____	4:00
	Sunday Night	Kansas City _____ at Atlanta _____	(TNT) 8:00
	Monday, September 19	Detroit _____ at Dallas _____	(ABC) 8:00

FOURTH WEEK
Open Dates: Arizona,
Dallas, New York Giants,
Philadelphia

Sunday, September 25	Atlanta ____ at Washington ____		1:00
(NBC-TV National Weekend)	Cincinnati ____ at Houston ____		3:00
	Cleveland ____ at Indianapolis ____		12:00
	Los Angeles Rams ____ at Kansas City ____		12:00
	Miami ____ at Minnesota ____		12:00
	New England ____ at Detroit ____		4:00
	New Orleans ____ at San Francisco ____		1:00
	Pittsburgh ____ at Seattle ____		1:00
	San Diego ____ at Los Angeles Raiders ____		1:00
	Tampa Bay ____ at Green Bay ____		12:00
Sunday Night	Chicago ____ at New York Jets ____		(TNT) 8:00
Monday, September 26	Denver ____ at Buffalo ____		(ABC) 9:00

FIFTH WEEK
Open Dates: Denver,
Kansas City, Los Angeles
Raiders, San Diego

Sunday, October 2	Atlanta ____ at Los Angeles Rams ____		1:00
(FOX-TV National Weekend)	Buffalo ____ at Chicago ____		3:00
	Dallas ____ at Washington ____		1:00
	Detroit ____ at Tampa Bay ____		1:00
	Green Bay ____ at New England ____		1:00
	Minnesota ____ at Arizona ____		1:00
	New York Giants ____ at New Orleans ____		3:00
	New York Jets ____ at Cleveland ____		1:00
	Philadelphia ____ at San Francisco ____		1:00
	Seattle ____ at Indianapolis ____		12:00
Sunday Night	Miami ____ at Cincinnati ____		(TNT) 8:00
Monday, October 3	Houston ____ at Pittsburgh ____		(ABC) 9:00

SIXTH WEEK
Open Dates: Cincinnati,
Cleveland, Houston,
Pittsburgh

Sunday, October 9	Arizona ____ at Dallas ____		3:00
(NBC-TV National Weekend)	Denver ____ at Seattle ____		1:00
	Indianapolis ____ at New York Jets ____		1:00
	Kansas City ____ at San Diego ____		1:00
	Los Angeles Raiders ____ at New England ____		4:00
	Los Angeles Rams ____ at Green Bay ____		12:00
	Miami ____ at Buffalo ____		1:00
	New Orleans ____ at Chicago ____		12:00
	San Francisco ____ at Detroit ____		1:00
	Tampa Bay ____ at Atlanta ____		1:00
Sunday Night	Washington ____ at Philadelphia ____		(TNT) 8:00
Monday, October 10	Minnesota ____ at New York Giants ____		(ABC) 9:00

SEVENTH WEEK
Open Dates: Chicago,
Detroit, Green Bay,
Minnesota, Seattle,
Tampa Bay

Thursday, October 13	Cleveland ____ at Houston ____		(TNT) 7:00
Sunday, October 16	Arizona ____ at Washington ____		1:00
(FOX-TV National Weekend)	Cincinnati ____ at Pittsburgh ____		1:00
	Indianapolis ____ at Buffalo ____		1:00
	Los Angeles Raiders ____ at Miami ____		1:00
	New England ____ at New York Jets ____		1:00
	New York Giants ____ at Los Angeles Rams ____		1:00
	Philadelphia ____ at Dallas ____		3:00
	San Diego ____ at New Orleans ____		3:00
	San Francisco ____ at Atlanta ____		1:00
Monday, October 17	Kansas City ____ at Denver ____		(ABC) 7:00

EIGHTH WEEK
Open Dates: Buffalo,
Miami, New England,
New York Jets

Thursday, October 20	Green Bay ____ at Minnesota ____		(TNT) 7:00
Sunday, October 23	Atlanta ____ at Los Angeles Raiders ____		1:00
(FOX-TV National Weekend)	Chicago ____ at Detroit ____		1:00
	Cincinnati ____ at Cleveland ____		1:00
	Dallas ____ at Arizona ____		1:00
	Denver ____ at San Diego ____		1:00
	Los Angeles Rams ____ at New Orleans ____		12:00
	Pittsburgh ____ at New York Giants ____		1:00
	Seattle ____ at Kansas City ____		12:00
	Tampa Bay ____ at San Francisco ____		1:00
	Washington ____ at Indianapolis ____		12:00
Monday, October 24	Houston ____ at Philadelphia ____		(ABC) 9:00

NINTH WEEK
Open Dates: Atlanta,
Los Angeles Rams,
New Orleans, San Francisco

Sunday, October 30	Cleveland _____ at Denver _____	2:00
(NBC-TV National Weekend)	Dallas _____ at Cincinnati _____	1:00
	Detroit _____ at New York Giants _____	1:00
	Houston _____ at Los Angeles Raiders _____	1:00
	Kansas City _____ at Buffalo _____	1:00
	Miami _____ at New England _____	1:00
	Minnesota _____ at Tampa Bay _____	4:00
	New York Jets _____ at Indianapolis _____	4:00
	Philadelphia _____ at Washington _____	1:00
	Seattle _____ at San Diego _____	1:00
Sunday Night	Pittsburgh _____ at Arizona _____	(TNT) 6:00
Monday, October 31	Green Bay _____ at Chicago _____	(ABC) 8:00

TENTH WEEK

Sunday, November 6	Arizona _____ at Philadelphia _____	4:00
(NBC-TV National Weekend)	Buffalo _____ at New York Jets _____	4:00
	Chicago _____ at Tampa Bay _____	1:00
	Cincinnati _____ at Seattle _____	1:00
	Denver _____ at Los Angeles Rams _____	1:00
	Detroit _____ vs. Green Bay _____ at Milwaukee	12:00
	Indianapolis _____ at Miami _____	1:00
	New England _____ at Cleveland _____	1:00
	New Orleans _____ at Minnesota _____	12:00
	Pittsburgh _____ at Houston _____	12:00
	San Diego _____ at Atlanta _____	1:00
	San Francisco _____ at Washington _____	1:00
Sunday Night	Los Angeles Raiders _____ at Kansas City _____	(ESPN) 7:00
Monday, November 7	New York Giants _____ at Dallas _____	(ABC) 8:00

ELEVENTH WEEK
Open Dates: Indianapolis,
Washington

Sunday, November 13	Arizona _____ at New York Giants _____	1:00
(FOX-TV National Weekend)	Atlanta _____ at New Orleans _____	12:00
	Chicago _____ at Miami _____	1:00
	Cleveland _____ at Philadelphia _____	1:00
	Dallas _____ at San Francisco _____	1:00
	Houston _____ at Cincinnati _____	1:00
	Los Angeles Raiders _____ at Los Angeles Rams _____	1:00
	Minnesota _____ at New England _____	1:00
	New York Jets _____ at Green Bay _____	3:00
	San Diego _____ at Kansas City _____	12:00
	Seattle _____ at Denver _____	2:00
Sunday Night	Tampa Bay _____ at Detroit _____	(ESPN) 8:00
Monday, November 14	Buffalo _____ at Pittsburgh _____	(ABC) 9:00

TWELFTH WEEK

Sunday, November 20	Atlanta _____ at Denver _____	2:00
(FOX-TV National Weekend)	Cleveland _____ at Kansas City _____	12:00
	Detroit _____ at Chicago _____	12:00
	Green Bay _____ at Buffalo _____	1:00
	Indianapolis _____ at Cincinnati _____	1:00
	Miami _____ at Pittsburgh _____	1:00
	New Orleans _____ at Los Angeles Raiders _____	1:00
	New York Jets _____ at Minnesota _____	3:00
	Philadelphia _____ at Arizona _____	2:00
	San Diego _____ at New England _____	1:00
	Tampa Bay _____ at Seattle _____	1:00
	Washington _____ at Dallas _____	12:00
Sunday Night	Los Angeles Rams _____ at San Francisco _____	(ESPN) 5:00
Monday, November 21	New York Giants _____ at Houston _____	(ABC) 8:00

THIRTEENTH WEEK	**Thursday, November 24**	Buffalo ___ at Detroit ___	(NBC) 12:30
		Green Bay ___ at Dallas ___	(FOX) 3:00
	Sunday, November 27	Chicago ___ at Arizona ___	2:00
	(NBC-TV National Weekend)	Cincinnati ___ at Denver ___	2:00
		Houston ___ at Cleveland ___	1:00
		Kansas City ___ at Seattle ___	1:00
		Los Angeles Rams ___ at San Diego ___	1:00
		Miami ___ at New York Jets ___	1:00
		New York Giants ___ at Washington ___	4:00
		Philadelphia ___ at Atlanta ___	1:00
		Pittsburgh ___ at Los Angeles Raiders ___	1:00
		Tampa Bay ___ at Minnesota ___	12:00
	Sunday Night	New England ___ at Indianapolis ___	(ESPN) 8:00
	Monday, November 28	San Francisco ___ at New Orleans ___	(ABC) 8:00

FOURTEENTH WEEKEND	**Thursday, December 1**	Chicago ___ at Minnesota ___	(ESPN) 7:00
	Sunday, December 4	Arizona ___ at Houston ___	3:00
	(FOX-TV National Weekend)	Atlanta ___ at San Francisco ___	1:00
		Dallas ___ at Philadelphia ___	1:00
		Denver ___ at Kansas City ___	3:00
		Green Bay ___ at Detroit ___	1:00
		Indianapolis ___ at Seattle ___	1:00
		New Orleans ___ at Los Angeles Rams ___	1:00
		New York Giants ___ at Cleveland ___	4:00
		New York Jets ___ at New England ___	1:00
		Pittsburgh ___ at Cincinnati ___	1:00
		Washington ___ at Tampa Bay ___	1:00
	Sunday Night	Buffalo ___ at Miami ___	(ESPN) 8:00
	Monday, December 5	Los Angeles Raiders ___ at San Diego ___	(ABC) 6:00

FIFTEENTH WEEK	**Saturday, December 10**	Cleveland ___ at Dallas ___	(NBC) 3:00
		Detroit ___ at New York Jets ___	(FOX) 12:30
	Sunday, December 11	Chicago ___ at Green Bay ___	12:00
	(FOX-TV National Weekend)	Cincinnati ___ at New York Giants ___	1:00
		Denver ___ at Los Angeles Raiders ___	1:00
		Indianapolis ___ at New England ___	1:00
		Los Angeles Rams ___ at Tampa Bay ___	1:00
		Minnesota ___ at Buffalo ___	1:00
		Philadelphia ___ at Pittsburgh ___	1:00
		San Francisco ___ at San Diego ___	1:00
		Seattle ___ at Houston ___	3:00
		Washington ___ at Arizona ___	2:00
	Sunday Night	New Orleans ___ at Atlanta ___	(ESPN) 8:00
	Monday, December 12	Kansas City ___ at Miami ___	(ABC) 9:00

SIXTEENTH WEEK	**Saturday, December 17**	Denver ___ at San Francisco ___	(NBC) 1:00
		Minnesota ___ at Detroit ___	(FOX) 12:30
	Sunday, December 18	Atlanta ___ vs. Green Bay ___ at Milwaukee	12:00
	(NBC-TV National Weekend)	Cincinnati ___ at Arizona ___	2:00
		Cleveland ___ at Pittsburgh ___	1:00
		Houston ___ at Kansas City ___	3:00
		Los Angeles Rams ___ at Chicago ___	12:00
		Miami ___ at Indianapolis ___	1:00
		New England ___ at Buffalo ___	1:00
		New York Giants ___ at Philadelphia ___	4:00
		San Diego ___ at New York Jets ___	1:00
		Tampa Bay ___ at Washington ___	1:00
	Sunday Night	Los Angeles Raiders ___ at Seattle ___	(ESPN) 5:00
	Monday, December 19	Dallas ___ at New Orleans ___	(ABC) 8:00

SEVENTEENTH WEEK	**Saturday, December 24** **(NBC-TV National Weekend)**		
		Arizona _____ at Atlanta _____	1:00
		Buffalo _____ at Indianapolis _____	1:00
		Dallas _____ at New York Giants _____	1:00
		Green Bay _____ at Tampa Bay _____	1:00
		Kansas City _____ at Los Angeles Raiders _____	1:00
		New England _____ at Chicago _____	12:00
		New Orleans _____ at Denver _____	2:00
		New York Jets _____ at Houston _____	3:00
		Philadelphia _____ at Cincinnati _____	1:00
		Pittsburgh _____ at San Diego _____	1:00
		Seattle _____ at Cleveland _____	1:00
		Washington _____ at Los Angeles Rams _____	1:00
	Sunday Night, December 25	Detroit _____ at Miami _____	(ESPN) 8:00
	Monday, December 26	San Francisco _____ at Minnesota _____	(ABC) 8:00

Wild Card Playoff Games
Site Priorities
Three Wild Card teams (division non-champions with best three records) from each conference and the division champion with the third-best record in each conference will enter the first round of the playoffs. The division champion with the third-best record will play host to the Wild Card team with the third-best record. The Wild Card team with the best record will play host to the Wild Card team with the second-best record. There are no restrictions on intra-division games.

Saturday, December 31, 1994 American Football Conference

_____ at _____ (ABC)

National Football Conference

_____ at _____ (ABC)

Sunday, January 1, 1995 American Football Conference

_____ at _____ (NBC)

National Football Conference

_____ at _____ (FOX)

Divisional Playoff Games
Site Priorities
In each conference, the two division champions with the highest won-lost-tied percentage during the regular season will play host to the Wild Card winners. The division champion with the best record in each conference is assured of playing the Wild Card survivor with the poorest record. There are no restrictions on intra-division games.

Saturday, January 7, 1995 American Football Conference

_____ at _____ (NBC)

National Football Conference

_____ at _____ (FOX)

Sunday, January 8, 1995 American Football Conference

_____ at _____ (NBC)

National Football Conference

_____ at _____ (FOX)

Championship Games
Site Priorities
for Championship Games
The home teams will be the surviving playoff winners with the best won-lost-tied percentage during the regular season. A Wild Card team cannot play host unless two Wild Card teams are in the game, in which case the Wild Card team with the best record will play host.

Sunday, January 15, 1995 American Football Conference

_____ at _____ (NBC)

National Football Conference

_____ at _____ (FOX)

Super Bowl XXIX **Sunday, January 29, 1995** Super Bowl XXIX at Joe Robbie Stadium, Miami, Florida

_____ at _____ (ABC)

AFC-NFC Pro Bowl **Sunday, February 5, 1995** AFC-NFC Pro Bowl at Honolulu, Hawaii

AFC _____ at NFC _____ (ABC)

POSTSEASON GAMES

Saturday, Dec. 31	AFC and NFC Wild Card Playoffs (ABC)
Sunday, January 1	AFC and NFC Wild Card Playoffs (NBC and FOX)
Saturday, January 7	AFC and NFC Divisional Playoffs (NBC and FOX)
Sunday, January 8	AFC and NFC Divisional Playoffs (NBC and FOX)
Sunday, January 15	AFC and NFC Championship Games (NBC and FOX)
Sunday, January 29	Super Bowl XXIX at Joe Robbie Stadium, Miami, Florida (ABC)
Sunday, February 5	AFC-NFC Pro Bowl at Honolulu, Hawaii (ABC)

1994 NATIONALLY TELEVISED GAMES

Regular Season

Sunday, September 4	Dallas at Pittsburgh (day, FOX)
	San Diego at Denver (night, TNT)
Monday, September 5	Los Angeles Raiders at San Francisco (night, ABC)
Sunday, September 11	Houston at Dallas (day, NBC)
	New York Giants at Arizona (night, TNT)
Monday, September 12	Chicago at Philadelphia (night, ABC)
Sunday, September 18	San Francisco at Los Angeles Rams (day, FOX)
	Kansas City at Atlanta (night, TNT)
Monday, September 19	Detroit at Dallas (night, ABC)
Sunday, September 25	San Diego at Los Angeles Raiders (day, NBC)
	Chicago at New York Jets (night, TNT)
Monday, September 26	Denver at Buffalo (night, ABC)
Sunday, October 2	Philadelphia at San Francisco (day, FOX)
	Miami at Cincinnati (night, TNT)
Monday, October 3	Houston at Pittsburgh (night, ABC)
Sunday, October 9	Kansas City at San Diego (day, NBC)
	Washington at Philadelphia (night, TNT)
Monday, October 10	Minnesota at New York Giants (night, ABC)
Thursday, October 13	Cleveland at Houston (night, TNT)
Sunday, October 16	Philadelphia at Dallas (day, FOX)
Monday, October 17	Kansas City at Denver (night, ABC)
Thursday, October 20	Green Bay at Minnesota (night, TNT)
Sunday, October 23	Dallas at Arizona (day, FOX)
Monday, October 24	Houston at Philadelphia (night, ABC)
Sunday, October 30	Houston at Los Angeles Raiders (day, NBC)
	Pittsburgh at Arizona (night, TNT)
Monday, October 31	Green Bay at Chicago (night, ABC)
Sunday, November 6	Buffalo at New York Jets (day, NBC)
	Los Angeles Raiders at Kansas City (night, ESPN)
Monday, November 7	New York Giants at Dallas (night, ABC)
Sunday, November 13	Dallas at San Francisco (day, FOX)
	Tampa Bay at Detroit (night, ESPN)
Monday, November 14	Buffalo at Pittsburgh (night, ABC)
Sunday, November 20	New Orleans at Los Angeles Raiders (day, FOX)
	Los Angeles Rams at San Francisco (night, ESPN)
Monday, November 21	New York Giants at Houston (night, ABC)
Thursday, November 24	Buffalo at Detroit (day, NBC)
	Green Bay at Dallas (day, FOX)
Sunday, November 27	Pittsburgh at Los Angeles Raiders (day, NBC)
	New England at Indianapolis (night, ESPN)
Monday, November 28	San Francisco at New Orleans (night, ABC)
Thursday, December 1	Chicago at Minnesota (night, ESPN)
Sunday, December 4	Arizona at Houston (day, FOX)
	Buffalo at Miami (night, ESPN)
Monday, December 5	Los Angeles Raiders at San Diego (night, ABC)
Saturday, December 10	Cleveland at Dallas (day, NBC)
	Detroit at New York Jets (day, FOX)
Sunday, December 11	San Francisco at San Diego (day, FOX)
	New Orleans at Atlanta (night, ESPN)
Monday, December 12	Kansas City at Miami (night, ABC)
Saturday, December 17	Denver at San Francisco (day, NBC)
	Minnesota at Detroit (day, FOX)
Sunday, December 18	Houston at Kansas City (day, NBC)
	Los Angeles Raiders at Seattle (night, ESPN)
Monday, December 19	Dallas at New Orleans (night, ABC)
Saturday, December 24	Kansas City at Los Angeles Raiders (day, NBC)
Sunday, December 25	Detroit at Miami (night, ESPN)
Monday, December 26	San Francisco at Minnesota (night, ABC)

1994 AFC-NFC INTERCONFERENCE GAMES

(All Times Local)

September 4	Dallas at Pittsburgh	4:00
	Kansas City at New Orleans	12:00
	Seattle at Washington	1:00
September 5	Los Angeles Raiders at San Francisco	6:00
September 11	Houston at Dallas	3:00
	Indianapolis at Tampa Bay	1:00
	Miami vs. Green Bay at Milwaukee	12:00
	San Francisco at Kansas City	12:00
September 18	Arizona at Cleveland	1:00
	Kansas City at Atlanta	8:00
September 25	Los Angeles Rams at Kansas City	12:00
	Miami at Minnesota	12:00
	New England at Detroit	4:00
	Chicago at New York Jets	8:00
October 2	Buffalo at Chicago	3:00
	Green Bay at New England	1:00
October 16	San Diego at New Orleans	3:00
October 23	Atlanta at Los Angeles Raiders	1:00
	Pittsburgh at New York Giants	1:00
	Washington at Indianapolis	12:00
October 24	Houston at Philadelphia	9:00
October 30	Dallas at Cincinnati	1:00
	Pittsburgh at Arizona	6:00
November 6	Denver at Los Angeles Rams	1:00
	San Diego at Atlanta	1:00
November 13	Chicago at Miami	1:00
	Cleveland at Philadelphia	1:00
	Los Angeles Raiders at Los Angeles Rams	1:00
	Minnesota at New England	1:00
	New York Jets at Green Bay	3:00
November 20	Atlanta at Denver	2:00
	Green Bay at Buffalo	1:00
	New Orleans at Los Angeles Raiders	1:00
	New York Jets at Minnesota	3:00
	Tampa Bay at Seattle	1:00
November 21	New York Giants at Houston	8:00
November 24	Buffalo at Detroit	12:30
November 27	Los Angeles Rams at San Diego	1:00
December 4	Arizona at Houston	3:00
	New York Giants at Cleveland	4:00
December 10	Cleveland at Dallas	3:00
	Detroit at New York Jets	12:30
December 11	Cincinnati at New York Giants	1:00
	Minnesota at Buffalo	1:00
	Philadelphia at Pittsburgh	1:00
	San Francisco at San Diego	1:00
December 17	Denver at San Francisco	1:00
December 18	Cincinnati at Arizona	2:00
December 24	New England at Chicago	12:00
	New Orleans at Denver	2:00
	Philadelphia at Cincinnati	1:00
December 25	Detroit at Miami	8:00

1994

July 5	Claiming period of 24 hours begins in waiver system. All waiver requests for the rest of the year are no-recall and no-withdrawal.
July 10	Los Angeles Raiders are first team to open training camp. Veteran players cannot be required to report earlier than 15 days prior to club's first preseason game or July 15, whichever is later.
July 15	Signing periods ends at 4 P.M., Eastern Daylight Time, for Unrestricted Free Agents to whom June 1 tender (or June 14 tender to Transition Player) was made by Old Club. After this date and through 4 P.M., Eastern Daylight Time, on November 8, Old Club has exclusive negotiating rights with its unsigned Unrestricted Free Agents.
July 30	Hall of Fame Game, Canton, Ohio: Atlanta vs. San Diego.
July 31	American Bowl, Barcelona, Spain: Denver vs. Los Angeles Raiders.
August 5	If a drafted rookie has not signed with his club by this date, he may not be traded to any other club in 1994.
August 6	American Bowl, Tokyo, Japan: Kansas City vs. Minnesota.
August 13	American Bowl, Berlin, Germany: New York Giants vs. San Diego.
August 15	American Bowl, Mexico City, Mexico: Dallas vs. Houston.
August 23	Roster cutdown to maximum of 60 players on Active List by 4 P.M., Eastern Daylight Time.
August 28	Roster cutdown to maximum of 53 players on Active/Inactive List by 4 P.M., Eastern Daylight Time. Clubs may dress minimum of 42 and maximum of 45 players and third quarterback for each regular season and postseason game.
August 29	After 4 P.M., Eastern Daylight Time, clubs may establish a Practice Squad of five players by signing free agents who do not have a season of free-agency credit, unless that season was achieved by spending an entire regular season on Reserve/Injured or Reserve/Physically Unable to Perform.
September 2	All clubs are required to identify their 49-player Active List by 7:00 P.M., Eastern Daylight Time, on this Friday and thereafter on each Friday before a regular-season Sunday game. No later than one hour and 15 minutes prior to kickoff, clubs must identify their 45-player Active List and third quarterback, if any.
September 4-5	Regular season opens.
September 20	Priority on multiple waiver claims is now based on the current season's standing.
September 28-29	Special League meeting on realignment and player-stocking for expansion teams, Dallas, Texas.
October 11	All trading ends at 4 P.M., Eastern Daylight Time.
October 12	Players with at least four previous pension credits are subject to the waiver system for the remainder of the regular season and post-season.
November 1-2	NFL Fall Meeting, Chicago, Illinois.
November 8	Deadline for clubs to sign by 4 P.M., Eastern Time, their Unrestricted Free Agents to whom June 1 tender was made. If still unsigned after this date, such players are prohibited from playing in NFL in 1994.
November 8	Deadline for clubs to sign by 4 P.M., Eastern Time, their Restricted Free Agents to whom June 1 tender was made. If such players remain unsigned, they are prohibited from playing in NFL in 1994.
November 8	Deadline for clubs to sign Drafted players by 4 P.M., Eastern Time. If such players remain unsigned, they are prohibited from playing in NFL in 1994.
November 26	Deadline for reinstatement of players in Reserve List categories of Retired and Did Not Report.
December 23	Deadline for waiver requests in 1994, except for "special waiver requests" by teams participating in playoffs.
December 27	Clubs may begin signing free-agent players for the 1995 season.
December 31	Wild Card Playoff Games.

1995

January 1	Wild Card Playoff Games.
January 7-8	Divisional Playoff Games.
January 15	AFC and NFC Championship Games.
January 29	Super Bowl XXIX at Joe Robbie Stadium, Miami, Florida.
February 5	AFC-NFC Pro Bowl, Honolulu, Hawaii.
February 9-13	Combine Timing and Testing, Hoosier Dome, Indianapolis, Indiana.
March 12-17	NFL Annual Meeting, Phoenix, Arizona.
Late April	Annual player selection meeting, New York, New York.
July 29	Hall of Fame Game, Canton, Ohio.
September 3-4	Regular season opens.
*December 30-31	Wild Card Playoff Games.

*1996

*January 6-7	Divisional Playoff Games.
*January 14	AFC and NFC Championship Games.
*January 28	Super Bowl XXX, Sun Devil Stadium, Tempe, Arizona
*February 4	AFC-NFC Pro Bowl, Honolulu, Hawaii.

*Tentatively scheduled.

11

WAIVERS

The waiver system is a procedure by which player contracts or NFL rights to players are made available by a club to other clubs in the League. During the procedure, the 27 other clubs either file claims to obtain the players or waive the opportunity to do so—thus the term "waiver." Claiming clubs are assigned players on a priority based on the inverse of won-and-lost standing. The claiming period normally is 10 days during the offseason and 24 hours from early July through December. In some circumstances, another 24 hours is added on to allow the original club to rescind its action (known as a recall of a waiver request) and/or the claiming club to do the same (known as withdrawal of a claim). If a player passes through waivers unclaimed and is not recalled by the original club, he becomes a free agent. All waivers from July through December are no recall and no withdrawal. Under the Collective Bargaining Agreement, from the beginning of the waiver system each year through the trading deadline (October 11, 1994), any veteran who has acquired four years of pension credit is not subject to the waiver system if the club desires to release him. After the trading deadline, such players are subject to the waiver system.

ACTIVE/INACTIVE LIST

The Active/Inactive List is the principal status for players participating for a club. It consists of all players under contract who are eligible for preseason, regular-season, and postseason games. In 1994, teams will be permitted to open training camp with no more than 80 players under contract and thereafter must meet two mandatory roster reductions prior to the season opener. Teams will be permitted an Active List of 45 players and an Inactive List of eight players for each regular-season and postseason game during the 1994 season. Provided that a club has two quarterbacks on its 45-player Active List, a third quarterback from its Inactive List is permitted to dress for the game, but if he participates in the game, the other two quarterbacks are thereafter prohibited from playing. Teams also are permitted to establish Practice Squads of up to five players who are eligible to participate in practice, but these players remain free agents and are eligible to sign with any other team in the league.

August 23 ....Roster reduction to 60 players
August 28 ....Roster reduction to 53 players
August 29 ....Teams establish a Practice Squad of up to five players

In addition to the squad limits described above, there also is an overall roster limit of 80 players that is applicable to players on a team's Active, Inactive, and Exempt Lists, and any players on the Practice Squad and on the Reserve List as Injured, Physically Unable to Perform, Non-Football Illness/Injury, and Suspended.

RESERVE LIST

The Reserve List is a status for players who, for reasons of injury, retirement, military service, or other circumstances, are not immediately available for participation with a club. Players on Reserve/Injured are not eligible to practice or return to the Active/Inactive List in the same season that they are placed on Reserve.

Players in the category of Reserve/Retired or Reserve/Did Not Report may not be reinstated during the period from 30 days before the end of the regular season through the postseason.

TRADES

Unrestricted trading between the AFC and NFC is allowed in 1994 through October 11, after which trading will end until 1995.

ANNUAL ACTIVE PLAYER LIMITS

NFL

Year(s)	Limit
1991-94	45**
1985-90	45
1983-84	49
1982	45†-49
1978-81	45
1975-77	43
1974	47
1964-73	40
1963	37
1961-62	36
1960	38
1959	36
1957-58	35
1951-56	33
1949-50	32
1948	35
1947	35*-34
1945-46	33

Year(s)	Limit
1943-44	28
1940-42	33
1938-39	30
1936-37	25
1935	24
1930-34	20
1926-29	18
1925	16

**45 plus a third quarterback
† 45 for first two games
* 35 for first three games

AFL

Year(s)	Limit
1966-69	40
1965	38
1964	34
1962-63	33
1960-61	35

The following procedures will be used to break standings ties for postseason playoffs and to determine regular-season schedules.

TO BREAK A TIE WITHIN A DIVISION

If, at the end of the regular season, two or more clubs in the same division finish with identical won-lost-tied percentages, the following steps will be taken until a champion is determined.

TWO CLUBS

1. Head-to-head (best won-lost-tied percentage in games between the clubs).
2. Best won-lost-tied percentage in games played within the division.
3. Best won-lost-tied percentage in games played within the conference.
4. Best won-lost-tied percentage in common games, if applicable.
5. Best net points in division games.
6. Best net points in all games.
7. Strength of schedule.
8. Best net touchdowns in all games.
9. Coin toss.

THREE OR MORE CLUBS

(Note: If two clubs remain tied after third or other clubs are eliminated during any step, tiebreaker reverts to step 1 of the two-club format).

1. Head-to-head (best won-lost-tied percentage in games among the clubs).
2. Best won-lost-tied percentage in games played within the division.
3. Best won-lost-tied percentage in games played within the conference.
4. Best won-lost-tied percentage in common games.
5. Best net points in division games.
6. Best net points in all games.
7. Strength of schedule.
8. Best net touchdowns in all games.
9. Coin toss.

TO BREAK A TIE FOR THE WILD CARD TEAM

If it is necessary to break ties to determine the three Wild Card clubs from each conference, the following steps will be taken.

1. If the tied clubs are from the same division, apply division tiebreaker.
2. If the tied clubs are from different divisions, apply the following steps.

TWO CLUBS

1. Head-to-head, if applicable.
2. Best won-lost-tied percentage in games played within the conference.
3. Best won-lost-tied percentage in common games, minimum of four.
4. Best average net points in conference games.
5. Best net points in all games.
6. Strength of schedule.
7 Best net touchdowns in all games.
8. Coin toss.

THREE OR MORE CLUBS

(Note: If two clubs remain tied after third or other clubs are eliminated, tiebreaker reverts to step 1 of applicable two-club format.)

1. Apply division tiebreaker to eliminate all but the highest ranked club in each division prior to proceeding to step 2. The original seeding within a division upon application of the division tiebreaker remains the same for all subsequent applications of the procedure that are necessary to identify the three Wild Card participants.
2. Head-to-head sweep. (Applicable only if one club has defeated each of the others or if one club has lost to each of the others).

3. Best won-lost-tied percentage in games played within the conference.
4. Best won-lost-tied percentage in common games, minimum of four.
5. Best average net points in conference games.
6. Best net points in all games.
7. Strength of schedule.
8. Best net touchdowns in all games.
9. Coin toss.

When the first Wild Card team has been identified, the procedure is repeated to name the second Wild Card, i.e., eliminate all but the highest-ranked club in each division prior to proceeding to step 2, and repeated a third time, if necessary, to identify the third Wild Card. In situations where three or more teams from the same division are involved in the procedure, the original seeding of the teams remains the same for subsequent applications of the tiebreaker if the top-ranked team in that division qualifies for a Wild Card berth.

OTHER TIE-BREAKING PROCEDURES

1. Only one club advances to the playoffs in any tie-breaking step. Remaining tied clubs revert to the first step of the applicable division or Wild Card tiebreakers. As an example, if two clubs remain tied in any tie-breaker step after all other clubs have been eliminated, the procedure reverts to step one of the two-club format to determine the winner. When one club wins the tie-breaker, all other clubs revert to step 1 of the applicable two-club or three-club format.
2. In comparing division and conference records or records against common opponents among tied teams, the best won-lost-tied percentage is the deciding factor since teams may have played an unequal number of games.
3. To determine home-field priority among division titlists, apply Wild Card tiebreakers.
4. To determine home-field priority for Wild Card qualifiers, apply division tiebreakers (if teams are from the same division) or Wild Card tiebreakers (if teams are from different divisions).

TIE-BREAKING PROCEDURE FOR SELECTION MEETING

If two or more clubs are tied in the selection order, the strength-of-schedule tie-breaker is applied, subject to the following exceptions for playoff clubs:

1. The Super Bowl winner is last and the Super Bowl loser next-to-last.
2. Any non-Super Bowl playoff club involved in a tie shall be assigned priority within its segment below that of non-playoff clubs and in the order that the playoff clubs exited from the playoffs. Thus, within a tied segment a playoff club that loses in the Wild Card game will have priority over a playoff club that loses in the Divisional playoff game, which in turn will have priority over a club that loses in the Conference Championship game. If two tied clubs exited the playoffs in the same round, the tie is broken by strength-of-schedule.

If any ties cannot be broken by strength-of-schedule, the divisional or conference tie-breakers, whichever are applicable, are applied. Any ties that still exist are broken by a coin flip.

NFL PASSER RATING SYSTEM

The NFL rates its passers for statistical purposes against a fixed performance standard based on statistical achievements of all qualified pro passers since 1960. The current system replaced one that rated passers in relation to their position in a total group based on various criteria. The current system, which was adopted in 1973, removes inequities that existed in the former method and, at the same time, provides a means of comparing passing performances from one season to the next.

It is important to remember that the system is used to rate **passers,** not **quarterbacks.** Statistics do not reflect leadership, play-calling, and other intangible factors that go into making a successful professional quarterback. Four categories are used as a basis for compiling a rating:

—Percentage of touchdown passes per attempt
—Percentage of completions per attempt
—Percentage of interceptions per attempt
—Average yards gained per attempt

The **average** standard is 1.000. The bottom is .000. To earn a 2.000 rating, a passer must perform at exceptional levels, i.e., 70 percent in completions, 10 percent in touchdowns, 1.5 percent in interceptions, and 11 yards average gain per pass attempt. The **maximum** a passer can receive in any category is 2.375.

For example, to gain a 2.375 in completion percentage, a passer would have to complete 77.5 percent of his passes. The NFL record is 70.55 by Ken Anderson (Cincinnati, 1982). To earn a 2.375 in percentage of touchdowns, a passer would have to achieve a percentage of 11.9. The record is 13.9 percent by Sid Luckman (Chicago, 1943). To gain 2.375 in percentage of interceptions, a passer would have to go the entire season without an interception. The 2.375 figure in average yards is 12.50, compared with the NFL record of 11.17 by Tommy O'Connell (Cleveland, 1957).

In order to make the rating more understandable, the point rating is then converted into a scale of 100. For instance, if a passer completes 11 of 23 passes for 114 yards, with 1 touchdown and no interceptions, the four components would be:

—**Percentage of Completions**—11 of 23 is 47.8 percent. The point rating is 0.890.

—**Percentage of Touchdown Passes**—1 touchdown in 23 attempts works out to 4.3 percent for a rating of 0.860.

—**Percentage of Interceptions**—You can't do better than zero, so the passer receives a maximum rating of 2.375.

—**Average Yards Gained Per Attempt**—114 yards divided by 23 attempts equals 4.96 yards per attempt for a corresponding rating of 0.490.

The sum of the four components is 4.615, which converts to a rating of 76.9. In order for a passer to achieve 100, his points would have to total 6.000. In rare cases, where statistical performance has been superior, it is possible for a passer to surpass 100.

The following is a list of qualifying passers who had a single-season passer rating of 100 or higher:

Player, Team	Season	Rating	Att.	Comp.	Pct.	Yds.	Avg.	TD	TD Pct.	Int.	Int. Pct.
Joe Montana, San Francisco	1989	112.4	386	271	70.2	3,521	9.12	26	6.7	8	2.1
Milt Plum, Cleveland	1960	110.4	250	151	60.4	2,297	9.19	21	8.4	5	2.0
Sammy Baugh, Washington	1945	109.9	182	128	70.3	1,669	9.17	11	6.0	4	2.2
Dan Marino, Miami	1984	108.9	564	362	64.2	5,084	9.01	48	8.5	17	3.0
Sid Luckman, Chicago Bears	1943	107.5	202	110	54.5	2,194	10.86	28	13.9	12	5.9
Steve Young, San Francisco	1992	107.0	402	268	66.7	3,465	8.62	25	6.2	7	1.7
Bart Starr, Green Bay	1966	105.0	251	156	62.2	2,257	8.99	14	5.6	3	1.2
Roger Staubach, Dallas	1971	104.8	211	126	59.7	1,882	8.92	15	7.1	4	1.9
Y.A. Tittle, N.Y. Giants	1963	104.8	367	221	60.2	3,145	8.57	36	9.8	14	3.8
Bart Starr, Green Bay	1968	104.3	171	109	63.7	1,617	9.46	15	8.8	8	4.7
Ken Stabler, Oakland	1976	103.4	291	194	66.7	2,737	9.41	27	9.3	17	5.8
Joe Montana, San Francisco	1984	102.9	432	279	64.6	3,630	8.40	28	6.5	10	2.3
Charlie Conerly, N.Y. Giants	1959	102.7	194	113	58.2	1,706	8.79	14	7.2	4	2.1
Bert Jones, Baltimore	1976	102.5	343	207	60.3	3,104	9.05	24	7.0	9	2.6
Joe Montana, San Francisco	1987	102.1	398	266	66.8	3,054	7.67	31	7.8	13	3.3
Steve Young, San Francisco	1991	101.8	279	180	64.5	2,517	9.02	17	6.1	8	2.9
Len Dawson, Kansas City	1966	101.7	284	159	56.0	2,527	8.90	26	9.2	10	3.5
Steve Young, San Francisco	1993	101.5	462	314	68.0	4,023	8.71	29	6.3	16	3.5
Jim Kelly, Buffalo	1990	101.2	346	219	63.3	2,829	8.18	24	6.9	9	2.6

ACTIVE COACHES' CAREER RECORDS (Order Based on Career Victories)

Start of 1994 Season

Coach	Team(s)	Yrs.	Regular Season Won	Lost	Tied	Pct.	Postseason Won	Lost	Tied	Pct.	Career Won	Lost	Tied	Pct.
Don Shula	Baltimore Colts, Miami Dolphins	31	309	143	6	.681	18	15	0	.545	327	158	6	.672
Chuck Knox	Los Angeles Rams, Buffalo Bills, Seattle Seahawks	21	182	135	1	.574	7	11	0	.389	189	146	1	.564
Dan Reeves	Denver Broncos, New York Giants	13	121	78	1	.608	8	7	0	.533	129	85	1	.602
Marv Levy	Kansas City Chiefs, Buffalo Bills	13	110	81	0	.576	10	6	0	.625	120	87	0	.580
Tom Flores	Oakland-Los Angeles Raiders, Seattle Seahawks	11	91	77	0	.542	8	3	0	.727	99	80	0	.553
Marty Schottenheimer	Cleveland Browns, Kansas City Chiefs	10	94	56	1	.626	5	8	0	.385	99	64	1	.607
Bill Parcells	New York Giants, New England Patriots	9	82	60	1	.577	8	3	0	.727	90	63	1	.588
Jack Pardee	Chicago Bears, Washington Redskins, Houston Oilers	10	86	68	0	.558	1	5	0	.167	87	73	0	.544
Jim Mora	New Orleans Saints	8	77	50	0	.606	0	4	0	.000	77	54	0	.588
Sam Wyche	Cincinnati Bengals, Tampa Bay Buccaneers	10	71	88	0	.447	3	2	0	.600	74	90	0	.451
George Seifert	San Francisco 49ers	5	62	18	0	.775	6	3	0	.667	68	21	0	.764
Ted Marchibroda	Baltimore-Indianapolis Colts	7	54	52	0	.509	0	3	0	.000	54	55	0	.495
Art Shell	Los Angeles Raiders	5	45	31	0	.592	2	3	0	.400	47	34	0	.580
Wayne Fontes	Detroit Lions	5	42	43	0	.494	1	2	0	.333	43	45	0	.489
Buddy Ryan	Philadelphia Eagles, Arizona Cardinals	5	43	35	1	.551	0	3	0	.000	43	38	1	.530
Rich Kotite	Philadelphia Eagles	3	29	19	0	.604	1	1	0	.500	30	20	0	.600
Bill Belichick	Cleveland Browns	3	20	28	0	.417	0	0	0	.000	20	28	0	.417
Bill Cowher	Pittsburgh Steelers	2	20	12	0	.625	0	2	0	.000	20	14	0	.588
Dennis Green	Minnesota Vikings	2	20	12	0	.625	0	2	0	.000	20	14	0	.588
Bobby Ross	San Diego Chargers	2	19	13	0	.594	1	1	0	.500	20	14	0	.588
Mike Holmgren	Green Bay Packers	2	18	14	0	.563	1	1	0	.500	19	15	0	.559
Wade Phillips	New Orleans Saints, Denver Broncos	2	10	10	0	.500	0	1	0	.000	10	11	0	.476
Dave Shula	Cincinnati Bengals	2	8	24	0	.250	0	0	0	.000	8	24	0	.250
Dave Wannstedt	Chicago Bears	1	7	9	0	.438	0	0	0	.000	7	9	0	.438
Pete Carroll	New York Jets	0	0	0	0	.000	0	0	0	.000	0	0	0	.000
June Jones	Atlanta Falcons	0	0	0	0	.000	0	0	0	.000	0	0	0	.000
Barry Switzer	Dallas Cowboys	0	0	0	0	.000	0	0	0	.000	0	0	0	.000
Norv Turner	Washington Redskins	0	0	0	0	.000	0	0	0	.000	0	0	0	.000

COACHES WITH 100 CAREER VICTORIES (Order Based on Career Victories)

Start of 1994 Season

Coach	Team(s)	Yrs.	Regular Season Won	Lost	Tied	Pct.	Postseason Won	Lost	Tied	Pct.	Career Won	Lost	Tied	Pct.
Don Shula	Baltimore Colts, Miami Dolphins	31	309	143	6	.681	18	15	0	.545	327	158	6	.672
George Halas	Chicago Bears	40	318	148	31	.671	6	3	0	.667	324	151	31	.671
Tom Landry	Dallas Cowboys	29	250	162	6	.605	20	16	0	.556	270	178	6	.601
Earl (Curly) Lambeau	Green Bay Packers, Chicago Cardinals, Washington Redskins	33	226	132	22	.624	3	2	0	.600	229	134	22	.623
Chuck Noll	Pittsburgh Steelers	23	193	148	1	.566	16	8	0	.667	209	156	1	.572
Chuck Knox	Los Angeles Rams, Buffalo Bills, Seattle Seahawks	21	182	135	1	.574	7	11	0	.389	189	146	1	.564
Paul Brown	Cleveland Browns, Cincinnati Bengals	21	166	100	6	.621	4	8	0	.333	170	108	6	.609
Bud Grant	Minnesota Vikings	18	158	96	5	.620	10	12	0	.455	168	108	5	.607
Steve Owen	New York Giants	23	151	100	17	.595	2	8	0	.200	153	108	17	.581
Joe Gibbs	Washington Redskins	12	124	60	0	.674	16	5	0	.762	140	65	0	.683
Hank Stram	Kansas City Chiefs, New Orleans Saints	17	131	97	10	.571	5	3	0	.625	136	100	10	.573
Weeb Ewbank	Baltimore Colts, New York Jets	20	130	129	7	.502	4	1	0	.800	134	130	7	.507
Dan Reeves	Denver Broncos, New York Giants	13	121	78	1	.608	8	7	0	.553	129	85	1	.602
Sid Gillman	Los Angeles Rams, Los Angeles-San Diego Chargers, Houston Oilers	18	122	99	7	.550	1	5	0	.167	123	104	7	.541
Marv Levy	Kansas City Chiefs, Buffalo Bills	13	110	81	0	.576	10	6	0	.625	120	87	0	.580
George Allen	Los Angeles Rams, Washington Redskins	12	116	47	5	.705	2	7	0	.222	118	54	5	.681
Don Coryell	St. Louis Cardinals, San Diego Chargers	14	111	83	1	.572	3	6	0	.333	114	89	1	.561
Mike Ditka	Chicago Bears	11	106	62	0	.631	6	6	0	.500	112	68	0	.622
John Madden	Oakland Raiders	10	103	32	7	.750	9	7	0	.563	112	39	7	.731
Ray (Buddy) Parker	Chicago Cardinals, Detroit Lions, Pittsburgh Steelers	15	104	75	9	.577	3	1	0	.750	107	76	9	.581
Vince Lombardi	Green Bay Packers, Washington Redskins	10	96	34	6	.728	9	1	0	.900	105	35	6	.740
Bill Walsh	San Francisco 49ers	10	92	59	1	.609	10	4	0	.714	102	63	1	.617

Active coaches in bold.

59th Annual NFL Draft, April 24-25, 1994

ARIZONA CARDINALS
(Drafted alternately 10-9-11)
1. Jamir Miller—10, LB, UCLA
2. Chuck Levy—38, RB, Arizona
   * Choice to Miami
3. Rich Braham—76, G, West Virginia
   Eric England—89, DE, Texas A&M, from Green Bay through Miami
4. Perry Carter—107, DB, Southern Mississippi, from New England
   John Reece—113, DB, Nebraska
   Terry Irving—115, LB, McNeese State, from San Diego through Miami
5. Anthony Redmon—139, G, Auburn
6. Terry Samuels—172, TE, Kentucky
7. Frank Harvey—204, RB, Georgia

ATLANTA FALCONS
(Drafted alternately 7-8)
1. Choice to San Francisco through Indianapolis and Los Angeles Rams
2. Choice to Philadelphia
   * Bert Emanuel—45, WR, Rice, from Minnesota
3. Anthony Phillips—72, DB, Texas A&M-Kingsville
   * Choice to Los Angeles Rams through Indianapolis
   Alai Kalaniuvalu—99, G, Oregon State, from Dallas through San Francisco and Denver
4. Perry Klein—111, QB, C.W. Post
   Mitch Davis—118, LB, Georgia, from Philadelphia
5. Harrison Houston—138, WR, Florida
6. Choice to Green Bay through Los Angeles Raiders
7. Jamal Anderson—201, RB, Utah

BUFFALO BILLS
(Drafted 27)
1. Jeff Burris—27, DB, Notre Dame
2.* Bucky Brooks—48, WR, North Carolina
   Lonnie Johnson—61, TE, Florida State
   * Sam Rogers—64, LB, Colorado
3.* Marlo Perry—81, LB, Jackson State
   Corey Louchiey—98, T, South Carolina
4. Sean Crocker—130, DB, North Carolina
5. A.J. Ofodile—158, TE, Missouri
6. Anthony Abrams—188, DE, Clark, Ga.
   * Kevin Knox—192, WR, Florida State
7. Filmel Johnson—221, DB, Illinois

CHICAGO BEARS
(Drafted alternately 11-10-9)
1. John Thierry—11, DE, Alcorn State
2. Marcus Spears—39, T, N.W. Louisiana
3. Jim Flanigan—74, DT, Notre Dame
4. Raymont Harris—114, RB, Ohio State
5. Choice to Pittsburgh
6. Lloyd Hill—170, WR, Texas Tech
7. Dennis Collier—205, DB, Colorado

CINCINNATI BENGALS
(Drafted 1)
1. Dan Wilkinson—1, DT, Ohio State
2. Darnay Scott—30, WR, San Diego State
3. Jeff Cothran—66, RB, Ohio State
   * Steve Shine—86, LB, Northwestern
4. Corey Sawyer—104, DB, Florida State
5. Trent Pollard—132, T, Eastern Washington
6. Kimo Von Oelhoffen—162, DT, Boise State
   Jerry Reynolds—184, T, Nevada-Las Vegas, from Los Angeles Raiders
7. Ramondo Stallings—195, DE, San Diego State

CLEVELAND BROWNS
(Drafted alternately 9-11-10)
1. Antonio Langham—9, DB, Alabama
   * Derrick Alexander—29, WR, Michigan, from Philadelphia
2. Choice to Minnesota through Philadelphia and Atlanta
3. Romeo Bandison—75, DT, Oregon
4. Choice to Miami
5. Issac Booth—141, DB, California

6. Robert Strait—171, RB, Baylor
7. Andre Hewitt—203, T, Clemson

DALLAS COWBOYS
(Drafted 28)
1. Shante Carver—23, DE, Arizona State, from San Francisco
   Choice to San Francisco
2.* Larry Allen—46, G, Sonoma State
   Choice to San Francisco
3. Choice to Atlanta through San Francisco and Denver
   * George Hegamin—102, T, North Carolina State
4. Willie Jackson—109, WR, Florida, from Tampa Bay
   DeWayne Dotson—131, LB, Mississippi
5. Choice to Los Angeles Raiders
6. Choice to Los Angeles Rams
   * Darren Studstill—191, DB, West Virginia, from Los Angeles Rams
7. Toddrick McIntosh—216, DT, Florida State, from Los Angeles Raiders
   Choice to New England

DENVER BRONCOS
(Drafted alternately 18-17-16-20-19)
1. Choice to Minnesota
2. Allen Aldridge—51, LB, Houston
3. Choice to San Francisco
4. Randy Fuller—123, DB, Tennessee State
5. Choice to Green Bay through San Francisco
6. Choice to Minnesota
7. Keith Burns—210, LB, Oklahoma State
   Butler By'not'e—212, RB, Ohio State, from Green Bay
   Tom Nalen—218, C, Boston College, from New York Giants

DETROIT LIONS
(Drafted alternately 21-23-22)
1. Johnnie Morton—21, WR, Southern California
2. Van Malone—57, DB, Texas
3. Shane Bonham—93, DT, Tennessee
4. Vaughn Bryant—124, DB, Stanford
5. Tony Semple—154, G, Memphis State
6. Jocelyn Borgella—183, DB, Cincinnati
7. Tom Beer—215, LB, Wayne State, Mich.

GREEN BAY PACKERS
(Drafted alternately 20-19-18-17-16)
1. Aaron Taylor—16, T, Notre Dame, from Miami
   Choice to Miami
2. Choice to San Francisco
3.* Le Shon Johnson—84, RB, Northern Illinois, from San Francisco
   Choice to Arizona through Miami
4. Choice to Los Angeles Raiders
   Gabe Wilkins—126, DE, Gardner-Webb, from San Francisco through Los Angeles Raiders
5. Terry Mickens—146, WR, Florida A&M
   Dorsey Levens—149, RB, Georgia Tech, from Denver through San Francisco
6. Jay Kearney—169, WR, West Virginia, from Atlanta through Los Angeles Raiders
   Ruffin Hamilton—175, LB, Tulane, from San Diego through San Francisco
   Bill Schroeder—181, WR, Wisconsin-LaCrosse
   * Paul Duckworth—190, LB, Connecticut, from Philadelphia through San Francisco
7. Choice to Denver

HOUSTON OILERS
(Drafted 26)
1. Henry Ford—26, DE, Arkansas
2. Jeremy Nunley—60, DE, Alabama
3. Choice to Washington
   * Malcolm Seabron—101, WR, Fresno State
4. Michael Davis—119, DB, Cincinnati, from Minnesota
   Sean Jackson—129, RB, Florida State
5. Roderick Lewis—157, TE, Arizona
   * Jim Reid—161, T, Virginia
6. Lee Gissendaner—187, WR, Northwestern

   * Barron Wortham—194, LB, Texas-El Paso
7. Lemanski Hall—220, LB, Alabama

INDIANAPOLIS COLTS
(Drafted alternately 2-3)
1. Marshall Faulk—2, RB, San Diego State
   Trev Alberts—5, LB, Nebraska, from Los Angeles Rams
2. Eric Mahlum—32, G, California
3. Jason Mathews—67, T, Texas A&M
4. Brad Banta—106, TE, Southern California
5. John Covington—133, DB, Notre Dame
6. Lamont Warren—164, RB, Colorado
7. Lance Teichelman—196, DT, Texas A&M

KANSAS CITY CHIEFS
(Drafted alternately 25-24)
1. Greg Hill—25, RB, Texas A&M
2. Donnell Bennett—58, RB, Miami
3. Lake Dawson—92, WR, Notre Dame, from San Francisco
   Chris Penn—96, WR, Tulsa
4. Bracey Walker—127, DB, North Carolina
5. James Burton—151, DB, Fresno State, from Minnesota
   Rob Waldrop—156, DT, Arizona
6. Anthony Daigle—185, RB, Fresno State
7. Steve Matthews—199, QB, Memphis State, from Los Angeles Rams
   Tracy Greene—219, TE, Grambling

LOS ANGELES RAIDERS
(Drafted alternately 22-21-23)
1. Rob Fredrickson—22, LB, Michigan State
2. James Folston—52, DE, N.E. Louisiana, from Minnesota
   Choice to Minnesota
3. Calvin Jones—80, RB, Nebraska, from New York Jets
   Choice to New York Jets
4. Austin Robbins—120, DT, North Carolina, from Green Bay
   Choice to Minnesota
5. Choice to New York Jets
   Roosevelt Patterson—159, G, Alabama, from Dallas
6. Choice to Cincinnati
7. Choice to Dallas
   Rob Holmberg—217, LB, Penn State, from San Francisco through Dallas

LOS ANGELES RAMS
(Drafted alternately 5-4-6)
1. Choice to Indianapolis
   Wayne Gandy—15, T, Auburn, from San Diego through San Francisco
2. Isaac Bruce—33, WR, Memphis State
   * Toby Wright—49, DB, Nebraska
   Brad Ottis—56, DT, Wayne State, Neb., from San Francisco
3. Keith Lyle—71, DB, Virginia
   * James Bostic—83, RB, Auburn, from Atlanta through Indianapolis
   * Ernest Jones—100, LB, Oregon, from Philadelphia through San Francisco
4. Chris Brantley—108, WR, Rutgers
5. Choice to New England through Arizona
6. Rickey Brady—167, TE, Oklahoma
   Ronald Edwards—189, T, North Carolina A&T, from Dallas
   * Choice to Dallas
7. Choice to Kansas City

MIAMI DOLPHINS
(Drafted alternately 16-20-19-18-17)
1. Choice to Green Bay
   Tim Bowens—20, DT, Mississippi, from Green Bay
2. Aubrey Beavers—54, LB, Oklahoma
   * Tim Ruddy—65, C, Notre Dame, from Arizona
3. Choice to New England
4. Ronnie Woolfork—112, LB, Colorado, from Cleveland
   Choice to New England through Arizona

5. William Gaines—147, DT, Florida
6. Brant Boyer—177, LB, Arizona
7. Sean Hill—214, DB, Montana State

MINNESOTA VIKINGS
(Drafted alternately 19-18-17-16-20)
1. DeWayne Washington—18, DB, North Carolina State, from Denver
   Todd Steussie—19, T, California
2. David Palmer—40, WR, Alabama, from Cleveland through Philadelphia and Atlanta
   * Choice to Atlanta
   Choice to Los Angeles Raiders
   Fernando Smith—55, DE, Jackson State, from Los Angeles Raiders
3. Choice to Pittsburgh
4. Choice to Houston
   Mike Wells—125, DT, Iowa, from Los Angeles Raiders
5. Shelly Hammonds—134, DB, Penn State, from Washington
   Choice to Kansas City
6. Andrew Jordan—179, TE, Western Carolina, from Denver
   Choice to Pittsburgh
7. Pete Bercich—211, LB, Notre Dame

NEW ENGLAND PATRIOTS
(Drafted alternately 4-6-5)
1. Willie McGinest—4, DE, Southern California
2. Kevin Lee—35, WR, Alabama
3. Choice to San Diego
   Ervin Collier—78, NT, Florida A&M, from San Diego
   Joe Burch—90, C, Texas Southern, from Miami
4. Choice to Arizona
   John Burke—121, TE, Virginia Tech, from Miami through Arizona
5. Pat O'Neill—135, P, Syracuse, from Los Angeles Rams through Arizona
   Choice to San Diego
6. Steve Hawkins—166, WR, Western Michigan
   Max Lane—168, T, Navy, from Seattle
7. Jay Walker—198, QB, Howard
   Marty Moore—222, LB, Kentucky, from Dallas

NEW ORLEANS SAINTS
(Drafted alternately 12-15-14-13)
1. Choice to New York Jets
   Joe Johnson—13, DE, Louisville, from New York Jets
2. Mario Bates—44, RB, Arizona State
3. Winfred Tubbs—79, LB, Texas
4. Doug Nussmeier—116, QB, Idaho
5. Herman Carroll—142, DE, Mississippi State
   Craig Novitsky—143, G, UCLA, from New York Jets
6. Derrell Mitchell—176, WR, Texas Tech
7. Lance Lundberg—213, T, Nebraska

NEW YORK GIANTS
(Drafted alternately 24-25)
1. Thomas Lewis—24, WR, Indiana
2.* Thomas Randolph—47, DB, Kansas State
   Jason Sehorn—59, DB, Southern California
3. Gary Downs—95, RB, North Carolina State
4. Chris Maumalanga—128, DT, Kansas
5. Chad Bratzke—155, DE, Eastern Kentucky
6. Jason Winrow—186, G, Ohio State
7. Choice to Denver

NEW YORK JETS
(Drafted alternately 13-12-15-14)
1. Aaron Glenn—12, DB, Texas A&M, from New Orleans
   Choice to New Orleans
2. Ryan Yarborough—41, WR, Wyoming
3. Choice to Los Angeles Raiders
   Lou Benfatti—94, DT, Penn State, from Los Angeles Raiders
4. Orlando Parker—117, WR, Troy State
5. Choice to New Orleans

Horace Morris—152, LB, Tennessee from Los Angeles Raiders
6. Fred Lester—173, RB, Alabama A&M
7. Glenn Foley—208, QB, Boston College

PHILADELPHIA EAGLES
(Drafted alternately 14-13-12-15)
1. Bernard Williams—14, T, Georgia
   * Choice to Cleveland
2. Bruce Walker—37, DT, UCLA, from Atlanta
   Charlie Garner—42, RB, Tennessee
3. Joe Panos—77, G, Wisconsin
   * Choice to Los Angeles Rams through San Francisco
   * Eric Zomalt—103, DB, California
4. Choice to Atlanta
5. Marvin Goodwin—144, DB, UCLA
6. Ryan McCoy—174, LB, Houston
   * Choice to Green Bay through San Francisco
   * Mitch Berger—193, P, Colorado
7. Mark Montgomery—206, RB, Wisconsin

PITTSBURGH STEELERS
(Drafted alternately 17-16-20-19-18)
1. Charles Johnson—17, WR, Colorado
2. Brentson Buckner—50, DE, Clemson
3. Jason Gildon—88, LB, Oklahoma State, from Minnesota
   Bam Morris—91, RB, Texas Tech
4. Taase Faumui—122, DE, Hawaii
5. Myron Bell—140, DB, Michigan State, from Chicago
   Gary Brown—148, T, Georgia Tech
6. Jim Miller—178, QB, Michigan State
   Eric Ravotti—180, LB, Penn State, from Minnesota
7. Brice Abrams—209, RB, Michigan State

SAN DIEGO CHARGERS
(Drafted alternately 15-14-13-12)
1. Choice to L.A. Rams through San Francisco
2. Isaac Davis—43, G, Arkansas
   * Vaughn Parker—63, G, UCLA
3. Andre Coleman—70, WR, Kansas State, from New England
   Choice to New England
   * Willie Clark—82, DB, Notre Dame
4. Choice to Arizona through Miami
5. Aaron Laing—137, TE, New Mexico State, from New England
   Rodney Harrison—145, DB, Western Illinois
   Darren Krein—150, DE, Miami, from Seattle
   * Tony Vinson—160, RB, Towson State
6. Choice to Green Bay through San Francisco
7. Zane Beehn—207, LB, Kentucky

SAN FRANCISCO 49ERS
(Drafted alternately 23-22-21)
1. Bryant Young—7, DT, Notre Dame, from Atlanta through Indianapolis and Los Angeles Rams
   Choice to Dallas
   William Floyd—28, RB, Florida State, from Dallas
2. Kevin Mitchell—53, LB, Syracuse, from Green Bay
   Choice to Los Angeles Rams
   Tyronne Drakeford—62, DB, Virginia Tech, from Dallas
3.* Choice to Green Bay
   * Doug Brien—85, K, California
   Cory Fleming—87, WR, Tennessee, from Denver
   Choice to Kansas City
4. Choice to Green Bay through Los Angeles Raiders
5. Tony Peterson—153, LB, Notre Dame
6. Lee Woodall—182, LB, West Chester, Pa.
7. Choice to Los Angeles Raiders through Dallas

SEATTLE SEAHAWKS
(Drafted alternately 8-7)
1. Sam Adams—8, DT, Texas A&M
2. Kevin Mawae—36, C, Louisiana State
3. Lamar Smith—73, RB, Houston
4. Larry Whigham —110, DB, N.E. Louisiana
5. Choice to San Diego
6. Choice to New England
7. Carlester Crumpler—202, TE, East Carolina

TAMPA BAY BUCCANEERS
(Drafted alternately 6-5-4)
1. Trent Dilfer—6, QB, Fresno State
2. Errict Rhett—34, RB, Florida
3. Harold Bishop—69, TE, Louisiana State
4. Choice to Dallas
5. Pete Pierson—136, T, Washington
6. Bernard Carter —165, LB, East Carolina
7. Jim Pyne—200, C, Virginia Tech

WASHINGTON REDSKINS
(Drafted alternately 3-2)
1. Heath Shuler—3, QB, Tennessee
2. Tre Johnson—31, T, Temple
3. Tydus Winans—68, WR, Fresno State
   Joseph Patton—97, G, Alabama A&M, from Houston
4. Kurt Haws—105, TE, Utah
5. Choice to Minnesota
6. Dexter Nottage—163, DE, Florida A&M
7. Gus Frerotte—197, QB, Tulsa

*Compensatory pick

NUMBER OF PLAYERS DRAFTED

BY POSITION:

Defensive Backs	34
Linebackers	33
Wide Receivers	29
Running Backs	28
Defensive Ends	18
Defensive Tackles	18
Tackles	18
Guards	13
Tight Ends	13
Quarterbacks	9
Centers	5
Punters	2
Kickers	1
Nose Tackles	1
Kick Returners	0

BY COLLEGE (3 or more players):

Notre Dame	10
Alabama	6
Colorado	6
Florida State	6
Texas A&M	6
California	5
Fresno State	5
Nebraska	5
Ohio State	5
Tennessee	5
UCLA	5
Arizona	4
Florida	4
Michigan State	4
North Carolina	4
Penn State	4
Southern California	4
Auburn	3
Florida A&M	3
Georgia	3
Houston	3
Kentucky	3
Memphis State	3
North Carolina State	3
San Diego State	3
Texas Tech	3
Virginia Tech	3
West Virginia	3

AFC ACTIVE STATISTICAL LEADERS

TOP ACTIVE PASSERS, AMERICAN FOOTBALL CONFERENCE
1,000 or more attempts

	Yrs.	Att.	Comp.	Pct. Comp.	Yards	Avg. Gain	TD	Pct. TD	Had Int.	Pct. Int.	Rating Pts.
Joe Montana, K.C.	14	4898	3110	63.5	37268	7.61	257	5.2	130	2.7	93.1
Dan Marino, Mia.	11	5434	3219	59.2	40720	7.49	298	5.5	168	3.1	88.1
Jim Kelly, Buff.	8	3494	2112	60.4	26413	7.56	179	5.1	126	3.6	86.0
Boomer Esiason, N.Y.J.	10	3851	2185	56.7	29092	7.55	190	4.9	140	3.6	82.1
Jeff Hostetler, Raiders	8	1051	601	57.2	7651	7.28	34	3.2	22	2.1	82.1
Bernie Kosar, Mia.	11	3213	1889	58.8	22314	6.94	119	3.7	81	2.5	81.9
Neil O'Donnell, Pitt.	3	1085	611	56.3	7454	6.87	38	3.5	23	2.1	80.5
Mark Rypien, Clev.	6	2207	1244	56.4	15928	7.22	101	4.6	75	3.4	80.2
John Elway, Den.	11	4890	2723	55.7	34246	7.00	183	3.7	167	3.4	75.9
Steve DeBerg, Mia.	18	4965	2844	57.3	33872	6.82	193	3.9	203	4.1	74.2
Jim Harbaugh, Ind.	7	1759	1023	58.2	11567	6.58	50	2.8	56	3.2	74.2
Don Majkowski, Ind.	7	1631	902	55.3	10975	6.73	56	3.4	57	3.5	73.1
Jay Schroeder, Cin.	9	2570	1293	50.3	18553	7.22	110	4.3	101	3.9	72.0
Vinny Testaverde, Clev.	7	2390	1256	52.6	16617	6.95	91	3.8	121	5.1	66.4
Mike Tomczak, Pitt.	9	1418	731	51.6	9828	6.93	53	3.7	68	4.8	66.4
Jack Trudeau, N.Y.J.	8	1536	812	52.9	9647	6.28	41	2.7	62	4.0	64.4
Vince Evans, Raiders	13	1182	586	49.6	8027	6.79	44	3.7	66	5.6	60.8

TOP ACTIVE RUSHERS, AFC
2,000 or more yards

	Yrs.	Att.	Yards	TD
1. Marcus Allen, K.C.	12	2296	9309	91
2. Thurman Thomas, Buff.	6	1731	7631	41
3. Earnest Byner, Clev.	10	1662	6663	48
4. John L. Williams, Pitt.	8	1148	4579	17
5. Marion Butts, N.E.	5	1031	4297	31
6. Lorenzo White, Hou.	6	809	3322	26
7. Johnny Johnson, N.Y.J.	4	806	3147	18
8. Kenneth Davis, Buff.	8	732	3132	25
9. Barry Foster, Pitt.	4	699	3092	21
10. Keith Byars, Mia.	8	814	2941	20

Other Leading Rushers

Bobby Humphrey	4	695	2857	15
Harold Green, Cin.	4	721	2843	5
Rod Bernstine, Den.	7	630	2823	21
Mark Higgs, Mia.	6	732	2764	14
Brad Baxter, N.Y.J.	5	634	2462	30
Leonard Russell, N.E.	3	689	2437	13
John Elway, Den.	11	538	2435	22
Ronnie Harmon, S.D.	8	500	2326	7
Derrick Fenner, Cin.	5	550	2149	27
Chris Warren, Sea.	4	513	2113	11
Blair Thomas, N.E.	4	468	2009	5

TOP ACTIVE PASS RECEIVERS, AFC
275 or more receptions

	Yrs.	No.	Yards	TD
1. Art Monk, N.Y.J.	14	888	12026	65
2. Andre Reed, Buff.	9	586	8233	58
3. Ernest Givins, Hou.	8	506	7414	45
4. Marcus Allen, K.C.	12	480	4496	21
5. Bill Brooks, Buff.	8	471	6532	33
John L. Williams, Pitt.	8	471	4151	16
7. Keith Byars, Mia.	8	432	4145	16
8. Irving Fryar, Mia.	10	427	6736	43
9. Webster Slaughter, Hou.	8	421	6224	36
10. Reggie Langhorne	9	411	5446	19

Other Leading Receivers

Vance Johnson, S.D.	9	403	5525	37
Ronnie Harmon, S.D.	8	401	4103	16
Earnest Byner, Clev.	10	389	3611	12
Haywood Jeffires, Hou.	7	386	4652	33
Anthony Miller, Den.	6	374	5582	37
Mark Carrier, Clev.	7	364	5764	30
Brian Blades, Sea.	6	335	4474	22
Willie Gault, Raiders	11	333	6635	44
Keith Jackson, Mia.	6	329	3963	31
Curtis Duncan, Hou.	7	322	3935	20
Tim McGee, Cin.	8	308	5028	27
Thurman Thomas, Buff.	6	295	3053	16
Pete Metzelaars, Buff.	12	280	2797	21

TOP ACTIVE SCORERS, AFC
250 or more points

	Yrs.	TD	FG	PAT	TP
1. Nick Lowery	15	0	329	486	1473
2. Gary Anderson, Pitt.	12	0	285	384	1239
3. Matt Bahr, N.E.	19	0	250	459	1209
4. Al Del Greco, Hou.	12	0	161	317	800
5. Dean Biasucci, Ind.	9	0	160	218	698
6. Marcus Allen, K.C.	12	113	0	0	678
7. Jeff Jaeger, Raiders	6	0	131	191	584
8. Pete Stoyanovich, Mia.	5	0	125	174	549
9. John Carney, S.D.	8	0	97	130	421
10. Art Monk, N.Y.J.	14	65	0	0	390

Other Leading Scorers

Steve Christie, Buff.	4	0	85	128	383
Earnest Byner, Clev.	10	61	0	0	366
Andre Reed, Buff.	9	59	0	0	354
Thurman Thomas, Buff.	6	57	0	0	342
Irving Fryar, Mia.	10	47	0	0	282
Ernest Givins, Hou.	8	46	0	0	276
Willie Gault, Raiders	11	45	0	0	270
Matt Stover, Clev.	3	0	53	98	257
John Kasay, Sea.	3	0	62	70	256

TOP ACTIVE INTERCEPTORS, AFC
20 or more interceptions

	Yrs.	No.	Yards	TD
1. Ronnie Lott, N.Y.J.	13	63	730	5
2. Gill Byrd, S.D.	10	42	546	2
3. Eugene Robinson, Sea.	9	38	536	0
Albert Lewis, Raiders	11	38	329	0
5. David Fulcher, Raiders	8	31	246	2
6. Dennis Smith, Den.	13	30	431	0
Mark Kelso	8	30	327	1
Lionel Washington, Raiders	11	30	292	2
9. Felix Wright	8	29	492	2
10. Rod Woodson, Pitt.	7	28	549	2

Other Leading Interceptors

Eugene Daniel, Ind.	10	27	240	1
Nate Odomes, Sea.	7	26	224	1
Cris Dishman, Hou.	6	23	250	0
Don Griffin, Clev.	8	22	49	0
Louis Oliver, Cin.	5	21	459	2
Gene Atkins, Mia.	7	21	324	0
Wilber Marshall, Hou.	10	21	271	3

TOP ACTIVE QUARTERBACK SACKERS, AFC (since 1982)
50 or more sacks

	Yrs.	No.
1. Greg Townsend, Raiders	11	107.5
2. Bruce Smith, Buff.	9	106.0
3. Simon Fletcher, Den.	9	85.5
4. Kevin Greene, Pitt.	9	85.0
5. Lee Williams, Hou.	10	82.5
6. Leonard Marshall	11	81.5
7. Leslie O'Neal, S.D.	7	80.5
8. Karl Mecklenburg, Den.	11	77.5
9. Ray Childress, Hou.	9	68.5
10. Derrick Thomas, K.C.	5	66.0

Other Leading Sackers

Jeff Bryant, Sea.	12	63.0
Clay Matthews, Clev.	16	62.0
Keith Willis, N.Y.J.	12	59.0
Bill Pickel, N.Y.J.	11	56.0
Neil Smith, K.C.	6	56.0
Duane Bickett	9	50.0

TOP ACTIVE PUNT RETURNERS, AFC
40 or more punt returns

	Yrs.	No.	Yards	Avg.	TD
1. Eric Metcalf, Clev.	5	92	993	10.8	3
2. Glyn Milburn, Den.	1	40	425	10.6	0
3. Tim Brown, Raiders	6	193	1960	10.2	2
4. Kelvin Martin, Sea.	7	170	1700	10.0	3
5. Irving Fryar, Mia.	10	206	2055	10.0	3
6. Dale Carter, K.C.	2	65	645	9.9	2
7. Rod Woodson, Pitt.	7	218	2043	9.4	2
8. Jeff Query, Cin.	5	76	712	9.4	0
9. Don Griffin, Clev.	8	74	667	9.0	1
10. Kitrick Taylor, Den.	6	63	568	9.0	0

Other Leading Punt Returners

Chris Warren, Sea.	4	94	819	8.7	1
Vance Johnson, S.D.	9	81	689	8.5	0
Willie Drewrey, Hou.	9	192	1597	8.3	0
Scott Miller, Mia.	3	52	423	8.1	0
Patrick Robinson, Cin.	1	43	305	7.1	0
Bill Brooks, Buff.	8	44	295	6.7	0

TOP ACTIVE KICKOFF RETURNERS, AFC
40 or more kick returns

	Yrs.	No.	Yards	Avg.	TD
1. Tim Brown, Raiders	6	47	1204	25.6	1
2. Anthony Miller, Den.	6	50	1269	25.4	2
3. Willie Gault, Raiders	11	45	1088	24.2	1
4. Vance Johnson, S.D.	9	45	1027	22.8	0
5. Jon Vaughn, Sea.	3	70	1561	22.3	2
6. Rod Woodson, Pitt.	7	205	4529	22.1	2
7. Tim McGee, Cin.	8	58	1249	21.5	0
8. Eric Ball, Cin.	5	73	1559	21.4	0
9. Steve Tasker, Buff.	11	42	896	21.3	0
10. Gene Atkins, Mia.	7	71	1508	21.2	0

Other Leading Kickoff Returners

Leonard Harris, Hou.	8	57	1193	20.9	0
Chris Warren, Sea.	4	86	1794	20.9	0
Randy Baldwin, Clev.	4	55	1133	20.6	0
Willie Drewrey, Hou.	9	102	2097	20.6	0
Harvey Williams, Raiders	3	48	982	20.5	0
Alexander Wright, Raiders	6	69	1399	20.3	2
Eric Metcalf, Clev.	5	130	2596	20.0	2
Ronnie Harmon, S.D.	8	58	1148	19.8	0
Aaron Craver, Mia.	2	40	789	19.7	0
Robert Delpino, Den.	6	68	1339	19.7	0
Dwight Stone, Pitt.	7	98	1904	19.4	1
Kelvin Martin, Sea.	7	54	1035	19.2	0
Kenneth Davis, Buff.	8	41	707	17.2	0
Mark Ingram, Mia.	7	47	742	15.8	0

TOP ACTIVE PUNTERS, AFC
50 or more punts

	Yrs.	No.	Avg.	LG
1. Tom Rouen, Den.	1	67	45.0	62
2. Rohn Stark, Ind.	12	912	43.9	72
3. Rick Tuten, Sea.	5	307	43.1	65
4. Rich Camarillo, Hou.	13	854	42.9	76
5. Jim Arnold, Mia.	11	820	42.5	71
6. Brian Hansen, N.Y.J.	9	689	42.3	73
7. Lee Johnson, Cin.	13	607	41.8	70
8. Mike Saxon, N.E.	9	664	41.6	64
9. Mark Royals, Pitt.	7	329	41.4	62
10. Jeff Gossett, Raiders	14	773	41.2	64

Other Leading Punters

John Kidd, S.D.	10	708	40.8	67
Chris Mohr, Buff.	5	272	40.1	61
Louie Aguiar, K.C.	4	210	39.6	71

TOP ACTIVE PASSERS, NATIONAL FOOTBALL CONFERENCE
1,000 or more attempts

	Yrs.	Att.	Comp.	Pct. Comp.	Yards	Avg. Gain	TD	Pct. TD	Had Int.	Pct. Int.	Rating Pts.
Steve Young, S.F.	9	1968	1222	62.1	15900	8.08	105	5.3	58	2.9	93.0
Dave Krieg, Det.	14	4178	2431	58-2	30485	7.30	217	5.2	163	3.9	82.0
Troy Aikman, Dall.	5	1920	1191	62.0	13627	7.10	69	3.6	66	3.4	81.0
Ken O'Brien	10	3602	2110	58.6	25094	6.97	128	3.6	98	2.7	80.4
Warren Moon, Minn.	10	4546	2632	57.9	33685	7.41	196	4.3	166	3.7	80.4
Randall Cunningham, Phil.	9	2751	1540	56.0	19043	6.92	131	4.8	87	3.2	80.3
Bobby Hebert, Atl.	8	2485	1465	59.0	17608	7.09	109	4.4	92	3.7	79.9
Jim McMahon, Ariz.	12	2525	1465	58.0	17884	7.08	99	3.9	87	3.4	78.7
Phil Simms, N.Y.G.	14	4647	2576	55.4	33462	7.20	199	4.3	157	3.4	78.5
Jim Everett, N.O.	8	3277	1847	56.4	23758	7.25	142	4.3	123	3.8	78.1
Steve Beuerlein, Ariz.	5	1028	551	53.6	7545	7.34	44	4.3	36	3.5	77.0
Wade Wilson, N.O.	12	2216	1261	56.9	15958	7.20	91	4.1	94	4.2	75.5
Chris Miller, Rams	7	2089	1129	54.0	14066	6.73	87	4.2	72	3.4	74.7
Rodney Peete, Dall.	5	1125	641	57.0	8164	7.26	38	3.4	49	4.4	72.9
Bubby Brister, Phil.	8	1786	957	53.6	12009	6.72	65	3.6	62	3.5	72.4
Rich Gannon, Wash.	6	1128	635	56.3	7161	6.35	43	3.8	43	3.8	72.3
Jeff George, Atl.	4	1532	874	57.0	9551	6.23	41	2.7	46	3.0	72.0
Chris Chandler, Rams	8	1066	585	54.9	6769	6.35	34	3.2	48	4.5	66.1

TOP ACTIVE RUSHERS, NFC
2,000 or more yards

	Yrs.	Att.	Yards	TD
1. Roger Craig, Minn.	11	1991	8189	56
2. Herschel Walker, Phil.	9	1794	7468	55
3. Barry Sanders, Det.	5	1432	6789	55
4. Neal Anderson	8	1515	6166	51
5. Emmitt Smith, Dall.	4	1262	5699	50
6. Dalton Hilliard, N.O.	8	1126	4164	39
7. Randall Cunningham, Phil.	9	591	4096	29
8. Rodney Hampton, N.Y.G.	4	914	3732	31
9. Gary Anderson, Det.	10	869	3409	16
10. Merril Hoge, Chi.	7	819	3115	21

Other Leading Rushers

Reggie Cobb, G.B.	4	878	3061	21
Barry Word, Minn.	6	705	2897	16
Steve Young, S.F.	9	431	2676	20
Cleveland Gary, Rams	5	667	2634	24
Brad Muster, N.O.	6	519	2228	23
Heath Sherman, Phil.	5	537	2130	10
Craig Heyward	6	500	2019	13

TOP ACTIVE PASS RECEIVERS, NFC
275 or more receptions

	Yrs.	No.	Yards	TD
1. Jerry Rice, S.F.	9	708	11770	118
2. Gary Clark, Ariz.	9	612	9560	62
3. Henry Ellard, Wash.	11	593	9761	48
4. Roger Craig, Minn.	11	566	4911	17
5. Eric Martin, N.O.	9	532	7854	48
6. Sterling Sharpe, G.B.	6	501	7015	47
7. Steve Jordan, Minn.	12	495	6284	28
8. Anthony Carter, Det.	9	478	7636	52
9. Ricky Sanders	8	414	5854	36
10. Herschel Walker, Phil.	9	410	3887	16

Other Leading Receivers

Andre Rison, Atl.	5	394	5365	52
Rodney Holman, Det.	12	343	4573	36
Michael Irvin, Dall.	6	337	5694	34
Mark Jackson, N.Y.G.	8	334	5454	28
Mark Bavaro, Phil.	8	334	4518	36
Cris Carter, Minn.	7	327	4577	42
Jay Novacek, Dall.	9	313	3450	23
Gary Anderson, Det.	10	302	2999	15
Neal Anderson	8	302	2763	20
Jessie Hester, Rams	8	298	4807	23
Tom Rathman, S.F.	8	294	2490	8
John Taylor, S.F.	7	277	4680	36

TOP ACTIVE SCORERS, NFC
250 or more points

	Yrs.	TD	FG	PAT	TP
1. Eddie Murray, Phil.	16	0	277	432	1263
2. Morten Andersen, N.O.	12	0	274	380	1202
3. Norm Johnson, Atl.	12	0	222	444	1110
4. Kevin Butler, Chi.	9	0	199	318	915
5. Tony Zendejas, Rams	9	0	165	283	778
6. Jerry Rice, S.F.	9	124	0	0	744
7. Chip Lohmiller, Wash.	6	0	155	232	697
8. Mike Cofer, S.F.	7	0	129	294	681
9. Fuad Reveiz, Minn.	10	0	128	293	677
10. Greg Davis, Ariz.	9	0	122	180	546

Other Leading Scorers

David Treadwell	5	0	124	160	532
Chris Jacke, G.B.	5	0	116	166	514
Roger Craig, Minn.	11	73	0	0	438
Herschel Walker, Phil.	9	72	0	0	432
Neal Anderson	8	71	0	0	426
Gary Clark, Ariz.	9	62	0	0	372
Barry Sanders, Det.	5	60	0	0	360
Anthony Carter, Det.	9	54	0	0	324
Dalton Hilliard, N.O.	8	53	0	0	318
Emmitt Smith, Dall.	4	53	0	0	318
Henry Ellard, Wash.	11	52	0	0	312
Andre Rison, Atl.	5	52	0	0	312
Eric Martin, N.O.	9	48	0	0	288
Sterling Sharpe, G.B.	6	48	0	0	288
Cris Carter, Minn.	7	43	0	0	258

TOP ACTIVE INTERCEPTORS, NFC
20 or more interceptions

	Yrs.	No.	Yards	TD
1. Darrell Green, Wash.	11	34	276	2
2. Eric Allen, Phil.	6	31	421	5
3. Kevin Ross, Atl.	10	30	551	2
Wes Hopkins	10	30	241	1
5. Carl Lee	11	29	349	2
Tim McKyer, Det.	8	29	136	1
6. Jerry Gray, T.B.	9	28	374	3
Mike Prior, G.B.	8	28	352	1
Scott Case, Atl.	10	28	255	1
9. Vencie Glenn, Minn.	10	26	398	1
10. Deion Sanders, Atl.	5	24	520	3

Other Leading Interceptors

Tim McDonald, S.F.	7	23	338	1
Terry Taylor, Rams	10	21	228	2
Thomas Everett, T.B.	7	20	229	0

TOP ACTIVE QUARTERBACK SACKERS, NFC (since 1982)
50 or more sacks

	Yrs.	No.
1. Reggie White, G.B.	9	137.0
2. Richard Dent, S.F.	11	124.5
3. Rickey Jackson, N.O.	13	115.0
4. Steve McMichael, G.B.	14	92.5
5. Chris Doleman, Atl.	9	88.5
Sean Jones, G.B.	10	88.5
7. Jim Jeffcoat, Dall.	11	86.5
8. Pat Swilling, Det.	8	83.0
9. Charles Mann	11	82.0
10. Clyde Simmons, Ariz.	8	76.0

Other Leading Sackers

Tim Harris, Phil.	8	75.0
Charles Haley, Dall.	8	73.5
Freddie Joe Nunn, Ariz.	9	66.5
Michael Cofer, Det.	10	62.5
William Fuller, Phil.	8	59.0
Keith Millard	10	58.0

TOP ACTIVE PUNT RETURNERS, NFC
40 or more punt returns

	Yrs.	No.	Yards	Avg.	TD
1. Mel Gray, Det.	8	160	1851	11.6	3
2. Henry Ellard, Wash.	11	135	1527	11.3	4
Darrell Green, Wash.	11	51	576	11.3	0
4. David Meggett, N.Y.G.	5	176	1907	10.8	4
5. John Taylor, S.F.	7	138	1461	10.6	2
6. Mitchell Price, Rams	9	50	513	10.3	2
7. Brian Mitchell, Wash.	4	115	1171	10.2	3
8. Johnny Bailey, Ariz.	4	127	1225	9.6	2
9. Anthony Parker, Minn.	5	42	400	9.5	0
10. Clifford Hicks, Rams	9	100	942	9.4	0

Other Leading Punt Returners

Terance Mathis, Atl.	4	50	445	8.9	1
Tony Smith, Atl.	2	48	410	8.5	0
Deion Sanders, Atl.	5	93	789	8.5	2

TOP ACTIVE KICKOFF RETURNERS, NFC
40 or more kick returns

	Yrs.	No.	Yards	Avg.	TD
1. Tony Smith, Atl.	2	45	1120	24.9	1
2. Mel Gray, Det.	8	264	6374	24.1	3
3. Corey Harris, G.B.	4	49	1173	23.9	0
4. Robert Brooks, G.B.	2	41	949	23.1	1
5. Deion Sanders, Atl.	5	147	3388	23.0	3
6. Nate Lewis, Rams	4	92	2047	22.3	1
7. Herschel Walker, Phil.	9	76	1676	22.1	1
8. Charles Wilson, T.B.	4	82	1797	21.9	1
9. Qadry Ismail, Minn.	1	42	902	21.5	0
10. Johnny Bailey, Ariz.	4	98	2063	21.1	0

Other Leading Kickoff Returners

David Meggett, N.Y.G.	5	117	2441	20.9	1
Marc Logan, S.F.	7	85	1760	20.7	1
Dexter Carter, S.F.	4	105	2171	20.7	1
Brian Mitchell, Wash.	4	103	2118	20.6	0

TOP ACTIVE PUNTERS, NFC
50 or more punts

	Yrs.	No.	Avg.	LG
1. Greg Montgomery, Det.	6	310	43.6	77
2. Reggie Roby, Wash.	11	633	43.4	77
Sean Landeta, Rams	9	568	43.4	71
4. Harold Alexander, Atl.	1	72	43.3	75
5. Tommy Barnhardt, N.O.	9	387	42.8	65
6. Harry Newsome	9	683	42.5	84
7. Mike Horan, N.Y.G.	11	601	42.3	75
8. John Jett, Dall.	1	56	41.8	59
9. Scott Fulhage, Atl.	6	399	41.4	65
10. Chris Gardocki, Chi.	3	159	40.7	61

Other Leading Punters

Bryan Wagner, G.B.	7	404	40.6	71
Jeff Feagles, Ariz.	6	478	40.4	77
Dan Stryzinski, T.B.	4	306	40.0	63
Klaus Wilmsmeyer, S.F.	2	91	40.0	61

Don Shula, celebrating his twenty-fifth season in Miami, enters his thirty-second overall season as an NFL head coach. Shula, the all-time winningest coach in NFL history with 327 career victories (including postseason), needs 10 regular-season wins to record the most regular-season victories in history, surpassing George Halas, who amassed 318 in 40 years as head coach of the Chicago Bears.

Tom Flores, Seattle, and **Marty Schottenheimer**, Kansas City, each need just 1 win to reach 100 career victories. Flores has recorded his 99 wins in 11 NFL seasons and Schottenheimer has 99 in 10.

Wayne Fontes, Detroit, needs 13 wins to become the Lions' all-time winningest coach, surpassing Buddy Parker (50), Potsy Clark (54), and George Wilson (55). Fontes has recorded 43 victories in six seasons as Lions head coach.

Jerry Rice, San Francisco, needs 3 touchdowns to become the NFL's all-time touchdown scoring leader, surpassing Jim Brown who tallied 126 in his nine-year NFL career, and Walter Payton, with 125 in 13 seasons. Rice has totaled 124 touchdowns (118 receiving, 6 rushing) during his nine-year NFL career.

Rice is the 49ers' all-time leader with 11,776 receiving yards and needs 224 yards to become the fifth receiver in NFL history to reach 12,000 career yards.

Dan Marino, Miami, needs 2,321 yards to move past Dan Fouts (43,040) into second place on the NFL's all-time passing yardage chart behind Fran Tarkenton (47,003). Marino has passed for 40,720 yards during his 11 NFL seasons. Marino (3,219 completions and 5,434 attempts) needs just 79 completions and 171 attempts to surpass Fouts in both categories and move into second place behind Tarkenton (3,686 completions and 6,467 attempts). Marino (298) also needs 2 touchdown passes to become only the second player in NFL history to reach 300 touchdown passes during a career. Tarkenton threw 342 scoring passes during his 18-year NFL career.

Marino (17) needs just one more game with at least 4 touchdown passes to break a tie for the NFL record with Johnny Unitas.

Emmitt Smith, Dallas, can become only the second player in history to win four consecutive rushing titles. Smith, who led the league with 1,486 yards in 1993, 1,713 yards in 1992, and 1,563 yards in 1991, would join Jim Brown, who won five consecutive rushing titles from 1957-61.

Steve Jordan, Minnesota, needs 47 receptions to pass Kellen Winslow (541) and move into second place on the NFL's all-time receiving list for tight ends. Jordan has 495 receptions in 12 NFL seasons. Ozzie Newsome is the NFL's all-time tight end leader with 662 receptions.

Joe Montana, Kansas City, needs 2,732 passing yards to become the fifth player in history to throw for 40,000 career yards, joining Fran Tarkenton (47,003), Dan Fouts (43,040), Dan Marino (40,720), and Johnny Unitas (40,239). Montana has passed for 37,268 yards in 15 NFL seasons.

Sterling Sharpe, Green Bay, enters 1994 with 501 receptions in his six seasons with the Packers and needs 30 more to pass James Lofton, the Packers' career leader with 530 catches. Sharpe became the first receiver in history to accumulate 100 receptions in two consecutive seasons (108 in 1992, 112 in 1993).

Marcus Allen, Kansas City, has scored 113 touchdowns (91 rushing, 21 receiving, and 1 return) in 12 NFL seasons to tie Lenny Moore for fifth on the all-time chart. With 14 touchdowns, Allen could become the all-time touchdown scorer in NFL history, surpassing Jim Brown (126), Walter Payton (125), Jerry Rice (124, active), and John Riggins (116).

John Elway, Denver, can tie Dan Marino's NFL record nine seasons passing for 3,000-or-more yards. Elway has posted eight 3,000-yard passing seasons in 11 years with the Broncos. Elway also has passed for 34,246 yards and needs 754 more to become the sixth quarterback to reach 35,000 career yards. Elway (183) also needs 17 touchdown passes to become the sixteenth quarterback to throw for 200 touchdowns.

Mel Gray, Detroit, needs 549 yards to surpass Ron Smith (6,922) as the NFL's all-time kickoff return yardage leader. Gray has amassed 6,374 kickoff return yards in eight NFL seasons. Gray (264) also needs 12 kickoff returns to pass Smith, who is the league's all-time leader with 275 career kickoff returns.

Andre Rison, Atlanta, needs 18 catches to surpass Alfred Jenkins (359 receptions) as the club's all-time reception leader . Rison has 342 receptions for 4,547 yards in four seasons with Atlanta.

Steve Young, San Francisco, can extend his NFL-record streak of three consecutive seasons with a passer rating of more than 100. Young, who achieved passer ratings of 101.8 in 1991 and 107.0 in 1992, completed 314 of 462 for a club single-season record 4,023 yards with 29 touchdowns and 16 interceptions for a passer rating of 101.5 in 1993.

Phil Simms, New York Giants, needs just 1 touchdown pass to become the sixteenth quarterback in history to throw for 200 scores. Simms has tallied his 199 touchdown passes in 15 NFL seasons.

Ernest Givins, Houston, needs 64 receiving yards to break Drew Hill's club-record 7,477. Givins has 7,414 receiving yards in eight seasons with the Oilers. Givins is the team's all-time pass-catcher with 506 receptions.

Troy Aikman, Dallas, has thrown for at least 3,000 yards in each of the past two seasons (3,445 in 1992 and 3,100 in 1993). With at least 3,000 yards in 1994, he would become the first quarterback in club history to throw for over 3,000 yards in 3 consecutive seasons.

Thurman Thomas, Buffalo, needs six more 100-yard rushing performances to exceed Hall of Fame running back O.J. Simpson's club-record 41. Thomas has rushed for more than 100 yards in 36 career games.

Warren Moon, Minnesota, needs 4 more touchdown passes to reach 200 in his career. Moon threw 196 touchdown passes in 10 seasons with the Houston Oilers.

Moon has passed for 33,685 yards and needs 1,315 to become the sixth quarterback in history to reach 35,000 passing yards.

Darrell Green, Washington, has 34 career interceptions in 11 seasons with the Redskins, 3 from surpassing the club's all-time leader, Brig Owens, who had 36 career interceptions.

Jim Kelly, Buffalo, needs 3 touchdown passes to become the Bills' all-time leader, surpassing Joe Ferguson (181). Kelly has thrown 179 touchdowns in his eight-year career with the Bills. Kelly (26,413 yards and 2,112 completions) also needs 1,178 yards and 77 completions to surpass club-leader Ferguson in those two categories.

Monte Coleman, Washington, needs to play in just six more games to pass Art Monk (205) in first place on the club's all-time list for games played. Coleman has played in 200 games during his 15-year career with the Redskins. In addition, Coleman will play his sixteenth season with the team, equaling Sammy Baugh's record of service with the Redskins.

Eric Green, Pittsburgh, needs 1 touchdown reception to break a tie with Bennie Cunningham (20) and move into first place on the club's all-time list for touchdowns by a tight end. Green (152 receptions and 2,063 yards) also needs 51 receptions and 817 yards to pass Cunningham in those two tight end categories.

Boomer Esiason, New York Jets, needs 908 yards to become the eighteenth quarterback in history to throw for 30,000 career passing yards. Esiason has passed for 29,092 yards in 10 NFL seasons.

Reggie Brooks, Washington, gained 1,063 rushing yards in his rookie season. Brooks can become the first Redskins' rusher to gain over 1,000 yards in each of his first two NFL seasons.

Chris Jacke, Green Bay, has made 116 field goals in five seasons with the Packers and needs 5 more to break Chester Marcol's club record of 120.

Paul Gruber, Tampa Bay, has started all 90 games in which he has played since being drafted in 1988. With 10 consecutive starts, Gruber would become the first Buccaneers player to start his first 100 games.

EXPANSION TEAMS TO BEGIN PLAY IN 1995

CAROLINA PANTHERS

Team Colors: Black, Panther Blue,
and Silver
Suite 1600
227 West Trade Street
Charlotte, North Carolina 28202
Telephone: (704) 358-7000

CLUB OFFICIALS
Founder/Owner: Jerry Richardson
President: Mike McCormack
General Manager: Bill Polian
Director of Business Operations:
Mark Richardson
Assistant Director of Business Operations:
Charles Waddell
Counsel: Richard Thigpen
Chief Financial Officer: Dave Olsen
Controller: Lisa Garber
Director of Stadium Operations:
Jon Richardson
Assistant General Manager: Joe Mack
Director Player Personnel: Dom Anile
Pro Scout: Mike Murphy
Scouts: Edwin Bailey, Boyd Dowler,
Ralph Hawkins

Director of Marketing/Communications:
Charlie Dayton
Director of Ticket Sales: Phil Youtsey
Director of Community Affairs/Player
Relations: Donnie Shell
Director of Family Programs: B.J. Waymer
Director of Information Systems:
Roger Goss
Video Director: Dave Sutherby
Trainer: John Kasik
1995 Stadium Site: Clemson Stadium•
Capacity: 82,000
Clemson, South Carolina
Stadium Beginning 1996:
Carolinas Stadium•
Capacity: 73,000
Charlotte, North Carolina 28202
Training Camp: Wofford College
Spartanburg, SC 29303

CAROLINAS STADIUM

N

JACKSONVILLE JAGUARS

Team Colors: Teal, Gold, and Black
One Stadium Place
Jacksonville, Florida 32202
Telephone: (904) 633-6000

CLUB OFFICIALS
Chairman and Chief Executive Officer:
Wayne Weaver
President and Chief Operating Officer:
David Seldin
Head Coach: Tom Coughlin
Vice President-Football Operations:
Michael Huyghue
Senior Vice President-Marketing:
Dan Connell
Vice President-Ticket Operations:
Judy Seldin
Vice President-Broadcasting and Creative
Services: Peter Scheurmier
Executive Director of Communications:
Dan Edwards
Executive Director of Administration:
John Jones
Defensive Assistant Coach: Randy Edsall
Defensive Assistant Coach: Steve Szabo
Offensive Assistant Coach:
Pete Carmichael
Offensive Assistant Coach: Jerald Ingram
Offensive Assistant Coach: Mike Maser
Director of College Scouting:
Richard Reiprish
Director of Pro Personnel: Ron Hill

Assistant Director of Pro Personnel:
Fran Foley
Scouts: Tim Mingey, Rick Mueller,
Gene Smith
Video Director: Mike Perkins
Head Trainer: Michael Ryan
Equipment Manager: Bob Monica
Director of Finance: David Blasic
Director of Special Events and Promotions:
Ann Carroll
Director of Corporate Sponsorship:
David Rowan
Manager of Contract Information:
Daren Anderson
Manager of Football Operations:
Joe Baker
Manager of Football Projects:
Ron Williams
Manager of Office Services: Karen Battle
Manager of Ticketholder Services:
Steve Greenfield
Manager of Stadium Club Programs:
Melissa Scott
Corporate Sponsorship Representative:
Macky Weaver

GATOR BOWL

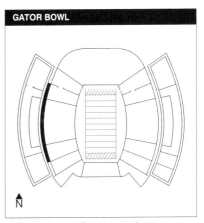

N

Public Relations Representative:
David Auchter
Production Assistant: Joe Bailey
Executive Assistant, Office of the
President: Sandy Dodd
Executive Assistant, Head Coach:
Joanna Raney
Executive Assistant, Vice President-
Football Operations: Pam Yonge
Stadium: Gator Bowl •**Capacity:** 73,000
One Stadium Place
Jacksonville, Florida 32202
Playing Surface: Grass
Training Camp: TBA

The AFC

American Football Conference
Eastern Division
Team Colors: Royal Blue, Scarlet Red, and White
One Bills Drive
Orchard Park, New York 14127-2296
Telephone: (716) 648-1800

CLUB OFFICIALS

President: Ralph C. Wilson
Exec. V.P./General Manager: John Butler
V.P./Administration: Jerry Foran
Corporate V.P.: Linda Bogdan
V.P./Head Coach: Marv Levy
Treasurer: Jeffrey C. Littmann
Asst. G.M./Business Operations: Bill Munson
Director of Business Operations: Jim Overdorf
Director of Marketing and Sales: John Livsey
Director of Merchandising: Christy Wilson Hofmann
Director of Player Personnel: Dwight Adams
Director of Pro Personnel: A.J. Smith
Director of Player/Alumni Relations: Jerry Butler
Director of Public/Community Relations: Denny Lynch
Director of Media Relations: Scott Berchtold
Director of Stadium Operations: George Koch
Stadium Operations Supervisor: Pete Reidy
Director of Security: Bill Bambach
Ticket Director: June Foran
Equipment Manager: Dave Hojnowski
Strength/Conditioning Coordinator: Rusty Jones
Trainers: Ed Abramoski, Bud Carpenter, Bill Ford
Video Director: Henry Kunttu
Stadium: Rich Stadium •**Capacity:** 80,437
  One Bills Drive
  Orchard Park, New York 14127-2296
Playing Surface: AstroTurf
Training Camp: Fredonia State University
                Fredonia, New York 14063

1994 SCHEDULE

PRESEASON
Aug. 8	**Washington**	8:00
Aug. 12	at Atlanta	7:00
Aug. 20	vs. Houston at San Antonio, Tex.	7:00
Aug. 26	**Kansas City**	8:00

REGULAR SEASON
Sept. 4	**New York Jets**	4:00
Sept. 11	at New England	1:00
Sept. 18	at Houston	12:00
Sept. 26	**Denver** (Monday)	9:00
Oct. 2	at Chicago	3:00
Oct. 9	**Miami**	1:00
Oct. 16	**Indianapolis**	1:00
Oct. 23	Open Date	
Oct. 30	**Kansas City**	1:00
Nov. 6	at New York Jets	4:00
Nov. 14	at Pittsburgh (Monday)	9:00
Nov. 20	**Green Bay**	1:00
Nov. 24	at Detroit (Thanksgiving)	12:30
Dec. 4	at Miami	8:00
Dec. 11	**Minnesota**	1:00
Dec. 18	**New England**	1:00
Dec. 24	at Indianapolis	1:00

RECORD HOLDERS

INDIVIDUAL RECORDS—CAREER
Category	Name	Performance
Rushing (Yds.)	O.J. Simpson, 1969-1977	10,183
Passing (Yds.)	Joe Ferguson, 1973-1984	27,590
Passing (TDs)	Joe Ferguson, 1973-1984	181
Receiving (No.)	Andre Reed, 1985-1993	586
Receiving (Yds.)	Andre Reed, 1985-1993	8,233
Interceptions	George (Butch) Byrd, 1964-1970	40
Punting (Avg.)	Paul Maguire, 1964-1970	42.1
Punt Return (Avg.)	Keith Moody, 1976-79	10.5
Kickoff Return (Avg.)	Wallace Francis, 1973-74	27.2
Field Goals	Scott Norwood, 1985-1991	133
Touchdowns (Tot.)	O.J. Simpson, 1969-1977	70
Points	Scott Norwood, 1985-1991	670

INDIVIDUAL RECORDS—SINGLE SEASON
Category	Name	Performance
Rushing (Yds.)	O.J. Simpson, 1973	2,003
Passing (Yds.)	Jim Kelly, 1991	3,844
Passing (TDs)	Jim Kelly, 1991	33
Receiving (No.)	Andre Reed, 1989	88
Receiving (Yds.)	Andre Reed, 1989	1,312
Interceptions	Billy Atkins, 1961	10
	Tom Janik, 1967	10
Punting (Avg.)	Billy Atkins, 1961	44.5
Punt Return (Avg.)	Keith Moody, 1977	13.1
Kickoff Return (Avg.)	Ed Rutkowski, 1963	30.2
Field Goals	Scott Norwood, 1988	32
Touchdowns (Tot.)	O.J. Simpson, 1975	23
Points	O.J. Simpson, 1975	138

INDIVIDUAL RECORDS—SINGLE GAME
Category	Name	Performance
Rushing (Yds.)	O.J. Simpson, 11-25-76	273
Passing (Yds.)	Joe Ferguson, 10-9-83	419
Passing (TDs)	Jim Kelly, 9-8-91	6
Receiving (No.)	Greg Bell, 9-8-85	13
	Andre Reed, 9-18-89	13
	Thurman Thomas, 9-15-91	13
Receiving (Yds.)	Jerry Butler, 9-23-79	255
Interceptions	Many Times	3
	Last time by Jeff Nixon, 9-7-80	
Field Goals	Pete Gogolak, 12-5-65	5
	Scott Norwood, 9-25-88	5
Touchdowns (Tot.)	Cookie Gilchrist, 12-8-63	5
Points	Cookie Gilchrist, 12-8-63	30

COACHING HISTORY
(247-269-8)
1960-61	Buster Ramsey	11-16-1
1962-65	Lou Saban	38-18-3
1966-68	Joe Collier*	13-17-1
1968	Harvey Johnson	1-10-1
1969-70	John Rauch	7-20-1
1971	Harvey Johnson	1-13-0
1972-76	Lou Saban**	32-29-1
1976-77	Jim Ringo	3-20-0
1978-82	Chuck Knox	38-38-0
1983-85	Kay Stephenson***	10-26-0
1985-86	Hank Bullough****	4-17-0
1986-93	Marv Levy	89-45-0

*Released after two games in 1968
**Resigned after five games in 1976
***Released after four games in 1985
****Released after nine games in 1986

RICH STADIUM

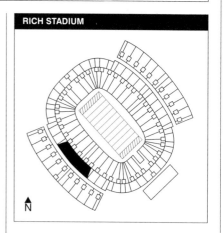

N

1993 TEAM RECORD

PRESEASON (2-3)

Date	Result		Opponents
7/30	L	7-14	at Detroit
8/7	L	6-20	vs. Minnesota at Berlin
8/12	W	30-7	at Kansas City
8/21	L	12-32	vs. Tampa Bay at Orlando
8/27	W	17-16	Atlanta

REGULAR SEASON (12-4)

Date	Result		Opponents	Att.
9/5	W	38-14	New England	79,751
9/12	W	13-10	at Dallas	63,226
9/26	L	13-22	Miami	79,635
10/3	W	17-14	N.Y. Giants	79,283
10/11	W	35-7	Houston	79,613
10/24	W	19-10	at N.Y. Jets	71,541
11/1	W	24-10	Washington	79,106
11/7	W	13-10	at New England (OT)	54,326
11/15	L	0-23	at Pittsburgh	60,265
11/21	W	23-9	Indianapolis	79,101
11/28	L	7-23	at Kansas City	74,452
12/5	L	24-25	L.A. Raiders	79,478
12/12	W	10-7	at Philadelphia	60,769
12/19	W	47-34	at Miami	71,597
12/26	W	16-14	N.Y. Jets	70,817
1/2	W	30-10	at Indianapolis	43,028

POSTSEASON (2-1)

Date	Result		Opponents	Att.
1/15	W	29-23	L.A. Raiders	61,923
1/23	W	30-13	Kansas City	76,642
1/30	L	13-30	Dallas	72,817

(OT) Overtime

SCORE BY PERIODS

Bills	64	113	51	98	3	—	329
Opponents	71	62	67	42	0	—	242

ATTENDANCE

Home 626,784   Away 499,204   Total 1,125,988
Single-game home record, 80,366 (9-29-91)
Single-season home record, 635,899 (1991)*
*NFL record

1993 TEAM STATISTICS

	Bills	Opp.
Total First Downs	316	331
Rushing	117	114
Passing	176	199
Penalty	23	18
Third Down: Made/Att	98/225	107/235
Third Down Pct.	43.6	45.5
Fourth Down: Made/Att	5/8	6/18
Fourth Down Pct.	62.5	33.3
Total Net Yards	5260	5554
Avg. Per Game	328.8	347.1
Total Plays	1078	1119
Avg. Per Play	4.9	5.0
Net Yards Rushing	1943	1921
Avg. Per Game	121.4	120.1
Total Rushes	550	500
Net Yards Passing	3317	3633
Avg. Per Game	207.3	227.1
Sacked/Yards Lost	31/218	37/256
Gross Yards	3535	3889
Att./Completions	497/304	582/323
Completion Pct.	61.2	55.5
Had Intercepted	18	23
Punts/Avg.	74/40.4	65/41.8
Net Punting Avg.	74/36.0	65/35.1
Penalties/Yards Lost	94/630	99/681
Fumbles/Ball Lost	26/17	35/24
Touchdowns	37	25
Rushing	12	7
Passing	20	18
Returns	5	0
Avg. Time of Possession	27:30	32:30

1993 INDIVIDUAL STATISTICS

PASSING	Att	Cmp	Yds.	Pct.	TD	Int	Tkld.	Rate
Kelly	470	288	3382	61.3	18	18	25/171	79.9
Reich	26	16	153	61.5	2	0	6/47	103.5
Thomas	1	0	0	0.0	0	0	0/0	39.6
Bills	497	304	3535	61.2	20	18	31/218	81.0
Opponents	582	323	3889	55.5	18	23	37/256	70.0

SCORING	TD R	TD P	TD Rt	PAT	FG	Saf	PTS
Christie	0	0	0	36/37	23/32	0	105
K. Davis	6	0	0	0/0	0/0	0	36
Reed	0	6	0	0/0	0/0	0	36
Thomas	6	0	0	0/0	0/0	0	36
Brooks	0	5	0	0/0	0/0	0	30
Metzelaars	0	4	0	0/0	0/0	0	24
Beebe	0	3	0	0/0	0/0	0	18
Jones	0	0	1	0/0	0/0	1	8
Copeland	0	0	1	0/0	0/0	0	6
Gardner	0	1	0	0/0	0/0	0	6
McKeller	0	1	0	0/0	0/0	0	6
Odomes	0	0	1	0/0	0/0	0	6
Talley	0	0	1	0/0	0/0	0	6
Washington	0	0	1	0/0	0/0	0	6
Bills	12	20	5	36/37	23/32	1	329
Opponents	7	18	0	23/25	23/35	0	242

RUSHING	No.	Yds.	Avg.	LG	TD
Thomas	355	1315	3.7	27	6
K. Davis	109	391	3.6	19	6
Kelly	36	102	2.8	17	0
Gardner	20	56	2.8	8	0
Turner	11	36	3.3	10	0
Brooks	3	30	10.0	15	0
Reed	9	21	2.3	15	0
Fina	1	-2	-2.0	-2	0
Reich	6	-6	-1.0	-1	0
Bills	550	1943	3.5	27	12
Opponents	500	1921	3.8	35	7

RECEIVING	No.	Yds.	Avg.	LG	TD
Metzelaars	68	609	9.0	51	4
Brooks	60	714	11.9	32	5
Reed	52	854	16.4	65t	6
Thomas	48	387	8.1	37	0
Beebe	31	504	16.3	65t	3
K. Davis	21	95	4.5	28	0
Copeland	13	242	18.6	60	0
Gardner	4	50	12.5	22	1
McKeller	3	35	11.7	13t	1
Tasker	2	26	13.0	22	0
Awalt	2	19	9.5	14	0
Bills	304	3535	11.6	65t	20
Opponents	323	3889	12.0	54t	18

INTERCEPTIONS	No.	Yds.	Avg.	LG	TD
Odomes	9	65	7.2	25	0
Talley	3	74	24.7	61t	1
Jones	2	92	46.0	85t	1
Darby	2	32	16.0	32	0
Williams	2	11	5.5	6	0
M. Patton	2	0	0.0	0	0
Washington	1	27	27.0	27t	1
Bennett	1	5	5.0	5	0
B. Smith	1	0	0.0	0	0
Bills	23	306	13.3	85t	3
Opponents	18	174	9.7	35	0

PUNTING	No.	Yds.	Avg.	In 20	LG
Mohr	74	2991	40.4	19	58
Bills	74	2991	40.4	19	58
Opponents	65	2719	41.8	20	58

PUNT RETURNS	No.	FC	Yds.	Avg.	LG	TD
Copeland	31	7	274	8.8	47t	1
Brooks	1	0	3	3.0	3	0
Tasker	1	0	0	0.0	0	0
Bills	33	7	277	8.4	47t	1
Opponents	29	24	247	8.5	27	0

KICKOFF RETURNS	No.	Yds.	Avg.	LG	TD
Copeland	24	436	18.2	28	0
Beebe	10	160	16.0	22	0
K. Davis	8	100	12.5	18	0
Lamb	2	40	20.0	23	0
Turner	1	10	10.0	10	0
Bills	45	746	16.6	28	0
Opponents	43	850	19.8	49	0

SACKS	No.
B. Smith	14.0
Bennett	5.0
Wright	4.5
Hansen	3.5
Barnett	2.0
Jones	2.0
Talley	2.0
Goganious	1.0
Parrella	1.0
M. Patton	1.0
Lodish	0.5
Washington	0.5
Bills	37.0
Opponents	31.0

1994 DRAFT CHOICES

Round	Name	Pos.	College
1	Jeff Burris	DB	Notre Dame
2	Bucky Brooks	WR	North Carolina
	Lonnie Johnson	TE	Florida State
	Sam Rogers	LB	Colorado
3	Marlo Perry	LB	Jackson State
	Corey Louchiey	T	South Carolina
4	Sean Crocker	DB	North Carolina
5	A.J. Ofodile	TE	Missouri
6	Anthony Abrams	DT	Clark, Ga.
	Kevin Knox	WR	Florida State
7	Filmel Johnson	DB	Illinois

BUFFALO BILLS

1994 VETERAN ROSTER

No.		Name	Pos.	Ht.	Wt.	Birthdate	NFL Exp.	College	Hometown	How Acq.	'93 Games/ Starts
86	#	Awalt, Rob	TE	6-5	242	4/9/64	8	San Diego State	Sacramento, Calif.	FA-'92	12/1
77		Barnett, Oliver	DE	6-3	292	4/9/66	5	Kentucky	Louisville, Ky.	RFA(Atl)-'93	16/6
82		Beebe, Don	WR	5-11	180	12/18/64	6	Chadron State	Sugar Grove, Ill.	D3-'89	14/14
97		Bennett, Cornelius	LB	6-2	238	8/25/65	8	Alabama	Birmingham, Ala.	T(Ind)-'87	16/16
80		Brooks, Bill	WR	6-0	189	4/6/64	9	Boston University	Framingham, Mass.	UFA(Ind)-'93	16/13
96		Brown, Monty	LB	6-0	228	4/13/70	2	Ferris State	Bridgeport, Mich.	FA-'93	13/0
2		Christie, Steve	K	6-0	185	11/13/67	5	William & Mary	Oakville, Canada	PB(TB)-'92	16/0
85		Copeland, Russell	WR	6-0	200	11/4/71	2	Memphis State	Tupelo, Miss.	D4-'93	16/2
66		Crafts, Jerry	T	6-6	351	1/6/68	3	Louisville	Tulsa, Okla.	FA-'93	16/0
43		Darby, Matt	S	6-1	200	11/19/68	3	UCLA	Virginia Beach, Va.	D5-'92	16/3
65		Davis, John	G	6-4	310	8/22/65	8	Georgia Tech	Ellijay, Ga.	PB(Hou)-'89	16/16
23		Davis, Kenneth	RB	5-10	208	4/16/62	9	Texas Christian	Temple, Tex.	PB(GB)-'89	16/0
62		Devlin, Mike	C	6-1	293	11/16/69	2	Iowa	Marlton, N.J.	D5a-'93	12/0
70		Fina, John	T-G	6-4	285	3/11/69	3	Arizona	Tucson, Ariz.	D1-'92	16/16
33		Fuller, Eddie	RB	5-9	198	6/22/68	5	Louisiana State	Leesville, La.	D4-'90	7/0
35		Gardner, Carwell	RB	6-2	244	11/27/66	5	Louisville	Louisville, Ky.	D2-'90	13/2
50		Goganious, Keith	LB	6-2	239	12/7/68	3	Penn State	Virginia Beach, Va.	D3-'92	16/7
26		Gulledge, David	S	6-1	203	10/26/67	2	Jacksonville State	Pell City, Ala.	FA-'94	0*
90		Hansen, Phil	DE	6-5	278	5/20/68	4	North Dakota State	Ellendale, N.D.	D2-'91	11/9
36	†	Henderson, Jerome	CB-S	5-10	189	8/8/69	4	Clemson	Statesville, N.C.	FA-'93	3/0*
67		Hull, Kent	C	6-5	284	1/13/61	9	Mississippi State	Greenwood, Miss.	FA-'86	14/13
20		Jones, Henry	S	5-11	197	12/29/67	4	Illinois	St. Louis, Mo.	D1-'91	16/16
12		Kelly, Jim	QB	6-3	226	2/14/60	9	Miami	East Brady, Pa.	D1b-'83	16/16
63		Lingner, Adam	C	6-4	268	11/2/60	12	Illinois	Rock Island, Ill.	PB(KC)-'89	16/0
73		Lodish, Mike	NT	6-3	280	8/11/67	5	UCLA	Birmingham, Mich.	D10-'90	15/1
55		Maddox, Mark	LB	6-1	233	3/23/68	4	Northern Michigan	Milwaukee, Wis.	D9-'91	11/8
84	#	McKeller, Keith	TE	6-4	242	7/9/64	8	Jacksonville State	Fairfield, Ala.	D9-'87	8/1
88		Metzelaars, Pete	TE	6-7	254	5/24/60	13	Wabash	Portage, Mich.	T(Sea)-'85	16/16
9		Mohr, Chris	P	6-5	215	5/11/66	5	Alabama	Thomson, Ga.	FA-'91	16/0
74	†	Parker, Glenn	G-T	6-5	305	4/22/66	5	Arizona	Huntington Beach, Calif.	D3-'90	16/9
92		Parrella, John	DE-NT	6-3	296	11/22/69	2	Nebraska	Topeka, Kan.	D2-'93	10/0
44		Paterra, Greg	RB	5-11	224	5/11/67	3	Slippery Rock	McKeesport, Pa.	FA-'94	0*
99		Patton, James	DE-NT	6-3	287	1/5/70	3	Texas	Houston, Tex.	D2-'92	2/0
53		Patton, Marvcus	LB	6-2	243	5/1/67	5	UCLA	Lawndale, Calif.	D8-'90	16/16
94		Pike, Mark	DE	6-4	272	12/27/63	9	Georgia Tech	Villa Hills, Ky.	D7b-'86	14/0
83		Reed, Andre	WR	6-2	190	1/29/64	10	Kutztown	Allentown, Pa.	D4a-'85	15/15
14		Reich, Frank	QB	6-4	205	12/4/61	10	Maryland	Lebanon, Pa.	D3a-'85	15/0
24		Schulz, Kurt	S	6-1	208	12/12/68	3	Eastern Washington	Yakima, Wash.	D7-'92	12/0
78		Smith, Bruce	DE	6-4	273	6/18/63	10	Virginia Tech	Norfolk, Va.	D1a-'85	16/16
28		Smith, Thomas	CB	5-11	188	12/5/70	2	North Carolina	Gates, N.C.	D1-'93	16/1
11		Strom, Rick	QB	6-2	197	3/11/65	6	Georgia Tech	Pittsburgh, Pa.	UFA(Pitt)-'94	0*
56		Talley, Darryl	LB	6-4	235	7/10/60	12	West Virginia	Cleveland, Ohio	D2-'83	16/16
89		Tasker, Steve	WR	5-9	181	4/10/62	10	Northwestern	Leoti, Kan.	W(Hou)-'86	15/0
34		Thomas, Thurman	RB	5-10	198	5/16/66	7	Oklahoma State	Missouri City, Tex.	D2-'88	16/16
21		Turner, Nate	RB	6-1	255	5/28/69	3	Nebraska	Chicago, Ill.	D6-'92	13/0
25		Washington, Mickey	CB	5-9	191	7/8/68	4	Texas A&M	Beaumont, Tex.	FA-'93	16/6
91		Wright, Jeff	NT	6-3	274	6/13/63	7	Central Missouri State	Lawrence, Kan.	D8b-'88	15/15

* Gulledge last active with Washington in '92; Henderson played 1 game with New England, 2 games with Buffalo in '93; Paterra on injured reserve with Buffalo in '91; Strom inactive for 16 games with Pittsburgh.

\# Unrestricted free agent; subject to developments.

† Restricted free agent; subject to developments.

Traded—CB-S James Williams to Arizona.

Players lost through free agency (4): T Howard Ballard (Sea; 16 games in '93), QB Gale Gilbert (SD; 1), LB Richard Harvey (Den; 15), CB Nate Odomes (Sea; 16).

Also played with Bills in '93—S Mark Kelso (14 games), WR Brad Lamb (1), G Tom Myslinski (1), CB David Pool (2), G Jim Ritcher (12), WR Chris Walsh (3), CB-S James Williams (15).

COACHING STAFF

Head Coach,
Marv Levy

Pro Career: Begins his eighth full season as Bills head coach. Led the Bills to their fourth consecutive AFC championship in 1993. Under Levy, the Bills recorded 13-3 records in 1990 and 1991, the best regular-season marks in club history. He guided the Bills to their second consecutive AFC East title with a 9-7 record in 1989. Finished 1988 season with a 12-4 record and a berth in the AFC Championship Game. In his first full year with Bills in 1987, he led team to a 7-8 record. Replaced Hank Bullough on November 3, 1986, and compiled a 2-5 record over the final seven weeks of the season. Previously served as head coach of the Kansas City Chiefs from 1978-1982 and produced a 31-42 mark. Levy began his pro coaching career in 1969 as an assistant with the Philadelphia Eagles. He joined George Allen and the Los Angeles Rams as an assistant one year later and followed Allen to Washington, where he remained with the Redskins through the 1972 season when Washington played in Super Bowl VII. He was named head coach of the Montreal Alouettes (CFL) in 1973 and posted a 50-34-4 record and two Grey Cup victories (1974, 1977) in five seasons in Canada. After two seasons away from football, he became head coach of the Chicago Blitz of the USFL in 1984. No pro playing experience. Career NFL record: 120-87.

Background: Running back at Coe College 1948-50. Coached at high school level for two years before returning to alma mater from 1953-55. Joined New Mexico staff in 1956 and served as head coach there in 1958-59. Head coach at California from 1960-63 before becoming head coach at William & Mary from 1964-68.

Personal: Born August 3, 1928, Chicago, Ill. Levy was Phi Beta Kappa at Coe College and earned master's degree in English history from Harvard. He lives with his wife Mary Frances in Hamburg, N.Y.

ASSISTANT COACHES

Tom Bresnahan, offensive coordinator-offensive line; born January 21, 1935, Springfield, Mass., lives in Hamburg, N.Y. Tackle Holy Cross 1953-55. No pro playing experience. College coach: Williams 1963-67, Columbia 1968-72, Navy 1973-80. Pro coach: Kansas City Chiefs 1981-82, New York Giants 1983-84, St. Louis/Phoenix Cardinals 1986-88, joined Bills in 1989.

Walt Corey, defensive coordinator-linebackers; born May 9, 1938, Latrobe, Pa., lives in West Seneca, N.Y. Defensive end Miami 1957-59. Pro linebacker Kansas City Chiefs 1960-66. College coach: Utah State 1967-69, Miami 1970-71. Pro coach: Kansas City Chiefs 1972-74, 1978-86, Cleveland Browns 1975-77, joined Bills in 1987.

Bruce DeHaven, special teams; born September 6, 1952, Trousdale, Kan., lives in East Aurora, N.Y. No college or pro playing experience. College coach: Kansas 1979-81, New Mexico State 1982. Pro coach: New Jersey Generals (USFL) 1983, Pittsburgh Maulers (USFL) 1984, Orlando Renegades (USFL) 1985, joined Bills in 1987.

Charlie Joiner, receivers; born October 14, 1947, Many, La., lives in Orchard Park, N.Y. Wide receiver Grambling 1965-68. Defensive back-wide receiver Houston Oilers 1969-72, Cincinnati Bengals 1972-75, San Diego Chargers 1976-86. Pro coach: San Diego Chargers 1987-91, joined Bills in 1992.

Rusty Jones, strength and conditioning; born August 14, 1953, Berwick, Maine, lives in Lakeview, N.Y. No college or pro playing experience. College coach: Springfield 1978-79. Pro coach: Pittsburgh Maulers (USFL) 1983-84, joined Bills in 1985.

Don Lawrence, offensive quality control-tight ends; born June 4, 1937, Cleveland, Ohio, lives in Orchard Park, N.Y. Offensive-defensive lineman Notre Dame 1957-58. Pro offensive-defensive lineman Washington Redskins 1959-61. College coach: Notre Dame 1961-63, Kansas State 1964-65, Cincinnati 1966, Virginia 1970-73 (head coach 1971-73), Texas Christian

1994 FIRST-YEAR ROSTER

Name	Pos.	Ht.	Wt.	Birthdate	College	Hometown	How Acq.
Abrams, Anthony	DT	6-3	298	2/16/71	Clark, Ga.	Warner Robins, Ga.	D6a
Bock, John	G	6-3	286	2/11/71	Indiana State	Berwyn, Ill.	FA
Branch, Darrick (1)	WR	5-11	195	2/10/70	Hawaii	Dallas, Tex.	FA
Brooks, Bucky	WR	6-0	190	1/22/71	North Carolina	Raleigh, N.C.	D2a
Bryant, Phil (1)	RB	5-10	208	3/27/70	Virginia Tech	Landover, Md.	FA
Burris, Jeff	CB-S	6-0	204	6/7/72	Notre Dame	Rock Hill, S.C.	D1
Collins, Mike	CB-S	5-11	195	4/25/71	West Virginia	Huntington, W. Va.	FA
Crocker, Sean	CB-S	5-9	191	6/14/71	North Carolina	Wakefield, Va.	D4
Evans, Greg	S	6-1	217	6/28/71	Texas Christian	Daingerfield, Tex.	FA
Feexico, Sonny	F	6-2	240	11/29/68	E. Central Oklahoma	Norman, Okla.	FA
Fieldings, Anthony (1)	LB	6-1	237	7/9/71	Morningside	Eustis, Fla.	FA
Hendrickson, Craig (1)	T	6-3	290	5/5/68	Minnesota	Tucson, Ariz.	FA
Herget, Todd	LB	6-2	226	8/9/69	Brigham Young	Lethbridge, Ala.	FA
Hoyem, Steve	T	6-7	287	11/12/70	Stanford	Boise, Idaho	FA
Johnson, Filmel	CB-S	5-10	187	12/24/70	Illinois	Detroit, Mich.	D7
Johnson, Lonnie	TE	6-3	230	2/14/71	Florida State	Miami, Fla.	D2b
Jourdain, Yonel (1)	RB	5-11	204	4/20/71	Southern Illinois	Evanston, Ill.	FA
Knox, Kevin	WR	6-3	195	1/30/71	Florida State	Miami, Fla.	D6b
Lacina, Corbin (1)	T	6-4	297	11/2/70	Augustana, S.D.	Woodbury, Minn.	D6-'93
Lawson, Shawn (1)	CB	5-11	176	9/27/70	Baylor	Longview, Tex.	FA
Louchiey, Corey	T	6-8	305	10/10/71	South Carolina	Greenville, S.C.	D3b
Marrow, Vince (1)	TE	6-3	251	8/17/68	Toledo	Youngstown, Ohio	D11-'92
McKay, Orlando (1)	WR	5-10	176	10/2/69	Washington	Mesa, Ariz.	FA
Ofodile, A.J.	TE	6-7	260	10/9/73	Missouri	Detroit, Mich.	D5
Ostroski, Jerry (1)	G	6-4	310	7/12/70	Tulsa	Collegeville, Pa.	FA
Perry, Mario	LB	6-4	250	8/25/72	Jackson State	Forest, Miss.	D3a
Philion, Ed	DT	6-2	273	3/27/70	Ferris State	Essex, Canada	FA
Rodgers, Matt (1)	QB	6-3	205	!/8/69	Iowa	Walpole, Mass.	D12-'92
Rogers, Sam	LB	6-3	245	5/30/70	Colorado	Pontiac, Mich.	D2c
Silvestri, Don (1)	K	6-4	210	12/25/68	Pittsburgh	Perkasie, Pa.	FA
Thomas, Damon	WR	6-2	215	12/15/70	Wayne State	Clovis, Calif.	FA
Tindale, Tim	RB	5-10	220	4/15/71	Western Ontario	London, Canada	FA
Young, Glenn (1)	LB	6-3	240	5/2/69	Syracuse	Scarborough, Canada	FA

The term NFL Rookie is defined as a player who is in his first season of professional football and has not been on the roster of another professional football team for any regular-season or postseason games. A Rookie is designated by an "R" on NFL rosters. Players who have been active in another professional football league or players who have NFL experience, including either preseason training camp or being on an Active List or Inactive List, or on Reserve/Injured or Reserve/Physically Unable to Perform for fewer than six regular-season games, are termed NFL First-Year Players. An NFL First-Year Player is designated by a "1" on NFL rosters. Thereafter, a player is credited with an additional year of experience for each season in which he accumulates six games on the Active List or Inactive List, or on Reserve/Injured or Reserve/Physically Unable to Perform.

NOTES

_____

_____

_____

_____

_____

_____

_____

1974-75, Missouri 1976-77. Pro coach: British Columbia Lions (CFL) 1978-79, Kansas City Chiefs 1980-82, 1987-88, Buffalo Bills 1983-84, Tampa Bay Buccaneers 1985-86, Winnipeg Blue Bombers (CFL) 1989, rejoined Bills in 1990.

Chuck Lester, administrative assistant to head coach, assistant linebackers coach; born May 18, 1955, Chicago, Ill., lives in Orchard Park, N.Y. Linebacker Oklahoma 1974. No pro playing experience. College coach: Iowa State 1980-81, Oklahoma 1982-84. Pro coach: Kansas City Chiefs 1984-86 (scout), joined Bills in 1987.

Elijah Pitts, assistant head coach-running backs; born February 3, 1938, Mayflower, Ark., lives in Orchard Park, N.Y. Running back Philander Smith 1957-60. Pro running back Green Bay Packers 1961-69, 1971, Los Angeles Rams 1970, Chicago Bears 1970, New Orleans Saints 1970. Pro coach: Los Angeles Rams 1974-77, Buffalo Bills 1978-80, Houston Oilers 1981-83, Hamilton Tiger-Cats (CFL) 1984, rejoined Bills in 1985.

Dick Roach, defensive backs; born August 23, 1937, Rapid City, S.D., lives in West Seneca, N.Y. Defensive back Black Hills State 1952-55. No pro playing experience. College coach: Montana State 1966-69, Oregon State 1970, Wyoming 1971-72,

Fresno State 1973, Washington State 1974-75. Pro coach: Montreal Alouettes (CFL) 1976-77, Kansas City Chiefs 1978-80, New England Patriots 1981, Michigan Panthers (USFL) 1983-84, Tampa Bay Buccaneers 1985-86, joined Bills in 1987.

Dan Sekanovich, defensive line; born July 27, 1933, West Hazelton, Pa., lives in Orchard Park, N.Y. End Tennessee 1951-53. Pro defensive end Montreal Alouettes (CFL) 1954. College coach: Susquehanna 1961-63, Connecticut 1964-67, Pittsburgh 1968, Navy 1969-70, Kentucky 1971-72. Pro coach: Montreal Alouettes (CFL) 1973-76, New York Jets 1977-82, Atlanta Falcons 1983-85, Miami Dolphins 1986-91, joined Bills in 1992.

Jim Shofner, quarterbacks; born December 18, 1935, Grapevine, Tex., lives in Orchard Park, N.Y. Running back Texas Christian 1955-57. Pro defensive back Cleveland Browns 1958-63. College coach: Texas Christian 1964-66, 1974-76 (head coach). Pro coach: San Francisco 49ers 1967-73, 1977, Cleveland Browns 1978-80, 1990-91 (head coach last 7 games in 1990, director of player personnel in 1991), Houston Oilers 1981-82, Dallas Cowboys 1983-85, St. Louis/Phoenix Cardinals 1986-89, joined Bills in 1992.

CINCINNATI BENGALS

American Football Conference
Central Division
Team Colors: Black, Orange, and White
200 Riverfront Stadium
Cincinnati, Ohio 45202
Telephone: (513) 621-3550

CLUB OFFICIALS

President/General Manager: Michael Brown
Vice President: John Sawyer
Assistant General Manager/Director of
    Player Personnel: Pete Brown
Secretary/Treasurer:Katherine Blackburn
Assistant Secretary/Assistant Treasurer, Scouting:
    Paul Brown
Assistant Director of Player Personnel:
    Frank Smouse
Scouting/Personnel: Jim Lippincott
Business Manager: Bill Connelly
Public Relations Directors: Allan Heim,
    Jack Brennan
Accountant: Jay Reis
Ticket Manager: Paul Kelly
Consultant: John Murdough, Bill Johnson
Trainer: Paul Sparling
Assistant Trainer: Rob Recker
Equipment Manager: Tom Gray
Video Director: Al Davis
Stadium: Riverfront Stadium •**Capacity:** 60,389
    200 Riverfront Stadium
    Cincinnati, Ohio 45202
Playing Surface: AstroTurf-8
Training Camp: Wilmington College
    Wilmington, Ohio 45177

1994 SCHEDULE
PRESEASON
Aug. 6	at Tampa Bay	7:30
Aug. 13	**Indianapolis**	7:30
Aug. 20	at Philadelphia	7:30
Aug. 26	**Detroit**	7:30

REGULAR SEASON
Sept. 4	**Cleveland**	1:00
Sept. 11	at San Diego	1:00
Sept. 18	**New England**	1:00
Sept. 25	at Houston	3:00
Oct. 2	**Miami**	8:00
Oct. 9	Open Date	
Oct. 16	at Pittsburgh	1:00
Oct. 23	at Cleveland	1:00
Oct. 30	**Dallas**	1:00
Nov. 6	at Seattle	1:00
Nov. 13	**Houston**	1:00
Nov. 20	**Indianapolis**	1:00
Nov. 27	at Denver	2:00
Dec. 4	**Pittsburgh**	1:00
Dec. 11	at New York Giants	1:00
Dec. 18	at Arizona	2:00
Dec. 24	**Philadelphia**	1:00

RECORD HOLDERS
INDIVIDUAL RECORDS—CAREER
Category	Name	Performance
Rushing (Yds.)	James Brooks, 1984-1991	6,447
Passing (Yds.)	Ken Anderson, 1971-1986	32,838
Passing (TDs)	Ken Anderson, 1971-1986	197
Receiving (No.)	Isaac Curtis, 1973-1984	420
Receiving (Yds.)	Isaac Curtis, 1973-1984	7,106
Interceptions	Ken Riley, 1969-1983	63
Punting (Avg.)	Dave Lewis, 1970-73	43.9
Punt Return (Avg.)	Mitchell Price, 1990-92	10.4
Kickoff Return (Avg.)	Lemar Parrish, 1970-78	24.7
Field Goals	Jim Breech, 1980-1992	225
Touchdowns (Tot.)	Pete Johnson, 1977-1983	70
Points	Jim Breech, 1980-1992	1,246

INDIVIDUAL RECORDS—SINGLE SEASON
Category	Name	Performance
Rushing (Yds.)	James Brooks, 1989	1,239
Passing (Yds.)	Boomer Esiason, 1986	3,959
Passing (TDs)	Ken Anderson, 1981	29
Receiving (No.)	Dan Ross, 1981	71
Receiving (Yds.)	Eddie Brown, 1988	1,273
Interceptions	Ken Riley, 1976	9
Punting (Avg.)	Dave Lewis, 1970	46.2
Punt Return (Avg.)	Mike Martin, 1984	15.7
Kickoff Return (Avg.)	Lemar Parrish, 1970	30.2
Field Goals	Horst Muhlmann, 1972	27
Touchdowns (Tot.)	Pete Johnson, 1981	16
Points	Jim Breech, 1985	120

INDIVIDUAL RECORDS—SINGLE GAME
Category	Name	Performance
Rushing (Yds.)	James Brooks, 12-23-90	201
Passing (Yds.)	Boomer Esiason, 10-7-90	490
Passing (TDs)	Boomer Esiason, 12-21-86	5
	Boomer Esiason, 10-29-89	5
Receiving (No.)	James Brooks, 12-25-89	12
Receiving (Yds.)	Eddie Brown, 11-6-88	216
Interceptions	Many times	3
	Last time by David Fulcher, 12-16-89	
Field Goals	Many times	3
	Last time by Doug Pelfrey, 10-10-93	
Touchdowns (Tot.)	Larry Kinnebrew, 10-28-84	4
Points	Larry Kinnebrew, 10-28-84	24

COACHING HISTORY
(187-212-1)
1968-75	Paul Brown	55-59-1
1976-78	Bill Johnson*	18-15-0
1978-79	Homer Rice	8-19-0
1980-83	Forrest Gregg	34-27-0
1984-91	Sam Wyche	64-68-0
1992-93	Dave Shula	8-24-0

*Resigned after five games in 1978

RIVERFRONT STADIUM

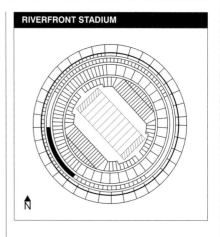

N

1993 TEAM RECORD

PRESEASON (2-2)

Date	Result		Opponents
8/7	L	16-27	N.Y. Giants
8/14	W	24-7	at Indianapolis
8/20	L	7-30	at Detroit
8/27	W	23-3	Philadelphia

REGULAR SEASON (3-13)

Date	Result		Opponents	Att.
9/5	L	14-27	at Cleveland	75,508
9/12	L	6-9	Indianapolis	50,299
9/19	L	7-34	at Pittsburgh	53,682
9/26	L	10-19	Seattle	46,880
10/10	L	15-17	at Kansas City	75,394
10/17	L	17-28	Cleveland	55,647
10/24	L	12-28	at Houston	50,039
11/7	L	16-24	Pittsburgh	51,202
11/14	L	3-38	Houston	42,347
11/21	L	12-17	at N.Y. Jets	64,264
11/28	W	16-10	L.A. Raiders	43,272
12/5	L	8-21	at San Francisco	60,039
12/12	L	2-7	at New England	29,794
12/19	W	15-3	L.A. Rams	36,612
12/26	W	21-17	Atlanta	27,014
1/2	L	13-20	at New Orleans	58,036

SCORE BY PERIODS

Bengals	41	74	18	54	0	—	187
Opponents	42	119	63	95	0	—	319

ATTENDANCE

Home 353,273   Away 466,756   Total 820,029
Single-game home record, 60,284 (10-17-71)
Single-season home record, 473,288 (1990)

1993 TEAM STATISTICS

	Bengals	Opp.
Total First Downs	239	306
Rushing	89	134
Passing	133	159
Penalty	17	13
Third Down: Made/Att	80/232	85/212
Third Down Pct.	34.5	40.1
Fourth Down: Made/Att	10/26	7/11
Fourth Down Pct.	38.5	63.6
Total Net Yards	4052	5018
Avg. Per Game	253.3	313.6
Total Plays	986	1000
Avg. Per Play	4.1	5.0
Net Yards Rushing	1511	2220
Avg. Per Game	94.4	138.8
Total Rushes	423	521
Net Yards Passing	2541	2798
Avg. Per Game	158.8	174.9
Sacked/Yards Lost	53/289	22/154
Gross Yards	2830	2952
Att./Completions	510/272	457/251
Completion Pct.	53.3	54.9
Had Intercepted	11	12
Punts/Avg.	90/43.9	74/42.2
Net Punting Avg.	90/36.6	74/36.2
Penalties/Yards Lost	105/773	73/567
Fumbles/Ball Lost	24/9	22/14
Touchdowns	16	37
Rushing	3	15
Passing	11	20
Returns	2	2
Avg. Time of Possession	28:58	31:02

1993 INDIVIDUAL STATISTICS

PASSING	Att	Cmp	Yds.	Pct.	TD	Int	Tkld.	Rate
Klingler	343	190	1935	55.4	6	9	40/202	66.6
Schroeder	159	78	832	49.1	5	2	13/87	70.0
Wilhelm	6	4	63	66.7	0	0	0/0	101.4
L. Johnson	1	0	0	0.0	0	0	0/0	39.6
Pickens	1	0	0	0.0	0	0	0/0	39.6
Bengals	510	272	2830	53.3	11	11	53/289	67.9
Opponents	457	251	2952	54.9	20	12	22/154	78.4

SCORING	TD R	TD P	TD Rt	PAT	FG	Saf	PTS
Pelfrey	0	0	0	13/16	24/31	0	85
Pickens	0	6	0	0/0	0/0	0	36
Query	0	4	0	0/0	0/0	0	24
Ball	1	0	0	0/0	0/0	0	6
Brim	0	0	1	0/0	0/0	0	6
Fenner	1	0	0	0/0	0/0	0	6
Miles	1	0	0	0/0	0/0	0	6
Thompson	0	1	0	0/0	0/0	0	6
D. Williams	0	0	1	0/0	0/0	0	6
A. Williams	0	0	0	0/0	0/0	1	2
Bengals	3	11	2	13/16	24/31	3	187
Opponents	15	20	2	37/37	20/28	0	319

RUSHING	Att.	Yds.	Avg.	LG	TD
Green	215	589	2.7	25	0
Fenner	121	482	4.0	26	1
Klingler	41	282	6.9	29	0
Miles	22	56	2.5	15	1
Schroeder	10	41	4.1	20	0
Ball	8	37	4.6	18	1
Query	2	13	6.5	8	0
Robinson	1	6	6.0	6	0
Benjamin	3	5	1.7	2	0
Bengals	423	1511	3.6	29	3
Opponents	521	2220	4.3	38t	15

RECEIVING	No.	Yds.	Avg.	LG	TD
Query	56	654	11.7	51	4
Fenner	48	427	8.9	40	0
McGee	44	525	11.9	37	0
Pickens	43	565	13.1	36	6
Green	22	115	5.2	16	0
Thompson	17	87	5.1	10	1
Rembert	8	101	12.6	21	0
Robinson	8	72	9.0	14	0
Miles	6	89	14.8	27	0
Carroll	6	81	13.5	28	0
Frisch	6	43	7.2	12	0
Ball	4	39	9.8	24	0
Thomason	2	8	4.0	5	0
Benjamin	1	16	16.0	16	0
Stegall	1	8	8.0	8	0
Bengals	272	2830	10.4	51	11
Opponents	251	2952	11.8	71t	20

INTERCEPTIONS	No.	Yds.	Avg.	LG	TD
Brim	3	74	24.7	30	1
D. Williams	2	126	63.0	97t	1
White	2	19	9.5	14	0
Francis	2	12	6.0	12	0
Grant	1	17	17.0	17	0
R. Jones	1	0	0.0	0	0
Tovar	1	0	0.0	0	0
Wheeler	0	24	—	24	0
Bengals	12	272	22.7	97t	2
Opponents	11	49	4.5	30	0

PUNTING	No.	Yds.	Avg.	In 20	LG
L. Johnson	90	3954	43.9	24	60
Bengals	90	3954	43.9	24	60
Opponents	74	3123	42.2	20	72

PUNT RETURNS	No.	FC	Yds.	Avg.	LG	TD
Robinson	43	6	305	7.1	36	0
Pickens	4	2	16	4.0	9	0
Simmons	1	0	0	0.0	0	0
Bengals	48	8	321	6.7	36	0
Opponents	47	13	416	8.9	39	0

KICKOFF RETURNS	No.	Yds.	Avg.	LG	TD
Robinson	30	567	18.9	42	0
Ball	23	501	21.8	45	0
Benjamin	4	78	19.5	24	0
Miles	4	65	16.3	24	0
Shaw	0	0	—	—	0
Bengals	61	1211	19.9	45	0
Opponents	38	831	21.9	66	0

SACKS	No.
Stubbs	5.0
A. Williams	4.0
Copeland	3.0
Krumrie	3.0
Francis	2.0
D. Williams	2.0
Frier	1.0
Hinkle	1.0
McDonald	1.0
Bengals	22.0
Opponents	53.0

1994 DRAFT CHOICES

Round	Name	Pos.	College
1	Dan Wilkinson	DT	Ohio State
2	Darnay Scott	WR	San Diego State
3	Jeff Cothran	RB	Ohio State
	Steve Shine	LB	Northwestern
4	Corey Sawyer	DB	Florida State
5	Trent Pollard	T	Eastern Washington
6	Kimo von Oelhoffen	DT	Boise State
	Jerry Reynolds	T	Nevada-Las Vegas
7	Ramondo Stallings	DE	San Diego State

CINCINNATI BENGALS

1994 VETERAN ROSTER

No.	Name	Pos.	Ht.	Wt.	Birthdate	NFL Exp.	College	Hometown	How Acq.	'93 Games/ Starts
42	Ball, Eric	RB	6-2	220	7/1/66	6	UCLA	Ypsilanti, Mich.	D2-'89	15/1
21	Benjamin, Ryan	RB	5-7	183	4/23/70	2	Pacific	Pixley, Calif.	FA-'93	1/0
60	Bradley, Chuck	T	6-5	296	4/9/70	2	Kentucky	Fern Creek, Ky.	W(Hou)-'93	1/0
65	Brilz, Darrick	G	6-3	287	2/14/64	8	Oregon	Pinole Valley, Calif.	UFA(Sea)-'94	0*
43	Brim, Mike	CB	6-0	192	1/23/66	7	Virginia Union	Danville, Va.	UFA(NYJ)-'93	16/16
33	Broussard, Steve	RB	5-7	201	2/22/67	5	Washington State	Los Angeles, Calif.	FA-'94	8/0*
72	Brumfield, Scott	T	6-8	320	8/19/70	2	Brigham Young	Spanish Fork, Utah	FA-'93	16/7
32	Carpenter, Ron	S	6-1	188	1/20/70	2	Miami, Ohio	Cincinnati, Ohio	W(Minn)-'93	13/0*
92	Copeland, John	DE	6-3	286	9/20/70	2	Alabama	Lanett, Ala.	D1-'93	14/14
44	Fenner, Derrick	RB	6-3	228	4/6/67	6	North Carolina	Oxon Hill, Md.	PB(Sea)-'92	15/14
50	Francis, James	LB	6-5	252	8/4/68	5	Baylor	Houston, Tex.	D1-'90	14/12
97	Frier, Mike	DE	6-5	299	3/20/69	3	Appalachian State	Jacksonville, N.C.	W(Sea)-'92	16/6
47	Frisch, David	TE	6-7	260	6/22/70	2	Colorado	House Springs, Mo.	FA-'93	11/2
58	Gordon, Alex	LB	6-5	245	9/14/64	8	Cincinnati	Jacksonville, Fla.	PB(Raid)-'91	16/3
24	Grant, Alan	CB	5-10	187	10/1/66	5	Stanford	Pasadena, Calif.	W(SF)-'93	12/1*
28	Green, Harold	RB	6-2	222	1/29/68	5	South Carolina	Ladson, S.C.	D2-'90	15/15
27	Gunn, Lance	S	6-3	222	1/9/70	2	Texas	Houston, Tex.	D7-'93	8/8
98	Hinkle, George	DE	6-5	288	3/17/65	7	Arizona	St. Louis, Mo.	FA-'93	13/9
12	Hollas, Donald	QB	6-3	215	11/22/67	3	Rice	Kingsville, Tex.	D4-'91	0*
71	Howe, Garry	NT	6-1	298	6/20/68	2	Colorado	Spencer, Iowa	FA-'93	1/0
68	Johnson, Donnell	T	6-7	310	12/24/69	2	Johnson C. Smith	Miami, Fla.	FA-'93	7/0
11	Johnson, Lee	P-K	6-2	200	11/27/61	10	Brigham Young	Conroe, Tex.	W(Clev)-'88	16/0
66	Jones, Dan	T	6-7	304	7/22/70	2	Maine	Malden, Mass.	FA-'93	15/5
25	Jones, Rod	CB	6-0	185	3/31/64	9	Southern Methodist	Dallas, Tex.	T(TB)-'90	16/16
7	Klingler, David	QB	6-3	205	2/17/69	3	Houston	Stratford, Tex.	D1a-'92	14/13
64	Kozerski, Bruce	G-C	6-4	287	4/2/62	11	Holy Cross	Plains, Pa.	D9-'84	15/15
69	Krumrie, Tim	NT	6-2	274	5/20/60	12	Wisconsin	Eau Claire, Wis.	D10-'83	16/16
56	McDonald, Ricardo	LB	6-2	235	11/8/69	3	Pittsburgh	Kingston, Jamaica	D4-'92	14/12
85	McGee, Tim	WR	5-10	183	8/7/64	9	Tennessee	Cleveland, Ohio	FA-'94	13/12*
82	McGee, Tony	TE	6-3	246	4/21/71	2	Michigan	Terre Haute, Ind.	D2-'93	15/15
59	McGill, Karmeeleyah	LB	6-3	224	1/11/71	2	Notre Dame	Clearwater, Fla.	FA-'93	4/0
36	Miles, Ostell	RB	6-0	236	8/6/71	3	Houston	Pueblo, Colo.	D9-'92	15/2
62	Moore, Eric	G	6-5	290	1/21/65	7	Indiana	Berkeley, Mo.	UFA(NYG)-'94	7/5*
73	Moyer, Ken	T	6-7	297	11/19/66	5	Toledo	Temperance, Mich.	FA-'89	16/14
29	Oliver, Louis	S	6-2	224	3/9/66	6	Florida	Belle Glade, Fla.	UFA(Mia)-'94	11/11*
93	Parten, Ty	NT	6-4	272	10/13/69	2	Arizona	Washington, D.C.	D3a-'93	11/1
9	Pelfrey, Doug	K	5-11	185	9/25/70	2	Kentucky	Ft. Thomas, Ky.	D8-'93	15/0
80	Pickens, Carl	WR	6-2	206	3/23/70	3	Tennessee	Murphy, N.C.	D2-'92	13/12
89	Query, Jeff	WR	6-0	165	3/7/67	6	Millikin	Maroa, Ill.	W(Hou)-'92	16/16
88	Rembert, Reggie	WR	6-5	200	12/25/66	4	West Virginia	Okeechobee, Fla.	FA-'94	3/0*
81	Robinson, Patrick	WR	5-8	176	10/3/69	2	Tennessee State	Memphis, Tenn.	W(Hou)-'93	15/3
87	Sadowski, Troy	TE	6-5	250	12/8/65	5	Georgia	Chamblee, Ga.	UFA(NYJ)-'94	13/1*
77	Sargent, Kevin	T	6-6	284	3/31/69	3	Eastern Washington	Bremerton, Wash.	FA-'92	1/1
10	Schroeder, Jay	QB	6-4	215	6/28/61	11	UCLA	Pacific Palisades, Calif.	UFA(Raid)0-'93	9/3
74	Scott, Tom	T	6-6	330	6/25/70	2	East Carolina	Burke County, N.C.	D6-'93	13/13
90	Shaw, Eric	LB	6-3	248	9/17/71	3	Louisiana Tech	Pensacola, Fla.	D12-'92	14/9
22	Simmons, Marcello	CB	6-1	180	8/8/71	2	Southern Methodist	Tomball, Tex.	D4-'93	16/2
91	Smith, Brad	LB	6-2	228	9/5/69	2	Texas Christian	Houston, Tex.	FA-'93	7/0
84	Stegall, Milt	WR	6-0	184	1/25/70	3	Miami, Ohio	Cincinnati, Ohio	FA-'92	4/0
53	Stephens, Santo	LB	6-4	232	6/16/69	2	Temple	Capital Heights, Md.	W(KC)-'94	16/0*
96	# Stubbs, Daniel	LB	6-4	264	1/3/65	7	Miami	Red Bank, N.J.	W(Dall)-'91	16/0
49	Thomason, Jeff	TE	6-4	233	12/30/69	3	Oregon	Newport Beach, Calif.	FA-'92	3/0
48	Thompson, Craig	TE	6-2	244	1/13/69	3	North Carolina A&T	Hartsville, S.C.	D5-'92	13/0
51	Tovar, Steve	LB	6-3	244	4/25/70	2	Ohio State	Elyria, Ohio	D3-'93	16/9
34	Vinson, Fernandus	S	6-0	197	11/3/68	4	North Carolina State	Montgomery, Ala.	D7-'91	16/7
63	Walter, Joe	T	6-7	292	6/18/63	10	Texas Tech	Dallas, Tex.	D7a-'85	16/16
37	Wheeler, Leonard	CB	5-11	189	1/15/69	3	Troy State	Toccoa, Ga.	D3-'92	16/2
4	Wilhelm, Erik	QB	6-3	217	11/19/65	5	Oregon State	Lake Oswego, Ore.	FA-'93	1/0
94	† Williams, Alfred	LB	6-6	240	11/6/68	4	Colorado	Houston, Tex.	D1-'91	16/16
31	Williams, Darryl	S	6-0	191	1/7/70	3	Miami	Miami, Fla.	D1a-'92	16/16

* Brilz played 16 games with Seattle in '93; Broussard played 8 games with Atlanta; Carpenter played 7 games with Minnesota; Grant played 3 games with San Francisco; Hollas missed '93 season due to injury; Tim McGee played 13 games with Washington; Moore played 7 games with N.Y. Giants; Oliver played 11 games with Miami; Rembert played 3 games with Cincinnati; Sadowski played 13 games with N.Y. Jets; Stephens played 16 games with Kansas City.

\# Unrestricted free agent; subject to developments.

† Restricted free agent; subject to developments.

Players lost through free agency (1): LB Randy Kirk (Ariz; 16 games in '93).

Also played with Bengals in '93—WR Wesley Carroll (12 games), WR Allen Degraffenreid (2), CB-S R.J. Kors (7), G Jack Linn (3), DE Roosevelt Nix (10), CB Mitchell Price (1), G Tom Rayam (10), WR Reggie Thornton (1), CB Sheldon White (8).

COACHING STAFF

Head Coach,
Dave Shula

Pro Career: Shula is in his third year as head coach of the Cincinnati Bengals. He became the sixth head coach in Bengals history on December 27, 1991. Shula was offensive coordinator and quarterbacks coach for Dallas in 1989-90 before joining Cincinnati in 1991 as receivers coach. Shula began his coaching career with the Miami Dolphins in 1982. In 1988, Shula was named assistant head coach with the Dolphins. He was a wide receiver and kick return specialist with the Baltimore Colts in 1981. Career record: 8-24.

Background: Outstanding wide receiver at Dartmouth where he was a two-time All-Ivy League selection.

Personal: Born May 28, 1959, Lexington, Ky. Dave and his wife, Leslie, live in Cincinnati, and have three sons—Daniel, Christopher, and Matthew.

ASSISTANT COACHES

Paul Alexander, tight ends; born February 12, 1960, Rochester, N.Y., lives in Cincinnati. Tackle Cortland State 1978-81. No pro playing experience. College coach: Penn State 1982-84, Michigan 1985-86, Central Michigan 1987-91. Pro coach: New York Jets 1992-93, joined Bengals in 1994.

Jim Anderson, running backs; born March 27, 1948, Harrisburg, Pa., lives in Cincinnati. Linebacker-defensive end Cal Western (U.S. International) 1967-70. No pro playing experience. College coach: Cal Western 1970-71, Scottsdale, Ariz., Community College 1973, Nevada-Las Vegas 1974-75, Southern Methodist 1976-80, Stanford 1981-83. Pro coach: Joined Bengals in 1984.

Ken Anderson, quarterbacks; born February 15, 1949, Batavia, Ill., lives in Lakeside Park, Ky. Quarterback Augustana (Ill.) 1967-70. Pro quarterback Cincinnati Bengals 1971-86. Pro coach: Joined Bengals in 1992.

Marv Braden, special teams; born January 25, 1938, Kansas City, Mo., lives in Cincinnati. Linebacker Southwest Missouri State 1956-59. No pro playing experience. College coach: Parsons 1963-66, Northeast Missouri State 1967-68 (head coach), Cal Western (U.S. International) 1969-72, Iowa State 1973, Southern Methodist 1974-75, Michigan State 1976. Pro coach: Denver Broncos 1977-80, San Diego Chargers 1981-85, St. Louis/Phoenix Cardinals 1986-89, joined Bengals in 1990.

Bruce Coslet, offensive coordinator; born August 5, 1946, Oakdale, Calif., lives in Cincinnati. Tight end University of Pacific 1965-67. Pro tight end Cincinnati Bengals 1969-76. Pro coach: San Francisco 49ers 1980, Cincinnati Bengals 1981-89, New York Jets (head coach) 1990-93, rejoined Bengals in 1994.

Bobby DePaul, defensive assistant; born January 29, 1963, Cheverly, Md., lives in Cincinnati. Linebacker Maryland 1982-83. No pro playing experience. College coach: Catholic University 1986-88. Pro coach: Washington Redskins 1989-93, joined Bengals in 1994.

Jim McNally, offensive line; born December 13, 1943, Buffalo, N.Y., lives in Cincinnati. Guard Buffalo 1961-65. No pro playing experience. College coach: Buffalo 1966-69, Marshall 1973-75, Boston College 1976-78, Wake Forest 1979. Pro coach: Joined Bengals in 1980.

Ron Meeks, defensive backfield; born August 27, 1954, Jacksonville, Fla., lives in Cincinnati. Defensive back Arkansas State 1975-76. Pro defensive back Hamilton Tiger-Cats (CFL) 1977-79, Ottawa Roughriders (CFL) 1979, Toronto Argonauts (CFL) 1980-81. College coach: Arkansas State 1984-85, Miami 1986-87, New Mexico State 1988, Fresno State 1989-90. Pro coach: Dallas Cowboys 1991, joined Bengals in 1992.

Joe Pascale, linebackers; born April 4, 1946, New York, N.Y., lives in Cincinnati. Linebacker Connecticut 1963-66. No pro playing experience. College coach: Connecticut 1967-68, Rhode Island 1969-73,

1994 FIRST-YEAR ROSTER

Name	Pos.	Ht.	Wt.	Birthdate	College	Hometown	How Acq.
Beckett, Andrew	DE	6-4	265	3/15/72	Rutgers	Barrington, N.J.	FA
Cothran, Jeff	RB	6-2	231	6/28/71	Ohio State	Middletown, Ohio	D3
Dickey, Troy	WR	6-3	226	4/8/71	Arizona	Houston, Tex.	FA
Duckett, Forey (1)	CB	6-3	195	2/5/70	Nevada-Reno	Pinole, Calif.	D5
Ford, Artis (1)	DE	6-3	275	9/30/71	Mississippi	Pahokee, Fla.	FA
Hill, Jeff	WR	5-11	178	9/24/72	Purdue	Cincinnati, Ohio	FA
Jefferson, Kevin	LB	6-2	232	1/14/74	Lehigh	Greensburg, Pa.	FA
Johnson, Lance	C	6-1	265	11/27/70	Notre Dame	Charlotte, N.C.	FA
Phillips, Jey	CB	6-2	183	12/21/71	Arizona	El Paso, Tex.	FA
Pollard, Trent	G-T	6-4	325	11/20/72	Eastern Washington	Seattle, Wash.	D5
Reynolds, Jerry	G-T	6-6	300	4/2/70	Nevada-Las Vegas	Ft. Thomas, Ky.	D6a
Richardson, Terry	RB	6-1	205	10/8/71	Syracuse	Ft. Lauderdale, Fla.	FA
Sawyer, Corey	CB	5-11	171	10/4/71	Florida State	Key West, Fla.	D4
Scott, Darnay	WR	6-1	180	7/7/72	San Diego State	St. Louis, Mo.	D2
Shine, Steve	LB	6-6	232	11/28/70	Northwestern	Kokomo, Ind.	D3a
Stallings, Ramondo	DE	6-7	285	11/21/71	San Diego State	Winston-Salem, N.C.	D7
Truitt, Gregg (1)	RB	6-0	235	12/8/65	Penn State	Sarasota, Fla.	FA
Turner, Elbert (1)	WR	5-11	165	3/19/68	Illinois	Gary, Ind.	FA
von Oelhoffen, Kimo	DT	6-4	300	1/30/71	Boise State	Molokai, Hawaii	D6
Wilkinson, Dan	DT	6-5	300	3/13/73	Ohio State	Dayton, Ohio	D1
Williams, Ronald (1)	RB	6-1	203	5/19/72	Clemson	Ninety Six, S.C.	FA
Woodside, Ray	G	6-4	280	8/22/72	Cincinnati	Oberlin, Ohio	FA

The term NFL Rookie is defined as a player who is in his first season of professional football and has not been on the roster of another professional football team for any regular-season or postseason games. A Rookie is designated by an "R" on NFL rosters. Players who have been active in another professional football league or players who have NFL experience, including either preseason training camp or being on an Active List or Inactive List, or on Reserve/Injured or Reserve/Physically Unable to Perform for fewer than six regular-season games, are termed NFL First-Year Players. An NFL First-Year Player is designated by a "1" on NFL rosters. Thereafter, a player is credited with an additional year of experience for each season in which he accumulates six games on the Active List or Inactive List, or on Reserve/Injured or Reserve/Physically Unable to Perform.

NOTES

Idaho State 1974-76 (head coach 1976), Princeton 1977-79. Pro coach: Montreal Alouettes (CFL) 1980-81. Ottawa Rough Riders (CFL) 1982-83, New Jersey Generals (USFL) 1984-85, St. Louis/Phoenix Cardinals 1986-93, joined Bengals in 1994.

Larry Peccatiello, defensive coordinator; born December 21, 1935, Newark, N.J., lives in Cincinnati. Receiver William & Mary 1955-58. No pro playing experience. College coach: William & Mary 1961-68, Navy 1969-70, Rice 1971. Pro coach: Houston Oilers 1972-75, Seattle Seahawks 1976-80, Washington Redskins 1981-93, joined Bengals in 1994.

Joe Wessel, defensive line; born January 5, 1962, Miami, Fla., lives in Cincinnati. Quarterback-safety Florida State 1981-84. No pro playing experience.

College coach: Louisiana State 1985-90, Notre Dame 1991-93. Pro coach: Joined Bengals in 1994.

Richard Williamson, wide receivers, born April 13, 1941, Ft. Deposit, Ala., lives in Cincinnati. Receiver Alabama 1961-62. No pro playing experience. College coach: Alabama 1963-67, 1970-71, Arkansas 1968-69, 1972-74, Memphis State 1975-80 (head coach). Pro coach: Kansas City Chiefs 1983-86, Tampa Bay Buccaneers 1987-91 (interim head coach final three games of 1990 season, head coach 1991), joined Bengals in 1992.

Kim Wood, strength; born July 12, 1945, Barrington, Ill., lives in Cincinnati. Running back Wisconsin 1965-68. No pro playing experience. Pro coach: Joined Bengals in 1975.

CLEVELAND BROWNS

American Football Conference
Central Division
Team Colors: Seal Brown, Orange, and White
80 First Avenue
Berea, Ohio 44017
Telephone: (216) 891-5000

CLUB OFFICIALS

President and Owner: Arthur B. Modell
Executive Vice President/Legal and
   Administration: Jim Bailey
Vice President/Assistant to President: David Modell
Vice President/Public Relations: Kevin Byrne
Director of Player Personnel: Michael Lombardi
Director of Pro Personnel: Ozzie Newsome
Treasurer: Mike Srsen
Director of Operations/Information: Bob Eller
Director of Business Operations: Pat Moriarty
Assistant Director of Public Relations:
   Francine Lubera
Player Relations/Media Services: Dino Lucarelli
Scouts: Tom Dimitroff, Ron Marciniak,
   Terry McDonough, Vince Newsome, Scott Pioli,
   Ernie Plank, Ellis Rainsberger, Phil Savage,
   Bill Shunkwiler, Lionel Vital
Head Trainer: Bill Tessendorf
Facilities Manager: Charley Cusick
Equipment Manager: Ed Carroll
Stadium: Cleveland Stadium • **Capacity:** 78,512
   West 3rd Street
   Cleveland, Ohio 44114
Playing Surface: Grass
Training Camp: 80 First Avenue
   Berea, Ohio 44017

1994 SCHEDULE

PRESEASON

Aug. 6	at New York Giants	8:00
Aug. 13	**Detroit**	7:30
Aug. 19	**Atlanta**	7:30
Aug. 25	at Indianapolis	7:30

REGULAR SEASON

Sept. 4	at Cincinnati	1:00
Sept. 11	**Pittsburgh**	1:00
Sept. 18	**Arizona**	1:00
Sept. 25	at Indianapolis	12:00
Oct. 2	**New York Jets**	1:00
Oct. 9	Open Date	
Oct. 13	at Houston (Thursday)	7:00
Oct. 23	**Cincinnati**	1:00
Oct. 30	at Denver	2:00
Nov. 6	**New England**	1:00
Nov. 13	at Philadelphia	1:00
Nov. 20	at Kansas City	12:00
Nov. 27	**Houston**	1:00
Dec. 4	**New York Giants**	4:00
Dec. 10	at Dallas (Saturday)	3:00
Dec. 18	at Pittsburgh	1:00
Dec. 24	**Seattle**	1:00

RECORD HOLDERS

INDIVIDUAL RECORDS—CAREER

Category	Name	Performance
Rushing (Yds.)	Jim Brown, 1957-1965	12,312
Passing (Yds.)	Brian Sipe, 1974-1983	23,713
Passing (TDs)	Brian Sipe, 1974-1983	154
Receiving (No.)	Ozzie Newsome, 1978-1990	662
Receiving (Yds.)	Ozzie Newsome, 1978-1990	7,980
Interceptions	Thom Darden, 1972-74, 1976-1981	45
Punting (Avg.)	Horace Gillom, 1950-56	43.8
Punt Return (Avg.)	Greg Pruitt, 1973-1981	11.8
Kickoff Return (Avg.)	Greg Pruitt, 1973-1981	26.3
Field Goals	Lou Groza, 1950-59, 1961-67	234
Touchdowns (Tot.)	Jim Brown, 1957-1965	*126
Points	Lou Groza, 1950-59, 1961-67	1,349

INDIVIDUAL RECORDS—SINGLE SEASON

Category	Name	Performance
Rushing (Yds.)	Jim Brown, 1963	1,863
Passing (Yds.)	Brian Sipe, 1980	4,132
Passing (TDs)	Brian Sipe, 1980	30
Receiving (No.)	Ozzie Newsome, 1983	89
	Ozzie Newsome, 1984	89
Receiving (Yds.)	Webster Slaughter, 1989	1,236
Interceptions	Thom Darden, 1978	10
Punting (Avg.)	Gary Collins, 1965	46.7
Punt Return (Avg.)	Leroy Kelly, 1965	15.6
Kickoff Return (Avg.)	Billy Reynolds, 1954	29.5
Field Goals	Matt Bahr, 1984	24
	Matt Bahr, 1988	24
Touchdowns (Tot.)	Jim Brown, 1965	21
Points	Jim Brown, 1965	126

INDIVIDUAL RECORDS—SINGLE GAME

Category	Name	Performance
Rushing (Yds.)	Jim Brown, 11-24-57	237
	Jim Brown, 11-19-61	237
Passing (Yds.)	Bernie Kosar, 1-3-87	489
Passing (TDs)	Frank Ryan, 12-12-64	5
	Bill Nelsen, 11-2-69	5
	Brian Sipe, 10-7-79	5
Receiving (No.)	Ozzie Newsome, 10-14-84	14
Receiving (Yds.)	Ozzie Newsome, 10-14-84	191
Interceptions	Many times	3
	Last time by Frank Minnifield, 11-22-87	
Field Goals	Don Cockroft, 10-19-75	5
Touchdowns (Tot.)	Dub Jones, 11-25-51	*6
Points	Dub Jones, 11-25-51	36

*NFL Record

COACHING HISTORY

(368-268-10)

1950-62	Paul Brown	115-49-5
1963-70	Blanton Collier	79-38-2
1971-74	Nick Skorich	30-26-2
1975-77	Forrest Gregg*	18-23-0
1977	Dick Modzelewski	0-1-0
1978-84	Sam Rutigliano**	47-52-0
1984-88	Marty Schottenheimer	46-31-0
1989-90	Bud Carson***	12-14-1
1990	Jim Shofner	1-6-0
1991-93	Bill Belichick	20-28-0

*Resigned after 13 games in 1977
**Released after eight games in 1984
***Released after nine games in 1990

CLEVELAND STADIUM

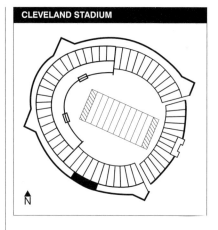

1993 TEAM RECORD

PRESEASON (2-2)

Date	Result		Opponents
8/9	L	12-41	at Washington
8/14	W	12-9	vs. New England at Toronto
8/21	W	21-10	L.A. Rams
8/27	L	20-23	at Tampa Bay

REGULAR SEASON (7-9)

Date	Result		Opponents	Att.
9/5	W	27-14	Cincinnati	75,508
9/13	W	23-13	San Francisco	78,218
9/19	W	19-16	at L.A. Raiders	48,617
9/26	L	10-23	at Indianapolis	59,654
10/10	L	14-24	Miami	78,138
10/17	W	28-17	at Cincinnati	55,647
10/24	W	28-23	Pittsburgh	78,118
11/7	L	14-29	Denver	77,818
11/14	L	5-22	at Seattle	54,622
11/21	L	20-27	Houston	71,668
11/28	L	14-17	at Atlanta	54,510
12/5	W	17-13	New Orleans	60,388
12/12	L	17-19	at Houston	58,720
12/19	L	17-20	New England	48,618
12/26	W	42-14	at L.A. Rams	34,155
1/2	L	9-16	at Pittsburgh	49,208

SCORE BY PERIODS

Browns	56	99	58	91	0	—	304
Opponents	64	110	52	81	0	—	307

ATTENDANCE

Home 568,474   Away 415,133   Total 983,607
Single-game home record, 85,073 (9-21-70)
Single-season home record, 620,496 (1980)

1993 TEAM STATISTICS

	Browns	Opp.
Total First Downs	264	290
Rushing	91	94
Passing	152	170
Penalty	21	26
Third Down: Made/Att	66/201	88/231
Third Down Pct.	32.8	38.1
Fourth Down: Made/Att	11/14	6/13
Fourth Down Pct.	78.6	46.2
Total Net Yards	4740	4778
Avg. Per Game	296.3	298.6
Total Plays	948	1040
Avg. Por Play	5.0	4.6
Net Yards Rushing	1701	1654
Avg. Per Game	106.3	103.4
Total Rushes	425	451
Net Yards Passing	3039	3124
Avg. Per Game	189.9	195.3
Sacked/Yards Lost	45/289	48/342
Gross Yards	3328	3466
Att./Completions	478/262	541/306
Completion Pct.	54.8	56.6
Had Intercepted	19	13
Punts/Avg.	84/43.2	85/42.4
Net Punting Avg.	84/35.6	85/34.1
Penalties/Yards Lost	121/842	105/821
Fumbles/Ball Lost	27/17	29/9
Touchdowns	36	30
Rushing	8	9
Passing	23	19
Returns	5	2
Avg. Time of Possession	29:32	30:28

1993 INDIVIDUAL STATISTICS

PASSING	Att	Cmp	Yds.	Pct.	TD	Int	Tkld.	Rate
Testaverde	230	130	1797	56.5	14	9	17/101	85.7
Kosar	138	79	807	57.2	5	3	21/128	77.2
Philcox	108	52	699	48.1	4	7	7/60	54.5
Hoard	1	0	0	0.0	0	0	0/0	39.6
Jackson	1	1	25	100.0	0	0	0/0	118.8
Browns	478	262	3328	54.8	23	19	45/289	76.2
Opponents	541	306	3466	56.6	19	13	48/342	77.6

SCORING	TD R	TD P	TD Rt	PAT	FG	Saf	PTS
Stover	0	0	0	36/36	16/22	0	84
Jackson	0	8	0	0/0	0/0	0	48
Carrier	1	3	1	0/0	0/0	0	30
Metcalf	1	2	2	0/0	0/0	0	30
McCardell	0	4	0	0/0	0/0	0	24
Vardell	3	1	0	0/0	0/0	0	24
Kinchen	0	2	0	0/0	0/0	0	12
Baldwin	0	1	0	0/0	0/0	0	6
J. Jones	1	0	0	0/0	0/0	0	6
Mack	1	0	0	0/0	0/0	0	6
Moore	0	0	1	0/0	0/0	0	6
Mustafaa	0	0	1	0/0	0/0	0	6
Philcox	1	0	0	0/0	0/0	0	6
Tillman	0	1	0	0/0	0/0	0	6
Wolfley	0	1	0	0/0	0/0	0	6
Pleasant	0	0	0	0/0	0/0	1	2
Riddick	0	0	0	0/0	0/0	1	2
Browns	8	23	5	36/36	16/22	2	304
Opponents	9	19	2	30/30	31/38	2	307

RUSHING	Att.	Yds.	Avg.	LG	TD
Vardell	171	644	3.8	54	3
Metcalf	129	611	4.7	55	1
Hoard	56	227	4.1	30	0
Testaverde	18	74	4.1	14	0
Baldwin	18	61	3.4	11	0
Mack	10	33	3.3	7	1
Carrier	4	26	6.5	15t	1
Kosar	14	19	1.4	10	0
Philcox	2	3	1.5	3t	1
J. Jones	2	2	1.0	1t	1
Jackson	1	1	1.0	1	0
Browns	425	1701	4.0	55	8
Opponents	451	1654	3.7	49	9

RECEIVING	No.	Yds.	Avg.	LG	TD
Metcalf	63	539	8.6	49t	2
Carrior	43	746	17.3	55	3
Jackson	41	756	18.4	62t	8
Hoard	35	351	10.0	41	0
Kinchen	29	347	12.0	40	2
Vardell	19	151	7.9	28t	1
McCardell	13	234	18.0	43	4
Tillman	5	68	13.6	18	1
Wolfley	5	25	5.0	9	1
Smith	4	55	13.8	17	0
Rowe	3	37	12.3	16	0
C. Williams	1	14	14.0	14	0
Baldwin	1	5	5.0	5t	1
Browns	262	3328	12.7	62t	23
Opponents	306	3466	11.3	56	19

INTERCEPTIONS	No.	Yds.	Avg.	LG	TD
Turner	5	25	5.0	19	0
S. Jones	3	0	0.0	0	0
Mustafaa	1	97	97.0	97t	1
Hilliard	1	54	54.0	54	0
Speer	1	22	22.0	22	0
Matthews	1	10	10.0	10	0
M. Johnson	1	0	0.0	0	0
Browns	13	208	16.0	97t	1
Opponents	19	246	12.9	69	0

PUNTING	No.	Yds.	Avg.	In 20	LG
Hansen	82	3632	44.3	15	72
Browns	84	3632	43.2	15	72
Opponents	85	3603	42.4	24	61

PUNT RETURNS	No.	FC	Yds.	Avg.	LG	TD
Metcalf	36	11	464	12.9	91t	2
Carrier	6	1	92	15.3	56t	1
Turner	0	0	7	—	7	0
Browns	42	12	563	13.4	91t	3
Opponents	49	14	438	8.9	36	0

KICKOFF RETURNS	No.	Yds.	Avg.	LG	TD
Baldwin	24	444	18.5	31	0
Metcalf	15	318	21.2	47	0
Hoard	13	286	22.0	39	0
Vardell	4	58	14.5	16	0
Kinchen	1	0	0.0	0	0
Smith	1	13	13.0	13	0
Browns	58	1119	19.3	47	0
Opponents	46	814	17.7	49	0

SACKS	No.
Pleasant	11.0
Burnett	9.0
Perry	6.0
J. Jones	5.5
Matthews	5.5
M. Johnson	4.0
Ball	3.0
Footman	1.0
P. Johnson	1.0
W. Johnson	1.0
Walls	1.0
Browns	48.0
Opponents	45.0

1994 DRAFT CHOICES

Round	Name	Pos.	College
1	Antonio Langham	CB	Alabama
	Derrick Alexander	WR	Michigan
3	Romeo Bandison	DT	Oregon
5	Issac Booth	CB	California
6	Robert Strait	RB	Baylor
7	Andre Hewitt	T	Clemson

CLEVELAND BROWNS

1994 VETERAN ROSTER

No.	Name	Pos.	Ht.	Wt.	Birthdate	NFL Exp.	College	Hometown	How Acq.	'93 Games/ Starts
73	Arvie, Herman	T	6-4	305	10/12/70	2	Grambling	Opelousas, La.	D5-'93	16/0
25	Briggs, Greg	S	6-3	210	10/19/68	2	Texas Southern	Meadville, Miss.	FA-'93	0*
77	Brown, Orlando	T	6-7	325	12/12/70	2	South Carolina State	Washington D.C.	FA-'93	0*
52	Brown, Richard	LB	6-3	240	9/21/65	7	San Diego State	Westminster, Calif.	PB(SD)-'91	0*
90	Burnett, Rob	DE	6-4	280	8/27/67	5	Syracuse	Coram, N.Y.	D5-'90	16/16
23	Byner, Earnest	RB	5-10	215	9/15/62	11	East Carolina	Milledgeville, Ga.	UFA(Wash)-'94	16/3*
56	Caldwell, Mike	LB	6-2	235	8/31/71	2	Middle Tennessee State	Oak Ridge, Tenn.	D3-'93	15/1
83	Carrier, Mark	WR	6-0	185	10/28/65	8	Nicholls State	Lafayette, La.	UFA(TB)-'93	16/16
72	Dahl, Bob	G	6-5	300	11/5/68	3	Notre Dame	Chagrin Falls, Ohio	FA-'92	16/16
51	Dixon, Gerald	LB	6-3	250	6/20/69	3	South Carolina	Rock Hill, S.C.	D3b-'92	11/0
61	Everitt, Steve	C	6-5	290	8/21/70	2	Michigan	Miami, Fla.	D1-'93	16/16
78	Footman, Dan	DE	6-5	290	1/13/69	2	Florida State	Tampa, Fla.	D2-'93	8/0
37	t- Frank, Donald	CB	6-0	192	10/24/65	5	Winston-Salem State	Tarboro, N.C.	T(SD)-'94	16/16*
8	Goebel, Brad	QB	6-3	198	10/13/67	4	Baylor	Cuero, Tex.	FA-'93	0*
28	Griffin, Don	CB	6-0	176	3/17/64	9	Middle Tennessee State	Camilla, Ga.	UFA(SF)-'94	12/12*
31	Hairston, Stacey	CB	5-9	180	8/16/67	2	Ohio Northern	Columbus, Ohio	FA-'93	16/0
55	Hill, Travis	LB	6-2	240	10/3/69	2	Nebraska	Houston, Tex.	D7-'93	0*
33	Hoard, Leroy	RB	5-11	225	5/15/68	5	Michigan	New Orleans, La.	D2-'90	16/7
64	Hoover, Houston	G	6-2	300	2/6/65	7	Jackson State	Yazoo City, Miss.	UFA(Atl)-'93	16/16
81	† Jackson, Michael	WR	6-4	195	4/12/69	4	Southern Mississippi	Kentwood, La.	D6-'91	15/11
94	Johnson, Bill	DE-DT	6-4	290	12/9/68	3	Michigan State	Chicago, Ill.	D3a-'92	10/0
53	# Johnson, Pepper	LB	6-3	248	7/29/64	9	Ohio State	Detroit, Mich.	FA-'93	16/11
47	Jones, David	TE	6-3	255	11/9/68	3	Delaware State	Hillside, N.J.	FA-'94	0*
96	† Jones, James	DT	6-2	290	2/6/69	4	Northern Iowa	Davenport, Iowa	D3-'91	16/12
22	Jones, Selwyn	CB	6-0	185	5/13/70	3	Colorado State	Missouri City, Tex.	D7-'92	11/2
66	Jones, Tony	T	6-5	295	5/24/66	7	Western Carolina	Cannesville, Ga.	FA-'88	16/16
88	Kinchen, Brian	TE	6-2	240	8/6/65	7	Louisiana State	Baton Rouge, La.	FA-'91	16/15
34	# Mack, Kevin	RB	6-0	225	8/9/62	9	Clemson	Kings Mountain, N.C.	SD1a-'84	4/0
57	# Matthews, Clay	LB	6-2	245	3/15/56	17	Southern California	New Trier, Ill.	D1a-'78	16/15
87	McCardell, Keenan	WR	6-1	175	1/6/70	3	Nevada-Las Vegas	Houston, Tex.	FA-'92	6/3
80	McLemore, Tom	TE	6-5	250	3/14/70	3	Southern	Shreveport, La.	W(Det)-'93	4/0
21	Metcalf, Eric	RB	5-10	190	1/23/68	6	Texas	Arlington, Tex.	D1-'89	16/9
65	Milstead, Rod	G	6-2	290	11/10/69	3	Delaware State	Bryans Road, Md.	T(Dall)-'92	0*
27	Moore, Stevon	S	5-11	210	2/9/67	6	Mississippi	Wiggins, Miss.	FA-'92	16/16
48	Mustafaa, Najee	CB	6-1	190	6/20/64	8	Georgia Tech	East Point, Ga.	UFA(Minn)-'93	14/14
92	Perry, Michael Dean	DT	6-1	285	8/27/65	7	Clemson	Aiken, S.C.	D2-'88	16/13
17	# Philcox, Todd	QB	6-4	225	9/25/66	5	Syracuse	Norwalk, Conn.	PB(Cin)-'91	5/4
98	Pleasant, Anthony	DE	6-5	280	1/27/68	5	Tennessee State	Century, Fla.	D3-'90	16/13
49	Reeves, Walter	TE	6-4	270	12/16/65	6	Auburn	Eugaula, Ala.	UFA(Ariz)-'94	16/15*
42	Riddick, Louis	S	6-2	215	3/15/69	3	Pittsburgh	Quakertown, Pa.	FA-'93	15/0
86	Rowe, Patrick	WR	6-1	195	2/17/69	3	San Diego State	San Diego, Calif.	D2-'92	5/0
11	Rypien, Mark	QB	6-4	234	10/2/62	8	Washington State	Spokane, Wash.	FA-'94	12/10*
75	† Sagapolutele, Pio	DE	6-6	297	11/28/69	4	San Diego State	Honolulu, Hawaii	D4-'91	8/0
84	Smith, Rico	WR	6-0	185	1/14/69	3	Colorado	Paramount, Calif.	D6a-'92	10/1
43	Speer, Del	S	6-0	200	2/1/70	2	Florida	Miami, Fla.	FA-'93	16/2
50	Stams, Frank	LB	6-2	230	7/17/66	6	Notre Dame	Akron, Ohio	T(Rams)-'92	14/0
3	Stover, Matt	K	5-11	178	1/27/68	5	Louisiana Tech	Dallas, Tex.	PB(NYG)-'91	16/0
54	Sutter, Ed	LB	6-3	235	10/3/69	2	Northwestern	Peoria, Ill.	W(NE)-'93	15/0
12	Testaverde, Vinny	QB	6-5	215	11/13/63	8	Miami	Floral Park, N.Y.	UFA(TB)-'93	10/6
85	# Tillman, Lawyer	WR	6-5	230	5/20/66	6	Auburn	Mobile, Ala.	D2-'89	7/0
7	Tupa, Tom	P-QB	6-4	230	2/6/66	6	Ohio State	Brecksville, Ohio	FA-'94	0*
29	Turner, Eric	S	6-1	207	9/20/68	4	UCLA	Ventura, Calif.	D1-'91	16/16
44	Vardell, Tommy	RB	6-2	230	2/20/69	3	Stanford	El Cajon, Calif.	D1-'92	16/12
62	† Williams, Gene	T-G	6-2	305	10/14/68	4	Iowa State	Omaha, Neb.	T(Mia)-'93	16/14
63	Williams, Wally	C	6-2	300	2/19/71	2	Florida A&M	Tallahassee, Fla.	FA-'93	2/0
60	Withycombe, Mike	G	6-5	300	11/18/64	6	Fresno State	Lemoore, Calif.	UFA(SD)-'94	0*

* Briggs last on injured list with Dallas in '92; O. Brown, R. Brown, and Hill missed '93 season due to injury; Byner played 16 games with Washington; Frank played 16 games with San Diego in '93; Goebel active for 3 games but did not play; Griffin played 12 games with San Francisco; D. Jones last active with L.A. Raiders in '92; Milstead inacitve for 11 games; Reeves played 16 games with Arizona; Rypien played 12 games with Washington; Tupa inactive for 2 games; Withycombe active for 3 games with San Diego but did not play.

\# Unrestricted free agent; subject to developments.

† Restricted free agent; subject to developments.

t- Browns traded for Frank (San Diego).

Players lost through free agency (3): P Brian Hansen (NYJ; 16 games in '93), CB Randy Hilliard (Den; 12), LB Mike Johnson (Det; 16).

Also played with Browns in '93—RB Randy Baldwin (14 games), DT Jerry Ball (16), LB David Brandon (6), CB Tim Jacobs (2), T-G Ed King (6), QB Bernie Kosar (7), S Erik McMillan (3), CB Terry Taylor (10), CB Everson Walls (7), TE Clarence Williams (7), RB Ron Wolfley (16), C Lance Zeno (2).

COACHING STAFF

Head Coach,
Bill Belichick

Pro Career: Became the Browns' tenth head coach on February 5, 1991. Belichick formerly was defensive coordinator of the New York Giants, who defeated the Buffalo Bills 20-19 in Super Bowl XXV. He also coordinated the Giants' defense that won Super Bowl XXI in 1986. Began coaching career at 23 as a special assistant to Ted Marchibroda with the Baltimore Colts in 1975. He tutored the Detroit Lions' tight ends, wide receivers, and special teams in 1976-77, before joining the Denver Broncos in 1978. He joined the Giants in 1979 as a defensive assistant and special teams coach, moved to linebackers in 1981-82, and became defensive coordinator in 1983. Career record: 20-28.

Background: Attended Annapolis (Maryland) High School and Phillips Academy in Andover, Mass. Played football and lacrosse at Wesleyan (Conn.) University. Earned a bachelor's degree in economics from Wesleyan in 1975.

Personal: Born April 16, 1952, in Nashville, Tenn. Bill and his wife, Debby, live in Brecksville, Ohio, and have three children—Amanda, Stephen, and Brian.

ASSISTANT COACHES

Ernie Adams, special assignments; born March 31, 1953, Waltham, Mass., lives in Lakewood, Ohio. No college or pro playing experience. College coach: Northwestern 1971-74. Pro coach: New England Patriots 1975-78, New York Giants 1979-81 (Pro Personnel Director 1982-85), joined Browns in 1991.

Jacob Burney, defensive line; born January 24, 1959, Chattanooga, Tenn., lives in Berea, Ohio. Defensive tackle Tennessee-Chattanooga 1977-80. No pro playing experience. College coach: New Mexico 1983-86, Tulsa 1987, Mississippi State 1988, Wisconsin 1989, UCLA 1990-92, Tennessee 1993. Pro coach: Joined Browns in 1994.

Steve Crosby, offensive coordinator; born July 3, 1950, Great Bend, Kan., lives in Strongsville, Ohio. Running back Fort Hays State 1969-72. Pro running back New York Giants 1974-76. Pro coach: Miami Dolphins 1979-82, Atlanta Falcons 1983-84, 1986-89, Cleveland Browns 1985, New England Patriots 1990, rejoined Browns in 1991.

Rod Dowhower, quarterbacks; born April 15, 1943, Ord, Neb., lives in Berea, Ohio. Quarterback San Diego State 1963-65. No pro playing experience. College coach: San Diego State 1966-72, UCLA 1974-75, Boise State 1976, Stanford 1977-79 (head coach 1979). Pro coach: St. Louis Cardinals 1973, 1982-84, Denver Broncos 1980-81, Indianapolis Colts 1985-86 (head coach), Atlanta Falcons 1987-89, Washington Redskins 1990-93, joined Browns in 1994.

Kirk Ferentz, offensive line; born August 1, 1955, Royal Oak, Mich., lives in North Royalton, Ohio. Linebacker Connecticut 1973-76. No pro playing experience. College coach: Connecticut 1977, Pittsburgh 1980, Iowa 1981-89, Maine 1990-92 (head coach). Pro coach: Joined Browns in 1993.

Pat Hill, tight ends-assistant offensive line; born December 17, 1951, Los Angeles, Calif., lives in Berea, Ohio. Center California-Riverside 1971-73. No pro playing experience. College coach: Los Angeles Valley Junior College 1974-76, Utah 1977-80, Nevada-Las Vegas 1981-82, Fresno State 1985-89, Arizona 1990-91. Pro coach: Calgary Stampeders (CFL) 1983-84, joined Browns in 1992.

Scott O'Brien, special teams; born June 25, 1957, Superior, Wis., lives in Strongsville, Ohio. Defensive end Wisconsin-Superior 1975-78. Pro defensive end Green Bay Packers 1979, Toronto Argonauts (CFL) 1979. College coach: Wisconsin-Superior 1980-82, Nevada-Las Vegas 1983-85, Rice 1986, Pittsburgh 1987-90. Pro coach: Joined Browns in 1991.

Nick Saban, defensive coordinator; born October 31, 1951, Fairmont, W. Va., lives in Medina, Ohio. Defensive back Kent State 1969-72. No pro playing experience. College coach: Kent State 1973-76,

Syracuse 1977, West Virginia 1978-79, Ohio State 1980-81, Navy 1982, Michigan State 1983-87, Toledo 1990 (head coach). Pro coach: Houston Oilers 1988-89, joined Browns in 1991.

Mike Sheppard, receivers; born October 29, 1951, Tulsa, Okla., lives in Strongsville, Ohio. Wide receiver Cal Lutheran 1969-72. No pro playing experience. College coach: Cal Lutheran 1974-76, Brigham Young 1977-78, U.S. International 1979, Idaho State 1980-81, Long Beach State 1982, 1984-86 (head coach), Kansas 1983, New Mexico 1987-91 (head coach), California 1992. Pro coach: Joined Browns in 1993.

Jerry Simmons, strength and conditioning; born June 15, 1954, Elkhart, Kan., lives in Strongsville, Ohio. Linebacker Fort Hays State 1976-77. No pro playing experience. College coach: Fort Hays State 1978, Clemson 1980, Rice 1981-82, Southern California 1983-87. Pro coach: New England Patriots 1988-90, joined Browns in 1991.

Kevin Spencer, offensive assistant; born November 2, 1953, Queens, N.Y., lives in Bay Village, Ohio. No college or pro playing experience. College coach: State University of New York 1975-76, Cornell 1979-80, Ithaca 1981-86, Wesleyan 1987-91 (head coach). Pro coach: Joined Browns in 1991.

Rick Venturi, defensive backs; born February 23, 1946, Taylorville, Ill., lives in Strongsville, Ohio. Quarterback-defensive back Northwestern 1965-67. No pro playing experience. College coach: Northwestern 1968-72, 1978-80 (head coach), Purdue 1973-76, Illinois 1977. Pro coach: Hamilton Tiger-Cats (CFL) 1981, Indianapolis Colts 1982-93 (interim head coach 1991), joined Browns in 1994.

Woody Widenhofer, linebackers; born January 20, 1943, Butler, Pa., lives in Berea, Ohio. Linebacker Missouri 1961-64. No pro playing experience. College coach: Michigan State 1969-70, Eastern Michigan 1971, Minnesota 1972, Missouri 1985-88 (head coach). Pro coach: Pittsburgh Steelers 1973-83, Oklahoma Outlaws (USFL) 1984 (head coach), Detroit Lions 1989-92, joined Browns in 1993.

1994 FIRST-YEAR ROSTER

Name	Pos.	Ht.	Wt.	Birthdate	College	Hometown	How Acq.
Alexander, Derrick	WR	6-2	195	11/6/71	Michigan	Detroit, Mich.	D1b
Bandison, Romeo	DT	6-5	290	2/12/71	Oregon	Mill Valley, Calif.	D3
Bomba, Matt (1)	DE-DT	6-5	275	5/22/68	Indiana	Bloomington, Ind.	FA
Booth, Isaac	CB-S	6-3	190	5/23/71	California	Indianapolis, Ind.	D5
Cobb, Robert	QB	6-2	217	2/7/71	Northeast Louisiana	Monroe, La.	FA
Derby, John (1)	LB	6-0	232	3/24/68	Iowa	Pittsburgh, Pa.	FA
Eichloff, Dan	K	6-0	215	6/3/72	Kansas	Ft. Lauderdale, Fla.	FA
Ferrell, Kerry (1)	WR	5-11	173	7/8/70	Syracuse	Piscataway, N.J.	FA
Gray, Jim (1)	DT	6-2	285	7/5/69	West Virginia	West Mifflin, Pa.	FA
Hartley, Frank (1)	TE	6-2	268	12/15/67	Illinois	Chicago, Ill.	FA
Hewitt, Andre	T	6-6	285	4/26/71	Clemson	Pittsburgh, Pa.	D7
Jacobs, Tim (1)	CB	5-10	185	4/5/70	Delaware	Landover, Md.	FA
Kalal, Tim (1)	P	6-3	205	9/13/67	Miami	Longview, Wash.	FA
Killian, P.J.	LB	6-2	242	5/19/71	Virginia	Pittsburgh, Pa.	FA
Langham, Antonio	CB	6-0	180	7/31/72	Alabama	Town Creek, Ala.	D1a
Lee, Marcus	RB	5-10	227	5/21/71	Syracuse	Springfield, Mass.	FA
Leomiti, Carlson	T-G	6-3	384	1/10/71	San Diego State	Carson, Calif.	FA
Lyle, Rick	DE-DT	6-5	275	2/26/71	Missouri	Kansas City, Mo.	FA
McKenzie, Rich (1)	LB	6-2	240	4/15/71	Penn State	Ft. Lauderdale, Fla.	D6-'93
Montford, Joe	LB	6-0	210	7/30/70	South Carolina State	Columbia, S.C.	FA
Myles, Tim	DE-DT	6-1	280	6/22/70	Vermillion J.C.	Duluth, Minn.	FA
Strait, Robert	RB	6-1	255	11/14/69	Baylor	Cuero, Tex.	D6
Toney, Eudean	S	6-1	208	4/13/72	Grambling	Monroe, La.	FA
Tremble, Greg	S	5-11	188	4/16/72	Georgia	Atlanta, Ga.	FA
Werdel, John	P	6-2	205	3/16/71	Washington	Bakersfield, Calif.	FA

The term NFL Rookie is defined as a player who is in his first season of professional football and has not been on the roster of another professional football team for any regular-season or postseason games. A Rookie is designated by an "R" on NFL rosters. Players who have been active in another professional football league or players who have NFL experience, including either preseason training camp or being on an Active List or Inactive List, or on Reserve/Injured or Reserve/Physically Unable to Perform for fewer than six regular-season games, are termed NFL First-Year Players. An NFL First-Year Player is designated by a "1" on NFL rosters. Thereafter, a player is credited with an additional year of experience for each season in which he accumulates six games on the Active List or Inactive List, or on Reserve/Injured or Reserve/Physically Unable to Perform.

NOTES

35

DENVER BRONCOS

American Football Conference
Western Division
Team Colors: Orange, Royal Blue, and White
13655 Broncos Parkway
Englewood, Colorado 80112
Telephone: (303) 649-9000

CLUB OFFICIALS

President-Chief Executive Officer:
  Pat Bowlen
General Manager: John Beake
Head Coach: Wade Phillips
Chief Financial Officer-Treasurer:
  Robert M. Hurley
Director of Football Operations/Player Personnel:
  Bob Ferguson
Director of Media Relations: Jim Saccomano
Assistant to the General Manager/Community
  Relations: Fred Fleming
Ticket Manager: Gail Stuckey
Director of Operations: Bill Harpole
Director of Marketing: Rosemary Manratty
Director of Player Relations: Bill Thompson
Trainer: Steve Antonopulos
Equipment Manager: Doug West
Video Director: Kent Erickson
Stadium: Denver Mile High Stadium
  •**Capacity:** 76,273
    1900 West Eliot
    Denver, Colorado 80204
Playing Surface: Grass (PAT)
Training Camp: University of Northern Colorado
                    Greeley, Colorado 80639

1994 SCHEDULE
PRESEASON

July 31	vs. L.A. Raiders at Barcelona	1:00
Aug. 6	**Atlanta**	7:00
Aug. 12	at San Francisco	5:00
Aug. 21	at Dallas	7:00
Aug. 25	**Arizona**	7:00

REGULAR SEASON

Sept. 4	**San Diego**	6:00
Sept. 11	at New York Jets	4:00
Sept. 18	**Los Angeles Raiders**	2:00
Sept. 26	at Buffalo (Monday)	9:00
Oct. 2	Open Date	
Oct. 9	at Seattle	1:00
Oct. 17	**Kansas City** (Monday)	7:00
Oct. 23	at San Diego	1:00
Oct. 30	**Cleveland**	2:00
Nov. 6	at Los Angeles Rams	1:00
Nov. 13	**Seattle**	2:00
Nov. 20	**Atlanta**	2:00
Nov. 27	**Cincinnati**	2:00
Dec. 4	at Kansas City	3:00
Dec. 11	at Los Angeles Raiders	1:00
Dec. 17	at San Francisco (Saturday)	1:00
Dec. 24	**New Orleans**	2:00

RECORD HOLDERS
INDIVIDUAL RECORDS—CAREER

Category	Name	Performance
Rushing (Yds.)	Floyd Little, 1967-1975	6,323
Passing (Yds.)	John Elway, 1983-1993	34,246
Passing (TDs)	John Elway, 1983-1993	183
Receiving (No.)	Lionel Taylor, 1960-66	543
Receiving (Yds.)	Lionel Taylor, 1960-66	6,872
Interceptions	Steve Foley, 1976-1986	44
Punting (Avg.)	Jim Fraser, 1962-64	45.2
Punt Return (Avg.)	Rick Upchurch, 1975-1983	12.1
Kickoff Return (Avg.)	Abner Haynes, 1965-66	26.3
Field Goals	Jim Turner, 1971-79	151
Touchdowns (Tot.)	Floyd Little, 1967-1975	54
Points	Jim Turner, 1971-79	742

INDIVIDUAL RECORDS—SINGLE SEASON

Category	Name	Performance
Rushing (Yds.)	Otis Armstrong, 1974	1,407
Passing (Yds.)	John Elway, 1993	4,030
Passing (TDs)	John Elway, 1993	25
Receiving (No.)	Lionel Taylor, 1961	100
Receiving (Yds.)	Steve Watson, 1981	1,244
Interceptions	Goose Gonsoulin, 1960	11
Punting (Avg.)	Jim Fraser, 1963	46.1
Punt Return (Avg.)	Floyd Little, 1967	16.9
Kickoff Return (Avg.)	Bill Thompson, 1969	28.5
Field Goals	Gene Mingo, 1962	27
	David Treadwell, 1989, 1991	27
Touchdowns (Tot.)	Sammy Winder, 1986	14
Points	Gene Mingo, 1962	137

INDIVIDUAL RECORDS—SINGLE GAME

Category	Name	Performance
Rushing (Yds.)	Otis Armstrong, 12-8-74	183
Passing (Yds.)	Frank Tripucka, 9-15-62	447
Passing (TDs)	Frank Tripucka, 10-28-62	5
	John Elway, 11-18-84	5
Receiving (No.)	Lionel Taylor, 11-29-64	13
	Bobby Anderson, 9-30-73	13
Receiving (Yds.)	Lionel Taylor, 11-27-60	199
Interceptions	Goose Gonsoulin, 9-18-60	*4
	Willie Brown, 11-15-64	*4
Field Goals	Gene Mingo, 10-6-63	5
	Rich Karlis, 11-20-83	5
Touchdowns (Tot.)	Many times	3
	Last time by Shannon Sharpe, 12-12-93	
Points	Gene Mingo, 12-10-60	21

*NFL Record

COACHING HISTORY
(250-259-10)

1960-61	Frank Filchock	7-20-1
1962-64	Jack Faulkner*	9-22-1
1964-66	Mac Speedie**	6-19-1
1966	Ray Malavasi	4-8-0
1967-71	Lou Saban***	20-42-3
1971	Jerry Smith	2-3-0
1972-76	John Ralston	34-33-3
1977-80	Robert (Red) Miller	42-25-0
1981-92	Dan Reeves	117-79-1
1993	Wade Phillips	9-8-0

  *Released after four games in 1964
 **Resigned after two games in 1966
***Resigned after nine games in 1971

DENVER MILE HIGH STADIUM

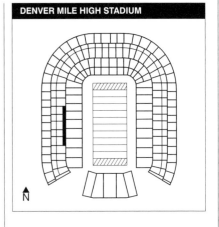

1993 TEAM RECORD

PRESEASON (2-2)

Date	Result		Opponents
8/7	W	23-7	at Tampa Bay
8/16	L	13-16	San Francisco
8/20	W	34-24	Miami
8/27	L	9-34	at Phoenix

REGULAR SEASON (9-7)

Date	Result		Opponents	Att.
9/5	W	26-20	at N.Y. Jets	68,130
9/12	W	34-17	San Diego	75,074
9/20	L	7-15	at Kansas City	78,453
10/3	W	35-13	Indianapolis	74,953
10/10	L	27-30	at Green Bay	58,943
10/18	L	20-23	L.A. Raiders	75,712
10/31	W	28-17	Seattle	73,644
11/7	W	29-14	at Cleveland	77,818
11/14	L	23-26	Minnesota	67,329
11/21	W	37-13	Pittsburgh	74,840
11/28	W	17-9	at Seattle	57,812
12/5	L	10-13	at San Diego	60,233
12/12	W	27-21	Kansas City	75,822
12/18	W	13-3	at Chicago	53,056
12/26	L	10-17	Tampa Bay	73,434
1/2	L	30-33	at L.A. Raiders (OT)	66,904

POSTSEASON (0-1)

1/9	L	24-42	at L.A. Raiders	65,314

SCORE BY PERIODS

Broncos	66	147	91	69	0	—	373
Opponents	53	82	62	84	3	—	284

ATTENDANCE

Home 590,808   Away 521,349   Total 1,112,157
Single-game home record, 76,105 (1-4-87)
Single-season home record, 598,224 (1981)

1993 TEAM STATISTICS

	Broncos	Opp.
Total First Downs	327	280
Rushing	105	86
Passing	187	181
Penalty	35	13
Third Down: Made/Att	98/225	71/215
Third Down Pct.	43.6	33.0
Fourth Down: Made/Att	2/11	8/17
Fourth Down Pct.	18.2	47.1
Total Net Yards	5461	5149
Avg. Per Game	341.3	321.8
Total Plays	1060	1005
Avg. Per Play	5.2	5.1
Net Yards Rushing	1693	1418
Avg. Per Game	105.8	88.6
Total Rushes	468	397
Net Yards Passing	3768	3731
Avg. Per Game	235.5	233.2
Sacked/Yards Lost	39/293	46/238
Gross Yards	4061	3969
Att./Completions	553/350	562/314
Completion Pct.	63.3	55.9
Had Intercepted	10	18
Punts/Avg.	68/44.4	81/43.7
Net Punting Avg.	68/37.1	81/36.0
Penalties/Yards Lost	112/822	128/1019
Fumbles/Ball Lost	29/18	27/13
Touchdowns	42	27
Rushing	13	6
Passing	27	21
Returns	2	0
Avg. Time of Possession	31:35	28:25

1993 INDIVIDUAL STATISTICS

PASSING

	Att.	Comp.	Yds.	Pct.	TD	Int.	Tkid.	Rate
Elway	551	348	4030	63.2	25	10	39/293	92.8
Maddox	1	1	1	100.0	1	0	0/0	118.8
Marshall	1	1	30	100.0	1	0	0/0	158.3
Broncos	553	350	4061	63.3	27	10	39/293	94.2
Opponents	562	314	3969	55.9	21	18	46/238	77.2

SCORING

	TD R	TD P	TD Rt	PAT	FG	Saf	PTS
Elam	0	0	0	41/42	26/35	0	119
Sharpe	0	9	0	0/0	0/0	0	54
Delpino	8	0	0	0/0	0/0	0	48
V. Johnson	0	5	0	0/0	0/0	0	30
Bernstine	4	0	0	0/0	0/0	0	24
Russell	0	3	1	0/0	0/0	0	24
Milburn	0	3	0	0/0	0/0	0	18
Rivers	1	1	0	0/0	0/0	1	14
Marshall	0	2	0	0/0	0/0	0	12
Tillman	0	2	0	0/0	0/0	0	12
Croel	0	0	1	0/0	0/0	0	6
R. Johnson	0	1	0	0/0	0/0	0	6
Wyman	0	1	0	0/0	0/0	0	6
Broncos	13	27	2	41/42	26/35	1	373
Opponents	6	21	0	27/27	31/36	1	284

RUSHING

	Att.	Yds.	Avg.	LG	TD
Bernstine	223	816	3.7	24	4
Delpino	131	445	3.4	18	8
Milburn	52	231	4.4	26	0
Elway	44	153	3.5	18	0
Rivers	15	50	3.3	14	1
Rouen	1	0	0.0	0	0
Maddox	2	-2	-1.0	-1	0
Broncos	468	1693	3.6	26	13
Opponents	397	1418	3.6	28	6

RECEIVING

	No.	Yds.	Avg.	LG	TD
Sharpe	81	995	12.3	63	9
Russell	44	719	16.3	43	3
Bernstine	44	372	8.5	41	0
Milburn	38	300	7.9	50	3
V. Johnson	36	517	14.4	56	5
Marshall	28	360	12.9	40	2
Delpino	26	195	7.5	25	0
R. Johnson	20	243	12.2	38	1
Tillman	17	193	11.4	30	2
Kimbrough	8	79	9.9	16	0
Rivers	6	59	9.8	17	1
K. Taylor	1	28	20.0	28	0
Wyman	1	1	1.0	1t	1
Broncos	350	4061	11.6	63	27
Opponents	314	3969	12.6	74t	21

INTERCEPTIONS

	No.	Yds.	Avg.	LG	TD
Smith	3	57	19.0	36	0
Braxton	3	37	12.3	25	0
Atwater	2	81	40.5	68	0
Dronett	2	13	6.5	7	0
Lang	2	4	2.0	4	0
Croel	1	22	22.0	22t	1
F. Robinson	1	13	13.0	13	0
Wyman	1	9	9.0	9	0
Bradford	1	0	0.0	0	0
Dimry	1	0	0.0	0	0
Hall	1	0	0.0	0	0
Broncos	18	236	13.1	68	1
Opponents	10	79	7.9	19	0

PUNTING

	No.	Yds.	Avg.	In 20	LG
Rouen	67	3017	45.0	17	62
Broncos	68	3017	44.4	17	62
Opponents	81	3541	43.7	22	61

PUNT RETURNS

	No.	FC	Yds.	Avg.	LG	TD
Milburn	40	1	425	10.6	54	0
Bradford	1	0	0	0.0	0	0
Broncos	41	11	425	10.4	54	0
Opponents	33	8	337	10.2	37	0

KICKOFF RETURNS

	No.	Yds.	Avg.	LG	TD
Russell	18	374	20.8	49	0
Milburn	12	188	15.7	26	0
Delpino	7	146	20.9	49	0
Meeks	1	9	9.0	9	0
Sharpe	1	0	0.0	0	0
Broncos	39	717	18.4	49	0
Opponents	63	1119	17.8	68	0

SACKS

	No.
Fletcher	13.5
Mecklenburg	9.0
Dronett	7.0
Croel	5.0
J. Robinson	3.5
Kragen	3.0
Wyman	2.0
Atwater	1.0
Oshodin	1.0
Williams	1.0
Broncos	46.0
Opponents	39.0

1994 DRAFT CHOICES

Round	Name	Pos.	College
2	Allen Aldridge	LB	Houston
4	Randy Fuller	DB	Tennessee State
7	Keith Burns	LB	Oklahoma State
	Butler By'not'e	RB	Ohio State
	Tom Nalen	C	Boston College

DENVER BRONCOS

1994 VETERAN ROSTER

No.		Name	Pos.	Ht.	Wt.	Birthdate	NFL Exp.	College	Hometown	How Acq.	'93 Games/ Starts
58		Alexander, Elijah	LB	6-2	230	8/8/70	3	Kansas State	Ft. Worth, Tex.	W(TB)-'93	16/0
27		Atwater, Steve	S	6-3	217	10/28/66	6	Arkansas	Chicago, Ill.	D1-'89	16/16
11		Ball, Michael	CB-S	6-1	215	8/5/64	7	Southern	New Orleans, La.	FA-'94	0*
33		Bernstine, Rod	RB	6-3	238	2/8/65	8	Texas A&M	Bryan, Tex.	UFA(SD)-'93	15/14
83		Bonner, Melvin	WR	6-3	207	2/18/70	2	Baylor	Hempstead, Tex.	D6-'93	3/0
23		Bradford, Ronnie	CB	5-10	188	10/1/70	2	Colorado	Commerce City, Colo.	FA-'93	10/3
10		Campbell, Jeff	WR	5-8	167	3/26/68	5	Colorado	Vail, Colo.	UFA(Det)-'94	10/0*
15		Carlson, Jeff	QB	6-3	212	5/23/66	4	Weber State	Long Beach, Calif.	FA-'94	0*
20		Crockett, Ray	CB	5-10	185	1/5/67	6	Baylor	Dallas, Tex.	UFA(Det)-'94	16/16*
51		Croel, Mike	LB	6-3	231	6/6/69	4	Nebraska	Detroit, Mich.	D1-'91	16/16
39		Delpino, Robert	RB	6-0	205	11/2/65	7	Missouri	Dodge City, Kan.	UFA(Rams)-'93	16/4
29	#	Dimry, Charles	CB	6-0	175	1/31/66	7	Nevada-Las Vegas	San Diego, Calif.	PB(Atl)-'91	12/11
54		Donahue, Mitch	LB	6-2	254	2/4/68	4	Wyoming	Billings, Mont.	W(SF)-'93	13/0
99		Dronett, Shane	DE	6-6	275	1/12/71	3	Texas	Orange, Tex.	D2-'92	16/16
97		Drozdov, Darren	NT	6-3	280	4/7/69	2	Maryland	Wilmington, Del.	FA-'93	6/2
1		Elam, Jason	K	5-11	192	3/8/70	2	Hawaii	Ft. Walton Beach, Fla.	D3b-'93	16/0
7		Elway, John	QB	6-3	215	6/28/60	12	Stanford	Port Angeles, Wash.	T(Balt)-'83	16/16
88		Evans, Jerry	TE	6-4	250	9/28/68	2	Toledo	Lorain, Ohio	FA-'93	14/2
73		Fletcher, Simon	LB	6-5	240	2/18/62	10	Houston	Bay City, Tex.	D2b-'85	16/16
68		Freeman, Russell	T	6-7	290	9/2/69	3	Georgia Tech	Homestead, Pa.	FA-'92	14/14
75		Habib, Brian	G	6-7	292	12/2/64	7	Washington	Ellensburg, Wash.	UFA(Minn)-'93	16/16
40		Hall, Darryl	S	6-2	210	8/1/66	2	Washington	Oscoda, Mich.	FA-'93	16/2
52		Harvey, Richard	LB	6-1	242	9/11/66	5	Tulane	Pascagoula, Miss.	UFA(Buff)-'94	15/0*
89	†	Johnson, Reggie	TE	6-2	256	1/27/68	4	Florida State	Pensacola, Fla.	D2-'91	13/12
31		Jones, Rondell	S	6-2	210	5/7/71	2	North Carolina	Sunderland, Mass.	D3a-'93	16/0
72		Kartz, Keith	C	6-4	270	5/5/63	8	California	Las Vegas, Nev.	FA-'87	12/10
80		Kimbrough, Tony	WR	6-2	192	9/17/70	2	Jackson State	Weir, Miss.	D7b-'93	15/0
21	#	Lang, Le-Lo	CB	5-11	185	1/23/67	5	Washington	Los Angeles, Calif.	D5b-'90	16/0
59	#	Lucas, Tim	LB	6-3	230	4/3/61	8	California	Stockton, Calif.	FA-'87	7/0
37		Lynn, Anthony	RB	6-3	230	12/21/68	2	Texas Tech	McKinney, Tex.	FA'-93	13/0
8		Maddox, Tommy	QB	6-4	195	9/2/71	3	UCLA	Shreveport, La.	D1-'92	16/0
78		Maggs, Don	T	6-5	290	11/1/61	9	Tulane	Youngstown, Ohio	UFA(Hou)-'93	7/2
77	#	Mecklenburg, Karl	LB	6-3	235	9/1/60	12	Minnesota	Edina, Minn.	D12-'83	16/16
61		Meeks, Bob	G	6-2	279	5/28/69	3	Auburn	Andulusia, Ala.	D10-'92	8/0
64	#	Melander, Jon	G	6-7	280	12/27/66	5	Minnesota	Fridley, Minn.	W(Cin)-'93	14/7
22		Milburn, Glyn	RB	5-8	177	2/19/71	2	Stanford	Santa Monica, Calif.	D2-'93	16/2
83		Miller, Anthony	WR	5-11	190	4/15/65	7	Tennessee	Pasadena, Calif.	RFA(SD)-'94	16/16*
52	#	Mills, Jeff	LB	6-3	238	10/8/68	5	Nebraska	Montclair, N.J.	W(SD)-'90	13/0
12		Moore, Shawn	QB	6-2	213	4/4/68	3	Virginia	Martinsville, Va.	D11-'91	0*
91		Oshodin, Willie	DE	6-4	260	9/16/69	4	Villanova	Benn City, Nigeria	FA-'92	15/5
81	t-	Pritchard, Mike	WR	5-10	190	10/26/69	4	Colorado	Las Vegas, Nev.	T(Atl)-'94	15/14*
38		Rivers, Reggie	RB	6-1	215	2/22/68	4	Southwest Texas State	Dayton, Ohio	FA-'91	16/2
36		Robinson, Frank	CB	5-11	174	1/11/69	3	Boise State	Newark, N.J.	D5-'92	16/2
94		Robinson, Jeff	DE	6-4	265	2/20/70	2	Idaho	Kennewick, Wash.	D4-'93	16/0
16		Rouen, Tom	P	6-3	215	6/9/68	2	Colorado	Hindsdale, Ill.	FA-'93	16/0
85		Russell, Derek	WR	6-0	179	6/22/69	4	Arkansas	Little Rock, Ark.	D4-'91	13/12
55		Sanders, Glenell	LB	6-1	237	11/4/66	2	Louisiana Tech	Clinton, La.	FA-'94	0*
76	#	Scrafford, Kirk	T	6-6	265	3/13/67	5	Montana	Billings, Mont.	W(Cin)-'93	16/0
84		Sharpe, Shannon	TE	6-2	230	6/26/68	5	Savannah State	Glennville, Ga.	D7-'90	16/12
26	t-	Smith, Ben	CB	5-11	185	5/14/67	5	Georgia	Warner Robins, Ga.	T(Phil)-'94	13/3*
49	#	Smith, Dennis	S	6-3	200	2/3/59	14	Southern California	Santa Monica, Calif.	D1-'81	14/14
95		Taylor, Alphonso	DT	6-3	350	9/7/69	2	Temple	Trenton, N.J.	W(Phx)-'93	3/0
81	#	Taylor, Kitrick	WR	5-11	189	7/22/64	6	Washington State	Pomona, Calif.	FA-'93	2/0
87		Tillman, Cedric	WR	6-2	204	7/22/70	3	Alcorn State	Gulfport, Miss.	D11-'92	14/3
98	t-	Washington, Ted	NT	6-4	295	4/13/68	4	Louisville	Tampa, Fla.	T(SF)-'94	12/12*
79		Widell, Dave	G-C	6-6	292	5/14/65	7	Boston College	Hartford, Conn.	T(Dall)-'91	15/15
90		Williams, Dan	DE	6-4	290	12/15/69	2	Toledo	Ypsilanti, Mich.	D1-'93	13/11
92		Wyman, Dave	LB	6-2	248	3/31/64	8	Stanford	San Diego, Calif.	UFA(Sea)-'93	16/16
65		Zimmerman, Gary	T	6-6	294	12/13/61	9	Oregon	Walnut, Calif.	T(Minn)-'94	16/16

* Ball last active with Indianapolis in '92; Campbell played 10 games with Detroit in '93; Carlson last active with New England in '92; Crockett played 16 games with Detroit; Harvey played 15 games with Buffalo; Miller played 16 games with San Diego; Moore inactive for 16 games; Pritchard played 15 games with Atlanta; Sanders last active with L.A. Rams in '92; B. Smith played 13 games with Philadelphia; Washington played 12 games with San Francisco.

\# Unrestricted free agent; subject to developments.

† Restricted free agent; subject to developments.

Traded—WR Arthur Marshall to N.Y. Giants.

t- Broncos traded for Pritchard (Atlanta), Smith (Philadelphia), Washington (San Francisco).

Players lost through free agency (3): CB Tyrone Braxton (Mia; 16 games in '93), WR Vance Johnson (SD; 10), CB David Pool (Minn; 0).

Also played with Broncos in '93—NT Greg Kragen (14 games), WR Arthur Marshall (16), WR Barry Rose (3).

COACHING STAFF

Head Coach,
Wade Phillips

Pro Career: Became the tenth head coach in Broncos history on January 25, 1993, moving into the head-coaching slot from his previous position as defensive coordinator. In his first year as the Broncos' head coach, Phillips had the youngest team in the NFL and still led Denver back into the playoffs with a 9-7 regular-season record. Under Phillips's leadership, the Broncos' defense led the American Football Conference in fewest points allowed in two of the past five seasons (1989 and 1991), and the 1991 Denver team was paced by a defensive unit that led the AFC in 12 different categories. In addition to his role as defensive coordinator with the Broncos, Phillips assumed the capacity of interim head coach during the 1990 preseason posting a win over Indianapolis. Going into his sixth season with Denver, Phillips came to the Broncos from Philadelphia, where he was the defensive coordinator and linebackers coach from 1986-88. He served as defensive coordinator at New Orleans from 1981-85 and was the interim head coach for the final four games of the 1985 season (1-3 record). Prior to joining the Saints, Phillips spent five seasons at Houston, coaching the linebackers (1976) and defensive line (1977-80). Career record: 10-11.

Background: Phillips began his coaching career at his alma mater, the University of Houston, in 1969, and then coached at Orange (Texas) High School for three years (1970-72) before moving to Oklahoma State (1973-74) and Kansas (1975).

Personal: The son of former NFL head coach Bum Phillips, Phillips was born in Orange, Texas on June 21, 1947. He attended Port Neches-Groves High School. He went on to be a three-year starter at linebacker at Houston under head coach Bill Yeoman. Wade and his wife, Laurie, live in Denver and have two children—Tracy and Wesley.

ASSISTANT COACHES

Vernon Banks, strength and conditioning; born May 24, 1956, Alvin, Tex., lives in Denver. Defensive back-running back Blinn Junior College 1976-77, Texas A&M 1978-79. No pro playing experience. College coach: Texas A&M 1981-83, Houston 1985, Wyoming 1986-87, 1992, Stanford 1987-89, Colorado 1990-91. Pro coach: Joined Broncos in 1993.

Barney Chavous, defensive assistant; born March 22, 1951, Aiken, S.C., lives in Englewood, Colo. Defensive end South Carolina State 1969-72. Pro defensive end Denver Broncos 1973-85. Pro coach: Joined Broncos in 1989.

Jim Fassel, assistant head coach-offensive coordinator; born August 31, 1949, Anaheim, Calif., lives in Greenwood Village, Colo. Quarterback Southern California 1969-70, Long Beach State 1971. Pro quarterback Chicago Bears 1972, Houston Oilers 1972, San Diego Chargers 1972. College coach: Fullerton (Calif.) Junior College 1973, Utah 1976, 1985-89 (head coach), Weber State 1977-78, Stanford 1979-83. Pro coach: Hawaii (WFL) 1974, Portland Breakers (USFL) 1984, New York Giants 1990-92, joined Broncos in 1993.

Mo Forte, wide receivers; born March 1, 1947, Hannibal, Mo., lives in Littleton, Colo. Running back Minnesota 1965-68. No pro playing experience. College coach: Minnesota 1970-75, Duke 1976-77, Michigan State 1978-79, Arizona State 1980-81, North Carolina A&T 1982-87 (head coach). Pro coach: Joined Broncos in 1988.

Leon Fuller, defensive backs; born July 28, 1938, Nederland, Tex., lives in Denver. Linebacker Alabama 1957-60. No pro playing experience. College coach: Alabama 1962, Oklahoma State 1963-66, Kentucky 1967-68, New Mexico 1969-73, West Texas State 1974, Wyoming 1975-76, Texas 1977-81, 1989-93, Colorado State 1982-88 (head coach). Pro coach: Joined Broncos in 1994.

Bishop Harris, running backs; born November 23, 1941, Phoenix City, Ala., lives in Denver. Defensive back North Carolina College 1960-64. No pro play-

ing experience. College coach: Duke 1972-75, North Carolina State 1977-79, Louisiana State 1980-83, Notre Dame 1984-85, Minnesota 1986-90, North Carolina Central 1991-92 (head coach). Pro coach: Joined Broncos in 1993.

John Levra, offensive line; born October 2, 1937, Arma, Kan., lives in Englewood, Colo. Guard-linebacker Pittsburg (Kan.) State 1963-65. No pro playing experience. College coach: Stephen F. Austin 1971-74, Kansas 1975-78, North Texas State 1979. Pro coach: British Columbia Lions (CFL) 1980, New Orleans Saints 1981-85, Chicago Bears 1986-92, joined Broncos in 1993.

Rex Norris, defensive line; born December 10, 1939, Tipton, Ind., lives in Denver. Linebacker San Angelo (Texas) Junior College 1959-60, East Texas State 1961-62. No pro playing experience. College coach: Navarro (Texas) Junior College 1970-71, Texas A&M 1972, Oklahoma 1973-83, Arizona State 1984, Florida 1988-89, Tennessee 1990-91, Texas 1992-93. Pro coach: Detroit Lions 1985-87, joined Broncos in 1994.

Alvin Reynolds, assistant defensive backs/quality control; born June 24, 1959, Pineville, La., lives in Aurora, Colo. Safety Indiana State 1978-81. No pro playing experience. College coach: Indiana State 1982-92. Pro coach: Joined Broncos in 1993.

Harold Richardson, special assistant to head coach/offense; born September 27, 1944, Houston, Tex., lives in Englewood, Colo. Tight end Southern Methodist 1964-67. No pro playing experience. College coach: Southern Methodist 1971-72, Oklahoma State 1973-76, Texas Christian 1977-78, North Texas

State 1979-80, Colorado State 1986-88. Pro coach: New Orleans Saints 1981-85, joined Broncos in 1989.

Richard Smith, special teams/linebackers; born October 17, 1955, Los Angeles, Calif., lives in Denver. Offensive lineman Rio Hondo (Calif.) Junior College 1975-76, Fresno State 1977-78. No pro playing experience. College coach: Rio Hondo (Calif.) Junior College 1979-80, Cal State-Fullerton 1981-83, California 1984-86, Arizona 1987. Pro coach: Houston Oilers 1988-92, joined Broncos in 1993.

Les Steckel, H-backs-tight ends; born July 1, 1946, North Hampton, Pa., lives in Louisville, Colo. Running back Kansas 1964-68. No pro playing experience. College coach: Colorado 1972-76, 1991-92, Navy 1977, Brown 1989. Pro coach: San Francisco 49ers 1978, Minnesota Vikings 1979-84 (head coach, 1984), New England Patriots 1985-88, joined Broncos in 1993.

Charlie Waters, defensive coordinator; born September 10, 1948, Miami, Fla., lives in Greenwood Village, Colo. Safety Clemson 1967-69. Pro safety Dallas Cowboys 1970-81. Pro coach: Joined Broncos in 1988.

John Paul Young, linebackers; born December 31, 1939, Dallas, Tex., lives in Denver. Linebacker Texas-El Paso 1959-61. No pro playing experience. College coach: Texas El-Paso 1962-63, Southern Methodist 1967-68, Oklahoma State 1969, Texas A&M 1970-77, Texas Tech 1989-91. Pro coach: Houston Oilers 1978-80, New Orleans Saints 1981-85, Kansas City Chiefs 1986-88, Dallas Texans (Arena League, head coach) 1992, joined Broncos in 1993.

1994 FIRST-YEAR ROSTER

Name	Pos.	Ht.	Wt.	Birthdate	College	Hometown	How Acq.
Aldridge, Allen	LB	6-1	245	5/30/72	Houston	Houston, Tex.	D2
Bell, Trumane	TE	6-3	235	11/26/71	Nebraska	Chicago, Ill.	FA
Burns, Keith	LB	6-2	245	5/16/72	Oklahoma State	Greeleyville, S.C.	D7a
By'not'e, Butler	RB	5-9	190	9/29/72	Ohio State	Louis, Miss.	D7b
Carswell, Dwayne	TE	6-3	261	1/18/72	Liberty	Jacksonville, Fla.	FA
Dyet, Brian	DE	6-4	257	12/12/70	Colorado	Denver, Colo.	FA
Farkas, Kevin	T	6-9	360	2/4/71	Appalachian State	Richmond, Va.	FA
Fowler, Carlos	DT	6-2	278	8/30/72	Wisconsin	Cleveland, Ohio	FA
Fuller, Randy	CB	5-9	173	6/2/70	Tennessee State	Columbus, Ga.	D4
Geter, Eric (1)	CB	5-11	190	6/24/70	Clemson	Gay, Ga.	FA
Hall, Kenny	G-T	6-4	315	7/15/71	Fresno State	Wallugan, Ill.	FA
Hampel, Olaf (1)	G	6-6	305	6/24/67	No College	Essen, Germany	FA
Hasselbach, Harald (1)	DT	6-6	280	9/22/67	Washington	Amsterdam, Holland	FA
Jacobs, Ray	LB	6-2	244	8/18/72	North Carolina	Hampstead, N.C.	FA
Lofton, Billy	DE	6-2	290	10/28/71	Kentucky	Wilmington, N.C.	FA
Mosley, Tim	WR	6-3	187	1/19/71	Northern Iowa	Ft. Dodge, Iowa	FA
Nalen, Tom	C	6-2	280	5/13/71	Boston College	Foxboro, Mass.	D7c
Redmond, Jamie (1)	CB	5-9	185	10/1/69	Middle Tennessee St.	Savannah, Ga.	FA
Rose, Barry	WR	6-0	185	7/28/68	Wis.-Stevens Point	Hudson, Wis.	FA
Savage, Sebastian (1)	CB	5-11	196	12/12/69	North Carolina State	Union, S.C.	FA
Smith, Rod	WR	6-0	183	5/15/70	Missouri Southern	Texarkana, Ark.	FA
Snowden, Chuck	RB	6-0	209	4/21/71	Northern Colorado	Washington, D.C.	FA
Strother, Deon	RB	5-11	213	4/12/72	Southern California	Saginaw, Mich.	FA
Swann, Charles (1)	WR	6-1	188	10/29/70	Indiana State	Memphis, Tenn.	FA
Vaughn, Scott	T	6-5	319	4/9/71	Rutgers	Easton, Pa.	FA

The term NFL Rookie is defined as a player who is in his first season of professional football and has not been on the roster of another professional football team for any regular-season or postseason games. A Rookie is designated by an "R" on NFL rosters. Players who have been active in another professional football league or players who have NFL experience, including either preseason training camp or being on an Active List or Inactive List, or on Reserve/Injured or Reserve/Physically Unable to Perform for fewer than six regular-season games, are termed NFL First-Year Players. An NFL First-Year Player is designated by a "1" on NFL rosters. Thereafter, a player is credited with an additional year of experience for each season in which he accumulates six games on the Active List or Inactive List, or on Reserve/Injured or Reserve/Physically Unable to Perform.

NOTES

HOUSTON OILERS

American Football Conference
Central Division
Team Colors: Columbia Blue, Scarlet, and White
6910 Fannin Street
Houston, Texas 77030
Telephone: (713) 797-9111

CLUB OFFICIALS

President: K.S. (Bud) Adams, Jr.
Exec. V.P./General Manager: Floyd Reese
Exec. V.P./Administration: Mike McClure
Exec. V.P./Finance: Scott Thompson
Exec. Assistant to President: Thomas S. Smith
Vice President/General Counsel: Steve Underwood
Vice President/Player Personnel and Scouting:
  Mike Holovak
Senior Vice President//Marketing and Broadcasting:
  Don MacLachlan
Director of Business Operations: Lewis Mangum
Director of Media Services: TBA
Director of Accounting Services: Marilan Logan
Controller: Jackie Curley
Director of Ticket Administration Services: Mike Mullis
Assistant Ticket Manager: Ralph Stolarski
Director of Security: Grady Sessums
Director of Computer Services: Steve Reese
Director of Player Relations: Willie Alexander
Head Trainer: Brad Brown
Assistant Trainer: Don Moseley
Equipment Manager: Dan Murray
Video Coordinator: Ken Sparacino
Stadium: Astrodome •**Capacity:** 59,905
    8400 Kirby Drive
    Houston, Texas 77054
Playing Surface: AstroTurf-8
Training Camp: Prassel Residence Hall
    Trinity University
    San Antonio, Texas 78212

1994 SCHEDULE
PRESEASON

July 31	at Kansas City	8:00
Aug. 6	vs. San Diego at San Antonio, Tex.	7:00
Aug. 15	vs. Dallas at Mexico City	9:00
Aug. 20	vs. Buffalo at San Antonio, Tex.	7:00
Aug. 27	**Los Angeles Raiders**	1:00

REGULAR SEASON

Sept. 4	at Indianapolis	12:00
Sept. 11	at Dallas	3:00
Sept. 18	**Buffalo**	12:00
Sept. 25	**Cincinnati**	3:00
Oct. 3	at Pittsburgh (Monday)	9:00
Oct. 9	Open Date	
Oct. 13	**Cleveland** (Thursday)	7:00
Oct. 24	at Philadelphia (Monday)	9:00
Oct. 30	at Los Angeles Raiders	1:00
Nov. 6	**Pittsburgh**	12:00
Nov. 13	at Cincinnati	1:00
Nov. 21	**New York Giants** (Monday)	8:00
Nov. 27	at Cleveland	1:00
Dec. 4	**Arizona**	3:00
Dec. 11	**Seattle**	3:00
Dec. 18	at Kansas City	3:00
Dec. 24	**New York Jets**	3:00

RECORD HOLDERS
INDIVIDUAL RECORDS—CAREER

Category	Name	Performance
Rushing (Yds.)	Earl Campbell, 1978-1984	8,574
Passing (Yds.)	Warren Moon, 1984-1993	33,685
Passing (TDs)	Warren Moon, 1984-1993	196
Receiving (No.)	Ernest Givins, 1986-1993	506
Receiving (Yds.)	Drew Hill, 1985-1991	7,477
Interceptions	Jim Norton, 1960-68	45
Punting (Avg.)	Greg Montgomery, 1988-1993	43.6
Punt Return (Avg.)	Billy Johnson, 1974-1980	13.2
Kickoff Return (Avg.)	Bobby Jancik, 1962-67	26.4
Field Goals	Tony Zendejas, 1985-1990	117
Touchdowns (Tot.)	Earl Campbell, 1978-1984	73
Points	George Blanda, 1960-66	596

INDIVIDUAL RECORDS—SINGLE SEASON

Category	Name	Performance
Rushing (Yds.)	Earl Campbell, 1980	1,934
Passing (Yds.)	Warren Moon, 1991	4,690
Passing (TDs)	George Blanda, 1961	36
Receiving (No.)	Charlie Hennigan, 1964	101
Receiving (Yds.)	Charlie Hennigan, 1961	*1,746
Interceptions	Fred Glick, 1963	12
	Mike Reinfeldt, 1979	12
Punting (Avg.)	Greg Montgomery, 1992	46.9
Punt Return (Avg.)	Billy Johnson, 1977	15.4
Kickoff Return (Avg.)	Ken Hall, 1960	31.2
Field Goals	Al Del Greco, 1993	29
Touchdowns (Tot.)	Earl Campbell, 1979	19
Points	Al Del Greco, 1993	126

INDIVIDUAL RECORDS—SINGLE GAME

Category	Name	Performance
Rushing (Yds.)	Billy Cannon, 12-10-61	216
Passing (Yds.)	Warren Moon, 12-16-90	527
Passing (TDs)	George Blanda, 11-19-61	*7
Receiving (No.)	Charlie Hennigan, 10-13-61	13
	Haywood Jeffires, 10-13-91	13
Receiving (Yds.)	Charlie Hennigan, 10-13-61	272
Interceptions	Many times	3
	Last time by Marcus Robertson, 11-21-93	
Field Goals	Skip Butler, 10-12-75	6
Touchdowns (Tot.)	Billy Cannon, 12-10-61	5
Points	Billy Cannon, 12-10-61	30

*NFL Record

COACHING HISTORY
(243-273-6)

1960-61	Lou Rymkus*	12-7-1
1961	Wally Lemm	10-0-0
1962-63	Frank (Pop) Ivy	17-12-0
1964	Sammy Baugh	4-10-0
1965	Hugh Taylor	4-10-0
1966-70	Wally Lemm	28-40-4
1971	Ed Hughes	4-9-1
1972-73	Bill Peterson**	1-18-0
1973-74	Sid Gillman	8-15-0
1975-80	O.A. (Bum) Phillips	59-38-0
1981-83	Ed Biles***	8-23-0
1983	Chuck Studley	2-8-0
1984-85	Hugh Campbell****	8-22-0
1985-89	Jerry Glanville	35-35-0
1990-93	Jack Pardee	43-26-0

 *Released after five games in 1961
 **Released after five games in 1973
 ***Resigned after six games in 1983
 ****Released after 14 games in 1985

ASTRODOME

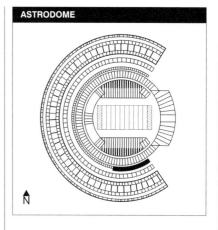

N

1993 TEAM RECORD

PRESEASON (1-3)

Date	Result		Opponents
8/7	L	28-37	vs. New Orleans at San Antonio
8/16	L	20-24	Detroit
8/21	W	23-20	vs. Dallas at San Antonio
8/28	L	10-20	Seattle

REGULAR SEASON (12-4)

Date	Result		Opponents	Att.
9/5	L	21-33	at New Orleans	69,029
9/12	W	30-0	Kansas City	59,780
9/19	L	17-18	at San Diego	58,519
9/26	L	13-28	L.A. Rams	53,072
10/11	L	7-35	at Buffalo	79,613
10/17	W	28-14	at New England	51,037
10/24	W	28-12	Cincinnati	50,039
11/7	W	24-14	Seattle	50,447
11/14	W	38-3	at Cincinnati	42,347
11/21	W	27-20	at Cleveland	71,668
11/28	W	23-3	Pittsburgh	61,238
12/5	W	33-17	Atlanta	58,186
12/12	W	19-17	Cleveland	58,720
12/19	W	26-17	at Pittsburgh	57,592
12/25	W	10-7	at San Francisco	61,744
1/2	W	24-0	N.Y. Jets	61,040

POSTSEASON (0-1)

Date	Result		Opponents	Att.
1/16	L	20-28	Kansas City	64,011

SCORE BY PERIODS

Oilers	68	131	75	94	0	—	368
Opponents	40	73	50	75	0	—	238

ATTENDANCE

Home 452,522   Away 491,549   Total 944,071
Single-game home record, 63,705 (9-6-92)
Single-season home record, 494,447 (1992)

1993 TEAM STATISTICS

	Oilers	Opp.
Total First Downs	330	289
Rushing	101	73
Passing	208	184
Penalty	21	32
Third Down: Made/Att	94/211	64/208
Third Down Pct.	44.5	30.8
Fourth Down: Made/Att	3/12	12/24
Fourth Down Pct.	25.0	50.0
Total Net Yards	5658	4874
Avg. Per Game	353.6	304.6
Total Plays	1066	1003
Avg. Per Play	5.3	4.9
Net Yards Rushing	1792	1273
Avg. Per Game	112.0	79.6
Total Rushes	409	369
Net Yards Passing	3866	3601
Avg. Per Game	241.6	225.1
Sacked/Yards Lost	43/279	52/313
Gross Yards	4145	3914
Att./Completions	614/357	582/302
Completion Pct.	58.1	51.9
Had Intercepted	25	26
Punts/Avg.	56/45.3	79/43.7
Net Punting Avg.	56/38.7	79/36.9
Penalties/Yards Lost	132/1005	103/791
Fumbles/Ball Lost	37/20	32/17
Touchdowns	40	26
Rushing	11	9
Passing	23	16
Returns	6	1
Avg. Time of Possession	31:48	28:12

1993 INDIVIDUAL STATISTICS

PASSING	Att.	Cmp.	Yds.	Pct.	TD	Int	Tkld.	Rate
Moon	520	303	3485	58.3	21	21	34/218	75.2
Carlson	90	51	605	56.7	2	4	8/53	66.2
Richardson	4	3	55	75.0	0	0	1/8	116.7
Oilers	614	357	4145	58.1	23	25	43/279	74.2
Opponents	582	302	3914	51.9	16	26	52/313	63.9

SCORING	TD R	TD P	TD Rt	PAT	FG	Saf	PTS
Del Greco	0	0	0	39/40	29/34	0	126
G. Brown	6	2	0	0/0	0/0	0	48
Jeffires	0	6	0	0/0	0/0	0	36
Slaughter	0	5	0	0/0	0/0	0	30
Givins	0	4	0	0/0	0/0	0	24
Duncan	0	3	0	0/0	0/0	0	18
Carlson	2	0	0	0/0	0/0	0	12
White	2	0	0	0/0	0/0	0	12
Childress	0	0	1	0/0	0/0	0	6
Dishman	0	0	1	0/0	0/0	0	6
Harris	0	1	0	0/0	0/0	0	6
Jackson	0	0	1	0/0	0/0	0	6
Lewis	0	0	1	0/0	0/0	0	6
Moon	1	0	0	0/0	0/0	0	6
Orlando	0	0	1	0/0	0/0	0	6
Robertson	0	0	1	0/0	0/0	0	6
Tillman	0	1	0	0/0	0/0	0	6
Wellman	0	1	0	0/0	0/0	0	6
Oilers	11	23	6	39/40	29/34	1	368
Opponents	9	16	1	25/26	19/28	0	238

RUSHING	Att.	Yds.	Avg.	LG	TD
G. Brown	195	1002	5.1	26	6
White	131	465	3.5	14	2
Moon	48	145	3.0	35	1
Tillman	9	94	10.4	34	0
Carlson	14	41	2.9	10t	2
Givins	6	19	3.2	16	0
Maston	1	10	10.0	10	0
Richardson	2	9	4.5	11	0
Wellman	2	6	3.0	4	0
Coleman	1	1	1.0	1	0
Oilers	409	1792	4.4	35	11
Opponents	369	1273	3.4	29	9

RECEIVING	No.	Yds.	Avg.	LG	TD
Slaughter	77	904	11.7	41	5
Givins	68	887	13.0	80t	4
Jeffires	66	753	11.4	66t	6
Duncan	41	456	11.1	47	3
White	34	229	6.7	20	0
Wellman	31	430	13.9	44	1
G. Brown	21	240	11.4	38t	2
Coleman	9	129	14.3	25	0
Harris	4	53	13.3	17t	1
R. Brown	2	30	15.0	26	0
Maston	1	14	14.0	14	0
Norgard	1	13	13.0	13	0
Tillman	1	4	4.0	4t	1
Drewrey	1	3	3.0	3	0
Oilers	357	4145	11.6	80t	23
Opponents	302	3914	13.0	53t	16

INTERCEPTIONS	No.	Yds.	Avg.	Long	TD
Robertson	7	137	19.6	69	0
Dishman	6	74	12.3	30	0
Jackson	5	54	10.8	22t	1
Orlando	3	68	22.7	38t	1
McDowell	3	31	10.3	13	0
Lewis	1	47	47.0	47t	1
Bishop	1	1	1.0	1	0
Oilers	26	412	15.8	69	3
Opponents	25	309	12.4	42	0

PUNTING	No.	Yds.	Avg.	In 20	LG
Gr. Montgomery	54	2462	45.6	13	77
Sullivan	2	73	36.5	1	37
Oilers	56	2535	45.3	14	77
Opponents	79	3454	43.7	15	71

PUNT RETURNS	No.	FC	Yds.	Avg.	LG	TD
Drewrey	41	19	275	6.7	18	0
Oilers	41	19	275	6.7	18	0
Opponents	28	5	249	8.9	30	0

KICKOFF RETURNS	No.	Yds.	Avg.	LG	TD
Drewrey	15	293	19.5	34	0
Mills	11	230	20.9	37	0
Coleman	3	37	12.3	16	0
Gl. Brown	2	29	14.5	16	0
Oilers	31	589	19.0	37	0
Opponents	60	1062	17.7	36	0

SACKS	No.
S. Jones	13.0
Fuller	10.0
Childress	9.0
Gl. Montgomery	6.0
L. Williams	3.0
Lathon	2.0
Marshall	2.0
Barrow	1.0
Bishop	1.0
Bowden	1.0
McDowell	1.0
Robinson	1.0
Teeter	1.0
Oilers	52.0
Opponents	43.0

1994 DRAFT CHOICES

Round	Name	Pos.	College
1	Henry Ford	DE	Arkansas
2	Jeremy Nunley	DE	Alabama
3	Malcolm Seabron	WR	Fresno State
4	Mike Davis	DB	Cincinnati
	Sean Jackson	RB	Florida State
5	Roderick Lewis	TE	Arizona
	Jim Reid	T	Virginia
6	Lee Gissendaner	WR	Northwestern
	Barron Wortham	LB	Texas-El Paso
7	Lemanski Hall	LB	Alabama

1994 VETERAN ROSTER

No.	Name	Pos.	Ht.	Wt.	Birthdate	NFL Exp.	College	Hometown	How Acq.	'93 Games/ Starts
51	Barrow, Micheal	LB	6-1	236	4/19/70	2	Miami	Homestead, Fla.	D2-'93	16/0
23	Bishop, Blaine	S-CB	5-8	197	7/24/70	2	Ball State	Indianapolis, Ind.	D8-'93	16/2
59	† Bowden, Joe	LB	5-11	230	2/25/70	3	Oklahoma	Mesquite, Tex.	D5a-'92	16/6
33	† Brown, Gary	RB	5-11	233	7/1/69	4	Penn State	Williamsport, Pa.	D8-'91	16/8
17	Brown, Reggie	WR	6-1	195	5/5/70	2	Alabama State	Miami, Fla.	FA-'93	4/0
22	Brown, Tony	CB	5-9	183	5/15/70	3	Fresno State	Granada Hills, Calif.	D5b-'92	16/0
16	Camarillo, Rich	P	5-11	195	11/29/59	14	Washington	Pico Rivera, Calif.	UFA(Ariz)-'94	16/0*
14	Carlson, Cody	QB	6-3	202	11/5/63	8	Baylor	San Antonio, Tex.	D3-'87	8/2
46	Carter, Pat	TE	6-4	258	8/1/66	7	Florida State	Sarasota, Fla.	UFA(Rams)-'94	11/10*
79	Childress, Ray	DT	6-6	272	10/20/62	10	Texas A&M	Richardson, Tex.	D1a-'85	16/16
87	Coleman, Pat	WR	5-7	176	4/8/67	4	Mississippi	Cleveland, Miss.	FA-'91	13/1
66	# Dawson, Doug	G	6-3	288	12/27/61	8	Texas	Houston, Tex.	FA-'90	16/16
3	Del Greco, Al	K	5-10	202	3/2/62	11	Auburn	Coral Gables, Fla.	FA-'91	16/0
28	† Dishman, Cris	CB	6-0	188	8/13/65	7	Purdue	Louisville, Ky.	D5a-'88	16/16
77	Donnalley, Kevin	T	6-5	305	6/10/68	4	North Carolina	Raleigh, N.C.	D3b-'91	16/6
38	† Dumas, Mike	S	5-11	181	3/18/69	4	Indiana	Lowell, Mich.	D2a-'91	0*
80	Duncan, Curtis	WR	5-11	184	1/26/65	8	Northwestern	Detroit, Mich.	D10-'87	12/12
55	† Flannery, John	G-C	6-3	304	1/13/69	4	Syracuse	Pottsville, Pa.	D2c-'91	0*
81	Givins, Ernest	WR	5-9	178	9/3/64	9	Louisville	St. Petersburg, Fla.	D2-'86	16/16
82	Hannah, Travis	WR	5-7	161	1/31/70	2	Southern California	Hawthorne, Calif.	D4-'93	12/0
27	# Hoage, Terry	S	6-2	201	4/11/62	11	Georgia	Huntsville, Tex.	FA-'93	7/0*
72	Hopkins, Brad	T	6-3	306	9/5/70	2	Illinois	Moline, Ill.	D1-'93	16/11
24	† Jackson, Steve	CB	5-8	182	4/8/69	4	Purdue	Houston, Tex.	D3a-'91	16/12
84	# Jeffires, Haywood	WR	6-2	201	12/12/64	8	North Carolina State	Greensboro, N.C.	D1b-'87	16/16
56	Kozak, Scott	LB	6-3	222	11/28/65	6	Oregon	Colton, Ore.	D2-'89	16/0
57	Lathon, Lamar	LB	6-3	252	12/23/67	5	Houston	Wharton, Tex.	D1-'90	13/1
29	† Lewis, Darryll	CB	5-9	183	12/16/68	4	Arizona	La Puente, Calif.	D2b-'91	4/4
58	# Marshall, Wilber	LB	6-1	240	4/18/62	11	Florida	Titusville, Fla.	T(Wash)-'93	10/10
47	Maston, Le'Shai	RB	6-1	215	10/7/70	2	Baylor	Dallas, Tex.	FA-'93	10/0
74	Matthews, Bruce	C	6-5	298	8/8/61	12	Southern California	Arcadia, Calif.	D1-'83	16/16
78	# McCants, Keith	DE	6-3	265	4/19/68	5	Alabama	Mobile, Ala.	FA-'93	13/0
25	McDowell, Bubba	S	6-1	198	11/4/66	6	Miami	Merritt Island, Fla.	D3-'89	14/14
48	Mills, John Henry	TE	6-0	222	10/31/69	2	Wake Forest	Tallahassee, Fla.	D5-'93	16/0
94	Montgomery, Glenn	DT	6-0	282	3/31/67	6	Houston	Gretna, La.	D5-'89	16/11
63	# Munchak, Mike	G	6-3	284	3/5/60	13	Penn State	Scranton, Pa.	D1-'82	12/12
64	Norgard, Erik	C-G	6-1	282	11/4/65	5	Colorado	Arlington, Wash.	FA-'90	16/4
26	Orlando, Bo	S	5-10	180	4/3/66	5	West Virginia	Berwick, Pa.	FA-'90	16/3
7	Richardson, Bucky	QB	6-1	228	2/7/69	3	Texas A&M	Baton Rouge, La.	D8-'92	2/0
68	Roberts, Tim	DT	6-6	318	4/14/69	3	Southern Mississippi	Atlanta, Ga.	D5c-'92	6/0
31	† Robertson, Marcus	S	5-11	197	10/2/69	4	Iowa State	Pasadena, Calif.	D4b-'91	13/13
50	Robinson, Eddie	LB	6-1	245	4/13/70	3	Alabama State	New Orleans, La.	D2-'92	16/15
12	Salisbury, Sean	QB	6-5	217	3/9/63	6	Southern California	Escondido, Calif.	UFA(Minn)-'94	11/4*
89	# Slaughter, Webster	WR	6-1	175	10/19/64	9	San Diego State	Stockton, Calif.	FA-'92	14/14
54	Smith, Al	LB	6-1	244	11/26/64	8	Utah State	Los Angeles, Calif.	D6a-'87	16/16
71	Teeter, Mike	DE	6-2	260	10/4/67	3	Michigan	Fruitport, Mich.	FA-'93	14/0
70	Thomas, Stan	T	6-5	295	10/28/68	4	Texas	San Diego, Calif.	FA-'93	14/0
32	Tillman, Spencer	RB	5-11	206	4/21/64	8	Oklahoma	Tulsa, Okla.	PB(SF)-'92	15/0
88	Wellman, Gary	WR	5-9	173	8/9/67	3	Southern California	Westlake Hills, Calif.	D5-'91	11/3
44	# White, Lorenzo	RB	5-11	222	4/12/66	7	Michigan State	Ft. Lauderdale, Fla.	D1-'88	8/8
73	Williams, David	T	6-5	292	6/21/66	6	Florida	Lakeland, Fla.	D1-'89	15/15
97	Williams, Lee	DT-DE	6-6	275	10/15/62	11	Bethune-Cookman	Ft. Lauderdale, Fla.	T(SD)-'91	14/5

* Camarillo played 16 games with Phoenix in '93; Carter played 11 games with L.A. Rams; Dumas and Flannery missed '93 season due to injury; Hoage played 4 games with San Francisco, 3 games with Houston; Salisbury played 11 games with Minnesota.

\# Unrestricted free agent; subject to developments.

† Restricted free agent; subject to developments.

Traded—QB Warren Moon to Minnesota.

Players lost through free agency (3): DE William Fuller (Phil; 16 games in '93), DE Sean Jones (GB; 16), P Greg Montgomery (Det; 15).

Also played with Oilers in '93—S Melvin Aldridge (1 game), DT Jeff Alm (2), WR Willie Drewrey (16), WR Leonard Harris (4), WR Tony Jones (2), CB Emanuel Martin (1), WR Damon Mays (1), QB Warren Moon (15), P Kent Sullivan (1), DE-DT Craig Veasey (1).

COACHING STAFF

Head Coach,
Jack Pardee

Pro Career: Named the Oilers' fourteenth head coach on January 9, 1990. Houston has qualified for playoffs in each of his four seasons with the Oilers. Accepted post after serving three years (1987-89) as head coach at University of Houston. While at Houston, Cougars set more than 100 NCAA/Southwest Conference records in 1988 and 1989. In 1986, was a scout for the Green Bay Packers. Prior to that, was head coach of successful Houston Gamblers of the USFL from 1984-85 as team led league in total offense and scoring in both seasons. Spent 1982 in private business after serving as defensive coordinator for San Diego Chargers in 1981. That season, Chargers won AFC's Western Division and advanced to AFC Championship Game. From 1978-80, was head coach of the Washington Redskins, earning NFL coach of the year honors in 1979. Was head coach of the Chicago Bears from 1975-77, earning NFC coach of the year accolades in 1976 and leading the club in 1977 to its first playoff berth in 14 years. Was general manager/head coach for Florida Blazers of the World Football League in 1974, winning division title and advancing to WFL title game. Began coaching career as Washington Redskins' assistant in 1973. Drafted by Los Angeles Rams in second round in 1957 and played 15 seasons at linebacker for Rams (1957-64, 1966-70) and Washington Redskins (1971-72). Was an all-pro selection in 1963 and 1971, and is a member of Rams' fortieth anniversary team. Career record: 87-73.

Background: Played linebacker and fullback in All-America and Academic All-America career for coach Paul (Bear) Bryant at Texas A&M (1953-56). Is a member of the Texas A&M Hall of Fame, National Football Foundation Hall of Fame, College Football Hall of Fame, Texas Sports Hall of Fame, and Senior Bowl Hall of Fame.

Personal: Born April 19, 1936, Exira, Iowa. Jack and his wife, Phyllis, live in Missouri City, Tex., and have two sons, Steven and Ted, and three daughters—Judee, Anne, and Susan.

ASSISTANT COACHES

Charlie Baggett, receivers; born January 21, 1953, Fayetteville, N.C., lives in Houston. Quarterback Michigan State 1972-75. No pro playing experience. College coach: Bowling Green 1977-80, Minnesota 1981-82, Michigan State 1983-92. Pro coach: Joined Oilers in 1993.

Tom Bettis, defensive backs; born March 17, 1933, Chicago, Ill., lives in Pearland, Tex. Linebacker-guard Purdue 1952-54. Pro linebacker Green Bay Packers 1955-61, Pittsburgh Steelers 1962, Chicago Bears 1963. Pro coach: Chicago Bears 1964-65 (scout), Kansas City Chiefs 1966-77 (interim head coach 1977), 1988, St. Louis Cardinals 1978-84, Cleveland Browns 1985, Houston Oilers 1986-87, Philadelphia Eagles 1989-90, Los Angeles Rams 1991, rejoined Oilers in 1993.

Frank Bush, quality control; born January 10, 1963, Athens, Ga., lives in Houston. Linebacker North Carolina State 1981-84. Pro linebacker Houston Oilers 1985-86. Pro coach: Joined Oilers in 1987 as scout, named assistant coach in 1992.

Dick Coury, offensive coordinator; born September 29, 1929, Athens, Ohio, lives in Missouri City, Tex. Quarterback Notre Dame 1950-54. No pro playing experience. College coach: Southern California 1967-69, Cal State-Fullerton 1970-71 (head coach). Pro coach: Denver Broncos 1972-73, Portland Storm (WFL) 1974 (head coach), San Diego Chargers 1975, Philadelphia Eagles 1976-81, Boston/New Orleans/Portland Breakers (USFL) 1983-85 (head coach), Los Angeles Rams 1986-90, New England Patriots 1991-92, Minnesota Vikings 1993, joined Oilers in 1994.

Jeff Fisher, defensive coordinator; born February 25, 1958, Culver City, Calif., lives in Sugar Land, Tex. Defensive back Southern California 1977-80. Pro defensive back Chicago Bears 1981-85. Pro coach: Philadelphia Eagles 1986-90, Los Angeles Rams 1991, San Francisco 49ers 1992-93, joined Oilers in 1994.

Kevin Gilbride, assistant head coach-offense; born August 27, 1951, New Haven, Conn., lives in Missouri City, Tex. Quarterback-tight end Southern Connecticut State 1970-73. No pro playing experience. College coach: Idaho State 1974-75, Tufts 1976-77, American International 1978-79, Southern Connecticut State 1980-84 (head coach), East Carolina 1987-88. Pro coach: Ottawa Rough Riders (CFL) 1985-86, joined Oilers in 1989.

Frank Novak, special teams-running backs; born May 18, 1938, Worcester, Mass., lives in Missouri City, Tex. Quarterback Northern Michigan 1959-61. No pro playing experience. College coach: Northern Michigan 1966-72, East Carolina 1973, Virginia 1974-75, Western Illinois 1976-77, Holy Cross 1978-83, Massachusetts 1986, Missouri 1988. Pro coach: Oklahoma Outlaws (USFL) 1984, Birmingham Stallions (USFL) 1985, joined Oilers in 1989.

Jim Stanley, defensive line; born June 22, 1934, Dunham, Ky., lives in Pearland, Tex. Guard-defensive tackle Texas A&M 1954-57. No pro playing experience. College coach: Southern Methodist 1961, Texas-El Paso 1962, Oklahoma State 1963-68, 1972-78 (head coach 1973-78), Navy 1969-70. Pro coach: Winnipeg Blue Bombers (CFL) 1971, New York Giants 1979, Atlanta Falcons 1980-82, Michigan Panthers (USFL) 1983-84 (head coach), Tampa Bay Buccaneers 1986, joined Oilers in 1990.

Steve Watterson, strength and rehabilitation; born November 27, 1956, Newport, R.I., lives in Sugar Land, Tex. Attended Rhode Island. No college or pro playing experience. Pro coach: Philadelphia Eagles 1984-85 (assistant trainer), joined Oilers in 1986 (elevated to assistant coach in 1988).

Gregg Williams, linebackers; born July 15, 1958, Excelsior Springs, Mo., lives in Katy, Tex. Quarterback Northeast Missouri State 1976-79. No pro playing experience. College coach: Houston 1988-89. Pro coach: Houston Oilers 1990-92 (quality control coordinator), named assistant coach in 1993.

Bob Young, offensive line; born September 3, 1942, Marshall, Tex., lives in Missouri City, Tex. Guard Texas 1960-61, Howard Payne 1962-63. Pro guard Denver Broncos 1966-70, Houston Oilers 1971, 1980, St. Louis Cardinals 1972-79, New Orleans Saints 1981. College coach: Houston 1987-89. Pro coach: Houston Gamblers (USFL) 1984-85, joined Oilers in 1990.

1994 FIRST-YEAR ROSTER

Name	Pos.	Ht.	Wt.	Birthdate	College	Hometown	How Acq.
Aldridge, Melvin (1)	S	6-2	195	7/22/70	Murray State	Pittsburg, Tex.	FA
Davis, Mike	CB	6-1	192	1/14/72	Cincinnati	Springfield, Ohio	D4a
Ford, Henry	DE	6-3	284	10/30/71	Arkansas	Ft. Worth, Tex.	D1
Gissendaner, Lee	WR	5-9	175	10/25/71	Northwestern	Stow, Ohio	D6a
Hall, Lemanski	LB	6-0	229	11/24/70	Alabama	Valley, Ala.	D7
Jackson, Sean	RB	6-1	222	2/6/71	Florida State	New Orleans, La.	D4b
Lewis, Roderick	TE	6-5	254	6/9/71	Arizona	Dallas, Tex.	D5a
Nunley, Jeremy	DE	6-5	278	9/19/71	Alabama	Winchester, Tenn.	D2
Reid, Jim	T	6-6	306	2/13/71	Virginia	Newport News, Va.	D5b
Seabron, Malcolm	WR	6-0	194	12/29/72	Fresno State	Sacramento, Calif.	D3
Wortham, Barron	LB	5-11	244	11/1/69	Texas-El Paso	Everman, Tex.	D6b

The term NFL Rookie is defined as a player who is in his first season of professional football and has not been on the roster of another professional football team for any regular-season or postseason games. A Rookie is designated by an "R" on NFL rosters. Players who have been active in another professional football league or players who have NFL experience, including either preseason training camp or being on an Active List or Inactive List, or on Reserve/Injured or Reserve/Physically Unable to Perform for fewer than six regular-season games, are termed NFL First-Year Players. An NFL First-Year Player is designated by a "1" on NFL rosters. Thereafter, a player is credited with an additional year of experience for each season in which he accumulates six games on the Active List or Inactive List, or on Reserve/Injured or Reserve/Physically Unable to Perform.

NOTES

American Football Conference
Eastern Division
Team Colors: Royal Blue and White
P.O. Box 535000
Indianapolis, Indiana 46253
Telephone: (317) 297-2658

CLUB OFFICIALS

President-Treasurer: Robert Irsay
Vice President-General Manager: James Irsay
Vice President-Director of Football Operations:
  Bill Tobin
Vice President-General Counsel: Michael G. Chernoff
Assistant General Manager: Bob Terpening
Director of Pro Personnel: Clyde Powers
Director of College Player Personnel:
  George Boone
Controller: Kurt Humphrey
Director of Operations: Pete Ward
Director of Public Relations: Craig Kelley
Ticket Manager: Larry Hall
Director of Sales: Rene Longoria
Assistant Directors of Public Relations:
  Rod St. Clair, Todd Stewart
Purchasing Administrator: David Filar
Administrative Assistant: Nicole Kucharski
Equipment Manager: Jon Scott
Assistant Equipment Manager: Mike Mays
Video Director: Marty Heckscher
Assistant Video Director: John Starliper
Head Trainer: Hunter Smith
Assistant Trainer: Dave Hammer
Team Physician and Orthopedic Surgeon:
  K. Donald Shelbourne
Orthopedic Surgeon: Arthur C. Rettig
Physician: Douglas Robertson
Stadium: Hoosier Dome •**Capacity:** 60,273
  100 South Capitol Avenue
  Indianapolis, Indiana 46225
Playing Surface: AstroTurf
Training Camp: Anderson University
  Anderson, Indiana 46011

1994 SCHEDULE
PRESEASON

Aug. 5	**Seattle**	7:30
Aug. 13	at Cincinnati	7:30
Aug. 20	at Pittsburgh	6:00
Aug. 25	**Cleveland**	7:30

REGULAR SEASON

Sept. 4	**Houston**	12:00
Sept. 11	at Tampa Bay	1:00
Sept. 18	at Pittsburgh	1:00
Sept. 25	**Cleveland**	12:00
Oct. 2	**Seattle**	12:00
Oct. 9	at New York Jets	1:00
Oct. 16	at Buffalo	1:00
Oct. 23	**Washington**	12:00
Oct. 30	**New York Jets**	4:00
Nov. 6	at Miami	1:00
Nov. 13	Open Date	
Nov. 20	at Cincinnati	1:00
Nov. 27	**New England**	8:00
Dec. 4	at Seattle	1:00
Dec. 11	at New England	1:00
Dec. 18	**Miami**	1:00
Dec. 24	**Buffalo**	1:00

RECORD HOLDERS
INDIVIDUAL RECORDS—CAREER

Category	Name	Performance
Rushing (Yds.)	Lydell Mitchell, 1972-77	5,487
Passing (Yds.)	Johnny Unitas, 1956-1972	39,768
Passing (TDs)	Johnny Unitas, 1956-1972	287
Receiving (No.)	Raymond Berry, 1955-1967	631
Receiving (Yds.)	Raymond Berry, 1955-1967	9,275
Interceptions	Bob Boyd, 1960-68	57
Punting (Avg.)	Rohn Stark, 1982-1993	43.9
Punt Return (Avg.)	Wendell Harris, 1964	12.6
Kickoff Return (Avg.)	Jim Duncan, 1969-1971	32.5
Field Goals	Dean Biasucci 1984, 1986-1993	160
Touchdowns (Tot.)	Lenny Moore, 1956-1967	113
Points	Dean Biasucci, 1984, 1986-1993	698

INDIVIDUAL RECORDS—SINGLE SEASON

Category	Name	Performance
Rushing (Yds.)	Eric Dickerson, 1988	1,659
Passing (Yds.)	Johnny Unitas, 1963	3,481
Passing (TDs)	Johnny Unitas, 1959	32
Receiving (No.)	Reggie Langhorne, 1993	85
Receiving (Yds.)	Raymond Berry, 1960	1,298
Interceptions	Tom Keane, 1953	11
Punting (Avg.)	Rohn Stark, 1985	45.9
Punt Return (Avg.)	Clarence Verdin, 1989	12.9
Kickoff Return (Avg.)	Jim Duncan, 1970	35.4
Field Goals	Raul Allegre, 1983	30
Touchdowns (Tot.)	Lenny Moore, 1964	20
Points	Lenny Moore, 1964	120

INDIVIDUAL RECORDS—SINGLE GAME

Category	Name	Performance
Rushing (Yds.)	Norm Bulaich, 9-19-71	198
Passing (Yds.)	Johnny Unitas, 9-17-67	401
Passing (TDs)	Gary Cuozzo, 11-14-65	5
	Gary Hogeboom, 10-4-87	5
Receiving (No.)	Lydell Mitchell, 12-15-74	13
	Joe Washington, 9-2-79	13
Receiving (Yds.)	Raymond Berry, 11-10-57	224
Interceptions	Many times	3
	Last time by Mike Prior, 12-20-92	
Field Goals	Many times	5
	Last time by Dean Biasucci, 9-25-88	
Touchdowns (Tot.)	Many times	4
	Last time by Eric Dickerson, 10-31-88	
Points	Many times	24
	Last time by Eric Dickerson, 10-31-88	

COACHING HISTORY
BALTIMORE 1953-1983
(289-302-7)

1953	Keith Molesworth	3-9-0
1954-62	Weeb Ewbank	61-52-1
1963-69	Don Shula	73-26-4
1970-72	Don McCafferty*	26-11-1
1972	John Sandusky	4-5-0
1973-74	Howard Schnellenberger**	4-13-0
1974	Joe Thomas	2-9-0
1975-79	Ted Marchibroda	41-36-0
1980-81	Mike McCormack	9-23-0
1982-84	Frank Kush***	11-28-1
1984	Hal Hunter	0-1-0
1985-86	Rod Dowhower****	5-24-0
1986-91	Ron Meyer#	36-36-0
1991	Rick Venturi	1-10-0
1992-93	Ted Marchibroda	13-19-0

*Released after five games in 1972
**Released after three games in 1974
***Resigned after 15 games in 1984
****Released after 13 games in 1986
#Released after five games in 1991

HOOSIER DOME

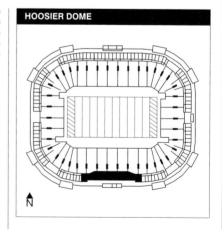

N

1993 TEAM RECORD

PRESEASON (2-2)

Date	Result		Opponents
8/7	W	16-13	at Seattle
8/14	L	7-24	Cincinnati
8/20	W	18-7	L.A. Raiders
8/27	L	10-41	at Green Bay

REGULAR SEASON (4-12)

Date	Result		Opponents	Att.
9/5	L	20-24	Miami	51,858
9/12	W	9-6	at Cincinnati	50,299
9/26	W	23-10	Cleveland	59,654
10/3	L	13-35	at Denver	74,953
10/10	L	3-27	Dallas	60,453
10/24	L	27-41	at Miami	57,301
10/31	W	9-6	New England	46,522
11/7	L	24-30	at Washington	50,523
11/14	L	17-31	N.Y. Jets	47,351
11/21	L	9-23	at Buffalo	79,101
11/29	L	0-31	San Diego	54,110
12/5	W	9-6	at N.Y. Jets	45,799
12/12	L	6-20	at N.Y. Giants	70,411
12/19	L	10-20	Philadelphia	44,952
12/26	L	0-38	at New England	26,571
1/2	L	10-30	Buffalo	43,028

SCORE BY PERIODS

Colts	19	60	29	81	0	—	189
Opponents	96	96	98	88	0	—	378

ATTENDANCE

Home 407,928   Away 454,958   Total 862,886
Single-game home record, 61,479 (11-13-83)
Single-season home record, 481,305 (1984)

1993 TEAM STATISTICS

	Colts	Opp.
Total First Downs	269	334
Rushing	71	151
Passing	180	166
Penalty	18	17
Third Down: Made/Att	61/209	85/206
Third Down Pct.	29.2	41.3
Fourth Down: Made/Att	9/22	8/12
Fourth Down Pct.	40.9	66.7
Total Net Yards	4705	5638
Avg. Por Game	294.1	352.4
Total Plays	988	1050
Avg. Per Play	4.8	5.4
Net Yards Rushing	1288	2521
Avg. Per Game	80.5	157.6
Total Rushes	365	575
Net Yards Passing	3417	3117
Avg. Per Game	213.6	194.8
Sacked/Yards Lost	29/206	21/121
Gross Yards	3623	3238
Att./Completions	594/332	454/270
Completion Pct.	55.9	59.5
Had Intercepted	15	10
Punts/Avg.	83/43.3	71/40.2
Net Punting Avg.	83/35.9	71/36.1
Penalties/Yards Lost	94/685	87/610
Fumbles/Ball Lost	34/20	25/11
Touchdowns	16	45
Rushing	4	20
Passing	10	22
Returns	2	3
Avg. Time of Possession	27:55	32:05

1993 INDIVIDUAL STATISTICS

PASSING	Att.	Cmp.	Yds.	Pct.	TD	Int.	Tkld.	Rate
George	407	234	2526	57.5	8	6	26/190	76.3
Trudeau	162	85	992	52.5	2	7	2/11	57.4
Majkowski	24	13	105	54.2	0	1	1/5	48.1
Johnson	1	0	0	0.0	0	1	0/0	0.0
Colts	594	332	3623	55.9	10	15	29/206	69.2
Opponents	454	270	3238	59.5	22	10	21/121	88.3

SCORING	TD R	TD P	TD Rt	PAT	FG	Saf	PTS
Biasucci	0	0	0	15/16	26/31	0	93
Culver	3	1	1	0/0	0/0	0	30
Cash	0	3	0	0/0	0/0	0	18
Langhorne	0	3	0	0/0	0/0	0	18
Dawkins	0	1	0	0/0	0/0	0	6
Herrod	0	0	1	0/0	0/0	0	6
Hester	0	1	0	0/0	0/0	0	6
Johnson	1	0	0	0/0	0/0	0	6
Verdin	0	1	0	0/0	0/0	0	6
Colts	4	10	2	15/16	26/31	0	189
Opponents	20	22	3	43/45	21/30	1	378

RUSHING	Att.	Yds.	Avg.	LG	TD
Potts	179	711	4.0	34	0
Johnson	95	331	3.5	14	1
Culver	65	150	2.3	9	3
George	13	39	3.0	14	0
Verdin	3	33	11.0	29	0
Stark	1	11	11.0	11	0
Toner	2	6	3.0	6	0
Majkowski	2	4	2.0	4	0
Trudeau	5	3	0.6	2	0
Colts	365	1288	3.5	34	4
Opponents	575	2521	4.4	57t	20

RECEIVING	No.	Yds.	Avg.	LG	TD
Langhorne	85	1038	12.2	72t	3
Hester	64	835	13.0	58	1
Johnson	55	443	8.1	36	0
Cash	43	402	9.3	37	3
Dawkins	26	430	16.5	68	1
Potts	26	189	7.3	24	0
Arbuckle	15	90	6.0	23	0
Culver	11	112	10.2	26	1
Cox	4	59	14.8	24	0
Verdin	2	20	10.0	19	1
Toner	1	5	5.0	5	0
Colts	332	3623	10.9	72t	10
Opponents	270	3238	12.0	77	22

INTERCEPTIONS	No.	Yds.	Avg.	LG	TD
Buchanan	4	45	11.3	28	0
Baylor	3	11	3.7	7	0
Herrod	1	29	29.0	29	0
Daniel	1	17	17.0	17	0
Belser	1	14	14.0	11	0
Colts	10	116	11.6	29	0
Opponents	15	247	16.5	56t	1

PUNTING	No.	Yds.	Avg.	In 20	LG
Stark	83	3595	43.3	18	65
Colts	83	3595	43.3	18	65
Opponents	71	2855	40.2	30	59

PUNT RETURNS	No.	FC	Yds.	Avg.	LG	TD
Verdin	30	17	173	5.8	24	0
Colts	30	17	173	5.8	24	0
Opponents	41	12	352	8.6	71t	1

KICKOFF RETURNS	No.	Yds.	Avg.	LG	TD
Verdin	50	1050	21.0	38	0
Culver	3	51	17.0	20	0
Butcher	2	2	1.0	2	0
Cash	1	11	11.0	11	0
Radecic	1	10	10.0	10	0
Colts	57	1124	19.7	38	0
Opponents	37	551	14.9	37	0

SACKS	No.
Hand	5.5
Bickett	3.5
Herrod	2.0
Peguese	2.0
McClendon	1.5
Siragusa	1.5
Clancy	1.0
Coryatt	1.0
Emtman	1.0
Sims	1.0
Stargell	1.0
Colts	21.0
Opponents	29.0

1994 DRAFT CHOICES

Round	Name	Pos.	College
1	Marshall Faulk	RB	San Diego State
	Trev Alberts	LB	Nebraska
2	Eric Mahlum	G	California
3	Jason Mathews	T	Texas A&M
4	Brad Banta	TE	Southern California
5	John Covington	DB	Notre Dame
6	Lamont Warren	RB	Colorado
7	Lance Teichelman	DT	Texas A&M

1994 VETERAN ROSTER

No.	Name	Pos.	Ht.	Wt.	Birthdate	NFL Exp.	College	Hometown	How Acq.	'93 Games/ Starts
33	Ambrose, Ashley	CB-S	5-10	177	9/17/70	3	Mississippi Valley State	New Orleans, La.	D2-'92	14/6
81	Arbuckle, Charles	TE	6-3	248	9/13/68	4	UCLA	Beaumont, Tex.	FA-'92	16/2
86	Baker, Shannon	WR	5-9	185	7/20/71	2	Florida State	Lakeland, Fla.	FA-'93	0*
36	# Baylor, John	CB-S	6-0	208	3/5/65	7	Southern Mississippi	Meridian, Miss.	D5-'88	16/11
29	Belser, Jason	CB-S	5-9	187	5/28/70	3	Oklahoma	Kansas City, Mo.	D8a-'92	16/16
56	Bennett, Tony	LB	6-2	243	7/1/67	5	Mississippi	Clarksdale, Miss.	UFA(GB)-'94	10/7*
4	Biasucci, Dean	K	6-0	190	7/25/62	10	Western Carolina	Niagara Falls, N.Y.	FA-'86	16/0
99	Brandon, Michael	DE	6-4	290	7/30/68	2	Florida	Berry, Fla.	FA-'93	15/0
34	Buchanan, Ray	CB-S	5-9	193	9/29/71	2	Louisville	Chicago, Ill.	D3-'93	16/5
53	# Butcher, Paul	LB	6-0	230	11/8/63	8	Wayne State	Dearborn, Mich.	FA-'93	16/0
71	Call, Kevin	T	6-7	308	11/13/61	11	Colorado State	Boulder, Colo.	D5b-'84	10/0
88	† Cash, Kerry	TE	6-4	252	8/7/69	4	Texas	San Antonio, Tex.	D5-'91	16/14
55	Coryatt, Quentin	LB	6-3	250	8/1/70	3	Texas A&M	St. Croix, Virgin Islands	D1b-'92	16/16
80	Cox, Aaron	WR	5-10	178	3/13/65	7	Arizona State	Los Angeles, Calif.	UFA(Rams)-'92	11/0
35	Culver, Rodney	RB	5-9	224	12/23/69	3	Notre Dame	Detroit, Mich.	D4a-'92	16/1
38	Daniel, Eugene	CB-S	5-11	188	5/4/61	11	Louisiana State	Baton Rouge, La.	D8-'84	16/16
87	Dawkins, Sean	WR	6-4	213	2/3/71	2	California	Red Bank, N.J.	D1-'93	16/7
69	Dixon, Randy	G	6-3	305	3/12/65	8	Pittsburgh	Clewiston, Fla.	D4-'87	15/15
90	Emtman, Steve	DT	6-4	300	4/16/70	3	Washington	Spokane, Wash.	D1a-'92	5/5
48	Etheredge, Carlos	TE	6-5	236	8/10/70	2	Miami	Albuquerque, N.M.	D6-'93	0*
37	# Goode, Chris	CB-S	6-0	199	9/17/63	8	Alabama	Town Creek, Ala.	D10-'87	14/10
59	Grant, Stephen	LB	6-0	231	12/23/69	3	West Virginia	Miami, Fla.	D10-'92	16/0
75	Gray, Cecil	T	6-4	292	2/16/68	5	North Carolina	Norfolk, Va.	FA-'93	6/2
30	Gray, Derwin	CB-S	5-10	190	4/9/71	2	Brigham Young	San Antonio, Tex.	D4a-'93	11/0
78	Hand, Jon	DE	6-7	301	11/13/63	9	Alabama	Sylacauga, Ala.	D1-'86	15/14
12	Harbaugh, Jim	QB	6-3	215	12/23/63	8	Michigan	Ann Arbor, Mich.	FA-'94	15/15
54	Herrod, Jeff	LB	6-0	249	7/29/66	7	Mississippi	Birmingham, Ala.	D9-'88	14/14
25	Humphrey, Ronald	RB	5-10	201	3/3/69	2	Mississippi Valley State	Marland, Tex.	FA-'93	0*
23	# Johnson, Anthony	RB	6-0	222	10/25/67	5	Notre Dame	Indianapolis, Ind.	D2-'90	13/8
63	Lowdermilk, Kirk	C	6-4	280	4/10/63	10	Ohio State	Canton, Ohio	UFA(Minn)-'93	16/16
7	Majkowski, Don	QB	6-3	203	2/25/64	8	Virginia	Depew, N.Y.	FA-'93	3/0
61	McCoy, Tony	NT	6-0	279	6/10/69	3	Florida	Orlando, Fla.	D4b-'92	6/0
57	McDonald, Devon	LB	6-4	240	11/8/69	2	Notre Dame	Kingston, Jamaica	D4b-'93	16/0
73	Moss, Zefross	T	6-6	338	8/17/66	6	Alabama State	Tuscaloosa, Ala.	T(Dall)-'89	16/16
32	O'Neal, Robert	CB-S	6-1	194	1/2/71	2	Clemson	Atlanta, Ga.	FA-'93	0*
96	# Peguese, Willis	DE	6-4	273	12/18/66	5	Miami	Miami, Fla.	FA-'93	13/4
42	Potts, Roosevelt	RB	6-0	258	1/8/71	2	Northeast Louisiana	Rayville, La.	D2-'93	16/15
52	Ratigan, Brian	LB	6-4	226	12/27/70	2	Notre Dame	Council Bluffs, Iowa	FA-'93	0*
74	Schultz, William	T	6-5	305	5/1/67	5	Southern California	Granada Hills, Calif.	D4b-'90	14/14
92	Sims, Thomas	NT	6-2	291	4/18/67	5	Pittsburgh	Detroit, Mich.	FA-'93	5/3
98	Siragusa, Tony	NT	6-3	303	5/14/67	5	Pittsburgh	Kenilworth, N.J.	FA-'90	14/14
3	Stark, Rohn	P	6-3	203	5/4/59	13	Florida State	Minneapolis, Minn.	D2b-'82	16/0
79	† Staysniak, Joe	T	6-4	296	12/8/66	4	Ohio State	Elyria, Ohio	FA-'92	14/1
94	Thomas, Marquise	LB	6-4	255	5/25/71	2	Mississippi	Fresno, Calif.	D8-'93	0*
28	Toner, Ed	RB	6-0	240	3/22/68	3	Boston College	Lynn, Mass.	FA-'92	16/1
85	Turner, Floyd	WR	5-11	198	5/29/66	6	Northwestern Louisiana	Mansfield, La.	UFA(NO)-'94	10/2*
72	Vander Poel, Mark	T	6-7	303	3/5/68	3	Colorado	Upland, Calif.	D4-'91	0*
67	Wolford, Will	T	6-5	300	5/18/64	9	Vanderbilt	Louisville, Ky.	RFA(Buff)-'93	12/12

* Baker active for 14 games but did not play; Bennett played 10 games with Green Bay in '93; Etheredge, Humphrey, Radigan, and Vander Poel missed '93 season due to injury; O'Neal active for 10 games but did not play; Thomas active for 1 game but did not play; Turner played 10 games with New Orleans.

Unrestricted free agent; subject to developments.

† Restricted free agent; subject to developments.

Traded—QB Jeff George to Atlanta.

Players lost through free agency (2): C Trevor Matich (Wash; 16 games in '93); CB Tony Stargell (TB; 16).

Also played with Colts in '93—CB-S Michael Ball (5 games), LB Duane Bickett (15), DE Sam Clancy (16), QB Jeff George (13), WR Jessie Hester (16), WR Reggie Langhorne (16), DE-DT Skip McClendon (16), WR Eddie Miller (1), LB Scott Radecic (16), QB Jack Trudeau (5), WR Clarence Verdin (16), RB Warren Williams (5).

COACHING STAFF

Head Coach,
Ted Marchibroda

Pro Career: Marchibroda ranks as the third-winningest head coach in Colts history with a 54-55 record. He returned to the Colts on January 28, 1992, after serving as head coach with the team from 1975-79. Marchibroda's first tenure produced a 41-36 overall record and three AFC Eastern Divisional titles (1975, 10-4; 1976, 11-3; and 1977, 10-4). He took over a Colts team that was 2-12 in 1974 and produced an eight-game improvement, then the best one-season turnaround in NFL history. It marked the first time a coach had taken a team from last to first place in one season. Marchibroda authored a 9-7 record two years ago, thus his 1975 and 1992 Colts squads posted two of the four eight-game seasonal turnarounds in NFL history. The Colts were 4-12 in 1993. His three divisional championships represent the most titles won by a Colts head coach. Prior to returning to the Colts, Marchibroda served five years as an assistant with the Buffalo Bills, the last three as offensive coordinator. Marchibroda began his career as backfield coach with the Washington Redskins in 1961. He joined George Allen's staff with the Los Angeles Rams in 1966. He moved with Allen to the Redskins in 1971, where he served as offensive coordinator through the 1974 season. After his stint with the Colts, Marchibroda served as quarterback coach with Chicago in 1981, then moved on to Detroit as offensive coordinator from 1982-83. He served that same role in Philadelphia from 1984-85 before joining Buffalo in 1987. Marchibroda was the first draft pick of the Pittsburgh Steelers in 1953 and played one year before serving in the Army. He returned to Pittsburgh for the 1955-56 seasons. His top year was 1956, completing 124 of 275 passes for 1,585 yards and 12 touchdowns. Marchibroda's playing career ended with the Chicago Cardinals in 1957. Career record: 54-55.

Background: Quarterback at St. Bonaventure 1950-51 and University of Detroit 1952. Led nation in total offense at Detroit. He was a football, basketball (all-state selection), and baseball player at Franklin (Pa.) High School.

Personal: Born March 15, 1931, Franklin, Pa. Ted and his wife, Ann, reside in Indianapolis. They have two daughters, Jodi and Lonni, and two sons, Ted Jr. and Robert.

ASSISTANT COACHES

Tom Batta, special teams; born October 6, 1942, Youngstown, Ohio, lives in Indianapolis. Offensive-defensive line Kent State 1961-63. No pro playing experience. College coach: Akron 1973, Colorado 1974-78, Kansas 1979-82, North Carolina State 1983. Pro coach: Minnesota Vikings 1984-93, joined Colts in 1994.

Greg Blache, defensive line; born March 9, 1949, New Orleans, La., lives in Indianapolis. No college or pro playing experience. College coach: Notre Dame 1973-75, 1981-83, Tulane 1976, Southern University 1986, Kansas 1987. Pro coach: Jacksonville Bulls (USFL) 1984-85, Green Bay Packers 1988-93, joined Colts in 1994.

Ron Blackledge, offensive line; born April 15, 1938, Canton, Ohio, lives in Indianapolis. Tight end-defensive end Bowling Green 1957-59. No pro playing experience. College coach: Ashland 1968-69, Cincinnati 1970-72, Kentucky 1973-75, Princeton 1976, Kent State 1977-81 (head coach 1979-81). Pro coach: Pittsburgh Steelers 1982-91, joined Colts in 1992.

Fred Bruney, defensive assistant; born December 30, 1931, Martins Ferry, Ohio, lives in Indianapolis. Running back-defensive back Ohio State 1950-52. Pro defensive back San Francisco 49ers 1953-56, Pittsburgh Steelers 1957, Los Angeles Rams 1958, Boston Patriots 1960-62. College coach: Ohio State 1959. Pro coach: Boston Patriots 1962-63, Philadelphia Eagles 1964-68, 1977-85, Atlanta Falcons 1969-76, 1986-89, Tampa Bay Buccaneers 1990, New York Giants 1991-92, joined Colts in 1993.

Gene Huey, running backs; born July 20, 1947, Uniontown, Pa., lives in Indianapolis. Defensive back-wide receiver Wyoming 1966-69. No pro playing experience. College coach: Wyoming 1970-74, New Mexico 1975-77, Nebraska 1978-87, Ohio State 1988-91. Pro coach: Joined Colts in 1992.

Jim Johnson, linebackers; born May 26, 1941, Maywood, Ill., lives in Indianapolis. Quarterback Missouri 1959-62. Pro tight end Buffalo Bills 1963-64. College coach: Missouri Southern 1967-68 (head coach), Drake 1969-72, Indiana 1973-76, Notre Dame 1977-80. Pro coach: Oklahoma Outlaws (USFL) 1984, Jacksonville Bulls (USFL) 1985, Phoenix Cardinals 1986-93, joined Colts in 1994.

Hank Kuhlman, tight ends; born October 6, 1937, Webster Groves, Mo., lives in Indianapolis. Running back Missouri 1956-59. No pro playing experience. College coach: Missouri 1962-70, Notre Dame 1975-77. Pro coach: Green Bay Packers 1972-74, Chicago Bears 1978-82, Birmingham Stallions (USFL) 1983-85, Phoenix Cardinals 1986-90 (scout, 1990), Tampa Bay Buccaneers 1991, joined Colts in 1994.

Nick Nicolau, offensive coordinator; born May 5, 1933, New York, N.Y., lives in Indianapolis. Running back Southern Connecticut 1957-59. No pro playing experience. College coach: Southern Connecticut 1960, Springfield 1961, Bridgeport 1962-69 (head coach 1965-69), Massachusetts 1970, Connecticut 1971-72, Kentucky 1973-75, Kent State 1976. Pro coach: Hamilton Tiger-Cats (CFL) 1977, Montreal

Alouettes (CFL) 1978-79, New Orleans Saints 1980, Denver Broncos 1981-87, Los Angeles Raiders 1988, Buffalo Bills 1989-91, joined Colts in 1992.

Jimmy Robinson, wide receivers; born January 3, 1953, Atlanta, Ga., lives in Indianapolis. Wide receiver Georgia Tech 1972-74. Pro wide receiver Atlanta Falcons 1975, New York Giants 1976-79, San Francisco 49ers 1980, Denver Broncos 1981. College coach: Georgia Tech 1986-89. Pro coach: Memphis Showboats (USFL) 1984-85, Atlanta Falcons 1990-93, joined Colts in 1994.

Pat Thomas, secondary; born September 1, 1954, Plano, Tex., lives in Indianapolis. Cornerback Texas A&M 1972-75. Pro cornerback Los Angeles Rams 1976-82. College coach: Houston 1987-89. Pro coach Houston Gamblers (USFL) 1984-85, Houston Oilers 1990-92, joined Colts in 1994.

Vince Tobin, defensive coordinator; born September 29, 1943, Burlington Junction, Mo., lives in Indianapolis. Defensive back-running back Missouri 1961-64. No pro playing experience. College coach: Missouri 1967-76. Pro coach: British Columbia Lions (CFL) 1977-82, Philadelphia/Baltimore Stars (USFL) 1983-85, Chicago Bears 1986-92, joined Colts in 1994.

Tom Zupancic, strength and conditioning; born September 14, 1955, Indianapolis, lives in Indianapolis. Defensive tackle-offensive tackle Indiana Central 1975-78. No pro playing experience. Pro coach: Joined Colts in 1984.

1994 FIRST-YEAR ROSTER

Name	Pos.	Ht.	Wt.	Birthdate	College	Hometown	How Acq.
Alberts, Trev	LB	6-4	243	8/8/70	Nebraska	Cedar Falls, Iowa	D1b
Allen, Russell	DE	6-6	296	4/8/71	Oklahoma	Oklahoma City, Okla.	FA
Bailey, Aaron	WR	5-10	184	10/24/71	Louisville	Ann Arbor, Mich.	FA
Banta, Brad	TE	6-6	254	12/14/70	Southern California	Baton Rouge, La.	D4
Borrelli, Marc	T	6-5	286	4/30/71	Boston College	Philadelphia, Pa.	FA
Campbell, Darnell	RB	6-1	224	4/2/70	Boston College	Brockton, Mass.	FA
Cook, Mike (1)	WR	6-4	205	3/20/71	Stanford	Fountain Valley, Calif.	FA
Courtney, Marvin	RB	6-0	204	1/15/71	Mississippi	Greenville, Miss.	FA
Covington, John	CB-S	6-0	198	4/22/72	Notre Dame	Winter Haven, Fla.	D5
Ericson, Todd	CB-S	6-3	205	6/28/71	Montana	Butte, Mont.	FA
Faulk, Marshall	RB	5-10	200	2/26/73	San Diego State	New Orleans, La.	D1a
Houston, William	RB	6-1	260	3/18/71	Ohio State	Trotwood, Ohio	FA
Jordan, Todd	QB-P	6-2	231	6/18/70	Mississippi State	Tupelo, Miss.	FA
Justin, Paul (1)	QB	6-4	202	5/19/68	Arizona State	Schaumberg, Ill.	FA
Mahlum, Eric	G	6-4	285	12/6/70	California	San Diego, Calif.	D2
Mathews, Jason	T	6-5	284	2/9/71	Texas A&M	Orange, Tex.	D3
McEntyre, Kenny	CB-S	5-9	181	12/7/70	Kansas State	Dallas, Tex.	FA
Orton, Jason	CB-S	5-11	175	4/25/71	Indiana	Terre Haute, Ind.	FA
Pointer, Deron	WR	5-11	175	9/9/71	Washington State	Tacoma, Wash.	FA
Ray, John (1)	T	6-8	350	4/26/69	West Virginia	South Charleston, W.Va.	FA
Simon, Jose	DT	6-3	291	6/24/72	Texas A&I	Middletown, Calif.	FA
Smith, Terry	WR	6-0	200	4/20/71	Clemson	Clemson, S.C.	FA
Stablein, Brian (1)	WR	6-1	185	4/14/70	Ohio State	Erie, Pa.	FA
Starks, Glenn	RB	6-1	205	2/14/72	Central Oklahoma St.	Covington, Tenn.	FA
Teichelman, Lance	DE-DT	6-4	274	10/21/70	Texas A&M	San Antonio, Tex.	D7
Vickers, Kipp (1)	G-T	6-2	275	8/27/69	Miami	Holiday, Fla.	FA
Ware, Cassius	LB	5-11	243	6/8/71	Mississippi	Batesville, Miss.	FA
Warren, Lamont	RB	5-11	194	1/4/73	Colorado	Indianapolis, Ind.	D6
Whittington, Bernard	DE	6-6	257	7/20/71	Indiana	St. Louis, Mo.	FA

The term NFL Rookie is defined as a player who is in his first season of professional football and has not been on the roster of another professional football team for any regular-season or postseason games. A Rookie is designated by an "R" on NFL rosters. Players who have been active in another professional football league or players who have NFL experience, including either preseason training camp or being on an Active List or Inactive List, or on Reserve/Injured or Reserve/Physically Unable to Perform for fewer than six regular-season games, are termed NFL First-Year Players. An NFL First-Year Player is designated by a "1" on NFL rosters. Thereafter, a player is credited with an additional year of experience for each season in which he accumulates six games on the Active List or Inactive List, or on Reserve/Injured or Reserve/Physically Unable to Perform.

NOTES

American Football Conference
Western Division
Team Colors: Red, Gold, and White
One Arrowhead Drive
Kansas City, Missouri 64129
Telephone: (816) 924-9300

CLUB OFFICIALS

Founder: Lamar Hunt
Chairman of the Board: Jack Steadman
President/General Manager and Chief Operating
    Officer: Carl Peterson
Executive Vice President: Tim Connolly
Vice President/Player Personnel: Lynn Stiles
Assistant General Manager: Dennis Thum
Secretary: Jim Seigfreid
Director of Finance/Treasurer: Dale Young
Director of Public Relations: Bob Moore
Director of Operations: Jeff Klein
Director of Marketing & Sales: Dennis Watley
Director of Development: Ken Blume
Assistant Director of Public Relations: Jim Carr
Director of Promotions: Phil Thomas
Community Relations Manager: Brenda Sniezek
Ticket Manager: Dave Hopkins
Equipment Manager: Mike Davidson
Asst. Equipment Managers: Allen Wright, Darin Kerns
Trainer: Dave Kendall
Assistant Trainer: Bud Epps
Video Coordinator: Mike Dennis
Assistant Video Coordinator: Mike Kirk
Stadium: Arrowhead Stadium •**Capacity:** 78,067
    One Arrowhead Drive
    Kansas City, Missouri 64129
Playing Surface: Grass
Training Camp: University of
    Wisconsin-River Falls
    River Falls, Wisconsin 54022

1994 SCHEDULE
PRESEASON

July 31	**Houston**	8:00
Aug. 6	vs. Minnesota at Tokyo	10:00
Aug. 12	at Washington	8:00
Aug. 22	**Chicago**	7:00
Aug. 26	at Buffalo	8:00

REGULAR SEASON

Sept. 4	at New Orleans	12:00
Sept. 11	**San Francisco**	12:00
Sept. 18	at Atlanta	8:00
Sept. 25	**Los Angeles Rams**	12:00
Oct. 2	Open Date	
Oct. 9	at San Diego	1:00
Oct. 17	at Denver (Monday)	7:00
Oct. 23	**Seattle**	12:00
Oct. 30	at Buffalo	1:00
Nov. 6	**Los Angeles Raiders**	7:00
Nov. 13	**San Diego**	12:00
Nov. 20	**Cleveland**	12:00
Nov. 27	at Seattle	1:00
Dec. 4	**Denver**	3:00
Dec. 12	at Miami (Monday)	9:00
Dec. 18	**Houston**	3:00
Dec. 24	at Los Angeles Raiders	1:00

RECORD HOLDERS
INDIVIDUAL RECORDS—CAREER

Category	Name	Performance
Rushing (Yds.)	Christian Okoye, 1987-1992	4,897
Passing (Yds.)	Len Dawson, 1962-1975	28,507
Passing (TDs)	Len Dawson, 1962-1975	237
Receiving (No.)	Henry Marshall, 1976-1987	416
Receiving (Yds.)	Otis Taylor, 1965-1975	7,306
Interceptions	Emmitt Thomas, 1966-1978	58
Punting (Avg.)	Jerrel Wilson, 1963-1977	43.5
Punt Return (Avg.)	J.T. Smith, 1979-1984	10.6
Kickoff Return (Avg.)	Noland Smith, 1967-69	26.8
Field Goals	Nick Lowery, 1980-1993	329
Touchdowns (Tot.)	Otis Taylor, 1965-1975	60
Points	Nick Lowery, 1980-1993	1,466

INDIVIDUAL RECORDS—SINGLE SEASON

Category	Name	Performance
Rushing (Yds.)	Christian Okoye, 1989	1,480
Passing (Yds.)	Bill Kenney, 1983	4,348
Passing (TDs)	Len Dawson, 1964	30
Receiving (No.)	Carlos Carson, 1983	80
Receiving (Yds.)	Carlos Carson, 1983	1,351
Interceptions	Emmitt Thomas, 1974	12
Punting (Avg.)	Jerrel Wilson, 1965	46.0
Punt Return (Avg.)	Abner Haynes, 1960	15.4
Kickoff Return (Avg.)	Dave Grayson, 1962	29.7
Field Goals	Nick Lowery, 1990	34
Touchdowns (Tot.)	Abner Haynes, 1962	19
Points	Nick Lowery, 1990	139

INDIVIDUAL RECORDS—SINGLE GAME

Category	Name	Performance
Rushing (Yds.)	Barry Word, 10-14-90	200
Passing (Yds.)	Len Dawson, 11-1-64	435
Passing (TDs)	Len Dawson, 11-1-64	6
Receiving (No.)	Ed Podolak, 10-7-73	12
Receiving (Yds.)	Stephone Paige, 12-22-85	309
Interceptions	Bobby Ply, 12-16-62	*4
	Bobby Hunt, 12-4-64	*4
	Deron Cherry, 9-29-85	*4
Field Goals	Many times.	5
	Last time by Nick Lowery, 9-20-93	
Touchdowns (Tot.)	Abner Haynes, 11-26-61	5
Points	Abner Haynes, 11-26-61	30

*NFL Record

COACHING HISTORY
DALLAS TEXANS 1960-62
(263-241-12)

1960-74	Hank Stram	129-79-10
1975-77	Paul Wiggin*	11-24-0
1977	Tom Bettis	1-6-0
1978-82	Marv Levy	31-42-0
1983-86	John Mackovic	30-35-0
1987-88	Frank Gansz	8-22-1
1989-93	Marty Schottenheimer	53-33-1

*Released after seven games in 1977

ARROWHEAD STADIUM

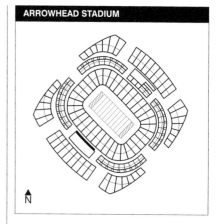

1993 TEAM RECORD

PRESEASON (3-1)

Date	Result		Opponents
8/7	W	29-21	vs. Green Bay at Milw.
8/12	L	7-30	Buffalo
8/21	W	27-20	Minnesota
8/27	W	27-20	at New England

REGULAR SEASON (11-5)

Date	Result		Opponents	Att.
9/5	W	27-3	at Tampa Bay	63,378
9/12	L	0-30	at Houston	59,780
9/20	W	15-7	Denver	78,453
10/3	W	24-9	L.A. Raiders	77,395
10/10	W	17-15	Cincinnati	75,394
10/17	W	17-14	at San Diego	60,729
10/31	L	10-30	at Miami	67,765
11/8	W	23-16	Green Bay	76,742
11/14	W	31-20	at L.A. Raiders	66,553
11/21	L	17-19	Chicago	76,872
11/28	W	23-7	Buffalo	74,452
12/5	W	31-16	at Seattle	58,551
12/12	L	21-27	at Denver	75,822
12/19	W	28-24	San Diego	74,778
12/26	L	10-30	at Minnesota	59,236
1/2	W	34-24	Seattle	72,136

POSTSEASON (2-1)

Date	Result		Opponents	Att.
1/8	W	27-24	Pittsburgh (OT)	74,515
1/16	W	28-20	at Houston	64,011
1/23	L	13-30	at Buffalo	76,642

(OT) Overtime

SCORE BY PERIODS

Chiefs	71	108	82	67	0	—	328
Opponents	51	86	50	104	0	—	291

ATTENDANCE

Home 606,222   Away 511,814   Total 1,118,036
Single-game home record, 82,094 (11-5-72)
Single-season home record, 612,773 (1992)

1993 TEAM STATISTICS

	Chiefs	Opp.
Total First Downs	300	300
Rushing	94	103
Passing	180	161
Penalty	26	36
Third Down: Made/Att	82/203	86/210
Third Down Pct.	40.4	41.0
Fourth Down: Made/Att	4/9	3/13
Fourth Down Pct.	44.4	23.1
Total Net Yards	4835	4771
Avg. Per Game	302.2	298.2
Total Plays	970	1013
Avg. Per Play	5.0	4.7
Net Yards Rushing	1655	1620
Avg. Per Game	103.4	101.3
Total Rushes	445	453
Net Yards Passing	3180	3151
Avg. Per Game	198.8	196.9
Sacked/Yards Lost	35/204	35/228
Gross Yards	3384	3379
Att./Completions	490/287	525/312
Completion Pct.	58.6	59.4
Had Intercepted	10	21
Punts/Avg.	77/42.1	68/44.6
Net Punting Avg.	77/35.4	68/37.8
Penalties/Yards Lost	121/969	127/1015
Fumbles/Ball Lost	28/18	30/17
Touchdowns	37	30
Rushing	14	11
Passing	20	18
Returns	3	1
Avg. Time of Possession	29:28	30:32

1993 INDIVIDUAL STATISTICS

PASSING

	Att.	Cmp.	Yds.	Pct.	TD	Int.	Tkld.	Rate
Montana	298	181	2144	60.7	13	7	12/61	87.4
Krieg	189	105	1238	55.6	7	3	22/138	81.4
Blundin	3	1	2	33.3	0	0	0/0	42.4
Anders	0	0	0	—	0	0	1/5	-1.0
Chiefs	490	287	3384	58.6	20	10	35/204	84.8
Opponents	525	312	3379	59.4	18	21	35/228	73.2

SCORING

	TD R	TD P	TD Rt	PAT	FG	Saf	PTS
Lowery	0	0	0	37/37	23/29	0	106
Allen	12	3	0	0/0	0/0	0	90
Davis	0	7	0	0/0	0/0	0	42
Cash	0	4	0	0/0	0/0	0	24
Birden	0	2	0	0/0	0/0	0	12
McNair	2	0	0	0/0	0/0	0	12
Anders	0	1	0	0/0	0/0	0	6
Barnett	0	1	0	0/0	0/0	0	6
Hayes	0	1	0	0/0	0/0	0	6
A. Lewis	0	0	1	0/0	0/0	0	6
Saleaumua	0	0	1	0/0	0/0	0	6
Thomas	0	0	1	0/0	0/0	0	6
Valerio	0	1	0	0/0	0/0	0	6
Chiefs	14	20	3	37/37	23/29	0	328
Opponents	11	18	1	27/30	28/32	0	291

RUSHING

	Att.	Yds.	Avg.	LG	TD
Allen	206	764	3.7	39	12
Anders	75	291	3.9	18	0
McNair	51	278	5.5	47	2
J. Stephens	6	18	3.0	7	0
H. Williams	42	149	3.5	19	0
Montana	25	64	2.6	17	0
F. Jones	5	34	6.8	13	0
E. Thompson	11	28	2.5	14	0
Krieg	21	24	1.1	20	0
Barnett	1	3	3.0	3	0
Carter	1	2	2.0	2	0
Cash	1	0	0.0	0	0
Chiefs	445	1655	3.7	47	14
Opponents	453	1620	3.6	38	11

RECEIVING

	No.	Yds.	Avg.	LG	TD
Davis	52	909	17.5	66t	7
Birden	51	721	14.1	50t	5
Anders	40	326	8.2	27	1
Allen	34	238	7.0	18t	3
Hayes	24	331	13.0	19	1
Cash	24	242	10.1	24	4
Barnett	17	182	10.7	25	1
McNair	10	74	7.4	24	0
F. Jones	9	111	12.3	19	0
H. Jones	7	91	13.0	22	0
Dyal	7	83	11.9	31	0
H. Williams	7	42	6.0	14	0
E. Thompson	4	33	8.3	13	0
Valerio	1	1	1.0	1t	1
Chiefs	287	3384	11.8	66t	20
Opponents	312	3379	10.8	77t	18

INTERCEPTIONS

	No.	Yds.	Avg.	LG	TD
A. Lewis	6	61	10.2	24	0
Mincy	5	44	8.8	20	0
Ross	2	49	24.5	48	0
Bayless	2	14	7.0	16	0
Terry	1	21	21.0	21	0
Marts	1	20	20.0	20	0
Saleaumua	1	13	13.0	13	0
Smith	1	3	3.0	3	0
Carter	1	0	0.0	0	0
Taylor	1	0	0.0	0	0
Chiefs	21	225	10.7	48	0
Opponents	10	111	11.1	48	0

PUNTING

	No.	Yds.	Avg.	In 20	LG
Barker	76	3240	42.6	19	59
Chiefs	77	3240	42.1	19	59
Opponents	68	3035	44.6	23	67

PUNT RETURNS

	No.	FC	Yds.	Avg.	LG	TD
Carter	27	4	247	9.1	30	0
Birden	5	3	43	8.6	12	0
Hughes	3	0	49	16.3	29	0
Mincy	2	0	9	4.5	9	0
Chiefs	37	7	348	9.4	30	0
Opponents	43	15	352	8.2	54	0

KICKOFF RETURNS

	No.	Yds.	Avg.	LG	TD
Hughes	14	266	19.0	30	0
Dickerson	11	237	21.5	44	0
F. Jones	9	156	17.3	29	0
J. Stephens	5	88	17.6	25	0
H. Williams	3	53	17.7	26	0
Anders	1	47	47.0	47	0
Marts	1	0	0.0	0	0
McNair	1	28	28.0	28	0
Birden	0	0	—	—	0
Chiefs	45	875	19.4	47	0
Opponents	49	1007	20.6	60	0

SACKS

	No.
Smith	15.0
Thomas	8.0
Saleaumua	3.5
Marts	2.0
Phillips	1.5
Bayless	1.0
Mickell	1.0
Newton	1.0
Terry	1.0
Ross	0.5
B.Thompson	0.5
Chiefs	35.0
Opponents	35.0

1994 DRAFT CHOICES

Round	Name	Pos.	College
1	Greg Hill	RB	Texas A&M
2	Donnell Bennett	RB	Miami
3	Lake Dawson	WR	Notre Dame
	Chris Penn	WR	Tulsa
4	Bracey Walker	DB	North Carolina
5	James Burton	DB	Fresno State
	Rob Waldrop	DT	Arizona
6	Anthony Daigle	RB	Fresno State
7	Steve Matthews	QB	Memphis State
	Tracy Greene	TE	Grambling

KANSAS CITY CHIEFS

1994 VETERAN ROSTER

No.	Name	Pos.	Ht.	Wt.	Birthdate	NFL Exp.	College	Hometown	How Acq.	'93 Games/ Starts
5	Aguiar, Louie	P	6-2	215	6/30/66	4	Utah State	Livermore, Calif.	FA-'94	16/0*
32	Allen, Marcus	RB	6-2	210	3/26/60	13	Southern California	San Diego, Calif.	UFA(Raid)-'93	16/10
76	† Alt, John	T	6-8	307	5/30/62	11	Iowa	Columbia Heights, Minn.	D1b-'84	16/16
38	Anders, Kimble	RB	5-11	221	9/10/66	4	Houston	Galveston, Tex.	FA-'91	16/13
50	Anderson, Erick	LB	6-1	235	10/7/68	3	Michigan	Glenbrook, Ill.	D7-'92	8/1
82	Barnett, Tim	WR	6-1	200	4/19/68	4	Jackson State	Rosedale, Miss.	D3-'91	16/0
87	Bartrum, Mike	TE	6-4	234	6/23/70	2	Marshall	Pomeroy, Ohio	FA-'93	3/0
30	# Bayless, Martin	S	6-2	219	10/11/62	11	Bowling Green	Dayton, Ohio	PB(SD)-'92	16/10
88	Birden, J.J.	WR	5-9	165	5/16/65	6	Oregon	Portland, Ore.	FA-'90	16/16
14	Blundin, Matt	QB	6-5	233	3/7/69	3	Virginia	Ridley, Pa.	D2-'92	1/0
13	t- Bono, Steve	QB	6-4	215	5/11/62	10	UCLA	Norristown, Pa.	T(SF)-'94	8/0*
34	Carter, Dale	CB-KR	6-1	188	11/28/69	3	Tennessee	Covington, Ga.	D1-'92	15/11
89	Cash, Keith	TE	6-4	240	8/7/69	3	Texas	San Antonio, Tex.	PB(Pitt)-'92	15/0
99	Casillas, Tony	DT	6-3	273	10/26/63	9	Oklahoma	Tulsa, Okla.	UFA(Dall)-'94	15/14*
22	Cobb, Trevor	RB	5-9	190	11/20/70	2	Rice	Pasadena, Tex.	FA-'93	0*
24	Collins, Mark	CB	5-10	190	1/16/64	9	Cal State-Fullerton	San Bernardino, Calif.	UFA(NYG)-'94	16/16*
84	Davis, Willie	WR	6-0	172	5/16/65	3	Central Arkansas	Altheimer, Ark.	FA-'92	16/15
23	Dickerson, Ron	RB	6-0	211	8/31/71	2	Arkansas	State College, Pa.	FA-'93	6/0
2	Elliot, Lin	K	6-0	182	11/11/68	2	Texas Tech	Waco, Tex.	FA-'94	2/0*
59	Fields, Jaime	LB	5-11	230	8/28/70	2	Washington	Lynwood, Calif.	D4-'93	6/0
74	Graham, Derrick	T	6-4	306	3/18/67	5	Appalachian State	Groveland, Fla.	D5a-'90	11/2
61	Grunhard, Tim	C	6-2	299	5/17/68	5	Notre Dame	Chicago, Ill.	D2-'90	16/16
83	Hughes, Danan	WR	6-1	201	12/11/70	2	Iowa	Bayonne, N.J.	D7-'93	6/0
91	Johnson, Jimmie	TE	6-2	248	10/6/66	6	Howard	Augusta, Ga.	FA-'94	6/4*
65	Knapp, Lindsay	G-T	6-5	280	2/25/70	2	Notre Dame	Deerfield, Ill.	D5-'93	0*
8	Lowery, Nick	K	6-4	207	5/27/56	15	Dartmouth	Washington, D.C.	FA-'80	16/0
77	McDaniels, Pellom	DE	6-3	278	2/21/68	2	Oregon State	San Jose, Calif.	FA-'93	10/0
92	Mickell, Darren	DT	6-4	280	8/3/70	3	Florida	Miami, Fla.	SD2-'92	16/1
42	† Mincy, Charles	S	5-11	197	12/16/69	4	Washington	Los Angeles, Calif.	D5-'91	16/4
19	Montana, Joe	QB	6-2	205	6/11/56	16	Notre Dame	Monongahela, Pa.	T(SF)-'93	11/11
96	Newton, Tim	DT	6-0	269	3/23/63	9	Florida	Orlando, Fla.	FA-'94	16/0
75	Phillips, Joe	DT	6-5	300	7/15/63	8	Southern Methodist	Vancouver, Wash.	FA-'92	16/16
39	Pickens, Bruce	CB	5-11	190	5/9/68	4	Nebraska	Kansas City, Mo.	FA-'93	7/4*
52	# Rogers, Tracy	LB	6-2	241	8/13/67	5	Fresno State	Taft, Calif.	FA-'90	14/14
97	† Saleaumua, Dan	DT	6-0	300	11/25/64	8	Arizona State	San Diego, Calif.	PB(Det)-'89	16/16
68	Shields, Will	G	6-2	296	9/15/71	2	Nebraska	Lawton, Okla.	D3-'93	16/15
66	Siglar, Ricky	T	6-7	304	6/14/66	3	San Jose State	Manzano, N.M.	FA-'93	14/14
54	Simien, Tracy	LB	6-2	250	5/21/67	4	Texas Christian	Bay City, Tex.	FA-'91	16/14
90	Smith, Neil	DE	6-4	273	4/10/66	7	Nebraska	New Orleans, La.	D1-'88	16/15
21	Stephens, John	RB	6-1	215	2/23/66	7	Northwestern Louisiana	Springhill, La.	FA-'93	12/5*
79	Szott, Dave	G	6-4	290	12/12/67	5	Penn State	Clifton, N.J.	D7-'90	14/13
27	Taylor, Jay	CB	5-10	170	11/8/67	6	San Jose State	San Diego, Calif.	T(Phx)-'93	15/1
25	Terry, Doug	S	5-11	197	12/12/69	3	Kansas	Liberal, Kan.	FA-'92	15/8
58	Thomas, Derrick	LB	6-3	242	1/1/67	6	Alabama	Miami, Fla.	D1-'89	16/15
45	Thompson, Ernie	RB	5-11	257	10/25/69	2	Indiana	Terre Haute, Ind.	FA-'93	16/2
94	Traylor, Keith	DE	6-2	290	9/3/69	3	Central Oklahoma	Malvern, Ark.	FA-'94	5/0*
73	Valerio, Joe	G-C	6-5	295	2/11/69	4	Pennsylvania	Ridley, Pa.	D2-'91	13/0
72	Villa, Danny	G	6-5	300	9/21/64	8	Arizona State	Nogales, Ariz.	UFA(Phx)-'93	13/3
26	Watson, Tim	S	6-1	213	8/13/70	2	Howard	Ft. Valley, Ga.	FA-'93	4/0
41	Whitmore, David	S	6-0	232	7/6/67	5	Stephen F. Austin	Daingerfield, Tex.	T(SF)-'93	6/6
47	Wilburn, Barry	CB	6-3	186	12/9/63	7	Mississippi	Memphis, Tenn.	FA-'94	0*

* Aguiar played 16 games with N.Y. Jets in '93; Bono played 8 games with San Francisco; Casillas played 15 games with Dallas; Cobb missed '93 season due to injury; Collins played 16 games with N.Y. Giants; Elliott played 2 games with Dallas; Johnson played 6 games with Detroit; Knapp inactive for 16 games; Pickens played 4 games with Atlanta, 3 games with Kansas City; Stephens played 5 games with Green Bay, 7 games with Kansas City; Traylor played 5 games with Green Bay; Wilburn last active with Cleveland in '92.

\# Unrestricted free agent; subject to developments.

† Restricted free agent; subject to developments.

t- Chiefs trade for Bono (San Francisco).

Players lost through free agency (4): QB Dave Krieg (Det; 12 games in '93), CB Albert Lewis (Raid; 14), LB Lonnie Marts (TB; 16), CB Kevin Ross (Atl; 15).

Also played with Chiefs in '93—P Bryan Barker (16 games), TE Mike Dyal (6), DE Leonard Griffin (4), TE Jonathan Hayes (16), WR Fred Jones (10), WR Hassan Jones (8), CB Garry Lewis (1), G Reggie McElroy (8), S Erik McMillan (1), RB Todd McNair (15), CB-S Muhammed Oliver (2), G Tom Ricketts (3), LB Santo Stephens (16), S Bennie Thompson (16), RB Harvey Williams (7).

COACHING STAFF

Head Coach,
Marty Schottenheimer

Pro Career: In five seasons as head coach of the Kansas City Chiefs, Schottenheimer has established the highest winning percentage in franchise history (.632). Moreover, his .626 regular-season winning percentage is third highest among active NFL coaches. He has directed the Chiefs to five of their seven winning seasons since 1974 and has taken Kansas City to the playoffs four consecutive years, a team record. He is the only coach that has taken his team to the playoffs eight times since 1985 and has missed the playoffs only once as an NFL head coach. As head coach of the Cleveland Browns from midseason in 1984 through 1988, he led the club to four playoff berths, three AFC Central Division titles, two AFC Championship Game appearances, and captured AFC coach of the years honors (1986). He first joined the Browns in 1980 as defensive coordinator after serving as linebackers coach of the Detroit Lions in 1978-79. His first NFL coaching job came with the New York Giants, where he was linebackers coach and later defensive coordinator from 1975-77. He also served as an assistant coach with the Portland Storm (WFL) in 1974. A seventh-round draft choice of the Buffalo Bills in 1965, he played linebacker with the Bills until 1968 and finished his pro playing career with the Boston Patriots in 1969-70. Career record: 99-64-1.

Background: Schottenheimer was an All-America linebacker at the University of Pittsburgh 1962-64. Following his retirement from pro football, he worked as a real estate developer in both Miami and Denver from 1971-74.

Personal: Born September 23, 1943, Canonsburg, Pa. Marty and his wife, Patricia, live in Overland Park, Kan., and have one daughter, Kristen, and one son, Brian.

ASSISTANT COACHES

Dave Adolph, defensive coordinator-linebackers; born June 6, 1937, Akron, Ohio, lives in Overland Park, Kan. Guard-linebacker Akron 1955-58. No pro playing experience. College coach: Akron 1963-64, Connecticut 1965-68, Kentucky 1969-72, Illinois 1970-76, Ohio State 1977-78. Pro coach: Cleveland Browns 1979-84, 1986-88, San Diego Chargers 1985, Los Angeles Raiders 1989-91, joined Chiefs in 1992.

Russ Ball, assistant strength and conditioning; born August 28, 1959, Moberly, Mo., lives in Kansas City. Center Central Missouri State 1977-80. No pro playing experience. College coach: Missouri 1981-88. Pro coach: Joined Chiefs in 1989.

John Bunting, defensive assistant; born July 15, 1950, Portland, Me., lives in Kansas City. Linebacker North Carolina 1968-71. Pro linebacker Philadelphia Eagles 1972-82, Philadelphia Stars (USFL) 1983-84. College coach: Brown 1986, Rowan College 1987-92 (head coach 1988-92). Pro coach: Baltimore Stars (USFL) 1985, joined Chiefs in 1993.

Herman Edwards, defensive backs; born April 27, 1954, Ft. Monmouth, N.J., lives in Blue Springs, Mo. Defensive back California 1972-75, San Diego State 1976. Pro cornerback Philadelphia Eagles 1977-85, Los Angeles Rams 1986, Atlanta Falcons 1986. Pro scout: Kansas City Chiefs 1989-91. Pro coach: Joined Chiefs in 1992.

Alex Gibbs, offensive line; born February 11, 1941, Morganton, N.C., lives in Kansas City. Running back-defensive back Davidson College 1959-63. No pro playing experience. College coach: Duke 1969-70, Kentucky 1971-72, West Virginia 1973-74, Ohio State 1975-78, Auburn 1979-81, Georgia 1982-83. Pro coach: Denver Broncos 1984-87, Los Angeles Raiders 1988-89, San Diego Chargers 1990-91, Indianapolis Colts 1992, joined Chiefs in 1993.

Paul Hackett, offensive coordinator-quarterbacks; born July 5, 1947, Burlington, Vt., lives in Overland Park, Kan. Quarterback Cal-Davis 1965-68. No pro playing experience. College coach: Cal-Davis 1970-71, California 1972-75, Southern California 1976-80,

1994 FIRST-YEAR ROSTER

Name	Pos.	Ht.	Wt.	Birthdate	College	Hometown	How Acq.
Ale, Arnold (1)	LB	6-2	230	6/17/70	UCLA	Carson, Calif.	FA
Alexander, Ken	LB	6-3	254	12/15/71	Florida State	Austin, Tex.	FA
Anderson, Dunstan	DE	6-4	260	12/31/70	Tulsa	Ft. Worth, Tex.	FA
Bennett, Donnell	RB	5-11	241	9/14/72	Miami	Ft. Lauderdale, Fla.	D2
Booker, Vaughn (1)	DE	6-5	290	2/24/68	Cincinnati	Cincinnati, Ohio	FA
Boyd, Larry	DE	6-2	285	1/3/71	Arizona State	Glimer, Tex.	FA
Burton, James	CB	5-9	185	4/22/71	Fresno State	Long Beach, Calif.	D5a
Daigle, Anthony	RB	5-10	198	4/5/70	Fresno State	Benicia, Calif.	D6
Dawson, Lake	WR	6-1	204	1/2/72	Notre Dame	Federal Way, Wash.	D3a
DeGraffenreid, Allen (1)	WR	6-3	200	5/1/70	Ohio State	Cincinnati, Ohio	FA
Freese, Jerry	LB	6-2	221	5/25/70	N.E. Oklahoma	Melbourne, Fla.	FA
Gaddy, Robert	T	6-4	295	6/22/71	Alcorn State	Coila, Miss.	FA
Gay, Matt (1)	S	5-11	180	4/3/70	Kansas	Chicago, Ill.	FA
Greene, Tracy	TE-T	6-4	276	11/5/72	Grambling	Grambling, La.	D7b
Grow, Monty	S	6-3	214	9/4/71	Florida	Inverness, Fla.	FA
Hill, Greg	RB	5-11	207	2/23/72	Texas A&M	Dallas, Tex.	D1
Kwarta, Bret	G	6-2	290	1/28/71	California-Davis	Mullica, N.J.	FA
Ma'afala, Nick (1)	DT	6-2	295	4/13/67	Hawaii	Honolulu, Hawaii	FA
Martin, Emerson	G	6-2	293	5/6/71	Hampton	Elizabethtown, N.C.	FA
Matthews, Steve	QB	6-2	217	10/13/70	Memphis State	Tullahoma, Tenn.	D7a
McCullough, Russ (1)	T	6-10	315	10/31/68	Missouri	Olathe, Kan.	FA
Montgomery, Fred (1)	WR	6-0	183	8/30/71	New Mexico State	Greenville, Miss.	FA
Penn, Chris	WR	6-0	195	4/20/71	Tulsa	Lenapah, Okla.	D3b
Randall, Brian	CB	6-0	185	1/28/71	Delaware State	Swedesboro, N.J.	FA
Shufelt, Pete (1)	LB	6-2	241	10/28/69	Texas-El Paso	Tucson, Ariz.	FA
Stephens, Michael	WR	6-1	195	10/9/72	Nevada	Gardena, Calif.	FA
Van Pelt, Alex (1)	QB	6-1	219	5/1/70	Pittsburgh	San Antonio, Tex.	FA
Waldrop, Rob	DT	6-1	276	12/1/71	Arizona	Scottsdale, Ariz.	D5b
Walker, Bracey	S	5-10	200	10/28/70	North Carolina	Pine Forest, N.C.	D4

The term NFL Rookie is defined as a player who is in his first season of professional football and has not been on the roster of another professional football team for any regular-season or postseason games. A Rookie is designated by an "R" on NFL rosters. Players who have been active in another professional football league or players who have NFL experience, including either preseason training camp or being on an Active List or Inactive List, or on Reserve/Injured or Reserve/Physically Unable to Perform for fewer than six regular-season games, are termed NFL First-Year Players. An NFL First-Year Player is designated by a "1" on NFL rosters. Thereafter, a player is credited with an additional year of experience for each season in which he accumulates six games on the Active List or Inactive List, or on Reserve/Injured or Reserve/Physically Unable to Perform.

NOTES

Pittsburgh 1989-92 (head coach 1990-92). Pro coach: Cleveland Browns 1981-82, San Francisco 49ers 1983-85, Dallas Cowboys 1986-88, joined Chiefs in 1993.

Mike McCarthy, offensive assistant-quality control; born November 10, 1963, Pittsburgh, Pa., lives in Overland Park, Kan. Tight end Baker University 1985-86. No pro playing experience. College coach: Fort Hays State 1987-88, Pittsburgh 1989-92. Pro coach: Joined Chiefs in 1993.

Tom Pratt, defensive line; born June 21, 1935, Edgerton, Wis., lives in Overland Park, Kan. Linebacker Miami 1953-56. No pro playing experience. College coach: Miami 1957-59, Southern Mississippi 1960-62. Pro coach: Kansas City Chiefs 1963-77, New Orleans Saints 1978-80, Cleveland Browns 1981-88, rejoined Chiefs in 1989.

Jimmy Raye, running backs; born March 26, 1946, Fayetteville, N.C., lives in Kansas City. Quarterback Michigan State 1965-67. Pro defensive back Philadelphia Eagles 1969. College coach: Michigan State 1971-75, Wyoming 1976. Pro coach: San Francisco 49ers 1977, Detroit Lions 1978-79, Atlanta Falcons 1980-82, 1987-89, Los Angeles Rams 1983-84, 1991, Tampa Bay Buccaneers 1985-86, New England Patriots 1990, joined Chiefs in 1992.

Dave Redding, strength and conditioning; born June 14, 1952, North Platte, Neb., lives in Kansas

City. Defensive end Nebraska 1972-75. No pro playing experience. College coach: Nebraska 1976, Washington State 1977, Missouri 1978-81. Pro coach: Cleveland Browns 1982-88, joined Chiefs in 1989.

Al Saunders, assistant head coach-receivers; born February 1, 1947, London, England, lives in Kansas City. Defensive back San Jose State 1966-68. No pro playing experience. College coach: Southern California 1970-71, Missouri 1972, Utah State 1973-75, California 1976-81, Tennessee 1982. Pro coach: San Diego Chargers 1983-88 (head coach 1986-88), joined Chiefs in 1989.

Kurt Schottenheimer, special teams; born October 1, 1949, McDonald, Pa., lives in Kansas City. Defensive back Miami 1969-70. No pro playing experience. College coach: William Patterson 1974, Michigan State 1978-82, Tulane 1983, Louisiana State 1984-85, Notre Dame 1986. Pro coach: Cleveland Browns 1987-88, joined Chiefs in 1989.

Darvin Wallis, special assistant-quality control; born February 14, 1949, Ft. Branch, Ind., lives in Overland Park, Kan. Defensive end Arizona 1970-71. No pro playing experience. College coach: Adams State 1976-77, Tulane 1978-79, Mississippi 1980-81. Pro coach: Cleveland Browns 1982-88, joined Chiefs in 1989.

LOS ANGELES RAIDERS

American Football Conference
Western Division
Team Colors: Silver and Black
332 Center Street
El Segundo, California 90245
Telephone: (310) 322-3451

CLUB OFFICIALS

President of the Managing General Partner:
  Al Davis
Executive Assistant: Al LoCasale
Pro Football Scout: George Karras
Legal Affairs: Jeff Birren, Amy Trask
Finance: Klaus Leitenbauer
Senior Administrator: Morris Bradshaw
Business Manager: John Novak
Senior Executive: John Herrera
Publications: Mike Taylor
Community Relations: Gil Lafferty-Hernandez
Administrative Assistants: Mario Perez,
  Marc McKinney
Ticket Operations: Peter Eiges
Trainers: George Anderson, H. Rod Martin,
  Jonathan Jones
Equipment Manager: Richard Romanski
Assistant Equipment Manager: Bob Romanski
Stadium: Los Angeles Memorial Coliseum
  •Capacity: 67,800
  3911 South Figueroa Street
  Los Angeles, California 90037
Playing Surface: Grass
Training Camp: Radisson Hotel
  Oxnard, California 93030

1994 SCHEDULE
PRESEASON

July 31	vs. Denver at Barcelona	1:00
Aug. 7	at Dallas	8:00
Aug. 13	at Pittsburgh	6:00
Aug. 20	at Los Angeles Rams	7:00
Aug. 27	at Houston	1:00

REGULAR SEASON

Sept. 5	at San Francisco (Monday)	6:00
Sept. 11	**Seattle**	1:00
Sept. 18	at Denver	2:00
Sept. 25	**San Diego**	1:00
Oct. 2	Open Date	
Oct. 9	at New England	4:00
Oct. 16	at Miami	1:00
Oct. 23	**Atlanta**	1:00
Oct. 30	**Houston**	1:00
Nov. 6	at Kansas City	7:00
Nov. 13	at Los Angeles Rams	1:00
Nov. 20	**New Orleans**	1:00
Nov. 27	**Pittsburgh**	1:00
Dec. 5	at San Diego (Monday)	6:00
Dec. 11	**Denver**	1:00
Dec. 18	at Seattle	5:00
Dec. 24	**Kansas City**	1:00

RECORD HOLDERS
INDIVIDUAL RECORDS—CAREER

Category	Name	Performance
Rushing (Yds.)	Marcus Allen, 1982-1992	8,545
Passing (Yds.)	Ken Stabler, 1970-79	19,078
Passing (TDs)	Ken Stabler, 1970-79	150
Receiving (No.)	Fred Biletnikoff, 1965-1978	589
Receiving (Yds.)	Fred Biletnikoff, 1965-1978	8,974
Interceptions	Willie Brown, 1967-1978	39
	Lester Hayes, 1977-1986	39
Punting (Avg.)	Ray Guy, 1973-1986	42.5
Punt Return (Avg.)	Claude Gibson, 1963-65	12.6
Kickoff Return (Avg.)	Jack Larscheid, 1960-61	28.4
Field Goals	George Blanda, 1967-1975	156
Touchdowns (Tot.)	Marcus Allen, 1982-1992	98
Points	George Blanda, 1967-1975	863

INDIVIDUAL RECORDS—SINGLE SEASON

Category	Name	Performance
Rushing (Yds.)	Marcus Allen, 1985	1,759
Passing (Yds.)	Ken Stabler, 1979	3,615
Passing (TDs)	Daryle Lamonica, 1969	34
Receiving (No.)	Todd Christensen, 1986	95
Receiving (Yds.)	Art Powell, 1964	1,361
Interceptions	Lester Hayes, 1980	13
Punting (Avg.)	Ray Guy, 1973	45.3
Punt Return (Avg.)	Claude Gibson, 1964	14.4
Kickoff Return (Avg.)	Harold Hart, 1975	30.5
Field Goals	Jeff Jaeger, 1993	*35
Touchdowns (Tot.)	Marcus Allen, 1984	18
Points	Jeff Jaeger, 1993	132

INDIVIDUAL RECORDS—SINGLE GAME

Category	Name	Performance
Rushing (Yds.)	Bo Jackson, 11-30-87	221
Passing (Yds.)	Jeff Hostetler, 10-31-93	424
Passing (TDs)	Tom Flores, 12-22-63	6
	Daryle Lamonica, 10-19-69	6
Receiving (No.)	Dave Casper, 10-3-76	12
Receiving (Yds.)	Art Powell, 12-22-63	247
Interceptions	Many times	3
	Last time by Charles Phillips, 12-8-75	
Field Goals	Many times	4
	Last time by Jeff Jaeger, 1-2-94	
Touchdowns (Tot.)	Art Powell, 12-22-63	4
	Marcus Allen, 9-24-84	4
Points	Art Powell, 12-22-63	24
	Marcus Allen, 9-24-84	24

*NFL Record

COACHING HISTORY
OAKLAND 1960-1981
(325-200-11)

1960-61	Eddie Erdelatz*	6-10-0
1961-62	Marty Feldman**	2-15-0
1962	Red Conkright	1-8-0
1963-65	Al Davis	23-16-3
1966-68	John Rauch	35-10-1
1969-78	John Madden	112-39-7
1979-87	Tom Flores	91-56-0
1988-89	Mike Shanahan***	8-12-0
1989-93	Art Shell	47-34-0

 *Released after two games in 1961
 **Released after five games in 1962
 ***Released after four games in 1989

LOS ANGELES MEMORIAL COLISEUM

1993 TEAM RECORD

PRESEASON (2-3)

Date	Result		Opponents
7/31	W	19-3	vs. Green Bay at Canton
8/8	L	0-27	vs. San Francisco at Stanford Stadium
8/14	L	7-13	at Dallas
8/20	L	7-18	at Indianapolis
8/28	W	20-19	at L.A. Rams

REGULAR SEASON (10-6)

Date	Result		Opponents	Att.
9/5	W	24-7	Minnesota	44,120
9/12	W	17-13	at Seattle	58,836
9/19	L	16-19	Cleveland	48,617
10/3	L	9-24	at Kansas City	77,395
10/10	W	24-20	N.Y. Jets	41,627
10/18	W	23-20	at Denver	75,712
10/31	L	23-30	San Diego	45,122
11/7	W	16-14	at Chicago	59,750
11/14	L	20-31	Kansas City	66,553
11/21	W	12-7	at San Diego	60,615
11/28	L	10-16	at Cincinnati	43,272
12/5	W	25-24	at Buffalo	79,478
12/12	W	27-23	Seattle	38,161
12/19	W	27-20	Tampa Bay	40,532
12/26	L	0-28	at Green Bay	54,482
1/2	W	33-30	Denver (OT)	66,904

POSTSEASON (1-1)

1/9	W	42-24	Denver	65,314
1/15	L	23-29	at Buffalo	61,923

(OT) Overtime

SCORE BY PERIODS

Raiders	77	93	50	83	3	—	306
Opponents	34	108	57	127	0	—	326

ATTENDANCE

Home 391,636   Away 509,540   Total 901,176
Single-game home record, 91,494 (9-29-91)
Single-season home record, 516,205 (1986)

1993 TEAM STATISTICS

	Raiders	Opp.
Total First Downs	292	302
Rushing	95	111
Passing	168	154
Penalty	29	37
Third Down: Made/Att	74/202	74/204
Third Down Pct.	36.6	36.3
Fourth Down: Made/Att	1/8	5/9
Fourth Down Pct.	12.5	55.6
Total Net Yards	5014	4723
Avg. Per Game	313.4	295.2
Total Plays	978	996
Avg. Per Play	5.1	4.7
Net Yards Rushing	1425	1865
Avg. Per Game	89.1	116.6
Total Rushes	433	494
Net Yards Passing	3589	2858
Avg. Per Game	224.3	178.6
Sacked/Yards Lost	50/293	45/283
Gross Yards	3882	3141
Att./Completions	495/281	457/258
Completion Pct.	56.8	56.5
Had Intercepted	14	14
Punts/Avg.	71/41.8	80/42.1
Net Punting Avg.	71/35.1	80/34.3
Penalties/Yards Lost	148/1181	105/801
Fumbles/Ball Lost	23/11	23/9
Touchdowns	29	37
Rushing	10	17
Passing	17	17
Returns	2	3
Avg. Time of Possession	30:21	29:39

1993 INDIVIDUAL STATISTICS

PASSING	Att.	Cmp.	Yds.	Pct.	TD	Int.	Tkld.	Rate
Hostetler	419	236	3242	56.3	14	10	38/206	82.5
Evans	76	45	640	59.2	3	4	12/87	77.7
Raiders	495	281	3882	56.8	17	14	50/293	81.7
Opponents	457	258	3141	56.5	17	14	45/283	77.4

SCORING	TD R	TD P	TD Rt	PAT	FG	Saf	PTS
Jaeger	0	0	0	27/29	35/44	0	132
Brown	0	7	1	0/0	0/0	0	48
Hostetler	5	0	0	0/0	0/0	0	30
A. Wright	0	4	0	0/0	0/0	0	24
Jett	0	3	0	0/0	0/0	0	18
McCallum	3	0	0	0/0	0/0	0	18
Bell	1	0	0	0/0	0/0	0	6
Glover	0	1	0	0/0	0/0	0	6
Horton	0	1	0	0/0	0/0	0	6
Ismail	0	1	0	0/0	0/0	0	6
McDaniel	0	0	1	0/0	0/0	0	6
Robinson	1	0	0	0/0	0/0	0	6
Raiders	10	17	2	27/29	35/44	0	306
Opponents	17	17	3	37/37	21/33	2	326

RUSHING	Att.	Yds.	Avg.	LG	TD
Robinson	156	591	3.8	16	1
Hostetler	55	202	3.7	19	5
Bell	67	180	2.7	12	1
S. Smith	47	156	3.3	13	0
McCallum	37	114	3.1	14	3
Montgomery	37	106	2.9	15	0
Evans	14	51	3.6	17	0
R. Jordan	12	33	2.8	12	0
Brown	2	7	3.5	14	0
Jett	1	0	0.0	0	0
Ismail	4	-5	-1.2	10	0
Gossett	1	-10	-10.0	-10	0
Raiders	433	1425	3.3	19	10
Opponents	494	1865	3.8	60t	17

RECEIVING	No.	Yds.	Avg.	LG	TD
Brown	80	1180	14.8	71t	7
Horton	43	467	10.9	32	1
Jett	33	771	23.4	74t	3
A. Wright	27	462	17.1	68t	4
Ismail	26	353	13.6	43t	1
S. Smith	18	187	10.4	22	0
Robinson	15	142	9.5	58	0
Bell	11	111	10.1	18	0
Montgomery	10	43	4.3	9	0
Gault	8	64	8.0	12	0
Glover	4	55	13.8	26	1
R. Jordan	4	42	10.5	33	0
McCallum	2	5	2.5	3	0
Raiders	281	3882	13.8	74t	17
Opponents	258	3141	12.2	66t	17

INTERCEPTIONS	No.	Yds.	Avg.	LG	TD
McDaniel	5	87	17.4	36t	1
Anderson	2	52	26.0	27	0
Hoskins	2	34	17.0	20	0
Washington	2	0	0.0	0	0
McGlockton	1	19	19.0	19	0
Trapp	1	7	7.0	7	0
Bates	1	0	0.0	0	0
Raiders	14	199	14.2	36t	1
Opponents	14	289	20.6	102t	2

PUNTING	No.	Yds.	Avg.	In 20	LG
Gossett	71	2971	41.8	19	61
Raiders	71	2971	41.8	19	61
Opponents	80	3369	42.1	13	56

PUNT RETURNS	No.	FC	Yds.	Avg.	LG	TD
Brown	40	20	465	11.6	74t	1
Raiders	40	20	465	11.6	74t	1
Opponents	35	7	301	8.6	28	0

KICKOFF RETURNS	No.	Yds.	Avg.	LG	TD
Ismail	25	605	24.2	66	0
A. Wright	10	167	16.7	28	0
Gault	7	187	26.7	60	0
Robinson	4	57	14.3	33	0
Peat	2	18	9.0	10	0
K. Smith	2	15	7.5	8	0
McCallum	1	12	12.0	12	0
Turk	1	0	0.0	0	0
Raiders	52	1061	20.4	66	0
Opponents	45	783	17.4	49	0

SACKS	No.
A. Smith	12.5
Townsend	7.5
McGlockton	7.0
Long	6.0
Harrison	3.0
Bruce	2.0
Wallace	2.0
Anderson	1.0
Broughton	1.0
Kelly	1.0
Washington	1.0
Raiders	45.0
Opponents	50.0

1994 DRAFT CHOICES

Round	Name	Pos.	College
1	Rob Fredrickson	LB	Michigan State
2	James Folston	DE	N.E. Louisiana
3	Calvin Jones	RB	Nebraska
4	Austin Robbins	DT	North Carolina
5	Roosevelt Patterson	G	Alabama
7	Rob Holmberg	LB	Penn State

LOS ANGELES RAIDERS

1994 VETERAN ROSTER

No.	Name	Pos.	Ht.	Wt.	Birthdate	NFL Exp.	College	Hometown	How Acq.	'93 Games/ Starts
33	Anderson, Eddie	S	6-1	210	7/22/63	9	Fort Valley State	Warner Robins, Ga.	FA-'87	16/16
29	Bates, Patrick	S	6-3	220	11/27/70	2	Texas A&M	Galveston, Tex.	D1-'93	13/0
43	† Bell, Nick	RB	6-2	255	8/19/68	4	Iowa	Las Vegas, Nev.	D2-'91	10/3
54	Biekert, Greg	LB	6-2	240	3/14/69	2	Colorado	Longmont, Colo.	D7-'93	16/0
97	Broughton, Willie	DT	6-5	285	9/9/64	8	Miami	Ft. Pierce, Fla.	FA-'92	15/0
81	Brown, Tim	WR	6-0	195	7/22/66	7	Notre Dame	Dallas, Tex.	D1-'88	16/16
56	Bruce, Aundray	DE	6-5	260	1/30/66	7	Auburn	Montgomery, Ala.	PB(Atl)-'92	16/0
92	Collons, Ferric	DT	6-6	295	12/4/69	2	California	Sacramento, Calif.	FA-'92	0*
31	Dixon, Rickey	S	5-11	185	12/26/66	7	Oklahoma	Dallas, Tex.	T(Cin)-'93	9/0
46	Dorn, Torin	CB	6-0	190	2/28/68	5	North Carolina	Southfield, Mich.	D4-'90	15/0
11	Evans, Vince	QB	6-2	215	6/19/55	14	Southern California	Greensboro, N.C.	FA-'92	8/1
45	# Fulcher, David	LB	6-3	245	9/28/64	9	Arizona State	Los Angeles, Calif.	FA-'93	3/0
34	t- Gainer, Derrick	RB	5-11	240	8/15/66	4	Florida A&M	Plant City, Fla.	T(Dall)-'94	11/0*
83	Gault, Willie	WR	6-1	175	9/5/60	12	Tennessee	Griffin, Ga.	T(Chi)-'91	15/0
87	Glover, Andrew	TE	6-6	245	8/12/67	4	Grambling	Geismar, La.	D10-'91	15/0
66	Gogan, Kevin	G	6-7	325	11/2/64	8	Washington	Pacifica, Calif.	UFA(Dall)-'94	16/16*
7	Gossett, Jeff	P	6-2	195	1/25/57	13	Eastern Illinois	Charleston, Ill.	T(Hou)-'88	16/0
74	Harrison, Nolan	DT	6-5	285	1/25/69	4	Indiana	Flossmoor, Ill.	D6-'91	16/14
80	Hobbs, Daryl	WR	6-2	175	5/23/68	2	Pacific	Los Angeles, Calif.	FA-'93	3/0
12	Hobert, Billy Joe	QB	6-3	230	1/8/71	2	Washington	Puyallup, Wash.	D3-'93	0*
20	Hoskins, Derrick	S	6-2	205	11/16/70	3	Southern Mississippi	Philadelphia, Miss.	D5-'92	16/16
15	Hostetler, Jeff	QB	6-3	220	4/22/61	11	West Virginia	Davidsville, Pa.	UFA(NYG)-'93	15/15
86	Ismail, Raghib	WR	5-10	180	11/16/69	2	Notre Dame	Wilkes-Barre, Pa.	D4-'90	13/0
18	Jaeger, Jeff	K	5-11	190	11/28/64	8	Washington	Kent, Wash.	PB(Clev)-'89	16/0
82	Jett, James	WR	5-10	165	12/28/70	2	West Virginia	Charlestown, W. Va.	FA-'93	16/1
52	Jones, Mike	LB	6-1	230	4/15/69	4	Missouri	Kansas City, Mo.	FA-'91	16/2
85	Jordan, Charles	WR	5-10	175	10/9/69	2	Long Beach City College	Inglewood, Calif.	FA-'93	0*
23	Jordan, Randy	RB	5-10	210	6/6/70	2	North Carolina	Manson, N.C.	FA-'93	10/2
25	Land, Dan	CB	6-0	195	7/3/65	6	Albany State	Donalsonville, Ga.	FA-'89	15/0
79	# Lanier, Ken	T	6-3	290	7/8/59	14	Florida State	Columbus, Ohio	UFA(Den)-'93	2/2
24	Lewis, Albert	CB	6-2	195	10/6/60	12	Grambling	Mansfield, La.	UFA(KC)-'94	14/13*
41	McCallum, Napoleon	RB	6-2	225	10/6/63	6	Navy	Milford, Ohio	FA-'92	13/1
36	McDaniel, Terry	CB	5-10	180	2/8/65	7	Tennessee	Saginaw, Mich.	D1-'88	16/16
91	McGlockton, Chester	DT	6-4	315	9/16/69	3	Clemson	Whiteville, Miss.	D1-'92	16/16
21	Montgomery, Tyrone	RB	6-0	190	8/3/70	2	Mississippi	Greenville, Miss.	FA-'93	12/0
65	# Montoya, Max	G	6-5	295	5/2/56	16	UCLA	La Puente, Calif.	PB(Cin)-'90	16/16
72	Mosebar, Don	C	6-6	300	9/11/61	12	Southern California	Visalia, Calif.	D1-'83	16/16
99	Moss, Winston	LB	6-3	240	12/24/65	8	Miami	Miami, Fla.	T(TB)-'91	16/16
64	# Peat, Todd	G	6-2	305	5/20/64	6	Northern Illinois	Champaign, Ill.	FA-'92	16/0
71	Perry, Gerald	T	6-6	300	11/12/64	7	Southern	Columbia, S.C.	UFA(Rams)-'93	15/15
96	# Powers, Warren	DT	6-5	285	2/1/65	5	Maryland	Baltimore, Md.	FA-'93	0*
28	Robinson, Greg	RB	5-10	200	8/7/69	2	Northeast Louisiana	Grenada, Miss.	D8-'93	12/12
78	Skrepenak, Greg	G	6-6	310	1/31/70	3	Michigan	Wilkes-Barre, Pa.	D2-'92	0*
94	Smith, Anthony	DE	6-3	260	6/28/67	5	Arizona	Elizabeth City, N.C.	D1-'90	16/2
39	Smith, Kevin	TE	6-4	255	7/25/69	2	UCLA	Oakland, Calif.	D7-'91	10/1
77	Stephens, Rich	T	6-7	300	11/1/65	2	Tulsa	St. Louis, Mo.	FA-'92	16/1
93	Townsend, Greg	DE	6-3	275	11/3/61	12	Texas Christian	Compton, Calif.	D4-'83	16/16
37	Trapp, James	CB	6-0	180	12/28/69	2	Clemson	Lawton, Okla.	D3-'93	14/2
67	Turk, Dan	C	6-4	290	8/25/62	10	Wisconsin	Milwaukee, Wis.	FA-'89	16/0
51	Wallace, Aaron	LB	6-3	240	4/17/67	5	Texas A&M	Dallas, Tex.	D2-'90	16/14
48	Washington, Lionel	CB	6-0	185	10/21/60	12	Tulane	New Orleans, La.	T(StL)-'87	16/16
68	Wilkerson, Bruce	T	6-5	295	7/28/64	8	Tennessee	Philadelphia, Tenn.	D2-'87	14/14
22	Williams, Harvey	RB	6-2	220	4/22/67	4	Louisiana State	Hempstead, Tex.	UFA(KC)-'94	7/6*
88	Williams, Jamie	TE	6-4	240	4/25/60	12	Nebraska	Davenport, Iowa	UFA(SF)-'94	16/0*
76	Wisniewski, Steve	G	6-4	285	4/7/67	6	Penn State	Houston, Tex.	D2-'89	16/16
89	Wright, Alexander	WR	6-0	190	7/19/67	5	Auburn	Albany, Ga.	T(Dall)-'92	15/15

* Collons inactive for 16 games in '93; Gogan played 16 games with Dallas; Gainer played 11 games with Dallas; Hobert active for 1 game but did not play; C. Jordan inactive for 16 games; Lewis played 14 games with Kansas City; Powers last active with L.A. Rams in '92; Skrepenak inactive for 16 games; H. Williams played 7 games with Kansas City; J. Williams played 16 games with San Francisco.

\# Unrestricted free agent; subject to developments.

† Restricted free agent; subject to developments.

Retired—Howie Long, 13-year defensive end, 16 games in '93; Steve Wright, 11-year tackle, 0 games in '93.

Traded—CB-S Elvis Patterson to Dallas.

t- Raiders traded for Gainer.

Players lost through free agency (2): TE Ethan Horton (Wash; 16 games in '93), LB Joe Kelly (Rams; 16).

Also played with Raiders in '93—TE John Duff (1 game), S Elvis Patterson (3), RB Steve Smith (16).

COACHING STAFF

Head Coach,
Art Shell

Pro Career: Named ninth head coach in Raiders' history on October 3, 1989. Had been Raiders' offensive line coach for seven years, including 1983 world championship season. He first joined the coaching staff in 1983 after 15 seasons as one of the greatest offensive tackles in pro football history. Came to Raiders in 1968 as a third-round draft choice out of Maryland State (now Maryland-Eastern Shore). Went on to play in 207 league games, including first 156 in a row, and 24 playoff games for the Raiders. Starting left tackle in Super Bowl XI and XV victories. Selected to Pro Bowl eight times—most by any Raiders player. Inducted into Pro Football Hall of Fame on August 5, 1989. Also named to state of South Carolina Sports Hall of Fame. Career record: 47-34.

Background: All-America tackle as junior and senior and three-year All-Conference on both offense and defense at Maryland State 1965-67. Also lettered in basketball.

Personal: Born November 26, 1946, Charleston, S.C. Art and wife, Janice, live in Palos Verdes, California, with their sons—Arthur III and Christopher.

ASSISTANT COACHES

Fred Biletnikoff, wide receivers; born February 23, 1943, Erie, Pa., lives in El Segundo, Calif. Wide receiver Florida State 1962-64. Pro wide receiver Oakland Raiders 1965-78, Montreal Alouettes (CFL) 1980. College coach: Palomar, Calif., J.C. 1983, Diablo Valley, Calif., J.C. 1984, 1986. Pro coach: Oakland Invaders (USFL) 1985, Calgary Stampeders (CFL) 1987-88, joined Raiders in 1989.

Gunther Cunningham, defensive line; born June 19, 1946, Munich, Germany, lives in Palos Verdes, Calif. Linebacker Oregon 1965-67. No pro playing experience. College coach: Oregon 1969-71, Arkansas 1972, Stanford 1973-76, California 1977-80. Pro coach: Hamilton Tiger-Cats (CFL) 1981, Baltimore/Indianapolis Colts 1982-84, San Diego Chargers 1985-90, joined Raiders in 1991.

John Fox, defensive coordinator; born February 8, 1955, Virginia Beach, Va., lives in Palos Verdes, Calif. Defensive back San Diego State 1975-77. No pro playing experience. College coach: U.S. International 1979, Boise State 1980, Long Beach State 1981, Utah 1982, Kansas 1983, 1985, Iowa State 1984, Pittsburgh 1986-88. Pro coach: Los Angeles Express (USFL) 1985, Pittsburgh Steelers 1989-91, San Diego Chargers 1992-93, joined Raiders in 1994.

Ray Hamilton, defensive line; born January 20, 1951, Omaha, Neb., lives in Culver City, Calif. Nose tackle Oklahoma 1969-72. Pro nose tackle-defensive end New England Patriots 1973-81. College coach: Tennessee 1992. Pro coach: New England Patriots 1985-89, Tampa Bay Buccaneers 1991, joined Raiders in 1993.

Jim Haslett, linebackers; born December 9, 1955, Pittsburgh, Pa., lives in Palos Verdes, Calif. Defensive end Indiana University (Pa.) 1975-78. Linebacker Buffalo Bills 1979-86, New York Jets 1987. College coach: Buffalo 1988-90. Pro coach: Sacramento Surge (World League) 1991-92, joined Raiders in 1993.

Odis McKinney, defensive backs; born May 19, 1957, Detroit, Mich., lives in Manhattan Beach, Calif. Defensive back Colorado 1976-77. Pro defensive back New York Giants 1978-79, Oakland/Los Angeles Raiders 1980-85, Kansas City Chiefs 1985, Los Angeles Raiders 1986. Pro coach: Joined Raiders in 1990.

Bill Meyers, offensive line-tight ends; born October 8, 1946, Chippewa Falls, Wis., lives in Surfside, Calif. Tackle Stanford 1970-71. No pro playing experience. College coach: California 1972-73, 1977-78, Santa Clara 1974-76, Notre Dame 1979-81, Missouri 1985-86, Pittsburgh 1987-92. Pro coach: Green Bay Packers 1982-83, Pittsburgh Steelers 1984, joined Raiders in 1993.

Steve Ortmayer, football operations-special teams;
born February 13, 1944, Painesville, Ohio, lives in Palos Verdes Estates, Calif. La Verne College 1966. No college or pro playing experience. College coach: Colorado 1967-73, Georgia Tech 1974. Pro coach: Kansas City Chiefs 1975-77, Oakland/Los Angeles Raiders 1978-86, San Diego Chargers 1987-89 (Director of Football Operations), rejoined Raiders in 1990.

Jack Reilly, offensive backfield; born May 22, 1945, Boston, Mass., lives in El Segundo, Calif. Quarterback Washington State 1963, Santa Monica, Calif., J.C. 1964, Long Beach State 1965-66. No pro playing experience. College coach: El Camino, Calif., J.C. 1980-84 (head coach 1981-84), Utah 1985-89. Pro coach: San Diego Chargers 1990-93, joined Raiders in 1994.

Jack Stanton, defensive backs; born June 6, 1938, Bridgeville, Pa., lives in El Segundo, Calif. Running back North Carolina State 1959-60. Pro running back Pittsburgh Steelers 1961, Toronto Argonauts (CFL) 1962-63. College coach: George Washington 1966, North Carolina State 1968-72, Florida State 1973, 1976-83, North Carolina 1974-75, Purdue

1986, New Mexico 1987-88. Pro coach: Atlanta Falcons 1984-85, joined Raiders in 1989.

Tom Walsh, offense; born April 16, 1949, Vallejo, Calif., lives in Manhattan Beach, Calif. UC-Santa Barbara 1971. No college or pro playing experience. College coach: University of San Diego 1972-76, U.S. International 1979 (head coach), Murray State 1980, Cincinnati 1981. Pro coach: Joined Raiders in 1982.

Mike White, offensive line; born January 4, 1936, Berkeley, Calif., lives in Newport Beach, Calif. Offensive end California 1955-57. No pro playing experience. College coach: California 1958-63, 1972-77 (head coach), Stanford 1964-71, Illinois 1980-87 (head coach). Pro coach: San Francisco 49ers 1978-79, joined Raiders in 1990.

Arthur Whittington, assistant; born September 4, 1955, Cuero, Tex; lives in El Segundo, Calif. Running back Southern Methodist 1974-77. Pro running back Oakland Raiders 1978-81, Oakland Invaders (USFL) 1983-85. College coach: Southern Methodist 1986. Pro coach: Joined Raiders in 1994.

1994 FIRST-YEAR ROSTER

Name	Pos.	Ht.	Wt.	Birthdate	College	Hometown	How Acq.
Brabham, Cary (1)	S	6-0	195	8/11/70	Southern Methodist	Hughes Springs, Tex.	FA
Butler, Darren (1)	CB	5-10	175	1/19/70	Alcorn State	Tylertown, Miss.	FA
Duff, John (1)	TE	6-7	250	7/31/67	New Mexico	Tustin, Calif.	FA
Elliott, Matt	G	6-4	285	5/27/71	Northern Arizona	Yorba Linda, Calif.	FA
Folston, James	LB	6-3	240	8//14/71	Northeast Louisiana	Cocoa, Fla.	D2
Fredrickson, Rob	LB	6-4	235	5/13/71	Michigan State	St. Joseph, Mich.	D1
Gallatin, Donovan	S	6-1	210	2/16/71	UCLA	El Segundo, Calif.	FA
Hill, James	RB	5-11	215	2/20/70	Colorado	Colorado Springs, Colo.	FA
Holmberg, Rob	LB	6-3	225	5/6/71	Penn State	Mt. Pleasant, Pa.	D7
Johnson, Billy	RB	5-10	200	9/21/70	Arizona	San Jose, Calif.	FA
Jones, Brian (1)	LB	6-3	245	1/22/68	Texas	Lubbock, Tex.	FA
Jones, Calvin	RB	5-11	215	11/27/70	Nebraska	Omaha, Neb.	D3
Kralik, Joe	WR	5-11	185	12/14/70	Washington	Puyallup, Wash.	FA
Morris, Cree	QB	6-7	235	12/17/70	St. Mary's	Escondido, Calif.	FA
Morton, John (1)	WR	6-0	185	9/24/69	Western Michigan	Auburn Hills, Mich.	FA
Neujahr, Quentin	C	6-4	285	1/30/71	Kansas State	Ulysses, Neb.	FA
Patterson, Roosevelt	G	6-3	310	7/12/70	Alabama	Prichard, Ala.	D5
Ridley, Lester (1)	CB	6-1	180	11/15/70	Iowa State	Omaha, Neb.	FA
Robbins, Austin	DT	6-6	300	3/1/71	North Carolina	Washington, D.C.	D4
Skartvedt, Doug	T	6-3	305	7/2/71	Iowa State	Hubbard, Iowa	FA
Stubbins, Willie	T	6-5	290	5/23/67	Texas Southern	Tifton, Ga.	FA
White, Alberto (1)	DE	6-3	240	4/3/71	Texas Southern	Miami, Fla.	FA

The term NFL Rookie is defined as a player who is in his first season of professional football and has not been on the roster of another professional football team for any regular-season or postseason games. A Rookie is designated by an "R" on NFL rosters. Players who have been active in another professional football league or players who have NFL experience, including either preseason training camp or being on an Active List or Inactive List, or on Reserve/Injured or Reserve/Physically Unable to Perform for fewer than six regular-season games, are termed NFL First-Year Players. An NFL First-Year Player is designated by a "1" on NFL rosters. Thereafter, a player is credited with an additional year of experience for each season in which he accumulates six games on the Active List or Inactive List, or on Reserve/Injured or Reserve/Physically Unable to Perform.

NOTES

MIAMI DOLPHINS

American Football Conference
Eastern Division
Team Colors: Aqua, Coral, and White
Joe Robbie Stadium
2269 N.W. 199th Street
Miami, Florida 33056
Telephone: (305) 620-5000

CLUB OFFICIALS

President: Timothy J. Robbie
Executive Vice President: Daniel T. Robbie
Executive Vice President: Janet Robbie
Executive VP/General Manager: Eddie J. Jones
General Counsel: Jann M. Iliff
Treasurer: Jill R. Strafaci
Assistant General Manager: Bryan Wiedmeier
Head Coach: Don Shula
Director of Player Personnel: Tom Heckert
Director of College Scouting: Tom Braatz
Director of Facility Operations: John Glode
Director of Media Relations: Harvey Greene
Media Relations Assistant: Scott Stone
Marketing Director: David Evans
Community Relations Director: Fudge Browne
Ticket Director: Lamar Vernon
Sales Director: Lynn Abramson
Trainer: Ryan Vermillion
Equipment Manager: Bob Monica
Stadium: Joe Robbie Stadium •**Capacity:** 74,916
2269 N.W. 199th Street
Miami, Florida 33056
Playing Surface: Grass (PAT)
Training Camp: Nova University
7500 S.W. 30th Street
Davie, Florida 33314

1994 SCHEDULE
PRESEASON

July 30	at New York Giants	8:00
Aug. 6	**Pittsburgh**	8:00
Aug. 13	vs. Green Bay at Milwaukee	7:00
Aug. 20	**Tampa Bay**	8:00
Aug. 26	at Minnesota	7:00

REGULAR SEASON

Sept. 4	**New England**	4:00
Sept. 11	vs. Green Bay at Milwaukee	12:00
Sept. 18	**New York Jets**	1:00
Sept. 25	at Minnesota	12:00
Oct. 2	at Cincinnati	8:00
Oct. 9	at Buffalo	1:00
Oct. 16	**Los Angeles Raiders**	1:00
Oct. 23	Open Date	
Oct. 30	at New England	1:00
Nov. 6	**Indianapolis**	1:00
Nov. 13	**Chicago**	1:00
Nov. 20	at Pittsburgh	1:00
Nov. 27	at New York Jets	1:00
Dec. 4	**Buffalo**	8:00
Dec. 12	**Kansas City** (Monday)	9:00
Dec. 18	at Indianapolis	1:00
Dec. 25	**Detroit**	8:00

RECORD HOLDERS
INDIVIDUAL RECORDS—CAREER

Category	Name	Performance
Rushing (Yds.)	Larry Csonka, 1968-1974, 1979	6,737
Passing (Yds.)	Dan Marino, 1983-1993	40,720
Passing (TDs)	Dan Marino, 1983-1993	298
Receiving (No.)	Mark Clayton, 1983-1992	550
Receiving (Yds.)	Mark Duper, 1982-1992	8,869
Interceptions	Jake Scott, 1970-75	35
Punting (Avg.)	Reggie Roby, 1983-1992	43.3
Punt Return (Avg.)	Freddie Solomon, 1975-77	11.4
Kickoff Return (Avg.)	Mercury Morris, 1969-1975	26.5
Field Goals	Garo Yepremian, 1970-78	165
Touchdowns (Tot.)	Mark Clayton, 1983-1992	82
Points	Garo Yepremian, 1970-78	830

INDIVIDUAL RECORDS—SINGLE SEASON

Category	Name	Performance
Rushing (Yds.)	Delvin Williams, 1978	1,258
Passing (Yds.)	Dan Marino, 1984	*5,084
Passing (TDs)	Dan Marino, 1984	*48
Receiving (No.)	Mark Clayton, 1988	86
Receiving (Yds.)	Mark Clayton, 1984	1,389
Interceptions	Dick Westmoreland, 1967	10
Punting (Avg.)	Reggie Roby, 1991	45.7
Punt Return (Avg.)	Freddie Solomon, 1975	12.3
Kickoff Return (Avg.)	Duriel Harris, 1976	32.9
Field Goals	Pete Stoyanovich, 1991	31
Touchdowns (Tot.)	Mark Clayton, 1984	18
Points	Pete Stoyanovich, 1992	124

INDIVIDUAL RECORDS—SINGLE GAME

Category	Name	Performance
Rushing (Yds.)	Mercury Morris, 9-30-73	197
Passing (Yds.)	Dan Marino, 10-23-88	521
Passing (TDs)	Bob Griese, 11-24-77	6
	Dan Marino, 9-21-86	6
Receiving (No.)	Jim Jensen, 11-6-88	12
Receiving (Yds.)	Mark Duper, 11-10-85	217
Interceptions	Dick Anderson, 12-3-73	*4
Field Goals	Garo Yepremian, 9-26-71	5
Touchdowns (Tot.)	Paul Warfield, 12-15-73	4
Points	Paul Warfield, 12-15-73	24

*NFL Record

COACHING HISTORY
(269-171-4)

1966-69	George Wilson	15-39-2
1970-93	Don Shula	254-132-2

JOE ROBBIE STADIUM

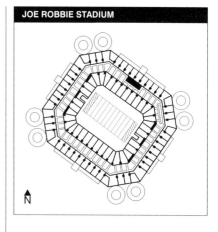

1993 TEAM RECORD

PRESEASON (3-1)

Date	Result		Opponents
8/6	W	28-27	at Atlanta
8/14	W	19-10	Washington
8/20	L	24-34	at Denver
8/28	W	23-17	N.Y. Giants

REGULAR SEASON (9-7)

Date	Result		Opponents	Att.
9/5	W	24-20	at Indianapolis	51,858
9/12	L	14-24	N.Y. Jets	70,314
9/26	W	22-13	at Buffalo	79,635
10/4	W	17-10	Washington	68,568
10/10	W	24-14	at Cleveland	78,138
10/24	W	41-27	Indianapolis	57,301
10/31	W	30-10	Kansas City	67,765
11/7	L	10-27	at N.Y. Jets	71,306
11/14	W	19-14	at Philadelphia	64,213
11/21	W	17-13	New England	59,982
11/25	W	16-14	at Dallas	60,198
12/5	L	14-19	N.Y. Giants	72,161
12/13	L	20-21	Pittsburgh	70,232
12/19	L	34-47	Buffalo	71,597
12/27	L	20-45	at San Diego	60,311
1/2	L	27-33	at New England (OT)	53,883

(OT) Overtime

SCORE BY PERIODS

Dolphins	100	76	85	88	0	—	349
Opponents	56	126	71	92	6	—	351

ATTENDANCE

Home 537,920   Away 519,542   Total 1,057,462
Single-game home record, 72,161 (12-5-93)
Single-season home record, 537,920 (1993)

1993 TEAM STATISTICS

	Dolphins	Opp.
Total First Downs	309	332
Rushing	85	103
Passing	207	205
Penalty	17	24
Third Down: Made/Att	100/218	103/229
Third Down Pct.	45.9	45.0
Fourth Down: Made/Att	8/17	3/10
Fourth Down Pct.	47.1	30.0
Total Net Yards	5812	5150
Avg. Per Game	303.3	321.9
Total Plays	1030	1061
Avg. Per Play	5.6	4.9
Net Yards Rushing	1459	1665
Avg. Per Game	91.2	104.1
Total Rushes	419	460
Net Yards Passing	4353	3485
Avg. Per Game	272.1	217.8
Sacked/Yards Lost	30/211	29/197
Gross Yards	4564	3682
Att./Completions	581/342	572/350
Completion Pct.	58.9	61.2
Had Intercepted	18	13
Punts/Avg.	58/39.7	76/41.3
Net Punting Avg.	58/32.2	76/34.9
Penalties/Yards Lost	81/663	92/650
Fumbles/Ball Lost	32/16	30/14
Touchdowns	40	43
Rushing	10	12
Passing	27	26
Returns	3	5
Avg. Time of Possession	28:59	31:01

1993 INDIVIDUAL STATISTICS

PASSING	Att.	Cmp.	Yds.	Pct.	TD	Int.	Tkld.	Rate
Mitchell	233	133	1773	57.1	12	8	7/49	84.2
DeBerg	188	113	1521	60.1	6	7	15/116	81.0
Marino	150	91	1218	60.7	8	3	7/42	95.9
Pederson	8	4	41	50.0	0	0	1/4	65.1
Byars	2	1	11	50.0	1	0	0/0	106.3
Dolphins	581	342	4564	58.9	27	18	30/211	86.4
Opponents	572	350	3682	61.2	26	13	29/197	85.6

SCORING	TD R	TD P	TD Rt	PAT	FG	Saf	PTS
Stoyanovich	0	0	0	37/37	24/32	0	109
Byars	3	3	0	0/0	0/0	0	36
Ingram	0	6	0	0/0	0/0	0	36
K. Jackson	0	6	0	0/0	0/0	0	36
Kirby	3	3	0	0/0	0/0	0	36
Fryar	0	5	0	0/0	0/0	0	30
Higgs	3	0	0	0/0	0/0	0	18
Martin	0	3	0	0/0	0/0	0	18
McDuffie	0	0	2	0/0	0/0	0	12
Baty	0	1	0	0/0	0/0	0	6
Marino	1	0	0	0/0	0/0	0	6
L. Oliver	0	0	1	0/0	0/0	0	6
Dolphins	10	27	3	37/40	24/32	0	349
Opponents	12	26	5	40/42	17/27	1	351

RUSHING	Att.	Yds.	Avg.	LG	TD
Higgs	186	693	3.7	31	3
Kirby	119	390	3.3	20	3
Byars	64	269	4.2	77t	3
Mitchell	21	89	4.2	32	0
Parmalee	4	16	4.0	12	0
Saxon	5	13	2.6	9	0
Martin	1	6	6.0	6	0
Pederson	2	-1	-0.5	0	0
DeBerg	4	-4	-1.0	-1	0
Fryar	3	-4	-1.3	2	0
Marino	9	-4	-0.4	4t	1
McDuffie	1	-4	-4.0	-4	0
Dolphins	419	1459	3.5	77t	10
Opponents	460	1665	3.6	65t	12

RECEIVING	No.	Yds.	Avg.	LG	TD
Kirby	75	874	11.7	47	3
Fryar	64	1010	15.8	65t	5
Byars	61	613	10.0	27	3
Ingram	44	707	16.1	77t	6
K. Jackson	39	613	15.7	57t	6
Martin	20	347	17.4	80t	3
McDuffie	19	197	10.4	18	0
Higgs	10	72	7.2	15	0
Baty	5	78	15.6	32	1
Miller	2	15	7.5	8	0
Banks	1	26	26.0	26	0
M. Williams	1	11	11.0	11	0
Parmalee	1	1	1.0	1	0
Dolphins	342	4564	13.3	80t	27
Opponents	350	3682	10.5	54	26

INTERCEPTIONS	No.	Yds.	Avg.	LG	TD
Brown	5	43	8.6	29	0
L. Oliver	2	60	30.0	56t	1
Vincent	2	29	14.5	23	0
Green	2	0	0.0	0	0
Cox	1	26	26.0	26	0
Hobley	1	17	17.0	17	0
Dolphins	13	175	13.5	56t	1
Opponents	18	329	18.3	97t	2

PUNTING	No.	Yds.	Avg.	In 20	LG
Hatcher	58	2304	39.7	13	56
Dolphins	58	2304	39.7	13	56
Opponents	76	3135	41.3	19	60

PUNT RETURNS	No.	FC	Yds.	Avg.	LG	TD
McDuffie	28	22	317	11.3	72t	2
Vincent	0	0	9	—	9	0
Dolphins	28	22	326	11.6	72t	2
Opponents	32	12	359	11.2	64t	1

KICKOFF RETURNS	No.	Yds.	Avg.	LG	TD
McDuffie	32	755	23.6	48	0
M. Williams	8	180	22.5	39	0
Kirby	4	85	21.3	26	0
Miller	2	22	11.0	16	0
Baty	1	7	7.0	7	0
Fryar	1	10	10.0	10	0
Saxon	1	7	7.0	7	0
Vincent	0	2	—	2	0
Dolphins	49	1068	21.8	48	0
Opponents	62	1239	20.0	40	0

SACKS	No.
Cross	10.5
Coleman	5.5
Cox	5.0
Hunter	3.0
Veasey	2.0
Klingbeil	1.5
Alexander	1.0
Griggs	0.5
Dolphins	29.0
Opponents	30.0

1994 DRAFT CHOICES

Round	Name	Pos.	College
1	Tim Bowens	DT	Mississippi
2	Aubrey Beavers	LB	Oklahoma
	Tim Ruddy	C	Notre Dame
4	Ronnie Woolfork	LB	Colorado
5	William Gaines	DT	Florida
6	Brant Boyer	LB	Arizona
7	Sean Hill	DB	Montana State

MIAMI DOLPHINS

1994 VETERAN ROSTER

No.	Name	Pos.	Ht.	Wt.	Birthdate	NFL Exp.	College	Hometown	How Acq.	'93 Games/ Starts
32	# Alexander, Bruce	CB	5-8	178	9/17/65	6	Stephen F. Austin	Lufkin, Tex.	PB(Det)-'92	14/0
6	Arnold, Jim	P	6-3	211	1/31/61	12	Vanderbilt	Dalton, Ga.	UFA(Det)-'94	16/0*
28	Atkins, Gene	S	5-11	200	11/22/64	8	Florida A&M	Tallahassee, Fla.	UFA(NO)-'94	16/16*
84	# Baty, Greg	TE	6-6	240	8/28/64	8	Stanford	Sparta, N.J.	FA-'90	16/1
66	Blake, Eddie	G	6-3	315	12/18/68	2	Auburn	Fayetteville, Tenn.	D2-'92	0*
34	Braxton, Tyrone	CB	5-11	185	12/17/64	8	North Dakota State	Madison, Wis.	UFA(Den)-'94	16/16*
37	Brown, J.B.	CB	6-0	190	1/5/67	6	Maryland	Washington, D.C.	D12-'89	16/16
41	Byars, Keith	RB	6-1	256	10/14/63	9	Ohio State	Dayton, Ohio	UFA(Phil)-'93	16/16
90	Coleman, Marco	DE	6-3	262	12/18/69	3	Georgia Tech	Dayton, Ohio	D1b-'92	15/15
51	Cox, Bryan	LB	6-4	242	2/17/68	4	Western Illinois	East St. Louis, Ill.	D5a-'91	16/16
49	Craver, Aaron	RB	6-0	220	12/18/68	4	Fresno State	Compton, Calif.	D3-'91	0*
91	Cross, Jeff	DE	6-4	273	3/25/66	7	Missouri	Blythe, Calif.	D9-'88	16/16
17	# DeBerg, Steve	QB	6-3	220	1/19/54	18	San Jose State	Anaheim, Calif.	FA-'93	8/5*
65	Dellenbach, Jeff	T-C	6-5	290	2/14/63	10	Wisconsin	Wausau, Wis.	D4b-'85	16/16
74	# Dennis, Mark	T	6-6	296	4/15/65	8	Illinois	Washington, Ill.	D8b-'87	16/0
80	Fryar, Irving	WR	6-0	200	9/28/62	11	Nebraska	Mount Holly, N.J.	T(NE)-'93	16/16
62	Gray, Chris	G-T	6-4	289	6/19/70	2	Auburn	Birmingham, Ala.	D5-'93	5/0
42	Green, Chris	S-CB	5-11	192	2/26/68	4	Illinois	Lawrenceburg, Ind.	D7-'91	14/0
59	# Grimsley, John	LB	6-2	236	2/25/62	11	Kentucky	Canton, Ohio	T(Hou)-'91	13/9
45	# Harden, Bobby	S	6-0	205	2/8/67	5	Miami	Fort Lauderdale, Fla.	D12-'90	8/0
73	Heller, Ron	T	6-6	293	8/25/62	11	Penn State	Farmingdale, N.Y.	UFA(Phil)-'93	16/16
21	Higgs, Mark	RB	5-7	196	4/11/66	7	Kentucky	Owensboro, Ky.	PB(Phil)-'90	16/8
50	Hollier, Dwight	LB	6-2	250	4/21/69	3	North Carolina	Hampton, Va.	D4-'92	16/10
82	Ingram, Mark	WR	5-11	190	8/23/68	8	Michigan State	Flint, Mich.	UFA(NYG)-'93	16/16
88	Jackson, Keith	TE	6-2	254	4/19/65	7	Oklahoma	Little Rock, Ark.	UFA(Phil)-'92	15/15
24	# Jackson, Vestee	CB	6-0	186	8/14/63	9	Washington	Fresno, Calif.	T(Chi)-'91	16/5
43	Kirby, Terry	RB	6-1	219	1/20/70	2	Virginia	Tabb, Va.	D3-'93	16/8
99	† Klingbeil, Chuck	NT	6-1	289	11/2/65	4	Northern Michigan	Houghton, Mich.	FA-'91	16/16
19	Kosar, Bernie	QB	6-5	215	11/25/63	10	Miami	Boardman, Ohio	UFA(Dall)-'94	11/7*
47	Malone, Darrell	CB	5-10	182	11/23/67	3	Jacksonville State	Jacksonville, Ala.	FA-'92	16/1
13	Marino, Dan	QB	6-4	224	9/15/61	12	Pittsburgh	Pittsburgh, Pa.	D1-'83	5/5
81	McDuffie, O.J.	WR	5-10	185	12/2/69	2	Penn State	Gates Mills, Ohio	D1-'93	16/0
15	# Millen, Hugh	QB	6-5	216	11/22/63	9	Washington	Seattle, Wash.	FA-'93	0*
93	# Odom, Cliff	LB	6-2	236	8/15/58	14	Texas-Arlington	Beaumont, Tex.	PB(Ind)-'90	14/1
56	# Offerdahl, John	LB	6-3	238	8/17/64	9	Western Michigan	Fort Atkinson, Wis.	D2-'86	9/8
20	Oliver, Muhammad	CB-S	5-11	180	3/12/69	3	Oregon	Brooklyn, N.Y.	FA-'93	4/0*
30	Parmalee, Bernie	RB	5-11	204	9/16/67	3	Ball State	Jersey City, N.J.	FA-'92	16/0
14	Pederson, Doug	QB	6-3	209	1/31/68	2	Northeast Louisiana	Ferndale, Wash.	FA-'93	7/0
22	Saxon, James	RB	5-11	237	3/23/66	7	San Jose State	Burton, S.C.	PB(KC)-'92	16/0
69	Sims, Keith	G	6-3	303	6/17/67	5	Iowa State	Watchung, N.J.	D2-'90	16/16
55	Singleton, Chris	LB	6-2	242	2/2/67	5	Arizona	Parsippany, N.J.	FA-'93	17/4*
29	Smith, Frankie	CB	5-9	186	10/8/68	2	Baylor	Groesbeck, Tex.	FA-'93	5/1
33	Stewart, Michael	S	6-0	199	7/12/65	8	Fresno State	Bakersfield, Calif.	UFA(Rams)-'94	16/14*
11	Stouffer, Kelly	QB	6-3	214	7/6/64	6	Colorado State	Rushville, Neb.	FA-'94	0*
10	Stoyanovich, Pete	K	5-11	195	4/28/67	6	Indiana	Dearborn Heights, Mich.	D8-'89	16/0
57	Thayer, Tom	C-G	6-4	284	8/16/61	10	Notre Dame	Catholic, Ill.	FA-'93	3/0
94	Veasey, Craig	NT	6-2	300	12/25/66	5	Houston	Houston, Tex.	FA-'93	14/0
23	Vincent, Troy	CB	6-0	192	6/8/70	3	Wisconsin	Trenton, N.J.	D1a-'92	13/13
78	Webb, Richmond	T	6-6	302	1/11/67	5	Texas A&M	Dallas, Tex.	D1-'90	16/16
79	Webster, Larry	DT	6-5	288	1/18/69	3	Maryland	Elkton, Md.	D3-'92	13/9
60	# Weidner, Bert	G-C	6-2	290	1/20/66	5	Kent State	Eden, N.Y.	D11-'89	16/11
26	# Williams, Jarvis	S	5-11	200	5/16/65	7	Florida	Palatka, Fla.	D2-'88	16/14
87	Williams, Mike	WR	5-11	187	10/9/66	3	Northeastern	Katonah, N.Y.	FA-'91	13/0
85	Williams, Ronnie	TE	6-3	259	1/19/66	3	Oklahoma State	North Natchez, Miss.	FA-'93	11/0

* Arnold played 16 games with Detroit in '93; Atkins played 16 games with New Orleans; Blake inactive for 16 games; Braxton played 16 games with Denver; Craver missed '93 season due to injury; DeBerg played 3 games with Tampa Bay, 5 games with Miami; Kosar played 7 games with Cleveland, 4 games with Dallas; Millen was inactive for 8 games with Dallas, 7 games with Miami; Oliver played 2 games with Kansas City, 2 games with Green Bay; Singleton played 8 games with New England, 9 games with Miami; Stewart played 16 games with L.A. Rams; Stouffer last active with Seattle in '92.

\# Unrestricted free agent; subject to developments.

† Restricted free agent; subject to developments.

Traded—WR Tony Martin to San Diego.

Players lost through free agency (5): DE-LB David Griggs (SD; 9 games in '93), DE Jeffrey Hunter (TB; 5), QB Scott Mitchell (Det; 13), S Louis Oliver (Cin; 11), C Jeff Uhlenhake (NO; 5).

Also played with Dolphins in '93—WR Fred Banks (2 games), S-CB Stephen Braggs (11), LB Chuck Bullough (3), NT Mike Golic (15), P Dale Hatcher (16), S Liffort Hobley (4), WR Tony Martin (12), LB David Merritt (4), WR Scott Miller (3), DT Karl Wilson (2).

COACHING STAFF

Head Coach,
Don Shula

Pro Career: Begins his thirty-second season as an NFL head coach, and twenty-fifth with the Dolphins. Miami has won or shared first place in the AFC East in 14 of his 24 years and has earned 14 playoff berths in that span. Has most wins (327) in NFL history, surpassing George Halas's 324 in 1993. Captured back-to-back NFL championships, defeating Washington 14-7 in Super Bowl VII and Minnesota 24-7 in Super Bowl VIII. Lost to Dallas 24-3 in Super Bowl VI, to Washington 27-17 in Super Bowl XVII, and to San Francisco 38-16 in Super Bowl XIX. His 17-0 team in 1972 is the only team in NFL history to go undefeated throughout the regular season and postseason. Started his pro playing career with Cleveland Browns as defensive back in 1951. After two seasons with Browns, spent 1953-56 with Baltimore Colts and 1957 with Washington Redskins. Joined Detroit Lions as defensive coach in 1960 and was named head coach of the Colts in 1963. Baltimore had a 13-1 record in 1968 and captured NFL championship before losing to New York Jets in Super Bowl III. Career record: 327-158-6.

Background: Outstanding offensive player at John Carroll University in Cleveland before becoming defensive specialist as a pro. His alma mater awarded him a doctorate in humanities in May, 1973. Served as assistant coach at Virginia in 1958 and at Kentucky in 1959.

Personal: Born January 4, 1930, in Painesville, Ohio. Don and his wife, Mary Anne, live in Miami. He has five children— Dave, Donna, Sharon, Annie, and Mike. Dave is Cincinnati's head coach and Mike is tight ends coach with Chicago.

ASSISTANT COACHES

Joel Collier, staff assistant; born December 25, 1963, Buffalo, N.Y., lives in Miami. Linebacker Northern Colorado 1984-87. No pro playing experience. College coach: Syracuse 1988-89. Pro coach: Tampa Bay Buccaneers 1990, New England Patriots 1991-93, joined Dolphins in 1994.

John Gamble, strength; born June 26, 1957, Richmond, Va., lives in Miami. Linebacker Hampton Institute 1975-78. No pro playing experience. College coach: Virginia 1982-93. Pro coach: Joined Dolphins in 1994.

Joe Greene, defensive line; born September 24, 1946, Temple, Tex., lives in Miami. Defensive tackle North Texas State 1966-68. Pro defensive tackle Pittsburgh Steelers 1969-81. Inducted into Pro Football Hall of Fame in 1987. Pro coach: Pittsburgh Steelers 1987-91, joined Dolphins in 1992.

George Hill, linebackers; born April 28, 1933, Bay Village, Ohio. No pro playing experience. College coach: Findlay 1959, Denison 1960-64, Cornell 1965, Duke 1966-70, Ohio State 1971-78. Pro coach: Philadelphia Eagles 1979-84, Indianapolis Colts 1985-88, joined Dolphins in 1989.

Rich McGeorge, assistant offensive line-tight ends; born September 14, 1948, Roanoke, Va., lives in Miami. Tight end Elon College 1966-69. Pro tight end Green Bay Packers 1970-78. College coach: Duke 1981-82, 1987-89, Florida 1990-92. Pro coach: Birmingham Stallions (USFL) 1983-84, Tampa Bay Bandits (USFL) 1985, joined Dolphins in 1993.

Tony Nathan, offensive backs; born December 14, 1956, Birmingham, Ala., lives in Miami. Running back Alabama 1975-78. Pro running back Miami Dolphins 1979-87. Pro coach: Joined Dolphins in 1988.

Tom Olivadotti, defense; born September 22, 1945, Long Branch, N.J., lives in Cooper City, Fla. Defensive back-wide receiver Upsala 1963-66. No pro playing experience. College coach: Princeton 1975-77, Boston College 1978-79, Miami 1980-83. Pro coach: Cleveland Browns 1985-86, joined Dolphins in 1987.

Mel Phillips, defensive backs; born January 6, 1942, Shelby, N.C., lives in Miami Lakes, Fla. Defensive back-running back North Carolina A&T 1964-65.

1994 FIRST-YEAR ROSTER

Name	Pos.	Ht.	Wt.	Birthdate	College	Hometown	How Acq.
Albright, Ethan	T	6-5	285	5/1/71	North Carolina	Greensboro, N.C.	FA
Araguz, Leo	P	6-0	185	1/18/70	Stephen F. Austin	Harlingen, Tex.	FA
Ballard, Jim	QB	6-3	223	4/16/72	Mount Union	Cuyahoga Falls, Ohio	FA
Barnett, Ja'Karl	LB	6-0	235	11/16/70	Jacksonville State	Opelika, Ala.	FA
Beavers, Aubrey	LB	6-3	233	8/30/71	Oklahoma	Houston, Tex.	D2a
Borgognone, Dirk (1)	K	6-2	220	1/9/68	Pacific	Reno, Nev.	FA
Bowens, Tim	DT	6-4	317	2/7/73	Mississippi	Okolona, Miss.	D1
Boyer, Brant	LB	6-0	233	6/27/71	Arizona	Ogden, Utah	D6
Brothen, Kevin (1)	C	6-1	284	11/16/69	Vanderbilt	Chicago, Ill.	FA
Brown, Reggie (1)	WR	5-11	175	6/1/68	Mesa, Colo.	Denver, Colo.	FA
Bullough, Chuck (1)	LB	6-1	234	3/3/69	Michigan State	Orchard Park, N.Y.	FA
Caesar, Mark (1)	DT	6-2	295	1/12/70	Miami	Newark, N.J.	FA
Cartwright, Ricardo (1)	CB	5-10	185	5/27/65	Florida A&M	Freeport, Bahamas	FA
Coons, Rob (1)	TE	6-5	245	9/18/69	Pittsburgh	Brea, Calif.	FA
Covington, Leevary	LB	6-0	246	6/10/71	North Carolina A&T	Rockingham, N.C.	FA
Davis, Dwayne	S	6-1	203	9/27/70	Colorado	Gulfport, Miss.	FA
Davis, Robert	CB	5-9	188	8/6/72	Vanderbilt	Nashville, Tenn.	FA
Dixon, Johnny	S	5-11	204	2/13/71	Mississippi	Harvey, La.	FA
Foxx, Dion	LB	6-3	249	6/11/71	James Madison	Richmond, Va.	FA
Francisco, Paul	TE	6-6	236	10/14/69	Boston University	Dorchester, Mass.	FA
Gaines, William	DT	6-5	300	6/20/71	Florida	Jackson, Miss.	D5
Hill, Sean	CB	5-10	176	8/14/71	Montana State	Ft. Carson, Colo.	D7
Hopkins, Jimmie	DE	6-5	255	1/5/71	Arizona	Brawley, Calif.	FA
Johnson, Demeris (1)	WR	6-0	183	8/26/69	Western Illinois	Detroit, Mich.	FA
Letcher, Morris	WR	5-9	167	11/8/70	East Carolina	Kansas City, Kan.	FA
Mash, Alex	LB	6-0	256	12/16/70	Georgia Southern	Thomasville, Ga.	FA
McGuire, Stephen (1)	RB	5-10	236	11/20/69	Miami	Brooklyn, N.Y.	FA
Middleton, Mike (1)	S	5-11	224	12/4/69	Indiana	Cincinnati, Ohio	FA
Novak, Jeff (1)	T	6-5	295	7/27/67	Southwest Texas State	Cook County, Ill.	FA
Quarles, Shelton	LB	6-1	234	9/11/71	Vanderbilt	Whites Creek, Tenn.	FA
Richardson, Sean	RB	5-10	248	6/10/71	Jacksonville State	Auburn, Ala.	FA
Rooks, George (1)	DT	6-3	298	8/9/70	Syracuse	White Plains, N.Y.	FA
Rowell, Tony (1)	G	6-4	293	7/24/69	Florida	Melbourne, Fla.	FA
Rowley, Bryan	WR	5-10	176	11/2/70	Utah	Orem, Utah	FA
Ruddy, Tim	C	6-3	286	4/27/72	Notre Dame	Scranton, Pa.	D2b
Schulte, Scott	RB	5-10	200	11/13/71	Hillsdale College	Delphos, Ohio	FA
Seigler, Dexter	CB	5-9	178	1/11/72	Miami	Avon Park, Fla.	FA
Spikes, Irving	RB	5-8	215	12/20/70	Northeast Louisiana	Ocean Springs, Miss.	FA
Spralding, Melvin	LB	6-1	235	10/9/69	South Carolina State	Alachua, Fla.	FA
Sturdivant, Mark	DE	6-3	274	7/2/71	Maryland	Silver Spring, Md.	FA
Williams, Jay	DE	6-3	266	10/13/71	Wake Forest	Washington, D.C.	FA
Woolfork, Ronnie	LB	6-3	256	12/21/70	Colorado	Detroit, Mich.	D4

The term NFL Rookie is defined as a player who is in his first season of professional football and has not been on the roster of another professional football team for any regular-season or postseason games. A Rookie is designated by an "R" on NFL rosters. Players who have been active in another professional football league or players who have NFL experience, including either preseason training camp or being on an Active List or Inactive List, or on Reserve/Injured or Reserve/Physically Unable to Perform for fewer than six regular-season games, are termed NFL First-Year Players. An NFL First-Year Player is designated by a "1" on NFL rosters. Thereafter, a player is credited with an additional year of experience for each season in which he accumulates six games on the Active List or Inactive List, or on Reserve/Injured or Reserve/Physically Unable to Perform.

NOTES

_____
_____
_____
_____
_____
_____

Pro defensive back San Francisco 49ers 1966-77. Pro coach: Detroit Lions 1980-84, joined Dolphins in 1985.

John Sandusky, assistant head coach-offensive line; born December 28, 1925, Philadelphia, Pa., lives in Hollywood, Fla. Tackle Villanova 1946-49. Pro tackle Cleveland Browns 1950-55, Green Bay Packers 1956. College coach: Villanova 1957-58. Pro coach: Baltimore Colts 1959-72 (head coach 1972), Philadelphia Eagles 1973-75, joined Dolphins in 1976.

Larry Seiple, wide receivers; born February 14, 1945, Allentown, Pa., lives in Miami Lakes, Fla. Running back-receiver-punter Kentucky 1964-66. Pro punter-tight end-receiver-running back Miami Dolphins 1967-77. College coach: Miami 1978-79. Pro coach: Detroit Lions 1980-84, Tampa Bay Buccaneers 1985-86, joined Dolphins in 1988.

Gary Stevens, offense-quarterbacks; born March 19, 1943, Cleveland, Ohio, lives in Kendall, Fla. Running back John Carroll 1963-65. No playing experience. College coach: Louisville 1971-74, Kent State 1975, West Virginia 1976-79, Miami 1980-88. Pro coach: Joined Dolphins in 1989.

Junior Wade, strength and conditioning; born February 2, 1947, Bath, S.C., lives in Miami. South Carolina State 1969. No college or pro playing experience. Pro coach: Joined Dolphins in 1975, coach since 1983.

Mike Westhoff, special teams; born January 10, 1948, Pittsburgh, Pa., lives in Ft. Lauderdale, Fla. Center-linebacker Wichita State 1967-69. No pro playing experience. College coach: Indiana 1974-75, Dayton 1976, Indiana State 1977, Northwestern 1978-80, Texas Christian 1981. Pro coach: Baltimore/Indianapolis Colts 1982-84, Arizona Outlaws (USFL) 1985, joined Dolphins in 1986.

American Football Conference
Eastern Division
Team Colors: Blue, Red, Silver, and White
Foxboro Stadium
60 Washington Street
Foxboro, Massachusetts 02035
Telephone: (508) 543-8200

CLUB OFFICIALS

President/Chief Executive Officer: Robert K. Kraft
Vice President-Owner's Repesentative:
  Jonathan A. Kraft
Vice President-Business Operations:
  Andrew Wasynczuk
Vice President-Football Operations: Patrick Forté
Vice President-Finance: James Hausmann
Vice President-Event Management:
  Brian O'Donovan
Corporate Marketing and Sales: Daniel A. Kraft
Director of Public and Community Relations:
  Donald Lowery
Assistant Director of Public Relations: Stacey James
Director of Player Resources: Andre Tippett
Controller: Virginia Widman
Director of Pro Scouting: Bobby Grier
Director of College Scouting: Charles Armey
Director of Data Processing: Peg Myers
Director of Ticketing: Ken Sternfeld
Marketing Manager: Mitch Hardin
National Accounts Manager: Richard Doucette
Assistant General Manager Foxboro Stadium:
  Raymond J. Cantwell
Head Trainer: Ron O'Neil
Equipment Manager: Don Brocher
Video Director: Ken Deininger
Stadium: Foxboro Stadium •**Capacity:** 60,290
  60 Washington Street
  Foxboro, Massachusetts 02035
Playing Surface: Grass
Training Camp: Bryant College
  Route 7
  Smithfield, Rhode Island 02917

1994 SCHEDULE
PRESEASON
Aug. 5	**New Orleans**	8:00
Aug. 13	at Los Angeles Rams	7:00
Aug. 18	**Washington**	7:00
Aug. 26	at Green Bay	7:00

REGULAR SEASON
Sept. 4	at Miami	4:00
Sept. 11	**Buffalo**	1:00
Sept. 18	at Cincinnati	1:00
Sept. 25	at Detroit	4:00
Oct. 2	**Green Bay**	1:00
Oct. 9	**Los Angeles Raiders**	4:00
Oct. 16	at New York Jets	1:00
Oct. 23	Open Date	
Oct. 30	**Miami**	1:00
Nov. 6	at Cleveland	1:00
Nov. 13	**Minnesota**	1:00
Nov. 20	**San Diego**	1:00
Nov. 27	at Indianapolis	8:00
Dec. 4	**New York Jets**	1:00
Dec. 11	**Indianapolis**	1:00
Dec. 18	at Buffalo	1:00
Dec. 24	at Chicago	12:00

RECORD HOLDERS
INDIVIDUAL RECORDS—CAREER
Category	Name	Performance
Rushing (Yds.)	Sam Cunningham, 1973-79, 1981-82	5,453
Passing (Yds.)	Steve Grogan, 1975-1990	26,886
Passing (TDs)	Steve Grogan, 1975-1990	182
Receiving (No.)	Stanley Morgan, 1977-1989	534
Receiving (Yds.)	Stanley Morgan, 1977-1989	10,352
Interceptions	Raymond Clayborn, 1977-1989	36
Punting (Avg.)	Rich Camarillo, 1981-87	42.6
Punt Return (Avg.)	Mack Herron, 1973-75	12.0
Kickoff Return (Avg.)	Horace Ivory, 1977-1981	27.6
Field Goals	Gino Cappelletti, 1960-1970	176
Touchdowns (Tot.)	Stanley Morgan, 1977-1989	68
Points	Gino Cappelletti, 1960-1970	1,130

INDIVIDUAL RECORDS—SINGLE SEASON
Category	Name	Performance
Rushing (Yds.)	Jim Nance, 1966	1,458
Passing (Yds.)	Vito (Babe) Parilli, 1964	3,465
Passing (TDs)	Vito (Babe) Parilli, 1964	31
Receiving (No.)	Stanley Morgan, 1986	84
Receiving (Yds.)	Stanley Morgan, 1986	1,491
Interceptions	Ron Hall, 1964	11
Punting (Avg.)	Rich Camarillo, 1983	44.6
Punt Return (Avg.)	Mack Herron, 1974	14.8
Kickoff Return (Avg.)	Raymond Clayborn, 1977	31.0
Field Goals	Tony Franklin, 1986	32
Touchdowns (Tot.)	Steve Grogan, 1976	13
	Stanley Morgan, 1979	13
Points	Gino Cappelletti, 1964	155

INDIVIDUAL RECORDS—SINGLE GAME
Category	Name	Performance
Rushing (Yds.)	Tony Collins, 9-18-83	212
Passing (Yds.)	Tony Eason, 9-21-86	414
Passing (TDs)	Vito (Babe) Parilli, 11-15-64	5
	Vito (Babe) Parilli, 10-15-67	5
	Steve Grogan, 9-9-79	5
Receiving (No.)	Art Graham, 11-20-66	11
	Tony Collins, 11-29-87	11
Receiving (Yds.)	Stanley Morgan, 11-8-81	182
Interceptions	Many times	3
	Last time by Roland James, 10-23-83	
Field Goals	Gino Cappelletti, 10-4-64	6
Touchdowns (Tot.)	Many times	3
	Last time by Stanley Morgan, 9-21-86	
Points	Gino Cappelletti, 12-18-65	28

*NFL Record

COACHING HISTORY
BOSTON 1960-1970
(225-276-9)
1960-61	Lou Saban*	7-12-0
1961-68	Mike Holovak	53-47-9
1969-70	Clive Rush**	5-16-0
1970-72	John Mazur***	9-21-0
1972	Phil Bengtson	1-4-0
1973-78	Chuck Fairbanks****	46-41-0
1978	Hank Bullough-Ron Erhardt#	0-1-0
1979-81	Ron Erhardt	21-27-0
1982-84	Ron Meyer##	18-16-0
1984-89	Raymond Berry	51-41-0
1990	Rod Rust	1-15-0
1991-92	Dick MacPherson	8-24-0
1993	Bill Parcells	5-11-0

*Released after five games in 1961
**Released after seven games in 1970
***Resigned after nine games in 1972
****Suspended for final regular-season game in 1978
#Co-coaches
##Released after eight games in 1984

FOXBORO STADIUM

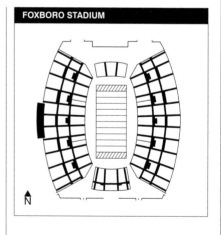

1993 TEAM RECORD

PRESEASON (1-3)

Date	Result		Opponents
8/7	L	7-13	at San Diego
8/14	L	9-12	vs. Cleveland at Toronto
8/20	W	21-17	Green Bay
8/27	L	20-27	Kansas City

REGULAR SEASON (5-11)

Date	Result		Opponents	Att.
9/5	L	14-38	at Buffalo	79,751
9/12	L	16-19	Detroit (OT)	54,151
9/19	L	14-17	Seattle	50,392
9/26	L	7-45	at New York Jets	64,836
10/10	W	23-21	at Phoenix	36,115
10/17	L	14-28	Houston	51,037
10/24	L	9-10	at Seattle	56,526
10/31	L	6-9	at Indianapolis	46,522
11/7	L	10-13	Buffalo (OT)	54,326
11/21	L	13-17	at Miami	59,982
11/28	L	0-6	New York Jets	42,810
12/5	L	14-17	at Pittsburgh	51,358
12/12	W	7-2	Cincinnati	29,794
12/19	W	20-17	at Cleveland	48,618
12/26	W	38-0	Indianapolis	26,571
1/2	W	33-27	Miami (OT)	53,883

(OT) Overtime

SCORE BY PERIODS

Patriots	33	60	54	85	6	—	238
Opponents	41	103	26	110	6	—	286

ATTENDANCE

Home 362,964   Away 443,708   Total 806,672
Single-game home record, 61,457 (12-5-71)
Single-season home record, 482,572 (1986)

1993 TEAM STATISTICS

	Patriots	Opp.
Total First Downs	315	269
Rushing	116	97
Passing	169	161
Penalty	30	11
Third Down: Made/Att	92/237	96/231
Third Down Pct.	38.8	41.6
Fourth Down: Made/Att	13/27	5/13
Fourth Down Pct.	48.1	38.5
Total Net Yards	5065	4796
Avg. Per Game	316.6	299.8
Total Plays	1091	1013
Avg. Per Play	4.6	4.7
Net Yards Rushing	1780	1951
Avg. Per Game	111.3	121.9
Total Rushes	502	505
Net Yards Passing	3285	2845
Avg. Per Game	205.3	177.8
Sacked/Yards Lost	23/127	34/242
Gross Yards	3412	3087
Att./Completions	566/289	474/280
Completion Pct.	51.1	59.1
Had Intercepted	24	13
Punts/Avg.	76/40.7	90/41.2
Net Punting Avg.	76/34.8	90/34.7
Penalties/Yards Lost	64/468	111/803
Fumbles/Ball Lost	30/10	20/9
Touchdowns	26	32
Rushing	9	9
Passing	17	20
Returns	0	3
Avg. Time of Possession	29:43	30:17

1993 INDIVIDUAL STATISTICS

PASSING	Att.	Cmp.	Yds.	Pct.	TD	Int.	Tkld.	Rate
Bledsoe	429	214	2494	49.9	15	15	16/99	65.0
Secules	134	75	918	56.0	2	9	7/28	54.3
Zolak	2	0	0	0.0	0	0	0/0	39.6
Turner	1	0	0	0.0	0	0	0/0	39.6
Patriots	566	289	3412	51.1	17	24	23/127	62.1
Opponents	474	280	3087	59.1	20	13	34/242	81.1

SCORING	TD R	TD P	TD Rt	PAT	FG	Saf	PTS
Sisson	0	0	0	15/15	14/26	0	57
Coates	0	8	0	0/0	0/0	0	48
Russell	7	0	0	0/0	0/0	0	42
Bahr	0	0	0	10/10	5/5	0	25
Brisby	0	2	0	0/0	0/0	0	12
Timpson	0	2	0	0/0	0/0	0	12
Turner	0	2	0	0/0	0/0	0	12
Cook	0	1	0	0/0	0/0	0	6
Crittenden	0	1	0	0/0	0/0	0	6
Croom	1	0	0	0/0	0/0	0	6
Gash	1	0	0	0/0	0/0	0	6
McMurtry	1	0	0	0/0	0/0	0	6
Patriots	9	17	0	25/25	19/31	0	238
Opponents	9	20	3	32/32	20/24	1	286

RUSHING	Att.	Yds.	Avg.	LG	TD
Russell	300	1088	3.6	21	7
Turner	50	231	4.6	49	0
Croom	60	198	3.3	22	1
Gash	48	149	3.1	14	1
Bledsoe	32	82	2.6	15	0
Secules	8	33	4.1	13	0
Saxon	2	2	1.0	2	0
Zolak	1	0	0.0	0	0
Crittenden	1	-3	-3.0	-3	0
Patriots	502	1780	3.5	49	9
Opponents	505	1951	3.9	57	9

RECEIVING	No.	Yds.	Avg.	LG	TD
Coates	53	659	12.4	54t	8
Brisby	45	626	13.9	39	2
Timpson	42	654	15.6	48	2
Turner	39	333	8.5	26	2
Russell	26	245	9.4	69	0
McMurtry	22	241	11.0	20	1
Cook	22	154	7.0	17	1
Crittenden	16	293	18.3	44	1
Gash	14	03	6 6	15	0
Croom	8	92	11.5	21	0
T. Brown	2	22	11.0	14	0
Patriots	289	3412	11.8	82	17
Opponents	280	3087	11.0	56	20

INTERCEPTIONS	No.	Yds.	Avg.	LG	TD
Hurst	4	53	13.3	24	0
Wren	3	-7	-2.3	2	0
Barnett	1	40	40.0	40	0
V. Brown	1	24	24.0	24	0
Collins	1	8	8.0	8	0
Thompson	1	4	4.0	4	0
Lambert	1	0	0.0	0	0
Ray	1	0	0.0	0	0
Patriots	13	122	9.4	40	0
Opponents	24	201	8.4	34	1

PUNTING	No.	Yds.	Avg.	In 20	LG
Saxon	73	3096	42.4	25	59
Patriots	76	3096	40.7	25	59
Opponents	90	3709	41.2	19	58

PUNT RETURNS	No.	FC	Yds.	Avg.	LG	TD
T. Brown	25	9	224	9.0	19	0
Harris	23	4	201	8.7	21	0
Crittenden	2	1	37	18.5	30	0
Smith	1	0	0	0.0	0	0
Patriots	51	14	462	9.1	30	0
Opponents	34	6	313	9.2	47t	1

KICKOFF RETURNS	No.	Yds.	Avg.	LG	TD
Crittenden	23	478	20.8	44	0
T. Brown	15	243	16.2	29	0
Harris	6	90	15.0	19	0
Sabb	2	0	0.0	0	0
Cook	1	8	8.0	8	0
Coates	0	0	—	—	0
Patriots	47	819	17.4	44	0
Opponents	44	921	20.9	42	0

SACKS	No.
Slade	9.0
Tippett	8.5
A. Jones	3.5
Pitts	3.0
Sabb	2.0
Williams	2.0
Agnew	1.5
V. Brown	1.0
Collins	1.0
Hurst	1.0
Thompson	1.0
Goad	0.5
Patriots	34.0
Opponent	23.0

1994 DRAFT CHOICES

Round	Name	Pos.	College
1	Willie McGinest	DE	Southern California
2	Kevin Lee	WR	Alabama
3	Ervin Collier	NT	Florida A&M
	Joe Burch	C	Texas Southern
4	John Burke	TE	Virginia Tech
5	Pat O'Neill	P	Syracuse
6	Steve Hawkins	WR	Western Michigan
	Max Lane	T	Navy
7	Jay Walker	QB	Howard
	Marty Moore	LB	Kentucky

NEW ENGLAND PATRIOTS

1994 VETERAN ROSTER

No.	Name	Pos.	Ht.	Wt.	Birthdate	NFL Exp.	College	Hometown	How Acq.	'93 Games/ Starts
92	Agnew, Ray	DE	6-3	272	12/9/67	5	North Carolina State	Winston-Salem, N.C.	D1b-'90	16/1
78	Armstrong, Bruce	T	6-4	284	9/7/65	8	Louisville	Miami, Fla.	D1-'87	16/16
65	Arthur, Mike	C	6-3	280	5/7/68	4	Texas A&M	Houston, Tex.	W(Cin)-'93	13/11
3	Bahr, Matt	K	5-10	175	7/6/56	16	Penn State	Langhorne, Pa.	W(Phil)-'93	14/0*
42	Barnett, Harlon	S	5-11	200	1/2/67	5	Michigan State	Cincinnati, Ohio	W(Clev)-'93	14/12
52	Bavaro, David	LB	6-1	228	3/27/67	3	Syracuse	Danvers, Mass.	FA-'93	12/0
11	Bledsoe, Drew	QB	6-5	233	2/14/72	2	Washington State	Walla Walla, Wash.	D1-'93	13/12
82	Brisby, Vincent	WR	6-1	186	1/25/71	2	Northeast Louisiana	Lake Charles, La.	D2c-'93	16/12
30	Brown, Corwin	S	6-1	192	4/25/70	2	Michigan	Chicago, Ill.	D4b-'93	15/12
80	Brown, Troy	WR-KR	5-9	183	7/2/71	2	Marshall	Blackville, S.C.	D8-'93	12/0
59	Brown, Vincent	LB	6-2	245	1/9/65	7	Mississippi Valley State	Decatur, Ga.	D2-'88	16/16
44	t- Butts, Marion	RB	6-1	248	8/1/66	6	Florida State	Sylvester, Ga.	T(SD)-'94	16/16*
99	Carthen Jason	LB	6-3	255	11/16/70	2	Ohio University	Toledo, Ohio	W(Buff)-'93	5/0
69	Chung, Eugene	G	6-4	295	6/14/69	3	Virginia Tech	Oakton, Va.	D1-'92	16/16
87	Coates, Ben	TE	6-5	245	8/16/69	4	Livingstone College	Greenwood, S.C.	D5b-'91	16/10
54	Collins, Todd	LB	6-2	242	5/27/70	3	Carson-Newman	New Market, Tenn.	D3a-'92	16/12
81	Crittenden, Ray	WR	6-1	188	3/1/70	2	Virginia Tech	Washington, D.C.	FA-'93	16/2
26	Croom, Corey	RB	5-11	212	5/22/71	2	Ball State	Sandusky, Ohio	FA-'93	14/1
50	DeOssie, Steve	LB	6-2	248	11/22/62	11	Boston College	Roslindale, Mass.	UFA(NYJ)-'94	15/0*
33	Gash, Sam	RB	6-1	224	3/7/69	3	Penn State	Hendersonville, N.C.	D8b-'92	15/4
67	Gisler, Mike	G	6-4	300	8/26/69	2	Houston	Range, Tex.	FA-'93	12/0
72	Goad, Tim	NT	6-3	280	2/28/66	7	North Carolina	Stuart, Va.	D4a-'88	16/15
88	Griffith, Richard	TE	6-5	256	7/31/69	2	Arizona	Tucson, Ariz.	D5b-'93	3/0
29	Guyton, Myron	S	6-1	205	8/26/67	6	Eastern Kentucky	Thomasville, Ga.	UFA(NYG)-'94	16/16*
77	Harlow, Pat	T	6-6	290	3/16/69	4	Southern California	Norco, Calif.	D1a-'91	16/16
37	Hurst, Maurice	CB	5-10	185	9/17/67	6	Southern	New Orleans, La.	D4a-'89	16/16
98	Johnson, Mario	NT	6-3	288	1/30/70	3	Missouri	Florissant, Mo.	W(NYJ)-'93	6/0
97	Jones, Aaron	DE	6-5	267	12/18/66	7	Eastern Kentucky	Orlando, Fla.	UFA(Pitt)-'93	11/1
61	Kratch, Bob	G	6-3	288	1/6/66	6	Iowa	Mahwah, N.J.	UFA(NYG)-'94	16/16*
28	Lambert, Dion	S	6-1	185	2/12/69	3	UCLA	Lake View Terrace, Calif.	D4a-'92	14/4
35	Legette, Burnie	RB	6-1	243	12/5/70	2	Michigan	Colorado Springs, Colo.	FA-'93	7/0
75	Lewis, Bill	C	6-6	290	7/12/63	9	Nebraska	Sioux City, Iowa	UFA(Phx)-'93	7/5
43	Lewis, Vernon	CB	5-10	192	10/27/70	2	Pittsburgh	Houston, Tex.	FA-'93	10/0
70	Moore, Brandon	T	6-6	290	6/21/70	2	Duke	Bowling Springs, Pa.	FA-'93	16/0
93	Pitts, Mike	DE	6-5	277	9/25/60	12	Alabama	Baltimore, Md.	UFA(Phil)-'93	16/15
23	Ray, Terry	S	6-1	205	10/12/69	3	Oklahoma	Killeen, Tex.	W(Atl)-'93	15/1
	Reynolds, Ricky	CB	5-11	190	1/19/65	8	Washington State	Sacramento, Calif.	UFA(TB)-'94	14/13*
71	Rucci, Todd	G	6-5	291	7/14/70	2	Penn State	Upper Darby, Pa.	D2b-'93	2/1
32	† Russell, Leonard	RB	6-2	235	11/17/69	4	Arizona State	Long Beach, Calif.	D1b-'91	16/15
95	Sabb, Dwayne	LB	6-4	248	10/9/69	3	New Hampshire	Union, N.J.	D5-'92	14/7
7	Saxon, Mike	P	6-3	202	7/10/62	10	San Diego State	Whittier, Calif	FA-'93	16/0
9	Sisson, Scott	K	6-1	197	7/21/71	2	Georgia Tech	Marietta, Ga.	D5-'93	13/0
68	Skene, Doug	G	6-6	295	6/17/70	2	Michigan	Fairview, Tex.	FA-'93	0*
53	Slade, Chris	LB	6-4	232	1/30/71	2	Virginia	Newport News, Va.	D2a-'93	16/5
22	Smith, Rod	CB	5-11	187	3/12/70	3	Notre Dame	Roseville, Minn.	D2-'92	16/9
66	Staten, Mark	G	6-6	308	10/8/70	2	Miami, Ohio	Dowagiac, Mich.	FA-'93	0*
31	Thomas, Blair	RB	5-10	202	10/7/67	5	Penn State	Philadelphia, Pa.	UFA(NYJ)-'94	11/5*
83	# Timpson, Michael	WR	5-10	175	6/6/67	6	Penn State	Hialeah, Fla.	D4-'89	16/7
34	Turner, Kevin	RB	6-1	224	6/12/69	3	Alabama	Prattville, Ala.	D3b-'92	16/9
76	Washington, John	DE	6-4	290	2/20/63	9	Oklahoma State	Houston, Tex.	UFA(Atl)-'93	16/13
51	White, David	LB	6-2	235	2/27/70	2	Nebraska	New Orleans, La.	W(Buff)-'93	6/0
27	Wren, Darryl	CB	6-1	188	1/25/67	4	Pittsburg State, Kan.	Tulsa, Okla.	W(Buff)-'93	12/5
16	Zolak, Scott	QB	6-5	222	12/13/67	4	Maryland	Monongahela, Pa.	D4-'91	3/0

* Bahr played 11 games with Philadelphia, 3 games with New England in '93; Butts played 16 games with San Diego; DeOssie played 8 games with N.Y. Giants, 7 games with N.Y. Jets; Guyton played 16 games with N.Y. Giants; Kratch played 16 games with N.Y. Giants; Reynolds played 14 games with Tampa Bay; Skene inactive for 8 games; Staten inactive for 9 games; Thomas played 11 games with N.Y. Jets.

\# Unrestricted free agent; subject to developments.

† Restricted free agent; subject to developments.

t- Patriots traded for Butts (San Diego).

Retired—Andre Tippett, 12-year linebacker, 16 games in '93.

Players lost through free agency (2): WR Greg McMurtry (Rams; 16 games in '93), DE Brent Williams (Sea; 13).

Also played with Patriots in '93—G Rich Baldinger (15 games), TE Marv Cook (16), DE Chris Gannon (4), CB Jerome Henderson (1), C Todd Jones (4), RB Scott Lockwood (2), QB Scott Secules (12), LB Chris Singleton (8), CB Reyna Thompson (15), CB S Adrian White (5).

COACHING STAFF

Head Coach,
Bill Parcells

Pro Career: On January 21, 1993, Parcells became the franchise's thirteenth head coach since the Patriots' inception in 1960. He enters the 1994 season on a four-game winning streak. Season-ending victory knocked the Miami Dolphins out of the playoffs and gave the Patriots a fourth-place finish in the AFC East. Parcells made his NFL coaching debut with the New England Patriots as the linebackers coach on Ron Erhardt's staff in 1980. He accepted the same position on the New York Giants staff in 1981 and was named the Giants head coach in 1983. In eight seasons at the helm of the Giants, Parcells led his teams to two Super Bowl championships. His first title came in 1986, with a 39-20 victory over the Denver Broncos. Four years later, the Giants claimed another championship with a 20-19 victory over the Buffalo Bills. On May 15, 1991, health concerns caused Parcells to resign from the Giants. During his two seasons away from coaching, Parcells entertained football audiences from the broadcast booth, in 1991 as a studio analyst and in 1992 as a color commentator for NBC Sports. Career record: 90-63-1.

Background: Linebacker at Wichita State 1961-63. College assistant Hastings (Neb.) 1964, Wichita State 1965, Army 1966-69, Florida State 1970-72, Vanderbilt 1973-74, Texas Tech 1975-77, Air Force 1978 (head coach).

Personal: Born August 22, 1941, Englewood, N.J. Bill and his wife, Judy, live in Foxboro, Mass., and have three daughters—Suzy, Jill, and Dallas.

ASSISTANT COACHES

Maurice Carthon, offensive assistant; born April 24, 1961, Chicago, Ill., lives in Foxboro, Mass. Running back Arkansas State 1979-82. Pro running back New Jersey Generals (USFL) 1983-85, New York Giants 1985-91, Indianapolis Colts 1992. Pro coach: Joined Patriots in 1994.

Romeo Crennel, defensive line; born June 18, 1947, Lynchburg, Va., lives in Foxboro, Mass. Defensive tackle, linebacker Western Kentucky 1966-69. No pro playing experience. College coach: Western Kentucky 1970-74, Texas Tech 1975-77, Mississippi 1978-79, Georgia Tech 1980. Pro coach: New York Giants 1981-92, joined Patriots in 1993.

Al Groh, defensive coordinator; born July 13, 1944, New York City, lives in Foxboro, Mass. Defensive end Virginia 1964-67. No pro playing experience. College coach: Army 1968-69, Virginia 1970-72, North Carolina 1973-77, Air Force 1978-79, Texas Tech 1980, Wake Forest 1981-86 (head coach), South Carolina 1988. Pro coach: Atlanta Falcons 1987, New York Giants 1989-91, Cleveland Browns 1992, joined Patriots in 1993.

Fred Hoaglin, offensive line; born January 28, 1944, Alliance, Ohio, lives in Cumberland, R.I. Center Pittsburgh 1962-65. Pro center Cleveland Browns 1966-72, Baltimore Colts 1973, Houston Oilers 1974-75, Seattle Seahawks 1976. Pro coach: Detroit Lions 1978-84, New York Giants 1985-92, joined Patriots in 1993.

Chris Palmer, wide receivers; born September 23, 1949, Mt. Kisco, N.Y., lives in Foxboro, Mass. Quarterback Southern Connecticut State 1968-71. No pro playing experience. College coach: Connecticut 1972-74, Lehigh 1975, Colgate 1976-82, New Haven 1986-87 (head coach), Boston University 1988-89 (head coach). Pro coach: Montreal Concordes (CFL) 1983, New Jersey Generals (USFL) 1984-85, Houston Oilers 1990-92, joined Patriots in 1993.

Johnny Parker, strength and conditioning; born February 1, 1947, Greenville, S.C., lives in Foxboro, Mass. Graduate of Mississippi, master's degree from Delta State University. No college or pro playing experience. College coach: South Carolina 1974-76, Indiana 1977-79, Louisiana State 1980, Mississippi 1981-83. Pro coach: New York Giants 1984-92, joined Patriots in 1993.

Ray Perkins, offensive coordinator, born November 6, 1941, Mount Olive, Miss., lives in Foxboro, Mass.

1994 FIRST-YEAR ROSTER

Name	Pos.	Ht.	Wt.	Birthdate	College	Hometown	How Acq.
Ballard, Gregory	WR	6-3	190	5/5/71	Kansas	Lawrence, Kan.	FA
Barnett, Troy	DE	6-4	282	5/24/71	North Carolina	Jacksonville, N.C.	FA
Basham, Bernard	DE	6-6	281	6/23/71	Virginia Tech	Roanoke, Va.	FA
Botkin, Kirk	TE	6-2	233	3/19/71	Arkansas	Baytown, Tex.	FA
Boyd, Jean	S	5-11	185	6/12/71	Arizona State	Paramount, Calif.	FA
Burch, Joe	C	6-2	278	8/8/71	Texas Southern	Dallas, Tex.	D3b
Burke, John	TE	6-3	258	9/7/71	Virginia Tech	Holmdel, N.J.	D4
Collier, Ervin	NT	6-3	287	5/12/71	Florida A&M	Jacksonville, Fla.	D3a
Dixon, Todd	WR	5-10	175	6/8/71	Wake Forest	Billerica, Mass.	FA
Durkin, Bill	G	6-5	281	3/18/71	Massachusetts	Stratford, Conn.	FA
Glenn, Kevin	WR	6-1	166	10/5/71	Illinois State	Brandon, Fla.	FA
Green, Damacio	CB	5-10	183	2/1/71	Virginia State	Miami, Fla.	FA
Hawkins, Steve	WR	6-5	207	3/16/71	Western Michigan	Detroit, Mich.	D6a
Harris, Ronnie (1)	WR	5-10	170	6/4/70	Oregon	San Jose, Calif.	FA
Henry, Mario	WR	6-1	184	9/14/71	Rutgers	Medford, N.J.	FA
Hooks, Bryan (1)	DE	6-3	286	9/15/70	Arizona State	Tempe, Ariz.	FA
Kerr, Mike (1)	LB	6-5	236	10/10/69	Florida	Miami, Fla.	FA
Lane, Max	T	6-6	295	2/22/71	Navy	Norborne, Mo.	D6b
Lee, Kevin	WR	6-1	194	1/1/71	Alabama	Mobile, Ala.	D2
McGinest, Willie	LB	6-4	255	12/11/71	Southern California	Long Beach, Calif.	D1
Moore, Marty	LB	6-1	242	3/19/71	Kentucky	Ft. Thomas, Ky.	D7b
O'Neill, Pat	P-K	6-1	195	2/9/71	Syracuse	Harrisburg, Pa.	D5
Reynolds, Don (1)	DE	6-3	278	11/25/69	Virginia	Axton, Va.	FA
Stanley, Sylvester	NT	6-2	283	5/14/70	Michigan	Youngstown, Ohio	FA
Stephens, Eric	CB	5-10	170	12/19/70	Jacksonville State	Walterboro, S.C.	FA
Tylski, Rich	G	6-4	287	2/27/71	Utah State	San Diego, Calif.	FA
Walker, Jay	QB	6-3	230	1/24/72	Howard	Los Angeles, Calif.	D7a
Washington, Jerrod	RB	6-1	205	3/10/72	Virginia	Philadelphia, Pa.	FA
Witherspoon, Derrick	RB	5-10	198	2/14/71	Clemson	Sumter, S.C.	FA

The term NFL Rookie is defined as a player who is in his first season of professional football and has not been on the roster of another professional football team for any regular-season or postseason games. A Rookie is designated by an "R" on NFL rosters. Players who have been active in another professional football league or players who have NFL experience, including either preseason training camp or being on an Active List or Inactive List, or on Reserve/Injured or Reserve/Physically Unable to Perform for fewer than six regular-season games, are termed NFL First-Year Players. An NFL First-Year Player is designated by a "1" on NFL rosters. Thereafter, a player is credited with an additional year of experience for each season in which he accumulates six games on the Active List or Inactive List, or on Reserve/Injured or Reserve/Physically Unable to Perform.

NOTES

Wide receiver Alabama 1964-66. Pro receiver Baltimore Colts 1967-71. College coach: Mississippi State 1973, Alabama 1983-86 (head coach), Arkansas State 1992 (head coach). Pro coach: New England Patriots 1974-77, San Diego Chargers 1978, New York Giants 1979-82 (head coach), Tampa Bay Buccaneers 1987-90 (head coach), rejoined Patriots in 1993.

Michael Pope, running backs; born March 15, 1942, Monroe, N.C., lives in Foxboro, Mass. Quarterback Lenoir Rhyne 1962-64. No pro playing experience. College coach: Florida State 1970-74, Texas Tech 1975-77, Mississippi 1978-82. Pro coach: New York Giants 1983-91, Cincinnati Bengals 1992-93, joined Patriots in 1994.

Dante Scarnecchia, special assistant, born February 15, 1948, Los Angeles, Calif., lives in Wrentham, Mass. Center-guard California Western 1968-70. No pro playing experience. College coach: California Western (now U.S. International) 1970-72, Iowa State 1973, Southern Methodist 1975-76, 1980-81, Pacific 1977-78, Northern Arizona 1979. Pro coach: New England Patriots 1982-89, Indianapolis Colts 1990, rejoined Patriots in 1991.

Mike Sweatman, special teams, born October 23, 1947, Kansas City, Mo., lives in Foxboro, Mass. Linebacker Kansas 1964-67. No pro playing experience. College coach: Kansas 1973-74, 1979-82, Tulsa 1977-78, Tennessee 1983. Pro coach: Minnesota Vikings 1984, New York Giants 1985-92, joined Patriots in 1993.

Bob Trott, defensive backs, born March 19, 1954, Kannapolis, N.C., lives in Franklin, Mass. Defensive back North Carolina 1973-75. No pro playing experience. College coach: North Carolina 1976-77, Air Force 1978-83, Arkansas 1984-89, Clemson 1990. Pro coach: New York Giants 1990-92, joined Patriots in 1993.

Charlie Weis, tight ends, born March 30, 1956, Trenton, N.J., lives in Foxboro, Mass. Graduate of Notre Dame. No college or pro playing experience. College coach: South Carolina 1985-88. Pro coach: New York Giants 1990-92, joined Patriots in 1993.

NEW YORK JETS

American Football Conference
Eastern Division
Team Colors: Kelly Green and White
1000 Fulton Avenue
Hempstead, New York 11550
Telephone: (516) 538-6600

CLUB OFFICIALS
Chairman of the Board: Leon Hess
President: Steve Gutman
V.P./General Manager: Dick Steinberg
Director of Player Personnel: Dick Haley
Assistant General Manager: James Harris
Pro Personnel Director: Jim Royer
Assistant Pro Personnel Director: Pat Kirwan
Talent Scouts: Joe Collins, Don Grammer,
   Sid Hall, Ron Nay, Marv Sunderland
College Scouting Coordinator: John Griffin
Director of Public Relations: Frank Ramos
Asst. Director of Public Relations: Brooks Thomas
Public Relations Assistants: Ken Ilchuk,
   Sharon Kelleher, Doug Miller
Travel Coordinator: Kevin Coyle
Treasurer & C.F.O.: Mike Gerstle
Controller: Mike Minarczyk
Director of Operations: Mike Kensil
Exec. Director of Business Operations: Bob Parente
Marketing Manager: Bruce Popko
Ticket Manager: Gerry Parravano
Video Director: Jim Pons
Assistant Video Director: John Seiter
Trainer: Bob Reese
Assistant Trainers: Joe Patten, Darryl Conway
Equipment Manager: Bill Hampton
Assistant Equipment Manager: Clay Hampton
Stadium: Giants Stadium •**Capacity:** 77,121
   East Rutherford, New Jersey 07073
Playing Surface: AstroTurf
Training Center: 1000 Fulton Avenue
   Hempstead, New York 11550

1994 SCHEDULE
PRESEASON
Aug. 5	at Detroit	7:30
Aug. 13	at Philadelphia	7:30
Aug. 20	**New York Giants**	8:00
Aug. 26	at Tampa Bay	7:30

REGULAR SEASON
Sept. 4	at Buffalo	4:00
Sept. 11	**Denver**	4:00
Sept. 18	at Miami	1:00
Sept. 25	**Chicago**	8:00
Oct. 2	at Cleveland	1:00
Oct. 9	**Indianapolis**	1:00
Oct. 16	**New England**	1:00
Oct. 23	Open Date	
Oct. 30	at Indianapolis	4:00
Nov. 6	**Buffalo**	4:00
Nov. 13	at Green Bay	3:00
Nov. 20	at Minnesota	3:00
Nov. 27	**Miami**	1:00
Dec. 4	at New England	1:00
Dec. 10	**Detroit** (Saturday)	12:30
Dec. 18	**San Diego**	1:00
Dec. 24	at Houston	3:00

RECORD HOLDERS
INDIVIDUAL RECORDS—CAREER
Category	Name	Performance
Rushing (Yds.)	Freeman McNeil, 1981-1992	8,074
Passing (Yds.)	Joe Namath, 1965-1976	27,057
Passing (TDs)	Joe Namath, 1965-1976	170
Receiving (No.)	Don Maynard, 1960-1972	627
Receiving (Yds.)	Don Maynard, 1960-1972	11,732
Interceptions	Bill Baird, 1963-69	34
Punting (Avg.)	Curley Johnson, 1961-68	42.8
Punt Return (Avg.)	Dick Christy, 1961-63	16.2
Kickoff Return (Avg.)	Bobby Humphery, 1984-89	22.8
Field Goals	Pat Leahy, 1974-1991	304
Touchdowns (Tot.)	Don Maynard, 1960-1972	88
Points	Pat Leahy, 1974-1991	1,470

INDIVIDUAL RECORDS—SINGLE SEASON
Category	Name	Performance
Rushing (Yds.)	Freeman McNeil, 1985	1,331
Passing (Yds.)	Joe Namath, 1967	4,007
Passing (TDs)	Al Dorow, 1960	26
	Joe Namath, 1967	26
Receiving (No.)	Al Toon, 1988	93
Receiving (Yds.)	Don Maynard, 1967	1,434
Interceptions	Dainard Paulson, 1964	12
Punting (Avg.)	Curley Johnson, 1965	45.3
Punt Return (Avg.)	Dick Christy, 1961	21.3
Kickoff Return (Avg.)	Bobby Humphery, 1984	30.7
Field Goals	Jim Turner, 1968	34
Touchdowns (Tot.)	Art Powell, 1960	14
	Don Maynard, 1965	14
	Emerson Boozer, 1972	14
Points	Jim Turner, 1968	145

INDIVIDUAL RECORDS—SINGLE GAME
Category	Name	Performance
Rushing (Yds.)	Freeman McNeil, 9-15-85	192
Passing (Yds.)	Joe Namath, 9-24-72	496
Passing (TDs)	Joe Namath, 9-24-72	6
Receiving (No.)	Clark Gaines, 9-21-80	17
Receiving (Yds.)	Don Maynard, 11-17-68	228
Interceptions	Many times	3
	Last time by Erik McMillan, 10-23-88	
Field Goals	Jim Turner, 11-3-68	6
	Bobby Howfield, 12-3-72	6
Touchdowns (Tot.)	Wesley Walker, 9-21-86	4
Points	Wesley Walker, 9-21-86	24

COACHING HISTORY
New York Titans 1960-62
(226-277-8)
1960-61	Sammy Baugh	14-14-0
1962	Clyde (Bulldog) Turner	5-9-0
1963-73	Weeb Ewbank	73-78-6
1974-75	Charley Winner*	9-14-0
1975	Ken Shipp	1-4-0
1976	Lou Holtz**	3-10-0
1976	Mike Holovak	0-1-0
1977-82	Walt Michaels	41-49-1
1983-89	Joe Walton	54-59-1
1990-93	Bruce Coslet	26-39-0

*Released after nine games in 1975
**Resigned after 13 games in 1976

GIANTS STADIUM
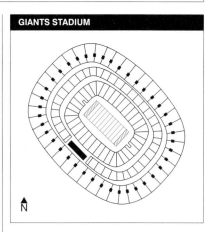

1993 TEAM RECORD

PRESEASON (0-4)

Date	Result		Opponents
8/7	L	13-17	at Pittsburgh
8/13	L	13-24	Philadelphia
8/21	L	13-14	at N.Y. Giants
8/27	L	3-17	at Washington

REGULAR SEASON (8-8)

Date	Result		Opponents	Att.
9/5	L	20-26	Denver	68,130
9/12	W	24-14	at Miami	70,314
9/26	W	45-7	New England	64,836
10/3	L	30-35	Philadelphia	72,593
10/10	L	20-24	at L.A. Raiders	41,627
10/24	L	10-19	Buffalo	71,541
10/31	W	10-6	at N.Y. Giants	71,659
11/7	W	27-10	Miami	71,306
11/14	W	31-17	at Indianapolis	47,351
11/21	W	17-12	Cincinnati	64,264
11/28	W	6-0	at New England	42,810
12/5	L	6-9	Indianapolis	45,799
12/11	W	3-0	at Washington	47,970
12/18	L	7-28	Dallas	73,233
12/26	L	14-16	at Buffalo	70,817
1/2	L	0-24	at Houston	61,040

SCORE BY PERIODS

Jets	65	105	37	63	0	—	270
Opponents	36	77	68	66	0	—	247

ATTENDANCE

Home 531,702 Away 453,588 Total 985,290
Single-game home record, 75,945 (9-20-92)
Single-season home record, 603,619 (1992)

1993 TEAM STATISTICS

	Jets	Opp.
Total First Downs	304	266
Rushing	106	93
Passing	173	161
Penalty	25	12
Third Down: Made/Att	92/220	81/200
Third Down Pct.	41.8	40.5
Fourth Down: Made/Att	10/21	9/19
Fourth Down Pct.	47.6	47.4
Total Net Yards	5212	4712
Avg. Per Game	325.8	294.5
Total Plays	1031	949
Avg. Per Play	5.1	5.0
Net Yards Rushing	1880	1473
Avg. Per Game	117.5	92.1
Total Rushes	521	420
Net Yards Passing	3332	3239
Avg. Per Game	208.3	202.4
Sacked/Yards Lost	21/160	32/195
Gross Yards	3492	3434
Att./Completions	489/294	497/296
Completion Pct.	60.1	59.6
Had Intercepted	12	19
Punts/Avg.	73/38.4	66/43.3
Net Punting Avg.	73/34.4	66/37.6
Penalties/Yards Lost	86/555	86/661
Fumbles/Ball Lost	38/16	30/18
Touchdowns	31	26
Rushing	14	8
Passing	16	15
Returns	1	3
Avg. Time of Possession	32:16	27:44

1993 INDIVIDUAL STATISTICS

PASSING

	Att.	Cmp.	Yds.	Pct.	TD	Int.	Tkld.	Rate
Esiason	473	288	3421	60.9	16	11	18/139	84.5
Nagle	14	6	71	42.9	0	0	3/21	58.9
Aguiar	2	0	0	0.0	0	1	0/0	0.0
Jets	489	294	3492	60.1	16	12	21/160	82.6
Opponents	497	296	3434	59.6	15	19	32/195	74.6

SCORING

	TD R	TD P	TD Rt	PAT	FG	Saf	PTS
Blanchard	0	0	0	31/31	17/26	0	82
B. Baxter	7	0	0	0/0	0/0	0	42
Mitchell	0	6	0	0/0	0/0	0	36
Burkett	0	4	0	0/0	0/0	0	24
J. Johnson	3	1	0	0/0	0/0	0	24
Thornton	0	2	0	0/0	0/0	0	12
F. Baxter	0	1	0	0/0	0/0	0	6
Chaffey	0	1	0	0/0	0/0	0	6
Esiason	1	0	0	0/0	0/0	0	6
Mathis	1	0	0	0/0	0/0	0	6
Moore	0	1	0	0/0	0/0	0	6
Murrell	1	0	0	0/0	0/0	0	6
B. Thomas	1	0	0	0/0	0/0	0	6
B. Washington	0	0	1	0/0	0/0	0	6
Jets	14	16	1	31/31	17/26	1	270
Opponents	8	15	3	26/26	21/26	1	247

Rushing

	Att.	Yds.	Avg.	LG	TD
J. Johnson	198	821	4.1	57t	3
B. Baxter	174	559	3.2	16	7
B. Thomas	59	221	3.7	24	1
Murrell	34	157	4.6	37t	1
Esiason	45	118	2.6	17	1
Mathis	2	20	10.0	17t	1
Chaffey	5	17	3.4	7	0
Moore	1	-6	-6.0	-6	0
Aguiar	3	-27	-9.0	5	0
Jets	521	1880	3.6	57t	14
Opponents	420	1473	3.5	29	8

RECEIVING

	No.	Yds.	Avg.	LG	TD
J. Johnson	67	641	9.6	48	1
Moore	64	843	13.2	51	1
Burkett	40	531	13.3	77	4
Mitchell	39	630	16.2	65t	6
Mathis	24	352	14.7	46	0
B. Baxter	20	158	7.9	24	0
Thornton	12	108	9.0	22	2
B. Thomas	7	25	3.6	7	0
Carpenter	6	83	13.8	18	0
Murrell	5	12	2.4	8	0
Chaffey	4	55	13.8	20t	1
F. Baxter	3	48	16.0	25	1
Sadowski	2	14	7.0	11	0
Esiason	1	-8	-8.0	-8	0
Jets	294	3492	11.9	77	16
Opponents	296	3434	11.6	68t	15

INTERCEPTIONS

	No.	Yds.	Avg.	LG	TD
B. Washington	6	128	21.3	62t	1
Lott	3	35	11.7	29	0
Hasty	2	22	11.0	22	0
E. Thomas	2	20	10.0	20	0
Lewis	2	4	2.0	3	0
Lageman	1	15	15.0	15	0
Young	1	6	6.0	6	0
Clifton	1	3	3.0	3	0
Houston	1	0	0.0	0	0
Jets	19	233	12.3	62t	1
Opponents	12	310	25.8	94t	3

PUNTING

	No.	Yds.	Avg.	In 20	LG
Aguiar	73	2806	38.4	21	71
Jets	73	2806	38.4	21	71
Opponents	66	2859	43.3	17	68

PUNT RETURNS

	No.	FC	Yds.	Avg.	LG	TD
Hicks	17	4	157	9.2	20	0
Mathis	14	8	99	7.1	16	0
Jets	31	12	256	8.3	20	0
Opponents	26	12	156	6.0	36	0

KICKOFF RETURNS

	No.	Yds.	Avg.	LG	TD
Murrell	23	342	14.9	23	0
Prior	9	126	14.0	27	0
Mathis	7	102	14.6	28	0
R. Anderson	4	66	16.5	22	0
B. Thomas	2	39	19.5	28	0
Sadowski	1	0	0.0	0	0
Jets	46	675	14.7	28	0
Opponents	47	911	19.4	45	0

SACKS

	No.
Lageman	8.5
M. Washington	5.5
Lewis	4.0
Houston	3.0
Marshall	2.0
Clifton	1.0
Frase	1.0
D. Jones	1.0
Lott	1.0
Mersereau	1.0
Turner	1.0
Young	1.0
Team	2.0
Jets	32.0
Opponents	21.0

1994 DRAFT CHOICES

Round	Name	Pos.	College
1	Aaron Glenn	DB	Texas A&M
2	Ryan Yarborough	WR	Wyoming
3	Lou Benfatti	DT	Penn State
4	Orlando Parker	WR	Troy State
5	Horace Morris	LB	Tennessee
6	Fred Lester	RB	Alabama A&M
7	Glenn Foley	QB	Boston College

NEW YORK JETS

1994 VETERAN ROSTER

No.	Name	Pos.	Ht.	Wt.	Birthdate	NFL Exp.	College	Hometown	How Acq.	'93 Games/ Starts
20	Anderson, Richie	RB	6-2	215	9/13/71	2	Penn State	Sandy Spring, Md.	D6-'93	7/0
98	Barber, Kurt	LB	6-4	241	1/5/69	3	Southern California	Paducah, Ky.	D2-'92	13/0
6	Baumann, Charlie	K	6-1	200	8/25/67	3	West Virginia	Erie, Pa.	FA-'94	0*
30	Baxter, Brad	RB	6-1	235	5/5/67	5	Alabama State	Slocomb, Ala.	FA-'89	16/13
84	Baxter, Fred	TE	6-3	250	6/14/71	2	Auburn	Brundidge, Ala.	D5a-'93	7/0
9	Blake, Jeff	QB	6-0	202	12/4/70	3	East Carolina	Sanford, Fla.	D6b-'92	0*
10	Blanchard, Cary	K	6-1	225	11/5/68	3	Oklahoma State	Hurst, Tex.	W(NO)-'92	16/0
76	Brown, James	T	6-6	321	1/3/70	2	Virginia State	Philadelphia, Pa.	W(Ind)-'92	14/1
66	# Cadigan, Dave	G	6-4	285	4/6/65	7	Southern California	Newport Beach, Calif.	D1-'88	16/16
50	Cadrez, Glenn	LB	6-3	240	1/2/70	3	Houston	El Centro, Calif.	D6a-'92	16/0
82	Carpenter, Rob	WR	6-2	190	8/1/68	4	Syracuse	Amityville, N.Y.	PB(NE)-'92	16/0
28	Chaffey, Pat	RB	6-1	220	4/19/67	4	Oregon State	Aurora, Ore.	PB(Atl)-'92	3/0
59	Clifton, Kyle	LB	6-4	236	8/23/62	11	Texas Christian	Bridgeport, Tex.	D3-'84	16/16
69	Criswell, Jeff	T	6-7	291	3/7/64	7	Graceland, Iowa	Searsboro, Iowa	FA-'88	16/16
52	Dixon, Cal	C	6-4	284	10/11/69	3	Florida	Merritt Island, Fla.	D5-'92	16/0
62	Duffy, Roger	G-C	6-3	285	7/16/67	5	Penn State	Canton, Ohio	D8-'90	16/1
7	Esiason, Boomer	QB	6-5	220	4/17/61	11	Maryland	East Islip, N.Y.	T(Cin)-'93	16/16
60	Evans, Donald	DT-DE	6-2	282	3/14/64	7	Winston-Salem State	Raleigh, N.C.	UFA(Pitt)-'94	16/16*
91	Frase, Paul	DT-DE	6-5	270	5/5/65	6	Syracuse	Barrington, N.H.	D6-'88	16/4
21	Green, Victor	CB	5-9	195	12/8/69	2	Akron	Americus, Ga.	FA-'93	11/0
96	† Gunn, Mark	DT-DE	6-5	279	7/24/68	4	Pittsburgh	Cleveland, Ohio	D4-'91	12/0
11	Hansen, Brian	P	6-4	215	10/26/60	10	Sioux Falls	Hawarden, Iowa	UFA(Clev)-'94	16/0*
40	Hasty, James	CB	6-0	201	5/23/65	7	Washington State	Seattle, Wash.	D3b-'88	16/16
55	Houston, Bobby	LB	6-2	239	10/26/67	4	North Carolina State	Hyattsville, Md.	PB(Atl)-'91	16/14
39	Johnson, Johnny	RB	6-3	220	6/11/68	5	San Jose State	Santa Cruz, Calif.	T(Phx)-'93	15/9
49	Johnson, Troy	LB	6-2	236	11/10/64	6	Oklahoma	Houston, Tex.	FA-'94	0*
54	Jones, Marvin	LB	6-2	240	6/28/72	2	Florida State	Miami, Fla.	D1-'93	9/0
56	Lageman, Jeff	DE	6-5	266	7/18/67	6	Virginia	Great Falls, Va.	D1-'89	16/16
57	Lewis, Mo	LB	6-3	250	10/21/69	4	Georgia	Peachtree, Ga.	D3-'91	16/16
42	Lott, Ronnie	S	6-1	203	5/8/59	14	Southern California	Rialto, Calif.	UFA(Raid)-'93	16/16
75	Malamala, Siupeli	T	6-5	308	1/15/69	3	Washington	Kalaheo, Hawaii	D3-'92	15/15
70	Marshall, Leonard	DT	6-4	288	10/22/61	12	Louisiana State	Franklin, La.	UFA(NYG)-'93	12/12
86	Mitchell, Johnny	TE	6-3	237	1/20/71	3	Nebraska	Chicago, Ill.	D1-'92	14/14
81	Monk, Art	WR	6-3	210	12/5/57	15	Syracuse	White Plains, N.Y.	FA-'94	16/5*
85	† Moore, Rob	WR	6-3	205	9/27/68	5	Syracuse	Hempstead, N.Y.	SD1-'90	13/13
29	Murrell, Adrian	RB	5-11	205	10/16/70	2	West Virginia	Wahiawa, Hawaii	D5b-'93	16/0
95	Oglesby, Alfred	DT	6-4	276	1/27/67	4	Houston	Weimer, Tex.	FA-'94	0*
71	# Pickel, Bill	DT	6-5	265	11/5/59	12	Rutgers	Maspeth, N.Y.	PB(Raid)-'91	16/3
37	Prior, Anthony	CB-S	5-11	185	3/27/70	2	Washington State	Riverside, Calif.	FA-'93	16/0
92	Rudolph, Coleman	DE-DT	6-4	270	10/22/70	2	Georgia Tech	Valdosta, Ga.	D2-'93	4/0
53	Sweeney, Jim	C-G	6-4	286	8/8/62	11	Pittsburgh	Pittsburgh, Pa.	D2a-'84	16/16
27	Terrell, Pat	S	6-2	210	3/18/68	5	Notre Dame	St. Petersburg, Fla.	UFA(Rams)-'94	13/3*
80	Thornton, James	TE	6-2	242	2/8/65	7	Cal State-Fullerton	Santa Rosa, Calif.	UFA(Chi)-'93	13/6
16	Trudeau, Jack	QB	6-3	227	9/9/62	9	Illinois	Livermore, Calif.	FA-'94	5/5*
23	Turner, Marcus	CB-S	6-0	190	1/13/66	6	UCLA	Long Beach, Calif.	PB(Phx)-'92	16/0
68	Ware, David	G-T	6-6	285	2/21/70	2	Virginia	Roanoke, Va.	D4-'93	0*
48	Washington, Brian	S	6-1	206	9/10/65	6	Nebraska	Richmond, Va.	W(Clev)-'89	16/16
97	Washington, Marvin	DE	6-6	272	10/22/65	6	Idaho	Dallas, Tex.	D6a-'89	16/16
67	White, Dwayne	G	6-2	315	2/10/67	5	Alcorn State	Philadelphia, Pa.	D7a-'90	15/15
22	Williams, Perry	CB	6-2	203	5/12/61	12	North Carolina State	Rockingham, N.C.	UFA(NYG)-'94	8/6*
77	Willig, Matt	T	6-8	305	1/21/69	2	Southern California	Santa Fe Springs, Calif.	FA-'92	3/0
31	# Young, Lonnie	S-CB	6-1	196	7/18/63	10	Michigan State	Flint, Mich.	T(Phx)-'91	9/2

* Baumann last active with New England in '92; Blake and Ware inactive for 16 games; Evans played 16 games with Pittsburgh in '93; Hansen played 16 games with Cleveland; T. Johnson last active with Detroit in '92; Monk played 16 games with Washington; Ogelsby inactive for 1 game; Terrell played 13 games with L.A. Rams; Trudeau played 5 games with Indianapolis; Williams played 8 games with N.Y. Giants.

\# Unrestricted free agent; subject to developments.

† Restricted free agent; subject to developments.

Retired—Chris Burkett, 9-year veteran wide receiver, 16 games in '93.

Players lost through free agency (4): LB Steve DeOssie (NE; 7 games in '93), WR-KR Terance Mathis (Atl; 16), TE Troy Sadowski (Cin; 13), RB Blair Thomas (NE; 11).

Also played with Jets in '93—P Louie Aguiar (16 games), WR Dale Dawkins (4), CB-KR Clifford Hicks (10), LB Don Jones (6), LB Mike Merriweather (1), DT Scott Mersereau (13), QB Browning Nagle (3), S Damon Pieri (5), CB Eric Thomas (16), DT-DE Karl Wilson (5).

COACHING STAFF

Head Coach,
Pete Carroll

Pro Career: Became New York's ninth head coach on January 7, 1994. Carroll, one of the most respected young coaches in the NFL, spent the past four seasons as the Jets' defensive coordinator. His aggressive, attacking schemes helped turn the Jets' defense into one of the NFL's finest units. Carroll entered the pro ranks as defensive backs coach with the Buffalo Bills in 1984. He coached the Minnesota Vikings defensive backs from 1985-89. Carroll joined the Jets in 1990.

Background: Defensive back at the University of the Pacific from 1969-72. No pro playing experience. College coach: Arkansas 1977, Iowa State 1978, Ohio State 1979, North Carolina State 1980-82, Pacific 1983.

Personal: Born September 15, 1951, in San Francisco. Pete and his wife, Glena, live on Long Island, and have three children—Brennan, Nathan, and Jaime.

ASSISTANT COACHES

Larry Beightol, offensive line; born November 21, 1942, Morrisdale, Pa., lives on Long Island. Guard-linebacker Catawba College 1961-63. No pro playing experience. College coach: William & Mary 1968-71, North Carolina State 1972-75, Auburn 1976, Arkansas 1977-78, 1980-82, Louisiana Tech 1979 (head coach), Missouri 1983-84. Pro coach: Atlanta Falcons 1985-86, Tampa Bay Buccaneers 1987-88, San Diego Chargers 1989, joined Jets in 1990.

Don Breaux, tight ends; born August 3, 1940, Jennings, La., lives on Long Island. Quarterback McNeese State 1959-61. Pro quarterback Denver Broncos 1963, San Diego Chargers 1964-65. College coach: Florida State 1966-67, Arkansas 1968-71, 1977-80, Florida 1973-74, Texas 1975-76. Pro coach: Washington Redskins 1981-1993, joined Jets in 1994.

Larry Coyer, defensive line; born April 19, 1943, Huntington, W. Va., lives on Long Island. Quarterback-defensive back Marshall 1961-65. No pro playing experience. College coach: Marshall 1965-67, Bowling Green 1973, Iowa 1974-77, Oklahoma State 1978, Iowa State 1979-83, UCLA 1987-89, Houston 1990, Ohio State 1991-92, East Carolina 1993. Pro coach: Michigan Panthers (USFL) 1984-85, Memphis Showboats (USFL) 1986, joined Jets in 1994.

Ed Donatell, defensive backs; born February 4, 1957, Akron, Ohio, lives on Long Island. Safety Glenville State 1975-78. No pro playing experience. College coach: Kent State 1979-80, Washington 1981-82, Pacific 1983-85, Idaho 1986-88, Cal State-Fullerton 1989. Pro coach: Joined Jets in 1990.

Foge Fazio, linebackers; born February 28, 1939, Dawmont, W.Va., lives on Long Island. Linebacker-center Pittsburgh 1957-60. No pro playing experience. College coach: Boston University 1967, Harvard 1968, Pittsburgh 1969-72, 1977-81, 1982-85 (head coach), Cincinnati 1973-76, Notre Dame 1986-87. Pro coach: Atlanta Falcons 1988-89, joined Jets in 1990.

Walt Harris, quarterbacks; born November 9, 1946, Modesto, Calif., lives on Long Island. Defensive back Pacific 1966-67. No pro playing experience. College coach: Pacific 1970-73, 1989-91 (head coach), California 1974-77, Michigan State 1978-79, Illinois 1980-82, Tennessee 1983-88. Pro coach: Joined Jets in 1992.

Greg Mackrides, strength and conditioning; born July 9, 1954, Philadelphia, Pa., lives on Long Island. No college or pro playing experience. College coach: Villanova 1984-85, Fairfield 1986-88. U.S. Olympic Wrestling team 1988, U.S. Pan American and World touring teams 1986-88. Pro coach: New York Knicks (NBA) 1987-90, joined Jets in 1990.

Richard Mann, receivers; born April 20, 1947, Aliquippa, Pa., lives on Long Island. Wide receiver Arizona State 1966-68. No pro playing experience. College coach: Arizona State 1974-79, Louisville 1980-81. Pro coach: Baltimore/Indianapolis Colts 1982-84, Cleveland Browns 1985-93, joined Jets in 1994.

Greg Robinson, defensive coordinator; born October 9, 1951, Los Angeles, Calif., lives on Long Island. Linebacker-tight end Pacific 1972-73. No pro playing experience. College coach: Cal State-Fullerton 1977-79, North Carolina State 1980-81, UCLA 1982-89. Pro coach: Joined Jets in 1990.

Johnny Roland, running backs; born May 21, 1943, Corpus Christi, Tex., lives on Long Island. Running back Missouri 1963-65. Pro running back St. Louis Cardinals 1966-72, New York Giants 1973. College coach: Notre Dame 1975. Pro coach: Green Bay Packers 1974, Philadelphia Eagles 1976-78, Chicago Bears 1983-92, joined Jets in 1993.

Brad Seely, special teams; born September 6, 1956, Vinton, Iowa, lives on Long Island. Tackle-guard South Dakota State 1974-77. No pro playing experience. College coach: Colorado State 1980, Southern Methodist 1981, North Carolina State 1982, Pacific 1983, Oklahoma State 1984-88. Pro coach: Indianapolis Colts 1989-93, joined Jets in 1994.

Ray Sherman, offensive coordinator; born November 27, 1951, Berkeley, Calif., lives on Long Island. Wide receiver Laney, Calif., J.C. 1969-70, Fresno State 1971-72. Pro defensive back Green Bay Packers 1973. College coach: San Jose State 1974, California 1975, 1981, Michigan State 1976-77, Wake Forest 1978-80, Purdue 1982-85, Georgia 1986-87. Pro coach: Houston Oilers 1988-89, Atlanta Falcons 1990, San Francisco 49ers 1991-93, joined Jets in 1994.

Steve Trimble, defensive assistant-quality control; born May 11, 1958, Cumberland, Md., lives on Long Island. Defensive back Maryland 1976-80. Pro defensive back Denver Broncos 1981-1983, Denver Gold (USFL) 1984-85, Chicago Bears 1987. College coach: New Mexico Highlands 1986-87, Colorado 1988-90, Howard 1991-92. Pro coach: Detroit Drive (Arena League) 1988-89, Cincinnati Rockers (Arena League) 1993, joined Jets in 1994.

Sparky Woods, offensive assistant; born December 20, 1953, Oneida, Tenn., lives on Long Island. Quarterback-defensive back Carson-Newman 1972-75. No pro playing experience. College coach: Tennessee 1976, Kansas 1977, North Alabama 1978, Iowa State 1979-82, Appalachian State 1983, 1984-88, South Carolina 1989-93 (head coach). Pro coach: Joined Jets in 1994.

1994 FIRST-YEAR ROSTER

Name	Pos.	Ht.	Wt.	Birthdate	College	Hometown	How Acq.
Adams, Kyle	G	6-4	290	5/7/71	Syracuse	Webster, N.Y.	FA
Alipate, Tuineau (1)	LB	6-1	234	8/21/67	Washington State	Union City, Calif.	FA
Allen, Alan	WR	6-1	191	8/9/71	Idaho	Tacoma, Wash.	FA
Anderson, Mike	LB	6-0	235	10/5/70	Nebraska	Grand Island, Neb.	FA
Anderson, Stevie (1)	WR	6-5	205	5/12/70	Grambling	Jonesboro, La.	FA
Ball, LaVar	TE	6-5	273	10/23/68	Cal State-Los Angeles	Canoga Park, Calif.	FA
Beckford, Gary	CB-S	5-11	200	10/18/72	Bowie State	Wheaton, Md.	FA
Benfatti, Lou	DT	6-4	280	3/9/71	Penn State	Green Pond, N.J.	D3
Burke, Paul	TE	6-3	248	2/16/67	Idaho	Detroit, Mich.	FA
Chapman, Lindsey	RB	5-8	197	1/1/71	California	Marrero, La.	FA
Cooke, Jeff	DT	6-1	271	6/3/71	East Carolina	Sanford, N.C.	FA
Crisp, Jackie	T	6-7	296	7/18/72	Colorado Mines	Cheyenne, Wyo.	FA
Davis, Rob (1)	DT	6-3	275	12/10/68	Shippensburg State	District Heights, Md.	FA
Doggette, Cecil (1)	CB-S	5-8	185	11/15/70	West Virginia	Queens, N.Y.	FA
Fisher, Bill	DT	6-2	278	7/30/70	Rowan	Cherry Hill, N.J.	FA
Foley, Glenn	QB	6-2	205	10/10/70	Boston College	Cherry Hill, N.J.	D7
Glenn, Aaron	CB-S	5-9	185	9/16/72	Texas A&M	Aldine, Tex.	D1
Hales, Ross	TE	6-6	262	10/20/70	Indiana	Elkhart, Ind.	FA
Lester, Fred	RB	6-0	241	8/1/71	Alabama A&M	Miami, Fla.	D6
McIver, Everett (1)	T	6-6	309	8/5/70	Elizabeth City State	Fayetteville, N.C.	FA
Mitter, Craig (1)	RB	5-9	200	1/25/70	Rutgers	Matawan, N.J.	FA
Morris, Horace	LB	6-2	230	5/29/71	Tennessee	Miami, Fla.	D5
Nelson, Chico	CB-S	6-0	200	12/25/69	Ohio State	Sarasota, Fla.	FA
Papasedero, Fran	DT	6-2	275	3/2/69	Springfield	Boston, Mass.	FA
Parker, Orlando	WR	5-11	183	3/7/72	Troy State	Montgomery, Ala.	D4
Pieri, Damon (1)	S	6-0	186	9/25/70	San Diego State	Phoenix, Ariz.	FA
Shale, Cris (1)	P	6-0	200	6/27/68	Bowling Green	Beaver Creek, Ohio	FA
Shedd, Kenny (1)	WR-KR	5-9	166	2/14/71	Northern Iowa	Davenport, Iowa	D5c-'93
Solari, Steve	LB	6-0	235	2/25/71	Texas A&M	Houston, Tex.	FA
Trice, Robert	RB	5-10	204	5/21/70	Cal State-Northridge	Burgaw, N.C.	FA
Wisdom, Terrence (1)	G	6-4	305	12/4/71	Syracuse	Roosevelt, N.Y.	FA
Yarborough, Ryan	WR	6-2	195	4/26/71	Wyoming	Park Forest, Ill.	D2
Yatkowski, Paul	DT	6-2	278	11/18/70	Tennessee	Winnipeg, Canada	FA

The term NFL Rookie is defined as a player who is in his first season of professional football and has not been on the roster of another professional football team for any regular-season or postseason games. A Rookie is designated by an "R" on NFL rosters. Players who have been active in another professional football league or players who have NFL experience, including either preseason training camp or being on an Active List or Inactive List, or on Reserve/Injured or Reserve/Physically Unable to Perform for fewer than six regular-season games, are termed NFL First-Year Players. An NFL First-Year Player is designated by a "1" on NFL rosters. Thereafter, a player is credited with an additional year of experience for each season in which he accumulates six games on the Active List or Inactive List, or on Reserve/Injured or Reserve/Physically Unable to Perform.

NOTES

American Football Conference
Central Division
Team Colors: Black and Gold
Three Rivers Stadium
300 Stadium Circle
Pittsburgh, Pennsylvania 15212
Telephone: (412) 323-1200

CLUB OFFICIALS

President: Daniel M. Rooney
Vice President: John R. McGinley
Vice President: Arthur J. Rooney, Jr.
Secretary and Counsel: Arthur J. Rooney II
Administration Advisor: Charles H. Noll
Director of Communications: Joe Gordon
Public Relations Coordinator: Rob Boulware
P.R. Assistant/Community Relations: Ron Miller
Controller: Michael J. Hagan
Assistant Controller: Dan Ferens
Assistant Controller: Jim Ellenberger
Director of Football Operations: Tom Donahoe
Football Business Manager: James A. Boston
College Personnel Coordinator: Tom Modrak
Pro Personnel Coordinator: Charles Bailey
College Scouts: Phil Kreidler, Bob Lane,
    Max McCartney, Bob Schmitz
Ticket Sales Manager: Geraldine R. Glenn
Player Development Coordinator: Anthony Griggs
Trainers: John Norwig, Rick Burkholder
Equipment Manager: Anthony Parisi
Field Manager: Rodgers Freyvogel
Stadium: Three Rivers Stadium
    •**Capacity:** 59,600
        300 Stadium Circle
        Pittsburgh, Pennsylvania 15212
Playing Surface: AstroTurf
Training Camp: St. Vincent College
        Latrobe, Pennsylvania 15650

1994 SCHEDULE

PRESEASON

Aug. 6	at Miami	8:00
Aug. 13	**Los Angeles Raiders**	6:00
Aug. 20	**Indianapolis**	6:00
Aug. 26	at Washington	8:00

REGULAR SEASON

Sept. 4	**Dallas**	4:00
Sept. 11	at Cleveland	1:00
Sept. 18	**Indianapolis**	1:00
Sept. 25	at Seattle	1:00
Oct. 3	**Houston** (Monday)	9:00
Oct. 9	Open Date	
Oct. 16	**Cincinnati**	1:00
Oct. 23	at New York Giants	1:00
Oct. 30	at Arizona	6:00
Nov. 6	at Houston	12:00
Nov. 14	**Buffalo** (Monday)	9:00
Nov. 20	**Miami**	1:00
Nov. 27	at Los Angeles Raiders	1:00
Dec. 4	at Cincinnati	1:00
Dec. 11	**Philadelphia**	1:00
Dec. 18	**Cleveland**	1:00
Dec. 24	at San Diego	1:00

RECORD HOLDERS

INDIVIDUAL RECORDS—CAREER

Category	Name	Performance
Rushing (Yds.)	Franco Harris, 1972-1983	11,950
Passing (Yds.)	Terry Bradshaw, 1970-1983	27,989
Passing (TDs)	Terry Bradshaw, 1970-1983	212
Receiving (No.)	John Stallworth, 1974-1987	537
Receiving (Yds.)	John Stallworth, 1974-1987	8,723
Interceptions	Mel Blount, 1970-1983	57
Punting (Avg.)	Bobby Joe Green, 1960-61	45.7
Punt Return (Avg.)	Bobby Gage, 1949-1950	14.9
Kickoff Return (Avg.)	Lynn Chandnois, 1950-56	29.6
Field Goals	Gary Anderson, 1982-1993	285
Touchdowns (Tot.)	Franco Harris, 1972-1983	100
Points	Gary Anderson, 1982-1993	1,239

INDIVIDUAL RECORDS—SINGLE SEASON

Category	Name	Performance
Rushing (Yds.)	Barry Foster, 1992	1,690
Passing (Yds.)	Terry Bradshaw, 1979	3,724
Passing (TDs)	Terry Bradshaw, 1978	28
Receiving (No.)	John Stallworth, 1984	80
Receiving (Yds.)	John Stallworth, 1984	1,395
Interceptions	Mel Blount, 1975	11
Punting (Avg.)	Bobby Joe Green, 1961	47.0
Punt Return (Avg.)	Bobby Gage, 1949	16.0
Kickoff Return (Avg.)	Lynn Chandnois, 1952	35.2
Field Goals	Gary Anderson, 1985	33
Touchdowns (Tot.)	Louis Lipps, 1985	15
Points	Gary Anderson, 1985	139

INDIVIDUAL RECORDS—SINGLE GAME

Category	Name	Performance
Rushing (Yds.)	John Fuqua, 12-20-70	218
Passing (Yds.)	Bobby Layne, 12-3-58	409
Passing (TDs)	Terry Bradshaw, 11-15-81	5
	Mark Malone, 9-8-85	5
Receiving (No.)	J.R. Wilburn, 10-22-67	12
Receiving (Yds.)	Buddy Dial, 10-22-61	235
Interceptions	Jack Butler, 12-13-53	*4
Field Goals	Gary Anderson, 10-23-88	6
Touchdowns (Tot.)	Ray Mathews, 10-17-54	4
	Roy Jefferson, 11-3-68	4
Points	Ray Mathews, 10-17-54	24
	Roy Jefferson, 11-3-68	24

*NFL Record

COACHING HISTORY

Pittsburgh Pirates 1933-1940
(390-426-20)

1933	Forrest (Jap) Douds	3-6-2
1934	Luby DiMelio	2-10-0
1935-36	Joe Bach	10-14-0
1937-39	Johnny Blood (McNally)*	6-19-0
1939-40	Walt Kiesling	3-13-3
1941	Bert Bell**	0-2-0
	Aldo (Buff) Donelli***	0-5-0
1941-44	Walt Kiesling****	13-20-2
1945	Jim Leonard	2-8-0
1946-47	Jock Sutherland	13-10-1
1948-51	Johnny Michelosen	20-26-2
1952-53	Joe Bach	11-13-0
1954-56	Walt Kiesling	14-22-0
1957-64	Raymond (Buddy) Parker	51-48-6
1965	Mike Nixon	2-12-0
1966-68	Bill Austin	11-28-3
1969-91	Chuck Noll	209-156-1
1992-93	Bill Cowher	20-14-0

*Released after three games in 1939
**Resigned after two games in 1941
***Released after five games in 1941
****Co-coach with Earle (Greasy) Neale in Philadelphia-
    Pittsburgh merger in 1943 and with Phil Handler in
    Chicago Cardinals-Pittsburgh merger in 1944

THREE RIVERS STADIUM

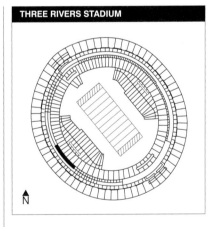

1993 TEAM RECORD

PRESEASON (2-3)

Date	Result		Opponents
8/1	L	14-21	vs. San Francisco at Barcelona
8/7	W	17-13	N.Y. Jets
8/14	W	23-17	at N.Y. Giants
8/22	L	3-10	Washington
8/26	L	13-30	at Minnesota

REGULAR SEASON (9-7)

Date	Result		Opponents	Att.
9/5	L	13-24	San Francisco	57,502
9/12	L	0-27	at L.A. Rams	50,588
9/19	W	34-7	Cincinnati	53,682
9/27	W	45-17	at Atlanta	65,477
10/10	W	16-3	San Diego	55,264
10/17	W	37-14	New Orleans	56,056
10/24	L	23-28	at Cleveland	78,118
11/7	W	24-16	at Cincinnati	51,202
11/15	W	23-0	Buffalo	60,265
11/21	L	13-37	at Denver	74,840
11/28	L	3-23	at Houston	61,238
12/5	W	17-14	New England	51,358
12/13	W	21-20	at Miami	70,232
12/19	L	17-26	Houston	57,592
12/26	L	6-16	at Seattle	51,814
1/2	W	16-9	Cleveland	49,208

POSTSEASON (0-1)

1/8	L	24-27	at Kansas City (OT)	74,515

(OT) Overtime

SCORE BY PERIOD

Steelers	38	110	79	81	0	—	308
Opponents	75	102	40	64	0	—	281

ATTENDANCE

Home 440,927   Away 503,509   Total 944,436
Single-game home record, 60,265 (11-15-93)
Single-season home record, 471,306 (1992)

1993 TEAM STATISTICS

	Steelers	Opp.
Total First Downs	307	267
Rushing	116	74
Passing	180	163
Penalty	11	30
Third Down: Made/Att	92/235	68/201
Third Down Pct.	39.1	33.8
Fourth Down: Made/Att	8/16	4/10
Fourth Down Pct.	50.0	40.0
Total Net Yards	5235	4531
Avg. Per Game	327.2	283.2
Total Plays	1079	962
Avg. Per Play	4.9	4.7
Net Yards Rushing	2003	1368
Avg. Per Game	125.2	85.5
Total Rushes	491	399
Net Yards Passing	3232	3163
Avg. Per Game	202.0	197.7
Sacked/Yards Lost	48/374	42/277
Gross Yards	3606	3440
Att./Completions	540/299	521/277
Completion Pct.	55.4	53.2
Had Intercepted	12	24
Punts/Avg.	89/42.5	82/43.9
Net Punting Avg.	89/34.2	82/38.1
Penalties/Yards Lost	100/861	77/652
Fumbles/Ball Lost	28/15	37/14
Touchdowns	32	30
Rushing	13	6
Passing	16	16
Returns	3	8
Avg. Time of Possession	32:15	27:45

1993 INDIVIDUAL STATISTICS

PASSING	Att.	Cmp.	Yds.	Pct.	TD	Int.	Tkld.	Rate
O'Donnell	486	270	3208	55.6	14	7	41/331	79.5
Tomczak	54	29	398	53.7	2	5	7/43	51.3
Steelers	540	299	3606	55.4	16	12	48/374	76.7
Opponents	521	277	3440	53.2	16	24	42/277	64.9

SCORING	TD R	TD P	TD Rt	PAT	FG	Saf	PTS
Anderson	0	0	0	32/32	28/30	0	116
Foster	8	1	0	0/0	0/0	0	54
Green	0	5	0	0/0	0/0	0	30
Hoge	1	4	0	0/0	0/0	0	30
Stone	1	2	0	0/0	0/0	0	18
Thigpen	0	3	0	0/0	0/0	0	18
Thompson	3	0	0	0/0	0/0	0	18
Davidson	0	0	1	0/0	0/0	0	6
Kirkland	0	0	1	0/0	0/0	0	6
Mills	0	1	0	0/0	0/0	0	6
Woodson	0	0	1	0/0	0/0	0	6
Steelers	13	16	3	32/32	28/30	0	308
Opponents	6	16	8	29/30	24/29	0	281

RUSHING	Att.	Yds.	Avg.	LG	TD
Thompson	205	763	3.7	36	3
Foster	177	711	4.0	38	8
Hoge	51	249	4.9	30	1
Stone	12	121	10.1	38t	1
O'Donnell	26	111	4.3	27	0
Worley	10	33	3.3	8	0
Mills	3	12	4.0	19	0
Cuthbert	1	7	7.0	7	0
Woodson	1	0	0.0	0	0
Tomczak	5	-4	-0.8	2	0
Steelers	491	2003	4.1	38t	13
Opponents	399	1368	3.4	37	6

RECEIVING	No.	Yds.	Avg.	LG	TD
Green	63	942	15.0	71t	5
Stone	41	587	14.3	44	2
Graham	38	579	15.2	51	0
Thompson	38	259	6.8	28	0
Hoge	33	247	7.5	18	4
Mills	29	386	13.3	30	1
Foster	27	217	8.0	21	1
Thigpen	9	154	17.1	39t	3
Cooper	9	112	12.4	38	0
Davenport	4	51	12.8	19	0
Hastings	3	44	14.7	18	0
Worley	3	10	4.0	0	0
Jorden	1	12	12.0	12	0
Cuthbert	1	3	3.0	3	0
Steelers	299	3606	12.1	71t	16
Opponents	277	3440	12.4	66t	16

INTERCEPTIONS	No.	Yds.	Avg.	LG	TD
Woodson	8	138	17.3	63t	1
Perry	4	61	15.3	30	0
Lake	4	31	7.8	26	0
Johnson	3	51	17.0	26	0
G. Jones	2	11	5.5	11	0
Figures	1	78	78.0	78	0
Henry	1	10	10.0	10	0
Davidson	1	6	6.0	6	0
Steelers	24	386	16.1	78	1
Opponents	12	216	18.0	97t	2

PUNTING	No.	Yds.	Avg.	In 20	LG
Royals	89	3781	42.5	28	61
Steelers	89	3781	42.5	28	61
Opponents	82	3600	43.9	23	58

PUNT RETURNS	No.	FC	Yds.	Avg.	LG	TD
Woodson	42	10	338	8.0	39	0
Figures	5	2	15	3.0	6	0
Steelers	47	12	353	7.5	39	0
Opponents	50	16	678	13.6	91t	3

KICKOFF RETURNS	No.	Yds.	Avg.	LG	TD
Woodson	15	294	19.6	44	0
Hastings	12	177	14.8	22	0
Stone	11	168	15.3	30	0
Thompson	4	77	19.3	27	0
Worley	4	85	21.3	26	0
Hoge	3	33	11.0	15	0
Cooper	1	2	2.0	2	0
Thigpen	1	23	23.0	23	0
W. Williams	1	19	19.0	19	0
Steelers	52	878	16.9	44	0
Opponents	54	1165	21.6	97t	1

SACKS	No.
Greene	12.5
Evans	6.5
Lloyd	6.0
Lake	5.0
Brown	3.0
Davidson	2.5
Woodson	2.0
Steed	1.5
Henry	1.0
Kirkland	1.0
G. Williams	1.0
Steelers	42.0
Opponents	48.0

1994 DRAFT CHOICES

Round	Name	Pos.	College
1	Charles Johnson	WR	Colorado
2	Brentson Buckner	DE	Clemson
3	Jason Gildon	LB	Oklahoma State
	Bam Morris	RB	Texas Tech
4	Taase Faumui	DE	Hawaii
5	Myron Bell	DB	Michigan State
	Gary Brown	T	Georgia Tech
6	Jim Miller	QB	Michigan State
	Eric Ravotti	LB	Penn State
7	Brice Abrams	RB	Michigan State

PITTSBURGH STEELERS

1994 VETERAN ROSTER

No.	Name	Pos.	Ht.	Wt.	Birthdate	NFL Exp.	College	Hometown	How Acq.	'93 Games/ Starts
1	Anderson, Gary	K	5-11	179	7/16/59	13	Syracuse	Durban, South Africa	W(Buff)-'82	16/0
50	Barnes, Reggie	LB	6-1	235	10/23/69	2	Oklahoma	Grand Prairie, Tex.	FA-'93	16/0
94	Brown, Chad	LB	6-2	240	7/12/70	2	Colorado	Pasadena, Calif.	D2-'93	16/9
42	Cuthbert, Randy	RB	6-2	225	1/16/70	2	Duke	Chalfont, Pa.	FA-'93	10/0
80	Davenport, Charles	WR	6-3	210	11/22/68	3	North Carolina State	Fayetteville, N.C.	D4-'92	16/0
64	# Davidson, Kenny	DE	6-5	275	8/17/67	5	Louisiana State	Shreveport, La.	D2-'90	16/9
63	Dawson, Dermontti	C	6-2	286	6/17/65	7	Kentucky	Lexington, Ky.	D2-'88	16/16
21	Figures, Deon	CB	6-0	200	1/10/70	2	Colorado	Compton, Calif.	D1-'93	15/4
79	Finn, Mike	T	6-4	290	9/26/67	2	Arkansas-Pine Bluff	Texarkana, Tex.	FA-'92	0*
29	Foster, Barry	RB	5-10	218	12/8/68	5	Arkansas	Duncanville, Tex.	D5-'90	9/9
60	Gammon, Kendall	C-G	6-4	286	10/23/68	3	Pittsburg State	Wichita, Kan.	D11-'92	16/0
86	Green, Eric	TE	6-5	280	6/22/67	5	Liberty	Savannah, Ga.	D1-'90	16/16
91	Greene, Kevin	LB	6-3	247	7/31/62	10	Auburn	Oxford, Ala.	UFA(Rams)-'93	16/16
28	Haller, Alan	CB	5-11	185	8/9/70	2	Michigan State	Lansing, Mich.	FA-'93	4/0
77	Haselrig, Carlton	G	6-1	295	1/22/66	5	Pittsburgh-Johnstown	Johnstown, Pa.	D12-'89	9/4
88	Hastings, Andre	WR	6-0	188	11/7/70	2	Georgia	Atlanta, Ga.	D3-'93	6/0
76	Henry, Kevin	DE	6-4	275	10/23/68	2	Mississippi State	Mound Bayou, Miss.	D4-'93	12/1
65	Jackson, John	T	6-6	297	1/4/65	7	Eastern Kentucky	Cincinnati, Ohio	D10-'88	16/16
25	Jones, Gary	S	6-1	214	11/30/67	5	Texas A&M	Tyler, Tex.	D9-'90	13/2
30	Jones, Victor	RB	5-8	215	12/5/67	5	Louisiana State	Zachary, La.	FA-'93	16/0
84	Jorden, Tim	TE	6-3	240	10/30/66	5	Indiana	Middletown, Ohio	FA-'92	16/1
62	Kalis, Todd	G	6-5	296	5/10/65	7	Arizona State	Phoenix, Ariz.	UFA(Minn)-'94	16/7*
87	Keith, Craig	TE	6-3	262	4/27/71	2	Lenoir-Rhyne	Raleigh, N.C.	D7b-'93	1/0
99	Kirkland, Levon	LB	6-1	252	2/17/69	3	Clemson	Lamar, S.C.	D2-'92	16/13
37	Lake, Carnell	S	6-1	210	7/15/67	6	UCLA	Inglewood, Calif.	D2-'89	14/14
95	Lloyd, Greg	LB	6-2	226	5/26/65	8	Ft. Valley State	Ft. Valley, Ga.	D6b-'87	15/15
67	Love, Duval	G	6-3	288	6/24/63	10	UCLA	Fountain Valley, Calif.	PB(Rams)-'92	16/16
56	Mack, Rico	LB	6-4	239	2/22/71	2	Appalachian State	Statham, Ga.	FA-'93	8/0
89	† Mills, Ernie	WR	5-11	192	10/28/68	4	Florida	Dunnellon, Fla.	D3-'91	14/5
14	O'Donnell, Neil	QB	6-3	230	7/3/66	5	Maryland	Madison, N.J.	D3a-'90	16/15
55	# Olsavsky, Jerry	LB	6-1	224	3/29/67	6	Pittsburgh	Youngstown, Ohio	D10-'89	7/7
66	Palelei, Siulagi	G	6-3	322	10/15/70	2	Nevada-Las Vegas	American Samoa	D5a-'93	3/0
39	Perry, Darren	S	5-11	196	12/29/68	3	Penn State	Deep Creek, Va.	D8a-'92	16/16
3	Royals, Mark	P	6-5	215	6/22/65	5	Appalachian State	Mathews, Va.	PB(TB)-'92	16/0
97	Seals, Ray	DE	6-3	290	6/17/65	7	No College	Syracuse, N.Y.	UFA(TB)-'94	16/11*
72	Searcy, Leon	T	6-3	304	12/21/69	3	Miami	Orlando, Fla.	D1-'92	16/16
24	Shelton, Richard	S	5-10	202	1/2/66	5	Liberty	Marietta, Ga.	FA-'91	9/2
69	Solomon, Ariel	C-G	6-5	290	7/16/68	4	Colorado	Boulder, Colo.	D10-'91	16/0
93	Steed, Joel	NT	6-2	295	2/17/69	3	Colorado	Denver, Colo.	D3-'92	14/12
20	Stone, Dwight	WR-RB	6-0	180	1/28/64	8	Middle Tennessee State	Florala, Ala.	FA-'87	16/15
73	Strzelczyk, Justin	T	6-5	295	8/18/68	5	Maine	Seneca, N.Y.	D11-'90	16/12
96	Sutton, Ricky	DE	6-2	281	4/27/71	2	Auburn	Tucker, Ga.	FA-'93	7/0
82	Thigpen, Yancey	WR	6-1	207	8/15/69	3	Winston-Salem State	Pinetops, N.C.	FA-'92	12/0
34	† Thompson, Leroy	RB	5-11	217	2/3/69	4	Penn State	Knoxville, Tenn.	D6-'91	15/6
18	Tomczak, Mike	QB	6-1	195	10/23/62	10	Ohio State	Calumet City, Ill.	UFA(Clev)-'93	7/1
98	Williams, Gerald	DE	6-3	288	9/8/63	9	Auburn	Lanett, Ala.	D2-'86	10/8
22	Williams, John L.	RB	5-11	231	11/23/64	9	Florida	Palatka, Fla.	UFA(Sea)-'94	16/9*
27	Williams, Willie	CB	5-9	188	12/26/70	2	Western Carolina	Columbia, S.C.	D6-'93	16/0
26	Woodson, Rod	CB	6-0	200	3/10/65	8	Purdue	Fort Wayne, Ind.	D1-'87	16/16
90	Zgonina, Jeff	DT	6-1	284	5/24/70	2	Purdue	Lake Grove, Ill.	D7a-'93	5/0

* Finn active with Steelers for 9 games in '93 but did not play; Kalis played 16 games with Minnesota; Seals played 16 games with Tampa Bay; J.L. Williams played 16 games with Seattle.

\# Unrestricted free agent; subject to developments.

† Restricted free agent; subject to developments.

Traded—TE Adrian Cooper to Minnesota, RB Tim Worley to Chicago, WR Jeff Graham to Chicago.

Retired—LB Bryan Hinkle, 13-year veteran, 12 games in '93.

Players lost through free agency (4): DE Donald Evans (NYJ; 16 games in '93), RB Merril Hoge (Chi; 16), CB D.J. Johnson (Atl; 16), QB Rick Strom (Buff; 0).

Also played with Steelers in '93—TE Adrian Cooper (14 games), G-T Dan Fike (3), WR Jeff Graham (15), S Larry Griffin (12), LB Dave Hoffmann (1), RB Tim Worley (5).

PITTSBURGH STEELERS

COACHING STAFF

Head Coach,
Bill Cowher

Pro Career: Became the fifteenth head coach in Steelers' history on January 21, 1992, succeeding the retired Chuck Noll. Cowher is the second-youngest head coach in the NFL. Named *AP* NFL Coach of the Year in 1992, after becoming one of only 12 coaches in NFL history to win 11 games in his first season. Began his NFL career as a free agent linebacker with the Philadelphia Eagles in 1979, and then signed with the Cleveland Browns the following year. Cowher played three seasons (1980-82) in Cleveland before being traded back to the Eagles, where he played two more years (1983-84). Cowher began his coaching career in 1985 at age 28 under Marty Schottenheimer with the Cleveland Browns. He was the Browns' special teams coach in 1985-86 and secondary coach in 1987-88 before following Schottenheimer to the Kansas City Chiefs in 1989 as defensive coordinator. Career record: 20-14.

Background: Excelled in football, basketball, and track for Carlynton High in Crafton, Pa. Was a three-year starter at linebacker for North Carolina State, serving as captain and earning team MVP honors as senior. Graduated in 1979 with education degree.

Personal: Born in Pittsburgh, Pa., on May 8, 1957. His wife Kaye, also a North Carolina State graduate, played professional basketball for the New York Stars of the Women's Professional Basketball League with twin sister Faye. Bill and Kaye live in Pittsburgh and have three daughters—Meagan Lyn, Lauren Marie, and Lindsay Morgan.

ASSISTANT COACHES

Bobby April, Jr., special teams; born April 15, 1953, New Orleans, La., lives in Pittsburgh. Defensive end/linebacker Nicholls State 1972-75. No pro playing experience. College coach: Tulane 1979, Arizona 1980-86, Southern California 1987-90. Pro coach: Atlanta Falcons 1991-93, joined Steelers in 1994.

Dom Capers, defensive coordinator; born August 7, 1950, Cambridge, Ohio, lives in Pittsburgh. Defensive back Mount Union College 1968-71. No pro playing experience. College coach: Hawaii 1975-76, San Jose State 1977, California 1978-79, Tennessee 1980-81, Ohio State 1982-83. Pro coach: Philadelphia/Baltimore Stars (USFL) 1984-85, New Orleans Saints 1986-91, joined Steelers in 1992.

Ron Erhardt, offensive coordinator; born February 27, 1931, Mandan, N.D., lives in Pittsburgh. Quarterback Jamestown (N.D.) College 1951-54. No pro playing experience. College coach: North Dakota State 1963-72 (head coach 1966-72). Pro coach: New England Patriots 1973-81 (head coach 1979-81), New York Giants 1982-91, joined Steelers in 1992.

Chan Gailey, wide receivers; born January 5, 1952, Gainesville, Ga., lives in Pittsburgh. Quarterback Florida 1970-73. No pro playing experience. College coach: Troy State 1976-78, 1983-84, Air Force 1979-82, Samford (head coach) 1992. Pro coach: Denver Broncos 1985-90, Birmingham Fire (WL) 1991-92, joined Steelers in 1994.

Dick Hoak, running backs; born December 8, 1939, Jeannette, Pa., lives in Greensburg, Pa. Halfback-quarterback Penn State 1958-60. Pro running back Pittsburgh Steelers 1961-70. Pro coach: Joined Steelers in 1972.

Pat Hodgson, tight ends; born January 30, 1944, Columbus, Ga., lives in Pittsburgh. Tight end Georgia 1963-65. Pro tight end Washington Redskins 1966, Minnesota Vikings 1967. College coach: Georgia 1968-70, 1972-77, Florida State 1971, Texas Tech 1978. Pro coach: San Diego Chargers 1978, New York Giants 1979-87, joined Steelers in 1992.

Dick LeBeau, defensive backs; born September 9, 1937, London, Ohio, lives in Pittsburgh. Defensive back-offensive back Ohio State 1954-57. Pro cornerback Detroit Lions 1959-72. Pro coach: Philadelphia Eagles 1972-75, Green Bay Packers 1976-79, Cincinnati Bengals 1980-91, joined Steelers in 1992.

Marvin Lewis, linebackers; born September 23,

1958, McDonald, Pa., lives in Pittsburgh. Linebacker Idaho State 1977-80. No pro playing experience. College coach: Idaho State 1981-84, Long Beach State 1985-86, New Mexico 1987-89, Pittsburgh 1990-91. Pro coach: Joined Steelers in 1992.

John Mitchell, defensive line; born October 15, 1951, Mobile, Ala., lives in Pittsburgh. Defensive end Eastern Arizona J.C. 1969-70, Alabama 1971-72. No pro playing experience. College coach: Alabama 1973-76, Arkansas 1977-82, Temple 1986, Louisiana State 1987-90. Pro coach: Birmingham Stallions (USFL) 1983-85, Cleveland Browns 1991-1993, joined Steelers in 1994.

Kent Stephenson, offensive line; born February 4, 1942, Anita, Iowa, lives in Pittsburgh. Guard-nose tackle Northern Iowa 1962-64. No pro playing experience. College coach: Wayne State 1965-68, North Dakota 1969-71, Southern Methodist 1972-73, Iowa 1974-76, Oklahoma State 1977-78, Kansas 1979-82. Pro coach: Michigan Panthers (USFL) 1983-84, Seattle Seahawks 1985-91, joined Steelers in 1992.

1994 FIRST-YEAR ROSTER

Name	Pos.	Ht.	Wt.	Birthdate	College	Hometown	How Acq.
Abrams, Brice	RB	6-1	258	8/10/71	Michigan State	Detroit, Mich.	FA
Adams, Frank	CB	5-8	176	11/7/70	South Carolina	Gastonia, N.C.	FA
Allen, Andre	C-G	6-0	310	2/28/71	Jacksonville State	Oxford, Ala.	FA
Avery, Steve (1)	RB	6-2	226	8/18/66	Northern Michigan	Brookfield, Wis.	FA
Baker, Mike	WR	6-0	188	1/9/69	West Virginia	Waverly, Ga.	FA
Bell, Myron	S	5-11	203	9/15/71	Michigan State	Toledo, Ohio	D5a
Brown, Gary	T	6-4	288	6/25/71	Georgia Tech	Brentwood, N.Y.	D5b
Buckner, Brentson	DE	6-2	305	9/30/71	Clemson	Columbus, Ga.	D2
Calloway, Dominic	CB	6-0	182	4/24/72	Memphis State	Anniston, Ala.	FA
Dukes, Chuckie (1)	RB	5-9	202	5/16/70	Boston College	Albany, N.Y.	FA
Edwards, Pheathur	DE	6-2	281	1/3/71	Jackson State	Boligee, Ala.	FA
Faumui, Taase	DE	6-3	278	3/19/71	Hawaii	Honolulu, Hawaii	D4
Foggie, Fred (1)	CB-S	6-0	200	6/10/69	Minnesota	Laurens, S.C.	FA
Gildon, Jason	LB	6-3	237	7/31/72	Oklahoma State	Altus, Okla.	D3a
Hoffmann, Dave (1)	LB	6-2	233	7/24/70	Washington	San Jose, Calif.	FA
Holliday, Corey	WR	6-2	208	1/31/71	North Carolina	Richmond, Va.	FA
Johnson, Charles	WR	6-0	189	1/3/72	Colorado	San Bernardino, Calif.	D1
Kelly, Andy (1)	QB	6-3	212	5/6/68	Tennessee	Dayton, Tenn.	FA
Kinsler, Latish	S	6-2	193	8/16/71	Cincinnati	Montclair, N.J.	FA
Miller, Jim	QB	6-2	226	2/9/71	Michigan State	Waterford, Mich.	D6a
Morris, Byron "Bam"	RB	6-0	235	1/13/72	Texas Tech	Cooper, Tex.	D3b
Parker, Curtis	T	6-3	312	3/8/71	North Carolina	Wingate, N.C.	FA
Rasby, Walter	TE	6-3	247	9/7/72	Wake Forest	Washington, N.C.	FA
Ravotti, Eric	LB	6-3	254	3/16/71	Penn State	Freeport, Pa.	D6b
Robinson, Ed	LB	6-0	228	12/7/70	Florida	DeFuniak Springs, Fla.	FA
Scott, Patrick	LB	6-4	229	6/4/71	South Carolina State	Durham, N.C.	FA
Shepherd, Leslie (1)	WR	5-11	189	11/3/69	Temple	Forestville, Md.	FA
Simpson, Tim (1)	G-C	6-2	296	3/5/69	Illinois	Peoria, Ill.	FA
Volpe, Jon (1)	RB	5-7	201	4/17/68	Stanford	Kincheloe, Mich.	FA
Williams, Chris	DE	6-3	281	8/8/70	Hampton	Houston, Tex.	FA

The term NFL Rookie is defined as a player who is in his first season of professional football and has not been on the roster of another professional football team for any regular-season or postseason games. A Rookie is designated by an "R" on NFL rosters. Players who have been active in another professional football league or players who have NFL experience, including either preseason training camp or being on an Active List or Inactive List, or on Reserve/Injured or Reserve/Physically Unable to Perform for fewer than six regular-season games, are termed NFL First-Year Players. An NFL First-Year Player is designated by a "1" on NFL rosters. Thereafter, a player is credited with an additional year of experience for each season in which he accumulates six games on the Active List or Inactive List, or on Reserve/Injured or Reserve/Physically Unable to Perform.

NOTES

SAN DIEGO CHARGERS

American Football Conference
Western Division
Team Colors: Navy Blue, White, and Gold
San Diego Jack Murphy Stadium
P.O. Box 609609
San Diego, California 92160-9609
Telephone: (619) 280-2111

CLUB OFFICIALS

Chairman of the Board/President: Alex G. Spanos
Vice Chairman: Dean A. Spanos
General Manager: Bobby Beathard
Vice President-Finance: Jeremiah T. Murphy
Assistant General Manager: Dick Daniels
Director of Player Personnel: Billy Devaney
Director of Pro Personnel: Rudy Feldman
Director of College Scouting: John Hinek
Coordinator of Football Operations: Marty Hurney
Director of Public Relations: Bill Johnston
Chief Financial Officer: Jeanne Bonk
Business Manager: Pat Curran
Director of Marketing: Rich Israel
Director of Ticket Operations: Joe Scott
Video Director: Gene Leff
Head Trainer: Keoki Kamau
Equipment Manager: Sid Brooks
Stadium: San Diego Jack Murphy Stadium
       Capacity: 60,789
       9449 Friars Road
       San Diego, California 92108
Playing Surface: Grass
Training Camp: University of California-San Diego
       Third College
       La Jolla, California 92037

1994 SCHEDULE

PRESEASON

July 30	vs. Atlanta at Canton, Ohio	12:00
Aug. 6	vs. Houston at San Antonio, Tex.	7:00
Aug. 13	vs. N.Y. Giants at Berlin	1:30
Aug. 18	**San Francisco**	5:00
Aug. 25	**Los Angeles Rams**	7:00

REGULAR SEASON

Sept. 4	at Denver	6:00
Sept. 11	**Cincinnati**	1:00
Sept. 18	at Seattle	1:00
Sept. 25	at Los Angeles Raiders	1:00
Oct. 2	Open Date	
Oct. 9	**Kansas City**	1:00
Oct. 16	at New Orleans	3:00
Oct. 23	**Denver**	1:00
Oct. 30	**Seattle**	1:00
Nov. 6	at Atlanta	1:00
Nov. 13	at Kansas City	12:00
Nov. 20	at New England	1:00
Nov. 27	**Los Angeles Rams**	1:00
Dec. 5	**Los Angeles Raiders** (Monday)	6:00
Dec. 11	**San Francisco**	1:00
Dec. 18	at New York Jets	1:00
Dec. 24	**Pittsburgh**	1:00

RECORD HOLDERS

INDIVIDUAL RECORDS—CAREER

Category	Name	Performance
Rushing (Yds.)	Paul Lowe, 1960-67	4,963
Passing (Yds.)	Dan Fouts, 1973-1987	43,040
Passing (TDs)	Dan Fouts, 1973-1987	254
Receiving (No.)	Charlie Joiner, 1976-1986	586
Receiving (Yds.)	Lance Alworth, 1962-1970	9,585
Interceptions	Gill Byrd, 1983-1992	42
Punting (Avg.)	Ralf Mojsiejenko, 1985-88	42.9
Punt Return (Avg.)	Leslie (Speedy) Duncan, 1964-1970	12.3
Kickoff Return (Avg.)	Leslie (Speedy) Duncan, 1964-1970	25.2
Field Goals	Rolf Benirschke, 1977-1986	146
Touchdowns (Tot.)	Lance Alworth, 1962-1970	83
Points	Rolf Benirschke, 1977-1986	766

INDIVIDUAL RECORDS—SINGLE SEASON

Category	Name	Performance
Rushing (Yds.)	Marion Butts, 1990	1,225
Passing (Yds.)	Dan Fouts, 1981	4,802
Passing (TDs)	Dan Fouts, 1981	33
Receiving (No.)	Kellen Winslow, 1980	89
Receiving (Yds.)	Lance Alworth, 1965	1,602
Interceptions	Charlie McNeil, 1961	9
Punting (Avg.)	Dennis Partee, 1969	44.6
Punt Return (Avg.)	Leslie (Speedy) Duncan, 1965	15.5
Kickoff Return (Avg.)	Keith Lincoln, 1962	28.4
Field Goals	John Carney, 1993	31
Touchdowns (Tot.)	Chuck Muncie, 1981	19
Points	John Carney, 1993	124

INDIVIDUAL RECORDS—SINGLE GAME

Category	Name	Performance
Rushing (Yds.)	Gary Anderson, 12-18-88	217
Passing (Yds.)	Dan Fouts, 10-19-80	444
	Dan Fouts, 12-11-82	444
Passing (TDs)	Dan Fouts, 11-22-81	6
Receiving (No.)	Kellen Winslow, 10-7-84	15
Receiving (Yds.)	Wes Chandler, 12-20-82	260
Interceptions	Many times	3
	Last time by Pete Shaw, 11-2-80	
Field Goals	John Carney, 9-5-93	6
	John Carney, 9-18-93	6
Touchdowns (Tot.)	Kellen Winslow, 11-22-81	5
Points	Kellen Winslow, 11-22-81	30

COACHING HISTORY

(250-253-11)

1960-69	Sid Gillman*	83-51-6
1969-70	Charlie Waller	9-7-3
1971	Sid Gillman**	4-6-0
1971-73	Harland Svare***	7-17-2
1973	Ron Waller	1-5-0
1974-78	Tommy Prothro****	21-39-0
1978-86	Don Coryell#	72-60-0
1986-88	Al Saunders	17-22-0
1989-91	Dan Henning	16-32-0
1992-93	Bobby Ross	20-14-0

  *Retired after nine games in 1969
  **Resigned after 10 games in 1971
  ***Resigned after eight games in 1973
  ****Resigned after four games in 1978
  #Resigned after eight games in 1986

SAN DIEGO JACK MURPHY STADIUM

1993 TEAM RECORD,

PRESEASON (3-1)

Date	Result		Opponents
8/7	W	13-7	New England
8/14	W	23-17	at L.A. Rams
8/21	W	10-3	Phoenix
8/28	L	14-30	at San Francisco

REGULAR SEASON (8-8)

Date	Result		Opponents	Att.
9/5	W	18-12	Seattle	58,039
9/12	L	17-34	at Denver	75,074
9/19	W	18-17	Houston	58,519
10/3	L	14-31	at Seattle	54,778
10/10	L	3-16	at Pittsburgh	55,264
10/17	L	14-17	Kansas City	60,729
10/31	W	30-23	at L.A. Raiders	45,122
11/7	W	30-17	at Minnesota	55,527
11/14	L	13-16	Chicago	58,459
11/21	L	7-12	L.A. Raiders	60,615
11/29	W	31-0	at Indianapolis	54,110
12/5	W	13-10	Denver	60,233
12/12	L	13-20	Green Bay	57,930
12/19	L	24-28	at Kansas City	74,778
12/27	W	45-20	Miami	60,311
1/2	W	32-17	at Tampa Bay	35,587

SCORE BY PERIODS

Chargers	66	76	67	113	0	—	322
Opponents	50	102	83	55	0	—	290

ATTENDANCE

Home 474,835   Away 450,240   Total 925,075
Single-game home record, 64,411 (12-15-84)
Single-season home record, 494,103 (1988)

1993 TEAM STATISTICS

	Chargers	Opp.
Total First Downs	313	299
Rushing	120	86
Passing	171	192
Penalty	22	21
Third Down: Made/Att	89/224	83/210
Third Down Pct.	39.7	39.5
Fourth Down: Made/Att	6/15	4/8
Fourth Down Pct.	40.0	50.0
Total Net Yards	4967	5066
Avg. Per Game	310.4	316.6
Total Plays	1050	1002
Avg. Per Play	4.7	5.1
Net Yards Rushing	1824	1314
Avg. Per Game	114.0	82.1
Total Rushes	455	414
Net Yards Passing	3143	3752
Avg. Per Game	196.4	234.5
Sacked/Yards Lost	32/240	32/206
Gross Yards	3383	3958
Att./Completions	563/301	556/329
Completion Pct.	53.5	59.2
Had Intercepted	14	22
Punts/Avg.	74/42.3	72/42.1
Net Punting Avg.	74/36.4	72/35.5
Penalties/Yards Lost	87/699	94/724
Fumbles/Ball Lost	13/5	19/12
Touchdowns	33	30
Rushing	14	10
Passing	18	17
Returns	1	3
Average Time of Possession	29:52	30:08

1993 INDIVIDUAL STATISTICS

PASSING	Att.	Cmp.	Yds.	Pct.	TD	Int.	Tkld.	Rate
Humphries	324	173	1981	53.4	12	10	18/142	71.5
Friesz	238	128	1402	53.8	6	4	14/98	72.8
Means	1	0	0	0.0	0	0	0/0	39.6
Chargers	563	301	3383	53.5	18	14	32/240	72.0
Opponents	556	329	3958	59.2	17	22	32/206	74.8

SCORING	TD R	TD P	TD Rt	PAT	FG	Saf	PTS
Carney	0	0	0	31/33	31/40	0	124
Means	8	0	0	0/0	0/0	0	48
A. Miller	0	7	0	0/0	0/0	0	42
Butts	4	0	0	0/0	0/0	0	24
Lewis	0	4	0	0/0	0/0	0	24
Harmon	0	2	0	0/0	0/0	0	12
Jefferson	0	2	0	0/0	0/0	0	12
Young	0	2	0	0/0	0/0	0	12
Bieniemy	1	0	0	0/0	0/0	0	6
Frank	0	0	1	0/0	0/0	0	6
Kidd	1	0	0	0/0	0/0	0	6
Walker	0	1	0	0/0	0/0	0	6
Chargers	14	18	1	31/33	31/40	0	322
Opponents	10	17	3	30/30	26/33	1	290

RUSHING	Att.	Yds.	Avg.	LG	TD
Butts	185	746	4.0	27	4
Means	160	645	4.0	65t	8
Harmon	46	216	4.7	19	0
Bieniemy	33	135	4.1	12	1
Jefferson	5	53	10.6	33	0
Humphries	8	37	4.6	27	0
Friesz	10	3	0.3	2	0
Lewis	3	2	0.7	7	0
Hendrickson	1	0	0.0	0	0
A. Miller	1	0	0.0	0	0
Kidd	3	-13	-4.3	2t	1
Chargers	455	1824	4.0	65t	14
Opponents	414	1314	3.2	19	10

RECEIVING	No.	Yds.	Avg.	LG	TD
A. Miller	84	1162	13.8	66t	7
Harmon	73	671	9.2	37	2
Lewis	38	463	12.2	47	4
Jefferson	30	391	13.0	39t	2
Walker	21	212	10.1	25t	1
Butts	15	105	7.0	23	0
Pupunu	13	142	10.9	28	0
Barnes	10	137	13.7	21	0
Means	10	59	5.9	11	0
Young	6	41	6.8	12t	2
Bieniemy	1	0	0.0	0	0
Chargers	301	3383	11.2	66t	18
Opponents	329	3958	12.0	71t	17

INTERCEPTIONS	No.	Yds.	Avg.	LG	TD
Carrington	7	104	14.9	28	0
Frank	3	119	39.7	102t	1
Seau	2	58	29.0	42	0
Pope	2	14	7.0	12	0
Plummer	2	7	3.5	6	0
Vanhorse	2	0	0.0	0	0
Hendrickson	1	16	16.0	16	0
Gordon	1	3	3.0	3	0
Davis	1	0	0.0	0	0
Richard	1	-2	-2.0	-2	0
Chargers	22	319	14.5	102t	1
Opponents	14	271	19.4	68	2

PUNTING	No.	Yds.	Avg.	In 20	LG
Kidd	57	2431	42.6	16	67
Sullivan	13	541	41.6	3	50
Carney	4	155	38.8	1	46
Chargers	74	3127	42.3	20	67
Opponents	72	3031	42.1	23	77

PUNT RETURNS	No.	FC	Yds.	Avg.	LG	TD
Gordon	31	15	395	12.7	54	0
Lewis	3	2	17	5.7	7	0
Chargers	34	17	412	12.1	54	0
Opponents	36	21	292	8.1	30	0

KICKOFF RETURNS	No.	Yds.	Avg.	LG	TD
Lewis	33	684	20.7	60	0
Bieniemy	7	110	15.7	18	0
Hendrickson	2	25	12.5	13	0
Means	2	22	11.0	14	0
A. Miller	2	42	21.0	29	0
Harmon	1	18	18.0	18	0
Chargers	47	901	19.2	60	0
Opponents	64	1063	16.6	48	0

SACKS	No.
O'Neal	12.0
Mims	7.0
Grossman	4.5
Lee	3.0
Richard	2.0
Winter	2.0
Carrington	1.0
Pope	0.5
Chargers	32.0
Opponents	32.0

1994 DRAFT CHOICES

Round	Name	Pos.	College
2	Isaac Davis	G	Arkansas
	Vaughn Parker	G	UCLA
3	Andre Coleman	WR	Kansas State
	Willie Clark	DB	Notre Dame
5	Aaron Laing	TE	New Mexico State
	Rodney Harrison	DB	Western Illinois
	Darren Krein	DE	Miami
	Tony Vinson	RB	Towson State
7	Zane Beehn	LB	Kentucky

1994 VETERAN ROSTER

No.		Name	Pos.	Ht.	Wt.	Birthdate	NFL Exp.	College	Hometown	How Acq.	'93 Games/ Starts
52	#	Anno, Sam	LB	6-3	240	1/26/65	8	Southern California	Santa Monica, Calif.	PB(TB)-'92	16/0
85		Barnes, Johnnie	WR	6-1	180	7/21/68	3	Hampton	Suffolk, Va.	FA-'92	14/0
37		Boles, Eric	TE	6-3	210	4/29/70	2	Central Washington	Tacoma, Wash.	FA-'94	0*
67		Brock, Stan	T	6-6	295	6/8/58	15	Colorado	Portland, Ore.	UFA(NO)-'93	16/16
58		Bush, Lewis	LB	6-2	245	12/2/69	2	Washington State	Tacoma, Wash.	D4b-'93	16/0
22	#	Byrd, Gill	CB-S	5-11	198	2/20/61	12	San Jose State	San Francisco, Calif.	D1c-'83	0*
3		Carney, John	K	5-11	170	4/20/64	5	Notre Dame	West Palm Beach, Fla.	FA-'90	16/0
29		Carrington, Darren	S	6-2	200	10/10/66	6	Northern Arizona	Bronx, N.Y.	FA-'91	16/14
44		Castle, Eric	S	6-3	212	3/15/70	2	Oregon	Lebanon, Ore.	D6-'93	5/0
68		Cocozzo, Joe	G	6-4	300	8/7/70	2	Michigan	Mechanicville, N.Y.	D3-'93	16/5
51		Crews, Terry	LB	6-2	245	7/30/68	3	Western Michigan	Flint, Mich.	FA-'94	10/0*
93		Davis, Reuben	DT	6-5	340	5/7/67	7	North Carolina	Greensboro, N.C.	UFA(Ariz)-'94	16/15*
23		Dunson, Walter	WR	5-9	173	10/24/70	2	Middle Tennessee State	Carrollton, Ga.	D5-'93	0*
84		Dyal, Mike	TE	6-2	240	5/20/66	7	Texas A&I	Kerrville, Tex.	FA-'93	10/0*
40		Fuller, James	S	6-0	208	8/5/69	3	Portland State	Tacoma, Wash.	D8-'92	10/0
56		Gibson, Dennis	LB	6-2	240	2/8/64	8	Iowa State	Ankeny, Iowa	UFA(Det)-'94	15/15*
5		Gilbert, Gale	QB	6-3	210	12/20/61	9	California	Red Bluff, Calif.	UFA(Buff)-'94	1/0*
21		Gordon, Darrien	CB	5-11	182	11/14/70	2	Stanford	Shawnee, Okla.	D1-'93	16/7
7		Green, Trent	QB	6-3	211	7/9/70	2	Indiana	St. Louis, Mo.	D8-'93	0*
92		Griggs, David	LB	6-3	250	2/5/67	5	Virginia	Miami Beach, Fla.	UFA(Mia)-'94	9/0*
53		Hall, Courtney	C-G	6-1	281	8/26/68	6	Rice	Wilmington, Calif.	D2a-'89	16/16
33		Harmon, Ronnie	RB	5-11	207	5/7/64	9	Iowa	Queens, N.Y.	PB(Buff)-'90	16/1
28		Harper, Dwayne	CB	5-11	175	3/29/66	7	South Carolina State	Orangeburg, S.C.	UFA(Sea)-'94	14/14*
34	#	Hendrickson, Steve	RB-LB	6-0	250	8/30/66	6	California	Napa, Calif.	FA-'90	16/10
12		Humphries, Stan	QB	6-2	223	4/14/65	6	Northeast Louisiana	Shreveport, La.	T(Wash)-'92	12/10
80		Jefferson, Shawn	WR	5-11	172	2/22/69	4	Central Florida	Jacksonville, Fla.	T(Hou)-'91	16/4
99		Johnson, Raylee	DE	6-3	245	6/1/70	2	Arkansas	Fordyce, Ark.	D4a-'93	9/0
89		Johnson, Vance	WR	5-11	180	3/13/63	10	Arizona	Tucson, Ariz.	UFA(Den)-'94	10/8*
74		Jonassen, Eric	T	6-5	310	8/16/68	3	Bloomsburg, Pa.	Glen Burnie, Md.	D5c-'92	16/2
10	#	Kidd, John	P	6-3	208	8/22/61	11	Northwestern	Findlay, Ohio	PB(Buff)-'90	14/0
98		Lee, Shawn	DT	6-2	300	10/24/66	7	North Alabama	Brooklyn, N.Y.	FA-'92	16/15
81	t-	Martin, Tony	WR	6-0	181	9/5/65	5	Mesa, Colo.	Miami, Fla.	T(Mia)-'94	12/0*
88		May, Deems	TE	6-4	263	3/6/69	3	North Carolina	Lexington, N.C.	D7-'92	15/1
20		Means, Natrone	RB	5-10	245	4/26/72	2	North Carolina	Harrisburg, N.C.	D2-'93	16/0
71		Milinichik, Joe	G	6-5	300	3/30/63	9	North Carolina State	Emmaus, Pa.	UFA(Rams)-'93	10/10
54		Miller, Doug	LB	6-3	232	10/29/69	2	South Dakota State	Sturgis, S.D.	D7-'93	8/0
94		Mims, Chris	DE-DT	6-5	290	9/29/70	3	Tennessee	Los Angeles, Calif.	D1-'92	16/7
77	†	Moten, Eric	G-T	6-2	306	4/11/68	4	Michigan State	Cleveland Heights, Ohio	D2c-'91	4/4
91		O'Neal, Leslie	DE	6-4	265	5/7/64	9	Oklahoma State	Little Rock, Ark.	D1a-'86	16/16
86		Pupunu, Alfred	TE	6-2	255	10/17/69	3	Weber State	Salt Lake City, Utah	W(KC)-'92	16/7
24		Richard, Stanley	S	6-2	197	10/21/67	4	Texas	Hawkins, Tex.	D1-'91	16/16
55		Seau, Junior	LB	6-3	250	1/19/69	5	Southern California	Oceanside, Calif.	D1-'90	16/16
82		Seay, Mark	WR	6-0	175	4/11/67	2	Long Beach State	San Bernardino, Calif.	W(SF)-'93	1/0
72		Swayne, Harry	T	6-5	295	2/2/65	8	Rutgers	Philadelphia, Pa.	PB(TB)-'91	11/11
25		Vanhorse, Sean	CB	5-10	180	7/22/68	5	Howard	Baltimore, Md.	PB(Det)-'92	15/10
90		White, Reggie	DT	6-4	300	3/22/70	3	North Carolina A&T	Mulford Mills, Md.	D6-'92	8/0
64		Whitley, Curtis	C	6-1	285	5/10/69	3	Clemson	Smithfield, N.C.	D5a-'92	15/0
57	#	Williams, Jerrol	LB	6-4	240	7/5/67	6	Purdue	Las Vegas, Nev.	RFA(Pitt)-'93	6/5
87		Young, Duane	TE	6-1	270	5/29/68	4	Michigan State	Kalamazoo, Mich.	D5-'91	16/15

* Boles on injured reserve for 16 games with Jets in '93; Byrd and Dunson missed '93 season due to injury; Crews played 10 games with San Diego; Davis played 16 games with Phoenix; Dyal played 6 games with Kansas City, 4 games with San Diego; Gibson played 15 games with Detroit; Gilbert played 1 game with Buffalo; Green inactive for 16 games; Griggs played 9 games with Miami; Harper played 14 games with Seattle; Johnson played 10 games with Denver; Martin played 12 games with Miami.

\# Unrestricted free agent; subject to developments.

† Restricted free agent; subject to developments.

Traded—RB Marion Butts to New England, CB Donald Frank to Cleveland, DE Burt Grossman to Philadelphia, WR Nate Lewis to L.A. Rams, CB Marquez Pope to L.A. Rams.

t- Chargers traded for Martin (Miami).

Players lost through free agency (5): QB John Friesz (Wash; 12 games in '93), WR Anthony Miller (Den; 16), LB Gary Plummer (SF; 16), T Mike Withycombe (Clev; 0), G Mike Zandofsky (Atl; 16).

Also played with Chargers in '93—RB Eric Bieniemy (16 games), LB Jeff Brady (3), RB Marion Butts (16), CB Brian Davis (11), S Floyd Fields (13), CB Donald Frank (16), DE Burt Grossman (10), WR Nate Lewis (15), T Mike Mooney (1), CB Marquez Pope (16), G-T Raymond Smoot (2), P Kent Sullivan (2), TE Derrick Walker (12), DT Blaise Winter (16).

COACHING STAFF

Head Coach,
Bobby Ross

Pro Career: Begins third season as San Diego's head coach. In 1992, led the Chargers to an 11-5 regular-season record and the team's first AFC Western Division title since 1981. Named ninth head coach in Chargers' history on January 2, 1992. Ross began his pro coaching career in 1978 as an assistant with the Kansas City Chiefs, where he coached special teams and defense in 1978-79 and offensive backs in 1980-81. No pro playing experience. Career record: 20-14.

Background: Played quarterback and defensive back for Virginia Military Institute. Began coaching career in 1965 at VMI. Moved on as an assistant at William & Mary 1967-70, Rice 1971, and Maryland 1972. Head coach at The Citadel 1973-77. Compiled 39-19-1 (.672) record as he led Maryland (1982-86) to three Atlantic Coast Conference titles and made four bowl game appearances in five seasons. Guided Georgia Tech (1987-91) to first ACC title in school history. Under Ross, the Yellow Jackets won first national championship as the country's only undefeated team (11-0-1) in 1990. Named consensus national coach of the year in 1990. Career collegiate head coaching record: 94-76-2.

Personal: Born December 23, 1936, Richmond, Va. Bobby and wife, Alice, live in San Diego and have five children—Chris, Kevin, Robbie, Mary, and Teresa.

ASSISTANT COACHES

Bill Arnsparger, defensive coordinator; born December 16, 1926, Paris, Ky., lives in San Diego. Tackle Miami (Ohio) 1946-49. No pro playing experience. College coach: Miami (Ohio) 1950, Ohio State 1951-53, Kentucky 1954-61, Tulane 1962-63, Louisiana State 1984-86, Florida 1987-91 (athletic director). Pro coach: Baltimore Colts 1964-69, Miami Dolphins 1970-73, 1976-83, New York Giants 1974-76 (head coach), joined Chargers in 1992.

Sylvester Croom, offensive backs; born September 25, 1954, Tuscaloosa, Ala., lives in San Diego. Center Alabama 1971-74. Pro center New Orleans Saints 1975. College coach: Alabama 1976-86. Pro coach: Tampa Bay Buccaneers 1987-90, Indianapolis Colts 1991, joined Chargers in 1992.

John Dunn, strength and conditioning; born July 22, 1956, Hillsdale, N.Y., lives in San Diego. Guard Penn State 1974-77. No pro playing experience. College coach: Penn State 1978. Pro coach: Washington Redskins 1984-86, Los Angeles Raiders 1987-89, joined Chargers in 1990.

Frank Falks, H-Backs-tight ends; born March 9, 1943, Tampa, Fla., lives in San Diego. Linebacker Joplin (Missouri) J.C. 1963-64, Parsons College 1965-66. No pro playing experience. College coach: Parsons College 1967-69, Kansas State 1970-72, Arkansas 1973-77, Wyoming 1978-79, San Diego State 1980, Oklahoma State 1981-82, Southern California 1983-86, Arizona State 1987-91, Ohio State 1992-93. Pro coach: Joined Chargers in 1994.

Ralph Friedgen, offensive coordinator; born April 4, 1947, Harrison, N.Y., lives in San Diego. Guard Maryland 1967-68. No pro playing experience. College coach: The Citadel 1973-79, William & Mary 1980, Murray State 1981, Maryland 1982-86, Georgia Tech 1987-91. Pro coach: Joined Chargers in 1992.

Dale Lindsey, linebackers; born January 18, 1943, Bedford, Ind., lives in San Diego. Linebacker Western Kentucky 1961-64. Pro linebacker Cleveland Browns 1965-73. College coach: Southern Methodist 1988-89. Pro coach: Cleveland Browns 1974, Portland Storm (WFL) 1975, Toronto Argonauts (CFL) 1979-82, Boston Breakers (USFL) 1983, New Jersey Generals (USFL) 1984-85, Green Bay Packers 1986-87, New England Patriots 1990, Tampa Bay Buccaneers 1991, joined Chargers in 1992.

Carl Mauck, offensive line; born July 7, 1947, McLeansboro, Ill., lives in San Diego. Linebacker-center Southern Illinois 1966-68. Pro center Baltimore Colts 1969, Miami Dolphins 1970, San Diego Chargers 1971-74, Houston Oilers 1975-81. Pro

1994 FIRST-YEAR ROSTER

Name	Pos.	Ht.	Wt.	Birthdate	College	Hometown	How Acq.
Beeching, Todd	T	6-7	305	3/15/71	Southern Mississippi	Stockbridge, Ga.	FA
Beehn, Zane	LB	6-4	252	9/28/71	Kentucky	Owensboro, Ky.	D7
Bennett, Darren (1)	P	6-5	235	1/9/65	No College	Western Australia	FA
Berger, Blaine	DE	6-5	285	12/28/70	Utah	Idaho Falls, Idaho	FA
Binn, David	TE	6-3	234	2/6/72	California	San Mateo, Calif.	FA
Breedlove, Brad	WR	5-10	175	10/30/69	Duke	Lecanto, Fla.	FA
Brohm, Jeff	QB	6-1	200	4/24/71	Louisville	Louisville, Ky.	FA
Caldwell, Henry	RB	5-10	216	8/7/71	Central Missouri State	Daytona Beach, Fla.	FA
Carter, Grant	LB	6-2	222	12/30/70	Pacific	Lake Oswego, Ore.	FA
Clark, Willie	CB	5-10	186	1/6/72	Notre Dame	Wheatland, Calif.	D3b
Coleman, Andre	WR-KR	5-9	165	1/18/71	Kansas State	Hermitage, Pa.	D3a
Currie, Herschel	CB	6-1	190	9/8/65	Oregon State	San Jose, Calif.	FA
Davis, Isaac	G	6-3	325	4/8/72	Arkansas	Malvern, Ark.	D2a
Engel, Greg	C	6-3	293	1/18/71	Illinois	Bloomington, Ill.	FA
Greene, Ernest	T	6-5	294	2/25/71	Savannah State	Savannah, Ga.	FA
Gregory, James	DT	6-3	283	7/26/71	Alabama	St. Louis, Mo.	FA
Harrison, Rodney	S	6-0	201	12/15/72	Western Illinois	Marion, Ill.	D5b
Hocker, Shawn	G	6-4	288	7/27/71	North Carolina	Sarasota, Fla.	FA
Hollis, Mike	K	5-7	164	5/22/72	Idaho	Spokane, Wash.	FA
Johnson, Chris	S	6-0	205	8/7/71	San Diego State	San Diego, Calif.	FA
Johnson, Tom	LB	6-4	245	12/28/70	Georgia Tech	Huntsville, Ala.	FA
Krein, Darren	DE	6-4	258	7/7/71	Miami	Aurora, Colo.	D5c
Laing, Aaron	TE	6-3	264	7/19/71	New Mexico State	Houston, Tex.	D5a
Lane, Greg	CB	5-9	181	10/31/71	Notre Dame	Austin, Tex.	FA
Long, Juan	LB	6-2	245	11/21/71	Mississippi State	Tupelo, Miss.	FA
McAlister, Scott (1)	P	6-3	210	3/30/69	North Carolina	Greensboro, N.C.	FA
Mitchell, Shannon	TE	6-2	245	3/28/72	Georgia	Alcoa, Tenn.	FA
Munoz, Jose	G	6-3	280	5/7/71	Ball State	Merrillville, Ind.	FA
Parker, Vaughn	G-T	6-3	296	6/5/71	UCLA	Buffalo, N.Y.	D2b
Ramaekers, Kevin	DT	6-4	278	12/18/69	Nebraska	Norfolk, Neb.	FA
Rivers, Ron	RB	5-8	200	11/13/71	Fresno State	Highland, Calif.	FA
Rodahaffer, Chris	T	6-5	295	4/30/71	San Diego State	Lodi, Calif.	FA
Smoot, Raymond (1)	G-T	6-4	305	7/24/70	Louisiana State	Leesville, La.	FA
Snyder, Sean (1)	P	6-2	190	9/21/69	Kansas State	Greenville, Tex.	FA
Stanley, Israel (1)	DE	6-2	250	4/21/70	Arizona State	San Diego, Calif.	FA
Sullivan, Kent (1)	P	6-0	202	5/15/67	California-Lutheran	Middlebury, Ind.	FA
Thomas, Chris (1)	WR	6-1	180	7/16/71	Cal Poly-SLO	Ventura, Calif.	FA
Thomas, Cornell	DE	6-3	250	11/11/72	West Georgia State	Norcross, Ga.	FA
Thomas, Sean	CB	6-1	189	1/22/72	Duke	Westerville, Ohio	FA
Thompson, Chris	LB	6-0	253	6/17/69	Bowie State	Adelphi, Md.	FA
Vinson, Tony	RB	6-1	229	3/13/71	Towson State	Denbigh, Va.	D5d
Ward, Jim	DT	6-3	288	9/2/71	Slippery Rock	Munhall, Pa.	FA
Watson, Darrius	S	6-0	193	6/11/71	Louisville	Torrance, Calif.	FA
Wilbert, Patrick	DT	6-4	330	8/24/71	Angelo State	Big Spring, Tex.	FA
Williams, Michael (1)	CB-S	5-10	185	5/28/70	UCLA	Los Angeles, Calif.	FA
Wyatt, Earnest	WR	5-8	175	4/9/70	Northeast Louisiana	Monroe, La.	FA

The term NFL Rookie is defined as a player who is in his first season of professional football and has not been on the roster of another professional football team for any regular-season or postseason games. A Rookie is designated by an "R" on NFL rosters. Players who have been active in another professional football league or players who have had NFL experience, including either preseason training camp or being on an Active List or Inactive List, or on Reserve/Injured or Reserve/Physically Unable to Perform for fewer than six regular-season games, are termed NFL First-Year Players. An NFL First-Year Player is designated by a "1" on NFL rosters. Thereafter, a player is credited with an additional year of experience for each season in which he accumulates six games on the Active List or Inactive List, or on Reserve/Injured or Reserve/Physically Unable to Perform.

NOTES

coach: New Orleans Saints 1982-85, Kansas City Chiefs 1986-88, Tampa Bay Buccaneers 1991, joined Chargers in 1992.

John Misciagna, quality control; born December 11, 1954, Brooklyn, N.Y., lives in San Diego. Guard Dickinson College 1973-76. No pro playing experience. College coach: Indiana (Pa.) University 1977, Columbia 1978-79, Maryland 1980-88, Georgia Tech 1989-91. Pro coach: Joined Chargers in 1992.

Dennis Murphy, defensive line; born October 22, 1940, Endicott, N.Y., lives in San Diego. Tight end-defensive lineman Notre Dame 1959-61. No pro playing experience. College coach: Notre Dame 1968-74, Colgate 1975, Holy Cross 1976-77, Eastern Michigan 1978-81, Maryland 1982-91, Navy 1992-93. Pro coach: Joined Chargers in 1994.

Chuck Priefer, special teams; born July 26, 1941, Cleveland, Ohio, lives in San Diego. No college or pro playing experience. College coach: Miami (Ohio) 1977, North Carolina 1978-83, Kent State 1986, Georgia Tech 1987-91. Pro coach: Green Bay Packers 1984-85, joined Chargers in 1992.

Dwain Painter, quarterbacks; born February 13,

1942, Monroeville, Pa., lives in San Diego. Quarterback-defensive back Rutgers 1961-64. No pro playing experience. College coach: San Jose State 1971-72, UCLA 1976-78, Northern Arizona 1979-81 (head coach), Georgia Tech 1982-85, Texas 1986, Illinois 1987. Pro coach: Pittsburgh Steelers 1988-91, Indianapolis Colts 1992-93, joined Chargers in 1994.

Willie Shaw, defensive backs; born January 11, 1944, San Diego, Calif., lives in San Diego. Cornerback New Mexico 1966-68. No pro playing experience. College coach: San Diego City College 1970-73, Stanford 1974-76, 1989-91, Long Beach State 1977-78, Oregon 1979, Arizona State 1980-84. Pro coach: Detroit Lions 1985-88, Minnesota Vikings 1992-93, joined Chargers in 1994.

Jerry Sullivan, wide receivers; born July 13, 1944, Miami, Fla., lives in San Diego. Quarterback Florida State 1963-64. No pro playing experience. College coach: Kansas State 1971-72, Texas Tech 1973-75, South Carolina 1976-82, Indiana 1983, Louisiana State 1984-90, Ohio State 1991. Pro coach: Joined Chargers in 1992.

American Football Conference
Western Division
Team Colors: Blue, Green, and Silver
11220 N.E. 53rd Street
Kirkland, Washington 98033
Telephone: (206) 827-9777

CLUB OFFICIALS

Owner: Ken Behring
President: David Behring
General Manager/Head Coach: Tom Flores
Executive Vice President: Mickey Loomis
Vice President/Football Operations:
  Chuck Allen
Vice President/Administration and Public
  Relations: Gary Wright
Player Personnel Director: Mike Allman
Publicity Director: Dave Neubert
Community Relations Director: Sandy Gregory
Sales and Marketing Director: Reggie McKenzie
Data Processing Director: Sterling Monroe
Ticket Manager: James Nagaoka
Trainer: Jim Whitesel
Equipment Manager: Terry Sinclair
Team Physicians: Dr. Kevin Auld,
  Dr. Pierce Scranton, Dr. James Trombold,
  Dr. Pete Van Patten
Stadium: Kingdome •**Capacity:** 66,400
      201 South King Street
      Seattle, Washington 98104
Playing Surface: AstroTurf
Training Camp: 11220 N.E. 53rd Street
      Kirkland, Washington 98033

1994 SCHEDULE
PRESEASON

Aug. 5	at Indianapolis	7:30
Aug. 13	**Tampa Bay**	6:00
Aug. 20	**Minnesota**	7:00
Aug. 26	at San Francisco	6:00

REGULAR SEASON

Sept. 4	at Washington	1:00
Sept. 11	at Los Angeles Raiders	1:00
Sept. 18	**San Diego**	1:00
Sept. 25	**Pittsburgh**	1:00
Oct. 2	at Indianapolis	12:00
Oct. 9	**Denver**	1:00
Oct. 16	Open Date	
Oct. 23	at Kansas City	12:00
Oct. 30	at San Diego	1:00
Nov. 6	**Cincinnati**	1:00
Nov. 13	at Denver	2:00
Nov. 20	**Tampa Bay**	1:00
Nov. 27	**Kansas City**	1:00
Dec. 4	**Indianapolis**	1:00
Dec. 11	at Houston	3:00
Dec. 18	**Los Angeles Raiders**	5:00
Dec. 24	at Cleveland	1:00

RECORD HOLDERS
INDIVIDUAL RECORDS—CAREER

Category	Name	Performance
Rushing (Yds.)	Curt Warner, 1983-89	6,705
Passing (Yds.)	Dave Krieg, 1980-1991	26,132
Passing (TDs)	Dave Krieg, 1980-1991	195
Receiving (No.)	Steve Largent, 1976-1989	819
Receiving (Yds.)	Steve Largent, 1976-1989	13,089
Interceptions	Dave Brown, 1976-1986	50
Punting (Avg.)	Rick Tuten, 1991-93	44.0
Punt Return (Avg.)	Paul Johns, 1981-84	11.4
Kickoff Return (Avg.)	Bobby Joe Edmonds, 1986-88	22.1
Field Goals	Norm Johnson, 1982-1990	159
Touchdowns (Tot.)	Steve Largent, 1976-1989	101
Points	Norm Johnson, 1982-1990	810

INDIVIDUAL RECORDS—SINGLE SEASON

Category	Name	Performance
Rushing (Yds.)	Curt Warner, 1986	1,481
Passing (Yds.)	Dave Krieg, 1984	3,671
Passing (TDs)	Dave Krieg, 1984	32
Receiving (No.)	Brian Blades, 1993	80
Receiving (Yds.)	Steve Largent, 1985	1,287
Interceptions	John Harris, 1981	10
	Kenny Easley, 1984	10
Punting (Avg.)	Rick Tuten, 1993	44.5
Punt Return (Avg.)	Bobby Joe Edmonds, 1987	12.6
Kickoff Return (Avg.)	Al Hunter, 1978	24.1
Field Goals	John Kasay, 1991	25
Touchdowns (Tot.)	David Sims, 1978	15
	Sherman Smith, 1979	15
	Derrick Fenner, 1990	15
Points	Norm Johnson, 1984	110

INDIVIDUAL RECORDS—SINGLE GAME

Category	Name	Performance
Rushing (Yds.)	Curt Warner, 11-27-83	207
Passing (Yds.)	Dave Krieg, 11-20-83	418
Passing (TDs)	Dave Krieg, 12-2-84	5
	Dave Krieg, 9-15-85	5
	Dave Krieg, 11-28-88	5
Receiving (No.)	Steve Largent, 10-18-87	15
Receiving (Yds.)	Steve Largent, 10-18-87	261
Interceptions	Kenny Easley, 9-3-84	3
	Eugene Robinson, 12-6-92	3
Field Goals	Norm Johnson, 9-20-87	5
	Norm Johnson, 12-18-88	5
Touchdowns (Tot.)	Daryl Turner, 9-15-85	4
	Curt Warner, 12-11-88	4
Points	Daryl Turner, 9-15-85	24
	Curt Warner, 12-11-88	24

*NFL Record

COACHING HISTORY
(130-153-0)

1976-82	Jack Patera*	35-59-0
1982	Mike McCormack	4-3-0
1983-91	Chuck Knox	83-67-0
1992-93	Tom Flores	8-24-0

*Released after two games in 1982

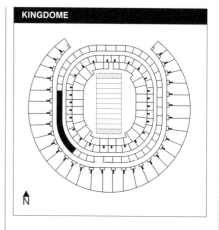

KINGDOME

1993 TEAM RECORD,

PRESEASON (2-2)

Date	Result		Opponents
8/7	L	13-16	Indianapolis
8/14	L	10-23	at Minnesota
8/21	W	30-0	San Francisco
8/28	W	20-10	at Houston

REGULAR SEASON (6-10)

Date	Result		Opponents	Att.
9/5	L	12-18	at San Diego	58,039
9/12	L	13-17	L.A. Raiders	58,836
9/19	W	17-14	at New England	50,392
9/26	W	19-10	at Cincinnati	46,880
10/3	W	31-14	San Diego	54,778
10/17	L	10-30	at Detroit	60,801
10/24	W	10-9	New England	56,526
10/31	L	17-28	at Denver	73,644
11/7	L	14-24	at Houston	50,447
11/14	W	22-5	Cleveland	54,622
11/28	L	9-17	Denver	57,812
12/5	L	16-31	Kansas City	58,551
12/12	L	23-27	at L.A. Raiders	38,161
12/19	L	27-30	Phoenix (OT)	45,737
12/26	W	16-6	Pittsburgh	51,814
1/2	L	24-34	at Kansas City	72,136

(OT) Overtime

SCORE BY PERIODS

Seahawks	72	64	45	99	0	—	280
Opponents	65	104	66	76	3	—	314

ATTENDANCE

Home 438,676   Away 450,500   Total 889,176
Single-game home record, 64,673 (11-8-92)
Single-season home record, 514,984 (1992)

1993 TEAM STATISTICS

	Seahawks	Opp.
Total First Downs	279	322
Rushing	114	106
Passing	144	193
Penalty	21	23
Third Down: Made/Att	80/224	91/229
Third Down Pct.	35.7	39.7
Fourth Down: Made/Att	6/14	6/13
Fourth Down Pct.	42.9	46.2
Total Net Yards	4669	5313
Avg. Per Game	291.8	332.1
Total Plays	1019	1085
Avg. Per Play	4.6	4.9
Net Yards Rushing	2015	1660
Avg. Per Game	125.9	103.8
Total Rushes	473	452
Net Yards Passing	2654	3653
Avg. Per Game	165.9	228.3
Sacked/Yards Lost	48/242	38/244
Gross Yards	2896	3897
Att./Completions	498/280	595/333
Completion Pct.	56.2	56.0
Had Intercepted	18	22
Punts/Avg.	91/44.0	73/42.4
Net Punting Avg.	91/37.3	73/35.6
Penalties/Yards Lost	99/745	109/818
Fumbles/Ball Lost	25/13	23/15
Touchdowns	29	32
Rushing	13	12
Passing	13	16
Returns	3	4
Avg. Time of Possession	29:03	30:57

1993 INDIVIDUAL STATISTICS

PASSING	Att.	Cmp.	Yds.	Pct.	TD	Int.	Tkld.	Rate
Mirer	486	274	2833	56.4	12	17	47/235	67.0
Gelbaugh	5	3	39	60.0	0	1	1/7	45.0
McGwire	5	3	24	60.0	1	0	0/0	111.7
Tuten	1	0	0	0.0	0	0	0/0	39.6
Williams	1	0	0	0.0	0	0	0/0	39.6
Seahawks	498	280	2896	56.2	13	18	48/242	66.8
Opponents	595	333	3897	56.0	16	22	38/244	69.6

SCORING	TD R	TD P	TD Rt	PAT	FG	Saf	PTS
Kasay	0	0	0	29/29	23/28	0	98
C. Warren	7	0	0	0/0	0/0	0	42
Martin	0	5	0	0/0	0/0	0	30
Williams	3	1	0	0/0	0/0	0	24
Blades	0	3	0	0/0	0/0	0	18
Mirer	3	0	0	0/0	0/0	0	18
Edmunds	0	2	0	0/0	0/0	0	12
Stephens	0	0	1	0/0	0/0	2	10
Blackmon	0	0	1	0/0	0/0	0	6
Green	0	1	0	0/0	0/0	0	6
Johnson	0	1	0	0/0	0/0	0	6
Nash	0	0	1	0/0	0/0	0	6
Edwards	0	0	0	0/0	0/0	1	2
Seahawks	13	13	3	29/29	23/28	4	280
Opponents	12	16	4	31/32	29/39	2	314

RUSHING	Att.	Yds.	Avg.	LG	TD
C. Warren	273	1072	3.9	45t	7
Williams	82	371	4.5	38	3
Mirer	68	343	5.0	33	3
Vaughn	36	153	4.3	37	0
Blades	5	52	10.4	26	0
Bates	2	12	6.0	6	0
Johnson	2	8	4.0	5	0
D. Thomas	1	4	4.0	4	0
Mayes	1	2	2.0	2	0
Martin	1	0	0.0	0	0
Gelbaugh	1	-1	-1.0	-1	0
McGwire	1	-1	-1.0	-1	0
Seahawks	473	2015	4.3	45t	13
Opponents	452	1660	3.7	30t	12

RECEIVING	No.	Yds.	Avg.	LG	TD
Blades	80	945	11.8	41	3
Williams	58	450	7.8	25	1
Martin	57	798	14.0	53t	5
Edmunds	24	230	10.0	32	2
Green	23	178	7.7	20	1
C. Warren	15	99	6.6	21	0
D. Thomas	11	95	8.6	20	0
R. Thomas	7	67	9.6	16	0
Johnson	3	15	5.0	8	1
Bates	1	6	6.0	6	0
Roberts	1	4	4.0	4	0
Seahawks	280	2896	10.3	53t	13
Opponents	333	3897	11.7	58t	16

INTERCEPTIONS	No.	Yds.	Avg.	LG	TD
E. Robinson	9	80	8.9	28	0
Hunter	4	54	13.5	34	0
Gray	3	33	11.0	16	0
Blackmon	2	0	0.0	0	0
Nash	1	13	13.0	13t	1
Jefferson	1	12	12.0	12	0
Porter	1	4	4.0	4	0
Harper	1	0	0.0	0	0
Seahawks	22	196	8.9	34	1
Opponents	18	159	8.8	40	0

PUNTING	No.	Yds.	Avg.	In 20	LG
Tuten	90	4007	44.5	21	64
Seahawks	91	4007	44.0	21	64
Opponents	73	3097	42.4	19	60

PUNT RETURNS	No.	FC	Yds.	Avg.	LG	TD
Martin	32	15	270	8.4	33	0
McCloughan	1	0	10	10.0	10	0
Seahawks	33	15	280	8.5	33	0
Opponents	47	21	475	10.1	74t	1

KICKOFF RETURNS	No.	Yds.	Avg.	LG	TD
Bates	30	603	20.1	46	0
Vaughn	16	280	17.5	31	0
Martin	3	38	12.7	15	0
Tuatagaloa	1	10	10.0	10	0
Seahawks	50	931	18.6	46	0
Opponents	52	967	18.6	95t	1

SACKS	No.
Sinclair	8.0
Kennedy	6.5
McCrary	4.0
Tuatagaloa	3.5
Edwards	3.0
Stephens	2.5
Wooden	2.5
E. Robinson	2.0
R. Robinson	1.5
Bryant	1.0
Gray	1.0
Porter	1.0
Rodgers	1.0
Nash	0.5
Seahawks	38.0
Opponents	48.0

1994 DRAFT CHOICES

Round	Name	Pos.	College
1	Sam Adams	DT	Texas A&M
2	Kevin Mawae	C	Louisiana State
3	Lamar Smith	RB	Houston
4	Larry Whigham	DB	N.E. Louisiana
7	Carlester Crumpler	TE	East Carolina

SEATTLE SEAHAWKS

1994 VETERAN ROSTER

No.	Name	Pos.	Ht.	Wt.	Birthdate	NFL Exp.	College	Hometown	How Acq.	'93 Games/ Starts
39	Allred, Brian	CB	5-10	175	3/16/69	2	Sacramento State	Columbia Md.	FA-'93	4/0
75	Ballard, Howard	T	6-6	336	11/3/63	7	Alabama A&M	Ashland, Ala.	UFA(Buff)-'94	16/16*
15	t- Barrett, Reggie	WR	6-3	215	8/14/69	4	Texas-El Paso	Corpus Christi, Tex.	T(Det)-'94	13/2*
81	Bates, Michael	WR	5-10	189	12/19/69	2	Arizona	Tucson, Ariz.	D6-'92	16/1
25	Blackmon, Robert	S	6-0	197	5/12/67	5	Baylor	Van Vleck, Tex.	D2b-'90	16/16
69	Blackshear, Jeff	G	6-6	315	3/29/69	2	Northeast Louisiana	Ft. Pierce, Fla.	D8a-'93	15/2
89	† Blades, Brian	WR	5-11	189	7/24/66	7	Miami	Ft. Lauderdale, Fla.	D2-'88	16/16
51	Brandon, David	LB	6-4	230	2/9/65	8	Memphis State	Memphis, Tenn.	FA-'93	13/0*
77	# Bryant, Jeff	DE	6-5	281	5/22/60	13	Clemson	Decatur, Ga.	D1-'82	16/15
79	Childs, Jason	T	6-4	285	1/6/69	2	North Dakota	Plymouth, Minn.	W(SF)-'93	0*
50	Davis, Anthony	LB	6-0	231	3/7/69	2	Utah	Pasco, Wash.	FA-'92	10/0
53	Donaldson, Ray	C	6-3	300	5/18/58	15	Georgia	Rome, Ga.	FA-'93	16/16
82	Edmunds, Ferrell	TE	6-6	254	4/16/65	7	Maryland	Danville, Va.	UFA(Mia)-'93	16/16
67	Edwards, Antonio	DE	6-3	270	3/10/70	2	Valdosta State	Moultrie, Ga.	D8b-'93	9/0
59	Frerotte, Mitch	G	6-3	286	3/30/65	7	Penn State	Kittanning, Pa.	UFA(Buff)-'93	0*
18	Gelbaugh, Stan	QB	6-3	207	12/4/62	6	Maryland	Mechanicsburg, Pa.	PB(Phx)-'92	1/0
7	Graham, Jeff	QB	6-5	220	2/5/66	3	Long Beach State	Costa Mesa, Calif.	FA-'92	0*
26	Gray, Carlton	CB	6-0	191	6/26/71	2	UCLA	Cincinnati, Ohio	D2-'93	10/2
87	Green, Paul	TE	6-3	230	10/8/66	3	Southern California	Clovis, Calif.	FA-'92	15/8
76	Hitchcock, Bill	G	6-6	291	8/26/65	4	Purdue	Kirkland, Canada	FA-'91	14/14
27	Hunter, Patrick	CB	5-11	186	10/24/64	9	Nevada	San Francisco, Calif.	D3-'86	15/15
43	Johnson, Tracy	RB	6-0	230	11/29/66	6	Clemson	Kannapolis, N.C.	PB(Atl)-'92	16/1
93	# Junior, E.J.	LB	6-3	242	12/8/59	14	Alabama	Nashville, Tenn.	FA-'92	4/0
83	# Junkin, Trey	TE	6-2	237	1/23/61	12	Louisiana Tech	Winfield, La.	FA-'90	16/1
4	† Kasay, John	K	5-10	189	10/27/69	4	Georgia	Athens, Ga.	D4-'91	16/0
78	Keim, Mike	T	6-7	301	11/12/65	2	Brigham Young	Springerville, Ariz.	FA-'92	3/0
96	Kennedy, Cortez	DT	6-3	293	8/23/68	5	Miami	Rivercrest, Ark.	D1-'90	16/16
84	Martin, Kelvin	WR	5-9	162	5/14/65	8	Boston College	Jacksonville, Fla.	UFA(Dall)-'93	16/14
44	† McCloughan, Dave	S	6-1	185	11/20/66	4	Colorado	Loveland, Colo.	T(GB)-'93	15/1
92	McCrary, Michael	DE	6-4	250	7/7/70	2	Wake Forest	Vienna, Va.	D7-'93	15/0
10	McGwire, Dan	QB	6-8	239	12/18/67	4	San Diego State	Claremont, Calif.	D1-'91	2/0
3	Mirer, Rick	QB	6-2	216	3/19/70	2	Notre Dame	Goshen, Ind.	D1-'93	16/16
98	Murphy, Kevin	LB	6-2	235	9/8/63	9	Oklahoma	Richardson, Tex.	UFA(SD)-'93	14/10
72	# Nash, Joe	DT	6-3	278	10/11/60	13	Boston College	Dorchester, Mass.	FA-'82	16/16
37	Odomes, Nate	CB	5-10	188	8/25/65	8	Wisconsin	Columbus, Ga.	UFA(Buff)-'94	16/15*
97	Porter, Rufus	LB	6-1	227	5/18/65	7	Southern	Baton Rouge, La.	FA-'88	7/6
73	Roberts, Ray	T	6-6	304	6/3/69	3	Virginia	Asheville, N.C.	D1-'92	16/16
41	Robinson, Eugene	S	6-0	191	5/28/63	10	Colgate	Hartford, Conn.	FA-'85	16/16
37	Robinson, Rafael	S	5-11	200	6/19/69	3	Wisconsin	Jefferson, Tex.	FA-'92	16/1
91	Rodgers, Tyrone	DT	6-3	266	4/27/69	3	Washington	Wilmington, Calif.	FA-'92	16/0
71	Shaw, Rickie	T	6-4	294	12/26/69	2	North Crolina	Whiteville, N.C.	W(NO)-'93	0*
70	Sinclair, Michael	DE	6-4	271	1/31/68	3	Eastern New Mexico	Beaumont, Tex.	D6-'91	9/1
58	Spitulski, Bob	LB	6-3	235	9/10/69	3	Central Florida	Orlando, Fla.	D3-'92	6/0
94	Stephens, Rod	LB	6-1	237	6/14/66	5	Georgia Tech	Atlanta, Ga.	FA-'90	13/13
86	# Thomas, Robb	WR	5-11	175	3/29/66	6	Oregon State	Corvallis, Ore.	FA-'92	16/0
56	Tofflemire, Joe	C	6-3	273	7/7/65	6	Arizona	Post Falls, Idaho	D2-'89	0*
99	# Tuatagaloa, Natu	DE	6-4	274	5/25/66	6	California	San Rafael, Calif.	FA-'92	16/15
14	Tuten, Rick	P	6-2	218	1/5/65	5	Florida State	Ocala, Fla.	FA-'91	16/0
22	† Vaughn, Jon	RB	5-9	203	3/12/70	4	Michigan	Florissant, Mo.	T(NE)-'93	16/2
42	Warren, Chris	RB	6-2	225	1/24/67	5	Ferrum	Burke, Va.	D4-'90	14/14
88	Warren, Terrence	WR	6-1	200	8/2/69	2	Hampton	Suffolk, Va.	D5-'93	2/0
95	Wells, Dean	LB	6-3	238	7/20/70	2	Kentucky	Louisville, Ky.	D4-'93	14/1
64	Williams, Brent	DE	6-4	285	10/23/64	9	Toledo	Flint, Mich.	UFA(NE)-'94	13/2*
90	Wooden, Terry	LB	6-3	239	1/14/67	5	Syracuse	Farmington, Conn.	D2a-'90	16/16

* Ballard played 16 games with Buffalo in '93; Barrett active for 16 games with Detroit; Brandon played 6 games with Cleveland, 7 games with Seattle; Childs active for 2 games but did not play; Frerotte inactive for 5 games; Graham inactive for 16 games; Odomes played 16 games with Buffalo; Shaw active for 2 games but did not play; Tofflemire active for 13 games but did not play; Williams played 13 games with New England.

\# Unrestricted free agent; subject to developments.

† Restricted free agent; subject to developments.

t- Seahawks traded for Barrett (Detroit).

Retired—C Grant Feasel, 11-year veteran, 0 games in '93; RB Rueben Mayes, 8-year veteran, 1 game in '93.

Players lost through free agency (4): G Darrick Brilz (Cin; 16 games in '93), CB Dwayne Harper (SD; 14), T Andy Heck (Chi; 16), RB John L. Williams (Pitt; 16).

Also played with Seahawks in '93—LB Ray Berry (7 games), LB Dino Hackett (3), CB James Jefferson (10), WR Doug Thomas (16).

COACHING STAFF

Head Coach,
Tom Flores

Pro Career: Named the fourth head coach in the history of the Seahawks on January 6, 1992. Had served as president and general manager from February 22, 1989. Flores previously served as the head coach of the Oakland/Los Angeles Raiders from 1979 through 1987. He won two Super Bowl titles with the Raiders, 27-10 over the Philadelphia Eagles in Super Bowl XV after the 1980 season, and 38-9 over the Washington Redskins in Super Bowl XVIII in 1983. Those are the only Super Bowl triumphs by an AFC team in the 1980s. The 1980 Raiders are the only Wild Card team to win the Super Bowl. Flores was a member of the Raiders' organization for 22 seasons, as a quarterback (1960-61, 1963-66), assistant coach (1972-78), and head coach (1979-87). Also played for the Buffalo Bills (1967-68) and Kansas City Chiefs (1969-70), and coached with the Bills (1971) before returning to the Raiders as a coach. Is one of two players in league history to have Super Bowl rings as a player (Kansas City, Super Bowl IV), assistant coach (Raiders, Super Bowl XI) and head coach (Raiders, Super Bowls XV and XVIII). Still holds the Raiders' record with six touchdown passes in a 1963 game. Career record: 99-80-0.
Background: Quarterback at Fresno, California, Junior College 1954-55 and the College of the Pacific 1956-57. Coached at his alma mater in 1959 before joining the Raiders as a quarterback in 1960.
Personal: Born March 21, 1937, in Fresno, California. Tom and his wife, Barbara, live in Kirkland, Washington, and have twin sons, Mark and Scott, and a daughter, Kim.

ASSISTANT COACHES

Tommy Brasher, defensive line; born December 30, 1940, El Dorado, Ark., lives in Redmond, Wash. Linebacker Arkansas 1962-63. No pro playing experience. College coach: Arkansas 1970, Virginia Tech 1971, Northeast Louisiana 1974, 1976, Southern Methodist 1977-81. Pro coach: Shreveport Steamer (WFL) 1975, New England Patriots 1982-84, Philadelphia Eagles 1985, Atlanta Falcons 1986-89, Tampa Bay Buccaneers 1990, joined Seahawks in 1992.

Bob Bratkowski, wide receivers; born December 2, 1955, San Angelo, Tex., lives in Redmond, Wash. Wide receiver Washington State 1974, 1976-77. No pro playing experience. College coach: Missouri 1978-80, Weber State 1981-85, Wyoming 1986, Washington State 1987-88, Miami 1989-91. Pro coach: Joined Seahawks in 1992.

Dave Brown, defensive assistant; born January 16, 1953, Akron, Ohio, lives in Woodinville, Wash. Defensive back Michigan 1972-74. Pro defensive back Pittsburgh Steelers 1975, Seattle Seahawks 1976-86, Green Bay Packers 1987-90. Pro coach: Joined Seahawks in 1992.

Tom Catlin, quality control; born September 8, 1931, Ponca City, Okla., lives in Redmond, Wash. Center-linebacker Oklahoma 1950-52. Pro linebacker Cleveland Browns 1953-54, 1957-58, Philadelphia Eagles 1959. College coach: Army 1956. Pro coach: Dallas Texans-Kansas City Chiefs 1960-65, Los Angeles Rams 1966-77, Buffalo Bills 1978-82, joined Seahawks in 1983.

Larry Kennan, offensive coordinator-quarterbacks; born June 13, 1944, Pomona, Calif., lives in Kirkland, Wash. Quarterback La Verne College 1962-65. No pro playing experience. College coach: Colorado 1969-71, Nevada-Las Vegas 1973-75, Southern Methodist 1976-78, Lamar 1979-81 (head coach). Pro coach: Los Angeles Raiders 1982-87, Denver Broncos 1988, Indianapolis Colts 1989-90, London Monarchs (World League) 1991 (head coach), joined Seahawks in 1992.

Arnie Matsumoto, staff assistant; born December 18, 1962, Isesaki, Gumma, Japan, lives in Kirkland, Wash. No college or pro playing experience. Pro coach: Joined Seahawks in 1989.

Paul Moyer, defensive backfield; born July 26, 1961, Villa Park, Calif., lives in Renton, Wash. Safety Fullerton, Calif., J.C. 1979-80, Arizona State 1981-82. Pro safety Seattle Seahawks 1983-89. Pro coach: Joined Seahawks in 1990.

Howard Mudd, offensive line; born February 10, 1942, Midland, Mich., lives in Kirkland, Wash. Guard Hillsdale College 1961-63. Pro guard San Francisco 49ers 1964-69, Chicago Bears 1969-71. College coach: California 1972-73. Pro coach: San Diego Chargers 1974-76, San Francisco 49ers 1977, Seattle Seahawks 1978-82, Cleveland Browns 1983-88, Kansas City Chiefs 1989-92, rejoined Seahawks in 1993.

Russ Purnell, special teams-tight ends; born June 12, 1948, Chicago, Ill., lives in Bellevue, Wash. Center Orange Coast, Calif., J.C. 1966-67, Whittier College 1968-69. No pro playing experience. College coach: Whittier 1970-71, Southern California 1982-85. Pro coach: Joined Seahawks in 1986.

Frank Raines, strength and conditioning; born November 29, 1960, Portsmouth, Va., lives in Renton, Wash. No college or pro playing experience. Pro coach: Washington Redskins 1986-89, joined Seahawks in 1990.

Clarence Shelmon, running backs; born September 17, 1952, Bossier, La., lives in Kirkland, Wash. Running back Houston 1971-75. No pro playing experience. College coach: Army 1978-80, Indiana 1981-83, Arizona 1984-86, Southern California 1987-90. Pro coach: Los Angeles Rams 1991, joined Seahawks in 1992.

Rusty Tillman, defensive coordinator-linebackers; born February 27, 1948, Beloit, Wis., lives in Redmond, Wash. Linebacker Northern Arizona 1967-69. Pro linebacker Washington Redskins 1970-77. Pro coach: Joined Seahawks in 1979.

1994 FIRST-YEAR ROSTER

Name	Pos.	Ht.	Wt.	Birthdate	College	Hometown	How Acq.
Adams, Sam	DT	6-3	285	6/13/73	Texas A&M	Houston, Tex.	D1
Atkins, James (1)	G	6-6	291	1/28/70	S.W. Louisiana	Amite, La.	FA
Atkinson, Jason	LB	6-3	230	10/11/70	Texas A&M	Houston, Tex.	FA
Bellamy, Jay	S	5-11	177	7/8/72	Rutgers	Matawan, N.J.	FA
Bryant, Steve	LB	6-3	240	7/2/71	Nevada	Sparks, Nev.	FA
Butler, Hillary	LB	6-2	240	1/5/71	Washington	Tacoma, Wash.	FA
Carter, Marcus	WR	5-11	205	8/18/71	S.W. Louisiana	Mansfield, La.	FA
Crumpler, Carlester	TE	6-6	255	9/5/71	East Carolina	Greenville, N.C.	D7
DeVries, Jed	T	6-5	282	1/6/71	Utah State	Plain City, Utah	FA
Gordon, Steve (1)	C	6-3	279	4/15/69	California	Nevada City, Calif.	FA
Hamilton, Bobby	DE	6-4	266	7/1/71	Southern Mississippi	East Marion, Miss.	FA
Kegarise, Mike	T	6-5	310	6/19/71	Edinboro	Milan, Ohio	FA
Mawae, Kevin	C	6-4	288	1/23/71	Louisiana State	Savannah, Ga.	D2
McDaniel, Curtis	DT	6-3	283	2/12/70	Jacksonville State	Ft. Payne, Ala.	FA
McKnight, James	WR	6-0	181	6/17/72	Liberty	Apopka, Fla.	FA
Seegars, Stacy	G	6-3	337	4/26/71	Clemson	Kershaw, N.C.	FA
Shamsid-Deen, M. (1)	RB	5-11	200	11/16/69	Tenn.-Chattanooga	Decatur, Ga.	D8-'92
Smith, Lamar	RB	5-11	230	11/29/70	Houston	Ft. Wayne, Ind.	D3
Strong, Mack (1)	RB	6-0	211	9/11/71	Georgia	Columbus, Ga.	FA
Tinner, Glenn	G	6-5	292	3/3/70	Temple	Hanover, Pa.	FA
Watters, Orlando	CB	5-11	177	10/26/71	Arkansas	Anniston, Ala.	FA
Werner, Matt	DT	6-3	265	6/14/71	UCLA	Anaheim, Calif.	FA
Whigham, Larry	S	6-2	202	6/23/72	Southeast Louisiana	Hattiesburg, Miss.	D4
Wood, Rick	RB	6-2	242	7/19/71	Norfolk State	Washington, D.C.	FA

The term NFL Rookie is defined as a player who is in his first season of professional football and has not been on the roster of another professional football team for any regular-season or postseason games. A Rookie is designated by an "R" on NFL rosters. Players who have been active in another professional football league or players who have NFL experience, including either preseason training camp or being on an Active List or Inactive List, or on Reserve/Injured or Reserve/Physically Unable to Perform for fewer than six regular-season games, are termed NFL First-Year Players. An NFL First-Year Player is designated by a "1" on NFL rosters. Thereafter, a player is credited with an additional year of experience for each season in which he accumulates six games on the Active List or Inactive List, or on Reserve/Injured or Reserve/Physically Unable to Perform.

NOTES

The NFC

ARIZONA CARDINALS

National Football Conference
Eastern Division
Team Colors: Cardinal Red, Black, and White
P.O. Box 888
Phoenix, Arizona 85001-0888
Telephone: (602) 379-0101

CLUB OFFICIALS

President: William V. Bidwill
Head Coach and General Manager: Buddy Ryan
Executive Vice President: Joe Rhein
Vice President: Larry Wilson
Secretary and General Counsel:
  Thomas J. Guilfoil
Treasurer and Chief Financial Officer:
  Charley Schlegel
Assistant General Manager: Bob Ackles
Director of Broadcast Sales: John Shean
Public Relations Director: Paul Jensen
Media Coordinator: Greg Gladysiewski
Director of Community Relations: Adele Harris
Director of Marketing: Joe Castor
Ticket Manager: Steve Walsh
Trainer: John Omohundro
Assistant Trainers: Jim Shearer, Jeff Herndon
Equipment Manager: Mark Ahlemeier
Assistant Equipment Manager: Steve Christensen
Stadium: Sun Devil Stadium •**Capacity:** 73,377
  Fifth Street
  Tempe, Arizona 85287
Playing Surface: Grass
Training Camp: Northern Arizona University
  Flagstaff, Arizona 86011

1994 SCHEDULE
PRESEASON

Aug. 5	**San Francisco**	6:30
Aug. 13	**Chicago**	6:00
Aug. 19	at Detroit	7:30
Aug. 25	at Denver	7:00

REGULAR SEASON

Sept. 4	at Los Angeles Rams	1:00
Sept. 11	**New York Giants**	5:00
Sept. 18	at Cleveland	1:00
Sept. 25	Open Date	
Oct. 2	**Minnesota**	1:00
Oct. 9	at Dallas	3:00
Oct. 16	at Washington	1:00
Oct. 23	**Dallas**	1:00
Oct. 30	**Pittsburgh**	6:00
Nov. 6	at Philadelphia	4:00
Nov. 13	at New York Giants	1:00
Nov. 20	**Philadelphia**	2:00
Nov. 27	**Chicago**	2:00
Dec. 4	at Houston	3:00
Dec. 11	**Washington**	2:00
Dec. 18	**Cincinnati**	2:00
Dec. 24	at Atlanta	1:00

RECORD HOLDERS
INDIVIDUAL RECORDS—CAREER

Category	Name	Performance
Rushing (Yds.)	Ottis Anderson, 1979-1986	7,999
Passing (Yds.)	Jim Hart, 1966-1983	34,639
Passing (TDs)	Jim Hart, 1966-1983	209
Receiving (No.)	Roy Green, 1979-1990	522
Receiving (Yds.)	Roy Green, 1979-1990	8,497
Interceptions	Larry Wilson, 1960-1972	52
Punting (Avg.)	Jerry Norton, 1959-1961	44.9
Punt Return (Avg.)	Charley Trippi, 1947-1955	13.7
Kickoff Return (Avg.)	Ollie Matson, 1952, 1954-58	28.5
Field Goals	Jim Bakken, 1962-1978	282
Touchdowns (Tot.)	Roy Green, 1979-1990	70
Points	Jim Bakken, 1962-1978	1,380

INDIVIDUAL RECORDS—SINGLE SEASON

Category	Name	Performance
Rushing (Yds.)	Ottis Anderson, 1979	1,605
Passing (Yds.)	Neil Lomax, 1984	4,614
Passing (TDs)	Charley Johnson, 1963	28
	Neil Lomax, 1984	28
Receiving (No.)	J.T. Smith, 1987	91
Receiving (Yds.)	Roy Green, 1984	1,555
Interceptions	Bob Nussbaumer, 1949	12
Punting (Avg.)	Jerry Norton, 1960	45.6
Punt Return (Avg.)	John (Red) Cochran, 1949	20.9
Kickoff Return (Avg.)	Ollie Matson, 1958	35.5
Field Goals	Jim Bakken, 1967	27
Touchdowns (Tot.)	John David Crow, 1962	17
Points	Jim Bakken, 1967	117
	Neil O'Donoghue, 1984	117

INDIVIDUAL RECORDS—SINGLE GAME

Category	Name	Performance
Rushing (Yds.)	John David Crow, 12-18-60	203
Passing (Yds.)	Neil Lomax, 12-16-84	468
Passing (TDs)	Jim Hardy, 10-2-50	6
	Charley Johnson, 9-26-65	6
	Charley Johnson, 11-2-69	6
Receiving (No.)	Sonny Randle, 11-4-62	16
Receiving (Yds.)	Sonny Randle, 11-4-62	256
Interceptions	Bob Nussbaumer, 11-13-49	*4
	Jerry Norton, 11-20-60	*4
Field Goals	Jim Bakken, 9-24-67	*7
Touchdowns (Tot.)	Ernie Nevers, 11-28-29	*6
Points	Ernie Nevers, 11-28-29	*40

*NFL Record

COACHING HISTORY
Chicago 1920-1959, St. Louis 1960-1987,
Phoenix 1988-1993
(386-526-39)

1920-22	John (Paddy) Driscoll	17-8-4
1923-24	Arnold Horween	13-8-1
1925-26	Norman Barry	16-8-2
1927	Guy Chamberlin	3-7-1
1928	Fred Gillies	1-5-0
1929	Dewey Scanlon	6-6-1
1930	Ernie Nevers	5-6-2
1931	LeRoy Andrews*	0-1-0
1931	Ernie Nevers	5-3-0
1932	Jack Chevigny	2-6-2
1933-34	Paul Schissler	6-15-1
1935-38	Milan Creighton	16-26-4
1939	Ernie Nevers	1-10-0
1940-42	Jimmy Conzelman	8-22-3
1943-45	Phil Handler**	1-29-0
1946-48	Jimmy Conzelman	27-10-0
1949	Phil Handler-Buddy Parker***	2-4-0
1949	Raymond (Buddy) Parker	4-1-1
1950-51	Earl (Curly) Lambeau****	7-15-0
1951	Phil Handler-Cecil Isbell#	1-1-0
1952	Joe Kuharich	4-8-0
1953-54	Joe Stydahar	3-20-1
1955-57	Ray Richards	14-21-1
1958-61	Frank (Pop) Ivy##	17-29-2
1961	Chuck Drulis-Ray Prochaska-	
	Ray Willsey###	2-0-0
1962-65	Wally Lemm	27-26-3
1966-70	Charley Winner	35-30-5
1971-72	Bob Hollway	8-18-2
1973-77	Don Coryell	42-29-1
1978-79	Bud Wilkinson####	9-20-0

SUN DEVIL STADIUM

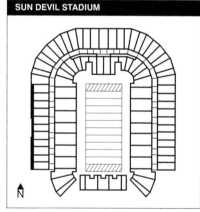

1979	Larry Wilson	2-1-0
1980-85	Jim Hanifan	39-50-1
1986-89	Gene Stallings@	23-34-1
1989	Hank Kuhlmann	0-5-0
1990-93	Joe Bugel	20-44-0

* Resigned after one game in 1931
** Co-coach with Walt Kiesling in Chicago Cardinals-Pittsburgh merger in 1944
*** Co-coaches for first six games in 1949
**** Resigned after 10 games in 1951
# Co-coaches
Resigned after 12 games in 1961
Co-coaches
Released after 13 games in 1979
@ Released after 11 games in 1989

1993 TEAM RECORD

PRESEASON (3-1)

Date	Result		Opponents
8/7	W	24-13	L.A. Rams
8/14	W	11-10	at Chicago
8/21	L	3-10	at San Diego
8/27	W	34-9	Denver

REGULAR SEASON (7-9)

Date	Result		Opponents	Att.
9/5	L	17-23	at Philadelphia	59,831
9/12	L	17-10	at Washington	53,525
9/19	L	10-17	Dallas	73,025
9/26	L	20-26	at Detroit	57,180
10/10	L	21-23	New England	36,115
10/17	L	36-6	Washington	48,143
10/24	L	14-28	at San Francisco	62,020
10/31	L	17-20	New Orleans	36,778
11/7	W	16-3	Philadelphia	41,634
11/14	L	15-20	at Dallas	64,224
11/28	L	17-19	at N.Y. Giants	59,979
12/5	W	38-10	L.A. Rams	33,964
12/12	L	14-21	Detroit	39,393
12/19	W	30-27	at Seattle (OT)	45,737
12/26	W	17-6	N.Y. Giants	53,414
1/2	W	27-10	at Atlanta	44,360

(OT) Overtime

SCORE BY PERIODS

Cardinals	54	98	79	92	3	—	326
Opponents	58	84	53	74	0	—	269

ATTENDANCE

Home 362,466   Away 446,856   Total 809,322
Single-game home record, 71,628 (11-22-92)
Single-season home record, 472,937 (1988)

1993 TEAM STATISTICS

	Cardinals	Opp.
Total First Downs	295	278
Rushing	107	106
Passing	173	158
Penalty	15	14
Third Down: Made/Att	102/221	76/206
Third Down Pct.	46.2	36.9
Fourth Down: Made/Att	7/14	1/5
Fourth Down Pct.	50.0	20.0
Total Net Yards	5213	5167
Avg. Per Game	325.8	322.9
Total Plays	1007	962
Avg. Per Play	5.2	5.4
Net Yards Rushing	1809	1861
Avg. Per Game	113.1	116.3
Total Rushes	452	433
Net Yards Passing	3404	3306
Avg. Per Game	212.8	206.6
Sacked/Yards Lost	33/231	34/205
Gross Yards	3635	3511
Att./Completions	522/310	495/281
Completion Pct.	59.4	56.8
Had Intercepted	20	9
Punts/Avg.	73/43.7	78/42.7
Net Punting Avg.	73/37.8	78/36.8
Penalties/Yards Lost	77/644	95/730
Fumbles/Ball Lost	23/11	27/17
Touchdowns	37	27
Rushing	12	13
Passing	21	14
Returns	4	0
Avg. Time of Possession	31:54	28:06

1993 INDIVIDUAL STATISTICS

PASSING	Att	Cmp	Yds.	Pct.	TD	Int	Tkld.	Rate
Beuerlein	418	258	3164	61.7	18	17	29/206	82.5
Chandler	103	52	471	50.5	3	2	4/25	64.8
Hearst	1	0	0	0.0	0	1	0/0	0.0
Cardinals	522	310	3635	59.4	21	20	33/231	78.0
Opponents	495	281	3511	56.8	14	9	34/205	80.8

SCORING	TD R	TD P	TD Rt	PAT	FG	Saf	PTS
G. Davis	0	0	0	37/37	21/28	0	100
Moore	9	0	0	0/0	0/0	0	54
Proehl	0	7	0	0/0	0/0	0	42
Clark	0	4	0	0/0	0/0	0	24
R. Hill	0	4	0	0/0	0/0	0	24
Centers	0	3	0	0/0	0/0	0	18
Bailey	1	0	1	0/0	0/0	0	12
Williams	0	0	2	0/0	0/0	0	12
Blount	1	0	0	0/0	0/0	0	6
Edwards	0	1	0	0/0	0/0	0	6
Hearst	1	0	0	0/0	0/0	0	6
Lynch	0	0	1	0/0	0/0	0	6
Reeves	0	1	0	0/0	0/0	0	6
Rolle	0	1	0	0/0	0/0	0	6
Swann	0	0	0	0/0	0/0	1	2
Cardinals	12	21	4	37/37	21/28	2	326
Opponents	13	14	0	27/27	26/35	1	269

RUSHING	Att.	Yds.	Avg.	LG	TD
Moore	263	1018	3.9	20	9
Hearst	76	264	3.5	57	1
Bailey	49	253	5.2	31	1
Centers	25	152	6.1	33	0
Proehl	8	47	5.9	17	0
Beuerlein	22	45	2.0	20	0
Blount	5	28	5.6	7	1
Chandler	3	2	0.7	1	0
Camarillo	1	0	0.0	0	0
Cardinals	452	1809	4.0	57	12
Opponents	433	1861	4.3	48	13

RECEIVING	No.	Yds.	Avg.	LG	TD
Centers	66	603	9.1	29	3
Proehl	65	877	13.5	51t	7
Clark	63	818	13.0	55	4
R. Hill	35	519	14.8	58t	4
Bailey	32	243	7.6	30	0
Edwards	13	326	25.1	65t	1
Rolle	10	67	6.7	22	1
Reeves	9	67	7.4	18	1
Hearst	6	18	3.0	9	0
Blount	5	36	7.2	9	0
Ware	3	45	15.0	27	0
Moore	3	16	5.3	6	0
Cardinals	310	3635	11.7	65t	21
Opponents	281	3511	12.5	86	14

INTERCEPTIONS	No.	Yds.	Avg.	LG	TD
Lynch	3	13	4.3	13	0
Williams	2	87	43.5	46t	1
Booty	2	24	12.0	19	0
Oldham	1	0	0.0	0	0
Zordich	1	0	0.0	0	0
Cardinals	9	124	13.8	46t	1
Opponents	20	143	7.2	37	0

PUNTING	No.	Yds.	Avg.	In 20	LG
Camarillo	73	3189	43.7	23	61
Cardinals	73	3189	43.7	23	61
Opponents	78	3333	42.7	23	62

PUNT RETURNS	No.	FC	Yds.	Avg.	LG	TD
Bailey	35	5	282	8.1	58t	1
Blount	9	3	90	10.0	25	0
Edwards	3	3	12	4.0	11	0
Cardinals	47	11	384	8.2	58t	1
Opponents	30	19	267	8.9	33	0

KICKOFF RETURNS	No.	Yds.	Avg.	LG	TD
Bailey	31	699	22.5	48	0
Blount	8	163	20.4	27	0
Edwards	3	51	17.0	20	0
Lofton	1	18	18.0	18	0
Moore	1	9	9.0	9	0
Smith	1	11	11.0	11	0
Cardinals	45	951	21.1	48	0
Opponents	51	994	19.5	61	0

SACKS	No.
Harvey	9.5
Nunn	6.5
Swann	3.5
Bankston	3.0
Booty	3.0
M. Jones	3.0
Stowe	1.5
R. Davis	1.0
E. Hill	1.0
Lynch	1.0
Oldham	1.0
Cardinals	34.0
Opponents	33.0

1994 DRAFT CHOICES

Round	Name	Pos.	College
1	Jamir Miller	LB	UCLA
2	Chuck Levy	RB	Arizona
3	Rich Braham	G	West Virginia
	Eric England	DE	Texas A&M
4	Perry Carter	DB	Southern Mississippi
	John Reece	DB	Nebraska
	Terry Irving	LB	McNeese State
5	Anthony Redmon	G	Auburn
6	Terry Samuels	TE	Kentucky
7	Frank Harvey	RB	Georgia

ARIZONA CARDINALS

1994 VETERAN ROSTER

No.	Name	Pos.	Ht.	Wt.	Birthdate	NFL Exp.	College	Hometown	How Acq.	'93 Games/ Starts
63	Bankston, Michael	DE-DT	6-2	290	3/12/70	3	Sam Houston State	East Bernard, Tex.	D4b-'92	16/12
7	Beuerlein, Steve	QB	6-2	209	3/7/65	8	Notre Dame	Hollywood, Calif.	UFA(Dall)-'93	16/14
25	Blount, Eric	RB-KR	5-9	190	9/22/70	3	North Carolina	Ayden, N.C.	D8-'92	6/0
42	Booty, John	S	6-0	180	10/9/65	7	Texas Christian	Carthage, Tex.	UFA(Phil)-'93	12/12
54	# Braxton, David	LB	6-2	230	5/26/65	6	Wake Forest	Jacksonville, N.C.	FA-'90	16/0
78	Brown, Chad	DE	6-7	265	7/9/71	2	Mississippi	Thomasville, Ga.	D8a-'93	5/0
26	Cecil, Chuck	S	6-0	190	11/8/64	7	Arizona	San Diego, Calif.	UFA(GB)-'93	15/7
37	Centers, Larry	RB	6-0	200	6/1/68	5	Stephen F. Austin	Tatum, Tex.	D5-'90	16/9
84	Clark, Gary	WR	5-9	173	5/1/62	10	James Madison	Dublin, Va.	UFA(Wash)-'93	14/10
62	Coleman, Ben	G	6-6	335	5/18/71	2	Wake Forest	South Hill, Va.	D2-'93	12/0
59	Cunningham, Ed	C	6-3	290	8/17/69	3	Washington	Alexandria, Va.	D3-'92	15/15
64	Cunningham, Rick	T	6-6	307	1/4/67	4	Texas A&M	Los Angeles, Calif.	FA-'92	16/16
5	Davis, Greg	K	6-0	200	10/29/65	7	Citadel	Atlanta, Ga.	PB(Atl)-'91	16/0
65	Dye, Ernest	G	6-6	325	7/15/71	2	South Carolina	Greenwood, S.C.	D1b-'93	7/1
83	Edwards, Anthony	WR	5-9	190	5/26/66	6	New Mexico Highlands	Casa Grande, Ariz.	FA-'91	16/0
80	Fann, Chad	TE	6-3	250	6/7/70	2	Florida A&M	Jacksonville, Fla.	FA-'93	1/0
10	Feagles, Jeff	P	6-1	205	3/7/66	7	Miami	Scottsdale, Ariz.	UFA(Phil)-'94	16/0*
2	Furrer, Will	QB	6-3	210	2/5/68	3	Virginia Tech	Pullman, Wash.	W(Chi)-'93	0*
31	# Harris, Odie	S	6-0	190	4/1/66	7	Sam Houston State	Bryan, Tex.	W(Clev)-'92	16/0
23	Hearst, Garrison	RB	5-11	215	1/4/71	2	Georgia	Lincolnton, Ga.	D1a-'93	6/5
58	Hill, Eric	LB	6-2	250	11/14/66	6	Louisiana State	Galveston, Tex.	D1-'89	13/12
81	† Hill, Randal	WR	5-10	177	9/21/69	4	Miami	Miami, Fla.	T(Mia)-'91	16/8
97	Hyche, Steve	LB	6-2	226	6/12/63	5	Livingston	Cordova, Ala.	FA-'91	2/0
53	# Jax, Garth	LB	6-3	240	9/16/63	9	Florida State	Houston, Tex.	PB(Dall)-'89	16/0
72	Johnson, Chuckie	DT	6-4	310	3/5/69	2	Auburn	Fayetteville, N.C.	FA-'93	5/0
75	† Jones, Mike	DE-DT	6-4	285	8/25/69	4	North Carolina State	Columbia, S.C.	D2-'91	16/2
59	Joyner, Seth	LB	6-2	235	11/18/64	9	Texas-El Paso	Spring Valley, N.Y.	UFA(Phil)-'94	16/16*
57	Kirk, Randy	LB	6-2	231	12/27/64	7	San Diego State	San Diego, Calif.	UFA(Cin)-'94	16/0*
28	Lofton, Steve	CB	5-9	180	11/26/68	4	Texas A&M	Jacksonville, Miss.	FA-'91	13/0
29	# Lynch, Lorenzo	CB	5-10	200	4/6/63	8	Cal State-Sacramento	Oakland, Calif.	PB(Chi)-'90	16/15
9	McMahon, Jim	QB	6-1	195	8/21/59	13	Brigham Young	Jersey City, N.J.	FA-'94	12/12*
94	Merritt, David	LB	6-1	237	9/8/71	2	North Carolina State	Raleigh, N.C.	FA-'93	3/0
30	Moore, Ron	RB	5-10	220	11/26/70	2	Pittsburg State	Spencer, Okla.	D4-'93	16/11
27	† Oldham, Chris	CB	5-9	183	10/28/68	4	Oregon	Sacramento, Calif.	FA-'92	16/6
87	Proehl, Ricky	WR	6-0	190	3/7/68	5	Wake Forest	Hillsborough, N.J.	D3-'90	16/16
79	Rucker, Keith	DE-DT	6-3	325	11/20/68	3	Ohio Wesleyan	University Park, Ill.	FA-'92	16/15
67	Sharpe, Luis	T	6-5	295	6/16/60	13	UCLA	Detroit, Mich.	D1-'82	16/16
96	Simmons, Clyde	DE	6-6	280	8/4/64	9	Western Carolina	Wilmington, N.C.	UFA(Phil)-'94	16/16*
90	Stowe, Tyronne	LB	6-1	249	5/30/65	8	Rutgers	Passaic, N.J.	PB(Pitt)-'91	15/15
98	Swann, Eric	DE-DT	6-4	310	8/16/70	4	No College	Swann Station, N.C.	D1-'91	9/9
71	Tucker, Mark	C	6-3	290	4/29/68	2	Southern California	Los Angeles, Calif.	FA-'93	0*
52	Wallerstedt, Brett	LB	6-1	240	11/24/70	2	Arizona State	Manhattan, Kan.	D6-'93	7/0
85	Ware, Derek	RB-TE	6-2	255	9/17/67	3	Central State, Ohio	Sacramento, Calif.	D7-'92	16/1
35	† Williams, Aeneas	CB	5-10	187	1/29/69	4	Southern	New Orleans, La.	D3-'91	16/16
21	t- Williams, James	CB	5-10	185	3/30/67	5	Fresno State	Coalinga, Calif.	T(Buff)-'94	15/11*
68	Wolf, Joe	G	6-6	295	12/28/66	6	Boston College	Allentown, Pa.	D1b-'89	8/5
38	# Zordich, Michael	S	6-1	200	10/12/63	8	Penn State	Youngstown, Ohio	PB(NYJ)-'89	16/9

* Feagles played 16 games with Philadelphia in '93; Furrer active for 1 game but did not play; Joyner played 16 games with Philadelphia; Kirk played 16 games with Cincinnati; McMahon played 12 games with Minnesota; Simmons played 16 games with Philadelphia; Tucker active for 4 games but did not play; Williams played 15 games with Buffalo.

\# Unrestricted free agent; subject to developments.

† Restricted free agent; subject to developments.

t- Cardinals traded for J. Williams (Buffalo).

Players lost through free agency (7): P Rich Camarillo (Hou; 16 games in '93), QB Chris Chandler (Rams; 4), DE Reuben Davis (SD; 16), LB Ken Harvey (Wash; 16), CB Robert Massey (Det; 10), TE Walter Reeves (Clev; 16), G Lance Smith (NYG; 16).

Also played with Cardinals in '93—RB Johnny Bailey (13 games), TE Pat Beach (15), CB Dexter Davis (6), S Dave Duerson (16), LB Jock Jones (7), C Kani Kauahi (1), G Mark May (11), LB Freddie Joe Nunn (16), TE Butch Rolle (16).

COACHING STAFF

Head Coach,
Buddy Ryan

Pro Career: Named head coach and general manager on February 3, 1994. Became thirty-second head coach in the history of the franchise dating back to 1920. Known as one of the game's top defensive minds, he devised the "46 defense" with its multiple variations of alignments and coverages. Served as defensive coordinator for Houston Oilers' in 1993. Defense set a club record with 52 quarterback sacks and ranked first in the league in both rushing defense (79.6 yards per game) and interceptions (26). Posted 43-35-1 record as head coach for Philadelphia Eagles from 1986-1990, a span which included consecutive playoff berths his final three seasons with records of 10-6, 11-5, and 10-6, highlighted by the NFC East title in 1988, the Eagles' first divisional crown since 1980. Defensive coordinator of the Chicago Bears from 1978-1985 as the Bears' defense set an NFL record with 72 quarterback sacks in 1984, then a year later led the league in nine defensive categories. In Chicago's Super Bowl XX victory over New England, Chicago held the Patriots to a Super Bowl record fewest first downs (7) and fewest rushing first downs (1), while allowing just 123 total yards. En route to the Super Bowl, Chicago posted playoff shutouts against the Los Angeles Rams and New York Giants, an unprecedented accomplishment in NFL postseason annals. Served as defensive line coach for Bud Grant's Minnesota Vikings in 1976-77 as the "Purple People Eaters" line of Carl Eller, Alan Page, and Jim Marshall helped the Vikings reach Super Bowl XI. Ryan was a member of the New York Jets defensive staff from 1968-1975 under Hall of Fame coach Weeb Ewbank, when Jets upset heavily-favored Baltimore Colts in Super Bowl III. Career record: 43-35-1.

Background: Ryan was a four-year letterman at Oklahoma State from 1952-55 as a guard. While serving in the U.S. Army in Korea, Ryan played on the Fourth Army championship team in Japan. He began his coaching career at the high school level in Texas at Gainesville (1957-59) and Marshall (1960), then was a college assistant at Buffalo (1961-65), Vanderbilt (1966), and Pacific (1967). Has a master's degree in education from Middle Tennessee State.

Personal: Born February 17, 1934, in Frederick, Oklahoma. Buddy and his wife, Joan, live in Phoenix and have three sons—twins Rex and Rob, and Jim.

ASSISTANT COACHES

David Atkins, offensive coordinator-running backs; born May 18, 1949, Victoria, Tex., lives in Phoenix. Running back Texas-El Paso 1970-72. Pro running back San Francisco 49ers 1973, Honolulu (WFL) 1974, San Diego Chargers 1975. College coach: Texas-El Paso 1979-80, San Diego State 1981-85. Pro coach: Philadelphia Eagles 1986-92, New England Patriots 1993, joined Cardinals in 1994.

Matt Cavanaugh, quarterbacks; born October 27, 1956, Youngstown, Ohio, lives in Phoenix. Quarterback Pittsburgh 1974-77. Pro quarterback New England Patriots 1978-82, San Francisco 49ers 1983-85, Philadelphia Eagles 1986-89, New York Giants 1990-91. College coach: Pittsburgh 1993. Pro coach: Joined Cardinals in 1994.

Ted Cottrell, linebackers; born June 13, 1947, Chester, Pa., lives in Phoenix. Linebacker Delaware Valley College 1966-68. Pro linebacker Atlanta Falcons 1969-70, Winnipeg Blue Bombers (CFL) 1971. College coach: Rutgers 1973-80, 1983. Pro coach: Kansas City Chiefs 1981-82, New Jersey Generals (USFL) 1983-84, Buffalo Bills 1986-89, joined Cardinals in 1990.

Ronnie Jones, defensive coordinator; born October 17, 1955, Dumas, Tex., lives in Phoenix. Running back Northwestern Oklahoma, State 1974-77. No pro playing experience. College coach: Northeastern Oklahoma State 1979-83, Tulsa 1984, Arizona State 1985-86. Pro coach: Philadelphia Eagles 1987-90, Los Angeles Rams 1991, Los Angeles Raiders 1992, Houston Oilers 1993, joined Cardinals in 1994.

George Martinez, quality control; born August 5, 1961, Fort Bragg, N.C., lives in Phoenix. Quarterback Northwestern Oklahoma State 1969-72. No pro playing experience. College coach: East Central Oklahoma 1981-87, Panhandle State 1988, New Mexico Highlands 1989-91 (head coach). Pro coach: Joined Cardinals in 1994.

Guy Morriss, offensive line assistant; born May 13, 1951, Colorado City, Tex., lives in Phoenix. Guard Texas Christian 1969-72. Pro guard Philadelphia Eagles 1973-83, New England Patriots 1984-87. College coach: Valdosta State 1992-93. Pro coach: New England Patriots 1988-89, joined Cardinals in 1994.

Dan Neal, offensive line; born August 30, 1949, Corbin, Ky., lives in Phoenix. Center Kentucky 1970-72. Pro center Baltimore Colts 1973-74, Chicago Bears 1975-83. Pro coach: Philadelphia Eagles 1986-91, joined Cardinals in 1994.

Ted Plumb, receivers-tight ends; born August 20, 1939, Reno, Nev., lives in Phoenix. Wide receiver Baylor 1960-61. Pro wide receiver Buffalo Bills 1962. College coach: Cerritos, Calif., J.C. 1966-67, Texas Christian 1968-70, Tulsa 1971, Kansas 1972-73. Pro coach: New York Giants 1974-76, Atlanta Falcons 1977-79, Chicago Bears 1980-85, Philadelphia Eagles 1986-89, joined Cardinals in 1990.

Al Roberts, special teams; born January 6, 1944, Fresno, Calif., lives in Phoenix. Running back Washington 1964-65, Puget Sound 1967-68. No pro playing experience. College coach: Washington 1977-82, Purdue 1986, Wyoming 1987. Pro coach: Los Angeles Express (USFL) 1983-84, Houston Oilers 1984-85, Philadelphia Eagles 1988-90, New York Jets 1991-93, joined Cardinals in 1994.

Bob Rogucki, strength and conditioning; born September 27, 1953, Clarksburg, W. Va., lives in Phoenix. No college or pro playing experience. College coach: Penn State 1981, Weber State 1982, Army 1983-89. Pro coach: Joined Cardinals in 1990.

Rex Ryan, defensive line; born December 13, 1962, Ardmore, Okla., lives in Phoenix. Defensive end Southwest Oklahoma State 1983-86. No pro playing experience. College coach: Eastern Kentucky 1987-88, New Mexico Highlands 1989, Morehead State 1990-93. Pro coach: Joined Cardinals in 1994.

Robert Ryan, defensive backs; born December 13, 1962, Ardmore, Okla., lives in Phoenix. Defensive end-linebacker Southwest Oklahoma State 1983-86. No pro playing experience. College coach: Western Kentucky 1987, Ohio State 1988, Tennessee State 1989-93. Pro coach: Joined Cardinals in 1994.

1994 FIRST-YEAR ROSTER

Name	Pos.	Ht.	Wt.	Birthdate	College	Hometown	How Acq.
Alexander, Brent	S	5-10	184	7/10/71	Tennessee State	Gallatin, Tenn.	FA
Braham, Rich	G	6-4	290	11/6/70	West Virginia	Morgantown, W. Va.	D3a
Bruere, Carl	WR	6-2	185	11/14/68	New Mexico Highlands	Albuquerque, N.M.	FA
Carter, Perry	CB	5-11	194	8/15/71	Southern Mississippi	McComb, Miss.	D4a
Ciaccio, Tom	QB	6-1	190	8/28/69	Holy Cross	Gloversville, N.Y.	FA
England, Eric	DE	6-2	283	3/25/71	Texas A&M	Sugar Land, Tex.	D3b
Faulkner, Greg	T	6-4	305	4/29/72	Millersville, Pa.	Royersford, Pa.	FA
Gardner, Gerome	DT	6-0	260	3/31/72	Tennessee State	Columbus, Ga.	FA
Harvey, Frank	RB	6-0	245	1/19/71	Georgia	Dawson, Ga.	D7
Henesey, Brian	RB	5-10	215	12/10/69	Bucknell	Radnor, Pa.	FA
Irving, Terry	LB	6-0	224	7/3/71	McNeese State	Galveston, Tex.	D4c
Jenkins, Lennie	DT	6-2	257	10/4/71	Northeast Louisiana	Media, Pa.	FA
Kurinsky, York	T	6-3	286	11/11/71	Valdosta State	St. Charles, Ill.	FA
Levy, Chuck	QB-RB	6-0	197	1/7/72	Arizona	Torrance, Calif.	D2
Lopez, Kenny	DE	6-2	275	1/10/70	Miami	Key West, Fla.	FA
McLeod, David	WR	5-11	172	8/15/71	James Madison	Richmond, Va.	FA
Miller, Jamir	LB	6-4	242	11/19/73	UCLA	Oakland, Calif.	D1
Moody, Mike (1)	T	6-5	285	5/9/69	Southern California	San Francisco, Calif.	FA
Owens, Anthony (1)	WR	6-0	194	3/8/69	Tennessee State	Nashville, Tenn.	FA
Pinckney, Jon (1)	WR	6-0	189	5/6/69	Stanford	Bethlehem, Pa.	FA
Redmon, Anthony	G	6-4	308	4/6/71	Auburn	Brewton, Ala.	D5
Reece, John	CB	6-0	203	1/24/71	Nebraska	Crowell, Tex.	D4b
Reeves, Bryan	WR	5-11	195	7/10/70	Nevada	Los Angeles, Calif.	FA
Richardson, Mose	CB	6-2	180	11/22/71	Indiana	Dayton, Ohio	FA
Samuels, Terry	TE	6-2	254	9/27/70	Kentucky	Louisville, Ky.	D6
Shadwick, Richard	DE	6-4	255	7/20/70	Morehead State	Nicholasville, Ky.	FA
Tate, Will	WR	5-10	170	2/5/71	San Diego State	San Diego, Calif.	FA
Wallace, Sean	S	5-8	185	11/13/72	Southern	New Orleans, La.	FA

The term NFL Rookie is defined as a player who is in his first season of professional football and has not been on the roster of another professional football team for any regular-season or postseason games. A Rookie is designated by an "R" on NFL rosters. Players who have been active in another professional football league or players who have NFL experience, including either preseason training camp or being on an Active List or Inactive List, or on Reserve/Injured or Reserve/Physically Unable to Perform for fewer than six regular-season games, are termed NFL First-Year Players. An NFL First-Year Player is designated by a "1" on NFL rosters. Thereafter, a player is credited with an additional year of experience for each season in which he accumulates six games on the Active List or Inactive List, or on Reserve/Injured or Reserve/Physically Unable to Perform.

NOTES

ATLANTA FALCONS

**National Football Conference
Western Division
Team Colors:** Black, Red, Silver, and White
**2745 Burnette Road
Suwanee, Georgia 30174
Telephone:** (404) 945-1111

CLUB OFFICIALS

Chairman of the Board: Rankin M. Smith, Sr.
President: Taylor Smith
Vice President & Chief Financial Officer: Jim Hay
Vice President of Player Personnel: Ken Herock
Director of Player Development: Tommy Nobis
Director of Public Relations: Charlie Taylor
Director of Administration: Rob Jackson
Asst. Director of Public Relations: Frank Kleha
Public Relations Assistant: Gary Glenn
Marketing Reps: Todd Marble, John Knox
Director of Community Relations: Carol Breeding
Director of Ticket Operations: Jack Ragsdale
Asst. Director of Ticket Operations: Mike Jennings
Administrative Asst./Finance: Kevin Anthony
Administrative Asst./Player Personnel: Danny Mock
Scouts: Bill Baker, Scott Campbell, Dick Corrick,
    Elbert Dubenion, Bill Groman
Director of Pro Personnel: Chuck Connor
Controller: Wallace Norman
Trainer: Ron Medlin
Assistant Trainer: Arnold Gamber
Equipment Manager: Whitey Zimmerman
Assistant Equipment Manager: Horace Daniel
Equipment Assistant: Craig Campanozzi
Video Director: Tom Atcheson
Assistant Video Director: Lou Crocker
Stadium: Georgia Dome •**Capacity:** 71,594
    One Georgia Dome Drive
    Atlanta, Georgia 30313
Playing Surface: Artificial turf
Training Camp: 2745 Burnette Road
    Suwanee, Georgia 30174

1994 SCHEDULE

PRESEASON

July 30	vs. San Diego at Canton, Ohio	12:00
Aug. 6	at Denver	7:00
Aug. 12	**Buffalo**	7:00
Aug. 19	at Cleveland	7:30
Aug. 26	**Philadelphia**	7:00

REGULAR SEASON

Sept. 4	at Detroit	1:00
Sept. 11	**Los Angeles Rams**	1:00
Sept. 18	**Kansas City**	8:00
Sept. 25	at Washington	1:00
Oct. 2	at Los Angeles Rams	1:00
Oct. 9	**Tampa Bay**	1:00
Oct. 16	**San Francisco**	1:00
Oct. 23	at Los Angeles Raiders	1:00
Oct. 30	Open Date	
Nov. 6	**San Diego**	1:00
Nov. 13	at New Orleans	12:00
Nov. 20	at Denver	2:00
Nov. 27	**Philadelphia**	1:00
Dec. 4	at San Francisco	1:00
Dec. 11	**New Orleans**	8:00
Dec. 18	vs. Green Bay at Milwaukee	12:00
Dec. 24	**Arizona**	1:00

RECORD HOLDERS

INDIVIDUAL RECORDS—CAREER

Category	Name	Performance
Rushing (Yds.)	Gerald Riggs, 1982-88	6,631
Passing (Yds.)	Steve Bartkowski, 1975-1985	23,468
Passing (TDs)	Steve Bartkowski, 1975-1985	154
Receiving (No.)	Alfred Jenkins, 1975-1983	359
Receiving (Yds.)	Alfred Jenkins, 1975-1983	6,257
Interceptions	Rolland Lawrence, 1973-1980	39
Punting (Avg.)	Rick Donnelly, 1985-89	42.6
Punt Return (Avg.)	Al Dodd, 1973-74	11.8
Kickoff Return (Avg.)	Ron Smith, 1966-67	24.3
Field Goals	Mick Luckhurst, 1981-87	115
Touchdowns (Tot.)	Gerald Riggs, 1982-88	48
	Andre Rison, 1990-93	48
Points	Mick Luckhurst, 1981-87	558

INDIVIDUAL RECORDS—SINGLE SEASON

Category	Name	Performance
Rushing (Yds.)	Gerald Riggs, 1985	1,719
Passing (Yds.)	Steve Bartkowski, 1981	3,830
Passing (TDs)	Steve Bartkowski, 1980	31
Receiving (No.)	Andre Rison, 1992	93
Receiving (Yds.)	Alfred Jenkins, 1981	1,358
Interceptions	Scott Case, 1988	10
Punting (Avg.)	Billy Lothridge, 1968	44.3
Punt Return (Avg.)	Gerald Tinker, 1974	13.9
Kickoff Return (Avg.)	Sylvester Stamps, 1987	27.5
Field Goals	Nick Mike-Mayer, 1973	26
	Norm Johnson, 1993	26
Touchdowns (Tot.)	Andre Rison, 1993	15
Points	Mick Luckhurst, 1981	114

INDIVIDUAL RECORDS—SINGLE GAME

Category	Name	Performance
Rushing (Yds.)	Gerald Riggs, 9-2-84	202
Passing (Yds.)	Steve Bartkowski, 11-15-81	416
Passing (TDs)	Wade Wilson, 12-13-92	5
Receiving (No.)	William Andrews, 11-15-81	15
Receiving (Yds.)	Alfred Jackson, 12-2-84	193
Interceptions	Many times	2
	Last time by Deion Sanders, 12-11-93	
Field Goals	Nick Mike-Mayer, 11-4-73	5
	Tim Mazzetti, 10-30-78	5
Touchdowns (Tot.)	Many times	3
	Last time by Andre Rison, 9-19-93	
Points	Many times	18
	Last time by Andre Rison, 9-19-93	

COACHING HISTORY

(158-259-5)

1966-68	Norb Hecker*	4-26-1
1968-74	Norm Van Brocklin**	37-49-3
1974-76	Marion Campbell***	6-19-0
1976	Pat Peppler	3-6-0
1977-82	Leeman Bennett	47-44-0
1983-86	Dan Henning	22-41-1
1987-89	Marion Campbell****	11-32-0
1989	Jim Hanifan	0-4-0
1990-93	Jerry Glanville	28-38-0

*Released after three games in 1968
**Released after eight games in 1974
***Released after five games in 1976
****Retired after 12 games in 1989

GEORGIA DOME

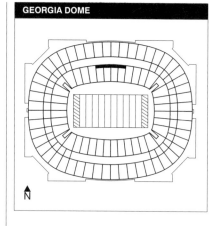

N

1993 TEAM RECORD

PRESEASON (1-3)

Date	Result		Opponents
8/6	L	27-28	Miami
8/14	W	20-10	Tampa Bay
8/21	L	20-37	at Philadelphia
8/27	L	16-17	at Buffalo

REGULAR SEASON (6-10)

Date	Result		Opponents	Att.
9/5	L	13-30	at Detroit	56,216
9/12	L	31-34	New Orleans	64,287
9/19	L	30-37	at San Francisco	63,032
9/27	L	17-45	Pittsburgh	65,477
10/3	L	0-6	at Chicago	57,441
10/14	W	30-24	L.A. Rams	45,231
10/24	W	26-15	at New Orleans	69,043
10/31	L	24-31	Tampa Bay	50,647
11/14	W	13-0	at L.A. Rams	37,073
11/21	W	27-14	Dallas	67,337
11/28	W	17-14	Cleveland	54,510
12/5	L	17-33	at Houston	58,186
12/11	W	27-24	San Francisco	64,688
12/19	L	17-30	at Washington	50,192
12/26	L	17-21	at Cincinnati	27,014
1/2	L	10-27	Phoenix	44,360

SCORE BY PERIODS

Falcons	60	77	68	111	0	—	316
Opponents	78	116	100	91	0	—	385

ATTENDANCE

Home 456,537   Away 418,197   Total 874,734
Single-game home record, 69,898 (11-9-92)
Single-season home record, 553,979 (1992)

1993 TEAM STATISTICS

	Falcons	Opp.
Total First Downs	292	278
Rushing	91	79
Passing	185	180
Penalty	16	19
Third Down: Made/Att.	80/209	73/200
Third Down: Pct	38.3	36.5
Fourth Down: Made/Att.	10/18	7/16
Fourth Down: Pct	55.6	43.8
Total Net Yards	5110	5421
Avg. Per Game	319.4	338.8
Total Plays	1008	951
Avg. Per Play	5.1	5.7
Net Yards Rushing	1590	1784
Avg. Per Game	99.4	111.5
Total Rushes	395	419
Net Yards Passing	3520	3637
Avg. Per Game	220.0	227.3
Sacked/Yards Lost	40/267	27/149
Gross Yards	3787	3786
Att./Completions	573/334	505/308
Completion Pct.	58.3	61.0
Had Intercepted	25	13
Punts/Avg.	72/43.3	74/40.9
Net Punting Avg.	72/37.6	74/35.9
Penalties/Yards Lost	111/838	100/874
Fumbles/Ball Lost	31/17	25/11
Touchdowns	34	46
Rushing	4	14
Passing	28	27
Returns	2	5
Avg. Time of Possession	31:23	28:37

1993 INDIVIDUAL STATISTICS

Passing	Att.	Comp.	Yds.	Pct.	TD	Int.	Tkld.	Rate
Hebert	430	263	2978	61.2	24	17	29/190	84.0
Tolliver	76	39	464	51.3	3	5	3/15	56.0
Miller	66	32	345	48.5	1	3	8/62	50.4
Sanders	1	0	0	0.0	0	0	0/0	39.6
Falcons	573	334	3787	58.3	28	25	40/267	76.3
Opponents	505	308	3786	61.0	27	13	27/149	91.2

SCORING	TD R	TD P	TD Rt	PAT	FG	Saf	PTS
Johnson	0	0	0	34/34	26/27	0	112
Rison	0	15	0	0/0	0/0	0	90
Pritchard	0	7	0	0/0	0/0	0	42
Haynes	0	4	0	0/0	0/0	0	24
Pegram	3	0	0	0/0	0/0	0	18
Broussard	1	0	0	0/0	0/0	0	6
Clark	0	0	1	0/0	0/0	0	6
Mims	0	1	0	0/0	0/0	0	6
Sanders	0	1	0	0/0	0/0	0	6
T. Smith	0	0	1	0/0	0/0	0	6
Falcons	4	28	2	34/34	26/27	0	316
Opponents	14	27	5	45/46	20/31	2	385

RUSHING	Att.	Yds.	Avg.	LG	TD
Pegram	292	1185	4.1	29	3
Broussard	39	206	5.3	26	1
Dickerson	26	91	3.5	10	0
Hebert	24	49	2.0	14	0
Tolliver	7	48	6.9	24	0
Miller	2	11	5.5	6	0
Pritchard	2	4	2.0	4	0
Mims	1	3	3.0	3	0
Alexander	2	-7	-3.5	0	0
Falcons	395	1590	4.0	29	4
Opponents	419	1784	4.3	74t	14

RECEIVING	No.	Yds.	Avg.	LG	TD
Rison	86	1242	14.4	53t	15
Pritchard	74	736	9.9	34	7
Haynes	72	778	10.8	98t	4
Hill	34	384	11.3	30	0
Pegram	33	302	9.2	30	0
Mims	12	107	8.9	19	1
Lyons	8	63	7.9	14	0
Sanders	6	106	17.7	70t	1
Dickerson	6	58	9.7	30	0
Phillips	1	15	15.0	15	0
Broussard	1	4	4.0	4	0
Hinton	1	-8	-8.0	-8	0
Falcons	334	3787	11.3	98t	28
Opponents	308	3786	12.3	72	27

INTERCEPTIONS	No.	Yds.	Avg.	LG	TD
Sanders	7	91	13.0	41	0
Walker	3	7	2.3	7	0
Clark	2	59	29.5	38	0
Eaton	1	0	0.0	0	0
Case	0	3	—	3	0
Falcons	13	160	12.3	44	0
Opponents	25	345	13.8	78	2

PUNTING	No.	Yds.	Avg.	In 20	LG
Alexander	72	3114	43.3	21	75
Falcons	72	3114	43.3	21	75
Opponents	74	3029	40.9	23	66

PUNT RETURNS	No.	FC	Yds.	Avg.	LG	TD
T. Smith	32	17	255	8.0	51	0
Sanders	2	1	21	10.5	16	0
Clark	1	0	0	0.0	0	0
Falcons	35	18	276	7.9	51	0
Opponents	41	17	350	8.5	30	0

KICKOFF RETURNS	No.	Yds.	Avg.	LG	TD
T. Smith	38	948	24.9	97t	1
Sanders	7	169	24.1	31	0
Pegram	4	63	15.8	28	0
Montgomery	2	53	26.5	33	0
Phillips	2	38	19.0	29	0
Mims	1	22	22.0	22	0
Ruether	1	7	7.0	7	0
Falcons	55	1300	23.6	97t	1
Opponents	55	1064	19.3	65	0

SACKS	No.
Holt	6.5
Geathers	3.5
C. Smith	3.5
Agee	2.5
Gardner	2.0
Tuggle	2.0
Case	1.5
Conner	1.5
Gann	1.0
George	1.0
Logan	1.0
Falcons	26.0
Opponents	40.0

1994 DRAFT CHOICES

Round	Name	Pos.	College
2	Bert Emanuel	WR	Rice
3	Anthony Phillips	DB	Texas A&M-Kingsville
	Alai Kalaniuvalu	G	Oregon State
4	Perry Klein	QB	C.W. Post
	Mitch Davis	LB	Georgia
5	Harrison Houston	WR	Florida
7	Jamal Anderson	RB	Utah

ATLANTA FALCONS

1994 VETERAN ROSTER

No.		Name	Pos.	Ht.	Wt.	Birthdate	NFL Exp.	College	Hometown	How Acq.	'93 Games/ Starts
98		Age, Louis	T	6-7	360	2/1/70	2	Southwest Louisiana	New Orleans. La.	FA-'94	0*
68		Agee, Mel	DE-DT	6-5	298	11/22/68	3	Illinois	Chicago, Ill.	FA-'92	11/7
5		Alexander, Harold	P	6-2	224	10/20/70	2	Appalachian State	Pickens, S.C.	D3-'93	16/0
92		Archambeau, Lester	DE	6-5	275	6/27/67	5	Stanford	Montville, N.J.	T(GB)-'93	15/11
25	#	Case, Scott	S	6-1	188	5/17/62	11	Oklahoma	Edmond, Okla.	D2-'84	16/16
27		Clark, Vinnie	CB	6-0	194	1/22/69	4	Ohio State	Cincinnati, Ohio	T(GB)-'93	15/9
56	#	Conner, Darion	LB	6-2	245	9/28/67	5	Jackson State	Prairie Point, Miss.	D2-'90	14/10
51		Dinkins, Howard	LB	6-1	230	4/26/69	3	Florida State	Jacksonville, Fla.	D3-'92	3/0
59	t-	Doleman, Chris	DE	6-5	275	10/16/61	10	Pittsburgh	York, Pa.	T(Minn)-'94	16/16*
49		Figaro, Cedric	LB	6-3	255	8/17/66	6	Notre Dame	Lafayette, La.	FA-'94	0*
48		Ford, Darryl	LB	6-1	225	6/22/66	3	New Mexico State	Dallas, Tex.	FA-'94	11/0*
65		Fortin, Roman	G-C	6-5	295	2/26/67	5	San Diego State	Ventura, Calif.	PB(Det)-'92	16/1
14	#	Gagliano, Bob	QB	6-3	205	9/5/58	10	Utah State	Los Angeles, Calif.	FA-'93	0*
76		Gann, Mike	DE	6-5	270	10/19/63	10	Notre Dame	Lakewood, Colo.	D2-'85	8/8
67		Gardner, Moe	NT	6-2	261	8/10/68	4	Illinois	Indianapolis, Ind.	D4-'91	16/16
97		Geathers, Jumpy	DT	6-7	290	6/26/60	11	Wichita State	Lafayette Hills, Pa.	UFA(Wash)-'93	14/0
1	t-	George, Jeff	QB	6-4	218	12/8/67	5	Illinois	Indianapolis, Ind.	T(Ind)-'94	13/11*
50		George, Ron	LB	6-2	225	3/20/70	2	Stanford	Heidelberg, Germany	D5-'93	12/4
53		Gordon, Dwayne	LB	6-1	231	11/2/69	2	New Hampshire	LaGrangeville, N.Y.	FA-'93	5/0
47		Harper, Roger	S	6-2	223	10/26/70	2	Ohio State	Columbus, Ohio	D2-'93	16/12
83		Harris, Leonard	WR	5-8	166	11/27/60	9	Texas Tech	McKinney, Tex.	FA-'94	4/2*
3		Hebert, Bobby	QB	6-4	215	8/19/60	9	Northwestern Louisiana	Mandeville, La.	UFA(NO)-'93	14/12
95		Holt, Pierce	DE	6-4	275	1/1/62	7	Angelo State	Marlin, Tex.	RFA(SF)-'93	16/15
44		Johnson, D.J.	CB	6-0	183	7/14/66	6	Kentucky	Louisville, Ky.	UFA(Pitt)-'94	16/15*
9		Johnson, Norm	K	6-2	203	5/31/60	13	UCLA	Garden Grove, Calif.	FA-'91	15/0
85		Jones, Tony	WR	5-7	145	12/30/65	5	Texas	Grapeland, Tex.	FA-'94	2/0*
78		Kenn, Mike	T	6-7	286	2/9/56	17	Michigan	Evanston, Ill.	D1-'78	16/16
66		Kennedy, Lincoln	G-T	6-6	335	2/12/71	2	Washington	San Diego, Calif.	D1-'93	16/16
88		Le Bel, Harper	TE	6-4	248	7/14/63	6	Colorado State	Sherman Oaks, Calif.	PB(Phil)-'91	16/0
73		Logan, Ernie	DE	6-3	285	5/18/68	4	East Carolina	Fayetteville, N.C.	FA-'93	8/1
86		Lyons, Mitch	TE	6-4	255	5/13/70	2	Michigan State	Grand Rapids, Mich.	D6-'93	16/8
81		Mathis, Terance	WR	5-10	177	6/7/67	5	New Mexico	Stone Mountain, Ga.	UFA(NYJ)-'94	16/3*
22		Montgomery, Alton	S	6-0	202	6/16/68	5	Houston	Griffin, Ga.	T(Den)-'93	8/0
33		Pegram, Erric	RB	5-9	188	1/7/69	4	North Texas State	Dallas, Tex.	D6-'91	16/14
82	#	Phillips, Jason	WR	5-7	166	10/11/66	6	Houston	Houston, Tex.	PB(Det)-'91	6/0
96		Richardson, Huey	DE	6-4	243	2/3/68	3	Florida	Atlanta, Ga.	FA-'94	0*
80		Rison, Andre	WR	6-1	188	3/18/67	6	Michigan State	Flint, Mich.	T(Ind)-'90	16/16
35		Ross, Kevin	S	5-9	182	1/16/62	11	Temple	Paulsboro, N.J.	UFA(KC)-'94	15/15*
55	#	Ruether, Mike	G-C	6-4	286	9/20/62	9	Texas	Shawnee Mission, Kan.	FA-'90	16/0
21	†	Sanders, Deion	CB	6-1	185	8/9/67	6	Florida State	Ft. Myers, Fla.	D1-'89	11/10
83		Sanders, Ricky	WR	5-11	178	8/30/62	9	Southwest Texas State	Temple, Tex.	FA-'94	16/11*
37	#	Shelley, Elbert	CB	6-1	185	12/24/64	8	Arkansas State	Tyronza, Ark.	D11-'87	16/0
90		Smith, Chuck	LB-DE	6-2	254	12/21/69	3	Tennessee	Athens, Ga.	D2-'92	15/1
28		Smith, Tony	RB	6-1	224	6/29/70	3	Southern Mississippi	Vicksburg, Miss.	D1b-'92	15/0
32	#	Stinson, Lemuel	CB	5-9	180	5/10/66	7	Texas Tech	Houston, Tex.	FA-'93	0*
52	#	Tippins, Ken	LB	6-1	235	7/22/66	6	Middle Tennessee State	Adel, Ga.	FA-'90	14/1
11	#	Tolliver, Billy Joe	QB	6-1	218	2/7/66	6	Texas Tech	Boyd, Tex.	T(SD)-'91	7/2
58		Tuggle, Jessie	LB	5-11	230	2/14/65	8	Valdosta State	Spalding, Ga.	FA-'87	16/16
45		Walker, Darnell	CB	5-8	164	1/17/70	2	Oklahoma	St. Louis, Mo.	D7-'93	15/8
48		Washington, Charles	S	6-1	217	10/8/66	5	Cameron	Dallas, Tex.	FA-'93	6/0
70		Whitfield, Bob	T	6-5	308	10/18/71	3	Stanford	Carson, Calif.	D1a-'92	16/16
94		Wilkins, David	DE-LB	6-4	240	2/24/69	2	Eastern Kentucky	Cincinnati, Ohio	FA-'94	0*
72		Zandofsky, Mike	C-G	6-2	305	11/30/65	6	Washington	Corvallis, Ore.	UFA(SD)-'94	16/16*

* Age last active with Chicago in '92; Doleman played 16 games with Minnesota in '93; Figaro last active with Cleveland in '92; Ford played 11 games with Detroit; Gagliano active for 2 games but did not play; J. George played 13 games with Indianapolis; Harris played 4 games with Houston; D. Johnson played 16 games with Pittsburgh; Jones played 2 games with Houston; Mathis played 16 games with N.Y. Jets; Richardson last active with Washington in '92; Ross played 15 games with Kansas City; R. Sanders played 16 games with Washington; Stinson inactive for 10 games; Wilkins last active with San Francisco in '92; Zandofsky played 16 games with San Diego.

\# Unrestricted free agent; subject to developments.

† Restricted free agent; subject to developments.

Retired—RB Eric Dickerson, 11-year veteran, 4 games in '93.

Traded—CB Bruce Pickens to Green Bay, WR Mike Pritchard to Denver.

t- Falcons traded for Doleman (Minnesota), J. George (Indianapolis).

Players lost through free agency (3): WR Michael Haynes (NO; 16 games in '93), T Chris Hinton (Minn; 16), QB Chris Miller (Rams; 3).

Also played with Falcons in '93—G Keith Alex (14 games), RB Steve Broussard (8), DE Rick Bryan (2), S Jeff Donaldson (13), C Jamie Dukes (16), S Tracey Eaton (16), NT Tory Epps (2), NT Bill Goldberg (5), DE Tim Green (9), WR Drew Hill (16), CB Melvin Jenkins (14), WR David Mims (15), CB Brian Mitchell (5), CB Bruce Pickens (4), WR Mike Pritchard (15), LB Jesse Solomon (16).

COACHING STAFF

Head Coach,
June Jones

Pro Career: Became the eighth head coach in Falcons history on January 24, 1994, succeeding Jerry Glanville. Most recently was Falcons' assistant head coach-offense since 1991. He played four seasons (1977-79, 1981) in NFL mainly as a backup quarterback to Falcons' all-time leading passer Steve Bartkowski. He was a member of the Falcons' first-ever playoff team in 1978. Jones began his coaching career as wide receivers coach of Houston Gamblers of the USFL in 1984. He became the offensive coordinator of the Denver Gold (USFL) in 1985 and then moved on to Ottawa Roughriders of the CFL in 1986. He was quarterbacks coach of the Houston Oilers in 1987-89. Was the quarterbacks and receivers coach for Detroit Lions in 1989-90.

Background: Guided Portland State to back-to-back 8-3 seasons, serving as team captain during his senior year, after also playing at Hawaii and Oregon. Jones and new Redskins head coach, Norv Turner, were backups to Hall of Famer quarterback Dan Fouts at Oregon. Jones has been a winning member of a Grey Cup team, a division titlist with Jim Kelly in the USFL, and has advanced to the postseason in both NFL conferences.

Personal: Born on February 19, 1953, in Portland, Oregon. June and his wife, Diane, live in Lake Lanier, Ga., and have three daughters—Jennifer, Kellie, Nicole, and son June, IV.

ASSISTANT COACHES

Keith Armstrong, outside linebackers; born December 15, 1963, Philadelphia, Pa., lives in Atlanta. Running back Temple 1983-86. No pro playing experience. College coach: Akron 1989, Oklahoma State 1990-92, Notre Dame 1993. Pro coach: Joined Falcons in 1994.

Jim Bates, defensive coordinator; born May 31, 1946, Pontiac, Mich., lives in Atlanta. Linebacker Tennessee 1964-67. No pro playing experience. College coach: Tennessee 1968, 1989, Southern Mississippi 1972, Villanova 1973-74, Kansas State 1975-76, West Virginia 1977, Texas Tech 1978-83, Florida 1990. Pro coach: San Antonio Gunslingers (USFL) 1984-85 (head coach 1985), Detroit Drive (Arena Football) 1988, Cleveland Browns 1991-93, joined Falcons in 1994.

Greg Brown, secondary; born October 10, 1957, Denver, Colo., lives in Atlanta. No college or pro playing experience. College coach: Wyoming 1987-88, Purdue 1989-90, Colorado 1991-93. Pro coach: Denver Gold (USFL) 1983-84, Tampa Bay Buccaneers 1984-86, joined Falcons in 1994.

Darrell "Mouse" Davis, quarterbacks; born September 6, 1932, Palouse, Wash., lives in Atlanta. Quarterback Western Oregon State 1952-55. No pro playing experience. College coach: Portland State 1974-80 (head coach 1975-80). Pro coach: Toronto Argonauts (CFL) 1982-83, Houston Gamblers (USFL) 1984, Denver Gold (USFL) 1985, Detroit Lions 1989-90, NY/NJ Knights (WL) 1991-92, joined Falcons in 1994.

Frank Gansz, assistant head coach-offense; born November 22, 1938, Altoona, Pa., lives in Atlanta. Center-linebacker Navy 1957-59. No pro playing experience. College coach: Air Force 1964, Colgate 1968, Navy 1969, Oklahoma State 1973, 1975, Army 1974, UCLA 1976-77. Pro coach: San Francisco 49ers 1978, Cincinnati Bengals 1979-80, Kansas City Chiefs 1981-82, 1986-88 (head coach 1987-88), Philadelphia Eagles 1983-85, Detroit Lions 1989-93, joined Falcons in 1994.

Joe Haering, linebackers; born February 1, 1946, Pittsburgh, Pa., lives in Atlanta. Linebacker Bucknell 1961-65. No pro playing experience. College coach: Bucknell 1969, Kentucky 1970-72, Boston University 1973-74, Kent State 1975-77. Pro coach: New York Jets 1978-79, Hamilton Tiger-Cats (CFL) 1980, Chicago Blitz (USFL) 1982-83, Pittsburgh Maulers (USFL) 1984, Denver Gold (USFL) 1985, NY/NJ Knights (WL) 1992, joined Falcons in 1994.

1994 FIRST-YEAR ROSTER

Name	Pos.	Ht.	Wt.	Birthdate	College	Hometown	How Acq.
Addison, Bryan (1)	S	6-0	200	4/13/70	Hawaii	Los Angeles, Calif.	FA
Alex, Keith (1)	G	6-4	307	6/9/69	Texas A&M	Beaumont, Tex.	FA
Anderson, Jamal	RB	5-10	246	3/6/72	Utah	El Camino, Calif.	D7
Barber, Rudy	G	6-2	286	9/21/71	Miami	Miami, Fla.	FA
Bedosky, Mike	G	6-4	289	2/13/71	Missouri	Jefferson City, Mo.	FA
Davis, Mitch	LB	6-3	238	7/7/71	Georgia	Mobile, Ala.	D4
Dixon, Corey	WR	5-7	155	2/16/72	Nebraska	Dallas, Tex.	FA
Earle, John (1)	G	6-4	290	7/3/69	Western Illinois	Blue Springs, Mo.	FA
Emanuel, Bert	WR	5-10	171	10/27/70	Rice	Houston, Tex.	D2
Ferguson, Reggie	WR	5-9	180	10/7/71	Louisville	Jacksonville, Fla.	FA
Goldberg, Bill (1)	DT	6-2	266	12/29/69	Georgia	Tulsa, Okla.	FA
Guiles, Jonathan	DE	6-4	270	7/27/71	South Carolina State	Georgetown, S.C.	FA
Harrison, Tony	WR	5-10	188	9/25/71	Texas A&M	Houston, Tex.	FA
Hatch, Lawrence (1)	CB	5-11	194	5/22/71	Florida	Tucker, Ga.	FA
Heidenreich, Jon (1)	G	6-5	285	6/28/69	Northeast Louisiana	Duluth, Ga.	FA
Houston, Harrison	WR	5-9	174	1/26/72	Florida	Pensacola, Fla.	D5
Jack, Eric	CB	5-10	177	4/19/72	New Mexico	El Paso, Tex.	FA
Jack, Keith	WR	5-9	177	5/11/71	Houston	Daly City, Calif.	FA
Jackson, Tyoka	DE	6-1	266	11/22/71	Penn State	Forestville, Md.	FA
James, John (1)	T-G	6-3	294	3/28/70	Mississippi State	Atlanta, Ga.	FA
Johnson, Clint	WR	5-7	178	1/6/72	Notre Dame	Altamonte Springs, Fla.	FA
Johnson, Pat	S	6-1	201	6/10/72	Purdue	Mineral Point, Mo.	FA
Kalaniuvalu, Alal	G	6-3	302	10/23/71	Oregon State	Seattle, Wash.	D3
Klein, Perry	QB	6-2	218	3/25/71	C.W. Post	Santa Monica, Calif.	D4
Lowery, Tim (1)	RB	5-11	247	11/29/70	Clark, Ga.	Effingham, Calif.	FA
Mims, David (1)	WR	5-8	191	7/7/70	Baylor	Daingerfield, Tex.	FA
Paulk, Tim (1)	LB	6-0	232	4/3/68	Florida	Miami, Fla.	FA
Peterson, Todd (1)	K	5-10	176	2/4/70	Georgia	Valdosta, Ga.	FA
Phillips, Anthony	CB	6-0	217	10/5/70	Texas A&M-Kingsville	Galveston, Tex.	D3
Rogers, Joe	WR	5-7	161	5/23/71	Texas Southern	Miami, Fla.	FA
Sally, Lamar (1)	DE	6-5	281	8/11/70	Central Michigan	Detroit, Mich.	FA
Spencer, Darryl (1)	WR	5-8	172	3/21/70	Miami	Merritt Island, Fla.	FA
Tobeck, Robbie (1)	C	6-4	275	3/6/70	Washington State	Tarpon Springs, Fla.	FA
Tyner, Scott	P-K	6-1	189	4/11/72	Oklahoma State	Edgewood, Tex.	FA
Wallace, Anthony (1)	RB	6-0	191	7/8/69	California	Pasadena, Calif.	FA
Walton, Tim	CB	5-11	180	3/11/71	Ohio State	Columbus, Ga.	FA
White, Stan	QB	6-2	202	8/14/71	Auburn	Birmingham, Ala.	FA
Williams, Thomas	DT	6-3	274	12/19/70	Wyoming	Pueblo, Colo.	FA

The term NFL Rookie is defined as a player who is in his first season of professional football and has not been on the roster of another professional football team for any regular-season or postseason games. A Rookie is designated by an "R" on NFL rosters. Players who have been active in another professional football league or players who have NFL experience, including either preseason training camp or being on an Active List or Inactive List, or on Reserve/Injured or Reserve/Physically Unable to Perform for fewer than six regular-season games, are termed NFL First-Year Players. An NFL First-Year Player is designated by a "1" on NFL rosters. Thereafter, a player is credited with an additional year of experience for each season in which he accumulates six games on the Active List or Inactive List, or on Reserve/Injured or Reserve/Physically Unable to Perform.

NOTES

_____
_____
_____
_____
_____
_____
_____
_____
_____

Milt Jackson, receivers; born October 16, 1943, Groesbeck, Tex., lives in Atlanta. Defensive back Tulsa 1965-66. Pro defensive back San Francisco 49ers 1967. College coach: Oregon State 1973, Rice 1974, California 1975-76, Oregon 1977-78, UCLA 1979. Pro coach: San Francisco 49ers 1980-82, Buffalo Bills 1983-84, Philadelphia Eagles 1985, Houston Oilers 1986-88, Indianapolis Colts 1989-91, Los Angeles Rams 1992-93, joined Falcons in 1994.

Tim Jorgensen, strength and conditioning; born April 21, 1955, St. Louis, Mo., lives in Snellville, Ga. Guard Southwest Missouri State 1974-76. No pro playing experience. College coach: Southwest Missouri State 1977-78, Alabama 1979, Louisiana State 1980-83. Pro coach: Philadelphia Eagles 1984-86, joined Falcons in 1987.

Bill Kollar, defensive line; born November 12, 1952, Warren, Ohio, lives in Atlanta. Defensive end Montana State 1971-74. Pro defensive end Cincinnati Bengals 1974-76, Tampa Bay Buccaneers 1977-81. College coach: Illinois 1985-87, Purdue 1988-89. Pro coach: Tampa Bay Buccaneers 1984, joined Falcons in 1990.

Bob Palcic, offensive line; born July 2, 1948, Dunkirk, N.Y., lives in Atlanta. Linebacker Dayton 1968-70. No pro playing experience. College coach: Dayton 1974-75, Ball State 1976-77, Wisconsin 1978-81, Arizona 1984-85, Ohio State 1986-91, Southern California 1992, UCLA 1993. Pro coach: Joined Falcons in 1994.

Ollie Wilson, running backs; born March 31, 1951, Worcester, Mass., lives in Atlanta. Wide receiver Springfield 1971-73. No pro playing experience. College coach: Springfield 1975, Northeastern 1976-82, California 1983-90. Pro coach: Joined Falcons in 1991.

National Football Conference
Central Division
Team Colors: Navy Blue, Orange, and White
Halas Hall, 250 North Washington
Lake Forest, Illinois 60045
Telephone: (708) 295-6600

CLUB OFFICIALS

Chairman of the Board: Edward W. McCaskey
President and CEO: Michael B. McCaskey
Secretary: Virginia H. McCaskey
Vice President: Tim McCaskey
Vice President of Operations: Ted Phillips
Director of Player Personnel: Rod Graves
Director of Administration: Tim LeFevour
Director of Community Relations: Pat McCaskey
Player Liaison: Brian McCaskey
Director of Marketing/Communications:
　Ken Valdiserri
Manager of Promotions: John Bostrom
Manager of Sales: Jack Trompeter
Director of Public Relations: Bryan Harlan
Asst. Director of Public Relations: Doug Green
Ticket Manager: George McCaskey
Computer Systems: Greg Gershuny
Video Director: Dean Pope
Trainer: Fred Caito
Strength Coordinator: Clyde Emrich
Physical Dev. Coordinator: Russ Reiderer
Equipment Manager: Gary Haeger
Assistant Equipment Manager: Tony Medlin
Scouts: Gary Smith, Jeff Shiver, Charlie Mackey,
　Bobby Riggle, Mike McCartney
Stadium: Soldier Field • **Capacity:** 66,950
　　425 McFetridge Place
　　Chicago, Illinois 60605
Playing Surface: Grass
Training Camp: University of Wisconsin-Platteville
　　　Platteville, Wisconsin 53818

1994 SCHEDULE
PRESEASON

Aug. 5	**Philadelphia**	7:00
Aug. 13	at Arizona	6:00
Aug. 22	at Kansas City	7:00
Aug. 27	**New York Giants**	7:00

REGULAR SEASON

Sept. 4	**Tampa Bay**	12:00
Sept. 12	at Philadelphia (Monday)	9:00
Sept. 18	**Minnesota**	12:00
Sept. 25	at New York Jets	8:00
Oct. 2	**Buffalo**	3:00
Oct. 9	**New Orleans**	12:00
Oct. 16	Open Date	
Oct. 23	at Detroit	1:00
Oct. 31	**Green Bay** (Monday)	8:00
Nov. 6	at Tampa Bay	1:00
Nov. 13	at Miami	1:00
Nov. 20	**Detroit**	12:00
Nov. 27	at Arizona	2:00
Dec. 1	at Minnesota (Thursday)	7:00
Dec. 11	at Green Bay	12:00
Dec. 18	**Los Angeles Rams**	12:00
Dec. 24	**New England**	12:00

COACHING HISTORY
Decatur Staleys 1920,
Chicago Staleys 1921
(586-384-42)

1920-29	George Halas	84-31-19
1930-32	Ralph Jones	24-10-7
1933-42	George Halas*	88-24-4
1942-45	Hunk Anderson- Luke Johnsos**	24-12-2
1946-55	George Halas	76-43-2
1956-57	John (Paddy) Driscoll	14-10-1
1958-67	George Halas	76-53-6
1968-71	Jim Dooley	20-36-0
1972-74	Abe Gibron	11-30-1
1975-77	Jack Pardee	20-23-0
1978-81	Neill Armstrong	30-35-0
1982-92	Mike Ditka	112-68-0
1993	Dave Wannstedt	7-9-0

　*Retired after five games to enter U.S. Navy
**Co-coaches

RECORD HOLDERS
INDIVIDUAL RECORDS—CAREER

Category	Name	Performance
Rushing (Yds.)	Walter Payton, 1975-1987	*16,726
Passing (Yds.)	Sid Luckman, 1939-1950	14,686
Passing (TDs)	Sid Luckman, 1939-1950	137
Receiving (No.)	Walter Payton, 1975-1987	492
Receiving (Yds.)	Johnny Morris, 1958-1967	5,059
Interceptions	Gary Fencik, 1976-1987	38
Punting (Avg.)	George Gulyanics, 1947-1952	44.5
Punt Return (Avg.)	Ray (Scooter) McLean, 1940-47	14.8
Kickoff Return (Avg.)	Gale Sayers, 1965-1971	30.6
Field Goals	Kevin Butler, 1985-1993	197
Touchdowns (Tot.)	Walter Payton, 1975-1987	125
Points	Kevin Butler, 1985-1993	915

INDIVIDUAL RECORDS—SINGLE SEASON

Category	Name	Performance
Rushing (Yds.)	Walter Payton, 1977	1,852
Passing (Yds.)	Bill Wade, 1962	3,172
Passing (TDs)	Sid Luckman, 1943	28
Receiving (No.)	Johnny Morris, 1964	93
Receiving (Yds.)	Johnny Morris, 1964	1,200
Interceptions	Mark Carrier, 1990	10
Punting (Avg.)	Bobby Joe Green, 1963	46.5
Punt Return (Avg.)	Harry Clark, 1943	15.8
Kickoff Return (Avg.)	Gale Sayers, 1967	37.7
Field Goals	Kevin Butler, 1985	31
Touchdowns (Tot.)	Gale Sayers, 1965	**22
Points	Kevin Butler, 1985	**144

INDIVIDUAL RECORDS—SINGLE GAME

Category	Name	Performance
Rushing (Yds.)	Walter Payton, 11-20-77	*275
Passing (Yds.)	Johnny Lujack, 12-11-49	468
Passing (TDs)	Sid Luckman, 11-14-43	*7
Receiving (No.)	Jim Keane, 10-23-49	14
Receiving (Yds.)	Harlon Hill, 10-31-54	214
Interceptions	Many times	3
	Last time by Mark Carrier, 12-9-90	
Field Goals	Roger LeClerc, 12-3-61	5
	Mac Percival, 10-20-68	5
Touchdowns (Tot.)	Gale Sayers, 12-12-65	*6
Points	Gale Sayers, 12-12-65	36

　*NFL Record
**NFL Rookie Record

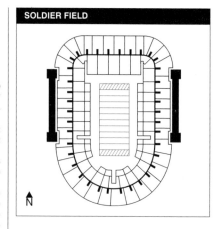

SOLDIER FIELD

1993 TEAM RECORD

PRESEASON (1-3)

Date	Result		Opponents
8/8	L	9-13	at Philadelphia
8/14	L	10-11	Phoenix
8/23	L	14-20	at New Orleans
8/27	W	23-21	Dallas

REGULAR SEASON (7-9)

Date	Result		Opponents	Att.
9/5	L	20-26	N.Y. Giants	66,900
9/12	L	7-10	at Minnesota	57,921
9/26	W	47-17	Tampa Bay	58,329
10/3	W	6-0	Atlanta	57,441
10/10	W	17-6	at Philadelphia	63,601
10/25	L	12-19	Minnesota	64,677
10/31	L	3-17	at Green Bay	58,945
11/7	L	14-16	L.A. Raiders	59,750
11/14	W	16-13	at San Diego	58,459
11/21	W	19-17	at Kansas City	76,872
11/25	W	10-6	at Detroit	76,699
12/5	W	30-17	Green Bay	62,236
12/12	L	10-13	at Tampa Bay	56,667
12/18	L	3-13	Denver	53,056
12/26	L	14-20	Detroit	43,443
1/2	L	6-20	at L.A. Rams	39,147

SCORE BY PERIODS

Bears	37	85	56	56	0	—	234
Opponents	45	83	38	64	0	—	230

ATTENDANCE

Home 465,832   Away 488,311   Total 954,143
Single-game home record, 66,900 (9-5-93)
Single-season home record, 528,465 (1992)

1993 TEAM STATISTICS

	Bears	Opp.
Total First Downs	226	289
Rushing	98	112
Passing	113	163
Penalty	15	14
Third Down: Made/Att	73/211	80/214
Third Down Pct.	34.6	37.4
Fourth Down: Made/Att	4/14	6/15
Fourth Down Pct.	28.6	40.0
Total Net Yards	3717	4653
Avg. Per Game	232.3	290.8
Total Plays	913	1026
Avg. Per Play	4.1	4.5
Net Yards Rushing	1677	1835
Avg. Per Game	104.8	114.7
Total Rushes	477	476
Net Yards Passing	2040	2818
Avg. Per Game	127.5	176.1
Sacked/Yards Lost	48/230	46/287
Gross Yards	2270	3105
Att./Completions	388/230	504/306
Completion Pct.	59.3	60.7
Had Intercepted	16	18
Punts/Avg.	80/38.5	78/41.4
Net Punting Avg.	80/36.6	78/36.2
Penalties/Yards Lost	68/587	91/783
Fumbles/Ball Lost	29/14	24/12
Touchdowns	22	22
Rushing	10	9
Passing	7	12
Returns	5	1
Avg. Time of Possession	28:36	31:24

1993 INDIVIDUAL STATISTICS

PASSING

	Att	Cmp	Yds.	Pct.	TD	Int	Tkld.	Rate
Harbaugh	325	200	2002	61.5	7	11	43/210	72.1
Willis	60	30	268	50.0	0	5	5/20	27.6
Gardocki	2	0	0	0.0	0	0	0/0	39.6
Anderson	1	0	0	0.0	0	0	0/0	39.6
Bears	388	230	2270	59.3	7	16	48/230	64.7
Opponents	504	306	3105	60.7	12	18	46/287	71.4

SCORING

	TD R	TD P	TD Rt	PAT	FG	Saf	PTS
Butler	0	0	0	21/22	27/36	0	102
Anderson	4	0	0	0/0	0/0	0	24
Harbaugh	4	0	0	0/0	0/0	0	24
Obee	0	3	0	0/0	0/0	0	18
Baker	0	0	2	0/0	0/0	0	12
Conway	0	2	0	0/0	0/0	0	12
Worley	2	0	0	0/0	0/0	0	12
Carrier	0	0	1	0/0	0/0	0	6
Jones	0	0	1	0/0	0/0	0	6
Lincoln	0	0	1	0/0	0/0	0	6
Waddle	0	1	0	0/0	0/0	0	6
Wetnight	0	1	0	0/0	0/0	0	6
Bears	10	7	5	21/22	27/36	0	234
Opponents	9	12	1	20/22	26/34	0	230

RUSHING

	Att.	Yds.	Avg.	LG	TD
Anderson	202	646	3.2	45	4
Worley	110	437	4.0	28	2
Harbaugh	60	277	4.6	25	4
Heyward	68	206	3.0	11	0
Conway	5	44	8.8	18	0
Green	15	29	1.9	10	0
Christian	8	19	2.4	12	0
Lewis	7	13	1.9	3	0
Willis	2	6	3.0	6	0
Bears	477	1677	3.5	45	10
Opponents	476	1835	3.9	26t	9

RECEIVING

	No.	Yds.	Avg.	LG	TD
Waddle	44	552	12.5	38	1
Anderson	31	160	5.2	35	0
Obee	26	351	13.5	48	3
Conway	19	231	12.2	38t	2
Christian	16	160	10.0	36	0
Heyward	16	132	8.3	20	0
Jennings	14	150	10.7	29	0
Green	13	63	4.8	9	0
Davis	12	132	11.0	17	0
Gedney	10	98	9.8	24	0
Wetnight	9	93	10.3	25t	1
Worley	8	49	6.1	15	0
Whitaker	6	53	8.8	18	0
Lewis	4	26	6.5	18	0
Banks	1	19	19.0	19	0
Harbaugh	1	1	1.0	1	0
Bears	230	2270	9.9	48	7
Opponents	306	3105	10.1	67	12

INTERCEPTIONS

	No.	Yds.	Avg.	Long	TD
Carrier	4	94	23.5	34t	1
Jones	4	52	13.0	22	0
Lincoln	3	109	36.3	80t	1
Woolford	2	18	9.0	18	0
Blaylock	2	3	1.5	3	0
Dent	1	24	24.0	24	0
Mangum	1	0	0.0	0	0
McMichael	1	0	0.0	0	0
Bears	18	300	16.7	86t	2
Opponents	16	105	6.6	25	1

PUNTING

	No.	Yds.	Avg.	In	LG
Gardocki	80	3080	38.5	28	58
Bears	80	3080	38.5	28	58
Opponents	78	3231	41.4	22	75

PUNT RETURNS

	No.	FC	Yds.	Avg.	LG	TD
Obee	35	20	289	8.3	28	0
Bears	35	20	289	8.3	28	0
Opponents	22	38	115	5.2	34	0

KICKOFF RETURNS

	No.	Yds.	Avg.	LG	TD
Conway	21	450	21.4	55	0
Green	9	141	15.7	30	0
Obee	9	159	17.7	34	0
Worley	2	36	18.0	24	0
A. Fontenot	1	8	8.0	8	0
Heyward	1	12	12.0	12	0
Mangum	1	0	0.0	0	0
Ryan	1	5	5.0	5	0
Bears	45	811	18.0	55	0
Opponents	53	918	17.3	35	0

SACKS

	No.
Dent	12.5
Armstrong	11.5
Zorich	7.0
McMichael	6.0
Spellman	2.5
Cox	2.0
A. Fontenot	1.0
Gayle	1.0
Jones	1.0
Simpson	0.5
Bears	46.0
Opponents	48.0

1994 DRAFT CHOICES

Round	Name	Pos.	College
1	John Thierry	DE	Alcorn State
2	Marcus Spears	T	N.W. Louisiana
3	Jim Flanigan	DT	Notre Dame
4	Raymont Harris	RB	Ohio State
6	Lloyd Hill	WR	Texas Tech
7	Dennis Collier	DB	Colorado

CHICAGO BEARS

1994 VETERAN ROSTER

No.	Name	Pos.	Ht.	Wt.	Birthdate	NFL Exp.	College	Hometown	How Acq.	'93 Games/ Starts
35	# Anderson, Neal	RB	5-11	215	8/14/64	9	Florida	Graceville, Fla.	D1-'86	15/11
93	Armstrong, Trace	DE	6-4	265	10/5/65	6	Florida	Birmingham, Ala.	D1b-'89	16/16
70	Auzenne, Troy	T	6-7	290	6/26/69	3	California	Baldwin Park, Calif.	D2-'92	11/11
91	Baker, Myron	LB	6-1	228	1/6/71	2	Louisiana Tech	Haughton, La.	D4b-'93	16/0
47	Blaylock, Anthony	CB	5-10	185	2/21/65	7	Winston-Salem State	Raleigh, N.C.	UFA(SD)-'93	9/9
62	Bortz, Mark	G	6-6	282	2/12/61	12	Iowa	Pardeeville, Wis.	D8-'83	16/16
6	# Butler, Kevin	K	6-1	204	7/24/62	10	Georgia	Redan, Ga.	D4-'85	16/0
59	Cain, Joe	LB	6-1	233	6/11/65	6	Oregon Tech	Compton, Calif.	RFA(Sea)-'93	15/15
20	Carrier, Mark	S	6-1	192	4/28/68	5	Southern California	Long Beach, Calif.	D1-'90	16/16
44	Christian, Bob	RB	5-10	225	11/14/68	2	Northwestern	St. Louis, Mo.	FA-'92	14/1
80	Conway, Curtis	WR-KR	6-0	185	3/13/71	2	Southern California	Hawthorne, Calif.	D1-'93	16/7
86	Cook, Marv	TE	6-4	234	2/24/66	6	Iowa	West Branch, Iowa	FA-'94	16/12*
54	# Cox, Ron	LB	6-2	235	2/27/68	5	Fresno State	Fresno, Calif.	D2b-'90	16/2
82	# Davis, Wendell	WR	6-0	188	1/3/66	7	Louisiana State	Shreveport, La.	D1-'88	5/4
95	# Dent, Richard	DE	6-5	265	12/13/60	12	Tennessee State	Atlanta, Ga.	D8-'83	16/16
37	Douglass, Maurice	CB	5-11	202	2/12/64	8	Kentucky	Dayton, Ohio	D8-'86	16/1
65	Epps, Tory	DT	6-1	280	5/28/67	5	Memphis State	Uniontown, Pa.	FA-'93	5/0*
74	Fontenot, Albert	DE	6-4	265	9/17/70	2	Baylor	Houston, Tex.	D4c-'93	16/0
67	Fontenot, Jerry	G-C	6-3	287	11/21/66	6	Texas A&M	Lafayette, La.	D3-'89	16/16
17	Gardocki, Chris	P-K	6-1	188	2/7/70	4	Clemson	Stone Mountain, Calif.	D3-'91	16/0
23	# Gayle, Shaun	S	5-11	202	3/8/62	11	Ohio State	Bethel, Va.	D10-'84	16/16
84	Gedney, Chris	TE	6-5	262	8/9/70	2	Syracuse	Liverpool, N.Y.	D3-'93	7/4
81	t- Graham, Jeff	WR	6-1	193	2/14/69	4	Ohio State	Dayton, Ohio	T(Pitt)-'94	15/12*
22	Green, Robert	RB	5-8	209	9/10/70	3	William & Mary	Ft. Washington, Md.	W(Wash)-'93	16/0
64	Heck, Andy	T	6-6	298	1/1/67	6	Notre Dame	Fairfax, Va.	RFA(Sea)-'93	16/16*
33	Hoge, Merril	RB	6-2	230	1/26/65	8	Idaho State	Pocatello, Idaho	UFA(Pitt)-'94	16/13*
85	Jennings, Keith	TE	6-4	265	5/19/66	5	Clemson	Summerville, S.C.	FA-'91	13/10
25	Johnson, Keshon	CB	5-10	179	7/17/70	2	Arizona	Fresno, Calif.	D7-'93	15/0
53	Jones, Dante	LB	6-2	230	3/23/65	7	Oklahoma	Dallas, Tex.	D2-'88	16/16
12	Kramer, Erik	QB	6-1	199	11/6/64	5	North Carolina State	Burbank, Calif.	UFA(Det)-'94	5/4*
58	Leeuwenburg, Jay	G-C	6-2	288	6/18/69	3	Colorado	Kirkwood, Mo.	W(KC)-'92	16/16
39	Lincoln, Jeremy	CB	5-10	180	4/7/69	3	Tennessee	Toledo, Ohio	D3-'92	16/7
26	Mangum, John	S	5-10	182	3/16/67	5	Alabama	Magee, Miss.	D7-'90	12/1
9	Matthews, Shane	QB	6-3	197	6/1/70	2	Florida	Pascagoula, Miss.	FA-'93	0*
60	McGuire, Gene	C	6-2	286	7/17/70	3	Notre Dame	Lynn Haven, Fla.	W(NO)-'93	9/0
24	Miniefield, Kevin	CB	5-9	178	3/2/70	2	Arizona State	Phoenix, Ariz.	FA-'93	8/0
92	Minter, Barry	LB	6-2	242	1/28/70	2	Tulsa	Mt. Pleasant, Tex.	T(Dall)-'93	2/0
69	Myslinski, Tom	G	6-2	293	12/7/68	2	Tennessee	Rome, N.Y.	FA-'93	1/0
83	Obee, Terry	WR	5-10	180	6/15/68	2	Oregon	Richmond, Calif.	UFA(Minn)-'93	16/5
75	Perry, Todd	G	6-5	298	11/28/70	2	Kentucky	Elizabethtown, Ky.	D4a-'93	13/3
99	Ryan, Tim	DT	6-4	265	9/8/67	5	Southern California	San Jose, Calif.	D3a-'90	11/0
98	Simpson, Carl	DT	6-2	282	4/18/70	2	Florida State	Appling County, Ga.	D2-'93	11/0
55	Smith, Vinson	LB	6-2	236	7/3/65	7	East Carolina	Statesville, N.C.	T(Dall)-'93	16/13
96	Snow, Percy	LB	6-2	245	11/5/67	5	Michigan State	Canton, Ohio	W(KC)-'93	10/0
90	Spellman, Alonzo	DE	6-4	282	9/27/71	3	Ohio State	Rancocas, N.J.	D1-'92	16/0
27	Tillman, Lewis	RB	6-0	195	4/16/66	6	Jackson State	Oklahoma City, Okla.	UFA(NYG)-'94	16/7*
78	# Van Horne, Keith	T	6-6	290	11/6/57	14	Southern California	Fullerton, Calif.	D1-'81	13/3
87	Waddle, Tom	WR	6-0	185	2/20/67	5	Boston College	Cincinnati, Ohio	FA-'89	15/15
4	Walsh, Steve	QB	6-3	210	12/1/66	6	Miami	St. Paul, Minn.	FA-'94	2/1*
89	Wetnight, Ryan	TE	6-2	228	11/5/70	2	Stanford	Fresno, Calif.	FA-'93	10/1
71	Williams, James	T	6-7	330	3/29/68	4	Cheyney State	Allderdice, Pa.	FA-'91	3/0
21	Woolford, Donnell	CB	5-9	188	1/6/66	6	Clemson	Byrd, N.C.	D1a-'89	16/16
38	t- Worley, Tim	RB	6-2	226	9/24/66	5	Georgia	Lumberton, N.C.	T(Pitt)-'93	15/3*
97	Zorich, Chris	DT	6-1	275	3/13/69	4	Notre Dame	Chicago, Ill.	D2-'91	16/16

* Cook played 16 games with New England in '93; Epps played 2 games with Atlanta, 3 games with Chicago; Graham played 15 games with Pittsburgh; Heck played 16 games with Seattle; Hoge played 16 games with Pittsburgh; Kramer played 5 games with Detroit; Matthews inactive for 12 games; Tillman played 16 games with N.Y. Giants; Walsh played 2 games with New Orleans; Worley played 5 games with Pittsburgh, 10 games with Chicago.

\# Unrestricted free agent; subject to developments.

† Restricted free agent; subject to developments.

t- Bears traded for Graham (Pittsburgh), Worley (Pittsburgh).

Also played with Bears in '93—WR Fred Banks (8 games), QB Jim Harbaugh (15), RB Craig Heyward (16), RB John Ivlow (2), RB Darren Lewis (2), DT Steve McMichael (16), WR Anthony Morgan (1), LB Jim Morrissey (2), S Markus Paul (8), DT William Perry (7), G Vernice Smith (6), TE Danta Whitaker (5), QB Peter Tom Willis (5), G John Wojciechowski (14).

COACHING STAFF

Head Coach,
Dave Wannstedt

Pro Career: Led Bears to a 7-9 record in rookie season. Named Chicago's head coach on January 19, 1993. He was an integral part of one of the most successful turnarounds in NFL history, helping to turn the 1989 Dallas Cowboys, which finished the season 1-15, into Super Bowl champions four years later. In January, 1992, he was named Dallas's assistant head coach and defensive coordinator. He was the defensive coordinator for the Cowboys in 1989. Selected by the Green Bay Packers in the fifteenth round of the 1974 draft, but spent the entire season on injured reserve. Career record: 7-9.

Background: Played offensive tackle at the University of Pittsburgh from 1970-73. Began coaching career at Pittsburgh in 1975 and was part of the staff that led the Panthers to a 12-0 record and the NCAA championship in 1976. In 1979, he took a job with Jimmy Johnson at Oklahoma State as defensive line coach. After two seasons, he was promoted to defensive coordinator. In 1983, Wannstedt was the defensive line coach for Southern California before rejoining Johnson at the University of Miami as the Hurricanes' defensive coordinator. In his first year (1986), Miami went 11-0 before losing to Penn State in the Fiesta Bowl. The following season Miami was crowned NCAA champion with a perfect 12-0 record.

Personal: Born May 21, 1952, Pittsburgh, Pa. Dave and his wife, Jan, live in Lake Forest, Ill. and have two children—Keri and Jami.

ASSISTANT COACHES

Danny Abramowicz, special teams; born July 13, 1945, Steubenville, Ohio, lives in Lake Forest, Ill. Wide receiver Xavier 1964-66. Pro wide receiver New Orleans Saints 1967-73, San Francisco 49ers 1973-74. Pro coach: Joined Bears in 1992.

Clarence Brooks, defensive line; born May 20, 1951, New York, N.Y., lives in Lake Forest, Ill. Guard Massachusetts 1970-73. No pro playing experience. College coach: Massachusetts 1976-80, Syracuse 1981-89, Arizona 1990-92. Pro coach: Joined Bears in 1993.

Ivan Fears, wide receivers; born November 15, 1954, Portsmouth, Va., lives in Lake Forest, Ill. Running back William and Mary 1973-75. No pro playing experience. College coach: William and Mary 1977-80, Syracuse 1981-90. Pro coach: New England Patriots 1991-92, joined Bears in 1993.

Carlos Mainord, defensive assistant; born August 26, 1944, Greenville, Tex., lives in Lake Forest, Ill. Linebacker Navarro (Tex.) Junior College 1962-63, McMurry College 1964-65. No pro playing experience. College coach: McMurry College 1966-68, Texas Tech 1969, 1983-85, 1987-92, Ranger (Tex.) Junior College 1970-71, 1972-77 (head coach), Rice 1978-82, Miami 1986. Pro coach: Joined Bears in 1993.

David McGinnis, linebackers; born August 7, 1951, Independence, Kan., lives in Lake Forest, Ill. Defensive back Texas Christian 1970-72. No pro playing experience. College coach: Texas Christian 1973-74, 1982, Missouri 1975-77, Indiana State 1978-81, Kansas State 1983-85. Pro coach: Joined Bears in 1986.

Joe Pendry, running backs; born August 5, 1947, Matheny, W. Va., lives in Lake Forest, Ill. Tight end West Virginia 1966-67. No pro playing experience. College coach: West Virginia 1967-74, 1976-77, Kansas State 1975, Pittsburgh 1978-79, Michigan State 1980-81. Pro coach: Philadelphia Stars (USFL) 1983, Pittsburgh Maulers (USFL) 1984 (head coach), Cleveland Browns 1985-88, Kansas City Chiefs 1989-92, joined Bears in 1993.

Mike Shula, tight ends; born June 23, 1965, Baltimore, Md., lives in Lake Forest, Ill. Quarterback Alabama 1984-87. Pro quarterback Tampa Bay Buccaneers 1987. Pro coach: Tampa Bay Buccaneers 1988-90, Miami Dolphins 1991-92, joined Bears in 1993.

Bob Slowik, defensive coordinator-defensive backs; born May 16, 1954, Pittsburgh, Pa., lives in Lake Forest, Ill. Cornerback Delaware 1973-76. No pro playing experience. College coach: Delaware 1977, Florida 1978-81, Drake 1982, Rutgers 1983, East Carolina 1984-91. Pro coach: Dallas Cowboys 1992, joined Bears in 1993.

Ron Turner, offensive coordinator-quarterbacks; born December 5, 1953, Martinez, Calif., lives in Lake Forest, Ill. Running back-defensive back Pacific 1973-76. No pro playing experience. College coach: Pacific 1977, Arizona 1978-80, Northwestern 1981-82, Pittsburgh 1983-84, Southern California 1985-87, Texas A&M 1988, Stanford 1989-91, San Jose State 1992 (head coach). Pro coach: Joined Bears in 1993.

Tony Wise, offensive line; born December 28, 1951, Albany, N.Y., lives in Lake Forest, Ill. Offensive lineman Ithaca College 1971-72. No pro playing experience. College coach: Albany State 1973, Bridgeport 1974, Central Connecticut State 1975, Washington State 1976, Pittsburgh 1977-78, Oklahoma State 1979-83, Syracuse 1984, Miami 1985-88. Pro coach: Dallas Cowboys 1989-92, joined Bears in 1993.

1994 FIRST-YEAR ROSTER

Name	Pos.	Ht.	Wt.	Birthdate	College	Hometown	How Acq.
Acorn, Daron (1)	K	6-2	235	5/12/71	Akron	Vancouver, Wash.	FA
Bass, Robert	LB	6-1	239	11/10/70	Miami	Tilden, N.Y.	FA
Brooks, Anthony (1)	WR	5-11	193	8/3/68	East Texas State	Irving, Tex.	FA
Brooks, Donny	CB	5-11	188	1/26/70	Texas Tech	Rockdale, Tex.	FA
Burger, Todd (1)	G	6-3	296	3/20/70	Penn State	Clark, N.J.	FA
Bussie, Arthur	DE	6-4	258	2/25/70	Northeast Louisiana	Camden, N.J.	FA
Carter, Antonio	RB	5-11	216	8/23/72	Minnesota	Columbus, Ohio	FA
Collier, Dennis	S	5-9	187	5/17/71	Colorado	San Bernardino, Calif.	D7
Dunning, Josh	G	6-3	302	12/5/71	Washington State	Eatonville, Wash.	FA
Durgin, Marcus	CB	6-1	191	7/29/72	Samford, Ala.	Prichard, Ala.	FA
Flanigan, Jim	DT	6-2	280	8/27/71	Notre Dame	Green Bay, Wis.	D3
Frier, Matt	WR	5-11	190	9/1/71	Florida State	Live Oak, Fla.	FA
Givens, Reggie (1)	LB	6-1	220	10/3/71	Penn State	Sussex, Va.	FA
Harris, Raymont	RB	6-1	225	12/23/70	Ohio State	Lorain, Ohio	D4
Hawkins, Garland (1)	DE	6-3	253	2/19/70	Syracuse	Washington, D.C.	FA
Hightower, Mike	RB	5-9	191	8/17/71	East Texas State	Paris, Tex.	FA
Hill, Lloyd	WR	6-1	189	1/16/72	Texas Tech	Hobbs, N.M.	D6
Ireland, Darwin	LB	5-11	240	5/26/71	Arkansas	Pine Bluff, Tex.	FA
Kmet, Frank (1)	G	6-3	294	3/13/70	Purdue	Arlington Heights, Ill.	FA
Marshall, Anthony	S	6-1	205	9/16/70	Louisiana State	Mobile, Ala.	FA
Martin, John	RB	5-7	185	8/31/71	Memphis State	Homestead, Fla.	FA
Norman, Todd	T	6-5	300	9/11/71	Notre Dame	Huntington Beach, Calif.	FA
Primus, Greg (1)	WR	5-11	190	10/20/70	Colorado State	Denver, Colo.	FA
Sanders, Steven	WR	5-8	161	9/26/72	Virginia Tech	Virginia Beach, Fla.	FA
Schwantz, Jim (1)	LB	6-2	232	1/23/70	Purdue	Palatine, Ill.	FA
Shorten, Oscar	DT	6-3	285	1/27/71	Abilene Christian	Tascosa, Tex.	FA
Spears, Marcus	T	6-4	300	9/28/71	N.W. Louisiana	Baton Rouge, La.	D2
Thierry, John	DE	6-4	260	9/4/71	Alcorn State	Opelousas, La.	D1
Thompson, Aubrey	TE	6-1	230	2/19/71	Utah State	Atlanta, Ga.	FA
Walker, Cedric	S	6-1	205	2/16/71	Stephen F. Austin	Lufkin, Tex.	FA

The term NFL Rookie is defined as a player who is in his first season of professional football and has not been on the roster of another professional football team for any regular-season or postseason games. A Rookie is designated by an "R" on NFL rosters. Players who have been active in another professional football league or players who have NFL experience, including either preseason training camp or being on an Active List or Inactive List, or on Reserve/Injured or Reserve/Physically Unable to Perform for fewer than six regular-season games, are termed NFL First-Year Players. An NFL First-Year Player is designated by a "1" on NFL rosters. Thereafter, a player is credited with an additional year of experience for each season in which he accumulates six games on the Active List or Inactive List, or on Reserve/Injured or Reserve/Physically Unable to Perform.

NOTES

National Football Conference
Eastern Division
Team Colors: Royal Blue, Metallic Silver
      Blue, and White
Cowboys Center
One Cowboys Parkway
Irving, Texas 75063
Telephone: (214) 556-9900

CLUB OFFICIALS

Owner/President/General Manager:
  Jerry Jones
Vice President: Stephen Jones
Vice President: Mike McCoy
Vice President/Marketing: George Hays
Treasurer: Jack Dixon
Marketing and Special Events Coordinator:
  Charlotte Anderson
Public Relations Director: Rich Dalrymple
Assistant Director of Public Relations:
  Brett Daniels
Director of College Scouting: Larry Lacewell
Director of Operations: Bruce Mays
Trainer: Kevin O'Neill
Equipment Manager: Mike McCord
Video Director: Robert Blackwell
Cheerleader Director: Kelli McGonagill
Stadium: Texas Stadium • **Capacity:** 65,846
     Irving, Texas 75062
Playing Surface: Texas Turf
Training Camp: St. Edward's University
     Austin, Texas 78704

1994 SCHEDULE

PRESEASON

July 31	**Minnesota**	8:00
Aug. 7	**Los Angeles Raiders**	8:00
Aug. 15	vs. Houston at Mexico City	9:00
Aug. 21	**Denver**	7:00
Aug. 25	at New Orleans	7:00

REGULAR SEASON

Sept. 4	at Pittsburgh	4:00
Sept. 11	**Houston**	3:00
Sept. 19	**Detroit** (Monday)	8:00
Sept. 25	Open Date	
Oct. 2	at Washington	1:00
Oct. 9	**Arizona**	3:00
Oct. 16	**Philadelphia**	3:00
Oct. 23	at Arizona	1:00
Oct. 30	at Cincinnati	1:00
Nov. 7	**New York Giants** (Monday)	8:00
Nov. 13	at San Francisco	1:00
Nov. 20	**Washington**	12:00
Nov. 24	**Green Bay** (Thanksgiving)	3:00
Dec. 4	at Philadelphia	1:00
Dec. 10	**Cleveland** (Saturday)	3:00
Dec. 19	at New Orleans (Monday)	8:00
Dec. 24	at New York Giants	1:00

RECORD HOLDERS

INDIVIDUAL RECORDS—CAREER

Category	Name	Performance
Rushing (Yds.)	Tony Dorsett, 1977-1987	12,036
Passing (Yds.)	Roger Staubach, 1969-1979	22,700
Passing (TDs)	Danny White, 1976-1988	155
Receiving (No.)	Drew Pearson, 1973-1983	489
Receiving (Yds.)	Tony Hill, 1977-1986	7,988
Interceptions	Mel Renfro, 1964-1977	52
Punting (Avg.)	Mike Saxon, 1985-1992	41.5
Punt Return (Avg.)	Bob Hayes, 1965-1974	11.1
Kickoff Return (Avg.)	Mel Renfro, 1964-1977	26.4
Field Goals	Rafael Septien, 1978-1986	162
Touchdowns (Tot.)	Tony Dorsett, 1977-1987	86
Points	Rafael Septien, 1978-1986	874

INDIVIDUAL RECORDS—SINGLE SEASON

Category	Name	Performance
Rushing (Yds.)	Emmitt Smith, 1992	1,713
Passing (Yds.)	Danny White, 1983	3,980
Passing (TDs)	Danny White, 1983	29
Receiving (No.)	Michael Irvin, 1991	93
Receiving (Yds.)	Michael Irvin, 1991	1,523
Interceptions	Everson Walls, 1981	11
Punting (Avg.)	Sam Baker, 1962	45.4
Punt Return (Avg.)	Bob Hayes, 1968	20.8
Kickoff Return (Avg.)	Mel Renfro, 1965	30.0
Field Goals	Eddie Murray, 1993	28
Touchdowns (Tot.)	Emmitt Smith, 1992	19
Points	Rafael Septien, 1983	123

INDIVIDUAL RECORDS—SINGLE GAME

Category	Name	Performance
Rushing (Yds.)	Emmitt Smith, 10-31-93	237
Passing (Yds.)	Don Meredith, 11-10-63	460
Passing (TDs)	Many times	5
	Last time by Danny White, 10-30-83	
Receiving (No.)	Lance Rentzel, 11-19-67	13
Receiving (Yds.)	Bob Hayes, 11-13-66	246
Interceptions	Herb Adderley, 9-26-71	3
	Lee Roy Jordan, 11-4-73	3
	Dennis Thurman, 12-13-81	3
Field Goals	Roger Ruzek, 12-21-87	5
	Eddie Murray, 10-3-93	5
Touchdowns (Tot.)	Many times	4
	Last time by Emmitt Smith, 11-18-90	
Points	Many times	24
	Last time by Emmitt Smith, 11-18-90	

COACHING HISTORY
(321-215-6)

1960-88	Tom Landry	270-178-6
1989-93	Jimmy Johnson	51-37-0

TEXAS STADIUM

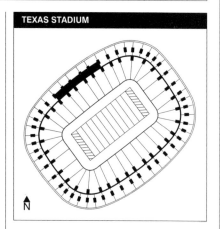

1993 TEAM RECORD

PRESEASON (1-3-1)

Date	Result		Opponents
8/1	L	7-13	Minnesota
8/8	T	13-13	vs. Detroit at London (OT)
8/14	W	13-7	L.A. Raiders
8/21	L	20-23	vs. Houston at San Antonio
8/27	L	21-23	at Chicago

REGULAR SEASON (12-4)

Date	Result		Opponents	Att.
9/6	L	16-35	at Washington	56,345
9/12	L	10-13	Buffalo	63,226
9/19	W	17-10	at Phoenix	73,025
10/3	W	36-14	Green Bay	63,568
10/10	W	27-3	at Indianapolis	60,453
10/17	W	26-17	San Francisco	65,099
10/31	W	23-10	at Philadelphia	61,912
11/7	W	31-9	N.Y. Giants	64,735
11/14	W	20-15	Phoenix	64,224
11/21	L	14-27	at Atlanta	67,337
11/25	L	14-16	Miami	60,198
12/6	W	23-17	Philadelphia	64,521
12/12	W	37-20	at Minnesota	63,321
12/18	W	28-7	at N.Y. Jets	73,233
12/26	W	38-3	Washington	64,497
1/2	W	16-13	at N.Y. Giants (OT)	77,356

POSTSEASON (3-0)

Date	Result		Opponents	Att.
1/16	W	27-17	Green Bay	64,790
1/23	W	38-21	San Francisco	64,902
1/30	W	30-13	Buffalo	72,817

(OT) Overtime

SCORE BY PERIODS

Cowboys	76	124	86	87	3	—	376
Opponents	43	46	79	61	0	—	229

ATTENDANCE

Home 510,068   Away 532,982   Total 1,043,050
Single-game home record, 80,259 (11-24-66)
Single-season home record, 511,541 (1981)

1993 TEAM STATISTICS

	Cowboys	Opp.
Total First Downs	322	297
Rushing	120	94
Passing	172	176
Penalty	30	27
Third Down: Made/Att	83/198	87/219
Third Down Pct.	41.9	39.7
Fourth Down: Made/Att	7/12	6/17
Fourth Down Pct.	58.3	35.3
Total Net Yards	5615	4767
Avg. Per Game	350.9	297.9
Total Plays	994	1012
Avg. Per Play	5.6	4.7
Net Yards Rushing	2161	1651
Avg. Per Game	135.1	103.2
Total Rushes	490	423
Net Yards Passing	3454	3116
Avg. Per Game	215.9	194.8
Sacked/Yards Lost	29/163	34/231
Gross Yards	3617	3347
Att./Completions	475/317	555/334
Completion Pct.	66.7	60.2
Had Intercepted	6	14
Punts/Avg.	56/41.8	78/41.3
Net Punting Avg.	56/37.7	78/34.8
Penalties/Yards Lost	94/744	87/653
Fumbles/Ball Lost	33/16	22/14
Touchdowns	41	23
Rushing	20	7
Passing	18	14
Returns	3	2
Avg. Time of Possession	30:56	29:04

1993 INDIVIDUAL STATISTICS

PASSING	Att.	Comp.	Yds.	Pct.	TD	Int.	Tkld.	Rate
Aikman	392	271	3100	69.1	15	6	26/153	99.0
Kosar	63	36	410	57.1	3	0	2/4	92.7
Garrett	19	9	61	47.4	0	0	1/6	54.9
Harper	1	1	46	100.0	0	0	0/0	118.8
Cowboys	475	317	3617	66.7	18	6	29/163	96.8
Opponents	555	334	3347	60.2	14	14	34/231	75.3

SCORING	TD R	TD P	TD Rt	PAT	FG	Saf	PTS
Murray	0	0	0	38/38	28/33	0	122
E. Smith	9	1	0	0/0	0/0	0	60
Irvin	0	7	0	0/0	0/0	0	42
K. Williams	2	2	2	0/0	0/0	0	36
Harper	0	5	0	0/0	0/0	0	30
Johnston	3	1	0	0/0	0/0	0	24
Lassic	3	0	0	0/0	0/0	0	18
Coleman	2	0	0	0/0	0/0	0	12
Novacek	1	1	0	0/0	0/0	0	12
Elliott	0	0	0	2/3	2/4	0	8
Galbraith	0	1	0	0/0	0/0	0	6
K. Smith	0	0	1	0/0	0/0	0	6
Cowboys	20	18	3	40/41	30/37	0	376
Opponents	7	14	2	23/23	22/27	1	229

RUSHING	Att.	Yds.	Avg.	LG	TD
E. Smith	283	1486	5.3	62t	9
Lassic	75	269	3.6	15	3
Coleman	34	132	3.9	16	2
Aikman	32	125	3.9	20	0
Johnston	24	74	3.1	11	3
Gainer	9	29	3.2	8	0
K. Williams	7	26	3.7	12	2
Agee	6	13	2.2	6	0
Kosar	9	7	0.8	4	0
Irvin	2	6	3.0	9	0
Novacek	1	2	2.0	2t	1
Garrett	8	-8	-1.0	0	0
Cowboys	490	2161	4.4	62t	20
Opponents	423	1651	3.9	77t	7

RECEIVING	No.	Yds.	Avg.	LG	TD
Irvin	88	1330	15.1	61t	7
E. Smith	57	414	7.3	86	1
Johnston	50	372	7.4	20	1
Novacek	44	445	10.1	30	1
Harper	36	777	21.6	80t	5
K. Williams	20	161	7.6	33	2
Lassic	9	37	4.1	9	0
Gainer	6	37	6.2	8	0
Coleman	4	24	6.0	10	0
T. Williams	1	25	25.0	25	0
Price	1	4	4.0	4	0
Galbraith	1	1	1.0	1t	1
Cowboys	317	3617	11.4	86	18
Opponents	334	3347	10.0	70t	14

INTERCEPTIONS	No.	Yds.	Avg.	LG	TD
K. Smith	6	56	9.3	32t	1
Bates	2	25	12.5	22	0
Everett	2	25	12.5	17	0
Washington	1	38	38.0	24	0
Norton	1	25	25.0	25	0
Marion	1	2	2.0	2	0
Gant	1	0	0.0	0	0
Cowboys	14	171	12.2	32t	1
Opponents	6	47	7.8	26	0

PUNTING	No.	Yds.	Avg.	In 20	LG
Jett	56	2342	41.8	22	59
Cowboys	56	2342	41.8	22	59
Opponents	78	3219	41.3	21	60

PUNT RETURNS	No.	FC	Yds.	Avg.	LG	TD
K. Williams	36	14	381	10.6	64t	2
Washington	1	0	0	0.0	0	0
Cowboys	37	14	381	10.3	64t	2
Opponents	32	12	169	5.3	20	0

KICKOFF RETURNS	No.	Yds.	Avg.	LG	TD
K. Williams	31	689	22.2	49	0
Gant	1	18	18.0	18	0
Hennings	1	7	7.0	7	0
R. Jones	1	12	12.0	12	0
Novacek	1	-1	-1.0	-1	0
K. Smith	1	33	33.0	33	0
Vanderbeek	0	0	—	0	0
Cowboys	36	758	21.1	49	0
Opponents	66	1225	18.6	95t	1

SACKS	No.
Tolbert	7.5
Jeffcoat	6.0
J. Jones	5.5
Haley	4.0
Maryland	2.5
Casillas	2.0
Norton	2.0
Roper	2.0
Edwards	1.5
D. Smith	1.0
Cowboys	34.0
Opponents	29.0

1994 DRAFT CHOICES

Round	Name	Pos.	College
1	Shante Carver	DE	Arizona State
2	Larry Allen	G	Sonoma State
3	George Hegamin	T	North Carolina State
4	Willie Jackson	WR	Florida
	DeWayne Dotson	LB	Mississippi
6	Darren Studstill	DB	West Virginia
7	Toddrick McIntosh	DT	Florida State

DALLAS COWBOYS

1994 VETERAN ROSTER

No.	Name	Pos.	Ht.	Wt.	Birthdate	NFL Exp.	College	Hometown	How Acq.	'93 Games/ Starts
34	# Agee, Tommie	RB	6-0	235	2/22/64	8	Auburn	Maplesville, Ala.	FA-'93	12/0
8	Aikman, Troy	QB	6-4	228	11/21/66	6	UCLA	Henryetta, Okla.	D1-'89	14/14
40	# Bates, Bill	S	6-1	205	6/6/61	12	Tennessee	Knoxville, Tenn.	FA-'83	16/0
24	Brown, Larry	CB	5-11	182	11/30/69	4	Texas Christian	Los Angeles, Calif.	D12-'91	16/16
44	Coleman, Lincoln	RB	6-1	249	8/12/69	2	Baylor	Dallas, Tex.	FA-'93	7/0
56	Collins, Roosevelt	LB	6-4	244	1/25/68	2	Texas Christian	Shreveport, La.	FA-'94	0*
68	# Cornish, Frank	C-G	6-4	287	9/24/67	5	UCLA	Chicago, Ill.	PB(SD)-'92	14/3
81	Daniel, Tim	WR	5-11	192	9/14/69	3	Florida A&M	Atlanta, Ga.	D11-'92	0*
58	Edwards, Dixon	LB	6-1	222	3/25/68	4	Michigan State	Cincinnati, Ohio	D2-'91	16/15
46	Fishback, Joe	S	6-0	212	11/29/67	5	Carson-Newman	Knoxville, Tenn.	FA-'93	6/0
89	# Galbraith, Scott	TE	6-1	255	1/7/67	5	Southern California	Sacramento, Calif.	FA-'93	7/0
29	Gant, Kenneth	S	5-11	189	4/18/67	5	Albany State	Lakeland, Fla.	D9-'90	12/1
17	Garrett, Jason	QB	6-2	195	3/28/66	2	Princeton	Chagrin, Ohio	FA-'93	5/1
94	Haley, Charles	DE	6-5	250	1/6/64	9	James Madison	Campbell County, Va.	T(SF)-'92	14/11
80	Harper, Alvin	WR	6-3	208	7/6/67	4	Tennessee	Frostproof, Fla.	D1b-'91	16/15
70	# Hellestrae, Dale	G-C	6-5	275	7/11/62	10	Southern Methodist	Scottsdale, Ariz.	T(Raid)-'90	16/0
95	Hennings, Chad	DT	6-6	286	10/20/65	3	Air Force	Elberon, Iowa	D11-'88	13/0
47	Holmes, Clayton	CB	5-10	181	8/23/69	3	Carson-Newman	Florence, S.C.	D3a-'92	0*
88	Irvin, Michael	WR	6-2	205	3/5/66	7	Miami	Ft. Lauderdale, Fla.	D1-'88	16/16
77	Jeffcoat, Jim	DE	6-5	280	4/1/61	12	Arizona State	Cliffwood, N.J.	D1-'83	16/3
19	Jett, John	P	6-0	184	11/11/68	2	East Carolina	Reedville, Va.	FA-'93	16/0
48	Johnston, Daryl	RB	6-2	238	2/10/66	6	Syracuse	Youngstown, N.Y.	D2-'89	16/16
55	Jones, Robert	LB	6-2	237	9/27/69	3	East Carolina	Nottoway, Va.	D1b-'92	13/3
60	Kennard, Derek	G	6-3	300	9/9/62	9	Nevada-Reno	Stockton, Calif.	UFA(NO)-'94	16/16*
25	Lassic, Derrick	RB	5-10	188	1/26/70	2	Alabama	North Rockland, N.Y.	D4a-'93	10/3
78	Lett, Leon	DE-DT	6-6	285	10/12/68	4	Emporia State	Fair Hope, Ala.	D7-'91	11/6
31	Marion, Brock	S	5-11	189	6/11/70	2	Nevada-Reno	Bakersfield, Calif.	D7-'93	15/0
67	Maryland, Russell	DT	6-1	279	3/22/69	4	Miami	Chicago, Ill.	D1a-'91	16/12
98	Myles, Godfrey	LB	6-1	242	9/22/68	4	Florida	Miami, Fla.	D3a-'91	10/0
61	Newton, Nate	G	6-3	325	12/20/61	9	Florida A&M	Orlando, Fla.	FA-'86	16/16
84	Novacek, Jay	TE	6-4	232	10/24/62	10	Wyoming	Gothenburg, Neb.	PB(Phx)-'90	16/16
43	t- Patterson, Elvis	CB-S	5-11	195	10/21/60	11	Kansas	Houston, Tex.	T(Raid)-'93	11/0
9	Peete, Rodney	QB	6-0	193	3/16/66	6	Southern California	Shawnee Mission, Kan.	UFA(Det)-'94	10/10*
89	t- Price, Jim	TE	6-4	247	10/2/66	4	Stanford	Pine Brook, N.J.	T(Rams)-'93	8/0*
74	Rentie, Caesar	T-G	6-3	323	11/10/64	2	Oklahoma	Hartshorne, Okla.	FA-'94	0*
59	Smith, Darrin	LB	6-1	227	4/15/70	2	Miami	Miami, Fla.	D2b-'93	16/13
22	Smith, Emmitt	RB	5-9	209	5/15/69	5	Florida	Escambia, Fla.	D1-'90	14/13
82	Smith, Jimmy	WR	6-1	205	2/9/69	3	Jackson State	Jackson, Miss.	D2a-'92	0*
26	Smith, Kevin	CB	5-11	180	4/7/70	3	Texas A&M	Orange, Tex.	D1a-'92	16/16
53	# Stepnoski, Mark	C	6-2	264	1/20/67	6	Pittsburgh	Erie, Pa.	D3a-'89	13/13
65	Stone, Ron	T	6-5	309	7/20/71	2	Boston College	West Roxbury, Mass.	D4b-'93	0*
41	Thomas, Dave	CB	6-2	208	8/25/68	2	Tennessee	Miami, Fla.	D8a-'93	12/0
92	Tolbert, Tony	DE	6-6	263	12/29/67	6	Texas-El Paso	Englewood, N.J.	D4-'89	16/16
71	Tuinei, Mark	T	6-5	305	3/31/60	12	Hawaii	Honolulu, Hawaii	FA-'83	16/16
91	# Vanderbeek, Matt	LB-DE	6-3	243	8/16/67	5	Michigan State	Upland, Calif.	W(Ind)-'93	16/0
37	Washington, James	S	6-1	209	1/10/65	7	UCLA	Los Angeles, Calif.	PB(Rams)-'90	14/1
79	Williams, Erik	T	6-6	324	9/7/68	4	Central State, Ohio	Philadelphia, Pa.	D3c-'91	16/16
85	Williams, Kevin	WR	5-9	192	1/25/71	2	Miami	Dallas, Tex.	D2a-'93	16/1
86	Williams, Tyrone	WR	6-5	220	3/26/70	2	Western Ontario	Halifax, Nova Scotia	FA-'92	5/0
42	Wilson, Robert	RB	6-0	258	1/13/69	2	Texas A&M	Houston, Tex.	FA-'94	0*
28	Woodson, Darren	S	6-1	215	4/25/69	3	Arizona State	Phoenix, Ariz.	D2b-'92	16/15

* Collins inactive for 2 games with Miami in '93; Daniel active for 16 games; Holmes, J. Smith, and Wilson missed '93 season due to injury; Kennard played 16 games with New Orleans in '93; Price played 5 games with L.A. Rams, 3 games with Dallas; Rentie last active with Chicago in '88; Stone active for 4 games but did not play.

\# Unrestricted free agent; subject to developments.

† Restricted free agent; subject to developments.

Traded—S Thomas Everett to Tampa Bay, RB Derrick Gainer to L.A. Raiders.

t- Cowboys traded for Patterson (L.A. Raiders), Price (L.A. Rams).

Players lost through free agency (7): DT Tony Casillas (KC; 15 games in '93), G John Gesek (Wash; 14), G-T Kevin Gogan (Raid; 16), DT Jimmie Jones (Rams; 15), QB Bernie Kosar (Mia; 8 with Cleveland, 4 with Dallas), K Eddie Murray (Phil; 14), LB Ken Norton (SF; 16).

Also played with Cowboys in '93—LB Bobby Abrams (5 games), TE Kelly Blackwell (2), K Lin Elliot (2), S Thomas Everett (16), S Chris Hall (1), Hugh Millen (0), LB John Roper (3), S Robert Williams (4).

COACHING STAFF

Head Coach,
Barry Switzer

Pro Career: Named the third head coach in Cowboys history on March 30, 1994. No pro playing experience.

Background: Played at Arkansas from 1955-59 before beginning his assistant coaching career at his alma mater in 1962. Moved on to Oklahoma in 1966, and was named the Sooners' offensive coordinator in 1967. As head coach at Oklahoma from 1973-88, Switzer registered a career record of 157-29-4. His .837 winning percentage at Oklahoma is the fourth highest mark in college history, behind only Notre Dame's Knute Rockne (.881) and Frank Leahy (.864) and Carlisle's George Woodruff (.846). He guided the Sooners to 28 consecutive wins from 1973-75 and went 37 straight games without a defeat. Switzer's Oklahoma teams won national championships (1974, 1975, and 1985) and 12 Big Eight Conference championships.

Personal: Born October 5, 1937, Crossett, Arkansas. Switzer lives in Irving, Texas. He has two sons—Greg and Doug and one daughter Kathy.

ASSISTANT COACHES

Hubbard Alexander, wide receivers; born February 14, 1939, Winston-Salem, N.C., lives in Coppell, Tex. Center Tennessee State 1958-61. No pro playing experience. College coach: Tennessee State 1962-63, Vanderbilt 1974-78, Miami 1979-88. Pro coach: Joined Cowboys in 1989.

Joe Avezzano, special teams; born November 17, 1943, Yonkers, N.Y., lives in Coppell, Tex. Guard Florida State 1961-65. Pro center Boston Patriots 1966. College coach: Florida State 1968, Iowa State 1969-72, Pittsburgh 1973-76, Tennessee 1977-79, Oregon State 1980-84 (head coach), Texas 1985-88. Pro coach: Joined Cowboys in 1990.

John Blake, defensive line; born March 6, 1961, Sand Springs, Okla., lives in Irving, Tex. Nose tackle Oklahoma 1980-83. No pro playing experience. College coach: Oklahoma 1986-87, 1989-92, Tulsa 1988. Pro coach: Joined Cowboys in 1993.

Joe Brodsky, running backs; born June 9, 1934, Miami, Fla., lives in Coppell, Tex. Fullback-linebacker Florida 1953-56. No pro playing experience. College coach: Miami 1978-88. Pro coach: Joined Cowboys in 1989.

Dave Campo, defensive backs; born July 18, 1947, New London, Conn., lives in Coppell, Tex. Defensive back Central Connecticut State 1967-70. No pro playing experience. College coach: Central Connecticut State 1971-72, Albany State 1973, Bridgeport 1974, Pittsburgh 1975, Washington State 1976, Boise State 1977-79, Oregon State 1980, Weber State 1981-82, Iowa State 1983, Syracuse 1984-86, Miami 1987-88. Pro coach: Joined Cowboys in 1989.

Butch Davis, defensive coordinator; born November 17, 1951, Tahlequah, Okla., lives in Coppell, Tex. Defensive end Arkansas 1971-74. No pro playing experience. College coach: Oklahoma State 1979-83, Miami 1984-88. Pro coach: Joined Cowboys in 1989.

Jim Eddy, linebackers; born May 2, 1939, Checotah, Okla., lives in Irving, Tex. Defensive back-running back New Mexico State 1956-59. No pro playing experience. College coach: New Mexico State 1965-70, Texas El-Paso 1971-72, Houston 1987-89. Pro coach: Saskatchewan Rough Riders (CFL) 1974-78 (head coach 1977-78), Hamilton Tiger Cats (CFL) 1979-80, Montreal Alouettes (CFL) 1981 (head coach), Toronto Argonauts (CFL) 1982-83, Houston Gamblers (USFL) 1984-85, Houston Oilers 1990-92, joined Cowboys in 1993.

Robert Ford, tight ends; born June 21, 1951, Belton, Tex., lives in Coppell, Tex. Wide receiver Houston 1970-72. No pro playing experience. College coach: Western Illinois 1974-76, New Mexico 1977-79, Oregon State 1980-81, Mississippi State 1982-83, Kansas 1986, Texas Tech 1987-88, Texas A&M 1989-90. Pro coach: Houston Gamblers (USFL) 1985, joined Cowboys in 1991.

Steve Hoffman, kickers-research and development;

1994 FIRST-YEAR ROSTER

Name	Pos.	Ht.	Wt.	Birthdate	College	Hometown	How Acq.
Allen, Larry	G	6-3	325	11/27/71	Sonoma State	Napa, Calif.	D2
Batiste, Michael	DT	6-3	301	12/24/70	Tulane	Beaumont, Tex.	FA
Bell, Coleman (1)	TE	6-2	232	4/22/70	Miami	Tampa, Fla.	FA
Boniol, Chris	K	5-11	159	12/9/71	Louisiana Tech	Alexandria, La.	FA
Bretz, Brad (1)	QB	6-4	208	8/17/70	Cal State-Hayward	San Jose, Calif.	FA
Burch, Alfie	CB	6-0	196	3/24/71	Michigan	Warren, Ohio	FA
Carver, Shante	DE	6-5	240	2/12/71	Arizona State	Stockton, Calif.	D1
Cunningham, Richie	K	5-10	165	8/18/70	Southwest Louisiana	Houma, La.	FA
Dotson, Dewayne	LB	6-1	250	6/10/71	Mississippi	Hendersonville, Tenn.	D4b
Fayak, Craig	K	6-1	188	7/22/72	Penn State	Belle Vernon, Pa.	FA
Garrett, Judd (1)	RB	6-2	214	6/25/67	Princeton	Monmouth Beach, N.J.	FA
Hegamin, George	T	6-7	355	2/14/73	North Carolina State	Camden, N.J.	D3
Hill, Shelby	WR	6-0	207	8/29/71	Syracuse	Phoenix, Ariz.	FA
Jackson, Willie	WR	6-1	205	8/16/71	Florida	Gainesville, Fla.	D4a
Jones, Tommy	CB	5-8	167	1/21/71	Fresno State	Lemoore, Calif.	FA
Joyce, Matt	T-G	6-7	283	3/30/72	Richmond	St. Petersburg, Fla.	FA
Mason, Mark	RB	5-7	189	4/25/72	Maryland	Potomac, Md.	FA
Mays, Marvin	DE	6-3	262	9/16/69	S.E. Oklahoma	Senatobia, Miss.	FA
McClanahan, Anthony	LB	6-1	238	4/3/71	Washington State	Bakersfield, Calif.	FA
McCormack, Hurvin	DT	6-5	271	4/6/72	Indiana	Brooklyn, N.Y.	FA
McIntosh, Toddrick	DT	6-3	277	1/22/72	Florida State	Richardson, Tex.	D7
Mills, Toby	C	6-0	270	12/29/71	Arizona State	Henderson, Tex.	FA
Mundy, Aaron	TE	6-5	252	11/9/71	Virginia	Hampton, Va.	FA
Parrish, James (1)	T	6-6	310	5/19/68	Temple	Baltimore, Md.	FA
Powe, Keith (1)	DE	6-4	265	6/5/69	Texas-El Paso	Houston, Tex.	FA
Richardson, Tony	RB	6-1	224	12/17/71	Auburn	Daleville, Ala.	FA
Schorp, Greg	TE	6-3	242	9/6/71	Texas A&M	San Antonio, Tex.	FA
Studstill, Darren	CB-S	6-1	186	8/9/70	West Virginia	Palm Beach Garden, Fla.	D6
Wagner, Keith	T	6-4	302	1/22/70	Abilene Christian	Corpus Christi, Tex.	FA
Wilkins, Jeff	K	6-1	180	4/19/72	Youngstown State	Austintown, Ohio	FA
Younger, Jermaine	LB	6-0	262	6/1/71	Utah State	Hayward, Calif.	FA

The term NFL Rookie is defined as a player who is in his first season of professional football and has not been on the roster of another professional football team for any regular-season or postseason games. A Rookie is designated by an "R" on NFL rosters. Players who have been active in another professional football league or players who have NFL experience, including either preseason training camp or being on an Active List or Inactive List, or on Reserve/Injured or Reserve/Physically Unable to Perform for fewer than six regular-season games, are termed NFL First-Year Players. An NFL First-Year Player is designated by a "1" on NFL rosters. Thereafter, a player is credited with an additional year of experience for each season in which he accumulates six games on the Active List or Inactive List, or on Reserve/Injured or Reserve/Physically Unable to Perform.

NOTES

born September 8, 1958, Camden, N.J., lives in Coppell, Tex. Quarterback-running back-wide receiver Dickinson College 1979-82. Pro punter Washington Federals (USFL) 1983. College coach: Miami 1985-87. Pro coach: Joined Cowboys in 1989.

Hudson Houck, offensive line; born January 7, 1943, Los Angeles, Calif., lives in Irving, Tex. Center Southern California 1962-64. No pro playing experience. College coach: Southern California 1970-72, 1976-82, Stanford 1973-75. Pro coach: Los Angeles Rams 1983-91, Seattle Seahawks 1992, joined Cowboys in 1993.

Mike Woicik, strength and conditioning; born September 26, 1956, Westwood, Mass., lives in Coppell, Tex. Boston College 1974-78. No college or pro playing experience. College coach: Springfield 1978-80,

Syracuse 1980-89. Pro coach: Joined Cowboys in 1990.

Ernie Zampese, offensive coordinator; born March 12, 1936, Santa Barbara, Calif., lives in Mission Viejo, Calif. Halfback Southern California 1956-58. No pro playing experience. College coach: Hancock, Calif., J.C. 1962-65, Cal Poly-SLO 1966, San Diego State 1967-75. Pro coach: San Diego Chargers 1976, 1979-86, New York Jets 1977-78 (scout), Los Angeles Rams 1987-93, joined Cowboys in 1994.

Mike Zimmer, defensive assistant; born June 5, 1956, Peoria, Ill., lives in Irving, Tex. Quarterback-linebacker Illinois State 1974-76. No pro playing experience. College coach: Missouri 1979-80, Weber State 1981-88, Washington State 1989-93. Pro coach: Joined Cowboys in 1994.

DETROIT LIONS

National Football Conference
Central Division
Team Colors: Honolulu Blue and Silver
Pontiac Silverdome
1200 Featherstone Road
Pontiac, Michigan 48342
Telephone: (313) 335-4131

CLUB OFFICIALS

President-Owner: William Clay Ford
Executive Vice President-COO: Chuck Schmidt
Vice President Administration/Communications:
  Bill Keenist
Director of Player Personnel: Ron Hughes
Director of Pro Personnel: Kevin Colbert
Scouts: Milt Davis, Dirk Dierking, Tom Dimitroff,
  Allen Hughes, Scott McEwen, Jim Owens,
  Rick Spielman, John Trump
Director of Player Programs/Pro Scouting Assistant:
  Larry Lee
Controller/Travel Coordinator: Tom Lesnau
Director of Marketing, Sales, and Ticket Operations:
  Fred Otto
Director of Marketing: Steve Harms
Director of Community Relations and Detroit Lions
  Charities: Tim Pendell
Media Relations Coordinator: Mike Murray
Media Relations Assistant: James Petrylka
Strength and Conditioning: Bert Hill
Trainer: Kent Falb
Equipment Manager: Dan Jaroshewich
Video Director: Steve Hermans
Stadium: Pontiac Silverdome •**Capacity:** 80,368
        1200 Featherstone Road
        Pontiac, Michigan 48342
Playing Surface: AstroTurf
Training Camp: Pontiac Silverdome
        1200 Featherstone Road
        Pontiac, Michigan 48342

1994 SCHEDULE
PRESEASON
Aug. 5	**New York Jets**	7:30
Aug. 13	at Cleveland	7:30
Aug. 19	**Arizona**	7:30
Aug. 26	at Cincinnati	7:30

REGULAR SEASON
Sept. 4	**Atlanta**	1:00
Sept. 11	at Minnesota	12:00
Sept. 19	at Dallas (Monday)	8:00
Sept. 25	**New England**	4:00
Oct. 2	at Tampa Bay	1:00
Oct. 9	**San Francisco**	1:00
Oct. 16	Open Date	
Oct. 23	**Chicago**	1:00
Oct. 30	at New York Giants	1:00
Nov. 6	vs. Green Bay at Milwaukee	12:00
Nov. 13	**Tampa Bay**	8:00
Nov. 20	at Chicago	12:00
Nov. 24	**Buffalo** (Thanksgiving)	12:30
Dec. 4	**Green Bay**	1:00
Dec. 10	at New York Jets (Saturday)	12:30
Dec. 17	**Minnesota** (Saturday)	12:30
Dec. 25	at Miami	8:00

RECORD HOLDERS
INDIVIDUAL RECORDS—CAREER
Category	Name	Performance
Rushing (Yds.)	Barry Sanders, 1989-1993	6,789
Passing (Yds.)	Bobby Layne, 1950-58	15,710
Passing (TDs)	Bobby Layne, 1950-58	118
Receiving (No.)	Charlie Sanders, 1968-1977	336
Receiving (Yds.)	Gail Cogdill, 1960-68	5,220
Interceptions	Dick LeBeau, 1959-1972	62
Punting (Avg.)	Yale Lary, 1952-53, 1956-1964	44.3
Punt Return (Avg.)	Jack Christiansen, 1951-58	12.8
Kickoff Return (Avg.)	Pat Studstill, 1961-67	25.7
Field Goals	Eddie Murray, 1980-1991	243
Touchdowns (Tot.)	Barry Sanders, 1989-1993	60
Points	Eddie Murray, 1980-1991	1,113

INDIVIDUAL RECORDS—SINGLE SEASON
Category	Name	Performance
Rushing (Yds.)	Barry Sanders, 1991	1,548
Passing (Yds.)	Gary Danielson, 1980	3,223
Passing (TDs)	Bobby Layne, 1951	26
Receiving (No.)	James Jones, 1984	77
Receiving (Yds.)	Pat Studstill, 1966	1,266
Interceptions	Don Doll, 1950	12
	Jack Christiansen, 1953	12
Punting (Avg.)	Yale Lary, 1963	48.9
Punt Return (Avg.)	Jack Christiansen, 1952	21.5
Kickoff Return (Avg.)	Tom Watkins, 1965	34.4
Field Goals	Jason Hanson, 1993	34
Touchdowns (Tot.)	Barry Sanders, 1991	17
Points	Jason Hanson, 1993	130

INDIVIDUAL RECORDS—SINGLE GAME
Category	Name	Performance
Rushing (Yds.)	Barry Sanders, 11-24-91	220
Passing (Yds.)	Bobby Layne, 11-5-50	374
Passing (TDs)	Gary Danielson, 12-9-78	5
Receiving (No.)	Cloyce Box, 12-3-50	12
	James Jones, 9-28-86	12
Receiving (Yds.)	Cloyce Box, 12-3-50	302
Interceptions	Don Doll, 10-23-49	*4
Field Goals	Garo Yepremian, 11-13-66	6
Touchdowns (Tot.)	Cloyce Box, 12-3-50	4
Points	Cloyce Box, 12-3-50	24

*NFL Record

COACHING HISTORY
Portsmouth Spartans 1930-33
(409-421-32)
1930	Hal (Tubby) Griffen	5-6-3
1931-36	George (Potsy) Clark	49-20-6
1937-38	Earl (Dutch) Clark	14-8-0
1939	Elmer (Gus) Henderson	6-5-0
1940	George (Potsy) Clark	5-5-1
1941-42	Bill Edwards*	4-9-1
1942	John Karcis	0-8-0
1943-47	Charles (Gus) Dorais	20-31-2
1948-50	Alvin (Bo) McMillin	12-24-0
1951-56	Raymond (Buddy) Parker	50-24-2
1957-64	George Wilson	55-45-6
1965-66	Harry Gilmer	10-16-2
1967-72	Joe Schmidt	43-35-7
1973	Don McCafferty	6-7-1
1974-76	Rick Forzano**	15-17-0
1976-77	Tommy Hudspeth	11-13-0
1978-84	Monte Clark	43-63-1
1985-88	Darryl Rogers***	18-40-0
1988-93	Wayne Fontes	43-45-0

  *Released after three games in 1942
 **Resigned after four games in 1976
***Released after 11 games in 1988

PONTIAC SILVERDOME

1993 TEAM RECORD

PRESEASON (4-0-1)

Date	Result		Opponents
7/30	W	14-7	Buffalo
8/8	T	13-13	vs. Dallas at London (OT)
8/16	W	24-20	at Houston
8/20	W	30-7	Cincinnati
8/27	W	17-16	at New Orleans

REGULAR SEASON (10-6)

Date	Result		Opponents	Att.
9/5	W	30-13	Atlanta	56,216
9/12	W	19-16	at New England (OT)	54,151
9/19	L	3-14	at New Orleans	69,039
9/26	W	26-20	Phoenix	57,180
10/3	L	10-27	at Tampa Bay	40,794
10/17	W	30-10	Seattle	60,801
10/24	W	16-13	at L.A. Rams	43,850
10/31	W	30-27	at Minnesota	53,428
11/7	W	23-0	Tampa Bay	65,295
11/21	L	17-26	at Green Bay	55,119
11/25	L	6-10	Chicago	76,699
12/5	L	0-13	Minnesota	63,216
12/12	W	21-14	at Phoenix	39,393
12/19	L	17-55	San Francisco	77,052
12/26	W	20-14	at Chicago	43,443
1/2	W	30-20	Green Bay	77,510

POSTSEASON (0-1)

1/8	L	24-28	Green Bay	68,479

(OT) Overtime

SCORE BY PERIODS

Lions	44	102	62	87	3	—	298
Opponents	61	86	78	67	0	—	292

ATTENDANCE

Home 533,969   Away 399,217   Total 933,186
Single-game home record, 80,444 (12-20-81)
Single-season home record, 622,593 (1980)

1993 TEAM STATISTICS

	Lions	Opp.
Total First Downs	248	279
Rushing	101	108
Passing	139	154
Penalty	8	17
Third Down: Made/Att	73/211	92/225
Third Down Pct.	34.6	40.9
Fourth Down: Made/Att	5/12	7/11
Fourth Down Pct.	41.7	63.6
Total Net Yards	4658	4669
Avg. Per Game	291.1	291.8
Total Plays	937	990
Avg. Per Play	5.0	4.7
Net Yards Rushing	1944	1649
Avg. Per Game	121.5	103.1
Total Rushes	456	433
Net Yards Passing	2714	3020
Avg. Per Game	169.6	188.8
Sacked/Yards Lost	46/229	43/253
Gross Yards	2943	3273
Att./Completions	435/264	514/309
Completion Pct.	60.7	60.1
Had Intercepted	19	19
Punts/Avg.	72/44.5	81/43.1
Net Punting Avg.	72/36.8	81/37.0
Penalties/Yards Lost	93/665	73/500
Fumbles/Ball Lost	29/13	34/16
Touchdowns	28	32
Rushing	9	12
Passing	15	19
Returns	4	1
Avg. Time of Possession	29:27	30:33

1993 INDIVIDUAL STATISTICS

PASSING	Att	Cmp	Yds.	Pct.	TD	Int	Tkld.	Rate
Peete	252	157	1670	62.3	6	14	34/174	66.4
Kramer	138	87	1002	63.0	8	3	5/35	95.1
Ware	45	20	271	44.4	1	2	7/20	53.1
Lions	435	264	2943	60.7	15	19	46/229	74.1
Opponents	514	309	3273	60.1	19	19	43/253	75.6

SCORING	TD R	TD P	TD Rt	PAT	FG	Saf	PTS
Hanson	0	0	0	28/28	34/43	0	130
H. Moore	0	6	0	0/0	0/0	0	36
D. Moore	3	1	0	0/0	0/0	0	24
Sanders	3	0	0	0/0	0/0	0	18
Clay	0	0	2	0/0	0/0	0	12
Green	0	2	0	0/0	0/0	0	12
Hallock	0	2	0	0/0	0/0	0	12
Holman	0	2	0	0/0	0/0	0	12
Lynch	2	0	0	0/0	0/0	0	12
Perriman	0	2	0	0/0	0/0	0	12
Gray	0	0	1	0/0	0/0	0	6
Jamison	0	0	1	0/0	0/0	0	6
Peete	1	0	0	0/0	0/0	0	6
Lions	9	15	4	28/28	34/43	0	298
Opponents	12	19	1	31/32	23/30	0	292

RUSHING	Att.	Yds.	Avg.	LG	TD
Sanders	243	1115	4.6	42	3
D. Moore	88	405	4.6	48	3
Lynch	53	207	3.9	15	2
Peete	45	165	3.7	28	1
Ware	7	23	3.3	8	0
Perriman	4	16	4.0	16	0
Matthews	2	7	3.5	9	0
Kramer	10	5	0.5	4	0
C. Richards	4	1	0.3	1	0
Lions	456	1944	4.3	48	9
Opponents	433	1649	3.8	50t	12

RECEIVING	No.	Yds.	Avg.	LG	TD
H. Moore	61	935	15.3	93t	6
Perriman	49	496	10.1	34	2
Sanders	36	205	5.7	17	0
Green	28	462	16.5	47	2
Holman	25	244	9.8	28t	2
D. Moore	21	169	8.0	20	1
Lynch	13	82	6.3	11	0
Matthews	11	171	15.5	40	0
Hallock	8	88	11.0	24	2
Campbell	7	55	7.9	12	0
Johnson	2	18	9.0	9	0
Thompson	1	15	15.0	15	0
Turner	1	7	7.0	7	0
Fralic	1	-4	-4.0	-4	0
Lions	264	2943	11.1	93t	15
Opponents	309	3273	10.6	80t	19

INTERCEPTIONS	No.	Yds.	Avg.	LG	TD
Swilling	3	16	5.3	14	0
Jamison	2	48	24.0	35t	1
Crockett	2	31	15.5	31	0
Colon	2	28	14.0	27	0
McNeil	2	19	9.5	16	0
McKyer	2	10	5.0	10	0
Spielman	2	-2	-1.0	0	0
White	1	5	5.0	5	0
Owens	1	1	1.0	1	0
Gibson	1	0	0.0	0	0
Scroggins	1	0	0.0	0	0
Lions	19	156	8.2	35t	1
Opponents	19	177	9.3	63t	1

PUNTING	No.	Yds.	Avg.	In 20	LG
Arnold	72	3207	44.5	15	68
Lions	72	3207	44.5	15	68
Opponents	81	3489	43.1	25	57

PUNT RETURNS	No.	FC	Yds.	Avg.	LG	TD
Gray	23	14	197	8.6	35	0
Turner	17	4	152	8.9	53	0
Lions	40	18	349	8.7	53	0
Opponents	45	5	377	8.4	21	0

KICKOFF RETURNS	No.	Yds.	Avg.	LG	TD
Gray	28	688	24.6	95t	1
Anderson	3	51	17.0	24	0
Turner	15	330	22.0	46	0
Clay	2	34	17.0	20	0
Hallock	1	11	11.0	11	0
Jamison	1	0	0.0	0	0
Lynch	1	22	22.0	22	0
D. Moore	1	68	68.0	68	0
V. Jones	0	0	—	—	0
Lions	52	1204	23.2	95t	1
Opponents	30	609	20.3	64	0

SACKS	No.
Porcher	8.5
Scroggins	8.0
Swilling	6.5
Pritchett	4.0
Owens	3.0
Hayworth	2.0
Jamison	2.0
Spindler	2.0
White	1.5
Clay	1.0
Colon	1.0
Crockett	1.0
Gibson	1.0
London	1.0
Spielman	0.5
Lions	43.0
Opponents	46.0

1994 DRAFT CHOICES

Round	Name	Pos.	College
1	Johnnie Morton	WR	Southern California
2	Van Malone	DB	Texas
3	Shane Bonham	DT	Tennessee
4	Vaughn Bryant	DB	Stanford
5	Tony Semple	G	Memphis State
6	Jocelyn Borgella	DB	Cincinnati
7	Thomas Beer	LB	Wayne State, Mich.

DETROIT LIONS

1994 VETERAN ROSTER

No.		Name	Pos.	Ht.	Wt.	Birthdate	NFL Exp.	College	Hometown	How Acq.	'93 Games/ Starts
43	#	Anderson, Gary	RB	6-1	190	4/18/61	9	Arkansas	Columbia, Mo.	FA-'93	10/1*
36		Blades, Bennie	S	6-1	221	9/3/66	7	Miami	Ft. Lauderdale, Fla.	D1-'88	4/4
66		Bouwens, Shawn	G	6-4	290	5/25/68	4	Nebraska-Wesleyan	Lincoln, Neb.	FA-'91	15/1
75		Brown, Lomas	T	6-4	287	3/30/63	10	Florida	Miami, Fla.	D1-'85	11/11
68		Burton, Leonard	C	6-3	275	6/18/64	8	South Carolina	Memphis, Tenn.	FA-'94	0*
50	#	Caston, Toby	LB	6-1	243	7/17/65	8	Louisiana State	Monroe, La.	FA-'93	9/0
32		Clay, Willie	CB	5-9	184	9/5/70	3	Georgia Tech	Pittsburgh, Pa.	D8-'92	16/1
21	†	Colon, Harry	S	6-0	203	2/14/69	4	Missouri	Kansas City, Kan.	FA-'92	15/11
77		Compton, Mike	C-G	6-6	297	9/18/70	2	West Virginia	Glenwood, Iowa	D3b-'93	8/0
76		Conover, Scott	T	6-4	285	9/27/68	4	Purdue	Freehold, N.J.	D5-'91	1/0
53		Glover, Kevin	C	6-2	282	6/17/63	10	Maryland	Upper Marlboro, Md.	D2-'85	16/16
23		Gray, Mel	WR-KR	5-9	171	3/16/61	9	Purdue	Williamsburg, Va.	FA-'89	11/0
86		Green, Willie	WR	6-2	181	4/2/66	5	Mississippi	Athens, Ga.	D8a-'90	16/6
89		Hall, Ron	TE	6-4	245	3/15/64	8	Hawaii	Escondido, Calif.	UFA(TB)-'94	16/16*
49		Hallock, Ty	TE	6-3	249	4/30/71	2	Michigan State	Greenville, Mich.	D7-'93	16/4
4		Hanson, Jason	K	5-11	183	6/17/70	3	Washington State	Spokane, Wash.	D2b-'92	16/0
99		Hayworth, Tracy	LB	6-3	260	12/18/67	5	Tennessee	Franklin, Tenn.	D7-'90	11/2
81	#	Holman, Rodney	TE	6-3	238	4/20/60	13	Tulane	Ypsilanti, Mich.	UFA(Cin)-'93	16/16
58	#	Jamison, George	LB	6-1	235	9/30/62	9	Cincinnati	Bridgeton, N.J.	SD2-'84	16/16
25		Jeffries, Greg	CB	5-9	184	10/16/71	2	Virginia	High Point, N.C.	D6-'93	7/0
51		Johnson, Mike	LB	6-1	230	11/26/62	9	Virginia Tech	Hyattsville, Md.	UFA(Clev)-'94	16/16*
57	#	Jones, Victor	LB	6-2	250	10/19/66	7	Virginia Tech	Rockville, Md.	FA-'89	16/1
52		Kowalkowski, Scott	LB	6-2	228	8/23/68	4	Notre Dame	Orchard Lake, Mich.	FA-'94	0*
17		Krieg, Dave	QB	6-1	202	10/20/58	15	Milton	Schofield, Wis.	UFA(KC)-'94	12/5*
55		London, Antonio	LB	6-2	234	4/14/71	2	Alabama	Tullahoma, Tenn.	D3a-'93	14/0
16		Long, Chuck	QB	6-4	217	2/18/63	8	Iowa	Wheaton, Ill.	FA-'94	0*
73		Lutz, Dave	G-T	6-6	305	12/20/59	12	Georgia Tech	Peachland, N.C.	UFA(KC)-'93	16/16
40		Massey, Robert	CB	5-11	195	2/16/67	6	North Carolina Central	Charlotte, N.C.	UFA(Ariz)-'94	10/10*
83	#	Matthews, Aubrey	WR	5-7	165	9/15/62	9	Delta State	Pascaguola, Miss.	FA-'90	14/2
33	#	McKyer, Tim	CB	6-0	174	9/5/63	9	Texas-Arlington	Port Arthur, Tex.	UFA(Atl)-'93	15/4
47		McNeil, Ryan	CB	6-0	175	10/4/70	2	Miami	Ft. Pierce, Fla.	D2-'93	16/2
19		Mitchell, Scott	QB	6-6	230	1/2/68	5	Utah	Springville, Utah	UFA(Mia)-'94	13/7*
9		Montgomery, Greg	P	6-4	215	10/29/64	6	Michigan State	Red Bank, N.J.	UFA(Hou)-'94	15/0*
31		Moore, Derrick	RB	6-1	227	10/13/67	3	Northeast Oklahoma St.	Albany, Ga.	W(Atl)-'93	13/3
84		Moore, Herman	WR	6-3	210	10/20/69	4	Virginia	Danville, Va.	D1-'91	15/15
90	†	Owens, Dan	DE	6-3	280	3/16/67	5	Southern California	Whittier, Calif.	D2-'90	15/11
80		Perriman, Brett	WR	5-9	180	10/10/65	7	Miami	Miami, Fla.	T(NO)-'91	15/15
91		Porcher, Robert	DE	6-3	283	7/30/69	3	South Carolina State	Wendo, S.C.	D1-'92	16/4
94	†	Pritchett, Kelvin	DE	6-2	281	10/24/69	2	Mississippi	Atlanta, Ga.	T(Dall)-'91	16/5
67		Richards, Dave	G	6-5	310	4/11/66	7	UCLA	Dallas, Tex.	UFA(SD)-'93	15/15
63	#	Rodenhauser, Mark	C	6-5	280	6/1/61	7	Illinois State	Addison, Ill.	FA-'93	16/0
20		Sanders, Barry	RB	5-8	203	7/16/68	6	Oklahoma State	Wichita, Kan.	D1-'89	11/11
38	†	Scott, Kevin	CB	5-9	175	5/19/69	4	Stanford	Phoenix, Ariz.	D4-'91	12/10
59		Scroggins, Tracy	LB	6-2	255	9/11/69	3	Tulsa	Chectah, Okla.	D2a-'92	16/0
54		Spielman, Chris	LB	6-0	247	10/11/65	7	Ohio State	Massilon, Ohio	D2b-'88	16/16
93		Spindler, Marc	DE	6-5	290	11/28/69	5	Pittsburgh	West Scranton, Pa.	D3-'90	16/16
56		Swilling, Pat	LB	6-3	242	10/25/64	9	Georgia Tech	Toccoa, Ga.	T(NO)-'93	14/14
71		Tharpe, Larry	T	6-4	299	11/19/70	3	Tennessee State	Macon, Ga.	D6-'92	5/3
81		Thompson, Marty	TE	6-3	243	12/9/69	2	Fresno State	Mammoth Lakes, Calif.	FA-'93	6/2
35		White, William	S	5-10	191	2/19/66	7	Ohio State	Lima, Ohio	D4-'88	16/16

* Anderson played 6 games with Tampa Bay, 4 games with Detroit in '93; Burton last active with Detroit in '92; Hall played 16 games with Tampa Bay; Johnson played 16 games with Cleveland; Kowalkowski missed '93 season due to injury; Krieg played 12 games with Kansas City; Long on injured reserve with Detroit in '92; Massey played 10 games with Arizona; Mitchell played 13 games with Miami; Montgomery played 15 games with Houston.

\# Unrestricted free agent; subject to developments.

† Restricted free agent; subject to developments.

Traded—WR Reggie Barnett to Seattle.

Retired—Lawrence Pete, 6-year nose tackle, 12 games in '93.

Players lost through free agency (7): P Jim Arnold (Mia; 16 games in '93), WR Jeff Campbell (Den; 10), CB Ray Crockett (Den; 16), LB Dennis Gibson (SD; 15), QB Erik Kramer (Chi; 5), QB Rodney Peete (Dall; 10), QB Andre Ware (Minn; 5).

Also played with Lions in '93—LB Darryl Ford (11 games in '93), G Bill Fralic (16), CB Melvin Jenkins (1), TE Jimmy Johnson (6), T Jack Linn (3), RB Eric Lynch (4), (6), RB Curvin Richards (1), NT Mack Travis (4), WR Vernon Turner (7).

COACHING STAFF

Head Coach,
Wayne Fontes

Pro Career: Became the Lions' seventeenth head coach on December, 22, 1988, after serving five weeks as interim head coach (2-3 record). Has led the Lions to two Central Division championships in the last three seasons. The Lions captured the NFC Central title with a 10-6 record in 1993, but were eliminated in the first round of the playoffs. Detroit finished 5-11 in 1992. In 1991, Fontes led the Lions to a 12-4 record and the team's first NFC Central Division title since 1983. The Lions notched their first playoff victory since 1957 and reached the NFC Championship Game in 1991. The Lions were 6-10 in 1990. In 1989, Fontes's first full season, the Lions finished 7-9, including five consecutive season-ending wins. He began the 1988 season as Detroit's defensive coordinator and secondary coach, following a nine-year stint with the Tampa Bay Buccaneers. A former defensive back with the New York Jets, Fontes advanced from secondary coach to defensive coordinator to assistant head coach of the Buccaneers during his years with Tampa Bay. As a player with the Jets, his brief pro career was cut short by a broken leg after two seasons (1963-64). However, his 83-yard interception return against Houston (12-15-63) did stand as the Jets' team record until it was broken in 1989 by Erik McMillan's 93-yard return. Career record: 43-45.

Background: A former two-sport star (football and baseball) at Michigan State, Fontes earned all-Big Ten honors at defensive back for the Spartans. He earned his bachelor's degree in education and biological science and later earned his master's degree in administration, all from Michigan State. Fontes became defensive backfield coach at Dayton in 1968. He also served in the same capacity at Iowa (1969-71) and Southern California (1972-75).

Personal: Born February 17, 1939, New Bedford, Mass. Fontes and his wife, Evelyn, live in Rochester Hills, Mich., and have three children—Mike, Scott, and Kim.

ASSISTANT COACHES

Paul Boudreau, offensive line; born December 30, 1949, Somerville, Mass., lives in Rochester Hills, Mich. Guard Boston College 1971-73. No pro playing experience. College coach: Boston College 1974-76, Maine 1977-78, Dartmouth 1979-81, Navy 1983. Pro coach: Edmonton Eskimos (CFL) 1983-86, New Orleans Saints 1987-93, joined Lions in 1994.

Don Clemons, outside linebackers; born February 15, 1954, Newark, N.J., lives in Rochester, Mich. Defensive end Muehlenberg College 1973-76. No pro playing experience. College coach: Kutztown State 1977-78, New Mexico 1979, Arizona State 1980-84. Pro coach: Joined Lions in 1985.

John Fontes, defensive backs; born June 24, 1949, New Bedford, Mass., lives in Rochester Hills, Mich. Defensive back Iowa 1969-70. No pro playing experience. College coach: Iowa 1971-72, Oregon State 1976-80, Northwestern 1985, Miami 1986, Louisiana State 1987-89. Pro coach: Tampa Bay Storm (Arena League) 1991, Sacramento Surge (World League) 1992, joined Lions in 1992.

Steve Kazor, special teams; born February 24, 1948, New Kensington, Pa., lives in Oxford, Mich. Nose tackle Westminster College 1967-70. No pro playing experience. College coach: Emporia State 1973 (head coach), Texas Arlington 1974, Colorado State 1975, Wyoming 1976, Texas 1977-78, Texas-El Paso 1979-80, Iowa Wesleyan 1993 (head coach). Pro coach: Chicago Bears 1982-92, joined Lions in 1994.

Lamar Leachman, defensive line; born August 7, 1934, Cartersville, Ga., lives in Pontiac, Mich. Center-linebacker Tennessee 1952-55. No pro playing experience. College coach: Richmond 1966-67, Georgia Tech 1968-71, Memphis State 1972, South Carolina 1973. Pro coach: New York Stars (WFL) 1974, Toronto Argonauts (CFL) 1975-77, Montreal Alou-

ettes (CFL) 1978-79, New York Giants 1980-89, joined Lions in 1990.

Dave Levy, assistant head coach-offensive coordinator; born October 25, 1932, Carrollton, Mo., lives in Southfield, Mich. Guard UCLA 1952-53. No pro playing experience. College coach: UCLA 1954, Long Beach City College 1955, Southern California 1960-75. Pro coach: San Diego Chargers 1980-88, joined Lions in 1989.

Billie Matthews, running backs; born March 15, 1930, Houston, Tex., lives in Rochester, Mich. Quarterback Southern University 1948-51. No pro playing experience. College coach: Kansas 1970, UCLA 1971-78. Pro coach: San Francisco 49ers 1979-82, Philadelphia Eagles 1983-84, Indianapolis Colts 1985-86, Kansas City Chiefs 1987-88, joined Lions in 1989.

Tom Moore, quarterbacks; born November 7, 1938, Owatanna, Minn., lives in Rochester Hills, Mich. Quarterback Iowa 1957-60. No pro playing experience. College coach: Iowa 1961-62, Dayton 1965-68, Wake Forest 1969, Georgia Tech 1970-71, Minnesota 1972-73, 1975-76. Pro coach: New York Stars (WFL) 1974, Pittsburgh Steelers 1977-89, Minnesota Vikings 1990-93, joined Lions in 1994.

Herb Paterra, defensive coordinator; born Novem-

ber 8, 1940, Glassport, Pa., lives in Rochester Hills, Mich. Offensive guard-linebacker Michigan State 1960-62. Pro linebacker Buffalo Bills 1963-64, Hamilton Tiger-Cats (CFL) 1965-68. College coach: Michigan State 1969-71, Wyoming 1972-74. Pro coach: Charlotte Hornets (WFL) 1975, Hamilton Tiger-Cats (CFL) 1978-79, Los Angeles Rams 1980-82, Edmonton Eskimos (CFL) 1983, Green Bay Packers 1984-85, Buffalo Bills 1986, Tampa Bay Buccaneers 1987-88, joined Lions in 1989.

Charlie Sanders, receivers; born August 25, 1946, Greensboro, N.C., lives in Rochester, Mich. Tight end Minnesota 1966-67. Pro tight end Detroit Lions 1968-77. Pro coach: Joined Lions in 1989.

Howard Tippett, linebackers; born September 23, 1938, Tallassee, Ala., lives in Rochester Hills, Mich. Quarterback-safety East Tennessee State 1956-58. No pro playing experience. College coach: Tulane 1963-65, West Virginia 1966, 1970-71, Houston 1967-69, Wake Forest 1972, Mississippi State 1973, 1979, Washington State 1976, Oregon 1977-78, UCLA 1980, Illinois 1987. Pro coach: Jacksonville Express (WFL) 1974-75, Tampa Bay Buccaneers 1981-86, Green Bay Packers 1988-91, Los Angeles Rams 1992-93, joined Lions in 1994.

1994 FIRST-YEAR ROSTER

Name	Pos.	Ht.	Wt.	Birthdate	College	Hometown	How Acq.
Batiste, Raymond	G	6-4	305	11/3/71	N.E. Louisiana	New Orleans, La.	FA
Beer, Tom	LB	6-1	237	3/27/69	Wayne State	Bay Port, Mich.	D7
Bonham, Shane	DE	6-4	260	10/18/70	Tennessee	Fairbanks, Alaska	D3
Borgella, Jocelyn	CB	5-10	180	8/26/71	Cincinnati	Miami, Fla.	D6
Brown, Ernie	DE	6-2	280	3/14/71	Syracuse	Pittsburgh, Pa.	FA
Bryant, Vaughn	CB	5-9	187	3/20/72	Stanford	Detroit, Mich.	D4
Butland, Josh	P	6-5	240	5/6/69	Michigan State	Troy, Mich.	FA
Green, Eric	WR-KR	5-10	170	4/7/71	Illinois-Benedictine	Plainfield, N.J.	FA
Jones, Jason	G	6-3	282	5/16/70	Hampton	Williamsburg, Va.	FA
Kaplan, Scott (1)	K	6-0	190	2/17/70	Pittsburgh	Coral Springs, Fla.	FA
Lynch, Eric (1)	RB	5-10	224	5/16/70	Grand Valley State	Woodhaven, Mich.	FA
Mack, Travis (1)	NT	6-1	280	7/3/70	California	Las Vegas, Nev.	FA
Malone, Van	S	5-11	188	7/1/70	Texas	Houston, Tex.	D2
Moore, Kyle (1)	DE	6-3	250	2/27/71	Kansas State	Newark, N.J.	FA
Morton, Johnnie	WR	5-9	190	10/7/71	Southern California	Torrance, Calif.	D1
Oglesby, John	RB	6-0	230	12/31/70	Texas Christian	Detroit, Mich.	FA
Powers, Ricky	RB	6-0	205	11/30/71	Michigan	Akron, Ohio	FA
Roberts, Ray	TE	6-2	251	3/6/71	Northern Illinois	Chicago, Ill.	FA
Ryans, Larry (1)	WR	5-11	182	7/28/71	Clemson	Greenwood, S.C.	FA
Semple, Tony	G	6-4	286	12/20/70	Memphis State	Lincoln, Ill.	D5
Wilson, James	DE	6-3	253	1/10/70	Tennessee	Hampton, Va.	FA
Woodley, Richard	WR	5-9	180	1/13/72	Texas Christian	Texas City, Tex.	FA

The term NFL Rookie is defined as a player who is in his first season of professional football and has not been on the roster of another professional football team for any regular-season or postseason games. A Rookie is designated by an "R" on NFL rosters. Players who have been active in another professional football league or players who have NFL experience, including either preseason training camp or being on an Active List or Inactive List, or on Reserve/Injured or Reserve/Physically Unable to Perform for fewer than six regular-season games, are termed NFL First-Year Players. An NFL First-Year Player is designated by a "1" on NFL rosters. Thereafter, a player is credited with an additional year of experience for each season in which he accumulates six games on the Active List or Inactive List, or on Reserve/Injured or Reserve/Physically Unable to Perform.

NOTES

National Football Conference
Central Division
Team Colors: Dark Green, Gold, and White
1265 Lombardi Avenue
Green Bay, Wisconsin 54304
Telephone: (414) 496-5700

CLUB OFFICIALS
President, CEO: Robert E. Harlan
Vice President: John Fabry
Secretary: Peter M. Platten III
Treasurer: John R. Underwood
Vice President-Administration: Michael R. Reinfeldt
Exec. V.P. and General Manager: Ron Wolf
Exec. Assistant to the President: Phil Pionek
Exec. Director of Public Relations: Lee Remmel
Director of Marketing: Jeff Cieply
Asst. Director of Public Relations: Jeff Blumb
Dir. of Community Relations: Mark Schiefelbein
General Legal Counsel: Lance Lopes
Director of Pro Personnel: Ted Thompson
Director of College Scouting: John Math
Green Bay Ticket Director: Mark Wagner
Milwaukee Ticket Director: Marge Paget
Controller: Dick Blasczyk
Dir. of Computer Operations: Wayne A. Wichlacz
Video Director: Al Treml
Trainer: Pepper Burruss
Equipment Manager: Gordon Batty
Corporate Security Officer: Jerry Parins
Stadium Supervisor: Ted Eisenreich
Stadium: Lambeau Field •**Capacity:** 59,543
      1265 Lombardi Avenue
      Green Bay, Wisconsin 54304
      Milwaukee County Stadium
      •**Capacity:** 56,051
      201 South 46th Street
      Milwaukee, Wisconsin 53214
Playing Surfaces: Grass
Training Camp: St. Norbert College
      West De Pere, Wisconsin 54115

1994 SCHEDULE
PRESEASON
Aug. 6	vs. L.A. Rams at Madison, Wis.	12:00
Aug. 13	vs. Miami at Milwaukee	7:00
Aug. 19	at New Orleans	7:00
Aug. 26	**New England**	7:00

REGULAR SEASON
Sept. 4	**Minnesota**	12:00
Sept. 11	**Miami** at Milwaukee	12:00
Sept. 18	at Philadelphia	1:00
Sept. 25	**Tampa Bay**	12:00
Oct. 2	at New England	1:00
Oct. 9	**Los Angeles Rams**	12:00
Oct. 16	Open Date	
Oct. 20	at Minnesota (Thursday)	7:00
Oct. 31	at Chicago (Monday)	8:00
Nov. 6	**Detroit** at Milwaukee	12:00
Nov. 13	**New York Jets**	3:00
Nov. 20	at Buffalo	1:00
Nov. 24	at Dallas (Thanksgiving)	3:00
Dec. 4	at Detroit	1:00
Dec. 11	**Chicago**	12:00
Dec. 18	**Atlanta** at Milwaukee	12:00
Dec. 24	at Tampa Bay	1:00

RECORD HOLDERS
INDIVIDUAL RECORDS—CAREER
Category	Name	Performance
Rushing (Yds.)	Jim Taylor, 1958-1966	8,207
Passing (Yds.)	Bart Starr, 1956-1971	23,718
Passing (TDs)	Bart Starr, 1956-1971	152
Receiving (No.)	James Lofton, 1978-1986	530
Receiving (Yds.)	James Lofton, 1978-1986	9,656
Interceptions	Bobby Dillon, 1952-59	52
Punting (Avg.)	Dick Deschaine, 1955-57	42.6
Punt Return (Avg.)	Billy Grimes, 1950-52	13.2
Kickoff Return (Avg.)	Travis Williams, 1967-1970	26.7
Field Goals	Chester Marcol, 1972-1980	120
Touchdowns (Tot.)	Don Hutson, 1935-1945	105
Points	Don Hutson, 1935-1945	823

INDIVIDUAL RECORDS—SINGLE SEASON
Category	Name	Performance
Rushing (Yds.)	Jim Taylor, 1962	1,474
Passing (Yds.)	Lynn Dickey, 1983	4,458
Passing (TDs)	Lynn Dickey, 1983	32
Receiving (No.)	Sterling Sharpe, 1993	*112
Receiving (Yds.)	Sterling Sharpe, 1992	1,461
Interceptions	Irv Comp, 1943	10
Punting (Avg.)	Jerry Norton, 1963	44.7
Punt Return (Avg.)	Billy Grimes, 1950	19.1
Kickoff Return (Avg.)	Travis Williams, 1967	*41.1
Field Goals	Chester Marcol, 1972	33
Touchdowns (Tot.)	Jim Taylor, 1962	19
Points	Paul Hornung, 1960	*176

INDIVIDUAL RECORDS—SINGLE GAME
Category	Name	Performance
Rushing (Yds.)	Jim Taylor, 12-3-61	186
Passing (Yds.)	Lynn Dickey, 10-12-80	418
Passing (TDs)	Many times	5
	Last time by Lynn Dickey, 9-4-83	
Receiving (No.)	Don Hutson, 11-22-42	14
Receiving (Yds.)	Bill Howton, 10-21-56	257
Interceptions	Bobby Dillon, 11-26-53	*4
	Willie Buchanon, 9-24-78	*4
Field Goals	Chris Jacke, 11-11-90	5
Touchdowns (Tot.)	Paul Hornung, 12-12-65	5
Points	Paul Hornung, 10-8-61	33

*NFL Record

COACHING HISTORY
(508-428-36)
1921-49	Earl (Curly) Lambeau	212-106-21
1950-53	Gene Ronzani*	14-31-1
1953	Hugh Devore-	
	Ray (Scooter) McLean**	0-2-0
1954-57	Lisle Blackbourn	17-31-0
1958	Ray (Scooter) McLean	1-10-1
1959-67	Vince Lombardi	98-30-4
1968-70	Phil Bengtson	20-21-1
1971-74	Dan Devine	25-28-4
1975-83	Bart Starr	53-77-3
1984-87	Forrest Gregg	25-37-1
1988-91	Lindy Infante	24-40-0
1992-93	Mike Holmgren	19-15-0

*Released after 10 games in 1953
**Co-coaches

MILWAUKEE/LAMBEAU FIELD

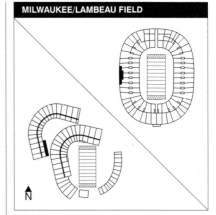

1993 TEAM RECORD

PRESEASON (1-4)

Date	Result		Opponents
7/31	L	3-19	vs. L.A. Raiders at Canton
8/7	L	21-29	Kansas City at Milw.
8/14	L	17-26	vs. New Orleans at Madison
8/21	L	17-21	at New England
8/27	W	41-10	Indianapolis

REGULAR SEASON (9-7)

Date	Result		Opponents	Att.
9/5	W	36-6	L.A. Rams	54,648
9/12	L	17-20	Philadelphia	59,061
9/26	L	13-15	at Minnesota	61,746
10/3	L	14-36	at Dallas	63,568
10/10	W	30-27	Denver	58,943
10/24	W	37-14	at Tampa Bay	47,354
10/31	W	17-3	Chicago	58,945
11/8	L	16-23	at Kansas City	76,742
11/14	W	19-17	at New Orleans	69,043
11/21	W	26-17	Detroit	55,119
11/28	W	13-10	Tampa Bay	56,995
12/5	L	17-30	at Chicago	62,236
12/12	W	20-13	at San Diego	57,930
12/19	L	17-21	Minnesota	54,773
12/26	W	28-0	L.A. Raiders	54,482
1/2	L	20-30	at Detroit	77,510

POSTSEASON (1-1)

1/8	W	28-24	at Detroit	68,479
1/16	L	17-27	at Dallas	64,790

SCORE BY PERIODS

Packers	97	95	77	71	0	—	340
Opponents	29	76	90	87	0	—	282

ATTENDANCE

Home 452,966   Away 516,129   Total 969,095
Single-game home record, 59,061 (9-12-93, Lambeau Field), 56,258 (9-28-80, Milwaukee County Stadium)
Single-season home record, 456,944 (1992)

1993 TEAM STATISTICS

	Packers	Opp.
Total First Downs	282	261
Rushing	98	88
Passing	166	157
Penalty	18	16
Third Down: Made/Att	81/218	70/217
Third Down Pct.	37.2	32.3
Fourth Down: Made/Att	9/16	3/19
Fourth Down Pct.	56.3	15.8
Total Net Yards	4750	4482
Avg. Per Game	296.9	280.1
Total Plays	1006	999
Avg. Per Play	4.7	4.5
Net Yards Rushing	1619	1582
Avg. Per Game	101.2	98.9
Total Rushes	448	424
Net Yards Passing	3131	2900
Avg. Per Game	195.7	181.3
Sacked/Yards Lost	30/199	46/301
Gross Yards	3330	3201
Att./Completions	528/322	529/290
Completion Pct.	61.0	54.8
Had Intercepted	24	18
Punts/Avg.	74/42.9	79/40.2
Net Punting Avg.	74/36.3	79/34.3
Penalties/Yards Lost	85/734	85/712
Fumbles/Ball Lost	26/10	33/15
Touchdowns	35	27
Rushing	14	6
Passing	19	16
Returns	2	5
Avg. Time of Possession	30:53	29:07

1993 INDIVIDUAL STATISTICS

PASSING	Att	Cmp	Yds.	Pct.	TD	Int	Tkld.	Rate
Favre	522	318	3303	60.9	19	24	30/199	72.2
Detmer	5	3	26	60.0	0	0	0/0	73.8
Sharpe	1	1	1	100.0	0	0	0/0	79.2
Packers	528	322	3330	61.0	19	24	30/199	72.2
Opponents	529	290	3201	54.8	16	18	46/301	68.9

SCORING	TD R	TD P	TD Rt	PAT	FG	Saf	PTS
Jacke	0	0	0	35/35	31/37	0	128
Sharpe	0	11	0	0/0	0/0	0	66
E. Bennett	9	1	0	0/0	0/0	0	60
J. Harris	0	4	0	0/0	0/0	0	24
Clayton	0	3	0	0/0	0/0	0	18
Thompson	3	0	0	0/0	0/0	0	18
Brooks	0	0	1	0/0	0/0	0	6
Butler	0	0	1	0/0	0/0	0	6
Favre	1	0	0	0/0	0/0	0	6
Stephens	1	0	0	0/0	0/0	0	6
Packers	14	19	2	35/35	31/37	1	340
Opponents	6	16	5	27/27	31/40	0	282

RUSHING	Att.	Yds.	Avg.	LG	TD
Thompson	169	654	3.9	60t	3
E. Bennett	159	550	3.5	19	9
Favre	58	216	3.7	27	1
Stephens	48	173	3.6	22	1
Brooks	3	17	5.7	21	0
Sharpe	4	8	2.0	5	0
Wilson	6	3	0.5	5	0
Detmer	1	-2	-2.0	-2	0
Packers	448	1619	3.6	60t	14
Opponents	424	1582	3.7	60	6

RECEIVING	No.	Yds.	Avg.	LG	TD
Sharpe	112	1274	11.4	54	11
E. Bennett	59	457	7.7	39t	1
J. Harris	42	604	14.4	66t	4
Clayton	32	331	10.3	32	3
West	25	253	10.1	24	0
Brooks	20	180	9.0	25	0
Thompson	18	129	7.2	34	0
Stephens	5	31	6.2	10	0
Lewis	2	21	10.5	17	0
Wilson	2	18	9.0	11	0
Chmura	2	13	6.5	7	0
C. Harris	2	11	5.5	6	0
Morgan	1	8	8.0	8	0
Packers	322	3330	10.3	66t	19
Opponents	290	3201	11.0	67t	16

INTERCEPTIONS	No.	Yds.	Avg.	LG	TD
Butler	6	131	21.8	39	0
Holland	2	41	20.5	30	0
Buckley	2	31	15.5	31	0
Simmons	2	21	10.5	19	0
Teague	1	22	22.0	22	0
Paup	1	8	8.0	8	0
Prior	1	1	1.0	1	0
Brock	1	0	0.0	0	0
Evans	1	0	0.0	0	0
Mitchell	1	0	0.0	0	0
Packers	18	255	14.2	39	0
Opponents	24	437	18.2	86t	3

PUNTING	No.	Yds.	Avg.	In 20	LG
Wagner	74	3174	42.9	19	60
Packers	74	3174	42.9	19	60
Opponents	79	3176	40.2	20	58

PUNT RETURNS	No.	FC	Yds.	Avg.	LG	TD
Prior	17	3	194	11.4	24	0
Brooks	16	4	135	8.4	35	0
Buckley	11	5	76	6.9	39	0
Teague	1	0	-1	-1.0	-1	0
Packers	45	12	404	9.0	39	0
Opponents	38	12	350	9.2	35	0

KICKOFF RETURNS	No.	Yds.	Avg.	LG	TD
Brooks	23	611	26.6	95t	1
C. Harris	16	482	30.1	65	0
Thompson	9	171	19.0	42	0
Wilson	9	197	21.9	37	0
Jurkovic	2	22	11.0	13	0
Chmura	1	0	0.0	0	0
Packers	60	1483	24.7	95t	1
Opponents	70	1407	20.1	68	0

SACKS	No.
White	13.0
Paup	11.0
T. Bennett	6.5
Jurkovic	5.5
Koonce	3.0
Brock	2.0
Holland	2.0
Butler	1.0
Patterson	1.0
Simmons	1.0
Packers	46.0
Opponents	30.0

1994 DRAFT CHOICES

Round	Name	Pos.	College
1	Aaron Taylor	G	Notre Dame
3	LeShon Johnson	RB	Northern Illinois
4	Gabe Wilkins	DE	Gardner-Webb
5	Terry Mickens	WR	Florida A&M
	Dorsey Levens	RB	Georgia Tech
6	Jay Kearney	WR	West Virginia
	Ruffin Hamilton	LB	Tulane
	Bill Schroeder	WR	Wisconsin-LaCrosse
	Paul Duckworth	LB	Connecticut

GREEN BAY PACKERS

1994 VETERAN ROSTER

No.	Name	Pos.	Ht.	Wt.	Birthdate	NFL Exp.	College	Hometown	How Acq.	'93 Games/ Starts
51	Barker, Tony	LB	6-2	235	9/7/68	2	Rice	Wichita, Kan.	FA-'94	0*
34	Bennett, Edgar	RB	6-0	216	2/15/69	3	Florida State	Jacksonville, Fla.	D4-'92	16/14
62	# Brock, Matt	DE	6-5	280	1/14/66	6	Oregon	San Diego, Calif.	D3a-'89	16/13
87	Brooks, Robert	WR	6-0	174	6/23/70	3	South Carolina	Greenwood, S.C.	D3-'92	14/0
71	Brown, Gilbert	NT	6-2	330	2/22/71	2	Kansas	Detroit, Mich.	W(Minn)-'93	2/0
8	Brunell, Mark	QB	6-1	208	9/17/70	2	Washington	Santa Maria, Calif.	D5a-'93	0*
27	Buckley, Terrell	CB	5-9	174	6/7/71	3	Florida State	Pascagoula, Miss.	D1-'92	16/16
36	Butler, LeRoy	S	6-0	193	7/19/68	5	Florida State	Jacksonville, Fla.	D2-'90	16/16
63	Campen, James	C	6-2	280	6/11/64	8	Tulane	Shingle Springs, Calif.	PB(NO)-'89	4/4
89	Chmura, Mark	TE	6-5	242	2/22/69	3	Boston College	South Deerfield, Mass.	D6-'92	14/0
32	Cobb, Reggie	RB	6-0	215	7/7/68	5	Tennessee	Knoxville, Tenn.	UFA(TB)-'94	12/10*
54	Coleman, Keo	LB	6-1	255	5/1/70	3	Mississippi State	Milwaukee, Wis.	FA-'93	12/2
99	Davey, Don	DE	6-4	270	4/8/68	4	Wisconsin	Manitowoc, Wis.	FA-'92	9/0
11	Detmer, Ty	QB	6-0	190	10/30/67	3	Brigham Young	San Antonio, Tex.	D9a-'92	3/0
32	Dingle, Mike	RB	6-2	240	1/30/69	3	South Carolina	Moncks Corner, S.C.	FA-'94	0*
58	D'Onofrio, Mark	LB	6-2	235	3/17/69	2	Penn State	North Bergen, N.J.	D2-'92	0*
72	Dotson, Earl	T	6-3	315	12/17/70	2	Texas A&I	Beaumont, Tex.	D3-'93	13/0
33	Evans, Doug	CB	6-0	188	5/13/70	2	Louisiana Tech	Haynesville, La.	D6a-'93	16/0
93	Evans, Mike	DE	6-3	270	6/2/67	2	Michigan	Ashburnham, Mass.	FA-'94	0*
4	† Favre, Brett	QB	6-2	218	10/10/69	4	Southern Mississippi	Kiln, Miss.	T(Atl)-'92	16/16
76	Galbreath, Harry	G	6-1	275	1/1/65	7	Tennessee	Clarksville, Tenn.	UFA(Mia)-'93	16/16
30	Harris, Corey	CB	5-11	195	10/25/69	3	Vanderbilt	Indianapolis, Ind.	W(Hou)-'92	11/0
80	† Harris, Jackie	TE	6-3	243	1/4/68	5	Northeast Louisiana	Pine Bluff, Ark.	D4-'90	12/12
24	# Hauck, Tim	S	5-10	185	12/20/66	5	Montana	Big Timber, Mont.	PB(NE)-'91	13/0
67	Hutchins, Paul	T	6-4	335	2/11/70	2	Western Michigan	Chicago, Ill.	FA-'93	1/0
13	Jacke, Chris	K	6-0	200	3/12/66	6	Texas-El Paso	Richardson, Tex.	D6-'89	16/0
96	Jones, Sean	DE	6-7	268	12/19/62	11	Northeastern	Montclair, N.J.	UFA(Hou)-'94	16/16*
64	Jurkovic, John	NT	6-2	285	8/18/67	3	Eastern Illinois	Calumet City, Ill.	FA-'91	16/12
77	Jurkovic, Mirko	T	6-3	290	5/19/70	2	Notre Dame	Calumet City, Ill.	FA-'94	0*
53	Koonce, George	LB	6-1	238	10/15/68	3	Eastern Carolina	Vanceboro, N.C.	FA-'92	15/15
78	LaBounty, Matt	DE	6-3	254	1/3/69	2	Oregon	San Marin, Calif.	W(SF)-'93	6/0*
85	# Lewis, Ron	WR	5-11	189	3/25/68	5	Florida State	Jacksonville, Fla.	FA-'93	9/0
	McMichael, Steve	DT	6-2	268	10/17/57	15	Texas	Frees, Tex.	FA-'94	16/16*
44	McNabb, Dexter	RB	6-1	245	7/9/69	3	Florida State	DeFuniak Springs, Fla.	D5a-'92	16/0
97	Merriweather, Mike	LB	6-2	228	11/26/60	12	Pacific	Vallejo, Calif.	FA-'93	1/0*
94	Mersereau, Scott	NT	6-3	275	4/8/65	8	Southern Connecticut	Riverhead, N.Y.	FA-'94	13/13*
47	Mitchell, Roland	CB	5-11	195	3/15/64	7	Texas Tech	Bay City, Tex.	PB(Atl)-'91	16/16
81	Morgan, Anthony	WR	6-1	195	11/15/67	4	Tennessee	Cleveland, Ohio	W(Chi)-'93	3/0*
95	Paup, Bryce	LB	6-5	247	2/29/68	5	Northern Iowa	Scranton, Iowa	D6-'90	15/14
45	Prior, Mike	S	6-0	215	11/14/63	9	Illinois State	Chicago Heights, Ill.	UFA(Ind)-'93	16/4
73	# Robbins, Tootie	T	6-5	315	6/2/58	13	Eastern Carolina	Windsor, N.C.	FA-'93	12/11
75	Ruettgers, Ken	T	6-6	290	8/20/62	10	Southern California	Bakersfield, Calif.	D1-'85	16/16
84	Sharpe, Sterling	WR	6-1	210	4/6/65	7	South Carolina	Glennville, Ga.	D1-'88	16/16
59	Simmons, Wayne	LB	6-2	240	12/15/69	2	Clemson	Hilton Head, S.C.	D1a-'93	14/8
68	Sims, Joe	T	6-3	310	3/1/69	4	Nebraska	Sudbury, Mass.	FA-'92	13/5
31	Teague, George	S	6-1	187	2/18/71	2	Alabama	Montgomery, Ala.	D1b-'93	16/12
39	# Thompson, Darrell	RB	6-0	217	11/23/67	5	Minnesota	Rochester, Minn.	D1b-'90	16/11
9	Wagner, Bryan	P	6-2	200	3/28/62	7	Cal State-Northridge	Chula Vista, Calif.	FA-'92	16/0
23	Walker, Sammy	CB	5-11	203	1/20/69	4	Texas Tech	McKinney, Tex.	FA-'93	8/1
86	# West, Ed	TE	6-1	245	8/2/61	11	Auburn	Leighton, Ala.	FA-'93	16/7
92	White, Reggie	DE	6-5	290	12/19/61	10	Tennessee	Chattanooga, Tenn.	UFA(Phil)-'93	16/16
74	# Widell, Doug	G	6-4	280	9/23/66	6	Boston College	Hartford, Conn.	T(Den)-'93	16/9
20	Williams, Kevin	RB	6-1	215	2/17/70	2	UCLA	Spring, Tex.	FA-'93	3/0
56	Willis, James	LB	6-1	235	9/2/72	2	Auburn	Huntsville, Ga.	D5b-'93	13/0
29	Wilson, Marcus	RB	6-1	210	4/16/68	3	Virginia	Rochester, N.Y.	FA-'92	16/0
52	Winters, Frank	C-G	6-3	285	1/23/64	8	Western Illinois	Union City, N.J.	PB(KC)-'92	16/16
60	Zeno, Lance	C	6-4	279	4/15/67	3	UCLA	Fountain Valley, Calif.	W(TB)-'93	5/0

* Barker last active with Washington in '92; Brunell active for 1 game in '93 but did not play; Cobb played 12 games with Tampa Bay; Dingle on injured reserve with Cincinnati in '92; D'Onofrio missed '93 season due to injury; Evans last active with Kansas City in '92; Jones played 16 games with Houston; M. Jurkovic last active with Chicago in '92; LaBounty played 6 games with San Francisco; McMichael played 16 games with Chicago; Merriweather played 1 game with N.Y. Jets; Mersereau played 13 games with N.Y. Jets; Morgan played 1 game with Chicago.

\# Unrestricted free agent; subject to developments.

† Restricted free agent; subject to developments.

Retired: Johnny Holland, 7-year linebacker, 16 games in '93; Brian Noble, 9-year linebacker, 2 games in '93.

Traded—DE Lester Archambeau to Atlanta, RB John Stephens to Atlanta.

Players lost through free agency (1)—LB Tony Bennett (Ind; 10 games in '93).

Also played with the Packers in '93—WR Mark Clayton (16 games), WR Brett Collins (4), WR Shawn Collins (4), DE David Grant (7), T Tunch Ilkin (1), TE Darryl Ingram (2), NT Bill Maas (14), G Rich Moran (3), LB Jim Morrissey (6), LB Joe Mott (2), CB Muhammed Oliver (2), DE Shawn Patterson (5), CB Bruce Pickens (2), RB John Stephens (5), LB Keith Traylor (5).

COACHING STAFF

Head Coach,
Mike Holmgren

Pro Career: Became Packers' eleventh head coach on January 11, 1992. He led team to first back-to-back winning seasons (identical 9-7 records) since 1966-67 and first playoff berth (1993). Holmgren was offensive coordinator for the San Francisco 49ers under George Seifert (1989-91) after spending three previous seasons (1986-88) as quarterbacks coach under Bill Walsh. During his six-year tenure with San Francisco, the 49ers won five consecutive NFC Western Division championships (1986-1990) and back-to-back Super Bowls (XXIII and XXIV). In that span, San Francisco compiled the NFL's best overall record (71-23-1, a .753 percentage). The 49ers never ranked lower than third overall in his three years as offensive coordinator. Career record: 19-15.
Background: Quarterback at Southern California (1966-69) and was drafted by the St. Louis Cardinals in the eighth round of the 1970 NFL draft. He served as an assistant coach at San Francisco State (1981) and Brigham Young (1982-85) before his tenure with the 49ers. Earned his bachelor of science degree in business finance at Southern California (1970).
Personal: Born June 15, 1948, in San Francisco. He and his wife, Kathy, live in Green Bay and have four daughters—Calla, Jenny, Emily, and Gretchen.

ASSISTANT COACHES

Larry Brooks, defensive line; born June 10, 1950, Prince George, Va., lives in Green Bay. Defensive lineman Virginia State 1968-71. Pro defensive tackle Los Angeles Rams 1972-82. College coach: Virginia State 1992-93. Pro coach: Los Angeles Rams 1983-90, joined Packers in 1994.
Nolan Cromwell, special teams; born January 30, 1955, Smith Center, Kan., lives in Green Bay. Quarterback-safety Kansas 1973-76. Pro defensive back Los Angeles Rams 1977-87. Pro coach: Los Angeles Rams 1991, joined Packers in 1992.
Jon Gruden, wide receivers; born August 17, 1963, Sandusky, Ohio, lives in Green Bay. Quarterback Dayton 1983-85. No pro playing experience. College coach: Tennessee 1986-87, Southeast Missouri 1988, Pacific 1989, Pittsburgh 1991. Pro coach: San Francisco 49ers 1990, joined Packers in 1992.
Gil Haskell, running backs; born September 24, 1943, San Francisco, Calif., lives in Green Bay. Defensive back San Francisco State 1961, 1963-65. No pro playing exprience. College coach: Southern California 1978-82. Pro coach: Los Angeles Rams 1983-91, joined Packers in 1992.
Dick Jauron, defensive backs; born October 7, 1950, Peoria, Ill., lives in Green Bay. Defensive back Yale 1970-72. Pro defensive back Detroit Lions 1973-77, Cincinnati Bengals 1978-80. Pro coach: Buffalo Bills 1985, joined Packers in 1986.
Kent Johnston, strength and conditioning; born February 21, 1956, Mexia, Tex., lives in Green Bay. Defensive back Stephen F. Austin 1974-77. No pro playing experience. College coach: Northeast Louisiana 1979, Northwestern Louisiana 1980-81, Alabama 1983-86. Pro coach: Tampa Bay Buccaneers 1987-91, joined Packers in 1992.
Sherman Lewis, offensive coordinator; born June 29, 1942, Louisville, Ky., lives in Green Bay. Running back Michigan State 1961-63. Pro running back Toronto Argonauts (CFL) 1964-65, New York Jets 1966. College coach: Michigan State 1969-82. Pro coach: San Francisco 49ers 1983-91, joined Packers in 1992.
Jim Lind, defensive assistant-quality control; born November 11, 1947, Isle, Minn., lives in Green Bay. Linebacker Bethel College 1965-66; defensive back Bemidji State 1971-72. No pro playing experience. College coach: St. Cloud State 1977-78, St. John's (Minn.) 1979-80, Brigham Young 1981-82, Minnesota-Morris 1983-86 (head coach), Wisconsin-Eau Claire 1987-91 (head coach). Pro coach: Joined Packers in 1992.
Tom Lovat, offensive line; born December 28, 1938, Bingham, Utah, lives in Green Bay. Guard-linebacker

Utah 1958-60. No pro playing experience. College coach: Utah 1967, 1972-76 (head coach 1974-76), Idaho State 1968-70, Stanford 1977-79, Wyoming 1989. Pro coach: Saskatchewan Roughriders (CFL) 1971, Green Bay Packers 1980, St. Louis-Phoenix Cardinals 1981-84, 1990-91, Indianapolis Colts 1985-88, rejoined Packers in 1992.
Steve Mariucci, quarterbacks; born November 4, 1955, Iron Mountain, Mich., lives in Green Bay. Quarterback Northern Michigan 1974-77. No pro playing experience. College coach: Northern Michigan 1978-79, Cal State-Fullerton 1980-82, Louisville 1983-84, Southern California 1986, California 1987-91. Pro coach: Orlando Renegades (USFL) 1985, Los Angeles Rams 1985, joined Packers in 1992.
Andy Reid, tight ends-offensive line assistant; born March 19, 1958, Los Angeles, Calif., lives in Green Bay. Offensive tackle-guard Brigham Young 1978-80. No pro playing experience. College coach: San Francisco State 1983-85, Northern Arizona 1986, Texas-El Paso 1987, Missouri 1988-91. Pro

coach: Joined Packers in 1992.
Fritz Shurmur, defensive coordinator; born July 15, 1932, Riverview, Mich., lives in Green Bay. No pro playing experience. College coach: Albion 1956-61, Wyoming 1962-74 (head coach 1971-74). Pro coach: Detroit Lions 1975-77, New England Patriots 1978-81, Los Angeles Rams 1982-90, Phoenix Cardinals 1991-93, joined Packers in 1994.
Harry Sydney, general assistant, born June 26, 1959, Fayetteville, N.C., lives in Green Bay. Quarterback/running back Kansas 1978-81. Pro running back San Francisco 49ers 1987-91, Green Bay Packers 1992. Pro coach: Joined Packers in 1994.
Bob Valesente, linebackers; born July 19, 1940, Seneca Falls, N.Y., lives in Green Bay. Halfback Ithaca College 1958-61. No pro playing experience. College coach: Cornell 1964-74, Cincinnati 1975-76, Arizona 1977-79, Mississippi State 1980-81, Kansas 1984-87 (head coach, 1986-87), Maryland 1988, Pittsburgh 1989. Pro coach: Baltimore Colts 1982-83, Pittsburgh Steelers 1990-91, joined Packers in 1992.

1994 FIRST-YEAR ROSTER

Name	Pos.	Ht.	Wt.	Birthdate	College	Hometown	How Acq.
Bierman, Randy	T	6-5	298	4/30/71	Illinois	Waukegan, Ill.	FA
Brown, Victor	S	6-1	208	4/21/70	Tennessee	Junction City, Kan.	FA
Cotton, Curtis (1)	S	6-0	212	10/15/69	Nebraska	Omaha, Neb.	FA
Crawford, Lionel (1)	WR	5-10	185	12/24/69	Wisconsin	Houston, Tex.	FA
Dean, Charlie	TE	6-2	246	7/12/70	Florida	Inverness, Fla.	FA
Duckworth, Paul	LB	6-1	245	3/12/71	Connecticut	Danbury, Conn.	D6d
Eller, Matt (1)	DE	6-5	275	1/30/70	Bethel College, Minn.	Radcliffe, Iowa	FA
Fisher, John (1)	C	6-3	270	9/4/69	Tennessee	Milan, Tex.	FA
Frazier, Daryl	WR	6-1	181	1/23/71	Florida	Winter Haven, Fla.	FA
Hamilton, Ruffin	LB	6-1	230	3/2/71	Tulane	Zachary, La.	D6b
Harris, Willie (1)	WR	6-1	194	11/8/70	Mississippi State	Moss Point, Miss.	FA
Hentrich, Craig (1)	P-K	6-3	200	5/18/71	Notre Dame	Alton, Ill.	FA
Holt, Reggie	S	5-11	201	2/18/71	Wisconsin	Miami, Fla.	FA
Hope, Charles (1)	G-T	6-3	308	3/12/70	Central State, Ohio	New Castle, Del.	FA
Johnson, LeShon	RB	6-0	204	1/15/71	Northern Illinois	Haskell, Okla.	D3
Kearney, Jay	WR	6-1	194	9/29/71	West Virginia	Piscataway, N.J.	D6a
Levens, Dorsey	RB	6-1	231	5/21/70	Georgia Tech	Syracuse, N.Y.	D5b
McGill, Lenny	CB	6-1	194	5/31/71	Arizona State	Escondido, Calif.	FA
Mickens, Terry	WR	6-0	203	2/21/71	Florida A&M	Tallahassee, Fla.	D5a
Perez, Chris (1)	T	6-6	295	6/21/69	Kansas	Palatine, Ill.	FA
Schroeder, Bill	WR	6-1	195	1/9/71	Wisconsin-LaCrosse	Sheboygan, Wis.	D6c
Shackerford, Lamark	NT	6-0	255	3/12/72	Wisconsin	Gary, Ind.	FA
Showell, Malcolm (1)	DE	6-6	275	10/1/68	Delaware State	Baltimore, Md.	FA
Smith, LeRoy (1)	LB	6-0	230	1/6/69	Iowa	Atco, N.J.	FA
Taylor, Aaron	G	6-4	307	11/14/72	Notre Dame	Concord, Calif.	D1
Warner, Kurt	QB	6-2	198	6/22/71	Northern Iowa	Cedar Rapids, Iowa	FA
Wilkins, Gabe	DE	6-4	292	9/1/71	Gardner-Webb	Cowpens, S.C.	D4
Williams, Mark	LB	6-3	229	5/17/71	Ohio State	Upper Marlboro, Md.	FA
Wilner, Jeff	TE	6-4	253	12/31/71	Wesleyan, Conn.	Exeter, N.H.	FA

The term NFL Rookie is defined as a player who is in his first season of professional football and has not been on the roster of another professional football team for any regular-season or postseason games. A Rookie is designated by an "R" on NFL rosters. Players who have been active in another professional football league or players who have NFL experience, including either preseason training camp or being on an Active List or Inactive List, or on Reserve/Injured or Reserve/Physically Unable to Perform for fewer than six regular-season games, are termed NFL First-Year Players. An NFL First-Year Player is designated by a "1" on NFL rosters. Thereafter, a player is credited with an additional year of experience for each season in which he accumulates six games on the Active List or Inactive List, or on Reserve/Injured or Reserve/Physically Unable to Perform.

NOTES

LOS ANGELES RAMS

National Football Conference
Western Division
Team Colors: Royal Blue, Gold, and White
Business Address:
2327 West Lincoln Avenue
Anaheim, California 92801
Telephone: (714) 535-7267
Ticket Office:
Anaheim Stadium
1900 State College Boulevard
Anaheim, California 92806
Telephone: (714) 937-6767

CLUB OFFICIALS

Owner/President: Georgia Frontiere
Executive Vice President: John Shaw
Senior Vice President: Jay Zygmunt
Vice President-Head Coach: Chuck Knox
Vice President-Media and Community Relations:
　Marshall Klein
Director of Player Personel: John Becker
Administrator of Pro Personnel: Jack Faulkner
Executive Director: Mary Olson-Kromolowski
Treasurer: Jeff Brewer
Director of Player Relations: Paul (Tank) Younger
Director of Operations: John Oswald
Director of Public Relations: Rick Smith
Director of Ticket Operations: Don Nims
Trainer: Jim Anderson
Equipment Manager: Todd Hewitt
Video Director: Mickey Dukich
Scouts: Lawrence McCutcheon, David Razzano,
　Pete Russell, Harley Sewell, Frank Trump,
　Ron Waller
Stadium: Anaheim Stadium •**Capacity:** 69,008
　　　Anaheim, California 92806
Playing Surface: Grass
Training Camp: University of California-Irvine
　　　Irvine, California 92715

1994 SCHEDULE
PRESEASON

Aug. 6	vs. Green Bay at Madison, Wis.	12:00
Aug. 13	**New England**	7:00
Aug. 20	**Los Angeles Raiders**	7:00
Aug. 25	at San Diego	7:00

REGULAR SEASON

Sept. 4	**Arizona**	1:00
Sept. 11	at Atlanta	1:00
Sept. 18	**San Francisco**	1:00
Sept. 25	at Kansas City	12:00
Oct. 2	**Atlanta**	1:00
Oct. 9	al Green Bay	12:00
Oct. 16	**New York Giants**	1:00
Oct. 23	at New Orleans	12:00
Oct. 30	Open Date	
Nov. 6	**Denver**	1:00
Nov. 13	**Los Angeles Raiders**	1:00
Nov. 20	at San Francisco	5:00
Nov. 27	at San Diego	1:00
Dec. 4	**New Orleans**	1:00
Dec. 11	at Tampa Bay	1:00
Dec. 18	at Chicago	12:00
Dec. 24	**Washington**	1:00

COACHING HISTORY
Cleveland 1937-1945
(407-357-20)

1937-38	Hugo Bezdek*	1-13-0
1938	Art Lewis	4-4-0
1939-42	Earl (Dutch) Clark	16-26-2
1944	Aldo (Buff) Donelli	4-6-0
1945-46	Adam Walsh	16-5-1
1947	Bob Snyder	6-6-0
1948-49	Clark Shaughnessy	14-8-3
1950-52	Joe Stydahar**	19-9-0
1952-54	Hamp Pool	23-11-2
1955-59	Sid Gillman	28-32-1
1960-62	Bob Waterfield***	9-24-1
1962-65	Harland Svare	14-31-3
1966-70	George Allen	49-19-4
1971-72	Tommy Prothro	14-12-2
1973-77	Chuck Knox	57-20-1
1978-82	Ray Malavasi	43-36-0
1983-91	John Robinson	79-74-0
1992-93	Chuck Knox	11-21-0

*Released after three games in 1938
**Resigned after one game in 1952
***Resigned after eight games in 1962

RECORD HOLDERS
INDIVIDUAL RECORDS—CAREER

Category	Name	Performance
Rushing (Yds.)	Eric Dickerson, 1983-87	7,245
Passing (Yds.)	Jim Everett, 1986-1993	23,758
Passing (TDs)	Roman Gabriel, 1962-1972	154
Receiving (No.)	Henry Ellard, 1983-1993	593
Receiving (Yds.)	Henry Ellard, 1983-1993	9,761
Interceptions	Ed Meador, 1959-1970	46
Punting (Avg.)	Danny Villanueva, 1960-64	44.2
Punt Return (Avg.)	Henry Ellard, 1983-1992	11.3
Kickoff Return (Avg.)	Tom Wilson, 1956-1961	27.1
Field Goals	Mike Lansford, 1982-1990	158
Touchdowns (Tot.)	Eric Dickerson, 1983-87	58
Points	Mike Lansford, 1982-1990	789

INDIVIDUAL RECORDS—SINGLE SEASON

Category	Name	Performance
Rushing (Yds.)	Eric Dickerson, 1984	*2,105
Passing (Yds.)	Jim Everett, 1989	4,310
Passing (TDs)	Jim Everett, 1988	31
Receiving (No.)	Henry Ellard, 1988	86
Receiving (Yds.)	Elroy (Crazylegs) Hirsch, 1951	1,425
Interceptions	Dick (Night Train) Lane, 1952	*14
Punting (Avg.)	Danny Villanueva, 1962	45.5
Punt Return (Avg.)	Woodley Lewis, 1952	18.5
Kickoff Return (Avg.)	Verda (Vitamin T) Smith, 1950	33.7
Field Goals	David Ray, 1973	30
Touchdowns (Tot.)	Eric Dickerson, 1983	20
Points	David Ray, 1973	130

INDIVIDUAL RECORDS—SINGLE GAME

Category	Name	Performance
Rushing (Yds.)	Eric Dickerson, 1-4-86	248
Passing (Yds.)	Norm Van Brocklin, 9-28-51	*554
Passing (TDs)	Many times	5
	Last time by Jim Everett, 9-25-88	
Receiving (No.)	Tom Fears, 12-3-50	*18
Receiving (Yds.)	Willie Anderson, 11-26-89	*336
Interceptions	Many times	3
	Last time by Pat Thomas, 10-7-79	
Field Goals	Bob Waterfield, 12-9-51	5
Touchdowns (Tot.)	Bob Shaw, 12-11-49	4
	Elroy (Crazylegs) Hirsch, 9-28-51	4
	Harold Jackson, 10-14-73	4
Points	Bob Shaw, 12-11-49	24
	Elroy (Crazylegs) Hirsch, 9-28-51	24
	Harold Jackson, 10-14-73	24

*NFL Record

ANAHEIM STADIUM

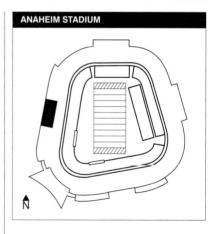

1993 TEAM RECORD

PRESEASON (0-4)

Date	Result		Opponents
8/7	L	13-24	at Phoenix
8/14	L	17-23	San Diego
8/21	L	10-21	at Cleveland
8/28	L	19-20	L.A. Raiders

REGULAR SEASON (5-11)

Date	Result		Opponents	Att.
9/5	L	6-36	at Green Bay	54,648
9/12	W	27-0	Pittsburgh	50,588
9/19	L	10-20	at N.Y. Giants	76,213
9/26	W	28-13	at Houston	53,072
10/3	L	6-37	New Orleans	50,709
10/14	L	24-30	at Atlanta	45,231
10/24	L	13-16	Detroit	43,850
10/31	L	17-40	at San Francisco	63,417
11/14	L	0-13	Atlanta	37,073
11/21	W	10-6	Washington	45,546
11/28	L	10-35	San Francisco	62,143
12/5	L	10-38	at Phoenix	33,964
12/12	W	23-20	at New Orleans	69,033
12/19	L	3-15	at Cincinnati	36,612
12/26	L	14-42	Cleveland	34,155
1/2	W	20-6	Chicago	39,147

SCORE BY PERIODS

Rams	52	40	40	89	0	—	221
Opponents	72	95	92	108	0	—	367

ATTENDANCE

Home 363,211   Away 432,190   Total 795,401
Single-game home record, 69,898 (11-9-92)
Single-season home record, 553,979 (1992)

1993 TEAM STATISTICS

	Rams	Opp.
Total First Downs	278	304
Rushing	117	117
Passing	147	179
Penalty	14	8
Third Down: Made/Att	79/202	102/218
Third Down Pct.	39.1	46.8
Fourth Down: Made/Att	5/11	10/17
Fourth Down Pct.	45.5	58.8
Total Net Yards	4804	5411
Avg. Per Game	300.3	338.2
Total Plays	953	1003
Avg. Per Play	5.0	5.4
Net Yards Rushing	2014	1851
Avg. Per Game	125.9	115.7
Total Rushes	449	480
Net Yards Passing	2790	3560
Avg. Per Game	174.4	222.5
Sacked/Yards Lost	31/231	35/203
Gross Yards	3021	3763
Att./Completions	473/247	488/299
Completion Pct.	52.2	61.3
Had Intercepted	19	11
Punts/Avg.	80/40.9	58/42.3
Net Punting Avg.	80/31.7	58/37.4
Penalties/Yards Lost	71/526	80/542
Fumbles/Ball Lost	20/11	26/9
Touchdowns	25	40
Rushing	8	18
Passing	16	17
Returns	1	5
Avg. Time of Possession	28:18	31:42

1993 INDIVIDUAL STATISTICS

PASSING

	Att	Cmp	Yds.	Pct.	TD	Int	Tkld.	Rate
Everett	274	135	1652	49.3	8	12	18/125	59.7
Rubley	189	108	1338	57.1	8	6	13/106	80.1
Pagel	9	3	23	33.3	0	1	0/0	2.8
Gary	1	1	8	100.0	0	0	0/0	100.0
Rams	473	247	3021	52.2	16	19	31/231	66.8
Opponents	488	299	3763	61.3	17	11	35/203	87.5

SCORING

	TD R	TD P	TD Rt	PAT	FG	Saf	PTS
Zendejas	0	0	0	23/25	16/23	0	71
Bettis	7	0	0	0/0	0/0	0	42
Anderson	0	4	0	0/0	0/0	0	24
Drayton	0	4	0	0/0	0/0	0	24
Ellard	0	2	0	0/0	0/0	0	12
Gary	1	1	0	0/0	0/0	0	12
Jones	0	2	0	0/0	0/0	0	12
Boykin	0	0	1	0/0	0/0	0	6
Carter	0	1	0	0/0	0/0	0	6
Kinchen	0	1	0	0/0	0/0	0	6
McNeal	0	1	0	0/0	0/0	0	6
Rams	8	16	1	23/25	16/23	0	221
Opponents	18	17	5	38/40	29/37	1	367

RUSHING

	Att.	Yds.	Avg.	LG	TD
Bettis	294	1429	4.9	71t	7
Gary	79	293	3.7	15	1
Rubley	29	102	3.5	13	0
Lester	11	74	6.7	26	0
Everett	19	38	2.0	14	0
Lang	9	29	3.2	28	0
Ellard	2	18	9.0	15	0
Kinchen	2	10	5.0	8	0
R. White	2	10	5.0	5	0
Drayton	1	7	7.0	7	0
Jones	1	4	4.0	4	0
Rams	449	2014	4.5	71t	8
Opponents	480	1851	3.9	35t	18

RECEIVING

	No.	Yds.	Avg.	LG	TD
Ellard	61	945	15.5	54	2
Anderson	37	552	14.9	56t	4
Gary	36	289	8.0	60t	1
Drayton	27	319	11.8	27	4
Bettis	26	244	9.4	28	0
Lester	18	154	8.6	21	0
Carter	14	166	11.9	38	1
Kinchen	8	137	17.1	35t	1
McNeal	8	75	9.4	22t	1
Jones	5	56	11.2	21t	2
Lang	4	45	11.3	21	0
LaChapelle	2	23	11.5	14	0
Lofton	1	16	16.0	16	0
Rams	247	3021	12.2	60t	16
Opponents	299	3763	12.6	80t	17

INTERCEPTIONS

	No.	Yds.	Avg.	LG	TD
Bailey	2	41	20.5	41	0
Rolling	2	21	10.5	12	0
Terrell	2	1	0.5	1	0
Lyght	2	0	0.0	0	0
Stewart	1	30	30.0	30	0
Conlan	1	28	28.0	28	0
Homco	1	6	6.0	6	0
Rams	11	127	11.5	41	0
Opponents	19	347	18.3	54	2

PUNTING

	No.	Yds.	Avg.	In 20	LG
Landeta	42	1825	43.5	7	66
McJulien	21	795	37.9	5	56
Bracken	17	651	38.3	3	51
Rams	80	3271	40.9	15	66
Opponents	58	2451	42.3	18	68

PUNT RETURNS

	No.	FC	Yds.	Avg.	LG	TD
Buchanan	8	1	41	5.1	12	0
Kinchen	7	4	32	4.6	8	0
Ellard	2	8	18	9.0	13	0
Henley	1	0	8	8.0	8	0
M. Price	1	2	3	3.0	3	0
Rams	19	15	102	5.4	13	0
Opponents	43	16	533	12.4	74t	2

KICKOFF RETURNS

	No.	Yds.	Avg.	LG	TD
Boykin	13	216	16.6	29	0
Griffith	8	169	21.1	29	0
M. Price	8	144	18.0	23	0
R. White	8	122	15.3	35	0
Kinchen	6	96	16.0	22	0
Israel	5	92	18.4	23	0
Drayton	1	-15	-15.0	-15	0
Rams	49	824	16.8	35	0
Opponents	47	984	20.9	45	0

SACKS

	No.
Gilbert	10.5
Stokes	9.5
Young	7.0
Robinson	3.0
Boutte	1.0
Henderson	1.0
Rocker	1.0
Stewart	1.0
Woods	1.0
Rams	35.0
Opponents	31.0

1994 DRAFT CHOICES

Round	Name	Pos.	College
1	Wayne Gandy	T	Auburn
2	Isaac Bruce	WR	Memphis State
	Toby Wright	DB	Nebraska
	Brad Ottis	DE	Wayne State, Neb.
3	Keith Lyle	DB	Virginia
	James Bostic	RB	Auburn
	Ernest Jones	LB	Oregon
4	Chris Brantley	WR	Rutgers
6	Rickey Brady	TE	Oklahoma
	Ronald Edwards	T	North Carolina A&T

LOS ANGELES RAMS

1994 VETERAN ROSTER

No.	Name	Pos.	Ht.	Wt.	Birthdate	NFL Exp.	College	Hometown	How Acq.	'93 Games/ Starts
83	Anderson, Willie	WR	6-0	172	3/7/65	7	UCLA	Paulsboro, N.J.	D2b-'88	15/15
77	Ashmore, Darryl	T	6-7	300	11/1/69	3	Northwestern	Peoria, Ill.	D7-'92	9/7
28	† Bailey, Robert	CB	5-9	176	9/3/68	4	Miami	Miami, Fla.	D4-'91	9/3
71	Belin, Chuck	G	6-2	312	10/27/70	2	Wisconsin	Milwaukee, Wis.	D5b-'93	0*
36	Bettis, Jerome	RB	5-11	243	2/16/72	2	Notre Dame	Detroit, Mich.	D1-'93	16/12
96	Boutte, Marc	DT	6-4	296	7/26/69	3	Louisiana State	Lake Charles, La.	D3a-'92	16/16
21	Boykin, Deral	S	5-11	196	9/2/70	2	Louisville	Kent, Ohio	D6-'93	16/0
61	Brostek, Bern	C	6-3	300	9/11/66	5	Washington	Honolulu, Hawaii	D1-'90	16/16
89	Buchanan, Richard	WR	5-10	178	5/8/69	2	Northwestern	Maywood, Ill.	FA-'93	5/0
51	# Bush, Blair	C	6-3	275	11/25/56	17	Washington	Palos Verdes, Calif.	PB(GB)-'92	16/0
17	Chandler, Chris	QB	6-4	225	10/12/65	7	Washington	Everett, Wash.	UFA(Ariz)-'94	4/2*
54	Collins, Brett	LB	6-1	234	10/8/68	3	Washington	Portland, Ore.	W(GB)-'93	14/0*
56	Conlan, Shane	LB	6-3	235	3/4/64	8	Penn State	Frewsburg, N.Y.	UFA(Buff)-'93	12/11
29	† Davis, Dexter	CB	5-10	185	3/20/70	5	Clemson	Sumter, S.C.	FA-'93	12/4*
84	Drayton, Troy	TE	6-3	255	6/29/70	2	Penn State	Steelton, Pa.	D2-'93	16/2
43	Gary, Cleveland	RB	6-0	226	5/4/66	6	Miami	Indiantown, Fla.	D1b-'89	15/4
90	Gilbert, Sean	DT	6-4	315	4/10/70	3	Pittsburgh	Aliquippa, Pa.	D1-'92	16/16
79	Goeas, Leo	G-T	6-4	292	8/15/66	5	Hawaii	Honolulu, Hawaii	T(SD)-'93	16/16
42	Griffin, Courtney	CB	5-10	180	12/19/66	2	Fresno State	Fresno, Calif.	FA-'92	7/1
30	Griffith, Howard	RB	6-0	226	11/17/67	2	Illinois	Chicago, Ill.	FA-'93	15/0
24	# Henderson, Wymon	CB	5-10	188	12/15/61	9	Nevada-Las Vegas	N. Miami Beach, Fla.	FA-'93	9/4
20	# Henley, Darryl	CB	5-9	172	10/30/66	5	UCLA	La Verne, Calif.	D2c-'89	5/4
23	Hicks, Clifford	S-CB	5-10	187	8/18/64	8	Oregon	San Diego, Calif.	UFA(NYJ)-'94	10/0*
57	Homco, Thomas	LB	6-0	245	1/8/70	2	Northwestern	Highland, Ind.	FA-'92	16/3
31	Israel, Steve	CB	5-11	186	3/16/69	3	Pittsburgh	Lawnside, N.J.	D2-'92	16/12
72	Jones, Clarence	T	6-6	280	5/6/68	4	Maryland	Brooklyn, N.Y.	FA-'94	4/0*
98	Jones, Jimmie	DT	6-4	276	1/9/66	5	Miami	Lake Okeechobee, Fla.	UFA(Dall)-'94	15/2*
52	Kelly, Joe	LB	6-2	235	12/11/64	9	Washington	Los Angeles, Calif.	FA-'94	16/14*
81	Kinchen, Todd	WR	6-0	187	1/7/69	3	Louisiana State	Baton Rouge, La.	D3b-'92	6/1
88	LaChapelle, Sean	WR	6-3	205	7/29/70	2	UCLA	Napa, Calif.	D5a-'93	10/0
5	Landeta, Sean	P	6-0	210	1/6/62	10	Towson State	Baltimore, Md.	FA-'93	16/0*
38	Lang, David	RB	5-11	213	3/28/67	4	Northern Arizona	San Bernardino, Calif.	D12-'90	6/0
34	Lester, Tim	RB	5-9	215	6/5/68	3	Eastern Kentucky	Miami, Fla.	D10-'92	16/14
87	t- Lewis, Nate	WR	5-11	198	10/19/66	5	Oregon Tech	Moultrie, Ga.	T(SD)-'94	15/9*
64	Loneker, Keith	G	6-3	330	6/21/71	2	Kansas	Roselle Park, N.J.	FA-'93	4/2
41	Lyght, Todd	CB	6-0	186	2/9/69	4	Notre Dame	Flint, Mich.	D1-'91	9/9
53	# Martin, Chris	LB	6-2	241	12/19/60	12	Auburn	Huntsville, Ala.	T(KC)-'93	16/4
86	McMurtry, Greg	WR	6-2	207	10/15/67	5	Michigan	Brockton, Mass.	UFA(NE)-'94	14/8*
82	# McNeal, Travis	TE	6-3	244	1/10/67	6	Tennessee-Chattanooga	Birmingham, Ala.	FA-'92	16/6
13	Miller, Chris	QB	6-2	212	8/9/65	8	Oregon	Eugene, Ore.	UFA(Atl)-'94	3/2*
66	Newberry, Tom	G	6-2	285	12/20/62	9	Wisconsin-LaCrosse	Onalaska, Wis.	D2-'86	9/9
26	Newman, Anthony	S	6-0	199	11/25/65	7	Oregon	Beaverton, Ore.	D2a-'88	16/16
69	Pahukoa, Jeff	G-T	6-2	298	2/9/69	4	Washington	Marysville, Wash.	D12a-'91	16/5
58	† Phifer, Roman	LB	6-2	230	3/5/68	4	UCLA	Pineville, N.C.	D2-'91	16/16
22	t- Pope, Marquez	S-CB	5-10	193	10/29/70	3	Fresno State	Nashville, Tenn.	T(SD)-'94	16/1*
27	Price, Mitchell	CB	5-9	181	5/10/67	5	Tulane	San Antonio, Tex.	FA-'93	6/0*
72	Robbins, Kevin	T	6-4	286	12/12/67	3	Michigan State	Washington, D.C.	FA-'93	1/0
97	Robinson, Gerald	DE	6-3	262	5/4/63	8	Auburn	Notasulga, Ala.	PB(SD)-'91	16/3
92	Rocker, David	DT	6-4	267	3/12/69	4	Auburn	Atlanta, Ga.	FA-'91	14/0
59	Rolling, Henry	LB	6-2	225	9/8/65	8	Nevada-Reno	Henderson, Nev.	UFA(SD)-'93	12/9
12	Rubley, T.J.	QB	6-3	205	11/29/68	3	Tulsa	Davenport, Iowa	D9-'92	9/7
78	Slater, Jackie	T	6-4	285	5/27/54	19	Jackson State	Jackson, Miss.	D3-'76	8/8
60	Stokes, Fred	DE	6-3	274	3/14/64	8	Georgia Southern	Vidalia, Ga.	UFA(Wash)-'93	15/15
99	Tanuvasa, Maa	DT	6-2	277	11/6/70	2	Hawaii	Mililani, Hawaii	D8b-'93	0*
37	Taylor, Terry	CB	5-10	185	7/18/61	10	Southern Illinois	Warren, Ohio	FA-'94	10/7*
55	White, Leon	LB	6-3	242	10/4/63	9	Brigham Young	La Mesa, Calif.	FA-'92	14/0
44	White, Russell	RB	5-11	216	12/15/70	2	California	Encino, Calif.	D3-'93	5/0
76	Young, Robert	DE	6-6	273	1/29/69	4	Mississippi State	Jackson, Miss.	D5-'91	6/6
10	Zendejas, Tony	K	5-8	165	5/15/60	10	Nevada-Reno	Chino, Calif.	PB(Hou)-'91	16/0

* Belin active for 5 games in '93 but did not play; Chandler played 4 games with Phoenix; Collins played 4 games with Green Bay, 10 games with L.A. Rams; Davis played 6 games with Phoenix, 6 games with L.A. Rams; Hicks played 10 games with N.Y. Jets; C. Jones played 4 games with N.Y. Jets; J. Jones played 15 games with Dallas; Kelly played 16 games with L.A. Raiders; Landeta played 8 games with N.Y. Giants, 8 games with L.A. Rams; Lewis played 15 games with San Diego; Miller played 3 games with Atlanta; McMurtry played 14 games with New England; Pope played 16 games with San Diego; Price played 1 game with Cincinnati; Taylor played 10 games with Cleveland; Tanuvasa missed '93 season due to injury.

Unrestricted free agent; subject to developments.

† Restricted free agent; subject to developments.

Traded —QB Jim Everett to New Orleans, TE Jim Price to Dallas.

t- Rams traded for Lewis (San Diego), Pope (San Diego).

Players lost through free agency (5): TE Pat Carter (Hou; 11 games in '93), WR Henry Ellard (Wash; 16), S Michael Stewart (Mia; 16), S Pat Terrell (NYJ; 13), DE Tony Woods (Wash; 14).

Also played with Rams in '93—P Don Bracken (3 games), LB Jeff Brady (6), T Irv Eatman (16), QB Jim Everett (10), T Robert Jenkins (8), WR Ernie Jones (10), WR James Lofton (1), P Paul McJulien (5), QB Mike Pagel (7), CB Sam Seale (1), LB Leon White (14).

COACHING STAFF

Head Coach,
Chuck Knox

Pro Career: Started his second tour of duty as Rams head coach on January 8, 1992, after serving as Seattle's head coach from 1983-91 and leading the Seahawks into the playoffs four times, including the AFC Western Division title in 1988. Previously served as head coach of Buffalo Bills 1978-82, leading them to the AFC East title in 1980. Led the Rams to five consecutive NFC West titles (1973-77) before taking over Bills. Pro assistant with New York Jets 1963-66, coaching offensive line, before moving to Detroit in 1967. Served Lions as offensive line coach until named head coach of Rams in 1973. No pro playing experience. Career record: 189-146-1.

Background: Played tackle for Juniata College in Huntingdon, Pa., 1950-53. Was an assistant coach at his alma mater in 1954, then spent 1955 season at Tyrone High in Tyrone, Pa. Was head coach at Ellwood City (Pa.) High School from 1956-58. Moved to Wake Forest as an assistant coach in 1959-60, then Kentucky in 1961-62.

Personal: Born April 27, 1932, in Sewickley, Pa. Chuck and his wife, Shirley live in Villa Park, Calif., and have four children—Chris, Kathy, Colleen, and Chuck.

ASSISTANT COACHES

Chris Clausen, strength and conditioning coordinator; born February 21, 1958, Evergreen Park, Ill., lives in Huntington Beach, Calif. Cornerback Indiana 1976-79. No pro playing experience. College coach: San Diego State 1987-88. Pro coach: San Diego Chargers 1989-91, joined Rams in 1992.

George Dyer, defensive coordinator; born May 4, 1940, Alhambra, Calif., lives in Villa Park, Calif. Center-linebacker U.C. Santa Barbara 1961-63. No pro playing experience. College coach: Humboldt State 1964-66, Coalinga (Calif.) J.C. 1967 (head coach), Portland State 1968-71, Idaho 1972, San Jose State 1973, Michigan State 1977-79, Arizona State 1980-81. Pro coach: Winnipeg Blue Bombers (CFL) 1974-76, Buffalo Bills 1982, Seattle Seahawks 1983-91, joined Rams in 1992.

Jim Erkenbeck, offensive line; born September 10, 1929, Los Angeles, Calif., lives in Anaheim Hills, Calif. Linebacker-end San Diego State 1949-52. No pro playing experience. College coach: San Diego State 1960-63, Grossmont (Calif.) J.C. 1964-67, Utah State 1968, Washington State 1969-71, California 1972-76. Pro coach: Winnipeg Blue Bombers (CFL) 1977, Montreal Alouettes (CFL) 1978-81, Calgary Stampeders (CFL) 1982, Philadelphia/Baltimore Stars (USFL) 1983-85, New Orleans Saints 1986, Dallas Cowboys 1987-88, Kansas City Chiefs 1989-91, joined Rams in 1992.

Greg Gaines, defensive assistant; born October 16, 1958, Martinsville, Va., lives in Mission Viejo, Calif. Linebacker Tennessee 1976-80. Pro linebacker Seatle Seahawks 1981-88, Kansas City Chiefs 1989. Pro coach: Joined Rams in 1992.

Chick Harris, offensive coordinator; born September 21, 1945, Durham, N.C., lives in Irvine, Calif. Running back Northern Arizona 1966-69. No pro playing experience. College coach: Colorado State 1970-72, Long Beach State 1973-74, Washington 1975-80. Pro coach: Buffalo Bills 1981-82, Seattle Seahawks 1983-91, joined Rams in 1992.

Chuck Knox, Jr., offensive assistant-running backs; born June 19, 1965, Englewood, N.J., lives in Villa Park, Calif. Running back Arizona 1984-88. No pro playing experience. Pro coach: Joined Rams in 1993.

Mike Martz, quarterbacks; born May 13, 1951, Sioux Falls, S.D., lives in Huntington Beach, Calif. Tight end San Diego Mesa (Calif.) Junior College 1969-70, U.C. Santa Barbara 1971, Fresno State 1972. No pro playing experience. College coach: San Diego Mesa (Calif.) Junior College 1974, 1976-77, San Jose State 1975, Santa Ana (Calif.) Junior College 1978-79, Fresno State 1979, Pacific 1980-81, Minnesota 1982-83, Arizona State 1984-91. Pro coach: Joined Rams in 1992.

Steve Moore, receivers; born August 19, 1947, Los Angeles, lives in Huntington Beach, Calif. Wide receiver U.C. Santa Barbara 1968-69. No pro playing experience. College coach: U.C. Santa Barbara 1970-71, Army 1975, Rice 1976-77. Pro coach: Buffalo Bills 1978-82, Seattle Seahawks 1983-88, joined Rams in 1994.

Rod Perry, defensive backfield; born September 11, 1953, Fresno, Calif., lives in Anaheim Hills, Calif. Defensive back Colorado 1972-74. Pro cornerback Los Angeles Rams 1975-82, Cleveland Browns 1983-84. College coach: Columbia 1985, Fresno City College 1986, Fresno State 1987-88. Pro coach: Seattle Seahawks 1989-91, joined Rams in 1992.

Dick Selcer, linebackers; born August 22, 1937, Cincinnati, Ohio, lives in Anaheim Hills, Calif. Running back Notre Dame 1955-58. No pro playing experience. College coach: Xavier, Ohio 1962-64, 1970-71 (head coach), Cincinnati, 1965-66, Brown 1967-69, Wisconsin 1972-74, Kansas State 1975-77, Southwestern Louisiana 1978-80. Pro coach: Houston Oilers 1981-83, Cincinnati Bengals 1984-91, joined Rams in 1992.

Wayne Sevier, special teams; born July 3, 1941, San Diego, Calif., lives in Newport Beach, Calif. Quarterback Chaffey, Calif., J.C. 1960, San Diego State 1961-62. No pro playing experience. College coach: California Western 1968-69. Pro coach: St. Louis Cardinals 1974-75, Atlanta Falcons 1976, San Diego Chargers 1979-80, 1987-88, Washington Redskins 1981-86, 1989-93, joined Rams in 1994.

Rennie Simmons, tight ends; born February 25, 1942, Poughkeepsie, N.Y., lives in Anaheim, Calif. Center San Diego State 1963-65. No pro playing experience. College coach: Cal State-Fullerton 1972-75, Cerritos, Calif., J.C. 1976-80. Pro coach: Washington Redskins 1981-93, joined Rams in 1994.

Joe Vitt, assistant head coach-safeties; born August 23, 1954, Camden, N.J., lives in Mission Viejo, Calif. Linebacker Towson State 1973-75. No pro playing experience. Pro coach: Baltimore Colts 1979-81, Seattle Seahawks 1982-91, joined Rams in 1992.

1994 FIRST-YEAR ROSTER

Name	Pos.	Ht.	Wt.	Birthdate	College	Hometown	How Acq.
Bostic, James	RB	5-11	230	3/13/72	Auburn	Ft. Lauderdale, Fla.	D3b
Brady, Rickey	TE	6-4	246	11/19/71	Oklahoma	Oklahoma City, Okla.	D6a
Brantley, Chris	WR	5-10	180	12/12/70	Rutgers	Teaneck, N.J.	D4
Brasher, Bob (1)	TE	6-5	244	4/30/70	Arizona State	San Diego, Calif.	FA
Bruce, Isaac	WR	6-0	178	11/10/72	Memphis State	Ft. Lauderdale, Fla.	D2a
Bryant, Beno	RB	5-9	170	1/1/71	Washington	Los Angeles, Calif.	FA
Buffaloe, Jeff (1)	P	6-1	194	9/18/70	Memphis State	Memphis, Tenn.	FA
Edwards, Ronald	T	6-5	311	9/18/71	North Carolina A&T	Temple Hill, Md.	D6b
Farmer, Willie (1)	WR	6-2	190	12/12/68	Virginia Union	Tampa, Fla.	FA
Farr, D'Marco	DT	6-1	270	6/9/71	Washington	Richmond, Calif.	FA
Gandy, Wayne	T	6-4	289	2/10/71	Auburn	Haines City, Fla.	D1
Jones, Ernest	LB	6-2	239	4/1/71	Oregon	Utica, N.Y.	D3c
Jones, Jeff (1)	WR	5-10	185	10/19/70	California	Irvine, Calif.	FA
Kirchoff, Jay (1)	K	6-4	198	5/28/70	Arizona	Plymouth, Minn.	FA
Lyle, Keith	S	6-2	204	4/17/72	Virginia	Vienna, Va.	D3a
Mason, Andy	LB	6-2	228	8/31/71	Washington	Longview, Wash.	FA
McDougal, Kevin	QB	6-2	182	5/29/72	Notre Dame	Pompano Beach, Fla.	FA
O'Bannon, Turhon	WR	6-0	195	3/23/70	New Mexico	Reseda, Calif.	FA
Ottis, Brad	DE	6-4	272	8/2/72	Wayne State, Neb.	Wahoo, Neb.	D2c
Patrick, Kevin	DE	6-3	255	7/30/71	Miami	West Palm Beach, Fla.	FA
Ross, Jermaine	WR	5-11	192	4/27/71	Purdue	Jeffersonville, Ind.	FA
Setzer, Rusty	RB	5-7	184	12/16/69	Grand Valley State	Gary, Ind.	FA
Starck, Justin	T	6-6	310	11/4/71	Oregon	Salem, Ore.	FA
Turk, Matt (1)	P	6-5	230	6/16/68	Wis.-Whitewater	Greenfield, Wis.	FA
Wilson, David (1)	S	5-10	192	6/10/70	California	Reseda, Calif.	FA
Wright, Toby	S	5-11	203	11/19/70	Nebraska	Phoenix, Ariz.	D2b

The term NFL Rookie is defined as a player who is in his first season of professional football and has not been on the roster of another professional football team for any regular-season or postseason games. A Rookie is designated by an "R" on NFL rosters. Players who have been active in another professional football league or players who have NFL experience, including either preseason training camp or being on an Active List or Inactive List, or on Reserve/Injured or Reserve/Physically Unable to Perform for fewer than six regular-season games, are termed NFL First-Year Players. An NFL First-Year Player is designated by a "1" on NFL rosters. Thereafter, a player is credited with an additional year of experience for each season in which he accumulates six games on the Active List or Inactive List, or on Reserve/Injured or Reserve/Physically Unable to Perform.

NOTES

MINNESOTA VIKINGS

National Football Conference
Central Division
Team Colors: Purple, Gold, and White
9520 Viking Drive
Eden Prairie, Minnesota 55344
Telephone: (612) 828-6500

CLUB OFFICERS
Chairman of the Board: John C. Skoglund
Vice Chairmen: Jaye F. Dyer, Philip S. Maas
Directors: N. Bud Grossman, Roger L. Headrick,
    James R. Jundt, Elizabeth MacMillan, Carol S.
    Sperry, Wheelock Whitney

CLUB OFFICIALS
President/CEO: Roger L. Headrick
Vice President Administration/Team Operations:
    Jeff Diamond
Vice President Player Personnel: Frank Gilliam
Assistant General Manager/College Scouting:
    Jerry Reichow
Assistant General Manager/Pro Personnel:
    Paul Wiggin
Director of Finance: Nick Valentine
Director of Research and Dev.: Mike Eayrs
Director of Marketing: Kernal Buhler
Director of Public Relations: David Pelletier
Director of Team Operations: Breck Spinner
Ticket Manager: Harry Randolph
Director of Security: Steve Rollins
Player Personnel Coordinator: Scott Studwell
Equipment Manager: Dennis Ryan
Trainer: Fred Zamberletti
Video Director: Larry Kohout
Stadium: Hubert H. Humphrey Metrodome
    •**Capacity:** 63,000
    500 11th Avenue South
    Minneapolis, Minnesota 55415
Playing Surface: AstroTurf
Training Camp: Mankato State University
    Mankato, Minnesota 56001

1994 SCHEDULE
PRESEASON
July 31	at Dallas	8:00
Aug. 6	vs. Kansas City at Tokyo	10:00
Aug. 13	**New Orleans**	7:00
Aug. 20	at Seattle	7:00
Aug. 26	**Miami**	7:00

REGULAR SEASON
Sept. 4	at Green Bay	12:00
Sept. 11	**Detroit**	12:00
Sept. 18	at Chicago	12:00
Sept. 25	**Miami**	12:00
Oct. 2	at Arizona	1:00
Oct. 10	at New York Giants (Monday)	9:00
Oct. 16	Open Date	
Oct. 20	**Green Bay** (Thursday)	7:00
Oct. 30	at Tampa Bay	4:00
Nov. 6	**New Orleans**	12:00
Nov. 13	at New England	1:00
Nov. 20	**New York Jets**	3:00
Nov. 27	**Tampa Bay**	12:00
Dec. 1	**Chicago** (Thursday)	7:00
Dec. 11	at Buffalo	1:00
Dec. 17	at Detroit (Saturday)	12:30
Dec. 26	**San Francisco** (Monday)	8:00

RECORD HOLDERS
INDIVIDUAL RECORDS—CAREER
Category	Name	Performance
Rushing (Yds.)	Chuck Foreman, 1973-79	5,879
Passing (Yds.)	Fran Tarkenton, 1961-66, 1972-78	33,098
Passing (TDs)	Fran Tarkenton, 1961-66, 1972-78	239
Receiving (No.)	Steve Jordan, 1982-1993	495
Receiving (Yds.)	Anthony Carter, 1985-1993	7,636
Interceptions	Paul Krause, 1968-1979	53
Punting (Avg.)	Harry Newsome, 1990-93	43.8
Punt Return (Avg.)	Tommy Mason, 1961-66	10.4
Kickoff Return (Avg.)	Bob Reed, 1962-63	27.1
Field Goals	Fred Cox, 1963-1977	282
Touchdowns (Tot.)	Bill Brown, 1962-1974	76
Points	Fred Cox, 1963-1977	1,365

INDIVIDUAL RECORDS—SINGLE SEASON
Category	Name	Performance
Rushing (Yds.)	Terry Allen, 1992	1,201
Passing (Yds.)	Tommy Kramer, 1981	3,912
Passing (TDs)	Tommy Kramer, 1981	26
Receiving (No.)	Rickey Young, 1978	88
Receiving (Yds.)	Anthony Carter, 1988	1,225
Interceptions	Paul Krause, 1975	10
Punting (Avg.)	Bobby Walden, 1964	46.4
Punt Return (Avg.)	Leo Lewis, 1987	12.5
Kickoff Return (Avg.)	John Gilliam, 1972	26.3
Field Goals	Rich Karlis, 1989	31
Touchdowns (Tot.)	Chuck Foreman, 1975	22
Points	Chuck Foreman, 1975	132

INDIVIDUAL RECORDS—SINGLE GAME
Category	Name	Performance
Rushing (Yds.)	Chuck Foreman, 10-24-76	200
Passing (Yds.)	Tommy Kramer, 11-2-86	490
Passing (TDs)	Joe Kapp, 9-28-69	*7
Receiving (No.)	Rickey Young, 12-16-79	15
Receiving (Yds.)	Sammy White, 11-7-76	210
Interceptions	Many times	3
	Last time by Jack Del Rio, 12-5-93	
Field Goals	Rich Karlis, 11-5-89	*7
Touchdowns (Tot.)	Chuck Foreman, 12-20-75	4
	Ahmad Rashad, 9-2-79	4
Points	Chuck Foreman, 12-20-75	24
	Ahmad Rashad, 9-2-79	24

*NFL Record

VIKINGS COACHING HISTORY
(275-232-9)
1961-66	Norm Van Brocklin	29-51-4
1967-83	Bud Grant	161-99-5
1984	Les Steckel	3-13-0
1985	Bud Grant	7-9-0
1986-91	Jerry Burns	55-46-0
1992-93	Dennis Green	20-14-0

HUBERT H. HUMPHREY METRODOME

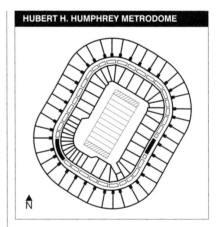

N

1993 TEAM RECORD
PRESEASON (4-1)

Date	Result		Opponents
8/1	W	13-7	at Dallas
8/7	W	20-6	vs. Buffalo at Berlin
8/14	W	23-10	Seattle
8/21	L	20-27	at Kansas City
8/26	W	30-13	Pittsburgh

REGULAR SEASON (9-7)

Date	Result		Opponents	Att.
9/5	L	7-24	at L.A. Raiders	44,120
9/12	W	10-7	Chicago	57,921
9/26	W	15-13	Green Bay	61,746
10/3	L	19-38	at San Francisco	63,071
10/10	W	15-0	Tampa Bay	54,215
10/25	W	19-12	at Chicago	64,677
10/31	L	27-30	Detroit	53,428
11/7	L	17-30	San Diego	55,527
11/14	W	26-23	at Denver	67,329
11/21	L	10-23	at Tampa Bay	40,848
11/28	L	14-17	New Orleans	53,030
12/5	W	13-0	at Detroit	63,216
12/12	L	20-37	Dallas	63,321
12/19	W	21-17	at Green Bay	54,773
12/26	W	30-10	Kansas City	59,236
12/31	W	14-9	at Washington	42,836

POSTSEASON (0-1)

Date	Result		Opponents	Att.
1/9	L	10-17	at N.Y. Giants	75,089

SCORE BY PERIODS

Vikings	49	81	83	64	0	—	277
Opponents	67	93	36	94	0	—	290

ATTENDANCE
Home 458,424   Away 440,870   Total 899,294
Single-game home record, 63,321 (12-12-93)
Single-season home record, 485,616 (1992)

1993 TEAM STATISTICS

	Vikings	Opp.
Total First Downs	283	259
Rushing	85	98
Passing	182	139
Penalty	16	22
Third Down Made/Att.	72/212	81/207
Third Down Pct.	34.0	39.1
Fourth Down: Made/Att.	4/7	3/6
Fourth Down Pct.	57.1	50.0
Total Net Yards	4824	4406
Avg. Per Game	301.5	275.4
Total Plays	1008	938
Avg. Per Play	4.8	4.7
Net Yards Rushing	1624	1536
Avg. Per Game	101.5	96.0
Total Rushes	447	415
Net Yards Passing	3200	2870
Avg. Per Game	200.0	179.4
Sacked/Yards Lost	35/181	45/276
Gross Yards	3381	3146
Att./Completions	526/315	478/310
Completion Pct.	59.9	64.9
Had Intercepted	14	24
Punts/Avg.	90/42.9	78/42.4
Net Punting Avg.	90/35.4	78/37.8
Penalties/Yards Lost	109/806	97/768
Fumbles/Ball Lost	15/10	24/10
Touchdowns	28	31
Rushing	8	14
Passing	18	11
Returns	2	6
Avg. Time of Possession	30:28	29:33

1993 INDIVIDUAL STATISTICS

PASSING

	Att	Cmp	Yds.	Pct.	TD	Int	Tkld.	Rate
McMahon	331	200	1968	60.4	9	8	23/104	76.2
Salisbury	195	115	1413	59.0	9	6	12/77	84.0
Vikings	526	315	3381	59.9	18	14	35/181	79.1
Opponents	478	310	3146	64.9	11	24	45/276	70.3

SCORING

	TD R	TD P	TD Rt	PAT	FG	Saf	PTS
Reveiz	0	0	0	27/28	26/35	0	105
C. Carter	0	9	0	0/0	0/0	0	54
A. Carter	0	5	0	0/0	0/0	0	30
Graham	3	0	0	0/0	0/0	0	18
Craig	1	1	0	0/0	0/0	0	12
Smith	2	0	0	0/0	0/0	0	12
Word	2	0	0	0/0	0/0	0	12
Ismail	0	1	0	0/0	0/0	0	6
Jordan	0	1	0	0/0	0/0	0	6
McGriggs	0	0	1	0/0	0/0	0	6
McMillian	0	0	1	0/0	0/0	0	6
Tice	0	1	0	0/0	0/0	0	6
Thomas	0	0	0	0/0	0/0	1	2
Vikings	8	18	2	27/28	26/35	2	277
Opponents	14	11	6	29/31	25/33	0	290

RUSHING

	Att.	Yds.	Avg.	LG	TD
Graham	118	488	4.1	31	3
Word	142	458	3.2	14	2
Smith	82	399	4.9	26t	2
Craig	38	119	3.1	11	1
McMahon	33	96	2.9	16	0
Evans	14	32	2.3	5	0
A. Carter	7	19	2.7	9	0
Ismail	3	14	4.7	6	0
Salisbury	10	-1	-0.1	6	0
Vikings	447	1624	3.6	31	8
Opponents	415	1536	3.7	45	14

RECEIVING

	No.	Yds.	Avg.	LG	TD
C. Carter	86	1071	12.5	58	9
A. Carter	60	775	12.9	39	5
Jordan	56	542	9.7	53	1
Smith	24	111	4.6	12	0
Ismail	19	212	11.2	37	1
Craig	19	169	8.9	31	1
Tennell	15	122	8.1	17	0
Word	9	105	11.7	27	0
Graham	7	46	6.6	11	0
Tice	6	39	6.5	21	1
Reed	5	65	13.0	18	0
Truitt	4	40	10.0	13	0
Evans	4	39	9.8	21	0
Guliford	1	45	45.0	45	0
Vikings	315	3381	10.7	58	18
Opponents	310	3146	10.1	93t	11

INTERCEPTIONS

	No.	Yds.	Avg.	LG	TD
Glenn	5	49	9.8	23	0
McMillian	4	45	11.3	22t	1
Del Rio	4	3	0.8	3	0
Lee	3	20	6.7	19	0
Scott	2	26	13.0	26	0
C. Jenkins	2	7	3.5	4	0
McGriggs	1	63	63.0	63t	1
Parker	1	1	1.0	1	0
Pearson	1	0	0.0	0	0
Doleman	1	-3	-3.0	-3	0
Vikings	24	211	8.8	63t	2
Opponents	14	166	11.9	41t	3

PUNTING

	No.	Yds.	Avg.	In 20	LG
Newsome	90	3862	42.9	25	64
Vikings	90	3862	42.9	25	64
Opponents	78	3307	42.4	23	59

PUNT RETURNS

	No.	FC	Yds.	Avg.	LG	TD
Guliford	29	15	212	7.3	50	0
Parker	9	6	64	7.1	20	0
Smith	1	2	4	4.0	4	0
Vikings	39	23	280	7.2	50	0
Opponents	46	22	560	12.2	72t	1

KICKOFF RETURNS

	No.	Yds.	Avg.	LG	TD
Ismail	42	902	21.5	47	0
Guliford	5	101	20.2	29	0
Smith	3	41	13.7	16	0
Craig	1	11	11.0	11	0
Del Rio	1	4	4.0	4	0
Evans	1	11	11.0	11	0
Graham	1	16	16.0	16	0
McMillian	1	0	0.0	0	0
Vikings	55	1086	19.7	47	0
Opponents	58	1420	24.5	99t	1

SACKS

	No.
Doleman	12.5
Randle	12.5
Thomas	9.0
Barker	6.0
C. Jenkins	2.5
R. Harris	1.0
Sheppard	1.0
Del Rio	0.5
Vikings	45.0
Opponents	35.0

1994 DRAFT CHOICES

Round	Name	Pos.	College
1	DeWayne Washington	DB	North Carolina State
	Todd Steussie	T	California
2	David Palmer	RB	Alabama
	Fernando Smith	DE	Jackson State
4	Mike Wells	DT	Iowa
5	Shelly Hammonds	DB	Penn State
6	Andrew Jordan	TE	Western Carolina
7	Pete Bercich	LB	Notre Dame

MINNESOTA VIKINGS

1994 VETERAN ROSTER

No.		Name	Pos.	Ht.	Wt.	Birthdate	NFL Exp.	College	Hometown	How Acq.	'93 Games/ Starts
50		Abrams, Bobby	LB	6-3	230	4/12/67	5	Michigan	Detroit, Mich.	FA-'93	4/0
72		Adams, Scott	G-T	6-5	293	9/28/66	3	Georgia	Lake City, Fla.	FA-'91	15/9
21		Allen, Terry	RB	5-10	197	2/21/68	5	Clemson	Commerce, Ga.	D9-'90	0*
4		Barker, Bryan	P	6-1	187	6/28/64	5	Santa Clara	Orinda, Calif.	FA-'94	16/0*
92		Barker, Roy	DT	6-4	280	2/14/69	3	North Carolina	New York, N.Y.	D4-'92	16/16
80		Carter, Cris	WR	6-3	197	11/25/65	8	Ohio State	Middletown, Ohio	W(Phil)-'90	16/16
62		Christy, Jeff	C	6-3	277	2/2/69	2	Pittsburgh	Freeport, Pa.	FA-'93	9/0
87	t-	Cooper, Adrian	TE	6-5	263	4/27/68	4	Oklahoma	Denver, Colo.	T(Pitt)-'94	14/3*
33	#	Craig, Roger	RB	6-0	211	7/10/60	12	Nebraska	Davenport, Iowa	PB(Raid)-'92	14/3
77		Culpepper, Brad	DT	6-1	260	5/8/68	3	Florida	Tallahassee, Fla.	D10-'92	15/0
75		Dafney, Bernard	T	6-5	331	11/1/69	3	Tennessee	Los Angeles, Calif.	FA-'92	16/4
55		Del Rio, Jack	LB	6-4	243	4/4/63	10	Southern California	Hayward, Calif.	PB(Dall)-'92	16/16
29		Evans, Charles	RB	6-1	226	4/16/67	2	Clark, Ga.	Augusta, Ga.	FA-'93	3/0
54		Garnett, Dave	LB	6-2	225	12/6/70	2	Stanford	Naperville, Ill.	FA-'93	16/0
66		Gerak, John	G	6-3	285	1/6/70	2	Penn State	Struthers, Ohio	D3a-'93	4/0
25		Glenn, Vencie	S	6-0	201	10/26/64	9	Indiana State	Silver Spring, Md.	PB(NO)-'92	16/16
31		Graham, Scottie	RB	5-9	215	3/28/69	2	Ohio State	Long Island, N.Y.	FA-'93	7/3
84		Guliford, Eric	WR	5-8	165	10/25/69	2	Arizona State	Peoria, Ariz.	FA-'93	10/0
99		Harris, James	DE	6-4	270	5/13/68	2	Temple	East St. Louis, Ill.	FA-'93	6/0
90		Harris, Robert	DE	6-4	285	6/13/69	2	Southern	Riviera Beach, Fla.	D2-'92	16/0
78		Hinton, Chris	T	6-4	305	7/31/61	12	Northwestern	Chicago, Ill.	FA-'94	16/16*
82		Ismail, Qadry	WR	6-0	192	11/8/70	2	Syracuse	Wilkes-Barre, Pa.	D2-'93	15/3
51		Jenkins, Carlos	LB	6-3	217	7/12/68	4	Michigan State	Lantana, Fla.	D3a-'91	16/16
14		Johnson, Brad	QB	6-5	221	9/13/68	2	Florida State	Black Mountain, N.C.	D9a-'92	0*
83	#	Jordan, Steve	TE	6-3	242	1/10/61	13	Brown	Phoenix, Ariz.	D7-'82	14/12
32		Lee, Amp	RB	5-11	200	10/1/71	3	Florida State	Chipley, Fla.	FA-'94	15/3*
61		Lindsay, Everett	G	6-4	290	9/18/70	2	Mississippi	Raleigh, N.C.	D5-'93	12/12
91		Manusky, Greg	LB	6-1	233	8/12/66	7	Colgate	Wilkes-Barre, Pa.	FA-'91	16/0*
58		McDaniel, Ed	LB	5-11	230	2/2/69	3	Clemson	Leesville, S.C.	D5-'92	7/1
64		McDaniel, Randall	G	6-3	280	12/19/64	7	Arizona State	Avondale, Ariz.	D1-'88	16/16
37	†	McGriggs, Lamar	S	6-3	210	5/9/68	4	Western Illinois	Harvey, Ill.	FA-'93	9/4
1	t-	Moon, Warren	QB	6-3	212	11/18/56	11	Washington	Los Angeles, Calif.	T(Hou)-'94	15/14*
68		Morris, Mike	C	6-5	284	2/22/61	7	Northeast Missouri State	Centerville, Iowa	FA-'91	16/0
85	#	Novoselsky, Brent	TE	6-2	237	1/8/66	7	Pennsylvania	Niles, Ill.	FA-'89	15/0
27		Parker, Anthony	CB	5-10	181	2/11/66	4	Arizona State	Tempe, Ariz.	PB(Ind)-'92	14/0
28		Pool, David	CB	5-9	182	12/20/66	5	Carson-Newman	Cincinnati, Ohio	UFA(Den)-'94	0*
93		Randle, John	DT	6-1	275	12/12/67	5	Texas A&I	Hearne, Tex.	FA-'90	16/16
86		Reed, Jake	WR	6-3	212	9/28/67	3	Grambling	Covington, Ga.	D3b-'91	10/1
7	#	Reveiz, Fuad	K	5-11	223	2/24/63	10	Tennessee	Miami, Fla.	FA-'90	16/0
60		Schreiber, Adam	C-G	6-4	288	2/20/62	11	Texas	Huntsville, Ala.	PB(NYJ)-'90	16/16
38		Scott, Todd	S	5-10	207	1/23/68	4	Southwestern Louisiana	Galveston, Tex.	D6-'91	13/12
59		Sheppard, Ashley	LB	6-3	243	1/21/69	2	Clemson	North Pitt, N.C.	D4-'93	10/0
26		Smith, Robert	RB	6-0	195	3/4/72	2	Ohio State	Euclid, Ohio	D1-'93	10/2
53	#	Strickland, Fred	LB	6-2	245	8/15/64	7	Purdue	Wanaque, N.J.	UFA(Rams)-'93	16/15
46		Tennell, Derek	TE	6-2	251	2/12/64	6	UCLA	West Covina, Calif.	FA-'93	16/6
97		Thomas, Henry	DT	6-2	277	1/12/65	8	Louisiana State	Houston, Tex.	D3-'87	13/13
94		Thornton, John	DT	6-0	303	10/25/68	2	Cincinnati	Flint, Mich.	FA-'94	0*
89		Truitt, Olanda	WR	6-0	186	1/4/71	2	Mississippi State	Birmingham, Ala.	W(Raid)-'93	8/0
95	†	Tuaolo, Esera	DT	6-2	274	7/11/68	4	Oregon State	Honolulu, Hawaii	FA-'92	11/3
15		Walsh, Chris	WR	6-1	185	12/12/68	2	Stanford	Concord, Calif.	FA-'94	3/0*
11		Ware, Andre	QB	6-2	205	7/31/68	5	Houston	Dickinson, Tex.	UFA(Det)-'94	5/2*
35		West, Ronnie	WR	6-2	215	6/23/68	3	Pittsburg State, Kan.	Wilcox, Ga.	D9b-'92	0*
23	#	Word, Barry	RB	6-2	242	1/17/63	6	Virginia	Long Island, Va.	T(KC)-'93	13/8

* Allen and West missed '93 season due to injury; B. Barker played 16 games with Kansas City in '93; Cooper played 14 games with Pittsburgh; Hinton played 16 games with Atlanta; Johnson inactive for 16 games; A. Lee played 15 games with San Francisco; Manusky played 16 games with Minnesota; Pool active for 2 games but did not play; Moon played 15 games with Houston; Thornton inactive for 2 games; Walsh played 3 games with Buffalo; Ware played 5 games with Detroit.

\# Unrestricted free agent; subject to developments.

† Restricted free agent; subject to developments.

Traded—DE Chris Doleman to Atlanta.

t- Vikings traded for Cooper (Pittsburgh), Moon (Houston).

Players lost through free agency (4): WR Anthony Carter (Det; 15 games in '93), T Tim Irwin (TB; 16), G Todd Kalis (Pitt; 16), QB Sean Salisbury (Hou; 11).

Also played with Vikings in '93—S Ron Carpenter (7 games), DE Chris Doleman (16), LB Bruce Holmes (1), CB Izel Jenkins (4), S Shawn Jones (1), CB Carl Lee (16), QB Jim McMahon (12), CB Audray McMillian (16), P Harry Newsome (16), CB Jayice Pearson (13), TE Mike Tice (16), QB Gino Torretta (1).

COACHING STAFF

Head Coach,
Dennis Green

Pro Career: Named the fifth head coach in Vikings history on January 10, 1992. In 1993 Green became only the eleventh head coach in the history of the NFL to lead his team to the playoffs in each of his first two seasons as a head coach in the league. Last year, he led the Vikings through a season of adversity to a 9-7 record and a postseason berth. In December, Minnesota compiled a 4-1 record despite playing four playoff teams, including three division winners. In his first season with the Vikings in 1992, Green became one of only eight coaches since the NFL merger in 1970 to lead a team to a division title in his first year as a head coach. He earned NFL coach of the year recognition from the Washington Touchdown Club and NFC coach of the year honors from *United Press International* and *College & Pro Football Newsweekly.* Coached special teams and receivers for the San Francisco 49ers in 1979. Returned to San Francisco from 1986-88 as receivers coach. Credited with the development of two of the game's premier wide receivers—Jerry Rice and John Taylor. Coached with 49ers in Super Bowl XXIII. Played one season for British Columbia Lions (CFL). Career record: 20-14.

Background: Running back at Iowa 1968-70. Began coaching career at Iowa as a graduate assistant in 1972. Moved to Dayton in 1973 as running backs and receivers coach before returning to Iowa from 1974-76 to coach receivers and quarterbacks. Running backs coach at Stanford from 1977-78. Returned to Stanford in 1980 as offensive coordinator. Head coach at Northwestern from 1981-85. Green earned Big Ten coach-of-the-year honors in 1982. In 1989, Green was named head coach at Stanford where he led the Cardinal to the 1991 Aloha Bowl, its first postseason appearance since 1986.

Personal: Born February 17, 1949, in Harrisburg, Pa. Graduated from Iowa with bachelor of science degree in recreation. Dennis, and his wife, Margie, live in Eden Prairie, Minn., and have two children—Patti and Jeremy.

ASSISTANT COACHES

Brian Billick, offensive coordinator/quarterbacks; born February 28, 1954, Redlands, Calif., lives in Eden Prairie, Minn. Tight end Brigham Young 1974-76. Pro tight end Dallas Cowboys 1977. College coach: Brigham Young 1978, Redlands 1979, San Diego State 1981-85, Utah State 1986-88, Stanford 1989-91. Pro coach: Joined Vikings in 1992.

Tony Dungy, defensive coordinator; born October 6, 1955, Jackson, Mich., lives in Eden Prairie, Minn. Quarterback Minnesota 1973-76. Pro safety Pittsburgh Steelers 1977-78, San Francisco 49ers 1979. College coach: Minnesota 1980. Pro coach: Pittsburgh Steelers 1981-88, Kansas City Chiefs 1989-91, joined Vikings in 1992.

Chris Foerster, offensive line assistant; born October 12, 1961, Milwaukee, Wis., lives in Maple Grove, Minn. Center Colorado State 1979-82. No pro playing experience. College coach: Colorado State 1983-87, Stanford 1988-91, Minnesota 1992. Pro coach: Joined Vikings in 1993.

Carl Hargrave, offensive assistant; born November 8, 1954, Frankfurt, Germany, lives in Eden Prairie, Minn. Defensive back Upper Iowa 1972-75. No pro playing experience. College coach: Upper Iowa 1977-80, Northwestern 1981-85, Pittsburgh 1986, Houston 1987-91, Iowa 1992-93. Pro coach: Joined Vikings in 1994.

Monte Kiffin, inside linebackers; born February 29, 1940, Lexington, Ky., lives in Bloomington, Minn. Offensive-defensive tackle Nebraska 1958-61. Pro defensive end Winnipeg Blue Bombers (CFL) 1965. College coach: Nebraska 1966-76, Arkansas 1977-79, North Carolina State 1980-82 (head coach). Pro coach: Green Bay Packers 1983, Buffalo Bills 1984-85, Minnesota Vikings 1986-89, New York Jets 1990, rejoined Vikings in 1991.

Jerry Rhome, receivers; born March 6, 1942, Dallas Tex., lives in Eden Prairie, Minn. Quarterback Southern Methodist 1960-61, Tulsa 1963-64. Pro quarterback Dallas Cowboys 1965-68, Cleveland Browns 1969, Houston Oilers 1970, Los Angeles Rams 1971-72. College coach: Tulsa 1973-75. Pro coach: Seattle Seahawks 1976-82, Washington Redskins 1983-87, San Diego Chargers 1988, Dallas Cowboys 1989, Phoenix Cardinals 1990-93, joined Vikings in 1994.

Keith Rowen, offensive line; born September 2, 1952, New York, N.Y., lives in Eden Prairie, Minn. Offensive tackle Stanford 1972-74. No pro playing experience. College coach: Stanford 1975-76, Long Beach State 1977-78, Arizona 1979-82. Pro coach: Boston/New Orleans Breakers (USFL) 1983-84, Cleveland Browns 1984, Indianapolis Colts 1985-88, New England Patriots 1989, Atlanta Falcons 1990-93, joined Vikings in 1994.

Richard Solomon, defensive backs; born December 8, 1949, New Orleans, La., lives in Eden Prairie, Minn. Running back-defensive back Iowa 1970-73. No pro playing experience. College coach: Dubuque 1973-75, Southern Illinois 1976, Iowa 1977-78, Syracuse 1979, Illinois 1980-86. Pro coach: New York Giants 1987-91 (scout), joined Vikings in 1992.

John Teerlinck, defensive line; born April 9, 1951, Rochester, N.Y., lives in Eden Prairie, Minn. Defensive lineman Western Illinois 1970-73. Pro defensive tackle San Diego Chargers 1974-76. College coach: Iowa Lakes J.C. 1977, Eastern Illinois 1978-79, Illinois 1980-82. Pro coach: Chicago Blitz (USFL) 1983, Arizona Wranglers/Outlaws (USFL) 1984-85, Cleveland Browns 1989-90, Los Angeles Rams 1991, joined Vikings in 1992.

Trent Walters, outside linebackers; born November 20, 1943, Knoxville, Tenn., lives in Eden Prairie, Minn. Defensive back Indiana 1963-65. Pro defensive back Edmonton Eskimos (CFL) 1966-67. College coach: Indiana 1968-71, Louisville 1972, Indiana 1973-80, Washington 1981-83, Pittsburgh 1985, Louisville 1986-90, Texas A&M 1991-93. Pro coach: Cincinnati Bengals 1984, joined Vikings in 1994.

Steve Wetzel, strength and conditioning; born May 11, 1963, Washington D.C., lives in Eden Prairie, Minn. No college or pro playing experience. College coach: Maryland 1985-89, George Mason 1990. Pro coach: Washington Redskins 1990-91, joined Vikings in 1992.

Tyrone Willingham, running backs; born December 30, 1953, Jacksonville, N.C., lives in Deephaven, Minn. Quarterback Michigan State 1974-77. No pro playing experience. College coach: Michigan State 1977, 1980-82, Central Michigan 1978-79, North Carolina State 1983-85, Rice 1986-88, Stanford 1989-91. Pro coach: Joined Vikings in 1992.

Mike Wolf, assistant strength and conditioning; born May 15, 1965, Allentown, Pa., lives in Eden Prairie, Minn. Center Penn State 1983-87. No pro playing experience. College coach: Vanderbilt 1988-89, Lehigh 1990, Penn State 1991. Pro coach: Joined Vikings in 1992.

Gary Zauner, special teams; born November 2, 1950, Milwaukee, Wis., lives in Eden Prairie, Minn. Kicker Wisconsin-LaCrosse 1968-72. No pro playing experience. College coach: Brigham Young 1979-80, San Diego State 1981-86, New Mexico 1987-88, Long Beach State 1990-91. Pro coach: Joined Vikings in 1994.

1994 FIRST-YEAR ROSTER

Name	Pos.	Ht.	Wt.	Birthdate	College	Hometown	How Acq.
Bercich, Pete	LB	6-1	240	12/23/71	Notre Dame	Joliet, Ill.	D7
Boudreaux, Frank (1)	DT	6-5	273	6/20/70	Northwestern	Honolulu, Hawaii	FA
Boyd, Malik	CB	5-10	175	11/5/70	Southern	Houston, Tex.	FA
Boyd, Tracy (1)	T	6-4	296	8/27/67	Elizabeth City State	Crowley, La.	FA
Brown, Phil	RB	5-10	210	12/30/70	Texas	Commerce, Tex.	FA
Buck, Edward	S	5-11	175	2/6/71	Alcorn State	Brandon, Miss.	FA
Gray, Lance	RB	6-1	220	6/14/70	Nebraska	Owego, N.Y.	FA
Griffith, Robert (1)	CB-S	5-11	200	11/30/70	San Diego State	San Diego, Calif.	FA
Hammonds, Shelly	CB	5-10	187	2/13/71	Penn State	Barnwell, S.C.	D5
Harrison, Todd (1)	TE	6-4	260	3/20/69	North Carolina State	Gainesville, Fla.	FA
Jones, Richard (1)	P	6-3	198	3/25/65	Arizona State	Scottsdale, Ariz.	FA
Jordan, Andrew	TE	6-4	268	6/21/72	Western Carolina	Charlotte, N.C.	D6
Lasley, J.J. (1)	RB	6-0	220	2/9/70	Stanford	Encino, Calif.	FA
Lenseigne, Tony (1)	TE	6-4	235	8/7/69	Eastern Washington	Yakima, Wash.	FA
Palmer, David	RB	5-8	167	11/19/72	Alabama	Birmingham, Ala.	D2a
Riemer, Troy	T	6-5	287	12/1/70	Texas	Austin, Tex.	FA
Sims, William (1)	LB	6-3	265	12/30/70	S.W. Louisiana	Brooks County, Ga.	FA
Smith, Fernando	DE	6-6	270	8/2/71	Jackson State	Flint, Mich.	D2b
Staten, Robert (1)	RB	5-11	235	1/23/69	Jackson State	Shubuta, Miss.	FA
Steussie, Todd	T	6-5	298	12/1/70	California	Canoga Park, Calif.	D1b
Washington, DeWayne	CB	5-11	192	12/1/72	North Carolina State	Burham, N.C.	D1a
Wells, Mike	DT	6-3	287	1/6/71	Iowa	Arnold, Mo.	D4

The term NFL Rookie is defined as a player who is in his first season of professional football and has not been on the roster of another professional football team for any regular-season or postseason games. A Rookie is designated by an "R" on NFL rosters. Players who have been active in another professional football league or players who have NFL experience, including either preseason training camp or being on an Active List or Inactive List, or on Reserve/Injured or Reserve/Physically Unable to Perform for fewer than six regular-season games, are termed NFL First-Year Players. An NFL First-Year Player is designated by a "1" on NFL rosters. Thereafter, a player is credited with an additional year of experience for each season in which he accumulates six games on the Active List or Inactive List, or on Reserve/Injured or Reserve/Physically Unable to Perform.

NOTES

National Football Conference
Western Division
Team Colors: Old Gold, Black, and White
6928 Saints Drive
Metairie, Louisiana 70003
Telephone: (504) 733-0255

CLUB OFFICIALS

Owner: Tom Benson
Executive Vice President/Administration: Jim Miller
Vice President/Football Operations: Bill Kuharich
Vice President/Head Coach: Jim Mora
Vice President/Marketing: Greg Suit
Director of Pro Personnel: Chet Franklin
Treasurer: Bruce Broussard
Administrative Coordinator: Austin Dejan
Comptroller: Charleen Sharpe
Director of Corporate Sales: Bill Ferrante
Director of Media Relations: Rusty Kasmiersky
Assistant Director of Media Relations: Neal Gulkis
Data Processing Manager: Jay Romig
Director of Travel/Entertainment/Special Projects:
   Barra Birrcher
Director of Community Relations: Chanel Lagarde
Player Personnel Scouts: Bill Baker, Hamp Cook,
   Hokie Gajan, Tom Marino, Carmen Piccone
Ticket Manager: Sandy King
Trainer: Dean Kleinschmidt
Equipment Manager: Dan Simmons
Video Director: Albert Aucoin
Stadium: Louisiana Superdome
   •**Capacity:** 69,056
   1500 Poydras Street
   New Orleans, Louisiana 70112
Playing Surface: AstroTurf
Training Camp: University of Wisconsin-La Crosse
   La Crosse, Wisconsin 54601

1994 SCHEDULE
PRESEASON

Aug. 5	at New England	8:00
Aug. 13	at Minnesota	7:00
Aug. 19	**Green Bay**	7:00
Aug. 25	**Dallas**	7:00

REGULAR SEASON

Sept. 4	**Kansas City**	12:00
Sept. 11	**Washington**	3:00
Sept. 18	at Tampa Bay	1:00
Sept. 25	at San Francisco	1:00
Oct. 2	**New York Giants**	3:00
Oct. 9	at Chicago	12:00
Oct. 16	**San Diego**	3:00
Oct. 23	**Los Angeles Rams**	12:00
Oct. 30	Open Date	
Nov. 6	at Minnesota	12:00
Nov. 13	**Atlanta**	12:00
Nov. 20	at Los Angeles Raiders	1:00
Nov. 28	**San Francisco** (Monday)	8:00
Dec. 4	at Los Angeles Rams	1:00
Dec. 11	at Atlanta	8:00
Dec. 19	**Dallas** (Monday)	8:00
Dec. 24	at Denver	2:00

RECORD HOLDERS
INDIVIDUAL RECORDS—CAREER

Category	Name	Performance
Rushing (Yds.)	George Rogers, 1981-84	4,267
Passing (Yds.)	Archie Manning, 1971-1982	21,734
Passing (TDs)	Archie Manning, 1971-1982	115
Receiving (No.)	Eric Martin, 1985-1993	532
Receiving (Yds.)	Eric Martin, 1985-1993	7,854
Interceptions	Dave Waymer, 1980-89	37
Punting (Avg.)	Tommy Barnhardt, 1987, 1989-1993	42.9
Punt Return (Avg.)	Tyrone Hughes, 1993	13.6
Kickoff Return (Avg.)	Walter Roberts, 1967	26.3
Field Goals	Morten Andersen, 1982-1993	274
Touchdowns (Tot.)	Dalton Hilliard, 1986-1993	53
Points	Morten Andersen, 1982-1993	1,202

INDIVIDUAL RECORDS—SINGLE SEASON

Category	Name	Performance
Rushing (Yds.)	George Rogers, 1981	1,674
Passing (Yds.)	Archie Manning, 1980	3,716
Passing (TDs)	Archie Manning, 1980	23
Receiving (No.)	Eric Martin, 1988	85
Receiving (Yds.)	Eric Martin, 1989	1,090
Interceptions	Dave Whitsell, 1967	10
Punting (Avg.)	Tommy Barnhardt, 1992	44.0
Punt Return (Avg.)	Mel Gray, 1987	14.7
Kickoff Return (Avg.)	Don Shy, 1969	27.9
Field Goals	Morten Andersen, 1985	31
Touchdowns (Tot.)	Dalton Hilliard, 1989	18
Points	Morten Andersen, 1987	121

INDIVIDUAL RECORDS—SINGLE GAME

Category	Name	Performance
Rushing (Yds.)	George Rogers, 9-4-83	206
Passing (Yds.)	Archie Manning, 12-7-80	377
Passing (TDs)	Billy Kilmer, 11-2-69	6
Receiving (No.)	Tony Galbreath, 9-10-78	14
Receiving (Yds.)	Wes Chandler, 9-2-79	205
Interceptions	Tommy Myers, 9-3-78	3
	Dave Waymer, 10-6-85	3
	Reggie Sutton, 10-18-87	3
	Gene Atkins, 12-22-91	3
Field Goals	Morten Andersen, 12-1-85	5
	Morten Andersen, 11-15-87	5
	Morten Andersen, 12-3-92	5
Touchdowns (Tot.)	Many times	3
	Last time by Rueben Mayes, 9-23-90	
Points	Many times	18
	Last time by Rueben Mayes, 9-23-90	

COACHING HISTORY
(160-241-5)

1967-70	Tom Fears*	13-34-2
1970-72	J.D. Roberts	7-25-3
1973-75	John North**	11-23-0
1975	Ernie Hefferle	1-7-0
1976-77	Hank Stram	7-21-0
1978-80	Dick Nolan***	15-29-0
1980	Dick Stanfel	1-3-0
1981-85	O.A. (Bum) Phillips****	27-42-0
1985	Wade Phillips	1-3-0
1986-93	Jim Mora	77-54-0

  *Released after seven games in 1970
 **Released after six games in 1975
***Released after 12 games in 1980
****Resigned after 12 games in 1985

LOUISIANA SUPERDOME

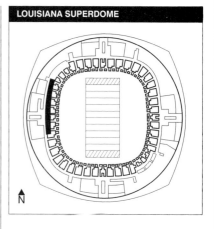

1993 TEAM RECORD

PRESEASON (4-1)

Date	Result		Opponents
7/31	W	28-16	vs. Philadelphia at Tokyo
8/7	W	37-28	vs. Houston at San Antonio
8/14	W	26-17	vs. Green Bay at Madison
8/23	W	20-14	Chicago
8/27	L	16-17	Detroit

REGULAR SEASON (8-8)

Date	Result		Opponents	Att.
9/5	W	33-21	Houston	69,029
9/12	W	34-31	at Atlanta	64,287
9/19	W	14-3	Detroit	69,039
9/26	W	16-13	San Francisco	69,041
10/3	W	37-6	at L.A. Rams	50,709
10/17	L	14-37	at Pittsburgh	56,056
10/24	L	15-26	Atlanta	69,043
10/31	W	20-17	at Phoenix	36,778
11/14	L	17-19	Green Bay	69,043
11/22	L	7-42	at San Francisco	66,500
11/28	W	17-14	at Minnesota	53,030
12/5	L	13-17	at Cleveland	60,388
12/12	L	20-23	L.A. Rams	69,033
12/20	L	14-24	N.Y. Giants	69,036
12/26	L	26-37	at Philadelphia	50,085
1/2	W	20-13	Cincinnati	58,036

SCORE BY PERIODS

Saints	66	80	60	111	0	—	317
Opponents	78	106	72	87	0	—	343

ATTENDANCE

Home 541,300 Away 437,833 Total 979,133
Single-game home record, 70,940 (11-4-79)
Single-season home record, 548,655 (1991)

1993 TEAM STATISTICS

	Saints	Opp.
Total First Downs	264	273
Rushing	94	116
Passing	158	145
Penalty	12	12
Third Down: Made/Att	72/203	92/227
Third Down Pct.	35.5	40.5
Fourth Down: Made/Att	7/11	9/16
Fourth Down Pct.	63.6	56.3
Total Net Yards	4707	4696
Avg. Per Game	294.2	293.5
Total Plays	935	1008
Avg. Per Play	5.0	4.7
Net Yards Rushing	1766	2090
Avg. Per Game	110.4	130.6
Total Rushes	414	513
Net Yards Passing	2941	2606
Avg. Per Game	183.8	162.9
Sacked/Yards Lost	40/242	51/318
Gross Yards	3183	2924
Att./Completions	481/274	444/259
Completion Pct.	57.0	58.3
Had Intercepted	21	10
Punts/Avg.	77/43.6	80/42.3
Net Punting Avg.	77/37.5	80/34.8
Penalties/Yards Lost	81/663	86/590
Fumbles/Ball Lost	24/13	30/20
Touchdowns	33	39
Rushing	10	7
Passing	18	22
Returns	5	10
Avg. Time of Possession	28:32	31:28

1993 INDIVIDUAL STATISTICS

PASSING

	Att	Cmp	Yds.	Pct.	TD	Int	Tkld.	Rate
Wilson	388	221	2457	57.0	12	15	37/225	70.1
M. Buck	54	32	448	59.3	4	3	3/17	87.6
Walsh	38	20	271	52.6	2	3	0/0	60.3
Barnhardt	1	1	7	100.0	0	0	0/0	95.8
Saints	481	274	3183	57.0	18	21	40/242	71.4
Opponents	444	259	2924	58.3	22	10	51/318	85.3

SCORING

	TD R	TD P	TD Rt	PAT	FG	Saf	PTS
Andersen	0	0	0	33/33	28/35	0	117
Early	0	6	0	0/0	0/0	0	36
Brown	2	1	0	0/0	0/0	0	18
Hilliard	2	1	0	0/0	0/0	0	18
Hughes	0	0	3	0/0	0/0	0	18
E. Martin	0	3	0	0/0	0/0	0	18
Muster	3	0	0	0/0	0/0	0	18
Smith	0	2	0	0/0	0/0	0	12
Brenner	0	1	0	0/0	0/0	0	6
Dowdell	0	1	0	0/0	0/0	0	6
McAfee	1	0	0	0/0	0/0	0	6
Mills	0	0	1	0/0	0/0	0	6
Neal	1	0	0	0/0	0/0	0	6
Ned	1	0	0	0/0	0/0	0	6
Newman	0	1	0	0/0	0/0	0	6
Small	0	1	0	0/0	0/0	0	6
Turner	0	1	0	0/0	0/0	0	6
Warren	0	0	1	0/0	0/0	0	6
Stowers	0	0	0	0/0	0/0	1	2
Saints	10	18	5	33/33	28/35	1	317
Opponents	7	22	10	35/39	24/30	1	343

RUSHING

	Att.	Yds.	Avg.	LG	TD
Brown	180	705	3.9	60	2
Wilson	31	230	7.4	44	0
Muster	64	214	3.3	18	3
Neal	21	175	8.3	74t	2
Hilliard	50	165	3.3	16	2
McAfee	51	160	3.1	27	1
Ned	9	71	7.9	35t	1
Early	2	32	16.0	26	0
Barnhardt	1	18	18.0	18	0
M. Buck	1	0	0.0	0	0
Walsh	4	-4	-1.0	-1	0
Saints	414	1766	4.3	74t	10
Opponents	513	2090	4.1	71t	7

RECEIVING

	No.	Yds.	Avg.	LG	TD
E. Martin	66	950	14.4	54t	3
Early	45	670	14.9	63t	6
Hilliard	40	296	7.4	34	1
Muster	23	195	8.5	31	0
Brown	21	170	8.1	19	1
Smith	16	180	11.3	23	2
Small	16	164	10.3	17	1
Turner	12	163	13.6	52	1
Brenner	11	171	15.5	27	1
Ned	9	54	6.0	14	0
Newman	8	121	15.1	32	1
Dowdell	6	46	7.7	11t	1
McAfee	1	3	3.0	3	0
Saints	274	3183	11.6	63t	18
Opponents	259	2924	11.3	98t	22

INTERCEPTIONS

	No.	Yds.	Avg.	LG	TD
Atkins	3	59	19.7	37	0
Taylor	2	32	16.0	30	0
V. Buck	2	28	14.0	28	0
Jones	1	12	12.0	12	0
Turnbull	1	2	2.0	2	0
Cook	1	0	0.0	0	0
Saints	10	133	13.3	37	0
Opponents	21	444	21.1	67t	6

PUNTING

	No.	Yds.	Avg.	In 20	LG
Barnhardt	77	3356	43.6	26	58
Saints	77	3356	43.6	26	58
Opponents	80	3384	42.3	20	60

PUNT RETURNS

	No.	FC	Yds.	Avg.	LG	TD
Hughes	37	21	503	13.6	83t	2
Newman	1	0	14	14.0	14	0
Saints	38	21	517	13.6	83t	2
Opponents	36	18	348	9.7	75t	1

KICKOFF RETURNS

	No.	Yds.	Avg.	LG	TD
Hughes	30	753	25.1	99t	1
McAfee	28	580	20.7	55	0
Brown	3	58	19.3	23	0
Hilliard	1	17	17.0	17	0
Dowdell	0	52	—	52	0
Saints	62	1460	23.5	99t	1
Opponents	40	788	19.7	47	0

SACKS

	No.
Turnbull	13.0
Jackson	11.5
Johnson	5.0
W. Martin	5.0
V. Buck	3.0
Miller	2.5
Goff	2.0
Mills	2.0
Williams	2.0
Atkins	1.0
Cook	1.0
Jones	1.0
Smeenge	1.0
Warren	1.0
Saints	51.0
Opponents	40.0

1994 DRAFT CHOICES

Round	Name	Pos.	College
1	Joe Johnson	DE	Louisville
2	Mario Bates	RB	Arizona State
3	Winfred Tubbs	LB	Texas
4	Doug Nussmeier	QB	Idaho
5	Herman Carroll	DE	Mississippi State
	Craig Novitsky	G	UCLA
6	Derrell Mitchell	WR	Texas Tech
7	Lance Lundberg	T	Nebraska

1994 VETERAN ROSTER

No.		Name	Pos.	Ht.	Wt.	Birthdate	NFL Exp.	College	Hometown	How Acq.	'93 Games/ Starts
7		Andersen, Morten	K	6-2	221	8/19/60	13	Michigan State	Indianapolis, Ind.	D4-'82	16/0
6		Barnhardt, Tommy	P	6-2	207	6/11/63	8	North Carolina	China Grove, N.C.	FA-'89	16/0
24		Brown, Derek	RB	5-9	186	4/15/71	2	Nebraska	Anaheim, Calif.	D4b-'93	13/12
16		Buck, Mike	QB	6-3	227	4/22/67	5	Maine	Sayville, N.Y.	D6a-'90	4/1
26		Buck, Vince	CB	6-0	198	1/12/68	5	Central State, Ohio	Owensboro, Ky.	D2-'90	16/16
40		Coghill, George	S	6-2	196	3/30/70	2	Wake Forest	Fredericksburg, Va.	FA-'93	0*
41	#	Cook, Toi	CB	5-11	188	12/3/64	8	Stanford	Van Nuys, Calif.	D8-'87	16/16
71		Cooper, Richard	T	6-5	290	11/1/64	5	Tennessee	Memphis, Tenn.	FA-'89	16/16
63		Davidson, Jeff	G	6-5	305	10/3/67	4	Ohio State	Akron, Ohio	FA-'94	0*
95		Dixon, Ronnie	NT	6-2	292	5/10/71	2	Cincinnati	Clinton, N.C.	D6-'93	2/0
72		Dombrowski, Jim	G	6-5	298	10/19/63	9	Virginia	Williamsville, N.Y.	D1-'86	16/2
80		Dowdell, Marcus	WR	5-10	179	5/22/70	2	Tennessee State	Birmingham, Ala.	D10-'92	9/1
63		Dunbar, Karl	DE	6-4	275	5/18/67	3	Louisiana State	Opelousas, La.	FA-'92	13/1
32		Dunbar, Vaughn	RB	5-10	204	9/4/68	3	Indiana	Ft. Wayne, Ind.	D1-'92	0*
89		Early, Quinn	WR	6-0	188	4/13/65	7	Iowa	South Great Neck, N.Y.	PB(SD)-'91	16/15
17	t-	Everett, Jim	QB	6-5	212	1/3/63	9	Purdue	Albuquerque, N.M.	T(Rams)-'94	10/9*
55		Freeman, Reggie	LB	6-1	233	5/8/70	2	Florida State	Clewiston, Fla.	D2-'93	10/0
66		Garten, Joe	C-G	6-2	290	8/13/68	3	Colorado	Valencia, Calif.	FA-'94	0*
91		Goff, Robert	NT	6-3	270	10/2/65	7	Auburn	Bradenton, Fla.	T(TB)-'90	16/9
81		Haynes, Michael	WR	6-0	184	12/24/65	7	Northern Arizona	New Orleans, La.	FA-'94	16/16*
38		Henderson, Othello	S	6-0	192	8/23/72	2	UCLA	Killeen, Tex.	D7-'93	5/1
61	#	Hilgenberg, Joel	C-G	6-2	252	7/10/62	11	Iowa	Iowa City, Iowa	D4-'84	9/9
21	#	Hilliard, Dalton	RB	5-8	204	1/21/64	9	Louisiana State	Patterson, La.	D2-'86	16/0
33		Hughes, Tyrone	CB	5-9	175	1/14/70	2	Nebraska	New Orleans, La.	D5-'93	16/0
57	#	Jackson, Rickey	LB	6-2	243	3/20/58	14	Pittsburgh	Pahokee, Fla.	D2-'81	16/16
53		Johnson, Vaughan	LB	6-3	235	3/24/62	9	North Carolina State	Morehead City, N.C.	SD1-'84	15/13
27		Jones, Reginald	CB	6-1	202	1/11/69	4	Memphis State	West Memphis, Ark.	D5-'91	12/2
43		Legette, Tyrone	CB	5-9	177	2/15/70	3	Nebraska	Columbia, S.C.	D3-'92	14/1
46		Lumpkin, Sean	S	6-0	206	1/4/70	3	Minnesota	St. Louis Park, Minn.	D4b-'92	12/0
84		Martin, Eric	WR	6-1	207	11/8/61	10	Louisiana State	Van Vleck, Tex.	D7-'85	16/13
93		Martin, Wayne	DE	6-5	275	10/26/65	6	Arkansas	Cherry Valley, Ark.	D1-'89	16/16
39	#	Maxie, Brett	S	6-2	194	1/13/62	10	Texas Southern	Dallas, Tex.	FA-'85	1/1
96		Mayfield, Corey	NT	6-3	290	2/25/70	2	Oklahoma	Tyler, Tex.	FA-'94	0*
69		Miller, Les	DE	6-7	285	3/1/65	8	Fort Hays State	Arkansas City, Kan.	PB(SD)-'91	13/11
51	#	Mills, Sam	LB	5-9	225	6/3/59	9	Montclair State	Long Branch, N.J.	FA-'86	9/7
22		Muster, Brad	RB	6-4	235	4/11/65	7	Stanford	Santa Rosa, Calif.	FA-'93	13/11
23		Neal, Lorenzo	RB	5-11	240	12/27/70	2	Fresno State	Lemoore, Calif.	D4a-'93	2/2
36		Ned, Derrick	RB	6-1	210	1/5/69	2	Grambling State	Eunice, La.	FA-'92	14/1
79		Nelson, Royce	G	6-4	315	8/9/70	2	Nicholls State	New Orleans, La.	FA-'93	0*
70		Port, Chris	G-T	6-5	290	11/2/67	4	Duke	Wanaque, N.J.	FA-'90	15/15
64		Ricketts, Tom	G	6-5	305	11/21/65	6	Pittsburgh	Murrysville, Pa.	FA-'94	3/0*
77		Roaf, William	T	6-5	300	4/18/70	2	Louisiana Tech	Pine Bluff, Ark.	D1a-'93	16/16
83		Small, Torrance	WR	6-3	201	9/6/70	3	Alcorn State	Tampa, Fla.	D5-'92	11/0
99		Smeenge, Joel	DE	6-5	250	4/1/68	4	Western Michigan	Grand Rapids, Mich.	D3-'90	16/2
82		Smith, Irv	TE	6-3	246	10/13/71	2	Notre Dame	Pemberton, N.J.	D1b-'93	16/8
37		Spencer, Jimmy	CB	5-9	180	3/29/69	3	Florida	South Bay, Fla.	FA-'92	16/3
52		Stonebreaker, Michael	LB	6-0	235	1/14/67	2	Notre Dame	Glencoe, Ill.	FA-'94	0*
34		Tillison, Ed	RB	5-10	229	12/12/69	3	N.W. Missouri State	Pearl River, La.	FA-'94	0*
97		Turnbull, Renaldo	DE	6-4	255	1/5/66	5	West Virginia	St. Thomas, Virgin Islands	D1-'90	15/14
62		Uhlenhake, Jeff	C	6-3	284	1/28/66	6	Ohio State	Newark, Ohio	UFA(Mia)-'94	5/5*
87		Wainright, Frank	TE	6-3	236	10/10/67	4	Northern Colorado	Arvada, Colo.	D8-'91	16/2
85		Walls, Wesley	TE	6-5	250	2/26/66	6	Mississippi	Pontotic, Miss.	UFA(SF)-'94	6/0*
73	#	Warren, Frank	DE	6-4	290	9/14/59	13	Auburn	Birmingham, Ala.	D3a-'81	8/7
94	#	Wilks, Jim	NT	6-5	275	3/12/58	14	San Diego State	Pasadena, Calif.	D12-'81	8/1
90		Williams, James	LB	6-0	230	10/10/68	5	Mississippi State	North Natchez, Miss.	D6b-'90	16/9
65		Williams, Willie	T	6-6	295	8/6/67	3	Louisiana State	Houston, Tex.	FA-'94	0*
18		Wilson, Wade	QB	6-3	206	2/1/59	14	East Texas State	Commerce, Tex.	FA-'93	14/14
92	#	Winston, DeMond	LB	6-2	239	9/14/68	5	Vanderbilt	Lansing, Mich.	D4-'90	16/0

* Coghill, V. Dunbar, Nelson, and Tillison missed '93 season due to injury; Davidson last active with Denver in '92; Everett played 10 games with L.A. Rams in '93; Garten on injured reserve with Green Bay in '92; Haynes played 16 games with Atlanta; Mayfield last active with Tampa Bay in '92; Ricketts played 3 games with Kansas City; Stonebreaker last active with Chicago in '91; Uhlenhake played 5 games with Miami; Walls played 6 games with San Francisco; Williams last active with Arizona in '91.

\# Unrestricted free agent; subject to developments.

† Restricted free agent; subject to developments.

t- Saints traded for Everett (L.A. Rams).

Players lost through free agency (4): S Gene Atkins (Mia; 16 games in '93), G Derek Kennard (Dall; 16) S Keith Taylor (Wash; 16), WR Floyd Turner (Ind; 10).

Also played with Saints in '93—TE Jesse Anderson (1 game), TE Hoby Brenner (10), DE Jeff Faulkner (1), C Jay Hilgenberg (9), CB Cedric Mack (1), RB Fred McAfee (15), WR Patrick Newman (16), TE Tommie Stowers (4).

COACHING STAFF

Vice President-Head Coach,
Jim Mora

Pro Career: Begins ninth year as an NFL head coach. Led Saints to a 12-4 record and their third straight playoff appearance in 1992. Guided Saints to an 11-5 mark and the club's first-ever NFC West title in 1991. Was named 1987 NFL coach of the year after leading Saints to a 12-3 record and the team's first playoff appearance. Came to New Orleans following a three-year career as the winningest coach in USFL history as head coach of the Philadelphia/Baltimore Stars. Directed Stars to championship game in each of his three seasons and won league championship in 1984 and 1985. He won USFL coach of the year honors following the 1984 season. Mora began his pro coaching career in 1978 as defensive line coach of the Seattle Seahawks. In 1982, he became defensive coordinator of the New England Patriots and played a vital role in the Patriots' march to the playoffs that year. No pro playing experience. Career record: 77-54.

Background: Played tight end and defensive end at Occidental College. Assistant coach at Occidental from 1960-63 and head coach from 1964-66. Linebacker coach at Stanford (1967) on a staff that included former Eagles head coach Dick Vermeil. Defensive assistant at Colorado 1968-73. Linebacker coach under Vermeil at UCLA 1974. Defensive coordinator at Washington 1975-77. Received bachelor's degree in physical education from Occidental in 1957. Also holds master's degree in education from Southern California.

Personal: Born May 24, 1935, in Glendale, Calif. Jim and his wife, Connie, live in Metairie, La., and have three sons—Michael, Stephen, and Jim (defensive backs coach for the Saints).

ASSISTANT COACHES

Vic Fangio, linebackers; born August 22, 1958, Dunmore, Pa., lives in Destrehan, La. Defensive back East Stroudsburg 1976-78. No pro playing experience. College coach: North Carolina 1983. Pro coach: Philadelphia/Baltimore Stars (USFL) 1984-85, joined Saints in 1986.

Joe Marciano, tight ends-special teams; born February 10, 1954, Scranton, Pa., lives in Kenner, La. Quarterback Temple 1972-75. No pro playing experience. College coach: East Stroudsburg 1977, Rhode Island 1978-79, Villanova 1980, Penn State 1981, Temple 1982. Pro coach: Philadelphia/Baltimore Stars (USFL) 1983-85, joined Saints in 1986.

John Matsko, offensive line; born February 2, 1951, Cleveland, Ohio, lives in Mandeville, La. Fullback Kent State 1970-73. No pro playing experience. College coach: Kent State 1973, Miami, Ohio 1974-75, 1977, North Carolina 1978-84, Navy 1985, Arizona 1986, Southern California 1987-91. Pro coach: Phoenix Cardinals 1992-93, joined Saints in 1994.

Jim Mora, defensive backs; born November 19, 1961, Los Angeles, Calif., lives in New Orleans. Defensive back Washington 1980-83. No pro playing experience. College coach: Washington 1984. Pro coach: San Diego Chargers 1985-91, joined Saints in 1992.

Chip Myers, offensive assistant; born July 9, 1945, Panama City, Fla., lives in Mandeville, La. Receiver Northwestern Oklahoma 1964-66. Pro receiver San Francisco 49ers 1967, Cincinnati Bengals 1969-76. College coach: Illinois 1980-82. Pro coach: Tampa Bay Buccaneers 1983-84, Indianapolis Colts 1985-88, New York Jets 1990-93, joined Saints in 1994.

Russell Paternostro, strength and conditioning; born July 21, 1940, New Orleans, La., lives in Covington, La. San Diego State. No college or pro playing experience. Pro coach: Joined Saints in 1981.

John Pease, defensive line; born October 14, 1943, Pittsburgh, Pa., lives in Kenner, La. Wingback Utah 1963-64. No pro playing experience. College coach: Fullerton, Calif., J.C. 1970-73, Long Beach State 1974-76, Utah 1977, Washington 1978-83. Pro coach: Philadelphia/Baltimore Stars (USFL) 1983-85, joined Saints in 1986.

1994 FIRST-YEAR ROSTER

Name	Pos.	Ht.	Wt.	Birthdate	College	Hometown	How Acq.
Backes, Tom (1)	T	6-4	273	3/19/68	Oklahoma	El Paso, Tex.	FA
Bates, Mario	RB	6-1	217	1/16/73	Arizona State	Tucson, Ariz.	D2
Bowden, Andre (1)	LB	6-3	240	4/4/68	Fayetteville State	Fuquay-Varina, N.C.	FA
Brown, Tim	LB	6-0	222	1/20/71	West Virginia	McKeesport, Pa.	FA
Byrd, Israel (1)	CB	5-11	184	2/1/71	Utah State	St. Louis, Mo.	FA
Caldwell, Mike	WR	6-0	200	3/28/71	California	San Ramon, Calif.	FA
Campbell, Matt	TE	6-5	256	7/14/72	South Carolina	North Augusta, S.C.	FA
Carroll, Herman	DE	6-4	265	6/20/71	Mississippi State	North Natchez, Miss.	D5a
Cooper, Hunkie (1)	WR	5-8	185	5/17/69	Nevada-Las Vegas	Palestine, Tex.	FA
Dawkins, Ralph	RB	5-8	195	10/20/70	Louisville	Jacksonville, Fla.	FA
Dixon, Ernest	LB	6-1	250	10/17/71	South Carolina	Ft. Mill, S.C.	FA
Hamilton, Brandon	CB	5-9	173	3/5/72	Tulane	Baton Rouge, La.	FA
Hanna, Jim	NT	6-4	255	8/10/71	Louisville	W. Palm Beach, Fla.	FA
Henry, Adam	WR	6-1	184	4/27/72	McNeese State	Beaumont, Tex.	FA
Jeffcoat, Jerold (1)	NT	6-2	285	8/30/69	Temple	Matawan, N.J.	FA
Johnson, Joe	DE	6-4	285	7/11/72	Louisville	St. Louis, Mo.	D1
Johnson, Tyrone	WR	5-11	171	9/4/71	Western State, Colo.	Aurora, Colo.	FA
Kline, Alan	T	6-5	277	5/25/71	Ohio State	Tiffin, Ohio	FA
Knight, Kelvin	S	6-0	203	1/7/71	Mississippi State	North Natchez, Miss.	FA
Lundberg, Lance	T	6-4	308	8/15/70	Nebraska	Wausa, Neb.	D7
McCleskey, J.J. (1)	WR	5-7	177	4/10/70	Tennessee	Knoxville, Tenn.	FA
McDaniels, Terry	T	6-3	287	4/24/71	Southern California	Pasadena, Calif.	FA
Milburn, Darryl (1)	DE	6-3	245	10/25/68	Grambling	Baton Rouge, La.	FA
Mitchell, Darrell	WR	5-9	190	9/16/71	Texas Tech	Miami, Fla.	D6
Novitsky, Craig	G	6-5	295	5/12/71	UCLA	Dumfries, Va.	D5b
Nussmeier, Doug	QB	6-3	211	12/11/70	Idaho	Lake Oswego, Ore.	D4
Orr, Thomas	CB	5-10	197	8/14/72	West Virginia	Elizabeth, N.J.	FA
Pahukoa, Shane (1)	S	6-2	202	11/25/70	Washington	Marysville, Calif.	FA
Rhem, Steve	WR	6-2	212	11/9/71	Minnesota	Ocala, Fla.	FA
Rollins, Baron (1)	G	6-4	335	7/23/70	Louisiana Tech	Winnsboro, La.	FA
Roth, Tom (1)	G	6-5	285	9/19/68	Southern Illinois	Godfrey, Ill.	FA
Thomas, Franklin (1)	TE	6-3	262	4/22/68	Grambling	New Orleans, La.	FA
Tubbs, Winfred	LB	6-4	250	9/24/70	Texas	Fairfield, Tex.	D3
Washington, Sean	CB	5-10	182	5/25/71	Rice	Houston, Tex.	FA
Wilson, Ray	S	6-2	202	8/26/71	New Mexico	Panama City, Fla.	FA
Young, Jim	CB	5-11	188	2/16/71	Purdue	Union, N.J.	FA

The term NFL Rookie is defined as a player who is in his first season of professional football and has not been on the roster of another professional football team for any regular-season or postseason games. A Rookie is designated by an "R" on NFL rosters. Players who have been active in another professional football league or players who have NFL experience, including either preseason training camp or being on an Active List or Inactive List, or on Reserve/Injured or Reserve/Physically Unable to Perform for fewer than six regular-season games, are termed NFL First-Year Players. An NFL First-Year Player is designated by a "1" on NFL rosters. Thereafter, a player is credited with an additional year of experience for each season in which he accumulates six games on the Active List or Inactive List, or on Reserve/Injured or Reserve/Physically Unable to Perform.

NOTES

Steve Sidwell, defensive coordinator; born August 30, 1944, Winfield, Kan., lives in New Orleans. Linebacker Colorado 1962-65. No pro playing experience. College coach: Colorado 1966-73, Nevada-Las Vegas 1974-75, Southern Methodist 1976-81. Pro coach: New England Patriots 1982-84, Indianapolis Colts 1985, joined Saints in 1986.

Jim Skipper, running backs; born January 23, 1949, Breaux Bridge, La., lives in Kenner, La. Defensive back Whittier College 1971-72. No pro playing experience. College coach: Cal Poly-Pomona 1974-76, San Jose State 1977-78, Pacific 1979, Oregon 1980-82. Pro coach: Philadelphia/Baltimore Stars (USFL) 1983-85, joined Saints in 1986.

Carl Smith, offensive coordinator-quarterbacks; born April 26, 1948, Wasco, Calif., lives in Kenner, La. Defensive back Cal Poly-SLO 1968-70. No pro playing experience. College coach: Cal Poly-SLO 1971,

Colorado 1972-73, Southwestern Louisiana 1974-78, Lamar 1979-81, North Carolina State 1982. Pro coach: Philadelphia/Baltimore Stars (USFL) 1983-85, joined Saints in 1986.

Steve Walters, wide receivers; born June 16, 1948, Jonesboro, Ark., lives in Destrehan, La. Quarterback-defensive back Arkansas 1967-70. No pro playing experience. College coach: Tampa 1973, Northeast Louisiana 1974-75, Morehead State 1976, Tulsa 1977-78, Memphis State 1979, Southern Methodist 1980-81, Alabama 1985. Pro coach: New England Patriots 1982-84, joined Saints in 1986.

Everett Withers, defensive assistant; born June 15, 1963, Charlotte, N.C., lives in Kenner, La. Defensive back Appalachian State 1983-86. No pro playing experience. College coach: Appalachian State 1987, Austin Peay 1988-90, Tulane 1991, Southern Mississippi 1992-93. Pro coach: Joined Saints in 1994.

National Football Conference
Eastern Division
Team Colors: Blue, Red, and White
Giants Stadium
East Rutherford, New Jersey 07073
Telephone: (201) 935-8111

CLUB OFFICIALS

President/Co-CEO: Wellington T. Mara
Chairman/Co-CEO: Preston Robert Tisch
Executive Vice President/General Counsel:
  John K. Mara, Esq.
Treasurer: Jonathan Tisch
Vice President-General Manager: George Young
Assistant General Manager: Harry Hulmes
Controller: John Pasquali
Director of Player Personnel: Tom Boisture
Director of Pro Personnel: Tim Rooney
Assistant Director of Player Personnel:
  Rick Donohue
Director of Administration: Tom Power
Senior Director of Marketing: Rusty Hawley
Director of Promotion: Frank Mara
Ticket Manager: John Gorman
Director of Public Relations: Pat Hanlon
Assistant Controller: Christine Prokops
Assistant Director of Public Relations: Aaron Salkin
Assistant Director of Marketing: Bill Smith
Head Trainer: Ronnie Barnes
Assistant Trainers: John Johnson, Michael Colello,
  Steve Kennelly
Equipment Manager: Ed Wagner, Jr.
Stadium: Giants Stadium •**Capacity:** 77,553
    East Rutherford, New Jersey 07073
Playing Surface: AstroTurf
Training Camp: Fairleigh Dickinson-Madison
    Florham Park, N.J. 07932

1994 SCHEDULE
PRESEASON

July 30	**Miami**	8:00
Aug. 6	**Cleveland**	8:00
Aug. 13	vs. San Diego at Berlin	1:30
Aug. 20	at New York Jets	8:00
Aug. 27	at Chicago	7:00

REGULAR SEASON

Sept. 4	**Philadelphia**	1:00
Sept. 11	at Arizona	5:00
Sept. 18	**Washington**	4:00
Sept. 25	Open Date	
Oct. 2	at New Orleans	3:00
Oct. 10	**Minnesota** (Monday)	9:00
Oct. 16	at Los Angeles Rams	1:00
Oct. 23	**Pittsburgh**	1:00
Oct. 30	**Detroit**	1:00
Nov. 7	at Dallas (Monday)	8:00
Nov. 13	**Arizona**	1:00
Nov. 21	at Houston (Monday)	8:00
Nov. 27	at Washington	4:00
Dec. 4	at Cleveland	4:00
Dec. 11	**Cincinnati**	1:00
Dec. 18	at Philadelphia	4:00

RECORD HOLDERS
INDIVIDUAL RECORDS—CAREER

Category	Name	Performance
Rushing (Yds.)	Joe Morris, 1982-88	5,296
Passing (Yds.)	Phil Simms, 1979-1993	33,462
Passing (TDs)	Phil Simms, 1979-1993	199
Receiving (No.)	Joe Morrison, 1959-1972	395
Receiving (Yds.)	Frank Gifford, 1952-1960, 1962-64	5,434
Interceptions	Emlen Tunnell, 1948-1958	74
Punting (Avg.)	Don Chandler, 1956-1964	43.8
Punt Return (Avg.)	David Meggett, 1989-1993	10.8
Kickoff Return (Avg.)	Rocky Thompson, 1971-72	27.2
Field Goals	Pete Gogolak, 1966-1974	126
Touchdowns (Tot.)	Frank Gifford, 1952-1960, 1962-64	78
Points	Pete Gogolak, 1966-1974	646

INDIVIDUAL RECORDS—SINGLE SEASON

Category	Name	Performance
Rushing (Yds.)	Joe Morris, 1986	1,516
Passing (Yds.)	Phil Simms, 1984	4,044
Passing (TDs)	Y.A. Tittle, 1963	36
Receiving (No.)	Earnest Gray 1983	78
Receiving (Yds.)	Homer Jones, 1967	1,209
Interceptions	Otto Schnellbacher, 1951	11
	Jim Patton, 1958	11
Punting (Avg.)	Don Chandler, 1959	46.6
Punt Return (Avg.)	Merle Hapes, 1942	15.5
Kickoff Return (Avg.)	John Salscheider, 1949	31.6
Field Goals	Ali Haji-Sheikh, 1983	35
Touchdowns (Tot.)	Joe Morris, 1985	21
Points	Ali Haji-Sheikh, 1983	127

INDIVIDUAL RECORDS—SINGLE GAME

Category	Name	Performance
Rushing (Yds.)	Gene Roberts, 11-12-50	218
Passing (Yds.)	Phil Simms, 10-13-85	513
Passing (TDs)	Y.A. Tittle, 10-28-62	*7
Receiving (No.)	Mark Bavaro, 10-13-85	12
Receiving (Yds.)	Del Shofner, 10-28-62	269
Interceptions	Many times	3
	Last time by Terry Kinard, 9-27-87	
Field Goals	Joe Danelo, 10-18-81	6
Touchdowns (Tot.)	Ron Johnson, 10-2-72	4
	Earnest Gray, 9-7-80	4
Points	Ron Johnson, 10-2-72	24
	Earnest Gray, 9-7-80	24

*NFL Record

Dec. 24	**Dallas**	1:00

COACHING HISTORY
(507-414-32)

1925	Bob Folwell	8-4-0
1926	Joe Alexander	8-4-1
1927-28	Earl Potteiger	15-8-3
1929-30	LeRoy Andrews*	24-5-1
1930	Benny Friedman	2-0-0
1930-53	Steve Owen	155-108-17
1954-60	Jim Lee Howell	55-29-4
1961-68	Allie Sherman	57-54-4
1969-73	Alex Webster	29-40-1
1974-76	Bill Arnsparger**	7-28-0
1976-78	John McVay	14-23-0
1979-82	Ray Perkins	24-35-0
1983-90	Bill Parcells	85-52-1
1991-92	Ray Handley	14-18-0
1993	Dan Reeves	12-6-0

*Released after 15 games in 1930
**Released after seven games in 1976

GIANTS STADIUM

N

1993 TEAM RECORD

PRESEASON (2-2)

Date	Result		Opponents
8/7	W	27-16	at Cincinnati
8/14	L	17-23	Pittsburgh
8/21	W	14-13	N.Y. Jets
8/28	L	17-23	at Miami

REGULAR SEASON (11-5)

Date	Result		Opponents	Att.
9/5	W	26-20	at Chicago	66,900
9/12	W	23-7	Tampa Bay	75,891
9/19	W	20-10	L.A. Rams	76,213
10/3	L	14-17	at Buffalo	79,283
10/10	W	41-7	at Washington	53,715
10/17	W	21-10	Philadelphia	76,050
10/31	L	6-10	N.Y. Jets	71,659
11/7	L	9-31	at Dallas	64,735
11/14	W	20-6	Washington	76,606
11/21	W	7-3	at Philadelphia	62,928
11/28	W	19-17	Phoenix	59,979
12/5	W	19-14	at Miami	72,161
12/12	W	20-6	Indianapolis	70,411
12/20	W	24-14	at New Orleans	69,036
12/26	L	6-17	at Phoenix	53,414
1/2	L	13-16	Dallas (OT)	77,356

POSTSEASON (1-1)

Date	Result		Opponents	Att.
1/9	W	17-10	Minnesota	75,089
1/15	L	3-44	at San Francisco	67,143

(OT) Overtime

SCORE BY PERIODS

Giants	61	112	43	72	0	—	288
Opponents	40	60	40	62	3	—	205

ATTENDANCE

Home 584,165   Away 522,172   Total 1,106,337
Single-game home record, 77,356 (1-2-94)
Single-season home record, 608,706 (1992)

1993 TEAM STATISTICS

	Giants	Opp.
Total First Downs	300	268
Rushing	127	89
Passing	153	161
Penalty	20	18
Third Down: Made/Att	90/221	67/196
Third Down Pct.	40.7	34.2
Fourth Down: Made/Att	5/11	12/23
Fourth Down Pct.	45.5	52.2
Total Net Yards	5145	4663
Avg. Per Game	321.6	291.4
Total Plays	1024	950
Avg. Per Play	5.0	4.9
Net Yards Rushing	2210	1547
Avg. Per Game	138.1	96.7
Total Rushes	560	395
Net Yards Passing	2935	3116
Avg. Per Game	183.4	194.8
Sacked/Yards Lost	40/245	41/238
Gross Yards	3180	3354
Att./Completions	424/257	514/298
Completion Pct.	60.6	58.0
Had Intercepted	9	18
Punts/Avg.	78/41.9	80/40.3
Net Punting Avg.	78/37.8	80/34.7
Penalties/Yards Lost	90/596	98/820
Fumbles/Ball Lost	19/8	27/10
Touchdowns	30	22
Rushing	11	7
Passing	17	13
Returns	2	2
Avg. Time of Possession	32:18	27:42

1993 INDIVIDUAL STATISTICS

PASSING

	Att	Cmp	Yds.	Pct.	TD	Int	Tkld.	Rate
Simms	400	247	3038	61.8	15	9	37/217	88.3
Graham	22	8	79	36.4	0	0	3/28	47.3
Meggett	2	2	63	100.0	2	0	0/0	158.3
Giants	424	257	3180	60.6	17	9	40/245	88.4
Opponents	514	298	3354	58.0	13	18	41/238	71.4

SCORING

	TD R	TD P	TD Rt	PAT	FG	Saf	PTS
Treadwell	0	0	0	28/29	25/31	0	103
Cross	0	5	0	0/0	0/0	0	30
Hampton	5	0	0	0/0	0/0	0	30
M. Jackson	0	4	0	0/0	0/0	0	24
Bunch	2	1	0	0/0	0/0	0	18
Calloway	0	3	0	0/0	0/0	0	18
Tillman	3	0	0	0/0	0/0	0	18
McCaffrey	0	2	0	0/0	0/0	0	12
Sherrard	0	2	0	0/0	0/0	0	12
Collins	0	0	1	0/0	0/0	0	6
Meggett	0	0	1	0/0	0/0	0	6
Rasheed	1	0	0	0/0	0/0	0	6
Daluiso	0	0	0	0/0	1/3	0	3
Hamilton	0	0	0	0/0	0/0	1	2
Giants	11	17	2	28/30	26/34	1	288
Opponents	7	13	2	22/22	17/23	0	205

RUSHING

	Att.	Yds.	Avg.	LG	TD
Hampton	292	1077	3.7	20	5
Tillman	121	585	4.8	58	3
Meggett	69	329	4.8	23	0
Bunch	33	128	3.9	13	2
Rasheed	9	42	4.7	23t	1
Simms	28	31	1.1	9	0
M. Jackson	3	25	8.3	20	0
Graham	2	-3	-1.5	-1	0
Da. Brown	3	-4	-1.3	-1	0
Giants	560	2210	3.9	58	11
Opponents	395	1547	3.9	46	7

RECEIVING

	No.	Yds.	Avg.	LG	TD
M. Jackson	58	708	12.2	40t	4
Meggett	38	319	8.4	50	0
Calloway	35	513	14.7	47	3
McCaffrey	27	335	12.4	31	2
Sherrard	24	433	18.0	55t	2
Cross	21	272	13.0	32	5
Hampton	18	210	11.7	02	0
Bunch	13	98	7.5	15	1
Pierce	12	212	17.7	54	0
De. Brown	7	56	8.0	14	0
Tillman	1	21	21.0	21	0
Crawford	1	6	6.0	6	0
Rasheed	1	3	3.0	3	0
Simms	1	-6	-6.0	-6	0
Giants	257	3180	12.4	62	17
Opponents	298	3354	11.3	58	13

INTERCEPTIONS

	No.	Yds.	Avg.	LG	TD
Collins	4	77	19.3	50t	1
G. Jackson	4	32	8.0	29	0
Guyton	2	34	17.0	19	0
Miller	2	18	9.0	11	0
Raymond	2	11	5.5	11	0
Tate	1	12	12.0	12	0
Armstead	1	0	0.0	0	0
Beamon	1	0	0.0	0	0
Campbell	1	0	0.0	0	0
Giants	18	184	10.2	50t	1
Opponents	9	175	19.4	85t	1

PUNTING

	No.	Yds.	Avg.	In 20	LG
Horan	44	1882	42.8	13	60
Landeta	33	1390	42.1	11	57
Giants	78	3272	41.9	24	60
Opponents	80	3224	40.3	23	54

PUNT RETURNS

	No.	FC	Yds.	Avg.	LG	TD
Meggett	32	20	331	10.3	75t	1
Giants	32	20	331	10.3	75t	1
Opponents	44	10	247	5.6	28	0

KICKOFF RETURNS

	No.	Yds.	Avg.	LG	TD
Meggett	24	403	16.8	35	0
Calloway	6	89	14.8	21	0
Cross	2	15	7.5	13	0
Giants	32	507	15.8	35	0
Opponents	29	646	22.3	68	0

SACKS

	No.
Hamilton	11.5
Miller	6.5
Taylor	6.0
Fox	4.5
Howard	3.5
Dillard	3.0
Bailey	1.5
McGhee	1.5
Brooks	1.0
Collins	1.0
Strahan	1.0
Giants	41.0
Opponents	40.0

1994 DRAFT CHOICES

Round	Name	Pos.	College
1	Thomas Lewis	WR	Indiana
2	Thomas Randolph	DB	Kansas State
	Jason Sehorn	DB	Southern California
3	Gary Downs	RB	North Carolina State
4	Chris Maumalanga	DT	Kansas
5	Chad Bratzke	DE	Eastern Kentucky
6	Jason Winrow	G	Ohio State

NEW YORK GIANTS

1994 VETERAN ROSTER

No.		Name	Pos.	Ht.	Wt.	Birthdate	NFL Exp.	College	Hometown	How Acq.	'93 Games/ Starts
98		Armstead, Jessie	LB	6-1	238	10/26/70	2	Miami	Dallas, Tex.	D8-'93	16/0
54		Bailey, Carlton	LB	6-3	235	12/15/64	7	North Carolina	Baltimore, Md.	UFA(Buff)-'93	16/16
21		Beamon, Willie	CB	5-11	170	6/14/70	2	Northern Iowa	Riviera Beach, Fla.	FA-'93	13/0
78		Bishop, Greg	T	6-5	298	5/2/71	2	Pacific	Lodi, Calif.	D4-'93	8/0
94		Brooks, Michael	LB	6-1	235	3/2/64	8	Louisiana State	Ruston, La.	UFA(Den)-'93	13/13
17		Brown, Dave	QB	6-5	215	2/25/70	3	Duke	Westfield, N.J.	SD1-'92	1/0
86		Brown, Derek	TE	6-6	252	3/31/70	3	Notre Dame	Fairfax, Va.	D1-'92	16/0
55		Buckley, Marcus	LB	6-3	235	2/3/71	2	Texas A&M	Ft. Worth, Tex.	D3-'93	16/2
33	†	Bunch, Jarrod	RB	6-2	248	8/9/68	4	Michigan	Ashtabula, Ohio	D1-'91	13/8
80	#	Calloway, Chris	WR	5-10	185	3/29/68	5	Michigan	Chicago, Ill.	FA-'92	16/9
37	†	Campbell, Jesse	S	6-1	215	4/11/69	4	North Carolina State	Vanceboro, N.C.	FA-'92	16/0
85		Crawford, Keith	WR	6-2	180	11/21/70	2	Howard Payne	Palestine, Tex.	FA-'93	7/0
87		Cross, Howard	TE	6-5	245	8/8/67	6	Alabama	Huntsville, Ala.	D6-'89	16/16
3	†	Daluiso, Brad	K	6-2	207	12/31/67	4	UCLA	San Diego, Calif.	FA-'93	15/0
62		Davis, Scott	G	6-3	289	1/29/70	2	Iowa	Glenwood, Iowa	D6-'93	4/0
58	#	Dent, Burnell	LB	6-2	235	3/16/63	8	Tulane	New Orleans, La.	FA-'93	0*
71		Dillard, Stacey	NT	6-5	288	9/17/68	3	Oklahoma	Clarksville, Tex.	D6-'92	16/16
76		Elliott, John	T	6-7	305	4/1/65	7	Michigan	Lake Ronkonkoma, N.Y.	D2-'88	11/11
95		Flythe, Mark	DE	6-7	290	10/4/68	2	Penn State	Philadelphia, Pa.	FA-'93	2/0
93		Fox, Mike	DE	6-6	275	8/5/67	5	West Virginia	Akron, Ohio	D2-'90	16/16
10		Graham, Kent	QB	6-5	220	11/1/68	3	Ohio State	Wheaton, Ill.	D8-'92	9/0
75		Hamilton, Keith	DE	6-6	280	5/25/71	3	Pittsburgh	Lynchburg, Va.	D4-'92	16/16
27		Hampton, Rodney	RB	5-11	215	4/3/69	5	Georgia	Houston, Tex.	D1-'90	12/10
2	#	Horan, Mike	P	5-11	190	2/1/59	10	Long Beach State	Orange, Calif.	FA-'93	8/0
74		Howard, Erik	NT	6-4	268	11/12/64	9	Washington State	San Jose, Calif.	D2a-'86	16/0
47	#	Jackson, Greg	S	6-1	200	8/20/66	6	Louisiana State	Hialeah, Fla.	D3a-'89	16/16
24	#	Jenkins, Izel	CB	5-10	190	5/27/64	7	North Carolina State	Wilson, N.C.	FA-'93	9/0*
69		Johnson, Chuck	T	6-3	280	5/22/69	2	Texas	Freeport, Tex.	FA-'94	0*
81	†	McCaffrey, Ed	WR	6-5	215	8/17/68	4	Stanford	Allentown, Pa.	D3-'91	16/1
30		Meggett, David	RB	5-7	180	4/30/66	6	Towson State	Charleston, S.C.	D5-'89	16/1
57		Miller, Corey	LB	6-2	255	10/25/68	4	South Carolina	Pageland, S.C.	D6-'91	16/14
65	#	Oates, Bart	C	6-3	265	12/16/58	10	Brigham Young	Albany, Ga.	FA-'85	16/15
84		Pierce, Aaron	TE	6-5	246	9/6/69	3	Washington	Seattle, Wash.	D3-'92	13/6
51		Powell, Andre	LB	6-1	226	6/5/69	2	Penn State	York, Pa.	FA-'93	15/1
44		Rasheed, Kenyon	RB	5-10	245	8/23/70	2	Oklahoma	Kansas City, Mo.	FA-'93	5/3
39		Raymond, Corey	CB	5-11	180	7/28/69	3	Louisiana State	New Iberia, La.	FA-'92	16/8
72		Riesenberg, Doug	T	6-5	275	7/22/65	8	California	Moscow, Idaho	D6a-'87	16/16
66	#	Roberts, William	G	6-5	280	8/5/62	10	Ohio State	Miami, Fla.	D1b-'84	16/16
88		Sherrard, Mike	WR	6-2	187	6/21/63	9	UCLA	Los Angeles, Calif.	UFA(SF)-'93	6/5
11		Simms, Phil	QB	6-3	214	11/3/55	16	Morehead State	Louisville, Ky.	D1-'79	16/16
28		Smith, Joey	CB-S	5-10	190	5/30/69	2	Louisville	Knoxville, Tenn.	FA-'94	0*
61		Smith, Lance	G	6-3	285	1/1/63	10	Louisiana State	Kannapolis, N.C.	UFA(Ariz)-'94	16/16*
22		Sparks, Phillippi	CB	5-11	186	4/15/69	3	Arizona State	Glendale, Calif.	D2-'92	5/3
92		Strahan, Michael	DE	6-4	253	11/21/71	2	Texas Southern	Westbury, Tex.	D2-'93	9/0
49	#	Tate, David	S	6-1	200	11/22/64	7	Colorado	Buffalo Grove, Ill.	FA-'93	14/1
97		Thigpen, Tommy	LB	6-2	242	3/17/71	2	North Carolina	Dumfries, Va.	D5-'93	0*
90		Widmer, Corey	LB	6-3	276	12/25/68	3	Montana State	Bozeman, Mont.	D7-'92	11/0
59		Williams, Brian	C	6-5	300	6/8/66	6	Minnesota	Mt. Lebanon, Pa.	D1-'89	16/1

* Dent inactive for 6 games in '93; Jenkins played 4 games with Minnesota, 5 games with N.Y. Giants; Johnson inactive for 1 game with Denver; Marshall played 16 games with Denver; J. Smith last active with N.Y. Giants in '92; L. Smith played 16 games with Phoenix in '93; Thigpen missed '93 season due to injury.

\# Unrestricted free agent; subject to developments.

† Restricted free agent; subject to developments.

t- Giants traded for Marshall (Denver).

Retired—LB Lawrence Taylor, 13-year veteran, 16 games in '93.

Players lost through free agency (6): CB Mark Collins (KC; 16 games in '93), S Myron Guyton (NE; 16), G Bob Kratch (NE; 16), T Eric Moore (Cin; 7), RB Lewis Tillman (Chi; 16), CB Perry Williams (NYJ; 8).

Also played with Giants in '93—LB Steve DeOssie (8 games), WR Mark Jackson (16), T Clarence Jones (4), P Sean Landeta (8), LB Kanavis McGhee (10), DE George Thornton (5), K David Treadwell (16).

COACHING STAFF

Head Coach,
Dan Reeves

Pro Career: After being named the fourteenth head coach in New York Giants history on January 27, 1993, Reeves led his squad to an 11-5 record and a berth in the playoffs as a Wild Card team in his first season with the Giants. Reeves's regular-season record of 11-5 is the best-ever for a first-year Giants coach. He became just the second head coach in Giants history to lead his team to the playoffs in his first season with the Giants. Reeves was named the *Associated Press* coach of the year after helping the Giants improve from a 6-10 record in 1992. Reeves came to the Giants after spending 12 years as head coach of the Denver Broncos. His 129 career victories going into the 1994 season gives him the thirteenth-most victories in NFL history and gives him the third-best among active head coaches in the NFL, behind Miami's Don Shula (327) and the Rams' Chuck Knox (190). He has participated in 45 NFL postseason games, 15 games as a head coach, 16 as an assistant, 6 as a player-coach, and 8 as a player. Reeves has played or coached in a record eight Super Bowls, including leading Denver to three Super Bowl appearances. He was the only AFC coach in the decade of the 1980s to lead his team to consecutive Super Bowl appearances, and he led Denver to seven 10-victory seasons in his 12 years there. Until taking the Denver post, Reeves had been a member of the Dallas coaching staff since 1970 when he spent two seasons as a player-coach. In 1972, he was a full-time assistant coach in charge of the offensive backfield. Reeves was in private business in 1973 before returning to the coaching ranks in 1974 as the backfield coach for the Cowboys. He remained in that position until 1977 when he was named offensive coordinator on Tom Landry's staff. Reeves's record of success dates back to his playing days with the Dallas Cowboys. Reeves began his professional football career as a free-agent running back for Dallas in 1965. Reeves was an all-purpose player during his eight seasons (1965-72) with Dallas (1,900 yards rushing with 25 touchdowns and 129 pass receptions for 1,693 yards and 17 touchdowns) and he finished his playing career as the fifth all-time rusher in Dallas history. In addition, he completed 30 passes, including two for touchdowns and also returned punts and kickoffs at various times as he played in the 1966, 1967, and 1970 NFL Championship Games. Career record: 129-85-1.

Background: Quarterback at South Carolina from 1962-64. He was inducted into the school's Hall of Fame in 1978.

Personal: Born January 19, 1944, Americus, Ga. Dan and his wife, Pam, live in East Rutherford, N.J., and have three children—Dana, Laura, and Lee. They also have two grandchildren-Caitlin and Ashley.

ASSISTANT COACHES

Don Blackmon, linebackers; born March 14, 1958, Pompano Beach, Fla., lives in Morristown, N.J. Linebacker Tulsa 1977-80. Pro linebacker New England Patriots 1981-87. Pro coach: New England Patriots 1988-90, Cleveland Browns 1991-92, joined Giants in 1993.

Dave Brazil, defensive quality control; born March 25, 1936, Detroit, Mich., lives in East Rutherford, N.J. No college or pro playing experience. College coach: Holy Cross 1968, Tulsa 1969-70, Eastern Michigan 1971-73, Boston College 1980, Kent State 1981-82. Pro coach: Detroit Wheels (WFL) 1974, Chicago Fire (WFL) 1975, Kansas City Chiefs 1984-88, Pittsburgh Steelers 1989-91, joined Giants in 1992.

James Daniel, tight ends; born January 17, 1953, Wetumpka, Ala., lives in Clifton, N.J. Offensive guard Alabama State 1970-73. No pro playing experience. College coach: Auburn 1981-92. Pro coach: Joined Giants in 1993.

Joe DeCamillis, special teams; born June 29, 1965, Arvada, Colo., lives in Morris Township, N.J. Wrestler

1994 FIRST-YEAR ROSTER

Name	Pos.	Ht.	Wt.	Birthdate	College	Hometown	How Acq.
Alexander, Mike	C	6-3	260	12/19/69	San Diego State	Wilmington, Calif.	FA
Bloedorn, Kurt (1)	P	6-5	207	10/20/67	Cal State-Fullerton	Brea, Calif.	FA
Brannon, Steve (1)	DE	6-3	265	11/27/68	Hampton	Georgetown, S.C.	FA
Bratzke, Chad	DE	6-4	262	9/15/71	Eastern Kentucky	Brandon, Fla.	D5
Brown, John	CB-S	5-9	183	9/2/70	Houston	Palo Duro, Tex.	FA
Brown, Leon	RB	5-10	190	5/16/70	Louisville	Jacksonville, Fla.	FA
Dillard, Ivory	G-T	6-3	299	8/15/71	Florida A&M	Dallas, Tex.	FA
Douglas, Donald	S	6-2	203	12/9/70	Houston	Liberty, Tex.	FA
Douglas, Omar	WR	5-10	170	6/3/72	Minnesota	New Orleans, La.	FA
Downs, Gary	RB	6-0	212	6/28/71	North Carolina State	Columbus, Ga.	D3
Elias, Keith	RB	5-9	191	2/3/72	Princeton	Lacey Township, N.J.	FA
Fox, Brian (1)	QB	6-4	214	12/23/70	Florida	Orlando, Fla.	FA
Gant, Eric	RB	6-2	245	10/13/70	Grambling	Lakeland, Fla.	FA
Jones, Milton	DE	6-5	270	3/24/71	Central State, Ohio	Detroit, Mich.	FA
Kozlowski, Brian (1)	TE	6-3	245	10/4/70	Connecticut	Rochester, N.Y.	FA
Lewis, Thomas	WR	6-1	185	1/10/72	Indiana	Akron, Ohio	D1
Marks, Duane	LB	6-4	238	11/19/70	Duke	Missouri City, Tex.	FA
Maumalanga, Chris	DT	6-2	288	12/15/71	Kansas	Redwood City, Calif.	D4
Pyne, Dave	C	6-4	292	10/25/70	Lafayette	Milford, Mass.	FA
Randolph, Thomas	CB	5-9	176	10/5/70	Kansas State	Norfolk, Va.	D2a
Ray, Leonard	DT	6-3	295	1/21/69	Louisville	Port St. Joe, Fla.	FA
Reese, Darren	G	6-4	285	10/25/70	Ohio	Elida, Ohio	FA
Sehorn, Jason	S	6-2	212	4/15/71	Southern California	Mt. Shasta, Calif.	D2b
Smith, Shawn	LB	6-2	236	7/5/71	San Diego State	Buena, N.J.	FA
Townes, William	DT	6-5	270	8/1/72	Nevada-Las Vegas	Dallas, Tex.	FA
Weir, Eric (1)	WR	6-2	175	7/15/70	Vanderbilt	Houston, Tex.	FA
Winrow, Jason	G	6-4	321	1/16/71	Ohio State	Bridgeton, N.J.	D6

The term NFL Rookie is defined as a player who is in his first season of professional football and has not been on the roster of another professional football team for any regular-season or postseason games. A Rookie is designated by an "R" on NFL rosters. Players who have been active in another professional football league or players who have NFL experience, including either preseason training camp or being on an Active List or Inactive List, or on Reserve/Injured or Reserve/Physically Unable to Perform for fewer than six regular-season games, are termed NFL First-Year Players. An NFL First-Year Player is designated by a "1" on NFL rosters. Thereafter, a player is credited with an additional year of experience for each season in which he accumulates six games on the Active List or Inactive List, or on Reserve/Injured or Reserve/Physically Unable to Perform.

NOTES

Wyoming 1983-87. No pro playing experience. College coach: Wyoming 1988. Pro coach: Denver Broncos 1989-92, joined Giants 1993.

Kerry Goode, assistant strength and conditioning; born July 28, 1965, Town Creek, Ala., lives in Mahwah, N.J. Tailback Alabama 1983-87. Pro running back Tampa Bay Buccaneers 1988, Denver Broncos 1989, Miami Dolphins 1990. Pro coach: Joined Giants in 1993.

George Henshaw, offensive coordinator-quarterbacks; born January 22, 1948, Midlothian, Va., lives in Smoke Rise, N.J. Defensive tackle West Virginia 1967-69. No pro playing experience. College coach: West Virginia 1970-75, Florida State 1976-82, Alabama 1983-86, Tulsa 1987 (head coach). Pro coach: Denver Broncos 1988-92, joined Giants in 1993.

Earl Leggett, defensive line, born March 5, 1935, Jacksonville, Fla., lives in Randolph, N.J. Tackle Hinds J.C. 1953-54, Louisiana State 1955-56. Pro defensive tackle Chicago Bears 1957-65, Los Angeles Rams 1966, New Orleans Saints 1967-68. College coach: Nicholls State 1971, Texas Christian 1972-73. Pro coach: Southern California Sun (WFL) 1974-75, Seattle Seahawks 1976-77, San Francisco 49ers 1978, Oakland/Los Angeles Raiders 1980-88, Denver Broncos 1989-92, joined Giants in 1993.

Pete Mangurian, offensive line; born June 17, 1955, Los Angeles, Calif., lives in Denville, N.J. Defensive lineman Louisiana State 1975-78. No pro playing experience. College coach: Southern Methodist 1979-80, New Mexico State 1981, Stanford 1982-83, Louisiana State 1984-87. Pro coach: Denver Broncos 1988-92, joined Giants in 1993.

Al Miller, strength and conditioning; born August 29,

1947, El Dorado, Ark., lives in Randolph, N.J. Wide receiver Northeast Louisiana 1965-69. No pro playing experience. College coach: Northwestern Louisiana 1974-78, Mississippi State 1980. Northeast Louisiana 1981, Alabama 1982-84. Pro coach: Denver Broncos 1987-92, joined Giants in 1993.

Mike Nolan, defensive coordinator, born March 7, 1959, Baltimore, Md., lives in Chatham, N.J. Safety Oregon 1977-80. No pro playing experience. College coach: Stanford 1982-83, Rice 1984-85, Louisiana State 1986. Pro coach: Denver Broncos 1987-92, joined Giants in 1993.

Dick Rehbein, wide receivers; born November 22, 1955, Green Bay, Wis., lives in Wayne, N.J. Center Ripon 1973-77. No pro playing experience. Pro coach: Green Bay Packers 1979-83, Los Angeles Express (USFL) 1984, Minnesota Vikings 1984-91, joined Giants in 1992.

George Sefcik, running backs; born December 27, 1939, Cleveland, Ohio, lives in Cranford, N.J. Halfback Notre Dame 1959-61. No pro playing experience. College coach: Notre Dame 1963-68, Kentucky 1969-72. Pro coach: Baltimore Colts 1973-74, Cleveland Browns 1975-77, 1989-90, Cincinnati Bengals 1978-83, Green Bay Packers 1984-87, Kansas City Chiefs 1988, joined Giants in 1991.

Zaven Yaralian, defensive backs, born February 5, 1952, Syria, lives in Mountain Lakes, N.J. Defensive back Nebraska 1972-73. Pro defensive back Green Bay Packers 1974, Philadelphia Bell (WFL) 1975. College coach: Nebraska 1975, Washington State 1976-77, Missouri 1978-83, Florida 1984-87, Colorado 1988-89. Pro coach: Chicago Bears 1990-92, joined Giants in 1993.

PHILADELPHIA EAGLES

National Football Conference
Eastern Division
Team Colors: Kelly Green, Silver, and White
Veterans Stadium
Broad Street and Pattison Avenue
Philadelphia, Pennsylvania 19148
Telephone: (215) 463-2500

CLUB OFFICIALS

Owner: Jeffrey Lurie
President-Chief Operating Officer: Harry Gamble
Vice President: Suzi Braman
V.P.-Chief Financial Officer: Mimi Box
V.P.-Sales and Development: Decker Uhlhorn
Vice President-Player Personnel/Operations:
    John Wooten
Asst. to Pres.: George Azar
Asst. to Pres.-General Counsel: Bob Wallace
Director of Pro Scouting: Tom Gamble
Director of Public Relations: Ron Howard
Asst. Director of Public Relations: Michael Gilbert
Director of Marketing: Leslie Stephenson-Matz
Dir. of Alumni Relations/Traveling Sec.:
    Jim Gallagher
Director of Administration: Vicki Chatley
Ticket Manager: Leo Carlin
Penthouse Suites Sales: Andrea Minassian
Asst. Director of Penthouse Sales: Ken Iman
Dir. Penthouse Operations: Christiana Noyalas
Trainer: Otho Davis
Asst. Trainer: David Price
Equipment Manager: Rusty Sweeney
Video Director: Mike Dougherty
Stadium: Veterans Stadium •**Capacity:** 65,178
        3501 South Broad Street
        Philadelphia, Pennsylvania 19148
Playing Surface: AstroTurf-8
Training Camp: West Chester University
            West Chester, Pennsylvania 19382

1994 SCHEDULE

PRESEASON

Aug. 5	at Chicago	7:00
Aug. 13	**New York Jets**	7:30
Aug. 20	**Cincinnati**	7:30
Aug. 26	at Atlanta	7:00

REGULAR SEASON

Sept. 4	at New York Giants	1:00
Sept. 12	**Chicago** (Monday)	9:00
Sept. 18	**Green Bay**	1:00
Sept. 25	Open Date	
Oct. 2	at San Francisco	1:00
Oct. 9	**Washington**	8:00
Oct. 16	at Dallas	3:00
Oct. 24	**Houston** (Monday)	9:00
Oct. 30	at Washington	1:00
Nov. 6	**Arizona**	4:00
Nov. 13	**Cleveland**	1:00
Nov. 20	at Arizona	2:00
Nov. 27	at Atlanta	1:00
Dec. 4	**Dallas**	1:00
Dec. 11	at Pittsburgh	1:00
Dec. 18	**New York Giants**	4:00
Dec. 24	at Cincinnati	4:00

RECORD HOLDERS

INDIVIDUAL RECORDS—CAREER

Category	Name	Performance
Rushing (Yds.)	Wilbert Montgomery, 1977-1984	6,538
Passing (Yds.)	Ron Jaworski, 1977-1986	26,963
Passing (TDs)	Ron Jaworski, 1977-1986	175
Receiving (No.)	Harold Carmichael, 1971-1983	589
Receiving (Yds.)	Harold Carmichael, 1971-1983	8,978
Interceptions	Bill Bradley, 1969-1976	34
Punting (Avg.)	Joe Muha, 1946-1950	42.9
Punt Return (Avg.)	Steve Van Buren, 1944-1951	13.9
Kickoff Return (Avg.)	Steve Van Buren, 1944-1951	26.7
Field Goals	Paul McFadden, 1984-87	91
Touchdowns (Tot.)	Harold Carmichael, 1971-1983	79
Points	Bobby Walston, 1951-1962	881

INDIVIDUAL RECORDS—SINGLE SEASON

Category	Name	Performance
Rushing (Yds.)	Wilbert Montgomery, 1979	1,512
Passing (Yds.)	Randall Cunningham, 1988	3,808
Passing (TDs)	Sonny Jurgensen, 1961	32
Receiving (No.)	Keith Jackson, 1988	81
	Keith Byars, 1990	81
Receiving (Yds.)	Mike Quick, 1983	1,409
Interceptions	Bill Bradley, 1971	11
Punting (Avg.)	Joe Muha, 1948	47.2
Punt Return (Avg.)	Steve Van Buren, 1944	15.3
Kickoff Return (Avg.)	Al Nelson, 1972	29.1
Field Goals	Paul McFadden, 1984	30
Touchdowns (Tot.)	Steve Van Buren, 1945	18
Points	Paul McFadden, 1984	116

INDIVIDUAL RECORDS—SINGLE GAME

Category	Name	Performance
Rushing (Yds.)	Steve Van Buren, 11-27-49	205
Passing (Yds.)	Bobby Thomason, 11-18-53	437
Passing (TDs)	Adrian Burk, 10-17-54	*7
Receiving (No.)	Don Looney, 12-1-40	14
Receiving (Yds.)	Tommy McDonald, 12-10-60	237
Interceptions	Russ Craft, 9-24-50	*4
Field Goals	Tom Dempsey, 11-12-72	6
Touchdowns (Tot.)	Many times	4
	Last time by Wilbert Montgomery, 10-7-79	
Points	Bobby Walston, 10-17-54	25

*NFL Record

COACHING HISTORY
(363-434-24)

1933-35	Lud Wray	9-21-1
1936-40	Bert Bell	10-44-2
1941-50	Earle (Greasy) Neale*	66-44-5
1951	Alvin (Bo) McMillin**	2-0-0
1951	Wayne Millner	2-8-0
1952-55	Jim Trimble	25-20-3
1956-57	Hugh Devore	7-16-1
1958-60	Lawrence (Buck) Shaw	20-16-1
1961-63	Nick Skorich	15-24-3
1964-68	Joe Kuharich	28-41-1
1969-71	Jerry Williams***	7-22-2
1971-72	Ed Khayat	8-15-2
1973-75	Mike McCormack	16-25-1
1976-82	Dick Vermeil	57-51-0
1983-85	Marion Campbell****	17-29-1
1985	Fred Bruney	1-0-0
1986-90	Buddy Ryan	43-38-1
1991-93	Rich Kotite	30-20-0

  *Co-coach with Walt Kiesling in Philadelphia-Pittsburgh
   merger in 1943
 **Retired after two games in 1951
***Released after three games in 1971
****Released after 15 games in 1985

VETERANS STADIUM

N

1993 TEAM RECORD

PRESEASON (3-2)

Date	Result		Opponents
7/31	L	16-28	vs. New Orleans at Tokyo
8/8	W	13-9	Chicago
8/13	W	24-13	at N.Y. Jets
8/21	W	37-20	Atlanta
8/27	L	3-23	at Cincinnati

REGULAR SEASON (8-8)

Date	Result		Opponents	Att.
9/5	W	23-17	Phoenix	59,831
9/12	W	20-17	at Green Bay	59,061
9/19	W	34-31	Washington	65,435
10/3	W	35-30	at N.Y. Jets	72,593
10/10	L	6-17	Chicago	63,601
10/17	L	10-21	at N.Y. Giants	76,050
10/31	L	10-23	Dallas	61,912
11/7	L	3-16	at Phoenix	41,634
11/14	L	14-19	Miami	64,213
11/21	L	3-7	N.Y. Giants	62,928
11/28	W	17-14	at Washington	46,663
12/6	L	17-23	at Dallas	64,521
12/12	L	7-10	Buffalo	60,769
12/19	W	20-10	at Indianapolis	44,952
12/26	W	37-26	New Orleans	50,085
1/3	W	37-34	at San Francisco (OT)	61,653

(OT) Overtime

SCORE BY PERIODS

Eagles	36	101	56	97	3	—	293
Opponents	65	94	55	101	0	—	315

ATTENDANCE

Home 488,774   Away 467,127   Total 955,901
Single-game home record, 72,111 (11-1-81)
Single-season home record, 557,325 (1980)

1993 TEAM STATISTICS

	Eagles	Opp.
Total First Downs	303	271
Rushing	104	91
Passing	184	155
Penalty	15	25
Third Down: Made/Att	92/224	66/205
Third Down Pct.	41.1	32.2
Fourth Down: Made/Att	7/16	15/20
Fourth Down Pct.	43.8	75.0
Total Net Yards	4922	5019
Avg. Per Game	307.6	313.7
Total Plays	1054	966
Avg. Per Play	4.7	5.2
Net Yards Rushing	1761	2080
Avg. Per Game	110.1	130.0
Total Rushes	456	467
Net Yards Passing	3161	2939
Avg. Per Game	197.6	183.7
Sacked/Yards Lost	42/302	36/214
Gross Yards	3463	3153
Att./Completions	556/328	463/251
Completion Pct.	59.0	54.2
Had Intercepted	13	20
Punts/Avg.	83/40.0	75/41.8
Net Punting Avg.	83/35.3	75/36.2
Penalties/Yards Lost	101/770	85/610
Fumbles/Ball Lost	32/21	33/15
Touchdowns	35	35
Rushing	7	11
Passing	23	22
Returns	5	2
Avg. Time of Possession	31:00	29:00

1993 INDIVIDUAL STATISTICS

PASSING	Att	Cmp	Yds.	Pct.	TD	Int	Tkld.	Rate
Brister	309	181	1905	58.6	14	5	19/148	84.9
O'Brien	137	71	708	51.8	4	3	15/116	67.4
Cunningham	110	76	850	69.1	5	5	7/33	88.1
Walker	0	0	0	—	0	0	1/5	-1.0
Eagles	556	328	3463	59.0	23	13	42/302	81.2
Opponents	463	251	3153	54.2	22	20	36/214	73.5

SCORING	TD R	TD P	TD Rt	PAT	FG	Saf	PTS
Williams	0	10	0	0/0	0/0	0	60
Bahr	0	0	0	18/19	8/13	0	42
Ruzek	0	0	0	13/16	8/10	0	37
Bavaro	0	6	0	0/0	0/0	0	36
Allen	0	0	4	0/0	0/0	0	24
Walker	1	3	0	0/0	0/0	0	24
Hebron	3	0	0	0/0	0/0	0	18
Sherman	2	0	0	0/0	0/0	0	12
Young	0	2	0	0/0	0/0	0	12
Bailey	0	1	0	0/0	0/0	0	6
Cunningham	1	0	0	0/0	0/0	0	6
Evans	0	0	1	0/0	0/0	0	6
Joseph	0	1	0	0/0	0/0	0	6
Flores	0	0	0	0/0	0/0	1	2
Eagles	7	23	5	31/35	16/23	2	293
Opponents	11	22	2	34/35	23/34	1	315

RUSHING	Att.	Yds.	Avg.	LG	TD
Walker	174	746	4.3	35	1
Sherman	115	406	3.5	19	2
Hebron	84	297	3.5	33	3
Joseph	39	140	3.6	12	0
Cunningham	18	110	6.1	26	1
Brister	20	39	2.0	13	0
O'Brien	4	17	4.3	11	0
Feagles	2	6	3.0	6	0
Eagles	456	1761	3.9	35	7
Opponents	467	2080	4.5	85t	11

RECEIVING	No.	Yds.	Avg.	LG	TD
Walker	75	610	8.1	55	3
Williams	60	725	12.1	80t	10
Bavaro	43	481	11.2	27	6
Bailey	41	545	13.3	58	1
Joseph	29	291	10.0	48	1
Barnett	17	170	10.0	21	0
Young	14	186	13.3	49t	2
Lofton	13	167	12.8	32	0
Sherman	12	78	6.5	21	0
Hebron	11	82	7.5	12	0
Johnson	10	81	8.1	17	0
Sydner	2	42	21.0	31	0
Lawrence	1	5	5.0	5	0
Eagles	328	3463	10.6	80t	23
Opponents	251	3153	12.6	69	22

INTERCEPTIONS	No.	Yds.	Avg.	LG	TD
Allen	6	201	33.5	94t	4
Miano	4	26	6.5	16	0
W. Thomas	2	39	19.5	21	0
McMillian	2	25	12.5	17	0
Hager	1	19	19.0	19	0
Evans	1	8	8.0	7	0
Joyner	1	6	6.0	6	0
Hopkins	1	0	0.0	0	0
Simmons	1	0	0.0	0	0
O. Smith	1	0	0.0	0	0
Eagles	20	324	16.2	94t	4
Opponents	13	107	8.2	41	0

PUNTING	No.	Yds.	Avg.	In 20	LG
Feagles	83	3323	40.0	31	60
Eagles	83	3323	40.0	31	60
Opponents	75	3137	41.8	28	59

PUNT RETURNS	No.	FC	Yds.	Avg.	LG	TD
Sikahema	33	20	275	8.3	25	0
O. Smith	0	0	9	—	9	0
Eagles	33	20	284	8.6	25	0
Opponents	35	19	311	8.9	83t	1

KICKOFF RETURNS	No.	Yds.	Avg.	LG	TD
Sikahema	30	579	19.3	35	0
Walker	11	184	16.7	30	0
Sydner	9	158	17.6	36	0
Hebron	3	35	11.7	18	0
Johnson	1	7	7.0	7	0
O. Smith	0	24	—	24	0
Eagles	54	987	18.3	36	0
Opponents	53	1133	21.4	60	0

SACKS	No.
Harmon	11.5
W. Thomas	6.5
Simmons	5.0
Millard	4.0
Flores	3.0
Allen	2.0
Joyner	2.0
Hager	1.0
Perry	1.0
Eagles	36.0
Opponents	42.0

1994 DRAFT CHOICES

Round	Name	Pos.	College
1	Bernard Williams	T	Georgia
2	Bruce Walker	DT	UCLA
	Charlie Garner	RB	Tennessee
3	Joe Panos	G	Wisconsin
	Eric Zomalt	DB	California
5	Marvin Goodwin	DB	UCLA
6	Ryan McCoy	LB	Houston
	Mitch Berger	P	Colorado
7	Mark Montgomery	RB	Wisconsin

PHILADELPHIA EAGLES

1994 VETERAN ROSTER

No.		Name	Pos.	Ht.	Wt.	Birthdate	NFL Exp.	College	Hometown	How Acq.	'93 Games/ Starts
72		Alexander, David	C	6-3	275	7/28/64	8	Tulsa	Broken Arrow, Okla.	D5-'87	16/16
21		Allen, Eric	CB	5-10	180	11/22/65	7	Arizona State	San Diego, Calif.	D2-'88	16/16
82		Bailey, Victor	WR	6-2	196	7/3/70	2	Missouri	Ft. Worth, Tex.	D2-'93	16/10
62	#	Baldinger, Brian	G-T	6-4	278	1/7/60	13	Duke	Indianapolis, Ind.	FA-'92	12/4
24		Barlow, Corey	CB	5-9	182	11/1/70	2	Auburn	Atlanta, Ga.	D5-'91	10/0
86		Barnett, Fred	WR	6-0	199	6/17/66	5	Arkansas State	Gunnison, Miss.	D3-'90	4/4
84		Bavaro, Mark	TE	6-4	245	4/28/63	9	Notre Dame	Danvers, Mass.	UFA(Clev)-'93	16/16
6		Brister, Bubby	QB	6-3	207	8/15/62	9	Northeast Louisiana	Alexandria, La.	FA-'93	10/8
39		Brooks, Tony	RB	6-0	230	8/17/69	2	Notre Dame	Tulsa, Okla.	D4a-'92	0*
71		Chalenski, Mike	DE-DT	6-5	288	1/28/70	2	UCLA	Elizabeth, N.J.	FA-'93	15/0
12		Cunningham, Randall	QB	6-4	205	3/27/63	10	Nevada-Las Vegas	Santa Barbara, Calif.	D2-'85	4/4
78		Davis, Antone	T	6-4	325	2/28/67	4	Tennessee	Ft. Valley, Ga.	D1-'91	16/16
56		Evans, Byron	LB	6-2	235	2/23/64	8	Arizona	Phoenix, Ariz.	D4-'87	11/10
95	†	Flores, Mike	DE	6-3	256	12/1/66	4	Louisville	Youngstown, Ohio	D11-'91	16/11
61	#	Floyd, Eric	G	6-5	310	10/28/65	5	Auburn	Rome, Ga.	PB(SD)-'92	3/3
33	#	Frizzell, William	S	6-3	206	9/8/62	11	North Carolina Central	Rose, N.C.	FA-'92	16/2
93		Fuller, William	DE	6-3	274	3/8/62	9	North Carolina	Chesapeake, Va.	UFA(Hou)-'94	16/16*
69	t-	Grossman, Burt	DE	6-4	275	4/10/67	6	Pittsburgh	Bala-Cynwyd, Pa.	T(SD)-'94	10/10*
54		Hager, Britt	LB	6-1	225	2/20/66	6	Texas	Odessa, Tex.	D3b-'89	16/7
65	#	Hallstrom, Ron	G	6-6	315	6/11/59	13	Iowa	Moline, Ill.	FA-'93	12/8
91		Harmon, Andy	DT	6-4	265	4/6/69	4	Kent State	Centerville, Ohio	D6-'91	16/15
97		Harris, Tim	DE	6-6	258	9/10/64	9	Memphis State	Memphis, Tenn.	UFA(SF)-'93	4/3
45		Hebron, Vaughn	RB	5-8	196	10/7/70	2	Virginia Tech	Baltimore, Md.	FA-'93	16/4
73		Holmes, Lester	G	6-3	301	9/27/69	2	Jackson State	Tylertown, Miss.	D1a-'93	12/6
76		Hudson, John	G-C	6-2	275	1/29/68	5	Auburn	Memphis, Tenn.	D11-'90	16/0
98		Jeter, Tommy	DT	6-5	282	9/20/69	3	Texas	Nacogdoches, Tex.	D3-'92	7/0
87		Johnson, Maurice	TE	6-2	243	1/9/67	4	Temple	Washington, D.C.	FA-'91	16/2
8		Jones, Preston	QB	6-3	223	7/3/70	2	Georgia	Anderson, S.C.	FA-'93	0*
32		Joseph, James	RB	6-2	222	10/28/67	4	Auburn	Phenix City, Ala.	D7-'91	16/5
68	#	McHale, Tom	G	6-4	290	2/25/63	8	Cornell	Gaithersburg, Md.	FA-'93	8/4
29		McMillian, Mark	CB	5-7	162	4/29/70	3	Alabama	Los Angeles, Calif.	D10-'92	16/12
38	#	Miano, Rich	S	6-1	200	9/3/62	10	Hawaii	Honolulu, Hawaii	FA-'91	16/14
3		Murray, Eddie	K	5-11	195	8/29/56	15	Tulane	Victoria, Canada	FA-'94	14/0*
58		Oden, Derrick	LB	5-11	230	9/29/70	2	Alabama	Hillcrest, Ala.	D6-'93	12/0
90		Perry, William	DT	6-2	335	12/16/62	10	Clemson	Aiken, S.C.	W(Chi)-'93	15/8*
42		Reid, Mike	S	6-1	218	11/24/70	2	North Carolina State	Spartanburg, S.C.	D3b-'93	9/0
94		Renfro, Leonard	DT	6-2	291	6/29/70	2	Colorado	Detroit, Mich.	D1b-'93	14/2
53	t-	Romanowski, Bill	LB	6-4	231	4/2/66	7	Boston College	Vernon, Conn.	T(SF)-'94	16/16*
55		Rose, Ken	LB	6-1	215	6/9/62	8	Nevada-Las Vegas	Sacramento, Calif.	FA-'90	5/0
79	#	Schad, Mike	G	6-5	290	10/2/63	9	Queens College, Canada	Bellville, Canada	PB(Rams)-'89	13/13
23		Sherman, Heath	RB	6-0	205	3/27/67	6	Texas A&I	El Campo, Tex.	D6-'89	15/7
30		Smith, Otis	CB	5-11	184	10/22/65	5	Missouri	Metairie, La.	FA-'90	15/0
85		Sydner, Jeff	WR-KR	5-6	170	11/11/69	3	Hawaii	Columbus, Ohio	D6-'92	4/0
46		Thomas, Markus	RB	5-10	192	7/12/70	2	Eastern Kentucky	Cincinnati, Ohio	FA-'93	0*
51	†	Thomas, William	LB	6-2	218	8/13/68	4	Texas A&M	Amarillo, Tex.	D4-'91	16/16
76		Thompson, Broderick	T	6-5	295	8/14/60	9	Kansas	Cerritos, Calif.	T(SD)-'93	10/10
34		Walker, Herschel	RB	6-1	225	3/3/62	9	Georgia	Wrightsville, Ga.	FA-'92	16/16
20	#	Waters, Andre	S	5-11	200	3/10/62	11	Cheyney State	Pahokee, Fla.	FA-'84	9/8
89		Williams, Calvin	WR	5-11	190	3/3/67	5	Purdue	Baltimore, Md.	D5-'90	16/14
83	#	Young, Michael	WR	6-1	183	2/21/62	10	UCLA	Hanford, Calif.	FA-'93	10/0

* Brooks missed '93 season due to injury; Fuller played 16 games with Houston in '93; Grossman played 10 games with San Diego; Jones active for 1 game but did not play; Murray played 14 games with Dallas; Perry played 7 games with Chicago, 8 games with Philadelphia; Romanowski played 16 games with San Francisco; M. Thomas inactive for 16 games.

\# Unrestricted free agent; subject to developments.

† Restricted free agent; subject to developments.

Traded—CB-S Ben Smith to Denver.

t- Eagles traded for Grossman (San Diego), Romanowski (San Francisco).

Players lost through free agency (3): P Jeff Feagles (Ariz; 16 games in '93), LB Seth Joyner (Ariz; 16), DE Clyde Simmons (Ariz; 16).

Also played with Eagles in '93—K Matt Bahr (11 games), LB Louis Cooper (11), S Wes Hopkins (15), WR Reggie Lawrence (1), WR James Lofton (9), S Erik McMillan (6), DT Keith Millard (14), DT Gerald Nichols (7), QB Ken O'Brien (5), WR Paul Richardson (1), LB John Roper (3), K Roger Ruzek (5), G Rob Selby (1), CB-S Ben Smith (13).

COACHING STAFF

Head Coach,
Rich Kotite

Pro Career: Became the eighteenth head coach in Eagles' history on January 8, 1991. After a 3-5 start in his rookie year as head coach, marked by a season-ending injury to quarterback Randall Cunningham on opening day and subsequent injuries to backup Jim McMahon, Kotite rallied the Eagles. Philadelphia narrowly missed the playoffs after winning seven of their last eight games on the strength of the league's best defense. In his second season, the Eagles returned to the playoffs for the fourth time in five years, recording an 11-5 mark along the way to give the club five consecutive seasons of 10-or-more wins. A year ago, Kotite led the Eagles to a blistering 4-0 start before a series of season-ending injuries to starters—including Pro Bowlers Cunningham and wide receiver Fred Barnett—brought on a skid. Kotite, however, nearly guided the club into the playoffs again by rallying the depleted Eagles to a three-game winning streak at season's end and an 8-8 finish that narrowly missed a playoff berth. Kotite originally served as the team's offensive coordinator in 1990 when the club led the NFL in rushing and topped the NFC in scoring and touchdown passes. Kotite had served previously as the New York Jets' offensive coordinator and receivers coach from 1985-89 after originally joining the club as receivers coach in 1983. In each of Kotite's years at the helm of the New York offense, the Jets finished near the top in the AFC in total offense, including a third-place ranking in 1985. Kotite began his pro coaching career with New Orleans in 1977 before joining Cleveland as receiver's coach from 1978-1982 and aiding in the development of perennial all-pro tight end Ozzie Newsome. During his playing career, he was known as a scrappy tight end and outstanding special teams performer with the New York Giants (1967, 1969-72) and Steelers (1968). Career record: 30-20.
Background: Attended Poly Prep in Brooklyn, N.Y. After a brief boxing career at the University of Miami where he was the school's heavyweight champ, he served as a sparring partner for Cassius Clay, later known as Muhammad Ali. Kotite became a Little All-America tight end at Wagner College in Staten Island, N.Y.
Personal: Born in Brooklyn on October 13, 1942. He and his wife, Elizabeth, live in Mt. Laurel, N.J. and have one daughter—Alexandra.

ASSISTANT COACHES

Zeke Bratkowski, offensive coordinator-quarterbacks; born October 20, 1931, Danville, Ill., lives in Mt. Laurel, N.J. Quarterback Georgia 1951-53. Pro quarterback Chicago Bears 1954, 1957-60, Los Angeles Rams 1961-63, Green Bay Packers 1963-68, 1971. Pro coach: Green Bay Packers 1969-70, 1975-81, Chicago Bears 1972-74, Baltimore-Indianapolis Colts 1982-84, New York Jets 1985-89, Cleveland Browns 1990, joined Eagles in 1991.
Lew Carpenter, receivers-tight ends; born January 12, 1932, Hayti, Mo., lives in Mt. Laurel, N.J. Running backend Arkansas 1950-52. Pro running back-defensive back-end Detroit Lions 1953-55, Cleveland Browns 1957-58, Green Bay Packers 1959-63. College coach: Southwest Texas State 1989. Pro coach: Minnesota Vikings 1964-66, Atlanta Falcons 1967-68, Washington Redskins 1969-70, St. Louis Cardinals 1971-72, Houston Oilers 1973-74, Green Bay Packers 1975-85, Detroit Lions 1986-88, joined Eagles in 1990.
Bud Carson, defensive coordinator-secondary; born April 28, 1931, Freeport, Pa., lives in Mt. Laurel, N.J. Defensive back North Carolina 1950-52. No pro playing experience. College coach: North Carolina 1957-64, South Carolina 1965, Georgia Tech 1966-71 (head coach 1967-71), Kansas 1984. Pro coach: Pittsburgh Steelers 1972-77, Los Angeles Rams 1978-81, Baltimore Colts 1982, Kansas City Chiefs 1983, New York Jets 1985-88, Cleveland Browns 1989-90 (head coach), joined Eagles in 1991.
Peter Giunta, defensive assistant; born August 11,

NOTES

1956, Salem, Mass., lives in Bensalem, Pa. Running back-defensive back Northeastern 1974-77. No pro playing experience. College coach: Penn State 1981-83, Brown 1984-87, Lehigh 1988-90. Pro coach: Joined Eagles in 1991.
Dale Haupt, defensive line; born April 12, 1929, Manitowoc, Wis., lives in Cherry Hill, N.J. Defensive lineman-linebacker Wyoming 1950-53. No pro playing experience. College coach: Tennessee 1960-63, Iowa State 1964-65, Richmond 1966-71, North Carolina State 1972-76, Duke 1977. Pro coach: Chicago Bears 1978-85, joined Eagles in 1986.
Bill Muir, offensive line; born October 26, 1942, Pittsburgh, Pa., lives in Mt. Laurel, N.J. Tackle Susquehanna 1962-64. No pro playing experience. College coach: Susquehanna 1965, Delaware Valley 1966-67, Rhode Island 1970-71, Idaho State 1972-73, Southern Methodist 1976-77. Pro coach: Orlando (Continental Football League) 1968-69, Houston-Shreveport Steamer (WFL) 1975, New England Patriots 1982-84, Detroit Lions 1985-88, Indianapolis Colts 1989-91, joined Eagles in 1992.
Larry Pasquale, special teams coordinator; born April 21, 1941, Brooklyn, N.Y., lives in Mt. Laurel, N.J. Quarterback Bridgeport 1961-63. No pro playing experience. College coach: Slippery Rock State 1967, Boston University 1968, Navy 1969-70, Massachusetts 1971-75, Idaho State 1976. Pro coach: Montreal Alouettes (CFL) 1977-78, Detroit Lions 1979, New

York Jets 1980-89, San Diego Chargers 1990-91, joined Eagles in 1992.
Jim Vechiarella, linebackers; born February 20, 1937, Youngstown, Ohio, lives in Mt. Laurel, N.J. Linebacker Youngstown State 1955-57. No pro playing experience. College coach: Youngstown State 1964-74, Southern Illinois 1976-77, Tulane 1978-80. Pro coach: Charlotte (WFL) 1975, Los Angeles Rams 1981-82, Kansas City Chiefs 1983-85, New York Jets 1986-89, Cleveland Browns 1990, joined Eagles in 1991.
Jim Williams, strength and conditioning; born March 29, 1948, Kingston, Pa., lives in Mt. Laurel, N.J. No college or pro playing experience. College coach: Nebraska 1972-74, Arkansas 1974-77, Wyoming 1977-79. Pro coach: New York Giants 1979-81, New York Jets 1982-89, joined Eagles in 1991.
Richard Wood, running backs; born February 2, 1936, Lanett, Ala., lives in Mt. Laurel, N.J. Quarterback Auburn 1956-59. Pro quarterback Baltimore Colts 1960-61, San Diego Chargers 1962, Denver Broncos 1962, New York Jets 1963-64, Oakland Raiders 1965, Miami Dolphins 1966. College coach: Georgia 1967-68, Mississippi 1971-73, Auburn 1986. Pro coach: Oakland Raiders 1969-70, Cleveland Browns 1974, New Orleans Saints 1976-77, Atlanta Falcons 1978-82, Philadelphia Eagles 1983, Kansas City Chiefs 1987-88, New England Patriots 1989-90, rejoined Eagles in 1991.

1994 FIRST-YEAR ROSTER

Name	Pos.	Ht.	Wt.	Birthdate	College	Hometown	How Acq.
Barnett, Alonza	CB	6-2	210	7/17/70	North Carolina A&T	Jacksonville, N.C.	FA
Berger, Mitch	P	6-2	231	6/24/72	Colorado	Kamloops, Canada	D6b
Brown, Curt (1)	DT	6-5	260	4/5/70	North Carolina	Virginia Beach, Va.	FA
Clapp, Darrell	G-T	6-5	300	10/13/70	Houston	Corpus Christi, Tex.	FA
Cummins, Jeff (1)	DE	6-6	270	5/25/69	Oregon	Torrance, Calif.	FA
Dausin, Chris	C	6-4	285	12/18/69	Texas A&M	San Antonio, Tex.	FA
Dixon, Mark	G	6-4	290	11/26/70	Virginia	Jamestown, N.C.	FA
Fiedler, Jay	QB	6-1	215	12/29/71	Dartmouth	Oceanside, N.Y.	FA
Frazier, Derrick (1)	CB	5-10	178	4/29/70	Texas A&M	Sugar Land, Tex.	D3a-'93
Gamble, David	WR	6-1	193	6/14/71	New Hampshire	Albany, N.Y.	FA
Garlick, Tom	WR	5-11	180	9/22/71	Fordham	Philadelphia, Pa.	FA
Garner, Charlie	RB	5-9	181	2/13/72	Tennessee	Falls Church, Va.	D2b
Goodwin, Marvin	S	6-0	199	9/21/72	UCLA	Camden, N.J.	D5
Hall, Ray	DT	6-4	267	3/2/71	Washington State	Seattle, Wash.	FA
Jackson, Al	CB	6-0	182	9/7/71	Georgia	Pensacola, Fla.	FA
Knight, Dewayne	S	6-2	206	10/8/70	Virginia Tech	Newport News, Va.	FA
Lawrence, Reggie (1)	WR	6-0	178	4/12/70	North Carolina State	Camden, N.J.	FA
Lewis, Darrell	S	6-0	205	3/24/71	San Diego State	San Diego, Calif.	FA
McCoy, Ryan	LB	6-2	237	3/13/72	Houston	Beaumont, Tex.	D6a
McGill, Jason (1)	WR	6-0	192	1/12/72	Georgia Tech	Miami, Fla.	FA
McKenzie, Mike	TE	6-2	247	9/18/70	Baylor	San Antonio, Tex.	FA
Mendez, Jaime	S	5-11	194	2/20/71	Kansas State	Youngstown, Ohio	FA
Miller, Derrick	WR	5-10	170	12/7/70	Virginia State	Steelton, Pa.	FA
Morrill, Matt	DE	6-3	261	8/13/71	Delaware	Neshanic, N.J.	FA
Montgomery, Mark	RB	5-11	220	2/19/72	Wisconsin	St. Paul, Minn.	D7
O'Neal, Brian	RB	6-0	233	2/25/70	Penn State	Cincinnati, Ohio	FA
Pale, Peter	G	6-3	279	12/30/71	Hawaii	Molokai, Hawaii	FA
Panos, Joe	G-C	6-2	296	1/24/71	Wisconsin	Brookfield, Wis.	D3a
Richardson, Paul (1)	WR	6-3	204	2/25/69	UCLA	Los Angeles, Calif.	FA
Schrock, Chris (1)	P	6-2	225	10/18/70	Boston University	Hamilton, Mass.	FA
Shankle, William	CB	5-10	195	4/28/70	Oklahoma	Houston, Tex.	FA
Simien, Eric	LB	6-2	233	12/31/70	Nevada-Las Vegas	Los Angeles, Calif.	FA
Smith, Herman	DE	6 5	242	1/25/71	Portland State	Portland, Ore.	FA
Smith, Jemone	WR	6-5	200	7/22/71	Indiana, Pa.	Harrisburg, Pa.	FA
Starcevich, Steve (1)	K	6-4	225	10/21/66	Philadelphia Textile	Northville, Mich.	FA
Walker, Bruce	DT	6-3	326	7/18/72	UCLA	Compton, Calif.	D2a
Williams, Bernard	T	6-8	317	7/18/72	Georgia	Memphis, Tenn.	D1
Woodard, Marc	LB	6-0	234	2/21/71	Mississippi State	Kosciusko, Miss.	FA
Wooten, Al	RB	5-11	232	9/9/70	Syracuse	Niagara Falls, N.Y.	FA
Zomalt, Eric	S	5-11	197	8/9/72	California	Los Angeles, Calif.	D3b

The term NFL Rookie is defined as a player who is in his first season of professional football and has not been on the roster of another professional football team for any regular-season or postseason games. A Rookie is designated by an "R" on NFL rosters. Players who have been active in another professional football league or players who have NFL experience, including either preseason training camp or being on an Active List or Inactive List, or on Reserve/Injured or Reserve/Physically Unable to Perform for fewer than six regular-season games, are termed NFL First-Year Players. An NFL First-Year Player is designated by a "1" on NFL rosters. Thereafter, a player is credited with an additional year of experience for each season in which he accumulates six games on the Active List or Inactive List, or on Reserve/Injured or Reserve/Physically Unable to Perform.

National Football Conference
Western Division
Team Colors: Forty Niners Gold and Scarlet
4949 Centennial Boulevard
Santa Clara, California 95054
Telephone: (408) 562-4949

CLUB OFFICIALS
Owner: Edward J. DeBartolo, Jr.
President: Carmen Policy
Vice President-Football Administration:
 John McVay
Vice President-Business Operations & C.F.O.:
 Keith Simon
Coordinator of Football Operations/Player
 Personnel: Dwight Clark
Director of Pro Personnel: Allan Webb
Director of College Scouting: Vinny Cerrato
Director of Public/Community Relations:
 Rodney Knox
Director of Marketing/Promotions:
 Laurie Albrecht
Coordinator of Football Operations: Neal Dahlen
Ticket Manager: Lynn Carrozzi
Director of Stadium Operations:
 Murlan (Mo) Fowell
Video Director: Robert Yanagi
Trainer: Lindsy McLean
Equipment Manager: Bronco Hinek
Stadium: Candlestick Park •**Capacity:** 69,423
 San Francisco, California 94124
Playing Surface: Grass
Training Camp: Sierra Community College
 Rocklin, California 95677

1994 SCHEDULE
PRESEASON

Aug. 5	at Arizona	6:30
Aug. 12	**Denver**	5:00
Aug. 18	at San Diego	5:00
Aug. 26	**Seattle**	6:00

REGULAR SEASON

Sept. 5	**Los Angeles Raiders** (Monday)	6:00
Sept. 11	at Kansas City	12:00
Sept. 18	at Los Angeles Rams	1:00
Sept. 25	**New Orleans**	1:00
Oct. 2	**Philadelphia**	1:00
Oct. 9	at Detroit	1:00
Oct. 16	at Atlanta	1:00
Oct. 23	**Tampa Bay**	1:00
Oct. 30	Open Date	
Nov. 6	at Washington	1:00
Nov. 13	**Dallas**	1:00
Nov. 20	**Los Angeles Rams**	5:00
Nov. 28	at New Orleans (Monday)	8:00
Dec. 4	**Atlanta**	1:00
Dec. 11	at San Diego	1:00
Dec. 17	**Denver** (Saturday)	1:00
Dec. 26	at Minnesota (Monday)	8:00

RECORD HOLDERS
INDIVIDUAL RECORDS—CAREER

Category	Name	Performance
Rushing (Yds.)	Joe Perry, 1950-1960, 1963	7,344
Passing (Yds.)	Joe Montana, 1979-1992	35,124
Passing (TDs)	Joe Montana, 1979-1992	244
Receiving (No.)	Jerry Rice, 1985-1993	708
Receiving (Yds.)	Jerry Rice, 1985-1993	11,776
Interceptions	Ronnie Lott, 1981-1990	51
Punting (Avg.)	Tommy Davis, 1959-1969	44.7
Punt Return (Avg.)	Manfred Moore, 1974-75	14.7
Kickoff Return (Avg.)	Abe Woodson, 1958-1964	29.4
Field Goals	Ray Wersching, 1977-1987	190
Touchdowns (Tot.)	Jerry Rice, 1985-1993	124
Points	Ray Wersching, 1977-1987	979

INDIVIDUAL RECORDS—SINGLE SEASON

Category	Name	Performance
Rushing (Yds.)	Roger Craig, 1988	1,502
Passing (Yds.)	Steve Young, 1993	4,023
Passing (TDs)	Joe Montana, 1987	31
Receiving (No.)	Jerry Rice, 1990	100
Receiving (Yds.)	Jerry Rice, 1986	1,570
Interceptions	Dave Baker, 1960	10
	Ronnie Lott, 1986	10
Punting (Avg.)	Tommy Davis, 1965	45.8
Punt Return (Avg.)	Dana McLemore, 1982	22.3
Kickoff Return (Avg.)	Joe Arenas, 1953	34.4
Field Goals	Mike Cofer, 1989	29
Touchdowns (Tot.)	Jerry Rice, 1987	23
Points	Jerry Rice, 1987	138

INDIVIDUAL RECORDS—SINGLE GAME

Category	Name	Performance
Rushing (Yds.)	Delvin Williams, 10-31-76	194
Passing (Yds.)	Joe Montana, 10-14-90	476
Passing (TDs)	Joe Montana, 10-14-90	6
Receiving (No.)	Jerry Rice, 10-14-90	13
Receiving (Yds.)	John Taylor, 12-11-89	286
Interceptions	Dave Baker, 12-4-60	*4
Field Goals	Ray Wersching, 10-16-83	6
Touchdowns (Tot.)	Jerry Rice, 10-14-90	5
Points	Jerry Rice, 10-14-90	30

*NFL Record

COACHING HISTORY
(350-284-13)

1950-54	Lawrence (Buck) Shaw	33-25-2
1955	Norman (Red) Strader	4-8-0
1956-58	Frankie Albert	19-17-1
1959-63	Howard (Red) Hickey*	27-27-1
1963-67	Jack Christiansen	26-38-3
1968-75	Dick Nolan	56-56-5
1976	Monte Clark	8-6-0
1977	Ken Meyer	5-9-0
1978	Pete McCulley**	1-8-0
1978	Fred O'Connor	1-6-0
1979-88	Bill Walsh	102-63-1
1989-93	George Seifert	68-21-0

 *Resigned after three games in 1963
 **Released after nine games in 1978

CANDLESTICK PARK

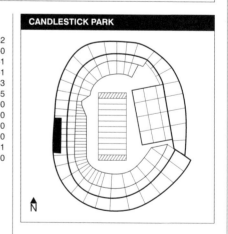

1993 TEAM RECORD

PRESEASON (4-1)

Date	Result		Opponents
8/1	W	21-14	vs. Pittsburgh at Barcelona
8/8	W	27-0	vs. L.A. Raiders at Stanford Stadium
8/16	W	16-13	at Denver
8/21	L	0-30	at Seattle
8/28	W	30-14	San Diego

REGULAR SEASON (10-6)

Date	Result		Opponents	Att.
9/5	W	24-13	at Pittsburgh	57,502
9/13	L	13-23	at Cleveland	78,218
9/19	W	37-30	Atlanta	63,032
9/26	L	13-16	at New Orleans	69,041
10/3	W	38-19	Minnesota	63,071
10/17	L	17-26	at Dallas	65,047
10/24	W	28-14	Phoenix	62,020
10/31	W	40-17	L.A. Rams	63,417
11/14	W	45-21	at Tampa Bay	43,835
11/22	W	42-7	New Orleans	66,500
11/28	W	35-10	at L.A. Rams	62,143
12/5	W	21-8	Cincinnati	60,039
12/11	L	24-27	at Atlanta	64,688
12/19	W	55-17	at Detroit	77,052
12/25	L	7-10	Houston	61,744
1/3	L	34-37	Philadelphia (OT)	61,653

POSTSEASON (1-1)

Date	Result		Opponents	Att.
1/15	W	44-3	N.Y. Giants	67,143
1/23	L	21-38	at Dallas	64,902

(OT) Overtime

SCORE BY PERIODS

49ers	97	158	108	110	0	—	473
Opponents	44	106	57	85	3	—	295

ATTENDANCE

Home 501,476   Away 517,578   Total 1,019,054
Single-game home record, 66,500 (11-22-93)
Single-season home record, 523,355 (1992)

1993 TEAM STATISTICS

	49ers	Opp.
Total First Downs	372	297
Rushing	134	109
Passing	212	171
Penalty	26	17
Third Down: Made/Att	89/186	87/214
Third Down Pct.	47.8	40.7
Fourth Down: Made/Att	10/16	9/20
Fourth Down Pct.	62.5	45.0
Total Net Yards	6435	4997
Avg. Per Game	402.2	312.3
Total Plays	1022	1012
Avg. Per Play	6.3	4.9
Net Yards Rushing	2133	1800
Avg. Per Game	133.3	112.5
Total Rushes	463	404
Net Yards Passing	4302	3197
Avg. Per Game	268.9	199.8
Sacked/Yards Lost	35/178	44/316
Gross Yards	4480	3513
Att./Completions	524/354	564/314
Completion Pct.	67.6	55.7
Had Intercepted	17	19
Punts/Avg.	42/40.9	68/43.9
Net Punting Avg.	42/34.5	68/36.4
Penalties/Yards Lost	95/800	99/743
Fumbles/Ball Lost	32/13	20/11
Touchdowns	61	30
Rushing	26	6
Passing	29	23
Returns	6	1
Avg. Time of Possession	30:24	29:36

1993 INDIVIDUAL STATISTICS

PASSING	Att	Cmp	Yds.	Pct.	TD	Int	Tkld.	Rate
Young	462	314	4023	68.0	29	16	31/160	101.5
Bono	61	39	416	63.9	0	1	4/18	76.9
J. Taylor	1	1	41	100.0	0	0	0/0	118.8
49ers	524	354	4480	67.6	29	17	35/178	98.9
Opponents	564	314	3513	55.7	23	19	44/316	74.0

	TD	TD	TD				
SCORING	R	P	Rt	PAT	FG	Saf	PTS
Cofer	0	0	0	59/61	16/26	0	107
Rice	1	15	0	0/0	0/0	0	96
Watters	10	1	0	0/0	0/0	0	66
Logan	7	0	0	0/0	0/0	0	42
J. Taylor	0	5	0	0/0	0/0	0	30
Jones	0	3	0	0/0	0/0	0	18
Lee	1	2	0	0/0	0/0	0	18
Rathman	3	0	0	0/0	0/0	0	18
Carter	1	0	1	0/0	0/0	0	12
Davis	0	0	2	0/0	0/0	0	12
Young	2	0	0	0/0	0/0	0	12
Beach	0	1	0	0/0	0/0	0	6
Bono	1	0	0	0/0	0/0	0	6
Hanks	0	0	1	0/0	0/0	0	6
McGruder	0	0	1	0/0	0/0	0	6
Singleton	0	1	0	0/0	0/0	0	6
Tamm	0	0	1	0/0	0/0	0	6
Williams	0	1	0	0/0	0/0	0	6
49ers	26	29	6	59/61	16/26	0	473
Opponents	6	23	1	30/30	27/30	2	295

RUSHING	Att.	Yds.	Avg.	LG	TD
Watters	208	950	4.6	39	10
Young	69	407	5.9	35	2
Logan	58	280	4.8	45	7
Lee	72	230	3.2	13	1
Rathman	19	80	4.2	19	3
Carter	10	72	7.2	50t	1
Rice	3	69	23.0	43t	1
J. Taylor	2	17	8.5	12	0
Walker	5	17	3.4	11	0
Bono	12	14	1.2	10	1
Wilmsmeyer	2	0	0.0	0	0
Musgrave	3	-3	-1.0	-1	0
49ers	463	2133	4.6	50t	26
Opponents	404	1800	4.5	41	6

RECEIVING	No.	Yds.	Avg.	LG	TD
Rice	98	1503	15.3	80t	15
Jones	68	735	10.8	29	3
J. Taylor	56	940	16.8	76t	5
Logan	37	348	9.4	24	0
Watters	31	326	10.5	48t	1
Williams	16	132	8.3	15	1
Lee	16	115	7.2	22	2
Rathman	10	86	8.6	17	0
Singleton	8	126	15.8	33	1
Beach	5	59	11.8	20t	1
Turner	3	64	21.3	32	0
Carter	3	40	13.3	14	0
Young	2	2	1.0	6	0
Walker	1	4	4.0	4	0
49ers	354	4480	12.7	80t	29
Opponents	314	3513	11.2	65t	23

INTERCEPTIONS	No.	Yds.	Avg.	LG	TD
McGruder	5	89	17.8	37	1
Davis	4	45	11.3	41t	1
Hanks	3	104	34.7	67t	1
McDonald	3	23	7.7	21	0
Griffin	3	6	2.0	3	0
Johnson	1	0	0.0	0	0
49ers	19	267	14.1	67t	3
Opponents	17	157	9.2	30	0

PUNTING	No.	Yds.	Avg.	In 20	LG
Wilmsmeyer	42	1718	40.9	11	61
49ers	42	1718	40.9	11	61
Opponents	68	2985	43.9	12	57

PUNT RETURNS	No.	FC	Yds.	Avg.	LG	TD
Carter	34	20	411	12.1	72t	1
Kelm	1	0	0	0.0	0	0
49ers	35	20	411	11.7	72t	1
Opponents	15	8	171	11.4	50	0

KICKOFF RETURNS	No.	Yds.	Avg.	LG	TD
Carter	25	494	19.8	60	0
Lee	10	160	16.0	28	0
Walker	3	51	17.0	30	0
Brandes	1	10	10.0	10	0
Kelm	1	0	0.0	0	0
Walls	0	0	—	—	0
Williams	0	0	—	—	0
49ers	40	715	17.9	60	0
Opponents	61	1196	19.6	50	0

SACKS	No.
Stubblefield	10.5
Harrison	6.0
Brown	5.5
T. Wilson	5.5
Romanowski	3.0
Washington	3.0
K. Wilson	3.0
Johnson	2.0
Roberts	1.5
Smith	1.5
Fagan	1.0
Kelly	1.0
Thomas	0.5
49ers	44.0
Opponents	35.0

1994 DRAFT CHOICES

Round	Name	Pos.	College
1	Bryant Young	DT	Notre Dame
	William Floyd	RB	Florida State
2	Kevin Mitchell	LB	Syracuse
	Tyronne Drakeford	DB	Virginia Tech
3	Doug Brien	K	California
	Cory Fleming	WR	Tennessee
5	Tony Peterson	LB	Notre Dame
6	Lee Woodall	LB	West Chester, Pa.

SAN FRANCISCO 49ERS

1994 VETERAN ROSTER

No.	Name	Pos.	Ht.	Wt.	Birthdate	NFL Exp.	College	Hometown	How Acq.	'93 Games/ Starts
79	Barton, Harris	G	6-4	286	4/19/64	8	North Carolina	Atlanta, Ga.	D1a-'87	15/15
83	Beach, Sanjay	WR	6-1	194	2/21/66	4	Colorado State	Chandler, Ariz.	FA-'94	9/0
65	Boatswain, Harry	T	6-4	295	6/26/69	4	New Haven	Brooklyn, N.Y.	D5b-'91	16/2
71	Bollinger, Brian	G	6-5	285	11/21/68	3	North Carolina	Indialantic, Fla.	D3-'92	16/0
85 #	Brandes, John	TE	6-2	249	4/2/64	8	Cameron	Arlington, Tex.	FA-'93	9/0
96	Brown, Dennis	DE	6-4	290	11/6/67	5	Washington	Long Beach, Calif.	D2a-'90	16/16
54 #	Caldwell, Ravin	LB	6-3	240	8/4/63	8	Arkansas	Ft. Smith, Ark.	FA-'93	0*
35	Carter, Dexter	RB	5-9	174	9/15/67	5	Florida State	Baxley, Ga.	D1-'90	16/0
6 #	Cofer, Mike	K	6-1	190	2/19/64	7	North Carolina State	Charlotte, N.C.	FA-'88	16/0
50	Dalman, Chris	G-C	6-3	285	3/15/70	2	Stanford	Salinas, Calif.	D6-'93	15/0
25	Davis, Eric	CB	5-11	178	1/26/68	5	Jacksonville State	Anniston, Ala.	D2b-'90	16/16
63	Deese, Derrick	G	6-3	270	5/17/70	3	Southern California	Culver City, Calif.	FA-'92	0*
75 #	Fagan, Kevin	DE	6-3	254	4/25/63	8	Miami	Lake Worth, Fla.	D4c-'86	7/7
67 #	Foster, Roy	G	6-4	290	5/24/60	13	Southern California	Los Angeles, Calif.	PB(Mia)-'91	1/0
18	Grbac, Elvis	QB	6-3	232	8/13/70	2	Michigan	Willoughby Hills, Ohio	D8-'93	0*
28	Hall, Dana	S	6-2	206	7/8/69	3	Washington	Diamond Bar, Calif.	D1-'92	13/7
36	Hanks, Merton	CB	6-2	185	3/12/68	4	Iowa	Dallas, Tex.	D5a-'91	16/14
45	Hardy, Adrian	CB	5-11	194	8/16/70	2	Northwestern Louisiana	New Orleans, La.	D2-'93	10/0
55	Johnson, John	LB	6-3	230	5/8/68	4	Clemson	La Grange, Ga.	D2c-'91	15/12
84	Jones, Brent	TE	6-4	230	2/12/63	8	Santa Clara	San Jose, Calif.	FA-'87	16/16
90 #	Jordan, Darin	LB	6-2	245	12/4/64	5	Northeastern	Stoughton, Mass.	PB(Raid)-'91	14/0
58	Kelly, Todd	LB	6-2	259	11/27/70	2	Tennessee	Hampton, Va.	D1b-'93	14/5
52 #	Kelm, Larry	LB	6-4	240	11/29/64	8	Texas A&M	Corpus Christi, Tex.	FA-'93	10/1
43	Logan, Marc	RB	6-0	212	5/9/65	7	Kentucky	Lexington, Ky.	PB(Mia)-'92	14/12
46	McDonald, Tim	S	6-2	215	1/26/65	8	Southern California	Fresno, Calif.	FA-'93	16/16
26 #	McGruder, Michael	CB	5-10	190	5/6/64	5	Kent State	Cleveland, Ohio	FA-'92	16/5
62 #	McIntyre, Guy	G	6-3	276	2/17/61	11	Georgia	Thomasville, Ga.	D3-'84	16/16
14	Musgrave, Bill	QB	6-2	205	11/11/67	4	Oregon	Grand Junction, Colo.	FA-'91	1/0
51	Norton, Ken	LB	6-2	241	9/29/66	7	UCLA	Los Angeles, Calif.	UFA(Dall)-'94	16/16*
50	Plummer, Gary	LB	6-2	247	1/26/60	9	California	Fremont, Calif.	UFA(SD)-'94	16/15*
44 #	Rathman, Tom	RB	6-1	232	10/7/62	9	Nebraska	Grand Island, Neb.	D3a-'86	8/4
80	Rice, Jerry	WR	6-2	200	10/13/62	10	Mississippi Valley State	Crawford, Miss.	D1-'85	16/16
91 #	Roberts, Larry	DE	6-3	275	6/2/63	9	Alabama	Dothan, Ala.	D2-'86	6/0
38	Russell, Damien	S	6-1	204	8/20/70	2	Virginia Tech	Washington, D.C.	D6-'92	16/0
61	Sapolu, Jesse	C	6-4	278	3/10/61	12	Hawaii	Honolulu, Hawaii	D11-'83	16/16
88	Singleton, Nate	WR	5-11	190	7/5/68	2	Grambling	Marrero, La.	FA-'93	16/0
95	Smith, Artie	DE	6-4	303	5/15/70	2	Louisiana Tech	Stillwater, Okla.	D5-'93	16/6
94	Stubblefield, Dana	DT	6-2	302	11/14/70	2	Kansas	Cleves, Ohio	D1a-'93	16/14
64	Tamm, Ralph	G-C	6-4	280	3/11/66	7	West Chester, Pa.	Philadelphia, Pa.	PB(Cin)-'92	16/16
82	Taylor, John	WR	6-1	185	3/31/62	9	Delaware State	Pennsauken, N.J.	D3c-'86	16/16
72	Thomas, Mark	DE	6-5	273	5/6/69	3	North Carolina State	Lilburn, Ga.	D4a-'92	11/1
74	Wallace, Steve	T	6-5	280	12/27/64	9	Auburn	Atlanta, Ga.	D4b-'86	15/15
99 #	Walter, Mike	LB	6-3	246	11/30/60	12	Oregon	Eugene, Ore.	FA-'84	15/9
32	Watters, Ricky	RB	6-1	212	4/7/69	4	Notre Dame	Harrisburg, Pa.	D2a-'91	13/13
10	Wilmsmeyer, Klaus	P	6-1	210	12/4/67	3	Louisville	Mississauga, Canada	FA-'92	15/0
77	Wilson, Karl	DE	6-5	277	9/10/64	7	Louisiana State	Amite, La.	FA-'93	12/2*
92	Wilson, Troy	DE	6-4	235	11/20/70	2	Pittsburg State, Kan.	Topeka, Kan.	D7-'93	10/0
8	Young, Steve	QB	6-2	205	10/11/61	10	Brigham Young	Greenwich, Conn.	T(TB)-'87	16/16

* Caldwell last active with Washington in '92; Deese inactive for 6 games in '93; Grbac inactive for 16 games; Norton played 16 games with Dallas; Plummer played 16 games with San Diego; Wilson played 5 games with N.Y. Jets, 2 games with Miami, 5 games with San Francisco.

\# Unrestricted free agent; subject to developments.

† Restricted free agent; subject to developments.

Traded—QB Steve Bono to Kansas City, LB Bill Romanowski to Philadelphia, NT Ted Washington to Denver.

Players lost through free agency (3): CB Don Griffin (Clev; 12 games in '93), TE Wesley Walls (NO; 6), TE Jamie Williams (Raid; 16).

Also played with 49ers in '93—QB Steve Bono (8 games), LB Keith DeLong (4), LB Brett Faryniarz (2), LB Antonio Goss (14), CB Alan Grant (3), DE Martin Harrison (11), S Terry Hoage (4), DE Matt LaBounty (6), T James Parrish (1), LB Bill Romanowski (16), WR Odessa Turner (7), RB Adam Walker (10), NT Ted Washington (12).

COACHING STAFF

Head Coach,
George Seifert

Pro Career: Named 49ers' head coach on January 26, 1989, after serving as the team's defensive coordinator since 1983. Immediately earned a place in league history, winning a record 17 games his first year and becoming only the second rookie head coach to lead his team to a Super Bowl title (Don Mc-Cafferty of Baltimore in 1970 was the first). Recorded the NFL's best won-loss mark in 1990, posting a 14-2 record and guided San Francisco to its fifth consecutive NFC West title. In 1991, the 49ers recorded a 10-6 mark, missing the playoffs for the first time since 1982. Again earned a trip to the NFC Championship Game in 1993, posting a 10-6 record mark and winning the NFC West. Joined 49ers as secondary coach in 1980. In only his second season in the pro ranks, San Francisco had the second best defense in the league and won a Super Bowl (XVI) title, despite starting three rookies in the defensive backfield. Appointed the team's defensive coordinator in 1983. Finished 1987 with the top defense in the NFL and a 13-2 record. No pro playing experience. Career record: 68-21.

Background: Linebacker at University of Utah (1960-62). Served a six-month tour of duty with the U.S. Army following graduation. Returned to Utah as a graduate assistant in 1964. Named head coach at Westminster College in Salt Lake City in 1965. Assistant at Iowa (1966), Oregon (1967-71), and Stanford (1972-74). Left Stanford to become head coach at Cornell (1975-76). Joined Bill Walsh's staff at Stanford in 1977 and helped the Cardinal to a two-year mark of 17-7, including victories in the Sun and Bluebonnet Bowls. Received bachelor's degree in zoology (1963) and master's degree in physical education (1966) from Utah.

Personal: Born January 22, 1940, in San Francisco. He and his wife, Linda, have two children—Eve and Jason—and live in Los Altos, Calif.

ASSISTANT COACHES

Jerry Attaway, conditioning; born January 3, 1946, Susanville, Calif., lives in San Jose, Calif. Defensive back Yuba, Calif., J.C. 1964-65, Cal-Davis 1967. No pro playing experience. College coach: Cal-Davis 1970-71, Idaho 1972-74, Utah State 1975-77, Southern California 1978-82. Pro coach: Joined 49ers in 1983.

Mike Barnes, conditioning assistant; born March 13, 1966, Rochester N.Y., lives in Walnut Creek, Calif. No college or pro playing experience. College coach: Texas A&M 1990, California 1991-93. Pro coach: Joined 49ers in 1994.

Dwaine Board, defensive line; born November 29, 1956, Rocky Mount, Va., lives in Redwood City, Calif. Defensive lineman North Carolina A&T 1974-77. Pro defensive lineman San Francisco 49ers 1979-87, New Orleans Saints 1988. Pro coach: Joined 49ers in 1991.

Tom Holmoe, defensive backs; born March 7, 1960, Glendale, Calif., lives in Foster City, Calif. Defensive back Brigham Young 1979-82. Pro defensive back San Francisco 49ers 1983-89. College coach: Brigham Young 1990-91, Stanford 1992-93. Pro coach: Joined 49ers in 1994.

Carl Jackson, running backs; born August 16, 1940, Bay City, Tex., lives in San Jose, Calif. Quarterback Prairie View A&M 1959-62. No pro playing experience. College coach: North Texas State 1976-78, Iowa 1979-91. Pro coach: Joined 49ers in 1992.

Larry Kirksey, wide receivers; born January 6, 1951, Harlan, Ky., lives in Pleasanton, Calif. Wide receiver Eastern Kentucky 1970-72. No pro playing experience. College coach: Miami, Ohio 1974-76, Kentucky 1977-81, Kansas 1982, Kentucky State 1983 (head coach), Florida 1984-88, Pittsburgh 1989, Alabama 1990-93. Pro coach: Joined 49ers in 1994.

Gary Kubiak, quarterbacks; born August 15, 1961, Houston, Tex., lives in Santa Clara, Calif. Quarterback Texas A&M 1979-82. Pro quarterback Denver Broncos 1983-91. College coach: Texas A&M 1992-93. Pro coach: Joined 49ers in 1994.

Alan Lowry, special teams; born November 21, 1950, Irving, Tex., lives in Danville, Calif. Defensive back-quarterback Texas 1970-72. No pro playing experience. College coach: Virginia Tech 1974, Wyoming 1975, Texas 1976-81. Pro coach: Dallas Cowboys 1982-90, Tampa Bay Buccaneers 1991, joined 49ers in 1992.

John Marshall, linebackers; born October 2, 1945, Arroyo Grande, Calif., lives in Pleasanton, Calif. Linebacker Washington State 1964. No pro playing experience. College coach: Oregon 1970-76, Southern California 1977-79. Pro coach: Green Bay Packers 1980-82, Atlanta Falcons 1983-85, Indianapolis Colts 1986-88, joined 49ers in 1989.

Bobb McKittrick, offensive line; born December 29, 1935, Baker, Ore., lives in San Mateo, Calif. Guard Oregon State 1955-57. No pro playing experience. College coach: Oregon State 1961-64, UCLA 1965-70. Pro coach: Los Angeles Rams 1971-72, San Diego Chargers 1974-78, joined 49ers in 1979.

Bill McPherson, assistant head coach; born October 24, 1931, Santa Clara, Calif., lives in San Jose, Calif. Tackle Santa Clara 1950-52. No pro playing experience. College coach: Santa Clara 1963-74, UCLA 1975-77. Pro coach: Philadelphia Eagles 1978, joined 49ers in 1979.

Brian Pariani, offensive coaches assistant; born July 2, 1965, San Francisco, Calif., lives in Menlo Park, Calif. No college or pro playing experience. College coach: UCLA 1989. Pro coach: Joined 49ers in 1991.

Ray Rhodes, defensive coordinator; born October 20, 1950, Mexia, Tex., lives in Pleasanton, Calif. Running back-wide receiver Texas Christian 1969-70, Tulsa 1972-73. Pro defensive back New York Giants 1974-79, San Francisco 49ers 1980. Pro coach: San Francisco 49ers 1980-91, Green Bay Packers 1992-93, rejoined 49ers in 1994.

Mike Shanahan, offensive coordinator; born August 24, 1952, Oak Park, Ill., lives in Saratoga, Calif. Quarterback Eastern Illinois 1970-73. No pro playing experience. College coach: Oklahoma 1975-76, Northern Arizona 1977, Eastern Illinois 1978, Minnesota 1979, Florida 1980-83. Pro coach: Denver Broncos 1984-87, 1989-91, Los Angeles Raiders 1988-89 (head coach), joined 49ers in 1992.

Mike Solari, tight ends-offensive line assistant; born January 16, 1955, Daly City, Calif., lives in Pleasanton, Calif. Offensive lineman San Diego State 1975-76. No pro playing experience. College coach: Mira Vista (Calif.) Junior College 1977-78, U.S. International 1979, Boise State 1980, Cincinnati 1981-82, Kansas 1983-85, Pittsburgh 1986, Alabama 1990-91. Pro coach: Dallas Cowboys 1987-88, Phoenix Cardinals 1989, joined 49ers in 1992.

1994 FIRST-YEAR ROSTER

Name	Pos.	Ht.	Wt.	Birthdate	College	Hometown	How Acq.
Barnes, Tomur (1)	CB	5-10	188	9/8/70	North Texas State	Baytown, Tex.	FA
Bridewell, Jeff (1)	QB	6-5	220	5/13/67	California-Davis	Napa, Calif.	FA
Brien, Doug	K	5-11	177	11/24/70	California	Concord, Calif.	D3a
Browning, Alfonzo	WR	6-2	203	7/27/72	Kentucky	San Francisco, Calif.	FA
Bryant, Junior (1)	DE	6-4	275	1/16/71	Notre Dame	Omaha, Neb.	FA
Burnett, Bryce (1)	TE	6-3	225	3/9/69	San Jose State	Flossmoor, Ill.	FA
Carolan, Brett	TE	6-3	241	3/10/71	Washington State	Novato, Calif.	FA
Collins, Ron	G	6-5	289	9/30/71	Fresno State	San Bernardino, Calif.	FA
Drakeford, Tyronne	CB	5-9	185	6/21/71	Virginia Tech	Camden, S.C.	D2b
Fleming, Cory	WR	6-1	207	3/19/71	Tennessee	Nashville, Tenn.	D3b
Floyd, William	RB	6-1	242	2/17/72	Florida State	St. Petersburg, Fla.	D1b
Fountaine, Jamal	DE	6-3	240	1/29/71	Washington	San Francisco, Calif.	FA
Hillman, Jay (1)	RB	6-0	230	3/10/68	Boston University	Oxford, Conn.	FA
Ivlow, John (1)	RB	5-11	226	1/26/70	Colorado State	Joliet, Ill.	FA
Jefferson, Anthony	CB	5-11	197	3/11/70	Sonoma State	Hawthorne, Calif.	FA
Kellogg, Jackie	CB	6-1	188	3/29/71	Eastern Washington	Tacoma, Wash.	FA
Millen, Alec (1)	T	6-7	285	9/25/70	Georgia	Atlanta, Ga.	FA
Mitchell, Kevin	LB	6-1	260	1/1/71	Syracuse	Harrisburg, Pa.	D2a
Owens, Darrick (1)	WR	6-2	216	11/5/70	Mississippi	Tallahassee, Fla.	FA
Pay, Gary (1)	C	6-4	285	1/20/68	Brigham Young	Glendale, Ariz.	FA
Popson, Ted (1)	TE	6-4	250	9/10/66	Portland State	Lake Tahoe, Calif.	FA
Peterson, Anthony	LB	6-0	223	1/23/72	Notre Dame	Monongahela, Pa.	D5
Preston, P.J.	LB	6-2	221	11/9/71	Virginia Tech	Martinsville, Va.	FA
Thompson, Tom	P	5-10	192	4/27/72	Oregon	Lompoc, Calif.	FA
Woodall, Lee	S	6-0	220	10/31/69	West Chester, Pa.	Carlisle, Pa.	D6
Young, Alan	DE	6-3	253	1/20/71	Vanderbilt	Woodstock, N.Y.	FA
Young, Bryant	DT	6-2	276	1/27/72	Notre Dame	Chicago Heights, Ill.	D1a

The term NFL Rookie is defined as a player who is in his first season of professional football and has not been on the roster of another professional football team for any regular-season or postseason games. A Rookie is designated by an "R" on NFL rosters. Players who have been active in another professional football league or players who have NFL experience, including either preseason training camp or being on an Active List or Inactive List, or on Reserve/Injured or Reserve/Physically Unable to Perform for fewer than six regular-season games, are termed NFL First-Year Players. An NFL First-Year Player is designated by a "1" on NFL rosters. Thereafter, a player is credited with an additional year of experience for each season in which he accumulates six games on the Active List or Inactive List, or on Reserve/Injured or Reserve/Physically Unable to Perform.

NOTES

National Football Conference
Central Division
Team Colors: Florida Orange, White, and Red
One Buccaneer Place
Tampa, Florida 33607
Telephone: (813) 870-2700

CLUB OFFICIALS

Owner: Hugh F. Culverhouse
V.P.-Football Administration: Rich McKay
Director of Player Personnel: Jerry Angelo
Director of College Scouting: Tim Ruskell
Director of Ticket Sales and Operations:
  Rick Odioso
Director of Public Relations: Chip Namias
Director of Corporate Sales/Broadcasting:
  Jim Overton
Director of Advertising & Sales: Paul Sickmon
Controller: Patrick Smith
College Scouts: Mike Ackerley, Brian Gardner
  Ruston Webster, Mike Yowarsky
Pro Personnel Asst.: John Garrett, John Idzik
Office Manager: Deb Matzke
Asst. Director/Ticket Operations: Lori Grimm
Asst. Director/Media Relations: Scott Smith
Computer Services Coordinator: Terri Kimbell
Assistant Director/Community Relations:
  Sherry Gruden
Media Relations Assistant: Jearl Lett
Assistant Director of Sales/Advertising:
  Jayne Portnoy
Corporate Sales Assistant: Heidi Soderholm
Trainer: Chris Smith
Assistant Trainer: Joe Joe Petrone
Equipment Manager: Frank Pupello
Video Director: Davy Levy
Assistant Video Director: Pat Brazil
Stadium: Tampa Stadium •**Capacity:** 74,321
  Tampa, Florida 33607
Playing Surface: Grass
Training Camp: University of Tampa
  Tampa, Florida 33606

1994 SCHEDULE
PRESEASON

Aug. 6	**Cincinnati**	7:30
Aug. 13	at Seattle	6:00
Aug. 20	at Miami	8:00
Aug. 26	**New York Jets**	7:30

REGULAR SEASON

Sept. 4	at Chicago	12:00
Sept. 11	**Indianapolis**	1:00
Sept. 18	**New Orleans**	1:00
Sept. 25	at Green Bay	12:00
Oct. 2	**Detroit**	1:00
Oct. 9	at Atlanta	1:00
Oct. 16	Open Date	
Oct. 23	at San Francisco	1:00
Oct. 30	**Minnesota**	4:00
Nov. 6	**Chicago**	1:00
Nov. 13	at Detroit	8:00
Nov. 20	at Seattle	1:00

RECORD HOLDERS
INDIVIDUAL RECORDS—CAREER

Category	Name	Performance
Rushing (Yds.)	James Wilder, 1981-89	5,957
Passing (Yds.)	Vinny Testaverde, 1987-1992	14,820
Passing (TDs)	Vinny Testaverde, 1987-1992	77
Receiving (No.)	James Wilder, 1981-89	430
Receiving (Yds.)	Mark Carrier, 1987-1992	5,018
Interceptions	Cedric Brown, 1977-1984	29
Punting (Avg.)	Frank Garcia, 1983-87	41.1
Punt Return (Avg.)	Willie Drewrey, 1989-1992	9.4
Kickoff Return (Avg.)	Isaac Hagins, 1976-1980	21.9
Field Goals	Donald Igwebuike, 1985-89	94
Touchdowns (Tot.)	James Wilder, 1981-89	46
Points	Donald Igwebuike, 1985-89	416

INDIVIDUAL RECORDS—SINGLE SEASON

Category	Name	Performance
Rushing (Yds.)	James Wilder, 1984	1,544
Passing (Yds.)	Doug Williams, 1981	3,563
Passing (TDs)	Doug Williams, 1980	20
	Vinny Testaverde, 1989	20
Receiving (No.)	Mark Carrier, 1989	86
Receiving (Yds.)	Mark Carrier, 1989	1,422
Interceptions	Cedric Brown, 1981	9
Punting (Avg.)	Larry Swider, 1981	42.7
Punt Return (Avg.)	Courtney Hawkins, 1993	11.1
Kickoff Return (Avg.)	Isaac Hagins, 1977	23.5
Field Goals	Steve Christie, 1990	23
Touchdowns (Tot.)	James Wilder, 1984	13
Points	Donald Igwebuike, 1989	99

INDIVIDUAL RECORDS—SINGLE GAME

Category	Name	Performance
Rushing (Yds.)	James Wilder, 11-6-83	219
Passing (Yds.)	Doug Williams, 11-16-80	486
Passing (TDs)	Steve DeBerg, 9-13-87	5
Receiving (No.)	James Wilder, 9-15-85	13
Receiving (Yds.)	Mark Carrier, 12-6-87	212
Interceptions	Many times	2
	Last time by Joe King and Milton Mack, 12-27-92	
Field Goals	Many times	4
	Last time by Steve Christie, 12-16-90	4
Touchdowns (Tot.)	Jimmie Giles, 10-20-85	4
Points	Jimmie Giles, 10-20-85	24

Nov. 27	at Minnesota	12:00
Dec. 4	**Washington**	1:00
Dec. 11	**Los Angeles Rams**	1:00
Dec. 18	at Washington	1:00
Dec. 24	**Green Bay**	1:00

COACHING HISTORY
(82-197-1)

1976-84	John McKay	45-91-1
1985-86	Leeman Bennett	4-28-0
1987-90	Ray Perkins*	19-41-0
1990-91	Richard Williamson	4-15-0
1992-93	Sam Wyche	10-22-0

*Released after 13 games in 1990

TAMPA STADIUM

N

1993 TEAM RECORD

PRESEASON (2-2)

Date	Result		Opponents
8/7	L	7-23	Denver
8/14	L	10-20	at Atlanta
8/21	W	32-12	vs. Buffalo at Orlando
8/27	W	23-20	Cleveland

REGULAR SEASON (5-11)

Date	Result		Opponents	Att.
9/5	L	3-27	Kansas City	63,378
9/12	L	7-23	at N.Y. Giants	75,891
9/26	L	17-47	at Chicago	58,329
10/3	W	27-10	Detroit	40,794
10/10	L	0-15	at Minnesota	54,215
10/24	L	14-37	Green Bay	47,354
10/31	W	31-24	at Atlanta	50,647
11/7	L	0-23	at Detroit	65,295
11/14	L	21-45	San Francisco	43,835
11/21	W	23-10	Minnesota	40,848
11/28	L	10-13	at Green Bay	56,995
12/5	L	17-23	Washington	49,035
12/12	W	13-10	Chicago	56,667
12/19	L	20-27	at L.A. Raiders	40,532
12/26	W	17-10	at Denver	73,434
1/2	L	17-32	San Diego	35,587

(OT) Overtime

SCORE BY PERIODS

Buccaneers	19	74	89	55	0	—	237
Opponents	72	133	75	96	0	—	376

ATTENDANCE

Home 377,498   Away 475,338   Total 852,836

Single-game home record, 72,077 (10-8-89)

Single-season home record, 545,980 (1979)

1993 TEAM STATISTICS

	Buccaneers	Opp.
Total First Downs	241	280
Rushing	80	109
Passing	141	152
Penalty	20	19
Third Down: Made/Att	74/213	85/224
Third Down Pct.	34.7	37.9
Fourth Down: Made/Att	3/12	5/16
Fourth Down Pct.	25.0	31.3
Total Net Yards	4311	5246
Avg. Per Game	269.4	327.9
Total Plays	949	1011
Avg. Per Play	4.5	5.2
Net Yards Rushing	1290	1994
Avg. Per Game	80.6	124.6
Total Rushes	402	479
Net Yards Passing	3021	3252
Avg. Per Game	188.8	203.3
Sacked/Yards Lost	39/274	29/132
Gross Yards	3295	3384
Att./Completions	508/262	503/300
Completion Pct.	51.6	59.6
Had Intercepted	25	9
Punts/Avg.	94/40.1	76/43.3
Net Punting Avg.	94/35.3	76/36.3
Penalties/Yards Lost	89/765	126/913
Fumbles/Ball Lost	28/11	27/13
Touchdowns	27	40
Rushing	6	15
Passing	19	22
Returns	2	3
Avg. Time of Possession	28:38	31:22

1993 INDIVIDUAL STATISTICS

PASSING	Att	Cmp	Yds.	Pct.	TD	Int	Tkld.	Rate
Erickson	457	233	3054	51.0	18	21	35/236	66.4
DeBerg	39	23	186	59.0	1	3	3/27	47.6
Weldon	11	6	55	54.5	0	1	1/11	30.5
Moore	1	0	0	0.0	0	0	0/0	39.6
Buccaneers	508	262	3295	51.6	19	25	39/274	64.1
Opponents	503	300	3384	59.6	22	9	29/132	86.9

SCORING	TD R	TD P	TD Rt	PAT	FG	Saf	PTS
Husted	0	0	0	27/27	16/22	0	75
Hawkins	0	5	0	0/0	0/0	0	30
Cobb	3	1	0	0/0	0/0	0	24
Copeland	0	4	0	0/0	0/0	0	24
Workman	2	2	0	0/0	0/0	0	24
L. Thomas	0	2	0	0/0	0/0	0	12
G. Anderson	0	1	0	0/0	0/0	0	6
Armstrong	0	1	0	0/0	0/0	0	6
Ro. Hall	0	1	0	0/0	0/0	0	6
Mack	0	0	1	0/0	0/0	0	6
McDowell	0	1	0	0/0	0/0	0	6
Moore	0	1	0	0/0	0/0	0	6
Royster	1	0	0	0/0	0/0	0	6
Seals	0	0	1	0/0	0/0	0	6
Buccaneers	6	19	2	27/27	16/22	0	237
Opponents	15	22	3	38/40	32/35	1	376

RUSHING	Att.	Yds.	Avg.	LG	TD
Cobb	221	658	3.0	16	3
Workman	78	284	3.6	21	2
Royster	33	115	3.5	19	1
Erickson	26	96	3.7	15	0
G. Anderson	28	56	2.0	13	0
Copeland	3	34	11.3	22	0
Harris	7	29	4.1	12	0
C. Wilson	2	7	3.5	4	0
McDowell	2	6	3.0	3	0
Armstrong	2	5	2.5	4	0
Buccaneers	402	1290	3.2	22	6
Opponents	479	1994	4.2	78t	15

RECEIVING	No.	Yds.	Avg.	LG	TD
Hawkins	62	933	15.0	67	5
Workman	54	411	7.6	42t	2
Copeland	30	633	21.1	67t	4
Ro. Hall	23	268	11.7	37t	1
C. Wilson	15	225	15.0	24	0
Dawsey	15	203	13.5	24	0
G. Anderson	11	89	8.1	28	1
Armstrong	9	86	9.6	29	1
Cobb	9	61	6.8	19	1
L. Thomas	8	186	23.3	62t	2
McDowell	8	26	3.3	9	1
Claiborne	5	61	12.2	16	0
Royster	5	18	3.6	10	0
Harris	4	48	12.0	25	0
Moore	4	47	11.8	19t	1
Buccaneers	262	3295	12.6	67t	19
Opponents	300	3384	11.3	53t	22

INTERCEPTIONS	No.	Yds.	Avg.	LG	TD
King	3	29	9.7	28	0
Mack	1	27	27.0	27t	1
D. Anderson	1	6	6.0	6	0
Nickerson	1	6	6.0	6	0
Reynolds	1	3	3.0	3	0
Carter	1	0	0.0	0	0
Seals	1	0	0.0	0t	1
Buccaneers	9	71	7.9	28	2
Opponents	25	280	11.2	59t	1

PUNTING	No.	Yds.	Avg.	In 20	LG
Stryzinski	93	3772	40.6	24	57
Buccaneers	94	3772	40.1	24	57
Opponents	76	3290	43.3	20	64

PUNT RETURNS	No.	FC	Yds.	Avg.	LG	TD
G. Anderson	17	1	113	6.6	15	0
Hawkins	15	8	166	11.1	35	0
Claiborne	6	6	32	5.3	13	0
Buccaneers	38	15	311	8.2	35	0
Opponents	53	23	394	7.4	54	0

KICKOFF RETURNS	No.	Yds.	Avg.	LG	TD
C. Wilson	23	454	19.7	42	0
Turner	6	61	10.2	19	0
G. Anderson	12	181	15.1	24	0
Royster	8	102	12.8	26	0
Workman	5	67	13.4	19	0
Claiborne	4	57	14.3	33	0
Buccaneers	58	922	15.9	42	0
Opponents	28	499	17.8	46	0

SACKS	No.
Seals	8.5
Curry	5.0
Dotson	5.0
Price	3.0
Wheeler	2.0
Ahanotu	1.5
Jones	1.0
Nickerson	1.0
Reynolds	1.0
B. Thomas	1.0
Buccaneers	29.0
Opponents	39.0

1994 DRAFT CHOICES

Round	Name	Pos.	College
1	Trent Dilfer	QB	Fresno State
2	Errict Rhett	RB	Florida
3	Harold Bishop	TE	Louisiana State
5	Pete Pierson	T	Washington
6	Bernard Carter	LB	East Carolina
7	Jim Pyne	C	Virginia Tech

TAMPA BAY BUCCANEERS

1994 VETERAN ROSTER

No.	Name	Pos.	Ht.	Wt.	Birthdate	NFL Exp.	College	Hometown	How Acq.	'93 Games/ Starts
72	Ahanotu, Chidi	DE-DT	6-2	280	10/11/70	2	California	Berkeley, Calif.	D6-'93	16/10
44	Anderson, Darren	CB	5-10	180	1/11/69	2	Toledo	Cincinnati, Ohio	FA-'92	14/1
86	Armstrong, Tyji	TE	6-4	250	10/3/70	3	Mississippi	Inkster, Mich.	D3b-'92	12/7
62	Beckles, Ian	G	6-1	295	7/20/67	5	Indiana	Montreal, Canada	D5-'90	14/14
53	Brady, Ed	LB	6-2	235	6/17/62	11	Illinois	Morris, Ill.	PB(Cin)-'92	16/0
28	Buckley, Curtis	CB-S	6-0	185	9/25/70	2	East Texas State	Silsbee, Tex.	FA-'93	10/2
27	Bussey, Barney	S	6-0	210	5/20/62	9	South Carolina State	Lincolnton, Ga.	UFA(Cin)-'93	16/7
23	Carter, Marty	S	6-1	200	12/17/69	4	Middle Tennessee State	La Grange, Ga.	D8-'91	16/14
89	Collins, Shawn	WR	6-2	205	2/20/67	6	Northern Arizona	San Diego, Calif.	FA-'93	4/0*
88	Copeland, Horace	WR	6-2	195	1/1/71	2	Miami	Orlando, Fla.	D4b-'93	14/8
25	Covington, Tony	S	5-11	195	12/26/67	4	Virginia	Winston-Salem, N.C.	D4-'91	0*
75	Curry, Eric	DE	6-5	270	2/3/70	2	Alabama	Thomasville, Ga.	D1-'93	10/10
80	Dawsey, Lawrence	WR	6-0	195	11/16/67	4	Florida State	Dothan, Ala.	D3-'91	4/4
76	Dill, Scott	T	6-5	290	4/5/66	7	Memphis State	Birmingham, Ala.	PB(Phx)-'90	16/16
71	Dotson, Santana	DE	6-5	270	12/19/69	3	Baylor	Houston, Tex.	D5b-'92	16/13
93	DuBose, Demetrius	LB	6-1	240	3/23/71	2	Notre Dame	Seattle, Wash.	D2-'93	15/4
7	Erickson, Craig	QB	6-2	205	5/17/69	3	Miami	West Palm Beach, Fla.	D4-'92	16/15
22	t- Everett, Thomas	S	5-9	185	11/21/64	8	Baylor	Daingerfield, Tex.	T(Dall)-'94	16/16*
20	# Gray, Jerry	S	6-0	195	12/16/62	10	Texas	Lubbock, Tex.	UFA(Hou)-'93	14/5
26	Green, Rogerick	CB	5-10	185	12/14/69	3	Kansas State	San Antonio, Tex.	D5-'92	0*
74	Gruber, Paul	T	6-5	290	2/24/65	7	Wisconsin	Prairie du Sac, Wis.	D1-'88	10/10
43	Harris, Rudy	RB	6-1	255	9/18/71	2	Clemson	Brockton, Mass.	D4a-'93	10/2
85	Hawkins, Courtney	WR	5-9	180	12/12/69	3	Michigan State	Flint, Mich.	D2-'92	16/12
95	Hill, Tony	DE	6-6	255	10/23/68	3	Tennessee-Chattanooga	Camak, Ga.	FA-'94	0*
5	Husted, Michael	K	6-0	190	6/16/70	2	Virginia	Hampton, Va.	FA-'93	16/0
78	Irwin, Tim	T	6-7	300	12/13/58	14	Tennessee	Knoxville, Tenn.	UFA(Minn)-'94	16/16*
24	† Jones, Roger	CB	5-9	175	4/22/69	4	Tennessee State	Nashville, Tenn.	FA-'92	16/5
41	King, Joe	S	6-2	195	5/7/68	4	Oklahoma State	Dallas, Tex.	PB(Clev)-'92	15/10
79	Love, Sean	G	6-3	290	9/6/68	2	Penn State	Tamaqua, Pa.	FA-'93	2/0
47	Lynch, John	S	6-2	220	9/25/71	2	Stanford	Solana Beach, Calif.	D3b-'93	15/4
21	Mack, Milton	CB	5-11	195	9/20/63	8	Alcorn State	Jackson, Miss.	PB(NO)-'92	12/3
97	Marts, Lonnie	LB	6-2	230	11/10/68	5	Tulane	New Orleans, La.	UFA(KC)-'94	16/15*
61	Mayberry, Tony	C	6-4	290	12/8/67	5	Wake Forest	Springfield, Va.	D4-'90	16/16
35	Mayhew, Martin	CB	5-8	175	10/8/65	7	Florida State	Tallahassee, Fla.	UFA(Wash)-'93	15/14
33	McDowell, Anthony	RB	5-11	235	11/12/68	3	Texas Tech	Killeen, Tex.	D8-'92	4/3
70	McRae, Charles	T	6-7	300	9/16/68	4	Tennessee	Clinton, Tenn.	D1-'91	13/4
83	Moore, Dave	TE	6-2	245	11/11/69	2	Pittsburgh	Roxbury, N.J.	FA-'92	15/1
56	Nickerson, Hardy	LB	6-2	230	9/1/65	8	California	Los Angeles, Calif.	UFA(Pitt)-'93	16/16
36	Paul, Markus	S	6-2	200	4/1/66	6	Syracuse	Osceola, Fla.	FA-'93	9/0*
92	Price, Shawn	DE-DT	6-5	260	3/28/70	2	Pacific	North Tahoe, Nev.	FA-'93	9/6
66	Reimers, Bruce	G	6-7	300	9/28/60	11	Iowa State	Humboldt, Iowa	PB(Cin)-'92	11/10
31	Royster, Mazio	RB	6-1	200	8/3/70	3	Southern California	Pomona, Calif.	D11-'92	14/0
64	Ryan, Tim	G	6-2	280	9/2/68	4	Notre Dame	Kansas City, Mo.	D5-'91	6/0
29	Stargell, Tony	CB-S	5-11	190	8/7/66	5	Tennessee State	La Grange, Ga.	UFA(Ind)-'94	16/1*
4	Stryzinski, Dan	P	6-1	195	5/15/65	5	Indiana	Indianapolis, Ind.	PB(Pitt)-'92	16/0
67	Sullivan, Mike	G	6-3	290	12/22/67	3	Miami	Chicago, Ill.	FA-'92	11/3
51	Thomas, Broderick	LB	6-4	250	2/20/67	6	Nebraska	Houston, Tex.	D1-'89	16/8
87	Thomas, Lamar	WR	6-1	170	2/12/70	2	Miami	Gainesville, Fla.	D3a-'93	14/2
30	Turner, Vernon	KR-WR	5-8	185	1/6/67	4	Carson-Newman	Staten Island, N.Y.	FA-'93	8/0*
13	Vlasic, Mark	QB	6-3	205	10/25/63	8	Iowa	Center Township, Pa.	UFA(KC)-'93	0*
11	Weldon, Casey	QB	6-1	200	2/3/68	3	Florida State	Tallahassee, Fla.	FA-'93	3/0
77	Wheeler, Mark	NT	6-2	280	4/1/70	3	Texas A&M	San Marcos, Tex.	D3a-'92	10/10
54	# Williams, Jimmy	LB	6-2	230	11/15/60	13	Nebraska	Washington, D.C.	T(Minn)-'92	11/8
96	Wilson, Bernard	NT	6-2	295	8/17/70	2	Tennessee State	Nashville, Tenn.	FA-'93	13/2
84	Wilson, Charles	WR	5-10	185	7/1/68	4	Memphis State	Tallahassee, Fla.	FA-'92	15/1
99	Winter, Blaise	DT	6-4	295	1/31/62	10	Syracuse	Blauvelt, N.Y.	FA-'94	16/16*
46	Workman, Vince	RB	5-10	205	5/9/68	6	Ohio State	Dublin, Ohio	RFA(GB)-'93	16/11

* Collins played 4 games with Green Bay in '93; Covington and Green missed '93 season due to injury; Everett played 16 games with Dallas; HIll last active with Dallas in '92; Irwin played 16 games with Minnesota; Marts played 16 games with Kansas City; Paul played 8 games with Chicago, 1 game with Tampa Bay; Stargell played 16 games with Indianapolis; Turner played 7 games with Detroit, 1 game with Tampa Bay; Vlasic inactive for 9 games; Winter played 16 games with San Diego.

\# Unrestricted free agent; subject to developments.

† Restricted free agent; subject to developments.

t- Buccaneers traded for Everett (Dallas).

Players lost through free agency (4): RB Reggie Cobb (GB; 12 games in '93), TE Ron Hall (Det; 16), CB Ricky Reynolds (NF; 14), DE Ray Seals (Pitt; 16).

Also played with Buccaneers in '93—T Theo Adams (7 games in '93), RB Gary Anderson (6), LB Darrick Brownlow (15), LB Reggie Burnette (5), WR Robert Claiborne (5), QB Steve DeBerg (3), DE-NT Eric Hayes (2), T Rob Taylor (16), G-T Pat Tomberlin (2).

COACHING STAFF

Head Coach,
Sam Wyche

Pro Career: Became the Buccaneers' fifth head coach on January 10, 1992, after eight seasons with the Cincinnati Bengals. Led the Bengals to the AFC championship in 1988 and Super Bowl XXIII against the San Francisco 49ers. Played quarterback with the Bengals 1968-70, Washington Redskins 1971-73, Detroit Lions 1974-75, St. Louis Cardinals 1976, and Buffalo Bills 1977. Quarterback coach with the San Francisco 49ers 1979-82. Career record: 74-90.

Background: Attended North Fulton High School in Atlanta. Quarterback at Furman University from 1963-65. Assistant coach at South Carolina in 1967. Head coach at Indiana in 1983.

Personal: Born January 5, 1945, in Atlanta, Georgia. Sam and wife, Jane, live in Tampa, and have two children—Zak and Kerry.

ASSISTANT COACHES

Maxie Baughan, linebackers; born August 3, 1938, Forkland, Ala., lives in Tampa. Center-linebacker Georgia Tech 1956-60. Pro linebacker Philadelphia Eagles 1960-65, Los Angeles Rams 1966-70, Washington Redskins 1971, 1974. College coach: Georgia Tech 1972-73, Cornell 1983-88 (head coach). Pro coach: Baltimore Colts 1975-79, Detroit Lions 1980-82, Minnesota Vikings 1990-91, joined Buccaneers in 1992.

Ken Clarke, defensive line; born August 28, 1956, Savannah, Ga., lives in Tampa. Defensive tackle Syracuse 1974-77. Pro defensive tackle Philadelphia Eagles 1978-87, Seattle Seahawks 1988, Minnesota Vikings 1989-91. Pro coach: Joined Buccaneers in 1994.

David Culley, receivers; born September 17, 1955, Sparta, Tenn., lives in Tampa. Quarterback Vanderbilt 1973, 1975-77. No pro playing experience. College coach: Austin Peay 1978, Vanderbilt 1979-81, Middle Tennessee State 1982, Tennessee-Chattanooga 1983, Western Kentucky 1984, Southwestern Louisiana 1985-89, Texas-El Paso 1989-90, Texas A&M 1991-93. Pro coach: Joined Buccaneers in 1994.

Johnny Lynn, defensive backs; born December 19, 1956, Los Angeles, Calif., lives in Tampa. Defensive back UCLA 1975-78. Pro defensive back New York Jets 1979-86. College coach: Arizona 1988-93. Pro coach: Joined Buccaneers in 1994.

Mike Mularkey, offensive assistant; born November 19, 1961, Ft. Lauderdale, Fla., lives in Tampa. Tight end Florida 1979-82. Pro tight end Minnesota 1983-88, Pittsburgh 1989-91. Pro coach: Joined Buccaneers in 1994.

Willie Peete, running backs; born July 14, 1937, Mesa, Ariz., lives in Tampa. Fullback Arizona 1956-59. No pro playing experience. College coach: Arizona 1960-62, 1971-82. Pro coach: Kansas City Chiefs 1983-86, Green Bay Packers 1987-91, joined Buccaneers in 1992.

Floyd Peters, defensive coordinator; born May 21, 1936, Council Bluffs, Iowa; lives in Tampa. Defensive lineman San Francisco State 1954-57. Defensive tackle Baltimore Colts 1958, Cleveland Browns 1959-62, Detroit Lions 1963, Philadelphia Eagles 1964-69, Washington Redskins 1970. Pro coach: Miami Dolphins 1971-73 (scout), New York Giants 1974-75, San Francisco 49ers 1976-77, Detroit Lions 1978-81, St. Louis Cardinals 1982-85, Minnesota Vikings 1986-90, joined Buccaneers in 1991.

Turk Schonert, quarterbacks; born January 15, 1957, Placentia, Calif., lives in Tampa. Quarterback Stanford 1976-79. Pro quarterback Cincinnati Bengals 1981-85, 1988-89, Atlanta Falcons 1986. Pro coach: Joined Buccaneers in 1992.

George Stewart, special teams; born December 29, 1958, Little Rock, Ark., lives in Tampa. Guard Arkansas 1977-80. No pro playing experience. College coach: Minnesota 1984-85, Notre Dame 1986-88. Pro coach: Pittsburgh Steelers 1989-91, joined Buccaneers in 1992.

1994 FIRST-YEAR ROSTER

Name	Pos.	Ht.	Wt.	Birthdate	College	Hometown	How Acq.
Allison, Joe	K	6-0	185	1/20/71	Memphis State	Miami, Fla.	FA
Bishop, Harold	TE	6-4	250	4/8/70	Louisiana State	Tuscaloosa, Ala.	D3
Carter, Bernard	LB	6-3	245	8/22/71	East Carolina	Tallahassee, Fla.	D6
Crisman, Joel	G	6-5	290	2/3/71	Southern California	Grundy Center, Iowa	FA
Davis, Tyree (1)	WR	5-9	165	9/23/70	Central Arkansas	Altheimer, Ark.	D7-'93
Dilfer, Trent	QB	6-4	230	3/13/72	Fresno State	Aptos, Calif.	D1
Ellison, Jerry	RB	5-11	195	12/20/71	Tenn.-Chatanooga	Augusta, Ga.	FA
Hadnot, Butch (1)	RB	6-1	230	3/31/70	Texas	Kirbyville, Tex.	FA
Holliday, Tommy	G	6-3	280	11/16/69	Southern	Baton Rouge, La.	FA
Holstein, Scott	P	6-5	210	6/6/71	Louisiana State	Baton Rouge, La.	FA
Mills, Vidal	S	5-11	190	7/21/72	Bethune-Cookman	Tampa, Fla.	FA
Pierson, Pete	T	6-5	285	2/4/71	Washington	Portland, Ore.	D5
Pyne, Jim	C	6-2	280	11/23/71	Virginia Tech	Milford, Mass.	D7
Rhett, Errict	RB	5-11	210	12/11/70	Florida	Pembroke Pines, Fla.	D2
Saunders, Cedric	TE	6-3	240	9/30/72	Ohio State	Sarasota, Fla.	FA
Small, Eddie	WR	6-1	200	12/9/72	Mississippi	Jacksonville, Fla.	FA
Smith, Dedric	WR	5-7	170	9/16/71	Savannah State	Atlanta, Ga.	FA
Warren, Corey	WR	5-10	195	11/9/71	Oklahoma	Houston, Tex.	FA
White, Paul	CB-S	5-9	185	11/8/71	Miami	Tampa, Fla.	FA
Williams, Germaine	RB	5-10	230	2/4/71	Louisiana State	Donaldsonville, La.	FA

The term NFL Rookie is defined as a player who is in his first season of professional football and has not been on the roster of another professional football team for any regular-season or postseason games. A Rookie is designated by an "R" on NFL rosters. Players who have been active in another professional football league or players who have NFL experience, including either preseason training camp or being on an Active List or Inactive List, or on Reserve/Injured or Reserve/Physically Unable to Perform for fewer than six regular-season games, are termed NFL First-Year Players. An NFL First-Year Player is designated by a "1" on NFL rosters. Thereafter, a player is credited with an additional year of experience for each season in which he accumulates six games on the Active List or Inactive List, or on Reserve/Injured or Reserve/Physically Unable to Perform.

NOTES

Bob Wylie, offensive line; born February 16, 1951, Providence, R.I., lives in Tampa. Linebacker Colorado 1969-71. No pro playing experience. College coach: Brown 1980-82, Holy Cross 1983-84, Ohio University 1985-87, Colorado State 1988-89. Pro coach: New York Jets 1990-91, joined Buccaneers in 1992.

™

National Football Conference
Eastern Division
Team Colors: Burgundy and Gold
Redskin Park
P.O. Box 17247
Washington, D.C. 20041
Telephone: (703) 478-8900

CLUB OFFICIALS

Chairman of the Board-CEO: Jack Kent Cooke
Executive Vice President: John Kent Cooke
House Counsel: Stuart Haney
Controller: Gregory Dillon
Board of Directors: Jack Kent Cooke, John Kent
 Cooke, Ralph Kent Cooke, James Lacher
General Manager: Charley Casserly
Assistant General Manager: Bobby Mitchell
Director of Pro Player Personnel: Kirk Mee
Director of College Scouting: George Saimes
Scouts: Chuck Banker, Gene Bates, Larry Bryan,
 Scott Cohen, Mike Hagen, Reed Johnson,
 Mel Kaufman, Miller McCalmon, Joe Mendes
Director of Communications: Rick Vaughn
Director of Media Relations: Mike McCall
Director of Information: John Autry
Director of Stadium Operations/Club Promotions:
 John Kent Cooke, Jr.
Assistant Promotions/Advertising Director:
 John Wagner
Video Director: Donnie Schoenmann
Asst. Video Director: Hugh McPhillips
Ticket Manager: Jeff Ritter
Head Trainer: Bubba Tyer
Assistant Trainers: Al Bellamy, Kevin Bastin
Equipment Manager: Jay Brunetti
Asst. Equipment Manager: Jeff Parsons
Stadium: RFK Stadium •**Capacity:** 56,454
 Washington, D.C. 20003
Playing Surface: Grass
Training Camp: Dickinson College
 Carlisle, Pennsylvania 17013

1994 SCHEDULE

PRESEASON

Aug. 8	at Buffalo	8:00
Aug. 12	**Kansas City**	8:00
Aug. 18	at New England	7:00
Aug. 26	**Pittsburgh**	8:00

REGULAR SEASON

Sept. 4	**Seattle**	1:00
Sept. 11	at New Orleans	3:00
Sept. 18	at New York Giants	4:00
Sept. 25	**Atlanta**	1:00
Oct. 2	**Dallas**	1:00
Oct. 9	at Philadelphia	8:00
Oct. 16	**Arizona**	1:00
Oct. 23	at Indianapolis	12:00
Oct. 30	**Philadelphia**	1:00
Nov. 6	**San Francisco**	1:00
Nov. 13	Open Date	
Nov. 20	at Dallas	12:00
Nov. 27	**New York Giants**	4:00
Dec. 4	at Tampa Bay	1:00
Dec. 11	at Arizona	2:00
Dec. 18	**Tampa Bay**	1:00
Dec. 24	at Los Angeles Rams	1:00

COACHING HISTORY

Boston 1932-36
(450-377-26)

1932	Lud Wray	4-4-2
1933-34	William (Lone Star) Dietz	11-11-2
1935	Eddie Casey	2-8-1
1936-42	Ray Flaherty	56-23-3
1943	Arthur (Dutch) Bergman	7-4-1
1944-45	Dudley DeGroot	14-6-1
1946-48	Glen (Turk) Edwards	16-18-1
1949	John Whelchel*	3-3-1
1949-51	Herman Ball**	4-16-0
1951	Dick Todd	5-4-0
1952-53	Earl (Curly) Lambeau	10-13-1
1954-58	Joe Kuharich	26-32-2
1959-60	Mike Nixon	4-18-2
1961-65	Bill McPeak	21-46-3
1966-68	Otto Graham	17-22-3
1969	Vince Lombardi	7-5-2
1970	Bill Austin	6-8-0
1971-77	George Allen	69-35-1

RECORD HOLDERS

INDIVIDUAL RECORDS—CAREER

Category	Name	Performance
Rushing (Yds.)	John Riggins, 1976-79, 1981-85	7,472
Passing (Yds.)	Joe Theismann, 1974-1985	25,206
Passing (TDs)	Sammy Baugh, 1937-1952	187
Receiving (No.)	Art Monk, 1980-1993	*888
Receiving (Yds.)	Art Monk, 1980-1993	12,028
Interceptions	Brig Owens, 1966-1977	36
Punting (Avg.)	Sammy Baugh, 1937-1952	*45.1
Punt Return (Avg.)	Johnny Williams, 1952-53	12.8
Kickoff Return (Avg.)	Bobby Mitchell, 1962-68	28.5
Field Goals	Mark Moseley, 1974-1986	263
Touchdowns (Tot.)	Charley Taylor, 1964-1977	90
Points	Mark Moseley, 1974-1986	1,206

INDIVIDUAL RECORDS—SINGLE SEASON

Category	Name	Performance
Rushing (Yds.)	John Riggins, 1983	1,347
Passing (Yds.)	Jay Schroeder, 1986	4,109
Passing (TDs)	Sonny Jurgensen, 1967	31
Receiving (No.)	Art Monk, 1984	106
Receiving (Yds.)	Bobby Mitchell, 1963	1,436
Interceptions	Dan Sandifer, 1948	13
Punting (Avg.)	Sammy Baugh, 1940	*51.4
Punt Return (Avg.)	Johnny Williams, 1952	15.3
Kickoff Return (Avg.)	Mike Nelms, 1981	29.7
Field Goals	Mark Moseley, 1983	33
Touchdowns (Tot.)	John Riggins, 1983	*24
Points	Mark Moseley, 1983	161

INDIVIDUAL RECORDS—SINGLE GAME

Category	Name	Performance
Rushing (Yds.)	Gerald Riggs, 9-17-89	221
Passing (Yds.)	Sammy Baugh, 10-31-43	446
Passing (TDs)	Sammy Baugh, 10-31-43, 11-23-47	6
	Mark Rypien, 11-10-91	6
Receiving (No.)	Art Monk, 12-15-85	13
	Kelvin Bryant, 12-7-86	13
	Art Monk, 11-4-90	13
Receiving (Yds.)	Anthony Allen, 10-4-87	255
Interceptions	Sammy Baugh, 11-14-43	*4
	Dan Sandifer, 10-31-48	*4
Field Goals	Many times	5
	Last time by Chip Lohmiller, 10-25-92	
Touchdowns (Tot.)	Dick James, 12-17-61	4
	Larry Brown, 12-4-73	4
Points	Dick James, 12-17-61	24
	Larry Brown, 12-4-73	24

*NFL Record

ROBERT F. KENNEDY STADIUM

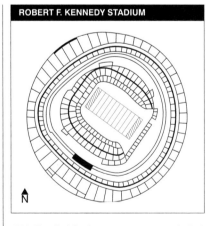

N

1978-80	Jack Pardee	24-24-0
1981-92	Joe Gibbs	140-65-0
1993	Richie Petitbon	4-12

*Released after seven games in 1949
**Released after three games in 1951

1993 TEAM RECORD

PRESEASON (3-1)

Date	Result		Opponents
8/9	W	41-12	Cleveland
8/14	L	10-19	at Miami
8/22	W	10-3	at Pittsburgh
8/27	W	17-3	N.Y. Jets

REGULAR SEASON (4-12)

Date	Result		Opponents	Att.
9/6	W	35-16	Dallas	56,345
9/12	L	10-17	Phoenix	53,525
9/19	L	31-34	at Philadelphia	65,435
10/4	L	10-17	at Miami	68,568
10/10	L	7-41	N.Y. Giants	53,715
10/17	L	6-36	at Phoenix	48,143
11/1	L	10-24	at Buffalo	79,106
11/7	W	30-24	Indianapolis	50,523
11/14	L	6-20	at N.Y. Giants	76,606
11/21	L	6-10	at L.A. Rams	45,546
11/28	L	14-17	Philadelphia	46,663
12/5	W	23-17	at Tampa Bay	49,035
12/11	L	0-3	N.Y. Jets	47,970
12/19	W	30-17	Atlanta	50,192
12/26	L	3-38	at Dallas	64,497
12/31	L	9-14	Minnesota	42,836

SCORE BY PERIODS

Redskins	23	77	59	71	0	—	230
Opponents	81	92	69	103	0	—	345

ATTENDANCE

Home 401,769   Away 496,936   Total 898,705
Single-game home record, 56,345 (9-6-93)
Single-season home record, 443,678 (1992)

1993 TEAM STATISTICS

	Redskins	Opp.
Total First Downs	255	304
Rushing	92	127
Passing	143	157
Penalty	20	20
Third Down: Made/Att.	74/213	92/215
Third Down: Pct	34.7	42.8
Fourth Down: Made/Att.	5/16	5/15
Fourth Down: Pct	31.3	33.3
Total Net Yards	4273	5499
Avg. Per Game	267.1	343.7
Total Plays	960	1027
Avg. Per Play	4.4	5.4
Net Yards Rushing	1728	2112
Avg. Per Game	108.0	132.0
Total Rushes	396	513
Net Yards Passing	2545	3387
Avg. Per Game	159.1	211.7
Sacked/Yards Lost	40/219	31/197
Gross Yards	2764	3584
Att./Completions	533/287	483/291
Completion Pct.	53.8	60.2
Had Intercepted	21	17
Punts/Avg.	83/43.9	73/41.0
Net Punting Avg/	83/37.4	73/36.6
Penalties/Yards Lost	90/597	100/782
Fumbles/Ball Lost	24/10	25/14
Touchdowns	26	42
Rushing	11	14
Passing	11	24
Returns	4	4
Avg. Time of Possession	27:58	32:02

1993 INDIVIDUAL STATISTICS

PASSING

	Att.	Comp.	Yds.	Pct.	TD	Int.	Tkld.	Rate
Rypien	319	166	1514	52.0	4	10	16/87	56.3
Gannon	125	74	704	59.2	3	7	16/87	59.6
Conklin	87	46	496	52.9	4	3	8/45	70.9
Mitchell	2	1	50	50.0	0	1	0/0	56.3
Redskins	533	287	2764	53.8	11	21	40/219	59.0
Opponents	483	291	3584	60.2	24	17	31/197	85.1

SCORING

	TD R	TD P	TD Rt	PAT	FG	Saf	PTS
Lohmiller	0	0	0	24/26	16/28	0	72
Sanders	0	4	0	0/0	0/0	0	24
Brooks	3	0	0	0/0	0/0	0	18
McGee	0	3	0	0/0	0/0	0	18
Mitchell	3	0	0	0/0	0/0	0	18
Rypien	3	0	0	0/0	0/0	0	18
Middleton	0	2	0	0/0	0/0	0	12
Monk	0	2	0	0/0	0/0	0	12
Byner	1	0	0	0/0	0/0	0	6
Coleman	0	0	1	0/0	0/0	0	6
Gannon	1	0	0	0/0	0/0	0	6
Gouveia	0	0	1	0/0	0/0	0	6
Green	0	0	1	0/0	0/0	0	6
A. Johnson	0	0	1	0/0	0/0	0	6
Redskins	11	11	4	24/26	16/28	1	230
Opponents	14	24	4	40/42	17/22	1	345

RUSHING

	Att.	Yds.	Avg.	LG	TD
Brooks	223	1063	4.8	85t	3
Mitchell	63	246	3.9	29t	3
Ervins	50	201	4.0	18	0
Byner	23	105	4.6	16	1
Gannon	21	88	4.2	12	1
Howard	2	17	8.5	9	0
Sanders	1	7	7.0	7	0
Rypien	9	4	0.4	5	3
Roby	1	0	0.0	0	0
Monk	1	-1	-1.0	-1	0
Conklin	2	-2	-1.0	-1	0
Redskins	396	1728	4.4	85t	11
Opponents	513	2112	4.1	35	14

RECEIVING

	No.	Yds.	Avg.	LG	TD
Sanders	58	638	11.0	50	4
Monk	41	398	9.7	29	2
McGee	39	500	12.8	54	3
Byner	27	194	7.2	20	0
Middleton	24	154	6.4	18	2
Howard	23	286	12.4	27	0
Brooks	21	186	8.9	43	0
Mitchell	20	157	7.9	18	0
Ervins	16	123	7.7	20	0
Wycheck	16	113	7.1	20	0
Clifton	2	15	7.5	10	0
Redskins	287	2764	9.6	54	11
Opponents	291	3584	12.3	80t	24

INTERCEPTIONS

	No.	Yds.	Avg.	LG	TD
Carter	6	54	9.0	29	0
Green	4	10	2.5	6	0
Coleman	2	27	13.5	14	0
A. Johnson	1	69	69.0	69t	1
Gouveia	1	59	59.0	59t	1
Edwards	1	17	17.0	17	0
A. Collins	1	5	5.0	5	0
Copeland	1	0	0.0	0	0
Redskins	17	241	14.2	69t	2
Opponents	21	209	10.0	30	2

PUNTING

	No.	Yds.	Avg.	In 20	LG
Roby	78	3447	44.2	25	60
Goodburn	5	197	39.4	3	49
Redskins	83	3644	43.9	28	60
Opponents	73	2995	41.0	20	65

PUNT RETURNS

	No.	FC	Yds.	Avg.	LG	TD
Mitchell	29	7	193	6.7	48	0
Howard	4	0	25	6.3	13	0
Green	1	1	27	27.0	24	0
Mays	1	0	0	0.0	0	0
Redskins	35	8	245	7.0	48	0
Opponents	34	23	343	10.1	62t	2

KICKOFF RETURNS

	No.	Yds.	Avg.	LG	TD
Mitchell	33	678	20.5	68	0
Howard	21	405	19.3	33	0
Ervins	2	29	14.5	18	0
Bowles	1	27	27.0	27	0
Brooks	1	12	12.0	12	0
Buck	1	15	15.0	15	0
Redskins	59	1166	19.8	68	0
Opponents	36	722	20.1	43	0

SACKS

	No.
Coleman	6.0
A. Collins	6.0
Palmer	4.5
T. Johnson	4.0
Noga	4.0
Wilson	2.0
Gouveia	1.5
Banks	1.0
Faulkner	1.0
Mann	1.0
Redskins	31.0
Opponents	40.0

1994 DRAFT CHOICES

Round	Name	Pos.	College
1	Heath Shuler	QB	Tennessee
2	Tre Johnson	T	Temple
3	Tydus Winans	WR	Fresno State
	Joe Patton	G	Alabama A&M
4	Kurt Haws	TE	Utah
6	Dexter Nottage	DE	Florida A&M
7	Gus Frerotte	QB	Tulsa

WASHINGTON REDSKINS

1994 VETERAN ROSTER

No.	Name	Pos.	Ht.	Wt.	Birthdate	NFL Exp.	College	Hometown	How Acq.	'93 Games/ Starts
40	Brooks, Reggie	RB	5-8	202	1/19/71	2	Notre Dame	Tulsa, Okla.	D2-'93	16/11
67	Brown, Ray	T	6-5	312	12/12/62	9	Arkansas State	Marion, Ark.	PB(Phx)-'89	16/14
99	# Buck, Jason	DE	6-4	274	7/27/63	8	Brigham Young	St. Anthony, Idaho	FA-'91	13/3
25	Carter, Tom	CB	5-11	181	9/5/72	2	Notre Dame	St. Petersburg, Fla.	D1-'93	14/11
51	# Coleman, Monte	LB	6-2	242	11/4/57	16	Central Arkansas	Pine Bluff, Ark.	D11-'79	14/4
55	Collins, Andre	LB	6-1	231	5/4/68	5	Penn State	Cinnaminson, N.J.	D2-'90	13/13
91	Collins, Shane	DE	6-3	267	4/11/69	3	Arizona State	Bozeman, Mont.	D2-'92	7/5
12	# Conklin, Cary	QB	6-4	225	2/29/68	5	Washington	Yakima, Wash.	D4-'90	4/2
26	Copeland, Danny	S	6-2	210	1/24/66	7	Eastern Kentucky	Thomasville, Ga.	PB(KC)-'91	14/14
27	Edwards, Brad	S	6-2	207	3/22/66	7	South Carolina	Fayetteville, N.C.	PB(Minn)-'90	16/16
24	Eilers, Pat	S	5-11	197	9/3/66	4	Notre Dame	St. Paul, Minn.	FA-'93	11/0
64	Elewonibi, Moe	T	6-4	286	12/16/65	5	Brigham Young	British Columbia, Canada	D3-'90	15/15
85	Ellard, Henry	WR	5-11	182	7/21/61	12	Fresno State	Fresno, Calif.	UFA(Rams)-'94	16/16*
52	Elliott, Matt	C	6-1	265	10/1/68	3	Michigan	Carmel, Ind.	D12-'92	0*
32	† Ervins, Ricky	RB	5-7	195	12/7/68	4	Southern California	Pasadena, Calif.	D3-'91	15/1
92	Faulkner, Jeff	DE	6-4	305	4/4/64	5	Southern	Miami, Fla.	FA-'93	5/3
17	Friesz, John	QB	6-4	218	5/19/67	5	Idaho	Coeur D'Alene, Idaho	UFA(SD)-'94	12/6*
16	# Gannon, Rich	QB	6-3	208	12/20/65	8	Delaware	Philadelphia, Pa.	T(Minn)-'93	8/4
75	Gesek, John	C	6-5	282	2/18/63	8	Cal State-Sacramento	Danville, Calif.	UFA(Dall)-'94	14/0*
54	Gouveia, Kurt	LB	6-1	233	9/14/64	9	Brigham Young	Honolulu, Hawaii	D8-'86	16/16
90	Graf, Rick	LB	6-5	244	8/29/64	8	Wisconsin	Madison, Wis.	UFA(Hou)-'93	5/0
28	Green, Darrell	CB	5-8	170	2/15/60	12	Texas A&I	Houston, Tex.	D1-'83	16/16
56	Hamilton, Rick	LB	6-2	241	4/19/70	2	Central Florida	Inverness, Fla.	D3a-'93	16/0
57	Harvey, Ken	LB	6-2	245	5/6/65	7	California	Austin, Tex.	UFA(Ariz)-'94	16/6*
86	Hobbs, Stephen	WR	5-11	200	11/14/65	7	North Alabama	Mendenhall, Miss.	PB(KC)-'89	0*
96	Hollinquest, Lamont	LB	6-3	245	10/24/70	2	Southern California	Downey, Calif.	D8-'93	16/0
89	Horton, Ethan	TE	6-4	240	12/19/62	8	North Carolina	Kannapolis, N.C.	UFA(Raid)-'94	16/16*
80	Howard, Desmond	WR	5-9	180	5/15/70	3	Michigan	Cleveland, Ohio	D1-'92	16/5
60	Huntington, Greg	C	6-3	287	9/22/70	2	Penn State	Birmingham, Pa.	D5-'93	9/0
88	Jenkins, James	TE	6-2	241	8/17/67	3	Rutgers	Staten Island, N.Y.	FA-'91	15/5
47	Johnson, AJ	CB	5-8	175	6/22/67	5	Southwest Texas State	San Antonio, Tex.	D6-'89	13/3
78	Johnson, Tim	DT	6-3	275	1/29/65	8	Penn State	Sarasota, Fla.	T(Pitt)-'90	15/15
79	Lachey, Jim	T	6-6	294	6/4/63	10	Ohio State	St. Henry, Ohio	T(Raid)-'88	0*
8	Lohmiller, Chip	K	6-3	215	7/16/66	7	Minnesota	Woodbury, Minn.	D2-'88	16/0
59	Matich, Trevor	C	6-4	297	10/9/61	10	Brigham Young	Sacramento, Calif.	UFA(Ind)-'94	16/4*
20	Mays, Alvoid	CB-S	5-9	172	7/10/66	5	West Virginia	Bradenton, Fla.	FA-'90	15/2
63	McKenzie, Raleigh	C-G	6-2	279	2/8/63	10	Tennessee	Knoxville, Tenn.	D11-'85	16/16
87	Middleton, Ron	TE	6-2	262	7/17/65	8	Auburn	Atmore, Ala.	PB(Clev)-'90	16/16
30	# Mitchell, Brian	RB	5-10	203	8/18/68	5	Southwestern Louisiana	Plaquemine, La.	D5-'90	16/4
62	Moore, Darryl	G	6-2	292	1/27/69	3	Texas-El Paso	Minden, La.	D8-'92	12/0
4	O'Hara, Pat	QB	6-3	205	9/27/68	3	Southern California	Santa Monica, Calif.	FA-'94	0*
89	# Orr, Terry	TE	6-2	235	9/27/61	10	Texas	Savannah, Ga.	FA-'91	4/0
97	Palmer, Sterling	DE	6-5	256	2/4/71	2	Florida State	Ft. Lauderdale, Fla.	D4-'93	14/10
1	Roby, Reggie	P	6-2	258	7/30/61	12	Iowa	East Waterloo, Iowa	FA-'93	15/0
69	Schlereth, Mark	G	6-3	278	1/25/66	6	Idaho	Anchorage, Alaska	D10-'89	9/8
74	Siever, Paul	G	6-5	294	8/10/69	3	Penn State	Coatesville, Pa.	FA-'93	0*
76	Simmons, Ed	T	6-5	300	12/31/63	8	Eastern Washington	Seattle, Wash.	D6-'87	13/13
61	Smith, Vernice	G	6-3	298	10/24/65	5	Florida A&M	Orlando, Fla.	FA-'93	14/8*
84	Stock, Mark	WR	6-0	180	4/27/66	4	Virginia Military Institute	Atlanta, Ga.	FA-'92	3/0
41	Thomas, Johnny	CB	5-9	191	8/3/64	7	Baylor	Houston, Tex.	FA-'92	16/0
77	# Wahler, Jim	DT	6-4	275	7/29/66	6	UCLA	San Jose, Calif.	FA-'92	8/0
94	† Wilson, Bobby	DT	6-2	297	3/4/68	4	Michigan State	Chicago, Ill.	D1-'91	12/9
98	Woods, Tony	DE	6-4	269	9/11/65	8	Pittsburgh	South Orange, N.J.	UFA(Rams)-'94	13/7*
22	Wycheck, Frank	RB	6-3	235	10/14/71	2	Maryland	Philadelphia, Pa.	D6b-'93	9/7

*   Ellard played 16 games with L.A. Rams in '93; Elliott, Hobbs, and Lachey missed '93 season due to injury; Friesz played 12 games with San Diego; Gesek played 14 games with Dallas; Harvey played 16 games with Phoenix; Horton played 16 games with L.A. Raiders; Matich played 16 games with Indianapolis; O'Hara last active with San Diego in '92; Siever active for 1 game but did not play; V. Smith played 6 games with Chicago, 8 games with Washington; Woods played 13 games with L.A. Rams.

\#   Unrestricted free agent; subject to developments.

†   Restricted free agent; subject to developments.

Players lost through free agency (1): RB Earnest Byner (Clev; 16 games in '93).

Also played with Redskins in '93—LB Carl Banks (15 games), C Guy Bingham (14), C Jeff Bostic (16), S Todd Bowles (10), P Kelly Goodburn (1), G-T Joe Jacoby (5), DE Charles Mann (12), WR Tim McGee (13), WR Art Monk (16), DT Gerald Nichols (2), DE Al Noga (16), C Marc Raab (2), TE Jim Riggs (3), QB Mark Rypien (12), WR Ricky Sanders (16), DT Eric Williams (4), DE Keith Willis (1).

COACHING STAFF

Head Coach,
Norv Turner

Pro Career: Enters his first seaon as head coach of the Washington Redskins after serving three years as the Dallas Cowboys' offensive coordinator. Turner guided the Cowboys' prolific offense during back-to-back Super Bowl championship seasons. He inherited a Cowboys offense that finished twenty-eighth in total offense in 1990, and a year later improved to ninth. The Cowboys finished fourth in the league offensively the past two seasons. In three seasons under Turner, quarterback Troy Aikman compiled a 91.7 rating, and running back Emmitt Smith won three consecutive NFL rushing titles. Prior to joining the Cowboys, Turner coached six seasons (1985-1990) with the Los Angeles Rams where he oversaw the passing game. Quarterback Jim Everett enjoyed his best seasons under Turner, while Willie Anderson led the NFL in yards per catch in 1989 and 1990, and Henry Ellard was the league's leading receiver in 1988.

Background: Turner played quarterback for three seasons at the University of Oregon (1972-74). He began his coaching career as a graduate assistant at Oregon in 1975. A year later, he moved to the University of Southern California, where he coached from 1976-1984.

Personal: Born May 17, 1952, in LeJeune, N.C. Turner and his wife, Nancy, live in Oakton, Va., and have three children—Scott, Stephanie, and Drew.

ASSISTANT COACHES

Jason Arapoff, assistant conditioning; born July 8, 1965, Weymouth, Mass., lives in Centreville,Va. Defensive back Springfield College 1985-88. No pro playing experience. Pro coach: Joined Redskins in 1992.

Cam Cameron, quarterbacks; born February 6, 1961, Chapel Hill, N.C., lives in Ashburn, Va. Quarterback Indiana 1980-83. No pro playing experience. College coach: Michigan 1984-93. Pro coach: Joined Redskins in 1994.

Russ Grimm, tight ends; born May 2, 1959, Scottdale, Pa., lives in Fairfax, Va. Guard-center Pittsburgh 1977-80. Pro guard Washington Redskins 1981-91. Pro coach: Joined Redskins in 1992.

Mike Haluchak, linebackers; born November 28, 1949, Concord, Calif., lives in Ashburn, Va. Line backer Southern California 1967-70. No pro playing experience. College coach: Southern California 1976-77, Cal State-Fullerton 1978, Pacific 1979-80, California 1981, North Carolina State 1982. Pro coach: Oakland Invaders (USFL) 1983-85, San Diego Chargers 1986-91, Cincinnati Bengals 1992-93, joined Redskins in 1994.

Jim Hanifan, offensive line; born September 21, 1933, Compton, Calif., lives in Ashburn, Va. Tight end California 1952-54. Pro tight end Toronto Argonauts (CFL) 1955. College coach: Glendale, Calif., J.C. 1964-66, Utah 1967-70, California 1971-72, San Diego State 1972-73. Pro coach: St. Louis Cardinals 1974-85 (head coach 1980-85), Atlanta Falcons 1987-89 (interim head coach last four games of 1989), joined Redskins in 1990.

Ray Horton, defensive assistant; born April 12, 1960, Tacoma, Wash., lives in Ashburn, Va. Defensive back Washington 1979-82. Pro defensive back Cincinnati Bengals 1983-88, Dallas Cowboys 1989-92. Pro coach: Joined Redskins in 1994.

Bobby Jackson, running backs; born February 16, 1940, Forsyth, Ga., lives in Sterling, Va. Linebacker-running back Samford (Ga.) 1959-62. No pro playing experience. College coach: Florida State 1965-69, Kansas State 1970-74, Louisville 1975-76, Tennessee 1977-82. Pro coach: Atlanta Falcons 1983-86, San Diego Chargers 1987-91, Phoenix Cardinals 1992-93, joined Redskins in 1994.

Bob Karmelowicz, defensive line; born July 22, 1949, New Britain, Conn., lives in Ashburn, Va. Nose tackle Bridgeport 1972. No pro playing experience. College coach: Arizona State 1974-79, Massachusetts 1979-80, Texas-El Paso 1980-81, Illinois

1982-87, Washington State 1987-89, Miami 1990-91. Pro coach: Cincinnati Bengals 1992-93, joined Redskins in 1994.

Ron Lynn, defensive coordinator, born December 6, 1944, Youngstown, Ohio, lives in Sterling, Va. Quarterback-defensive back Mt. Union (Ohio) 1963-65. No pro playing experience. College coach: Toledo 1966, Mt. Union (Ohio) 1967-73, Kent State 1974-76, San Jose State 1977-78, Pacific 1979, California 1980-82. Pro coach: Oakland Invaders (USFL) 1983-85, San Diego Chargers 1986-91, Cincinnati Bengals 1992-93, joined Redskins in 1994.

Dan Riley, conditioning; born October 19, 1949, Syracuse, N.Y., lives in Ashburn, Va. No college or pro playing experience. College coach: Army 1973-76, Penn State 1977-81. Pro coach: Joined Redskins in 1982.

Terry Robiskie, receivers; born November 12, 1954, New Orleans, La., lives in Clifton, Va. Running back Louisiana State 1973-76. Pro running back Oakland Raiders 1977-79, Miami Dolphins 1980-81. Pro

coach: Oakland/Los Angeles Raiders 1982-1993, joined Redskins in 1994.

Pete Rodriguez, special teams; born July 25, 1940, Chicago, Ill., lives in Sterling, Va. Guard-linebacker Denver University 1959-60, Western State, Colo. 1961-63. No pro playing experience. College coach: Western State, Colo. 1964, Arizona 1968-69, Western Illinois 1970-73, 1979-82 (head coach), Florida State 1974-75, Iowa State 1976-78, Northern Iowa 1986. Pro coach: Michigan Panthers (USFL) 1983-84, Denver Gold (USFL) 1985, Jacksonville Bulls (USFL) 1986, Ottawa Rough Riders (CFL) 1987, Los Angeles Raiders 1988-89, Phoenix Cardinals 1990-93, joined Redskins in 1994.

Emmitt Thomas, defensive backs; born June 4, 1943, Angleton,Tex., lives in Reston, Va. Quarterback-wide receiver Bishop (Tex.) College 1963-65. Pro defensive back Kansas City Chiefs 1966-78. College coach: Central Missouri State 1979-80. Pro coach: St. Louis Cardinals 1981-85, joined Redskins in 1986.

1994 FIRST-YEAR ROSTER

Name	Pos.	Ht.	Wt.	Birthdate	College	Hometown	How Acq.
Bell, William	RB	5-11	203	7/22/71	Georgia Tech	Miami, Fla.	FA
Clifton, Gregory (1)	WR	5-11	175	2/6/68	Johnson C. Smith	Charlotte, N.C.	FA
Cruz, Rick	LB	6-4	250	10/16/69	Portland State	Bakersfield, Calif.	FA
Dingle, Nate	LB	6-3	254	7/23/71	Cincinnati	Well, Maine	FA
Domingos, Steven	P-K	6-4	205	4/15/67	San Francisco State	Visalia, Calif.	FA
Duckett, Tico (1)	RB	5-10	195	2/4/70	Michigan State	Kalamazoo, Mich.	FA
Earle, Guy (1)	T	6-4	290	4/1/68	Chadron State	Keyport, N.J.	FA
Floyd, Gonzalo	LB	6-3	233	9/2/71	Texas-El Paso	Orange Park, Fla.	FA
Frerotte, Gus	QB	6-2	221	7/31/71	Tulsa	Ford Cliff, Pa.	D7
Hall, Chris (1)	S	6-2	184	4/25/70	East Carolina	Pemberton, N.J.	FA
Haws, Kurt	TE	6-5	248	9/25/69	Utah	Mesa, Ariz.	D4
Hinchcliff, Willie (1)	WR	6-0	195	9/13/69	Auckland Institute	Auckland, New Zealand	FA
Hochertz, Martin (1)	DE	6-5	269	10/21/68	Southern Illinois	Cary, Ill.	FA
Johnson, Tre	T	6-2	315	8/30/71	Temple	Peekskill, N.Y.	D2
Lawrence, Tyler	LB	6-4	248	2/7/70	North Carolina State	Greensboro, N.C.	FA
Mills, Lamar	DE	6-5	270	1/26/71	Indiana	Detroit, Mich.	FA
Morrison, Darryl (1)	CB	5-11	185	5/19/71	Arizona	Phoenix, Ariz.	D6a-'93
Nottage, Dexter	DE	6-4	273	11/14/70	Florida A&M	Miami, Fla.	D6
Olobia, Austin (1)	WR	5-11	195	7/18/69	Washington State	Belgin, Nigeria	FA
Owens, Dondre	CB	5-9	170	7/10/72	Howard	Lanham, Md.	FA
Patton, Joe	G	6-5	288	1/5/72	Alabama A&M	Birmingham, Ala.	D3b
Rowe, Ray (1)	TE	6-2	256	7/28/69	San Diego State	San Diego, Calif.	D6-'92
Rush, Tyrone	RB	5-11	196	2/5/71	North Alabama	Philadelphia, Miss.	FA
Satterfield, Brian	RB	6-0	204	12/22/69	North Alabama	Blue Ridge, Ga.	FA
Shuler, Heath	QB	6-2	221	12/31/71	Tennessee	Bryson City, N.C.	D1
Simmons, Jason	DE	6-5	250	12/20/70	Ohio State	Akron, Ohio	FA
Williams, Keith	WR	5-10	177	6/18/71	San Diego State	Lodi, Calif.	FA
Wilson, Pierre	DT	6-4	310	5/5/71	Clemson	Jackson, Miss.	FA
Winans, Tydus	WR	5-11	180	7/26/72	Fresno State	Los Angeles, Calif.	D6b
Wright, Damon	WR	5-9	159	10/30/71	Carson-Newman	High Springs, Fla.	FA

The term NFL Rookie is defined as a player who is in his first season of professional football and has not been on the roster of another professional football team for any regular-season or postseason games. A Rookie is designated by an "R" on NFL rosters. Players who have been active in another professional football league or players who have NFL experience, including either preseason training camp or being on an Active List or Inactive List, or on Reserve/Injured or Reserve/Physically Unable to Perform for fewer than six regular-season games, are termed NFL First-Year Players. An NFL First-Year Player is designated by a "1" on NFL rosters. Thereafter, a player is credited with an additional year of experience for each season in which he accumulates six games on the Active List or Inactive List, or on Reserve/Injured or Reserve/Physically Unable to Perform.

NOTES

1993 Season in Review

1993 INTERCONFERENCE TRADES

San Francisco's eighth-round selection in 1993 from San Francisco to San Diego for the Chargers' sixth-round selection in 1994. (4/26)

Quarterback **Hugh Millen** from New England to Dallas for the Cowboys' seventh-round selection in 1994. (4/28)

Linebacker **Chris Martin** from Kansas City to the Los Angeles Rams for the Rams' seventh-round selection in 1994. (5/7)

Wide receiver **Mervyn Fernandez** from the Los Angeles Raiders to San Francisco for the 49ers' fourth-round selection in 1994. (5/10)

Tackle **Rick Trumbull** from Cleveland to Tampa Bay for past consideration. (6/1)

Running back **Eric Dickerson** from the Los Angeles Raiders to Atlanta for the Falcons' sixth-round selection in 1994. (7/9)

Guard **Gene Williams** from Miami to Cleveland for the Browns' fifth-round selection in 1994. (7/14)

Defensive back **Rickey Dixon** from Cincinnati to the Los Angeles Raiders for the Raiders' seventh-round selection in 1994. (7/16)

Guard **Dan Fike** from Cleveland to Green Bay for the Packers' seventh-round selection in 1994. (8/5)

Guard **Doug Widell** from Denver to Green Bay for the Packers' seventh-round selection in 1994. (8/24)

Tackle **Gary Zimmerman** from Minnesota to Denver for the Broncos' first- and sixth-round selections in 1994 and the Broncos' second-round selection in 1995. (8/24)

Wide receiver **Vance Johnson** from Denver to Minnesota for the Vikings' seventh-round selection in 1994. (8/24)

Wide receiver **Sam Graddy** from the Los Angeles Raiders to the Los Angeles Rams for the Rams' sixth-round selection in 1995. (8/24)

Running back **Barry Word** from Kansas City to Minnesota for the Vikings' fifth-round selection in 1994. (8/30)

Defensive back **Elvis Patterson** and the Raiders' seventh-round selection in 1994 from the Los Angeles Raiders to Dallas for the Cowboys' fifth-round selection in 1994. (10/13)

Running back **Tim Worley** from Pittsburgh to Chicago for the Bears' fifth-round selection in 1994 and the Dallas Cowboys' sixth-round selection in 1995. (10/19)

1994 INTERCONFERENCE TRADES

Defensive back **James Williams** from Buffalo to Phoenix for the Cardinals' best fourth-round selection in 1995. (3/9)

Wide receiver **Nate Lewis** from San Diego to the Los Angeles Rams for the Rams' fourth-round selection in 1995. (3/18)

Tight end **Adrian Cooper** from Pittsburgh to Minnesota for the Vikings' third- and sixth-round selections in 1994. (3/21)

Quarterback **Jeff George** from Indianapolis to Atlanta for the Falcons' first- (seventh selection in round one) and third-round (seventh selection in round three) selections in 1994 and the Falcons' second-round selection in 1996. (3/24)

Defensive end **Burt Grossman** from San Diego to Philadelphia for the Eagles' sixth-round selection in 1995. (4/7)

Defensive back **Marquez Pope** from San Diego to the Los Angeles Rams for the Rams' sixth-round selection in 1995. (4/11)

Quarterback **Warren Moon** from Houston to Minnesota for the Vikings' fourth-round selection in 1994. (4/18)

Defensive back **Ben Smith** from Philadelphia to Denver for the Broncos' third-round selection in 1995. (4/18)

Defensive tackle **Ted Washington** and Dallas's third-round selection in 1994 from San Francisco to Denver for the Broncos' third-and fifth-round selections in 1994. (4/20)

Los Angeles Rams' first-round selection in 1994 to Indianapolis for the Colts' first-round choice from Atlanta and third-round compensatory selection from Atlanta in 1994. Indianapolis selected linebacker **Trev Alberts** (Nebraska). The Los Angeles Rams selected running back **James Bostic** (Auburn). (4/24)

New Orleans' first-round selection in 1994 to the New York Jets for the Jets' first- and fifth-round selections in 1994. New York selected defensive back **Aaron Glenn** (Texas A&M). New Orleans selected defensive end **Joe Johnson** (Louisville) and guard **Craig Novitsky** (UCLA). (4/24)

Miami's first-round selection in 1994 to Green Bay for the Packers' first- and third-round selections in 1994. Green Bay selected tackle **Aaron Taylor** (Notre Dame). Miami selected defensive tackle **Tim Bowens** (Mississippi). (4/24)

Philadelphia's compensatory first-round selection in 1994 to Cleveland for the Browns' second-round selection in 1994 and second-round selection in 1995. Cleveland selected wide receiver **Derrick Alexander** (Michigan). (4/24)

The Los Angeles Raiders' second- and fourth-round selections in 1994 to Minnesota for the Vikings' second-round selection in 1994. Los Angeles selected defensive end **James Folston** (Northeast Louisiana). Minnesota selected defensive end **Fernando Smith** (Jackson State) and defensive tackle **Mike Wells** (Iowa). (4/24)

Denver's third-round selection from Dallas in 1994 and first-round selection in 1995 to Atlanta for Falcons' wide receiver **Mike Pritchard** and Atlanta's seventh-round selection in 1995. Atlanta selected guard **Alai Kalaniuvalu** (Oregon State). (4/24)

Arizona's second-round compensatory selection in 1994 to Miami for the Dolphins' third-round selection from Green Bay, fourth-round selection from San Diego, and Miami's fourth-round selection in 1994. Miami selected center **Tim Ruddy** (Notre Dame). Arizona selected defensive end **Eric England** (Texas A&M), linebacker **Terry Irving** (McNeese State), and defensive back **Perry Carter** (Southern Mississippi). (4/24)

New England's fourth-round selection in 1994 to Arizona for the Cardinals' fourth-round selection from Miami and fifth-round selection from the Los Angeles Rams in 1994. Arizona selected defensive back **Perry Carter** (Southern Mississippi). New England selected tight end **John Burke** (Virginia Tech) and punter **Pat O'Neill** (Syracuse). (4/25)

Green Bay's fourth-round selection in 1994 to the Los Angeles Raiders for the Raiders' fourth-round selection from San Francisco and sixth-round selection from Atlanta. The Raiders selected defensive tackle **Austin Robbins** (North Carolina). Green Bay selected defensive end **Gabe Wilkins** (Gardner-Webb) and wide receiver **Jay Kearney** (West Virginia). (4/25)

The New York Giants' seventh-round selection in 1994 to Denver for Broncos' wide receiver **Arthur Marshall**. The Broncos selected center **Tom Nalen** (Boston College). (4/25)

San Francisco's seventh-round selection through Dallas in 1994 to the Los Angeles Raiders for past consideration. The Raiders selected linebacker **Rob Holmberg** (Penn State). (4/25)

1993 AFC TRADES

Defensive tackle **George Williams** from Cleveland to New England for linebacker **Rob McGovern**. (8/16)

Wide receiver **David Daniels** from Seattle to the New York Jets for the Jets' seventh-round selection in 1994. (8/23)

Tight end **David Jones** from the Los Angeles Raiders to Cleveland for past consideration. (8/24)

Running back **Jon Vaughn** from New England to Seattle for the Seahawks' sixth-round selection in 1994. (8/26)

Guard **Rich Baldinger** from Kansas City to New England for Dallas' seventh-round selection in 1994. (8/30)

1994 AFC TRADES

Defensive back **Donald Frank** from San Diego to Cleveland for the Browns' sixth-round selection in 1995. (3/4)

Wide receiver **Tony Martin** from Miami to San Diego for the Chargers' fourth-round selection in 1994. (3/24)

New England's third- and fifth-round selections in 1994 to San Diego for the Chargers' third-round selection and running back **Marion Butts**. San Diego selected wide receiver **Andre Coleman** (Kansas State) and tight end **Aaron Laing** (New Mexico State). New England selected defensive tackle **Ervin Collier** (Florida A&M). (4/25)

The New York Jets' third-round selection in 1994 to the Los Angeles Raiders for the Raiders' third- and fifth-round selections in 1994. The Raiders selected running back **Calvin Jones** (Nebraska). The Jets selected defensive tackle **Lou Benfatti** (Penn State) and linebacker **Horace Morris** (Tennessee). (4/25)

Seattle's fifth-round selection in 1994 to San Diego for the Chargers' fourth-round selection in 1995. The Chargers selected defensive end **Darren Krein** (Miami). (4/25)

1993 NFC TRADES

Defensive end **Lester Archambeau** from Green Bay to Atlanta for wide receiver **James Milling**. (6/3)

Defensive back **Chris Crooms** from the Los Angeles Rams to Green Bay for the Packers' fifth-round selection in 1994. (8/11)

Tackle **Stan Thomas** from Chicago to Atlanta for the Falcons' fifth-round selection in 1994. (8/17)

Tight end **Kelly Blackwell**, defensive back **Markus Paul**, and linebacker **John Roper** from Chicago to Dallas for linebackers **Barry Minter** and **Vinson Smith** and the Cowboys' sixth-round selection in 1995. (8/17)

Quarterback **Rich Gannon** from Minnesota to Washington for the Redskins' fifth-round selection in 1994. (8/20)

Wide receiver **Ernie Jones** from Phoenix to the Los Angeles Rams for the Rams' fifth-round selection in 1994. (8/26)

Punter **Tim Kalal** from Atlanta to Green Bay for New England's seventh-round selection in 1994, if available. (8/30)

Tight end **Jim Price** from the Los Angeles Rams to Dallas for the Cowboys' sixth-round pick in 1994. (10/5)

Defensive back **Bruce Pickens** from Atlanta to Green Bay for New England's seventh-round pick in 1994, if available. (10/12)

Running back **Eric Dickerson** from Atlanta to Green Bay for running back **John Stephens**. (10/12)

1994 NFC TRADES

Quarterback **Jim Everett** from the Los Angeles Rams to New Orleans for the Saints' seventh-round selection in 1995. (3/18)

Defensive back **Thomas Everett** from Dallas to Tampa Bay for the Buccaneers' fourth-round selection in 1994. (4/5)

Linebacker **Bill Romanowski** from San Francisco to Philadelphia for the Eagles' third-round compensatory selection and sixth-round compensatory selection in 1994. (4/24)

The Los Angeles Rams' first-round selection from Atlanta in 1994 to San Francisco for the 49ers' first-round selection from San Diego, second-round selection, and third-round compensatory selection from Philadelphia in 1994. San Francisco selected defensive tackle **Bryant Young** (Notre Dame). Los Angeles selected tackle **Wayne Gandy** (Auburn), defensive tackle **Brad Ottis** (Wayne State), and linebacker **Ernest Jones** (Oregon). (4/24)

San Francisco's first- and seventh-round selections in 1994 to Dallas for the Cowboys' first- and second-round selections in 1994. Dallas selected defensive end **Shante Carver** (Arizona State). San Francisco selected running back **William Floyd** (Florida State) and defensive back **Tyronne Drakeford** (Virginia Tech). (4/24)

Green Bay's second-round selection in 1994 to San Francisco for the 49ers' third-round compensatory selection, fifth-round selection from Denver, sixth-round selection from San Diego, and sixth-round compensatory selection from Philadelphia in 1994. San Francisco selected linebacker **Kevin Mitchell** (Syracuse). Green Bay selected running back **LeShon Johnson** (Northern Illinois), running back **Dorsey Levens** (Georgia Tech), linebacker **Ruffin Hamilton** (Tulane), and linebacker **Paul Duckworth** (Connecticut). (4/24)

Philadelphia's second-round selection from Cleveland and fourth-round selection in 1994 to Atlanta for the Falcons' second-round selection in 1994. Philadelphia selected defensive tackle **Bruce Walker** (UCLA). Atlanta selected linebacker **Mitch Davis** (Georgia). (4/24)

Defensive end **Chris Doleman** from Minnesota with the Vikings' second-round compensatory selection in 1994 to Atlanta for the Falcons' second-round selection from Cleveland in 1994 and first-round selection in 1995. Minnesota selected wide receiver **David Palmer** (Alabama). Atlanta selected wide receiver **Bert Emanuel** (Rice). (4/24)

The Los Angeles Rams' sixth-round compensatory selection in 1994 to Dallas for the Cowboys' fourth-round selection in 1995. The Cowboys selected defensive back **Darren Studstill** (West Virginia). (4/25)

FINAL STANDINGS

AMERICAN FOOTBALL CONFERENCE

Eastern Division	W	L	T	Pct.	Pts.	OP
Miami	3	1	0	.750	94	88
Indianapolis	2	2	0	.500	51	85
Buffalo***	2	3	0	.400	72	89
New England	1	3	0	.250	57	69
N.Y. Jets	0	4	0	.000	42	72
Central Division						
Cincinnati	2	2	0	.500	70	67
Cleveland	2	2	0	.500	65	83
Pittsburgh++	2	3	0	.400	70	91
Houston	1	3	0	.250	81	101
Western Division						
Kansas City	3	1	0	.750	90	91
San Diego	3	1	0	.750	60	57
Denver	2	2	0	.500	79	81
Seattle	2	2	0	.500	73	49
L.A. Raiders*	2	3	0	.400	53	80

NATIONAL FOOTBALL CONFERENCE

Eastern Division	W	L	T	Pct.	Pts.	OP
Phoenix	3	1	0	.750	72	42
Washington	3	1	0	.750	78	37
Philadelphia+	3	2	0	.600	93	93
N.Y. Giants	2	2	0	.500	75	75
Dallas**	1	3	1	.300	74	79
Central Division						
Detroit**	4	0	1	.900	98	63
Minnesota***	4	1	0	.800	106	63
Tampa Bay	2	2	0	.500	72	75
Chicago	1	3	0	.250	56	65
Green Bay*	1	4	0	.200	99	106
Western Division						
New Orleans+	4	1	0	.800	127	92
San Francisco++	4	1	0	.800	94	71
Atlanta	1	3	0	.250	83	92
L.A. Rams	0	4	0	.000	59	88

* includes Hall of Fame Game
** includes American Bowl '93 in London
*** includes American Bowl '93 in Berlin
+ includes American Bowl '93 in Tokyo
++ includes American Bowl '93 in Barcelona

AFC PRESEASON RECORDS—TEAM BY TEAM

BUFFALO (2-3)
16	* N.Y. Giants	27
7	Detroit	14
6	Minnesota (ABBe)	20
30	Kansas City	7
12	Tampa Bay (ORL)	32
17	* Atlanta	16
72		**89**

CINCINNATI (2-2)
16	* N.Y. Giants	27
24	Indianapolis	7
7	Detroit	30
23	* Philadelphia	3
70		**67**

CLEVELAND (2-2)
12	Washington	41
12	New England (TOR)	9
21	* L.A. Rams	10
20	Tampa Bay	23
65		**83**

DENVER (2-2)
23	Tampa Bay	7
13	* San Francisco	16
34	* Miami	24
9	Phoenix	34
79		**81**

HOUSTON (1-3)
28	New Orleans (SA)	37
20	* Detroit	24
23	Dallas (SA)	20
10	* Seattle	20
81		**101**

INDIANAPOLIS (2-2)
16	Seattle	13
7	* Cincinnati	24
18	* L.A. Raiders	7
10	Green Bay	41
51		**85**

KANSAS CITY (3-1)
29	Green Bay (MIL)	21
7	* Buffalo	30
27	* Minnesota	20
27	New England	20
90		**91**

L.A. RAIDERS (2-3)
19	Green Bay (HOF)	3
0	San Fran. (PAL)	27
7	Dallas	13
7	Indianapolis	18
20	L.A. Rams	19
53		**80**

MIAMI (3-1)
28	Atlanta	27
19	* Washington	10
24	Denver	34
23	* N.Y. Giants	17
94		**88**

NEW ENGLAND (1-3)
7	San Diego	13
9	Cleveland (TOR)	12
21	* Green Bay	17
20	* Kansas City	27
57		**69**

N.Y. JETS (0-4)
13	Pittsburgh	17
13	* Philadelphia	24
13	N.Y. Giants	14
3	Washington	17
42		**72**

PITTSBURGH (2-3)
14	San Fran. (ABBa)	21
17	* N.Y. Jets	13
23	N.Y. Giants	17
3	* Washington	10
13	Minnesota	30
70		**91**

SAN DIEGO (3-1)
13	* New England	7
23	L.A. Rams	17
10	* Phoenix	3
14	San Francisco	30
60		**57**

SEATTLE (2-2)
13	* Indianapolis	16
10	Minnesota	23
30	* San Francisco	0
20	Houston	10
73		**49**

NFC PRESEASON RECORDS—TEAM BY TEAM

ATLANTA (1-3)
27	* Miami	28
20	* Tampa Bay	10
20	Philadelphia	37
16	Buffalo	17
83		**92**

CHICAGO (1-3)
9	Philadelphia	13
10	* Phoenix	11
14	New Orleans	20
23	* Dallas	21
56		**65**

DALLAS (1-3-1)
7	* Minnesota	13
13	Detroit (ABL)(OT)	13
13	* L.A. Raiders	7
20	Houston (3A)	23
21	Chicago	23
74		**79**

DETROIT (4-0-1)
14	* Buffalo	7
13	Dallas (ABL)(OT)	13
24	Houston	20
30	* Cincinnati	7
17	New Orleans	16
98		**63**

GREEN BAY (1-4)
3	L.A. Raid. (HOF)	19
21	Kansas City (MIL)	29
17	N.O. (MAD)	26
17	New England	21
41	* Indianapolis	10
99		**106**

L.A. RAMS (0-4)
13	Phoenix	24
17	* San Diego	23
10	Cleveland	21
19	* L.A. Raiders	20
59		**88**

MINNESOTA (4-1)
13	Dallas	7
20	Buffalo (ABBe)	6
23	* Seattle	10
20	Kansas City	27
30	* Pittsburgh	13
106		**63**

NEW ORLEANS (4-1)
28	Phil. (ABT)	16
37	Houston (SA)	28
26	Green Bay (MAD)	17
20	* Chicago	14
16	* Detroit	17
127		**92**

N.Y. GIANTS (2-2)
27	Cincinnati	16
17	* Pittsburgh	23
14	* N.Y. Jets	13
17	Miami	23
75		**75**

PHILADELPHIA (3-2)
16	N.O. (ABT)	28
13	* Chicago	9
24	N.Y. Jets	13
37	Atlanta	20
3	Cincinnati	23
93		**93**

PHOENIX (3-1)
24	* L.A. Rams	13
11	Chicago	10
3	San Diego	10
34	* Denver	9
72		**42**

SAN FRANCISCO (4-1)
21	Pitts. (ABBa)	14
27	Raiders (PAL)	0
16	Denver	13
0	Seattle	30
30	* San Diego	14
94		**71**

TAMPA BAY (2-2)
7	* Denver	23
10	Atlanta	20
32	Buffalo (ORL)	12
23	* Cleveland	20
72		**75**

WASHINGTON (3-1)
41	* Cleveland	12
10	Miami	19
17	Pittsburgh	3
17	* N.Y. Jets	3
78		**37**

*denotes home game
(OT) denotes overtime
(HOF) denotes Hall of Fame Game
(ABBa) denotes American Bowl '93 in Barcelona
(ABBe) denotes American Bowl '93 in Berlin
(ABL) denotes American Bowl '93 in London
(ABT) denotes American Bowl '93 in Tokyo
(MAD) denotes game played in Madison, Wis.
(MIL) denotes game played in Milwaukee, Wis.
(ORL) denotes game played in Orlando, Fla.
(PAL) denotes game played in Palo Alto, Calif.
(SA) denotes game played in San Antonio, Tex.
(TOR) denotes game played in Toronto, Canada

FINAL STANDINGS

AMERICAN FOOTBALL CONFERENCE

Eastern Division

	W	L	T	Pct.	Pts.	OP
Buffalo	12	4	0	.750	329	242
Miami	9	7	0	.563	349	351
N.Y Jets	8	8	0	.500	270	247
New England	5	11	0	.313	238	286
Indianapolis	4	12	0	.250	189	378

Central Division

	W	L	T	Pct.	Pts.	OP
Houston	12	4	0	.750	368	238
*Pittsburgh	9	7	0	.563	308	281
Cleveland	7	9	0	.438	304	307
Cincinnati	3	13	0	.188	187	319

Western Division

	W	L	T	Pct.	Pts.	OP
Kansas City	11	5	0	.688	328	291
*L.A. Raiders	10	6	0	.625	306	326
*Denver	9	7	0	.563	373	284
San Diego	8	8	0	.500	322	290
Seattle	6	10	0	.375	280	314

NATIONAL FOOTBALL CONFERENCE

Eastern Division

	W	L	T	Pct.	Pts.	OP
Dallas	12	4	0	.750	376	229
*N.Y. Giants	11	5	0	.688	288	205
Philadelphia	8	8	0	.500	293	315
Phoenix	7	9	0	.438	326	269
Washington	4	12	0	.250	230	345

Central Division

	W	L	T	Pct.	Pts.	OP
Detroit	10	6	0	.625	298	292
*Minnesota	9	7	0	.563	277	290
*Green Bay	9	7	0	.563	340	282
Chicago	7	9	0	.438	234	230
Tampa Bay	5	11	0	.313	237	376

Western Division

	W	L	T	Pct.	Pts.	OP
San Francisco	10	6	0	.625	473	295
New Orleans	8	8	0	.500	317	343
Atlanta	6	10	0	.375	316	385
L.A. Rams	5	11	0	.313	221	367

*Wild-Card qualifier for playoffs
Minnesota finished ahead of Green Bay based on a head-to-head sweep (2-0)

WILD CARD PLAYOFFS

AFC
Kansas City 27, Pittsburgh 24 (OT), January 8, at Kansas City
Los Angeles Raiders 42, Denver 24, January 9, at Los Angeles

NFC
Green Bay 28, Detroit 24, January 8, at Detroit
New York Giants 17, Minnesota 10, January 9, at New York

DIVISIONAL PLAYOFFS

AFC
Buffalo 29, Los Angeles Raiders 23, January 15, at Buffalo
Kansas City 28, Houston 20, January 16, at Houston

NFC
San Francisco 44, New York Giants 3, January 15, at San Francisco
Dallas 27, Green Bay 17, January 16, at Dallas

CHAMPIONSHIP GAMES

AFC
Buffalo 30, Kansas City 13, January 23, at Buffalo

NFC
Dallas 38, San Francisco 21, January 23, at Dallas

SUPER BOWL XXVIII
Dallas 30, Buffalo 13, January 30, at Georgia Dome, Atlanta, Georgia

AFC-NFC PRO BOWL
NFC 17, AFC 3, February 6, at Aloha Stadium, Honolulu, Hawaii

AFC SEASON RECORDS—TEAM BY TEAM

BUFFALO (12-4)

38	*New England		14
13	at Dallas		10
	OPEN DATE		
13	*Miami		22
17	*N.Y. Giants		14
35	*Houston		7
	OPEN DATE		
19	at N.Y. Jets		10
24	*Washington		10
13	at New Eng. (OT)		10
0	at Pittsburgh		23
23	*Indianapolis		9
7	at Kansas City		23
24	*L.A. Raiders		25
10	at Philadelphia		7
47	at Miami		34
16	*N.Y. Jets		14
30	at Indianapolis		10
329			**242**

CINCINNATI (3-13)

14	at Cleveland		27
6	*Indianapolis		9
7	at Pittsburgh		34
10	*Seattle		19
15	at Kansas City		17
	OPEN DATE		
17	*Cleveland		28
12	at Houston		28
	OPEN DATE		
16	*Pittsburgh		24
3	*Houston		38
12	at N.Y. Jets		17
16	*L.A. Raiders		10
8	at San Francisco		21
2	at New England		7
15	*L.A. Rams		3
21	*Atlanta		17
13	at New Orleans		20
187			**319**

CLEVELAND (7-9)

27	*Cincinnati		14
23	*San Francisco		13
19	at L.A. Raiders		16
10	at Indianapolis		23
	OPEN DATE		
14	*Miami		24
28	at Cincinnati		17
28	*Pittsburgh		23
	OPEN DATE		
14	*Denver		29
5	at Seattle		22
20	*Houston		27
14	at Atlanta		17
17	*New Orleans		13
17	at Houston		19
17	*New England		20
42	at L.A. Rams		14
9	at Pittsburgh		16
304			**307**

DENVER (9-7)

26	at N.Y. Jets		20
34	*San Diego		17
7	at Kansas City		15
	OPEN DATE		
35	*Indianapolis		13
27	at Green Bay		30
20	*L.A. Raiders		23
	OPEN DATE		
28	*Seattle		17
29	at Cleveland		14
23	*Minnesota		26
37	*Pittsburgh		13
17	at Seattle		9
10	at San Diego		13
27	*Kansas City		21
13	at Chicago		3
10	*Tampa Bay		17
30	at L.A. Raiders (OT)		33
373			**284**

HOUSTON (12-4)

21	at New Orleans		33
30	*Kansas City		0
17	at San Diego		18
13	*L.A. Rams		28
	OPEN DATE		
7	at Buffalo		35
28	at New England		14
28	*Cincinnati		12
	OPEN DATE		
24	*Seattle		14
38	at Cincinnati		3
27	at Cleveland		20
23	*Pittsburgh		3
33	*Atlanta		17
19	*Cleveland		17
26	at Pittsburgh		17
10	at San Francisco		7
24	*N.Y. Jets		0
368			**238**

INDIANAPOLIS (4-12)

20	*Miami		24
9	at Cincinnati		6
	OPEN DATE		
23	*Cleveland		10
13	at Denver		35
3	*Dallas		27
	OPEN DATE		
27	at Miami		41
9	*New England		6
24	at Washington		30
17	*N.Y. Jets		31
9	at Buffalo		23
0	*San Diego		31
9	at N.Y. Jets		6
6	at N.Y. Giants		20
10	*Philadelphia		20
0	at New England		38
10	*Buffalo		30
189			**378**

KANSAS CITY (11-5)

27	at Tampa Bay		3
0	at Houston		30
15	*Denver		7
	OPEN DATE		
24	*L.A. Raiders		9
17	*Cincinnati		15
17	at San Diego		14
10	at Miami		30
23	*Green Bay		16
31	at L.A. Raiders		20
17	*Chicago		19
23	*Buffalo		7
31	at Seattle		16
21	at Denver		27
28	*San Diego		24
10	at Minnesota		30
34	*Seattle		24
328			**291**

L.A. RAIDERS (10-6)

24	*Minnesota		7
17	at Seattle		13
16	*Cleveland		19
	OPEN DATE		
9	at Kansas City		24
24	*N.Y. Jets		20
23	at Denver		20
	OPEN DATE		
23	*San Diego		30
16	at Chicago		14
20	*Kansas City		31
12	at San Diego		7
10	at Cincinnati		16
25	at Buffalo		24
27	*Tampa Bay		20
0	at Green Bay		28
33	*Denver (OT)		30
306			**326**

MIAMI (9-7)

24	at Indianapolis		20
14	*N.Y. Jets		24
	OPEN DATE		
22	at Buffalo		13
17	*Washington		10
24	at Cleveland		14
	OPEN DATE		
41	*Indianapolis		27
30	*Kansas City		10
10	at N.Y. Jets		27
19	at Philadelphia		14
17	*New England		13
14	*N.Y. Giants		19
20	*Pittsburgh		21
34	*Buffalo		47
20	at San Diego		45
27	at New Eng. (OT)		33
349			**351**

NEW ENGLAND (5-11)

14	at Buffalo		38
16	*Detroit (OT)		19
14	*Seattle		17
7	at N.Y. Jets		45
	OPEN DATE		
23	at Phoenix		21
14	*Houston		28
9	at Seattle		10
6	at Indianapolis		9
10	*Buffalo (OT)		13
	OPEN DATE		
13	at Miami		17
0	*N.Y. Jets		6
14	at Pittsburgh		17
7	*Cincinnati		2
20	at Cleveland		17
38	*Indianapolis		0
33	*Miami (OT)		27
238			**286**

N.Y. JETS (8-8)

20	*Denver		26
24	at Miami		14
	OPEN DATE		
45	*New England		7
30	*Philadelphia		35
20	at L.A. Raiders		24
	OPEN DATE		
10	*Buffalo		19
10	at N.Y. Giants		6
27	*Miami		10
31	at Indianapolis		17
17	*Cincinnati		12
6	at New England		0
6	*Indianapolis		9
3	at Washington		0
7	*Dallas		28
14	at Buffalo		16
0	at Houston		24
270			**247**

PITTSBURGH (9-7)

13	*San Francisco		24
0	at L.A. Rams		27
34	*Cincinnati		7
45	at Atlanta		17
	OPEN DATE		
16	*San Diego		3
37	*New Orleans		14
23	at Cleveland		28
	OPEN DATE		
24	at Cincinnati		16
23	*Buffalo		0
13	at Denver		37
3	at Houston		23
17	*New England		14
21	at Miami		20
17	*Houston		26
6	at Seattle		16
16	*Cleveland		9
308			**281**

SAN DIEGO (8-8)

18	*Seattle		12
17	at Denver		34
18	*Houston		17
	OPEN DATE		
14	at Seattle		31
3	at Pittsburgh		16
	OPEN DATE		
14	*Kansas City		17
30	at L.A. Raiders		23
30	at Minnesota		17
13	*Chicago		16
7	*L.A. Raiders		12
31	at Indianapolis		0
13	*Denver		10
13	*Green Bay		20
24	at Kansas City		28
45	*Miami		20
32	at Tampa Bay		17
322			**290**

SEATTLE (6-10)

12	at San Diego		18
13	*L.A. Raiders		17
17	at New England		14
19	at Cincinnati		10
31	*San Diego		14
	OPEN DATE		
10	at Detroit		30
10	*New England		9
17	at Denver		28
14	at Houston		24
22	*Cleveland		5
	OPEN DATE		
9	*Denver		17
16	*Kansas City		31
23	at L.A. Raiders		27
27	*Phoenix (OT)		30
16	*Pittsburgh		6
24	at Kansas City		34
280			**314**

NFC SEASON RECORDS—TEAM BY TEAM

ATLANTA (6-10)
13	at Detroit	30
31	* New Orleans	34
30	at San Francisco	37
17	* Pittsburgh	45
0	at Chicago	6
	OPEN DATE	
30	* L.A. Rams	24
26	at New Orleans	15
24	* Tampa Bay	31
	OPEN DATE	
13	at L.A. Rams	0
27	* Dallas	14
17	* Cleveland	14
17	at Houston	33
27	* San Francisco	24
17	at Washington	30
17	at Cincinnati	21
10	* Phoenix	27
316		**385**

GREEN BAY (9-7)
36	* L.A. Rams	6
17	* Philadelphia	20
	OPEN DATE	
13	at Minnesota	15
14	at Dallas	36
30	* Denver	27
	OPEN DATE	
37	at Tampa Bay	14
17	* Chicago	3
16	at Kansas City	23
19	at New Orleans	17
26	* Detroit	17
13	* Tampa Bay	10
17	at Chicago	30
20	at San Diego	13
17	* Minnesota	21
28	* L.A. Raiders	0
20	at Detroit	30
340		**282**

N.Y. GIANTS (11-5)
26	at Chicago	20
23	* Tampa Bay	7
20	* L.A. Rams	10
	OPEN DATE	
14	at Buffalo	17
41	at Washington	7
21	* Philadelphia	10
	OPEN DATE	
6	* N.Y. Jets	10
9	at Dallas	31
20	* Washington	6
7	at Philadelphia	3
19	* Phoenix	17
19	at Miami	14
20	* Indianapolis	6
24	at New Orleans	14
6	at Phoenix	17
13	* Dallas (OT)	16
288		**205**

TAMPA BAY (5-11)
3	* Kansas City	27
7	at N.Y. Giants	23
	OPEN DATE	
17	at Chicago	47
27	* Detroit	10
0	at Minnesota	15
	OPEN DATE	
14	* Green Bay	37
31	at Atlanta	24
0	at Detroit	23
21	* San Francisco	45
23	* Minnesota	10
10	at Green Bay	13
17	* Washington	23
13	* Chicago	10
20	at L.A. Raiders	27
17	at Denver	10
17	* San Diego	32
237		**376**

CHICAGO (7-9)
20	* N.Y. Giants	26
7	at Minnesota	10
	OPEN DATE	
47	* Tampa Bay	17
6	* Atlanta	0
17	at Philadelphia	6
	OPEN DATE	
12	* Minnesota	19
3	at Green Bay	17
14	* L.A. Raiders	16
16	at San Diego	13
19	at Kansas City	17
10	at Detroit	6
30	* Green Bay	17
10	at Tampa Bay	13
3	* Denver	13
14	* Detroit	20
6	at L.A. Rams	20
234		**230**

L.A. RAMS (5-11)
6	at Green Bay	36
27	* Pittsburgh	0
10	at N.Y. Giants	20
28	at Houston	13
6	* New Orleans	37
	OPEN DATE	
24	at Atlanta	30
13	* Detroit	16
17	at San Francisco	40
	OPEN DATE	
0	* Atlanta	13
10	* Washington	6
10	* San Francisco	35
10	at Phoenix	38
23	at New Orleans	20
3	at Cincinnati	15
14	* Cleveland	42
20	* Chicago	6
221		**367**

PHILADELPHIA (8-8)
23	* Phoenix	17
20	at Green Bay	17
34	* Washington	31
	OPEN DATE	
35	at N.Y. Jets	30
6	* Chicago	17
10	at N.Y. Giants	21
	OPEN DATE	
10	* Dallas	23
3	at Phoenix	16
14	* Miami	19
3	* N.Y. Giants	7
17	at Washington	14
17	at Dallas	23
7	* Buffalo	10
20	at Indianapolis	10
37	* New Orleans	26
37	at San Fran. (OT)	34
293		**315**

WASHINGTON (4-12)
35	* Dallas	16
10	* Phoenix	17
31	at Philadelphia	34
	OPEN DATE	
10	at Miami	17
7	* N.Y. Giants	41
6	at Phoenix	36
	OPEN DATE	
10	at Buffalo	24
30	* Indianapolis	24
6	at N.Y. Giants	20
6	at L.A. Rams	10
14	* Philadelphia	17
23	at Tampa Bay	17
0	* N.Y. Jets	3
30	* Atlanta	17
3	at Dallas	38
9	* Minnesota	14
230		**345**

DALLAS (12-4)
16	at Washington	35
10	* Buffalo	13
17	at Phoenix	10
	OPEN DATE	
36	* Green Bay	14
27	at Indianapolis	3
26	* San Francisco	17
	OPEN DATE	
23	at Philadelphia	10
31	* N.Y. Giants	9
20	* Phoenix	15
14	at Atlanta	27
14	* Miami	16
23	* Philadelphia	17
37	at Minnesota	20
28	at N.Y. Jets	7
38	* Washington	3
16	at N.Y. Giants (OT)	13
376		**229**

MINNESOTA (9-7)
7	at L.A. Raiders	24
10	* Chicago	7
	OPEN DATE	
15	* Green Bay	13
19	at San Francisco	38
15	* Tampa Bay	0
	OPEN DATE	
19	at Chicago	12
27	* Detroit	30
17	* San Diego	30
26	at Denver	23
10	at Tampa Bay	23
14	* New Orleans	17
13	at Detroit	0
20	* Dallas	37
21	at Green Bay	17
30	* Kansas City	10
14	at Washington	9
277		**290**

PHOENIX (7-9)
17	at Philadelphia	23
17	at Washington	10
10	* Dallas	17
20	at Detroit	26
	OPEN DATE	
21	* New England	23
36	* Washington	6
14	at San Francisco	28
17	* New Orleans	20
16	* Philadelphia	3
15	at Dallas	20
	OPEN DATE	
17	at N.Y. Giants	19
38	* L.A. Rams	10
14	* Detroit	21
30	at Seattle (OT)	27
17	* N.Y. Giants	6
27	at Atlanta	10
326		**269**

DETROIT (10-6)
30	* Atlanta	13
19	at New Eng. (OT)	16
3	at New Orleans	14
26	* Phoenix	20
10	at Tampa Bay	27
	OPEN DATE	
30	* Seattle	10
16	at L.A. Rams	13
30	at Minnesota	27
23	* Tampa Bay	0
	OPEN DATE	
17	at Green Bay	26
6	* Chicago	10
0	* Minnesota	13
21	at Phoenix	14
17	* San Francisco	55
20	at Chicago	14
30	* Green Bay	20
298		**292**

NEW ORLEANS (8-8)
33	* Houston	21
34	at Atlanta	31
14	* Detroit	3
16	* San Francisco	13
37	at L.A. Rams	6
	OPEN DATE	
14	at Pittsburgh	37
15	* Atlanta	26
20	at Phoenix	17
	OPEN DATE	
17	* Green Bay	19
7	at San Francisco	42
17	at Minnesota	14
13	at Cleveland	17
20	* L.A. Rams	23
14	* N.Y. Giants	24
26	at Philadelphia	37
20	* Cincinnati	13
317		**343**

SAN FRANCISCO (10-6)
24	at Pittsburgh	13
13	at Cleveland	23
37	* Atlanta	30
13	at New Orleans	16
38	* Minnesota	19
	OPEN DATE	
17	at Dallas	26
28	* Phoenix	14
40	* L.A. Rams	17
	OPEN DATE	
45	at Tampa Bay	21
42	* New Orleans	7
35	at L.A. Rams	10
21	* Cincinnati	8
24	at Atlanta	27
55	at Detroit	17
7	* Houston	10
34	* Philadelphia (OT)	37
473		**295**

*denotes home games
(OT) denotes overtime

Attendance figures as they appear in the following, and in the club-by-club sections starting on page 24, are turnstile counts and not paid attendance. Paid attendance totals are on page 217.

FIRST WEEK SUMMARIES

AMERICAN FOOTBALL CONFERENCE

Eastern Division	W	L	T	Pct.	Pts.	OP
Buffalo	1	0	0	1.000	38	14
Miami	1	0	0	1.000	24	20
Indianapolis	0	1	0	.000	20	24
New England	0	1	0	.000	14	38
N.Y. Jets	0	1	0	.000	20	26
Central Division						
Cleveland	1	0	0	1.000	27	14
Cincinnati	0	1	0	.000	14	27
Houston	0	1	0	.000	21	33
Pittsburgh	0	1	0	.000	13	24
Western Division						
Denver	1	0	0	1.000	26	20
Kansas City	1	0	0	1.000	27	3
L.A. Raiders	1	0	0	1.000	24	7
San Diego	1	0	0	1.000	18	12
Seattle	0	1	0	.000	12	18

NATIONAL FOOTBALL CONFERENCE

Eastern Division	W	L	T	Pct.	Pts.	OP
N.Y. Giants	1	0	0	1.000	26	20
Philadelphia	1	0	0	1.000	23	17
Washington	1	0	0	1.000	35	16
Dallas	0	1	0	.000	16	35
Phoenix	0	1	0	.000	17	23
Central Division						
Detroit	1	0	0	1.000	30	13
Green Bay	1	0	0	1.000	36	6
Chicago	0	1	0	.000	20	26
Minnesota	0	1	0	.000	7	24
Tampa Bay	0	1	0	.000	3	27
Western Division						
New Orleans	1	0	0	1.000	33	21
San Francisco	1	0	0	1.000	24	13
Atlanta	0	1	0	.000	13	30
L.A. Rams	0	1	0	.000	6	36

SUNDAY, SEPTEMBER 5

DETROIT 30, ATLANTA 13—at Silverdome, attendance 56,216. The Lions raced to a 24-3 halftime lead and coasted to the victory over the Falcons. Detroit took a 7-0 advantage just 3:05 into the game on a 26-yard touchdown run by Barry Sanders, which capped a 61-yard drive on the Lions' first possession. Linebacker George Jamison returned an interception 35 yards for a touchdown late in the first quarter, and Rodney Peete tossed a 21-yard touchdown pass to Herman Moore in the second period as the Lions turned the game into a rout. Forced to play catch-up, Falcons quarterback Chris Miller attempted 50 passes and completed 26 for 260 yards, including a 32-yard touchdown to Andre Rison. But Miller also was intercepted twice and sacked 6 times. Wide receiver Mike Pritchard caught 10 passes for Atlanta, and Rison finished with 106 yards on 6 receptions. Moore caught 4 passes for 113 yards for the Lions.

Atlanta	0	3	3	7	—	13
Detroit	14	10	3	3	—	30

Det — Sanders 26 run (Hanson kick)
Det — Jamison 35 interception return (Hanson kick)
Det — FG Hanson 44
Det — Moore 21 pass from Peete (Hanson kick)
Atl — FG Johnson 54
Atl — FG Johnson 20
Det — FG Hanson 37
Atl — Rison 32 pass from Miller (Johnson kick)
Det — FG Hanson 37

CLEVELAND 27, CINCINNATI 14—at Cleveland Stadium, attendance 75,508. The Browns spotted the Bengals a 14-point first-quarter lead, then rallied behind their defense to win. Cleveland sacked Cincinnati quarterback David Klingler 6 times, intercepted 2 passes, and returned a fumble for the clinching score in the fourth quarter. The Browns also executed a goal-line stand late in the game, keeping the Bengals out of the end zone after facing first-and-goal from the 1-yard line. Cleveland, which fell behind 14-0 in the game's initial 12 minutes, tied it by halftime on a 13-yard touchdown pass from Bernie Kosar to Michael Jackson and a 1-yard touchdown run by Tommy Vardell, the latter coming just 28 seconds before intermission. Matt Stover kicked a pair of field goals in the third quarter to put the Browns ahead 20-14, and cornerback Everson Walls made the key play of the game one minute into the final period. Walls sacked Klingler, forcing the fumble that safety Steven Moore recovered and returned 22 yards for a touchdown.

Cincinnati	14	0	0	0	—	14
Cleveland	0	14	6	7	—	27

Cin — Miles 4 run (Pelfrey kick)
Cin — Pickens 5 pass from Klingler (Pelfrey kick)
Cle — Jackson 13 pass from Kosar (Stover kick)
Cle — Vardell 1 run (Stover kick)
Cle — FG Stover 28
Cle — FG Stover 34
Cle — Moore 22 fumble recovery return (Stover kick)

DENVER 26, N.Y. JETS 20—at Giants Stadium, attendance 68,130. John Elway passed for 269 yards and 2 touchdowns and rookies Glyn Milburn and Jason Elam played key roles as the Broncos beat the Jets. Elway, who completed 20 of 29 passes, broke a 6-6 tie with a 3-yard touchdown pass to Cedric Tillman 27 seconds before halftime. He then marched his team 80 yards following the second-half kickoff to another touchdown, a 25-yard pass to Milburn. That score was set up when Milburn, a running back who was Denver's second-round draft choice, went 50 yards with a catch on third-and-19. Elam, a third-round pick, kicked 4 field goals in as many tries as the Broncos built a 26-6 advantage and withstood a pair of touchdown passes by New York's Boomer Esiason in the fourth quarter. Esiason, the veteran quarterback who was acquired from the Bengals in the offseason, completed 29 of 40 passes for 371 yards. Wide receiver Rob Moore had 9 receptions for 140 yards.

Denver	6	7	13	0	—	26
N.Y. Jets	0	6	0	14	—	20

Den — FG Elam 28
Den — FG Elam 30
Jets — FG Blanchard 22
Jets — FG Blanchard 43
Den — Tillman 3 pass from Elway (Elam kick)
Den — Milburn 25 pass from Elway (Elam kick)
Den — FG Elam 30
Den — FG Elam 41
Jets — Mitchell 5 pass from Esiason (Blanchard kick)
Jets — Moore 6 pass from Esiason (Blanchard kick)

KANSAS CITY 27, TAMPA BAY 3—at Tampa Stadium, attendance 63,378. Joe Montana threw 3 touchdown passes in his debut with Kansas City, leading the Chiefs to an easy victory over the Buccaneers. Montana, acquired from the 49ers in the offseason after missing most of the last two years with an elbow injury, completed his first 8 passes. He finished 14 of 21 for 246 yards before leaving the game with a sprained right wrist late in the third quarter. He gave Kansas City the lead for good with a 19-yard touchdown pass to Willie Davis 39 seconds into the second period. Later in the quarter, he threw a 50-yard touchdown pass to J.J. Birden, and he finished his day with a 12-yard scoring toss to running back Marcus Allen with 5:08 to go in the third quarter. Allen, the former Raiders running back who signed with the Chiefs as a free agent, also ran for 79 yards on 13 carries. Kansas City amassed 400 total yards while allowing Tampa Bay only 157.

Kansas City	0	17	7	3	—	27
Tampa Bay	3	0	0	0	—	3

TB — FG Husted 35
KC — W. Davis 19 pass from Montana (Lowery kick)
KC — FG Lowery 21
KC — Birden 50 pass from Montana (Lowery kick)
KC — Allen 12 pass from Montana (Lowery kick)
KC — FG Lowery 23

GREEN BAY 36, L.A. RAMS 6—at Milwaukee County Stadium, attendance 54,648. Brett Favre passed for 264 yards and 2 touchdowns and wide receiver Sterling Sharpe caught 7 passes for 120 yards and a touchdown as the Packers easily handled the Rams. Sharpe, who set an NFL record with 108 receptions in 1992, gave Green Bay a 9-3 lead with a 50-yard touchdown catch midway through the first quarter, and the Packers were not challenged after that. Favre's second touchdown pass, a 4-yard toss to Mark Clayton, came with 40 seconds remaining in the first half and made it 19-6. Edgar Bennett rushed for 2 touchdowns in the third quarter.

L.A. Rams	3	3	0	0	—	6
Green Bay	9	10	14	3	—	36

Rams — FG Zendejas 31
GB — Safety, Noble tackled Gary in end zone
GB — Sharpe 50 pass from Favre (Jacke kick)
GB — FG Jacke 51
Rams — FG Zendejas 32
GB — Clayton 3 pass from Favre (Jacke kick)
GB — Bennett 11 run (Jacke kick)
GB — Bennett 1 run (Jacke kick)
GB — FG Jacke 33

MIAMI 24, INDIANAPOLIS 20—at Hoosier Dome, attendance 51,858. Dan Marino's 1-yard touchdown pass to tight end Greg Baty with 35 seconds left lifted the Dolphins past the Colts. Indianapolis had rallied from a 17-10 deficit to take a 20-17 lead on a 25-yard touchdown pass from Jack Trudeau to rookie wide receiver Sean Dawkins and a 33-yard field goal by Dean Biasucci with 5:04 left in the game. Marino then marched Miami 80 yards in 13 plays, completing all 8 of his pass attempts on the drive. The winning pass came on third down. Cornerback Troy Vincent secured the victory by intercepting Trudeau's pass with 10 seconds remaining.

Miami	7	3	7	7	—	24
Indianapolis	7	0	3	10	—	20

Ind — Culver 56 fumble recovery return (Biasucci kick)
Mia — Jackson 40 pass from Marino (Stoyanovich kick)
Mia — FG Stoyanovich 20
Ind — FG Biasucci 26
Mia — Jackson 27 pass from Marino (Stoyanovich kick)
Ind — Dawkins 25 pass from Trudeau (Biasucci kick)
Ind — FG Biasucci 33
Mia — Baty 1 pass from Marino (Stoyanovich kick)

L.A. RAIDERS 24, MINNESOTA 7—at Los Angeles Memorial Coliseum, attendance 45,136. Jeff Hostetler completed 23 of 27 passes for 225 yards and 1 touchdown to lead the Raiders past the defending NFC Central Division champions. Los Angeles dominated the game from the opening kickoff, when rookie safety Patrick Bates recovered a fumble on his first play as a professional. Hostetler, who signed with the Raiders as a free agent in the offseason, took only three plays to get his new team in the end zone, completing his first pass attempt for 17 yards and a touchdown to Tim Brown. Los Angeles led 21-0 at the half and coasted to the victory. The Raiders outgained the Vikings 312-205 and maintained possession for more than 39 minutes. Minnesota's lone touchdown came in the final minute on a 1-yard run by Roger Craig.

Minnesota	0	0	0	7	—	7
L.A. Raiders	7	14	0	3	—	24

Raid — Brown 17 pass from Hostetler (Jaeger kick)
Raid — Robinson 1 run (Jaeger kick)
Raid — McDaniel 36 interception return (Jaeger kick)
Raid — FG Jaeger 21
Minn — Craig 1 run (Reveiz kick)

BUFFALO 38, NEW ENGLAND 14—at Rich Stadium, attendance 79,751. Jim Kelly threw 4 touchdown passes, 3 of them to wide receiver Andre Reed, and the Bills broke open a close game by scoring 3 times in a span of 6:26 of the fourth quarter. Buffalo led just 17-14 until Kelly teamed with Reed on a 22-yard touchdown pass on the first play of the fourth quarter. After safety Matt Darby recovered a fumble, Kelly found Reed for 14 yards and another touchdown, and rookie Russell Copeland finished the scoring spree by returning a punt 47 yards for a touchdown with 8:30 left in the game. Reed finished with 6 catches for 110 yards, while Bills running back Thurman Thomas ran for 114 yards on 24 carries. Patriots quarterback Drew Bledsoe, the top pick in the 1993 NFL draft, completed 14 of 30 passes for 148 yards and 2 scores, including a 54-yard touchdown to tight end Ben Coates. Buffalo won on opening day for the sixth consecutive year.

New England	0	7	7	0	—	14
Buffalo	0	17	0	21	—	38

Buff — FG Christie 28
Buff — Brooks 4 pass from Kelly (Christie kick)

NE	— Coates 54 pass from Bledsoe (Sisson kick)
Buff	— Reed 41 pass from Kelly (Christie kick)
NE	— McMurtry 2 pass from Bledsoe (Sisson kick)
Buff	— Reed 22 pass from Kelly (Christie kick)
Buff	— Reed 14 pass from Kelly (Christie kick)
Buff	— Copeland 47 punt return (Christie kick)

N.Y. GIANTS 26, CHICAGO 20—at Soldier Field, attendance 66,900. Phil Simms's 1-yard touchdown pass to running back Jarrod Bunch with 1:07 remaining gave the Giants the victory in a see-saw game in which the lead changed hands three times in the final quarter. Three of David Treadwell's four field goals staked New York to a 9-7 first-half advantage, before the Bears rallied to go ahead 17-9 midway through the third quarter. The Giants closed the deficit to 17-16 on Simms's 40-yard touchdown pass to Mark Jackson with 19 seconds to go in the third quarter, then went ahead on Treadwell's 36-yard field goal with 9:44 left in the game. Kevin Butler's 34-yard field goal gave Chicago its last lead at 20-19 with 3:07 left. But New York drove 80 yards in 8 plays to the winning touchdown. Simms passed 38 yards to Mike Sherrard to convert a third-and-18, and had a 24-yard completion to Chris Calloway on the march. The Giants also were aided by a pass interference penalty that positioned the ball on the 1. Simms finished with 24 completions in 34 attempts for 277 yards. Another veteran, linebacker Lawrence Taylor, made a successful return from the Achilles tendon injury that kept him out of the final seven games of 1992. Taylor had 2 sacks and forced and recovered a fumble to quell any hopes of a Bears' comeback in the final minute. Chicago had its NFL-best nine-game winning streak on opening day snapped.

N.Y. Giants	3	6	7	10	—	26
Chicago	0	7	10	3	—	20

Giants	— FG Treadwell 19
Giants	— FG Treadwell 35
Giants	— FG Treadwell 23
Chi	— Obee 2 pass from Harbaugh (Butler kick)
Chi	— Baker 5 blocked punt return (Butler kick)
Chi	— FG Butler 20
Giants	— M. Jackson 40 pass from Simms (Treadwell kick)
Giants	— FG Treadwell 36
Chi	— FG Butler 34
Giants	— Bunch 1 pass from Simms (Treadwell kick)

PHILADELPHIA 23, PHOENIX 17—at Veterans Stadium, attendance 59,831. Randall Cunningham passed for 192 yards and ran for 49, and the Eagles held off the Cardinals to win. Cunningham completed 18 of 29 passes and also scored on a 9-yard bootleg to give Philadelphia a 14-0 lead in the second quarter. Phoenix rallied in the second half on a 27-yard touchdown pass from Chris Chandler to running back Larry Centers and cornerback Lorenzo Lynch's 55-yard touchdown return of a fumble recovery, but it wasn't enough to overcome a slow start. The Eagles had 359 total yards and limited the Cardinals to 231. Chandler and starting quarterback Steve Beuerlein combined to complete only 15 of 39 passes for Phoenix.

Phoenix	0	3	7	7	—	17
Philadelphia	7	7	2	7	—	23

Phil	— Sherman 1 run (Ruzek kick)
Phil	— Cunningham 9 run (Ruzek kick)
Phx	— FG Davis 24
Phil	— Safety, Camarillo ran out of end zone
Phx	— Centers 27 pass from Chandler (Davis kick)
Phil	— Hebron 5 run (Ruzek kick)
Phx	— Lynch 55 fumble recovery return (Davis kick)

SAN FRANCISCO 24, PITTSBURGH 13—at Three Rivers Stadium, attendance 57,502. Steve Young shook off the effects of a broken thumb on his throwing hand to throw 3 touchdown passes in the 49ers' victory. Young, who suffered the injury in a preseason game against the Raiders one month earlier and was questionable for this game until midweek, completed 24 of 36 passes for 240 yards with 3 interceptions. He helped stake San Francisco to a 17-0 lead in the first half with 2 short touchdown passes to Jerry Rice, then put the game away with a 5-yard touchdown pass to tight end Brent Jones early in the fourth quarter. The latter came after Pittsburgh's ailing Neil O'Donnell, normally the starting quarterback but sidelined the first half with tendinitis in his elbow, relieved an ineffective Mike Tomczak and led the Steelers to 10 third-quarter points that trimmed the 49ers' advantage to 17-13. San Francisco sacked the Pittsburgh quarterbacks 5 times, including 2 by rookie defensive end Dana Stubblefield. Steelers cornerback Rod Woodson intercepted 2 passes.

San Francisco	10	7	0	7	—	24
Pittsburgh	0	3	10	0	—	13

SF	— FG Cofer 37
SF	— Rice 5 pass from Young (Cofer kick)
SF	— Rice 6 pass from Young (Cofer kick)
Pitt	— FG Anderson 29
Pitt	— Foster 5 run (Anderson kick)
Pitt	— FG Anderson 39
SF	— B. Jones 5 pass from Young (Cofer kick)

SAN DIEGO 18, SEATTLE 12—at San Diego Jack Murphy Stadium, attendance 58,039. John Carney's club-record 6 field goals provided the Chargers with all their points in a victory over the Seahawks. It was San Diego's first opening-day win in seven years. Carney's fourth field goal of the game, a 32-yard kick 3:21 before halftime, gave the defending AFC Western Division champions the lead for good at 12-10. He added kicks of 51 and 19 yards in the fourth quarter before the Chargers gave up a concession safety on the final play of the game. Seattle had taken a 7-0 advantage only 53 seconds into the game when defensive tackle Joe Nash intercepted a Stan Humphries pass that was tipped by Cortez Kennedy and ran 13 yards for a touchdown. But the Seahawks could muster little offense, totaling just 240 yards. Rookie quarterback Rick Mirer completed 20 of 27 passes, but for only 154 yards.

Seattle	7	3	0	2	—	12
San Diego	6	6	0	6	—	18

Sea	— Nash 13 interception return (Kasay kick)
SD	— FG Carney 26
SD	— FG Carney 44
Sea	— FG Kasay 27
SD	— FG Carney 50
SD	— FG Carney 32
SD	— FG Carney 51
SD	— FG Carney 19
Sea	— Safety, Kidd downed ball in end zone

SUNDAY NIGHT, SEPTEMBER 5

NEW ORLEANS 33, HOUSTON 21—at Louisiana Superdome, attendance 69,029. The Saints fell behind on the game's first possession, then dominated the Oilers to win easily. Wade Wilson passed for 206 yards, rookie Lorenzo Neal rushed for 89 yards, and Morten Andersen kicked 4 field goals for New Orleans. The Saints raced to a 33-7 advantage after Warren Moon's 6-yard touchdown pass to Haywood Jeffires 6:13 into the game. Dalton Hilliard's 2-yard touchdown run early in the second quarter put the Saints ahead for good, and Andersen's 47-yard field goal 11 seconds before halftime gave New Orleans a 13-7 lead. The Saints then marched 82 yards with the second-half kickoff, consuming 8:09 en route to another field goal by Andersen. They put the game out of reach when defensive end Frank Warren returned a fumble 47 yards for a touchdown early in the fourth quarter to make it 26-7. Moon completed 21 of 32 passes for 241 yards for Oilers, but he was sacked 3 times and intercepted once. Houston also lost 4 fumbles. Saints cornerback Toi Cook had 7 tackles, a sack, a fumble recovery, and an interception.

Houston	7	0	0	14	—	21
New Orleans	3	10	6	14	—	33

Hou	— Jeffires 6 pass from Moon (Del Greco kick)
NO	— FG Andersen 28
NO	— Hilliard 2 run (Andersen kick)
NO	— FG Andersen 37
NO	— FG Andersen 18
NO	— FG Andersen 47
NO	— Warren 47 fumble recovery return (Andersen kick)
NO	— D. Brown 2 run (Andersen kick)
Hou	— Carlson 1 run (Del Greco kick)
Hou	— Robertson 80 fumble recovery return (Del Greco kick)

MONDAY, SEPTEMBER 6

WASHINGTON 35, DALLAS 16—at RFK Stadium, attendance 56,345. Brian Mitchell ran for 116 yards and 2 touchdowns, and the Redskins stunned the defending Super Bowl champions with a lopsided victory. Washington put the game away with a back-breaking 99-yard touchdown drive in the third quarter, after Dallas had pulled within 21-13 on a 32-yard touchdown pass from Troy Aikman to Alvin Harper. Mitchell inadvertently downed the ensuing kickoff at the Redskins' 1-yard line, but Washington took 13 plays and more than seven minutes to march the length of the field. Mark Rypien capped the drive by throwing a 15-yard touchdown pass to Art Monk with six seconds left in the third quarter. Rypien directed a ball-control passing attack and completed 22 of 34 passes for 161 yards. The Cowboys' Troy Aikman passed for 267 yards but Dallas, playing without Emmitt Smith, the NFL's leading rusher in 1991 and 1992, managed only 91 rushing yards. The Cowboys also lost 4 fumbles, 2 on punts, that enabled the Redskins to build a 14-6 halftime lead.

Dallas	6	0	7	3	—	16
Washington	0	14	14	7	—	35

Dall	— Harper 80 pass from Aikman (kick failed)
Wash	— Sanders 15 pass from Rypien (Lohmiller kick)
Wash	— Mitchell 1 run (Lohmiller kick)
Wash	— Middleton 1 pass from Rypien (Lohmiller kick)
Dall	— Harper 32 pass from Aikman (Elliott kick)
Wash	— Monk 15 pass from Rypien (Lohmiller kick)
Dall	— FG Elliott 22
Wash	— Mitchell 29 run (Lohmiller kick)

SECOND WEEK SUMMARIES

AMERICAN FOOTBALL CONFERENCE

Eastern Division	W	L	T	Pct.	Pts.	OP
Buffalo	2	0	0	1.000	51	24
Indianapolis	1	1	0	.500	29	30
Miami	1	1	0	.500	38	44
N.Y. Jets	1	1	0	.500	44	40
New England	0	2	0	.000	30	57
Central Division						
Cleveland	2	0	0	1.000	50	27
Houston	1	1	0	.500	51	33
Cincinnati	0	2	0	.000	20	36
Pittsburgh	0	2	0	.000	13	51
Western Division						
Denver	2	0	0	1.000	60	37
L.A. Raiders	2	0	0	1.000	41	20
Kansas City	1	1	0	.500	27	33
San Diego	1	1	0	.500	35	46
Seattle	0	2	0	.000	25	35

NATIONAL FOOTBALL CONFERENCE

Eastern Division	W	L	T	Pct.	Pts.	OP
N.Y. Giants	2	0	0	1.000	49	27
Philadelphia	2	0	0	1.000	43	34
Phoenix	1	1	0	.500	34	33
Washington	1	1	0	.500	45	33
Dallas	0	2	0	.000	26	48
Central Division						
Detroit	2	0	0	1.000	49	29
Green Bay	1	1	0	.500	53	26
Minnesota	1	1	0	.500	17	31
Chicago	0	2	0	.000	27	36
Tampa Bay	0	2	0	.000	10	50
Western Division						
New Orleans	2	0	0	1.000	67	52
L.A. Rams	1	1	0	.500	33	36
San Francisco	1	1	0	.500	37	36
Atlanta	0	2	0	.000	44	64

SUNDAY, SEPTEMBER 12

BUFFALO 13, DALLAS 10—at Texas Stadium, attendance 63,226. Safety Matt Darby intercepted a pass at the goal line in the closing seconds to preserve the Bills' victory, handing the defending Super Bowl champions their second consecutive defeat. It was a dramatic reversal for Buffalo, which turned over the ball 9 times while being routed by the Cowboys 52-17 in Super Bowl XXVII eight months earlier. After the Bills' Steve Tasker recovered rookie Kevin Williams's fumbled punt return at Dallas's 34-yard line, Steve Christie kicked a 35-yard field goal to break a 10-10 tie with 2:49 left in the game. The Cowboys took over on their 20 and marched 69 yards to Buffalo's 11. But Troy Aikman's pass over the middle bounced off the shoulder pads of tight end Jay Novacek, who collided with Darby. The ball deflected in the air and Darby made a lunging interception at the 1. Dallas outgained the Bills 393-229 but was intercepted twice and lost a pair of fumbles. Aikman finished with 28 completions in a career-high 45 attempts for 297 yards. Cowboys wide receiver Michael Irvin caught 8 passes for 115 yards, while Novacek had 8 receptions for 106 yards.

Buffalo	7	3	0	3	—	13
Dallas	0	3	0	7	—	10

Buff — Gardner 10 pass from Kelly (Christie kick)
Buff — FG Christie 48
Dall — FG Elliott 43
Dall — K. Williams 5 run (Elliott kick)
Buff — FG Christie 35

MINNESOTA 10, CHICAGO 7—at Metrodome, attendance 56,285. Jim McMahon's 16-yard touchdown pass to Cris Carter midway through the fourth quarter lifted the Vikings over the Bears. Playing for the first time against the team that traded him five years earlier, McMahon completed 23 of 29 passes for 173 yards and was not intercepted. Running back Barry Word, acquired from the Chiefs to replace injured Terry Allen, supplied most of the rest of the offense, gaining 94 yards on 24 carries and catching 5 passes for 58 yards. But it was the Vikings' defense that made the difference, limiting Chicago to only 7 first downs and 140 total yards. Minnesota maintained possession for more than 37 of the game's 60 minutes.

Chicago	7	0	0	0	—	7
Minnesota	0	3	0	7	—	10

Chi — Harbaugh 1 run (Butler kick)
Minn — FG Reveiz 22
Minn — C. Carter 16 pass from McMahon (Reveiz kick)

DETROIT 19, NEW ENGLAND 16—at Foxboro Stadium, attendance 54,151. Jason Hanson's 38-yard field goal with 3:56 left in overtime won it for the Lions. The Patriots had forced the extra session when Drew Bledsoe threw a 2-yard touchdown pass to wide receiver Vincent Brisby with 12 seconds remaining in the fourth quarter. In the overtime, Detroit quarterback Rodney Peete marched his team 60 yards in 11 plays to the winning kick. Peete, who had thrown 3 interceptions, lost a fumble, and suffered 3 sacks earlier in the game, completed passes of 14 yards to Barry Sanders, 13 yards to Herman Moore, and 17 yards to Brett Perriman to position Hanson for his fourth field goal of the game. The Lions' only touchdown came 11 seconds into the game when cornerback Willie Clay returned a fumble on the opening kickoff 15 yards for a score. Bledsoe completed 28 of 49 passes for 239 yards for New England. Rookie linebacker Chris Slade had all 3 of the Patriots' sacks. Sanders ran for 148 yards on 32 carries for Detroit.

Detroit	7	0	3	6	3	—	19
New England	6	3	0	7	0	—	16

Det — Clay 15 fumble recovery return (Hanson kick)
NE — FG Sisson 26
NE — FG Sisson 21
NE — FG Sisson 32
Det — FG Hanson 22
Det — FG Hanson 26
Det — FG Hanson 23
NE — Brisby 2 pass from Bledsoe (Sisson kick)
Det — FG Hanson 38

INDIANAPOLIS 9, CINCINNATI 6—at Riverfront Stadium, attendance 50,299. Dean Biasucci kicked 3 field goals, including the winning 42-yard kick with three seconds remaining, as the Colts edged the Bengals. The decisive kick came four plays after Indianapolis linebacker Quentin Coryatt hit Cincinnati quarterback David Klingler as he threw, forcing a pass that cornerback John Baylor intercepted at midfield. Baylor returned the theft 7 yards, and the Bengals were penalized 15 yards for a facemask penalty that moved the ball to the 28-yard line to set up Biasucci's winning kick. Doug Pelfrey kicked a pair of field goals for Cincinnati, but also missed a 35-yard attempt with 2:18 to go in the game when the ball was tipped by Colts linebacker Scott Radecic.

Indianapolis	0	3	3	3	—	9
Cincinnati	3	0	3	0	—	6

Cin — FG Pelfrey 35
Ind — FG Biasucci 53
Cin — FG Pelfrey 23
Ind — FG Biasucci 31
Ind — FG Biasucci 42

HOUSTON 30, KANSAS CITY 0—at Astrodome, attendance 59,780. The Oilers rebounded from an opening-game loss to the Saints by blanking the Chiefs. Kansas City played without starting quarterback Joe Montana, who was nursing an injured wrist. Houston struggled offensively, accumulating only 57 rushing yards and 247 total yards,

but used 3 field goals by Al Del Greco and an opportunistic defense to hand the Chiefs their first shutout loss since 1987. Leading 16-0 in the fourth quarter, the Oilers put the game out of reach when cornerback Cris Dishman stripped the ball from Kansas City tight end Mike Dyal and raced 58 yards for a touchdown with 5:34 left to play. Safety Marcus Robertson set up the final touchdown, a 1-yard run by Lorenzo White, with his second interception of the game. He returned his first theft 48 yards to set up a field goal late in the first half. Houston forced 5 turnovers and sacked the Chiefs' Dave Krieg 4 times. Kansas City managed only 10 first downs, 46 rushing yards, and 206 total yards. Warren Moon completed 22 of 35 passes for 204 yards and a touchdown for the Oilers.

Kansas City	0	0	0	0	—	0
Houston	0	7	6	17	—	30

Hou — Duncan 2 pass from Moon (Del Greco kick)
Hou — FG Del Greco 25
Hou — FG Del Greco 22
Hou — FG Del Greco 50
Hou — Dishman 58 fumble recovery return (Del Greco kick)
Hou — White 1 run (Del Greco kick)

NEW ORLEANS 34, ATLANTA 31—at Georgia Dome, attendance 64,287. Morten Andersen kicked a 44-yard field goal as time expired and the Saints survived a 21-point fourth-quarter barrage to beat the Falcons. Wade Wilson threw 3 touchdown passes as New Orleans built a seemingly insurmountable 31-10 advantage through three quarters. But Atlanta rallied behind free-agent quarterback Bobby Hebert, who spent his first seven seasons with the Saints and was on the field for the first time with his new team. Hebert threw a 4-yard touchdown pass to Michael Haynes 2:34 into the fourth quarter, then tossed a club-record 98-yard scoring pass to the speedster 1:35 later to trim the Falcons' deficit to 31-24. His 3-yard touchdown pass to Mike Pritchard with 2:40 remaining in the game tied the score at 31-31. But after Atlanta got the ball back again, New Orleans linebacker Renaldo Turnbull stripped Hebert of the ball and recovered it on the Falcons' 32-yard line with 22 seconds left. Andersen's winning kick came three plays later. The usually conservative Saints amassed a club-record 557 yards, including a 74-yard run by rookie Lorenzo Neal on their first play from scrimmage. But Neal later broke his ankle and was lost for the season. Wilson, who played with the Falcons in 1992, completed 22 of 34 passes for 341 yards. Hebert was 14 of 18 for 243 yards for Atlanta, which had 380 total yards. Haynes caught 7 passes for 182 yards. Andersen kicked a 27-yard field goal in the first quarter to extend his consecutive streak to an NFL-record 25 in a row. But he missed his next two attempts, from 42 and 50 yards, before converting on the last play.

New Orleans	10	14	7	3	—	34
Atlanta	0	10	0	21	—	31

NO — Neal 74 run (Andersen kick)
NO — FG Andersen 27
Atl — Pegram 1 run (Johnson kick)
NO — Early 42 pass from Wilson (Andersen kick)
Atl — FG Johnson 20
NO — Early 18 pass from Wilson (Andersen kick)
NO — I. Smith 1 pass from Wilson (Andersen kick)
Atl — Haynes 4 pass from Hebert (Johnson kick)
Atl — Haynes 98 pass from Hebert (Johnson kick)
Atl — Pritchard 3 pass from Hebert (Johnson kick)
NO — FG Andersen 44

N.Y. JETS 24, MIAMI 14—at Joe Robbie Stadium, attendance 70,314. Boomer Esiason threw 2 touchdown passes and ran for another as the Jets upset the Dolphins. Esiason, who threw for more than 300 yards for the second consecutive week, set up Cary Blanchard's tie-breaking 39-yard field goal late in the third quarter with a 46-yard, flea-flicker pass to Terance Mathis. His 20-yard scoring toss to running back Pat Chaffey capped a 73-yard fourth-quarter drive and gave New York a 10-point advantage with 4:14 left. Dan Marino passed for 286 yards for Miami but had little help as the Dolphins could manage only 27 rushing yards. Marino became only the fourth player in NFL history to pass for more than 40,000 yards in his career, finishing the game at 40,024. Esiason completed 22 of 33 attempts for 323 yards.

N.Y. Jets	0	14	3	7	—	24
Miami	7	7	0	0	—	14

Mia — K. Jackson 57 pass from Marino (Stoyanovich kick)
Jets — Esiason 4 run (Blanchard kick)
Jets — Baxter 3 pass from Esiason (Blanchard kick)
Mia — Ingram 25 pass from Marino (Stoyanovich kick)
Jets — FG Blanchard 39
Jets — Chaffey 20 pass from Esiason (Blanchard kick)

PHILADELPHIA 20, GREEN BAY 17—at Lambeau Field, attendance 59,061. Roger Ruzek's 30-yard field goal with five seconds left lifted the Eagles to victory in a game that featured Packers defensive end Reggie White playing against his old teammates for the first time. White, the seven-time Pro Bowl defensive end who signed with Green Bay as a free agent in the offseason, had 2 sacks and forced a pair of fumbles in the first quarter. But Philadelphia stole the spotlight by rallying from a 10-point deficit in the fourth quarter. Ruzek's 27-yard field goal and Randall Cunningham's 40-yard touchdown pass to rookie wide receiver Victor Bailey with 4:14 left in the game tied the score at 17-17. After the Packers failed to make a first down, Vai Sikahema's 13-yard punt return positioned the Eagles at the Green Bay 45-yard line. Philadelphia then consumed most of the time remaining on the clock by marching 32 yards on the ground to the winning field goal. The game was played before a crowd of 59,061, the second largest ever at historic Lambeau Field.

Philadelphia	0	7	0	13	—	20
Green Bay	7	3	7	0	—	17

GB — Sharpe 2 pass from Favre (Jacke kick)
GB — FG Jacke 23
Phil — Bavaro 2 pass from Cunningham (Ruzek kick)
GB — J. Harris 15 pass from Favre (Jacke kick)
Phil — FG Ruzek 27
Phil — Bailey 40 pass from Cunningham (Ruzek kick)
Phil — FG Ruzek 30

PHOENIX 17, WASHINGTON 10—at RFK Stadium, attendance 53,525. The Cardinals built a 17-0 halftime lead and hung on to stun the Redskins. It was Phoenix's first victory at RFK Stadium in 15 years. Washington suffered a blow when quarterback Mark Rypien injured his knee while scrambling in the second quarter. He was expected to miss three to six weeks. Cary Conklin, who spent his first two NFL seasons on injured reserve and threw only 2 passes in 1992, replaced Rypien and threw a 9-yard touchdown pass to Ricky Sanders in the third quarter, but it wasn't enough. Johnny Bailey returned a punt 58 yards for a touchdown in the first quarter and rookie Garrison Hearst, the Cardinals' first-round draft choice, had 76 of his team's 152 rushing yards as the Cardinals controlled the ball on the ground. Phoenix outgained the Redskins 303-233 and maintained possession for 35:54.

Phoenix	10	7	0	0	—	17
Washington	0	0	7	3	—	10

Phx — Bailey 58 punt return (Davis kick)
Phx — FG Davis 53
Phx — Moore 18 run (Davis kick)
Wash — Sanders 9 pass from Conklin (Lohmiller kick)
Wash — FG Lohmiller 23

L.A. RAMS 27, PITTSBURGH 0—at Anaheim Stadium, attendance 50,588. The Rams rebounded from a lopsided loss to the Packers on opening day by blanking the defending AFC Central Division champions. Jim Everett passed for 221 yards and rookies Troy Drayton and Jerome Bettis scored their first NFL touchdowns. Tony Zendejas added a pair of long-range field goals, including a club-record 54-yard kick. Los Angeles amassed 314 total yards while limiting the Steelers to 175. Rams defensive tackle Sean Gilbert had 4 sacks. Wide receiver Henry Ellard caught 9 passes for 127 yards.

Pittsburgh	0	0	0	0	—	0
L.A. Rams	0	14	6	7	—	27

Rams — Drayton 22 pass from Everett (Zendejas kick)
Rams — Gary 6 run (Zendejas kick)
Rams — FG Zendejas 54
Rams — FG Zendejas 50
Rams — Bettis 29 run (Zendejas kick)

DENVER 34, SAN DIEGO 17—at Mile High Stadium, attendance 75,074. John Elway completed 24 of 34 passes for 294 yards and 2 touchdowns to lead the Broncos past the Chargers. The game was scoreless until Denver went to the No-Huddle offense at the outset of the second quarter. Two minutes into the period, Elway capped an 87-yard drive with a 34-yard touchdown pass to Arthur Marshall. San Diego fumbled two plays later and Broncos linebacker Karl Mecklenburg recovered at the Chargers' 25-yard line. A penalty moved the ball to the 12, and Elway's touchdown pass to Reggie Rivers made it 14-0. San Diego closed to 17-14 midway through the third quarter, turning an interception and a fumble recovery into touchdowns just 2:19 apart. Denver countered with a 12-play, 80-yard drive, capped by a 1-yard touchdown run by former Chargers running back Rod Bernstine. Elway made the key play on the march, scrambling on third-and-19 before finding Vance Johnson for a 46-yard gain to the 1. Stan Humphries passed for 298 yards for San Diego, which amassed 26 first downs and 390 total yards. Chargers wide receiver Nate Lewis caught 10 passes for 119 yards. Running back Ronnie Harmon had 10 catches for 81 yards.

San Diego	0	0	14	3	—	17
Denver	0	17	7	10	—	34

Den — Marshall 34 pass from Elway (Elam kick)
Den — Rivers 12 pass from Elway (Elam kick)
Den — FG Elam 20
SD — Walker 25 pass from Humphries (Carney kick)
SD — Lewis 24 pass from Humphries (Carney kick)
Den — Bernstine 1 run (Elam kick)
SD — FG Carney 30
Den — FG Elam 54
Den — Delpino 1 run (Elam kick)

N.Y. GIANTS 23, TAMPA BAY 7—at Giants Stadium, attendance 75,891. Rodney Hampton gained 134 yards on 29 carries and scored a touchdown as the Giants ground out a methodical victory over the Buccaneers. New York ran the football 41 times for 181 yards and maintained possession for 35:04 of the game's 60 minutes. The Giants led 17-7 at halftime and increased the lead to 20-7 early in the third quarter before Tampa Bay threatened to get back in the game. The Buccaneers drove 79 yards to New York's 1-yard line before Reggie Cobb was stopped short of the goal line on fourth down. David Treadwell added his third field goal of the game in the fourth quarter. Craig Erickson started his first game for Tampa Bay and completed 16 of 28 passes for 174 yards.

Tampa Bay	0	7	0	0	—	7
N.Y. Giants	7	10	3	3	—	23

Giants— Cross 18 pass from Simms (Treadwell kick)
Giants— Hampton 2 run (Treadwell kick)
TB — Armstrong 17 pass from Erickson (Husted kick)
Giants— FG Treadwell 33
Giants— FG Treadwell 22
Giants— FG Treadwell 46

SUNDAY NIGHT, SEPTEMBER 12

L.A. RAIDERS 17, SEATTLE 13—at Kingdome, attendance 58,836. Jeff Hostetler's 33-yard touchdown pass to Tim Brown broke a 10-10 tie 1:13 before halftime and the Raiders went on to beat the Seahawks. The decisive touchdown came three plays after Los Angeles linebacker Aaron Wallace recovered rookie quarterback Rick Mirer's fumble at the Raiders' 48-yard line. In the second half, Seattle managed only a 53-yard field goal by John Kasay with 7:49 left in the game. Los Angeles's defense limited the Seahawks to 232 total yards and harassed Mirer, sacking him 5 times, 4 of them by end Anthony Smith. Brown finished with 9 catches for 97 yards.

L.A. Raiders	7	10	0	0	—	17
Seattle	0	10	0	3	—	13

Raid — Hostetler 2 run (Jaeger kick)
Sea — Warren 6 run (Kasay kick)
Sea — FG Kasay 39
Raid — FG Jaeger 36
Raid — Brown 33 pass from Hostetler (Jaeger kick)
Sea — FG Kasay 53

MONDAY, SEPTEMBER 13

CLEVELAND 23, SAN FRANCISCO 13—at Cleveland Stadium, attendance 78,512. Bernie Kosar threw a 30-yard touchdown pass to Michael Jackson with 35 seconds left in the first half, and the Browns' defense shut out the 49ers in the second half to preserve the victory. San Francisco had 396 total yards but was stifled by 3 interceptions, a lost fumble, a blocked field-goal attempt, and a fumbled snap on another field-goal try. The loss snapped the 49ers' nine-game regular-season winning streak. Jackson finished with 5 catches for a career-high 105 yards for the Browns. Defensive tackle James Jones scored a touchdown on a 1-yard run after lining up as a blocking back in the second quarter.

San Francisco	6	7	0	0	—	13
Cleveland	3	17	3	0	—	23

SF — FG Cofer 46
Cle — FG Stover 47
SF — FG Cofer 28
Cle — J. Jones 1 run (Stover kick)
Cle — FG Stover 41
SF — Logan 4 run (Cofer kick)
Cle — Jackson 30 pass from Kosar (Stover kick)
Cle — FG Stover 33

THIRD WEEK SUMMARIES

AMERICAN FOOTBALL CONFERENCE

Eastern Division	W	L	T	Pct.	Pts.	OP
Buffalo	2	0	0	1.000	51	24
Indianapolis	1	1	0	.500	29	30
Miami	1	1	0	.500	38	44
N.Y. Jets	1	1	0	.500	44	40
New England	0	3	0	.000	44	74
Central Division						
Cleveland	3	0	0	1.000	69	43
Houston	1	2	0	.333	68	51
Pittsburgh	1	2	0	.333	47	58
Cincinnati	0	3	0	.000	27	70
Western Division						
Denver	2	1	0	.667	67	52
Kansas City	2	1	0	.667	42	40
L.A. Raiders	2	1	0	.667	57	39
San Diego	2	1	0	.667	53	63
Seattle	1	2	0	.333	42	49

NATIONAL FOOTBALL CONFERENCE

Eastern Division	W	L	T	Pct.	Pts.	OP
N.Y. Giants	3	0	0	1.000	69	37
Philadelphia	3	0	0	1.000	77	65
Dallas	1	2	0	.333	43	58
Phoenix	1	2	0	.333	44	50
Washington	1	2	0	.333	76	67
Central Division						
Detroit	2	1	0	.667	52	43
Green Bay	1	1	0	.500	53	26
Minnesota	1	1	0	.500	17	31
Chicago	0	2	0	.000	27	36
Tampa Bay	0	2	0	.000	10	50
Western Division						
New Orleans	3	0	0	1.000	81	55
San Francisco	2	1	0	.667	74	66
L.A. Rams	1	2	0	.333	43	56
Atlanta	0	3	0	.000	74	101

SUNDAY, SEPTEMBER 19

SAN FRANCISCO 37, ATLANTA 30—at Candlestick Park, attendance 63,032. Steve Young threw 3 touchdown pass and completed a key pass to himself as the 49ers beat Atlanta in a wild game. San Francisco trailed 20-16 late in the third quarter but had moved the ball to the Falcons' 8-yard line when Young, scrambling to avoid a sack, threw a pass that was batted in the air near the goal line. The ball bounced back to Young, who caught it and was tackled at the 2 after a 6-yard gain. Ricky Watters then ran for a touchdown on the next play to give San Francisco the lead for good. The two teams accounted for 859 total yards, including 478 by the 49ers, who never punted. San Francisco had 268 rushing yards, including 43 by wide receiver Jerry Rice on a fourth-quarter reverse for the clinching touchdown. Young completed 18 of 22 passes for 210 yards and Watters ran for 112 yards on 19 carries. Atlanta running back Erric Pegram, starting in place of injured Eric Dickerson, rushed for 192 yards on 27 carries. Quarterback Bobby Hebert, a free-agent signee making his first start for the Falcons, completed 23 of 38 passes for 199 yards and 3 touchdowns, all of them to Andre Rison.

Atlanta	3	10	7	10	—	30
San Francisco	3	6	14	14	—	37

Atl — FG Johnson 42
SF — FG Cofer 46
Atl — Rison 12 pass from Hebert (Johnson kick)
SF — Williams 9 pass from Young (kick failed)
Atl — FG Johnson 38
SF — Jones 20 pass from Young (Cofer kick)
Atl — Rison 3 pass from Hebert (Johnson kick)
SF — Watters 2 run (Cofer kick)
SF — Singleton 6 pass from Young (Cofer kick)
Atl — FG Johnson 27
SF — Rice 43 run (Cofer kick)
Atl — Rison 16 pass from Hebert (Johnson kick)

PITTSBURGH 34, CINCINNATI 7—at Three Rivers Stadium, attendance 53,682. The Steelers amassed 404 total yards and breezed to victory. It was the first win of the year for the defending AFC Central Division champions. Quarterback Neil O'Donnell, playing with tendinitis in his right elbow, completed 21 of 25 passes for 189 yards and 3 touchdowns. His 18-yard touchdown pass to Yancey Thigpen with 36 seconds left in the first half gave Pittsburgh a 17-7 lead. His 9-yard scoring toss to Dwight Stone late in the third quarter made it 27-7. Stone also ran 38 yards on a reverse for a touchdown. Cincinnati's David Klingler completed 17 of 21 passes, but the Bengals managed only 170 total yards. Klingler was 11 of 12 in the first half, including a 15-yard touchdown pass to Carl Pickens.

Cincinnati	0	7	0	0	—	7
Pittsburgh	7	10	10	7	—	34

Pitt — Mills 3 pass from O'Donnell (Anderson kick)
Pitt — FG Anderson 33
Cin — Pickens 15 pass from Klingler (Pelfrey kick)
Pitt — Thigpen 18 pass from O'Donnell (Anderson kick)
Pitt — FG Anderson 34
Pitt — Stone 9 pass from O'Donnell (Anderson kick)
Pitt — Stone 38 run (Anderson kick)

CLEVELAND 19, L.A. RAIDERS 16—at Los Angeles Memorial Coliseum, attendance 48,617. Eric Metcalf ran 1 yard for a touchdown with 2 seconds left, capping a 19-point fourth quarter and lifting the Browns to a dramatic come-from-behind victory. Los Angeles led 13-0 at halftime behind the strength of its defense, which limited Cleveland to only 37 total yards in the first half and did not permit the Browns to cross midfield. But the Raiders could not put Cleveland away, settling for short field goals by Jeff Jaeger after interceptions had positioned them in first-and-goal situations. Then in the second half, Los Angeles managed only 17 total yards and 1 first down, which came via penalty. Still, the Raiders led 16-3 until backup quarterback Vinny Testaverde, who replaced an ineffective Bernie Kosar in the fourth quarter, marched the Browns 90 yards in 12 plays, the last a 12-yard touchdown pass to Lawyer Tillman to trim the deficit to 16-10 with 2:26 remaining. After failing to make a first down on their next possession, the Raiders elected to give up a safety rather than punt from their own end zone. But Metcalf returned the ensuing free kick 37 yards, and Cleveland began its winning drive from Los Angeles's 45-yard line. Testaverde completed passes of 17 and 16 yards to Mark Carrier, his former teammate at Tampa Bay, and Metcalf took a pitchout and ran for the winning score on second down, even though the Browns had no timeouts left. Metcalf, who scored 4 touchdowns in a victory over the Raiders at the Coliseum last year, had minus-3 yards rushing until his winning run.

Cleveland	0	0	0	19	—	19
L.A. Raiders	10	3	0	3	—	16

Raid — Glover 2 pass from Hostetler (Jaeger kick)
Raid — FG Jaeger 24
Raid — FG Jaeger 27
Cle — FG Stover 32
Raid — FG Jaeger 53
Cle — Tillman 12 pass from Testaverde (Stover kick)
Cle — Safety, Gossett ran out of end zone
Cle — Metcalf 1 run (Stover kick)

NEW ORLEANS 14, DETROIT 3—at Louisiana Superdome, attendance 69,039. Wade Wilson threw 2 touchdown passes, but it was the Saints' defense that keyed the victory over the Lions. New Orleans allowed Detroit only 9 first downs and 165 total yards, and sacked Lions quarterback Rodney Peete 5 times, knocking him out of the game with a knee sprain in the fourth quarter. Renaldo Turnbull, who took over for Pro Bowl linebacker Pat Swilling after Swilling was traded to the Lions, had 3 sacks, 2 of which forced fumbles that teammate Rickey Jackson recovered. One set up an 18-yard drive for the clinching touchdown in the third quarter. Detroit took a 3-0 lead on a 41-yard field goal by Jason Hanson in the second quarter, but the Saints countered with a 73-yard touchdown drive over the next 6:17 to take the lead for good on a 17-yard pass from Wilson to tight end Hoby Brenner. New Orleans got 121 rushing yards from rookie Derek Brown while limiting the Lions' Barry Sanders to 76.

Detroit	0	3	0	0	—	3
New Orleans	0	7	7	0	—	14

Det — FG Hanson 41
NO — Brenner 17 pass from Wilson (Andersen kick)
NO — Martin 12 pass from Wilson (Andersen kick)

SAN DIEGO 18, HOUSTON 17—at San Diego Jack Murphy Stadium, attendance 58,519. John Carney equaled his club record set two weeks earlier by kicking 6 field goals in as many attempts, including the game-winner from 27 yards with three seconds left. Carney, already 13-for-13 on the season, also ran his string of field goals to an NFL-record 29, dating back to the 1992 season. The previous mark was 25, which the Saints' Morten Andersen held for just one week. The Oilers trailed 15-14 until backup quarterback Cody Carlson rallied his team with an apparent go-ahead 8-yard touchdown pass to Haywood Jeffires. But officials ruled that Jeffires had caught the ball out of bounds, and Houston had to settle for a 27-yard field goal by Al Del Greco with 4:59 remaining. The Chargers took the ensuing kickoff and marched 75 yards in 13 plays to Carney's winning kick. Carney was the hero for the second time in three weeks. He also scored all of San Diego's points in an 18-12 victory over Seattle on opening day.

Houston	0	14	0	3	—	17
San Diego	3	6	3	6	—	18

SD — FG Carney 34
SD — FG Carney 34
SD — FG Carney 27
Hou — Slaughter 2 pass from Moon (Del Greco kick)
Hou — D. Lewis 47 interception return (Del Greco kick)
SD — FG Carney 27
SD — FG Carney 36
Hou — FG Del Greco 27
SD — FG Carney 27

N.Y. GIANTS 20, L.A. RAMS 10—at Giants Stadium, attendance 76,213. Rodney Hampton rushed for 134 yards on a career-high 41 carries to power the Giants past the Rams. Hampton capped a 60-yard drive on the first possession of the game when he ran 1 yard for a touchdown to give New York a lead it would never relinquish. The Giants led 13-3 at halftime. Cornerback Mark Collins helped seal the outcome with a 50-yard interception return for a touchdown with 4:32 left in the third quarter. The Giants iced the game by eating up large amounts of time on the strength of Hampton's running. New York finished with 146 rushing yards to only 45 for the Rams, ran 79 plays to only 41 for Los Angeles, and maintained possession for 43:29 of the game's 60 minutes. Phil Simms completed 21 of 27 passes for 217 yards for the Giants. The Rams' Jim Everett was just 11 of 28 for 135 yards, but did have a 51-yard touchdown pass to Willie Anderson early in the fourth quarter.

L.A. Rams	0	3	0	7	—	10
N.Y. Giants	7	6	7	0	—	20

Giants— Hampton 1 run (Treadwell kick)
Giants— FG Treadwell 34
Rams — FG Zendejas 52
Giants— FG Treadwell 19
Giants— Collins 50 interception return (Treadwell kick)
Rams — Anderson 51 pass from Everett (Zendejas kick)

SEATTLE 17, NEW ENGLAND 14—at Foxboro Stadium, attendance 50,392. The Seahawks built a 17-0 advantage through three quarters then held on to win when Scott Sisson's 54-yard field goal try in the final minute bounced off the crossbar. With the victory, Seattle snapped a six-game losing streak dating back to the 1992 season; the Patriots dropped their eighth in a row. Rick Mirer threw a 4-yard touchdown pass to Brian Blades to cap the opening drive of the game, and Chris Warren ran 15 yards for a touchdown late in the third quarter as the Seahawks built their 17-point advantage. But New England quarterback Drew Bledsoe, who passed for 240 yards, rallied his team to a pair of fourth-quarter touchdowns before Sisson's attempt to send the game into overtime. Warren rushed for 174 yards on a club-record 36 carries for Seattle.

Seattle	7	0	10	0	—	17
New England	0	0	0	14	—	14

Sea — Blades 4 pass from Mirer (Kasay kick)
Sea — FG Kasay 24
Sea — Warren 15 run (Kasay kick)
NE — Coates 25 pass from Bledsoe (Sisson kick)
NE — Gash 4 run (Sisson kick)

PHILADELPHIA 34, WASHINGTON 31—at Veterans Stadium, attendance 65,435. Randall Cunningham threw 3 touchdown passes to Calvin Williams, including the game-winner with 10 seconds left, as the Eagles remained undefeated by rallying from an 11-point second-half deficit. Philadelphia trailed 21-10 late in the third quarter, but cornerback Eric Allen's 29-yard interception return for a touchdown and Cunningham's 9-yard touchdown pass to Williams with 8:23 left helped tie the score at 24-24. That tie lasted only 21 seconds, however, because rookie running back Reggie Brooks raced 85 yards for a touchdown on the next play from scrimmage to put the Redskins back in front 31-24. The Eagles closed to within four points when Matt Bahr, signed two days earlier to replace injured Roger Ruzek, kicked a 42-yard field goal with 3:57 to go in the game. Philadelphia forced Washington to punt, then took over at its 17-yard line with 1:54 remaining. Cunningham accounted for all 83 yards on the winning drive, completing 6 of 9 passes for 74 yards and scrambling for 9 yards. He finished with a team-high 49 rushing yards and completed 25 of 39 passes for 360 yards. Williams had career highs with 8 catches and 181 yards. The Redskins' Cary Conklin, filling in for injured Mark Rypien, completed 17 of 36 passes for 218 yards and 3 touchdowns in his first career start. Brooks gained 154 yards on 22 carries.

Washington	0	14	7	10	—	31
Philadelphia	3	7	7	17	—	34

Phil — FG Bahr 27
Wash — McGee 11 pass from Conklin (Lohmiller kick)
Wash — Sanders 34 pass from Conklin (Lohmiller kick)
Phil — Williams 80 pass from Cunningham (Bahr kick)
Wash — Middleton 1 pass from Conklin (Lohmiller kick)
Phil — Allen 29 interception return (Bahr kick)
Wash — FG Lohmiller 38
Phil — Williams 9 pass from Cunningham (Bahr kick)
Wash — Brooks 85 run (Lohmiller kick)
Phil — FG Bahr 42
Phil — Williams 10 pass from Cunningham (Bahr kick)

SUNDAY NIGHT, SEPTEMBER 19

DALLAS 17, PHOENIX 10—at Sun Devil Stadium, attendance 73,025. Derrick Lassic ran for 2 touchdowns, Troy Aikman passed for 281 yards, and the Cowboys notched their first victory of the season. Running back Emmitt Smith also made his 1993 debut and rushed for 45 yards in less than one half of action. Lassic, starting in place of Smith, ran 8 yards for a touchdown in the first quarter and 2 yards for a score in the third quarter as Dallas built a 17-0 advantage and held on for the victory. Aikman completed 21 of 27 passes with no interceptions and no sacks. Wide receiver Alvin Harper caught 6 passes for 136 yards. Phoenix's Steve Beuerlein completed 20 of 27 passes for 218 yards and 1 touchdown against his former teammates. The crowd of more than 73,000 was the largest ever to see the Cardinals play in Sun Devil Stadium. There were only 90 no-shows.

Dallas	7	3	7	0	—	17
Phoenix	0	0	7	3	—	10

Dall — Lassic 8 run (Murray kick)
Dall — FG Murray 23
Dall — Lassic 2 run (Murray kick)
Phx — Proehl 12 pass from Beuerlein (G. Davis kick)
Phx — FG G. Davis 20

MONDAY, SEPTEMBER 20

KANSAS CITY 15, DENVER 7—at Arrowhead Stadium, attendance 78,453. Nick Lowery kicked 5 field goals to give the Chiefs the victory and upstage the quarterback duel between Kansas City's Joe Montana and the Broncos' John Elway. Lowery had 4 field goals by halftime as the Chiefs built a 12-0 advantage. It was 15-0 before Denver drove 91 yards to the game's lone touchdown, Elway's 2-yard pass to Vance Johnson with 1:24 left in the fourth quarter. Montana, back in the lineup after sitting out one week with an injured wrist, completed 21 of 36 passes for 273 yards. Kansas City's Willie Davis caught 6 passes for 139 yards, and Marcus Allen ran for 91 yards. Elway was 28 of 45 for 300 yards. But the Broncos managed only 35 rushing yards, turned over the ball 3 times, and were whistled for 14 penalties.

Denver	0	0	0	7	—	7
Kansas City	6	6	0	3	—	15

KC — FG Lowery 34
KC — FG Lowery 41
KC — FG Lowery 52
KC — FG Lowery 44
KC — FG Lowery 20
Den — V. Johnson 2 pass from Elway (Elam kick)

FOURTH WEEK SUMMARIES

AMERICAN FOOTBALL CONFERENCE

Eastern Division	W	L	T	Pct.	Pts.	OP
Buffalo	2	1	0	.667	64	46
Indianapolis	2	1	0	.667	52	40
Miami	2	1	0	.667	60	57
N.Y. Jets	2	1	0	.667	89	47
New England	0	4	0	.000	51	119
Central Division						
Cleveland	3	1	0	.750	79	66
Pittsburgh	2	2	0	.500	92	75
Houston	1	3	0	.250	81	79
Cincinnati	0	4	0	.000	37	89
Western Division						
Denver	2	1	0	.667	67	52
Kansas City	2	1	0	.667	42	40
L.A. Raiders	2	1	0	.667	57	39
San Diego	2	1	0	.667	53	63
Seattle	2	2	0	.500	61	59

NATIONAL FOOTBALL CONFERENCE

Eastern Division	W	L	T	Pct.	Pts.	OP
N.Y. Giants	3	0	0	1.000	69	37
Philadelphia	3	0	0	1.000	77	65
Dallas	1	2	0	.333	43	58
Washington	1	2	0	.333	76	67
Phoenix	1	3	0	.250	64	76
Central Division						
Detroit	3	1	0	.750	78	63
Minnesota	2	1	0	.667	32	44
Chicago	1	2	0	.333	74	53
Green Bay	1	2	0	.333	66	41
Tampa Bay	0	3	0	.000	27	97
Western Division						
New Orleans	4	0	0	1.000	97	68
L.A. Rams	2	2	0	.500	71	69
San Francisco	2	2	0	.500	87	82
Atlanta	0	4	0	.000	91	146

SUNDAY, SEPTEMBER 26

INDIANAPOLIS 23, CLEVELAND 10—at Hoosier Dome, attendance 59,654. The Colts scored 2 touchdowns in the closing minutes to hand the Browns their first loss of the season. Cleveland led 10-9 until Indianapolis embarked on a 65-yard drive that was capped by Anthony Johnson's 6-yard touchdown run with 3:14 left in the game. The Browns still had time to rally, but quarterback Vinny Testaverde, who replaced an ineffective Bernie Kosar for the second consecutive week, threw an interception and fumbled on Cleveland's next two possessions. The latter was recovered in the end zone by Colts linebacker Jeff Herrod for an insurance touchdown with 1:09 left. The fumble came after 1 of 5 Indianapolis sacks, and the third by linebacker Duane Bickett. Jack Trudeau passed for 260 yards and wide receiver Jessie Hester caught 7 passes for 110 yards for Indianapolis. The Colts improved to 2-1 and completed the month of September with a winning record for the first time since 1977.

Cleveland	0	0	7	3	—	10
Indianapolis	0	6	3	14	—	23

Ind — FG Biasucci 27
Ind — FG Biasucci 19
Cle — Kinchen 10 pass from Testaverde (Stover kick)
Ind — FG Biasucci 26
Cle — FG Stover 32
Ind — Johnson 6 run (Biasucci kick)
Ind — Herrod fumble recovery in end zone (Biasucci kick)

MINNESOTA 15, GREEN BAY 13—at Metrodome, attendance 61,077. Fuad Reveiz kicked 5 field goals, including the game-winner from 22 yards with four seconds left, to give the Vikings the victory. The winning kick was set up when Jim McMahon completed a 45-yard pass to wide receiver Eric Guliford on the previous play. It was the first down from scrimmage that Guliford, a rookie free agent, had played in his NFL career. Earlier, Reveiz's 49-yard field-goal attempt with 2:40 to go in the game bounced off the crossbar. He got another chance after Minnesota got the ball back at its 17-yard line with 1:53 remaining. McMahon had a key 19-yard completion to Cris Carter on fourth-and-8 on the winning drive. It was the second tough loss in a row for the Packers, who previously had fallen to the Eagles on a field goal with 10 seconds to go.

Green Bay	7	3	0	3	—	13
Minnesota	3	3	6	3	—	15

GB — Favre 2 run (Jacke kick)
Minn — FG Reveiz 35
Minn — FG Reveiz 19
GB — FG Jacke 49
Minn — FG Reveiz 29
Minn — FG Reveiz 51
GB — FG Jacke 20
Minn — FG Reveiz 22

L.A. RAMS 28, HOUSTON 13—at Astrodome, attendance 53,072. Jim Everett passed for 316 yards and 3 touchdowns as the Rams stunned the Oilers. Everett, who completed 19 of 28 passes, became the first quarterback in 31 games to throw for more than 300 yards against Houston's defense. He threw a 4-yard touchdown pass to Willie Anderson to open the scoring midway through the first quarter, then put the game out of reach with a pair of second-half scoring tosses. After the Oilers had trimmed a 14-0 deficit to 14-13 on a pair of field goals by Al Del Greco and an 80-yard bomb from Warren Moon to Ernest Givins, Los Angeles responded with a 9-play, 66-yard drive that ended with Everett's 22-yard touchdown pass to tight end Travis McNeal with 1:21 left in the third quarter. Two minutes and 21 seconds later, Everett teamed with wide receiver Henry Ellard on a 48-yard touchdown pass. Ellard finished with 6 catches for 132 yards. Moon passed for 310 yards, but completed only 19 of 42 attempts, was intercepted twice, and suffered 4 sacks.

L.A. Rams	7	7	7	7	—	28
Houston	0	3	10	0	—	13

Rams — Anderson 4 pass from Everett (Zendejas kick)
Rams — Bettis 1 run (Zendejas kick)
Hou — FG Del Greco 52
Hou — FG Del Greco 25
Hou — Givins 80 pass from Moon (Del Greco kick)
Rams — McNeal 22 pass from Everett (Zendejas kick)
Rams — Ellard 48 pass from Everett (Zendejas kick)

MIAMI 22, BUFFALO 13—at Rich Stadium, attendance 79,635. Dan Marino passed for 1 touchdown and ran for another as the Dolphins handled the Bills with ease. Miami built a 19-6 first-half advantage and never was seriously threatened. After Buffalo's Steve Christie had narrowed the margin to 19-6 with a 59-yard field goal on the final play of the first half, the Dolphins put the game away with a time-consuming drive that led to a field goal following the second-half kickoff. Miami held the ball for more than 12 minutes in the third quarter, including 8:23 on the opening march. Marino completed 20 of 32 passes for 282 yards and moved past Johnny Unitas into third place on the NFL's all-time list with 40,306 yards.

Miami	16	3	3	0	—	22
Buffalo	0	6	0	7	—	13

Mia — FG Stoyanovich 30
Mia — Fryar 36 pass from Marino (kick failed)
Mia — Marino 4 run (Stoyanovich kick)
Mia — FG Stoyanovich 23
Buff — FG Christie 40
Buff — FG Christie 59
Mia — FG Stoyanovich 24
Buff — Brooks 27 pass from Kelly (Christie kick)

DETROIT 26, PHOENIX 20—at Silverdome, attendance 57,180. Quarterback Andre Ware made his first start of the season and threw the go-ahead touchdown pass to Brett Perriman in the third quarter of the Lions' victory. Ware, given the starting nod over Rodney Peete, completed 11 of 24 passes for 194 yards. He directed a 66-yard, 4-play drive to open the third quarter, capped by his scoring toss to Perriman, to give Detroit the lead for good at 23-17 three minutes into the second half. Derrick Moore, who ran 1 yard for a touchdown in the second quarter, set up the touchdown pass with a 48-yard run. Jason Hanson kicked 4 field goals for Lions. He also missed a 43-yard try in the third quarter, his first miss in 31 attempts from inside 45 yards in his career. Steve Beuerlein completed 23 of 31 passes for 288 yards and 2 touchdowns for the Cardinals, who hurt themselves by losing 3 fumbles.

Phoenix	0	17	0	3	—	20
Detroit	6	10	7	3	—	26

Det — FG Hanson 44
Det — FG Hanson 22
Phx — Proehl 51 pass from Beuerlein (Davis kick)
Det — FG Hanson 33
Det — D. Moore 1 run (Hanson kick)
Phx — Reeves 2 pass from Beuerlein (Davis kick)
Phx — FG Davis 54
Det — Perriman 9 pass from Ware (Hanson kick)
Phx — FG Davis 30
Det — FG Hanson 38

NEW ORLEANS 16, SAN FRANCISCO 13—at Louisiana Superdome, attendance 69,041. Morten Andersen's 49-yard field goal with five seconds remaining lifted the Saints to their fourth consecutive victory. The 49ers' Mike Cofer tied the game at 13-13 on a 30-yard field goal with 1:14 left. That capped a 15-play, 68-yard drive that took 7:23. But New Orleans started its next possession on its 23-yard line and marched 45 yards to Andersen's winning kick. Wade Wilson passed for 37 yards and scrambled for 8 more on the drive. San Francisco accumulated 339 yards to the Saints' 264, but New Orleans's defense harassed 49ers quarterback Steve Young most of the day, sacking him 6 times and intercepting a pass. Saints linebacker Rickey Jackson had 3 sacks. San Francisco's Ricky Watters rushed for 135 yards on 25 carries.

San Francisco	0	3	7	3	—	13
New Orleans	3	7	3	3	—	16

NO — FG Andersen 33
NO — Brown 1 run (Andersen kick)
SF — FG Cofer 34
SF — Logan 23 run (Cofer kick)
NO — FG Andersen 39
SF — FG Cofer 30
NO — FG Andersen 39

SEATTLE 19, CINCINNATI 10—at Riverfront Stadium, attendance 46,880. Linebacker Rod Stephens recovered a fumble in the end zone with 4:38 remaining to give the Seahawks the victory. It was Seattle's second win of the season, matching its total for all of 1992. Cincinnati had rallied from a 9-0 deficit to take a 10-9 fourth-quarter advantage on Doug Pelfrey's 23-yard field goal and a 21-yard touchdown pass from Jay Schroeder to Carl Pickens with 8:21 to go. But on their next possession, the Bengals coughed up the football at their 4-yard line when linebacker Kevin Murphy hit running back Harold Green, and Stephens recovered for the winning score. John Kasay added his fourth field goal of the game, from 35 yards, with 2:27 left, after Cincinnati turned over the ball on downs.

Seattle	0	6	3	10	—	19
Cincinnati	0	0	0	10	—	10

Sea — FG Kasay 32
Sea — FG Kasay 35
Sea — FG Kasay 23
Cin — FG Pelfrey 23
Cin — Pickens 21 pass from Schroeder (Pelfrey kick)
Sea — Stephens fumble recovery in end zone (Kasay kick)
Sea — FG Kasay 35

CHICAGO 47, TAMPA BAY 17—at Soldier Field, attendance 58,329. The Bears forced 7 turnovers and routed the Buccaneers, giving rookie head coach Dave Wannstedt his first victory. Tampa Bay led 3-0 until Chicago broke the game open with 4 second-quarter touchdowns, 3 of them within a span of 4:04. Bears quarterback Jim Harbaugh ran 1 yard for a touchdown with 4:51 left in the first half, then threw a 25-yard touchdown pass to tight end Ryan Wetnight at the 1:10 mark. Defensive tackle Chris Zorich sacked Buccaneers quarterback Craig Erickson on the next play from scrimmage and end Trace Armstrong recovered at the Tampa Bay 17-yard line. Harbaugh then teamed with Tom Waddle on another touchdown pass 47 seconds before intermission. Tampa Bay countered with a 62-yard touchdown on a desperation pass to end the first half and close within 28-10, but the Buccaneers were not able to mount a serious challenge. Erickson passed for 240 yards but completed only 13 of 32 passes and was intercepted twice. Backups Steve DeBerg and Casey Weldon also threw interceptions, and Tampa Bay lost 3 fumbles, 1 of which was returned 8 yards for a touchdown by Chicago linebacker Myron Baker. Harbaugh completed 17 of 22 passes for 192 yards, and Bears running back Neal Anderson gained 104 yards on 23 carries.

Tampa Bay	3	7	0	7	—	17
Chicago	0	28	3	16	—	47

TB — FG Husted 20
Chi — Anderson 1 run (Butler kick)
Chi — Harbaugh 1 run (Butler kick)
Chi — Wetnight 25 pass from Harbaugh (Butler kick)
Chi — Waddle 17 pass from Harbaugh (Butler kick)
TB — L. Thomas 62 pass from Erickson (Husted kick)
Chi — FG Butler 33
Chi — FG Butler 40
Chi — Baker 8 fumble return (Butler kick)
Chi — FG Butler 32
TB — McDowell 3 pass from DeBerg (Husted kick)
Chi — FG Butler 31

SUNDAY NIGHT, SEPTEMBER 26

N.Y. JETS 45, NEW ENGLAND 7—at Giants Stadium, attendance 64,836. The Jets scored on all five of their first-half possessions and blasted the Patriots, spoiling the return of Bill Parcells to Giants Stadium. Parcells, who led the New York Giants to two Super Bowl titles in his eight seasons as that club's head coach, remained winless in his first year as New England's head coach. The Jets marched 73 yards in 10 plays the first time they had the ball, capping the drive with a 1-yard touchdown run by Brad Baxter 6:40 into the first quarter. Baxter had 2 of New York's 5 rushing touchdowns. Jets quarterback Boomer Esiason completed his first 13 passes and set a club record with 18 consecutive completions over a two-game span. He finished the night with 17 completions in 21 attempts for 217 yards and 1 touchdown, with no interceptions or sacks. New York amassed 388 total yards, and limited the Patriots to 211. With the victory, the Jets moved into a four-way tie for first place in the AFC East.

New England	0	0	0	7	—	7
N.Y. Jets	14	21	0	10	—	45

Jets — B. Baxter 1 run (Blanchard kick)
Jets — Johnson 6 run (Blanchard kick)
Jets — B. Baxter 4 run (Blanchard kick)
Jets — Thornton 13 pass from Esiason (Blanchard kick)
Jets — Mathis 17 run (Blanchard kick)
Jets — FG Blanchard 42
Jets — Murrell 37 run (Blanchard kick)
NE — Russell 5 run (Sisson kick)

MONDAY, SEPTEMBER 27

PITTSBURGH 45, ATLANTA 17—at Georgia Dome, attendance 65,477. Barry Foster ran for 3 touchdowns and Neil O'Donnell passed for 2 as the Steelers kept the Falcons winless. Atlanta led 17-10 five minutes into the second quarter, thanks to touchdowns by the special teams (Tony Smith's 97-yard kickoff return) and defense (cornerback Vinnie Clark's 46-yard fumble return). But Pittsburgh rallied to go up 24-17 at halftime on Foster's 7-yard touchdown run and O'Donnell's 4-yard scoring pass to Dwight Stone. The latter was set up when rookie cornerback Deon Figures returned an interception 78 yards to the 1-yard line. O'Donnell's 7-yard touchdown pass to Yancey Thigpen and Foster's third touchdown run, from 1 yard early in the fourth quarter, turned the game into a rout. O'Donnell finished with 19 completions in 25 attempts for 259 yards. Cornerback Rod Woodson had 2 interceptions for the Steelers, who forced 6 turnovers.

Pittsburgh	7	17	7	14	—	45
Atlanta	14	3	0	0	—	17

Pitt — Foster 30 run (Anderson kick)
Atl — T. Smith 97 kickoff return (N. Johnson kick)
Atl — Clark 46 fumble return (N. Johnson kick)
Pitt — FG Anderson 21

Atl — FG N. Johnson 49
Pitt — Foster 7 run (Anderson kick)
Pitt — Stone 4 pass from O'Donnell (Anderson kick)
Pitt — Thigpen 7 pass from O'Donnell (Anderson kick)
Pitt — Foster 1 run (Anderson kick)
Pitt — Davidson 18 fumble return (Anderson kick)

FIFTH WEEK SUMMARIES
AMERICAN FOOTBALL CONFERENCE

Eastern Division	W	L	T	Pct.	Pts.	OP
Buffalo	3	1	0	.750	81	60
Miami	3	1	0	.750	77	67
Indianapolis	2	2	0	.500	65	75
N.Y. Jets	2	2	0	.500	119	82
New England	0	4	0	.000	51	119
Central Division						
Cleveland	3	1	0	.750	79	66
Pittsburgh	2	2	0	.500	92	75
Houston	1	3	0	.250	81	79
Cincinnati	0	4	0	.000	37	89
Western Division						
Denver	3	1	0	.750	102	65
Kansas City	3	1	0	.750	66	49
Seattle	3	2	0	.600	92	73
L.A. Raiders	2	2	0	.500	66	63
San Diego	2	2	0	.500	67	94

NATIONAL FOOTBALL CONFERENCE

Eastern Division	W	L	T	Pct.	Pts.	OP
Philadelphia	4	0	0	1.000	112	95
N.Y. Giants	3	1	0	.750	83	54
Dallas	2	2	0	.500	79	72
Phoenix	1	3	0	.250	64	76
Washington	1	3	0	.250	86	84
Central Division						
Detroit	3	2	0	.600	88	90
Chicago	2	2	0	.500	80	53
Minnesota	2	2	0	.500	51	82
Green Bay	1	3	0	.250	80	77
Tampa Bay	1	3	0	.250	54	107
Western Division						
New Orleans	5	0	0	1.000	134	74
San Francisco	3	2	0	.600	125	101
L.A. Rams	2	3	0	.400	77	106
Atlanta	0	5	0	.000	91	152

SUNDAY, OCTOBER 3

CHICAGO 6, ATLANTA 0—at Soldier Field, attendance 57,441. Kevin Butler kicked 2 field goals and the Bears thwarted the Falcons' in the closing minutes to win. Butler's field goals included a 52-yard kick in the third quarter, matching his career high. Late in the game, Atlanta drove to Chicago's 8-yard line, but turned over the ball on downs with 1:25 to play. The Falcons outgained the Bears 271-220, but suffered 3 turnovers and were whistled for 11 penalties. Atlanta quarterback Bobby Hebert left the game after three quarters with an elbow injury.

Atlanta	0	0	0	0	—	0
Chicago	0	3	3	0	—	6

Chi — FG Butler 48
Chi — FG Butler 52

TAMPA BAY 27, DETROIT 10—at Tampa Stadium, attendance 40,794. The Buccaneers spotted the Lions a 10-point first-half lead, then rallied to win. Detroit wasted little time getting on the scoreboard, taking the opening kickoff and marching 80 yards in only 5 plays, the last a 20-yard touchdown run by Barry Sanders 2:06 into the game. Jason Hanson's 30-yard field goal early in the second quarter made it 10-0, but Tampa Bay closed to 10-3 on Michael Husted's 52-yard field goal as time ran out in the first half. In the third quarter, the Buccaneers erupted for touchdowns on three consecutive possessions. Craig Erickson capped an 80-yard drive with a 15-yard touchdown pass to Courtney Hawkins to tie the score, and cornerback Darren Anderson intercepted an Andre Ware pass to set up Reggie Cobb's 3-yard touchdown run. Erik Kramer relieved Ware at quarterback for the Lions but was intercepted by safety Joe King, setting up Erickson's 37-yard touchdown pass to tight end Ron Hall. Erickson, making only his third NFL start, completed 14 of 25 passes for 210 yards, and Cobb rushed for 113 yards on 25 carries. Sanders, who had 50 yards on Detroit's opening drive, finished with 130 yards on 22 carries.

Detroit	7	3	0	0	—	10
Tampa Bay	0	3	21	3	—	27

Det — Sanders 20 run (Hanson kick)

Det — FG Hanson 30
TB — FG Husted 52
TB — Hawkins 15 pass from Erickson (Husted kick)
TB — Cobb 3 run (Husted kick)
TB — Hall 37 pass from Erickson (Husted kick)
TB — FG Husted 46

DALLAS 36, GREEN BAY 14—at Texas Stadium, attendance 63,568. Troy Aikman passed for 317 yards and Eddie Murray kicked 5 field goals as the Cowboys easily handled the Packers. After Dallas fell behind 7-0, Aikman brought his team even with a 61-yard touchdown pass to Michael Irvin midway through the first quarter. The Cowboys then relied on Murray to build a 19-7 advantage, and put the game out of reach on Emmitt Smith's 22-yard touchdown run 7:11 into the second half. Aikman completed 18 of 23 passes and was not intercepted. Irvin caught 7 passes for 155 yards, and Smith rushed for 71 yards in his first start of the season. Robert Brooks returned a kickoff 95 yards for a touchdown for the Packers, who lost their third straight game.

Green Bay	7	0	7	0	—	14
Dallas	10	6	13	7	—	36

GB — Bennett 1 run (Jacke kick)
Dall — Irvin 61 pass from Aikman (Murray kick)
Dall — FG Murray 33
Dall — FG Murray 19
Dall — FG Murray 19
Dall — FG Murray 50
Dall — E. Smith 22 run (Murray kick)
GB — Brooks 95 kickoff return (Jacke kick)
Dall — FG Murray 48
Dall — Lassic 1 run (Murray kick)

DENVER 35, INDIANAPOLIS 13—at Mile High Stadium, attendance 74,953. The Broncos scored on their first four possessions and routed the Colts. With John Elway completing 13 of 17 passes for 156 yards, including touchdowns of 3 yards to Glyn Milburn and 22 yards to Shannon Sharpe, Denver built a 28-0 advantage midway through the second quarter. Indianapolis tried to rally, pulling within 28-13 on a pair of Dean Biasucci field goals and Jack Trudeau's 4-yard touchdown pass to tight end Kerry Cash 10 seconds before halftime. But the Broncos used a trick play to score the clinching touchdown with nine seconds left in the third quarter. Wide receiver Arthur Marshall tossed a 30-yard touchdown pass to Derek Russell on a fake reverse to make it 35-13. Robert Delpino rushed for 83 yards and a touchdown and Rod Bernstine added 60 yards and a score as Denver amassed 196 rushing yards en route to 454 total yards. Elway finished with 20 completions in 30 attempts for 230 yards.

Indianapolis	0	10	3	0	—	13
Denver	21	7	7	0	—	35

Den — Delpino 2 run (Elam kick)
Den — Bernstine 9 run (Elam kick)
Den — Milburn 3 pass from Elway (Elam kick)
Den — Sharpe 22 pass from Elway (Elam kick)
Ind — FG Biasucci 24
Ind — Cash 4 pass from Trudeau (Biasucci kick)
Ind — FG Biasucci 28
Den — Russell 30 pass from Marshall (Elam kick)

KANSAS CITY 24, L.A. RAIDERS 9—at Arrowhead Stadium, attendance 77,395. Joe Montana threw 2 touchdown passes before injuring a hamstring in the Chiefs' victory. Montana capped Kansas City's first drive with a 1-yard touchdown pass to tackle-eligible Joe Valerio, and threw a 15-yard scoring pass to Willie Davis on the next series. The veteran quarterback completed 7 of 9 passes for 68 yards, but had to leave the game in the second quarter when he was injured while scrambling out of bounds. Raiders linebacker Aaron Wallace was assessed a late-hit penalty on the play, 1 of 16 infractions for 168 yards whistled against Los Angeles. Marcus Allen, playing against his former teammates for the first time, capped that same drive with a 4-yard touchdown run for a 21-3 lead. Allen became only the tenth player in NFL history to score 100 touchdowns. Former Notre Dame and Canadian Football League star Raghib (Rocket) Ismail made his NFL debut for the Raiders and caught 4 passes for 75 yards, including a 43-yard touchdown in the fourth quarter. Los Angeles played without injured starting quarterback Jeff Hostetler. Backup Vince Evans completed 15 of 26 passes for 192 yards and was not intercepted. But he was sacked 6 times, 4 by de-

fensive end Neil Smith and 2 by linebacker Derrick Thomas.

L.A. Raiders	0	3	0	6	—	9
Kansas City	14	7	3	0	—	24

KC — Valerio 1 pass from Montana (Lowery kick)
KC — Davis 15 pass from Montana (Lowery kick)
Raid — FG Jaeger 27
KC — Allen 4 run (Lowery kick)
KC — FG Lowery 29
Raid — Ismail 43 pass from Evans (kick blocked)

SAN FRANCISCO 38, MINNESOTA 19—at Candlestick Park, attendance 63,071. Defense and special teams made the key plays in the 49ers' victory over the Vikings. San Francisco led 14-7 in the second quarter when cornerback Eric Davis increased the advantage to 14 points with a 41-yard interception return for a touchdown. After Minnesota closed to within 24-19 early in the fourth quarter, the 49ers' Dexter Carter returned a punt 22 yards. That led to a 56-yard touchdown drive, capped by Ricky Watters' 3-yard run with 5:54 to play. Carter put the game away just 68 seconds later with a 72-yard punt return for a touchdown. San Francisco managed only 254 total yards, but the 49ers added 131 yards on 5 punt returns. The Vikings' Jim McMahon completed 25 of 45 passes for 223 yards and 2 touchdowns.

Minnesota	7	2	3	7	—	19
San Francisco	7	14	3	14	—	38

Minn — Tice 3 pass from McMahon (Reveiz kick)
SF — Rice 39 pass from Young (Cofer kick)
SF — Logan 1 run (Cofer kick)
SF — Davis 41 interception return (Cofer kick)
Minn — Safety, H. Thomas tackled Young in end zone
SF — FG Cofer 22
Minn — FG Reveiz 21
Minn — C. Carter 9 pass from McMahon (Reveiz kick)
SF — Watters 3 run (Cofer kick)
SF — D. Carter 72 punt return (Cofer kick)

NEW ORLEANS 37, L.A. RAMS 6—at Anaheim Stadium, attendance 50,709. The Saints broke open a close game with 3 fourth-quarter touchdowns and raised their record to 5-0. New Orleans led just 16-6 early in the final period when the Rams marched to the Saints' 34-yard line. But New Orleans linebacker Rickey Jackson sacked Los Angeles quarterback Jim Everett, forcing a fumble that defensive end Wayne Martin recovered at the 45. Five plays later, Wade Wilson threw a 30-yard touchdown pass to Patrick Newman to give the Saints a 17-point cushion with 13:51 left. Less than three minutes later, Tyrone Hughes returned a punt 74 yards for a touchdown to break open the game. Wilson completed 15 of 25 passes for 205 yards and also had a 15-yard scoring toss to Derek Brown in the first quarter. Everett, who had directed an upset of Houston one week earlier, completed only 10 of 26 passes for 126 yards with 1 interception. Rams rookie running back Jerome Bettis gained 102 yards on 22 carries. Kicker Tony Zendejas converted a 53-yard field goal late in the first quarter, his ninth successful kick in a row from 50 yards or more.

New Orleans	10	3	3	21	—	37
L.A. Rams	3	0	3	0	—	6

NO — Brown 15 pass from Wilson (Andersen kick)
NO — FG Andersen 48
Rams — FG Zendejas 53
NO — FG Andersen 25
Rams — FG Zendejas 37
NO — FG Andersen 43
NO — Newman 30 pass from Wilson (Andersen kick)
NO — Hughes 74 punt return (Andersen kick)
NO — Ned 35 run (Andersen kick)

PHILADELPHIA 35, N.Y. JETS 30—at Giants Stadium, attendance 72,593. Cornerback Eric Allen returned a fourth-quarter interception 94 yards for the winning touchdown as the Eagles rallied from a 21-point deficit to defeat the Jets and remain unbeaten. It was a costly victory for Philadelphia, however, which was hit hard by injuries, most notably a broken leg suffered by starting quarterback Randall Cunningham, who was expected to miss at least two months. Wide receiver Fred Barnett, the team's leading pass catcher in 1992, and Jeff Sydner, a special teams star, were lost for the season with knee injuries. Nevertheless, the Eagles rallied to win for the third consecutive game. Quarterback Boomer Esiason staked New York to a 21-0 first-half advantage with 3 touchdown passes, 2 to tight end Johnny Mitchell. Philadelphia closed to 21-14 by intermission, but Esiason and Mitchell teamed for another touchdown, a 65-yard pass, on the Jets' first play of the second half. Bubby Brister, Cunningham's replacement, threw his second touchdown pass and rookie Vaughn Hebron ran 1 yard for a touchdown to tie the game at 28-28 early in the fourth quarter. After New York regained the lead with a safety, Allen won the game with his interception with 8:43 to go. Brister finished with 11 completions in 16 attempts for 108 yards. Mitchell caught 7 passes for 146 yards and Chris Burkett had 4 receptions for 103 yards for the Jets, who amassed 417 total yards but turned over the ball 3 times. Esiason completed 19 of 33 attempts for 297 yards and 4 touchdowns.

Philadelphia	0	14	7	14	—	35
N.Y. Jets	14	7	7	2	—	30

Jets — Thornton 7 pass from Esiason (Blanchard kick)
Jets — Mitchell 14 pass from Esiason (Blanchard kick)
Jets — Mitchell 12 pass from Esiason (Blanchard kick)
Phil — Walker 8 run (Bahr kick)
Phil — Bavaro 10 pass from Brister (Bahr kick)
Jets — Mitchell 65 pass from Esiason (Blanchard kick)
Phil — Williams 11 pass from Brister (Bahr kick)
Phil — Hebron 1 run (Bahr kick)
Jets — Safety, Brister intentionally grounded ball in end zone
Phil — Allen 94 interception return (Bahr kick)

SEATTLE 31, SAN DIEGO 14—at Kingdome, attendance 54,778. Rookie quarterback Rick Mirer passed for 282 yards as the Seahawks upset the Chargers. Seattle, which won only two games in 1992, won its third in a row and improved to 3-2. Defending AFC Western Division champion San Diego fell to 2-2. Mirer, the second overall selection in the 1993 draft, completed 25 of 40 passes. But one of the key plays of the game was made by backup quarterback Dan McGwire in the closing seconds of the first half. After Mirer sprained his ankle when hit by Chargers linebacker Junior Seau 21 seconds before intermission, McGwire tossed a 17-yard touchdown pass to Brian Blades with 10 seconds left in the first half, giving the Seahawks a 17-7 lead. Chris Warren's 1-yard run and Kelvin Martin's 18-yard touchdown catch made it 31-7 before reserve quarterback John Friesz led San Diego to a touchdown late in the game. Chargers wide receiver Anthony Miller caught 10 passes for 123 yards. Blades had 10 receptions for 132 yards for Seattle. Defensive end Michael Sinclair had 3 sacks.

San Diego	7	0	0	7	—	14
Seattle	7	10	7	7	—	31

Sea — Mirer 2 run (Kasay kick)
SD — Butts 2 run (Carney kick)
Sea — FG Kasay 33
Sea — Blades 17 pass from McGwire (Kasay kick)
Sea — C. Warren 1 run (Kasay kick)
Sea — Martin 18 pass from Mirer (Kasay kick)
SD — Miller 11 pass from Friesz (Carney kick)

SUNDAY NIGHT, OCTOBER 3

BUFFALO 17, N.Y. GIANTS 14—at Rich Stadium, attendance 79,813. Jim Kelly's 8-yard touchdown pass to tight end Pete Metzelaars lifted the Bills past the Giants. It was the first time the two teams had met since New York beat Buffalo in Super Bowl XXV. The Bills jumped out to a 10-point lead in the first quarter, but the Giants rallied to take a 14-10 halftime advantage behind a pair of short touchdown passes by Phil Simms. It remained that way until Buffalo marched 73 yards in 11 plays to the winning score. Thurman Thomas rushed for 122 yards on 26 carries for Buffalo. The Bills intercepted 3 of Simms's passes, including an 85-yard touchdown return by safety Henry Jones.

N.Y. Giants	0	14	0	0	—	14
Buffalo	10	0	0	7	—	17

Buff — FG Christie 24
Buff — Jones 85 interception return (Christie kick)
Giants— Calloway 5 pass from Simms (Treadwell kick)
Giants— M. Jackson 3 pass from Simms (Treadwell kick)
Buff — Metzelaars 8 pass from Kelly (Christie kick)

MONDAY, OCTOBER 4

MIAMI 17, WASHINGTON 10—at Joe Robbie Stadium, attendance 68,568. Dan Marino passed for 253 yards and a touchdown as the Dolphins handed the Redskins their third consecutive defeat. Marino teamed with Tony Martin on the third play of the game for an 80-yard touchdown pass, then directed a 73-yard drive to Mark Higgs's 1-yard run for a 14-0 lead just 7:39 into the game. Washington closed within 4 points on a 28-yard field goal by Chip Lohmiller and backup quarterback Rich Gannon's 12-yard touchdown pass to Ricky Sanders with 11:08 left in the game. But the Redskins never got a chance to take the lead, because Miami held the ball for the next 13 plays and 7:10 before Pete Stoyanovich kicked a 37-yard field goal with 3:58 remaining. Washington's last chance ended when Troy Vincent intercepted a pass from Gannon in the final minute. The Dolphins outgained an ineffective Redskins' offense 354-232. Rookie running back Terry Kirby gained 94 yards on 16 carries and had 3 catches for 36 yards in his first NFL start. He had an 18-yard run and a 34-yard reception on the second touchdown drive. The Redskins, who had not won since beating defending Super Bowl-champion Dallas in the opener, lost three in a row for the first time since 1988.

Washington	0	3	0	7	—	10
Miami	14	0	0	3	—	17

Mia — Martin 80 pass from Marino (Stoyanovich kick)
Mia — Higgs 1 run (Stoyanovich kick)
Wash — FG Lohmiller 28
Wash — Sanders 12 pass from Gannon (Lohmiller kick)
Mia — FG Stoyanovich 37

SIXTH WEEK SUMMARIES

AMERICAN FOOTBALL CONFERENCE

Eastern Division	W	L	T	Pct.	Pts.	OP
Buffalo	4	1	0	.800	116	67
Miami	4	1	0	.800	101	81
Indianapolis	2	3	0	.400	68	102
N.Y. Jets	2	3	0	.400	139	106
New England	1	4	0	.200	74	140
Central Division						
Cleveland	3	2	0	.600	93	90
Pittsburgh	3	2	0	.600	108	78
Houston	1	4	0	.200	88	114
Cincinnati	0	5	0	.000	52	106
Western Division						
Kansas City	4	1	0	.800	83	64
Denver	3	2	0	.600	129	95
L.A. Raiders	3	2	0	.600	90	83
Seattle	3	2	0	.600	92	73
San Diego	2	3	0	.400	70	110

NATIONAL FOOTBALL CONFERENCE

Eastern Division	W	L	T	Pct.	Pts.	OP
N.Y. Giants	4	1	0	.800	124	61
Philadelphia	4	1	0	.800	118	112
Dallas	3	2	0	.600	106	75
Phoenix	1	4	0	.200	85	99
Washington	1	4	0	.200	93	125
Central Division						
Chicago	3	2	0	.600	97	59
Detroit	3	2	0	.600	88	90
Minnesota	3	2	0	.600	66	82
Green Bay	2	3	0	.400	110	104
Tampa Bay	1	4	0	.200	54	122
Western Division						
New Orleans	5	0	0	1.000	134	74
San Francisco	3	2	0	.600	125	101
L.A. Rams	2	3	0	.400	77	106
Atlanta	0	5	0	.000	91	152

SUNDAY, OCTOBER 10

CHICAGO 17, PHILADELPHIA 6—at Veterans Stadium, attendance 63,601. Defensive end Richard Dent had 2 sacks and an interception as the Bears moved into a tie for first place in the NFC Central by winning their third consecutive game and handing the Eagles their first defeat. Dent's interception came midway through the first quarter of a scoreless tie. He returned the ball 24 yards to Philadelphia's 30-yard line, setting up Kevin Butler's 37-yard field goal. On the Eagles' next possession, Chicago defensive end Trace Armstrong forced a fumble that linebacker Dante Jones recovered, and three plays later Jim Harbaugh teamed with rookie wide receiver Curtis Conway on a 32-yard touchdown pass. Philadelphia, which started the season 4-0, averted a shutout when Bubby Brister threw a 7-yard touchdown pass to Calvin Williams with 23 seconds left. It was not a productive day for Brister, who was replacing injured Randall Cunningham as the Eagles' quarterback. Brister completed 18 of 33 passes for 209 yards, but was intercepted twice, lost 2 fumbles, and was sacked 7 times. Philadelphia had its 11-game winning streak at Veterans Stadium snapped.

Chicago	10	7	0	0	—	17
Philadelphia	0	0	0	6	—	6

Chi — FG Butler 37
Chi — Conway 32 pass from Harbaugh (Butler kick)
Chi — Harbaugh 1 run (Butler kick)
Phil — Williams 7 pass from Brister (kick failed)

KANSAS CITY 17, CINCINNATI 15—at Arrowhead Stadium, attendance 75,394. Nick Lowery's 37-yard field goal with 2:43 remaining lifted the Chiefs to victory over the winless Bengals. Cincinnati had taken a 15-14 lead on the last of rookie Doug Pelfrey's club-record tying 5 field goals, from 34 yards with 5:59 to play. But Kansas City quarterback Dave Krieg, playing in place of injured Joe Montana, moved his team into Bengals territory with a 28-yard completion to J.J. Birden, and Lowery converted the winning kick moments later. The Chiefs managed only 203 total yards (Cincinnati had 277), but won their third consecutive game and moved into sole possession of first place in the AFC Western Division.

Cincinnati	3	9	0	3	—	15
Kansas City	0	7	7	3	—	17

Cin — FG Pelfrey 23
Cin — FG Pelfrey 24
Cin — FG Pelfrey 42
KC — Barnett 8 pass from Krieg (Lowery kick)
Cin — FG Pelfrey 47
KC — Allen 9 run (Lowery kick)
Cin — FG Pelfrey 34
KC — FG Lowery 37

DALLAS 27, INDIANAPOLIS 3—at Hoosier Dome, attendance 60,453. Emmitt Smith rushed for 104 yards and 1 touchdown, and Troy Aikman passed for 245 yards and another score to lead the Cowboys to their third consecutive victory. Leading 14-3 in the third quarter, Dallas put the game out of reach when tight end Jay Novacek, the holder on field-goal attempts, took the snap in field-goal formation and ran 2 yards for a touchdown. Eddie Murray added a pair of field goals in the fourth quarter. The Colts amassed 361 total yards, including 113 rushing yards by rookie Roosevelt Potts, but were victimized by 4 turnovers. Indianapolis also suffered a severe blow when defensive tackle Steve Emtman suffered a season-ending injury to his right knee in the second quarter. Emtman, the top overall pick in the 1992 draft, missed the final seven games of his rookie year when he injured his left knee.

Dallas	14	0	7	6	—	27
Indianapolis	0	3	0	0	—	3

Dall — Johnston 1 pass from Aikman (Murray kick)
Dall — E. Smith 20 run (Murray kick)
Ind — FG Biasucci 27
Dall — Novacek 2 run (Murray kick)
Dall — FG Murray 30
Dall — FG Murray 32

MIAMI 24, CLEVELAND 14—at Cleveland Stadium, attendance 78,138. Scott Mitchell replaced injured Dan Marino and threw a pair of third-quarter touchdown passes to rally the Dolphins past the Browns. Marino, who started his 145th consecutive game for Miami, tore his Achilles tendon in the second quarter and was lost for the season. Mitchell's first pass was intercepted by Cleveland cornerback Najee Mustafaa, who returned it a club-record 97 yards for a touchdown to give the Browns a 14-10 halftime advantage. In the third quarter, Mitchell teamed with wide receiver Tony Martin (19 yards) and tight end Keith Jackson (3 yards) for touchdowns. Marino completed 14 of 19 passes for 161 yards and a touchdown before being injured, while Mitchell was 10 of 16 for 118 yards. The Browns could muster only 202 total yards, and for the third consecutive game, starting quarterback Bernie Kosar was relieved by backup Vinny Testaverde. Kosar completed 15 of 19 passes, but for only 82 yards, and was sacked 5 times. Testaverde did not fare any better, completing only 6 of 13 for 44 yards, but was sacked only once and earned the starting assignment against Cincinnati the following week.

Miami	0	10	14	0	—	24
Cleveland	7	7	0	0	—	14

Cle — M. Jackson 14 pass from Kosar (Stover kick)
Mia — FG Stoyanovich 52
Mia — Ingram 13 pass from Marino (Stoyanovich kick)
Cle — Mustafaa 97 interception return (Stover kick)
Mia — Martin 19 pass from Mitchell (Stoyanovich kick)
Mia — K. Jackson 3 pass from Mitchell (Stoyanovich kick)

NEW ENGLAND 23, PHOENIX 21—at Sun Devil Stadium, attendance 36,115. Backup quarterback Scott Secules threw a 2-yard touchdown pass to tight end Ben Coates with 3:56 remaining, lifting the Patriots past the Cardinals. It was New England's first victory of the season and snapped a nine-game losing streak dating back to 1992. Phoenix lost its third in a row. The Cardinals took a 21-16 lead on Steve Beuerlein's third touchdown pass of the game, a 30-yard toss to Randal Hill with 7:35 to go. But the Patriots won by marching 84 yards in just 3 plays for the winning score. The key blow was running back Leonard Russell's 69-yard run with a lateral from running back Kevin Turner, after Turner had caught a 13-yard pass from Secules. Russell was tackled at the 2-yard line, but Secules teamed with Coates for the winning score on the next play. Secules, who entered the game in the closing seconds of the first half after starter Drew Bledsoe sprained his knee, completed 12 of 20 passes for 214 yards. Russell ran for 116 yards on 28 carries. New England, which entered the game ranked twenty-third in the league in total offense, finished with 432 yards.

New England	0	13	3	7	—	23
Phoenix	0	14	0	7	—	21

NE — Coates 4 pass from Bledsoe (Sisson kick)
Phx — Proehl 6 pass from Beuerlein (Davis kick)
Phx — Proehl 15 pass from Beuerlein (Davis kick)
NE — FG Sisson 29
NE — FG Sisson 23
NE — FG Sisson 31
Phx — R. Hill 30 pass from Beuerlein (Davis kick)
NE — Coates 2 pass from Secules (Sisson kick)

N.Y. GIANTS 41, WASHINGTON 7—at RFK Stadium, attendance 53,715. Phil Simms threw 3 touchdown passes and the Giants built a 27-0 first-half lead en route to handing the Redskins their worst defeat at home in 45 years. Simms, who completed his first 10 passes, finished 14 of 17 for 182 yards. Tight end Howard Cross and wide receiver Mike Sherrard each caught 2 touchdown passes, David Meggett threw a touchdown pass on a halfback option play, and Lewis Tillman and rookie Kenyon Rasheed ran for scores. Tillman, who replaced injured Rodney Hampton in the lineup, gained a career-high 104 yards on 29 carries. He got New York rolling with a 3-yard touchdown run to cap the Giants' first possession, a 13-play, 89-yard drive. New York then scored on each of its next three possessions to turn the game into a rout. Washington's lone score came on a 12-yard touchdown pass from Mark Rypien to Tim McGee with 53 seconds left in the first half. Rypien, playing for the first time since injuring his knee in week 2, completed 21 of 35 passes for 220 yards but could not prevent the Redskins' fourth consecutive defeat.

N.Y. Giants	7	20	0	14	—	41
Washington	0	7	0	0	—	7

Giants — Tillman 3 run (Treadwell kick)
Giants — Cross 7 pass from Simms (kick failed)
Giants — Sherrard 42 pass from Meggett (Treadwell kick)
Giants — Cross 17 pass from Simms (Treadwell kick)
Wash — McGee 12 pass from Rypien (Lohmiller kick)
Giants — Sherrard 55 pass from Simms (Treadwell kick)
Giants — Rasheed 23 run (Treadwell kick)

L.A. RAIDERS 24, N.Y. JETS 20—at Los Angeles Memorial Coliseum, attendance 41,627. Nick Bell ran 1 yard for a touchdown with four seconds left to give the Raiders a dramatic come-from-behind victory. After rallying from a 17-0 first-half deficit to tie the game, Los Angeles fell behind again when the Jets' Cary Blanchard kicked a 20-yard field goal with 4:29 remaining. But the Raiders responded by marching 72 yards in 11 plays to the winning score. Quarterback Vince Evans passed for 57 yards on the drive, including a 6-yard completion to Tim Brown to position the ball on the 1-yard line. With no timeouts left, Raiders coaches were signaling for a pass into the ground to stop the clock and set up a game-tying field goal, but Evans did not see them. Instead, he handed off to Bell, who scored behind a block by tackle Gerald Perry. The Jets built their first-half lead on a 6-yard run by Blair Thomas, a 62-yard interception return by Brian Washington, and Blanchard's 25-yard field goal. After Washington's interception return, which came 3:51 into the second quarter, Raiders quarterback Jeff Hostetler, still not fully recovered from the sprained ankle that kept him out of the previous game, was replaced by Evans. The 38-year-old quarterback completed 14 of 22 passes for 247 yards, including touchdowns of 42 yards to James Jett and 68 yards to Alexander Wright.

N.Y. Jets	0	17	0	3	—	20
L.A. Raiders	0	7	10	7	—	24

Jets — B. Thomas 6 run (Blanchard kick)
Jets — B. Washington 62 interception return (Blanchard kick)
Jets — FG Blanchard 25
Raid — Jett 42 pass from Evans (Jaeger kick)
Raid — Wright 68 pass from Evans (Jaeger kick)
Raid — FG Jaeger 42
Jets — FG Blanchard 20
Raid — Bell 1 run (Jaeger kick)

PITTSBURGH 16, SAN DIEGO 3—at Three Rivers Stadium, attendance 55,264. Linebacker Levon Kirkland returned a fumble 16 yards for the only touchdown of the game as the Steelers won their third straight game. Pittsburgh's offense accumulated 304 total yards, but could manage only 3 field goals by Gary Anderson. So the Steelers relied on their defense, which limited the Chargers to 138 total yards, including just 19 on the ground in 20 attempts. San Diego's only score came on John Carney's 33-yard field goal three seconds before halftime, and their best chance for a touchdown was thwarted by safety Darren Perry's goal-line interception in the third quarter. On that play, Chargers quarterback John Friesz was knocked out of the game when hit by Pittsburgh linebacker Kevin Greene. Stan Humphries replaced Friesz, and on his first series was sacked by linebacker Greg Lloyd. The ball came loose, and Kirkland converted the fumble into the clinching score. Barry Foster led the Steelers with 110 yards on 23 carries.

San Diego	0	3	0	0	—	3
Pittsburgh	3	3	7	3	—	16

Pitt — FG Anderson 37
Pitt — FG Anderson 34
SD — FG Carney 33
Pitt — Kirkland 16 fumble return (Anderson kick)
Pitt — FG Anderson 35

MINNESOTA 15, TAMPA BAY 0—at Metrodome, attendance 53,562. The Vikings' defense dominated this one, limiting the Buccaneers to 169 total yards and forcing 5 turnovers. Safety Vencie Glenn had 2 of Minnesota's 4 interceptions, and defensive tackle Roy Barker pressured Tampa Bay quarterback Craig Erickson into an intentional grounding call in the end zone for a safety that gave the Vikings a 5-0 lead with 6:19 left in the second quarter. Barry Word ran 1 yard for a touchdown 4:24 later to increase the advantage to 12-0. Minnesota was not threatened after that. The Vikings won for the ninth consecutive time against an NFC Central opponent and moved into a three-way tie for first place in the division.

Tampa Bay	0	0	0	0	—	0
Minnesota	0	12	0	3	—	15

Minn — FG Reveiz 26
Minn — Safety, Erickson called for intentional grounding in end zone
Minn — Word 1 run (Reveiz kick)
Minn — FG Reveiz 25

SUNDAY NIGHT, OCTOBER 10

GREEN BAY 30, DENVER 27—at Lambeau Field, attendance 58,943. The Packers snapped their three-game losing streak by building a 30-7 halftime lead, then holding on to win. Green Bay manufactured its big advantage by scoring on all six of its first-half possessions. The Broncos' lone score of the half came on a 14-yard pass from John Elway to Vance Johnson 3:27 into the second quarter, trimming the Packers' lead to 17-7. But Green Bay quarterback Brett Favre countered just 24 seconds later with a 66-yard touchdown pass to tight end Jackie Harris. Denver chipped away at its deficit in the second half, and pulled within three points on Jason Elam's 37-yard field goal with 8:31 left in the game. The Broncos had a chance to win or tie after cornerback Le-Lo Lang's interception gave them the ball at the Packers' 43-yard line with 2:05 to go. But Green Bay defensive end Reggie White had sacks of Elway on consecutive plays to secure the victory. Favre finished with 20 completions in 32 attempts for 235 yards, with 3 interceptions. The Packers' Sterling Sharpe caught 10 passes for 70 yards and Harris had 5 receptions for 128 yards. Denver's Elway completed 33 of 59 passes for 367 yards. Vance Johnson had 10 catches for 148 yards.

Denver	0	7	14	6	—	27
Green Bay	17	13	0	0	—	30

GB — FG Jacke 28
GB — Stephens 1 run (Jacke kick)
GB — Bennett 1 run (Jacke kick)
Den — V. Johnson 14 pass from Elway (Elam kick)
GB — Harris 66 pass from Favre (Jacke kick)
GB — FG Jacke 32
GB — FG Jacke 21
Den — Croel 22 interception return (Elam kick)
Den — Bernstine 2 run (Elam kick)
Den — FG Elam 47
Den — FG Elam 37

MONDAY, OCTOBER 11

BUFFALO 35, HOUSTON 7—at Rich Stadium, attendance 79,928. Jim Kelly broke a 7-7 tie with a pair of touchdown passes to Andre Reed, and the Bills went on to hand the Oilers their third consecutive defeat. Kelly, who also threw a 34-yard touchdown pass to Don Beebe in the first quarter, teamed with Reed on scoring tosses of 24 and 39 yards just 3:51 apart in the second quarter. Thurman Thomas's 7-yard run 3:34 before halftime turned the game into a rout. Buffalo's defense bore out after that and finished the night with 7 turnovers. Kelly had 15 completions in 25 attempts for 247 yards, while Thomas rushed for 92 yards, including 90 before intermission. Houston managed 329 total yards, but stymied itself with the turnovers, 12 penalties, and 4 sacks. The game was a rematch of the 1992 AFC Wild Card Game, in which Buffalo rallied from a 35-3 third-quarter deficit to win 41-38 in overtime.

Houston	7	0	0	0	—	7
Buffalo	7	21	0	7	—	35

Buff — Beebe 34 pass from Kelly (Christie kick)
Hou — L. Harris 17 pass from Moon (Del Greco kick)
Buff — Reed 24 pass from Kelly (Christie kick)
Buff — Reed 39 pass from Kelly (Christie kick)
Buff — Thomas 7 run (Christie kick)
Buff — K. Davis 3 run (Christie kick)

SEVENTH WEEK SUMMARIES
AMERICAN FOOTBALL CONFERENCE

Eastern Division	W	L	T	Pct.	Pts.	OP
Buffalo	4	1	0	.800	116	67
Miami	4	1	0	.800	101	81
Indianapolis	2	3	0	.400	68	102
N.Y. Jets	2	3	0	.400	139	106
New England	1	5	0	.167	88	168
Central Division						
Cleveland	4	2	0	.667	121	107
Pittsburgh	4	2	0	.667	145	92
Houston	2	4	0	.333	116	128
Cincinnati	0	6	0	.000	69	134
Western Division						
Kansas City	5	1	0	.833	100	78
L.A. Raiders	4	2	0	.667	113	103
Denver	3	3	0	.500	149	118
Seattle	3	3	0	.500	102	103
San Diego	2	4	0	.333	84	127

NATIONAL FOOTBALL CONFERENCE

Eastern Division	W	L	T	Pct.	Pts.	OP
N.Y. Giants	5	1	0	.833	145	71
Dallas	4	2	0	.667	132	92
Philadelphia	4	2	0	.667	128	133
Phoenix	2	4	0	.333	121	105
Washington	1	5	0	.167	99	161

Central Division						
Detroit	4	2	0	.667	118	100
Chicago	3	2	0	.600	97	59
Minnesota	3	2	0	.600	66	82
Green Bay	2	3	0	.400	110	104
Tampa Bay	1	4	0	.200	54	122
Western Division						
New Orleans	5	1	0	.833	148	111
San Francisco	3	3	0	.500	142	127
L.A. Rams	2	4	0	.333	101	136
Atlanta	1	5	0	.167	121	176

THURSDAY, OCTOBER 14

ATLANTA 30, L.A. RAMS 24—at Georgia Dome, attendance 45,231. Billy Joe Tolliver threw a career-high 3 touchdown passes and the Falcons rallied from a 14-point deficit to win their first game of the season. A 56-yard touchdown pass from Jim Everett and a 2-yard run by Jerome Bettis helped stake the Rams to a 17-3 lead late in the first half. But Tolliver, Atlanta's third-string quarterback who was starting because of injuries to Bobby Hebert and Chris Miller, threw a 21-yard touchdown pass to Andre Rison 1:50 before intermission to trim the Falcons' deficit to 17-10. Los Angeles led 24-20 until Tolliver and Rison teamed again, this time on a 42-yard touchdown pass that gave Atlanta the lead for the first time with 4:40 remaining in the game. The Falcons added a field goal 1:11 later after recovering a fumble on the ensuing kickoff. Everett passed for 294 yards, but also threw 2 interceptions that led to Atlanta's second-half touchdowns. He marched the Rams from their 20-yard line to the Falcons' 27 with less than a minute to go, but threw 4 consecutive incompletions from there. Bettis ran for 85 yards for Los Angeles, which averaged nearly 7 yards per play and piled up 456 total yards. Tolliver completed 18 of 34 passes for 213 yards.

L.A. Rams	10	7	7	0	—	24
Atlanta	3	7	7	13	—	30

Rams — Anderson 56 pass from Everett (Zendejas kick)
Atl — FG Johnson 28
Rams — FG Zendejas 52
Rams — Bettis 2 run (Zendejas kick)
Atl — Rison 21 pass from Tolliver (Johnson kick)
Atl — Mims 3 pass from Tolliver (Johnson kick)
Rams — Gary 60 pass from Everett (Zendejas kick)
Atl — FG Johnson 32
Atl — Rison 42 pass from Tolliver (Johnson kick)
Atl — FG Johnson 34

SUNDAY, OCTOBER 17

CLEVELAND 28, CINCINNATI 17—at Riverfront Stadium, attendance 55,647. Vinny Testaverde led the Browns to the victory by throwing 3 touchdown passes in his first start of the season. Testaverde, who had come off the bench to replace Bernie Kosar each of the past three games, completed only 11 of 24 passes for 127 yards, but he staked his team to a 21-0 lead by throwing all of his scoring passes in the game's first 21 minutes. Wide receiver Mark Carrier's 15-yard run on a reverse put the game out of reach after the Bengals had closed within 21-10. Tommy Vardell led Cleveland with 98 rushing yards. Cincinnati managed only 34 rushing yards and 194 total yards.

Cleveland	7	14	0	7	—	28
Cincinnati	0	7	3	7	—	17

Cle — Vardell 28 pass from Testaverde (Stover kick)
Cle — Baldwin 5 pass from Testaverde (Stover kick)
Cle — Kinchen 1 pass from Testaverde (Stover kick)
Cin — Query 11 pass from Schroeder (Pelfrey kick)
Cin — FG Pelfrey 49
Cle — Carrier 15 run (Stover kick)
Cin — Pickens 24 pass from Schroeder (Pelfrey kick)

HOUSTON 28, NEW ENGLAND 14—at Foxboro Stadium, attendance 51,037. Warren Moon came off the bench to throw 2 touchdown passes as the Oilers snapped a three-game losing streak. The game was scoreless until Houston quarterback Cody Carlson, making his first start of the season, scrambled 10 yards for a touchdown midway through the second quarter. But Carlson pulled a groin muscle on the run and was replaced by Moon during the Oilers' next drive. That 57-yard march ended when Moon threw a 7-yard touchdown pass to Webster Slaughter to make it 14-0 15 seconds before halftime. After the Patriots closed the deficit to 7 points early in the second half, Moon directed an 85-yard drive that took nearly 10 minutes and culminated in his second scoring toss to Slaughter, this one from 2 yards. Cornerback Steve Jackson returned an interception 22 yards for the clinching touchdown with 9:58 left in the game. Moon completed 16 of 21 passes for 102 yards. New England quarterback Scott Secules, starting in place of injured Drew Bledsoe, completed 23 of 40 attempts for 280 yards and a touchdown, but was intercepted 3 times.

Houston	0	14	7	7	—	28
New England	0	0	7	7	—	14

Hou — Carlson 10 run (Del Greco kick)
Hou — Slaughter 7 pass from Moon (Del Greco kick)
NE — Turner 7 pass from Secules (Sisson kick)
Hou — Slaughter 2 pass from Moon (Del Greco kick)
Hou — Jackson 22 interception return (Del Greco kick)
NE — Russell 1 run (Sisson kick)

KANSAS CITY 17, SAN DIEGO 14—at San Diego Jack Murphy Stadium, attendance 60,729. Marcus Allen's 1-yard touchdown run with 1:57 remaining capped an 80-yard drive and gave the Chiefs the victory. The Chargers had taken a 14-10 early in the fourth quarter on John Friesz's 4-yard touchdown pass to Anthony Miller. But later in the quarter, Chiefs defensive end Neil Smith blocked John Carney's 31-yard field goal try (Smith also swatted away Carney's 46-yard attempt in the third quarter), and Kansas City took over at its 20-yard line with 3:27 left. Montana completed a 22-yard pass to tight end Keith Cash, and a 15-yard penalty for roughing the passer on the same play put the ball at the Chargers' 43. Still there on fourth-and-10, Montana threw 12 yards to Willie Davis to keep the drive alive. Later, Allen's 18-yard run on a draw play moved the ball to the 1 and set up the winning score. Montana, questionable for the game because of a hamstring injury suffered two weeks earlier against the Raiders, completed 21 of 39 passes for 284 yards. Kansas City won for the fifth time in six games, its best start in 22 years.

Kansas City	7	3	0	7	—	17
San Diego	0	7	0	7	—	14

KC — Allen 15 pass from Montana (Lowery kick)
SD — Means 7 run (Carney kick)
KC — FG Lowery 37
SD — Miller 4 pass from Friesz (Carney kick)
KC — Allen 1 run (Lowery kick)

PITTSBURGH 37, NEW ORLEANS 14—at Three Rivers Stadium, attendance 56,056. Cornerback Rod Woodson returned an interception 63 yards for a touchdown just 1:39 into the game, and the Steelers went on to hand the Saints, the league's last unbeaten team, their first loss of the season. Woodson intercepted his second pass of the game later in the first quarter, setting up Neil O'Donnell's 20-yard touchdown pass to Barry Foster. Foster ran 1 yard for a touchdown to make it 24-0 with 2:29 left in the first half, and to that point New Orleans had yet to record a first down. Pittsburgh went on to build a 37-0 advantage before backup quarterback Mike Buck threw 2 touchdown passes in the last 4:15 for the Saints. New Orleans's starting quarterback, Wade Wilson, entered the game with a string of 107 pass attempts without an interception, but was picked off 3 times while completing only 6 of 26 passes for 85 yards. Leroy Thompson ran for 101 yards, and Barry Foster had 75 for the Steelers. Pittsburgh's defense forced 5 turnovers.

New Orleans	0	0	0	14	—	14
Pittsburgh	14	10	6	7	—	37

Pitt — Woodson 63 interception return (Anderson kick)
Pitt — Foster 20 pass from O'Donnell (Anderson kick)
Pitt — FG Anderson 40
Pitt — Foster 1 run (Anderson kick)
Pitt — FG Anderson 22
Pitt — FG Anderson 29
Pitt — Green 26 pass from Tomczak (Anderson kick)
NO — Small 3 pass from Buck (Andersen kick)
NO — Early 63 pass from Buck (Andersen kick)

N.Y. GIANTS 21, PHILADELPHIA 10—at Giants Stadium, attendance 76,050. Lewis Tillman ran for a career-high 169 yards and 2 touchdowns, and the Giants moved into sole possession of first place in the NFC Eastern Division by beating the Eagles. Philadelphia led 3-0 until Phil Simms's 17-yard touchdown pass to Ed McCaffrey 4:53 into the second quarter gave New York the lead for good. Tillman, who ran for more than 100 yards for the second consecutive week while replacing injured starter Rodney Hampton, scored on a 1-yard run 3:53 before halftime. He put the game out of reach by running 10 yards for another touchdown with 10:07 left in the game. The Giants amassed 210 of their 347 total yards on the ground. Tillman averaged nearly 8.5 yards on his 20 carries.

Philadelphia	0	3	0	7	—	10
N.Y. Giants	0	14	0	7	—	21

Phil — FG Bahr 47
Giants— McCaffrey 17 pass from Simms (Treadwell kick)
Giants— Tillman 1 run (Treadwell kick)
Giants— Tillman 10 run (Treadwell kick)
Phil — Bavaro 13 pass from O'Brien (Bahr kick)

DALLAS 26, SAN FRANCISCO 17—at Texas Stadium, attendance 65,099. Michael Irvin caught 12 passes for 168 yards and a touchdown to lead the Cowboys past the 49ers in a rematch of the 1992 NFC Championship Game, also won by Dallas. Irvin made the key play of the game as time ran out in the third quarter, making a juggling 36-yard touchdown catch with San Francisco cornerback Michael McGruder in close pursuit, giving the Cowboys the lead for good. Trailing 23-17, the 49ers marched to Dallas's 6-yard line, but could not score when the drive stalled and the snap on a short field-goal attempt went awry. Eddie Murray's 18-yard field goal, his fourth of the game, clinched it with 4:21 to go. San Francisco quarterback Steve Young completed 24 of 33 passes for 267 yards, and the 49ers rolled up 25 first downs and 403 total yards, but managed only 1 offensive touchdown. Troy Aikman completed 21 of 35 passes for 243 yards for the Cowboys, who won their fourth straight game.

San Francisco	10	0	7	0	—	17
Dallas	3	13	7	3	—	26

SF — Davis 47 fumble return (Cofer kick)
Dall — FG Murray 48
SF — FG Cofer 25
Dall — FG Murray 39
Dall — E. Smith 1 run (Murray kick)
Dall — FG Murray 29
SF — B. Jones 12 pass from Young (Cofer kick)
Dall — Irvin 36 pass from Aikman (Murray kick)
Dall — FG Murray 18

DETROIT 30, SEATTLE 10—at Silverdome, attendance 60,801. Mel Gray's 95-yard kickoff return for a touchdown broke open a close game and helped the Lions take over first place in the NFC Central Division. John Kasay's 19-yard field goal 4:56 into the second half had pulled the Seahawks within 14-10. But Gray, whose fumble on the opening kickoff led to Seattle's first score, countered with his big return. Jason Hanson added 3 field goals to keep the game out of reach. Rodney Peete, back in as Detroit's starting quarterback, threw second-quarter touchdown passes of 13 and 11 yards to Herman Moore, and Barry Sanders rushed for 101 yards on 22 carries.

Seattle	7	0	3	0	—	10
Detroit	0	14	13	3	—	30

Sea — Martin 6 pass from Mirer (Kasay kick)
Det — Moore 13 pass from Peete (Hanson kick)
Det — Moore 11 pass from Peete (Hanson kick)
Sea — FG Kasay 19
Det — Gray 95 kickoff return (Hanson kick)
Det — FG Hanson 34
Det — FG Hanson 32
Det — FG Hanson 35

PHOENIX 36, WASHINGTON 6—at Sun Devil Stadium, attendance 48,143. The Cardinals swept the season series from Washington for the first time since 1974 and handed the Redskins their fifth consecutive defeat. Steve Beuerlein passed for 250 yards, including a 42-yard touchdown to Ricky Proehl that put Phoenix ahead 20-3 early in the second half. Defensive end Eric Swann and linebacker Freddie Joe Nunn each had 2 sacks as the Cardinals' defense limited Washington to 2 field goals. Swann also recorded a safety, tackling Redskins running back Reggie Brooks in the end zone one minute into the fourth quarter.

Washington	3	0	3	0	—	6
Phoenix	0	13	7	16	—	36

Wash — FG Lohmiller 43
Phx — FG Davis 23
Phx — FG Davis 45
Phx — Hearst 1 run (Davis kick)
Phx — Proehl 42 pass from Beuerlein (Davis kick)
Wash — FG Lohmiller 38
Phx — Safety, Swann tackled Brooks in end zone
Phx — Bailey 14 run (Davis kick)
Phx — Moore 1 run (Davis kick)

MONDAY, OCTOBER 18

L.A. RAIDERS 23, DENVER 20—at Mile High Stadium, attendance 75,712. Jeff Jaeger's 53-yard field goal with 16 seconds left gave the Raiders the victory and spoiled another of John Elway's comeback efforts. The Broncos trailed 13-3 early in the fourth quarter until Elway threw a 27-yard touchdown pass to Arthur Marshall to trim the deficit to 3 points with 11:47 remaining. Raiders quarterback Jeff Hostetler fumbled the snap on the next play from scrimmage, and nose tackle Greg Kragen's recovery at the 5-yard line set up Elway's 2-yard touchdown pass to tight end Reggie Johnson, giving Denver its first lead at 17-13 with 10:48 to go. But the Broncos' advantage lasted only 23 seconds because Hostetler teamed with rookie James Jett on a 74-yard touchdown pass that put Los Angeles back in front. Jason Elam kicked a 37-yard field goal on Denver's next possession to tie the game, but the Raiders held the Broncos the next time they had the ball, then used a 20-yard completion from Hostetler to Tim Brown to set up Jaeger's winning kick. Hostetler completed 15 of 24 passes for 264 yards and 2 touchdowns. Russell had 5 catches for 111 yards for the Broncos, and Rod Bernstine ran for 101 yards on 23 carries.

L.A. Raiders	10	3	0	10	—	23
Denver	0	0	3	17	—	20

Raid — Wright 11 pass from Hostetler (Jaeger kick)
Raid — FG Jaeger 32
Raid — FG Jaeger 49
Den — FG Elam 40
Den — Marshall 27 pass from Elway (Elam kick)
Den — R. Johnson 2 pass from Elway (Elam kick)
Raid — Jett 74 pass from Hostetler (Jaeger kick)
Den — FG Elam 37
Raid — FG Jaeger 53

EIGHTH WEEK SUMMARIES
AMERICAN FOOTBALL CONFERENCE

Eastern Division	W	L	T	Pct.	Pts.	OP
Buffalo	4	1	0	.800	116	67
Miami	4	1	0	.800	101	81
Indianapolis	2	3	0	.400	68	102
N.Y. Jets	2	3	0	.400	139	106
New England	1	5	0	.167	88	168
Central Division						
Cleveland	4	2	0	.667	121	107
Pittsburgh	4	2	0	.667	145	92
Houston	2	4	0	.333	116	128
Cincinnati	0	6	0	.000	69	134
Western Division						
Kansas City	5	1	0	.833	100	78
L.A. Raiders	4	2	0	.667	113	103
Denver	3	3	0	.500	149	118
Seattle	3	3	0	.500	102	103
San Diego	2	4	0	.333	84	127

NATIONAL FOOTBALL CONFERENCE

Eastern Division	W	L	T	Pct.	Pts.	OP
N.Y. Giants	5	1	0	.833	145	71
Dallas	4	2	0	.667	132	92
Philadelphia	4	2	0	.667	128	133
Phoenix	2	4	0	.333	121	105
Washington	1	5	0	.167	99	161
Central Division						
Detroit	4	2	0	.667	118	100
Chicago	3	2	0	.600	97	59
Minnesota	3	2	0	.600	66	82
Green Bay	2	3	0	.400	110	104
Tampa Bay	1	4	0	.200	54	122

WESTERN DIVISION

New Orleans	5	1	0	.833	148	111
San Francisco	3	3	0	.500	142	127
L.A. Rams	2	4	0	.333	101	136
Atlanta	1	5	0	.167	121	176

SUNDAY, OCTOBER 24

ATLANTA 26, NEW ORLEANS 15—at Louisiana Superdome, attendance 69,043. Ailing Bobby Hebert completed 13 of 16 passes, 2 for touchdowns, to lead the Falcons' upset of the Saints. Hebert, who threw for 163 yards, was not expected to play against his former teammates because of an elbow injury. But with Chris Miller sidelined by injury and Billy Joe Tolliver suffering a sprained shoulder less than five minutes into the game, Hebert was pressed into duty. He responded by throwing short touchdown passes to Andre Rison and Michael Haynes in the second quarter as Atlanta built a 17-6 halftime lead. Running back Erric Pegram helped keep New Orleans at a distance by rushing for 132 yards on 34 carries as the Falcons maintained possession for more than 36 of the game's 60 minutes. That was uncharacteristic of the Saints, who were forced to take to the air to play catchup. New Orleans quarterback Wade Wilson completed 27 of 45 passes for 277 yards, but was intercepted twice.

Atlanta	0	17	3	6	—	26
New Orleans	3	3	7	2	—	15

NO — FG Andersen 40
Atl — FG Johnson 19
Atl — Rison 5 pass from Hebert (Johnson kick)
Atl — Haynes 9 pass from Hebert (Johnson kick)
NO — FG Andersen 27
Atl — FG Johnson 32
NO — Early 23 pass from Wilson (Andersen kick)
Atl — FG Johnson 38
Atl — FG Johnson 30
NO — Safety, Alexander ran out of end zone

BUFFALO 19, N.Y. JETS 10—at Giants Stadium, attendance 71,541. Linebacker Darryl Talley made the key play, returning an interception 61 yards for a touchdown in the third quarter, as the Bills won their third in a row. The Jets took the opening kickoff and held the ball for 7:58, marching 80 yards in 16 plays, the last a 1-yard touchdown run by Brad Baxter. New York led 7-6 midway through the third quarter and had the ball at Buffalo's 39-yard line after an interception and 22-yard return by cornerback James Hasty. But on the first play following the turnover, Talley intercepted Boomer Esiason's pass and gave the Bills the lead for good. Steve Christie kicked 4 field goals, including the clincher from 30 yards with 3:37 remaining. That came 6 plays after the first interception of defensive end Bruce Smith's nine-year career. Despite failing to score an offensive touchdown, Buffalo held substantial advantages over the Jets in first downs (27-15), total yards (413-237), plays (81-49), and time of possession (37:16-22:44). Bills quarterback Jim Kelly passed for 224 yards, and Thurman Thomas rushed for 117 yards and caught 7 passes for 67 yards.

Buffalo	0	6	7	6	—	19
N.Y. Jets	7	0	3	0	—	10

Jets — B. Baxter 1 run (Blanchard kick)
Buff — FG Christie 37
Buff — FG Christie 33
Buff — Talley 61 interception return (Christie kick)
Buff — FG Christie 22
Jets — FG Blanchard 33
Buff — FG Christie 30

HOUSTON 28, CINCINNATI 12—at Astrodome, attendance 50,039. Warren Moon passed for 253 yards and 2 touchdowns and the Oilers handed the Bengals their seventh consecutive defeat of 1993 and thirteenth in 14 games dating to 1992. Moon completed 24 of 34 passes as Houston amassed 369 total yards. Still, the Oilers struggled against winless Cincinnati and trailed 12-7 late in the third quarter until Lorenzo White capped a 71-yard drive with a 4-yard touchdown run. Houston put the game out of reach with a pair of fourth-quarter touchdowns.

Cincinnati	0	9	3	0	—	12
Houston	7	0	7	14	—	28

Hou — Wellman 9 pass from Moon (Del Greco kick)
Cin — Query 8 pass from Schroeder (kick failed)
Cin — FG Pelfrey 53
Cin — FG Pelfrey 50
Hou — White 4 run (Del Greco kick)
Hou — Jeffires 11 pass from Moon (Del Greco kick)
Hou — Brown 25 run (Del Greco kick)

DETROIT 16, L.A. RAMS 13—at Anaheim Stadium, attendance 43,850. Jason Hanson's 18-yard field goal with four seconds left gave the Lions the victory and spoiled a fourth-quarter comeback by the Rams that was engineered by backup quarterback T.J. Rubley. Detroit built a 13-0 lead midway through the fourth quarter on 2 field goals by Hanson and a 5-yard touchdown run by Barry Sanders. But Rubley, who replaced an ineffective Jim Everett in the third quarter, threw a 4-yard touchdown pass to Ernie Jones with 4:19 to go in the game, then capped a 68-yard drive with a 21-yard touchdown pass to Jones with 1:52 left. Tony Zendejas's extra-point try following the second touchdown bounced off the left upright, leaving the game tied at 13-13. Ex-Rams player Vernon Turner, in the game because Pro Bowl kick returner Mel Gray was injured, returned the ensuing kickoff 45 yards to give the Lions possession at Los Angeles's 44-yard line. Rodney Peete sandwiched passes of 13 yards to Sanders and 25 yards to tight end Rodney Holman around a 5-yard run by Sanders, positioning Hanson for his winning kick. Peete completed 15 of 25 passes for 249 yards, and Detroit wide receiver Herman Moore caught 6 passes for 120 yards. Rubley was 12 of 17 for 151 yards and scrambled 3 times for 24 yards in his NFL debut. Rams rookie Jerome Bettis ran for 113 yards on 23 carries. Los Angeles tackle Jackie Slater played in his 245th NFL game, equaling the all-time record for offensive linemen held by Jeff Van Note and Mike Webster. But Slater left the game in the first half with a torn shoulder muscle.

Detroit	0	3	3	10	—	16
L.A. Rams	0	0	0	13	—	13

Det — FG Hanson 25
Det — FG Hanson 24
Det — Sanders 5 run (Hanson kick)
Rams — Jones 4 pass from Rubley (Zendejas kick)
Rams — Jones 21 pass from Rubley (kick failed)
Det — FG Hanson 18

GREEN BAY 37, TAMPA BAY 14—at Tampa Stadium, attendance 47,354. Sterling Sharpe caught 4 touchdown passes to lead the Packers' rout of the Buccaneers. Sharpe had 3 of his scoring catches in the first half as Green Bay built a 24-0 lead at intermission. He was instrumental on the Packers' third touchdown drive, catching 3 passes for 41 yards, including a 10-yard touchdown, and lining up as a quarterback for two plays that resulted in a 5-yard gain on a keeper and his 1-yard completion to Mark Clayton. Brett Favre completed 20 of 35 passes for 268 yards and Darrell Thompson rushed for 105 yards for Green Bay, which accumulated 421 yards of total offense. Sharpe finished with 10 catches for 147 yards. Tampa Bay's Craig Erickson teamed with rookie wide receiver Horace Copeland on touchdowns of 26 and 67 yards in the second half.

Green Bay	7	17	6	7	—	37
Tampa Bay	0	0	7	7	—	14

GB — Sharpe 7 pass from Favre (Jacke kick)
GB — Sharpe 30 pass from Favre (Jacke kick)
GB — Sharpe 10 pass from Favre (Jacke kick)
GB — FG Jacke 50
GB — FG Jacke 44
GB — FG Jacke 24
TB — Copeland 26 pass from Erickson (Husted kick)
GB — Sharpe 32 pass from Favre (Jacke kick)
TB — Copeland 67 pass from Erickson (Husted kick)

SEATTLE 10, NEW ENGLAND 9—at Kingdome, attendance 56,526. Rick Mirer threw a 1-yard touchdown pass to Brian Blades with 25 seconds remaining to lift the Seahawks past the Patriots. New England, behind 3 field goals by Scott Sisson, led 9-3 when Seattle took possession at its 46-yard line with 3:30 to play. Mirer completed 7 of 10 passes for 39 yards on the ensuing march to the winning touchdown. He finished with 22 completions in 43 attempts for 203 yards. Blades caught 9 passes for 70 yards. The Patriots' Leonard Russell rushed for 97 yards on 21 carries.

New England	0	0	3	6	—	9
Seattle	0	3	0	7	—	10

Sea — FG Kasay 30

NE — FG Sisson 36
NE — FG Sisson 25
NE — FG Sisson 19
Sea — Blades 1 pass from Mirer (Kasay kick)

SAN FRANCISCO 28, PHOENIX 14—at Candlestick Park, attendance 62,020. Steve Young passed for 247 yards and 2 touchdowns to lead the 49ers to a methodical victory over the Cardinals. San Francisco pulled within one game of the lead in the NFC Western Division by building a 28-0 advantage before Phoenix's Steve Beuerlein threw a pair of scoring passes in the final quarter. Young teamed with Jerry Rice on both of his touchdown throws. Rice, who caught 9 passes for 155 yards, moved past Lenny Moore and into fourth place on the NFL's all-time list with 114 career touchdowns. Ricky Watters ran for 95 yards as San Francisco rolled up 428 total yards. Phoenix actually outgained the 49ers, rushing for 107 yards and passing for 322, but was victimized by 3 interceptions, including 1 by San Francisco cornerback Eric Davis at the 1-yard line. Beuerlein completed 26 of 50 passes for 334 yards.

Phoenix	0	0	0	14	—	14
San Francisco	0	14	0	14	—	28

SF — Logan 1 run (Cofer kick)
SF — Rice 8 pass from Young (Cofer kick)
SF — Rice 7 pass from Young (Cofer kick)
SF — Watters 19 run (Cofer kick)
Phx — Edwards 65 pass from Beuerlein (G. Davis kick)
Phx — Proehl 4 pass from Beuerlein (G. Davis kick)

CLEVELAND 28, PITTSBURGH 23—at Cleveland Stadium, attendance 78,118. The Browns' Eric Metcalf stunned the Steelers with a 75-yard punt return for the winning touchdown with 2:05 remaining. Metcalf, who returned a punt 91 yards for a score in the second quarter, became the seventh player in NFL history to return 2 punts for touchdowns in the same game. After a scoreless first quarter, things heated up in the battle for first place in the AFC Central Division. Two big plays—Vinny Testaverde's 62-yard touchdown pass to Michael Jackson and Metcalf's long punt return—staked Cleveland to a 14-0 lead, but the Steelers countered with a pair of long scoring drives, capped by short touchdown runs by Barry Foster, to tie the score at 14-14. Pittsburgh, which dominated much of the game, drove to 3 field goals in the second half, the last of which put the Steelers ahead 23-21 with 7:51 remaining. The Browns began to move the ball on their next possession, but Testaverde suffered a slightly separated shoulder when scrambling for a first down with 7:27 to play. Bernie Kosar replaced Testaverde, but the drive stalled and Cleveland was forced to punt. The Browns' defense then held Pittsburgh without a first down, setting the stage for Metcalf's heroics. Neil O'Donnell completed 25 of 39 passes for a career-high 355 yards for the Steelers, who amassed 444 total yards to just 245 for Cleveland.

Pittsburgh	0	14	6	3	—	23
Cleveland	0	14	7	7	—	28

Cle — Jackson 62 pass from Testaverde (Stover kick)
Cle — Metcalf 91 punt return (Stover kick)
Pitt — Foster 4 run (Anderson kick)
Pitt — Foster 1 run (Anderson kick)
Pitt — FG Anderson 30
Cle — Wolfley 4 pass from Testaverde (Stover kick)
Pitt — FG Anderson 46
Pitt — FG Anderson 30
Cle — Metcalf 75 punt return (Stover kick)

SUNDAY NIGHT, OCTOBER 24
MIAMI 41, INDIANAPOLIS 27—at Joe Robbie Stadium, attendance 57,301. Quarterback Scott Mitchell was impressive in his starting debut, and rookies Terry Kirby and O.J. McDuffie scored their first career touchdowns as the Dolphins won their fourth consecutive game and handed the Colts their third straight defeat. Mitchell, starting because Dan Marino was lost for the season with an Achilles tendon injury one week earlier, completed 12 of 19 passes for 190 yards and 1 touchdown, with no interceptions. His 44-yard touchdown pass to Kirby gave Miami a 17-0 first-quarter lead. Earlier in the period, McDuffie raced 71 yards with a punt return for a touchdown. Kirby also had a 14-yard touchdown run late in the third quarter as the Dolphins built a 34-13 advantage. Still, Indianapolis battled, closing to within 34-20 on Jeff George's 6-yard touchdown pass to Reggie Langhorne with 9:56 left. But Miami safety Louis Oliver put the game out of reach by returning an in-

terception 56 yards for a touchdown 2:48 later. George completed 27 of 44 passes for 260 yards and 2 touchdowns, but was intercepted 3 times. The Dolphins' Mark Higgs ran for 114 yards on 17 carries to help Miami head coach Don Shula record his 323rd career victory, just 1 short of the NFL record held by the legendary George Halas.

Indianapolis	0	6	7	14	—	27
Miami	17	3	14	7	—	41

Mia — FG Stoyanovich 23
Mia — McDuffie 71 punt return (Stoyanovich kick)
Mia — Kirby 44 pass from Mitchell (Stoyanovich kick)
Ind — Culver 3 pass from George (kick failed)
Mia — FG Stoyanovich 39
Ind — Culver 1 run (Biasucci kick)
Mia — Fryar 11 pass from Byars (Stoyanovich kick)
Mia — Kirby 14 run (Stoyanovich kick)
Ind — Langhorne 6 pass from George (Biasucci kick)
Mia — Oliver 56 interception return (Stoyanovich kick)
Ind — Culver 3 run (Biasucci kick)

MONDAY, OCTOBER 25
MINNESOTA 19, CHICAGO 12—at Soldier Field, attendance 64,677. Cornerback Audray McMillian returned an interception 22 yards for a touchdown, and linebacker Jack Del Rio picked off a pass at the goal line with three seconds remaining to preserve the Vikings' victory. The Bears did little offensively until taking over at their 4-yard line and advancing to Minnesota's 25 late in the game. But Del Rio's interception was the last in a series of big plays by the Vikings' top-ranked defense, which also forced a fumble to set up Robert Smith's 26-yard touchdown run in the first quarter. Minnesota harassed Chicago quarterback Jim Harbaugh all night, sacking him 8 times, including 3½ by defensive tackle John Randle. Smith, the Vikings' first-round pick in the 1993 draft, ran for 80 yards while Barry Word added 78. Kevin Butler kicked 4 field goals, including a career-best 55-yard boot, to account for all of the Bears' points.

Minnesota	10	3	6	0	—	19
Chicago	3	6	0	3	—	12

Chi — FG Butler 37
Minn — FG Reveiz 39
Minn — R. Smith 26 run (Reveiz kick)
Chi — FG Butler 39
Chi — FG Butler 55
Minn — FG Reveiz 26
Minn — McMillian 22 interception return (kick failed)
Chi — FG Butler 35

NINTH WEEK SUMMARIES
AMERICAN FOOTBALL CONFERENCE

Eastern Division	W	L	T	Pct.	Pts.	OP
Buffalo	6	1	0	.857	159	87
Miami	6	1	0	.857	172	118
Indianapolis	3	4	0	.429	104	149
N.Y. Jets	3	4	0	.429	159	131
New England	1	7	0	.125	103	187
Central Division						
Cleveland	5	2	0	.714	149	130
Pittsburgh	4	3	0	.571	168	120
Houston	3	4	0	.429	144	140
Cincinnati	0	7	0	.000	81	162
Western Division						
Kansas City	5	2	0	.714	110	108
Denver	4	3	0	.571	177	135
L.A. Raiders	4	3	0	.571	136	133
Seattle	4	4	0	.500	129	140
San Diego	4	4	0	.429	114	150

NATIONAL FOOTBALL CONFERENCE

Eastern Division	W	L	T	Pct.	Pts.	OP
Dallas	5	2	0	.714	155	102
N.Y. Giants	5	2	0	.714	151	81
Philadelphia	4	3	0	.571	138	156
Phoenix	2	6	0	.250	152	153
Washington	1	6	0	.143	109	185
Central Division						
Detroit	6	2	0	.750	164	140
Green Bay	4	3	0	.571	164	121
Minnesota	4	3	0	.571	112	124
Chicago	3	4	0	.429	112	95
Tampa Bay	2	5	0	.286	99	183
Western Division						
New Orleans	6	2	0	.750	183	154
San Francisco	5	3	0	.625	210	158
Atlanta	2	6	0	.250	171	222
L.A. Rams	2	6	0	.250	131	192

SUNDAY, OCTOBER 31
GREEN BAY 17, CHICAGO 3—at Lambeau Field, attendance 58,945. Defensive end Reggie White became the NFL's all-time sack leader by recording 2 of the Packers' 7 sacks in a victory over the Bears. White, who joined Green Bay as a free agent in 1993 after eight seasons with Philadelphia, improved his career total to 130½ sacks, 1 better than Giants linebacker Lawrence Taylor. But it was a fourth-quarter sack by the Packers' LeRoy Butler that was the key play against Chicago. The Bears trailed 10-3 while driving to Green Bay's 12-yard line early in the period. Butler blitzed and sacked Bears quarterback Jim Harbaugh, forcing a fumble that the Packers' safety recovered. Later in the quarter, Darrell Thompson ran 17 yards for the clinching touchdown. Green Bay's offense managed only 261 total yards against Chicago's stingy defense. But the Bears continued to struggle offensively, and extended a dubious string of 10 quarters without a touchdown. Harbaugh completed 15 of his 19 passes, but for only 149 yards. Chicago had just 230 total yards.

Chicago	0	3	0	0	—	3
Green Bay	3	7	0	7	—	17

GB — FG Jacke 40
GB — Sharpe 21 pass from Favre (Jacke kick)
Chi — FG Butler 33
GB — Thompson 17 run (Jacke kick)

DALLAS 23, PHILADELPHIA 10—at Veterans Stadium, attendance 61,912. Emmitt Smith rushed for a club-record 237 yards, including a clinching 62-yard touchdown run in the fourth quarter, to power the Cowboys past the Eagles in a driving rain. Smith, who averaged 7.9 yards on his 30 carries, broke Dallas's single-game mark of 206 yards, set by Tony Dorsett in 1977, also against the Eagles. Smith's performance was the sixth best in league history. The Cowboys built a 10-0 lead in the second quarter on a field goal by Eddie Murray and wide receiver Kevin Williams's 11-yard touchdown run on a reverse. Philadelphia closed within 10-7 on a 3-yard touchdown pass from Ken O'Brien to Herschel Walker 1:25 before halftime. Murray kicked 2 more field goals in the second half to give Dallas a 16-10 edge, and Smith's touchdown run put the game out of reach with 3:45 remaining. The Cowboys won their fifth in a row to pull into a tie for first place in the NFC East, while the Eagles dropped their third straight after beginning the season 4-0.

Dallas	3	7	3	10	—	23
Philadelphia	0	7	0	3	—	10

Dall — FG Murray 35
Dall — K. Williams 11 run (Murray kick)
Phil — Walker 3 pass from O'Brien (Bahr kick)
Dall — FG Murray 23
Phil — FG Bahr 33
Dall — FG Murray 40
Dall — E. Smith 62 run (Murray kick)

MIAMI 30, KANSAS CITY 10—at Joe Robbie Stadium, attendance 67,765. Scott Mitchell threw 3 touchdown passes to help Dolphins coach Don Shula win his 324th career victory, equaling the legendary George Halas's NFL record. Mitchell, who completed 22 of 33 passes for 344 yards, threw touchdown passes of 27 yards to Irving Fryar and 8 yards to Keith Byars as Miami built a 13-3 halftime lead. The Dolphins put the game out of reach when Mitchell teamed with Mark Ingram on a 77-yard touchdown pass just 28 seconds into the second half. Miami controlled the clock after that, finishing with 139 rushing yards while maintaining possession for nearly 37 of the game's 60 minutes. The Chiefs, who had their four-game winning streak snapped, managed 305 total yards but lost 3 fumbles. Quarterback Joe Montana completed his 3,000th pass of his career, but left the game in the second quarter with a hamstring injury. Shula's career record improved to 324-152-6 (a .678 winning percentage) in 31 seasons with the Dolphins and Baltimore Colts. Halas was 324-151-31 (.671) in 40 years with the Bears.

Kansas City	0	3	0	7	— 10
Miami	6	7	14	3	— 30

Mia — Fryar 27 pass from Mitchell (pass failed)
Mia — Byars 8 pass from Mitchell (Stoyanovich kick)
KC — FG Lowery 47
Mia — Ingram 77 pass from Mitchell (Stoyanovich kick)
Mia — Kirby 1 run (Stoyanovich kick)
Mia — FG Stoyanovich 34
KC — Cash 6 pass from Krieg (Lowery kick)

SAN FRANCISCO 40, L.A. RAMS 17—at Candlestick Park, attendance 63,417. Steve Young passed for 245 yards and the 49ers' defense harassed Rams quarterback T.J. Rubley in his first NFL start. Young completed 22 of 34 passes and tossed a 15-yard touchdown pass to John Taylor on the game's pivotal play in the second quarter. San Francisco led just 6-3 when Young's pass bounced off the hands of Rams cornerback Steve Israel, who had an open field ahead of him. Taylor made a juggling catch and gave the 49ers a 13-3 lead. Meanwhile, San Francisco's defense exerted heavy pressure on Rubley, who got the starting nod over veteran Jim Everett. Rubley was sacked 7 times, pressured on numerous occasions, and intercepted twice. He completed only 2 of 6 passes for 20 while the 49ers built a commanding 23-3 lead at halftime. Rubley fared better in the second half and finished 15 of 26 for 158 yards, including a 35-yard touchdown pass to Todd Kinchen in the third quarter. Mark Logan had 2 short touchdown runs for San Francisco.

L.A. Rams	3	0	7	7	— 17
San Francisco	6	17	7	10	— 40

Rams — FG Zendejas 50
SF — Watters 1 run (kick failed)
SF — Taylor 15 pass from Young (Cofer kick)
SF — Logan 1 run (Cofer kick)
SF — FG Cofer 25
Rams — Kinchen 35 pass from Rubley (Zendejas kick)
SF — Logan 1 run (Cofer kick)
Rams — Bettis 1 run (Zendejas kick)
SF — FG Cofer 28
SF — McGruder 32 interception return (Cofer kick)

INDIANAPOLIS 9, NEW ENGLAND 6—at Hoosier Dome, attendance 46,522. Dean Biasucci kicked 3 field goals, including the winner from 37 yards with 2:42 left, as Indianapolis snapped a four-game losing streak. The Patriots, who fell to 1-7, lost their fourth game by 3 points or fewer. New England managed 363 total yards against Indianapolis, but had three drives stalled by turnovers. Its last threat ended when Colts rookie defensive back Ray Buchanan intercepted a pass with 1:55 to go. Jeff George completed 18 of 26 passes for 200 yards for the Colts. The Patriots' Scott Secules was 23 of 37 for 279 yards. Tight end Ben Coates caught 6 passes for 108 yards. This was the second consecutive game between these teams that failed to produce a touchdown. Biasucci accounted for all the points with 2 field goals in Indianapolis's 6-0 victory over New England late in the 1992 season.

New England	0	3	0	3	— 6
Indianapolis	3	0	0	6	— 9

Ind — FG Biasucci 27
NE — FG Sisson 40
Ind — FG Biasucci 38
NE — FG Sisson 26
Ind — FG Biasucci 37

NEW ORLEANS 20, PHOENIX 17—at Sun Devil Stadium, attendance 36,778. The Saints rallied from a 10-point halftime deficit to beat the Cardinals and maintain their hold on first place in the NFC West. Phoenix managed only 143 total yards—just 38 in the second half—against the Saints, but took a 17-7 lead on the strength of its defense. Cornerback Aeneas Williams scooped up a fumble and ran 20 yards for a touchdown late in the first quarter, then intercepted a pass and returned it 46 yards for another touchdown in the second. But Morten Andersen's 48-yard field goal and Wade Wilson's 25-yard touchdown pass to Quinn Early 3:10 into the fourth quarter tied the game at 17-17. Moments later, safety Gene Atkins intercepted a pass at the Cardinals' 24-yard line to position Andersen for the decisive field goal with 7:34 remaining. Linebacker Renaldo Turnbull had 3 of New Orleans's 6 sacks.

New Orleans	7	0	3	10	— 20
Phoenix	10	7	0	0	— 17

NO — Muster 1 run (Andersen kick)

Phx — FG Davis 28
Phx — Williams 20 fumble return (Davis kick)
Phx — Williams 46 interception return (Davis kick)
NO — FG Andersen 48
NO — Early 25 pass from Wilson (Andersen kick)
NO — FG Andersen 38

N.Y. JETS 10, N.Y. GIANTS 6—at Giants Stadium, attendance 71,659. Brad Baxter ran 2 yards for a touchdown late in the third quarter and the Jets held on to beat the Giants. The Giants led 6-3 at halftime, but the Jets put together an 18-play, 79-yard touchdown drive that consumed 11:15 of the third quarter. Along the way, they converted 3 third-down opportunities and a fourth-down try. Baxter's score came with 2:04 left in the quarter and was the first touchdown against the Giants' defense all season. The Jets, who snapped a three-game losing streak, had failed to hold second-half leads in all three of the defeats. The Giants threatened to extend that string, moving from their 33-yard line to a first-and-goal at the Jets' 6 with 1:05 to go. But on fourth down from the 11, Phil Simms's end-zone pass fell incomplete. The loss dropped the Giants into a tie for first place in the NFC East.

N.Y. Jets	0	3	7	0	— 10
N.Y. Giants	3	3	0	0	— 6

Giants — FG Treadwell 28
Jets — FG Blanchard 21
Giants — FG Treadwell 23
Jets — B. Baxter 2 run (Blanchard kick)

SAN DIEGO 30, L.A. RAIDERS 23—at Los Angeles Memorial Coliseum, attendance 45,122. Defensive back Donald Frank returned an interception 102 yards for a touchdown, breaking a 17-17 tie in the third quarter and lifting the Chargers past the Raiders. Los Angeles quarterback Jeff Hostetler, who passed for a club-record 424 yards, had just teamed with James Jett on a 55-yard pass play that gave the Raiders a first-and-goal at San Diego's 5-yard line. After a running play moved the ball to the 3, Hostetler tried to find Tim Brown on a slant pattern in the end zone. But Frank stepped in front of the pass and returned it untouched for the go-ahead score with 3:24 left in the third period. Moments later, linebacker Gary Plummer intercepted Hostetler's pass in Chargers' territory, setting up a 47-yard drive to a 36-yard field goal by John Carney 1:22 into the fourth quarter. Los Angeles could not get closer than seven points after that. Hostetler, who finished with 20 completions in 32 attempts, broke the Raiders' record of 419 yards held by Cotton Davidson. Brown caught 5 passes for 156 yards and 2 touchdowns, including a 71-yard bomb on the Raiders' first play from scrimmage. But Los Angeles was ineffective rushing the ball, gaining only 65 yards on the ground. Meanwhile, San Diego's Natrone Means (68 yards) and Marion Butts (64) combined for 132 of their team's 177 rushing yards.

San Diego	7	3	14	6	— 30
L.A. Raiders	10	0	7	6	— 23

Raid — Brown 71 pass from Hostetler (Jaeger kick)
SD — A. Miller 29 pass from Friesz (Carney kick)
Raid — FG Jaeger 38
SD — FG Carney 45
Raid — Brown 38 pass from Hostetler (Jaeger kick)
SD — Butts 12 run (Carney kick)
SD — Frank 102 interception return (Carney kick)
SD — FG Carney 36
Raid — FG Jaeger 21
SD — FG Carney 38
Raid — FG Jaeger 31

DENVER 28, SEATTLE 17—at Mile High Stadium, attendance 73,644. John Elway threw 2 touchdown passes and Robert Delpino ran for 2 to lead the Broncos to their twentieth victory in the last 23 games at Mile High Stadium. Seattle converted an interception on Denver's first play into an early touchdown, but the Broncos responded by scoring touchdowns on three consecutive drives in the second quarter. Elway, who completed 23 of 36 passes for 255 yards, capped an 80-yard drive with a 20-yard touchdown pass to Vance Johnson, Delpino ran 2 yards for a score, and Elway tossed a 5-yard touchdown pass to Shannon Sharpe. The latter came 44 seconds before halftime and came 9 plays after cornerback Tyrone Braxton's interception and 12-yard return to Denver's 35-yard line.

Seattle	7	0	3	7	— 17
Denver	0	21	7	0	— 28

Sea — J. Williams 10 run (Kasay kick)
Den — V. Johnson 20 pass from Elway (Elam kick)
Den — Delpino 2 run (Elam kick)
Den — Sharpe 5 pass from Elway (Elam kick)
Sea — FG Kasay 53
Den — Delpino 1 run (Elam kick)
Sea — J. Williams 2 run (Kasay kick)

TAMPA BAY 31, ATLANTA 24—at Georgia Dome, attendance 50,647. Craig Erickson threw 4 touchdown passes as the Buccaneers built a 31-3 lead, then withstood a furious rally by the Falcons to win. Erickson completed 18 of 28 passes for 318 yards. His 44-yard touchdown pass to rookie Horace Copeland with 2:21 left in the third quarter gave Tampa Bay its 28-point advantage. But Atlanta's Tony Smith returned the ensuing kickoff 46 yards, and on the next play, Bobby Hebert threw a 53-yard touchdown pass to Andre Rison to make it 31-10. Smith's 51-yard punt return set up Hebert's 9-yard touchdown pass to Rison 10 seconds into the fourth quarter, and when Hebert teamed with Mike Pritchard on a 5-yard touchdown pass with 9:37 to go, the Falcons trailed by only 7 points. Atlanta had a chance to tie the game, moving to the Buccaneers' 9-yard line in the closing minute, but Hebert's fourth-down pass was tipped away by Tampa Bay defensive lineman Chidi Ahanotu. Hebert finished with 25 completions in 47 attempts for 277 yards. Rison caught 11 passes for 147 yards. The Buccaneers' Copeland caught 2 touchdown passes for the second consecutive week.

Tampa Bay	7	10	14	0	— 31
Atlanta	0	0	10	14	— 24

TB — Workman 42 pass from Erickson (Husted kick)
TB — Cobb 5 pass from Erickson (Husted kick)
TB — FG Husted 24
Atl — FG Johnson 34
TB — Copeland 60 pass from Erickson (Husted kick)
TB — Copeland 44 pass from Erickson (Husted kick)
Atl — Rison 53 pass from Hebert (Johnson kick)
Atl — Rison 9 pass from Hebert (Johnson kick)
Atl — Pritchard 5 pass from Hebert (Johnson kick)

SUNDAY NIGHT, OCTOBER 31

DETROIT 30, MINNESOTA 27—at Metrodome, attendance 53,739. Derrick Moore's 1-yard touchdown run with 40 seconds remaining gave the Lions the come-from-behind victory in a battle for first place in the NFC Central Division. Vikings quarterback Sean Salisbury, who entered the game in the first quarter after starter Jim McMahon suffered a shoulder injury, threw 2 touchdown passes to help Minnesota take a 27-13 lead into the fourth quarter. But on the first play of the period, Detroit quarterback Rodney Peete took advantage of a breakdown in coverage to find Herman Moore all alone for a 93-yard touchdown pass. Jason Hanson's third field goal of the game, from 32 yards with 5:20 to go, trimmed the Lions' deficit to 27-23, and after holding the Vikings without a first down, Detroit marched 61 yards to the winning score. It appeared Minnesota had stopped the drive on fourth-and-8 from the 12-yard line, when Peete's pass for Brett Perriman was tipped away by Anthony Parker at the goal line. But Parker was whistled for pass interference, and Moore scored on the next play. Peete finished with 20 completions in 28 attempts for 273 yards. Salisbury was 25 of 37 for 234 yards and ignited the Vikings' offense, which had not scored more than 19 points in a game all season.

Detroit	7	6	0	17	— 30
Minnesota	7	10	10	0	— 27

Minn — A. Carter 10 pass from Salisbury (Reveiz kick)
Det — Clay 39 fumble return (Hanson kick)
Det — FG Hanson 34
Minn — C. Carter 5 pass from Salisbury (Reveiz kick)
Det — FG Hanson 44
Minn — FG Reveiz 44
Minn — R. Smith 1 run (Reveiz kick)
Minn — FG Reveiz 37
Det — H. Moore 93 pass from Peete (Hanson kick)

Det — FG Hanson 32
Det — D. Moore 1 run (Hanson kick)

MONDAY, NOVEMBER 1

BUFFALO 24, WASHINGTON 10—at Rich Stadium, attendance 79,106. Jim Kelly threw 2 touchdown passes and the Bills intercepted 4 passes while completing a season sweep of the teams that defeated them in the last three Super Bowls. Kelly completed 18 of 24 passes for 238 yards and got Buffalo off to a good start by throwing a 65-yard touchdown pass to Andre Reed six minutes into the game. Kelly's 11-yard touchdown pass to Bill Brooks with 10 seconds left in the first quarter broke a 7-7 tie and gave the Bills the lead for good. Thurman Thomas helped put the game out of reach with a 1-yard touchdown run in the third quarter. Thomas ran for 129 yards on 28 carries, and Reed finished with 7 receptions for 159 yards as Buffalo amassed 402 total yards. Cornerback Nate Odomes intercepted 2 of Mark Rypien's passes, and the Bills stopped four consecutive drives with interceptions to keep the Redskins from closing their deficit. The game was the first between these two teams since Washington's 37-24 victory in Super Bowl XXVI following the 1991 season. Earlier this year, Buffalo avenged its losses to the Giants and Cowboys in Super Bowl XXV and XXVII.

Washington	7	3	0	0	—	10
Buffalo	14	0	7	3	—	24

Buff — Reed 65 pass from Kelly (Christie kick)
Wash — R. Brooks 7 run (Lohmiller kick)
Buff — B. Brooks 11 pass from Kelly (Christie kick)
Wash — FG Lohmiller 19
Buff — Thomas 1 run (Christie kick)
Buff — FG Christie 45

TENTH WEEK SUMMARIES

AMERICAN FOOTBALL CONFERENCE

Eastern Division	W	L	T	Pct.	Pts.	OP
Buffalo	7	1	0	.875	172	97
Miami	6	2	0	.750	182	145
N.Y. Jets	4	4	0	.500	186	141
Indianapolis	3	5	0	.375	128	179
New England	1	8	0	.111	113	200
Central Division						
Cleveland	5	3	0	.625	163	159
Pittsburgh	5	3	0	.625	192	136
Houston	4	4	0	.500	168	154
Cincinnati	0	8	0	.000	97	186
Western Division						
Kansas City	6	2	0	.750	133	124
Denver	5	3	0	.625	206	149
L.A. Raiders	5	3	0	.625	152	147
San Diego	4	4	0	.500	144	167
Seattle	4	5	0	.444	143	164

NATIONAL FOOTBALL CONFERENCE

Eastern Division	W	L	T	Pct.	Pts.	OP
Dallas	6	2	0	.750	186	111
N.Y. Giants	5	3	0	.625	160	112
Philadelphia	4	4	0	.500	141	172
Phoenix	3	6	0	.333	168	156
Washington	2	6	0	.250	139	209
Central Division						
Detroit	7	2	0	.778	187	140
Green Bay	4	4	0	.500	180	144
Minnesota	4	4	0	.500	129	154
Chicago	3	5	0	.375	126	111
Tampa Bay	2	6	0	.250	99	206
Western Division						
New Orleans	6	2	0	.750	183	154
San Francisco	5	3	0	.625	210	158
Atlanta	2	6	0	.250	171	222
L.A. Rams	2	6	0	.250	131	192

SUNDAY, NOVEMBER 7

BUFFALO 13, NEW ENGLAND 10—at Foxboro Stadium, attendance 54,326. Steve Christie tied the game by kicking a 27-yard field goal with 14 seconds left in regulation, then won it with a 30-yard field goal 9:22 into overtime. The Bills rallied from a 10-point deficit in the fourth quarter to post their fifth consecutive victory. First, Jim Kelly capped an 80-yard drive with a 9-yard touchdown pass to tight end Pete Metzelaars with 7:48 remaining. After moving into field-goal range on its next possession only to lose a fumble, Buffalo got the ball back at its 13-yard line with 1:04 remaining. In 50 seconds, the Bills moved 78 yards to the tying field goal, the big play a 56-yard pass from Kelly to Russell Copeland. Another long pass, Kelly's 46-yard completion to Andre Reed, set up the winning kick in overtime. Kelly completed 29 of 46 passes for 317 yards, and Thurman

Thomas ran for 111 yards for Buffalo, which outgained the Patriots 432-284 but stymied itself with 3 lost fumbles. New England dropped its fourth in a row to fall to 1-8, but five of the eight losses have come by 3 points or less.

Buffalo	0	0	0	10	3	—	13
New England	0	0	7	3	0	—	10

NE — Russell 2 run (Sisson kick)
NE — FG Sisson 27
Buff — Metzelaars 9 pass from Kelly (Christie kick)
Buff — FG Christie 27
Buff — FG Christie 30

DENVER 29, CLEVELAND 14—at Cleveland Stadium, attendance 77,818. John Elway threw for 244 yards and 3 touchdowns to lead the Broncos past the Browns. After a scoreless first quarter, Denver broke the game open with 16 points in a span of less than five minutes in the second quarter. First, Elway's 56-yard completion to Vance Johnson set up a 2-yard touchdown pass to running back Glyn Milburn 3:54 into the period. On Cleveland's next possession, reserve running back Reggie Rivers broke through to block a punt out of the end zone for a safety and a 9-0 lead. Moments later, Elway capped the scoring spree with a 38-yard touchdown pass to Derek Russell 6:07 before halftime. After the Browns pulled within 16-7 early in the second half, Elway teamed with tight end Shannon Sharpe on a 33-yard touchdown pass. Rookie Jason Elam added a pair of field goals in the fourth quarter. Elway finished with 17 completions in 23 attempts while beating the Browns for the ninth time in 11 tries in his career. The Broncos' balanced offense also produced 159 rushing yards, including 82 from Rod Bernstine. Bernie Kosar threw a pair of touchdown passes to Michael Jackson in what would be his last game with the Browns. Kosar, whose final pass was a 38-yard touchdown to Jackson with 12 seconds remaining, completed 16 of 30 passes for 226 yards but was sacked 6 times.

Denver	0	16	7	6	—	29
Cleveland	0	0	7	7	—	14

Den — Milburn 2 pass from Elway (Elam kick)
Den — Safety, Rivers blocked punt out of end zone
Den — Russell 38 pass from Elway (Elam kick)
Cle — Jackson 8 pass from Kosar (Stover kick)
Den — Sharpe 33 pass from Elway (Elam kick)
Den — FG Elam 22
Den — FG Elam 38
Cle — Jackson 38 pass from Kosar (Stover kick)

L.A. RAIDERS 16, CHICAGO 14—at Soldier Field, attendance 59,750. The Raiders escaped with the victory when Kevin Butler's 30-yard field-goal try as time expired hooked wide left. Los Angeles appeared comfortably ahead 16-7 late in the game. But Chicago, the third-period touchdown of which was its first in 13 quarters, pulled within 2 points by marching 66 yards to Jim Harbaugh's 13-yard touchdown pass to Terry Obee with 1:13 to go. After the Bears recovered the ensuing onside kick, quarterback Jim Harbaugh scrambled 25 yards. When the Raiders were penalized for a late hit on the same play, Chicago was in position for the go-ahead field goal. But Butler, who entered the game 10-for-10 inside 40 yards this season before misfiring on a 21-yard try early in the fourth quarter, failed to convert the kick. Cold weather and swirling winds limited the effectiveness of both teams' passing offenses, but Los Angeles, which entered the game ranked twenty-sixth in the NFL in rushing, ran for 179 yards. Three backs had 50 yards or more, topped by Greg Robinson's 70 yards on 12 carries. Neal Anderson ran for 75 yards and a touchdown on 28 carries for the Bears.

L.A. Raiders	3	10	0	3	—	16
Chicago	0	0	7	7	—	14

Raid — FG Jaeger 31
Raid — McCallum 1 run (Jaeger kick)
Raid — FG Jaeger 21
Chi — Anderson 3 run (Butler kick)
Raid — FG Jaeger 21
Chi — Obee 13 pass from Harbaugh (Butler kick)

N.Y. JETS 27, MIAMI 10—at Giants Stadium, attendance 71,306. Boomer Esiason threw 3 touchdown passes and the Jets beat the Dolphins for the second time this season. New York took the opening kickoff and scored on Esiason's 17-yard touchdown pass to tight end Johnny Mitchell 4:51 into the game. Moments later, Lonnie Young intercepted Scott Mitchell's pass, setting up Cary Blanchard for a 37-yard field goal and a 10-0 Jets' lead. Esiason's second

touchdown pass to Mitchell (2 yards) came 19 seconds before halftime and made it 17-3. After Scott Mitchell threw a 65-yard touchdown pass to Irving Fryar to pull Miami within 20-10 late in the third quarter, New York countered with a 13-play, 70-yard drive to the clinching touchdown, Esiason's 12-yard pass to Chris Burkett with 8:43 left in the game. Esiason finished with 23 completions in 32 attempts for 256 yards. The Dolphins managed only 48 rushing yards, taking to the air after falling behind early. Mitchell completed 23 of 44 passes for 297 yards. Fryar caught 7 passes for 111 yards. Miami's Don Shula remained tied with George Halas for the most coaching wins in NFL history.

Miami	0	3	7	0	—	10
N.Y. Jets	10	7	3	7	—	27

Jets — Mitchell 17 pass from Esiason (Blanchard kick)
Jets — FG Blanchard 37
Mia — FG Stoyanovich 48
Jets — Mitchell 2 pass from Esiason (Blanchard kick)
Jets — FG Blanchard 43
Mia — Fryar 65 pass from Mitchell (Stoyanovich kick)
Jets — Burkett 12 pass from Esiason (Blanchard kick)

DALLAS 31, N.Y. GIANTS 9—at Texas Stadium, attendance 64,735. The Cowboys rolled to their sixth consecutive victory in impressive fashion and took over sole possession of first place in the NFC Eastern Division. Troy Aikman completed his first 10 passes, including 28- and 50-yard scoring strikes to Alvin Harper, as Dallas built a 17-6 halftime advantage. But Aikman, who finished 11 of 13 for 162 yards, was forced to leave the game after straining a hamstring while scrambling with 9:30 remaining in the third quarter. Reserve quarterback Jason Garrett took over and directed a pair of scoring drives, each of which ended in short touchdown runs by Emmitt Smith. Garrett was 5 of 6 for 34 yards, while Smith ran for 117 yards on 24 carries. Harper positioned the Cowboys for Smith's 2-yard touchdown run with 9:02 left when he took a handoff and then completed a 46-yard pass to Michael Irvin.

N.Y. Giants	0	6	0	3	—	9
Dallas	10	7	0	14	—	31

Dall — FG Murray 34
Dall — Harper 28 pass from Aikman (Murray kick)
Giants — FG Treadwell 22
Dall — Harper 50 pass from Aikman (Murray kick)
Giants — FG Treadwell 45
Dall — E. Smith 1 run (Murray kick)
Dall — E. Smith 2 run (Murray kick)
Giants — FG Treadwell 29

PHOENIX 16, PHILADELPHIA 3—at Sun Devil Stadium, attendance 41,634. Rookie Ron Moore rushed for 160 yards as the Cardinals handed the Eagles their fourth consecutive defeat. Phoenix dominated on the ground, rushing for 243 of their 359 total yards. Moore, playing in place of injured starter and 1993 first-round draft choice Garrison Hearst, equaled a club record with 36 carries. The game's lone touchdown came 7 plays after Cardinals cornerback Aeneas Williams returned an interception 41 yards to Philadelphia's 34-yard line midway through the second quarter. Moore ran 4 yards on fourth-and-1 and also had a 10-yard run on the short drive, which was capped by Chris Chandler's 10-yard touchdown pass to Gary Clark. Larry Centers ran for 59 yards and caught 4 passes for 46 yards for Phoenix, which controlled the ball for more than 38 minutes. The Eagles managed only 65 yards on the ground and 205 yards in all.

Philadelphia	3	0	0	0	—	3
Phoenix	3	13	0	0	—	16

Phil — FG Bahr 27
Phx — FG Davis 23
Phx — FG Davis 20
Phx — Clark 10 pass from Chandler (Davis kick)
Phx — FG Davis 29

PITTSBURGH 24, CINCINNATI 16—at Riverfront Stadium, attendance 51,202. The Steelers spotted the winless Bengals 16 points, then roared back to the victory to move into a tie for first place in the AFC Central Division. Safety Darryl Williams returned an interception 97 yards for a touchdown and Cincinnati recovered a fumbled snap to help build its 16-0 lead 3:50 before halftime. But Pittsburgh quarterback Neil O'Donnell shook off the mistakes and completed a 71-yard touchdown pass to tight end Eric Green 2:49 before halftime. After three straight incomplete passes, the Bengals punted, and the Steelers marched 60 yards to pull within 16-14 on O'Donnell's 9-yard touchdown pass to Merril Hoge with eight seconds remaining in the half. Barry Foster ran 1 yard for a touchdown 1:22 into the fourth quarter to put Pittsburgh ahead for the first time. Foster finished with 120 yards on 25 carries. The Steelers had 390 total yards, Cincinnati just 199.

Pittsburgh	0	14	0	10	—	24
Cincinnati	3	13	0	0	—	16

Cin — FG Pelfrey 32
Cin — Williams 97 interception return (kick failed)
Cin — Query 7 pass from Schroeder (Pelfrey kick)
Pitt — Green 71 pass from O'Donnell (Anderson kick)
Pitt — Hoge 9 pass from O'Donnell (Anderson kick)
Pitt — Foster 1 run (Anderson kick)
Pitt — FG Anderson 23

SAN DIEGO 30, MINNESOTA 17—at Metrodome, attendance 54,960. John Friesz threw 2 touchdown passes and rookie Natrone Means ran for 105 yards to lead the Chargers past the Vikings. Minnesota rallied from a 16-3 deficit to take a 17-16 lead on Barry Word's 1-yard touchdown run late in the third quarter. But on the Vikings' next possession, San Diego cornerback Sean Vanhorse intercepted Sean Salisbury's pass at the Chargers' 39-yard line. San Diego then marched 61 yards in 7 plays, taking the lead on a 7-yard touchdown run by Means with 10:12 left in the game. Minnesota rookie Qadry Ismail fumbled the ensuing kickoff, and it took the Chargers just three plays to capitalize, the touchdown coming when Friesz threw 18 yards to Shawn Jefferson. Friesz completed 20 of 32 passes for 268 yards for San Diego. Anthony Miller caught 7 passes for 142 yards, including a 66-yard touchdown. Salisbury completed 29 of 47 passes for 347 yards for the Vikings, but Minnesota was hurt by the lack of a running game. The Vikings gained only 20 yards on the ground, the lowest single-game total in franchise history. Anthony Carter caught 10 passes for 164 yards.

San Diego	7	3	6	14	—	30
Minnesota	0	3	14	0	—	17

SD — Butts 3 run (Carney kick)
SD — FG Carney 36
Minn — FG Reveiz 20
SD — Miller 66 pass from Friesz (kick failed)
Minn — A. Carter 9 pass from Salisbury (Reveiz kick)
Minn — Word 1 run (Reveiz kick)
SD — Means 7 run (Carney kick)
SD — Jefferson 18 pass from Friesz (Carney kick)

HOUSTON 24, SEATTLE 14—at Astrodome, attendance 50,447. Warren Moon completed 36 of 55 passes for 369 yards and 2 touchdowns, and the Oilers won their third consecutive game. Moon completed all 7 of his attempts on the game's opening drive, a 79-yard march capped by his 3-yard touchdown pass to Webster Slaughter 6:55 into the first quarter. After a 53-yard touchdown pass from Rick Mirer to Kelvin Martin tied the game, Houston took the lead for good when Moon teamed with Ernest Givins on a 14-yard scoring toss with 20 seconds left in the period. Al Del Greco added 3 field goals in the second quarter. The Oilers rolled up 26 first downs and 458 total yards while maintaining possession for more than 40 of the game's 60 minutes. Slaughter caught 9 passes for 135 yards.

Seattle	7	0	0	7	—	14
Houston	13	9	2	0	—	24

Hou — Slaughter 3 pass from Moon (Del Greco kick)
Sea — Martin 53 pass from Mirer (Kasay kick)
Hou — Givins 14 pass from Moon (kick failed)
Hou — FG Del Greco 33
Hou — FG Del Greco 51
Hou — FG Del Greco 39
Hou — Safety, Mirer called for intentionally grounding in the end zone
Sea — Warren 10 run (Kasay kick)

DETROIT 23, TAMPA BAY 0—at Pontiac Silverdome, attendance 65,295. Barry Sanders ran for 187 yards on 29 carries to lead the Lions to their seventh victory in nine games this season, their best start in 31 years. Detroit's defense was dominant, limiting the Buccaneers to only 6 first downs and 146 total yards while posting its first shutout since 1983. Quarterback Rodney Peete completed 16 of 22 passes for 134 yards without an interception. He completed all 4 of his attempts for 54 yards and ran 9 yards for a touchdown on the decisive drive of the game early in the third quarter. Leading just 6-0, the Lions marched 81 yards in 10 plays the first time they had the ball in the second half to open up a 13-point advantage.

Tampa Bay	0	0	0	0	—	0
Detroit	3	3	7	10	—	23

Det — FG Hanson 29
Det — FG Hanson 49
Det — Peete 9 run (Hanson kick)
Det — Moore 1 run (Hanson kick)
Det — FG Hanson 37

SUNDAY NIGHT, NOVEMBER 7

WASHINGTON 30, INDIANAPOLIS 24—at RFK Stadium, attendance 50,523. The Redskins used takeaways and big plays to halt their losing streak at six. The game was scoreless until Washington safety Darrell Green scooped up a loose ball and returned it 79 yards for a touchdown 2:03 into the second quarter. The fumble was forced when linebacker Kurt Gouveia tackled Colts running back Roosevelt Potts, who had caught a short pass from Jeff George. Moments later, linebacker Andre Collins intercepted George's pass. Though forced to punt following that turnover, the Redskins got a break when Indianapolis's Clarence Verdin muffed the kick. Washington's Rick Hamilton recovered the ball at the Colts' 6-yard line, and two plays later, quarterback Mark Rypien ran 1 yard for a touchdown and a 14-0 lead. Rypien set up his 1-yard touchdown run in the third quarter with a 42-yard pass to Tim McGee, then positioned the Redskins for a field goal in the fourth quarter with a 43-yard completion to Reggie Brooks. Brooks also ran for 105 yards on 21 carries. George completed 37 of 59 passes for 376 yards and 3 touchdowns as Indianapolis had sizable advantages in plays (78-60) and total yards (405-275). But 2 of his scoring passes came in the final 1:50 with the game out of reach.

Indianapolis	0	10	0	14	—	24
Washington	0	14	6	10	—	30

Wash — Green 79 fumble return (Lohmiller kick)
Wash — Rypien 1 run (Lohmiller kick)
Ind — Langhorne 72 pass from George (Biasucci kick)
Ind — FG Biasucci 22
Wash — Rypien 1 run (kick failed)
Wash — FG Lohmiller 24
Wash — Mitchell 2 run (Lohmiller kick)
Ind — Cash 9 pass from George (Biasucci kick)
Ind — Verdin 1 pass from George (Biasucci kick)

MONDAY, NOVEMBER 8

KANSAS CITY 23, GREEN BAY 16—at Arrowhead Stadium, attendance 76,742. Defensive tackle Dan Saleaumua returned a fumble for a touchdown, then forced a key fumble in the fourth quarter as the Chiefs ended the Packers' three-game winning streak. Kansas City trailed 9-3 until linebacker Derrick Thomas stripped the ball from Green Bay quarterback Brett Favre on the Packers' first play from scrimmage in the second half. Saleaumua picked up the loose ball and ran 16 yards for the touchdown that put the Chiefs ahead for good. Nick Lowery's field goal and a 1-yard touchdown run by Marcus Allen extended Kansas City's advantage to 20-9 1:06 into the fourth quarter. But Green Bay countered just 55 seconds after Allen's score with a 35-yard touchdown pass from Favre to tight end Jackie Harris. The Packers appeared to be on the verge of taking the lead the next time they had the ball. But Saleaumua's jarring hit on running back Darrell Thompson forced a fumble at the Chiefs' 2-yard line, and Kansas City linebacker Tracy Rogers recovered in the end zone to end the threat. After Lowery added another field goal with 3:26 to go, Green Bay's last chance was foiled when safety Martin Bayless intercepted a pass with 1:40 to play. It was the sixth turnover of the game for Packers, who did not force any. Favre completed 20 of 34 passes for 213 yards, but was intercepted 3 times. Dave Krieg, starting while Joe Montana nursed an injured hamstring, completed 17 of 30 passes for 170 yards for the Chiefs. He was sacked 4 times, 3 times by Bryce Paup.

Green Bay	3	6	0	7	—	16
Kansas City	3	0	10	10	—	23

KC — FG Lowery 23
GB — FG Jacke 23
GB — FG Jacke 51
GB — FG Jacke 19
KC — Saleaumua 16 fumble return (Lowery kick)
KC — FG Lowery 34
KC — Allen 1 run (Lowery kick)
GB — Harris 35 pass from Favre (Jacke kick)
KC — FG Lowery 40

ELEVENTH WEEK SUMMARIES

AMERICAN FOOTBALL CONFERENCE

Eastern Division	W	L	T	Pct.	Pts.	OP
Buffalo	7	2	0	.778	172	120
Miami	7	2	0	.778	201	159
N.Y. Jets	5	4	0	.556	217	158
Indianapolis	3	6	0	.333	145	210
New England	1	8	0	.111	113	200
Central Division						
Pittsburgh	6	3	0	.667	215	136
Cleveland	5	4	0	.556	168	181
Houston	5	4	0	.556	206	157
Cincinnati	0	9	0	.000	100	224
Western Division						
Kansas City	7	2	0	.778	164	144
Denver	5	4	0	.556	229	175
L.A. Raiders	5	4	0	.556	172	178
Seattle	5	5	0	.500	165	169
San Diego	4	5	0	.444	157	183

NATIONAL FOOTBALL CONFERENCE

Eastern Division	W	L	T	Pct.	Pts.	OP
Dallas	7	2	0	.778	206	126
N.Y. Giants	6	3	0	.667	180	118
Philadelphia	4	5	0	.444	155	191
Phoenix	3	7	0	.300	183	176
Washington	2	7	0	.222	145	229
Central Division						
Detroit	7	2	0	.778	187	140
Green Bay	5	4	0	.556	199	161
Minnesota	5	4	0	.556	155	177
Chicago	4	5	0	.444	142	124
Tampa Bay	2	7	0	.222	120	251
Western Division						
New Orleans	6	3	0	.667	200	173
San Francisco	6	3	0	.667	255	179
Atlanta	3	6	0	.333	184	222
L.A. Rams	2	7	0	.222	131	205

SUNDAY, NOVEMBER 14

ATLANTA 13, L.A. RAMS 0—at Anaheim Stadium, attendance 37,073. Six Falcons recorded 1 sack each as Atlanta posted its first shutout on the road in 16 years, handing the Rams their fifth consecutive defeat. Erric Pegram rushed for 128 yards on 27 carries and Bobby Hebert threw a 31-yard touchdown pass to Andre Rison in the third quarter, but it was the Falcons' defense that made the difference, limiting Los Angeles to 260 total yards. Rams quarterback Jim Everett completed 20 of 41 passes for 203 yards but was intercepted twice, lost a fumble, and was sacked for 38 yards in losses. Atlanta entered the game with the league's lowest-rated defense and had allowed more points than any other team in the NFL. The Falcons had just 10 sacks in their first eight games. The Rams were shut out for the first time since 1987.

Atlanta	3	3	7	0	—	13
L.A. Rams	0	0	0	0	—	0

Atl — FG Johnson 46
Atl — FG Johnson 44
Atl — Rison 31 pass from Hebert (Johnson kick)

SEATTLE 22, CLEVELAND 5—at Kingdome, attendance 54,622. The Seahawks recovered 5 fumbles and intercepted 2 passes en route to knocking the Browns out of first place in the AFC Central Division. Cleveland was playing its first game without long-time quarterback Bernie Kosar, who was waived earlier in the week. The Browns turned to Todd Philcox, who was making only the second start of his four-year career. Philcox completed just 9 of 20 passes for 85 yards, with 2 interceptions. He also fumbled twice, including 1 on the game's first play from scrimmage. Seattle safety Robert Blackmon picked up the loose ball and returned it 5 yards for a touchdown just 14 seconds into the first quarter, giving the Seahawks all the points they would need. Cleveland dominated the first half, maintaining possession for nearly 22 minutes and limiting Seattle to 2 first downs and 38 total yards, but still trailed 7-5. Two more fumbles and an interception, all in the shadow of the Seahawks' goal line, stymied Browns' scoring opportunities. In the second half, Seattle's offense came to life and put the game out of reach. Chris Warren finished the game with 112 rushing yards, all but 5 coming after intermission. Safety Eugene Robinson had both of the Seahawks' interceptions and recovered a fumble.

Cleveland	2	3	0	0	—	5
Seattle	7	0	7	8	—	22

Sea — Blackmon 5 fumble return (Kasay kick)
Cle — Safety, Pleasant tackled Mirer in end zone
Cle — FG Stover 25
Sea — J. Williams 23 pass from Mirer (Kasay kick)
Sea — FG Kasay 42
Sea — FG Kasay 47
Sea — Safety, Edwards tackled Philcox in end zone

GREEN BAY 19, NEW ORLEANS 17—at Louisiana Superdome, attendance 69,043. Chris Jacke's fourth field goal of the game, from 36 yards with three seconds left, gave the Packers their fourth victory in the last five games. Jacke's winning kick was set up by wide receiver Sterling Sharpe, who caught a 54-yard pass from Brett Favre to position the ball on the Saints' 19-yard line. Up to that point, Green Bay had done little offensively. The Packers managed only 13 first downs and 194 total yards, and Favre was sacked 6 times, including 3 by New Orleans linebacker Rickey Jackson. But Green Bay stayed close by converting 3 of the Saints' 5 turnovers into 13 points. Linebacker Johnny Holland's interception and 11-yard return early in the fourth quarter positioned Jacke for a 44-yard field goal that gave the Packers a 16-14 lead with 8:01 remaining. But New Orleans's Fred McAfee returned the ensuing kickoff 55 yards, and seven plays later, Morten Andersen's 27-yard field goal put the Saints back in front with 3:38 to go. After an exchange of punts, Green Bay drove to the winning field goal. New Orleans rookie Derek Brown led all rushers with 106 yards on 21 carries.

Green Bay	3	7	3	6	—	19
New Orleans	0	14	0	3	—	17

GB — FG Jacke 38
NO — Early 24 pass from Wilson (Andersen kick)
GB — Harris 1 pass from Favre (Jacke kick)
NO — Dowdell 11 pass from Wilson (Andersen kick)
GB — FG Jacke 20
GB — FG Jacke 44
NO — FG Andersen 27
GB — FG Jacke 36

HOUSTON 38, CINCINNATI 3—at Riverfront Stadium, attendance 42,347. Warren Moon threw 4 touchdown passes, Gary Brown rushed for 166 yards, and the Oilers dominated the Bengals while winning their fourth in a row. Moon, who completed 23 of 31 passes for 225 yards, threw 3 of his touchdown passes to Haywood Jeffires, the last of which was a 12-yard collaboration that put Houston ahead 35-0 6:04 into the second half. With Lorenzo White nursing a pulled hamstring, Brown got the first start of his three-year career and carried 26 times. His 4-yard touchdown run in the second quarter capped a 7-play, 70-yard drive. The Oilers had 32 first downs to just 9 for Cincinnati, and amassed 462 total yards to 165. Houston's balanced attack produced 240 rushing yards and 222 passing yards. Bengals quarterbacks David Klingler and Jay Schroeder combined to complete only 8 of 28 passes for 80 yards. Cincinnati fell to 0-9, the worst start in franchise history.

Houston	7	21	10	0	—	38
Cincinnati	0	0	3	0	—	3

Hou — Duncan 3 pass from Moon (Del Greco kick)
Hou — Brown 4 run (Del Greco kick)
Hou — Jeffires 21 pass from Moon (Del Greco kick)
Hou — Jeffires 6 pass from Moon (Del Greco kick)
Hou — Jeffires 12 pass from Moon (Del Greco kick)
Hou — FG Del Greco 39
Cin — FG Pelfrey 46

KANSAS CITY 31, L.A. RAIDERS 20—at Los Angeles Memorial Coliseum, attendance 66,553. Dave Krieg threw 3 touchdown passes, and Marcus Allen ran for a key touchdown in his return to Los Angeles, spurring the Chiefs to the victory. Krieg, playing in place of injured Joe Montana, completed just 12 of 27 passes for 178 yards. But his 66-yard touchdown pass to Willie Davis late in the third quarter put Kansas City ahead for good, and his 4-yard scoring toss to tight end Keith Cash with 2:52 remaining in the game clinched the victory. He also had a 15-yard touchdown pass to running back Kimble Anders in the second quarter. That capped a 13-play, 80-yard drive and trimmed the Raiders' lead to 14-7. It was 17-7 at halftime, before Allen's 39-yard run in the third quarter set up his own score from 4 yards to make it 17-14. Allen, appearing for the first time in a Chiefs' uniform in the stadium in which he played four years at USC and 11 with the Raiders, rushed for 85 yards on 17 carries. Kansas City outgained Los Angeles 338-280, but the margin was 218-65 after intermission. Davis caught 5 passes for 115 yards. Krieg became the seventeenth quarterback in NFL history to surpass 30,000 career passing yards.

Kansas City	0	7	14	10	—	31
L.A. Raiders	7	10	0	3	—	20

Raid — McCallum 4 run (Jaeger kick)
Raid — Horton 8 pass from Hostetler (Jaeger kick)
KC — Anders 15 pass from Krieg (Lowery kick)
Raid — FG Jaeger 35
KC — Allen 4 run (Lowery kick)
KC — Davis 66 pass from Krieg (Lowery kick)
Raid — FG Jaeger 30
KC — FG Lowery 29
KC — Cash 4 pass from Krieg (Lowery kick)

MIAMI 19, PHILADELPHIA 14—at Veterans Stadium, attendance 64,213. Don Shula became the winningest head coach in NFL history by guiding the Dolphins past the Eagles. The victory was the 325th of Shula's 31-year coaching career. George Halas had 324 wins in his 40 years as coach of the Chicago Bears. To get Shula his milestone victory, Miami had to overcome a 14-13 halftime deficit with a reserve quarterback who never had thrown an NFL pass before. Doug Pederson, a former World League player, took over when Scott Mitchell separated his shoulder with the Dolphins trailing by a point. Mitchell was starting in place of Dan Marino, who was lost for the season with an Achilles tendon injury suffered five weeks earlier. With Pederson at the helm, Miami played conservatively, settling for a pair of second-half field goals by Pete Stoyanovich to win. Pederson completed 3 of 6 passes for 34 yards, including 11-yard strikes to O.J. McDuffie and Terry Kirby on a 45-yard march to Stoyanovich's fourth-quarter field goal. The victory was not secured, however, until Eagles quarterback Ken O'Brien lost his grip on the football while attempting to pass, and the Dolphins recovered with just over two minutes left. That stymied a drive that had reached Miami's 22-yard line. Shula, who coached seven years with the Baltimore Colts before joining the Dolphins in 1970, raised his career record to 325-153-6. Halas was 324-151-31 in four separate 10-year stints with the Bears.

Miami	6	7	3	3	—	19
Philadelphia	0	14	0	0	—	14

Mia — Kirby 8 pass from Mitchell (kick failed)
Phil — Williams 11 pass from O'Brien (Bahr kick)
Mia — Higgs 1 run (Stoyanovich kick)
Phil — Williams 8 pass from O'Brien (Bahr kick)
Mia — FG Stoyanovich 46
Mia — FG Stoyanovich 45

MINNESOTA 26, DENVER 23—at Mile High Stadium, attendance 67,329. Sean Salisbury passed for a career-high 366 yards and 2 touchdowns as the Vikings erased a 17-point deficit to beat the Broncos. John Elway's 2 touchdown passes helped Denver to a 20-3 lead midway through the second quarter. But Salisbury countered with scoring strikes of 9 yards to Cris Carter and 17 yards to Roger Craig just 3:08 apart to pull Minnesota within 20-17 at halftime. Fuad Reveiz kicked 3 field goals in the second half, including a 43-yard kick with 2:49 left in the game, to complete the comeback. The victory was sealed in the final minute when the Vikings recovered Glyn Milburn's fumble to thwart a Broncos' drive that had reached Minnesota's 21-yard line. Salisbury finished with 19 completions in 37 attempts, and Cris Carter caught 6 passes for 134 yards. Anthony Carter had 111 yards on his 4 receptions. Tackle Tim Irwin blocked 2 kicks, an extra point attempt and a 26-yard field-goal try in the third quarter. Elway completed 30 of 40 passes for 290 yards for Denver. Tight end Shannon Sharpe caught 7 passes for 104 yards. The two teams were whistled for 23 penalties, including 13 on the Vikings.

Minnesota	3	14	3	6	—	26
Denver	6	14	0	3	—	23

Den — Russell 4 pass from Elway (kick blocked)
Minn — FG Reveiz 25
Den — Delpino 3 run (Elam kick)
Den — V. Johnson 15 pass from Elway (Elam kick)
Minn — C. Carter 9 pass from Salisbury (Reveiz kick)
Minn — Craig 17 pass from Salisbury (Reveiz kick)
Minn — FG Reveiz 19
Minn — FG Reveiz 35
Den — FG Elam 53
Minn — FG Reveiz 43

N.Y. JETS 31, INDIANAPOLIS 17—at Hoosier Dome, attendance 47,351. Johnny Johnson rushed for 141 yards, including the game-clinching 57-yard touchdown run late in the fourth quarter, to lead the Jets to their third consecutive victory. Johnson averaged nearly 7 yards on his 21 carries and keyed a rushing attack that produced 202 yards. New York had 458 total yards, including 256 passing from Boomer Esiason. Indianapolis, meanwhile, mustered only 215 total yards, most of it coming on Reggie Langhorne's 8 catches for 112 yards. Still, the Colts trailed only 24-17 and had the Jets pinned at their 2-yard line after Rohn Stark's punt midway through the fourth quarter. But New York covered 98 yards on a 9-play drive capped by Johnson's touchdown with 2:22 remaining.

N.Y. Jets	7	10	7	7	—	31
Indianapolis	3	7	7	0	—	17

Ind — FG Biasucci 41
Jets — B. Baxter 1 run (Blanchard kick)
Jets — Burkett 15 pass from Esiason (Blanchard kick)
Ind — Cash 3 pass from George (Biasucci kick)
Jets — FG Blanchard 22
Jets — Burkett 4 pass from Esiason (Blanchard kick)
Ind — Culver 1 run (Biasucci kick)
Jets — Johnson 57 run (Blanchard kick)

DALLAS 20, PHOENIX 15—at Texas Stadium, attendance 64,224. Bernie Kosar, released earlier in the week by the Browns, came off the bench to throw for 199 yards and a touchdown in the Cowboys' seventh consecutive victory. With Troy Aikman nursing a hamstring injury, Kosar took over for Jason Garrett 10:11 into the game with Dallas leading 3-0. By halftime, he had completed 7 of 8 passes for 152 yards and directed touchdown drives of 65 and 86 yards. His 1-yard touchdown pass to tight end Jay Novacek gave the Cowboys a 17-0 lead at intermission. The Cardinals rallied in the second half, but could pull no closer than the final score. Dallas safety Kenneth Gant's interception with 57 seconds left sealed the victory. Cowboys running back Emmitt Smith rushed for 80 yards on 24 carries and caught 4 passes for 102 yards. Kosar finished with 13 completions in 21 attempts. His 86-yard completion to Smith, who took a short pass and turned it into a big gain, was the fifth-longest in franchise history. Chris Chandler completed 27 of 46 passes for 214 yards and a touchdown for Phoenix.

Phoenix	0	0	10	5	—	15
Dallas	3	14	0	3	—	20

Dall — FG Murray 44
Dall — Smith 4 run (Murray kick)
Dall — Novacek 1 pass from Kosar (Murray kick)
Phx — FG Davis 19
Phx — Centers 17 pass from Chandler (Davis kick)
Dall — FG Murray 43
Phx — Safety, Kosar called for intentionally grounding in the end zone
Phx — FG Davis 47

SAN FRANCISCO 45, TAMPA BAY 21—at Tampa Stadium, attendance 43,835. Jerry Rice caught 8 passes for 172 yards and 4 touchdowns in the 49ers' rout of the Buccaneers. Rice's 12-yard touchdown grab 5:16 into the game gave San Francisco a lead it would never relinquish, and his 2 second-period touchdowns put the game out of reach. The 49ers led 17-0 until Tampa Bay quarterback Craig Erickson threw 2 touchdown passes in a 14-second span to trim the Buccaneers' deficit to 3 points. But San Francisco took just two plays to counter, with quarterback Steve Young and Rice teaming on a 51-yard touchdown pass 6:19 before halftime. Rice's third touchdown, on a 9-yard reception, came in the final minute of the second quarter and made it 31-14 at the half. That gave him 117 career touchdowns, moving him past John Riggins and into third place on the NFL's all-time list. Number 118 came on a 26-yard scoring catch late in the third quarter. Young completed 23 of 29 passes for 311 yards while directing 8 possessions, 6 of which resulted in touchdowns. Ricky Watters ran for 88 yards and caught 5 passes for 35 yards as San Francisco rolled up 448 total yards. Erickson completed 17 of 27 passes for 239 yards for the Buccaneers.

San Francisco	10	21	7	7	—	45
Tampa Bay	0	14	7	0	—	21

SF — Rice 12 pass from Young (Cofer kick)
SF — FG Cofer 44
SF — Tamm 1 run (Cofer kick)
TB — G. Anderson 14 pass from Erickson (Husted kick)
TB — Workman 18 pass from Erickson (Husted kick)
SF — Rice 51 pass from Young (Cofer kick)
SF — Rice 9 pass from Young (Cofer kick)
TB — Workman 3 run (Husted kick)
SF — Rice 26 pass from Young (Cofer kick)
SF — Watters 1 run (Cofer kick)

N.Y. GIANTS 20, WASHINGTON 6—at Giants Stadium, attendance 76,606. Rodney Hampton, back in the lineup for the first time in more than a month, ran for 78 yards and a touchdown as the Giants ground out a victory over the Redskins. New York took the opening kickoff and held the ball for 7:44, marching 80 yards in 12 plays, the last of which was Hampton's 1-yard touchdown run. The Giants never trailed and kept the ball mostly on the ground; 38 of their 57 plays were rushes, and 152 of their 262 total yards came via the running game. Quarterback Phil Simms attempted only 15 passes, completing 9 for 100 yards. Running back David Meggett, who threw a 42-yard touchdown pass on a halfback-option play in a 41-7 victory over Washington earlier in the year, tossed a 21-yard scoring strike to Chris Calloway on a similar play in this one. Mark Rypien threw for 239 yards, and Reggie Brooks ran for 91 for the Redskins, who fell to 2-7, their worst start in 30 years.

Washington	0	0	3	3	—	6
N.Y. Giants	7	7	3	3	—	20

Giants— Hampton 1 run (Treadwell kick)
Giants— Calloway 21 pass from Meggett (Treadwell kick)
Giants— FG Treadwell 43
Wash — FG Lohmiller 27
Giants— FG Treadwell 39
Wash — FG Lohmiller 33

SUNDAY NIGHT, NOVEMBER 14

CHICAGO 16, SAN DIEGO 13—at San Diego Jack Murphy Stadium, attendance 58,459. Jim Harbaugh threw a 38-yard touchdown pass to Curtis Conway, and the Bears hung on to upset the Chargers. The decisive scoring pass came with 4:08 remaining in the third quarter and San Diego leading 10-9. It came one play after Chicago's Terry Obee returned a punt 25 yards. The Chargers then held the ball for more than eight minutes on a 19-play drive, but managed only a 26-yard field goal by John Carney to pull within three points 3:55 into the fourth quarter. San Diego had a chance to tie the game with 71 seconds remaining, but Carney's 41-yard field-goal try was wide left.

Chicago	0	6	10	0	—	16
San Diego	3	7	0	3	—	13

SD — FG Carney 28
SD — Kidd 2 run (Carney kick)
Chi — FG Butler 33
Chi — FG Butler 54
Chi — FG Butler 20
Chi — Conway 38 pass from Harbaugh (Butler kick)
SD — FG Carney 26

MONDAY, NOVEMBER 15

PITTSBURGH 23, BUFFALO 0—at Three Rivers Stadium, attendance 60,265. Leroy Thompson rushed for 108 yards and a touchdown as the Steelers ended the Bills' five-game winning streak with surprising ease. Thompson, who replaced Barry Foster at running back after Foster sprained an ankle on Pittsburgh's first possession, carried 30 times and gave the Steelers all the points they would need on a 9-yard touchdown run 9:24 into the game. Neil O'Donnell threw a 1-yard touchdown pass to tight end Eric Green in the third quarter, and Gary Anderson kicked 3 field goals. A stifling defense did the rest, limiting Buffalo to 9 first downs and 157 total yards while knocking quarterback Jim Kelly (concussion) and wide receivers Andre Reed (broken bone in his wrist) and Don Beebe (concussion) out of the game. Pittsburgh had 400 total yards and maintained possession for 44:51 of the game's 60 minutes.

Buffalo	0	0	0	0	—	0
Pittsburgh	7	3	10	3	—	23

Pitt — Thompson 9 run (Anderson kick)
Pitt — FG Anderson 37
Pitt — Green 1 pass from O'Donnell (Anderson kick)
Pitt — FG Anderson 19
Pitt — FG Anderson 31

TWELFTH WEEK SUMMARIES

AMERICAN FOOTBALL CONFERENCE

Eastern Division	**W**	**L**	**T**	**Pct.**	**Pts.**	**OP**
Buffalo	8	2	0	.800	195	129
Miami	8	2	0	.800	218	172
N.Y. Jets	6	4	0	.600	234	170
Indianapolis	3	7	0	.300	154	233
New England	1	9	0	.100	126	217
Central Division						
Houston	6	4	0	.600	233	177
Pittsburgh	6	4	0	.600	228	173
Cleveland	5	5	0	.500	188	208
Cincinnati	0	10	0	.000	112	241
Western Division						
Kansas City	7	3	0	.700	181	163
Denver	6	4	0	.600	266	188
L.A. Raiders	6	4	0	.600	184	185
Seattle	5	5	0	.500	165	169
San Diego	4	6	0	.400	164	195

NATIONAL FOOTBALL CONFERENCE

Eastern Division	**W**	**L**	**T**	**Pct.**	**Pts.**	**OP**
Dallas	7	3	0	.700	220	153
N.Y. Giants	7	3	0	.700	187	121
Philadelphia	4	6	0	.400	158	198
Phoenix	3	7	0	.300	183	176
Washington	2	8	0	.200	151	239
Central Division						
Detroit	7	3	0	.700	204	166
Green Bay	6	4	0	.600	225	178
Chicago	5	5	0	.500	161	141
Minnesota	5	5	0	.500	165	200
Tampa Bay	3	7	0	.300	143	261
Western Division						
San Francisco	7	3	0	.700	297	186
New Orleans	6	4	0	.600	207	215
Atlanta	4	6	0	.400	211	236
L.A. Rams	3	7	0	.300	141	211

SUNDAY, NOVEMBER 21

CHICAGO 19, KANSAS CITY 17—at Arrowhead Stadium, attendance 76,872. Neal Anderson ran 1 yard for a touchdown with 3:09 remaining as the Bears snapped the Chiefs' 10-game winning streak at home. Kansas City jumped out to a 14-0 lead on the strength of 2 rushing touchdowns by Marcus Allen. But Chicago pulled within 17-12, and Bears cornerback Jeremy Lincoln made the key play of the game late in the fourth quarter. From his 2-yard line, Chiefs quarterback Dave Krieg threw a pass to Jonathan Hayes. Kansas City's tight end bobbled the low throw, and Lincoln picked it off at the 12. He returned the theft 8 yards, and three plays later Anderson ran for the winning score. Allen, who rushed for 78 yards, became the ninth player in NFL history to run for 9,000 yards in his career. His 2 touchdowns raised his career total to 107, sixth on the league's all-time chart.

Chicago	0	6	6	7	—	19
Kansas City	7	7	3	0	—	17

KC — Allen 2 run (Lowery kick)
KC — Allen 8 run (Lowery kick)
Chi — FG Butler 32
Chi — FG Butler 45
Chi — Worley 25 run (kick blocked)
KC — FG Lowery 20
Chi — Anderson 1 run (Butler kick)

N.Y. JETS 17, CINCINNATI 12—at Giants Stadium, attendance 64,264. Brad Baxter and Johnny Johnson capped long drives with touchdown runs in the second quarter, and the Jets went on to record their fourth consecutive victory. The winless Bengals led 3-0 until New York embarked on a 19-play, 94-yard drive that culminated in Baxter's 5-yard touchdown run 4:13 before halftime. Quarterback Boomer Esiason got the drive going by completing a 12-yard pass to Johnson on third-and-6 from the Jets' 12-yard line, then had a 26-yard completion to Johnson later in the drive and converted a fourth-and-1 by sneaking 2 yards for a first down. He teamed with Johnson again the next time New York had the ball, completing a 48-yard pass to the running back to key an 80-yard drive. Johnson's 6-yard touchdown run with 57 seconds left in the second quarter capped that march and made it 14-3. Cincinnati closed within 17-10 on David Klingler's 4-yard touchdown pass to Jeff Query with 2:09 remaining in the game, but the Jets ran all but one second off the clock before giving up a concession safety.

Cincinnati	3	0	0	9	—	12
N.Y. Jets	0	14	0	3	—	17

Cin — FG Pelfrey 28
Jets — B. Baxter 5 run (Blanchard kick)
Jets — Johnson 6 run (Blanchard kick)
Jets — FG Blanchard 42
Cin — Query 4 pass from Klingler (Pelfrey kick)
Cin — Safety, Aguiar threw ball out of back of end zone

ATLANTA 27, DALLAS 14—at Georgia Dome, attendance 71,253. Bobby Hebert threw 3 touchdown passes and the Falcons stunned the Cowboys, snapping the defending Super Bowl champions' seven-game winning streak. Atlanta dominated from the outset, taking the opening kickoff and marching 73 yards to Norm Johnson's 26-yard field goal. The 14-play drive consumed 8:48. After forcing a punt, the Falcons drove to another field goal by Johnson the next time they had the ball. At that point, Atlanta had amassed 133 total yards to 1 for Dallas, and had run 29 plays to 3. The Falcons didn't let up, driving 87 yards to Hebert's 13-yard touchdown pass to Mike Pritchard 4:37 before halftime, then opening up a 20-0 advantage when the pair teamed again on an 11-yard touchdown pass midway through the third quarter. The Cowboys, already playing without injured starting quarterback Troy Aikman, lost running back Emmitt Smith for the rest of the game with a bruised right quadriceps suffered shortly before halftime. Smith left having gained only 1 yard on 1 carry and 9 yards on 4 receptions. Bernie Kosar, making his first start for Dallas, completed 22 of 39 passes for 186 yards. Hebert was 24 of 32 for 315 yards as Atlanta outgained the Cowboys 400-230. Cornerback Deion Sanders lined up at wide receiver late in the game and turned a short pass from Hebert into a 70-yard touchdown.

Dallas	0	0	7	7	—	14
Atlanta	3	10	7	7	—	27

Atl — FG Johnson 26
Atl — FG Johnson 24
Atl — Pritchard 13 pass from Hebert (Johnson kick)
Atl — Pritchard 11 pass from Hebert (Johnson kick)
Dall — Galbraith 1 pass from Kosar (Murray kick)
Atl — Sanders 70 pass from Hebert (Johnson kick)
Dall — K. Williams 28 pass from Kosar (Murray kick)

GREEN BAY 26, DETROIT 17—at Milwaukee County Stadium, attendance 55,119. Edgar Bennett scored 2 touchdowns and Chris Jacke kicked 4 field goals as the Packers pulled within one game of the first-place Lions in the NFC Central Division. Trailing 17-16 early in the fourth quarter, Green Bay drove to Jacke's fourth field goal, from 34 yards, to take a 19-17 advantage with 9:03 left in the game. Later in the period, Packers safety LeRoy Butler intercepted Rodney Peete's pass at Detroit's 36-yard line and returned it 22 yards to the 14. That set up the game-clinching 2-yard touchdown run by Bennett with 1:51 to go. Bennett also had a 1-yard touchdown run to open the scoring 3:37 into the game. Brett Favre completed 24 of 33 passes for 259 yards for the Packers, who rolled up 404 total yards while limiting the Lions to just 205. Detroit's Barry Sanders ran for 75 yards and joined Eric Dickerson and Tony Dorsett as the only players in NFL history to rush for more than 1,000 yards in each of their first five seasons.

Detroit	0	10	7	0	—	17
Green Bay	10	3	3	10	—	26

GB — E. Bennett 1 run (Jacke kick)
GB — FG Jacke 27
Det — Green 17 pass from Peete (Hanson kick)
Det — FG Hanson 50
GB — FG Jacke 52
Det — Hallock 1 pass from Peete (Hanson kick)

GB — FG Jacke 20
GB — FG Jacke 34
GB — E. Bennett 2 run (Jacke kick)

HOUSTON 27, CLEVELAND 20—at Cleveland Stadium, attendance 71,668. Gary Brown rushed for 194 yards on 34 carries to lead the Oilers to their fifth consecutive victory. Brown, making his second consecutive start in place of injured Lorenzo White, followed his 166-yard effort against Cincinnati one week earlier with the best single-game performance by a Houston runner in 13 years. He capped a 76-yard drive 3:07 into the second quarter with an 11-yard touchdown run to give the Oilers a lead they would never relinquish. Warren Moon threw a 4-yard touchdown pass to Curtis Duncan and ran 4 yards for another touchdown to help Houston build a 27-10 advantage in the fourth quarter. Browns quarterback Todd Philcox completed 22 of 47 passes for a career-high 316 yards, but was intercepted 4 times. Cleveland also had a punt blocked, which led to a field goal. Marcus Robertson equaled a club record with 3 interceptions for the Oilers.

Houston	0	14	3	10	—	27
Cleveland	3	7	0	10	—	20

Cle — FG Stover 21
Hou — Brown 11 run (Del Greco kick)
Hou — Duncan 4 pass from Moon (Del Greco kick)
Cle — Metcalf 13 pass from Philcox (Stover kick)
Hou — FG Del Greco 28
Hou — Moon 4 run (Del Greco kick)
Hou — FG Del Greco 30
Cle — Carrier 24 pass from Philcox (Stover kick)
Cle — FG Stover 44

BUFFALO 23, INDIANAPOLIS 9—at Rich Stadium, attendance 79,101. A second-quarter safety led to the deciding touchdowns in the Bills' victory. Indianapolis led 6-0 after 2 lengthy drives that stalled inside Buffalo's 10-yard line resulted in field goals by Dean Biasucci. But midway through the second quarter, the Bills' Henry Jones sacked Colts quarterback Jeff George in the end zone for a safety. After the ensuing free kick, Buffalo drove 55 yards and took a 9-6 lead on Kenneth Davis's 1-yard run 2:35 before halftime. Then the Bills' Richard Harvey stripped the ball from Indianapolis's Clarence Verdin on the following kickoff and Keith Goganious recovered for Buffalo at the Colts' 26. It took the Bills only 2 plays to convert that into Jim Kelly's 23-yard touchdown pass to Bill Brooks with 1:55 remaining in the second quarter. After Biasucci's third field goal pulled Indianapolis within 16-9 midway through the third period, Kelly capped an 80-yard drive with a 13-yard touchdown pass to tight end Keith McKeller for the game's final points. The Colts, who failed to score a touchdown for the fourth time in 10 games this season, had two drives thwarted in the end zone in the fourth quarter, one on a fourth-down incompletion and one on cornerback Nate Odomes's interception. Kelly passed for 274 yards and Thurman Thomas rushed for 116 for Buffalo. George threw for 262 yards for Indianapolis.

Indianapolis	3	3	3	0	—	9
Buffalo	0	16	7	0	—	23

Ind — FG Biasucci 26
Ind — FG Biasucci 22
Buff — Safety, Jones tackled George in end zone
Buff — Davis 1 run (Christie kick)
Buff — Brooks 23 pass from Kelly (Christie kick)
Ind — FG Biasucci 37
Buff — McKeller 13 pass from Kelly (Christie kick)

L.A. RAIDERS 12, SAN DIEGO 7—at San Diego Jack Murphy Stadium, attendance 60,615. Jeff Jaeger's 4 field goals kept the Raiders within a game of first place in the AFC West. Los Angeles dominated from the outset, taking the opening kickoff and marching 86 yards on a 19-play drive that chewed up 11:22. That drive stalled at the Chargers' 2-yard line, and Jaeger kicked a 20-yard field goal. A 13-play, 89-yard drive stalled at the 3 late in the second quarter, and Jaeger kicked another 20-yard field goal. It was 12-0 before Stan Humphries got San Diego on the board by completing 6 consecutive passes on a 73-yard drive that culminated in his 9-yard touchdown toss to Nate Lewis with 1:53 left in the game. But an onside kick attempt failed, and the Chargers did not get the ball back until only 14 seconds remained. The Raiders fin-

ished the game with substantial advantages in total yards (421-154) and time of possession (41:48-18:12). Jeff Hostetler passed for 270 yards and Greg Robinson rushed for 89. James Jett caught 7 passes for 138 yards.

L.A. Raiders	3	3	3	3	—	12
San Diego	0	0	0	7	—	7

Raid — FG Jaeger 20
Raid — FG Jaeger 20
Raid — FG Jaeger 37
Raid — FG Jaeger 27
SD — Lewis 9 pass from Humphries (Carney kick)

MIAMI 17, NEW ENGLAND 13—at Joe Robbie Stadium, attendance 59,982. Seventeen-year veteran Steve DeBerg rallied the Dolphins past the Patriots by throwing 2 touchdown passes in the fourth quarter. New England led 6-3 until DeBerg gave Miami the lead for the first time by teaming with running back Keith Byars on an 11-yard touchdown pass with 9:28 left in the game. He threw a 44-yard scoring strike to Irving Fryar for the clinching points with 2:49 to go. Drew Bledsoe's 40-yard touchdown pass to Ray Crittenden with 71 seconds left made it close, but the Dolphins recovered the ensuing onside kickoff. DeBerg, at 39 the oldest player in the NFL, started for the fifth different team in his career. He was acquired less than two weeks earlier as a free agent and finished with 16 completions in 27 attempts for 252 yards. Mark Higgs complemented DeBerg's passing by rushing for 108 yards. Bledsoe threw for 275 yards for the Patriots, who lost their fifth straight game.

New England	3	0	3	7	—	13
Miami	0	0	3	14	—	17

NE — FG Sisson 28
Mia — FG Stoyanovich 23
NE — FG Sisson 40
Mia — Byars 11 pass from DeBerg (Stoyanovich kick)
Mia — Fryar 44 pass from DeBerg (Stoyanovich kick)
NE — Crittenden 40 pass from Bledsoe (Sisson kick)

N.Y. GIANTS 7, PHILADELPHIA 3—at Veterans Stadium, attendance 62,928. Phil Simms's 26-yard touchdown pass to Mark Jackson on the first play of the fourth quarter lifted the Giants to their first victory at Veterans Stadium since 1987. New York, which pulled into a tie with Dallas for first place in the NFC East, managed only 292 total yards but struck quickly for the game's lone touchdown, moving 80 yards in only 3 plays. Simms's 50-yard completion to running back David Meggett was the big blow. The veteran quarterback completed 13 of 22 passes for 187 yards. Rodney Hampton rushed for 101 yards on 24 carries. Eagles quarterbacks Ken O'Brien and Bubby Brister combined to complete only 13 of 32 passes for 130 yards.

N.Y. Giants	0	0	0	7	—	7
Philadelphia	0	0	3	0	—	3

Phil — FG Bahr 35
Giants — M. Jackson 26 pass from Simms (Treadwell kick)

DENVER 37, PITTSBURGH 13—at Mile High Stadium, attendance 74,840. John Elway passed for 276 yards to lead the Broncos' rout of the Steelers. Pittsburgh entered the game with the league's leading defense, but Elway had 230 passing yards by halftime as Denver scored on four of its first five possessions to build a comfortable 20-0 lead. The key blow was a 95-yard touchdown drive after Steelers running back Leroy Thompson lost a fumble at the Broncos' 5-yard line with his team trailing only 3-0. Elway completed passes of 31 yards to Reggie Johnson and 27 yards to Leonard Russell on the 9-play march, which was capped by the first of Robert Delpino's two 1-yard touchdown runs. Elway added a 13-yard touchdown pass to Vance Johnson midway through the third quarter.

Pittsburgh	0	0	6	7	—	13
Denver	10	10	14	3	—	37

Den — FG Elam 48
Den — Delpino 1 run (Elam kick)
Den — Russell recovered fumble in end zone (Elam kick)
Den — FG Elam 27
Pitt — FG Anderson 37
Den — Delpino 1 run (Elam kick)
Den — V. Johnson 13 pass from Elway (Elam kick)
Pitt — FG Anderson 38

Den — FG Elam 28
Pitt — Thigpen 39 pass from Tomczak (Anderson kick)

L.A. RAMS 10, WASHINGTON 6—at Anaheim Stadium, attendance 45,546. T.J. Rubley came off the bench to lead the Rams to 10 fourth-quarter points and the victory over the Redskins. With Los Angeles trailing 6-0 and starting quarterback Jim Everett ineffective, Rubley entered the game on the last play of the third quarter. He took only four plays to get the Rams in the end zone, completing a 38-yard pass to tight end Pat Carter on third-and-11 and a 25-yard pass to rookie tight end Troy Drayton for the touchdown with 13:31 left in the game. Rubley's 29-yard pass to Willie Anderson set up Tony Zendejas's 23-yard field goal with 3:10 to go. Washington tried to rally, driving to Los Angeles's 27-yard line in the closing moments, but safety Michael Stewart preserved the win for the Rams by intercepting Rich Gannon's pass. Rubley completed 5 of 6 passes for 112 yards in his short stint. Gannon was 25 of 40 for the Redskins, but for only 172 yards.

Washington	3	0	3	0	—	6
L.A. Rams	0	0	0	10	—	10

Wash — FG Lohmiller 19
Wash — FG Lohmiller 34
Rams — Drayton 25 pass from Rubley (Zendejas kick)
Rams — FG Zendejas 23

SUNDAY NIGHT, NOVEMBER 21

TAMPA BAY 23, MINNESOTA 10—at Tampa Stadium, attendance 40,848. Vince Workman gained 123 yards from scrimmage and scored on a 1-yard run in the fourth quarter to lead the Buccaneers' upset of the Vikings. Minnesota led 7-6 at halftime, but 52 seconds into the third quarter, Tampa Bay cornerback Milton Mack intercepted Sean Salisbury's pass and returned it 27 yards for the touchdown that gave the Buccaneers the lead for good. Workman, who rushed for 58 yards and caught 7 passes for 65 yards, scored the clinching touchdown 4:40 into the fourth quarter after Craig Erickson completed a 27-yard pass to Horace Copeland. Erickson was 19 of 32 for 239 yards. Wide receiver Anthony Carter supplied most of Minnesota's offense by catching 9 passes for 104 yards.

Minnesota	0	7	3	0	—	10
Tampa Bay	3	3	10	7	—	23

TB — FG Husted 26
TB — FG Husted 54
Minn — A. Carter 2 pass from Salisbury (Reveiz kick)
TB — Mack 27 interception return (Husted kick)
TB — FG Husted 21
Minn — FG Reveiz 43
TB — Workman 1 run (Husted kick)

MONDAY, NOVEMBER 22

SAN FRANCISCO 42, NEW ORLEANS 7—at Candlestick Park, attendance 66,500. Steve Young threw 3 touchdown passes and ran for another as the 49ers blasted the Saints to take over first place in the NFC West. Safety Merton Hanks returned an interception 67 yards for a touchdown 6:54 into the game, and San Francisco turned the game into a rout by scoring touchdowns on five consecutive possessions in the second and third quarters. Two of Young's scoring tosses went to Jerry Rice, including 1 of 14 yards that gave the 49ers a 42-0 lead with 5:54 to go in the third quarter. Young completed 14 of 21 passes for 205 yards. Ricky Watters ran for 116 yards on 16 carries. San Francisco amassed 25 first downs and 455 total yards, while intercepting 4 passes and sending New Orleans to its fourth loss in five games.

New Orleans	0	0	0	7	—	7
San Francisco	7	21	14	0	—	42

SF — Hanks 67 interception return (Cofer kick)
SF — J. Taylor 26 pass from Young (Cofer kick)
SF — Rice 11 pass from Young (Cofer kick)
SF — Young 7 run (Cofer kick)
SF — Logan 5 run (Cofer kick)
SF — Rice 14 pass from Young (Cofer kick)
NO — F. Turner 6 pass from M. Buck (Andersen kick)

THIRTEENTH WEEK SUMMARIES

AMERICAN FOOTBALL CONFERENCE

Eastern Division	W	L	T	Pct.	Pts.	OP
Miami	9	2	0	.818	234	186
Buffalo	8	3	0	.727	202	152
N.Y. Jets	7	4	0	.636	240	170
Indianapolis	3	8	0	.273	154	264
New England	1	10	0	.091	126	223
Central Division						
Houston	7	4	0	.636	256	180
Pittsburgh	6	5	0	.545	231	196
Cleveland	5	6	0	.455	202	225
Cincinnati	1	10	0	.091	128	251
Western Division						
Kansas City	8	3	0	.727	204	170
Denver	7	4	0	.636	283	197
L.A. Raiders	6	5	0	.545	194	201
San Diego	5	6	0	.455	195	195
Seattle	5	6	0	.455	174	186

NATIONAL FOOTBALL CONFERENCE

Eastern Division	W	L	T	Pct.	Pts.	OP
N.Y. Giants	8	3	0	.727	206	138
Dallas	7	4	0	.636	234	169
Philadelphia	5	6	0	.455	175	212
Phoenix	3	8	0	.273	200	195
Washington	2	9	0	.182	165	256
Central Division						
Detroit	7	4	0	.636	210	176
Green Bay	7	4	0	.636	238	188
Chicago	6	5	0	.545	171	147
Minnesota	5	6	0	.455	179	217
Tampa Bay	3	8	0	.273	153	274
Western Division						
San Francisco	8	3	0	.727	332	196
New Orleans	7	4	0	.636	224	229
Atlanta	5	6	0	.455	228	250
L.A. Rams	3	8	0	.273	151	246

THURSDAY, NOVEMBER 25

CHICAGO 10, DETROIT 6—at Pontiac Silverdome, attendance 76,699. Jim Harbaugh's 42-yard pass to Terry Obee provided the game's only touchdown, but it was a key play by punter Chris Gardocki that helped preserve the Bears' win. Ahead 10-6 late in the third quarter, Chicago lined up to punt at its 35-yard line, and but the snap sailed over Gardocki's head and toward the end zone. Gardocki scooped up the loose ball and kicked it while off balance and being chased behind his own goal line. The result was only a 4-yard punt from the original line of scrimmage, but instead of a safety, touchdown, or field position deep inside Bears' territory, the Lions took over at the 39. Cornerback Jeremy Lincoln snuffed that threat with an interception, and Chicago went on to win its third in succession on the road. Defensive end Trace Armstrong set up all of the Bears' points by recovering 2 fumbles.

Chicago	0	10	0	0	—	10
Detroit	0	3	3	0	—	6

Chi — FG Butler 27
Det — FG Hanson 39
Chi — Obee 42 pass from Harbaugh (Butler kick)
Det — FG Hanson 27

MIAMI 16, DALLAS 14—at Texas Stadium, attendance 60,198. Pete Stoyanovich kicked a 19-yard field goal as time ran out to cap a wild finish and give the Dolphins an improbable victory. The Cowboys appeared to have won the game when Stoyanovich's 41-yard field goal try in the final seconds was blocked by defensive end Jimmie Jones. But defensive tackle Leon Lett muffed the ball while trying to recover it at the 7-yard line and Miami center Jeff Dellenbach fell on it at the 1 with three seconds remaining. Had no Dallas player touched the loose football, the Cowboys would have taken over possession. Instead, the Dolphins made the most of their reprieve by kicking the winning field goal on the next play. The game was played in freezing temperatures, and an unexpected snowstorm in Dallas covered the field with sleet and made footing treacherous and tackling difficult. Miami's Keith Byars equaled a club record for the longest touchdown run from scrimmage when he rambled 77 yards in the first quarter. Cowboys rookie Kevin Williams scored both of his team's touchdown. The victory, coupled with Buffalo's loss to Kansas City later in the weekend, gave the Dolphins sole possession of first in the AFC East.

Miami	7	0	3	6	—	16
Dallas	0	14	0	0	—	14

Mia — Byars 77 run (Stoyanovich kick)
Dall — K. Williams 4 pass from Aikman (Murray kick)
Dall — K. Williams 64 punt return (Murray kick)
Mia — FG Stoyanovich 20
Mia — FG Stoyanovich 31
Mia — FG Stoyanovich 19

SUNDAY, NOVEMBER 28

KANSAS CITY 23, BUFFALO 7—at Arrowhead Stadium, attendance 74,452. Joe Montana, starting for the first time in four weeks, threw 2 touchdown passes to lead the Chiefs over the Bills. After spotting Buffalo a 7-0 lead in the first quarter, Kansas City dominated the rest of the way. Montana, apparently recovered from a nagging hamstring injury, completed 18 of 32 passes for 208 yards, including touchdowns of 18 yards to running back Marcus Allen and 1 yard to tight end Keith Cash. Allen rushed for 74 yards on 22 carries, and caught 2 passes for 28 yards. The Chiefs' defense took care of the rest, forcing 4 turnovers and limiting the Bills to 43 rushing yards. Buffalo quarterback Jim Kelly completed 23 of 36 passes for 214 yards but was intercepted 3 times, while Thurman Thomas was held to a season-low 25 yards on 15 carries.

Buffalo	7	0	0	0	—	7
Kansas City	7	3	10	3	—	23

Buff — Davis 9 run (Christie kick)
KC — Allen 18 pass from Montana (Lowery kick)
KC — FG Lowery 30
KC — Cash 1 pass from Montana (Lowery kick)
KC — FG Lowery 22
KC — FG Lowery 34

ATLANTA 17, CLEVELAND 14—at Georgia Dome, attendance 54,510. Bobby Hebert threw 2 touchdown passes in the first half as the Falcons built a 17-point lead, then hung on to win. The victory was the fifth in six games for Atlanta, which started the season 0-5. The Browns, who lost their fourth in a row, managed only 42 total yards while falling behind 17-0 at halftime. But Cleveland rallied in the second half, getting on the scoreboard when Todd Philcox threw a 35-yard touchdown pass to Mark Carrier on the final play of the third quarter. Philcox's 3-yard touchdown run on a quarterback draw with 3:31 left in the game pulled his team within 3 points, but the next time the Browns got the ball back, it was on their 34-yard line with no timeouts and just 53 seconds remaining. Falcons defensive end Chuck Smith sacked Philcox on the first play to end Cleveland's hopes. Hebert, who completed 13 of 18 passes for 144 yards in the first half, finished 21 of 29 for 214 yards. Philcox was 14 of 26 for 206 yards.

Cleveland	0	0	7	7	—	14
Atlanta	10	7	0	0	—	17

Atl — FG Johnson 51
Atl — Rison 14 pass from Hebert (Johnson kick)
Atl — Pritchard 8 pass from Hebert (Johnson kick)
Cle — Carrier 35 pass from Philcox (Stover kick)
Cle — Philcox 3 run (Stover kick)

DENVER 17, SEATTLE 9—at Kingdome, attendance 57,812. The Broncos kept pace with first-place Kansas City in the AFC West by beating the Seahawks in Seattle for the first time since 1989. Denver quarterback John Elway made the key play of the game, ducking underneath blitzing linebacker David Brandon and completing a 50-yard touchdown pass to Shannon Sharpe on the first play of the second quarter. That put the Broncos ahead 7-0 and they never trailed. The Seahawks managed to pull within 1 point in the fourth quarter when Rick Mirer completed a 10-yard touchdown pass to Kelvin Martin with 7:55 remaining. But Denver countered with an 80-yard drive that culminated in Rod Bernstine's clinching 2-yard touchdown run with 4:06 left. The victory was not without cost for the Broncos, however, who lost wide receiver Vance Johnson for the remainder of the season when he fractured his ankle. The defense-oriented game featured 20 punts, including a club-record 12 by Seattle's Rick Tuten.

Denver	0	7	3	7	—	17
Seattle	0	0	2	7	—	9

Den — Sharpe 50 pass from Elway (Elam kick)
Sea — Safety, Stephens tackled Elway in end zone
Den — FG Elam 25
Sea — Martin 10 pass from Mirer (Kasay kick)
Den — Bernstine 2 run (Elam kick)

CINCINNATI 16, L.A. RAIDERS 10—at Riverfront Stadium, attendance 43,272. Eric Ball ran 1 yard for a touchdown and rookie Doug Pelfrey kicked 3 field goals as the Bengals stunned the Raiders for their first victory after opening the season with 10 consecutive losses. The defeat was costly for the 6-5 Raiders, who fell two games behind first-place Kansas City in the AFC West and into a battle for a wild-card playoff berth. The game began amid snow flurries and a swirling wind, and the icy conditions contributed to Los Angeles's 4 missed field goals, a lost fumble, and an interception. Quarterback Jeff Hostetler completed only 12 of 32 passes for 220 yards, but was victimized by numerous dropped balls. Cincinnati quarterback David Klingler, meanwhile, was efficient and error-free, completing 14 of 20 attempts for 157 yards. The Bengals also ran for 131 yards and did not commit a turnover.

L.A. Raiders	0	0	0	10	—	10
Cincinnati	3	7	3	3	—	16

Cin — FG Pelfrey 45
Cin — Ball 1 run (Pelfrey kick)
Cin — FG Pelfrey 34
Raid — Hostetler 4 run (Jaeger kick)
Cin — FG Pelfrey 44
Raid — FG Jaeger 34

NEW ORLEANS 17, MINNESOTA 14—at Metrodome, attendance 53,030. Saints rookie Tyrone Hughes tied the game by returning a kickoff 99 yards for a touchdown on the last play of the third quarter and Morten Andersen won it with a 24-yard field goal five minutes into the fourth quarter. New Orleans marched 76 yards to a touchdown following the game's opening kickoff, and the Vikings countered with an 80-yard drive to tie the score. It remained 7-7 until Minnesota quarterback Sean Salisbury threw his second touchdown pass of the game, a 7-yard toss to Cris Carter with six seconds left in the third quarter. But Hughes, a reserve cornerback, tied it again by becoming the first New Orleans player since 1989 to return a kickoff for a touchdown. The Saints then drove 73 yards to Andersen's winning kick the next time they had the ball. The key play of the drive was quarterback Wade Wilson's 28-yard run. Wilson, who also scrambled 13 yards for a first down on New Orleans's opening drive, was playing in the Metrodome for the first time since being released by the Vikings in 1992. Minnesota drove to an apparent game-tying 41-yard field goal by Fuad Reveiz in the final minute, but the Vikings' Fred Strickland was cited for holding. Reveiz's subsequent 51-yard try was blocked by Jim Wilks.

New Orleans	7	0	7	3	—	17
Minnesota	7	0	7	0	—	14

NO — McAfee 3 run (Andersen kick)
Minn — Jordan 14 pass from Salisbury(Reveiz kick)
Minn — C. Carter 7 pass from Salisbury (Reveiz kick)
NO — Hughes 99 kickoff return (Andersen kick)
NO — FG Andersen 24

N.Y. JETS 6, NEW ENGLAND 0—at Foxboro Stadium, attendance 42,810. Cary Blanchard kicked a pair of field goals, and the Jets won their fifth in a row by recording their first shutout in 11 years. Scoring was kept low by torrential rains and winds that gusted up to 68 miles per hour. Still, the Patriots had chances to win, driving inside New York's 20-yard line twice in the fourth quarter. But Scott Sisson's 28-yard field goal attempt with 5:25 remaining was blocked, and wide receiver Michael Timpson fumbled at the 7 when hit by free safety Lonnie Young after catching a pass with 1:28 to play. Strong safety Brian Washington recovered to secure the victory for the Jets. Hard-luck New England fell to 1-10 but lost for the seventh time by 6 points or less. Patriots running back Leonard Russell accounted for the majority of his team's 289 total yards by rushing 27 times for 147 yards.

N.Y. Jets	3	3	0	0	—	6
New England	0	0	0	0	—	0

Jets — FG Blanchard 33
Jets — FG Blanchard 23

PHILADELPHIA 17, WASHINGTON 14—at RFK Stadium, attendance 46,663. The Eagles snapped their six-game losing streak when running back James Joseph caught a 2-yard touchdown pass from Bubby Brister with 46 seconds remaining. The winning play negated a fourth-quarter rally by the Redskins. Washington entered the fourth period trailing 10-0, but scored 2 touchdowns in a span of 5:36 to take a 14-10 lead. Tim McGee sparked the comeback by catching a 17-yard touchdown pass from

Rich Gannon 3:40 into the final quarter, and then turning a short pass into a 54-yard gain on Washington's next possession, a 77-yard march that ended with Gannon's 6-yard touchdown pass to Art Monk with 5:44 to go. But Philadelphia drove 75 yards in 12 plays to the winning score, completing its first season sweep of the Redskins in 13 years.

| Philadelphia | 3 | 7 | 0 | 7 | — | 17 |
| Washington | 0 | 0 | 0 | 14 | — | 14 |

Phil — FG Bahr 22
Phil — Hebron 1 run (Bahr kick)
Wash — McGee 17 pass from Gannon (Lohmiller kick)
Wash — Monk 6 pass from Gannon (Lohmiller kick)
Phil — Joseph 2 pass from Brister (Bahr kick)

N.Y. GIANTS 19, PHOENIX 17—at Giants Stadium, attendance 59,979. Brad Daluiso's 54-yard field goal with 32 seconds remaining lifted the Giants to the victory and into first place in the NFC's Eastern Division. It was another heartbreaking defeat for the Cardinals, who got 2 touchdown passes from Steve Beuerlein and limited New York's top-ranked rushing offense to 46 yards, but could not prevent their tenth consecutive loss at Giants Stadium. Beuerlein's second touchdown pass, a 17-yard toss to Ricky Proehl late in the third quarter, gave Phoenix a 17-13 lead. But David Treadwell, New York's primary kicker, booted a 22-yard field-goal 2:04 into the fourth quarter to trim the Giants' deficit to 17-16. Later in the quarter, New York drove 30 yards, converting a second-and-29 situation along the way. On fourth-and-10 from the Cardinals' 37-yard line, New York elected to go with Daluiso, whose strong leg earned him a spot on the roster as a kickoff and long field-goal specialist.

| Phoenix | 10 | 0 | 7 | 0 | — | 17 |
| N.Y. Giants | 3 | 3 | 7 | 6 | — | 19 |

Phx — FG G. Davis 47
Phx — Rolle 1 pass from Beuerlein (G. Davis kick)
Giants — FG Treadwell 22
Giants — FG Treadwell 37
Giants — McCaffrey 20 pass from Simms (Treadwell kick)
Phx — Proehl 17 pass from Beuerlein (G. Davis kick)
Giants — FG Treadwell 22
Giants — FG Daluiso 54

SAN FRANCISCO 35, L.A. RAMS 10—at Anaheim Stadium, attendance 62,143. Steve Young passed for a career-high 462 yards and 4 touchdowns to lead the 49ers to their fifth consecutive victory. Young completed 26 of 32 passes, most of them to wide receivers Jerry Rice (8 catches for 166 yards and 2 touchdowns) and John Taylor (6 for 150 yards and 1 touchdown). Running back Ricky Watters scored 2 touchdowns, 1 on a 48-yard catch 1:50 before halftime to give San Francisco a 21-3 advantage at intermission. The 49ers then put the game out of reach when Young threw a 76-yard touchdown pass to Taylor on the second play of the third quarter. San Francisco amassed 539 total yards and averaged 8.2 yards per play while beating the Rams in Anaheim Stadium for the seventh consecutive time and twelfth time in the last 13 years. Rice upped his league-leading total to 1,048 receiving yards, and broke the NFL record for consecutive 1,000-yard seasons with eight. Rams tackle Jackie Slater played in his 246th career game, the most ever by an offensive lineman. He helped lead the way for rookie Jerome Bettis, who gained a career-high 133 yards on 18 carries.

| San Francisco | 7 | 14 | 7 | 7 | — | 35 |
| L.A. Rams | 3 | 0 | 0 | 7 | — | 10 |

SF — Watters 6 run (Cofer kick)
Rams — FG Zendejas 25
SF — Rice 39 pass from Young (Cofer kick)
SF — Watters 48 pass from Young (Cofer kick)
SF — Taylor 76 pass from Young (Cofer kick)
SF — Rice 7 pass from Young (Cofer kick)
Rams — Ellard 14 pass from Rubley (Zendejas kick)

GREEN BAY 13, TAMPA BAY 10—at Lambeau Field, attendance 56,995. Brett Favre's 2-yard touchdown pass to Sterling Sharpe with 1:16 remaining lifted the Packers to the victory. Green Bay won for the sixth time in the last seven games and moved into a tie for first place in the NFC Central Division. The Buccaneers appeared on the verge of an upset when quarterback Craig Erickson and wide receiver Courtney Hawkins teamed on a 9-yard touchdown pass with 7:33 to go, giving Tampa Bay a 10-6 advantage.

But the Packers, who had managed fewer than 200 total yards and only a pair of field goals to that point, marched 75 yards in 15 plays to the winning score. Sharpe caught 3 passes on the drive, and Mark Clayton converted a second-and-20 with a 28-yard reception.

| Tampa Bay | 0 | 0 | 3 | 7 | — | 10 |
| Green Bay | 0 | 3 | 3 | 7 | — | 13 |

GB — FG Jacke 24
TB — FG Husted 30
GB — FG Jacke 36
TB — Hawkins 9 pass from Erickson (Husted kick)
GB — Sharpe 2 pass from Favre (Jacke kick)

SUNDAY NIGHT, NOVEMBER 28

HOUSTON 23, PITTSBURGH 3—at Astrodome, attendance 61,238. Houston won its sixth in a row and moved into sole possession of first place in the AFC Central by beating the division-rival Steelers. The Oilers began the season 1-4 but the victory over Pittsburgh gave them their longest winning streak in 31 years. Warren Moon completed 21 of 34 passes for 295 yards and a touchdown. After Pittsburgh's Gary Anderson tied the game at 3-3 on a 42-yard field goal with 2:23 remaining in the first half, Houston marched 79 yards in seven plays to take the lead for good. Moon completed passes of 25, 24, and 18 yards to Ernest Givins on the 93-second drive, which was capped by Gary Brown's 3-yard touchdown run 50 seconds before intermission. Moon's 66-yard touchdown pass to Haywood Jeffires came only five plays into the second half and helped break the game open. Jeffires finished with 7 catches for 139 yards. Givins had 5 receptions to raise his career total to 484, surpassing Drew Hill (480) for the most in Oilers' history.

| Pittsburgh | 0 | 3 | 0 | 0 | — | 3 |
| Houston | 0 | 10 | 10 | 3 | — | 23 |

Hou — FG Del Greco 43
Pitt — FG Anderson 42
Hou — Brown 3 run (Del Greco kick)
Hou — Jeffires 66 pass from Moon (Del Greco kick)
Hou — FG Del Greco 21
Hou — FG Del Greco 28

MONDAY, NOVEMBER 29

SAN DIEGO 31, INDIANAPOLIS 0—at Hoosier Dome, attendance 54,110. Stan Humphries passed for 216 yards and 2 touchdowns to lead a balanced attack as the Chargers blanked the Colts. Humphries, who backed up John Friesz the previous six weeks because of a shoulder injury suffered in the preseason, regained his starting job and completed passes to eight different receivers, finishing with 16 completions in 25 attempts. He sparked San Diego's sluggish offense by throwing second-quarter touchdown passes to Shawn Jefferson and Nate Lewis. The Chargers' 14 points before intermission was the most they had scored in the first half of any game this year. San Diego's rushing attack also was effective, amassing 247 yards. Marion Butts ran for 80 yards, Natrone Means had 74, and Eric Bieniemy 64. Butts and Bieniemy put the game out of reach with short fourth-quarter touchdown runs. The Chargers outgained the Colts 474-262.

| San Diego | 0 | 14 | 3 | 14 | — | 31 |
| Indianapolis | 0 | 0 | 0 | 0 | — | 0 |

SD — Jefferson 39 pass from Humphries (Carney kick)
SD — Lewis 8 pass from Humphries (Carney kick)
SD — FG Carney 36
SD — Butts 1 run (Carney kick)
SD — Bieniemy 4 run (Carney kick)

FOURTEENTH WEEK SUMMARIES
AMERICAN FOOTBALL CONFERENCE

Eastern Division	W	L	T	Pct.	Pts.	OP
Miami	9	3	0	.750	248	205
Buffalo	8	4	0	.667	226	177
N.Y. Jets	7	5	0	.583	246	179
Indianapolis	4	8	0	.333	163	270
New England	1	11	0	.083	140	240
Central Division						
Houston	8	4	0	.667	289	197
Pittsburgh	7	5	0	.583	248	210
Cleveland	6	6	0	.500	219	238
Cincinnati	1	11	0	.083	136	272
Western Division						
Kansas City	9	3	0	.750	235	186
Denver	7	5	0	.583	293	210
L.A. Raiders	7	5	0	.583	219	225
San Diego	6	6	0	.500	208	205
Seattle	5	7	0	.417	190	217

NATIONAL FOOTBALL CONFERENCE

Eastern Division	W	L	T	Pct.	Pts.	OP
N.Y. Giants	9	3	0	.750	225	152
Dallas	8	4	0	.667	257	186
Philadelphia	5	7	0	.417	192	235
Phoenix	4	8	0	.333	238	205
Washington	3	9	0	.250	188	273
Central Division						
Chicago	7	5	0	.583	201	164
Detroit	7	5	0	.583	210	189
Green Bay	7	5	0	.583	255	218
Minnesota	6	6	0	.500	192	217
Tampa Bay	3	9	0	.250	170	297
Western Division						
San Francisco	9	3	0	.750	353	204
New Orleans	7	5	0	.583	237	246
Atlanta	5	7	0	.417	245	283
L.A. Rams	3	9	0	.250	161	284

SUNDAY, DECEMBER 5

HOUSTON 33, ATLANTA 17—at Astrodome, attendance 58,186. Warren Moon threw for 342 yards and 1 touchdown, and the Oilers forced 7 turnovers while rallying to their seventh consecutive victory. The Falcons took a 14-6 advantage when Bobby Hebert threw touchdown passes on their last possession of the first half and first possession of the second. But it took Houston only four plays to drive 80 yards and close within 14-13 on Moon's 25-yard touchdown pass to Webster Slaughter, and San Destructed after that. First, Oilers defensive end William Fuller sacked Hebert, forcing a fumble that tackle Ray Childress recovered in the end zone for the go-ahead touchdown 25 seconds before the end of the third quarter. Moments later, cornerback Steve Jackson intercepted Hebert's pass and returned it 16 yards to the Falcons' 9-yard line, setting up Al Del Greco's field goal to put Houston ahead 23-14 2:44 into the fourth quarter. Three plays after that, cornerback Cris Dishman intercepted a pass and returned it 20 yards to Atlanta's 22. It took the Oilers six plays to score from there, with Gary Brown's 1-yard touchdown run with 9:09 left putting the game out of reach. Moon finished with 24 completions in 42 attempts, while Slaughter caught 8 passes for 108 yards. Hebert completed 30 of 52 passes for 317 yards, but the Falcons could not overcome his 6 interceptions. Jackson had 2 of the thefts for Houston.

| Atlanta | 0 | 7 | 7 | 3 | — | 17 |
| Houston | 3 | 3 | 14 | 13 | — | 33 |

Hou — FG Del Greco 50
Hou — FG Del Greco 43
Atl — Pritchard 9 pass from Hebert (Johnson kick)
Atl — Rison 6 pass from Hebert (Johnson kick)
Hou — Slaughter 25 pass from Moon (Del Greco kick)
Hou — Childress recovered fumble in end zone (Del Greco kick)
Hou — FG Del Greco 21
Hou — G. Brown 1 run (Del Greco kick)
Atl — FG Johnson 30
Hou — FG Del Greco 36

SAN DIEGO 13, DENVER 10—at San Diego Jack Murphy Stadium, attendance 60,233. John Carney kicked a 34-yard field goal with three seconds left and the Chargers overcame a 10-point halftime deficit to beat the Broncos and keep their playoff hopes alive. Denver forged a 10-0 lead at intermission on a 30-yard field goal by Jason Elam and a 1-yard touchdown pass from holder Tommy Maddox to linebacker David Wyman on a fake field goal attempt. It was the first touchdown of the seven-year veteran's NFL career. But San Diego rallied to tie the game on Carney's 27-yard field goal and Natrone Means's 1-yard touchdown run with 11:32 remaining in the game. The Broncos countered with a 56-yard drive that took more than six minutes, but Jason Elam missed a 42-yard field-goal attempt. The Chargers started their winning drive from their 5-yard line with 2:57 to go. Stan Humphries completed 7 of 10 passes for 72 yards on the 12-play, 79-yard march. He was 22 of 39 for 229 yards in all. Denver quarterback John Elway completed only 14 of 32 passes for 171 yards and failed to throw a touchdown pass for the first time in 1993.

Denver	3	7	0	0	—	10
San Diego	0	0	3	10	—	13

Den — FG Elam 30
Den — Wyman 1 pass from Maddox (Elam kick)
SD — FG Carney 27
SD — Means 1 run (Carney kick)
SD — FG Carney 34

CHICAGO 30, GREEN BAY 17—at Soldier Field, attendance 62,236. Linebacker Dante Jones returned a fumble for 1 touchdown and intercepted a pass that resulted in another as the Bears climbed into a three-way tie for first place in the NFC Central Division by winning their fourth consecutive game. Chicago was outgained 466-210, and the Bears' offense failed to produce a touchdown. But the defense, led by Jones, put the ball in the end zone three times. The first time came 7:04 into the game, when Jones intercepted Brett Favre's pass and returned it 6 yards before lateraling to cornerback Jeremy Lincoln, who raced 80 yards for a touchdown. Early in the second half, Jones picked up a fumble by Favre and returned it 32 yards for a touchdown and a 17-7 lead. The Packers quickly rallied to tie on Chris Jacke's 26-yard field goal and Favre's 22-yard touchdown pass to Mark Clayton after Keo Coleman recovered Curtis Conway's fumble on the ensuing kickoff. The Bears' offense didn't get on the field in the second half until less than five minutes remained in the third quarter, but they marched to Kevin Butler's 24-yard field goal on that initial possession to regain the lead at 20-17. After Butler's 29-yard field goal made it 23-17 with 5:19 remaining, Chicago's defense came up with two more big plays, stopping Green Bay on fourth-and-1 from the the Bears' 26, and then forcing an interception that Mark Carrier returned 34 yards for the clinching touchdown with 1:41 to play. The Packers' Favre completed 36 of 54 passes for 402 yards and 2 touchdowns, but also threw 3 interceptions. Sterling Sharpe caught 10 passes for 114 yards and 1 touchdown.

Green Bay	7	0	10	0	—	17
Chicago	7	3	10	10	—	30

Chi — Lincoln 80 interception return on lateral from D. Jones (Butler kick)
GB — Sharpe 18 pass from Favre (Jacke kick)
Chi — FG Butler 29
Chi — D. Jones 32 fumble return (Butler kick)
GB — FG Jacke 26
GB — Clayton 22 pass from Favre (Jacke kick)
Chi — FG Butler 24
Chi — FG Butler 29
Chi — Carrier 34 interception return (Butler kick)

INDIANAPOLIS 9, N.Y. JETS 6—at Giants Stadium, attendance 45,799. Dean Biasucci kicked 3 field goals, including the game-winner from 38 yards with one second left, and the Colts snapped the Jets' five-game winning streak. Indianapolis was 1 of 13 on third-down conversions and managed only 7 first downs and 169 total yards. But following interceptions, the Colts had to drive a total of only 1 yard to their 2 fourth-quarter field goals. The first theft came late in the third period with Indianapolis trailing 6-3, when defensive back Ray Buchanan picked off Boomer Esiason's pass and returned it 28 yards to the Jets' 6-yard line. Three plays netted only 1 yard, but Biasucci kicked a 24-yard field goal six seconds into the fourth quarter to tie the score. Late in the game, the Colts drove to New York's 31-yard line, only to be stopped on downs. But cornerback Eugene Daniel intercepted Esiason on the next play, and returned the ball 17 yards to the Jets' 36 with 61 seconds remaining. A personal foul penalty moved the ball to the 21, and from there Biasucci converted the kick that gave Indianapolis its third 9-6 victory of the season and its fifth consecutive win over the Jets in New York. With his 3 field goals, Biasucci moved past Pro Football Hall of Fame running back Lenny Moore and into first place on the Colts' all-time scoring list.

Indianapolis	0	3	0	6	—	9
N.Y. Jets	0	3	3	0	—	6

Jets — FG Blanchard 28
Ind — FG Biasucci 42
Jets — FG Blanchard 19
Ind — FG Biasucci 24
Ind — FG Biasucci 38

KANSAS CITY 31, SEATTLE 16—at Kingdome, attendance 58,551. Marcus Allen ran for 3 touchdowns and linebacker Derrick Thomas returned a fumble for a score to help the Chiefs open up a two-game lead in the AFC West. Kansas City led just 10-3 and the Seahawks were driving early in the second quarter when Chiefs defensive end Darren Mickell sacked quarterback Rick Mirer, forcing a fumble. Thomas scooped up the loose ball and raced 86 yards for a touchdown. Kansas City, which led 17-6 at halftime, broke open the game when Allen scored 2 third-quarter touchdowns following turnovers. First, cornerback Albert Lewis intercepted Rick Mirer's pass and returned it 24 yards to Seattle's 13-yard line. Kimble Anders ran 12 yards to the 1, and Allen scored on the next play to make it 24-6 3:07 into the second half. On the Seahawks' next possession, Lewis recovered Kelvin Martin's fumble at Seattle's 47, and two plays later Allen ran 30 yards for the touchdown that put the game out of reach. The Chiefs won for the sixth time in the seven games that Joe Montana had started at quarterback. Montana completed 20 of 30 passes for 239 yards. Rick Mirer was 18 of 30 for 287 yards for the Seahawks, who produced a season-high 365 total yards. Brian Blades caught 7 passes for 134 yards.

Kansas City	10	7	14	0	—	31
Seattle	3	3	7	3	—	16

Sea — FG Kasay 22
KC — Allen 1 run (Lowery kick)
KC — FG Lowery 47
KC — Thomas 86 fumble return (Lowery kick)
Sea — FG Kasay 26
KC — Allen 1 run (Lowery kick)
KC — Allen 30 run (Lowery kick)
Sea — Warren 1 run (Kasay kick)
Sea — FG Kasay 37

L.A. RAIDERS 25, BUFFALO 24—at Rich Stadium, attendance 79,478. Jeff Hostetler passed for 289 yards, including the game-winning touchdown on a 29-yard pass to Tim Brown with 4:58 remaining, as the Raiders bounced back from a dismal loss to the Bengals to beat the Bills. Buffalo led 24-16 until Los Angeles scored 10 points in the final nine minutes. First, Raiders cornerback Terry McDaniel intercepted a Jim Kelly pass and returned it 35 yards to Buffalo's 12-yard line. Though Los Angeles moved backwards to the 30, Jeff Jaeger kicked a 47-yard field goal to trim the Raiders' deficit to 24-19 with 8:47 to go. Then, after a punt, the Raiders took over at their 43. On successive plays, Hostetler completed passes of 18 yards to Nick Bell and 10 yards to James Jett before teaming with Brown on the winning touchdown pass. Brown caught 10 passes for 183 yards and helped the Raiders, who had been struggling offensively, amass 399 total yards. Greg Robinson (56 yards), Bell (44), and Hostetler (39, including an 11-yard touchdown) combined to rush for 138 yards. Buffalo wide receiver Don Beebe caught 4 passes for 115 yards, including a 65-yard touchdown in the final minute of the first half. Thomas ran for 74 yards and became the eighth player in NFL history to rush for more than 1,000 yards in five consecutive seasons.

L.A. Raiders	3	7	6	9	—	25
Buffalo	0	14	3	7	—	24

Raid — FG Jaeger 37
Buff — Thomas 3 run (Christie kick)
Raid — Hostetler 11 run (Jaeger kick)
Buff — Beebe 65 pass from Kelly (Christie kick)
Raid — FG Jaeger 34
Buff — FG Christie 35
Raid — FG Jaeger 26
Buff — Thomas 1 run (Christie kick)
Raid — FG Jaeger 47
Raid — Brown 29 pass from Hostetler (kick blocked)

PHOENIX 38, L.A. RAMS 10—at Sun Devil Stadium, attendance 33,964. Ron Moore rushed for 126 yards and a club-record 4 touchdowns on 29 carries to power the Cardinals past the Rams. Phoenix started the rout early, taking the opening kickoff and marching 78 yards to a touchdown, Moore's 1-yard run 5:26 into the game. It was 14-3 at halftime, and the rookie running back broke open the game with 19- and 1-yard touchdown runs in the third quarter. His final touchdown, another 1-yard run in the fourth quarter, made it 38-3. Steve Beuerlein complemented Moore's running by completing 14 of 25 passes for 250 yards and 1 touchdown, a 22-yarder to Gary Clark in the second quarter. Clark caught 8 passes for 159 yards. Rams rookie Jerome Bettis rushed for 115 yards on 16 carries.

L.A. Rams	3	0	0	7	—	10
Phoenix	7	7	14	10	—	38

Phx — Moore 1 run (G. Davis kick)
Rams — FG Zendejas 22
Phx — Clark 22 pass from Beuerlein (G. Davis kick)
Phx — Moore 19 run (G. Davis kick)
Phx — Moore 1 run (G. Davis kick)
Phx — FG G. Davis 27
Phx — Moore 1 run (G. Davis kick)
Rams — Drayton 4 pass from Everett (Zendejas kick)

MINNESOTA 13, DETROIT 0—at Pontiac Silverdome, attendance 63,216. Quarterback Jim McMahon returned to the Vikings' lineup, but it was Minnesota's defense that made the difference in this one, creating a logjam atop the NFC Central. The Lions' loss, coupled with the Bears' victory over the Packers, left Detroit, Chicago, and Green Bay tied for first place, with the Vikings just one game behind. Against the Lions, Minnesota relied on its defense, which limited Detroit to 219 total yards and intercepted 5 passes. Safety Lamar McGriggs returned 1 of them 63 yards for the clinching touchdown with 2:19 left in the game. Linebacker Jack Del Rio, who entered the 1993 season with 5 interceptions in eight years in the league, picked off 3. Lions quarterback Rodney Peete completed 18 of 30 passes, but for only 138 yards. He suffered 4 of the interceptions and was lifted in favor of Andre Ware after McGriggs' touchdown. McMahon, out more than a month with a dislocated shoulder, completed just 15 of 32 passes for 145 yards, but set up Minnesota's 2 first-half field goals with completions of 26 yards to Anthony Carter and 31 yards to Roger Craig.

Minnesota	3	3	0	7	—	13
Detroit	0	0	0	0	—	0

Minn — FG Reveiz 37
Minn — FG Reveiz 29
Minn — McGriggs 63 interception return (Reveiz kick)

PITTSBURGH 17, NEW ENGLAND 14—at Three Rivers Stadium, attendance 51,358. Linebacker Levon Kirkland stopped quarterback Drew Bledsoe on fourth-and-goal from inside the 1-yard line in the closing seconds to preserve the Steelers' victory. Bledsoe, who completed 18 of 48 passes for 296 yards, was intercepted 5 times in the second half to thwart drives inside Pittsburgh territory, and also lost a fumble late in the first half that led to the Steelers' go-ahead touchdown. But in the closing 3:47, he drove the Patriots from their 5-yard line to within a foot of the goal line on a lengthy, 16-play drive. But with 17 seconds remaining, his sneak attempt was stopped by Kirkland inches short of the end zone. Bledsoe's 3-yard touchdown pass to tight end Ben Coates and Leonard Russell's 3-yard run staked New England to a 14-0 first-quarter lead. But Pittsburgh countered Russell's touchdown with an 80-yard march capped by Neil O'Donnell's 5-yard touchdown pass to Merril Hoge 3:13 into the second quarter. Gary Anderson's 35-yard field goal and O'Donnell's 1-yard touchdown pass to Hoge 10 seconds before halftime completed the scoring. The latter touchdown came seven plays after defensive lineman Jeff Zgonina recovered Bledsoe's fumble at the Patriots' 18.

New England	14	0	0	0	—	14
Pittsburgh	0	17	0	0	—	17

NE — Coates 3 pass from Bledsoe (Sisson kick)
NE — Russell 3 run (Sisson kick)
Pitt — Hoge 5 pass from O'Donnell (Anderson kick)
Pitt — FG Anderson 35
Pitt — Hoge 1 pass from O'Donnell (Anderson kick)

CLEVELAND 17, NEW ORLEANS 13—at Municipal Stadium, attendance 60,388. The Browns recorded a club-record 9 sacks and shut down the Saints' offense in the second half to snap a four-game losing streak. Todd Philcox started the game at quarterback for Cleveland, but was replaced in the second quarter by Vinny Testaverde, who played for the first time since separating his shoulder against the Steelers six weeks earlier. Each threw a touchdown pass to Michael Jackson, with Testaverde's 4-yard toss breaking a 10-10 tie late in the third quarter and providing the winning points. The Browns relied primarily on their defense, however, which held New Orleans to only 22 yards in the second half, including minus-6 in the fourth quarter. Saints quarterback Wade Wilson completed 15 of 29 passes for 119 yards, but the 9 sacks dropped New Orleans's net-passing total to just 48 yards. The Saints could muster only 79 yards on the ground. Defensive ends Anthony Pleasant and Rob Burnett each had 2 sacks for Cleveland.

New Orleans	7	0	3	3	—	13
Cleveland	10	0	7	0	—	17

Cle — Jackson 8 pass from Philcox (Stover kick)
NO — Martin 10 pass from Wilson (Andersen kick)
Cle — FG Stover 43
NO — FG Andersen 41
Cle — Jackson 4 pass from Testaverde (Stover kick)
NO — FG Andersen 27

N.Y. GIANTS 19, MIAMI 14—at Joe Robbie Stadium, attendance 72,161. Phil Simms passed for 257 yards to lead the Giants to the victory in a battle of division leaders. Simms completed 17 of 24 passes and directed an 86-yard touchdown march shortly before halftime that put New York ahead for good. He accounted for all but 3 of the yards on the drive by completing 5 of 6 passes, including a 20-yard touchdown to tight end Howard Cross to break a 7-7 tie 1:12 before intermission. David Treadwell's 42-yard field goal and a safety gave the Giants a 12-point cushion that rendered meaningless Steve DeBerg's 25-yard touchdown pass to Tony Martin with 61 seconds left in the game. The Dolphins amassed 408 total yards but suffered 3 sacks, 2 interceptions, a lost fumble, and a blocked field goal. DeBerg completed 26 of 41 passes for 365 yards. New York's victory was the first during the regular season by an NFC team at Joe Robbie Stadium, which opened in 1987.

N.Y. Giants	7	7	3	2	—	19
Miami	7	0	0	7	—	14

Giants— Hampton 14 run (Treadwell kick)
Mia — Byars 6 run (Stoyanovich kick)
Giants— H. Cross 20 pass from Simms (Treadwell kick)
Giants— FG Treadwell 42
Giants— Safety, Hamilton sacked DeBerg in end zone
Mia — Martin 25 pass from DeBerg (Stoyanovich kick)

WASHINGTON 23, TAMPA BAY 17—at Tampa Stadium, attendance 49,035. Reggie Brooks rushed for 128 yards, including a 78-yard touchdown, to spark the Redskins to the victory. Washington led 10-0 at halftime, then Brooks helped break open the game with his long scoring run on the first play of the second half. The Buccaneers tried to rally, scoring 10 points within an 88-second span of the third quarter to pull within 17-10, but Redskins linebacker Kurt Gouveia intercepted Craig Erickson's pass and returned it 59 yards for the clinching touchdown with 1:43 left in the third quarter. Washington cornerback Darrell Green had 2 interceptions, 1 of which set up Chip Lohmiller's 51-yard field goal as time expired in the first half.

Washington	7	3	13	0	—	23
Tampa Bay	0	0	10	7	—	17

Wash — Gannon 1 run (Lohmiller kick)
Wash — FG Lohmiller 51
Wash — Brooks 78 run (Lohmiller kick)
TB — FG Husted 31
TB — Seals interception in end zone (Husted kick)
Wash — Gouveia 59 interception return (kick failed)
TB — Hawkins 4 pass from Erickson (Husted kick)

SUNDAY NIGHT, DECEMBER 5

SAN FRANCISCO 21, CINCINNATI 8—at Candlestick Park, attendance 60,039. Ricky Watters ran for 3 touchdowns and the 49ers won their sixth in a row despite struggling against the 1-11 Bengals. Cincinnati entered the game ranked last in the league in total offense, while San Francisco ranked first. But the Bengals outgained the 49ers 339-284 and maintained possession for more than 36 of the game's 60 minutes. San Francisco struck quickly, driving 55 yards following the opening kickoff to a touchdown 2:01 into the game. Steve Young completed a 43-yard pass to Jerry Rice on the first play, and Watters eventually scored from 2 yards out. Cincinnati rallied to take an 8-7 lead at halftime on a safety and 2 field goals by Doug Pelfrey. But the key play of the game came early in the fourth quarter, when the Bengals faked a punt near midfield. Punter Lee Johnson's pass was batted down by Amp Lee, and the 49ers took over possession at Cincinnati's 44-yard line. Seven plays later, Watters ran 2 yards for the touchdown that put San Francisco ahead for good. After holding the Bengals without a first down and forcing a punt, the 49ers then marched 56 yards in 11 plays to an insurance touchdown, Watters's 4-yard run on the first play of the fourth quarter.

Cincinnati	2	6	0	0	—	8
San Francisco	7	0	7	7	—	21

SF — Watters 2 run (Cofer kick)
Cin — Safety, A. Williams tackled Young in end zone
Cin — FG Pelfrey 38
Cin — FG Pelfrey 29
SF — Watters 2 run (Cofer kick)
SF — Watters 4 run (Cofer kick)

MONDAY, DECEMBER 6

DALLAS 23, PHILADELPHIA 17—at Texas Stadium, attendance 64,521. Emmitt Smith rushed for 172 yards on 23 carries to pace the Cowboys past the Eagles. Troy Aikman threw an 11-yard touchdown pass to Michael Irvin, and Eddie Murray kicked 3 field goals to help Dallas forge a 16-0 first-half lead. But the Eagles pulled within 6 points on Matt Bahr's 25-yard field goal on the last play of the first half, and Bubby Brister's 2-yard touchdown pass to tight end Mark Bavaro. Then Smith, who ran for a club-record 237 yards in a 23-10 victory over the Eagles five weeks earlier, broke off a 57-yard run to set up Daryl Johnston for the game-clinching, 2-yard touchdown run 5:44 into the fourth quarter. Brister added another touchdown pass late in the fourth quarter for the Eagles, and finished with 27 completions in 45 attempts for 248 yards.

Philadelphia	0	3	7	7	—	17
Dallas	7	9	0	7	—	23

Dall — Irvin 11 pass from Aikman (Murray kick)
Dall — FG Murray 23
Dall — FG Murray 19
Dall — FG Murray 47
Phil — FG Bahr 25
Phil — Bavaro 2 pass from Brister (Bahr kick)
Dall — Johnston 2 run (Murray kick)
Phil — Bavaro 8 pass from Brister (Bahr kick)

FIFTEENTH WEEK SUMMARIES

AMERICAN FOOTBALL CONFERENCE

Eastern Division	W	L	T	Pct.	Pts.	OP
Buffalo	9	4	0	.692	236	184
Miami	9	4	0	.692	268	226
N.Y. Jets	8	5	0	.615	249	179
Indianapolis	4	9	0	.308	169	290
New England	2	11	0	.154	147	242
Central Division						
Houston	9	4	0	.692	308	214
Pittsburgh	8	5	0	.615	269	230
Cleveland	6	7	0	.462	236	257
Cincinnati	1	12	0	.077	138	279
Western Division						
Kansas City	9	4	0	.692	256	213
Denver	8	5	0	.615	320	231
L.A. Raiders	8	5	0	.615	246	248
San Diego	6	7	0	.462	221	225
Seattle	5	8	0	.385	213	244

NATIONAL FOOTBALL CONFERENCE

Eastern Division	W	L	T	Pct.	Pts.	OP
N.Y. Giants	10	3	0	.769	245	158
Dallas	9	4	0	.692	294	206
Philadelphia	5	8	0	.385	199	245
Phoenix	4	9	0	.308	252	226
Washington	3	10	0	.231	188	276
Central Division						
Detroit	8	5	0	.615	231	203
Green Bay	8	5	0	.615	275	231
Chicago	7	6	0	.538	211	177
Minnesota	6	7	0	.462	212	254
Tampa Bay	4	9	0	.308	183	307
Western Division						
San Francisco	9	4	0	.692	377	231
New Orleans	7	6	0	.538	257	269
Atlanta	6	7	0	.462	272	307
L.A. Rams	4	9	0	.308	184	304

SATURDAY, DECEMBER 11

N.Y. JETS 3, WASHINGTON 0—at RFK Stadium, attendance 47,970. Cary Blanchard's 45-yard field goal late in the first quarter accounted for the only points in the Jets' victory. New York failed to score a touchdown for the third consecutive week, but won for the second time in that span. The drought started with a 6-0 victory over the Patriots, followed by a 9-6 loss to the Colts. Blanchard accounted for all the points in the stretch with 5 field goals. Still, the Jets remained in the thick of the playoff hunt and pulled within one game of first place in the AFC East. They limited the Redskins to only 7 first downs while outgaining them 308-150, and maintained possession for 41 minutes. Johnny Johnson rushed for 155 yards on 32 carries. Washington quarterbacks Rich Gannon and Mark Rypien combined to complete only 9 of 23 passes for 79 yards.

N.Y. Jets	3	0	0	0	—	3
Washington	0	0	0	0	—	0

Jets — FG Blanchard 45

ATLANTA 27, SAN FRANCISCO 24—at Georgia Dome, attendance 64,688. The Falcons stayed alive in the race for a wild-card playoff berth by rallying for 20 points in the fourth quarter to beat the 49ers. San Francisco appeared on the verge of its seventh consecutive victory when quarterback Steve Young, who passed for 268 yards and a touchdown, increased his team's lead to 24-7 by running 10 yards for a touchdown with 2:22 left in the third quarter. But Atlanta took the ensuing kickoff and marched 80 yards in 9 plays, the last a 1-yard touchdown pass from Bobby Hebert to Michael Haynes 1:23 into the fourth quarter. Midway through the period, 49ers return specialist Dexter Carter muffed a punt, giving Atlanta possession on San Francisco's 6-yard line. Three plays later, Hebert's 6-yard touchdown pass to Andre Rison pulled the Falcons within 24-21 with 6:48 to go. Norm Johnson's 47-yard field goal tied the game at 2:12 mark, and when Carter lost a fumble on the subsequent kickoff, Johnson was positioned for the winning field goal from 37 yards with 28 seconds left. Hebert completed 24 of 39 passes for 290 yards and 3 touchdowns. Two of his scoring tosses went to Andre Rison, who caught 6 passes for 107 yards. The 49ers' Jerry Rice caught 6 passes for 105 yards. Atlanta's Deion Sanders intercepted Young on San Francisco's first and last possessions of the game. The Falcons won for the sixth time in their last eight games.

San Francisco	7	10	7	0	—	24
Atlanta	7	0	0	20	—	27

SF — Lee 6 pass from Young (Cofer kick)
Atl — Rison 5 pass from Hebert (Johnson kick)
SF — Rathman 2 run (Cofer kick)
SF — FG Cofer 32
SF — Young 10 run (Cofer kick)
Atl — Haynes 1 pass from Hebert (Johnson kick)
Atl — Rison 6 pass from Hebert (Johnson kick)
Atl — FG Johnson 47
Atl — FG Johnson 37

SUNDAY, DECEMBER 12

BUFFALO 10, PHILADELPHIA 7—at Veterans Stadium, attendance 60,769. Steve Christie's 34-yard field goal with 2:18 remaining lifted the Bills past the Eagles. Buffalo's victory, coupled with Miami's loss to the Steelers the next night, left the Bills and Dolphins tied atop the AFC East. Philadelphia, which lost for the eighth time in its past nine games, led 7-0 and was driving toward another score in the fourth quarter when running back Heath Sherman fumbled at Buffalo's 29-yard line. Bills cornerback Mickey Washington recovered, and Buffalo marched 71 yards to the tying score, Frank Reich's 2-yard touchdown pass to tight end Pete Metzelaars with 3:44 remaining. Vai Sikahema fumbled on the ensuing kickoff, and Jerome Henderson recovered for the Bills at the Eagles' 22-yard line. Christie, who had missed 3 field-goal tries earlier in the game, converted his winning kick three plays later. Buffalo made its fourth-quarter rally without starting quarterback Jim Kelly and running back Thurman Thomas. Kelly, who completed 17 of 27 passes for 210 yards, sprained an ankle and left the game early in the final period. Thomas bruised his left forearm in the first quarter and gave way to Kenneth Davis, who ran for 70 yards on 18 carries. Wide receiver Bill Brooks had 10 receptions for 90 yards. Bubby Brister completed 28 of 48 passes for 299 yards and a touchdown for the Eagles, who had 366 total yards but were stymied by 4 lost fumbles. Running back Herschel Walker caught a career-high 11 passes for 109 yards.

Buffalo	0	0	0	10	—	10
Philadelphia	0	0	7	0	—	7

Phil — C. Williams 19 pass from Brister (Bahr kick)
Buff — Metzelaars 2 pass from Reich (Christie kick)
Buff — FG Christie 34

TAMPA BAY 13, CHICAGO 10—at Tampa Stadium, attendance 56,667. The Buccaneers snapped Chicago's four-game winning streak, knocking the Bears out of a first-place tie in the NFC Central Division. Tampa Bay's Courtney Hawkins returned a punt 34 yards to set up Mazio Royster's 4-yard touchdown run in the second quarter, and Michael Husted kicked 2 field goals, including the decisive 42-yard kick late in the third quarter. The Bears' best chance after that was thwarted when running back Tim Worley was stopped on fourth-and-1 at the Buccaneers' 36-yard line with 9:26 left in the game. Chicago's only touchdown came after a 39-yard pass interference penalty positioned Neal Anderson for a 1-yard touchdown run. Kevin Butler had a 55-yard field goal to equal his career long. Bears starting quarterback Jim Harbaugh sat out the second half after bruising his throwing hand in the second quarter. He completed 11 of 18 passes for 81 yards in his abbreviated appearance. Backup Peter Tom Willis completed 11 of 18 for 86 yards.

Chicago	0	3	7	0	—	10
Tampa Bay	3	7	3	0	—	13

TB — FG Husted 38
TB — Royster 4 run (Husted kick)
Chi — FG Butler 55
Chi — Anderson 1 run (Butler kick)
TB — FG Husted 42

NEW ENGLAND 7, CINCINNATI 2—at Foxboro Stadium, attendance 29,794. Drew Bledsoe's 8-yard pass to tight end Ben Coates 44 seconds before halftime accounted for the game's only touchdown and was enough for the Patriots to edge the Bengals. Cincinnati managed only 11 first downs and 165 total yards, but still had a chance to tie the score late in the game after New England punter Mike Saxon mishandled a snap from center. His hurried kick was blocked and the Bengals recovered at the Patriots' 30-yard line. They marched to the 1, but on fourth-and-goal with 1:21 remaining, running back Eric Ball was stopped for a 1-yard loss. Moments later, Saxon lined up to punt again, but Marv Cook intentionally snapped the ball out of the end zone for a safety with 19 seconds left.

Cincinnati	0	0	0	2	—	2
New England	0	7	0	0	—	7

NE — Coates 8 pass from Bledsoe (Sisson kick)
Cin — Safety, ball snapped out of end zone

HOUSTON 19, CLEVELAND 17—at Astrodome, attendance 63,016. Al Del Greco kicked 4 field goals and the Oilers overcame an early 10-point deficit to win their eighth consecutive game. The Browns fell to 6-7 and clung only to slim wild-card playoff hopes. Cleveland scored on its first play from scrimmage, a 49-yard touchdown pass from Vinny Testaverde to running back Eric Metcalf, then added a 53-yard field goal by Matt Stover to take a 10-0 lead just 5:50 into the game. Houston rallied to go on top 16-10 at halftime, but Testaverde's second touchdown pass, a 28-yard toss to Mark Carrier 3:36 into the third quarter, put the Browns back on top 17-16. It still was a one-point game early in the fourth quarter when cornerback Cris Dishman intercepted Testaverde's pass at Cleveland's 39-yard line with 13:08 to go. A 20-yard pass interference penalty accounted for most of the yards on the Oilers' 32-yard march to Del Greco's 25-yard field goal with 10:39 remaining. Stover had a chance to win the game with a long field goal, but his 56-yard try in the final minutes was wide right. Houston won despite sputtering on offense in the second half. The Oilers managed only 257 total yards for the game, just 56 after intermission. Gary Brown rushed for 109 yards on 23 carries. The Browns, meanwhile, amassed 410 total yards, but turned the ball over 3 times. Testaverde, making his first start since separating his shoulder seven weeks earlier, completed 19 of 37 passes for 319 yards. Metcalf ran for 82 yards on 18 carries and caught 5 passes for 101 yards.

Cleveland	10	0	7	0	—	17
Houston	3	13	0	3	—	19

Cle — Metcalf 49 pass from Testaverde (Stover kick)
Cle — FG Stover 53
Hou — FG Del Greco 27
Hou — FG Del Greco 48
Hou — Tillman 4 pass from Moon (Del Greco kick)
Hou — FG Del Greco 49
Cle — Carrier 28 pass from Testaverde (Stover kick)
Hou — FG Del Greco 25

DALLAS 37, MINNESOTA 20—at Metrodome, attendance 63,321. Emmitt Smith rushed for 104 yards and a touchdown, and Michael Irvin caught 8 passes for 125 yards and a score to power the Cowboys past the Vikings. Dallas scored on seven of its first eight possessions to build a 37-13 lead 5:30 into the fourth quarter. Minnesota led 6-3 until Irvin caught a 10-yard touchdown pass from Troy Aikman early in the second quarter to give the Cowboys the lead for good. That capped a 5-play, 74-yard drive on which Irvin had the key gain, a 37-yard reception. He had a 22-yard catch on Dallas's next series, another 74-yard march that culminated in Smith's 4-yard touchdown run with 5:15 left in the first half. Eddie Murray kicked a 52-yard field goal as time expired for a 20-6 lead at intermission. Daryl Johnston capped another lengthy drive, a 12-play, 73-yard march, with a 1-yard touchdown run midway through the third quarter to put the game out of reach. Aikman finished with 19 completions in 29 attempts for 208 yards, with no interceptions and no sacks. Minnesota quarterbacks Jim McMahon and Sean Salisbury combined to complete 20 of 25 passes for 178 yards. But the Vikings squandered their best chances early in the game, driving inside the Cowboys' 5-yard line on each of their first two possessions, but coming away with only 6 points on a pair of field goals by Fuad Reveiz.

Dallas	3	17	7	10	—	37
Minnesota	6	0	7	7	—	20

Minn — FG Reveiz 19
Dall — FG Murray 51
Minn — FG Reveiz 21
Dall — Irvin 10 pass from Aikman (Murray kick)
Dall — E. Smith 4 run (Murray kick)
Dall — FG Murray 52
Dall — Johnston 1 run (Murray kick)
Minn — Graham 1 run (Reveiz kick)
Dall — FG Murray 46
Dall — Coleman 1 run (Murray kick)
Minn — A. Carter 9 pass from Salisbury (Reveiz kick)

DETROIT 21, PHOENIX 14—at Sun Devil Stadium, attendance 39,393. Erik Kramer, making his first start of the season, completed 19 of 25 passes for 257 yards and 3 touchdowns as the Lions remained tied with the Packers for first place in the NFC Central. Kramer, elevated to starter over Rodney Peete and Andre Ware earlier in the week, threw scoring passes of 6 yards to Herman Moore, 28 yards to tight end Rodney Holman, and 43 yards to Willie Green. The scoring pass to Green came 49 seconds into the fourth quarter and proved to be the decisive points. Late in the game, the Cardinals drove from their 9-yard to Detroit's 1, but failed to score. Defensive end Kelvin Pritchett threw Ron Moore for a 3-yard loss on second down, and cornerback Ryan McNeil intercepted Steve Beuerlein's pass at the goal line on fourth down. Beuerlein completed 23 of 35 passes for 219 yards, but was intercepted 3 times and sacked 4 times. Pritchett and end Robert Porcher each had 2 sacks. Dexter Moore rushed for 107 yards on 20 carries and caught 7 passes for 54 yards for the Lions.

Detroit	0	7	7	7	—	21
Phoenix	0	7	7	0	—	14

Phx — Blount 6 run (Davis kick)
Det — H. Moore 6 pass from Kramer (Hanson kick)
Phx — R. Moore 1 run (Davis kick)
Det — Holman 28 pass from Kramer (Hanson kick)
Det — Green 43 pass from Kramer (Hanson kick)

N.Y. GIANTS 20, INDIANAPOLIS 6—at Giants Stadium, attendance 70,411. The Giants became the first team to clinch a playoff berth by methodically pounding the Colts. Rodney Hampton ran for a career-high 173 yards on 33 carries as New York garnered 205 of its 290 total yards on the ground, exploiting the NFL's lowest-rated rushing defense. The Giants marched 70 and 67 yards, most of it on the ground, to touchdowns the first two times they had the ball. Hampton had 116 yards on 16 carries as New York built a 13-6 advantage at halftime. The Giants then maintained possession for nearly 12 minutes of the third quarter, and finished the scoring on Jarrod Bunch's 2-yard touchdown run on the first play of the fourth quarter. Jeff George completed 22 of 38 passes for 254 yards for the Colts, but could not get his team into the end zone. New York qualified for the playoffs for the first time since 1990, when they went on to win Super Bowl XXV.

Indianapolis	0	6	0	0	—	6
N.Y. Giants	7	6	0	7	—	20

Giants— Hampton 1 run (Treadwell kick)
Giants— Calloway 17 pass from Simms (kick failed)
Ind — FG Biasucci 21
Ind — FG Biasucci 26
Giants— Bunch 2 run (Treadwell kick)

DENVER 27, KANSAS CITY 21—at Mile High Stadium, attendance 75,822. John Elway's 3 touchdown passes to tight end Shannon Sharpe helped the Broncos pull within one game of the first-place Chiefs in the AFC West. Kansas City, trying to avoid its eleventh consecutive defeat at Mile High Stadium, jumped out to a 14-3 lead in the second quarter and still led 21-17 after Joe Montana teamed with Willie Davis on a 29-yard touchdown pass with 2:59 left in the third quarter. But early in the fourth period, Denver's Reggie Rivers blocked Bryan Barker's punt from the Chiefs' 42-yard line, and the Broncos took over on the 11. Three plays later, Elway's 6-yard touchdown pass to Sharpe gave the Broncos the lead for good. Jason Elam added a 53-yard field goal with 2:26 to go, and Kansas City could not get past its 46 on its final possession. Elway completed 20 of 30 passes for 221 yards and Rod Bernstine rushed for 90 yards on 23 carries for Denver. Sharpe caught 10 passes for 65 yards. Montana was 17 of 30 for 237 yards and 2 touchdowns for the Chiefs.

Kansas City	7	7	7	0	—	21
Denver	3	7	7	10	—	27

KC — Hayes 11 pass from Montana (Lowery kick)
Den — FG Elam 36
KC — Allen 4 run (Lowery kick)
Den — Sharpe 9 pass from Elway (Elam kick)
Den — Sharpe 14 pass from Elway (Elam kick)
KC — Davis 29 pass from Montana (Lowery kick)
Den — Sharpe 6 pass from Elway (Elam kick)
Den — FG Elam 53

L.A. RAMS 23, NEW ORLEANS 20—at Louisiana Superdome, attendance 69,033. Rookie Jerome Bettis ran for 212 yards and a touchdown as the Rams stunned the Saints. Bettis averaged 7.6 yards on his 28 attempts while becoming the eighth rookie in NFL history to rush for more than 200 yards in a game. Among the previous seven, only Jim Brown (237 yards), Tom Wilson (223), and Bo Jackson (221) had more productive days. Remarkably, Bettis compiled his big numbers in only three quarters of play. He ran for 125 yards in the first quarter, including a 71-yard touchdown, but suffered a bruised abdomen and sat out the second period. While he was on the bench, New Orleans got a pair of field goals from Morten Andersen to take a 13-10 lead at halftime. But Fred McAfee fumbled the second-half kickoff and Rams rookie Deral Boykin picked up the loose ball and ran 6 yards for the go-ahead touchdown. Later in the quarter, Bettis carried 10 times for 51 yards on an 80-yard touchdown drive that gave Los Angeles a 23-13 advantage. Rams quarterback T.J. Rubley completed only 5 of 13 passes for 47 yards, but capped that march with an 11-yard touchdown pass to tight end Pat Carter. The Saints pulled within 3 points on Dalton Hilliard's 2-yard run 4:37 into the fourth quarter but could get no closer. The victory snapped Los Angeles's seven-game losing streak to the Saints. New Orleans dropped its sixth decision in eight games since starting the season 5-0.

L.A. Rams	10	0	13	0	—	23
New Orleans	7	6	0	7	—	20

NO — Mills 30 fumble return (Andersen kick)
Rams — FG Zendejas 22
Rams — Bettis 71 run (Zendejas kick)
NO — FG Andersen 18
NO — FG Andersen 32
Rams — Boykin 6 fumble return (Zendejas kick)
Rams — Carter 11 pass from Rubley (kick failed)
NO — Hilliard 2 run (Andersen kick)

L.A. RAIDERS 27, SEATTLE 23—at Los Angeles Memorial Coliseum, attendance 38,161. Jeff Hostetler passed for 278 yards and a touchdown and the Raiders built a 27-9 lead in the third quarter, then withstood the Seahawks' comeback attempt. Los Angeles trailed 9-3 until taking the lead for good on Hostetler's 4-yard run with 32 seconds left in the first half. Just 1:45 into the second half, Tim Brown returned a punt 74 yards for a touchdown. Jeff Jaeger's 48-yard field goal and a 56-yard bomb from Hostetler to James Jett came just 98 seconds apart and gave the Raiders a seemingly insurmountable 18-point lead. But after Jaeger missed a 50-yard field-goal try early in the fourth quarter, Seattle quarterback Rick Mirer rallied his team, capping a 13-play, 68-yard drive by running 2 yards for a touchdown with 6:24 remaining. Cornerback James Jefferson intercepted a pass on Los Angeles's next possession, and the Seahawks launched another 13-play drive, this time for 57 yards to Mirer's 7-yard touchdown pass to Kelvin Martin. That cut Seattle's deficit to 4 points with 1:17 to go, and the Seahawks appeared to have a chance to win when safety Eugene Robinson recovered the ensuing onside kickoff. But Robinson was ruled to have gone out of bounds before recovering the ball, and the Raiders covered the subsequent try. Hostetler completed 18 of 25 attempts before leaving early in the fourth quarter with a twisted knee.

Seattle	0	9	0	14	—	23
L.A. Raiders	3	7	17	0	—	27

Raid — FG Jaeger 24
Sea — C. Warren 1 run (Kasay kick)
Sea — Safety, Stephens tackled Bell in end zone
Raid — Hostetler 4 run (Jaeger kick)
Raid — Brown 74 punt return (Jaeger kick)
Raid — FG Jaeger 48
Raid — Jett 56 pass from Hostetler (Jaeger kick)
Sea — Mirer 2 run (Kasay kick)
Sea — Martin 7 pass from Mirer (Kasay kick)

SUNDAY NIGHT, DECEMBER 12

GREEN BAY 20, SAN DIEGO 13—at San Diego Jack Murphy Stadium, attendance 57,930. The Packers maintained a share of first place in the NFC Central Division while all but eliminating the defending AFC Western Division-champion Chargers from the playoff picture. Edgar Bennett's short touchdown run and a pair of field goals by Chris Jacke staked Green Bay to a 13-6 halftime lead. San Diego marched to the Packers' 34-yard line on its first possession of the second half, but linebacker Tony Bennett sacked quarterback Stan Humphries for an 11-yard loss on fourth-and-4, and Green Bay took over on its 45-yard line. Twelve plays later, Darrell Thompson ran 5 yards for the touchdown that proved to be the decisive score. The Packers converted three consecutive third-down situations on the 55-yard drive. The Chargers tried to rally behind the passing of Humphries, who completed 27 of a career-high 51 attempts for 257 yards. But Humphries also was intercepted 3 times, and suffered from the absence of a running attack. After his 10-yard touchdown pass to Nate Lewis in the final minute of the third quarter trimmed San Diego's deficit to 7 points, the Chargers best chance to tie the game was thwarted when Natrone Means was stopped for no gain on fourth-and-1 from the Packers' 37 with 4:42 to go. Interceptions by Terrell Buckley and Mike Prior ended San Diego's hopes after that.

Green Bay	7	6	7	0	—	20
San Diego	3	3	7	0	—	13

GB — E. Bennett 3 run (Jacke kick)
SD — FG Carney 47
GB — FG Jacke 51
GB — FG Jacke 42
SD — FG Carney 43
GB — Thompson 5 run (Jacke kick)
SD — Lewis 10 pass from Humphries (Carney kick)

MONDAY, DECEMBER 13

PITTSBURGH 21, MIAMI 20—at Joe Robbie Stadium, attendance 73,882. Running back Leroy Thompson had 142 yards from scrimmage and the Steelers held off a fourth-quarter rally to defeat the Dolphins. Thompson, playing in place of injured Barry Foster, ran for 81 yards on 28 carries and caught 4 passes for 61 yards. He had touchdown runs of 1 and 3 yards as Pittsburgh built a 21-6 advantage early in the fourth quarter. But Dolphins quarterback Steve DeBerg threw a 3-yard touchdown pass to tight end Keith Jackson 4:30 into the final period, and when rookie O.J. McDuffie returned a punt 72 yards for a touchdown with 6:37 remaining, Miami trailed by only a point. The Dolphins had two chances after that, but a sack by safety Carnell Lake and cornerback Rod Woodson's interception ended the threats. The 39-year-old DeBerg completed 27 of 44 passes for 344 yards, but was intercepted twice and pressured throughout the game. Linebacker Greg Lloyd had 2 of the Steelers' 5 sacks.

Pittsburgh	0	7	7	7	—	21
Miami	3	3	0	14	—	20

Mia — FG Stoyanovich 31
Pitt — Thompson 1 run (Anderson kick)
Mia — FG Stoyanovich 22
Pitt — Thompson 3 run (Anderson kick)
Pitt — Hoge 2 pass from O'Donnell (Anderson kick)
Mia — K. Jackson 3 pass from DeBerg (Stoyanovich kick)
Mia — McDuffie 72 punt return (Stoyanovich kick)

SIXTEENTH WEEK SUMMARIES

AMERICAN FOOTBALL CONFERENCE

Eastern Division	W	L	T	Pct.	Pts.	OP
Buffalo	10	4	0	.714	283	218
Miami	9	5	0	.643	302	273
N.Y. Jets	8	6	0	.571	256	207
Indianapolis	4	10	0	.286	179	310
New England	3	11	0	.214	167	259
Central Division						
Houston	10	4	0	.714	334	231
Pittsburgh	8	6	0	.571	286	256
Cleveland	6	8	0	.429	253	277
Cincinnati	2	12	0	.143	153	282
Western Division						
Kansas City	10	4	0	.714	284	237
Denver	9	5	0	.643	333	234
L.A. Raiders	9	5	0	.643	273	268
San Diego	6	8	0	.429	245	253
Seattle	5	9	0	.357	240	274

NATIONAL FOOTBALL CONFERENCE

Eastern Division	W	L	T	Pct.	Pts.	OP
N.Y. Giants	11	3	0	.786	269	172
Dallas	10	4	0	.714	322	213
Philadelphia	6	8	0	.429	219	255
Phoenix	5	9	0	.357	282	253
Washington	4	10	0	.286	218	293
Central Division						
Detroit	8	6	0	.571	248	258
Green Bay	8	6	0	.571	292	252
Chicago	7	7	0	.500	214	190
Minnesota	7	7	0	.500	233	271
Tampa Bay	4	10	0	.286	203	334
Western Division						
San Francisco	10	4	0	.714	432	248
New Orleans	7	7	0	.500	271	293
Atlanta	6	8	0	.429	289	337
L.A. Rams	4	10	0	.286	187	319

SATURDAY, DECEMBER 18

DENVER 13, CHICAGO 3—at Soldier Field, attendance 53,056. Rod Bernstine rushed for 103 yards in the rain and the mud at Soldier Field as the Broncos moved a step closer to the playoffs by beating the Bears. Bernstine's 15-yard run late in the first half set up the only touchdown of the game, Robert Delpino's 1-yard run 1:24 before halftime. That broke a 3-3 tie and came after linebacker Mike Croel sacked Chicago quarterback Peter Tom Willis and recovered Willis's fumble at the Bears' 16-yard line. Chicago turned over the ball 5 times, including 3 on interceptions thrown by Willis, who was playing because Jim Harbaugh was nursing a bruised hand. Willis completed just 14 of 29 passes for 120 yards and was sacked 4 times as the Bears could muster only 185 total yards. Denver didn't fare much better, totaling only 234 yards, but the Broncos scored 10 points off the turnovers. They tied the score at 3-3 midway through the second quarter after linebacker David Wyman recovered Tim Worley's fumble at Chicago's 11. Though Denver was unable to move the ball, Jason Elam kicked a 29-yard field goal. Elam added a 24-yard field goal with 7:02 left in the third quarter.

Denver	0	10	3	0	—	13
Chicago	3	0	0	0	—	3

Chi — FG Butler 31
Den — FG Elam 29
Den — Delpino 1 run (Elam kick)
Den — FG Elam 24

DALLAS 28, N.Y. JETS 7—at Giants Stadium, attendance 73,109. Troy Aikman threw for 252 yards and 2 touchdowns as the defending Super Bowl-champion Cowboys wrapped up a playoff berth by beating the Jets. Though he was intercepted 3 times, Aikman completed 21 of 27 passes, and broke a scoreless tie by throwing a 42-yard touchdown pass to Michael Irvin 36 seconds before intermission. The pair hooked up again at the end of a 95-yard drive late in the third quarter, this time on a 3-yard touchdown with 1:23 to go in the period. Fifty-one seconds later, cornerback Kevin Smith put the game out of reach by intercepting Boomer Esiason's pass and returning it 32 yards for a touchdown. Brad Baxter's 1-yard scoring run 3:32 into the fourth quarter was New York's first touchdown in four games.

Dallas	0	7	14	7	—	28
N.Y. Jets	0	0	0	7	—	7

Dall — Irvin 42 pass from Aikman (Murray kick)
Dall — Irvin 3 pass from Aikman (Murray kick)
Dall — K. Smith 32 interception return (Murray kick)
Jets — B. Baxter 1 run (Blanchard kick)
Dall — Johnston 4 run (Murray kick)

SUNDAY, DECEMBER 19

WASHINGTON 30, ATLANTA 17—at RFK Stadium, attendance 50,192. Cornerback AJ Johnson and linebacker Monte Coleman scored touchdowns as the Redskins dealt the Falcons' playoff hopes a severe blow. Atlanta entered the game with six wins in eight games since an 0-5 start, but left clinging to slim chances for a wild-card berth despite dominating Washington statistically. The Falcons doubled the Redskins in first downs (22-8), plays (85-42), total yards (378-167), and time of possession (40:40-19:20). But they also committed 6 turnovers (to Washington's 2), and were whistled for 10 penalties (Washington had none). Coleman, whose 29-yard touchdown return of quarterback Bobby Hebert's fumble sealed the victory with 2:11 remaining in the game, also recorded a safety, tackling Atlanta punter Harold Alexander after Harper Le Bel's snap from the 26-yard line sailed high. Quarterback Mark Rypien's 1-yard run and Johnson's 69-yard interception return with nine seconds left in the first half put the Redskins ahead 16-7. The Falcons rallied to go back in front on Steve Broussard's 2-yard touchdown run and Norm Johnson's 41-yard field goal with 4:39 to go in the game. But Desmond Howard returned the ensuing kickoff 33 yards, then caught a 17-yard pass from Rypien to set up Earnest Byner's 8-yard touchdown run at the 3:06 mark. Fifty-five seconds later, defensive end Sterling Palmer sacked Hebert, forcing the fumble that Coleman returned for a touchdown. Hebert completed 24 of 42 passes for 233 yards and a touchdown for Atlanta, but suffered 4 interceptions and 7 sacks. Broussard rushed for 162 yards on 26 carries, and Mike Pritchard caught 8 passes for 92 yards and a touchdown. Coleman, Palmer, and defensive end Al Noga each had 2 sacks for Washington.

Atlanta	7	0	7	3	—	17
Washington	0	16	0	14	—	30

Atl — Pritchard 29 pass from Hebert (Johnson kick)
Wash — Safety, Coleman tackled Alexander in end zone
Wash — Rypien 1 run (Lohmiller kick)
Wash — Johnson 69 interception return (Lohmiller kick)
Atl — Broussard 2 run (Johnson kick)
Atl — FG Johnson 41
Wash — Byner 8 run (Lohmiller kick)
Wash — Coleman 29 fumble return (Lohmiller kick)

BUFFALO 47, MIAMI 34—at Joe Robbie Stadium, attendance 71,597. Kenneth Davis rushed for 3 touchdowns and the Bills converted 5 takeaways into 28 points while routing the Dolphins in a battle for first place in the AFC East. Miami led 17-16 until Steve Christie's 32-yard field goal with 1:27 remaining in the first half gave Buffalo the lead for good and started an avalanche of points. Eight seconds after Christie's field goal, cornerback Mickey Washington intercepted Scott Mitchell's pass and returned it 27 yards for a touchdown and a 26-17 advantage. The Dolphins' Pete Stoyanovich kicked an 18-yard field goal as time ran out in the first half to trim the margin to six points, but the Bills scored 3 touchdowns in the first 5:59 of the second half to turn the game into a rout. On the first play of the third quarter, linebacker Darryl Talley stripped the ball from Miami tight end Keith Jackson. Cornerback Nate Odomes picked up the loose ball and returned it 25 yards for a touchdown. Two plays later, safety Matt Darby's interception and 32-yard return set up Davis's third touchdown of the game, a 1-yard run for a 40-20 lead. Four plays after that, running back Keith Byars fumbled and Buffalo nose tackle Mike Lodish recovered at the Dolphins' 37-yard line. Jim Kelly's 28-yard touchdown pass to Don Beebe made it 47-20. In all, the Bills scored 31 points in a span of 7:26, with each touchdown resulting from a turnover. Steve DeBerg tried to rally Miami with 2 touchdown passes, but after the Dolphins drove to Buffalo's 27-yard line midway through the fourth quarter, an interception by Odomes secured the victory for the Bills. Miami rolled up 424 total yards, but managed only 23 yards on the ground. Mitchell threw for 156 yards, and DeBerg completed 20 of 35 passes for 273 yards in less than two quarters of play. Running back Terry Kirby caught 9 passes for 148 yards. Kelly completed 20 of 30 passes for 245 yards for the Bills. Davis rushed for 64 yards on 13 carries.

Buffalo	9	17	21	0	—	47
Miami	7	13	7	7	—	34

Buff — K. Davis 1 run (kick failed)
Mia — Ingram 14 pass from Mitchell (Stoyanovich kick)
Buff — FG Christie 38
Mia — FG Stoyanovich 41
Mia — Jackson 16 pass from Mitchell (Stoyanovich kick)
Buff — K. Davis 12 run (Christie kick)
Buff — FG Christie 32
Buff — M. Washington 27 interception return (Christie kick)
Mia — FG Stoyanovich 18
Buff — Odomes 25 fumble return (Christie kick)
Buff — K. Davis 1 run (Christie kick)
Buff — Beebe 28 pass from Kelly (Christie kick)
Mia — Kirby 30 pass from DeBerg (Stoyanovich kick)
Mia — Ingram 7 pass from DeBerg (Stoyanovich kick)

HOUSTON 26, PITTSBURGH 17—at Three Rivers Stadium, attendance 57,592. The Oilers completed a dramatic turnaround by beating the Steelers to clinch the AFC Central title. After starting the season 1-4, Houston won its ninth consecutive game, six of them against division rivals. The Oilers quieted the Three Rivers Stadium crowd early in this one, marching 80 yards in 8 plays, the last a 38-yard screen pass from Warren Moon to Gary Brown, to take a 7-0 lead just 3:53 into the game. Three plays later, Houston safety Bo Orlando intercepted Neil O'Donnell's pass and returned it 38 yards for a touchdown and a 14-0 advantage. The Oilers led 20-0 before 1992 division champ Pittsburgh scored. Brown rushed for 100 yards on 20 carries and caught 4 passes for 80 yards. Moon passed for 268 yards. O'Donnell and Mike Tomczak combined for 400 passing yards for the Steelers, but completed only 24 of 57 passes and were intercepted twice. Jeff Graham caught 7 passes for 192 yards. Houston's victory was tempered by the death of defensive tackle Jeff Alm earlier in the week.

Houston	14	6	3	3	—	26
Pittsburgh	0	3	7	7	—	17

Hou — G. Brown 38 pass from Moon (Del Greco kick)
Hou — Orlando 38 interception return (Del Greco kick)
Hou — FG Del Greco 34
Hou — FG Del Greco 22
Pitt — FG Anderson 26
Hou — FG Del Greco 33
Pitt — Green 36 pass from O'Donnell (Anderson kick)
Hou — FG Del Greco 21
Pitt — Hoge 5 run (Anderson kick)

CINCINNATI 15, L.A. RAMS 3—at Riverfront Stadium, attendance 36,612. David Klingler passed for a career-high 223 yards and the Bengals compiled a season-high 393 total yards en route to beating the Rams. Cincinnati, which entered the game 1-12 and ranked last in the league in total offense, got a season-high 170 yards on the ground to complement Klingler's passing. Derrick Fenner rushed for 89 yards on 15 carries and Harold Green added 76 yards on 18 attempts. Fenner scored the game's only touchdown on a 1-yard run in the second quarter. Doug Pelfrey kicked 3 field goals, 2 in the second half to secure the victory. Los Angeles' Jerome Bettis had his fourth consecutive 100-yard game, gaining 124 yards on 24 attempts. The rookie took over the league lead with 1,227 yards.

L.A. Rams	0	3	0	0	—	3
Cincinnati	3	6	3	3	—	15

Cin — FG Pelfrey 43
Cin — Fenner 1 run (kick failed)
Rams — FG Zendejas 32
Cin — FG Pelfrey 28
Cin — FG Pelfrey 25

MINNESOTA 21, GREEN BAY 17—at Milwaukee County Stadium, attendance 54,773. Jim McMahon threw 3 touchdown passes as the Vikings kept their playoff hopes alive by beating the Packers. McMahon, who completed 22 of 31 passes for 207 yards, erased Minnesota's 10-7 halftime deficit by teaming with Cris Carter on scoring plays of 6 and 25 yards. The veteran quarterback also tossed a 6-yard touchdown pass to Qadry Ismail early in the second quarter. Down 21-10 in the fourth quarter, Green Bay rallied, pulling within 4 points on Brett Favre's 11-yard touch-

down pass to Mark Clayton with 5:51 left in the game. Minutes later, the Packers marched to a first-and-goal at the Vikings' 2-yard line. But Minnesota held, with safety Vencie Glenn knocking down Favre's fourth-down pass in the end zone with 1:14 remaining. Glenn also had an interception in the final minute to wrap up the victory. Vikings running back Scottie Graham, pressed into duty because of injuries, carried 30 times for 139 yards, just 6 short of his season total. Carter caught 6 passes for 106 yards. Green Bay wide receiver Sterling Sharpe also caught 6 passes for 106 yards. Favre completed 20 of 33 passes for 256 yards.

Minnesota	0	7	7	7	—	21
Green Bay	3	7	0	7	—	17

GB — FG Jacke 20
Minn — Ismail 6 pass from McMahon (Reveiz kick)
GB — Sharpe 37 pass from Favre (Jacke kick)
Minn — C. Carter 6 pass from McMahon (Reveiz kick)
Minn — C. Carter 25 pass from McMahon (Reveiz kick)
GB — Clayton 11 pass from Favre (Jacke kick)

NEW ENGLAND 20, CLEVELAND 17—at Municipal Stadium, attendance 48,618. Leonard Russell's 4-yard touchdown run with 2:02 remaining lifted the Patriots to the victory and knocked the Browns out of the playoff picture. Cleveland led 17-13 and was driving to the apparent game-clinching touchdown when Vinny Testaverde's pass in the end zone was intercepted by New England safety Dion Lambert with 4:50 remaining. The Patriots then embarked on the winning 10-play, 80-yard drive, the key gain a 49-yard pass by Kevin Turner. After Russell's touchdown run, any Browns' hopes were quashed when cornerback Maurice Hurst intercepted Testaverde's pass on the next play from scrimmage. Despite the 2 late thefts, Testaverde was productive, completing 21 of 31 passes for 297 yards and 2 touchdowns. Cleveland running back Eric Metcalf rushed for 48 yards and caught 8 passes for 81 yards. The Browns lost for the sixth time in the last seven games and missed the playoffs despite a 5-2 start.

New England	0	10	3	7	—	20
Cleveland	7	7	0	3	—	17

Cle — McCardell 10 pass from Testaverde (Stover kick)
NE — FG Bahr 23
Cle — McCardell 10 pass from Testaverde (Stover kick)
NE — K. Turner 6 pass from Bledsoe (Bahr kick)
NE — FG Bahr 34
Cle — FG Stover 23
NE — Russell 4 run (Bahr kick)

PHOENIX 30, SEATTLE 27—at Kingdome, attendance 45,737. Greg Davis tied the game with a club-record 55-yard field goal as time ran out in regulation, then won it with a 41-yard kick 6:45 into overtime. Davis also kicked a 50-yard field goal to give the Cardinals a 24-20 lead with 5:09 to go in the fourth quarter. The Seahawks rallied, marching 93 yards in 15 plays to take a 27-24 advantage on quarterback Rick Mirer's 1-yard sneak for a touchdown. But 1:22 still remained, and Steve Beuerlein's 17-yard pass to Gary Clark positioned Davis for the tying kick. Phoenix took the kickoff in the extra session and drove 57 yards in 13 plays to the winning score. Beuerlein teamed with Clark and Anthony Edwards on key third-down completions. The Cardinals' quarterback completed 34 of 53 passes for 431 yards and 3 touchdowns. Clark caught 12 passes for 152 yards. Chris Warren carried 27 times for 168 yards, including a 45-yard touchdown run 1:13 into the fourth quarter for Seattle. Mirer passed for 165 yards, giving him 2,576 yards for the season. He broke former Seahawks quarterback Jim Zorn's NFL record for passing yards by a rookie.

Phoenix	7	0	7	13	3	—	30
Seattle	10	10	0	7	0	—	27

Sea — Warren 45 run (Kasay kick)
Sea — FG Kasay 37
Phx — R. Hill 58 pass from Beuerlein (G. Davis kick)
Sea — FG Kasay 47
Sea — Edmunds 1 run from Mirer (Kasay kick)
Phx — Clark 20 pass from Beuerlein (G. Davis kick)
Phx — Centers 16 pass from Beuerlein (G. Davis kick)
Phx — FG G. Davis 50
Sea — Mirer 1 run (Kasay kick)

Phx — FG G. Davis 55
Phx — FG G. Davis 41

KANSAS CITY 28, SAN DIEGO 24—at Arrowhead Stadium, attendance 74,778. The Chiefs rallied from a 17-point deficit to defeat the Chargers and maintain their hold on first place in the AFC West. San Diego jumped out to a 10-0 lead 3:47 into the game by converting an interception and a fumble recovery into Stan Humphries' 28-yard touchdown pass to Ronnie Harmon and John Carney's 38-yard field goal. Humphries was forced to leave the game with a concussion, but backup John Friesz threw a 3-yard touchdown pass to tight end Duane Young on the first play of the second quarter, increasing the Chargers' advantage to 17-0. Kansas City responded with touchdown drives of 77 and 66 yards to trim the margin to 17-14 by halftime, then took the lead for good on Joe Montana's 4-yard touchdown pass to J.J. Birden with 4:39 remaining in the third quarter. Montana also was forced from the game with a concussion, but Dave Krieg came on to throw a 28-yard touchdown pass to Willie Davis 2:06 into the fourth quarter for the decisive score.

San Diego	10	7	0	7	—	24
Kansas City	0	14	7	7	—	28

SD — Harmon 28 pass from Humphries (Carney kick)
SD — FG Carney 38
SD — Young 3 pass from Friesz (Carney kick)
KC — Allen 1 run (Lowery kick)
KC — Davis 9 pass from Montana (Lowery kick)
KC — Birden 4 pass from Montana (Lowery kick)
KC — Davis 28 pass from Krieg (Lowery kick)
SD — Means 2 run (Carney kick)

SAN FRANCISCO 55, DETROIT 17—at Pontiac Silverdome, attendance 77,052. Steve Young threw 4 touchdown passes and the 49ers exploded for 565 total yards while wrapping up their tenth division championship in the last 12 years. San Francisco dominated from the start, scoring on a 68-yard pass from Young to Taylor on its third play from scrimmage. The 49ers did not punt, and scored on every possession except the two when they ran out in the first half and in the game. Young completed 17 of 23 passes for 354 yards in less than three quarters of play. Jerry Rice caught 4 passes for 132 yards and a touchdown, while Taylor had 4 receptions for 115 yards. Amp Lee rushed for 66 yards and caught 6 passes for 50 yards, including a 12-yard touchdown. Tom Rathman had 2 short scoring runs. Erik Kramer passed for 220 yards and 2 touchdowns for the Lions, who remained tied with the Packers atop the NFC Central.

San Francisco	14	17	14	10	—	55
Detroit	0	10	0	7	—	17

SF — Taylor 68 pass from Young (Cofer kick)
SF — Beach 20 pass from Young (Cofer kick)
Det — FG Hanson 51
SF — Rice 80 pass from Young (Cofer kick)
SF — Rathman 2 run (Cofer kick)
SF — FG Cofer 43
Det — D. Moore 12 pass from Kramer (Hanson kick)
SF — Rathman 1 run (Cofer kick)
SF — Lee 12 pass from Young (Cofer kick)
SF — FG Cofer 21
Det — H. Moore 31 pass from Kramer (Hanson kick)
SF — Carter 50 run (Cofer kick)

L.A. RAIDERS 27, TAMPA BAY 20—at Los Angeles Memorial Coliseum, attendance 40,532. The Raiders converted a pair of fumble recoveries into the key touchdowns in their victory over the Buccaneers. Los Angeles led 7-0 in the first quarter when defensive end Greg Townsend sacked Tampa Bay quarterback Craig Erickson, forcing a fumble that was recovered by defensive tackle Chester McGlockton at the Buccaneers' 5-yard line. Napoleon McCallum ran for a touchdown on the next play to increase the Raiders' lead to 14-0. It was 20-10 in the fourth quarter when cornerback Torin Dorn forced Cobb to fumble, and end Aundray Bruce recovered at Tampa Bay's 16. Four plays later, Hostetler ran 1 yard for the decisive points. Los Angeles managed only 17 rushing yards, but Hostetler completed 19 of 30 passes for 260 yards. Alexander Wright caught 6 passes for 104 yards, including a 27-yard touchdown. Erickson completed 21 of 34 passes for 295 yards for the Buccaneers. Michael Husted's 57-yard field goal

10 seconds before halftime was the longest in franchise history.

Tampa Bay	0	10	0	10	—	20
L.A. Raiders	14	3	0	10	—	27

Raid — Wright 27 pass from Hostetler (Jaeger kick)
Raid — McCallum 5 run (Jaeger kick)
TB — Cobb 5 run (Husted kick)
Raid — FG Jaeger 50
TB — FG Husted 57
Raid — FG Jaeger 33
Raid — Hostetler 1 run (Jaeger kick)
TB — Cobb 2 run (Husted kick)
TB — FG Husted 31

SUNDAY NIGHT, DECEMBER 19

PHILADELPHIA 20, INDIANAPOLIS 10—at Hoosier Dome, attendance 44,952. The Eagles kept their slim play-off hopes alive by beating the Colts. Bubby Brister passed for 217 yards, including a 14-yard touchdown to Calvin Williams to break open the game. Philadelphia led 10-3 at halftime, but Eagles defensive tackle William Perry sacked Indianapolis quarterback Jeff George midway through the third quarter, forcing a fumble that linebacker William Thomas recovered. One play later, Brister and Williams teamed on the touchdown that made it 17-3. Philadelphia sacked George 4 times and forced 3 fumbles. The Eagles converted a first-quarter fumble by wide receiver Jessie Hester into a 21-yard field goal by Roger Ruzek. The Colts snapped a 20-quarter touchdown drought when George threw a 24-yard scoring pass to Reggie Langhorne with 4:18 to go in the game.

Philadelphia	10	0	7	3	—	20
Indianapolis	3	0	0	7	—	10

Phil — FG Ruzek 21
Phil — Sherman 1 run (Ruzek kick)
Ind — FG Biasucci 39
Phil — Williams 14 pass from Brister (Ruzek kick)
Phil — FG Ruzek 25
Ind — Langhorne 24 pass from George (Biasucci kick)

MONDAY, DECEMBER 20

N.Y. GIANTS 24, NEW ORLEANS 14—at Louisiana Superdome, attendance 69,036. Phil Simms threw 2 touchdown passes and David Meggett returned a punt 75 yards for a touchdown to lead the Giants past the slumping Saints. New York won its sixth in a row, while New Orleans lost its seventh in the last nine. After beginning the season 5-0, the Saints were in danger of falling out of the playoff chase. Simms, who completed 15 of 23 attempts for 166 yards, teamed with Mark Jackson on a 9-yard touchdown pass 10:15 into the game, then capped a 96-yard drive with a 17-yard touchdown pass to tight end Howard Cross to give the Giants a 14-0 advantage midway through the second quarter. It was 17-7 when Meggett effectively ended any doubts about the outcome with his punt return for a touchdown with 11:13 to go in the game.

N.Y. Giants	7	7	3	7	—	24
New Orleans	0	7	0	7	—	14

Giants — M. Jackson 9 pass from Simms (Treadwell kick)
Giants — Cross 17 pass from Simms (Treadwell kick)
NO — Muster 1 run (Andersen kick)
Giants — FG Treadwell 22
Giants — Meggett 75 punt return (Treadwell kick)
NO — Hilliard 5 pass from Buck (Andersen kick)

SEVENTEENTH WEEK SUMMARIES

AMERICAN FOOTBALL CONFERENCE

Eastern Division	W	L	T	Pct.	Pts.	OP
Buffalo	11	4	0	.733	299	232
Miami	9	6	0	.600	322	318
N.Y. Jets	8	7	0	.533	270	223
Indianapolis	4	11	0	.267	179	348
New England	4	11	0	.267	205	259
Central Division						
Houston	11	4	0	.733	344	238
Pittsburgh	8	7	0	.533	292	272
Cleveland	7	8	0	.467	295	291
Cincinnati	3	12	0	.200	174	299

Western Division						
Kansas City	10	5	0	.667	294	267
Denver	9	6	0	.600	343	251
L.A. Raiders	9	6	0	.600	273	296
San Diego	7	8	0	.467	290	273
Seattle	6	9	0	.400	256	280

NATIONAL FOOTBALL CONFERENCE

Eastern Division	W	L	T	Pct.	Pts.	OP
Dallas	11	4	0	.733	360	216
N.Y. Giants	11	4	0	.733	275	189
Philadelphia	7	8	0	.467	256	281
Phoenix	6	9	0	.400	299	259
Washington	4	11	0	.267	221	331
Central Division						
Detroit	9	6	0	.600	268	272
Green Bay	9	6	0	.600	320	252
Minnesota	8	7	0	.533	263	281
Chicago	7	8	0	.467	228	210
Tampa Bay	5	10	0	.333	220	344
Western Division						
San Francisco	10	5	0	.667	439	258
New Orleans	7	8	0	.467	297	330
Atlanta	6	9	0	.400	306	358
L.A. Rams	4	11	0	.267	201	361

SATURDAY, DECEMBER 25

HOUSTON 10, SAN FRANCISCO 7—at Candlestick Park, attendance 61,744. The game matched the NFL's two highest scoring teams, but it was defense that carried the Oilers to the victory. Al Del Greco kicked a 24-yard field goal and Warren Moon threw a 7-yard touchdown pass to Ernest Givins to give Houston all the points it needed in the second quarter. From there, the Oilers' defense took over, using a steady stream of blitzes to knock the 49ers' number-one ranked offense off-balance. San Francisco didn't score until backup quarterback Steve Bono took over for Steve Young late in the third quarter. Bono's first drive was a 12-play, 73-yard march that resulted in Amp Lee's 8-yard touchdown run 2:49 into the fourth quarter. But the 49ers could not score again, and did not get the ball back after punting with 6:49 remaining in the game. Young completed 15 of 29 passes for 178 yards and was intercepted twice. Bono was 11 of 13 for 79 yards in his limited duty. Jerry Rice caught 10 passes for 83 yards. Moon completed only 11 of 26 attempts for 158 yards, with 3 interceptions. Gary Brown rushed for 114 yards on 19 carries. The Oilers won their tenth consecutive game and snapped the 49ers' club-record 13-game regular-season home winning streak.

Houston	0	10	0	0	—	10
San Francisco	0	0	0	7	—	7

Hou — FG Del Greco 24
Hou — Givins 7 pass from Moon (Del Greco kick)
SF — Lee 8 run (Cofer kick)

SUNDAY, DECEMBER 26

CINCINNATI 21, ATLANTA 17—at Riverfront Stadium, attendance 47,014. David Klingler threw a career-high 3 touchdown passes, including the game winner to Carl Pickens with one minute left, to lift the Bengals to the victory. Pickens' 6-yard touchdown catch was his second of the game. He also had a 24-yard scoring reception to give Cincinnati a 14-7 advantage late in the first half. The Falcons, fighting to stay alive in the playoff race, rallied behind a 49-yard field goal by Norm Johnson and Erric Pegram's 1-yard touchdown run to take a 17-14 lead with 6:58 to go in the game. But the Bengals countered with the game-winning drive, which covered 70 yards in 8 plays, the key gain Klingler's 26-yard scramble. Cincinnati cornerback Rod Jones ended Atlanta's last threat with an interception in the closing seconds. Klingler finished with 16 completions in 30 attempts for 174 yards. Pegram led all rushers with 180 yards on 37 carries. The Bengals won their third in a row at Riverfront Stadium. The Falcons, who won six of seven games after an 0-5 start to climb into playoff contention, were eliminated from the wild-card chase.

Atlanta	7	0	3	7	—	17
Cincinnati	7	7	0	7	—	21

Atl — Rison 21 pass from Hebert (Johnson kick)
Cin — Thompson 3 pass from Klingler (Pelfrey kick)
Cin — Pickens 24 pass from Klingler (Pelfrey kick)
Atl — FG Johnson 49
Cin — Pickens 6 pass from Klingler (Pelfrey kick)
Atl — Pegram 1 run (Johnson kick)

CLEVELAND 42, L.A. RAMS 14—at Anaheim Stadium, attendance 34,155. Vinny Testaverde set an NFL record by completing 21 of 23 passes in the Browns' victory. Testaverde's completion percentage of .913 broke the old mark of .909 held by Cincinnati's Ken Anderson, who was 20 of 22 in a game against Pittsburgh in 1974. Testaverde passed for 216 yards, including touchdowns of 8 and 28 yards to Keenan McCardell, helping stake Cleveland to a 21-7 lead through three quarters. The Browns broke open the game with 3 touchdowns in a span of 4:13 early in the fourth period. Mark Carrier returned a punt 56 yards for a touchdown with 8:04 left in the game, Randy Hilliard's interception and 54-yard return set up Tommy Vardell's 1-yard touchdown run with 6:14 to go, and Selwyn Jones's fumble recovery on the ensuing kickoff positioned Kevin Mack for a 1-yard touchdown run with 3:51 remaining. The Rams outgained Cleveland 382-315, but much of that came after the issue was decided. Los Angeles quarterback T.J. Rubley completed 24 of 32 passes for 294 yards, including a 23-yard touchdown pass to Willie Anderson. Henry Ellard caught 8 passes for 114 yards. Jerome Bettis, who entered the game as the NFL's leading rusher, was limited to 56 yards on 16 carries.

Cleveland	7	7	7	21	—	42
L.A. Rams	7	0	0	7	—	14

Rams — Bettis 1 run (Zendejas kick)
Cle — Vardell 1 run (Stover kick)
Cle — McCardell 8 pass from Testaverde (Stover kick)
Cle — McCardell 28 pass from Testaverde (Stover kick)
Cle — Carrier 56 punt return (Stover kick)
Cle — Vardell 1 run (Stover kick)
Cle — Mack 1 run (Stover kick)
Rams — Anderson 23 pass from Rubley (Zendejas kick)

DETROIT 20, CHICAGO 14—at Soldier Field, attendance 43,443. Erik Kramer's 1-yard touchdown pass to tight end Ty Hallock with 3:04 remaining clinched a playoff berth for the Lions, eliminated the Bears, and set up Detroit's show-down with the Packers for the NFC Central Division title one week later. Quarterback Jim Harbaugh's 1-yard dive 4:39 into the fourth quarter had given Chicago a 14-13 lead. But the Lions countered with a 12-play, 80-yard drive that took 7:17 off the clock, capping the march with Kramer's second touchdown pass of the game. The division rivals squared off in 13-degree temperatures with a wind-chill factor of minus-1. The Bears took the opening kickoff and maintained possession for 10:19, driving 65 yards in 16 plays to Tim Worley's 1-yard touchdown run. Detroit didn't get the ball until only 4:41 remained in the first quarter, but promptly reeled off a touchdown drive that lasted nearly seven minutes, finishing it off with Kramer's 20-yard scoring pass to Brett Perriman early in the second quarter. Despite the freezing conditions, Kramer completed 23 of 31 passes for 223 yards. Eric Lynch, playing only because of injuries to Barry Sanders and Derrick Moore, rushed for 85 yards and caught 7 passes for 46 yards. Chicago's offense faltered after its impressive opening drive, finishing with only 187 total yards.

Detroit	0	10	3	7	—	20
Chicago	7	0	0	7	—	14

Chi — Worley 1 run (Butler kick)
Det — Perriman 20 pass from Kramer (Hanson kick)
Det — FG Hanson 40
Det — FG Hanson 37
Chi — Harbaugh 1 run (Butler kick)
Det — Hallock 1 pass from Kramer (Hanson kick)

NEW ENGLAND 38, INDIANAPOLIS 0—at Foxboro Stadium, attendance 26,571. Leonard Russell ran for 2 touchdowns and Drew Bledsoe passed for 2 as the Patriots posted their biggest rout in 14 years. Russell gained 97 yards in the first quarter and finished with 138 yards on 26 carries. Backfield mate Corey Croom rushed for 93 yards on 21 carries. Bolstered by 257 rushing yards, Bledsoe attempted only 11 passes. He completed 9 for 143 yards, including touchdowns of 1 yard to tight end Marv Cook and 30 yards to Michael Timpson. The statistics reflected the one-sidedness of the game: New England had 24 first downs to 7 for the Colts, limited Indianapolis to only 37 rushing yards and 99 passing yards, outgained the Colts 400-136, and maintained possession for 38:28. Wind gusts of up to 43 miles per hour produced a wind-chill factor of minus-21.

Indianapolis	0	0	0	0	—	0
New England	7	10	14	7	—	38

NE — Russell 2 run (Bahr kick)
NE — FG Bahr 19
NE — Cook 1 pass from Bledsoe (Bahr kick)
NE — Timpson 30 pass from Bledsoe (Bahr kick)
NE — Russell 3 run (Bahr kick)
NE — Croom 5 run (Bahr kick)

GREEN BAY 28, L.A. RAIDERS 0—at Lambeau Field, attendance 54,482. The Packers sealed a playoff berth by breaking open a close game in the second half and beating the Raiders in zero-degree temperature. The game was scoreless until late in the first half, when Edgar Bennett capped a 48-yard drive with a 1-yard touchdown run just 1:01 before intermission. Green Bay then marched 74 yards with its first possession of the third quarter, increasing its lead to 14-0 on Brett Favre's 23-yard touchdown pass to Sterling Sharpe, who had 7 catches for 119 yards. Sharpe raised his season total to 106 receptions and became the first player in NFL history to record two seasons of more than 100. He also was on pace to break his season mark of 108 catches, which he set in 1992. Turnovers resulted in Green Bay's last 2 touchdowns, which came 1:50 apart early in the fourth quarter. Defensive end Reggie White scooped up a fumble forced by safety LeRoy Butler and ran 10 yards before lateraling to Butler, who scampered the remaining 25 yards for a score. Linebacker Wayne Simmons's interception preceded Darrell Thompson's 60-yard touchdown run. Thompson finished with 101 yards on 21 carries. Raiders quarterback Jeff Hostetler completed only 7 of 18 passes for 56 yards before leaving the game with a slight concussion early in the third quarter. Hostetler and backup Vince Evans were sacked 8 times. White, nose tackle John Jurkovic, and linebacker Tony Bennett each were credited with 2.5 sacks.

L.A. Raiders	0	0	0	0	—	0
Green Bay	0	7	7	14	—	28

GB — E. Bennett 1 run (Jacke kick)
GB — Sharpe 23 pass from Favre (Jacke kick)
GB — Butler 25 fumble return (Jacke kick)
GB — Thompson 60 run (Jacke kick)

PHILADELPHIA 37, NEW ORLEANS 26—at Veterans Stadium, attendance 50,085. Eagles cornerback Eric Allen returned 2 interceptions for touchdowns and the Saints' slide continued. Allen returned thefts 33 yards and 25 yards for scores, giving him an NFL-record-tying 4 interception returns for touchdowns on the season. New Orleans, which began the season 5-0 but now was on the brink of elimination after falling to 7-8, sputtered all day offensively and managed only 158 total yards. Still, the Saints led 9-0 13 minutes into the game and trailed only 15-12 shortly before halftime because Morten Andersen kicked 4 field goals after short drives following poor punts, a bad punt snap, and a recovered fumble. But Roger Ruzek kicked a 46-yard field goal five seconds before intermission, and Allen returned his first interception for a touchdown 5:21 into the second half as Philadelphia increased its margin to 24-12. After New Orleans's Brad Muster closed the gap to 24-19 with a 2-yard touchdown run, the Eagles put the game away with a 17-play, 82-yard drive that resulted in Bubby Brister's 6-yard touchdown pass to tight end Mark Bavaro 1:28 into the fourth quarter. Less than a minute later, Allen scored his second touchdown to make it 37-19. Saints quarterback Mike Buck made his first NFL start in place of injured Wade Wilson but completed only 1 of 7 passes for 14 yards. He was relieved in the third quarter by Steve Walsh, who did not fare much better, completing only 5 of 11 attempts for 78 yards, with 2 interceptions.

New Orleans	9	3	7	7	—	26
Philadelphia	0	18	6	13	—	37

NO — FG Andersen 41
NO — FG Andersen 56
NO — FG Andersen 35
Phil — Safety, Thomas sacked M. Buck in end zone
Phil — Young 49 pass from Brister (kick blocked)
Phil — Walker 11 pass from Brister (Ruzek kick)
NO — FG Andersen 37
Phil — FG Ruzek 46
Phil — Allen 33 interception return (kick failed)
NO — Muster 2 run (Andersen kick)
Phil — Bavaro 6 pass from Brister (kick failed)
Phil — Allen 25 interception return (Ruzek kick)
NO — Hughes 83 punt return (Andersen kick)

PHOENIX 17, N.Y. GIANTS 6—at Sun Devil Stadium, attendance 53,414. Ron Moore rushed for 2 second-half touchdowns to lead the Cardinals to an upset victory over the Giants. New York dominated the first half, holding a 224-85 edge in total offense and maintaining possession for more than 20 minutes. But the Giants managed only a pair of field goals by David Treadwell and led just 6-0 at intermission. Phoenix halved its deficit on a 20-yard field goal by Greg Davis 8:48 into the second half, then took the lead for good by marching 57 yards in 6 plays, the last of which was Moore's 19-yard touchdown run with 2:01 remaining in the third quarter. Moore's 1-yard run 2:51 into the fourth period put the game out of reach. The rookie running back finished with 135 yards on 23 carries. The Cardinals limited New York to 69 total yards in the second half and held the Giants' powerful rushing attack to only 78 yards for the game.

N.Y. Giants	3	3	0	0	—	6
Phoenix	0	0	10	7	—	17

Giants— FG Treadwell 19
Giants— FG Treadwell 22
Phx — FG G. Davis 20
Phx — R. Moore 19 run (G. Davis kick)
Phx — R. Moore 1 run (G. Davis kick)

BUFFALO 16, N.Y. JETS 14—at Rich Stadium, attendance 70,817. The Bills clinched the AFC Eastern Division title when Steve Christie kicked a 40-yard field goal with 3:48 remaining and the Jets' Cary Blanchard missed a 42-yard try in the final minute. It's Buffalo's fifth division crown in the last six years; four times they clinched against New York. The Bills started quickly, taking the opening kickoff and driving 71 yards in 10 plays to Thurman Thomas's 2-yard touchdown run. But the Jets tied it later in the quarter on Boomer Esiason's 24-yard touchdown pass to running back Johnny Johnson. Esiason's second touchdown pass, a 6-yard toss to Chris Burkett, gave New York its only lead of the game, 14-13 midway through the third quarter. That held up until Christie's winning kick. Christie also converted 38- and 36-yard field goal tries despite swirling winds and a wind-chill factor of minus-23. Blanchard, however, was unsuccessful on attempts from 27 and 41 yards, in addition to his miss from 42. Jim Kelly passed for 256 yards for Buffalo. Johnson rushed for 94 yards and caught 8 passes for 81 yards for the Jets.

N.Y. Jets	7	0	7	0	—	14
Buffalo	7	6	0	3	—	16

Buff — T. Thomas 2 run (Christie kick)
Jets — J. Johnson 24 pass from Esiason (Blanchard kick)
Buff — FG Christie 38
Buff — FG Christie 36
Jets — Burkett 6 pass from Esiason (Blanchard kick)
Buff — FG Christie 40

SEATTLE 16, PITTSBURGH 6—at Kingdome, attendance 51,814. Jon Vaughn ran for a career-high 131 yards as the Seahawks shredded the league's top-ranked rushing defense and put a dent in the Steelers' playoff hopes. Pittsburgh entered the game allowing only 74 yards per game on the ground. But in addition to Vaughn, playing because Chris Warren was out with a strained abdomen, John L. Williams rushed for 86 yards and quarterback Rick Mirer had 44 as Seattle ran for 267 yards on 45 attempts. Mirer had a 33-yard run on the Seahawks' first touchdown drive, which ended with his 2-yard touchdown pass to tight end Paul Green. After that, John Kasay kicked 3 field goals, and Seattle's defense limited the Steelers to 2 field goals by Gary Anderson. Quarterback Neil O'Donnell threw for 285 yards and Pittsburgh amassed 380 total yards, but could not crack the end zone. Tight end Eric Green caught 7 passes for 119 yards.

Pittsburgh	0	3	0	3	—	6
Seattle	7	3	3	3	—	16

Sea — Green 2 pass from Mirer (Kasay kick)
Sea — FG Kasay 32
Pitt — FG Anderson 42
Sea — FG Kasay 48
Pitt — FG Anderson 43
Sea — FG Kasay 35

TAMPA BAY 17, DENVER 10—at Mile High Stadium, attendance 73,434. Craig Erickson threw 2 touchdown passes as the Buccaneers stunned the Broncos at Mile High Stadium. Despite the defeat, Denver qualified for the playoffs when Pittsburgh and the Jets also lost. The Broncos struck first, driving 84 yards to a touchdown the first time they had the ball, but Erickson's 19-yard touchdown pass to tight end Dave Moore and Michael Husted's 48-yard field goal 32 seconds before halftime put Tampa Bay ahead 10-7. The Buccaneers' first drive of the second half stalled, but Denver's Glyn Milburn fumbled the ensuing punt and Tampa Bay recovered at the Broncos' 15-yard line. Three plays later, Erickson teamed with Courtney Hawkins, who caught 8 passes for 105 yards, on a 14-yard touchdown pass for a 17-7 lead. Denver pulled within a touchdown, but could get no closer. The Broncos' last drive ended on downs with 1:23 remaining after reaching the Buccaneers' 29. Tampa Bay ended a 20-game losing streak to AFC teams on the road.

Tampa Bay	0	10	7	0	—	17
Denver	7	0	3	0	—	10

Den — Rivers 5 run (Elam kick)
TB — Moore 19 pass from Erickson (Husted kick)
TB — FG Husted 48
TB — Hawkins 14 pass from Erickson (Husted kick)
Den — FG Elam 24

DALLAS 38, WASHINGTON 3—at Texas Stadium, attendance 64,497. Emmitt Smith rushed for 153 yards on 21 carries as the Cowboys blasted the Redskins to set up a showdown against the Giants for the NFC East title. Washington led 3-0 early on Chip Lohmiller's 32-yard field goal 4:30 into the game. But Dallas answered with an 80-yard touchdown march capped by Smith's 1-yard run, and the Cowboys never trailed after that. Troy Aikman threw a pair of touchdown passes in the second quarter to break open the game, and rookie Kevin Williams returned a punt 62 yards for a touchdown in the third period. Aikman passed for 193 yards as Dallas rolled up 380 total yards. The Redskins could muster only 198 yards. Mark Rypien completed just 12 of 30 passes for 91 yards and was intercepted twice. The 35-point margin of victory was the largest in the history of the 68-game series that began in 1960.

Washington	3	0	0	0	—	3
Dallas	7	14	14	3	—	38

Wash — FG Lohmiller 32
Dall — E. Smith 1 run (Murray kick)
Dall — Irvin 8 pass from Aikman (Murray kick)
Dall — Harper 15 pass from Aikman (Murray kick)
Dall — Coleman 1 run (Murray kick)
Dall — K. Williams 62 punt return (Murray kick)
Dall — FG Murray 38

SUNDAY NIGHT, DECEMBER 26

MINNESOTA 30, KANSAS CITY 10—at Metrodome, attendance 59,236. Scottie Graham ran for 166 yards and the Vikings turned 3 Chiefs turnovers into 13 points while taking a big step toward the playoffs. Though out of the race for the division title, Minnesota put itself in position to clinch the remaining wild-card playoff berth with a victory the following week at Washington. Because of losses by Denver and the Raiders earlier in the day, Kansas City had already clinched the AFC West title by the time it took the field, but the Chiefs fell behind Houston and Buffalo in the race for home-field advantage. Vikings cornerback Anthony Parker intercepted Joe Montana's pass on the second play from scrimmage and 11 plays later Minnesota took a lead it would never relinquish on Fuad Reveiz's 22-yard field goal. A pair of touchdown passes from Jim McMahon to Cris Carter helped turn the game into a rout, and Graham, who tied a club record with 33 carries, added a 6-yard touchdown run in the fourth quarter. McMahon completed 17 of 25 passes for 219 yards, and the Vikings outgained Kansas City 424-220.

Kansas City	0	3	0	7	—	10
Minnesota	3	7	10	10	—	30

Minn — FG Reveiz 22
Minn — C. Carter 31 pass from McMahon (Reveiz kick)
KC — FG Lowery 42
Minn — C. Carter 29 pass from McMahon (Reveiz kick)
Minn — FG Reveiz 19
Minn — Graham 6 run (Reveiz kick)
Minn — FG Reveiz 34
KC — Cash 2 pass from Krieg (Lowery kick)

MONDAY, DECEMBER 27

SAN DIEGO 45, MIAMI 20—at San Diego Jack Murphy Stadium, attendance 60,311. Stan Humphries broke open a close game with touchdown passes on 3 consecutive possessions, and the Chargers handed the Dolphins their fourth consecutive loss. Humphries and Anthony Miller teamed on a 41-yard touchdown pass as time ran out in the first half to give San Diego a 24-13 halftime lead. Humphries's desperation heave bounced off two Miami defenders and into the hands of Miller in the corner of the end zone. The Chargers' Nate Lewis then returned the second-half kickoff 40 yards and it took Humphries only three plays to toss a 21-yard touchdown pass to running back Ronnie Harmon, making it 31-13. It was 38-13 after Humphries and Miller teamed on a 14-yard touchdown 8:40 into the third quarter. Humphries finished with 19 completions in 29 attempts for 248 yards, while Miller caught 7 passes for 110 yards. Natrone Means had 118 of San Diego's 220 rushing yards. Dolphins quarterback Scott Mitchell completed 24 of 40 passes for 260 yards, but was intercepted 3 times. The 3 thefts—2 by safety Darren Carrington and 1 by cornerback Donald Frank—led to 17 points for the Chargers.

Miami	3	10	7	0	—	20
San Diego	10	14	14	7	—	45

SD — FG Carney 32
Mia — FG Stoyanovich 31
SD — Means 1 run (Carney kick)
Mia — FG Stoyanovich 50
SD — Means 65 run (Carney kick)
Mia — Byars 1 run (Stoyanovich kick)
SD — A. Miller 41 pass from Humphries (Carney kick)
SD — Harmon 21 pass from Humphries (Carney kick)
SD — A. Miller 14 pass from Humphries (Carney kick)
Mia — Byars 13 pass from Mitchell (Stoyanovich kick)
SD — Means 2 run (Carney kick)

EIGHTEENTH WEEK SUMMARIES

AMERICAN FOOTBALL CONFERENCE

Eastern Division	W	L	T	Pct.	Pts.	OP
Buffalo	12	4	0	.750	329	242
Miami	9	7	0	.563	349	351
N.Y. Jets	8	8	0	.500	270	247
New England	5	11	0	.313	238	286
Indianapolis	4	12	0	.250	189	378
Central Division						
Houston	12	4	0	.750	368	238
Pittsburgh	9	7	0	.563	308	281
Cleveland	7	9	0	.438	304	307
Cincinnati	3	13	0	.188	187	319
Western Division						
Kansas City	11	5	0	.688	328	291
L.A. Raiders	10	6	0	.625	306	326
Denver	9	7	0	.563	373	284
San Diego	8	8	0	.500	322	290
Seattle	6	10	0	.375	280	314

NATIONAL FOOTBALL CONFERENCE

Eastern Division	W	L	T	Pct.	Pts.	OP
Dallas	12	4	0	.750	376	229
N.Y. Giants	11	5	0	.688	288	205
Philadelphia	8	8	0	.500	293	315
Phoenix	7	9	0	.438	326	269
Washington	4	12	0	.250	230	345
Central Division						
Detroit	10	6	0	.625	298	292
Minnesota	9	7	0	.563	277	290
Green Bay	9	7	0	.563	340	282
Chicago	7	9	0	.438	234	230
Tampa Bay	5	11	0	.313	237	376
Western Division						
San Francisco	10	6	0	.625	473	295
New Orleans	8	8	0	.500	317	343
Atlanta	6	10	0	.375	316	385
L.A. Rams	5	11	0	.313	221	367

FRIDAY, DECEMBER 31

MINNESOTA 14, WASHINGTON 9—at RFK Stadium, attendance 42,836. Jim McMahon passed for 225 yards and the decisive touchdown in the third quarter as the Vikings nailed down the final wild-card playoff berth in the NFC. Minnesota was clinging to a 7-6 advantage before marching 76 yards to McMahon's 11-yard touchdown pass to Anthony Carter in the final minute of the third quarter. The veteran quarterback converted four third-down situations with pass completions on the 14-play drive. The Redskins pulled within 5 points on Chip Lohmiller's third field goal of the game, from 34 yards 5:35 into the fourth quarter, but could get no closer. Their final possession reached the Vikings' 41-yard line inside of two minutes remaining before defensive end Roy Barker sacked quarterback Mark Rypien and recovered the Washington quarterback's fum-

ble. McMahon, who was supported by only 45 rushing yards, completed 19 of 32 passes for 225 yards. Cris Carter caught 7 passes for 113 yards, including 24- and 30-yard receptions to set up each of Minnesota's touchdowns. Redskins rookie Reggie Brooks rushed for 68 yards to push his season total to 1,063. But Washington finished the season at 4-12, its worst record in 30 years.

Minnesota	0	7	7	0	—	14
Washington	0	3	3	3	—	9

Minn — Graham 1 run (Reveiz kick)
Wash — FG Lohmiller 37
Wash — FG Lohmiller 35
Minn — A. Carter 11 pass from McMahon (Reveiz kick)
Wash — FG Lohmiller 34

SUNDAY, JANUARY 2, 1994

BUFFALO 30, INDIANAPOLIS 10—at Hoosier Dome, attendance 43,028. Thurman Thomas rushed for 110 yards and the Bills clinched home-field advantage throughout the AFC playoffs by handing the Colts their eighth loss in nine games. Thomas's 3-yard touchdown run 45 seconds before halftime broke a 3-3 tie and gave Buffalo the lead for good. After Steve Christie kicked 2 field goals in the third quarter, the Bills put the game away with a pair of touchdowns in a span of 1:40 early in the fourth quarter. Jim Kelly threw a 1-yard touchdown pass to tight end Pete Metzelaars with 13:22 to play, and backup quarterback Frank Reich tossed a 30-yard scoring strike to Bill Brooks to make it 30-3 at the 11:42 mark. The final score came after Buffalo recovered 1 of Indianapolis's 4 lost fumbles. The Colts' lone touchdown came on Jeff George's 10-yard pass to Jessie Hester midway through the fourth quarter. It was just the second touchdown in the last seven games for Indianapolis. The Colts outgained the Bills 402-297, but were victimized by 4 sacks and 4 turnovers. George completed 30 of 48 passes for 338 yards.

Buffalo	3	7	6	14	—	30
Indianapolis	0	3	0	7	—	10

Buff — FG Christie 39
Buff — Thomas 3 run (Christie kick)
Ind — FG Biasucci 22
Buff — FG Christie 49
Buff — FG Christie 40
Buff — Metzelaars 1 pass from Kelly (Christie kick)
Buff — Brooks 30 pass from Reich (Christie kick)
Ind — Hester 10 pass from George (Biasucci kick)

L.A. RAMS 20, CHICAGO 6—at Anaheim Stadium, attendance 39,147. Jerome Bettis carried a club-record 39 times for 116 yards to power the Rams past the Bears. Bettis finished the season with 1,429 rushing yards, second in the NFL and the sixth-highest total ever by a rookie. He did most of the damage on this game's decisive drive, which came after Chicago had pulled within 13-6 on Kevin Butler's 53-yard field goal with 8:20 left in the game. Bettis had a 13-yard run and a 25-yard reception on the ensuing 10-play, 78-yard drive, which he capped with a 4-yard scoring run with 1:56 to go. T.J. Rubley completed 18 of 28 passes for 213 yards for the Rams, who amassed 394 total yards to 163 for the Bears. Chicago converted just 1 of 9 third-down opportunities and maintained possession for only 19:20 of the game's 60 minutes.

Chicago	0	3	0	3	—	6
L.A. Rams	3	3	0	14	—	20

Rams — FG Zendejas 29
Rams — FG Zendejas 29
Chi — FG Butler 27
Rams — Drayton 11 pass from Rubley (Zendejas kick)
Chi — FG Butler 53
Rams — Bettis 4 run (Zendejas kick)

NEW ORLEANS 20, CINCINNATI 13—at Louisiana Superdome, attendance 58,036. Steve Walsh, making his first start in more than two years, threw a 54-yard touchdown pass to Eric Martin 3:54 into the fourth quarter to provide the winning margin in the Saints' victory. The Bengals had rallied from a 13-3 deficit to tie the game on two scores just 14 seconds apart: a 31-yard field goal by Doug Pelfrey and safety Mike Brim's 23-yard interception return for a touchdown. But moments later, New Orleans's Tyrone Hughes returned a punt 34 yards to set up the winning score. Walsh finished with 15 completions in 27 attempts for 193 yards and 2 touchdowns. Martin caught 5 passes for 120 yards. The Saints finished the season at 8-8, becoming

only the third team since the AFL-NFL merger in 1970 to miss the playoffs after starting the season 5-0.

Cincinnati	0	3	0	10	—	13
New Orleans	0	6	7	7	—	20

NO — FG Andersen 43
NO — FG Andersen 49
Cin — FG Pelfrey 22
NO — Smith 9 pass from Walsh (Andersen kick)
Cin — FG Pelfrey 31
Cin — Brim 23 interception return (Pelfrey kick)
NO — E. Martin 54 pass from Walsh (Andersen kick)

PITTSBURGH 16, CLEVELAND 9—at Three Rivers Stadium, attendance 49,208. Neil O'Donnell's fourth-quarter touchdown pass to tight end Eric Green lifted the Steelers past the Browns and, coupled with losses by the Dolphins and Jets, into the playoffs. After 3 Matt Stover field goals enabled Cleveland to forge a 9-3 halftime lead, Pittsburgh pulled within 9-6 on Gary Anderson's 38-yard field goal 8:07 into the second half. The Steelers then marched 80 yards in 13 plays to O'Donnell's 14-yard touchdown pass to Green with 7:16 remaining in the game. It was Pittsburgh's first touchdown in eight quarters. Anderson's third field goal of the game, from 26 yards with 1:11 to go, increased the Steelers' advantage to 7 points. That held up despite the efforts of Browns quarterback Vinny Testaverde, who drove his team to Pittsburgh's 13-yard line, but had his fourth-down pass in the end zone broken up by cornerback D.J. Johnson with two seconds left. Testaverde passed for 249 yards and wide receiver Mark Carrier caught 4 passes for 118 yards for the Browns. O'Donnell threw for 226 yards but was sacked 7 times. Cleveland defensive end Anthony Pleasant had 3 of the sacks.

Cleveland	0	9	0	0	—	9
Pittsburgh	0	3	3	10	—	16

Pitt — FG Anderson 36
Cle — FG Stover 36
Cle — FG Stover 47
Cle — FG Stover 44
Pitt — FG Anderson 38
Pitt — Green 14 pass from O'Donnell (Anderson kick)
Pitt — FG Anderson 26

DALLAS 16, N.Y. GIANTS 13—at Giants Stadium, attendance 77,356. Eddie Murray's 41-yard field goal 10:44 into overtime lifted the Cowboys to a dramatic victory in a showdown for the NFC Eastern Division title and home-field advantage throughout the playoffs. Dallas running back Emmitt Smith, who separated his shoulder when hit late in the first half, remained in the game and finished with 168 rushing yards on 32 carries and 61 yards on 10 receptions. He had an 11-yard run and an 11-yard catch on the winning field-goal drive, which covered 52 yards in 10 plays. The Giants had rallied from a 13-0 halftime deficit to tie the game on Jarrod Bunch's 1-yard touchdown run and a pair of field goals by David Treadwell, the second of which came from 32 yards with 10 seconds remaining in regulation. The Cowboys forged their first-half lead while outgaining New York 238-68 with a healthy Smith in the backfield. Dallas quarterback Troy Aikman completed 24 of 30 passes, but for only 180 yards. Most of his completions were dumpoffs to Smith, fullback Daryl Johnston (6 catches for 47 yards), or tight end Jay Novacek (4 for 19). Smith became only the fourth player to win three consecutive NFL rushing titles, finishing the season with 1,486 yards. Phil Simms passed for 207 yards and Rodney Hampton ran for 114 for the Giants. Hampton raised his season total to 1,077 yards and became the first player in franchise history to rush for more than 1,000 yards three straight years. Despite the loss, the Giants were assured of hosting a wild-card playoff game.

Dallas	3	10	0	0	3	—	16
N.Y. Giants	0	0	10	3	0	—	13

Dall — FG Murray 32
Dall — E. Smith 5 pass from Aikman (Murray kick)
Dall — FG Murray 38
Giants — Bunch 1 run (Treadwell kick)
Giants — FG Treadwell 29
Giants — FG Treadwell 32
Dall — FG Murray 41

L.A. RAIDERS 33, DENVER 30—at Los Angeles Memorial Coliseum, attendance 66,904. The Raiders battled back from the verge of playoff extinction to beat the Broncos on

Jeff Jaeger's 47-yard field goal 7:10 into overtime. Needing at least a tie to qualify for postseason play, Los Angeles fell behind by 17 points on two occasions, the last time at 30-13 after Denver drove 71 yards to a field goal following the second-half kickoff. The Broncos had scored on each of their six possessions to that point, but the Raiders' defense stiffened and shut out Denver the rest of the way. Meanwhile, Los Angeles quarterback Jeff Hostetler was rallying his team with a 24-yard touchdown pass to Tim Brown and a dramatic 4-yard touchdown pass to Alexander Wright sandwiched around another field goal by Jaeger. The latter touchdown capped a 14-play, 70-yard drive and came as time expired in regulation. Jaeger's extra point tied the score and forced the extra session. Denver, assured of a playoff berth but needing a victory to host a wild-card game, won the toss in overtime and marched to a 41-yard field-goal attempt by Jason Elam, but the rookie's kick hooked wide. The Raiders countered with their winning field-goal drive and earned the right to host the Broncos in the playoffs one week later. The wide-open game featured 671 passing yards between Denver's John Elway and Hostetler. Elway completed 25 of 36 passes for 361 yards and 3 touchdowns, 2 to tight end Shannon Sharpe, who caught 6 passes for 115 yards. Hostetler was 25 of 41 for 310 yards and 3 scores. Brown caught 11 passes for 173 yards and 2 touchdowns. Jaeger tied an NFL single-season record with 35 field goals.

Denver	10	17	3	0	0	— 30
L.A. Raiders	0	13	7	10	3	— 33

Den — FG Elam 52
Den — Tillman 27 pass from Elway (Elam kick)
Den — FG Elam 25
Raid — Brown 4 pass from Hostetler (Jaeger kick)
Den — Sharpe 54 pass from Elway (Elam kick)
Raid — FG Jaeger 43
Den — Sharpe 1 pass from Elway (Elam kick)
Raid — FG Jaeger 50
Den — FG Elam 27
Raid — Brown 24 pass from Hostetler (Jaeger kick)
Raid — FG Jaeger 39
Raid — Wright 4 pass from Hostetler (Jaeger kick)
Raid — FG Jaeger 47

DETROIT 30, GREEN BAY 20—at Pontiac Silverdome, attendance 77,510. Free-agent running back Eric Lynch rushed for 115 yards and 2 touchdowns as the Lions beat the Packers to decide the NFC Central Division champion and set up a rematch in the same stadium one week later in the first round of the playoffs. Lynch, playing because Barry Sanders was nursing a knee injury and backup Derrick Moore had sore ribs, carried 30 times and scored on runs of 5 yards in the second quarter and 1 yard in the fourth. The latter came with 11:50 to go in the game and gave Detroit the lead for good at 23-20. Moments later, Lions linebacker Pat Swilling intercepted Brett Favre's pass, setting up Erik Kramer's 8-yard touchdown pass to tight end Rodney Holman with 9:19 left. Another interception thwarted Green Bay's last threat, which reached Detroit's 23-yard line. Favre completed 23 of 37 passes for 190 yards, including a 39-yard touchdown to Edgar Bennett in the first quarter, but was picked off 4 times. Packers wide receiver Sterling Sharpe caught 6 passes to raise his season total to an NFL-record 112, surpassing his own mark of 108 receptions that he set in 1992.

Green Bay	7	3	10	0	— 20
Detroit	0	10	6	14	— 30

GB — E. Bennett 39 pass from Favre (Jacke kick)
Det — Lynch 5 run (Hanson kick)
GB — FG Jacke 54
Det — FG Hanson 37
Det — FG Hanson 53
GB — E. Bennett 2 run (Jacke kick)
Det — FG Hanson 48
GB — FG Jacke 47
Det — Lynch 1 run (Hanson kick)
Det — Holman 8 pass from Kramer (Hanson kick)

NEW ENGLAND 33, MIAMI 27—at Foxboro Stadium, attendance 53,883. The Patriots' Drew Bledsoe threw a 36-yard touchdown pass to Michael Timpson 4:44 into overtime to stun the Dolphins. The loss was Miami's fifth in a row and, coupled with the Raiders' victory over Denver later in the day, knocked the Dolphins out of the playoffs. Before the losing skid started, Miami had the NFL's best record at 9-2. In this one, the lead see-sawed in a fourth quarter that began with the Patriots leading 17-10. It was 20-17 when the Dolphins' Terry Kirby ran 15 yards for a touchdown to give his team a 24-20 advantage with 4:40 remaining in the game. That lasted only 2:36, the time it took for New England to drive 75 yards and take back the lead on Bledsoe's 11-yard touchdown pass to tight end Ben Coates with 1:04 to go. Miami rallied again, as quarterback Scott Mitchell completed passes of 18 yards to running back O.J. McDuffie and 23 yards to Mark Ingram to march to a first-and-goal at the Patriots' 6-yard line. Three passes into the end zone fell incomplete, and Pete Stoyanovich kicked a 24-yard field goal to tie the game at 27-27 with six seconds left in regulation. In overtime, Bledsoe completed a short pass from his 32-yard line to Vincent Brisby. Brisby fumbled at the 42, but the ball was picked up by running back Leonard Russell, who scampered 22 yards to the Dolphins' 36. The winning touchdown pass came on the next play. Bledsoe completed 27 of 43 passes for 329 yards and 4 touchdowns. Mitchell completed 22 of 40 passes for 259 yards. New England closed the season with four consecutive victories.

Miami	0	7	3	17	0	— 27
New England	3	7	7	10	6	— 33

NE — FG Bahr 31
NE — Coates 11 pass from Bledsoe (Bahr kick)
Mia — Higgs 5 run (Stoyanovich kick)
Mia — FG Stoyanovich 29
NE — Brisby 11 pass from Bledsoe (Bahr kick)
Mia — Ingram 9 pass from Mitchell (Stoyanovich kick)
NE — FG Bahr 37
Mia — Kirby 15 run (Stoyanovich kick)
NE — Coates 11 pass from Bledsoe (Bahr kick)
Mia — FG Stoyanovich 24
NE — Timpson 36 pass from Bledsoe

PHOENIX 27, ATLANTA 10—at Georgia Dome, attendance 44,360. Steve Beuerlein threw 3 touchdown passes as the Cardinals closed the season with their fourth victory in the last five games. Beuerlein, who set a club record by completing 14 passes in a row to start the game, finished 27 of 33 for 278 yards. Two of his scoring tosses went to Randal Hill in the first half and helped Phoenix build a 17-3 advantage at intermission. Gary Clark had 9 receptions for 121 yards, including a 20-yard score in the fourth quarter. Cardinals running back Ron Moore gained 96 yards to finish the season at 1,018. He didn't start until the sixth game of the year, when he took over for injured Garrison Hearst. The Falcons, who began the season with five consecutive losses before climbing into the playoff picture by winning six of their next eight, lost their third in a row.

Phoenix	7	10	3	7	— 27
Atlanta	3	0	7	0	— 10

Phx — Hill 7 pass from Beuerlein (Davis kick)
Atl — FG Johnson 24
Phx — Hill 9 pass from Beuerlein (Davis kick)
Phx — FG Davis 29
Atl — Pegram 19 run (Johnson kick)
Phx — FG Davis 20
Phx — Clark 20 pass from Beuerlein (Davis kick)

SAN DIEGO 32, TAMPA BAY 17—at Tampa Stadium, attendance 35,587. The defending AFC Western Division-champion Chargers closed a disappointing season at 8-8 by beating the Buccaneers. John Carney kicked 4 field goals, including a 45-yard kick with 6:17 remaining in the game that put San Diego ahead for good at 19-17. Subsequent interceptions by cornerbacks Darrien Gordon and Brian Davis set up touchdowns just 44 seconds apart to secure the victory. Tampa Bay had rallied from a 13-3 halftime deficit behind 2 touchdown passes from Craig Erickson, the second of which covered 42 yards to Courtney Hawkins 6:34 into the final quarter. But the Buccaneers' 17-16 advantage lasted only 2:09, the time it took the Chargers to drive 52 yards to Carney's go-ahead field goal. San Diego quarterback Stan Humphries completed 18 of 30 passes for 272 yards and 2 touchdowns. Anthony Miller caught 7 passes for 119 yards. Erickson was 21 of 41 for 272 yards, but was intercepted 3 times. Horace Copeland caught 7 passes for 101 yards.

San Diego	10	3	3	16	— 32
Tampa Bay	0	3	7	7	— 17

SD — FG Carney 48
SD — Miller 48 pass from Humphries (Carney kick)
TB — FG Husted 21
SD — FG Carney 38
TB — Thomas 20 pass from Erickson (Husted kick)
SD — FG Carney 43
TB — Hawkins 42 pass from Erickson (Husted kick)
SD — FG Carney 45
SD — Young 12 pass from Humphries (kick failed)
SD — Means 15 run (Carney kick)

KANSAS CITY 34, SEATTLE 24—at Arrowhead Stadium, attendance 72,136. Joe Montana threw for 210 yards and a touchdown as the Chiefs tuned up for the playoffs by beating the Seahawks. Montana's 14-yard touchdown pass to Willie Davis in the first quarter helped stake Kansas City to a 27-10 lead at halftime. Seattle rallied in the fourth quarter, pulling within 3 points on John L. Williams's 23-yard run and Rick Mirer's 4-yard touchdown pass to tight end Ferrell Edmunds with 6:27 remaining. But on the Seahawks' next possession, Chiefs linebacker Lonnie Marts sacked Mirer, forcing a fumble that defensive tackle Tim Newton recovered at the 11-yard line. Five plays later, Todd McNair ran 2 yards for the clinching touchdown with 46 seconds left.

Seattle	3	7	0	14	— 24
Kansas City	10	17	0	7	— 34

Sea — FG Kasay 55
KC — Davis 14 pass from Montana (Lowery kick)
KC — FG Lowery 23
KC — McNair 3 run (Lowery kick)
KC — Lewis recovered blocked punt in end zone (Lowery kick)
Sea — Johnson 2 pass from Mirer (Kasay kick)
KC — FG Lowery 47
Sea — Williams 23 run (Kasay kick)
Sea — Edmunds 4 pass from Mirer (Kasay kick)
KC — McNair 2 run (Lowery kick)

SUNDAY NIGHT, JANUARY 2, 1994

HOUSTON 24, N.Y. JETS 0—at Astrodome, attendance 61,040. The Oilers routed the Jets to win their eleventh consecutive game and knock New York out of the playoffs. Reserve quarterback Cody Carlson, playing in place of injured Warren Moon, completed 23 of 38 passes for 247 yards, including touchdowns of 22 yards to Ernest Givins and 8 yards to Gary Brown to stake Houston to a 14-0 halftime advantage. Brown, subbing for the injured Lorenzo White the second half of the season, scored on a 16-yard touchdown run in the fourth quarter and rushed for 85 yards to finish the season at 1,002 despite starting only seven games. Wide receiver Gary Wellman, whose playing time increased after Webster Slaughter was lost for the season two weeks earlier, caught 8 passes for 106 yards. The Oilers' defense was dominant, limiting the Jets to 9 first downs and 164 total yards, and setting a club record with 6 sacks. Defensive end Ray Childress had 2.5 sacks and linebacker Lee Williams added 2. Miami's loss earlier in the day opened the door for the Jets to make the playoffs, but New York lost its third straight and finished at .500. Houston won 12 regular-season games for the first time.

N.Y. Jets	0	0	0	0	— 0
Houston	7	7	3	7	— 24

Hou — Givins 22 pass from Carlson (Del Greco kick)
Hou — Brown 8 pass from Carlson (Del Greco kick)
Hou — FG Del Greco 38
Hou — Brown 16 run (Del Greco kick)

MONDAY, JANUARY 3, 1994

PHILADELPHIA 37, SAN FRANCISCO 34—at Candlestick Park, attendance 61,653. Roger Ruzek kicked a second-chance, 28-yard field goal after time had expired in overtime to lift the Eagles past the 49ers. Ruzek's winning kick came after he pushed a 38-yard attempt wide right as the final seconds ticked off the clock. But San Francisco's Merton Hanks was called for roughing the kicker on the play and Ruzek made good on his next try. Philadelphia, which won its last three games to finish the season at .500, jumped to a 24-3 lead in the first half and still led 34-24 late in the game. But the 49ers, playing with most of its starters on the bench, pulled within 3 points when quarterback Steve Bono scored on a 1-yard sneak with 4:41 remaining in regulation, then forced the overtime when Mike Cofer capped an 82-yard drive in the final two minutes by kicking a 29-yard field goal with 12 seconds left. San Francisco took the opening kickoff in the extra session and marched quickly to a 32-yard field-goal attempt to win the game, but Cofer's kick hooked wide left. The Eagles' winning score was set up by Bubby Brister's scramble and 32-yard completion to 37-year-old wide receiver James Lofton. It was Lofton's only catch of the game and enabled him to become the first player in league history to accumulate more than 14,000 career receiving yards. Brister finished with 26 completions in 43 attempts for 350 yards and 3 touchdowns. The 49ers' Steve Young completed 15 of 19 passes for 165 yards and gave way to Bono after throwing a 38-yard touchdown pass to John Taylor to tie the game at 24-24 midway through the third quarter. Young became the first player to win three consecutive NFL passing titles.

Philadelphia	10	14	10	0	3	—	37
San Francisco	3	7	14	10	0	—	34

Phil — FG Ruzek 34
Phil — Evans 30 fumble return (Ruzek kick)
SF — FG Cofer 30
Phil — C. Williams 13 pass from Brister (Ruzek kick)
Phil — M. Young 8 pass from Brister (Ruzek kick)
SF — Rice 3 pass from S. Young (Cofer kick)
SF — Watters 11 run (Cofer kick)
SF — Taylor 38 pass from S. Young (Cofer kick)
Phil — Walker 21 pass from Brister (Ruzek kick)
Phil — FG Ruzek 32
SF — Bono 1 run (Cofer kick)
SF — FG Cofer 29
Phil — FG Ruzek 28

NINETEENTH WEEK SUMMARIES
SATURDAY, JANUARY 8, 1994

GREEN BAY 28, DETROIT 24—at Pontiac Silverdome, attendance 68,479. Brett Favre's 40-yard touchdown pass to Sterling Sharpe with 55 seconds remaining lifted the Packers to victory in their first playoff game in 11 years. Favre, unable to find intended receiver Mark Clayton, scrambled left and threw across the field to Sharpe, who had gotten behind cornerback Kevin Scott down the right sideline. The quarterback's heroics offset brilliant individual performances by the Lions' Barry Sanders and Brett Perriman. Sanders, playing for first time since injuring his knee against the Bears on Thanksgiving Day, rushed for 169 yards on 27 carries. Perriman caught 10 passes for 150 yards, including a 1-yard touchdown from Erik Kramer late in the second quarter to give Detroit a 10-7 edge at halftime. The Lions increased that advantage to 17-7 when cornerback Melvin Jenkins intercepted Favre's pass and returned it 15 yards for a touchdown 6:40 into the third period. After Green Bay countered with a 28-yard touchdown pass from Favre to Sharpe, Detroit appeared poised to score again, driving to the Packers' 5-yard line. But Kramer's pass in the end zone was intercepted by rookie safety George Teague, who raced a playoff-record 101 yards to give Green Bay a 21-17 lead with 1:40 to go in the third quarter. The Lions then pieced together a 15-play, 89-yard drive that consumed more than 8 minutes, taking the lead for the last time on Derrick Moore's 5-yard touchdown run 6:33 into the fourth quarter. Kramer finished with 22 completions in 31 attempts for 248 yards for Detroit, which amassed 410 total yards but could not overcome the Packers' big plays. Sharpe, who set an NFL record with 112 receptions during the regular season, caught only 5 passes but made the most of them, gaining 101 yards and scoring 3 times.

Green Bay	0	7	14	7	—	28
Detroit	3	7	7	7	—	24

Det — FG Hanson 47
GB — Sharpe 12 pass from Favre (Jacke kick)
Det — Perriman 1 pass from Kramer (Hanson kick)
Det — Jenkins 15 interception return (Hanson kick)
GB — Sharpe 28 pass from Favre (Jacke kick)
GB — Teague 101 interception return (Jacke kick)
Det — D. Moore 5 run (Hanson kick)
GB — Sharpe 40 pass from Favre (Jacke kick)

KANSAS CITY 27, PITTSBURGH 24—at Arrowhead Stadium, attendance 74,515. Nick Lowery kicked a 32-yard field goal 11:03 into overtime to give the Chiefs the come-from-behind victory. Kansas City rallied from a 10-point

halftime deficit to tie the game at 17-17 in the fourth quarter, only to fall behind again before forcing the extra session when Joe Montana threw a 7-yard touchdown pass to Tim Barnett with 1:43 remaining in regulation. That came four plays after the Chiefs' Keith Cash blocked a punt and teammate Fred Jones returned it 31 yards to the Steelers' 9-yard line. Two running plays and an incomplete pass netted only 2 yards, but Montana teamed with Barnett on fourth down. Pittsburgh led 17-7 at intermission largely on the strength of 2 touchdown passes from Neil O'Donnell, the second of which was a 26-yard strike to Ernie Mills 18 seconds before halftime. That came six plays after the Steelers stopped Kansas City on downs near midfield. Lowery's 23-yard field goal and Marcus Allen's 2-yard run 6:02 into the fourth quarter tied the game, but Pittsburgh answered with a 74-yard drive capped by O'Donnell's 22-yard pass to tight end Eric Green to take back the lead. The Chiefs had a chance to win the game in regulation, forcing the Steelers to punt just 29 seconds after Barnett's touchdown catch. Montana quickly directed a 47-yard drive, setting up Lowery's 43-yard field-goal try in the closing seconds, but the kick was wide right. The teams exchanged punts in overtime, then Kansas City drove 66 yards in 11 plays to win it. Montana started slowly, completing only 1 of his first 8 passes, but wound up 28 of 43 for 276 yards. Backup Dave Krieg subbed briefly when Montana hurt his ribs in the first quarter, and completed his only pass attempt for a 23-yard touchdown to J.J. Birden. O'Donnell completed 23 of 42 attempts for 286 yards and 3 touchdowns. Pittsburgh nose tackle Gerald Williams had 3 sacks. There were no turnovers in the game.

Pittsburgh	7	10	0	7	0	—	24
Kansas City	7	0	3	14	3	—	27

Pitt — Cooper 10 pass from O'Donnell (Anderson kick)
KC — Birden 23 pass from Krieg (Lowery kick)
Pitt — FG Anderson 30
Pitt — Mills 26 pass from O'Donnell (Anderson kick)
KC — FG Lowery 23
KC — Allen 2 run (Lowery kick)
Pitt — Green 22 pass from O'Donnell (Anderson kick)
KC — Barnett 7 pass from Montana (Lowery kick)
KC — FG Lowery 32

SUNDAY, JANUARY 9, 1994

L.A. RAIDERS 42, DENVER 24—at Los Angeles Memorial Coliseum, attendance 65,314. Napoleon McCallum rushed for 3 second-half touchdowns to decide what began as a shootout between quarterbacks Jeff Hostetler and John Elway. A wild first half ended in a 21-21 tie after the Raiders' Hostetler and the Broncos' Elway each traded 3 touchdown passes. But field position played a big role early in the third quarter: Los Angeles pinned Denver deep in its territory with a Jeff Gossett punt that was downed inside the 5, and moments later the Raiders took over at the Broncos' 35 after a short punt by Tom Rouen. Three plays later, McCallum turned a third-and-1 into a touchdown, scampering 26 yards—the team's longest run from scrimmage all year—for the score that put Los Angeles ahead for good with 8:08 left in the period. Another short punt set up McCallum's 2-yard touchdown run at the 4:27 mark, the key play on the 52-yard drive Hostetler's 33-yard completion to tight end Ethan Horton. After the Broncos closed within 35-24 early in the fourth quarter, the Raiders put the game out of reach with a time-consuming, 76-yard drive that culminated in McCallum's 1-yard run with 6:43 remaining in the game. McCallum finished with 81 yards on 13 carries and tied an NFL postseason record with his 3 touchdowns. Hostetler averaged better than 15 yards per attempt, throwing for 294 yards while completing 13 of 19 passes. James Jett had 111 yards on just 3 receptions, including a difficult over-the-shoulder grab to complete a 54-yard touchdown in the second quarter. Elway completed 29 of 47 passes for 302 yards. Tight end Shannon Sharpe tied a postseason record with 13 catches for 156 yards. The two teams combined for 814 total yards, including 427 by the Raiders.

Denver	7	14	0	3	—	24
L.A. Raiders	14	7	14	7	—	42

Raid — Horton 9 pass from Hostetler (Jaeger kick)
Den — Sharpe 23 pass from Elway (Elam kick)
Raid — Brown 65 pass from Hostetler (Jaeger kick)
Den — R. Johnson 16 pass from Elway (Elam kick)
Raid — Jett 54 pass from Hostetler (Jaeger kick)
Den — Russell 6 pass from Elway (Elam kick)
Raid — McCallum 26 run (Jaeger kick)
Raid — McCallum 2 run (Jaeger kick)
Den — FG Elam 33
Raid — McCallum 1 run (Jaeger kick)

N.Y. GIANTS 17, MINNESOTA 10—at Giants Stadium, attendance 75,089. Rodney Hampton's 2 third-quarter touchdown runs erased a 7-point halftime deficit and lifted the Giants to the victory. Freezing temperatures and blustery winds limited the effectiveness of each team's offense, so much so that all the points in the game were scored by the team that had the wind at its back. New York, trailing 10-3, had such conditions in the third quarter when it rallied to win. The Giants tied the score on their first possession of the second half, as Hampton barreled over right end for 51 yards and a touchdown just 2:54 into the third period. Shortly after that, a 21-yard punt positioned New York at Minnesota's 26-yard line, and six plays later, Hampton ran 2 yards for the game's deciding score. Primarily on the strength of Hampton, the Giants controlled the game by rushing 41 times for 176 yards and maintaining possession for 35:23 of the game's 60 minutes. Vikings quarterbacks Jim McMahon and Sean Salisbury combined to complete only 15 of 34 passes for 192 yards.

Minnesota	0	10	0	0	—	10
N.Y. Giants	3	0	14	0	—	17

Giants — FG Treadwell 26
Minn — C. Carter 40 pass from McMahon (Reveiz kick)
Minn — FG Reveiz 52
Giants — Hampton 51 run (Treadwell kick)
Giants — Hampton 2 run (Treadwell kick)

TWENTIETH WEEK SUMMARIES
SATURDAY, JANUARY 15, 1994

BUFFALO 29, L.A. RAIDERS 23—at Rich Stadium, attendance 61,923. Jim Kelly threw 2 second-half touchdown passes to Bill Brooks and the Bills overcame an 11-point deficit to advance to the AFC Championship Game for the fifth time in six years. Napoleon McCallum scored on a pair of 1-yard touchdown runs for the Raiders, the second of which gave Los Angeles a 17-6 advantage with 1:57 remaining in the first half. But Buffalo took only 67 seconds to march 76 yards and trim the deficit to 4 points at intermission. A 37-yard pass interference penalty preceded Thurman Thomas's 8-yard touchdown run with 50 seconds remaining in the second quarter. That set up a flurry of activity that saw the lead change three times in a span of 6:18 late in the third and early in the fourth quarters. Kelly gave the Bills a 19-17 edge with a 25-yard touchdown pass to Brooks with 3:23 left in the third period. Moments later, Buffalo safety Henry Jones recovered McCallum's fumble on the Raiders' 30-yard line, setting up Steve Christie's 29-yard field goal 59 seconds before the end of the quarter. Two plays after that, Raiders wide receiver Tim Brown took a short pass from a scrambling Jeff Hostetler and turned it into an 86-yard touchdown that put Los Angeles back on top 23-22. But the Bills responded by driving 71 yards to Kelly's 22-yard touchdown pass to Brooks 2:55 into the fourth quarter. That held up for the winning points as Buffalo's defense shut down the Raiders. After gaining 14 first downs in the first half, Los Angeles managed only 1 in the second half, that coming on the long touchdown pass. Kelly completed 27 of 37 passes for 287 yards for the Bills, while Brooks caught 6 passes for 96 yards. Hostetler was 14 of 20 for 230 yards for the Raiders. The game was played in frigid conditions. Temperature at kickoff was zero degrees, with the wind-chill at minus-32.

L.A. Raiders	0	17	6	0	—	23
Buffalo	0	13	9	7	—	29

Raid — FG Jaeger 30
Buff — Davis 1 run (kick failed)
Raid — McCallum 1 run (Jaeger kick)
Raid — McCallum 1 run (Jaeger kick)
Buff — Thomas 8 run (Christie kick)
Buff — Brooks 25 pass from Kelly (kick failed)
Buff — FG Christie 29
Raid — Brown 86 pass from Hostetler (kick failed)
Buff — Brooks 22 pass from Kelly (Christie kick)

SAN FRANCISCO 44, N.Y. GIANTS 3—at Candlestick Park, attendance 67,143. Ricky Watters scored an NFL playoff-record 5 touchdowns to key the 49ers' victory. Watters ran for 118 yards on 24 carries, caught 5 passes for 46 yards, and scored all of his touchdowns on short runs. No player had scored more than 3 touchdowns in a postseason game. San Francisco started the rout early, with quarterback Steve Young completing all 4 of his passes for 63 yards on an 8-play, 80-yard touchdown drive following the opening kickoff, a march capped by Watters's 1-yard run 4:27 into the game. The Giants failed to make a first down on their initial possession, and the 49ers' Dexter Carter returned the ensuing punt 31 yards to set up Mike Cofer's 29-yard field goal. Safety Tim McDonald intercepted Phil Simms's pass on the next play, leading to another 1-yard touchdown run by Watters, and San Francisco led 16-0 two seconds into the second quarter. It was 23-3 at halftime and the 49ers never were threatened. Young completed 17 of 22 passes for 226 yards as San Francisco amassed 413 total yards to just 194 for the Giants. New York, which led the NFL by averaging 138 rushing yards per game during the regular season, managed only 41 yards on the ground. The 49ers' defense also recorded 4 sacks, including 2 by rookie end Dana Stubblefield.

N.Y. Giants	0	3	0	0	—	3
San Francisco	9	14	14	7	—	44

SF — Watters 1 run (kick failed)
SF — FG Cofer 29
SF — Watters 1 run (Cofer kick)
SF — Watters 2 run (Cofer kick)
Giants— FG Treadwell 25
SF — Watters 6 run (Cofer kick)
SF — Watters 2 run (Cofer kick)
SF — Logan 2 run (Cofer kick)

SUNDAY, JANUARY 16, 1994

DALLAS 27, GREEN BAY 17—at Texas Stadium, attendance 64,790. Troy Aikman passed for 302 yards and 3 touchdowns, and the Cowboys scored 10 points in a span of 18 seconds shortly before halftime to break open a close game. Aikman's 25-yard touchdown pass to Alvin Harper 5:53 into the second quarter put Dallas ahead 7-3, a lead the Cowboys would not relinquish. After Eddie Murray kicked a 41-yard field goal 23 seconds before halftime to stretch the advantage to 10-3, Kenneth Gant made the key play of the game on the ensuing kickoff. Gant knocked the ball loose from Packers kick returner Corey Harris, and Dallas's Joe Fishback recovered at Green Bay's 14-yard line. Aikman completed an 8-yard pass to Michael Irvin, then teamed with tight end Jay Novacek on a 6-yard touchdown pass with five seconds left in the first half to make it 17-3. Aikman's 19-yard touchdown pass to Michael Irvin 9:05 into the third quarter put the game out of reach. Aikman finished with 28 completions in 37 attempts, while Irvin caught 9 passes for 126 yards. Packers quarterback Brett Favre completed 28 of 45 passes for 331 yards, but most of it came after the issue was decided. Running back Edgar Bennett caught 9 passes. Wide receiver Sterling Sharpe had 6 receptions for 128 yards.

Green Bay	3	0	7	7	—	17
Dallas	0	17	7	3	—	27

GB — FG Jacke 30
Dall — Harper 25 pass from Aikman (Murray kick)
Dall — FG Murray 41
Dall — Novacek 6 pass from Aikman (Murray kick)
Dall — Irvin 19 pass from Aikman (Murray kick)
GB — Brooks 13 pass from Favre (Jacke kick)
Dall — FG Murray 38
GB — Sharpe 29 pass from Favre (Jacke kick)

KANSAS CITY 28, HOUSTON 20—at Astrodome, attendance 64,011. Joe Montana threw 3 second-half touchdown passes, including 2 just 54 seconds apart in the fourth quarter, to rally the Chiefs past the Oilers. Houston, which entered the game with an 11-game winning streak, jumped out to a 10-0 lead in the opening quarter and still led 13-7 after Al Del Greco's 43-yard field goal with 9:37 remaining in the fourth quarter. But Kansas City marched 71 yards in only 59 seconds, the key play a 38-yard pass interference penalty against Oilers cornerback Cris Dishman, to take the lead for the first time on Montana's 11-yard touchdown pass to J.J. Birden. On the next play from scrimmage, Chiefs linebacker Derrick Thomas sacked Houston quarterback Warren Moon, forcing a fumble that defensive tackle Dan Saleaumua recovered at the Oilers' 12-yard line. On third down, Montana's 18-yard touchdown pass to Willie Davis put Kansas City ahead 21-13 with 7:44 left. Houston drove 80 yards to a touchdown to pull within 1 point with 3:45 to go, but Marcus Allen's 21-yard touchdown run at the 1:55 mark sealed the Oilers' fate. The key play on the Chiefs' 79-yard march came on third-and-1 from Kansas City's 30-yard line. Montana's arm was hit as he threw, but his wobbly pass was caught by tight end Keith Cash, who rumbled 41 yards to Houston's 29. Cash also had a 7-yard touchdown reception in the third quarter. Montana finished with 22 completions in 38 attempts for 299 yards. Allen rushed for 74 yards on only 14 carries. Moon completed 32 of 43 passes for 306 yards for the Oilers. But without the benefit of an effective rushing attack (Houston ran for only 39 yards), he was under pressure all afternoon and was sacked 9 times. Thomas, Joe Phillips, Albert Lewis, and Bennie Thompson each had 2 sacks for the Chiefs, who equaled the NFL record for sacks in a postseason game.

Kansas City	0	0	7	21	—	28
Houston	10	0	0	10	—	20

Hou — FG Del Greco 49
Hou — Brown 2 run (Del Greco kick)
KC — Cash 7 pass from Montana (Lowery kick)
Hou — FG Del Greco 43
KC — Birden 11 pass from Montana (Lowery kick)
KC — Davis 18 pass from Montana (Lowery kick)
Hou — Givins 7 pass from Moon (Del Greco kick)
KC — Allen 21 run (Lowery kick)

TWENTY-FIRST WEEK SUMMARIES

SUNDAY, JANUARY 23, 1994

BUFFALO 30, KANSAS CITY 13—at Rich Stadium, attendance 76,642. Thurman Thomas rushed for 186 yards and 3 touchdowns as the Bills qualified for an unprecedented fourth consecutive Super Bowl. Thomas, who ran for 129 yards in the first two quarters, helped stake Buffalo to a 20-6 advantage at intermission by scoring on touchdown runs of 12 and 3 yards. The Chiefs had an opportunity to cut that deficit in half, marching 75 yards to the Bills' 5-yard line in the closing seconds of the first half. But Joe Montana's pass to a wide-open Kimble Anders near the goal line bounced off the running back's hands and was intercepted in the end zone by Buffalo safety Henry Jones. Montana, who completed only 9 of 23 passes for 125 yards, sat out most of the second half after suffering a concussion on the third play of the third quarter. Backup Dave Krieg, who completed 16 of 29 passes for 198 yards, came on and led a 90-yard touchdown drive that pulled Kansas City within 20-13 late in the third quarter. But Buffalo answered with a 14-play, 79-yard march capped by Steve Christie's 18-yard field goal 3:05 into the fourth quarter. Thomas's third touchdown, a 3-yard run with 5:30 remaining, put the game out of reach. Thomas averaged 5.6 yards on his 33 carries as the Bills overwhelmed the Chiefs on the ground, outrushing them 229 yards to 52.

Kansas City	6	0	7	0	—	13
Buffalo	7	13	0	10	—	30

Buff — Thomas 12 run (Christie kick)
KC — FG Lowery 31
KC — FG Lowery 31
Buff — Thomas 3 run (Christie kick)
Buff — FG Christie 23
Buff — FG Christie 25
KC — Allen 1 run (Lowery kick)
Buff — FG Christie 18
Buff — Thomas 3 run (Christie kick)

DALLAS 38, SAN FRANCISCO 21—at Texas Stadium, attendance 64,902. Troy Aikman threw 2 touchdown passes and Emmitt Smith scored twice as the Cowboys scored on four of their first five possessions and easily handled the 49ers to win the NFC title. Dallas struck quickly, taking the opening kickoff and marching 75 yards in 11 plays to Smith's 5-yard touchdown run 6:19 into the game. San Francisco tied it when running back Tom Rathman caught a 7-yard touchdown pass from Steve Young on the first play of the second quarter, but the Cowboys broke open the game by scoring touchdowns the next three times they had the ball. They countered Rathman's score with an 11-play, 80-yard drive capped by Daryl Johnston's 4-yard touchdown run 5:12 into the second quarter. Three plays later, safety Thomas Everett intercepted a pass that was tipped by San Francisco's John Taylor, and returned it 14 yards to the 49ers' 24-yard line. It took Dallas only four plays to convert that into Aikman's 11-yard touchdown pass to Smith 6:04 before intermission. Aikman teamed with tight end Jay Novacek on a 19-yard touchdown pass in the final minute of the first half to give the Cowboys a 28-7 lead. San Francisco tried to make a game of it, pulling within 14 points on a 4-yard touchdown run by Ricky Watters, but Dallas put the game out of reach when Bernie Kosar teamed with Alvin Harper on a 42-yard touchdown pass with 2:24 remaining in the third quarter. Kosar, in the game because Aikman suffered a concussion early in the second half, kept the drive alive with a 12-yard completion to Michael Irvin on third-and-9 from the Cowboys' 19, and also had a 20-yard completion to Novacek on the 7-play, 82-yard drive. Aikman, who did not return, completed 14 of 18 passes for 177 yards. Kosar was 5 of 9 for 83 yards. Smith rushed for 88 yards on 23 carries and caught 7 passes for 85 yards. 49ers quarterback Steve Young completed 27 of 45 passes for 287 yards and led his team with 38 rushing yards. But he also suffered 4 sacks and was supported by only 46 yards from San Francisco's running backs. Dallas, which beat the 49ers 30-20 in the 1992 NFC Championship Game, qualified for its seventh Super Bowl, extending its NFL record. San Francisco lost in the NFC title game for the third time in four years.

San Francisco	0	7	7	7	—	21
Dallas	7	21	7	3	—	38

Dall — E. Smith 5 run (Murray kick)
SF — Rathman 7 pass from Young (Cofer kick)
Dall — Johnston 4 run (Murray kick)
Dall — E. Smith 11 pass from Aikman (Murray kick)
Dall — Novacek 19 pass from Aikman (Murray kick)
SF — Watters 4 run (Cofer kick)
Dall — Harper 42 pass from Kosar (Murray kick)
Dall — FG Murray 50
SF — Young 1 run (Cofer kick)

TWENTY-SECOND WEEK SUMMARY

SUNDAY, JANUARY 30, 1994
SUPER BOWL XXVIII
ATLANTA, GEORGIA

DALLAS 30, BUFFALO 13—at Georgia Dome, attendance 72,817. Emmitt Smith rushed for 132 yards and 2 second-half touchdowns to power the Cowboys to their second consecutive NFL title. By winning, Dallas joined San Francisco and Pittsburgh as the only franchises with four Super Bowl victories. The Bills, meanwhile, extended a dubious string by losing in the Super Bowl for the fourth consecutive year. To win, the Cowboys had to rally from a 13-6 halftime deficit. Buffalo had forged its lead on Thurman Thomas's 4-yard touchdown run and a pair of field goals by Steve Christie, including a 54-yard kick, the longest in Super Bowl history. But just 55 seconds into the second half, Thomas was stripped of the ball by Dallas defensive tackle Leon Lett. Safety James Washington recovered and weaved his way 46 yards for a touchdown to tie the game at 13-13. After forcing the Bills to punt, the Cowboys began their next possession on their 36-yard line and Smith, the game's most valuable player, took over. He carried 7 times for 61 yards on the ensuing 8-play, 64-yard drive, capping the march with a 15-yard touchdown run to give Dallas the lead for good with 8:42 remaining in the third quarter. Early in the fourth quarter, Washington intercepted Jim Kelly's pass and returned it 12 yards to Buffalo's 34. A penalty moved the ball back to the 39, but Smith carried twice for 10 yards and caught a screen pass for 9, and quarterback Troy Aikman completed a 16-yard pass to Alvin Harper to give the Cowboys a first-and-goal at the 6. Smith took it from there, cracking the end zone on fourth-and-goal from the 1 to put Dallas ahead 27-13 with 9:50 remaining. Eddie Murray's third field goal, from 20 yards with 2:50 left, ended any doubt about the game's outcome. Smith had 30 carries in all, with 19 of his attempts and 92 yards coming after intermission. Washington, normally a reserve who played most of the game because the Cowboys used five defensive backs to combat the Bills' No-Huddle offense, had 11 tackles and forced another fumble by Thomas in the first quarter. Aikman completed 19 of 27 passes for 207 yards. Buffalo's Kelly completed a Super Bowl-record 31 passes in 50 attempts for 260 yards. Thomas and Bill Brooks each caught 7 passes, while Andre Reed and Don Beebe added 6 receptions each. Dallas, the first team in NFL history to begin the regular season 0-2 and go on to win the Super Bowl, also became the fifth to win back-to-back titles, following Green Bay, Miami, Pittsburgh (the Steelers did it twice), and San Francisco. Buffalo became the third team, along with Minnesota and Denver, to lose four

Super Bowls. The Cowboys' victory was the tenth in succession for NFC teams over AFC teams in the Super Bowl.

Dallas	6	0	14	10	—	30
Buffalo	3	10	0	0	—	13

Dall — FG Murray 41
Buff — FG Christie 54
Dall — FG Murray 24
Buff — Thomas 4 run (Christie kick)
Buff — FG Christie 28
Dall — Washington 46 fumble return (Murray kick)
Dall — E. Smith 15 run (Murray kick)
Dall — E. Smith 1 run (Murray kick)
Dall — FG Murray 20

TWENTY-THIRD WEEK SUMMARY
SUNDAY, FEBRUARY 6, 1994
PRO BOWL
HONOLULU, HAWAII

NFC 17, AFC 3—at Aloha Stadium, attendance 50,026. The NFC converted a blocked punt and a fumble recovery into touchdowns just 2:20 apart in the second half of its victory over the AFC. With the score tied 3-3 late in the third quarter, Saints linebacker Renaldo Turnbull deflected a punt by the Oilers' Greg Montgomery, and the NFC took possession at the AFC's 48-yard line. A 32-yard pass from Bobby Hebert to Falcons teammate Andre Rison positioned Rams running back Jerome Bettis for a 4-yard touchdown run with 1:27 left in the third quarter. Moments later, Rams defensive tackle Sean Gilbert recovered a fumble by Oilers quarterback Warren Moon at the AFC's 19. Hebert then teamed with the Vikings' Cris Carter on a 15-yard touchdown pass 53 seconds into the fourth period. The NFC kept the AFC out of the end zone by maintaining possession for more than 38 minutes and forcing 6 turnovers. Rison earned the Dan McGuire Trophy as the player of the game by catching 6 passes for 86 yards. The victory was the fourth in the last six years for the NFC, which leads the series 14-10.

NFC	3	0	7	7	—	17
AFC	0	3	0	0	—	3

NFC — FG N. Johnson 35
AFC — FG G. Anderson 25
NFC — Bettis 4 run (N. Johnson kick)
NFC — C. Carter 15 pass from Hebert (N. Johnson kick)

1993 PRO FOOTBALL AWARDS

	NFL	AFC	NFC
PRO FOOTBALL WRITERS OF AMERICA			
Most Valuable Player	Emmitt Smith		
Rookie of the Year	Jerome Bettis		
Coach of the Year	Dan Reeves		
ASSOCIATED PRESS			
Most Valuable Player	Emmitt Smith		
Offensive Player of the Year	Jerry Rice		
Defensive Player of the Year	Rod Woodson		
Offensive Rookie of the Year	Jerome Bettis		
Defensive Rookie of the Year	Dana Stubblefield		
Coach of the Year	Dan Reeves		
UNITED PRESS INTERNATIONAL			
Offensive Player of the Year		John Elway	Emmitt Smith
Defensive Player of the Year		Rod Woodson	Eric Allen
Coach of the Year		Marv Levy	Dan Reeves
Rookie of the Year		Rick Mirer	Jerome Bettis
THE SPORTING NEWS			
Player of the Year	Emmitt Smith		
Rookie of the Year	Jerome Bettis		
Coach of the Year	Dan Reeves		
FOOTBALL NEWS			
Player of the Year		John Elway	Emmitt Smith
Coach of the Year		Don Shula	Dan Reeves
PRO FOOTBALL WEEKLY			
Most Valuable Player	Emmitt Smith		
Offensive Player of the Year	Emmitt Smith		
Defensive Player of the Year	Bruce Smith		
Offensive Rookie of the Year	Jerome Bettis		
Defensive Rookie of the Year	Dana Stubblefield		
Coach of the Year	Dan Reeves		
FOOTBALL DIGEST			
Player of the Year	Emmitt Smith		
Defensive Player of the Year	Deion Sanders		
Offensive Rookie of the Year	Rick Mirer		
Defensive Rookie of the Year	Dana Stubblefield		
Coach of the Year	Dan Reeves		
MAXWELL CLUB PLAYER OF THE YEAR			
(Bert Bell Trophy)	Emmitt Smith		
MAXWELL CLUB COACH OF THE YEAR			
(Earle "Greasy" Neale Trophy)	Dan Reeves		
SUPER BOWL MOST VALUABLE PLAYER			
(Pete Rozelle Trophy)	Emmitt Smith		
AFC-NFC PRO BOWL PLAYER OF THE GAME			
(Dan McGuire Award)	Andre Rison		

1993 AFC PLAYERS OF THE WEEK

Offense

Week	1	QB	Joe Montana, Kansas City
Week	2	QB	Boomer Esiason, N.Y. Jets
Week	3	RB	Chris Warren, Seattle
Week	4	QB	Dan Marino, Miami
Week	5	QB	Rick Mirer, Seattle
Week	6	QB	Scott Mitchell, Miami
Week	7	QB	Joe Montana, Kansas City
Week	8	QB	Warren Moon, Houston
Week	9	QB	Scott Mitchell, Miami
Week	10	QB	John Elway, Denver
Week	11	RB	Gary Brown, Houston
Week	12	QB	John Elway, Denver
Week	13	QB	Joe Montana, Kansas City
Week	14	WR	Tim Brown, L.A. Raiders
Week	15	TE	Shannon Sharpe, Denver
Week	16	RB	Gary Brown, Houston
Week	17	QB	Vinny Testaverde, Cleveland
Week	18	QB	Jeff Hostetler, L.A. Raiders

Defense

DE	Anthony Smith, L.A. Raiders
S	Marcus Robertson, Houston
LB	Junior Seau, San Diego
LB	Duane Bickett, Indianapolis
DE	Neil Smith, Kansas City
LB	Greg Lloyd, Pittsburgh
CB	Rod Woodson, Pittsburgh
DE	Bruce Smith, Buffalo
CB	Donald Frank, San Diego
DT	Dan Saleaumua, Kansas City
S	Eugene Robinson, Seattle
S	Marcus Robertson, Houston
DE	William Fuller, Houston
CB	Steve Jackson, Houston
LB	Greg Lloyd, Pittsburgh
CB	Nate Odomes, Buffalo
S	Blaine Bishop, Houston
DT	Ray Childress, Houston

Special Teams

K	John Carney, San Diego
WR	Steve Tasker, Buffalo
K	John Carney, San Diego
KR	Rod Woodson, Pittsburgh
P	Rick Tuten, Seattle
P	Mike Saxon, New England
P	Greg Montgomery, Houston
PR	Eric Metcalf, Cleveland
K	Dean Biasucci, Indianapolis
LB	Kurt Barber, N.Y. Jets
P	Mark Royals, Pittsburgh
P	Dale Hatcher, Miami
K	Doug Pelfrey, Cincinnati
K	Dean Biasucci, Indianapolis
RB	Reggie Rivers, Denver
K	Jeff Jaeger, L.A. Raiders
K	Steve Christie, Buffalo
K	Jeff Jaeger, L.A. Raiders

1993 AFC PLAYERS OF THE MONTH

Offense

September	QB	Boomer Esiason, N.Y. Jets
October	QB	Scott Mitchell, Miami
November	RB	Gary Brown, Houston
Dec.-Jan.	WR	Tim Brown, L.A. Raiders

Defense

DE	Anthony Smith, L.A. Raiders
DE	Bruce Smith, Buffalo
LB	Mo Lewis, N.Y. Jets
CB	Cris Dishman, Houston

Special Teams

K	John Carney, San Diego
PR	Eric Metcalf, Cleveland
K	Al Del Greco, Houston
K	Jeff Jaeger, L.A. Raiders

1993 NFC PLAYERS OF THE WEEK

Offense

Week	1	QB	Mark Rypien, Washington
Week	2	QB	Wade Wilson, New Orleans
Week	3	WR	Calvin Williams, Philadelphia
Week	4	QB	Jim Everett, L.A. Rams
Week	5	QB	Troy Aikman, Dallas
Week	6	TE	Jackie Harris, Green Bay
Week	7	WR	Michael Irvin, Dallas
Week	8	WR	Sterling Sharpe, Green Bay
Week	9	RB	Emmitt Smith, Dallas
Week	10	RB	Barry Sanders, Detroit
Week	11	WR	Jerry Rice, San Francisco
Week	12	QB	Bobby Hebert, Atlanta
Week	13	QB	Steve Young, San Francisco
Week	14	RB	Ron Moore, Phoenix
Week	15	RB	Jerome Bettis, L.A. Rams
Week	16	QB	Steve Young, San Francisco
Week	17	RB	Ron Moore, Phoenix
Week	18	RB	Emmitt Smith, Dallas

Defense

LB	Lawrence Taylor, N.Y. Giants
DT	Sean Gilbert, L.A. Rams
LB	Renaldo Turnbull, New Orleans
LB	Vaughan Johnson, New Orleans
CB	Eric Allen, Philadelphia
DE	Richard Dent, Chicago
DE	Eric Swann, Phoenix
DT	John Randle, Minnesota
LB	Hardy Nickerson, Tampa Bay
CB	Darrell Green, Washington
DE	Reggie White, Green Bay
CB	Merton Hanks, San Francisco
DE	Trace Armstrong, Chicago
LB	Dante Jones, Chicago
CB	Deion Sanders, Atlanta
CB	Kevin Smith, Dallas
CB	Eric Allen, Philadelphia
CB	Ray Crockett, Detroit

Special Teams

K	Jason Hanson, Detroit
KR	Johnny Bailey, Phoenix
P	Tommy Barnhardt, New Orleans
K	Morten Andersen, New Orleans
KR	Dexter Carter, San Francisco
K	Chris Jacke, Green Bay
LB	Darion Conner, Atlanta
K	Norm Johnson, Atlanta
KR	Vernon Turner, Detroit
KR	Kevin Williams, Dallas
LB	Jessie Armstead, N.Y. Giants
P	Sean Landeta, L.A. Rams
KR	Tyrone Hughes, New Orleans
K	Brad Daluiso, N.Y. Giants
K	Eddie Murray, Dallas
RB	David Meggett, N.Y. Giants
CB	Roger Jones, Tampa Bay
P	Jim Arnold, Detroit

1993 NFC PLAYERS OF THE MONTH

Offense

September	QB	Randall Cunningham, Philadelphia
October	QB	Troy Aikman, Dallas
November	QB	Steve Young, San Francisco
Dec.-Jan.	RB	Emmitt Smith, Dallas

Defense

LB	Renaldo Turnbull, New Orleans
CB	Eric Davis, San Francisco
CB	Deion Sanders, Atlanta
DE	Chris Doleman, Minnesota

Special Teams

S	Pat Eilers, Washington
K	Jason Hanson, Detroit
LB	Jessie Armstead, N.Y. Giants
K	Jason Hanson, Detroit

1993 ALL-PRO TEAMS

1993 PFWA ALL-PRO TEAM

Selected by the Professional Football Writers of America

Offense

Jerry Rice, San Francisco	Wide Receiver
Sterling Sharpe, Green Bay	Wide Receiver
Shannon Sharpe, Denver	Tight End
Erik Williams, Dallas	Tackle
Harris Barton, San Francisco	Tackle
Randall McDaniel, Minnesota	Guard
Steve Wisniewski, Los Angeles Raiders	Guard
Bruce Matthews, Houston	Center
Steve Young, San Francisco	Quarterback
Jerome Bettis, Los Angeles Rams	Running Back
Emmitt Smith, Dallas	Running Back

Defense

Bruce Smith, Buffalo	End
Neil Smith, Kansas City	End
Cortez Kennedy, Seattle	Tackle
John Randle, Minnesota	Tackle
Greg Lloyd, Pittsburgh	Linebacker
Seth Joyner, Philadelphia	Linebacker
Junior Seau, San Diego	Linebacker
Hardy Nickerson, Tampa Bay	Linebacker
Rod Woodson, Pittsburgh	Cornerback
Deion Sanders, Atlanta	Cornerback
LeRoy Butler, Green Bay	Safety
Eugene Robinson, Seattle	Safety

Specialists

Norm Johnson, Atlanta	Kicker
Greg Montgomery, Houston	Punter
Tyrone Hughes, New Orleans	Kick Returner
Eric Metcalf, Cleveland	Punt Returner
Steve Tasker, Buffalo	Special Teams Player

1993 ASSOCIATED PRESS ALL-PRO TEAM

Offense

Jerry Rice, San Francisco	Wide Receiver
Sterling Sharpe, Green Bay	Wide Receiver
Shannon Sharpe, Denver	Tight End
Erik Williams, Dallas	Tackle
Harris Barton, San Francisco	Tackle
Randall McDaniel, Minnesota	Guard
Chris Hinton, Atlanta	Guard
Dermontti Dawson, Pittsburgh	Center
Steve Young, San Francisco	Quarterback
Jerome Bettis, L.A. Rams	Running Back
Emmitt Smith, Dallas	Running Back

Defense

Bruce Smith, Buffalo	End
Neil Smith, Kansas City	End
Cortez Kennedy, Seattle	Tackle
John Randle, Minnesota	Tackle
Greg Lloyd, Pittsburgh	Linebacker
Renaldo Turnbull, New Orleans	Linebacker
Junior Seau, San Diego	Linebacker
Hardy Nickerson, Tampa Bay	Linebacker
Rod Woodson, Pittsburgh	Cornerback
Deion Sanders, Atlanta	Cornerback
LeRoy Butler, Green Bay	Safety
Marcus Robertson, Houston	Safety

Specialists

Chris Jacke, Green Bay	Kicker
Greg Montgomery, Atlanta	Punter
Eric Metcalf, Cleveland	Kick Returner

1993 ALL-NFL TEAM

Selected by the Associated Press and the Professional Football Writers of America

Offense

Jerry Rice, San Francisco (AP, PFWA)	Wide Receiver
Sterling Sharpe, Green Bay (AP, PFWA)	Wide Receiver
Shannon Sharpe, Denver (AP, PFWA)	Tight End
Erik Williams, Dallas (AP, PFWA)	Tackle
Harris Barton, San Francisco (AP, PFWA)	Tackle
Randall McDaniel, Minnesota (AP, PFWA)	Guard
Chris Hinton, Atlanta (AP)	Guard
Steve Wisniewski, L.A. Raiders (PFWA)	Guard
Dermontti Dawson, Pittsburgh (AP)	Center
Bruce Matthews, Houston (PFWA)	Center
Steve Young, San Francisco (AP, PFWA)	Quarterback
Jerome Bettis, L.A. Rams (AP, PFWA)	Running Back
Emmitt Smith, Dallas (AP, PFWA)	Running Back

Defense

Bruce Smith, Buffalo (AP, PFWA)	End
Neil Smith, Kansas City (AP, PFWA)	End
Cortez Kennedy, Seattle (AP, PFWA)	Tackle
John Randle, Minnesota (AP, PFWA)	Tackle
Greg Lloyd, Pittsburgh (AP, PFWA)	Linebacker
Renaldo Turnbull (AP)	Linebacker
Seth Joyner, Philadelphia (PFWA)	Linebacker
Junior Seau, San Diego (AP, PFWA)	Linebacker
Hardy Nickerson, Tampa Bay (AP, PFWA)	Linebacker
Rod Woodson, Pittsburgh (AP, PFWA)	Cornerback
Deion Sanders, Atlanta (AP, PFWA)	Cornerback
LeRoy Butler, Green Bay (AP, PFWA)	Safety
Marcus Robertson, Houston (AP)	Safety
Eugene Robinson, Seattle (PFWA)	Safety

Specialists

Chris Jacke, Green Bay (AP)	Kicker
Norm Johnson, Atlanta (PFWA)	Kicker
Greg Montgomery, Houston (AP, PFWA)	Punter
Eric Metcalf, Cleveland (AP)	Kick Returner
Tyrone Hughes, New Orleans (PFWA)	Kick Returner
Eric Metcalf, Cleveland (PFWA)	Punt Returner
Steve Tasker, Buffalo (PFWA)	Special Teams Player

1993 UPI ALL-AFC TEAM
Selected by United Press International
Offense

Tim Brown, L.A. Raiders	Wide Receiver
Anthony Miller, San Diego	Wide Receiver
Shannon Sharpe, Denver	Tight End
Richmond Webb, Miami	Tackle
Howard Ballard, Buffalo	Tackle
Mike Munchak, Houston	Guard
Steve Wisniewski, L.A. Raiders	Guard
Bruce Matthews, Houston	Center
John Elway, Denver	Quarterback
Thurman Thomas, Buffalo	Running Back
Marcus Allen, Kansas City	Running Back

Defense

Bruce Smith, Buffalo	End
Neil Smith, Kansas City	End
Cortez Kennedy, Seattle	Tackle
Ray Childress, Houston	Tackle
Junior Seau, San Diego	Linebacker
Greg Lloyd, Pittsburgh	Linebacker
Derrick Thomas, Kansas City	Linebacker
Rod Woodson, Pittsburgh	Cornerback
Nate Odomes, Buffalo	Cornerback
Marcus Robertson, Houston	Safety
Steve Atwater, Denver	Safety

Specialists

Gary Anderson, Pittsburgh	Kicker
Greg Montgomery, Houston	Punter
Eric Metcalf, Cleveland	Kick Returner

1993 UPI ALL-NFC TEAM
Selected by United Press International
Offense

Sterling Sharpe, Green Bay	Wide Receiver
Jerry Rice, San Francisco	Wide Receiver
Brent Jones, San Francisco	Tight End
Erik Williams, Dallas	Tackle
Harris Barton, San Francisco	Tackle
Randall McDaniel, Minnesota	Guard
Chris Hinton, Atlanta	Guard
Mark Stepnoski, Dallas	Center
Steve Young, San Francisco	Quarterback
Jerome Bettis, Los Angeles Rams	Running Back
Emmitt Smith, Dallas	Running Back

Defense

Reggie White, Green Bay	End
Chris Doleman, Minnesota	End
John Randle, Minnesota	Tackle
Sean Gilbert, Los Angeles Rams	Tackle
Renaldo Turnbull, New Orleans	Linebacker
Rickey Jackson, New Orleans	Linebacker
Michael Brooks, New York Giants	Linebacker
Deion Sanders, Atlanta	Cornerback
Eric Allen, Philadelphia	Cornerback
LeRoy Butler, Green Bay	Safety
Tim McDonald, San Francisco	Safety

Specialists

Norm Johnson, Atlanta	Kicker
Rich Camarillo, Phoenix	Punter
Tyrone Hughes, New Orleans	Kick Returner

1993 PFWA ALL-ROOKIE TEAM
Selected by the Professional Football Writers of America
Offense

James Jett, Los Angeles Raiders	Wide Receiver
Vincent Brisby, New England	Wide Receiver
Tony McGee, Cincinnati	Tight End
William Roaf, New Orleans	Tackle
Brad Hopkins, Houston	Tackle
Lincoln Kennedy, Atlanta	Guard
Will Shields, Kansas City	Guard
Steve Everitt, Cleveland	Center
Rick Mirer, Seattle	Quarterback
Jerome Bettis, Los Angeles Rams	Running Back
Reggie Brooks, Washington	Running Back

Defense

John Copeland, Cincinnati	End
Eric Curry, Tampa Bay	End
Dana Stubblefield, San Francisco	Tackle
Leonard Renfro, Philadelphia	Tackle
Darrin Smith, Dallas	Linebacker
Wayne Simmons, Green Bay	Linebacker
Chad Brown, Pittsburgh	Linebacker
Steve Tovar, Cincinnati	Linebacker
Tom Carter, Washington	Cornerback
Darrien Gordon, San Diego	Cornerback
George Teague, Green Bay	Safety
Roger Harper, Atlanta	Safety

Specialists

Jason Elam, Denver	Kicker
Tyrone Hughes, New Orleans	Punt and Kick Returner
Jessie Armstead, New York Giants	Special Teams Player

TEN BEST RUSHING PERFORMANCES, 1993

	Att.	Yards	TD
1. Emmitt Smith			
Dallas vs. Philadelphia, October 31	30	237	1
2. Jerome Bettis			
L.A. Rams vs. New Orleans, December 12	28	212	1
3. Gary Brown			
Houston vs. Cleveland, November 21	34	194	1
4. Erric Pegram			
Atlanta vs. San Francisco, September 19	27	192	0
5. Barry Sanders			
Detroit vs. Tampa Bay, November 7	29	187	0
6. Erric Pegram			
Atlanta vs. Cincinnati, December 26	37	180	1
7. Chris Warren			
Seattle vs. New England, September 19	36	174	1
8. Rodney Hampton			
N.Y. Giants vs. Indianapolis, December 12	33	173	1
9. Emmitt Smith			
Dallas vs. Philadelphia, December 6	23	172	0
10. Lewis Tillman			
N.Y. Giants vs. Philadelphia, October 17	20	169	2

100-YARD RUSHING PERFORMANCES, 1993

First Week
Brian Mitchell, Washington — 116 yards vs. Dallas
Thurman Thomas, Buffalo — 114 yards vs. New England

Second Week
Barry Sanders, Detroit — 148 yards vs. New England
Rodney Hampton, N.Y. Giants — 134 yards vs. Tampa Bay

Third Week
Erric Pegram, Atlanta — 192 yards vs. San Francisco
Chris Warren, Seattle — 174 yards vs. New England
Reggie Brooks, Washington — 154 yards vs. Philadelphia
Rodney Hampton, N.Y. Giants — 134 yards vs. L.A. Rams
Derek Brown, New Orleans — 125 yards vs. Detroit
Ricky Watters, San Francisco — 112 yards vs. Atlanta
Tommy Vardell, Cleveland — 104 yards vs. L.A. Raiders
Barry Foster, Pittsburgh — 103 yards vs. Cincinnati

Fourth Week
Ricky Watters, San Francisco — 135 yards vs. New Orleans
Neal Anderson, Chicago — 104 yards vs. Tampa Bay

Fifth Week
Barry Sanders, Detroit — 130 yards vs. Tampa Bay
Thurman Thomas, Buffalo — 122 yards vs. N.Y. Giants
Reggie Cobb, Tampa Bay — 113 yards vs. Detroit
Jerome Bettis, L.A. Rams — 102 yards vs. New Orleans

Sixth Week
Leonard Russell, New England — 116 yards vs. Phoenix
Roosevelt Potts, Indianapolis — 113 yards vs. Dallas
Barry Foster, Pittsburgh — 110 yards vs. San Diego
Emmitt Smith, Dallas — 104 yards vs. Indianapolis
Lewis Tillman, N.Y. Giants — 104 yards vs. Washington

Seventh Week
Lewis Tillman, N.Y. Giants — 169 yards vs. Philadelphia
Rod Bernstine, Denver — 101 yards vs. L.A. Raiders
Barry Sanders, Detroit — 101 yards vs. Seattle
Leroy Thompson, Pittsburgh — 101 yards vs. New Orleans

Eighth Week
Erric Pegram, Atlanta — 132 yards vs. New Orleans
Thurman Thomas, Buffalo — 117 yards vs. N.Y. Jets
Mark Higgs, Miami — 114 yards vs. Indianapolis
Jerome Bettis, L.A. Rams — 113 yards vs. Detroit
Darrell Thompson, Green Bay — 105 yards vs. Tampa Bay

Ninth Week
Emmitt Smith, Dallas — 237 yards vs. Philadelphia
Thurman Thomas, Buffalo — 129 yards vs. Washington
Reggie Brooks, Washington — 117 yards vs. Buffalo
Robert Smith, Minnesota — 115 yards vs. Detroit

Tenth Week
Barry Sanders, Detroit — 187 yards vs. Tampa Bay
Ron Moore, Phoenix — 160 yards vs. Philadelphia
Barry Foster, Pittsburgh — 120 yards vs. Cincinnati
Emmitt Smith, Dallas — 117 yards vs. N.Y. Giants
Thurman Thomas, Buffalo — 111 yards vs. New England
Reggie Brooks, Washington — 105 yards vs. Indianapolis
Natrone Means, San Diego — 105 yards vs. Minnesota

Eleventh Week
Gary Brown, Houston — 166 yards vs. Cincinnati
Johnny Johnson, N.Y. Jets — 141 yards vs. Indianapolis
Erric Pegram, Atlanta — 128 yards vs. L.A. Rams
Chris Warren, Seattle — 112 yards vs. Cleveland
Leroy Thompson, Pittsburgh — 108 yards vs. Buffalo
Derek Brown, New Orleans — 106 yards vs. Green Bay

Twelfth Week
Gary Brown, Houston — 194 yards vs. Cleveland
Thurman Thomas, Buffalo — 116 yards vs. Indianapolis
Ricky Watters, San Francisco — 116 yards vs. New Orleans
Mark Higgs, Miami — 108 yards vs. New England
Rodney Hampton, N.Y. Giants — 101 yards vs. Philadelphia

Thirteenth Week
Leonard Russell, New England — 147 yards vs. N.Y. Jets
Jerome Bettis, L.A. Rams — 133 yards vs. San Francisco

Fourteenth Week
Emmitt Smith, Dallas — 172 yards vs. Philadelphia
Reggie Brooks, Washington — 128 yards vs. Tampa Bay
Ron Moore, Phoenix — 126 yards vs. L.A. Rams
Jerome Bettis, L.A. Rams — 115 yards vs. Phoenix

Fifteenth Week
Jerome Bettis, L.A. Rams — 212 yards vs. New Orleans
Rodney Hampton, N.Y. Giants — 173 yards vs. Indianapolis
Johnny Johnson, N.Y. Jets — 155 yards vs. Washington
Gary Brown, Houston — 109 yards vs. Cleveland
Derrick Moore, Detroit — 107 yards vs. Phoenix
Emmitt Smith, Dallas — 104 yards vs. Minnesota

Sixteenth Week
Chris Warren, Seattle — 168 yards vs. Phoenix
Steve Broussard, Atlanta — 162 yards vs. Washington
Scottie Graham, Minnesota — 139 yards vs. Green Bay
Jerome Bettis, L.A. Rams — 124 yards vs. Cincinnati
Gary Brown, Houston — 100 yards vs. Pittsburgh

Seventeenth Week
Erric Pegram, Atlanta — 180 yards vs. Cincinnati
Scottie Graham, Minnesota — 166 yards vs. Kansas City
Emmitt Smith, Dallas — 153 yards vs. Washington
Leonard Russell, New England — 138 yards vs. Indianapolis
Ron Moore, Phoenix — 135 yards vs. N.Y. Giants
Jon Vaughn, Seattle — 131 yards vs. Pittsburgh
Natrone Means, San Diego — 118 yards vs. Miami
Darrell Thompson, Green Bay — 101 yards vs. L.A. Raiders

Eighteenth Week
Emmitt Smith, Dallas — 168 yards vs. N.Y. Giants
Jerome Bettis, L.A. Rams — 146 yards vs. Chicago
Eric Lynch, Detroit — 115 yards vs. Green Bay
Rodney Hampton, N.Y. Giants — 114 yards vs. Dallas
Thurman Thomas, Buffalo — 110 yards vs. Indianapolis
John L. Williams, Seattle — 102 yards vs. Kansas City
Roosevelt Potts, Indianapolis — 100 yards vs. Buffalo

Times 100 or More (86)
Bettis, E. Smith, T. Thomas, 7; Hampton, 5; Brooks, G. Brown, Pegram, Sanders, 4; Foster, R. Moore, Russell, C. Warren, Watters, 3; D. Brown, Graham, Higgs, J. Johnson, Means, Potts, D. Thompson, L. Thompson, Tillman, 2.

TEN BEST PASSING PERFORMANCES, 1993

	Att.	Comp.	Yards	TD
1. Steve Young				
San Francisco vs. L.A. Rams, November 28	32	26	462	4
2. Steve Beuerlein				
Phoenix vs. Seattle, December 19	53	34	431	3
3. Jeff Hostetler				
L.A. Raiders vs. San Diego, October 31	32	20	424	2
4. Brett Favre				
Green Bay vs. Chicago, December 5	54	36	402	2
5. Jeff George				
Indianapolis vs. Washington, November 7	59	37	376	3
6. Boomer Esiason				
N.Y. Jets vs. Denver, September 5	40	29	371	2
7. Warren Moon				
Houston vs. Seattle, November 7	55	36	369	2
8. John Elway				
Denver vs. Green Bay, October 10	59	33	367	1
9. Sean Salisbury				
Minnesota vs. Denver, November 14	37	19	366	2
10. Steve DeBerg				
Miami vs. N.Y. Giants, December 5	41	26	365	1

300-YARD PASSING PERFORMANCES, 1993

First Week
Boomer Esiason, N.Y. Jets — 371 yards vs. Denver
Second Week
Wade Wilson, New Orleans — 341 yards vs. Atlanta
Boomer Esiason, N.Y. Jets — 323 yards vs. Miami
Third Week
Randall Cunningham, Philadelphia — 360 yards vs. Washington
John Elway, Denver — 300 yards vs. Kansas City
Fourth Week
Jim Everett, L.A. Rams — 316 yards vs. Houston
Warren Moon, Houston — 310 yards vs. L.A. Rams
Fifth Week
Troy Aikman, Dallas — 317 yards vs. Green Bay
Sixth Week
John Elway, Denver — 367 yards vs. Green Bay
Seventh Week
None
Eighth Week
Neil O'Donnell, Pittsburgh — 355 yards vs. Cleveland
Steve Beuerlein, Phoenix — 334 yards vs. San Francisco
Ninth Week
Jeff Hostetler, L.A. Raiders — 424 yards vs. San Diego
Scott Mitchell, Miami — 344 yards vs. Kansas City
Craig Erickson, Tampa Bay — 318 yards vs. Atlanta
Tenth Week
Jeff George, Indianapolis — 376 yards vs. Washington
Warren Moon, Houston — 369 yards vs. Seattle
Sean Salisbury, Minnesota — 347 yards vs. San Diego
Jim Kelly, Buffalo — 317 yards vs. New England
Eleventh Week
Sean Salisbury, Minnesota — 366 yards vs. Denver
Steve Young, San Francisco — 311 yards vs. Tampa Bay
Twelfth Week
Todd Philcox, Cleveland — 316 yards vs. Houston
Bobby Hebert, Atlanta — 315 yards vs. Dallas
Thirteenth Week
Steve Young, San Francisco — 462 yards vs. L.A. Rams
Phil Simms, N.Y. Giants — 337 yards vs. Phoenix
Fourteenth Week
Brett Favre, Green Bay — 402 yards vs. Chicago
Steve DeBerg, Miami — 365 yards vs. N.Y. Giants
Warren Moon, Houston — 342 yards vs. Atlanta
Bobby Hebert, Atlanta — 317 yards vs. Houston

Fifteenth Week
Steve DeBerg, Miami — 344 yards vs. Pittsburgh
Vinny Testaverde, Cleveland — 319 yards vs. Houston
Sixteenth Week
Steve Beuerlein, Phoenix — 431 yards vs. Seattle
Steve Young, San Francisco — 354 yards vs. Detroit
Seventeenth Week
None
Eighteenth Week
John Elway, Denver — 361 yards vs. L.A. Raiders
Bubby Brister, Philadelphia — 350 yards vs. San Francisco
Jeff George, Indianapolis — 330 yards vs. Buffalo
Drew Bledsoe, New England — 329 yards vs. Miami
Jeff Hostetler, L.A. Raiders — 310 yards vs. Denver

Times 300 or More (37)
Elway, Moon, Young, 3; Beuerlein, DeBerg, Esiason, George, Hebert, Hostetler, Salisbury, 2.

TEN BEST RECEIVING PERFORMANCES, 1993

	Yards	No.	TD
1. Reggie Langhorne Indianapolis vs. Washington, November 7	203	12	1
2. Jeff Graham Pittsburgh vs. Houston, December 19	192	7	0
3. Tim Brown L.A. Raiders vs. Buffalo, December 5	183	10	1
4. Michael Haynes Atlanta vs. New Orleans, September 12	182	7	2
5. Calvin Williams Philadelphia vs. Washington, September 19	181	8	3
6. Tim Brown L.A. Raiders vs. Denver, January 2	173	11	2
7. Jerry Rice San Francisco vs. Tampa Bay, November 14	172	8	4
8. Michael Irvin Dallas vs. San Francisco, October 17	168	12	1
9. Jerry Rice San Francisco vs. L.A. Rams, November 28	166	8	2
10. Anthony Carter Minnesota vs. San Diego, November 7	164	10	1

100-YARD RECEIVING PERFORMANCES, 1993

First Week
Alvin Harper, Dallas — 140 yards vs. Washington
Rob Moore, N.Y. Jets — 140 yards vs. Denver
Sterling Sharpe, Green Bay — 120 yards vs. L.A. Rams
Herman Moore, Detroit — 113 yards vs. Atlanta
Eric Martin, New Orleans — 111 yards vs. Houston
Andre Reed, Buffalo — 110 yards vs. New England
Andre Rison, Atlanta — 106 yards vs. Detroit

Second Week
Michael Haynes, Atlanta — 182 yards vs. New Orleans
Henry Ellard, L.A. Rams — 127 yards vs. Pittsburgh
Rob Moore, N.Y. Jets — 124 yards vs. Miami
Nate Lewis, San Diego — 119 yards vs. Denver
Michael Irvin, Dallas — 115 yards vs. Buffalo
Jay Novacek, Dallas — 106 yards vs. Buffalo
Michael Jackson, Cleveland — 105 yards vs. San Francisco

Third Week
Calvin Williams, Philadelphia — 181 yards vs. Washington
Willie Davis, Kansas City — 139 yards vs. Denver
Alvin Harper, Dallas — 136 yards vs. Phoenix
Derek Russell, Denver — 104 yards vs. Kansas City

Fourth Week
Henry Ellard, L.A. Rams — 132 yards vs. Houston
Jessie Hester, Indianapolis — 110 yards vs. Cleveland
Ernest Givins, Houston — 107 yards vs. L.A. Rams
Irving Fryar, Miami — 103 yards vs. Buffalo
Willie Green, Detroit — 102 yards vs. Phoenix
Tony McGee, Cincinnati — 102 yards vs. Seattle
Lawrence Dawsey, Tampa Bay — 101 yards vs. Chicago

Fifth Week
Michael Irvin, Dallas — 155 yards vs. Green Bay
Johnny Mitchell, N.Y. Jets — 146 yards vs. Philadelphia
Brian Blades, Seattle — 132 yards vs. San Diego
Anthony Miller, San Diego — 123 yards vs. Seattle
Tony Martin, Miami — 110 yards vs. Washington
Chris Burkett, N.Y. Jets — 103 yards vs. Philadelphia

Sixth Week
Vance Johnson, Denver — 148 yards vs. Green Bay
Sean Dawkins, Indianapolis — 144 yards vs. Dallas
Jackie Harris, Green Bay — 128 yards vs. Denver
Mike Sherrard, N.Y. Giants — 124 yards vs. Washington
Michael Irvin, Dallas — 112 yards vs. Indianapolis

Seventh Week
Michael Irvin, Dallas — 168 yards vs. San Francisco
Tim Brown, L.A. Raiders — 116 yards vs. Denver
Ricky Proehl, Phoenix — 115 yards vs. Washington
Derek Russell, Denver — 111 yards vs. L.A. Raiders
Anthony Miller, San Diego — 105 yards vs. Kansas City

Eighth Week
Jerry Rice, San Francisco — 155 yards vs. Phoenix
Sterling Sharpe, Green Bay — 147 yards vs. Tampa Bay
Carl Pickens, Cincinnati — 127 yards vs. Houston
Herman Moore, Detroit — 120 yards vs. L.A. Rams
Anthony Edwards, Phoenix — 112 yards vs. San Francisco
Eric Green, Pittsburgh — 108 yards vs. Cleveland
Michael Jackson, Cleveland — 106 yards vs. Pittsburgh

Ninth Week
Andre Reed, Buffalo — 159 yards vs. Washington
Tim Brown, L.A. Raiders — 156 yards vs. San Diego
Andre Rison, Atlanta — 147 yards vs. Tampa Bay
Herman Moore, Detroit — 113 yards vs. Minnesota
Ben Coates, New England — 108 yards vs. Indianapolis
Horace Copeland, Tampa Bay — 104 yards vs. Atlanta
Mark Ingram, Miami — 103 yards vs. Kansas City

Tenth Week
Reggie Langhorne, Indianapolis — 203 yards vs. Washington
Anthony Carter, Minnesota — 164 yards vs. San Diego
Anthony Miller, San Diego — 142 yards vs. Minnesota
Webster Slaughter, Houston — 135 yards vs. Seattle
Irving Fryar, Miami — 111 yards vs. N.Y. Jets

Eleventh Week
Jerry Rice, San Francisco — 172 yards vs. Tampa Bay
Cris Carter, Minnesota — 134 yards vs. Denver
Andre Rison, Atlanta — 120 yards vs. L.A. Rams
Willie Davis, Kansas City — 115 yards vs. L.A. Raiders
Reggie Langhorne, Indianapolis — 112 yards vs. N.Y. Jets
Anthony Carter, Minnesota — 111 yards vs. Denver
Shannon Sharpe, Denver — 104 yards vs. Minnesota
Emmitt Smith, Dallas — 102 yards vs. Phoenix

Twelfth Week
James Jett, L.A. Raiders — 138 yards vs. San Diego
Mark Carrier, Cleveland — 123 yards vs. Houston
Anthony Carter, Minnesota — 104 yards vs. Tampa Bay

Thirteenth Week
Jerry Rice, San Francisco — 166 yards vs. L.A. Rams
John Taylor, San Francisco — 150 yards vs. L.A. Rams
Haywood Jeffires, Houston — 139 yards vs. Pittsburgh
James Jett, L.A. Raiders — 117 yards vs. Cincinnati
Mark Jackson, N.Y. Giants — 113 yards vs. Phoenix
Herschel Walker, Philadelphia — 103 yards vs. Washington
Jeff Graham, Pittsburgh — 102 yards vs. Houston

Fourteenth Week
Tim Brown, L.A. Raiders — 183 yards vs. Buffalo
Gary Clark, Phoenix — 159 yards vs. L.A. Rams
Brian Blades, Seattle — 134 yards vs. Kansas City
Don Beebe, Buffalo — 115 yards vs. L.A. Raiders
Sterling Sharpe, Green Bay — 114 yards vs. Chicago
Courtney Hawkins, Tampa Bay — 112 yards vs. Washington
Webster Slaughter, Houston — 108 yards vs. Atlanta

Fifteenth Week
Michael Irvin, Dallas — 125 yards vs. Minnesota
Herschel Walker, Philadelphia — 109 yards vs. Buffalo
Terry Kirby, Miami — 107 yards vs. Pittsburgh
Andre Rison, Atlanta — 107 yards vs. San Francisco
Jerry Rice, San Francisco — 105 yards vs. Atlanta
Anthony Miller, San Diego — 103 yards vs. Green Bay
Eric Metcalf, Cleveland — 101 yards vs. Houston

Sixteenth Week

Jeff Graham, Pittsburgh	192 yards vs. Houston
Gary Clark, Phoenix	152 yards vs. Seattle
Terry Kirby, Miami	148 yards vs. Buffalo
Jerry Rice, San Francisco	132 yards vs. Detroit
John Taylor, San Francisco	115 yards vs. Detroit
Cris Carter, Minnesota	106 yards vs. Green Bay
Sterling Sharpe, Green Bay	106 yards vs. Minnesota
Calvin Williams, Philadelphia	105 yards vs. Indianapolis
Alexander Wright, L.A. Raiders	104 yards vs. Tampa Bay

Seventeenth Week

Eric Green, Pittsburgh	119 yards vs. Seattle
Sterling Sharpe, Green Bay	119 yards vs. L.A. Raiders
Henry Ellard, L.A. Rams	114 yards vs. Cleveland
Anthony Miller, San Diego	110 yards vs. Miami
Courtney Hawkins, Tampa Bay	105 yards vs. Denver
Dwight Stone, Pittsburgh	100 yards vs. Seattle

Eighteenth Week

Tim Brown, L.A. Raiders	173 yards vs. Denver
Gary Clark, Phoenix	121 yards vs. Atlanta
Eric Martin, New Orleans	120 yards vs. Cincinnati
Anthony Miller, San Diego	119 yards vs. Tampa Bay
Mark Carrier, Cleveland	118 yards vs. Pittsburgh
Shannon Sharpe, Denver	115 yards vs. L.A. Raiders
James Joseph, Philadelphia	109 yards vs. San Francisco
Gary Wellman, Houston	106 yards vs. N.Y. Jets
Horace Copeland, Tampa Bay	101 yards vs. San Diego

Times 100 or More (116)

Miller, 6; Irvin, Rice, Sterling Sharpe, 5; Brown, Rison, 4; A. Carter, Clark, Ellard, H. Moore, 3; Blades, Carrier, C. Carter, Copeland, Davis, Fryar, Graham, Green, Harper, Hawkins, Michael Jackson, Jett, Kirby, Langhorne, E. Martin, R. Moore, Reed, Russell, Shannon Sharpe, Slaughter, J. Taylor, Walker, Williams, 2.

TOP QUARTERBACK SACK PERFORMANCES, 1993
(2.5 or More Sacks Per Game Needed to Qualify)

First Week

Robert Young, L.A. Rams	3.0 vs. Green Bay

Second Week

Sean Gilbert, L.A. Rams	4.0 vs. Pittsburgh
Anthony Smith, L.A. Raiders	4.0 vs. Seattle
Keith Hamilton, N.Y. Giants	3.0 vs. Tampa Bay
Ken Harvey, Phoenix	3.0 vs. Washington
Chris Slade, New England	3.0 vs. Detroit

Third Week

Renaldo Turnbull, New Orleans	3.0 vs. Detroit

Fourth Week

Duane Bickett, Indianapolis	3.0 vs. Cleveland

Fifth Week

Neil Smith, Kansas City	4.0 vs. L.A. Raiders
Michael Sinclair, Seattle	3.0 vs. San Diego
Henry Thomas, Minnesota	3.0 vs. San Francisco
Martin Harrison, San Francisco	2.5 vs. Minnesota

Sixth Week

Jeff Cross, Miami	3.0 vs. Cleveland
Reggie White, Green Bay	3.0 vs. Denver
Richard Dent, Chicago	2.5 vs. Philadelphia

Seventh Week

Andre Collins, Washington	3.0 vs. Phoenix
Greg Townsend, L.A. Raiders	3.0 vs. Denver

Eighth Week

John Randle, Minnesota	3.0 vs. Chicago

Ninth Week

Renaldo Turnbull, New Orleans	3.0 vs. Phoenix
Troy Wilson, San Francisco	3.0 vs. L.A. Rams

Tenth Week

Bryce Paup, Green Bay	3.0 vs. Kansas City

Eleventh Week

Jeff Cross, Miami	3.0 vs. Philadelphia
Rickey Jackson, New Orleans	3.0 vs. Green Bay

Twelfth Week

Trace Armstrong, Chicago	2.5 vs. Kansas City

Thirteenth Week

William Fuller, Houston	4.0 vs. Pittsburgh
Chester McGlockton, L.A. Raiders	3.0 vs. Cincinnati

Fourteenth Week

John Randle, Minnesota	3.0 vs. Detroit
Andy Harmon, Philadelphia	2.5 vs. Dallas

Fifteenth Week

None

Sixteenth Week

None

Seventeenth Week

Kevin Greene, Pittsburgh	3.0 vs. Seattle
Tony Bennett, Green Bay	2.5 vs. L.A. Raiders
John Jurkovic, Green Bay	2.5 vs. L.A. Raiders
Reggie White, Green Bay	2.5 vs. L.A. Raiders

Eighteenth Week

Ray Childress, Houston	3.0 vs. N.Y. Jets
Andy Harmon, Philadelphia	3.0 vs. San Francisco
Anthony Pleasant, Cleveland	3.0 vs. Pittsburgh
Marvin Washington, N.Y. Jets	2.5 vs. Houston

AMERICAN FOOTBALL CONFERENCE OFFENSE

	Buff.	Cin.	Clev.	Den.	Hou.	Ind.	K.C.	Raid.	Mia.	N.E.	N.Y.J.	Pitt.	S.D.	Sea.
First Downs	316	239	264	327	330	269	300	292	309	315	304	307	313	279
Rushing	117	89	91	105	101	71	94	95	85	116	106	116	120	114
Passing	176	133	152	187	208	180	180	168	207	169	173	180	171	144
Penalty	23	17	21	35	21	18	26	29	17	30	25	11	22	21
Rushes	550	423	425	468	409	365	445	433	419	502	521	491	455	473
Net Yds. Gained	1943	1511	1701	1693	1792	1288	1655	1425	1459	1780	1880	2003	1824	2015
Avg. Gain	3.5	3.6	4.0	3.6	4.4	3.5	3.7	3.3	3.5	3.5	3.6	4.1	4.0	4.3
Avg. Yds. per Game	121.4	94.4	106.3	105.8	112.0	80.5	103.4	89.1	91.2	111.3	117.5	125.2	114.0	125.9
Passes Attempted	497	510	478	553	614	594	490	495	581	566	489	540	563	498
Completed	304	272	262	350	357	332	287	281	342	289	294	299	301	280
% Completed	61.2	53.3	54.8	63.3	58.1	55.9	58.6	56.8	58.9	51.1	60.1	55.4	53.5	56.2
Total Yds. Gained	3535	2830	3328	4061	4145	3623	3384	3882	4564	3412	3492	3606	3383	2896
Times Sacked	31	53	45	39	43	29	35	50	30	23	21	48	32	48
Yds. Lost	218	289	289	293	279	206	204	293	211	127	160	374	240	242
Net Yds. Gained	3317	2541	3039	3768	3866	3417	3180	3589	4353	3285	3332	3232	3143	2654
Avg. Yds. per Game	207.3	158.8	189.9	235.5	241.6	213.6	198.8	224.3	272.1	205.3	208.3	202.0	196.4	165.9
Net Yds. per Pass Play	6.28	4.51	5.81	6.36	5.88	5.48	6.06	6.59	7.12	5.58	6.53	5.50	5.28	4.86
Yds. Gained per Comp.	11.63	10.40	12.70	11.60	11.61	10.91	11.79	13.81	13.35	11.81	11.88	12.06	11.24	10.34
Combined Net Yds. Gained	5260	4052	4740	5461	5658	4705	4835	5014	5812	5065	5212	5235	4967	4669
% Total Yds. Rushing	36.9	37.3	35.9	31.0	31.7	27.4	34.2	28.4	25.1	35.1	36.1	38.3	36.7	43.2
% Total Yds. Passing	63.1	62.7	64.1	69.0	68.3	72.6	65.8	71.6	74.9	64.9	63.9	61.7	63.3	56.8
Avg. Yds. per Game	328.8	253.3	296.3	341.3	353.6	294.1	302.2	313.4	363.3	316.6	325.8	327.2	310.4	291.8
Ball Control Plays	1078	986	948	1060	1066	988	970	978	1030	1091	1031	1079	1050	1019
Avg. Yds. per Play	4.9	4.1	5.0	5.2	5.3	4.8	5.0	5.1	5.6	4.6	5.1	4.9	4.7	4.6
Avg. Time of Poss.	27:30	28:58	29:32	31:35	31:48	27:55	29:28	30:21	28:59	29:43	32:16	32:15	29:52	29:03
Third Down Efficiency	43.6	34.5	32.8	43.6	44.5	29.2	40.4	36.6	45.9	38.8	41.8	39.1	39.7	35.7
Had Intercepted	18	11	19	10	25	15	10	14	18	24	12	12	14	18
Yds. Opp. Returned	174	49	246	79	309	247	111	289	329	201	310	216	271	159
Ret. by Opp. for TD	0	0	0	0	0	1	0	2	2	1	3	2	2	0
Punts	74	90	84	68	56	83	77	71	58	76	73	89	74	91
Yds. Punted	2991	3954	3632	3017	2535	3595	3240	2971	2304	3096	2806	3781	3127	4007
Avg. Yds. per Punt	40.4	43.9	43.2	44.4	45.3	43.3	42.1	41.8	39.7	40.7	38.4	42.5	42.3	44.0
Punt Returns	33	48	42	41	41	30	37	40	28	51	31	47	34	33
Yds. Returned	277	321	563	425	275	173	348	465	326	462	256	353	412	280
Avg. Yds. per Return	8.4	6.7	13.4	10.4	6.7	5.8	9.4	11.6	11.6	9.1	8.3	7.5	12.1	8.5
Returned for TD	1	0	3	0	0	0	0	1	2	0	0	0	0	0
Kickoff Returns	45	61	58	39	31	57	45	52	49	47	46	52	47	50
Yds. Returned	746	1211	1119	717	589	1124	875	1061	1068	819	675	878	901	931
Avg. Yds. per Return	16.6	19.9	19.3	18.4	19.0	19.7	19.4	20.4	21.8	17.4	14.7	16.9	19.2	18.6
Returned for TD	0	0	0	0	0	0	0	0	0	0	0	0	0	0
Fumbles	26	24	27	29	37	34	28	23	32	30	38	28	13	25
Lost	17	9	17	18	20	20	18	11	16	10	16	15	5	13
Out of Bounds	0	2	2	1	5	3	3	1	1	1	2	4	1	2
Own Rec. for TD	0	0	0	1	0	0	0	0	0	0	0	0	0	0
Opp. Rec. by	24	14	9	13	17	11	17	9	14	9	18	14	12	15
Opp. Rec. for TD	1	0	1	0	3	2	2	0	0	0	0	2	0	2
Penalties	94	105	121	112	132	94	121	148	81	64	86	100	87	99
Yds. Penalized	630	773	842	822	1005	685	969	1181	663	468	555	861	699	745
Total Points Scored	329	187	304	373	368	189	328	306	349	238	270	308	322	280
Total TDs	37	16	36	42	40	16	37	29	40	26	31	32	33	29
TDs Rushing	12	3	8	13	11	4	14	10	10	9	14	13	14	13
TDs Passing	20	11	23	27	23	10	20	17	27	17	16	16	18	13
TDs on Ret. and Rec.	5	2	5	2	6	2	3	2	3	0	1	3	1	3
Extra Points	36	13	36	41	39	15	37	27	37	25	31	32	31	29
Safeties	1	3	2	1	1	0	0	0	0	0	1	0	0	4
Field Goals Made	23	24	16	26	29	26	23	35	24	19	17	28	31	23
Field Goals Attempted	32	31	22	35	34	31	29	44	32	31	26	30	40	28
% Successful	71.9	77.4	72.7	74.3	85.3	83.9	79.3	79.5	75.0	61.3	65.4	93.3	77.5	82.1

AMERICAN FOOTBALL CONFERENCE DEFENSE

	Buff.	Cin.	Clev.	Den.	Hou.	Ind.	K.C.	Raid.	Mia.	N.E.	N.Y.J.	Pitt.	S.D.	Sea.
First Downs	331	306	290	280	289	334	300	302	332	269	266	267	299	322
Rushing	114	134	94	86	73	151	103	111	103	97	93	74	86	106
Passing	199	159	170	181	184	166	161	154	205	161	161	163	192	193
Penalty	18	13	26	13	32	17	36	37	24	11	12	30	21	23
Rushes	500	521	451	397	369	575	453	494	460	505	420	399	414	452
Net Yds. Gained	1921	2220	1654	1418	1273	2521	1620	1865	1665	1951	1473	1368	1314	1660
Avg. Gain	3.8	4.3	3.7	3.6	3.4	4.4	3.6	3.8	3.6	3.9	3.5	3.4	3.2	3.7
Avg. Yds. per Game	120.1	138.8	103.4	88.6	79.6	157.6	101.3	116.6	104.1	121.9	92.1	85.5	82.1	103.8
Passes Attempted	582	457	541	562	582	454	525	457	572	474	497	521	556	595
Completed	323	251	306	314	302	270	312	258	350	280	296	277	329	333
% Completed	55.5	54.9	56.6	55.9	51.9	59.5	59.4	56.5	61.2	59.1	59.6	53.2	59.2	56.0
Total Yds. Gained	3889	2952	3466	3969	3914	3238	3379	3141	3682	3087	3434	3440	3958	3897
Times Sacked	37	22	48	46	52	21	35	45	29	34	32	42	32	38
Yds. Lost	256	154	342	238	313	121	228	283	197	242	195	277	206	244
Net Yds. Gained	3633	2798	3124	3731	3601	3117	3151	2858	3485	2845	3239	3163	3752	3653
Avg. Yds. per Game	227.1	174.9	195.3	233.2	225.1	194.8	196.9	178.6	217.8	177.8	202.4	197.7	234.5	228.3
Net Yds. per Pass Play	5.87	5.84	5.30	6.14	5.68	6.56	5.63	5.69	5.80	5.60	6.12	5.62	6.38	5.77
Yds. Gained per Comp.	12.04	11.76	11.33	12.64	12.96	11.99	10.83	12.17	10.52	11.03	11.60	12.42	12.03	11.70
Combined Net														
Yds. Gained	5554	5018	4778	5149	4874	5638	4771	4723	5150	4796	4712	4531	5066	5313
% Total Yds. Rushing	34.6	44.2	34.6	27.5	26.1	44.7	34.0	39.5	32.3	40.7	31.3	30.2	25.9	31.2
% Total Yds. Passing	65.4	55.8	65.4	72.5	73.9	55.3	66.0	60.5	67.7	59.3	68.7	69.8	74.1	68.8
Avg. Yds. per Game	347.1	313.6	298.6	321.8	304.6	352.4	298.2	295.2	321.9	299.8	294.5	283.2	316.6	332.1
Ball Control Plays	1119	1000	1040	1005	1003	1050	1013	996	1061	1013	949	962	1002	1085
Avg. Yds. per Play	5.0	5.0	4.6	5.1	4.9	5.4	4.7	4.7	4.9	4.7	5.0	4.7	5.1	4.9
Avg. Time of Poss.	32:30	31:02	30:28	28:25	28:12	32:05	30:32	29:39	31:01	30:17	27:44	27:45	30:08	30:57
Third Down Efficiency	45.5	40.1	38.1	33.0	30.8	41.3	41.0	36.3	45.0	41.6	40.5	33.8	39.5	39.7
Intercepted By	23	12	13	18	26	10	21	14	13	13	19	24	22	22
Yds. Returned By	306	272	208	236	412	116	225	199	175	122	233	386	319	196
Returned for TD	3	2	1	1	3	0	0	1	1	0	1	1	1	1
Punts	65	74	85	81	79	71	68	80	76	90	66	82	72	73
Yds. Punted	2719	3123	3603	3541	3454	2855	3035	3369	3135	3709	2859	3600	3031	3097
Avg. Yds. per Punt	41.8	42.2	42.4	43.7	43.7	40.2	44.6	42.1	41.3	41.2	43.3	43.9	42.1	42.4
Punt Returns	29	47	49	33	28	41	43	35	32	34	26	50	36	47
Yds. Returned	247	416	438	337	249	352	352	301	359	313	156	678	292	475
Avg. Yds. per Return	8.5	8.9	8.9	10.2	8.9	8.6	8.2	8.6	11.2	9.2	6.0	13.6	8.1	10.1
Returned for TD	0	0	0	0	0	1	0	0	1	1	0	3	0	1
Kickoff Returns	43	38	46	63	60	37	49	45	62	44	47	54	64	52
Yds. Returned	850	831	814	1119	1062	551	1007	783	1239	921	911	1165	1063	967
Avg. Yds. per Return	19.8	21.9	17.7	17.8	17.7	14.9	20.6	17.4	20.0	20.9	19.4	21.6	16.6	18.6
Returned for TD	0	0	0	0	0	0	0	0	0	0	0	1	0	1
Fumbles	35	22	29	27	32	25	30	23	30	20	30	37	19	23
Lost	24	14	9	13	17	11	17	9	14	9	18	14	12	15
Out of Bounds	0	3	5	1	3	1	2	1	1	3	0	1	0	2
Own Rec. for TD	0	0	0	0	0	0	0	0	0	0	0	1	0	0
Opp. Rec. by	17	9	17	18	20	20	18	11	16	10	16	15	5	13
Opp. Rec. for TD	0	2	2	0	1	1	1	1	2	1	0	1	1	1
Penalties	99	73	105	128	103	87	127	105	92	111	86	77	94	109
Yds. Penalized	681	567	821	1019	791	610	1015	801	650	803	661	652	724	818
Total Points Scored	242	319	307	284	238	378	291	326	351	286	247	281	290	314
Total TDs	25	37	30	27	26	45	30	37	43	32	26	30	30	32
TDs Rushing	7	15	9	6	9	20	11	17	12	9	8	6	10	12
TDs Passing	18	20	19	21	16	22	18	17	26	20	15	16	17	16
TDs on Ret. and Rec.	0	2	2	0	1	3	1	3	5	3	3	8	3	4
Extra Points	23	37	30	27	25	43	27	37	40	32	26	29	30	31
Safeties	0	0	2	1	0	1	0	2	1	1	1	0	1	2
Field Goals Made	23	20	31	31	19	21	28	21	17	20	21	24	26	29
Field Goals Attempted	35	28	38	36	28	30	32	33	27	24	26	29	33	39
% Successful	65.7	71.4	81.6	86.1	67.9	70.0	87.5	63.6	63.0	83.3	80.8	82.8	78.8	74.4

NATIONAL FOOTBALL CONFERENCE OFFENSE

	Atl.	Chi.	Dall.	Det.	G.B.	Rams	Minn.	N.O.	N.Y.G.	Phil.	Phx.	S.F.	T.B.	Wash.
First Downs	292	226	322	248	282	278	283	264	300	303	295	372	241	255
Rushing	91	98	120	101	98	117	85	94	127	104	107	134	80	92
Passing	185	113	172	139	166	147	182	158	153	184	173	212	141	143
Penalty	16	15	30	8	18	14	16	12	20	15	15	26	20	20
Rushes	395	477	490	456	448	449	447	414	560	456	452	463	402	396
Net Yds. Gained	1590	1677	2161	1944	1619	2014	1624	1766	2210	1761	1809	2133	1290	1728
Avg. Gain	4.0	3.5	4.4	4.3	3.6	4.5	3.6	4.3	3.9	3.9	4.0	4.6	3.2	4.4
Avg. Yds. per Game	99.4	104.8	135.1	121.5	101.2	125.9	101.5	110.4	138.1	110.1	113.1	133.3	80.6	108.0
Passes Attempted	573	388	475	435	528	473	526	481	424	556	522	524	508	533
Completed	334	230	317	264	322	247	315	274	257	328	310	354	262	287
% Completed	58.3	59.3	66.7	60.7	61.0	52.2	59.9	57.0	60.6	59.0	59.4	67.6	51.6	53.8
Total Yds. Gained	3787	2270	3617	2943	3330	3021	3381	3183	3180	3463	3635	4480	3295	2764
Times Sacked	40	48	29	46	30	31	35	40	40	42	33	35	39	40
Yds. Lost	267	230	163	229	199	231	181	242	245	302	231	178	274	219
Net Yds. Gained	3520	2040	3454	2714	3131	2790	3200	2941	2935	3161	3404	4302	3021	2545
Avg. Yds. per Game	220.0	127.5	215.9	169.6	195.7	174.4	200.0	183.8	183.4	197.6	212.8	268.9	188.8	159.1
Net Yds. per Pass Play	5.74	4.68	6.85	5.64	5.61	5.54	5.70	5.64	6.33	5.29	6.13	7.70	5.52	4.44
Yds. Gained per Comp.	11.34	9.87	11.41	11.15	10.34	12.23	10.73	11.62	12.37	10.56	11.73	12.66	12.58	9.63
Combined Net Yds. Gained	5110	3717	5615	4658	4750	4804	4824	4707	5145	4922	5213	6435	4311	4273
% Total Yds. Rushing	31.1	45.1	38.5	41.7	34.1	41.9	33.7	37.5	43.0	35.8	34.7	33.1	29.9	40.4
% Total Yds. Passing	68.9	54.9	61.5	58.3	65.9	58.1	66.3	62.5	57.0	64.2	65.3	66.9	70.1	59.6
Avg. Yds. per Game	319.4	232.3	350.9	291.1	296.9	300.3	301.5	294.2	321.6	307.6	325.8	402.2	269.4	267.1
Ball Control Plays	1008	913	994	937	1006	953	1008	935	1024	1054	1007	1022	949	969
Avg. Yds. per Play	5.1	4.1	5.6	5.0	4.7	5.0	4.8	5.0	5.0	4.7	5.2	6.3	4.5	4.4
Avg. Time of Poss.	31:23	28:36	30:56	29:27	30:53	28:18	30:28	28:32	32:18	31:00	31:54	30:24	28:38	27:58
Third Down Efficiency	38.3	34.6	41.9	34.6	37.2	39.1	34.0	35.5	40.7	41.1	46.2	47.8	34.7	34.7
Had Intercepted	25	16	6	19	24	19	14	21	9	13	20	17	25	21
Yds. Opp Returned	345	105	47	177	437	347	166	444	175	107	143	157	280	209
Ret. by Opp. for TD	2	1	0	1	3	2	3	6	1	0	0	0	1	2
Punts	72	80	56	72	74	80	90	77	78	83	73	42	94	83
Yds. Punted	3114	3080	2342	3207	3174	3271	3862	3356	3272	3323	3189	1718	3772	3644
Avg. Yds. per Punt	43.3	38.5	41.8	44.5	42.9	40.9	42.9	43.6	41.9	40.0	43.7	40.9	40.1	43.9
Punt Returns	35	35	37	40	45	19	39	38	32	33	47	35	35	35
Yds. Returned	276	289	381	349	404	102	280	517	331	284	384	411	311	245
Avg. Yds. per Return	7.9	8.3	10.3	8.7	9.0	5.4	7.2	13.6	10.3	8.6	8.2	11.7	8.2	7.0
Returned for TD	0	0	2	0	0	0	0	2	1	0	1	1	0	0
Kickoff Returns	55	45	36	52	60	49	55	62	32	54	45	40	58	59
Yds. Returned	1300	811	758	1204	1483	824	1086	1460	507	987	951	715	922	1166
Avg. Yds. per Return	23.6	18.0	21.1	23.2	24.7	16.8	19.7	23.5	15.8	18.3	21.1	17.9	15.9	19.8
Returned for TD	1	0	0	1	1	0	0	1	0	0	0	0	0	0
Fumbles	31	29	33	29	26	20	15	24	19	32	23	32	28	24
Lost	17	14	16	13	10	11	10	13	8	21	11	13	11	10
Out of Bounds	1	1	3	4	1	1	1	0	1	1	1	3	1	0
Own Rec. for TD	0	0	0	0	0	0	0	0	0	0	1	0	0	0
Opp. Rec. by	11	12	14	16	15	9	10	20	10	15	17	11	13	14
Opp. Rec. for TD	1	2	0	2	1	1	0	2	0	1	2	1	0	2
Penalties	111	68	94	93	85	71	109	81	90	101	77	95	89	90
Yds. Penalized	838	587	744	665	734	526	806	663	596	770	644	800	765	597
Total Points Scored	316	234	376	298	340	221	277	317	288	293	326	473	237	230
Total TDs	34	22	41	28	35	25	28	33	30	35	37	61	27	26
TDs Rushing	4	10	20	9	14	8	8	10	11	7	12	26	6	11
TDs Passing	28	7	18	15	19	16	18	18	17	23	21	29	19	11
TDs on Ret. and Rec.	2	5	3	4	2	1	2	5	2	5	4	6	2	4
Extra Points	34	21	40	28	35	23	27	33	28	31	37	59	27	24
Safeties	0	0	0	0	1	0	2	1	1	2	2	0	0	1
Field Goals Made	26	27	30	34	31	16	26	28	26	16	21	16	16	16
Field Goals Attempted	27	36	37	43	37	23	35	35	34	23	28	26	22	28
% Successful	96.3	75.0	81.1	79.1	83.8	69.6	74.3	80.0	76.5	69.6	75.0	61.5	72.7	57.1

NATIONAL FOOTBALL CONFERENCE DEFENSE

	Atl.	Chi.	Dall.	Det.	G.B.	Rams	Minn.	N.O.	N.Y.G.	Phil.	Phx.	S.F.	T.B.	Wash.
First Downs	278	289	297	279	261	304	259	273	268	271	278	297	280	304
Rushing	79	112	94	108	88	117	98	116	89	91	106	109	109	127
Passing	180	163	176	154	157	179	139	145	161	155	158	171	152	157
Penalty	19	14	27	17	16	8	22	12	18	25	14	17	19	20
Rushes	419	476	423	433	424	480	415	513	395	467	433	404	479	513
Net Yds. Gained	1784	1835	1651	1649	1582	1851	1536	2090	1547	2080	1861	1800	1994	2112
Avg. Gain	4.3	3.9	3.9	3.8	3.7	3.9	3.7	4.1	3.9	4.5	4.3	4.5	4.2	4.1
Avg. Yds. per Game	111.5	114.7	103.2	103.1	98.9	115.7	96.0	130.6	96.7	130.0	116.3	112.5	124.6	132.0
Passes Attempted	505	504	555	514	529	488	478	444	514	463	495	564	503	483
Completed	308	306	334	309	290	299	310	259	298	251	281	314	300	291
% Completed	61.0	60.7	60.2	60.1	54.8	61.3	64.9	58.3	58.0	54.2	56.8	55.7	59.6	60.2
Total Yds. Gained	3786	3105	3347	3273	3201	3763	3146	2924	3354	3153	3511	3513	3384	3584
Times Sacked	27	46	34	43	46	35	45	51	41	36	34	44	29	31
Yds. Lost	149	287	231	253	301	203	276	318	238	214	205	316	132	197
Net Yds. Gained	3637	2818	3116	3020	2900	3560	2870	2606	3116	2939	3306	3197	3252	3387
Avg. Yds. per Game	227.3	176.1	194.8	188.8	181.3	222.5	179.4	162.9	194.8	183.7	206.6	199.8	203.3	211.7
Net Yds. per Pass Play	6.84	5.12	5.29	5.42	5.04	6.81	5.49	5.26	5.61	5.89	6.25	5.26	6.11	6.59
Yds. Gained per Comp.	12.29	10.15	10.02	10.59	11.04	12.59	10.15	11.29	11.26	12.56	12.49	11.19	11.28	12.32
Combined Net Yds. Gained	5421	4653	4767	4669	4482	5411	4406	4696	4663	5019	5167	4997	5246	5499
% Total Yds. Rushing	32.9	39.4	34.6	35.3	35.3	34.2	34.9	44.5	33.2	41.4	36.0	36.0	38.0	38.4
% Total Yds. Passing	67.1	60.6	65.4	64.7	64.7	65.8	65.1	55.5	66.8	58.6	64.0	64.0	62.0	61.6
Avg. Yds. per Game	338.8	290.8	297.9	291.8	280.1	338.2	275.4	293.5	291.4	313.7	322.9	312.3	327.9	343.7
Ball Control Plays	951	1026	1012	990	999	1003	938	1008	950	966	962	1012	1011	1027
Avg. Yds. per Play	5.7	4.5	4.7	4.7	4.5	5.4	4.7	4.7	4.9	5.2	5.4	4.9	5.2	5.4
Avg. Time of Poss.	28:37	31:24	29:04	30:33	29:07	31:42	29:33	31:28	27:42	29:00	28:06	29:36	31:22	32:02
Third Down Efficiency	36.5	37.4	39.7	40.9	32.3	46.8	39.1	40.5	34.2	32.2	36.9	40.7	37.9	42.8
Intercepted By	13	18	14	19	18	11	24	10	18	20	9	19	9	17
Yds. Returned By	160	300	171	156	255	127	211	133	184	324	124	267	71	241
Returned for TD	0	2	1	1	0	0	2	0	1	4	1	3	2	2
Punts	74	78	78	81	79	58	78	80	80	75	78	68	76	73
Yds. Punted	3029	3231	3219	3489	3176	2451	3307	3384	3224	3137	3333	2985	3290	2995
Avg. Yds. per Punt	40.9	41.4	41.3	43.1	40.2	42.3	42.4	42.3	40.3	41.8	42.7	43.9	43.3	41.0
Punt Returns	41	22	32	45	38	43	46	36	44	35	30	15	53	34
Yds. Returned	350	115	169	377	350	533	560	348	247	311	267	171	394	343
Avg. Yds. per Return	8.5	5.2	5.3	8.4	9.2	12.4	12.2	9.7	5.6	8.9	8.9	11.4	7.4	10.1
Returned for TD	0	0	0	0	0	2	1	1	0	1	0	0	0	2
Kickoff Returns	55	53	66	30	70	47	58	40	29	53	51	61	28	36
Yds. Returned	1064	918	1225	609	1407	984	1420	788	646	1133	994	1196	499	722
Avg. Yds. per Return	19.3	17.3	18.6	20.3	20.1	20.9	24.5	19.7	22.3	21.4	19.5	19.6	17.8	20.1
Returned for TD	0	0	1	0	0	0	1	0	0	0	0	0	0	0
Fumbles	25	24	22	34	33	26	24	30	27	33	27	20	27	25
Lost	11	12	14	16	15	9	10	20	10	15	17	11	13	14
Out of Bounds	5	0	1	2	2	0	1	1	4	0	2	1	4	1
Own Rec. for TD	0	0	0	0	0	0	0	0	0	0	0	0	1	0
Opp. Rec. by	17	14	16	13	10	11	10	13	8	21	11	13	11	10
Opp. Rec. for TD	3	0	1	0	2	1	1	3	0	1	0	1	1	0
Penalties	100	91	87	73	85	80	97	86	98	85	95	99	126	100
Yds. Penalized	874	783	653	500	712	542	768	590	820	610	730	743	913	782
Total Points Scored	385	230	229	292	282	367	290	343	205	315	269	295	376	345
Total TDs	46	22	23	32	27	40	31	39	22	35	27	30	40	42
TDs Rushing	14	9	7	12	6	18	14	7	7	11	13	6	15	14
TDs Passing	27	12	14	19	16	17	11	22	13	22	14	23	22	24
TDs on Ret. and Rec.	5	1	2	1	5	5	6	10	2	2	0	1	3	4
Extra Points	45	20	23	31	27	38	29	35	22	34	27	30	38	40
Safeties	2	0	1	0	0	1	0	1	0	1	1	2	1	1
Field Goals Made	20	26	22	23	31	29	25	24	17	23	26	27	32	17
Field Goals Attempted	31	34	27	30	40	37	33	30	23	34	35	30	35	22
% Successful	64.5	76.5	81.5	76.7	77.5	78.4	75.8	80.0	73.9	67.6	74.3	90.0	91.4	77.3

AFC, NFC, AND NFL SUMMARY

	AFC Offense Total	AFC Offense Average	AFC Defense Total	AFC Defense Average	NFC Offense Total	NFC Offense Average	NFC Defense Total	NFC Defense Average	NFL Total	NFL Average
First Downs	4164	297.4	4187	299.1	3961	282.9	3938	281.3	8125	290.2
Rushing	1420	101.4	1425	101.8	1448	103.4	1443	103.1	2868	102.4
Passing	2428	173.4	2449	174.9	2268	162.0	2247	160.5	4696	167.7
Penalty	316	22.6	313	22.4	245	17.5	248	17.7	561	20.0
Rushes	6379	455.6	6410	457.9	6305	450.4	6274	448.1	12684	453.0
Net Yds. Gained	23969	1712.1	23923	1708.8	25326	1809.0	25372	1812.3	49295	1760.5
Avg. Gain	——	3.8	——	3.7	——	4.0	——	4.0	——	3.9
Avg. Yds. per Game	——	107.0	——	106.8	——	113.1	——	113.3	——	110.0
Passes Attempted	7468	533.4	7375	526.8	6946	496.1	7039	502.8	14414	514.8
Completed	4250	303.6	4201	300.1	4101	292.9	4150	296.4	8351	298.3
% Completed	——	56.9	——	57.0	——	59.0	——	59.0	——	57.9
Total Yds. Gained	50141	3581.5	49446	3531.9	46349	3310.6	47044	3360.3	96490	3446.1
Times Sacked	527	37.6	513	36.6	528	37.7	542	38.7	1055	37.7
Yds. Lost	3425	244.6	3296	235.4	3191	227.9	3320	237.1	6616	236.3
Net Yds. Gained	46716	3336.9	46150	3296.4	43158	3082.7	43724	3123.1	89874	3209.8
Avg. Yds. per Game	——	208.6	——	206.0	——	192.7	——	195.2	——	200.6
Net Yds. per Pass Play	——	5.84	——	5.85	——	5.77	——	5.77	——	5.81
Yds. Gained per Comp.	——	11.80	——	11.77	——	11.30	——	11.34	——	11.55
Combined Net Yds. Gained	70685	5048.9	70073	5005.2	68484	4891.7	69096	4935.4	139169	4970.3
% Total Yds. Rushing	——	33.9	——	34.1	——	37.0	——	36.7	——	35.4
% Total Yds. Passing	——	66.1	——	65.9	——	63.0	——	63.3	——	64.6
Avg. Yds. per Game	——	315.6	——	312.8	——	305.7	——	308.5	——	310.6
Ball Control Plays	14374	1026.7	14298	1021.3	13779	984.2	13855	989.6	28153	1005.5
Avg. Yds. per Play	——	4.9	——	4.9	——	5.0	——	5.0	——	4.9
Third Down Efficiency	——	39.1	——	39.1	——	38.5	——	38.5	——	38.8
Interceptions	220	15.7	250	17.9	249	17.8	219	15.6	469	16.8
Yds. Returned	2990	213.6	3405	243.2	3139	224.2	2724	194.6	6129	218.9
Returned for TD	13	0.9	16	1.1	22	1.6	19	1.4	35	1.3
Punts	1064	76.0	1062	75.9	1054	75.3	1056	75.4	2118	75.6
Yds. Punted	45056	3218.3	45130	3223.6	44324	3166.0	44250	3160.7	89380	3192.1
Avg. Yds. per Punt	——	42.3	——	42.5	——	42.1	——	41.9	——	42.2
Punt Returns	536	38.3	530	37.9	508	36.3	514	36.7	1044	37.3
Yds. Returned	4936	352.6	4965	354.6	4564	326.0	4535	323.9	9500	339.3
Avg. Yds. per Return	——	9.2	——	9.4	——	9.0	——	8.8	——	9.1
Returned for TD	7	0.5	7	0.5	7	0.5	7	0.5	14	0.5
Kickoff Returns	679	48.5	704	50.3	702	50.1	677	48.4	1381	49.3
Yds. Returned	12714	908.1	13283	948.8	14174	1012.4	13605	971.8	26888	960.3
Avg. Yds. per Return	——	18.7	——	18.9	——	20.2	——	20.1	——	19.5
Returned for TD	0	0.0	2	0.1	4	0.3	2	0.1	4	0.1
Fumbles	394	28.1	382	27.3	365	26.1	377	26.9	759	27.1
Lost	205	14.6	196	14.0	178	12.7	187	13.4	383	13.7
Out of Bounds	28	2.0	23	1.6	19	1.4	24	1.7	47	1.7
Own Rec. for TD	1	0.1	1	0.1	1	0.1	1	0.1	2	0.1
Opp. Rec.	196	14.0	205	14.6	187	13.4	178	12.7	383	13.7
Opp. Rec. for TD	13	0.9	14	1.0	15	1.1	14	1.0	28	1.0
Penalties	1444	103.1	1396	99.7	1254	89.6	1302	93.0	2698	96.4
Yds. Penalized	10898	778.4	10613	758.1	9735	695.4	10020	715.7	20633	736.9
Total Points Scored	4151	296.5	4154	296.7	4226	301.9	4223	301.6	8377	299.2
Total TDs	444	31.7	450	32.1	462	33.0	456	32.6	906	32.4
TDs Rushing	148	10.6	151	10.8	156	11.1	153	10.9	304	10.9
TDs Passing	258	18.4	261	18.6	259	18.5	256	18.3	517	18.5
TDs on Ret. and Rec.	38	2.7	38	2.7	47	3.4	47	3.4	85	3.0
Extra Points	429	30.6	437	31.2	447	31.9	439	31.4	876	31.3
Safeties	13	0.9	12	0.9	10	0.7	11	0.8	23	0.8
Field Goals Made	344	24.6	331	23.6	329	23.5	342	24.4	673	24.0
Field Goals Attempted	445	31.8	438	31.3	434	31.0	441	31.5	879	31.4
% Successful	——	77.3	——	75.6	——	75.8	——	77.6	——	76.6

CLUB LEADERS

First Downs	Offense	Defense
	S.F. 372	Minn. 259
Rushing	S.F. 134	Hou. 73
Passing	S.F. 212	Minn. 139
Penalty	Den. 35	Rams 8
Rushes	N.Y.G. 560	Hou. 369
Net Yds. Gained	N.Y.G. 2210	Hou. 1273
Avg. Gain	S.F. 4.6	S.D. 3.2
Passes Attempted	Hou. 614	N.O. 444
Completed	Hou. 357	Cin. & Phil. 251
% Completed	S.F. 67.6	Hou. 51.9
Total Yds. Gained	Mia. 4564	N.O. 2924
Times Sacked	N.Y.J. 21	Hou. 52
Yds. Lost	N.E. 127	Clev. 342
Net Yds. Gained	Mia. 4353	N.O. 2606
Net Yds. per Pass Play	S.F. 7.70	G.B. 5.04
Yds. Gained per Comp.	Raid. 1381	Dall. 10.02
Combined Net Yds. Gained	S.F. 6435	Minn. 4406
% Total Yds. Rushing	Chi. 45.1	S.D. 25.9
% Total Yds. Passing	Mia. 74.9	Ind. 55.3
Ball Control Plays	N.E. 1091	Minn. 938
Avg. Yds. per Play	S.F. 6.30	G.B. 4.49
Avg. Time of Poss.	N.Y.G. 32:18	—
Third Down Efficiency	S.F. 47.8	Hou. 30.8
Interceptions	—	Hou. 26
Yds. Returned	—	Hou. 412
Returned for TD	—	Phil. 4
Punts	T.B. 94	—
Yds. Punted	Sea. 4007	—
Avg. Yds. per Punt	Hou. 45.3	—
Punt Returns	N.E. 51	S.F. 15
Yds. Returned	Clev. 563	Chi. 115
Avg. Yds. per Return	N.O. 13.6	Chi. 5.2
Returned for TD	Clev. 3	—
Kickoff Returns	N.O. 62	T.B. 28
Yds. Returned	G.B. 1483	T.B. 499
Avg. Yds. per Return	G.B. 24.7	Ind. 14.9
Returned for TD	Four with 1	—
Total Points Scored	S.F. 473	N.Y.G. 205
Total TDs	S.F. 61	Chi. & N.Y.G. 22
TDs Rushing	S.F. 26	Four with 6
TDs Passing	S.F. 29	Minn. 11
TDs on Ret. and Rec.	Hou. & S.F. 6	Buff., Den., & Phx. 0
Extra Points	S.F. 59	Chi. 20
Safeties	Sea. 4	
Field Goals Made	Raid. 35	Mia., N.Y.G., & Wash. 17
Field Goals Attempted	Raid. 44	Wash. 22
% Successful	Atl. 96.3	Mia. 63.0

NFL CLUB RANKINGS BY YARDS

	Offense			Defense		
	Total	Rush	Pass	Total	Rush	Pass
Atlanta	11	23	6	25	15	25
Buffalo	6	8	11	27	21	24
Chicago	28	19	28	4	17	3
Cincinnati	27	24	27	16	27	2
Cleveland	20	17	19	12	12	13
Dallas	4	2	7	10	11	10T
Denver	5	18	4	19	4	27
Detroit	24	7	24	6	10	9
Green Bay	19	22	18	2	8	7
Houston	3	12	3	14	*1	23
Indianapolis	22	28	8	28	28	12
Kansas City	16	20	15	11	9	14
L.A. Rams	18	5	23	24	18	22
L.A. Raiders	13	26	5	9	20	5
Miami	2	25	*1	20	14	21
Minnesota	17	21	14	*1	6	6
New England	12	13	12	13	22	4
New Orleans	21	14	21	7	25	*1
N.Y. Giants	10	*1	22	5	7	10T
N.Y. Jets	9	9	10	8	5	17
Philadelphia	15	15	16	17	24	8
Phoenix	8	11	9	21	19	19
Pittsburgh	7	6	13	3	3	15
San Diego	14	10	17	18	2	28
San Francisco	*1	3	2	15	16	16
Seattle	23	4	25	23	13	26
Tampa Bay	25	27	20	22	23	18
Washington	26	16	26	26	26	20

T = Tied for position
* = League Leader

AFC TAKEAWAYS/GIVEAWAYS

	Takeaways			Giveaways			Net
	Int	Fum	Total	Int	Fum	Total	Diff.
San Diego	22	12	34	14	5	19	+15
Buffalo	23	24	47	18	17	35	+12
Pittsburgh	24	14	38	12	15	27	+11
Kansas City	21	17	38	10	18	28	+10
N.Y. Jets	19	18	37	12	16	28	+9
Seattle	22	15	37	18	13	31	+6
Cincinnati	12	14	26	11	9	20	+6
Denver	18	13	31	10	18	28	+3
L.A. Raiders	14	9	23	14	11	25	-2
Houston	26	17	43	25	20	45	-2
Miami	13	14	27	18	16	34	-7
New England	13	9	22	24	10	34	-12
Indianapolis	10	11	21	15	20	35	-14
Cleveland	13	9	22	19	17	36	-14

NFC TAKEAWAYS/GIVEAWAYS

	Takeaways			Giveaways			Net
	Int	Fum	Total	Int	Fum	Total	Diff.
N.Y. Giants	18	10	28	9	8	17	+11
Minnesota	24	10	34	14	10	24	+10
Dallas	14	14	28	6	16	22	+6
Detroit	19	16	35	19	13	32	+3
Philadelphia	20	15	35	13	21	34	+1
San Francisco	19	11	30	17	13	30	0
Washington	17	14	31	21	10	31	0
Chicago	18	12	30	16	14	30	0
Green Bay	18	15	33	24	10	34	-1
New Orleans	10	20	30	21	13	34	-4
Phoenix	9	17	26	20	11	31	-5
L.A. Rams	11	9	20	19	11	30	-10
Tampa Bay	9	13	22	25	11	36	-14
Atlanta	13	11	24	25	17	42	-18

SCORING

Points
- **AFC:** 132—Jeff Jaeger, Raiders
- **NFC:** 130—Jason Hanson Detroit

Touchdowns
- **NFC:** 16—Jerry Rice, San Francisco
- **AFC:** 15—Marcus Allen, Kansas City

Extra Points
- **NFC:** 59—Mike Cofer, San Francisco
- **AFC:** 41—Jason Elam, Denver

Field Goals
- **AFC:** 35—Jeff Jaeger, Raiders
- **NFC:** 34—Jason Hanson, Detroit

Field Goal Attempts
- **AFC:** 44—Jeff Jaeger, Raiders
- **NFC:** 43—Jason Hanson, Detroit

Longest Field Goal
- **AFC:** 59—Steve Christie, Buffalo vs. Miami, September 26
- **NFC:** 57—Michael Husted, Tampa Bay at Raiders, December 19

Most Points, Game
- **NFC:** 24—Sterling Sharpe, Green Bay at Tampa Bay, October 24, (4 TD)
  Jerry Rice, San Francisco at Tampa Bay, November 14, (4 TD)
  Ron Moore, Phoenix vs. Rams, December 5, (4 TD)
- **AFC:** 18—Andre Reed, Buffalo vs. New England, September 5, (3 TD)
  John Carney, San Diego vs. Seattle, September 5, (6 FG)
  John Carney, San Diego vs. Houston, September 19, (6 FG)
  Barry Foster, Pittsburgh at Atlanta, September 27, (3 TD)
  Johnny Mitchell, Jets vs. Philadelphia, October 3, (3 TD)
  Rodney Culver, Indianapolis at Miami, October 24, (3 TD)
  Haywood Jeffires, Houston at Cincinnati, November 14, (3 TD)
  Marcus Allen, Kansas City at Seattle, December 5, (3 TD)
  Shannon Sharpe, Denver vs. Kansas City, December 12, (3 TD)
  Kenneth Davis, Buffalo at Miami, December 19, (3 TD)
  Natrone Means, San Diego vs. Miami, December 27, (3 TD)

Team Leaders, Points
- **AFC:** BUFFALO: 105, Steve Christie; CINCINNATI: 85, Doug Pelfrey; CLEVELAND: 84, Matt Stover; DENVER: 119, Jason Elam; HOUSTON: 126, Al Del Greco; INDIANAPOLIS: 93, Dean Biasucci; KANSAS CITY: 106, Nick Lowery; L.A. RAIDERS: 132, Jeff Jaeger; MIAMI: 109, Pete Stoyanovich; NEW ENGLAND: 57, Scott Sisson; N.Y. JETS: 82, Cary Blanchard; PITTSBURGH: 116, Gary Anderson; SAN DIEGO: 124, John Carney; SEATTLE: 98, John Kasay
- **NFC:** ATLANTA: 112, Norm Johnson; CHICAGO: 102, Kevin Butler; DALLAS: 122, Ed Murray; DETROIT: 130, Jason Hanson ; GREEN BAY: 128, Chris Jacke ; L.A. RAMS: 71, Tony Zendejas; MINNESOTA: 105, Fuad Reveiz; NEW ORLEANS: 117, Morten Andersen; N.Y. GIANTS: 103, David Treadwell; PHILADELPHIA: 60, Calvin Williams; PHOENIX: 100, Greg Davis; SAN FRANCISCO: 107, Mike Cofer; TAMPA BAY: 75, Michael Husted; WASHINGTON: 72, Chip Lohmiller

Team Champion
- **NFC:** 473—San Francisco
- **AFC:** 373—Denver

AFC SCORING—TEAM

	TD	TDR	TDP	TDM	XP	XPA	FG	FGA	SAF	TP
Denver	42	13	27	2	41	42	26	35	1	373
Houston	40	11	23	6	39	40	29	34	1	368
Miami	40	10	27	3	37	40	24	32	0	349
Buffalo	37	12	20	5	36	37	23	32	1	329
Kansas City	37	14	20	3	37	37	23	29	0	328
San Diego	33	14	18	1	31	33	31	40	0	322
Pittsburgh	32	13	16	3	32	32	28	30	0	308
L.A. Raiders	29	10	17	2	27	29	35	44	0	306
Cleveland	36	8	23	5	36	36	16	22	2	304
Seattle	29	13	13	3	29	29	23	28	4	280
N.Y. Jets	31	14	16	1	31	31	17	26	1	270
New England	26	9	17	0	25	25	19	31	0	238
Indianapolis	16	4	10	2	15	16	26	31	0	189
Cincinnati	16	3	11	2	13	16	24	31	3	187
AFC Total	444	148	258	38	429	443	344	445	13	4151
AFC Average	31.7	10.6	18.4	2.7	30.6	31.6	24.6	31.8	0.9	296.5

NFC SCORING—TEAM

	TD	TDR	TDP	TDM	XP	XPA	FG	FGA	SAF	TP
San Francisco	61	26	29	6	59	61	16	26	0	473
Dallas	41	20	18	3	40	41	30	37	0	376
Green Bay	35	14	19	2	35	35	31	37	1	340
Phoenix	37	12	21	4	37	37	21	28	2	326
New Orleans	33	10	18	5	33	33	28	35	1	317
Atlanta	34	4	28	2	34	34	26	27	0	316
Detroit	28	9	15	4	28	28	34	43	0	298
Philadelphia	35	7	23	5	31	35	16	23	2	293
N.Y. Giants	30	11	17	2	28	30	26	34	1	288
Minnesota	28	8	18	2	27	28	26	35	2	277
Tampa Bay	27	6	19	2	27	27	16	22	0	237
Chicago	22	10	7	5	21	22	27	36	0	234
Washington	26	11	11	4	24	26	16	28	1	230
L.A. Rams	25	8	16	1	23	25	16	23	0	221
NFC Total	462	156	259	47	447	462	329	434	10	4226
NFC Average	33.0	11.1	18.5	3.4	31.9	33.0	23.5	31.0	0.7	301.9
NFL Total	906	304	517	85	876	905	673	879	23	8377
NFL Average	32.4	10.9	18.5	3.0	31.3	32.3	24.0	31.4	0.8	299.2

NFL TOP TEN SCORERS—TOUCHDOWNS

	TD	TDR	TDP	TDM	PTS
Rice, Jerry, S.F.	16	1	15	0	96
Allen, Marcus, K.C.	15	12	3	0	90
Rison, Andre, Atl.	15	0	15	0	90
Sharpe, Sterling, G.B.	11	0	11	0	66
Watters, Ricky, S.F.	11	10	1	0	66
Smith, Emmitt, Dall.	10	9	1	0	60
Bennett, Edgar, G.B.	10	9	1	0	60
Williams, Calvin, Phil.	10	0	10	0	60
Moore, Ron, Phx.	9	9	0	0	54
Carter, Cris, Minn.	9	0	9	0	54
Foster, Barry, Pitt.	9	8	1	0	54
Sharpe, Shannon, Den.	9	0	9	0	54

NFL TOP TEN SCORERS—KICKERS

	XP	XPA	FG	FGA	PTS
Jaeger, Jeff, Raid.	27	29	35	44	132
Hanson, Jason, Det.	28	28	34	43	130
Jacke, Chris, G.B.	35	35	31	37	128
Del Greco, Al, Hou.	39	40	29	34	126
Carney, John, S.D.	31	33	31	40	124
Murray, Eddie, Dall.	38	38	28	33	122
Elam, Jason, Den.	41	42	26	35	119
Andersen, Morten, N.O.	33	33	28	35	117
Anderson, Gary, Pitt.	32	32	28	30	116
Johnson, Norm, Atl.	34	34	26	27	112

AFC SCORERS—INDIVIDUAL

Kickers

	XP	XPA	FG	FGA	PTS
Jaeger, Jeff, Raid.	27	29	35	44	132
Del Greco, Al, Hou.	39	40	29	34	126
Carney, John, S.D.	31	33	31	40	124
Elam, Jason, Den.	41	42	26	35	119
Anderson, Gary, Pitt.	32	32	28	30	116
Stoyanovich, Pete, Mia.	37	37	24	32	109
Lowery, Nick, K.C.	37	37	23	29	106
Christie, Steve, Buff.	36	37	23	32	105
Kasay, John, Sea.	29	29	23	28	98
Biasucci, Dean, Ind.	15	16	26	31	93
Pelfrey, Doug, Cinn.	13	16	24	31	85
Stover, Matt, Clev.	36	36	16	22	84
Blanchard, Cary, N.Y.J.	31	31	17	26	82
Bahr, Matt, Phil.-N.E.	28	29	13	18	67
Sisson, Scott, N.E.	15	15	14	26	57

Non-kickers

	TD	TDR	TDP	TDM	PTS
Allen, Marcus, K.C.	15	12	3	0	90
Foster, Barry, Pitt.	9	8	1	0	54
Sharpe, Shannon, Den.	9	0	9	0	54
Brown, John, Hou.	8	6	2	0	48
Brown, Tim, Raid.	8	0	7	1	48
Coates, Ben, N.E.	8	0	8	0	48
Delpino, Robert, Den.	8	8	0	0	48
Jackson, Michael, Clev.	8	0	8	0	48
Means, Natrone, S.D.	8	8	0	0	48
Baxter, Brad, N.Y.J.	7	7	0	0	42
Davis, Willie, K.C.	7	0	7	0	42

	TD	TDR	TDP	TDM	PTS
Miller, Anthony, S.D.	7	0	7	0	42
Russell, Leonard, N.E.	7	7	0	0	42
Warren, Chris, Sea.	7	7	0	0	42
Byars, Keith, Mia.	6	3	3	0	36
Davis, Kenneth, Buff.	6	6	0	0	36
Ingram, Mark, Mia.	6	0	6	0	36
Jackson, Keith, Mia.	6	0	6	0	36
Jeffires, Haywood, Hou.	6	0	6	0	36
Kirby, Terry, Mia.	6	3	3	0	36
Mitchell, Johnny, N.Y.J.	6	0	6	0	36
Pickens, Carl, Cinn.	6	0	6	0	36
Reed, Andre, Buff.	6	0	6	0	36
Thomas, Thurman, Buff.	6	6	0	0	36
Brooks, Bill, Buff.	5	0	5	0	30
Carrier, Mark, Clev.	5	1	3	1	30
Culver, Rodney, Ind.	5	3	1	1	30
Fryar, Irving, Mia.	5	0	5	0	30
Green, Eric, Pitt.	5	0	5	0	30
Hoge, Merril, Pitt.	5	1	4	0	30
Hostetler, Jeff, Raid.	5	5	0	0	30
Johnson, Vance, Den.	5	0	5	0	30
Martin, Kelvin, Sea.	5	0	5	0	30
Metcalf, Eric, Clev.	5	1	2	2	30
Slaughter, Webster, Hou.	5	0	5	0	30
Bernstine, Rod, Den.	4	4	0	0	24
Burkett, Chris, N.Y.J..	4	0	4	0	24
Butts, Marion, S.D.	4	4	0	0	24
Cash, Keith, K.C.	4	0	4	0	24
Givins, Ernest, Hou.	4	0	4	0	24
Johnson, Johnny, N.Y.J.	4	3	1	0	24
Lewis, Nate, S.D.	4	0	4	0	24
McCardell, Keenan, Clev.	4	0	4	0	24
Metzelaars, Pete, Buff.	4	0	4	0	24
Query, Jeff, Cinn.	4	0	4	0	24
Russell, Derek, Den.	4	0	3	1	24
Vardell, Tommy, Clev.	4	3	1	0	24
Williams, John L., Sea.	4	3	1	0	24
Wright, Alexander, Raid.	4	0	4	0	24
Beebe, Don, Buff.	3	0	3	0	18
Blades, Brian, Sea.	3	0	3	0	18
Cash, Kerry, Ind.	3	0	3	0	18
Duncan, Curtis, Hou.	3	0	3	0	18
Higgs, Mark, Mia.	3	3	0	0	18
Jett, James, Raid.	3	0	3	0	18
Langhorne, Reggie, Ind.	3	0	3	0	18
Martin, Tony, Mia.	3	0	3	0	18
McCallum, Napoleon, Raid.	3	3	0	0	18
Milburn, Glyn, Den.	3	0	3	0	18
Mirer, Rick, Sea.	3	3	0	0	18
Stone, Dwight, Pitt.	3	1	2	0	18
Thigpen, Yancey, Pitt.	3	0	3	0	18
Thompson, Leroy, Pitt.	3	3	0	0	18
Rivers, Reggie, Den.	2	1	1	0	*14
Birden, J. J., K.C.	2	0	2	0	12
Brisby, Vincent, N.E.	2	0	2	0	12
Carlson, Cody, Hou.	2	2	0	0	12
Edmunds, Ferrell, Sea.	2	0	2	0	12
Harmon, Ronnie, S.D.	2	0	2	0	12
Jefferson, Shawn, S.D.	2	0	2	0	12
Kinchen, Brian, Clev.	2	0	2	0	12
Marshall, Arthur, Den.	2	0	2	0	12
McDuffie, O. J., Mia.	2	0	0	2	12
McNair, Todd, K.C.	2	2	0	0	12
Thornton, James, N.Y.J.	2	0	2	0	12
Timpson, Michael, N.E.	2	0	2	0	12
Turner, Kevin, N.E.	2	0	2	0	12
White, Lorenzo, Hou.	2	2	0	0	12
Young, Duane, S.D.	2	0	2	0	12
Stephens, Rod, Sea.	1	0	0	1	*10
Jones, Henry, Buff.	1	0	0	1	*8
Anders, Kimble, K.C.	1	0	1	0	6
Baldwin, Randy, Clev.	1	0	1	0	6
Ball, Eric, Cinn.	1	1	0	0	6
Barnett, Tim, K.C.	1	0	1	0	6
Baty, Greg, Mia.	1	0	1	0	6
Baxter, Fred, N.Y.J.	1	0	1	0	6
Bell, Nick, Raid.	1	1	0	0	6
Bieniemy, Eric, S.D.	1	1	0	0	6
Blackmon, Robert, Sea.	1	0	0	1	6
Brim, Michael, Cinn.	1	0	0	1	6
Chaffey, Pat, N.Y.J.	1	0	1	0	6

	TD	TDR	TDP	TDM	PTS
Childress, Ray, Hou.	1	0	0	1	6
Cook, Marv, N.E.	1	0	1	0	6
Copeland, Russell, Buff.	1	0	0	1	6
Crittenden, Ray, N.E.	1	0	1	0	6
Croel, Mike, Den.	1	0	0	1	6
Croom, Corey, N.E.	1	1	0	0	6
Davidson, Kenny, Pitt.	1	0	0	1	6
Dawkins, Sean, Ind.	1	0	1	0	6
Dishman, Cris, Hou.	1	0	0	1	6
Esiason, Boomer, N.Y.J.	1	1	0	0	6
Fenner, Derrick, Cinn.	1	1	0	0	6
Frank, Donald, S.D.	1	0	0	1	6
Gardner, Carwell, Buff.	1	0	1	0	6
Gash, Sam, N.E.	1	1	0	0	6
Glover, Andrew, Raid.	1	0	1	0	6
Green, Paul, Sea.	1	0	1	0	6
Harris, Leonard, Hou.	1	0	1	0	6
Hayes, Jonathan, K.C.	1	0	1	0	6
Herrod, Jeff, Ind.	1	0	0	1	6
Hester, Jessie, Ind.	1	0	1	0	6
Horton, Ethan, Raid.	1	0	1	0	6
Ismail, Raghib, Raid.	1	0	1	0	6
Jackson, Steve, Hou.	1	0	0	1	6
Johnson, Anthony, Ind.	1	1	0	0	6
Johnson, Reggie, Den.	1	0	1	0	6
Johnson, Tracy, Sea.	1	0	1	0	6
Jones, James, Clev.	1	1	0	0	6
Kidd, John, S.D.	1	1	0	0	6
Kirkland, Levon, Pitt.	1	0	0	1	6
Lewis, Albert, K.C.	1	0	0	1	6
Lewis, Darryll, Hou.	1	0	0	1	6
Mack, Kevin, Clev.	1	1	0	0	6
Marino, Dan, Mia.	1	1	0	0	6
Mathis, Terance, N.Y.J.	1	1	0	0	6
McDaniel, Terry, Raid.	1	0	0	1	6
McKeller, Keith, Buff.	1	0	1	0	6
McMurtry, Greg, N.E.	1	0	1	0	6
Miles, Ostell, Cinn.	1	1	0	0	6
Mills, Ernie, Pitt.	1	0	1	0	6
Moon, Warren, Hou.	1	1	0	0	6
Moore, Rob, N.Y.J.	1	0	1	0	6
Moore, Stevon, Clev.	1	0	0	1	6
Murrell, Adrian, N.Y.J.	1	1	0	0	6
Mustafaa, Najee, Clev.	1	0	0	1	6
Nash, Joe, Sea.	1	0	0	1	6
Odomes, Nate, Buff.	1	0	0	1	6
Oliver, Louis, Mia.	1	0	0	1	6
Orlando, Bo, Hou.	1	0	0	1	6
Philcox, Todd, Clev.	1	1	0	0	6
Robertson, Marcus, Hou.	1	0	0	1	6
Robinson, Greg, Raid.	1	1	0	0	6
Saleaumua, Dan, K.C.	1	0	0	1	6
Talley, Darryl, Buff.	1	0	0	1	6
Thomas, Blair, N.Y.J.	1	1	0	0	6
Thomas, Derrick, K.C.	1	0	0	1	6
Thompson, Craig, Cinn.	1	0	1	0	6
Tillman, Lawyer, Clev.	1	0	1	0	6
Tillman, Spencer, Hou.	1	0	1	0	6
Valerio, Joe, K.C.	1	0	1	0	6
Verdin, Clarence, Ind.	1	0	1	0	6
Walker, Derrick, S.D.	1	0	1	0	6
Washington, Brian, N.Y.J.	1	0	0	1	6
Washington, Mickey, Buff.	1	0	0	1	6
Wellman, Gary, Hou.	1	0	1	0	6
Williams, Darryl, Cinn.	1	0	0	1	6
Wolfley, Ron, Clev.	1	0	1	0	6
Woodson, Rod, Pitt.	1	0	0	1	6
Wyman, David, Den.	1	0	1	0	6
Edwards, Antonio, Sea.	0	0	0	0	*2
Pleasant, Anthony, Clev.	0	0	0	0	*2
Riddick, Louis, Clev.	0	0	0	0	*2
Williams, Alfred, Cinn.	0	0	0	0	*2

* Safety
Team Safeties credited to Cincinnati (2), Houston, New York Jets and Seattle

NFC SCORERS—INDIVIDUAL
Kickers

	XP	XPA	FG	FGA	PTS
Hanson, Jason, Det.	28	28	34	43	130
Jacke, Chris, G.B.	35	35	31	37	128
Murray, Eddie, Dall.	38	38	28	33	122

	XP	XPA	FG	FGA	PTS
Andersen, Morten, N.O.	33	33	28	35	117
Johnson, Norm, Atl.	34	34	26	27	112
Cofer, Mike, S.F.	59	61	16	26	107
Reveiz, Fuad, Minn.	27	28	26	35	105
Treadwell, David, N.Y.G.	28	29	25	31	103
Butler, Kevin, Chi.	21	22	27	36	102
Davis, Greg, Phx.	37	37	21	28	100
Husted, Michael, T.B.	27	27	16	22	75
Lohmiller, Chip, Wash.	24	26	16	28	72
Zendejas, Tony, Rams	23	25	16	23	71
Ruzek, Roger, Phil.	13	16	8	10	37
Elliott, Lin, Dall.	2	3	2	4	8
Daluiso, Brad, N.Y.G.	0	0	1	3	3

Non-kickers

	TD	TDR	TDP	TDM	PTS
Rice, Jerry, S.F.	16	1	15	0	96
Rison, Andre, Atl.	15	0	15	0	90
Sharpe, Sterling, G.B.	11	0	11	0	66
Watters, Ricky, S.F.	11	10	1	0	66
Bennett, Edgar, G.B.	10	9	1	0	60
Smith, Emmitt, Dall.	10	9	1	0	60
Williams, Calvin, Phil.	10	0	10	0	60
Carter, Cris, Minn.	9	0	9	0	54
Moore, Ron, Phx.	9	9	0	0	54
Bettis, Jerome, Rams	7	7	0	0	42
Irvin, Michael, Dall.	7	0	7	0	42
Logan, Marc, S.F.	7	7	0	0	42
Pritchard, Mike, Atl.	7	0	7	0	42
Proehl, Ricky, Phx.	7	0	7	0	42
Bavaro, Mark, Phil.	6	0	6	0	36
Early, Quinn, N.O.	6	0	6	0	36
Moore, Herman, Det.	6	0	6	0	36
Williams, Kevin, Dall.	6	2	2	2	36
Carter, Anthony, Minn.	5	0	5	0	30
Cross, Howard, N.Y.G.	5	0	5	0	30
Hampton, Rodney, N.Y.G.	5	5	0	0	30
Harper, Alvin, Dall.	5	0	5	0	30
Hawkins, Courtney, T.B.	5	0	5	0	30
Taylor, John, S.F.	5	0	5	0	30
Allen, Eric, Phil.	4	0	0	4	24
Anderson, Neal, Chi.	4	4	0	0	24
Anderson, Willie, Rams	4	0	4	0	24
Clark, Gary, Phx.	4	0	4	0	24
Cobb, Reggie, T.B.	4	3	1	0	24
Copeland, Horace, T.B.	4	0	4	0	24
Drayton, Troy, Rams	4	0	4	0	24
Harbaugh, Jim, Chi.	4	4	0	0	24
Harris, Jackie, G.B.	4	0	4	0	24
Haynes, Michael, Atl.	4	0	4	0	24
Hill, Randal, Phx.	4	0	4	0	24
Jackson, Mark, N.Y.G.	4	0	4	0	24
Johnston, Daryl, Dall.	4	3	1	0	24
Moore, Derrick, Det.	4	3	1	0	24
Sanders, Ricky, Wash.	4	0	4	0	24
Walker, Herschel, Phil.	4	1	3	0	24
Workman, Vince, T.B.	4	2	2	0	24
Brooks, Reggie, Wash.	3	3	0	0	18
Brown, Derek, N.O.	3	2	1	0	18
Bunch, Jarrod, N.Y.G.	3	2	1	0	18
Calloway, Chris, N.Y.G.	3	0	3	0	18
Centers, Larry, Phx.	3	0	3	0	18
Clayton, Mark, G.B.	3	0	3	0	18
Graham, Scottie, Minn.	3	3	0	0	18
Hebron, Vaughn, Phil.	3	3	0	0	18
Hilliard, Dalton, N.O.	3	2	1	0	18
Hughes, Tyrone, N.O.	3	0	0	3	18
Jones, Brent, S.F.	3	0	3	0	18
Lassic, Derrick, Dall.	3	3	0	0	18
Lee, Amp, S.F.	3	1	2	0	18
Martin, Eric, N.O.	3	0	3	0	18
McGee, Tim, Wash.	3	0	3	0	18
Mitchell, Brian, Wash.	3	3	0	0	18
Muster, Brad, N.O.	3	3	0	0	18
Obee, Terry, Chi.	3	0	3	0	18
Pegram, Erric, Atl.	3	3	0	0	18
Rathman, Tom, S.F.	3	3	0	0	18
Rypien, Mark, Wash.	3	3	0	0	18
Sanders, Barry, Det.	3	3	0	0	18
Thompson, Darrell, G.B.	3	3	0	0	18
Tillman, Lewis, N.Y.G.	3	3	0	0	18
Bailey, Johnny, Phx.	2	1	0	1	12

	TD	TDR	TDP	TDM	PTS
Baker, Myron, Chi.	2	0	0	2	12
Carter, Dexter, S.F.	2	1	0	1	12
Clay, Willie, Det.	2	0	0	2	12
Coleman, Lincoln, Dall.	2	2	0	0	12
Conway, Curtis, Chi.	2	0	2	0	12
Craig, Roger, Minn.	2	1	1	0	12
Davis, Eric, S.F.	2	0	0	2	12
Ellard, Henry, Rams	2	0	2	0	12
Gary, Cleveland, Rams	2	1	1	0	12
Green, Willie, Det.	2	0	2	0	12
Hallock, Ty, Det.	2	0	2	0	12
Holman, Rodney, Det.	2	0	2	0	12
Jones, Ernie, Rams	2	0	2	0	12
Lynch, Eric, Det.	2	2	0	0	12
McCaffrey, Ed, N.Y.G.	2	0	2	0	12
Middleton, Ron, Wash.	2	0	2	0	12
Monk, Art, Wash.	2	0	2	0	12
Novacek, Jay, Dall.	2	1	1	0	12
Perriman, Brett, Det.	2	0	2	0	12
Sherman, Heath, Phil.	2	2	0	0	12
Sherrard, Mike, N.Y.G.	2	0	2	0	12
Smith, Irv, N.O.	2	0	2	0	12
Smith, Robert, Minn.	2	2	0	0	12
Thomas, Lamar, T.B.	2	0	2	0	12
Williams, Aeneas, Phx.	2	0	0	2	12
Word, Barry, Minn.	2	2	0	0	12
Worley, Tim, Chi.	2	2	0	0	12
Young, Steve, S.F.	2	2	0	0	12
Young, Mike, Phil.	2	0	2	0	12
Anderson, Gary, T.B.	1	0	1	0	6
Armstrong, Tyji, T.B.	1	0	1	0	6
Bailey, Victor, Phil.	1	0	1	0	6
Beach, Sanjay, S.F.	1	0	1	0	6
Blount, Eric, Phx.	1	1	0	0	6
Bono, Steve, S.F.	1	1	0	0	6
Boykin, Deral, Rams	1	0	0	1	6
Brenner, Hoby, N.O.	1	0	1	0	6
Brooks, Robert, G.B.	1	0	0	1	6
Broussard, Steven, Atl.	1	1	0	0	6
Butler, LeRoy, G.B.	1	0	0	1	6
Byner, Earnest, Wash.	1	1	0	0	6
Carrier, Mark, Chi.	1	0	0	1	6
Carter, Pat, Rams	1	0	1	0	6
Clark, Vinnie, Atl.	1	0	0	1	6
Coleman, Monte, Wash.	1	0	0	1	6
Collins, Mark, N.Y.G.	1	0	0	1	6
Cunningham, Randall, Phil.	1	1	0	0	6
Dowdell, Marcus, N.O.	1	0	1	0	6
Edwards, Anthony, Phx.	1	0	1	0	6
Evans, Byron, Phil.	1	0	0	1	6
Favre, Brett, G.B.	1	1	0	0	6
Galbraith, Scott, Dall.	1	0	1	0	6
Gannon, Rich, Wash.	1	1	0	0	6
Gouveia, Kurt, Wash.	1	0	0	1	6
Gray, Mel, Det.	1	0	0	1	6
Green, Darrell, Wash.	1	0	0	1	6
Hall, Ron, T.B.	1	0	1	0	6
Hanks, Merton, S.F.	1	0	0	1	6
Hearst, Garrison, Phx.	1	1	0	0	6
Ismail, Qadry, Minn.	1	0	1	0	6
Jamison, George, Det.	1	0	0	1	6
Johnson, A. J., Wash.	1	0	0	1	6
Jones, Dante, Chi.	1	0	0	1	6
Jordan, Steve, Minn.	1	0	1	0	6
Joseph, James, Phil.	1	0	1	0	6
Kinchen, Todd, Rams	1	0	1	0	6
Lincoln, Jeremy, Chi.	1	0	0	1	6
Lynch, Lorenzo, Phx.	1	0	0	1	6
Mack, Milton, T.B.	1	0	0	1	6
McAfee, Fred, N.O.	1	1	0	0	6
McDowell, Anthony, T.B.	1	0	1	0	6
McGriggs, Lamar, Minn.	1	0	0	1	6
McGruder, Michael, S.F.	1	0	0	1	6
McMillian, Audray, Minn.	1	0	0	1	6
McNeal, Travis, Rams	1	0	1	0	6
Meggett, David, N.Y.G.	1	0	0	1	6
Mills, Sam, N.O.	1	0	0	1	6
Mims, David, Atl.	1	0	1	0	6
Moore, Dave, T.B.	1	0	1	0	6
Neal, Lorenzo, N.O.	1	1	0	0	6
Ned, Derrick, N.O.	1	1	0	0	6
Newman, Pat, N.O.	1	0	1	0	6

	TD	TDR	TDP	TDM	PTS
Peete, Rodney, Det.	1	1	0	0	6
Rasheed, Kenyon, N.Y.G.	1	1	0	0	6
Reeves, Walter, Phx.	1	0	1	0	6
Rolle, Butch, Phx.	1	0	1	0	6
Royster, Mazio, T.B.	1	1	0	0	6
Sanders, Deion, Atl.	1	0	1	0	6
Seals, Ray, T.B.	1	0	0	1	6
Singleton, Nate, S.F.	1	0	1	0	6
Small, Torrance, N.O.	1	0	1	0	6
Smith, Kevin, Dall.	1	0	0	1	6
Smith, Tony, Atl.	1	0	0	1	6
Stephens, John, G.B.	1	1	0	0	6
Tamm, Ralph, S.F.	1	0	0	1	6
Tice, Mike, Minn.	1	0	1	0	6
Turner, Floyd, N.O.	1	0	1	0	6
Waddle, Tom, Chi.	1	0	1	0	6
Warren, Frank, N.O.	1	0	0	1	6
Wetnight, Ryan, Chi.	1	0	1	0	6
Williams, Jamie, S.F.	1	0	1	0	6
Flores, Mike, Phil.	0	0	0	0	*2
Hamilton, Keith, N.Y.G.	0	0	0	0	*2
Stowers, Tommie, N.O.	0	0	0	0	*2
Swann, Eric, Phx.	0	0	0	0	*2
Thomas, Henry, Minn.	0	0	0	0	*2

* Indicates safety
Team Safeties credited to Green Bay, Minnesota, Philadelphia, Phoenix, and Washington.

FIELD GOALS

Field Goal Percentage
NFC: .963—Norm Johnson, Atlanta
AFC: .933—Gary Anderson, Pittsburgh

Field Goals
AFC: 35—Jeff Jaeger, Raiders
NFC: 34—Jason Hanson, Detroit

Field Goal Attempts
AFC: 44—Jeff Jaeger, Raiders
NFC: 43—Jason Hanson, Detroit

Longest Field Goal
AFC: 59—Steve Christie, Buffalo vs. Miami, September 26
NFC: 57—Michael Husted, Tampa Bay at Raiders, December 19

Average Yards Made
NFC: 37.1—Tony Zendejas, Rams
AFC: 36.6—Steve Christie, Buffalo

AFC FIELD GOALS—TEAM

	FG	FGA	Pct.	Long
Pittsburgh	28	30	.933	46
Houston	29	34	.853	52
Indianapolis	26	31	.839	53
Seattle	23	28	.821	55
L.A. Raiders	35	44	.795	53
Kansas City	23	29	.793	52
San Diego	31	40	.775	51
Cincinnati	24	31	.774	53
Miami	24	32	.750	52
Denver	26	35	.743	54
Cleveland	16	22	.727	53
Buffalo	23	32	.719	59
N.Y. Jets	17	26	.654	45
New England	19	31	.613	40
AFC Total	344	445	——	59
AFC Average	24.6	31.8	.773	—

NFC FIELD GOALS—TEAM

	FG	FGA	Pct.	Long
Atlanta	26	27	.963	54
Green Bay	31	37	.838	54
Dallas	30	37	.811	52
New Orleans	28	35	.800	56
Detroit	34	43	.791	53
N.Y. Giants	26	34	.765	54
Phoenix	21	28	.750	55
Chicago	27	36	.750	55
Minnesota	26	35	.743	51
Tampa Bay	16	22	.727	57
Philadelphia	16	23	.696	48
L.A. Rams	16	23	.696	54
San Francisco	16	26	.615	46
Washington	16	28	.571	51
NFC Total	329	434	——	57
NFC Average	23.5	31.0	.758	—
League Total	673	879	——	59
League Average	24.0	31.4	.766	—

AFC FIELD GOALS—INDIVIDUAL

	1-19 Yards	20-29 Yards	30-39 Yards	40-49 Yards	50 or Longer	Totals	Avg. Yds. Att.	Avg. Yds. Made	Avg. Yds. Miss	Long
Anderson, Gary, Pitt.	1-1	8-9	14-14	5-6	0-0	28-30	33.3	33.3	34.5	46
	1.000	.889	1.000	.833	—	.933				
Del Greco, Al, Hou.	0-0	13-13	8-9	4-5	4-7	29-34	35.9	34.0	46.6	52
	—	1.000	.889	.800	.571	.853				
Biasucci, Dean, Ind.	1-1	14-14	7-8	3-6	1-2	26-31	33.3	30.8	46.2	53
	1.000	1.000	.875	.500	.500	.839				
Kasay, John, Sea.	1-1	5-5	10-11	4-6	3-5	23-28	37.9	36.1	46.2	55
	1.000	1.000	.909	.667	.600	.821				
Jaeger, Jeff, Raid.	0-0	12-12	13-15	6-10	4-7	35-44	36.5	34.5	44.2	53
	—	1.000	.867	.600	.571	.795				
Lowery, Nick, K.C.	0-0	8-8	7-9	7-11	1-1	23-29	35.5	33.8	42.2	52
	—	1.000	.778	.636	1.000	.793				
Carney, John, S.D.	1-1	7-7	14-17	7-12	2-3	31-40	37.4	35.8	42.7	51
	1.000	1.000	.824	.583	.667	.775				
Pelfrey, Doug, Cinn.	0-0	8-8	6-10	8-10	2-3	24-31	37.0	36.2	40.0	53
	—	1.000	.600	.800	.667	.774				
Stoyanovich, Pete, Mia.	2-2	9-10	7-11	4-7	2-2	24-32	33.2	31.7	37.6	52
	1.000	.900	.636	.571	1.000	.750				
Elam, Jason, Den.	0-0	11-12	7-7	4-10	4-6	26-35	36.7	34.8	42.4	54
	—	.917	1.000	.400	.667	.743				
Stover, Matt, Clev.	0-0	4-4	5-6	6-8	1-4	16-22	39.9	36.4	49.2	53
	—	1.000	.833	.750	.250	.727				
Bahr, Matt, Phil.-N.E.	1-1	5-7	5-5	2-5	0-0	13-18	32.6	31.0	36.8	48
	1.000	.714	1.000	.400	—	.722				
Christie, Steve, Buff.	0-0	4-5	12-12	6-9	1-6	23-32	39.4	36.6	46.7	59
	—	.800	1.000	.667	.167	.719				
Blanchard, Cary, N.Y.J.	1-1	7-8	4-5	5-10	0-2	17-26	35.6	31.6	43.1	45
	1.000	.875	.800	.500	.000	.654				
Sisson, Scott, N.E.	1-1	8-13	3-4	2-6	0-2	14-26	33.1	28.8	38.2	40
	1.000	.615	.750	.333	.000	.538				
AFC Totals	9-9	119-129	120-141	71-116	25-50	344-445	36.0	34.0	42.8	59
	1.000	.922	.851	.612	.500	.773				
League Totals	28-28	229-246	219-263	136-222	61-120	673-879	36.2	34.1	43.3	59
	1.000	.931	.833	.613	.508	.766				

Leader based on percentage, minimum 16 field goal attempts

NFC FIELD GOALS—INDIVIDUAL

	1-19 Yards	20-29 Yards	30-39 Yards	40-49 Yards	50 or Longer	Totals	Avg. Yds. Att.	Avg. Yds. Made	Avg. Yds. Miss	Long
Johnson, Norm, Atl.	1-1 1.000	7-7 1.000	9-10 .900	7-7 1.000	2-2 1.000	26-27 .963	35.4	35.3	38.0	54
Murray, Eddie, Dall.	4-4 1.000	4-4 1.000	9-12 .750	8-8 1.000	3-5 .600	28-33 .848	36.5	35.5	42.0	52
Jacke, Chris, G.B.	1-1 1.000	12-12 1.000	6-10 .600	6-7 .857	6-7 .857	31-37 .838	35.4	34.8	38.5	54
Treadwell, David, NYG	3-3 1.000	11-12 .917	7-10 .700	4-6 .667	0-0 —	25-31 .806	31.2	29.6	37.7	46
Andersen, Morten, N.O.	2-2 1.000	7-7 1.000	7-7 1.000	11-14 .786	1-5 .200	28-35 .800	38.7	36.5	47.7	56
Hanson, Jason, Det.	1-1 1.000	8-8 1.000	15-15 1.000	7-12 .583	3-7 .429	34-43 .791	38.3	35.6	48.8	53
Butler, Kevin, Chi.	0-0 —	7-8 .875	12-13 .923	3-7 .429	5-8 .625	27-36 .750	38.1	36.5	42.9	55
Davis, Greg, Phx.	1-1 1.000	11-11 1.000	1-1 1.000	4-10 .400	4-5 .800	21-28 .750	36.6	33.5	45.9	55
Reveiz, Fuad, Minn.	4-4 1.000	12-12 1.000	6-6 1.000	3-7 .429	1-6 .167	26-35 .743	34.7	29.4	50.0	51
Husted, Michael, T.B.	0-0 —	5-5 1.000	5-6 .833	3-6 .500	3-5 .600	16-22 .727	39.1	36.0	47.3	57
Zendejas, Tony, Rams	0-0 —	6-7 .857	4-5 .800	0-3 .000	6-8 .750	16-23 .696	38.8	37.1	42.7	54
Cofer, Mike, S.F.	0-0 —	7-9 .778	5-7 .714	4-7 .571	0-3 .000	16-26 .615	35.9	32.5	41.4	46
Lohmiller, Chip, Wash.	2-2 1.000	4-4 1.000	8-12 .667	1-4 .250	1-6 .167	16-28 .571	37.9	32.2	45.6	51
Nonqualifiers:										
Ruzek, Roger, Phil.	0-0 —	4-4 1.000	3-5 .600	1-1 1.000	0-0 —	8-10 .800	30.6	30.4	31.5	46
Elliott, Lin, Dall.	0-0 —	1-1 1.000	0-1 .000	1-2 .500	0-0 —	2-4 .500	36.0	32.5	39.5	43
Daluiso, Brad, NYG	0-0 —	0-0 —	0-0 —	0-0 —	1-3 .333	1-3 .333	52.0	54.0	51.0	54
NFC Totals	19-19 1.000	110-117 .940	99-122 .811	65-106 .613	36-70 .514	329-434 .758	36.5	34.2	43.9	57
League Totals	28-28 1.000	229-246 .931	219-263 .833	136-222 .613	61-120 .508	673-879 .766	36.2	34.1	43.3	59

Leader based on percentage, minimum 16 field goal attempts

RUSHING

Yards
- **NFC:** 1486—Emmitt Smith, Dallas
- **AFC:** 1315—Thurman Thomas, Buffalo

Yards, Game
- **NFC:** 237—Emmitt Smith, Dallas at Philadelphia, October 31, (30 attempts, TD)
- **AFC:** 194—Gary Brown, Houston at Cleveland, November 21, (34 attempts, TD)

Longest
- **NFC:** 85—Reggie Brooks, Washington at Philadelphia, September 19 - TD
- **AFC:** 77—Keith Byars, Miami at Dallas, November 25 - TD

Attempts
- **AFC:** 355—Thurman Thomas, Buffalo
- **NFC:** 294—Jerome Bettis, Rams

Attempts, Game
- **NFC:** 41—Rodney Hampton, Giants vs. Rams, September 19, (134 yards)
- **AFC:** 36—Chris Warren, Seattle at New England, September 19, (174 yards)

Yards Per Attempt
- **NFC:** 5.3—Emmitt Smith, Dallas
- **AFC:** 5.1—Gary Brown, Houston

Touchdowns
- **AFC:** 12—Marcus Allen, Kansas City
- **NFC:** 10—Ricky Watters, San Francisco

Team Leaders, Yards
- **AFC:** BUFFALO: 1315, Thurman Thomas; CINCINNATI: 589, Harold Green; CLEVELAND: 644, Tommy Vardell; DENVER: 816, Rod Bernstine; HOUSTON: 1002, Gary Brown; INDIANAPOLIS: 711, Roosevelt Potts; KANSAS CITY: 764, Marcus Allen; L.A. RAIDERS: 591, Greg Robinson; MIAMI: 693, Mark Higgs; NEW ENGLAND: 1088, Leonard Russell; N.Y. JETS: 821, Johnny Johnson; PITTSBURGH: 763, Leroy Thompson; SAN DIEGO: 746, Marion Butts; SEATTLE: 1072, Chris Warren

- **NFC:** ATLANTA: 1185, Erric Pegram; CHICAGO: 646, Neal Anderson; DALLAS: 1486, Emmitt Smith; DETROIT: 1115, Barry Sanders; GREEN BAY: 654, Darrell Thompson; L.A. RAMS: 1429, Jerome Bettis; MINNESOTA: 487, Scottie Graham; NEW ORLEANS: 705, Derek Brown; N.Y. GIANTS: 1077, Rodney Hampton; PHILADELPHIA: 746, Herschel Walker; PHOENIX: 1018, Ron Moore; SAN FRANCISCO: 950, Ricky Watters; TAMPA BAY: 658, Reggie Cobb; WASHINGTON: 1063, Reggie Brooks

Team Champion
- **NFC:** 2210—Giants
- **AFC:** 2015—Seattle

AFC RUSHING—TEAM

	Att	Yards	Avg	Long	TD
Seattle	473	2015	4.3	45t	13
Pittsburgh	491	2003	4.1	38t	13
Buffalo	550	1943	3.5	27	12
N.Y. Jets	521	1880	3.6	57t	14
San Diego	455	1824	4.0	65t	14
Houston	409	1792	4.4	35	11
New England	502	1780	3.5	49	9
Cleveland	425	1701	4.0	55	8
Denver	468	1693	3.6	26	13
Kansas City	445	1655	3.7	47	14
Cincinnati	423	1511	3.6	29	3
Miami	419	1459	3.5	77t	10
L.A. Raiders	433	1425	3.3	19	10
Indianapolis	365	1288	3.5	34	4
AFC Total	6379	23969	3.8	77t	148
AFC Average	455.6	1712.1	3.8	—	10.6

NFC RUSHING—TEAM

	Att.	Yards	Avg.	Long	TD
N.Y. Giants	560	2210	3.9	58	11
Dallas	490	2161	4.4	62t	20
San Francisco	463	2133	4.6	50t	26
L.A. Rams	449	2014	4.5	71t	8
Detroit	456	1944	4.3	48	9
Phoenix	452	1809	4.0	57	12
New Orleans	414	1766	4.3	74t	10
Philadelphia	456	1761	3.9	35	7
Washington	396	1728	4.4	85t	11
Chicago	477	1677	3.5	45	10
Minnesota	447	1624	3.6	31	8
Green Bay	448	1619	3.6	60t	14
Atlanta	395	1590	4.0	29	4
Tampa Bay	402	1290	3.2	22	6
NFC Total	6305	25326	4.0	85t	156
NFC Average	450.4	1809.0	4.0	—	11.1
League Total	12684	49295	—	85t	304
League Average	453.0	1760.5	3.9	—	10.9

NFL TOP TEN RUSHERS

	Att.	Yards	Avg.	Long	TD
Smith, Emmitt, Dall.	283	1486	5.3	62t	9
Bettis, Jerome, Rams	294	1429	4.9	71t	7
Thomas, Thurman, Buff.	355	1315	3.7	27	6
Pegram, Erric, Atl.	292	1185	4.1	29	3
Sanders, Barry, Det.	243	1115	4.6	42	3
Russell, Leonard, N.E.	300	1088	3.6	21	7
Hampton, Rodney, N.Y.G.	292	1077	3.7	20	5
Warren, Chris, Sea.	273	1072	3.9	45t	7
Brooks, Reggie, Wash.	223	1063	4.8	85t	3
Moore, Ron, Phx.	263	1018	3.9	20	9

AFC RUSHERS—INDIVIDUAL

	Att.	Yards	Avg.	Long	TD
Thomas, Thurman, Buff.	355	1315	3.7	27	6
Russell, Leonard, N.E.	300	1088	3.6	21	7
Warren, Chris, Sea.	273	1072	3.9	45t	7
Brown, Gary, Hou.	195	1002	5.1	26	6
Johnson, Johnny, N.Y.J.	198	821	4.1	57t	3
Bernstine, Rod, Den.	223	816	3.7	24	4
Allen, Marcus, K.C.	206	764	3.7	39	12
Thompson, Leroy, Pitt.	205	763	3.7	36	3
Butts, Marion, S.D.	185	746	4.0	27	4
Foster, Barry, Pitt.	177	711	4.0	38	8
Potts, Roosevelt, Ind.	179	711	4.0	34	0
Higgs, Mark, Mia.	186	693	3.7	31	3
Means, Natrone, S.D.	160	645	4.0	65t	8
Vardell, Tommy, Clev.	171	644	3.8	54	3
Metcalf, Eric, Clev.	129	611	4.7	55	1
Robinson, Greg, Raid.	156	591	3.8	16	1
Green, Harold, Cinn.	215	589	2.7	25	0
Baxter, Brad, N.Y.J.	174	559	3.2	16	7
Fenner, Derrick, Cinn.	121	482	4.0	26	1
White, Lorenzo, Hou.	131	465	3.5	14	2
Delpino, Robert, Den.	131	445	3.4	18	8
Davis, Kenneth, Buff.	109	391	3.6	19	6
Kirby, Terry, Mia.	119	390	3.3	20	3
Williams, John L., Sea.	82	371	4.5	38	3
Mirer, Rick, Sea.	68	343	5.0	33	3
Johnson, Anthony, Ind.	95	331	3.5	14	1
Anders, Kimble, K.C.	75	291	3.9	18	0
Klingler, David, Cinn.	41	282	6.9	29	0
McNair, Todd, K.C.	51	278	5.5	47	2
Byars, Keith, Mia.	64	269	4.2	77t	3
Hoge, Merril, Pitt.	51	249	4.9	30	1
Milburn, Glyn, Den.	52	231	4.4	26	0
Turner, Kevin, N.E.	50	231	4.6	49	0
Hoard, Leroy, Clev.	56	227	4.1	30	0
Thomas, Blair, N.Y.J.	59	221	3.7	24	1
Harmon, Ronnie, S.D.	46	216	4.7	19	0
Hostetler, Jeff, Raid.	55	202	3.7	19	5
Croom, Corey, N.E.	60	198	3.3	22	1
Stephens, John, G.B.-K.C.	54	191	3.5	22	1
Bell, Nick, Raid.	67	180	2.7	12	1
Murrell, Adrian, N.Y.J.	34	157	4.6	37t	1
Smith, Steve, Raid.	47	156	3.3	13	0
Elway, John, Den.	44	153	3.5	18	0

	Att.	Yards	Avg.	Long	TD
Vaughn, Jon, Sea.	36	153	4.3	37	0
Culver, Rodney, Ind.	65	150	2.3	9	3
Gash, Sam, N.E.	48	149	3.1	14	1
Williams, Harvey, K.C.	42	149	3.5	19	0
Moon, Warren, Hou.	48	145	3.0	35	1
Bieniemy, Eric, S.D.	33	135	4.1	12	1
Stone, Dwight, Pitt.	12	121	10.1	38t	1
Esiason, Boomer, N.Y.J.	45	118	2.6	17	1
McCallum, Napoleon, Raid.	37	114	3.1	14	3
O'Donnell, Neil, Pitt.	26	111	4.3	27	0
Montgomery, Tyrone, Raid.	37	106	2.9	15	0
Kelly, Jim, Buff.	36	102	2.8	17	0
Tillman, Spencer, Hou.	9	94	10.4	34	0
Mitchell, Scott, Mia.	21	89	4.2	32	0
Bledsoe, Drew, N.E.	32	82	2.6	15	0
Testaverde, Vinny, Clev.	18	74	4.1	14	0
Montana, Joe, K.C.	25	64	2.6	17	0
Baldwin, Randy, Clev.	18	61	3.4	11	0
Gardner, Carwell, Buff.	20	56	2.8	8	0
Miles, Ostell, Cinn.	22	56	2.5	15	1
Jefferson, Shawn, S.D.	5	53	10.6	33	0
Blades, Brian, Sea.	5	52	10.4	26	0
Evans, Vince, Raid.	14	51	3.6	17	0
Rivers, Reggie, Den.	15	50	3.3	14	1
Carlson, Cody, Hou.	14	41	2.9	10t	2
Schroeder, Jay, Cinn.	10	41	4.1	20	0
George, Jeff, Ind.	13	39	3.0	14	0
Ball, Eric, Cinn.	8	37	4.6	18	1
Humphries, Stan, S.D.	8	37	4.6	27	0
Turner, Nate, Buff.	11	36	3.3	10	0
Jones, Fred, K.C.	5	34	6.8	13	0
Jordan, Randy, Raid.	12	33	2.8	12	0
Mack, Kevin, Clev.	10	33	3.3	7	1
Secules, Scott, N.E.	8	33	4.1	13	0
Verdin, Clarence, Ind.	3	33	11.0	29	0
Brooks, Bill, Buff.	3	30	10.0	15	0
Thompson, Ernie, K.C.	11	28	2.5	14	0
Carrier, Mark, Clev.	4	26	6.5	15t	1
Krieg, Dave, K.C.	21	24	1.1	20	0
Reed, Andre, Buff.	9	21	2.3	15	0
Mathis, Terance, N.Y.J.	2	20	10.0	17t	1
Givins, Ernest, Hou.	6	19	3.2	16	0
Chaffey, Pat, N.Y.J.	5	17	3.4	7	0
Parmalee, Bernie, Mia.	4	16	4.0	12	0
Query, Jeff, Cinn.	2	13	6.5	8	0
Saxon, James, Mia.	5	13	2.6	9	0
Bates, Michael, Sea.	2	12	6.0	6	0
Mills, Ernie, Pitt.	3	12	4.0	19	0
Stark, Rohn, Ind.	1	11	11.0	11	0
Maston, Le'Shai, Hou.	1	10	10.0	10	0
Richardson, Bucky, Hou.	2	9	4.5	11	0
Johnson, Tracy, Sea.	2	8	4.0	5	0
Brown, Tim, Raid.	2	7	3.5	14	0
Cuthbert, Randy, Pitt.	1	7	7.0	7	0
Martin, Tony, Mia.	1	6	6.0	6	0
Robinson, Patrick, Cinn.	1	6	6.0	6	0
Toner, Ed, Ind.	2	6	3.0	6	0
Wellman, Gary, Hou.	2	6	3.0	4	0
Benjamin, Ryan, Cinn.	3	5	1.7	2	0
Majkowski, Don, Ind.	2	4	2.0	4	0
Thomas, Doug, Sea.	1	4	4.0	4	0
Barnett, Tim, K.C.	1	3	3.0	3	0
Friesz, John, S.D.	10	3	0.3	2	0
Philcox, Todd, Clev.	2	3	1.5	3t	1
Trudeau, Jack, Ind.	5	3	0.6	2	0
Carter, Dale, K.C.	1	2	2.0	2	0
Jones, James, Clev.	2	2	1.0	1t	1
Lewis, Nate, S.D.	3	2	0.7	7	0
Mayes, Rueben, Sea.	1	2	2.0	2	0
Saxon, Mike, N.E.	2	2	1.0	2	0
Coleman, Pat, Hou.	1	1	1.0	1	0
Jackson, Michael, Clev.	1	1	1.0	1	0
Cash, Keith, K.C.	1	0	0.0	0	0
Hendrickson, Steve, S.D.	1	0	0.0	0	0
Jett, James, Raid.	1	0	0.0	0	0
Martin, Kelvin, Sea.	1	0	0.0	0	0
Miller, Anthony, S.D.	1	0	0.0	0	0
Rouen, Tom, Den.	1	0	0.0	0	0
Woodson, Rod, Pitt.	1	0	0.0	0	0
Zolak, Scott, N.E.	1	0	0.0	0	0
Gelbaugh, Stan, Sea.	1	-1	-1.0	-1	0
McGwire, Dan, Sea.	1	-1	-1.0	-1	0

	Att.	Yards	Avg.	Long	TD
Pederson, Doug, Mia.	2	-1	-.5	0	0
Fina, John, Buff.	1	-2	-2.0	-2	0
Maddox, Tommy, Den.	2	-2	-1.0	-1	0
Crittenden, Ray, N.E.	1	-3	-3.0	-3	0
DeBerg, Steve, Mia.	4	-4	-1.0	-1	0
Fryar, Irving, Mia.	3	-4	-1.3	2	0
Marino, Dan, Mia.	9	-4	-.4	4t	1
McDuffie, O. J., Mia.	1	-4	-4.0	-4	0
Tomczak, Mike, Pitt.	5	-4	-.8	2	0
Ismail, Raghib, Raid.	4	-5	-1.2	10	0
Moore, Rob, N.Y.J.	1	-6	-6.0	-6	0
Reich, Frank, Buff.	6	-6	-1.0	-1	0
Gossett, Jeff, Raid.	1	-10	-10.0	-10	0
Kidd, John, S.D.	3	-13	-4.3	2t	1
Aguiar, Louie, N.Y.J.	3	-27	-9.0	5	0

t = Touchdown
Leader based on most yards gained

NFC RUSHERS—INDIVIDUAL

	Att.	Yards	Avg.	Long	TD
Smith, Emmitt, Dall.	283	1486	5.3	62t	9
Bettis, Jerome, Rams	294	1429	4.9	71t	7
Pegram, Erric, Atl.	292	1185	4.1	29	3
Sanders, Barry, Det.	243	1115	4.6	42	3
Hampton, Rodney, N.Y.G.	292	1077	3.7	20	5
Brooks, Reggie, Wash.	223	1063	4.8	85t	3
Moore, Ron, Phx.	263	1018	3.9	20	9
Watters, Ricky, S.F.	208	950	4.6	39	10
Walker, Herschel, Phil.	174	746	4.3	35	1
Brown, Derek, N.O.	180	705	3.9	60	2
Cobb, Reggie, T.B.	221	658	3.0	16	3
Thompson, Darrell, G.B.	169	654	3.9	60t	3
Anderson, Neal, Chi.	202	646	3.2	45	4
Tillman, Lewis, N.Y.G.	121	585	4.8	58	3
Bennett, Edgar, G.B.	159	550	3.5	19	9
Graham, Scottie, Minn.	118	488	4.1	31	3
Worley, Tim, Pitt.-Chi.	120	470	3.9	28	2
Word, Barry, Minn.	142	458	3.2	14	2
Young, Steve, S.F.	69	407	5.9	35	2
Sherman, Heath, Phil.	115	406	3.5	19	2
Moore, Derrick, Det.	88	405	4.6	48	3
Smith, Robert, Minn.	82	399	4.9	26t	2
Meggett, David, N.Y.G.	69	329	4.8	23	0
Hebron, Vaughn, Phil.	84	297	3.5	33	3
Gary, Cleveland, Rams	79	293	3.7	15	1
Workman, Vince, T.B.	78	284	3.6	21	2
Logan, Marc, S.F.	58	280	4.8	45	7
Harbaugh, Jim, Chi.	60	277	4.6	25	4
Lassic, Derrick, Dall.	75	269	3.6	15	3
Hearst, Garrison, Phx.	76	264	3.5	57	1
Bailey, Johnny, Phx.	49	253	5.2	31	1
Mitchell, Brian, Wash.	63	246	3.9	29t	3
Lee, Amp, S.F.	72	230	3.2	13	1
Wilson, Wade, N.O.	31	230	7.4	44	0
Favre, Brett, G.B.	58	216	3.7	27	1
Muster, Brad, N.O.	64	214	3.3	18	3
Lynch, Eric, Det.	53	207	3.9	15	2
Broussard, Steven, Atl.	39	206	5.3	26	1
Heyward, Craig, Chi.	68	206	3.0	11	0
Ervins, Ricky, Wash.	50	201	4.0	18	0
Neal, Lorenzo, N.O.	21	175	8.3	74t	1
Hilliard, Dalton, N.O.	50	165	3.3	16	2
Peete, Rodney, Det.	45	165	3.7	28	1
McAfee, Fred, N.O.	51	160	3.1	27	1
Centers, Larry, Phx.	25	152	6.1	33	0
Joseph, James, Phil.	39	140	3.6	12	0
Coleman, Lincoln, Dall.	34	132	3.9	16	2
Bunch, Jarrod, N.Y.G.	33	128	3.9	13	2
Aikman, Troy, Dall.	32	125	3.9	20	0
Craig, Roger, Minn.	38	119	3.1	11	1
Royster, Mazio, T.B.	33	115	3.5	19	1
Cunningham, Randall, Phil.	18	110	6.1	26	1
Byner, Earnest, Wash.	23	105	4.6	16	1
Rubley, T. J., Rams	29	102	3.5	13	0
Erickson, Craig, T.B.	26	96	3.7	15	0
McMahon, Jim, Minn.	33	96	2.9	16	0
Dickerson, Eric, Atl.	26	91	3.5	10	0
Gannon, Rich, Wash.	21	88	4.2	12	1
Rathman, Tom, S.F.	19	80	4.2	19	3
Johnston, Daryl, Dall.	24	74	3.1	11	3
Lester, Tim, Rams	11	74	6.7	26	0

	Att.	Yards	Avg.	Long	TD
Carter, Dexter, S.F.	10	72	7.2	50t	1
Ned, Derrick, N.O.	9	71	7.9	35t	1
Rice, Jerry, S.F.	3	69	23.0	43t	1
Anderson, Gary, T.B.	28	56	2.0	13	0
Hebert, Bobby, Atl.	24	49	2.0	14	0
Tolliver, Billy Joe, Atl.	7	48	6.9	24	0
Proehl, Ricky, Phx.	8	47	5.9	17	0
Beuerlein, Steve, Phx.	22	45	2.0	20	0
Conway, Curtis, Chi.	5	44	8.8	18	0
Rasheed, Kenyon, N.Y.G.	9	42	4.7	23t	1
Brister, Bubby, Phil.	20	39	2.0	13	0
Everett, Jim, Rams	19	38	2.0	14	0
Copeland, Horace, T.B.	3	34	11.3	22	0
Early, Quinn, N.O.	2	32	16.0	26	0
Evans, Chuck, Minn.	14	32	2.3	5	0
Simms, Phil, N.Y.G.	28	31	1.1	9	0
Gainer, Derrick, Dall.	9	29	3.2	8	0
Green, Robert, Chi.	15	29	1.9	10	0
Harris, Rudy, T.B.	7	29	4.1	12	0
Lang, David, Rams	9	29	3.2	28	0
Blount, Eric, Phx.	5	28	5.6	7	1
Kosar, Bernie, Clev.-Dall.	23	26	1.1	10	0
Williams, Kevin, Dall.	7	26	3.7	12	2
Jackson, Mark, N.Y.G.	3	25	8.3	20	0
Ware, Andre, Det.	7	23	3.3	8	0
Carter, Anthony, Minn.	7	19	2.7	9	0
Christian, Bob, Chi.	8	19	2.4	12	0
Barnhardt, Tommy, N.O.	1	18	18.0	18	0
Ellard, Henry, Rams	2	18	9.0	15	0
Brooks, Robert, G.B.	3	17	5.7	21	0
Howard, Desmond, Wash.	2	17	8.5	9	0
O'Brien, Ken, Phil.	4	17	4.3	11	0
Taylor, John, S.F.	2	17	8.5	12	0
Walker, Adam, S.F.	5	17	3.4	11	0
Perriman, Brett, Det.	4	16	4.0	16	0
Bono, Steve, S.F.	12	14	1.2	10	1
Ismail, Qadry, Minn.	3	14	4.7	6	0
Agee, Tommie, Dall.	6	13	2.2	6	0
Lewis, Darren, Chi.	7	13	1.9	3	0
Miller, Chris, Atl.	2	11	5.5	6	0
Kinchen, Todd, Rams	2	10	5.0	8	0
White, Russell, Rams	2	10	5.0	5	0
Sharpe, Sterling, G.B.	4	8	2.0	5	0
Drayton, Troy, Rams	1	7	7.0	7	0
Matthews, Aubrey, Det.	2	7	3.5	9	0
Sanders, Ricky, Wash.	1	7	7.0	7	0
Wilson, Charles, T.B.	2	7	3.5	4	0
Feagles, Jeff, Phil.	2	6	3.0	6	0
Irvin, Michael, Dall.	2	6	3.0	9	0
McDowell, Anthony, T.B.	2	6	3.0	3	0
Willis, Peter Tom, Chi.	2	6	3.0	6	0
Armstrong, Tyji, T.B.	2	5	2.5	4	0
Kramer, Erik, Det.	10	5	0.5	4	0
Jones, Ernie, Rams	1	4	4.0	4	0
Pritchard, Mike, Atl.	2	4	2.0	4	0
Rypien, Mark, Wash.	9	4	0.4	5	3
Mims, David, Atl.	1	3	3.0	3	0
Wilson, Marcus, G.B.	6	3	0.5	5	0
Chandler, Chris, Phx.	3	2	0.7	1	0
Novacek, Jay, Dall.	1	2	2.0	2t	1
Richards, Curvin, Det.	4	1	0.3	1	0
Buck, Mike, N.O.	1	0	0.0	0	0
Camarillo, Rich, Phx.	1	0	0.0	0	0
Roby, Reggie, Wash.	1	0	0.0	0	0
Wilmsmeyer, Klaus, S.F.	2	0	0.0	0	0
Monk, Art, Wash.	1	-1	-1.0	-1	0
Salisbury, Sean, Minn.	10	-1	-0.1	6	0
Conklin, Cary, Wash.	2	-2	-1.0	-1	0
Detmer, Ty, G.B.	1	-2	-2.0	-2	0
Graham, Kent, N.Y.G.	2	-3	-1.5	-1	0
Musgrave, Bill, S.F.	3	-3	-1.0	-1	0
Brown, Dave, N.Y.G.	3	-4	-1.3	-1	0
Walsh, Steve, N.O.	4	-4	-1.0	-1	0
Alexander, Harold, Atl.	2	-7	-3.5	0	0
Garrett, Jason, Dall.	8	-8	-1.0	0	0

t = Touchdown
Leader based on most yards gained

PASSING

Highest Rating
NFC: 101.5—Steve Young, San Francisco
AFC: 92.8—John Elway, Denver

Completion Percentage
NFC: 69.1—Troy Aikman, Dallas
AFC: 63.2—John Elway, Denver

Attempts
AFC: 551—John Elway, Denver
NFC: 522—Brett Favre, Green Bay

Completions
AFC: 348—John Elway, Denver
NFC: 318—Brett Favre, Green Bay

Yards
AFC: 4030—John Elway, Denver
NFC: 4023—Steve Young, San Francisco

Yards, Game
NFC: 462—Steve Young, San Francisco at Rams, November 28, (26-32, 4 TD)
AFC: 424—Jeff Hostetler, Raiders vs. San Diego, October 31, (20-32, 2 TD)

Longest
NFC: 98—Bobby Hebert (to Michael Haynes), Atlanta vs. New Orleans, September 12 - TD
AFC: 82—Scott Secules (to Kevin Turner {13 yds} lateral to Leonard Russell {69 yds}), New England at Phoenix, October 10

Yards Per Attempt
NFC: 8.71—Steve Young, San Francisco
AFC: 7.81—Vinny Testaverde, Cleveland

Touchdown Passes
NFC: 29—Steve Young, San Francisco
AFC: 25—John Elway, Denver

Touchdown Passes, Game
AFC: 4—Jim Kelly, Buffalo vs. New England, September 5, (13-22, 167 yards)
Boomer Esiason, Jets vs. Philadelphia, October 3, (19-33, 297 yards)
Warren Moon, Houston at Cincinnati, November 14, (23-31, 225 yards)
Drew Bledsoe, New England vs. Miami, January 2, (27-43, 329 yards) (OT)
NFC: 4—Brett Favre, Green Bay at Tampa Bay, October 24, (20-35, 268 yards)
Craig Erickson, Tampa Bay at Atlanta, October 31, (18-28, 318 yards)
Steve Young, San Francisco at Tampa Bay. November 14, (23-29, 311 yards)
Steve Young, San Francisco at Rams, November 28, (26-32, 462 yards)
Steve Young, San Francisco at Detroit, December 19, (17-23, 354 yards)

Lowest Interception Percentage
AFC: 1.4—Neil O'Donnell, Pittsburgh
NFC: 1.5—Troy Aikman, Dallas

Team Champion (Most Net Yards)
AFC: 4353—Miami
NFC: 4302—San Francisco

AFC PASSING—TEAM

	Att.	Comp.	Pct. Comp.	Gross Yards	Sacked	Yds. Lost	Net Yards	Yds./ Att.	Yds./ Comp.	TD	Pct. TD	Long	Int.	Pct. Int.
Miami	581	342	58.9	4564	30	211	4353	7.86	13.35	27	4.65	80t	18	3.1
Houston	614	357	58.1	4145	43	279	3866	6.75	11.61	23	3.75	80t	25	4.1
Denver	553	350	63.3	4061	39	293	3768	7.34	11.60	27	4.88	63	10	1.8
L.A. Raiders	495	281	56.8	3882	50	293	3589	7.84	13.81	17	3.43	74t	14	2.8
Indianapolis	594	332	55.9	3623	29	206	3417	6.10	10.91	10	1.68	72t	15	2.5
Pittsburgh	540	299	55.4	3606	48	374	3232	6.68	12.06	16	2.96	71t	12	2.2
Buffalo	497	304	61.2	3535	31	218	3317	7.11	11.63	20	4.02	65t	18	3.6
N.Y. Jets	489	294	60.1	3492	21	160	3332	7.14	11.88	16	3.27	77	12	2.5
New England	566	289	51.1	3412	23	127	3285	6.03	11.81	17	3.00	82	24	4.2
Kansas City	490	287	58.6	3384	35	204	3180	6.91	11.79	20	4.08	66t	10	2.0
San Diego	563	301	53.5	3383	32	240	3143	6.01	11.24	18	3.20	66t	14	2.5
Cleveland	478	262	54.8	3328	45	289	3039	6.96	12.70	23	4.81	62t	19	4.0
Seattle	498	280	56.2	2896	48	242	2654	5.82	10.34	13	2.61	53t	18	3.6
Cincinnati	510	272	53.3	2830	53	289	2541	5.55	10.40	11	2.16	51	11	2.2
AFC Total	7468	4250	—	50141	527	3425	46716	—	—	258	—	82	220	—
AFC Average	533.4	303.6	56.9	3581.5	37.6	244.6	3336.9	6.71	11.80	18.4	3.5	—	15.7	2.9

NFC PASSING—TEAM

	Att.	Comp.	Pct. Comp.	Gross Yards	Sacked	Yds. Lost	Net Yards	Yds./ Att.	Yds./ Comp.	TD	Pct. TD	Long	Int.	Pct. Int.
San Francisco	524	354	67.6	4480	35	178	4302	8.55	12.66	29	5.53	80t	17	3.2
Atlanta	573	334	58.3	3787	40	267	3520	6.61	11.34	28	4.89	98t	25	4.4
Phoenix	522	310	59.4	3635	33	231	3404	6.96	11.73	21	4.02	65t	20	3.8
Dallas	475	317	66.7	3617	29	163	3454	7.61	11.41	18	3.79	86	6	1.3
Philadelphia	556	328	59.0	3463	42	302	3161	6.23	10.56	23	4.14	80t	13	2.3
Minnesota	526	315	59.9	3381	35	181	3200	6.43	10.73	18	3.42	58	14	2.7
Green Bay	528	322	61.0	3330	30	199	3131	6.31	10.34	19	3.60	66t	24	4.5
Tampa Bay	508	262	51.6	3295	39	274	3021	6.49	12.58	19	3.74	67t	25	4.9
New Orleans	481	274	57.0	3183	40	242	2941	6.62	11.62	18	3.74	63t	21	4.4
N.Y. Giants	424	257	60.6	3180	40	245	2935	7.50	12.37	17	4.01	62	9	2.1
L.A. Rams	473	247	52.2	3021	31	231	2790	6.39	12.23	16	3.38	60t	19	4.0
Detroit	435	264	60.7	2943	46	229	2714	6.77	11.15	15	3.45	93t	19	4.4
Washington	533	287	53.8	2764	40	219	2545	5.19	9.63	11	2.06	54	21	3.9
Chicago	388	230	59.3	2270	48	230	2040	5.85	9.87	7	1.80	48	16	4.1
NFC Total	6946	4101	—	46349	528	3191	43158	—	—	259	—	98t	249	—
NFC Average	496.1	292.9	59.0	3310.6	37.7	227.9	3082.7	6.67	11.30	18.5	3.7	—	17.8	3.6
League Total	14414	8351	—	96490	1055	6616	89874	—	—	517	—	98t	460	—
League Average	514.8	298.3	57.9	3446.1	37.7	236.3	3209.8	6.69	11.55	18.5	3.6	—	16.8	3.3

Leader based on net yards

NFL TOP TEN PASSERS

	Att.	Comp.	Pct. Comp.	Yds.	Avg. Gain	TD	Pct. TD	Long	Int.	Pct. Int.	Sack	Yds. Lost	Rating Points
Young, Steve, S.F.	462	314	68.0	4023	8.71	29	6.3	80t	16	3.5	31	160	101.5
Aikman, Troy, Dall.	392	271	69.1	3100	7.91	15	3.8	80t	6	1.5	26	153	99.0
Elway, John, Den.	551	348	63.2	4030	7.31	25	4.5	63	10	1.8	39	293	92.8
Simms, Phil, N.Y.G.	400	247	61.8	3038	7.60	15	3.8	62	9	2.3	37	217	88.3
Montana, Joe, K.C.	298	181	60.7	2144	7.19	13	4.4	50t	7	2.3	12	61	87.4
Testaverde, Vinny, Clev.	230	130	56.5	1797	7.81	14	6.1	62t	9	3.9	17	101	85.7
Brister, Bubby, Phil.	309	181	58.6	1905	6.17	14	4.5	58	5	1.6	19	148	84.9
Esiason, Boomer, N.Y.J.	473	288	60.9	3421	7.23	16	3.4	77	11	2.3	18	139	84.5
Mitchell, Scott, Mia.	233	133	57.1	1773	7.61	12	5.2	77t	8	3.4	7	49	84.2
Hebert, Bobby, Atl.	430	263	61.2	2978	6.93	24	5.6	98t	17	4.0	29	190	84.0

AFC PASSING—INDIVIDUAL

	Att.	Comp.	Pct. Comp.	Yds.	Avg. Gain	TD	Pct. TD	Long	Int.	Pct. Int.	Sack	Yds. Lost	Rating Points
Elway, John, Den.	551	348	63.2	4030	7.31	25	4.5	63	10	1.8	39	293	92.8
Montana, Joe, K.C.	298	181	60.7	2144	7.19	13	4.4	50t	7	2.3	12	61	87.4
Testaverde, Vinny, Clev.	230	130	56.5	1797	7.81	14	6.1	62t	9	3.9	17	101	85.7
Esiason, Boomer, N.Y.J.	473	288	60.9	3421	7.23	16	3.4	77	11	2.3	18	139	84.5
Mitchell, Scott, Mia.	233	133	57.1	1773	7.61	12	5.2	77t	8	3.4	7	49	84.2
Hostetler, Jeff, Raid.	419	236	56.3	3242	7.74	14	3.3	74t	10	2.4	38	206	82.5
Kelly, Jim, Buff.	470	288	61.3	3382	7.20	18	3.8	65t	18	3.8	25	171	79.9
O'Donnell, Neil, Pitt.	486	270	55.6	3208	6.60	14	2.9	71t	7	1.4	41	331	79.5
George, Jeff, Ind.	407	234	57.5	2526	6.21	8	2.0	72t	6	1.5	26	190	76.3
DeBerg, Steve, T.B.-Mia.	227	136	59.9	1707	7.52	7	3.1	47	10	4.4	18	143	75.3
Moon, Warren, Hou.	520	303	58.3	3485	6.70	21	4.0	80t	21	4.0	34	218	75.2
Friesz, John, S.D.	238	128	53.8	1402	5.89	6	2.5	66t	4	1.7	14	98	72.8
Humphries, Stan, S.D.	324	173	53.4	1981	6.11	12	3.7	48t	10	3.1	18	142	71.5
Mirer, Rick, Sea.	486	274	56.4	2833	5.83	12	2.5	53t	17	3.5	47	235	67.0
Klingler, David, Cinn.	343	190	55.4	1935	5.64	6	1.7	51	9	2.6	40	202	66.6
Bledsoe, Drew, N.E.	429	214	49.9	2494	5.81	15	3.5	54t	15	3.5	16	99	65.0

Nonqualifiers

	Att.	Comp.	Pct. Comp.	Yds.	Avg. Gain	TD	Pct. TD	Long	Int.	Pct. Int.	Sack	Yds. Lost	Rating Points
Reich, Frank, Buff.	26	16	61.5	153	5.88	2	7.7	30t	0	0.0	6	47	103.5
Marino, Dan, Mia.	150	91	60.7	1218	8.12	8	5.3	80t	3	2.0	7	42	95.9
Krieg, Dave, K.C.	189	105	55.6	1238	6.55	7	3.7	66t	3	1.6	22	138	81.4
Evans, Vince, Raid.	76	45	59.2	640	8.42	3	3.9	68t	4	5.3	12	87	77.7
Schroeder, Jay, Cinn.	159	78	49.1	832	5.23	5	3.1	37	2	1.3	13	87	70.0
Carlson, Cody, Hou.	90	51	56.7	605	6.72	2	2.2	47	4	4.4	8	53	66.2
Nagle, Browning, N.Y.J.	14	6	42.9	71	5.07	0	0.0	18	0	0.0	3	21	58.9
Trudeau, Jack, Ind.	162	85	52.5	992	6.12	2	1.2	68	7	4.3	2	11	57.4
Philcox, Todd, Clev.	108	52	48.1	699	6.47	4	3.7	56	7	6.5	7	60	54.5
Secules, Scott, N.E.	134	75	56.0	918	6.85	2	1.5	82	9	6.7	7	28	54.3
Tomczak, Mike, Pitt.	54	29	53.7	398	7.37	2	3.7	39t	5	9.3	7	43	51.3
Majkowski, Don, Ind.	24	13	54.2	105	4.38	0	0.0	17	1	4.2	1	5	48.1

Fewer than 10 attempts

	Att.	Comp.	Pct. Comp.	Yds.	Avg. Gain	TD	Pct. TD	Long	Int.	Pct. Int.	Sack	Yds. Lost	Rating Points
Aguiar, Louie, N.Y.J.	2	0	0.0	0	0.00	0	0.0	0	1	50.0	0	0	0.0
Anders, Kimble, K.C.	0	0	—	0	—	0	—	—	0	—	1	5	—
Blundin, Matt, K.C.	3	1	33.3	2	0.67	0	0.0	2	0	0.0	0	0	42.4
Byars, Keith, Mia.	2	1	50.0	11	5.50	1	50.0	11t	0	0.0	0	0	106.3
Gelbaugh, Stan, Sea.	5	3	60.0	39	7.80	0	0.0	22	1	20.0	1	7	45.0
Hoard, Leroy, Clev.	1	0	0.0	0	0.00	0	0.0	0	0	0.0	0	0	39.6
Jackson, Michael, Clev.	1	1	100.0	25	25.00	0	0.0	25	0	0.0	0	0	118.8
Johnson, Anthony, Ind.	1	0	0.0	0	0.00	0	0.0	0	1	100.0	0	0	0.0
Johnson, Lee, Cinn.	1	0	0.0	0	0.00	0	0.0	0	0	0.0	0	0	39.6
Maddox, Tommy, Den.	1	1	100.0	1	1.00	1	100.0	1t	0	0.0	0	0	118.8
Marshall, Arthur, Den.	1	1	100.0	30	30.00	1	100.0	30t	0	0.0	0	0	158.3
McGwire, Dan, Sea.	5	3	60.0	24	4.80	1	20.0	17t	0	0.0	0	0	111.7
Means, Natrone, S.D.	1	0	0.0	0	0.00	0	0.0	0	0	0.0	0	0	39.6
Pederson, Doug, Mia.	8	4	50.0	41	5.13	0	0.0	12	0	0.0	1	4	65.1
Pickens, Carl, Cinn.	1	0	0.0	0	0.00	0	0.0	0	0	0.0	0	0	39.6
Richardson, Bucky, Hou.	4	3	75.0	55	13.75	0	0.0	34	0	0.0	1	8	116.7
Thomas, Thurman, Buff.	1	0	0.0	0	0.00	0	0.0	0	0	0.0	0	0	39.6
Turner, Kevin, N.E.	1	0	0.0	0	0.00	0	0.0	0	0	0.0	0	0	39.6
Tuten, Rick, Sea.	1	0	0.0	0	0.00	0	0.0	0	0	0.0	0	0	39.6
Wilhelm, Erik, Cinn.	6	4	66.7	63	10.50	0	0.0	27	0	0.0	0	0	101.4
Williams, John L., Sea.	1	0	0.0	0	0.00	0	0.0	0	0	0.0	0	0	39.6
Zolak, Scott, N.E.	2	0	0.0	0	0.00	0	0.0	0	0	0.0	0	0	39.6

t = Touchdown
Leader based on rating points, minimum 224 attempts

NFC PASSING—INDIVIDUAL

	Att.	Comp.	Pct. Comp.	Yds.	Avg. Gain	TD	Pct. TD	Long	Int.	Pct. Int.	Sack	Yds. Lost	Rating Points
Young, Steve, S.F.	462	314	68.0	4023	8.71	29	6.3	80t	16	3.5	31	160	101.5
Aikman, Troy, Dall.	392	271	69.1	3100	7.91	15	3.8	80t	6	1.5	26	153	99.0
Simms, Phil, N.Y.G.	400	247	61.8	3038	7.60	15	3.8	62	9	2.3	37	217	88.3
Brister, Bubby, Phil.	309	181	58.6	1905	6.17	14	4.5	58	5	1.6	19	148	84.9
Hebert, Bobby, Atl.	430	263	61.2	2978	6.93	24	5.6	98t	17	4.0	29	190	84.0
Beuerlein, Steve, Phx.	418	258	61.7	3164	7.57	18	4.3	65t	17	4.1	29	206	82.5
McMahon, Jim, Minn.	331	200	60.4	1968	5.95	9	2.7	58	8	2.4	23	104	76.2
Favre, Brett, G.B.	522	318	60.9	3303	6.33	19	3.6	66t	24	4.6	30	199	72.2
Harbaugh, Jim, Chi.	325	200	61.5	2002	6.16	7	2.2	48	11	3.4	43	210	72.1
Wilson, Wade, N.O.	388	221	57.0	2457	6.33	12	3.1	42t	15	3.9	37	225	70.1
Erickson, Craig, T.B.	457	233	51.0	3054	6.68	18	3.9	67t	21	4.6	35	236	66.4
Peete, Rodney, Det.	252	157	62.3	1670	6.63	6	2.4	93t	14	5.6	34	174	66.4
Everett, Jim, Rams	274	135	49.3	1652	6.03	8	2.9	60t	12	4.4	18	125	59.7
Rypien, Mark, Wash.	319	166	52.0	1514	4.75	4	1.3	43	10	3.1	16	87	56.3
Nonqualifiers													
Kramer, Erik, Det.	138	87	63.0	1002	7.26	8	5.8	48	3	2.2	5	35	95.1
Cunningham, Randall, Phil.	110	76	69.1	850	7.73	5	4.5	80t	5	4.5	7	33	88.1
Buck, Mike, N.O.	54	32	59.3	448	8.30	4	7.4	63t	3	5.6	3	17	87.6
Salisbury, Sean, Minn.	195	115	59.0	1413	7.25	9	4.6	55	6	3.1	12	77	84.0
Kosar, Bernie, Clev.-Dall.	201	115	57.2	1217	6.05	8	4.0	86	3	1.5	23	132	82.0
Rubley, T. J., Rams	189	108	57.1	1338	7.08	8	4.2	54	6	3.2	13	106	80.1
Bono, Steve, S.F.	61	39	63.9	416	6.82	0	0.0	33	1	1.6	4	18	76.9
Conklin, Cary, Wash.	87	46	52.9	496	5.70	4	4.6	34t	3	3.4	8	45	70.9
O'Brien, Ken, Phil.	137	71	51.8	708	5.17	4	2.9	41	3	2.2	15	116	67.4
Chandler, Chris, Phx.	103	52	50.5	471	4.57	3	2.9	27t	2	1.9	4	25	64.8
Walsh, Steve, N.O.	38	20	52.6	271	7.13	2	5.3	54t	3	7.9	0	0	60.3
Gannon, Rich, Wash.	125	74	59.2	704	5.63	3	2.4	54	7	5.6	16	87	59.6
Tolliver, Billy Joe, Atl.	76	39	51.3	464	6.11	3	3.9	42t	5	6.6	3	15	56.0
Garrett, Jason, Dall.	19	9	47.4	61	3.21	0	0.0	16	0	0.0	1	6	54.9
Ware, Andre, Det.	45	20	44.4	271	6.02	1	2.2	47	2	4.4	7	20	53.1
Miller, Chris, Atl.	66	32	48.5	345	5.23	1	1.5	32t	3	4.5	8	62	50.4
Graham, Kent, N.Y.G.	22	8	36.4	79	3.59	0	0.0	18	0	0.0	3	28	47.3
Weldon, Casey, T.B.	11	6	54.5	55	5.00	0	0.0	20	1	9.1	1	11	30.5
Willis, Peter Tom, Chi.	60	30	50.0	268	4.47	0	0.0	29	5	8.3	5	20	27.6
Fewer than 10 attempts													
Anderson, Neal, Chi.	1	0	0.0	0	0.00	0	0.0	0	0	0.0	0	0	39.6
Barnhardt, Tommy, N.O.	1	1	100.0	7	7.00	0	0.0	7	0	0.0	0	0	95.8
Detmer, Ty, G.B.	5	3	60.0	26	5.20	0	0.0	25	0	0.0	0	0	73.8
Gardocki, Chris, Chi.	2	0	0.0	0	0.00	0	0.0	0	0	0.0	0	0	39.6
Gary, Cleveland, Rams	1	1	100.0	8	8.00	0	0.0	8	0	0.0	0	0	100.0
Harper, Alvin, Dall.	1	1	100.0	46	46.00	0	0.0	46	0	0.0	0	0	118.8
Hearst, Garrison, Phx.	1	0	0.0	0	0.00	0	0.0	0	1	100.0	0	0	0.0
Meggett, David, N.Y.G.	2	2	100.0	63	31.50	2	100.0	42t	0	0.0	0	0	158.3
Mitchell, Brian, Wash.	2	1	50.0	50	25.00	0	0.0	50	1	50.0	0	0	56.3
Moore, Dave, T.B.	1	0	0.0	0	0.00	0	0.0	0	0	0.0	0	0	39.6
Pagel, Mike, Rams	9	3	33.3	23	2.56	0	0.0	10	1	11.1	0	0	2.8
Sanders, Deion, Atl.	1	0	0.0	0	0.00	0	0.0	0	0	0.0	0	0	39.6
Sharpe, Sterling, G.B.	1	1	100.0	1	1.00	0	0.0	1	0	0.0	0	0	79.2
Taylor, John, S.F.	1	1	100.0	41	41.00	0	0.0	41	0	0.0	0	0	118.8
Walker, Herschel, Phil.	0	0	—	0	—	0	—	—	0	—	1	5	—

t = Touchdown
Leader based on rating points, minimum 224 attempts

PASS RECEIVING

Receptions
NFC: 112—Sterling Sharpe, Green Bay
AFC: 85—Reggie Langhorne, Indianapolis

Receptions, Game
AFC: 12—Reggie Langhorne, Indianapolis at Washington, November 7, (203 yards - TD)
NFC: 12—Michael Irvin, Dallas vs. San Francisco, October 17, (168 yards - TD)
Gary Clark, Phoenix at Seattle, December 19, (152 yards - TD) (OT)

Yards
NFC: 1503—Jerry Rice, San Francisco
AFC: 1180—Tim Brown, Raiders

Yards, Game
AFC: 203—Reggie Langhorne, Indianapolis at Washington, November 7, (12 receptions - TD)
NFC: 182—Michael Haynes, Atlanta vs. New Orleans, September 12, (7 receptions - 2 TD)

Longest
NFC: 98—Michael Haynes (from Bobby Hebert), Atlanta vs. New Orleans, September 12 - TD
AFC: 82—Kevin Turner {13 yds} lateral to Leonard Russell {69 yds} (from Scott Secules), New England at Phoenix, October 10

Yards Per Reception
AFC: 23.4—James Jett, Raiders
NFC: 21.6—Alvin Harper, Dallas

Touchdowns
NFC: 15—Jerry Rice, San Francisco
Andre Rison, Atlanta
AFC: 9—Shannon Sharpe, Denver

Team Leaders, Receptions
AFC: BUFFALO: 68, Pete Metzelaars; CINCINNATI: 56, Jeff Query; CLEVELAND: 63, Eric Metcalf; DENVER: 81, Shannon Sharpe; HOUSTON: 77, Webster Slaughter; INDIANAPOLIS: 85, Reggie Langhorne; KANSAS CITY: 52, Willie Davis; L.A. RAIDERS: 80, Tim Brown; MIAMI: 75, Terry Kirby; NEW ENGLAND: 53, Ben Coates; N.Y. JETS: 67, Johnny Johnson; PITTSBURGH: 63, Eric Green; SAN DIEGO: 84, Anthony Miller; SEATTLE: 80, Brian Blades

NFC: ATLANTA: 86, Andre Rison; CHICAGO: 44, Tom Waddle; DALLAS: 88, Michael Irvin; DETROIT: 61, Herman Moore; GREEN BAY: 112, Sterling Sharpe; L.A. RAMS: 61, Henry Ellard; MINNESOTA: 86, Cris Carter; NEW ORLEANS: 66, Eric Martin; N.Y. GIANTS: 58, Mark Jackson; PHILADELPHIA: 75, Herschel Walker; PHOENIX: 66, Larry Centers; SAN FRANCISCO: 98, Jerry Rice; TAMPA BAY: 62, Courtney Hawkins; WASHINGTON: 58, Ricky Sanders

NFL TOP TEN PASS RECEIVERS

	No.	Yards	Avg.	Long	TD
Sharpe, Sterling, G.B.	112	1274	11.4	54	11
Rice, Jerry, S.F.	98	1503	15.3	80t	15
Irvin, Michael, Dall.	88	1330	15.1	61t	7
Carter, Cris, Minn.	86	1071	12.5	58	9
Rison, Andre, Atl.	86	1242	14.4	53t	15
Langhorne, Reggie, Ind.	85	1038	12.2	72t	3
Miller, Anthony, S.D.	84	1162	13.8	66t	7
Sharpe, Shannon, Den.	81	995	12.3	63	9
Blades, Brian, Sea.	80	945	11.8	41	3
Brown, Tim, Raid.	80	1180	14.8	71t	7

NFL TOP TEN RECEIVERS BY YARDS

	Yards	No.	Avg.	Long	TD
Rice, Jerry, S.F.	1503	98	15.3	80t	15
Irvin, Michael, Dall.	1330	88	15.1	61t	7
Sharpe, Sterling, G.B.	1274	112	11.4	54	11
Rison, Andre, Atl.	1242	86	14.4	53t	15
Brown, Tim, Raid.	1180	80	14.8	71t	7
Miller, Anthony, S.D.	1162	84	13.8	66t	7
Carter, Cris, Minn.	1071	86	12.5	58	9
Langhorne, Reggie, Ind.	1038	85	12.2	72t	3
Fryar, Irving, Mia.	1010	64	15.8	65t	5
Sharpe, Shannon, Den.	995	81	12.3	63	9

AFC RECEIVERS—INDIVIDUAL

	No.	Yards	Avg.	Long	TD
Langhorne, Reggie, Ind.	85	1038	12.2	72t	3
Miller, Anthony, S.D.	84	1162	13.8	66t	7
Sharpe, Shannon, Den.	81	995	12.3	63	9
Brown, Tim, Raid.	80	1180	14.8	71t	7
Blades, Brian, Sea.	80	945	11.8	41	3
Slaughter, Webster, Hou.	77	904	11.7	41	5
Kirby, Terry, Mia.	75	874	11.7	47	3
Harmon, Ronnie, S.D.	73	671	9.2	37	2

	No.	Yards	Avg.	Long	TD
Givins, Ernest, Hou.	68	887	13.0	80t	4
Metzelaars, Pete, Buff.	68	609	9.0	51	4
Johnson, Johnny, N.Y.J.	67	641	9.6	48	1
Jeffires, Haywood, Hou.	66	753	11.4	66t	6
Fryar, Irving, Mia.	64	1010	15.8	65t	5
Moore, Rob, N.Y.J.	64	843	13.2	51	1
Hester, Jessie, Ind.	64	835	13.0	58	1
Green, Eric, Pitt.	63	942	15.0	71t	5
Metcalf, Eric, Clev.	63	539	8.6	49t	2
Byars, Keith, Mia.	61	613	10.0	27	3
Brooks, Bill, Buff.	60	714	11.9	32	5
Williams, John L., Sea.	58	450	7.8	25	1
Martin, Kelvin, Sea.	57	798	14.0	53t	5
Query, Jeff, Cinn.	56	654	11.7	51	4
Johnson, Anthony, Ind.	55	443	8.1	36	0
Coates, Ben, N.E.	53	659	12.4	54t	8
Davis, Willie, K.C.	52	909	17.5	66t	7
Reed, Andre, Buff.	52	854	16.4	65t	6
Birden, J. J., K.C.	51	721	14.1	50t	2
Fenner, Derrick, Cinn.	48	427	8.9	40	0
Thomas, Thurman, Buff.	48	387	8.1	37	0
Brisby, Vincent, N.E.	45	626	13.9	39	2
Russell, Derek, Den.	44	719	16.3	43	3
Ingram, Mark, Mia.	44	707	16.1	77t	6
McGee, Tony, Cinn.	44	525	11.9	37	0
Bernstine, Rod, Den.	44	372	8.5	41	0
Carrier, Mark, Clev.	43	746	17.3	55	3
Pickens, Carl, Cinn.	43	565	13.1	36	6
Horton, Ethan, Raid.	43	467	10.9	32	1
Cash, Kerry, Ind.	43	402	9.3	37	3
Timpson, Michael, N.E.	42	654	15.6	48	2
Jackson, Michael, Clev.	41	756	18.4	62t	8
Stone, Dwight, Pitt.	41	587	14.3	44	2
Duncan, Curtis, Hou.	41	456	11.1	47	3
Burkett, Chris, N.Y.J.	40	531	13.3	77	4
Anders, Kimble, K.C.	40	326	8.2	27	1
Mitchell, Johnny, N.Y.J.	39	630	16.2	65t	6
Jackson, Keith, Mia.	39	613	15.7	57t	6
Turner, Kevin, N.E.	39	333	8.5	26	2
Graham, Jeffrey, Pitt.	38	579	15.2	51	0
Lewis, Nate, S.D.	38	463	12.2	47	4
Milburn, Glyn, Den.	38	300	7.9	50	3
Thompson, Leroy, Pitt.	38	259	6.8	28	0
Johnson, Vance, Den.	36	517	14.4	56	1
Hoard, Leroy, Clev.	35	351	10.0	41	0
Allen, Marcus, K.C.	34	238	7.0	18t	3
White, Lorenzo, Hou.	34	229	6.7	20	0
Jett, James, Raid.	33	771	23.4	74t	3
Hoge, Merril, Pitt.	33	247	7.5	18	4
Beebe, Don, Buff.	31	504	16.3	65t	3
Wellman, Gary, Hou.	31	430	13.9	44	1
Jefferson, Shawn, S.D.	30	391	13.0	39t	2
Mills, Ernie, Pitt.	29	386	13.3	30	1
Kinchen, Brian, Clev.	29	347	12.0	40	2
Marshall, Arthur, Den.	28	360	12.9	40	2
Wright, Alexander, Raid.	27	462	17.1	68t	4
Foster, Barry, Pitt.	27	217	8.0	21	1
Dawkins, Sean, Ind.	26	430	16.5	68	1
Ismail, Raghib, Raid.	26	353	13.6	43t	1
Russell, Leonard, N.E.	26	245	9.4	69	0
Delpino, Robert, Den.	26	195	7.5	25	0
Potts, Roosevelt, Ind.	26	189	7.3	24	0
Mathis, Terance, N.Y.J.	24	352	14.7	46	0
Hayes, Jonathan, K.C.	24	331	13.8	49	1
Cash, Keith, K.C.	24	242	10.1	24	4
Edmunds, Ferrell, Sea.	24	239	10.0	32	2
Green, Paul, Sea.	23	178	7.7	20	1
McMurtry, Greg, N.E.	22	241	11.0	20	1
Cook, Marv, N.E.	22	154	7.0	17	1
Green, Harold, Cinn.	22	115	5.2	16	0
Brown, Gary, Hou.	21	240	11.4	38t	2
Walker, Derrick, S.D.	21	212	10.1	25t	1
Davis, Kenneth, Buff.	21	95	4.5	28	0
Martin, Tony, Mia.	20	347	17.4	80t	3
Johnson, Reggie, Den.	20	243	12.2	38	1
Baxter, Brad, N.Y.J.	20	158	7.9	24	0
McDuffie, O. J., Mia.	19	197	10.4	18	0
Vardell, Tommy, Clev.	19	151	7.9	28t	1
Smith, Steve, Raid.	18	187	10.4	22	0
Tillman, Cedric, Den.	17	193	11.4	30	2
Barnett, Tim, K.C.	17	182	10.7	25	1
Thompson, Craig, Cinn.	17	87	5.1	10	1

	No.	Yards	Avg.	Long	TD
Crittenden, Ray, N.E.	16	293	18.3	44	1
Robinson, Greg, Raid.	15	142	9.5	58	0
Butts, Marion, S.D.	15	105	7.0	23	0
Warren, Chris, Sea.	15	99	6.6	21	0
Arbuckle, Charles, Ind.	15	90	6.0	23	0
Gash, Sam, N.E.	14	93	6.6	15	0
Copeland, Russell, Buff.	13	242	18.6	60	0
McCardell, Keenan, Clev.	13	234	18.0	43	4
Pupunu, Alfred, S.D.	13	142	10.9	28	0
Thornton, James, N.Y.J.	12	108	9.0	22	2
Culver, Rodney, Ind.	11	112	10.2	26	1
Bell, Nick, Raid.	11	111	10.1	18	0
Thomas, Doug, Sea.	11	95	8.6	20	0
Barnes, Johnnie, S.D.	10	137	13.7	21	0
McNair, Todd, K.C.	10	74	7.4	24	0
Higgs, Mark, Mia.	10	72	7.2	15	0
Means, Natrone, S.D.	10	59	5.9	11	0
Montgomery, Tyrone, Raid.	10	43	4.3	9	0
Thigpen, Yancey, Pitt.	9	154	17.1	39t	3
Coleman, Pat, Hou.	9	129	14.3	25	0
Cooper, Adrian, Pitt.	9	112	12.4	38	0
Jones, Fred, K.C.	9	111	12.3	19	0
Rembert, Reggie, Cinn.	8	101	12.6	21	0
Croom, Corey, N.E.	8	92	11.5	21	0
Kimbrough, Tony, Den.	8	79	9.9	16	0
Robinson, Patrick, Cinn.	8	72	9.0	14	0
Gault, Willie, Raid.	8	64	8.0	12	0
Jones, Hassan, K.C.	7	91	13.0	22	0
Dyal, Mike, K.C.	7	83	11.9	31	0
Thomas, Robb, Sea.	7	67	9.6	16	0
Williams, Harvey, K.C.	7	42	6.0	14	0
Thomas, Blair, N.Y.J.	7	25	3.6	7	0
Miles, Ostell, Cinn.	6	89	14.8	27	0
Carpenter, Rob, N.Y.J.	6	83	13.8	18	0
Carroll, Wesley, Cinn.	6	81	13.5	28	0
Rivers, Reggie, Den.	6	59	9.8	17	1
Frisch, David, Cinn.	6	43	7.2	12	0
Young, Duane, S.D.	6	41	6.8	12t	2
Baty, Greg, Mia.	5	78	15.6	32	1
Tillman, Lawyer, Clev.	5	68	13.6	18	1
Wolfley, Ron, Clev.	5	25	5.0	9	1
Murrell, Adrian, N.Y.J.	5	12	2.4	8	0
Cox, Aaron, Ind.	4	59	14.8	24	0
Chaffey, Pat, N.Y.J.	4	55	13.8	20t	1
Glover, Andrew, Raid.	4	55	13.8	26	1
Smith, Rico, Clev.	4	55	13.8	17	0
Harris, Leonard, Hou.	4	53	13.3	17t	1
Davenport, Charles, Pitt.	4	51	12.8	19	0
Gardner, Carwell, Buff.	4	50	12.5	22	1
Jordan, Randy, Raid.	4	42	10.5	33	0
Ball, Eric, Cinn.	4	39	9.8	24	0
Thompson, Ernie, K.C.	4	33	8.3	13	0
Baxter, Fred, N.Y.J.	3	48	16.0	25	1
Hastings, Andre, Pitt.	3	44	14.7	18	0
Rowe, Patrick, Clev.	3	37	12.3	16	0
McKeller, Keith, Buff.	3	35	11.7	13t	1
Johnson, Tracy, Sea.	3	15	5.0	8	1
Brown, Reggie, Hou.	2	30	15.0	26	0
Tasker, Steve, Buff.	2	26	13.0	22	0
Brown, Troy, N.E.	2	22	11.0	14	0
Verdin, Clarence, Ind.	2	20	10.0	19	1
Awalt, Robert, Buff.	2	19	9.5	10	0
Miller, Scott, Mia.	2	15	7.5	8	0
Sadowski, Troy, N.Y.J.	2	14	7.0	11	0
Thomason, Jeff, Cinn.	2	8	4.0	5	0
McCallum, Napoleon, Raid.	2	5	2.5	3	0
Taylor, Kitrick, Den.	1	28	28.0	28	0
Benjamin, Ryan, Cinn.	1	16	16.0	16	0
Maston, Le'Shai, Hou.	1	14	14.0	14	0
Williams, Clarence, Clev.	1	14	14.0	14	0
Norgard, Erik, Hou.	1	13	13.0	13	0
Jorden, Tim, Pitt.	1	12	12.0	12	0
Williams, Mike, Mia.	1	11	11.0	11	0
Stegall, Milt, Cinn.	1	8	8.0	8	0
Bates, Michael, Sea.	1	6	6.0	6	0
Baldwin, Randy, Clev.	1	5	5.0	5t	1
Toner, Ed, Ind.	1	5	5.0	5	0
Roberts, Ray, Sea.	1	4	4.0	4	0
Tillman, Spencer, Hou.	1	4	4.0	4t	1
Cuthbert, Randy, Pitt.	1	3	3.0	3	0
Drewrey, Willie, Hou.	1	3	3.0	3	0
Parmalee, Bernie, Mia.	1	1	1.0	1	0

	No.	Yards	Avg.	Long	TD
Valerio, Joe, K.C.	1	1	1.0	1t	1
Wyman, David, Den.	1	1	1.0	1t	1
Bieniemy, Eric, S.D.	1	0	0.0	0	0
Esiason, Boomer, N.Y.J.	1	-8	-8.0	-8	0

t = Touchdown
Leader based on receptions

NFC RECEIVERS—INDIVIDUAL

	No.	Yards	Avg.	Long	TD
Sharpe, Sterling, G.B.	112	1274	11.4	54	11
Rice, Jerry, S.F.	98	1503	15.3	80t	15
Irvin, Michael, Dall.	88	1330	15.1	61t	7
Rison, Andre, Atl.	86	1242	14.4	53t	15
Carter, Cris, Minn.	86	1071	12.5	58	9
Walker, Herschel, Phil.	75	610	8.1	55	3
Pritchard, Mike, Atl.	74	736	9.9	34	7
Haynes, Michael, Atl.	72	778	10.8	98t	4
Jones, Brent, S.F.	68	735	10.8	29	3
Martin, Eric, N.O.	66	950	14.4	54t	3
Centers, Larry, Phx.	66	603	9.1	29	3
Proehl, Ricky, Phx.	65	877	13.5	51t	7
Clark, Gary, Phx.	63	818	13.0	55	4
Hawkins, Courtney, T.B.	62	933	15.0	67	5
Ellard, Henry, Rams	61	945	15.5	54	2
Moore, Herman, Det.	61	935	15.3	93t	6
Carter, Anthony, Minn.	60	775	12.9	39	5
Williams, Calvin, Phil.	60	725	12.1	80t	10
Bennett, Edgar, G.B.	59	457	7.7	39t	1
Jackson, Mark, N.Y.G.	58	708	12.2	40t	4
Sanders, Ricky, Wash.	58	638	11.0	50	4
Smith, Emmitt, Dall.	57	414	7.3	86	1
Taylor, John, S.F.	56	940	16.8	76t	5
Jordan, Steve, Minn.	56	542	9.7	53	1
Workman, Vince, T.B.	54	411	7.6	42t	2
Johnston, Daryl, Dall.	50	372	7.4	20	1
Perriman, Brett, Det.	49	496	10.1	34	2
Early, Quinn, N.O.	45	670	14.9	63t	6
Waddle, Tom, Chi.	44	552	12.5	38	1
Novacek, Jay, Dall.	44	445	10.1	30	1
Bavaro, Mark, Phil.	43	481	11.2	27	6
Harris, Jackie, G.B.	42	604	14.4	66t	4
Bailey, Victor, Phil.	41	545	13.3	58	1
Monk, Art, Wash.	41	398	9.7	29	2
Hilliard, Dalton, N.O.	40	296	7.4	34	1
McGee, Tim, Wash.	39	500	12.8	54	3
Meggett, David, N.Y.G.	38	319	8.4	50	0
Anderson, Willie, Rams	37	552	14.9	56t	4
Logan, Marc, S.F.	37	348	9.4	24	0
Harper, Alvin, Dall.	36	777	21.6	80t	5
Gary, Cleveland, Rams	36	289	8.0	60t	1
Sanders, Barry, Det.	36	205	5.7	17	0
Hill, Randal, Phx.	35	519	14.8	58t	4
Calloway, Chris, N.Y.G.	35	513	14.7	47	3
Hill, Drew, Atl.	34	384	11.3	30	0
Pegram, Erric, Atl.	33	302	9.2	30	0
Clayton, Mark, G.B.	32	331	10.3	32	3
Bailey, Johnny, Phx.	32	243	7.6	30	0
Watters, Ricky, S.F.	31	326	10.5	48t	1
Anderson, Neal, Chi.	31	160	5.2	35	0
Copeland, Horace, T.B.	30	633	21.1	67t	4
Joseph, James, Phil.	29	291	10.0	48	1
Green, Willie, Det.	28	462	16.5	47	2
McCaffrey, Ed, N.Y.G.	27	335	12.4	31	2
Drayton, Troy, Rams	27	319	11.8	27	4
Byner, Earnest, Wash.	27	194	7.2	20	0
Obee, Terry, Chi.	26	351	13.5	48	3
Bettis, Jerome, Rams	26	244	9.4	28	0
West, Ed, G.B.	25	253	10.1	24	0
Holman, Rodney, Det.	25	244	9.8	28t	2
Sherrard, Mike, N.Y.G.	24	433	18.0	55t	2
Middleton, Ron, Wash.	24	154	6.4	18	2
Smith, Robert, Minn.	24	111	4.6	12	0
Howard, Desmond, Wash.	23	286	12.4	27	0
Hall, Ron, T.B.	23	268	11.7	37t	1
Muster, Brad, N.O.	23	195	8.5	31	0
Cross, Howard, N.Y.G.	21	272	13.0	32	5
Brooks, Reggie, Wash.	21	186	8.9	43	0
Brown, Derek, N.O.	21	170	8.1	19	1
Moore, Derrick, Det.	21	169	8.0	20	1
Brooks, Robert, G.B.	20	180	9.0	25	0
Mitchell, Brian, Wash.	20	157	7.9	18	0

	No.	Yards	Avg.	Long	TD
Williams, Kevin, Dall.	20	151	7.6	33	2
Conway, Curtis, Chi.	19	231	12.2	38t	2
Ismail, Qadry, Minn.	19	212	11.2	37	1
Craig, Roger, Minn.	19	169	8.9	31	1
Hampton, Rodney, N.Y.G.	18	210	11.7	62	0
Lester, Tim, Rams	18	154	8.6	21	0
Thompson, Darrell, G.B.	18	129	7.2	34	0
Barnett, Fred, Phil.	17	170	10.0	21	0
Smith, Irv, N.O.	16	180	11.3	23	2
Small, Torrance, N.O.	16	164	10.3	17	1
Christian, Bob, Chi.	16	160	10.0	36	0
Heyward, Craig, Chi.	16	132	8.3	20	0
Williams, Jamie, S.F.	16	132	8.3	15	1
Ervins, Ricky, Wash.	16	123	7.7	20	0
Lee, Amp, S.F.	16	115	7.2	22	2
Wycheck, Frank, Wash.	16	113	7.1	20	0
Wilson, Charles, T.B.	15	225	15.0	24	0
Dawsey, Lawrence, T.B.	15	203	13.5	24	0
Tennell, Derek, Minn.	15	122	8.1	17	0
Young, Mike, Phil.	14	186	13.3	49t	2
Lofton, James, Rams-Phil.	14	183	13.1	32	0
Carter, Pat, Rams	14	166	11.9	38	1
Jennings, Keith, Chi.	14	150	10.7	29	0
Edwards, Anthony, Phx.	13	326	25.1	65t	1
Bunch, Jarrod, N.Y.G.	13	98	7.5	15	1
Lynch, Eric, Det.	13	82	6.3	11	0
Green, Robert, Chi.	13	63	4.8	9	0
Pierce, Aaron, N.Y.G.	12	212	17.7	54	0
Turner, Floyd, N.O.	12	163	13.6	52	1
Davis, Wendell, Chi.	12	132	11.0	17	0
Mims, David, Atl.	12	107	8.9	19	1
Sherman, Heath, Phil.	12	78	6.5	21	0
Brenner, Hoby, N.O.	11	171	15.5	27	1
Matthews, Aubrey, Det.	11	171	15.5	40	0
Anderson, Gary, T.B.	11	89	8.1	28	1
Hebron, Vaughn, Phil.	11	82	7.5	12	0
Worley, Tim, Pitt.-Chi.	11	62	5.6	15	0
Gedney, Chris, Chi.	10	98	9.8	24	0
Rathman, Tom, S.F.	10	86	8.6	17	0
Johnson, Maurice, Phil.	10	81	8.1	17	0
Rolle, Butch, Phx.	10	67	6.7	22	1
Word, Barry, Minn.	9	105	11.7	27	0
Wetnight, Ryan, Chi.	9	93	10.3	25t	1
Armstrong, Tyji, T.B.	9	86	9.6	29	1
Reeves, Walter, Phx.	9	67	7.4	18	1
Cobb, Reggie, T.B.	9	61	6.8	19	1
Ned, Derrick, N.O.	9	54	6.0	14	0
Lassic, Derrick, Dall.	9	37	4.1	9	0
Thomas, Lamar, T.B.	8	186	23.3	62t	2
Kinchen, Todd, Rams	8	137	17.1	35t	1
Singleton, Nate, S.F.	8	126	15.8	33	1
Newman, Pat, N.O.	8	121	15.1	32	1
Hallock, Ty, Det.	8	88	11.0	24	2
McNeal, Travis, Rams	8	75	9.4	22t	1
Lyons, Mitch, Atl.	8	63	7.9	14	0
McDowell, Anthony, T.B.	8	26	3.3	9	1
Brown, Derek, N.Y.G.	7	56	8.0	14	0
Campbell, Jeff, Det.	7	55	7.9	12	0
Graham, Scottie, Minn.	7	46	6.6	11	0
Sanders, Deion, Atl.	6	106	17.7	70t	1
Dickerson, Eric, Atl.	6	58	9.7	30	0
Whitaker, Danta, Chi.	6	53	8.8	18	0
Dowdell, Marcus, N.O.	6	46	7.7	11t	1
Tice, Mike, Minn.	6	39	6.5	21	1
Gainer, Derrick, Dall.	6	37	6.2	8	0
Hearst, Garrison, Phx.	6	18	3.0	9	0
Reed, Jake, Minn.	5	65	13.0	18	0
Claiborne, Robert, T.B.	5	61	12.2	16	0
Beach, Sanjay, S.F.	5	59	11.8	20t	1
Jones, Ernie, Rams	5	56	11.2	21t	2
Blount, Eric, Phx.	5	36	7.2	9	0
Stephens, John, G.B.	5	31	6.2	10	0
Royster, Mazio, T.B.	5	18	3.6	10	0
Harris, Rudy, T.B.	4	48	12.0	25	0
Moore, Dave, T.B.	4	47	11.8	19t	1
Lang, David, Rams	4	45	11.3	21	0
Truitt, Olanda, Minn.	4	40	10.0	13	0
Evans, Chuck, Minn.	4	39	9.8	21	0
Lewis, Darren, Chi.	4	26	6.5	18	0
Coleman, Lincoln, Dall.	4	24	6.0	10	0
Turner, Odessa, S.F.	3	64	21.3	32	0
Ware, Derek, Phx.	3	45	15.0	27	0

	No.	Yards	Avg.	Long	TD
Carter, Dexter, S.F.	3	40	13.3	14	0
Moore, Ron, Phx.	3	16	5.3	6	0
Banks, Fred, Mia.-Chi.	2	45	22.5	26	0
Sydner, Jeff, Phil.	2	42	21.0	31	0
LaChapelle, Sean, Rams	2	23	11.5	14	0
Lewis, Ron, G.B.	2	21	10.5	17	0
Johnson, Jimmy, Det.	2	18	9.0	9	0
Wilson, Marcus, G.B.	2	18	9.0	11	0
Clifton, Gregory, Wash.	2	15	7.5	10	0
Chmura, Mark, G.B.	2	13	6.5	7	0
Harris, Corey, G.B.	2	11	5.5	6	0
Young, Steve, S.F.	2	2	1.0	6	0
Guliford, Eric, Minn.	1	45	45.0	45	0
Williams, Tyrone, Dall.	1	25	25.0	25	0
Tillman, Lewis, N.Y.G.	1	21	21.0	21	0
Phillips, Jason, Atl.	1	15	15.0	15	0
Thompson, Marty, Det.	1	15	15.0	15	0
Morgan, Anthony, G.B.	1	8	8.0	8	0
Turner, Vernon, Det.	1	7	7.0	7	0
Crawford, Keith, N.Y.G.	1	6	6.0	6	0
Lawrence, Reggie, Phil.	1	5	5.0	5	0
Broussard, Steven, Atl.	1	4	4.0	4	0
Price, Jim, Dall.	1	4	4.0	4	0
Walker, Adam, S.F.	1	4	4.0	4	0
McAfee, Fred, N.O.	1	3	3.0	3	0
Rasheed, Kenyon, N.Y.G.	1	3	3.0	3	0
Galbraith, Scott, Dall.	1	1	1.0	1t	1
Harbaugh, Jim, Chi.	1	1	1.0	1	0
Fralic, Bill, Det.	1	-4	-4.0	-4	0
Simms, Phil, N.Y.G.	1	-6	-6.0	-6	0
Hinton, Chris, Atl.	1	-8	-8.0	-8	0

t = Touchdown
Leader based on receptions

INTERCEPTIONS

Interceptions
AFC: 9—Nate Odomes, Buffalo
Eugene Robinson, Seattle
NFC: 7—Deion Sanders, Atlanta

Interceptions, Game
AFC: 3—Marcus Robertson, Houston at Cleveland, November 21
NFC: 3—Jack Del Rio, Minnesota at Detroit, December 5

Yards
NFC: 201—Eric Allen, Philadelphia
AFC: 138—Rod Woodson, Pittsburgh

Longest
AFC: 102—Donald Frank, San Diego at Raiders, October 31 - TD
NFC: 94—Eric Allen, Philadelphia at Jets, October 3 - TD

Touchdowns
NFC: 4—Eric Allen, Philadelphia
AFC: 1—Mike Brim, Cincinnati
Mike Croel, Denver
Donald Frank, San Diego
Steve Jackson, Houston
Henry Jones, Buffalo
Darryll Lewis, Houston
Terry McDaniel, Raiders
Najee Mustafaa, Cleveland
Joe Nash, Seattle
Louis Oliver, Miami
Bo Orlando, Houston
Darryl Talley, Buffalo
Brian Washington, Jets
Mickey Washington, Buffalo
Darryl Williams, Cincinnati
Rod Woodson, Pittsburgh

Team Leaders, Interceptions
AFC: BUFFALO: 9, Nate Odomes; CINCINNATI: 3, Mike Brim; CLEVELAND: 5, Eric Turner; DENVER: 3, Tyrone Braxton, Dennis Smith; HOUSTON: 7, Marcus Robertson; INDIANAPOLIS: 4, Ray Buchanan; KANSAS CITY: 6, Albert Lewis; L.A. RAIDERS: 5, Terry McDaniel; MIAMI: 5, J.B. Brown; NEW ENGLAND: 4, Maurice Hurst; N.Y. JETS: 6, Brian Washington; PITTSBURGH: 8, Rod Woodson; SAN DIEGO: 7, Darren Carrington; SEATTLE: 9, Eugene Robinson
NFC: ATLANTA: 7, Deion Sanders; CHICAGO: 4, Mark Carrier, Dante Jones; DALLAS: 6, Kevin Smith; DETROIT: 3, Pat Swilling; GREEN BAY: 6, LeRoy Butler; L.A. RAMS: 2, Robert Bailey, Todd Lyght, Henry Rolling, Pat Terrell; MINNESOTA: 5, Vencie Glenn; NEW ORLEANS: 3, Gene Atkins; N.Y. GIANTS: 4, Mark Collins, Greg Jackson; PHILADELPHIA: 6, Eric Allen ; PHOENIX: 3, Lorenzo Lynch; SAN FRANCISCO : 5, Michael McGruder; TAMPA BAY: 3, Joe King; WASHINGTON: 6, Tom Carter

Team Champions

AFC:	26—Houston
NFC:	24—Minnesota

AFC INTERCEPTIONS—TEAM

	No.	Yards	Avg.	Long	TD
Houston	26	412	15.8	69	3
Pittsburgh	24	386	16.1	78	1
Buffalo	23	306	13.3	85t	3
San Diego	22	319	14.5	102t	1
Seattle	22	196	8.9	34	1
Kansas City	21	225	10.7	48	0
N.Y. Jets	19	233	12.3	62t	1
Denver	18	236	13.1	68	1
L.A. Raiders	14	199	14.2	36t	1
New England	13	122	9.4	40	0
Miami	13	175	13.5	56t	1
Cleveland	13	208	16.0	97t	1
Cincinnati	12	272	22.7	97t	2
Indianapolis	10	116	11.6	29	0
AFC Total	250	3405	13.6	102t	16
AFC Average	17.9	243.2	13.6	—	1.1

NFC INTERCEPTIONS—TEAM

	No.	Yards	Avg.	Long	TD
Minnesota	24	211	8.8	63t	2
Philadelphia	20	324	16.2	94t	4
San Francisco	19	267	14.1	67t	3
Detroit	19	156	8.2	35t	1
Chicago	18	300	16.7	86t	2
N.Y. Giants	18	184	10.2	50t	1
Green Bay	18	255	14.2	39	0
Washington	17	241	14.2	69t	2
Dallas	14	171	12.2	32t	1
Atlanta	13	160	12.3	44	0
L.A. Rams	11	127	11.5	41	0
New Orleans	10	133	13.3	37	0
Tampa Bay	9	71	7.9	28	2
Phoenix	9	124	13.8	46t	1
NFC Total	219	2724	12.4	94t	19
NFC Average	15.6	194.6	12.4	—	1.4
League Total	469	6129	—	102t	35
League Average	16.8	218.9	13.1	—	1.3

NFL TOP TEN INTERCEPTORS

	No.	Yards	Avg.	Long	TD
Odomes, Nate, Buff.	9	65	7.2	25	0
Robinson, Eugene, Sea.	9	80	8.9	28	0
Woodson, Rod, Pitt.	8	138	17.3	63t	1
Carrington, Darren, S.D.	7	104	14.9	28	0
Robertson, Marcus, Hou.	7	137	19.6	69	0
Sanders, Deion, Atl.	7	91	13.0	41	0
Allen, Eric, Phil.	6	201	33.5	94t	4
Butler, LeRoy, G.B.	6	131	21.8	39	0
Carter, Tom, Wash.	6	54	9.0	29	0
Dishman, Cris, Hou.	6	74	12.3	30	0
Lewis, Albert, K.C.	6	61	10.2	24	0
Smith, Kevin, Dall.	6	56	9.3	32t	1
Washington, Brian, N.Y.J.	6	128	21.3	62t	1

AFC INTERCEPTIONS—INDIVIDUAL

	No.	Yards	Avg.	Long	TD
Robinson, Eugene, Sea.	9	80	8.9	28	0
Odomes, Nate, Buff.	9	65	7.2	25	0
Woodson, Rod, Pitt.	8	138	17.3	63t	1
Robertson, Marcus, Hou.	7	137	19.6	69	0
Carrington, Darren, S.D.	7	104	14.9	28	0
Washington, Brian, N.Y.J.	6	128	21.3	62t	1
Dishman, Cris, Hou.	6	74	12.3	30	0
Lewis, Albert, K.C.	6	61	10.2	24	0
McDaniel, Terry, Raid.	5	87	17.4	36t	1
Jackson, Steve, Hou.	5	54	10.8	22t	1
Mincy, Charles, K.C.	5	44	8.8	20	0
Brown, J. B., Mia.	5	43	8.6	29	0
Turner, Eric, Clev.	5	25	5.0	19	0
Perry, Darren, Pitt.	4	61	15.3	30	0
Hunter, Patrick, Sea.	4	54	13.5	34	0

	No.	Yards	Avg.	Long	TD
Hurst, Maurice, N.E.	4	53	13.3	24	0
Buchanan, Ray, Ind.	4	45	11.3	28	0
Lake, Carnell, Pitt.	4	31	7.8	26	0
Frank, Donald, S.D.	3	119	39.7	102t	1
Brim, Michael, Cinn.	3	74	24.7	30	1
Talley, Darryl, Buff.	3	74	24.7	61t	1
Orlando, Bo, Hou.	3	68	22.7	38t	1
Smith, Dennis, Den.	3	57	19.0	36	0
Johnson, David, Pitt.	3	51	17.0	26	0
Braxton, Tyrone, Den.	3	37	12.3	25	0
Lott, Ronnie, N.Y.J.	3	35	11.7	29	0
Gray, Carlton, Sea.	3	33	11.0	16	0
McDowell, Bubba, Hou.	3	31	10.3	13	0
Baylor, John, Ind.	3	11	3.7	7	0
Jones, Selwyn, Clev.	3	0	0.0	0	0
Wren, Darryl, N.E.	3	-7	-2.3	2	0
Williams, Darryl, Cinn.	2	126	63.0	97t	1
Jones, Henry, Buff.	2	92	46.0	85t	1
Atwater, Steve, Den.	2	81	40.5	68	0
Oliver, Louis, Mia.	2	60	30.0	56t	1
Seau, Junior, S.D.	2	58	29.0	42	0
Anderson, Eddie, Raid.	2	52	26.0	27	0
Ross, Kevin, K.C.	2	49	24.5	48	0
Hoskins, Derrick, Raid.	2	34	17.0	20	0
Darby, Matt, Buff.	2	32	16.0	32	0
Vincent, Troy, Mia.	2	29	14.5	23	0
Hasty, James, N.Y.J.	2	22	11.0	22	0
Thomas, Eric, N.Y.J.	2	20	10.0	20	0
White, Sheldon, Cinn.	2	19	9.5	14	0
Bayless, Martin, K.C.	2	14	7.0	16	0
Pope, Marquez, S.D.	2	14	7.0	12	0
Dronett, Shane, Den.	2	13	6.5	7	0
Francis, James, Cinn.	2	12	6.0	12	0
Jones, Gary, Pitt.	2	11	5.5	11	0
Williams, James, Buff.	2	11	5.5	6	0
Plummer, Gary, S.D.	2	7	3.5	6	0
Lang, Le-Lo, Den.	2	4	2.0	4	0
Lewis, Mo, N.Y.J.	2	4	2.0	3	0
Blackmon, Robert, Sea.	2	0	0.0	0	0
Green, Chris, Mia.	2	0	0.0	0	0
Patton, Marvcus, Buff.	2	0	0.0	0	0
Vanhorse, Sean, S.D.	2	0	0.0	0	0
Washington, Lionel, Raid.	2	0	0.0	0	0
Mustafaa, Najee, Clev.	1	97	97.0	97t	1
Figures, Deon, Pitt.	1	78	78.0	78	0
Hilliard, Randy, Clev.	1	54	54.0	54	0
Lewis, Darryll, Hou.	1	47	47.0	47t	1
Barnett, Harlon, N.E.	1	40	40.0	40	0
Herrod, Jeff, Ind.	1	29	29.0	29	0
Washington, Mickey, Buff.	1	27	27.0	27t	1
Cox, Bryan, Mia.	1	26	26.0	26	0
Brown, Vincent, N.E.	1	24	24.0	24	0
Croel, Mike, Den.	1	22	22.0	22t	1
Speer, Del, Clev.	1	22	22.0	22	0
Terry, Doug, K.C.	1	21	21.0	21	0
Marts, Lonnie, K.C.	1	20	20.0	20	0
McGlockton, Chester, Raid.	1	19	19.0	19	0
Daniel, Eugene, Ind.	1	17	17.0	17	0
Grant, Alan, Cinn.	1	17	17.0	17	0
Hobley, Liffort, Mia.	1	17	17.0	17	0
Hendrickson, Steve, S.D.	1	16	16.0	16	0
Lageman, Jeff, N.Y.J.	1	15	15.0	15	0
Belser, Jason, Ind.	1	14	14.0	11	0
Nash, Joe, Sea.	1	13	13.0	13t	1
Robinson, Frank, Den.	1	13	13.0	13	0
Saleaumua, Dan, K.C.	1	13	13.0	13	0
Jefferson, James, Sea.	1	12	12.0	12	0
Henry, Kevin, Pitt.	1	10	10.0	10	0
Matthews, Clay Jr., Clev.	1	10	10.0	10	0
Wyman, David, Den.	1	9	9.0	9	0
Collins, Todd, N.E.	1	8	8.0	8	0
Trapp, James, Raid.	1	7	7.0	7	0
Davidson, Kenny, Pitt.	1	6	6.0	6	0
Young, Lonnie, N.Y.J.	1	6	6.0	6	0
Bennett, Cornelius, Buff.	1	5	5.0	5	0
Porter, Rufus, Sea.	1	4	4.0	4	0
Thompson, Reyna, N.E.	1	4	4.0	4	0
Clifton, Kyle, N.Y.J.	1	3	3.0	3	0
Gordon, Darrien, S.D.	1	3	3.0	3	0
Smith, Neil, K.C.	1	3	3.0	3	0
Bishop, Blaine, Hou.	1	1	1.0	1	0
Bates, Patrick, Raid.	1	0	0.0	0	0

	No.	Yards	Avg.	Long	TD
Bradford, Ronnie, Den.	1	0	0.0	0	0
Carter, Dale, K.C.	1	0	0.0	0	0
Davis, Brian, S.D.	1	0	0.0	0	0
Dimry, Charles, Den.	1	0	0.0	0	0
Hall, Darryl, Den.	1	0	0.0	0	0
Harper, Dwayne, Sea.	1	0	0.0	0	0
Houston, Bobby, N.Y.J.	1	0	0.0	0	0
Johnson, Mike, Clev.	1	0	0.0	0	0
Jones, Rod, Cinn.	1	0	0.0	0	0
Lambert, Dion, N.E.	1	0	0.0	0	0
Ray, Terry, N.E.	1	0	0.0	0	0
Smith, Bruce, Buff.	1	0	0.0	0	0
Taylor, Jay, K.C.	1	0	0.0	0	0
Tovar, Steve, Cinn.	1	0	0.0	0	0
Richard, Stanley, S.D.	1	-2	-2.0	-2	0
Wheeler, Leonard, Cinn.	0	24	—	24	0

t = Touchdown
Leader based on interceptions

NFC INTERCEPTIONS—INDIVIDUAL

	No.	Yards	Avg.	Long	TD
Sanders, Deion, Atl.	7	91	13.0	41	0
Allen, Eric, Phil.	6	201	33.5	94t	4
Butler, LeRoy, G.B.	6	131	21.8	39	0
Smith, Kevin, Dall.	6	56	9.3	32t	1
Carter, Tom, Wash.	6	54	9.0	29	0
McGruder, Michael, S.F.	5	89	17.8	37	1
Glenn, Vencie, Minn.	5	49	9.8	23	0
Carrier, Mark, Chi.	4	94	23.5	34t	1
Collins, Mark, N.Y.G.	4	77	19.3	50t	1
Jones, Dante, Chi.	4	52	13.0	22	0
Davis, Eric, S.F.	4	45	11.3	41t	1
McMillian, Audray, Minn.	4	45	11.3	22t	1
Jackson, Greg, N.Y.G.	4	32	8.0	29	0
Miano, Rich, Phil.	4	26	6.5	16	0
Green, Darrell, Wash.	4	10	2.5	6	0
Del Rio, Jack, Minn.	4	3	0.8	3	0
Lincoln, Jeremy, Chi.	3	109	36.3	80t	1
Hanks, Merton, S.F.	3	104	34.7	67t	1
Atkins, Gene, N.O.	3	59	19.7	37	0
King, Joe, T.B.	3	29	9.7	28	0
McDonald, Tim, S.F.	3	23	7.7	21	0
Lee, Carl, Minn.	3	20	6.7	19	0
Swilling, Pat, Det.	3	16	5.3	14	0
Lynch, Lorenzo, Phx.	3	13	4.3	13	0
Walker, Darnell, Atl.	3	7	2.3	7	0
Griffin, Don, S.F.	3	6	2.0	3	0
Williams, Aeneas, Phx.	2	87	43.5	46t	1
Clark, Vinnie, Atl.	2	59	29.5	38	0
Jamison, George, Det.	2	48	24.0	35t	1
Bailey, Robert, Rams	2	41	20.5	41	0
Holland, Johnny, G.B.	2	41	20.5	30	0
Thomas, William, Phil.	2	39	19.5	21	0
Guyton, Myron, N.Y.G.	2	34	17.0	19	0
Taylor, Keith, N.O.	2	32	16.0	30	0
Buckley, Terrell, G.B.	2	31	15.5	31	0
Crockett, Ray, Det.	2	31	15.5	31	0
Buck, Vince, N.O.	2	28	14.0	28	0
Colon, Harry, Det.	2	28	14.0	27	0
Coleman, Monte, Wash.	2	27	13.5	14	0
Scott, Todd, Minn.	2	26	13.0	26	0
Bates, Bill, Dall.	2	25	12.5	22	0
Everett, Thomas, Dall.	2	25	12.5	17	0
McMillian, Mark, Phil.	2	25	12.5	17	0
Booty, John, Phx.	2	24	12.0	19	0
Rolling, Henry, Rams	2	21	10.5	12	0
Simmons, Wayne, G.B.	2	21	10.5	19	0
McNeil, Ryan, Det.	2	19	9.5	16	0
Miller, Corey, N.Y.G.	2	18	9.0	11	0
Woolford, Donnell, Chi.	2	18	9.0	18	0
Raymond, Corey, N.Y.G.	2	11	5.5	11	0
McKyer, Tim, Det.	2	10	5.0	10	0
Jenkins, Carlos, Minn.	2	7	3.5	4	0
Blaylock, Anthony, Chi.	2	3	1.5	3	0
Terrell, Pat, Rams	2	1	0.5	1	0
Lyght, Todd, Rams	2	0	0.0	0	0
Spielman, Chris, Det.	2	-2	-1.0	0	0
Johnson, A. J., Wash.	1	69	69.0	69t	1
McGriggs, Lamar, Minn.	1	63	63.0	63t	1
Gouveia, Kurt, Wash.	1	59	59.0	59t	1
Washington, James, Dall.	1	38	38.0	24	0

	No.	Yards	Avg.	Long	TD
Stewart, Michael, Rams	1	30	30.0	30	0
Conlan, Shane, Rams	1	28	28.0	28	0
Mack, Milton, T.B.	1	27	27.0	27t	1
Norton, Ken, Dall.	1	25	25.0	25	0
Dent, Richard, Chi.	1	24	24.0	24	0
Teague, George, G.B.	1	22	22.0	22	0
Hager, Britt, Phil.	1	19	19.0	19	0
Edwards, Brad, Wash.	1	17	17.0	17	0
Jones, Reggie, N.O.	1	12	12.0	12	0
Tate, David, N.Y.G.	1	12	12.0	12	0
Evans, Byron, Phil.	1	8	8.0	7	0
Paup, Bryce, G.B.	1	8	8.0	8	0
Anderson, Darren, T.B.	1	6	6.0	6	0
Homco, Thomas, Rams	1	6	6.0	6	0
Joyner, Seth, Phil.	1	6	6.0	6	0
Nickerson, Hardy, T.B.	1	6	6.0	6	0
Collins, Andre, Wash.	1	5	5.0	5	0
White, William, Det.	1	5	5.0	5	0
Reynolds, Ricky, T.B.	1	3	3.0	3	0
Marion, Brock, Dall.	1	2	2.0	2	0
Turnbull, Renaldo, N.O.	1	2	2.0	2	0
Owens, Dan, Det.	1	1	1.0	1	0
Parker, Anthony, Minn.	1	1	1.0	1	0
Prior, Mike, G.B.	1	1	1.0	1	0
Armstead, Jessie, N.Y.G.	1	0	0.0	0	0
Beamon, Willie, N.Y.G.	1	0	0.0	0	0
Brock, Matt, G.B.	1	0	0.0	0	0
Campbell, Jesse, N.Y.G.	1	0	0.0	0	0
Carter, Marty, T.B.	1	0	0.0	0	0
Cook, Toi, N.O.	1	0	0.0	0	0
Copeland, Danny, Wash.	1	0	0.0	0	0
Eaton, Tracey, Atl.	1	0	0.0	0	0
Evans, Doug, G.B.	1	0	0.0	0	0
Gant, Kenneth, Dall.	1	0	0.0	0	0
Gibson, Dennis, Det.	1	0	0.0	0	0
Hopkins, Wes, Phil.	1	0	0.0	0	0
Johnson, John, S.F.	1	0	0.0	0	0
Mangum, John, Chi.	1	0	0.0	0	0
McMichael, Steve, Chi.	1	0	0.0	0	0
Mitchell, Roland, G.B.	1	0	0.0	0	0
Oldham, Chris, Phx.	1	0	0.0	0	0
Pearson, J. C., Minn.	1	0	0.0	0	0
Scroggins, Tracy, Det.	1	0	0.0	0	0
Seals, Ray, T.B.	1	0	0.0	0t	1
Simmons, Clyde, Phil.	1	0	0.0	0	0
Smith, Otis, Phil.	1	0	0.0	0	0
Zordich, Mike, Phx.	1	0	0.0	0	0
Doleman, Chris, Minn.	1	-3	-3.0	-3	0
Case, Scott, Atl.	0	0	—	3	0

t = Touchdown
Leader based on interceptions

PUNTING

Average Yards Per Punt
AFC: 45.6—Greg Montgomery, Houston
NFC: 44.5—Jim Arnold, Detroit

Net Average Yards Per Punt
NFC: 39.9—Mike Horan, Giants
AFC: 39.1—Greg Montgomery, Houston

Longest
AFC: 77—Greg Montgomery, Houston at San Diego, September 19
NFC: 75—Harold Alexander, Atlanta at Chicago, October 3

Punts
NFC: 93—Dan Stryzinski, Tampa Bay
AFC: 90—Rick Tuten, Seattle
         Lee Johnson, Cincinnati

Punts, Game
AFC: 12—Rick Tuten, Seattle vs. Denver, November 28, (559 yards)
NFC: 10—Tommy Barnhardt, New Orleans at Cleveland, December 5, (428 yards)
         Dan Stryzinski, Tampa Bay at Green Bay, November 28, (336 yards)

Team Champion
AFC: 45.3—Houston
NFC: 44.5—Detroit

AFC PUNTING—TEAM

	Total Punts	Yards	Long	Avg.	TB	Blk.	Opp. Ret.	Return Yards	Inside the 20	Net. Avg.
Houston	56	2535	77	45.3	6	0	28	249	14	38.7
Denver	68	3017	62	44.4	8	1	33	337	17	37.1
Seattle	91	4007	64	44.0	7	1	47	475	21	37.3
Cincinnati	90	3954	60	43.9	12	0	47	416	24	36.6
Indianapolis	83	3595	65	43.3	13	0	41	352	18	35.9
Cleveland	84	3632	72	43.2	10	2	49	438	15	35.6
Pittsburgh	89	3781	61	42.5	3	0	50	678	28	34.2
San Diego	74	3127	67	42.3	7	0	36	292	20	36.4
Kansas City	77	3240	59	42.1	8	1	43	352	19	35.4
L.A. Raiders	71	2971	61	41.8	9	0	35	301	19	35.1
New England	76	3096	59	40.7	7	3	34	313	25	34.8
Buffalo	74	2991	58	40.4	4	0	29	247	19	36.0
Miami	58	2304	56	39.7	4	0	32	359	13	32.2
N.Y. Jets	73	2806	71	38.4	7	0	26	156	21	34.4
AFC Total	1064	45056	77	——	105	8	530	4965	273	——
AFC Average	76.0	3218.3	—	42.3	7.5	0.6	37.9	354.6	19.5	35.7

NFC PUNTING—TEAM

	Total Punts	Yards	Long	Avg.	TB	Blk.	Opp. Ret.	Return Yards	Inside the 20	Net. Avg.
Detroit	72	3207	68	44.5	9	0	45	377	15	36.8
Washington	83	3644	60	43.9	10	0	34	343	28	37.4
Phoenix	73	3189	61	43.7	8	0	30	267	23	37.8
New Orleans	77	3356	58	43.6	6	0	36	348	26	37.5
Atlanta	72	3114	75	43.3	3	0	41	350	21	37.6
Minnesota	90	3862	64	42.9	6	0	46	560	25	35.4
Green Bay	74	3174	60	42.9	7	0	38	350	19	36.3
N.Y. Giants	78	3272	60	41.9	4	1	44	247	24	37.8
Dallas	56	2342	59	41.8	3	0	32	169	22	37.7
San Francisco	42	1718	61	40.9	5	0	15	171	11	34.5
L.A. Rams	80	3271	66	40.9	10	0	43	533	15	31.7
Tampa Bay	94	3772	57	40.1	3	1	53	394	24	35.3
Philadelphia	83	3323	60	40.0	4	0	35	311	31	35.3
Chicago	80	3080	58	38.5	2	0	22	115	28	36.6
NFC Total	1054	44324	75	——	80	2	514	4535	312	——
NFC Average	75.3	3166.0	—	42.1	5.7	0.1	36.7	323.9	22.3	36.2
League Total	2118	89380	77	——	185	10	1044	9500	585	——
League Average	75.6	3192.1	—	42.2	6.6	0.4	37.3	339.3	20.9	36.0

NFL TOP TEN PUNTERS

	No.	Yards	Long	Avg.	Total Punts	TB	Blk.	Opp. Ret.	Ret. Yds.	In 20	Net. Avg.
Montgomery, Greg, Hou.	54	2462	77	45.6	54	5	0	28	249	13	39.1
Rouen, Tom, Den.	67	3017	62	45.0	68	8	1	33	337	17	37.1
Arnold, Jim, Det.	72	3207	68	44.5	72	9	0	45	377	15	36.8
Tuten, Rick, Sea.	90	4007	64	44.5	91	7	1	47	475	21	37.3
Hansen, Brian, Clev.	82	3632	72	44.3	84	10	2	49	438	15	35.6
Roby, Reggie, Wash.	78	3447	60	44.2	78	10	0	31	343	25	37.2
Johnson, Lee, Cinn.	90	3954	60	43.9	90	12	0	47	416	24	36.6
Camarillo, Rich, Phx.	73	3189	61	43.7	73	8	0	30	267	23	37.8
Barnhardt, Tommy, N.O.	77	3356	58	43.6	77	6	0	36	348	26	37.5
Stark, Rohn, Ind.	83	3595	65	43.3	83	13	0	41	352	18	35.9

AFC PUNTERS—INDIVIDUAL

	No.	Yards	Long	Avg.	Total Punts	TB	Blk.	Opp. Ret.	Ret. Yds.	In 20	Net. Avg.
Montgomery, Greg, Hou.	54	2462	77	45.6	54	5	0	28	249	13	39.1
Rouen, Tom, Den.	67	3017	62	45.0	68	8	1	33	337	17	37.1
Tuten, Rick, Sea.	90	4007	64	44.5	91	7	1	47	475	21	37.3
Hansen, Brian, Clev.	82	3632	72	44.3	84	10	2	49	438	15	35.6
Johnson, Lee, Cinn.	90	3954	60	43.9	90	12	0	47	416	24	36.6
Stark, Rohn, Ind.	83	3595	65	43.3	83	13	0	41	352	18	35.9
Kidd, John, S.D.	57	2431	67	42.6	57	7	0	28	243	16	35.9
Barker, Bryan, K.C.	76	3240	59	42.6	77	8	1	43	352	19	35.4
Royals, Mark, Pitt.	89	3781	61	42.5	89	3	0	50	678	28	34.2
Saxon, Mike, N.E.	73	3096	59	42.4	76	7	3	34	313	25	34.8
Gossett, Jeff, Raid.	71	2971	61	41.8	71	9	0	35	301	19	35.1
Mohr, Chris, Buff.	74	2991	58	40.4	74	4	0	29	247	19	36.0
Hatcher, Dale, Mia.	58	2304	56	39.7	58	4	0	32	359	13	32.2
Aguiar, Louie, N.Y.J.	73	2806	71	38.4	73	7	0	26	156	21	34.4
Nonqualifiers											
Sullivan, Kent, S.D.-Hou.-S.D.	15	614	50	40.9	15	1	0	6	33	4	37.4
Carney, John, S.D.	4	155	46	38.8	4	0	0	2	16	1	34.8

Leader based on average, minimum 40 punts

NFC PUNTERS—INDIVIDUAL

	No.	Yards	Long	Avg.	Total Punts	TB	Blk.	Opp. Ret.	Ret. Yds.	In 20	Net. Avg.
Arnold, Jim, Det.	72	3207	68	44.5	72	9	0	45	377	15	36.8
Roby, Reggie, Wash.	78	3447	60	44.2	78	10	0	31	343	25	37.2
Camarillo, Rich, Phx.	73	3189	61	43.7	73	8	0	30	267	23	37.8
Barnhardt, Tommy, N.O.	77	3356	58	43.6	77	6	0	36	348	26	37.5
Alexander, Harold, Atl.	72	3114	75	43.3	72	3	0	41	350	21	37.6
Newsome, Harry, Minn.	90	3862	64	42.9	90	6	0	46	560	25	35.4

	No.	Yards	Long	Avg.	Total Punts	TB	Blk	Opp. Ret.	Ret. Yds.	In 20	Net. Avg.
Wagner, Bryan, G.B.	74	3174	60	42.9	74	7	0	38	350	19	36.3
Landeta, Sean, N.Y.G.-Rams	75	3215	66	42.9	76	10	1	44	444	18	33.8
Horan, Mike, N.Y.G.	44	1882	60	42.8	44	1	0	25	107	13	39.9
Jett, John, Dall.	56	2342	59	41.8	56	3	0	32	169	22	37.7
Wilmsmeyer, Klaus, S.F.	42	1718	61	40.9	42	5	0	15	171	11	34.5
Stryzinski, Dan, T.B.	93	3772	57	40.6	94	3	1	53	394	24	35.3
Feagles, Jeff, Phil.	83	3323	60	40.0	83	4	0	35	311	31	35.3
Gardocki, Chris, Chi.	80	3080	58	38.5	80	2	0	22	115	28	36.6
Nonqualifiers											
McJulien, Paul, Rams	21	795	56	37.9	21	3	0	10	143	5	28.2
Bracken, Don, Rams	17	651	51	38.3	17	0	0	8	86	3	33.2
Goodburn, Kelly, Wash.	5	197	49	39.4	5	0	0	3	0	3	39.4

Leader based on average, minimum 40 punts

PUNT RETURNS

Yards Per Return
  NFC: 13.6—Tyrone Hughes, New Orleans
  AFC: 12.9—Eric Metcalf, Cleveland
Yards
  NFC: 503—Tyrone Hughes, New Orleans
  AFC: 465—Tim Brown, Raiders
Yards, Game
  AFC: 166—Eric Metcalf, Cleveland vs. Pittsburgh, October 24,
        (2 returns - 2 TD)
  NFC: 131—Dexter Carter, San Francisco vs. Minnesota, October 3,
        (5 returns - TD)
Longest
  AFC: 91—Eric Metcalf, Cleveland vs. Pittsburgh, October 24 - TD
  NFC: 83—Tyrone Hughes, New Orleans at Philadelphia
        December 26 - TD
Returns
  AFC: 43—Patrick Robinson, Cincinnati
  NFC: 37—Tyrone Hughes, New Orleans
Returns, Game
  AFC: 10—Ron Harris, New England at Pittsburgh, December 5,
        (74 yards)
  NFC: 6—Mel Gray, Detroit vs. Atlanta, September 5, (52 yards)
        Vernon Turner, Detroit vs. Tampa Bay, November 7,
        (17 yards)
        Brian Mitchell, Washington at Rams, November 21,
        (30 yards)
        Vai Sikahema, Philadelphia vs. Giants, November 21,
        (29 yards)
        Robert Brooks, Green Bay vs. Tampa Bay, November 28,
        (39 yards)
Fair Catches
  AFC: 22—O.J. McDuffie, Miami
  NFC: 21—Tyrone Hughes, New Orleans
Touchdowns
  AFC: 2—O.J. McDuffie, Miami
        Eric Metcalf, Cleveland
  NFC: 2—Tyrone Hughes, New Orleans
        Kevin Williams, Dallas
Team Champion
  NFC: 13.6—New Orleans
  AFC: 13.4—Cleveland

AFC PUNT RETURNS—TEAM

	No.	FC	Yards	Avg.	Long	TD
Cleveland	42	12	563	13.4	91t	3
San Diego	34	17	412	12.1	54	0
Miami	28	22	326	11.6	72t	2
L.A. Raiders	40	20	465	11.6	74t	1
Denver	41	11	425	10.4	54	0
Kansas City	37	7	348	9.4	30	0
New England	51	14	462	9.1	30	0
Seattle	33	15	280	8.5	33	0
Buffalo	33	7	277	8.4	47t	1
N.Y. Jets	31	12	256	8.3	20	0
Pittsburgh	47	12	353	7.5	39	0
Houston	41	19	275	6.7	18	0
Cincinnati	48	8	321	6.7	36	0
Indianapolis	30	17	173	5.8	24	0
AFC Total	536	193	4936	9.2	91t	7
AFC Average	38.3	13.8	352.6	9.2	—-	0.5

NFC PUNT RETURNS—TEAM

	No.	FC	Yards	Avg.	Long	TD
New Orleans	38	21	517	13.6	83t	2
San Francisco	35	20	411	11.7	72t	1
N.Y. Giants	32	20	331	10.3	75t	1
Dallas	37	14	381	10.3	64t	2
Green Bay	45	12	404	9.0	39	0
Detroit	40	18	349	8.7	53	0
Philadelphia	33	20	284	8.6	25	0
Chicago	35	20	289	8.3	28	0
Tampa Bay	38	15	311	8.2	35	0
Phoenix	47	11	384	8.2	58t	1
Atlanta	35	18	276	7.9	51	0
Minnesota	39	23	280	7.2	50	0
Washington	35	8	245	7.0	48	0
L.A. Rams	19	15	102	5.4	13	0
NFC Total	508	235	4564	9.0	83t	7
NFC Average	36.3	16.8	326.0	9.0	—-	0.5
League Total	1044	428	9500	—-	91t	14
League Average	37.3	15.3	339.3	9.1	—-	0.5

NFL TOP TEN PUNT RETURNERS

	No.	FC	Yards	Avg.	Long	TD
Hughes, Tyrone, N.O.	37	21	503	13.6	83t	2
Metcalf, Eric, Clev.	36	11	464	12.9	91t	2
Gordon, Darrien, S.D.	31	15	395	12.7	54	0
Carter, Dexter, S.F.	34	20	411	12.1	72t	1
Brown, Tim, Raid.	40	20	465	11.6	74t	1
McDuffie, O. J., Mia.	28	22	317	11.3	72t	2
Milburn, Glyn, Den.	40	11	425	10.6	54	0
Williams, Kevin, Dall.	36	14	381	10.6	64t	2
Meggett, David, N.Y.G.	32	20	331	10.3	75t	1
Carter, Dale, K.C.	27	4	247	9.1	30	0

AFC - INDIVIDUAL PUNT RETURNERS

	No.	FC	Yards	Avg.	Long	TD
Metcalf, Eric, Clev.	36	11	464	12.9	91t	2
Gordon, Darrien, S.D.	31	15	395	12.7	54	0
Brown, Tim, Raid.	40	20	465	11.6	74t	1
McDuffie, O. J., Mia.	28	22	317	11.3	72t	2
Milburn, Glyn, Den.	40	11	425	10.6	54	0
Carter, Dale, K.C.	27	4	247	9.1	30	0
Brown, Troy, N.E.	25	9	224	9.0	19	0
Copeland, Russell, Buff.	31	7	274	8.8	47t	1
Harris, Ronnie, N.E.	23	4	201	8.7	21	0
Martin, Kelvin, Sea.	32	15	270	8.4	33	0
Woodson, Rod, Pitt.	42	10	338	8.0	39	0
Robinson, Patrick, Cinn.	43	6	305	7.1	36	0
Drewrey, Willie, Hou.	41	19	275	6.7	18	0
Verdin, Clarence, Ind.	30	17	173	5.8	24	0
Nonqualifiers						
Hicks, Cliff, N.Y.J.	17	4	157	9.2	20	0
Mathis, Terance, N.Y.J.	14	8	99	7.1	16	0
Carrier, Mark, Clev.	6	1	92	15.3	56t	1
Birden, J. J., K.C.	5	3	43	8.6	12	0
Figures, Deon, Pitt.	5	2	15	3.0	6	0
Pickens, Carl, Cinn.	4	2	16	4.0	9	0
Hughes, Danan, K.C.	3	0	49	16.3	29	0
Lewis, Nate, S.D.	3	2	17	5.7	7	0
Crittenden, Ray, N.E.	2	1	37	18.5	30	0

	No.	FC	Yards	Avg.	Long	TD
Mincy, Charles, K.C.	2	0	9	4.5	9	0
McCloughan, Dave, Sea.	1	0	10	10.0	10	0
Brooks, Bill, Buff.	1	0	3	3.0	3	0
Bradford, Ronnie, Den.	1	0	0	0.0	0	0
Simmons, Marcello, Cinn.	1	0	0	0.0	0	0
Smith, Rod, N.E.	1	0	0	0.0	0	0
Tasker, Steve, Buff.	1	0	0	0.0	0	0
Vincent, Troy, Mia.	0	0	9	—	9	0
Turner, Eric, Clev.	0	0	7	—	7	0

t = Touchdown
Leader based on average return, minimum 20 returns

NFC - INDIVIDUAL PUNT RETURNERS

	No.	FC	Yards	Avg.	Long	TD
Hughes, Tyrone, N.O.	37	21	503	13.6	83t	2
Carter, Dexter, S.F.	34	20	411	12.1	72t	1
Williams, Kevin, Dall.	36	14	381	10.6	64t	2
Meggett, David, N.Y.G.	32	20	331	10.3	75t	1
Gray, Mel, Det.	23	14	197	8.6	35	0
Sikahema, Vai, Phil.	33	20	275	8.3	25	0
Obee, Terry, Chi.	35	20	289	8.3	28	0
Bailey, Johnny, Phx.	35	5	282	8.1	58t	1
Smith, Tony, Atl.	32	17	255	8.0	51	0
Guliford, Eric, Minn.	29	15	212	7.3	50	0
Mitchell, Brian, Wash.	29	7	193	6.7	48	0
Nonqualifiers						
Prior, Mike, G.B.	17	3	194	11.4	24	0
Turner, Vernon, Det.	17	4	152	8.9	53	0
Anderson, Gary, T.B.	17	1	113	6.6	15	0
Brooks, Robert, G.B.	16	4	135	8.4	35	0
Hawkins, Courtney, T.B.	15	8	166	11.1	35	0
Buckley, Terrell, G.B.	11	5	76	6.9	39	0
Blount, Eric, Phx.	9	3	90	10.0	25	0
Parker, Anthony, Minn.	9	6	64	7.1	20	0
Buchanan, Richard, Rams	8	1	41	5.1	12	0
Kinchen, Todd, Rams	7	4	32	4.6	8	0
Claiborne, Robert, T.B.	6	6	32	5.3	13	0
Howard, Desmond, Wash.	4	0	25	6.3	13	0
Edwards, Anthony, Phx.	3	3	12	4.0	11	0
Sanders, Deion, Atl.	2	1	21	10.5	16	0
Ellard, Henry, Rams	2	8	18	9.0	13	0
Green, Darrell, Wash.	1	1	27	27.0	24	0
Newman, Pat, N.O.	1	0	14	14.0	14	0
Henley, Darryl, Rams	1	0	8	8.0	8	0
Smith, Robert, Minn.	1	2	4	4.0	4	0
Price, Mitchell, Rams	1	2	3	3.0	3	0
Clark, Vinnie, Atl.	1	0	0	0.0	0	0
Kelm, Larry, S.F.	1	0	0	0.0	0	0
Mays, Alvoid, Wash.	1	0	0	0.0	0	0
Washington, James, Dall.	1	0	0	0.0	0	0
Teague, George, G.B.	1	0	-1	-1.0	-1	0
Smith, Otis, Phil.	0	0	9	—	9	0

t = Touchdown
Leader based on average return, minimum 20 returns

KICKOFF RETURNS

Yards Per Return
NFC: 26.6—Robert Brooks, Green Bay
AFC: 24.2—Raghib Ismail, Raiders
Yards
AFC: 1050—Clarence Verdin, Indianapolis
NFC: 948—Tony Smith, Atlanta
Yards, Game
NFC: 249—Tony Smith, Atlanta vs. Pittsburgh, September 27, (6 returns - TD)
AFC: 117—Nate Lewis, San Diego at Kansas City, December 19, (4 returns)
Longest
NFC: 99—Tyrone Hughes, New Orleans at Minnesota, November 28 - TD
AFC: 66—Raghib Ismail, Raiders at Cincinnati, November 28
Returns
AFC: 50—Clarence Verdin, Indianapolis
NFC: 42—Qadry Ismail, Minnesota

Returns, Game
NFC: 7—Johnny Bailey, Phoenix at Seattle, December 19, (137 yards)
AFC: 6—Adrian Murrell, Jets vs. Denver, September 5, (83 yards)
Clarence Verdin, Indianapolis at Miami, October 24, (151 yards)
Eric Ball, Cincinnati vs. Houston, November 14, (121 yards)
Michael Bates, Seattle vs. Kansas City, December 5, (164 yards)
O.J. McDuffie, Miami at New England, January 2, (150 yards)
Touchdowns
NFC: 1—Robert Brooks, Green Bay
Mel Gray, Detroit
Tyrone Hughes, New Orleans
Tony Smith, Atlanta
AFC: None
Team Champion
NFC: 24.7—Green Bay
AFC: 21.8—Miami

AFC KICKOFF RETURNS—TEAM

	No.	Yards	Avg.	Long	TD
Miami	49	1068	21.8	48	0
L.A. Raiders	52	1061	20.4	66	0
Cincinnati	61	1211	19.9	45	0
Indianapolis	57	1124	19.7	38	0
Kansas City	45	875	19.4	47	0
Cleveland	58	1119	19.3	47	0
San Diego	47	901	19.2	60	0
Houston	31	589	19.0	37	0
Seattle	50	931	18.6	46	0
Denver	39	717	18.4	49	0
New England	47	819	17.4	44	0
Pittsburgh	52	878	16.9	44	0
Buffalo	45	746	16.6	28	0
N.Y. Jets	46	675	14.7	28	0
AFC Total	679	12714	18.7	66	0
AFC Average	48.5	908.1	18.7	—	0.0

NFC KICKOFF RETURNS—TEAM

	No.	Yards	Avg.	Long	TD
Green Bay	60	1483	24.7	95t	1
Atlanta	55	1300	23.6	97t	1
New Orleans	62	1460	23.5	99t	1
Detroit	52	1204	23.2	95t	1
Phoenix	45	951	21.1	48	0
Dallas	36	758	21.1	49	0
Washington	59	1166	19.8	68	0
Minnesota	55	1086	19.7	47	0
Philadelphia	54	987	18.3	36	0
Chicago	45	811	18.0	55	0
San Francisco	40	715	17.9	60	0
L.A. Rams	49	824	16.8	35	0
Tampa Bay	58	922	15.9	42	0
N.Y. Giants	32	507	15.8	35	0
NFC Total	702	14174	20.2	99t	4
NFC Average	50.1	1012.4	20.2	—	0.3
League Total	1381	26888	—	99t	4
League Average	49.3	960.3	19.5	—	0.1

TOP TEN KICKOFF RETURNERS

	No.	Yards	Avg.	Long	TD
Brooks, Robert, G.B.	23	611	26.6	95t	1
Hughes, Tyrone, N.O.	30	753	25.1	99t	1
Smith, Tony, Atl.	38	948	24.9	97t	1
Gray, Mel, Det.	28	688	24.6	95t	1
Ismail, Raghib, Raid.	25	605	24.2	66	0
McDuffie, O. J., Mia.	32	755	23.6	48	0
Bailey, Johnny, Phx.	31	699	22.5	48	0
Williams, Kevin, Dall.	31	689	22.2	49	0
Ball, Eric, Cinn.	23	501	21.8	45	0
Ismail, Qadry, Minn.	42	902	21.5	47	0

AFC KICKOFF RETURNERS—INDIVIDUAL

	No.	Yards	Avg.	Long	TD
Ismail, Raghib, Raid.	25	605	24.2	66	0
McDuffie, O. J., Mia.	32	755	23.6	48	0
Ball, Eric, Cinn.	23	501	21.8	45	0
Verdin, Clarence, Ind.	50	1050	21.0	38	0
Crittenden, Ray, N.E.	23	478	20.8	44	0
Lewis, Nate, S.D.	33	684	20.7	60	0
Bates, Michael, Sea.	30	603	20.1	46	0
Robinson, Patrick, Cinn.	f30	567	18.9	42	0
Baldwin, Randy, Clev.	24	444	18.5	31	0
Copeland, Russell, Buff.	24	436	18.2	28	0
Murrell, Adrian, N.Y.J.	23	342	14.9	23	0
Nonqualifiers					
Russell, Derek, Den.	18	374	20.8	49	0
Vaughn, Jon, Sea.	16	280	17.5	31	0
Metcalf, Eric, Clev.	15	318	21.2	47	0
Woodson, Rod, Pitt.	15	294	19.6	44	0
Drewrey, Willie, Hou.	15	293	19.5	34	0
Brown, Troy, N.E.	15	243	16.2	29	0
Hughes, Danan, K.C.	14	266	19.0	30	0
Hoard, Leroy, Clev.	13	286	22.0	39	0
Milburn, Glyn, Den.	12	188	15.7	26	0
Hastings, Andre, Pitt.	12	177	14.8	22	0
Dickerson, Ron, K.C.	11	237	21.5	44	0
Mills, John Henry, Hou.	11	230	20.9	37	0
Stone, Dwight, Pitt.	11	168	15.3	30	0
Wright, Alexander, Raid.	10	167	16.7	28	0
Beebe, Don, Buff.	10	160	16.0	22	0
Jones, Fred, K.C.	9	156	17.3	29	0
Prior, Anthony, N.Y.J.	9	126	14.0	27	0
Williams, Mike, Mia.	8	180	22.5	39	0
Davis, Kenneth, Buff.	8	100	12.5	18	0
Gault, Willie, Raid.	7	187	26.7	60	0
Delpino, Robert, Den.	7	146	20.9	49	0
Bieniemy, Eric, S.D.	7	110	15.7	18	0
Mathis, Terance, N.Y.J.	7	102	14.6	28	0
Harris, Ronnie, N.E.	6	90	15.0	19	0
Stephens, John, K.C.	5	88	17.6	25	0
Kirby, Terry, Mia.	4	85	21.3	26	0
Benjamin, Ryan, Cinn.	4	78	19.5	24	0
Thompson, Leroy, Pitt.	4	77	19.3	27	0
Anderson, Richie, N.Y.J.	4	66	16.5	22	0
Miles, Ostell, Cinn.	4	65	16.3	24	0
Vardell, Tommy, Clev.	4	58	14.5	16	0
Robinson, Greg, Raid.	4	57	14.3	33	0
Williams, Harvey, K.C.	3	53	17.7	26	0
Culver, Rodney, Ind.	3	51	17.0	20	0
Martin, Kelvin, Sea.	3	38	12.7	15	0
Coleman, Pat, Hou.	3	37	12.3	10	0
Hoge, Merril, Pitt.	3	33	11.0	15	0
Miller, Anthony, S.D.	2	42	21.0	29	0
Lamb, Brad, Buff.	2	40	20.0	23	0
Thomas, Blair, N.Y.J.	2	39	19.5	28	0
Brown, Gary, Hou.	2	29	14.5	16	0
Hendrickson, Steve, S.D.	2	25	12.5	13	0
Means, Natrone, S.D.	2	22	11.0	14	0
Miller, Scott, Mia.	2	22	11.0	16	0
Peat, Todd, Raid.	2	18	9.0	10	0
Smith, Kevin, Raid.	2	15	7.5	8	0
Butcher, Paul, Ind.	2	2	1.0	2	0
Sabb, Dwayne, N.E.	2	0	0.0	0	0
Anders, Kimble, K.C.	1	47	47.0	47	0
McNair, Todd, K.C.	1	28	28.0	28	0
Thigpen, Yancey, Pitt.	1	23	23.0	23	0
Williams, Willie, Pitt.	1	19	19.0	19	0
Harmon, Ronnie, S.D.	1	18	18.0	18	0
Smith, Rico, Clev.	1	13	13.0	13	0
McCallum, Napoleon, Raid.	1	12	12.0	12	0
Cash, Kerry, Ind.	1	11	11.0	11	0
Fryar, Irving, Mia.	1	10	10.0	10	0
Radecic, Scott, Ind.	1	10	10.0	10	0
Tuatagaloa, Natu, Sea.	1	10	10.0	10	0
Turner, Nate, Buff.	1	10	10.0	10	0
Meeks, Bob, Den.	1	9	9.0	9	0
Cook, Marv, N.E.	1	8	8.0	8	0
Baty, Greg, Mia.	1	7	7.0	7	0
Saxon, James, Mia.	1	7	7.0	7	0
Cooper, Adrian, Pitt.	1	2	2.0	2	0
Kinchen, Brian, Clev.	1	0	0.0	0	0
Marts, Lonnie, K.C.	1	0	0.0	0	0
Sadowski, Troy, N.Y.J.	1	0	0.0	0	0
Sharpe, Shannon, Den.	1	0	0.0	0	0

	No.	Yards	Avg.	Long	TD
Turk, Daniel, Raid.	1	0	0.0	0	0
Vincent, Troy, Mia.	0	2	—	2	0
Birden, J. J., K.C.	f0	0	—	—	0
Coates, Ben, N.E.	f0	0	—	—	0
Shaw, Eric, Cinn.	f0	0	—	—	0

t = Touchdown
f = Fair Catch (Shaw, Eric, Cinn.: 2 fair catches)
Leader based on average return, minimum 20 returns

NFC KICKOFF RETURNERS—INDIVIDUAL

	No.	Yards	Avg.	Long	TD
Brooks, Robert, G.B.	23	611	26.6	95t	1
Hughes, Tyrone, N.O.	30	753	25.1	99t	1
Smith, Tony, Atl.	38	948	24.9	97t	1
Gray, Mel, Det.	28	688	24.6	95t	1
Bailey, Johnny, Phx.	31	699	22.5	48	0
Williams, Kevin, Dall.	31	689	22.2	49	0
Ismail, Qadry, Minn.	42	902	21.5	47	0
Conway, Curtis, Chi.	21	450	21.4	55	0
McAfee, Fred, N.O.	28	580	20.7	55	0
Mitchell, Brian, Wash.	33	678	20.5	68	0
Carter, Dexter, S.F.	f25	494	19.8	60	0
Wilson, Charles, T.B.	f23	454	19.7	42	0
Sikahema, Vai, Phil.	30	579	19.3	35	0
Howard, Desmond, Wash.	21	405	19.3	33	0
Turner, Vernon, Det.-T.B.	21	391	18.6	46	0
Meggett, David, N.Y.G.	f24	403	16.8	35	0
Nonqualifiers					
Harris, Corey, G.B.	16	482	30.1	65	0
Anderson, Gary, T.B.-Det.	15	232	15.5	24	0
Boykin, Deral, Rams	13	216	16.6	29	0
Walker, Herschel, Phil.	11	184	16.7	30	0
Lee, Amp, S.F.	10	160	16.0	28	0
Wilson, Marcus, G.B.	9	197	21.9	37	0
Thompson, Darrell, G.B.	9	171	19.0	42	0
Obee, Terry, Chi.	9	159	17.7	34	0
Sydner, Jeff, Phil.	9	158	17.6	36	0
Green, Robert, Chi.	9	141	15.7	30	0
Griffith, Howard, Rams	8	169	21.1	29	0
Blount, Eric, Phx.	8	163	20.4	27	0
Price, Mitchell, Rams	8	144	18.0	23	0
White, Russell, Rams	8	122	15.3	35	0
Royster, Mazio, T.B.	8	102	12.8	26	0
Sanders, Deion, Atl.	7	169	24.1	31	0
Worley, Tim, Pitt.-Chi.	6	121	20.2	26	0
Kinchen, Todd, Rams	6	96	16.0	22	0
Calloway, Chris, N.Y.G.	6	89	14.8	21	0
Guliford, Eric, Minn.	5	101	20.2	29	0
Israel, Steve, Rams	5	92	18.4	23	0
Workman, Vince, T.B.	5	67	13.4	19	0
Pegram, Erric, Atl.	4	63	15.8	28	0
Claiborne, Robert, T.B.	4	57	14.3	33	0
Brown, Derek, N.O.	3	58	19.3	23	0
Edwards, Anthony, Phx.	3	51	17.0	20	0
Walker, Adam, S.F.	3	51	17.0	30	0
Smith, Robert, Minn.	3	41	13.7	16	0
Hebron, Vaughn, Phil.	3	35	11.7	18	0
Montgomery, Alton, Atl.	2	53	26.5	33	0
Phillips, Jason, Atl.	2	38	19.0	29	0
Clay, Willie, Det.	2	34	17.0	20	0
Ervins, Ricky, Wash.	2	29	14.5	18	0
Jurkovic, John, G.B.	2	22	11.0	13	0
Cross, Howard, N.Y.G.	2	15	7.5	13	0
Moore, Derrick, Det.	1	68	68.0	68	0
Smith, Kevin, Dall.	1	33	33.0	33	0
Bowles, Todd, Wash.	1	27	27.0	27	0
Lynch, Eric, Det.	1	22	22.0	22	0
Mims, David, Atl.	1	22	22.0	22	0
Gant, Kenneth, Dall.	1	18	18.0	18	0
Lofton, Steve, Phx.	1	18	18.0	18	0
Hilliard, Dalton, N.O.	1	17	17.0	17	0
Graham, Scottie, Minn.	1	16	16.0	16	0
Buck, Jason, Wash.	1	15	15.0	15	0
Brooks, Reggie, Wash.	1	12	12.0	12	0
Heyward, Craig, Chi.	1	12	12.0	12	0
Jones, Robert, Dall.	1	12	12.0	12	0
Craig, Roger, Minn.	1	11	11.0	11	0
Evans, Chuck, Minn.	1	11	11.0	11	0
Hallock, Ty, Det.	1	11	11.0	11	0
Smith, Lance, Phx.	1	11	11.0	11	0
Brandes, John, S.F.	1	10	10.0	10	0

	No.	Yards	Avg.	Long	TD
Moore, Ron, Phx.	1	9	9.0	9	0
Fontenot, Albert, Chi.	1	8	8.0	8	0
Hennings, Chad, Dall.	1	7	7.0	7	0
Johnson, Maurice, Phil.	1	7	7.0	7	0
Ruether, Mike, Atl.	1	7	7.0	7	0
Ryan, Tim, Chi.	1	5	5.0	5	0
Del Rio, Jack, Minn.	1	4	4.0	4	0
Chmura, Mark, G.B.	1	0	0.0	0	0
Jamison, George, Det.	1	0	0.0	0	0
Kelm, Larry, S.F.	1	0	0.0	0	0
Mangum, John, Chi.	1	0	0.0	0	0
McMillian, Audray, Minn.	1	0	0.0	0	0
Novacek, Jay, Dall.	1	-1	-1.0	-1	0
Drayton, Troy, Rams	1	-15	-15.0	-15	0
Dowdell, Marcus, N.O.	0	52	—	52	0
Smith, Otis, Phil.	0	24	—	24	0
Jones, Victor, Det.	f0	0	—	—	0
Vanderbeek, Matt, Dall.	f0	0	—	—	0
Walls, Wesley, S.F.	f0	0	—	—	0
Williams, Jamie, S.F.	f0	0	—	—	0

t = Touchdown
f = Fair Catch (Vanderbeek, Matt, Dall.: 2 fair catches)
Leader based on average return, minimum 20 returns

FUMBLES
Most Fumbles
NFC: 15—Jim Harbaugh, Chicago
AFC: 13—Boomer Esiason, Jets
Rick Mirer, Seattle
Warren Moon, Houston
Most Fumbles, Game
AFC: 3—David Klingler, Cincinnati at Cleveland, September 5
Vince Evans, Raiders at Kansas City, October 3
Rick Mirer, Seattle at Detroit, October 17
Scott Secules, New England at Indianapolis, October 31
Leroy Thompson, Pittsburgh at Denver, November 21
Drew Bledsoe, New England at Pittsburgh, December 5
Glyn Milburn, Denver vs. Tampa Bay, December 26
Boomer Esiason, Jets at Houston, January 2
Leroy Hoard, Cleveland at Pittsburgh, January 2
NFC: 3—Jim Harbaugh, Chicago vs. Giants, September 5
Randall Cunningham, Philadelphia at Green Bay, September 12
Rodney Peete, Detroit at New Orleans, September 19
Bobby Hebert, Atlanta vs. Pittsburgh, September 27
Brett Favre, Green Bay at Kansas City, November 8
Craig Erickson, Tampa Bay at Denver, December 26
Mark Rypien, Washington vs. Minnesota, December 31
Own Fumbles Recovered
NFC: 6—Craig Erickson, Tampa Bay
AFC: 5—Drew Bledsoe, New England
John Elway, Denver
Boomer Esiason, Jets
Rick Mirer, Seattle
Warren Moon, Houston
Most Own Fumbles Recovered, Game
NFC: 3—Craig Erickson, Tampa Bay at Denver, December 26
AFC: 2—Drew Bledsoe, New England at Buffalo, September 5
Dan Marino, Miami at Indianapolis, September 5
Terry Kirby, Miami vs. Jets, September 12
Nate Lewis, San Diego at Pittsburgh, October 10
Jim Kelly, Buffalo vs. Houston, October 11
Rick Mirer, Seattle vs. New England, October 24
Scott Secules, New England at Indianapolis, October 31
Boomer Esiason, Jets vs. Miami, November 7
John Elway, Denver at Seattle, November 28
Warren Moon, Houston vs. Pittsburgh, November 28
Drew Bledsoe, New England at Pittsburgh, December 5
Opponents' Fumbles Recovered
NFC: 5—Michael Bankston, Phoenix
AFC: 4—Bryan Cox, Miami
Andre Tippett, New England

Most Opponents' Fumbles Recovered, Game
AFC: 2—Bill Pickel, Jets at Raiders, October 10
Bryan Cox, Miami vs. Kansas City, October 31
Andre Tippett, New England vs. Buffalo, November 7 (OT)
Patrick Hunter, Seattle vs. Cleveland, November 14
Tim Newton, Kansas City vs. Seattle, January 2
NFC: 2—Lorenzo Lynch, Phoenix at Philadelphia, September 5
Jimmy Spencer, New Orleans vs. Houston, September 5
Pat Eilers, Washington vs. Dallas, September 6
Rickey Jackson, New Orleans vs. Detroit, September 19
Myron Baker, Chicago vs. Tampa Bay, September 26
Michael Bankston, Phoenix vs. Washington, October 17
Trace Armstrong, Chicago at Detroit, November 25
Yards
AFC: 107—Marcus Robertson, Houston
NFC: 86—Darrell Green, Washington
Longest
AFC: 86—Derrick Thomas, Kansas City at Seattle, December 5 - TD
NFC: 78—Darrell Green, Washington vs. Indianapolis, November 7 - TD

AFC FUMBLES—TEAM

	Fum.	Own. Rec.	Fum. OB	TD	Opp. Rec.	TD	Fum. Yards	Tot. Rec.
San Diego	13	7	1	0	12	0	29	19
L.A. Raiders	23	11	1	0	9	0	4	20
Cincinnati	24	13	2	0	14	0	-24	27
Seattle	25	10	2	0	15	2	-6	25
Buffalo	26	9	0	0	24	1	87	33
Cleveland	27	8	2	0	9	1	12	17
Pittsburgh	28	9	4	0	14	2	57	23
Kansas City	28	7	3	0	17	2	122	24
Denver	29	10	1	1	13	0	-24	23
New England	30	19	1	0	9	0	-29	28
Miami	32	15	1	0	14	0	-23	29
Indianapolis	34	11	3	0	11	2	45	22
Houston	37	12	5	0	17	3	178	29
N.Y. Jets	38	20	2	0	18	0	22	38
AFC Total	394	161	28	1	196	13	450	357
AFC Average	28.1	11.5	2.0	0.1	14.0	0.9	32.1	25.5

NFC FUMBLES—TEAM

	Fum.	Own. Rec.	Fum. OB	TD	Opp. Rec.	TD	Fum. Yards	Tot. Rec.
Minnesota	15	4	1	0	10	0	-12	14
N.Y. Giants	19	10	1	0	10	0	-17	20
L.A. Rams	20	8	1	0	9	1	61	17
Phoenix	23	11	1	0	17	2	56	28
New Orleans	24	11	0	0	20	2	118	31
Washington	24	14	0	0	14	2	114	28
Green Bay	26	15	1	0	15	1	34	30
Tampa Bay	28	16	1	0	13	0	7	29
Chicago	29	14	1	0	12	2	42	26
Detroit	29	12	4	0	16	2	110	28
Atlanta	31	13	1	0	11	1	11	24
San Francisco	32	16	3	1	11	1	56	27
Philadelphia	32	10	1	0	15	1	29	25
Dallas	33	14	3	0	14	0	14	28
NFC Total	365	168	19	1	187	15	623	355
NFC Average	26.1	12.0	1.4	0.1	13.4	1.1	44.5	25.4
League Total	759	329	47	2	383	28	1073	712
League Average	27.1	11.8	1.7	0.1	13.7	1.0	38.3	25.4

Fum OB = Fumbled out of bounds, includes fumbled through the end zone.
Yards includes aborted plays, own recoveries, and oppponents' recoveries.

AFC FUMBLES - INDIVIDUAL

	Fum.	Own Rec.	Opp. Rec.	Yards	Tot. Rec.
Aguiar, Louie, N.Y.J.	2	1	0	-10	1
Alexander, Bruce, Mia.	0	0	1	0	1
Allen, Marcus, K.C.	4	1	0	0	1
Anders, Kimble, K.C.	1	0	0	0	0
Anderson, Eddie, Raid.	0	0	1	0	1
Anderson, Richie, N.Y.J.	1	1	0	0	1
Arbuckle, Charles, Ind.	1	0	0	0	0
Armstrong, Bruce, N.E.	0	1	0	0	1

Name	Fum.	Own Rec.	Opp. Rec.	Yards	Tot. Rec.
Arthur, Mike, N.E.	0	1	0	0	1
Baldwin, Randy, Clev.	2	1	0	0	1
Bates, Michael, Sea.	1	0	2	3	2
Bavaro, David, N.E.	0	1	1	0	2
Baxter, Brad, N.Y.J.	3	2	0	0	2
Beebe, Don, Buff.	1	1	0	0	1
Bell, Nick, Raid.	2	0	0	0	0
Belser, Jason, Ind.	0	0	3	0	3
Bennett, Cornelius, Buff.	1	1	1	40	2
Bernstine, Rod, Den.	3	1	0	0	1
Bickett, Duane, Ind.	0	0	1	0	1
Bieniemy, Eric, S.D.	1	0	0	0	0
Birden, J. J., K.C.	1	0	0	0	0
Bishop, Blaine, Hou.	1	0	1	0	1
Blackmon, Robert, Sea.	0	0	1	5	1
Blades, Brian, Sea.	1	0	0	0	0
Bledsoe, Drew, N.E.	8	5	0	-23	5
Bowden, Joe, Hou.	0	0	1	0	1
Bradford, Ronnie, Den.	1	0	0	0	0
Brady, Jeff, S.D.	0	0	1	0	1
Braxton, Tyrone, Den.	0	0	2	6	2
Brim, Michael, Cinn.	0	1	1	0	2
Brisby, Vincent, N.E.	1	1	0	0	1
Brown, Corwin, N.E.	0	0	1	0	1
Brown, Gary, Hou.	4	2	0	4	2
Brown, J. B., Mia.	1	0	0	0	0
Brown, Tim, Raid.	1	0	0	0	0
Brown, Troy, N.E.	2	1	0	0	1
Bruce, Aundray, Raid.	0	0	1	0	1
Burkett, Chris, N.Y.J.	1	0	0	0	0
Burnett, Rob, Clev.	0	0	2	0	2
Byars, Keith, Mia.	3	0	0	0	0
Caldwell, Mike, Clev.	0	0	1	0	1
Carlson, Cody, Hou.	3	2	0	-2	2
Carrington, Darren, S.D.	1	0	1	0	1
Carter, Dale, K.C.	4	2	0	0	2
Cash, Keith, K.C.	1	1	1	0	2
Cash, Kerry, Ind.	2	1	0	0	1
Childress, Ray, Hou.	0	0	3	0	3
Clancy, Sam, Ind.	0	0	1	0	1
Clifton, Kyle, N.Y.J.	0	0	2	0	2
Collins, Todd, N.E.	0	0	1	2	1
Cook, Marv, N.E.	1	0	0	-2	0
Cooper, Adrian, Pitt.	1	0	0	0	0
Copeland, Russell, Buff.	1	0	0	0	0
Cox, Bryan, Mia.	0	0	4	1	4
Croel, Mike, Den.	0	0	2	0	2
Croom, Corey, N.E.	1	0	0	0	0
Cross, Jeff, Mia.	0	0	2	0	2
Culver, Rodney, Ind.	3	1	1	56	2
Dahl, Bob, Clev.	0	1	0	0	1
Darby, Matt, Buff.	0	0	1	0	1
Davidson, Kenny, Pitt.	0	0	1	18	1
Davis, Kenneth, Buff.	3	1	0	0	1
Dawson, Dermontti, Pitt.	1	0	0	0	0
DeBerg, Steve, T.B.-Mia.	2	0	0	0	0
Dellenbach, Jeff, Mia.	1	0	1	-6	1
Delpino, Robert, Den.	1	0	0	0	0
Dennis, Mark, Mia.	0	1	0	0	1
Dishman, Cris, Hou.	0	0	2	69	2
Donaldson, Ray, Sea.	1	0	0	-7	0
Drewrey, Willie, Hou.	2	1	0	0	1
Duffy, Roger, N.Y.J.	0	1	0	0	1
Dyal, Mike, K.C.	1	0	0	0	0
Edmunds, Ferrell, Sea.	1	0	0	0	0
Elway, John, Den.	8	5	0	-5	5
Esiason, Boomer, N.Y.J.	13	5	0	-10	5
Evans, Vince, Raid.	4	0	0	0	0
Everitt, Steve, Clev.	0	2	0	0	2
Fenner, Derrick, Cinn.	1	2	0	0	2
Figures, Deon, Pitt.	2	0	2	6	2
Fletcher, Simon, Den.	0	0	1	0	1
Foster, Barry, Pitt.	3	0	0	0	0
Francis, James, Cinn.	0	0	1	0	1
Frase, Paul, N.Y.J.	0	0	2	0	2
Friesz, John, S.D.	2	1	0	-3	1
Gardner, Carwell, Buff.	1	0	0	0	0
Gash, Sam, N.E.	1	0	0	0	0
Gelbaugh, Stan, Sea.	1	0	0	0	0
George, Jeff, Ind.	4	0	0	-1	0
Givins, Ernest, Hou.	2	0	0	0	0
Goad, Tim, N.E.	0	0	1	0	1
Goganious, Keith, Buff.	0	0	1	0	1
Gordon, Darrien, S.D.	4	1	1	-2	2
Gray, Derwin, Ind.	0	0	1	0	1
Green, Eric, Pitt.	3	0	0	0	0
Green, Harold, Cinn.	3	0	0	0	0
Greene, Kevin, Pitt.	0	0	3	5	3
Grossman, Burt, S.D.	0	0	1	0	1
Grunhard, Tim, K.C.	1	0	0	-1	0
Gunn, Lance, Cinn.	0	0	1	0	1
Harper, Dwayne, Sea.	0	0	1	0	1
Harris, Ronnie, N.E.	2	1	0	0	1
Harrison, Nolan, Raid.	0	0	1	5	1
Hasty, James, N.Y.J.	0	0	2	28	2
Hayes, Jonathan, K.C.	1	0	0	0	0
Heck, Andy, Sea.	0	2	0	0	2
Heller, Ron, Mia.	0	1	0	0	1
Henderson, Jerome, Buff.	0	0	1	0	1
Hendrickson, Steve, S.D.	0	0	1	0	1
Herrod, Jeff, Ind.	0	0	1	0	1
Hester, Jessie, Ind.	1	0	0	0	0
Hicks, Cliff, N.Y.J.	2	1	0	0	1
Higgs, Mark, Mia.	1	0	0	0	0
Hoard, Leroy, Clev.	4	0	0	0	0
Hoge, Merril, Pitt.	0	1	0	4	1
Hollier, Dwight, Mia.	0	0	1	0	1
Hoover, Houston, Clev.	0	1	0	0	1
Horton, Ethan, Raid.	0	1	0	0	1
Hoskins, Derrick, Raid.	0	0	1	0	1
Hostetler, Jeff, Raid.	6	2	0	-1	2
Houston, Bobby, N.Y.J.	0	0	1	0	1
Humphries, Stan, S.D.	2	1	0	0	1
Hunter, Patrick, Sea.	0	0	3	0	3
Ingram, Mark, Mia.	3	1	0	0	1
Ismail, Raghib, Raid.	0	1	0	0	1
Jackson, John, Pitt.	0	1	0	0	1
Jackson, Keith, Mia.	2	0	0	0	0
Jackson, Michael, Clev.	1	0	1	0	1
Jeffires, Haywood, Hou.	5	0	0	0	0
Jett, James, Raid.	1	0	0	0	0
Johnson, Anthony, Ind.	5	2	0	0	2
Johnson, Johnny, N.Y.J.	5	2	0	0	2
Johnson, Reggie, Den.	1	0	0	0	0
Jones, Fred, K.C.	1	0	0	0	0
Jones, Gary, Pitt.	0	1	0	0	1
Jones, Henry, Buff.	0	1	1	0	2
Jones, Marvin, N.Y.J.	0	0	1	0	1
Jones, Rod, Cinn.	0	0	1	0	1
Jones, Sean, Hou.	0	0	2	0	2
Jones, Selwyn, Clev.	0	0	1	0	1
Jordan, Randy, Raid.	2	0	0	0	0
Jorden, Tim, Pitt.	0	1	0	2	1
Junior, E. J., Sea.	0	1	0	0	1
Kartz, Keith, Den.	2	0	0	-17	0
Kasay, John, Sea.	0	0	1	0	1
Kelly, Jim, Buff.	7	3	0	-17	3
Kelly, Joe, Raid.	0	0	1	0	1
Kelso, Mark, Buff.	0	0	1	0	1
Kennedy, Cortez, Sea.	0	0	1	0	1
Kinchen, Brian, Clev.	1	0	0	0	0
Kirby, Terry, Mia.	5	4	0	0	4
Kirkland, Levon, Pitt.	0	0	2	24	2
Klingler, David, Cinn.	7	2	0	-10	2
Kozerski, Bruce, Cinn.	3	1	0	-14	1
Kragen, Greg, Den.	0	0	1	0	1
Krieg, Dave, K.C.	6	1	0	0	1
Lake, Carnell, Pitt.	0	0	2	0	2
Langhorne, Reggie, Ind.	4	1	1	0	2
Lathon, Lamar, Hou.	0	0	1	0	1
Lee, Shawn, S.D.	0	0	1	0	1
Lewis, Albert, K.C.	0	0	2	0	2
Lewis, Bill, N.E.	2	0	0	-43	0
Lewis, Nate, S.D.	2	2	0	0	2
Lloyd, Greg, Pitt.	0	0	1	0	1
Lodish, Mike, Buff.	0	0	1	0	1
Lott, Ronnie, N.Y.J.	0	0	2	0	2
Lowdermilk, Kirk, Ind.	0	1	0	0	1
Maddox, Mark, Buff.	0	0	2	0	2
Majkowski, Don, Ind.	1	1	0	-7	1
Malamala, Siupeli, N.Y.J.	0	1	0	0	1
Marino, Dan, Mia.	4	2	0	-13	2

	Fum.	Own Rec.	Opp. Rec.	Yards	Tot. Rec.
Marshall, Leonard, N.Y.J.	0	0	1	0	1
Marshall, Wilber, Hou.	0	0	1	0	1
Martin, Kelvin, Sea.	1	1	0	0	1
Martin, Tony, Mia.	1	0	0	0	0
Marts, Lonnie, K.C.	0	0	1	0	1
Maston, Le'Shai, Hou.	1	0	0	0	0
Mathis, Terance, N.Y.J.	5	1	0	0	1
McCallum, Napoleon, Raid.	1	0	0	0	0
McClendon, Skip, Ind.	0	0	2	0	2
McDuffie, O. J., Mia.	4	1	0	0	1
McGee, Tony, Cinn.	1	0	0	0	0
McGlockton, Chester, Raid.	0	0	1	0	1
McMurtry, Greg, N.E.	1	1	0	0	1
McNair, Todd, K.C.	2	0	0	0	0
Means, Natrone, S.D.	1	1	0	0	1
Mecklenburg, Karl, Den.	0	0	2	0	2
Metcalf, Eric, Clev.	4	0	0	0	0
Metzelaars, Pete, Buff.	1	0	0	0	0
Mickell, Darren, K.C.	0	0	1	0	1
Milburn, Glyn, Den.	9	1	0	0	1
Mims, Chris, S.D.	0	0	2	0	2
Mincy, Charles, K.C.	0	0	2	0	2
Mirer, Rick, Sea.	13	5	0	-14	5
Mitchell, Scott, Mia.	3	1	0	-4	1
Mohr, Chris, Buff.	1	1	0	0	1
Montana, Joe, K.C.	1	0	0	-1	0
Montgomery, Glenn, Hou.	0	0	3	0	3
Montgomery, Tyrone, Raid.	2	1	0	0	1
Moon, Warren, Hou.	13	5	0	-7	5
Moore, Rob, N.Y.J.	2	0	0	0	0
Moore, Stevon, Clev.	0	0	1	22	1
Murrell, Adrian, N.Y.J.	4	2	0	0	2
Newton, Tim, K.C.	0	0	3	0	3
Norgard, Erik, Hou.	0	1	0	0	1
Odomes, Nate, Buff.	0	0	1	25	1
O'Donnell, Neil, Pitt.	5	0	0	-2	0
Oliver, Louis, Mia.	0	0	1	0	1
O'Neal, Leslie, S.D.	0	0	1	13	1
Patton, Marvcus, Buff.	0	0	3	5	3
Pederson, Doug, Mia.	2	1	0	-1	1
Perry, Gerald, Raid.	0	1	0	0	1
Perry, Michael Dean, Clev.	0	0	2	4	2
Philcox, Todd, Clev.	2	0	0	-1	0
Pickel, Bill, N.Y.J.	0	0	3	7	3
Pickens, Carl, Cinn.	1	0	0	0	0
Pool, David, Buff.	0	0	1	12	1
Potts, Roosevelt, Ind.	8	2	0	0	2
Prior, Anthony, N.Y.J.	0	1	0	0	1
Pupunu, Alfred, S.D.	0	1	0	0	1
Query, Jeff, Cinn.	1	0	0	0	0
Rayam, Thomas, Cinn.	0	2	0	0	2
Reed, Andre, Buff.	3	0	0	0	0
Richard, Stanley, S.D.	0	0	1	0	1
Rivers, Reggie, Den.	0	0	1	0	1
Robertson, Marcus, Hou.	0	0	3	107	3
Robinson, Eugene, Sea.	0	0	2	7	2
Robinson, Greg, Raid.	3	1	0	0	1
Robinson, Jeff, Den.	1	0	1	-10	1
Robinson, Patrick, Cinn.	2	1	0	0	1
Robinson, Rafael, Sea.	0	0	1	0	1
Rogers, Tracy, K.C.	0	0	1	0	1
Ross, Kevin, K.C.	0	0	1	22	1
Rowe, Patrick, Clev.	1	0	0	0	0
Russell, Derek, Den.	1	1	0	0	1
Russell, Leonard, N.E.	4	2	0	22	2
Saleaumua, Dan, K.C.	0	0	1	16	1
Saxon, Mike, N.E.	1	1	0	0	1
Schroeder, Jay, Cinn.	5	1	0	0	1
Scott, Tom, Cinn.	0	2	0	0	2
Searcy, Leon, Pitt.	0	1	0	0	1
Seau, Junior, S.D.	0	0	1	21	1
Secules, Scott, N.E.	4	2	0	-5	2
Sharpe, Shannon, Den.	1	0	0	0	0
Shaw, Eric, Cinn.	0	0	1	0	1
Shields, Will, K.C.	0	2	0	0	2
Sims, Keith, Mia.	0	1	0	0	1
Slade, Chris, N.E.	0	0	1	0	1
Slaughter, Webster, Hou.	4	0	0	0	0
Smith, Bruce, Buff.	0	0	1	0	1
Smith, Neil, K.C.	0	0	3	0	3
Smith, Steve, Raid.	1	3	0	0	3

	Fum.	Own Rec.	Opp. Rec.	Yards	Tot. Rec.
Smith, Thomas, Buff.	0	0	1	0	1
Speer, Del, Clev.	1	0	1	0	1
Steed, Joel, Pitt.	0	0	1	0	1
Stephens, John, G.B.-K.C.	1	1	0	0	1
Stephens, Rod, Sea.	0	0	1	0	1
Stone, Dwight, Pitt.	2	1	0	0	1
Strzelczyk, Justin, Pitt.	0	0	1	0	1
Stubbs, Danny, Cinn.	0	0	1	0	1
Talley, Darryl, Buff.	0	0	2	4	2
Tasker, Steve, Buff.	1	0	1	0	1
Testaverde, Vinny, Clev.	4	0	0	0	0
Thomas, Blair, N.Y.J.	0	1	0	0	1
Thomas, Derrick, K.C.	0	0	1	86	1
Thomas, Eric, N.Y.J.	0	1	0	0	1
Thomas, Thurman, Buff.	6	1	0	0	1
Thompson, Craig, Cinn.	0	1	0	0	1
Thompson, Leroy, Pitt.	7	1	0	0	1
Tillman, Cedric, Den.	1	1	0	0	1
Timpson, Michael, N.E.	1	0	0	0	0
Tippett, Andre, N.E.	0	0	4	14	4
Tomczak, Mike, Pitt.	2	1	0	0	1
Tovar, Steve, Cinn.	0	0	1	0	1
Trudeau, Jack, Ind.	2	1	0	-3	1
Tuatagaloa, Natu, Sea.	0	0	1	0	1
Turk, Daniel, Raid.	0	0	1	0	1
Turner, Kevin, N.E.	1	2	0	6	2
Turner, Marcus, N.Y.J.	0	0	1	7	1
Vardell, Tommy, Clev.	3	0	0	0	0
Vaughn, Jon, Sea.	1	0	0	0	0
Verdin, Clarence, Ind.	3	1	0	0	1
Vincent, Troy, Mia.	0	0	1	0	1
Vinson, Fernandus, Cinn.	0	0	3	0	3
Wallace, Aaron, Raid.	0	0	2	0	2
Warren, Chris, Sea.	3	0	0	0	0
Washington, Brian, N.Y.J.	0	0	1	0	1
Washington, Mickey, Buff.	0	0	2	6	2
Webster, Larry, Mia.	0	0	1	0	1
Weidner, Bert, Mia.	0	0	1	0	1
Wellman, Gary, Hou.	1	0	0	0	0
Wheeler, Leonard, Cinn.	0	0	1	0	1
White, Lorenzo, Hou.	1	0	0	0	0
White, Sheldon, Cinn.	0	0	1	0	1
Wilkerson, Bruce, Raid.	0	1	0	0	1
Williams, Dan, Den.	0	0	1	0	1
Williams, Darryl, Cinn.	0	0	2	0	2
Williams, David, Hou.	0	1	0	7	1
Williams, Harvey, K.C.	3	0	0	0	0
Williams, James, Buff.	0	0	2	12	2
Williams, Jarvis, Mia.	0	0	2	0	2
Williams, John L., Sea.	2	1	0	0	1
Williams, Mike, Mia.	1	0	0	0	0
Williams, Ronnie, Mia.	0	1	0	0	1
Wilson, Karl, N.Y.J.	0	0	1	0	1
Winter, Blaise, S.D.	0	0	1	0	1
Wooden, Terry, Sea.	0	0	1	0	1
Woodson, Rod, Pitt.	2	1	0	0	1
Wright, Jeff, Buff.	0	0	1	0	1
Wyman, David, Den.	0	0	2	2	2
Young, Lonnie, N.Y.J.	0	0	1	0	1
Zgonina, Jeff, Pitt.	0	0	1	0	1
Zimmerman, Gary, Den.	0	1	0	0	1

Yards includes aborted plays, own recoveries, and opponents' recoveries.

NFC FUMBLES - INDIVIDUAL

	Fum.	Own Rec.	Opp. Rec.	Yards	Tot. Rec.
Aikman, Troy, Dall.	7	3	0	-3	3
Alexander, Harold, Atl.	0	1	0	0	1
Anderson, Neal, Chi.	2	1	0	0	1
Anderson, Gary, T.B.-Det.	4	0	0	0	0
Anderson, Willie, Rams	0	1	0	0	1
Armstrong, Trace, Chi.	0	0	3	3	3
Atkins, Gene, N.O.	0	0	2	4	2
Bailey, Carlton, N.Y.G.	1	1	0	0	1
Bailey, Johnny, Phx.	4	0	0	0	0
Baker, Myron, Chi.	0	0	2	8	2
Bankston, Michael, Phx.	0	0	5	16	5
Barker, Roy, Minn.	0	0	1	0	1
Barlow, Corey, Phil.	0	1	0	0	1
Barnett, Fred, Phil.	1	0	0	0	0

	Fum.	Own Rec.	Opp. Rec.	Yards	Tot. Rec.
Bates, Bill, Dall.	0	0	1	0	1
Beach, Sanjay, S.F.	0	0	1	0	1
Beckles, Ian, T.B.	0	1	0	0	1
Bennett, Edgar, G.B.	0	1	0	0	1
Bettis, Jerome, Rams	4	0	0	0	0
Beuerlein, Steve, Phx.	8	2	0	0	2
Bingham, Guy, Wash.	1	0	0	-9	0
Bortz, Mark, Chi.	0	1	0	0	1
Boutte, Marc, Rams	0	0	1	0	1
Bowles, Todd, Wash.	0	0	1	0	1
Boykin, Deral, Rams	1	1	1	6	2
Brandes, John, S.F.	1	0	1	0	1
Brister, Bubby, Phil.	3	0	0	0	0
Brock, Matt, G.B.	0	0	1	0	1
Brooks, Michael, N.Y.G.	0	0	1	0	1
Brooks, Reggie, Wash.	4	1	0	0	1
Brooks, Robert, G.B.	1	1	0	0	1
Brostek, Bern, Rams	1	0	0	0	0
Brown, Derek, N.O.	1	0	0	0	0
Buck, Mike, N.O.	2	0	0	-8	0
Buck, Vince, N.O.	0	0	2	6	2
Buckley, Marcus, N.Y.G.	0	0	1	0	1
Buckley, Terrell, G.B.	1	0	0	0	0
Bunch, Jarrod, N.Y.G.	2	0	0	0	0
Bussey, Barney, T.B.	0	0	1	0	1
Butler, LeRoy, G.B.	0	0	1	25	1
Byner, Earnest, Wash.	0	1	0	0	1
Calloway, Chris, N.Y.G.	0	1	0	0	1
Camarillo, Rich, Phx.	0	1	0	0	1
Campen, James, G.B.	0	1	0	0	1
Carter, Anthony, Minn.	1	0	0	0	0
Carter, Cris, Minn.	0	1	0	0	1
Carter, Dexter, S.F.	5	1	0	0	1
Carter, Marty, T.B.	0	0	2	0	2
Casillas, Tony, Dall.	0	0	1	0	1
Centers, Larry, Phx.	1	2	0	0	2
Chandler, Chris, Phx.	2	0	0	0	0
Chmura, Mark, G.B.	1	1	0	0	1
Claiborne, Robert, T.B.	2	0	0	0	0
Clark, Gary, Phx.	1	0	0	0	0
Clark, Vinnie, Atl.	1	0	1	46	1
Clay, Willie, Det.	0	0	2	54	2
Cobb, Reggie, T.B.	5	1	0	0	1
Coleman, Keo, G.B.	0	0	1	0	1
Coleman, Lincoln, Dall.	1	0	0	0	0
Coleman, Monte, Wash.	0	0	2	29	2
Collins, Shane, Wash.	0	0	1	0	1
Conklin, Cary, Wash.	1	0	0	0	0
Conway, Curtis, Chi.	1	0	0	0	0
Cook, Toi, N.O.	0	0	3	0	3
Cooper, Richard, N.O.	0	1	0	0	1
Cox, Ron, Chi.	0	0	1	0	1
Craig, Roger, Minn.	1	0	0	0	0
Crockett, Ray, Det.	0	0	1	0	1
Cross, Howard, N.Y.G.	0	0	1	0	1
Cunningham, Randall, Phil.	3	0	0	0	0
Cunningham, Rick, Phx.	0	1	0	0	1
Curry, Eric, T.B.	0	0	1	0	1
Dalman, Chris, S.F.	0	1	0	0	1
Davis, Eric, S.F.	0	0	1	47	1
Davis, Reuben, Phx.	0	0	1	0	1
DeLong, Keith, S.F.	0	0	1	0	1
Dickerson, Eric, Atl.	0	1	0	0	1
Dill, Scott, T.B.	0	1	0	0	1
Doleman, Chris, Minn.	0	0	1	0	1
Dowdell, Marcus, N.O.	1	0	0	0	0
Drayton, Troy, Rams	1	0	0	0	0
Dukes, Jamie, Atl.	0	0	1	0	1
Early, Quinn, N.O.	1	0	0	0	0
Eatman, Irv, Rams	0	1	0	0	1
Edwards, Brad, Wash.	0	0	1	0	1
Edwards, Dixon, Dall.	0	0	1	0	1
Eilers, Pat, Wash.	0	0	3	0	3
Elewonibi, Mohammed, Wash.	0	2	0	10	2
Erickson, Craig, T.B.	9	6	0	-2	6
Ervins, Ricky, Wash.	2	0	0	0	0
Evans, Byron, Phil.	0	0	3	30	3
Evans, Doug, G.B.	0	0	2	0	2
Everett, Jim, Rams	7	1	0	-1	1
Favre, Brett, G.B.	14	2	0	-1	2
Feagles, Jeff, Phil.	0	1	0	0	1
Flores, Mike, Phil.	0	0	1	0	1
Floyd, Eric, Phil.	0	1	0	5	1
Fontenot, Jerry, Chi.	0	1	0	0	1
Fox, Mike, N.Y.G.	0	0	1	2	1
Gannon, Rich, Wash.	3	1	0	0	1
Gardocki, Chris, Chi.	1	1	0	0	1
Garrett, Jason, Dall.	1	0	0	-2	0
Gary, Cleveland, Rams	1	0	0	0	0
Gedney, Chris, Chi.	1	0	0	0	0
Gibson, Dennis, Det.	0	0	1	2	1
Gordon, Dwayne, Atl.	1	0	0	0	0
Gray, Jerry, T.B.	0	1	0	3	1
Gray, Mel, Det.	3	0	0	0	0
Green, Darrell, Wash.	0	0	2	86	2
Guliford, Eric, Minn.	1	0	0	0	0
Guyton, Myron, N.Y.G.	0	1	0	0	1
Haley, Charles, Dall.	0	0	1	0	1
Hamilton, Keith, N.Y.G.	0	0	1	10	1
Hamilton, Rick, Wash.	0	0	1	0	1
Hampton, Rodney, N.Y.G.	2	1	0	0	1
Hanks, Merton, S.F.	0	1	0	0	1
Harbaugh, Jim, Chi.	15	4	0	-1	4
Harmon, Andy, Phil.	0	0	2	0	2
Harper, Alvin, Dall.	1	0	0	0	0
Harper, Roger, Atl.	1	0	1	0	1
Hauck, Tim, G.B.	0	0	1	0	1
Hawkins, Courtney, T.B.	2	0	0	0	0
Haynes, Michael, Atl.	1	0	0	0	0
Hearst, Garrison, Phx.	2	0	0	0	0
Hebert, Bobby, Atl.	11	3	0	-9	3
Hebron, Vaughn, Phil.	5	1	0	0	1
Henley, Darryl, Rams	0	0	1	0	1
Heyward, Craig, Chi.	1	0	0	0	0
Hilgenberg, Jay, N.O.	1	0	0	-2	0
Hilgenberg, Joel, N.O.	1	0	0	-19	0
Hill, Eric, Phx.	0	0	1	0	1
Hilliard, Dalton, N.O.	2	3	0	0	3
Holland, Johnny, G.B.	2	0	2	0	2
Holman, Rodney, Det.	1	0	0	0	0
Holmes, Lester, Phil.	0	1	0	0	1
Hopkins, Wes, Phil.	0	0	2	8	2
Hudson, John, Phil.	1	0	0	-14	0
Irwin, Tim, Minn.	0	1	0	0	1
Ismail, Qadry, Minn.	1	0	0	0	0
Jackson, Greg, N.Y.G.	0	1	2	3	3
Jackson, Mark, N.Y.G.	1	0	0	0	0
Jackson, Rickey, N.O.	0	0	3	3	3
Joffrion, Greg, Det.	0	1	0	0	1
Jenkins, Carlos, Minn.	0	0	1	0	1
Jenkins, Mel, Atl.	0	0	1	0	1
Jennings, Keith, Chi.	1	1	0	0	1
Johnson, A. J., Wash.	0	1	0	0	1
Johnson, John, S.F.	0	0	1	7	1
Johnson, Maurice, Phil.	1	1	0	0	1
Johnson, Tim, Wash.	0	0	1	0	1
Johnston, Daryl, Dall.	1	1	0	0	1
Jones, Brent, S.F.	2	2	0	0	2
Jones, Dante, Chi.	1	1	2	32	3
Jones, Roger, T.B.	0	1	2	12	3
Kauahi, Kani, Phx.	1	0	0	-35	0
Kelm, Larry, S.F.	1	1	0	0	1
Kennedy, Lincoln, Atl.	0	1	0	0	1
Kinchen, Todd, Rams	1	0	0	0	0
King, Joe, T.B.	0	0	2	0	2
Koonce, George, G.B.	0	0	1	0	1
Kosar, Bernie, Clev.-Dall.	6	3	0	-13	3
Kramer, Erik, Det.	1	0	0	0	0
Lassic, Derrick, Dall.	2	1	0	0	1
LeBel, Harper, Atl.	1	0	0	-26	0
Lee, Amp, S.F.	1	0	0	0	0
Lee, Carl, Minn.	0	0	1	0	1
Lett, Leon, Dall.	1	0	0	0	0
Logan, Marc, S.F.	2	1	0	0	1
Lyght, Todd, Rams	0	0	1	13	1
Lynch, Eric, Det.	1	0	0	0	0
Lynch, Lorenzo, Phx.	0	0	3	55	3
Marion, Brock, Dall.	0	0	1	0	1
Martin, Chris, Rams	0	0	1	0	1
Martin, Wayne, N.O.	0	0	2	7	2
Maryland, Russell, Dall.	0	0	2	0	2
Massey, Robert, Phx.	0	0	2	0	2

213

	Fum.	Own Rec.	Opp. Rec.	Yards	Tot. Rec.
May, Mark, Phx.	0	1	0	0	1
Mayberry, Tony, T.B.	1	1	0	-6	1
Mays, Alvoid, Wash.	1	0	0	0	0
McAfee, Fred, N.O.	3	0	0	0	0
McDonald, Tim, S.F.	0	0	1	15	1
McDowell, Anthony, T.B.	2	1	0	0	1
McIntyre, Guy, S.F.	0	2	0	0	2
McKyer, Tim, Det.	0	0	1	23	1
McMahon, Jim, Minn.	4	1	0	-7	1
McMichael, Steve, Chi.	0	0	2	0	2
McMillian, Audray, Minn.	0	0	1	0	1
McMillian, Mark, Phil.	1	0	1	0	1
McNeal, Travis, Rams	0	1	0	0	1
Meggett, David, N.Y.G.	1	1	0	0	1
Miano, Rich, Phil.	0	0	1	0	1
Middleton, Ron, Wash.	0	1	0	0	1
Millard, Keith, Phil.	0	0	1	0	1
Miller, Chris, Atl.	2	0	0	0	0
Miller, Corey, N.Y.G.	1	0	2	0	2
Mills, Sam, N.O.	0	0	1	30	1
Mitchell, Brian, Wash.	3	1	0	0	1
Moore, Dave, T.B.	0	0	1	0	1
Moore, Derrick, Det.	4	3	0	0	3
Moore, Herman, Det.	2	0	0	0	0
Moore, Ron, Phx.	3	1	0	0	1
Morrissey, Jim, G.B.	0	0	1	0	1
Muster, Brad, N.O.	0	0	1	0	1
Neal, Lorenzo, N.O.	1	0	0	0	0
Ned, Derrick, N.O.	1	0	0	0	0
Newberry, Tom, Rams	0	1	0	0	1
Nickerson, Hardy, T.B.	0	0	1	0	1
Noble, Brian, G.B.	0	0	1	0	1
Noga, Al, Wash.	0	0	1	0	1
Norton, Ken, Dall.	0	0	1	3	1
Novacek, Jay, Dall.	3	1	0	0	1
Nunn, Freddie Joe, Phx.	0	0	1	0	1
Obee, Terry, Chi.	1	1	0	0	1
O'Brien, Ken, Phil.	4	0	0	0	0
Owens, Dan, Det.	0	0	2	17	2
Peete, Rodney, Det.	11	4	0	-8	4
Pegram, Erric, Atl.	6	4	0	0	4
Perriman, Brett, Det.	1	0	0	0	0
Pete, Lawrence, Det.	0	0	2	0	2
Phifer, Roman, Rams	0	0	2	10	2
Pierce, Aaron, N.Y.G.	2	0	0	0	0
Port, Chris, N.O.	0	1	0	0	1
Prior, Mike, G.B.	3	2	0	0	2
Pritchard, Mike, Atl.	1	0	0	0	0
Proehl, Ricky, Phx.	1	0	0	0	0
Reeves, Walter, Phx.	0	1	0	0	1
Rice, Jerry, S.F.	3	1	0	0	1
Richards, David, Det.	0	1	0	0	1
Rison, Andre, Atl.	2	0	0	0	0
Roberts, William, N.Y.G.	0	1	0	0	1
Roby, Reggie, Wash.	0	1	0	0	1
Romanowski, Bill, S.F.	0	0	1	0	1
Roper, John, Phil.	0	0	1	0	1
Rose, Ken, Phil.	0	1	0	0	1
Rubley, T. J., Rams	4	2	0	-18	2
Rucker, Keith, Phx.	0	0	1	0	1
Ruettgers, Ken, G.B.	0	2	0	0	2
Russell, Damien, S.F.	0	0	1	0	1
Rypien, Mark, Wash.	7	0	0	-2	0
Salisbury, Sean, Minn.	3	1	0	-9	1
Sanders, Barry, Det.	3	3	0	0	3
Sanders, Ricky, Wash.	1	1	0	0	1
Schad, Mike, Phil.	0	1	0	0	1
Schlereth, Mark, Wash.	0	1	0	0	1
Scott, Kevin, Det.	0	0	1	22	1
Scott, Todd, Minn.	0	0	1	0	1
Scroggins, Tracy, Det.	0	0	1	0	1
Seals, Ray, T.B.	0	0	1	0	1
Sharpe, Sterling, G.B.	1	0	0	0	0
Sherman, Heath, Phil.	3	0	0	0	0
Sikahema, Vai, Phil.	4	0	0	0	0
Simmons, Ed, Wash.	0	1	0	0	1
Simmons, Wayne, G.B.	0	1	0	0	1
Simms, Phil, N.Y.G.	7	3	0	-13	3
Smith, Chuck, Atl.	0	0	2	0	2
Smith, Darrin, Dall.	0	0	1	0	1
Smith, Emmitt, Dall.	4	3	0	0	3
Smith, Irv, N.O.	1	1	0	0	1
Smith, Kevin, Dall.	0	0	1	14	1
Smith, Lance, Phx.	0	2	0	0	2
Smith, Tony, Atl.	4	1	0	0	1
Solomon, Jesse, Atl.	0	0	1	0	1
Spencer, Jimmy, N.O.	0	0	3	53	3
Spielman, Chris, Det.	0	0	2	0	2
Spindler, Marc, Det.	0	0	2	0	2
Stepnoski, Mark, Dall.	1	0	0	-1	0
Stokes, Fred, Rams	0	0	2	51	2
Strickland, Fred, Minn.	0	0	4	4	4
Swann, Eric, Phx.	0	0	1	0	1
Swilling, Pat, Det.	0	0	1	0	1
Sydner, Jeff, Phil.	3	0	0	0	0
Tamm, Ralph, S.F.	0	1	0	1	1
Tate, David, N.Y.G.	1	0	0	0	0
Taylor, John, S.F.	1	0	0	0	0
Taylor, Keith, N.O.	0	1	0	0	1
Taylor, Lawrence, N.Y.G.	0	0	1	0	1
Teague, George, G.B.	0	0	2	0	2
Thomas, Broderick, T.B.	0	0	1	0	1
Thomas, Johnny, Wash.	0	1	1	0	2
Thomas, Mark, S.F.	0	0	1	0	1
Thomas, William, Phil.	0	0	3	0	3
Thompson, Darrell, G.B.	2	1	0	0	1
Tice, Mike, Minn.	1	0	0	0	0
Tillman, Lewis, N.Y.G.	1	0	0	-19	0
Tippins, Kenny, Atl.	0	0	1	0	1
Tuggle, Jessie, Atl.	0	0	1	0	1
Tuinei, Mark, Dall.	0	1	0	0	1
Turnbull, Renaldo, N.O.	0	0	2	0	2
Turner, Odessa, S.F.	1	0	0	0	0
Turner, Vernon, Det.	1	0	0	0	0
Walker, Herschel, Phil.	3	2	0	0	2
Wallace, Steve, S.F.	0	0	1	0	1
Walls, Wesley, S.F.	0	1	0	0	1
Warren, Frank, N.O.	0	0	1	47	1
Washington, Charles, Atl.	0	0	2	0	2
Washington, James, Dall.	1	0	1	0	1
Washington, Ted, S.F.	0	0	1	0	1
Watters, Ricky, S.F.	5	1	0	0	1
White, Reggie, G.B.	0	1	1	10	2
Whitfield, Bob, Atl.	0	2	0	0	2
Williams, Aeneas, Phx.	0	0	2	20	2
Williams, Jimmy, T.B.	0	0	1	0	1
Williams, Kevin, Dall.	8	4	0	0	4
Willis, James, G.B.	0	1	0	0	1
Willis, Peter Tom, Chi.	2	1	0	0	1
Wilmsmeyer, Klaus, S.F.	2	1	0	-10	1
Wilson, Charles, T.B.	1	2	0	0	2
Wilson, Marcus, G.B.	1	0	1	0	1
Wilson, Wade, N.O.	9	4	0	-3	4
Wojciechowski, John, Chi.	0	2	0	0	2
Woodson, Darren, Dall.	0	0	3	3	3
Word, Barry, Minn.	3	0	0	0	0
Workman, Vince, T.B.	2	1	0	0	1
Worley, Tim, Chi.	3	0	0	0	0
Wycheck, Frank, Wash.	1	1	0	0	1
Young, Steve, S.F.	8	2	0	-4	2
Zorich, Chris, Chi.	0	0	2	0	2

Yards includes aborted plays, own recoveries, and opponents' recoveries.

SACKS

Most Sacks

AFC:	15.0—Neil Smith, Kansas City
NFC:	13.0—Renaldo Turnbull, New Orleans
	Reggie White, Green Bay

Most Sacks, Game

AFC:	4.0—Anthony Smith, Raiders at Seattle, September 12
	Neil Smith, Kansas City vs. Raiders, October 3
	William Fuller, Houston vs. Pittsburgh, November 28
NFC:	4.0—Sean Gilbert, Rams vs. Pittsburgh, September 12

Team Champion

AFC:	52—Houston
NFC:	51—New Orleans

AFC SACKS—TEAM

	Sacks	Yards
Houston	52	313
Cleveland	48	342
Denver	46	238
L.A. Raiders	45	283
Pittsburgh	42	277
Seattle	38	244
Buffalo	37	256
Kansas City	35	228
New England	34	242
San Diego	32	206
N.Y. Jets	32	195
Miami	29	197
Cincinnati	22	154
Indianapolis	21	121
AFC Total	513	3296
AFC Average	36.6	235.4

NFC SACKS—TEAM

	Sacks	Yards
New Orleans	51	318
Green Bay	46	301
Chicago	46	287
Minnesota	45	276
San Francisco	44	316
Detroit	43	253
N.Y. Giants	41	238
Philadelphia	36	214
L.A. Rams	35	203
Phoenix	34	205
Dallas	34	231
Washington	31	197
Tampa Bay	29	132
Atlanta	27	149
NFC Total	542	3320
NFC Average	38.7	237.1
League Total	1055	6616
League Average	37.7	236.3

NFL TOP TEN LEADERS - SACKS

	Total
Smith, Neil, K.C.	15.0
Smith, Bruce, Buff.	14.0
Fletcher, Simon, Den.	13.5
Jones, Sean, Hou.	13.0
Turnbull, Renaldo, N.O.	13.0
White, Reggie, G.B.	13.0
Dent, Richard, Chi.	12.5
Doleman, Chris, Minn.	12.5
Greene, Kevin, Pitt.	12.5
Randle, John, Minn.	12.5
Smith, Anthony, Raid.	12.5

AFC SACKS—INDIVIDUAL

Smith, Neil, K.C.	15.0
Smith, Bruce, Buff.	14.0
Fletcher, Simon, Den.	13.5
Jones, Sean, Hou.	13.0
Greene, Kevin, Pitt.	12.5
Smith, Anthony, Raid.	12.5
O'Neal, Leslie, S.D.	12.0
Pleasant, Anthony, Clev.	11.0
Cross, Jeff, Mia.	10.5
Fuller, William, Hou.	10.0
Burnett, Rob, Clev.	9.0
Childress, Ray, Hou.	9.0
Mecklenburg, Karl, Den.	9.0
Slade, Chris, N.E.	9.0
Lageman, Jeff, N.Y.J.	8.5
Tippett, Andre, N.E.	8.5
Sinclair, Mike, Sea.	8.0
Thomas, Derrick, K.C.	8.0
Townsend, Greg, Raid.	7.5
Dronett, Shane, Den.	7.0
McGlockton, Chester, Raid.	7.0
Mims, Chris, S.D.	7.0
Evans, Donald, Pitt.	6.5
Kennedy, Cortez, Sea.	6.5
Lloyd, Greg, Pitt.	6.0
Long, Howie, Raid.	6.0
Montgomery, Glenn, Hou.	6.0
Perry, Michael Dean, Clev.	6.0
Coleman, Marco, Mia.	5.5
Hand, Jon, Ind.	5.5
Jones, James, Clev.	5.5
Matthews, Clay, Clev.	5.5
Washington, Marvin, N.Y.J.	5.5
Bennett, Cornelius, Buff.	5.0
Cox, Bryan, Mia.	5.0
Croel, Mike, Den.	5.0
Lake, Carnell, Pitt.	5.0
Stubbs, Danny, Cinn.	5.0
Grossman, Burt, S.D.	4.5
Wright, Jeff, Buff.	4.5
Johnson, Mike, Clev.	4.0
Lewis, Mo, N.Y.J.	4.0
McCrary, Michael, Sea.	4.0
Williams, Alfred, Cinn.	4.0
Bickett, Duane, Ind.	3.5
Hansen, Phil, Buff.	3.5
Jones, Aaron, N.E.	3.5
Robinson, Jeff, Den.	3.5
Saleaumua, Dan, K.C.	3.5
Tuatagaloa, Natu, Sea.	3.5
Ball, Jerry, Clev.	3.0
Brown, Chad, Pitt.	3.0
Copeland, John, Cinn.	3.0
Edwards, Antonio, Sea.	3.0
Harrison, Nolan, Raid.	3.0
Houston, Bobby, N.Y.J.	3.0
Hunter, Jeff, Mia.	3.0
Kragen, Greg, Den.	3.0
Krumrie, Tim, Cinn.	3.0
Lee, Shawn, S.D.	3.0
Pitts, Mike, N.E.	3.0
Williams, Lee, Hou.	3.0
Davidson, Kenny, Pitt.	2.5
Stephens, Rod, Sea.	2.5
Wooden, Terry, Sea.	2.5
Barnett, Oliver, Buff.	2.0
Bruce, Aundray, Raid.	2.0
Francis, James, Cinn.	2.0
Herrod, Jeff, Ind.	2.0
Jones, Henry, Buff.	2.0
Lathon, Lamar, Hou.	2.0
Marshall, Leonard, N.Y.J.	2.0
Marshall, Wilber, Hou.	2.0
Marts, Lonnie, K.C.	2.0
Peguese, Willis, Ind.	2.0
Richard, Stanley, S.D.	2.0
Robinson, Eugene, Sea.	2.0
Sabb, Dwayne, N.E.	2.0
Talley, Darryl, Buff.	2.0
Veasey, Craig, Mia.	2.0
Wallace, Aaron, Raid.	2.0
Williams, Brent, N.E.	2.0
Williams, Darryl, Cinn.	2.0
Winter, Blaise, S.D.	2.0
Woodson, Rod, Pitt.	2.0
Wyman, David, Den.	2.0
Agnew, Ray, N.E.	1.5
Klingbeil, Chuck, Mia.	1.5
McClendon, Skip, Ind.	1.5
Phillips, Joe, K.C.	1.5
Robinson, Rafael, Sea.	1.5
Siragusa, Tony, Ind.	1.5
Steed, Joel, Pitt.	1.5
Alexander, Bruce, Mia.	1.0
Anderson, Eddie, Raid.	1.0
Atwater, Steve, Den.	1.0
Barrow, Micheal, Hou.	1.0
Bayless, Martin, K.C.	1.0
Bishop, Blaine, Hou.	1.0
Bowden, Joe, Hou.	1.0
Broughton, Willie, Raid.	1.0
Brown, Vincent, N.E.	1.0
Bryant, Jeff, Sea.	1.0
Carrington, Darren, S.D.	1.0
Clancy, Sam, Ind.	1.0
Clifton, Kyle, N.Y.J.	1.0
Collins, Todd, N.E.	1.0
Coryatt, Quentin, Ind.	1.0
Emtman, Steve, Ind.	1.0
Footman, Dan, Clev.	1.0
Frase, Paul, N.Y.J.	1.0
Frier, Mike, Cinn.	1.0
Goganious, Keith, Buff.	1.0
Gray, Carlton, Sea.	1.0
Henry, Kevin, Pitt.	1.0
Hinkle, George, Cinn.	1.0
Hurst, Maurice, N.E.	1.0
Johnson, Pepper, N.Y.J.	1.0
Johnson, William, Clev.	1.0
Jones, Don, N.Y.J.	1.0
Kelly, Joe, Raid.	1.0
Kirkland, Levon, Pitt.	1.0
Lott, Ronnie, N.Y.J.	1.0
McDonald, Ricardo, Cinn.	1.0
McDowell, Bubba, Hou.	1.0
Mersereau, Scott, N.Y.J.	1.0
Mickell, Darren, K.C.	1.0
Newton, Tim, K.C.	1.0
Oshodin, Willie, Den.	1.0
Parrella, John, Buff.	1.0
Patton, Marvcus, Buff.	1.0
Porter, Rufus, Sea.	1.0
Robinson, Eddie, Hou.	1.0
Rodgers, Tyrone, Sea.	1.0
Sims, Tom, Ind.	1.0
Stargell, Tony, Ind.	1.0
Teeter, Mike, Hou.	1.0
Terry, Doug, K.C.	1.0
Thompson, Reyna, N.E.	1.0
Turner, Marcus, N.Y.J.	1.0
Walls, Everson, Clev.	1.0
Washington, Lionel, Raid.	1.0
Williams, Dan, Den.	1.0
Williams, Gerald, Pitt.	1.0
Young, Lonnie, N.Y.J.	1.0
Goad, Tim, N.E.	0.5
Griggs, David, Mia.	0.5
Lodish, Mike, Buff.	0.5
Nash, Joe, Sea.	0.5
Pope, Marquez, S.D.	0.5
Ross, Kevin, K.C.	0.5
Thompson, Bennie, K.C.	0.5
Washington, Mickey, Buff.	0.5

NFC SACKS—INDIVIDUAL

Turnbull, Renaldo, N.O.	13.0
White, Reggie, G.B.	13.0
Dent, Richard, Chi.	12.5
Doleman, Chris, Minn.	12.5
Randle, John, Minn.	12.5
Armstrong, Trace, Chi.	11.5
Hamilton, Keith, N.Y.G.	11.5
Harmon, Andy, Phil.	11.5
Jackson, Rickey, N.O.	11.5
Paup, Bryce, G.B.	11.0

215

Gilbert, Sean, Rams	10.5	Case, Scott, Atl.	1.5
Stubblefield, Dana, S.F.	10.5	Conner, Darion, Atl.	1.5
Harvey, Ken, Phx.	9.5	Edwards, Dixon, Dall.	1.5
Stokes, Fred, Rams	9.5	Gouveia, Kurt, Wash.	1.5
Thomas, Henry, Minn.	9.0	McGhee, Kanavis, N.Y.G.	1.5
Porcher, Robert, Det.	8.5	Roberts, Larry, S.F.	1.5
Seals, Ray, T.B.	8.5	Smith, Artie, S.F.	1.5
Scroggins, Tracy, Det.	8.0	Stowe, Tyronne, Phx.	1.5
Tolbert, Tony, Dall.	7.5	White, William, Det.	1.5
Young, Robert, Rams	7.0	Atkins, Gene, N.O.	1.0
Zorich, Chris, Chi.	7.0	Banks, Carl, Wash.	1.0
Bennett, Tony, G.B.	6.5	Boutte, Marc, Rams	1.0
Holt, Pierce, Atl.	6.5	Brooks, Michael, N.Y.G.	1.0
Miller, Corey, N.Y.G.	6.5	Butler, LeRoy, G.B.	1.0
Nunn, Freddie Joe, Phx.	6.5	Clay, Willie, Det.	1.0
Swilling, Pat, Det.	6.5	Collins, Mark, N.Y.G.	1.0
Thomas, William, Phil.	6.5	Colon, Harry, Det.	1.0
Barker, Roy, Minn.	6.0	Cook, Toi, N.O.	1.0
Coleman, Monte, Wash.	6.0	Crockett, Ray, Det.	1.0
Collins, Andre, Wash.	6.0	Davis, Reuben, Phx.	1.0
Harrison, Martin, S.F.	6.0	Fagan, Kevin, S.F.	1.0
Jeffcoat, Jim, Dall.	6.0	Faulkner, Jeff, Wash.	1.0
McMichael, Steve, Chi.	6.0	Fontenot, Albert, Chi.	1.0
Taylor, Lawrence, N.Y.G.	6.0	Gann, Mike, Atl.	1.0
Brown, Dennis, S.F.	5.5	Gayle, Shaun, Chi.	1.0
Jones, Jimmie, Dall.	5.5	George, Ron, Atl.	1.0
Jurkovic, John, G.B.	5.5	Gibson, Dennis, Det.	1.0
Wilson, Troy, S.F.	5.5	Hager, Britt, Phil.	1.0
Curry, Eric, T.B.	5.0	Harris, Robert, Minn.	1.0
Dotson, Santana, T.B.	5.0	Henderson, Wymon, Rams	1.0
Johnson, Vaughan, N.O.	5.0	Hill, Eric, Phx.	1.0
Martin, Wayne, N.O.	5.0	Jones, Dante, Chi.	1.0
Simmons, Clyde, Phil.	5.0	Jones, Reggie, N.O.	1.0
Fox, Mike, N.Y.G.	4.5	Jones, Roger, T.B.	1.0
Palmer, Sterling, Wash.	4.5	Kelly, Todd, S.F.	1.0
Haley, Charles, Dall.	4.0	Logan, Ernie, Atl.	1.0
Johnson, Tim, Wash.	4.0	London, Antonio, Det.	1.0
Millard, Keith, Phil.	4.0	Lynch, Lorenzo, Phx.	1.0
Noga, Al, Wash.	4.0	Mann, Charles, Wash.	1.0
Pritchett, Kelvin, Det.	4.0	Nickerson, Hardy, T.B.	1.0
Geathers, James, Atl.	3.5	Oldham, Chris, Phx.	1.0
Howard, Erik, N.Y.G.	3.5	Patterson, Shawn, G.B.	1.0
Smith, Chuck, Atl.	3.5	Perry, William, Phil.	1.0
Swann, Eric, Phx.	3.5	Reynolds, Ricky, T.B.	1.0
Bankston, Michael, Phx.	3.0	Rocker, David, Rams	1.0
Booty, John, Phx.	3.0	Sheppard, Ashley, Minn.	1.0
Buck, Vince, N.O.	3.0	Simmons, Wayne, G.B.	1.0
Dillard, Stacey, N.Y.G.	3.0	Smeenge, Joel, N.O.	1.0
Flores, Mike, Phil.	3.0	Smith, Darrin, Dall.	1.0
Jones, Mike, Phx.	3.0	Stewart, Michael, Rams	1.0
Koonce, George, G.B.	3.0	Strahan, Michael, N.Y.G.	1.0
Owens, Dan, Det.	3.0	Thomas, Broderick, T.B.	1.0
Price, Shawn, T.B.	3.0	Warren, Frank, N.O.	1.0
Robinson, Gerald, Rams	3.0	Woods, Tony, Rams	1.0
Romanowski, Bill, S.F.	3.0	Del Rio, Jack, Minn.	0.5
Washington, Ted, S.F.	3.0	Simpson, Carl, Chi.	0.5
Wilson, Karl, S.F.	3.0	Spielman, Chris, Det.	0.5
Agee, Mel, Atl.	2.5	Thomas, Mark, S.F.	0.5
Jenkins, Carlos, Minn.	2.5		
Maryland, Russell, Dall.	2.5		
Miller, Les, N.O.	2.5		
Spellman, Alonzo, Chi.	2.5		
Allen, Eric, Phil.	2.0		
Brock, Matt, G.B.	2.0		
Casillas, Tony, Dall.	2.0		
Cox, Ron, Chi.	2.0		
Gardner, Moe, Atl.	2.0		
Goff, Robert, N.O.	2.0		
Hayworth, Tracy, Det.	2.0		
Holland, Johnny, G.B.	2.0		
Jamison, George, Det.	2.0		
Johnson, John, S.F.	2.0		
Joyner, Seth, Phil.	2.0		
Mills, Sam, N.O.	2.0		
Norton, Ken, Dall.	2.0		
Roper, John, Dall.	2.0		
Spindler, Marc, Det.	2.0		
Tuggle, Jessie, Atl.	2.0		
Wheeler, Mark, T.B.	2.0		
Williams, James, N.O.	2.0		
Wilson, Bobby, Wash.	2.0		
Ahanotu, Chidi, T.B.	1.5		
Bailey, Carlton, N.Y.G.	1.5		

1993 NFL PAID ATTENDANCE BREAKDOWN

	Games	Attendance	Average
AFC Preseason	10	517,195	51,720
NFC Preseason	14	755,187	53,942
AFC-NFC Preseason, Interconference	37	1,897,999	51,297
NFL Preseason Total	**61**	**3,170,381**	**51,973**
AFC Regular Season	86	5,474,280	63,654
NFC Regular Season	86	5,264,255	61,212
AFC-NFC Regular Season, Interconference	52	3,228,308	62,083
NFL Regular Season Total	**224**	***13,966,843**	***62,352**
AFC Wild Card Playoffs	2		
Denver at Los Angeles Raiders		63,236	
Pittsburgh at Kansas City		77,588	
AFC Divisional Playoffs	2		
Los Angeles Raiders at Buffalo		71,123	
Kansas City at Houston		63,712	
AFC Championship Game	1		
Kansas City at Buffalo		77,824	
NFC Wild Card Playoffs	2		
Minnesota at New York Giants		76,828	
Green Bay at Detroit		69,789	
NFC Divisional Playoffs	2		
Green Bay at Dallas		64,142	
New York Giants at San Francisco		67,130	
NFC Championship Game	1		
San Francisco at Dallas		64,552	
Super Bowl XXVIII at Atlanta, Georgia	1		
Buffalo vs. Dallas		70,783	
AFC-NFC Pro Bowl at Honolulu, Hawaii	1	47,900	
NFL Postseason Total	**12**	**814,607**	**67,884**
NFL All Games	**297**	***17,951,831**	**60,444**

All-time record

ONE MILLION PLUS CLUB

During the 1993 season, 10 clubs drew a combined home and away paid attendance of more than 1 million. The Kansas City Chiefs drew an NFL-leading 1,144,109 fans in 1993.

Team	Total Paid Home Attendance	Total Paid Visiting Attendance	Total Paid Attendance
Kansas City	617,795	526,314	1,144,109
Buffalo	624,349	518,636	1,142,985
New York Giants	611,057	525,806	1,136,863
Denver	585,986	544,542	1,130,528
Miami	561,627	531,982	1,093,609
New York Jets	606,377	486,045	1,092,422
San Francisco	537,718	527,824	1,065,542
Dallas	505,422	536,434	1,041,856
Chicago	527,515	508,313	1,035,828
Cleveland	572,281	451,307	1,023,588
New Orleans	533,407	475,918	1,009,325
Philadelphia	521,804	483,083	1,004,887
Pittsburgh	473,910	529,669	1,003,579

Note: *For complete year-by-year paid attendance and attendance records, see page 337.*

Inside the Numbers

75 NOTES FOR THE NFL'S 75TH SEASON

1. Phil Simms of the New York Giants needs 1 touchdown pass to become the sixteenth player to throw 200 touchdown passes in his NFL career.
2. In the first change in scoring rules in NFL history, teams may opt for a 2-point conversion following touchdowns this season.
3. With 3 more touchdowns, San Francisco's Jerry Rice would break Jim Brown's all-time NFL record of 126 touchdowns.
4. If he recovers 4 more opponents' fumbles, the Saints' Rickey Jackson would break the all-time record of 29 held by Jim Marshall.
5. Five NFL teams have new head coaches: Arizona, Buddy Ryan; Atlanta, June Jones; Dallas, Barry Switzer; New York Jets, Pete Carroll; Washington, Norv Turner.
6. The Pro Football Hall of Fame enshrines six former players and coaches this year: Tony Dorsett, Bud Grant, Jimmy Johnson, Leroy Kelly, Jackie Smith, and Randy White.
7. The Houston Oilers are the only NFL team that has reached the playoffs in each of the past 7 seasons.
8. Eight Super Bowl champions have failed to reach the playoffs the following season, most recently the New York Giants in 1991.
9. With 9 more rushing touchdowns, Kansas City's Marcus Allen would become just the fourth player in NFL history to score 100 touchdowns on the ground.
10. The New York Giants have allowed the fewest points in the league in 10 different seasons, an all-time NFL record.
11. Minnesota's Roger Craig needs 11 more carries to become the eleventh player in NFL history with 2,000 career carries.
12. With 12 more kickoff returns, Detroit's Mel Gray would break the all-time NFL record of 275 kickoff returns held by Ron Smith.
13. The San Francisco 49ers have won 13 division titles since the 1970 AFL-NFL merger, the most by any team.
14. The most successful 2-point conversions in any one season in the 10-year history of the American Football League was 14 in 1961.
15. Buffalo's Thurman Thomas has scored 15 touchdowns in postseason play, 2 shy of the NFL record held by Franco Harris.
16. The AFC-NFC Pro Bowl will be played in Honolulu for the sixteenth consecutive year on February 5, 1995.
17. The 1994 regular season will be played over 17 weeks, with each team having only one bye week, instead of two as in 1993.
18. The Cleveland Browns have finished the regular season in first place in their division or conference 18 times, an all-time NFL record.
19. This is the nineteenth season for the Seattle Seahawks and Tampa Bay Buccaneers, the most recent expansion teams prior to the Carolina Panthers and Jacksonville Jaguars, who were selected in 1993.
20. The San Diego Chargers are the only NFL team that did not allow a 20-yard rushing play last season.
21. The youngest player to appear in the NFL in 1993 was Tom Carter of the Washington Redskins; he turned 21 last September 5.
22. Morten Andersen of the New Orleans Saints has made 22 field goals of 50-or-more yards, the highest career total by any player in NFL history.
23. The New York Giants have reached postseason play 23 times, the most such appearances by any team in NFL history.
24. There have been 24 games played in the AFC-NFC Pro Bowl series, with the NFC holding a 14-10 series advantage.
25. This is the twenty-fifth season of ABC's NFL Monday Night Football, the longest-running prime-time series in the history of the ABC network.
26. The Dallas Cowboys have won 26 postseason games since the 1970 AFL-NFL merger, the most by any team.
27. The Miami Dolphins won an NFL-record 27 consecutive home games, 1971-74. In the 20 years since, the longest streak is 18 by Dallas, 1979-1981.
28. The Saints' Morten Andersen has scored in 158 consecutive games; that's 28 games shy of the NFL record, held by Jim Breech.
29. The Green Bay Packers allowed only 29 points in the first quarter last season, the fewest by any NFL team.
30. The Raiders have won 30 games on ABC's NFL Monday Night Football, the most by any team in the history of the series.
31. Philadelphia's Jeff Feagles's 31 punts inside-the-20 were the most by any player in the NFL in 1993.
32. Miami's Don Shula is in his thirty-second season as an NFL head coach, 8 years shy of George Halas's record.
33. Paul Hornung's NFL single-season scoring record of 176 points, established in a 12-game schedule in 1960, has survived for 33 years.
34. There have been 34 players in NFL history who have passed for 25,000-or-more yards; Jim Everett (23,758) of the Saints could be the next to reach that mark.
35. Steve DeBerg needs 35 more passes to become the sixth player in NFL history with 5,000 career passes.
36. The Bills' Thurman Thomas has 36 career 100-yard rushing games, the most by any active NFL player.
37. The San Francisco 49ers have retired uniform number 37 in honor of former defensive back Jimmy Johnson, a 1994 Hall of Fame inductee.
38. Phil Simms of the Giants, who turned 38 during the 1993 season, was the oldest NFL player to start every game last season.
39. At age 39, Steve DeBerg was the oldest player in the NFL in 1993; he turned 40 on January 19, 1994.
40. 1994 Pro Football Hall of Fame inductee Jackie Smith had 40 touchdown receptions in his NFL career.
41. Dick (Night Train) Lane's NFL single-season record of 14 interceptions, set in a 12-game schedule in 1952, has survived for 41 years.
42. The Buffalo Bills allowed only 42 points in the fourth quarter last season, the fewest by any team in the NFL.
43. Kansas City's Joe Montana has thrown 43 touchdown passes in post-season play; no other player in NFL history has thrown more than 30.
44. Miami's Dan Marino starts the season with 298 touchdown passes; that's 44 behind the total of all-time NFL record-holder Fran Tarkenton.
45. Kansas City's Nick Lowery needs 45 more field goals to break the NFL record of 373, established by Hall of Famer Jan Stenerud.
46. Once again in 1994, NFL teams will be permitted to dress 46 players (including an emergency quarterback) for each NFL game.
47. The Buffalo Bills led the NFL with 47 takeaways last season.
48. Dan Marino threw an NFL-record 48 touchdown passes in 1984. The only other over-40 total in NFL history: Marino's 44 in 1986.
49. In 1949, two NFL players rushed for 1,000-or-more yards in a season for the first time: Philadelphia's Steve Van Buren and Green Bay's Tony Canadeo.
50. Winning teams (335.6 yards per game) averaged 50 more yards per game than did losing teams (285.7) in the NFL in 1993.
51. It has been 51 years since the NFL's last scoreless tie was played between the Giants and the Lions on November 7, 1943.
52. Of 201 regular-season overtime games over the past 20 years, 52 have ended on touchdowns, 135 on field goals, 1 on a safety, and 13 have ended tied.
53. Elmer Layden was named the first Commissioner of the NFL 53 years ago.
54. 1994 Pro Football Hall of Fame inductee Randy White wore uniform number 54 during his career with the Dallas Cowboys.
55. The San Francisco 49ers scored 55 points at Detroit last December 19, the highest single-game total by any NFL team in 1993.
56. All 56 teams that have played in a Super Bowl played their home games (that season) in an outdoor stadium.
57. Michael Husted's 57-yard field goal in 1993 was the longest in the history of the Tampa Bay Buccaneers.
58. Of the NFL's 224 regular-season games in 1994, 58 have been designated for national television.
59. Jerry Rice of the 49ers needs 59 more yards on receptions to surpass Don Maynard's career total of 11,834 and move into fifth place in NFL history.
60. The first Thanksgiving Day game hosted by the Detroit Lions was played 60 years ago. The visiting Chicago Bears won 19-16 on November 29, 1934.
61. The San Francisco 49ers scored 61 touchdowns in 1993, leading the NFL in that category for the second year in a row.
62. The San Francisco 49ers have won an NFL-high 62 games over the past 5 seasons, 4 more than the runner-up Buffalo Bills.
63. In 13 seasons in the NFL, Ronnie Lott of the New York Jets has made 63 interceptions, the highest total by any active NFL player.
64. Only 64 penalties were enforced against the New England Patriots last season, the fewest against any NFL team.
65. An NFL team has scored 65-or-more points in a regular-season NFL game 4 times; the Los Angeles Rams did it in consecutive weeks in 1950.
66. The NFL record for most takeaways in one season is 66 by the San Diego Chargers in a 14-game season in 1961.
67. In 1967, the NFL adopted as standard the single-stem style of goalpost and a 6-foot border around the playing field.
68. Six feet, eight inches is the height of Seattle Seahawks quarterback Dan McGwire; he's the tallest active quarterback in the NFL.
69. Troy Aikman completed 69 percent of his passes in 1993, the highest rating by any quarterback in the NFL.
70. The New York Giants are in their seventieth season in the NFL. They made their debut on October 11, 1925.
71. Bob Hayes holds the Dallas Cowboys record with 71 touchdown receptions; Michael Irvin, with 34, is less than halfway to that mark.
72. An NFL team played a turnover-free game 72 times last season, or slightly less than one-sixth of the time.
73. The Chicago Bear's 73-0 win over the Washington Redskins in the 1940 NFL Championship Game represents the NFL record for points in a postseason game.
74. 1994 Pro Football Hall of Fame inductee Leroy Kelly scored 74 rushing touchdowns in his career, tied for eleventh place on the all-time list.
75. Chicago is the only city that has been represented in each of the NFL's 75 seasons.

COMPARISON OF JOE MONTANA'S CAREER STATISTICS WITH HALL OF FAME QUARTERBACKS WHOSE CAREERS ENDED SINCE 1945

PASSING	Att.	Comp.	Pct.	Yds.	Avg.	Lng.	TD	Pct.	Int.	Pct.	Rating
Joe Montana	4898	3110	63.5	37,268	7.61	96t	257	5.2	130	2.7	93.1
Sammy Baugh	2995	1693	56.5	21,886	7.31	86t	187	6.2	203	6.8	72.0
George Blanda	4007	1911	47.7	26,920	6.72	95t	236	5.9	277	6.9	60.8
Terry Bradshaw	3901	2025	51.9	27,989	7.17	90t	212	5.4	210	5.4	70.9
Len Dawson	3741	2136	57.1	28,711	7.67	92t	239	6.4	183	4.9	82.6
Dan Fouts	5604	3297	58.8	43,040	7.68	81t	254	4.5	242	4.3	80.2
Otto Graham	1565	872	55.7	13,499	8.63	81t	88	5.6	94	6.0	78.1
Bob Griese	3429	1926	56.2	25,092	7.32	86t	192	5.6	172	5.0	77.1
Arnie Herber*	1175	481	40.9	8,041	6.84	92t	78	6.6	106	9.0	49.3
Sonny Jurgensen	4262	2433	57.1	32,224	7.56	99t	255	6.0	189	4.4	82.8
Bobby Layne	3700	1814	49.0	26,768	7.23	97t	196	5.3	243	6.6	63.4
Sid Luckman	1744	904	51.8	14,686	8.42	86t	137	7.9	132	7.6	75.0
Joe Namath	3762	1886	50.1	27,663	7.35	91	173	4.6	220	5.8	65.6
Bart Starr	3149	1808	57.4	24,718	7.85	91t	152	4.8	138	4.4	80.5
Roger Staubach	2958	1685	57.0	22,700	7.67	91t	153	5.2	109	3.7	83.4
Fran Tarkenton	6467	3686	57.0	47,003	7.27	89t	342	5.3	266	4.1	80.4
Y.A. Tittle	3817	2118	55.5	28,339	7.42	78t	212	5.6	221	5.8	73.8
Johnny Unitas	5186	2830	54.6	40,239	7.76	89t	290	5.6	253	4.9	78.2
Norm Van Brocklin	2895	1553	53.6	23,611	8.16	91t	173	6.0	178	6.1	75.3
Bob Waterfield	1617	814	50.3	11,849	7.33	91t	97	6.0	128	7.9	61.6

RUSHING	Years	Last Year	Games	Att.	Yds.	Avg.	Lng.	TD
Joe Montana	14	1993	178	439	1659	3.8	21	20
Sammy Baugh	16	1952	165	324	325	1.0	41t	9
George Blanda	26	1975	340	135	344	2.5	19	9
Terry Bradshaw	14	1983	168	444	2257	5.1	39	32
Len Dawson	19	1975	211	294	1293	4.4	43	9
Dan Fouts	15	1987	142	224	476	2.1	32	13
Otto Graham	6	1955	72	306	682	2.2	36	33
Bob Griese	14	1980	161	261	994	3.8	35	7
Arnie Herber*	13	1945	x	250	116	0.5	x	2
Sonny Jurgensen	18	1974	218	181	492	2.7	33	15
Bobby Layne	15	1962	175	611	2451	4.0	36	25
Sid Luckman	12	1950	128	204	−239	−1.2	40t	4
Joe Namath	13	1977	140	71	140	2.0	39	7
Bart Starr	16	1971	196	247	1308	5.3	39	15
Roger Staubach	11	1979	131	410	2264	5.5	33	20
Fran Tarkenton	18	1978	246	675	3674	5.4	52t	32
Y.A. Tittle	15	1964	178	291	999	3.4	45	33
Johnny Unitas	18	1973	211	450	1777	3.9	34	13
Norm Van Brocklin	12	1960	140	102	40	0.4	16	11
Bob Waterfield	8	1952	91	75	21	0.3	25	13

*statistics do not include 1930-31 seasons. xUnavailable.

JOE MONTANA'S GAME-BY-GAME POSTSEASON CAREER

Date	Game	Opponent	Att.	Comp.	Pct.	Yds.	Avg.	TD	Int.	Rating
Jan. 3, 1982	NFC Divisional Playoff	N.Y. Giants	31	20	64.5	304	9.81	2	1	104.8
Jan. 10, 1982	NFC Championship Game	Dallas	35	22	62.9	286	8.17	3	3	81.4
Jan. 24, 1982	Super Bowl XVI	Cincinnati	22	14	63.6	157	7.14	1	0	100.0
Dec. 31, 1983	NFC Divisional Playoff	Detroit	31	18	58.1	201	6.48	1	1	74.8
Jan. 8, 1984	NFC Championship Game	Washington	48	27	56.3	347	7.23	3	1	91.2
Dec. 29, 1984	NFC Divisional Playoff	N.Y. Giants	39	25	64.1	309	7.92	3	3	82.1
Jan. 6, 1985	NFC Championship Game	Chicago	34	18	52.9	233	6.85	1	2	60.0
Jan. 20, 1985	Super Bowl XIX	Miami	35	24	68.6	331	9.46	3	0	127.2
Dec. 29, 1985	NFC First-Round Game	N.Y. Giants	47	26	55.3	296	6.30	0	1	65.6
Jan. 4, 1987	NFC Divisional Playoff	N.Y. Giants	15	8	53.3	98	6.53	0	2	34.2
Jan. 9, 1988	NFC Divisional Playoff	Minnesota	26	12	46.2	109	4.19	0	1	42.0
Jan. 1, 1989	NFC Divisional Playoff	Minnesota	27	16	59.3	178	6.59	3	1	100.5
Jan. 8, 1989	NFC Championship Game	Chicago	27	17	63.0	288	10.67	3	0	136.0
Jan. 22, 1989	Super Bowl XXIII	Cincinnati	36	23	63.9	357	9.92	2	0	115.2
Jan. 6, 1990	NFC Divisional Playoff	Minnesota	24	17	70.8	241	10.04	4	0	142.5
Jan. 14, 1990	NFC Championship Game	L.A. Rams	30	26	86.7	262	8.73	2	0	125.3
Jan. 28, 1990	Super Bowl XXIV	Denver	29	22	75.9	297	10.24	5	0	147.6
Jan. 12, 1991	NFC Divisional Playoff	Washington	31	22	71.0	274	8.84	2	1	106.1
Jan. 20, 1991	NFC Championship Game	N.Y. Giants	26	18	69.2	190	7.31	1	0	103.0
Jan. 8, 1994	AFC First-Round Game	Pittsburgh	43	28	65.1	276	6.42	1	0	90.8
Jan. 16, 1994	AFC Divisional Playoff	Houston	38	22	57.9	299	7.87	3	2	87.5
Jan. 23, 1994	AFC Championship Game	Buffalo	23	9	39.1	125	5.43	0	1	39.2
Totals (22 games)			697	434	62.3	5458	7.83	43	20	95.2

HIGHEST NFL POSTSEASON PASSER RATINGS (MINIMUM: 150 ATTEMPTS)

	Games	Att.	Comp.	Pct.	Yds.	Avg. Gain	TD	Int.	Rating
Troy Aikman	7	187	133	71.1	1595	8.53	13	4	111.2
Bart Starr	10	213	130	61.0	1753	8.23	15	3	104.8
Joe Montana	22	697	434	62.3	5458	7.83	43	20	95.2
Ken Anderson	6	166	110	66.3	1321	7.96	9	6	93.5
Joe Theismann	10	211	128	60.7	1782	8.45	11	7	91.4
Steve Young	12	156	106	67.9	1261	8.08	5	5	89.7
Warren Moon	9	351	230	65.5	2578	7.34	15	12	87.3
Ken Stabler	13	351	203	57.8	2641	7.52	19	13	84.2

Bernie Kosar	9	269	151	56.1	1943	7.22	16	10	83.3
Terry Bradshaw	19	456	261	57.2	3833	8.41	30	26	83.0

HIGHEST NFL POSTSEASON PASSER RATINGS, ACTIVE PLAYERS (MINIMUM: 150 ATTEMPTS)

	Games	Att.	Comp.	Pct.	Yds.	Avg.	TD	Int.	Rating
Troy Aikman	7	187	133	71.1	1595	8.53	13	4	111.2
Joe Montana	22	697	434	62.3	5458	7.83	43	20	95.2
Steve Young	12	156	106	67.9	1261	8.08	5	5	89.7
Warren Moon	9	351	230	65.5	2578	7.34	15	12	87.3
Bernie Kosar	9	269	151	56.1	1943	7.22	16	10	83.3
Dan Marino	10	387	212	54.8	2659	6.87	22	14	80.2
Phil Simms	10	279	157	56.3	1679	6.02	10	6	77.0
Jim McMahon	8	155	82	52.9	1112	7.17	5	4	76.1
John Elway	14	431	229	53.1	3321	7.71	19	18	75.8
Wade Wilson	6	185	99	53.5	1322	7.15	7	6	75.6

ALL-TIME RANKINGS OF PLAYERS IN FOUR CATEGORIES THAT DETERMINE NFL PASSER RATING

Minimum: 1500 Attempts

COMPLETION PERCENTAGE

	Pct.	Att.	Comp.
Joe Montana	63.50	4898	3110
Steve Young	62.09	1968	1222
Troy Aikman	62.03	1920	1191
Jim Kelly	60.45	3494	2112
Ken Stabler	59.85	3793	2270
Danny White	59.69	2950	1761
Ken Anderson	59.31	4475	2654
Dan Marino	59.24	5434	3219
Bobby Hebert	58.95	2485	1465
Dan Fouts	58.83	5604	3297

TOUCHDOWN PERCENTAGE

	Pct.	Att.	TD
Sid Luckman	7.86	1744	137
Frank Ryan	6.99	2133	149
Len Dawson	6.39	3741	239
Daryle Lamonica	6.31	2601	164
Sammy Baugh	6.24	2995	187
Charley Conerly	6.11	2833	173
Bob Waterfield	6.00	1617	97
Earl Morrall	5.99	2689	161
Sonny Jurgensen	5.98	4262	255
Norm Van Brocklin	5.98	2895	173

AVERAGE YARDS PER PASS

	Avg.	Att.	Yards
Otto Graham	8.63	1565	13,499
Sid Luckman	8.42	1744	14,686
Norm Van Brocklin	8.16	2895	23,611
Steve Young	8.08	1968	15,900
Ed Brown	7.85	1987	15,600
Bart Starr	7.85	3149	24,718
Johnny Unitas	7.76	5186	40,239
Earl Morrall	7.74	2689	20,809
Dan Fouts	7.68	5604	43,040
Len Dawson	7.67	3741	28,711

INTERCEPTION PERCENTAGE

	Pct.	Att.	Int.
Bernie Kosar	2.52	3213	81
Joe Montana	2.65	4898	130
Ken O'Brien	2.72	3602	98
Neil Lomax	2.85	3153	90
Steve Young	2.95	1968	58
Jeff George	3.00	1532	46
Dan Marino	3.09	5434	168
Randall Cunningham	3.16	2751	87
Jim Harbaugh	3.18	1759	56
Tony Eason	3.26	1564	51

TEAMS THAT FINISHED IN FIRST PLACE IN THEIR DIVISION THE SEASON AFTER FINISHING IN LAST PLACE

Season	Team	Record	Previous Season
1967	Houston	9 - 4 - 1	*3 - 11
1968	Minnesota	8 - 6	3 - 8 - 3
1970	Cincinnati	8 - 6	4 - 9 - 1
1970	San Francisco	10 - 3 - 1	4 - 8 - 2
1972	Green Bay	10 - 4	4 - 8 - 2
1975	Baltimore	10 - 4	2 - 12
1979	Tampa Bay	10 - 6	5 - 11
1981	Cincinnati	12 - 4	6 - 10
1987	Indianapolis	9 - 6	3 - 13
1988	Cincinnati	12 - 4	4 - 11

1990	Cincinnati	9 - 7	8 - 8
1991	Denver	12 - 4	5 - 11
1992	San Diego	11 - 5	4 - 12
1993	Detroit	10 - 6	5 - 11

*tied for last place

RECORDS OF NFL TEAMS, 1984-93

AFC	W - L - T	Pct.	Division Titles	Playoff Berths	Postseason Record	Super Bowl Record
Denver	98 - 60 - 1	.619	5	6	7-6	0-3
Miami	96 - 63 - 0	.604	3	4	5-4	0-1
L.A. Raiders	89 - 70 - 0	.560	2	5	2-5	0-0
Buffalo	85 - 74 - 0	.535	5	6	10-6	0-4
Houston	83 - 76 - 0	.522	2	7	3-7	0-0
Kansas City	82 - 75 - 2	.522	1	5	3-5	0-0
Pittsburgh	80 - 79 - 0	.503	2	4	2-4	0-0
Seattle	79 - 80 - 0	.497	1	3	1-3	0-0
Cleveland	77 - 81 - 1	.487	4	5	3-5	0-0
N.Y. Jets	72 - 86 - 1	.456	0	3	1-3	0-0
Cincinnati	69 - 90 - 0	.434	2	2	3-2	0-1
San Diego	68 - 91 - 0	.428	1	1	1-1	0-0
New England	67 - 92 - 0	.421	1	2	3-2	0-1
Indianapolis	59 - 100 - 0	.371	1	1	0-1	0-0

NFC	W - L - T	Pct.	Division Titles	Playoff Berths	Postseason Record	Super Bowl Record
San Francisco	120 - 38 - 1	.758	8	9	12-6	3-0
Chicago	102 - 57 - 0	.642	6	7	6-6	1-0
N.Y. Giants	99 - 60 - 0	.623	3	6	9-4	2-0
Washington	98 - 61 - 0	.616	3	6	10-4	2-0
New Orleans	89 - 70 - 0	.560	1	4	0-4	0-0
Philadelphia	85 - 72 - 2	.541	1	4	1-4	0-0
Minnesota	82 - 77 - 0	.516	2	5	3-5	0-0
Dallas	80 - 79 - 0	.503	3	4	7-2	2-0
L.A. Rams	77 - 82 - 0	.484	1	5	3-5	0-0
Green Bay	67 - 91 - 1	.425	0	1	1-1	0-0
Detroit	64 - 94 - 1	.406	2	2	1-2	0-0
Arizona	57 - 101 - 1	.362	0	0	0-0	0-0
Atlanta	53 - 105 - 1	.336	0	1	1-1	0-0
Tampa Bay	43 - 116 - 0	.270	0	0	0-0	0-0

Arizona totals include St. Louis, 1984-87, and Phoenix, 1988-93

HOME RECORDS, 1984-93

AFC	W - L - T	Pct.	NFC	W - L - T	Pct.
Denver	62-18-0	.775	San Francisco	60-19-0	.759
Kansas City	54-25-0	.684	N.Y. Giants	59-21-0	.738
Houston	53-26-0	.671	Chicago	58-22-0	.725
Miami	53-26-0	.671	Washington	56-23-0	.709
Buffalo	52-28-0	.650	Minnesota	48-32-0	.600
Pittsburgh	51-28-0	.646	New Orleans	47-32-0	.595
L.A. Raiders	50-30-0	.625	Philadelphia	47-32-1	.594
Seattle	48-32-0	.600	Dallas	43-36-0	.544
Cincinnati	44-36-0	.550	L.A. Rams	41-38-0	.519
Cleveland	42-36-1	.538	Green Bay	38-41-1	.481
San Diego	39-40-0	.494	Detroit	35-43-1	.449
New England	39-41-0	.488	Atlanta	34-45-1	.431
N.Y. Jets	38-41-1	.481	Arizona	34-45-0	.430
Indianapolis	32-48-0	.400	Tampa Bay	29-50-0	.367

ROAD RECORDS, 1984-93

AFC	W - L - T	Pct.	NFC	W - L - T	Pct.
Miami	43-37-0	.538	San Francisco	60-19-1	.756
L.A. Raiders	39-40-0	.494	Chicago	44-35-0	.557
Denver	36-42-1	.462	New Orleans	42-38-0	.525
Cleveland	35-45-0	.438	Washington	42-38-0	.525
N.Y. Jets	34-45-0	.430	N.Y. Giants	40-39-0	.506
Buffalo	33-46-0	.418	Philadelphia	38-40-1	.487

AFC			NFC		
Seattle	31-48-0	.392	Dallas	37-43-0	.463
Houston	30-50-0	.375	L.A. Rams	36-44-0	.450
Kansas City	28-50-2	.363	Minnesota	34-45-0	.430
Pittsburgh	29-51-0	.363	Green Bay	29-50-0	.367
San Diego	29-51-0	.363	Detroit	29-51-0	.363
New England	28-51-0	.354	Arizona	23-56-1	.294
Indianapolis	27-52-0	.342	Atlanta	19-60-0	.241
Cincinnati	25-54-0	.316	Tampa Bay	14-66-0	.175

RECORDS BY MONTHS, 1984-93

AFC	Sept. W-L-T	Oct. W-L-T	Nov. W-L-T	Dec. W-L-T	Total W-L-T	Pct.
Denver	26-11-1	26-14	26-16	20-19	98-60-1	.619
Miami	22-15	27-13	26-17	21-18	96-63-0	.604
L.A. Raiders	21-17	26-15	20-21	22-17	89-70-0	.560
Buffalo	22-16	21-17	25-19	17-22	85-74-0	.535
Houston	16-22	21-19	24-18	22-17	83-76-0	.522
Kansas City	23-15	14-26-1	19-21-1	26-13	82-75-2	.522
Pittsburgh	16-21	20-21	22-21	22-16	80-79-0	.503
Seattle	18-20	24-18	18-22	19-20	79-80-0	.497
Cleveland	17-21	23-17	19-22-1	18-21	77-81-1	.487
N.Y. Jets	21-17	18-21-1	22-22	11-26	72-86-1	.456
Cincinnati	15-21	17-25	17-25	20-19	69-90-0	.434
San Diego	13-25	14-27	23-19	18-20	68-91-0	.428
New England	13-25	18-22	19-23	17-22	67-92-0	.421
Indianapolis	9-28	17-23	14-29	19-20	59-100-0	.371

NFC	Sept. W-L-T	Oct. W-L-T	Nov. W-L-T	Dec. W-L-T	Total W-L-T	Pct.
San Francisco	27-11	30-9-1	30-11	33-7	120-38-1	.758
Chicago	29-9	28-11	29-15	16-22	102-57-0	.642
N.Y. Giants	24-13	25-15	27-15	23-17	99-60-0	.623
Washington	23-14	24-15	26-19	25-13	98-61-0	.616
New Orleans	23-15	21-19	25-17	20-19	89-70-0	.560
Philadelphia	17-20	21-19	24-18-1	23-15-1	85-72-2	.541
Minnesota	22-16	16-24	25-19	19-18	82-77-0	.516
Dallas	21-16	21-20	20-25	18-18	80-79-0	.503
L.A. Rams	24-14	17-23	18-24	18-21	77-82-0	.484
Green Bay	9-28-1	17-22	22-21	19-20	67-91-1	.425
Detroit	15-24	17-22	15-28-1	17-20	64-94-1	.406
Arizona	15-23	15-26	14-29	13-23-1	57-101-1	.362
Atlanta	13-25	13-26-1	15-27	12-27	53-105-1	.336
Tampa Bay	13-25	9-31	11-32	10-28	43-116-0	.270

Arizona totals include St. Louis, 1984-87, and Phoenix, 1988-93
December totals include January

TAKEAWAYS/GIVEAWAYS IN 1984-93

AFC	Takeaways Int.	Fum.	Total	Giveaways Int.	Fum.	Total	Net.Diff.
Kansas City	212	166	378	105	146	311	67
Pittsburgh	228	152	380	187	148	335	45
Denver	204	161	365	186	138	324	41
N.Y. Jets	190	157	347	159	159	318	29
Seattle	204	176	380	214	151	365	15
Cincinnati	178	148	326	175	143	318	8
Cleveland	180	134	314	159	158	317	-3
Indianapolis	160	163	323	199	142	341	-18
Houston	197	154	351	209	163	372	-21
San Diego	199	135	334	216	143	359	-25
New England	171	160	331	207	153	360	-29
Buffalo	188	155	343	205	176	381	-38
Miami	169	127	296	191	151	342	-46
L.A. Raiders	168	127	295	202	149	351	-56

NFC	Takeaways Int.	Fum.	Total	Giveaways Int.	Fum.	Total	Net.Diff.
San Francisco	215	137	352	137	138	275	77
Philadelphia	233	164	397	177	149	326	71
N.Y. Giants	191	137	328	144	129	273	55
Minnesota	228	149	377	198	133	331	46
New Orleans	193	172	365	198	144	342	23
Chicago	231	136	367	189	163	352	15
Washington	215	125	340	187	139	326	14
L.A. Rams	185	145	330	176	164	340	-10
Detroit	180	160	340	208	156	364	-24
Green Bay	189	174	363	224	170	394	-31
Dallas	172	146	318	206	144	350	-32
Atlanta	175	141	316	200	159	359	-43
Arizona	148	142	290	204	144	348	-58
Tampa Bay	172	163	335	253	154	407	-72

Arizona totals include St. Louis, 1984-87, and Phoenix, 1988-93

HIGH AND LOW SINGLE-GAME YARDAGE TOTALS, 1984-93

Most Total Yards, Game
- 676 Washington vs. Detroit, Nov. 4, 1990 (OT)
- 621 Cincinnati vs. N.Y. Jets, Dec. 21, 1986
- 598 San Francisco vs. Buffalo, Sept. 13, 1992
- 597 N.Y. Jets vs. Miami, Nov. 27, 1988
- 593 San Diego vs. L.A. Raiders, Nov. 10, 1985 (OT)

Fewest Total Yards, Game
- 53 Pittsburgh vs. Cleveland, Sept. 10, 1989
- 60 Detroit vs. Minnesota, Nov. 24, 1988
- 62 Seattle vs. Dallas, Oct. 11, 1992
- 65 Tampa Bay vs. Green Bay, Dec. 1, 1985
- 65 Seattle vs. New England, Dec. 4, 1988

Most Yards Rushing, Game
- 356 L.A. Raiders vs. Seattle, Nov. 30, 1987
- 315 Buffalo vs. Atlanta, Nov. 22, 1992
- 310 Kansas City vs. Detroit, Oct. 14, 1990
- 307 Washington vs. Atlanta, Nov. 3, 1985
- 305 Pittsburgh vs. Miami, Dec. 18, 1988

Fewest Yards Rushing, Game
- 0 Buffalo vs. Chicago, Oct. 2, 1988
- 1 Tampa Bay vs. Washington, Oct. 22, 1989
- 2 New England vs. New Orleans, Nov. 30, 1986
- 4 Indianapolis vs. Detroit, Sept. 22, 1991
- 6 N.Y. Giants vs. L.A. Rams, Nov. 12, 1989

Most Yards Passing, Game
- 521 Miami vs. N.Y. Jets, Oct. 23, 1988
- 505 Houston vs. Kansas City, Dec. 16, 1990
- 494 San Diego vs. Seattle, Sept. 15, 1985
- 483 Cincinnati vs. L.A. Rams, Oct. 7, 1990
- 482 Washington vs. Detroit, Nov. 4, 1990 (OT)

Fewest Yards Passing, Game
- −22 Atlanta vs. Chicago, Nov. 24, 1985
- −13 Cincinnati vs. San Diego, Oct. 4, 1987
- 4 St. Louis vs. New Orleans, Oct. 11, 1987
- 11 Tampa Bay vs. Green Bay, Dec. 1, 1985
- 15 New England vs. Atlanta, Nov. 29, 1992

NFL INDIVIDUAL LEADERS, 1984-93

Points	Touchdowns	Field Goals
1,099, Morten Andersen	124, Jerry Rice	254, Morten Andersen
1,068, Gary Anderson	87, Marcus Allen	248, Gary Anderson
1,064, Nick Lowery	83, Mark Clayton	240, Nick Lowery
964, Norm Johnson	76, Eric Dickerson	199, Kevin Butler
915, Kevin Butler	72, Herschel Walker	194, Norm Johnson

Rushes	Rushing Yards	Rushing TDs
2,606, Eric Dickerson	11,451, Eric Dickerson	72, Eric Dickerson
1,870, Marcus Allen	7,631, Thurman Thomas	71, Marcus Allen
1,815, Roger Craig	7,168, Herschel Walker	56, Gerald Riggs
1,811, Gerald Riggs	7,464, Roger Craig	55, Barry Sanders
1,794, Herschel Walker	7,452, Gerald Riggs	55, Herschel Walker

Passes	Completions	Passing Yards
5,138, Dan Marino	3,046, Dan Marino	38,510, Dan Marino
4,631, John Elway	2,632, Warren Moon	33,685, Warren Moon
4,546, Warren Moon	2,600, John Elway	32,583, John Elway
3,851, Boomer Esiason	2,185, Boomer Esiason	29,092, Boomer Esiason
3,743, Dave Krieg	2,171, Dave Krieg	27,237, Phil Simms

TD Passes	Receptions	Reception Yards
278, Dan Marino	708, Jerry Rice	11,776, Jerry Rice
196, Warren Moon	692, Art Monk	9,560, Gary Clark
190, Boomer Esiason	612, Gary Clark	9,493, Henry Ellard
190, Dave Krieg	588, Drew Hill	9,142, Art Monk
179, Jim Kelly	586, Andre Reed	8,874, Drew Hill
179, Joe Montana		

Receiving TDs	Interceptions	Sacks
118, Jerry Rice	50, Ronnie Lott	137.0, Reggie White
83, Mark Clayton	44, Dave Waymer	121.5, Richard Dent
62, Gary Clark	42, Deron Cherry	116.0, Lawrence Taylor
58, Andre Reed	41, Gil Byrd	106.0, Bruce Smith
54, Drew Hill	38, Eugene Robinson	98.5, Rickey Jackson

RECORDS FOR EACH CURRENT NFL TEAM FOR MOST POINTS IN A GAME (REGULAR SEASON ONLY)

Note: When the record has been achieved more than once, only the most recent game is shown; summaries are listed in alphabetical order by conference. Bold face indicates team holding record.

BUFFALO BILLS
September 18, 1966, at Buffalo

Miami	3	7	0	14	—	24
Buffalo	21	27	3	7	—	58

TDs: Buff—Bobby Burnett 2, Butch Byrd 2, Jack Spikes 2, Bobby Crockett, Jack Kemp; Mia—Dave Kocourek, Bo Roberson, John Roderick. TD Passes: Buff—Jack Kemp, Daryle Lamonica; Mia—George Wilson 3. FGs: Buff—Booth Lusteg; Mia—Gene Mingo.

CINCINNATI BENGALS
December 17, 1989, at Cincinnati

Houston	0	0	0	7	—	7
Cincinnati	21	10	21	9	—	61

TDs: Cin—Eddie Brown 2, Eric Ball, James Brooks, Ira Hillary, Rodney Holman, Tim McGee, Craig Taylor; Hou—Lorenzo White. TD Passes: Cin—Boomer Esiason 4, Erik Wilhelm. FGs: Cin—Jim Breech 2.

CLEVELAND BROWNS
November 7, 1954, at Cleveland

Washington	0	3	0	0	—	3
Cleveland	13	14	21	14	—	62

TDs: Clev—Darrell Brewster 2, Mo Bassett, Ken Gorgal, Otto Graham, Dub Jones, Dante Lavelli, Curley Morrison. TD Passes: Clev—George Ratterman 3, Otto Graham. FGs: Clev—Lou Groza 2; Wash—Vic Janowicz.

DENVER BRONCOS
October 6, 1963, at Denver

San Diego	13	7	0	14	—	34
Denver	3	14	9	24	—	50

TDs: Den—Lionel Taylor 2, Goose Gonsoulin, Gene Prebola, Donnie Stone; SD—Keith Lincoln 2, Lance Alworth, Paul Lowe, Jacque MacKinnon. TD Passes: Den—John McCormick 3; SD—Tobin Rote, John Hadl 2. FGs: Den—Gene Mingo 5.

HOUSTON OILERS
December 9, 1990, at Houston

Cleveland	0	7	7	0	—	14
Houston	14	31	7	6	—	58

TDs: Hou—Lorenzo White 4, Ernest Givins, Drew Harris, Tony Jones, Terry Kinard; Clev—Eric Metcalf 2. TD Passes: Hou—Warren Moon 2, Cody Carlson; Clev—Bernie Kosar. FG: Hou—Teddy Garcia.

INDIANAPOLIS COLTS
December 12, 1976, at Baltimore

Buffalo	3	3	7	7	—	20
Baltimore Colts	7	13	28	10	—	58

TDs: Balt—Roger Carr, Raymond Chester, Glenn Doughty, Roosevelt Leaks, Derrel Luce, Lydell Mitchell, Howard Stevens; Buff—Bob Chandler, O.J. Simpson. TD Passes: Balt—Bert Jones 3; Buff—Gary Marangi. FGs: Balt—Toni Linhart 3; Buff—George Jakowenko 2.

KANSAS CITY CHIEFS
September 7, 1963, at Denver

Kansas City	14	14	21	10	—	59
Denver	0	7	0	0	—	7

TDs: KC—Chris Burford 2, Frank Jackson 2, Dave Grayson, Abner Haynes, Sherrill Headrick, Curtis McClinton; Den—Lionel Taylor. TD Passes: KC—Len Dawson 4, Curtis McClinton; Den—Mickey Slaughter. FG: KC—Tommy Brooker.

LOS ANGELES RAIDERS
December 22, 1963, at Oakland

Houston	14	21	14	0	—	49
Oakland Raiders	7	28	7	10	—	52

TDs: Oak—Art Powell 4, Clem Daniels, Claude Gibson, Ken Herock; Hou—Willard Dewveall 2, Dave Smith 2, Charley Hennigan, Bob McLeod, Charley Tolar. TD Passes: Oak—Tom Flores 6; Hou—George Blanda 5. FG: Oak—Mike Mercer.

MIAMI DOLPHINS
November 24, 1977, at St. Louis

Miami	14	14	20	7	—	55
St. Louis	7	0	0	7	—	14

TDs: Mia—Nat Moore 3, Gary Davis, Duriel Harris, Leroy Harris, Benny Malone, Andre Tillman; StL—Ike Harris, Terry Metcalf. TD Passes: Mia—Bob Griese 6; StL—Jim Hart.

NEW ENGLAND PATRIOTS
September 9, 1979, at New England

New York Jets	3	0	0	0	—	3
New England	14	21	7	14	—	56

TDs: NE—Harold Jackson 3, Stanley Morgan 2, Allan Clark, Andy Johnson, Don Westbrook. TD Passes: NE—Steve Grogan 5, Tom Owen. FG: NYJ—Pat Leahy.

NEW YORK JETS
November 17, 1985, at New York

Tampa Bay	14	7	7	0	—	28
New York Jets	17	24	14	7	—	62

TDs: NYJ—Mickey Shuler 3, Johnny Hector 2, Tony Paige, Al Toon, Wesley Walker; TB—James Wilder 2, Kevin House, Calvin Magee. TD Passes: NYJ—Ken O'Brien 5; TB—Steve DeBerg 2. FGs: NYJ—Pat Leahy 2.

PITTSBURGH STEELERS
November 30, 1952, at Pittsburgh

New York Giants	0	0	7	0	—	7
Pittsburgh	14	14	7	28	—	63

TDs: Pitt—Lynn Chandnois 2, Dick Hensley 2, Jack Butler, George Hays, Ray Mathews, Ed Modzelewski, Elbie Nickel; NYG—Bill Stribling. TD Passes: Pitt—Jim Finks 4, Gary Kerkorian; NYG—Tom Landry.

SAN DIEGO CHARGERS
December 22, 1963, at San Diego

Denver	7	10	3	0	—	20
San Diego	10	16	10	22	—	58

TDs: SD—Paul Lowe 2, Chuck Allen, Bobby Jackson, Dave Kocourek, Keith Lincoln, Jacque MacKinnon; Den—Billy Joe, Donnie Stone. TD Passes: SD—John Hadl, Tobin Rote; Den—Don Breaux. FGs: SD—George Blair 3; Den—Gene Mingo 2.

SEATTLE SEAHAWKS
October 30, 1977, at Seattle

Buffalo	3	0	7	7	—	17
Seattle	14	28	7	7	—	56

TDs: Sea—Steve Largent 2, Duke Fergerson, Al Hunter, David Sims, Sherman Smith, Don Testerman, Jim Zorn; Buff—Joe Ferguson, John Kimbrough. TD Passes: Sea—Jim Zorn 4; Buff—Joe Ferguson. FG: Buff—Carson Long.

ARIZONA CARDINALS
November 14, 1949, at New York

Chicago Cardinals	7	31	14	13	—	65
New York Bulldogs	7	0	6	7	—	20

TDs: Chi—Red Cochran 2, Pat Harder 2, Bill Dewell, Mel Kutner, Bob Ravensburg, Vic Schwall, Charlie Trippi; NY—Joe Golding, Frank Muehlheuser, Johnny Rauch. TD Passes: Chi—Paul Christman 3, Jim Hardy 3; NY—Bobby Layne. FG: Chi—Pat Harder.

ATLANTA FALCONS
September 16, 1973, at New Orleans

Atlanta	0	24	21	17	—	62
New Orleans	0	0	7	0	—	7

TDs: Atl—Ken Burrow 2, Eddie Ray 2, Wes Chesson, Tom Hayes, Art Malone, Joe Profit; NO—Bill Butler. TD Passes: Atl—Dick Shiner 2, Bob Lee; NO—Archie Manning. FGs: Atl—Nick Mike-Mayer 2.

CHICAGO BEARS
December 7, 1980, at Chicago

Green Bay	0	7	0	0	—	7
Chicago	0	28	13	20	—	61

TDs: Chi—Walter Payton 3, Brian Baschnagel, Robin Earl, Roland Harper, Willie McClendon, Len Walterscheid, Rickey Watts; GB—James Lofton. TD Passes: Chi—Vince Evans 3; GB—Lynn Dickey.

DALLAS COWBOYS
October 12, 1980, at Dallas

San Francisco	0	7	0	7	—	14
Dallas	14	24	14	7	—	59

TDs: Dall—Drew Pearson 3, Ron Springs 2, Tony Dorsett, Billy Joe DuPree, Robert Newhouse; SF—Dwight Clark 2. TD Passes: Dall—Danny White 4; SF—Steve DeBerg 2. FG: Dall—Rafael Septien.

DETROIT LIONS
October 26, 1952, at Green Bay

Detroit	14	14	14	10	—	52
Green Bay	7	3	7	0	—	17

TDs: Det—Jug Girard 2, Bob Hoernschemeyer 2, Jack Christiansen, Jim Smith, Bill Swiacki; GB—Billy Howton, Jim Keane. TD Passes: Det—Bobby Layne 3; GB—Babe Parilli, Tobin Rote. FGs: Det—Pat Harder; GB—Bill Reichardt.

GREEN BAY PACKERS
October 7, 1945, at Milwaukee

Detroit	0	7	7	7	—	21
Green Bay	0	41	9	7	—	57

TDs: GB—Don Hutson 4, Charley Brock, Irv Comp, Ted Fritsch, Clyde Goodnight; Det—Chuck Fenenbock, John Greene, Bob Westfall. TD Passes: GB—Tex McKay 4, Lou Brock, Irv Comp; Det—Dave Ryan.

LOS ANGELES RAMS
October 22, 1950, at Los Angeles

Baltimore	13	0	7	7	—	27
Los Angeles	21	14	14	21	—	70

TDs: LA—Bob Boyd 2, Vitamin T. Smith 2, Tom Fears, Elroy (Crazylegs) Hirsch, Dick Hoerner, Ralph Pasquariello, Dan Towler, Bob Waterfield; Balt—Chet Mutryn 2, Adrian Burk, Billy Stone. TD Passes: LA—Norm Van Brocklin 2, Bob Waterfield, Glenn Davis; Balt—Adrian Burk 3.

MINNESOTA VIKINGS
October 18, 1970, at Minnesota

Dallas	3	3	0	7	—	13
Minnesota	14	20	17	3	—	54

TDs: Minn—Clint Jones 2, Ed Sharockman 2, John Beasley, Dave Osborn; Dall—Calvin Hill. TD Pass: Minn—Gary Cuozzo. FGs: Minn—Fred Cox 4; Dall—Mike Clark 2.

NEW ORLEANS SAINTS
November 21, 1976, at Seattle

New Orleans	3	17	28	3	—	51
Seattle	6	0	7	14	—	27

TDs: NO—Bobby Douglass 2, Tony Galbreath, Chuck Muncie, Tom Myers, Elex Price; Sea—Sherman Smith 2, Steve Largent, Jim Zorn. TD Pass: Sea—Bill Munson. FGs: NO—Rich Szaro 3.

NEW YORK GIANTS
November 26, 1972, at New York

Philadelphia	3	7	0	0	—	10
New York Giants	14	24	10	14	—	62

TDs: NYG—Don Herrmann 2, Ron Johnson 2, Bob Tucker 2, Randy Johnson; Phil—Harold Jackson. TD Passes: NYG—Norm Snead 3, Randy Johnson 2; Phil—John Reaves. FGs: NYG—Pete Gogolak 2; Phil—Tom Dempsey.

PHILADELPHIA EAGLES
November 6, 1934, at Philadelphia

Cincinnati Reds	0	0	0	0	—	0
Philadelphia	26	6	12	20	—	64

TDs: Phil—Joe Carter 3, Swede Hanson 3, Marvin Ellstrom, Roger Kirkman, Ed Matesic, Ed Storm. TD Passes: Phil—Ed Matesic 2, Albert Weiner 2, Marvin Elstrom.

SAN FRANCISCO 49ERS
October 18, 1992, at San Francisco

Atlanta	7	3	0	7	—	17
San Francisco	21	21	14	0	—	56

TDs: SF—Jerry Rice 3, Ricky Watters 3, Brent Jones, Tom Rathman; Atl—Michael Haynes, Jason Phillips. TD Passes: SF—Steve Young 3; Atl—Chris Miller, Wade Wilson. FG: Atl—Norm Johnson.

TAMPA BAY BUCCANEERS
September 13, 1987, at Tampa Bay

Atlanta	0	3	0	7	—	10
Tampa Bay	14	13	7	14	—	48

TDs: TB—Gerald Carter 2, Cliff Austin, Steve Bartalo, Mark Carrier, Phil Freeman, Calvin Magee; Atl—Stacey Bailey. TD Passes: TB—Steve DeBerg 5; Atl—Scott Campbell. FG: Atl—Mick Luckhurst.

WASHINGTON REDSKINS
November 27, 1966, at Washington

New York Giants	0	14	14	13	—	41
Washington	13	21	14	24	—	72

TDs: Wash—A.D. Whitfield 3, Brig Owens 2, Charley Taylor 2, Rickie Harris, Joe Don Looney, Bobby Mitchell; NYG—Allen Jacobs, Homer Jones, Dan Lewis, Joe Morrison, Aaron Thomas, Gary Wood. TD Passes: Wash—Sonny Jurgensen 3; NYG—Gary Wood 2, Tom Kennedy. FG: Wash—Charlie Gogolak.

NFL GAMES IN WHICH A TEAM HAS SCORED 60 OR MORE POINTS

(Home team in capitals)

Regular Season

WASHINGTON 72, New York Giants 41 ....November 27, 1966
LOS ANGELES RAMS 70, Baltimore 27 ....October 22, 1950
Chicago Cardinals 65, NEW YORK BULLDOGS 20 ....November 13, 1949
LOS ANGELES RAMS 65, Detroit 24 ....October 29, 1950
PHILADELPHIA 64, Cincinnati 0 ....November 6, 1934
CHICAGO CARDINALS 63, New York Giants 35 ....October 17, 1948
AKRON 62, Oorang 0 ....October 29,1922
PITTSBURGH 62, New York Giants 7 ....November 30, 1952
CLEVELAND 62, New York Giants 14 ....December 6, 1953
CLEVELAND 62, Washington 3 ....November 7, 1954
NEW YORK GIANTS 62, Philadelphia 10 ....November 26, 1972
Atlanta 62, NEW ORLEANS 7 ....September 16, 1973
NEW YORK JETS 62, Tampa Bay 28 ....November 17, 1985
CHICAGO 61, San Francisco 20 ....December 12, 1965
Cincinnati 61, HOUSTON 17 ....December 17, 1972
CHICAGO 61, Green Bay 7 ....December 7, 1980
CINCINNATI 61, Houston 7 ....December 17, 1989
ROCK ISLAND 60, Evansville 0 ....October 15, 1922
CHICAGO CARDINALS 60, Rochester 0 ....October 7, 1923

Postseason

Chicago Bears 73, WASHINGTON 0 ....December 8, 1940

YOUNGEST AND OLDEST PLAYERS IN NFL IN 1993

Ten Youngest Players	Birthdate	Games	Starts	Position
Tom Carter, Washington	9/5/72	14	11	CB
James Willis, Green Bay	9/2/72	13	0	LB
Othello Henderson, New Orleans	8/23/72	5	1	DB
Marvin Jones, N.Y. Jets	6/28/72	9	0	LB
Natrone Means, San Diego	4/26/72	16	0	RB
Robert Smith, Minnesota	3/4/72	10	2	RB
Jerome Bettis, L.A. Rams	2/16/72	16	12	RB
Drew Bledsoe, New England	2/14/72	13	12	QB
Michael Strahan, N.Y. Giants	11/21/71	9	0	DE
Russell Copeland, Buffalo	11/4/71	16	2	WR

Ten Oldest Players	Birthdate	Games	Starts	Position
Steve DeBerg, Tampa Bay-Miami	1/19/54	8	5	QB
Jackie Slater, L.A. Rams	5/27/54	8	8	T
Vince Evans, L.A. Raiders	6/14/55	8	1	QB
Phil Simms, N.Y. Giants	11/3/55	16	16	QB
Mike Kenn, Atlanta	2/9/56	16	16	T
Clay Matthews, Cleveland	3/15/56	16	15	LB
Max Montoya, L.A. Raiders	5/12/56	16	16	G
Nick Lowery, Kansas City	5/27/56	16	0	K
Joe Montana, Kansas City	6/11/56	11	11	QB
James Lofton, L.A. Rams-Phil.	7/5/56	10	2	WR

YOUNGEST AND OLDEST REGULAR STARTERS BY POSITION IN 1993

Minimum: 8 Games Started

	Youngest	Oldest
QB	2/14/72 Drew Bledsoe, N.E.	11/3/55 Phil Simms, N.Y. Giants
RB	2/16/72 Jerome Bettis, L.A. Rams	3/26/60 Marcus Allen, K.C.
WR	1/25/71 Vincent Brisby, N.E.	9/17/60 Anthony Carter, Minn.
TE	10/13/71 Irv Smith, N.O.	2/2/59 Mike Tice, Minn.
C	8/21/70 Steve Everitt, Clev.	5/18/58 Ray Donaldson, Sea.
G	9/15/71 Will Shields, K.C.	5/12/56 Max Montoya, L.A. Raiders
T	10/18/71 Bob Whitfield, Atl.	5/27/54 Jackie Slater, L.A. Rams
DE	5/25/71 Keith Hamilton, N.Y. Giants	1/6/60 Howie Long, L.A. Raiders
DT	11/14/70 Dana Stubblefield, S.F.	10/17/57 Steve McMichael, Chi.
LB	9/17/71 Eric Shaw, Cin.	3/15/56 Clay Matthews, Clev.
CB	9/2/72 Tom Carter, Wash.	2/15/60 Darrell Green, Wash.
S	2/18/71 George Teague, G.B.	2/3/59 Dennis Smith, Den.

MARCUS ALLEN'S CAREER RUSHING VS. EACH OPPONENT

Opponent	Games	Rushes	Yards	Yards Per Rush	Yards Per Game	TD
Arizona	2	22	96	4.4	48.0	1
Atlanta	3	47	230	4.9	76.7	1
Buffalo	7	120	412	3.4	58.9	4
Chicago	4	61	252	4.1	63.0	4
Cincinnati	8	101	363	3.6	45.4	5
Cleveland	4	55	224	4.1	56.0	0
Dallas	3	25	93	3.7	31.0	1
Denver	20	281	1,189	4.2	59.5	7
Detroit	3	46	153	3.3	51.0	2
Green Bay	4	75	269	3.6	67.3	5
Houston	5	74	281	3.8	56.2	3
Indianapolis	2	28	141	5.0	70.5	0

Opponent	Games	Rushes	Yards	Yards Per Rush	Yards Per Game	TD
Kansas City	17	264	961	3.6	56.5	8
L.A. Raiders	2	34	109	3.2	54.5	2
L.A. Rams	3	63	269	4.3	89.7	3
Miami	6	87	451	5.2	75.2	6
Minnesota	4	44	150	3.4	37.5	1
New England	2	37	139	3.8	69.5	1
New Orleans	3	53	234	4.4	78.0	2
N.Y. Giants	4	30	117	3.9	29.3	1
N.Y. Jets	2	30	119	4.0	59.5	2
Philadelphia	2	30	82	2.7	41.0	0
Pittsburgh	2	24	82	3.4	41.0	1
San Diego	20	315	1,297	4.1	64.9	20
San Francisco	3	49	233	4.8	77.7	1
Seattle	22	260	1,140	4.4	51.8	10
Tampa Bay	1	13	79	6.1	79.0	0
Washington	3	28	144	5.1	48.0	0
Totals	161	2,296	9,309	4.1	57.8	91

Arizona totals include one game vs. St. Louis, one game vs. Phoenix

EMMITT SMITH'S CAREER RUSHING VS. EACH OPPONENT

Opponent	Games	Rushes	Yards	Yards Per Rush	Yards Per Game	TD
Arizona	8	162	716	4.4	89.5	11
Atlanta	4	73	369	5.1	92.3	4
Chicago	1	20	131	6.6	131.0	1
Cincinnati	1	19	62	3.3	62.0	1
Cleveland	1	32	112	3.5	112.0	0
Denver	1	26	62	2.4	62.0	1
Detroit	2	35	133	3.8	66.5	3
Green Bay	2	45	193	4.3	96.5	1
Houston	1	12	49	4.1	49.0	0
Indianapolis	1	25	104	4.2	104.0	1
Kansas City	1	24	95	4.0	95.0	1
L.A. Raiders	1	29	152	5.2	152.0	3
L.A. Rams	2	40	134	3.4	67.0	1
Miami	1	16	51	3.2	51.0	0
Minnesota	1	19	104	5.5	104.0	1
New Orleans	2	47	197	4.2	98.5	1
N.Y. Giants	8	149	697	4.7	87.1	6
N.Y. Jets	2	35	146	4.2	73.0	0
Philadelphia	8	168	871	5.2	108.9	2
Pittsburgh	1	32	109	3.4	109.0	1
San Diego	1	2	2	1.0	2.0	0
San Francisco	2	33	132	4.0	66.0	1
Seattle	1	22	78	3.5	78.0	2
Tampa Bay	2	39	169	4.3	84.5	1
Washington	7	158	831	5.3	118.7	7
Totals	62	1,262	5,699	4.5	91.9	50

Arizona totals include eight games vs. Phoenix

BARRY SANDERS'S CAREER RUSHING VS. EACH OPPONENT

Opponent	Games	Rushes	Yards	Yards Per Rush	Yards Per Game	TD
Arizona	2	32	161	5.0	80.5	1
Atlanta	3	64	303	4.7	101.0	5
Buffalo	1	26	108	4.2	108.0	1
Chicago	9	171	784	4.6	87.1	6
Cincinnati	2	47	265	5.6	132.5	2
Cleveland	2	58	232	4.0	116.0	1
Dallas	2	39	163	4.2	81.5	0
Denver	1	23	147	6.4	147.0	1
Green Bay	9	175	834	4.8	92.7	4
Houston	2	41	145	3.5	72.5	3
Indianapolis	1	30	179	6.0	179.0	2
Kansas City	1	16	90	5.6	90.0	1
L.A. Raiders	1	25	176	7.0	176.0	2
L.A. Rams	2	52	148	2.8	74.0	1
Miami	1	32	143	4.5	143.0	0
Minnesota	9	169	820	4.9	91.1	7
New England	1	32	148	4.6	148.0	0
New Orleans	4	57	194	3.4	48.5	2
N.Y. Giants	2	23	126	5.5	63.0	1
N.Y. Jets	1	20	114	5.7	114.0	2
Pittsburgh	2	26	95	3.7	47.5	1
San Francisco	2	26	130	5.0	65.0	0
Seattle	2	31	124	4.0	62.0	1
Tampa Bay	9	192	1022	5.3	113.6	10
Washington	2	25	138	5.5	69.0	1
Totals	73	1,432	6,789	4.7	93.0	55

Arizona totals include two games vs. Phoenix

THURMAN THOMAS'S CAREER RUSHING VS. EACH OPPONENT

Opponent	Games	Rushes	Yards	Yards Per Rush	Yards Per Game	TD
Arizona	1	26	112	4.3	112.0	0
Atlanta	2	34	198	5.8	99.0	1
Chicago	2	30	129	4.3	64.5	1
Cincinnati	3	50	234	4.7	78.0	0
Cleveland	1	17	58	3.4	58.0	2
Dallas	1	25	75	3.0	75.0	0
Denver	3	50	194	3.9	64.7	1
Green Bay	2	47	222	4.7	111.0	1
Houston	4	69	301	4.4	75.3	2
Indianapolis	12	213	936	4.4	78.0	6
Kansas City	2	28	76	2.7	38.0	0
L.A. Raiders	5	79	356	4.5	71.2	3
L.A. Rams	2	46	208	4.5	104.0	3
Miami	11	218	997	4.6	90.6	4
Minnesota	1	18	86	4.8	86.0	1
New England	12	265	1,207	4.6	100.6	7
New Orleans	2	40	155	3.9	77.5	2
N.Y. Giants	2	47	182	3.9	91.0	1
N.Y. Jets	12	208	1,094	5.3	91.2	3
Philadelphia	2	31	84	2.7	42.0	0
Pittsburgh	4	81	351	4.3	87.8	1
San Francisco	2	25	92	3.7	46.0	1
Seattle	2	27	100	3.7	50.0	0
Tampa Bay	2	24	55	2.3	27.5	0
Washington	2	33	129	3.9	64.5	1
Totals	94	1,731	7,631	4.4	81.2	41

Arizona totals include one game vs. Phoenix

JOE MONTANA'S CAREER PASSING VS. EACH OPPONENT

Opponent	Games	Att.	Cmp.	Pct.	Yards	Avg. Gain	TD	Int.	Sacked
Arizona	6	141	95	67.4	1,389	9.85	13	5	7/53
Atlanta	21	567	370	65.3	4,436	7.82	36	17	33/235
Buffalo	3	96	61	63.5	589	6.14	4	1	6/46
Chicago	7	162	90	55.6	1,023	6.31	5	4	20/144
Cincinnati	4	141	90	63.8	923	6.55	7	6	9/75
Cleveland	4	140	88	62.9	1,003	7.16	7	6	6/48
Dallas	5	126	84	66.7	1,114	8.84	9	3	7/48
Denver	6	172	96	55.8	1,289	7.49	6	4	10/72
Detroit	6	141	89	63.1	839	5.95	4	2	10/63
Green Bay	5	149	104	69.8	1,264	8.48	7	2	8/50
Houston	4	135	95	70.4	1,164	8.62	10	4	5/31
Indianapolis	1	26	15	57.7	233	8.96	1	0	3/29
Kansas City	2	69	43	62.3	488	7.07	2	2	3/16
L.A. Raiders	5	105	58	55.2	727	6.92	6	1	11/92
L.A. Rams	23	693	446	64.4	5,632	8.13	37	15	47/297
Miami	3	47	29	61.7	357	7.60	1	0	3/22
Minnesota	6	128	83	64.8	950	7.42	9	5	8/34
New England	4	108	69	63.9	791	7.32	6	2	6/39
New Orleans	20	508	314	61.8	3,704	7.29	31	14	38/225
N.Y. Giants	8	210	132	62.9	1,435	6.83	10	3	7/38
N.Y. Jets	3	79	48	60.8	538	6.81	3	3	3/17
Philadelphia	3	54	35	64.8	546	10.11	5	2	9/52
Pittsburgh	4	150	100	66.7	919	6.13	4	8	3/20
San Diego	5	139	84	60.4	1,079	7.76	9	4	7/32
Seattle	5	120	75	62.5	988	8.23	7	5	4/25
Tampa Bay	9	275	190	69.1	2,106	7.66	11	6	12/76
Washington	6	217	127	58.5	1,742	8.03	7	6	9/84
Totals	178	4,898	3,110	63.5	37,268	7.61	257	130	294/1,963

Arizona totals include six games vs. St. Louis.
L.A. Raiders totals include one game vs. Oakland

PHIL SIMMS'S CAREER PASSING VS. EACH OPPONENT

Opponent	Games	Att.	Cmp.	Pct.	Yards	Avg. Gain	TD	Int.	Sacked
Arizona	18	509	263	51.7	3,404	6.69	29	10	47/294
Atlanta	4	116	66	56.9	910	7.84	4	3	12/81
Buffalo	2	38	18	47.4	219	5.76	2	3	3/7
Chicago	3	91	58	63.7	678	7.45	5	0	13/82
Cincinnati	2	106	66	62.3	809	7.63	4	2	10/88
Cleveland	1	37	23	62.2	289	7.81	1	2	4/22
Dallas	23	604	322	53.3	4,804	7.95	34	29	59/427
Denver	3	78	43	55.1	519	6.65	1	1	8/64
Detroit	4	112	78	69.6	935	8.35	6	0	11/73
Green Bay	5	156	97	62.2	1,302	8.35	11	4	16/111
Houston	2	41	28	68.3	434	10.59	3	1	1/8
Indianapolis	3	50	33	66.0	324	6.48	2	5	5/33
Kansas City	3	82	42	51.2	587	7.16	5	5	7/52
L.A. Raiders	3	84	50	59.5	604	7.19	2	3	8/62

L.A. Rams	8	262	152	58.0	1,782	6.80	7	6	32/257
Miami	2	49	30	61.2	439	8.96	1	0	4/19
Minnesota	3	58	33	56.9	428	7.38	1	2	4/27
New Orleans	6	178	105	59.0	1,177	6.61	7	7	17/110
N.Y. Jets	5	165	98	59.4	1,070	6.48	5	3	22/168
Philadelphia	21	595	296	49.7	4,111	6.91	24	23	58/414
Pittsburgh	1	16	10	62.5	106	6.63	1	1	3/24
San Diego	3	99	54	54.5	667	6.74	1	4	8/72
San Francisco	8	295	163	55.3	2,025	6.86	8	9	35/212
Seattle	3	78	43	55.1	487	6.24	3	5	9/59
Tampa Bay	8	217	123	56.7	1,264	5.82	7	6	20/201
Washington	20	531	282	53.1	4,088	7.70	25	23	61/451
Totals	164	4,647	2,576	55.4	33,462	7.20	199	157	477/3,418

Arizona totals include 12 games vs. St. Louis, six games vs. Phoenix
Indianapolis totals include one game vs. Baltimore

DAN MARINO'S CAREER PASSING VS. EACH OPPONENT

Opponent	Games	Att.	Cmp.	Pct.	Yards	Avg. Gain	TD	Int.	Sacked
Arizona	2	61	42	68.9	634	10.39	5	0	1/9
Atlanta	2	80	40	50.0	553	6.91	2	4	1/2
Buffalo	20	681	432	63.4	5,375	7.89	39	27	25/210
Chicago	3	79	39	49.4	566	7.16	5	3	6/36
Cincinnati	4	136	84	61.8	1,026	7.54	7	1	5/39
Cleveland	6	205	126	61.5	1,661	8.10	11	5	4/33
Dallas	3	115	66	57.4	860	7.48	6	3	4/36
Denver	1	43	25	58.1	390	9.07	3	0	3/25
Detroit	2	78	39	50.0	421	5.40	2	2	3/28
Green Bay	4	146	95	65.1	1,151	7.88	9	6	4/22
Houston	7	220	116	52.7	1,464	6.65	10	11	7/36
Indianapolis	21	687	412	60.0	5,108	7.44	37	11	16/115
Kansas City	4	148	84	56.8	1,031	6.97	8	3	2/20
L.A. Raiders	6	204	116	56.9	1,469	7.20	12	6	8/70
L.A. Rams	3	121	75	62.0	905	7.48	9	3	1/4
Minnesota	1	37	20	54.1	264	7.14	2	3	0/0
New England	19	649	376	57.9	4,544	7.00	30	29	13/101
New Orleans	3	105	65	61.9	650	6.19	5	2	6/42
N.Y. Giants	1	30	14	46.7	115	3.83	0	2	1/7
N.Y. Jets	19	712	417	58.6	5,724	8.04	49	22	28/153
Philadelphia	3	127	72	56.7	987	7.77	6	2	5/45
Pittsburgh	6	175	110	62.9	1,333	7.62	9	9	1/4
San Diego	4	163	103	63.2	1,243	7.63	9	2	6/42
San Francisco	3	106	61	57.5	687	6.48	3	4	4/36
Seattle	2	68	40	58.8	504	7.41	3	4	3/21
Tampa Bay	3	117	74	63.2	875	7.48	7	1	1/10
Washington	4	141	76	53.9	1,180	8.37	10	3	2/7
Totals	156	5,434	3,219	59.2	40,720	7.49	298	168	160/1,157

Arizona totals include one game vs. St. Louis, one game vs. Phoenix
Indianapolis totals include two games vs. Baltimore

JOHN ELWAY'S CAREER PASSING VS. EACH OPPONENT

Opponent	Games	Att.	Cmp.	Pct.	Yards	Avg. Gain	TD	Int.	Sacked
Arizona	2	62	39	62.9	492	7.94	3	5	3/16
Atlanta	2	64	35	54.7	526	8.22	4	2	4/26
Buffalo	4	109	55	50.5	739	6.78	5	4	8/70
Chicago	5	118	65	55.1	763	6.47	3	4	12/73
Cincinnati	3	75	48	64.0	617	8.23	6	1	2/13
Cleveland	8	210	117	55.7	1,656	7.89	12	7	15/120
Dallas	1	24	12	50.0	200	8.33	3	0	1/2
Detroit	3	88	56	63.6	699	7.94	2	2	7/72
Green Bay	4	153	88	57.5	913	5.97	2	5	5/38
Houston	3	98	54	55.1	749	7.64	6	4	11/109
Indianapolis	7	213	118	55.4	1,545	7.25	8	2	17/129
Kansas City	20	626	341	54.5	4,311	6.89	17	29	52/388
L.A. Raiders	19	560	306	54.6	3,811	6.81	22	23	51/417
L.A. Rams	2	74	39	52.7	501	6.77	5	2	3/24
Miami	1	37	18	48.6	250	6.76	0	1	3/24
Minnesota	5	130	84	64.6	923	7.10	10	2	13/100
New England	6	192	108	56.3	1,286	6.70	7	4	8/54
New Orleans	2	79	46	58.2	519	6.57	4	2	4/35
N.Y. Giants	3	103	58	56.3	724	7.03	2	3	3/19
N.Y. Jets	3	90	51	56.7	675	7.50	3	3	7/42
Philadelphia	4	102	52	51.0	626	6.14	4	6	16/119
Pittsburgh	7	192	105	54.7	1,366	7.11	6	5	14/109
San Diego	21	646	357	55.3	4,327	6.70	17	26	50/340
San Francisco	2	81	41	50.6	425	5.25	3	3	5/43
Seattle	20	656	369	56.3	4,968	7.57	28	20	47/329
Tampa Bay	1	41	26	63.4	225	5.49	0	0	1/0
Washington	2	67	35	52.2	410	6.12	1	2	8/59
Totals	160	4,890	2,723	55.7	34,246	7.00	183	167	370/2,770

Arizona totals include two games vs. Phoenix

BOOMER ESIASON'S CAREER PASSING VS. EACH OPPONENT

Opponent	Games	Att.	Cmp.	Pct.	Yards	Avg. Gain	TD	Int.	Sacked
Arizona	2	38	24	63.2	356	9.37	4	1	3/22
Atlanta	3	67	34	50.7	367	5.48	1	2	3/3
Buffalo	8	183	109	59.6	1,410	7.70	8	6	8/72
Chicago	3	95	48	50.5	568	5.98	5	5	9/88
Cincinnati	1	26	17	65.4	192	7.38	0	0	2/15
Cleveland	16	369	198	53.7	2,561	6.94	18	13	19/134
Dallas	4	122	69	56.6	855	7.01	6	3	5/35
Denver	3	90	61	67.8	883	9.81	6	5	5/37
Detroit	3	91	55	60.4	630	6.92	3	4	5/24
Green Bay	2	47	26	55.3	335	7.13	4	2	3/24
Houston	17	461	266	57.7	3,740	8.11	25	21	36/255
Indianapolis	6	153	84	54.9	1,059	6.92	6	6	9/72
Kansas City	4	121	67	55.4	940	7.77	5	3	7/71
L.A. Raiders	6	147	81	55.1	1,029	7.00	5	2	8/70
L.A. Rams	1	45	31	68.9	490	10.89	3	0	1/7
Miami	5	151	92	60.9	1,196	7.92	7	2	6/69
Minnesota	3	100	59	59.0	747	7.47	4	8	9/78
New England	8	241	133	55.2	1,968	8.17	13	7	11/79
New Orleans	3	75	33	44.0	309	4.12	3	2	9/71
N.Y. Giants	3	71	44	62.0	526	7.41	4	0	4/36
N.Y. Jets	7	180	93	51.7	1,410	7.83	12	8	16/123
Philadelphia	3	83	49	59.0	770	9.28	9	5	5/45
Pittsburgh	16	437	261	59.7	3,589	8.21	18	17	28/230
San Diego	3	97	56	57.7	748	7.71	8	5	10/84
San Francisco	2	49	26	53.1	294	6.00	2	2	5/28
Seattle	6	167	90	53.9	1,093	6.54	2	6	14/109
Tampa Bay	1	28	17	60.7	197	7.04	5	0	1/1
Washington	4	117	62	53.0	861	7.36	4	3	9/72
Totals	143	3,851	2,185	56.7	29,092	7.55	190	140	248/1,954

Arizona totals include one game vs. St. Louis, one game vs. Phoenix

WARREN MOON'S CAREER PASSING VS. EACH OPPONENT

Opponent	Games	Att.	Cmp.	Pct.	Yards	Avg. Gain	TD	Int.	Sacked
Arizona	2	61	31	50.8	453	7.43	4	2	3/21
Atlanta	4	156	87	55.8	1,189	7.62	9	5	9/43
Buffalo	7	172	96	55.8	1,267	7.37	7	9	12/94
Chicago	2	55	28	50.9	521	9.47	3	3	5/49
Cincinnati	19	606	357	58.9	4,608	7.60	35	22	36/301
Cleveland	18	561	316	56.3	4,048	7.22	23	21	41/308
Dallas	3	111	67	60.4	873	7.86	2	4	16/105
Denver	3	87	50	57.5	777	8.93	5	2	9/66
Detroit	2	76	51	67.1	743	9.78	3	4	0/0
Green Bay	1	21	14	66.7	218	10.38	2	1	0/0
Indianapolis	7	255	160	62.7	2,156	8.45	13	7	14/97
Kansas City	8	207	100	02.2	2,006	7.51	10	7	26/180
L.A. Raiders	4	138	68	49.3	1,004	7.28	6	5	13/115
L.A. Rams	4	157	85	54.1	1,163	7.41	4	7	10/71
Miami	5	111	76	68.5	910	8.20	5	6	9/97
Minnesota	3	95	58	61.1	592	6.23	2	2	14/106
New England	3	94	50	53.2	597	6.35	5	4	4/31
New Orleans	4	113	63	55.8	737	6.52	3	3	8/65
N.Y. Giants	2	83	48	57.8	566	6.82	3	2	5/46
N.Y. Jets	3	121	85	70.2	1,011	8.36	6	2	7/60
Philadelphia	1	46	24	52.2	262	5.70	0	0	4/36
Pittsburgh	19	591	333	56.3	4,208	7.12	22	27	41/315
San Diego	6	201	108	53.7	1,362	6.78	7	6	10/71
San Francisco	4	128	71	55.5	903	7.05	7	8	8/46
Seattle	3	115	73	63.5	783	6.81	4	4	5/34
Tampa Bay	1	23	14	60.9	149	6.48	2	0	0/0
Washington	3	102	53	52.0	579	5.68	4	3	6/46
Totals	141	4,546	2,632	57.9	33,685	7.41	196	166	315/2,403

Arizona totals include one game vs. St. Louis, one game vs. Phoenix

JIM KELLY'S CAREER PASSING VS. EACH OPPONENT

Opponent	Games	Att.	Cmp.	Pct.	Yards	Avg. Gain	TD	Int.	Sacked
Arizona	2	26	17	65.4	270	10.38	4	1	5/34
Atlanta	2	37	24	64.9	324	8.76	4	2	3/18
Chicago	2	66	39	59.1	576	8.73	3	1	9/79
Cincinnati	4	99	65	65.7	1,008	10.18	10	7	5/49
Cleveland	3	93	56	60.2	737	7.93	5	0	6/31
Dallas	1	27	16	59.3	155	5.74	1	1	4/26
Denver	4	124	71	57.3	813	6.56	3	7	8/58
Green Bay	2	49	27	55.1	312	6.37	3	2	5/23
Houston	6	179	110	61.5	1,435	8.02	14	6	19/141
Indianapolis	15	407	241	59.2	3,015	7.41	26	10	14/112
Kansas City	4	131	81	61.8	884	6.75	3	7	12/101
L.A. Raiders	6	208	125	60.1	1,550	7.45	8	5	12/89
L.A. Rams	1	19	13	68.4	106	5.58	2	1	1/0

Miami	14	450	286	63.6	3,358	7.46	17	12	22/173
Minnesota	1	31	17	54.8	204	6.58	0	1	1/8
New England	15	426	252	59.2	3,235	7.59	20	19	41/329
New Orleans	2	63	30	47.6	346	5.49	2	4	3/16
N.Y. Giants	2	36	21	58.3	257	7.14	2	1	5/30
N.Y. Jets	15	472	281	59.5	3,566	7.56	26	18	24/170
Philadelphia	3	98	56	57.1	698	7.12	4	5	3/26
Pittsburgh	5	149	95	63.8	1,129	7.58	11	3	9/62
San Francisco	2	75	48	64.0	668	8.91	3	4	5/32
Seattle	2	48	26	54.2	324	6.75	1	2	2/21
Tampa Bay	3	114	72	63.2	913	8.01	4	3	5/54
Washington	2	67	43	64.2	530	7.91	3	4	3/33
Totals	118	3,494	2,112	60.4	26,413	7.56	179	126	226/1,715

Arizona totals include one game vs. St. Louis, one game vs. Phoenix

TROY AIKMAN'S CAREER PASSING VS. EACH OPPONENT

Opponent	Games	Att.	Cmp.	Pct.	Yards	Avg. Gain	TD	Int.	Sacked
Arizona	8	210	131	62.4	1,726	8.22	8	8	12/85
Atlanta	2	44	31	70.5	480	10.91	4	2	0/0
Buffalo	1	45	28	62.2	297	6.60	2	1	1/7
Chicago	1	20	10	50.0	78	3.90	0	0	1/2
Cincinnati	1	22	14	63.6	276	12.55	1	2	1/12
Cleveland	1	37	24	64.9	274	7.41	2	0	2/9
Denver	1	35	25	71.4	231	6.60	3	0	2/9
Detroit	2	67	44	65.7	545	8.13	2	3	2/16
Green Bay	3	92	67	72.8	729	7.92	2	4	4/29
Houston	1	39	24	61.5	260	6.67	1	0	3/19
Indianapolis	1	28	21	75.0	245	8.75	1	0	2/14
Kansas City	1	29	21	72.4	192	6.62	1	2	1/9
L.A. Raiders	1	25	16	64.0	234	9.36	0	0	5/27
L.A. Rams	3	103	58	56.3	754	7.32	7	2	4/25
Miami	2	76	53	69.7	442	5.82	2	2	0/0
Minnesota	1	29	19	65.5	208	7.17	1	0	0/0
New Orleans	2	56	32	57.1	357	6.38	1	2	4/46
N.Y. Giants	10	231	155	67.1	1,587	6.87	9	5	15/91
N.Y. Jets	2	67	46	68.7	501	7.48	2	5	6/40
Philadelphia	9	232	121	52.2	1,295	5.58	6	11	31/191
San Diego	1	29	13	44.8	193	6.66	1	1	5/32
San Francisco	2	56	30	53.6	339	6.05	1	1	4/29
Seattle	1	23	15	65.2	173	7.52	0	2	1/3
Tampa Bay	2	53	30	56.6	332	6.26	2	2	5/38
Washington	9	272	163	59.9	1,879	6.91	12	10	28/199
Totals	68	1,920	1,191	62.0	13,627	7.10	69	66	139/932

Arizona totals include eight games vs. Phoenix

JERRY RICE'S CAREER RECEIVING VS. EACH OPPONENT

Opponent	Games	Rec.	Yards	Yards Per Rec.	Yards Per Game	TD
Arizona	5	25	465	18.6	93.0	5
Atlanta	17	89	1,523	17.1	89.6	17
Buffalo	2	6	72	12.0	36.0	1
Chicago	5	24	424	17.7	84.8	7
Cincinnati	3	16	269	16.8	89.7	2
Cleveland	3	19	275	14.5	91.7	4
Dallas	4	28	368	13.1	92.0	2
Denver	2	7	145	20.7	72.5	0
Detroit	5	17	267	15.7	53.4	2
Green Bay	4	23	432	18.8	108.0	4
Houston	3	23	238	10.3	79.3	4
Indianapolis	2	12	335	27.9	167.5	4
Kansas City	2	8	100	12.5	50.0	2
L.A. Raiders	3	11	193	17.5	64.3	0
L.A. Rams	18	84	1,527	18.2	84.8	11
Miami	2	10	155	15.5	77.5	3
Minnesota	7	32	552	17.3	78.9	6
New England	3	13	207	15.9	69.0	3
New Orleans	18	86	1,280	14.9	75.3	9
N.Y. Giants	6	27	454	16.8	75.7	4
N.Y. Jets	3	15	265	17.7	88.3	2
Philadelphia	5	25	424	17.0	84.8	5
Pittsburgh	3	19	215	11.3	71.7	3
San Diego	2	15	321	21.4	160.5	4
Seattle	3	14	272	19.4	90.7	4
Tampa Bay	6	39	615	15.8	102.5	10
Washington	4	21	383	18.2	95.8	2
Totals	140	708	11,776	16.6	84.1	118

Arizona totals include one game vs. St. Louis, four games vs. Phoenix

ART MONK'S CAREER RECEIVING VS. EACH OPPONENT

Opponent	Games	Rec.	Yards	Yards Per Rec.	Yards Per Game	TD
Arizona	27	112	1,555	13.9	59.6	14
Atlanta	9	42	600	14.3	66.7	7
Buffalo	5	31	305	9.8	61.0	2
Chicago	7	36	496	13.8	70.9	4
Cincinnati	3	21	366	17.4	122.0	1
Cleveland	3	11	146	13.3	48.7	1
Dallas	24	94	1,334	14.2	55.6	3
Denver	4	21	261	12.4	65.3	2
Detroit	8	39	426	10.9	53.3	2
Green Bay	3	10	148	14.8	49.3	1
Houston	3	16	147	9.2	49.0	0
Indianapolis	4	22	351	16.0	87.8	5
Kansas City	1	2	19	9.5	19.0	0
L.A. Raiders	5	14	258	18.4	51.6	1
L.A. Rams	5	16	310	19.4	62.0	2
Miami	4	20	219	11.0	54.8	2
Minnesota	5	21	243	11.6	48.6	1
New England	3	9	100	11.1	33.3	0
New Orleans	7	32	440	13.8	62.9	2
N.Y. Giants	26	101	1,313	13.0	50.5	3
N.Y. Jets	2	6	94	15.7	47.0	0
Philadelphia	27	101	1,299	12.9	48.1	9
Pittsburgh	3	23	281	12.2	93.7	1
San Diego	4	23	361	15.7	90.3	0
San Francisco	6	40	583	14.6	97.2	2
Seattle	4	12	226	18.8	56.5	0
Tampa Bay	3	13	145	11.2	48.3	0
Totals	205	888	12,026	13.5	58.7	65

Arizona totals include 15 games vs. St. Louis, 12 games vs. Phoenix
Indianapolis totals include one game vs. Baltimore
L.A. Raiders totals include one game vs. Oakland

ANDRE REED'S CAREER RECEIVING VS. EACH OPPONENT

Opponent	Games	Rec.	Yards	Yards Per Rec.	Yards Per Game	TD
Arizona	2	0	0	—	0.0	0
Atlanta	2	9	170	18.9	85.0	1
Chicago	2	11	131	11.9	65.5	0
Cincinnati	5	11	171	15.5	42.8	2
Cleveland	4	16	250	15.6	62.5	1
Dallas	1	1	10	10.0	10.0	0
Denver	4	21	258	12.3	64.5	1
Detroit	1	2	31	15.5	31.0	1
Green Bay	2	6	58	9.7	29.0	1
Houston	7	35	536	15.3	76.6	5
Indianapolis	17	78	1,065	13.7	62.6	13
Kansas City	4	21	262	12.5	65.5	2
L.A. Raiders	5	28	406	14.5	81.2	1
L.A. Rams	2	10	135	13.5	67.5	1
Miami	18	80	1,103	13.8	68.9	7
Minnesota	2	9	86	9.6	43.0	0
New England	16	67	1,041	15.5	65.1	5
New Orleans	2	6	54	9.0	27.0	0
N.Y. Giants	2	7	95	13.6	47.5	1
N.Y. Jets	18	74	1,016	13.7	56.4	8
Philadelphia	3	15	161	10.7	53.7	3
Pittsburgh	6	22	295	13.4	49.2	2
San Diego	2	9	138	15.3	69.0	0
San Francisco	2	20	259	13.0	129.5	0
Seattle	2	5	116	23.2	58.0	1
Tampa Bay	3	8	119	14.9	39.7	0
Washington	3	15	267	17.8	89.0	2
Totals	137	586	8,233	14.0	60.1	58

Arizona totals include one game vs. St. Louis, one game vs. Phoenix

MICHAEL IRVIN'S CAREER RECEIVING VS. EACH OPPONENT

Opponent	Games	Rec.	Yards	Yards Per Rec.	Yards Per Game	TD
Arizona	10	30	623	20.8	77.9	4
Atlanta	6	24	406	16.9	67.7	2
Buffalo	1	8	115	14.4	115.0	0
Chicago	1	5	46	9.2	46.0	0
Cincinnati	2	10	242	24.2	121.0	0
Cleveland	2	11	160	14.5	80.0	1
Denver	1	6	62	10.3	62.0	2
Detroit	2	13	257	19.8	128.5	1
Green Bay	3	18	296	16.4	98.7	2
Houston	2	8	106	13.3	53.0	1
Indianapolis	1	7	112	16.0	112.0	0
Kansas City	1	6	84	14.0	84.0	0

Opponent	Games	Rec.	Yards	Yards Per Rec.	Yards Per Game	TD
L.A. Raiders	1	3	54	18.0	54.0	0
L.A. Rams	2	10	239	23.9	119.5	2
Miami	1	3	31	10.3	31.0	0
Minnesota	2	10	167	16.7	83.5	1
New Orleans	4	11	197	17.9	49.3	0
N.Y. Giants	9	32	497	15.5	62.1	3
N.Y. Jets	2	10	184	18.4	92.0	2
Philadelphia	10	25	427	17.1	53.4	2
Pittsburgh	2	11	230	20.9	115.0	2
San Francisco	3	19	238	12.5	79.3	1
Seattle	1	6	113	18.8	113.0	0
Tampa Bay	2	2	42	21.0	21.0	1
Washington	9	49	766	15.6	85.1	7
Totals	80	337	5,694	16.9	71.2	34

Arizona totals include 10 games vs. Phoenix

STARTING RECORDS OF ACTIVE NFL QUARTERBACKS

Minimum: 10 starts

	W- L- T	Pct.
Joe Montana	108- 42	.720
Cody Carlson	10- 4	.714
Jim McMahon	67- 29	.698
Stan Humphries	20- 10	.667
Jeff Hostetler	26- 14	.650
Erik Kramer	11- 6	.647
Jim Kelly	76- 42	.644
Dan Marino	97- 57	.630
Jay Schroeder	57- 34	.626
Mark Rypien	45- 27	.625
Randall Cunningham	55- 33 -1	.624
John Elway	98- 59 -1	.623
Bobby Hebert	53- 34	.609
Phil Simms	95- 64	.597
Dave Krieg	83- 57	.593
Brett Favre	17- 12	.586
Mike Tomczak	27- 20	.574
Neil O'Donnell	20- 15	.571
Troy Aikman	38- 30	.559
Steve Young	39- 32	.549
Steve Beuerlein	18- 15	.545
Bob Gagliano	7- 6	.538
Jim Harbaugh	35- 30	.538
Wade Wilson	35- 30	.538
Rich Gannon	20- 19	.513
Bernie Kosar	53- 52 -1	.505
Warren Moon	70- 69	.504
Boomer Esiason	66- 68	.493
Bubby Brister	32- 33	.492
Billy Joe Tolliver	13- 15	.464
Ken O'Brien	50- 59 -1	.459
Don Majkowski	22- 26 -1	.459
Steve Walsh	11- 13	.458
Rodney Peete	21- 26	.447
Jim Everett	46- 59	.438
Drew Bledsoe	5- 7	.417
Steve DeBerg	53- 85 -1	.385
Chris Chandler	15- 24	.385
Jack Trudeau	18- 29	.383
Rick Mirer	6- 10	.375
Vince Evans	13- 23	.361
Chris Miller	23- 43	.348
Vinny Testaverde	27- 51	.346
Craig Erickson	5- 10	.333
Hugh Millen	7- 16	.304
Jeff George	14- 35	.286
John Friesz	6- 17	.261
David Klingler	4- 13	.235
Browning Nagle	3- 10	.231
Chuck Long	4- 17	.190
Stan Gelbaugh	0- 11	.000

NFL INDIVIDUAL LEADERS OVER RECENT SEASONS

Last 2 Seasons	Last 3 Seasons	Last 4 Seasons
Points		
237, Morten Andersen	354, Pete Stoyanovich	472, Chip Lohmiller
237, John Carney	350, Morten Andersen	460, Nick Lowery
233, Pete Stoyanovich	341, Chip Lohmiller	454, Pete Stoyanovich
230, Al Del Greco	329, Gary Anderson	442, Morten Andersen
229, Gary Anderson	325, John Carney	421, Gary Anderson

Touchdowns

Last 2 Seasons	Last 3 Seasons	Last 4 Seasons
29, Emmitt Smith	42, Emmitt Smith	54, Jerry Rice
27, Jerry Rice	41, Jerry Rice	53, Emmitt Smith
26, Andre Rison	38, Andre Rison	48, Andre Rison
24, Sterling Sharpe	30, Barry Sanders	46, Barry Sanders
22, Ricky Watters	30, Thurman Thomas	43, Thurman Thomas

Field Goals

Last 2 Seasons	Last 3 Seasons	Last 4 Seasons
57, Morten Andersen	85, Pete Stoyanovich	107, Chip Lohmiller
57, John Carney	82, Morten Andersen	106, Pete Stoyanovich
56, Gary Anderson	79, Gary Anderson	104, Nick Lowery
55, Jason Hanson	79, Jeff Jaeger	103, Morten Andersen
54, Pete Stoyanovich	77, Chip Lohmiller	99, Gary Anderson

Rushes

Last 2 Seasons	Last 3 Seasons	Last 4 Seasons
667, Thurman Thomas	1021, Emmitt Smith	1262, Emmitt Smith
656, Emmitt Smith	955, Thurman Thomas	1226, Thurman Thomas
567, Barry Foster	897, Barry Sanders	1152, Barry Sanders
555, Barry Sanders	805, Rodney Hampton	914, Rodney Hampton
549, Rodney Hampton	727, Reggie Cobb	878, Reggie Cobb

Rushing Yards

Last 2 Seasons	Last 3 Seasons	Last 4 Seasons
3199, Emmitt Smith	4762, Emmitt Smith	5699, Emmitt Smith
2802, Thurman Thomas	4209, Thurman Thomas	5506, Thurman Thomas
2467, Barry Sanders	4015, Barry Sanders	5319, Barry Sanders
2401, Barry Foster	3277, Rodney Hampton	3732, Rodney Hampton
2218, Rodney Hampton	2889, Barry Foster	3614, Marion Butts

Rushing TDs

Last 2 Seasons	Last 3 Seasons	Last 4 Seasons
27, Emmitt Smith	39, Emmitt Smith	50, Emmitt Smith
19, Barry Foster	29, Rodney Hampton	41, Barry Sanders
19, Rodney Hampton	28, Barry Sanders	33, Thurman Thomas
19, Ricky Watters	24, Brad Baxter	31, Rodney Hampton
15, Thurman Thomas	22, Thurman Thomas	30, Brad Baxter

Passes

Last 2 Seasons	Last 3 Seasons	Last 4 Seasons
993, Brett Favre	1521, Warren Moon	2105, Warren Moon
932, Jim Kelly	1406, Jim Kelly	1820, John Elway
867, John Elway	1318, John Elway	1793, Jim Everett
866, Warren Moon	1253, Dan Marino	1784, Dan Marino
865, Troy Aikman	1239, Jim Everett	1752, Jim Kelly

Completions

Last 2 Seasons	Last 3 Seasons	Last 4 Seasons
620, Brett Favre	931, Warren Moon	1293, Warren Moon
582, Steve Young	861, Jim Kelly	1080, Jim Kelly
573, Troy Aikman	810, Troy Aikman	1058, John Elway
557, Jim Kelly	764, John Elway	1045, Dan Marino
527, Warren Moon	762, Steve Young	1036, Troy Aikman

Passing Yards

Last 2 Seasons	Last 3 Seasons	Last 4 Seasons
7488, Steve Young	10696, Warren Moon	15385, Warren Moon
6839, Jim Kelly	10683, Jim Kelly	13512, Jim Kelly
6545, Troy Aikman	10005, Steve Young	13051, John Elway
6530, Brett Favre	9525, John Elway	12867, Dan Marino
6272, John Elway	9304, Dan Marino	12402, Jim Everett

Touchdown Passes

Last 2 Seasons	Last 3 Seasons	Last 4 Seasons
54, Steve Young	74, Jim Kelly	98, Jim Kelly
43, Bobby Hebert	71, Steve Young	95, Warren Moon
41, Jim Kelly	62, Warren Moon	78, Dan Marino
39, Warren Moon	57, Dan Marino	73, Steve Young
38, Troy Aikman	52, Bobby Hebert	64, Boomer Esiason
		64, Jim Everett

Receptions

Last 2 Seasons	Last 3 Seasons	Last 4 Seasons
220, Sterling Sharpe	289, Sterling Sharpe	362, Jerry Rice
182, Jerry Rice	262, Jerry Rice	356, Sterling Sharpe
179, Andre Rison	260, Andre Rison	342, Andre Rison
166, Michael Irvin	259, Michael Irvin	330, Haywood Jeffires
156, Haywood Jeffires	256, Haywood Jeffires	279, Michael Irvin
156, Anthony Miller		

Reception Yards

Last 2 Seasons	Last 3 Seasons	Last 4 Seasons
2735, Sterling Sharpe	4249, Michael Irvin	5412, Jerry Rice
2726, Michael Irvin	3910, Jerry Rice	4801, Sterling Sharpe
2704, Jerry Rice	3696, Sterling Sharpe	4662, Michael Irvin
2361, Andre Rison	3337, Andre Rison	4545, Andre Rison
2222, Anthony Miller	3070, Gary Clark	4182, Gary Clark

Receiving Touchdowns

Last 2 Seasons	Last 3 Seasons	Last 4 Seasons
26, Andre Rison	39, Jerry Rice	52, Jerry Rice
25, Jerry Rice	38, Andre Rison	48, Andre Rison
24, Sterling Sharpe	28, Sterling Sharpe	34, Sterling Sharpe
17, Calvin Williams	25, Michael Haynes	30, Haywood Jeffires
15, three players	22, Michael Irvin	29, Calvin Williams
	22, Haywood Jeffires	

Interceptions

Last 2 Seasons	Last 3 Seasons	Last 4 Seasons
16, Eugene Robinson	21, Eugene Robinson	24, Eugene Robinson
14, Nate Odomes	19, Nate Odomes	20, Nate Odomes
13, Darren Carrington	16, Darren Carrington	20, Rod Woodson
12, Audray McMillian	16, Audray McMillian	19, Cris Dishman
12, Brian Washington	16, Deion Sanders	19, Audray McMillian
12, Rod Woodson		19, Deion Sanders

Sacks

Last 2 Seasons	Last 3 Seasons	Last 4 Seasons
29.5, Simon Fletcher	43.0, Simon Fletcher	56.0, Derrick Thomas
29.5, Neil Smith	42.0, Reggie White	56.0, Reggie White
29.0, Leslie O'Neal	38.0, Leslie O'Neal	54.0, Simon Fletcher
28.0, Bruce Smith	37.5, Neil Smith	51.5, Leslie O'Neal
27.0, Chris Doleman	37.0, Clyde Simmons	48.5, Bruce Smith
27.0, Reggie White		

NFL TEAM LEADERS OVER RECENT SEASONS

Highest Won-Lost Percentage

Last 2 Seasons	Last 3 Seasons	Last 4 Seasons
.781, Dallas	.750, Buffalo	.766, Buffalo
.750, San Francisco	.750, Dallas	.750, San Francisco
.719, Buffalo	.708, San Francisco	.672, Dallas
.688, Houston	.688, Houston	.656, Houston
.656, Kansas City	.646, Kansas City	.656, Kansas City
	.646, New Orleans	

Most Points

Last 2 Seasons	Last 3 Seasons	Last 4 Seasons
904, San Francisco	1297, San Francisco	1650, San Francisco
785, Dallas	1168, Buffalo	1596, Buffalo
720, Houston	1127, Dallas	1511, Houston
710, Buffalo	1106, Houston	1396, Washington
689, Miami	1032, Miami	1371, Dallas

Most Total Yards

Last 2 Seasons	Last 3 Seasons	Last 4 Seasons
12630, San Francisco	18488, San Francisco	24383, San Francisco
11313, Houston	17405, Buffalo	23522, Houston
11312, Miami	17300, Houston	22681, Buffalo
11221, Dallas	16553, Miami	21600, Miami
11153, Buffalo	16322, Dallas	20466, Washington

Most Rushing Yards

Last 2 Seasons	Last 3 Seasons	Last 4 Seasons
4448, San Francisco	6760, Buffalo	8840, Buffalo
4379, Buffalo	6351, N.Y. Giants	8400, N.Y. Giants
4287, N.Y. Giants	6309, San Francisco	8204, San Diego
4282, Dallas	5993, Dallas	8101, Philadelphia
4159, Pittsburgh	5947, San Diego	8027, San Francisco

Most Passing Yards

Last 2 Seasons	Last 3 Seasons	Last 4 Seasons
8328, Miami	12516, Houston	17321, Houston
8182, San Francisco	12217, Miami	16356, San Francisco
7895, Houston	12179, San Francisco	15729, Miami
7153, Atlanta	10645, Buffalo	14063, Atlanta
6939, Dallas	10602, Atlanta	13841, Buffalo

Fewest Turnovers

Last 2 Seasons	Last 3 Seasons	Last 4 Seasons
40, N.Y. Giants	63, N.Y. Giants	77, N.Y. Giants
46, Dallas	70, Dallas	90, Kansas City
47, Cincinnati	71, Kansas City	103, Dallas
49, Kansas City	78, Washington	106, Washington
52, San Diego	80, San Diego	112, San Diego
52, San Francisco		

Fewest Points Allowed

Last 2 Seasons	Last 3 Seasons	Last 4 Seasons
472, Dallas	747, Houston	1009, San Francisco
496, Houston	756, New Orleans	1031, New Orleans
506, Pittsburgh	770, San Francisco	1054, Houston
525, Buffalo	782, Dallas	1080, N.Y. Giants
531, San Diego	804, Philadelphia	1082, Kansas City
531, San Francisco		

Fewest Total Yards Allowed

Last 2 Seasons	Last 3 Seasons	Last 4 Seasons
8698, Dallas	12704, New Orleans	17582, New Orleans
8771, New Orleans	12979, Philadelphia	17639, Philadelphia
8921, Minnesota	13764, Dallas	18379, Dallas
9085, Houston	13842, Houston	18472, Pittsburgh
9095, Kansas City	13937, Minnesota	18477, Houston

Fewest Rushing Yards Allowed

2709, San Diego	4375, San Diego	5866, Philadelphia
2895, Dallas	4447, Houston	5890, San Diego
2907, Houston	4466, Dallas	5988, San Francisco
3209, Pittsburgh	4697, Philadelphia	6022, Houston
3218, San Francisco	4730, San Francisco	6406, Pittsburgh

Fewest Passing Yards Allowed

5076, New Orleans	7796, New Orleans	11115, New Orleans
5652, Minnesota	8282, Philadelphia	11474, Minnesota
5688, Kansas City	8749, Chicago	11664, L.A. Raiders
5691, L.A. Raiders	8817, Indianapolis	11669, Chicago
5803, Dallas	8831, Minnesota	11768, N.Y. Giants

Most Opponents' Turnovers

82, Buffalo	120, Philadelphia	155, Kansas City
81, Pittsburgh	119, Buffalo	154, Buffalo
77, Kansas City	116, New Orleans	153, Pittsburgh
76, Minnesota	113, N.Y. Jets	150, Philadelphia
76, N.Y. Jets	112, Houston	145, Houston

RECORDS OF TEAMS ON OPENING DAY, 1933-93

AFC	W	L	T	Pct.	Longest W Strk.	Longest L Strk.	Current Streak
Denver	21	12	1	.636	3	4	W-3
L.A. Raiders	20	14	0	.588	5	5	W-1
Cleveland	25	19	0	.568	5	5	W-1
Kansas City	19	15	0	.559	5	4	W-4
San Diego	19	15	0	.559	6	6	W-1
Pittsburgh	29	26	4	.527	4	3	L-1
Indianapolis	21	20	0	.512	8	8	L-1
Cincinnati	13	13	0	.500	4	4	L-1
Houston	17	17	0	.500	4	3	L-2
Miami	13	14	1	.481	4	5	W-2
New England	16	18	0	.471	6	3	L-2
Buffalo	15	19	0	.441	6	5	W-6
N.Y. Jets	14	20	0	.412	3	5	L-2
Seattle	4	14	0	.222	3	8	L-5

NFC	W	L	T	Pct.	Longest W Strk.	Longest L Strk.	Current Streak
Dallas	25	8	1	.758	17	3	L-1
N.Y. Giants	34	23	4	.596	4	3	W-1
Chicago	35	25	1	.583	9	6	L-1
Minnesota	18	14	1	.563	4	2	L-1
Atlanta	15	13	0	.536	5	3	L-1
Washington	30	27	4	.526	6	5	W-1
Detroit	31	28	2	.525	7	4	W-1
L.A. Rams	29	27	0	.518	5	6	L-4
Green Bay	30	28	3	.517	5	6	W-1
San Francisco	21	22	1	.488	4	3	W-2
Arizona	26	33	1	.441	6	6	L-2
Philadelphia	25	34	1	.424	5	9	W-3
Tampa Bay	7	11	0	.389	3	5	L-1
New Orleans	7	20	0	.259	1	6	W-1

NOTE: All tied games occurred prior to 1972, when calculation of ties in percentages as half-win, half-loss was begun.

OLDEST INDIVIDUAL SINGLE-SEASON OR SINGLE-GAME RECORDS IN NFL RECORD & FACT BOOK
Regular-Season Records That Have Not Been Surpassed or Tied

Most Points, Game—40, Ernie Nevers, Chi. Cardinals vs. Chi. Bears, Nov. 28, 1929 (6-td, 4-pat)

Most Touchdowns Rushing, Game—6, Ernie Nevers, Chi. Cardinals vs. Chi. Bears, Nov. 28, 1929

Highest Punting Average, Season (Qualifiers)—51.40, Sammy Baugh, Washington, 1940 (35-1,799)

Highest Punting Average, Game (minimum: 4 punts)—61.75, Bob Cifers, Detroit vs. Chi. Bears, Nov. 24, 1946 (4-247)

Highest Average Gain, Pass Receptions, Season (minimum: 24 receptions)—32.58, Don Currivan, Boston, 1947 (24-782)

Highest Average Gain, Passing, Game (minimum: 20 passes)—18.58, Sammy Baugh, Washington vs. Boston, Oct. 31, 1948 (24-446)

Most Touchdowns, Fumble Recoveries, Game—2, Fred (Dippy) Evans, Chi. Bears vs. Washington, Nov. 28, 1948

Most Yards Gained, Intercepted Passes, Rookie, Season—301, Don Doll, Detroit, 1949

Most Passes Had Intercepted, Game—8, Jim Hardy, Chi. Cardinals vs. Philadelphia, Sept. 24, 1950

Highest Average Gain, Rushing, Game (minimum: 10 attempts)—17.09, Marion Motley, Cleveland vs. Pittsburgh, Oct. 29, 1950 (11-188)

Most Yards Gained, Kickoff Returns, Game—294, Wally Triplett, Detroit vs. Los Angeles, Oct. 29, 1950

Highest Kickoff Return Average, Game (minimum: 3 returns)—73.50, Wally Triplett, Detroit vs. Los Angeles, Oct. 29, 1950 (4-294)

Most Pass Receptions, Game—18, Tom Fears, Los Angeles vs. Green Bay, Dec. 3, 1950

Highest Punt Return Average, Season (Qualifiers)—23.00, Herb Rich, Baltimore, 1950 (12-276)

Highest Punt Return Average, Rookie, Season (Qualifiers)—23.00, Herb Rich, Baltimore, 1950 (12-276)

Most Yards Passing, Game—554, Norm Van Brocklin, Los Angeles vs. N.Y. Yanks, Sept. 28, 1951

Most Touchdowns, Punt Returns, Rookie, Season—4, Jack Christiansen, Detroit, 1951

Most Interceptions By, Season—14, Dick (Night Train) Lane, Los Angeles, 1952

Most Interceptions By, Rookie, Season—14, Dick (Night Train) Lane, Los Angeles, 1952

Highest Average Gain, Passing, Season (Qualifiers)—11.17, Tommy O'Connell, Cleveland, 1957 (110-1,229)

Most Points, Season—176, Paul Hornung, Green Bay, 1960 (15-td, 41-pat,15-fg)

Most Yards Gained, Pass Receptions, Rookie, Season—1,473, Bill Groman, Houston, 1960

LARGEST TRADES IN NFL HISTORY
(Based on number of players or draft choices involved)

18—October 13, 1989—RB Herschel Walker from the Dallas Cowboys to Minnesota. Dallas also traded its third-round choice in 1990, its tenth-round choice in 1990, and its third-round choice in 1991 to Minnesota. Minnesota traded LB Jesse Solomon, LB David Howard, CB Issiac Holt, and DE Alex Stewart along with its first-round choice in 1990, its second-round choice in 1990, its sixth-round choice in 1990, its first-round choice in 1991, its second-round choice in 1991, its first-round choice in 1992, its second-round choice in 1992, and its third-round choice in 1992 to Dallas. Minnesota traded RB Darrin Nelson to Dallas, which traded Nelson to San Diego for the Chargers' fifth-round choice in 1990, which Dallas then sent to Minnesota.

15—March 26, 1953—T Mike McCormack, DT Don Colo, LB Tom Catlin, DB John Petitbon, and G Herschell Forester from Baltimore to Cleveland for DB Don Shula, DB Bert Rechichar, DB Carl Taseff, LB Ed Sharkey, E Gern Nagler, QB Harry Agganis, T Dick Batten, T Stu Sheets, G Art Spinney, and G Elmer Willhoite.

15—January 28, 1971—LB Marlin McKeever, first- and third-round choices in 1971, and third-, fourth-, fifth-, sixth-, and seventh-round choices in 1972 from Washington to the Los Angeles Rams for LB Maxie Baughan, LB Jack Pardee, LB Myron Pottios, RB Jeff Jordan, G John Wilbur, DT Diron Talbert, and a fifth-round choice in 1971.

12—June 13, 1952—Selection rights to Les Richter from the Dallas Texans to the Los Angeles Rams for RB Dick Hoerner, DB Tom Keane, DB George Sims, C Joe Reid, HB Billy Baggett, T Jack Halliday, FB Dick McKissack, LB Vic Vasicek, E Richard Wilkins, C Aubrey Phillips, and RB Dave Anderson.

10—March 23, 1959—HB Ollie Matson from the Chicago Cardinals to the Los Angeles Rams for T Frank Fuller, DE Glenn Holtzman, T Ken Panfil, DT Art Hauser, E John Tracey, FB Larry Hickman, HB Don Brown, the Rams second-round choice in 1960, and a player to be delivered during the 1959 training camp.

10—October 31, 1987—RB Eric Dickerson from the Los Angeles Rams to Indianapolis. The rights to LB Cornelius Bennett from Indianapolis to Buffalo. Indianapolis running back Owen Gill and the Colts' first- and second-round choices in 1988 and second-round choice in 1989, plus Bills running back Greg Bell and Buffalo's first-round choice in 1988 and first- and second-round choices in 1989 to the Rams.

RETIRED UNIFORM NUMBERS IN NFL
AFC

Buffalo:	None	
Cincinnati:	Bob Johnson	54
Cleveland:	Otto Graham	14
	Jim Brown	32
	Ernie Davis	45
	Don Fleming	46
	Lou Groza	76
Denver:	Frank Tripucka	18
	Floyd Little	44
Houston:	Earl Campbell	34
	Jim Norton	43
	Elvin Bethea	65
Indianapolis:	Johnny Unitas	19
	Buddy Young	22
	Lenny Moore	24
	Art Donovan	70
	Jim Parker	77
	Raymond Berry	82
	Gino Marchetti	89

Kansas City: ....Jan Stenerud 3
Len Dawson 16
Abner Haynes.....................................28
Stone Johnson 33
Mack Lee Hill 36
Willie Lanier......................................63
Bobby Bell 78
Buck Buchanan 86
Los Angeles Raiders: ....None
Miami:.....................................Bob Griese 12
New England:...........................Gino Cappelletti 20
Steve Nelson....................................57
John Hannah.....................................73
Jim Hunt...79
Bob Dee 89
New York Jets: ....Joe Namath 12
Don Maynard 13
Pittsburgh:...............................None
San Diego: ....Dan Fouts.......................................14
Seattle: ...."Fans/the twelfth man"...................12
NFC
Arizona: ....Larry Wilson 8
Stan Mauldin 77
J.V. Cain 88
Marshall Goldberg 99
Atlanta: ....Steve Bartowski 10
William Andrews.................................31
Jeff Van Note 57
Tommy Nobis 60
Chicago:..................................Bronko Nagurski 3
George McAfee 5
George Halas 7
Willie Galimore 28
Walter Payton 34
Brian Piccolo....................................41
Sid Luckman 42
Bill Hewitt 56
Bill George 61
Bulldog Turner..................................66
Red Grange......................................77
Dallas: ....None
Detroit:....................................Dutch Clark 7
Bobby Layne 22
Doak Walker.....................................37
Joe Schmidt 56
Chuck Hughes 85
Charlie Sanders 88
Green Bay: ....Tony Canadeo 3
Don Hutson.....................................14
Bart Starr.......................................15
Ray Nitschke....................................66
Los Angeles Rams: ....Bob Waterfield....................................7
Merlin Olsen.....................................74
Minnesota:...............................Fran Tarkenton 10
Alan Page.......................................88
New Orleans: ....Jim Taylor.......................................31
Doug Atkins.....................................81
New York Giants:......................Ray Flaherty 1
Mel Hein...7
Y.A. Tittle.......................................14
Al Blozis..32
Joe Morrison 40
Charlie Conerly 42
Ken Strong......................................50
Philadelphia: ....Steve Van Buren 15
Tom Brookshier..................................40
Pete Retzlaff 44
Chuck Bednarik 60
Al Wistert 70
Jerome Brown....................................99
San Francisco: ....John Brodie......................................12
Joe Perry.......................................34
Jimmy Johnson..................................37
Hugh McElhenny 39
Charlie Krueger..................................70
Leo Nomellini 73
Dwight Clark.....................................87
Tampa Bay: ....Lee Roy Selmon.................................63
Washington ....Sammy Baugh 33

1993 NFL SCORE BY QUARTERS

AFC Offense	1	2	3	4	OT	PTS
Denver	66	147	91	69	0	373
Houston	68	131	75	94	0	368
Miami	100	76	85	88	0	349
Buffalo	64	113	51	98	3	329
Kansas City	71	108	82	67	0	328
San Diego	66	76	67	113	0	322
Pittsburgh	38	110	79	81	0	308
L.A. Raiders	77	93	50	83	3	306
Cleveland	56	99	58	91	0	304
Seattle	72	64	45	99	0	280
N.Y. Jets	65	105	37	63	0	270
New England	33	60	54	85	6	238
Indianapolis	19	60	29	81	0	189
Cincinnati	41	74	18	54	0	187

NFC Offense	1	2	3	4	OT	PTS
San Francisco	97	158	108	110	0	473
Dallas	76	124	86	87	3	376
Green Bay	97	95	77	71	0	340
Phoenix	54	98	79	92	3	326
New Orleans	66	80	60	111	0	317
Atlanta	60	77	68	111	0	316
Detroit	44	102	62	87	3	298
Philadelphia	36	101	56	97	3	293
N.Y. Giants	61	112	43	72	0	288
Minnesota	49	81	83	64	0	277
Tampa Bay	19	74	89	55	0	237
Chicago	37	85	56	56	0	234
Washington	23	77	59	71	0	230
L.A. Rams	52	40	40	89	0	221

AFC Defense	1	2	3	4	OT	PTS
Houston	40	73	50	75	0	238
Buffalo	71	62	67	42	0	242
N.Y. Jets	36	77	68	66	0	247
Pittsburgh	75	102	40	64	0	281
Denver	53	82	62	84	3	284
New England	41	103	26	110	6	286
San Diego	50	102	83	55	0	290
Kansas City	51	86	50	104	0	291
Cleveland	64	110	52	81	0	307
Seattle	65	104	66	76	3	314
Cincinnati	42	119	63	95	0	319
L.A. Raiders	34	108	57	127	0	326
Miami	56	126	71	92	6	351
Indianapolis	96	96	98	88	0	378

NFC Defense	1	2	3	4	OT	PTS
N.Y. Giants	40	60	40	62	3	205
Dallas	43	46	79	61	0	229
Chicago	45	83	38	64	0	230
Phoenix	58	84	53	74	0	269
Green Bay	29	76	90	87	0	282
Minnesota	67	93	36	94	0	290
Detroit	61	86	78	67	0	292
San Francisco	44	106	57	85	3	295
Philadelphia	65	94	55	101	0	315
New Orleans	78	106	72	87	0	343
Washington	81	92	69	103	0	345
L.A. Rams	72	95	92	108	0	367
Tampa Bay	72	133	75	96	0	376
Atlanta	78	116	100	91	0	385

NFL Totals	1	2	3	4	OT	PTS
	1,607	2,620	1,787	2,339	24	8,377

TEAM LEADERS

Offense	Most Scored	Fewest Scored
1st Quarter	100, Miami	19, Ind. & T.B.
2nd Quarter	158, San Francisco	40, L.A. Rams
3rd Quarter	108, San Francisco	18, Cincinnati
4th Quarter	113, San Diego	54, Cincinnati

Defense	Most Allowed	Fewest Allowed
1st Quarter	96, Indianapolis	29, Green Bay
2nd Quarter	133, Tampa Bay	46, Dallas
3rd Quarter	100, Atlanta	26, New England
4th Quarter	127, L.A. Raiders	42, Buffalo

GREATEST COMEBACKS IN NFL HISTORY
(Most Points Overcome To Win Game)

REGULAR SEASON GAMES

FROM 28 POINTS BEHIND TO WIN:
December 7, 1980, at San Francisco

New Orleans	14	21	0	0	0	— 35
San Francisco	0	7	14	14	3	— 38

NO — Harris 33 pass from Manning (Ricardo kick)
NO — Childs 21 pass from Manning (Ricardo kick)
NO — Holmes 1 run (Ricardo kick)
SF — Solomon 57 punt return (Wersching kick)
NO — Holmes 1 run (Ricardo kick)
NO — Harris 41 pass from Manning (Ricardo kick)
SF — Montana 1 run (Wersching kick)
SF — Clark 71 pass from Montana (Wersching kick)
SF — Solomon 14 pass from Montana (Wersching kick)
SF — Elliott 7 run (Wersching kick)
SF — FG Wersching 36

	N.O.	S.F.
First Downs	27	24
Total Yards	519	430
Yards Rushing	143	176
Yards Passing	376	254
Turnovers	3	0

FROM 25 POINTS BEHIND TO WIN:
November 8, 1987, at St. Louis

Tampa Bay	7	7	14	0	— 28
St. Louis	0	3	0	28	— 31

TB — Carrier 5 pass from DeBerg (Igwebuike kick)
TB — Carter 3 pass from DeBerg (Igwebuike kick)
StL — FG Gallery 31
TB — Smith 34 pass from DeBerg (Igwebuike kick)
TB — Smith 3 run (Igwebuike kick)
StL — Awalt 4 pass from Lomax (Gallery kick)
StL — Noga 23 fumble recovery (Gallery kick)
StL — J. Smith 11 pass from Lomax (Gallery kick)
StL — J. Smith 17 pass from Lomax (Gallery kick)

	T.B.	St.L.
First Downs	26	26
Total Yards	377	415
Yards Rushing	83	137
Yards Passing	294	278
Turnovers	1	2

FROM 24 POINTS BEHIND TO WIN:
October 27, 1946, at Washington

Philadelphia	0	0	14	14	— 28
Washington	10	14	0	0	— 24

Wash — Rosato 2 run (Poillon kick)
Wash — FG Poillon 28
Wash — Rosato 4 run (Poillon kick)
Wash — Lapka recovered fumble in end zone (Poillon kick)
Phil — Steele 1 run (Lio kick)
Phil — Pritchard 45 pass from Thompson (Lio kick)
Phil — Steinke 7 pass from Thompson (Lio kick)
Phil — Ferrante 30 pass from Thompson (Lio kick)

	Phil.	Wash.
First Downs	14	8
Total Yards	262	127
Yards Rushing	34	66
Yards Passing	228	61
Turnovers	6	3

FROM 24 POINTS BEHIND TO WIN:
October 20, 1957, at Detroit

Baltimore	7	14	6	0	— 27
Detroit	0	3	7	21	— 31

Balt — Mutscheller 15 pass from Unitas (Rechichar kick)
Det — FG Martin 47
Balt — Moore 72 pass from Unitas (Rechichar kick)
Balt — Mutscheller 52 pass from Unitas (Rechichar kick)
Balt — Moore 4 pass from Unitas (kick failed)
Det — Junker 14 pass from Rote (Layne kick)
Det — Cassady 26 pass from Layne (Layne kick)
Det — Johnson 1 run (Layne kick)
Det — Cassady 29 pass from Layne (Layne kick)

	Balt.	Det.
First Downs	15	20
Total Yards	322	369
Yards Rushing	117	178
Yards Passing	205	191
Turnovers	6	4

FROM 24 POINTS BEHIND TO WIN:
October 25, 1959, at Chicago

Philadelphia	0	0	21	7	— 28
Chicago Cardinals	7	10	7	0	— 24

Cardinals — Crow 10 pass from Roach (Conrad kick)
Cardinals — J. Hill 77 blocked field goal return (Conrad kick)
Cardinals — FG Conrad 15
Cardinals — Lane 37 interception return (Conrad kick)
Phil — Barnes 1 run (Walston kick)
Phil — McDonald 29 pass from Van Brocklin (Walston kick)
Phil — Barnes 2 run (Walston kick)
Phil — McDonald 22 pass from Van Brocklin (Walston kick)

	Phil.	Cardinals
First Downs	22	14
Total Yards	399	313
Yards Rushing	168	163
Yards Passing	231	150
Turnovers	2	6

FROM 24 POINTS BEHIND TO WIN:
October 23, 1960, at Denver

Boston	10	7	7	0	— 24
Denver	0	0	14	17	— 31

Bos — FG Cappelletti 12
Bos — Colclough 10 pass from Songin (Cappelletti kick)
Bos — Wells 6 pass from Songin (Cappelletti kick)
Bos — Miller 47 pass from Songin (Cappelletti kick)
Den — Carmichael 21 pass from Tripucka (Mingo kick)
Den — Jessup 19 pass from Tripucka (Mingo kick)
Den — Carmichael 35 lateral from Taylor, pass from Tripucka (Mingo kick)
Den — Taylor 8 pass from Tripucka (Mingo kick)
Den — FG Mingo 9

	Bos.	Den.
First Downs	19	16
Total Yards	434	326
Yards Rushing	211	65
Yards Passing	223	261
Turnovers	7	4

FROM 24 POINTS BEHIND TO WIN:
December 15, 1974, at Miami

New England	21	3	0	3	— 27
Miami	0	17	7	10	— 34

NE — Hannah recovered fumble in end zone (J. Smith kick)
NE — Sanders 23 interception return (J. Smith kick)
NE — Herron 4 pass from Plunkett (J. Smith kick)
NE — FG J. Smith 46
Mia — Nottingham 1 run (Yepremian kick)
Mia — Baker 37 pass from Morrall (Yepremian kick)
Mia — FG Yepremian 28
Mia — Baker 46 pass from Morrall (Yepremian kick)
NE — FG J. Smith 34
Mia — Nottingham 2 run (Yepremian kick)
Mia — FG Yepremian 40

	N.E.	Mia.
First Downs	18	18

Total Yards	333	333
Yards Rushing	114	61
Yards Passing	219	272
Turnovers	3	4

FROM 24 POINTS BEHIND TO WIN:
December 4, 1977, at Minnesota

San Francisco	0	10	14	3	— 27
Minnesota	0	0	7	21	— 28

SF — Delvin Williams 2 run (Wersching kick)
SF — FG Wersching 31
SF — Dave Williams 80 kickoff return (Wersching kick)
SF — Delvin Williams 5 run (Wersching kick)
Minn — McClanahan 15 pass from Lee (Cox kick)
Minn — Rashad 8 pass from Kramer (Cox kick)
Minn — Tucker 9 pass from Kramer (Cox kick)
SF — FG Wersching 31
Minn — S. White 69 pass from Kramer (Cox kick)

	S.F.	Minn.
First Downs	19	18
Total Yards	243	309
Yards Rushing	196	52
Yards Passing	47	257
Turnovers	2	5

FROM 24 POINTS BEHIND TO WIN:
September 23, 1979, at Denver

Seattle	10	10	14	0	— 34
Denver	0	10	21	6	— 37

Sea — FG Herrera 28
Sea — Doornink 5 run (Herrera kick)
Den — FG Turner 27
Sea — Doornink 5 run (Herrera kick)
Den — Armstrong 2 run (Turner kick)
Sea — FG Herrera 22
Sea — McCullum 13 pass from Zorn (Herrera kick)
Sea — Smith 1 run (Herrera kick)
Den — Studdard 2 pass from Morton (Turner kick)
Den — Moses 11 pass from Morton (Turner kick)
Den — Upchurch 35 pass from Morton (Turner kick)
Den — Lytle 1 run (kick failed)

	Sea.	Den.
First Downs	22	23
Total Yards	350	344
Yards Rushing	153	90
Yards Passing	197	254
Turnovers	4	3

FROM 24 POINTS BEHIND TO WIN:
September 23, 1979, at Cincinnati

Houston	0	10	17	0	3	—30
Cincinnati	14	10	0	3	0	—27

Cin — Johnson 1 run (Bahr kick)
Cin — Alexander 2 run (Bahr kick)
Cin — Johnson 1 run (Bahr kick)
Cin — FG Bahr 52
Hou — Burrough 35 pass from Pastorini (Fritsch kick)
Hou — FG Fritsch 33
Hou — Campbell 8 run (Fritsch kick)
Hou — Caster 22 pass from Pastorini (Fritsch kick)
Hou — FG Fritsch 47
Cin — FG Bahr 55
Hou — FG Fritsch 29

	Hou.	Cin.
First Downs	19	21
Total Yards	361	265
Yards Rushing	177	165
Yards Passing	184	100
Turnovers	3	2

FROM 24 POINTS BEHIND TO WIN:
November 22, 1982, at Los Angeles

San Diego	10	14	0	0	— 24
L.A. Raiders	0	7	14	7	— 28

SD — FG Benirschke 19
SD — Scales 29 pass from Fouts (Benirschke kick)
SD — Muncie 2 run (Benirschke kick)
SD — Muncie 1 run (Benirschke kick)
Raiders — Christensen 1 pass from Plunkett (Bahr kick)

Raiders — Allen 3 run (Bahr kick)
Raiders — Allen 6 run (Bahr kick)
Raiders — Hawkins 1 run (Bahr kick)

	S.D.	Raiders
First Downs	26	23
Total Yards	411	326
Yards Rushing	72	181
Yards Passing	339	145
Turnovers	4	2

FROM 24 POINTS BEHIND TO WIN:
September 26, 1988, at Denver

L.A. Raiders	0	0	14	13	3	— 30
Denver	7	17	0	3	0	— 27

Den — Dorsett 1 run (Karlis kick)
Den — Dorsett 1 run (Karlis kick)
Den — Sewell 7 pass from Elway (Karlis kick)
Den — FG Karlis 39
Raiders — Smith 40 pass from Schroeder (Bahr kick)
Raiders — Smith 42 pass from Schroeder (Bahr kick)
Raiders — FG Bahr 28
Raiders — Allen 4 run (Bahr kick)
Den — FG Karlis 25
Raiders — FG Bahr 44
Raiders — FG Bahr 35

	Raiders	Den.
First Downs	20	23
Total Yards	363	398
Yards Rushing	128	189
Yards Passing	235	209
Turnovers	1	5

FROM 24 POINTS BEHIND TO WIN:
December 6, 1992, at Tampa

L.A. Rams	0	3	21	7	— 31
Tampa Bay	6	21	0	0	— 27

TB — FG Murray 34
TB — FG Murray 47
TB — Armstrong 81 pass from Testaverde (Murray kick)
TB — Jones 26 fumble recovery (Murray kick)
Rams — FG Zendejas 18
TB — Carrier 10 pass from Testaverde (Murray kick)
Rams — Anderson 40 pass from Everett (Zendejas kick)
Rams — Chadwick 27 pass from Everett (Zendejas kick)
Rams — Lang 1 run (Zendejas kick)
Rams — Carter 8 pass from Everett (Zendejas kick)

	Rams	T.B.
First Downs	21	16
Total Yards	405	313
Yards Rushing	63	150
Yards Passing	342	163
Turnovers	3	3

POSTSEASON GAMES

FROM 32 POINTS BEHIND TO WIN:
AFC First-Round Playoff Game
January 3, 1993, at Buffalo

Houston	7	21	7	3	0	— 38
Buffalo	3	0	28	7	3	— 41

Hou — Jeffires 3 pass from Moon (Del Greco kick)
Buff — FG Christie 36
Hou — Slaughter 7 pass from Moon (Del Greco kick)
Hou — Duncan 26 pass from Moon (Del Greco kick)
Hou — Jeffires 27 pass from Moon (Del Greco kick)
Hou — McDowell 58 interception return (Del Greco kick)
Buff — Davis 1 run (Christie kick)
Buff — Beebe 38 pass from Reich (Christie kick)
Buff — Reed 26 pass from Reich (Christie kick)
Buff — Reed 18 pass from Reich (Christie kick)
Buff — Reed 17 pass from Reich (Christie kick)
Hou — FG Del Greco 26
Buff — FG Christie 32

	Hou.	Buff.
First Downs	27	19
Total Yards	429	366
Yards Rushing	82	98
Yards Passing	347	268
Turnovers	2	1

FROM 20 POINTS BEHIND TO WIN:
Western Conference Playoff Game
December 22, 1957, at San Francisco

Detroit	0	7	14	10	— 31
San Francisco	14	10	3	0	— 27

SF — Owens 34 pass from Tittle (Soltau kick)
SF — McElhenny 47 pass from Tittle (Soltau kick)
Det — Junker 4 pass from Rote (Martin kick)
SF — Wilson 12 pass from Tittle (Soltau kick)
SF — FG Soltau 25
SF — FG Soltau 10
Det — Tracy 2 run (Martin kick)
Det — Tracy 58 run (Martin kick)

Det — Gedman 3 run (Martin kick)
Det — FG Martin 14

	Det.	S.F.
First Downs	22	20
Total Yards	324	351
Yards Rushing	129	127
Yards Passing	195	224
Turnovers	5	4

FROM 18 POINTS BEHIND TO WIN:
NFC Divisional Playoff Game
December 23, 1972, at San Francisco

Dallas	3	10	0	17	— 30
San Francisco	7	14	7	0	— 28

SF — Washington 97 kickoff return (Gossett kick)
Dall — FG Fritsch 37
SF — Schreiber 1 run (Gossett kick)
SF — Schreiber 1 run (Gossett kick)
Dall — FG Fritsch 45
Dall — Alworth 28 pass from Morton (Fritsch kick)
SF — Schreiber 1 run (Gossett kick)
Dall — FG Fritsch 27
Dall — Parks 20 pass from Staubach (Fritsch kick)
Dall — Sellers 10 pass from Staubach (Fritsch kick)

	Dall.	S.F.
First Downs	22	13
Total Yards	402	255
Yards Rushing	165	105
Yards Passing	237	150
Turnovers	5	3

FROM 18 POINTS BEHIND TO WIN:
AFC Divisional Playoff Game
January 4, 1986, at Miami

Cleveland	7	7	7	0	— 21
Miami	3	0	14	7	— 24

Mia — FG Reveiz 51
Clev — Newsome 16 pass from Kosar (Bahr kick)
Clev — Byner 21 run (Bahr kick)
Clev — Byner 66 run (Bahr kick)
Mia — Moore 6 pass from Marino (Reveiz kick)
Mia — Davenport 31 run (Reveiz kick)
Mia — Davenport 1 run (Reveiz kick)

	Clev.	Mia.
First Downs	17	20
Total Yards	313	330
Yards Rushing	251	92
Yards Passing	62	238
Turnovers	1	1

RECORDS OF NFL TEAMS SINCE 1970 AFL-NFL MERGER

AFC	W - L - T	Pct.	Division Titles	Playoff Berths	Post-season Record	Super Bowl Record	NFC	W - L - T	Pct.	Division Titles	Playoff Berths	Post-season Record	Super Bowl Record
Miami	238-120-2	.664	10	14	16-12	2-3	Dallas	227-133-0	.631	11	17	26-13	4-3
L.A. Raiders	227-127-6	.640	9	15	18-12	3-0	Washington	225-134-1	.627	5	13	18-10	3-2
Pittsburgh	212-147-1	.590	10	14	16-10	4-0	San Francisco	212-145-3	.593	13	14	18-10	4-0
Denver	202-152-6	.570	7	10	9-10	0-4	Minnesota	210-148-2	.589	11	15	11-15	0-3
Cleveland	178-179-3	.499	6	9	3-9	0-0	L.A. Rams	203-153-4	.570	8	14	10-14	0-1
Cincinnati	175-185-0	.486	5	7	5-7	0-2	Chicago	186-173-1	.519	6	9	6-8	1-0
Kansas City	168-185-7	.476	2	6	3-6	0-0	Philadelphia	171-183-6	.483	2	8	4-8	0-1
Buffalo	169-189-2	.472	6	9	11-9	0-4	N.Y. Giants	169-189-2	.472	3	7	10-5	2-0
Seattle*	127-149-0	.460	1	4	3-4	0-0	Detroit	160-196-4	.450	3	5	1-5	0-0
Houston	164-194-2	.458	2	10	7-10	0-0	Arizona	151-203-6	.427	2	3	0-3	0-0
San Diego	159-196-5	.448	4	5	4-5	0-0	Green Bay	150-202-8	.427	1	3	2-3	0-0
New England	158-202-0	.439	2	5	3-5	0-1	New Orleans	148-208-4	.416	1	4	0-4	0-0
N.Y. Jets	152-206-2	.425	0	5	3-5	0-0	Atlanta	144-212-4	.405	1	4	2-4	0-0
Indianapolis	148-210-2	.414	5	6	4-5	1-0	Tampa Bay*	81-194-1	.295	2	3	1-3	0-0

*entered NFL in 1976.
Indianapolis totals include Baltimore, 1970-83.
L.A. Raiders totals include Oakland, 1970-81.
Arizona totals include St. Louis, 1970-87, and Phoenix, 1988-93.

Tie games before 1972 are not calculated in won-lost percentage.
In 1982, due to players' strike, the divisional format was abandoned.
(L.A. Raiders and Washington won regular-season conference titles, not included in "Division Titles" totals listed above. Sixteen teams were awarded playoff berths, included in totals listed above.)

LONGEST WINNING STREAKS SINCE 1970

Regular-season games

16	Miami, 1971-73	(1 in 1971, 14 in 1972, 1 in 1973)
16	Miami, 1983-84	(5 in 1983, 11 in 1984)
15	San Francisco, 1989-90	(5 in 1989, 10 in 1990)
14	Oakland, 1976-77	(10 in 1976, 4 in 1977)
13	Minnesota, 1974-75	(3 in 1974, 10 in 1975)
13	Chicago, 1984-85	(1 in 1984, 12 in 1985)
13	N.Y. Giants, 1989-90	(3 in 1989, 10 in 1990)
12	Washington, 1990-91	(1 in 1990, 11 in 1991)
11	Pittsburgh, 1975	
11	Baltimore, 1975-76	(9 in 1975, 2 in 1976)
11	Chicago, 1986-87	(7 in 1986, 4 in 1987)
10	Miami, 1973	
10	Pittsburgh, 1976-77	(9 in 1976, 1 in 1977)
10	Denver, 1984	
10	Houston, 1993	

NFL PLAYOFF APPEARANCES BY SEASONS

Team	Number of Seasons in Playoffs
N.Y. Giants	23
Cleveland	22
L.A. Rams	22
Dallas	21
Chicago	20
Washington	19
L.A. Raiders	18
Minnesota	17
Houston	15
Pittsburgh	15
San Francisco	15
Green Bay	14
Miami	14
Buffalo	13
Philadelphia	12
Indianapolis	11
Denver	10
Detroit	10
Kansas City	10
San Diego	10
Cincinnati	7
N.Y. Jets	7
New England	6
Arizona	5
Atlanta	4
New Orleans	4
Seattle	4
Tampa Bay	3

TEAMS IN SUPER BOWL CONTENTION, 1978-93

	With 3 Weeks to Play	With 2 Weeks to Play	With 1 Week to Play
1993	20	18	16
1992	20	16	14
1991	20	18	13
1990	23	20	15
1989	21	18	17
1988	21	18	15
1987	19	19	15
1986	19	17	14
1985	21	18	13
1984	18	14	13
1983	24	19	15
1982	20	17	16
1981	21	20	16
1980	20	14	12
1979	19	15	13
1978	20	17	12

GAMES DECIDED BY 7 POINTS OR LESS AND 3 POINTS OR LESS (1970-93)

	Games Decided by 7 Points or Less	Games Decided by 3 Points or Less
1970	59 of 182 (32.4%)	34 of 182 (18.7%)
1971	76 of 182 (41.8%)	35 of 182 (19.2%)
1972	71 of 182 (39.0%)	38 of 182 (20.9%)
1973	60 of 182 (32.9%)	28 of 182 (15.4%)
1974	91 of 182 (50.0%)	37 of 182 (20.3%)
1975	62 of 182 (34.1%)	35 of 182 (19.2%)
1976	73 of 196 (37.2%)	38 of 196 (19.4%)
1977	85 of 196 (43.4%)	36 of 196 (18.4%)
1978	108 of 224 (48.2%)	49 of 224 (21.9%)
1979	104 of 224 (46.4%)	51 of 224 (22.8%)
1980	108 of 224 (48.2%)	58 of 224 (25.9%)
1981	91 of 224 (40.6%)	60 of 224 (26.8%)
1982	61 of 126 (48.4%)	33 of 126 (26.2%)
1983	106 of 224 (47.3%)	54 of 224 (24.1%)
1984	95 of 224 (42.4%)	58 of 224 (25.9%)
1985	87 of 224 (38.8%)	38 of 224 (17.0%)
1986	106 of 224 (47.3%)	48 of 224 (21.4%)
1987	99 of 210 (47.1%)	40 of 210 (19.0%)
1988	113 of 224 (50.4%)	62 of 224 (27.7%)
1989	107 of 224 (47.8%)	55 of 224 (24.6%)
1990	97 of 224 (43.3%)	54 of 224 (24.1%)
1991	112 of 224 (50.0%)	57 of 224 (25.4%)
1992	88 of 224 (39.3%)	48 of 224 (21.4%)
1993	105 of 224 (46.9%)	53 of 224 (23.7%)

1993 RECORDS OF TEAMS IN CLOSE GAMES

AFC	Overall Record	Decided by 7 Pts. or Less	Decided By 3 Pts. or Less
Buffalo	12-4	5-1	5-1
Cincinnati	3-13	2-5	0-2
Cleveland	7-9	3-5	1-3
Denver	9-7	2-6	0-5
Houston	12-4	3-1	2-1
Indianapolis	4-12	3-2	3-0
Kansas City	11-5	4-2	2-1
L.A. Raiders	10-6	9-3	4-1
Miami	9-7	5-3	1-1
New England	5-11	4-8	2-6
N.Y. Jets	8-8	4-5	1-2
Pittsburgh	9-7	3-1	2-0
San Diego	8-8	4-5	2-2
Seattle	6-10	2-4	2-1

NFC	Overall Record	Decided by 7 Pts. or Less	Decided By 3 Pts. or Less
Atlanta	6-10	3-5	2-1
Chicago	7-9	4-6	2-3
Dallas	12-4	4-2	1-2
Detroit	10-6	6-1	3-0
Green Bay	9-7	4-4	3-2
L.A. Rams	5-11	2-2	1-1
Minnesota	9-7	6-2	2-2
New Orleans	8-8	5-3	4-2
N.Y. Giants	11-5	4-3	1-2
Philadelphia	8-8	6-4	4-1
Phoenix	7-9	2-8	1-3
San Francisco	10-6	1-4	0-4
Tampa Bay	5-11	3-3	2-1
Washington	4-12	2-7	0-3

SUPER BOWL CHAMPIONS WHO DID NOT MAKE PLAYOFFS THE FOLLOWING YEAR

N.Y. Giants—Super Bowl XXV champions did not make playoffs in the 1991 season.

Washington—Super Bowl XXII champions did not make playoffs in the 1988 season.

N.Y. Giants—Super Bowl XXI champions did not make playoffs in the 1987 season.

San Francisco—Super Bowl XVI champions did not make playoffs in the 1982 season.

Oakland—Super Bowl XV champions did not make playoffs in the 1981 season.

Pittsburgh—Super Bowl XIV champions did not make playoffs in the 1980 season.

Kansas City—Super Bowl IV champions did not make playoffs in the 1970 season.

Green Bay—Super Bowl II champions did not make playoffs in the 1968 season.

ALL-TIME RECORDS OF CURRENT NFL TEAMS

AFC

BUFFALO BILLS

	All Games			Home Games			Road Games		
Season	W	L	T	W	L	T	W	L	T
1960	5	8	1	3	4		2	4	1
1961	6	8		2	5		4	3	
1962	7	6	1	3	3	1	4	3	
1963	7	6	1	4	2	1	3	4	
1964	12	2		6	1		6	1	
1965	10	3	1	5	2		5	1	1
1966	9	4	1	4	2	1	5	2	
1967	4	10		2	5		2	5	
1968	1	12	1	1	6		0	6	1
1969	4	10		4	3		0	7	
1970	3	10	1	1	6		2	4	1
1971	1	13		1	6		0	7	
1972	4	9	1	2	4	1	2	5	
1973	9	5		5	2		4	3	
1974	9	5		5	2		4	3	
1975	8	6		3	4		5	2	
1976	2	12		1	6		1	6	
1977	3	11		1	6		2	5	
1978	5	11		4	4		1	7	
1979	7	9		3	5		4	4	
1980	11	5		6	2		5	3	
1981	10	6		7	1		3	5	
1982	4	5		4	1		0	4	
1983	8	8		3	5		5	3	
1984	2	14		2	6		0	8	
1985	2	14		2	6		0	8	
1986	4	12		3	5		1	7	
1987	7	8		4	4		3	4	
1988	12	4		8	0		4	4	
1989	9	7		6	2		3	5	
1990	13	3		8	0		5	3	
1991	13	3		7	1		6	2	
1992	11	5		6	2		5	3	
1993	12	4		6	2		6	2	
Total	234	258	8	132	115	4	102	143	4

CINCINNATI BENGALS

	All Games			Home Games			Road Games		
Season	W	L	T	W	L	T	W	L	T
1968	3	11		2	5		1	6	
1969	4	9	1	4	3		0	6	1
1970	8	6		5	2		3	4	
1971	4	10		3	4		1	6	
1972	8	6		4	3		4	3	
1973	10	4		7	0		3	4	
1974	7	7		4	3		3	4	
1975	11	3		6	1		5	2	
1976	10	4		6	1		4	3	
1977	8	6		5	2		3	4	
1978	4	12		3	5		1	7	
1979	4	12		4	4		0	8	
1980	6	10		3	5		3	5	
1981	12	4		6	2		6	2	
1982	7	2		4	0		3	2	
1983	7	9		4	4		3	5	
1984	8	8		5	3		3	5	
1985	7	9		5	3		2	6	
1986	10	6		6	2		4	4	
1987	4	11		1	7		3	4	
1988	12	4		8	0		4	4	
1989	8	8		5	3		3	5	
1990	9	7		5	3		4	4	
1991	3	13		3	5		0	8	
1992	5	11		3	5		2	6	
1993	3	13		3	5		0	8	
Total	182	205	1	114	80		68	125	1

CLEVELAND BROWNS

	All Games			Home Games			Road Games		
Season	W	L	T	W	L	T	W	L	T
1950	10	2		5	1		5	1	
1951	11	1		6	0		5	1	
1952	8	4		4	2		4	2	
1953	11	1		6	0		5	1	
1954	9	3		5	1		4	2	
1955	9	2	1	5	1		4	1	1
1956	5	7		1	5		4	2	

Season	All Games W	L	T	Home Games W	L	T	Road Games W	L	T
1957	9	2	1	6	0		3	2	1
1958	9	3		4	2		5	1	
1959	7	5		3	3		4	2	
1960	8	3	1	4	2		4	1	1
1961	8	5	1	4	3		4	2	1
1962	7	6	1	4	2	1	3	4	
1963	10	4		5	2		5	2	
1964	10	3	1	5	1	1	5	2	
1965	11	3		5	2		6	1	
1966	9	5		5	2		4	3	
1967	9	5		6	1		3	4	
1968	10	4		5	2		5	2	
1969	10	3	1	5	1	1	5	2	
1970	7	7		4	3		3	4	
1971	9	5		4	3		5	2	
1972	10	4		4	3		6	1	
1973	7	5	2	5	1	1	2	4	1
1974	4	10		3	4		1	6	
1975	3	11		3	4		0	7	
1976	9	5		6	1		3	4	
1977	6	8		2	5		4	3	
1978	8	8		5	3		3	5	
1979	9	7		5	3		4	4	
1980	11	5		6	2		5	3	
1981	5	11		3	5		2	6	
1982	4	5		2	2		2	3	
1983	9	7		6	2		3	5	
1984	5	11		2	6		3	5	
1985	8	8		5	3		3	5	
1986	12	4		6	2		6	2	
1987	10	5		5	2		5	3	
1988	10	6		6	2		4	4	
1989	9	6	1	5	2	1	4	4	
1990	3	13		2	6		1	7	
1991	6	10		3	5		3	5	
1992	7	9		4	4		3	5	
1993	7	9		4	4		3	5	
Total	358	250	10	193	110	5	165	140	5

DENVER BRONCOS

Season	All Games W	L	T	Home Games W	L	T	Road Games W	L	T
1960	4	9	1	2	4	1	2	5	
1961	3	11		2	5		1	6	
1962	7	7		3	4		4	3	
1963	2	11	1	2	5		0	6	1
1964	2	11	1	2	4	1	0	7	
1965	4	10		2	5		2	5	
1966	4	10		3	4		1	6	
1967	3	11		1	6		2	5	
1968	5	9		3	4		2	5	
1969	5	8	1	4	2	1	1	6	
1970	5	8	1	3	3	1	2	5	
1971	4	9	1	2	4	1	2	5	
1972	5	9		3	4		2	5	
1973	7	5	2	3	3	1	4	2	1
1974	7	6	1	3	3	1	4	3	
1975	6	8		5	2		1	6	
1976	9	5		6	1		3	4	
1977	12	2		6	1		6	1	
1978	10	6		6	2		4	4	
1979	10	6		6	2		4	4	
1980	8	8		4	4		4	4	
1981	10	6		8	0		2	6	
1982	2	7		1	4		1	3	
1983	9	7		6	2		3	5	
1984	13	3		7	1		6	2	
1985	11	5		6	2		5	3	
1986	11	5		7	1		4	4	
1987	10	4	1	7	1		3	3	1
1988	8	8		6	2		2	6	
1989	11	5		6	2		5	3	
1990	5	11		4	4		1	7	
1991	12	4		7	1		5	3	
1992	8	8		7	1		1	7	
1993	9	7		5	3		4	4	
Total	241	249	10	148	96	7	93	153	3

HOUSTON OILERS

Season	All Games W	L	T	Home Games W	L	T	Road Games W	L	T
1960	10	4		6	1		4	3	
1961	10	3	1	6	1		4	2	1
1962	11	3		6	1		5	2	
1963	6	8		4	3		2	5	
1964	4	10		3	4		1	6	
1965	4	10		3	4		1	6	
1966	3	11		3	4		0	7	
1967	9	4	1	5	2		4	2	1
1968	7	7		3	4		4	3	
1969	6	6	2	4	2	1	2	4	1
1970	3	10	1	1	6		2	4	1
1971	4	9	1	3	3	1	1	6	
1972	1	13		1	6		0	7	
1973	1	13		0	7		1	6	
1974	7	7		3	4		4	3	
1975	10	4		5	2		5	2	
1976	5	9		3	4		2	5	
1977	8	6		5	2		3	4	
1978	10	6		5	3		5	3	
1979	11	5		6	2		5	3	
1980	11	5		6	2		5	3	
1981	7	9		5	3		2	6	
1982	1	8		1	4		0	4	
1983	2	14		2	6		0	8	
1984	3	13		2	6		1	7	
1985	5	11		4	4		1	7	
1986	5	11		4	4		1	7	
1987	9	6		5	2		4	4	
1988	10	6		7	1		3	5	
1989	9	7		6	2		3	5	
1990	9	7		6	2		3	5	
1991	11	5		7	1		4	4	
1992	10	6		5	3		5	3	
1993	12	4		7	1		5	3	
Total	234	260	6	142	106	2	92	154	4

INDIANAPOLIS COLTS*

Season	All Games W	L	T	Home Games W	L	T	Road Games W	L	T
1953	3	9		2	4		1	5	
1954	3	9		2	4		1	5	
1955	5	6	1	4	1	1	1	5	
1956	5	7		4	2		1	5	
1957	7	5		4	2		3	3	
1958	9	3		6	0		3	3	
1959	9	3		4	2		5	1	
1960	6	6		4	2		2	4	
1961	8	6		5	2		3	4	
1962	7	7		3	4		4	3	
1963	8	6		4	3		4	3	
1964	12	2		7	1		5	1	
1965	10	3	1	5	2		5	1	1
1966	9	5		5	2		4	3	
1967	11	1	2	6	0	1	5	1	1
1968	13	1		6	1		7	0	
1969	8	5	1	4	2	1	4	3	
1970	11	2	1	5	1	1	6	1	
1971	10	4		5	2		5	2	
1972	5	9		2	5		3	4	
1973	4	10		3	4		1	6	
1974	2	12		0	7		2	5	
1975	10	4		5	2		5	2	
1976	11	3		6	1		5	2	
1977	10	4		6	1		4	3	
1978	5	11		2	6		3	5	
1979	5	11		3	5		2	6	
1980	7	9		2	6		5	3	
1981	2	14		1	7		1	7	
1982	0	8	1	0	3	1	0	5	
1983	7	9		3	5		4	4	
1984	4	12		2	6		2	6	
1985	5	11		4	4		1	7	
1986	3	13		1	7		2	6	
1987	9	6		4	4		5	2	
1988	9	7		6	2		3	5	
1989	8	8		6	2		2	6	
1990	7	9		3	5		4	4	
1991	1	15		0	8		1	7	
1992	9	7		4	4		5	3	
1993	4	12		2	6		2	6	
Total	281	294	7	150	137	5	131	157	2

*includes Baltimore Colts (1953-83).

KANSAS CITY CHIEFS*

Season	All Games W	L	T	Home Games W	L	T	Road Games W	L	T
1960	8	6		5	2		3	4	
1961	6	8		4	3		2	5	
1962	11	3		6	1		5	2	
1963	5	7	2	4	3		1	4	2
1964	7	7		4	3		3	4	
1965	7	5	2	5	2		2	3	2
1966	11	2	1	4	2	1	7	0	
1967	9	5		4	3		5	2	
1968	12	2		6	1		6	1	
1969	11	3		6	1		5	2	
1970	7	5	2	4	1	2	3	4	
1971	10	3	1	7	0		3	3	1
1972	8	6		3	4		5	2	
1973	7	5	2	5	1	1	2	4	1
1974	5	9		1	6		4	3	
1975	5	9		3	4		2	5	
1976	5	9		1	6		4	3	
1977	2	12		1	6		1	6	
1978	4	12		3	5		1	7	
1979	7	9		3	5		4	4	
1980	8	8		3	5		5	3	
1981	9	7		5	3		4	4	
1982	3	6		2	2		1	4	
1983	6	10		5	3		1	7	
1984	8	8		5	3		3	5	
1985	6	10		5	3		1	7	
1986	10	6		6	2		4	4	
1987	4	11		3	4		1	7	
1988	4	11	1	4	4		0	7	1
1989	8	7	1	5	3		3	4	1
1990	11	5		6	2		5	3	
1991	10	6		6	2		4	4	
1992	10	6		7	1		3	5	
1993	11	5		7	1		4	4	
Total	255	233	12	148	97	4	107	136	8

*includes Dallas Texans (1960-62).

LOS ANGELES RAIDERS*

Season	All Games W	L	T	Home Games W	L	T	Road Games W	L	T
1960	6	8		3	4		3	4	
1961	2	12		1	6		1	6	
1962	1	13		1	6		0	7	
1963	10	4		6	1		4	3	
1964	5	7	2	5	2		0	5	2
1965	8	5	1	5	2		3	3	1
1966	8	5	1	3	3	1	5	2	
1967	13	1		7	0		6	1	
1968	12	2		6	1		6	1	
1969	12	1	1	7	0		5	1	1
1970	8	4	2	6	1		2	3	2
1971	8	4	2	5	1	1	3	3	1
1972	10	3	1	5	1	1	5	2	
1973	9	4	1	5	2		4	2	1
1974	12	2		6	1		6	1	
1975	11	3		6	1		5	2	
1976	13	1		7	0		6	1	
1977	11	3		6	1		5	2	
1978	9	7		4	4		5	3	
1979	9	7		6	2		3	5	
1980	11	5		6	2		5	3	
1981	7	9		4	4		3	5	
1982	8	1		4	0		4	1	
1983	12	4		6	2		6	2	
1984	11	5		6	2		5	3	
1985	12	4		7	1		5	3	
1986	8	8		3	5		5	3	
1987	5	10		3	5		2	5	
1988	7	9		3	5		4	4	
1989	8	8		7	1		1	7	
1990	12	4		6	2		6	2	
1991	9	7		5	3		4	4	

Season	All Games W	L	T	Home Games W	L	T	Road Games W	L	T
1992	7	9		5	3		2	6	
1993	10	6		5	3		5	3	
Total	304	185	11	170	77	3	134	108	8

includes Oakland Raiders (1960-81).

MIAMI DOLPHINS

Season	All Games W	L	T	Home Games W	L	T	Road Games W	L	T
1966	3	11		2	5		1	6	
1967	4	10		4	3		0	7	
1968	5	8	1	1	5	1	4	3	
1969	3	10	1	2	4	1	1	6	
1970	10	4		6	1		4	3	
1971	10	3	1	6	1		4	2	1
1972	14	0		7	0		7	0	
1973	12	2		7	0		5	2	
1974	11	3		7	0		4	3	
1975	10	4		5	2		5	2	
1976	6	8		3	4		3	4	
1977	10	4		6	1		4	3	
1978	11	5		7	1		4	4	
1979	10	6		6	2		4	4	
1980	8	8		5	3		3	5	
1981	11	4	1	6	1	1	5	3	
1982	7	2		4	0		3	2	
1983	12	4		7	1		5	3	
1984	14	2		7	1		7	1	
1985	12	4		8	0		4	4	
1986	8	8		4	4		4	4	
1987	8	7		4	3		4	4	
1988	6	10		4	4		2	6	
1989	8	8		4	4		4	4	
1990	12	4		7	1		5	3	
1991	8	8		5	3		3	5	
1992	11	5		6	2		5	3	
1993	9	7		4	4		5	3	
Total	253	159	4	144	60	3	109	99	1

NEW ENGLAND PATRIOTS*

Season	All Games W	L	T	Home Games W	L	T	Road Games W	L	T
1960	5	9		3	4		2	5	
1961	9	4	1	4	2	1	5	2	
1962	9	4	1	6	1		3	3	1
1963	7	6	1	5	1	1	2	5	
1964	10	3	1	4	2	1	6	1	
1965	4	8	2	1	4	2	3	4	
1966	8	4	2	4	2	1	4	2	1
1967	3	10	1	2	4	1	1	6	1
1968	4	10		2	5		2	5	
1969	4	10		2	5		2	5	
1970	2	12		1	6		1	6	
1971	6	8		5	2		1	6	
1972	3	11		2	5		1	6	
1973	5	9		3	4		2	5	
1974	7	7		3	4		4	3	
1975	3	11		2	5		1	6	
1976	11	3		6	1		5	2	
1977	9	5		6	1		3	4	
1978	11	5		5	3		6	2	
1979	9	7		6	2		3	5	
1980	10	6		6	2		4	4	
1981	2	14		2	6		0	8	
1982	5	4		3	1		2	3	
1983	8	8		5	3		3	5	
1984	9	7		5	3		4	4	
1985	11	5		7	1		4	4	
1986	11	5		4	4		7	1	
1987	8	7		5	3		3	4	
1988	9	7		7	1		2	6	
1989	5	11		3	5		2	6	
1990	1	15		0	8		1	7	
1991	6	10		4	4		2	6	
1992	2	14		1	7		1	7	
1993	5	11		3	5		2	6	
Total	221	270	9	127	116	6	94	154	3

includes Boston Patriots (1960-70).

NEW YORK JETS*

Season	All Games W	L	T	Home Games W	L	T	Road Games W	L	T
1960	7	7		3	4		4	3	
1961	7	7		5	2		2	5	
1962	5	9		2	5		3	4	
1963	5	8	1	4	2	1	1	6	
1964	5	8	1	5	1	1	0	7	
1965	5	8	1	3	3	1	2	5	
1966	6	6	2	4	3		2	3	2
1967	8	5	1	4	2	1	4	3	
1968	11	3		6	1		5	2	
1969	10	4		5	2		5	2	
1970	4	10		2	5		2	5	
1971	6	8		4	3		2	5	
1972	7	7		4	3		3	4	
1973	4	10		2	4		2	6	
1974	7	7		3	4		4	3	
1975	3	11		1	6		2	5	
1976	3	11		2	5		1	6	
1977	3	11		1	6		2	5	
1978	8	8		4	4		4	4	
1979	8	8		6	2		2	6	
1980	4	12		2	6		2	6	
1981	10	5	1	6	2		4	3	1
1982	6	3		3	1		3	2	
1983	7	9		2	6		5	3	
1984	7	9		3	5		4	4	
1985	11	5		7	1		4	4	
1986	10	6		5	3		5	3	
1987	6	9		4	4		2	5	
1988	8	7	1	5	2	1	3	5	
1989	4	12		1	7		3	5	
1990	6	10		3	5		3	5	
1991	8	8		4	4		4	4	
1992	4	12		3	5		1	7	
1993	8	8		3	5		5	3	
Total	221	271	8	121	123	5	100	148	3

includes New York Titans (1960-62).

PITTSBURGH STEELERS*

Season	All Games W	L	T	Home Games W	L	T	Road Games W	L	T
1933	3	6	2	2	3		1	3	2
1934	2	10		1	5		1	5	
1935	4	8		2	5		2	3	
1936	6	6		4	1		2	5	
1937	4	7		2	4		2	3	
1938	2	9		0	5		2	4	
1939	1	9	1	1	4		0	5	1
1940	2	7	2	1	2	2	1	5	
1941	1	9	1	1	4		0	5	1
1942	7	4		3	2		4	2	
1945	2	8		1	4		1	4	
1946	5	5	1	4	1		1	4	1
1947	8	4		5	1		3	3	
1948	4	8		4	2		0	6	
1949	6	5	1	3	2	1	3	3	
1950	6	6		2	4		4	2	
1951	4	7	1	1	4	1	3	3	
1952	5	7		2	4		3	3	
1953	6	6		3	3		3	3	
1954	5	7		4	2		1	5	
1955	4	8		3	2		1	6	
1956	5	7		3	3		2	4	
1957	6	6		4	2		2	4	
1958	7	4	1	5	1		2	3	1
1959	6	5	1	3	2	1	3	3	
1960	5	6	1	4	2	1	1	4	1
1961	6	8		4	3		2	5	
1962	9	5		4	3		5	2	
1963	7	4	3	5	0	2	2	4	1
1964	5	9		2	5		3	4	
1965	2	12		1	6		1	6	
1966	5	8	1	3	3	1	2	5	
1967	4	9	1	1	6		3	3	1
1968	2	11	1	1	6		1	5	1
1969	1	13		1	6		0	7	
1970	5	9		4	3		1	6	
1971	6	8		5	2		1	6	
1972	11	3		7	0		4	3	
1973	10	4		7	1		3	3	
1974	10	3	1	5	2		5	1	1

Season	All Games W	L	T	Home Games W	L	T	Road Games W	L	T
1975	12	2		6	1		6	1	
1976	10	4		6	1		4	3	
1977	9	5		6	1		3	4	
1978	14	2		7	1		7	1	
1979	12	4		8	0		4	4	
1980	9	7		6	2		3	5	
1981	8	8		5	3		3	5	
1982	6	3		4	0		2	3	
1983	10	6		4	4		6	2	
1984	9	7		6	2		3	5	
1985	7	9		5	3		2	6	
1986	6	10		4	4		2	6	
1987	8	7		4	3		4	4	
1988	5	11		4	4		1	7	
1989	9	7		4	4		5	3	
1990	9	7		6	2		3	5	
1991	7	9		5	3		2	6	
1992	11	5		7	1		4	4	
1993	9	7		6	2		3	5	
Total	369	400	19	221	161	8	148	239	11

includes Pittsburgh Pirates (1933-40).

SAN DIEGO CHARGERS*

Season	All Games W	L	T	Home Games W	L	T	Road Games W	L	T
1960	10	4		5	2		5	2	
1961	12	2		6	1		6	1	
1962	4	10		3	4		1	6	
1963	11	3		6	1		5	2	
1964	8	5	1	4	3		4	2	1
1965	9	2	3	4	1	2	5	1	1
1966	7	6	1	5	2		2	4	1
1967	8	5	1	5	2	1	3	3	
1968	9	5		4	3		5	2	
1969	8	6		5	2		3	4	
1970	5	6	3	2	3	2	3	3	1
1971	6	8		6	1		0	7	
1972	4	9	1	2	5		2	4	1
1973	2	11	1	2	5		0	6	1
1974	5	9		3	4		2	5	
1975	2	12		1	6		1	6	
1976	6	8		3	4		3	4	
1977	7	7		3	4		4	3	
1978	9	7		5	3		4	4	
1979	12	4		7	1		5	3	
1980	11	5		6	2		5	3	
1981	10	6		5	3		5	3	
1982	6	3		3	1		3	2	
1983	6	10		4	4		2	6	
1984	7	9		4	4		3	5	
1985	8	8		6	2		2	6	
1986	4	12		2	6		2	6	
1987	8	7		4	3		4	4	
1988	6	10		3	5		3	5	
1989	6	10		4	4		2	6	
1990	6	10		3	5		3	5	
1991	4	12		3	5		1	7	
1992	11	5		6	2		5	3	
1993	8	8		4	4		4	4	
Total	245	244	11	138	107	5	107	137	6

includes Los Angeles Chargers (1960).

SEATTLE SEAHAWKS

Season	All Games W	L	T	Home Games W	L	T	Road Games W	L	T
1976	2	12		1	6		1	6	
1977	5	9		3	4		2	5	
1978	9	7		5	3		4	4	
1979	9	7		5	3		4	4	
1980	4	12		0	8		4	4	
1981	6	10		5	3		1	7	
1982	4	5		3	2		1	3	
1983	9	7		5	3		4	4	
1984	12	4		7	1		5	3	
1985	8	8		5	3		3	5	
1986	10	6		7	1		3	5	
1987	9	6		6	2		3	4	
1988	9	7		5	3		4	4	
1989	7	9		5	3		2	6	
1990	9	7		5	3		4	4	
1991	7	9		5	3		2	6	

Season	All Games W	L	T	Home Games W	L	T	Road Games W	L	T
1992	2	14		1	7		1	7	
1993	6	10		4	4		2	6	
Total	127	149		75	64		52	85	

NFC
ARIZONA CARDINALS*

Season	All Games W	L	T	Home Games W	L	T	Road Games W	L	T
1920	6	2	2	5	1	1	1	1	1
1921	3	3	2	3	3	1	0	0	1
1922	8	3		8	3		0	0	
1923	8	4		8	3		0	1	
1924	5	4	1	5	3	1	0	1	
1925	11	2	1	11	2		0	0	1
1926	5	6	1	3	3		2	3	1
1927	3	7	1	2	3	1	1	4	
1928	1	5		1	1		0	4	
1929	6	6	1	3	2		3	4	1
1930	5	6	2	3	2		2	4	2
1931	5	4		3	0		2	4	
1932	2	6	2	1	2	1	1	4	1
1933	1	9	1	0	4	1	1	5	
1934	5	6		2	2		3	4	
1935	6	4	2	2	2		4	2	2
1936	3	8	1	3	1	1	0	7	
1937	5	5	1	1	3		4	2	1
1938	2	9		1	4		1	5	
1939	1	10		0	4		1	6	
1940	2	7	2	2	1	1	0	6	1
1941	3	7	1	0	3	1	3	4	
1942	3	8		2	2		1	6	
1943	0	10		0	3		0	7	
1945	1	9		0	3		1	6	
1946	6	5		2	2		4	3	
1947	9	3		5	0		4	3	
1948	11	1		5	1		6	0	
1949	6	5	1	2	3	1	4	2	
1950	5	7		3	3		2	4	
1951	3	9		1	5		2	4	
1952	4	8		2	4		2	4	
1953	1	10	1	0	5	1	1	5	
1954	2	10		2	4		0	6	
1955	4	7	1	3	2	1	1	5	
1956	7	5		4	2		3	3	
1957	3	9		0	6		3	3	
1958	2	9	1	1	4	1	1	5	
1959	2	10		2	4		0	6	
1960	6	5	1	3	2	1	3	3	
1961	7	7		3	4		4	3	
1962	4	9	1	2	4	1	2	5	
1963	9	5		3	4		6	1	
1964	9	3	2	4	1	1	5	2	1
1965	5	9		2	5		3	4	
1966	8	5	1	5	1	1	3	4	
1967	6	7	1	3	3	1	3	4	
1968	9	4	1	4	2	1	5	2	
1969	4	9	1	3	4		1	5	1
1970	8	5	1	6	1		2	4	1
1971	4	9	1	1	5	1	3	4	
1972	4	9	1	2	5		2	4	1
1973	4	9	1	2	4	1	2	5	
1974	10	4		5	2		5	2	
1975	11	3		6	1		5	2	
1976	10	4		6	1		4	3	
1977	7	7		4	3		3	4	
1978	6	10		3	5		3	5	
1979	5	11		3	5		2	6	
1980	5	11		2	6		3	5	
1981	7	9		5	3		2	6	
1982	5	4		1	3		4	1	
1983	8	7	1	4	3	1	4	4	
1984	9	7		5	3		4	4	
1985	5	11		4	4		1	7	
1986	4	11	1	3	5		1	6	1
1987	7	8		4	3		3	5	
1988	7	9		4	4		3	5	
1989	5	11		2	6		3	5	
1990	5	11		3	5		2	6	
1991	4	12		2	6		2	6	
1992	4	12		3	5		1	7	
1993	7	9		4	4		3	5	
Total	383	514	39	217	227	22	166	287	17

*includes Chicago Cardinals (1920-59), St. Louis Cardinals (1960-87), and Phoenix Cardinals (1988-1993).

ATLANTA FALCONS

Season	All Games W	L	T	Home Games W	L	T	Road Games W	L	T
1966	3	11		1	6		2	5	
1967	1	12	1	1	5	1	0	7	
1968	2	12		1	6		1	6	
1969	6	8		4	3		2	5	
1970	4	8	2	3	4		1	4	2
1971	7	6	1	4	3		3	3	1
1972	7	7		4	3		3	4	
1973	9	5		4	3		5	2	
1974	3	11		2	5		1	6	
1975	4	10		3	4		1	6	
1976	4	10		3	4		1	6	
1977	7	7		4	3		3	4	
1978	9	7		7	1		2	6	
1979	6	10		3	5		3	5	
1980	12	4		6	2		6	2	
1981	7	9		4	4		3	5	
1982	5	4		2	3		3	1	
1983	7	9		4	4		3	5	
1984	4	12		2	6		2	6	
1985	4	12		3	5		1	7	
1986	7	8	1	2	5	1	5	3	
1987	3	12		2	6		1	6	
1988	5	11		2	6		3	5	
1989	3	13		3	5		0	8	
1990	5	11		5	3		0	8	
1991	10	6		6	2		4	4	
1992	6	10		5	3		1	7	
1993	6	10		4	4		2	6	
Total	156	255	5	94	113	2	62	142	3

CHICAGO BEARS*

Season	All Games W	L	T	Home Games W	L	T	Road Games W	L	T
1920	10	1	2	6	0	1	4	1	1
1921	9	1	1	9	1	1	0	0	
1922	9	3		7	1		2	2	
1923	9	2	1	7	1	1	2	1	
1924	6	1	4	5	0	3	1	1	1
1925	9	5	3	7	1	1	2	4	2
1926	12	1	3	10	0	2	2	1	1
1927	9	3	2	7	1	1	2	2	1
1928	7	5	1	6	3		1	2	1
1929	4	9	2	1	5	2	3	4	
1930	9	4	1	5	2	1	4	2	
1931	8	5		6	3		2	2	
1932	7	1	6	6	1	1	1	0	5
1933	10	2	1	6	0		4	2	1
1934	13	0		5	0		8	0	
1935	6	4	2	1	2	2	5	2	
1936	9	3		3	1		6	2	
1937	9	1	1	4	1		5	0	1
1938	6	5		2	3		4	2	
1939	8	3		4	1		4	2	
1940	8	3		5	0		3	3	
1941	10	1		5	1		5	0	
1942	11	0		6	0		5	0	
1943	8	1	1	5	0		3	1	1
1944	6	3	1	4	0	1	2	3	
1945	3	7		2	3		1	4	
1946	8	2	1	4	1	1	4	1	
1947	8	4		4	2		4	2	
1948	10	2		5	1		5	1	
1949	9	3		5	1		4	2	
1950	9	3		6	0		3	3	
1951	7	5		3	3		4	2	
1952	5	7		3	3		2	4	
1953	3	8	1	1	4	1	2	4	
1954	8	4		4	2		4	2	
1955	8	4		5	1		3	3	
1956	9	2	1	6	0		3	2	1
1957	5	7		2	4		3	3	
1958	8	4		5	1		3	3	
1959	8	4		4	2		4	2	
1960	5	6	1	4	2		1	4	1
1961	8	6		5	2		3	4	
1962	9	5		4	3		5	2	
1963	11	1	2	6	0	1	5	1	1
1964	5	9		2	5		3	4	
1965	9	5		5	2		4	3	
1966	5	7	2	4	1	2	1	6	
1967	7	6	1	3	3	1	4	3	
1968	7	7		2	5		5	2	
1969	1	13		1	6		0	7	
1970	6	8		3	4		3	4	
1971	6	8		4	3		2	5	
1972	4	9	1	1	5	1	3	4	
1973	3	11		1	6		2	5	
1974	4	10		4	3		0	7	
1975	4	10		3	4		1	6	
1976	7	7		4	3		3	4	
1977	9	5		5	2		4	3	
1978	7	9		4	4		3	5	
1979	10	6		6	2		4	4	
1980	7	9		5	3		2	6	
1981	6	10		4	4		2	6	
1982	3	6		2	2		1	4	
1983	8	8		5	3		3	5	
1984	10	6		6	2		4	4	
1985	15	1		8	0		7	1	
1986	14	2		7	1		7	1	
1987	11	4		6	2		5	2	
1988	12	4		7	1		5	3	
1989	6	10		4	4		2	6	
1990	11	5		7	1		4	4	
1991	11	5		6	2		5	3	
1992	5	11		4	4		1	7	
1993	7	9		3	5		4	4	
Total	573	371	42	336	155	24	237	216	18

*includes Decatur Staleys (1920) and Chicago Staleys (1921).

DALLAS COWBOYS

Season	All Games W	L	T	Home Games W	L	T	Road Games W	L	T
1960	0	11	1	0	6		0	5	1
1961	4	9	1	2	4	1	2	5	
1962	5	8	1	2	4	1	3	4	
1963	4	10		3	4		1	6	
1964	5	8	1	2	4	1	3	4	
1965	7	7		5	2		2	5	
1966	10	3	1	6	1		4	2	1
1967	9	5		5	2		4	3	
1968	12	2		5	2		7	0	
1969	11	2	1	6	0	1	5	2	
1970	10	4		6	1		4	3	
1971	11	3		6	1		5	2	
1972	10	4		5	2		5	2	
1973	10	4		6	1		4	3	
1974	8	6		5	2		3	4	
1975	10	4		5	2		5	2	
1976	11	3		6	1		5	2	
1977	12	2		6	1		6	1	
1978	12	4		7	1		5	3	
1979	11	5		6	2		5	3	
1980	12	4		8	0		4	4	
1981	12	4		8	0		4	4	
1982	6	3		3	2		3	1	
1983	12	4		6	2		6	2	
1984	9	7		5	3		4	4	
1985	10	6		7	1		3	5	
1986	7	9		3	5		4	4	
1987	7	8		3	4		4	4	
1988	3	13		1	7		2	6	
1989	1	15		0	8		1	7	
1990	7	9		5	3		2	6	
1991	11	5		6	2		5	3	
1992	13	3		7	1		6	2	
1993	12	4		6	2		6	2	
Total	294	198	6	162	83	4	132	115	2

DETROIT LIONS*

Season	All Games W	L	T	Home Games W	L	T	Road Games W	L	T
1930	5	6	3	5	1	2	0	5	1

Season	All Games W	L	T	Home Games W	L	T	Road Games W	L	T
1931	11	3		8	0		3	3	
1932	6	2	4	3	0	2	3	2	2
1933	6	5		4	1		2	4	
1934	10	3		6	2		4	1	
1935	7	3	2	5	0	1	2	3	1
1936	8	4		5	1		3	3	
1937	7	4		4	2		3	2	
1938	7	4		4	3		3	1	
1939	6	5		4	2		2	3	
1940	5	5	1	3	3		2	2	1
1941	4	6	1	3	2		1	4	1
1942	0	11		0	7		0	4	
1943	3	6	1	2	2	1	1	4	
1944	6	3	1	4	2		2	1	1
1945	7	3		4	1		3	2	
1946	1	10		1	5		0	5	
1947	3	9		2	4		1	5	
1948	2	10		2	4		0	6	
1949	4	8		2	4		2	4	
1950	6	6		4	2		2	4	
1951	7	4	1	3	3	1	4	1	
1952	9	3		6	1		3	2	
1953	10	2		5	1		5	1	
1954	9	2	1	5	0	1	4	2	
1955	3	9		3	4		0	5	
1956	9	3		5	1		4	2	
1957	8	4		5	1		3	3	
1958	4	7	1	2	4		2	3	1
1959	3	8	1	2	4		1	4	1
1960	7	5		5	1		2	4	
1961	8	5	1	2	5		6	0	1
1962	11	3		7	0		4	3	
1963	5	8	1	3	3	1	2	5	
1964	7	5	2	3	3	1	4	2	1
1965	6	7	1	2	4	1	4	3	
1966	4	9	1	3	4		1	5	1
1967	5	7	2	3	4		2	3	2
1968	4	8	2	1	4	2	3	4	
1969	9	4	1	5	2		4	2	1
1970	10	4		6	1		4	3	
1971	7	6	1	3	4		4	2	1
1972	8	5	1	5	2		3	3	1
1973	6	7	1	4	3		2	4	1
1974	7	7		5	2		2	5	
1975	7	7		4	3		3	4	
1976	6	8		5	2		1	6	
1977	6	8		5	2		1	6	
1978	7	9		5	3		2	6	
1979	2	14		2	6		0	8	
1980	9	7		6	2		3	5	
1981	8	8		7	1		1	7	
1982	4	5		2	3		2	2	
1983	9	7		6	2		3	5	
1984	4	11	1	2	5	1	2	6	
1985	7	9		6	2		1	7	
1986	5	11		1	7		4	4	
1987	4	11		1	6		3	5	
1988	4	12		2	6		2	6	
1989	7	9		4	4		3	5	
1990	6	10		3	5		3	5	
1991	12	4		8	0		4	4	
1992	5	11		3	5		2	6	
1993	10	6		5	3		5	3	
Total	402	415	32	245	176	14	157	239	18

*includes Portsmouth Spartans (1930-33)

GREEN BAY PACKERS

Season	All Games W	L	T	Home Games W	L	T	Road Games W	L	T
1921	3	2	1	2	1		1	1	1
1922	4	3	3	4	1	1	0	2	2
1923	7	2	1	4	2	1	3	0	
1924	7	4		5	0		2	4	
1925	8	5		6	0		2	5	
1926	7	3	3	4	1	2	3	2	1
1927	7	2	1	6	1		1	1	1
1928	6	4	3	2	2	2	4	2	1
1929	12	0	1	5	0		7	0	1
1930	10	3	1	6	0		4	3	1
1931	12	2		8	0		4	2	
1932	10	3	1	5	0	1	5	3	

Season	All Games W	L	T	Home Games W	L	T	Road Games W	L	T
1933	5	7	1	3	2	1	2	5	
1934	7	6		4	2		3	4	
1935	8	4		5	2		3	2	
1936	10	1	1	5	1		5	0	1
1937	7	4		3	2		4	2	
1938	8	3		4	2		4	1	
1939	9	2		4	1		5	1	
1940	6	4	1	4	2		2	2	1
1941	10	1		4	1		6	0	
1942	8	2	1	4	1		4	1	1
1943	7	2	1	2	1	1	5	1	
1944	8	2		5	0		3	2	
1945	6	4		4	1		2	3	
1946	6	5		2	3		4	2	
1947	6	5	1	4	2		2	3	1
1948	3	9		2	4		1	5	
1949	2	10		1	5		1	5	
1950	3	9		3	3		0	6	
1951	3	9		2	4		1	5	
1952	6	6		3	3		3	3	
1953	2	9	1	1	5		1	4	1
1954	4	8		2	4		2	4	
1955	6	6		5	1		1	5	
1956	4	8		2	4		2	4	
1957	3	9		1	5		2	4	
1958	1	10	1	1	4	1	0	6	
1959	7	5		4	2		3	3	
1960	8	4		4	2		4	2	
1961	11	3		6	1		5	2	
1962	13	1		7	0		6	1	
1963	11	2	1	6	1		5	1	1
1964	8	5	1	4	3		4	2	1
1965	10	3	1	6	1		4	2	1
1966	12	2		6	1		6	1	
1967	9	4	1	4	2	1	5	2	
1968	6	7	1	2	5		4	2	1
1969	8	6		5	2		3	4	
1970	6	8		4	3		2	5	
1971	4	8	2	3	3	1	1	5	1
1972	10	4		4	3		6	1	
1973	5	7	2	3	2	2	2	5	
1974	6	8		4	3		2	5	
1975	4	10		3	4		1	6	
1976	5	9		4	3		1	6	
1977	4	10		2	5		2	5	
1978	8	7	1	5	2	1	3	5	
1979	5	11		4	4		1	7	
1980	5	10	1	4	4		1	6	1
1981	8	8		4	4		4	4	
1982	5	3	1	3	1		2	2	1
1983	8	8		5	3		3	5	
1984	8	8		5	3		3	5	
1985	8	8		5	3		3	5	
1986	4	12		1	7		3	5	
1987	5	9	1	2	5	1	3	4	
1988	4	12		2	6		2	6	
1989	10	6		6	2		4	4	
1990	6	10		3	5		3	5	
1991	4	12		2	6		2	6	
1992	9	7		6	2		3	5	
1993	9	7		6	2		3	5	
Total	494	422	36	281	178	16	213	244	20

LOS ANGELES RAMS*

Season	All Games W	L	T	Home Games W	L	T	Road Games W	L	T
1937	1	10		0	5		1	5	
1938	4	7		2	2		2	5	
1939	5	5	1	3	2	1	2	3	
1940	4	6	1	3	1	1	1	5	
1941	2	9		1	4		1	5	
1942	5	6		3	2		2	4	
1944	4	6		1	2		3	4	
1945	9	1		4	0		5	1	
1946	6	4	1	3	2		3	2	1
1947	6	6		3	3		3	3	
1948	6	5	1	3	2	1	3	3	
1949	8	2	2	5	1		3	1	2
1950	9	3		5	1		4	2	
1951	8	4		5	2		3	2	
1952	9	3		5	1		4	2	

Season	All Games W	L	T	Home Games W	L	T	Road Games W	L	T
1953	8	3	1	5	1		3	2	1
1954	6	5	1	3	2	1	3	3	
1955	8	3	1	5	1		3	2	1
1956	4	8		4	2		0	6	
1957	6	6		5	1		1	5	
1958	8	4		4	2		4	2	
1959	2	10		0	6		2	4	
1960	4	7	1	2	3	1	2	4	
1961	4	10		4	3		0	7	
1962	1	12	1	0	7		1	5	1
1963	5	9		3	4		2	5	
1964	5	7	2	3	2	2	2	5	
1965	4	10		3	4		1	6	
1966	8	6		5	2		3	4	
1967	11	1	2	5	1	1	6	0	1
1968	10	3	1	5	2		5	1	1
1969	11	3		5	2		6	1	
1970	9	4	1	3	3	1	6	1	
1971	8	5	1	4	2	1	4	3	
1972	6	7	1	4	3		2	4	1
1973	12	2		7	0		5	2	
1974	10	4		6	1		4	3	
1975	12	2		6	1		6	1	
1976	10	3	1	5	2		5	1	1
1977	10	4		7	0		3	4	
1978	12	4		6	2		6	2	
1979	9	7		4	4		5	3	
1980	11	5		6	2		5	3	
1981	6	10		4	4		2	6	
1982	2	7		1	4		1	3	
1983	9	7		5	3		4	4	
1984	10	6		5	3		5	3	
1985	11	5		6	2		5	3	
1986	10	6		6	2		4	4	
1987	6	9		3	4		3	5	
1988	10	6		4	4		6	2	
1989	11	5		6	2		5	3	
1990	5	11		2	6		3	5	
1991	3	13		2	6		1	7	
1992	6	10		4	4		2	6	
1993	5	11		3	5		2	6	
Total	394	337	20	216	144	10	178	193	10

*includes Cleveland Rams (1937-42, 1944-45).

MINNESOTA VIKINGS

Season	All Games W	L	T	Home Games W	L	T	Road Games W	L	T
1961	3	11		3	4		0	7	
1962	2	11	1	1	5	1	1	6	
1963	5	8	1	3	4		2	4	1
1964	8	5	1	4	3		4	2	1
1965	7	7		2	5		5	2	
1966	4	9	1	2	5		2	4	1
1967	3	8	3	1	4	2	2	4	1
1968	8	6		4	3		4	3	
1969	12	2		7	0		5	2	
1970	12	2		7	0		5	2	
1971	11	3		5	2		6	1	
1972	7	7		3	4		4	3	
1973	12	2		7	0		5	2	
1974	10	4		4	3		6	1	
1975	12	2		7	0		5	2	
1976	11	2	1	6	0	1	5	2	
1977	9	5		5	2		4	3	
1978	8	7	1	5	3		3	4	1
1979	7	9		5	3		2	6	
1980	9	7		5	3		4	4	
1981	7	9		5	3		2	6	
1982	5	4		4	1		1	3	
1983	8	8		3	5		5	3	
1984	3	13		2	6		1	7	
1985	7	9		4	4		3	5	
1986	9	7		5	3		4	4	
1987	8	7		5	3		3	4	
1988	11	5		7	1		4	4	
1989	10	6		8	0		2	6	
1990	6	10		4	4		2	6	
1991	8	8		4	4		4	4	
1992	11	5		5	3		6	2	
1993	9	7		4	4		5	3	
Total	262	215	9	146	94	4	116	121	5

NEW ORLEANS SAINTS

Season	All Games W	L	T	Home Games W	L	T	Road Games W	L	T
1967	3	11		2	5		1	6	
1968	4	9	1	3	4		1	5	1
1969	5	9		3	4		2	5	
1970	2	11	1	2	5		0	6	1
1971	4	8	2	2	4	1	2	4	1
1972	2	11	1	2	5		0	6	1
1973	5	9		5	2		0	7	
1974	5	9		4	3		1	6	
1975	2	12		2	5		0	7	
1976	4	10		2	5		2	5	
1977	3	11		2	5		1	6	
1978	7	9		3	5		4	4	
1979	8	8		3	5		5	3	
1980	1	15		0	8		1	7	
1981	4	12		2	6		2	6	
1982	4	5		2	3		2	2	
1983	8	8		5	3		3	5	
1984	7	9		3	5		4	4	
1985	5	11		3	5		2	6	
1986	7	9		4	4		3	5	
1987	12	3		6	1		6	2	
1988	10	6		5	3		5	3	
1989	9	7		5	3		4	4	
1990	8	8		5	3		3	5	
1991	11	5		6	2		5	3	
1992	12	4		6	2		6	2	
1993	8	8		4	4		4	4	
Total	160	237	5	91	109	1	69	128	4

NEW YORK GIANTS

Season	All Games W	L	T	Home Games W	L	T	Road Games W	L	T
1925	8	4		7	2		1	2	
1926	8	4	1	5	2	1	3	2	
1927	11	1	1	7	1		4	0	1
1928	4	7	2	1	2	2	3	5	
1929	13	1	1	7	1		6	0	1
1930	13	4		6	2		7	2	
1931	7	6	1	4	2	1	3	4	
1932	4	6	2	3	2	1	1	4	1
1933	11	3		7	0		4	3	
1934	8	5		5	1		3	4	
1935	9	3		4	2		5	1	
1936	5	6	1	3	3	1	2	3	
1937	6	3	2	4	2	1	2	1	1
1938	8	2	1	6	1		2	1	1
1939	9	1	1	6	0		3	1	1
1940	6	4	1	4	3		2	1	1
1941	8	3		5	2		3	1	
1942	5	5	1	3	2	1	2	3	
1943	6	3	1	4	2		2	1	1
1944	8	1	1	5	1		3	0	1
1945	3	6	1	2	4		1	2	1
1946	7	3	1	5	1	1	2	2	
1947	2	8	2	2	3	1	0	5	1
1948	4	8		2	4		2	4	
1949	6	6		2	4		4	2	
1950	10	2		5	1		5	1	
1951	9	2	1	5	1		4	1	1
1952	7	5		2	4		5	1	
1953	3	9		2	4		1	5	
1954	7	5		4	2		3	3	
1955	6	5	1	4	1	1	2	4	
1956	8	3	1	4	1	1	4	2	
1957	7	5		3	3		4	2	
1958	9	3		5	1		4	2	
1959	10	2		5	1		5	1	
1960	6	4	2	1	3	2	5	1	
1961	10	3	1	4	2	1	6	1	
1962	12	2		6	1		6	1	
1963	11	3		5	2		6	1	
1964	2	10	2	2	5		0	5	2
1965	7	7		3	4		4	3	
1966	1	12	1	1	6		0	6	1
1967	7	7		5	2		2	5	
1968	7	7		3	4		4	3	
1969	6	8		5	2		1	6	
1970	9	5		5	2		4	3	
1971	4	10		1	6		3	4	
1972	8	6		4	3		4	3	
1973	2	11	1	2	4	1	0	7	
1974	2	12		0	7		2	5	
1975	5	9		2	5		3	4	
1976	3	11		3	4		0	7	
1977	5	9		3	4		2	5	
1978	6	10		5	3		1	7	
1979	6	10		4	4		2	6	
1980	4	12		2	6		2	6	
1981	9	7		4	4		5	3	
1982	4	5		2	3		2	2	
1983	3	12	1	1	7		2	5	1
1984	9	7		6	2		3	5	
1985	10	6		6	2		4	4	
1986	14	2		8	0		6	2	
1987	6	9		5	3		1	6	
1988	10	6		5	3		5	3	
1989	12	4		7	1		5	3	
1990	13	3		7	1		6	2	
1991	8	8		5	3		3	5	
1992	6	10		4	4		2	6	
1993	11	5		6	2		5	3	
Total	493	396	32	280	182	16	213	214	16

PHILADELPHIA EAGLES

Season	All Games W	L	T	Home Games W	L	T	Road Games W	L	T
1933	3	5	1	2	3	1	1	2	
1934	4	7		2	4		2	3	
1935	2	9		0	5		2	4	
1936	1	11		1	6		0	5	
1937	2	8	1	0	5	1	2	3	
1938	5	6		2	3		3	3	
1939	1	9	1	1	3	1	0	6	
1940	1	10		1	4		0	6	
1941	2	8	1	1	4	1	1	4	
1942	2	9		0	5		2	4	
1944	7	1	2	3	1	2	4	0	
1945	7	3		6	0		1	3	
1946	6	5		3	2		3	3	
1947	8	4		6	1		2	3	
1948	9	2	1	6	0		3	2	1
1949	11	1		6	0		5	1	
1950	6	6		2	4		4	2	
1951	4	8		1	5		3	3	
1952	7	5		4	2		3	3	
1953	7	4	1	5	0	1	2	4	
1954	7	4	1	5	1		2	3	1
1955	4	7	1	4	2		0	5	1
1956	3	8	1	2	3	1	1	5	
1957	4	8		3	3		1	5	
1958	2	9	1	2	4		0	5	1
1959	6	5		4	1		2	4	
1960	10	2		5	1		5	1	
1961	10	4		5	2		5	2	
1962	3	10	1	2	5		1	5	1
1963	2	10	2	1	5	1	1	5	1
1964	6	8		3	4		3	4	
1965	5	9		2	5		3	4	
1966	9	5		5	2		4	3	
1967	6	7	1	5	2		1	5	1
1968	2	12		1	6		1	6	
1969	4	9	1	2	5		2	4	1
1970	3	10	1	3	3	1	0	7	
1971	6	7	1	3	4		3	3	1
1972	2	11	1	0	6	1	2	5	
1973	5	8	1	4	3		1	5	1
1974	7	7		5	2		2	5	
1975	4	10		2	5		2	5	
1976	4	10		2	5		2	5	
1977	5	9		4	3		1	6	
1978	9	7		5	3		4	4	
1979	11	5		5	3		6	2	
1980	12	4		7	1		5	3	
1981	10	6		6	2		4	4	
1982	3	6		1	4		2	2	
1983	5	11		1	7		4	4	
1984	6	9	1	5	3		1	6	1
1985	7	9		4	4		3	5	
1986	5	10	1	2	5	1	3	5	
1987	7	8		4	4		3	4	
1988	10	6		5	3		5	3	
1989	11	5		6	2		5	3	
1990	10	6		6	2		4	4	
1991	10	6		4	4		6	2	
1992	11	5		8	0		3	5	
1993	8	8		3	5		5	3	
Total	349	421	23	198	191	12	151	230	11

SAN FRANCISCO 49ERS

Season	All Games W	L	T	Home Games W	L	T	Road Games W	L	T
1950	3	9		3	3		0	6	
1951	7	4	1	5	1		2	3	1
1952	7	5		3	3		4	2	
1953	9	3		5	1		4	2	
1954	7	4	1	4	2		3	2	1
1955	4	8		2	4		2	4	
1956	5	6	1	3	3		2	3	1
1957	8	4		5	1		3	3	
1958	6	6		4	2		2	4	
1959	7	5		4	2		3	3	
1960	7	5		3	3		4	2	
1961	7	6	1	5	1	1	2	5	
1962	6	8		1	6		5	2	
1963	2	12		2	5		0	7	
1964	4	10		3	4		1	6	
1965	7	6	1	4	2	1	3	4	
1966	6	6	2	4	2	1	2	4	1
1967	7	7		3	4		4	3	
1968	7	6	1	3	3	1	4	3	
1969	4	8	2	3	3	1	1	5	1
1970	10	3	1	5	1	1	5	2	
1971	9	5		4	3		5	2	
1972	8	5	1	4	2	1	4	3	
1973	5	9		3	4		2	5	
1974	6	8		3	4		3	4	
1975	5	9		2	5		3	4	
1976	8	6		4	3		4	3	
1977	5	9		3	4		2	5	
1978	2	14		2	6		0	8	
1979	2	14		2	6		0	8	
1980	6	10		4	4		2	6	
1981	13	3		7	1		6	2	
1982	3	6		0	5		3	1	
1983	10	6		4	4		6	2	
1984	15	1		7	1		8	0	
1985	10	6		5	3		5	3	
1986	10	5	1	6	2		4	3	1
1987	13	2		6	1		7	1	
1988	10	6		4	4		6	2	
1989	14	2		6	2		8	0	
1990	14	2		6	2		8	0	
1991	10	6		7	1		3	5	
1992	14	2		7	1		7	1	
1993	10	6		6	2		4	4	
Total	332	273	13	176	126	7	156	147	6

TAMPA BAY BUCCANEERS

Season	All Games W	L	T	Home Games W	L	T	Road Games W	L	T
1976	0	14		0	7		0	7	
1977	2	12		1	6		1	6	
1978	5	11		3	5		2	6	
1979	10	6		5	3		5	3	
1980	5	10	1	2	5	1	3	5	
1981	9	7		6	2		3	5	
1982	5	4		4	1		1	3	
1983	2	14		1	7		1	7	
1984	6	10		6	2		0	8	
1985	2	14		2	6		0	8	
1986	2	14		1	7		1	7	
1987	4	11		2	5		2	6	
1988	5	11		3	5		2	6	
1989	5	11		2	6		3	5	
1990	6	10		4	4		2	6	
1991	3	13		3	5		0	8	
1992	5	11		3	5		2	6	
1993	5	11		3	5		2	6	
Total	81	194	1	51	86	1	30	108	

WASHINGTON REDSKINS*

Season	All Games			Home Games			Road Games		
	W	L	T	W	L	T	W	L	T
1932	4	4	2	2	3	1	2	1	1
1933	5	5	2	4	2		1	3	2
1934	6	6		4	3		2	3	
1935	2	8	1	2	5		0	3	1
1936	7	5		4	3		3	2	
1937	8	3		4	2		4	1	
1938	6	3	2	3	1	1	3	2	1
1939	8	2	1	5	0	1	3	2	
1940	9	2		6	0		3	2	
1941	6	5		4	2		2	3	
1942	10	1		5	1		5	0	
1943	6	3	1	4	2		2	1	1
1944	6	3	1	4	2		2	1	1
1945	8	2		6	0		2	2	
1946	5	5	1	3	2	1	2	3	
1947	4	8		4	2		0	6	
1948	7	5		4	2		3	3	
1949	4	7	1	3	3		1	4	1
1950	3	9		1	5		2	4	
1951	5	7		2	4		3	3	
1952	4	8		1	5		3	3	
1953	6	5	1	3	3		3	2	1
1954	3	9		3	3		0	6	
1955	8	4		3	3		5	1	
1956	6	6		4	2		2	4	
1957	5	6	1	2	3	1	3	3	
1958	4	7	1	3	2	1	1	5	
1959	4	8		2	4		2	4	
1960	1	9	2	1	4	1	0	5	1
1961	1	12	1	1	6		0	6	1
1962	5	7	2	3	4		2	3	2
1963	3	11		1	6		2	5	
1964	6	8		4	3		2	5	
1965	6	8		3	4		3	4	
1966	7	7		4	3		3	4	
1967	5	6	3	2	4	1	3	2	2
1968	5	9		3	4		2	5	
1969	7	5	2	4	2	1	3	3	1
1970	6	8		4	3		2	5	
1971	9	4	1	4	2	1	5	2	
1972	11	3		6	1		5	2	
1973	10	4		7	0		3	4	
1974	10	4		6	1		4	3	
1975	8	6		5	2		3	4	
1976	10	4		5	2		5	2	
1977	9	5		5	2		4	3	
1978	8	8		5	3		3	5	
1979	10	6		6	2		4	4	
1980	6	10		4	4		2	6	
1981	8	8		5	3		3	5	
1982	8	1		3	1		5	0	
1983	14	2		7	1		7	1	
1984	11	5		7	1		4	4	
1985	10	6		5	3		5	3	
1986	12	4		7	1		5	3	
1987	11	4		6	1		5	3	
1988	7	9		4	4		3	5	
1989	10	6		4	4		6	2	
1990	10	6		7	1		3	5	
1991	14	2		7	1		7	1	
1992	9	7		6	2		3	5	
1993	4	12		3	5		1	7	
Total	430	362	26	249	159	10	181	203	16

*includes Boston Braves (1932) and Boston Redskins (1933-36).

History

The Professional Football Hall of Fame is located in Canton, Ohio, site of the organizational meeting on September 17, 1920, from which the National Football League evolved. The NFL recognized Canton as the Hall of Fame site on April 27, 1961. Canton area individuals, foundations, and companies donated almost $400,000 in cash and services to provide funds for the construction of the original two-building complex, which was dedicated on September 7, 1963. The original Hall of Fame complex was almost doubled in size with the completion of a $620,000 expansion project that was dedicated on May 10, 1971. A second expansion project was completed on November 20, 1978. It now features four exhibition areas and a theater twice the size of the original one.

The Hall represents the sport of pro football in many ways—through four large and colorful exhibition galleries, in the twin enshrinement halls, with numerous fan-participation electronic devices, a research library, and a museum store.

In recent years, the Pro Football Hall of Fame has become an extremely popular tourist attraction. At the end of 1993, a total of 5,466,279 fans had visited the Hall of Fame.

New members of the Pro Football Hall of Fame are elected annually by a 34-member National Board of Selectors, made up of media representatives from every league city, 5 at-large representatives, and a representative of the Pro Football Writers of America. Between four and seven new members are elected each year. An affirmative vote of approximately 80 percent is needed for election.

Any fan may nominate any eligible player or contributor simply by writing to the Pro Football Hall of Fame. Players must be retired five years to be eligible, while a coach need only be retired with no time limit specified. Contributors (administrators, owners, et al.) may be elected while they are still active.

The charter class of 17 enshrinees was elected in 1963 and the honor roll now stands at 175 with the election of a six-man class in 1994. That class consists of Tony Dorsett, Bud Grant, Jimmy Johnson, Leroy Kelly, Jackie Smith, and Randy White.

ROSTER OF MEMBERS

HERB ADDERLEY
Defensive back. 6-1, 200. Born in Philadelphia, Pennsylvania, June 8, 1939. Michigan State. Inducted in 1980. 1961-69 Green Bay Packers, 1970-72 Dallas Cowboys.

LANCE ALWORTH
Wide receiver. 6-0, 184. Born in Houston, Texas, August 3, 1940. Arkansas. Inducted in 1978. 1962-70 San Diego Chargers, 1971-72 Dallas Cowboys.

DOUG ATKINS
Defensive end. 6-8, 275. Born in Humboldt, Tennessee, May 8, 1930. Tennessee. Inducted in 1982. 1953-54 Cleveland Browns, 1955-66 Chicago Bears, 1967-69 New Orleans Saints.

MORRIS (RED) BADGRO
End. 6-0, 190. Born in Orilla, Washington, December 1, 1902. Southern California. Inducted in 1981. 1927 New York Yankees, 1930-35 New York Giants, 1936 Brooklyn Dodgers.

LEM BARNEY
Cornerback. 6-0, 190. Born in Gulfport, Mississippi, September 9, 1945. Jackson State. Inducted in 1992. 1967-77 Detroit Lions.

CLIFF BATTLES
Halfback. 6-1, 201. Born in Akron, Ohio, May 1, 1910. Died April 28, 1981. West Virginia Wesleyan. Inducted in 1968. 1932 Boston Braves, 1933-36 Boston Redskins, 1937 Washington Redskins.

SAMMY BAUGH
Quarterback. 6-2, 180. Born in Temple, Texas, March 17, 1914. Texas Christian. Inducted in 1963. 1937-52 Washington Redskins.

CHUCK BEDNARIK
Center-linebacker. 6-3, 230. Born in Bethlehem, Pennsylvania, May 1, 1925. Pennsylvania. Inducted in 1967. 1949-62 Philadelphia Eagles.

BERT BELL
Team owner. Commissioner. Born in Philadelphia, Pennsylvania, February 25, 1895. Died October 11, 1959. Pennsylvania. Inducted in 1963. 1933-40 Philadelphia Eagles, 1941-42 Pittsburgh Steelers, 1943 Phil-Pitt, 1944-46 Pittsburgh Steelers. Commissioner, 1946-59.

BOBBY BELL
Linebacker. 6-4, 225. Born in Shelby, North Carolina, June 17, 1940. Minnesota. Inducted in 1983. 1963-74 Kansas City Chiefs.

RAYMOND BERRY
End. 6-2, 187. Born in Corpus Christi, Texas, February 27, 1933. Southern Methodist. Inducted in 1973. 1955-67 Baltimore Colts.

CHARLES W. BIDWILL, SR.
Team owner. Born in Chicago, Illinois, September 16, 1895. Died April 19, 1947. Loyola of Chicago. Inducted in 1967. 1933-43 Chicago Cardinals, 1944 Card-Pitt, 1945-47 Chicago Cardinals.

FRED BILETNIKOFF
Wide receiver. 6-1, 190. Born in Erie, Pennsylvania, February 23, 1943. Florida State. Inducted in 1988. 1965-78 Oakland Raiders.

GEORGE BLANDA
Quarterback-kicker. 6-2, 215. Born in Youngwood, Pennsylvania, September 17, 1927. Kentucky. Inducted in 1981. 1949-58 Chicago Bears, 1950 Baltimore Colts, 1960-66 Houston Oilers, 1967-75 Oakland Raiders.

MEL BLOUNT
Cornerback. 6-3, 205. Born in Vidalia, Georgia, April 10, 1948. Southern University. Inducted in 1989. 1970-83 Pittsburgh Steelers.

TERRY BRADSHAW
Quarterback. 6-3, 210. Born in Shreveport, Louisiana, September 2, 1948. Louisiana Tech. Inducted in 1989. 1970-83 Pittsburgh Steelers.

JIM BROWN
Fullback. 6-2, 232. Born in St. Simons, Georgia, February 17, 1936. Syracuse. Inducted in 1971. 1957-65 Cleveland Browns.

PAUL BROWN
Coach. Born in Norwalk, Ohio, September 7, 1908. Died August 5, 1991. Miami, Ohio. Inducted in 1967. 1946-49 Cleveland Browns (AAFC), 1950-62 Cleveland Browns, 1968-75 Cincinnati Bengals.

ROOSEVELT BROWN
Tackle. 6-3, 255. Born in Charlottesville, Virginia, October 20, 1932. Morgan State. Inducted in 1975. 1953-65 New York Giants.

WILLIE BROWN
Defensive back. 6-1, 210. Born in Yazoo City, Mississippi, December 2, 1940. Grambling. Inducted in 1984. 1963-66 Denver Broncos, 1967-78 Oakland Raiders.

BUCK BUCHANAN
Defensive tackle. 6-7, 274. Born in Gainesville, Alabama, September 10, 1940. Grambling. Inducted in 1990. 1963-75 Kansas City Chiefs.

DICK BUTKUS
Linebacker. 6-3, 245. Born in Chicago, Illinois, December 9, 1942. Illinois. Inducted in 1979. 1965-73 Chicago Bears.

EARL CAMPBELL
Running back. 5-11, 233. Born in Tyler, Texas, March 29, 1955. Texas. Inducted in 1991. 1978-84 Houston Oilers, 1984-85 New Orleans Saints.

TONY CANADEO
Halfback. 5-11, 195. Born in Chicago, Illinois, May 5, 1919. Gonzaga. Inducted in 1974. 1941-44, 1946-52 Green Bay Packers.

JOE CARR
NFL president. Born in Columbus, Ohio, October 22, 1880. Died May 20, 1939. Did not attend college. Inducted in 1963. President, 1921-39 National Football League.

GUY CHAMBERLIN
End. Coach. 6-2, 210. Born in Blue Springs, Nebraska, January 16, 1894. Died April 4, 1967. Nebraska. Inducted in 1965. 1920 Decatur Staleys, 1921 Chicago Staleys, player-coach 1922-23 Canton Bulldogs, 1924 Cleveland Bulldogs, 1925-26 Frankford Yellow Jackets, 1927 Chicago Cardinals.

JACK CHRISTIANSEN
Defensive back. 6-1, 185. Born in Sublette, Kansas, December 20, 1928. Died June 29, 1986. Colorado State. Inducted in 1970. 1951-58 Detroit Lions.

EARL (DUTCH) CLARK
Quarterback. 6-0, 185. Born in Fowler, Colorado, October 11, 1906. Died August 5, 1978. Colorado College. Inducted in 1963. 1931-32 Portsmouth Spartans, 1934-38 Detroit Lions.

GEORGE CONNOR
Tackle-linebacker. 6-3, 240. Born in Chicago, Illinois, January 21, 1925. Holy Cross, Notre Dame. Inducted in 1975. 1948-55 Chicago Bears.

JIMMY CONZELMAN
Quarterback. Coach. Team owner. 6-0, 180. Born in St. Louis, Missouri, March 6, 1898. Died July 31, 1970. Washington, Missouri. Inducted in 1964. 1920 Decatur Staleys, 1921-22 Rock Island, Ill., Independents, 1923-24 Milwaukee Badgers; owner-coach, 1925-26 Detroit Panthers; player-coach 1927-29, coach 1930 Providence Steam Roller; coach, 1940-42 Chicago Cardinals, 1946-48 Chicago Cardinals.

LARRY CSONKA
Running back. 6-3, 235. Born in Stow, Ohio, December 25, 1946. Syracuse. Inducted in 1987. Miami Dolphins 1968-74, 1979, New York Giants 1976-78.

AL DAVIS
Team, League Administrator. Born in Brockton, Massachusetts, July 4, 1929. Wittenberg, Syracuse. Inducted in 1992. 1963-81 Oakland Raiders, 1982-92 Los Angeles Raiders, 1966 American Football League.

WILLIE DAVIS
Defensive end. 6-3, 245. Born in Lisbon, Louisiana, July 24, 1934. Grambling. Inducted in 1981. 1958-59 Cleveland Browns, 1960-69 Green Bay Packers.

LEN DAWSON
Quarterback. 6-0, 190. Born in Alliance, Ohio, June 20, 1935. Purdue. Inducted in 1987. 1957-59 Pittsburgh Steelers, 1960-61 Cleveland Browns, 1962 Dallas Texans, 1963-75 Kansas City Chiefs.

MIKE DITKA
Tight end. 6-3, 225. Born in Carnegie, Pennsylvania, October 18, 1939. Pittsburgh. Inducted in 1988. 1961-66 Chicago Bears, 1967-68 Philadelphia Eagles, 1969-72 Dallas Cowboys.

ART DONOVAN
Defensive tackle. 6-3, 265. Born in Bronx, New York, June 5, 1925. Boston College. Inducted in 1968. 1950 Baltimore Colts, 1951 New York Yanks, 1952 Dallas Texans, 1953-61 Baltimore Colts.

TONY DORSETT
Running back. 5-11, 184. Born in Rochester, Pennsylvania, April 7, 1954. Pittsburgh. Inducted in 1994. 1977-87 Dallas Cowboys, 1988 Denver Broncos.

JOHN (PADDY) DRISCOLL
Quarterback. 5-11, 160. Born in Evanston, Illinois, January 11, 1896. Died June 29, 1968. Northwestern. Inducted in 1965. 1920 Decatur Sta-

leys, 1920-25 Chicago Cardinals, 1926-29 Chicago Bears. Coach, 1956-57 Chicago Bears.

BILL DUDLEY
Halfback. 5-10, 176. Born in Bluefield, Virginia, December 24, 1921. Virginia. Inducted in 1966. 1942, 1945-46 Pittsburgh Steelers, 1947-49 Detroit Lions, 1950-51, 1953 Washington Redskins.

GLEN (TURK) EDWARDS
Tackle. 6-2, 260. Born in Mold, Washington, September 28, 1907. Died January 12, 1973. Washington State. Inducted in 1969. 1932 Boston Braves, 1933-36 Boston Redskins, 1937-40 Washington Redskins.

WEEB EWBANK
Coach. Born in Richmond, Indiana, May 6, 1907. Miami, Ohio. Inducted in 1978. 1954-62 Baltimore Colts, 1963-73 New York Jets.

TOM FEARS
End. 6-2, 215. Born in Los Angeles, California, December 3, 1923. Santa Clara, UCLA. Inducted in 1970. 1948-56 Los Angeles Rams.

RAY FLAHERTY
End. Coach. Born in Spokane, Washington, September 1, 1904. Gonzaga. Inducted in 1976. 1926 Los Angeles Wildcats (AFL), 1927-28 New York Yankees, 1928-29, 1931-35 New York Giants. Coach, 1936 Boston Redskins, 1937-42 Washington Redskins, 1946-48 New York Yankees (AAFC), 1949 Chicago Hornets (AAFC).

LEN FORD
End. 6-5, 260. Born in Washington, D.C., February 18, 1926. Died March 14, 1972. Michigan. Inducted in 1976. 1948-49 Los Angeles Dons (AAFC), 1950-57 Cleveland Browns, 1958 Green Bay Packers.

DAN FORTMANN
Guard. 6-0, 207. Born in Pearl River, New York, April 11, 1916. Colgate. Inducted in 1965. 1936-43 Chicago Bears.

DAN FOUTS
Quarterback. 6-3, 210. Born in San Francisco, California, June 10, 1951. Oregon. Inducted in 1993. 1973-1987 San Diego Chargers.

FRANK GATSKI
Center. 6-3, 240. Born in Farmington, West Virginia, March 18, 1922. Marshall, Auburn. Inducted in 1985. 1946-49 Cleveland Browns (AAFC), 1950-56 Cleveland Browns, 1957 Detroit Lions.

BILL GEORGE
Linebacker. 6-2, 230. Born in Waynesburg, Pennsylvania, October 27, 1930. Died September 30, 1982. Wake Forest. Inducted in 1974. 1952-65 Chicago Bears, 1966 Los Angeles Rams.

FRANK GIFFORD
Halfback. 6-1, 195. Born in Santa Monica, California, August 16, 1930. Southern California. Inducted in 1977. 1952-60, 1962-64 New York Giants.

SID GILLMAN
Coach. Born in Minneapolis, Minnesota, October 26, 1911. Ohio State. Inducted in 1983. 1955-59 Los Angeles Rams, 1960 Los Angeles Chargers, 1961-69 San Diego Chargers, 1973-74 Houston Oilers.

OTTO GRAHAM
Quarterback. 6-1, 195. Born in Waukegan, Illinois, December 6, 1921. Northwestern. Inducted in 1965. 1946-49 Cleveland Browns (AAFC), 1950-55 Cleveland Browns.

HAROLD (RED) GRANGE
Halfback. 6-0, 185. Born in Forksville, Pennsylvania, June 13, 1903. Died January 28, 1991. Illinois. Inducted in 1963. 1925 Chicago Bears, 1926 New York Yankees (AFL), 1927 New York Yankees, 1929-34 Chicago Bears.

BUD GRANT
Coach. Born in Superior, Wisconsin, May 20, 1927. Minnesota. Inducted in 1994. 1967-83, 1985 Minnesota Vikings.

JOE GREENE
Defensive tackle. 6-4, 260. Born in Temple, Texas, September 24, 1946. North Texas State. Inducted in 1987. 1969-81 Pittsburgh Steelers.

FORREST GREGG
Tackle. 6-4, 250. Born in Birthright, Texas, October 18, 1933. Southern Methodist. Inducted in 1977. 1956, 1958-70 Green Bay Packers, 1971 Dallas Cowboys.

BOB GRIESE
Quarterback. 6-1, 190. Born in Evansville, Indiana, February 3, 1945. Purdue. Inducted in 1990. 1967-80 Miami Dolphins.

LOU GROZA
Tackle-kicker. 6-3, 250. Born in Martin's Ferry, Ohio, January 25, 1924. Ohio State. Inducted in 1974. 1946-49 Cleveland Browns (AAFC), 1950-59, 1961-67 Cleveland Browns.

JOE GUYON
Halfback. 6-1, 180. Born in Mahnomen, Minnesota, November 26, 1892. Died November 27, 1971. Carlisle, Georgia Tech. Inducted in 1966. 1920 Canton Bulldogs, 1921 Cleveland Indians, 1922-23 Oorang Indians, 1924 Rock Island, Ill., Independents, 1924-25 Kansas City Cowboys, 1927 New York Giants.

GEORGE HALAS
End. Coach. Team owner. Born in Chicago, Illinois, February 2, 1895. Died October 31, 1983. Illinois. Inducted in 1963. 1920 Decatur Staleys, 1921 Chicago Staleys, 1922-29 Chicago Bears; coach, 1933-42, 1946-55, 1958-67 Chicago Bears.

JACK HAM
Linebacker. 6-1, 225. Born in Johnstown, Pennsylvania, December 23, 1948. Penn State. Inducted in 1988. 1971-82 Pittsburgh Steelers.

JOHN HANNAH
Guard. 6-3, 265. Born in Canton, Georgia, April 4, 1951. Alabama. Inducted in 1991. 1973-85 New England Patriots.

FRANCO HARRIS
Running back. 6-2, 225. Born in Fort Dix, New Jersey, March 7, 1950. Penn State. Inducted in 1990. 1972-83 Pittsburgh Steelers, 1984 Seattle Seahawks.

ED HEALEY
Tackle. 6-3, 220. Born in Indian Orchard, Massachusetts, December 28, 1894. Died December 9, 1978. Dartmouth. Inducted in 1964. 1920-22 Rock Island, Ill., Independents, 1922-27 Chicago Bears.

MEL HEIN
Center. 6-2, 225. Born in Redding, California, August 22, 1909. Died January 31, 1992. Washington State. Inducted in 1963. 1931-45 New York Giants.

TED HENDRICKS
Linebacker. 6-7, 235. Born in Guatemala City, Guatemala, November 1, 1947. Miami. Inducted in 1990. 1969-73 Baltimore Colts, 1974 Green Bay Packers, 1975-81 Oakland Raiders, 1982-83 Los Angeles Raiders.

WILBUR (PETE) HENRY
Tackle. 6-0, 250. Born in Mansfield, Ohio, October 31, 1897. Died February 7, 1952. Washington & Jefferson. Inducted in 1963. 1920-23, 1925-26 Canton Bulldogs, 1927 New York Giants, 1927-28 Pottsville Maroons.

ARNIE HERBER
Quarterback. 6-1, 200. Born in Green Bay, Wisconsin, April 2, 1910. Died October 14, 1969. Wisconsin, Regis College. Inducted in 1966. 1930-40 Green Bay Packers, 1944-45 New York Giants.

BILL HEWITT
End. 5-11, 191. Born in Bay City, Michigan, October 8, 1909. Died January 14, 1947. Michigan. Inducted in 1971. 1932-36 Chicago Bears, 1937-39 Philadelphia Eagles, 1943 Phil-Pitt.

CLARKE HINKLE
Fullback. 5-11, 201. Born in Toronto, Ohio, April 10, 1909. Died November 9, 1988. Bucknell. Inducted in 1964. 1932-41 Green Bay Packers.

ELROY (CRAZYLEGS) HIRSCH
Halfback-end. 6-2, 190. Born in Wausau, Wisconsin, June 17, 1923. Wisconsin, Michigan. Inducted in 1968. 1946-48 Chicago Rockets (AAFC), 1949-57 Los Angeles Rams.

PAUL HORNUNG
Halfback. 6-2, 220. Born in Louisville, Kentucky, December 23, 1935. Notre Dame. Inducted in 1986. 1957-62, 1964-66 Green Bay Packers.

KEN HOUSTON
Safety. 6-3, 198. Born in Lufkin, Texas, November 12, 1944. Prairie View A&M. Inducted in 1986. 1967-72 Houston Oilers, 1973-80 Washington Redskins.

CAL HUBBARD
Tackle. 6-5, 250. Born in Keytesville, Missouri, October 31, 1900. Died October 17, 1977. Centenary, Geneva. Inducted in 1963. 1927-28 New York Giants, 1929-33, 1935 Green Bay Packers, 1936 New York Giants, 1936 Pittsburgh Pirates.

SAM HUFF
Linebacker. 6-1, 230. Born in Morgantown, West Virginia, October 4, 1934. West Virginia. Inducted in 1982. 1956-63 New York Giants, 1964-67, 1969 Washington Redskins.

LAMAR HUNT
Team owner. Born in El Dorado, Arkansas, August 2, 1932. Southern Methodist. Inducted in 1972. 1960-62 Dallas Texans, 1963-90 Kansas City Chiefs.

DON HUTSON
End. 6-1, 180. Born in Pine Bluff, Arkansas, January 31, 1913. Alabama. Inducted in 1963. 1935-45 Green Bay Packers.

JIMMY JOHNSON
Cornerback. 6-2, 187. Born in Dallas, Texas, March 31, 1938. UCLA. Inducted in 1994. 1961-76 San Francisco 49ers.

JOHN HENRY JOHNSON
Fullback. 6-2, 225. Born in Waterproof, Louisiana, November 24, 1929. St. Mary's, Arizona State. Inducted in 1987. 1954-56 San Francisco 49ers, 1957-59 Detroit Lions, 1960-65 Pittsburgh Steelers, 1966 Houston Oilers.

DAVID (DEACON) JONES
Defensive end. 6-5, 250. Born in Eatonville, Florida, December 9, 1938. Mississippi Vocational. Inducted in 1980. 1961-71 Los Angeles Rams, 1972-73 San Diego Chargers, 1974 Washington Redskins.

STAN JONES
Guard-defensive tackle. 6-1, 250. Born in Altoona, Pennsylvania, November 24, 1931. Maryland. Inducted in 1991. 1954-65 Chicago Bears, 1966 Washington Redskins.

SONNY JURGENSEN
Quarterback. 6-0, 203. Born in Wilmington, North Carolina, August 23, 1934. Duke. Inducted in 1983. 1957-63 Philadelphia Eagles, 1964-74 Washington Redskins.

LEROY KELLY
Running back. 6-0, 205. Born in Philadelphia, Pennsylvania, May 20, 1942. Morgan State. Inducted in 1994. 1964-73 Cleveland Browns.

WALT KIESLING
Guard. Coach. 6-2, 245. Born in St. Paul, Minnesota, March 27, 1903. Died March 2, 1962. St. Thomas (Minnesota). Inducted in 1966. 1926-27 Duluth Eskimos, 1928 Pottsville Maroons, 1929-33 Chicago Cardinals, 1934 Chicago Bears, 1935-36 Green Bay Packers, 1937-38 Pittsburgh Pirates; coach, 1939-42 Pittsburgh Steelers;

co-coach, 1943 Phil-Pitt, 1944 Card-Pitt; coach, 1954-56 Pittsburgh Steelers.

FRANK (BRUISER) KINARD
Tackle. 6-1, 210. Born in Pelahatchie, Mississippi, October 23, 1914. Died September 7, 1985. Mississippi. Inducted in 1971. 1938-44 Brooklyn Dodgers-Tigers, 1946-47 New York Yankees (AAFC).

EARL (CURLY) LAMBEAU
Coach. Born in Green Bay, Wisconsin, April 9, 1898. Died June 1, 1965. Notre Dame. Inducted in 1963. 1919-49 Green Bay Packers, 1950-51 Chicago Cardinals, 1952-53 Washington Redskins.

JACK LAMBERT
Linebacker. 6-4, 220. Born in Mantua, Ohio, July 8, 1952. Kent State. Inducted in 1990. 1974-84 Pittsburgh Steelers.

TOM LANDRY
Coach. Born in Mission, Texas, September 11, 1924. Texas. Inducted in 1990. 1960-88 Dallas Cowboys.

DICK (NIGHT TRAIN) LANE
Defensive back. 6-2, 210. Born in Austin, Texas, April 16, 1928. Scottsbluff Junior College. Inducted in 1974. 1952-53 Los Angeles Rams, 1954-59 Chicago Cardinals, 1960-65 Detroit Lions.

JIM LANGER
Center. 6-2, 255. Born in Little Falls, Minnesota, May 16, 1948. South Dakota State. Inducted in 1987. 1970-79 Miami Dolphins, 1980-81 Minnesota Vikings.

WILLIE LANIER
Linebacker. 6-1, 245. Born in Clover, Virginia, August 21, 1945. Morgan State. Inducted in 1986. 1967-77 Kansas City Chiefs.

YALE LARY
Defensive back-punter. 5-11, 189. Born in Fort Worth, Texas, November 24, 1930. Texas A&M. Inducted in 1979. 1952-53, 1956-64 Detroit Lions.

DANTE LAVELLI
End. 6-0, 199. Born in Hudson, Ohio, February 23, 1923. Ohio State. Inducted in 1975. 1946-49 Cleveland Browns (AAFC), 1950-56 Cleveland Browns.

BOBBY LAYNE
Quarterback. 6-2, 190. Born in Santa Anna, Texas, December 19, 1926. Died December 1, 1986. Texas. Inducted in 1967. 1948 Chicago Bears, 1949 New York Bulldogs, 1950-58 Detroit Lions, 1958-62 Pittsburgh Steelers.

ALPHONSE (TUFFY) LEEMANS
Fullback. 6-0, 200. Born in Superior, Wisconsin, November 12, 1912. Died January 19, 1979. George Washington. Inducted in 1978. 1936-43 New York Giants.

BOB LILLY
Defensive tackle. 6-5, 260. Born in Olney, Texas, July 26, 1939. Texas

Christian. Inducted in 1980. 1961-74 Dallas Cowboys.

LARRY LITTLE
Guard. 6-1, 255. Born in Groveland, Georgia, November 2, 1945. Bethune-Cookman. Inducted in 1993. 1967-68 San Diego Chargers, 1969-80 Miami Dolphins.

VINCE LOMBARDI
Coach. Born in Brooklyn, New York, June 11, 1913. Died September 3, 1970. Fordham. Inducted in 1971. 1959-67 Green Bay Packers, 1969 Washington Redskins.

SID LUCKMAN
Quarterback. 6-0, 195. Born in Brooklyn, New York, November 21, 1916. Columbia. Inducted in 1965. 1939-50 Chicago Bears.

ROY (LINK) LYMAN
Tackle. 6-2, 252. Born in Table Rock, Nebraska, November 30, 1898. Died December 16, 1972. Nebraska. Inducted in 1964. 1922-23, 1925 Canton Bulldogs, 1924 Cleveland Bulldogs, 1925 Frankford Yellow Jackets, 1926-28, 1930-31, 1933-34 Chicago Bears.

JOHN MACKEY
Tight end. 6-2, 224. Born in New York, New York, September 24, 1941. Syracuse. Inducted in 1992. 1963-71 Baltimore Colts, 1972 San Diego Chargers.

TIM MARA
Team owner. Born in New York, New York, July 29, 1887. Died February 17, 1959. Did not attend college. Inducted in 1963. 1925-59 New York Giants.

GINO MARCHETTI
Defensive end. 6-4, 245. Born in Smithers, West Virginia, January 2, 1927. San Francisco. Inducted in 1972. 1952 Dallas Texans, 1953-64, 1966 Baltimore Colts.

GEORGE PRESTON MARSHALL
Team owner. Born in Grafton, West Virginia, October 11, 1897. Died August 9, 1969. Randolph-Macon. Inducted in 1963. 1932 Boston Braves, 1933-36 Boston Redskins, 1937-69 Washington Redskins.

OLLIE MATSON
Halfback. 6-2, 220. Born in Trinity, Texas, May 1, 1930. San Francisco. Inducted in 1972. 1952, 1954-58 Chicago Cardinals, 1959-62 Los Angeles Rams, 1963 Detroit Lions, 1964-66 Philadelphia Eagles.

DON MAYNARD
Wide receiver. 6-1, 175. Born in Crosbyton, Texas, January 25, 1935. Texas Western. Inducted in 1987. 1958 New York Giants, 1960-62 New York Titans, 1963-72 New York Jets, 1973 St. Louis Cardinals.

GEORGE McAFEE
Halfback. 6-0, 177. Born in Ironton, Ohio, March 13, 1918. Duke. Inducted in 1966. 1940-41, 1945-50 Chicago Bears.

MIKE McCORMACK
Tackle. 6-4, 248. Born in Chicago, Illinois, June 21, 1930. Kansas. Inducted in 1984. 1951 New York Yanks, 1954-62 Cleveland Browns.

HUGH McELHENNY
Halfback. 6-1, 198. Born in Los Angeles, California, December 31, 1928. Washington. Inducted in 1970. 1952-60 San Francisco 49ers, 1961-62 Minnesota Vikings, 1963 New York Giants, 1964 Detroit Lions.

JOHNNY BLOOD (McNALLY)
Halfback. 6-0, 185. Born in New Richmond, Wisconsin, November 27, 1903. Died November 28, 1985. St. John's (Minnesota). Inducted in 1963. 1925-26 Milwaukee Badgers, 1926-27 Duluth Eskimos, 1928 Pottsville Maroons, 1929-33, 1935-36 Green Bay Packers, 1934 Pittsburgh Pirates; player-coach, 1937-39 Pittsburgh Pirates.

MIKE MICHALSKE
Guard. 6-0, 209. Born in Cleveland, Ohio, April 24, 1903. Died October 26, 1983. Penn State. Inducted in 1964. 1926 New York Yankees (AFL), 1927-28 New York Yankees, 1929-35, 1937 Green Bay Packers.

WAYNE MILLNER
End. 6-0, 191. Born in Roxbury, Massachusetts, January 31, 1913. Died November 19, 1976. Notre Dame. Inducted in 1968. 1936 Boston Redskins, 1937-41, 1945 Washington Redskins.

BOBBY MITCHELL
Running back-wide receiver. 6-0, 195. Born in Hot Springs, Arkansas, June 6, 1935. Illinois. Inducted in 1983. 1958-61 Cleveland Browns, 1962-68 Washington Redskins.

RON MIX
Tackle. 6-4, 250. Born in Los Angeles, California, March 10, 1938. Southern California. Inducted in 1979. 1960 Los Angeles Chargers, 1961-69 San Diego Chargers, 1971 Oakland Raiders.

LENNY MOORE
Back. 6-1, 198. Born in Reading, Pennsylvania, November 25, 1933. Penn State. Inducted in 1975. 1956-67 Baltimore Colts.

MARION MOTLEY
Fullback. 6-1, 238. Born in Leesburg, Georgia, June 5, 1920. South Carolina State, Nevada. Inducted in 1968. 1946-49 Cleveland Browns (AAFC), 1950-53 Cleveland Browns, 1955 Pittsburgh Steelers.

GEORGE MUSSO
Guard-tackle. 6-2, 270. Born in Collinsville, Illinois. April 8, 1910. Millikin. Inducted in 1982. 1933-44 Chicago Bears.

BRONKO NAGURSKI
Fullback. 6-2, 225. Born in Rainy River, Ontario, Canada, November 3, 1908. Died January 7, 1990. Minnesota. Inducted in 1963. 1930-37, 1943 Chicago Bears.

JOE NAMATH
Quarterback. 6-2, 200. Born in Beaver Falls, Pennsylvania, May 31, 1943. Alabama. Inducted in 1985. 1965-76 New York Jets, 1977 Los Angeles Rams.

EARLE (GREASY) NEALE
Coach. Born in Parkersburg, West Virginia, November 5, 1891. Died November 2, 1973. West Virginia Wesleyan. Inducted in 1969. 1941-42, 1944-50 Philadelphia Eagles; co-coach, Phil-Pitt 1943.

ERNIE NEVERS
Fullback. 6-1, 205. Born in Willow River, Minnesota, June 11, 1903. Died May 3, 1976. Stanford. Inducted in 1963. 1926-27 Duluth Eskimos, 1929-31 Chicago Cardinals.

RAY NITSCHKE
Linebacker. 6-3, 235. Born in Elmwood Park, Illinois, December 29, 1936. Illinois. Inducted in 1978. 1958-72 Green Bay Packers.

CHUCK NOLL
Coach. Born in Cleveland, Ohio, January 5, 1932. Dayton. Inducted in 1993. 1969-91 Pittsburgh Steelers.

LEO NOMELLINI
Defensive tackle. 6-3, 250. Born in Lucca, Italy, June 19, 1924. Minnesota. Inducted in 1969. 1950-63 San Francisco 49ers.

MERLIN OLSEN
Defensive tackle. 6-5, 270. Born in Logan, Utah, September 15, 1940. Utah State. Inducted in 1982. 1962-76 Los Angeles Rams.

JIM OTTO
Center. 6-2, 255. Born in Wausau, Wisconsin, January 5, 1938. Miami. Inducted in 1980. 1960-74 Oakland Raiders.

STEVE OWEN
Tackle. Coach. 6-0, 235. Born in Cleo Springs, Oklahoma, April 21, 1898. Died May 17, 1964. Phillips. Inducted in 1966. 1924-25 Kansas City Cowboys, 1926-30 New York Giants; coach, 1931-53 New York Giants.

ALAN PAGE
Defensive tackle. 6-4, 225. Born in Canton, Ohio, August 7, 1945. Notre Dame. Inducted in 1988. 1967-78 Minnesota Vikings, 1978-81 Chicago Bears.

CLARENCE (ACE) PARKER
Quarterback. 5-11, 168. Born in Portsmouth, Virginia, May 17, 1912. Inducted in 1972. 1937-41 Brooklyn Dodgers, 1945 Boston Yanks, 1946 New York Yankees (AAFC).

JIM PARKER
Guard-tackle. 6-3, 273. Born in Macon, Georgia, April 3, 1934. Ohio State. Inducted in 1973. 1957-67 Baltimore Colts.

WALTER PAYTON
Running back. 5-10, 202. Born in Columbia, Mississippi, July 25, 1954.

Jackson State. Inducted in 1993. 1975-87 Chicago Bears.

JOE PERRY
Fullback. 6-0, 200. Born in Stevens, Arkansas, January 22, 1927. Compton Junior College. Inducted in 1969. 1948-49 San Francisco 49ers (AAFC), 1950-60, 1963 San Francisco 49ers, 1961-62 Baltimore Colts.

PETE PIHOS
End. 6-1, 210. Born in Orlando, Florida, October 22, 1923. Indiana. Inducted in 1970. 1947-55 Philadelphia Eagles.

HUGH (SHORTY) RAY
Supervisor of officials 1938-56. Born in Highland Park, Illinois, September 21, 1884. Died September 16, 1956. Illinois. Inducted in 1966.

DAN REEVES
Team owner. Born in New York, New York, June 30, 1912. Died April 15, 1971. Georgetown. Inducted in 1967. 1941-45 Cleveland Rams, 1946-71 Los Angeles Rams.

JOHN RIGGINS
Running back. 6-2, 240. Born in Seneca, Kansas, August 4, 1949. Kansas. Inducted in 1992. 1971-75 New York Jets, 1976-79, 1981-85 Washington Redskins.

JIM RINGO
Center. 6-1, 235. Born in Orange, New Jersey, November 21, 1931. Syracuse. Inducted in 1981. 1953-63 Green Bay Packers, 1964-67 Philadelphia Eagles.

ANDY ROBUSTELLI
Defensive end. 6-0, 230. Born in Stamford, Connecticut, December 6, 1925. Arnold College. Inducted in 1971. 1951-55 Los Angeles Rams, 1956-64 New York Giants.

ART ROONEY
Team owner. Born in Coulterville, Pennsylvania, January 27, 1901. Died August 25, 1988. Georgetown, Duquesne. Inducted in 1964. 1933-40 Pittsburgh Pirates, 1941-42, 1945-88 Pittsburgh Steelers, 1943 Phil-Pitt, 1944 Card-Pitt.

PETE ROZELLE
Commissioner. Born in South Gate, California, March 1, 1926. San Francisco. Inducted in 1985. Commissioner, 1960-89.

BOB ST. CLAIR
Tackle. 6-9, 265. Born in San Francisco, California, February 18, 1931. San Francisco, Tulsa. Inducted in 1990. 1953-63 San Francisco 49ers.

GALE SAYERS
Running back. 6-0, 200. Born in Wichita, Kansas, May 30, 1943. Kansas. Inducted in 1977. 1965-71 Chicago Bears.

JOE SCHMIDT
Linebacker. 6-0, 222. Born in Pittsburgh, Pennsylvania, January 19,1932. Pittsburgh. Inducted in 1973. 1953-65 Detroit Lions.

TEX SCHRAMM
Team president-general manager. Born in San Gabriel, California, June 2, 1920. Texas. Inducted in 1991. 1947-57 Los Angeles Rams. 1960-88 Dallas Cowboys.

ART SHELL
Tackle. 6-5, 285. Born in Charleston, South Carolina, November 25, 1946. Maryland State-Eastern Shore. Inducted in 1989. 1968-81 Oakland Raiders, 1982 Los Angeles Raiders.

O.J. SIMPSON
Running back. 6-1, 212. Born in San Francisco, California, July 9, 1947. Southern California. Inducted in 1985. 1969-77 Buffalo Bills, 1978-79 San Francisco 49ers.

JACKIE SMITH
Tight end. 6-4, 232. Born in Columbia, Mississippi, February 23, 1940. Northwestern Louisiana. Inducted in 1994. 1963-77 St. Louis Cardinals, 1978 Dallas Cowboys.

BART STARR
Quarterback. 6-1, 200. Born in Montgomery, Alabama, January 9, 1934. Alabama. Inducted in 1977. 1956-71 Green Bay Packers.

ROGER STAUBACH
Quarterback. 6-3, 202. Born in Cincinnati, Ohio, February 5, 1942. Navy. Inducted in 1985. 1969-79 Dallas Cowboys.

ERNIE STAUTNER
Defensive tackle. 6-2, 235. Born in Prinzing-by-Cham, Bavaria, Germany, April 20, 1925. Boston College. Inducted in 1969. 1950-63 Pittsburgh Steelers.

JAN STENERUD
Kicker. 6-2, 190. Born in Fetound, Norway, November 26, 1942. Montana State. Inducted in 1991. 1967-79 Kansas City Chiefs, 1980-83 Green Bay Packers, 1984-85 Minnesota Vikings.

KEN STRONG
Halfback. 5-11, 210. Born in New Haven, Connecticut, August 6, 1906. Died October 5, 1979. New York University. Inducted in 1967. 1929-32 Staten Island Stapletons, 1933-35, 1939, 1944-47 New York Giants, 1936-37 New York Yanks (AFL).

JOE STYDAHAR
Tackle. 6-4, 230. Born in Kaylor,Pennsylvania, March 3, 1912. Died March 23, 1977. West Virginia. Inducted in 1967. 1936-42, 1945-46 Chicago Bears.

FRAN TARKENTON
Quarterback. 6-0, 185. Born in Richmond, Virginia, February 3, 1940. Georgia. Inducted in 1986. 1961-66, 1972-78 Minnesota Vikings, 1967-71 New York Giants.

CHARLEY TAYLOR
Running back-wide receiver. 6-3, 210. Born in Grand Prairie, Texas, September 28, 1941. Arizona State. Inducted

in 1984. 1964-75, 1977 Washington Redskins.

JIM TAYLOR
Fullback. 6-0, 216. Born in Baton Rouge, Louisiana, September 20, 1935. Louisiana State. Inducted in 1976. 1958-66 Green Bay Packers, 1967 New Orleans Saints.

JIM THORPE
Halfback. 6-1, 190. Born in Prague, Oklahoma, May 28, 1888. Died March 28, 1953. Carlisle. Inducted in 1963. 1915-17, 1919-20, 1926 Canton Bulldogs, 1921 Cleveland Indians, 1922-23 Oorang Indians, 1924 Rock Island, Ill., Independents, 1925 New York Giants, 1928 Chicago Cardinals.

Y.A. TITTLE
Quarterback. 6-0, 200. Born in Marshall, Texas, October 24, 1926. Louisiana State. Inducted in 1971. 1948-49 Baltimore Colts (AAFC), 1950 Baltimore Colts, 1951-60 San Francisco 49ers, 1961-64 New York Giants.

GEORGE TRAFTON
Center. 6-2, 235. Born in Chicago, Illinois, December 6, 1896. Died September 5, 1971. Notre Dame. Inducted in 1964. 1920 Decatur Staleys, 1921 Chicago Staleys, 1922-32 Chicago Bears.

CHARLEY TRIPPI
Halfback. 6-0, 185. Born in Pittston, Pennsylvania, December 14, 1922. Georgia. Inducted in 1968. 1947-55 Chicago Cardinals.

EMLEN TUNNELL
Safety. 6-1, 200. Born in Bryn Mawr, Pennsylvania, March 29, 1925. Died July 23, 1975. Toledo, Iowa. Inducted in 1967. 1948-58 New York Giants, 1959-61 Green Bay Packers.

CLYDE (BULLDOG) TURNER
Center. 6-2, 235. Born in Sweetwater, Texas, November 10, 1919. Hardin-Simmons. Inducted in 1966. 1940-52 Chicago Bears.

JOHNNY UNITAS
Quarterback. 6-1, 195. Born in Pittsburgh, Pennsylvania, May 7, 1933. Louisville. Inducted in 1979. 1956-72 Baltimore Colts, 1973 San Diego Chargers.

GENE UPSHAW
Guard. 6-5, 255. Born in Robstown, Texas, August 15, 1945. Texas A & I. Inducted in 1987. 1967-81 Oakland Raiders.

NORM VAN BROCKLIN
Quarterback. 6-1, 190. Born in Eagle Butte, South Dakota, March 15, 1926. Died May 2, 1983. Oregon. Inducted in 1971. 1949-57 Los Angeles Rams, 1958-60 Philadelphia Eagles.

STEVE VAN BUREN
Halfback. 6-1, 200. Born in La Ceiba, Honduras, December 28, 1920. Louisiana State. Inducted in 1965. 1944-51 Philadelphia Eagles.

DOAK WALKER
Halfback. 5-10, 172. Born in Dallas,

Texas, January 1, 1927. Southern Methodist. Inducted in 1986. 1950-55 Detroit Lions.

BILL WALSH
Coach. Born in Los Angeles, California, November 30, 1931. San Jose State. Inducted in 1993. 1979-88 San Francisco 49ers.

PAUL WARFIELD
Wide receiver. 6-0, 188. Born in Warren, Ohio, November 28, 1942. Ohio State. Inducted in 1983. 1964-69, 1976-77 Cleveland Browns, 1970-74 Miami Dolphins.

BOB WATERFIELD
Quarterback. 6-2, 200. Born in Elmira, New York, July 26, 1920. Died March 25, 1983. UCLA. Inducted in 1965. 1945 Cleveland Rams, 1946-52 Los Angeles Rams.

ARNIE WEINMEISTER
Defensive tackle. 6-4, 235. Born in Rhein, Saskatchewan, Canada, March 23, 1923. Washington. Inducted in 1984. 1948-49 New York Yankees (AAFC), 1950-53 New York Giants.

RANDY WHITE
Defensive tackle. 6-4, 265. Born in Wilmington, Delaware, January 15, 1953. Maryland. Inducted in 1994. 1975-88 Dallas Cowboys.

BILL WILLIS
Guard. 6-2, 215. Born in Columbus, Ohio, October 5, 1921. Ohio State. Inducted in 1977. 1946-49 Cleveland Browns (AAFC), 1950-53 Cleveland Browns.

LARRY WILSON
Safety. 6-0, 190. Born in Rigby, Idaho, March 24, 1938. Utah. Inducted in 1978. 1960-72 St. Louis Cardinals.

ALEX WOJCIECHOWICZ
Center. 6-0, 235. Born in South River, New Jersey, August 12, 1915. Fordham. Inducted in 1968. 1938-46 Detroit Lions, 1946-50 Philadelphia Eagles.

WILLIE WOOD
Safety. 5-10, 190. Born in Washington, D.C., December 23, 1936. Southern California. Inducted in 1989. 1960-71 Green Bay Packers.

1869

Rutgers and Princeton played a college soccer football game, the first ever, November 6. The game used modified London Football Association rules. During the next seven years, rugby gained favor with the major eastern schools over soccer, and modern football began to develop from rugby.

1876

At the Massasoit convention, the first rules for American football were written. Walter Camp, who would become known as the father of American football, first became involved with the game.

1892

In an era in which football was a major attraction of local athletic clubs, an intense competition between two Pittsburgh-area clubs, the Allegheny Athletic Association (AAA) and the Pittsburgh Athletic Club (PAC), led to the making of the first professional football player. Former Yale All-America guard William (Pudge) Heffelfinger was paid $500 by the AAA to play in a game against the PAC, becoming the first person to be paid to play football, November 12. The AAA won the game 4-0 when Heffelfinger picked up a PAC fumble and ran 25 yards for a touchdown.

1893

The Pittsburgh Athletic Club signed one of its players, probably halfback Grant Dibert, to the first known pro football contract, which covered all of the PAC's games for the year.

1895

John Brallier became the first football player to openly turn pro, accepting $10 and expenses to play for the Latrobe YMCA against the Jeannette Athletic Club.

1896

The Allegheny Athletic Association team fielded the first completely professional team for its abbreviated two-game season.

1897

The Latrobe Athletic Association football team went entirely professional, becoming the first team to play a full season with only professionals.

1898

A touchdown was changed from four points to five.

1899

Chris O'Brien formed a neighborhood team, which played under the name the Morgan Athletic Club, on the south side of Chicago. The team later became known as the Normals, then the Racine (for a street in Chicago) Cardinals, the Chicago Cardinals, the St. Louis Cardinals, the Phoenix Cardinals, and, in 1994, the Arizona Cardinals. The team remains the oldest continuing operation in pro football.

1900

William C. Temple took over the team payments for the Duquesne Country

and Athletic Club, becoming the first known individual club owner.

1902

Baseball's Philadelphia Athletics, managed by Connie Mack, and the Philadelphia Phillies formed professional football teams, joining the Pittsburgh Stars in the first attempt at a pro football league, named the National Football League. The Athletics won the first night football game ever played, 39-0 over Kanaweola AC at Elmira, New York, November 21.

All three teams claimed the pro championship for the year, but the league president, Dave Berry, named the Stars the champions. Pitcher Rube Waddell was with the Athletics, and pitcher Christy Mathewson a fullback for Pittsburgh.

The first World Series of pro football, actually a five-team tournament, was played among a team made up of players from both the Athletics and the Phillies, but simply named New York; the New York Knickerbockers; the Syracuse AC; the Warlow AC; and the Orange (New Jersey) AC at New York's original Madison Square Garden. New York and Syracuse played the first indoor football game before 3,000, December 28. Syracuse, with Glen (Pop) Warner at guard, won 6-0 and went on to win the tournament.

1903

The Franklin (Pa.) Athletic Club won the second and last World Series of pro football over the Oreos AC of Asbury Park, New Jersey; the Watertown Red and Blacks; and the Orange AC.

Pro football was popularized in Ohio when the Massillon Tigers, a strong amateur team, hired four Pittsburgh pros to play in the season-ending game against Akron. At the same time, pro football declined in the Pittsburgh area, and the emphasis on the pro game moved west from Pennsylvania to Ohio.

1904

A field goal was changed from five points to four.

Ohio had at least seven pro teams, with Massillon winning the Ohio Independent Championship, that is, the pro title. Talk surfaced about forming a state-wide league to end spiraling salaries brought about by constant bidding for players and to write universal rules for the game. The feeble attempt to start the league failed.

Halfback Charles Follis signed a contract with the Shelby AC, making him the first known black pro football player.

1905

The Canton AC, later to become known as the Bulldogs, became a professional team. Massillon again won the Ohio League championship.

1906

The forward pass was legalized. The first authenticated pass completion in a pro game came on October 27, when George (Peggy) Parratt of Massillon threw a completion to Dan (Bullet) Riley in a victory over a combined Benwood-Moundsville team.

Arch-rivals Canton and Massillon, the two best pro teams in America, played twice, with Canton winning the first game but Massillon winning the second and the Ohio League championship. A betting scandal and the financial disaster wrought upon the two clubs by paying huge salaries caused a temporary decline in interest in pro football in the two cities and, somewhat, throughout Ohio.

1909

A field goal dropped from four points to three.

1912

A touchdown was increased from five points to six.

Jack Cusack revived a strong pro team in Canton.

1913

Jim Thorpe, a former football and track star at the Carlisle Indian School (Pa.) and a double gold medal winner at the 1912 Olympics in Stockholm, played for the Pine Village Pros in Indiana.

1915

Massillon again fielded a major team, reviving the old rivalry with Canton. Cusack signed Thorpe to play for Canton for $250 a game.

1916

With Thorpe and former Carlisle teammate Pete Calac starring, Canton went 9-0-1, won the Ohio League championship, and was acclaimed the pro football champion.

1917

Despite an upset by Massillon, Canton again won the Ohio League championship.

1919

Canton again won the Ohio League championship, despite the team having been turned over from Cusack to Ralph Hay. Thorpe and Calac were joined in the backfield by Joe Guyon.

Earl (Curly) Lambeau and George Calhoun organized the Green Bay Packers. Lambeau's employer at the Indian Packing Company provided $500 for equipment and allowed the team to use the company field for practices. The Packers went 10-1.

1920

Pro football was in a state of confusion due to three major problems: dramatically rising salaries; players continually jumping from one team to another following the highest offer; and the use of college players still enrolled in school. A league in which all the members would follow the same rules seemed the answer. An organizational meeting, at which the Akron Pros, Canton Bulldogs, Cleveland Indians, and Dayton Triangles were represented, was held in Canton, Ohio, August 20. This meeting resulted in the formation of the American Professional Football Conference.

A second organizational meeting was held in Canton, September 17. The teams were from four states—Akron, Canton, Cleveland, and Dayton

from Ohio; the Hammond Pros and Muncie Flyers from Indiana; the Rochester Jeffersons from New York; and the Rock Island Independents, Decatur Staleys, and Racine Cardinals from Illinois. The name of the league was changed to the American Professional Football Association. Hoping to capitalize on his fame, the members elected Thorpe president; Stanley Cofall of Cleveland was elected vice president. A membership fee of $100 per team was charged to give an appearance of respectability, but no team ever paid it. Scheduling was left up to the teams, and there were wide variations, both in the overall number of games played and in the number played against APFA member teams.

Four other teams—the Buffalo All-Americans, Chicago Tigers, Columbus Panhandles, and Detroit Heralds—joined the league sometime during the year. On September 26, the first game featuring an APFA team was played at Rock Island's Douglas Park. A crowd of 800 watched the Independents defeat the St. Paul Ideals 48-0. A week later, October 3, the first game matching two APFA teams was held. At Triangle Park, Dayton defeated Columbus 14-0, with Lou Partlow of Dayton scoring the first touchdown in a game between Association teams. The same day, Rock Island defeated Muncie 45-0.

By the beginning of December, most of the teams in the APFA had abandoned their hopes for a championship, and some of them, including the Chicago Tigers and the Detroit Heralds, had finished their seasons, disbanded, and had their franchises canceled by the Association. Four teams—Akron, Buffalo, Canton, and Decatur—still had championship aspirations, but a series of late-season games among them left Akron as the only undefeated team in the Association. At one of these games, Akron sold tackle Bob Nash to Buffalo for $300 and five percent of the gate receipts—the first APFA player deal.

1921

At the league meeting in Akron, April 30, the championship of the 1920 season was awarded to the Akron Pros. The APFA was reorganized, with Joe Carr of the Columbus Panhandles named president and Carl Storck of Dayton secretary-treasurer. Carr moved the Association's headquarters to Columbus, drafted a league constitution and by-laws, gave teams territorial rights, restricted player movements, developed membership criteria for the franchises, and issued standings for the first time, so that the APFA would have a clear champion.

The Association's membership increased to 22 teams, including the Green Bay Packers, who were awarded to John Clair of the Acme Packing Company.

Thorpe moved from Canton to the Cleveland Indians, but he was hurt early in the season and played very little.

A.E. Staley turned the Decatur Staleys over to player-coach George Halas, who moved the team to Cubs Park in Chicago. Staley paid Halas

$5,000 to keep the name Staleys for one more year. Halas made halfback Ed (Dutch) Sternaman his partner.

The Staleys claimed the APFA championship with a 9-1-1 record, as did Buffalo at 9-1-2. Carr ruled in favor of the Staleys, giving Halas his first championship.

1922

After admitting the use of players who had college eligibility remaining during the 1921 season, Clair and the Green Bay management withdrew from the APFA, January 28. Curly Lambeau promised to obey league rules and then used $50 of his own money to buy back the franchise. Bad weather and low attendance plagued the Packers, and Lambeau went broke, but local merchants arranged a $2,500 loan for the club. A public non-profit corporation was set up to operate the team, with Lambeau as head coach and manager.

The American Professional Football Association changed its name to the National Football League, June 24. The Chicago Staleys became the Chicago Bears.

The NFL fielded 18 teams, including the new Oorang Indians of Marion, Ohio, an all-Indian team featuring Thorpe, Joe Guyon, and Pete Calac, and sponsored by the Oorang dog kennels.

Canton, led by player-coach Guy Chamberlin and tackles Link Lyman and Wilbur (Pete) Henry, emerged as the league's first true powerhouse, going 10-0-2.

1923

For the first time, all of the franchises considered to be part of the NFL fielded teams. Thorpe played first for Oorang, then for the Toledo Maroons. Against the Bears, Thorpe fumbled, and Halas picked up the ball and returned it 98 yards for a touchdown, a record that would last until 1972.

Canton had its second consecutive undefeated season, going 11-0-1 for the NFL title.

1924

The league had 18 franchises, including new ones in Kansas City, Kenosha, and Frankford, a section of Philadelphia. League champion Canton, successful on the field but not at the box office, was purchased by the owner of the Cleveland franchise, who kept the Canton franchise inactive, while using the best players for his Cleveland team, which he renamed the Bulldogs. Cleveland won the title with a 7-1-1 record.

1925

Five new franchises were admitted to the NFL—the New York Giants, who were awarded to Tim Mara and Billy Gibson for $500; the Detroit Panthers, featuring Jimmy Conzelman as owner, coach, and tailback; the Providence Steam Roller; a new Canton Bulldogs team; and the Pottsville Maroons, who had been perhaps the most successful independent pro team. The NFL established its first player limit, at 16 players.

Late in the season, the NFL made its greatest coup in gaining national recognition. Shortly after the University of Illinois season ended in November, All-America halfback Harold (Red) Grange signed a contract to play with the Chicago Bears. On Thanksgiving Day, a crowd of 36,000—the largest in pro football history—watched Grange and the Bears play the Chicago Cardinals to a scoreless tie at Wrigley Field. At the beginning of December, the Bears left on a barnstorming tour that saw them play eight games in 12 days, in St. Louis, Philadelphia, New York City, Washington, Boston, Pittsburgh, Detroit, and Chicago. A crowd of 73,000 watched the game against the Giants at the Polo Grounds, helping assure the future of the troubled NFL franchise in New York. The Bears then played nine more games in the South and West, including a game in Los Angeles, in which 75,000 fans watched them defeat the Los Angeles Tigers in the Los Angeles Memorial Coliseum.

Pottsville and the Chicago Cardinals were the top contenders for the league title, with Pottsville winning a late-season meeting 21-7. Pottsville scheduled a game against a team of former Notre Dame players for Shibe Park in Philadelphia. Frankford lodged a protest not only because the game was in Frankford's protected territory, but because it was being played the same day as a Yellow Jackets home game. Carr gave three different notices forbidding Pottsville to play the game, but Pottsville played anyway, December 12. That day, Carr fined the club, suspended it from all rights and privileges (including the right to play for the NFL championship), and returned its franchise to the league. The Cardinals, who ended the season with the best record in the league, were named the 1925 champions.

1926

Grange's manager, C.C. Pyle, told the Bears that Grange wouldn't play for them unless he was paid a five-figure salary and given one-third ownership of the team. The Bears refused. Pyle leased Yankee Stadium in New York City, then petitioned for an NFL franchise. After he was refused, he started the first American Football League. It lasted one season and included Grange's New York Yankees and eight other teams. The AFL champion Philadelphia Quakers played a December game against the New York Giants, seventh in the NFL, and the Giants won 31-0. At the end of the season, the AFL folded.

Halas pushed through a rule that prohibited any team from signing a player whose college class had not graduated.

The NFL grew to 22 teams, including the Duluth Eskimos, who signed All-America fullback Ernie Nevers of Stanford, giving the league a gate attraction to rival Grange. The 15-member Eskimos, dubbed the Iron Men of the North, played 29 exhibition and league games, 28 on the road, and Nevers played in all but 29 minutes of them.

Frankford edged the Bears for the championship, despite Halas having obtained John (Paddy) Driscoll from the Cardinals. On December 4, the Yellow Jackets scored in the final two minutes to defeat the Bears 7-6 and move ahead of them in the standings.

1927

At a special meeting in Cleveland, April 23, Carr decided to secure the NFL's future by eliminating the financially weaker teams and consolidating the quality players onto a limited number of more successful teams. The new-look NFL dropped to 12 teams, and the center of gravity of the league left the Midwest, where the NFL had started, and began to emerge in the large cities of the East. One of the new teams was Grange's New York Yankees, but Grange suffered a knee injury and the Yankees finished in the middle of the pack. The NFL championship was won by the cross-town rival New York Giants, who posted 10 shutouts in 13 games.

1928

Grange and Nevers both retired from pro football, and Duluth disbanded, as the NFL was reduced to only 10 teams. The Providence Steam Roller of Jimmy Conzelman and Pearce Johnson won the championship, playing in the Cycledrome, a 10,000-seat oval that had been built for bicycle races.

1929

Chris O'Brien sold the Chicago Cardinals to David Jones, July 27.

The NFL added a fourth official, the field judge, July 28.

Grange and Nevers returned to the NFL. Nevers scored six rushing touchdowns and four extra points as the Cardinals beat Grange's Bears 40-6, November 28. The 40 points set a record that remains the NFL's oldest.

Providence became the first NFL team to host a game at night under floodlights, against the Cardinals, November 3.

The Packers added back Johnny Blood (McNally), tackle Cal Hubbard, and guard Mike Michalske, and won their first NFL championship, edging the Giants, who featured quarterback Benny Friedman.

1930

Dayton, the last of the NFL's original franchises, was purchased by John Dwyer, moved to Brooklyn, and renamed the Dodgers. The Portsmouth, Ohio, Spartans entered the league.

The Packers edged the Giants for the title, but the most improved team was the Bears. Halas retired as a player and replaced himself as coach of the Bears with Ralph Jones, who refined the T-formation by introducing wide ends and a halfback in motion. Jones also introduced rookie All-America fullback-tackle Bronko Nagurski.

The Giants defeated a team of former Notre Dame players coached by Knute Rockne 22-0 before 55,000 at the Polo Grounds, December 14. The proceeds went to the New York Unemployment Fund to help those suffering because of the Great Depression, and the easy victory helped give the NFL credibility with the press and the public.

1931

The NFL decreased to 10 teams, and halfway through the season the Frankford franchise folded. Carr fined the Bears, Packers, and Portsmouth $1,000 each for using players whose college classes had not graduated.

The Packers won an unprecedented third consecutive title, beating out the Spartans, who were led by rookie backs Earl (Dutch) Clark and Glenn Presnell.

1932

George Preston Marshall, Vincent Bendix, Jay O'Brien, and M. Dorland Doyle were awarded a franchise for Boston, July 9. Despite the presence of two rookies—halfback Cliff Battles and tackle Glen (Turk) Edwards—the new team, named the Braves, lost money and Marshall was left as the sole owner at the end of the year.

NFL membership dropped to eight teams, the lowest in history. Official statistics were kept for the first time. The Bears and the Spartans finished the season in the first-ever tie for first place. After the season finale, the league office arranged for the first playoff game in NFL history. The game was moved indoors to Chicago Stadium because of bitter cold and heavy snow. The arena allowed only an 80-yard field that came right to the walls. The goal posts were moved from the end lines to the goal lines and, for safety, inbounds lines or hashmarks where the ball would be put in play were drawn 10 yards from the walls that butted against the sidelines. The Bears won 9-0, December 18, scoring the winning touchdown on a two-yard pass from Nagurski to Grange. The Spartans claimed Nagurski's pass was thrown from less than five yards behind the line of scrimmage, violating the existing passing rule, but the play stood.

1933

The NFL, which long had followed the rules of college football, made a number of significant changes from the college game for the first time and began to develop rules serving its needs and the style of play it preferred. The innovations from the 1932 championship game—inbounds line or hashmarks and goal posts on the goal lines—were adopted. Also the forward pass was legalized from anywhere behind the line of scrimmage, February 25.

Marshall and Halas pushed through a proposal that divided the NFL into two divisions, with the winners to meet in an annual championship game, July 8.

Three new franchises joined the league—the Pittsburgh Pirates of Art Rooney, the Philadelphia Eagles of Bert Bell and Lud Wray, and the Cincinnati Reds. The Staten Island Stapletons suspended operations for a year, but never returned to the league.

Halas bought out Sternaman, became sole owner of the Bears, and reinstated himself as head coach. Marshall changed the name of the Boston Braves to the Redskins. David Jones sold the Chicago Cardinals to Charles W. Bidwill.

In the first NFL Championship Game scheduled before the season, the Western Division champion Bears defeated the Eastern Division champion Giants 23-21 at Wrigley Field, December 17.

1934

G.A. (Dick) Richards purchased the Portsmouth Spartans, moved them to Detroit, and renamed them the Lions.

Professional football gained new prestige when the Bears were matched against the best college football players in the first Chicago College All-Star Game, August 31. The game ended in a scoreless tie before 79,432 at Soldier Field.

The Cincinnati Reds lost their first eight games, then were suspended from the league for defaulting on payments. The St. Louis Gunners, an independent team, joined the NFL by buying the Cincinnati franchise and went 1-2 the last three weeks.

Rookie Beattie Feathers of the Bears became the NFL's first 1,000-yard rusher, gaining 1,004 on 101 carries. The Thanksgiving Day game between the Bears and the Lions became the first NFL game broadcast nationally, with Graham McNamee the announcer for CBS radio.

In the championship game, on an extremely cold and icy day at the Polo Grounds, the Giants trailed the Bears 13-3 in the third quarter before changing to basketball shoes for better footing. The Giants won 30-13 in what has come to be known as the Sneakers Game, December 9.

The player waiver rule was adopted, December 10.

1935

The NFL adopted Bert Bell's proposal to hold an annual draft of college players, to begin in 1936, with teams selecting in an inverse order of finish, May 19. The inbounds line or hashmarks were moved nearer the center of the field, 15 yards from the sidelines.

All-America end Don Hutson of Alabama joined Green Bay. The Lions defeated the Giants 26-7 in the NFL Championship Game, December 15.

1936

There were no franchise transactions for the first year since the formation of the NFL. It also was the first year in which all member teams played the same number of games.

The Eagles made University of Chicago halfback and Heisman Trophy winner Jay Berwanger the first player ever selected in the NFL draft, February 8. The Eagles traded his rights to the Bears, but Berwanger never played pro football. The first player selected to actually sign was the number-two pick, Riley Smith of Alabama, who was selected by Boston.

A rival league was formed, and it became the second to call itself the American Football League. The Boston Shamrocks were its champions.

Because of poor attendance, Marshall, the owner of the host team, moved the Championship Game from Boston to the Polo Grounds in New York. Green Bay defeated the Redskins 21-6, December 13.

1937

Homer Marshman was granted a Cleveland franchise, named the Rams, February 12. Marshall moved the Redskins to Washington, D.C., February 13. The Redskins signed TCU All-America tailback Sammy Baugh, who led them to a 28-21 victory over the Bears in the NFL Championship Game, December 12.

The Los Angeles Bulldogs had an 8-0 record to win the AFL title, but then the 2-year-old league folded.

1938

At the suggestion of Halas, Hugh (Shorty) Ray became a technical advisor on rules and officiating to the NFL. A new rule called for a 15-yard penalty for roughing the passer.

Rookie Byron (Whizzer) White of the Pittsburgh Pirates led the NFL in rushing. The Giants defeated the Packers 23-17 for the NFL title, December 11.

Marshall, *Los Angeles Times* sports editor Bill Henry, and promoter Tom Gallery established the Pro Bowl game between the NFL champion and a team of pro all-stars.

1939

The New York Giants defeated the Pro All-Stars 13-10 in the first Pro Bowl, at Wrigley Field, Los Angeles, January 15.

Carr, NFL president since 1921, died in Columbus, May 20. Carl Storck was named acting president, May 25.

An NFL game was televised for the first time when NBC broadcast the Brooklyn Dodgers-Philadelphia Eagles game from Ebbets Field to the approximately 1,000 sets then in New York.

Green Bay defeated New York 27-0 in the NFL Championship Game, December 10 at Milwaukee. NFL attendance exceeded 1 million in a season for the first time, reaching 1,071,200.

1940

A six-team rival league, the third to call itself the American Football League, was formed, and the Columbus Bullies won its championship.

Halas's Bears, with additional coaching by Clark Shaughnessy of Stanford, defeated the Redskins 73-0 in the NFL Championship Game, December 8. The game, which was the most decisive victory in NFL history, popularized the Bears' T-formation with a man-in-motion. It was the first championship carried on network radio, broadcast by Red Barber to 120 stations of the Mutual Broadcasting System, which paid $2,500 for the rights.

Art Rooney sold the Pittsburgh franchise to Alexis Thompson, December 9, then bought part interest in the Philadelphia Eagles.

1941

Elmer Layden was named the first Commissioner of the NFL, March 1; Storck, the acting president, resigned, April 5. NFL headquarters were moved to Chicago.

Bell and Rooney traded the Eagles to Thompson for the Pirates, then re-named their new team the Steelers. Homer Marshman sold the Rams to Daniel F. Reeves and Fred Levy, Jr.

The league by-laws were revised to provide for playoffs in case there were ties in division races, and sudden-death overtimes in case a playoff game was tied after four quarters. An official *NFL Record Manual* was published for the first time.

Columbus again won the championship of the AFL, but the two-year-old league then folded.

The Bears and the Packers finished in a tie for the Western Division championship, setting up the first divisional playoff game in league history. The Bears won 33-14, then defeated the Giants 37-9 for the NFL championship, December 21.

1942

Players departing for service in World War II depleted the rosters of NFL teams. Halas left the Bears in midseason to join the Navy, and Luke Johnsos and Heartley (Hunk) Anderson served as co-coaches as the Bears went 11-0 in the regular season. The Redskins defeated the Bears 14-6 in the NFL Championship Game, December 13.

1943

The Cleveland Rams, with co-owners Reeves and Levy in the service, were granted permission to suspend operations for one season, April 6. Levy transferred his stock in the team to Reeves, April 16.

The NFL adopted free substitution, April 7. The league also made the wearing of helmets mandatory and approved a 10-game schedule for all teams.

Philadelphia and Pittsburgh were granted permission to merge for one season, June 19. The team, known as Phil-Pitt (and called the Steagles by fans), divided home games between the two cities, and Earle (Greasy) Neale of Philadelphia and Walt Kiesling of Pittsburgh served as co-coaches. The merger automatically dissolved the last day of the season, December 5.

Ted Collins was granted a franchise for Boston, to become active in 1944.

Sammy Baugh led the league in passing, punting, and interceptions. He led the Redskins to a tie with the Giants for the Eastern Division title, and then to a 28-0 victory in a divisional playoff game. The Bears beat the Redskins 41-21 in the NFL Championship Game, December 26.

1944

Collins, who had wanted a franchise in Yankee Stadium in New York, named his new team the Boston Yanks. Cleveland resumed operations. The Brooklyn Dodgers changed their name to the Tigers.

Coaching from the bench was legalized, April 20.

The Cardinals and the Steelers were granted permission to merge for one year under the name Card-Pitt, April 21. Phil Handler of the Cardinals and Walt Kiesling of the Steelers

served as co-coaches. The merger automatically dissolved the last day of the season, December 3.

In the NFL Championship Game, Green Bay defeated the New York Giants 14-7, December 17.

1945

The inbounds lines or hashmarks were moved from 15 yards away from the sidelines to nearer the center of the field—20 yards from the sidelines.

Brooklyn and Boston merged into a team that played home games in both cities and was known simply as The Yanks. The team was coached by former Boston head coach Herb Kopf. In December, the Brooklyn franchise withdrew from the NFL to join the new All-America Football Conference; all the players on its active and reserve lists were assigned to The Yanks, who once again became the Boston Yanks.

Halas rejoined the Bears late in the season after service with the U.S. Navy. Although Halas took over much of the coaching duties, Anderson and Johnsos remained the coaches of record throughout the season.

Steve Van Buren of Philadelphia led the NFL in rushing, kickoff returns, and scoring.

After the Japanese surrendered ending World War II, a count showed that the NFL service roster, limited to men who had played in league games, totaled 638, 21 of whom had died in action.

Rookie quarterback Bob Waterfield led Cleveland to a 15-14 victory over Washington in the NFL Championship Game, December 16.

1946

The contract of Commissioner Layden was not renewed, and Bert Bell, the co-owner of the Steelers, replaced him, January 11. Bell moved the league headquarters from Chicago to the Philadelphia suburb of Bala-Cynwyd.

Free substitution was withdrawn and substitutions were limited to no more than three men at a time. Forward passes were made automatically incomplete upon striking the goal posts, January 11.

The NFL took on a truly national appearance for the first time when Reeves was granted permission by the league to move his NFL champion Rams to Los Angeles.

The rival All-America Football Conference began play with eight teams. The Cleveland Browns, coached by Paul Brown, won the AAFC's first championship, defeating the New York Yankees 14-9.

Bill Dudley of the Steelers led the NFL in rushing, interceptions, and punt returns, and won the league's most valuable player award.

Backs Frank Filchock and Merle Hapes of the Giants were questioned about an attempt by a New York man to fix the championship game with the Bears. Bell suspended Hapes but allowed Filchock to play; he played well, but Chicago won 24-14, December 15.

1947

The NFL added a fifth official, the back judge.

A bonus choice was made for the first time in the NFL draft. One team each year would select the special choice before the first round began. The Chicago Bears won a lottery and the rights to the first choice and drafted back Bob Fenimore of Oklahoma A&M.

The Cleveland Browns again won the AAFC title, defeating the New York Yankees 14-3.

Charles Bidwill, Sr., owner of the Cardinals, died April 19, but his wife and sons retained ownership of the team. On December 28, the Cardinals won the NFL Championship Game 28-21 over the Philadelphia Eagles, who had beaten Pittsburgh 21-0 in a playoff.

1948

Plastic helmets were prohibited. A flexible artificial tee was permitted at the kickoff. Officials other than the referee were equipped with whistles, not horns, January 14.

Fred Mandel sold the Detroit Lions to a syndicate headed by D. Lyle Fife, January 15.

Halfback Fred Gehrke of the Los Angeles Rams painted horns on the Rams' helmets, the first modern helmet emblems in pro football.

The Cleveland Browns won their third straight championship in the AAFC, going 14-0 and then defeating the Buffalo Bills 49-7.

In a blizzard, the Eagles defeated the Cardinals 7-0 in the NFL Championship Game, December 19.

1949

Alexis Thompson sold the champion Eagles to a syndicate headed by James P. Clark, January 15. The Boston Yanks became the New York Bulldogs, sharing the Polo Grounds with the Giants.

Free substitution was adopted for one year, January 20.

The NFL had two 1,000-yard rushers in the same season for the first time—Steve Van Buren of Philadelphia and Tony Canadeo of Green Bay.

The AAFC played its season with a one-division, seven-team format. On December 9, Bell announced a merger agreement in which three AAFC franchises—Cleveland, San Francisco, and Baltimore—would join the NFL in 1950. The Browns won their fourth consecutive AAFC title, defeating the 49ers 21-7, December 11.

In a heavy rain, the Eagles defeated the Rams 14-0 in the NFL Championship Game, December 18.

1950

Unlimited free substitution was restored, opening the way for the era of two platoons and specialization in pro football, January 20.

Curly Lambeau, founder of the franchise and Green Bay's head coach since 1921, resigned under fire, February 1.

The name National Football League was restored after about three months as the National-American Football League. The American and National conferences were created to replace the Eastern and Western divisions, March 3.

The New York Bulldogs became the Yanks and divided the players of the former AAFC Yankees with the Giants. A special allocation draft was held in which the 13 teams drafted the remaining AAFC players, with special consideration for Baltimore, which received 15 choices compared to 10 for other teams.

The Los Angeles Rams became the first NFL team to have all of its games—both home and away—televised. The Washington Redskins followed the Rams in arranging to televise their games; other teams made deals to put selected games on television.

In the first game of the season, former AAFC champion Cleveland defeated NFL champion Philadelphia 35-10. For the first time, deadlocks occurred in both conferences and playoffs were necessary. The Browns defeated the Giants in the American and the Rams defeated the Bears in the National. Cleveland defeated Los Angeles 30-28 in the NFL Championship Game, December 24.

1951

The Pro Bowl game, dormant since 1942, was revived under a new format matching the all-stars of each conference at the Los Angeles Memorial Coliseum. The American Conference defeated the National Conference 28-27, January 14.

Abraham Watner returned the Baltimore franchise and its player contracts back to the NFL for $50,000. Baltimore's former players were made available for drafting at the same time as college players, January 18.

A rule was passed that no tackle, guard, or center would be eligible to catch a forward pass, January 18.

The Rams reversed their television policy and televised only road games.

The NFL Championship Game was televised coast-to-coast for the first time, December 23. The DuMont Network paid $75,000 for the rights to the game, in which the Rams defeated the Browns 24-17.

1952

Ted Collins sold the New York Yanks' franchise back to the NFL, January 19. A new franchise was awarded to a group in Dallas after it purchased the assets of the Yanks, January 24. The new Texans went 1-11, with the owners turning the franchise back to the league in midseason. For the last five games of the season, the commissioner's office operated the Texans as a road team, using Hershey, Pennsylvania, as a home base. At the end of the season the franchise was canceled, the last time an NFL team failed.

The Pittsburgh Steelers abandoned the Single-Wing for the T-formation, the last pro team to do so.

The Detroit Lions won their first NFL championship in 17 years, defeating the Browns 17-7 in the title game, December 28.

1953

A Baltimore group headed by Carroll Rosenbloom was granted a franchise and was awarded the holdings of the defunct Dallas organization, January 23. The team, named the Colts, put together the largest trade in league history, acquiring 10 players from Cleveland in exchange for five.

The names of the American and National conferences were changed to the Eastern and Western conferences, January 24.

Jim Thorpe died, March 28.

Mickey McBride, founder of the Cleveland Browns, sold the franchise to a syndicate headed by Dave R. Jones, June 10.

The NFL policy of blacking out home games was upheld by Judge Allan K. Grim of the U.S. District Court in Philadelphia, November 12.

The Lions again defeated the Browns in the NFL Championship Game, winning 17-16, December 27.

1954

The Canadian Football League began a series of raids on NFL teams, signing quarterback Eddie LeBaron and defensive end Gene Brito of Washington and defensive tackle Arnie Weinmeister of the Giants, among others.

Fullback Joe Perry of the 49ers became the first player in league history to gain 1,000 yards rushing in consecutive seasons.

Cleveland defeated Detroit 56-10 in the NFL Championship Game, December 26.

1955

The sudden-death overtime rule was used for the first time in a preseason game between the Rams and Giants at Portland, Oregon, August 28. The Rams won 23-17 three minutes into overtime.

A rule change declared the ball dead immediately if the ball carrier touched the ground with any part of his body except his hands or feet while in the grasp of an opponent.

The Baltimore Colts made an 80-cent phone call to Johnny Unitas and signed him as a free agent. Another quarterback, Otto Graham, played his last game as the Browns defeated the Rams 38-14 in the NFL Championship Game, December 26. Graham had quarterbacked the Browns to 10 championship-game appearances in 10 years.

NBC replaced DuMont as the network for the title game, paying a rights fee of $100,000.

1956

The NFL Players Association was founded.

Grabbing an opponent's facemask (other than the ball carrier) was made illegal. Using radio receivers to communicate with players on the field was prohibited. A natural leather ball with white end stripes replaced the white ball with black stripes for night games.

The Giants moved from the Polo Grounds to Yankee Stadium.

Halas retired as coach of the Bears, and was replaced by Paddy Driscoll.

CBS became the first network to broadcast some NFL regular-season games to selected television markets across the nation.

The Giants routed the Bears 47-7 in the NFL Championship Game, December 30.

1957

Pete Rozelle was named general manager of the Rams. Anthony J. Morabito, founder and co-owner of the 49ers, died of a heart attack during a game against the Bears at Kezar Stadium, October 28. An NFL-record crowd of 102,368 saw the 49ers-Rams game at the Los Angeles Memorial Coliseum, November 10.

The Lions came from 20 points down to post a 31-27 playoff victory over the 49ers, December 22. Detroit defeated Cleveland 59-14 in the NFL Championship Game, December 29.

1958

The bonus selection in the draft was eliminated, January 29. The last selection was quarterback King Hill of Rice by the Chicago Cardinals.

Halas reinstated himself as coach of the Bears.

Jim Brown of Cleveland gained an NFL-record 1,527 yards rushing. In a divisional playoff game, the Giants held Brown to eight yards and defeated Cleveland 10-0.

Baltimore, coached by Weeb Ewbank, defeated the Giants 23-17 in the first sudden-death overtime in an NFL Championship Game, December 28. The game ended when Colts fullback Alan Ameche scored on a one-yard touchdown run after 8:15 of overtime.

1959

Vince Lombardi was named head coach of the Green Bay Packers, January 28. Tim Mara, the co-founder of the Giants, died, February 17.

Lamar Hunt of Dallas announced his intentions to form a second pro football league. The first meeting was held in Chicago, August 14, and consisted of Hunt representing Dallas; Bob Howsam, Denver; K.S. (Bud) Adams, Houston; Barron Hilton, Los Angeles; Max Winter and Bill Boyer, Minneapolis; and Harry Wismer, New York City. They made plans to begin play in 1960.

The new league was named the American Football League, August 22. Buffalo, owned by Ralph Wilson, became the seventh franchise, October 28. Boston, owned by William H. Sullivan, became the eighth team, November 22. The first AFL draft, lasting 33 rounds, was held, November 22. Joe Foss was named AFL Commissioner, November 30. An additional draft of 20 rounds was held by the AFL, December 2.

NFL Commissioner Bert Bell died of a heart attack suffered at Franklin Field, Philadelphia, during the last two minutes of a game between the Eagles and the Steelers, October 11. Treasurer Austin Gunsel was named president in the office of the commissioner, October 14.

The Colts again defeated the Giants in the NFL Championship Game, 31-16, December 27.

1960

Pete Rozelle was elected NFL Commissioner as a compromise choice on the twenty-third ballot, January 26. Rozelle moved the league offices to New York City.

Hunt was elected AFL president for

1960, January 26. Minneapolis withdrew from the AFL, January 27, and the same ownership was given an NFL franchise for Minnesota (to start in 1961), January 28. Dallas received an NFL franchise for 1960, January 28. Oakland received an AFL franchise, January 30.

The AFL adopted the two-point option on points after touchdown, January 28. A no-tampering verbal pact, relative to players' contracts, was agreed to between the NFL and AFL, February 9.

The NFL owners voted to allow the transfer of the Chicago Cardinals to St. Louis, March 13.

The AFL signed a five-year television contract with ABC, June 9.

The Boston Patriots defeated the Buffalo Bills 28-7 before 16,000 at Buffalo in the first AFL preseason game, July 30. The Denver Broncos defeated the Patriots 13-10 before 21,597 at Boston in the first AFL regular-season game, September 9.

Philadelphia defeated Green Bay 17-13 in the NFL Championship Game, December 26.

1961

The Houston Oilers defeated the Los Angeles Chargers 24-16 before 32,183 in the first AFL Championship Game, January 1.

Detroit defeated Cleveland 17-16 in the first Playoff Bowl, or Bert Bell Benefit Bowl, between second-place teams in each conference in Miami, January 7.

End Willard Dewveall of the Bears played out his option and joined the Oilers, becoming the first player to move deliberately from one league to the other, January 14.

Ed McGah, Wayne Valley, and Robert Osborne bought out their partners in the ownership of the Raiders, January 17. The Chargers were transferred to San Diego, February 10. Dave R. Jones sold the Browns to a group headed by Arthur B. Modell, March 22. The Howsam brothers sold the Broncos to a group headed by Calvin Kunz and Gerry Phipps, May 26.

NBC was awarded a two-year contract for radio and television rights to the NFL Championship Game for $615,000 annually, $300,000 of which was to go directly into the NFL Player Benefit Plan, April 5.

Canton, Ohio, where the league that became the NFL was formed in 1920, was chosen as the site of the Pro Football Hall of Fame, April 27. Dick McCann, a former Redskins executive, was named executive director.

A bill legalizing single-network television contracts by professional sports leagues was introduced in Congress by Representative Emanuel Celler. It passed the House and Senate and was signed into law by President John F. Kennedy, September 30.

Houston defeated San Diego 10-3 for the AFL championship, December 24. Green Bay won its first NFL championship since 1944, defeating the New York Giants 37-0, December 31.

1962

The Western Division defeated the Eastern Division 47-27 in the first AFL All-Star Game, played before 20,973 in San Diego, January 7.

Both leagues prohibited grabbing any player's facemask. The AFL voted to make the scoreboard clock the official timer of the game.

The NFL entered into a single-network agreement with CBS for telecasting all regular-season games for $4.65 million annually, January 10.

Judge Roszel Thompson of the U.S. District Court in Baltimore ruled against the AFL in its antitrust suit against the NFL, May 21. The AFL had charged the NFL with monopoly and conspiracy in areas of expansion, television, and player signings. The case lasted two and a half years, the trial two months.

McGah and Valley acquired controlling interest in the Raiders, May 24. The AFL assumed financial responsibility for the New York Titans, November 8. With Commissioner Rozelle as referee, Daniel F. Reeves regained the ownership of the Rams, outbidding his partners in sealed-envelope bidding for the team, November 27.

The Dallas Texans defeated the Oilers 20-17 for the AFL championship at Houston after 17 minutes, 54 seconds of overtime on a 25-yard field goal by Tommy Brooker, December 23. The game lasted a record 77 minutes, 54 seconds.

Judge Edward Weinfeld of the U.S. District Court in New York City upheld the legality of the NFL's television blackout within a 75-mile radius of home games and denied an injunction that would have forced the championship game between the Giants and the Packers to be televised in the New York City area, December 28. The Packers beat the Giants 16-7 for the NFL title, December 30.

1963

The Dallas Texans transferred to Kansas City, becoming the Chiefs, February 8. The New York Titans were sold to a five-man syndicate headed by David (Sonny) Werblin, March 28. Weeb Ewbank became the Titans' new head coach and the team's name was changed to the Jets, April 15. They began play in Shea Stadium.

NFL Properties, Inc., was founded to serve as the licensing arm of the NFL.

Rozelle indefinitely suspended Green Bay halfback Paul Hornung and Detroit defensive tackle Alex Karras for placing bets on their own teams and on other NFL games; he also fined five other Detroit players $2,000 each for betting on one game in which they did not participate, and the Detroit Lions Football Company $2,000 on each of two counts for failure to report information promptly and for lack of sideline supervision.

Paul Brown, head coach of the Browns since their inception, was fired and replaced by Blanton Collier. Don Shula replaced Weeb Ewbank as head coach of the Colts.

The AFL allowed the Jets and Raiders to select players from other franchises in hopes of giving the league more competitive balance, May 11.

NBC was awarded exclusive network broadcasting rights for the 1963 AFL Championship Game for $926,000, May 23.

The Pro Football Hall of Fame was dedicated at Canton, Ohio, September 7.

The U.S. Fourth Circuit Court of Appeals reaffirmed the lower court's finding for the NFL in the $10-million suit brought by the AFL, ending three and a half years of litigation, November 21.

Jim Brown of Cleveland rushed for an NFL single-season record 1,863 yards.

Boston defeated Buffalo 26-8 in the first divisional playoff game in AFL history, December 28.

The Bears defeated the Giants 14-10 in the NFL Championship Game, a record sixth and last title for Halas in his thirty-sixth season as the Bears' coach, December 29.

1964

The Chargers defeated the Patriots 51-10 in the AFL Championship Game, January 5.

William Clay Ford, the Lions' president since 1961, purchased the team, January 10. A group representing the late James P. Clark sold the Eagles to a group headed by Jerry Wolman, January 21. Carroll Rosenbloom, the majority owner of the Colts since 1953, acquired complete ownership of the team, January 23.

The AFL signed a five-year, $36-million television contract with NBC to begin with the 1965 season, January 29.

Commissioner Rozelle negotiated an agreement on behalf of the NFL clubs to purchase Ed Sabol's Blair Motion Pictures, which was renamed NFL Films, March 5.

Hornung and Karras were reinstated by Rozelle, March 16.

CBS submitted the winning bid of $14.1 million per year for the NFL regular-season television rights for 1964 and 1965, January 24. CBS acquired the rights to the championship games for 1964 and 1965 for $1.8 million per game, April 17.

Pete Gogolak of Cornell signed a contract with Buffalo, becoming the first soccer-style kicker in pro football.

Buffalo defeated San Diego 20-7 in the AFL Championship Game, December 26. Cleveland defeated Baltimore 27-0 in the NFL Championship Game, December 27.

1965

The NFL teams pledged not to sign college seniors until completion of all their games, including bowl games, and empowered the Commissioner to discipline the clubs up to as much as the loss of an entire draft list for a violation of the pledge, February 15.

The NFL added a sixth official, the line judge, February 19. The color of the officials' penalty flags was changed from white to bright gold, April 5.

Atlanta was awarded an NFL franchise for 1966, with Rankin Smith, Sr., as owner, June 30. Miami was awarded an AFL franchise for 1966, with Joe Robbie and Danny Thomas as owners, August 16.

Green Bay defeated Baltimore 13-10 in sudden-death overtime in a Western Conference playoff game. Don Chandler kicked a 25-yard field goal for the Packers after 13 minutes, 39 seconds of overtime, December 26. The Packers then defeated the Browns 23-12 in the NFL Championship Game, January 2.

In the AFL Championship Game, the Bills again defeated the Chargers, 23-0, December 26.

CBS acquired the rights to the NFL regular-season games in 1966 and 1967, with an option for 1968, for $18.8 million per year, December 29.

1966

The AFL-NFL war reached its peak, as the leagues spent a combined $7 million to sign their 1966 draft choices. The NFL signed 75 percent of its 232 draftees, the AFL 46 percent of its 181. Of the 111 common draft choices, 79 signed with the NFL, 28 with the AFL, and 4 went unsigned.

The rights to the 1966 and 1967 NFL Championship Games were sold to CBS for $2 million per game, February 14.

Foss resigned as AFL Commissioner, April 7. Al Davis, the head coach and general manager of the Raiders, was named to replace him, April 8.

Goal posts offset from the goal line, painted bright yellow, and with uprights 20 feet above the cross-bar were made standard in the NFL, May 16.

A series of secret meetings regarding a possible AFL-NFL merger were held in the spring between Hunt of Kansas City and Tex Schramm of Dallas. Rozelle announced the merger, June 8. Under the agreement, the two leagues would combine to form an expanded league with 24 teams, to be increased to 26 in 1968 and to 28 by 1970 or soon thereafter. All existing franchises would be retained, and no franchises would be transferred outside their metropolitan areas. While maintaining separate schedules through 1969, the leagues agreed to play an annual AFL-NFL World Championship Game beginning in January, 1967, and to hold a combined draft, also beginning in 1967. Preseason games would be held between teams of each league starting in 1967. Official regular-season play would start in 1970 when the two leagues would officially merge to form one league with two conferences. Rozelle was named Commissioner of the expanded league setup.

Davis rejoined the Raiders, and Milt Woodard was named president of the AFL, July 25.

The St. Louis Cardinals moved into newly constructed Busch Memorial Stadium.

Barron Hilton sold the Chargers to a group headed by Eugene Klein and Sam Schulman, August 25.

Congress approved the AFL-NFL merger, passing legislation exempting the agreement itself from antitrust action, October 21.

New Orleans was awarded an NFL franchise to begin play in 1967, November 1. John Mecom, Jr., of Houston was designated majority stockholder and president of the franchise, December 15.

The NFL was realigned for the 1967-69 seasons into the Capitol and Century Divisions in the Eastern Conference and the Central and Coastal Divisions in the Western Conference, December 2. New Orleans and the New York Giants agreed to switch divisions in 1968 and return to the 1967 alignment in 1969.

The rights to the Super Bowl for four years were sold to CBS and NBC for $9.5 million, December 13.

1967

Green Bay earned the right to represent the NFL in the first AFL-NFL World Championship Game by defeating Dallas 34-27, January 1. The same day, Kansas City defeated Buffalo 31-7 to represent the AFL. The Packers defeated the Chiefs 35-10 before 61,946 fans at the Los Angeles Memorial Coliseum in the first game between AFL and NFL teams, January 15. The winning players' share for the Packers was $15,000 each, and the losing players' share for the Chiefs was $7,500 each. The game was televised by both CBS and NBC.

The "sling-shot" goal post and a six-foot-wide border around the field were made standard in the NFL, February 22.

Baltimore made Bubba Smith, a Michigan State defensive lineman, the first choice in the first combined AFL-NFL draft, March 14.

The AFL awarded a franchise to begin play in 1968 to Cincinnati, May 24. A group with Paul Brown as part owner, general manager, and head coach, was awarded the Cincinnati franchise, September 27.

Arthur B. Modell, the president of the Cleveland Browns, was elected president of the NFL, May 28.

An AFL team defeated an NFL team for the first time, when Denver beat Detroit 13-7 in a preseason game, August 5.

Green Bay defeated Dallas 21-17 for the NFL championship on a last-minute 1-yard quarterback sneak by Bart Starr in 13-below-zero temperature at Green Bay, December 31. The same day, Oakland defeated Houston 40-7 for the AFL championship.

1968

Green Bay defeated Oakland 33-14 in Super Bowl II at Miami, January 14. The game had the first $3-million gate in pro football history.

Vince Lombardi resigned as head coach of the Packers, but remained as general manager, January 28.

Werblin sold his shares in the Jets to his partners Don Lillis, Leon Hess, Townsend Martin, and Phil Iselin, May 21. Lillis assumed the presidency of the club, but then died July 23. Iselin was appointed president, August 6.

Halas retired for the fourth and last time as head coach of the Bears, May 27.

The Oilers left Rice Stadium for the Astrodome and became the first NFL team to play its home games in a domed stadium.

The movie "Heidi" became a footnote in sports history when NBC didn't show the last 1:05 of the Jets-Raiders game in order to permit the children's special to begin on time. The Raiders scored two touchdowns in the last 42 seconds to win 43-32, November 17.

Ewbank became the first coach to win titles in both the NFL and AFL when his Jets defeated the Raiders 27-23 for the AFL championship, December 29. The same day, Baltimore defeated Cleveland 34-0.

1969

The AFL established a playoff format for the 1969 season, with the winner in one division playing the runner-up in the other, January 11.

An AFL team won the Super Bowl for the first time, as the Jets defeated the Colts 16-7 at Miami, January 12 in Super Bowl III. The title Super Bowl was recognized by the NFL for the first time.

Vince Lombardi became part owner, executive vice-president, and head coach of the Washington Redskins, February 7.

Wolman sold the Eagles to Leonard Tose, May 1.

Baltimore, Cleveland, and Pittsburgh agreed to join the AFL teams to form the 13-team American Football Conference of the NFL in 1970, May 17. The NFL also agreed on a playoff format that would include one "wild-card" team per conference—the second-place team with the best record.

Monday Night Football was signed for 1970. ABC acquired the rights to televise 13 NFL regular-season Monday night games in 1970, 1971, and 1972.

George Preston Marshall, president emeritus of the Redskins, died at 72, August 9.

The NFL marked its fiftieth year by the wearing of a special patch by each of the 16 teams.

1970

Kansas City defeated Minnesota 23-7 in Super Bowl IV at New Orleans, January 11. The gross receipts of approximately $3.8 million were the largest ever for a one-day sports event.

Four-year television contracts, under which CBS would televise all NFC games and NBC all AFC games (except Monday night games) and the two would divide televising the Super Bowl and AFC-NFC Pro Bowl games, were announced, January 26.

Art Modell resigned as president of the NFL, March 12. Milt Woodard resigned as president of the AFL, March 13. Lamar Hunt was elected president of the AFC and George Halas was elected president of the NFC, March 19.

The merged 26-team league adopted rules changes putting names on the backs of players' jerseys, making a point after touchdown worth only one point, and making the scoreboard clock the official timing device of the game, March 18.

The Players Negotiating Committee and the NFL Players Association announced a four-year agreement guaranteeing approximately $4,535,000 annually to player pension and insurance benefits, August 3. The owners also agreed to contribute $250,000 annually to improve or implement items such as disability payments, widows' benefits, maternity benefits, and dental benefits. The agreement also provided for increased preseason game and per diem payments, averaging approximately $2.6 million annually.

The Pittsburgh Steelers moved into Three Rivers Stadium. The Cincinnati Bengals moved to Riverfront Stadium.

Lombardi died of cancer at 57, September 3.

Tom Dempsey of New Orleans kicked a game-winning NFL-record 63-yard field goal against Detroit, November 8.

1971

Baltimore defeated Dallas 16-13 on Jim O'Brien's 32-yard field goal with five seconds to go in Super Bowl V at Miami, January 17. The NBC telecast was viewed in an estimated 23,980,000 homes, the largest audience ever for a one-day sports event.

The NFC defeated the AFC 27-6 in the first AFC-NFC Pro Bowl at Los Angeles, January 24.

The Boston Patriots changed their name to the New England Patriots, March 25. Their new stadium, Schaefer Stadium, was dedicated in a 20-14 preseason victory over the Giants.

The Philadelphia Eagles left Franklin Field and played their games at the new Veterans Stadium.

The San Francisco 49ers left Kezar Stadium and moved their games to Candlestick Park.

Daniel F. Reeves, the president and general manager of the Rams, died at 58, April 15.

The Dallas Cowboys moved from the Cotton Bowl into their new home, Texas Stadium, October 24.

Miami defeated Kansas City 27-24 in sudden-death overtime in an AFC Divisional Playoff Game, December 25. Garo Yepremian kicked a 37-yard field goal for the Dolphins after 22 minutes, 40 seconds of overtime, as the game lasted 82 minutes, 40 seconds overall, making it the longest game in history.

1972

Dallas defeated Miami 24-3 in Super Bowl VI at New Orleans, January 16. The CBS telecast was viewed in an estimated 27,450,000 homes, the top-rated one-day telecast ever.

The inbounds lines or hashmarks were moved nearer the center of the field, 23 yards, 1 foot, 9 inches from the sidelines, March 23. The method of determining won-lost percentage in standings changed. Tie games, previously not counted in the standings, were made equal to a half-game won and a half-game lost, May 24.

Robert Irsay purchased the Los Angeles Rams and transferred ownership of the club to Carroll Rosenbloom in exchange for the Baltimore Colts, July 13.

William V. Bidwill purchased the stock of his brother Charles (Stormy) Bidwill to become the sole owner of the St. Louis Cardinals, September 2.

The National District Attorneys Association endorsed the position of professional leagues in opposing proposed legalization of gambling on professional team sports, September 28.

Franco Harris's "Immaculate Reception" gave the Steelers their first postseason win ever, 13-7 over the Raiders, December 23.

1973

Rozelle announced that all Super Bowl VII tickets were sold and that the game would be telecast in Los Angeles, the site of the game, on an experimental basis, January 3.

Miami defeated Washington 14-7 in Super Bowl VII at Los Angeles, completing a 17-0 season, the first perfect-record regular-season and post-season mark in NFL history, January 14. The NBC telecast was viewed by approximately 75 million people.

The AFC defeated the NFC 33-28 in the Pro Bowl in Dallas, the first time since 1942 that the game was played outside Los Angeles, January 21.

A jersey numbering system was adopted, April 5: 1-19 for quarterbacks and specialists, 20-49 for running backs and defensive backs, 50-59 for centers and linebackers, 60-79 for defensive linemen and interior offensive linemen other than centers, and 80-89 for wide receivers and tight ends. Players who had been in the NFL in 1972 could continue to use old numbers.

NFL Charities, a nonprofit organization, was created to derive an income from monies generated from NFL Properties' licensing of NFL trademarks and team names, June 26. NFL Charities was set up to support education and charitable activities and to supply economic support to persons formerly associated with professional football who were no longer able to support themselves.

Congress adopted experimental legislation (for three years) requiring any NFL game that had been declared a sellout 72 hours prior to kickoff to be made available for local televising, September 14. The legislation provided for an annual review to be made by the Federal Communications Commission.

The Buffalo Bills moved their home games from War Memorial Stadium to Rich Stadium in nearby Orchard Park. The Giants tied the Eagles 23-23 in the final game in Yankee Stadium, September 23. The Giants played the rest of their home games at the Yale Bowl in New Haven, Connecticut.

A rival league, the World Football League, was formed and was reported in operation, October 2. It had plans to start play in 1974.

O.J. Simpson of Buffalo became the first player to rush for more than 2,000 yards in a season, gaining 2,003.

1974

Miami defeated Minnesota 24-7 in Super Bowl VIII at Houston, the second consecutive Super Bowl championship for the Dolphins, January 13. The CBS telecast was viewed by approximately 75 million people.

Rozelle was given a 10-year contract effective January 1, 1973, February 27.

Tampa Bay was awarded a franchise to begin operation in 1976, April 24.

Sweeping rules changes were adopted to add action and tempo to games: one sudden-death overtime period was added for preseason and regular-season games; the goal posts were moved from the goal line to the end lines; kickoffs were moved from the 40- to the 35-yard line; after missed field goals from beyond the 20, the ball was to be returned to the line of scrimmage; restrictions were placed on members of the punting team to open up return possibilities; roll-blocking and cutting of wide receivers was eliminated; the extent of downfield contact a defender could have with an eligible receiver was restricted; the penalties for offensive holding, illegal use of the hands, and tripping were reduced from 15 to 10 yards; wide receivers blocking back toward the ball within three yards of the line of scrimmage were prevented from blocking below the waist, April 25.

The Toronto Northmen of the WFL signed Larry Csonka, Jim Kiick, and Paul Warfield of Miami, March 31.

Seattle was awarded an NFL franchise to begin play in 1976, June 4. Lloyd W. Nordstrom, president of the Seattle Seahawks, and Hugh Culverhouse, president of the Tampa Bay Buccaneers, signed franchise agreements, December 5.

The Birmingham Americans defeated the Florida Blazers 22-21 in the WFL World Bowl, winning the league championship, December 5.

1975
Pittsburgh defeated Minnesota 16-6 in Super Bowl IX at New Orleans, the Steelers' first championship since entering the NFL in 1933. The NBC telecast was viewed by approximately 78 million people.

The divisional winners with the highest won-loss percentage were made the home team for the divisional playoffs, and the surviving winners with the highest percentage made home teams for the championship games, June 26.

Referees were equipped with wireless microphones for all preseason, regular-season, and playoff games.

The Lions moved to the new Pontiac Silverdome. The Giants played their home games in Shea Stadium. The Saints moved into the Louisiana Superdome.

The World Football League folded, October 22.

1976
Pittsburgh defeated Dallas 21-17 in Super Bowl X in Miami. The Steelers joined Green Bay and Miami as the only teams to win two Super Bowls; the Cowboys became the first wild-card team to play in the Super Bowl. The CBS telecast was viewed by an estimated 80 million people, the largest television audience in history.

Lloyd Nordstrom, the president of the Seahawks, died at 66, January 20. His brother Elmer succeeded him as majority representative of the team.

The owners awarded Super Bowl

XII, to be played on January 15, 1978, to New Orleans. They also adopted the use of two 30-second clocks for all games, visible to both players and fans to note the official time between the ready-for-play signal and snap of the ball, March 16.

A veteran player allocation was held to stock the Seattle and Tampa Bay franchises with 39 players each, March 30-31. In the college draft, Seattle and Tampa Bay each received eight extra choices, April 8-9.

The Giants moved into new Giants Stadium in East Rutherford, New Jersey.

The Steelers defeated the College All-Stars in a storm-shortened Chicago College All-Star Game, the last of the series, July 23. St. Louis defeated San Diego 20-10 in a preseason game before 38,000 in Korakuen Stadium, Tokyo, in the first NFL game outside of North America, August 16.

1977
Oakland defeated Minnesota 32-14 before a record crowd of 100,421 in Super Bowl XI at Pasadena, January 9. The paid attendance was a pro record 103,438. The NBC telecast was viewed by 81.9 million people, the largest ever to view a sports event. The victory was the fifth consecutive for the AFC in the Super Bowl.

The NFL Players Association and the NFL Management Council ratified a collective bargaining agreement extending until 1982, covering five football seasons while continuing the pension plan—including years 1974, 1975, and 1976—with contributions totaling more than $55 million. The total cost of the agreement was estimated at $107 million. The agreement called for a college draft at least through 1986; contained a no-strike, no-suit clause; established a 43-man active player limit; reduced pension vesting to four years; provided for increases in minimum salaries and preseason and postseason pay; improved insurance, medical, and dental benefits; modified previous practices in player movement and control; and reaffirmed the NFL Commissioner's disciplinary authority. Additionally, the agreement called for the NFL member clubs to make payments totaling $16 million the next 10 years to settle various legal disputes, February 25.

The San Francisco 49ers were sold to Edward J. DeBartolo, Jr., March 28.

A 16-game regular season, 4-game preseason was adopted to begin in 1978, March 29. A second wild-card team was adopted for the playoffs beginning in 1978, with the wild-card teams to play each other and the winners advancing to a round of eight postseason games.

The Seahawks were permanently aligned in the AFC Western Division and the Buccaneers in the NFC Central Division, March 31.

The owners awarded Super Bowl XIII, to be played on January 21, 1979, to Miami, to be played in the Orange Bowl; Super Bowl XIV, to be played January 20, 1980, was awarded to Pasadena, to be played in the Rose Bowl, June 14.

Rules changes were adopted to

open up the passing game and to cut down on injuries. Defenders were permitted to make contact with eligible receivers only once; the head slap was outlawed; offensive linemen were prohibited from thrusting their hands to an opponent's neck, face, or head; and wide receivers were prohibited from clipping, even in the legal clipping zone.

Rozelle negotiated contracts with the three television networks to televise all NFL regular-season and postseason games, plus selected preseason games, for four years beginning with the 1978 season. ABC was awarded yearly rights to 16 Monday night games, four prime-time games, the AFC-NFC Pro Bowl, and the Hall of Fame game. CBS received the rights to all NFC regular-season and postseason games (except those in the ABC package) and to Super Bowls XIV and XVI. NBC received the rights to all AFC regular-season and postseason games (except those in the ABC package) and to Super Bowls XIII and XV. Industry sources considered it the largest single television package ever negotiated, October 12.

Chicago's Walter Payton set a single-game rushing record with 275 yards (40 carries) against Minnesota, November 20.

1978
Dallas defeated Denver 27-10 in Super Bowl XII, held indoors for the first time, at the Louisiana Superdome in New Orleans, January 15. The CBS telecast was viewed by more than 102 million people, meaning the game was watched by more viewers than any other show of any kind in the history of television. Dallas's victory was the first for the NFC in six years.

According to a Louis Harris Sports Survey, 70 percent of the nation's sports fans said they followed football, compared to 54 percent who followed baseball. Football increased its lead as the country's favorite, 26 percent to 16 percent for baseball, January 19.

A seventh official, the side judge, was added to the officiating crew, March 14.

The NFL continued a trend toward opening up the game. Rules changes permitted a defender to maintain contact with a receiver within five yards of the line of scrimmage, but restricted contact beyond that point. The pass-blocking rule was interpreted to permit the extending of arms and open hands, March 17.

A study on the use of instant replay as an officiating aid was made during seven nationally televised preseason games.

The NFL played for the first time in Mexico City, with the Saints defeating the Eagles 14-7 in a preseason game, August 5.

Bolstered by the expansion of the regular-season schedule from 14 to 16 weeks, NFL paid attendance exceeded 12 million (12,771,800) for the first time. The per-game average of 57,017 was the third-highest in league history and the most since 1973.

1979
Pittsburgh defeated Dallas 35-31 in

Super Bowl XIII at Miami to become the first team ever to win three Super Bowls, January 21. The NBC telecast was viewed in 35,090,000 homes, by an estimated 96.6 million fans.

The owners awarded three future Super Bowl sites: Super Bowl XV to the Louisiana Superdome in New Orleans, to be played on January 25, 1981; Super Bowl XVI to the Pontiac Silverdome in Pontiac, Michigan, to be played on January 24, 1982; and Super Bowl XVII to Pasadena's Rose Bowl, to be played on January 30, 1983, March 13.

NFL rules changes emphasized additional player safety. The changes prohibited players on the receiving team from blocking below the waist during kickoffs, punts, and field-goal attempts; prohibited the wearing of torn or altered equipment and exposed pads that could be hazardous; extended the zone in which there could be no crackback blocks; and instructed officials to quickly whistle a play dead when a quarterback was clearly in the grasp of a tackler, March 16.

Rosenbloom, the president of the Rams, drowned at 72, April 2. His widow, Georgia, assumed control of the club.

1980
Pittsburgh defeated the Los Angeles Rams 31-19 in Super Bowl XIV at Pasadena to become the first team to win four Super Bowls, January 20. The game was viewed in a record 35,330,000 homes.

The AFC-NFC Pro Bowl, won 37-27 by the NFC, was played before 48,060 fans at Aloha Stadium in Honolulu, Hawaii. It was the first time in the 30-year history of the Pro Bowl that the game was played in a non-NFL city.

Rules changes placed greater restrictions on contact in the area of the head, neck, and face. Under the heading of "personal foul," players were prohibited from directly striking, swinging, or clubbing on the head, neck, or face. Starting in 1980, a penalty could be called for such contact whether or not the initial contact was made below the neck area.

CBS, with a record bid of $12 million, won the national radio rights to 26 NFL regular-season games and all 10 postseason games for the 1980-83 seasons.

The Los Angeles Rams moved their home games to Anaheim Stadium in nearby Orange County, California.

The Oakland Raiders joined the Los Angeles Coliseum Commission's antitrust suit against the NFL. The suit contended the league violated antitrust laws in declining to approve a proposed move by the Raiders from Oakland to Los Angeles.

NFL regular-season attendance of nearly 13.4 million set a record for the third year in a row. The average paid attendance for the 224-game 1980 regular season was 59,787, the highest in the league's 61-year history. NFL games in 1980 were played before 92.4 percent of total stadium capacity.

Television ratings in 1980 were the second-best in NFL history, trailing only the combined ratings of the 1976 season. All three networks posted gains, and NBC's 15.0 rating was its best ever. CBS and ABC had their best ratings since 1977, with 15.3 and 20.8 ratings, respectively. CBS Radio reported a record audience of 7 million for Monday night and special games.

1981

Oakland defeated Philadelphia 27-10 in Super Bowl XV at the Louisiana Superdome in New Orleans, to become the first wild-card team to win a Super Bowl, January 25.

Edgar F. Kaiser, Jr., purchased the Denver Broncos from Gerald and Allan Phipps, February 26.

The owners adopted a disaster plan for re-stocking a team should the club be involved in a fatal accident, March 20.

The owners awarded Super Bowl XVIII to Tampa, to be played in Tampa Stadium on January 22, 1984, June 3.

A CBS-New York Times poll showed that 48 percent of sports fans preferred football to 31 percent for baseball.

The NFL teams hosted 167 representatives from 44 predominantly black colleges during training camps for a total of 289 days. The program was adopted for renewal during each training camp period.

NFL regular-season attendance— 13.6 million for an average of 60,745— set a record for the fourth year in a row. It also was the first time the per-game average exceeded 60,000. NFL games in 1981 were played before 93.8 percent of total stadium capacity.

ABC and CBS set all-time rating highs. ABC finished with a 21.7 rating and CBS with a 17.5 rating. NBC was down slightly to 13.9.

1982

San Francisco defeated Cincinnati 26-21 in Super Bowl XVI at the Pontiac Silverdome, in the first Super Bowl held in the North, January 24. The CBS telecast achieved the highest rating of any televised sports event ever, 49.1 with a 73.0 share. The game was viewed by a record 110.2 million fans. CBS Radio reported a record 14 million listeners for the game.

The NFL signed a five-year contract with the three television networks (ABC, CBS, and NBC) to televise all NFL regular-season and postseason games starting with the 1982 season.

The owners awarded the 1983, 1984, and 1985 AFC-NFC Pro Bowls to Honolulu's Aloha Stadium.

A jury ruled against the NFL in the antitrust trial brought by the Los Angeles Coliseum Commission and the Oakland Raiders, May 7. The verdict cleared the way for the Raiders to move to Los Angeles, where they defeated Green Bay 24-3 in their first preseason game, August 29.

The 1982 season was reduced from a 16-game schedule to nine as the result of a 57-day players' strike. The strike was called by the NFLPA at midnight on Monday, September 20, following the Green Bay at New York Giants game. Play resumed November 21-22 following ratification of the Collective Bargaining Agreement by NFL owners, November 17 in New York.

Under the Collective Bargaining Agreement, which was to run through the 1986 season, the NFL draft was extended through 1992 and the veteran free-agent system was left basically unchanged. A minimum salary schedule for years of experience was established; training camp and postseason pay were increased; players' medical, insurance, and retirement benefits were increased; and a severance-pay system was introduced to aid in career transition, a first in professional sports.

Despite the players' strike, the average paid attendance in 1982 was 58,472, the fifth-highest in league history.

The owners awarded the sites of two Super Bowls, December 14: Super Bowl XIX, to be played on January 20, 1985, to Stanford University Stadium in Stanford, California, with San Francisco as host team; and Super Bowl XX, to be played on January 26, 1986, to the Louisiana Superdome in New Orleans.

1983

Because of the shortened season, the NFL adopted a format of 16 teams competing in a Super Bowl Tournament for the 1982 playoffs. The NFC's number-one seed, Washington, defeated the AFC's number-two seed, Miami, 27-17 in Super Bowl XVII at the Rose Bowl in Pasadena, January 30.

Super Bowl XVII was the second-highest rated live television program of all time, giving the NFL a sweep of the top 10 live programs in television history. The game was viewed in more than 40 million homes, the largest ever for a live telecast.

Halas, the owner of the Bears and the last surviving member of the NFL's second organizational meeting, died at 88, October 31.

1984

The Los Angeles Raiders defeated Washington 38-9 in Super Bowl XVIII at Tampa Stadium, January 22. The game achieved a 46.4 rating and 71.0 share.

An 11-man group headed by H.R. (Bum) Bright purchased the Dallas Cowboys from Clint Murchison, Jr., March 20. Club president Tex Schramm was designated as managing general partner.

Patrick Bowlen purchased a majority interest in the Denver Broncos from Edgar Kaiser, Jr., March 21.

The Colts relocated to Indianapolis, March 28. Their new home became the Hoosier Dome.

The owners awarded two Super Bowl sites at their May 23-25 meetings: Super Bowl XXI, to be played on January 25, 1987, to the Rose Bowl in Pasadena; and Super Bowl XXII, to be played on January 31, 1988, to San Diego Jack Murphy Stadium.

The New York Jets moved their home games to Giants Stadium in East Rutherford, New Jersey.

Alex G. Spanos purchased a majority interest in the San Diego Chargers from Eugene V. Klein, August 28.

Houston defeated Pittsburgh 23-20 to mark the one-hundredth overtime game in regular-season play since overtime was adopted in 1974, December 2.

On the field, many all-time records were set: Dan Marino of Miami passed for 5,084 yards and 48 touchdowns; Eric Dickerson of the Los Angeles Rams rushed for 2,105 yards; Art Monk of Washington caught 106 passes; and Walter Payton of Chicago broke Jim Brown's career rushing mark, finishing the season with 13,309 yards.

According to a CBS Sports/New York Times survey, 53 percent of the nation's sports fans said they most enjoyed watching football, compared to 18 percent for baseball, December 2-4.

NFL paid attendance exceeded 13 million for the fifth consecutive complete regular season when 13,398,112, an average of 59,813, attended games. The figure was the second-highest in league history. Teams averaged 42.4 points per game, the second-highest total since the 1970 merger.

1985

San Francisco defeated Miami 38-16 in Super Bowl XIX at Stanford Stadium in Stanford, California, January 20. The game was viewed on television by more people than any other live event in history. President Ronald Reagan, who took his second oath of office before tossing the coin for the game, was one of 115,936,000 viewers. The game drew a 46.4 rating and a 63.0 share. In addition, 6 million people watched the Super Bowl in the United Kingdom and a similar number in Italy. Super Bowl XIX had a direct economic impact of $113.5 million on the San Francisco Bay area.

NBC Radio and the NFL entered into a two-year agreement granting NBC the radio rights to a 37-game package in each of the 1985-86 seasons, March 6. The package included 27 regular-season games and 10 postseason games.

The owners awarded two Super Bowl sites at their annual meeting, March 10-15: Super Bowl XXIII, to be played on January 22, 1989, to the proposed Dolphins Stadium in Miami; and Super Bowl XXIV, to be played on January 28, 1990, to the Louisiana Superdome in New Orleans.

Norman Braman, in partnership with Edward Leibowitz, bought the Philadelphia Eagles from Leonard Tose, April 29.

Bruce Smith, a Virginia Tech defensive lineman selected by Buffalo, was the first player chosen in the fiftieth NFL draft, April 30.

A group headed by Tom Benson, Jr., was approved to purchase the New Orleans Saints from John W. Mecom, Jr., June 3.

The NFL owners adopted a resolution calling for a series of overseas preseason games, beginning in 1986, with one game to be played in England/Europe and/or one game in Japan each year. The game would be a fifth preseason game for the clubs involved and all arrangements and selection of the clubs would be under the control of the Commissioner, May 23.

The league-wide conversion to videotape from movie film for coaching study was approved.

Commissioner Rozelle was authorized to extend the commitment to Honolulu's Aloha Stadium for the AFC-NFC Pro Bowl for 1988, 1989, and 1990, October 15.

The NFL set a single-weekend paid attendance record when 902,657 tickets were sold for the weekend of October 27-28.

A Louis Harris poll in December revealed that pro football remained the sport most followed by Americans. Fifty-nine percent of those surveyed followed pro football, compared with 54 percent who followed baseball.

The Chicago-Miami Monday game had the highest rating, 29.6, and share, 46.0, of any prime-time game in NFL history, December 2. The game was viewed in more than 25 million homes.

The NFL showed a ratings increase on all three networks for the season, gaining 4 percent on NBC, 10 on CBS, and 16 on ABC.

1986

Chicago defeated New England 46-10 in Super Bowl XX at the Louisiana Superdome, January 26. The Patriots had earned the right to play the Bears by becoming the first wild-card team to win three consecutive games on the road. The NBC telecast replaced the final episode of M*A*S*H as the most-viewed television program in history, with an audience of 127 million viewers, according to A.C. Nielsen figures. In addition to drawing a 48.3 rating and a 70 percent share in the United States, Super Bowl XX was televised to 59 foreign countries and beamed via satellite to the QE II. An estimated 300 million Chinese viewed a tape delay of the game in March. NBC Radio figures indicated an audience of 10 million for the game.

Super Bowl XX injected more than $100 million into the New Orleans-area economy, and fans spent $250 per day and a record $17.69 per person on game day.

The owners adopted limited use of instant replay as an officiating aid, prohibited players from wearing or otherwise displaying equipment, apparel, or other items that carry commercial names, names of organizations, or personal messages of any type, March 11.

After an 11-week trial, a jury in U.S. District Court in New York awarded the United States Football League one dollar in its $1.7 billion antitrust suit against the NFL. The jury rejected all of the USFL's television-related claims, which were the self-proclaimed heart of the USFL's case, July 29.

Chicago defeated Dallas 17-6 at Wembley Stadium in London in the first American Bowl. The game drew a sellout crowd of 82,699 and the NBC national telecast in this country produced a 12.4 rating and 36 percent share, making it the second-highest-rated daytime preseason game and highest daytime preseason television audience ever with 10.65-million viewers, August 3.

Monday Night Football became the longest-running prime-time series in the history of the ABC network.

Instant replay was used to reverse two plays in 31 preseason games. During the regular season, 374 plays were closely reviewed by replay officials, leading to 38 reversals in 224 games. Eighteen plays were closely reviewed by instant replay in 10 postseason games with three reversals.

1987

The New York Giants defeated Denver 39-20 in Super Bowl XXI and captured their first NFL title since 1956. The game, played in Pasadena's Rose Bowl, drew a sellout crowd of 101,063. According to A.C. Nielsen figures, the CBS broadcast of the game was viewed in the U.S. on television by 122.64-million people, making the telecast the second most-watched television show of all-time behind Super Bowl XX. The game was watched live or on tape in 55 foreign countries and NBC Radio's broadcast of the game was heard by a record 10.1 million people.

The NFL set an all-time paid attendance mark of 17,304,463 for all games, including preseason, regular-season, and postseason. Average regular-season game attendance (60,663) exceeded the 60,000 figure for only the second time in league history.

New three-year TV contracts with ABC, CBS, and NBC were announced for 1987-89 at the NFL annual meeting in Maui, Hawaii, March 15. Commissioner Rozelle and Broadcast Committee Chairman Art Modell also announced a three-year contract with ESPN to televise 13 prime-time games each season. The ESPN contract was the first with a cable network. However, NFL games on ESPN also were scheduled for regular television in the city of the visiting team and in the home city if the game was sold out 72 hours in advance.

Owners also voted to continue in effect for one year the instant replay system used during the 1986 season.

A special payment program was adopted to benefit nearly 1,000 former NFL players who participated in the League before the current Bert Bell NFL Pension Plan was created and made retroactive to the 1959 season. Players covered by the new program spent at least five years in the League and played all or part of their career prior to 1959. Each vested player would receive $60 per month for each year of service in the League for life.

Possible sites for Super Bowl XXV were reduced to five locations by the NFL Super Bowl XXV Site Selection Committee: Anaheim Stadium, Los Angeles Memorial Coliseum, Joe Robbie Stadium, San Diego Jack Murphy Stadium, and Tampa Stadium.

NFL and CBS Radio jointly announced agreement granting CBS the radio rights to a 40-game package in each of the next three NFL seasons, 1987-89, April 7.

NFL owners awarded Super Bowl XXV, to be played on January 27, 1991, to Tampa Stadium, May 20.

Over 400 former NFL players from the pre-1959 era received first payments from NFL owners, July 1.

The NFL's debut on ESPN produced the two highest-rated and most-watched sports programs in basic cable history. The Chicago at Miami game on August 16 drew an 8.9 rating in 3.81 million homes. Those records fell two weeks later when the Los Angeles Raiders at Dallas game achieved a 10.2 cable rating in 4.36 million homes.

Fifty-eight preseason games drew a record paid attendance of 3,116,870.

The 1987 season was reduced from a 16-game season to 15 as the result of a 24-day players' strike. The strike was called by the NFLPA on Tuesday, September 22, following the New England at New York Jets game. Games scheduled for the third weekend were canceled but the games of weeks four, five, and six were played with replacement teams. Striking players returned for the seventh week of the season, October 25.

In a three-team deal involving 10 players and/or draft choices, the Los Angeles Rams traded running back Eric Dickerson to the Indianapolis Colts for six draft choices and two players. Buffalo obtained the rights to linebacker Cornelius Bennett from Indianapolis, sending Greg Bell and three draft choices to the Rams. The Colts added Owen Gill and three draft choices of their own to complete the deal with the Rams, October 31.

The Chicago at Minnesota game became the highest-rated and most-watched sports program in basic cable history when it drew a 14.4 cable rating in 6.5 million homes, December 6.

Instant replay was used to reverse eight plays in 52 preseason games. During the strike-shortened 210-game regular season, 490 plays were closely reviewed by replay officials, leading to 57 reversals. Eighteen plays were closely reviewed by instant replay in 10 postseason games, with three reversals.

1988

Washington defeated Denver 42-10 in Super Bowl XXII to earn its second victory this decade in the NFL Championship Game. The game, played for the first time in San Diego Jack Murphy Stadium, drew a sellout crowd of 73,302. According to A.C. Nielsen figures, the ABC broadcast of the game was viewed in the U.S. on television by 115,000,000 people. The game was seen live or on tape in 60 foreign countries, including the People's Republic of China, and CBS's radio broadcast of the game was heard by 13.7 million people.

A total of 811 players shared in the postseason pool of $16.9 million, the most ever distributed in a single season.

In a unanimous 3-0 decision, the 2nd Circuit Court of Appeals in New York upheld the verdict of the jury that in July, 1986, had awarded the United States Football League one dollar in its $1.7 billion antitrust suit against the NFL. In a 91-page opinion, Judge Ralph K. Winter said the USFL sought

through court decree the success it failed to gain among football fans, March 10.

By a 23-5 margin, owners voted to continue the instant replay system for the third consecutive season with the Instant Replay Official to be assigned to a regular seven-man, on-the-field crew. At the NFL annual meeting in Phoenix, Arizona, a 45-second clock was also approved to replace the 30-second clock. For a normal sequence of plays, the interval between plays was changed to 45 seconds from the time the ball is signaled dead until it is snapped on the succeeding play.

NFL owners approved the transfer of the Cardinals' franchise from St. Louis to Phoenix; approved two supplemental drafts each year—one prior to training camp and one prior to the regular season; and voted to initiate an annual series of games in Japan/Asia as early as the 1989 preseason, March 14-18.

The NFL Annual Selection Meeting returned to a separate two-day format and for the first time originated on a Sunday. ESPN drew a 3.6 rating during their seven-hour coverage of the draft, which was viewed in 1.6 million homes, April 24-25.

Art Rooney, founder and owner of the Steelers, died at 87, August 25.

Paid and average attendance of 934,271 and 66,734 at 14 games on October 16-17 set single weekend records.

Commissioner Rozelle announced that two teams would play a preseason game as part of the American Bowl series on August 6, 1989, in the Korakuen Tokyo Dome in Japan, December 16.

NFL regular-season paid attendance of 13,535,335 and the average of 60,427 was the third highest all-time. Buffalo set an NFL team single-season, in-house attendance mark of 622,793.

1989

San Francisco defeated Cincinnati 20-16 in Super Bowl XXIII. The game, played for the first time at Joe Robbie Stadium in Miami, was attended by a sellout crowd of 75,129. NBC's telecast of the game was watched by an estimated 110,780,000 viewers, according to A.C. Nielsen, making it the sixth most-watched program in television history. The game was seen live or on tape in 60 foreign countries, including an estimated 300 million in China. The CBS Radio broadcast of the game was heard by 11.2 million people.

Commissioner Rozelle announced his retirement, pending the naming of a successor, March 22 at the NFL annual meeting in Palm Desert, California.

Following the announcement, AFC president Lamar Hunt and NFC president Wellington Mara announced the formation of a six-man search committee composed of Art Modell, Robert Parins, Dan Rooney, and Ralph Wilson. Hunt and Mara served as co-chairmen.

By a 24-4 margin, owners voted to continue the instant replay system for the fourth straight season. A strength-

ened policy regarding anabolic steroids and masking agents was announced by Commissioner Rozelle. NFL clubs called for strong disciplinary measures in cases of feigned injuries and adopted a joint proposal by the Long-Range Planning and Finance committees regarding player personnel rules, March 19-23.

Two hundred twenty-nine unconditional free agents signed with new teams under management's Plan B system, April 1.

Jerry Jones purchased a majority interest in the Dallas Cowboys from H.R. (Bum) Bright, April 18.

Tex Schramm was named president of the new World League of American Football to work with a six-man committee of Dan Rooney, chairman; Norman Braman, Lamar Hunt, Victor Kiam, Mike Lynn, and Bill Walsh, April 18.

NFL and CBS Radio jointly announced agreement extending CBS's radio rights to an annual 40-game package through the 1994 season, April 18.

NFL owners awarded Super Bowl XXVI, to be played on January 26, 1992, to Minneapolis, May 24.

As of opening day, September 10, of the 229 Plan B free agents, 111 were active and 23 others were on teams' reserve lists. Ninety-two others were waived and three retired.

Art Shell was named head coach of the Los Angeles Raiders making him the NFL's first black head coach since Fritz Pollard coached the Akron Pros in 1921, October 3.

The site of the New England Patriots at San Francisco 49ers game scheduled for Candlestick Park on October 22 was switched to Stanford Stadium in the aftermath of the Bay Area earthquake of October 17. The change was announced on October 19.

Paul Tagliabue became the seventh chief executive of the NFL on October 26 when he was chosen to succeed Commissioner Pete Rozelle on the sixth ballot of a three-day meeting in Cleveland, Ohio.

In all, 12 ballots were required to select Tagliabue. Two were conducted at a meeting in Chicago on July 6, and four at a meeting in Dallas on October 10-11. On the twelfth ballot, with Seattle absent, Tagliabue received more than the 19 affirmative votes required for election from among the 27 clubs present.

The transfer from Commissioner Rozelle to Commissioner Tagliabue took place at 12:01 A.M. on Sunday, November 5.

NFL Charities donated $1 million through United Way to benefit Bay Area earthquake victims, November 6.

NFL paid attendance of 17,399,538 was the highest total in league history. This included a total of 13,625,662 for an average of 60,829—both NFL records—for the 224-game regular season.

1990

San Francisco defeated Denver 55-10 in Super Bowl XXIV at the Louisiana Superdome, January 28. San Francisco joined Pittsburgh as the NFL's only teams to win four Super Bowls.

The NFL announced revisions in its

1990 draft eligibility rules. College juniors became eligible but must renounce their collegiate football eligibility before applying for the NFL Draft, February 16.

Commissioner Tagliabue announced NFL teams will play their 16-game schedule over 17 weeks in 1990 and 1991 and 16 games over 18 weeks in 1992 and 1993, February 27.

The NFL revised its playoff format to include two additional wild-card teams (one per conference).

Commissioner Tagliabue and Broadcast Committee Chairman Art Modell announced a four-year contract with Turner Broadcasting to televise nine Sunday-night games.

New four-year TV agreements were ratified for 1990-93 for ABC, CBS, NBC, ESPN, and TNT at the NFL annual meeting in Orlando, Florida, March 12. The contracts totaled $3.6 billion, the largest in TV history.

The NFL announced plans to expand its American Bowl series of preseason games. In addition to games in London and Tokyo, American Bowl games were scheduled for Berlin, Germany, and Montreal, Canada, in 1990.

For the fifth straight year, NFL owners voted to continue a limited system of Instant Replay. Beginning in 1990, the replay official will have a two-minute time limit to make a decision. The vote was 21-7, March 12.

Commissioner Tagliabue announced the formation of a Committee on Expansion and Realignment, March 13. He also named a Player Advisory Council, comprised of 12 former NFL players, March 14.

One-hundred eighty-four Plan B unconditional free agents signed with new teams, April 2.

Commissioner Tagliabue appointed Dr. John Lombardo as the League's Drug Advisor for Anabolic Steroids, April 25 and named Dr. Lawrence Brown as the League's Advisor for Drugs of Abuse, May 17.

NFL owners awarded Super Bowl XXVIII, to be played in 1994, in the proposed Georgia Dome, May 23.

Commissioner Tagliabue named NFL referee Jerry Seeman as NFL Director of Officiating, replacing Art McNally, who announced his retirement, July 12.

NFL International Week was celebrated with four preseason games in seven days in Tokyo, London, Berlin, and Montreal. More than 200,000 fans on three continents attended the four games, August 4-11.

Commissioner Tagliabue announced the NFL Teacher of the Month program in which the League furnishes grants and scholarships in recognition of teachers who provided a positive influence upon NFL players in elementary and secondary schools, September 20.

For the first time since 1957, every NFL club won at least one of its first four games, October 1.

NFL total paid attendance of 17,665,671 was the highest total in League history. The regular-season total paid attendance of 13,959,896 and average of 62,321 for 224 games were the highest ever, surpassing the previous records set in the 1989 season.

1991

The New York Giants defeated Buffalo 20-19 in Super Bowl XXV to capture their second title in five years. The game was played before a sellout crowd of 73,813 at Tampa Stadium and became the first Super Bowl decided by one point, January 26. The ABC broadcast of the game was seen by more than 112-million people in the United States and was seen live or taped in 60 other countries.

NFL playoff games earned the top television rating spot of the week for each week of the month-long playoffs, January 29.

A total of 693 players shared in the postseason pool of $14.9 million.

New York businessman Robert Tisch purchased a 50 percent interest in the New York Giants from Mrs. Helen Mara Nugent and her children, Tim Mara and Maura Mara Concannon, February 2.

Commissioner Tagliabue named Neil Austrian to the newly created position of President of the NFL to be chief operating officer for League-wide business and financial operations, February 27.

NFL clubs voted to continue a limited system of Instant Replay for the sixth consecutive year. The vote was 21-7, March 19.

The NFL launched the World League of American Football, the first sports league to operate on a weekly basis on two separate continents, March 23.

NFL Charities presented a $250,000 donation to the United Service Organization. The donation was the second largest single grant ever by NFL Charities, April 5.

Commissioner Tagliabue named Harold Henderson as Executive Vice President for Labor Relations and Chairman of the NFL Management Council Executive Committee, April 8.

Russell Maryland, a University of Miami defensive lineman, was selected by Dallas, becoming the first player chosen in the 1991 NFL draft, April 21.

NFL clubs approved a recommendation by the Expansion and Realignment Committee to add two teams for the 1994 season, resulting in six divisions of five teams each, May 22.

NFL clubs awarded Super Bowl XXIX, to be played on January 29, 1995, to Miami, May 23.

"NFL International Week" featured six 1990 playoff teams playing nationally televised games in London, Berlin, and Tokyo on July 28 and August 3-4. The games drew more than 150,000 fans.

Paul Brown, founder of the Cleveland Browns and Cincinnati Bengals, died at age 82, August 5.

NFL clubs approved a resolution establishing an international division, reporting to the President of the NFL. A three-year financial plan for the World League was approved by NFL clubs at a meeting in Dallas, October 23.

1992

The NFL agreed to provide a minimum of $2.5 million in financial support to the NFL Alumni Association and assistance to NFL Alumni-related programs. The agreement included con-

tributions from NFL Charities to the Pre-59ers and Dire Need Programs for former players, January 25.

The Washington Redskins defeated the Buffalo Bills 37-24 in Super Bowl XXVI to capture their third world championship in 10 years, January 26. The game was played before a sellout crowd of 63,130 at the Hubert H. Humphrey Metrodome in Minneapolis and attracted the second largest television audience in Super Bowl history. The CBS broadcast was seen by more than 123 million people nationally, second only to the 127 million who viewed Super Bowl XX.

For the third consecutive season, NFL total paid attendance reached a record level. Total paid attendance was 17,752,139 for the 296 preseason, regular-season, and postseason games, February 3.

The use in officiating of a limited system of Instant Replay for a seventh consecutive year was not approved. The vote was 17-11 in favor of approval (21 votes were required), March 18.

Steve Emtman, a University of Washington defensive lineman, was selected by Indianapolis, becoming the first player chosen in the 1992 NFL draft, April 26.

St. Louis businessman James Orthwein purchased controlling interest in the New England Patriots from Victor Kiam, May 11.

In a Harris Poll taken during the NFL offseason, professional football again was declared the nation's most popular sport. Professional football finished atop similar surveys conducted by Harris in 1985 and 1989, May 23.

NFL clubs accepted the report of the Expansion Committee at a league meeting in Pasadena. The report names five cities as finalists for the two expansion teams—Baltimore, Charlotte, Jacksonville, Memphis, and St. Louis, May 19.

At a league meeting in Dallas, NFL clubs approved a proposal by the World League Board of Directors to restructure the World League and place future emphasis on its international success, September 17.

1993

The NFL and lawyers for the players announced a settlement of various lawsuits and an agreement on the terms of a seven-year deal that included a new player system to be in place through the 1999 season, January 6.

Commissioner Tagliabue announced the establishment of the "NFL World Partnership Program" to develop amateur football internationally through a series of clinics conducted by former NFL players and coaches, January 14.

As part of Super Bowl XXVII, the NFL announced the creation of the first NFL Youth Education Town, a facility located in south central Los Angeles for inner city youth. January 25.

The Dallas Cowboys defeated the Buffalo Bills 52-17 in Super Bowl XXVII to capture their first NFL title since 1978. The game was played before a crowd of 98,374 at the Rose Bowl in Pasadena, California. The NBC broadcast of the game was the most

watched program in television history and was seen by 133,400,000 people in the United States. The game also was seen live or taped in 101 other countries. The rating for the game was 45.1, the tenth highest for any televised sports event, January 31.

A total of 695 players shared in the postseason pool of $14.9 million, February 15.

For the fourth consecutive season, the NFL total paid attendance reached a record level. Total paid attendance was 17,784,354 for the 296 preseason, regular-season, and postseason games, March 4.

NFL clubs awarded Super Bowl XXX to the city of Phoenix, to be played on January 28, 1996, at Sun Devil Stadium, March 23.

Drew Bledsoe, a quarterback from Washington State, was selected by New England, becoming the first player chosen in the 1993 NFL draft, April 25.

The NFL and the NFL Players Association officially signed a 7-year Collective Bargaining Agreement in Washington, D.C., which guarantees more than $1 billion in pension, health, and post-career benefits for current and retired players—the most extensive benefits plan in pro sports. It was the NFL's first CBA since the 1982 agreement expired in 1987, June 29.

Ron Bernard was named president of NFL Enterprises, a newly formed division of the NFL responsible for NFL Films, home video, and special domestic and international television programming, August 19.

NFL announced plans to allow fans, for the first time ever, to join players and coaches in selecting the annual AFC and NFC Pro Bowl teams, October 12.

NFL clubs unanimously awarded the league's twenty-ninth franchise to the Carolina Panthers at a meeting in Chicago. NFL clubs also awarded Super Bowl XXXI to New Orleans and Super Bowl XXXII to San Diego, October 26.

At the same meeting in Chicago, NFL clubs approved a plan to form a European league with joint venture partners, October 27.

Don Shula became the winningest coach in NFL history when Miami beat Philadelphia to give Shula his 325th victory, one more than George Halas, November 14.

NFL clubs awarded the league's thirtieth franchise to the Jacksonville Jaguars at a meeting in Chicago, November 30.

The NFL announced new 4-year television agreements with ABC, ESPN, TNT, and NFL newcomer FOX, which took over the NFC package from CBS, December 18.

The NFL completed its new TV agreements by announcing that NBC would retain the rights to the AFC package, December 20.

1994

The NFL announced that a regular-season paid attendance record was set in 1993. Attendance averaged 62,354, topping the previous record of 62,321 set in 1990, January 6.

The Dallas Cowboys defeated the Buffalo Bills 30-13 in Super Bowl

255

XXVIII to become the fifth team to win back-to-back Super Bowl titles. The game was viewed by the largest U.S. audience in television history—134.8 million people. The game's 45.5 rating was the highest for a Super Bowl since 1987 and the tenth highest-rated Super Bowl ever, January 30.

NFL clubs unanimously approved the transfer of the New England Patriots from James Orthwein to Robert Kraft at a meeting in Orlando, February 22.

In an effort to increase offensive production, NFL clubs at the league's annual meeting in Orlando adopted a package of changes, including modifications in line play, chucking rules, and the roughing-the-passer rule, plus the adoption of the two-point conversion and moving the spot of the kickoff back to the 30-yard line, March 22.

NFL clubs approved the transfer of the majority interest in the Miami Dolphins from the Robbie family to H. Wayne Huizenga, March 23.

The NFL and FOX announced the formation of a joint venture to create a six-team World League to begin play in Europe in April, 1995, March 23.

The NFL announced a total paid attendance record for the fifth consecutive year, with 17,951,831 in paid attendance for all 1993 games, March 23.

Dan Wilkinson, a defensive tackle from Ohio State, was selected by Cincinnati as the first overall selection in the draft, April 24.

The Carolina Panthers earned the right to select first in the 1995 NFL draft by winning a coin toss with the Jacksonville Jaguars. The Jaguars received the second selection in the 1995 draft, April 24.

NFL clubs approved the transfer of the Philadelphia Eagles from Norman Braman to Jeffrey Lurie, May 6.

The NFL launched "NFL Sunday Ticket," a new season subscription service for satellite television dish owners, June 1.

NFL COMMISSIONERS AND PRESIDENTS*

1920	Jim Thorpe, President
1921-39	Joe Carr, President
1939-41	Carl Storck, President
1941-46	Elmer Layden, Commissioner
1946-59	Bert Bell, Commissioner
1960-89	Pete Rozelle, Commissioner
1989-present	Paul Tagliabue, Commissioner

NFL treasurer Austin Gunsel served as president in the office of the commissioner following the death of Bert Bell (Oct. 11, 1959) until the election of Pete Rozelle (Jan. 26, 1960).

1993

AMERICAN CONFERENCE

Eastern Division

	W	L	T	Pct.	Pts.	OP
Buffalo	12	4	0	.750	329	242
Miami	9	7	0	.563	349	351
N.Y. Jets	8	8	0	.500	270	247
New England	5	11	0	.313	238	286
Indianapolis	4	12	0	.250	189	378

Central Division

	W	L	T	Pct.	Pts.	OP
Houston	12	4	0	.750	368	238
Pittsburgh*	9	7	0	.563	308	281
Cleveland	7	9	0	.438	304	307
Cincinnati	3	13	0	.188	187	319

Western Division

	W	L	T	Pct.	Pts.	OP
Kansas City	11	5	0	.688	328	291
L.A. Raiders*	10	6	0	.625	306	326
Denver*	9	7	0	.563	373	284
San Diego	8	8	0	.500	322	290
Seattle	6	10	0	.375	280	314

NATIONAL CONFERENCE

Eastern Division

	W	L	T	Pct.	Pts.	OP
Dallas	12	4	0	.750	376	229
N.Y. Giants*	11	5	0	.688	288	205
Philadelphia	8	8	0	.500	293	315
Phoenix	7	9	0	.438	326	269
Washington	4	12	0	.250	230	345

Central Division

	W	L	T	Pct.	Pts.	OP
Detroit	10	6	0	.625	298	292
Minnesota*	9	7	0	.563	277	290
Green Bay*	9	7	0	.563	340	282
Chicago	7	9	0	.438	234	230
Tampa Bay	5	11	0	.313	237	376

Western Division

	W	L	T	Pct.	Pts.	OP
San Francisco	10	6	0	.625	473	295
New Orleans	8	8	0	.500	317	343
Atlanta	6	10	0	.375	316	385
L.A. Rams	5	11	0	.313	221	367

*Wild-Card qualifier for playoffs

Minnesota finished ahead of Green Bay based on a head-to-head sweep (2-0).

Wild Card playoffs: KANSAS CITY 27, Pittsburgh 24 (OT); L.A. RAIDERS 42, Denver 24
Divisional playoffs: BUFFALO 29, L.A. Raiders 23; Kansas City 28, HOUSTON 20
AFC championship: BUFFALO 30, Kansas City 13
Wild Card playoffs: Green Bay 28, DETROIT 24; N.Y. GIANTS 17, Minnesota 10
Divisional playoffs: SAN FRANCISCO 44, N.Y. Giants 3; DALLAS 27, Green Bay 17
NFC championship: DALLAS 38, San Francisco 21
Super Bowl XXVIII: Dallas (NFC) 30, Buffalo (AFC) 13, at Georgia Dome, Atlanta, Georgia

In Past Standings section, home teams in playoff games are indicated by capital letters.

1992

AMERICAN CONFERENCE

Eastern Division

	W	L	T	Pct.	Pts.	OP
Miami	11	5	0	.688	340	281
Buffalo*	11	5	0	.688	381	283
Indianapolis	9	7	0	.563	216	302
N.Y. Jets	4	12	0	.250	220	315
New England	2	14	0	.125	205	363

Central Division

	W	L	T	Pct.	Pts.	OP
Pittsburgh	11	5	0	.688	299	225
Houston*	10	6	0	.625	352	258
Cleveland	7	9	0	.438	272	275
Cincinnati	5	11	0	.313	274	304

Western Division

	W	L	T	Pct.	Pts.	OP
San Diego	11	5	0	.688	335	241
Kansas City*	10	6	0	.625	348	282
Denver	8	8	0	.500	262	329
L.A. Raiders	7	9	0	.438	249	281
Seattle	2	14	0	.125	140	312

NATIONAL CONFERENCE

Eastern Division

	W	L	T	Pct.	Pts.	OP
Dallas	13	3	0	.813	409	243
Philadelphia*	11	5	0	.688	354	245
Washington*	9	7	0	.563	300	255
N.Y. Giants	6	10	0	.375	306	367
Phoenix	4	12	0	.250	243	332

Central Division

	W	L	T	Pct.	Pts.	OP
Minnesota	11	5	0	.688	374	249
Green Bay	9	7	0	.563	276	296
Tampa Bay	5	11	0	.313	267	365
Chicago	5	11	0	.313	206	361
Detroit	5	11	0	.313	273	332

Western Division

	W	L	T	Pct.	Pts.	OP
San Francisco	14	2	0	.875	431	236
New Orleans*	12	4	0	.750	330	202
Atlanta	6	10	0	.375	327	414
L.A. Rams	6	10	0	.375	313	383

*Wild-Card qualifier for playoffs

Miami finished ahead of Buffalo based on better conference record (9-3 to 7-5). Tampa Bay finished ahead of Chicago and Detroit based on better conference record (5-9 to Bears' 4-8 and Lions' 3-9). Atlanta finished ahead of L.A. Rams based on better record versus common opponents (5-7 to 4-8).

Wild Card playoffs: SAN DIEGO 17, Kansas City 0; BUFFALO 41, Houston 38 (OT)
Divisional playoffs: Buffalo 24, PITTSBURGH 3; MIAMI 31, San Diego 0
AFC championship: Buffalo 29, MIAMI 10
Wild Card playoffs: Washington 24, MINNESOTA 7; Philadelphia 36, NEW ORLEANS 20
Divisional playoffs: SAN FRANCISCO 20, Washington 13; DALLAS 34, Philadelphia 10
NFC championship: Dallas 30, SAN FRANCISCO 20
Super Bowl XXVII: Dallas (NFC) 52, Buffalo (AFC) 17, at Rose Bowl, Pasadena, California.

1991

AMERICAN CONFERENCE

Eastern Division

	W	L	T	Pct.	Pts.	OP
Buffalo	13	3	0	.813	458	318
N.Y. Jets*	8	8	0	.500	314	293
Miami	8	8	0	.500	343	349
New England	6	10	0	.375	211	305
Indianapolis	1	15	0	.063	143	381

Central Division

	W	L	T	Pct.	Pts.	OP
Houston	11	5	0	.688	386	251
Pittsburgh	7	9	0	.438	292	344
Cleveland	6	10	0	.375	293	298
Cincinnati	3	13	0	.188	263	435

Western Division

	W	L	T	Pct.	Pts.	OP
Denver	12	4	0	.750	304	235
Kansas City*	10	6	0	.625	322	252
L.A. Raiders*	9	7	0	.563	298	297
Seattle	7	9	0	.438	276	261
San Diego	4	12	0	.250	274	342

NATIONAL CONFERENCE

Eastern Division

	W	L	T	Pct.	Pts.	OP
Washington	14	2	0	.875	485	224
Dallas*	11	5	0	.688	342	310
Philadelphia	10	6	0	.625	285	244
N.Y. Giants	8	8	0	.500	281	297
Phoenix	4	12	0	.250	196	344

Central Division

	W	L	T	Pct.	Pts.	OP
Detroit	12	4	0	.750	339	295
Chicago*	11	5	0	.688	299	269
Minnesota	8	8	0	.500	301	306
Green Bay	4	12	0	.250	273	313
Tampa Bay	3	13	0	.188	199	365

Western Division

	W	L	T	Pct.	Pts.	OP
New Orleans	11	5	0	.688	341	211
Atlanta*	10	6	0	.625	361	338
San Francisco	10	6	0	.625	393	239
L.A. Rams	3	13	0	.188	234	390

*Wild-Card qualifiers for playoffs

New York Jets finished ahead of Miami based on head-to-head sweep (2-0). Atlanta finished ahead of San Francisco based on head-to-head sweep (2-0).

Wild Card playoffs: KANSAS CITY 10, L.A. Raiders 6; HOUSTON 17, N.Y. Jets 10
Divisional playoffs: DENVER 26, Houston 24; BUFFALO 37, Kansas City 14
AFC championship: BUFFALO 10, Denver 7
Wild Card playoffs: Atlanta 27, NEW ORLEANS 20; Dallas 17, CHICAGO 13
Divisional playoffs: WASHINGTON 24, Atlanta 7; DETROIT 38, Dallas 6
NFC championship: WASHINGTON 41, Detroit 10
Super Bowl XXVI: Washington (NFC) 37, Buffalo (AFC) 24, at Hubert H. Humphrey Metrodome, Minneapolis, Minnesota.

1990

AMERICAN CONFERENCE

Eastern Division

	W	L	T	Pct.	Pts.	OP
Buffalo	13	3	0	.813	428	263
Miami*	12	4	0	.750	336	242
Indianapolis	7	9	0	.438	281	353
N.Y. Jets	6	10	0	.375	295	345
New England	1	15	0	.063	181	446

Central Division

	W	L	T	Pct.	Pts.	OP
Cincinnati	9	7	0	.563	360	352
Houston*	9	7	0	.563	405	307
Pittsburgh	9	7	0	.563	292	240
Cleveland	3	13	0	.188	228	462

Western Division

	W	L	T	Pct.	Pts.	OP
L.A. Raiders	12	4	0	.750	337	268
Kansas City*	11	5	0	.688	369	257
Seattle	9	7	0	.563	306	286
San Diego	6	10	0	.375	315	281
Denver	5	11	0	.313	331	374

NATIONAL CONFERENCE

Eastern Division

	W	L	T	Pct.	Pts.	OP
N.Y. Giants	13	3	0	.813	335	211
Philadelphia*	10	6	0	.625	396	299
Washington*	10	6	0	.625	381	301
Dallas	7	9	0	.438	244	308
Phoenix	5	11	0	.313	268	396

Central Division

	W	L	T	Pct.	Pts.	OP
Chicago	11	5	0	.688	348	280
Tampa Bay	6	10	0	.375	264	367
Detroit	6	10	0	.375	373	413
Green Bay	6	10	0	.375	271	347
Minnesota	6	10	0	.375	351	326

Western Division

	W	L	T	Pct.	Pts.	OP
San Francisco	14	2	0	.875	353	239
New Orleans*	8	8	0	.500	274	275
L.A. Rams	5	11	0	.313	345	412
Atlanta	5	11	0	.313	348	365

*Wild-Card qualifiers for playoffs

Cincinnati won AFC Central title based on best head-to-head record (3-1) vs. Houston (2-2) and Pittsburgh (1-3). Houston was Wild Card based on better conference record (8-4) than Seattle (7-5) and Pittsburgh (6-6). Philadelphia finished second in the NFC East based on better division record (5-3) than Washington (4-4). Tampa Bay was second in NFC Central based on 5-1 record vs. Detroit, Green Bay, and Minnesota. Detroit finished third based on best net division points (minus 8) vs. Green Bay (minus 40) in fourth. Minnesota was fifth based on 4-8 conference record. The Los Angeles Rams finished third in NFC West based on net points in division (plus 1) vs. Atlanta (minus 31).

Wild Card playoffs: MIAMI 17, Kansas City 16; CINCINNATI 41, Houston 14
Divisional playoffs: BUFFALO 44, Miami 34; L.A. RAIDERS 20, Cincinnati 10
AFC championship: BUFFALO 51, L.A. Raiders 3
Wild Card playoffs: Washington 20, PHILADELPHIA 6; CHICAGO 16, New Orleans 6
Divisional playoffs: SAN FRANCISCO 28, Washington 10; N.Y. GIANTS 31, Chicago 3
NFC championship: N.Y. Giants 15, SAN FRANCISCO 13
Super Bowl XXV: N.Y. Giants (NFC) 20, Buffalo (AFC) 19, at Tampa Stadium, Tampa, Florida.

1989

AMERICAN CONFERENCE

Eastern Division

	W	L	T	Pct.	Pts.	OP
Buffalo	9	7	0	.563	409	317
Indianapolis	8	8	0	.500	298	301
Miami	8	8	0	.500	331	379
New England	5	11	0	.313	297	391
N.Y. Jets	4	12	0	.250	253	411

Central Division

	W	L	T	Pct.	Pts.	OP
Cleveland	9	6	1	.594	334	254
Houston*	9	7	0	.563	365	412
Pittsburgh*	9	7	0	.563	265	326
Cincinnati	8	8	0	.500	404	285

Western Division

	W	L	T	Pct.	Pts.	OP
Denver	11	5	0	.688	362	226
Kansas City	8	7	1	.531	318	286
L.A. Raiders	8	8	0	.500	315	297
Seattle	7	9	0	.438	241	327
San Diego	6	10	0	.375	266	290

NATIONAL CONFERENCE

Eastern Division

	W	L	T	Pct.	Pts.	OP
N.Y. Giants	12	4	0	.750	348	252
Philadelphia*	11	5	0	.688	342	274
Washington	10	6	0	.625	386	308
Phoenix	5	11	0	.313	258	377
Dallas	1	15	0	.063	204	393

Central Division

	W	L	T	Pct.	Pts.	OP
Minnesota	10	6	0	.625	351	275
Green Bay	10	6	0	.625	362	356
Detroit	7	9	0	.438	312	364
Chicago	6	10	0	.375	358	377
Tampa Bay	5	11	0	.313	320	419

Western Division

	W	L	T	Pct.	Pts.	OP
San Francisco	14	2	0	.875	442	253
L.A. Rams*	11	5	0	.688	426	344
New Orleans	9	7	0	.563	386	301
Atlanta	3	13	0	.188	279	437

Wild-Card qualifiers for playoffs

Indianapolis finished ahead of Miami in AFC East because of better conference record (7-5 vs. 6-8). Houston finished ahead of Pittsburgh in AFC Central because of head-to-head sweep (2-0). Minnesota finished ahead of Green Bay in NFC Central because of better division record (6-2 vs. 5-3).

Wild Card playoff: Pittsburgh 26, HOUSTON 23 (OT)
Divisional playoffs: CLEVELAND 34, Buffalo 30; DENVER 24, Pittsburgh 23
AFC championship: DENVER 37, Cleveland 21
Wild Card playoff: L.A. Rams 21, PHILADELPHIA 7
Divisional playoffs: L.A. Rams 19, N.Y. GIANTS 13 (OT);
    SAN FRANCISCO 41, Minnesota 13
NFC championship: SAN FRANCISCO 30, L.A. Rams 3
Super Bowl XXIV: San Francisco (NFC) 55, Denver (AFC) 10, at Louisiana Superdome, New Orleans, Louisiana.

1988

AMERICAN CONFERENCE

Eastern Division

	W	L	T	Pct.	Pts.	OP
Buffalo	12	4	0	.750	329	237
Indianapolis	9	7	0	.563	354	315
New England	9	7	0	.563	250	284
N.Y. Jets	8	7	1	.531	372	354
Miami	6	10	0	.375	319	380

Central Division

	W	L	T	Pct.	Pts.	OP
Cincinnati	12	4	0	.750	448	329
Cleveland*	10	6	0	.625	304	288
Houston*	10	6	0	.625	424	365
Pittsburgh	5	11	0	.313	336	421

Western Division

	W	L	T	Pct.	Pts.	OP
Seattle	9	7	0	.563	339	329
Denver	8	8	0	.500	327	352
L.A. Raiders	7	9	0	.438	325	369
San Diego	6	10	0	.375	231	332
Kansas City	4	11	1	.281	254	320

NATIONAL CONFERENCE

Eastern Division

	W	L	T	Pct.	Pts.	OP
Philadelphia	10	6	0	.625	379	319
N.Y. Giants	10	6	0	.625	359	304
Washington	7	9	0	.438	345	387
Phoenix	7	9	0	.438	344	398
Dallas	3	13	0	.188	265	381

Central Division

	W	L	T	Pct.	Pts.	OP
Chicago	12	4	0	.750	312	215
Minnesota*	11	5	0	.688	406	233
Tampa Bay	5	11	0	.313	261	350
Detroit	4	12	0	.250	220	313
Green Bay	4	12	0	.250	240	315

Western Division

	W	L	T	Pct.	Pts.	OP
San Francisco	10	6	0	.625	369	294
L.A. Rams*	10	6	0	.625	407	293
New Orleans	10	6	0	.625	312	283
Atlanta	5	11	0	.313	244	315

Wild-Card qualifiers for playoffs

Indianapolis finished second in AFC East on basis of better record versus common opponents (7-5) over New England (6-6). Cleveland gained first AFC Wild-Card position based on better division record (4-2) over Houston (3-3). Philadelphia finished first in NFC East on basis of head-to-head sweep over New York Giants. Washington finished third in NFC East on basis of better division record (4-4) over Phoenix (3-5). Detroit finished fourth in NFC Central on basis of head-to-head sweep over Green Bay. San Francisco finished first in NFC West based on better head-to-head record (3-1) over Los Angeles Rams (2-2) and New Orleans (1-3). Los Angeles Rams finished second in NFC West on basis of better division record (4-2) over New Orleans (3-3) and earned Wild-Card position based on better conference record (8-4) over New York Giants (9-5) and New Orleans (6-6).

Wild Card playoff: Houston 24, CLEVELAND 23
Divisional playoffs: CINCINNATI 21, Seattle 13; BUFFALO 17, Houston 10
AFC championship: CINCINNATI 21, Buffalo 10
Wild Card playoff: MINNESOTA 28, Los Angeles Rams 17
Divisional playoffs: CHICAGO 20, Philadelphia 12
    SAN FRANCISCO 34, Minnesota 9
NFC championship: San Francisco 28, CHICAGO 3
Super Bowl XXIII: San Francisco (NFC) 20, Cincinnati (AFC) 16, at Joe Robbie Stadium, Miami, Florida.

1987

AMERICAN CONFERENCE

Eastern Division

	W	L	T	Pct.	Pts.	OP
Indianapolis	9	6	0	.600	300	238
New England	8	7	0	.533	320	293
Miami	8	7	0	.533	362	335
Buffalo	7	8	0	.467	270	305
N.Y. Jets	6	9	0	.400	334	360

Central Division

	W	L	T	Pct.	Pts.	OP
Cleveland	10	5	0	.667	390	239
Houston*	9	6	0	.600	345	349
Pittsburgh	8	7	0	.533	285	299
Cincinnati	4	11	0	.267	285	370

Western Division

	W	L	T	Pct.	Pts.	OP
Denver	10	4	1	.700	379	288
Seattle*	9	6	0	.600	371	314
San Diego	8	7	0	.533	253	317
L.A. Raiders	5	10	0	.333	301	289
Kansas City	4	11	0	.267	273	388

NATIONAL CONFERENCE

Eastern Division

	W	L	T	Pct.	Pts.	OP
Washington	11	4	0	.733	379	285
Dallas	7	8	0	.467	340	348
St. Louis	7	8	0	.467	362	368
Philadelphia	7	8	0	.467	337	380
N.Y. Giants	6	9	0	.400	280	312

Central Division

	W	L	T	Pct.	Pts.	OP
Chicago	11	4	0	.733	356	282
Minnesota*	8	7	0	.533	336	335
Green Bay	5	9	1	.367	255	300
Tampa Bay	4	11	0	.267	286	360
Detroit	4	11	0	.267	269	384

Western Division

	W	L	T	Pct.	Pts.	OP
San Francisco	13	2	0	.867	459	253
New Orleans*	12	3	0	.800	422	283
L.A. Rams	6	9	0	.400	317	361
Atlanta	3	12	0	.200	205	436

Wild-Card qualifiers for playoffs

Houston gained first AFC Wild-Card position on better conference record (7-4) over Seattle (5-6).

Wild Card playoff: HOUSTON 23, Seattle 20 (OT)
Divisional playoffs: CLEVELAND 38, Indianapolis 21; DENVER 34, Houston 10
AFC championship: DENVER 38, Cleveland 33
Wild Card playoff: Minnesota 44, NEW ORLEANS 10
Divisional playoffs: Minnesota 36, SAN FRANCISCO 24; Washington 21, CHICAGO 17
NFC championship: WASHINGTON 17, Minnesota 10
Super Bowl XXII: Washington (NFC) 42, Denver (AFC) 10, at San Diego Jack Murphy Stadium, San Diego, California.
Note: 1987 regular season was reduced from 16 to 15 games for each team due to players' strike.

1986

AMERICAN CONFERENCE

Eastern Division

	W	L	T	Pct.	Pts.	OP
New England	11	5	0	.688	412	307
N.Y. Jets*	10	6	0	.625	364	386
Miami	8	8	0	.500	430	405
Buffalo	4	12	0	.250	287	348
Indianapolis	3	13	0	.188	229	400

Central Division

	W	L	T	Pct.	Pts.	OP
Cleveland	12	4	0	.750	391	310
Cincinnati	10	6	0	.625	409	394
Pittsburgh	6	10	0	.375	307	336
Houston	5	11	0	.313	274	329

Western Division

	W	L	T	Pct.	Pts.	OP
Denver	11	5	0	.688	378	327
Kansas City*	10	6	0	.625	358	326
Seattle	10	6	0	.625	366	293
L.A. Raiders	8	8	0	.500	323	346
San Diego	4	12	0	.250	335	396

NATIONAL CONFERENCE

Eastern Division

	W	L	T	Pct.	Pts.	OP
N.Y. Giants	14	2	0	.875	371	236
Washington*	12	4	0	.750	368	296
Dallas	7	9	0	.438	346	337
Philadelphia	5	10	1	.344	256	312
St. Louis	4	11	1	.281	218	351

Central Division

	W	L	T	Pct.	Pts.	OP
Chicago	14	2	0	.875	352	187
Minnesota	9	7	0	.563	398	273
Detroit	5	11	0	.313	277	326
Green Bay	4	12	0	.250	254	418
Tampa Bay	2	14	0	.125	239	473

Western Division

	W	L	T	Pct.	Pts.	OP
San Francisco	10	5	1	.656	374	247
L.A. Rams*	10	6	0	.625	309	267
Atlanta	7	8	1	.469	280	280
New Orleans	7	9	0	.438	288	287

Wild-Card qualifiers for playoffs

New York Jets gained first AFC Wild-Card position on better conference record (8-4) over Kansas City (9-5), Seattle (7-5), and Cincinnati (7-5). Kansas City gained second Wild Card based on better conference record (7-5) over Seattle (7-5) and Cincinnati (7-5).

Wild Card playoff: NEW YORK JETS 35, Kansas City 15
Divisional playoffs: CLEVELAND 23, New York Jets 20 (OT)
    DENVER 22, New England 17
AFC championship: Denver 23, CLEVELAND 20 (OT)
Wild Card playoff: WASHINGTON 19, Los Angeles Rams 7
Divisional playoffs: Washington 27, CHICAGO 13
    NEW YORK GIANTS 49, San Francisco 3
NFC championship: NEW YORK GIANTS 17, Washington 0
Super Bowl XXI: New York Giants (NFC) 39, Denver (AFC) 20, at Rose Bowl, Pasadena, California.

1985

AMERICAN CONFERENCE
Eastern Division

	W	L	T	Pct.	Pts.	OP
Miami	12	4	0	.750	428	320
N.Y. Jets*	11	5	0	.688	393	264
New England*	11	5	0	.688	362	290
Indianapolis	5	11	0	.313	320	386
Buffalo	2	14	0	.125	200	381

Central Division

	W	L	T	Pct.	Pts.	OP
Cleveland	8	8	0	.500	287	294
Cincinnati	7	9	0	.438	441	437
Pittsburgh	7	9	0	.438	379	355
Houston	5	11	0	.313	284	412

Western Division

	W	L	T	Pct.	Pts.	OP
L.A. Raiders	12	4	0	.750	354	308
Denver	11	5	0	.688	380	329
Seattle	8	8	0	.500	349	303
San Diego	8	8	0	.500	467	435
Kansas City	6	10	0	.375	317	360

NATIONAL CONFERENCE
Eastern Division

	W	L	T	Pct.	Pts.	OP
Dallas	10	6	0	.625	357	333
N.Y. Giants*	10	6	0	.625	399	283
Washington	10	6	0	.625	297	312
Philadelphia	7	9	0	.438	286	310
St. Louis	5	11	0	.313	278	414

Central Division

	W	L	T	Pct.	Pts.	OP
Chicago	15	1	0	.938	456	198
Green Bay	8	8	0	.500	337	355
Minnesota	7	9	0	.438	346	359
Detroit	7	9	0	.438	307	366
Tampa Bay	2	14	0	.125	294	448

Western Division

	W	L	T	Pct.	Pts.	OP
L.A. Rams	11	5	0	.688	340	277
San Francisco*	10	6	0	.625	411	263
New Orleans	5	11	0	.313	294	401
Atlanta	4	12	0	.250	282	452

*Wild-Card qualifiers for playoffs

New York Jets gained first AFC Wild-Card position on better conference record (9-3) over New England (8-4) and Denver (8-4). New England gained second AFC Wild-Card position based on better record vs. common opponents (4-2) than Denver (3-3). Dallas won NFC Eastern Division title based on better record (4-0) vs. New York Giants (1-3) and Washington (1-3). New York Giants gained first NFC Wild Card position based on better conference record (8-4) over San Francisco (7-5) and Washington (6-6). San Francisco gained second NFC Wild-Card position based on head-to-head victory over Washington.
Wild Card playoff: New England 26, NEW YORK JETS 14
Divisional playoffs: MIAMI 24, Cleveland 21;
    New England 27, LOS ANGELES RAIDERS 20
AFC championship: New England 31, MIAMI 14
Wild Card playoff: NEW YORK GIANTS 17, San Francisco 3
Divisional playoffs: LOS ANGELES RAMS 20, Dallas 0;
    CHICAGO 21, New York Giants 0
NFC championship: CHICAGO 24, Los Angeles Rams 0
Super Bowl XX: Chicago (NFC) 46, New England (AFC) 10, at Louisiana
    Superdome, New Orleans, Louisiana.

1984

AMERICAN CONFERENCE
Eastern Division

	W	L	T	Pct.	Pts.	OP
Miami	14	2	0	.875	513	298
New England	9	7	0	.563	362	352
N.Y. Jets	7	9	0	.438	332	364
Indianapolis	4	12	0	.250	239	414
Buffalo	2	14	0	.125	250	454

Central Division

	W	L	T	Pct.	Pts.	OP
Pittsburgh	9	7	0	.563	387	310
Cincinnati	8	8	0	.500	339	339
Cleveland	5	11	0	.313	250	297
Houston	3	13	0	.188	240	437

Western Division

	W	L	T	Pct.	Pts.	OP
Denver	13	3	0	.813	353	241
Seattle*	12	4	0	.750	418	282
L.A. Raiders*	11	5	0	.688	368	278
Kansas City	8	8	0	.500	314	324
San Diego	7	9	0	.438	394	413

NATIONAL CONFERENCE
Eastern Division

	W	L	T	Pct.	Pts.	OP
Washington	11	5	0	.688	426	310
N.Y. Giants*	9	7	0	.563	299	301
St. Louis	9	7	0	.563	423	345
Dallas	9	7	0	.563	308	308
Philadelphia	6	9	1	.406	278	320

Central Division

	W	L	T	Pct.	Pts.	OP
Chicago	10	6	0	.625	325	248
Green Bay	8	8	0	.500	390	309
Tampa Bay	6	10	0	.375	335	380
Detroit	4	11	1	.281	283	408
Minnesota	3	13	0	.188	276	484

Western Division

	W	L	T	Pct.	Pts.	OP
San Francisco	15	1	0	.938	475	227
L.A. Rams*	10	6	0	.625	346	316
New Orleans	7	9	0	.438	298	361
Atlanta	4	12	0	.250	281	382

*Wild-Card qualifiers for playoffs

New York Giants clinched Wild-Card berth based on 3-1 record vs. St. Louis's 2-2 and Dallas's 1-3. St. Louis finished ahead of Dallas based on better division record (5-3 to 3-5).
Wild Card playoff: SEATTLE 13, Los Angeles Raiders 7
Divisional playoffs: MIAMI 31, Seattle 10; Pittsburgh 24, DENVER 17
AFC championship: MIAMI 45, Pittsburgh 28
Wild Card playoff: New York Giants 16, LOS ANGELES RAMS 13
Divisional playoffs: SAN FRANCISCO 21, New York Giants 10;
    Chicago 23, WASHINGTON 19
NFC championship: SAN FRANCISCO 23, Chicago 0
Super Bowl XIX: San Francisco (NFC) 38, Miami (AFC) 16, at Stanford Stadium,
    Stanford, California.

1983

AMERICAN CONFERENCE
Eastern Division

	W	L	T	Pct.	Pts.	OP
Miami	12	4	0	.750	389	250
New England	8	8	0	.500	274	289
Buffalo	8	8	0	.500	283	351
Baltimore	7	9	0	.438	264	354
N.Y. Jets	7	9	0	.438	313	331

Central Division

	W	L	T	Pct.	Pts.	OP
Pittsburgh	10	6	0	.625	355	303
Cleveland	9	7	0	.563	356	342
Cincinnati	7	9	0	.438	346	302
Houston	2	14	0	.125	288	460

Western Division

	W	L	T	Pct.	Pts.	OP
L.A. Raiders	12	4	0	.750	442	338
Seattle*	9	7	0	.563	403	397
Denver*	9	7	0	.563	302	327
San Diego	6	10	0	.375	358	462
Kansas City	6	10	0	.375	386	367

NATIONAL CONFERENCE
Eastern Division

	W	L	T	Pct.	Pts.	OP
Washington	14	2	0	.875	541	332
Dallas*	12	4	0	.750	479	360
St. Louis	8	7	1	.531	374	428
Philadelphia	5	11	0	.313	233	322
N.Y. Giants	3	12	1	.219	267	347

Central Division

	W	L	T	Pct.	Pts.	OP
Detroit	9	7	0	.563	347	286
Green Bay	8	8	0	.500	429	439
Chicago	8	8	0	.500	311	301
Minnesota	8	8	0	.500	316	348
Tampa Bay	2	14	0	.125	241	380

Western Division

	W	L	T	Pct.	Pts.	OP
San Francisco	10	6	0	.625	432	293
L.A. Rams*	9	7	0	.563	361	344
New Orleans	8	8	0	.500	319	337
Atlanta	7	9	0	.438	370	389

*Wild-Card qualifiers for playoffs

Seattle and Denver gained Wild-Card berths over Cleveland because of their victories over the Browns.
Wild Card playoff: SEATTLE 31, Denver 7
Divisional playoffs: Seattle 27, MIAMI 20; LOS ANGELES RAIDERS 38, Pittsburgh 10
AFC championship: LOS ANGELES RAIDERS 30, Seattle 14
Wild Card playoff: Los Angeles Rams 24, DALLAS 17
Divisional playoffs: SAN FRANCISCO 24, Detroit 23; WASHINGTON 51, L.A. Rams 7
NFC championship: WASHINGTON 24, San Francisco 21
Super Bowl XVIII: Los Angeles Raiders (AFC) 38, Washington (NFC) 9, at Tampa
    Stadium, Tampa, Florida.

1982

AMERICAN CONFERENCE

	W	L	T	Pct.	Pts.	OP
L.A. Raiders	8	1	0	.889	260	200
Miami	7	2	0	.778	198	131
Cincinnati	7	2	0	.778	232	177
Pittsburgh	6	3	0	.667	204	146
San Diego	6	3	0	.667	288	221
N.Y. Jets	6	3	0	.667	245	166
New England	5	4	0	.556	143	157
Cleveland	4	5	0	.444	140	182
Buffalo	4	5	0	.444	150	154
Seattle	4	5	0	.444	127	147
Kansas City	3	6	0	.333	176	184
Denver	2	7	0	.222	148	226
Houston	1	8	0	.111	136	245
Baltimore	0	8	1	.056	113	236

NATIONAL CONFERENCE

	W	L	T	Pct.	Pts.	OP
Washington	8	1	0	.889	190	128
Dallas	6	3	0	.667	226	145
Green Bay	5	3	1	.611	226	169
Minnesota	5	4	0	.556	187	198
Atlanta	5	4	0	.556	183	199
St. Louis	5	4	0	.556	135	170
Tampa Bay	5	4	0	.556	158	178
Detroit	4	5	0	.444	181	176
New Orleans	4	5	0	.444	129	160
N.Y. Giants	4	5	0	.444	164	160
San Francisco	3	6	0	.333	209	206
Chicago	3	6	0	.333	141	174
Philadelphia	3	6	0	.333	191	195
L.A. Rams	2	7	0	.222	200	250

As the result of a 57-day players' strike, the 1982 NFL regular season schedule was reduced from 16 weeks to 9. At the conclusion of the regular season, the NFL conducted a 16-team postseason Super Bowl Tournament. Eight teams from each conference were seeded 1-8 based on their records during the season.

Miami finished ahead of Cincinnati based on better conference record (6-1 to 6-2). Pittsburgh won common games tie-breaker with San Diego (3-1 to 2-1) after New York Jets were eliminated from three-way tie based on conference record (Pittsburgh and San Diego 5-3 vs. Jets 2-3). Cleveland finished ahead of Buffalo and Seattle based on better conference record (4-3 to 3-3 to 3-5). Minnesota (4-1), Atlanta (4-3), St. Louis (5-4), Tampa Bay (3-3) seeds were determined by best won-lost record in conference games. Detroit finished ahead of New Orleans and the New York Giants based on better conference record (4-4 to 3-5 to 3-5).

First round playoff: MIAMI 28, New England 13
    LOS ANGELES RAIDERS 27, Cleveland 10
    New York Jets 44, CINCINNATI 17
    San Diego 31, PITTSBURGH 28
Second round playoff: New York Jets 17, LOS ANGELES RAIDERS 14
    MIAMI 34, San Diego 13
AFC championship: MIAMI 14, New York Jets 0
First round playoff: WASHINGTON 31, Detroit 7
    GREEN BAY 41, St. Louis 16
    MINNESOTA 30, Atlanta 24
    DALLAS 30, Tampa Bay 17
Second round playoff: WASHINGTON 21, Minnesota 7
    DALLAS 37, Green Bay 26
NFC championship: WASHINGTON 31, Dallas 17
Super Bowl XVII: Washington (NFC) 27, Miami (AFC) 17, at Rose Bowl,
    Pasadena, California.

1981

AMERICAN CONFERENCE

Eastern Division

	W	L	T	Pct.	Pts.	OP
Miami	11	4	1	.719	345	275
N.Y. Jets*	10	5	1	.656	355	287
Buffalo*	10	6	0	.625	311	276
Baltimore	2	14	0	.125	259	533
New England	2	14	0	.125	322	370

Central Division

	W	L	T	Pct.	Pts.	OP
Cincinnati	12	4	0	.750	421	304
Pittsburgh	8	8	0	.500	356	297
Houston	7	9	0	.438	281	355
Cleveland	5	11	0	.313	276	375

Western Division

	W	L	T	Pct.	Pts.	OP
San Diego	10	6	0	.625	478	390
Denver	10	6	0	.625	321	289
Kansas City	9	7	0	.563	343	290
Oakland	7	9	0	.438	273	343
Seattle	6	10	0	.375	322	388

NATIONAL CONFERENCE

Eastern Division

	W	L	T	Pct.	Pts.	OP
Dallas	12	4	0	.750	367	277
Philadelphia*	10	6	0	.625	368	221
N.Y. Giants*	9	7	0	.563	295	257
Washington	8	8	0	.500	347	349
St. Louis	7	9	0	.438	315	408

Central Division

	W	L	T	Pct.	Pts.	OP
Tampa Bay	9	7	0	.563	315	268
Detroit	8	8	0	.500	397	322
Green Bay	8	8	0	.500	324	361
Minnesota	7	9	0	.438	325	369
Chicago	6	10	0	.375	253	324

Western Division

	W	L	T	Pct.	Pts.	OP
San Francisco	13	3	0	.813	357	250
Atlanta	7	9	0	.438	426	355
Los Angeles	6	10	0	.375	303	351
New Orleans	4	12	0	.250	207	378

Wild-Card qualifiers for playoffs

San Diego won AFC Western title over Denver on the basis of a better division record (6-2 to 5-3). Buffalo won a Wild-Card playoff berth over Denver as the result of a 9-7 victory in head-to-head competition.

Wild Card playoff: Buffalo 31, NEW YORK JETS 27

Divisional playoffs: San Diego 41, MIAMI 38 (OT); CINCINNATI 28, Buffalo 21

AFC championship: CINCINNATI 27, San Diego 7

Wild Card playoff: New York Giants 27, PHILADELPHIA 21

Divisional playoffs: DALLAS 38, Tampa Bay 0; SAN FRANCISCO 38, New York Giants 24

NFC championship: SAN FRANCISCO 28, Dallas 27

Super Bowl XVI: San Francisco (NFC) 26, Cincinnati (AFC) 21, at Silverdome, Pontiac, Michigan.

1980

AMERICAN CONFERENCE

Eastern Division

	W	L	T	Pct.	Pts.	OP
Buffalo	11	5	0	.688	320	260
New England	10	6	0	.625	441	325
Miami	8	8	0	.500	266	305
Baltimore	7	9	0	.438	355	387
N.Y. Jets	4	12	0	.250	302	395

Central Division

	W	L	T	Pct.	Pts.	OP
Cleveland	11	5	0	.688	357	310
Houston*	11	5	0	.688	295	251
Pittsburgh	9	7	0	.563	352	313
Cincinnati	6	10	0	.375	244	312

Western Division

	W	L	T	Pct.	Pts.	OP
San Diego	11	5	0	.688	418	327
Oakland*	11	5	0	.688	364	306
Kansas City	8	8	0	.500	319	336
Denver	8	8	0	.500	310	323
Seattle	4	12	0	.250	291	408

NATIONAL CONFERENCE

Eastern Division

	W	L	T	Pct.	Pts.	OP
Philadelphia	12	4	0	.750	384	222
Dallas*	12	4	0	.750	454	311
Washington	6	10	0	.375	261	293
St. Louis	5	11	0	.313	299	350
N.Y. Giants	4	12	0	.250	249	425

Central Division

	W	L	T	Pct.	Pts.	OP
Minnesota	9	7	0	.563	317	308
Detroit	9	7	0	.563	334	272
Chicago	7	9	0	.438	304	264
Tampa Bay	5	10	1	.344	271	341
Green Bay	5	10	1	.344	231	371

Western Division

	W	L	T	Pct.	Pts.	OP
Atlanta	12	4	0	.750	405	272
Los Angeles*	11	5	0	.688	424	289
San Francisco	6	10	0	.375	320	415
New Orleans	1	15	0	.063	291	487

Wild-Card qualifiers for playoffs

Philadelphia won division title over Dallas on the basis of best net points in division games (plus 84 net points to plus 50). Minnesota won division title because of a better conference record than Detroit (8-4 to 9-5). Cleveland won division title because of a better conference record than Houston (8-4 to 7-5). San Diego won division title over Oakland on the basis of best net points in division games (plus 60 net points to plus 37).

Wild Card playoff: OAKLAND 27, Houston 7

Divisional playoffs: SAN DIEGO 20, Buffalo 14; Oakland 14, CLEVELAND 12

AFC championship: Oakland 34, SAN DIEGO 27

Wild Card playoff: DALLAS 34, Los Angeles 13

Divisional playoffs: PHILADELPHIA 31, Minnesota 16; Dallas 30, ATLANTA 27

NFC championship: PHILADELPHIA 20, Dallas 7

Super Bowl XV: Oakland (AFC) 27, Philadelphia (NFC) 10, at Louisiana Superdome, New Orleans, Louisiana.

1979

AMERICAN CONFERENCE

Eastern Division

	W	L	T	Pct.	Pts.	OP
Miami	10	6	0	.625	341	257
New England	9	7	0	.563	411	326
N.Y. Jets	8	8	0	.500	337	383
Buffalo	7	9	0	.438	268	279
Baltimore	5	11	0	.313	271	351

Central Division

	W	L	T	Pct.	Pts.	OP
Pittsburgh	12	4	0	.750	416	262
Houston*	11	5	0	.688	362	331
Cleveland	9	7	0	.563	359	352
Cincinnati	4	12	0	.250	337	421

Western Division

	W	L	T	Pct.	Pts.	OP
San Diego	12	4	0	.750	411	246
Denver*	10	6	0	.625	289	262
Seattle	9	7	0	.563	378	372
Oakland	9	7	0	.563	365	337
Kansas City	7	9	0	.438	238	262

NATIONAL CONFERENCE

Eastern Division

	W	L	T	Pct.	Pts.	OP
Dallas	11	5	0	.688	371	313
Philadelphia*	11	5	0	.688	339	282
Washington	10	6	0	.625	348	295
N.Y. Giants	6	10	0	.375	237	323
St. Louis	5	11	0	.313	307	358

Central Division

	W	L	T	Pct.	Pts.	OP
Tampa Bay	10	6	0	.625	273	237
Chicago*	10	6	0	.625	306	249
Minnesota	7	9	0	.438	259	337
Green Bay	5	11	0	.313	246	316
Detroit	2	14	0	.125	219	365

Western Division

	W	L	T	Pct.	Pts.	OP
Los Angeles	9	7	0	.563	323	309
New Orleans	8	8	0	.500	370	360
Atlanta	6	10	0	.375	300	388
San Francisco	2	14	0	.125	308	416

Wild-Card qualifiers for playoffs

Dallas won division title because of a better conference record than Philadelphia (10-2 to 9-3). Tampa Bay won division title because of a better division record than Chicago (6-2 to 5-3). Chicago won a Wild-Card berth over Washington on the basis of best net points in all games (plus 57 net points to plus 53).

Wild Card playoff: HOUSTON 13, Denver 7

Divisional playoffs: Houston 17, SAN DIEGO 14; PITTSBURGH 34, Miami 14

AFC championship: PITTSBURGH 27, Houston 13

Wild Card playoff: PHILADELPHIA 27, Chicago 17

Divisional playoffs: TAMPA BAY 24, Philadelphia 17; Los Angeles 21, DALLAS 19

NFC championship: Los Angeles 9, TAMPA BAY 0

Super Bowl XIV: Pittsburgh (AFC) 31, Los Angeles (NFC) 19, at Rose Bowl, Pasadena, California.

1978

AMERICAN CONFERENCE

Eastern Division

	W	L	T	Pct.	Pts.	OP
New England	11	5	0	.688	358	286
Miami*	11	5	0	.688	372	254
N.Y. Jets	8	8	0	.500	359	364
Buffalo	5	11	0	.313	302	354
Baltimore	5	11	0	.313	239	421

Central Division

	W	L	T	Pct.	Pts.	OP
Pittsburgh	14	2	0	.875	356	195
Houston*	10	6	0	.625	283	298
Cleveland	8	8	0	.500	334	356
Cincinnati	4	12	0	.250	252	284

Western Division

	W	L	T	Pct.	Pts.	OP
Denver	10	6	0	.625	282	198
Oakland	9	7	0	.563	311	283
Seattle	9	7	0	.563	345	358
San Diego	9	7	0	.563	355	309
Kansas City	4	12	0	.250	243	327

NATIONAL CONFERENCE

Eastern Division

	W	L	T	Pct.	Pts.	OP
Dallas	12	4	0	.750	384	208
Philadelphia*	9	7	0	.563	270	250
Washington	8	8	0	.500	273	283
St. Louis	6	10	0	.375	248	296
N.Y. Giants	6	10	0	.375	264	298

Central Division

	W	L	T	Pct.	Pts.	OP
Minnesota	8	7	1	.531	294	306
Green Bay	8	7	1	.531	249	269
Detroit	7	9	0	.438	290	300
Chicago	7	9	0	.438	253	274
Tampa Bay	5	11	0	.313	241	259

Western Division

	W	L	T	Pct.	Pts.	OP
Los Angeles	12	4	0	.750	316	245
Atlanta*	9	7	0	.563	240	290
New Orleans	7	9	0	.438	281	298
San Francisco	2	14	0	.125	219	350

Wild-Card qualifiers for playoffs

New England won division title on the basis of a better division record than Miami (6-2 to 5-3). Minnesota won division title because of a better head-to-head record against Green Bay (1-0-1).

Wild Card playoff: Houston 17, MIAMI 9

Divisional playoffs: Houston 31, NEW ENGLAND 14; PITTSBURGH 33, Denver 10

AFC championship: PITTSBURGH 34, Houston 5

Wild Card playoff: ATLANTA 14, Philadelphia 13

Divisional playoffs: DALLAS 27, Atlanta 20; LOS ANGELES 34, Minnesota 10

NFC championship: Dallas 28, LOS ANGELES 0

Super Bowl XIII: Pittsburgh (AFC) 35, Dallas (NFC) 31, at Orange Bowl, Miami, Florida.

1977

AMERICAN CONFERENCE

Eastern Division

	W	L	T	Pct.	Pts.	OP
Baltimore	10	4	0	.714	295	221
Miami	10	4	0	.714	313	197
New England	9	5	0	.643	278	217
N.Y. Jets	3	11	0	.214	191	300
Buffalo	3	11	0	.214	160	313

Central Division

	W	L	T	Pct.	Pts.	OP
Pittsburgh	9	5	0	.643	283	243
Houston	8	6	0	.571	299	230
Cincinnati	8	6	0	.571	238	235
Cleveland	6	8	0	.429	269	267

Western Division

	W	L	T	Pct.	Pts.	OP
Denver	12	2	0	.857	274	148
Oakland*	11	3	0	.786	351	230
San Diego	7	7	0	.500	222	205
Seattle	5	9	0	.357	282	373
Kansas City	2	12	0	.143	225	349

NATIONAL CONFERENCE

Eastern Division

	W	L	T	Pct.	Pts.	OP
Dallas	12	2	0	.857	345	212
Washington	9	5	0	.643	196	189
St. Louis	7	7	0	.500	272	287
Philadelphia	5	9	0	.357	220	207
N.Y. Giants	5	9	0	.357	181	265

Central Division

	W	L	T	Pct.	Pts.	OP
Minnesota	9	5	0	.643	231	227
Chicago*	9	5	0	.643	255	253
Detroit	6	8	0	.429	183	252
Green Bay	4	10	0	.286	134	219
Tampa Bay	2	12	0	.143	103	223

Western Division

	W	L	T	Pct.	Pts.	OP
Los Angeles	10	4	0	.714	302	146
Atlanta	7	7	0	.500	179	129
San Francisco	5	9	0	.357	220	260
New Orleans	3	11	0	.214	232	336

Wild-Card qualifier for playoffs

Baltimore won division title on the basis of a better conference record than Miami (9-3 to 8-4). Chicago won a Wild-Card berth over Washington on the basis of best net points in conference games (plus 48 net points to plus 4).

Divisional playoffs: DENVER 34, Pittsburgh 21; Oakland 37, BALTIMORE 31 (OT)
AFC championship: DENVER 20, Oakland 17
Divisional playoffs: DALLAS 37, Chicago 7; Minnesota 14, LOS ANGELES 7
NFC championship: DALLAS 23, Minnesota 6
Super Bowl XII: Dallas (NFC) 27, Denver (AFC) 10, at Louisiana Superdome, New Orleans, Louisiana.

1976

AMERICAN CONFERENCE

Eastern Division

	W	L	T	Pct.	Pts.	OP
Baltimore	11	3	0	.786	417	246
New England*	11	3	0	.786	376	236
Miami	6	8	0	.429	263	264
N.Y. Jets	3	11	0	.214	169	383
Buffalo	2	12	0	.143	245	363

Central Division

	W	L	T	Pct.	Pts.	OP
Pittsburgh	10	4	0	.714	342	138
Cincinnati	10	4	0	.714	335	210
Cleveland	9	5	0	.643	267	287
Houston	5	9	0	.357	222	273

Western Division

	W	L	T	Pct.	Pts.	OP
Oakland	13	1	0	.929	350	237
Denver	9	5	0	.643	315	206
San Diego	6	8	0	.429	248	285
Kansas City	5	9	0	.357	290	376
Tampa Bay	0	14	0	.000	125	412

NATIONAL CONFERENCE

Eastern Division

	W	L	T	Pct.	Pts.	OP
Dallas	11	3	0	.786	296	194
Washington*	10	4	0	.714	291	217
St. Louis	10	4	0	.714	309	267
Philadelphia	4	10	0	.286	165	286
N.Y. Giants	3	11	0	.214	170	250

Central Division

	W	L	T	Pct.	Pts.	OP
Minnesota	11	2	1	.821	305	176
Chicago	7	7	0	.500	253	216
Detroit	6	8	0	.429	262	220
Green Bay	5	9	0	.357	218	299

Western Division

	W	L	T	Pct.	Pts.	OP
Los Angeles	10	3	1	.750	351	190
San Francisco	8	6	0	.571	270	190
Atlanta	4	10	0	.286	172	312
New Orleans	4	10	0	.286	253	346
Seattle	2	12	0	.143	229	429

Wild-Card qualifier for playoffs

Baltimore won division title on the basis of a better division record than New England (7-1 to 6-2). Pittsburgh won division title because of a two-game sweep over Cincinnati. Washington won Wild-Card berth over St. Louis because of a two-game sweep over Cardinals.

Divisional playoffs: OAKLAND 24, New England 21; Pittsburgh 40, BALTIMORE 14
AFC championship: OAKLAND 24, Pittsburgh 7
Divisional playoffs: MINNESOTA 35, Washington 20; Los Angeles 14, DALLAS 12
NFC championship: MINNESOTA 24, Los Angeles 13
Super Bowl XI: Oakland (AFC) 32, Minnesota (NFC) 14, at Rose Bowl, Pasadena, California.

1975

AMERICAN CONFERENCE

Eastern Division

	W	L	T	Pct.	Pts.	OP
Baltimore	10	4	0	.714	395	269
Miami	10	4	0	.714	357	222
Buffalo	8	6	0	.571	420	355
New England	3	11	0	.214	258	358
N.Y. Jets	3	11	0	.214	258	433

Central Division

	W	L	T	Pct.	Pts.	OP
Pittsburgh	12	2	0	.857	373	162
Cincinnati*	11	3	0	.786	340	246
Houston	10	4	0	.714	293	226
Cleveland	3	11	0	.214	218	372

Western Division

	W	L	T	Pct.	Pts.	OP
Oakland	11	3	0	.786	375	255
Denver	6	8	0	.429	254	307
Kansas City	5	9	0	.357	282	341
San Diego	2	12	0	.143	189	345

NATIONAL CONFERENCE

Eastern Division

	W	L	T	Pct.	Pts.	OP
St. Louis	11	3	0	.786	356	276
Dallas*	10	4	0	.714	350	268
Washington	8	6	0	.571	325	276
N.Y. Giants	5	9	0	.357	216	306
Philadelphia	4	10	0	.286	225	302

Central Division

	W	L	T	Pct.	Pts.	OP
Minnesota	12	2	0	.857	377	180
Detroit	7	7	0	.500	245	262
Chicago	4	10	0	.286	191	379
Green Bay	4	10	0	.286	226	285

Western Division

	W	L	T	Pct.	Pts.	OP
Los Angeles	12	2	0	.857	312	135
San Francisco	5	9	0	.357	255	286
Atlanta	4	10	0	.286	240	289
New Orleans	2	12	0	.143	165	360

Wild-Card qualifier for playoffs

Baltimore won division title on the basis of a two-game sweep over Miami.

Divisional playoffs: PITTSBURGH 28, Baltimore 10; OAKLAND 31, Cincinnati 28
AFC championship: PITTSBURGH 16, Oakland 10
Divisional playoffs: LOS ANGELES 35, St. Louis 23; Dallas 17, MINNESOTA 14
NFC championship: Dallas 37, LOS ANGELES 7
Super Bowl X: Pittsburgh (AFC) 21, Dallas (NFC) 17, at Orange Bowl, Miami, Florida.

1974

AMERICAN CONFERENCE

Eastern Division

	W	L	T	Pct.	Pts.	OP
Miami	11	3	0	.786	327	216
Buffalo*	9	5	0	.643	264	244
New England	7	7	0	.500	348	289
N.Y. Jets	7	7	0	.500	279	300
Baltimore	2	12	0	.143	190	329

Central Division

	W	L	T	Pct.	Pts.	OP
Pittsburgh	10	3	1	.750	305	189
Cincinnati	7	7	0	.500	283	259
Houston	7	7	0	.500	236	282
Cleveland	4	10	0	.286	251	344

Western Division

	W	L	T	Pct.	Pts.	OP
Oakland	12	2	0	.857	355	228
Denver	7	6	1	.536	302	294
Kansas City	5	9	0	.357	233	293
San Diego	5	9	0	.357	212	285

NATIONAL CONFERENCE

Eastern Division

	W	L	T	Pct.	Pts.	OP
St. Louis	10	4	0	.714	285	218
Washington*	10	4	0	.714	320	196
Dallas	8	6	0	.571	297	235
Philadelphia	7	7	0	.500	242	217
N.Y. Giants	2	12	0	.143	195	299

Central Division

	W	L	T	Pct.	Pts.	OP
Minnesota	10	4	0	.714	310	195
Detroit	7	7	0	.500	256	270
Green Bay	6	8	0	.429	210	206
Chicago	4	10	0	.286	152	279

Western Division

	W	L	T	Pct.	Pts.	OP
Los Angeles	10	4	0	.714	263	181
San Francisco	6	8	0	.429	226	236
New Orleans	5	9	0	.357	166	263
Atlanta	3	11	0	.214	111	271

Wild-Card qualifier for playoffs

St. Louis won division title because of a two-game sweep over Washington.

Divisional playoffs: OAKLAND 28, Miami 26; PITTSBURGH 32, Buffalo 14
AFC championship: Pittsburgh 24, OAKLAND 13
Divisional playoffs: MINNESOTA 30, St. Louis 14; LOS ANGELES 19, Washington 10
NFC championship: MINNESOTA 14, Los Angeles 10
Super Bowl IX: Pittsburgh (AFC) 16, Minnesota (NFC) 6, at Tulane Stadium, New Orleans, Louisiana.

1973

AMERICAN CONFERENCE

Eastern Division

	W	L	T	Pct.	Pts.	OP
Miami	12	2	0	.857	343	150
Buffalo	9	5	0	.643	259	230
New England	5	9	0	.357	258	300
Baltimore	4	10	0	.286	226	341
N.Y. Jets	4	10	0	.286	240	306

Central Division

	W	L	T	Pct.	Pts.	OP
Cincinnati	10	4	0	.714	286	231
Pittsburgh*	10	4	0	.714	347	210
Cleveland	7	5	2	.571	234	255
Houston	1	13	0	.071	199	447

Western Division

	W	L	T	Pct.	Pts.	OP
Oakland	9	4	1	.679	292	175
Denver	7	5	2	.571	354	296
Kansas City	7	5	2	.571	231	192
San Diego	2	11	1	.179	188	386

NATIONAL CONFERENCE

Eastern Division

	W	L	T	Pct.	Pts.	OP
Dallas	10	4	0	.714	382	203
Washington*	10	4	0	.714	325	198
Philadelphia	5	8	1	.393	310	393
St. Louis	4	9	1	.321	286	365
N.Y. Giants	2	11	1	.179	226	362

Central Division

	W	L	T	Pct.	Pts.	OP
Minnesota	12	2	0	.857	296	168
Detroit	6	7	1	.464	271	247
Green Bay	5	7	2	.429	202	259
Chicago	3	11	0	.214	195	334

Western Division

	W	L	T	Pct.	Pts.	OP
Los Angeles	12	2	0	.857	388	178
Atlanta	9	5	0	.643	318	224
New Orleans	5	9	0	.357	163	312
San Francisco	5	9	0	.357	262	319

Wild-Card qualifier for playoffs

Cincinnati won division title on the basis of a better conference record than Pittsburgh (8-3 to 7-4). Dallas won division title on the basis of a better point differential vs. Washington (net 13 points).

Divisional playoffs: OAKLAND 33, Pittsburgh 14; MIAMI 34, Cincinnati 16
AFC championship: MIAMI 27, Oakland 10
Divisional playoffs: MINNESOTA 27, Washington 20; DALLAS 27, Los Angeles 16
NFC championship: Minnesota 27, DALLAS 10
Super Bowl VIII: Miami (AFC) 24, Minnesota (NFC) 7, at Rice Stadium, Houston, Texas.

1972

AMERICAN CONFERENCE

Eastern Division

	W	L	T	Pct.	Pts.	OP
Miami	14	0	0	1.000	385	171
N.Y. Jets	7	7	0	.500	367	324
Baltimore	5	9	0	.357	235	252
Buffalo	4	9	1	.321	257	377
New England	3	11	0	.214	192	446

Central Division

	W	L	T	Pct.	Pts.	OP
Pittsburgh	11	3	0	.786	343	175
Cleveland*	10	4	0	.714	268	249
Cincinnati	8	6	0	.571	299	229
Houston	1	13	0	.071	164	380

Western Division

	W	L	T	Pct.	Pts.	OP
Oakland	10	3	1	.750	365	248
Kansas City	8	6	0	.571	287	254
Denver	5	9	0	.357	325	350
San Diego	4	9	1	.321	264	344

NATIONAL CONFERENCE

Eastern Division

	W	L	T	Pct.	Pts.	OP
Washington	11	3	0	.786	336	218
Dallas*	10	4	0	.714	319	240
N.Y. Giants	8	6	0	.571	331	247
St. Louis	4	9	1	.321	193	303
Philadelphia	2	11	1	.179	145	352

Central Division

	W	L	T	Pct.	Pts.	OP
Green Bay	10	4	0	.714	304	226
Detroit	8	5	1	.607	339	290
Minnesota	7	7	0	.500	301	252
Chicago	4	9	1	.321	225	275

Western Division

	W	L	T	Pct.	Pts.	OP
San Francisco	8	5	1	.607	353	249
Atlanta	7	7	0	.500	269	274
Los Angeles	6	7	1	.464	291	286
New Orleans	2	11	1	.179	215	361

Wild-Card qualifier for playoffs

Divisional playoffs: PITTSBURGH 13, Oakland 7; MIAMI 20, Cleveland 14
AFC championship: Miami 21, PITTSBURGH 17
Divisional playoffs: Dallas 30, SAN FRANCISCO 28; WASHINGTON 16, Green Bay 3
NFC championship: WASHINGTON 26, Dallas 3
Super Bowl VII: Miami (AFC) 14, Washington (NFC) 7, at Memorial Coliseum, Los Angeles, California.

1971

AMERICAN CONFERENCE

Eastern Division

	W	L	T	Pct.	Pts.	OP
Miami	10	3	1	.769	315	174
Baltimore*	10	4	0	.714	313	140
New England	6	8	0	.429	238	325
N.Y. Jets	6	8	0	.429	212	299
Buffalo	1	13	0	.071	184	394

Central Division

	W	L	T	Pct.	Pts.	OP
Cleveland	9	5	0	.643	285	273
Pittsburgh	6	8	0	.429	246	292
Houston	4	9	1	.308	251	330
Cincinnati	4	10	0	.286	284	265

Western Division

	W	L	T	Pct.	Pts.	OP
Kansas City	10	3	1	.769	302	208
Oakland	8	4	2	.667	344	278
San Diego	6	8	0	.429	311	341
Denver	4	9	1	.308	203	275

NATIONAL CONFERENCE

Eastern Division

	W	L	T	Pct.	Pts.	OP
Dallas	11	3	0	.786	406	222
Washington*	9	4	1	.692	276	190
Philadelphia	6	7	1	.462	221	302
St. Louis	4	9	1	.308	231	279
N.Y. Giants	4	10	0	.286	228	362

Central Division

	W	L	T	Pct.	Pts.	OP
Minnesota	11	3	0	.786	245	139
Detroit	7	6	1	.538	341	286
Chicago	6	8	0	.429	185	276
Green Bay	4	8	2	.333	274	298

Western Division

	W	L	T	Pct.	Pts.	OP
San Francisco	9	5	0	.643	300	216
Los Angeles	8	5	1	.615	313	260
Atlanta	7	6	1	.538	274	277
New Orleans	4	8	2	.333	266	347

Wild-Card qualifier for playoffs

Divisional playoffs: Miami 27, KANSAS CITY 24 (OT); Baltimore 20, CLEVELAND 3
AFC championship: MIAMI 21, Baltimore 0
Divisional playoffs: Dallas 20, MINNESOTA 12; SAN FRANCISCO 24, Washington 20
NFC championship: DALLAS 14, San Francisco 3
Super Bowl VI: Dallas (NFC) 24, Miami (AFC) 3, at Tulane Stadium, New Orleans, Louisiana.

1970

AMERICAN CONFERENCE

Eastern Division

	W	L	T	Pct.	Pts.	OP
Baltimore	11	2	1	.846	321	234
Miami*	10	4	0	.714	297	228
N.Y. Jets	4	10	0	.286	255	286
Buffalo	3	10	1	.231	204	337
Boston Patriots	2	12	0	.143	149	361

Central Division

	W	L	T	Pct.	Pts.	OP
Cincinnati	8	6	0	.571	312	255
Cleveland	7	7	0	.500	286	265
Pittsburgh	5	9	0	.357	210	272
Houston	3	10	1	.231	217	352

Western Division

	W	L	T	Pct.	Pts.	OP
Oakland	8	4	2	.667	300	293
Kansas City	7	5	2	.583	272	244
San Diego	5	6	3	.455	282	278
Denver	5	8	1	.385	253	264

NATIONAL CONFERENCE

Eastern Division

	W	L	T	Pct.	Pts.	OP
Dallas	10	4	0	.714	299	221
N.Y. Giants	9	5	0	.643	301	270
St. Louis	8	5	1	.615	325	228
Washington	6	8	0	.429	297	314
Philadelphia	3	10	1	.231	241	332

Central Division

	W	L	T	Pct.	Pts.	OP
Minnesota	12	2	0	.857	335	143
Detroit*	10	4	0	.714	347	202
Chicago	6	8	0	.429	256	261
Green Bay	6	8	0	.429	196	293

Western Division

	W	L	T	Pct.	Pts.	OP
San Francisco	10	3	1	.769	352	267
Los Angeles	9	4	1	.692	325	202
Atlanta	4	8	2	.333	206	261
New Orleans	2	11	1	.154	172	347

Wild-Card qualifier for playoffs

Divisional playoffs: BALTIMORE 17, Cincinnati 0; OAKLAND 21, Miami 14
AFC championship: BALTIMORE 27, Oakland 17
Divisional playoffs: DALLAS 5, Detroit 0; San Francisco 17, MINNESOTA 14
NFC championship: Dallas 17, SAN FRANCISCO 10
Super Bowl V: Baltimore (AFC) 16, Dallas (NFC) 13, at Orange Bowl, Miami, Florida.

1969 NFL

EASTERN CONFERENCE

Capitol Division

	W	L	T	Pct.	Pts.	OP
Dallas	11	2	1	.846	369	223
Washington	7	5	2	.583	307	319
New Orleans	5	9	0	.357	311	393
Philadelphia	4	9	1	.308	279	377

Century Division

	W	L	T	Pct.	Pts.	OP
Cleveland	10	3	1	.769	351	300
N.Y. Giants	6	8	0	.429	264	298
St. Louis	4	9	1	.308	314	389
Pittsburgh	1	13	0	.071	218	404

WESTERN CONFERENCE

Coastal Division

	W	L	T	Pct.	Pts.	OP
Los Angeles	11	3	0	.786	320	243
Baltimore	8	5	1	.615	279	268
Atlanta	6	8	0	.429	276	268
San Francisco	4	8	2	.333	277	319

Central Division

	W	L	T	Pct.	Pts.	OP
Minnesota	12	2	0	.857	379	133
Detroit	9	4	1	.692	259	188
Green Bay	8	6	0	.571	269	221
Chicago	1	13	0	.071	210	339

Conference championships: Cleveland 38, DALLAS 14; MINNESOTA 23, Los Angeles 20
NFL championship: MINNESOTA 27, Cleveland 7
Super Bowl IV: Kansas City (AFL) 23, Minnesota (NFL) 7, at Tulane Stadium, New Orleans, Louisiana

1969 AFL

EASTERN DIVISION	W	L	T	Pct.	Pts.	OP
N.Y. Jets	10	4	0	.714	353	269
Houston	6	6	2	.500	278	279
Boston Patriots	4	10	0	.286	266	316
Buffalo	4	10	0	.286	230	359
Miami	3	10	1	.231	233	332

WESTERN DIVISION	W	L	T	Pct.	Pts.	OP
Oakland	12	1	1	.923	377	242
Kansas City	11	3	0	.786	359	177
San Diego	8	6	0	.571	288	276
Denver	5	8	1	.385	297	344
Cincinnati	4	9	1	.308	280	367

Divisional playoffs: Kansas City 13, N.Y. JETS 6; OAKLAND 56, Houston 7
AFL championship: Kansas City 17, OAKLAND 7

1968 NFL

EASTERN CONFERENCE

Capitol Division	W	L	T	Pct.	Pts.	OP
Dallas	12	2	0	.857	431	186
N.Y. Giants	7	7	0	.500	294	325
Washington	5	9	0	.357	249	358
Philadelphia	2	12	0	.143	202	351

Century Division	W	L	T	Pct.	Pts.	OP
Cleveland	10	4	0	.714	394	273
St. Louis	9	4	1	.692	325	289
New Orleans	4	9	1	.308	246	327
Pittsburgh	2	11	1	.154	244	397

WESTERN CONFERENCE

Coastal Division	W	L	T	Pct.	Pts.	OP
Baltimore	13	1	0	.929	402	144
Los Angeles	10	3	1	.769	312	200
San Francisco	7	6	1	.538	303	310
Atlanta	2	12	0	.143	170	389

Central Division	W	L	T	Pct.	Pts.	OP
Minnesota	8	6	0	.571	282	242
Chicago	7	7	0	.500	250	333
Green Bay	6	7	1	.462	281	227
Detroit	4	8	2	.333	207	241

Conference championships: CLEVELAND 31, Dallas 20; BALTIMORE 24, Minnesota 14
NFL championship: Baltimore 34, CLEVELAND 0
Super Bowl III: N.Y. Jets (AFL) 16, Baltimore (NFL) 7, at Orange Bowl, Miami, Florida.

1968 AFL

EASTERN DIVISION	W	L	T	Pct.	Pts.	OP
N.Y. Jets	11	3	0	.786	419	280
Houston	7	7	0	.500	303	248
Miami	5	8	1	.385	276	355
Boston Patriots	4	10	0	.286	229	406
Buffalo	1	12	1	.077	199	367

WESTERN DIVISION	W	L	T	Pct.	Pts.	OP
Oakland	12	2	0	.857	453	233
Kansas City	12	2	0	.857	371	170
San Diego	9	5	0	.643	382	310
Denver	5	9	0	.357	255	404
Cincinnati	3	11	0	.214	215	329

Western Division playoff: OAKLAND 41, Kansas City 6
AFL championship: N.Y. JETS 27, Oakland 23

1967 NFL

EASTERN CONFERENCE

Capitol Division	W	L	T	Pct.	Pts.	OP
Dallas	9	5	0	.643	342	268
Philadelphia	6	7	1	.462	351	409
Washington	5	6	3	.455	347	353
New Orleans	3	11	0	.214	233	379

Century Division	W	L	T	Pct.	Pts.	OP
Cleveland	9	5	0	.643	334	297
N.Y. Giants	7	7	0	.500	369	379
St. Louis	6	7	1	.462	333	356
Pittsburgh	4	9	1	.308	281	320

WESTERN CONFERENCE

Coastal Division	W	L	T	Pct.	Pts.	OP
Los Angeles	11	1	2	.917	398	196
Baltimore	11	1	2	.917	394	198
San Francisco	7	7	0	.500	273	337
Atlanta	1	12	1	.077	175	422

Central Division	W	L	T	Pct.	Pts.	OP
Green Bay	9	4	1	.692	332	209
Chicago	7	6	1	.538	239	218
Detroit	5	7	2	.417	260	259
Minnesota	3	8	3	.273	233	294

Los Angeles won division title on the basis of advantage in points (58-34) in two games vs. Baltimore.
Conference championships: DALLAS 52, Cleveland 14; GREEN BAY 28, Los Angeles 7
NFL championship: GREEN BAY 21, Dallas 17
Super Bowl II: Green Bay (NFL) 33, Oakland (AFL) 14, at Orange Bowl, Miami, Florida.

1967 AFL

EASTERN DIVISION	W	L	T	Pct.	Pts.	OP
Houston	9	4	1	.692	258	199
N.Y. Jets	8	5	1	.615	371	329
Buffalo	4	10	0	.286	237	285
Miami	4	10	0	.286	219	407
Boston Patriots	3	10	1	.231	280	389

WESTERN DIVISION	W	L	T	Pct.	Pts.	OP
Oakland	13	1	0	.929	468	233
Kansas City	9	5	0	.643	408	254
San Diego	8	5	1	.615	360	352
Denver	3	11	0	.214	256	409

AFL championship: OAKLAND 40, Houston 7

1966 NFL

EASTERN CONFERENCE

	W	L	T	Pct.	Pts.	OP
Dallas	10	3	1	.769	445	239
Cleveland	9	5	0	.643	403	259
Philadelphia	9	5	0	.643	326	340
St. Louis	8	5	1	.615	264	265
Washington	7	7	0	.500	351	355
Pittsburgh	5	8	1	.385	316	347
Atlanta	3	11	0	.214	204	437
N.Y. Giants	1	12	1	.077	263	501

WESTERN CONFERENCE

	W	L	T	Pct.	Pts.	OP
Green Bay	12	2	0	.857	335	163
Baltimore	9	5	0	.643	314	226
Los Angeles	8	6	0	.571	289	212
San Francisco	6	6	2	.500	320	325
Chicago	5	7	2	.417	234	272
Detroit	4	9	1	.308	206	317
Minnesota	4	9	1	.308	292	304

NFL championship: Green Bay 34, DALLAS 27
Super Bowl I: Green Bay (NFL) 35, Kansas City (AFL) 10, at Memorial Coliseum, Los Angeles, California.

1966 AFL

EASTERN DIVISION	W	L	T	Pct.	Pts.	OP
Buffalo	9	4	1	.692	358	255
Boston Patriots	8	4	2	.677	315	283
N.Y. Jets	6	6	2	.500	322	312
Houston	3	11	0	.214	335	396
Miami	3	11	0	.214	213	362

WESTERN DIVISION	W	L	T	Pct.	Pts.	OP
Kansas City	11	2	1	.846	448	276
Oakland	8	5	1	.615	315	288
San Diego	7	6	1	.538	335	284
Denver	4	10	0	.286	196	381

AFL championship: Kansas City 31, BUFFALO 7

1965 NFL

EASTERN CONFERENCE

	W	L	T	Pct.	Pts.	OP
Cleveland	11	3	0	.786	363	325
Dallas	7	7	0	.500	325	280
N.Y. Giants	7	7	0	.500	270	338
Washington	6	8	0	.429	257	301
Philadelphia	5	9	0	.357	363	359
St. Louis	5	9	0	.357	296	309
Pittsburgh	2	12	0	.143	202	397

WESTERN CONFERENCE

	W	L	T	Pct.	Pts.	OP
Green Bay	10	3	1	.769	316	224
Baltimore	10	3	1	.769	389	284
Chicago	9	5	0	.643	409	275
San Francisco	7	6	1	.538	421	402
Minnesota	7	7	0	.500	383	403
Detroit	6	7	1	.462	257	295
Los Angeles	4	10	0	.286	269	328

Western Conference playoff: GREEN BAY 13, Baltimore 10 (OT)
NFL championship: GREEN BAY 23, Cleveland 12

1965 AFL

EASTERN DIVISION	W	L	T	Pct.	Pts.	OP
Buffalo	10	3	1	.769	313	226
N.Y. Jets	5	8	1	.385	285	303
Boston Patriots	4	8	2	.333	244	302
Houston	4	10	0	.286	298	429

WESTERN DIVISION	W	L	T	Pct.	Pts.	OP
San Diego	9	2	3	.818	340	227
Oakland	8	5	1	.615	298	239
Kansas City	7	5	2	.583	322	285
Denver	4	10	0	.286	303	392

AFL championship: Buffalo 23, SAN DIEGO 0

1964 NFL

EASTERN CONFERENCE

	W	L	T	Pct.	Pts.	OP
Cleveland	10	3	1	.769	415	293
St. Louis	9	3	2	.750	357	331
Philadelphia	6	8	0	.429	312	313
Washington	6	8	0	.429	307	305
Dallas	5	8	1	.385	250	289
Pittsburgh	5	9	0	.357	253	315
N.Y. Giants	2	10	2	.167	241	399

WESTERN CONFERENCE

	W	L	T	Pct.	Pts.	OP
Baltimore	12	2	0	.857	428	225
Green Bay	8	5	1	.615	342	245
Minnesota	8	5	1	.615	355	296
Detroit	7	5	2	.583	280	260
Los Angeles	5	7	2	.417	283	339
Chicago	5	9	0	.357	260	379
San Francisco	4	10	0	.286	236	330

NFL championship: CLEVELAND 27, Baltimore 0

1964 AFL

EASTERN DIVISION	W	L	T	Pct.	Pts.	OP
Buffalo	12	2	0	.857	400	242
Boston Patriots	10	3	1	.769	365	297
N.Y. Jets	5	8	1	.385	278	315
Houston	4	10	0	.286	310	355

WESTERN DIVISION	W	L	T	Pct.	Pts.	OP
San Diego	8	5	1	.615	341	300
Kansas City	7	7	0	.500	366	306
Oakland	5	7	2	.417	303	350
Denver	2	11	1	.154	240	438

AFL championship: BUFFALO 20, San Diego 7

1963 NFL

EASTERN CONFERENCE

	W	L	T	Pct.	Pts.	OP
N.Y. Giants	11	3	0	.786	448	280
Cleveland	10	4	0	.714	343	262
St. Louis	9	5	0	.643	341	283
Pittsburgh	7	4	3	.636	321	295
Dallas	4	10	0	.286	305	378
Washington	3	11	0	.214	279	398
Philadelphia	2	10	2	.167	242	381

WESTERN CONFERENCE

	W	L	T	Pct.	Pts.	OP
Chicago	11	1	2	.917	301	144
Green Bay	11	2	1	.846	369	206
Baltimore	8	6	0	.571	316	285
Detroit	5	8	1	.385	326	265
Minnesota	5	8	1	.385	309	390
Los Angeles	5	9	0	.357	210	350
San Francisco	2	12	0	.143	198	391

NFL championship: CHICAGO 14, N.Y. Giants 10

1963 AFL

EASTERN DIVISION	W	L	T	Pct.	Pts.	OP	WESTERN DIVISION	W	L	T	Pct.	Pts.	OP
Boston Patriots	7	6	1	.538	327	257	San Diego	11	3	0	.786	399	256
Buffalo	7	6	1	.538	304	291	Oakland	10	4	0	.714	363	288
Houston	6	8	0	.429	302	372	Kansas City	5	7	2	.417	347	263
N.Y. Jets	5	8	1	.385	249	399	Denver	2	11	1	.154	301	473

Eastern Division playoff: Boston 26, BUFFALO 8
AFL championship: SAN DIEGO 51, Boston 10

1962 NFL

EASTERN CONFERENCE	W	L	T	Pct.	Pts.	OP	WESTERN CONFERENCE	W	L	T	Pct.	Pts.	OP
N.Y. Giants	12	2	0	.857	398	283	Green Bay	13	1	0	.929	415	148
Pittsburgh	9	5	0	.643	312	363	Detroit	11	3	0	.786	315	177
Cleveland	7	6	1	.538	291	257	Chicago	9	5	0	.643	321	287
Washington	5	7	2	.417	305	376	Baltimore	7	7	0	.500	293	288
Dallas Cowboys	5	8	1	.385	398	402	San Francisco	6	8	0	.429	282	331
St. Louis	4	9	1	.308	287	361	Minnesota	2	11	1	.154	254	410
Philadelphia	3	10	1	.231	282	356	Los Angeles	1	12	1	.077	220	334

NFL championship: Green Bay 16, N.Y. GIANTS 7

1962 AFL

EASTERN DIVISION	W	L	T	Pct.	Pts.	OP	WESTERN DIVISION	W	L	T	Pct.	Pts.	OP
Houston	11	3	0	.786	387	270	Dallas Texans	11	3	0	.786	389	233
Boston Patriots	9	4	1	.692	346	295	Denver	7	7	0	.500	353	334
Buffalo	7	6	1	.538	309	272	San Diego	4	10	0	.286	314	392
N.Y. Titans	5	9	0	.357	278	423	Oakland	1	13	0	.071	213	370

AFL championship: Dallas Texans 20, HOUSTON 17 (OT)

1961 NFL

EASTERN CONFERENCE	W	L	T	Pct.	Pts.	OP	WESTERN CONFERENCE	W	L	T	Pct.	Pts.	OP
N.Y. Giants	10	3	1	.769	368	220	Green Bay	11	3	0	.786	391	223
Philadelphia	10	4	0	.714	361	297	Detroit	8	5	1	.615	270	258
Cleveland	8	5	1	.615	319	270	Baltimore	8	6	0	.571	302	307
St. Louis	7	7	0	.500	279	267	Chicago	8	6	0	.571	326	302
Pittsburgh	6	8	0	.429	295	287	San Francisco	7	6	1	.538	346	272
Dallas Cowboys	4	9	1	.308	236	380	Los Angeles	4	10	0	.286	263	333
Washington	1	12	1	.077	174	392	Minnesota	3	11	0	.214	285	407

NFL championship: GREEN BAY 37, N.Y. Giants 0

1961 AFL

EASTERN DIVISION	W	L	T	Pct.	Pts.	OP	WESTERN DIVISION	W	L	T	Pct.	Pts.	OP
Houston	10	3	1	.769	513	242	San Diego	12	2	0	.857	396	219
Boston Patriots	9	4	1	.692	413	313	Dallas Texans	6	8	0	.429	334	343
N.Y. Titans	7	7	0	.500	301	390	Denver	3	11	0	.214	251	432
Buffalo	6	8	0	.429	294	342	Oakland	2	12	0	.143	237	458

AFL championship: Houston 10, SAN DIEGO 3

1960 NFL

EASTERN CONFERENCE	W	L	T	Pct.	Pts.	OP	WESTERN CONFERENCE	W	L	T	Pct.	Pts.	OP
Philadelphia	10	2	0	.833	321	246	Green Bay	8	4	0	.667	332	209
Cleveland	8	3	1	.727	362	217	Detroit	7	5	0	.583	239	212
N.Y. Giants	6	4	2	.600	271	261	San Francisco	7	5	0	.583	208	205
St. Louis	6	5	1	.545	288	230	Baltimore	6	6	0	.500	288	234
Pittsburgh	5	6	1	.455	240	275	Chicago	5	6	1	.455	194	299
Washington	1	9	2	.100	178	309	L.A. Rams	4	7	1	.364	265	297
							Dallas Cowboys	0	11	1	.000	177	369

NFL championship: PHILADELPHIA 17, Green Bay 13

1960 AFL

EASTERN CONFERENCE	W	L	T	Pct.	Pts.	OP	WESTERN CONFERENCE	W	L	T	Pct.	Pts.	OP
Houston	10	4	0	.714	379	285	L.A. Chargers	10	4	0	.714	373	336
N.Y. Titans	7	7	0	.500	382	399	Dallas Texans	8	6	0	.571	362	253
Buffalo	5	8	1	.385	296	303	Oakland	6	8	0	.429	319	388
Boston	5	9	0	.357	286	349	Denver	4	9	1	.308	309	393

AFL championship: HOUSTON 24, L.A. Chargers 16

1959

EASTERN CONFERENCE	W	L	T	Pct.	Pts.	OP	WESTERN CONFERENCE	W	L	T	Pct.	Pts.	OP
N.Y. Giants	10	2	0	.833	284	170	Baltimore	9	3	0	.750	374	251
Cleveland	7	5	0	.583	270	214	Chi. Bears	8	4	0	.667	252	196
Philadelphia	7	5	0	.583	268	278	Green Bay	7	5	0	.583	248	246
Pittsburgh	6	5	1	.545	257	216	San Francisco	7	5	0	.583	255	237
Washington	3	9	0	.250	185	350	Detroit	3	8	1	.273	203	275
Chi. Cardinals	2	10	0	.167	234	324	Los Angeles	2	10	0	.167	242	315

NFL championship: BALTIMORE 31, N.Y. Giants 16

1958

EASTERN CONFERENCE	W	L	T	Pct.	Pts.	OP	WESTERN CONFERENCE	W	L	T	Pct.	Pts.	OP
N.Y. Giants	9	3	0	.750	246	183	Baltimore	9	3	0	.750	381	203
Cleveland	9	3	0	.750	302	217	Chi. Bears	8	4	0	.667	298	230
Pittsburgh	7	4	1	.636	261	230	Los Angeles	8	4	0	.667	344	278
Washington	4	7	1	.364	214	268	San Francisco	6	6	0	.500	257	324
Chi. Cardinals	2	9	1	.182	261	356	Detroit	4	7	1	.364	261	276
Philadelphia	2	9	1	.182	235	306	Green Bay	1	10	1	.091	193	382

Eastern Conference playoff: N.Y. GIANTS 10, Cleveland 0
NFL championship: Baltimore 23, N.Y. GIANTS 17 (OT)

1957

EASTERN CONFERENCE	W	L	T	Pct.	Pts.	OP	WESTERN CONFERENCE	W	L	T	Pct.	Pts.	OP
Cleveland	9	2	1	.818	269	172	Detroit	8	4	0	.667	251	231
N.Y. Giants	7	5	0	.583	254	211	San Francisco	8	4	0	.667	260	264
Pittsburgh	6	6	0	.500	161	178	Baltimore	7	5	0	.583	303	235
Washington	5	6	1	.455	251	230	Los Angeles	6	6	0	.500	307	278
Philadelphia	4	8	0	.333	173	230	Chi. Bears	5	7	0	.417	203	211
Chi. Cardinals	3	9	0	.250	200	299	Green Bay	3	9	0	.250	218	311

Western Conference playoff: Detroit 31, SAN FRANCISCO 27
NFL championship: DETROIT 59, Cleveland 14

1956

EASTERN CONFERENCE	W	L	T	Pct.	Pts.	OP	WESTERN CONFERENCE	W	L	T	Pct.	Pts.	OP
N.Y. Giants	8	3	1	.727	264	197	Chi. Bears	9	2	1	.818	363	246
Chi. Cardinals	7	5	0	.583	240	182	Detroit	9	3	0	.750	300	188
Washington	6	6	0	.500	183	225	San Francisco	5	6	1	.455	233	284
Cleveland	5	7	0	.417	167	177	Baltimore	5	7	0	.417	270	322
Pittsburgh	5	7	0	.417	217	250	Green Bay	4	8	0	.333	264	342
Philadelphia	3	8	1	.273	143	215	Los Angeles	4	8	0	.333	291	307

NFL championship: N.Y. GIANTS 47, Chi. Bears 7

1955

EASTERN CONFERENCE	W	L	T	Pct.	Pts.	OP	WESTERN CONFERENCE	W	L	T	Pct.	Pts.	OP
Cleveland	9	2	1	.818	349	218	Los Angeles	8	3	1	.727	260	231
Washington	8	4	0	.667	246	222	Chi. Bears	8	4	0	.667	294	251
N.Y. Giants	6	5	1	.545	267	223	Green Bay	6	6	0	.500	258	276
Chi. Cardinals	4	7	1	.364	224	252	Baltimore	5	6	1	.455	214	239
Philadelphia	4	7	1	.364	248	231	San Francisco	4	8	0	.333	216	298
Pittsburgh	4	8	0	.333	195	285	Detroit	3	9	0	.250	230	275

NFL championship: Cleveland 38, LOS ANGELES 14

1954

EASTERN CONFERENCE	W	L	T	Pct.	Pts.	OP	WESTERN CONFERENCE	W	L	T	Pct.	Pts.	OP
Cleveland	9	3	0	.750	336	162	Detroit	9	2	1	.818	337	189
Philadelphia	7	4	1	.636	284	230	Chi. Bears	8	4	0	.667	301	279
N.Y. Giants	7	5	0	.583	293	184	San Francisco	7	4	1	.636	313	251
Pittsburgh	5	7	0	.417	219	263	Los Angeles	6	5	1	.545	314	285
Washington	3	9	0	.250	207	432	Green Bay	4	8	0	.333	234	251
Chi. Cardinals	2	10	0	.167	183	347	Baltimore	3	9	0	.250	131	279

NFL championship: CLEVELAND 56, Detroit 10

1953

EASTERN CONFERENCE	W	L	T	Pct.	Pts.	OP	WESTERN CONFERENCE	W	L	T	Pct.	Pts.	OP
Cleveland	11	1	0	.917	348	162	Detroit	10	2	0	.833	271	205
Philadelphia	7	4	1	.636	352	215	San Francisco	9	3	0	.750	372	237
Washington	6	5	1	.545	208	215	Los Angeles	8	3	1	.727	366	236
Pittsburgh	6	6	0	.500	211	263	Chi. Bears	3	8	1	.273	218	262
N.Y. Giants	3	9	0	.250	179	277	Baltimore	3	9	0	.250	182	350
Chi. Cardinals	1	10	1	.091	190	337	Green Bay	2	9	1	.182	200	338

NFL championship: DETROIT 17, Cleveland 16

1952

AMERICAN CONFERENCE	W	L	T	Pct.	Pts.	OP	NATIONAL CONFERENCE	W	L	T	Pct.	Pts.	OP
Cleveland	8	4	0	.667	310	213	Detroit	9	3	0	.750	344	192
N.Y. Giants	7	5	0	.583	234	231	Los Angeles	9	3	0	.750	349	234
Philadelphia	7	5	0	.583	252	271	San Francisco	7	5	0	.583	285	221
Pittsburgh	5	7	0	.417	300	273	Green Bay	6	6	0	.500	295	312
Chi. Cardinals	4	8	0	.333	172	221	Chi. Bears	5	7	0	.417	245	326
Washington	4	8	0	.333	240	287	Dallas Texans	1	11	0	.083	182	427

National Conference playoff: DETROIT 31, Los Angeles 21
NFL championship: Detroit 17, CLEVELAND 7

1951

AMERICAN CONFERENCE	W	L	T	Pct.	Pts.	OP
Cleveland	11	1	0	.917	331	152
N.Y. Giants	9	2	1	.818	254	161
Washington	5	7	0	.417	183	296
Pittsburgh	4	7	1	.364	183	235
Philadelphia	4	8	0	.333	234	264
Chi. Cardinals	3	9	0	.250	210	287

NATIONAL CONFERENCE	W	L	T	Pct.	Pts.	OP
Los Angeles	8	4	0	.667	392	261
Detroit	7	4	1	.636	336	259
San Francisco	7	4	1	.636	255	205
Chi. Bears	7	5	0	.583	286	282
Green Bay	3	9	0	.250	254	375
N.Y. Yanks	1	9	2	.100	241	382

NFL championship: LOS ANGELES 24, Cleveland 17

1950

AMERICAN CONFERENCE	W	L	T	Pct.	Pts.	OP
Cleveland	10	2	0	.833	310	144
N.Y. Giants	10	2	0	.833	268	150
Philadelphia	6	6	0	.500	254	141
Pittsburgh	6	6	0	.500	180	195
Chi. Cardinals	5	7	0	.417	233	287
Washington	3	9	0	.250	232	326

NATIONAL CONFERENCE	W	L	T	Pct.	Pts.	OP
Los Angeles	9	3	0	.750	466	309
Chi. Bears	9	3	0	.750	279	207
N.Y. Yanks	7	5	0	.583	366	367
Detroit	6	6	0	.500	321	285
Green Bay	3	9	0	.250	244	406
San Francisco	3	9	0	.250	213	300
Baltimore	1	11	0	.083	213	462

American Conference playoff: CLEVELAND 8, N.Y. Giants 3
National Conference playoff: LOS ANGELES 24, Chi. Bears 14
NFL championship: CLEVELAND 30, Los Angeles 28

1949

EASTERN DIVISION	W	L	T	Pct.	Pts.	OP
Philadelphia	11	1	0	.917	364	134
Pittsburgh	6	5	1	.545	224	214
N.Y. Giants	6	6	0	.500	287	298
Washington	4	7	1	.364	268	339
N.Y. Bulldogs	1	10	1	.091	153	365

WESTERN DIVISION	W	L	T	Pct.	Pts.	OP
Los Angeles	8	2	2	.800	360	239
Chi. Bears	9	3	0	.750	332	218
Chi. Cardinals	6	5	1	.545	360	301
Detroit	4	8	0	.333	237	259
Green Bay	2	10	0	.167	114	329

NFL championship: Philadelphia 14, LOS ANGELES 0

1948

EASTERN DIVISION	W	L	T	Pct.	Pts.	OP
Philadelphia	9	2	1	.818	376	156
Washington	7	5	0	.583	291	287
N.Y. Giants	4	8	0	.333	297	388
Pittsburgh	4	8	0	.333	200	243
Boston	3	9	0	.250	174	372

WESTERN DIVISION	W	L	T	Pct.	Pts.	OP
Chi. Cardinals	11	1	0	.917	395	226
Chi. Bears	10	2	0	.833	375	151
Los Angeles	6	5	1	.545	327	269
Green Bay	3	9	0	.250	154	290
Detroit	2	10	0	.167	200	407

NFL championship: PHILADELPHIA 7, Chi. Cardinals 0

1947

EASTERN DIVISION	W	L	T	Pct.	Pts.	OP
Philadelphia	8	4	0	.667	308	242
Pittsburgh	8	4	0	.667	240	259
Boston	4	7	1	.364	168	256
Washington	4	8	0	.333	295	367
N.Y. Giants	2	8	2	.200	190	309

WESTERN DIVISION	W	L	T	Pct.	Pts.	OP
Chi. Cardinals	9	3	0	.750	300	201
Chi. Bears	8	4	0	.667	363	241
Green Bay	6	5	1	.545	274	210
Los Angeles	6	6	0	.500	259	214
Detroit	3	9	0	.250	231	305

Eastern Division playoff: Philadelphia 21, PITTSBURGH 0
NFL championship: CHI. CARDINALS 28, Philadelphia 21

1946

EASTERN DIVISION	W	L	T	Pct.	Pts.	OP
N.Y. Giants	7	3	1	.700	236	162
Philadelphia	6	5	0	.545	231	220
Washington	5	5	1	.500	171	191
Pittsburgh	5	5	1	.500	136	117
Boston	2	8	1	.200	189	273

WESTERN DIVISION	W	L	T	Pct.	Pts.	OP
Chi. Bears	8	2	1	.800	289	193
Los Angeles	6	4	1	.600	277	257
Green Bay	6	5	0	.545	148	158
Chi. Cardinals	6	5	0	.545	260	198
Detroit	1	10	0	.091	142	310

NFL championship: Chi. Bears 24, N.Y. GIANTS 14

1945

EASTERN DIVISION	W	L	T	Pct.	Pts.	OP
Washington	8	2	0	.800	209	121
Philadelphia	7	3	0	.700	272	133
N.Y. Giants	3	6	1	.333	179	198
Boston	3	6	1	.333	123	211
Pittsburgh	2	8	0	.200	79	220

WESTERN DIVISION	W	L	T	Pct.	Pts.	OP
Cleveland	9	1	0	.900	244	136
Detroit	7	3	0	.700	195	194
Green Bay	6	4	0	.600	258	173
Chi. Bears	3	7	0	.300	192	235
Chi. Cardinals	1	9	0	.100	98	228

NFL championship: CLEVELAND 15, Washington 14

1944

EASTERN DIVISION	W	L	T	Pct.	Pts.	OP
N.Y. Giants	8	1	1	.889	206	75
Philadelphia	7	1	2	.875	267	131
Washington	6	3	1	.667	169	180
Boston	2	8	0	.200	82	233
Brooklyn	0	10	0	.000	69	166

WESTERN DIVISION	W	L	T	Pct.	Pts.	OP
Green Bay	8	2	0	.800	238	141
Chi. Bears	6	3	1	.667	258	172
Detroit	6	3	1	.667	216	151
Cleveland	4	6	0	.400	188	224
Card-Pitt	0	10	0	.000	108	328

NFL championship: Green Bay 14, N.Y. GIANTS 7

1943

EASTERN DIVISION	W	L	T	Pct.	Pts.	OP
Washington	6	3	1	.667	229	137
N.Y. Giants	6	3	1	.667	197	170
Phil-Pitt	5	4	1	.556	225	230
Brooklyn	2	8	0	.200	65	234

WESTERN DIVISION	W	L	T	Pct.	Pts.	OP
Chi. Bears	8	1	1	.889	303	157
Green Bay	7	2	1	.778	264	172
Detroit	3	6	1	.333	178	218
Chi. Cardinals	0	10	0	.000	95	238

Eastern Division playoff: Washington 28, N.Y. GIANTS 0
NFL championship: CHI. BEARS 41, Washington 21

1942

EASTERN DIVISION	W	L	T	Pct.	Pts.	OP
Washington	10	1	0	.909	227	102
Pittsburgh	7	4	0	.636	167	119
N.Y. Giants	5	5	1	.500	155	139
Brooklyn	3	8	0	.273	100	168
Philadelphia	2	9	0	.182	134	239

WESTERN DIVISION	W	L	T	Pct.	Pts.	OP
Chi. Bears	11	0	0	1.000	376	84
Green Bay	8	2	1	.800	300	215
Cleveland	5	6	0	.455	150	207
Chi. Cardinals	3	8	0	.273	98	209
Detroit	0	11	0	.000	38	263

NFL championship: WASHINGTON 14, Chi. Bears 6

1941

EASTERN DIVISION	W	L	T	Pct.	Pts.	OP
N.Y. Giants	8	3	0	.727	238	114
Brooklyn	7	4	0	.636	158	127
Washington	6	5	0	.545	176	174
Philadelphia	2	8	1	.200	119	218
Pittsburgh	1	9	1	.100	103	276

WESTERN DIVISION	W	L	T	Pct.	Pts.	OP
Chi. Bears	10	1	0	.909	396	147
Green Bay	10	1	0	.909	258	120
Detroit	4	6	1	.400	121	195
Chi. Cardinals	3	7	1	.300	127	197
Cleveland	2	9	0	.182	116	244

Western Division playoff: CHI. BEARS 33, Green Bay 14
NFL championship: CHI. BEARS 37, N.Y. Giants 9

1940

EASTERN DIVISION	W	L	T	Pct.	Pts.	OP
Washington	9	2	0	.818	245	142
Brooklyn	8	3	0	.727	186	120
N.Y. Giants	6	4	1	.600	131	133
Pittsburgh	2	7	2	.222	60	178
Philadelphia	1	10	0	.091	111	211

WESTERN DIVISION	W	L	T	Pct.	Pts.	OP
Chi. Bears	8	3	0	.727	238	152
Green Bay	6	4	1	.600	238	155
Detroit	5	5	1	.500	138	153
Cleveland	4	6	1	.400	171	191
Chi. Cardinals	2	7	2	.222	139	222

NFL championship: Chi. Bears 73, WASHINGTON 0

1939

EASTERN DIVISION	W	L	T	Pct.	Pts.	OP
N.Y. Giants	9	1	1	.900	168	85
Washington	8	2	1	.800	242	94
Brooklyn	4	6	1	.400	108	219
Philadelphia	1	9	1	.100	105	200
Pittsburgh	1	9	1	.100	114	216

WESTERN DIVISION	W	L	T	Pct.	Pts.	OP
Green Bay	9	2	0	.818	233	153
Chi. Bears	8	3	0	.727	298	157
Detroit	6	5	0	.545	145	150
Cleveland	5	5	1	.500	195	164
Chi. Cardinals	1	10	0	.091	84	254

NFL championship: GREEN BAY 27, N.Y. Giants 0

1938

EASTERN DIVISION	W	L	T	Pct.	Pts.	OP
N.Y. Giants	8	2	1	.800	194	79
Washington	6	3	2	.667	148	154
Brooklyn	4	4	3	.500	131	161
Philadelphia	5	6	0	.455	154	164
Pittsburgh	2	9	0	.182	79	169

WESTERN DIVISION	W	L	T	Pct.	Pts.	OP
Green Bay	8	3	0	.727	223	118
Detroit	7	4	0	.636	119	108
Chi. Bears	6	5	0	.545	194	148
Cleveland	4	7	0	.364	131	215
Chi. Cardinals	2	9	0	.182	111	168

NFL championship: N.Y. GIANTS 23, Green Bay 17

1937

EASTERN DIVISION	W	L	T	Pct.	Pts.	OP
Washington	8	3	0	.727	195	120
N.Y. Giants	6	3	2	.667	128	109
Pittsburgh	4	7	0	.364	122	145
Brooklyn	3	7	1	.300	82	174
Philadelphia	2	8	1	.200	86	177

WESTERN DIVISION	W	L	T	Pct.	Pts.	OP
Chi. Bears	9	1	1	.900	201	100
Green Bay	7	4	0	.636	220	122
Detroit	7	4	0	.636	180	105
Chi. Cardinals	5	5	1	.500	135	165
Cleveland	1	10	0	.091	75	207

NFL championship: Washington 28, CHI. BEARS 21

PAST STANDINGS

1936

EASTERN DIVISION

	W	L	T	Pct.	Pts.	OP
Boston	7	5	0	.583	149	110
Pittsburgh	6	6	0	.500	98	187
N.Y. Giants	5	6	1	.455	115	163
Brooklyn	3	8	1	.273	92	161
Philadelphia	1	11	0	.083	51	206

WESTERN DIVISION

	W	L	T	Pct.	Pts.	OP
Green Bay	10	1	1	.909	248	118
Chi. Bears	9	3	0	.750	222	94
Detroit	8	4	0	.667	235	102
Chi. Cardinals	3	8	1	.273	74	143

NFL championship: Green Bay 21, Boston 6, at Polo Grounds, N.Y.

1935

EASTERN DIVISION

	W	L	T	Pct.	Pts.	OP
N. Y. Giants	9	3	0	.750	180	96
Brooklyn	5	6	1	.455	90	141
Pittsburgh	4	8	0	.333	100	209
Boston	2	8	1	.200	65	123
Philadelphia	2	9	0	.182	60	179

WESTERN DIVISION

	W	L	T	Pct.	Pts.	OP
Detroit	7	3	2	.700	191	111
Green Bay	8	4	0	.667	181	96
Chi. Bears	6	4	2	.600	192	106
Chi. Cardinals	6	4	2	.600	99	97

NFL championship: DETROIT 26, N.Y. Giants 7
One game between Boston and Philadelphia was canceled.

1934

EASTERN DIVISION

	W	L	T	Pct.	Pts.	OP
N.Y. Giants	8	5	0	.615	147	107
Boston	6	6	0	.500	107	94
Brooklyn	4	7	0	.364	61	153
Philadelphia	4	7	0	.364	127	85
Pittsburgh	2	10	0	.167	51	206

WESTERN DIVISION

	W	L	T	Pct.	Pts.	OP
Chi. Bears	13	0	0	1.000	286	86
Detroit	10	3	0	.769	238	59
Green Bay	7	6	0	.538	156	112
Chi. Cardinals	5	6	0	.455	80	84
St. Louis	1	2	0	.333	27	61
Cincinnati	0	8	0	.000	10	243

NFL championship: N.Y. GIANTS 30, Chi. Bears 13

1933

EASTERN DIVISION

	W	L	T	Pct.	Pts.	OP
N.Y. Giants	11	3	0	.786	244	101
Brooklyn	5	4	1	.556	93	54
Boston	5	5	2	.500	103	97
Philadelphia	3	5	1	.375	77	158
Pittsburgh	3	6	2	.333	67	208

WESTERN DIVISION

	W	L	T	Pct.	Pts.	OP
Chi. Bears	10	2	1	.833	133	82
Portsmouth	6	5	0	.545	128	87
Green Bay	5	7	1	.417	170	107
Cincinnati	3	6	1	.333	38	110
Chi. Cardinals	1	9	1	.100	52	101

NFL championship: CHI. BEARS 23, N.Y. Giants 21

1932

	W	L	T	Pct.
Chicago Bears	7	1	6	.875
Green Bay Packers	10	3	1	.769
Portsmouth Spartans	6	2	4	.750
Boston Braves	4	4	2	.500
New York Giants	4	6	2	.400
Brooklyn Dodgers	3	9	0	.250
Chicago Cardinals	2	6	2	.250
Staten Island Stapletons	2	7	3	.222

Chicago Bears and Portsmouth finished regularly scheduled games tied for first place. Bears won playoff game, which counted in standings, 9-0.

1931

	W	L	T	Pct.
Green Bay Packers	12	2	0	.857
Portsmouth Spartans	11	3	0	.786
Chicago Bears	8	5	0	.615
Chicago Cardinals	5	4	0	.556
New York Giants	7	6	1	.538
Providence Steam Roller	4	4	3	.500
Staten Island Stapletons	4	6	1	.400
Cleveland Indians	2	8	0	.200
Brooklyn Dodgers	2	12	0	.143
Frankford Yellow Jackets	1	6	1	.143

1930

	W	L	T	Pct.
Green Bay Packers	10	3	1	.769
New York Giants	13	4	0	.765
Chicago Bears	9	4	1	.692
Brooklyn Dodgers	7	4	1	.636
Providence Steam Roller	6	4	1	.600
Staten Island Stapletons	5	5	2	.500
Chicago Cardinals	5	6	2	.455
Portsmouth Spartans	5	6	3	.455
Frankford Yellow Jackets	4	13	1	.222
Minneapolis Red Jackets	1	7	1	.125
Newark Tornadoes	1	10	1	.091

1929

	W	L	T	Pct.
Green Bay Packers	12	0	1	1.000
New York Giants	13	1	1	.929
Frankford Yellow Jackets	9	4	5	.692
Chicago Cardinals	6	6	1	.500
Boston Bulldogs	4	4	0	.500
Orange Tornadoes	3	4	4	.429
Staten Island Stapletons	3	4	3	.429
Providence Steam Roller	4	6	2	.400
Chicago Bears	4	9	2	.308
Buffalo Bisons	1	7	1	.125
Minneapolis Red Jackets	1	9	0	.100
Dayton Triangles	0	6	0	.000

1928

	W	L	T	Pct.
Providence Steam Roller	8	1	2	.889
Frankford Yellow Jackets	11	3	2	.786
Detroit Wolverines	7	2	1	.778
Green Bay Packers	6	4	3	.600
Chicago Bears	7	5	1	.583
New York Giants	4	7	2	.364
New York Yankees	4	8	1	.333
Pottsville Maroons	2	8	0	.200
Chicago Cardinals	1	5	0	.167
Dayton Triangles	0	7	0	.000

1927

	W	L	T	Pct.
New York Giants	11	1	1	.917
Green Bay Packers	7	2	1	.778
Chicago Bears	9	3	2	.750
Cleveland Bulldogs	8	4	1	.667
Providence Steam Roller	8	5	1	.615
New York Yankees	7	8	1	.467
Frankford Yellow Jackets	6	9	3	.400
Pottsville Maroons	5	8	0	.385
Chicago Cardinals	3	7	1	.300
Dayton Triangles	1	6	1	.143
Duluth Eskimos	1	8	0	.111
Buffalo Bisons	0	5	0	.000

1926

	W	L	T	Pct.
Frankford Yellow Jackets	14	1	1	.933
Chicago Bears	12	1	3	.923
Pottsville Maroons	10	2	1	.833
Kansas City Cowboys	8	3	0	.727
Green Bay Packers	7	3	3	.700
Los Angeles Buccaneers	6	3	1	.667
New York Giants	8	4	1	.667
Duluth Eskimos	6	5	3	.545
Buffalo Rangers	4	4	2	.500
Chicago Cardinals	5	6	1	.455
Providence Steam Roller	5	7	1	.417
Detroit Panthers	4	6	2	.400
Hartford Blues	3	7	0	.300
Brooklyn Lions	3	8	0	.273
Milwaukee Badgers	2	7	0	.222
Akron Pros	1	4	3	.200
Dayton Triangles	1	4	1	.200
Racine Tornadoes	1	4	0	.200
Columbus Tigers	1	6	0	.143
Canton Bulldogs	1	9	3	.100
Hammond Pros	0	4	0	.000
Louisville Colonels	0	4	0	.000

1925

	W	L	T	Pct.
Chicago Cardinals	11	2	1	.846
Pottsville Maroons	10	2	0	.833
Detroit Panthers	8	2	2	.800
New York Giants	8	4	0	.667
Akron Indians	4	2	2	.667
Frankford Yellow Jackets	13	7	0	.650
Chicago Bears	9	5	3	.643
Rock Island Independents	5	3	3	.625
Green Bay Packers	8	5	0	.615
Providence Steam Roller	6	5	1	.545
Canton Bulldogs	4	4	0	.500
Cleveland Bulldogs	5	8	1	.385
Kansas City Cowboys	2	5	1	.286
Hammond Pros	1	4	0	.200
Buffalo Bisons	1	6	2	.143
Duluth Kelleys	0	3	0	.000
Rochester Jeffersons	0	6	1	.000
Milwaukee Badgers	0	6	0	.000
Dayton Triangles	0	7	1	.000
Columbus Tigers	0	9	0	.000

1924

	W	L	T	Pct.
Cleveland Bulldogs	7	1	1	.875
Chicago Bears	6	1	4	.857
Frankford Yellow Jackets	11	2	1	.846
Duluth Kelleys	5	1	0	.833
Rock Island Independents	6	2	2	.750
Green Bay Packers	7	4	0	.636
Racine Legion	4	3	3	.571
Chicago Cardinals	5	4	1	.556
Buffalo Bisons	6	5	0	.545
Columbus Tigers	4	4	0	.500
Hammond Pros	2	2	1	.500
Milwaukee Badgers	5	8	0	.385
Akron Indians	2	6	0	.250
Dayton Triangles	2	6	0	.250
Kansas City Blues	2	7	0	.222
Kenosha Maroons	0	5	1	.000
Minneapolis Marines	0	6	0	.000
Rochester Jeffersons	0	7	0	.000

1923

	W	L	T	Pct.
Canton Bulldogs	11	0	1	1.000
Chicago Bears	9	2	1	.818
Green Bay Packers	7	2	1	.778
Milwaukee Badgers	7	2	3	.778
Cleveland Indians	3	1	3	.750
Chicago Cardinals	8	4	0	.667
Duluth Kelleys	4	3	0	.571
Columbus Tigers	5	4	1	.556
Buffalo All-Americans	4	4	3	.500
Racine Legion	4	4	2	.500
Toledo Maroons	2	3	2	.400
Rock Island Independents	2	3	3	.400
Minneapolis Marines	2	5	2	.286
St. Louis All-Stars	1	4	2	.200
Hammond Pros	1	5	1	.167
Dayton Triangles	1	6	1	.143
Akron Indians	1	6	0	.143
Oorang Indians	1	10	0	.091
Rochester Jeffersons	0	2	0	.000
Louisville Brecks	0	3	0	.000

1922

	W	L	T	Pct.
Canton Bulldogs	10	0	2	1.000
Chicago Bears	9	3	0	.750
Chicago Cardinals	8	3	0	.727
Toledo Maroons	5	2	2	.714
Rock Island Independents	4	2	1	.667
Racine Legion	6	4	1	.600
Dayton Triangles	4	3	1	.571
Green Bay Packers	4	3	3	.571
Buffalo All-Americans	5	4	1	.556
Akron Pros	3	5	2	.375
Milwaukee Badgers	2	4	3	.333
Oorang Indians	2	6	0	.250
Minneapolis Marines	1	3	0	.250
Louisville Brecks	1	3	0	.250
Evansville Crimson Giants	0	3	0	.000
Rochester Jeffersons	0	4	1	.000
Hammond Pros	0	5	1	.000
Columbus Panhandles	0	7	0	.000

1921

	W	L	T	Pct.
Chicago Staleys	9	1	1	.900
Buffalo All-Americans	9	1	2	.900
Akron Pros	8	3	1	.727
Canton Bulldogs	5	2	3	.714
Rock Island Independents	4	2	1	.667
Evansville Crimson Giants	3	2	0	.600
Green Bay Packers	3	2	1	.600
Dayton Triangles	4	4	1	.500
Chicago Cardinals	3	3	2	.500
Rochester Jeffersons	2	3	0	.400
Cleveland Indians	3	5	0	.375
Washington Senators	1	2	0	.333
Cincinnati Celts	1	3	0	.250
Hammond Pros	1	3	1	.250
Minneapolis Marines	1	3	1	.250
Detroit Heralds	1	5	1	.167
Columbus Panhandles	1	8	0	.111
Tonawanda Kardex	0	1	0	.000
Muncie Flyers	0	2	0	.000
Louisville Brecks	0	2	0	.000
New York Giants	0	2	0	.000

1920*

	W	L	T	Pct.
Akron Pros	8	0	3	1.000
Decatur Staleys	10	1	2	.909
Buffalo All-Americans	9	1	1	.900
Chicago Cardinals	6	2	2	.750
Rock Island Independents	6	2	2	.750
Dayton Triangles	5	2	2	.714
Rochester Jeffersons	6	3	2	.667
Canton Bulldogs	7	4	2	.636
Detroit Heralds	2	3	3	.400
Cleveland Tigers	2	4	2	.333
Chicago Tigers	2	5	1	.286
Hammond Pros	2	5	0	.286
Columbus Panhandles	2	6	2	.250
Muncie Flyers	0	1	0	.000

**No official standing was maintained for the 1920 season, and the championship was awarded to the Akron Pros in a League meeting on April 30, 1921. Clubs played schedules which included games against non-league opponents. Records of clubs against all opponents are listed above.*

RS=REGULAR SEASON
PS=POSTSEASON
*ARIZONA vs. ATLANTA
RS: Cardinals lead series, 11-5
1966—Falcons, 16-10 (A)
1968—Cardinals, 17-12 (StL)
1971—Cardinals, 26-9 (A)
1973—Cardinals, 32-10 (A)
1975—Cardinals, 23-20 (StL)
1978—Cardinals, 42-21 (StL)
1980—Falcons, 33-27 (StL) OT
1981—Falcons, 41-20 (A)
1982—Cardinals, 23-20 (A)
1986—Falcons, 33-13 (A)
1987—Cardinals, 34-21 (A)
1989—Cardinals, 34-20 (P)
1990—Cardinals, 24-13 (A)
1991—Cardinals, 16-10 (P)
1992—Falcons, 20-17 (A)
1993—Cardinals, 27-10 (A)
(RS Pts.—Cardinals 385, Falcons 309)
Franchise known as Phoenix prior to 1994 and in St. Louis prior to 1988
*ARIZONA vs. BUFFALO
RS: Series tied, 3-3
1971—Cardinals, 28-23 (B)
1975—Bills, 32-14 (StL)
1981—Cardinals, 24-0 (StL)
1984—Cardinals, 37-7 (StL)
1986—Bills, 17-10 (B)
1990—Bills, 45-14 (B)
(RS Pts.—Cardinals 127, Bills 124)
Franchise known as Phoenix prior to 1994 and in St. Louis prior to 1988
*ARIZONA vs. **CHICAGO
RS: Bears lead series, 51-25-6
(NP denotes Normal Park;
Wr denotes Wrigley Field;
Co denotes Comiskey Park;
So denotes Soldier Field;
all Chicago)
1920—Cardinals, 7-6 (NP)
    Staleys, 10-0 (Wr)
1921—Tie, 0-0 (Wr)
1922—Cardinals, 6-0 (Co)
    Cardinals, 9-0 (Co)
1923—Bears, 3-0 (Wr)
1924—Bears, 6-0 (Wr)
    Bears, 21-0 (Co)
1925—Cardinals, 9-0 (Co)
    Tie, 0-0 (Wr)
1926—Bears, 16-0 (Wr)
    Bears, 10-0 (So)
    Tie, 0-0 (Wr)
1927—Bears, 9-0 (NP)
    Cardinals, 3-0 (Wr)
1928—Bears, 15-0 (NP)
    Bears, 34-0 (Wr)
1929—Tie, 0-0 (Wr)
    Cardinals, 40-6 (Co)
1930—Bears, 32-6 (Co)
    Bears, 6-0 (Wr)
1931—Bears, 26-13 (Wr)
    Bears, 18-7 (Wr)
1932—Tie, 0-0 (Wr)
    Bears, 34-0 (Wr)
1933—Bears, 12-9 (Wr)
    Bears, 22-6 (Wr)
1934—Bears, 20-0 (Wr)
    Bears, 17-6 (Wr)
1935—Tie, 7-7 (Wr)
    Bears, 13-0 (Wr)
1936—Bears, 7-3 (Wr)
    Cardinals, 14-7 (Wr)
1937—Bears, 16-7 (Wr)
    Bears, 42-28 (Wr)
1938—Bears, 16-13 (So)
    Bears, 34-28 (Wr)
1939—Bears, 44-7 (Wr)
    Bears, 48-7 (Co)
1940—Cardinals, 21-7 (Co)
    Bears, 31-23 (Wr)
1941—Bears, 53-7 (Wr)

Bears, 34-24 (Co)
1942—Bears, 41-14 (Wr)
    Bears, 21-7 (Co)
1943—Bears, 20-0 (Wr)
    Bears, 35-24 (Co)
1945—Cardinals, 16-7 (Wr)
    Bears, 28-20 (Co)
1946—Bears, 34-17 (Co)
    Cardinals, 35-28 (Wr)
1947—Cardinals, 31-7 (Co)
    Cardinals, 30-21 (Wr)
1948—Bears, 28-17 (Co)
    Cardinals, 24-21 (Wr)
1949—Bears, 17-7 (Co)
    Bears, 52-21 (Wr)
1950—Bears, 27-6 (Wr)
    Cardinals, 20-10 (Co)
1951—Cardinals, 28-14 (Co)
    Cardinals, 24-14 (Wr)
1952—Cardinals, 21-10 (Co)
    Bears, 10-7 (Wr)
1953—Cardinals, 24-17 (Wr)
1954—Bears, 29-7 (Co)
1955—Cardinals, 53-14 (Co)
1956—Bears, 10-3 (Wr)
1957—Bears, 14-6 (Co)
1958—Bears, 30-14 (Wr)
1959—Bears, 31-7 (So)
1965—Bears, 34-13 (Wr)
1966—Cardinals, 24-17 (StL)
1967—Bears, 30-3 (Wr)
1969—Cardinals, 20-17 (StL)
1972—Bears, 27-10 (StL)
1975—Cardinals, 34-20 (So)
1977—Cardinals, 16-13 (StL)
1978—Bears, 17-10 (StL)
1979—Bears, 42-6 (So)
1982—Cardinals, 10-7 (So)
1984—Cardinals, 38-21 (StL)
1990—Bears, 31-21 (P)
(RS Pts.—Bears 1,548, Cardinals 998)
Franchise known as Phoenix prior to 1994, in St. Louis prior to 1988, and in Chicago prior to 1960
**Franchise in Decatur prior to 1921 and known as Staleys prior to 1922*
*ARIZONA vs. CINCINNATI
RS: Bengals lead series, 3-1
1973—Bengals, 42-24 (C)
1979—Bengals, 34-28 (C)
1985—Cardinals, 41-27 (StL)
1988—Bengals, 21-14 (C)
(RS Pts.—Bengals 124, Cardinals 107)
Franchise known as Phoenix prior to 1994 and in St. Louis prior to 1988
*ARIZONA vs. CLEVELAND
RS: Browns lead series, 31-10-3
1950—Browns, 34-24 (Cle)
    Browns, 10-7 (Chi)
1951—Browns, 34-17 (Chi)
    Browns, 49-28 (Cle)
1952—Browns, 28-13 (Cle)
    Browns, 10-0 (Chi)
1953—Browns, 27-7 (Chi)
    Browns, 27-16 (Cle)
1954—Browns, 31-7 (Cle)
    Browns, 35-3 (Chi)
1955—Browns, 26-20 (Chi)
    Browns, 35-24 (Cle)
1956—Cardinals, 9-7 (Chi)
    Cardinals, 24-7 (Cle)
1957—Browns, 17-7 (Chi)
    Browns, 31-0 (Cle)
1958—Browns, 35-28 (Chi)
    Browns, 38-24 (Chi)
1959—Browns, 34-7 (Chi)
    Browns, 17-7 (Cle)
1960—Browns, 28-27 (Cle)
    Tie, 17-17 (StL)
1961—Browns, 20-17 (Cle)
    Browns, 21-10 (StL)
1962—Browns, 34-7 (StL)
    Browns, 38-14 (Cle)

1963—Cardinals, 20-14 (Cle)
    Browns, 24-10 (StL)
1964—Tie, 33-33 (Cle)
    Cardinals, 28-19 (StL)
1965—Cardinals, 49-13 (Cle)
    Browns, 27-24 (StL)
1966—Cardinals, 34-28 (Cle)
    Browns, 38-10 (StL)
1967—Browns, 20-16 (Cle)
    Browns, 20-16 (StL)
1968—Cardinals, 27-21 (Cle)
    Cardinals, 27-16 (StL)
1969—Tie, 21-21 (Cle)
    Browns, 27-21 (StL)
1974—Cardinals, 29-7 (StL)
1979—Browns, 38-20 (StL)
1985—Cardinals, 27-24 (Cle) OT
1988—Browns, 29-21 (P)
(RS Pts.—Browns 1,109, Cardinals 797)
Franchise known as Phoenix prior to 1994, in St. Louis prior to 1988, and in Chicago prior to 1960
*ARIZONA vs. DALLAS
RS: Cowboys lead series, 40-22-1
1960—Cardinals, 12-10 (StL)
1961—Cardinals, 31-17 (D)
    Cardinals, 31-13 (StL)
1962—Cardinals, 28-24 (D)
    Cardinals, 52-20 (StL)
1963—Cardinals, 34-7 (D)
    Cowboys, 28-24 (StL)
1964—Cardinals, 16-6 (D)
    Cowboys, 31-13 (StL)
1965—Cardinals, 20-13 (StL)
    Cowboys, 27-13 (D)
1966—Tie, 10-10 (StL)
    Cowboys, 31-17 (D)
1967—Cowboys, 46-21 (D)
1968—Cowboys, 27-10 (StL)
1969—Cowboys, 24-3 (D)
1970—Cardinals, 20-7 (StL)
    Cardinals, 38-0 (D)
1971—Cowboys, 16-13 (StL)
    Cowboys, 31-12 (D)
1972—Cowboys, 33-24 (D)
    Cowboys, 27-6 (StL)
1973—Cowboys, 45-10 (D)
    Cowboys, 30-3 (StL)
1974—Cardinals, 31-28 (StL)
    Cowboys, 17-14 (D)
1975—Cowboys, 37-31 (D) OT
    Cardinals, 31-17 (StL)
1976—Cardinals, 21-17 (StL)
    Cowboys, 19-14 (D)
1977—Cowboys, 30-24 (StL)
    Cardinals, 24-17 (D)
1978—Cowboys, 21-12 (StL)
    Cowboys, 24-21 (StL) OT
1979—Cowboys, 22-21 (StL)
    Cowboys, 22-13 (D)
1980—Cowboys, 27-24 (StL)
    Cowboys, 31-21 (D)
1981—Cowboys, 30-17 (D)
    Cardinals, 20-17 (StL)
1982—Cowboys, 24-7 (StL)
1983—Cowboys, 34-17 (StL)
    Cowboys, 35-17 (D)
1984—Cardinals, 31-20 (D)
    Cowboys, 24-17 (StL)
1985—Cardinals, 21-10 (StL)
    Cowboys, 35-17 (D)
1986—Cowboys, 31-7 (StL)
    Cowboys, 37-6 (D)
1987—Cardinals, 24-13 (StL)
    Cowboys, 21-16 (D)
1988—Cowboys, 17-14 (P)
    Cardinals, 16-10 (D)
1989—Cardinals, 19-10 (D)
    Cardinals, 24-20 (P)
1990—Cardinals, 20-3 (P)
    Cowboys, 41-10 (D)
1991—Cowboys, 17-9 (P)
    Cowboys, 27-7 (D)

1992—Cowboys, 31-20 (D)
    Cowboys, 16-10 (P)
1993—Cowboys, 17-10 (P)
    Cowboys, 20-15 (D)
(RS Pts.—Cowboys 1,412, Cardinals 1,154)
Franchise known as Phoenix prior to 1994 and in St. Louis prior to 1988
*ARIZONA vs. DENVER
RS: Broncos lead series, 3-0-1
1973—Tie, 17-17 (StL)
1977—Broncos, 7-0 (D)
1989—Broncos, 37-0 (P)
1991—Broncos, 24-19 (D)
(RS Pts.—Broncos 85, Cardinals 36)
Franchise known as Phoenix prior to 1994 and in St. Louis prior to 1988
*ARIZONA vs. **DETROIT
RS: Lions lead series, 27-16-5
1930—Tie, 0-0 (Port)
    Cardinals, 23-0 (C)
1931—Cardinals, 20-19 (C)
1932—Tie, 7-7 (C)
1933—Spartans, 7-6 (Port)
1934—Lions, 6-0 (C)
    Lions, 17-13 (C)
1935—Tie, 10-10 (D)
    Lions, 7-6 (C)
1936—Lions, 39-0 (D)
    Lions, 14-7 (C)
1937—Lions, 16-7 (C)
    Lions, 16-7 (D)
1938—Lions, 10-0 (C)
    Lions, 7-3 (C)
1939—Lions, 21-3 (D)
    Lions, 17-3 (C)
1940—Tie, 0-0 (Buffalo)
    Lions, 43-14 (C)
1941—Tie, 14-14 (C)
    Lions, 21-3 (D)
1942—Cardinals, 13-0 (C)
    Cardinals, 7-0 (D)
1943—Lions, 35-17 (D)
    Lions, 7-0 (C)
1945—Lions, 10-0 (D)
    Lions, 26-0 (D)
1946—Cardinals, 34-14 (C)
    Cardinals, 36-14 (D)
1947—Cardinals, 45-21 (C)
    Cardinals, 17-7 (D)
1948—Cardinals, 50-20 (C)
    Cardinals, 28-14 (D)
1949—Lions, 24-7 (C)
    Cardinals, 42-19 (D)
1959—Lions, 45-21 (D)
1961—Lions, 45-14 (StL)
1967—Cardinals, 38-28 (StL)
1969—Lions, 20-0 (D)
1970—Lions, 16-3 (D)
1973—Lions, 20-16 (StL)
1975—Cardinals, 24-13 (D)
1978—Cardinals, 21-14 (StL)
1980—Lions, 20-7 (D)
    Cardinals, 24-23 (StL)
1989—Cardinals, 16-13 (D)
1993—Lions, 26-20 (D)
    Lions, 21-14 (Phx)
(RS Pts.—Lions 806, Cardinals 676)
Franchise known as Phoenix prior to 1994, in St. Louis prior to 1988, and in Chicago prior to 1960
**Franchise in Portsmouth prior to 1934 and known as the Spartans*
*ARIZONA vs. GREEN BAY
RS: Packers lead series, 39-21-4
PS: Packers lead series, 1-0
1921—Tie, 3-3 (C)
1922—Cardinals, 16-3 (C)
1924—Cardinals, 3-0 (C)
1925—Cardinals, 9-6 (C)
1926—Cardinals, 13-7 (GB)
    Packers, 3-0 (C)
1927—Packers, 13-0 (GB)
    Tie, 6-6 (C)

1928—Packers, 20-0 (GB)
1929—Packers, 9-2 (GB)
    Packers, 7-6 (C)
    Packers, 12-0 (C)
1930—Packers, 14-0 (GB)
    Cardinals, 13-6 (C)
1931—Packers, 26-7 (GB)
    Cardinals, 21-13 (C)
1932—Packers, 15-7 (GB)
    Packers, 19-9 (C)
1933—Packers, 14-6 (C)
1934—Packers, 15-0 (GB)
    Cardinals, 9-0 (Mil)
    Cardinals, 6-0 (C)
1935—Cardinals, 7-6 (GB)
    Cardinals, 3-0 (Mil)
    Cardinals, 9-7 (C)
1936—Packers, 10-7 (GB)
    Packers, 24-0 (Mil)
    Tie, 0-0 (C)
1937—Cardinals, 14-7 (GB)
    Packers, 34-13 (Mil)
1938—Packers, 28-7 (Mil)
    Packers, 24-22 (Buffalo)
1939—Packers, 14-10 (GB)
    Packers, 27-20 (Mil)
1940—Packers, 31-6 (C)
    Packers, 28-7 (C)
1941—Packers, 14-13 (Mil)
    Packers, 17-9 (GB)
1942—Packers, 17-13 (C)
    Packers, 55-24 (GB)
1943—Packers, 28-7 (C)
    Packers, 35-14 (Mil)
1945—Packers, 33-14 (GB)
1946—Packers, 19-7 (C)
    Cardinals, 24-6 (GB)
1947—Cardinals, 14-10 (GB)
    Cardinals, 21-20 (C)
1948—Cardinals, 17-7 (Mil)
    Cardinals, 42-7 (C)
1949—Cardinals, 39-17 (Mil)
    Cardinals, 41-21 (C)
1955—Packers, 31-14 (C)
1956—Packers, 24-21 (C)
1962—Packers, 17-0 (Mil)
1963—Packers, 30-7 (StL)
1967—Packers, 31-23 (StL)
1969—Packers, 45-28 (GB)
1971—Tie, 16-16 (StL)
1973—Packers, 25-21 (GB)
1976—Cardinals, 29-0 (StL)
1982—**Packers, 41-16 (GB)
1984—Packers, 24-23 (GB)
1985—Cardinals, 43-28 (StL)
1988—Packers, 26-17 (P)
1990—Packers, 24-21 (P)
(RS Pts.—Packers 1,078, Cardinals 823)
(PS Pts.—Packers 41, Cardinals 16)
*Franchise known as Phoenix prior to
1994, in St. Louis prior to 1988,
and in Chicago prior to 1960
**NFC First-Round Playoff
ARIZONA vs. HOUSTON
RS: Cardinals lead series, 3-2
1970—Cardinals, 44-0 (StL)
1974—Cardinals, 31-27 (H)
1979—Cardinals, 24-17 (H)
1985—Oilers, 20-10 (StL)
1988—Oilers, 38-20 (H)
(RS Pts.—Cardinals 129, Oilers 102)
*Franchise known as Phoenix prior to
1994 and in St. Louis prior to 1988
ARIZONA vs. **INDIANAPOLIS
RS: Cardinals lead series, 6-5
1961—Colts, 16-0 (B)
1964—Colts, 47-27 (B)
1968—Colts, 27-0 (B)
1972—Cardinals, 10-3 (B)
1976—Cardinals, 24-17 (StL)
1978—Colts, 30-17 (StL)
1980—Cardinals, 17-10 (B)
1981—Cardinals, 35-24 (B)

1984—Cardinals, 34-33 (I)
1990—Cardinals, 20-17 (P)
1992—Colts, 16-13 (I)
(RS Pts.—Colts 240, Cardinals 197)
*Franchise known as Phoenix prior to
1994 and in St. Louis prior to 1988
**Franchise in Baltimore prior to 1984
ARIZONA vs. KANSAS CITY
RS: Chiefs lead series, 3-1-1
1970—Tie, 6-6 (KC)
1974—Chiefs, 17-13 (StL)
1980—Chiefs, 21-13 (StL)
1983—Chiefs, 38-14 (KC)
1986—Cardinals, 23-14 (StL)
(RS Pts.—Chiefs 96, Cardinals 69)
*Franchise known as Phoenix prior to
1994 and in St. Louis prior to 1988
ARIZONA vs. **L. A. RAIDERS
RS: Raiders lead series, 2-1
1973—Raiders, 17-10 (StL)
1983—Cardinals, 34-24 (LA)
1989—Raiders, 16-14 (LA)
(RS Pts.—Raiders 58, Raiders 57)
*Franchise known as Phoenix prior to
1994 and in St. Louis prior to 1988
**Franchise in Oakland prior to 1982
ARIZONA vs. **L.A. RAMS
RS: Rams lead series, 22-19-2
PS: Rams lead series, 1-0
1937—Cardinals, 6-0 (Clev)
    Cardinals, 13-7 (Chi)
1938—Cardinals, 7-6 (Clev)
    Cardinals, 31-17 (Chi)
1939—Rams, 24-0 (Chi)
    Rams, 14-0 (Clev)
1940—Rams, 26-14 (Clev)
    Cardinals, 17-7 (Chi)
1941—Rams, 10-6 (Clev)
    Cardinals, 7-0 (Chi)
1942—Cardinals, 7-0 (Chi)
    Rams, 7-3 (Clev)
1945—Cardinals, 21-0 (Clev)
    Rams, 35-21 (Chi)
1946—Cardinals, 34-10 (Chi)
    Rams, 17-14 (LA)
1947—Rams, 27-7 (LA)
    Cardinals, 17-10 (Chi)
1948—Cardinals, 27-22 (LA)
    Cardinals, 27-24 (Chi)
1949—Tie, 28-28 (Chi)
    Cardinals, 31-27 (LA)
1951—Rams, 45-21 (LA)
1953—Tie, 24-24 (Chi)
1954—Rams, 28-17 (LA)
1958—Rams, 20-14 (Chi)
1960—Cardinals, 43-21 (LA)
1965—Rams, 27-3 (StL)
1968—Rams, 24-13 (StL)
1970—Rams, 34-13 (LA)
1972—Cardinals, 24-14 (StL)
1975—***Rams, 35-23 (LA)
1976—Cardinals, 30-28 (LA)
1979—Rams, 21-0 (LA)
1980—Rams, 21-13 (StL)
1984—Rams, 16-13 (StL)
1985—Rams, 46-14 (LA)
1986—Rams, 16-10 (StL)
1987—Cardinals, 27-24 (StL)
1988—Cardinals, 41-27 (LA)
1989—Rams, 37-14 (LA)
1991—Cardinals, 24-14 (LA)
1992—Cardinals, 20-14 (LA)
1993—Cardinals, 38-10 (P)
(RS Pts.—Rams 853, Cardinals 730)
(PS Pts.—Rams 35, Cardinals 23)
*Franchise known as Phoenix prior to
1994, in St. Louis prior to 1988,
and in Chicago prior to 1960
**Franchise in Cleveland prior to 1946
***NFC Divisional Playoff
ARIZONA vs. MIAMI
RS: Dolphins lead series, 6-0
1972—Dolphins, 31-10 (M)

1977—Dolphins, 55-14 (StL)
1978—Dolphins, 24-10 (M)
1981—Dolphins, 20-7 (StL)
1984—Dolphins, 36-28 (StL)
1990—Dolphins, 23-3 (M)
(RS Pts.—Dolphins 189, Cardinals 72)
*Franchise known as Phoenix prior to
1994 and in St. Louis prior to 1988
ARIZONA vs. MINNESOTA
RS: Cardinals lead series, 7-4
PS: Vikings lead series, 1-0
1963—Cardinals, 56-14 (M)
1967—Cardinals, 34-24 (M)
1969—Vikings, 27-10 (StL)
1972—Cardinals, 19-17 (M)
1974—Vikings, 28-24 (StL)
    **Vikings, 30-14 (M)
1977—Cardinals, 27-7 (M)
1979—Cardinals, 37-7 (StL)
1981—Cardinals, 30-17 (StL)
1983—Cardinals, 41-31 (StL)
1991—Vikings, 34-7 (M)
    Vikings, 28-0 (P)
(RS Pts.—Cardinals 285, Vikings 234)
(PS Pts.—Vikings 30, Cardinals 14)
*Franchise known as Phoenix prior to
1994 and in St. Louis prior to 1988
**NFC Divisional Playoff
ARIZONA vs. **NEW ENGLAND
RS: Cardinals lead series, 6-2
1970—Cardinals, 31-0 (StL)
1975—Cardinals, 24-17 (StL)
1978—Patriots, 16-6 (StL)
1981—Cardinals, 27-20 (NE)
1984—Cardinals, 33-10 (NE)
1990—Cardinals, 34-14 (P)
1991—Cardinals, 24-10 (P)
1993—Patriots, 23-21 (P)
(RS Pts.—Cardinals 200, Patriots 110)
*Franchise known as Phoenix prior to
1994 and in St. Louis prior to 1988
**Franchise in Boston prior to 1971
ARIZONA vs. NEW ORLEANS
RS: Cardinals lead series, 10-9
1967—Cardinals, 31-20 (StL)
1968—Cardinals, 21-20 (NO)
    Cardinals, 31-17 (StL)
1969—Saints, 51-42 (StL)
1970—Cardinals, 24-17 (StL)
1974—Saints, 14-0 (NO)
1977—Cardinals, 49-31 (StL)
1980—Cardinals, 40-7 (NO)
1981—Cardinals, 30-3 (StL)
1982—Cardinals, 21-7 (NO)
1983—Saints, 28-17 (NO)
1984—Saints, 34-24 (NO)
1985—Cardinals, 28-16 (StL)
1986—Saints, 16-7 (StL)
1987—Cardinals, 24-19 (StL)
1990—Saints, 28-7 (NO)
1991—Saints, 27-3 (P)
1992—Saints, 30-21 (P)
1993—Saints, 20-17 (P)
(RS Pts.—Cardinals 437, Saints 405)
*Franchise known as Phoenix prior to
1994 and in St. Louis prior to 1988
ARIZONA vs. N.Y. GIANTS
RS: Giants lead series, 65-35-2
1926—Giants, 20-0 (NY)
1927—Giants, 28-7 (NY)
1929—Giants, 24-21 (NY)
1930—Giants, 25-12 (NY)
    Giants, 13-7 (C)
1935—Cardinals, 14-13 (NY)
1936—Giants, 14-6 (NY)
1938—Giants, 6-0 (NY)
1939—Giants, 17-7 (NY)
1941—Cardinals, 10-7 (NY)
1942—Giants, 21-7 (NY)
1943—Giants, 24-13 (NY)
1946—Giants, 28-24 (NY)
1947—Giants, 35-31 (NY)
1948—Cardinals, 63-35 (NY)

1949—Giants, 41-38 (C)
1950—Giants, 17-3 (C)
    Giants, 51-21 (NY)
1951—Giants, 28-17 (NY)
    Giants, 10-0 (C)
1952—Cardinals, 24-23 (NY)
    Giants, 28-6 (C)
1953—Giants, 21-7 (NY)
    Giants, 23-20 (C)
1954—Giants, 41-10 (C)
    Giants, 31-17 (NY)
1955—Cardinals, 28-17 (C)
    Giants, 10-0 (NY)
1956—Cardinals, 35-27 (C)
    Giants, 23-10 (NY)
1957—Giants, 27-14 (NY)
    Giants, 28-21 (C)
1958—Giants, 37-7 (Buffalo)
    Cardinals, 23-6 (NY)
1959—Giants, 9-3 (NY)
    Giants, 30-20 (Minn)
1960—Giants, 35-14 (StL)
    Cardinals, 20-13 (NY)
1961—Cardinals, 21-10 (NY)
    Giants, 24-9 (StL)
1962—Giants, 31-14 (StL)
    Giants, 31-28 (NY)
1963—Giants, 38-21 (StL)
    Cardinals, 24-17 (NY)
1964—Giants, 34-17 (NY)
    Tie, 10-10 (StL)
1965—Cardinals, 14-10 (NY)
    Giants, 28-15 (StL)
1966—Cardinals, 24-19 (StL)
    Cardinals, 20-17 (NY)
1967—Cardinals, 37-20 (StL)
    Giants, 37-14 (NY)
1968—Cardinals, 28-21 (NY)
1969—Cardinals, 42-17 (StL)
    Giants, 49-6 (NY)
1970—Giants, 35-17 (NY)
    Giants, 34-17 (StL)
1971—Giants, 21-20 (StL)
    Cardinals, 24-7 (NY)
1972—Cardinals, 27-21 (NY)
    Giants, 13-7 (StL)
1973—Cardinals, 35-27 (StL)
    Giants, 24-13 (New Haven)
1974—Cardinals, 23-21 (New Haven)
    Cardinals, 26-14 (StL)
1975—Cardinals, 26-14 (StL)
    Cardinals, 20-13 (NY)
1976—Cardinals, 27-21 (StL)
    Cardinals, 17-14 (NY)
1977—Cardinals, 28-0 (StL)
    Giants, 27-7 (NY)
1978—Cardinals, 20-10 (StL)
    Giants, 17-0 (NY)
1979—Cardinals, 27-14 (NY)
    Cardinals, 29-20 (StL)
1980—Giants, 41-35 (StL)
    Cardinals, 23-7 (NY)
1981—Giants, 34-14 (NY)
    Giants, 20-10 (StL)
1982—Cardinals, 24-21 (StL)
1983—Tie, 20-20 (StL) OT
    Cardinals, 10-6 (StL)
1984—Giants, 16-10 (NY)
    Cardinals, 31-21 (StL)
1985—Giants, 27-17 (NY)
    Giants, 34-3 (StL)
1986—Giants, 13-6 (StL)
    Giants, 27-7 (NY)
1987—Giants, 30-7 (NY)
    Cardinals, 27-24 (StL)
1988—Cardinals, 24-17 (P)
    Giants, 44-7 (NY)
1989—Giants, 35-7 (P)
    Giants, 20-13 (P)
1990—Giants, 20-19 (NY)
    Giants, 24-21 (P)
1991—Giants, 20-9 (NY)
    Giants, 21-14 (P)

1992—Giants, 31-21 (NY)
  Cardinals, 19-0 (P)
1993—Giants, 19-17 (NY)
  Cardinals, 17-6 (P)
(RS Pts.—Giants 2,277, Cardinals 1,753)
*Franchise known as Phoenix prior to 1994, in St. Louis prior to 1988, and in Chicago prior to 1960

ARIZONA vs. N.Y. JETS
RS: Cardinals lead series, 2-1
1971—Cardinals, 17-10 (StL)
1975—Cardinals, 37-6 (NY)
1978—Jets, 23-10 (NY)
(RS Pts.—Cardinals 64, Jets 39)
*Franchise known as Phoenix prior to 1994 and in St. Louis prior to 1988

ARIZONA vs. PHILADELPHIA
RS: Cardinals lead series, 44-43-5
PS: Series tied, 1-1
1935—Cardinals, 12-3 (C)
1936—Cardinals, 13-0 (C)
1937—Tie, 6-6 (P)
1938—Eagles, 7-0 (Erie, Pa.)
1941—Eagles, 21-14 (P)
1945—Eagles, 21-6 (P)
1947—Cardinals, 45-21 (P)
  **Cardinals, 28-21 (C)
1948—Cardinals, 21-14 (C)
  **Eagles, 7-0 (P)
1949—Eagles, 28-3 (P)
1950—Eagles, 45-7 (C)
  Cardinals, 14-10 (P)
1951—Eagles, 17-14 (P)
1952—Eagles, 10-7 (P)
  Cardinals, 28-22 (C)
1953—Eagles, 56-17 (C)
  Eagles, 38-0 (P)
1954—Eagles, 35-16 (C)
  Eagles, 30-14 (P)
1955—Tie, 24-24 (C)
  Eagles, 27-3 (P)
1956—Cardinals, 20-6 (P)
  Cardinals, 28-17 (C)
1957—Eagles, 38-21 (C)
  Cardinals, 31-27 (P)
1958—Tie, 21-21 (C)
  Eagles, 49-21 (P)
1959—Eagles, 28-24 (Minn)
  Eagles, 27-17 (P)
1960—Eagles, 31-27 (P)
  Eagles, 20-6 (StL)
1961—Cardinals, 30-27 (P)
  Eagles, 20-7 (StL)
1962—Cardinals, 27-21 (P)
  Cardinals, 45-35 (StL)
1963—Cardinals, 28-24 (P)
  Cardinals, 38-14 (StL)
1964—Cardinals, 38-13 (P)
  Cardinals, 36-34 (StL)
1965—Eagles, 34-27 (P)
  Eagles, 28-24 (StL)
1966—Cardinals, 16-13 (StL)
  Cardinals, 41-10 (P)
1967—Cardinals, 48-14 (StL)
  Cardinals, 45-17 (P)
1968—Cardinals, 45-17 (P)
1969—Eagles, 34-30 (StL)
1970—Cardinals, 35-20 (P)
  Cardinals, 23-14 (StL)
1971—Eagles, 37-20 (StL)
  Eagles, 19-7 (P)
1972—Tie, 6-6 (P)
  Cardinals, 24-23 (StL)
1973—Cardinals, 34-23 (P)
  Eagles, 27-24 (StL)
1974—Cardinals, 7-3 (StL)
  Cardinals, 13-3 (P)
1975—Cardinals, 31-20 (StL)
  Cardinals, 24-23 (StL)
1976—Cardinals, 33-14 (StL)
  Cardinals, 17-14 (P)
1977—Cardinals, 21-17 (P)
  Cardinals, 21-16 (StL)
1978—Cardinals, 16-10 (P)

Eagles, 14-10 (StL)
1979—Eagles, 24-20 (StL)
  Eagles, 16-13 (P)
1980—Cardinals, 24-14 (StL)
  Eagles, 17-3 (P)
1981—Eagles, 52-10 (StL)
  Eagles, 38-0 (P)
1982—Cardinals, 23-20 (P)
1983—Cardinals, 14-11 (P)
  Cardinals, 31-7 (StL)
1984—Cardinals, 34-14 (P)
  Cardinals, 17-16 (StL)
1985—Eagles, 30-7 (P)
  Eagles, 24-14 (StL)
1986—Cardinals, 13-10 (StL)
  Tie, 10-10 (P) OT
1987—Eagles, 28-23 (StL)
  Cardinals, 31-19 (P)
1988—Eagles, 31-21 (P)
  Eagles, 23-17 (Phx)
1989—Eagles, 17-5 (Phx)
  Eagles, 31-14 (P)
1990—Cardinals, 23-21 (P)
  Eagles, 23-21 (Phx)
1991—Cardinals, 26-10 (P)
  Eagles, 34-14 (Phx)
1992—Eagles, 31-14 (Phx)
  Eagles, 7-3 (P)
1993—Eagles, 23-17 (P)
  Cardinals, 16-3 (Phx)
(RS Pts.—Eagles 1,972, Cardinals 1,832)
(PS Pts.—Tie 28, 28)
*Franchise known as Phoenix prior to 1994, in St. Louis prior to 1988, and in Chicago prior to 1960
**NFL Championship

ARIZONA vs. **PITTSBURGH
RS: Steelers lead series, 29-21-3
1933—Pirates, 14-13 (C)
1935—Pirates, 17-13 (P)
1936—Cardinals, 14-6 (C)
1937—Cardinals, 13-7 (P)
1939—Cardinals, 10-0 (P)
1940—Tie, 7-7 (P)
1942—Steelers, 19-3 (P)
1945—Steelers, 23-0 (P)
1946—Steelers, 14-7 (P)
1948—Cardinals, 24-7 (P)
1950—Steelers, 28-17 (C)
  Steelers, 28-7 (P)
1951—Steelers, 28-14 (C)
1952—Steelers, 34-28 (C)
  Steelers, 17-14 (P)
1953—Steelers, 31-28 (P)
  Steelers, 21-17 (C)
1954—Cardinals, 17-14 (C)
  Steelers, 20-17 (P)
1955—Steelers, 14-7 (P)
  Cardinals, 27-13 (C)
1956—Steelers, 14-7 (P)
  Cardinals, 38-27 (C)
1957—Steelers, 29-20 (P)
  Steelers, 27-2 (C)
1958—Steelers, 27-20 (C)
  Steelers, 38-21 (P)
1959—Cardinals, 45-24 (C)
  Steelers, 35-20 (P)
1960—Steelers, 27-14 (P)
  Cardinals, 38-7 (StL)
1961—Steelers, 30-27 (P)
  Cardinals, 20-0 (StL)
1962—Steelers, 26-17 (StL)
  Steelers, 19-7 (P)
1963—Steelers, 23-10 (P)
  Cardinals, 24-23 (StL)
1964—Cardinals, 34-30 (StL)
  Cardinals, 21-20 (P)
1965—Cardinals, 20-7 (P)
  Cardinals, 21-17 (StL)
1966—Steelers, 30-9 (P)
  Cardinals, 6-3 (StL)
1967—Cardinals, 28-14 (P)
  Tie, 14-14 (StL)

1968—Tie, 28-28 (StL)
  Cardinals, 20-10 (P)
1969—Cardinals, 27-14 (P)
  Cardinals, 47-10 (StL)
1972—Steelers, 25-19 (StL)
1979—Steelers, 24-21 (StL)
1985—Steelers, 23-10 (P)
1988—Cardinals, 31-14 (Phx)
(RS Pts.—Steelers 1,021, Cardinals 983)
*Franchise known as Phoenix prior to 1994, in St. Louis prior to 1988, and in Chicago prior to 1960
**Steelers known as Pirates prior to 1941

ARIZONA vs. SAN DIEGO
RS: Chargers lead series, 5-1
1971—Chargers, 20-17 (SD)
1976—Chargers, 43-24 (SD)
1983—Chargers, 44-14 (SD)
1987—Chargers, 28-24 (SD)
1989—Chargers, 24-13 (P)
1992—Chargers, 27-21 (P)
(RS Pts.—Chargers 156, Cardinals 143)
*Franchise known as Phoenix prior to 1994, in St. Louis prior to 1988,

ARIZONA vs. SAN FRANCISCO
RS: 49ers lead series, 10-9
1951—Cardinals, 27-21 (SF)
1957—Cardinals, 20-10 (SF)
1962—49ers, 24-17 (StL)
1964—Cardinals, 23-13 (SF)
1968—49ers, 35-17 (SF)
1971—49ers, 26-14 (StL)
1974—Cardinals, 34-9 (SF)
1976—Cardinals, 23-20 (StL) OT
1978—Cardinals, 16-10 (SF)
1979—Cardinals, 13-10 (StL)
1980—49ers, 24-21 (SF) OT
1982—49ers, 31-20 (StL)
1983—49ers, 42-27 (StL)
1986—49ers, 43-17 (SF)
1987—49ers, 34-28 (SF)
1988—Cardinals, 24-23 (P)
1991—49ers, 14-10 (SF)
1992—Cardinals, 24-14 (P)
1993—49ers, 28-14 (SF)
(RS Pts.—49ers 431, Cardinals 389)
*Franchise known as Phoenix prior to 1994, in St. Louis prior to 1988, and in Chicago prior to 1960

ARIZONA vs. SEATTLE
RS: Cardinals lead series, 4-0
1976—Cardinals, 30-24 (S)
1983—Cardinals, 33-28 (StL)
1989—Cardinals, 34-24 (S)
1993—Cardinals, 30-27 (S) OT
(RS Pts.—Cardinals 127, Seahawks 103)
*Franchise known as Phoenix prior to 1994 and in St. Louis prior to 1988

ARIZONA vs. TAMPA BAY
RS: Series tied, 6-6
1977—Buccaneers, 17-7 (TB)
1981—Buccaneers, 20-10 (TB)
1983—Cardinals, 34-27 (TB)
1985—Buccaneers, 16-0 (TB)
1986—Cardinals, 30-19 (TB)
  Cardinals, 21-17 (StL)
1987—Cardinals, 31-28 (StL)
  Cardinals, 31-14 (TB)
1988—Cardinals, 30-24 (TB)
1989—Buccaneers, 14-13 (P)
1992—Buccaneers, 23-7 (TB)
  Buccaneers, 7-3 (P)
(RS Pts.—Buccaneers 226, Cardinals 217)
*Franchise known as Phoenix prior to 1994 and in St. Louis prior to 1988

ARIZONA vs. **WASHINGTON
RS: Redskins lead series, 61-36-2
1932—Cardinals, 9-0 (B)
  Braves, 8-6 (C)
1933—Redskins, 10-0 (C)
  Tie, 0-0 (B)
1934—Redskins, 9-0 (B)

1935—Cardinals, 6-0 (B)
1936—Redskins, 13-10 (B)
1937—Cardinals, 21-14 (W)
1939—Redskins, 28-7 (W)
1940—Redskins, 28-21 (W)
1942—Redskins, 28-0 (W)
1943—Redskins, 13-7 (W)
1945—Redskins, 24-21 (W)
1947—Redskins, 45-21 (W)
1949—Cardinals, 38-7 (C)
1950—Redskins, 38-28 (W)
1951—Redskins, 7-3 (C)
  Redskins, 20-17 (W)
1952—Redskins, 23-7 (C)
  Cardinals, 17-6 (W)
1953—Redskins, 24-13 (C)
  Redskins, 28-17 (W)
1954—Cardinals, 38-16 (C)
  Redskins, 37-20 (W)
1955—Cardinals, 24-10 (W)
  Redskins, 31-0 (C)
1956—Cardinals, 31-3 (W)
  Redskins, 17-14 (C)
1957—Redskins, 37-14 (C)
  Cardinals, 44-14 (W)
1958—Cardinals, 37-10 (C)
  Redskins, 45-31 (W)
1959—Cardinals, 49-21 (C)
  Redskins, 23-14 (W)
1960—Cardinals, 44-7 (StL)
  Cardinals, 26-14 (W)
1961—Cardinals, 24-0 (W)
  Cardinals, 38-24 (StL)
1962—Redskins, 24-14 (W)
  Tie, 17-17 (StL)
1963—Cardinals, 21-7 (W)
  Cardinals, 24-20 (StL)
1964—Cardinals, 23-17 (W)
  Cardinals, 38-24 (StL)
1965—Redskins, 37-16 (W)
  Redskins, 24-20 (StL)
1966—Cardinals, 23-7 (StL)
  Redskins, 26-20 (W)
1967—Cardinals, 27-21 (W)
1968—Redskins, 41-14 (StL)
1969—Redskins, 33-17 (W)
1970—Cardinals, 27-17 (StL)
  Redskins, 28-27 (W)
1971—Redskins, 24-17 (StL)
  Redskins, 20-0 (W)
1972—Redskins, 24-10 (W)
  Redskins, 33-3 (StL)
1973—Cardinals, 34-27 (StL)
  Redskins, 31-13 (W)
1974—Cardinals, 17-10 (W)
  Cardinals, 23-20 (StL)
1975—Redskins, 27-17 (W)
  Cardinals, 20-17 (StL) OT
1976—Redskins, 20-10 (W)
  Redskins, 16-10 (StL)
1977—Cardinals, 24-14 (W)
  Redskins, 26-20 (StL)
1978—Redskins, 28-10 (StL)
  Cardinals, 27-17 (W)
1979—Cardinals, 17-7 (StL)
  Redskins, 30-28 (W)
1980—Redskins, 23-0 (W)
  Redskins, 31-7 (StL)
1981—Cardinals, 40-30 (StL)
  Redskins, 42-21 (W)
1982—Redskins, 12-7 (StL)
  Redskins, 28-0 (W)
1983—Redskins, 38-14 (StL)
  Redskins, 45-7 (W)
1984—Cardinals, 26-24 (StL)
  Redskins, 29-27 (W)
1985—Redskins, 27-10 (W)
  Redskins, 27-16 (StL)
1986—Redskins, 28-21 (W)
  Redskins, 20-17 (StL)
1987—Redskins, 28-21 (W)
  Redskins, 34-17 (StL)
1988—Cardinals, 30-21 (P)

Redskins, 33-17 (W)
1989—Redskins, 30-28 (W)
Redskins, 29-10 (P)
1990—Redskins, 31-0 (W)
Redskins, 38-10 (P)
1991—Redskins, 34-0 (W)
Redskins, 20-14 (P)
1992—Cardinals, 27-24 (P)
Redskins, 41-3 (W)
1993—Cardinals, 17-10 (W)
Cardinals, 36-6 (P)
(RS Pts.—Redskins 2,161, Cardinals 1,826)
*Franchise known as Phoenix prior to
1994, in St. Louis prior to 1988,
and in Chicago prior to 1960
**Franchise in Boston prior to 1937 and
known as Braves prior to 1933

ATLANTA vs. ARIZONA
RS: Cardinals lead series, 11-5;
See Arizona vs. Atlanta
ATLANTA vs. BUFFALO
RS: Series tied, 3-3
1973—Bills, 17-6 (A)
1977—Bills, 3-0 (B)
1980—Falcons, 30-14 (B)
1983—Falcons, 31-14 (A)
1989—Falcons, 30-28 (A)
1992—Bills, 41-14 (B)
(RS Pts.—Bills 117, Falcons 111)
ATLANTA vs. CHICAGO
RS: Series tied, 9-9
1966—Bears, 23-6 (C)
1967—Bears, 23-14 (A)
1968—Falcons, 16-13 (C)
1969—Falcons, 48-31 (A)
1970—Bears, 23-14 (A)
1972—Falcons, 37-21 (C)
1973—Falcons, 46-6 (A)
1974—Falcons, 13-10 (A)
1976—Falcons, 10-0 (C)
1977—Falcons, 16-10 (C)
1978—Bears, 13-7 (C)
1980—Bears, 28-17 (A)
1983—Falcons, 20-17 (C)
1985—Bears, 36-0 (C)
1986—Bears, 13-10 (A)
1990—Bears, 30-24 (A)
1992—Bears, 41-31 (C)
1993—Bears, 6-0 (C)
(RS Pts.—Falcons 340, Bears 333)
ATLANTA vs. CINCINNATI
RS: Bengals lead series, 6-2
1971—Falcons, 9-6 (C)
1975—Bengals, 21-14 (A)
1978—Bengals, 37-7 (C)
1981—Bengals, 30-28 (A)
1984—Bengals, 35-14 (C)
1987—Bengals, 16-10 (A)
1990—Falcons, 38-17 (A)
1993—Bengals, 21-17 (C)
(RS Pts.—Bengals 183, Falcons 137)
ATLANTA vs. CLEVELAND
RS: Browns lead series, 8-2
1966—Browns, 49-17 (A)
1968—Browns, 30-7 (C)
1971—Falcons, 31-14 (C)
1976—Browns, 20-17 (A)
1978—Browns, 24-16 (A)
1981—Browns, 28-17 (C)
1984—Browns, 23-7 (A)
1987—Browns, 38-3 (C)
1990—Browns, 13-10 (C)
1993—Falcons, 17-14 (A)
(RS Pts.—Browns 253, Falcons 142)
ATLANTA vs. DALLAS
RS: Cowboys lead series, 9-6
PS: Cowboys lead series, 2-0
1966—Cowboys, 47-14 (A)
1967—Cowboys, 37-7 (D)
1969—Cowboys, 24-17 (A)
1970—Cowboys, 13-0 (D)
1974—Cowboys, 24-0 (A)

1976—Falcons, 17-10 (A)
1978—*Cowboys, 27-20 (D)
1980—*Cowboys, 30-27 (A)
1985—Cowboys, 24-10 (D)
1986—Falcons, 37-35 (D)
1987—Falcons, 21-10 (D)
1988—Cowboys, 26-20 (D)
1989—Falcons 27-21 (A)
1990—Falcons, 26-7 (A)
1991—Cowboys, 31-27 (D)
1992—Cowboys, 41-17 (A)
1993—Falcons, 27-14 (A)
(RS Pts.—Cowboys 364, Falcons 267)
(PS Pts.—Cowboys 57, Falcons 47)
*NFC Divisional Playoff
ATLANTA vs. DENVER
RS: Broncos lead series, 4-3
1970—Broncos, 24-10 (D)
1972—Falcons, 23-20 (A)
1975—Falcons, 35-21 (A)
1979—Broncos, 20-17 (A) OT
1982—Falcons, 34-27 (D)
1985—Broncos, 44-28 (A)
1988—Broncos, 30-14 (D)
(RS Pts.—Broncos 186, Falcons 161)
ATLANTA vs. DETROIT
RS: Lions lead series, 17-5
1966—Lions, 28-10 (D)
1967—Lions, 24-3 (D)
1968—Lions, 24-7 (A)
1969—Lions, 27-21 (D)
1971—Lions, 41-38 (D)
1972—Lions, 26-23 (A)
1973—Lions, 31-6 (D)
1975—Lions, 17-14 (A)
1976—Lions, 24-10 (D)
1977—Falcons, 17-6 (D)
1978—Falcons, 14-0 (A)
1979—Lions, 24-23 (D)
1980—Falcons, 43-28 (A)
1983—Falcons, 30-14 (D)
1984—Lions, 27-24 (A) OT
1985—Lions, 28-27 (A)
1986—Falcons, 20-6 (D)
1987—Lions, 30-13 (A)
1988—Falcons, 31-17 (D)
1989—Lions, 31-24 (A)
1990—Lions, 21-14 (D)
1993—Lions, 30-13 (D)
(RS Pts.—Lions 518, Falcons 411)
ATLANTA vs. GREEN BAY
RS: Series tied, 9-9
1966—Packers, 56-3 (Mil)
1967—Packers, 23-0 (Mil)
1968—Packers, 38-7 (A)
1969—Packers, 28-10 (GB)
1970—Packers, 27-24 (GB)
1971—Falcons, 28-21 (A)
1972—Falcons, 10-9 (Mil)
1974—Falcons, 10-3 (A)
1975—Packers, 22-13 (GB)
1976—Packers, 24-20 (A)
1979—Falcons, 25-7 (A)
1981—Falcons, 31-17 (GB)
1982—Packers, 38-7 (A)
1983—Falcons, 47-41 (A) OT
1988—Falcons, 20-0 (A)
1989—Packers, 23-21 (Mil)
1991—Falcons, 35-31 (A)
1992—Falcons, 24-10 (A)
(RS Pts.—Packers 418, Falcons 335)
ATLANTA vs. HOUSTON
RS: Falcons lead series, 5-3
1972—Falcons, 20-10 (A)
1976—Oilers, 20-14 (H)
1978—Falcons, 20-14 (A)
1981—Falcons, 31-27 (H)
1984—Falcons, 42-10 (A)
1987—Oilers, 37-33 (H)
1990—Falcons, 47-27 (A)
1993—Oilers, 33-17 (H)
(RS Pts.—Falcons 224, Oilers 178)
ATLANTA vs. *INDIANAPOLIS

RS: Colts lead series, 10-0
1966—Colts, 19-7 (A)
1967—Colts, 38-31 (B)
Colts, 49-7 (A)
1968—Colts, 28-20 (A)
Colts, 44-0 (B)
1969—Colts, 21-14 (A)
Colts, 13-6 (B)
1974—Colts, 17-7 (A)
1986—Colts, 28-23 (A)
1989—Colts, 13-9 (I)
(RS Pts.—Colts 270, Falcons 124)
*Franchise in Baltimore prior to 1984
ATLANTA vs. KANSAS CITY
RS: Chiefs lead series, 3-0
1972—Chiefs, 17-14 (A)
1985—Chiefs, 38-10 (KC)
1991—Chiefs, 14-3 (KC)
(RS Pts.—Chiefs 69, Falcons 27)
ATLANTA vs. *L.A. RAIDERS
RS: Raiders lead series, 4-3
1971—Falcons, 24-13 (A)
1975—Raiders, 37-34 (O) OT
1979—Raiders, 50-19 (O)
1982—Raiders, 38-14 (A)
1985—Raiders, 34-24 (A)
1988—Falcons, 12-6 (A)
1991—Falcons, 21-17 (A)
(RS Pts.—Raiders 195, Falcons 148)
*Franchise in Oakland prior to 1982
ATLANTA vs. L.A. RAMS
RS: Rams lead series, 36-16-2
1966—Rams, 19-14 (A)
1967—Rams, 31-3 (A)
Rams, 20-3 (LA)
1968—Rams, 27-14 (LA)
Rams, 17-10 (A)
1969—Rams, 17-7 (LA)
Rams, 38-6 (A)
1970—Tie, 10-10 (LA)
Rams, 17-7 (A)
1971—Tie, 20-20 (LA)
Rams, 24-16 (A)
1972—Falcons, 31-3 (A)
Rams, 20-7 (LA)
1973—Rams, 31-0 (LA)
Falcons, 15-13 (A)
1974—Rams, 21-0 (LA)
Rams, 30-7 (A)
1975—Rams, 22-7 (LA)
Rams, 16-7 (A)
1976—Rams, 30-14 (A)
Rams, 59-0 (LA)
1977—Falcons, 17-6 (A)
Rams, 23-7 (LA)
1978—Rams, 10-0 (LA)
Falcons, 15-7 (A)
1979—Rams, 20-14 (LA)
Rams, 34-13 (A)
1980—Falcons, 13-10 (A)
Rams, 20-17 (LA) OT
1981—Rams, 37-35 (A)
Rams, 21-16 (LA)
1982—Falcons, 34-17 (A)
1983—Rams, 27-21 (LA)
Rams, 36-13 (A)
1984—Falcons, 30-28 (LA)
Rams, 24-10 (A)
1985—Rams, 17-6 (LA)
Falcons, 30-14 (A)
1986—Falcons, 26-14 (A)
Rams, 14-7 (LA)
1987—Falcons, 24-20 (A)
Rams, 33-0 (LA)
1988—Rams, 33-0 (A)
Rams, 22-7 (LA)
1989—Rams, 31-21 (A)
Rams, 26-14 (LA)
1990—Rams, 44-24 (LA)
Falcons, 20-13 (A)
1991—Falcons, 31-14 (A)
Falcons, 31-14 (LA)
1992—Falcons, 30-28 (A)

Rams, 38-27 (LA)
1993—Rams, 30-24 (A)
Falcons, 13-0 (LA)
(RS Pts.—Rams 1,204, Falcons 794)
ATLANTA vs. MIAMI
RS: Dolphins lead series, 5-1
1970—Dolphins, 20-7 (A)
1974—Dolphins, 42-7 (M)
1980—Dolphins, 20-17 (A)
1983—Dolphins, 31-24 (M)
1986—Falcons, 20-14 (M)
1992—Dolphins, 21-17 (M)
(RS Pts.—Dolphins 148, Falcons 92)
ATLANTA vs. MINNESOTA
RS: Vikings lead series, 11-6
PS: Vikings lead series, 1-0
1966—Falcons, 20-13 (M)
1967—Falcons, 21-20 (A)
1968—Vikings, 47-7 (M)
1969—Falcons, 10-3 (A)
1970—Vikings, 37-7 (A)
1971—Vikings, 24-7 (M)
1973—Falcons, 20-14 (A)
1974—Vikings, 23-10 (M)
1975—Vikings, 38-0 (M)
1977—Vikings, 14-7 (A)
1980—Vikings, 24-23 (M)
1981—Falcons, 31-30 (A)
1982—*Vikings, 30-24 (M)
1984—Vikings, 27-20 (M)
1985—Falcons, 14-13 (A)
1987—Vikings, 24-13 (M)
1989—Vikings, 43-17 (M)
1991—Vikings, 20-19 (A)
(RS Pts.—Vikings 414, Falcons 246)
(PS Pts.—Vikings 30, Falcons 24)
*NFC First-Round Playoff
ATLANTA vs. NEW ENGLAND
RS: Falcons lead series, 4-3
1972—Patriots, 21-20 (NE)
1977—Patriots, 16-10 (A)
1980—Falcons, 37-21 (NE)
1983—Falcons, 24-13 (A)
1986—Patriots, 25-17 (NE)
1989—Falcons, 16-15 (A)
1992—Falcons, 34-0 (A)
(RS Pts.—Falcons 158, Patriots 111)
ATLANTA vs. NEW ORLEANS
RS: Falcons lead series, 27-22
PS: Falcons lead series, 1-0
1967—Saints, 27-24 (NO)
1969—Falcons, 45-17 (A)
1970—Falcons, 14-3 (NO)
Falcons, 32-14 (A)
1971—Falcons, 28-6 (A)
Falcons, 24-20 (NO)
1972—Falcons, 21-14 (NO)
Falcons, 36-20 (A)
1973—Falcons, 62-7 (NO)
Falcons, 14-10 (A)
1974—Falcons, 14-13 (NO)
Saints, 13-3 (A)
1975—Falcons, 14-7 (A)
Saints, 23-7 (NO)
1976—Saints, 30-0 (NO)
Falcons, 23-20 (A)
1977—Saints, 21-20 (NO)
Falcons, 35-7 (A)
1978—Falcons, 20-17 (NO)
Falcons, 20-17 (A)
1979—Falcons, 40-34 (NO) OT
Saints, 37-6 (A)
1980—Falcons, 41-14 (NO)
Falcons, 31-13 (A)
1981—Falcons, 27-0 (A)
Falcons, 41-10 (NO)
1982—Falcons, 35-0 (A)
Saints, 35-6 (NO)
1983—Saints, 19-17 (A)
Saints, 27-10 (NO)
1984—Falcons, 36-28 (NO)
Saints, 17-13 (A)
1985—Falcons, 31-24 (A)

Falcons, 16-10 (NO)
1986—Falcons, 31-10 (NO)
Saints, 14-9 (A)
1987—Saints, 38-0 (A)
1988—Saints, 29-21 (A)
Saints, 10-9 (NO)
1989—Saints, 20-13 (NO)
Saints, 26-17 (A)
1990—Falcons, 28-27 (A)
Saints, 10-7 (NO)
1991—Saints, 27-6 (A)
Falcons, 23-20 (NO) OT
*Falcons, 27-20 (NO)
1992—Saints, 10-7 (A)
Saints, 22-14 (NO)
1993—Saints, 34-31 (A)
Falcons, 26-15 (NO)
(RS Pts.—Falcons 1,047, Saints 887)
(PS Pts.—Falcons 27, Saints 20)
*NFC First-Round Playoff

ATLANTA vs. N.Y. GIANTS
RS: Series tied, 6-6
1966—Falcons, 27-16 (NY)
1968—Falcons, 24-21 (A)
1971—Giants, 21-17 (A)
1974—Falcons, 14-7 (New Haven)
1977—Falcons, 17-3 (A)
1978—Falcons, 23-20 (A)
1979—Giants, 24-3 (NY)
1981—Giants, 27-24 (A) OT
1982—Falcons, 16-14 (NY)
1983—Giants, 16-13 (A) OT
1984—Giants, 19-7 (A)
1988—Giants, 23-16 (A)
(RS Pts.—Giants 211, Falcons 201)

ATLANTA vs. N.Y. JETS
RS: Series tied, 3-3
1973—Falcons, 28-20 (NY)
1980—Jets, 14-7 (A)
1983—Falcons, 27-21 (NY)
1986—Jets, 28-14 (A)
1989—Jets, 27-7 (NY)
1992—Falcons, 20-17 (A)
(RS Pts.—Jets 127, Falcons 103)

ATLANTA vs. PHILADELPHIA
RS: Eagles lead series, 8-6-1
PS: Falcons lead series, 1-0
1966—Eagles, 23-10 (P)
1967—Eagles, 38-7 (A)
1969—Falcons, 27-3 (P)
1970—Tie, 13-13 (P)
1973—Falcons, 44-27 (P)
1976—Eagles, 14-13 (A)
1978—*Falcons, 14-13 (A)
1979—Falcons, 14-10 (P)
1980—Falcons, 20-17 (P)
1981—Eagles, 16-13 (P)
1983—Eagles, 28-24 (A)
1984—Falcons, 26-10 (A)
1985—Eagles, 23-17 (P) OT
1986—Falcons, 16-0 (A)
1988—Falcons, 27-24 (P)
1990—Eagles, 24-23 (A)
(RS Pts.—Eagles 286, Falcons 278)
(PS Pts.—Falcons 14, Eagles 13)
*NFC First-Round Playoff

ATLANTA vs. PITTSBURGH
RS: Steelers lead series, 9-1
1966—Steelers, 57-33 (A)
1968—Steelers, 41-21 (A)
1970—Falcons, 27-16 (A)
1974—Steelers, 24-17 (A)
1978—Steelers, 31-7 (P)
1981—Steelers, 34-20 (A)
1984—Steelers, 35-10 (P)
1987—Steelers, 28-12 (A)
1990—Steelers, 21-9 (P)
1993—Steelers, 45-17 (A)
(RS Pts.—Steelers 332, Falcons 173)

ATLANTA vs. SAN DIEGO
RS: Falcons lead series, 3-1
1973—Falcons, 41-0 (SD)
1979—Falcons, 28-26 (SD)

1988—Chargers, 10-7 (A)
1991—Falcons, 13-10 (SD)
(RS Pts.—Falcons 89, Chargers 46)

ATLANTA vs. SAN FRANCISCO
RS: 49ers lead series, 32-21-1
1966—49ers, 44-7 (A)
1967—49ers, 38-7 (SF)
49ers, 34-28 (A)
1968—49ers, 28-13 (SF)
49ers, 14-12 (A)
1969—Falcons, 24-12 (A)
Falcons, 21-7 (SF)
1970—Falcons, 21-20 (A)
49ers, 24-20 (SF)
1971—Falcons, 20-17 (A)
49ers, 24-3 (SF)
1972—Falcons, 49-14 (A)
49ers, 20-0 (SF)
1973—49ers, 13-9 (A)
Falcons, 17-3 (SF)
1974—49ers, 16-10 (A)
49ers, 27-0 (SF)
1975—Falcons, 17-3 (SF)
Falcons, 31-9 (A)
1976—49ers, 15-0 (SF)
Falcons, 21-16 (A)
1977—Falcons, 7-0 (SF)
49ers, 10-3 (A)
1978—Falcons, 20-17 (SF)
Falcons, 21-10 (A)
1979—49ers, 20-15 (SF)
Falcons, 31-21 (A)
1980—Falcons, 20-17 (SF)
Falcons, 35-10 (A)
1981—Falcons, 34-17 (A)
49ers, 17-14 (SF)
1982—Falcons, 17-7 (SF)
1983—49ers, 24-20 (SF)
Falcons, 28-24 (A)
1984—49ers, 14-5 (SF)
49ers, 35-17 (A)
1985—49ers, 35-16 (SF)
49ers, 38-17 (A)
1986—Tie, 10-10 (A) OT
49ers, 20-0 (SF)
1987—49ers, 25-17 (A)
49ers, 35-7 (SF)
1988—Falcons, 34-17 (SF)
49ers, 13-3 (A)
1989—49ers, 45-3 (SF)
49ers, 23-10 (A)
1990—49ers, 19-13 (SF)
49ers, 45-35 (A)
1991—Falcons, 39-34 (SF)
Falcons, 17-14 (A)
1992—49ers, 56-17 (SF)
49ers, 41-3 (A)
1993—49ers, 37-30 (SF)
Falcons, 27-24 (A)
(RS Pts.—49ers 1,207, Falcons 880)

ATLANTA vs. SEATTLE
RS: Seahawks lead series, 4-1
1976—Seahawks, 30-13 (S)
1979—Seahawks, 31-28 (A)
1985—Seahawks, 30-26 (S)
1988—Seahawks, 31-20 (A)
1991—Falcons, 26-13 (A)
(RS Pts.—Seahawks 135, Falcons 113)

ATLANTA vs. TAMPA BAY
RS: Series tied, 6-6
1977—Falcons, 17-0 (TB)
1978—Buccaneers, 14-9 (TB)
1979—Falcons, 17-14 (A)
1981—Buccaneers, 24-23 (TB)
1984—Buccaneers, 23-6 (TB)
1986—Falcons, 23-20 (TB) OT
1987—Buccaneers, 48-10 (TB)
1988—Falcons, 17-10 (A)
1990—Buccaneers, 23-17 (TB)
1991—Falcons, 43-7 (A)
1992—Falcons, 35-7 (TB)
1993—Buccaneers, 31-24 (A)
(RS Pts.—Falcons 241, Buccaneers 221)

ATLANTA vs. WASHINGTON
RS: Redskins lead series, 13-3-1
PS: Redskins lead series, 1-0
1966—Redskins, 33-20 (W)
1967—Tie, 20-20 (A)
1969—Redskins, 27-20 (W)
1972—Redskins, 24-13 (W)
1975—Redskins, 30-27 (A)
1977—Redskins, 10-6 (W)
1978—Falcons, 20-17 (A)
1979—Redskins, 16-7 (A)
1980—Falcons, 10-6 (A)
1983—Redskins, 37-21 (W)
1984—Redskins, 27-14 (W)
1985—Redskins, 44-10 (A)
1987—Falcons, 21-20 (A)
1989—Redskins, 31-30 (A)
1991—Redskins, 56-17 (W)
*Redskins, 24-7 (W)
1992—Redskins, 24-17 (A)
1993—Redskins, 30-17 (W)
(RS Pts.—Redskins 452, Falcons 290)
(PS Pts.—Redskins 24, Falcons 7)
*NFC Divisional Playoff

BUFFALO vs. ARIZONA
RS: Series tied, 3-3;
See Arizona vs. Buffalo

BUFFALO vs. ATLANTA
RS: Series tied 3-3;
See Atlanta vs. Buffalo

BUFFALO vs. CHICAGO
RS: Bears lead series, 3-2
1970—Bears, 31-13 (C)
1974—Bills, 16-6 (B)
1979—Bears, 7-0 (B)
1988—Bears, 24-3 (C)
1991—Bills, 35-20 (B)
(RS Pts.—Bears 88, Bills 67)

BUFFALO vs. CINCINNATI
RS: Bengals lead series, 9-7
PS: Bengals lead series, 2-0
1968—Bengals, 34-23 (C)
1969—Bills, 16-13 (B)
1970—Bengals, 43-14 (B)
1973—Bengals, 16-13 (B)
1975—Bengals, 33-24 (C)
1978—Bills, 5-0 (B)
1979—Bills, 51-24 (B)
1980—Bills, 14-0 (C)
1981—Bengals, 27-24 (C) OT
*Bengals, 28-21 (C)
1983—Bills, 10-6 (C)
1984—Bengals, 52-21 (C)
1985—Bengals, 23-17 (B)
1986—Bengals, 36-33 (C) OT
1988—Bengals, 35-21 (C)
**Bengals, 21-10 (C)
1989—Bills, 24-7 (B)
1991—Bills, 35-16 (B)
(RS Pts.—Bengals 365, Bills 345)
(PS Pts.—Bengals 49, Bills 31)
*AFC Divisional Playoff
**AFC Championship

BUFFALO vs. CLEVELAND
RS: Browns lead series, 7-3
PS: Browns lead series, 1-0
1972—Browns, 27-10 (C)
1974—Bills, 15-10 (C)
1977—Browns, 27-16 (B)
1978—Browns, 41-20 (C)
1981—Bills, 22-13 (B)
1984—Browns, 13-10 (B)
1985—Browns, 17-7 (C)
1986—Browns, 21-17 (B)
1987—Browns, 27-21 (C)
1989—*Browns, 34-30 (C)
1990—Bills, 42-0 (C)
(RS Pts.—Browns 196, Bills 180)
(PS Pts.—Browns 34, Bills 30)
*AFC Divisional Playoff

BUFFALO vs. DALLAS
RS: Cowboys lead series, 3-2

PS: Cowboys lead series, 2-0
1971—Cowboys, 49-37 (B)
1976—Cowboys, 17-10 (D)
1981—Cowboys, 27-14 (D)
1984—Bills, 14-3 (B)
1992—*Cowboys, 52-17 (Pasadena)
1993—Bills, 13-10 (D)
**Cowboys, 30-13 (Atlanta)
(RS Pts.—Cowboys 106, Bills 88)
(PS Pts.—Cowboys 82, Bills 30)
*Super Bowl XXVII
**Super Bowl XXVIII

BUFFALO vs. DENVER
RS: Bills lead series, 16-10-1
PS: Bills lead series, 1-0
1960—Broncos, 27-21 (B)
Tie, 38-38 (D)
1961—Broncos, 22-10 (B)
Bills, 23-10 (D)
1962—Broncos, 23-20 (B)
Bills, 45-38 (D)
1963—Bills, 30-28 (D)
Bills, 27-17 (B)
1964—Bills, 30-13 (B)
Bills, 30-19 (D)
1965—Bills, 30-15 (D)
Bills, 31-13 (B)
1966—Bills, 38-21 (B)
1967—Bills, 17-16 (D)
Broncos, 21-20 (B)
1968—Broncos, 34-32 (D)
1969—Bills, 41-28 (B)
1970—Broncos, 25-10 (B)
1975—Bills, 38-14 (B)
1977—Broncos, 26-6 (D)
1979—Broncos, 19-16 (B)
1981—Bills, 9-7 (B)
1984—Broncos, 37-7 (B)
1987—Bills, 21-14 (B)
1989—Broncos, 28-14 (B)
1990—Bills, 29-28 (B)
1991—*Bills, 10-7 (B)
1992—Bills, 27-17 (B)
(RS Pts.—Bills 660, Broncos 598)
(PS Pts.—Bills 10, Broncos 7)
*AFC Championship

BUFFALO vs. DETROIT
RS: Lions lead series, 2-1-1
1972—Tie, 21-21 (B)
1976—Lions, 27-14 (D)
1979—Bills, 20-17 (D)
1991—Lions, 17-14 (B) OT
(RS Pts.—Lions 82, Bills 69)

BUFFALO vs. GREEN BAY
RS: Bills lead series, 4-1
1974—Bills, 27-7 (GB)
1979—Bills, 19-12 (B)
1982—Packers, 33-21 (Mil)
1988—Bills, 28-0 (B)
1991—Bills, 34-24 (Mil)
(RS Pts.—Bills 129, Packers 76)

BUFFALO vs. HOUSTON
RS: Oilers lead series, 20-12
PS: Bills lead series, 2-0
1960—Bills, 25-24 (B)
Oilers, 31-23 (H)
1961—Bills, 22-12 (H)
Oilers, 28-16 (B)
1962—Oilers, 28-23 (B)
Oilers, 17-14 (H)
1963—Oilers, 31-20 (B)
Oilers, 28-14 (H)
1964—Bills, 48-17 (H)
Bills, 24-10 (B)
1965—Oilers, 19-17 (B)
Bills, 29-18 (H)
1966—Bills, 27-20 (B)
Bills, 42-20 (H)
1967—Oilers, 20-3 (B)
Oilers, 10-3 (H)
1968—Oilers, 30-7 (B)
Oilers, 35-6 (H)
1969—Oilers, 17-3 (B)

Oilers, 28-14 (H)
1971—Oilers, 20-14 (B)
1974—Oilers, 21-9 (B)
1976—Oilers, 13-3 (B)
1978—Oilers, 17-10 (H)
1983—Bills, 30-13 (B)
1985—Bills, 20-0 (B)
1986—Oilers, 16-7 (H)
1987—Bills, 34-30 (B)
1988—*Bills, 17-10 (B)
1989—Bills, 47-41 (H) OT
1990—Oilers, 27-24 (H)
1992—Oilers, 27-3 (H)
    **Bills, 41-38 (B) OT
1993—Bills, 35-7 (B)
(RS Pts.—Oilers 675, Bills 616)
(PS Pts.—Bills 58, Oilers 48)
*AFC Divisional Playoff
**AFC First-Round Game
BUFFALO vs. *INDIANAPOLIS
RS: Bills lead series, 26-20-1
1970—Tie, 17-17 (Balt)
    Colts, 20-14 (Buff)
1971—Colts, 43-0 (Buff)
    Colts, 24-0 (Balt)
1972—Colts, 17-0 (Buff)
    Colts, 35-7 (Balt)
1973—Bills, 31-13 (Buff)
    Bills, 24-17 (Balt)
1974—Bills, 27-14 (Balt)
    Bills, 6-0 (Buff)
1975—Bills, 38-31 (Balt)
    Colts, 42-35 (Buff)
1976—Colts, 31-13 (Buff)
    Colts, 58-20 (Balt)
1977—Colts, 17-14 (Balt)
    Colts, 31-13 (Buff)
1978—Bills, 24-17 (Buff)
    Bills, 21-14 (Balt)
1979—Bills, 31-13 (Balt)
    Colts, 14-13 (Buff)
1980—Colts, 17-12 (Buff)
    Colts, 28-24 (Balt)
1981—Bills, 35-3 (Balt)
    Bills, 23-17 (Buff)
1982—Bills, 20-0 (Buff)
1983—Bills, 28-23 (Buff)
    Bills, 30-7 (Balt)
1984—Colts, 31-17 (I)
    Bills, 21-15 (Buff)
1985—Colts, 49-17 (I)
    Bills, 21-9 (Buff)
1986—Bills, 24-13 (Buff)
    Colts, 24-14 (I)
1987—Colts, 47-6 (Buff)
    Bills, 27-3 (I)
1988—Bills, 34-23 (Buff)
    Colts, 17-14 (I)
1989—Colts, 37-14 (I)
    Bills, 30-7 (Buff)
1990—Bills, 26-10 (Buff)
    Bills, 31-7 (I)
1991—Bills, 42-6 (Buff)
    Bills, 35-7 (I)
1992—Bills, 38-0 (Buff)
    Colts, 16-13 (I) OT
1993—Bills, 23-9 (Buff)
    Bills, 30-10 (I)
(RS Pts.—Bills 997, Colts 903)
*Franchise in Baltimore prior to 1984
BUFFALO vs. *KANSAS CITY
RS: Bills lead series, 15-13-1
PS: Bills lead series, 2-1
1960—Texans, 45-28 (B)
    Texans, 24-7 (D)
1961—Bills, 27-24 (B)
    Bills, 30-20 (D)
1962—Texans, 41-21 (D)
    Bills, 23-14 (B)
1963—Tie, 27-27 (B)
    Bills, 35-26 (KC)
1964—Bills, 34-17 (B)
    Bills, 35-22 (KC)

1965—Bills, 23-7 (KC)
    Bills, 34-25 (B)
1966—Chiefs, 42-20 (B)
    Bills, 29-14 (KC)
    **Chiefs, 31-7 (B)
1967—Chiefs, 23-13 (KC)
1968—Chiefs, 18-7 (B)
1969—Chiefs, 29-7 (B)
    Chiefs, 22-19 (KC)
1971—Chiefs, 22-9 (KC)
1973—Bills, 23-14 (B)
1976—Bills, 50-17 (B)
1978—Bills, 28-13 (B)
    Chiefs, 14-10 (KC)
1982—Bills, 14-9 (B)
1983—Bills, 14-9 (KC)
1986—Chiefs, 20-17 (B)
    Bills, 17-14 (KC)
1991—Chiefs, 33-6 (KC)
    ***Bills, 37-14 (B)
1993—Chiefs, 23-7 (KC)
    ****Bills, 30-13 (B)
(RS Pts.—Chiefs 633, Bills 609)
(PS Pts.—Bills 74, Chiefs 58)
*Franchise in Dallas prior to 1963 and
known as Texans
**AFL Championship
***AFC Divisional Playoff
****AFC Championship
BUFFALO vs. *L.A. RAIDERS
RS: Raiders lead series, 15-14
PS: Bills lead series, 2-0
1960—Bills, 38-9 (B)
    Raiders, 20-7 (O)
1961—Raiders, 31-22 (B)
    Bills, 26-21 (O)
1962—Bills, 14-6 (B)
    Bills, 10-6 (O)
1963—Raiders, 35-17 (O)
    Bills, 12-0 (B)
1964—Bills, 23-20 (B)
    Raiders, 16-13 (O)
1965—Bills, 17-12 (B)
    Bills, 17-14 (O)
1966—Bills, 31-10 (O)
1967—Raiders, 24-20 (B)
    Raiders, 28-21 (O)
1968—Raiders, 48-6 (B)
    Raiders, 13-10 (O)
1969—Raiders, 50-21 (O)
1972—Raiders, 28-16 (O)
1974—Bills, 21-20 (B)
1977—Raiders, 34-13 (O)
1980—Bills, 24-7 (B)
1983—Bills, 27-24 (B)
1987—Raiders, 34-21 (LA)
1988—Bills, 37-21 (B)
1990—Bills, 38-24 (B)
    **Bills, 51-3 (B)
1991—Bills, 30-27 (LA) OT
1992—Raiders, 20-3 (LA)
1993—Raiders, 25-24 (B)
    ***Bills, 29-23 (B)
(RS Pts.—Raiders 630, Bills 576)
(PS Pts.—Bills 80, Raiders 26)
*Franchise in Oakland prior to 1982
**AFC Championship
***AFC Divisional Playoff
BUFFALO vs. L.A. RAMS
RS: Series tied, 3-3
1970—Rams, 19-0 (LA)
1974—Rams, 13-0 (LA)
1980—Bills, 10-7 (B) OT
1983—Rams, 41-17 (LA)
1989—Bills, 23-20 (B)
1992—Bills, 40-7 (B)
(RS Pts.—Rams 113, Bills 104)
BUFFALO vs. MIAMI
RS: Dolphins lead series, 37-18-1
PS: Bills lead series, 2-0
1966—Bills, 58-24 (B)
    Bills, 29-0 (M)
1967—Bills, 35-13 (B)

Dolphins, 17-14 (M)
1968—Tie, 14-14 (M)
    Dolphins, 21-17 (B)
1969—Dolphins, 24-6 (M)
    Bills, 28-3 (B)
1970—Dolphins, 33-14 (B)
    Dolphins, 45-7 (M)
1971—Dolphins, 29-14 (B)
    Dolphins, 34-0 (M)
1972—Dolphins, 24-23 (M)
    Dolphins, 30-16 (B)
1973—Dolphins, 27-6 (M)
    Dolphins, 17-0 (B)
1974—Dolphins, 24-16 (B)
    Dolphins, 35-28 (M)
1975—Dolphins, 35-30 (B)
    Dolphins, 31-21 (M)
1976—Dolphins, 30-21 (B)
    Dolphins, 45-27 (M)
1977—Dolphins, 13-0 (B)
    Dolphins, 31-14 (M)
1978—Dolphins, 31-24 (M)
    Dolphins, 25-24 (B)
1979—Dolphins, 9-7 (B)
    Dolphins, 17-7 (M)
1980—Bills, 17-7 (B)
    Dolphins, 17-14 (M)
1981—Bills, 31-21 (B)
    Dolphins, 16-6 (M)
1982—Dolphins, 9-7 (B)
    Dolphins, 27-10 (M)
1983—Dolphins, 12-0 (B)
    Bills, 38-35 (M) OT
1984—Dolphins, 21-17 (B)
    Dolphins, 38-7 (M)
1985—Dolphins, 23-14 (B)
    Dolphins, 28-0 (M)
1986—Dolphins, 27-14 (M)
    Dolphins, 34-24 (B)
1987—Bills, 34-31 (M) OT
    Bills, 27-0 (B)
1988—Bills, 9-6 (B)
    Bills, 31-6 (M)
1989—Bills, 27-24 (M)
    Bills, 31-17 (B)
1990—Dolphins, 30-7 (M)
    Bills, 24-14 (B)
    *Bills, 44-34 (B)
1991—Bills, 35-31 (B)
    Bills, 41-27 (M)
1992—Dolphins, 37-10 (B)
    Bills, 26-20 (M)
    **Bills, 29-10 (M)
1993—Dolphins, 22-13 (B)
    Bills, 47-34 (M)
(RS Pts.—Dolphins 1,295, Bills 1,061)
(PS Pts.—Bills 73, Dolphins 44)
*AFC Divisional Playoff
**AFC Championship
BUFFALO vs. MINNESOTA
RS: Vikings lead series, 4-2
1971—Vikings, 19-0 (M)
1975—Vikings, 35-13 (B)
1979—Vikings, 10-3 (M)
1982—Bills, 23-22 (B)
1985—Vikings, 27-20 (B)
1988—Bills, 13-10 (B)
(RS Pts.—Vikings 123, Bills 72)
BUFFALO vs. *NEW ENGLAND
RS: Series tied, 33-33-1
PS: Patriots lead series, 1-0
1960—Bills, 13-0 (B)
    Bills, 38-14 (Buff)
1961—Patriots, 23 21 (Buff)
    Patriots, 52-21 (Bos)
1962—Tie, 28-28 (Buff)
    Patriots, 21-10 (Bos)
1963—Bills, 28-21 (Buff)
    Patriots, 17-7 (Bos)
    **Patriots, 26-8 (Buff)
1964—Patriots, 36-28 (Buff)
    Bills, 24-14 (Bos)
1965—Bills, 24-7 (Buff)

Bills, 23-7 (Bos)
1966—Patriots, 20-10 (Buff)
    Patriots, 14-3 (Bos)
1967—Patriots, 23-0 (Buff)
    Bills, 44-16 (Bos)
1968—Patriots, 16-7 (Buff)
    Patriots, 23-6 (Bos)
1969—Bills, 23-16 (Buff)
    Patriots, 35-21 (Bos)
1970—Bills, 45-10 (Bos)
    Patriots, 14-10 (Buff)
1971—Patriots, 38-33 (NE)
    Bills, 27-20 (Buff)
1972—Bills, 38-14 (Buff)
    Bills, 27-24 (NE)
1973—Bills, 31-13 (NE)
    Bills, 37-13 (Buff)
1974—Bills, 30-28 (Buff)
    Bills, 29-28 (NE)
1975—Bills, 45-31 (Buff)
    Bills, 34-14 (NE)
1976—Patriots, 26-22 (Buff)
    Patriots, 20-10 (NE)
1977—Bills, 24-14 (NE)
    Patriots, 20-7 (Buff)
1978—Patriots, 14-10 (Buff)
    Patriots, 26-24 (NE)
1979—Patriots, 26-6 (NE)
    Bills, 16-13 (NE) OT
1980—Bills, 31-13 (NE)
    Patriots, 24-2 (NE)
1981—Bills, 20-17 (Buff)
    Bills, 19-10 (NE)
1982—Patriots, 30-19 (NE)
1983—Patriots, 31-0 (NE)
    Patriots, 21-7 (NE)
1984—Patriots, 21-17 (Buff)
    Patriots, 38-10 (NE)
1985—Patriots, 17-14 (Buff)
    Patriots, 14-3 (NE)
1986—Patriots, 23-3 (Buff)
    Patriots, 22-19 (NE)
1987—Patriots, 14-7 (Buff)
    Patriots, 13-7 (NE)
1988—Bills, 16-14 (NE)
    Bills, 23-20 (Buff)
1989—Bills, 31-10 (Buff)
    Patriots, 33-24 (NE)
1990—Bills, 27-10 (NE)
    Bills, 14-0 (Buff)
1991—Bills, 22-17 (Buff)
    Patriots, 16-13 (NE)
1992—Bills, 41-7 (NE)
    Bills, 16-7 (Buff)
1993—Bills, 38-14 (Buff)
    Bills, 13-10 (NE) OT
(RS Pts.—Bills 1,340, Patriots 1,275)
(PS Pts.—Patriots 26, Bills 8)
*Franchise in Boston prior to 1971
**Division Playoff
BUFFALO vs. NEW ORLEANS
RS: Bills lead series, 3-2
1973—Saints, 13-0 (NO)
1980—Bills, 35-26 (NO)
1983—Bills, 27-21 (B)
1989—Saints, 22-19 (B)
1992—Bills, 20-16 (NO)
(RS Pts.—Bills 101, Saints 98)
BUFFALO vs. N.Y. GIANTS
RS: Bills lead series, 4-2
PS: Giants lead series, 1-0
1970—Giants, 20-6 (NY)
1975—Giants, 17-14 (B)
1978—Bills, 41-17 (B)
1987—Bills, 6-3 (B) OT
1990—Bills, 17-13 (NY)
    *Giants, 20-19 (Tampa)
1993—Bills, 17-14 (B)
(RS Pts.—Bills 101, Giants 84)
(PS Pts.—Giants 20, Bills 19)
*Super Bowl XXV
BUFFALO vs. *N.Y. JETS
RS: Bills lead series, 37-29

PS: Bills lead series, 1-0
1960—Titans, 27-3 (NY)
    Titans, 17-13 (B)
1961—Bills, 41-31 (B)
    Titans, 21-14 (NY)
1962—Titans, 17-6 (B)
    Bills, 20-3 (NY)
1963—Bills, 45-14 (B)
    Bills, 19-10 (NY)
1964—Bills, 34-24 (B)
    Bills, 20-7 (NY)
1965—Bills, 33-21 (B)
    Jets, 14-12 (NY)
1966—Bills, 33-23 (NY)
    Bills, 14-3 (B)
1967—Bills, 20-17 (B)
    Jets, 20-10 (NY)
1968—Bills, 37-35 (B)
    Jets, 25-21 (NY)
1969—Jets, 33-19 (B)
    Jets, 16-6 (NY)
1970—Bills, 34-31 (B)
    Bills, 10-6 (NY)
1971—Jets, 28-17 (NY)
    Jets, 20-7 (B)
1972—Bills, 41-24 (B)
    Jets, 41-3 (NY)
1973—Bills, 9-7 (B)
    Bills, 34-14 (NY)
1974—Bills, 16-12 (B)
    Jets, 20-10 (NY)
1975—Bills, 42-14 (B)
    Bills, 24-23 (NY)
1976—Jets, 17-14 (NY)
    Jets, 19-14 (B)
1977—Jets, 24-19 (B)
    Bills, 14-10 (NY)
1978—Jets, 21-20 (B)
    Jets, 45-14 (NY)
1979—Bills, 46-31 (B)
    Bills, 14-12 (NY)
1980—Bills, 20-10 (B)
    Bills, 31-24 (NY)
1981—Bills, 31-0 (B)
    Jets, 33-14 (NY)
    **Bills, 31-27 (NY)
1983—Jets, 34-10 (B)
    Bills, 24-17 (NY)
1984—Jets, 28-26 (B)
    Jets, 21-17 (NY)
1985—Jets, 42-3 (NY)
    Jets, 27-7 (B)
1986—Jets, 28-24 (B)
    Jets, 14-13 (NY)
1987—Jets, 31-28 (B)
    Bills, 17-14 (NY)
1988—Bills, 37-14 (NY)
    Bills, 9-6 (B) OT
1989—Bills, 34-3 (B)
    Bills, 37-0 (NY)
1990—Bills, 30-7 (NY)
    Bills, 30-27 (B)
1991—Bills, 23-20 (NY)
    Bills, 24-13 (B)
1992—Bills, 24-20 (NY)
    Jets, 24-17 (B)
1993—Bills, 19-10 (NY)
    Bills, 16-14 (B)
(RS Pts.—Bills, 1,370, Jets 1,295)
(PS Pts.—Bills 31, Jets 27)
*Jets known as Titans prior to 1963
**AFC First-Round Playoff
BUFFALO vs. PHILADELPHIA
RS: Eagles lead series, 4-3
1973—Bills, 27-26 (B)
1981—Eagles, 20-14 (B)
1984—Eagles, 27-17 (B)
1985—Eagles, 21-17 (P)
1987—Eagles, 17-7 (P)
1990—Bills, 30-23 (B)
1993—Bills, 10-7 (P)
(RS Pts.—Eagles 141, Bills 122)
BUFFALO vs. PITTSBURGH

RS: Bills lead series, 7-6
PS: Series tied, 1-1
1970—Steelers, 23-10 (P)
1972—Steelers, 38-21 (B)
1974—*Steelers, 32-14 (P)
1975—Bills, 30-21 (P)
1978—Steelers, 28-17 (B)
1979—Steelers, 28-0 (P)
1980—Bills, 28-13 (B)
1982—Bills, 13-0 (B)
1985—Steelers, 30-24 (P)
1986—Bills, 16-12 (B)
1988—Bills, 36-28 (B)
1991—Bills, 52-34 (B)
1992—Bills, 28-20 (B)
    *Bills, 24-3 (P)
1993—Steelers, 23-0 (P)
(RS Pts.—Steelers 298, Bills 275)
(PS Pts.—Bills 38, Steelers 35)
*AFC Divisional Playoff
BUFFALO vs. *SAN DIEGO
RS: Chargers lead series, 16-7-2
PS: Bills lead series, 2-1
1960—Chargers, 24-10 (B)
    Bills, 32-3 (LA)
1961—Chargers, 19-11 (B)
    Chargers, 28-10 (SD)
1962—Bills, 35-10 (B)
    Bills, 40-20 (SD)
1963—Chargers, 14-10 (SD)
    Chargers, 23-13 (B)
1964—Bills, 30-3 (B)
    Bills, 27-24 (SD)
    **Bills, 20-7 (B)
1965—Bills, 34-3 (B)
    Tie, 20-20 (SD)
    **Bills, 23-0 (SD)
1966—Chargers, 27-7 (SD)
    Tie, 17-17 (B)
1967—Chargers, 37-17 (B)
1968—Chargers, 21-6 (B)
1969—Chargers, 45-6 (SD)
1971—Chargers, 20-3 (SD)
1973—Chargers, 34-7 (SD)
1976—Chargers, 34-13 (B)
1979—Chargers, 27-19 (SD)
1980—Bills, 26-24 (SD)
    ***Chargers, 20-14 (SD)
1981—Bills, 28-27 (SD)
1985—Chargers, 14-9 (B)
    Chargers, 40-7 (SD)
(RS Pts.—Chargers 589, Bills 406)
(PS Pts.—Bills 57, Chargers 27)
*Franchise in Los Angeles prior to 1961
**AFL Championship
***AFC Divisional Playoff
BUFFALO vs. SAN FRANCISCO
RS: Bills lead series 3-2
1972—Bills, 27-20 (B)
1980—Bills, 18-13 (SF)
1983—49ers, 23-10 (B)
1989—49ers, 21-10 (SF)
1992—Bills, 34-31 (SF)
(RS Pts.—49ers 108, Bills 99)
BUFFALO vs. SEATTLE
RS: Seahawks lead series, 3-1
1977—Seahawks, 56-17 (S)
1984—Seahawks, 31-28 (S)
1988—Bills, 13-3 (S)
1989—Seahawks, 17-16 (S)
(RS Pts.—Seahawks 107, Bills 74)
BUFFALO vs. TAMPA BAY
RS: Buccaneers lead series, 4-2
1976—Bills, 14-9 (TB)
1978—Buccaneers, 31-10 (TB)
1982—Buccaneers, 24-23 (TB)
1986—Buccaneers, 34-28 (TB)
1988—Buccaneers, 10-5 (TB)
1991—Bills, 17-10 (TB)
(RS Pts.—Buccaneers 118, Bills 97)
BUFFALO vs. WASHINGTON
RS: Redskins lead series, 4-3
PS: Redskins lead series, 1-0

1972—Bills, 24-17 (W)
1977—Redskins, 10-0 (B)
1981—Bills, 21-14 (B)
1984—Redskins, 41-14 (W)
1987—Redskins, 27-7 (B)
1990—Redskins, 29-14 (W)
1991—*Redskins, 37-24 (Minneapolis)
1993—Bills, 24-10 (B)
(RS Pts.—Redskins 148, Bills 104)
(PS Pts.—Redskins 37, Bills 24)
*Super Bowl XXVI

CHICAGO vs. ARIZONA
RS: Bears lead series, 51-25-6;
See Arizona vs. Chicago
CHICAGO vs. ATLANTA
RS: Series tied, 9-9;
See Atlanta vs. Chicago
CHICAGO vs. BUFFALO
RS: Bears lead series, 3-2;
See Buffalo vs. Chicago
CHICAGO vs. CINCINNATI
RS: Bengals lead series, 3-2
1972—Bengals, 13-3 (Chi)
1980—Bengals, 17-14 (Chi) OT
1986—Bears, 44-7 (Cin)
1989—Bears, 17-14 (Chi)
1992—Bengals, 31-28 (Chi) OT
(RS Pts.—Bears 106, Bengals 82)
CHICAGO vs. CLEVELAND
RS: Browns lead series, 8-3
1951—Browns, 42-21 (Cle)
1954—Browns, 39-10 (Chi)
1960—Browns, 42-0 (Cle)
1961—Bears, 17-14 (Chi)
1967—Browns, 24-0 (Cle)
1969—Browns, 28-24 (Chi)
1972—Bears, 17-0 (Cle)
1980—Browns, 27-21 (Cle)
1986—Bears, 41-31 (Chi)
1989—Browns, 27-7 (Cle)
1992—Browns, 27-14 (Cle)
(RS Pts.—Browns 301, Bears 172)
CHICAGO vs. DALLAS
RS: Cowboys lead series, 8-6
PS: Cowboys lead series, 2-0
1960—Bears, 17-7 (C)
1962—Bears, 34-33 (D)
1964—Cowboys, 24-10 (C)
1968—Cowboys, 34-3 (C)
1971—Bears, 23-19 (C)
1973—Cowboys, 20-17 (C)
1976—Cowboys, 31-21 (D)
1977—*Cowboys, 37-7 (D)
1979—Cowboys, 24-20 (D)
1981—Cowboys, 10-9 (D)
1984—Cowboys, 23-14 (C)
1985—Bears, 44-0 (D)
1986—Bears, 24-10 (D)
1988—Bears, 17-7 (C)
1991—**Cowboys, 17-13 (C)
1992—Cowboys, 27-14 (D)
(RS Pts.—Cowboys 269, Bears 267)
(PS Pts.—Cowboys 54, Bears 20)
*NFC Divisional Playoff
**NFC First-Round Playoff
CHICAGO vs. DENVER
RS: Series tied, 5-5
1971—Broncos, 6-3 (D)
1973—Bears, 33-14 (D)
1976—Broncos, 28-14 (C)
1978—Broncos, 16-7 (D)
1981—Bears, 35-24 (C)
1983—Bears, 31-14 (C)
1984—Bears, 27-0 (C)
1987—Broncos, 31-29 (D)
1990—Bears, 16-13 (D) OT
1993—Broncos, 13-3 (C)
(RS Pts.—Bears 198, Broncos 159)
CHICAGO vs. *DETROIT
RS: Bears lead series, 74-49-5
1930—Spartans, 7-6 (P)
    Bears, 14-6 (C)

1931—Bears, 9-6 (C)
    Spartans, 3-0 (P)
1932—Tie, 13-13 (C)
    Tie, 7-7 (P)
    Bears, 9-0 (C)
1933—Bears, 17-14 (C)
    Bears, 17-7 (P)
1934—Bears, 19-16 (D)
    Bears, 10-7 (C)
1935—Tie, 20-20 (C)
    Lions, 14-2 (D)
1936—Bears, 12-10 (C)
    Lions, 13-7 (D)
1937—Bears, 28-20 (C)
    Bears, 13-0 (D)
1938—Lions, 13-7 (C)
    Lions, 14-7 (D)
1939—Lions, 10-0 (C)
    Bears, 23-13 (D)
1940—Bears, 7-0 (C)
    Lions, 17-14 (D)
1941—Bears, 49-0 (C)
    Bears, 24-7 (D)
1942—Bears, 16-0 (C)
    Bears, 42-0 (D)
1943—Bears, 27-21 (D)
    Bears, 35-14 (C)
1944—Tie, 21-21 (C)
    Lions, 41-21 (D)
1945—Lions, 16-10 (C)
    Lions, 35-28 (C)
1946—Bears, 42-6 (C)
    Bears, 45-24 (D)
1947—Bears, 33-24 (C)
    Bears, 34-14 (D)
1948—Bears, 28-0 (C)
    Bears, 42-14 (D)
1949—Bears, 27-24 (C)
    Bears, 28-7 (D)
1950—Bears, 35-21 (D)
    Bears, 6-3 (C)
1951—Bears, 28-23 (D)
    Lions, 41-28 (C)
1952—Bears, 24-23 (C)
    Lions, 45-21 (D)
1953—Lions, 20-16 (C)
    Lions, 13-7 (D)
1954—Lions, 48-23 (C)
    Bears, 28-24 (C)
1955—Bears, 24-14 (D)
    Bears, 21-20 (C)
1956—Lions, 42-10 (D)
    Bears, 38-21 (C)
1957—Bears, 27-7 (D)
    Lions, 21-13 (C)
1958—Bears, 20-7 (D)
    Bears, 21-16 (C)
1959—Bears, 24-14 (D)
    Bears, 25-14 (C)
1960—Bears, 28-7 (C)
    Lions, 36-0 (D)
1961—Bears, 31-17 (D)
    Lions, 16-15 (C)
1962—Lions, 11-3 (D)
    Bears, 3-0 (C)
1963—Bears, 37-21 (D)
    Bears, 24-14 (C)
1964—Lions, 10-0 (C)
    Bears, 27-24 (D)
1965—Bears, 38-10 (C)
    Bears, 17-10 (D)
1966—Lions, 14-3 (D)
    Tie, 10-10 (C)
1967—Bears, 14-3 (C)
    Bears, 27-13 (D)
1968—Lions, 42-0 (D)
    Lions, 28-10 (C)
1969—Lions, 13-7 (D)
    Lions, 20-3 (C)
1970—Lions, 28-14 (D)
    Lions, 16-10 (C)
1971—Bears, 28-23 (D)
    Lions, 28-3 (C)

1972—Lions, 38-24 (C)
Lions, 14-0 (D)
1973—Lions, 30-7 (C)
Lions, 40-7 (D)
1974—Bears, 17-9 (C)
Lions, 34-17 (D)
1975—Lions, 27-7 (D)
Bears, 25-21 (C)
1976—Bears, 10-3 (C)
Lions, 14-10 (D)
1977—Bears, 30-20 (C)
Bears, 31-14 (D)
1978—Bears, 19-0 (C)
Lions, 21-17 (C)
1979—Bears, 35-7 (C)
Lions, 20-0 (D)
1980—Bears, 24-7 (C)
Bears, 23-17 (D) OT
1981—Lions, 48-17 (D)
Lions, 23-7 (C)
1982—Lions, 17-10 (D)
Bears, 20-17 (C)
1983—Lions, 31-17 (D)
Lions, 38-17 (C)
1984—Bears, 16-14 (C)
Bears, 30-13 (D)
1985—Bears, 24-3 (C)
Bears, 37-17 (D)
1986—Bears, 13-7 (C)
Bears, 16-13 (D)
1987—Bears, 30-10 (C)
1988—Bears, 24-7 (D)
Bears, 13-12 (C)
1989—Bears, 47-27 (D)
Lions, 27-17 (C)
1990—Bears, 23-17 (C) OT
Lions, 38-21 (D)
1991—Bears, 20-10 (C)
Lions, 16-6 (D)
1992—Bears, 27-24 (C)
Lions, 16-3 (D)
1993—Bears, 10-6 (D)
Lions, 20-14 (C)
(RS Pts.—Bears 2,386, Lions 2,156)
*Franchise in Portsmouth prior to 1934
and known as the Spartans
CHICAGO vs. GREEN BAY
RS: Bears lead series, 81-59-6
PS: Bears lead series, 1-0
1921—Staleys, 20-0 (C)
1923—Bears, 3-0 (GB)
1924—Bears, 3-0 (C)
1925—Packers, 14-10 (GB)
Bears, 21-0 (C)
1926—Tie, 6-6 (GB)
Bears, 19-13 (C)
Tie, 3-3 (C)
1927—Bears, 7-6 (GB)
Bears, 14-6 (C)
1928—Tie, 12-12 (GB)
Packers, 16-6 (C)
Packers, 6-0 (C)
1929—Packers, 23-0 (GB)
Packers, 14-0 (C)
Packers, 25-0 (C)
1930—Packers, 7-0 (GB)
Packers, 13-12 (C)
Bears, 21-0 (C)
1931—Packers, 7-0 (GB)
Packers, 6-2 (C)
Bears, 7-6 (C)
1932—Tie, 0-0 (GB)
Packers, 2-0 (C)
Bears, 9-0 (C)
1933—Bears, 14-7 (GB)
Bears, 10-7 (C)
Bears, 7-6 (C)
1934—Bears, 24-10 (GB)
Bears, 27-14 (C)
1935—Packers, 7-0 (GB)
Packers, 17-14 (C)
1936—Bears, 30-3 (GB)
Packers, 21-10 (C)

1937—Bears, 14-2 (GB)
Packers, 24-14 (C)
1938—Bears, 2-0 (GB)
Packers, 24-17 (C)
1939—Packers, 21-16 (GB)
Bears, 30-27 (C)
1940—Bears, 41-10 (GB)
Bears, 14-7 (C)
1941—Bears, 25-17 (GB)
Packers, 16-14 (C)
**Bears, 33-14 (C)
1942—Bears, 44-28 (GB)
Bears, 38-7 (C)
1943—Tie, 21-21 (GB)
Bears, 21-7 (C)
1944—Packers, 42-28 (GB)
Bears, 21-0 (C)
1945—Packers, 31-21 (GB)
Bears, 28-24 (C)
1946—Bears, 30-7 (GB)
Bears, 10-7 (C)
1947—Packers, 29-20 (GB)
Bears, 20-17 (C)
1948—Bears, 45-7 (GB)
Bears, 7-6 (C)
1949—Bears, 17-0 (GB)
Bears, 24-3 (C)
1950—Packers, 31-21 (GB)
Bears, 28-14 (C)
1951—Bears, 31-20 (GB)
Bears, 24-13 (C)
1952—Bears, 24-14 (GB)
Packers, 41-28 (C)
1953—Packers, 17-13 (GB)
Tie, 21-21 (C)
1954—Bears, 10-3 (GB)
Bears, 28-23 (C)
1955—Packers, 24-3 (GB)
Bears, 52-31 (C)
1956—Bears, 37-21 (GB)
Bears, 38-14 (C)
1957—Packers, 21-17 (GB)
Bears, 21-14 (C)
1958—Bears, 34-20 (GB)
Bears, 24-10 (C)
1959—Packers, 9-6 (GB)
Bears, 28-17 (C)
1960—Bears, 17-14 (GB)
Packers, 41-13 (C)
1961—Packers, 24-0 (GB)
Packers, 31-28 (C)
1962—Packers, 49-0 (GB)
Packers, 38-7 (C)
1963—Bears, 10-3 (GB)
Bears, 26-7 (C)
1964—Packers, 23-12 (GB)
Packers, 17-3 (C)
1965—Packers, 23-14 (GB)
Bears, 31-10 (C)
1966—Packers, 17-0 (C)
Packers, 13-6 (GB)
1967—Packers, 13-10 (GB)
Packers, 17-13 (C)
1968—Bears, 13-10 (GB)
Packers, 28-27 (C)
1969—Packers, 17-0 (GB)
Packers, 21-3 (C)
1970—Packers, 20-19 (GB)
Bears, 35-17 (C)
1971—Packers, 17-14 (C)
Packers, 31-10 (GB)
1972—Packers, 20-17 (GB)
Packers, 23-17 (C)
1973—Bears, 31-17 (GB)
Packers, 21-0 (C)
1974—Bears, 10-9 (C)
Packers, 20-3 (Mil)
1975—Bears, 27-14 (C)
Packers, 28-7 (GB)
1976—Bears, 24-13 (C)
Bears, 16-10 (GB)
1977—Bears, 26-0 (GB)
Bears, 21-10 (C)

1978—Packers, 24-14 (GB)
Bears, 14-0 (C)
1979—Bears, 6-3 (C)
Bears, 15-14 (GB)
1980—Packers, 12-6 (GB) OT
Bears, 61-7 (C)
1981—Packers, 16-9 (C)
Packers, 21-17 (GB)
1983—Packers, 31-28 (GB)
Bears, 23-21 (C)
1984—Bears, 9-7 (GB)
Packers, 20-14 (C)
1985—Bears, 23-7 (C)
Bears, 16-10 (GB)
1986—Bears, 25-12 (GB)
Bears, 12-10 (C)
1987—Bears, 26-24 (C)
Bears, 23-10 (C)
1988—Bears, 24-6 (GB)
Bears, 16-0 (C)
1989—Packers, 14-13 (GB)
Packers, 40-28 (C)
1990—Bears, 31-13 (GB)
Bears, 27-13 (C)
1991—Bears, 10-0 (GB)
Bears, 27-13 (C)
1992—Bears, 30-10 (GB)
Packers, 17-3 (C)
1993—Packers, 17-3 (GB)
Bears, 30-17 (C)
(RS Pts.—Bears 2,478, Packers 2,130)
(PS Pts.—Bears 33, Packers 14)
*Bears known as Staleys prior to 1922
**Division Playoff
CHICAGO vs. HOUSTON
RS: Oilers lead series, 4-2
1973—Bears, 35-14 (C)
1977—Oilers, 47-0 (H)
1980—Oilers, 10-6 (C)
1986—Bears, 20-7 (H)
1989—Oilers, 33-28 (C)
1992—Oilers, 24-7 (H)
(RS Pts.—Oilers 135, Bears 96)
CHICAGO vs. *INDIANAPOLIS
RS: Colts lead series, 21-16
1953—Colts, 13-9 (B)
Colts, 16-14 (C)
1954—Bears, 28-9 (C)
Bears, 28-13 (B)
1955—Colts, 23-17 (B)
Bears, 38-10 (C)
1956—Colts, 28-21 (B)
Bears, 58-27 (C)
1957—Colts, 21-10 (B)
Colts, 29-14 (C)
1958—Colts, 51-38 (B)
Colts, 17-0 (C)
1959—Bears, 26-21 (B)
Colts, 21-7 (C)
1960—Colts, 42-7 (B)
Colts, 24-20 (C)
1961—Bears, 24-10 (C)
Bears, 21-20 (B)
1962—Bears, 35-15 (C)
Bears, 57-0 (B)
1963—Bears, 10-3 (C)
Bears, 17-7 (B)
1964—Colts, 52-0 (C)
Colts, 40-24 (C)
1965—Bears, 26-21 (C)
Bears, 13-0 (B)
1966—Bears, 27-17 (C)
Colts, 21-16 (B)
1967—Colts, 24-3 (C)
1968—Colts, 28-7 (B)
1969—Colts, 24-21 (C)
1970—Colts, 21-20 (B)
1975—Colts, 35-7 (C)
1983—Colts, 22-19 (B) OT
1985—Bears, 17-10 (C)
1988—Bears, 17-13 (I)
1991—Bears, 31-17 (I)
(RS Pts.—Colts 770, Bears 742)

*Franchise in Baltimore prior to 1984
CHICAGO vs. KANSAS CITY
RS: Bears lead series, 4-2
1973—Chiefs, 19-7 (KC)
1977—Bears, 28-27 (C)
1981—Bears, 16-13 (KC) OT
1987—Bears, 31-28 (C)
1990—Chiefs, 21-10 (C)
1993—Bears, 19-17 (KC)
(RS Pts.—Chiefs 125, Bears 111)
CHICAGO vs. *L.A. RAIDERS
RS: Raiders lead series, 5-3
1972—Raiders, 28-21 (O)
1976—Raiders, 28-27 (C)
1978—Raiders, 25-19 (C) OT
1981—Bears, 23-6 (O)
1984—Bears, 17-6 (C)
1987—Bears, 6-3 (LA)
1990—Raiders, 24-10 (LA)
1993—Raiders, 16-14 (C)
(RS Pts.—Bears 137, Raiders 136)
*Franchise in Oakland prior to 1982
CHICAGO vs. *L.A. RAMS
RS: Bears lead series, 44-29-3
PS: Series tied, 1-1
1937—Bears, 20-2 (Clev)
Bears, 15-7 (C)
1938—Rams, 14-7 (C)
Rams, 23-21 (Clev)
1939—Bears, 30-21 (Clev)
Bears, 35-21 (C)
1940—Bears, 21-14 (Clev)
Bears, 47-25 (C)
1941—Bears, 48-21 (Clev)
Bears, 31-13 (C)
1942—Bears, 21-7 (Clev)
Bears, 47-0 (C)
1944—Rams, 19-7 (Clev)
Bears, 28-21 (C)
1945—Rams, 17-0 (Clev)
Rams, 41-21 (C)
1946—Tie, 28-28 (C)
Bears, 27-21 (LA)
1947—Rams, 41-21 (LA)
Rams, 17-14 (C)
1948—Bears, 42-21 (C)
Bears, 21-6 (LA)
1949—Rams, 31-16 (C)
Rams, 27-24 (LA)
1950—Bears, 24-20 (LA)
Bears, 24-14 (C)
**Rams, 24-14 (LA)
1951—Rams, 42-17 (C)
1952—Rams, 31-7 (LA)
Rams, 40-24 (C)
1953—Rams, 38-24 (LA)
Bears, 24-21 (C)
1954—Rams, 42-38 (LA)
Bears, 24-13 (C)
1955—Bears, 31-20 (LA)
Bears, 24-3 (C)
1956—Bears, 35-24 (LA)
Bears, 30-21 (C)
1957—Bears, 34-26 (C)
Bears, 16-10 (LA)
1958—Bears, 31-10 (C)
Rams, 41-35 (LA)
1959—Bears, 28-21 (C)
Bears, 26-21 (LA)
1960—Bears, 34-27 (C)
Tie, 24-24 (LA)
1961—Bears, 21-17 (LA)
Bears, 28-24 (C)
1962—Bears, 27-23 (LA)
Bears, 30-14 (C)
1963—Bears, 52-14 (LA)
Bears, 6-0 (C)
1964—Bears, 38-17 (C)
Bears, 34-24 (LA)
1965—Rams, 30-28 (LA)
Bears, 31-6 (C)
1966—Rams, 31-17 (LA)
Bears, 17-10 (C)

1967—Rams, 28-17 (C)
1968—Rams, 17-16 (LA)
1969—Rams, 9-7 (C)
1971—Rams, 17-3 (LA)
1972—Tie, 13-13 (C)
1973—Rams, 26-0 (C)
1975—Rams, 38-10 (LA)
1976—Rams, 20-12 (LA)
1977—Bears, 24-23 (C)
1979—Bears, 27-23 (C)
1981—Rams, 24-7 (C)
1982—Bears, 34-26 (LA)
1983—Rams, 21-14 (LA)
1984—Rams, 29-13 (LA)
1985—***Bears, 24-0 (C)
1986—Rams, 20-17 (C)
1988—Rams, 23-3 (LA)
1989—Bears, 20-10 (C)
1990—Bears, 38-9 (C)
1993—Rams, 20-6 (LA)
(RS Pts.—Bears 1,770, Rams 1,559)
(PS Pts.—Bears 38, Rams 24)
*Franchise in Cleveland prior to 1946
**Conference Playoff
***NFC Championship
CHICAGO vs. MIAMI
RS: Dolphins lead series, 5-1
1971—Dolphins, 34-3 (M)
1975—Dolphins, 46-13 (C)
1979—Dolphins, 31-16 (M)
1985—Dolphins, 38-24 (M)
1988—Bears, 34-7 (C)
1991—Dolphins, 16-13 (C) OT
(RS Pts.—Dolphins 172, Bears 103)
CHICAGO vs. MINNESOTA
RS: Vikings lead series, 34-29-2
1961—Vikings, 37-13 (M)
Bears, 52-35 (C)
1962—Bears, 13-0 (M)
Bears, 31-30 (C)
1963—Bears, 28-7 (M)
Tie, 17-17 (C)
1964—Bears, 34-28 (M)
Vikings, 41-14 (C)
1965—Bears, 45-37 (M)
Vikings, 24-17 (C)
1966—Bears, 13-10 (M)
Bears, 41-28 (C)
1967—Bears, 17-7 (M)
Tie, 10-10 (C)
1968—Bears, 27-17 (M)
Bears, 26-24 (C)
1969—Bears, 31-0 (C)
Vikings, 31-14 (M)
1970—Vikings, 24-0 (C)
Vikings, 16-13 (M)
1971—Bears, 20-17 (M)
Vikings, 27-10 (C)
1972—Bears, 13-10 (C)
Vikings, 23-10 (M)
1973—Bears, 22-13 (C)
Vikings, 31-13 (M)
1974—Vikings, 11-7 (M)
Vikings, 17-0 (C)
1975—Vikings, 28-3 (M)
Vikings, 13-9 (C)
1976—Vikings, 20-19 (M)
Bears, 14-13 (C)
1977—Vikings, 22-16 (M) OT
Bears, 10-7 (C)
1978—Vikings, 24-20 (C)
Vikings, 17-14 (M)
1979—Bears, 26-7 (C)
Vikings, 30-27 (M)
1980—Vikings, 34-14 (C)
Vikings, 13-7 (M)
1981—Vikings, 24-21 (M)
Bears, 10-9 (C)
1982—Vikings, 35-7 (M)
1983—Vikings, 23-14 (C)
Bears, 19-13 (M)
1984—Bears, 16-7 (C)
Bears, 34-3 (M)

1985—Bears, 33-24 (M)
Bears, 27-9 (C)
1986—Bears, 23-0 (C)
Vikings, 23-7 (M)
1987—Bears, 27-7 (C)
Bears, 30-24 (M)
1988—Vikings, 31-7 (C)
Vikings, 28-27 (M)
1989—Bears, 38-7 (C)
Vikings, 27-16 (M)
1990—Bears, 19-16 (C)
Vikings, 41-13 (M)
1991—Bears, 10-6 (C)
Bears, 34-17 (M)
1992—Vikings, 21-20 (M)
Vikings, 38-10 (C)
1993—Vikings, 10-7 (M)
Vikings, 19-12 (C)
(RS Pts.—Vikings 1,302, Bears 1,171)
CHICAGO vs. NEW ENGLAND
RS: Patriots lead series, 3-2
PS: Bears lead series, 1-0
1973—Patriots, 13-10 (C)
1979—Patriots, 27-7 (C)
1982—Bears, 26-13 (C)
1985—Bears, 20-7 (C)
*Bears, 46-10 (New Orleans)
1988—Patriots, 30-7 (NE)
(RS Pts.—Patriots 100, Bears 70)
(PS Pts.—Bears 46, Patriots 10)
*Super Bowl XX
CHICAGO vs. NEW ORLEANS
RS: Bears lead series, 8-6
PS: Bears lead series, 1-0
1968—Bears, 23-17 (NO)
1970—Bears, 24-3 (NO)
1971—Bears, 35-14 (C)
1973—Saints, 21-16 (NO)
1974—Bears, 24-10 (C)
1975—Bears, 42-17 (NO)
1977—Saints, 42-24 (C)
1980—Bears, 22-3 (C)
1982—Saints, 10-0 (C)
1983—Saints, 34-31 (NO) OT
1984—Bears, 20-7 (C)
1987—Saints, 19-17 (C)
1990—*Bears, 16-6 (C)
1991—Bears, 20-17 (NO)
1992—Saints, 20-6 (NO)
(RS Pts.—Bears 304, Saints 242)
(PS Pts.—Bears 16, Saints 6)
*NFC First-Round Playoff
CHICAGO vs. N.Y. GIANTS
RS: Bears lead series, 24-16-2
PS: Bears lead series, 5-3
1925—Bears, 19-7 (NY)
Giants, 9-0 (C)
1926—Bears, 7-0 (C)
1927—Giants, 13-7 (NY)
1928—Bears, 13-0 (C)
1929—Bears, 26-14 (C)
Giants, 34-0 (NY)
Giants, 14-9 (C)
1930—Giants, 12-0 (C)
Bears, 12-0 (NY)
1931—Bears, 6-0 (C)
Bears, 12-6 (NY)
Giants, 25-6 (C)
1932—Bears, 28-8 (NY)
Bears, 6-0 (C)
1933—Bears, 14-10 (C)
Giants, 3-0 (NY)
*Bears, 23-21 (C)
1934—Bears, 27-7 (C)
Bears, 10-9 (NY)
*Giants, 30-13 (NY)
1935—Bears, 20-3 (NY)
Giants, 3-0 (C)
1936—Bears, 25-7 (NY)
1937—Tie, 3-3 (NY)
1939—Giants, 16-13 (NY)
1940—Bears, 37-21 (NY)
1941—*Bears, 37-9 (C)

1942—Bears, 26-7 (NY)
1943—Bears, 56-7 (NY)
1946—Giants, 14-0 (NY)
*Bears, 24-14 (NY)
1948—Bears, 35-14 (C)
1949—Giants, 35-28 (NY)
1956—Tie, 17-17 (NY)
*Giants, 47-7 (NY)
1962—Giants, 26-24 (C)
1963—*Bears, 14-10 (C)
1965—Bears, 35-14 (NY)
1967—Bears, 34-7 (C)
1969—Giants, 28-24 (NY)
1970—Bears, 24-16 (NY)
1974—Bears, 16-13 (C)
1977—Bears, 12-9 (NY) OT
1985—**Bears, 21-0 (C)
1987—Bears, 34-19 (C)
1990—**Giants, 31-3 (NY)
1991—Bears, 20-17 (C)
1992—Giants, 27-14 (C)
1993—Giants, 26-20 (C)
(RS Pts.—Bears 707, Giants 532)
(PS Pts.—Giants 162, Bears 142)
*NFL Championship
**NFC Divisional Playoff
CHICAGO vs. N.Y. JETS
RS: Bears lead series, 3-1
1974—Jets, 23-21 (C)
1979—Bears, 23-13 (C)
1985—Bears, 19-6 (NY)
1991—Bears, 19-13 (C) OT
(RS Pts.—Bears 82, Jets 55)
CHICAGO vs. PHILADELPHIA
RS: Bears lead series, 23-3-1
PS: Series tied, 1-1
1933—Tie, 3-3 (P)
1935—Bears, 39-0 (P)
1936—Bears, 17-0 (P)
Bears, 28-7 (P)
1938—Bears, 28-6 (P)
1939—Bears, 27-14 (C)
1941—Bears, 49-14 (P)
1942—Bears, 45-14 (C)
1944—Bears, 28-7 (P)
1946—Bears, 21-14 (C)
1947—Bears, 40-7 (C)
1948—Eagles, 12-7 (P)
1949—Bears, 38-21 (C)
1955—Bears, 17-10 (C)
1961—Eagles, 16-14 (P)
1963—Bears, 16-7 (C)
1968—Bears, 29-16 (P)
1970—Bears, 20-16 (C)
1972—Bears, 21-12 (P)
1975—Bears, 15-13 (C)
1979—*Eagles, 27-17 (P)
1980—Eagles, 17-14 (P)
1983—Bears, 7-6 (P)
Bears, 17-14 (C)
1986—Bears, 13-10 (C) OT
1987—Bears, 35-3 (P)
1988—**Bears, 20-12 (C)
1989—Bears, 27-13 (C)
1993—Bears, 17-6 (P)
(RS Pts.—Bears 632, Eagles 278)
(PS Pts.—Eagles 39, Bears 37)
*NFC First-Round Playoff
**NFC Divisional Playoff
CHICAGO vs. *PITTSBURGH
RS: Bears lead series, 16-4-1
1934—Bears, 28-0 (P)
1935—Bears, 23-7 (P)
1936—Bears, 27-9 (P)
Bears, 26-6 (C)
1937—Bears, 7-0 (P)
1939—Bears, 32-0 (P)
1941—Bears, 34-7 (C)
1945—Bears, 28-7 (P)
1947—Bears, 49-7 (C)
1949—Bears, 30-21 (C)
1958—Steelers, 24-10 (P)
1959—Bears, 27-21 (C)

1963—Tie, 17-17 (P)
1967—Steelers, 41-13 (P)
1969—Bears, 38-7 (C)
1971—Bears, 17-15 (C)
1975—Steelers, 34-3 (P)
1980—Steelers, 38-3 (P)
1986—Bears, 13-10 (C) OT
1989—Bears, 20-0 (P)
1992—Bears, 30-6 (C)
(RS Pts.—Bears 475, Steelers 277)
*Steelers known as Pirates prior to 1941
CHICAGO vs. SAN DIEGO
RS: Chargers lead series, 4-2
1970—Chargers, 20-7 (C)
1974—Chargers, 28-21 (SD)
1978—Chargers, 40-7 (SD)
1981—Bears, 20-17 (C) OT
1984—Chargers, 20-7 (SD)
1993—Bears, 16-13 (SD)
(RS Pts.—Chargers 138, Bears 78)
CHICAGO vs. SAN FRANCISCO
RS: Series tied, 25-25-1
PS: 49ers lead series, 2-0
1950—Bears, 32-20 (C)
Bears, 17-0 (C)
1951—Bears, 13-7 (C)
1952—49ers, 40-16 (C)
Bears, 20-17 (SF)
1953—49ers, 35-28 (C)
49ers, 24-14 (SF)
1954—49ers, 31-24 (C)
Bears, 31-27 (SF)
1955—49ers, 20-19 (C)
Bears, 34-23 (SF)
1956—Bears, 31-7 (C)
Bears, 38-21 (SF)
1957—49ers, 21-17 (C)
49ers, 21-17 (SF)
1958—Bears, 28-6 (C)
Bears, 27-14 (SF)
1959—49ers, 20-17 (SF)
Bears, 14-3 (C)
1960—Bears, 27-10 (C)
49ers, 25-7 (SF)
1961—Bears, 31-0 (C)
49ers, 41-31 (SF)
1962—Bears, 30-14 (C)
49ers, 34-27 (SF)
1963—Bears, 20-14 (SF)
Bears, 27-7 (C)
1964—49ers, 31-21 (SF)
Bears, 23-21 (C)
1965—49ers, 52-24 (SF)
Bears, 61-20 (C)
1966—Tie, 30-30 (C)
49ers, 41-14 (SF)
1967—Bears, 28-14 (SF)
1968—Bears, 27-19 (C)
1969—49ers, 42-21 (SF)
1970—Bears, 37-16 (C)
1971—49ers, 13-0 (SF)
1972—Bears, 34-21 (C)
1974—Bears, 34-0 (C)
1975—49ers, 31-3 (SF)
1976—Bears, 19-12 (SF)
1978—Bears, 16-13 (SF)
1979—Bears, 28-27 (SF)
1981—49ers, 28-17 (SF)
1983—Bears, 13-3 (C)
1984—*49ers, 23-0 (SF)
1985—Bears, 26-10 (SF)
1987—49ers, 41-0 (SF)
1988—Bears, 10-9 (C)
*49ers, 28-3 (C)
1989—49ers, 26-0 (C)
1991—49ers, 52-14 (SF)
(RS Pts.—49ers 1,148, Bears 1,063)
(PS Pts.—49ers 51, Bears 3)
*NFC Championship
CHICAGO vs. SEATTLE
RS: Seahawks lead series, 4-2
1976—Bears, 34-7 (S)
1978—Seahawks, 31-29 (C)

1982—Seahawks, 20-14 (S)
1984—Seahawks, 38-9 (S)
1987—Seahawks, 34-21 (C)
1990—Bears, 17-0 (C)
(RS Pts.—Seahawks 130, Bears 124)
CHICAGO vs. TAMPA BAY
RS: Bears lead series, 24-8
1977—Bears, 10-0 (TB)
1978—Buccaneers, 33-19 (TB)
    Bears, 14-3 (C)
1979—Buccaneers, 17-13 (C)
    Bears, 14-0 (TB)
1980—Bears, 23-0 (C)
    Bears, 14-13 (TB)
1981—Bears, 28-17 (C)
    Buccaneers, 20-10 (TB)
1982—Buccaneers, 26-23 (TB) OT
1983—Bears, 17-10 (C)
    Bears, 27-0 (TB)
1984—Bears, 34-14 (C)
    Bears, 44-9 (TB)
1985—Bears, 38-28 (C)
    Bears, 27-19 (TB)
1986—Bears, 23-3 (TB)
    Bears, 48-14 (C)
1987—Bears, 20-3 (C)
    Bears, 27-26 (TB)
1988—Bears, 28-10 (C)
    Bears, 27-15 (TB)
1989—Buccaneers, 42-35 (TB)
    Buccaneers, 32-31 (C)
1990—Bears, 26-6 (TB)
    Bears, 27-14 (C)
1991—Bears, 21-20 (TB)
    Bears, 27-0 (C)
1992—Bears, 31-14 (C)
    Buccaneers, 20-17 (TB)
1993—Bears, 47-17 (C)
    Buccaneers, 13-10 (TB)
(RS Pts.—Bears 800, Buccaneers 458)
CHICAGO vs. *WASHINGTON
RS: Bears lead series, 18-12-1
PS: Redskins lead series, 4-3
1932—Tie, 7-7 (B)
1933—Bears, 7-0 (C)
    Redskins, 10-0 (B)
1934—Bears, 21-0 (B)
1935—Bears, 30-14 (B)
1936—Bears, 26-0 (B)
1937—**Redskins, 28-21 (C)
1938—Bears, 31-7 (C)
1940—Redskins, 7-3 (W)
    **Bears, 73-0 (W)
1941—Bears, 35-21 (C)
1942—**Redskins, 14-6 (W)
1943—Redskins, 21-7 (W)
    **Bears, 41-21 (C)
1945—Redskins, 28-21 (W)
1946—Bears, 24-20 (C)
1947—Bears, 56-20 (W)
1948—Bears, 48-13 (C)
1949—Bears, 31-21 (W)
1951—Bears, 27-0 (W)
1953—Bears, 27-24 (W)
1957—Redskins, 14-3 (W)
1964—Redskins, 27-20 (W)
1968—Redskins, 38-28 (C)
1971—Bears, 16-15 (C)
1974—Redskins, 42-0 (W)
1976—Bears, 33-7 (C)
1978—Bears, 14-10 (W)
1980—Bears, 35-21 (C)
1981—Redskins, 24-7 (C)
1984—***Bears, 23-19 (W)
1985—Bears, 45-10 (C)
1986—***Redskins, 27-13 (C)
1987—***Redskins, 21-17 (C)
1988—Bears, 34-14 (W)
1989—Redskins, 38-14 (W)
1990—Redskins, 10-9 (W)
1991—Redskins, 20-7 (C)
(RS Pts.—Bears 666, Redskins 503)
(PS Pts.—Bears 194, Redskins 130)

Franchise in Boston prior to 1937 and known as Braves prior to 1933
**NFL Championship
***NFC Divisional Playoff

CINCINNATI vs. ARIZONA
RS: Bengals lead series, 3-1;
See Arizona vs. Cincinnati
CINCINNATI vs. ATLANTA
RS: Bengals lead series, 6-2;
See Atlanta vs. Cincinnati
CINCINNATI vs. BUFFALO
RS: Bengals lead series, 9-7
PS: Bengals lead series, 2-0;
See Buffalo vs. Cincinnati
CINCINNATI vs. CHICAGO
RS: Bengals lead series, 3-2;
See Chicago vs. Cincinnati
CINCINNATI vs. CLEVELAND
RS: Bengals lead series, 24-23
1970—Browns, 30-27 (Cle)
    Bengals, 14-10 (Cin)
1971—Browns, 27-24 (Cin)
    Browns, 31-27 (Cle)
1972—Browns, 27-6 (Cle)
    Browns, 27-24 (Cin)
1973—Browns, 17-10 (Cle)
    Bengals, 34-17 (Cin)
1974—Bengals, 33-7 (Cin)
    Bengals, 34-24 (Cle)
1975—Bengals, 24-17 (Cin)
    Browns, 35-23 (Cle)
1976—Bengals, 45-24 (Cle)
    Bengals, 21-6 (Cin)
1977—Browns, 13-3 (Cin)
    Bengals, 10-7 (Cle)
1978—Browns, 13-10 (Cle) OT
    Bengals, 48-16 (Cin)
1979—Browns, 28-27 (Cle)
    Bengals, 16-12 (Cin)
1980—Browns, 31-7 (Cle)
    Browns, 27-24 (Cin)
1981—Browns, 20-17 (Cin)
    Bengals, 41-21 (Cle)
1982—Bengals, 23-10 (Cin)
1983—Browns, 17-7 (Cin)
    Bengals, 28-21 (Cin)
1984—Bengals, 12-9 (Cin)
    Bengals, 20-17 (Cle) OT
1985—Bengals, 27-10 (Cin)
    Browns, 24-6 (Cle)
1986—Bengals, 30-13 (Cle)
    Browns, 34-3 (Cin)
1987—Browns, 34-0 (Cin)
    Browns, 38-24 (Cle)
1988—Bengals, 24-17 (Cin)
    Browns, 23-16 (Cle)
1989—Bengals, 21-14 (Cin)
    Bengals, 21-0 (Cle)
1990—Bengals, 34-13 (Cle)
    Bengals, 21-14 (Cin)
1991—Browns, 14-13 (Cle)
    Bengals, 23-21 (Cin)
1992—Bengals, 30-10 (Cin)
    Browns, 37-21 (Cle)
1993—Browns, 27-14 (Cle)
    Browns, 28-17 (Cin)
(RS Pts.—Bengals 984, Browns 932)
CINCINNATI vs. DALLAS
RS: Cowboys lead series, 3-2
1973—Cowboys, 38-10 (D)
1979—Cowboys, 38-13 (D)
1985—Bengals, 50-24 (C)
1988—Bengals, 38-24 (D)
1991—Cowboys, 35-23 (D)
(RS Pts.—Cowboys 159, Bengals 134)
CINCINNATI vs. DENVER
RS: Broncos lead series, 10-6
1968—Bengals, 24-10 (C)
    Broncos, 10-7 (D)
1969—Broncos, 30-23 (C)
    Broncos, 27-16 (D)
1971—Bengals, 24-10 (D)

1972—Bengals, 21-10 (C)
1973—Broncos, 28-10 (D)
1975—Bengals, 17-16 (D)
1976—Bengals, 17-7 (C)
1977—Broncos, 24-13 (C)
1979—Broncos, 10-0 (D)
1981—Bengals, 38-21 (C)
1983—Broncos, 24-17 (D)
1984—Broncos, 20-17 (D)
1986—Broncos, 34-28 (D)
1991—Broncos, 45-14 (D)
(RS Pts.—Broncos 326, Bengals 286)
CINCINNATI vs. DETROIT
RS: Series tied, 3-3
1970—Lions, 38-3 (D)
1974—Lions, 23-19 (D)
1983—Bengals, 17-9 (C)
1986—Bengals, 24-17 (D)
1989—Bengals, 42-7 (C)
1992—Lions, 19-13 (C)
(RS Pts.—Bengals 118, Lions 113)
CINCINNATI vs. GREEN BAY
RS: Bengals lead series, 4-3
1971—Packers, 20-17 (GB)
1976—Bengals, 28-7 (C)
1977—Bengals, 17-7 (Mil)
1980—Packers, 14-9 (GB)
1983—Bengals, 34-14 (C)
1986—Bengals, 34-28 (Mil)
1992—Packers, 24-23 (GB)
(RS Pts.—Bengals 162, Packers 114)
CINCINNATI vs. HOUSTON
RS: Oilers lead series, 25-24-1
PS: Bengals lead series, 1-0
1968—Oilers, 27-17 (C)
1969—Tie, 31-31 (H)
1970—Oilers, 20-13 (C)
    Bengals, 30-20 (H)
1971—Oilers, 10-6 (H)
    Bengals, 28-13 (C)
1972—Bengals, 30-7 (C)
    Bengals, 61-17 (H)
1973—Bengals, 24-10 (C)
    Bengals, 27-24 (H)
1974—Oilers, 34-21 (C)
    Oilers, 20-3 (H)
1975—Bengals, 21-19 (H)
    Bengals, 23-19 (C)
1976—Bengals, 27-7 (H)
    Bengals, 31-27 (C)
1977—Bengals, 13-10 (C) OT
    Oilers, 21-16 (H)
1978—Bengals, 28-13 (C)
    Oilers, 17-10 (H)
1979—Oilers, 30-27 (C) OT
    Oilers, 42-21 (H)
1980—Bengals, 13-10 (C)
    Oilers, 23-3 (H)
1981—Oilers, 17-10 (H)
    Bengals, 34-21 (C)
1982—Bengals, 27-6 (C)
    Bengals, 35-27 (H)
1983—Bengals, 55-14 (H)
    Bengals, 38-10 (C)
1984—Bengals, 13-3 (C)
    Bengals, 31-13 (H)
1985—Oilers, 44-27 (H)
    Bengals, 45-27 (C)
1986—Bengals, 31-28 (C)
    Oilers, 32-28 (H)
1987—Oilers, 31-29 (C)
    Oilers, 21-17 (H)
1988—Bengals, 44-21 (C)
    Oilers, 41-6 (H)
1989—Oilers, 26-24 (H)
    Bengals, 61-7 (H)
1990—Oilers, 48-17 (H)
    Bengals, 40-20 (C)
    *Bengals, 41-14 (C)
1991—Oilers, 30-7 (C)
    Oilers, 35-3 (H)
1992—Oilers, 38-24 (C)
    Oilers, 26-10 (H)

1993—Oilers, 28-12 (H)
    Oilers, 38-3 (C)
(RS Pts.—Bengals 1,192, Oilers 1,126)
(PS Pts.—Bengals 41, Oilers 14)
*AFC First Round Playoff
CINCINNATI vs. *INDIANAPOLIS
RS: Colts lead series, 8-5
PS: Colts lead series, 1-0
1970—**Colts, 17-0 (B)
1972—Colts, 20-19 (C)
1974—Bengals, 24-14 (B)
1976—Colts, 28-27 (C)
1979—Colts, 38-28 (B)
1980—Bengals, 34-33 (C)
1981—Bengals, 41-19 (B)
1982—Bengals, 20-17 (B)
1983—Colts, 34-31 (C)
1987—Bengals, 23-21 (I)
1989—Colts, 23-12 (C)
1990—Colts, 34-20 (C)
1992—Colts, 21-17 (C)
1993—Colts, 9-6 (C)
(RS Pts.—Colts 311, Bengals 302)
(PS Pts.—Colts 17, Bengals 0)
*Franchise in Baltimore prior to 1984
**AFC Divisional Playoff
CINCINNATI vs. KANSAS CITY
RS: Chiefs lead series, 11-9
1968—Chiefs, 13-3 (KC)
    Chiefs, 16-9 (KC)
1969—Bengals, 24-19 (C)
    Chiefs, 42-22 (KC)
1970—Chiefs, 27-19 (C)
1972—Bengals, 23-16 (KC)
1973—Bengals, 14-6 (C)
1974—Bengals, 33-6 (C)
1976—Bengals, 27-24 (KC)
1977—Bengals, 27-7 (KC)
1978—Chiefs, 24-23 (C)
1979—Chiefs, 10-7 (C)
1980—Bengals, 20-6 (KC)
1983—Chiefs, 20-15 (C)
1984—Chiefs, 27-22 (C)
1986—Chiefs, 24-14 (KC)
1987—Bengals, 30-27 (C) OT
1988—Chiefs, 31-28 (KC)
1989—Bengals, 21-17 (KC)
1993—Chiefs, 17-15 (KC)
(RS Pts.—Bengals 396, Chiefs 379)
CINCINNATI vs. *L.A. RAIDERS
RS: Raiders lead series, 14-7
PS: Raiders lead series, 2-0
1968—Bengals, 31-10 (O)
    Raiders, 34-0 (C)
1969—Bengals, 31-17 (C)
    Raiders, 37-17 (O)
1970—Bengals, 31-21 (O)
1971—Raiders, 31-27 (O)
1972—Bengals, 20-14 (C)
1974—Raiders, 30-27 (O)
1975—Bengals, 14-10 (C)
    **Raiders, 31-28 (O)
1976—Raiders, 35-20 (O)
1978—Raiders, 34-21 (C)
1980—Raiders, 28-17 (O)
1982—Bengals, 31-17 (C)
1983—Raiders, 20-10 (C)
1985—Raiders, 13-6 (LA)
1988—Bengals, 45-21 (LA)
1989—Raiders, 28-7 (LA)
1990—Raiders, 24-7 (LA)
    **Raiders, 20-10 (LA)
1991—Raiders, 38-14 (C)
1992—Bengals, 24-21 (C) OT
1993—Bengals, 16-10 (C)
(RS Pts.—Raiders 520, Bengals 389)
(PS Pts.—Raiders 51, Bengals 38)
*Franchise in Oakland prior to 1982
**AFC Divisional Playoff
CINCINNATI vs. L.A. RAMS
RS: Bengals lead series, 5-2
1972—Rams, 15-12 (LA)
1976—Bengals, 20-12 (C)

1978—Bengals, 20-19 (LA)
1981—Bengals, 24-10 (C)
1984—Rams, 24-14 (C)
1990—Bengals, 34-31 (LA) OT
1993—Bengals, 15-3 (C)
(RS Pts.—Bengals 139, Rams 114)

CINCINNATI vs. MIAMI
RS: Dolphins lead series, 9-3
PS: Dolphins lead series, 1-0
1968—Dolphins, 24-22 (C)
    Bengals, 38-21 (M)
1969—Bengals, 27-21 (C)
1971—Dolphins, 23-13 (C)
1973—*Dolphins, 34-16 (M)
1974—Dolphins, 24-3 (M)
1977—Bengals, 23-17 (C)
1978—Dolphins, 21-0 (M)
1980—Dolphins, 17-16 (M)
1983—Dolphins, 38-14 (M)
1987—Dolphins, 20-14 (C)
1989—Dolphins, 20-13 (C)
1991—Dolphins, 37-13 (M)
(RS Pts.—Dolphins 317, Bengals 212)
(PS Pts.—Dolphins 34, Bengals 16)
*AFC Divisional Playoff

CINCINNATI vs. MINNESOTA
RS: Vikings lead series, 4-3
1973—Bengals, 27-0 (C)
1977—Vikings, 42-10 (M)
1980—Bengals, 14-0 (C)
1983—Vikings, 20-14 (M)
1986—Bengals, 24-20 (C)
1989—Vikings, 29-21 (M)
1992—Vikings, 42 7 (C)
(RS Pts.—Vikings 153, Bengals 117)

CINCINNATI vs. *NEW ENGLAND
RS: Patriots lead series, 8-7
1968—Patriots, 33-14 (B)
1969—Patriots, 25-14 (C)
1970—Bengals, 45-7 (C)
1972—Bengals, 31-7 (NE)
1975—Bengals, 27-10 (C)
1978—Patriots, 10-3 (C)
1979—Patriots, 20-14 (C)
1984—Patriots, 20-14 (NE)
1985—Patriots, 34-23 (NE)
1986—Bengals, 31-7 (NE)
1988—Patriots, 27-21 (NE)
1990—Bengals, 41-7 (C)
1991—Bengals, 29-7 (C)
1992—Bengals, 20-10 (C)
1993—Patriots, 7-2 (NE)
(RS Pts.—Bengals 329, Patriots 231)
*Franchise in Boston prior to 1971

CINCINNATI vs. NEW ORLEANS
RS: Saints lead series, 5-3
1970—Bengals, 26-6 (C)
1975—Bengals, 21-0 (NO)
1978—Saints, 20-18 (C)
1981—Saints, 17-7 (NO)
1984—Bengals, 24-21 (NO)
1987—Saints, 41-24 (C)
1990—Saints, 21-7 (C)
1993—Saints, 20-13 (NO)
(RS Pts.—Saints 146, Bengals 140)

CINCINNATI vs. N.Y. GIANTS
RS: Bengals lead series, 4-0
1972—Bengals, 13-10 (C)
1977—Bengals, 30-13 (C)
1985—Bengals, 35-30 (C)
1991—Bengals, 27-24 (C)
(RS Pts.—Bengals 105, Giants 77)

CINCINNATI vs. N.Y. JETS
RS: Jets lead series, 9-6
PS: Jets lead series, 1-0
1968—Jets, 27-14 (NY)
1969—Jets, 21-7 (C)
    Jets, 40-7 (NY)
1971—Jets, 35-21 (NY)
1973—Bengals, 20-14 (C)
1976—Bengals, 42-3 (NY)
1981—Bengals, 31-30 (NY)
1982—*Jets, 44-17 (C)

1984—Jets, 43-23 (NY)
1985—Jets, 29-20 (C)
1986—Bengals, 52-21 (C)
1987—Jets, 27-20 (NY)
1988—Bengals, 36-19 (C)
1990—Bengals, 25-20 (C)
1992—Jets, 17-14 (NY)
1993—Jets, 17-12 (NY)
(RS Pts.—Jets 363, Bengals 344)
(PS Pts.—Jets 44, Bengals 17)
*AFC First-Round Playoff

CINCINNATI vs. PHILADELPHIA
RS: Bengals lead series, 5-1
1971—Bengals, 37-14 (C)
1975—Bengals, 31-0 (P)
1979—Bengals, 37-13 (C)
1982—Bengals, 18-14 (P)
1988—Bengals, 28-24 (P)
1991—Eagles, 17-10 (P)
(RS Pts.—Bengals 161, Eagles 82)

CINCINNATI vs. PITTSBURGH
RS: Steelers lead series, 26-21
1970—Steelers, 21-10 (P)
    Bengals, 34-7 (C)
1971—Steelers, 21-10 (P)
    Steelers, 21-13 (C)
1972—Bengals, 15-10 (C)
    Steelers, 40-17 (P)
1973—Bengals, 19-7 (C)
    Steelers, 20-13 (P)
1974—Bengals, 17-10 (C)
    Steelers, 27-3 (P)
1975—Steelers, 30-24 (C)
    Steelers, 35-14 (P)
1976—Steelers, 23-6 (P)
    Steelers, 7-3 (C)
1977—Steelers, 20-14 (P)
    Bengals, 17-10 (C)
1978—Steelers, 28-3 (C)
    Steelers, 7-6 (P)
1979—Bengals, 34-10 (C)
    Steelers, 37-17 (P)
1980—Bengals, 30-28 (C)
    Bengals, 17-16 (P)
1981—Bengals, 34-7 (C)
    Bengals, 17-10 (P)
1982—Steelers, 26-20 (P) OT
1983—Steelers, 24-14 (C)
    Bengals, 23-10 (P)
1984—Steelers, 38-17 (P)
    Bengals, 22-20 (C)
1985—Bengals, 37-24 (P)
    Bengals, 26-21 (C)
1986—Bengals, 24-22 (C)
    Steelers, 30-9 (P)
1987—Steelers, 23-20 (P)
    Steelers, 30-16 (C)
1988—Bengals, 17-12 (C)
    Bengals, 42-7 (P)
1989—Bengals, 41-10 (C)
    Bengals, 26-16 (P)
1990—Bengals, 27-3 (C)
    Bengals, 16-12 (P)
1991—Steelers, 33-27 (C) OT
    Steelers, 17-10 (P)
1992—Steelers, 20-0 (C)
    Bengals, 21-9 (C)
1993—Steelers, 34-7 (P)
    Steelers, 24-16 (C)
(RS Pts.—Steelers 929, Bengals 853)

CINCINNATI vs. SAN DIEGO
RS: Chargers lead series, 12-8
PS: Bengals lead series, 1-0
1968—Chargers, 29-13 (SD)
    Chargers, 31-10 (C)
1969—Bengals, 34-20 (C)
    Chargers, 21-14 (SD)
1970—Bengals, 17-14 (SD)
1971—Bengals, 31-0 (C)
1973—Bengals, 20-13 (SD)
1974—Chargers, 20-17 (C)
1975—Bengals, 47-17 (C)
1977—Chargers, 24-3 (SD)

1978—Chargers, 22-13 (SD)
1979—Chargers, 26-24 (C)
1980—Chargers, 31-14 (C)
1981—Bengals, 40-17 (SD)
    *Bengals, 27-7 (C)
1982—Chargers, 50-34 (SD)
1985—Chargers, 44-41 (C)
1987—Chargers, 10-9 (C)
1988—Bengals, 27-10 (C)
1990—Bengals, 21-16 (SD)
1992—Chargers, 27-10 (SD)
(RS Pts.—Chargers 442, Bengals 439)
(PS Pts.—Bengals 27, Chargers 7)
*AFC Championship

CINCINNATI vs. SAN FRANCISCO
RS: 49ers lead series, 6-1
PS: 49ers lead series, 2-0
1974—Bengals, 21-3 (SF)
1978—49ers, 28-12 (SF)
1981—49ers, 21-3 (C)
    *49ers, 26-21 (Detroit)
1984—49ers, 23-17 (SF)
1987—49ers, 27-26 (C)
1988—**49ers, 20-16 (Miami)
1990—49ers, 20-17 (C)
1993—49ers, 21-8 (SF)
(RS Pts.—49ers 143, Bengals 104)
(PS Pts.—49ers 46, Bengals 37)
*Super Bowl XVI
**Super Bowl XXIII

CINCINNATI vs. SEATTLE
RS: Series tied, 6-6
PS: Bengals lead series, 1-0
1977—Bengals, 42-20 (C)
1981—Bengals, 27-21 (C)
1982—Bengals, 24-10 (C)
1984—Seahawks, 26-6 (C)
1985—Seahawks, 28-24 (C)
1986—Bengals, 34-7 (C)
1987—Bengals, 17-10 (S)
1988—*Bengals, 21-13 (C)
1989—Seahawks, 24-17 (C)
1990—Seahawks, 31-16 (S)
1991—Seahawks, 13-7 (C)
1992—Bengals, 21-3 (S)
1993—Seahawks, 19-10 (C)
(RS Pts.—Bengals 245, Seahawks 212)
(PS Pts.—Bengals 21, Seahawks 13)
*AFC Divisional Playoff

CINCINNATI vs. TAMPA BAY
RS: Bengals lead series, 3-1
1976—Bengals, 21-0 (C)
1980—Buccaneers, 17-12 (C)
1983—Bengals, 23-17 (TB)
1989—Bengals, 56-23 (C)
(RS Pts.—Bengals 112, Buccaneers 57)

CINCINNATI vs. WASHINGTON
RS: Redskins lead series, 4-2
1970—Redskins, 20-0 (W)
1974—Bengals, 28-17 (C)
1979—Redskins, 28-14 (W)
1985—Redskins, 27-24 (W)
1988—Bengals, 20-17 (C) OT
1991—Redskins, 34-27 (C)
(RS Pts.—Redskins 143, Bengals 113)

CLEVELAND vs. ARIZONA
RS: Browns lead series, 31-10-3;
See Arizona vs. Cleveland

CLEVELAND vs. ATLANTA
RS: Browns lead series, 8-2;
See Atlanta vs. Cleveland

CLEVELAND vs. BUFFALO
RS: Browns lead series, 7-3
PS: Browns lead series, 1-0;
See Buffalo vs. Cleveland

CLEVELAND vs. CHICAGO
RS: Browns lead series, 8-3;
See Chicago vs. Cleveland

CLEVELAND vs. CINCINNATI
RS: Bengals lead series, 24-23;
See Cincinnati vs. Cleveland

CLEVELAND vs. DALLAS

RS: Browns lead series, 14-9
PS: Browns lead series, 2-1
1960—Browns, 48-7 (D)
1961—Browns, 25-7 (C)
    Browns, 38-17 (D)
1962—Browns, 19-10 (C)
    Cowboys, 45-21 (D)
1963—Browns, 41-24 (D)
    Browns, 27-17 (C)
1964—Browns, 27-6 (C)
    Browns, 20-16 (D)
1965—Browns, 23-17 (C)
    Browns, 24-17 (D)
1966—Browns, 30-21 (C)
    Cowboys, 26-14 (D)
1967—Cowboys, 21-14 (C)
    *Cowboys, 52-14 (D)
1968—Cowboys, 28-7 (C)
    *Browns, 31-20 (C)
1969—Browns, 42-10 (C)
    *Browns, 38-14 (D)
1970—Cowboys, 6-2 (C)
1974—Cowboys, 41-17 (D)
1979—Browns, 26-7 (C)
1982—Cowboys, 31-14 (D)
1985—Cowboys, 20-7 (D)
1988—Browns, 24-21 (C)
1991—Cowboys, 26-14 (C)
(RS Pts.—Browns 524, Cowboys 441)
(PS Pts.—Cowboys 86, Browns 83)
*Conference Championship

CLEVELAND vs. DENVER
RS: Broncos lead series, 12-5
PS: Broncos lead series, 3-0
1970—Browns, 27-13 (D)
1971—Broncos, 27-0 (C)
1972—Browns, 27-20 (D)
1974—Browns, 23-21 (C)
1975—Broncos, 16-15 (D)
1976—Broncos, 44-13 (D)
1978—Broncos, 19-7 (C)
1980—Broncos, 19-16 (C)
1981—Broncos, 23-20 (D) OT
1983—Broncos, 27-6 (D)
1984—Broncos, 24-14 (C)
1986—*Broncos, 23-20 (C) OT
1987—*Broncos, 38-33 (D)
1988—Broncos, 30-7 (D)
1989—Browns, 16-13 (C)
    *Broncos, 37-21 (D)
1990—Browns, 30-29 (D)
1991—Broncos, 17-7 (C)
1992—Broncos, 12-0 (C)
1993—Broncos, 29-14 (C)
(RS Pts.—Broncos 383, Browns 242)
(PS Pts.—Broncos 98, Browns 74)
*AFC Championship

CLEVELAND vs. DETROIT
RS: Lions lead series, 11-3
PS: Lions lead series, 3-1
1952—Lions, 17-6 (D)
    *Lions, 17-7 (C)
1953—*Lions, 17-16 (D)
1954—Lions, 14-10 (C)
    *Browns, 56-10 (C)
1957—Lions, 20-7 (D)
    *Lions, 59-14 (D)
1958—Lions, 30-10 (C)
1963—Lions, 38-10 (D)
1964—Browns, 37-21 (D)
1967—Lions, 31-14 (D)
1969—Lions, 28-21 (D)
1970—Lions, 41-24 (D)
1975—Lions, 21-10 (D)
1983—Browns, 31-26 (D)
1986—Browns, 24-21 (C)
1989—Lions, 13-10 (D)
1992—Lions, 24-14 (D)
(RS Pts.—Lions 345, Browns 228)
(PS Pts.—Lions 103, Browns 93)
*NFL Championship

CLEVELAND vs. GREEN BAY
RS: Packers lead series, 7-6

PS: Packers lead series, 1-0
1953—Browns, 27-0 (Mil)
1955—Browns, 41-10 (C)
1956—Browns, 24-7 (Mil)
1961—Packers, 49-17 (C)
1964—Packers, 28-21 (Mil)
1965—*Packers, 23-12 (GB)
1966—Packers, 21-20 (C)
1967—Packers, 55-7 (Mil)
1969—Browns, 20-7 (C)
1972—Packers, 26-10 (C)
1980—Browns, 26-21 (C)
1983—Packers, 35-21 (Mil)
1986—Packers, 17-14 (C)
1992—Browns, 17-6 (C)
(RS Pts.—Packers 282, Browns 265)
(PS Pts.—Packers 23, Browns 12)
*NFL Championship
CLEVELAND vs. HOUSTON
RS: Browns lead series, 27-20
PS: Oilers lead series, 1-0
1970—Browns, 28-14 (C)
  Browns, 21-10 (H)
1971—Browns, 31-0 (C)
  Browns, 37-24 (H)
1972—Browns, 23-17 (C)
  Browns, 20-0 (H)
1973—Browns, 42-13 (C)
  Browns, 23-13 (H)
1974—Browns, 20-7 (C)
  Oilers, 28-24 (H)
1975—Oilers, 40-10 (C)
  Oilers, 21-10 (H)
1976—Browns, 21-7 (H)
  Browns, 13-10 (C)
1977—Browns, 24-23 (H)
  Oilers, 19-15 (C)
1978—Oilers, 16-13 (C)
  Oilers, 14-10 (H)
1979—Oilers, 31-10 (H)
  Browns, 14-7 (C)
1980—Oilers, 16-7 (C)
  Browns, 17-14 (H)
1981—Oilers, 9-3 (C)
  Oilers, 17-13 (H)
1982—Browns, 20-14 (H)
1983—Browns, 25-19 (C) OT
  Oilers, 34-27 (H)
1984—Browns, 27-10 (C)
  Browns, 27-20 (H)
1985—Browns, 21-6 (H)
  Browns, 28-21 (C)
1986—Browns, 23-20 (H)
  Browns, 13-10 (C) OT
1987—Oilers, 15-10 (C)
  Browns, 40-7 (H)
1988—Oilers, 24-17 (H)
  Browns, 28-23 (C)
  *Oilers, 24-23 (C)
1989—Browns, 28-17 (C)
  Browns, 24-20 (H)
1990—Oilers, 35-23 (C)
  Oilers, 58-14 (H)
1991—Oilers, 28-24 (C)
  Oilers, 17-14 (C)
1992—Browns, 24-14 (H)
  Oilers, 17-14 (C)
1993—Oilers, 27-20 (C)
  Oilers, 19-17 (H)
(RS Pts.—Browns 957, Oilers 845)
(PS Pts.—Oilers 24, Browns 23)
*AFC First-Round Playoff
CLEVELAND vs. *INDIANAPOLIS
RS: Browns lead series, 12-7
PS: Series tied, 2-2
1956—Colts, 21-7 (C)
1959—Browns, 38-31 (B)
1962—Colts, 36-14 (C)
1964—**Browns, 27-0 (C)
1968—Browns, 30-20 (B)
  **Colts, 34-0 (C)
1971—Browns, 14-13 (B)
  ***Colts, 20-3 (C)

1973—Browns, 24-14 (C)
1975—Colts, 21-7 (B)
1978—Browns, 45-24 (B)
1979—Browns, 13-10 (C)
1980—Browns, 28-27 (B)
1981—Browns, 42-28 (C)
1983—Browns, 41-23 (C)
1986—Browns, 24-9 (I)
1987—Colts, 9-7 (C)
  ***Browns, 38-21 (C)
1988—Browns, 23-17 (C)
1989—Colts, 23-17 (I) OT
1991—Browns, 31-0 (I)
1992—Colts, 14-3 (I)
1993—Colts, 23-10 (I)
(RS Pts.—Browns 418, Colts 363)
(PS Pts.—Colts 75, Browns 68)
*Franchise in Baltimore prior to 1984
**NFL Championship
***AFC Divisional Playoff
CLEVELAND vs. KANSAS CITY
RS: Browns lead series, 7-6-2
1971—Chiefs, 13-7 (KC)
1972—Chiefs, 31-7 (C)
1973—Tie, 20-20 (KC)
1975—Browns, 40-14 (C)
1976—Chiefs, 39-14 (KC)
1977—Browns, 44-7 (C)
1978—Chiefs, 17-3 (KC)
1979—Browns, 27-24 (KC)
1980—Browns, 20-13 (C)
1984—Chiefs, 10-6 (KC)
1986—Browns, 20-7 (C)
1988—Browns, 6-3 (KC)
1989—Tie, 10-10 (C) OT
1990—Browns, 34-0 (KC)
1991—Browns, 20-15 (C)
(RS Pts.—Chiefs 257, Browns 244)
CLEVELAND vs. *L.A.RAIDERS
RS: Raiders lead series, 8-4
PS: Raiders lead series, 2-0
1970—Raiders, 23-20 (O)
1971—Raiders, 34-20 (C)
1973—Browns, 7-3 (O)
1974—Raiders, 40-24 (C)
1975—Raiders, 38-17 (O)
1977—Raiders, 26-10 (C)
1979—Raiders, 19-14 (O)
1980—**Raiders, 14-12 (C)
1982—***Raiders, 27-10 (LA)
1985—Raiders, 21-20 (C)
1986—Raiders, 27-14 (LA)
1987—Browns, 24-17 (LA)
1992—Browns, 28-16 (LA)
1993—Browns, 19-16 (LA)
(RS Pts.—Raiders 280, Browns 217)
(PS Pts.—Raiders 41, Browns 22)
*Franchise in Oakland prior to 1982
**AFC Divisional Playoff
***AFC First-Round Playoff
CLEVELAND vs. L.A. RAMS
RS: Browns lead series, 8-7
PS: Browns lead series, 2-1
1950—*Browns, 30-28 (LA)
1951—Browns, 38-23 (LA)
  *Rams, 24-17 (LA)
1952—Browns, 37-7 (C)
1955—*Browns, 38-14 (LA)
1957—Browns, 45-31 (C)
1958—Browns, 30-27 (LA)
1963—Browns, 20-6 (C)
1965—Rams, 42-7 (LA)
1968—Rams, 24-6 (C)
1973—Rams, 30-17 (LA)
1977—Rams, 9-0 (C)
1978—Browns, 30-19 (C)
1981—Browns, 27-16 (LA)
1984—Rams, 20-17 (LA)
1987—Browns, 30-17 (C)
1990—Rams, 38-23 (C)
1993—Browns, 42-14 (LA)
(RS Pts.—Browns 358, Rams 334)
(PS Pts.—Browns 85, Rams 66)

*NFL Championship
CLEVELAND vs. MIAMI
RS: Dolphins lead series, 6-4
PS: Dolphins lead series, 2-0
1970—Browns, 28-0 (M)
1972—*Dolphins, 20-14 (M)
1973—Dolphins, 17-9 (C)
1976—Browns, 17-13 (C)
1979—Browns, 30-24 (C) OT
1985—*Dolphins, 24-21 (M)
1986—Browns, 26-16 (C)
1988—Dolphins, 38-31 (M)
1989—Dolphins, 13-10 (M) OT
1990—Dolphins, 30-13 (C)
1992—Dolphins, 27-23 (C)
1993—Dolphins, 24-14 (C)
(RS Pts.—Dolphins 202, Browns 201)
(PS Pts.—Dolphins 44, Browns 35)
*AFC Divisional Playoff
CLEVELAND vs. MINNESOTA
RS: Vikings lead series, 7-3
PS: Vikings lead series, 1-0
1965—Vikings, 27-17 (C)
1967—Browns, 14-10 (C)
1969—Vikings, 51-3 (M)
  *Vikings, 27-7 (M)
1973—Vikings, 26-3 (M)
1975—Vikings, 42-10 (C)
1980—Vikings, 28-23 (M)
1983—Vikings, 27-21 (C)
1986—Browns, 23-20 (M)
1989—Browns, 23-17 (C) OT
1992—Vikings, 17-13 (M)
(RS Pts.—Vikings 265, Browns 150)
(PS Pts.—Vikings 27, Browns 7)
*NFL Championship
CLEVELAND vs. NEW ENGLAND
RS: Browns lead series, 9-3
1971—Browns, 27-7 (C)
1974—Browns, 21-14 (NE)
1977—Browns, 30-27 (C) OT
1980—Patriots, 34-17 (NE)
1982—Browns, 10-7 (C)
1983—Browns, 30-0 (NE)
1984—Patriots, 17-16 (C)
1985—Browns, 24-20 (C)
1987—Browns, 20-10 (NE)
1991—Browns, 20-0 (NE)
1992—Browns, 19-17 (NE)
1993—Patriots, 20-17 (C)
(RS Pts.—Browns 251, Patriots 173)
CLEVELAND vs. NEW ORLEANS
RS: Browns lead series, 9-3
1967—Browns, 42-7 (NO)
1968—Browns, 24-10 (NO)
  Browns, 35-17 (C)
1969—Browns, 27-17 (NO)
1971—Browns, 21-17 (NO)
1975—Browns, 17-16 (C)
1978—Browns, 24-16 (NO)
1981—Browns, 20-17 (C)
1984—Saints, 16-14 (C)
1987—Saints, 28-21 (NO)
1990—Saints, 25-20 (NO)
1993—Browns, 17-13 (C)
(RS Pts.—Browns 282, Saints 199)
CLEVELAND vs. N.Y. GIANTS
RS: Browns lead series, 25-16-2
PS: Series tied, 1-1
1950—Giants, 6-0 (C)
  Giants, 17-13 (NY)
  *Browns, 8-3 (C)
1951—Browns, 14-13 (C)
  Browns, 10-0 (NY)
1952—Giants, 17-9 (C)
  Giants, 37-34 (NY)
1953—Browns, 7-0 (NY)
  Browns, 62-14 (C)
1954—Browns, 24-14 (C)
  Browns, 16-7 (NY)
1955—Browns, 24-14 (C)
  Tie, 35-35 (NY)
1956—Giants, 21-9 (C)

  Browns, 24-7 (NY)
1957—Browns, 6-3 (C)
  Browns, 34-28 (NY)
1958—Giants, 21-17 (C)
  Giants, 13-10 (NY)
  *Giants, 10-0 (NY)
1959—Giants, 10-6 (C)
  Giants, 48-7 (NY)
1960—Giants, 17-13 (C)
  Browns, 48-34 (NY)
1961—Giants, 37-21 (C)
  Tie, 7-7 (NY)
1962—Browns, 17-7 (C)
  Giants, 17-13 (NY)
1963—Browns, 35-24 (NY)
  Giants, 33-6 (C)
1964—Browns, 42-20 (C)
  Browns, 52-20 (NY)
1965—Browns, 38-14 (NY)
  Browns, 34-21 (C)
1966—Browns, 28-7 (NY)
  Browns, 49-40 (NY)
1967—Giants, 38-34 (NY)
  Browns, 24-14 (C)
1968—Browns, 45-10 (C)
1969—Browns, 28-17 (C)
  Giants, 27-14 (NY)
1973—Browns, 12-10 (C)
1977—Browns, 21-7 (NY)
1985—Browns, 35-33 (NY)
1991—Giants, 13-10 (NY)
(RS Pts.—Browns 987, Giants 792)
(PS Pts.—Giants 13, Browns 8)
*Conference Playoff
CLEVELAND vs. N.Y. JETS
RS: Browns lead series, 8-6
PS: Browns lead series, 1-0
1970—Browns, 31-21 (C)
1972—Browns, 26-10 (NY)
1976—Browns, 38-17 (C)
1978—Browns, 37-34 (C) OT
1979—Browns, 25-22 (NY) OT
1980—Browns, 17-14 (C)
1981—Jets, 14-13 (C)
1983—Browns, 10-7 (C)
1984—Jets, 24-20 (C)
1985—Jets, 37-10 (NY)
1986—*Browns, 23-20 (C) OT
1988—Jets, 23-3 (C)
1989—Browns, 38-24 (C)
1990—Jets, 24-21 (NY)
1991—Jets, 17-14 (C)
(RS Pts.—Browns 303, Jets 288)
(PS Pts.—Browns 23, Jets 20)
*AFC Divisional Playoff
CLEVELAND vs. PHILADELPHIA
RS: Browns lead series, 30-12-1
1950—Browns, 35-10 (P)
  Browns, 13-7 (C)
1951—Browns, 20-17 (C)
  Browns, 24-9 (P)
1952—Browns, 49-7 (C)
  Eagles, 28-20 (C)
1953—Browns, 37-13 (C)
  Eagles, 42-27 (P)
1954—Eagles, 28-10 (P)
  Browns, 6-0 (C)
1955—Browns, 21-17 (C)
  Eagles, 33-17 (P)
1956—Browns, 16-0 (C)
  Browns, 17-14 (P)
1957—Browns, 24-7 (C)
  Eagles, 17-7 (P)
1958—Browns, 28-14 (C)
  Browns, 21-14 (P)
1959—Browns, 28-7 (C)
  Browns, 28-21 (P)
1960—Browns, 41-24 (P)
  Eagles, 31-29 (C)
1961—Eagles, 27-20 (P)
  Browns, 45-24 (C)
1962—Eagles, 35-7 (P)
  Tie, 14-14 (C)

1963—Browns, 37-7 (C)
Browns, 23-17 (P)
1964—Browns, 28-20 (P)
Browns, 38-24 (C)
1965—Browns, 35-17 (P)
Browns, 38-34 (C)
1966—Browns, 27-7 (C)
Eagles, 33-21 (P)
1967—Eagles, 28-24 (P)
1968—Browns, 47-13 (C)
1969—Browns, 27-20 (P)
1972—Browns, 27-17 (P)
1976—Browns, 24-3 (C)
1979—Browns, 24-19 (P)
1982—Eagles, 24-21 (C)
1988—Browns, 19-3 (C)
1991—Eagles, 32-30 (C)
(RS Pts.—Browns 1,094, Eagles 778)

CLEVELAND vs. PITTSBURGH
RS: Browns lead series, 52-36
1950—Browns, 30-17 (P)
Browns, 45-7 (C)
1951—Browns, 17-0 (C)
Browns, 28-0 (P)
1952—Browns, 21-20 (P)
Browns, 29-28 (C)
1953—Browns, 34-16 (C)
Browns, 20-16 (P)
1954—Steelers, 55-27 (P)
Browns, 42-7 (C)
1955—Browns, 41-14 (C)
Browns, 30-7 (P)
1956—Browns, 14-10 (P)
Steelers, 24-16 (C)
1957—Browns, 23-12 (P)
Browns, 24-0 (C)
1958—Browns, 45-12 (P)
Browns, 27-10 (C)
1959—Steelers, 17-7 (P)
Steelers, 21-20 (C)
1960—Browns, 28-20 (C)
Steelers, 14-10 (P)
1961—Browns, 30-28 (P)
Steelers, 17-13 (C)
1962—Browns, 41-14 (P)
Browns, 35-14 (C)
1963—Browns, 35-23 (C)
Steelers, 9-7 (P)
1964—Steelers, 23-7 (C)
Browns, 30-17 (P)
1965—Browns, 24-19 (C)
Browns, 42-21 (P)
1966—Browns, 41-10 (C)
Steelers, 16-6 (P)
1967—Browns, 21-10 (C)
Browns, 34-14 (P)
1968—Browns, 31-24 (C)
Browns, 45-24 (P)
1969—Browns, 42-31 (C)
Browns, 24-3 (P)
1970—Browns, 15-7 (C)
Steelers, 28-9 (P)
1971—Browns, 27-17 (C)
Steelers, 26-9 (P)
1972—Browns, 26-24 (C)
Steelers, 30-0 (P)
1973—Steelers, 33-6 (P)
Browns, 21-16 (C)
1974—Steelers, 20-16 (P)
Steelers, 26-16 (C)
1975—Steelers, 42-6 (C)
Steelers, 31-17 (P)
1976—Steelers, 31-14 (P)
Browns, 18-16 (C)
1977—Steelers, 28-14 (C)
Steelers, 35-31 (P)
1978—Steelers, 15-9 (P) OT
Steelers, 34-14 (C)
1979—Steelers, 51-35 (C)
Steelers, 33-30 (P) OT
1980—Browns, 27-26 (C)
Steelers, 16-13 (P)
1981—Steelers, 13-7 (P)

Steelers, 32-10 (C)
1982—Browns, 10-9 (C)
Steelers, 37-21 (P)
1983—Steelers, 44-17 (P)
Browns, 30-17 (C)
1984—Browns, 20-10 (C)
Steelers, 23-20 (P)
1985—Browns, 17-7 (C)
Steelers, 10-9 (P)
1986—Browns, 27-24 (P)
Browns, 37-31 (C) OT
1987—Browns, 34-10 (C)
Browns, 19-13 (P)
1988—Browns, 23-9 (P)
Browns, 27-7 (C)
1989—Browns, 51-0 (P)
Steelers, 17-7 (C)
1990—Browns, 13-3 (C)
Steelers, 35-0 (P)
1991—Browns, 17-14 (C)
Steelers, 17-10 (P)
1992—Browns, 17-9 (C)
Steelers, 23-13 (P)
1993—Browns, 28-23 (C)
Steelers, 16-9 (P)
(RS Pts.—Browns 1,952, Steelers 1,682)

CLEVELAND vs. SAN DIEGO
RS: Chargers lead series, 8-6-1
1970—Chargers, 27-10 (C)
1972—Browns, 21-17 (SD)
1973—Tie, 16-16 (C)
1974—Chargers, 36-35 (SD)
1976—Browns, 21-17 (C)
1977—Chargers, 37-14 (SD)
1981—Chargers, 44-14 (C)
1982—Chargers, 30-13 (C)
1983—Browns, 30-24 (SD) OT
1985—Browns, 21-7 (SD)
1986—Browns, 47-17 (C)
1987—Chargers, 27-24 (SD) OT
1990—Browns, 24-14 (C)
1991—Browns, 30-24 (SD) OT
1992—Chargers, 14-13 (C)
(RS Pts.—Chargers 361, Browns 323)

CLEVELAND vs. SAN FRANCISCO
RS: Browns lead series, 9-6
1950—Browns, 34-14 (C)
1951—49ers, 24-10 (SF)
1953—Browns, 23-21 (C)
1955—Browns, 38-3 (SF)
1959—49ers, 21-20 (C)
1962—Browns, 13-10 (SF)
1968—Browns, 33-21 (SF)
1970—49ers, 34-31 (SF)
1974—Browns, 7-0 (C)
1978—Browns, 24-7 (C)
1981—Browns, 15-12 (SF)
1984—49ers, 41-7 (C)
1987—49ers, 38-24 (SF)
1990—49ers, 20-17 (SF)
1993—Browns, 23-13 (C)
(RS Pts.—Browns 319, 49ers 279)

CLEVELAND vs. SEATTLE
RS: Seahawks lead series, 9-3
1977—Seahawks, 20-19 (S)
1978—Seahawks, 47-24 (S)
1979—Seahawks, 29-24 (C)
1980—Browns, 27-3 (S)
1981—Seahawks, 42-21 (S)
1982—Browns, 21-7 (S)
1983—Seahawks, 24-9 (C)
1984—Seahawks, 33-0 (S)
1985—Seahawks, 31-13 (S)
1988—Seahawks, 16-10 (C)
1989—Browns, 17-7 (S)
1993—Seahawks, 22-5 (S)
(RS Pts.—Seahawks 281, Browns 190)

CLEVELAND vs. TAMPA BAY
RS: Browns lead series, 4-0
1976—Browns, 24-7 (TB)
1980—Browns, 34-27 (TB)
1983—Browns, 20-0 (C)
1989—Browns, 42-31 (TB)

(RS Pts.—Browns 120, Buccaneers 65)
CLEVELAND vs. WASHINGTON
RS: Browns lead series, 32-9-1
1950—Browns, 20-14 (C)
Browns, 45-21 (W)
1951—Browns, 45-0 (C)
1952—Browns, 19-15 (C)
Browns, 48-24 (W)
1953—Browns, 30-14 (W)
Browns, 27-3 (C)
1954—Browns, 62-3 (C)
Browns, 34-14 (W)
1955—Redskins, 27-17 (C)
Browns, 24-14 (W)
1956—Redskins, 20-9 (W)
Redskins, 20-17 (C)
1957—Browns, 21-17 (C)
Tie, 30-30 (W)
1958—Browns, 20-10 (W)
Browns, 21-14 (C)
1959—Browns, 34-7 (C)
Browns, 31-17 (W)
1960—Browns, 31-10 (W)
Browns, 27-16 (C)
1961—Browns, 31-7 (C)
Browns, 17-6 (W)
1962—Redskins, 17-16 (C)
Redskins, 17-9 (W)
1963—Browns, 37-14 (C)
Browns, 27-20 (W)
1964—Browns, 27-13 (W)
Browns, 34-24 (C)
1965—Browns, 17-7 (W)
Browns, 24-16 (C)
1966—Browns, 38-14 (W)
Browns, 14-3 (C)
1967—Browns, 42-37 (C)
1968—Browns, 24-21 (W)
1969—Browns, 27-23 (C)
1971—Browns, 20-13 (W)
1975—Redskins, 23-7 (C)
1979—Redskins, 13-9 (C)
1985—Redskins, 14-7 (C)
1988—Browns, 17-13 (W)
1991—Redskins, 42-17 (W)
(RS Pts.—Browns 1,073, Redskins 667)

DALLAS vs. ARIZONA
RS: Cowboys lead series, 40-22-1;
See Arizona vs. Dallas
DALLAS vs. ATLANTA
RS: Cowboys lead series, 9-6
PS: Cowboys lead series, 2-0;
See Atlanta vs. Dallas
DALLAS vs. BUFFALO
RS: Cowboys lead series, 3-2
PS: Cowboys lead series, 2-0;
See Buffalo vs. Dallas
DALLAS vs. CHICAGO
RS: Cowboys lead series, 8-6
PS: Cowboys lead series, 2-0;
See Chicago vs. Dallas
DALLAS vs. CINCINNATI
RS: Cowboys lead series, 3-2;
See Cincinnati vs. Dallas
DALLAS vs. CLEVELAND
RS: Browns lead series, 14-9
PS: Browns lead series, 2-1;
See Cleveland vs. Dallas
DALLAS vs. DENVER
RS: Cowboys lead series, 3-2
PS: Cowboys lead series, 1-0
1973—Cowboys, 22-10 (Den)
1977—Cowboys, 14-6 (Dal)
*Cowboys, 27-10 (New Orleans)
1980—Broncos, 41-20 (Den)
1986—Broncos, 29-14 (Den)
1992—Cowboys, 31-27 (Den)
(RS Pts.—Broncos 113, Cowboys 101)
(PS Pts.—Cowboys 27, Broncos 10)
*Super Bowl XII
DALLAS vs. DETROIT
RS: Cowboys lead series, 7-5

PS: Series tied, 1-1
1960—Lions, 23-14 (Det)
1963—Cowboys, 17-14 (Dal)
1968—Cowboys, 59-13 (Dal)
1970—*Cowboys, 5-0 (Dal)
1972—Cowboys, 28-24 (Dal)
1975—Cowboys, 36-10 (Dal)
1977—Cowboys, 37-0 (Dal)
1981—Lions, 27-24 (Det)
1985—Lions, 26-21 (Det)
1986—Cowboys, 31-7 (Det)
1987—Lions, 27-17 (Det)
1991—Lions, 34-10 (Det)
*Lions, 38-6 (Det)
1992—Cowboys, 37-3 (Det)
(RS Pts.—Cowboys 331, Lions 208)
(PS Pts.—Lions 38, Cowboys 11)
*NFC Divisional Playoff
DALLAS vs. GREEN BAY
RS: Packers lead series, 8-6
PS: Series tied, 2-2
1960—Packers, 41-7 (GB)
1964—Packers, 45-21 (D)
1965—Packers, 13-3 (Mil)
1966—*Packers, 34-27 (D)
1967—*Packers, 21-17 (GB)
1968—Packers, 28-17 (D)
1970—Cowboys, 16-3 (D)
1972—Packers, 16-13 (Mil)
1975—Packers, 19-17 (D)
1978—Cowboys, 42-14 (Mil)
1980—Cowboys, 28-7 (Mil)
1982—**Cowboys, 37-26 (D)
1984—Cowboys, 20-6 (D)
1989—Packers, 31-13 (GB)
Packers, 20-10 (D)
1991—Cowboys, 20-17 (Mil)
1993—Cowboys, 36-14 (D)
***Cowboys, 27-17 (D)
(RS Pts.—Packers 274, Cowboys 263)
(PS Pts.—Cowboys 108, Packers 98)
*NFL Championship
**NFC Second-Round Playoff
***NFC Divisional Playoff
DALLAS vs. HOUSTON
RS: Cowboys lead series, 4-3
1970—Cowboys, 52-10 (D)
1974—Cowboys, 10-0 (H)
1979—Oilers, 30-24 (D)
1982—Cowboys, 37-7 (H)
1985—Cowboys, 17-10 (H)
1988—Oilers, 25-17 (D)
1991—Oilers, 26-23 (H) OT
(RS Pts.—Cowboys 180, Oilers 108)
DALLAS vs. *INDIANAPOLIS
RS: Cowboys lead series, 7-2
PS: Colts lead series, 1-0
1960—Colts, 45-7 (D)
1967—Colts, 23-17 (B)
1969—Cowboys, 27-10 (D)
1970—**Colts, 16-13 (Miami)
1972—Cowboys, 21-0 (D)
1976—Cowboys, 30-27 (D)
1978—Cowboys, 38-0 (D)
1981—Cowboys, 37-13 (B)
1984—Cowboys, 22-3 (D)
1993—Cowboys, 27-3 (I)
(RS Pts.—Cowboys 226, Colts 124)
(PS Pts.—Colts 16, Cowboys 13)
*Franchise in Baltimore prior to 1984
**Super Bowl V
DALLAS vs. KANSAS CITY
RS: Cowboys lead series, 3-2
1970—Cowboys, 27-16 (KC)
1975—Chiefs, 34-31 (D)
1983—Cowboys, 41-21 (D)
1989—Chiefs, 36-28 (KC)
1992—Cowboys, 17-10 (D)
(RS Pts.—Cowboys 144, Chiefs 117)
DALLAS vs. *L.A. RAIDERS
RS: Raiders lead series, 3-2
1974—Raiders, 27-23 (O)
1980—Cowboys, 19-13 (O)

1983—Raiders, 40-38 (D)
1986—Raiders, 17-13 (D)
1992—Cowboys, 28-13 (LA)
(RS Pts.—Cowboys 121, Raiders 110)
*Franchise in Oakland prior to 1982

DALLAS vs. L.A. RAMS
RS: Rams lead series, 9-8
PS: Series tied, 4-4
1960—Rams, 38-13 (D)
1962—Cowboys, 27-17 (LA)
1967—Rams, 35-13 (D)
1969—Rams, 24-23 (LA)
1971—Cowboys, 28-21 (D)
1973—Rams, 37-31 (LA)
　　　*Cowboys, 27-16 (D)
1975—Cowboys, 18-7 (D)
　　　**Cowboys, 37-7 (LA)
1976—*Rams, 14-12 (D)
1978—Rams, 27-14 (LA)
　　　**Cowboys, 28-0 (LA)
1979—Cowboys, 30-6 (D)
　　　*Rams, 21-19 (D)
1980—Rams, 38-14 (LA)
　　　***Cowboys, 34-13 (D)
1981—Cowboys, 29-17 (D)
1983—***Rams, 24-17 (D)
1984—Cowboys, 20-13 (LA)
1985—*Rams, 20-0 (LA)
1986—Rams, 29-10 (LA)
1987—Cowboys, 29-21 (LA)
1989—Rams, 35-31 (D)
1990—Cowboys, 24-21 (LA)
1992—Rams, 27-23 (D)
(RS Pts.—Rams 413, Cowboys 377)
(PS Pts.—Cowboys 174, Rams 115)
*NFC Divisional Playoff
**NFC Championship
***NFC First-Round Playoff

DALLAS vs. MIAMI
RS: Dolphins lead series, 6-1
PS: Cowboys lead series, 1-0
1971—*Cowboys, 24-3 (New Orleans)
1973—Dolphins, 14-7 (D)
1978—Dolphins, 23-16 (M)
1981—Cowboys, 28-27 (D)
1984—Dolphins, 28-21 (M)
1987—Dolphins, 20-14 (D)
1989—Dolphins, 17-14 (D)
1993—Dolphins, 16-14 (D)
(RS Pts.—Dolphins 145, Cowboys 114)
(PS Pts.—Cowboys 24, Dolphins 3)
*Super Bowl VI

DALLAS vs. MINNESOTA
RS: Cowboys lead series, 8-6
PS: Cowboys lead series, 3-1
1961—Cowboys, 21-7 (D)
　　　Cowboys, 28-0 (M)
1966—Cowboys, 28-17 (D)
1968—Cowboys, 20-7 (M)
1970—Vikings, 54-13 (M)
1971—*Cowboys, 20-12 (M)
1973—**Vikings, 27-10 (D)
1974—Vikings, 23-21 (D)
1975—*Cowboys, 17-14 (M)
1977—Cowboys, 16-10 (M) OT
　　　**Cowboys, 23-6 (D)
1978—Vikings, 21-10 (D)
1979—Cowboys, 36-20 (M)
1982—Vikings, 31-27 (M)
1983—Cowboys, 37-24 (M)
1987—Vikings, 44-38 (D) OT
1988—Vikings, 43-3 (D)
1993—Cowboys, 37-20 (M)
(RS Pts.—Cowboys 335, Vikings 321)
(PS Pts.—Cowboys 70, Vikings 59)
*NFC Divisional Playoff
**NFC Championship

DALLAS vs. NEW ENGLAND
RS: Cowboys lead series, 6-0
1971—Cowboys, 44-21 (D)
1975—Cowboys, 34-31 (NE)
1978—Cowboys, 17-10 (D)
1981—Cowboys, 35-21 (NE)

1984—Cowboys, 20-17 (D)
1987—Cowboys, 23-17 (NE) OT
(RS Pts.—Cowboys 173, Patriots 117)

DALLAS vs. NEW ORLEANS
RS: Cowboys lead series, 13-3
1967—Cowboys, 14-10 (D)
　　　Cowboys, 27-10 (NO)
1968—Cowboys, 17-3 (NO)
1969—Cowboys, 21-17 (NO)
　　　Cowboys, 33-17 (D)
1971—Saints, 24-14 (NO)
1973—Cowboys, 40-3 (NO)
1976—Cowboys, 24-6 (NO)
1978—Cowboys, 27-7 (D)
1982—Cowboys, 21-7 (D)
1983—Cowboys, 21-20 (D)
1984—Cowboys, 30-27 (D) OT
1988—Saints, 20-17 (NO)
1989—Saints, 28-0 (NO)
1990—Cowboys, 17-13 (D)
1991—Cowboys, 23-14 (D)
(RS Pts.—Cowboys 346, Saints 226)

DALLAS vs. N.Y. GIANTS
RS: Cowboys lead series, 40-21-2
1960—Tie, 31-31 (NY)
1961—Giants, 31-10 (D)
　　　Cowboys, 17-16 (NY)
1962—Giants, 41-10 (D)
　　　Giants, 41-31 (NY)
1963—Giants, 37-21 (NY)
　　　Giants, 34-27 (D)
1964—Tie, 13-13 (D)
　　　Cowboys, 31-21 (NY)
1965—Cowboys, 31-2 (D)
　　　Cowboys, 38-20 (NY)
1966—Cowboys, 52-7 (D)
　　　Cowboys, 17-7 (NY)
1967—Cowboys, 38-24 (D)
1968—Giants, 27-21 (D)
　　　Cowboys, 28-10 (NY)
1969—Cowboys, 25-3 (D)
1970—Cowboys, 28-10 (D)
　　　Giants, 23-20 (NY)
1971—Cowboys, 20-13 (D)
　　　Cowboys, 42-14 (NY)
1972—Cowboys, 23-14 (NY)
　　　Giants, 23-3 (D)
1973—Cowboys, 45-28 (D)
　　　Cowboys, 23-10 (New Haven)
1974—Giants, 14-6 (D)
　　　Cowboys, 21-7 (New Haven)
1975—Cowboys, 13-7 (NY)
　　　Cowboys, 14-3 (D)
1976—Cowboys, 24-14 (NY)
　　　Cowboys, 9-3 (D)
1977—Cowboys, 41-21 (D)
　　　Cowboys, 24-10 (NY)
1978—Cowboys, 34-24 (NY)
　　　Cowboys, 24-3 (D)
1979—Cowboys, 16-14 (NY)
　　　Cowboys, 28-7 (D)
1980—Cowboys, 24-3 (D)
　　　Giants, 38-35 (NY)
1981—Cowboys, 18-10 (D)
　　　Giants, 13-10 (NY) OT
1983—Cowboys, 28-13 (D)
　　　Cowboys, 38-20 (NY)
1984—Giants, 28-7 (NY)
　　　Giants, 19-7 (D)
1985—Cowboys, 30-29 (NY)
　　　Cowboys, 28-21 (D)
1986—Cowboys, 31-28 (D)
　　　Giants, 17-14 (NY)
1987—Cowboys, 16-14 (NY)
　　　Cowboys, 33-24 (D)
1988—Giants, 12-10 (D)
　　　Giants, 29-21 (NY)
1989—Giants, 30-13 (D)
　　　Giants, 15-0 (NY)
1990—Giants, 28-7 (D)
　　　Giants, 31-17 (NY)
1991—Cowboys, 21-16 (D)
　　　Giants, 22-9 (NY)

1992—Cowboys, 34-28 (NY)
　　　Cowboys, 30-3 (D)
1993—Cowboys, 31-9 (D)
　　　Cowboys, 16-13 (NY) OT
(RS Pts.—Cowboys 1,427, Giants 1,140)

DALLAS vs. N.Y. JETS
RS: Cowboys lead series, 5-1
1971—Cowboys, 52-10 (D)
1975—Cowboys, 31-21 (NY)
1978—Cowboys, 30-7 (NY)
1987—Cowboys, 38-24 (NY)
1990—Jets, 24-9 (NY)
1993—Cowboys, 28-7 (NY)
(RS Pts.—Cowboys 188, Jets 93)

DALLAS vs. PHILADELPHIA
RS: Cowboys lead series, 40-26
PS: Series tied, 1-1
1960—Eagles, 27-25 (D)
1961—Eagles, 43-7 (D)
　　　Eagles, 35-13 (P)
1962—Cowboys, 41-19 (D)
　　　Eagles, 28-14 (P)
1963—Eagles, 24-21 (P)
　　　Cowboys, 27-20 (D)
1964—Eagles, 17-14 (D)
　　　Eagles, 24-14 (P)
1965—Eagles, 35-24 (D)
　　　Cowboys, 21-19 (P)
1966—Cowboys, 56-7 (D)
　　　Eagles, 24-23 (P)
1967—Eagles, 21-14 (P)
　　　Cowboys, 38-17 (D)
1968—Cowboys, 45-13 (D)
　　　Cowboys, 34-14 (P)
1969—Cowboys, 38-7 (P)
　　　Cowboys, 49-14 (D)
1970—Cowboys, 17-7 (D)
　　　Cowboys, 21-17 (D)
1971—Cowboys, 42-7 (P)
　　　Cowboys, 20-7 (D)
1972—Cowboys, 28-6 (D)
　　　Cowboys, 28-7 (P)
1973—Eagles, 30-16 (P)
　　　Cowboys, 31-10 (D)
1974—Eagles, 13-10 (P)
　　　Cowboys, 31-24 (D)
1975—Cowboys, 20-17 (P)
　　　Cowboys, 27-17 (D)
1976—Cowboys, 27-7 (D)
　　　Cowboys, 26-7 (P)
1977—Cowboys, 16-10 (P)
　　　Cowboys, 24-14 (D)
1978—Cowboys, 14-7 (D)
　　　Cowboys, 31-13 (P)
1979—Eagles, 31-21 (D)
　　　Cowboys, 24-17 (P)
1980—Eagles, 17-10 (P)
　　　Cowboys, 35-27 (D)
　　　*Eagles, 20-7 (P)
1981—Cowboys, 17-14 (P)
　　　Cowboys, 21-10 (D)
1982—Eagles, 24-20 (D)
1983—Cowboys, 37-7 (D)
　　　Cowboys, 27-20 (P)
1984—Cowboys, 23-17 (D)
　　　Cowboys, 26-10 (P)
1985—Eagles, 16-14 (P)
　　　Cowboys, 34-17 (D)
1986—Cowboys, 17-14 (P)
　　　Eagles, 23-21 (D)
1987—Cowboys, 41-22 (D)
　　　Eagles, 37-20 (P)
1988—Eagles, 24-23 (P)
　　　Eagles, 23-7 (D)
1989—Eagles, 27-0 (D)
　　　Eagles, 20-10 (P)
1990—Eagles, 21-20 (D)
　　　Eagles, 17-3 (P)
1991—Eagles, 24-0 (D)
　　　Cowboys, 25-13 (P)
1992—Eagles, 31-7 (P)
　　　Cowboys, 20-10 (D)
　　　**Cowboys, 34-10 (D)

1993—Cowboys, 23-10 (P)
　　　Cowboys, 23-17 (D)
(RS Pts.—Cowboys 1,516, Eagles 1,188)
(PS Pts.—Cowboys 41, Eagles 30)
*NFC Championship
**NFC Divisional Playoff

DALLAS vs. PITTSBURGH
RS: Cowboys lead series, 12-11
PS: Steelers lead series, 2-0
1960—Steelers, 35-28 (D)
1961—Cowboys, 27-24 (D)
　　　Steelers, 37-7 (P)
1962—Steelers, 30-28 (D)
　　　Cowboys, 42-27 (P)
1963—Steelers, 27-21 (P)
　　　Steelers, 24-19 (D)
1964—Steelers, 23-17 (P)
　　　Cowboys, 17-14 (D)
1965—Steelers, 22-13 (P)
　　　Cowboys, 24-17 (D)
1966—Cowboys, 52-21 (D)
　　　Cowboys, 20-7 (P)
1967—Cowboys, 24-21 (P)
1968—Cowboys, 28-7 (D)
1969—Cowboys, 10-7 (P)
1972—Cowboys, 17-13 (D)
1975—*Steelers, 21-17 (Miami)
1977—Steelers, 28-13 (P)
1978—**Steelers, 35-31 (Miami)
1979—Steelers, 14-3 (P)
1982—Steelers, 36-28 (D)
1985—Cowboys, 27-13 (D)
1988—Steelers, 24-21 (P)
1991—Cowboys, 20-10 (D)
(RS Pts.—Cowboys 506, Steelers 481)
(PS Pts.—Steelers 56, Cowboys 48)
*Super Bowl X
**Super Bowl XIII

DALLAS vs. SAN DIEGO
RS: Cowboys lead series, 4-1
1972—Cowboys, 34-28 (SD)
1980—Cowboys, 42-31 (D)
1983—Chargers, 24-23 (SD)
1986—Cowboys, 24-21 (SD)
1990—Cowboys, 17-14 (D)
(RS Pts.—Cowboys 140, Chargers 118)

DALLAS vs. SAN FRANCISCO
RS: 49ers lead series, 9-6-1
PS: Cowboys lead series, 5-1
1960—49ers, 26-14 (D)
1963—49ers, 31-24 (SF)
1965—Cowboys, 39-31 (D)
1967—49ers, 24-16 (SF)
1969—Tie, 24-24 (D)
1970—*Cowboys, 17-10 (SF)
1971—*Cowboys, 14-3 (D)
1972—49ers, 31-10 (D)
　　　**Cowboys, 30-28 (SF)
1974—Cowboys, 20-14 (D)
1977—Cowboys, 42-35 (SF)
1979—Cowboys, 21-13 (SF)
1980—Cowboys, 59-14 (D)
1981—49ers, 45-14 (SF)
　　　*49ers, 28-27 (SF)
1983—49ers, 42-17 (SF)
1985—49ers, 31-16 (SF)
1989—49ers, 31-14 (D)
1990—49ers, 24-6 (D)
1992—**Cowboys, 30-20 (SF)
1993—Cowboys, 26-17 (D)
　　　*Cowboys, 38-21 (D)
(RS Pts.—49ers 433, Cowboys 362)
(PS Pts.—Cowboys 156, 49ers 110)
*NFC Championship
**NFC Divisional Playoff

DALLAS vs. SEATTLE
RS: Cowboys lead series, 4-1
1976—Cowboys, 28-13 (S)
1980—Cowboys, 51-7 (S)
1983—Cowboys, 35-10 (S)
1986—Seahawks, 31-14 (D)
1992—Cowboys, 27-0 (D)
(RS Pts.—Cowboys 155, Seahawks 61)

DALLAS vs. TAMPA BAY
RS: Cowboys lead series, 6-0
PS: Cowboys lead series, 2-0
1977—Cowboys, 23-7 (D)
1980—Cowboys, 28-17 (D)
1981—*Cowboys, 38-0 (D)
1982—Cowboys, 14-9 (D)
　　　**Cowboys, 30-17 (D)
1983—Cowboys, 27-24 (D) OT
1990—Cowboys, 14-10 (D)
　　　Cowboys, 17-13 (TB)
(RS Pts.—Cowboys 123, Buccaneers 80)
(PS Pts.—Cowboys 68, Buccaneers 17)
*NFC Divisional Playoff
**NFC First-Round Playoff

DALLAS vs. WASHINGTON
RS: Cowboys lead series, 37-27-2
PS: Redskins lead series, 2-0
1960—Redskins, 26-14 (W)
1961—Tie, 28-28 (D)
　　　Redskins, 34-24 (W)
1962—Tie, 35-35 (D)
　　　Cowboys, 38-10 (W)
1963—Redskins, 21-17 (W)
　　　Cowboys, 35-20 (D)
1964—Cowboys, 24-18 (D)
　　　Redskins, 28-16 (W)
1965—Cowboys, 27-7 (D)
　　　Redskins, 34-31 (W)
1966—Cowboys, 31-30 (W)
　　　Redskins, 34-31 (D)
1967—Cowboys, 17-14 (W)
　　　Redskins, 27-20 (D)
1968—Cowboys, 44-24 (W)
　　　Cowboys, 29-20 (D)
1969—Cowboys, 41-28 (W)
　　　Cowboys, 20-10 (D)
1970—Cowboys, 45-21 (W)
　　　Cowboys, 34-0 (D)
1971—Redskins, 20-16 (D)
　　　Cowboys, 13-0 (W)
1972—Redskins, 24-20 (W)
　　　Cowboys, 34-24 (D)
　　　*Redskins, 26-3 (W)
1973—Redskins, 14-7 (W)
　　　Cowboys, 27-7 (D)
1974—Redskins, 28-21 (W)
　　　Cowboys, 24-23 (D)
1975—Redskins, 30-24 (W) OT
　　　Cowboys, 31-10 (D)
1976—Cowboys, 20-7 (W)
　　　Redskins, 27-14 (D)
1977—Cowboys, 34-16 (D)
　　　Cowboys, 14-7 (W)
1978—Redskins, 9-5 (W)
　　　Cowboys, 37-10 (D)
1979—Redskins, 34-20 (W)
　　　Cowboys, 35-34 (D)
1980—Cowboys, 17-3 (W)
　　　Cowboys, 14-10 (D)
1981—Cowboys, 26-10 (W)
　　　Cowboys, 24-10 (D)
1982—Cowboys, 24-10 (W)
　　　*Redskins, 31-17 (W)
1983—Cowboys, 31-30 (W)
　　　Redskins, 31-10 (D)
1984—Redskins, 34-14 (W)
　　　Redskins, 30-28 (D)
1985—Cowboys, 44-14 (W)
　　　Cowboys, 13-7 (W)
1986—Cowboys, 30-6 (D)
　　　Redskins, 41-14 (W)
1987—Redskins, 13-7 (D)
　　　Redskins, 24-20 (W)
1988—Redskins, 35-17 (D)
　　　Cowboys, 24-17 (W)
1989—Redskins, 30-7 (D)
　　　Cowboys, 13-3 (W)
1990—Redskins, 19-15 (W)
　　　Cowboys, 27-17 (D)
1991—Redskins, 33-31 (D)
　　　Cowboys, 24-21 (W)
1992—Cowboys, 23-10 (D)

Redskins, 20-17 (W)
1993—Redskins, 35-16 (W)
　　　Cowboys, 38-3 (D)
(RS Pts.—Cowboys, 1,565, Redskins 1,309)
(PS Pts.—Redskins 57, Cowboys 20)
*NFC Championship

DENVER vs. ARIZONA
RS: Broncos lead series, 3-0-1;
See Arizona vs. Denver

DENVER vs. ATLANTA
RS: Broncos lead series, 4-3;
See Atlanta vs. Denver

DENVER vs. BUFFALO
RS: Bills lead series, 16-10-1
PS: Bills lead series, 1-0;
See Buffalo vs. Denver

DENVER vs. CHICAGO
RS: Series tied, 5-5;
See Chicago vs. Denver

DENVER vs. CINCINNATI
RS: Broncos lead series, 10-6;
See Cincinnati vs. Denver

DENVER vs. CLEVELAND
RS: Broncos lead series, 12-5
PS: Broncos lead series, 3-0;
See Cleveland vs. Denver

DENVER vs. DALLAS
RS: Cowboys lead series, 3-2
PS: Cowboys lead series, 1-0;
See Dallas vs. Denver

DENVER vs. DETROIT
RS: Broncos lead series, 4-3
1971—Lions, 24-20 (Den)
1974—Broncos, 31-27 (Det)
1978—Lions, 17-14 (Det)
1981—Broncos, 27-21 (Den)
1984—Broncos, 28-7 (Det)
1987—Broncos, 34-0 (Den)
1990—Lions, 40-27 (Det)
(RS Pts.—Broncos 181, Lions 136)

DENVER vs. GREEN BAY
RS: Broncos lead series, 4-2-1
1971—Packers, 34-13 (Mil)
1975—Broncos, 23-13 (D)
1978—Broncos, 16-3 (D)
1984—Broncos, 17-14 (D)
1987—Tie, 17-17 (Mil) OT
1990—Broncos, 22-13 (D)
1993—Packers, 30-27 (GB)
(RS Pts.—Broncos 135, Packers 124)

DENVER vs. HOUSTON
RS: Oilers lead series, 19-11-1
PS: Broncos lead series, 2-1
1960—Oilers, 45-25 (D)
　　　Oilers, 20-10 (H)
1961—Oilers, 55-14 (D)
　　　Oilers, 45-14 (H)
1962—Broncos, 20-10 (D)
　　　Oilers, 34-17 (H)
1963—Oilers, 20-14 (H)
　　　Oilers, 33-24 (D)
1964—Oilers, 38-17 (D)
　　　Oilers, 34-15 (H)
1965—Broncos, 28-17 (D)
　　　Broncos, 31-21 (H)
1966—Oilers, 45-7 (H)
　　　Broncos, 40-38 (D)
1967—Oilers, 10-6 (H)
　　　Oilers, 20-18 (D)
1968—Oilers, 38-17 (H)
1969—Oilers, 24-21 (H)
　　　Tie, 20-20 (D)
1970—Oilers, 31-21 (H)
1972—Broncos, 30-17 (D)
1973—Broncos, 48-20 (H)
1974—Broncos, 37-14 (D)
1976—Oilers, 17-3 (H)
1977—Broncos, 24-14 (H)
1979—*Oilers, 13-7 (H)
1980—Oilers, 20-16 (D)
1983—Broncos, 26-14 (H)
1985—Broncos, 31-20 (D)

1987—Oilers, 40-10 (D)
　　　**Oilers, 34-10 (D)
1991—Oilers, 42-14 (H)
　　　**Broncos, 26-24 (D)
1992—Broncos, 27-21 (D)
(RS Pts.—Oilers 837, Broncos 645)
(PS Pts.—Broncos 67, Oilers 47)
*AFC First-Round Playoff
**AFC Divisional Playoff

DENVER vs. *INDIANAPOLIS
RS: Broncos lead series, 9-2
1974—Broncos, 17-6 (B)
1977—Broncos, 27-13 (D)
1978—Colts, 7-6 (B)
1981—Broncos, 28-10 (D)
1983—Broncos, 17-10 (B)
　　　Broncos, 21-19 (D)
1985—Broncos, 15-10 (I)
1988—Colts, 55-23 (I)
1989—Broncos, 14-3 (D)
1990—Broncos, 27-17 (I)
1993—Broncos, 35-13 (D)
(RS Pts.—Broncos 230, Colts 163)
*Franchise in Baltimore prior to 1984

DENVER vs. *KANSAS CITY
RS: Chiefs lead series, 38-29
1960—Texans, 17-14 (D)
　　　Texans, 34-7 (Dal)
1961—Texans, 19-12 (D)
　　　Texans, 49-21 (Dal)
1962—Texans, 24-3 (D)
　　　Texans, 17-10 (Dal)
1963—Chiefs, 59-7 (D)
　　　Chiefs, 52-21 (KC)
1964—Broncos, 33-27 (D)
　　　Chiefs, 49-39 (KC)
1965—Chiefs, 31-23 (D)
　　　Chiefs, 45-35 (KC)
1966—Chiefs, 37-10 (KC)
　　　Chiefs, 56-10 (D)
1967—Chiefs, 52-9 (KC)
　　　Chiefs, 38-24 (D)
1968—Chiefs, 34-2 (KC)
　　　Chiefs, 30-7 (D)
1969—Chiefs, 26-13 (D)
　　　Chiefs, 31-17 (KC)
1970—Broncos, 26-13 (D)
　　　Chiefs, 16-0 (KC)
1971—Chiefs, 16-3 (D)
　　　Chiefs, 28-10 (KC)
1972—Chiefs, 45-24 (D)
　　　Chiefs, 24-21 (KC)
1973—Chiefs, 16-14 (KC)
　　　Broncos, 14-10 (D)
1974—Broncos, 17-14 (KC)
　　　Chiefs, 42-34 (D)
1975—Broncos, 37-33 (D)
　　　Chiefs, 26-13 (KC)
1976—Broncos, 35-26 (KC)
　　　Broncos, 17-16 (D)
1977—Broncos, 23-7 (D)
　　　Broncos, 14-7 (KC)
1978—Broncos, 23-17 (KC) OT
　　　Broncos, 24-3 (D)
1979—Broncos, 24-10 (KC)
　　　Broncos, 20-3 (D)
1980—Chiefs, 23-17 (D)
　　　Chiefs, 31-14 (KC)
1981—Chiefs, 28-14 (KC)
　　　Broncos, 16-13 (D)
1982—Chiefs, 37-16 (D)
1983—Broncos, 27-24 (D)
　　　Chiefs, 48-17 (KC)
1984—Broncos, 21-0 (D)
　　　Chiefs, 16-13 (KC)
1985—Broncos, 30-10 (KC)
　　　Broncos, 14-13 (D)
1986—Broncos, 38-17 (D)
　　　Chiefs, 37-10 (KC)
1987—Broncos, 26-17 (KC)
　　　Broncos, 20-17 (D)
1988—Chiefs, 20-13 (KC)
　　　Broncos, 17-11 (D)

1989—Broncos, 34-20 (D)
　　　Broncos, 16-13 (KC)
1990—Broncos, 24-23 (D)
　　　Chiefs, 31-20 (KC)
1991—Broncos, 19-16 (D)
　　　Broncos, 24-20 (KC)
1992—Broncos, 20-19 (D)
　　　Chiefs, 42-20 (KC)
1993—Chiefs, 15-7 (KC)
　　　Broncos, 27-21 (D)
(RS Pts.—Chiefs 1,681, Broncos 1,244)
*Franchise in Dallas prior to 1963 and
known as Texans

DENVER vs. *L.A. RAIDERS
RS: Raiders lead series, 46-19-2
PS: Series tied, 1-1
1960—Broncos, 31-14 (D)
　　　Raiders, 48-10 (O)
1961—Raiders, 33-19 (O)
　　　Broncos, 27-24 (D)
1962—Broncos, 44-7 (D)
　　　Broncos, 23-6 (O)
1963—Raiders, 26-10 (D)
　　　Raiders, 35-31 (O)
1964—Raiders, 40-7 (O)
　　　Tie, 20-20 (D)
1965—Raiders, 28-20 (D)
　　　Raiders, 24-13 (O)
1966—Raiders, 17-3 (D)
　　　Raiders, 28-10 (O)
1967—Raiders, 51-0 (O)
　　　Raiders, 21-17 (D)
1968—Raiders, 43-7 (D)
　　　Raiders, 33-27 (O)
1969—Raiders, 24-14 (D)
　　　Raiders, 41-10 (O)
1970—Raiders, 35-23 (O)
　　　Raiders, 24-19 (D)
1971—Raiders, 27-16 (D)
　　　Raiders, 21-13 (O)
1972—Broncos, 30-23 (O)
　　　Raiders, 37-20 (D)
1973—Tie, 23-23 (D)
　　　Raiders, 21-17 (O)
1974—Raiders, 28-17 (D)
　　　Broncos, 20-17 (O)
1975—Raiders, 42-17 (D)
　　　Raiders, 17-10 (O)
1976—Raiders, 17-10 (D)
　　　Raiders, 19-6 (O)
1977—Broncos, 30-7 (O)
　　　Raiders, 24-14 (D)
　　　**Broncos, 20-17 (D)
1978—Broncos, 14-6 (D)
　　　Raiders, 21-6 (O)
1979—Raiders, 27-3 (O)
　　　Raiders, 14-10 (D)
1980—Raiders, 9-3 (O)
　　　Raiders, 24-21 (D)
1981—Broncos, 9-7 (D)
　　　Broncos, 17-0 (O)
1982—Raiders, 27-10 (LA)
1983—Raiders, 22-7 (D)
　　　Raiders, 22-20 (LA)
1984—Broncos, 16-13 (D)
　　　Broncos, 22-19 (LA) OT
1985—Raiders, 31-28 (LA) OT
　　　Raiders, 17-14 (D) OT
1986—Broncos, 38-36 (D)
　　　Broncos, 21-10 (LA)
1987—Broncos, 30-14 (D)
　　　Broncos, 23-17 (LA)
1988—Raiders, 30-27 (D) OT
　　　Raiders, 21-20 (LA)
1989—Broncos, 31-21 (D)
　　　Raiders, 16-13 (LA) OT
1990—Raiders, 14-9 (LA)
　　　Broncos, 23-20 (D)
1991—Raiders, 16-13 (LA)
　　　Raiders, 17-16 (D)
1992—Broncos, 17-13 (D)
　　　Raiders, 24-0 (LA)
1993—Raiders, 23-20 (D)

Raiders, 33-30 (LA) OT
***Raiders, 42-24 (LA)
(RS Pts.—Raiders 1,517, Broncos 1,171)
(PS Pts.—Raiders 59, Broncos 44)
*Franchise in Oakland prior to 1982
**AFC Championship
***AFC First-Round Playoff

DENVER vs. L.A. RAMS
RS: Series tied, 3-3
1972—Broncos, 16-10 (LA)
1974—Rams, 17-10 (D)
1979—Rams, 13-9 (D)
1982—Broncos, 27-24 (LA)
1985—Rams, 20-16 (LA)
1988—Broncos, 35-24 (D)
(RS Pts.—Broncos 113, Rams 108)

DENVER vs. MIAMI
RS: Dolphins lead series, 5-2-1
1966—Dolphins, 24-7 (M)
Broncos, 17-7 (D)
1967—Dolphins, 35-21 (M)
1968—Broncos, 21-14 (D)
1969—Dolphins, 27-24 (M)
1971—Tie, 10-10 (D)
1975—Dolphins, 14-13 (M)
1985—Dolphins, 30-26 (D)
(RS Pts.—Dolphins 161, Broncos 139)

DENVER vs. MINNESOTA
RS: Vikings lead series, 5-3
1972—Vikings, 23-20 (D)
1978—Vikings, 12-9 (M) OT
1981—Broncos, 19-17 (D)
1984—Broncos, 42-21 (D)
1987—Vikings, 34-27 (M)
1990—Vikings, 27-22 (M)
1991—Broncos, 13-6 (M)
1993—Vikings, 26-23 (D)
(RS Pts.—Broncos 175, Vikings 166)

DENVER vs. *NEW ENGLAND
RS: Broncos lead series, 16-12
PS: Broncos lead series, 1-0
1960—Broncos, 13-10 (B)
Broncos, 31-24 (D)
1961—Patriots, 45-17 (B)
Patriots, 28-24 (D)
1962—Patriots, 41-16 (B)
Patriots, 33-29 (D)
1963—Broncos, 14-10 (B)
Patriots, 40-21 (B)
1964—Patriots, 39-10 (D)
Patriots, 12-7 (B)
1965—Broncos, 27-10 (B)
Patriots, 28-20 (D)
1966—Patriots, 24-10 (D)
Broncos, 17-10 (B)
1967—Broncos, 26-21 (D)
1968—Patriots, 20-17 (D)
Broncos, 35-14 (B)
1969—Broncos, 35-7 (D)
1972—Broncos, 45-21 (D)
1976—Patriots, 38-14 (NE)
1979—Broncos, 45-10 (D)
1980—Patriots, 23-14 (NE)
1984—Broncos, 26-19 (D)
1986—Broncos, 27-20 (D)
**Broncos, 22-17 (D)
1987—Broncos, 31-20 (D)
1988—Broncos, 21-10 (D)
1991—Broncos, 9-6 (NE)
Broncos, 20-3 (D)
(RS Pts.—Broncos 621, Patriots 586)
(PS Pts.—Broncos 22, Patriots 17)
*Franchise in Boston prior to 1971
**AFC Divisional Playoff

DENVER vs. NEW ORLEANS
RS: Broncos lead series, 4-1
1970—Broncos, 31-6 (NO)
1974—Broncos, 33-17 (D)
1979—Broncos, 10-3 (D)
1985—Broncos, 34-23 (D)
1988—Saints, 42-0 (NO)
(RS Pts.—Broncos 108, Saints 91)

DENVER vs. N.Y. GIANTS

RS: Series tied, 3-3
PS: Giants lead series, 1-0
1972—Giants, 29-17 (NY)
1976—Broncos, 14-13 (D)
1980—Broncos, 14-9 (D)
1986—Giants, 19-16 (NY)
*Giants, 39-20 (Pasadena)
1989—Giants, 14-7 (D)
1992—Broncos, 27-13 (D)
(RS Pts.—Giants 97, Broncos 95)
(PS Pts.—Giants 39, Broncos 20)
*Super Bowl XXI

DENVER vs. *N.Y. JETS
RS: Broncos lead series, 12-11-1
1960—Titans, 28-24 (NY)
Titans, 30-27 (D)
1961—Titans, 35-28 (NY)
Broncos, 27-10 (D)
1962—Broncos, 32-10 (NY)
Titans, 46-45 (D)
1963—Tie, 35-35 (NY)
Jets, 14-9 (D)
1964—Jets, 30-6 (NY)
Broncos, 20-16 (D)
1965—Broncos, 16-13 (D)
Jets, 45-10 (NY)
1966—Jets, 16-7 (D)
1967—Jets, 38-24 (D)
Broncos, 33-24 (NY)
1968—Broncos, 21-13 (NY)
1969—Broncos, 21-19 (D)
1973—Broncos, 40-28 (NY)
1976—Broncos, 46-3 (D)
1978—Jets, 31-28 (D)
1980—Broncos, 31-24 (D)
1986—Jets, 22-10 (NY)
1992—Broncos, 27-16 (D)
1993—Broncos, 26-20 (NY)
(RS Pts.—Broncos 593, Jets 566)
*Jets known as Titans prior to 1963

DENVER vs. PHILADELPHIA
RS: Eagles lead series, 5-2
1971—Eagles, 17-16 (P)
1975—Broncos, 25-10 (D)
1980—Eagles, 27-6 (P)
1983—Eagles, 13-10 (D)
1986—Broncos, 33-7 (P)
1989—Eagles, 28-24 (D)
1992—Eagles, 30-0 (P)
(RS Pts.—Eagles 132, Broncos 114)

DENVER vs. PITTSBURGH
RS: Broncos lead series, 10-5-1
PS: Series tied, 2-2
1970—Broncos, 16-13 (D)
1971—Broncos, 22-10 (P)
1973—Broncos, 23-13 (P)
1974—Tie, 35-35 (D) OT
1975—Steelers, 20-9 (P)
1977—Broncos, 21-7 (D)
*Broncos, 34-21 (D)
1978—Steelers, 21-17 (D)
*Steelers, 33-10 (P)
1979—Steelers, 42-7 (P)
1983—Broncos, 14-10 (D)
1984—*Steelers, 24-17 (D)
1985—Broncos, 31-23 (P)
1986—Broncos, 21-10 (P)
1988—Steelers, 39-21 (P)
1989—Broncos, 34-7 (D)
*Broncos, 24-23 (D)
1990—Steelers, 34-17 (D)
1991—Broncos, 20-13 (D)
1993—Broncos, 37-13 (D)
(RS Pts. Broncos 345, Steelers 310)
(PS Pts.—Steelers 101, Broncos 85)
*AFC Divisional Playoff

DENVER vs. *SAN DIEGO
RS: Broncos lead series, 35-32-1
1960—Chargers, 23-19 (D)
Chargers, 41-33 (LA)
1961—Chargers, 37-0 (SD)
Chargers, 19-16 (D)
1962—Broncos, 30-21 (D)

Broncos, 23-20 (SD)
1963—Broncos, 50-34 (D)
Chargers, 58-20 (SD)
1964—Chargers, 42-14 (SD)
Chargers, 31-20 (D)
1965—Chargers, 34-31 (SD)
Chargers, 33-21 (D)
1966—Chargers, 24-17 (SD)
Broncos, 20-17 (D)
1967—Chargers, 38-21 (D)
Chargers, 24-20 (SD)
1968—Chargers, 55-24 (SD)
Chargers, 47-23 (D)
1969—Broncos, 13-0 (D)
Chargers, 45-24 (SD)
1970—Chargers, 24-21 (SD)
Tie, 17-17 (D)
1971—Broncos, 20-16 (D)
Chargers, 45-17 (SD)
1972—Chargers, 37-14 (SD)
Broncos, 38-13 (D)
1973—Broncos, 30-19 (D)
Broncos, 42-28 (SD)
1974—Broncos, 27-7 (D)
Chargers, 17-0 (SD)
1975—Broncos, 27-17 (SD)
Broncos, 13-10 (D) OT
1976—Broncos, 26-0 (D)
Broncos, 17-0 (SD)
1977—Broncos, 17-14 (D)
Broncos, 17-9 (D)
1978—Broncos, 27-14 (D)
Chargers, 23-0 (SD)
1979—Broncos, 7-0 (D)
Chargers, 17-7 (SD)
1980—Chargers, 30-13 (D)
Broncos, 20-13 (SD)
1981—Broncos, 42-24 (D)
Chargers, 34-17 (SD)
1982—Chargers, 23-3 (D)
Chargers, 30-20 (SD)
1983—Broncos, 14-6 (D)
Chargers, 31-7 (SD)
1984—Broncos, 16-13 (SD)
Broncos, 16-13 (D)
1985—Chargers, 30-10 (SD)
Broncos, 30-24 (D) OT
1986—Broncos, 31-14 (SD)
Chargers, 9-3 (D)
1987—Broncos, 31-17 (SD)
Broncos, 24-0 (D)
1988—Broncos, 34-3 (D)
Broncos, 12-0 (SD)
1989—Broncos, 16-10 (D)
Chargers, 19-16 (SD)
1990—Chargers, 19-7 (SD)
Broncos, 20-10 (D)
1991—Broncos, 27-19 (D)
Broncos, 17-14 (SD)
1992—Broncos, 21-13 (D)
Chargers, 24-21 (SD)
1993—Broncos, 34-17 (D)
Chargers, 13-10 (SD)
(RS Pts.—Chargers 1,442, Broncos 1,355)
*Franchise in Los Angeles prior to 1961

DENVER vs. SAN FRANCISCO
RS: Broncos lead series, 4-2
PS: 49ers lead series, 1-0
1970—49ers, 19-14 (SF)
1973—49ers, 36-34 (D)
1979—Broncos, 38-28 (SF)
1982—Broncos, 24-21 (D)
1985—Broncos, 17-16 (D)
1988—Broncos, 16-13 (SF) OT
1989—*49ers, 55-10 (New Orleans)
(RS Pts.—Broncos 143, 49ers 133)
(PS Pts.—49ers 55, Broncos 10)
*Super Bowl XXIV

DENVER vs. SEATTLE
RS: Broncos lead series, 20-13
PS: Seahawks lead series, 1-0
1977—Broncos, 24-13 (S)
1978—Broncos, 28-7 (D)

Broncos, 20-17 (S) OT
1979—Broncos, 37-34 (D)
Seahawks, 28-23 (S)
1980—Broncos, 36-20 (D)
Broncos, 25-17 (S)
1981—Seahawks, 13-10 (S)
Broncos, 23-13 (D)
1982—Seahawks, 17-10 (D)
Seahawks, 13-11 (S)
1983—Seahawks, 27-19 (S)
Broncos, 38-27 (D)
*Seahawks, 31-7 (S)
1984—Seahawks, 27-24 (D)
Broncos, 31-14 (S)
1985—Broncos, 13-10 (D) OT
Broncos, 27-24 (S)
1986—Broncos, 20-13 (D)
Seahawks, 41-16 (S)
1987—Broncos, 40-17 (D)
Seahawks, 28-21 (S)
1988—Seahawks, 21-14 (D)
Seahawks, 42-14 (S)
1989—Broncos, 24-21 (S) OT
Broncos, 41-14 (D)
1990—Broncos, 34-31 (D) OT
Seahawks, 17-12 (S)
1991—Broncos, 16-10 (D)
Seahawks, 13-10 (S)
1992—Seahawks, 16-13 (S) OT
Broncos, 10-6 (D)
1993—Broncos, 28-17 (D)
Broncos, 17-9 (S)
(RS Pts.—Broncos 729, Seahawks 637)
(PS Pts.—Seahawks 31, Broncos 7)
*AFC First-Round Playoff

DENVER vs. TAMPA BAY
RS: Broncos lead series, 2-1
1976—Broncos, 48-13 (D)
1981—Broncos, 24-7 (TB)
1993—Buccaneers, 17-10 (D)
(RS Pts.—Broncos 82, Buccaneers 37)

DENVER vs. WASHINGTON
RS: Series tied, 3-3
PS: Redskins lead series, 1-0
1970—Redskins, 19-3 (D)
1974—Redskins, 30-3 (W)
1980—Broncos, 20-17 (D)
1986—Broncos, 31-30 (D)
1987—*Redskins, 42-10 (San Diego)
1989—Broncos, 14-10 (W)
1992—Redskins, 34-3 (W)
(RS Pts.—Redskins 140, Broncos 74)
(PS Pts.—Redskins 42, Broncos 10)
*Super Bowl XXII

DETROIT vs. ARIZONA
RS: Lions lead series, 27-16-5;
See Arizona vs. Detroit

DETROIT vs. ATLANTA
RS: Lions lead series, 17-5;
See Atlanta vs. Detroit

DETROIT vs. BUFFALO
RS: Lions lead series, 2-1-1;
See Buffalo vs. Detroit

DETROIT vs. CHICAGO
RS: Bears lead series, 74-49-5;
See Chicago vs. Detroit

DETROIT vs. CINCINNATI
RS: Series tied, 3-3;
See Cincinnati vs. Detroit

DETROIT vs. CLEVELAND
RS: Lions lead series, 11 3
PS: Lions lead series, 3-1;
See Cleveland vs. Detroit

DETROIT vs. DALLAS
RS: Cowboys lead series, 7-5
PS: Series tied, 1-1;
See Dallas vs. Detroit

DETROIT vs. DENVER
RS: Broncos lead series, 4-3;
See Denver vs. Detroit

*DETROIT vs. GREEN BAY
RS: Packers lead series, 64-56-7

PS: Packers lead series, 1-0
1930—Packers, 47-13 (GB)
  Tie, 6-6 (P)
1932—Packers, 15-10 (GB)
  Spartans, 19-0 (P)
1933—Packers, 17-0 (GB)
  Spartans, 7-0 (P)
1934—Lions, 3-0 (GB)
  Packers, 3-0 (D)
1935—Packers, 13-9 (Mil)
  Packers, 31-7 (GB)
  Lions, 20-10 (D)
1936—Packers, 20-18 (GB)
  Packers, 26-17 (D)
1937—Packers, 26-6 (GB)
  Packers, 14-13 (D)
1938—Lions, 17-7 (GB)
❢ Packers, 28-7 (D)
1939—Packers, 26-7 (GB)
  Packers, 12-7 (D)
1940—Lions, 23-14 (GB)
  Packers, 50-7 (D)
1941—Packers, 23-0 (GB)
  Packers, 24-7 (D)
1942—Packers, 38-7 (Mil)
  Packers, 28-7 (D)
1943—Packers, 35-14 (GB)
  Packers, 27-6 (D)
1944—Packers, 27-6 (Mil)
  Packers, 14-0 (D)
1945—Packers, 57-21 (Mil)
  Lions, 14-3 (D)
1946—Packers, 10-7 (Mil)
  Packers, 9-0 (D)
1947—Packers, 34-17 (GB)
  Packers, 35-14 (D)
1948—Packers, 33-21 (GB)
  Lions, 24-20 (D)
1949—Packers, 16-14 (Mil)
  Lions, 21-7 (D)
1950—Lions, 45-7 (GB)
  Lions, 24-21 (D)
1951—Lions, 24-17 (GB)
  Lions, 52-35 (D)
1952—Lions, 52-17 (GB)
  Lions, 48-24 (D)
1953—Lions, 14-7 (GB)
  Lions, 34-15 (D)
1954—Lions, 21-17 (GB)
  Lions, 28-24 (D)
1955—Packers, 20-17 (GB)
  Lions, 24-10 (D)
1956—Lions, 20-16 (GB)
  Packers, 24-20 (D)
1957—Lions, 24-14 (GB)
  Lions, 18-6 (D)
1958—Tie, 13-13 (GB)
  Lions, 24-14 (D)
1959—Packers, 28-10 (GB)
  Packers, 24-17 (D)
1960—Packers, 28-9 (GB)
  Lions, 23-10 (D)
1961—Lions, 17-13 (Mil)
  Packers, 17-9 (D)
1962—Packers, 9-7 (GB)
  Lions, 26-14 (D)
1963—Packers, 31-10 (Mil)
  Tie, 13-13 (D)
1964—Packers, 14-10 (D)
  Packers, 30-7 (D)
1965—Packers, 31-21 (D)
  Lions, 12-7 (GB)
1966—Packers, 23-14 (GB)
  Packers, 31-7 (D)
1967—Tie, 17-17 (GB)
  Packers, 27-17 (D)
1968—Lions, 23-17 (GB)
  Tie, 14-14 (D)
1969—Packers, 28-17 (D)
  Lions, 16-10 (GB)
1970—Lions, 40-0 (GB)
  Lions, 20-0 (D)
1971—Lions, 31-28 (D)

Tie, 14-14 (Mil)
1972—Packers, 24-23 (D)
  Packers, 33-7 (GB)
1973—Tie, 13-13 (GB)
  Lions, 34-0 (D)
1974—Packers, 21-19 (Mil)
  Lions, 19-17 (D)
1975—Lions, 30-16 (Mil)
  Lions, 13-10 (D)
1976—Packers, 24-14 (GB)
  Lions, 27-6 (D)
1977—Lions, 10-6 (D)
  Packers, 10-9 (GB)
1978—Packers, 13-7 (D)
  Packers, 35-14 (Mil)
1979—Packers, 24-16 (Mil)
  Packers, 18-13 (D)
1980—Lions, 29-7 (Mil)
  Lions, 24-3 (D)
1981—Lions, 31-27 (D)
  Packers, 31-17 (GB)
1982—Lions, 30-10 (GB)
  Lions, 27-24 (D)
1983—Lions, 38-14 (D)
  Lions, 23-20 (Mil) OT
1984—Packers, 41-9 (GB)
  Lions, 31-28 (D)
1985—Packers, 43-10 (GB)
  Packers, 26-23 (D)
1986—Lions, 21-14 (GB)
  Packers, 44-40 (D)
1987—Lions, 19-16 (GB) OT
  Packers, 34-33 (D)
1988—Lions, 19-9 (Mil)
  Lions, 30-14 (D)
1989—Packers, 23-20 (Mil) OT
  Lions, 31-22 (D)
1990—Packers, 24-21 (D)
  Lions, 24-17 (GB)
1991—Lions, 23-14 (D)
  Lions, 21-17 (GB)
1992—Packers, 27-13 (D)
  Packers, 38-10 (Mil)
1993—Packers, 26-17 (Mil)
  Lions, 30-20 (D)
  **Packers, 28-24 (D)
(RS Pts.—Packers 2,487, Lions 2,271)
(PS Pts.—Packers 28, Lions 24)
*Franchise in Portsmouth prior to 1934
and known as the Spartans
**NFC First-Round Playoff

DETROIT vs. HOUSTON
RS: Oilers lead series, 4-2
1971—Lions, 31-7 (H)
1975—Oilers, 24-8 (H)
1983—Oilers, 27-17 (H)
1986—Lions, 24-13 (D)
1989—Oilers, 35-31 (H)
1992—Oilers, 24-21 (D)
(RS Pts.—Lions 132, Oilers 130)

DETROIT vs. *INDIANAPOLIS
RS: Series tied, 17-17-2
1953—Lions, 27-17 (B)
  Lions, 17-7 (D)
1954—Lions, 35-0 (D)
  Lions, 27-3 (B)
1955—Colts, 28-13 (B)
  Lions, 24-14 (D)
1956—Lions, 31-14 (B)
  Lions, 27-3 (D)
1957—Colts, 34-14 (B)
  Lions, 31-27 (D)
1958—Colts, 28-15 (B)
  Colts, 40-14 (D)
1959—Colts, 21-9 (B)
  Colts, 31-24 (D)
1960—Lions, 30-17 (D)
  Lions, 20-15 (B)
1961—Lions, 16-15 (B)
  Colts, 17-14 (D)
1962—Lions, 29-20 (B)
  Lions, 21-14 (D)
1963—Colts, 25-21 (D)

Colts, 24-21 (B)
1964—Colts, 34-0 (D)
  Lions, 31-14 (B)
1965—Colts, 31-7 (B)
  Tie, 24-24 (D)
1966—Colts, 45-14 (B)
  Lions, 20-14 (D)
1967—Colts, 41-7 (B)
1968—Colts, 27-10 (D)
1969—Tie, 17-17 (B)
1973—Colts, 29-27 (D)
1977—Lions, 13-10 (B)
1980—Colts, 10-9 (D)
1985—Colts, 14-6 (I)
1991—Lions, 33-24 (I)
(RS Pts.—Colts 748, Lions 698)
*Franchise in Baltimore prior to 1984

DETROIT vs. KANSAS CITY
RS: Chiefs lead series, 4-3
1971—Lions, 32-21 (D)
1975—Chiefs, 24-21 (KC) OT
1980—Chiefs, 20-17 (KC)
1981—Lions, 27-10 (D)
1987—Chiefs, 27-20 (D)
1988—Lions, 7-6 (KC)
1990—Chiefs, 43-24 (KC)
(RS Pts.—Chiefs 151, Lions 148)

DETROIT vs. *L.A. RAIDERS
RS: Raiders lead series, 5-2
1970—Lions, 28-14 (D)
1974—Raiders, 35-13 (O)
1978—Raiders, 29-17 (O)
1981—Lions, 16-0 (D)
1984—Raiders, 24-3 (D)
1987—Raiders, 27-7 (LA)
1990—Raiders, 38-31 (D)
(RS Pts.—Raiders 167, Lions 115)
*Franchise in Oakland prior to 1982
**Conference Playoff

DETROIT vs. *L.A. RAMS
RS: Rams lead series, 39-35-1
PS: Lions lead series, 1-0
1937—Lions, 28-0 (C)
  Lions, 27-7 (D)
1938—Rams, 21-17 (C)
  Lions, 6-0 (D)
1939—Lions, 15-7 (D)
  Rams, 14-3 (C)
1940—Lions, 6-0 (D)
  Rams, 24-0 (C)
1941—Lions, 17-7 (D)
  Lions, 14-0 (C)
1942—Rams, 14-0 (D)
  Rams, 27-7 (C)
1944—Rams, 20-17 (D)
  Lions, 26-14 (C)
1945—Rams, 28-21 (D)
  Rams, 45-14 (LA)
1946—Rams, 35-14 (LA)
  Rams, 41-20 (D)
1947—Rams, 27-13 (D)
  Rams, 28-17 (LA)
1948—Rams, 44-7 (LA)
  Rams, 34-27 (D)
1949—Rams, 27-24 (LA)
  Rams, 21-10 (D)
1950—Rams, 30-28 (D)
  Rams, 65-24 (LA)
1951—Rams, 27-21 (D)
  Lions, 24-22 (LA)
1952—Lions, 17-14 (LA)
  Lions, 24-16 (D)
  **Lions, 31-21 (D)
1953—Rams, 31-19 (D)
  Rams, 37-24 (LA)
1954—Lions, 21-3 (D)
  Lions, 27-24 (LA)
1955—Rams, 17-10 (D)
  Rams, 24-13 (LA)
1956—Lions, 24-21 (D)
  Lions, 16-7 (LA)
1957—Lions, 10-7 (D)
  Rams, 35-17 (LA)
1958—Rams, 42-28 (D)
  Lions, 41-24 (LA)

1959—Lions, 17-7 (LA)
  Lions, 23-17 (D)
1960—Rams, 48-35 (LA)
  Lions, 12-10 (D)
1961—Lions, 14-13 (D)
  Lions, 28-10 (LA)
1962—Lions, 13-10 (D)
  Lions, 12-3 (LA)
1963—Lions, 23-2 (LA)
  Rams, 28-21 (D)
1964—Tie, 17-17 (LA)
  Lions, 37-17 (D)
1965—Lions, 20-0 (D)
  Lions, 31-7 (LA)
1966—Rams, 14-7 (D)
  Rams, 23-3 (LA)
1967—Rams, 31-7 (D)
1968—Rams, 10-7 (LA)
1969—Lions, 28-0 (D)
1970—Lions, 28-23 (LA)
1971—Rams, 21-13 (D)
1972—Lions, 34-17 (LA)
1974—Rams, 16-13 (LA)
1975—Rams, 20-0 (D)
1976—Rams, 20-17 (D)
1980—Lions, 41-20 (LA)
1981—Rams, 20-13 (LA)
1982—Lions, 19-14 (LA)
1983—Lions, 21-10 (LA)
1986—Rams, 14-10 (LA)
1987—Rams, 37-16 (D)
1988—Rams, 17-10 (LA)
1991—Lions, 21-10 (D)
1993—Lions, 16-13 (LA)
(RS Pts.—Rams 1,436, Lions 1,340)
(PS Pts.—Lions 31, Rams 21)
*Franchise in Cleveland prior to 1946
**Conference Playoff

DETROIT vs. MIAMI
RS: Series tied, 2-2
1973—Dolphins, 34-7 (M)
1979—Dolphins, 28-10 (D)
1985—Lions, 31-21 (D)
1991—Lions, 17-13 (D)
(RS Pts.—Dolphins 96, Lions 65)

DETROIT vs. MINNESOTA
RS: Vikings lead series, 40-23-2
1961—Lions, 37-10 (M)
  Lions, 13-7 (D)
1962—Lions, 17-6 (M)
  Lions, 37-23 (D)
1963—Lions, 28-10 (D)
  Vikings, 34-31 (M)
1964—Lions, 24-20 (M)
  Tie, 23-23 (D)
1965—Lions, 31-29 (M)
  Vikings, 29-7 (D)
1966—Lions, 32-31 (M)
  Vikings, 28-16 (D)
1967—Tie, 10-10 (M)
  Lions, 14-3 (D)
1968—Vikings, 24-10 (M)
  Vikings, 13-6 (D)
1969—Vikings, 24-10 (M)
  Vikings, 27-0 (D)
1970—Vikings, 30-17 (D)
  Vikings, 24-20 (M)
1971—Vikings, 16-13 (D)
  Vikings, 29-10 (M)
1972—Vikings, 34-10 (D)
  Vikings, 16-14 (M)
1973—Vikings, 23-9 (D)
  Vikings, 28-7 (M)
1974—Vikings, 7-6 (D)
  Lions, 20-16 (M)
1975—Vikings, 25-19 (M)
  Lions, 17-10 (D)
1976—Vikings, 10-9 (D)
  Vikings, 31-23 (M)
1977—Vikings, 14-7 (M)
  Vikings, 30-21 (D)
1978—Vikings, 17-7 (M)
  Lions, 45-14 (D)

1979—Vikings, 13-10 (D)
    Vikings, 14-7 (M)
1980—Lions, 27-7 (D)
    Vikings, 34-0 (M)
1981—Vikings, 26-24 (M)
    Lions, 45-7 (D)
1982—Vikings, 34-31 (D)
1983—Vikings, 20-17 (M)
    Lions, 13-2 (D)
1984—Vikings, 29-28 (D)
    Lions, 16-14 (M)
1985—Vikings, 16-13 (M)
    Lions, 41-21 (D)
1986—Lions, 13-10 (M)
    Vikings, 24-10 (D)
1987—Vikings, 34-19 (M)
    Vikings, 17-14 (D)
1988—Vikings, 44-17 (M)
    Vikings, 23-0 (D)
1989—Vikings, 24-17 (M)
    Vikings, 20-7 (D)
1990—Lions, 34-27 (M)
    Vikings, 17-7 (D)
1991—Lions, 24-20 (D)
    Lions, 34-14 (M)
1992—Lions, 31-17 (D)
    Vikings, 31-14 (M)
1993—Lions, 30-27 (M)
    Vikings, 13-0 (D)
(RS Pts.—Vikings 1,327, Lions 1,163)

DETROIT vs. NEW ENGLAND
RS: Lions lead series, 3-2
1971—Lions, 34-7 (NE)
1976—Lions, 30-10 (D)
1979—Patriots, 24-17 (NE)
1985—Patriots, 23-6 (NE)
1993—Lions, 19-16 (NE) OT
(RS Pts.—Lions 106, Patriots 80)

DETROIT vs. NEW ORLEANS
RS: Saints lead series, 7-6-1
1968—Tie, 20-20 (D)
1970—Saints, 19-17 (NO)
1972—Lions, 27-14 (D)
1973—Saints, 20-13 (NO)
1974—Lions, 19-14 (D)
1976—Saints, 17-16 (NO)
1977—Lions, 23-19 (D)
1979—Saints, 17-7 (NO)
1980—Lions, 24-13 (D)
1988—Saints, 22-14 (D)
1989—Lions, 21-14 (D)
1990—Lions, 27-10 (NO)
1992—Saints, 13-7 (D)
1993—Saints, 14-3 (NO)
(RS Pts.—Lions 238, Saints 226)

*DETROIT vs. N.Y. GIANTS
RS: Lions lead series, 17-15-1
PS: Lions lead series, 1-0
1930—Giants, 19-6 (P)
1931—Spartans, 14-6 (P)
    Giants, 14-0 (NY)
1932—Spartans, 7-0 (P)
    Spartans, 6-0 (NY)
1933—Spartans, 17-7 (P)
    Giants, 13-10 (NY)
1934—Lions, 9-0 (D)
1935—**Lions, 26-7 (D)
1936—Giants, 14-7 (NY)
    Lions, 38-0 (D)
1937—Lions, 17-0 (NY)
1939—Lions, 18-14 (D)
1941—Giants, 20-13 (NY)
1943—Tie, 0-0 (D)
1945—Giants, 35-14 (NY)
1947—Lions, 35-7 (D)
1949—Lions, 45-21 (NY)
1953—Lions, 27-16 (NY)
1955—Giants, 24-19 (D)
1958—Giants, 19-17 (D)
1962—Giants, 17-14 (NY)
1964—Lions, 26-3 (D)
1967—Lions, 30-7 (NY)
1969—Lions, 24-0 (D)

1972—Lions, 30-16 (D)
1974—Lions, 20-19 (D)
1976—Giants, 24-10 (NY)
1982—Giants, 13-6 (D)
1983—Lions, 15-9 (D)
1988—Giants, 30-10 (NY)
    Giants, 13-10 (D) OT
1989—Giants, 24-14 (NY)
1990—Giants, 20-0 (NY)
(RS Pts.—Lions, 528, Giants 424)
(PS Pts.—Lions 26, Giants 7)
*Franchise in Portsmouth prior to 1934
and known as the Spartans*
**NFL Championship

DETROIT vs. N.Y. JETS
RS: Series tied, 3-3
1972—Lions, 37-20 (D)
1979—Jets, 31-10 (NY)
1982—Jets, 28-13 (D)
1985—Lions, 31-20 (D)
1988—Jets, 17-10 (D)
1991—Lions, 34-20 (D)
(RS Pts.—Jets 136, Lions 135)

*DETROIT vs. PHILADELPHIA
RS: Lions lead series, 12-9-2
1933—Spartans, 25-0 (P)
1934—Lions, 10-0 (P)
1935—Lions, 35-0 (D)
1936—Lions, 23-0 (P)
1938—Eagles, 21-7 (D)
1940—Lions, 21-0 (P)
1941—Lions, 21-17 (D)
1945—Lions, 28-24 (D)
1948—Eagles, 45-21 (P)
1949—Eagles, 22-14 (D)
1951—Lions, 28-10 (P)
1954—Tie, 13-13 (D)
1957—Lions, 27-16 (P)
1960—Eagles, 28-10 (P)
1961—Eagles, 27-24 (P)
1965—Lions, 35-28 (P)
1968—Eagles, 12-0 (D)
1971—Eagles, 23-20 (D)
1974—Eagles, 28-17 (P)
1977—Lions, 17-13 (D)
1979—Eagles, 44-7 (P)
1984—Tie, 23-23 (D) OT
1986—Lions, 13-11 (P)
(RS Pts.—Lions 439, Eagles 405)
*Franchise in Portsmouth prior to 1934
and known as the Spartans*

DETROIT vs. *PITTSBURGH
RS: Lions lead series, 13-11-1
1934—Lions, 40-7 (D)
1936—Lions, 28-3 (D)
1937—Lions, 7-3 (D)
1938—Lions, 16-7 (D)
1940—Pirates, 10-7 (D)
1942—Steelers, 35-7 (D)
1946—Lions, 17-7 (D)
1947—Steelers, 17-10 (P)
1948—Lions, 17-14 (D)
1949—Steelers, 14-7 (P)
1950—Lions, 10-7 (D)
1952—Lions, 31-6 (P)
1953—Lions, 38-21 (D)
1955—Lions, 31-28 (P)
1956—Lions, 45-7 (D)
1959—Tie, 10-10 (P)
1962—Lions, 45-7 (D)
1966—Steelers, 17-3 (P)
1967—Steelers, 24-14 (D)
1969—Steelers, 16-13 (P)
1973—Steelers, 24-10 (D)
1983—Lions, 45-3 (D)
1986—Steelers, 27-17 (P)
1989—Steelers, 23-3 (D)
1992—Steelers, 17-14 (P)
(RS Pts.—Lions 485, Steelers 354)
Steelers known as Pirates prior to 1941

DETROIT vs. SAN DIEGO
RS: Lions lead series, 3-2
1972—Lions, 34-20 (D)

1977—Lions, 20-0 (D)
1978—Lions, 31-14 (D)
1981—Chargers, 28-23 (SD)
1984—Chargers, 27-24 (SD)
(RS Pts.—Lions 132, Chargers 89)

DETROIT vs. SAN FRANCISCO
RS: 49ers lead series, 26-25-1
PS: Series tied, 1-1
1950—Lions, 24-7 (D)
    49ers, 28-27 (SF)
1951—49ers, 20-10 (D)
    49ers, 21-17 (SF)
1952—49ers, 17-3 (SF)
    49ers, 28-0 (D)
1953—Lions, 24-21 (D)
    Lions, 14-10 (SF)
1954—49ers, 37-31 (SF)
    Lions, 48-7 (D)
1955—49ers, 27-24 (D)
    49ers, 38-21 (SF)
1956—Lions, 20-17 (D)
    Lions, 17-13 (SF)
1957—49ers, 35-31 (SF)
    Lions, 31-10 (D)
    *Lions, 31-27 (SF)
1958—49ers, 24-21 (SF)
    Lions, 35-21 (D)
1959—49ers, 34-13 (D)
    49ers, 33-7 (SF)
1960—49ers, 14-10 (D)
    Lions, 24-0 (SF)
1961—49ers, 49-0 (D)
    Tie, 20-20 (SF)
1962—Lions, 45-24 (D)
    Lions, 38-24 (SF)
1963—Lions, 26-3 (D)
    Lions, 45-7 (SF)
1964—Lions, 26-17 (SF)
    Lions, 24-7 (D)
1965—49ers, 27-21 (D)
    49ers, 17-14 (SF)
1966—49ers, 27-24 (SF)
    49ers, 41-14 (D)
1967—Lions, 45-3 (SF)
1968—49ers, 14-7 (D)
1969—Lions, 26-14 (SF)
1970—Lions, 28-7 (D)
1971—49ers, 31-27 (SF)
1973—Lions, 30-20 (D)
1974—Lions, 17-13 (D)
1975—Lions, 28-17 (SF)
1977—49ers, 28-7 (SF)
1978—Lions, 33-14 (D)
1980—Lions, 17-13 (D)
1981—Lions, 24-17 (D)
1983—**49ers, 24-23 (SF)
1984—Lions, 30-27 (D)
1985—Lions, 23-21 (D)
1988—49ers, 20-13 (SF)
1991—49ers, 35-3 (SF)
1992—49ers, 24-6 (SF)
1993—49ers, 55-17 (D)
(RS Pts.—Lions 1,127, 49ers 1,101)
(PS Pts.—Lions 54, 49ers 51)
Conference Playoff
**NFC Divisional Playoff

DETROIT vs. SEATTLE
RS: Seahawks lead series, 4-2
1976—Lions, 41-14 (S)
1978—Seahawks, 28-16 (S)
1984—Seahawks, 38-17 (S)
1987—Seahawks, 37-14 (D)
1990—Seahawks, 30-10 (S)
1993—Lions, 30-10 (D)
(RS Pts.—Seahawks 157, Lions 128)

DETROIT vs. TAMPA BAY
RS: Series tied, 16-16
1977—Lions, 16-7 (D)
1978—Lions, 15-7 (D)
    Lions, 34-23 (D)
1979—Buccaneers, 31-16 (TB)
    Buccaneers, 16-14 (D)
1980—Lions, 24-10 (TB)

    Lions, 27-14 (D)
1981—Buccaneers, 28-10 (TB)
    Buccaneers, 20-17 (D)
1982—Buccaneers, 23-21 (TB)
1983—Lions, 11-0 (TB)
    Lions, 23-20 (D)
1984—Buccaneers, 21-17 (TB)
    Lions, 13-7 (D) OT
1985—Lions, 30-9 (D)
    Buccaneers, 19-16 (TB) OT
1986—Buccaneers, 24-20 (D)
    Lions, 38-17 (TB)
1987—Buccaneers, 31-27 (D)
    Lions, 20-10 (TB)
1988—Buccaneers, 23-20 (D)
    Buccaneers, 21-10 (TB)
1989—Lions, 17-16 (TB)
    Lions, 33-7 (D)
1990—Buccaneers, 38-21 (D)
    Buccaneers, 23-20 (TB)
1991—Lions, 31-3 (D)
    Buccaneers, 30-21 (TB)
1992—Buccaneers, 27-23 (D)
    Lions, 38-7 (TB)
1993—Buccaneers, 27-10 (TB)
    Lions, 23-0 (D)
(RS Pts.—Lions 676, Buccaneers 559)

*DETROIT vs. **WASHINGTON
RS: Redskins lead series, 22-8
PS: Redskins lead series, 2-0
1932—Spartans, 10-0 (P)
1933—Spartans, 13-0 (B)
1934—Lions, 24-0 (D)
1935—Lions, 17-7 (B)
1938—Redskins, 7-5 (D)
1939—Redskins, 31-7 (W)
1940—Redskins, 20-14 (D)
1942—Redskins, 15-3 (D)
1943—Redskins, 42-20 (W)
1946—Redskins, 17-16 (W)
1947—Lions, 38-21 (D)
1948—Redskins, 46-21 (W)
1951—Lions, 35-17 (D)
1956—Redskins, 18-17 (W)
1965—Lions, 14-10 (D)
1968—Redskins, 14-3 (W)
1970—Redskins, 31-10 (W)
1973—Redskins, 20-0 (D)
1976—Redskins, 20-7 (W)
1978—Redskins, 21-19 (D)
1979—Redskins, 27-24 (D)
1981—Redskins, 33-31 (W)
1982—***Redskins, 31-7 (W)
1983—Redskins, 38-17 (W)
1984—Redskins, 28-14 (W)
1985—Redskins, 24-3 (W)
1987—Redskins, 20-13 (W)
1990—Redskins, 41-38 (D)
1991—Redskins, 45-0 (W)
    ****Redskins, 41-10 (W)
1992—Redskins, 13-10 (W)
(RS Pts.—Redskins 626, Lions 457)
(PS Pts.—Redskins 72, Lions 17)
*Franchise in Portsmouth prior to 1934
and known as the Spartans.*
**Franchise in Boston prior to 1937
***NFC First-Round Playoff
****NFC Championship

GREEN BAY vs. ARIZONA
RS: Packers lead series, 39-21-4
PS: Packers lead series, 1-0;
See Arizona vs. Green Bay

GREEN BAY vs. ATLANTA
RS: Series tied, 9-9;
See Atlanta vs. Green Bay

GREEN BAY vs. BUFFALO
RS: Bills lead series, 4-1;
See Buffalo vs. Green Bay

GREEN BAY vs. CHICAGO
RS: Bears lead series, 81-59-6
PS: Bears lead series, 1-0;

See Chicago vs. Green Bay

GREEN BAY vs. CINCINNATI
RS: Bengals lead series, 4-3;
See Cincinnati vs. Green Bay

GREEN BAY vs. CLEVELAND
RS: Packers lead series, 7-6
PS: Packers lead series, 1-0;
See Cleveland vs. Green Bay

GREEN BAY vs. DALLAS
RS: Packers lead series, 8-6
PS: Series tied, 2-2;
See Dallas vs. Green Bay

GREEN BAY vs. DENVER
RS: Broncos lead series, 4-2-1;
See Denver vs. Green Bay

GREEN BAY vs. DETROIT
RS: Packers lead series, 64-56-7
PS: Packers lead series, 1-0;
See Detroit vs. Green Bay

GREEN BAY vs. HOUSTON
RS: Series tied, 3-3
1972—Packers, 23-10 (H)
1977—Oilers, 16-10 (GB)
1980—Oilers, 22-3 (GB)
1983—Packers, 41-38 (H) OT
1986—Oilers, 31-3 (GB)
1992—Packers, 16-14 (H)
(RS Pts.—Oilers 131, Packers 96)

GREEN BAY vs. *INDIANAPOLIS
RS: Series tied, 18-18-1
PS: Packers lead series, 1-0
1953—Packers, 37-14 (GB)
    Packers, 35-24 (B)
1954—Packers, 7-6 (B)
    Packers, 24-13 (Mil)
1955—Colts, 24-20 (Mil)
    Colts, 14-10 (B)
1956—Packers, 38-33 (Mil)
    Colts, 28-21 (B)
1957—Colts, 45-17 (Mil)
    Packers, 24-21 (B)
1958—Colts, 24-17 (Mil)
    Colts, 56-0 (B)
1959—Colts, 38-21 (B)
    Colts, 28-24 (Mil)
1960—Packers, 35-21 (GB)
    Colts, 38-24 (B)
1961—Packers, 45-7 (GB)
    Colts, 45-21 (B)
1962—Packers, 17-6 (B)
    Packers, 17-13 (GB)
1963—Packers, 31-20 (GB)
    Packers, 34-20 (B)
1964—Colts, 21-20 (GB)
    Colts, 24-21 (B)
1965—Packers, 20-17 (Mil)
    Packers, 42-27 (B)
    **Packers, 13-10 (GB) OT
1966—Packers, 24-3 (Mil)
    Packers, 14-10 (B)
1967—Colts, 13-10 (B)
1968—Colts, 16-3 (GB)
1969—Colts, 14-6 (B)
1970—Colts, 13-10 (Mil)
1974—Colts, 20-13 (B)
1982—Tie, 20-20 (B) OT
1985—Colts, 37-10 (I)
1988—Colts, 20-13 (GB)
1991—Packers, 14-10 (Mil)
(RS Pts.—Colts 796, Packers 766)
(PS Pts.—Packers 13, Colts 10)
*Franchise in Baltimore prior to 1984
**Conference Playoff

GREEN BAY vs. KANSAS CITY
RS: Chiefs lead series, 4-1-1
PS: Packers lead series, 1-0
1966—*Packers, 35-10 (Los Angeles)
1973—Tie, 10-10 (Mil)
1977—Chiefs, 20-10 (KC)
1987—Packers, 23-3 (KC)
1989—Chiefs, 21-3 (GB)
1990—Chiefs, 17-3 (GB)
1993—Chiefs, 23-16 (KC)

(RS Pts.—Chiefs 94, Packers 65)
(PS Pts.—Packers 35, Chiefs 10)
*Super Bowl I

GREEN BAY vs. *L.A. RAIDERS
RS: Raiders lead series, 5-2
PS: Packers lead series, 1-0
1967—**Packers, 33-14 (Miami)
1972—Raiders, 20-14 (GB)
1976—Raiders, 18-14 (O)
1978—Raiders, 28-3 (GB)
1984—Raiders, 28-7 (LA)
1987—Raiders, 20-0 (GB)
1990—Packers, 29-16 (LA)
1993—Packers, 28-0 (GB)
(RS Pts.—Raiders 130, Packers 95)
(PS Pts.—Packers 33, Raiders 14)
*Franchise in Oakland prior to 1982
**Super Bowl II

GREEN BAY vs. *L.A. RAMS
RS: Rams lead series, 42-36-2
PS: Packers lead series, 1-0
1937—Packers, 35-10 (C)
    Packers, 35-7 (GB)
1938—Packers, 26-17 (GB)
    Packers, 28-7 (C)
1939—Rams, 27-24 (GB)
    Packers, 7-6 (C)
1940—Packers, 31-14 (GB)
    Tie, 13-13 (C)
1941—Packers, 24-7 (Mil)
    Packers, 17-14 (C)
1942—Packers, 45-28 (GB)
    Packers, 30-12 (C)
1944—Packers, 30-21 (GB)
    Packers, 42-7 (C)
1945—Rams, 27-14 (GB)
    Rams, 20-7 (C)
1946—Rams, 21-17 (Mil)
    Rams, 38-17 (LA)
1947—Packers, 17-14 (Mil)
    Packers, 30-10 (LA)
1948—Packers, 16-0 (GB)
    Rams, 24-10 (LA)
1949—Packers, 48-7 (GB)
    Rams, 35-7 (LA)
1950—Rams, 45-14 (Mil)
    Rams, 51-14 (LA)
1951—Rams, 20-0 (Mil)
    Rams, 42-14 (LA)
1952—Rams, 30-28 (Mil)
    Rams, 45-27 (LA)
1953—Rams, 38-20 (Mil)
    Rams, 33-17 (LA)
1954—Packers, 35-17 (Mil)
    Rams, 35-27 (LA)
1955—Packers, 30-28 (Mil)
    Rams, 31-17 (LA)
1956—Packers, 42-17 (Mil)
    Rams, 49-21 (LA)
1957—Rams, 31-27 (Mil)
    Rams, 42-17 (LA)
1958—Rams, 20-7 (GB)
    Rams, 34-20 (LA)
1959—Rams, 45-6 (Mil)
    Packers, 38-20 (LA)
1960—Rams, 33-31 (Mil)
    Packers, 35-21 (LA)
1961—Packers, 35-17 (GB)
    Packers, 24-17 (LA)
1962—Packers, 41-10 (Mil)
    Packers, 20-17 (LA)
1963—Packers, 42-10 (GB)
    Packers, 31-14 (LA)
1964—Rams, 27-17 (Mil)
    Tie, 24-24 (LA)
1965—Packers, 6-3 (Mil)
    Rams, 21-10 (LA)
1966—Packers, 24-13 (GB)
    Packers, 27-23 (LA)
1967—Rams, 27-24 (LA)
    **Packers, 28-7 (Mil)
1968—Rams, 16-14 (Mil)
1969—Rams, 34-21 (LA)

1970—Rams, 31-21 (GB)
1971—Rams, 30-13 (LA)
1973—Rams, 24-7 (LA)
1974—Packers, 17-6 (Mil)
1975—Rams, 22-5 (LA)
1977—Rams, 24-6 (Mil)
1978—Rams, 31-14 (LA)
1980—Rams, 51-21 (LA)
1981—Rams, 35-23 (LA)
1982—Packers, 35-23 (Mil)
1983—Packers, 27-24 (Mil)
1984—Packers, 31-6 (Mil)
1985—Rams, 34-17 (LA)
1988—Rams, 34-7 (GB)
1989—Rams, 41-38 (LA)
1990—Packers, 36-24 (GB)
1991—Rams, 23-21 (LA)
1992—Packers, 28-13 (GB)
1993—Packers, 36-6 (Mil)
(RS Pts.—Rams 1,917, Packers 1,779)
(PS Pts.—Packers 28, Rams 7)
*Franchise in Cleveland prior to 1946
**Conference Championship

GREEN BAY vs. MIAMI
RS: Dolphins lead series, 7-0
1971—Dolphins, 27-6 (Mia)
1975—Dolphins, 31-7 (GB)
1979—Dolphins, 27-7 (Mia)
1985—Dolphins, 34-24 (GB)
1988—Dolphins, 24-17 (Mia)
1989—Dolphins, 23-20 (Mia)
1991—Dolphins, 16-13 (Mia)
(RS Pts.—Dolphins 182, Packers 94)

GREEN BAY vs. MINNESOTA
RS: Vikings lead series, 33-31-1
1961—Packers, 33-7 (Minn)
    Packers, 28-10 (Mil)
1962—Packers, 34-7 (GB)
    Packers, 48-21 (Minn)
1963—Packers, 37-28 (Minn)
    Packers, 28-7 (GB)
1964—Vikings, 24-23 (GB)
    Packers, 42-13 (Minn)
1965—Packers, 38-13 (Minn)
    Packers, 24-19 (GB)
1966—Vikings, 20-17 (GB)
    Packers, 28-16 (Minn)
1967—Vikings, 10-7 (Minn)
    Packers, 30-27 (Minn)
1968—Vikings, 26-13 (Mil)
    Vikings, 14-10 (Minn)
1969—Vikings, 19-7 (Minn)
    Vikings, 9-7 (Mil)
1970—Packers, 13-10 (Mil)
    Vikings, 10-3 (Minn)
1971—Vikings, 24-13 (GB)
    Vikings, 3-0 (Minn)
1972—Vikings, 27-13 (GB)
    Packers, 23-7 (Minn)
1973—Vikings, 11-3 (Minn)
    Vikings, 31-7 (GB)
1974—Vikings, 32-17 (GB)
    Packers, 19-7 (Minn)
1975—Vikings, 28-17 (GB)
    Vikings, 24-3 (Minn)
1976—Vikings, 17-10 (Mil)
    Vikings, 20-9 (Minn)
1977—Vikings, 19-7 (Minn)
    Vikings, 13-6 (GB)
1978—Vikings, 21-7 (Minn)
    Tie, 10-10 (GB) OT
1979—Vikings, 27-21 (Minn) OT
    Packers, 19-7 (Mil)
1980—Packers, 16-3 (GB)
    Packers, 25-13 (Minn)
1981—Vikings, 30-13 (Mil)
    Packers, 35-23 (Minn)
1982—Packers, 26-7 (Mil)
1983—Vikings, 20-17 (GB) OT
    Packers, 29-21 (Minn)
1984—Packers, 45-17 (Mil)
    Packers, 38-14 (Minn)
1985—Packers, 20-17 (Mil)

    Packers, 27-17 (Minn)
1986—Vikings, 42-7 (Minn)
    Vikings, 32-6 (GB)
1987—Packers, 23-16 (Minn)
    Packers, 16-10 (Mil)
1988—Packers, 34-14 (Minn)
    Packers, 18-6 (GB)
1989—Vikings, 26-14 (Minn)
    Packers, 20-19 (Mil)
1990—Packers, 24-10 (Mil)
    Vikings, 23-7 (Minn)
1991—Vikings, 35-21 (GB)
    Packers, 27-7 (Minn)
1992—Vikings, 23-20 (GB) OT
    Vikings, 27-7 (Minn)
1993—Vikings, 15-13 (Minn)
    Vikings, 21-17 (Mil)
(RS Pts.—Packers 1,239, Vikings 1,146)

GREEN BAY vs. NEW ENGLAND
RS: Series tied, 2-2
1973—Patriots, 33-24 (NE)
1979—Packers, 27-14 (GB)
1985—Patriots, 26-20 (NE)
1988—Packers, 45-3 (Mil)
(RS Pts.—Packers 116, Patriots 76)

GREEN BAY vs. NEW ORLEANS
RS: Packers lead series, 12-4
1968—Packers, 29-7 (Mil)
1971—Saints, 29-21 (Mil)
1972—Packers, 30-20 (NO)
1973—Packers, 30-10 (Mil)
1975—Saints, 20-19 (NO)
1976—Packers, 32-27 (Mil)
1977—Packers, 24-20 (NO)
1978—Packers, 28-17 (Mil)
1979—Packers, 28-19 (Mil)
1981—Packers, 35-7 (NO)
1984—Packers, 23-13 (NO)
1985—Packers, 38-14 (Mil)
1986—Saints, 24-10 (NO)
1987—Saints, 33-24 (NO)
1989—Packers, 35-34 (GB)
1993—Packers, 19-17 (NO)
(RS Pts.—Packers 425, Saints 311)

GREEN BAY vs. N.Y. GIANTS
RS: Packers lead series, 21-20-2
PS: Packers lead series, 4-1
1928—Giants, 6-0 (GB)
    Packers, 7-0 (NY)
1929—Packers, 20-6 (NY)
1930—Packers, 14-7 (GB)
    Giants, 13-6 (NY)
1931—Packers, 27-7 (GB)
    Packers, 14-10 (NY)
1932—Packers, 13-0 (GB)
    Giants, 6-0 (NY)
1933—Giants, 10-7 (Mil)
    Giants, 17-6 (NY)
1934—Packers, 20-6 (Mil)
    Giants, 17-3 (NY)
1935—Packers, 16-7 (GB)
1936—Packers, 26-14 (NY)
1937—Giants, 10-0 (NY)
1938—Giants, 15-3 (NY)
    *Giants, 23-17 (NY)
1939—*Packers, 27-0 (Mil)
1940—Giants, 7-3 (NY)
1942—Tie, 21-21 (NY)
1943—Packers, 35-21 (NY)
1944—Giants, 24-0 (NY)
    *Packers, 14-7 (NY)
1945—Packers, 23-14 (NY)
1947—Tie, 24-24 (NY)
1948—Giants, 49-3 (Mil)
1949—Giants, 30-10 (GB)
1952—Packers, 17-3 (NY)
1957—Giants, 31-17 (GB)
1959—Giants, 20-3 (NY)
1961—Packers, 20-17 (Mil)
    *Packers, 37-0 (GB)
1962—*Packers, 16-7 (NY)
1967—Packers, 48-21 (NY)
1969—Packers, 20-10 (Mil)

1971—Giants, 42-40 (GB)
1973—Packers, 16-14 (New Haven)
1975—Packers, 40-14 (Mil)
1980—Giants, 27-21 (NY)
1981—Packers, 27-14 (NY)
    Packers, 26-24 (Mil)
1982—Packers, 27-19 (NY)
1983—Giants, 27-3 (NY)
1985—Giants, 23-20 (GB)
1986—Giants, 55-24 (NY)
1987—Giants, 20-10 (NY)
1992—Giants, 27-7 (NY)
(RS Pts.—Giants 746, Packers 690)
(PS Pts.—Packers 111, Giants 37)
*NFL Championship

GREEN BAY vs. N.Y. JETS
RS: Jets lead series, 5-1
1973—Packers, 23-7 (Mil)
1979—Jets, 27-22 (GB)
1981—Jets, 28-3 (NY)
1982—Jets, 15-13 (NY)
1985—Jets, 24-3 (Mil)
1991—Jets, 19-16 (NY) OT
(RS Pts.—Jets 120, Packers 80)

GREEN BAY vs. PHILADELPHIA
RS: Packers lead series, 19-7
PS: Eagles lead series, 1-0
1933—Packers, 35-9 (GB)
    Packers, 10-0 (P)
1934—Packers, 19-6 (GB)
1935—Packers, 13-6 (P)
1937—Packers, 37-7 (Mil)
1939—Packers, 23-16 (P)
1940—Packers, 27-20 (GB)
1942—Packers, 7-0 (P)
1946—Packers, 19-7 (P)
1947—Eagles, 28-14 (P)
1951—Packers, 37-24 (GB)
1952—Packers, 12-10 (Mil)
1954—Packers, 37-14 (P)
1958—Packers, 38-35 (GB)
1960—*Eagles, 17-13 (P)
1962—Packers, 49-0 (P)
1968—Packers, 30-13 (GB)
1970—Packers, 30-17 (Mil)
1974—Eagles, 36-14 (P)
1976—Packers, 28-13 (GB)
1978—Eagles, 10-3 (P)
1979—Eagles, 21-10 (GB)
1987—Packers, 16-10 (GB) OT
1990—Eagles, 31-0 (P)
1991—Eagles, 20-3 (GB)
1992—Packers, 27-24 (Mil)
1993—Eagles, 20-17 (GB)
(RS Pts.—Packers 555, Eagles 397)
(PS Pts.—Eagles 17, Packers 13)
*NFL Championship

GREEN BAY vs. *PITTSBURGH
RS: Packers lead series, 17-11
1933—Packers, 47-0 (GB)
1935—Packers, 27-0 (GB)
    Packers, 34-14 (P)
1936—Packers, 42-10 (Mil)
1938—Packers, 20-0 (GB)
1940—Packers, 24-3 (Mil)
1941—Packers, 54-7 (P)
1942—Packers, 24-21 (Mil)
1946—Packers, 17-7 (GB)
1947—Steelers, 18-17 (Mil)
1948—Steelers, 38-7 (P)
1949—Steelers, 30-7 (Mil)
1951—Packers, 35-33 (Mil)
    Steelers, 28-7 (P)
1953—Steelers, 31-14 (P)
1954—Steelers, 21-20 (GB)
1957—Packers, 27-10 (P)
1960—Packers, 19-13 (P)
1963—Packers, 33-14 (Mil)
1965—Packers, 41-9 (P)
1967—Steelers, 24-17 (GB)
1969—Packers, 38-34 (P)
1970—Packers, 20-12 (P)
1975—Steelers, 16-13 (Mil)

1980—Steelers, 22-20 (P)
1983—Steelers, 25-21 (GB)
1986—Steelers, 27-3 (P)
1992—Packers, 17-3 (GB)
(RS Pts.—Packers 665, Steelers 470)
*Steelers known as Pirates prior to 1941

GREEN BAY vs. SAN DIEGO
RS: Packers lead series, 4-1
1970—Packers, 22-20 (SD)
1974—Packers, 34-0 (GB)
1978—Packers, 24-3 (SD)
1984—Chargers, 34-28 (GB)
1993—Packers, 20-13 (SD)
(RS Pts.—Packers 128, Chargers 70)

GREEN BAY vs. SAN FRANCISCO
RS: 49ers lead series, 25-21-1
1950—Packers, 25-21 (GB)
    49ers, 30-14 (SF)
1951—49ers, 31-19 (SF)
1952—49ers, 24-14 (SF)
1953—49ers, 37-7 (Mil)
    49ers, 48-14 (SF)
1954—49ers, 23-17 (Mil)
    49ers, 35-0 (SF)
1955—Packers, 27-21 (Mil)
    Packers, 28-7 (SF)
1956—49ers, 17-16 (GB)
    49ers, 38-20 (SF)
1957—49ers, 24-14 (Mil)
    49ers, 27-20 (SF)
1958—49ers, 33-12 (Mil)
    49ers, 48-21 (SF)
1959—Packers, 21-20 (GB)
    Packers, 36-14 (SF)
1960—Packers, 41-14 (Mil)
    Packers, 13-0 (SF)
1961—Packers, 30-10 (GB)
    49ers, 22-21 (SF)
1962—Packers, 31-13 (Mil)
    Packers, 31-21 (SF)
1963—Packers, 28-10 (Mil)
    Packers, 21-17 (SF)
1964—Packers, 24-14 (Mil)
    49ers, 24-14 (SF)
1965—Packers, 27-10 (GB)
    Tie, 24-24 (SF)
1966—49ers, 21-20 (SF)
    Packers, 20-7 (Mil)
1967—Packers, 13-0 (GB)
1968—49ers, 27-20 (SF)
1969—Packers, 14-7 (Mil)
1970—Packers, 26-10 (GB)
1972—Packers, 34-24 (Mil)
1973—49ers, 20-6 (SF)
1974—49ers, 7-6 (SF)
1976—49ers, 26-14 (GB)
1977—Packers, 16-14 (Mil)
1980—Packers, 23-16 (Mil)
1981—49ers, 13-3 (Mil)
1986—49ers, 31-17 (Mil)
1987—49ers, 23-12 (GB)
1989—Packers, 21-17 (SF)
1990—49ers, 24-20 (GB)
(RS Pts.—49ers 980, Packers 899)

GREEN BAY vs. SEATTLE
RS: Series tied, 3-3
1976—Packers, 27-20 (Mil)
1978—Packers, 45-28 (Mil)
1981—Packers, 34-24 (GB)
1984—Seahawks, 30-24 (Mil)
1987—Seahawks, 24-13 (S)
1990—Seahawks, 20-14 (Mil)
(RS Pts.—Packers 157, Seahawks 146)

GREEN BAY vs. TAMPA BAY
RS: Packers lead series, 17-12-1
1977—Packers, 13-0 (TB)
1978—Packers, 9-7 (GB)
    Packers, 17-7 (TB)
1979—Buccaneers, 21-10 (GB)
    Buccaneers, 21-3 (TB)
1980—Tie, 14-14 (TB) OT
    Buccaneers, 20-17 (Mil)
1981—Buccaneers, 21-10 (GB)

    Buccaneers, 37-3 (TB)
1983—Packers, 55-14 (GB)
    Packers, 12-9 (TB) OT
1984—Buccaneers, 30-27 (TB) OT
    Packers, 27-14 (GB)
1985—Packers, 21-0 (GB)
    Packers, 20-17 (TB)
1986—Packers, 31-7 (Mil)
    Packers, 21-7 (TB)
1987—Buccaneers, 23-17 (Mil)
1988—Buccaneers, 13-10 (GB)
    Buccaneers, 27-24 (TB)
1989—Buccaneers, 23-21 (GB)
    Packers, 17-16 (TB)
1990—Buccaneers, 26-14 (TB)
    Packers, 20-10 (Mil)
1991—Packers, 15-13 (GB)
    Packers, 27-0 (TB)
1992—Buccaneers, 31-3 (TB)
    Packers, 19-14 (Mil)
1993—Packers, 37-14 (TB)
    Packers, 13-10 (GB)
(RS Pts.—Packers 547, Buccaneers 466)

GREEN BAY vs. *WASHINGTON
RS: Packers lead series, 13-12-1
PS: Series tied, 1-1
1932—Packers, 21-0 (B)
1933—Tie, 7-7 (GB)
    Redskins, 20-7 (B)
1934—Packers, 10-0 (B)
1936—Packers, 31-2 (Mil)
    Packers, 7-3 (B)
    **Packers, 21-6 (New York)
1937—Redskins, 14-6 (W)
1939—Packers, 24-14 (Mil)
1941—Packers, 22-17 (W)
1943—Redskins, 33-7 (Mil)
1946—Packers, 20-7 (W)
1947—Packers, 27-10 (Mil)
1948—Redskins, 23-7 (Mil)
1949—Redskins, 30-0 (W)
1950—Packers, 35-21 (Mil)
1952—Packers, 35-20 (Mil)
1958—Redskins, 37-21 (W)
1959—Packers, 21-0 (GB)
1968—Packers, 27-7 (W)
1972—Packers, 21-16 (W)
    ***Redskins, 16-3 (W)
1974—Redskins, 17-6 (GB)
1977—Redskins, 10-9 (W)
1979—Redskins, 38-21 (W)
1983—Packers, 48-47 (GB)
1986—Redskins, 16-7 (GB)
1988—Redskins, 20-17 (Mil)
(RS Pts.—Packers 459, Redskins 434)
(PS Pts.—Packers 24, Redskins 22)
*Franchise in Boston prior to 1937 and
known as Braves prior to 1933
**NFL Championship
***NFC Divisional Playoff

HOUSTON vs. ARIZONA
RS: Cardinals lead series, 3-2;
See Arizona vs. Houston
HOUSTON vs. ATLANTA
RS: Falcons lead series, 5-3;
See Atlanta vs. Houston
HOUSTON vs. BUFFALO
RS: Oilers lead series, 20-12
PS: Bills lead series, 2-0;
See Buffalo vs. Houston
HOUSTON vs. CHICAGO
RS: Oilers lead series, 4-2;
See Chicago vs. Houston
HOUSTON vs. CINCINNATI
RS: Oilers lead series, 25-24-1
PS: Bengals lead series, 1-0;
See Cincinnati vs. Houston
HOUSTON vs. CLEVELAND
RS: Browns lead series, 27-20
PS: Oilers lead series, 1-0;
See Cleveland vs. Houston
HOUSTON vs. DALLAS

RS: Cowboys lead series, 4-3;
See Dallas vs. Houston
HOUSTON vs. DENVER
RS: Oilers lead series, 19-11-1
PS: Broncos lead series, 2-1;
See Denver vs. Houston
HOUSTON vs. DETROIT
RS: Oilers lead series, 4-2;
See Detroit vs. Houston
HOUSTON vs. GREEN BAY
RS: Series tied, 3-3;
See Green Bay vs. Houston
HOUSTON vs. *INDIANAPOLIS
RS: Oilers lead series, 7-6
1970—Colts, 24-20 (B)
1973—Oilers, 31-27 (B)
1976—Colts, 38-14 (B)
1979—Oilers, 28-16 (B)
1980—Oilers, 21-16 (H)
1983—Colts, 20-10 (B)
1984—Colts, 35-21 (H)
1985—Colts, 34-16 (I)
1986—Oilers, 31-17 (H)
1987—Colts, 51-27 (I)
1988—Oilers, 17-14 (I) OT
1990—Oilers, 24-10 (H)
1992—Oilers, 20-10 (I)
(RS Pts.—Colts 312, Oilers 280)
*Franchise in Baltimore prior to 1984

HOUSTON vs. *KANSAS CITY
RS: Chiefs lead series, 21-17
PS: Chiefs lead series, 2-0
1960—Oilers, 20-10 (H)
    Texans, 24-0 (D)
1961—Texans, 26-21 (D)
    Oilers, 38-7 (H)
1962—Texans, 31-7 (H)
    Oilers, 14-6 (D)
    **Texans, 20-17 (H) OT
1963—Chiefs, 28-7 (KC)
    Oilers, 28-7 (H)
1964—Chiefs, 28-7 (KC)
    Chiefs, 28-19 (H)
1965—Chiefs, 52-21 (KC)
    Oilers, 38-36 (H)
1966—Chiefs, 48-23 (KC)
1967—Chiefs, 25-20 (H)
    Oilers, 24-19 (KC)
1968—Chiefs, 26-21 (H)
    Chiefs, 24-10 (KC)
1969—Chiefs, 24-0 (KC)
1970—Chiefs, 24-9 (KC)
1971—Chiefs, 20-16 (H)
1973—Chiefs, 38-14 (KC)
1974—Chiefs, 17-7 (H)
1975—Chiefs, 17-13 (KC)
1977—Oilers, 34-20 (H)
1978—Oilers, 20-17 (KC)
1979—Oilers, 20-6 (H)
1980—Chiefs, 21-20 (KC)
1981—Chiefs, 23-10 (KC)
1983—Chiefs, 13-10 (H) OT
1984—Oilers, 17-16 (KC)
1985—Chiefs, 23-20 (H)
1986—Chiefs, 27-13 (KC)
1988—Oilers, 7-6 (H)
1989—Chiefs, 34-0 (KC)
1990—Chiefs, 27-10 (KC)
1991—Oilers, 17-7 (H)
1992—Oilers, 23-20 (H) OT
1993—Oilers, 30-0 (H)
    ***Chiefs, 28-20 (H)
(RS Pts.—Chiefs 801, Oilers 652)
(PS Pts.—Chiefs 48, Oilers 37)
*Franchise in Dallas prior to 1963 and
known as Texans
**AFL Championship
***AFC Divisional Playoff

HOUSTON vs. *L.A. RAIDERS
RS: Raiders lead series, 19-13
PS: Raiders lead series, 3-0
1960—Oilers, 37-22 (O)
    Raiders, 14-13 (H)

1961—Oilers, 55-0 (H)
Oilers, 47-16 (O)
1962—Oilers, 28-20 (O)
Oilers, 32-17 (H)
1963—Raiders, 24-13 (H)
Raiders, 52-49 (H)
1964—Oilers, 42-28 (H)
Raiders, 20-10 (O)
1965—Raiders, 21-17 (O)
Raiders, 33-21 (H)
1966—Oilers, 31-0 (H)
Raiders, 38-23 (O)
1967—Raiders, 19-7 (H)
**Raiders, 40-7 (O)
1968—Raiders, 24-15 (H)
1969—Raiders, 21-17 (O)
***Raiders, 56-7 (O)
1971—Raiders, 41-21 (O)
1972—Raiders, 34-0 (H)
1973—Raiders, 17-6 (H)
1975—Oilers, 27-26 (O)
1976—Raiders, 14-13 (H)
1977—Raiders, 34-29 (O)
1978—Raiders, 21-17 (O)
1979—Oilers, 31-17 (H)
1980—****Raiders, 27-7 (O)
1981—Oilers, 17-16 (H)
1983—Raiders, 20-6 (LA)
1984—Raiders, 24-14 (H)
1986—Raiders, 28-17 (H)
1988—Oilers, 38-35 (H)
1989—Oilers, 23-7 (H)
1991—Oilers, 47-17 (H)
(RS Pts.—Oilers 763, Raiders 720)
(PS Pts.—Raiders 123, Oilers 21)
*Franchise in Oakland prior to 1982
**AFL Championship
***Inter-Divisional Playoff
****AFC First-Round Playoff
HOUSTON vs. L.A. RAMS
RS: Rams lead series, 5-2
1973—Rams, 31-26 (H)
1978—Rams, 10-6 (H)
1981—Oilers, 27-20 (LA)
1984—Rams, 27-16 (LA)
1987—Oilers, 20-16 (H)
1990—Rams, 17-13 (LA)
1993—Rams, 28-13 (H)
(RS Pts.—Rams 149, Oilers 121)
HOUSTON vs. MIAMI
RS: Series tied, 11-11
PS: Oilers lead series, 1-0
1966—Dolphins, 20-13 (H)
Dolphins, 29-28 (M)
1967—Oilers, 17-14 (H)
Oilers, 41-10 (M)
1968—Oilers, 24-10 (H)
Dolphins, 24-7 (H)
1969—Oilers, 22-10 (H)
Oilers, 32-7 (M)
1970—Dolphins, 20-10 (H)
1972—Dolphins, 34-13 (M)
1975—Oilers, 20-19 (H)
1977—Dolphins, 27-7 (M)
1978—Dolphins, 35-30 (H)
*Oilers, 17-9 (M)
1979—Oilers, 9-6 (M)
1981—Dolphins, 16-10 (H)
1983—Dolphins, 24-17 (H)
1984—Dolphins, 28-10 (M)
1985—Oilers, 26-23 (H)
1986—Dolphins, 28-7 (M)
1989—Oilers, 39-7 (H)
1991—Oilers, 17-13 (M)
1992—Dolphins, 19-16 (M)
(RS Pts.—Oilers 420, Dolphins 418)
(PS Pts.—Oilers 17, Dolphins 9)
*AFC First Round Playoff
HOUSTON vs. MINNESOTA
RS: Series tied, 3-3
1974—Vikings, 51-10 (M)
1980—Oilers, 20-16 (H)
1983—Vikings, 34-14 (M)

1986—Oilers, 23-10 (H)
1989—Vikings, 38-7 (M)
1992—Oilers, 17-13 (M)
(RS Pts.—Vikings 162, Oilers 91)
HOUSTON vs. *NEW ENGLAND
RS: Patriots lead series, 17-14-1
PS: Oilers lead series, 1-0
1960—Oilers, 24-10 (B)
Oilers, 37-21 (H)
1961—Tie, 31-31 (B)
Oilers, 27-15 (H)
1962—Patriots, 34-21 (B)
Oilers, 21-17 (H)
1963—Patriots, 45-3 (B)
Patriots, 46-28 (H)
1964—Patriots, 25-24 (B)
Patriots, 34-17 (H)
1965—Oilers, 31-10 (H)
Patriots, 42-14 (B)
1966—Patriots, 27-21 (B)
Patriots, 38-14 (H)
1967—Patriots, 18-7 (B)
Oilers, 27-6 (H)
1968—Oilers, 16-0 (B)
Oilers, 45-17 (H)
1969—Patriots, 24-0 (B)
Oilers, 27-23 (H)
1971—Patriots, 28-20 (NE)
1973—Patriots, 32-0 (H)
1975—Oilers, 7-0 (NE)
1978—Oilers, 26-23 (NE)
**Oilers, 31-14 (NE)
1980—Oilers, 38-34 (H)
1981—Patriots, 38-10 (NE)
1982—Patriots, 29-21 (NE)
1987—Patriots, 21-7 (H)
1988—Oilers, 31-6 (H)
1989—Patriots, 23-13 (NE)
1991—Patriots, 24-20 (NE)
1993—Oilers, 28-14 (NE)
(RS Pts.—Patriots 755, Oilers 656)
(PS Pts.—Oilers 31, Patriots 14)
*Franchise in Boston prior to 1971
**AFC Divisional Playoff
HOUSTON vs. NEW ORLEANS
RS: Saints lead series, 4-3-1
1971—Tie, 13-13 (H)
1976—Oilers, 31-26 (NO)
1978—Oilers, 17-12 (NO)
1981—Saints, 27-24 (H)
1984—Saints, 27-10 (H)
1987—Saints, 24-10 (NO)
1990—Saints, 23-10 (H)
1993—Saints, 33-21 (NO)
(RS Pts.—Saints 172, Oilers 149)
HOUSTON vs. N.Y. GIANTS
RS: Giants lead series, 4-0
1973—Giants, 34-14 (NY)
1982—Giants, 17-14 (NY)
1985—Giants, 35-14 (H)
1991—Giants, 24-20 (NY)
(RS Pts.—Giants 110, Oilers 62)
HOUSTON vs. *N.Y. JETS
RS: Oilers lead series, 17-12-1
PS: Oilers lead series, 1-0
1960—Oilers, 27-21 (H)
Oilers, 42-28 (NY)
1961—Oilers, 49-13 (H)
Oilers, 48-21 (NY)
1962—Oilers, 56-17 (H)
Oilers, 44-10 (NY)
1963—Jets, 24-17 (NY)
Oilers, 31-27 (H)
1964—Jets, 24-21 (NY)
Oilers, 33-17 (H)
1965—Oilers, 27-21 (H)
Jets, 41-14 (NY)
1966—Jets, 52-13 (NY)
Oilers, 24-0 (H)
1967—Tie, 28-28 (NY)
1968—Jets, 20-14 (H)
Jets, 26-7 (NY)
1969—Jets, 26-17 (NY)

Jets, 34-26 (H)
1972—Oilers, 26-20 (H)
1974—Oilers, 27-22 (NY)
1977—Oilers, 20-0 (H)
1979—Oilers, 27-24 (H) OT
1980—Jets, 31-28 (NY) OT
1981—Jets, 33-17 (NY)
1984—Oilers, 31-20 (H)
1988—Jets, 45-3 (NY)
1990—Jets, 17-12 (H)
1991—Oilers, 23-20 (NY)
**Oilers, 17-10 (H)
1993—Oilers, 24-0 (H)
(RS Pts.—Oilers 776, Jets 682)
(PS Pts.—Oilers 17, Jets 10)
*Jets known as Titans prior to 1963
**AFC First-Round Playoff
HOUSTON vs. PHILADELPHIA
RS: Eagles lead series, 5-0
1972—Eagles, 18-17 (H)
1979—Eagles, 26-20 (H)
1982—Eagles, 35-14 (P)
1988—Eagles, 32-23 (P)
1991—Eagles, 13-6 (H)
(RS Pts.—Eagles 124, Oilers 80)
HOUSTON vs. PITTSBURGH
RS: Steelers lead series, 29-18
PS: Steelers lead series, 3-0
1970—Oilers, 19-7 (P)
Steelers, 7-3 (H)
1971—Steelers, 23-16 (P)
Oilers, 29-3 (H)
1972—Steelers, 24-7 (P)
Steelers, 9-3 (H)
1973—Steelers, 36-7 (H)
Steelers, 33-7 (P)
1974—Steelers, 13-7 (H)
Oilers, 13-10 (P)
1975—Steelers, 24-17 (P)
Steelers, 32-9 (H)
1976—Steelers, 32-16 (P)
Steelers, 21-0 (H)
1977—Oilers, 27-10 (H)
Steelers, 27-10 (P)
1978—Oilers, 24-17 (P)
Steelers, 13-3 (H)
*Steelers, 34-5 (P)
1979—Steelers, 38-7 (P)
Oilers, 20-17 (H)
*Steelers, 27-13 (P)
1980—Steelers, 31-17 (P)
Oilers, 6-0 (H)
1981—Steelers, 26-13 (P)
Oilers, 21-20 (H)
1982—Steelers, 24-10 (H)
1983—Steelers, 40-28 (H)
Steelers, 17-10 (P)
1984—Steelers, 35-7 (P)
Oilers, 23-20 (H) OT
1985—Steelers, 20-0 (P)
Steelers, 30-7 (H)
1986—Steelers, 22-16 (H) OT
Steelers, 21-10 (P)
1987—Oilers, 23-3 (P)
Oilers, 24-16 (H)
1988—Oilers, 34-14 (P)
Steelers, 37-34 (H)
1989—Oilers, 27-0 (H)
Oilers, 23-16 (P)
**Steelers, 26-23 (H)
1990—Steelers, 20-9 (P)
Oilers, 34-14 (H)
1991—Steelers, 26-14 (P)
Oilers, 31-6 (H)
1992—Steelers, 29-24 (H)
Steelers, 21-20 (P)
1993—Oilers, 23-3 (H)
Oilers, 26-17 (P)
(RS Pts.—Steelers 924, Oilers 758)
(PS Pts.—Steelers 87, Oilers 41)
*AFC Championship
**AFC First-Round Playoff
HOUSTON vs. *SAN DIEGO

RS: Chargers lead series, 18-13-1
PS: Oilers lead series, 3-0
1960—Oilers, 38-28 (H)
Chargers, 24-21 (LA)
**Oilers, 24-16 (H)
1961—Chargers, 34-24 (SD)
Oilers, 33-13 (H)
**Oilers, 10-3 (SD)
1962—Oilers, 42-17 (SD)
Oilers, 33-27 (H)
1963—Chargers, 27-0 (SD)
Chargers 20-14 (H)
1964—Chargers, 27-21 (SD)
Chargers, 20-17 (H)
1965—Chargers, 31-14 (SD)
Chargers, 37-26 (H)
1966—Chargers, 28-22 (H)
1967—Chargers, 13-3 (SD)
Oilers, 24-17 (H)
1968—Chargers, 30-14 (SD)
1969—Chargers, 21-17 (H)
1970—Tie, 31-31 (SD)
1971—Oilers, 49-33 (H)
1972—Chargers, 34-20 (SD)
1974—Oilers, 21-14 (H)
1975—Oilers, 33-17 (H)
1976—Chargers, 30-27 (SD)
1978—Chargers, 45-24 (H)
1979—***Oilers, 17-14 (SD)
1984—Chargers, 31-14 (SD)
1985—Oilers, 37-35 (H)
1986—Chargers, 27-0 (SD)
1987—Oilers, 33-18 (H)
1989—Oilers, 34-27 (SD)
1990—Oilers, 17-7 (SD)
1992—Oilers, 27-0 (H)
1993—Chargers, 18-17 (SD)
(RS Pts.—Chargers 781, Oilers 747)
(PS Pts.—Oilers 51, Chargers 33)
*Franchise in Los Angeles prior to 1961
**AFL Championship
***AFC Divisional Playoff
HOUSTON vs. SAN FRANCISCO
RS: 49ers lead series, 5-3
1970—49ers, 30-20 (H)
1975—Oilers, 27-13 (SF)
1978—Oilers, 20-19 (H)
1981—49ers, 28-6 (SF)
1984—49ers, 34-21 (H)
1987—49ers, 27-20 (SF)
1990—49ers, 24-21 (H)
1993—Oilers, 10-7 (SF)
(RS Pts.—49ers 182, Oilers 145)
HOUSTON vs. SEATTLE
RS: Series tied, 4-4
PS: Oilers lead series, 1-0
1977—Oilers, 22-10 (S)
1979—Seahawks, 34-14 (S)
1980—Seahawks, 26-7 (H)
1981—Oilers, 35-17 (H)
1982—Oilers, 23-21 (H)
1987—*Oilers, 23-20 (H) OT
1988—Seahawks, 27-24 (S)
1990—Seahawks, 13-10 (S) OT
1993—Oilers, 24-14 (H)
(RS Pts.—Seahawks 162, Oilers 159)
(PS Pts.—Oilers 23, Seahawks 20)
*AFC First-Round Playoff
HOUSTON vs. TAMPA BAY
RS: Oilers lead series, 3-1
1976—Oilers, 20-0 (H)
1980—Oilers, 20-14 (H)
1983—Buccaneers, 33-24 (TB)
1989—Oilers, 20-17 (H)
(RS Pts.—Oilers 84, Buccaneers 64)
HOUSTON vs. WASHINGTON
RS: Series tied, 3-3
1971—Redskins, 22-13 (W)
1975—Oilers, 13-10 (W)
1979—Oilers, 29-27 (W)
1985—Redskins, 16-13 (W)
1988—Oilers, 41-17 (H)
1991—Redskins, 16-13 (W) OT

(RS Pts.—Oilers 122, Redskins 108)

INDIANAPOLIS vs. ARIZONA
RS: Cardinals lead series, 6-5;
See Arizona vs. Indianapolis

INDIANAPOLIS vs. ATLANTA
RS: Colts lead series, 10-0;
See Atlanta vs. Indianapolis

INDIANAPOLIS vs. BUFFALO
RS: Bills lead series, 26-20-1;
See Buffalo vs. Indianapolis

INDIANAPOLIS vs. CHICAGO
RS: Colts lead series, 21-16;
See Chicago vs. Indianapolis

INDIANAPOLIS vs. CINCINNATI
RS: Colts lead series, 8-5;
PS: Colts lead series, 1-0;
See Cincinnati vs. Indianapolis

INDIANAPOLIS vs. CLEVELAND
RS: Browns lead series, 12-7
PS: Series tied, 2-2;
See Cleveland vs. Indianapolis

INDIANAPOLIS vs. DALLAS
RS: Cowboys lead series, 7-2
PS: Colts lead series, 1-0;
See Dallas vs. Indianapolis

INDIANAPOLIS vs. DENVER
RS: Broncos lead series, 9-2;
See Denver vs. Indianapolis

INDIANAPOLIS vs. DETROIT
RS: Series tied, 17-17-2;
See Detroit vs. Indianapolis

INDIANAPOLIS vs. GREEN BAY
RS: Series tied, 18-18-1
PS: Packers lead series, 1-0;
See Green Bay vs. Indianapolis

INDIANAPOLIS vs. HOUSTON
RS: Oilers lead series, 7-6;
See Houston vs. Indianapolis

*INDIANAPOLIS vs. KANSAS CITY
RS: Chiefs lead series, 6-4
1970—Chiefs, 44-24 (B)
1972—Chiefs, 24-10 (KC)
1975—Colts, 28-14 (B)
1977—Colts, 17-6 (KC)
1979—Chiefs, 14-0 (KC)
    Chiefs, 10-7 (B)
1980—Colts, 31-24 (KC)
    Chiefs, 38-28 (B)
1985—Chiefs, 20-7 (KC)
1990—Colts, 23-19 (I)
(RS Pts.—Chiefs 213, Colts 175)
Franchise in Baltimore prior to 1984

*INDIANAPOLIS vs **L.A. RAIDERS
RS: Raiders lead series, 4-2
PS: Series tied, 1-1
1970—***Colts, 27-17 (B)
1971—Colts, 37-14 (O)
1973—Raiders, 34-21 (B)
1975—Raiders, 31-20 (B)
1977—****Raiders, 37-31 (B) OT
1984—Raiders, 21-7 (LA)
1986—Colts, 30-24 (LA)
1991—Raiders, 16-0 (LA)
(RS Pts.—Raiders 140, Colts 115)
(PS Pts.—Colts 58, Raiders 54)
Franchise in Baltimore prior to 1984
**Franchise in Oakland prior to 1982*
***AFC Championship*
****AFC Divisional Playoff*

*INDIANAPOLIS vs. L.A. RAMS
RS: Colts lead series, 20-16-2
1953—Rams, 21-13 (B)
    Rams, 45-2 (LA)
1954—Rams, 48-0 (B)
    Colts, 22-21 (LA)
1955—Tie, 17-17 (B)
    Rams, 20-14 (LA)
1956—Colts, 56-21 (B)
    Rams, 31-7 (LA)
1957—Colts, 31-14 (B)
    Rams, 37-21 (LA)
1958—Colts, 34-7 (B)

    Rams, 30-28 (LA)
1959—Colts, 35-21 (B)
    Colts, 45-26 (LA)
1960—Colts, 31-17 (B)
    Rams, 10-3 (LA)
1961—Colts, 27-24 (B)
    Rams, 34-17 (LA)
1962—Colts, 30-27 (B)
    Colts, 14-2 (LA)
1963—Rams, 17-16 (LA)
    Colts, 19-16 (B)
1964—Colts, 35-20 (B)
    Colts, 24-7 (LA)
1965—Colts, 35-20 (B)
    Colts, 20-17 (LA)
1966—Colts, 17-3 (LA)
    Rams, 23-7 (B)
1967—Tie, 24-24 (B)
    Rams, 34-10 (LA)
1968—Colts, 27-10 (B)
    Colts, 28-24 (LA)
1969—Rams, 27-20 (B)
    Colts, 13-7 (LA)
1971—Colts, 24-17 (B)
1975—Rams, 24-13 (LA)
1986—Rams, 24-7 (I)
1989—Rams, 31-17 (LA)
(RS Pts.—Rams 818, Colts 803)
Franchise in Baltimore prior to 1984

*INDIANAPOLIS vs. MIAMI
RS: Dolphins lead series, 34-14
PS: Dolphins lead series, 1-0
1970—Colts, 35-0 (B)
    Dolphins, 34-17 (M)
1971—Dolphins, 17-14 (M)
    Colts, 14-3 (B)
    **Dolphins, 21-0 (M)
1972—Dolphins, 23-0 (B)
    Dolphins, 16-0 (M)
1973—Dolphins, 44-0 (M)
    Colts, 16-3 (B)
1974—Dolphins, 17-7 (M)
    Dolphins, 17-16 (B)
1975—Colts, 33-17 (M)
    Colts, 10-7 (B) OT
1976—Colts, 28-14 (B)
    Colts, 17-16 (M)
1977—Colts, 45-28 (B)
    Dolphins, 17-6 (M)
1978—Dolphins, 42-0 (B)
    Dolphins, 26-8 (M)
1979—Dolphins, 19-0 (M)
    Dolphins, 28-24 (B)
1980—Colts, 30-17 (M)
    Dolphins, 24-14 (B)
1981—Dolphins, 31-28 (B)
    Dolphins, 27-10 (M)
1982—Dolphins, 24-20 (M)
    Dolphins, 34-7 (B)
1983—Dolphins, 21-7 (B)
    Dolphins, 37-0 (M)
1984—Dolphins, 44-7 (M)
    Dolphins, 35-17 (I)
1985—Dolphins, 30-13 (M)
    Dolphins, 34-20 (I)
1986—Dolphins, 30-10 (M)
    Dolphins, 17-13 (I)
1987—Dolphins, 23-10 (I)
    Colts, 40-21 (M)
1988—Colts, 15-13 (I)
    Colts, 31-28 (M)
1989—Dolphins, 19-13 (M)
    Colts, 42-13 (I)
1990—Dolphins, 27-7 (I)
    Dolphins, 23-17 (M)
1991—Dolphins, 17-6 (M)
    Dolphins, 10-6 (I)
1992—Colts, 31-20 (M)
    Dolphins, 28-0 (I)
1993—Dolphins, 24-20 (I)
    Dolphins, 41-27 (M)
(RS Pts.—Dolphins 1,100, Colts 751)
(PS Pts.—Dolphins 21, Colts 0)

Franchise in Baltimore prior to 1984
**AFC Championship*

*INDIANAPOLIS vs. MINNESOTA
RS: Colts lead series, 11-6-1
PS: Colts lead series, 1-0
1961—Colts, 34-33 (B)
    Vikings, 28-20 (M)
1962—Colts, 34-7 (M)
    Colts, 42-17 (B)
1963—Colts, 37-34 (M)
    Colts, 41-10 (B)
1964—Vikings, 34-24 (M)
    Colts, 17-14 (B)
1965—Colts, 35-16 (B)
    Colts, 41-21 (M)
1966—Colts, 38-23 (M)
    Colts, 20-17 (B)
1967—Tie, 20-20 (M)
1968—Colts, 21-9 (B)
    **Colts, 24-14 (B)
1969—Vikings, 52-14 (M)
1971—Vikings, 10-3 (M)
1982—Vikings, 13-10 (M)
1988—Vikings, 12-3 (M)
(RS Pts.—Colts 454, Vikings 370)
(PS Pts.—Colts 24, Vikings 14)
Franchise in Baltimore prior to 1984
**Conference Championship*

*INDIANAPOLIS vs. **NEW ENGLAND
RS: Patriots lead series, 27-20
1970—Colts, 14-6 (Bos)
    Colts, 27-3 (Balt)
1971—Colts, 23-3 (NE)
    Patriots, 21-17 (Balt)
1972—Colts, 24-17 (NE)
    Colts, 31-0 (Balt)
1973—Patriots, 24-16 (NE)
    Colts, 18-13 (Balt)
1974—Patriots, 42-3 (NE)
    Patriots, 27-17 (Balt)
1975—Patriots, 21-10 (NE)
    Colts, 34-21 (Balt)
1976—Colts, 27-13 (NE)
    Patriots, 21-14 (Balt)
1977—Patriots, 17-3 (NE)
    Colts, 30-24 (Balt)
1978—Colts, 34-27 (NE)
    Patriots, 35-14 (Balt)
1979—Patriots, 31-26 (Balt)
    Patriots, 50-21 (NE)
1980—Patriots, 37-21 (Balt)
    Patriots, 47-14 (NE)
1981—Colts, 29-28 (NE)
    Colts, 23-21 (Balt)
1982—Patriots, 24-13 (Balt)
1983—Colts, 29-23 (NE) OT
    Colts, 12-7 (Balt)
1984—Patriots, 50-17 (I)
    Patriots, 16-10 (NE)
1985—Patriots, 34-15 (NE)
    Patriots, 38-31 (I)
1986—Patriots, 33-3 (NE)
    Patriots, 30-21 (I)
1987—Colts, 30-16 (I)
    Patriots, 24-0 (NE)
1988—Patriots, 21-17 (NE)
    Colts, 24-21 (I)
1989—Patriots, 23-20 (I) OT
    Patriots, 22-16 (NE)
1990—Patriots, 16-14 (I)
    Colts, 13-10 (NE)
1991—Patriots, 16-7 (I)
    Patriots, 23-17 (NE) OT
1992—Patriots, 37-34 (I) OT
    Colts, 6-0 (NE)
1993—Colts, 9-6 (I)
    Patriots, 38-0 (NE)
(RS Pts.—Patriots 1,072, Colts 860)
Franchise in Baltimore prior to 1984
**Franchise in Boston prior to 1971*

*INDIANAPOLIS vs. NEW ORLEANS
RS: Colts lead series, 3-2
1967—Colts, 30-10 (B)

1969—Colts, 30-10 (NO)
1973—Colts, 14-10 (B)
1986—Saints, 17-14 (I)
1989—Saints, 41-6 (NO)
(RS Pts.—Colts 94, Saints 88)
Franchise in Baltimore prior to 1984

*INDIANAPOLIS vs. N.Y. GIANTS
RS: Series tied, 5-5
PS: Colts lead series, 2-0
1954—Colts, 20-14 (B)
1955—Giants, 17-7 (NY)
1958—Giants, 24-21 (NY)
    **Colts, 23-17 (NY) OT
1959—**Colts, 31-16 (B)
1963—Giants, 37-28 (B)
1968—Colts, 26-0 (NY)
1971—Colts, 31-7 (NY)
1975—Colts, 21-0 (NY)
1979—Colts, 31-7 (NY)
1990—Giants, 24-7 (I)
1993—Giants, 20-6 (NY)
(RS Pts.—Colts 198, Giants 150)
(PS Pts.—Colts 54, Giants 33)
Franchise in Baltimore prior to 1984
**NFL Championship*

*INDIANAPOLIS vs. N.Y. JETS
RS: Colts lead series, 27-20
PS: Jets lead series, 1-0
1968—**Jets 16-7 (Miami)
1970—Colts, 29-22 (NY)
    Colts, 35-20 (B)
1971—Colts, 22-0 (B)
    Colts, 14-13 (NY)
1972—Jets, 44-34 (B)
    Jets, 24-20 (NY)
1973—Jets, 34-10 (B)
    Jets, 20-17 (NY)
1974—Colts, 35-20 (NY)
    Jets, 45-38 (B)
1975—Colts, 45-28 (NY)
    Colts, 52-19 (B)
1976—Colts, 20-0 (NY)
    Colts, 33-16 (B)
1977—Colts, 20-12 (B)
    Colts, 33-12 (B)
1978—Jets, 33-10 (B)
    Jets, 24-16 (NY)
1979—Colts, 10-8 (B)
    Jets, 30-17 (NY)
1980—Colts, 17-14 (NY)
    Colts, 35-21 (B)
1981—Jets, 41-14 (B)
    Jets, 25-0 (NY)
1982—Jets, 37-0 (NY)
1983—Colts, 17-14 (NY)
    Jets, 10-6 (B)
1984—Jets, 23-14 (I)
    Colts, 9-5 (NY)
1985—Jets, 25-20 (NY)
    Jets, 35-17 (I)
1986—Jets, 26-7 (I)
    Jets, 31-16 (NY)
1987—Colts, 6-0 (I)
    Colts, 19-14 (NY)
1988—Colts, 38-14 (I)
    Jets, 34-16 (NY)
1989—Colts, 17-10 (NY)
    Colts, 27-10 (I)
1990—Colts, 17-14 (I)
    Colts, 29-21 (NY)
1991—Jets, 17-6 (I)
    Colts, 28-27 (NY)
1992—Colts, 6-3 (I) OT
    Colts, 10-6 (NY)
1993—Jets, 31-17 (I)
    Colts, 9-6 (NY)
(RS Pts.—Jets 938, Colts 927)
(PS Pts.—Jets 16, Colts 7)
Franchise in Baltimore prior to 1984
**Super Bowl III*

*INDIANAPOLIS vs. PHILADELPHIA
RS: Series tied, 6-6
1953—Eagles, 45-14 (P)

1965—Colts, 34-24 (B)
1967—Colts, 38-6 (P)
1969—Colts, 24-20 (B)
1970—Colts, 29-10 (B)
1974—Eagles, 30-10 (P)
1978—Eagles, 17-14 (B)
1981—Eagles, 38-13 (P)
1983—Colts, 22-21 (P)
1984—Eagles, 16-7 (P)
1990—Colts, 24-23 (P)
1993—Eagles, 20-10 (I)
(RS Pts.—Eagles 270, Colts 239)
*Franchise in Baltimore prior to 1984
INDIANAPOLIS vs. PITTSBURGH
RS: Steelers lead series, 10-4
PS: Steelers lead series, 2-0
1957—Steelers, 19-13 (B)
1968—Colts, 41-7 (P)
1971—Colts, 34-21 (B)
1974—Steelers, 30-0 (B)
1975—**Steelers, 28-10 (P)
1976—**Steelers, 40-14 (B)
1977—31-21 (P)
1978—Steelers, 35-13 (P)
1979—Steelers, 17-13 (P)
1980—Steelers, 20-17 (B)
1983—Steelers, 24-13 (B)
1984—Colts, 17-16 (I)
1985—Steelers, 45-3 (P)
1987—Steelers, 21-7 (P)
1991—Steelers, 21-3 (I)
1992—Steelers, 30-14 (P)
(RS Pts.—Steelers 327, Colts 219)
(PS Pts.—Steelers 68, Colts 24)
*Franchise in Baltimore prior to 1984
**AFC Divisional Playoff
INDIANAPOLIS vs. SAN DIEGO
RS: Chargers lead series, 9-5
1970—Colts, 16-14 (SD)
1972—Chargers, 23-20 (B)
1976—Colts, 37-21 (SD)
1981—Chargers, 43-14 (B)
1982—Chargers, 44-26 (SD)
1984—Chargers, 38-10 (I)
1986—Chargers, 17-3 (I)
1987—Chargers, 16-13 (I)
      Colts, 20-7 (SD)
1988—Colts, 16-0 (SD)
1989—Colts, 10-6 (I)
1992—Chargers, 34-14 (I)
      Chargers, 26-0 (SD)
1993—Chargers, 31-0 (I)
(RS Pts.—Chargers 320, Colts 199)
*Franchise in Baltimore prior to 1984
INDIANAPOLIS vs. SAN FRANCISCO
RS: Colts lead series, 21-16
1953—49ers, 38-21 (B)
      49ers, 45-14 (SF)
1954—Colts, 17-13 (B)
      49ers, 10-7 (SF)
1955—Colts, 26-14 (B)
      49ers, 35-24 (SF)
1956—49ers, 20-17 (B)
      49ers, 30-17 (SF)
1957—Colts, 27-21 (B)
      49ers, 17-13 (SF)
1958—Colts, 35-27 (B)
      49ers, 21-12 (SF)
1959—Colts, 45-14 (B)
      Colts, 34-14 (SF)
1960—49ers, 30-22 (B)
      49ers, 34-10 (SF)
1961—Colts, 20-17 (B)
      Colts, 27-24 (SF)
1962—49ers, 21-13 (B)
      Colts, 22-3 (SF)
1963—Colts, 20-14 (SF)
      Colts, 20-3 (B)
1964—Colts, 37-7 (B)
      Colts, 14-3 (SF)
1965—Colts, 27-24 (B)
      Colts, 34-28 (SF)
1966—Colts, 36-14 (B)

Colts, 30-14 (SF)
1967—Colts, 41-7 (B)
      Colts, 26-9 (SF)
1968—Colts, 27-10 (B)
      Colts, 42-14 (SF)
1969—49ers, 24-21 (B)
      49ers, 20-17 (SF)
1972—49ers, 24-21 (SF)
1986—49ers, 35-14 (SF)
1989—49ers, 30-24 (I)
(RS Pts.—Colts 874, 49ers 728)
*Franchise in Baltimore prior to 1984
INDIANAPOLIS vs. SEATTLE
RS: Colts lead series, 2-1
1977—Colts, 29-14 (S)
1978—Colts, 17-14 (S)
1991—Seahawks, 31-3 (S)
(RS Pts.—Seahawks 59, Colts 49)
*Franchise in Baltimore prior to 1984
INDIANAPOLIS vs. TAMPA BAY
RS: Colts lead series, 5-2
1976—Colts, 42-17 (B)
1979—Buccaneers, 29-26 (B) OT
1985—Colts, 31-23 (TB)
1987—Colts, 24-6 (I)
1988—Colts, 35-31 (I)
1991—Buccaneers, 17-3 (TB)
1992—Colts, 24-14 (TB)
(RS Pts.—Colts 185, Buccaneers 137)
*Franchise in Baltimore prior to 1984
INDIANAPOLIS vs. WASHINGTON
RS: Colts lead series, 16-7
1953—Colts, 27-17 (B)
1954—Redskins, 24-21 (W)
1955—Redskins, 14-13 (B)
1956—Colts, 19-17 (B)
1957—Colts, 21-17 (W)
1958—Colts, 35-10 (B)
1959—Redskins, 27-24 (B)
1960—Colts, 20-0 (B)
1961—Colts, 27-6 (W)
1962—Colts, 34-21 (B)
1963—Colts, 36-20 (W)
1964—Colts, 45-17 (B)
1965—Colts, 38-7 (W)
1966—Colts, 37-10 (B)
1967—Colts, 17-13 (W)
1969—Colts, 41-17 (B)
1973—Redskins, 22-14 (W)
1977—Colts, 10-3 (B)
1978—Colts, 21-17 (B)
1981—Redskins, 38-14 (W)
1984—Redskins, 35-7 (I)
1990—Colts, 35-28 (I)
1993—Redskins, 30-24 (W)
(RS Pts.—Colts 580, Redskins 410)
*Franchise in Baltimore prior to 1984

KANSAS CITY vs. ARIZONA
RS: Chiefs lead series, 3-1-1;
See Arizona vs. Kansas City
KANSAS CITY vs. ATLANTA
RS: Chiefs lead series, 3-0;
See Atlanta vs. Kansas City
KANSAS CITY vs. BUFFALO
RS: Bills lead series, 15-13-1
PS: Bills lead series, 2-1;
See Buffalo vs. Kansas City
KANSAS CITY vs. CHICAGO
RS: Bears lead series, 4-2;
See Chicago vs. Kansas City
KANSAS CITY vs. CINCINNATI
RS: Chiefs lead series, 11-9;
See Cincinnati vs. Kansas City
KANSAS CITY vs. CLEVELAND
RS: Browns lead series, 7-6-2;
See Cleveland vs. Kansas City
KANSAS CITY vs. DALLAS
RS: Cowboys lead series, 3-2;
See Dallas vs. Kansas City
KANSAS CITY vs. DENVER
RS: Chiefs lead series, 38-29;
See Denver vs. Kansas City

KANSAS CITY vs. DETROIT
RS: Chiefs lead series, 4-3;
See Detroit vs. Kansas City
KANSAS CITY vs. GREEN BAY
RS: Chiefs lead series, 4-1-1
PS: Packers lead series, 1-0;
See Green Bay vs. Kansas City
KANSAS CITY vs. HOUSTON
RS: Chiefs lead series, 21-17
PS: Chiefs lead series, 2-0;
See Houston vs. Kansas City
KANSAS CITY vs. INDIANAPOLIS
RS: Chiefs lead series, 6-4;
See Indianapolis vs. Kansas City
KANSAS CITY vs. **L.A. RAIDERS
RS: Raiders lead series, 35-30-2
PS: Chiefs lead series, 2-1
1960—Texans, 34-16 (O)
      Raiders, 20-19 (D)
1961—Texans, 42-35 (O)
      Texans, 43-11 (D)
1962—Texans, 26-16 (O)
      Texans, 35-7 (D)
1963—Raiders, 10-7 (O)
      Raiders, 22-7 (KC)
1964—Raiders, 21-9 (O)
      Chiefs, 42-7 (KC)
1965—Raiders, 37-10 (O)
      Chiefs, 14-7 (KC)
1966—Chiefs, 32-10 (O)
      Raiders, 34-13 (KC)
1967—Raiders, 23-21 (O)
      Raiders, 44-22 (KC)
1968—Raiders, 24-10 (KC)
      Raiders, 38-21 (O)
      ***Raiders, 41-6 (O)
1969—Raiders, 27-24 (KC)
      Raiders, 10-6 (O)
      ****Chiefs, 17-7 (O)
1970—Tie, 17-17 (KC)
      Raiders, 20-6 (O)
1971—Tie, 20-20 (O)
      Chiefs, 16-14 (KC)
1972—Chiefs, 27-14 (KC)
      Raiders, 26-3 (O)
1973—Chiefs, 16-3 (KC)
      Raiders, 37-7 (O)
1974—Raiders, 27-7 (O)
      Raiders, 7-6 (KC)
1975—Chiefs, 42-10 (KC)
      Raiders, 28-20 (O)
1976—Raiders, 24-21 (KC)
      Raiders, 21-10 (O)
1977—Raiders, 37-28 (KC)
      Raiders, 21-20 (O)
1978—Raiders, 28-6 (O)
      Raiders, 20-10 (KC)
1979—Chiefs, 35-7 (KC)
      Chiefs, 24-21 (O)
1980—Raiders, 27-14 (KC)
      Chiefs, 31-17 (O)
1981—Chiefs, 27-0 (KC)
      Chiefs, 28-17 (O)
1982—Raiders, 21-16 (KC)
1983—Raiders, 21-20 (LA)
      Raiders, 28-20 (KC)
1984—Raiders, 22-20 (KC)
      Raiders, 17-7 (LA)
1985—Chiefs, 36-20 (KC)
      Raiders, 19-10 (LA)
1986—Raiders, 24-17 (KC)
      Chiefs, 20-17 (LA)
1987—Raiders, 35-17 (LA)
      Chiefs, 16-10 (KC)
1988—Raiders, 27-17 (KC)
      Raiders, 17-10 (LA)
1989—Chiefs, 24-19 (KC)
      Raiders, 20-14 (LA)
1990—Chiefs, 9-7 (KC)
      Chiefs, 27-24 (LA)
1991—Chiefs, 24-21 (KC)
      Chiefs, 27-21 (LA)
      †Chiefs, 10-6 (KC)

1992—Chiefs, 27-7 (KC)
      Raiders, 28-7 (LA)
1993—Chiefs, 24-9 (KC)
      Chiefs, 31-20 (LA)
(RS Pts.—Chiefs 1,344, Raiders 1,310)
(PS Pts.—Raiders 54, Chiefs 33)
*Franchise in Dallas prior to 1963 and
known as Texans
**Franchise in Oakland prior to 1982
***Division Playoff
****AFL Championship
†AFC First-Round Playoff
KANSAS CITY vs. L.A. RAMS
RS: Rams lead series, 3-1
1973—Rams, 23-13 (KC)
1982—Rams, 20-14 (LA)
1985—Rams, 16-0 (KC)
1991—Chiefs, 27-20 (LA)
(RS Pts.—Rams 79, Chiefs 54)
KANSAS CITY vs. MIAMI
RS: Chiefs lead series, 10-7
PS: Dolphins lead series, 2-0
1966—Chiefs, 34-16 (KC)
      Chiefs, 19-18 (M)
1967—Chiefs, 24-0 (M)
      Chiefs, 41-0 (KC)
1968—Chiefs, 48-3 (M)
1969—Chiefs, 17-10 (KC)
1971—*Dolphins, 27-24 (KC) OT
1972—Dolphins, 20-10 (KC)
1974—Dolphins, 9-3 (M)
1976—Chiefs, 20-17 (M) OT
1981—Dolphins, 17-7 (KC)
1983—Dolphins, 14-6 (M)
1985—Dolphins, 31-0 (M)
1987—Dolphins, 42-0 (M)
1989—Chiefs, 26-21 (KC)
      Chiefs, 27-24 (M)
1990—**Dolphins, 17-16 (M)
1991—Chiefs, 42-7 (KC)
1993—Dolphins, 30-10 (M)
(RS Pts.—Chiefs 334, Dolphins 279)
(PS Pts.—Dolphins 44, Chiefs 40)
*AFC Divisional Playoff
**AFC First-Round Playoff
KANSAS CITY vs. MINNESOTA
RS: Vikings lead series, 3-2
PS: Chiefs lead series, 1-0
1969—*Chiefs, 23-7 (New Orleans)
1970—Vikings, 27-10 (M)
1974—Vikings, 35-15 (KC)
1981—Chiefs, 10-6 (M)
1990—Chiefs, 24-21 (KC)
1993—Vikings, 30-10 (M)
(RS Pts.—Vikings 119, Chiefs 69)
(PS Pts.—Chiefs 23, Vikings 7)
*Super Bowl IV
KANSAS CITY vs. **NEW ENGLAND
RS: Chiefs lead series, 13-7-3
1960—Patriots, 42-14 (B)
      Texans, 34-0 (D)
1961—Patriots, 18-17 (D)
      Patriots, 28-21 (B)
1962—Texans, 42-28 (D)
      Texans, 27-7 (B)
1963—Tie, 24-24 (B)
      Chiefs, 35-3 (KC)
1964—Patriots, 24-7 (B)
      Patriots, 31-24 (KC)
1965—Chiefs, 27-17 (KC)
      Tie, 10-10 (B)
1966—Chiefs, 43-24 (B)
      Tie, 27-27 (KC)
1967—Chiefs, 33-10 (B)
1968—Chiefs, 31-17 (KC)
1969—Chiefs, 31-0 (B)
1970—Chiefs, 23-10 (KC)
1973—Chiefs, 10-7 (NE)
1977—Patriots, 21-17 (NE)
1981—Patriots, 33-17 (NE)
1990—Chiefs, 37-7 (NE)
1992—Chiefs, 27-20 (NE)
(RS Pts.—Chiefs 578, Patriots 408)

Franchise located in Dallas prior to 1963 and known as Texans
Franchise in Boston prior to 1971

KANSAS CITY vs. NEW ORLEANS
RS: Saints lead series, 3-2
1972—Chiefs, 20-17 (NO)
1976—Saints, 27-17 (KC)
1982—Saints, 27-17 (NO)
1985—Chiefs, 47-27 (NO)
1991—Saints, 17-10 (KC)
(RS Pts.—Saints 115, Chiefs 111)

KANSAS CITY vs. N.Y. GIANTS
RS: Giants lead series, 6-1
1974—Giants, 33-27 (KC)
1978—Giants, 26-10 (NY)
1979—Giants, 21-17 (KC)
1983—Chiefs, 38-17 (KC)
1984—Giants, 28-27 (NY)
1988—Giants, 28-12 (NY)
1992—Giants, 35-21 (NY)
(RS Pts.—Giants 188, Chiefs 152)

***KANSAS CITY vs. **N.Y. JETS**
RS: Chiefs lead series, 14-12-1
PS: Series tied, 1-1
1960—Titans, 37-35 (D)
    Titans, 41-35 (NY)
1961—Titans, 28-7 (NY)
    Texans, 35-24 (D)
1962—Texans, 20-17 (D)
    Texans, 52-31 (NY)
1963—Jets, 17-0 (NY)
    Chiefs, 48-0 (KC)
1964—Jets, 27-14 (NY)
    Chiefs, 24-7 (KC)
1965—Chiefs, 14-10 (NY)
    Jets, 13-10 (KC)
1966—Chiefs, 32-24 (NY)
1967—Chiefs, 42-18 (NY)
    Chiefs, 21-7 (NY)
1968—Jets, 20-19 (KC)
1969—Chiefs, 34-16 (NY)
    ***Chiefs, 13-6 (NY)
1971—Jets, 13-10 (NY)
1974—Jets, 24-16 (KC)
1975—Jets, 30-24 (KC)
1982—Chiefs, 37-13 (KC)
1984—Jets, 17-16 (KC)
    Jets, 28-7 (NY)
1986—****Jets, 35-15 (NY)
1987—Jets, 16-9 (KC)
1988—Tie, 17-17 (NY)
    Chiefs, 38-34 (KC)
1992—Chiefs, 23-7 (NY)
(RS Pts.—Chiefs 647, Jets 528)
(PS Pts.—Jets 41, Chiefs 28)
Franchise in Dallas prior to 1963 and known as Texans
Jets known as Titans prior to 1963
***Inter-Divisional Playoff*
****AFC First-Round Playoff*

KANSAS CITY vs. PHILADELPHIA
RS: Series tied, 1-1
1972—Eagles, 21-20 (KC)
1992—Chiefs, 24-17 (KC)
(RS Pts.—Chiefs 44, Eagles 38)

KANSAS CITY vs. PITTSBURGH
RS: Steelers lead series, 13-5
PS: Chiefs lead series, 1-0
1970—Chiefs, 31-14 (P)
1971—Chiefs, 38-16 (KC)
1972—Steelers, 16-7 (P)
1974—Steelers, 34-24 (KC)
1975—Steelers, 28-3 (P)
1976—Steelers, 45-0 (KC)
1978—Steelers, 27-24 (P)
1979—Steelers, 30-3 (KC)
1980—Steelers, 21-16 (P)
1981—Chiefs, 37-33 (P)
1982—Steelers, 35-14 (P)
1984—Chiefs, 37-27 (P)
1985—Steelers, 36-28 (KC)
1986—Chiefs, 24-19 (P)
1987—Steelers, 17-16 (KC)

1988—Steelers, 16-10 (P)
1989—Steelers, 23-17 (P)
1992—Steelers, 27-3 (KC)
1993—*Chiefs, 27-24 (KC) OT
(RS Pts.—Steelers 464, Chiefs 332)
(PS Pts.—Chiefs 27, Steelers 24)
AFC First-Round Playoff

***KANSAS CITY vs. **SAN DIEGO**
RS: Chiefs lead series, 35-31-1
PS: Chargers lead series, 1-0
1960—Chargers, 21-20 (LA)
    Texans, 17-0 (D)
1961—Chargers, 26-10 (D)
    Chargers, 24-14 (SD)
1962—Chargers, 32-28 (SD)
    Texans, 26-17 (D)
1963—Chargers, 24-10 (SD)
    Chargers, 38-17 (KC)
1964—Chargers, 28-14 (KC)
    Chiefs, 49-6 (SD)
1965—Tie, 10-10 (SD)
    Chiefs, 31-7 (KC)
1966—Chiefs, 24-14 (KC)
    Chiefs, 27-17 (SD)
1967—Chargers, 45-31 (SD)
    Chargers, 17-16 (KC)
1968—Chiefs, 27-20 (KC)
    Chiefs, 40-3 (SD)
1969—Chiefs, 27-9 (SD)
    Chiefs, 27-3 (KC)
1970—Chiefs, 26-14 (KC)
    Chargers, 31-13 (SD)
1971—Chargers, 21-14 (SD)
    Chiefs, 31-10 (KC)
1972—Chiefs, 26-14 (KC)
    Chargers, 27-17 (KC)
1973—Chiefs, 19-0 (SD)
    Chiefs, 33-6 (KC)
1974—Chiefs, 24-14 (SD)
    Chargers, 14-7 (KC)
1975—Chiefs, 12-10 (SD)
    Chargers, 28-20 (KC)
1976—Chargers, 30-16 (KC)
    Chiefs, 23-20 (SD)
1977—Chargers, 23-7 (KC)
    Chiefs, 21-16 (SD)
1978—Chargers, 29-23 (SD) OT
    Chiefs, 23-0 (KC)
1979—Chargers, 20-14 (KC)
    Chargers, 28-7 (SD)
1980—Chargers, 24-7 (KC)
    Chargers, 20-7 (SD)
1981—Chargers, 42-31 (KC)
    Chargers, 22-20 (SD)
1982—Chiefs, 19-12 (KC)
1983—Chargers, 17-14 (KC)
    Chargers, 41-38 (SD)
1984—Chiefs, 31-13 (KC)
    Chiefs, 42-21 (SD)
1985—Chargers, 31-20 (KC)
    Chiefs, 38-34 (KC)
1986—Chiefs, 42-41 (KC)
    Chiefs, 24-23 (SD)
1987—Chiefs, 20-13 (KC)
    Chargers, 42-21 (SD)
1988—Chargers, 24-23 (KC)
    Chargers, 24-13 (SD)
1989—Chargers, 21-6 (SD)
    Chargers, 20-13 (KC)
1990—Chiefs, 27-10 (KC)
    Chiefs, 24-21 (SD)
1991—Chiefs, 14-13 (SD)
    Chiefs, 20-17 (KC) OT
1992—Chiefs, 24-10 (SD)
    Chiefs, 16-14 (KC)
    ***Chargers, 17-0 (SD)
1993—Chiefs, 17-14 (SD)
    Chiefs, 28-24 (KC)
(RS Pts.—Chiefs 1,440, Chargers 1,324)
(PS Pts.—Chargers 17, Chiefs 0)
Franchise in Dallas prior to 1963 and known as Texans
Franchise in Los Angeles prior to 1961

***AFC First-Round Playoff*
KANSAS CITY vs. SAN FRANCISCO
RS: 49ers lead series, 4-1
1971—Chiefs, 26-17 (SF)
1975—49ers, 20-3 (KC)
1982—49ers, 26-13 (KC)
1985—49ers, 31-3 (SF)
1991—49ers, 28-14 (SF)
(RS Pts.—49ers 122, Chiefs 59)

KANSAS CITY vs. SEATTLE
RS: Chiefs lead series, 19-12
1977—Seahawks, 34-31 (KC)
1978—Seahawks, 13-10 (KC)
    Seahawks, 23-19 (S)
1979—Chiefs, 24-6 (S)
    Chiefs, 37-21 (KC)
1980—Seahawks, 17-16 (KC)
    Chiefs, 31-30 (S)
1981—Chiefs, 20-14 (S)
    Chiefs, 40-13 (KC)
1983—Chiefs, 17-13 (KC)
    Seahawks, 51-48 (S) OT
1984—Seahawks, 45-0 (S)
    Chiefs, 34-7 (KC)
1985—Chiefs, 28-7 (KC)
    Seahawks, 24-6 (S)
1986—Seahawks, 23-17 (S)
    Chiefs, 27-7 (KC)
1987—Seahawks, 43-14 (S)
    Chiefs, 41-20 (KC)
1988—Seahawks, 31-10 (S)
    Chiefs, 27-24 (KC)
1989—Chiefs, 20-16 (S)
    Chiefs, 20-10 (KC)
1990—Seahawks, 19-7 (S)
    Seahawks, 17-16 (KC)
1991—Chiefs, 20-13 (KC)
    Chiefs, 19-6 (S)
1992—Chiefs, 26-7 (KC)
    Chiefs, 24-14 (S)
1993—Chiefs, 31-16 (S)
    Chiefs, 34-24 (KC)
(RS Pts.—Chiefs 714, Seahawks 608)

KANSAS CITY vs. TAMPA BAY
RS: Chiefs lead series, 5-2
1976—Chiefs, 28-19 (TB)
1978—Buccaneers, 30-13 (KC)
1979—Buccaneers, 3-0 (TB)
1981—Chiefs, 19-10 (KC)
1984—Chiefs, 24-20 (KC)
1986—Chiefs, 27-20 (KC)
1993—Chiefs, 27-3 (TB)
(RS Pts.—Chiefs 138, Buccaneers 105)

KANSAS CITY vs. WASHINGTON
RS: Chiefs lead series, 3-1
1971—Chiefs, 27-20 (KC)
1976—Chiefs, 33-30 (W)
1983—Redskins, 27-12 (W)
1992—Chiefs, 35-16 (KC)
(RS Pts.—Chiefs 107, Redskins 93)

L.A. RAIDERS vs. ARIZONA
RS: Raiders lead series, 2-1;
See Arizona vs. L.A. Raiders
L.A. RAIDERS vs. ATLANTA
RS: Raiders lead series, 4-3;
See Atlanta vs. L.A. Raiders
L.A. RAIDERS vs. BUFFALO
RS: Raiders lead series, 15-14
PS: Bills lead series, 2-0;
See Buffalo vs. L.A. Raiders
L.A. RAIDERS vs. CHICAGO
RS: Raiders lead series, 5-3;
See Chicago vs. L.A. Raiders
L.A. RAIDERS vs. CINCINNATI
RS: Raiders lead series, 14-7
PS: Raiders lead series, 2-0;
See Cincinnati vs. L.A. Raiders
L.A. RAIDERS vs. CLEVELAND
RS: Raiders lead series, 8-4
PS: Raiders lead series, 2-0;
See Cleveland vs. L.A. Raiders
L.A. RAIDERS vs. DALLAS

RS: Raiders lead series, 3-2;
See Dallas vs. L.A. Raiders
L.A. RAIDERS vs. DENVER
RS: Raiders lead series, 46-19-2
PS: Series tied, 1-1;
See Denver vs. L.A. Raiders
L.A. RAIDERS vs. DETROIT
RS: Raiders lead series, 5-2;
See Detroit vs. L.A. Raiders
L.A. RAIDERS vs. GREEN BAY
RS: Raiders lead series, 5-2
PS: Packers lead series, 1-0;
See Green Bay vs. L.A. Raiders
L.A. RAIDERS vs. HOUSTON
RS: Raiders lead series, 19-13
PS: Raiders lead series, 3-0;
See Houston vs. L.A. Raiders
L.A. RAIDERS vs. INDIANAPOLIS
RS: Raiders lead series, 4-2
PS: Series tied, 1-1;
See Indianapolis vs. L.A. Raiders
L.A. RAIDERS vs. KANSAS CITY
RS: Raiders lead series, 35-30-2
PS: Chiefs lead series, 2-1;
See Kansas City vs. L.A. Raiders
***L.A. RAIDERS vs. L.A. RAMS**
RS: Raiders lead series, 5-2
1972—Raiders, 45-17 (O)
1977—Rams, 20-14 (LA)
1979—Raiders, 24-17 (LA)
1982—Raiders, 37-31 (LA Raiders)
1985—Raiders, 16-6 (LA Rams)
1988—Rams, 22-17 (LA Raiders)
1991—Raiders, 20-17 (LA Raiders)
(RS Pts.—Raiders 173, Rams 130)
Franchise in Oakland prior to 1982

***L.A. RAIDERS vs. MIAMI**
RS: Raiders lead series, 14-4-1
PS: Raiders lead series, 2-1
1966—Raiders, 23-14 (M)
    Raiders, 21-10 (O)
1967—Raiders, 31-17 (O)
1968—Raiders, 47-21 (M)
1969—Raiders, 20-17 (O)
    Tie, 20-20 (M)
1970—Dolphins, 20-13 (M)
    **Raiders, 21-14 (O)
1973—Raiders, 12-7 (O)
    ***Dolphins, 27-10 (M)
1974—**Raiders, 28-26 (O)
1975—Raiders, 31-21 (M)
1978—Dolphins, 23-6 (M)
1979—Raiders, 13-3 (O)
1980—Raiders, 16-10 (O)
1981—Raiders, 33-17 (M)
1983—Raiders, 27-14 (LA)
1984—Raiders, 45-34 (M)
1986—Raiders, 30-28 (M)
1988—Dolphins, 24-14 (LA)
1990—Raiders, 13-10 (M)
1992—Dolphins, 20-7 (M)
(RS Pts.—Raiders 422, Dolphins 330)
(PS Pts.—Dolphins 67, Raiders 59)
Franchise in Oakland prior to 1982
AFC Divisional Playoff
***AFC Championship**

***L.A. RAIDERS vs. MINNESOTA**
RS: Raiders lead series, 6-2
PS: Raiders lead series, 1-0
1973—Vikings, 24-16 (M)
1976—**Raiders, 32-14 (Pasadena)
1977—Raiders, 35-13 (O)
1978—Raiders, 27-20 (O)
1981—Raiders, 36-10 (M)
1984—Raiders, 23-20 (LA)
1987—Vikings, 31-20 (M)
1990—Raiders, 28-24 (M)
1993—Raiders, 24-7 (LA)
(RS Pts.—Raiders 209, Vikings 149)
(PS Pts.—Raiders 32, Vikings 14)
Franchise in Oakland prior to 1982
Super Bowl XI

***L.A. RAIDERS vs. **NEW ENGLAND**

RS: Series tied, 12-12-1
PS: Series tied, 1-1
1960—Raiders, 27-14 (O)
      Patriots, 34-28 (B)
1961—Patriots, 20-17 (B)
      Patriots, 35-21 (O)
1962—Patriots, 26-16 (B)
      Raiders, 20-0 (O)
1963—Patriots, 20-14 (O)
      Patriots, 20-14 (B)
1964—Patriots, 17-14 (O)
      Tie, 43-43 (B)
1965—Raiders, 24-10 (B)
      Raiders, 30-21 (O)
1966—Patriots, 24-21 (B)
1967—Raiders, 35-7 (O)
      Raiders, 48-14 (B)
1968—Raiders, 41-10 (O)
1969—Raiders, 38-23 (B)
1971—Patriots, 20-6 (NE)
1974—Raiders, 41-26 (O)
1976—Patriots, 48-17 (NE)
    ***Raiders, 24-21 (O)
1978—Patriots, 21-14 (O)
1981—Raiders, 27-17 (O)
1985—Raiders, 35-20 (NE)
    ***Patriots, 27-20 (LA)
1987—Patriots, 26-23 (NE)
1989—Raiders, 24-21 (LA)
(RS Pts.—Raiders 638, Patriots 537)
(PS Pts.—Patriots 48, Raiders 44)
*Franchise in Oakland prior to 1982
**Franchise in Boston prior to 1971
***AFC Divisional Playoff
L.A. RAIDERS vs. NEW ORLEANS
RS: Raiders lead series, 3-2-1
1971—Tie, 21-21 (NO)
1975—Raiders, 48-10 (O)
1979—Raiders, 42-35 (NO)
1985—Raiders, 23-13 (LA)
1988—Saints, 20-6 (NO)
1991—Saints, 27-0 (NO)
(RS Pts.—Raiders 140, Saints 126)
*Franchise in Oakland prior to 1982
L.A. RAIDERS vs. N.Y. GIANTS
RS: Raiders lead series, 4-2
1973—Raiders, 42-0 (O)
1980—Raiders, 33-17 (NY)
1983—Raiders, 27-12 (LA)
1986—Giants, 14-9 (LA)
1989—Giants, 34-17 (NY)
1992—Raiders, 13-10 (LA)
(RS Pts.—Raiders 141, Giants 87)
*Franchise in Oakland prior to 1982
L.A. RAIDERS vs. **N.Y. JETS
RS: Raiders lead series, 14-9-2
PS: Jets lead series, 2-0
1960—Raiders, 28-27 (NY)
      Titans, 31-28 (O)
1961—Titans, 14-6 (O)
      Titans, 23-12 (NY)
1962—Titans, 28-17 (O)
      Titans, 31-21 (NY)
1963—Jets, 10-7 (NY)
      Raiders, 49-26 (O)
1964—Jets, 35-13 (NY)
      Raiders, 35-26 (O)
1965—Tie, 24-24 (NY)
      Raiders, 24-14 (O)
1966—Raiders, 24-21 (NY)
      Tie, 28-28 (O)
1967—Jets, 27-14 (NY)
      Raiders, 38-29 (O)
1968—Raiders, 43-32 (O)
    ***Jets, 27-23 (NY)
1969—Raiders, 27-14 (NY)
1970—Raiders, 14-13 (NY)
1972—Raiders, 24-16 (O)
1977—Raiders, 28-27 (NY)
1979—Jets, 28-19 (NY)
1982—****Jets, 17-14 (LA)
1985—Raiders, 31-0 (LA)
1989—Raiders, 14-7 (NY)

1993—Raiders, 24-20 (LA)
(RS Pts.—Raiders 592, Jets 551)
(PS Pts.—Jets 44, Raiders 37)
*Franchise in Oakland prior to 1982
**Jets known as Titans prior to 1963
***AFL Championship
****AFC Second-Round Playoff
L.A. RAIDERS vs. PHILADELPHIA
RS: Eagles lead series, 4-2
PS: Raiders lead series, 1-0
1971—Raiders, 34-10 (O)
1976—Raiders, 26-7 (P)
1980—Eagles, 10-7 (P)
    **Raiders, 27-10 (New Orleans)
1986—Eagles, 33-27 (LA) OT
1989—Eagles, 10-7 (P)
1992—Eagles, 31-10 (P)
(RS Pts.—Raiders 111, Eagles 101)
(PS Pts.—Raiders 27, Eagles 10)
*Franchise in Oakland prior to 1982
**Super Bowl XV
L.A. RAIDERS vs. PITTSBURGH
RS: Raiders lead series, 7-3
PS: Series tied, 3-3
1970—Raiders, 31-14 (O)
1972—Steelers, 34-28 (P)
    **Steelers, 13-7 (P)
1973—Steelers, 17-9 (O)
    **Raiders, 33-14 (O)
1974—Raiders, 17-0 (P)
    ***Steelers, 24-13 (O)
1975—***Steelers, 16-10 (P)
1976—Raiders, 31-28 (O)
    ***Raiders, 24-7 (O)
1977—Raiders, 16-7 (P)
1980—Raiders, 45-34 (P)
1981—Raiders, 30-27 (O)
1983—**Raiders, 38-10 (LA)
1984—Steelers, 13-7 (LA)
1990—Raiders, 20-3 (LA)
(RS Pts.—Raiders 234, Steelers 177)
(PS Pts.—Raiders 125, Steelers 84)
*Franchise in Oakland prior to 1982
**AFC Divisional Playoff
***AFC Championship
L.A. RAIDERS vs. **SAN DIEGO
RS: Raiders lead series, 41-25-2
PS: Raiders lead series, 1-0
1960—Chargers, 52-28 (LA)
      Chargers, 41-17 (O)
1961—Chargers, 44-0 (SD)
      Chargers, 41-10 (O)
1962—Chargers, 42-33 (O)
      Chargers, 31-21 (SD)
1963—Raiders, 34-33 (SD)
      Raiders, 41-27 (O)
1964—Chargers, 31-17 (O)
      Raiders, 21-20 (SD)
1965—Chargers, 17-6 (O)
      Chargers, 24-14 (SD)
1966—Chargers, 29-20 (O)
      Raiders, 41-19 (SD)
1967—Raiders, 51-10 (O)
      Raiders, 41-21 (SD)
1968—Chargers, 23-14 (O)
      Raiders, 34-27 (SD)
1969—Raiders, 24-12 (SD)
      Raiders, 21-16 (O)
1970—Tie, 27-27 (SD)
      Raiders, 20-17 (O)
1971—Raiders, 34-0 (SD)
      Raiders, 34-33 (O)
1972—Tie, 17-17 (O)
      Raiders, 21-19 (SD)
1973—Raiders, 27-17 (SD)
      Raiders, 31-3 (O)
1974—Raiders, 14-10 (SD)
      Raiders, 17-10 (O)
1975—Raiders, 6-0 (SD)
      Raiders, 25-0 (O)
1976—Raiders, 27-17 (SD)
      Raiders, 24-0 (O)
1977—Raiders, 24-0 (O)

      Chargers, 12-7 (SD)
1978—Raiders, 21-20 (SD)
      Chargers, 27-23 (O)
1979—Chargers, 30-10 (SD)
      Raiders, 45-22 (O)
1980—Chargers, 30-24 (SD) OT
      Raiders, 38-24 (O)
    ***Raiders, 34-27 (SD)
1981—Chargers, 55-21 (O)
      Chargers, 23-10 (SD)
1982—Raiders, 28-24 (LA)
      Raiders, 41-34 (SD)
1983—Raiders, 42-10 (SD)
      Raiders, 30-14 (LA)
1984—Raiders, 33-30 (LA)
      Raiders, 44-37 (SD)
1985—Raiders, 34-21 (LA)
      Chargers, 40-34 (SD) OT
1986—Raiders, 17-13 (LA)
      Raiders, 37-31 (SD) OT
1987—Chargers, 23-17 (LA)
      Chargers, 16-14 (SD)
1988—Raiders, 24-13 (LA)
      Raiders, 13-3 (SD)
1989—Raiders, 40-14 (LA)
      Chargers, 14-12 (SD)
1990—Raiders, 24-9 (SD)
      Raiders, 17-12 (LA)
1991—Chargers, 21-13 (LA)
      Raiders, 9-7 (SD)
1992—Chargers, 27-3 (SD)
      Chargers, 36-14 (LA)
1993—Chargers, 30-23 (LA)
      Raiders, 12-7 (SD)
(RS Pts.—Raiders 1,610, Chargers, 1,459)
(PS Pts.—Raiders 34, Chargers 27)
*Franchise in Oakland prior to 1982
**Franchise in Los Angeles prior to 1961
***AFC Championship
L.A. RAIDERS vs. SAN FRANCISCO
RS: Raiders lead series, 5-2
1970—49ers, 38-7 (O)
1974—Raiders, 35-24 (SF)
1979—Raiders, 23-10 (O)
1982—Raiders, 23-17 (SF)
1985—49ers, 34-10 (LA)
1988—Raiders, 9-3 (SF)
1991—Raiders, 12-6 (LA)
(RS Pts.—49ers 132, Raiders 110)
*Franchise in Oakland prior to 1982
L.A. RAIDERS vs. SEATTLE
RS: Raiders lead series, 18-14
PS: Series tied, 1-1
1977—Raiders, 44-7 (O)
1978—Seahawks, 27-7 (S)
      Seahawks, 17-16 (O)
1979—Seahawks, 27-10 (S)
      Seahawks, 29-24 (O)
1980—Raiders, 33-14 (O)
      Raiders, 19-17 (S)
1981—Raiders, 20-10 (O)
      Raiders, 32-31 (S)
1982—Raiders, 28-23 (LA)
1983—Seahawks, 38-36 (S)
      Seahawks, 34-21 (LA)
    **Raiders, 30-14 (LA)
1984—Raiders, 28-14 (LA)
      Seahawks, 17-14 (S)
    ***Seahawks, 13-7 (S)
1985—Seahawks, 33-3 (S)
      Raiders, 13-3 (LA)
1986—Raiders, 14-10 (LA)
      Seahawks, 37-0 (S)
1987—Seahawks, 35-13 (LA)
      Raiders, 37-14 (S)
1988—Seahawks, 35-27 (S)
      Seahawks, 43-37 (LA)
1989—Seahawks, 24-20 (LA)
      Seahawks, 23-17 (S)
1990—Raiders, 17-13 (S)
      Raiders, 24-17 (LA)
1991—Raiders, 23-20 (S) OT

      Raiders, 31-7 (LA)
1992—Raiders, 19-0 (S)
      Raiders, 20-3 (LA)
1993—Raiders, 17-13 (S)
      Raiders, 27-23 (LA)
(RS Pts.—Raiders 691, Seahawks 658)
(PS Pts.—Raiders 37, Seahawks 27)
*Franchise in Oakland prior to 1982
**AFC Championship
***AFC First-Round Playoff
L.A. RAIDERS vs. TAMPA BAY
RS: Raiders lead series, 3-0
1976—Raiders, 49-16 (O)
1981—Raiders, 18-16 (LA)
1993—Raiders, 27-20 (LA)
(RS Pts.—Raiders 94, Buccaneers 52)
*Franchise in Oakland prior to 1982
L.A. RAIDERS vs. WASHINGTON
RS: Raiders lead series, 5-2
PS: Raiders lead series, 1-0
1970—Raiders, 34-20 (O)
1975—Raiders, 26-23 (W) OT
1980—Raiders, 24-21 (O)
1983—Redskins, 37-35 (W)
    **Raiders, 38-9 (Tampa)
1986—Redskins, 10-6 (W)
1989—Raiders, 37-24 (LA)
1992—Raiders, 21-20 (W)
(RS Pts.—Raiders 183, Redskins 155)
(PS Pts.—Redskins 38, Redskins 9)
*Franchise in Oakland prior to 1982
**Super Bowl XVIII

L.A. RAMS vs. ARIZONA
RS: Rams lead series, 22-19-2
PS: Rams lead series, 1-0;
See Arizona vs. L.A. Rams
L.A. RAMS vs. ATLANTA
RS: Rams lead series, 36-16-2;
See Atlanta vs. L.A. Rams
L.A. RAMS vs. BUFFALO
RS: Series tied, 3-3;
See Buffalo vs. L.A. Rams
L.A. RAMS vs. CHICAGO
RS: Bears lead series, 44-29-3
PS: Series tied, 1-1;
See Chicago vs. L.A. Rams
L.A. RAMS vs. CINCINNATI
RS: Bengals lead series, 5-2;
See Cincinnati vs. L.A. Rams
L.A. RAMS vs. CLEVELAND
RS: Browns lead series, 8-7
PS: Browns lead series, 2-1;
See Cleveland vs. L.A. Rams
L.A. RAMS vs. DALLAS
RS: Rams lead series, 9-8
PS: Series tied, 4-4;
See Dallas vs. L.A. Rams
L.A. RAMS vs. DENVER
RS: Series tied, 3-3;
See Denver vs. L.A. Rams
L.A. RAMS vs. DETROIT
RS: Rams lead series, 39-35-1
PS: Lions lead series, 1-0;
See Detroit vs. L.A. Rams
L.A. RAMS vs. GREEN BAY
RS: Rams lead series, 42-36-2
PS: Packers lead series, 1-0;
See Green Bay vs. L.A. Rams
L.A. RAMS vs. HOUSTON
RS: Rams lead series, 5-2;
See Houston vs. L.A. Rams
L.A. RAMS vs. INDIANAPOLIS
RS: Colts lead series, 20-16-2;
See Indianapolis vs. L.A. Rams
L.A. RAMS vs. KANSAS CITY
RS: Rams lead series, 3-1;
See Kansas City vs. L.A. Rams
L.A. RAMS VS. L.A. RAIDERS
RS: Raiders lead series, 5-2;
See L.A. Raiders vs. L.A. Rams
L.A. RAMS vs. MIAMI
RS: Dolphins lead series, 5-1

1971—Dolphins, 20-14 (LA)
1976—Rams, 31-28 (M)
1980—Dolphins, 35-14 (LA)
1983—Dolphins, 30-14 (M)
1986—Dolphins, 37-31 (LA) OT
1992—Dolphins, 26-10 (M)
(RS Pts.—Dolphins 176, Rams 114)

L.A. RAMS vs. MINNESOTA
RS: Vikings lead series, 15-11-2
PS: Vikings lead series, 5-1
1961—Rams, 31-17 (LA)
　　　Vikings, 42-21 (M)
1962—Vikings, 38-14 (LA)
　　　Tie, 24-24 (M)
1963—Rams, 27-24 (LA)
　　　Vikings, 21-13 (M)
1964—Rams, 22-13 (LA)
　　　Vikings, 34-13 (M)
1965—Vikings, 38-35 (LA)
　　　Vikings, 24-13 (M)
1966—Vikings, 35-7 (M)
　　　Rams, 21-6 (LA)
1967—Rams, 39-3 (LA)
1968—Rams, 31-3 (M)
1969—Rams, 20-13 (LA)
　　　*Vikings, 23-20 (M)
1970—Vikings, 13-3 (M)
1972—Vikings, 45-41 (LA)
1973—Vikings, 10-9 (M)
1974—Rams, 20-17 (LA)
　　　**Vikings, 14-10 (M)
1976—Tie, 10-10 (M) OT
　　　**Vikings, 24-13 (M)
1977—Rams, 35-3 (LA)
　　　***Vikings, 14-7 (LA)
1978—Rams, 34-17 (M)
　　　***Rams, 34-10 (LA)
1979—Rams, 27-21 (LA) OT
1985—Rams, 13-10 (LA)
1987—Vikings, 21-16 (LA)
1988—****Vikings, 28-17 (M)
1989—Vikings, 23-21 (M) OT
1991—Vikings, 20-14 (M)
1992—Vikings, 31-17 (LA)
(RS Pts.—Rams 584, Vikings 583)
(PS Pts.—Vikings 113, Rams 101)
*Conference Championship
**NFC Championship
***NFC Divisional Playoff
****NFC First-Round Playoff

L.A. RAMS vs. NEW ENGLAND
RS: Series tied, 3-3
1974—Patriots, 20-14 (NE)
1980—Rams, 17-14 (NE)
1983—Patriots, 21-7 (LA)
1986—Patriots, 30-28 (LA)
1989—Rams, 24-20 (NE)
1992—Rams, 14-0 (LA)
(RS Pts.—Patriots 105, Rams 104)

L.A. RAMS vs. NEW ORLEANS
RS: Rams lead series, 27-21
1967—Rams, 27-13 (NO)
1969—Rams, 36-17 (LA)
1970—Rams, 30-17 (NO)
　　　Rams, 34-16 (LA)
1971—Saints, 24-20 (NO)
　　　Rams, 45-28 (LA)
1972—Rams, 34-14 (LA)
　　　Saints, 19-16 (NO)
1973—Rams, 29-7 (LA)
　　　Rams, 24-13 (NO)
1974—Rams, 24-0 (LA)
　　　Saints, 20-7 (NO)
1975—Rams, 38-14 (LA)
　　　Rams, 14-7 (NO)
1976—Rams, 16-10 (NO)
　　　Rams, 33-14 (LA)
1977—Rams, 14-7 (LA)
　　　Saints, 27-26 (NO)
1978—Rams, 26-20 (NO)
　　　Saints, 10-3 (LA)
1979—Rams, 35-17 (NO)
　　　Saints, 29-14 (LA)

1980—Rams, 45-31 (LA)
　　　Rams, 27-7 (NO)
1981—Saints, 23-17 (NO)
　　　Saints, 21-13 (LA)
1983—Rams, 30-27 (LA)
　　　Rams, 26-24 (NO)
1984—Rams, 28-10 (NO)
　　　Rams, 34-21 (LA)
1985—Rams, 28-10 (LA)
　　　Saints, 29-3 (NO)
1986—Saints, 6-0 (NO)
　　　Rams, 26-13 (LA)
1987—Saints, 37-10 (NO)
　　　Saints, 31-14 (LA)
1988—Rams, 12-10 (NO)
　　　Saints, 14-10 (LA)
1989—Saints, 40-21 (LA)
　　　Rams, 20-17 (NO) OT
1990—Saints, 24-20 (LA)
　　　Saints, 20-17 (NO)
1991—Saints, 24-7 (NO)
　　　Saints, 24-17 (LA)
1992—Saints, 13-10 (NO)
　　　Saints, 37-14 (LA)
1993—Saints, 37-6 (LA)
　　　Rams, 23-20 (NO)
(RS Pts.—Rams 1,023, Saints 913)

*L.A. RAMS vs. N.Y. GIANTS
RS: Rams lead series, 20-9
PS: Series tied, 1-1
1938—Giants, 28-0 (NY)
1940—Rams, 13-0 (NY)
1941—Giants, 49-14 (NY)
1945—Rams, 21-17 (NY)
1946—Rams, 31-21 (NY)
1947—Rams, 34-10 (LA)
1948—Rams, 52-37 (NY)
1953—Rams, 21-7 (LA)
1954—Rams, 17-16 (NY)
1959—Giants, 23-21 (LA)
1961—Giants, 24-14 (NY)
1966—Rams, 55-14 (LA)
1968—Rams, 24-21 (LA)
1970—Rams, 31-3 (NY)
1973—Rams, 40-6 (LA)
1976—Rams, 24-10 (LA)
1978—Rams, 20-17 (NY)
1979—Giants, 20-14 (LA)
1980—Rams, 28-7 (NY)
1981—Giants, 10-7 (NY)
1983—Rams, 16-6 (NY)
1984—Rams, 33-12 (LA)
　　　**Giants, 16-13 (LA)
1985—Giants, 24-19 (NY)
1988—Rams, 45-31 (NY)
1989—Rams, 31-10 (LA)
　　　***Rams, 19-13 (NY) OT
1990—Giants, 31-7 (LA)
1991—Giants, 19-13 (NY)
1992—Rams, 38-17 (LA)
1993—Giants, 20-10 (NY)
(RS Pts.—Rams 699, Giants 504)
(PS Pts.—Rams 32, Giants 29)
*Franchise in Cleveland prior to 1946
**NFC First-Round Playoff
***NFC Divisional Playoff

L.A. RAMS vs. N.Y. JETS
RS: Rams lead series, 5-2
1970—Jets, 31-20 (LA)
1974—Rams, 20-13 (NY)
1980—Rams, 38-13 (LA)
1983—Jets, 27-24 (NY) OT
1986—Rams, 17-3 (NY)
1989—Rams, 38-14 (LA)
1992—Rams, 18-10 (LA)
(RS Pts.—Rams 175, Jets 111)

*L.A. RAMS vs. PHILADELPHIA
RS: Rams lead series, 15-11-1
PS: Series tied, 1-1
1937—Rams, 21-3 (P)
1939—Rams, 35-13 (Colorado Springs)
1940—Rams, 21-13 (C)
1942—Rams, 24-14 (Akron)

1944—Eagles, 26-13 (P)
1945—Eagles, 28-14 (P)
1946—Eagles, 25-14 (LA)
1947—Eagles, 14-7 (P)
1948—Tie, 28-28 (LA)
1949—Eagles, 38-14 (P)
　　　**Eagles, 14-0 (LA)
1950—Eagles, 56-20 (P)
1955—Rams, 23-21 (P)
1956—Rams, 27-7 (LA)
1957—Rams, 17-13 (LA)
1959—Eagles, 23-20 (P)
1964—Rams, 20-10 (LA)
1967—Rams, 33-17 (LA)
1969—Rams, 23-17 (P)
1972—Rams, 34-3 (P)
1975—Rams, 42-3 (P)
1977—Rams, 20-0 (LA)
1978—Rams, 16-14 (P)
1983—Eagles, 13-9 (P)
1985—Rams, 17-6 (P)
1986—Eagles, 34-20 (P)
1988—Eagles, 30-24 (P)
1989—***Rams, 21-7 (P)
1990—Eagles, 27-21 (LA)
(RS Pts.—Rams 577, Eagles 496)
(PS Pts.—Rams 21, Eagles 21)
*Franchise in Cleveland prior to 1946
**NFL Championship
***NFC First-Round Playoff

*L.A. RAMS vs. **PITTSBURGH
RS: Rams lead series, 14-4-2
PS: Steelers lead series, 1-0
1938—Rams, 13-7 (New Orleans)
1939—Tie, 14-14 (C)
1941—Rams, 17-14 (Akron)
1947—Rams, 48-7 (P)
1948—Rams, 31-14 (LA)
1949—Tie, 7-7 (P)
1952—Rams, 28-14 (LA)
1955—Rams, 27-26 (LA)
1956—Steelers, 30-13 (P)
1961—Rams, 24-14 (LA)
1964—Rams, 26-14 (P)
1968—Rams, 45-10 (LA)
1971—Rams, 23-14 (P)
1975—Rams, 10-3 (LA)
1978—Rams, 10-7 (LA)
1979—***Steelers, 31-19 (Pasadena)
1981—Steelers, 24-0 (P)
1984—Steelers, 24-14 (P)
1987—Rams, 31-21 (LA)
1990—Steelers, 41-10 (P)
1993—Rams, 27-0 (LA)
(RS Pts.—Rams 418, Steelers 305)
(PS Pts.—Steelers 31, Rams 19)
*Franchise in Cleveland prior to 1946
**Steelers known as Pirates prior to 1941
***Super Bowl XIV

L.A. RAMS vs. SAN DIEGO
RS: Rams lead series, 3-2
1970—Rams, 37-10 (LA)
1975—Rams, 13-10 (SD) OT
1979—Chargers, 40-16 (LA)
1988—Chargers, 38-24 (LA)
1991—Rams, 30-24 (LA)
(RS Pts.—Chargers 122, Rams 120)

L.A. RAMS vs. SAN FRANCISCO
RS: Rams lead series, 48-38-2
PS: 49ers lead series, 1-0
1950—Rams, 35-14 (SF)
　　　Rams, 28-21 (LA)
1951—49ers, 44-17 (SF)
　　　Rams, 23-16 (LA)
1952—Rams, 35-9 (LA)
　　　Rams, 34-21 (SF)
1953—49ers, 31-30 (SF)
　　　49ers, 31-27 (LA)
1954—Tie, 24-24 (LA)
　　　Rams, 42-34 (SF)
1955—Rams, 23-14 (SF)
　　　Rams, 27-14 (LA)
1956—49ers, 33-30 (SF)

　　　Rams, 30-6 (LA)
1957—49ers, 23-20 (SF)
　　　Rams, 37-24 (LA)
1958—Rams, 33-3 (SF)
　　　Rams, 56-7 (LA)
1959—49ers, 34-0 (SF)
　　　49ers, 24-16 (LA)
1960—Rams, 13-9 (SF)
　　　49ers, 23-7 (LA)
1961—49ers, 35-0 (SF)
　　　Rams, 17-7 (LA)
1962—49ers, 28-14 (SF)
　　　49ers, 24-17 (LA)
1963—Rams, 28-21 (LA)
　　　Rams, 21-17 (SF)
1964—Rams, 42-14 (LA)
　　　49ers, 28-7 (SF)
1965—49ers, 45-21 (LA)
　　　49ers, 30-27 (SF)
1966—Rams, 34-3 (LA)
　　　49ers, 21-13 (SF)
1967—49ers, 27-24 (LA)
　　　Rams, 17-7 (SF)
1968—Rams, 24-10 (LA)
　　　Tie, 20-20 (SF)
1969—49ers, 27-21 (SF)
　　　Rams, 41-30 (LA)
1970—49ers, 20-6 (SF)
　　　Rams, 30-13 (LA)
1971—Rams, 20-13 (SF)
　　　Rams, 17-6 (LA)
1972—Rams, 31-7 (LA)
　　　Rams, 26-16 (SF)
1973—Rams, 40-20 (LA)
　　　Rams, 31-13 (LA)
1974—Rams, 37-14 (LA)
　　　Rams, 15-13 (SF)
1975—Rams, 23-14 (LA)
　　　49ers, 24-23 (LA)
1976—49ers, 16-0 (LA)
　　　Rams, 23-3 (SF)
1977—Rams, 34-14 (LA)
　　　Rams, 23-10 (SF)
1978—Rams, 27-10 (LA)
　　　Rams, 31-28 (SF)
1979—Rams, 27-24 (LA)
　　　Rams, 26-20 (SF)
1980—Rams, 48-26 (LA)
　　　Rams, 31-17 (SF)
1981—49ers, 20-17 (SF)
　　　49ers, 33-31 (LA)
1982—49ers, 30-24 (LA)
　　　Rams, 21-20 (SF)
1983—49ers, 10-7 (SF)
　　　49ers, 45-35 (LA)
1984—49ers, 33-0 (LA)
　　　49ers, 19-16 (SF)
1985—49ers, 28-14 (LA)
　　　Rams, 27-20 (SF)
1986—Rams, 16-13 (LA)
　　　49ers, 24-14 (SF)
1987—49ers, 31-10 (LA)
　　　49ers, 48-0 (SF)
1988—49ers, 24-21 (LA)
　　　Rams, 38-16 (SF)
1989—Rams, 13-12 (SF)
　　　49ers, 30-27 (LA)
　　　*49ers, 30-3 (SF)
1990—Rams, 28-17 (SF)
　　　49ers, 26-10 (LA)
1991—49ers, 27-10 (LA)
　　　49ers, 33-10 (LA)
1992—49ers, 27-24 (SF)
　　　49ers, 27-10 (LA)
1993—49ers, 40-17 (SF)
　　　49ers, 35-10 (LA)
(RS Pts.—Rams 2,013, 49ers 1,863)
(PS Pts.—49ers 30, Rams 3)
*NFC Championship

L.A. RAMS vs. SEATTLE
RS: Rams lead series, 4-1
1976—Rams, 45-6 (LA)
1979—Rams, 24-0 (S)

1985—Rams, 35-24 (S)
1988—Rams, 31-10 (LA)
1991—Seahawks, 23-9 (S)
(RS Pts.—Rams 144, Seahawks 63)
L.A. RAMS vs. TAMPA BAY
RS: Rams lead series, 8-2
PS: Rams lead series, 1-0
1977—Rams, 31-0 (LA)
1978—Rams, 26-23 (LA)
1979—Buccaneers, 21-6 (TB)
    *Rams, 9-0 (TB)
1980—Buccaneers, 10-9 (TB)
1984—Rams, 34-33 (TB)
1985—Rams, 31-27 (TB)
1986—Rams, 26-20 (LA) OT
1987—Rams, 35-3 (LA)
1990—Rams, 35-14 (TB)
1992—Rams, 31-27 (TB)
(RS Pts.—Rams 264, Buccaneers 178)
(PS Pts.—Rams 9, Buccaneers 0)
*NFC Championship
L.A. RAMS vs. WASHINGTON
RS: Redskins lead series, 14-5-1
PS: Series tied, 2-2
1937—Redskins, 16-7 (C)
1938—Redskins, 37-13 (W)
1941—Redskins, 17-13 (W)
1942—Redskins, 33-14 (W)
1944—Redskins, 14-10 (W)
1945—**Rams, 15-14 (C)
1948—Rams, 41-13 (W)
1949—Rams, 53-27 (LA)
1951—Redskins, 31-21 (W)
1962—Redskins, 20-14 (W)
1963—Redskins, 37-14 (LA)
1967—Tie, 28-28 (LA)
1969—Rams, 24-13 (W)
1971—Redskins, 38-24 (LA)
1974—Redskins, 23-17 (LA)
    ***Rams, 19-10 (LA)
1977—Redskins, 17-14 (W)
1981—Redskins, 30-7 (LA)
1983—Redskins, 42-20 (LA)
    ***Redskins, 51-7 (W)
1986—****Redskins, 19-7 (W)
1987—Rams, 30-26 (W)
1991—Redskins, 27-6 (LA)
1993—Rams, 10-6 (LA)
(RS Pts.—Redskins 495, Rams 380)
(PS Pts.—Redskins 94, Rams 48)
*Franchise in Cleveland prior to 1946
**NFL Championship
***NFC Divisional Playoff
****NFC First-Round Playoff

MIAMI vs. ARIZONA
RS: Dolphins lead series, 6-0;
See Arizona vs. Miami
MIAMI vs. ATLANTA
RS: Dolphins lead series, 5-1;
See Atlanta vs. Miami
MIAMI vs. BUFFALO
RS: Dolphins lead series, 37-18-1
PS: Bills lead series, 2-0;
See Buffalo vs. Miami
MIAMI vs. CHICAGO
RS: Dolphins lead series, 5-1;
See Chicago vs. Miami
MIAMI vs. CINCINNATI
RS: Dolphins lead series, 9-3
PS: Dolphins lead series, 1-0;
See Cincinnati vs. Miami
MIAMI vs. CLEVELAND
RS: Dolphins lead series, 6-4
PS: Dolphins lead series, 2-0;
See Cleveland vs. Miami
MIAMI vs. DALLAS
RS: Dolphins lead series, 6-1
PS: Cowboys lead series, 1-0;
See Dallas vs. Miami
MIAMI vs. DENVER
RS: Dolphins lead series, 5-2-1;
See Denver vs. Miami

MIAMI vs. DETROIT
RS: Series tied, 2-2;
See Detroit vs. Miami
MIAMI vs. GREEN BAY
RS: Dolphins lead series, 7-0;
See Green Bay vs. Miami
MIAMI vs. HOUSTON
RS: Series tied, 11-11
PS: Oilers lead series, 1-0;
See Houston vs. Miami
MIAMI vs. INDIANAPOLIS
RS: Dolphins lead series, 34-14
PS: Dolphins lead series, 1-0;
See Indianapolis vs. Miami
MIAMI vs. KANSAS CITY
RS: Chiefs lead series, 10-7
PS: Dolphins lead series, 2-0;
See Kansas City vs. Miami
MIAMI vs. L.A. RAIDERS
RS: Raiders lead series, 14-4-1
PS: Raiders lead series, 2-1;
See L.A. Raiders vs. Miami
MIAMI vs. L.A. RAMS
RS: Dolphins lead series, 5-1;
See L.A. Rams vs. Miami
MIAMI vs. MINNESOTA
RS: Dolphins lead series, 4-1
PS: Dolphins lead series, 1-0
1972—Dolphins, 16-14 (Minn)
1973—*Dolphins, 24-7 (Houston)
1976—Vikings, 29-7 (Mia)
1979—Dolphins, 27-12 (Minn)
1982—Dolphins, 22-14 (Mia)
1988—Dolphins, 24-7 (Mia)
(RS Pts.—Dolphins 96, Vikings 76)
(PS Pts.—Dolphins 24, Vikings 7)
*Super Bowl VIII
MIAMI vs. *NEW ENGLAND
RS: Dolphins lead series, 33-21
PS: Series tied, 1-1
1966—Patriots, 20-14 (M)
1967—Patriots, 41-10 (B)
    Dolphins, 41-32 (M)
1968—Dolphins, 34-10 (B)
    Dolphins, 38-7 (M)
1969—Dolphins, 17-16 (B)
    Patriots, 38-23 (Tampa)
1970—Patriots, 27-14 (B)
    Dolphins, 37-20 (M)
1971—Dolphins, 41-3 (M)
    Patriots, 34-13 (NE)
1972—Dolphins, 52-0 (M)
    Dolphins, 37-21 (NE)
1973—Dolphins, 44-23 (M)
    Dolphins, 30-14 (NE)
1974—Patriots, 34-24 (NE)
    Dolphins, 34-27 (M)
1975—Dolphins, 22-14 (NE)
    Dolphins, 20-7 (M)
1976—Patriots, 30-14 (NE)
    Dolphins, 10-3 (M)
1977—Dolphins, 17-5 (M)
    Patriots, 14-10 (NE)
1978—Patriots, 33-24 (NE)
    Dolphins, 23-3 (M)
1979—Patriots, 28-13 (NE)
    Dolphins, 39-24 (M)
1980—Patriots, 34-0 (NE)
    Dolphins, 16-13 (M) OT
1981—Dolphins, 30-27 (NE) OT
    Dolphins, 24-14 (M)
1982—Patriots, 3-0 (NE)
    **Dolphins, 28-13 (M)
1983—Dolphins, 34-24 (M)
    Patriots, 17-6 (NE)
1984—Dolphins, 28-7 (M)
    Dolphins, 44-24 (NE)
1985—Patriots, 17-13 (NE)
    Dolphins, 30-27 (M)
    ***Patriots, 31-14 (M)
1986—Patriots, 34-7 (NE)
    Patriots, 34-27 (M)
1987—Patriots, 28-21 (NE)

    Patriots, 24-10 (M)
1988—Patriots, 21-10 (NE)
    Patriots, 6-3 (M)
1989—Dolphins, 24-10 (NE)
    Dolphins, 31-10 (M)
1990—Dolphins, 27-24 (NE)
    Dolphins, 17-10 (M)
1991—Dolphins, 20-10 (NE)
    Dolphins, 30-20 (M)
1992—Dolphins, 38-17 (M)
    Dolphins, 16-13 (NE) OT
1993—Dolphins, 17-13 (M)
    Patriots, 33-27 (NE) OT
(RS Pts.—Dolphins 1,245, Patriots 1,042)
(PS Pts.—Patriots 44, Dolphins 42)
*Franchise in Boston prior to 1971
**AFC First-Round Playoff
***AFC Championship
MIAMI vs. NEW ORLEANS
RS: Dolphins lead series, 4-2
1970—Dolphins, 21-10 (M)
1974—Dolphins, 21-0 (NO)
1980—Dolphins, 21-16 (M)
1983—Saints, 17-7 (NO)
1986—Dolphins, 31-27 (NO)
1992—Saints, 24-13 (NO)
(RS Pts.—Dolphins 114, Saints 94)
MIAMI vs. N.Y. GIANTS
RS: Giants lead series, 2-1
1972—Dolphins, 23-13 (NY)
1990—Giants, 20-3 (NY)
1993—Giants, 19-14 (M)
(RS Pts.—Giants 52, Dolphins 40)
MIAMI vs. N.Y. JETS
RS: Jets lead series, 28-27-1
PS: Dolphins lead series, 1-0
1966—Jets, 19-14 (M)
    Jets, 30-13 (NY)
1967—Jets, 29-7 (NY)
    Jets, 33-14 (M)
1968—Jets, 35-17 (NY)
    Jets, 31-7 (M)
1969—Jets, 34-31 (NY)
    Jets, 27-9 (M)
1970—Dolphins, 20-6 (NY)
    Dolphins, 16-10 (M)
1971—Jets, 14-10 (M)
    Dolphins, 30-14 (NY)
1972—Dolphins, 27-17 (NY)
    Dolphins, 28-24 (M)
1973—Dolphins, 31-3 (M)
    Dolphins, 24-14 (NY)
1974—Dolphins, 21-17 (M)
    Jets, 17-14 (NY)
1975—Dolphins, 43-0 (NY)
    Dolphins, 27-7 (M)
1976—Dolphins, 16-0 (M)
    Dolphins, 27-7 (NY)
1977—Dolphins, 21-17 (M)
    Dolphins, 14-10 (NY)
1978—Jets, 33-20 (NY)
    Jets, 24-13 (M)
1979—Jets, 33-27 (NY)
    Jets, 27-24 (M)
1980—Jets, 17-14 (NY)
    Jets, 24-17 (M)
1981—Tie, 28-28 (M) OT
    Jets, 16-15 (NY)
1982—Dolphins, 45-28 (NY)
    Dolphins, 20-19 (M)
    *Dolphins, 14-0 (M)
1983—Dolphins, 32-14 (NY)
    Dolphins, 34-14 (M)
1984—Dolphins, 31-17 (NY)
    Dolphins, 28-17 (M)
1985—Jets, 23-7 (NY)
    Dolphins, 21-17 (M)
1986—Jets, 51-45 (NY) OT
    Dolphins, 45-3 (M)
1987—Jets, 37-31 (NY) OT
    Dolphins, 37-28 (M)
1988—Jets, 44-30 (M)
    Jets, 38-34 (NY)

1989—Jets, 40-33 (M)
    Dolphins, 31-23 (NY)
1990—Dolphins, 20-16 (M)
    Dolphins, 17-3 (NY)
1991—Jets, 41-23 (NY)
    Jets, 23-20 (M) OT
1992—Jets, 26-14 (NY)
    Dolphins, 19-17 (M)
1993—Jets, 24-14 (M)
    Jets, 27-10 (NY)
(RS Pts.—Dolphins 1,280, Jets 1,207)
(PS Pts.—Dolphins 14, Jets 0)
*AFC Championship
MIAMI vs. PHILADELPHIA
RS: Dolphins lead series, 6-2
1970—Eagles, 24-17 (P)
1975—Dolphins, 24-16 (M)
1978—Eagles, 17-3 (P)
1981—Dolphins, 13-10 (M)
1984—Dolphins, 24-23 (M)
1987—Dolphins, 28-10 (P)
1990—Dolphins, 23-20 (M) OT
1993—Dolphins, 19-14 (P)
(RS Pts.—Dolphins 151, Eagles 134)
MIAMI vs. PITTSBURGH
RS: Dolphins lead series, 7-5
PS: Dolphins lead series, 2-1
1971—Dolphins, 24-21 (M)
1972—*Dolphins, 21-17 (P)
1973—Dolphins, 30-26 (M)
1976—Steelers, 14-3 (P)
1979—**Steelers, 34-14 (P)
1980—Steelers, 23-10 (P)
1981—Dolphins, 30-10 (M)
1984—Dolphins, 31-7 (P)
    *Dolphins, 45-28 (M)
1985—Dolphins, 24-20 (M)
1987—Dolphins, 35-24 (M)
1988—Steelers, 40-24 (P)
1989—Steelers, 34-14 (M)
1990—Dolphins, 28-6 (P)
1993—Steelers, 21-20 (M)
(RS Pts.—Dolphins 273, Steelers 246)
(PS Pts.—Dolphins 80, Steelers 79)
*AFC Championship
**AFC Divisional Playoff
MIAMI vs. SAN DIEGO
RS: Chargers lead series, 10-5
PS: Dolphins lead series, 2-1
1966—Chargers, 44-10 (SD)
1967—Chargers, 24-0 (SD)
    Dolphins, 41-24 (M)
1968—Chargers, 34-28 (SD)
1969—Chargers, 21-14 (M)
1972—Chargers, 24-10 (M)
1974—Dolphins, 28-21 (SD)
1977—Chargers, 14-13 (M)
1978—Dolphins, 28-21 (SD)
1980—Chargers, 27-24 (M) OT
1981—*Chargers, 41-38 (M) OT
1982—**Dolphins, 34-13 (M)
1984—Chargers, 34-28 (SD) OT
1986—Chargers, 50-28 (SD)
1988—Dolphins, 31-28 (M)
1991—Chargers, 38-30 (SD)
1992—*Dolphins, 31-0 (M)
1993—Chargers, 45-20 (SD)
(RS Pts.—Chargers 435, Dolphins 347)
(PS Pts.—Dolphins 103, Chargers 54)
*AFC Divisional Playoff
**AFC Second-Round Playoff
MIAMI vs. SAN FRANCISCO
RS: Dolphins lead series, 4-2
PS: 49ers lead series, 1-0
1973—Dolphins, 21-13 (M)
1977—Dolphins, 19-15 (SF)
1980—Dolphins, 17-13 (M)
1983—Dolphins, 20-17 (SF)
1984—*49ers, 38-16 (Stanford)
1986—49ers, 31-16 (M)
1992—49ers, 27-3 (SF)
(RS Pts.—49ers 116, Dolphins 96)
(PS Pts.—49ers 38, Dolphins 16)

ALL-TIME TEAM VS. TEAM RESULTS

Super Bowl XIX
MIAMI vs. SEATTLE
RS: Dolphins lead series, 4-1
PS: Series tied, 1-1
1977—Dolphins, 31-13 (M)
1979—Dolphins, 19-10 (M)
1983—*Seahawks, 27-20 (M)
1984—*Dolphins, 31-10 (M)
1987—Seahawks, 24-20 (S)
1990—Dolphins, 24-17 (M)
1992—Dolphins, 19-17 (S)
(RS Pts.—Dolphins 113, Seahawks 81)
(PS Pts.—Dolphins 51, Seahawks 37)
AFC Divisional Playoff
MIAMI vs. TAMPA BAY
RS: Dolphins lead series, 4-1
1976—Dolphins, 23-20 (TB)
1982—Buccaneers, 23-17 (TB)
1985—Dolphins, 41-38 (M)
1988—Dolphins, 17-14 (TB)
1991—Dolphins, 33-14 (M)
(RS Pts.—Dolphins 131, Buccaneers 109)
MIAMI vs. WASHINGTON
RS: Dolphins lead series, 5-2
PS: Series tied, 1-1
1972—*Dolphins, 14-7 (Los Angeles)
1974—Redskins, 20-17 (W)
1978—Dolphins, 16-0 (W)
1981—Dolphins, 13-10 (M)
1982—**Redskins, 27-17 (Pasadena)
1984—Dolphins, 35-17 (W)
1987—Dolphins, 23-21 (M)
1990—Redskins, 42-20 (W)
1993—Dolphins, 17-10 (M)
(RS Pts.—Dolphins 141, Redskins 120)
(PS Pts.—Redskins 34, Dolphins 31)
Super Bowl VII
**Super Bowl XVII*

MINNESOTA vs. ARIZONA
RS: Cardinals lead series, 7-4
PS: Vikings lead series, 1-0;
See Arizona vs. Minnesota
MINNESOTA vs. ATLANTA
RS: Vikings lead series, 11-6
PS: Vikings lead series, 1-0;
See Atlanta vs. Minnesota
MINNESOTA vs. BUFFALO
RS: Vikings lead series, 4-2;
See Buffalo vs. Minnesota
MINNESOTA vs. CHICAGO
RS: Vikings lead series, 34-29-2;
See Chicago vs. Minnesota
MINNESOTA vs. CINCINNATI
RS: Vikings lead series, 4-3;
See Cincinnati vs. Minnesota
MINNESOTA vs. CLEVELAND
RS: Vikings lead series, 7-3
PS: Vikings lead series, 1-0;
See Cleveland vs. Minnesota
MINNESOTA vs. DALLAS
RS: Cowboys lead series, 8-6
PS: Cowboys lead series, 3-1;
See Dallas vs. Minnesota
MINNESOTA vs. DENVER
RS: Vikings lead series, 5-3;
See Denver vs. Minnesota
MINNESOTA vs. DETROIT
RS: Vikings lead series, 40-23-2;
See Detroit vs. Minnesota
MINNESOTA vs. GREEN BAY
RS: Vikings lead series, 33-31-1;
See Green Bay vs. Minnesota
MINNESOTA vs. HOUSTON
RS: Series tied, 3-3;
See Houston vs. Minnesota
MINNESOTA vs. INDIANAPOLIS
RS: Colts lead series, 11-6-1
PS: Colts lead series, 1-0;
See Indianapolis vs. Minnesota
MINNESOTA vs. KANSAS CITY
RS: Vikings lead series, 3-2

PS: Chiefs lead series, 1-0;
See Kansas City vs. Minnesota
MINNESOTA vs. L.A. RAIDERS
RS: Raiders lead series, 6-2
PS: Raiders lead series, 1-0;
See L.A. Raiders vs. Minnesota
MINNESOTA vs. L.A. RAMS
RS: Vikings lead series, 15-11-2
PS: Vikings lead series, 5-1;
See L.A. Rams vs. Minnesota
MINNESOTA vs. MIAMI
RS: Dolphins lead series, 4-1
PS: Dolphins lead series, 1-0;
See Miami vs. Minnesota
MINNESOTA vs. *NEW ENGLAND
RS: Patriots lead series, 3-2
1970—Vikings, 35-14 (B)
1974—Patriots, 17-14 (M)
1979—Patriots, 27-23 (NE)
1988—Vikings, 36-6 (M)
1991—Patriots, 26-23 (NE) OT
(RS Pts.—Vikings 131, Patriots 90)
Franchise in Boston prior to 1971
MINNESOTA vs. NEW ORLEANS
RS: Vikings lead series, 11-6
PS: Vikings lead series, 1-0
1968—Saints, 20-17 (NO)
1970—Vikings, 26-0 (M)
1971—Vikings, 23-10 (NO)
1972—Vikings, 37-6 (M)
1974—Vikings, 29-9 (M)
1975—Vikings, 20-7 (NO)
1976—Vikings, 40-9 (NO)
1978—Saints, 31-24 (NO)
1980—Vikings, 23-20 (NO)
1981—Vikings, 20-10 (M)
1983—Saints, 17-16 (NO)
1985—Saints, 30-23 (M)
1986—Vikings, 33-17 (M)
1987—*Vikings, 44-10 (NO)
1988—Vikings, 45-3 (M)
1990—Vikings, 32-3 (M)
1991—Saints, 26-0 (NO)
1993—Saints, 17-14 (M)
(RS Pts.—Vikings 422, Saints 235)
(PS Pts.—Vikings 44, Saints 10)
NFC First-Round Playoff
MINNESOTA vs. N.Y. GIANTS
RS: Vikings lead series, 6-4
PS: Giants lead series, 1-0
1964—Vikings, 30-21 (NY)
1965—Vikings, 40-14 (M)
1967—Vikings, 27-24 (M)
1969—Giants, 24-23 (NY)
1971—Vikings, 17-10 (NY)
1973—Vikings, 31-7 (New Haven)
1976—Vikings, 24-7 (M)
1986—Giants, 22-20 (M)
1989—Giants, 24-14 (NY)
1990—Giants, 23-15 (NY)
1993—*Giants, 17-10 (NY)
(RS Pts.—Vikings 241, Giants 176)
(PS Pts.—Giants 17, Vikings 10)
NFC First-Round Playoff
MINNESOTA vs. N.Y. JETS
RS: Jets lead series, 3-1
1970—Jets, 20-10 (NY)
1975—Vikings, 29-21 (M)
1979—Jets, 14-7 (NY)
1982—Jets, 42-14 (M)
(RS Pts.—Jets 97, Vikings 60)
MINNESOTA vs. PHILADELPHIA
RS: Vikings lead series, 10-6
PS: Eagles lead series, 1-0
1962—Vikings, 31-21 (M)
1963—Vikings, 34-13 (P)
1968—Vikings, 24-17 (P)
1971—Vikings, 13-0 (P)
1973—Vikings, 28-21 (M)
1976—Vikings, 31-12 (P)
1978—Vikings, 28-27 (M)
1980—Eagles, 42-7 (M)
    *Eagles, 31-16 (P)

1981—Vikings, 35-23 (M)
1984—Eagles, 19-17 (P)
1985—Vikings, 28-23 (P)
    Eagles, 37-35 (M)
1988—Vikings, 23-21 (M)
1989—Eagles, 10-9 (P)
1990—Eagles, 32-24 (P)
1992—Eagles, 28-17 (P)
(RS Pts.—Vikings 384, Eagles 346)
(PS Pts.—Eagles 31, Vikings 16)
NFC Divisional Playoff
MINNESOTA vs. PITTSBURGH
RS: Vikings lead series, 7-4
PS: Steelers lead series, 1-0
1962—Steelers, 39-31 (P)
1964—Vikings, 30-10 (M)
1967—Vikings, 41-27 (P)
1969—Vikings, 52-14 (M)
1972—Steelers, 23-10 (P)
1974—*Steelers, 16-6 (New Orleans)
1976—Vikings, 17-6 (M)
1980—Steelers, 23-17 (M)
1983—Vikings, 17-14 (P)
1986—Vikings, 31-7 (M)
1989—Steelers, 27-14 (P)
1992—Vikings, 6-3 (P)
(RS Pts.—Vikings 266, Steelers 193)
(PS Pts.—Steelers 16, Vikings 6)
Super Bowl IX
MINNESOTA vs. SAN DIEGO
RS: Chargers lead series, 4-3
1971—Chargers, 30-14 (SD)
1975—Vikings, 28-13 (M)
1978—Chargers, 13-7 (M)
1981—Vikings, 33-31 (SD)
1984—Chargers, 42-13 (M)
1985—Vikings, 21-17 (M)
1993—Chargers, 30-17 (M)
(RS Pts.—Chargers 176, Vikings 133)
MINNESOTA vs. SAN FRANCISCO
RS: Series tied, 15-15-1
PS: 49ers lead series, 3-1
1961—49ers, 38-24 (M)
    49ers, 38-28 (SF)
1962—49ers, 21-7 (SF)
    49ers, 35-12 (M)
1963—Vikings, 24-20 (SF)
    Vikings, 45-14 (M)
1964—Vikings, 27-22 (SF)
    Vikings, 24-7 (M)
1965—Vikings, 42-41 (SF)
    49ers, 45-24 (M)
1966—Tie, 20-20 (SF)
    Vikings, 28-3 (M)
1967—49ers, 27-21 (M)
1968—Vikings, 30-20 (SF)
1969—Vikings, 10-7 (M)
1970—*49ers, 17-14 (M)
1971—49ers, 13-9 (M)
1972—Vikings, 20-17 (SF)
1973—Vikings, 17-13 (SF)
1975—Vikings, 27-17 (M)
1976—Vikings, 20-16 (SF)
1977—Vikings, 28-27 (M)
1979—Vikings, 28-22 (M)
1983—49ers, 48-17 (M)
1984—49ers, 51-7 (SF)
1985—Vikings, 28-21 (M)
1986—Vikings, 27-24 (SF) OT
1987—*Vikings, 36-24 (SF)
1988—49ers, 24-21 (SF)
    *49ers, 34-9 (SF)
1989—*49ers, 41-13 (SF)
1990—49ers, 20-17 (SF)
1991—Vikings, 17-14 (M)
1992—49ers, 20-17 (M)
1993—49ers, 38-19 (SF)
(RS Pts.—49ers 750, Vikings 678)
(PS Pts.—49ers 116, Vikings 72)
NFC Divisional Playoff
MINNESOTA vs. SEATTLE
RS: Seahawks lead series, 3-2
1976—Vikings, 27-21 (M)

1978—Seahawks, 29-28 (S)
1984—Seahawks, 20-12 (M)
1987—Seahawks, 28-17 (S)
1990—Vikings, 24-21 (S)
(RS Pts.—Seahawks 119, Vikings 108)
MINNESOTA vs. TAMPA BAY
RS: Vikings lead series, 23-9
1977—Vikings, 9-3 (TB)
1978—Buccaneers, 16-10 (M)
    Vikings, 24-7 (TB)
1979—Buccaneers, 12-10 (M)
    Vikings, 23-22 (TB)
1980—Vikings, 38-30 (M)
    Vikings, 21-10 (TB)
1981—Buccaneers, 21-13 (TB)
    Vikings, 25-10 (M)
1982—Vikings, 17-10 (M)
1983—Vikings, 19-16 (TB) OT
    Buccaneers, 17-12 (M)
1984—Buccaneers, 35-31 (TB)
    Vikings, 27-24 (M)
1985—Vikings, 31-16 (TB)
    Vikings, 26-7 (M)
1986—Vikings, 23-10 (TB)
    Vikings, 45-13 (M)
1987—Buccaneers, 20-10 (TB)
    Vikings, 23-17 (M)
1988—Vikings, 14-13 (M)
    Vikings, 49-20 (TB)
1989—Vikings, 17-3 (M)
    Vikings, 24-10 (TB)
1990—Buccaneers, 23-20 (M) OT
    Buccaneers, 26-13 (TB)
1991—Vikings, 28-13 (M)
    Vikings, 26-24 (TB)
1992—Vikings, 26-20 (M)
    Vikings, 35-7 (TB)
1993—Vikings, 15-0 (M)
    Buccaneers, 23-10 (TB)
(RS Pts.—Vikings 714, Buccaneers 498)
MINNESOTA vs. WASHINGTON
RS: Redskins lead series, 6-4
PS: Redskins lead series, 3-2
1968—Vikings, 27-14 (M)
1970—Vikings, 19-10 (W)
1972—Redskins, 24-21 (M)
1973—*Vikings, 28-27 (M)
1975—Redskins, 31-30 (W)
1976—*Vikings, 35-20 (M)
1980—Vikings, 39-14 (W)
1982—**Redskins, 21-7 (W)
1984—Redskins, 31-17 (M)
1986—Redskins, 44-38 (W) OT
1987—Redskins, 27-24 (M) OT
    ***Redskins, 17-10 (W)
1992—Redskins, 15-13 (M)
    ****Redskins, 24-7 (M)
1993—Vikings, 14-9 (W)
(RS Pts.—Vikings 242, Redskins 219)
(PS Pts.—Redskins 102, Vikings 86)
NFC Divisional Playoff
**NFC Second-Round Playoff*
***NFC Championship*
****NFC First-Round Playoff*

NEW ENGLAND vs. ARIZONA
RS: Cardinals lead series, 6-2;
See Arizona vs. New England
NEW ENGLAND vs. ATLANTA
RS: Falcons lead series, 4-3;
See Atlanta vs. New England
NEW ENGLAND vs. BUFFALO
RS: Series tied, 33-33 1
PS: Patriots lead series, 1-0;
See Buffalo vs. New England
NEW ENGLAND vs. CHICAGO
RS: Patriots lead series, 3-2
PS: Bears lead series, 1-0;
See Chicago vs. New England
NEW ENGLAND vs. CINCINNATI
RS: Patriots lead series, 8-7;
See Cincinnati vs. New England
NEW ENGLAND vs. CLEVELAND

RS: Browns lead series, 9-3;
See Cleveland vs. New England
NEW ENGLAND vs. DALLAS
RS: Cowboys lead series, 6-0;
See Dallas vs. New England
NEW ENGLAND vs. DENVER
RS: Broncos lead series, 16-12
PS: Broncos lead series, 1-0;
See Denver vs. New England
NEW ENGLAND vs. DETROIT
RS: Lions lead series, 3-2;
See Detroit vs. New England
NEW ENGLAND vs. GREEN BAY
RS: Series tied, 2-2;
See Green Bay vs. New England
NEW ENGLAND vs. HOUSTON
RS: Patriots lead series, 17-14-1
PS: Oilers lead series, 1-0;
See Houston vs. New England
NEW ENGLAND vs. INDIANAPOLIS
RS: Patriots lead series, 27-20;
See Indianapolis vs. New England
NEW ENGLAND vs. KANSAS CITY
RS: Chiefs lead series, 13-7-3;
See Kansas City vs. New England
NEW ENGLAND vs. L.A. RAIDERS
RS: Series tied, 12-12-1
PS: Series tied, 1-1;
See L.A. Raiders vs. New England
NEW ENGLAND vs. L.A. RAMS
RS: Series tied, 3-3;
See L.A. Rams vs. New England
NEW ENGLAND vs. MIAMI
RS: Dolphins lead series, 33-21
PS: Series tied, 1-1;
See Miami vs. New England
NEW ENGLAND vs. MINNESOTA
RS: Patriots lead series, 3-2;
See Minnesota vs. New England
NEW ENGLAND vs. NEW ORLEANS
RS: Patriots lead series, 5-2
1972—Patriots, 17-10 (NO)
1976—Patriots, 27-6 (NE)
1980—Patriots, 38-27 (NO)
1983—Patriots, 7-0 (NE)
1986—Patriots, 21-20 (NO)
1989—Saints, 28-24 (NE)
1992—Saints, 31-14 (NE)
(RS Pts.—Patriots 148, Saints 122)
***NEW ENGLAND vs. N.Y. GIANTS**
RS: Giants lead series, 3-1
1970—Giants, 16-0 (B)
1974—Patriots, 28-20 (New Haven)
1987—Giants, 17-10 (NY)
1990—Giants, 13-10 (NE)
(RS Pts.—Giants 66, Patriots 48)
*Franchise in Boston prior to 1971
***NEW ENGLAND vs. **N.Y. JETS**
RS: Jets lead series, 38-28-1
PS: Patriots lead series, 1-0
1960—Patriots, 28-24 (NY)
        Patriots, 38-21 (B)
1961—Titans, 21-20 (B)
        Titans, 37-30 (NY)
1962—Patriots, 43-14 (NY)
        Patriots, 24-17 (B)
1963—Patriots, 38-14 (B)
        Jets, 31-24 (NY)
1964—Patriots, 26-10 (B)
        Jets, 35-14 (NY)
1965—Jets, 30-20 (B)
        Patriots, 27-23 (NY)
1966—Tie, 24-24 (B)
        Jets, 38-28 (NY)
1967—Jets, 30-23 (NY)
        Jets, 29-24 (B)
1968—Jets, 47-31 (Birmingham)
        Jets, 48-14 (NY)
1969—Jets, 23-14 (B)
        Jets, 23-17 (NY)
1970—Jets, 31-21 (B)
        Jets, 17-3 (NY)
1971—Patriots, 20-0 (NE)

Jets, 13-6 (NY)
1972—Jets, 41-13 (NE)
        Jets, 34-10 (NY)
1973—Jets, 9-7 (NE)
        Jets, 33-13 (NY)
1974—Patriots, 24-0 (NY)
        Jets, 21-16 (NE)
1975—Jets, 36-7 (NY)
        Jets, 30-28 (NE)
1976—Patriots, 41-7 (NE)
        Patriots, 38-24 (NY)
1977—Jets, 30-27 (NY)
        Patriots, 24-13 (NE)
1978—Patriots, 55-21 (NE)
        Patriots, 19-17 (NY)
1979—Patriots, 56-3 (NE)
        Jets, 27-26 (NY)
1980—Patriots, 21-11 (NY)
        Patriots, 34-21 (NE)
1981—Jets, 28-24 (NY)
        Jets, 17-6 (NE)
1982—Jets, 31-7 (NE)
1983—Patriots, 23-13 (NE)
        Jets, 26-3 (NY)
1984—Patriots, 28-21 (NY)
        Patriots, 30-20 (NE)
1985—Patriots, 20-13 (NE)
        Jets, 16-13 (NY) OT
        ***Patriots, 26-14 (NY)
1986—Patriots, 20-6 (NY)
        Jets, 31-24 (NE)
1987—Jets, 43-24 (NY)
        Patriots, 42-20 (NE)
1988—Patriots, 28-3 (NE)
        Patriots, 14-13 (NY)
1989—Patriots, 27-24 (NY)
        Jets, 27-26 (NE)
1990—Jets, 37-13 (NE)
        Jets, 42-7 (NY)
1991—Jets, 28-21 (NE)
        Patriots, 6-3 (NY)
1992—Jets, 30-21 (NY)
        Patriots, 24-3 (NE)
1993—Jets, 45-7 (NY)
        Jets, 6-0 (NE)
(RS Pts.—Jets 1,524, Patriots 1,474)
(PS Pts.—Patriots 26, Jets 14)
*Franchise in Boston prior to 1971
**Jets known as Titans prior to 1963
***AFC First-Round Playoff
NEW ENGLAND vs. PHILADELPHIA
RS: Eagles lead series, 5-2
1973—Eagles, 24-23 (P)
1977—Patriots, 14-6 (NE)
1978—Patriots, 24-14 (NE)
1981—Eagles, 13-3 (P)
1984—Eagles, 27-17 (P)
1987—Eagles, 34-31 (NE) OT
1990—Eagles, 48-20 (P)
(RS Pts.—Eagles 166, Patriots 132)
NEW ENGLAND vs. PITTSBURGH
RS: Steelers lead series, 9-3
1972—Steelers, 33-3 (P)
1974—Steelers, 21-17 (NE)
1976—Patriots, 30-27 (P)
1979—Steelers, 16-13 (NE) OT
1981—Steelers, 27-21 (P) OT
1982—Steelers, 37-14 (P)
1983—Patriots, 28-23 (P)
1986—Steelers, 34-0 (P)
1989—Steelers, 28-10 (P)
1990—Steelers, 24-3 (P)
1991—Steelers, 20-6 (P)
1993—Steelers, 17-14 (P)
(RS Pts.—Steelers 273, Patriots 193)
***NEW ENGLAND vs. **SAN DIEGO**
RS: Patriots lead series, 13-11-2
PS: Chargers lead series, 1-0
1960—Patriots, 35-0 (LA)
        Chargers, 45-16 (B)
1961—Chargers, 38-27 (B)
        Patriots, 41-0 (SD)
1962—Patriots, 24-20 (B)

Patriots, 20-14 (SD)
1963—Chargers, 17-13 (SD)
        Chargers, 7-6 (B)
        ***Chargers, 51-10 (SD)
1964—Patriots, 33-28 (SD)
        Chargers, 26-17 (B)
1965—Tie, 10-10 (B)
        Patriots, 22-6 (SD)
1966—Chargers, 24-0 (SD)
        Patriots, 35-17 (B)
1967—Chargers, 28-14 (SD)
        Tie, 31-31 (SD)
1968—Chargers, 27-17 (B)
1969—Chargers, 13-10 (B)
        Chargers, 28-18 (SD)
1970—Chargers, 16-14 (B)
1973—Patriots, 30-14 (NE)
1975—Patriots, 33-19 (SD)
1977—Patriots, 24-20 (SD)
1978—Patriots, 28-23 (NE)
1979—Patriots, 27-21 (NE)
1983—Patriots, 37-21 (NE)
(RS Pts.—Patriots 582, Chargers 513)
(PS Pts.—Chargers 51, Patriots 10)
*Franchise in Boston prior to 1971
**Franchise in Los Angeles prior to 1961
***AFL Championship
NEW ENGLAND vs. SAN FRANCISCO
RS: 49ers lead series, 6-1
1971—49ers, 27-10 (SF)
1975—Patriots, 24-16 (SF)
1980—49ers, 21-17 (SF)
1983—49ers, 33-13 (NE)
1986—49ers, 29-24 (NE)
1989—49ers, 37-20 (SF)
1992—49ers, 24-12 (NE)
(RS Pts.—49ers 187, Patriots 120)
NEW ENGLAND vs. SEATTLE
RS: Seahawks lead series, 7-6
1977—Patriots, 31-0 (NE)
1980—Patriots, 37-31 (S)
1982—Patriots, 16-0 (S)
1983—Seahawks, 24-6 (S)
1984—Patriots, 38-23 (NE)
1985—Patriots, 20-13 (S)
1986—Seahawks, 38-31 (NE)
1988—Patriots, 13-7 (NE)
1989—Seahawks, 24-3 (NE)
1990—Seahawks, 33-20 (NE)
1992—Seahawks, 10-6 (NE)
1993—Seahawks, 17-14 (NE)
        Seahawks, 10-9 (S)
(RS Pts.—Patriots 244, Seahawks 230)
NEW ENGLAND vs. TAMPA BAY
RS: Patriots lead series, 3-0
1976—Patriots, 31-14 (TB)
1985—Patriots, 32-14 (TB)
1988—Patriots, 10-7 (NE) OT
(RS Pts.—Patriots 73, Buccaneers 35)
NEW ENGLAND vs. WASHINGTON
RS: Redskins lead series, 4-1
1972—Patriots, 24-23 (NE)
1978—Redskins, 16-14 (NE)
1981—Redskins, 24-22 (W)
1984—Redskins, 26-10 (NE)
1990—Redskins, 25-10 (NE)
(RS Pts.—Redskins 114, Patriots 80)

───────────────

NEW ORLEANS vs. ARIZONA
RS: Cardinals lead series, 10-9;
See Arizona vs. New Orleans
NEW ORLEANS vs. ATLANTA
RS: Falcons lead series, 27-22
PS: Falcons lead series, 1-0;
See Atlanta vs. New Orleans
NEW ORLEANS vs. BUFFALO
RS: Bills lead series, 3-2;
See Buffalo vs. New Orleans
NEW ORLEANS vs. CHICAGO
RS: Bears lead series, 8-6
PS: Bears lead series, 1-0;
See Chicago vs. New Orleans
NEW ORLEANS vs. CINCINNATI

RS: Saints lead series, 5-3;
See Cincinnati vs. New Orleans
NEW ORLEANS vs. CLEVELAND
RS: Browns lead series, 9-3;
See Cleveland vs. New Orleans
NEW ORLEANS vs. DALLAS
RS: Cowboys lead series, 13-3;
See Dallas vs. New Orleans
NEW ORLEANS vs. DENVER
RS: Broncos lead series, 4-1;
See Denver vs. New Orleans
NEW ORLEANS vs. DETROIT
RS: Saints lead series, 7-6-1;
See Detroit vs. New Orleans
NEW ORLEANS vs. GREEN BAY
RS: Packers lead series, 12-4;
See Green Bay vs. New Orleans
NEW ORLEANS vs. HOUSTON
RS: Saints lead series, 4-3-1;
See Houston vs. New Orleans
NEW ORLEANS vs. INDIANAPOLIS
RS: Colts lead series, 3-2;
See Indianapolis vs. New Orleans
NEW ORLEANS vs. KANSAS CITY
RS: Saints lead series, 3-2;
See Kansas City vs. New Orleans
NEW ORLEANS vs. L.A. RAIDERS
RS: Raiders lead series, 3-2-1;
See L.A. Raiders vs. New Orleans
NEW ORLEANS vs. L.A. RAMS
RS: Rams lead series, 27-21;
See L.A. Rams vs. New Orleans
NEW ORLEANS vs. MIAMI
RS: Dolphins lead series, 4-2;
See Miami vs. New Orleans
NEW ORLEANS vs. MINNESOTA
RS: Vikings lead series, 11-6
PS: Vikings lead series, 1-0;
See Minnesota vs. New Orleans
NEW ORLEANS vs. NEW ENGLAND
RS: Patriots lead series, 5-2;
See New England vs. New Orleans
NEW ORLEANS vs. N.Y. GIANTS
RS: Giants lead series, 9-6
1967—Giants, 27-21 (NY)
1968—Giants, 38-21 (NY)
1969—Saints, 25-24 (NY)
1970—Saints, 14-10 (NO)
1972—Giants, 45-21 (NY)
1975—Giants, 28-14 (NY)
1978—Saints, 28-17 (NO)
1979—Saints, 24-14 (NO)
1981—Giants, 20-7 (NY)
1984—Saints, 10-3 (NY)
1985—Giants, 21-13 (NO)
1986—Giants, 20-17 (NY)
1987—Saints, 23-14 (NO)
1988—Giants, 13-12 (NO)
1993—Giants, 24-14 (NO)
(RS Pts.—Giants 318, Saints 264)
NEW ORLEANS vs. N.Y. JETS
RS: Jets lead series, 4-3
1972—Jets, 18-17 (NY)
1977—Jets, 16-13 (NY)
1980—Saints, 21-20 (NY)
1983—Jets, 31-28 (NO)
1986—Jets, 28-23 (NY)
1989—Saints, 29-14 (NO)
1992—Saints, 20-0 (NY)
(RS Pts.—Saints 151, Jets 127)
NEW ORLEANS vs. PHILADELPHIA
RS: Eagles lead series, 11-8
PS: Eagles lead series, 1-0
1967—Saints, 31-24 (NO)
        Eagles, 48-21 (P)
1968—Eagles, 29-17 (P)
1969—Eagles, 13-10 (P)
        Saints, 26-17 (NO)
1972—Saints, 21-3 (NO)
1974—Saints, 14-10 (NO)
1977—Eagles, 28-7 (P)
1978—Eagles, 24-17 (NO)
1979—Eagles, 26-14 (NO)

1980—Eagles, 34-21 (NO)
1981—Eagles, 31-14 (NO)
1983—Saints, 20-17 (P) OT
1985—Saints, 23-21 (NO)
1987—Eagles, 27-17 (P)
1989—Saints, 30-20 (NO)
1991—Saints, 13-6 (P)
1992—Eagles, 15-13 (P)
　　　*Eagles, 36-20 (NO)
1993—Eagles, 37-26 (P)
(RS Pts.—Eagles 430, Saints 355)
(PS Pts.—Eagles 36, Saints 20)
*NFC First-Round Playoff

NEW ORLEANS vs. PITTSBURGH
RS: Steelers lead series, 6-5
1967—Steelers, 14-10 (NO)
1968—Saints, 16-12 (P)
　　　Saints, 24-14 (NO)
1969—Saints, 27-24 (NO)
1974—Steelers, 28-7 (NO)
1978—Steelers, 20-14 (P)
1981—Saints, 20-6 (NO)
1984—Saints, 27-24 (NO)
1987—Saints, 20-16 (P)
1990—Steelers, 9-6 (NO)
1993—Steelers, 37-14 (P)
(RS Pts.—Steelers 218, Saints 171)

NEW ORLEANS vs. SAN DIEGO
RS: Chargers lead series, 4-1
1973—Chargers, 17-14 (SD)
1977—Chargers, 14-0 (NO)
1979—Chargers, 35-0 (NO)
1988—Saints, 23-17 (SD)
1991—Chargers, 24-21 (SD)
(RS Pts.—Chargers 107, Saints 58)

NEW ORLEANS vs. SAN FRANCISCO
RS: 49ers lead series, 33-14-2
1967—49ers, 27-13 (SF)
1969—Saints, 43-38 (NO)
1970—Tie, 20-20 (SF)
　　　49ers, 38-27 (NO)
1971—49ers, 38-20 (NO)
　　　Saints, 26-20 (SF)
1972—49ers, 37-2 (NO)
　　　Tie, 20-20 (SF)
1973—49ers, 40-0 (SF)
　　　Saints, 16-10 (NO)
1974—49ers, 17-13 (NO)
　　　49ers, 35-21 (SF)
1975—49ers, 35-21 (SF)
　　　49ers, 16-6 (NO)
1976—49ers, 33-3 (SF)
　　　49ers, 27-7 (NO)
1977—49ers, 10-7 (NO) OT
　　　49ers, 20-17 (SF)
1978—Saints, 14-7 (SF)
　　　Saints, 24-13 (NO)
1979—Saints, 30-21 (SF)
　　　Saints, 31-20 (NO)
1980—49ers, 26-23 (NO)
　　　49ers, 38-35 (SF) OT
1981—49ers, 21-14 (SF)
　　　49ers, 21-17 (NO)
1982—Saints, 23-20 (SF)
1983—49ers, 32-13 (NO)
　　　49ers, 27-0 (SF)
1984—49ers, 30-20 (SF)
　　　49ers, 35-3 (NO)
1985—Saints, 20-17 (SF)
　　　49ers, 31-19 (NO)
1986—49ers, 26-17 (SF)
　　　Saints, 23-10 (NO)
1987—49ers, 24-22 (NO)
　　　Saints, 26-24 (SF)
1988—49ers, 34-33 (NO)
　　　49ers, 30-17 (SF)
1989—49ers, 24-20 (NO)
　　　49ers, 31-13 (SF)
1990—49ers, 13-12 (NO)
　　　Saints, 13-10 (SF)
1991—Saints, 10-3 (NO)
　　　49ers, 38-24 (SF)
1992—49ers, 16-10 (NO)

　　　49ers, 21-20 (SF)
1993—Saints, 16-13 (NO)
　　　49ers, 42-7 (SF)
(RS Pts.—49ers, 1,199, Saints 851)

NEW ORLEANS vs. SEATTLE
RS: Saints lead series, 3-2
1976—Saints, 51-27 (S)
1979—Seahawks, 38-24 (S)
1985—Seahawks, 27-3 (NO)
1988—Saints, 20-19 (S)
1991—Saints, 27-24 (NO)
(RS Pts.—Seahawks 135, Saints 125)

NEW ORLEANS vs. TAMPA BAY
RS: Saints lead series, 11-4
1977—Buccaneers, 33-14 (NO)
1978—Saints, 17-10 (TB)
1979—Saints, 42-14 (TB)
1981—Buccaneers, 31-14 (NO)
1982—Buccaneers, 13-10 (NO)
1983—Saints, 24-21 (TB)
1984—Saints, 17-13 (NO)
1985—Saints, 20-13 (NO)
1986—Saints, 38-7 (NO)
1987—Saints, 44-34 (NO)
1988—Saints, 13-9 (NO)
1989—Buccaneers, 20-10 (TB)
1990—Saints, 35-7 (NO)
1991—Saints, 23-7 (NO)
1992—Saints, 23-21 (NO)
(RS Pts.—Saints 344, Buccaneers 253)

NEW ORLEANS vs. WASHINGTON
RS: Redskins lead series, 11-5
1967—Redskins, 30-10 (NO)
　　　Saints, 30-14 (W)
1968—Saints, 37-17 (NO)
1969—Redskins, 26-20 (NO)
　　　Redskins, 17-14 (W)
1971—Redskins, 24-14 (W)
1973—Redskins, 19-3 (NO)
1975—Redskins, 41-3 (W)
1979—Saints, 14-10 (W)
1980—Redskins, 22-14 (W)
1982—Redskins, 27-10 (NO)
1986—Redskins, 14-6 (NO)
1988—Redskins, 27-24 (W)
1989—Redskins, 16-14 (NO)
1990—Redskins, 31-17 (W)
1992—Saints, 20-3 (NO)
(RS Pts.—Redskins 322, Saints 266)

N.Y. GIANTS vs. ARIZONA
RS: Giants lead series, 65-35-2;
See Arizona vs. N.Y. Giants

N.Y. GIANTS vs. ATLANTA
RS: Series tied, 6-6;
See Atlanta vs. N.Y. Giants

N.Y. GIANTS vs. BUFFALO
RS: Bills lead series, 4-2
PS: Giants lead series, 1-0;
See Buffalo vs. N.Y. Giants

N.Y. GIANTS vs. CHICAGO
RS: Bears lead series, 24-16-2
PS: Bears lead series, 5-3;
See Chicago vs. N.Y. Giants

N.Y. GIANTS vs. CINCINNATI
RS: Bengals lead series, 4-0;
See Cincinnati vs. N.Y. Giants

N.Y. GIANTS vs. CLEVELAND
RS: Browns lead series, 25-16-2
PS: Series tied, 1-1;
See Cleveland vs. N.Y. Giants

N.Y. GIANTS vs. DALLAS
RS: Cowboys lead series, 40-21-2;
See Dallas vs. N.Y. Giants

N.Y. GIANTS vs. DENVER
RS: Series tied, 3-3
PS: Giants lead series, 1-0;
See Denver vs. N.Y. Giants

N.Y. GIANTS vs. DETROIT
RS: Lions lead series, 17-15-1
PS: Lions lead series, 1-0;
See Detroit vs. N.Y. Giants

N.Y. GIANTS vs. GREEN BAY

RS: Packers lead series, 21-20-2
PS: Packers lead series, 4-1;
See Green Bay vs. N.Y. Giants

N.Y. GIANTS vs. HOUSTON
RS: Giants lead series, 4-0;
See Houston vs. N.Y. Giants

N.Y. GIANTS vs. INDIANAPOLIS
RS: Series tied, 5-5
PS: Colts lead series, 2-0;
See Indianapolis vs. N.Y. Giants

N.Y. GIANTS vs. KANSAS CITY
RS: Giants lead series, 6-1;
See Kansas City vs. N.Y. Giants

N.Y. GIANTS vs. L.A. RAIDERS
RS: Raiders lead series, 4-2;
See L.A. Raiders vs. N.Y. Giants

N.Y. GIANTS vs. L.A. RAMS
RS: Rams lead series, 20-9
PS: Series tied, 1-1;
See L.A. Rams vs. N.Y. Giants

N.Y. GIANTS vs. MIAMI
RS: Giants lead series, 2-1;
See Miami vs. N.Y. Giants

N.Y. GIANTS vs. MINNESOTA
RS: Vikings lead series, 6-4
PS: Giants lead series, 1-0;
See Minnesota vs. N.Y. Giants

N.Y. GIANTS vs. NEW ENGLAND
RS: Giants lead series, 3-1;
See New England vs. N.Y. Giants

N.Y. GIANTS vs. NEW ORLEANS
RS: Giants lead series, 9-6;
See New Orleans vs. N.Y. Giants

N.Y. GIANTS vs. N.Y. JETS
RS: Jets lead series, 4-3
1970—Giants, 22-10 (NYJ)
1974—Jets, 26-20 (New Haven) OT
1981—Jets, 26-7 (NYG)
1984—Giants, 20-10 (NYJ)
1987—Giants, 20-7 (NYG)
1988—Jets, 27-21 (NYJ)
1993—Jets, 10-6 (NYG)
(RS Pts.—Giants 116, Jets 116)

N.Y. GIANTS vs. PHILADELPHIA
RS: Giants lead series, 62-54-2
PS: Giants lead series, 1-0
1933—Giants, 56-0 (NY)
　　　Giants, 20-14 (P)
1934—Giants, 17-0 (NY)
　　　Eagles, 6-0 (P)
1935—Giants, 10-0 (NY)
　　　Giants, 21-14 (P)
1936—Eagles, 10-7 (P)
　　　Giants, 21-17 (NY)
1937—Giants, 16-7 (P)
　　　Giants, 21-0 (NY)
1938—Eagles, 14-10 (P)
　　　Giants, 17-7 (NY)
1939—Giants, 13-3 (P)
　　　Giants, 27-10 (NY)
1940—Giants, 20-14 (P)
　　　Giants, 17-7 (NY)
1941—Giants, 24-0 (P)
　　　Giants, 16-0 (NY)
1942—Giants, 35-17 (NY)
　　　Giants, 14-0 (P)
1944—Eagles, 24-17 (NY)
　　　Tie, 21-21 (P)
1945—Eagles, 38-17 (P)
　　　Giants, 28-21 (NY)
1946—Eagles, 24-14 (P)
　　　Giants, 45-17 (NY)
1947—Eagles, 23-0 (P)
　　　Eagles, 41-24 (NY)
1948—Eagles, 45-0 (P)
　　　Eagles, 35-14 (NY)
1949—Eagles, 24-3 (NY)
　　　Eagles, 17-3 (P)
1950—Giants, 7-3 (NY)
　　　Giants, 9-7 (P)
1951—Eagles, 26-24 (NY)
　　　Giants, 23-7 (P)
1952—Giants, 31-7 (P)

　　　Eagles, 14-10 (NY)
1953—Eagles, 30-7 (P)
　　　Giants, 37-28 (NY)
1954—Giants, 27-14 (NY)
　　　Eagles, 29-14 (P)
1955—Eagles, 27-17 (P)
　　　Giants, 31-7 (NY)
1956—Giants, 20-3 (NY)
　　　Giants, 21-7 (P)
1957—Giants, 24-20 (P)
　　　Giants, 13-0 (NY)
1958—Eagles, 27-24 (P)
　　　Giants, 24-10 (NY)
1959—Giants, 49-21 (P)
　　　Giants, 24-7 (NY)
1960—Eagles, 17-10 (NY)
　　　Eagles, 31-23 (P)
1961—Giants, 38-21 (NY)
　　　Giants, 28-24 (P)
1962—Giants, 29-13 (P)
　　　Giants, 19-14 (NY)
1963—Giants, 37-14 (P)
　　　Giants, 42-14 (NY)
1964—Eagles, 38-7 (P)
　　　Giants, 23-17 (NY)
1965—Giants, 16-14 (P)
　　　Giants, 35-27 (NY)
1966—Eagles, 35-17 (P)
　　　Eagles, 31-3 (NY)
1967—Giants, 44-7 (NY)
1968—Giants, 7-6 (NY)
1969—Eagles, 23-20 (NY)
1970—Giants, 30-23 (NY)
　　　Eagles, 23-20 (P)
1971—Eagles, 23-7 (P)
　　　Eagles, 41-28 (NY)
1972—Giants, 27-12 (P)
　　　Giants, 62-10 (NY)
1973—Tie, 23-23 (NY)
　　　Eagles, 20-16 (P)
1974—Eagles, 35-7 (P)
　　　Eagles, 20-7 (New Haven)
1975—Giants, 23-14 (P)
　　　Eagles, 13-10 (NY)
1976—Eagles, 20-7 (P)
　　　Eagles, 10-0 (NY)
1977—Eagles, 28-10 (NY)
　　　Eagles, 17-14 (P)
1978—Eagles, 19-17 (NY)
　　　Eagles, 20-3 (P)
1979—Eagles, 23-17 (P)
　　　Eagles, 17-13 (NY)
1980—Eagles, 35-3 (P)
　　　Eagles, 31-16 (NY)
1981—Eagles, 24-10 (P)
　　　Giants, 20-10 (P)
　　　*Giants, 27-21 (P)
1982—Giants, 23-7 (NY)
　　　Eagles, 26-24 (P)
1983—Eagles, 17-13 (NY)
　　　Giants, 23-0 (P)
1984—Giants, 28-27 (NY)
　　　Eagles, 24-10 (P)
1985—Giants, 21-0 (NY)
　　　Giants, 16-10 (P) OT
1986—Giants, 35-3 (NY)
　　　Giants, 17-14 (P)
1987—Giants, 20-17 (P)
　　　Giants, 23-20 (NY) OT
1988—Eagles, 24-13 (P)
　　　Eagles, 23-17 (NY) OT
1989—Eagles, 21-19 (P)
　　　Eagles, 24-17 (NY)
1990—Giants, 27-20 (NY)
　　　Eagles, 31-13 (P)
1991—Eagles, 30-7 (P)
　　　Eagles, 19-14 (NY)
1992—Eagles, 47-34 (NY)
　　　Eagles, 20-10 (P)
1993—Eagles, 21-10 (NY)
　　　Giants, 7-3 (P)
(RS Pts.—Giants 2,248, Eagles 2,113)

(PS Pts.—Giants 27, Eagles 21)
*NFC First-Round Playoff
N.Y. GIANTS vs. *PITTSBURGH
RS: Giants lead series, 42-26-3
1933—Giants, 23-2 (P)
　　　Giants, 27-3 (NY)
1934—Giants, 14-12 (P)
　　　Giants, 17-7 (NY)
1935—Giants, 42-7 (P)
　　　Giants, 13-0 (NY)
1936—Pirates, 10-7 (P)
1937—Giants, 10-7 (P)
　　　Giants, 17-0 (NY)
1938—Giants, 27-14 (P)
　　　Pirates, 13-10 (NY)
1939—Giants, 14-7 (P)
　　　Giants, 23-7 (NY)
1940—Tie, 10-10 (P)
　　　Giants, 12-0 (NY)
1941—Giants, 37-10 (P)
　　　Giants, 28-7 (NY)
1942—Steelers, 13-10 (P)
　　　Steelers, 17-9 (NY)
1945—Giants, 34-6 (P)
　　　Steelers, 21-7 (NY)
1946—Giants, 17-14 (P)
　　　Giants, 7-0 (NY)
1947—Steelers, 38-21 (NY)
　　　Steelers, 24-7 (P)
1948—Giants, 34-27 (NY)
　　　Steelers, 38-28 (P)
1949—Steelers, 28-7 (P)
　　　Steelers, 21-17 (NY)
1950—Giants, 18-7 (P)
　　　Steelers, 17-6 (NY)
1951—Tie, 13-13 (P)
　　　Giants, 14-0 (NY)
1952—Steelers, 63-7 (P)
1953—Steelers, 24-14 (P)
　　　Steelers, 14-10 (NY)
1954—Giants, 30-6 (P)
　　　Giants, 24-3 (NY)
1955—Steelers, 30-23 (P)
　　　Steelers, 19-17 (NY)
1956—Giants, 38-10 (NY)
　　　Giants, 17-14 (P)
1957—Giants, 35-0 (NY)
　　　Steelers, 21-10 (P)
1958—Giants, 17-6 (NY)
　　　Steelers, 31-10 (P)
1959—Giants, 21-16 (P)
　　　Steelers, 14-9 (NY)
1960—Giants, 19-17 (P)
　　　Giants, 27-24 (NY)
1961—Giants, 17-14 (P)
　　　Giants, 42-21 (NY)
1962—Giants, 31-27 (P)
　　　Steelers, 20-17 (NY)
1963—Steelers, 31-0 (P)
　　　Giants, 33-17 (NY)
1964—Steelers, 27-24 (P)
　　　Steelers, 44-17 (NY)
1965—Giants, 23-13 (P)
　　　Giants, 35-10 (NY)
1966—Tie, 34-34 (P)
　　　Steelers, 47-28 (NY)
1967—Giants, 27-24 (P)
　　　Giants, 28-20 (NY)
1968—Giants, 34-20 (P)
1969—Giants, 10-7 (NY)
　　　Giants, 21-17 (P)
1971—Steelers, 17-13 (P)
1976—Steelers, 27-0 (NY)
1985—Giants, 28-10 (NY)
1991—Giants, 23-20 (P)
(RS Pts.—Giants 1,393, Steelers 1,179)
*Steelers known as Pirates prior to 1941
N.Y. GIANTS vs. SAN DIEGO
RS: Giants lead series, 4-2
1971—Giants, 35-17 (NY)
1975—Giants, 35-24 (NY)
1980—Chargers, 44-7 (SD)
1983—Chargers, 41-34 (NY)

1986—Giants, 20-7 (NY)
1989—Giants, 20-13 (SD)
(RS Pts.—Giants 151, Chargers 146)
N.Y. GIANTS vs. SAN FRANCISCO
RS: Giants lead series, 11-10
PS: Series tied, 3-3
1952—Giants, 23-14 (NY)
1956—Giants, 38-21 (SF)
1957—49ers, 27-17 (NY)
1960—Giants, 21-19 (SF)
1963—Giants, 48-14 (NY)
1968—49ers, 26-10 (NY)
1972—Giants, 23-17 (SF)
1975—Giants, 26-23 (SF)
1977—Giants, 20-17 (NY)
1978—Giants, 27-10 (NY)
1979—Giants, 32-16 (NY)
1980—49ers, 12-0 (SF)
1981—49ers, 17-10 (SF)
　　　*49ers, 38-24 (SF)
1984—49ers, 31-10 (NY)
　　　*49ers, 21-10 (SF)
1985—**Giants, 17-3 (NY)
1986—Giants, 21-17 (SF)
　　　*Giants, 49-3 (NY)
1987—49ers, 41-21 (NY)
1988—49ers, 20-17 (NY)
1989—49ers, 34-24 (SF)
1990—49ers, 7-3 (SF)
　　　***Giants, 15-13 (SF)
1991—Giants, 16-14 (NY)
1992—49ers, 31-14 (NY)
1993—*49ers, 44-3 (SF)
(RS Pts.—49ers 431, Giants 421)
(PS Pts.—49ers 119, Giants 118)
*NFC Divisional Playoff
**NFC First-Round Playoff
***NFC Championship
N.Y. GIANTS vs. SEATTLE
RS: Giants lead series, 5-2
1976—Giants, 28-16 (NY)
1980—Giants, 27-21 (S)
1981—Giants, 32-0 (S)
1983—Seahawks, 17-12 (NY)
1986—Seahawks, 17-12 (S)
1989—Giants, 15-3 (NY)
1992—Giants, 23-10 (NY)
(RS Pts.—Giants 149, Seahawks 84)
N.Y. GIANTS vs. TAMPA BAY
RS: Giants lead series, 8-3
1977—Giants, 10-0 (TB)
1978—Giants, 19-13 (TB)
　　　Giants, 17-14 (NY)
1979—Giants, 17-14 (NY)
　　　Buccaneers, 31-3 (TB)
1980—Buccaneers, 30-13 (TB)
1984—Giants, 17-14 (NY)
　　　Buccaneers, 20-17 (TB)
1985—Giants, 22-20 (NY)
1991—Giants, 21-14 (TB)
1993—Giants, 23-7 (NY)
(RS Pts.—Giants 179, Buccaneers 177)
N.Y. GIANTS vs. *WASHINGTON
RS: Giants lead series, 69-50-3
PS: Series tied, 1-1
1932—Braves, 14-6 (B)
　　　Tie, 0-0 (NY)
1933—Redskins, 21-20 (B)
　　　Giants, 7-0 (NY)
1934—Giants, 16-13 (B)
　　　Giants, 3-0 (NY)
1935—Giants, 20-12 (B)
　　　Giants, 17-6 (NY)
1936—Giants, 7-0 (B)
　　　Redskins, 14-0 (NY)
1937—Redskins, 13-3 (W)
　　　Redskins, 49-14 (NY)
1938—Giants, 10-7 (W)
　　　Giants, 36-0 (NY)
1939—Tie, 0-0 (W)
　　　Giants, 9-7 (NY)
1940—Redskins, 21-7 (W)
　　　Giants, 21-7 (NY)

1941—Giants, 17-10 (W)
　　　Giants, 20-13 (NY)
1942—Giants, 14-7 (W)
　　　Redskins, 14-7 (NY)
1943—Giants, 14-10 (NY)
　　　Giants, 31-7 (W)
　　　**Redskins, 28-0 (NY)
1944—Giants, 16-13 (NY)
　　　Giants, 31-0 (W)
1945—Redskins, 24-14 (NY)
　　　Redskins, 17-0 (W)
1946—Redskins, 24-14 (W)
　　　Giants, 31-0 (NY)
1947—Redskins, 28-20 (W)
　　　Giants, 35-10 (W)
1948—Redskins, 41-10 (W)
　　　Redskins, 28-21 (NY)
1949—Giants, 45-35 (W)
　　　Giants, 23-7 (NY)
1950—Giants, 21-17 (W)
　　　Giants, 24-21 (NY)
1951—Giants, 35-14 (W)
　　　Giants, 28-14 (NY)
1952—Giants, 14-10 (W)
　　　Redskins, 27-17 (NY)
1953—Redskins, 13-9 (W)
　　　Redskins, 24-21 (NY)
1954—Giants, 51-21 (W)
　　　Giants, 24-7 (NY)
1955—Giants, 35-7 (NY)
　　　Giants, 27-20 (W)
1956—Redskins, 33-7 (W)
　　　Giants, 28-14 (NY)
1957—Giants, 24-20 (W)
　　　Redskins, 31-14 (NY)
1958—Giants, 21-14 (W)
　　　Giants, 30-0 (NY)
1959—Giants, 45-14 (NY)
　　　Giants, 24-10 (W)
1960—Tie, 24-24 (NY)
　　　Giants, 17-3 (W)
1961—Giants, 24-21 (W)
　　　Giants, 53-0 (NY)
1962—Giants, 49-34 (NY)
　　　Giants, 42-24 (W)
1963—Giants, 24-14 (W)
　　　Giants, 44-14 (NY)
1964—Giants, 13-10 (W)
　　　Redskins, 36-21 (W)
1965—Redskins, 23-7 (NY)
　　　Giants, 27-10 (W)
1966—Giants, 13-10 (NY)
　　　Redskins, 72-41 (W)
1967—Redskins, 38-34 (W)
1968—Giants, 48-21 (NY)
　　　Giants, 13-10 (W)
1969—Redskins, 20-14 (W)
1970—Giants, 35-33 (NY)
　　　Giants, 27-24 (W)
1971—Redskins, 30-3 (NY)
　　　Redskins, 23-7 (W)
1972—Redskins, 23-16 (NY)
　　　Redskins, 27-13 (W)
1973—Redskins, 21-3 (New Haven)
　　　Redskins, 27-24 (W)
1974—Redskins, 13-10 (New Haven)
　　　Redskins, 24-3 (W)
1975—Redskins, 49-13 (W)
　　　Redskins, 21-13 (NY)
1976—Redskins, 19-17 (W)
　　　Giants, 12-9 (NY)
1977—Giants, 20-17 (NY)
　　　Giants, 17-6 (W)
1978—Giants, 17-6 (NY)
　　　Redskins, 16-13 (W) OT
1979—Redskins, 27-0 (W)
　　　Giants, 14-6 (NY)
1980—Redskins, 23-21 (NY)
　　　Redskins, 16-13 (W)
1981—Giants, 17-7 (W)
　　　Redskins, 30-27 (NY) OT
1982—Redskins, 27-17 (NY)
　　　Redskins, 15-14 (W)

1983—Redskins, 33-17 (NY)
　　　Redskins, 31-22 (W)
1984—Redskins, 30-14 (W)
　　　Giants, 37-13 (NY)
1985—Giants, 17-3 (NY)
　　　Redskins, 23-21 (W)
1986—Giants, 27-20 (NY)
　　　Giants, 24-14 (W)
　　　***Giants, 17-0 (NY)
1987—Redskins, 38-12 (NY)
　　　Redskins, 23-19 (W)
1988—Giants, 27-20 (NY)
　　　Giants, 24-23 (W)
1989—Giants, 27-24 (W)
　　　Giants, 20-17 (NY)
1990—Giants, 24-20 (W)
　　　Giants, 21-10 (NY)
1991—Redskins, 17-13 (NY)
　　　Redskins, 34-17 (W)
1992—Giants, 24-7 (W)
　　　Redskins, 28-10 (NY)
1993—Giants, 41-7 (W)
　　　Giants, 20-6 (NY)
(RS Pts.—Giants 2,430, Redskins 2,167)
(PS Pts.—Redskins 28, Giants 17)
*Franchise in Boston prior to 1937 and
known as Braves prior to 1933
**Division Playoff
***NFC Championship

N.Y. JETS vs. ARIZONA
RS: Cardinals lead series, 2-1;
See Arizona vs. N.Y. Jets
N.Y. JETS vs. ATLANTA
RS: Series tied, 3-3;
See Atlanta vs. N.Y. Jets
N.Y. JETS vs. BUFFALO
RS: Bills lead series, 37-29
PS: Bills lead series, 1-0;
See Buffalo vs. N.Y. Jets
N.Y. JETS vs. CHICAGO
RS: Bears lead series, 3-1;
See Chicago vs. N.Y. Jets
N.Y. JETS vs. CINCINNATI
RS: Jets lead series, 9-6
PS: Jets lead series, 1-0;
See Cincinnati vs. N.Y. Jets
N.Y. JETS vs. CLEVELAND
RS: Browns lead series, 8-6
PS: Browns lead series, 1-0;
See Cleveland vs. N.Y. Jets
N.Y. JETS vs. DALLAS
RS: Cowboys lead series, 5-1;
See Dallas vs. N.Y. Jets
N.Y. JETS vs. DENVER
RS: Broncos lead series, 12-11-1;
See Denver vs. N.Y. Jets
N.Y. JETS vs. DETROIT
RS: Series tied, 3-3;
See Detroit vs. N.Y. Jets
N.Y. JETS vs. GREEN BAY
RS: Jets lead series, 5-1;
See Green Bay vs. N.Y. Jets
N.Y. JETS vs. HOUSTON
RS: Oilers lead series, 17-12-1
PS: Oilers lead series, 1-0;
See Houston vs. N.Y. Jets
N.Y. JETS vs. INDIANAPOLIS
RS: Colts lead series, 27-20
PS: Jets lead series, 1-0;
See Indianapolis vs. N.Y. Jets
N.Y. JETS vs. KANSAS CITY
RS: Chiefs lead series, 14-12-1
PS: Series tied, 1-1;
See Kansas City vs. N.Y. Jets
N.Y. JETS vs. L.A. RAIDERS
RS: Raiders lead series, 14-9-2
PS: Jets lead series, 2-0;
See L.A. Raiders vs. N.Y. Jets
N.Y. JETS vs. L.A. RAMS
RS: Rams lead series, 5-2;
See L.A. Rams vs. N.Y. Jets
N.Y. JETS vs. MIAMI

RS: Jets lead series, 28-27-1
PS: Dolphins lead series, 1-0;
See Miami vs. N.Y. Jets

N.Y. JETS vs. MINNESOTA
RS: Jets lead series, 3-1;
See Minnesota vs. N.Y. Jets

N.Y. JETS vs. NEW ENGLAND
RS: Jets lead series, 38-28-1
PS: Patriots lead series, 1-0;
See New England vs. N.Y. Jets

N.Y. JETS vs. NEW ORLEANS
RS: Jets lead series, 4-3;
See New Orleans vs. N.Y. Jets

N.Y. JETS vs. N.Y. GIANTS
RS: Jets lead series, 34-0;
See N.Y. Giants vs. N.Y. Jets

N.Y. JETS vs. PHILADELPHIA
RS: Eagles lead series, 5-0
1973—Eagles, 24-23 (P)
1977—Eagles, 27-0 (P)
1978—Eagles, 17-9 (P)
1987—Eagles, 38-27 (NY)
1993—Eagles, 35-30 (NY)
(RS Pts.—Eagles 141, Jets 89)

N.Y. JETS vs. PITTSBURGH
RS: Steelers lead series, 12-1
1970—Steelers, 21-17 (P)
1973—Steelers, 26-14 (P)
1975—Steelers, 20-7 (NY)
1977—Steelers, 23-20 (NY)
1978—Steelers, 28-17 (NY)
1981—Steelers, 38-10 (P)
1983—Steelers, 34-7 (NY)
1984—Steelers, 23-17 (NY)
1986—Steelers, 45-24 (NY)
1988—Jets, 24-20 (NY)
1989—Steelers, 13-0 (NY)
1990—Steelers, 24-7 (NY)
1992—Steelers, 27-10 (P)
(RS Pts.—Steelers 342, Jets 174)

*N.Y. JETS vs. **SAN DIEGO
RS: Chargers lead series, 16-9-1
1960—Chargers, 21-7 (NY)
    Chargers, 50-43 (LA)
1961—Chargers, 25-10 (NY)
    Chargers, 48-13 (SD)
1962—Chargers, 40-14 (SD)
    Titans, 23-3 (NY)
1963—Chargers, 24-20 (SD)
    Chargers, 53-7 (NY)
1964—Tie, 17-17 (NY)
    Chargers, 38-3 (SD)
1965—Chargers, 34-9 (NY)
    Chargers, 38-7 (SD)
1966—Jets, 17-16 (NY)
    Chargers, 42-27 (SD)
1967—Jets, 42-31 (SD)
1968—Jets, 23-20 (NY)
    Jets, 37-15 (SD)
1969—Chargers, 34-27 (SD)
1971—Chargers, 49-21 (SD)
1974—Jets, 27-14 (NY)
1975—Chargers, 24-16 (SD)
1983—Jets, 41-29 (SD)
1989—Jets, 20-17 (SD)
1990—Chargers, 39-3 (NY)
    Chargers, 38-17 (SD)
1991—Jets, 24-3 (NY)
(RS Pts.—Chargers 762, Jets 515)
*Jets known as Titans prior to 1963
**Franchise in Los Angeles prior to 1961

N.Y. JETS vs. SAN FRANCISCO
RS: 49ers lead series, 6-1
1971—49ers, 24-21 (NY)
1976—49ers, 17-6 (SF)
1980—49ers, 37-27 (NY)
1983—Jets, 27-13 (SF)
1986—49ers, 24-10 (SF)
1989—49ers, 23-10 (NY)
1992—49ers, 31-14 (NY)
(RS Pts.—49ers 169, Jets 115)

N.Y. JETS vs. SEATTLE
RS: Seahawks lead series, 8-3

1977—Seahawks, 17-0 (NY)
1978—Seahawks, 24-17 (NY)
1979—Seahawks, 30-7 (S)
1980—Seahawks, 27-17 (NY)
1981—Seahawks, 19-3 (NY)
    Seahawks, 27-23 (S)
1983—Seahawks, 17-10 (NY)
1985—Jets, 17-14 (NY)
1986—Jets, 38-7 (S)
1987—Jets, 30-14 (NY)
1991—Seahawks, 20-13 (S)
(RS Pts.—Seahawks 216, Jets 175)

N.Y. JETS vs. TAMPA BAY
RS: Jets lead series, 5-1
1976—Jets, 34-0 (NY)
1982—Jets, 32-17 (NY)
1984—Buccaneers, 41-21 (TB)
1985—Jets, 62-28 (NY)
1990—Jets, 16-14 (TB)
1991—Jets, 16-13 (NY)
(RS Pts.—Jets 181, Buccaneers 113)

N.Y. JETS vs. WASHINGTON
RS: Redskins lead series, 4-1
1972—Redskins, 35-17 (NY)
1976—Redskins, 37-16 (NY)
1978—Redskins, 23-3 (W)
1987—Redskins, 17-16 (W)
1993—Jets, 3-0 (W)
(RS Pts.—Redskins 112, Jets 55)

PHILADELPHIA vs. ARIZONA
RS: Cardinals lead series, 44-43-5
PS: Series tied, 1-1;
See Arizona vs. Philadelphia

PHILADELPHIA vs. ATLANTA
RS: Eagles lead series, 8-6-1
PS: Falcons lead series, 1-0;
See Atlanta vs. Philadelphia

PHILADELPHIA vs. BUFFALO
RS: Eagles lead series, 4-3;
See Buffalo vs. Philadelphia

PHILADELPHIA vs. CHICAGO
RS: Bears lead series, 23-3-1
PS: Series tied, 1-1;
See Chicago vs. Philadelphia

PHILADELPHIA vs. CINCINNATI
RS: Bengals lead series, 5-1;
See Cincinnati vs. Philadelphia

PHILADELPHIA vs. CLEVELAND
RS: Browns lead series, 30-12-1;
See Cleveland vs. Philadelphia

PHILADELPHIA vs. DALLAS
RS: Cowboys lead series, 40-26
PS: Series tied, 1-1;
See Dallas vs. Philadelphia

PHILADELPHIA vs. DENVER
RS: Eagles lead series, 5-2;
See Denver vs. Philadelphia

PHILADELPHIA vs. DETROIT
RS: Lions lead series, 12-9-2;
See Detroit vs. Philadelphia

PHILADELPHIA vs. GREEN BAY
RS: Packers lead series, 19-7
PS: Eagles lead series, 1-0;
See Green Bay vs. Philadelphia

PHILADELPHIA vs. HOUSTON
RS: Eagles lead series, 5-0;
See Houston vs. Philadelphia

PHILADELPHIA vs. INDIANAPOLIS
RS: Series tied, 6-6;
See Indianapolis vs. Philadelphia

PHILADELPHIA vs. KANSAS CITY
RS: Series tied, 1-1;
See Kansas City vs. Philadelphia

PHILADELPHIA vs. L.A. RAIDERS
RS: Eagles lead series, 4-2
PS: Raiders lead series, 1-0;
See L.A. Raiders vs. Philadelphia

PHILADELPHIA vs. L.A. RAMS
RS: Rams lead series, 15-11-1
PS: Series tied, 1-1;
See L.A. Rams vs. Philadelphia

PHILADELPHIA vs. MIAMI

RS: Dolphins lead series, 6-2;
See Miami vs. Philadelphia

PHILADELPHIA vs. MINNESOTA
RS: Vikings lead series, 10-6
PS: Eagles lead series, 1-0;
See Minnesota vs. Philadelphia

PHILADELPHIA vs. NEW ENGLAND
RS: Eagles lead series, 5-2;
See New England vs. Philadelphia

PHILADELPHIA vs. NEW ORLEANS
RS: Eagles lead series, 11-8
PS: Eagles lead series, 1-0;
See New Orleans vs. Philadelphia

PHILADELPHIA vs. N.Y. GIANTS
RS: Giants lead series, 62-54-2
PS: Giants lead series, 1-0;
See N.Y. Giants vs. Philadelphia

PHILADELPHIA vs. N.Y. JETS
RS: Eagles lead series, 5-0;
See N.Y. Jets vs. Philadelphia

PHILADELPHIA vs. *PITTSBURGH
RS: Eagles lead series, 43-25-3
PS: Eagles lead series, 1-0
1933—Eagles, 25-6 (Phila)
1934—Eagles, 17-0 (Pitt)
    Pirates, 9-7 (Phila)
1935—Pirates, 17-7 (Phila)
    Eagles, 17-6 (Pitt)
1936—Pirates, 17-0 (Pitt)
    Pirates, 6-0 (Johnstown, Pa.)
1937—Pirates, 27-14 (Pitt)
    Pirates, 16-7 (Phila)
1938—Eagles, 27-7 (Buffalo)
    Eagles, 14-7 (Charleston, W. Va.)
1939—Eagles, 17-14 (Phila)
    Pirates, 24-12 (Pitt)
1940—Pirates, 7-3 (Pitt)
    Eagles, 7-0 (Phila)
1941—Eagles, 10-7 (Pitt)
    Tie, 7-7 (Phila)
1942—Eagles, 24-14 (Pitt)
    Steelers, 14-0 (Phila)
1945—Eagles, 45-3 (Pitt)
    Eagles, 30-6 (Phila)
1946—Steelers, 10-7 (Pitt)
    Eagles, 10-7 (Phila)
1947—Steelers, 35-24 (Pitt)
    Eagles, 21-0 (Phila)
    **Eagles, 21-0 (Pitt)
1948—Eagles, 34-7 (Pitt)
    Eagles, 17-0 (Phila)
1949—Eagles, 38-7 (Pitt)
    Eagles, 34-17 (Phila)
1950—Eagles, 17-10 (Pitt)
    Steelers, 9-7 (Phila)
1951—Eagles, 34-13 (Pitt)
    Steelers, 17-13 (Phila)
1952—Eagles, 31-25 (Pitt)
    Eagles, 26-21 (Phila)
1953—Eagles, 23-17 (Phila)
    Eagles, 35-7 (Pitt)
1954—Eagles, 24-22 (Phila)
    Steelers, 17-7 (Pitt)
1955—Steelers, 13-7 (Pitt)
    Eagles, 24-0 (Phila)
1956—Eagles, 35-21 (Phila)
    Eagles, 14-7 (Phila)
1957—Steelers, 6-0 (Pitt)
    Eagles, 7-6 (Phila)
1958—Steelers, 24-3 (Pitt)
    Steelers, 31-24 (Phila)
1959—Eagles, 28-24 (Phila)
    Steelers, 31-0 (Pitt)
1960—Eagles, 34-7 (Phila)
    Steelers, 27-21 (Pitt)
1961—Eagles, 21-16 (Pitt)
    Eagles, 35-24 (Phila)
1962—Steelers, 13-7 (Pitt)
    Steelers, 26-17 (Phila)
1963—Tie, 21-21 (Phila)
    Tie, 20-20 (Pitt)
1964—Eagles, 21-7 (Phila)
    Eagles, 34-10 (Pitt)

1965—Steelers, 20-14 (Phila)
    Eagles, 47-13 (Pitt)
1966—Steelers, 31-14 (Pitt)
    Eagles, 27-23 (Phila)
1967—Eagles, 34-24 (Phila)
1968—Steelers, 6-3 (Pitt)
1969—Eagles, 41-27 (Phila)
1970—Eagles, 30-20 (Phila)
1974—Steelers, 27-0 (Pitt)
1979—Eagles, 17-14 (Phila)
1988—Eagles, 27-26 (Pitt)
1991—Eagles, 23-14 (Phila)
(RS Pts.—Eagles 1,359, Steelers 1,007)
(PS Pts.—Eagles 21, Steelers 0)
*Steelers known as Pirates prior to 1941
**Division Playoff

PHILADELPHIA vs. SAN DIEGO
RS: Chargers lead series, 3-2
1974—Eagles, 13-7 (SD)
1980—Chargers, 22-21 (SD)
1985—Chargers, 20-14 (SD)
1986—Eagles, 23-7 (P)
1989—Chargers, 20-17 (SD)
(RS Pts.—Eagles 88, Chargers 76)

PHILADELPHIA vs. SAN FRANCISCO
RS: 49ers lead series, 13-5-1
1951—Eagles, 21-14 (P)
1953—49ers, 31-21 (SF)
1956—Tie, 10-10 (P)
1958—49ers, 30-24 (P)
1959—49ers, 24-14 (SF)
1964—49ers, 28-24 (P)
1966—Eagles, 35-34 (SF)
1967—49ers, 28-27 (P)
1969—49ers, 14-13 (SF)
1971—49ers, 31-3 (P)
1973—49ers, 38-28 (SF)
1975—Eagles, 27-17 (P)
1983—Eagles, 22-17 (SF)
1984—49ers, 21-9 (P)
1985—49ers, 24-13 (SF)
1989—49ers, 38-28 (P)
1991—49ers, 23-7 (P)
1992—49ers, 20-14 (SF)
1993—Eagles, 37-34 (SF) OT
(RS Pts.—49ers 476, Eagles 377)

PHILADELPHIA vs. SEATTLE
RS: Eagles lead series, 4-1
1976—Eagles, 27-10 (P)
1980—Eagles, 27-20 (S)
1986—Seahawks, 24-20 (S)
1989—Eagles, 31-7 (P)
1992—Eagles, 20-17 (S) OT
(RS Pts.—Eagles 125, Seahawks 78)

PHILADELPHIA vs. TAMPA BAY
RS: Eagles lead series, 3-1
PS: Buccaneers lead series, 1-0
1977—Eagles, 13-3 (P)
1979—*Buccaneers, 24-17 (TB)
1981—Eagles, 20-10 (P)
1988—Eagles, 41-14 (TB)
1991—Buccaneers, 14-13 (TB)
(RS Pts.—Eagles 87, Buccaneers 41)
(PS Pts.—Buccaneers 24, Eagles 17)
*NFC Divisional Playoff

PHILADELPHIA vs. *WASHINGTON
RS: Redskins lead series, 66-46-5
PS: Redskins lead series, 1-0
1934—Redskins, 6-0 (B)
    Redskins, 14-7 (P)
1935—Eagles, 7-6 (P)
1936—Redskins, 26-3 (P)
    Redskins, 17-7 (B)
1937—Eagles, 14-0 (W)
    Redskins, 10-7 (P)
1938—Redskins, 26-23 (P)
    Redskins, 20-14 (W)
1939—Redskins, 7-0 (P)
    Redskins, 7-6 (P)
1940—Redskins, 34-17 (P)
    Redskins, 13-6 (W)
1941—Redskins, 21-17 (P)
    Redskins, 20-14 (W)

1942—Redskins, 14-10 (P)
    Redskins, 30-27 (W)
1944—Tie, 31-31 (P)
    Eagles, 37-7 (W)
1945—Redskins, 24-14 (W)
    Eagles, 16-0 (P)
1946—Eagles, 28-24 (W)
    Redskins, 27-10 (W)
1947—Eagles, 45-42 (P)
    Eagles, 38-14 (W)
1948—Eagles, 45-0 (W)
    Eagles, 42-21 (P)
1949—Eagles, 49-14 (P)
    Eagles, 44-21 (W)
1950—Eagles, 35-3 (P)
    Eagles, 33-0 (W)
1951—Redskins, 27-23 (P)
    Eagles, 35-21 (W)
1952—Eagles, 38-20 (P)
    Redskins, 27-21 (W)
1953—Tie, 21-21 (P)
    Redskins, 10-0 (W)
1954—Eagles, 49-21 (W)
    Eagles, 41-33 (P)
1955—Redskins, 31-30 (P)
    Redskins, 34-21 (W)
1956—Eagles, 13-9 (P)
    Redskins, 19-17 (W)
1957—Eagles, 21-12 (P)
    Redskins, 42-7 (W)
1958—Redskins, 24-14 (P)
    Redskins, 20-0 (W)
1959—Eagles, 30-23 (P)
    Eagles, 34-14 (W)
1960—Eagles, 19-13 (P)
    Eagles, 38-28 (W)
1961—Eagles, 14-7 (P)
    Eagles, 27-24 (W)
1962—Redskins, 27-21 (P)
    Eagles, 37-14 (W)
1963—Eagles, 37-24 (W)
    Redskins, 13-10 (P)
1964—Redskins, 35-20 (W)
    Redskins, 21-10 (P)
1065—Redskins, 23-21 (W)
    Eagles, 21-14 (P)
1966—Redskins, 27-13 (P)
    Eagles, 37-28 (W)
1967—Eagles, 35-24 (P)
    Tie, 35-35 (W)
1968—Redskins, 17-14 (W)
    Redskins, 16-10 (P)
1969—Tie, 28-28 (W)
    Redskins, 34-29 (P)
1970—Redskins, 33-21 (P)
    Redskins, 24-6 (W)
1971—Tie, 7-7 (W)
    Redskins, 20-13 (P)
1972—Redskins, 14-0 (W)
    Redskins, 23-7 (P)
1973—Redskins, 28-7 (P)
    Redskins, 38-20 (W)
1974—Redskins, 27-20 (P)
    Redskins, 26-7 (W)
1975—Eagles, 26-10 (P)
    Eagles, 26-3 (W)
1976—Redskins, 20-17 (P) OT
    Redskins, 24-0 (W)
1977—Redskins, 23-17 (W)
    Redskins, 17-14 (P)
1978—Redskins, 35-30 (W)
    Eagles, 17-10 (P)
1979—Eagles, 28-17 (P)
    Redskins, 17-7 (W)
1980—Eagles, 24-14 (P)
    Eagles, 24-0 (W)
1981—Eagles, 36-13 (P)
    Redskins, 15-13 (W)
1982—Redskins, 37-34 (P) OT
    Redskins, 13-9 (W)
1983—Redskins, 23-13 (P)
    Redskins, 28-24 (W)
1984—Redskins, 20-0 (W)

Eagles, 16-10 (P)
1985—Eagles, 19-6 (W)
    Redskins, 17-12 (P)
1986—Redskins, 41-14 (W)
    Redskins, 21-14 (P)
1987—Redskins, 34-24 (W)
    Eagles, 31-27 (P)
1988—Redskins, 17-10 (W)
    Redskins, 20-19 (P)
1989—Eagles, 42-37 (W)
    Redskins, 10-3 (P)
1990—Redskins, 13-7 (W)
    Eagles, 28-14 (P)
    **Redskins, 20-6 (P)
1991—Redskins, 23-0 (W)
    Eagles, 24-22 (W)
1992—Redskins, 16-12 (W)
    Eagles, 17-13 (P)
1993—Eagles, 34-31 (P)
    Eagles, 17-14 (W)
(RS Pts.—Eagles 2,347, Redskins 2,324)
(PS Pts.—Redskins 20, Eagles 6)
*Franchise in Boston prior to 1937
**NFC First-Round Playoff

PITTSBURGH vs. ARIZONA
RS: Steelers lead series, 29-21-3;
See Arizona vs. Pittsburgh
PITTSBURGH vs. ATLANTA
RS: Steelers lead series, 9-1;
See Atlanta vs. Pittsburgh
PITTSBURGH vs. BUFFALO
RS: Bills lead series, 7-6
PS: Series tied, 1-1;
See Buffalo vs. Pittsburgh
PITTSBURGH vs. CHICAGO
RS: Bears lead series, 16-4-1;
See Chicago vs. Pittsburgh
PITTSBURGH vs. CINCINNATI
RS: Steelers lead series, 26-21;
See Cincinnati vs. Pittsburgh
PITTSBURGH vs. CLEVELAND
RS: Browns lead series, 52-36;
See Cleveland vs. Pittsburgh
PITTSBURGH vs. DALLAS
RS: Cowboys lead series, 12-11
PS: Steelers lead series, 2-0;
See Dallas vs. Pittsburgh
PITTSBURGH vs. DENVER
RS: Broncos lead series, 10-5-1
PS: Series tied, 2-2;
See Denver vs. Pittsburgh
PITTSBURGH vs. DETROIT
RS: Lions lead series, 13-11-1;
See Detroit vs. Pittsburgh
PITTSBURGH vs. GREEN BAY
RS: Packers lead series, 17-11;
See Green Bay vs. Pittsburgh
PITTSBURGH vs. HOUSTON
RS: Steelers lead series, 29-18
PS: Steelers lead series, 3-0;
See Houston vs. Pittsburgh
PITTSBURGH vs. INDIANAPOLIS
RS: Steelers lead series, 10-4
PS: Steelers lead series, 2-0;
See Indianapolis vs. Pittsburgh
PITTSBURGH vs. KANSAS CITY
RS: Steelers lead series, 13-5
PS: Chiefs lead series, 1-0;
See Kansas City vs. Pittsburgh
PITTSBURGH vs. L.A. RAIDERS
RS: Raiders lead series, 7-3
PS: Series tied, 3-3;
See L.A. Raiders vs. Pittsburgh
PITTSBURGH vs. L.A. RAMS
RS: Rams lead series, 14-4-2
PS: Steelers lead series, 1-0;
See L.A. Rams vs. Pittsburgh
PITTSBURGH vs. MIAMI
RS: Dolphins lead series, 7-5
PS: Dolphins lead series, 2-1;
See Miami vs. Pittsburgh
PITTSBURGH vs. MINNESOTA

RS: Vikings lead series, 7-4
PS: Steelers lead series, 1-0;
See Minnesota vs. Pittsburgh
PITTSBURGH vs. NEW ENGLAND
RS: Steelers lead series, 9-3;
See New England vs. Pittsburgh
PITTSBURGH vs. NEW ORLEANS
RS: Steelers lead series, 6-5;
See New Orleans vs. Pittsburgh
PITTSBURGH vs. N.Y. GIANTS
RS: Giants lead series, 42-26-3;
See N.Y. Giants vs. Pittsburgh
PITTSBURGH vs. N.Y. JETS
RS: Steelers lead series, 12-1;
See N.Y. Jets vs. Pittsburgh
PITTSBURGH vs. PHILADELPHIA
RS: Eagles lead series, 43-25-3
PS: Eagles lead series, 1-0;
See Philadelphia vs. Pittsburgh
PITTSBURGH vs. SAN DIEGO
RS: Steelers lead series, 14-4
PS: Chargers lead series, 1-0
1971—Steelers, 21-17 (P)
1972—Steelers, 24-2 (SD)
1973—Steelers, 38-21 (P)
1975—Steelers, 37-0 (SD)
1976—Steelers, 23-0 (P)
1977—Steelers, 10-9 (SD)
1979—Chargers, 35-7 (SD)
1980—Chargers, 26-17 (SD)
1982—*Chargers, 31-28 (P)
1983—Steelers, 26-3 (P)
1984—Steelers, 52-24 (P)
1985—Chargers, 54-44 (SD)
1987—Steelers, 20-16 (SD)
1988—Chargers, 20-14 (SD)
1989—Steelers, 20-17 (P)
1990—Steelers, 36-14 (P)
1991—Steelers, 26-20 (P)
1992—Steelers, 23-6 (SD)
1993—Steelers,.16-3 (P)
(RS Pts.—Steelers 454, Chargers 287)
(PS Pts.—Chargers 31, Steelers 28)
*AFC First-Round Playoff
PITTSBURGH vs. SAN FRANCISCO
RS: 49ers lead series, 8-7
1951—49ers, 28-24 (P)
1952—Steelers, 24-7 (SF)
1954—49ers, 31-3 (SF)
1958—49ers, 23-20 (SF)
1961—Steelers, 20-10 (P)
1965—49ers, 27-17 (SF)
1968—49ers, 45-28 (P)
1973—Steelers, 37-14 (SF)
1977—Steelers, 27-0 (P)
1978—Steelers, 24-7 (SF)
1981—49ers, 17-14 (P)
1984—Steelers, 20-17 (SF)
1987—Steelers, 30-17 (P)
1990—49ers, 27-7 (SF)
1993—49ers, 24-13 (P)
(RS Pts.—Steelers 308, 49ers 294)
PITTSBURGH vs. SEATTLE
RS: Series tied, 5-5
1977—Steelers, 30-20 (P)
1978—Steelers, 21-10 (P)
1981—Seahawks, 24-21 (S)
1982—Seahawks, 16-0 (S)
1983—Steelers, 27-21 (S)
1986—Seahawks, 30-0 (S)
1987—Steelers, 13-9 (P)
1991—Seahawks, 27-7 (P)
1992—Steelers, 20-14 (P)
1993—Seahawks, 16-6 (S)
(RS Pts.—Seahawks 187, Steelers 145)
PITTSBURGH vs. TAMPA BAY
RS: Steelers lead series, 4-0
1976—Steelers, 42-0 (P)
1980—Steelers, 24-21 (TB)
1983—Steelers, 17-12 (P)
1989—Steelers, 31-22 (TB)
(RS Pts.—Steelers 114, Buccaneers 55)
***PITTSBURGH vs. **WASHINGTON**

RS: Redskins lead series, 42-27-3
1933—Redskins, 21-6 (P)
    Pirates, 16-14 (B)
1934—Redskins, 7-0 (P)
    Redskins, 39-0 (B)
1935—Pirates, 6-0 (P)
    Redskins, 13-3 (B)
1936—Pirates, 10-0 (P)
    Redskins, 30-0 (B)
1937—Redskins, 34-20 (W)
    Pirates, 21-13 (P)
1938—Redskins, 7-0 (P)
    Redskins, 15-0 (W)
1939—Redskins, 44-14 (W)
    Redskins, 21-14 (P)
1940—Redskins, 40-10 (P)
    Redskins, 37-10 (W)
1941—Redskins, 24-20 (P)
    Redskins, 23-3 (W)
1942—Redskins, 28-14 (P)
    Redskins, 14-0 (P)
1945—Redskins, 14-0 (P)
    Redskins, 24-0 (W)
1946—Tie, 14-14 (W)
    Steelers, 14-7 (P)
1947—Redskins, 27-26 (W)
    Steelers, 21-14 (W)
1948—Redskins, 17-14 (W)
    Steelers, 10-7 (P)
1949—Redskins, 27-14 (P)
    Redskins, 27-14 (W)
1950—Steelers, 26-7 (W)
    Redskins, 24-7 (P)
1951—Redskins, 22-7 (P)
    Steelers, 20-10 (W)
1952—Redskins, 28-24 (P)
    Steelers, 24-23 (W)
1953—Redskins, 17-9 (P)
    Steelers, 14-13 (W)
1954—Steelers, 37-7 (P)
    Redskins, 17-14 (W)
1955—Redskins, 23-14 (W)
    Redskins, 28-17 (W)
1956—Steelers, 30-13 (P)
    Steelers, 23-0 (W)
1957—Steelers, 28-7 (P)
    Redskins, 10-3 (W)
1958—Redskins, 24-16 (P)
    Tie, 14-14 (W)
1959—Redskins, 23-17 (P)
    Steelers, 27-6 (W)
1960—Tie, 27-27 (W)
    Steelers, 22-10 (P)
1961—Steelers, 20-0 (P)
    Steelers, 30-14 (W)
1962—Steelers, 23-21 (P)
    Steelers, 27-24 (W)
1963—Steelers, 38-27 (P)
    Steelers, 34-28 (W)
1964—Redskins, 30-0 (P)
    Steelers, 14-7 (W)
1965—Redskins, 31-3 (P)
    Redskins, 35-14 (W)
1966—Redskins, 33-27 (P)
    Redskins, 24-10 (W)
1967—Redskins, 15-10 (P)
1968—Redskins, 16-13 (W)
1969—Redskins, 14-7 (P)
1973—Steelers, 21-16 (P)
1979—Steelers, 38-7 (P)
1985—Redskins, 30-23 (W)
1988—Redskins, 30-29 (W)
1991—Redskins, 41-14 (P)
(RS Pts.—Redskins 1,390, Steelers 1,117)
*Steelers known as Pirates prior to 1941
**Franchise in Boston prior to 1937

SAN DIEGO vs. ARIZONA
RS: Chargers lead series, 5-1;
See Arizona vs. San Diego
SAN DIEGO vs. ATLANTA
RS: Falcons lead series, 3-1;

See Atlanta vs. San Diego

SAN DIEGO vs. BUFFALO
RS: Chargers lead series, 16-7-2
PS: Bills lead series, 2-1;
See Buffalo vs. San Diego

SAN DIEGO vs. CHICAGO
RS: Chargers lead series, 4-2;
See Chicago vs. San Diego

SAN DIEGO vs. CINCINNATI
RS: Chargers lead series, 12-8
PS: Bengals lead series, 1-0;
See Cincinnati vs. San Diego

SAN DIEGO vs. CLEVELAND
RS: Chargers lead series, 8-6-1;
See Cleveland vs. San Diego

SAN DIEGO vs. DALLAS
RS: Cowboys lead series, 4-1;
See Dallas vs. San Diego

SAN DIEGO vs. DENVER
RS: Broncos lead series, 35-32-1;
See Denver vs. San Diego

SAN DIEGO vs. DETROIT
RS: Lions lead series, 3-2;
See Detroit vs. San Diego

SAN DIEGO vs. GREEN BAY
RS: Packers lead series, 4-1;
See Green Bay vs. San Diego

SAN DIEGO vs. HOUSTON
RS: Chargers lead series, 18-13-1
PS: Oilers lead series, 3-0;
See Houston vs. San Diego

SAN DIEGO vs. INDIANAPOLIS
RS: Chargers lead series, 9-5;
See Indianapolis vs. San Diego

SAN DIEGO vs. KANSAS CITY
RS: Chiefs lead series, 35-31-1
PS: Chargers lead series, 1-0;
See Kansas City vs. San Diego

SAN DIEGO vs. L.A. RAIDERS
RS: Raiders lead series, 41-25-2
PS: Raiders lead series, 1-0;
See L.A. Raiders vs. San Diego

SAN DIEGO vs. L.A. RAMS
RS: Rams lead series, 3-2;
See L.A. Rams vs. San Diego

SAN DIEGO vs. MIAMI
RS: Chargers lead series, 10-5
PS: Dolphins lead series, 2-1;
See Miami vs. San Diego

SAN DIEGO vs. MINNESOTA
RS: Chargers lead series, 4-3;
See Minnesota vs. San Diego

SAN DIEGO vs. NEW ENGLAND
RS: Patriots lead series, 13-11-2
PS: Chargers lead series, 1-0;
See New England vs. San Diego

SAN DIEGO vs. NEW ORLEANS
RS: Chargers lead series, 4-1;
See New Orleans vs. San Diego

SAN DIEGO vs. N.Y. GIANTS
RS: Giants lead series, 4-2;
See N.Y. Giants vs. San Diego

SAN DIEGO vs. N.Y. JETS
RS: Chargers lead series, 16-9-1;
See N.Y. Jets vs. San Diego

SAN DIEGO vs. PHILADELPHIA
RS: Chargers lead series, 3-2;
See Philadelphia vs. San Diego

SAN DIEGO vs. PITTSBURGH
RS: Steelers lead series, 14-4
PS: Chargers lead series, 1-0;
See Pittsburgh vs. San Diego

SAN DIEGO vs. SAN FRANCISCO
RS: Series tied, 3-3
1972—49ers, 34-3 (SF)
1976—Chargers, 13-7 (SD) OT
1979—Chargers, 31-9 (SD)
1982—49ers, 41-37 (SF)
1988—49ers, 48-10 (SD)
1991—49ers, 34-14 (SF)
(RS Pts.—49ers 169, Chargers 112)

SAN DIEGO vs. SEATTLE
RS: Series tied, 15-15

1977—Chargers, 30-28 (S)
1978—Chargers, 24-20 (S)
     Chargers, 37-10 (SD)
1979—Chargers, 33-16 (S)
     Chargers, 20-10 (SD)
1980—Chargers, 34-13 (S)
     Chargers, 21-14 (SD)
1981—Chargers, 24-10 (SD)
     Seahawks, 44-23 (S)
1983—Seahawks, 34-31 (S)
     Chargers, 28-21 (SD)
1984—Seahawks, 31-17 (S)
     Seahawks, 24-0 (SD)
1985—Seahawks, 49-35 (SD)
     Seahawks, 26-21 (S)
1986—Seahawks, 33-7 (S)
     Seahawks, 34-24 (SD)
1987—Seahawks, 34-3 (S)
1988—Chargers, 17-6 (SD)
     Seahawks, 17-14 (S)
1989—Seahawks, 17-16 (SD)
     Seahawks, 10-7 (S)
1990—Chargers, 31-14 (S)
     Seahawks, 13-10 (SD) OT
1991—Seahawks, 20-9 (S)
     Chargers, 17-14 (SD)
1992—Chargers, 17-6 (SD)
     Chargers, 31-14 (S)
1993—Chargers, 18-12 (SD)
     Seahawks, 31-14 (S)
(RS Pts.—Seahawks 625, Chargers 613)

SAN DIEGO vs. TAMPA BAY
RS: Chargers lead series, 6-0
1976—Chargers, 23-0 (TB)
1981—Chargers, 24-23 (TB)
1987—Chargers, 17-13 (SD)
1990—Chargers, 41-10 (SD)
1992—Chargers, 29-14 (SD)
1993—Chargers, 32-17 (TB)
(RS Pts.—Chargers 166, Buccaneers 77)

SAN DIEGO vs. WASHINGTON
RS: Redskins lead series, 5-0
1973—Redskins, 38-0 (W)
1980—Redskins, 40-17 (W)
1983—Redskins, 27-24 (SD)
1986—Redskins, 30-27 (SD)
1989—Redskins, 26-21 (W)
(RS Pts.—Redskins 161, Chargers 89)

SAN FRANCISCO vs. ARIZONA
RS: 49ers lead series, 10-9;
See Arizona vs. San Francisco

SAN FRANCISCO vs. ATLANTA
RS: 49ers lead series, 32-21-1;
See Atlanta vs. San Francisco

SAN FRANCISCO vs. BUFFALO
RS: Bills lead series, 3-2;
See Buffalo vs. San Francisco

SAN FRANCISCO vs. CHICAGO
RS: Series tied, 25-25-1
PS: 49ers lead series, 2-0;
See Chicago vs. San Francisco

SAN FRANCISCO vs. CINCINNATI
RS: 49ers lead series, 6-1
PS: 49ers lead series, 2-0;
See Cincinnati vs. San Francisco

SAN FRANCISCO vs. CLEVELAND
RS: Browns lead series, 9-6;
See Cleveland vs. San Francisco

SAN FRANCISCO vs. DALLAS
RS: 49ers lead series, 9-6-1
PS: Cowboys lead series, 5-1;
See Dallas vs. San Francisco

SAN FRANCISCO vs. DENVER
RS: Broncos lead series, 4-2
PS: 49ers lead series, 1-0;
See Denver vs. San Francisco

SAN FRANCISCO vs. DETROIT
RS: 49ers lead series, 26-25-1
PS: Series tied, 1-1;
See Detroit vs. San Francisco

SAN FRANCISCO vs. GREEN BAY
RS: 49ers lead series, 25-21-1;

See Green Bay vs. San Francisco

SAN FRANCISCO vs. HOUSTON
RS: 49ers lead series, 5-3;
See Houston vs. San Francisco

SAN FRANCISCO vs. INDIANAPOLIS
RS: Colts lead series, 21-16;
See Indianapolis vs. San Francisco

SAN FRANCISCO vs. KANSAS CITY
RS: 49ers lead series, 4-1;
See Kansas City vs. San Francisco

SAN FRANCISCO vs. L.A RAIDERS
RS: Raiders lead series, 5-2;
See L.A. Raiders vs. San Francisco

SAN FRANCISCO vs. L.A. RAMS
RS: Rams lead series, 48-38-2
PS: 49ers lead series, 1-0;
See L.A. Rams vs. San Francisco

SAN FRANCISCO vs. MIAMI
RS: Dolphins lead series, 4-2
PS: 49ers lead series, 1-0;
See Miami vs. San Francisco

SAN FRANCISCO vs. MINNESOTA
RS: Series tied, 15-15-1
PS: 49ers lead series, 3-1;
See Minnesota vs. San Francisco

SAN FRANCISCO vs. NEW ENGLAND
RS: 49ers lead series, 6-1;
See New England vs. San Francisco

SAN FRANCISCO vs. NEW ORLEANS
RS: 49ers lead series, 33-14-2;
See New Orleans vs. San Francisco

SAN FRANCISCO vs. N.Y. GIANTS
RS: Giants lead series, 11-10
PS: Series tied, 3-3;
See N.Y. Giants vs. San Francisco

SAN FRANCISCO vs. N.Y. JETS
RS: 49ers lead series, 6-1;
See N.Y. Jets vs. San Francisco

SAN FRANCISCO vs. PHILADELPHIA
RS: 49ers lead series, 13-5-1;
See Philadelphia vs. San Francisco

SAN FRANCISCO vs. PITTSBURGH
RS: 49ers lead series, 8-7;
See Pittsburgh vs. San Francisco

SAN FRANCISCO vs. SAN DIEGO
RS: Series tied, 3-3;
See San Diego vs. San Francisco

SAN FRANCISCO vs. SEATTLE
RS: 49ers lead series, 4-1
1976—49ers, 37-21 (S)
1979—Seahawks, 35-24 (SF)
1985—49ers, 19-6 (SF)
1988—49ers, 38-7 (S)
1991—49ers, 24-22 (S)
(RS Pts.—49ers 142, Seahawks 91)

SAN FRANCISCO vs. TAMPA BAY
RS: 49ers lead series, 11-1
1977—49ers, 20-10 (SF)
1978—49ers, 6-3 (SF)
1979—49ers, 23-7 (SF)
1980—Buccaneers, 24-23 (SF)
1983—49ers, 35-21 (SF)
1984—49ers, 24-17 (SF)
1986—49ers, 31-7 (TB)
1987—49ers, 24-10 (TB)
1989—49ers, 20-16 (TB)
1990—49ers, 31-7 (SF)
1992—49ers, 21-14 (SF)
1993—49ers, 45-21 (TB)
(RS. Pts.—49ers 303, Buccaneers 157)

SAN FRANCISCO vs. WASHINGTON
RS: 49ers lead series, 9-6-1
PS: 49ers lead series, 3-1
1952—49ers, 23-17 (W)
1954—49ers, 41-7 (SF)
1955—Redskins, 7-0 (W)
1961—49ers, 35-3 (SF)
1967—Redskins, 31-28 (W)
1969—Tie, 17-17 (SF)
1970—49ers, 26-17 (SF)
1971—*49ers, 24-20 (SF)
1973—Redskins, 33-9 (W)
1976—Redskins, 24-21 (SF)

1978—Redskins, 38-20 (W)
1981—49ers, 30-17 (W)
1983—**Redskins, 24-21 (W)
1984—49ers, 37-31 (SF)
1985—49ers, 35-8 (W)
1986—Redskins, 14-6 (W)
1988—49ers, 37-21 (SF)
1990—49ers, 26-13 (SF)
     *49ers, 28-10 (SF)
1992—*49ers, 20-13 (SF)
(RS Pts.—49ers 391, Redskins 298)
(PS Pts.—49ers 93, Redskins 67)
*NFC Divisional Playoff
**NFC Championship

SEATTLE vs. ARIZONA
RS: Cardinals lead series, 4-0;
See Arizona vs. Seattle

SEATTLE vs. ATLANTA
RS: Seahawks lead series, 4-1;
See Atlanta vs. Seattle

SEATTLE vs. BUFFALO
RS: Seahawks lead series, 3-1;
See Buffalo vs. Seattle

SEATTLE vs. CHICAGO
RS: Seahawks lead series, 4-2;
See Chicago vs. Seattle

SEATTLE vs. CINCINNATI
RS: Series tied, 6-6
PS: Bengals lead series, 1-0;
See Cincinnati vs. Seattle

SEATTLE vs. CLEVELAND
RS: Seahawks lead series, 9-3;
See Cleveland vs. Seattle

SEATTLE vs. DALLAS
RS: Cowboys lead series, 4-1;
See Dallas vs. Seattle

SEATTLE vs. DENVER
RS: Broncos lead series, 20-13
PS: Seahawks lead series, 1-0;
See Denver vs. Seattle

SEATTLE vs. DETROIT
RS: Seahawks lead series, 4-2;
See Detroit vs. Seattle

SEATTLE vs. GREEN BAY
RS: Series tied, 3-3;
See Green Bay vs. Seattle

SEATTLE vs. HOUSTON
RS: Series tied, 4-4
PS: Oilers lead series, 1-0;
See Houston vs. Seattle

SEATTLE vs. INDIANAPOLIS
RS: Colts lead series, 2-1;
See Indianapolis vs. Seattle

SEATTLE vs. KANSAS CITY
RS: Chiefs lead series, 19-12;
See Kansas City vs. Seattle

SEATTLE vs. L.A. RAIDERS
RS: Raiders lead series, 18-14
PS: Series tied, 1-1;
See L.A. Raiders vs. Seattle

SEATTLE vs. L.A. RAMS
RS: Rams lead series, 4-1;
See L.A. Rams vs. Seattle

SEATTLE vs. MIAMI
RS: Dolphins lead series, 4-1
PS: Series tied, 1-1;
See Miami vs. Seattle

SEATTLE vs. MINNESOTA
RS: Seahawks lead series, 3-2;
See Minnesota vs. Seattle

SEATTLE vs. NEW ENGLAND
RS: Seahawks lead series, 7-6;
See New England vs. Seattle

SEATTLE vs. NEW ORLEANS
RS: Saints lead series, 3-2;
See New Orleans vs. Seattle

SEATTLE vs. N.Y. GIANTS
RS: Giants lead series, 5-2;
See N.Y. Giants vs. Seattle

SEATTLE vs. N.Y. JETS
RS: Seahawks lead series, 8-3;
See N.Y. Jets vs. Seattle

SEATTLE vs. PHILADELPHIA
RS: Eagles lead series, 4-1;
See Philadelphia vs. Seattle
SEATTLE vs. PITTSBURGH
RS: Series tied, 5-5;
See Pittsburgh vs. Seattle
SEATTLE vs. SAN DIEGO
RS: Series tied, 15-15;
See San Diego vs. Seattle
SEATTLE vs. SAN FRANCISCO
RS: 49ers lead series, 4-1;
See San Francisco vs. Seattle
SEATTLE vs. TAMPA BAY
RS: Seahawks lead series, 2-0
1976—Seahawks, 13-10 (TB)
1977—Seahawks, 30-23 (S)
(RS Pts.—Seahawks 43, Buccaneers 33)
SEATTLE vs. WASHINGTON
RS: Redskins lead series, 5-1
1976—Redskins, 31-7 (W)
1980—Seahawks, 14-0 (W)
1983—Redskins, 27-17 (S)
1986—Redskins, 19-14 (W)
1989—Redskins, 29-0 (S)
1992—Redskins, 16-3 (S)
(RS Pts.—Redskins 122, Seahawks 55)

TAMPA BAY vs. ARIZONA
RS: Series tied, 6-6;
See Arizona vs. Tampa Bay
TAMPA BAY vs. ATLANTA
RS: Series tied,6-6;
See Atlanta vs. Tampa Bay
TAMPA BAY vs. BUFFALO
RS: Buccaneers lead series, 4-2;
See Buffalo vs. Tampa Bay
TAMPA BAY vs. CHICAGO
RS: Bears lead series, 24-8;
See Chicago vs. Tampa Bay
TAMPA BAY vs. CINCINNATI
RS: Bengals lead series, 3-1;
See Cincinnati vs. Tampa Bay
TAMPA BAY vs. CLEVELAND
RS: Browns lead series, 4-0;
See Cleveland vs. Tampa Bay
TAMPA BAY vs. DALLAS
RS: Cowboys lead series, 0-0
PS: Cowboys lead series, 2-0;
See Dallas vs. Tampa Bay
TAMPA BAY vs. DENVER
RS: Broncos lead series, 2-1;
See Denver vs. Tampa Bay
TAMPA BAY vs. DETROIT
RS: Series tied, 16-16;
See Detroit vs. Tampa Bay
TAMPA BAY vs. GREEN BAY
RS: Packers lead series, 17-12-1;
See Green Bay vs. Tampa Bay
TAMPA BAY vs. HOUSTON
RS: Oilers lead series, 3-1;
See Houston vs. Tampa Bay
TAMPA BAY vs. INDIANAPOLIS
RS: Colts lead series, 5-2;
See Indianapolis vs. Tampa Bay
TAMPA BAY vs. KANSAS CITY
RS: Chiefs lead series, 5-2;
See Kansas City vs. Tampa Bay
TAMPA BAY vs. L.A. RAIDERS
RS: Raiders lead series, 3-0;
See L.A. Raiders vs. Tampa Bay
TAMPA BAY vs. L.A. RAMS
RS: Rams lead series, 8-2
PS: Rams lead series, 1-0;
See L.A. Rams vs. Tampa Bay
TAMPA BAY vs. MIAMI
RS: Dolphins lead series, 4-1;
See Miami vs. Tampa Bay
TAMPA BAY vs. MINNESOTA
RS: Vikings lead series, 23-9;
See Minnesota vs. Tampa Bay
TAMPA BAY vs. NEW ENGLAND
RS: Patriots lead series, 3-0;

See New England vs. Tampa Bay
TAMPA BAY vs. NEW ORLEANS
RS: Saints lead series, 11-4;
See New Orleans vs. Tampa Bay
TAMPA BAY vs. N.Y. GIANTS
RS: Giants lead series, 8-3;
See N.Y. Giants vs. Tampa Bay
TAMPA BAY vs. N.Y. JETS
RS: Jets lead series, 5-1;
See N.Y. Jets vs. Tampa Bay
TAMPA BAY vs. PHILADELPHIA
RS: Eagles lead series, 3-1
PS: Buccaneers lead series, 1-0;
See Philadelphia vs. Tampa Bay
TAMPA BAY vs. PITTSBURGH
RS: Steelers lead series, 4-0;
See Pittsburgh vs. Tampa Bay
TAMPA BAY vs. SAN DIEGO
RS: Chargers lead series, 6-0;
See San Diego vs. Tampa Bay
TAMPA BAY vs. SAN FRANCISCO
RS: 49ers lead series, 11-1;
See San Francisco vs. Tampa Bay
TAMPA BAY vs. SEATTLE
RS: Seahawks lead series, 2-0;
See Seattle vs. Tampa Bay
TAMPA BAY vs. WASHINGTON
RS: Redskins lead series, 4-0
1977—Redskins, 10-0 (TB)
1982—Redskins, 21-13 (TB)
1989—Redskins, 32-28 (W)
1993—Redskins, 23-17 (TB)
(RS Pts.—Redskins 86, Buccaneers 58)

WASHINGTON vs. ARIZONA
RS: Redskins lead series, 61-36-2;
See Arizona vs. Washington
WASHINGTON vs. ATLANTA
RS: Redskins lead series, 13-3-1
PS: Redskins lead series, 1-0;
See Atlanta vs. Washington
WASHINGTON vs. BUFFALO
RS: Redskins lead series, 4-3
PS: Redskins lead series, 1-0;
See Buffalo vs. Washington
WASHINGTON vs. CHICAGO
RS: Bears lead series, 18-12-1
PS: Redskins lead series, 4-3;
See Chicago vs. Washington
WASHINGTON vs. CINCINNATI
RS: Redskins lead series, 4-2;
See Cincinnati vs. Washington
WASHINGTON vs. CLEVELAND
RS: Browns lead series, 32-9-1;
See Cleveland vs. Washington
WASHINGTON vs. DALLAS
RS: Cowboys lead series, 37-27-2
PS: Redskins lead series, 2-0;
See Dallas vs. Washington
WASHINGTON vs. DENVER
RS: Series tied 3-3
PS: Redskins lead series, 1-0;
See Denver vs. Washington
WASHINGTON vs. DETROIT
RS: Redskins lead series, 22-8
PS: Redskins lead series, 2-0;
See Detroit vs. Washington
WASHINGTON vs. GREEN BAY
RS: Packers lead series, 13-12-1
PS: Series tied 1-1;
See Green Bay vs. Washington
WASHINGTON vs. HOUSTON
RS: Series tied 3-3;
See Houston vs. Washington
WASHINGTON vs. INDIANAPOLIS
RS: Colts lead series, 16-7;
See Indianapolis vs. Washington
WASHINGTON vs. KANSAS CITY
RS: Chiefs lead series, 3-1;
See Kansas City vs. Washington
WASHINGTON vs. L.A. RAIDERS
RS: Raiders lead series, 5-2
PS: Raiders lead series, 1-0;

See L.A. Raiders vs. Washington
WASHINGTON vs. L.A. RAMS
RS: Redskins lead series, 14-5-1
PS: Series tied 2-2;
See L.A. Rams vs. Washington
WASHINGTON vs. MIAMI
RS: Dolphins lead series, 5-2
PS: Series tied 1-1;
See Miami vs. Washington
WASHINGTON vs. MINNESOTA
RS: Redskins lead series, 6-4
PS: Redskins lead series, 3-2;
See Minnesota vs. Washington
WASHINGTON vs. NEW ENGLAND
RS: Redskins lead series, 4-1;
See New England vs. Washington
WASHINGTON vs. NEW ORLEANS
RS: Redskins lead series, 11-5;
See New Orleans vs. Washington
WASHINGTON vs. N.Y. GIANTS
RS: Giants lead series, 69-50-3
PS: Series tied 1-1;
See N.Y. Giants vs. Washington
WASHINGTON vs. N.Y. JETS
RS: Redskins lead series, 4-1;
See N.Y. Jets vs. Washington
WASHINGTON vs. PHILADELPHIA
RS: Redskins lead series, 66-46-5
PS: Redskins lead series, 1-0;
See Philadelphia vs. Washington
WASHINGTON vs. PITTSBURGH
RS: Redskins lead series, 42-27-3;
See Pittsburgh vs. Washington
WASHINGTON vs. SAN DIEGO
RS: Redskins lead series, 5-0;
See San Diego vs. Washington
WASHINGTON vs. SAN FRANCISCO
RS: 49ers lead series, 9-6-1
PS: 49ers lead series, 3-1;
See San Francisco vs. Washington
WASHINGTON vs. SEATTLE
RS: Redskins lead series, 5-1;
See Seattle vs. Washington
WASHINGTON vs. TAMPA BAY
RS: Redskins lead series, 4-0;
See Tampa Bay vs. Washington

RESULTS

Season	Date	Winner (Share)	Loser (Share)	Score	Site	Attendance
XXVIII	1-30-94	Dallas ($38,000)	Buffalo ($23,500)	30-13	Atlanta	72,817
XXVII	1-31-93	Dallas ($36,000)	Buffalo ($18,000)	52-17	Pasadena	98,374
XXVI	1-26-92	Washington ($36,000)	Buffalo ($18,000)	37-24	Minneapolis	63,130
XXV	1-27-91	N.Y. Giants ($36,000)	Buffalo ($18,000)	20-19	Tampa	73,813
XXIV	1-28-90	San Francisco ($36,000)	Denver ($18,000)	55-10	New Orleans	72,919
XXIII	1-22-89	San Francisco ($36,000)	Cincinnati ($18,000)	20-16	Miami	75,129
XXII	1-31-88	Washington ($36,000)	Denver ($18,000)	42-10	San Diego	73,302
XXI	1-25-87	N.Y. Giants ($36,000)	Denver ($18,000)	39-20	Pasadena	101,063
XX	1-26-86	Chicago ($36,000)	New England ($18,000)	46-10	New Orleans	73,818
XIX	1-20-85	San Francisco ($36,000)	Miami ($18,000)	38-16	Stanford	84,059
XVIII	1-22-84	L.A. Raiders ($36,000)	Washington ($18,000)	38-9	Tampa	72,920
XVII	1-30-83	Washington ($36,000)	Miami ($18,000)	27-17	Pasadena	103,667
XVI	1-24-82	San Francisco ($18,000)	Cincinnati ($9,000)	26-21	Pontiac	81,270
XV	1-25-81	Oakland ($18,000)	Philadelphia ($9,000)	27-10	New Orleans	76,135
XIV	1-20-80	Pittsburgh ($18,000)	Los Angeles ($9,000)	31-19	Pasadena	103,985
XIII	1-21-79	Pittsburgh ($18,000)	Dallas ($9,000)	35-31	Miami	79,484
XII	1-15-78	Dallas ($18,000)	Denver ($9,000)	27-10	New Orleans	75,583
XI	1-9-77	Oakland ($15,000)	Minnesota ($7,500)	32-14	Pasadena	103,438
X	1-18-76	Pittsburgh ($15,000)	Dallas ($7,500)	21-17	Miami	80,187
IX	1-12-75	Pittsburgh ($15,000)	Minnesota ($7,500)	16-6	New Orleans	80,997
VIII	1-13-74	Miami ($15,000)	Minnesota ($7,500)	24-7	Houston	71,882
VII	1-14-73	Miami ($15,000)	Washington ($7,500)	14-7	Los Angeles	90,182
VI	1-16-72	Dallas ($15,000)	Miami ($7,500)	24-3	New Orleans	81,023
V	1-17-71	Baltimore ($15,000)	Dallas ($7,500)	16-13	Miami	79,204
IV	1-11-70	Kansas City ($15,000)	Minnesota ($7,500)	23-7	New Orleans	80,562
III	1-12-69	N.Y. Jets ($15,000)	Baltimore ($7,500)	16-7	Miami	75,389
II	1-14-68	Green Bay ($15,000)	Oakland ($7,500)	33-14	Miami	75,546
I	1-15-67	Green Bay ($15,000)	Kansas City ($7,500)	35-10	Los Angeles	61,946

SUPER BOWL COMPOSITE STANDINGS

	W	L	Pct.	Pts.	OP
Pittsburgh Steelers	4	0	1.000	103	73
San Francisco 49ers	4	0	1.000	139	63
Green Bay Packers	2	0	1.000	68	24
New York Giants	2	0	1.000	59	39
Chicago Bears	1	0	1.000	46	10
New York Jets	1	0	1.000	16	7
Oakland/L.A. Raiders	3	1	.750	111	66
Washington Redskins	3	2	.600	122	103
Dallas Cowboys	4	3	.571	194	115
Baltimore Colts	1	1	.500	23	29
Kansas City Chiefs	1	1	.500	33	42
Miami Dolphins	2	3	.400	74	103
Los Angeles Rams	0	1	.000	19	31
New England Patriots	0	1	.000	10	46
Philadelphia Eagles	0	1	.000	10	27
Cincinnati Bengals	0	2	.000	37	46
Buffalo Bills	0	4	.000	73	139
Denver Broncos	0	4	.000	50	163
Minnesota Vikings	0	4	.000	34	95

SUPER BOWL MOST VALUABLE PLAYERS*

Super Bowl I — QB Bart Starr, Green Bay
Super Bowl II — QB Bart Starr, Green Bay
Super Bowl III — QB Joe Namath, N.Y. Jets
Super Bowl IV — QB Len Dawson, Kansas City
Super Bowl V — LB Chuck Howley, Dallas
Super Bowl VI — QB Roger Staubach, Dallas
Super Bowl VII — S Jake Scott, Miami
Super Bowl VIII — RB Larry Csonka, Miami
Super Bowl IX — RB Franco Harris, Pittsburgh
Super Bowl X — WR Lynn Swann, Pittsburgh
Super Bowl XI — WR Fred Biletnikoff, Oakland
Super Bowl XII — DT Randy White and
 DE Harvey Martin, Dallas
Super Bowl XIII — QB Terry Bradshaw, Pittsburgh
Super Bowl XIV — QB Terry Bradshaw, Pittsburgh
Super Bowl XV — QB Jim Plunkett, Oakland
Super Bowl XVI — QB Joe Montana, San Francisco
Super Bowl XVII — RB John Riggins, Washington
Super Bowl XVIII — RB Marcus Allen, L.A. Raiders
Super Bowl XIX — QB Joe Montana, San Francisco
Super Bowl XX — DE Richard Dent, Chicago
Super Bowl XXI — QB Phil Simms, N.Y. Giants
Super Bowl XXII — QB Doug Williams, Washington
Super Bowl XXIII — WR Jerry Rice, San Francisco

Super Bowl XXIV — QB Joe Montana, San Francisco
Super Bowl XXV — RB Ottis Anderson, N.Y. Giants
Super Bowl XXVI — QB Mark Rypien, Washington
Super Bowl XXVII — QB Troy Aikman, Dallas
Super Bowl XXVIII — RB Emmitt Smith, Dallas
Award named Pete Rozelle Trophy since Super Bowl XXV.

SUPER BOWL XXVIII

Georgia Dome, Atlanta, Georgia
January 30, 1994, Attendance: 72,817

DALLAS 30, BUFFALO 13—Emmitt Smith rushed for 132 yards and 2 second-half touchdowns to power the Cowboys to their second consecutive NFL title. By winning, Dallas joined San Francisco and Pittsburgh as the only franchises with four Super Bowl victories. The Bills, meanwhile, extended a dubious string by losing in the Super Bowl for the fourth consecutive year. To win, the Cowboys had to rally from a 13-6 halftime deficit. Buffalo had forged its lead on Thurman Thomas's 4-yard touchdown run and a pair of field goals by Steve Christie, including a 54-yard kick, the longest in Super Bowl history. But just 55 seconds into the second half, Thomas was stripped of the ball by Dallas defensive tackle Leon Lett. Safety James Washington recovered and weaved his way 46 yards for a touchdown to tie the game at 13-13. After forcing the Bills to punt, the Cowboys began their next possession on their own 36-yard line and Smith, the game's most valuable player, took over. He carried 7 times for 61 yards on the ensuing 8-play, 64-yard drive, capping the march with a 15-yard touchdown run to give Dallas the lead for good with 8:42 remaining in the third quarter. Early in the fourth quarter, Washington intercepted Jim Kelly's pass and returned it 12 yards to Buffalo's 34. A penalty moved the ball back to the 39, but Smith carried twice for 10 yards and caught a screen pass for 9, and quarterback Troy Aikman completed a 16-yard pass to Alvin Harper to give the Cowboys a first-and-goal at the 6. Smith took it from there, cracking the end zone on fourth-and-goal from the 1 to put Dallas ahead 20-13 with 9:50 remaining. Eddie Murray's third field goal, from 20 yards with 2:50 left, ended any doubt about the game's outcome. Smith had 30 carries in all, with 19 of his attempts and 92 yards coming after intermission. Washington, normally a reserve who played most of the game because the Cowboys used five defensive backs to combat the Bills' No-Huddle offense, had 11 tackles

and forced another fumble by Thomas in the first quarter. Aikman completed 19 of 27 passes for 207 yards. Buffalo's Kelly completed a Super Bowl-record 31 passes in 50 attempts for 260 yards. Dallas, the first team in NFL history to begin the regular season 0-2 and go on to win the Super Bowl, also became the fifth to win back-to-back titles, following Green Bay, Miami, Pittsburgh (the Steelers did it twice), and San Francisco. Buffalo became the third team, along with Minnesota and Denver, to lose four Super Bowls. The Cowboys' victory was the tenth in succession for the NFC over the AFC.

Dallas (30)	Offense	Buffalo (13)
Alvin Harper	WR	Don Beebe
Mark Tuinei	LT	John Fina
Nate Newton	LG	Glenn Parker
John Gesek	C	Kent Hull
Kevin Gogan	RG	John Davis
Erik Williams	RT	Howard Ballard
Jay Novacek	TE	Pete Metzelaars
Michael Irvin	WR	Bill Brooks
Troy Aikman	QB	Jim Kelly
Emmitt Smith	RB	Thurman Thomas
Daryl Johnston	RB-WR	Andre Reed
	Defense	
Tony Tolbert	LE	Phil Hansen
Tony Casillas	LT-NT	Jeff Wright
Leon Lett	RT-RE	Bruce Smith
Charles Haley	RE-RILB	Cornelius Bennett
Darrin Smith	LLB-RILB	Mark Maddox
Darren Woodson	DB-LOLB	Marvcus Patton
Ken Norton	RLB-LOLB	Darryl Talley
Kevin Smith	LCB	Mickey Washington
Larry Brown	RCB	Nate Odomes
Thomas Everett	SS	Henry Jones
James Washington	FS	Mark Kelso

SUBSTITUTIONS

Dallas—Offense: K—Eddie Murray. P—John Jett. QB—Bernie Kosar. RB—Lincoln Coleman, Derrick Gainer. WR—Kevin Williams. TE—Scott Galbraith. G-C—Frank Cornish, Dale Hellestrae. Defense: E—Jim Jeffcoat. T—Chad Hennings, Russell Maryland. DL—Jimmie Jones. DB—Bill Bates, Joe Fishback, Elvis Patterson. LB—Dixon Edwards, Robert Jones, Godfrey Myles, Matt Vanderbeek. CB—Dave Thomas. S—Kenneth Gant. DNP: RB—Derrick Lassic.

Buffalo—Offense: K—Steve Christie. P—Chris

Mohr. QB—Frank Reich. RB—Kenneth Davis, Carwell Gardner. WR—Russell Copeland, Steve Tasker. TE—Keith McKeller. T—Jerry Crafts. G—Jim Ritcher. C—Mike Devlin, Adam Lingner. Defense: E—Oliver Barnett, Mark Pike. NT—Mike Lodish. LB—Monty Brown, Keith Goganious, Richard Harvey. CB—Jerome Henderson, Thomas Smith. S—Matt Darby, Kurt Schulz. DNP: RB—Nate Turner.

OFFICIALS

Referee—Bob McElwee. Umpire—Art Demmas. Head Linesman—Sid Semon. Line Judge—Tom Barnes. Back Judge—Al Jury. Field Judge—Don Orr. Side Judge—Nate Jones.

SCORING

Dallas (NFC)	6	0	14	10	—	30
Buffalo (AFC)	3	10	0	0	—	13

Dall — FG Murray 41
Buff — FG Christie 54
Dall — FG Murray 24
Buff — Thomas 4 run (Christie kick)
Buff — FG Christie 28
Dall — Washington 46 fumble return (Murray kick)
Dall — E. Smith 15 run (Murray kick)
Dall — E. Smith 1 run (Murray kick)
Dall — FG Murray 20

TEAM STATISTICS

	Dallas	Buffalo
Total First Downs	20	22
Rushing	6	6
Passing	14	15
Penalty	0	1
Total Net Yardage	341	314
Total Offensive Plays	64	80
Average Gain per Offensive Play	5.3	3.9
Rushes	35	27
Yards Gained Rushing (Net)	137	87
Average Yards per Rush	3.9	3.2
Passes Attempted	27	50
Passes Completed	19	31
Had Intercepted	1	1
Tackled Attempting to Pass	2	3
Yards Lost Attempting to Pass	3	33
Yards Gained Passing (Net)	204	227
Punts	4	5
Average Distance	43.8	37.6
Punt Returns	1	1
Punt Return Yardage	5	5
Kickoff Returns	2	6
Kickoff Return Yardage	72	144
Interception Return Yardage	12	41
Total Return Yardage	89	190
Fumbles	0	3
Own Fumbles Recovered	0	1
Opponent Fumbles Recovered	2	0
Penalties	6	1
Yards Penalized	50	10
Total Points Scored	30	13
Touchdowns	3	1
Rushing	2	1
Passing	0	0
Returns	1	0
Extra Points	3	1
Field Goals	3	2
Field Goals Attempted	3	2
Safeties	0	0
Third-Down Efficiency	5/13	5/17
Fourth-Down Efficiency	1/1	2/3
Time of Possession	34:29	25:31

INDIVIDUAL STATISTICS

Rushing

Dallas	No.	Yds.	LG	TD
E. Smith	30	132	15t	2
K. Williams	1	6	6	0
Aikman	1	3	3	0
Johnston	1	0	0	0
Kosar	1	-1	-1	0
Coleman	1	-3	-3	0
Buffalo	No.	Yds.	LG	TD
Thomas	16	37	6	1
K. Davis	9	38	11	0

| Kelly | 2 | 12 | 8 | 0 |

Passing

Dallas	Att.	Comp.	Yds.	TD	Int.
Aikman	27	19	207	0	1
Buffalo	Att.	Comp.	Yds.	TD	Int.
Kelly	50	31	260	0	1

Receiving

Dallas	No.	Yds.	LG	TD
Irvin	5	66	20	0
Novacek	5	26	9	0
E. Smith	4	26	10	0
Harper	3	75	35	0
Johnston	2	14	11	0
Buffalo	No.	Yds.	LG	TD
Brooks	7	63	15	0
Thomas	7	52	24	0
Reed	6	75	22	0
Beebe	6	60	18	0
K. Davis	3	-5	7	0
Metzelaars	1	8	8	0
McKeller	1	7	7	0

Interceptions

Dallas	No.	Yds.	LG	TD
Washington	1	12	12	0
Buffalo	No.	Yds.	LG	TD
Odomes	1	41	41	0

Punting

Dallas	No.	Avg.	LG	Blk.
Jett	4	43.8	47	0
Buffalo	No.	Avg.	LG	Blk.
Mohr	5	37.6	52	0

Punt Returns

Dallas	No.	FC	Yds.	LG	TD
K. Williams	1	1	5	5	0
Buffalo	No.	FC	Yds.	LG	TD
Copeland	1	1	5	5	0

Kickoff Returns

Dallas	No.	Yds.	LG	TD
K. Williams	1	50	50	0
Gant	1	22	22	0
Buffalo	No.	Yds.	LG	TD
Copeland	4	82	22	0
Beebe	2	62	34	0

SUPER BOWL XXVII

Rose Bowl, Pasadena, California
January 31, 1993, Attendance: 98,374
DALLAS 52, BUFFALO 17—Troy Aikman threw 4 touchdown passes, Emmitt Smith rushed for 108 yards, and the Cowboys converted 9 turnovers into 35 points while coasting to the victory. Dallas's win was its third in its record sixth Super Bowl appearance; the Bills became the first team to drop three in succession. Buffalo led 7-0 until the first 2 of its record number of turnovers helped the Cowboys take the lead for good late in the opening quarter. First, Dallas safety James Washington intercepted a Jim Kelly pass and returned it 13 yards to the Bills' 47, setting up Aikman's 23-yard touchdown pass to tight end Jay Novacek with 1:36 remaining in the period. On the next play from scrimmage, Kelly was sacked by Charles Haley and fumbled at the Bills' 2-yard line where the Cowboys' Jimmie Jones picked up the loose ball and ran 2 yards for a touchdown. Dallas, which recovered 5 fumbles and intercepted 4 passes, struck just as quickly late in the first half, when Aikman tossed 19- and 18-yard touchdown passes to Michael Irvin 15 seconds apart to give the Cowboys a 28-10 lead at intermission. The second score was set up when Bills running back Thurman Thomas lost a fumble at his 19-yard line. Buffalo scored for the last time when backup quarterback Frank Reich, playing because Kelly was injured while attempting to pass midway through the second quarter, threw a 40-yard touchdown pass to Don Beebe on the final play of the third period to trim the deficit to 31-17. But Dallas put the game out of reach by scoring three times in a span of 2:33 of the fourth quarter. Aikman, the game's most valuable player, completed 22 of 30 passes for 273 yards and was not intercepted. The victory was the ninth in succession for the NFC over the AFC.

Buffalo (AFC)	7	3	7	0	—	17
Dallas (NFC)	14	14	3	21	—	52

Buff — Thomas 2 run (Christie kick)
Dall — Novacek 23 pass from Aikman (Elliott kick)
Dall — J. Jones 2 fumble recovery return (Elliott kick)
Buff — FG Christie 21
Dall — Irvin 19 pass from Aikman (Elliott kick)
Dall — Irvin 18 pass from Aikman (Elliott kick)
Dall — FG Elliott 20
Buff — Beebe 40 pass from Reich (Christie kick)
Dall — Harper 45 pass from Aikman (Elliott kick)
Dall — E. Smith 10 run (Elliott kick)
Dall — Norton 9 fumble recovery return (Elliott kick)

SUPER BOWL XXVI

Metrodome, Minneapolis, Minnesota
January 26, 1992, Attendance: 63,130
WASHINGTON 37, BUFFALO 24—Mark Rypien passed for 292 yards and 2 touchdowns as the Redskins overwhelmed the Bills to win their third Super Bowl in the past 10 years. Rypien, the game's most valuable player, completed 18 of 33 passes, including a 10-yard scoring strike to Earnest Byner and a 30-yard touchdown to Gary Clark. The latter came late in the third quarter after Buffalo had trimmed a 24-0 deficit to 24-10, and effectively put the game out of reach. Washington went on to lead by as much as 37-10 before the Bills made it close wih a pair of touchdowns in the final six minutes. Though the Redskins struggled early, converting their first three drives inside the Bills' 20-yard line into only 3 points, they built a 17-0 halftime lead. And they made it 24-0 just 16 seconds into the second half, after Kurt Gouveia intercepted Buffalo quarterback Jim Kelly's pass on the first play of the third quarter and returned it 23 yards to the Bills' 2. One play later, Gerald Riggs scored his second touchdown of the game to make it 24-0. Kelly, forced to bring Buffalo from behind, completed 28 of a Super Bowl-record 58 passes for 275 yards and 2 touchdowns, but was intercepted 4 times. Bills running back Thurman Thomas, who had an AFC-high 1,407 yards rushing and an NFL-best 2,038 total yards from scrimmage during the regular season, ran for only 13 yards on 10 carries and was limited to 27 yards on 4 receptions. Clark had 7 catches for 114 yards and Art Monk added 7 for 113 for the Redskins, who amassed 417 yards of total offense while limiting the explosive Bills to 283. Washington's Joe Gibbs became only the third head coach to win three Super Bowls.

Washington (NFC)	0	17	14	6	—	37
Buffalo (AFC)	0	0	10	14	—	24

Wash — FG Lohmiller 34
Wash — Byner 10 pass from Rypien (Lohmiller kick)
Wash — Riggs 1 run (Lohmiller kick)
Wash — Riggs 2 run (Lohmiller kick)
Buff — FG Norwood 21
Buff — Thomas 1 run (Norwood kick)
Wash — Clark 30 pass from Rypien (Lohmiller kick)
Wash — FG Lohmiller 25
Wash — FG Lohmiller 39
Buff — Metzelaars 2 pass from Kelly (Norwood kick)
Buff — Beebe 4 pass from Kelly (Norwood kick)

SUPER BOWL XXV

Tampa Stadium, Tampa, Florida
January 27, 1991, Attendance: 73,813
NEW YORK GIANTS 20, BUFFALO 19—The NFC champion New York Giants won their second Super Bowl in five years with a 20-19 victory over AFC titlist Buffalo. New York, employing its ball-control offense, had possession for 40 minutes, 33 seconds, a Super Bowl record. The Bills, who scored 95 points in their previous two playoff games leading to Super Bowl XXV, had the ball for less than eight minutes in the second half and just 19:27 for the game. Fourteen of New York's 73 plays came on its initial drive of the third quarter, which covered 75 yards and consumed a Super Bowl-record 9:29 before running back Ottis Anderson ran 1 yard for a touchdown. Giants

quarterback Jeff Hostetler kept the long drive going by converting three third-down plays—an 11-yard pass to running back David Meggett on third-and-eight, a 14-yard toss to wide receiver Mark Ingram on third-and-13, and a 9-yard pass to Howard Cross on third-and-four—to give New York a 17-12 lead in the third quarter. Buffalo jumped to a 12-3 lead midway through the second quarter before Hostetler completed a 14-yard scoring strike to wide receiver Stephen Baker to close the score to 12-10 at halftime. Buffalo's Thurman Thomas ran 31 yards for a touchdown on the opening play of the fourth quarter to help Buffalo recapture the lead 19-17. Matt Bahr's 21-yard field goal gave the Giants a 20-19 lead, but Buffalo's Scott Norwood had a chance to win the game with seconds remaining before his 47-yard field-goal attempt sailed wide right. Hostetler completed 20 of 32 passes for 222 yards and 1 touchdown. Anderson rushed 21 times for 102 yards and 1 touchdown to capture the most-valuable-player honors. Thomas totaled 190 scrimmage yards, rushing 15 times for 135 yards and catching 5 passes for 55 yards.

Buffalo (AFC)	3	9	0	7 —	19
N.Y. Giants (NFC)	3	7	7	3 —	20

NYG — FG Bahr 28
Buff — FG Norwood 23
Buff — D. Smith 1 run (Norwood kick)
Buff — Safety, B. Smith tackled Hostetler in end zone
NYG — Baker 14 pass from Hostetler (Bahr kick)
NYG — Anderson 1 run (Bahr kick)
Buff — Thomas 31 run (Norwood kick)
NYG — FG Bahr 21

SUPER BOWL XXIV

Louisiana Superdome, New Orleans, Louisiana
January 28, 1990, Attendance: 72,919
SAN FRANCISCO 55, DENVER 10—NFC titlist San Francisco won its fourth Super Bowl championship with a 55-10 victory over AFC champion Denver. The 49ers, who also won Super Bowls XVI, XIX, and XXIII, tied the Pittsburgh Steelers for most Super Bowl victories. The Steelers captured Super Bowls IX, X, XIII, and XIV. San Francisco's 55 points broke the previous Super Bowl scoring mark of 46 points by Chicago in Super Bowl XX. San Francisco scored touchdowns on four of its six first-half possessions to hold a 27-3 lead at halftime. Interceptions by Michael Walter and Chet Brooks ended the Broncos' first two possessions of the second half. San Francisco quarterback Joe Montana was named the Super Bowl most valuable player for a record third time. Montana completed 22 of 29 passes for 297 yards and a Super Bowl-record 5 touchdowns. Jerry Rice, Super Bowl XXIII most valuable player, caught 7 passes for 148 yards and three touchdowns. The 49ers' domination included first downs (28 to 12), net yards (461 to 167), and time of possession (39:31 to 20:29).

San Francisco (NFC)	13	14	14	14 —	55
Denver (AFC)	3	0	7	0 —	10

SF — Rice 20 pass from Montana (Cofer kick)
Den — FG Treadwell 42
SF — Jones 7 pass from Montana (kick failed)
SF — Rathman 1 run (Cofer kick)
SF — Rice 38 pass from Montana (Cofer kick)
SF — Rice 28 pass from Montana (Cofer kick)
SF — Taylor 35 pass from Montana (Cofer kick)
Den — Elway 3 run (Treadwell kick)
SF — Rathman 3 run (Cofer kick)
SF — Craig 1 run (Cofer kick)

SUPER BOWL XXIII

Joe Robbie Stadium, Miami, Florida
January 22, 1989, Attendance: 75,129
SAN FRANCISCO 20, CINCINNATI 16—NFC champion San Francisco captured its third Super Bowl of the 1980s by defeating AFC champion Cincinnati 20-16. The 49ers, who also won Super Bowls XVI and XIX, are the first NFC team to win three Super Bowls. Pittsburgh, with four Super Bowl titles (IX, X, XIII, and XIV), and the Oakland/Los Angeles Raiders, with three (XI, XV, and XVIII), lead

AFC franchises. Even though San Francisco held an advantage in total net yards (453 to 229), the 49ers found themselves trailing the Bengals late in the game. With the score 13-13, Cincinnati took a 16-13 lead on Jim Breech's 40-yard field goal with 3:20 remaining. It was Breech's third field goal of the day, following earlier successes from 34 and 43 yards. The 49ers started their winning drive at their 8-yard line. Over the next 11 plays, San Francisco covered 92 yards with the decisive score coming on a 10-yard pass from quarterback Joe Montana to wide receiver John Taylor with 34 seconds remaining. At halftime, the score was 3-3, the first time in Super Bowl history the game was tied at intermission. After the teams traded third-period field goals, the Bengals jumped ahead 13-6 on Stanford Jennings's 93-yard kickoff return for a touchdown with 34 seconds remaining in the quarter. The 49ers didn't waste any time coming back as they covered 85 yards in four plays, concluding with Montana's 14-yard scoring pass to Jerry Rice 57 seconds into the final stanza. Rice was named the game's most valuable player after compiling 11 catches for a Super Bowl-record 215 yards. Montana completed 23 of 36 passes for a Super Bowl-record 357 yards and 2 touchdowns.

Cincinnati (AFC)	0	3	10	3 —	16
San Francisco (NFC)	3	0	3	14 —	20

SF — FG Cofer 41
Cin — FG Breech 34
Cin — FG Breech 43
SF — FG Cofer 32
Cin — Jennings 93 kickoff return (Breech kick)
SF — Rice 14 pass from Montana (Cofer kick)
Cin — FG Breech 40
SF — Taylor 10 pass from Montana (Cofer kick)

SUPER BOWL XXII

San Diego Jack Murphy Stadium, San Diego, California
January 31, 1988, Attendance: 73,302
WASHINGTON 42, DENVER 10—NFC champion Washington won Super Bowl XXII and its second NFL championship of the 1980s with a 42-10 decision over AFC champion Denver. The Redskins, who also won Super Bowl XVII, enjoyed a record-setting second quarter en route to the victory. The Broncos broke in front 10-0 when quarterback John Elway threw a 56-yard touchdown pass to wide receiver Ricky Nattiel on the Broncos' first play from scrimmage. Following a Washington punt, Denver's Rich Karlis kicked a 24-yard field goal to cap a seven-play, 61-yard scoring drive. The Redskins then erupted for 35 points on five straight possessions in the second period and coasted thereafter. The 35 points established an NFL postseason mark for most points in a period, bettering the previous total of 21 by San Francisco in Super Bowl XIX and Chicago in Super Bowl XX. Redskins quarterback Doug Williams led the second-period explosion by throwing a Super Bowl record-tying 4 touchdown passes, including 80- and 50-yard passes to wide receiver Ricky Sanders, a 27-yard toss to wide receiver Gary Clark, and an 8-yard pass to tight end Clint Didier. Washington scored 5 touchdowns in 18 plays with total time of possession of only 5:47. Overall, Williams completed 18 of 29 passes for 340 yards and was named the game's most valuable player. His pass-yardage total eclipsed the Super Bowl record of 331 yards by Joe Montana of San Francisco in Super Bowl XIX. Sanders ended with 193 yards on 8 catches, breaking the previous Super Bowl yardage record of 161 yards by Lynn Swann of Pittsburgh in Game X. Rookie running back Timmy Smith was the game's leading rusher with 22 carries for a Super Bowl-record 204 yards, breaking the previous mark of 191 yards by Marcus Allen of the Raiders in Game XVIII. Smith also scored twice on runs of 58 and 4 yards. Washington's 6 touchdowns and 602 total yards gained also set Super Bowl records. Redskins cornerback Barry Wilburn had 2 of the team's 3 interceptions, and strong safety Alvin Walton had 2 of Washington's 5 sacks.

Washington (NFC)	0	35	0	7 —	42
Denver (AFC)	10	0	0	0 —	10

Den — Nattiel 56 pass from Elway (Karlis kick)
Den — FG Karlis 24
Wash — Sanders 80 pass from Williams (Haji-Sheikh kick)
Wash — Clark 27 pass from Williams (Haji-Sheikh kick)
Wash — Smith 58 run (Haji-Sheikh kick)
Wash — Sanders 50 pass from Williams (Haji-Sheikh kick)
Wash — Didier 8 pass from Williams (Haji-Sheikh kick)
Wash — Smith 4 run (Haji-Sheikh kick)

SUPER BOWL XXI

Rose Bowl, Pasadena, California
January 25, 1987, Attendance: 101,063
NEW YORK GIANTS 39, DENVER 20—The NFC champion New York Giants captured their first NFL title since 1956 when they downed the AFC champion Denver Broncos 39-20 in Super Bowl XXI. The victory marked the NFC's fifth NFL title in the past six seasons. The Broncos, behind the passing of quarterback John Elway, who was 13 of 20 for 187 yards in the first half, held a 10-9 lead at intermission, the narrowest halftime margin in Super Bowl history. Denver's Rich Karlis opened the scoring with a Super Bowl record-tying 48-yard field goal. New York took a 7-3 lead on quarterback Phil Simms's 6-yard touchdown pass to tight end Zeke Mowatt. The Broncos came right back with a 58-yard scoring drive on six plays capped by Elway's 4-yard touchdown run. The only scoring in the second period was the sack of Elway in the end zone by defensive end George Martin for a New York safety. The Giants produced a key defensive stand early in the second quarter when the Broncos had a first down at the New York 1-yard line, but failed to score on three running plays and Karlis's 23-yard missed field-goal attempt. The Giants took command of the game in the third period en route to a 30-point second half, the most ever scored in one half of Super Bowl play. New York took the lead for good on tight end Mark Bavaro's 13-yard touchdown catch 4:52 into the third period. The nine-play, 63-yard scoring drive included the successful conversion of a fourth-and-1 play on the New York 46-yard line. Denver was limited to only 2 net yards on 10 offensive plays in the third quarter. Simms set Super Bowl records for most consecutive completions (10) and highest completion percentage (88 percent on 22 completions in 25 attempts). He also passed for 268 yards and 3 touchdowns and was named the game's most valuable player. New York running back Joe Morris was the game's leading rusher with 20 carries for 67 yards. Denver wide receiver Vance Johnson led all receivers with 5 catches for 121 yards. The Giants defeated their three playoff opponents by a cumulative total of 82 points (New York 105, opponents 23), the largest such margin by a Super Bowl winner.

Denver (AFC)	10	0	0	10 —	20
N.Y. Giants (NFC)	7	2	17	13 —	39

Den — FG Karlis 48
NYG — Mowatt 6 pass from Simms (Allegre kick)
Den — Elway 4 run (Karlis kick)
NYG — Safety, Martin tackled Elway in end zone
NYG — Bavaro 13 pass from Simms (Allegre kick)
NYG — FG Allegre 21
NYG — Morris 1 run (Allegre kick)
NYG — McConkey 6 pass from Simms (Allegre kick)
Den — FG Karlis 28
NYG — Anderson 2 run (kick failed)
Den — V. Johnson 47 pass from Elway (Karlis kick)

SUPER BOWL XX

Louisiana Superdome, New Orleans, Louisiana
January 26, 1986, Attendance: 73,818
CHICAGO 46, NEW ENGLAND 10—The NFC champion Chicago Bears, seeking their first NFL title since 1963, scored a Super Bowl-record 46 points in downing AFC champion New England 46-10 in Super Bowl XX. The previous record for most points in a Super Bowl was 38, shared by San Francisco in XIX and the Los Angeles Raiders in XVIII. The Bears' league-leading defense tied the Super Bowl record for sacks (7) and limited the Patriots to a record-low 7 rushing yards. New England took the quickest lead in Super Bowl history when Tony Franklin kicked a 36-yard field goal with 1:19 elapsed in the first period. The score came about because of Larry Mc-Grew's fumble recovery at the Chicago 19-yard line. However, the Bears rebounded for a 23-3 first-half lead, while building a yardage advantage of 236 total yards to New England's minus 19. Running back Matt Suhey rushed 8 times for 37 yards, including an 11-yard touchdown run, and caught 1 pass for 24 yards in the first half. After the Patriots first drive of the second half ended with a punt to the Bears' 4-yard line, Chicago marched 96 yards in nine plays with quarterback Jim McMahon's 1-yard scoring run capping the drive. McMahon became the first quarterback in Super Bowl history to rush for a pair of touchdowns. The Bears completed their scoring via a 28-yard interception return by reserve cornerback Reggie Phillips, a 1-yard run by defensive tackle/fullback William Perry, and a safety when defensive end Henry Waechter tackled Patriots quarterback Steve Grogan in the end zone. Bears defensive end Richard Dent became the fourth defender to be named the game's most valuable player after contributing 1½ sacks. The Bears' victory margin of 36 points was the largest in Super Bowl history, bettering the previous mark of 29 by the Los Angeles Raiders when they topped Washington 38-9 in Game XVIII. McMahon completed 12 of 20 passes for 256 yards before leaving the game in the fourth period with a wrist injury. The NFL's all-time leading rusher, Bears running back Walter Payton, carried 22 times for 61 yards. Wide receiver Willie Gault caught 4 passes for 129 yards, the fourth-most receiving yards in a Super Bowl. Chicago coach Mike Ditka became the second man (Tom Flores of Raiders was the other) who played in a Super Bowl and coached a team to a victory in the game.

Chicago (NFC)	13	10	21	2 —	46
New England (AFC)	3	0	0	7 —	10

NE — FG Franklin 36
Chi — FG Butler 28
Chi — FG Butler 24
Chi — Suhey 11 run (Butler kick)
Chi — McMahon 2 run (Butler kick)
Chi — FG Butler 24
Chi — McMahon 1 run (Butler kick)
Chi — Phillips 28 interception return (Butler kick)
Chi — Perry 1 run (Butler kick)
NE — Fryar 8 pass from Grogan (Franklin kick)
Chi — Safety, Waechter tackled Grogan in end zone

SUPER BOWL XIX

Stanford Stadium, Stanford, California
January 20, 1985, Attendance: 84,059
SAN FRANCISCO 38, MIAMI 16—The San Francisco 49ers captured their second Super Bowl title with a dominating offense and a defense that tamed Miami's explosive passing attack. The Dolphins held a 10-7 lead at the end of the first period, which represented the most points scored by two teams in an opening quarter of a Super Bowl. However, the 49ers used excellent field position in the second period to build a 28-16 halftime lead. Running back Roger Craig set a Super Bowl record by scoring 3 touchdowns on pass receptions of 8 and 16 yards and a run of 2 yards. San Francisco's Joe Montana was voted the game's most valuable player. He joined Green Bay's Bart Starr and Pittsburgh's Terry Bradshaw as the only two-time Super Bowl most valuable players. Montana completed 24 of 35 passes for a Super Bowl-record 331 yards and 3 touchdowns, and rushed 5 times for 59 yards, including a 6-yard touchdown. Craig had 58 yards on 15 carries and caught 7 passes for 77 yards. Wendell Tyler rushed 13 times for 65 yards and had 4 catches for 70 yards. Dwight Clark had 6 receptions for 77 yards, while Russ Francis had 5 for 60. San Francisco's 537 total net yards bettered the previous Super Bowl record of 429 yards by Oakland in Super Bowl XI. The 49ers also held a time of possession advantage over the Dolphins of 37:11 to 22:49.

Miami (AFC)	10	6	0	0 —	16
San Francisco (NFC)	7	21	10	0 —	38

Mia — FG von Schamann 37
SF — Monroe 33 pass from Montana (Wersching kick)
Mia — D. Johnson 2 pass from Marino (von Schamann kick)
SF — Craig 8 pass from Montana (Wersching kick)
SF — Montana 6 run (Wersching kick)
SF — Craig 2 run (Wersching kick)
Mia — FG von Schamann 31
Mia — FG von Schamann 30
SF — FG Wersching 27
SF — Craig 16 pass from Montana (Wersching kick)

SUPER BOWL XVIII

Tampa Stadium, Tampa, Florida
January 22, 1984, Attendance: 72,920
LOS ANGELES RAIDERS 38, WASHINGTON 9—The Los Angeles Raiders dominated the Washington Redskins from the beginning in Super Bowl XVIII and achieved the most lopsided victory in Super Bowl history, surpassing Green Bay's 35-10 win over Kansas City in Super Bowl I. The Raiders took a 7-0 lead 4:52 into the game when Derrick Jensen blocked a Jeff Hayes punt and recovered it in the end zone for a touchdown. With 9:14 remaining in the first half, Raiders quarterback Jim Plunkett threw a 12-yard touchdown pass to wide receiver Cliff Branch to complete a three-play, 65-yard drive. Washington cut the Raiders' lead to 14-3 on a 24-yard field goal by Mark Moseley. With seven seconds left in the first half, Raiders linebacker Jack Squirek intercepted a Joe Theismann pass at the Redskins' 5-yard line and ran it in for a touchdown to give Los Angeles a 21-3 halftime lead. In the third period, running back Marcus Allen, who rushed for a Super Bowl-record 191 yards on 20 carries, increased the Raiders' lead to 35-9 on touchdown runs of 5 and 74 yards, the latter erasing the Super Bowl record of 58 yards set by Baltimore's Tom Matte in Game III. Allen was named the game's most valuable player. The victory over Washington raised Raiders coach Tom Flores' playoff record to 8-1, including a 27-10 win against Philadelphia in Super Bowl XV. The 38 points scored by the Raiders were the highest total by a Super Bowl team. The previous high was 35 points by Green Bay in Game I.

Washington (NFC)	0	3	6	0 —	9
L.A. Raiders (AFC)	7	14	14	3 —	38

Raiders — Jensen recovered blocked punt in end zone (Bahr kick)
Raiders — Branch 12 pass from Plunkett (Bahr kick)
Wash — FG Moseley 24
Raiders — Squirek 5 interception return (Bahr kick)
Wash — Riggins 1 run (kick blocked)
Raiders — Allen 5 run (Bahr kick)
Raiders — Allen 74 run (Bahr kick)
Raiders — FG Bahr 21

SUPER BOWL XVII

Rose Bowl, Pasadena, California
January 30, 1983, Attendance: 103,667
WASHINGTON 27, MIAMI 17—Fullback John Riggins ran for a Super Bowl-record 166 yards on 38 carries to spark Washington to a 27-17 victory over AFC champion Miami. It was Riggins' fourth straight 100-yard rushing game during the playoffs, also a record. The win marked Washington's first NFL title since 1942, and was only the second time in Super Bowl history NFL/NFC teams scored consecutive victories (Green Bay did it in Super Bowls I and II and San Francisco won Super Bowl XVI). The Redskins, under second-year head coach Joe Gibbs, used a balanced offense that accounted for 400 total yards (a Super Bowl-record 276 yards rushing and 124 passing), second in Super Bowl history to 429 yards by Oakland in Super Bowl XI. The Dolphins built a 17-10 halftime lead on a 76-yard touchdown pass from quarterback David Woodley to wide receiver Jimmy Cefalo 6:49 into the first period, a 20-yard field goal by Uwe von Schamann with 6:00 left in the half, and a Super Bowl-record 98-yard kickoff return by Fulton Walker with 1:38 remaining. Washington had tied the score at 10-10 with 1:51 left on a four-yard touchdown pass from Joe Theismann to wide receiver Alvin Garrett. Mark Moseley started the Redskins' scoring with a 31-yard field goal late in the first period, and added a 20-yarder midway through the third period to cut the Dolphins' lead to 17-13. Riggins, who was voted the game's most valuable player, gave Washington its first lead of the game with 10:01 left when he ran 43 yards off left tackle for a touchdown in a fourth-and-1 situation. Wide receiver Charlie Brown caught a six-yard scoring pass from Theismann with 1:55 left to complete the scoring. The Dolphins managed only 176 yards (142 in first half). Theismann completed 15 of 23 passes for 143 yards, with 2 touchdowns and 2 interceptions. For Miami, Woodley was 4 of 14 for 97 yards, with 1 touchdown, and 1 interception. Don Strock was 0 for 3 in relief.

Miami (AFC)	7	10	0	0 —	17
Washington (NFC)	0	10	3	14 —	27

Mia — Cefalo 76 pass from Woodley (von Schamann kick)
Wash — FG Moseley 31
Mia — FG von Schamann 20
Wash — Garrett 4 pass from Theismann (Moseley kick)
Mia — Walker 98 kickoff return (von Schamann kick)
Wash — FG Moseley 20
Wash — Riggins 43 run (Moseley kick)
Wash — Brown 6 pass from Theismann (Moseley kick)

SUPER BOWL XVI

Pontiac Silverdome, Pontiac, Michigan
January 24, 1982, Attendance: 81,270
SAN FRANCISCO 26, CINCINNATI 21—Ray Wersching's Super Bowl record-tying 4 field goals and Joe Montana's controlled passing helped lift the San Francisco 49ers to their first NFL championship with a 26-21 victory over Cincinnati. The 49ers built a game-record 20-0 halftime lead via Montana's 1-yard touchdown run, which capped an 11-play, 68-yard drive; fullback Earl Cooper's 11-yard scoring pass from Montana, which climaxed a Super Bowl record 92-yard drive on 12 plays; and Wersching's 22- and 26-yard field goals. The Bengals rebounded in the second half, closing the gap to 20-14 on quarterback Ken Anderson's 5-yard run and Dan Ross's 4-yard reception from Anderson, who established Super Bowl passing records for completions (25) and completion percentage (73.5 percent on 25 of 34). Wersching added early fourth-period field goals of 40 and 23 yards to increase the 49ers' lead to 26-14. The Bengals managed to score on an Anderson-to-Ross 3-yard pass with only 16 seconds remaining. Ross set a Super Bowl record with 11 receptions for 104 yards. Montana, the game's most valuable player, completed 14 of 22 passes for 157 yards. Cincinnati compiled 356 yards to San Francisco's 275, which marked the first time in Super Bowl history that the team that gained the most yards from scrimmage lost the game.

San Francisco (NFC)	7	13	0	6 —	26
Cincinnati (AFC)	0	0	7	14 —	21

SF — Montana 1 run (Wersching kick)
SF — Cooper 11 pass from Montana (Wersching kick)

SF — FG Wersching 22
SF — FG Wersching 26
Cin — Anderson 5 run (Breech kick)
Cin — Ross 4 pass from Anderson (Breech kick)
SF — FG Wersching 40
SF — FG Wersching 23
Cin — Ross 3 pass from Anderson (Breech kick)

SUPER BOWL XV

Louisiana Superdome, New Orleans, Louisiana
January 25, 1981, Attendance: 76,135
OAKLAND 27, PHILADELPHIA 10—Jim Plunkett threw 3 touchdown passes, including an 80-yard strike to Kenny King, as the Raiders became the first wild-card team to win the Super Bowl. Plunkett's touchdown bomb to King—the longest play in Super Bowl history—gave Oakland a decisive 14-0 lead with nine seconds left in the first period. Linebacker Rod Martin had set up Oakland's first touchdown, a 2-yard reception by Cliff Branch, with a 17-yard interception return to the Eagles' 30-yard line. The Eagles never recovered from that early deficit, managing only a Tony Franklin field goal (30 yards) and an 8-yard touchdown pass from Ron Jaworski to Keith Krepfle. Plunkett, who became a starter in the sixth game of the season, completed 13 of 21 for 261 yards and was named the game's most valuable player. Oakland won 9 of 11 games with Plunkett starting, but that was good enough only for second place in the AFC West, although they tied division winner San Diego with an 11-5 record. The Raiders, who had previously won Super Bowl XI over Minnesota, had to win three playoff games to get to the championship game. Oakland defeated Houston 27-7 at home followed by road victories over Cleveland (14-12) and San Diego (34-27). Oakland's Mark van Eeghen was the game's leading rusher with 75 yards on 18 carries. Philadelphia's Wilbert Montgomery led all receivers with 6 receptions for 91 yards. Branch had 5 for 67 and Harold Carmichael of Philadelphia 5 for 83. Martin finished the game with 3 interceptions, a Super Bowl record.

Oakland (AFC)	14	0	10	3	— 27
Philadelphia (NFC)	0	3	0	7	— 10

Oak — Branch 2 pass from Plunkett (Bahr kick)
Oak — King 80 pass from Plunkett (Bahr kick)
Phil — FG Franklin 30
Oak — Branch 29 pass from Plunkett (Bahr kick)
Oak — FG Bahr 46
Phil — Krepfle 8 pass from Jaworski (Franklin kick)
Oak — FG Bahr 35

SUPER BOWL XIV

Rose Bowl, Pasadena, California
January 20, 1980, Attendance: 103,985
PITTSBURGH 31, LOS ANGELES 19—Terry Bradshaw completed 14 of 21 passes for 309 yards and set two passing records as the Steelers became the first team to win four Super Bowls. Despite 3 interceptions by the Rams, Bradshaw kept his poise and brought the Steelers from behind twice in the second half. Trailing 13-10 at halftime, Pittsburgh went ahead 17-13 when Bradshaw hit Lynn Swann with a 47-yard touchdown pass after 2:48 of the third quarter. On the Rams' next possession Vince Ferragamo, who completed 15 of 25 passes for 212 yards, responded with a 50-yard pass to Billy Waddy that moved Los Angeles from its 26 to the Steelers' 24. On the following play, Lawrence McCutcheon connected with Ron Smith on a halfback option pass that gave the Rams a 19-17 lead. On Pittsburgh's initial possession of the final period, Bradshaw lofted a 73-yard scoring pass to John Stallworth to put the Steelers in front to stay 24-19. Franco Harris scored on a 1-yard run later in the quarter to seal the verdict. A 45-yard pass from Bradshaw to Stallworth was the key play in the drive to Harris's score. Bradshaw, the game's most valuable player for the second straight year, set career Super Bowl records for most touchdown passes (9) and most passing yards (932). Larry Anderson gave the Steelers excellent field position throughout the game with 5 kickoff returns for

a record 162 yards.

Los Angeles (NFC)	7	6	6	0	— 19
Pittsburgh (AFC)	3	7	7	14	— 31

Pitt — FG Bahr 41
LA — Bryant 1 run (Corral kick)
Pitt — Harris 1 run (Bahr kick)
LA — FG Corral 31
LA — FG Corral 45
Pitt — Swann 47 pass from Bradshaw (Bahr kick)
LA — Smith 24 pass from McCutcheon (kick failed)
Pitt — Stallworth 73 pass from Bradshaw (Bahr kick)
Pitt — Harris 1 run (Bahr kick)

SUPER BOWL XIII

Orange Bowl, Miami, Florida
January 21, 1979, Attendance: 79,484
PITTSBURGH 35, DALLAS 31—Terry Bradshaw threw a record 4 touchdown passes to lead the Steelers to victory. The Steelers became the first team to win three Super Bowls, mostly because of Bradshaw's accurate arm. Bradshaw, voted the game's most valuable player, completed 17 of 30 passes for 318 yards, a personal high. Four of those passes went for touchdowns—2 to John Stallworth and the third, with 26 seconds remaining in the second period, to Rocky Bleier for a 21-14 halftime lead. The Cowboys scored twice before intermission on Roger Staubach's 39-yard pass to Tony Hill and a 37-yard fumble return by linebacker Mike Hegman, who stole the ball from Bradshaw. The Steelers broke open the contest with 2 touchdowns in a span of 19 seconds midway through the final period. Franco Harris rambled 22 yards up the middle to give the Steelers a 28-17 lead with 7:10 left. Pittsburgh got the ball right back when Randy White fumbled the kickoff and Dennis Winston recovered for the Steelers. On first down, Bradshaw fired his fourth touchdown pass, an 18-yard pass to Lynn Swann to boost the Steelers' lead to 35-17 with 6:51 to play. The Cowboys refused to let the Steelers run away with the contest. Staubach connected with Billy Joe DuPree on a 7-yard scoring pass with 2:23 left. Then the Cowboys recovered an onside kick and Staubach took them in for another score, passing 4 yards to Butch Johnson with 22 seconds remaining. Bleier recovered another onside kick with 17 seconds left to seal the victory for the Steelers.

Pittsburgh (AFC)	7	14	0	14	— 35
Dallas (NFC)	7	7	3	14	— 31

Pitt — Stallworth 28 pass from Bradshaw (Gerela kick)
Dall — Hill 39 pass from Staubach (Septien kick)
Dall — Hegman 37 fumble recovery return (Septien kick)
Pitt — Stallworth 75 pass from Bradshaw (Gerela kick)
Pitt — Bleier 7 pass from Bradshaw (Gerela kick)
Dall — FG Septien 27
Pitt — Harris 22 run (Gerela kick)
Pitt — Swann 18 pass from Bradshaw (Gerela kick)
Dall — DuPree 7 pass from Staubach (Septien kick)
Dall — B. Johnson 4 pass from Staubach (Septien kick)

SUPER BOWL XII

Louisiana Superdome, New Orleans, Louisiana
January 15, 1978, Attendance: 75,583
DALLAS 27, DENVER 10—The Cowboys evened their Super Bowl record at 2-2 by defeating Denver before a sellout crowd of 75,583, plus 102,010,000 television viewers, the largest audience ever to watch a sporting event. Dallas converted 2 interceptions into 10 points and Efren Herrera added a 35-yard field goal for a 13-0 halftime advantage. In the third period Craig Morton engineered a drive to the Cowboys' 30 and Jim Turner's 47-yard field goal made the score 13-3. After an exchange of punts, Butch Johnson made a spectacular diving catch in the end zone to complete a 45-yard pass from Roger

Staubach and put the Cowboys ahead 20-3. Following Rick Upchurch's 67-yard kickoff return, Norris Weese guided the Broncos to a touchdown to cut the Dallas lead to 20-10. Dallas clinched the victory when running back Robert Newhouse threw a 29-yard touchdown pass to Golden Richards with 7:04 remaining in the game. It was the first pass thrown by Newhouse since 1975. Harvey Martin and Randy White, who were named co-most valuable players, led the Cowboys' defense, which recovered 4 fumbles and intercepted 4 passes.

Dallas (NFC)	10	3	7	7	— 27
Denver (AFC)	0	0	10	0	— 10

Dall — Dorsett 3 run (Herrera kick)
Dall — FG Herrera 35
Dall — FG Herrera 43
Den — FG Turner 47
Dall — Johnson 45 pass from Staubach (Herrera kick)
Den — Lytle 1 run (Turner kick)
Dall — Richards 29 pass from Newhouse (Herrera kick)

SUPER BOWL XI

Rose Bowl, Pasadena, California
January 9, 1977, Attendance: 103,438
OAKLAND 32, MINNESOTA 14—The Raiders won their first NFL championship before a record Super Bowl crowd plus 81 million television viewers, the largest audience ever to watch a sporting event. The Raiders gained a record-breaking 429 yards, including running back Clarence Davis's 137 rushing yards. Wide receiver Fred Biletnikoff made 4 key receptions, which earned him the game's most valuable player trophy. Oakland scored on three successive possessions in the second quarter to build a 16-0 halftime lead. Errol Mann's 24-yard field goal opened the scoring, then the AFC champions put together drives of 64 and 35 yards, scoring on a 1-yard pass from Ken Stabler to Dave Casper and a 1-yard run by Pete Banaszak. The Raiders increased their lead to 19-0 on a 40-yard field goal in the third quarter, but Minnesota responded with a 12-play, 58-yard drive late in the period, with Fran Tarkenton passing 8 yards to wide receiver Sammy White to cut the deficit to 19-7. Two fourth-quarter interceptions clinched the title for the Raiders. One set up Banaszak's second touchdown run, the other resulted in cornerback Willie Brown's Super Bowl-record 75-yard interception return.

Oakland (AFC)	0	16	3	13	— 32
Minnesota (NFC)	0	0	7	7	— 14

Oak — FG Mann 24
Oak — Casper 1 pass from Stabler (Mann kick)
Oak — Banaszak 1 run (kick failed)
Oak — FG Mann 40
Minn — S. White 8 pass from Tarkenton (Cox kick)
Oak — Banaszak 2 run (Mann kick)
Oak — Brown 75 interception return (kick failed)
Minn — Voigt 13 pass from Lee (Cox kick)

SUPER BOWL X

Orange Bowl, Miami, Florida
January 18, 1976, Attendance: 80,187
PITTSBURGH 21, DALLAS 17—The Steelers won the Super Bowl for the second year in a row on Terry Bradshaw's 64-yard touchdown pass to Lynn Swann and an aggressive defense that snuffed out a late rally by the Cowboys with an end-zone interception on the final play of the game. In the fourth quarter, Pittsburgh ran on fourth down and gave up the ball on the Cowboys' 39 with 1:22 to play. Roger Staubach ran and passed for 2 first downs but his last desperation pass was picked off by Glen Edwards. Dallas's scoring was the result of 2 touchdown passes by Staubach, one to Drew Pearson for 29 yards and the other to Percy Howard for 34 yards. Toni Fritsch had a 36-yard field goal. The Steelers scored on 2 touchdown passes by Bradshaw, 1 to Randy Grossman for 7 yards and the long bomb to Swann. Roy Gerela had 36- and 18-yard field goals. Reggie Harrison blocked a punt through the end zone for a safety. Swann set a Super Bowl record by

gaining 161 yards on his 4 receptions.

Dallas (NFC)	7	3	0	7 —	17
Pittsburgh (AFC)	7	0	0	14 —	21

Dall — D. Pearson 29 pass from Staubach (Fritsch kick)
Pitt — Grossman 7 pass from Bradshaw (Gerela kick)
Dall — FG Fritsch 36
Pitt — Safety, Harrison blocked Hoopes's punt through end zone
Pitt — FG Gerela 36
Pitt — FG Gerela 18
Pitt — Swann 64 pass from Bradshaw (kick failed)
Dall — P. Howard 34 pass from Staubach (Fritsch kick)

SUPER BOWL IX

Tulane Stadium, New Orleans, Louisiana
January 12, 1975, Attendance: 80,997
PITTSBURGH 16, MINNESOTA 6—AFC champion Pittsburgh, in its initial Super Bowl appearance, and NFC champion Minnesota, making a third bid for its first Super Bowl title, struggled through a first half in which the only score was produced by the Steelers' defense when Dwight White downed Vikings' quarterback Fran Tarkenton in the end zone for a safety 7:49 into the second period. The Steelers forced another break and took advantage on the second-half kickoff when Minnesota's Bill Brown fumbled and Marv Kellum recovered for Pittsburgh on the Vikings' 30. After Rocky Bleier failed to gain on first down, Franco Harris carried 3 consecutive times for 24 yards, a loss of 3, and a 9-yard touchdown and a 9-0 lead. Though its offense was completely stymied by Pittsburgh's defense, Minnesota managed to move into a threatening position after 4:27 of the final period when Matt Blair blocked Bobby Walden's punt and Terry Brown recovered the ball in the end zone for a touchdown. Fred Cox's kick failed and the Steelers led 9-6. Pittsburgh wasted no time putting the victory away. The Steelers took the ensuing kickoff and marched 66 yards in 11 plays, climaxed by Terry Bradshaw's 4-yard scoring pass to Larry Brown with 3:31 left. Pittsburgh's defense permitted Minnesota only 119 yards total offense, including a Super Bowl low of 17 rushing yards. The Steelers, meanwhile, gained 333 yards, including Harris's record 158 yards on 34 carries.

Pittsburgh (AFC)	0	2	7	7 —	16
Minnesota (NFC)	0	0	0	6 —	6

Pitt — Safety, White downed Tarkenton in end zone
Pitt — Harris 9 run (Gerela kick)
Minn — T. Brown recovered blocked punt in end zone (kick failed)
Pitt — L. Brown 4 pass from Bradshaw (Gerela kick)

SUPER BOWL VIII

Rice Stadium, Houston, Texas
January 13, 1974, Attendance: 71,882
MIAMI 24, MINNESOTA 7—The defending NFL champion Dolphins, representing the AFC for the third straight year, scored the first two times they had possession on marches of 62 and 56 yards while the Miami defense limited the Vikings to only seven plays in the first period. Larry Csonka climaxed the initial 10-play drive with a 5-yard touchdown bolt through right guard after 5:27 had elapsed. Four plays later, Miami began another 10-play scoring drive, which ended with Jim Kiick bursting 1 yard through the middle for another touchdown after 13:38 of the period. Garo Yepremian added a 28-yard field goal midway in the second period for a 17-0 Miami lead. Minnesota then drove from its 20 to a second-and-2 situation on the Miami 7 yard line with 1:18 left in the half. But on two plays, Miami limited Oscar Reed to 1 yard. On fourth-and-1 from the 6, Reed went over right tackle, but Dolphins middle linebacker Nick Buoniconti jarred the ball loose and Jake Scott recovered for Miami to halt the Minnesota threat. The Vikings were unable to muster enough

offense in the second half to threaten the Dolphins. Csonka rushed 33 times for a Super Bowl-record 145 yards. Bob Griese of Miami completed 6 of 7 passes for 73 yards.

Minnesota (NFC)	0	0	0	7 —	7
Miami (AFC)	14	3	7	0 —	24

Mia — Csonka 5 run (Yepremian kick)
Mia — Kiick 1 run (Yepremian kick)
Mia — FG Yepremian 28
Mia — Csonka 2 run (Yepremian kick)
Minn — Tarkenton 4 run (Cox kick)

SUPER BOWL VII

Memorial Coliseum, Los Angeles, California
January 14, 1973, Attendance: 90,182
MIAMI 14, WASHINGTON 7—The Dolphins played virtually perfect football in the first half as their defense permitted the Redskins to cross midfield only once and their offense turned good field position into 2 touchdowns. On its third possession, Miami opened its first scoring drive from the Dolphins' 37 yard line. An 18-yard pass from Bob Griese to Paul Warfield preceded by three plays Griese's 28-yard touchdown pass to Howard Twilley. After Washington moved from its 17 to the Miami 48 with two minutes remaining in the first half, Dolphins linebacker Nick Buoniconti intercepted a Billy Kilmer pass at the Miami 41 and returned it to the Washington 27. Jim Kiick ran for 3 yards, Larry Csonka for 3, Griese passed to Jim Mandich for 19, and Kiick gained 1 to the 1-yard line. With 18 seconds left until intermission, Kiick scored from the 1. Washington's only touchdown came with 2:07 left in the game and resulted from a misplayed field-goal attempt and fumble by Garo Yepremian, with the Redskins' Mike Bass picking the ball out of the air and running 49 yards for the score. Dolphins safety Jake Scott, who had 2 interceptions, including 1 in the end zone to kill a Redskins' drive, was voted the game's most valuable player.

Miami (AFC)	7	7	0	0 —	14
Washington (NFC)	0	0	0	7 —	7

Mia — Twilley 28 pass from Griese (Yepremian kick)
Mia — Kiick 1 run (Yepremian kick)
Wash — Bass 49 fumble recovery return (Knight kick)

SUPER BOWL VI

Tulane Stadium, New Orleans, Louisiana
January 16, 1972, Attendance: 81,023
DALLAS 24, MIAMI 3—The Cowboys rushed for a record 252 yards and their defense limited the Dolphins to a low of 185 yards while not permitting a touchdown for the first time in Super Bowl history. Dallas converted Chuck Howley's recovery of Larry Csonka's first fumble of the season into a 3-0 advantage and led at halftime 10-3. After Dallas received the second-half kickoff, Duane Thomas led a 71-yard march in eight plays for a 17-3 margin. Howley intercepted Bob Griese's pass at the 50 and returned it to the Miami 9 early in the fourth period, and three plays later Roger Staubach passed 7 yards to Mike Ditka for the final touchdown. Thomas rushed for 95 yards and Walt Garrison gained 74. Staubach, voted the game's most valuable player, completed 12 of 19 passes for 119 yards and 2 touchdowns.

Dallas (NFC)	3	7	7	7 —	24
Miami (AFC)	0	3	0	0 —	3

Dall — FG Clark 9
Dall — Alworth 7 pass from Staubach (Clark kick)
Mia — FG Yepremian 31
Dall — D. Thomas 3 run (Clark kick)
Dall — Ditka 7 pass from Staubach (Clark kick)

SUPER BOWL V

Orange Bowl, Miami, Florida
January 17, 1971, Attendance: 79,204
BALTIMORE 16, DALLAS 13—A 32-yard field goal by rookie kicker Jim O'Brien brought the Baltimore Colts a victory over the Dallas Cowboys in the final five seconds of Super Bowl V. The game between the champions of the AFC and NFC was played on artificial turf for the first time. Dallas led 13-6 at the half but interceptions by Rick Volk and Mike Curtis set up a Baltimore touchdown and O'Brien's decisive kick in the fourth period. Earl Morrell relieved an injured Johnny Unitas late in the first half, although Unitas completed the Colts' only scoring pass. It caromed off receiver Eddie Hinton's fingertips, off Dallas defensive back Mel Renfro, and finally settled into the grasp of John Mackey, who went 45 yards to score on a 75-yard play.

Baltimore (AFC)	0	6	0	10 —	16
Dallas (NFC)	3	10	0	0 —	13

Dall — FG Clark 14
Dall — FG Clark 30
Balt — Mackey 75 pass from Unitas (kick blocked)
Dall — Thomas 7 pass from Morton (Clark kick)
Balt — Nowatzke 2 run (O'Brien kick)
Balt — FG O'Brien 32

SUPER BOWL IV

Tulane Stadium, New Orleans, Louisiana
January 11, 1970, Attendance: 80,562
KANSAS CITY 23, MINNESOTA 7—The AFL squared the Super Bowl at two games apiece with the NFL, building a 16-0 halftime lead behind Len Dawson's superb quarterbacking and a powerful defense. Dawson, the fourth consecutive quarterback to be chosen the Super Bowl's top player, called an almost flawless game, completing 12 of 17 passes and hitting Otis Taylor on a 46-yard play for the final Chiefs touchdown. The Kansas City defense limited Minnesota's strong rushing game to 67 yards and had 3 interceptions and 2 fumble recoveries. The crowd of 80,562 set a Super Bowl record, as did the gross receipts of $3,817,872.69.

Minnesota (NFL)	0	0	7	0 —	7
Kansas City (AFL)	3	13	7	0 —	23

KC — FG Stenerud 48
KC — FG Stenerud 32
KC — FG Stenerud 25
KC — Garrett 5 run (Stenerud kick)
Minn — Osborn 4 run (Cox kick)
KC — Taylor 46 pass from Dawson (Stenerud kick)

SUPER BOWL III

Orange Bowl, Miami, Florida
January 12, 1969, Attendance: 75,389
NEW YORK JETS 16, BALTIMORE 7—Jets quarterback Joe Namath "guaranteed" victory on the Thursday before the game, then went out and led the AFL to its first Super Bowl victory over a Baltimore team that had lost only once in 16 games all season. Namath, chosen the outstanding player, completed 17 of 28 passes for 206 yards and directed a steady attack that dominated the NFL champions after the Jets' defense had intercepted Colts quarterback Earl Morrall 3 times in the first half. The Jets had 337 total yards, including 121 rushing yards by Matt Snell. Johnny Unitas, who had missed most of the season with a sore elbow, came off the bench and led Baltimore to its only touchdown late in the fourth quarter after New York led 16-0.

New York Jets (AFL)	0	7	6	3 —	16
Baltimore (NFL)	0	0	0	7 —	7

NYJ — Snell 4 run (Turner kick)
NYJ — FG Turner 32
NYJ — FG Turner 30
NYJ — FG Turner 9
Balt — Hill 1 run (Michaels kick)

SUPER BOWL II

Orange Bowl, Miami, Florida
January 14, 1968, Attendance: 75,546
GREEN BAY 33, OAKLAND 14—Green Bay, after winning its third consecutive NFL championship, won the Super Bowl title for the second straight year, defeating the AFL champion Raiders in a game that drew the first $3-million gate in football history. Bart Starr again was chosen the game's most valuable player as he completed 13 of 24 passes for 202 yards and 1 touchdown and directed a Packers attack that was in control all the way after building a 16-7 halftime lead. Don Chandler kicked 4 field goals and all-pro cornerback Herb Adderley capped the Green Bay scoring with a 60-yard interception return. The game marked the last for Vince Lombardi as Packers coach, ending nine years at Green Bay in which he won six Western Conference championships, five NFL championships, and two Super Bowls.

Green Bay (NFL)	3	13	10	7	—	33
Oakland (AFL)	0	7	0	7	—	14

GB — FG Chandler 39
GB — FG Chandler 20
GB — Dowler 62 pass from Starr (Chandler kick)
Oak — Miller 23 pass from Lamonica (Blanda kick)
GB — FG Chandler 43
GB — Anderson 2 run (Chandler kick)
GB — FG Chandler 31
GB — Adderley 60 interception return (Chandler kick)
Oak — Miller 23 pass from Lamonica (Blanda kick)

SUPER BOWL I

Memorial Coliseum, Los Angeles, California
January 15, 1967, Attendance: 61,946
GREEN BAY 35, KANSAS CITY 10—The Green Bay Packers opened the Super Bowl series by defeating the AFL champion Chiefs behind the passing of Bart Starr, the receiving of Max McGee, and a key interception by all-pro safety Willie Wood. Green Bay broke open the game with 3 second-half touchdowns, the first of which was set up by Wood's 50-yard return of an interception to the Chiefs' 5 yard line. McGee, filling in for ailing Boyd Dowler after having caught only 4 passes all season, caught 7 from Starr for 138 yards and 2 touchdowns. Elijah Pitts ran for two other scores. The Chiefs' 10 points came in the second quarter, the only touchdown on a 7-yard pass from Len Dawson to Curtis McClinton. Starr completed 16 of 23 passes for 250 yards and 2 touchdowns and was chosen the most valuable player. The Packers collected $15,000 per man and the Chiefs $7,500—the largest single-game shares in the history of team sports.

Kansas City (AFL)	0	10	0	0	—	10
Green Bay (NFL)	7	7	14	7	—	35

GB — McGee 37 pass from Starr (Chandler kick)
KC — McClinton 7 pass from Dawson (Mercer kick)
GB — Taylor 14 run (Chandler kick)
KC — FG Mercer 31
GB — Pitts 5 run (Chandler kick)
GB — McGee 13 pass from Starr (Chandler kick)
GB — Pitts 1 run (Chandler kick)

AFC CHAMPIONSHIP GAME RESULTS

Includes AFL Championship Games (1960-69)

Season	Date	Winner (Share)	Loser (Share)	Score	Site	Attendance
1993	Jan. 23	Buffalo ($23,500)	Kansas City ($23,500)	30-13	Buffalo	76,642
1992	Jan. 17	Buffalo ($18,000)	Miami ($18,000)	29-10	Miami	72,703
1991	Jan. 12	Buffalo ($18,000)	Denver ($18,000)	10-7	Buffalo	80,272
1990	Jan. 20	Buffalo ($18,000)	L.A. Raiders ($18,000)	51-3	Buffalo	80,325
1989	Jan. 14	Denver ($18,000)	Cleveland ($18,000)	37-21	Denver	76,046
1988	Jan. 8	Cincinnati ($18,000)	Buffalo ($18,000)	21-10	Cincinnati	59,747
1987	Jan. 17	Denver ($18,000)	Cleveland ($18,000)	38-33	Denver	76,197
1986	Jan. 11	Denver ($18,000)	Cleveland ($18,000)	23-20*	Cleveland	79,973
1985	Jan. 12	New England ($18,000)	Miami ($18,000)	31-14	Miami	75,662
1984	Jan. 6	Miami ($18,000)	Pittsburgh ($18,000)	45-28	Miami	76,029
1983	Jan. 8	L.A. Raiders ($18,000)	Seattle ($18,000)	30-14	Los Angeles	91,445
1982	Jan. 23	Miami ($18,000)	N.Y. Jets ($18,000)	14-0	Miami	67,396
1981	Jan. 10	Cincinnati ($9,000)	San Diego ($9,000)	27-7	Cincinnati	46,302
1980	Jan. 11	Oakland ($9,000)	San Diego ($9,000)	34-27	San Diego	52,675
1979	Jan. 6	Pittsburgh ($9,000)	Houston ($9,000)	27-13	Pittsburgh	50,475
1978	Jan. 7	Pittsburgh ($9,000)	Houston ($9,000)	34-5	Pittsburgh	50,725
1977	Jan. 1	Denver ($9,000)	Oakland ($9,000)	20-17	Denver	75,044
1976	Dec. 26	Oakland ($8,500)	Pittsburgh ($5,500)	24-7	Oakland	53,821
1975	Jan. 4	Pittsburgh ($8,500)	Oakland ($5,500)	16-10	Pittsburgh	50,609
1974	Dec. 29	Pittsburgh ($8,500)	Oakland ($5,500)	24-13	Oakland	53,800
1973	Dec. 30	Miami ($8,500)	Oakland ($5,500)	27-10	Miami	79,325
1972	Dec. 31	Miami ($8,500)	Pittsburgh ($5,500)	21-17	Pittsburgh	50,845
1971	Jan. 2	Miami ($8,500)	Baltimore ($5,500)	21-0	Miami	76,622
1970	Jan. 3	Baltimore ($8,500)	Oakland ($5,500)	27-17	Baltimore	54,799
1969	Jan. 4	Kansas City ($7,755)	Oakland ($6,252)	17-7	Oakland	53,564
1968	Dec. 29	N.Y. Jets ($7,007)	Oakland ($5,349)	27-23	New York	62,627
1967	Dec. 31	Oakland ($6,321)	Houston ($4,996)	40-7	Oakland	53,330
1966	Jan. 1	Kansas City ($5,309)	Buffalo ($3,799)	31-7	Buffalo	42,080
1965	Dec. 26	Buffalo ($5,189)	San Diego ($3,447)	23-0	San Diego	30,361
1964	Dec. 26	Buffalo ($2,668)	San Diego ($1,738)	20-7	Buffalo	40,242
1963	Jan. 5	San Diego ($2,498)	Boston ($1,596)	51-10	San Diego	30,127
1962	Dec. 23	Dallas ($2,206)	Houston ($1,471)	20-17*	Houston	37,981
1961	Dec. 24	Houston ($1,792)	San Diego ($1,111)	10-3	San Diego	29,556
1960	Jan. 1	Houston ($1,025)	L.A. Chargers ($718)	24-16	Houston	32,183

*Sudden death overtime.

AFC CHAMPIONSHIP GAME COMPOSITE STANDINGS

	W	L	Pct.	Pts.	OP
Cincinnati Bengals	2	0	1.000	48	17
Denver Broncos	4	1	.800	125	101
Buffalo Bills	6	2	.750	180	92
Kansas City Chiefs*	3	1	.750	81	61
Miami Dolphins	5	2	.714	152	115
Pittsburgh Steelers	4	3	.571	153	131
Baltimore Colts	1	1	.500	27	38
New England Patriots**	1	1	.500	41	65
New York Jets	1	1	.500	27	37
Houston Oilers	2	4	.333	76	140
Oakland/L.A. Raiders	4	8	.333	228	264
San Diego Chargers***	1	6	.143	111	148
Seattle Seahawks	0	1	.000	14	30
Cleveland Browns	0	3	.000	74	98

*One game played when franchise was in Dallas (Texans). (Won 20-17)
**One game played when franchise was in Boston. (Lost 51-10)
***One game played when franchise was in Los Angeles. (Lost 24-16)

1993 AFC CHAMPIONSHIP GAME

Rich Stadium, Buffalo, New York
January 23, 1994, Attendance: 76,642

BUFFALO 30, KANSAS CITY 13—Thurman Thomas rushed for 186 yards and 3 touchdowns as the Bills qualified for an unprecedented fourth consecutive Super Bowl. Thomas, who ran for 129 yards in the first two quarters, helped stake Buffalo to a 20-6 advantage at intermission by scoring on touchdown runs of 12 and 3 yards. The Chiefs had an opportunity to cut that deficit in half, marching 75 yards to the Bills' 5-yard line in the closing seconds of the first half. But Joe Montana's pass to a wide-open Kimble Anders near the goal line bounced off the running back's hands and was intercepted in the end zone by Buffalo safety Henry Jones. Montana, who completed only 9 of 23 passes for 125 yards, sat out most of the second half after suffering a concussion on the third play of the third quarter. Backup Dave Krieg, who completed 16 of 29 passes for 198 yards, came

on and led a 90-yard touchdown drive that pulled Kansas City within 20-13 late in the third quarter. But Buffalo answered with a 14-play, 79-yard march capped by Steve Christie's 18-yard field goal 3:05 into the fourth quarter. Thomas's third touchdown, a 3-yard run with 5:30 remaining, put the game out of reach. Thomas averaged 5.6 yards on his 33 carries as the Bills overwhelmed the Chiefs on the ground, outrushing them 229 yards to 52.

Kansas City (13)	Offense	Buffalo (30)
J.J. Birden	WR	Don Beebe
John Alt	LT	John Fina
David Szott	LG	Glenn Parker
Tim Grunhard	C	Kent Hull
Will Shields	RG	John Davis
Rickey Siglar	RT	Howard Ballard
Jonathan Hayes	TE	Pete Metzelaars
Keith Cash	TE-WR	Andre Reed
Joe Montana	QB	Jim Kelly
Marcus Allen	RB	Thurman Thomas
Willie Davis	WR	Bill Brooks
	Defense	
Neil Smith	LE	Phil Hansen
Joe Phillips	NT	Jeff Wright
Dan Saleaumua	RE	Bruce Smith
Derrick Thomas	LOLB	Cornelius Bennett
Martin Bayless	MLB-LILB	Marvcus Patton
Lonnie Marts	ROLB-RILB	Mark Maddox
Charles Mincy	DB-ROLB	Darryl Talley
Albert Lewis	LCB	Mickey Washington
Jay Taylor	RCB	Nate Odomes
Bruce Pickens	SS	Henry Jones
Kevin Ross	FS	Mark Kelso

SUBSTITUTIONS

Kansas City—Offense: K—Nick Lowery. P—Bryan Barker. QB—Dave Krieg. RB—Kimble Anders, Todd McNair, John Stephens, Ernie Thompson. WR—Tim Barnett, Danan Hughes, Fred Jones. T—Derrick Graham, Joe Valerio. G—Danny Villa. Defense: E—Pellom McDaniels. DT—Darren Mickell, Tim Newton.

LB—Erick Anderson, Tracy Rogers, Tracy Simien, Santo Stephens. S—Bennie Thompson, Tim Watson, Felix Wright. DNP: None.

Buffalo—Offense: K—Steve Christie. P—Chris Mohr. QB—Frank Reich. RB—Kenneth Davis, Carwell Gardner. WR—Russell Copeland, Steve Tasker. TF—Keith McKeller. T—Jerry Crafts. G—Jim Ritcher. C—Mike Devlin, Adam Lingner. Defense: E—Oliver Barnett, Mark Pike. NT—Mike Lodish. LB—Monty Brown, Keith Goganious, Keith Harvey. CB—Thomas Smith, James Williams. S—Matt Darby, Kurt Schulz. DNP: RB—Nate Turner.

OFFICIALS

Referee—Johnny Grier. Umpire—Ron Botchan. Head Linesman—Ron Phares. Line Judge—Jim Quirk. Back Judge—Dick Creed. Field Judge—Phil Luckett. Side Judge—Tom Fincken.

SCORING

Kansas City	6	0	7	0	–	13
Buffalo	7	13	0	10	–	30

Buff — Thomas 12 run (Christie kick)
KC — FG Lowery 31
KC — FG Lowery 31
Buff — Thomas 3 run (Christie kick)
Buff — FG Christie 23
Buff — FG Christie 25
KC — Allen 1 run (Lowery kick)
Buff — FG Christie 18
Buff — Thomas 3 run (Christie kick)

TEAM STATISTICS

	Kansas City	Buffalo
Total First Downs	22	30
Rushing	3	17
Passing	18	9
Penalty	1	4
Total Net Yardage	338	389
Total Offensive Plays	77	73
Average Gain per Offensive Play	4.4	5.3
Rushes	21	46

Yards Gained Rushing (Net)	52	229
Average Yards per Rush	2.5	5.0
Passes Attempted	52	27
Passes Completed	25	17
Had Intercepted	2	0
Tackled Attempting to Pass	4	0
Yards Lost Attempting to Pass	37	0
Yards Gained Passing (Net)	286	160
Punts	6	4
Average Distance	40.8	33.3
Punt Returns	1	5
Punt Return Yardage	11	70
Kickoff Returns	5	4
Kickoff Return Yardage	89	68
Interception Return Yardage	0	15
Total Return Yardage	100	153
Fumbles	1	1
Own Fumbles Recovered	0	0
Opponents Fumbles Recovered	1	0
Penalties	6	2
Yards Penalized	29	10
Total Points Scored	13	30
Touchdowns	1	3
Rushing	1	3
Passing	0	0
Returns	0	0
Extra Points	1	3
Field Goals	2	3
Field Goals Attempted	2	3
Safeties	0	0
Third-Down Efficiency	7/17	5/12
Fourth-Down Efficiency	1/1	0/0
Time of Possession	29:20	30:40

INDIVIDUAL STATISTICS

Rushing

Kansas City	No.	Yds.	LG	TD
Allen	18	50	24	1
Anders	2	1	3	0
Montana	1	1	1	0

Buffalo	No.	Yds.	LG	TD
Thomas	33	186	33	3
K. Davis	10	32	15	0
Reed	1	8	8	0
Kelly	2	3	4	0

Passing

Kansas City	Att.	Comp.	Yds.	TD	Int.
Krieg	29	16	198	0	1
Montana	23	9	125	0	1

Buffalo	Att.	Comp.	Yds.	TD	Int.
Kelly	27	17	160	0	0

Receiving

Kansas City	No.	Yds.	LG	TD
Cash	6	87	19	0
W. Davis	5	57	17	0
Birden	4	60	26	0
Allen	2	36	27	0
McNair	2	33	31	0
Hayes	2	14	10	0
E. Thompson	1	12	12	0
Hughes	1	11	11	0
Anders	1	7	7	0
Szott	1	6	6	0

Buffalo	No.	Yds.	LG	TD
Reed	4	49	28	0
Brooks	4	34	11	0
Metzelaars	4	29	12	0
Thomas	2	22	15	0
Beebe	2	19	11	0
McKeller	1	7	7	0

Interceptions

Kansas City	No.	Yds.	LG	TD
None				

Buffalo	No.	Yds.	LG	TD
Jones	1	15	15	0
Williams	1	0	0	0

Punting

Kansas City	No.	Avg.	LG	Blk.
Barker	6	40.8	51	0

Buffalo	No.	Avg.	LG	Blk.
Mohr	4	33.3	41	0

Punt Returns

Kansas City	No.	FC	Yds.	LG	TD
Hughes	1	1	11	11	0

Buffalo	No.	FC	Yds.	LG	TD
Copeland	5	0	70	26	0

Kickoff Returns

Kansas City	No.	Yds.	LG	TD
J. Stephens	5	89	31	0

Buffalo	No.	Yds.	LG	TD
Copeland	4	68	22	0

NFC CHAMPIONSHIP GAME RESULTS

Includes NFL Championship Games (1933-69)

Season	Date	Winner (Share)	Loser (Share)	Score	Site	Attendance
1993	Jan. 23	Dallas ($23,500)	San Francisco ($23,500)	38-21	Dallas	64,902
1992	Jan. 17	Dallas ($18,000)	San Francisco ($18,000)	30-20	San Francisco	64,920
1991	Jan. 12	Washington ($18,000)	Detroit ($18,000)	41-10	Washington	55,585
1990	Jan. 20	N.Y. Giants ($18,000)	San Francisco ($18,000)	15-13	San Francisco	65,750
1989	Jan. 14	San Francisco ($18,000)	L.A. Rams ($18,000)	30-3	San Francisco	65,634
1988	Jan. 8	San Francisco ($18,000)	Chicago ($18,000)	28-3	Chicago	66,946
1987	Jan. 17	Washington ($18,000)	Minnesota ($18,000)	17-10	Washington	55,212
1986	Jan. 11	New York Giants ($18,000)	Washington ($18,000)	17-0	East Rutherford	76,891
1985	Jan. 12	Chicago ($18,000)	L.A. Rams ($18,000)	24-0	Chicago	66,030
1984	Jan. 6	San Francisco ($18,000)	Chicago ($18,000)	23-0	San Francisco	61,336
1983	Jan. 8	Washington ($18,000)	San Francisco ($18,000)	24-21	Washington	55,363
1982	Jan. 22	Washington ($18,000)	Dallas ($18,000)	31-17	Washington	55,045
1981	Jan. 10	San Francisco ($9,000)	Dallas ($9,000)	28-27	San Francisco	60,525
1980	Jan. 11	Philadelphia ($9,000)	Dallas ($9,000)	20-7	Philadelphia	71,522
1979	Jan. 6	Los Angeles ($9,000)	Tampa Bay ($9,000)	9-0	Tampa Bay	72,033
1978	Jan. 7	Dallas ($9,000)	Los Angeles ($9,000)	28-0	Los Angeles	71,086
1977	Jan. 1	Dallas ($9,000)	Minnesota ($9,000)	23-6	Dallas	64,293
1976	Dec. 26	Minnesota ($8,500)	Los Angeles ($5,500)	24-13	Minnesota	48,379
1975	Jan. 4	Dallas ($8,500)	Los Angeles ($5,500)	37-7	Los Angeles	88,919
1974	Dec. 29	Minnesota ($8,500)	Los Angeles ($5,500)	14-10	Minnesota	48,444
1973	Dec. 30	Minnesota ($8,500)	Dallas ($5,500)	27-10	Dallas	64,422
1972	Dec. 31	Washington ($8,500)	Dallas ($5,500)	26-3	Washington	53,129
1971	Jan. 2	Dallas ($8,500)	San Francisco ($5,500)	14-3	Dallas	63,409
1970	Jan. 3	Dallas ($8,500)	San Francisco ($5,500)	17-10	San Francisco	59,364
1969	Jan. 4	Minnesota ($7,930)	Cleveland ($5,118)	27-7	Minnesota	46,503
1968	Dec. 29	Baltimore ($9,306)	Cleveland ($5,963)	34-0	Cleveland	78,410
1967	Dec. 31	Green Bay ($7,950)	Dallas ($5,299)	21-17	Green Bay	50,861
1966	Jan. 1	Green Bay ($9,813)	Dallas ($6,527)	34-27	Dallas	74,152
1965	Jan. 2	Green Bay ($7,819)	Cleveland ($5,288)	23-12	Green Bay	50,777
1964	Dec. 27	Cleveland ($8,052)	Baltimore ($5,571)	27-0	Cleveland	79,544
1963	Dec. 29	Chicago ($5,899)	New York ($4,218)	14-10	Chicago	45,801
1962	Dec. 30	Green Bay ($5,888)	New York ($4,166)	16-7	New York	64,892
1961	Dec. 31	Green Bay ($5,195)	New York ($3,339)	37-0	Green Bay	39,029
1960	Dec. 26	Philadelphia ($5,116)	Green Bay ($3,105)	17-13	Philadelphia	67,325
1959	Dec. 27	Baltimore ($4,674)	New York ($3,083)	31-16	Baltimore	57,545
1958	Dec. 28	Baltimore ($4,718)	New York ($3,111)	23-17*	New York	64,185
1957	Dec. 29	Detroit ($4,295)	Cleveland ($2,750)	59-14	Detroit	55,263
1956	Dec. 30	New York ($3,779)	Chi. Bears ($2,485)	47-7	New York	56,836
1955	Dec. 26	Cleveland ($3,508)	Los Angeles ($2,316)	38-14	Los Angeles	85,693
1954	Dec. 26	Cleveland ($2,478)	Detroit ($1,585)	56-10	Cleveland	43,827
1953	Dec. 27	Detroit ($2,424)	Cleveland ($1,654)	17-16	Detroit	54,577
1952	Dec. 28	Detroit ($2,274)	Cleveland ($1,712)	17-7	Cleveland	50,934

Season	Date	Winner (Share)	Loser (Share)	Score	Site	Attendance
1951	Dec. 23	Los Angeles ($2,108)	Cleveland ($1,483)	24-17	Los Angeles	57,522
1950	Dec. 24	Cleveland ($1,113)	Los Angeles ($686)	30-28	Cleveland	29,751
1949	Dec. 18	Philadelphia ($1,094)	Los Angeles ($739)	14-0	Los Angeles	27,980
1948	Dec. 19	Philadelphia ($1,540)	Chi. Cardinals ($874)	7-0	Philadelphia	36,309
1947	Dec. 28	Chi. Cardinals ($1,132)	Philadelphia ($754)	28-21	Chicago	30,759
1946	Dec. 15	Chi. Bears ($1,975)	New York ($1,295)	24-14	New York	58,346
1945	Dec. 16	Cleveland ($1,469)	Washington ($902)	15-14	Cleveland	32,178
1944	Dec. 17	Green Bay ($1,449)	New York ($814)	14-7	New York	46,016
1943	Dec. 26	Chi. Bears ($1,146)	Washington ($765)	41-21	Chicago	34,320
1942	Dec. 13	Washington ($965)	Chi. Bears ($637)	14-6	Washington	36,006
1941	Dec. 21	Chi. Bears ($430)	New York ($288)	37-9	Chicago	13,341
1940	Dec. 8	Chi. Bears ($873)	Washington ($606)	73-0	Washington	36,034
1939	Dec. 10	Green Bay ($703.97)	New York ($455.57)	27-0	Milwaukee	32,279
1938	Dec. 11	New York ($504.45)	Green Bay ($368.81)	23-17	New York	48,120
1937	Dec. 12	Washington ($225.90)	Chi. Bears ($127.78)	28-21	Chicago	15,870
1936	Dec. 13	Green Bay ($250)	Boston ($180)	21-6	New York	29,545
1935	Dec. 15	Detroit ($313.35)	New York ($200.20)	26-7	Detroit	15,000
1934	Dec. 9	New York ($621)	Chi. Bears ($414.02)	30-13	New York	35,059
1933	Dec. 17	Chi. Bears ($210.34)	New York ($140.22)	23-21	Chicago	26,000

*Sudden death overtime.

NFC CHAMPIONSHIP GAME COMPOSITE STANDINGS

	W	L	Pct.	Pts.	OP
Green Bay Packers	8	2	.800	223	116
Philadelphia Eagles	4	1	.800	79	48
Baltimore Colts	3	1	.750	88	60
Detroit Lions	4	2	.667	139	141
Minnesota Vikings	4	2	.667	108	80
Washington Redskins*	7	5	.583	222	255
Chicago Bears	7	6	.538	286	245
Dallas Cowboys	7	7	.500	295	254
Phoenix Cardinals**	1	1	.500	28	28
San Francisco 49ers	4	6	.400	197	171
Cleveland Browns	4	7	.364	224	253
New York Giants	5	11	.313	240	322
Los Angeles Rams***	3	9	.250	123	270
Tampa Bay Buccaneers	0	1	.000	0	9

*One game played when franchise was in Boston. (Lost 21-6)
**Both games played when franchise was in Chicago. (Won 28-21, lost 7-0)
***One game played when franchise was in Cleveland. (Won 15-14)

1993 NFC CHAMPIONSHIP GAME

Texas Stadium, Irving, Texas
January 23, 1994, Attendance: 64,902
DALLAS 38, SAN FRANCISCO 21—Troy Aikman threw 2 touchdown passes and Emmitt Smith scored twice as the Cowboys scored on four of their first five possessions and easily handled the 49ers to win the NFC title. Dallas struck quickly, taking the opening kickoff and marching 75 yards in 11 plays to Smith's 5-yard touchdown run 6:19 into the game. San Francisco tied it when running back Tom Rathman caught a 7-yard touchdown pass from Steve Young on the first play of the second quarter, but the Cowboys broke open the game by scoring touchdowns the next three times they had the ball. They countered Rathman's score with an 11-play, 80-yard drive capped by Daryl Johnston's 4-yard touchdown run 5:12 into the second quarter. Three plays later, safety Thomas Everett intercepted a pass that was tipped by San Francisco's John Taylor, and returned it 14 yards to the 49ers' 24-yard line. It took Dallas only four plays to convert that into Aikman's 11-yard touchdown pass to Smith 6:04 before intermission. Aikman teamed with tight end Jay Novacek on a 19-yard touchdown pass in the final minute of the first half to give the Cowboys a 28-7 lead. San Francisco pulled within 14 points on a 4-yard touchdown run by Ricky Watters, but Dallas put the game out of reach when Bernie Kosar teamed with Alvin Harper on a 42-yard touchdown pass with 2:24 remaining in the third quarter. Kosar, in the game because Aikman suffered a concussion early in the second half, kept the drive alive with a 12-yard completion to Michael Irvin on third-and-9 from the Cowboys' 19, and also had a 20-yard completion to Novacek on the 7-play, 82-yard drive. Aikman, who did not return, completed 14 of 18 passes for 177 yards. Kosar was 5 of 9

for 83 yards. Smith rushed for 88 yards on 23 carries and caught 7 passes for 85 yards. 49ers quarterback Steve Young completed 27 of 45 passes for 287 yards and led his team with 38 rushing yards. But he also suffered 4 sacks and was supported by only 46 yards from San Francisco's running backs. Dallas, which beat the 49ers 30-20 in the 1992 NFC Championship Game, qualified for its seventh Super Bowl, extending its NFL record. San Francisco lost in the NFC title game for the third time in four years.

San Francisco (21)	Offense	Dallas (38)
John Taylor	WR	Alvin Harper
Steve Wallace	LT	Mark Tuinei
Guy McIntyre	LG	Nate Newton
Jesse Sapolu	C	John Gesek
Ralph Tamm	RG	Kevin Gogan
Harris Barton	RT	Erik Williams
Brent Jones	TE	Jay Novacek
Jerry Rice	WR	Michael Irvin
Steve Young	QB	Troy Aikman
Ricky Watters	RD	Emmitt Smith
Tom Rathman	FB	Daryl Johnston
	Defense	
Dennis Brown	LE	Tony Tolbert
Dana Stubblefield	LT	Tony Casillas
Ted Washington	RT	Leon Lett
Karl Wilson	RE	Charles Haley
John Johnson	LLB	Dixon Edwards
Michael Walter	MLB	Ken Norton
Bill Romanowski	RLB	Darrin Smith
Eric Davis	LCB	Kevin Smith
Don Griffin	RCB	Larry Brown
Tim McDonald	SS	Darren Woodson
Merton Hanks	FS	Thomas Everett

SUBSTITUTIONS

San Francisco—Offense: K—Mike Cofer. P—Klaus Wilmsmeyer. QB—Steve Bono. RB—Dexter Carter, Amp Lee, Marc Logan. WR—Sanjay Beach, Odessa Turner. TE—John Brandes, Jamie Williams. T—Harry Boatswain. G—Brian Bollinger, Chris Dalman. Defense: E—Larry Roberts, Artie Smith, Troy Wilson. LB—Ravin Caldwell, Antonio Goss, Todd Kelly, Larry Kelm. CB—Michael McGruder. S—Dana Hall, Damien Russell. DNP: None.
Dallas—Offense: K—Eddie Murray. P—John Jett. QB—Bernie Kosar. RB—Derrick Gainer, Derrick Lassic. WR—Kevin Williams. TE—Scott Galbraith. C—Frank Cornish. T—Dale Hellestrae. Defense: E—Jim Jeffcoat. T—Jimmie Jones, Russell Maryland. DB—Bill Bates, Joe Fishback, Brock Marion, Elvis Patterson. LB—Robert Jones, Godfrey Myles, Matt Vanderbeek. CB—Dave Thomas. S—Kenneth Gant, James Washington. DNP: RB—Lincoln Coleman.

OFFICIALS

Referee—Jerry Markbreit. Umpire—Bob Boylston. Head Linesman—John Schleyer. Line Judge—Dale Orem. Back Judge—Jim Poole. Field Judge—Donnie Hampton. Side Judge—Mike Carey.

SCORING

San Francisco	0	7	7	7	— 21
Dallas	7	21	7	3	— 38

Dall — E. Smith 5 run (Murray kick)
SF — Rathman 7 pass from Young (Cofer kick)
Dall — Johnston 4 run (Murray kick)
Dall — E. Smith 11 pass from Aikman (Murray kick)
Dall — Novacek 19 pass from Aikman (Murray kick)
SF — Watters 4 run (Cofer kick)
Dall — Harper 42 pass from Kosar (Murray kick)
Dall — FG Murray 50
SF — Young 1 run (Cofer kick)

TEAM STATISTICS

	San Francisco	Dallas
Total First Downs	23	24
Rushing	5	9
Passing	15	15
Penalty	3	0
Total Net Yardage	359	377
Total Offensive Plays	70	63
Average Gain per Offensive Play	5.1	6.0
Rushes	21	33
Yards Gained Rushing (Net)	84	124
Average Yards per Rush	4.0	3.8
Passes Attempted	45	28
Passes Completed	27	19
Had Intercepted	1	0
Tackled Attempting to Pass	4	2
Yards Lost Attempting to Pass	12	7
Yards Gained Passing (Net)	275	253
Punts	4	4
Average Distance	45.5	41.0
Punt Returns	1	1
Punt Return Yardage	9	6
Kickoff Returns	6	2
Kickoff Return Yardage	82	29
Interception Return Yardage	0	14
Total Return Yardage	91	49
Fumbles	2	0
Own Fumbles Recovered	2	0
Opponents Fumbles Recovered	0	0
Penalties	6	4
Yards Penalized	40	29
Total Points Scored	21	38
Touchdowns	3	5
Rushing	2	2
Passing	1	3
Returns	0	0
Extra Points	3	5
Field Goals	0	1
Field Goals Attempted	0	1
Safeties	0	0

PLAYOFF GAMES SUMMARIES

	5/15	8/13
Third-Down Efficiency	5/15	8/13
Fourth-Down Efficiency	1/2	0/0
Time of Possession	26:27	33:33

INDIVIDUAL STATISTICS

Rushing

San Francisco	No.	Yds.	LG	TD
Watters	12	37	8	1
Young	7	38	18	1
Rathman	2	9	6	0
Dallas	**No.**	**Yds.**	**LG**	**TD**
E. Smith	23	88	9	1
Aikman	3	25	12	0
Johnston	4	13	4t	1
Lassic	1	1	1	0
Kosar	2	-3	-1	0

Passing

San Francisco	Att.	Comp.	Yds.	TD	Int.
Young	45	27	287	1	1
Dallas	**Att.**	**Comp.**	**Yds.**	**TD**	**Int.**
Aikman	18	14	177	2	0
Kosar	9	5	83	1	0
Harper	1	0	0	0	0

Receiving

San Francisco	No.	Yds.	LG	TD
Watters	7	33	9	0
Rice	6	83	23	0
J. Taylor	3	61	22	0
J. Williams	3	44	25	0
Jones	3	26	13	0
Logan	3	21	8	0
Turner	1	12	12	0
Rathman	1	7	7t	1
Dallas	**No.**	**Yds.**	**LG**	**TD**
E. Smith	7	85	28	1
Harper	4	78	42t	1
Novacek	4	57	20	1
Irvin	2	23	12	0
Johnston	2	17	9	0

Interceptions

San Francisco	No.	Yds.	LG	TD
None	—	—	—	—
Dallas	**No.**	**Yds.**	**LG**	**TD**
Everett	1	14	14	0

Punting

San Francisco	No.	Avg.	LG	Blk.
Wilmsmeyer	4	45.5	52	0
Dallas	**No.**	**Avg.**	**LG**	**Blk.**
Jett	4	41.0	46	0

Punt Returns

San Francisco	No.	FC	Yds.	LG	TD
Carter	1	1	9	9	0
Dallas	**No.**	**FC**	**Yds.**	**LG**	**TD**
K. Williams	1	2	6	6	0

Kickoff Returns

San Francisco	No.	Yds.	LG	TD
Carter	4	62	20	0
Logan	2	20	14	0
Dallas	**No.**	**Yds.**	**LG**	**TD**
Marion	1	15	15	0
K. Williams	1	14	14	0

AFC DIVISIONAL PLAYOFFS RESULTS

Includes Second-Round Playoff Games (1982), AFC Inter-Divisional Games (1969), and special playoff games to break ties for AFL Division Championships (1963, 1968)

Season	Date	Winner (Share)	Loser (Share)	Score	Site	Attendance
1993	Jan. 16	Kansas City ($12,000)	Houston ($12,000)	28-20	Houston	64,011
	Jan. 15	Buffalo ($12,000)	L.A. Raiders ($12,000)	29-23	Buffalo	61,923
1992	Jan. 10	Miami ($10,000)	San Diego ($10,000)	31-0	Miami	71,224
	Jan. 9	Buffalo ($10,000)	Pittsburgh ($10,000)	24-3	Pittsburgh	60,407
1991	Jan. 5	Buffalo ($10,000)	Kansas City ($10,000)	37-14	Buffalo	80,182
	Jan. 4	Denver ($10,000)	Houston ($10,000)	26-24	Denver	75,301
1990	Jan. 13	L.A. Raiders ($10,000)	Cincinnati ($10,000)	20-10	Los Angeles	92,045
	Jan. 12	Buffalo ($10,000)	Miami ($10,000)	44-34	Buffalo	77,087
1989	Jan. 7	Denver ($10,000)	Pittsburgh ($10,000)	24-23	Denver	75,477
	Jan. 6	Cleveland ($10,000)	Buffalo ($10,000)	34-30	Cleveland	78,921
1988	Jan. 1	Buffalo ($10,000)	Houston ($10,000)	17-10	Buffalo	79,532
	Dec. 31	Cincinnati ($10,000)	Seattle ($10,000)	21-13	Cincinnati	58,560
1987	Jan. 10	Denver ($10,000)	Houston ($10,000)	34-10	Denver	75,440
	Jan. 9	Cleveland ($10,000)	Indianapolis ($10,000)	38-21	Cleveland	79,372
1986	Jan. 4	Denver ($10,000)	New England ($10,000)	22-17	Denver	75,262
	Jan. 3	Cleveland ($10,000)	N.Y. Jets ($10,000)	23-20*	Cleveland	79,720
1985	Jan. 5	New England ($10,000)	L.A. Raiders ($10,000)	27-20	Los Angeles	87,163
	Jan. 4	Miami ($10,000)	Cleveland ($10,000)	24-21	Miami	74,667
1984	Dec. 30	Pittsburgh ($10,000)	Denver ($10,000)	24-17	Denver	74,981
	Dec. 29	Miami ($10,000)	Seattle ($10,000)	31-10	Miami	73,469
1983	Jan. 1	L.A. Raiders ($10,000)	Pittsburgh ($10,000)	38-10	Los Angeles	90,380
	Dec. 31	Seattle ($10,000)	Miami ($10,000)	27-20	Miami	74,136
1982	Jan. 16	Miami ($10,000)	San Diego ($10,000)	34-13	Miami	71,383
	Jan. 15	N.Y. Jets ($10,000)	L.A. Raiders ($10,000)	17-14	Los Angeles	90,038
1981	Jan. 3	Cincinnati ($5,000)	Buffalo ($5,000)	28-21	Cincinnati	55,420
	Jan. 2	San Diego ($5,000)	Miami ($5,000)	41-38*	Miami	73,735
1980	Jan. 4	Oakland ($5,000)	Cleveland ($5,000)	14-12	Cleveland	78,245
	Jan. 3	San Diego ($5,000)	Buffalo ($5,000)	20-14	San Diego	52,253
1979	Dec. 30	Pittsburgh ($5,000)	Miami ($5,000)	34-14	Pittsburgh	50,214
	Dec. 29	Houston ($5,000)	San Diego ($5,000)	17-14	San Diego	51,192
1978	Dec. 31	Houston ($5,000)	New England ($5,000)	31-14	New England	60,735
	Dec. 30	Pittsburgh ($5,000)	Denver ($5,000)	33-10	Pittsburgh	50,230
1977	Dec. 24	Oakland ($5,000)	Baltimore ($5,000)	37-31*	Baltimore	59,925
	Dec. 24	Denver ($5,000)	Pittsburgh ($5,000)	34-21	Denver	75,059
1976	Dec. 19	Pittsburgh ($)	Baltimore ($)	40-14	Baltimore	59,296
	Dec. 18	Oakland ($)	New England ($)	24-21	Oakland	53,050
1975	Dec. 28	Oakland ($)	Cincinnati ($)	31-28	Oakland	53,030
	Dec. 27	Pittsburgh ($)	Baltimore ($)	28-10	Pittsburgh	49,557
1974	Dec. 22	Pittsburgh ($)	Buffalo ($)	32-14	Pittsburgh	49,841
	Dec. 21	Oakland ($)	Miami ($)	28-26	Oakland	53,023
1973	Dec. 23	Miami ($)	Cincinnati ($)	34-16	Miami	78,928
	Dec. 22	Oakland ($)	Pittsburgh ($)	33-14	Oakland	52,646
1972	Dec. 24	Miami ($)	Cleveland ($)	20-14	Miami	78,916
	Dec. 23	Pittsburgh ($)	Oakland ($)	13-7	Pittsburgh	50,327
1971	Dec. 26	Baltimore ($)	Cleveland ($)	20-3	Cleveland	70,734
	Dec. 25	Miami ($)	Kansas City ($)	27-24*	Kansas City	45,822
1970	Dec. 27	Oakland ($)	Miami ($)	21-14	Oakland	52,594
	Dec. 26	Baltimore ($)	Cincinnati ($)	17-0	Baltimore	49,694
1969	Dec. 21	Oakland ($)	Houston ($)	56-7	Oakland	53,539
	Dec. 20	Kansas City ($)	N.Y. Jets ($)	13-6	New York	62,977
1968	Dec. 22	Oakland ($)	Kansas City ($)	41-6	Oakland	53,605
1963	Dec. 28	Boston ($)	Buffalo ($)	26-8	Buffalo	33,044

Sudden Death Overtime.

$ *Players received 1/14 of annual salary for playoff appearances.*

1993 AFC DIVISIONAL PLAYOFF GAMES

Rich Stadium, Buffalo, New York
January 15, 1994, Attendance: 61,923
BUFFALO 29, L.A. RAIDERS 23—Jim Kelly threw 2 second-half touchdown passes to Bill Brooks and the Bills overcame an 11-point deficit to advance to the AFC Championship Game for the fifth time in six years. Napoleon McCallum scored on a pair of 1-yard touchdown runs for the Raiders, the second of which gave Los Angeles a 17-6 advantage with 1:57 remaining in the first half. But Buffalo took only 67 seconds to march 76 yards and trim the deficit to 4 points at intermission. A 37-yard pass interference penalty preceded Thurman Thomas's 8-yard touchdown run with 50 seconds remaining in the second quarter. That set up a flurry of activity that saw the lead change three times in a span of 6:18 late in the third and early in the fourth quarters. Kelly gave the Bills a 19-17 edge with a 25-yard touchdown pass to Brooks with 3:23 left in the third period. Moments later, Buffalo safety Henry Jones recovered McCallum's fumble on the Raiders' 30-yard line, setting up Steve Christie's 29-yard field goal 59 seconds before the end of the quarter. Two plays after that, Raiders wide receiver Tim Brown took a short pass from a scrambling Jeff Hostetler and turned it into an 86-yard touchdown that put Los Angeles back on top 23-22. But the Bills responded by driving 71 yards to Kelly's 22-yard touchdown pass to Brooks 2:55 into the fourth quarter. That held up for the winning points as Buffalo's defense shut down the Raiders. After gaining 14 first downs in the first half, Los Angeles managed only 1 in the second half, that coming on the long touchdown pass. Kelly completed 27 of 37 passes for 287 yards for the Bills, while Brooks caught 6 passes for 96 yards. Hostetler was 14 of 20

for 230 yards for the Raiders. The game was played in frigid conditions. Temperature at kickoff was zero degrees, with the wind-chill at minus-32.

| L.A. Raiders | 0 | 17 | 6 | 0 | — | 23 |
| Buffalo | 0 | 13 | 9 | 7 | — | 29 |

Raid — FG Jaeger 30
Buff — Davis 1 run (kick failed)
Raid — McCallum 1 run (Jaeger kick)
Raid — McCallum 1 run (Jaeger kick)
Buff — Thomas 8 run (Christie kick)
Buff — Brooks 25 pass from Kelly (kick failed)
Buff — FG Christie 29
Raid — Brown 86 pass from Hostetler (kick failed)
Buff — Brooks 22 pass from Kelly (Christie kick)

Astrodome, Houston, Texas
January 16, 1994, Attendance: 64,011
KANSAS CITY 28, HOUSTON 20—Joe Montana threw 3 second-half touchdown passes, including 2 just 54 seconds apart in the fourth quarter, to rally the Chiefs past the Oilers. Houston, which entered the game with an 11-game winning streak, jumped out to a 10-0 lead in the opening quarter and still led 13-7 after Al Del Greco's 43-yard field goal with 9:37 remaining in the fourth quarter. But Kansas City marched 71 yards in only 59 seconds, the key play a 38-yard pass interference penalty against Oilers cornerback Cris Dishman, to take the lead for the first time on Montana's 11-yard touchdown pass to J.J. Birden. On the next play from scrimmage, Chiefs linebacker Derrick Thomas sacked Houston quarterback Warren Moon, forcing a fumble that defensive tackle Dan Saleaumua recovered at the Oilers' 12-yard line. On third down, Montana's 18-yard touchdown pass to Willie Davis put Kansas City ahead

21-13 with 7:44 left. Houston drove 80 yards to a touchdown to pull within 1 point with 3:45 to go, but Marcus Allen's 21-yard touchdown run at the 1:55 mark sealed the Oilers' fate. The key play on the Chiefs' 79-yard march came on third-and-1 from Kansas City's 30-yard line. Montana's arm was hit as he threw, but his wobbly pass was caught by tight end Keith Cash, who rumbled 41 yards to Houston's 29. Cash also had a 7-yard touchdown reception in the third quarter. Montana finished with 22 completions in 38 attempts for 299 yards. Allen rushed for 74 yards on only 14 carries. Moon completed 32 of 43 passes for 306 yards for the Oilers. But without the benefit of an effective rushing attack (Houston ran for only 39 yards), he was under pressure all afternoon and was sacked 9 times. Thomas, Joe Phillips, Albert Lewis, and Bennie Thompson each had 2 sacks for the Chiefs, who equaled the NFL record for sacks in a postseason game.

| Kansas City | 0 | 0 | 7 | 21 | — | 28 |
| Houston | 10 | 0 | 0 | 10 | — | 20 |

Hou — FG Del Greco 49
Hou — Brown 2 run (Del Greco kick)
KC — Cash 7 pass from Montana (Lowery kick)
Hou — FG Del Greco 43
KC — Birden 11 pass from Montana (Lowery kick)
KC — Davis 18 pass from Montana (Lowery kick)
Hou — Givins 7 pass from Moon (Del Greco kick)
KC — Allen 21 run (Lowery kick)

NFC DIVISIONAL PLAYOFFS RESULTS

Includes Second-Round Playoff Games (1982), NFL Conference Championship Games (1967-69), and special playoff games to break ties for NFL Division or Conference Championships (1941, 1943, 1947, 1950, 1952, 1957, 1958, 1965)

Season	Date	Winner (Share)	Loser (Share)	Score	Site	Attendance
1993	Jan. 16	Dallas ($12,000)	Green Bay ($12,000)	27-17	Dallas	64,790
	Jan. 15	San Francisco ($12,000)	N.Y. Giants ($12,000)	44-3	San Francisco	67,143
1992	Jan. 10	Dallas ($10,000)	Philadelphia ($10,000)	34-10	Dallas	63,721
	Jan. 9	San Francisco ($10,000)	Washington ($10,000)	20-13	San Francisco	64,991
1991	Jan. 5	Detroit ($10,000)	Dallas ($10,000)	38-6	Detroit	78,290
	Jan. 4	Washington ($10,000)	Atlanta ($10,000)	24-7	Washington	55,181
1990	Jan. 13	N.Y. Giants ($10,000)	Chicago ($10,000)	31-3	East Rutherford	77,025
	Jan. 12	San Francisco ($10,000)	Washington ($10,000)	28-10	San Francisco	65,292
1989	Jan. 7	L.A. Rams ($10,000)	N.Y. Giants ($10,000)	19-13*	East Rutherford	76,526
	Jan. 6	San Francisco ($10,000)	Minnesota ($10,000)	41-13	San Francisco	64,910
1988	Jan. 1	San Francisco ($10,000)	Minnesota ($10,000)	34-9	San Francisco	61,848
	Dec. 31	Chicago ($10,000)	Philadelphia ($10,000)	20-12	Chicago	65,534
1987	Jan. 10	Washington ($10,000)	Chicago ($10,000)	21-17	Chicago	65,268
	Jan. 9	Minnesota ($10,000)	San Francisco ($10,000)	36-24	San Francisco	63,008
1986	Jan. 4	N.Y. Giants ($10,000)	San Francisco ($10,000)	49-3	East Rutherford	75,691
	Jan. 3	Washington ($10,000)	Chicago ($10,000)	27-13	Chicago	65,524
1985	Jan. 5	Chicago ($10,000)	N.Y. Giants ($10,000)	21-0	Chicago	65,670
	Jan. 4	L.A. Rams ($10,000)	Dallas ($10,000)	20-0	Anaheim	66,581
1984	Dec. 30	Chicago ($10,000)	Washington ($10,000)	23-19	Washington	55,431
	Dec. 29	San Francisco ($10,000)	N.Y. Giants ($10,000)	21-10	San Francisco	60,303
1983	Jan. 1	Washington ($10,000)	L.A. Rams ($10,000)	51-7	Washington	54,440
	Dec. 31	San Francisco ($10,000)	Detroit ($10,000)	24-23	San Francisco	59,979
1982	Jan. 16	Dallas ($10,000)	Green Bay ($10,000)	37-26	Dallas	63,972
	Jan. 15	Washington ($10,000)	Minnesota ($10,000)	21-7	Washington	54,593
1981	Jan. 3	San Francisco ($5,000)	N.Y. Giants ($5,000)	38-24	San Francisco	58,360
	Jan. 2	Dallas ($5,000)	Tampa Bay ($5,000)	38-0	Dallas	64,848
1980	Jan. 4	Dallas ($5,000)	Atlanta ($5,000)	30-27	Atlanta	59,793
	Jan. 3	Philadelphia ($5,000)	Minnesota ($5,000)	31-16	Philadelphia	70,178
1979	Dec. 30	Los Angeles ($5,000)	Dallas ($5,000)	21-19	Dallas	64,792
	Dec. 29	Tampa Bay ($5,000)	Philadelphia ($5,000)	24-17	Tampa Bay	71,402
1978	Dec. 31	Los Angeles ($5,000)	Minnesota ($5,000)	34-10	Los Angeles	70,436
	Dec. 30	Dallas ($5,000)	Atlanta ($5,000)	27-20	Dallas	63,406
1977	Dec. 26	Dallas ($5,000)	Chicago ($5,000)	37-7	Dallas	63,260
	Dec. 26	Minnesota ($5,000)	Los Angeles ($5,000)	14-7	Los Angeles	70,203
1976	Dec. 19	Los Angeles ($)	Dallas ($)	14-12	Dallas	63,283
	Dec. 18	Minnesota ($)	Washington ($)	35-20	Minnesota	47,466
1975	Dec. 28	Dallas ($)	Minnesota ($)	17-14	Minnesota	48,050
	Dec. 27	Los Angeles ($)	St. Louis ($)	35-23	Los Angeles	73,459
1974	Dec. 22	Los Angeles ($)	Washington ($)	19-10	Los Angeles	77,925
	Dec. 21	Minnesota ($)	St. Louis ($)	30-14	Minnesota	48,150
1973	Dec. 23	Dallas ($)	Los Angeles ($)	27-16	Dallas	63,272

Year	Date	Winner	Loser	Score	Site	Attendance
1972	Dec. 22	Minnesota ($)	Washington ($)	27-20	Minnesota	48,040
	Dec. 24	Washington ($)	Green Bay ($)	16-3	Washington	52,321
	Dec. 23	Dallas ($)	San Francisco ($)	30-28	San Francisco	59,746
1971	Dec. 26	San Francisco ($)	Washington ($)	24-20	San Francisco	45,327
	Dec. 25	Dallas ($)	Minnesota ($)	20-12	Minnesota	47,307
1970	Dec. 27	San Francisco ($)	Minnesota ($)	17-14	Minnesota	45,103
	Dec. 26	Dallas ($)	Detroit ($)	5-0	Dallas	69,613
1969	Dec. 28	Cleveland ($)	Dallas ($)	38-14	Dallas	69,321
	Dec. 27	Minnesota ($)	Los Angeles ($)	23-20	Minnesota	47,900
1968	Dec. 22	Baltimore ($)	Minnesota ($)	24-14	Baltimore	60,238
	Dec. 21	Cleveland ($)	Dallas ($)	31-20	Cleveland	81,497
1967	Dec. 24	Dallas ($)	Cleveland ($)	52-14	Dallas	70,786
	Dec. 23	Green Bay ($)	Los Angeles ($)	28-7	Milwaukee	49,861
1965	Dec. 26	Green Bay ($)	Baltimore ($)	13-10*	Green Bay	50,484
1958	Dec. 21	N.Y. Giants (#)	Cleveland (#)	10-0	New York	61,274
1957	Dec. 22	Detroit (#)	San Francisco (#)	31-27	San Francisco	60,118
1952	Dec. 21	Detroit (#)	Los Angeles (#)	31-21	Detroit	47,645
1950	Dec. 17	Los Angeles (#)	Chicago Bears (#)	24-14	Los Angeles	83,501
	Dec. 17	Cleveland (#)	N.Y. Giants (#)	8-3	Cleveland	33,054
1947	Dec. 21	Philadelphia (#)	Pittsburgh (#)	21-0	Pittsburgh	35,729
1943	Dec. 19	Washington (¢)	N.Y. Giants (¢)	28-0	New York	42,800
1941	Dec. 14	Chicago Bears (¢)	Green Bay (¢)	33-14	Chicago	43,425

* Sudden Death Overtime.
$ Players received 1/14 of annual salary for playoff appearances.
# Players received 1/12 of annual salary for playoff appearances.
¢ Players received 1/10 of annual salary for playoff appearances.

1993 NFC DIVISIONAL PLAYOFF GAMES

Candlestick Park, San Francisco, California
January 15, 1994, Attendance: 67,143

SAN FRANCISCO 44, N.Y. GIANTS 3—Ricky Watters scored an NFL playoff-record 5 touchdowns to key the 49ers' victory. Watters ran for 118 yards on 24 carries, caught 5 passes for 46 yards, and scored all of his touchdowns on short runs. No player had scored more than 3 touchdowns in a postseason game. San Francisco started the rout early, with quarterback Steve Young completing all 4 of his passes for 63 yards on an 8-play, 80-yard touchdown drive following the opening kickoff, a march capped by Watters's 1-yard run to open the game. The Giants failed to make a first down on their initial possession, and the 49ers' Dexter Carter returned the ensuing punt 31 yards to set up Mike Cofer's 29-yard field goal. Safety Tim McDonald intercepted Phil Simms's pass on the next play, leading to another 1-yard touchdown run by Watters, and San Francisco led 16-0 two seconds into the second quarter. It was 23-3 at halftime and the 49ers never were threatened. Young completed 17 of 22 passes for 226 yards as San Francisco amassed 413 total yards to just 194 for the Giants. New York, which led the NFL by averaging 138 rushing yards per game during the regular season, managed only 41 yards on the ground. The 49ers' defense also recorded 4 sacks, including 2 by rookie end Dana Stubblefield.

	1	2	3	4	
N.Y. Giants	0	3	0	0	— 3
San Francisco	9	14	14	7	— 44

SF — Watters 1 run (kick failed)
SF — FG Cofer 29
SF — Watters 1 run (Cofer kick)
SF — Watters 2 run (Cofer kick)
NYG — FG Treadwell 25
SF — Watters 6 run (Cofer kick)
SF — Watters 2 run (Cofer kick)
SF — Logan 2 run (Cofer kick)

Texas Stadium, Irving, Texas
January 16, 1994, Attendance: 64,790

DALLAS 27, GREEN BAY 17—Troy Aikman passed for 302 yards and 3 touchdowns, and the Cowboys scored 10 points in a span of 18 seconds shortly before halftime to break open a close game. Aikman's 25-yard touchdown pass to Alvin Harper 5:53 into the second quarter put Dallas ahead 7-3, a lead the Cowboys would not relinquish. After Eddie Murray kicked a 41-yard field goal 23 seconds before halftime to stretch the advantage to 10-3, Kenneth Gant made the key play of the game on the ensuing kickoff. Gant knocked the ball loose from Packers kick returner Corey Harris, and Dallas's Joe Fishback recovered at Green Bay's 14-yard line. Aikman completed an 8-yard pass to Michael Irvin, then teamed with tight end Jay Novacek on a 6-yard touchdown pass with five seconds left in the first half to make it 17-3. Aikman's 19-yard touchdown pass to Michael Irvin 9:05 into the third quarter put the game out of reach. Aikman finished with 28 completions in 37 attempts, while Irvin caught 9 passes for 126 yards. Packers quarterback Brett Favre completed 28 of 45 passes for 331 yards, but most of it came after the issue was decided. Running back Edgar Bennett caught 9 passes. Wide receiver Sterling Sharpe had 6 receptions for 128 yards.

	1	2	3	4	
Green Bay	3	0	7	7	— 17
Dallas	0	17	7	3	— 27

GB — FG Jacke 30
Dall — Harper 25 pass from Aikman (Murray kick)
Dall — FG Murray 41
Dall — Novacek 6 pass from Aikman (Murray kick)
Dall — Irvin 19 pass from Aikman (Murray kick)
GB — Brooks 13 pass from Favre (Jacke kick)
Dall — FG Murray 38
GB — Sharpe 29 pass from Favre (Jacke kick)

AFC WILD CARD PLAYOFF GAMES RESULTS

Season	Date	Winner (Share)	Loser (Share)	Score	Site	Attendance
1993	Jan. 9	L.A. Raiders ($7,500)	Denver ($7,500)	42-24	Los Angeles	65,314
	Jan. 8	Kansas City ($12,000)	Pittsburgh ($7,500)	27-24*	Kansas City	74,515
1992	Jan. 3	Buffalo ($6,000)	Houston ($6,000)	41-38*	Buffalo	75,141
	Jan. 2	San Diego ($10,000)	Kansas City ($6,000)	17-0	San Diego	58,278
1991	Dec. 29	Houston ($10,000)	N.Y. Jets ($6,000)	17-10	Houston	61,485
	Dec. 28	Kansas City ($6,000)	L.A. Raiders ($6,000)	10-6	Kansas City	75,827
1990	Jan. 6	Cincinnati ($10,000)	Houston ($6,000)	41-14	Cincinnati	60,012
	Jan. 5	Miami ($6,000)	Kansas City ($6,000)	17-16	Miami	67,276
1989	Dec. 31	Pittsburgh ($6,000)	Houston ($6,000)	26-23*	Houston	59,406
1988	Dec. 26	Houston ($6,000)	Cleveland ($6,000)	24-23	Cleveland	75,896
1987	Jan. 3	Houston ($6,000)	Seattle ($6,000)	23-20*	Houston	50,519
1986	Dec. 28	N.Y. Jets ($6,000)	Kansas City ($6,000)	35-15	East Rutherford	75,210
1985	Dec. 28	New England ($6,000)	N.Y. Jets ($6,000)	26-14	East Rutherford	75,945
1984	Dec. 22	Seattle ($6,000)	L.A. Raiders ($6,000)	13-7	Seattle	62,049
1983	Dec. 24	Seattle ($6,000)	Denver ($6,000)	31-7	Seattle	64,275
1982	Jan. 9	N.Y. Jets ($6,000)	Cincinnati ($6,000)	44-17	Cincinnati	57,560
	Jan. 9	San Diego ($6,000)	Pittsburgh ($6,000)	31-28	Pittsburgh	53,546
	Jan. 8	L.A. Raiders ($6,000)	Cleveland ($6,000)	27-10	Los Angeles	56,555
	Jan. 8	Miami ($6,000)	New England ($6,000)	28-13	Miami	68,842
1981	Dec. 27	Buffalo ($3,000)	N.Y. Jets ($3,000)	31-27	New York	57,050
1980	Dec. 28	Oakland ($3,000)	Houston ($3,000)	27-7	Oakland	53,333
1979	Dec. 23	Houston ($3,000)	Denver ($3,000)	13-7	Houston	48,776
1978	Dec. 24	Houston ($3,000)	Miami ($3,000)	17-9	Miami	72,445

*Sudden death overtime.

1993 AFC WILD CARD PLAYOFF GAMES

Arrowhead Stadium, Kansas City, Missouri
January 8, 1994, Attendance: 74,515

KANSAS CITY 27, PITTSBURGH 24—Nick Lowery kicked a 32-yard field goal 11:03 into overtime to give the Chiefs the come-from-behind victory. Kansas City rallied from a 10-point halftime deficit to tie the game at 17-17 in the fourth quarter, only to fall behind again before forcing the extra session when Joe Montana threw a 7-yard touchdown pass to Tim Barnett with 1:43 remaining in regulation. That came four plays after the Chiefs' Keith Cash blocked a punt and teammate Fred Jones returned it 31 yards to the Steelers' 9-yard line. Two running plays and an incomplete pass netted only 2 yards, but Montana teamed with Barnett on fourth down. Pittsburgh led 17-7 at intermission largely on the strength of 2 touchdown passes from Neil O'Donnell, the second of which was a 26-yard strike to Ernie Mills 18 seconds before halftime. That came six plays after the Steelers stopped Kansas City on downs near midfield. Lowery's 23-yard field goal and Marcus Allen's 2-yard run 6:02 into the fourth quarter tied the game, but Pittsburgh answered with a 74-yard drive capped by O'Donnell's 22-yard pass to tight end Eric Green to take back the lead. The Chiefs had a chance to win the game in regulation, forcing the Steelers to punt just 29 seconds after Barnett's touchdown catch. Montana quickly directed a 47-yard drive, setting up Lowery's 43-yard field-goal try in the closing seconds, but the kick was wide right. The teams exchanged punts in overtime, then Kansas City drove 66 yards in 11 plays to win it. Montana started slowly, completing only 1 of his first 8 passes, but wound up 28 of 43 for 276 yards. Backup Dave Krieg subbed briefly when Montana hurt his ribs in the first quarter, and completed his only pass attempt for a 23-yard touchdown to J.J. Birden. O'Donnell completed 23 of 42 attempts for 286 yards and 3 touchdowns. Pittsburgh nose tackle Gerald Williams had 3 sacks. There were no turnovers in the game.

Pittsburgh	7	10	0	7	0	— 24
Kansas City	7	0	3	14	3	— 27

Pitt	—	Cooper 10 pass from O'Donnell (Anderson kick)
KC	—	Birden 23 pass from Krieg (Lowery kick)
Pitt	—	FG Anderson 30
Pitt	—	Mills 26 pass from O'Donnell (Anderson kick)
KC	—	FG Lowery 23
KC	—	Allen 2 run (Lowery kick)
Pitt	—	Green 22 pass from O'Donnell (Anderson kick)
KC	—	Barnett 7 pass from Montana (Lowery kick)
KC	—	FG Lowery 32

Memorial Coliseum, Los Angeles, California
January 9, 1994, Attendance: 65,314

L.A. RAIDERS 42, DENVER 24—Napoleon McCallum rushed for 3 second-half touchdowns to decide what began as a shootout between quarterbacks Jeff Hostetler and John Elway. A wild first half ended in a 21-21 tie after the Raiders' Hostetler and the Broncos' Elway each traded 3 touchdown passes. But field position played a big role early in the third quarter: Los Angeles pinned Denver deep in its territory with a Jeff Gossett punt that was downed inside the 5, and moments later the Raiders took over at the Broncos' 35 after a short punt by Tom Rouen. Three plays later, McCallum turned a third-and-1 into a touchdown, scampering 26 yards—the team's longest run from scrimmage all year—for the score that put Los Angeles ahead for good with 8:08 left in the period. Another short punt set up McCallum's 2-yard touchdown run at the 4:27 mark, the key play on the 52-yard drive Hostetler's 33-yard completion to tight end Ethan Horton. After the Broncos closed within 35-24 early in the fourth quarter, the Raiders put the game out of reach with a time-consuming, 76-yard drive that culminated in McCallum's 1-yard run with 6:43 remaining in the game. McCallum finished with 81 yards on 13 carries and tied an NFL postseason record with his 3 touchdowns. Hostetler averaged better than 15 yards per attempt, throwing for 294 yards while completing 13 of 19 passes. James Jett had 111 yards on just 3 receptions, including a difficult over-the-shoulder grab to complete a 54-yard touchdown in the second quarter. Elway completed 29 of 47 passes for 302 yards. Tight end Shannon Sharpe tied a postseason record with 13 catches for 156 yards. The two teams combined for 814 total yards, including 427 by the Raiders.

Denver	7	14	0	3	— 24
L.A. Raiders	14	7	14	7	— 42

Raid	—	Horton 9 pass from Hostetler (Jaeger kick)
Den	—	Sharpe 23 pass from Elway (Elam kick)
Raid	—	Brown 65 pass from Hostetler (Jaeger kick)
Den	—	R. Johnson 16 pass from Elway (Elam kick)
Raid	—	Jett 54 pass from Hostetler (Jaeger kick)
Den	—	Russell 6 pass from Elway (Elam kick)
Raid	—	McCallum 26 run (Jaeger kick)
Raid	—	McCallum 2 run (Jaeger kick)
Den	—	FG Elam 33
Raid	—	McCallum 1 run (Jaeger kick)

NFC WILD CARD PLAYOFF GAMES RESULTS

Season	Date	Winner (Share)	Loser (Share)	Score	Site	Attendance
1993	Jan. 9	N.Y. Giants ($7,500)	Minnesota ($7,500)	17-10	East Rutherford	75,089
	Jan. 8	Green Bay ($7,500)	Detroit ($12,000)	28-24	Detroit	68,479
1992	Jan. 3	Philadelphia ($6,000)	New Orleans ($6,000)	36-20	New Orleans	68,893
	Jan. 2	Washington ($6,000)	Minnesota ($10,000)	24-7	Minneapolis	57,353
1991	Dec. 29	Dallas ($6,000)	Chicago ($6,000)	17-13	Chicago	62,594
	Dec. 28	Atlanta ($6,000)	New Orleans ($10,000)	27-20	New Orleans	68,794
1990	Jan. 6	Chicago ($10,000)	New Orleans ($6,000)	16-6	Chicago	60,767
	Jan. 5	Washington ($6,000)	Philadelphia ($6,000)	20-6	Philadelphia	65,287
1989	Dec. 31	L.A. Rams ($6,000)	Philadelphia ($6,000)	21-7	Philadelphia	65,479
1988	Dec. 26	Minnesota ($6,000)	L.A. Rams ($6,000)	28-17	Minnesota	61,204
1987	Jan. 3	Minnesota ($6,000)	New Orleans ($6,000)	44-10	New Orleans	68,546
1986	Dec. 28	Washington ($6,000)	L.A. Rams ($6,000)	19-7	Washington	54,567
1985	Dec. 29	N.Y. Giants ($6,000)	San Francisco ($6,000)	17-3	East Rutherford	75,131
1984	Dec. 23	N.Y. Giants ($6,000)	L.A. Rams ($6,000)	16-3	Anaheim	67,037
1983	Dec. 26	L.A. Rams ($6,000)	Dallas ($6,000)	24-17	Dallas	62,118
1982	Jan. 9	Dallas ($6,000)	Tampa Bay ($6,000)	30-17	Dallas	65,042
	Jan. 9	Minnesota ($6,000)	Atlanta ($6,000)	30-24	Minnesota	60,560
	Jan. 8	Green Bay ($6,000)	St. Louis ($6,000)	41-16	Green Bay	54,282
	Jan. 8	Washington ($6,000)	Detroit ($6,000)	31-7	Washington	55,045
1981	Dec. 27	N.Y. Giants ($3,000)	Philadelphia ($3,000)	27-21	Philadelphia	71,611
1980	Dec. 28	Dallas ($3,000)	Los Angeles ($3,000)	34-13	Dallas	63,052
1979	Dec. 23	Philadelphia ($3,000)	Chicago ($3,000)	27-17	Philadelphia	69,397
1978	Dec. 24	Atlanta ($3,000)	Philadelphia ($3,000)	14-13	Atlanta	59,403

1993 NFC WILD CARD PLAYOFF GAMES

Silverdome, Pontiac, Michigan
January 8, 1994, Attendance: 68,479

GREEN BAY 28, DETROIT 24—Brett Favre's 40-yard touchdown pass to Sterling Sharpe with 55 seconds remaining lifted the Packers to victory in their first playoff game in 11 years. Favre, unable to find intended receiver Mark Clayton, scrambled left and threw across the field to Sharpe, who had gotten behind cornerback Kevin Scott down the right sideline. The quarterback's heroics offset brilliant individual performances by the Lions' Barry Sanders and Brett Perriman. Sanders, playing for first time since injuring his knee against the Bears on Thanksgiving Day, rushed for 169 yards on 27 carries. Perriman caught 10 passes for 150 yards, including a 1-yard touchdown from Erik Kramer late in the second quarter to give Detroit a 10-7 edge at halftime. The Lions increased that advantage to 17-7 when cornerback Melvin Jenkins intercepted Favre's pass and returned it 15 yards for a touchdown 6:40 into the third period. After Green Bay countered with a 28-yard touchdown pass from Favre to Sharpe, Detroit appeared poised to score again, driving to the Packers' 5-yard line. But Kramer's pass in the end zone was intercepted by rookie safety George Teague, who raced a playoff-record 101 yards to give Green Bay a 21-17 lead with 1:40 to go in the third quarter. The Lions then pieced together a 15-play, 89-yard drive that consumed more than 8 minutes, taking the lead for the last time on Derrick Moore's 5-yard touchdown run 6:33 into the fourth quarter. Kramer finished with 22 completions in 31 attempts for 248 yards for Detroit, which amassed 410 total yards but could not overcome the Packers' big plays. Sharpe, who set an NFL record with 112 receptions during the regular season, caught only 5 passes but made the most of them, gaining 101 yards and scoring 3 times.

Green Bay	0	7	14	7	— 28
Detroit	3	7	7	7	— 24

Det	—	FG Hanson 47
GB	—	Sharpe 12 pass from Favre (Jacke kick)
Det	—	Perriman 1 pass from Kramer (Hanson kick)
Det	—	Jenkins 15 interception return (Hanson kick)
GB	—	Sharpe 28 pass from Favre (Jacke kick)
GB	—	Teague 101 interception return (Jacke kick)
Det	—	D. Moore 5 run (Hanson kick)
GB	—	Sharpe 40 pass from Favre (Jacke kick)

Giants Stadium, East Rutherford, New Jersey
January 9, 1994, Attendance: 75,089

N.Y. GIANTS 17, MINNESOTA 10—Rodney Hampton's 2 third-quarter touchdown runs erased a 7-point halftime deficit and lifted the Giants to the victory. Freezing temperatures and blustery winds limited the effectiveness of each team's offense, so much so that all the points in the game were scored by the team that had the wind at its back. New York, trailing 10-3, had such conditions in the third quarter when it rallied to win. The Giants tied the score on their first possession of the second half, as Hampton barreled over right end for 51 yards and a touchdown just 2:54 into the third period. Shortly after that, a 21-yard punt positioned New York at Minnesota's 26-yard line, and six plays later, Hampton ran 2 yards for the game's deciding score. Primarily on the strength of Hampton, the Giants controlled the game by rushing 41 times for 176 yards and maintaining possession for 35:23 of the game's 60 minutes. Vikings quarterbacks Jim McMahon and Sean Salisbury combined to complete only 15 of 34 passes for 192 yards.

Minnesota	0	10	0	0	—	10
N.Y. Giants	3	0	14	0	—	17

NYG	—	FG Treadwell 26
Minn	—	C. Carter 40 pass from McMahon (Reveiz kick)
Minn	—	FG Reveiz 52
NYG	—	Hampton 51 run (Treadwell kick)
NYG	—	Hampton 2 run (Treadwell kick)

AFC-NFC PRO BOWL AT A GLANCE RESULTS (1971-1994)

NFC leads series, 14-10

Year	Date	Winner (Share)	Loser (Share)	Score	Site	Attendance
1994	Feb. 6	NFC ($20,000)	AFC ($10,000)	17-3	Honolulu	50,026
1993	Feb. 7	AFC ($10,000)	NFC ($5,000)	23-20 (OT)	Honolulu	50,007
1992	Feb. 2	NFC ($10,000)	AFC ($5,000)	21-15	Honolulu	50,209
1991	Feb. 3	AFC ($10,000)	NFC ($5,000)	23-21	Honolulu	50,345
1990	Feb. 4	NFC ($10,000)	AFC ($5,000)	27-21	Honolulu	50,445
1989	Jan. 29	NFC ($10,000)	AFC ($5,000)	34-3	Honolulu	50,113
1988	Feb. 7	AFC ($10,000)	NFC ($5,000)	15-6	Honolulu	50,113
1987	Feb. 1	AFC ($10,000)	NFC ($5,000)	10-6	Honolulu	50,101
1986	Feb. 2	NFC ($10,000)	AFC ($5,000)	28-24	Honolulu	50,101
1985	Jan. 27	AFC ($10,000)	NFC ($5,000)	22-14	Honolulu	50,385
1984	Jan. 29	NFC ($10,000)	AFC ($5,000)	45-3	Honolulu	50,445
1983	Feb. 6	NFC ($10,000)	AFC ($5,000)	20-19	Honolulu	49,883
1982	Jan. 31	AFC ($5,000)	NFC ($2,500)	16-13	Honolulu	50,402
1981	Feb. 1	NFC ($5,000)	AFC ($2,500)	21-7	Honolulu	50,360
1980	Jan. 27	NFC ($5,000)	AFC ($2,500)	37-27	Honolulu	49,800
1979	Jan. 29	NFC ($5,000)	AFC ($2,500)	13-7	Los Angeles	46,281
1978	Jan. 23	NFC ($5,000)	AFC ($2,500)	14-13	Tampa	51,337
1977	Jan. 17	AFC ($2,000)	NFC ($1,500)	24-14	Seattle	64,752
1976	Jan. 26	NFC ($2,000)	AFC ($1,500)	23-20	New Orleans	30,546
1975	Jan. 20	NFC ($2,000)	AFC ($1,500)	17-10	Miami	26,484
1974	Jan. 20	AFC ($2,000)	NFC ($1,500)	15-13	Kansas City	66,918
1973	Jan. 21	AFC ($2,000)	NFC ($1,500)	33-28	Dallas	37,091
1972	Jan. 23	AFC ($2,000)	NFC ($1,500)	26-13	Los Angeles	53,647
1971	Jan. 24	NFC ($2,000)	AFC ($1,500)	27-6	Los Angeles	48,222

1994 AFC-NFC PRO BOWL

Aloha Stadium, Honolulu, Hawaii
February 6, 1994, Attendance: 50,026

NFC 17, AFC 3—The NFC converted a blocked punt and a fumble recovery into touchdowns just 2:20 apart in the second half of its victory over the AFC. With the score tied 3-3 late in the third quarter, Saints linebacker Renaldo Turnbull deflected a punt by the Oilers' Greg Montgomery, and the NFC took possession at the AFC's 48-yard line. A 32-yard pass from Bobby Hebert to Falcons teammate Andre Rison positioned Rams running back Jerome Bettis for a 4-yard touchdown run with 1:27 left in the third quarter. Moments later, Rams defensive tackle Sean Gilbert recovered a fumble by Oilers quarterback Warren Moon at the AFC's 19. Hebert then teamed with the Vikings' Cris Carter on a 15-yard touchdown pass 53 seconds later in the fourth period. The NFC kept the AFC out of the end zone by maintaining possession for more than 38 minutes and forcing 6 turnovers. Rison earned the Dan McGuire Trophy as the player of the game for catching 6 passes for 86 yards. The victory was the fourth in the last six years for the NFC, which leads the series 14-10.

NFC (17)	Offense	AFC (3)
Jerry Rice (San Francisco)	WR	Tim Brown (L.A. Raiders)
Erik Williams (Dallas)	LT	Richmond Webb (Miami)
Nate Newton (Dallas)	LG	Keith Sims (Miami)
Jesse Sapolu (San Francisco)	C	Bruce Matthews (Houston)
Randall McDaniel (Minnesota)	RG	Steve Wisniewski (L.A. Raiders)
Harris Barton (San Francisco)	RT	Howard Ballard (Buffalo)
Jay Novacek (Dallas)	TE	Shannon Sharpe (Denver)
Michael Irvin (Dallas)	WR	Anthony Miller (San Diego)
Steve Young (San Francisco)	QB	John Elway (Denver)
Jerome Bettis (L.A. Rams)	RB	Thurman Thomas (Buffalo)
Daryl Johnston (Dallas)	RB	Marcus Allen (Kansas City)
	Defense	
Reggie White (Green Bay)	LE	Neil Smith (Kansas City)
Sean Gilbert (L.A. Rams)	LT	Cortez Kennedy (Seattle)
John Randle (Minnesota)	RT	Ray Childress (Houston)
Richard Dent (Chicago)	RE	Howie Long (L.A. Raiders)
Rickey Jackson (New Orleans)	LOLB	Derrick Thomas (Kansas City)
Hardy Nickerson (Tampa Bay)	LILB	Junior Seau (San Diego)
Renaldo Turnbull (New Orleans)	ROLB	Greg Lloyd (Pittsburgh)
Deion Sanders (Atlanta)	LCB	Rod Woodson (Pittsburgh)
Eric Allen (Philadelphia)	RCB	Nate Odomes (Buffalo)
Tim McDonald (San Francisco)	SS	Dennis Smith (Denver)
Mark Carrier (Chicago)	FS	Steve Atwater (Denver)

SUBSTITUTIONS

NFC—Offense: K—Norm Johnson (Atlanta). P—Rich Camarillo (Phoenix). QB—Brett Favre (Green Bay), Bobby Hebert (Atlanta). RB—Rodney Hampton (N.Y. Giants), Ricky Watters (San Francisco). WR—Cris Carter (Minnesota), Andre Rison (Atlanta). TE—Brent Jones (San Francisco). ST—Elbert Shelley (Atlanta). KR—Tyrone Hughes (New Orleans). T—Lomas Brown (Detroit). G—Guy McIntyre (San Francisco). C—Bart Oates (N.Y. Giants). Defense: E—Chris Doleman (Minnesota). T—Russell Maryland (Dallas). LB—Seth Joyner (Philadelphia), Ken Norton (Dallas), Pat Swilling (Detroit), CB—Donnell Woolford (Chicago). S—LeRoy Butler (Green Bay). DNP—None.

AFC—Offense: K—Gary Anderson (Pittsburgh). P—Greg Montgomery (Houston). QB—Boomer Esiason (N.Y. Jets), Warren Moon (Houston). RB—Keith Byars (Miami), Chris Warren (Seattle). WR—Irving Fryar (Miami), Haywood Jeffires (Houston). TE—Eric Green (Pittsburgh). ST—Steve Tasker (Buffalo). KR—Eric Metcalf (Cleveland). T—John Alt (Kansas City). G—Max Montoya (L.A. Raiders). C—Dermontti Dawson (Pittsburgh). Defense: E—Sean Jones (Houston), Leslie O'Neal (San Diego). T—Michael Dean Perry (Cleveland). LB—Cornelius Bennett (Buffalo), Karl Mecklenburg (Denver). CB—Terry McDaniel (L.A. Raiders). S—Eugene Robinson (Seattle). DNP—None.

HEAD COACHES

NFC—George Seifert (San Francisco)
AFC—Marty Schottenheimer (Kansas City)

OFFICIALS

Referee –Gordon McCarter. Umpire—Dave Hamilton. Head Linesman—Tom Johnson. Line Judge—Bama Glass. Back Judge—Jim Daopoulos. Field Judge—Pat Mallette. Side Judge—Howard Slavin.

SCORING

NFC	3	0	7	7 —	17
AFC	0	3	0	0 —	3

NFC — FG Johnson 35
AFC — FG Anderson 25
NFC — Bettis 4 run (Johnson kick)
NFC — Carter 15 pass from Hebert (Johnson kick)

TEAM STATISTICS

	NFC	AFC
Total First Downs	27	16
Rushing	10	3
Passing	13	11
Penalty	4	2
Total Net Yardage	350	271
Total Offensive Plays	82	60
Average Gain per Offensive Play	4.3	4.7
Rushes	37	14
Yards Gained Rushing (Net)	110	81
Average Yards per Rush	3.0	5.8
Passes Attempted	44	43
Passes Completed	22	21
Had Intercepted	2	4
Tackled Attempting to Pass	1	3
Yards Lost Attempting to Pass	11	10
Yards Gained Passing (Net)	240	190
Punts	5	5
Average Distance	43.0	42.4
Punt Returns	3	3
Punt Return Yardage	3	36
Kickoff Returns	1	4
Kickoff Return Yardage	24	80
Interception Return Yardage	13	103
Total Return Yardage	40	219
Fumbles	1	2
Own Fumbles Recovered	1	0
Opponent Fumbles Recovered	2	0
Penalties	9	9
Yards Penalized	42	48
Total Points Scored	17	3
Touchdowns	2	0
Rushing	1	0
Passing	1	0
Returns	0	0
Extra Points	2	0
Field Goals	1	1
Field Goals Attempted	3	1
Safeties	0	0
Third-Down Efficiency	6/17	2/13
Fourth-Down Efficiency	2/2	1/1
Time of Possession	38:22	21:38

INDIVIDUAL STATISTICS

Rushing

NFC	No.	Yds.	LG	TD
Bettis	14	49	10	1
Watters	11	25	8	0
Rice	1	12	12	0
Hampton	5	11	5	0
Young	1	7	7	0
Johnston	3	5	3	0
Favre	1	2	2	0
Hebert	1	-1	-1	0
AFC	No.	Yds.	LG	TD
Warren	4	64	39	0
Thomas	4	11	5	0
Byars	3	8	4	0
Moon	1	3	3	0
Esiason	1	2	2	0
Allen	1	-7	-7	0

Passing

NFC	Att.	Comp.	Yds.	TD	Int.
Favre	24	14	135	0	2
Young	14	4	48	0	2
Hebert	6	4	68	1	0
AFC	Att.	Comp.	Yds.	TD	Int.
Esiason	22	13	129	0	2
Elway	13	5	45	0	2
Moon	8	3	26	0	0

Receiving

NFC	No.	Yds.	LG	TD
Rison	6	86	32	0
Carter	3	52	22	1
Novacek	3	21	9	0
Hampton	3	13	6	0
Rice	2	30	19	0
Jones	1	13	13	0
Irvin	1	12	12	0
Bettis	1	10	10	0
Watters	1	9	5	0
Johnston	1	5	5	0
AFC	No.	Yds.	LG	TD
Byars	6	53	19	0
Sharpe	3	28	11	0
Green	2	35	26	0
Fryar	2	20	11	0
Brown	2	19	12	0
Miller	2	19	11	0
Allen	2	14	12	0
Metcalf	1	9	9	0
Jeffires	1	3	3	0

Interceptions

NFC	No.	Yds.	LG	TD
Jackson	1	7	7	0
Sanders	1	6	6	0
Allen	1	0	0	0
Woolford	1	0	0	0
AFC	No.	Yds.	LG	TD
McDaniel	1	20	20	0
Robinson	1	10	10	0
Woodson	0	73	73	0

Punting

NFC	No.	Avg.	LG	Blk.
Camarillo	5	43.0	51	0
AFC	No.	Avg.	LG	Blk.
Montgomery	5	42.4	53	0

Punt Returns

NFC	No.	FC	Yds.	LG	TD
Hughes	2	0	6	5	0
Sanders	1	0	-3	-3	0
AFC	No.	FC	Yds.	LG	TD
Metcalf	3	0	36	13	0

Kickoff Returns

NFC	No.	Yds.	LG	TD
Sanders	1	24	24	0
AFC	No.	Yds.	LG	TD
Metcalf	4	80	31	0

1993 AFC-NFC PRO BOWL
Aloha Stadium, Honolulu, Hawaii
February 7, 1993, Attendance: 50,007

AFC 23, NFC 20—Nick Lowery's 33-yard field goal 4:09 into overtime gave the American Conference all-stars an unlikely 23-20 victory over the National Conference. Despite being overwhelmed by the NFC in first downs (30-9), total yards (471-114), and time of possession (10:19-23:50), the AFC won because it forced 6 turnovers, bocked a pair of field goals (1 of which was returned for a touchdown), and returned an interception for a score. Special-teams star Steve Tasker of the Bills earned the Dan McGuire Trophy as the player of the game for making 4 tackles, forcing a fumble, and blocking a field goal. The block came with eight minutes left in regulation and the game tied at 13-13. The Raiders' Terry McDaniel picked up the loose ball and ran 28 yards for a touchdown and a 20-13 AFC lead. The NFC rallied behind 49ers quarterback Steve Young, whose fourth-down, 23-yard touchdown pass to Giants running back Rodney Hampton tied the game at 20-20 with 10 seconds left in regulation. Young completed 18 of 32 passes for 196 yards but was intercepted 3 times and lost a fumble when sacked in overtime. Raiders defensive end Howie Long fell on that fumble at the NFC 28-yard line, and five plays later, Lowery converted the winning field goal.

AFC	0	10	3	7	3 — 23
NFC	3	10	0	7	0 — 20

NFC — FG Andersen 27
AFC — Seau 31 interception return (Lowery kick)
NFC — FG Andersen 37
NFC — Irvin 9 pass from Aikman (Andersen kick)
AFC — FG Lowery 42
AFC — FG Lowery 29
AFC — McDaniel 28 blocked field goal return (Lowery kick)
NFC — Hampton 23 pass from Young (Andersen kick)
AFC — FG Lowery 33

1992 AFC-NFC PRO BOWL
Aloha Stadium, Honolulu, Hawaii
February 2, 1992, Attendance: 50,209

NFC 21, AFC 15—Atlanta's Chris Miller threw an 11-yard touchdown pass to San Francisco's Jerry Rice with 4:04 remaining in the game to lift the NFC over the AFC. It was the NFC's thirteenth win in the 22-game series. The AFC had taken a 15-14 lead when the Raiders' Jeff Jaeger kicked a 27-yard field goal 1:49 into the fourth quarter. But the NFC, aided by a key roughing-the-passer penalty on a third-down incompletion from the AFC 24-yard line, drove 85 yards to the winning score. The Cowboys' Michael Irvin, playing in his first Pro Bowl, caught 8 passes for 125 yards, including a 13-yard touchdown in the first quarter, and was named the player of the game. Rice had a 15-14 lead and 7 catches for 77 yards. Mark Rypien of Washington, the Super Bowl most valuable player one week earlier, completed 11 of 18 passes for 165 yards and 2 touchdowns for the NFC, including a 35-yard pass to Redskins teammate Gary Clark just 26 seconds before halftime. Miller completed 7 of his 10 attempts for 85 yards.

NFC	7	7	0	7	— 21
AFC	7	5	0	3	— 15

AFC — Clayton 4 pass from Kelly (Jaeger kick)
NFC — Irvin 13 pass from Rypien (Lohmiller kick)
AFC — Safety, Townsend tackled Byner in end zone
AFC — FG Jaeger 48
NFC — Clark 35 pass from Rypien (Lohmiller kick)
AFC — FG Jaeger 27
NFC — Rice 11 pass from Miller (Lohmiller kick)

1991 AFC-NFC PRO BOWL
Aloha Stadium, Honolulu, Hawaii
February 3, 1991, Attendance: 50,345

AFC 23, NFC 21—Buffalo's Jim Kelly and Houston's Ernest Givins combined for a 13-yard scoring pass late in the fourth quarter to rally the AFC over the NFC. Phoenix rookie Johnny Johnson scored on runs of 1 and 9 yards to put the NFC ahead 14-3 in the third quarter. Buffalo's Andre Reed, who led all receivers with 4 catches for 80 yards, caught a 20-yard scoring reception from Kelly early in the fourth quarter to move the AFC to within 1 point. Barry Sanders ran 22 yards for a touchdown to increase the NFC's lead to 21-13. Miami's Jeff Cross blocked a 46-yard field-goal attempt by New Orleans's Morten Andersen with seven seconds remaining to preserve the win. Buffalo's Bruce Smith recorded 3 sacks and also had a blocked field goal. Kelly, who completed 13 of 19 passes for 210 yards and 2 touchdowns, was presented the Dan McGuire Award as player of the game. The AFC's victory narrowed the NFC's Pro Bowl series lead to 12-9.

AFC	3	0	3	17	— 23
NFC	0	7	7	7	— 21

AFC — FG Lowery 26
NFC — J. Johnson 1 run (Andersen kick)
AFC — FG Lowery 43
NFC — J. Johnson 9 run (Andersen kick)
AFC — Reed 20 pass from Kelly (Lowery kick)
NFC — Sanders 22 run (Andersen kick)
AFC — FG Lowery 34
AFC — Givins 13 pass from Kelly (Lowery kick)

1990 AFC-NFC PRO BOWL
Aloha Stadium, Honolulu, Hawaii
February 4, 1990, Attendance: 50,445

NFC 27, AFC 21—The NFC captured its second straight Pro Bowl as the defense accounted for a pair of touchdowns and forced 5 turnovers before the eleventh consecutive sellout crowd at Aloha Stadium. The AFC held a 7-6 halftime edge on a 1-yard scoring run by Christian Okoye of the Chiefs. The NFC then rallied with 21 unanswered points in the third quarter. David Meggett of the Giants began the comeback with an 11-yard touchdown reception from Philadelphia's Randall Cunningham. The Rams' Jerry Gray followed with a 51-yard interception return for a score and the Vikings' Keith Millard added an 8-yard fumble return for a touchdown four minutes later to give the NFC a commanding 27-7 lead. Seattle's Dave Krieg rallied the AFC with a 5-yard touchdown pass to Miami's Ferrell Edmunds. Cleveland's Mike Johnson then returned an interception 22 yards for a score to pull the AFC to within 27-21. Gray, who was credited with 7 tackles, was given the Dan McGuire Award as player of the game. Krieg led all quarterbacks by completing 15 of 23 for 148 yards and 1 touchdown. Buffalo's Thurman Thomas topped all receivers with 5 catches for 47 yards, while Indianapolis's Eric Dickerson led all rushers with 46 yards on 15 carries. The win gave the NFC a 12-8 advantage in Pro Bowl games since 1971.

NFC	3	3	21	0	— 27
AFC	0	7	0	14	— 21

NFC — FG Murray 23
NFC — FG Murray 41
AFC — Okoye 1 run (Treadwell kick)
NFC — Meggett 11 pass from Cunningham (Murray kick)
NFC — Gray 51 interception return (Murray kick)
NFC — Millard 8 fumble recovery return (Murray kick)
AFC — Edmunds 5 pass from Krieg (Treadwell kick)
AFC — M. Johnson 22 interception return (Treadwell kick)

1989 AFC-NFC PRO BOWL
Aloha Stadium, Honolulu, Hawaii
January 29, 1989, Attendance: 50,113

NFC 34, AFC 3—The NFC scored 34 unanswered points to snap a two-game losing streak to the AFC before the tenth straight sellout crowd in Honolulu's Aloha Stadium. Bills kicker Scott Norwood provided the AFC's only points on a 38-yard field goal 6:23 into the game. Touchdown runs by Dallas's Herschel Walker (4 yards) and Atlanta's John Settle (1) brought the NFC a 14-3 halftime lead. Walker added a 7-yard scoring run, the Saints' Morten Andersen kicked field goals of 27 and 51 yards, and Los Angeles Rams' wide receiver Henry Ellard caught an 8-yard scoring pass from Minnesota quarterback Wade Wilson in the second half to complete the scoring. Chicago running back Neal Anderson and Philadelphia quarterback Randall Cunningham, who were both appearing in their first Pro Bowl, also played major roles in the NFC's victory. Anderson rushed 13 times for 85 yards and had 2 receptions for 17. Cunningham, who was voted the game's outstanding player, completed 10 of 14 passes for 63 yards and rushed for 49 yards. The NFC, which had 5 takeaways, outgained the AFC 355 yards to 167 and held a time-of-possession advantage of 35:18 to 24:42. Houston quarterback Warren Moon completed 13 of 20 passes for 134 yards for the AFC. The win gave the NFC an 11-8 advantage in Pro Bowl games.

AFC	3	0	0	0	—	3
NFC	7	7	10	10	—	34

AFC — FG Norwood 38
NFC — Walker 4 run (Andersen kick)
NFC — Settle 1 run (Andersen kick)
NFC — FG Andersen 27
NFC — Walker 7 run (Andersen kick)
NFC — FG Andersen 51
NFC — Ellard 8 pass from Wilson (Andersen kick)

1988 AFC-NFC PRO BOWL
Aloha Stadium, Honolulu, Hawaii
February 7, 1988, Attendance: 50,113
AFC 15, NFC 6—Led by a tenacious pass rush, the AFC defeated the NFC for the second consecutive year before the ninth straight sellout crowd in Honolulu's Aloha Stadium. Buffalo quarterback Jim Kelly scored the game's lone touchdown on a 1-yard run for a 7-6 halftime lead. Colts kicker Dean Biasucci added field goals from 37 and 30 yards to complete the AFC's scoring. Saints kicker Morten Andersen had 25- and 36-yard field goals to account for the NFC's points. AFC defenders held the NFC to 213 yards and recorded 8 sacks. Bills defensive end Bruce Smith, who had 2 sacks among his 5 tackles, was voted the game's outstanding player. Oilers running back Mike Rozier led all rushers with 49 yards on 9 carries. Jets wide receiver Al Toon had 5 receptions for 75 yards. The AFC generated 341 yards total offense and held a time-of-possession advantage of 34:14 to 25:46. By winning, the AFC cut the NFC's lead in the Pro Bowl series to 10-8.

NFC	0	6	0	0	—	6
AFC	0	7	6	2	—	15

NFC — FG Andersen 25
AFC — Kelly 1 run (Biasucci kick)
NFC — FG Andersen 36
AFC — FG Biasucci 37
AFC — FG Biasucci 30
AFC — Safety, Montana forced out of end zone

1987 AFC-NFC PRO BOWL
Aloha Stadium, Honolulu, Hawaii
February 1, 1987, Attendance: 50,101
AFC 10, NFC 6—The AFC defeated the NFC in the lowest-scoring game in AFC-NFC Pro Bowl history. The AFC took a 10-0 halftime lead on Broncos quarterback John Elway's 10-yard touchdown pass to Raiders tight end Todd Christensen and Patriots kicker Tony Franklin's 26-yard field goal. The AFC defense made the lead stand by forcing the NFC to settle for a pair of field goals from 38 and 19 yards by Saints kicker Morten Andersen after the NFC had first downs at the AFC 31-, 7-, 16-, 15-, 5-, and 7-yard lines. Both AFC scores were set up by fumble recoveries by Seahawks linebacker Fredd Young and Dolphins linebacker John Offerdahl, respectively. Eagles defensive end Reggie White, who tied a Pro Bowl record with 4 sacks among his 7 solo tackles, was voted the game's outstanding player. The AFC victory cut the NFC's lead in the Pro Bowl series to 10-7.

AFC	7	3	0	0	—	10
NFC	0	0	3	3	—	6

AFC — Christensen 10 pass from Elway (Franklin kick)
AFC — FG Franklin 26
NFC — FG Andersen 38

NFC — FG Andersen 19

1986 AFC-NFC PRO BOWL
Aloha Stadium, Honolulu, Hawaii
February 2, 1986, Attendance: 50,101
NFC 28, AFC 24—New York Giants quarterback Phil Simms brought the NFC back from a 24-7 halftime deficit to defeat the AFC. Simms, who completed 15 of 27 passes for 212 yards and 3 touchdowns, was named the most valuable player of the game. The AFC had taken its first-half lead behind a 2-yard run by Los Angeles Raiders running back Marcus Allen, who also threw a 51-yard scoring pass to San Diego wide receiver Wes Chandler, an 11-yard touchdown catch by Pittsburgh wide receiver Louis Lipps, and a 34-yard field goal by Steelers kicker Gary Anderson. Minnesota's Joey Browner accounted for the NFC's only score before halftime with a 48-yard interception return. After intermission, the NFC blanked the AFC while scoring 3 touchdowns via a 15-yard catch by Washington wide receiver Art Monk, a 2-yard reception by Dallas tight end Doug Cosbie, and a 15-yard catch by Tampa Bay tight end Jimmie Giles with 2:47 remaining in the game. The victory gave the NFC a 10-6 Pro Bowl record against the AFC.

NFC	0	7	7	14	—	28
AFC	7	17	0	0	—	24

AFC — Allen 2 run (Anderson kick)
NFC — Browner 48 interception return (Andersen kick)
AFC — Chandler 51 pass from Allen (Anderson kick)
AFC — FG Anderson 34
AFC — Lipps 11 pass from O'Brien (Anderson kick)
NFC — Monk 15 pass from Simms (Andersen kick)
NFC — Cosbie 2 pass from Simms (Andersen kick)
NFC — Giles 15 pass from Simms (Andersen kick)

1985 AFC-NFC PRO BOWL
Aloha Stadium, Honolulu, Hawaii
January 27, 1985, Attendance: 50,385
AFC 22, NFC 14—Defensive end Art Still of the Kansas City Chiefs recovered a fumble and returned it 83 yards for a touchdown to clinch the AFC's victory over the NFC. Still's touchdown came in the fourth period with the AFC trailing 14-12 and was one of several outstanding defensive plays in a Pro Bowl dominated by two record-breaking defenses. The teams combined for a Pro Bowl-record 17 sacks, including 4 by New York Jets defensive end Mark Gastineau, who was named the game's outstanding player. The AFC's first score came on a safety when Gastineau tackled running back Eric Dickerson of the Los Angeles Rams in the end zone. The AFC's second score, a 6-yard pass from Miami's Dan Marino to Los Angeles Raiders running back Marcus Allen, was set up by a partial block of a punt by Seahawks linebacker Fredd Young. The NFC leads the series 9-6.

AFC	0	9	0	13	—	22
NFC	0	0	7	7	—	14

AFC — Safety, Gastineau tackled Dickerson in end zone
AFC — Allen 6 pass from Marino (Johnson kick)
NFC — Lofton 13 pass from Montana (Stenerud kick)
NFC — Payton 1 run (Stenerud kick)
AFC — FG Johnson 33
AFC — Still 83 fumble recovery return (Johnson kick)
AFC — FG Johnson 22

1984 AFC-NFC PRO BOWL
Aloha Stadium, Honolulu, Hawaii
January 29, 1984, Attendance: 50,445
NFC 45, AFC 3—The NFC won its sixth Pro Bowl in the last seven seasons by routing the AFC. The NFC was led by the passing of most valuable player Joe Theismann of Washington, who completed 21 of 27 passes for 242 yards and 3 touchdowns. Theismann set Pro Bowl records for completions and touchdown

passes. The NFC established Pro Bowl marks for most points scored and fewest points allowed. Running back William Andrews of Atlanta had 6 carries for 43 yards and caught 4 passes for 49 yards, including scoring receptions of 16 and 2 yards. Los Angeles Rams rookie Eric Dickerson gained 46 yards on 11 carries, including a 14-yard touchdown run, and had 45 yards on 5 catches. Rams safety Nolan Cromwell had a 44-yard interception return for a touchdown early in the third period to give the NFC a commanding 24-3 lead. Green Bay wide receiver James Lofton caught an 8-yard touchdown pass, while tight end teammate Paul Coffman had a 6-yard scoring catch.

NFC	3	14	14	14	—	45
AFC	0	3	0	0	—	3

NFC — FG Haji-Sheikh 23
NFC — Andrews 16 pass from Theismann (Haji-Sheikh kick)
NFC — Andrews 2 pass from Montana (Haji-Sheikh kick)
AFC — FG Anderson 43
NFC — Cromwell 44 interception return (Haji-Sheikh kick)
NFC — Lofton 8 pass from Theismann (Haji-Sheikh kick)
NFC — Coffman 6 pass from Theismann (Haji-Sheikh kick)
NFC — Dickerson 14 run (Haji-Sheikh kick)

1983 AFC-NFC PRO BOWL
Aloha Stadium, Honolulu, Hawaii
February 6, 1983, Attendance: 49,883
NFC 20, AFC 19—Dallas's Danny White threw an 11-yard touchdown pass to the Packers' John Jefferson with 35 seconds remaining to rally the NFC over the AFC. White, who completed 14 of 26 passes for 162 yards, kept the winning 65-yard drive alive with a 14-yard completion to Jefferson on a fourth-and-7 play at the AFC 25. The AFC was ahead 12-10 at halftime and increased the lead to 19-10 in the third period, when Marcus Allen scored on a 1-yard run. San Diego's Dan Fouts, who attempted 30 passes, set Pro Bowl records for most completions (17) and yards (274). Pittsburgh's John Stallworth was the AFC's leading receiver with 7 catches for 67 yards. William Andrews topped the NFC with 5 receptions for 48 yards. Fouts and Jefferson were co-winners of the player of the game award.

AFC	9	3	7	0	—	19
NFC	0	10	0	10	—	20

AFC — Walker 34 pass from Fouts (Benirschke kick)
AFC — Safety, Still tackled Theismann in end zone
NFC — Andrews 3 run (Moseley kick)
NFC — FG Moseley 35
AFC — FG Benirschke 29
AFC — Allen 1 run (Benirschke kick)
NFC — FG Moseley 41
NFC — Jefferson 11 pass from D. White (Moseley kick)

1982 AFC-NFC PRO BOWL
Aloha Stadium, Honolulu, Hawaii
January 31, 1982, Attendance: 50,402
AFC 16, NFC 13—Nick Lowery of Kansas City kicked a 23-yard field goal with three seconds remaining to give the AFC a last-second victory over the NFC. Lowery's kick climaxed a 69-yard drive directed by quarterback Dan Fouts. The NFC gained a 13-13 tie with 2:43 to go when Dallas's Tony Dorsett ran 4 yards for a touchdown. In the drive to the winning field goal, Fouts completed 3 passes, including a 23-yard toss to San Diego teammate Kellen Winslow that put the ball on the NFC's 5-yard line. Two plays later, Lowery kicked the field goal. Winslow, who caught 6 passes for 86 yards, was named co-player of the game along with Tampa Bay defensive end Lee Roy Selmon.

NFC	0	6	0	7	—	13
AFC	0	0	13	3	—	16

NFC — Giles 4 pass from Montana (kick blocked)
AFC — Muncie 2 run (kick failed)
AFC — Campbell 1 run (Lowery kick)

NFC — Dorsett 4 run (Septien kick)
AFC — FG Lowery 23

1981 AFC-NFC PRO BOWL

Aloha Stadium, Honolulu, Hawaii
February 1, 1981, Attendance: 50,360
NFC 21, AFC 7—Eddie Murray kicked 4 field goals and Steve Bartkowski fired a 55-yard scoring pass to Alfred Jenkins to lead the NFC to its fourth straight victory over the AFC and a 7-4 edge in the series. Murray was named the game's most valuable player and missed tying Garo Yepremian's Pro Bowl record of 5 field goals when a 37-yard attempt hit the crossbar with 22 seconds remaining. The AFC's only score came on a 9-yard pass from Brian Sipe to Stanley Morgan in the second period. Bartkowski completed 9 of 21 passes for 173 yards, while Sipe connected on 10 of 15 for 142 yards. Ottis Anderson led all rushers with 70 yards on 10 carries. Earl Campbell, the NFL's leading rusher in 1980, was limited to 24 yards on 8 attempts.

AFC	0	7	0	0	— 7
NFC	3	6	0	12	— 21

NFC — FG Murray 31
AFC — Morgan 9 pass from Sipe (J. Smith kick)
NFC — FG Murray 31
NFC — FG Murray 34
NFC — Jenkins 55 pass from Bartkowski (Murray kick)
NFC — FG Murray 36
NFC — Safety, Shell called for holding in end zone

1980 AFC-NFC PRO BOWL

Aloha Stadium, Honolulu, Hawaii
January 27, 1980, Attendance: 49,800
NFC 37, AFC 27—Running back Chuck Muncie of New Orleans ran for 2 touchdowns and threw a 25-yard option pass for another score to give the NFC its third consecutive victory over the AFC. Muncie, who was selected the game's most valuable player, snapped a 3-3 tie on a 1-yard touchdown run at 1:41 of the second quarter, then scored on an 11-yard run in the fourth quarter for the NFC's final touchdown. Two scoring records were set in the game— 37 points by the NFC, eclipsing the 33 by the AFC in 1973, and the 64 points by both teams, surpassing the 61 scored in 1973.

NFC	3	20	7	7	— 37
AFC	3	7	10	7	— 27

NFC — FG Moseley 37
AFC — FG Fritsch 19
NFC — Muncie 1 run (Moseley kick)
AFC — Pruitt 1 pass from Bradshaw (Fritsch kick)
NFC — D. Hill 13 pass from Manning (kick failed)
NFC — T. Hill 25 pass from Muncie (Moseley kick)
NFC — Henry 86 punt return (Moseley kick)
AFC — Campbell 2 run (Fritsch kick)
AFC — FG Fritsch 29
NFC — Muncie 11 run (Moseley kick)
AFC — Campbell 1 run (Fritsch kick)

1979 AFC-NFC PRO BOWL

Memorial Coliseum, Los Angeles, California
January 29, 1979, Attendance: 46,281
NFC 13, AFC 7—Roger Staubach completed 9 of 15 passes for 125 yards, including the winning touchdown on a 19-yard strike to Dallas Cowboys teammate Tony Hill in the third period. The winning drive began at the AFC's 45-yard line after a shanked punt. Staubach hit Ahmad Rashad with passes of 15 and 17 yards to set up Hill's decisive catch. The victory gave the NFC a 5-4 advantage in Pro Bowl games. Rashad, who accounted for 89 yards on 5 receptions, was named the player of the game. The AFC led 7-6 at halftime on Bob Griese's 8-yard scoring toss to Steve Largent late in the second quarter. Largent finished the game with 5 receptions for 75 yards. The NFC scored first as Archie Manning marched his team 70 yards in 11 plays, capped by Wilbert Montgomery's 2-yard touchdown run. The AFC's Earl Campbell was the game's leading rusher with 66 yards on 12 carries.

AFC	0	7	0	0	— 7
NFC	0	6	7	0	— 13

NFC — Montgomery 2 run (kick failed)

AFC — Largent 8 pass from Griese (Yepremian kick)
NFC — T. Hill 19 pass from Staubach (Corral kick)

1978 AFC-NFC PRO BOWL

Tampa Stadium, Tampa, Florida
January 23, 1978, Attendance: 51,337
NFC 14, AFC 13—Walter Payton, the NFL's leading rusher in 1977, sparked a second-half comeback to give the NFC the win and tie the series between the two conferences at four victories each. Payton, who was the game's most valuable player, gained 77 yards on 13 carries and scored the tying touchdown on a 1-yard burst with 7:37 left in the game. Efren Herrera kicked the winning extra point. The AFC dominated the first half of the game, taking a 13-0 lead on field goals of 21 and 39 yards by Toni Linhart and a 10-yard touchdown pass from Ken Stabler to Oakland teammate Cliff Branch. On the NFC's first possession of the second half, Pat Haden put together the first touchdown drive after Eddie Brown returned Ray Guy's punt to the AFC 46-yard line. Haden connected on all 4 of his passes on that drive, finally hitting Terry Metcalf with a 4-yard scoring toss. The NFC continued to rally and, with Jim Hart at quarterback, moved 63 yards in 12 plays for the go-ahead score. During the winning drive, Hart completed 5 of 6 passes for 38 yards and Payton picked up 20 more on the ground.

AFC	3	10	0	0	— 13
NFC	0	0	7	7	— 14

AFC — FG Linhart 21
AFC — Branch 10 pass from Stabler (Linhart kick)
AFC — FG Linhart 39
NFC — Metcalf 4 pass from Haden (Herrera kick)
NFC — Payton 1 run (Herrera kick)

1977 AFC-NFC PRO BOWL

Kingdome, Seattle, Washington
January 17, 1977, Attendance: 64,752
AFC 24, NFC 14—O.J. Simpson's 3-yard touchdown burst at 7:03 of the first quarter gave the AFC a lead it would not surrender, the victory breaking a two-game NFC win streak and giving the American Conference stars a 4-3 series lead. The AFC took a 17-7 lead midway through the second period on the first of 2 Ken Anderson touchdown passes, a 12-yard toss to Charlie Joiner. But the NFC mounted a 73-yard drive capped by Lawrence McCutcheon's 1-yard touchdown plunge to pull within 17-14 at the half. Following a scoreless third quarter, player of the game Mel Blount thwarted a possible NFC score when he intercepted Jim Hart's pass in the end zone. Less than three minutes later, Blount again picked off a Hart pass, returning it 16 yards to the NFC 27. That set up Anderson's 27-yard touchdown strike to the Raiders' Cliff Branch for the final score.

NFC	0	14	0	0	— 14
AFC	10	7	0	7	— 24

AFC — Simpson 3 run (Linhart kick)
AFC — FG Linhart 31
NFC — Thomas 15 run (Bakken kick)
AFC — Joiner 12 pass from Anderson (Linhart kick)
NFC — McCutcheon 1 run (Bakken kick)
AFC — Branch 27 pass from Anderson (Linhart kick)

1976 AFC-NFC PRO BOWL

Superdome, New Orleans, Louisiana
January 26, 1976, Attendance: 30,546
NFC 23, AFC 20—Mike Boryla, a late substitute who did not enter the game until 5:39 remained, lifted the National Football Conference to the victory over the American Football Conference with 2 touchdown passes in the final minutes. It was the second straight NFC win, squaring the series at 3-3. Until Boryla started firing the ball the AFC was in control, leading 13-0 at the half. Boryla entered the game after Billy Johnson had raced 90 yards with a punt to make the score 20-9 in favor of the AFC. He floated a 14-yard touchdown pass to Terry Metcalf and later fired an 8-yard scoring pass to Mel Gray for the winner.

AFC	0	13	0	7	— 20
NFC	0	0	9	14	— 23

AFC — FG Stenerud 20
AFC — FG Stenerud 35
AFC — Burrough 64 pass from Pastorini (Stenerud kick)
NFC — FG Bakken 42
NFC — Foreman 4 pass from Hart (kick blocked)
AFC — Johnson 90 punt return (Stenerud kick)
NFC — Metcalf 14 pass from Boryla (Bakken kick)
NFC — Gray 8 pass from Boryla (Bakken kick)

1975 AFC-NFC PRO BOWL

Orange Bowl, Miami, Florida
January 20, 1975, Attendance: 26,484
NFC 17, AFC 10—Los Angeles quarterback James Harris, who took over the NFC offense after Jim Hart of St. Louis suffered a laceration above his right eye in the second period, threw 2 touchdown passes early in the fourth period to pace the NFC to its second victory in the five-game Pro Bowl series. The NFC win snapped a three-game AFC victory string. Harris, who was named the player of the game, connected with St. Louis's Mel Gray for an 8-yard touchdown 2:03 into the final period. One minute and 24 seconds later, following a fumble recovery by Washington's Ken Houston, Harris tossed another 8-yard scoring pass to Washington's Charley Taylor for the decisive points.

NFC	0	3	0	14	— 17
AFC	0	0	10	0	— 10

NFC — FG Marcol 33
AFC — Warfield 32 pass from Griese (Gerela kick)
AFC — FG Gerela 33
NFC — Gray 8 pass from J. Harris (Marcol kick)
NFC — Taylor 8 pass from J. Harris (Marcol kick)

1974 AFC-NFC PRO BOWL

Arrowhead Stadium, Kansas City, Missouri
January 20, 1974, Attendance: 66,918
AFC 15, NFC 13—Miami's Garo Yepremian's fifth field goal—a 42-yard kick with 21 seconds remaining—gave the AFC its third straight victory since the NFC won the inaugural game following the 1970 season. The field goal by Yepremian, who was voted the game's outstanding player, offset a 21-yard field goal by Atlanta's Nick Mike-Mayer that had given the NFC a 13-12 advantage with 1:41 remaining. The only touchdown in the game was scored by the NFC on a 14-yard pass from Philadelphia's Roman Gabriel to Lawrence McCutcheon of the Los Angeles Rams.

NFC	0	10	0	3	— 13
AFC	3	3	3	6	— 15

AFC — FG Yepremian 16
NFC — FG Mike-Mayer 27
NFC — McCutcheon 14 pass from Gabriel (Mike-Mayer kick)
AFC — FG Yepremian 37
AFC — FG Yepremian 27
AFC — FG Yepremian 41
NFC — FG Mike-Mayer 21
AFC — FG Yepremian 42

1973 AFC-NFC PRO BOWL

Texas Stadium, Irving, Texas
January 21, 1973, Attendance: 37,091
AFC 33, NFC 28—Paced by the rushing and receiving of player of the game O.J. Simpson, the AFC erased a 14-0 first period deficit and built a commanding 33-14 lead midway through the fourth period before the NFC managed 2 touchdowns in the final minute of play. Simpson rushed for 112 yards and caught 3 passes for 58 more to gain unanimous recognition in the balloting for player of the game. John Brockington scored 3 touchdowns for the NFC.

AFC	0	10	10	13	— 33
NFC	14	0	0	14	— 28

NFC — Brockington 1 run (Marcol kick)
NFC — Brockington 3 pass from Kilmer (Marcol kick)
AFC — Simpson 7 run (Gerela kick)
AFC — FG Gerela 18
AFC — FG Gerela 22

AFC — Hubbard 11 run (Gerela kick)
AFC — O. Taylor 5 pass from Lamonica (kick failed)
AFC — Bell 12 interception return (Gerela kick)
NFC — Brockington 1 run (Marcol kick)
NFC — Kwalick 12 pass from Snead (Marcol kick)

1972 AFC-NFC PRO BOWL

Memorial Coliseum, Los Angeles, California
January 23, 1972, Attendance: 53,647
AFC 26, NFC 13—Kansas City's Jan Stenerud kicked 4 field goals to lead the AFC from a 6-0 deficit to victory. The AFC defense picked off 3 passes. Stenerud was selected as the outstanding offensive player and his Kansas City teammate, linebacker Willie Lanier, was the game's outstanding defensive player.

AFC	0	3	13	10	— 26
NFC	0	6	0	7	— 13

NFC — Grim 50 pass from Landry (kick failed)
AFC — FG Stenerud 25
AFC — FG Stenerud 23
AFC — FG Stenerud 48
AFC — Morin 5 pass from Dawson (Stenerud kick)
AFC — FG Stenerud 42
NFC — V. Washington 2 run (Knight kick)
AFC — F. Little 6 run (Stenerud kick)

1971 AFC-NFC PRO BOWL

Memorial Coliseum, Los Angeles, California
January 24, 1971, Attendance: 48,222
NFC 27, AFC 6—Mel Renfro of Dallas broke open the first meeting between the American Football Conference and National Football Conference all-star teams as he returned a pair of punts 82 and 56 yards for touchdowns in the final period to clinch the NFC victory over the AFC. Renfro was voted the game's outstanding back and linebacker Fred Carr of Green Bay the outstanding lineman.

AFC	0	3	3	0	— 6
NFC	0	3	10	14	— 27

AFC — FG Stenerud 37
NFC — FG Cox 13
NFC — Osborn 23 pass from Brodie (Cox kick)
NFC — FG Cox 35
AFC — FG Stenerud 16
NFC — Renfro 82 punt return (Cox kick)
NFC — Renfro 56 punt return (Cox kick)

PRO BOWL ALL-TIME RESULTS

Date	Result	Site (attendance)	Honored players
Jan. 15, 1939	New York Giants 13, Pro All-Stars 10	Wrigley Field, Los Angeles (20,000)	
Jan. 14, 1940	Green Bay 16, NFL All-Stars 7	Gilmore Stadium, Los Angeles (18,000)	
Dec. 29, 1940	Chicago Bears 28, NFL All-Stars 14	Gilmore Stadium, Los Angeles (21,624)	
Jan. 4, 1942	Chicago Bears 35, NFL All-Stars 24	Polo Grounds, New York (17,725)	
Dec. 27, 1942	NFL All-Stars 17, Washington 14	Shibe Park, Philadelphia (18,671)	
Jan. 14, 1951	American Conf. 28, National Conf. 27	Los Angeles Memorial Coliseum (53,676)	Otto Graham, Cleveland, player of the game
Jan. 12, 1952	National Conf. 30, American Conf. 13	Los Angeles Memorial Coliseum (19,400)	Dan Towler, Los Angeles, player of the game
Jan. 10, 1953	National Conf. 27, American Conf. 7	Los Angeles Memorial Coliseum (34,208)	Don Doll, Detroit, player of the game
Jan. 17, 1954	East 20, West 9	Los Angeles Memorial Coliseum (44,214)	Chuck Bednarik, Philadelphia, player of the game
Jan. 16, 1955	West 26, East 19	Los Angeles Memorial Coliseum (43,972)	Billy Wilson, San Francisco, player of the game
Jan. 15, 1956	East 31, West 30	Los Angeles Memorial Coliseum (37,867)	Ollie Matson, Chi. Cardinals, player of the game
Jan. 13, 1957	West 19, East 10	Los Angeles Memorial Coliseum (44,177)	Bert Rechichar, Baltimore, outstanding back
			Ernie Stautner, Pittsburgh, outstanding lineman
Jan. 12, 1958	West 26, East 7	Los Angeles Memorial Coliseum (66,634)	Hugh McElhenny, San Francisco, outstanding back
			Gene Brito, Washington, outstanding lineman
Jan. 11, 1959	East 28, West 21	Los Angeles Memorial Coliseum (72,250)	Frank Gifford, N.Y. Giants, outstanding back
			Doug Atkins, Chi. Bears, outstanding lineman
Jan. 17, 1960	West 38, East 21	Los Angeles Memorial Coliseum (56,876)	Johnny Unitas, Baltimore, outstanding back
			Gene (Big Daddy) Lipscomb, Baltimore, outstanding lineman
Jan. 15, 1961	West 35, East 31	Los Angeles Memorial Coliseum (62,971)	Johnny Unitas, Baltimore, outstanding back
			Sam Huff, N.Y. Giants, outstanding lineman
Jan. 7, 1962	AFL West 47, East 27	Balboa Stadium, San Diego (20,973)	Cotton Davidson, Dallas Texans, player of the game
Jan. 14, 1962	NFL West 31, East 30	Los Angeles Memorial Coliseum (57,409)	Jim Brown, Cleveland, outstanding back
			Henry Jordan, Green Bay, outstanding lineman
Jan. 13, 1963	AFL West 21, East 14	Balboa Stadium, San Diego (27,641)	Curtis McClinton, Dallas Texans, outstanding offensive player
			Earl Faison, San Diego, outstanding defensive player
Jan. 13, 1963	NFL East 30, West 20	Los Angeles Memorial Coliseum (61,374)	Jim Brown, Cleveland, outstanding back
			Gene (Big Daddy) Lipscomb, Pittsburgh, outstanding lineman
Jan. 12, 1964	NFL West 31, East 17	Los Angeles Memorial Coliseum (67,242)	Johnny Unitas, Baltimore, player of the game
			Gino Marchetti, Baltimore, outstanding lineman
Jan. 19, 1964	AFL West 27, East 24	Balboa Stadium, San Diego (20,016)	Keith Lincoln, San Diego, outstanding offensive player
			Archie Matsos, Oakland, outstanding defensive player
Jan. 10, 1965	NFL West 34, East 14	Los Angeles Memorial Coliseum (60,598)	Fran Tarkenton, Minnesota, outstanding back
			Terry Barr, Detroit, outstanding lineman
Jan. 16, 1965	AFL West 38, East 14	Jeppesen Stadium, Houston (15,446)	Keith Lincoln, San Diego, outstanding offensive player
			Willie Brown, Denver, outstanding defensive player
Jan. 15, 1966	AFL All-Stars 30, Buffalo 19	Rice Stadium, Houston (35,572)	Joe Namath, N.Y. Jets, most valuable player, offense
			Frank Buncom, San Diego, most valuable player, defense
Jan. 15, 1966	NFL East 36, West 7	Los Angeles Memorial Coliseum (60,124)	Jim Brown, Cleveland, outstanding back
			Dale Meinert, St. Louis, outstanding lineman
Jan. 21, 1967	AFL East 30, West 23	Oakland-Alameda County Coliseum (18,876)	Babe Parilli, Boston, outstanding offensive player
			Verlon Biggs, N.Y. Jets, outstanding defensive player
Jan. 22, 1967	NFL East 20, West 10	Los Angeles Memorial Coliseum (15,062)	Gale Sayers, Chicago, outstanding back
			Floyd Peters, Philadelphia, outstanding lineman
Jan. 21, 1968	AFL East 25, West 24	Gator Bowl, Jacksonville, Fla. (40,103)	Joe Namath and Don Maynard, N.Y. Jets, out. off. players
			Leslie (Speedy) Duncan, San Diego, out. def. player
Jan. 21, 1968	NFL West 38, East 20	Los Angeles Memorial Coliseum (53,289)	Gale Sayers, Chicago, outstanding back
			Dave Robinson, Green Bay, outstanding lineman
Jan. 19, 1969	AFL West 38, East 25	Gator Bowl, Jacksonville, Fla. (41,058)	Len Dawson, Kansas City, outstanding offensive player
			George Webster, Houston, outstanding defensive player
Jan. 19, 1969	NFL West 10, East 7	Los Angeles Memorial Coliseum (32,050)	Roman Gabriel, Los Angeles, outstanding back
			Merlin Olsen, Los Angeles, outstanding lineman
Jan. 17, 1970	AFL West 26, East 3	Astrodome, Houston (30,170)	John Hadl, San Diego, player of the game
Jan. 18, 1970	NFL West 16, East 13	Los Angeles Memorial Coliseum (57,786)	Gale Sayers, Chicago, outstanding back
			George Andrie, Dallas, outstanding lineman
Jan. 24, 1971	NFC 27, AFC 6	Los Angeles Memorial Coliseum (48,222)	Mel Renfro, Dallas, outstanding back
			Fred Carr, Green Bay, outstanding lineman
Jan. 23, 1972	AFC 26, NFC 13	Los Angeles Memorial Coliseum (53,647)	Jan Stenerud, Kansas City, outstanding offensive player
			Willie Lanier, Kansas City, outstanding defensive player
Jan. 21, 1973	AFC 33, NFC 28	Texas Stadium, Irving (37,091)	O.J. Simpson, Buffalo, player of the game
Jan. 20, 1974	AFC 15, NFC 13	Arrowhead Stadium, Kansas City (66,918)	Garo Yepremian, Miami, player of the game
Jan. 20, 1975	NFC 17, AFC 10	Orange Bowl, Miami (26,484)	James Harris, Los Angeles, player of the game
Jan. 26, 1976	NFC 23, AFC 20	Louisiana Superdome, New Orleans (30,546)	Billy Johnson, Houston, player of the game
Jan. 17, 1977	AFC 24, NFC 14	Kingdome, Seattle (64,752)	Mel Blount, Pittsburgh, player of the game
Jan. 23, 1978	NFC 14, AFC 13	Tampa Stadium (51,337)	Walter Payton, Chicago, player of the game
Jan. 29, 1979	NFC 13, AFC 7	Los Angeles Memorial Coliseum (46,281)	Ahmad Rashad, Minnesota, player of the game
Jan. 27, 1980	NFC 37, AFC 27	Aloha Stadium, Honolulu (49,800)	Chuck Muncie, New Orleans, player of the game
Feb. 1, 1981	NFC 21, AFC 7	Aloha Stadium, Honolulu (50,360)	Eddie Murray, Detroit, player of the game
Jan. 31, 1982	AFC 16, NFC 13	Aloha Stadium, Honolulu (50,402)	Kellen Winslow, San Diego, and Lee Roy Selmon, Tampa Bay, players of the game
Feb. 6, 1983	NFC 20, AFC 19	Aloha Stadium, Honolulu (49,883)	Dan Fouts, San Diego, and John Jefferson, Green Bay, players of the game
Jan. 29, 1984	NFC 45, AFC 3	Aloha Stadium, Honolulu (50,445)	Joe Theismann, Washington, player of the game
Jan. 27, 1985	AFC 22, NFC 14	Aloha Stadium, Honolulu (50,385)	Mark Gastineau, N.Y. Jets, player of the game
Feb. 2, 1986	NFC 28, AFC 24	Aloha Stadium, Honolulu (50,101)	Phil Simms, N.Y. Giants, player of the game
Feb. 1, 1987	AFC 10, NFC 6	Aloha Stadium, Honolulu (50,101)	Reggie White, Philadelphia, player of the game
Feb. 7, 1988	AFC 15, NFC 6	Aloha Stadium, Honolulu (50,113)	Bruce Smith, Buffalo, player of the game
Jan. 29, 1989	NFC 34, AFC 3	Aloha Stadium, Honolulu (50,113)	Randall Cunningham, Philadelphia, player of the game
Feb. 4, 1990	NFC 27, AFC 21	Aloha Stadium, Honolulu (50,445)	Jerry Gray, L.A. Rams, player of the game
Feb. 3, 1991	AFC 23, NFC 21	Aloha Stadium, Honolulu (50,345)	Jim Kelly, Buffalo, player of the game
Feb. 2, 1992	NFC 21, AFC 15	Aloha Stadium, Honolulu (50,209)	Michael Irvin, Dallas, player of the game
Feb. 7, 1993	AFC 23, NFC 20 (OT)	Aloha Stadium, Honolulu (50,007)	Steve Tasker, Buffalo, player of the game
Feb. 6, 1994	NFC 17, AFC 3	Aloha Stadium, Honolulu (50,026)	Andre Rison, Atlanta, player of the game

PRO FOOTBALL HALL OF FAME GAME

1962	New York Giants 21, St. Louis Cardinals 21
1963	Pittsburgh Steelers 16, Cleveland Browns 7
1964	Baltimore Colts 48, Pittsburgh Steelers 17
1965	Washington Redskins 20, Detroit Lions 3
1966	No game
1967	Philadelphia Eagles 28, Cleveland Browns 13
1968	Chicago Bears 30, Dallas Cowboys 24
1969	Green Bay Packers 38, Atlanta Falcons 24
1970	New Orleans Saints 14, Minnesota Vikings 13
1971	Los Angeles Rams (NFC) 17, Houston Oilers (AFC) 6
1972	Kansas City Chiefs (AFC) 23, New York Giants (NFC) 17
1973	San Francisco 49ers (NFC) 20, New England Patriots (AFC) 7
1974	St. Louis Cardinals (NFC) 21, Buffalo Bills (AFC) 13
1975	Washington Redskins (NFC) 17, Cincinnati Bengals (AFC) 9
1976	Denver Broncos (AFC) 10, Detroit Lions (NFC) 7
1977	Chicago Bears (NFC) 20, New York Jets (AFC) 6
1978	Philadelphia Eagles (NFC) 17, Miami Dolphins (AFC) 3
1979	Oakland Raiders (AFC) 20, Dallas Cowboys (NFC) 13
1980*	San Diego Chargers (AFC) 0, Green Bay Packers (NFC) 0
1981	Cleveland Browns (AFC) 24, Atlanta Falcons (NFC) 10
1982	Minnesota Vikings (NFC) 30, Baltimore Colts (AFC) 14
1983	Pittsburgh Steelers (AFC) 27, New Orleans Saints (NFC) 14
1984	Seattle Seahawks (AFC) 38, Tampa Bay Buccaneers (NFC) 0
1985	New York Giants (NFC) 21, Houston Oilers (AFC) 20
1986	New England Patriots (AFC) 21, St. Louis Cardinals (NFC) 16
1987	San Francisco 49ers (NFC) 20, Kansas City Chiefs (AFC) 7
1988	Cincinnati Bengals (AFC) 14, Los Angeles Rams (NFC) 7
1989	Washington Redskins (NFC) 31, Buffalo Bills (AFC) 6
1990	Chicago Bears (NFC) 13, Cleveland Browns (AFC) 0
1991	Detroit Lions (NFC) 14, Denver Broncos (AFC) 3
1992	New York Jets (AFC) 41, Philadelphia Eagles (NFC) 14
1993	Los Angeles Raiders (AFC) 19, Green Bay Packers (NFC) 3

*Game called with 5:29 remaining due to severe thunder and lightning.

NFL INTERNATIONAL GAMES

Date	Site	Teams
Aug. 12, 1950	Ottawa, Canada	N.Y. Giants 27, Ottawa Roughriders 6
Aug. 11, 1951	Ottawa, Canada	N.Y. Giants 41, Ottawa Roughriders 18
Aug. 5, 1959	Toronto, Canada	Chi. Cardinals 55, Tor. Argonauts 26
Aug. 3, 1960	Toronto, Canada	Pittsburgh 43, Toronto Argonauts 16
Aug. 15, 1960	Toronto, Canada	Chicago 16, N.Y. Giants 7
Aug. 2, 1961	Toronto, Canada	St. Louis 36, Toronto Argonauts 7
Aug. 5, 1961	Montreal, Canada	Chicago 34, Montreal Allouettes 16
Aug. 8, 1961	Hamilton, Canada	Hamilton Tiger-Cats 38, Buffalo 21
Sept. 11, 1969	Montreal, Canada	Pittsburgh 17, N.Y. Giants 13
Aug. 25, 1969	Montreal, Canada	Detroit 22, Boston 9
Aug. 16, 1976	Tokyo, Japan	St. Louis 20, San Diego 10
Aug. 5, 1978	Mexico City, Mexico	New Orleans 14, Philadelphia 7
Aug. 6, 1983	London, England	Minnesota 28, St. Louis 10
*Aug. 3, 1986	London, England	Chicago 17, Dallas 6
*Aug. 9, 1987	London, England	L.A. Rams 28, Denver 27
*July 31, 1988	London, England	Miami 27, San Francisco 21
Aug. 14, 1988	Goteborg, Sweden	Minnesota 28, Chicago 21
Aug. 18, 1988	Montreal, Canada	N.Y. Jets 11, Cleveland 7
*Aug. 5, 1989	Tokyo, Japan	L.A. Rams 16, San Francisco 13 (OT)
*Aug. 6, 1989	London, England	Philadelphia 17, Cleveland 13
*Aug. 4, 1990	Tokyo, Japan	Denver 10, Seattle 7
*Aug. 5, 1990	London, England	New Orleans 17, L.A. Raiders 10
*Aug. 9, 1990	Montreal, Canada	Pittsburgh 30, New England 14
*Aug. 11, 1990	Berlin, Germany	L.A. Rams 19, Kansas City 3
*July 28, 1991	London, England	Buffalo 17, Philadelphia 13
*Aug. 3, 1991	Berlin, Germany	San Francisco 21, Chicago 7
*Aug. 3, 1991	Tokyo, Japan	Miami 19, L.A. Raiders 17
*Aug. 1, 1992	Tokyo, Japan	Houston 34, Dallas 23
*Aug. 15, 1992	Berlin, Germany	Miami 31, Denver 27
*Aug. 16, 1992	London, England	San Francisco 17, Washington 15
*July 31, 1993	Tokyo, Japan	New Orleans 28, Philadelphia 16
*Aug. 1, 1993	Barcelona, Spain	San Francisco 21, Pittsburgh 14
*Aug. 7, 1993	Berlin, Germany	Minnesota 20, Buffalo 6
*Aug. 8, 1993	London, England	Dallas 13, Detroit 13 (OT)
Aug. 14, 1993	Toronto, Canada	Cleveland 12, New England 9

*American Bowl Game

CHICAGO ALL-STAR GAME

Pro teams won 31, lost 9, and tied 2. The game was discontinued after 1976.

Year	Date	Winner	Loser	Attendance
1976*	July 23	Pittsburgh 24	All-Stars 0	52,895
1975	Aug. 1	Pittsburgh 21	All-Stars 14	54,103
1974		No game was played		
1973	July 27	Miami 14	All-Stars 3	54,103
1972	July 28	Dallas 20	All-Stars 7	54,162
1971	July 30	Baltimore 24	All-Stars 17	52,289
1970	July 31	Kansas City 24	All-Stars 3	69,940
1969	Aug. 1	N.Y. Jets 26	All-Stars 24	74,208
1968	Aug. 2	Green Bay 34	All-Stars 17	69,917
1967	Aug. 4	Green Bay 27	All-Stars 0	70,934
1966	Aug. 5	Green Bay 38	All-Stars 0	72,000
1965	Aug. 6	Cleveland 24	All-Stars 16	68,000
1964	Aug. 7	Chicago 28	All-Stars 17	65,000
1963	Aug. 2	All-Stars 20	Green Bay 17	65,000
1962	Aug. 3	Green Bay 42	All-Stars 20	65,000
1961	Aug. 4	Philadelphia 28	All-Stars 14	66,000
1960	Aug. 12	Baltimore 32	All-Stars 7	70,000
1959	Aug. 14	Baltimore 29	All-Stars 0	70,000
1958	Aug. 15	All-Stars 35	Detroit 19	70,000
1957	Aug. 9	N.Y. Giants 22	All-Stars 12	75,000
1956	Aug. 10	Cleveland 26	All-Stars 0	75,000
1955	Aug. 12	All-Stars 30	Cleveland 27	75,000
1954	Aug. 13	Detroit 31	All-Stars 6	93,470
1953	Aug. 14	Detroit 24	All-Stars 10	93,818
1952	Aug. 15	Los Angeles 10	All-Stars 7	88,316
1951	Aug. 17	Cleveland 33	All-Stars 0	92,180
1950	Aug. 11	All-Stars 17	Philadelphia 7	88,885
1949	Aug. 12	Philadelphia 38	All-Stars 0	93,780
1948	Aug. 20	Chi. Cardinals 28	All-Stars 0	101,220
1947	Aug. 22	All-Stars 16	Chi. Bears 0	105,840
1946	Aug. 23	All-Stars 16	Los Angeles 0	97,380
1945	Aug. 30	Green Bay 19	All-Stars 7	92,753
1944	Aug. 30	Chi. Bears 24	All-Stars 21	48,769
1943	Aug. 25	All-Stars 27	Washington 7	48,471
1942	Aug. 28	Chi. Bears 21	All-Stars 0	101,100
1941	Aug. 28	Chi. Bears 37	All-Stars 13	98,203
1940	Aug. 29	Green Bay 45	All-Stars 28	84,567
1939	Aug. 30	N.Y. Giants 9	All-Stars 0	81,456
1938	Aug. 31	All-Stars 28	Washington 16	74,250
1937	Sept. 1	All-Stars 6	Green Bay 0	84,560
1936	Sept. 3	All-Stars 7	Detroit 7 (tie)	76,000
1935	Aug. 29	Chi. Bears 5	All-Stars 0	77,450
1934	Aug. 31	Chi. Bears 0	All-Stars 0 (tie)	79,432

*Game shortened due to thunderstorms.

NFL PLAYOFF BOWL

Western Conference won 8, Eastern Conference won 2.
All games played at Miami's Orange Bowl.

1970	Los Angeles Rams 31, Dallas Cowboys 0
1969	Dallas Cowboys 17, Minnesota Vikings 13
1968	Los Angeles Rams 30, Cleveland Browns 6
1967	Baltimore Colts 20, Philadelphia Eagles 14
1966	Baltimore Colts 35, Dallas Cowboys 3
1965	St. Louis Cardinals 24, Green Bay Packers 17
1964	Green Bay Packers 40, Cleveland Browns 23
1963	Detroit Lions 17, Pittsburgh Steelers 10
1962	Detroit Lions 28, Philadelphia Eagles 10
1961	Detroit Lions 17, Cleveland Browns 16

INTERCONFERENCE GAMES

AFC VS. NFC (REGULAR SEASON), 1970-1993

	1970	1971	1972	1973	1974	1975	1976	1977	1978	1979	1980	1981	1982	1983	1984	1985	1986	1987	1988	1989	1990	1991	1992	1993	Totals
Miami	2-1	3-0	3-0	3-0	2-1	3-0	0-2	2-0	3-1	4-0	4-0	3-1	1-1	3-1	4-0	3-1	2-2	3-0	3-1	2-0	2-2	3-1	2-2	3-1	63-18
L.A. Raiders	1-2	1-1-1	3-0	2-1	3-0	3-0	3-0	1-1	4-0	4-0	2-2	2-2	3-0	2-2	3-1	3-1	1-3	2-2	1-3	2-2	3-1	2-2	2-2	3-1	56-29-1
Pittsburgh	0-3	1-2	2-1	3-0	3-0	2-1	1-1	2-0	3-1	3-1	4-0	3-1	1-0	2-2	3-1	1-3	2-2	2-2	1-3	3-1	3-1	0-4	1-3	2-2	48-35
Cincinnati	1-2	1-2	2-1	2-1	2-1	3-0	2-0	2-1	2-2	2-2	2-2	2-2	1-0	3-1	2-2	2-2	3-1	1-2	4-0	2-2	1-3	1-3	1-3	2-2	46-37
Denver	2-2	1-3	1-3	0-3-1	2-2	2-1	2-0	1-1	2-2	3-1	3-1	3-1	2-1	0-2	3-1	3-1	3-1	2-1-1	3-1	2-2	1-3	2-0	1-3	1-3	45-39-2
Cleveland	0-3	2-1	1-2	1-2	1-2	1-3	2-0	1-1	4-0	3-1	3-1	3-1	0-2	2-2	1-3	1-3	2-2	2-2	4-0	3-1	1-3	0-4	2-2	3-1	43-42
San Diego	1-2	2-1	0-3	1-2	1-2	0-3	2-0	1-1	2-2	3-1	2-2	2-2	1-0	2-2	4-0	1-1	0-4	2-0	2-2	2-2	1-1	1-3	2-0	2-2	37-38
Kansas City	0-2-1	2-1	2-1	1-1-1	1-2	2-1	1-1	1-1	0-2	0-2	2-0	2-2	0-3	2-2	1-1	2-2	1-1	1-?	0-2	2-0	4-0	2-2	2-2	2-2	33-35-2
Buffalo	0-3	0-3	2-0-1	2-1	2-1	1-2	0-2	1-1	1-1	2-2	3-1	1-3	1-2	1-3	1-3	0-2	1-1	1-2	2-2	1-3	3-1	3-1	4-0	4-0	37-40-1
Seattle								1-0	3-1	3-1	1-3	0-2	1-0	1-3	4-0	2-2	3-1	4-0	1-3	0-4	2-2	1-3	0-4	0-2	27-31
N.Y. Jets	2-1	0-3	1-2	0-3	2-1	0-3	0-2	1-1	1-3	3-1	1-3	2-0	4-0	3-1	0-2	2-2	2-2	0-4	2-0	1-3	2-0	2-2	0-4	2-2	33-45
Houston	0-3	0-2-1	0-3	0-3	0-3	3-0	2-0	2-0	2-2	2-2	4-0	1-3	0-3	1-3	0-4	1-3	2-2	2-2	3-1	3-1	1-3	1-3	3-1	2-2	35-49-1
Indianapolis	3-0	2-1	0-3	2-1	1-2	2-1	0-2	1-1	2-2	1-1	1-1	0-4	0-1-1	2-0	0-4	3-1	1-3	1-0	2-2	1-3	2-2	0-4	2-0	0-4	29-43-1
New England	0-3	0-3	3-0	2-1	3-0	1-2	1-1	2-0	2-2	3-1	1-3	0-4	0-1	2-2	0-4	3-1	3-1	0-3	2-2	0-4	0-4	1-1	0-4	1-1	30-48
Tampa Bay							0-1																		0-1
TOTALS	12-27-1	15-23-2	20-19-1	19-19-2	23-17	23-17	16-12	19-9	31-21	36-16	33-19	24-28	15-14-1	26-26	26-26	27-25	26-26	23-22-1	30-22	24-28	26-26	19-33	22-30	27-25	562-530-8

NFC VS. AFC (REGULAR SEASON), 1970-1993

	1970	1971	1972	1973	1974	1975	1976	1977	1978	1979	1980	1981	1982	1983	1984	1985	1986	1987	1988	1989	1990	1991	1992	1993	Totals
Dallas	3-0	3-0	3-0	2-1	2-1	2-1	2-0	1-1	3-1	1-3	3-1	4-0	2-1	2-2	2-2	3-1	1-3	2-1	0-4	0-2	1-1	3-1	4-0	2-2	51-29
Philadelphia	2-1	1-2	2-1	2-1	2-1	0-3	0-2	1-1	3-1	2-2	3-1	3-1	2-1	1-1	3-1	1-1	2-2	3-1	2-2	3-1	1-3	4-0	3-1	2-2	48-33
San Francisco	4-0	2-1	2-1	1-2	0-3	1-2	1-1	0-2	1-3	0-4	2-2	3-1	1-3	2-2	3-1	3-1	4-0	3-1	2-2	4-0	4-0	3-1	3-1	2-2	51-36
Washington	2-1	1-2	1-2	2-1	2-1	1-2	1-1	1-1	2-2	2-2	1-3	2-2		4-0	3-1	4-0	3-1	2-1	1-3	2-2	3-1	4-0	2-2	1-3	47-34
L.A. Rams	2-1	1-2	1-2	3-0	3-1	3-0	1-1	2-0	2-2	2-2	2-2	1-3	1-2	1-3	3-1	3-1	2-2	1-2	2-2	3-1	2-2	1-3	2-2	2-2	46-39
N.Y. Giants	3-0	1-2	1-2	1-2	1-2	2-1	0-2	0-2	1-1	1-1	1-3	1-1	1-0	0-4	2-0	2-2	3-1	2-1	1-1	4-0	3-1	3-1	2-2	2-2	38-34
Minnesota	2-1	2-1	1-2	2-1	2-1	4-0	2-0	1-1	1-3	1-3	1-3	1-3	1-3	4-0	0-4	2-0	1-3	2-1	2-2	2-2	2-2	0-2	3-1	2-2	41-41
Arizona	2-0-1	2-1	1-2	0-2-1	2-1	2-1	1-1	0-2	0-4	1-3	1-1	3-1		3-1	3-1	2-2	1-1	0-1	1-3	1-3	2-2	1-1	0-2	1-1	30-37-2
Chicago	1-2	1-2	1-2	2-2	0-3	0-3	0-2	1-1	0-4	2-2	0-4	4-0	1-1	1-1	2-2	3-1	4-0	2-2	3-1	2-2	2-2	1-3	2-2		37-46
Detroit	3-0	4-0	2-0-1	0-3	1-2	1-2	2-0	2-0	2-2	0-4	0-2	2-2	0-1	1-3	0-4	2-2	1-3	0-4	1-1	1-3	1-3	4-0	2-2	2-0	34-43-1
New Orleans	0-3	0-1-2	0-3	1-2	0-3	0-3	1-2	0-2	1-3	0-4	1-3	2-2	1-0	1-3	3-1	0-4	1-3	4-0	4-0	4-0	2-2	3-1	3-1	2-2	34-48-2
Atlanta	1-2	3-0	2-2	2-1	0-3	1-2	0-2	0-2	1-3	1-3	2-2	1-3	1-1	3-1	1-3	0-4	1-3	0-4	1-3	2-2	2-2	3-1	2-2	1-3	31-54
Green Bay	2-1	2-1	2-1	1-1-1	2-1	0-3	0-2	0-3	2-2	1-3	1-3	1-1	1-1-1	2-2	0-4	0-4	1-3	1-2-1	1-3	0-2	1-3	1-3	3-1	3-1	28-51-3
Tampa Bay								0-1	2-0	2-0	1-3	0-4	2-1	1-3	1-1	0-4	1-1	0-2	1-3	0-4	0-2	1-3	0-2	1-3	13-37
Seattle							1-0																		1-0
TOTALS	27-12-1	23-15-2	19-20-1	19-19-2	17-23	17-23	12-16	9-19	21-31	16-36	19-33	28-24	14-15-1	26-26	26-26	25-27	26-26	22-23-1	22-30	28-24	26-26	33-19	30-22	25-27	530-562-8

1993 INTERCONFERENCE GAMES

(Home Team in capital letters)

AFC 27, NFC 25

AFC Victories

Kansas City 27, TAMPA BAY 3
LOS ANGELES RAIDERS 24, Minnesota 7
Buffalo 13, DALLAS 10
CLEVELAND 23, San Francisco 13
Pittsburgh 45, ATLANTA 17
BUFFALO 17, New York Giants 14
MIAMI 17, Washington 10
New England 23, PHOENIX 21
PITTSBURGH 37, New Orleans 14
New York Jets 10, NEW YORK GIANTS 6
BUFFALO 24, Washington 10
Los Angeles Raiders 16, CHICAGO 14
San Diego 30, MINNESOTA 17
KANSAS CITY 23, Green Bay 16
Miami 19, PHILADELPHIA 14
Miami 16, DALLAS 14
HOUSTON 33, Atlanta 17
CLEVELAND 17, New Orleans 13
New York Jets 3, WASHINGTON 0
Buffalo 10, PHILADELPHIA 7
Denver 13, CHICAGO 3
CINCINNATI 15, Los Angeles Rams 3
LOS ANGELES RAIDERS 27, Tampa Bay 20
Houston 10, SAN FRANCISCO 7
CINCINNATI 21, Atlanta 17
Cleveland 42, LOS ANGELES RAMS 14
San Diego 32, TAMPA BAY 17

NFC Victories

NEW ORLEANS 33, Houston 21
San Francisco 24, PITTSBURGH 13
Detroit 19, NEW ENGLAND 16 (OT)
LOS ANGELES RAMS 27, Pittsburgh 0
Los Angeles Rams 28, HOUSTON 13
Philadelphia 35, NEW YORK JETS 30
Dallas 27, INDIANAPOLIS 3
GREEN BAY 30, Denver 27
DETROIT 30, Seattle 10
WASHINGTON 30, Indianapolis 24
Chicago 16, SAN DIEGO 13
Minnesota 26, DENVER 23
Chicago 19, KANSAS CITY 17
ATLANTA 17, Cleveland 14
SAN FRANCISCO 21, Cincinnati 8
New York Giants 19, MIAMI 14
Green Bay 20, SAN DIEGO 13
NEW YORK GIANTS 20, Indianapolis 6
Dallas 28, NEW YORK JETS 7
Philadelphia 20, INDIANAPOLIS 10
Phoenix 30, SEATTLE 27 (OT)
MINNESOTA 30, Kansas City 10
GREEN BAY 28, Los Angeles Raiders 0
Tampa Bay 17, DENVER 10
NEW ORLEANS 20, Cincinnati 13

REGULAR SEASON INTERCONFERENCE RECORDS, 1970-1993

AMERICAN FOOTBALL CONFERENCE

Eastern Division	W	L	T	Pct.
Miami	63	18	0	.778
Buffalo	37	40	1	.481
New York Jets	33	45	0	.423
Indianapolis	29	43	1	.404
New England	30	48	0	.385
Central Division				
Pittsburgh	48	35	0	.578
Cincinnati	46	37	0	.554
Cleveland	43	42	0	.506
Houston	35	49	1	.418
Western Division				
Los Angeles Raiders	56	29	1	.657
Denver	45	39	2	.535
San Diego	37	38	0	.493
Kansas City	33	35	2	.486
Seattle	27	31	0	.466

NATIONAL FOOTBALL CONFERENCE

Eastern Division	W	L	T	Pct.
Dallas	51	29	0	.638
Philadelphia	48	33	0	.593
Washington	47	34	0	.580
New York Giants	38	34	0	.528
Arizona	30	37	2	.449
Central Division				
Minnesota	41	41	0	.500
Chicago	37	46	0	.446
Detroit	34	43	1	.442
Green Bay	28	51	3	.360
Tampa Bay	13	37	0	.260
Western Division				
San Francisco	51	36	0	.586
Los Angeles Rams	46	39	0	.541
New Orleans	34	48	2	.417
Atlanta	31	54	0	.365

INTERCONFERENCE VICTORIES, 1970-1993

REGULAR SEASON	AFC	NFC	Tie	PRESEASON	AFC	NFC	Tie
1970	12	27	1	1970	21	28	1
1971	15	23	2	1971	28	28	3
1972	20	19	1	1972	27	25	4
1973	19	19	2	1973	23	35	2
1974	23	17	0	1974	35	25	0
1975	23	17	0	1975	30	26	1
1976	16	12	0	1976	30	31	0
1977	19	9	0	1977	38	25	0
1978	31	21	0	1978	20	19	0
1979	36	16	0	1979	25	18	0
1980	33	19	0	1980	22	20	1
1981	24	28	0	1981	18	19	0
1982	15	14	1	1982	25	16	0
1983	26	26	0	1983	15	24	0
1984	26	26	0	1984	16	19	0
1985	27	25	0	1985	10	22	1
1986	26	26	0	1986	22	17	0
1987	23	22	1	1987	22	22	0
1988	30	22	0	1988	23	16	1
1989	24	28	0	1989	16	27	0
1990	26	26	0	1990	15	29	0
1991	19	33	0	1991	19	27	0
1992	22	30	0	1992	30	22	0
1993	27	25	0	1993	17	22	0
Total	562	530	8	Total	547	562	14

MONDAY NIGHT FOOTBALL, 1970-1993

(Home Team in capitals, games listed in chronological order.)

1993
WASHINGTON 35, Dallas 16
CLEVELAND 23, San Francisco 13
KANSAS CITY 15, Denver 7
Pittsburgh 45, ATLANTA 17
MIAMI 17, Washington 10
BUFFALO 35, Houston 7
Los Angeles Raiders 23, DENVER 20
Minnesota 19, CHICAGO 12
BUFFALO 24, Washington 10
KANSAS CITY 23, Green Bay 16
PITTSBURGH 23, Buffalo 0
SAN FRANCISCO 42, New Orleans 7
San Diego 31, INDIANAPOLIS 0
DALLAS 23, Philadelphia 17
Pittsburgh 21, MIAMI 20
New York Giants 24, NEW ORLEANS 14
SAN DIEGO 45, Miami 20
Philadelphia 37, SAN FRANCISCO 34 (OT)

1992
DALLAS 23, Washington 10
Miami 27, CLEVELAND 23
New York Giants 27, CHICAGO 14
KANSAS CITY 27, Los Angeles Raiders 7
PHILADELPHIA 31, Dallas 7
WASHINGTON 34, Denver 3
PITTSBURGH 20, Cincinnati 0
Buffalo 24, NEW YORK JETS 20
Minnesota 38, CHICAGO 10
San Francisco 41, ATLANTA 3
Buffalo 26, MIAMI 20
NEW ORLEANS 20, Washington 3
SEATTLE 16, Denver 13 (OT)
HOUSTON 24, Chicago 7
MIAMI 20, Los Angeles Raiders 7
Dallas 41, ATLANTA 17
SAN FRANCISCO 24, Detroit 6

1991
NEW YORK GIANTS 16, San Francisco 14
Washington 33, DALLAS 31
HOUSTON 17, Kansas City 7
CHICAGO 19, New York Jets 13 (OT)
WASHINGTON 23, Philadelphia 0
KANSAS CITY 33, Buffalo 6
New York Giants 23, PITTSBURGH 20
BUFFALO 35, Cincinnati 16
KANSAS CITY 24, Los Angeles Raiders 21
PHILADELPHIA 30, New York Giants 7
Chicago 34, MINNESOTA 17
Buffalo 41, MIAMI 27
San Francisco 33, LOS ANGELES RAMS 10
Philadelphia 13, HOUSTON 6
MIAMI 37, Cincinnati 13
NEW ORLEANS 27, Los Angeles Raiders 0
SAN FRANCISCO 52, Chicago 14

1990
San Francisco 13, NEW ORLEANS 12
DENVER 24, Kansas City 23
Buffalo 30, NEW YORK JETS 7
SEATTLE 31, Cincinnati 16
Cleveland 30, DENVER 29
PHILADELPHIA 32, Minnesota 24
Cincinnati 34, CLEVELAND 13
PITTSBURGH 41, Los Angeles Rams 10
New York Giants 24, INDIANAPOLIS 7
PHILADELPHIA 28, Washington 14
Los Angeles Raiders 13, MIAMI 10
HOUSTON 27, Buffalo 24
SAN FRANCISCO 7, New York Giants 3
Los Angeles Raiders 38, DETROIT 31
San Francisco 26, LOS ANGELES RAMS 10
NEW ORLEANS 20, Los Angeles Rams 17

1989
New York Giants 27, WASHINGTON 24
Denver 28, BUFFALO 14

CINCINNATI 21, Cleveland 14
CHICAGO 27, Philadelphia 13
Los Angeles Raiders 14, NEW YORK JETS 7
BUFFALO 23, Los Angeles Rams 20
CLEVELAND 27, Chicago 7
NEW YORK GIANTS 24, Minnesota 14
SAN FRANCISCO 31, New Orleans 13
HOUSTON 26, Cincinnati 24
Denver 14, WASHINGTON 10
SAN FRANCISCO 34, New York Giants 24
SEATTLE 17, Buffalo 16
San Francisco 30, LOS ANGELES RAMS 27
NEW ORLEANS 30, Philadelphia 20
MINNESOTA 29, Cincinnati 21

1988
NEW YORK GIANTS 27, Washington 20
Dallas 17, PHOENIX 14
CLEVELAND 23, Indianapolis 17
Los Angeles Raiders 30, DENVER 27 (OT)
NEW ORLEANS 20, Dallas 17
PHILADELPHIA 24, New York Giants 13
Buffalo 37, NEW YORK JETS 14
CHICAGO 10, San Francisco 9
INDIANAPOLIS 55, Denver 23
HOUSTON 24, Cleveland 17
Buffalo 31, MIAMI 6
SAN FRANCISCO 37, Washington 21
SEATTLE 35, Los Angeles Raiders 27
LOS ANGELES RAMS 23, Chicago 3
MIAMI 38, Cleveland 31
MINNESOTA 28, Chicago 27

1987
CHICAGO 34, New York Giants 19
NEW YORK JETS 43, New England 24
San Francisco 41, NEW YORK GIANTS 21
DENVER 30, Los Angeles Raiders 14
Washington 13, DALLAS 7
CLEVELAND 30, Los Angeles Rams 17
MINNESOTA 34, Denver 27
DALLAS 33, New York Giants 24
NEW YORK JETS 30, Seattle 14
DENVER 31, Chicago 29
Los Angeles Rams 30, WASHINGTON 26
Los Angeles Raiders 37, SEATTLE 14
MIAMI 37, New York Jets 28
SAN FRANCISCO 41, Chicago 0
Dallas 29, LOS ANGELES RAMS 21
New England 24, MIAMI 10

1986
DALLAS 31, New York Giants 28
Denver 21, PITTSBURGH 10
Chicago 25, GREEN BAY 12
Dallas 31, ST. LOUIS 7
SEATTLE 33, San Diego 7
CINCINNATI 24, Pittsburgh 22
NEW YORK JETS 22, Denver 10
NEW YORK GIANTS 27, Washington 20
Los Angeles Rams 20, CHICAGO 17
CLEVELAND 26, Miami 16
MIAMI 45, New York Jets 3
New York Giants 21, SAN FRANCISCO 17
SEATTLE 37, Los Angeles Raiders 0
Chicago 16, DETROIT 13
New England 34, MIAMI 27

1985
DALLAS 44, Washington 14
CLEVELAND 17, Pittsburgh 7
Los Angeles Rams 35, SEATTLE 24
Cincinnati 37, PITTSBURGH 24
WASHINGTON 27, St. Louis 10
NEW YORK JETS 23, Miami 7
CHICAGO 23, Green Bay 7
LOS ANGELES RAIDERS 34, San Diego 21
ST. LOUIS 21, Dallas 10
DENVER 17, San Francisco 16
WASHINGTON 23, New York Giants 21
SAN FRANCISCO 19, Seattle 6
MIAMI 38, Chicago 24

Los Angeles Rams 27, SAN FRANCISCO 20
MIAMI 30, New England 27
L.A. Raiders 16, L.A. RAMS 6

1984
Dallas 20, LOS ANGELES RAMS 13
SAN FRANCISCO 37, Washington 31
Miami 21, BUFFALO 17
LOS ANGELES RAIDERS 33, San Diego 30
PITTSBURGH 38, Cincinnati 17
San Francisco 31, NEW YORK GIANTS 10
DENVER 17, Green Bay 14
Los Angeles Rams 24, ATLANTA 10
Seattle 24, SAN DIEGO 0
WASHINGTON 27, Atlanta 14
SEATTLE 17, Los Angeles Raiders 14
NEW ORLEANS 27, Pittsburgh 24
MIAMI 28, New York Jets 17
SAN DIEGO 20, Chicago 7
Los Angeles Raiders 24, DETROIT 3
MIAMI 28, Dallas 21

1983
Dallas 31, WASHINGTON 30
San Diego 17, KANSAS CITY 14
LOS ANGELES RAIDERS 27, Miami 14
NEW YORK GIANTS 27, Green Bay 3
New York Jets 34, BUFFALO 10
Pittsburgh 24, CINCINNATI 14
GREEN BAY 48, Washington 47
ST. LOUIS 20, New York Giants 20 (OT)
Washington 27, SAN DIEGO 24
DETROIT 15, New York Giants 9
Los Angeles Rams 36, ATLANTA 13
New York Jets 31, NEW ORLEANS 28
MIAMI 38, Cincinnati 14
DETROIT 13, Minnesota 2
Green Bay 12, TAMPA BAY 9 (OT)
SAN FRANCISCO 42, Dallas 17

1982
Pittsburgh 36, DALLAS 28
Green Bay 27, NEW YORK GIANTS 19
LOS ANGELES RAIDERS 28, San Diego 24
TAMPA BAY 23, Miami 17
New York Jets 28, DETROIT 13
Dallas 37, HOUSTON 7
SAN DIEGO 50, Cincinnati 34
MIAMI 27, Buffalo 10
MINNESOTA 31, Dallas 27

1981
San Diego 44, CLEVELAND 14
Oakland 36, MINNESOTA 10
Dallas 35, NEW ENGLAND 21
Los Angeles 24, CHICAGO 7
PHILADELPHIA 13, Atlanta 13
BUFFALO 31, Miami 21
DETROIT 48, Chicago 17
PITTSBURGH 26, Houston 13
DENVER 19, Minnesota 17
DALLAS 27, Buffalo 14
SEATTLE 44, San Diego 23
ATLANTA 31, Minnesota 30
MIAMI 13, Philadelphia 10
OAKLAND 30, Pittsburgh 27
LOS ANGELES 21, Atlanta 16
SAN DIEGO 23, Oakland 10

1980
Dallas 17, WASHINGTON 3
Houston 16, CLEVELAND 7
PHILADELPHIA 35, New York Giants 3
NEW ENGLAND 23, Denver 14
CHICAGO 23, Tampa Bay 0
DENVER 20, Washington 17
Oakland 45, PITTSBURGH 34
NEW YORK JETS 17, Miami 14
CLEVELAND 27, Chicago 21
HOUSTON 38, New England 34
Oakland 19, SEATTLE 17
Los Angeles 27, NEW ORLEANS 7
OAKLAND 9, Denver 3

MIAMI 16, New England 13 (OT)
LOS ANGELES 38, Dallas 14
SAN DIEGO 26, Pittsburgh 17

1979
Pittsburgh 16, NEW ENGLAND 13 (OT)
Atlanta 14, PHILADELPHIA 10
WASHINGTON 27, New York Giants 0
CLEVELAND 26, Dallas 7
GREEN BAY 27, New England 14
OAKLAND 13, Miami 3
NEW YORK JETS 14, Minnesota 7
PITTSBURGH 42, Denver 7
Seattle 31, ATLANTA 28
Houston 9, MIAMI 6
Philadelphia 31, DALLAS 21
LOS ANGELES 20, Atlanta 14
SEATTLE 30, New York Jets 7
Oakland 42, NEW ORLEANS 35
HOUSTON 20, Pittsburgh 17
SAN DIEGO 17, Denver 7

1978
DALLAS 38, Baltimore 0
MINNESOTA 12, Denver 9 (OT)
Baltimore 34, NEW ENGLAND 27
Minnesota 24, CHICAGO 20
WASHINGTON 9, Dallas 5
MIAMI 21, Cincinnati 0
DENVER 16, Chicago 7
Houston 24, PITTSBURGH 17
ATLANTA 15, Los Angeles 7
BALTIMORE 21, Washington 17
Oakland 34, CINCINNATI 21
HOUSTON 35, Miami 30
Pittsburgh 24, SAN FRANCISCO 7
SAN DIEGO 40, Chicago 7
Cincinnati 20, LOS ANGELES 19
MIAMI 23, New England 3

1977
PITTSBURGH 27, San Francisco 0
CLEVELAND 30, New England 27 (OT)
Oakland 37, KANSAS CITY 28
CHICAGO 24, Los Angeles 23
PITTSBURGH 20, Cincinnati 14
LOS ANGELES 35, Minnesota 3
ST. LOUIS 28, New York Giants 0
BALTIMORE 10, Washington 3
St. Louis 24, DALLAS 17
WASHINGTON 10, Green Bay 9
OAKLAND 34, Buffalo 13
MIAMI 17, Baltimore 6

Dallas 42, SAN FRANCISCO 35

1976
Miami 30, BUFFALO 21
Oakland 24, KANSAS CITY 21
Washington 20, PHILADELPHIA 17 (OT)
MINNESOTA 17, Pittsburgh 6
San Francisco 16, LOS ANGELES 0
NEW ENGLAND 41, New York Jets 7
WASHINGTON 20, St. Louis 10
BALTIMORE 38, Houston 14
CINCINNATI 20, Los Angeles 12
DALLAS 17, Buffalo 10
Baltimore 17, MIAMI 16
SAN FRANCISCO 20, Minnesota 16
OAKLAND 35, Cincinnati 20

1975
Oakland 31, MIAMI 21
DENVER 23, Green Bay 13
Dallas 36, DETROIT 10
WASHINGTON 27, St. Louis 17
New York Giants 17, BUFFALO 14
Minnesota 13, CHICAGO 9
Los Angeles 42, PHILADELPHIA 3
Kansas City 34, DALLAS 31
CINCINNATI 33, Buffalo 24
Pittsburgh 32, HOUSTON 9
MIAMI 20, New England 7
OAKLAND 17, Denver 10
SAN DIEGO 24, New York Jets 16

1974
BUFFALO 21, Oakland 20
PHILADELPHIA 13, Dallas 10
WASHINGTON 30, Denver 3
MIAMI 21, New York Jets 17
DETROIT 17, San Francisco 13
CHICAGO 10, Green Bay 9
PITTSBURGH 24, Atlanta 17
Los Angeles 15, SAN FRANCISCO 13
Minnesota 28, ST. LOUIS 24
Kansas City 42, DENVER 34
Pittsburgh 28, NEW ORLEANS 7
MIAMI 24, Cincinnati 3
Washington 23, LOS ANGELES 17

1973
GREEN BAY 23, New York Jets 7
DALLAS 40, New Orleans 3
DETROIT 31, Atlanta 6
WASHINGTON 14, Dallas 7
Miami 17, CLEVELAND 9

DENVER 23, Oakland 23
BUFFALO 23, Kansas City 14
PITTSBURGH 21, Washington 16
KANSAS CITY 19, Chicago 7
ATLANTA 20, Minnesota 14
SAN FRANCISCO 20, Green Bay 6
MIAMI 30, Pittsburgh 26
LOS ANGELES 40, New York Giants 6

1972
Washington 24, MINNESOTA 21
Kansas City 20, NEW ORLEANS 17
New York Giants 27, PHILADELPHIA 12
Oakland 34, HOUSTON 0
Green Bay 24, DETROIT 23
CHICAGO 13, Minnesota 10
DALLAS 28, Detroit 24
Baltimore 24, NEW ENGLAND 17
Cleveland 21, SAN DIEGO 17
WASHINGTON 24, Atlanta 13
MIAMI 31, St. Louis 10
Los Angeles 26, SAN FRANCISCO 16
OAKLAND 24, New York Jets 16

1971
Minnesota 16, DETROIT 13
ST. LOUIS 17, New York Jets 10
Oakland 34, CLEVELAND 20
DALLAS 20, New York Giants 13
KANSAS CITY 38, Pittsburgh 16
MINNESOTA 10, Baltimore 3
GREEN BAY 14, Detroit 14
BALTIMORE 24, Los Angeles 17
SAN DIEGO 20, St. Louis 17
ATLANTA 28, Green Bay 21
MIAMI 34, Chicago 3
Kansas City 26, SAN FRANCISCO 17
Washington 38, LOS ANGELES 24

1970
CLEVELAND 31, New York Jets 21
Kansas City 44, BALTIMORE 24
DETROIT 28, Chicago 14
Green Bay 22, SAN DIEGO 20
OAKLAND 34, Washington 20
MINNESOTA 13, Los Angeles 3
PITTSBURGH 21, Cincinnati 10
Baltimore 13, GREEN BAY 10
St. Louis 38, DALLAS 0
PHILADELPHIA 23, New York Giants 20
Miami 20, ATLANTA 7
Cleveland 21, HOUSTON 10
Detroit 28, LOS ANGELES 23

MONDAY NIGHT SYNDROME
1993
Of the 17 winning teams:
    8 won the next week
    5 lost the next week
    0 tied the next week
    4 had an Open Date the next week

Of the 17 losing teams:
    7 won the next week
    8 lost the next week
    0 tied the next week
    2 had an Open Date the next week

Of the 34 NFL teams:
    15 won the next week
    13 lost the next week
    0 tied the next week
    6 had an Open Date the next week

1970-1993
Of the 338 winning teams:
    195 won the next week
    132 lost the next week
    3 tied the next week
    8 had Open Dates the next week

Of the 338 losing teams:
    182 won the next week
    151 lost the next week
    1 tied the next week
    4 had Open Dates the next week

Of the 6 tying teams:
    5 won the next week
    1 lost the next week
    0 tied the next week

Of the 682 NFL teams:
    382 won the next week
    284 lost the next week
    4 tied the next week
    12 had Open Dates the next week

MONDAY NIGHT FOOTBALL

MONDAY NIGHT WON-LOST RECORDS, 1970-1992

AMERICAN FOOTBALL CONFERENCE

	Buff.	Cin.	Clev.	Den.	Hou.	Ind.	K.C.	Raid.	Mia.	N.E.	N.Y.J.	Pitt.	S.D.	Sea.
Total	13-14	7-16	13-9	12-17-1	11-8	9-7	12-6	30-10-1	28-19	4-12	9-16	19-14	12-9	11-5
1993	2-1		1-0	0-2	0-1	0-1	2-0	1-0	1-2			3-0	2-0	
1992	2-0	0-1	0-1	0-2	1-0		1-0	0-2	2-1		0-1	1-0		1-0
1991	2-1	0-2			1-1			2-1	0-2	1-1	0-1	0-1		
1990	1-1	1-1	1-1	1-1	1-0	0-1	0-1	2-0	0-1		0-1	1-0		1-0
1989	1-2	1-2	1-1	2-0	1-0			1-0			0-1			1-0
1988	2-0		1-2	0-2	1-0	1-1		1-1	1-1		0-1			1-0
1987			1-0	2-1				1-1	1-1	1-1	2-1			0-2
1986		1-0	1-0	1-1				0-1	1-2	1-0	1-1	0-2	0-1	2-0
1985		1-0	1-0	1-0				2-0	2-1	0-1	1-0	0-2	0-1	0-2
1984	0-1	0-1		1-0				2-1	3-0		0-1	1-1	1-2	2-0
1983	0-1	0-2					0-1	1-0	1-1		2-0	1-0	1-1	
1982	0-1	0-1			0-1			1-0	1-1		1-0	1-0	1-1	
1981	1-1		0-1	1-0	0-1			2-1	1-1	0-1		1-1	2-1	1-0
1980		1-1	1-2	2-0				3-0	1-1	1-2	1-0	0-2	1-0	0-1
1979			1-0	0-2	2-0			2-0	0-2	0-2	1-1	2-1	1-0	2-0
1978		1-2		1-1	2-0	2-1		1-0	2-1	0-2		1-1	1-0	
1977	0-1	0-1	1-0			1-1	0-1	2-0	1-0	0-1		2-0		
1976	0-2	1-1			0-1	2-0	0-1	2-0	1-1	1-0	0-1	0-1		
1975	0-2	1-0		1-1	0-1			1-0	2-0	1-1	0-1	1-0	1-0	
1974	1-0	0-1		0-2				1-0	0-1	2-0	0-1	2-0		
1973	1-0		0-1	0-0-1			1-1	0-0-1	2-0		0-1	1-1		
1972		1-0			0-1	1-0	1-0	2-0	1-0		0-1		0-1	
1971			0-1			1-1	2-0	1-0	1-0		0-1	0-1	1-0	
1970		0-1	2-0		0-1	1-1	1-0	1-0	1-0		0-1	1-0	0-1	

NATIONAL FOOTBALL CONFERENCE

	Atl.	Chi.	Dall.	Det.	G.B.	Rams	Minn.	N.O.	N.Y.G.	Phil.	Phx.	S.F.	T.B.	Wash.
Total	5-14	12-23	22-19	7-9-1	7-11-1	17-20	14-13	6-10	13-18-1	12-9	5-8-1	21-14	1-2	22-21
1993	0-1	0-1	1-1		0-1		1-0	0-2	1-0	1-1		1-2		1-2
1992	0-2	0-3	2-1	0-1			1-0	1-0	1-0	1-0		2-0		1-2
1991		2-1	0-1				0-1	0-1	1-0	2-1	2-1	2-1		2-0
1990				0-1			0-3	0-1	1-1	1-1	2-0	3-0		0-1
1989		1-1					0-2	1-1	1-1	2-1	0-2	3-0		0-2
1988		1-2	1-1				1-0	1-0	1-0	1-0	0-1	1-1		0-2
1987		1-2	2-1				1-2	1-0	0-3			2-0		1-1
1986		2-1	2-0	0-1	0-1	1-0			2-1		0-1	0-2		1-1
1985		1-1	1-1		0-1	2-1			0-1		1-1	1-2		2-1
1984	0-2	0-1	1-1	0-1	0-1	1-1		1-0	0-1			2-0		1-1
1983	0-1		1-1	2-0	2-1	1-0	0-1	0-1	1-1-1		0-0-1	1-0	0-1	1-2
1982		1-2	0-1	1-0			1-0		0-1		1-1		1-0	
1981	1-2	0-2	2-0	1-0		2-0	0-3				1-1			
1980		1-1	1-1				2-0	0-1	0-1	1-0			0-1	0-2
1979	1-2		0-2		1-0	1-0	0-1	0-1	1-1					1-0
1978	1-0	0-3	1-1			0-2	2-0					2-0	0-1	1-1
1977		1-0	1-1		0-1	1-1	0-1		0-1		0-1	0-2		1-1
1976		1-0					0-2	1-1			0-1	0-1	2-0	2-0
1975		0-1	1-1	0-1	0-1	1-0	1-0		1-0	0-1	0-1			1-0
1974	0-1	1-0	0-1	1-0	0-1	1-1	1-0	0-1		1-0		0-2		2-0
1973	1-1	0-1	1-1	1-0	1-1	1-0	0-1	0-1	0-1		0-1	1-0		1-1
1972	0-1	1-0	1-0	0-2	1-0	1-0	0-2	0-1		1-0	0-1	1-1	0-1	2-0
1971	1-0	0-1	1-0	0-1-1	0-1-1	0-2	2-0		0-1			1-0	0-1	1-0
1970	0-1	0-1	0-1	2-0	1-1	0-2	1-0		0-1	1-0				0-1

THURSDAY-SUNDAY NIGHT FOOTBALL, 1974-1993

(Home Team in capitals, games listed in chronological order.)

1993
NEW ORLEANS 33, Houston 21 (Sun.)
Los Angeles Raiders 17, SEATTLE 13 (Sun.)
Dallas 17, PHOENIX 10 (Sun.)
NEW YORK JETS 45, New England 7 (Sun.)
BUFFALO 17, New York Giants 14 (Sun.)
GREEN BAY 30, Denver 27 (Sun.)
ATLANTA 30, Los Angeles Rams 24 (Thurs.)
MIAMI 41, Indianapolis 27 (Sun.)
Detroit 30, MINNESOTA 27 (Sun.)
WASHINGTON 30, Indianapolis 24 (Sun.)
Chicago 16, SAN DIEGO 13 (Sun.)
TAMPA BAY 23, Minnesota 10 (Sun.)
HOUSTON 23, Pittsburgh 3 (Sun.)
SAN FRANCISCO 21, Cincinnati 8 (Sun.)
Green Bay 20, SAN DIEGO 13 (Sun.)
Philadelphia 20, INDIANAPOLIS 10 (Sun.)
MINNESOTA 30, Kansas City 10 (Sun.)
HOUSTON 24, New York Jets 0 (Sun.)

1992
DENVER 17, Los Angeles Raiders 13 (Sun.)
Philadelphia 31, PHOENIX 14 (Sun.)
BUFFALO 38, Indianapolis 0 (Sun.)
San Francisco 16, NEW ORLEANS 10 (Sun.)
NEW YORK JETS 30, New England 21 (Sun.)
NEW ORLEANS 13, Los Angeles Rams 10 (Sun.)
MINNESOTA 31, Detroit 14 (Thurs.)
Pittsburgh 27, KANSAS CITY 3 (Sun.)
New York Giants 24, WASHINGTON 7 (Sun.)
Cincinnati 31, CHICAGO 28 (OT) (Sun.)
DENVER 27, New York Giants 13 (Sun.)
Kansas City 24, SEATTLE 14 (Sun.)
Houston 24, DETROIT 21 (Thurs.)
DALLAS 30, New York Giants 3 (Thurs.)
SAN DIEGO 27, Los Angeles Raiders 3 (Sun.)
NEW ORLEANS 22, Atlanta 14 (Thurs.)
Los Angeles Rams 31, TAMPA BAY 27 (Sun.)
Green Bay 16, HOUSTON 14 (Sun.)
MIAMI 19, New York Jets 17 (Sun.)
Los Angeles Raiders 21, WASHINGTON 20 (Sat.)
HOUSTON 27, Buffalo 3 (Sun.)

1991
WASHINGTON 45, Detroit 0 (Sun.)
Houston 30, CINCINNATI 7 (Sun.)
NEW ORLEANS 24, Los Angeles Rams 7 (Sun.)
Dallas 17, PHOENIX 9 (Sun.)
Denver 13, MINNESOTA 6 (Sun.)
Pittsburgh 21, INDIANAPOLIS 3 (Sun.)
Los Angeles Raiders 23, SEATTLE 20 (Sun.)
Chicago 10, GREEN BAY 0 (Thurs.)
Washington 17, NEW YORK GIANTS 13 (Sun.)
DENVER 20, Pittsburgh 13 (Sun.)
MIAMI 30, New England 20 (Sun.)
HOUSTON 28, Cleveland 24 (Sun.)
Atlanta 23, NEW ORLEANS 20 (OT) (Sun.)
Los Angeles Raiders 9, SAN DIEGO 7 (Sun.)
Minnesota 26, TAMPA BAY 24 (Sun.)
Buffalo 35, INDIANAPOLIS 7 (Sun.)
SEATTLE 23, Los Angeles Rams 9 (Sun.)

1990
NEW YORK GIANTS 27, Philadelphia 20 (Sun.)
PITTSBURGH 20, Houston 9 (Sun.)
TAMPA BAY 23, Detroit 20 (Sun.)
Washington 38, PHOENIX 10 (Sun.)
BUFFALO 38, Los Angeles Raiders 24 (Sun.)
CHICAGO 38, Los Angeles Rams 9 (Sun.)
MIAMI 17, New England 10 (Thurs.)
ATLANTA 38, Cincinnati 17 (Sun.)
MINNESOTA 27, Denver 22 (Sun.)
San Francisco 24, DALLAS 6 (Sun.)
CINCINNATI 27, Pittsburgh 3 (Sun.)
Seattle 13, SAN DIEGO 10 (Sun.)
MINNESOTA 23, Green Bay 7 (Sun.)
MIAMI 23, Philadelphia 20 (Sun.)
DETROIT 38, Chicago 21 (Sun.)
INDIANAPOLIS 35, Washington 28 (Sat.)
SEATTLE 17, Denver 12 (Sun.)
HOUSTON 34, Pittsburgh 14 (Sun.)

1989
Dallas 13, WASHINGTON 3 (Sun.)

SAN DIEGO 14, Los Angeles Raiders 12 (Sun.)
INDIANAPOLIS 27, New York Jets 10 (Sun.)
Los Angeles Rams 20, NEW ORLEANS 17 (Sun.)
MINNESOTA 27, Chicago 16 (Sun.)
MIAMI 31, New England 10 (Sun.)
SEATTLE 23, Los Angeles Raiders 17 (Sun.)
Cleveland 24, HOUSTON 20 (Sat.)

1988
HOUSTON 41, Washington 17 (Sun.)
Los Angeles Raiders 13, SAN DIEGO 3 (Sun.)
Minnesota 34, DALLAS 3 (Sun.)
New England 6, MIAMI 3 (Sun.)
New York Giants 13, NEW ORLEANS 12 (Sun.)
Pittsburgh 37, HOUSTON 34 (Sun.)
SEATTLE 42, Denver 14 (Sun.)
Los Angeles Rams 38, SAN FRANCISCO 16 (Sun.)

1987
NEW YORK GIANTS 17, New England 10 (Sun.)
SAN DIEGO 16, Los Angeles Raiders 14 (Sun.)
Miami 20, DALLAS 14 (Sun.)
SAN FRANCISCO 38, Cleveland 24 (Sun.)
Chicago 30, MINNESOTA 24 (Sun.)
SEATTLE 28, Denver 21 (Sun.)
MIAMI 23, Washington 21 (Sun.)
SAN FRANCISCO 48, Los Angeles Rams 0 (Sun.)

1986
New England 20, NEW YORK JETS 6 (Thurs.)
Cincinnati 30, CLEVELAND 13 (Thurs.)
Los Angeles Raiders 37, SAN DIEGO 31 (OT) (Thurs.)
LOS ANGELES RAMS 29, Dallas 10 (Sun.)
SAN FRANCISCO 24, Los Angeles Rams 14 (Fri.)

1985
KANSAS CITY 36, Los Angeles Raiders 20 (Thurs.)
Chicago 33, MINNESOTA 24 (Thurs.)
Dallas 30, NEW YORK GIANTS 29 (Sun.)
SAN DIEGO 54, Pittsburgh 44 (Sun.)
Denver 27, SEATTLE 24 (Fri.)

1984
Pittsburgh 23, NEW YORK JETS 17 (Thurs.)
Denver 24, CLEVELAND 14 (Sun.)
DALLAS 30, New Orleans 27 (Sun.)
Washington 31, MINNESOTA 17 (Thurs.)
SAN FRANCISCO 19, Los Angeles Rams 16 (Fri.)

1983
San Francisco 48, MINNESOTA 17 (Thurs.)
CLEVELAND 17, Cincinnati 7 (Thurs.)
Los Angeles Raiders 40, DALLAS 38 (Sun.)
Los Angeles Raiders 42, SAN DIEGO 10 (Thurs.)
MIAMI 34, New York Jets 14 (Fri.)

1982
BUFFALO 23, Minnesota 22 (Thurs.)
SAN FRANCISCO 30, Los Angeles Rams 24 (Thurs.)
ATLANTA 17, San Francisco 7 (Sun.)

1981
MIAMI 30, Pittsburgh 10 (Thurs.)
Philadelphia 20, BUFFALO 14 (Thurs.)
DALLAS 29, Los Angeles 17 (Sun.)
HOUSTON 17, Cleveland 13 (Thurs.)

1980
TAMPA BAY 10, Los Angeles 9 (Thurs.)
DALLAS 42, San Diego 31 (Sun.)
San Diego 27, MIAMI 24 (OT) (Thurs.)
HOUSTON 6, Pittsburgh 0 (Thurs.)

1979
Los Angeles 13, DENVER 9 (Thurs.)
DALLAS 30, Los Angeles 6 (Sun.)
OAKLAND 45, San Diego 22 (Thurs.)
MIAMI 39, New England 24 (Thurs.)

1978
New England 21, OAKLAND 14 (Sun.)
Minnesota 21, DALLAS 10 (Thurs.)
LOS ANGELES 10, Pittsburgh 7 (Sun.)
Denver 21, OAKLAND 6 (Sun.)

1977
Minnesota 30, DETROIT 21 (Sat.)

1976
Los Angeles 20, DETROIT 17 (Sat.)

1975
LOS ANGELES 10, Pittsburgh 3 (Sat.)

1974
OAKLAND 27, Dallas 23 (Sat.)

329

OVERTIME GAMES

HISTORY OF OVERTIME GAMES

PRESEASON

Aug. 28, 1955	Los Angeles 23, New York Giants 17, at Portland, Oregon
Aug. 24, 1962	Denver 27, Dallas Texans 24, at Fort Worth, Texas
Aug. 10, 1974	San Diego 20, New York Jets 14, at San Diego
Aug. 17, 1974	Pittsburgh 33, Philadelphia 30, at Philadelphia
Aug. 17, 1974	Dallas 19, Houston 13, at Dallas
Aug. 17, 1974	Cincinnati 13, Atlanta 7, at Atlanta
Sept. 6, 1974	Buffalo 23, New York Giants 17, at Buffalo
Aug. 9, 1975	Baltimore 23, Denver 20, at Denver
Aug. 30, 1975	New England 20, Green Bay 17, at Milwaukee
Sept. 13, 1975	Minnesota 14, San Diego 14, at San Diego
Aug. 1, 1976	New England 13, New York Giants 7, at New England
Aug. 2, 1976	Kansas City 9, Houston 3, at Kansas City
Aug. 20, 1976	New Orleans 26, Baltimore 20, at Baltimore
Sept. 4, 1976	Dallas 26, Houston 20, at Dallas
Aug. 13, 1977	Seattle 23, Dallas 14, at Seattle
Aug. 28, 1977	New England 13, Pittsburgh 10, at New England
Aug. 28, 1977	New York Giants 24, Buffalo 21, at East Rutherford, N.J.
Aug. 2, 1979	Seattle 12, Minnesota 9, at Minnesota
Aug. 4, 1979	Los Angeles 20, Oakland 14, at Los Angeles
Aug. 24, 1979	Denver 20, New England 17, at Denver
Aug. 23, 1980	Tampa Bay 20, Cincinnati 14, at Tampa Bay
Aug. 5, 1981	San Francisco 27, Seattle 24, at Seattle
Aug. 29, 1981	New Orleans 20, Detroit 17, at New Orleans
Aug. 28, 1982	Miami 17, Kansas City 17, at Kansas City
Sept. 3, 1982	Miami 16, New York Giants 13, at Miami
Aug. 6, 1983	L.A. Raiders 26, San Francisco 23, at Los Angeles
Aug. 6, 1983	Atlanta 13, Washington 10, at Atlanta
Aug. 13, 1983	St. Louis 27, Chicago 24, at St. Louis
Aug. 18, 1983	New York Jets 20, Cincinnati 17, at Cincinnati
Aug. 27, 1983	Chicago 20, Kansas City 17, at Chicago
Aug. 11, 1984	Pittsburgh 20, Philadelphia 17, at Pittsburgh
Aug. 9, 1985	Buffalo 10, Detroit 10, at Pontiac, Mich.
Aug. 10, 1985	Minnesota 16, Miami 13, at Miami
Aug. 17, 1985	Dallas 27, San Diego 24, at San Diego
Aug. 24, 1985	N.Y. Giants 34, N.Y. Jets 31, at East Rutherford, N.J.
Aug. 15, 1986	Washington 27, Pittsburgh 24, at Washington
Aug. 15, 1986	Detroit 30, Seattle 27, at Detroit
Aug. 23, 1986	Los Angeles Rams 20, San Diego 17, at Anaheim
Aug. 30, 1986	Minnesota 23, Indianapolis 20, at Indianapolis
Aug. 23, 1987	Philadelphia 19, New England 13, at New England
Sept. 5, 1987	Cleveland 30, Green Bay 24, at Milwaukee
Sept. 6, 1987	Kansas City 13, St. Louis 10, at Memphis, Tenn.
Aug. 11, 1988	Seattle 16, Detroit 13, at Detroit
Aug. 19, 1988	Miami 16, Denver 13, at Miami
Aug. 19, 1988	Green Bay 21, Kansas City 21, at Milwaukee
Aug. 20, 1988	Houston 20, Los Angeles Rams 17, at Anaheim
Aug. 21, 1988	Minnesota 19, Phoenix 16, at Phoenix
Aug. 5, 1989	Los Angeles Rams 16, San Francisco 13, at Tokyo, Japan
Aug. 26, 1989	Denver 24, Dallas 21, at Denver
Sept. 1, 1989	N.Y. Jets 15, Kansas City 13, at Kansas City
Aug. 24, 1990	Cincinnati 13, New England 10, at New England
Aug. 16, 1991	Cleveland 24, Washington 21, at Washington
Aug. 17, 1991	Cincinnati 27, Minnesota 24, at Cincinnati
Aug. 23, 1991	Dallas 20, Atlanta 17, at Dallas
Aug. 24, 1991	Cincinnati 19, Green Bay 16, at Green Bay
Aug. 22, 1992	Los Angeles Rams 16, Green Bay 13, at Anaheim
Aug. 8, 1993	Dallas 13, Detroit 13, at London, England

REGULAR SEASON

Sept. 22, 1974—Pittsburgh 35, Denver 35, at Denver; Steelers win toss. Gilliam's pass intercepted and returned by Rowser to Denver's 42. Turner misses 41-yard field goal. Walden punts and Greer returns to Broncos' 39. Van Heusen punts and Edwards returns to Steelers' 16. Game ends with Steelers on own 26.

Nov. 10, 1974—New York Jets 26, New York Giants 20, at New Haven, Conn.; Giants win toss. Gogolak misses 42-yard field goal. Namath passes to Boozer for five yards and touchdown at 6:53.

Sept. 28, 1975—Dallas 37, St. Louis 31, at Dallas; Cardinals win toss. Hart's pass intercepted and returned by Jordan to Cardinals' 37. Staubach passes to DuPree for three yards and touchdown at 7:53.

Oct. 12, 1975—Los Angeles 13, San Diego 10, at San Diego; Chargers win toss. Partee punts to Rams' 14. Dempsey kicks 22-yard field goal at 9:27.

Nov. 2, 1975—Washington 30, Dallas 24, at Washington; Cowboys win toss. Staubach's pass intercepted and returned by Houston to Cowboys' 35. Kilmer runs one yard for touchdown at 6:34.

Nov. 16, 1975—St. Louis 20, Washington 17, at St. Louis; Cardinals win toss. Bakken kicks 37-yard field goal at 7:00.

Nov. 23, 1975—Kansas City 24, Detroit 21, at Kansas City; Lions win toss. Chiefs take over on downs at own 38. Stenerud kicks 26-yard field goal at 6:44.

Nov. 23, 1975—Oakland 26, Washington 23, at Washington; Redskins win toss. Bragg punts to Raiders' 42. Blanda kicks 27-yard field goal at 7:13.

Nov. 30, 1975—Denver 13, San Diego 10, at Denver; Broncos win toss. Turner kicks 25-yard field goal at 4:13.

Nov. 30, 1975—Oakland 37, Atlanta 34, at Oakland; Falcons win toss. James punts to Raiders' 16. Guy punts and Herron returns to Falcons' 41. Nick Mike-Mayer misses 45-yard field goal. Guy punts into Falcons' end zone. James punts to Raiders' 39. Blanda kicks 36-yard field goal at 15:00.

Dec. 14, 1975—Baltimore 10, Miami 7, at Baltimore; Dolphins win toss. Seiple punts to Colts' 4. Linhart kicks 31-yard field goal at 12:44.

Sept. 19, 1976—Minnesota 10, Los Angeles 10, at Minnesota; Vikings win toss. Tarkenton's pass intercepted by Monte Jackson and returned to Minnesota 16. Allen blocks Dempsey's 30-yard field goal attempt, ball rolls into end zone for touchback. Clabo punts and Scribner returns to Rams' 20. Rusty Jackson punts to Vikings' 35. Tarkenton's pass intercepted by Kay at Rams' 1, no return. Game ends with Rams on own 3.

*Sept. 27, 1976—Washington 20, Philadelphia 17, at Philadelphia; Eagles win toss. Jones punts and E. Brown loses one yard on return to Redskins' 40. Bragg punts 51 yards into end zone for touchback. Jones punts and E. Brown returns to Redskins' 42. Bragg punts and Marshall returns to Eagles' 41. Boryla's pass intercepted by Dusek at Redskins' 37, no return. Bragg punts and Bradley returns. Philadelphia holding penalty moves ball back to Eagles' 8. Boryla pass intercepted by E. Brown and returned to Eagles' 22. Moseley kicks 29-yard field goal at 12:49.

Oct. 17, 1976—Kansas City 20, Miami 17, at Miami; Chiefs win toss. Wilson punts into end zone for touchback. Bulaich fumbles into Kansas City end zone, Collier recovers for touchback. Stenerud kicks 34-yard field goal at 14:48.

Oct. 31, 1976—St. Louis 23, San Francisco 20, at St. Louis; Cardinals win toss. Joyce punts and Leonard fumbles on return, Jones recovers at 49ers' 43. Bakken kicks 21-yard field goal at 6:42.

Dec. 5, 1976—San Diego 13, San Francisco 7, at San Diego; Chargers win toss. Morris runs 13 yards for touchdown at 5:12.

Sept. 18, 1977—Dallas 16, Minnesota 10, at Minnesota; Vikings win toss. Dallas starts on Vikings' 47 after a punt early in the overtime period. Staubach scores seven plays later on a four-yard run at 6:14.

*Sept. 26, 1977—Cleveland 30, New England 27, at Cleveland; Browns win toss. Sipe throws a 22-yard pass to Logan at Patriots' 19. Cockroft kicks 35-yard field goal at 4:45.

Oct. 16, 1977—Minnesota 22, Chicago 16, at Minnesota; Bears win toss. Parsons punts 53 yards to Vikings' 18. Minnesota drives to Bears' 11. On a first-and-10, Vikings fake a field goal and holder Krause hits Voigt with a touchdown pass at 6:45.

Oct. 30, 1977—Cincinnati 13, Houston 10, at Cincinnati; Bengals win toss. Bahr kicks a 22-yard field goal at 5:51.

Nov. 13, 1977—San Francisco 10, New Orleans 7, at New Orleans; Saints win toss. Saints fail to move ball and Blanchard punts to 49ers' 41. Wersching kicks a 33-yard field goal at 6:33.

Dec. 18, 1977—Chicago 12, New York Giants 9, at East Rutherford, N.J.; Giants win toss. The ball changes hands eight times before Thomas kicks a 28-yard field goal at 14:51.

Sept. 10, 1978—Cleveland 13, Cincinnati 10, at Cleveland; Browns win toss. Collins returns kickoff 41 yards to Browns' 47. Cockroft kicks 27-yard field goal at 4:30.

*Sept. 11, 1978—Minnesota 12, Denver 9, at Minnesota; Vikings win toss. Danmeier kicks 44-yard field goal at 2:56.

Sept. 24, 1978—Pittsburgh 15, Cleveland 9, at Pittsburgh; Steelers win toss. Cunningham scores on a 37-yard "gadget" pass from Bradshaw at 3:43. Steelers start winning drive on their 21.

Sept. 24, 1978—Denver 23, Kansas City 17, at Kansas City; Broncos win toss. Dilts punts to Kansas City 20. Chiefs advance to Broncos' 40 where Reed fails to make first down on fourth-and-one situation. Broncos march downfield. Preston scores two-yard touchdown at 10:28.

Oct. 1, 1978—Oakland 25, Chicago 19, at Chicago; Bears win toss. Both teams punt on first possession. On Chicago's second offensive series, Colzie intercepts Avellini's pass and returns it to Bears' 3. Three plays later, Whittington runs two yards for a touchdown at 5:19.

Oct. 15, 1978—Dallas 24, St. Louis 21, at St. Louis; Cowboys win toss. Dallas drives from its 23 into field goal range. Septien kicks 27-yard field goal at 3:28.

Oct. 29, 1978—Denver 20, Seattle 17, at Seattle; Broncos win toss. Ball changes hands four times before Turner kicks 18-yard field goal at 12:59.

Nov. 12, 1978—San Diego 29, Kansas City 23, at San Diego; Chiefs win toss. Fouts hits Jefferson for decisive 14-yard touchdown pass on the last play (15:00) of overtime period.

Nov. 12, 1978—Washington 16, New York Giants 13, at Washington; Redskins win toss. Moseley kicks winning 45-yard field goal at 8:32 after missing first down field goal attempt of 35 yards at 4:50.

Nov. 26, 1978—Green Bay 10, Minnesota 10, at Green Bay; Packers win toss. Both teams have possession of the ball four times.

Dec. 9, 1978—Cleveland 37, New York Jets 34, at Cleveland; Browns win toss. Cockroft kicks 22-yard field goal at 3:07.

Sept. 2, 1979—Atlanta 40, New Orleans 34, at New Orleans; Falcons win toss. Bartkowski's pass intercepted by Myers and returned to Falcons' 46. Erxleben punts to Falcons' 4. James punts to Chandler on Saints' 43. Erxleben punts and Ryckman returns to Falcons' 28. James punts and Chandler returns to Saints' 36. Erxleben retrieves punt snap on Saints' 1 and attempts pass. Mayberry intercepts and returns six yards for touchdown at 8:22.

Sept. 2, 1979—Cleveland 25, New York Jets 22, at New York; Jets win toss. Leahy's 43-yard field goal attempt goes wide right at 4:41. Evans's punt blocked by Dykes is recovered by Newton. Ramsey punts into end zone for touchback. Evans punts and Harper returns to Jets' 24. Robinson's pass intercepted by Davis and returned 33 yards to Jets' 31. Cockroft kicks 27-yard field goal at 14:45.

*Sept. 3, 1979—Pittsburgh 16, New England 13, at Foxboro; Patriots win toss. Hare punts to Swann at Steelers' 31. Bahr kicks 41-yard field goal at 5:10.

Sept. 9, 1979—Tampa Bay 29, Baltimore 26, at Baltimore; Colts win toss. Landry fumbles, recovered by Kollar at Colts' 14. O'Donoghue kicks 31-yard, first-down field goal at 1:41.

Sept. 16, 1979—Denver 20, Atlanta 17, at Atlanta; Broncos win toss. Broncos march 65 yards to Falcons' 7. Turner kicks 24-yard field goal at 6:15.

Sept. 23, 1979—Houston 30, Cincinnati 27, at Cincinnati; Oilers win toss. Parsley punts and Lusby returns to Bengals' 33. Bahr's 32-yard field goal attempt is wide right at 8:05. Parsley's punt downed on Bengals' 5. McInally punts and Ellender returns to Bengals' 42. Fritsch's third down, 29-yard field goal attempt hits left upright and bounces through at 14:28.

Sept. 23, 1979—Minnesota 27, Green Bay 21, at Minnesota; Vikings win toss. Kramer throws 50-yard touchdown pass to Rashad at 3:18.

Oct. 28, 1979—Houston 27, New York Jets 24, at Houston; Oilers win toss. Oilers march 58 yards to Jets' 18. Fritsch kicks 35-yard field goal at 5:10.

Nov. 18, 1979—Cleveland 30, Miami 24, at Cleveland; Browns win toss. Sipe passes 39 yards to Rucker for touchdown at 1:59.

Nov. 25, 1979—Pittsburgh 33, Cleveland 30, at Pittsburgh; Browns win toss. Sipe's pass intercepted by Blount on Steelers' 4. Bradshaw pass intercepted by Bolton on Browns' 12. Evans punts and Bell returns to Steelers' 17. Bahr kicks 37-yard field goal at 14:51.

Nov. 25, 1979—Buffalo 16, New England 13, at Foxboro; Patriots win toss. Hare's punt downed on Bills' 38. Jackson punts and Morgan returns to Patriots' 20. Grogan's pass intercepted by Haslett and returned to Bills' 42. Ferguson's 51-yard pass to Butler sets up N. Mike-Mayer's 29-yard field goal at 9:15.

Dec. 2, 1979—Los Angeles 27, Minnesota 21, at Los Angeles; Rams win toss. Clark punts and Miller returns to Vikings' 25. Kramer's pass intercepted by Brown and returned to Rams' 40. Cromwell, holding for 22-yard field goal attempt, runs around left end untouched for winning score at 6:53.

Sept. 7, 1980—Green Bay 12, Chicago 6, at Green Bay; Bears win toss. Parsons punts and Nixon returns 16 yards. Five plays later, Marcol returns own blocked field goal attempt 24 yards for touchdown at 6:00.

Sept. 14, 1980—San Diego 30, Oakland 24, at San Diego; Raiders win toss. Pastorini's first-down pass intercepted by Edwards. Millen intercepts Fouts' first-down pass and returns to San Diego 46. Bahr's 50-yard field goal attempt partially blocked by Williams and recovered on Chargers' 32. Eight plays later, Fouts throws 24-yard touchdown pass to Jefferson at 8:09.

Sept. 14, 1980—San Francisco 24, St. Louis 21, at San Francisco; Cardinals win toss. Swider punts and Robinson returns to 49ers' 32. San Francisco drives 52 yards to St. Louis 16, where Wersching kicks 33-yard field goal at 4:12.

Oct. 12, 1900   Green Bay 14, Tampa Bay 14, at Tampa Bay; Packers win toss. Teams trade punts twice. Lee returns second Tampa Bay punt to Green Day 42. Dickey completes three passes to Buccaneers' 18, where Birney's 36-yard field goal attempt is wide right as time expires.

Nov. 9, 1980—Atlanta 33, St. Louis 27, at St. Louis; Falcons win toss. Strong runs 21 yards for touchdown at 4:20.

#Nov. 20, 1980—San Diego 27, Miami 24, at Miami; Chargers win toss. Partridge punts into end zone, Dolphins take over on their own 20. Woodley's pass for Nathan intercepted by Lowe and returned 28 yards to Dolphins' 12. Benirschke kicks 28-yard field goal at 7:14.

Nov. 23, 1980—New York Jets 31, Houston 28, at New York; Jets win toss. Leahy kicks 38-yard field goal at 3:58.

Nov. 27, 1980—Chicago 23, Detroit 17, at Detroit; Bears win toss. Williams returns kickoff 95 yards for touchdown at 0:21.

Dec. 7, 1980—Buffalo 10, Los Angeles 7, at Buffalo; Rams win toss. Corral punts and Hooks returns to Bills' 34. Ferguson's 30-yard pass to Lewis sets up N. Mike-Mayer's 30-yard field goal at 5:14.

Dec. 7, 1980—San Francisco 38, New Orleans 35, at San Francisco; Saints win toss. Erxleben's punt downed by Hardy on 49ers' 27. Wersching kicks 36-yard field goal at 7:40.

*Dec. 8, 1980—Miami 16, New England 13, at Miami; Dolphins win toss. Von Schamann kicks 23-yard field goal at 3:20.

Dec. 14, 1980—Cincinnati 17, Chicago 14, at Chicago; Bengals win toss. Breech kicks 28-yard field goal at 4:23.

Dec. 21, 1980—Los Angeles 20, Atlanta 17, at Los Angeles; Rams win toss. Corral's punt downed at Rams' 37. James punts into end zone for touchback. Corral's punt downed on Falcons' 17. Bartkowski fumbles when hit by Harris, recovered by Delaney. Corral kicks 23-yard field goal on first play of possession at 7:00.

Sept. 27, 1981—Cincinnati 27, Buffalo 24, at Cincinnati; Bills win toss. Cater punts into end zone for touchback. Bengals drive to the Bills' 10 where Breech kicks 28-yard field goal at 9:33.

Sept. 27, 1981—Pittsburgh 27, New England 21, at Pittsburgh; Patriots win toss. Hubach punts and Smith returns five yards to midfield. Four plays later Bradshaw throws 24-yard touchdown pass to Swann at 3:19.

Oct. 4, 1981—Miami 28, New York Jets 28, at Miami; Jets win toss. Teams trade punts twice. Leahy's 48-yard field goal attempt is wide right as time expires.

Oct. 25, 1981—New York Giants 27, Atlanta 24, at Atlanta; Giants win toss. Jennings' punt goes out of bounds at New York 47. Bright returns Atlanta punt to Giants' 14. Woerner fair catches punt at own 28. Andrews fumbles on first play, recovered by Van Pelt. Danelo kicks 40-yard field goal four plays later at 9:20.

Oct. 25, 1981—Chicago 20, San Diego 17, at Chicago; Bears win toss. Teams trade punts. Bears' second punt returned by Brooks to Chargers' 33. Fouts pass intercepted by Fencik and returned 32 yards to San Diego 27. Roveto kicks 27-yard field goal seven plays later at 9:30.

Nov. 8, 1981—Chicago 16, Kansas City 13, at Kansas City; Bears win toss. Teams trade punts. Kansas City takes over on downs on its own 38. Fuller's fumble recovered by Harris on Chicago 36. Roveto's 37-yard field goal wide, but Chiefs penalized for leverage. Roveto's 22-yard field goal attempt three plays later is good at 13:07.

Nov. 8, 1981—Denver 23, Cleveland 20, at Denver; Browns win toss. D. Smith recovers Hill's fumble at Denver 48. Morton's 33-yard pass to Upchurch and 6-yard run by Preston set up Steinfort's 30-yard field goal at 4:10.

Nov. 8, 1981—Miami 30, New England 27, at New England; Dolphins win toss. Orosz punts and Morgan returns six yards to New England 26. Grogan's pass intercepted by Brudzinski who returns 19 yards to Patriots' 26. Von Schamann kicks 30-yard field goal on first down at 7:09.

Nov. 15, 1981—Washington 30, New York Giants 27, at New York; Giants toss. Nelms returns Giants' punt 26 yards to New York 47. Five plays later Moseley kicks 48-yard field goal at 3:44.

Dec. 20, 1981—New York Giants 13, Dallas 10, at New York; Cowboys win toss and kick off. Jennings punts to Dallas 40. Taylor recovers Dorsett's fumble on second down. Danelo's 33-yard field goal attempt hits right upright and bounces back. White's pass for Pearson intercepted by Hunt and returned seven yards to Dallas 24. Four plays later Danelo kicks 35-yard field goal at 6:19.

Sept. 12, 1982—Washington 37, Philadelphia 34, at Philadelphia; Redskins win toss. Theismann completes five passes for 63 yards to set up Moseley's 26-yard field goal at 4:47.

Sept. 19, 1982—Pittsburgh 26, Cincinnati 20, at Pittsburgh; Bengals win toss. Anderson's pass intended for Kreider intercepted by Woodruff and returned 30 yards to Cincinnati 2. Bradshaw completes two-yard touchdown pass to Stallworth on first down at 1:08.

Dec. 19, 1982—Baltimore 20, Green Bay 20, at Baltimore; Packers win toss. K. Anderson intercepts Dickey's first-down pass and returns to Packers' 42. Miller's 44-yard field goal attempt blocked by G. Lewis. Teams trade punts before Stenerud's 47-yard field goal attempt is wide right. Teams trade punts again before time expires in Colts possession.

Jan. 2, 1983—Tampa Bay 26, Chicago 23, at Tampa; Bears win toss. Parsons punts to T. Bell at Buccaneers' 40. Capece kicks 33-yard field goal at 3:14.

Sept. 4, 1983—Baltimore 29, New England 23, at New England; Patriots win toss. Cooks runs 52 yards with fumble recovery three plays into overtime at 0:30.

Sept. 4, 1983—Green Bay 41, Houston 38, at Houston; Packers win toss. Stenerud kicks 42-yard field goal at 5:55.

Sept. 11, 1983—New York Giants 16, Atlanta 13, at Atlanta; Giants win toss. Dennis returns kickoff 54 yards to Atlanta 41. Haji-Sheikh kicks 30-yard field goal at 3:38.

Sept. 18, 1983—New Orleans 34, Chicago 31, at New Orleans; Bears win toss. Parsons punts and Groth returns five yards to New Orleans 34. Stabler pass intercepted by Schmidt at Chicago 47. Parsons punt downed by Gentry at New Orleans 2. Stabler gains 36 yards in four passes; Wilson 38 on six carries. Andersen kicks 41-yard field goal at 10:57.

Sept. 18, 1983—Minnesota 19, Tampa Bay 16, at Tampa; Vikings win toss. Coleman punts and Bell returns eight yards to Tampa Bay 47. Capece's 33-yard field goal attempt sails wide at 7:26. Dils and Young combine for 48-yard gain to Tampa Bay 27. Ricardo kicks 42-yard field goal at 9:27.

Sept. 25, 1983—Baltimore 22, Chicago 19, at Baltimore; Colts win toss. Allegre kicks 33-yard field goal nine plays later at 4:51.

Sept. 25, 1983—Cleveland 30, San Diego 24, at San Diego; Browns win toss. Walker returns kickoff 33 yards to Cleveland 37. Sipe completes 48-yard touchdown pass to Holt four plays later at 1:53.

Sept. 25, 1983—New York Jets 27, Los Angeles Rams 24, at New York; Jets win toss. Ramsey punts to Irvin who returns to 25 but penalty puts Rams on own 13. Holmes 30-yard interception return sets up Leahy's 26-yard field goal at 3:22.

Oct. 9, 1983—Buffalo 38, Miami 35, at Miami; Dolphins win toss. Von Schamann's 52-yard field goal attempt goes wide at 12:36. Cater punts to Clayton who loses 11 to own 13. Von Schamann's 43-yard field goal attempt sails wide at 5:15. Danelo kicks 36-yard field goal nine plays later at 13:58.

Oct. 9, 1983—Dallas 27, Tampa Bay 24, at Dallas; Cowboys win toss. Septien's 51-yard field goal attempt goes wide but Buccaneers penalized for roughing kicker. Septien kicks 42-yard field goal at 4:38.

Oct. 23, 1983—Kansas City 13, Houston 10, at Houston; Chiefs win toss. Lowery kicks 41-yard field goal 13 plays later at 7:41.

Oct. 23, 1983—Minnesota 20, Green Bay 17, at Green Bay; Packers win toss. Scribner's punt downed on Vikings' 42. Ricardo kicks 32-yard field goal eight plays later at 5:05.

*Oct. 24, 1983—New York Giants 20, St. Louis 20, at St. Louis; Cardinals win toss. Teams trade punts before O'Donoghue's 44-yard field goal attempt is wide left. Jennings' punt returned by Bird to St. Louis 21. Lomax pass intercepted by Haynes who loses six yards to New York 33. Jennings' punt downed on St. Louis 17. O'Donoghue's 19-yard field goal attempt is wide right. Rutledge's pass intercepted by L. Washington who returns 25 yards to New York 25. O'Donoghue's 42-yard field goal attempt is wide right. Rutledge's pass intercepted by W. Smith at St. Louis 33 to end game.

Oct. 30, 1983—Cleveland 25, Houston 19, at Cleveland; Oilers win toss. Teams trade punts. Nielsen's pass intercepted by Whitwell who returns to Houston 20. Green runs 20 yards for touchdown on first down at 6:34.

Nov. 20, 1983—Detroit 23, Green Bay 20, at Milwaukee; Packers win toss. Scribner punts and Jenkins returns 14 yards to Green Bay 45. Murray's 33-yard field goal attempt is wide left at 9:32. Whitehurst's pass intercepted by Watkins and returned to Green Bay 27. Murray kicks 37-yard field goal four plays later at 8:30.

Nov. 27, 1983—Atlanta 47, Green Bay 41, at Atlanta; Packers win toss. K. Johnson returns interception 31 yards for touchdown at 2:13.

Nov. 27, 1983—Seattle 51, Kansas City 48, at Seattle; Seahawks win toss. Dixon's 47-yard kickoff return sets up N. Johnson's 42-yard field goal at 1:36.

Dec. 11, 1983—New Orleans 20, Philadelphia 17, at Philadelphia; Eagles win toss. Runager punts to Groth who fair catches on New Orleans 32. Stabler completes two passes for 36 yards to Goodlow to set up Andersen's 50-yard field goal at 5:30.

*****Dec. 12, 1983—Green Bay 12, Tampa Bay 9,** at Tampa; Packers win toss. Stenerud kicks 23-yard field goal 11 plays later at 4:07.

Sept. 9, 1984—Detroit 27, Atlanta 24, at Atlanta; Lions win toss. Murray kicks 48-yard field goal nine plays later at 5:06.

Sept. 30, 1984—Tampa Bay 30, Green Bay 27, at Tampa; Packers win toss. Scribner punts 44 yards to Tampa Bay 2. Epps returns Garcia's punt three yards to Green Bay 27. Scribner's punt downed on Buccaneers' 33. Ariri kicks 46-yard field goal 11 plays later at 10:32.

Oct. 14, 1984—Detroit 13, Tampa Bay 7, at Detroit; Buccaneers win toss. Tampa Bay drives to Lions' 39 before Wilder fumbles. Five plays later Danielson hits Thompson with 37-yard touchdown pass at 4:34.

Oct. 21, 1984—Dallas 30, New Orleans 27, at Dallas; Cowboys win toss. Septien kicks 41-yard field goal eight plays later at 3:42.

Oct. 28, 1984—Denver 22, Los Angeles Raiders 19, at Los Angeles; Raiders win toss. Hawkins fumble recovered by Foley at Denver 7. Teams trade punts. Karlis's 42-yard field goal attempt is wide left. Teams trade punts. Wilson pass intercepted by R. Jackson at Los Angeles 45, returned 23 yards to Los Angeles 22. Karlis kicks 35-yard field goal two plays later at 15:00.

Nov. 4, 1984—Philadelphia 23, Detroit 23, at Detroit; Lions win toss. Lions drive to Eagles' 3 in eight plays. Murray's 21-yard field goal attempt hits left upright and bounces back. Jaworski's pass intercepted by Watkins at Detroit 8. Teams trade punts. Cooper returns Black's punt five yards to Eagles' 14. Time expires four plays later with Eagles on own 21.

Nov. 18, 1984—San Diego 34, Miami 28, at San Diego; Chargers win toss. McGee scores eight plays later on a 25-yard run at 3:17.

Dec. 2, 1984—Cincinnati 20, Cleveland 17, at Cleveland; Browns win toss. Simmons returns Cox's punt 30 yards to Cleveland 35. Breech kicks 35-yard field goal seven plays later at 4:34.

Dec. 2, 1984—Houston 23, Pittsburgh 20, at Houston; Oilers win toss. Cooper kicks 30-yard field goal 16 plays later at 5:53.

Sept. 8, 1985—St. Louis 27, Cleveland 24, at Cleveland; Cardinals win toss. O'Donoghue kicks 20-yard field goal nine plays later at 5:27.

Sept. 29, 1985—New York Giants 16, Philadelphia 10, at Philadelphia; Eagles win toss. Jaworski's pass tipped by Quick and intercepted by Patterson who returns 29 yards for touchdown at 0:55.

Oct. 20, 1985—Denver 13, Seattle 10, at Denver; Seahawks win toss. Teams trade punts twice. Krieg's pass intercepted by Hunter and returned to Seahawks' 15. Karlis kicks 24-yard field goal four plays later at 9:19.

Nov. 10, 1985—Philadelphia 23, Atlanta 17, at Philadelphia; Falcons win toss. Donnelly's 62-yard punt goes out of bounds at Eagles' 1. Jaworski completes 99-yard touchdown pass to Quick two plays later at 1:49.

Nov. 10, 1985—San Diego 40, Los Angeles Raiders 34, at San Diego; Chargers win toss. James scores on 17-yard run seven plays later at 3:44.

Nov. 17, 1985—Denver 30, San Diego 24, at Denver; Chargers win toss. Thomas' 40-yard field goal attempt blocked by Smith and returned 60 yards by Wright for touchdown at 4:45.

Nov. 24, 1985—New York Jets 16, New England 13, at New York; Jets win toss. Teams trade punts twice. Patriots' second punt returned 46 yards by Sohn to Patriots' 15. Leahy kicks 32-yard field goal one play later at 10:05.

Nov. 24, 1985—Tampa Bay 19, Detroit 16, at Tampa; Lions win toss. Teams trade punts. Lions' punt downed on Buccaneers' 38. Igwebuike kicks 24-yard field goal 11 plays later at 12:31.

Nov. 24, 1985—Los Angeles Raiders 31, Denver 28, at Los Angeles; Raiders win toss. Bahr kicks 32-yard field goal six plays later at 2:42.

Dec. 8, 1985—Los Angeles Raiders 17, Denver 14, at Denver; Broncos win toss. Teams trade punts twice. Elway's fumble recovered by Townsend at Broncos' 8. Bahr kicks 26-yard field goal one play later at 4:55.

Sept. 14, 1986—Chicago 13, Philadelphia 10, at Chicago; Eagles win toss. Crawford's fumble of kickoff recovered by Jackson at Eagles' 35. Butler kicks 23-yard field goal 10 plays later at 5:56.

Sept. 14, 1986—Cincinnati 36, Buffalo 33, at Cincinnati; Bills win toss. Zander intercepts Kelly's first-down pass and returns it to Bills' 17. Breech kicks 20-yard

field goal two plays later at 0:56.

Sept. 21, 1986—New York Jets 51, Miami 45, at New York; Jets win toss. O'Brien completes 43-yard touchdown pass to Walker five plays later at 2:35.

Sept. 28, 1986—Pittsburgh 22, Houston 16, at Houston; Oilers win toss. Johnson's punt returned 41 yards by Woods to Oilers' 15. Abercrombie scores on three-yard run three plays later at 2:35.

Sept. 28, 1986—Atlanta 23, Tampa Bay 20, at Tampa; Falcons win toss. Teams trade punts. Luckhurst kicks 34-yard field goal 10 plays later at 12:35.

Oct. 5, 1986—Los Angeles Rams 26, Tampa Bay 20, at Anaheim; Rams win toss. Dickerson scores four plays later on 42-yard run at 2:16.

Oct. 12, 1986—Minnesota 27, San Francisco 24, at San Francisco; Vikings win toss. C. Nelson kicks 28-yard field goal nine plays later at 4:27.

Oct. 19, 1986—San Francisco 10, Atlanta 10, at Atlanta; Falcons win toss. Teams trade punts twice. Donnelly punts to 49ers' 27. The following play Wilson recovers Rice's fumble at 49ers' 46 as time expires.

Nov. 2, 1986—Washington 44, Minnesota 38, at Washington; Redskins win toss. Schroeder completes 38-yard touchdown pass to Clark four plays later at 1:46.

Nov. 20, 1986—Los Angeles Raiders 37, San Diego 31, at San Diego; Raiders win toss. Teams trade punts. Allen scores five plays later on 28-yard run at 8:33.

Nov. 23, 1986—Cleveland 37, Pittsburgh 31, at Cleveland; Browns win toss. Teams trade punts. Six plays later Kosar hits Slaughter with 36-yard touchdown pass at 6:37.

Nov. 30, 1986—Chicago 13, Pittsburgh 10, at Chicago; Bears win toss and kick off. Newsome's punt returned by Barnes to Chicago 49. Butler kicks 42-yard field goal five plays later at 3:55.

Nov. 30, 1986—Philadelphia 33, Los Angeles Raiders 27, at Los Angeles; Eagles win toss. Teams trade punts. Long recovers Cunningham's fumble at Philadelphia 42. Waters returns Allen's fumble 81 yards to Los Angeles 4. Cunningham scores on one-yard run two plays later at 6:53.

Nov. 30, 1986—Cleveland 13, Houston 10, at Cleveland; Oilers win toss and kick off. Gossett punts to Houston 39. Luck's pass intercepted by Minnifield at Cleveland 21. Gossett punts to Houston 34. Luck's pass intercepted by Minnifield at Cleveland 43 who returns 20 yards to Houston 37. Moseley kicks 29-yard field goal nine plays later at 14:44.

Dec. 7, 1986—St. Louis 10, Philadelphia 10, at Philadelphia; Cardinals win toss. White blocks Schubert's 40-yard field goal attempt. Teams trade punts. McFadden's 43-yard field goal attempt is wide left. Schubert's 37-yard field goal attempt is wide right. Cavanaugh's pass intercepted by Carter and returned to Eagles' 48 to end game.

Dec. 14, 1986—Miami 37, Los Angeles Rams 31, at Anaheim; Dolphins win toss. Marino completes 20-yard touchdown pass to Duper six plays later at 3:04.

Sept. 20, 1987—Denver 17, Green Bay 17, at Milwaukee; Packers win toss. Del Greco's 47-yard field goal attempt is short. Teams trade punts. Elway intercepted by Noble who returns 10 yards to Green Bay 34. Davis fumbles on next play and Smith recovers. Two plays later, Karlis's 40-yard field goal attempt is wide left. Time expires two plays later with Packers on own 23.

Oct. 11, 1987—Detroit 19, Green Bay 16, at Green Bay; Lions win toss. Prindle's 42-yard field goal attempt is wide left. Packers punt downed on Detroit 17. Prindle kicks 31-yard field goal 16 plays later at 12:26.

Oct. 18, 1987—New York Jets 37, Miami 31, at New York; Jets win toss. Teams trade punts. Ryan intercepted by Hooper at Jets' 47 who returns 11 yards. Mackey intercepted by Haslett at Jets' 37 who returns 9 yards. Jets punt. Mackey intercepted by Radachowsky who returns 45 yards to Miami 24. Ryan completes eight-yard touchdown pass to Hunter five plays later at 14:26.

Oct. 18, 1987—Green Bay 16, Philadelphia 10, at Green Bay; Packers win toss. Hargrove scores on seven-yard run 10 plays later at 5:04.

Oct. 18, 1987—Buffalo 6, New York Giants 3, at Buffalo; Bills win toss. Schlopy's 28-yard field goal attempt is wide left. Teams trade punts. Rutledge intercepted by Clark who returns 23 yards to Buffalo 40. Schlopy kicks 27-yard field goal nine plays later at 14:41.

Oct. 25, 1987—Buffalo 34, Miami 31, at Miami; Bills win toss. Norwood kicks 27-yard field goal seven plays later at 4:12.

Nov. 1, 1987—San Diego 27, Cleveland 24, at San Diego; Browns win toss. Kosar intercepted by Glenn who returns 20 yards to Browns' 25. Abbott kicks 33-yard field goal three plays later at 2:16.

Nov. 15, 1987—Dallas 23, New England 17, at New England; Cowboys win toss. Walker scores on 60-yard run four plays later at 1:50.

Nov. 26, 1987—Minnesota 44, Dallas 38, at Dallas; Vikings win toss. Coleman's punt downed by Hilton at Cowboys' 37. White intercepted by Studwell who returns 12 yards to Vikings' 37. D. Nelson scores on 24-yard run seven plays later at 7:51.

Nov. 29, 1987—Philadelphia 34, New England 31, at New England; Patriots win toss. Ramsey intercepted by Joyner who returns 29 yards to Eagles' 32. Fryar fair catches Teltschik's punt at Patriots' 13. Franklin's 46-yard field goal attempt is short. McFadden's 39-yard field goal attempt is wide left. Tatupu fumbles on next play and Cobb recovers. McFadden kicks 38-yard field goal four plays later at 12:16.

Dec. 6, 1987—New York Giants 23, Philadelphia 20, at New York; Giants win toss and kick off. Teams trade punts. Teltschik's punt is returned 16 yards by McConkey to Eagles' 33. Three plays later, Allegre's 50-yard field goal attempt is blocked by Joyner and returned 25 yards by Hoage to Eagles' 30. McConkey returns Teltschik's punt four yards to Giants' 44. Allegre kicks 28-yard field goal four plays later at 10:42.

Dec. 6, 1987—Cincinnati 30, Kansas City 27, at Cincinnati; Bengals win toss. Teams trade punts. Breech kicks 32-yard field goal 16 plays later at 9:44.

Dec. 26, 1987—Washington 27, Minnesota 24, at Minnesota; Redskins win toss. Haji-Sheikh kicks 26-yard field goal six plays later at 2:09.

Sept. 4, 1988—Houston 17, Indianapolis 14, at Indianapolis; Colts win toss. Dickerson fumble recovered by Lyles who returns six yards to Colts' 42. Zendejas kicks 35-yard field goal six plays later at 3:51.

*****Sept. 26, 1988—Los Angeles Raiders 30, Denver 27,** at Denver; Broncos win toss. Teams trade punts twice. Elway intercepted by Lee who returns 20 yards to Broncos' 31. Bahr kicks 35-yard field goal four plays later at 12:35.

Oct. 2, 1988—New York Jets 17, Kansas City 17, at New York; Chiefs win toss. Chiefs punt goes into end zone for touchback. Leahy's 44-yard field goal attempt is wide right. Chiefs punt is returned by Townsell to Jets' 26. Burruss recovers McNeil's fumble at Chiefs' 11. DeBerg intercepted by Humphery at Jets' 49. Three plays later, time expires.

Oct. 9, 1988—Denver 16, San Francisco 13, at San Francisco; Broncos win toss and kick off. Young intercepted by Haynes at Broncos' 32. Denver punt downed at 49ers' 5. Young intercepted by Wilson who returns seven yards to 49ers' 5. Karlis kicks 22-yard field goal two plays later at 8:11.

Oct. 30, 1988—New York Giants 13, Detroit 10, at Detroit; Lions win toss. James's fumble recovered by Taylor at Lions' 22. Three plays later, McFadden kicks 33-yard field goal at 1:13.

Nov. 20, 1988—Buffalo 9, New York Jets 6, at Buffalo; Jets win toss. Vick's fumble recovered by Bennett at Bills' 32. Norwood kicks 30-yard field goal five plays later at 3:47.

Nov. 20, 1988—Philadelphia 23, New York Giants 17, at New York; Eagles win toss. Philadelphia's punt goes into end zone for touchback. Hostetler intercepted by Hoage who returns 11 yards to Giants' 41. Six plays later, Zendejas's 30-yard field-goal attempt is blocked and ball is recovered behind line of scrimmage by Eagles' Simmons, who runs 15 yards for touchdown at 3:09.

Dec. 11, 1988—New England 10, Tampa Bay 7, at New England; Buccaneers win toss and kick off. Staurovsky kicks 27-yard field goal six plays later at 3:08.

Dec. 17, 1988—Cincinnati 20, Washington 17, at Cincinnati; Bengals win toss. Cincinnati's punt returned by Oliphant to Redskins' 16. Grant recovers Williams's fumble at Redskins' 17. Breech kicks 20-yard field goal three plays later at 7:01.

Sept. 24, 1989—Buffalo 47, Houston 41, at Houston; Oilers win toss. Johnson returns Brady's kickoff 17 yards to Oilers' 19. Oilers drive to Buffalo 25, Zendejas's 37-yard field goal blocked, but Bills offsides and Zendejas's second attempt is wide left. Bills' ball and Kelly completes series of passes, including 28-yard game-winner to Andre Reed, at 8:42.

Oct. 8, 1989—Miami 13, Cleveland 10, at Miami; Browns win toss. Metcalf returns Stoyanovich's kickoff 20 yards to Browns' 28. Browns drive ball 46 yards in eight plays; Bahr wide left on 44-yard field goal attempt. Dolphins ball. Browns called for pass interference on Marino pass to Banks at Cleveland 47. Two plays later, Banks's 20-yard reception at Browns' 23 sets up winning 35-yard field goal by Stoyanovich at 0:23.

Oct. 22, 1989—Denver 24, Seattle 21, at Seattle; Seahawks win toss. Treadwell's 56-yard kickoff returned 18 yards by Jefferson to Seahawks' 27. Seahawks drive to Broncos' 22 in 10 plays, but Johnson's 40-yard field goal attempt wide left. Smith intercepts a Krieg pass and returns it 28 yards to Seahawks' 10. Treadwell kicks winning 27-yard field goal at 7:46.

Oct. 29, 1989—New England 23, Indianapolis 20, at Indianapolis; Patriots win toss. Biasucci kickoff returned 13 yards to Patriots' 23 by Martin. Holding penalty brings ball back to Patriots' 13. After six plays, Feagles punt returned 11 yards by Verdin to Colts' 28. Six plays later, Colts punt to Martin at Patriots' 12. Grogan completes three straight passes to Patriots' 44. Five consecutive runs put New England on Colts' 33. Davis kicks a 51-yard winning field goal for Patriots at 9:46.

Oct. 29, 1989—Green Bay 23, Detroit 20, at Milwaukee; Lions win toss. Sanders touchback on Jacke kickoff. On first play, Murphy intercepts Lions' Peete and returns it three yards to Lions' 26. Fullwood gains five yards on three plays to set up Jacke's 38-yard field goal at 2:14.

Nov. 5, 1989—Minnesota 23, Los Angeles Rams 21, at Minneapolis; Rams win toss. Karlis's kick returned 18 yards by Delpino to Rams' 19. Drive stops at Rams' 28. Merriweather blocks Hatcher's punt at 12. Ball rolls out of end zone for safety.

Nov. 19, 1989—Cleveland 10, Kansas City 10, at Cleveland; Browns win toss. Browns punt three times; Chiefs twice; before Kansas City's Lowery misses 47-yard field goal with 17 seconds remaining in overtime. Kosar's pass intercepted as time expired.

Nov. 26, 1989—Los Angeles Rams 20, New Orleans 17, at New Orleans; Saints win toss. Lansford's kickoff returned 27 yards to Saints' 30. After four plays, Barnhardt punts to Rams' 15. Saints penalized 35 yards for interference to Rams' 43. Three plays later, Everett hits Anderson with 14-yard pass to Saints' 40, then 26-yarder to put Rams in field goal position. Lansford kicks 31-yard field goal at 6:38.

Dec. 3, 1989—Los Angeles Raiders 16, Denver 13, at Los Angeles; Broncos win toss. Bell returns Jaeger kickoff 14 yards to Broncos' 18. Broncos' penalized for illegal block to Broncos' 9. Elway completes three passes for two first downs. On third and eight Elway sacked for 10-yard loss. Horan punts, Adams calls for fair catch at Raiders' 29. Dyal's 26-yard reception moves Raiders to Denver 43. Raiders move ball 34 yards in three plays to set up Jaeger's 26-yard

field goal at 7:02.

Dec. 10, 1989—Indianapolis 23, Cleveland 17, at Indianapolis; Browns win toss. Teams trade punts. McNeil returns Colts' punt 42 yards to 42. Seven plays later, Bahr misses 35-yard field goal attempt. Three plays later, Stark punts and McNeil returns ball to 50-yard line. Two plays later, Prior intercepts Kosar's pass at Colts' 42 and returns it 58 yards for touchdown at 10:54.

Dec. 17, 1989—Cleveland 23, Minnesota 17, at Cleveland; Browns win toss. Browns punt to Vikings' 18. Six plays later, Vikings punt to Browns' 22. Nine plays later, Bahr lines up to attempt 31-yard field goal. Holder Pagel takes snap and passes 14 yards to Waiters for touchdown at 9:30.

Sept. 23, 1990—Denver 34, Seattle 31, at Denver; Seahawks win toss. Loville returns kickoff 19 yards to Seahawks' 27. Seahawks drive to Broncos' 26, Johnson misses 44-yard field goal wide right. Broncos take over and Elway completes series of passes to set up Treadwell's 25-yard field goal at 9:14.

Sept. 30, 1990—Tampa Bay 23, Minnesota 20, at Minnesota; Vikings win toss. Vikings drive to Buccaneers' 31; Igwebuike's 48-yard field goal attempt wide left. Buccaneers drive to Vikings' 43 and punt. Gannon's pass is intercepted at Vikings' 26 by Wayne Haddix. Buccaneers drive to Vikings' 19 to set up Christie's 36-yard field goal at 9:11.

Oct. 7, 1990—Cincinnati 34, Los Angeles Rams 31, at Anaheim; Rams win toss. Berry returns kickoff to Rams' 21. After 3 plays, English punts and Green downs ball at Bengals' 25. After 3 plays, Johnson punts and Sutton downs ball at Rams' 29-yard line. After 3 plays, English punts and Price signals fair catch at Bengals' 47. Esiason completes series of passes to 26-yard line to set up Breech's 44-yard field goal at 11:56.

Nov. 4, 1990—Washington 41, Detroit 38, at Detroit; Redskins win toss. Howard downs kickoff on Redskins' 15. After 3 plays, Mojsiejenko punts to Redskins' 45. After 3 plays, Arnold punts to Redskins' 10. Rutledge completes series of passes to set up Lohmiller's 34-yard field goal at 9:10.

Nov. 18, 1990—Chicago 16, Denver 13, at Denver; Broncos win toss. Ezor returns kickoff to Broncos' 12. Both teams have ball twice and have to punt after each possession. Broncos punt after third possession of overtime and Bailey returns 20 yards to Broncos' 34. Harbaugh completes 10-yard pass to Thornton to set up Butler's 44-yard field goal at 13:14.

Nov. 25, 1990—Seattle 13, San Diego 10, at San Diego; Chargers win toss. Lewis returns kickoff to Chargers' 22. After 2 plays, Cox fumbles and ball is recovered by Porter at Chargers' 23. After two plays, Johnson kicks 40-yard field goal at 3:01.

Dec. 2, 1990—Chicago 23, Detroit 17, at Chicago; Lions win toss. Gray returns kickoff to Lions' 35. After 10 plays, Murray misses 35-yard field goal. Bears take possession at Chicago 20. Harbaugh completes 50-yard game-winning pass to Anderson at 10:57.

Dec. 2, 1990—Seattle 13, Houston 10, at Seattle; Seahawks win toss. Warren returns kickoff to Seahawks' 13. After 5 plays, Donnelly punts to Oilers' 23-yard line. Ford's fumble recovered by Wyman. Seahawks take possession at Oilers' 27. After 2 plays, Johnson kicks 42-yard field goal at 4:25.

Dec. 9, 1990—Miami 23, Philadelphia 20, at Miami; Eagles win toss. After 11 plays, Feagles punts to Dolphins' 26. After 6 plays, Roby punts to Eagles' 14 and Harris returns to 25. After 3 plays, Feagles punts to Dolphins' 43. Marino completes series of passes to Eagles' 22. Stoyanovich kicks 39-yard field goal at 12:32.

Dec. 9, 1990—San Francisco 20, Cincinnati 17, at Cincinnati; 49ers win toss. Carter returns kickoff to 49ers' 19. After 10 plays, Cofer kicks 23-yard field goal at 6:12.

Sept. 24, 1991—Chicago 19, New York Jets 13, at Chicago; Jets win toss. Mathis returns kickoff seven yards to New York's 12. Jets drive to New York 26; Bailey returns punt to Chicago 39. Bears drive to Jets' 44-yard line and punt in-to the end zone. Jets drive to Bears' 11 where Leahy's 28-yard field goal attempt is wide left. Bears drive from 20 to Jets' 1 where Harbaugh runs for touchdown at 14:42.

Oct. 13, 1991—Los Angeles Raiders 23, Seattle 20, at Seattle. Seahawks win toss. Seahawks begin on 20. After 5 plays, Tuten punts and Brown signals fair catch at Raiders' 24. After 3 plays, Gossett punts and Land downs ball at Seattle 9. After 1 play, Lott intercepts at Seahawks' 19 to set up Jaeger's game-winning 37-yard field goal at 6:37.

Oct. 20, 1991—Cleveland 30, San Diego 24, at San Diego; Chargers win toss. After kickoff, Chargers drive to Browns' 45 and punt to Browns' 6 where Hendrickson downs ball. Browns drive to 38 and punt; Taylor fair catches on Chargers' 14. After 3 plays, Brandon intercepts at Chargers' 30 and scores at 5:58.

Oct. 20, 1991—New England 26, Minnesota 23, at New England; Patriots win toss. Martin returns kickoff 18 yards to New England 22. Patriots drive to Minnesota 19. Staurovsky's 36-yard field goal attempt is wide left. Minnesota drives to the 50 where Newsome punts into end zone. On first play, McMillian intercepts at the 40 for Minnesota. After 2 plays, Marion causes Jordan fumble and Pool recovers at New England 20. New England drives to Minnesota 24 where Staurovsky kicks 42-yard field goal as time expires.

Nov. 3, 1991—New York Jets 19, Green Bay 16, at New York; Packers win toss. Thompson returns kickoff 30 yards to Packers' 39. Green Bay drives to New York 24 where Jacke's 42-yard field goal attempt is wide right. Jets drive to 50. Aguiar's punt is fumbled by Sikahema and recovered by New York at Packers' 23. After 2 plays, Leahy kicks 37-yard field goal at 9:40.

Nov. 3, 1991—Washington 16, Houston 13, at Washington; Redskins win toss. Mitchell returns kickoff 9 yards to Washington 14. After 4 plays, Goodburn punts and Givins returns to Houston 31. After 1 play, Moon's pass is intercepted by Green at Oilers' 35. After 3 plays, Lohmiller kicks 41-yard field goal at 4:01.

Nov. 10, 1991—Houston 26, Dallas 23, at Houston; Oilers win toss. Pinkett returns kickoff 20 yards to Houston 24. After 6 plays, Montgomery punts and Martin returns to Dallas 24. Cowboys drive to Oilers' 24 where Smith fumbles and McDowell recovers at Oilers' 15. Houston drives to Dallas 5 where Del Greco kicks 23-yard field goal at 14:31.

Nov. 10, 1991—Pittsburgh 33, Cincinnati 27, at Cincinnati; Pittsburgh wins toss. Woodson downs kickoff for touchback. After 3 plays, Stryzinski punts and Barber returns 7 yards to Cincinnati 38. Bengals drive to Pittsburgh 37 where Woods fumbles and Lloyd returns recovery to Cincinnati 44. After 2 plays, O'Donnell passes to Green for 26-yard touchdown at 6:32.

Nov. 24, 1991—Atlanta 23, New Orleans 20, at New Orleans; Atlanta wins toss. Falcons begin at 20. After 3 plays, Fulhage punts and Fenerty signals fair catch at New Orleans 43. After 3 plays, Barnhardt punts and Thompson downs ball at Atlanta 23. After 3 plays, Fulhage punts and Fenerty fair catches at New Orleans 25. Saints drive to Atlanta 38 where Andersen misses 55-yard field-goal attempt. After 1 play, Rozier fumbles and Martin recovers on 50. Saints drive to Atlanta 38 where Barnhardt punts to Falcons' 2. Atlanta drives to New Orleans 33 where Johnson kicks 50-yard field goal at 13:03.

Nov. 24, 1991—Miami 16, Chicago 13, at Chicago; Miami wins toss. Butler kicks to Miami 20 where Paige returns kickoff 15 yards to 35. Miami drives to Chicago 9 where Stoyanovich kicks 27-yard field goal at 4:11.

Dec. 8, 1991—Buffalo 30, Los Angeles Raiders 27, at Los Angeles; Raiders win toss. Daluiso kicks into end zone for touchback. On third play, Kelso intercepts for Buffalo and returns ball to Bills' 36. Bills drive to Los Angeles 24 where Norwood kicks 42-yard field goal at 2:34.

Dec. 8, 1991—Kansas City 20, San Diego 17, at Kansas City; Chiefs win toss. Carney kicks to Kansas City 10 where Stradford returns 23 yards to 33. After 3 plays, Barker punts to San Diego 4. Chargers drive to 40 where Kidd punts 60 yards into end zone for touchback. Kansas City drives to San Diego 39 where Barker punts 38 yards to 1. After 3 plays, Kidd punts 41 yards to San Diego 42 where Stradford returns 12 yards to 30. Chiefs drive to San Diego 1 where Lowery kicks 18-yard field goal at 11:26.

Dec. 8, 1991—New England 23, Indianapolis 17, at New England; Indianapolis wins toss. Baumann kicks off to Indianapolis 2 where Martin returns 23 yards to 25. After 3 downs, Stark punts to New England 17 where Henderson returns 8 yards to 25. New England drives to 50 where McCarthy punts and Prior signals fair catch at Indianapolis 15. After 3 plays, Stark punts to New England 40 where Henderson returns 7 yards to 47. After 2 plays, Millen passes to Timpson for 45-yard touchdown at 8:55.

Dec. 22, 1991—Detroit 17, Buffalo 14, at Buffalo; Detroit wins toss. Daluiso kicks off to Detroit 20 where Dozier returns 15 yards to Lions 35. Lions drive to Bills' 3 where Murray kicks 21-yard field goal at 4:23.

Dec. 22, 1991—New York Jets 23, Miami 20, at Miami; Jets win toss. Aguiar kicks to Miami's 30 where Logan returns 3 yards to the 33. After 4 downs, Stoyanovich punts to Jets' 15 where Baty returns 8 yards to 23. Jets drive to Miami 12 where Allegre kicks 30-yard field goal at 6:33.

Sept. 6, 1992—Minnesota 23, Green Bay 20, at Green Bay. Vikings win toss. Nelson returns kickoff 14 yards to the Minnesota 23. After 5 plays, Newsome punts 49 yards to Green Bay 21 where Brooks returns 12 yards to the 33. After 2 plays, Glenn intercepts pass at the Vikings' 48. On first play, Allen fumbles and Billups recovers at Green Bay 35. After 3 plays, McJulien punts 33 yards to Vikings' 35. After 3 plays, Newsome punts 52 yards for touchback. After 3 plays, McJulien punts and Parker returns 10 yards to Green Bay 48. Vikings drive to Packers' 9 where Reveiz kicks 26-yard field goal at 10:20.

Sept. 13, 1992—Cincinnati 24, Los Angeles Raiders 21, at Cincinnati. Raiders win toss. Land returns kickoff 13 yards but fumbles at Los Angeles' 20; ball recovered by Bengals' Bennett at Raiders' 21. After 1 play, Breech kicks 34-yard field goal at 1:01.

Sept. 20, 1992—Houston 23, Kansas City 20, at Houston. Chiefs win toss. Carter returns kickoff 25 yards to Kansas City 28. On third play of drive, Birden fumbles at Kansas City 34; ball recovered by Houston's D. Smith at Chiefs' 23. After one play, Del Greco kicks 39-yard field goal at 1:55.

Oct. 11, 1992—Indianapolis 6, New York Jets 3, at Indianapolis. Colts win toss. Verdin returns kickoff 33 yards to Colts' 36. Colts drive to Jets' 30 where Biasucci kicks 47-yard field goal at 3:01.

Nov. 8, 1992—Cincinnati 31, Chicago 28, at Chicago. Bears win toss. Lewis returns kickoff 22 yards to Chicago's 29. Bears drive to Chicago's 46 where Gardocki punts; fair catch by Wright at the Cincinnati 17. Bengals drive to Bears' 18 where Breech kicks 36-yard field goal at 8:39.

Nov. 15, 1992—New England 37, Indianapolis 34, at Indianapolis. Colts win toss. Verdin returns kickoff 10 yards to Colts' 20; holding penalty brings ball back to Colts' 10. After two plays, Henderson intercepts pass at Colts' 38 and returns it 9 yards to the 29. In three plays, Patriots drive to 1 where Baumann kicks 18-yard field goal at 3:25.

Nov. 29, 1992—Indianapolis 16, Buffalo 13, at Indianapolis. Colts win toss. Verdin returns kickoff 24 yards to Colts' 22. Colts drive to Buffalo 22 where Biasucci kicks 40-yard field goal at 3:51.

*Nov. 30, 1992—Seattle 16, Denver 13, at Seattle. Seahawks win toss. Daluiso kicks through end zone for touchback. After three plays, Tuten punts 53 yards to Denver 18 where Marshall returns for no gain. After three plays, Rodriguez punts 29 yards to Seattle 45 where Warren signals fair catch. Seahawks drive to

Denver 15 where Kasay's 33-yard field goal attempt misses. Broncos take over at Denver 20. After three plays, Rodriguez punts 43 yards to Seattle 38 where Warren signals for fair catch. After four plays, Tuten punts 39 yards to Denver 4 where Daniels downs punt. After three plays, Rodriguez punts 46 yards to Denver 48 where Warren returns 10 yards to the 38. Seahawks drive to Denver 14 where Kasay kicks 32-yard field goal at 11:10.

Dec. 13, 1992—Philadelphia 20, Seattle 17, at Seattle. Eagles win toss. Sydner returns kick 12 yards to Eagles' 16; illegal block penalty brings ball back to 8. Eagles drive to Philadelphia 45 where Feagles punts for a touchback. After 6 plays, Tuten punts 45 yards to Philadelphia 22 where Sydner returns 7 yards to 29. After 6 plays, Feagles punts 44 yards to Seattle 26 where Warren returns 5 yards to 31. After 5 plays, Tuten punts 32 yards to Philadelphia 20 where Sydner signals for fair catch. Eagles drive to Seattle 27 where Ruzek kicks 44-yard field goal with no time remaining.

Dec. 27, 1992—Miami 16, New England 13, at New England. Patriots win toss. Lockwood returns kickoff 15 yards to Patriots' 21. After three plays, McCarthy punts 39 yards to Miami 33 where Miller returns 2 yards to the 35. Miami drives to New England 18 where Stoyanovich kicks 35-yard field goal at 8:17.

Sept. 12, 1993—Detroit 19, New England 16, at New England. Patriots win toss. Patriots begin at 20. After 3 plays, Saxon returns 42 yards to Detroit 29 where Gray returns 12 yards to the 41. After 3 plays, Arnold punts 41 yards to New England 12 where Brown returns 16 yards to the 28. Patriots drive to Detroit 44 where Saxon punts into the end zone for a touchback. Detroit drives to New England 20 where Hanson kicks 38-yard field goal at 11:04.

Nov. 7, 1993—Buffalo 13, New England 10, at New England. Patriots win toss. T. Brown returns kickoff 27 yards to Patriots 30. Patriots drive to Buffalo 48 where Bills take over on downs. Bills drive to New England 25 where Metzelaars fumbles, and C. Brown recovers. After 3 plays, Saxon punts 46 yards to Buffalo 24 where Copeland returns 11 yards to the 35. Bills drive to New England 14 where Christie kicks 32-yard field goal at 9:22.

Dec. 19, 1993—Phoenix 30, Seattle 27, at Seattle. Cardinals win toss. Bailey returns kickoff 14 yards to Cardinals 20. Cardinals drive to Seattle 23 where Davis kicks 41-yard field goal at 6:45.

Jan. 2, 1994—Dallas 16, New York Giants 13, at New York. Giants win toss. Meggett returns kickoff 19 yards to Giants 19. After 6 plays, Horan punts 45 yards to Cowboys 25 where Widmer downs punt. Cowboys drive to Giants' 23 where Murray kicks 41-yard field goal at 10:44.

Jan. 2, 1994—New England 33, Miami 27, at New England. Dolphins win toss. McDuffie returns kickoff 21 yards to Miami 27. After 3 plays, Hatcher punts 43 yards to New England 29 where Harris returns 6 yards to the 35. After 2 plays, Brown intercepts pass from Bledsoe and returns 3 yards to Miami 49. After 3 plays, Hatcher punts 37 yards to New England 14 where Harris returns 18 yards to the 32. After 2 plays, Bledsoe passes 36 yards to Timpson for touchdown at 4:44.

Jan. 2, 1994—Los Angeles Raiders 33, Denver 30, at Los Angeles. Broncos win toss. Delpino returns kickoff 12 yards to Denver 25. Broncos drive to Los Angeles 22 where Elam's 40-yard field goal attempt is wide left. Raiders drive to Denver 29 where Jaeger kicks 47-yard field goal at 7:10.

*Jan. 3, 1994—Philadelphia 37, San Francisco 34, at San Francisco. 49ers win toss. Walker returns kickoff, 19 yards to San Francisco 27. 49ers drive to Philadelphia 14 where Cofer misses 32-yard field goal. Eagles start at their 20-yard line, and, after 3 plays, Feagles punts 48 yards to San Francisco 36 where Carter fumbles and 49ers recover. After 7 plays, Wilmsmeyer punts 57 yards to Philadelphia 6 where Sikahema returns 16 yards to the 22. Eagles drive to San Francisco 10 where Ruzek kicks 28-yard field goal with no time remaining.

*indicates Monday night game
#indicates Thursday night game

POSTSEASON

Dec. 28, 1958—Baltimore 23, New York Giants 17, at New York in NFL Championship Game. Giants win toss. Maynard returns kickoff to Giants' 20. Chandler punts and Taseff returns one yard to Colts' 20. Colts win at 8:15 on a 1-yard run by Ameche.

Dec. 23, 1962—Dallas Texans 20, Houston Oilers 17, at Houston in AFL Championship Game. Texans win toss and kick off. Jancik returns kickoff to Oilers' 33. Norton punts and Jackson makes fair catch on Texans' 22. Wilson punts and Jancik makes fair catch on Oilers' 45. Robinson intercepts Blanda's pass and returns 13 yards to Oilers' 47. Wilson's punt rolls dead at Oilers' 12. Hull intercepts Blanda's pass and returns 23 yards to midfield. Texans win at 17:54 on a 25-yard field goal by Brooker.

Dec. 26, 1965—Green Bay 13, Baltimore 10, at Green Bay in NFL Divisional Playoff Game. Packers win toss. Moore returns kickoff to Packers' 22. Chandler punts and Haymond returns nine yards to Colts' 41. Gilburg punts and Wood makes fair catch at Packers' 21. Chandler punts and Haymond returns one yard to Colts' 41. Michaels misses 47-yard field goal. Packers win at 13:39 on 25-yard field goal by Chandler.

Dec. 25, 1971—Miami 27, Kansas City 24, at Kansas City in AFC Divisional Playoff Game. Chiefs win toss. Podolak, after a lateral from Buchanan, returns kickoff to Chiefs' 46. Stenerud's 42-yard field goal is blocked. Seiple punts and Podolak makes fair catch at Chiefs' 17. Wilson punts and Scott returns 18 yards to Dolphins' 39. Yepremian misses 62-yard field goal. Scott intercepts Dawson's pass and returns 13 yards to Dolphins' 46. Seiple punts and Podolak loses one yard to Chiefs' 15. Wilson punts and Scott makes fair catch on Dolphins' 30. Dolphins win at 22:40 on a 37-yard field goal by Yepremian.

Dec. 24, 1977—Oakland 37, Baltimore 31, at Baltimore in AFC Divisional Play-off Game. Colts win toss. Raiders start on own 42 following a punt late in the first overtime. Oakland works way into field-goal range on Stabler's 19-yard pass to Branch at Colts' 26. Four plays later, on the second play of the second overtime, Stabler hits Casper with a 10-yard touchdown pass at 15:43.

Jan. 2, 1982—San Diego 41, Miami 38, at Miami in AFC Divisional Playoff Game. Chargers win toss. San Diego drives from its 13 to Miami 8. On second-and-goal, Benirschke misses 27-yard field goal attempt wide left at 9:15. Miami has the ball twice and San Diego twice more before the Dolphins get their third possession. Miami drives from the San Diego 46 to Chargers' 17 and on fourth-and-two, von Schamann's 34-yard field goal attempt is blocked by San Diego's Winslow after 11:27. Fouts then completes four of five passes, including a 39-yarder to Joiner that puts the ball on Dolphins' 10. On first down, Benirschke kicks a 29-yard field goal at 13:52. San Diego's winning drive covered 74 yards in six plays.

Jan. 3, 1987—Cleveland 23, New York Jets 20, at Cleveland in AFC Divisional Playoff Game. Jets win toss. Jets' punt downed at Browns' 26. Moseley's 23-yard field goal attempt is wide right. Teams trade punts. Jets' second punt downed at Browns' 31. First overtime period expires eight plays later with Browns in possession at Jets' 42. Moseley kicks 27-yard field goal four plays into second overtime at 17:02.

Jan. 11, 1987—Denver 23, Cleveland 20, at Cleveland in AFC Championship Game. Browns win toss. Broncos hold Browns on four downs. Browns' punt returned four yards to Denver's 25. Elway completes 22- and 28-yard passes to set up Karlis's 33-yard field goal nine plays into drive at 5:38.

Jan. 3, 1988—Houston 23, Seattle 20, at Houston in AFC Wild Card Game. Seahawks win toss. Rodriguez punts to K. Johnson who returns one yard to Houston 15. Zendejas kicks 32-yard field goal 12 plays later at 8:05.

Dec. 31, 1989—Pittsburgh 26, Houston 23, at Houston in AFC Wild Card Playoff Game. Steelers win toss. Steelers punt to Oilers. Oilers' fumble recovered by Woodson and returned three yards. Four plays and 13 yards later, Anderson kicks a 50-yard field goal at 3:26.

Jan. 7, 1990—Los Angeles Rams 19, New York Giants 13, at New York in NFC Wild Card Game. Rams win toss. Everett completes two passes to move ball to Giants' 48. White called for pass interference; ball spotted on Giants' 25. Everett hits Anderson with a 30-yard touchdown pass at 1:06.

Jan. 3, 1993—Buffalo 41, Houston 38, at Buffalo in AFC Wild Card Game. Houston wins toss. Oilers begin at 20. After 2 plays, Moon's pass is intercepted by Odomes who returns ball 2 yards to Houston 35. After 2 plays, Christie kicks 32-yard field goal at 3:06.

Jan. 8, 1994—Kansas City 27, Pittsburgh 24, at Kansas City. Kansas City wins toss. Hughes returns kickoff 20 yards to Kansas City 25. After 3 plays, Barker punts 48 yards to Pittsburgh 18 where Woodson returns 8 yards to the 26. After 6 plays, Royals punts 30 yards to Kansas City 20. Kansas City drives to Pittsburgh 14 where Lowery kicks 32-yard field goal at 11:03.

NFL POSTSEASON OVERTIME GAMES
(BY LENGTH OF GAME)

Date	Game	Time
Dec. 25, 1971	Miami 27, KANSAS CITY 24	82:40
Dec. 23, 1962	Dallas Texans 20, HOUSTON 17	77:54
Jan. 3, 1987	CLEVELAND 23, New York Jets 20	77:02
Dec. 24, 1977	Oakland 37, BALTIMORE 31	75:43
Jan. 2, 1982	San Diego 41, MIAMI 38	73:52
Dec. 26, 1965	GREEN BAY 13, Baltimore 10	73:39
Jan. 8, 1994	KANSAS CITY 27, Pittsburgh 24	71:03
Dec. 28, 1958	Baltimore 23, N.Y. GIANTS 17	68:15
Jan. 3, 1988	HOUSTON 23, Seattle 20	68:05
Jan. 11, 1987	Denver 23, CLEVELAND 20	65:38
Dec. 31, 1989	Pittsburgh 26, HOUSTON 23	63:26
Jan. 7, 1990	Los Angeles Rams 19, N.Y. GIANTS 13	61:06

Home team in CAPS

OVERTIME WON-LOST RECORDS, 1974-1993
(REGULAR SEASON)

AFC	W	L	T
Buffalo	9	4	0
Cincinnati	10	5	0
Cleveland	11	8	1
Denver	11	8	2
Houston	6	10	0
Indianapolis	6	5	1
Kansas City	4	6	2
Los Angeles Raiders	10	6	0
Miami	7	11	1
New England	6	13	0
New York Jets	8	6	2
Pittsburgh	7	3	1
San Diego	7	9	0
Seattle	4	7	0

NFC	W	L	T
Atlanta	5	7	1
Chicago	9	9	0
Dallas	7	4	0
Detroit	6	7	1
Green Bay	5	8	4
Los Angeles Rams	5	5	1
Minnesota	9	7	2
New Orleans	2	6	0
New York Giants	6	7	1
Philadelphia	6	8	2
Phoenix	4	4	2
San Francisco	4	5	1
Tampa Bay	5	7	1
Washington	9	3	0

OVERTIME GAMES BY YEAR
(REGULAR SEASON)

1993-7	1988- 9	1983-19	1978-11
1992-10	1987-13	1982- 4	1977- 6
1991-15	1986-16	1981-10	1976- 5
1990-10	1985-10	1980-13	1975- 9
1989-11	1984- 9	1979-12	1974- 2

OVERTIME GAME SUMMARY—1974-1993

There have been 201 overtime games in regular-season play since the rule was adopted in 1974 (7 in 1993 season). Breakdown follows:

150 (6) times both teams had at least one possession (75%)
  51 (1) times the team which won the toss drove for winning score
      (36 FG, 15 TD) (25%)
  94 (1) times the team which won the toss won the game (47%)
  94 (6) times the team which lost the toss won the game (47%)
135 (6) games were decided by a field goal (67%)
  52 (1) games were decided by a touchdown (26%)
   1 (0) game was decided by a safety (.5%)
  13 (0) games ended tied (6.5%). Last time: Nov. 19, 1989, Cleveland 10, Kansas City 10, at Cleveland

Note: The number in parentheses represents the 1993 season total in each category.

MOST OVERTIME GAMES, SEASON

5   Green Bay Packers, 1983
4   Denver Broncos, 1985
4   Cleveland Browns, 1989
3   By many teams, last time: New England Patriots, 1993

LONGEST CONSECUTIVE GAME STREAKS WITHOUT OVERTIME (Current)

60   Tampa Bay Buccaneers (last OT game, 9/30/90 vs. Minnesota)
60   Los Angeles Rams (last OT game, 10/7/90 vs. Cincinnati)
41   Cleveland Browns (last OT game, 10/20/91 vs. San Diego)
(Record: 110, Phoenix Cardinals, 12/7/86-12/19/93)

SHORTEST OVERTIME GAMES

0:21   (Chicago 23, Detroit 17; 11/27/80)—only kickoff return for TD
0:30   (Baltimore 29, New England 23; 9/4/83)
0:55   (New York Giants 16, Philadelphia 10; 9/29/85)

There have been 13 overtime postseason games dating back to 1958. In 12 cases, both teams had at least one possession. Last time: 1/8/94, Kansas City 27, Pittsburgh 24.

OVERTIME GAMES

LONGEST OVERTIME GAMES
(All Postseason Games)
22:40 Miami 27, Kansas City 24; 12/25/71
17:54 Dallas Texans 20, Houston 17; 12/23/62
17:02 Cleveland 23, New York Jets 20; 1/3/87

OVERTIME SCORING SUMMARY
135 were decided by a field goal
 22 were decided by a touchdown pass
 17 were decided by a touchdown run
  5 were decided by interceptions (Atlanta 40, New Orleans 34, 9/2/79; Atlanta 47, Green Bay 41, 11/27/83; New York Giants 16, Philadelphia 10, 9/29/85; Indianapolis 23, Cleveland 17, 12/10/89; Cleveland 30, San Diego 24, 10/20/91)
  2 were decided on a fake field goal/touchdown pass (Minnesota 22, Chicago 16, 10/16/77; Cleveland 23, Minnesota 17, 12/17/89)
  1 was decided by a kickoff return (Chicago 23, Detroit 17, 11/27/80)
  1 was decided by a fumble recovery (Baltimore 29, New England 23, 9/4/83)
  1 was decided on a fake field goal/touchdown run (Los Angeles Rams 27, Minnesota 21, 12/2/79)
  1 was decided on a blocked field goal (Denver 30, San Diego 24, 11/17/85)
  1 was decided on a blocked field goal/recovery by kicker (Green Bay 12, Chicago 6, 9/7/80)
  1 was decided on a blocked field goal/recovery by kicking team (Philadelphia 23, New York Giants 17, 11/20/88)
  1 was decided by a safety (Minnesota 23, Los Angeles Rams 21, 11/5/89)
 13 ended tied

OVERTIME RECORDS
Longest Touchdown Pass
99 Yards — Ron Jaworski to Mike Quick, Philadelphia 23, Atlanta 17 (11/10/85)
50 Yards — Tommy Kramer to Ahmad Rashad, Minnesota 27, Green Bay 21 (9/23/79)
50 Yards — Jim Harbaugh to Neal Anderson, Chicago 23, Detroit 17 (12/2/90)
Longest Touchdown Run
60 Yards — Herschel Walker, Dallas 23, New England 17 (11/15/87)
42 Yards — Eric Dickerson, Los Angeles Rams 26, Tampa Bay 20 (10/5/86)
28 Yards — Marcus Allen, Los Angeles Raiders 37, San Diego 31 (11/20/86)
Longest Field Goal
51 Yards — Greg Davis, New England 23, Indianapolis 20 (10/29/89)
50 Yards — Morten Andersen, New Orleans 20, Philadelphia 17 (12/11/83); Norm Johnson, Atlanta 23, New Orleans 20 (11/24/91)
48 Yards — Eddie Murray, Detroit 27, Atlanta 24 (9/9/84); Mark Moseley, Washington 30, New York Giants 27 (11/15/81)
Longest Touchdown Plays
99 Yards — (Pass) Ron Jaworski to Mike Quick, Philadelphia 23, Atlanta 17 (11/10/85)
60 Yards — (Blocked field goal return) Louis Wright, Denver 30, San Diego 24 (11/17/85)
 (Run) Herschel Walker, Dallas 23, New England 17 (11/15/87)
58 Yards — (Interception return) Mike Prior, Indianapolis 23, Cleveland 17 (12/10/89)

NFL PAID ATTENDANCE

For detailed 1993 attendance, see page 217.

Year	Regular Season		Average	Postseason	Total
1993	#13,966,843	(224 games)	#62,352	814,607 (12)	14,781,450
1992	13,828,887	(224 games)	61,736	815,910 (12)	14,644,797
1991	13,841,459	(224 games)	61,792	813,247 (12)	14,654,706
1990	13,959,896	(224 games)	62,321	847,543 (12)	14,807,439
1989	13,625,662	(224 games)	60,829	685,771 (10)	14,311,433
1988	13,539,848	(224 games)	60,446	658,317 (10)	14,198,165
1987	*11,406,166	(210 games)	54,315	656,977 (10)	12,063,143
1986	13,588,551	(224 games)	60,663	734,002 (10)	14,322,553
1985	13,345,047	(224 games)	59,567	710,768 (10)	14,055,815
1984	13,398,112	(224 games)	59,813	665,194 (10)	14,063,306
1983	13,277,222	(224 games)	59,273	675,513 (10)	13,952,735
1982	**7,367,438	(126 games)	58,472	1,033,153 (16)	8,400,591
1981	13,606,990	(224 games)	60,745	637,763 (10)	14,244,753
1980	13,392,230	(224 games)	59,787	624,430 (10)	14,016,660
1979	13,182,039	(224 games)	58,848	630,326 (10)	13,812,365
1978	12,771,800	(224 games)	57,017	624,388 (10)	13,396,188
1977	11,018,632	(196 games)	56,218	534,925 (8)	11,553,557
1976	11,070,543	(196 games)	56,482	492,884 (8)	11,563,427
1975	10,213,193	(182 games)	56,116	475,919 (8)	10,689,112
1974	10,236,322	(182 games)	56,244	438,664 (8)	10,674,986
1973	10,730,933	(182 games)	58,961	525,433 (8)	11,256,366
1972	10,445,827	(182 games)	57,395	483,345 (8)	10,929,172
1971	10,076,035	(182 games)	55,363	483,891 (8)	10,559,926
1970	9,533,333	(182 games)	52,381	458,493 (8)	9,991,826
1969	6,096,127	(112 games) NFL	54,430	162,279 (3)	6,258,406
	2,843,373	(70 games) AFL	40,620	167,088 (3)	3,010,461
1968	5,882,313	(112 games) NFL	52,521	215,902 (3)	6,098,215
	2,635,004	(70 games) AFL	37,643	114,438 (2)	2,749,442
1967	5,938,924	(112 games) NFL	53,026	166,208 (3)	6,105,132
	2,295,697	(63 games) AFL	36,439	53,330 (1)	2,349,027
1966	5,337,044	(105 games) NFL	50,829	74,152 (1)	5,411,196
	2,160,369	(63 games) AFL	34,291	42,080 (1)	2,202,449
1965	4,634,021	(98 games) NFL	47,286	100,304 (2)	4,734,325
	1,782,384	(56 games) AFL	31,828	30,361 (1)	1,812,745
1964	4,563,049	(98 games) NFL	46,562	79,544 (1)	4,642,593
	1,447,875	(56 games) AFL	25,855	40,242 (1)	1,488,117
1963	4,163,643	(98 games) NFL	42,486	45,801 (1)	4,209,444
	1,208,697	(56 games) AFL	21,584	63,171 (2)	1,271,868
1962	4,003,421	(98 games) NFL	40,851	64,892 (1)	4,068,313
	1,147,302	(56 games) AFL	20,487	37,981 (1)	1,185,283
1961	3,986,159	(98 games) NFL	40,675	39,029 (1)	4,025,188
	1,002,657	(56 games) AFL	17,904	29,556 (1)	1,032,213
1960	3,128,296	(78 games) NFL	40,106	67,325 (1)	3,195,621
	926,156	(56 games) AFL	16,538	32,183 (1)	958,339
1959	3,140,000	(72 games)	43,617	57,545 (1)	3,107,545
1958	3,006,124	(72 games)	41,752	123,659 (2)	3,129,783
1957	2,836,318	(72 games)	39,393	119,579 (2)	2,955,897
1956	2,551,263	(72 games)	35,434	56,836 (1)	2,608,099
1955	2,521,836	(72 games)	35,026	85,693 (1)	2,607,529
1954	2,190,571	(72 games)	30,425	43,827 (1)	2,234,398
1953	2,164,585	(72 games)	30,064	54,577 (1)	2,219,162
1952	2,052,126	(72 games)	28,502	97,507 (2)	2,149,633
1951	1,913,019	(72 games)	26,570	57,522 (1)	1,970,541
1950	1,977,500	(78 games)	25,356	136,647 (3)	2,114,400
1949	1,391,735	(60 games)	23,196	27,980 (1)	1,419,715
1948	1,525,243	(60 games)	25,421	36,309 (1)	1,561,552
1947	1,837,437	(60 games)	30,624	66,268 (2)	1,903,705
1946	1,732,135	(55 games)	31,493	58,346 (1)	1,790,481
1945	1,270,401	(50 games)	25,408	32,178 (1)	1,302,579
1944	1,019,649	(50 games)	20,393	46,016 (1)	1,065,665
1943	969,128	(40 games)	24,228	71,315 (2)	1,040,443
1942	887,920	(55 games)	16,144	36,006 (1)	923,926
1941	1,108,615	(55 games)	20,157	55,870 (2)	1,164,485
1940	1,063,025	(55 games)	19,328	36,034 (1)	1,099,059
1939	1,071,200	(55 games)	19,476	32,279 (1)	1,103,479
1938	937,197	(55 games)	17,040	48,120 (1)	985,317
1937	963,039	(55 games)	17,510	15,878 (1)	978,917
1936	816,007	(54 games)	15,111	29,545 (1)	845,552
1935	638,178	(53 games)	12,041	15,000 (1)	653,178
1934	492,684	(60 games)	8,211	35,059 (1)	527,743

Record

*Players' 24-day strike reduced 224-game schedule to 210 games.
**Players' 57-day strike reduced 224-game schedule to 126 games.

NFL'S 10 BIGGEST ATTENDANCE WEEKENDS
(Paid Count)

Weekend	Games	Attedance
October 16-17, 1988	14	934,211
September 1-2, 1991	14	922,076
November 8-9, 1992	14	917,384
November 4-5, 1990	14	916,127
October 29-30, 1989	14	915,401
November 17-18, 1990	14	905,486
October 27-28, 1985	14	902,128
October 12-13, 1980	14	898,223
September 12-13, 1993	14	898,703
September 23-24, 1984	14	894,402

NFL'S 10 HIGHEST SCORING WEEKENDS

Point Total	Date	Weekend
761	October 16-17, 1983	7th
736	October 25-26, 1987	7th
732	November 9-10, 1980	10th
725	November 24, 27-28, 1983	13th
714	September 17-18, 1989	2nd
711	November 26, 29-30, 1987	12th
710	November 28, December 1-2, 1985	13th
696	October 2-3, 1983	5th
693	September 24-25, 1989	3rd
676	September 21-22, 1980	3rd

TOP 10 TELEVISED SPORTS EVENTS OF ALL-TIME

(Based on A.C. Nielsen Figures)

Program	Date	Network	Share	Rating
Super Bowl XVI	1/24/82	CBS	73.0	49.1
Super Bowl XVII	1/30/83	NBC	69.0	48.6
Winter Olympics	2/23/94	CBS	64.0	48.5
Super Bowl XX	1/26/86	NBC	70.0	48.3
Super Bowl XII	1/15/78	CBS	67.0	47.2
Super Bowl XIII	1/21/79	NBC	74.0	47.1
Super Bowl XVIII	1/22/84	CBS	71.0	46.4
Super Bowl XIX	1/20/85	ABC	63.0	46.4
Super Bowl XIV	1/20/80	CBS	67.0	46.3
Super Bowl XXI	1/25/87	CBS	66.0	45.8

TEN MOST WATCHED TV PROGRAMS & ESTIMATED TOTAL NUMBER OF VIEWERS

(Based on A.C. Nielsen Figures)

Program	Date	Network	*Total Viewers
Super Bowl XXVIII	Jan. 30, 1994	NBC	134,800,000
Super Bowl XXVII	Jan. 31, 1993	NBC	133,400,000
Super Bowl XX	Jan. 26, 1986	NBC	127,000,000
Winter Olympics	Feb. 23, 1994	CBS	126,686,000
Super Bowl XXI	Jan. 25, 1987	CDC	122,640,000
M*A*S*H (Special)	Feb. 28, 1983	CBS	121,624,000
Winter Olympics	Feb. 25, 1994	CBS	119,900,000
Super Bowl XXVI	Jan. 26, 1992	CBS	119,680,000
Super Bowl XIX	Jan. 20, 1985	ABC	115,936,000
Super Bowl XXII	Jan. 31, 1988	ABC	115,000,000

*Watched some portion of the broadcast

NFL'S 10 BIGGEST TEAM SINGLE-SEASON HOME ATTENDANCE TOTALS
(Paid Count)

Year	Club	Games	Attendance
1980	Detroit Lions	8	634,204
1988	Buffalo Bills	8	631,818
1991	Buffalo Bills	8	631,786
1992	Buffalo Bills	8	630,978
1989	Buffalo Bills	8	626,399
1989	Cleveland Browns	8	625,240
1993	Buffalo Bills	8	624,349
1988	Cleveland Browns	8	624,154
1980	Cleveland Browns	8	623,351
1990	Buffalo Bills	8	621,528

NUMBER-ONE DRAFT CHOICES

Season	Team	Player	Position	College
1994	Cincinnati	Dan Wilkinson	DT	Ohio State
1993	New England	Drew Bledsoe	QB	Washington State
1992	Indianapolis	Steve Emtman	DT	Washington
1991	Dallas	Russell Maryland	DT	Miami
1990	Indianapolis	Jeff George	QB	Illinois
1989	Dallas	Troy Aikman	QB	UCLA
1988	Atlanta	Aundray Bruce	LB	Auburn
1987	Tampa Bay	Vinny Testaverde	QB	Miami
1986	Tampa Bay	Bo Jackson	RB	Auburn
1985	Buffalo	Bruce Smith	DE	Virginia Tech
1984	New England	Irving Fryar	WR	Nebraska
1983	Baltimore	John Elway	QB	Stanford
1982	New England	Kenneth Sims	DT	Texas
1981	New Orleans	George Rogers	RB	South Carolina
1980	Detroit	Billy Sims	RB	Oklahoma
1979	Buffalo	Tom Cousineau	LB	Ohio State
1978	Houston	Earl Campbell	RB	Texas
1977	Tampa Bay	Ricky Bell	RB	Southern California
1976	Tampa Bay	Lee Roy Selmon	DE	Oklahoma
1975	Atlanta	Steve Bartkowski	QB	California
1974	Dallas	Ed Jones	DE	Tennessee State
1973	Houston	John Matuszak	DE	Tampa
1972	Buffalo	Walt Patulski	DE	Notre Dame
1971	New England	Jim Plunkett	QB	Stanford
1970	Pittsburgh	Terry Bradshaw	QB	Louisiana Tech
1969	Buffalo (AFL)	O.J. Simpson	RB	Southern California
1968	Minnesota	Ron Yary	T	Southern California
1967	Baltimore	Bubba Smith	DT	Michigan State
1966	Atlanta	Tommy Nobis	LB	Texas
	Miami (AFL)	Jim Grabowski	RB	Illinois
1965	New York Giants	Tucker Frederickson	RB	Auburn
	Houston (AFL)	Lawrence Elkins	E	Baylor
1964	San Francisco	Dave Parks	E	Texas Tech
	Boston (AFL)	Jack Concannon	QB	Boston College
1963	Los Angeles	Terry Baker	QB	Oregon State
	Kansas City (AFL)	Buck Buchanan	DT	Grambling
1962	Washington	Ernie Davis	RB	Syracuse
	Oakland (AFL)	Roman Gabriel	QB	North Carolina State
1961	Minnesota	Tommy Mason	RB	Tulane
	Buffalo (AFL)	Ken Rice	G	Auburn
1960	Los Angeles	Billy Cannon	RB	Louisiana State
	(AFL had no formal first pick)			
1959	Green Bay	Randy Duncan	QB	Iowa
1958	Chicago Cardinals	King Hill	QB	Rice
1957	Green Bay	Paul Hornung	HB	Notre Dame
1956	Pittsburgh	Gary Glick	DB	Colorado A&M
1955	Baltimore	George Shaw	QB	Oregon
1954	Cleveland	Bobby Garrett	QB	Stanford
1953	San Francisco	Harry Babcock	E	Georgia
1952	Los Angeles	Bill Wade	QB	Vanderbilt
1951	New York Giants	Kyle Rote	HB	Southern Methodist
1950	Detroit	Leon Hart	E	Notre Dame
1949	Philadelphia	Chuck Bednarik	C	Pennsylvania
1948	Washington	Harry Gilmer	QB	Alabama
1947	Chicago Bears	Bob Fenimore	HB	Oklahoma A&M
1946	Boston	Frank Dancewicz	QB	Notre Dame
1945	Chicago Cardinals	Charley Trippi	HB	Georgia
1944	Boston	Angelo Bertelli	QB	Notre Dame
1943	Detroit	Frank Sinkwich	HB	Georgia
1942	Pittsburgh	Bill Dudley	HB	Virginia
1941	Chicago Bears	Tom Harmon	HB	Michigan
1940	Chicago Cardinals	George Cafego	HB	Tennessee
1939	Chicago Cardinals	Ki Aldrich	C	Texas Christian
1938	Cleveland	Corbett Davis	FB	Indiana
1937	Philadelphia	Sam Francis	FB	Nebraska
1936	Philadelphia	Jay Berwanger	HB	Chicago

Note: From 1947 through 1958, the first selection in the draft was a Bonus pick, awarded to the winner of a random draw. That club, in turn, forfeited its last-round draft choice. The winner of the Bonus choice was eliminated from future draws. The system was abolished after 1958, by which time all clubs had received a Bonus choice.

FIRST-ROUND SELECTIONS

If club had no first-round selection, first player drafted is listed with round in parentheses.

ARIZONA CARDINALS

Year	Player, College, Position
1936	Jim Lawrence, Texas Christian, B
1937	Ray Buivid, Marquette, B
1938	Jack Robbins, Arkansas, B
1939	Charles (Ki) Aldrich, Texas Christian, C
1940	George Cafego, Tennessee, B
1941	John Kimbrough, Texas A&M, B
1942	Steve Lach, Duke, B
1943	Glenn Dobbs, Tulsa, B
1944	Pat Harder, Wisconsin, B
1945	Charley Trippi, Georgia, B
1946	Dub Jones, Louisiana State, B
1947	DeWitt (Tex) Coulter, Army, T
1948	Jim Spavital, Oklahoma A&M, B
1949	Bill Fischer, Notre Dame, G
1950	Jack Jennings, Ohio State, T (2)
1951	Jerry Groom, Notre Dame, C
1952	Ollie Matson, San Francisco, B
1953	Johnny Olszewski, California, B
1954	Lamar McHan, Arkansas, B
1955	Max Boydston, Oklahoma, E
1956	Joe Childress, Auburn, B
1957	Jerry Tubbs, Oklahoma, C
1958	King Hill, Rice, B
	John David Crow, Texas A&M, B
1959	Bill Stacy, Mississippi State, B
1960	George Izo, Notre Dame, QB
1961	Ken Rice, Auburn, T
1962	Fate Echols, Northwestern, DT
	Irv Goode, Kentucky, C
1963	Jerry Stovall, Louisiana State, S
	Don Brumm, Purdue, DE
1964	Ken Kortas, Louisville, DT
1965	Joe Namath, Alabama, QB
1966	Carl McAdams, Oklahoma, LB
1967	Dave Williams, Washington, WR
1968	MacArthur Lane, Utah State, RB
1969	Roger Wehrli, Missouri, DB
1970	Larry Stegent, Texas A&M, RB
1971	Norm Thompson, Utah, CB
1972	Bobby Moore, Oregon, RB-WR
1973	Dave Butz, Purdue, DT
1974	J.V. Cain, Colorado, TE
1975	Tim Gray, Texas A&M, DB
1976	Mike Dawson, Arizona, DT
1977	Steve Pisarkiewicz, Missouri, QB
1978	Steve Little, Arkansas, K
	Ken Greene, Washington State, DB
1979	Ottis Anderson, Miami, RB
1980	Curtis Greer, Michigan, DE
1981	E.J. Junior, Alabama, LB
1982	Luis Sharpe, UCLA, T
1983	Leonard Smith, McNeese State, DB
1984	Clyde Duncan, Tennessee, WR
1985	Freddie Joe Nunn, Mississippi, LB
1986	Anthony Bell, Michigan State, LB
1987	Kelly Stouffer, Colorado State, QB
1988	Ken Harvey, California, LB
1989	Eric Hill, Louisiana State, LB
	Joe Wolf, Boston College, G
1990	Anthony Thompson, Indiana, RB (2)
1991	Eric Swann, No College, DE
1992	Tony Sacca, Penn State, QB (2)
1993	Garrison Hearst, Georgia, RB
	Ernest Dye, South Carolina, T
1994	Jamir Miller, UCLA, LB

ATLANTA FALCONS

Year	Player, College, Position
1966	Tommy Nobis, Texas, LB
	Randy Johnson, Texas A&I, QB
1967	Leo Carroll, San Diego State, DE (2)
1968	Claude Humphrey, Tennessee State, DE
1969	George Kunz, Notre Dame, T
1970	John Small, Citadel, LB
1971	Joe Profit, Northeast Louisiana, RB
1972	Clarence Ellis, Notre Dame, DB
1973	Greg Marx, Notre Dame, DT (2)

Year	Player, College, Position
1974	Gerald Tinker, Kent State, WR (2)
1975	Steve Bartkowski, California, QB
1976	Bubba Bean, Texas A&M, RB
1977	Warren Bryant, Kentucky, T
	Wilson Faumuina, San Jose State, DT
1978	Mike Kenn, Michigan, T
1979	Don Smith, Miami, DE
1980	Junior Miller, Nebraska, TE
1981	Bobby Butler, Florida State, DB
1982	Gerald Riggs, Arizona State, RB
1983	Mike Pitts, Alabama, DE
1984	Rick Bryan, Oklahoma, DT
1985	Bill Fralic, Pittsburgh, T
1986	Tony Casillas, Oklahoma, NT
	Tim Green, Syracuse, LB
1987	Chris Miller, Oregon, QB
1988	Aundray Bruce, Auburn, LB
1989	Deion Sanders, Florida State, DB
	Shawn Collins, Northern Arizona, WR
1990	Steve Broussard, Washington State, RB
1991	Bruce Pickens, Nebraska, DB
	Mike Pritchard, Colorado, WR
1992	Bob Whitfield, Stanford, T
	Tony Smith, Southern Mississippi, RB
1993	Lincoln Kennedy, Washington, T
1994	Bert Emanuel, Rice, WR (2)

BUFFALO BILLS

Year	Player, College, Position
1960	Richie Lucas, Penn State, QB
1961	Ken Rice, Auburn, T
1962	Ernie Davis, Syracuse, RB
1963	Dave Behrman, Michigan State, C
1964	Carl Eller, Minnesota, DE
1965	Jim Davidson, Ohio State, T
1966	Mike Dennis, Mississippi, RB
1967	John Pitts, Arizona State, S
1968	Haven Moses, San Diego State, WR
1969	O.J. Simpson, Southern California, RB
1970	Al Cowlings, Southern California, DE
1971	J.D. Hill, Arizona State, WR
1972	Walt Patulski, Notre Dame, DE
1973	Paul Seymour, Michigan, TE
	Joe DeLamielleure, Michigan State, G
1974	Reuben Gant, Oklahoma State, TE
1975	Tom Ruud, Nebraska, LB
1976	Mario Clark, Oregon, DB
1977	Phil Dokes, Oklahoma State, DT
1978	Terry Miller, Oklahoma State, RB
1979	Tom Cousineau, Ohio State, LB
	Jerry Butler, Clemson, WR
1980	Jim Ritcher, North Carolina State, C
1981	Booker Moore, Penn State, RB
1982	Perry Tuttle, Clemson, WR
1983	Tony Hunter, Notre Dame, TE
	Jim Kelly, Miami, QB
1984	Greg Bell, Notre Dame, RB
1985	Bruce Smith, Virginia Tech, DE
	Derrick Burroughs, Memphis State, DB
1986	Ronnie Harmon, Iowa, RB
	Will Wolford, Vanderbilt, T
1987	Shane Conlan, Penn State, LB
1988	Thurman Thomas, Oklahoma State, RB (2)
1989	Don Beebe, Chadron, Neb., WR (3)
1990	James Williams, Fresno State, DB
1991	Henry Jones, Illinois, DB
1992	John Fina, Arizona, T
1993	Thomas Smith, North Carolina, DB
1994	Jeff Burris, Notre Dame, DB

CHICAGO BEARS

Year	Player, College, Position
1936	Joe Stydahar, West Virginia, T
1937	Les McDonald, Nebraska, E
1938	Joe Gray, Oregon State, B
1939	Sid Luckman, Columbia, QB
	Bill Osmanski, Holy Cross, B
1940	Clyde (Bulldog) Turner, Hardin-Simmons, C
1941	Tom Harmon, Michigan, B
	Norm Standlee, Stanford, B
	Don Scott, Ohio State, B
1942	Frankie Albert, Stanford, B
1943	Bob Steber, Missouri, B

Year	Player, College, Position
1944	Ray Evans, Kansas, B
1945	Don Lund, Michigan, B
1946	Johnny Lujack, Notre Dame, QB
1947	Bob Fenimore, Oklahoma State, B
	Don Kindt, Wisconsin, B
1948	Bobby Layne, Texas, QB
	Max Bumgardner, Texas, E
1949	Dick Harris, Texas, C
1950	Chuck Hunsinger, Florida, B
	Fred Morrison, Ohio State, B
1951	Bob Williams, Notre Dame, B
	Billy Stone, Bradley, B
	Gene Schroeder, Virginia, E
1952	Jim Dooley, Miami, B
1953	Billy Anderson, Compton (Calif.) J.C., B
1954	Stan Wallace, Illinois, B
1955	Ron Drzewiecki, Marquette, B
1956	Menan (Tex) Schriewer, Texas, E
1957	Earl Leggett, Louisiana State, T
1958	Chuck Howley, West Virginia, G
1959	Don Clark, Ohio State, B
1960	Roger Davis, Syracuse, G
1961	Mike Ditka, Pittsburgh, E
1962	Ronnie Bull, Baylor, RB
1963	Dave Behrman, Michigan State, C
1964	Dick Evey, Tennessee, DT
1965	Dick Butkus, Illinois, LB
	Gale Sayers, Kansas, RB
	Steve DeLong, Tennessee, T
1966	George Rice, Louisiana State, DT
1967	Loyd Phillips, Arkansas, DE
1968	Mike Hull, Southern California, RB
1969	Rufus Mayes, Ohio State, T
1970	George Farmer, UCLA, WR (3)
1971	Joe Moore, Missouri, RB
1972	Lionel Antoine, Southern Illinois, T
	Craig Clemons, Iowa, DB
1973	Wally Chambers, Eastern Kentucky, DE
1974	Waymond Bryant, Tennessee State, LB
	Dave Gallagher, Michigan, DT
1975	Walter Payton, Jackson State, RB
1976	Dennis Lick, Wisconsin, T
1977	Ted Albrecht, California, T
1978	Brad Shearer, Texas, DT (3)
1979	Dan Hampton, Arkansas, DT
	Al Harris, Arizona State, DE
1980	Otis Wilson, Louisville, LB
1981	Keith Van Horne, Southern California, T
1982	Jim McMahon, Brigham Young, QB
1983	Jim Covert, Pittsburgh, T
	Willie Gault, Tennessee, WR
1984	Wilber Marshall, Florida, LB
1985	William Perry, Clemson, DT
1986	Neal Anderson, Florida, RB
1987	Jim Harbaugh, Michigan, QB
1988	Brad Muster, Stanford, RB
	Wendell Davis, Louisiana State, WR
1989	Donnell Woolford, Clemson, DB
	Trace Armstrong, Florida, DE
1990	Mark Carrier, Southern California, DB
1991	Stan Thomas, Texas, T
1992	Alonzo Spellman, Ohio State, DE
1993	Curtis Conway, Southern California, WR
1994	John Thierry, Alcorn State, DE

CINCINNATI BENGALS

Year	Player, College, Position
1968	Bob Johnson, Tennessee, C
1969	Greg Cook, Cincinnati, QB
1970	Mike Reid, Penn State, DT
1971	Vernon Holland, Tennessee State, T
1972	Sherman White, California, DE
1973	Isaac Curtis, San Diego State, WR
1974	Bill Kollar, Montana State, DT
1975	Glenn Cameron, Florida, LB
1976	Billy Brooks, Oklahoma, WR
	Archie Griffin, Ohio State, RB
1977	Eddie Edwards, Miami, DT
	Wilson Whitley, Houston, DT
	Mike Cobb, Michigan State, TE
1978	Ross Browner, Notre Dame, DT
	Blair Bush, Washington, C
1979	Jack Thompson, Washington State, QB

FIRST-ROUND SELECTIONS

	Charles Alexander, Louisiana State, RB
1980	Anthony Muñoz, Southern California, T
1981	David Verser, Kansas, WR
1982	Glen Collins, Mississippi State, DE
1983	Dave Rimington, Nebraska, C
1984	Ricky Hunley, Arizona, LB
	Pete Koch, Maryland, DE
	Brian Blados, North Carolina, T
1985	Eddie Brown, Miami, WR
	Emanuel King, Alabama, LB
1986	Joe Kelly, Washington, LB
	Tim McGee, Tennessee, WR
1987	Jason Buck, Brigham Young, DE
1988	Rickey Dixon, Oklahoma, DB
1989	Eric Ball, UCLA, RB (2)
1990	James Francis, Baylor, LB
1991	Alfred Williams, Colorado, LB
1992	David Klingler, Houston, QB
	Darryl Williams, Miami, DB
1993	John Copeland, Alabama, DE
1994	Dan Wilkinson, Ohio State, DT

CLEVELAND BROWNS

Year	Player, College, Position
1950	Ken Carpenter, Oregon State, B
1951	Ken Konz, Louisiana State, B
1952	Bert Rechichar, Tennessee, DB
	Harry Agganis, Boston U., QB
1953	Doug Atkins, Tennessee, DE
1954	Bobby Garrett, Stanford, QB
	John Bauer, Illinois, G
1955	Kurt Burris, Oklahoma, C
1956	Preston Carpenter, Arkansas, B
1957	Jim Brown, Syracuse, RB
1958	Jim Shofner, Texas Christian, DB
1959	Rich Kreitling, Illinois, DE
1960	Jim Houston, Ohio State, DE
1961	Bobby Crespino, Mississippi, TE
1962	Gary Collins, Maryland, WR
	Leroy Jackson, Western Illinois, RB
1963	Tom Hutchinson, Kentucky, WR
1964	Paul Warfield, Ohio State, WR
1965	James Garcia, Purdue, T (2)
1966	Milt Morin, Massachusetts, TE
1967	Bob Matheson, Duke, LB
1968	Marvin Upshaw, Trinity, Tex., DT-DE
1969	Ron Johnson, Michigan, RB
1970	Mike Phipps, Purdue, QB
	Bob McKay, Texas, T
1971	Clarence Scott, Kansas State, CB
1972	Thom Darden, Michigan, DB
1973	Steve Holden, Arizona State, WR
	Pete Adams, Southern California, T
1974	Billy Corbett, Johnson C. Smith, T (2)
1975	Mack Mitchell, Houston, DE
1976	Mike Pruitt, Purdue, RB
1977	Robert Jackson, Texas A&M, LB
1978	Clay Matthews, Southern California, LB
	Ozzie Newsome, Alabama, TE
1979	Willis Adams, Houston, WR
1980	Charles White, Southern California, RB
1981	Hanford Dixon, Southern Mississippi, DB
1982	Chip Banks, Southern California, LB
1983	Ron Brown, Arizona State, WR (2)
1984	Don Rogers, UCLA, DB
1985	Greg Allen, Florida State, RB (2)
1986	Webster Slaughter, San Diego State, WR (2)
1987	Mike Junkin, Duke, LB
1988	Clifford Charlton, Florida, LB
1989	Eric Metcalf, Texas, RB
1990	Leroy Hoard, Michigan, RB (2)
1991	Eric Turner, UCLA, DB
1992	Tommy Vardell, Stanford, RB
1993	Steve Everitt, Michigan, C
1994	Antonio Langham, Alabama, DB
	Derrick Alexander, Michigan, WR

DALLAS COWBOYS

Year	Player, College, Position
1960	None
1961	Bob Lilly, Texas Christian, DT
1962	Sonny Gibbs, Texas Christian, QB (2)
1963	Lee Roy Jordan, Alabama, LB

1964	Scott Appleton, Texas, DT
1965	Craig Morton, California, QB
1966	John Niland, Iowa, G
1967	Phil Clark, Northwestern, DB (3)
1968	Dennis Homan, Alabama, WR
1969	Calvin Hill, Yale, RB
1970	Duane Thomas, West Texas State, RB
1971	Tody Smith, Southern California, DE
1972	Bill Thomas, Boston College, RB
1973	Billy Joe DuPree, Michigan State, TE
1974	Ed (Too Tall) Jones, Tennessee State, DE
	Charley Young, North Carolina State, RB
1975	Randy White, Maryland, LB
	Thomas Henderson, Langston, LB
1976	Aaron Kyle, Wyoming, DB
1977	Tony Dorsett, Pittsburgh, RB
1978	Larry Bethea, Michigan State, DE
1979	Robert Shaw, Tennessee, C
1980	Bill Roe, Colorado, LB (3)
1981	Howard Richards, Missouri, T
1982	Rod Hill, Kentucky State, DB
1983	Jim Jeffcoat, Arizona State, DE
1984	Billy Cannon, Jr., Texas A&M, LB
1985	Kevin Brooks, Michigan, DE
1986	Mike Sherrard, UCLA, WR
1987	Danny Noonan, Nebraska, DT
1988	Michael Irvin, Miami, WR
1989	Troy Aikman, UCLA, QB
1990	Emmitt Smith, Florida, RB
1991	Russell Maryland, Miami, DT
	Alvin Harper, Tennessee, WR
	Kelvin Pritchett, Mississippi, DT
1992	Kevin Smith, Texas A&M, DB
	Robert Jones, East Carolina, LB
1993	Kevin Williams, Miami, WR (2)
1994	Shante Carver, Arizona State, DE

DENVER BRONCOS

Year	Player, College, Position
1960	Roger LeClerc, Trinity, Conn., C
1961	Bob Gaiters, New Mexico State, RB
1962	Merlin Olsen, Utah State, DT
1963	Kermit Alexander, UCLA, CB
1964	Bob Brown, Nebraska, T
1965	Dick Butkus, Illinois, LB (2)
1966	Jerry Shay, Purdue, DT
1967	Floyd Little, Syracuse, RB
1968	Curley Culp, Arizona State, DE (2)
1969	Grady Cavness, Texas-El Paso, DB (2)
1970	Bob Anderson, Colorado, RB
1971	Marv Montgomery, Southern California, T
1972	Riley Odoms, Houston, TE
1973	Otis Armstrong, Purdue, RB
1974	Randy Gradishar, Ohio State, LB
1975	Louis Wright, San Jose State, DB
1976	Tom Glassic, Virginia, G
1977	Steve Schindler, Boston College, G
1978	Don Latimer, Miami, DT
1979	Kelvin Clark, Nebraska, T
1980	Rulon Jones, Utah State, DE (2)
1981	Dennis Smith, Southern California, DB
1982	Gerald Willhite, San Jose State, RB
1983	Chris Hinton, Northwestern, G
1984	Andre Townsend, Mississippi, DE (2)
1985	Steve Sewell, Oklahoma, RB
1986	Jim Juriga, Illinois, T (4)
1987	Ricky Nattiel, Florida, WR
1988	Ted Gregory, Syracuse, NT
1989	Steve Atwater, Arkansas, DB
1990	Alton Montgomery, Houston, DB (2)
1991	Mike Croel, Nebraska, LB
1992	Tommy Maddox, UCLA, QB
1993	Dan Williams, Toledo, DE
1994	Allen Aldridge, Houston, LB (2)

DETROIT LIONS

Year	Player, College, Position
1936	Sid Wagner, Michigan State, G
1937	Lloyd Cardwell, Nebraska, B
1938	Alex Wojciechowicz, Fordham, C
1939	John Pingel, Michigan State, B
1940	Doyle Nave, Southern California, B
1941	Jim Thomason, Texas A&M, B

1942	Bob Westfall, Michigan, B
1943	Frank Sinkwich, Georgia, B
1944	Otto Graham, Northwestern, B
1945	Frank Szymanski, Notre Dame, C
1946	Bill Dellastatious, Missouri, B
1947	Glenn Davis, Army, B
1948	Y.A. Tittle, Louisiana State, B
1949	John Rauch, Georgia, B
1950	Leon Hart, Notre Dame, E
	Joe Watson, Rice, C
1951	Dick Stanfel, San Francisco, G (2)
1952	Yale Lary, Texas A&M, B (3)
1953	Harley Sewell, Texas, G
1954	Dick Chapman, Rice, T
1955	Dave Middleton, Auburn, B
1956	Hopalong Cassady, Ohio State, B
1957	Bill Glass, Baylor, G
1958	Alex Karras, Iowa, T
1959	Nick Pietrosante, Notre Dame, B
1960	John Robinson, Louisiana State, S
1961	Danny LaRose, Missouri, T (2)
1962	John Hadl, Kansas, QB
1963	Daryl Sanders, Ohio State, T
1964	Pete Beathard, Southern California, QB
1965	Tom Nowatzke, Indiana, RB
1966	Nick Eddy, Notre Dame, RB (2)
1967	Mel Farr, UCLA, RB
1968	Greg Landry, Massachusetts, QB
	Earl McCullouch, Southern California, WR
1969	Altie Taylor, Utah State, RB (2)
1970	Steve Owens, Oklahoma, RB
1971	Bob Bell, Cincinnati, DT
1972	Herb Orvis, Colorado, DE
1973	Ernie Price, Texas A&I, DE
1974	Ed O'Neil, Penn State, LB
1975	Lynn Boden, South Dakota State, G
1976	James Hunter, Grambling, DB
	Lawrence Gaines, Wyoming, RB
1977	Walt Williams, New Mexico State, DB (2)
1978	Luther Bradley, Notre Dame, DB
1979	Keith Dorney, Penn State, T
1980	Billy Sims, Oklahoma, RB
1981	Mark Nichols, San Jose State, WR
1982	Jimmy Williams, Nebraska, LB
1983	James Jones, Florida, RB
1984	David Lewis, California, TE
1985	Lomas Brown, Florida, T
1986	Chuck Long, Iowa, QB
1987	Reggie Rogers, Washington, DE
1988	Bennie Blades, Miami, DB
1989	Barry Sanders, Oklahoma State, RB
1990	Andre Ware, Houston, QB
1991	Herman Moore, Virginia, WR
1992	Robert Porcher, South Carolina State, DE
1993	Ryan McNeil, Miami, DB (2)
1994	Johnnie Morton, Southern California, WR

GREEN BAY PACKERS

Year	Player, College, Position
1936	Russ Letlow, San Francisco, G
1937	Eddie Jankowski, Wisconsin, B
1938	Cecil Isbell, Purdue, B
1939	Larry Buhler, Minnesota, B
1940	Harold Van Every, Minnesota, B
1941	George Paskvan, Wisconsin, B
1942	Urban Odson, Minnesota, T
1943	Dick Wildung, Minnesota, T
1944	Merv Pregulman, Michigan, G
1945	Walt Schlinkman, Texas Tech, B
1946	Johnny (Strike) Strzykalski, Marquette, B
1947	Ernie Case, UCLA, B
1948	Earl (Jug) Girard, Wisconsin, B
1949	Stan Heath, Nevada, B
1950	Clayton Tonnemaker, Minnesota, C
1951	Bob Gain, Kentucky, T
1952	Babe Parilli, Kentucky, QB
1953	Al Carmichael, Southern California, B
1954	Art Hunter, Notre Dame, T
	Veryl Switzer, Kansas State, B
1955	Tom Bettis, Purdue, G
1956	Jack Losch, Miami, B
1957	Paul Hornung, Notre Dame, B
	Ron Kramer, Michigan, E

Year	Player, College, Position
1958	Dan Currie, Michigan State, C
1959	Randy Duncan, Iowa, B
1960	Tom Moore, Vanderbilt, RB
1961	Herb Adderley, Michigan State, CB
1962	Earl Gros, Louisiana State, RB
1963	Dave Robinson, Penn State, LB
1964	Lloyd Voss, Nebraska, DT
1965	Donny Anderson, Texas Tech, RB
	Lawrence Elkins, Baylor, E
1966	Jim Grabowski, Illinois, RB
	Gale Gillingham, Minnesota, T
1967	Bob Hyland, Boston College, C
	Don Horn, San Diego State, QB
1968	Fred Carr, Texas-El Paso, LB
	Bill Lueck, Arizona, G
1969	Rich Moore, Villanova, DT
1970	Mike McCoy, Notre Dame, DT
	Rich McGeorge, Elon, TE
1971	John Brockington, Ohio State, RB
1972	Willie Buchanon, San Diego State, DB
	Jerry Tagge, Nebraska, QB
1973	Barry Smith, Florida State, WR
1974	Barty Smith, Richmond, RB
1975	Bill Bain, Southern California, G (2)
1976	Mark Koncar, Colorado, T
1977	Mike Butler, Kansas, DE
	Ezra Johnson, Morris Brown, DE
1978	James Lofton, Stanford, WR
	John Anderson, Michigan, LB
1979	Eddie Lee Ivery, Georgia Tech, RB
1980	Bruce Clark, Penn State, DE
	George Cumby, Oklahoma, LB
1981	Rich Campbell, California, QB
1982	Ron Hallstrom, Iowa, G
1983	Tim Lewis, Pittsburgh, DB
1984	Alphonso Carreker, Florida State, DE
1985	Ken Ruettgers, Southern California, T
1986	Kenneth Davis, Texas Christian, RB (2)
1987	Brent Fullwood, Auburn, RB
1988	Sterling Sharpe, South Carolina, WR
1989	Tony Mandarich, Michigan State, T
1990	Tony Bennett, Mississippi, LB
	Darrell Thompson, Minnesota, RB
1991	Vinnie Clark, Ohio State, DB
1992	Terrell Buckley, Florida State, DB
1993	Wayne Simmons, Clemson, LB
	George Teague, Alabama, DB
1994	Aaron Taylor, Notre Dame, T

HOUSTON OILERS

Year	Player, College, Position
1960	Billy Cannon, Louisiana State, RB
1961	Mike Ditka, Pittsburgh, E
1962	Ray Jacobs, Howard Payne, DT
1963	Danny Brabham, Arkansas, LB
1964	Scott Appleton, Texas, DT
1965	Lawrence Elkins, Baylor, WR
1966	Tommy Nobis, Texas, LB
1967	George Webster, Michigan State, LB
	Tom Regner, Notre Dame, G
1968	Mac Haik, Mississippi, WR (2)
1969	Ron Pritchard, Arizona State, LB
1970	Doug Wilkerson, N. Carolina Central, G
1971	Dan Pastorini, Santa Clara, QB
1972	Greg Sampson, Stanford, DE
1973	John Matuszak, Tampa, DE
	George Amundson, Iowa State, RB
1974	Steve Manstedt, Nebraska, LB (4)
1975	Robert Brazile, Jackson State, LB
	Don Hardeman, Texas A&I, RB
1976	Mike Barber, Louisiana Tech, TE (2)
1977	Morris Towns, Missouri, T
1978	Earl Campbell, Texas, RB
1979	Mike Stensrud, Iowa State, DE (2)
1980	Angelo Fields, Michigan State, T (2)
1981	Michael Holston, Morgan State, WR (3)
1982	Mike Munchak, Penn State, G
1983	Bruce Matthews, Southern California, T
1984	Dean Steinkuhler, Nebraska, T
1985	Ray Childress, Texas A&M, DE
	Richard Johnson, Wisconsin, DB
1986	Jim Everett, Purdue, QB
1987	Alonzo Highsmith, Miami, RB
	Haywood Jeffires, North Carolina St., WR
1988	Lorenzo White, Michigan State, RB
1989	David Williams, Florida, T
1990	Lamar Lathon, Houston, LB
1991	Mike Dumas, Indiana, DB (2)
1992	Eddie Robinson, Alabama State, LB (2)
1993	Brad Hopkins, Illinois, T
1994	Henry Ford, Arkansas, DE

INDIANAPOLIS COLTS

Year	Player, College, Position
1953	Billy Vessels, Oklahoma, B
1954	Cotton Davidson, Baylor, B
1955	George Shaw, Oregon, B
	Alan Ameche, Wisconsin, FB
1956	Lenny Moore, Penn State, B
1957	Jim Parker, Ohio State, G
1958	Lenny Lyles, Louisville, B
1959	Jackie Burkett, Auburn, C
1960	Ron Mix, Southern California, T
1961	Tom Matte, Ohio State, RB
1962	Wendell Harris, Louisiana State, S
1963	Bob Vogel, Ohio State, T
1964	Marv Woodson, Indiana, CB
1965	Mike Curtis, Duke, LB
1966	Sam Ball, Kentucky, T
1967	Bubba Smith, Michigan State, DT
	Jim Detwiler, Michigan, RB
1968	John Williams, Minnesota, G
1969	Eddie Hinton, Oklahoma, WR
1970	Norman Bulaich, Texas Christian, RB
1971	Don McCauley, North Carolina, RB
	Leonard Dunlap, North Texas State, DB
1972	Tom Drougas, Oregon, T
1973	Bert Jones, Louisiana State, QB
	Joe Ehrmann, Syracuse, DT
1974	John Dutton, Nebraska, DE
	Roger Carr, Louisiana Tech, WR
1975	Ken Huff, North Carolina, G
1976	Ken Novak, Purdue, DT
1977	Randy Burke, Kentucky, WR
1978	Reese McCall, Auburn, TE
1979	Barry Krauss, Alabama, LB
1980	Curtis Dickey, Texas A&M, RB
	Derrick Hatchett, Texas, DB
1981	Randy McMillan, Pittsburgh, RB
	Donnell Thompson, North Carolina, DT
1982	Johnie Cooks, Mississippi State, LB
	Art Schlichter, Ohio State, QB
1983	John Elway, Stanford, QB
1984	Leonard Coleman, Vanderbilt, DB
	Ron Solt, Maryland, G
1985	Duane Bickett, Southern California, LB
1986	Jon Hand, Alabama, DE
1987	Cornelius Bennett, Alabama, LB
1988	Chris Chandler, Washington, QB (3)
1989	Andre Rison, Michigan State, WR
1990	Jeff George, Illinois, QB
1991	Shane Curry, Miami, DE (2)
1992	Steve Emtman, Washington, DT
	Quentin Coryatt, Texas A&M, LB
1993	Sean Dawkins, California, WR
1994	Marshall Faulk, San Diego State, RB
	Trev Alberts, Nebraska, LB

KANSAS CITY CHIEFS

Year	Player, College, Position
1960	Don Meredith, Southern Methodist, QB
1961	E.J. Holub, Texas Tech, C
1962	Ronnie Bull, Baylor, RB
1963	Buck Buchanan, Grambling, DT
	Ed Budde, Michigan State, G
1964	Pete Beathard, Southern California, QB
1965	Gale Sayers, Kansas, RB
1966	Aaron Brown, Minnesota, DE
1967	Gene Trosch, Miami, DE-DT
1968	Mo Moorman, Texas A&M, G
	George Daney, Texas-El Paso, G
1969	Jim Marsalis, Tennessee State, CB
1970	Sid Smith, Southern California, T
1971	Elmo Wright, Houston, WR
1972	Jeff Kinney, Nebraska, RB
1973	Gary Butler, Rice, TE (2)
1974	Woody Green, Arizona State, RB
1975	Elmore Stephens, Kentucky, TE (2)
1976	Rod Walters, Iowa, G
1977	Gary Green, Baylor, DB
1978	Art Still, Kentucky, DE
1979	Mike Bell, Colorado State, DE
	Steve Fuller, Clemson, QB
1980	Brad Budde, Southern California, G
1981	Willie Scott, South Carolina, TE
1982	Anthony Hancock, Tennessee, WR
1983	Todd Blackledge, Penn State, QB
1984	Bill Maas, Pittsburgh, DT
	John Alt, Iowa, T
1985	Ethan Horton, North Carolina, RB
1986	Brian Jozwiak, West Virginia, T
1987	Paul Palmer, Temple, RB
1988	Neil Smith, Nebraska, DE
1989	Derrick Thomas, Alabama, LB
1990	Percy Snow, Michigan State, LB
1991	Harvey Williams, Louisiana State, RB
1992	Dale Carter, Tennessee, DB
1993	Will Shields, Nebraska, G (3)
1994	Greg Hill, Texas A&M, RB

LOS ANGELES RAIDERS

Year	Player, College, Position
1960	Dale Hackbart, Wisconsin, CB
1961	Joe Rutgens, Illinois, DT
1962	Roman Gabriel, North Carolina State, QB
1963	George Wilson, Alabama, RB (6)
1964	Tony Lorick, Arizona State, RB
1965	Harry Schuh, Memphis State, T
1966	Rodger Bird, Kentucky, S
1967	Gene Upshaw, Texas A&I, G
1968	Eldridge Dickey, Tennessee State, QB
1969	Art Thoms, Syracuse, DT
1970	Raymond Chester, Morgan State, TE
1971	Jack Tatum, Ohio State, S
1972	Mike Siani, Villanova, WR
1973	Ray Guy, Southern Mississippi, P
1974	Henry Lawrence, Florida A&M, T
1975	Neal Colzie, Ohio State, DB
1976	Charles Philyaw, Texas Southern, DT (2)
1977	Mike Davis, Colorado, DB (2)
1978	Dave Browning, Washington, DE (2)
1979	Willie Jones, Florida State, DE (2)
1980	Marc Wilson, Brigham Young, QB
1981	Ted Watts, Texas Tech, DB
	Curt Marsh, Washington, T
1982	Marcus Allen, Southern California, RB
1983	Don Mosebar, Southern California, T
1984	Sean Jones, Northeastern, DE (2)
1985	Jessie Hester, Florida State, WR
1986	Bob Buczkowski, Pittsburgh, DE
1987	John Clay, Missouri, T
1988	Tim Brown, Notre Dame, WR
	Terry McDaniel, Tennessee, DB
	Scott Davis, Illinois, DE
1989	Jeff Francis, Tennessee, QB (6)
1990	Anthony Smith, Arizona, DE
1991	Todd Marinovich, Southern California, QB
1992	Chester McGlockton, Clemson, DE
1993	Patrick Bates, Texas A&M, DB
1994	Rob Fredrickson, Michigan State, LB

LOS ANGELES RAMS

Year	Player, College, Position
1937	Johnny Drake, Purdue, B
1938	Corbett Davis, Indiana, B
1939	Parker Hall, Mississippi, B
1940	Ollie Cordill, Rice, B
1941	Rudy Mucha, Washington, C
1942	Jack Wilson, Baylor, B
1943	Mike Holovak, Boston College, B
1944	Tony Butkovich, Illinois, B
1945	Elroy (Crazylegs) Hirsch, Wisconsin, B
1946	Emil Sitko, Notre Dame, B
1947	Herman Wedemeyer, St. Mary's, Calif., B
1948	Tom Keane, West Virginia, B
1949	Bobby Thomason, Virginia Military, B
1950	Ralph Pasquariello, Villanova, B
	Stan West, Oklahoma, G
1951	Bud McFadin, Texas, G

1952	Bill Wade, Vanderbilt, QB
	Bob Carey, Michigan State, E
1953	Donn Moomaw, UCLA, C
	Ed Barker, Washington State, E
1954	Ed Beatty, Cincinnati, C
1955	Larry Morris, Georgia Tech, C
1956	Joe Marconi, West Virginia, B
	Charles Horton, Vanderbilt, B
1957	Jon Arnett, Southern California, B
	Del Shofner, Baylor, E
1958	Lou Michaels, Kentucky, T
	Jim Phillips, Auburn, E
1959	Dick Bass, Pacific, B
	Paul Dickson, Baylor, T
1960	Billy Cannon, Louisiana State, RB
1961	Marlin McKeever, So. California, E-LB
1962	Roman Gabriel, North Carolina State, QB
	Merlin Olsen, Utah State, DT
1963	Terry Baker, Oregon State, QB
	Rufus Guthrie, Georgia Tech, G
1964	Bill Munson, Utah State, QB
1965	Clancy Williams, Washington State, CB
1966	Tom Mack, Michigan, G
1967	Willie Ellison, Texas Southern, RB (2)
1968	Gary Beban, UCLA, QB (2)
1969	Larry Smith, Florida, RB
	Jim Seymour, Notre Dame, WR
	Bob Klein, Southern California, TE
1970	Jack Reynolds, Tennessee, LB
1971	Isiah Robertson, Southern, LB
	Jack Youngblood, Florida, DE
1972	Jim Bertelsen, Texas, RB (2)
1973	Cullen Bryant, Colorado, DB (2)
1974	John Cappelletti, Penn State, RB
1975	Mike Fanning, Notre Dame, DT
	Dennis Harrah, Miami, T
	Doug France, Ohio State, T
1976	Kevin McLain, Colorado State, LB
1977	Bob Brudzinski, Ohio State, LB
1978	Elvis Peacock, Oklahoma, RB
1979	George Andrews, Nebraska, LB
	Kent Hill, Georgia Tech, T
1980	Johnnie Johnson, Texas, DB
1981	Mel Owens, Michigan, LB
1982	Barry Redden, Richmond, RB
1983	Eric Dickerson, Southern Methodist, RB
1984	Hal Stephens, East Carolina, DE (5)
1985	Jerry Gray, Texas, DB
1986	Mike Schad, Queen's University, Canada, T
1987	Donald Evans, Winston-Salem, DE (2)
1988	Gaston Green, UCLA, RB
	Aaron Cox, Arizona State, WR
1989	Bill Hawkins, Miami, DE
	Cleveland Gary, Miami, RB
1990	Bern Brostek, Washington, C
1991	Todd Lyght, Notre Dame, DB
1992	Sean Gilbert, Pittsburgh, DE
1993	Jerome Bettis, Notre Dame, RB
1994	Wayne Gandy, Auburn, T

MIAMI DOLPHINS

Year	Player, College, Position
1966	Jim Grabowski, Illinois, RB
	Rick Norton, Kentucky, QB
1967	Bob Griese, Purdue, QB
1968	Larry Csonka, Syracuse, RB
	Doug Crusan, Indiana, T
1969	Bill Stanfill, Georgia, DE
1970	Jim Mandich, Michigan, TE (2)
1971	Otto Stowe, Iowa State, WR (2)
1972	Mike Kadish, Notre Dame, DT
1973	Chuck Bradley, Oregon, C (2)
1974	Donald Reese, Jackson State, DE
1975	Darryl Carlton, Tampa, T
1976	Larry Gordon, Arizona State, LB
	Kim Bokamper, San Jose State, LB
1977	A.J. Duhe, Louisiana State, DT
1978	Guy Benjamin, Stanford, QB (2)
1979	Jon Giesler, Michigan, T
1980	Don McNeal, Alabama, DB
1981	David Overstreet, Oklahoma, RB
1982	Roy Foster, Southern California, G
1983	Dan Marino, Pittsburgh, QB

1984	Jackie Shipp, Oklahoma, LB
1985	Lorenzo Hampton, Florida, RB
1986	John Offerdahl, Western Michigan, LB (2)
1987	John Bosa, Boston College, DE
1988	Eric Kumerow, Ohio State, DE
1989	Sammie Smith, Florida State, RB
	Louis Oliver, Florida, DB
1990	Richmond Webb, Texas A&M, T
1991	Randal Hill, Miami, WR
1992	Troy Vincent, Wisconsin, DB
	Marco Coleman, Georgia Tech, LB
1993	O.J. McDuffie, Penn State, WR
1994	Tim Bowens, Mississippi, DT

MINNESOTA VIKINGS

Year	Player, College, Position
1961	Tommy Mason, Tulane, RB
1962	Bill Miller, Miami, WR (3)
1963	Jim Dunaway, Mississippi, T
1964	Carl Eller, Minnesota, DE
1965	Jack Snow, Notre Dame, WR
1966	Jerry Shay, Purdue, DT
1967	Clint Jones, Michigan State, RB
	Gene Washington, Michigan State, WR
	Alan Page, Notre Dame, DT
1968	Ron Yary, Southern California, T
1969	Ed White, California, G (2)
1970	John Ward, Oklahoma State, DT
1971	Leo Hayden, Ohio State, RB
1972	Jeff Siemon, Stanford, LB
1973	Chuck Foreman, Miami, RB
1974	Fred McNeill, UCLA, LB
	Steve Riley, Southern California, T
1975	Mark Mullaney, Colorado State, DE
1976	James White, Oklahoma State, DT
1977	Tommy Kramer, Rice, QB
1978	Randy Holloway, Pittsburgh, DE
1979	Ted Brown, North Carolina State, RB
1980	Doug Martin, Washington, DT
1981	Mardye McDole, Mississippi State, WR (2)
1982	Darrin Nelson, Stanford, RB
1983	Joey Browner, Southern California, DB
1984	Keith Millard, Washington State, DE
1985	Chris Doleman, Pittsburgh, LB
1986	Gerald Robinson, Auburn, DE
1987	D.J. Dozier, Penn State, RB
1988	Randall McDaniel, Arizona State, G
1989	David Braxton, Wake Forest, LB (2)
1990	Mike Jones, Texas A&M, TE (3)
1991	Carlos Jenkins, Michigan State, LB (3)
1992	Robert Harris, Southern University, DE (2)
1993	Robert Smith, Ohio State, RB
1994	DeWayne Washington, N. Carolina St., DB
	Todd Steussie, California, T

NEW ENGLAND PATRIOTS

Year	Player, College, Position
1960	Ron Burton, Northwestern, RB
1961	Tommy Mason, Tulane, RB
1962	Gary Collins, Maryland, WR
1963	Art Graham, Boston College, WR
1964	Jack Concannon, Boston College, QB
1965	Jerry Rush, Michigan State, DE
1966	Karl Singer, Purdue, T
1967	John Charles, Purdue, S
1968	Dennis Byrd, North Carolina State, DE
1969	Ron Sellers, Florida State, WR
1970	Phil Olsen, Utah State, DE
1971	Jim Plunkett, Stanford, QB
1972	Tom Reynolds, San Diego State, WR (2)
1973	John Hannah, Alabama, G
	Sam Cunningham, So. California, RB
	Darryl Slingley, Purdue, WR
1974	Steve Corbett, Boston College, G (2)
1975	Russ Francis, Oregon, TE
1976	Mike Haynes, Arizona State, DB
	Pete Brock, Colorado, C
	Tim Fox, Ohio State, DB
1977	Raymond Clayborn, Texas, DB
	Stanley Morgan, Tennessee, WR
1978	Bob Cryder, Alabama, G
1979	Rick Sanford, South Carolina, DB
1980	Roland James, Tennessee, DB

	Vagas Ferguson, Notre Dame, RB
1981	Brian Holloway, Stanford, T
1982	Kenneth Sims, Texas, DT
	Lester Williams, Miami, DT
1983	Tony Eason, Illinois, QB
1984	Irving Fryar, Nebraska, WR
1985	Trevor Matich, Brigham Young, C
1986	Reggie Dupard, Southern Methodist, RB
1987	Bruce Armstrong, Louisville, T
1988	John Stephens, Northwestern St., La., RB
1989	Hart Lee Dykes, Oklahoma State, WR
1990	Chris Singleton, Arizona, LB
	Ray Agnew, North Carolina State, DE
1991	Pat Harlow, Southern California, T
	Leonard Russell, Arizona State, RB
1992	Eugene Chung, Virginia Tech, T
1993	Drew Bledsoe, Washington State, QB
1994	Willie McGinest, Southern California, DE

NEW ORLEANS SAINTS

Year	Player, College, Position
1967	Les Kelley, Alabama, RB
1968	Kevin Hardy, Notre Dame, DE
1969	John Shinners, Xavier, G
1970	Ken Burrough, Texas Southern, WR
1971	Archie Manning, Mississippi, QB
1972	Royce Smith, Georgia, G
1973	Derland Moore, Oklahoma, DE (2)
1974	Rick Middleton, Ohio State, LB
1975	Larry Burton, Purdue, WR
	Kurt Schumacher, Ohio State, T
1976	Chuck Muncie, California, RB
1977	Joe Campbell, Maryland, DE
1978	Wes Chandler, Florida, WR
1979	Russell Erxleben, Texas, P-K
1980	Stan Brock, Colorado, T
1981	George Rogers, South Carolina, RB
1982	Lindsay Scott, Georgia, WR
1983	Steve Korte, Arkansas, G (2)
1984	James Geathers, Wichita State, DE
1985	Alvin Toles, Tennessee, LB
1986	Jim Dombrowski, Virginia, T
1987	Shawn Knight, Brigham Young, DT
1988	Craig Heyward, Pittsburgh, RB
1989	Wayne Martin, Arkansas, DE
1990	Renaldo Turnbull, West Virginia, DE
1991	Wesley Carroll, Miami, WR (2)
1992	Vaughn Dunbar, Indiana, RB
1993	Willie Roaf, Louisiana Tech, T
	Irv Smith, Notre Dame, TE
1994	Joe Johnson, Louisville, DE

NEW YORK GIANTS

Year	Player, College, Position
1936	Art Lewis, Ohio U., T
1937	Ed Widseth, Minnesota, T
1938	George Karamatic, Gonzaga, B
1939	Walt Neilson, Arizona, B
1940	Grenville Lansdell, Southern California, B
1941	George Franck, Minnesota, B
1942	Merle Hapes, Mississippi, B
1943	Steve Filipowicz, Fordham, B
1944	Billy Hillenbrand, Indiana, B
1945	Elmer Barbour, Wake Forest, B
1946	George Connor, Notre Dame, T
1947	Vic Schwall, Northwestern, B
1948	Tony Minisi, Pennsylvania, B
1949	Paul Page, Southern Methodist, B
1950	Travis Tidwell, Auburn, B
1951	Kyle Rote, Southern Methodist, B
	Jim Spavital, Oklahoma A&M, B
1952	Frank Gifford, Southern California, B
1953	Bobby Marlow, Alabama, B
1954	Ken Buck, Pacific, C (2)
1955	Joe Heap, Notre Dame, B
1956	Henry Moore, Arkansas, B (2)
1957	Sam DeLuca, South Carolina, T (2)
1958	Phil King, Vanderbilt, B
1959	Lee Grosscup, Utah, B
1960	Lou Cordileone, Clemson, G
1961	Bruce Tarbox, Syracuse, G (2)
1962	Jerry Hillebrand, Colorado, LB
1963	Frank Lasky, Florida, T (2)

Year	Player, College, Position
1964	Joe Don Looney, Oklahoma, RB
1965	Tucker Frederickson, Auburn, RB
1966	Francis Peay, Missouri, T
1967	Louis Thompson, Alabama, DT (4)
1968	Dick Buzin, Penn State, T (2)
1969	Fred Dryer, San Diego State, DE
1970	Jim Files, Oklahoma, LB
1971	Rocky Thompson, West Texas State, WR
1972	Eldridge Small, Texas A&I, DB
	Larry Jacobson, Nebraska, DE
1973	Brad Van Pelt, Michigan State, LB (2)
1974	John Hicks, Ohio State, G
1975	Al Simpson, Colorado State, T (2)
1976	Troy Archer, Colorado, DE
1977	Gary Jeter, Southern California, DT
1978	Gordon King, Stanford, T
1979	Phil Simms, Morehead State, QB
1980	Mark Haynes, Colorado, DB
1981	Lawrence Taylor, North Carolina, LB
1982	Butch Woolfolk, Michigan, RB
1983	Terry Kinard, Clemson, DB
1984	Carl Banks, Michigan State, LB
	William Roberts, Ohio State, T
1985	George Adams, Kentucky, RB
1986	Eric Dorsey, Notre Dame, DE
1987	Mark Ingram, Michigan State, WR
1988	Eric Moore, Indiana, T
1989	Brian Williams, Minnesota, C-G
1990	Rodney Hampton, Georgia, RB
1991	Jarrod Bunch, Michigan, RB
1992	Derek Brown, Notre Dame, TE
1993	Michael Strahan, Texas Southern, DE (2)
1994	Thomas Lewis, Indiana, WR

NEW YORK JETS
Year	Player, College, Position
1960	George Izo, Notre Dame, QB
1961	Tom Brown, Minnesota, G
1962	Sandy Stephens, Minnesota, QB
1963	Jerry Stovall, Louisiana State, S
1964	Matt Snell, Ohio State, RB
1965	Joe Namath, Alabama, QB
	Tom Nowatzke, Indiana, RB
1966	Bill Yearby, Michigan, DT
1967	Paul Seiler, Notre Dame, T
1968	Lee White, Weber State, RB
1969	Dave Foley, Ohio State, T
1970	Steve Tannen, Florida, CB
1971	John Riggins, Kansas, RB
1972	Jerome Barkum, Jackson State, WR
	Mike Taylor, Michigan, LB
1973	Burgess Owens, Miami, DB
1974	Carl Barzilauskas, Indiana, DT
1975	Anthony Davis, Southern California, RB (2)
1976	Richard Todd, Alabama, QB
1977	Marvin Powell, Southern California, T
1978	Chris Ward, Ohio State, T
1979	Marty Lyons, Alabama, DE
1980	Johnny (Lam) Jones, Texas, WR
1981	Freeman McNeil, UCLA, RB
1982	Bob Crable, Notre Dame, LB
1983	Ken O'Brien, Cal-Davis, QB
1984	Russell Carter, Southern Methodist, DB
	Ron Faurot, Arkansas, DE
1985	Al Toon, Wisconsin, WR
1986	Mike Haight, Iowa, T
1987	Roger Vick, Texas A&M, RB
1988	Dave Cadigan, Southern California, T
1989	Jeff Lageman, Virginia, LB
1990	Blair Thomas, Penn State, RB
1991	Browning Nagle, Louisville, QB (2)
1992	Johnny Mitchell, Nebraska, TE
1993	Marvin Jones, Florida State, LB
1994	Aaron Glenn, Texas A&M, DB

PHILADELPHIA EAGLES
Year	Player, College, Position
1936	Jay Berwanger, Chicago, B
1937	Sam Francis, Nebraska, B
1938	Jim McDonald, Ohio State, B
1939	Davey O'Brien, Texas Christian, B
1940	George McAfee, Duke, B
1941	Art Jones, Richmond, B (2)

Year	Player, College, Position
1942	Pete Kmetovic, Stanford, B
1943	Joe Muha, Virginia Military, B
1944	Steve Van Buren, Louisiana State, B
1945	John Yonaker, Notre Dame, E
1946	Leo Riggs, Southern California, B
1947	Neill Armstrong, Oklahoma A&M, E
1948	Clyde (Smackover) Scott, Arkansas, B
1949	Chuck Bednarik, Pennsylvania, C
	Frank Tripucka, Notre Dame, B
1950	Harry (Bud) Grant, Minnesota, E
1951	Ebert Van Buren, Louisiana State, B
	Chet Mutryn, Xavier, B
1952	Johnny Bright, Drake, B
1953	Al Conway, Army, B (2)
1954	Neil Worden, Notre Dame, B
1955	Dick Bielski, Maryland, B
1956	Bob Pellegrini, Maryland, C
1957	Clarence Peaks, Michigan State, B
1958	Walt Kowalczyk, Michigan State, B
1959	J.D. Smith, Rice, T (2)
1960	Ron Burton, Northwestern, RB
1961	Art Baker, Syracuse, RB
1962	Pete Case, Georgia, G (2)
1963	Ed Budde, Michigan State, G
1964	Bob Brown, Nebraska, T
1965	Ray Rissmiller, Georgia, T (2)
1966	Randy Beisler, Indiana, DE
1967	Harry Jones, Arkansas, RB
1968	Tim Rossovich, Southern California, DE
1969	Leroy Keyes, Purdue, RB
1970	Steve Zabel, Oklahoma, TE
1971	Richard Harris, Grambling, DE
1972	John Reaves, Florida, QB
1973	Jerry Sisemore, Texas, T
	Charle Young, Southern California, TE
1974	Mitch Sutton, Kansas, DT (3)
1975	Bill Capraun, Miami, T (7)
1976	Mike Smith, Florida, DE (4)
1977	Skip Sharp, Kansas, DB (5)
1978	Reggie Wilkes, Georgia Tech, LB (3)
1979	Jerry Robinson, UCLA, LB
1980	Roynell Young, Alcorn State, DB
1981	Leonard Mitchell, Houston, DE
1982	Mike Quick, North Carolina State, WR
1983	Michael Haddix, Mississippi State, RB
1984	Kenny Jackson, Penn State, WR
1985	Kevin Allen, Indiana, T
1986	Keith Byars, Ohio State, RB
1987	Jerome Brown, Miami, DT
1988	Keith Jackson, Oklahoma, TE
1989	Jessie Small, Eastern Kentucky, LB (2)
1990	Ben Smith, Georgia, DB
1991	Antone Davis, Tennessee, T
1992	Siran Stacy, Alabama, RB (2)
1993	Lester Holmes, Jackson State, T
	Leonard Renfro, Colorado, DT
1994	Bernard Williams, Georgia, T

PITTSBURGH STEELERS
Year	Player, College, Position
1936	Bill Shakespeare, Notre Dame, B
1937	Mike Basrak, Duquesne, C
1938	Byron (Whizzer) White, Colorado, B
1939	Bill Patterson, Baylor, B (3)
1940	Kay Eakin, Arkansas, B
1941	Chet Gladchuk, Boston College, C (2)
1942	Bill Dudley, Virginia, B
1943	Bill Daley, Minnesota, B
1944	Johnny Podesto, St. Mary's, Calif., B
1945	Paul Duhart, Florida, B
1946	Felix (Doc) Blanchard, Army, B
1947	Hub Bechtol, Texas, E
1948	Dan Edwards, Georgia, E
1949	Bobby Gage, Clemson, B
1950	Lynn Chandnois, Michigan State, B
1951	Butch Avinger, Alabama, B
1952	Ed Modzelewski, Maryland, B
1953	Ted Marchibroda, St. Bonaventure, B
1954	Johnny Lattner, Notre Dame, B
1955	Frank Varrichione, Notre Dame, T
1956	Gary Glick, Colorado A&M, B
	Art Davis, Mississippi State, B
1957	Len Dawson, Purdue, B

Year	Player, College, Position
1958	Larry Krutko, West Virginia, B (2)
1959	Tom Barnett, Purdue, B (8)
1960	Jack Spikes, Texas Christian, RB
1961	Myron Pottios, Notre Dame, LB (2)
1962	Bob Ferguson, Ohio State, RB
1963	Frank Atkinson, Stanford, T (8)
1964	Paul Martha, Pittsburgh, S
1965	Roy Jefferson, Utah, WR (2)
1966	Dick Leftridge, West Virginia, RB
1967	Don Shy, San Diego State, RB (2)
1968	Mike Taylor, Southern California, T
1969	Joe Greene, North Texas State, DT
1970	Terry Bradshaw, Louisiana Tech, QB
1971	Frank Lewis, Grambling, WR
1972	Franco Harris, Penn State, RB
1973	J.T. Thomas, Florida State, DB
1974	Lynn Swann, Southern California, WR
1975	Dave Brown, Michigan, DB
1976	Bennie Cunningham, Clemson, TE
1977	Robin Cole, New Mexico, LB
1978	Ron Johnson, Eastern Michigan, DB
1979	Greg Hawthorne, Baylor, RB
1980	Mark Malone, Arizona State, QB
1981	Keith Gary, Oklahoma, DE
1982	Walter Abercrombie, Baylor, RB
1983	Gabriel Rivera, Texas Tech, DT
1984	Louis Lipps, Southern Mississippi, WR
1985	Darryl Sims, Wisconsin, DE
1986	John Rienstra, Temple, G
1987	Rod Woodson, Purdue, DB
1988	Aaron Jones, Eastern Kentucky, DE
1989	Tim Worley, Georgia, RB
	Tom Ricketts, Pittsburgh, T
1990	Eric Green, Liberty, TE
1991	Huey Richardson, Florida, DE
1992	Leon Searcy, Miami, T
1993	Deon Figures, Colorado, DB
1994	Charles Johnson, Colorado, WR

SAN DIEGO CHARGERS
Year	Player, College, Position
1960	Monty Stickles, Notre Dame, E
1961	Earl Faison, Indiana, DE
1962	Bob Ferguson, Ohio State, RB
1963	Walt Sweeney, Syracuse, G
1964	Ted Davis, Georgia Tech, LB
1965	Steve DeLong, Tennessee, DE
1966	Don Davis, Cal State-Los Angeles, DT
1967	Ron Billingsley, Wyoming, DE
1968	Russ Washington, Missouri, DT
	Jimmy Hill, Texas A&I, DB
1969	Marty Domres, Columbia, QB
	Bob Babich, Miami, Ohio, LB
1970	Walker Gillette, Richmond, WR
1971	Leon Burns, Long Beach State, RB
1972	Pete Lazetich, Stanford, DE (2)
1973	Johnny Rodgers, Nebraska, WR
1974	Bo Matthews, Colorado, RB
	Don Goode, Kansas, LB
1975	Gary Johnson, Grambling, DT
	Mike Williams, Louisiana State, DB
1976	Joe Washington, Oklahoma, RB
1977	Bob Rush, Memphis State, C
1978	John Jefferson, Arizona State, WR
1979	Kellen Winslow, Missouri, TE
1980	Ed Luther, San Jose State, QB (4)
1981	James Brooks, Auburn, RB
1982	Hollis Hall, Clemson, DB (7)
1983	Billy Ray Smith, Arkansas, LB
	Gary Anderson, Arkansas, WR
	Gill Byrd, San Jose State, DB
1984	Mossy Cade, Texas, DB
1985	Jim Lachey, Ohio State, G
1986	Leslie O'Neal, Oklahoma State, DE
	James FitzPatrick, Southern California, T
1987	Rod Bernstine, Texas A&M, TE
1988	Anthony Miller, Tennessee, WR
1989	Burt Grossman, Pittsburgh, DE
1990	Junior Seau, Southern California, LB
1991	Stanley Richard, Texas, DB
1992	Chris Mims, Tennessee, DE
1993	Darrien Gordon, Stanford, DB
1994	Isaac Davis, Arkansas, G (2)

FIRST-ROUND SELECTIONS

SAN FRANCISCO 49ERS

Year	Player, College, Position
1950	Leo Nomellini, Minnesota, T
1951	Y.A. Tittle, Louisiana State, B
1952	Hugh McElhenny, Washington, B
1953	Harry Babcock, Georgia, E
	Tom Stolhandske, Texas, E
1954	Bernie Faloney, Maryland, B
1955	Dickie Moegle, Rice, B
1956	Earl Morrall, Michigan State, B
1957	John Brodie, Stanford, B
1958	Jim Pace, Michigan, B
	Charlie Krueger, Texas A&M, T
1959	Dave Baker, Oklahoma, B
	Dan James, Ohio State, C
1960	Monty Stickles, Notre Dame, E
1961	Jimmy Johnson, UCLA, CB
	Bernie Casey, Bowling Green, WR
	Bill Kilmer, UCLA, QB
1962	Lance Alworth, Arkansas, WR
1963	Kermit Alexander, UCLA, CB
1964	Dave Parks, Texas Tech, WR
1965	Ken Willard, North Carolina, RB
	George Donnelly, Illinois, DB
1966	Stan Hindman, Mississippi, DE
1967	Steve Spurrier, Florida, QB
	Cas Banaszek, Northwestern, T
1968	Forrest Blue, Auburn, C
1969	Ted Kwalick, Penn State, TE
	Gene Washington, Stanford, WR
1970	Cedrick Hardman, North Texas State, DE
	Bruce Taylor, Boston U., DB
1971	Tim Anderson, Ohio State, DB
1972	Terry Beasley, Auburn, WR
1973	Mike Holmes, Texas Southern, DB
1974	Wilbur Jackson, Alabama, RB
	Bill Sandifer, UCLA, DT
1975	Jimmy Webb, Mississippi State, DT
1976	Randy Cross, UCLA, C (2)
1977	Elmo Boyd, Eastern Kentucky, WR (3)
1978	Ken MacAfee, Notre Dame, TE
	Dan Bunz, Cal State-Long Beach, LB
1979	James Owens, UCLA, WR (2)
1980	Earl Cooper, Rice, RB
	Jim Stuckey, Clemson, DT
1981	Ronnie Lott, Southern California, DB
1982	Bubba Paris, Michigan, T (2)
1983	Roger Craig, Nebraska, RB (2)
1984	Todd Shell, Brigham Young, LB
1985	Jerry Rice, Mississippi Valley State, WR
1986	Larry Roberts, Alabama, DE (2)
1987	Harris Barton, North Carolina, T
	Terrence Flagler, Clemson, RB
1988	Danny Stubbs, Miami, DE (2)
1989	Keith DeLong, Tennessee, LB
1990	Dexter Carter, Florida State, RB
1991	Ted Washington, Louisville, DT
1992	Dana Hall, Washington, DB
1993	Dana Stubblefield, Kansas, DT
	Todd Kelly, Tennessee, DE
1994	Bryant Young, Notre Dame, DT
	William Floyd, Florida State, RB

SEATTLE SEAHAWKS

Year	Player, College, Position
1976	Steve Niehaus, Notre Dame, DT
1977	Steve August, Tulsa, G
1978	Keith Simpson, Memphis State, DB
1979	Manu Tuiasosopo, UCLA, DT
1980	Jacob Green, Texas A&M, DE
1981	Ken Easley, UCLA, DB
1982	Jeff Bryant, Clemson, DE
1983	Curt Warner, Penn State, RB
1984	Terry Taylor, Southern Illinois, DR
1985	Owen Gill, Iowa, RB (2)
1986	John L. Williams, Florida, RB
1987	Tony Woods, Pittsburgh, LB
1988	Brian Blades, Miami, WR (2)
1989	Andy Heck, Notre Dame, T
1990	Cortez Kennedy, Miami, DT
1991	Dan McGwire, San Diego State, QB
1992	Ray Roberts, Virginia, T
1993	Rick Mirer, Notre Dame, QB

| 1994 | Sam Adams, Texas A&M, DT |

TAMPA BAY BUCCANEERS

Year	Player, College, Position
1976	Lee Roy Selmon, Oklahoma, DT
1977	Ricky Bell, Southern California, RB
1978	Doug Williams, Grambling, QB
1979	Greg Roberts, Oklahoma, G (2)
1980	Ray Snell, Wisconsin, G
1981	Hugh Green, Pittsburgh, LB
1982	Sean Farrell, Penn State, G
1983	Randy Grimes, Baylor, C (2)
1984	Keith Browner, Southern California, LB (2)
1985	Ron Holmes, Washington, DE
1986	Bo Jackson, Auburn, RB
	Roderick Jones, Southern Methodist, DB
1987	Vinny Testaverde, Miami, QB
1988	Paul Gruber, Wisconsin, T
1989	Broderick Thomas, Nebraska, LB
1990	Keith McCants, Alabama, LB
1991	Charles McRae, Tennessee, T
1992	Courtney Hawkins, Michigan State, WR (2)
1993	Eric Curry, Alabama, DE
1994	Trent Dilfer, Fresno State, QB

WASHINGTON REDSKINS

Year	Player, College, Position
1936	Riley Smith, Alabama, B
1937	Sammy Baugh, Texas Christian, B
1938	Andy Farkas, Detroit, B
1939	I.B. Hale, Texas Christian, T
1940	Ed Boell, New York U., B
1941	Forest Evashevski, Michigan, B
1942	Orban (Spec) Sanders, Texas, B
1943	Jack Jenkins, Missouri, B
1944	Mike Micka, Colgate, B
1945	Jim Hardy, Southern California, B
1946	Casl Rossi, UCLA, B*
1947	Casl Rossi, UCLA, B
1948	Harry Gilmer, Alabama, B
	Lowell Tew, Alabama, B
1949	Rob Goode, Texas A&M, B
1950	George Thomas, Oklahoma, B
1951	Leon Heath, Oklahoma, B
1952	Larry Isbell, Baylor, B
1953	Jack Scarbath, Maryland, B
1954	Steve Meilinger, Kentucky, E
1955	Ralph Guglielmi, Notre Dame, B
1956	Ed Vereb, Maryland, B
1957	Don Bosseler, Miami, B
1958	Mike Sommer, George Washington, B (2)
1959	Don Allard, Boston College, B
1960	Richie Lucas, Penn State, QB
1961	Norman Snead, Wake Forest, QB
	Joe Rutgens, Illinois, DT
1962	Ernie Davis, Syracuse, RB
1963	Pat Richter, Wisconsin, TE
1964	Charley Taylor, Arizona State, RB-WR
1965	Bob Breitenstein, Tulsa, T (2)
1966	Charlie Gogolak, Princeton, K
1967	Ray McDonald, Idaho, RB
1968	Jim Smith, Oregon, DB
1969	Eugene Epps, Texas-El Paso, DB (2)
1970	Bill Bundige, Colorado, DT (2)
1971	Cotton Speyrer, Texas, WR (2)
1972	Moses Denson, Maryland State, RB (8)
1973	Charles Cantrell, Lamar, G (5)
1974	Jon Keyworth, Colorado, TE (6)
1975	Mike Thomas, Nevada-Las Vegas, RB (6)
1976	Mike Hughes, Baylor, G (5)
1977	Duncan McColl, Stanford, DE (4)
1978	Tony Green, Florida, RB (6)
1979	Don Warren, San Diego State, TE (4)
1980	Art Monk, Syracuse, WR
1981	Mark May, Pittsburgh, T
1982	Vernon Dean, San Diego State, DB (2)
1983	Darrell Green, Texas A&I, DB
1984	Bob Slater, Oklahoma, DT (2)
1985	Tory Nixon, San Diego State, DB (2)
1986	Markus Koch, Boise State, DE (2)
1987	Brian Davis, Nebraska, DB (2)
1988	Chip Lohmiller, Minnesota, K (2)
1989	Tracy Rocker, Auburn, DT (3)

1990	Andre Collins, Penn State, LB (2)
1991	Bobby Wilson, Michigan State, DT
1992	Desmond Howard, Michigan, WR
1993	Tom Carter, Notre Dame, DB
1994	Heath Shuler, Tennessee, QB

Choice lost due to ineligibility

Records

Compiled by Elias Sports Bureau
The following records reflect all available official information on the National Football League from its formation in 1920 to date. Also included are all applicable records from the American Football League, 1960-69.

INDIVIDUAL RECORDS

SERVICE
Most Seasons
- 26   George Blanda, Chi. Bears, 1949, 1950-58; Baltimore, 1950; Houston, 1960-66; Oakland, 1967-75
- 21   Earl Morrall, San Francisco, 1956; Pittsburgh, 1957-58; Detroit, 1958-64; N.Y. Giants, 1965-67; Baltimore, 1968-71; Miami, 1972-76
- 20   Jim Marshall, Cleveland, 1960; Minnesota, 1961-79

Most Seasons, One Club
- 19   Jim Marshall, Minnesota, 1961-79
- 18   Jim Hart, St. Louis, 1966-83
-      Jeff Van Note, Atlanta, 1969-86
-      Pat Leahy, N.Y. Jets, 1974-91
-      Jackie Slater, L.A. Rams, 1976-93
- 17   Lou Groza, Cleveland, 1950-59, 1961-67
-      Johnny Unitas, Baltimore, 1956-72
-      John Brodie, San Francisco, 1957-73
-      Jim Bakken, St. Louis, 1962-78
-      Mick Tingelhoff, Minnesota, 1962-78

Most Games Played, Career
- 340   George Blanda, Chi. Bears, 1949, 1950-58; Baltimore, 1950; Houston, 1960-66; Oakland, 1967-75
- 282   Jim Marshall, Cleveland, 1960; Minnesota, 1961-79
- 263   Jan Stenerud, Kansas City, 1967-79; Green Bay, 1980-83; Minnesota, 1984-85

Most Consecutive Games Played, Career
- 282   Jim Marshall, Cleveland, 1960; Minnesota, 1961-79
- 240   Mick Tingelhoff, Minnesota, 1962-78
- 234   Jim Bakken, St. Louis, 1962-78

SCORING
Most Seasons Leading League
- 5   Don Hutson, Green Bay, 1940-44
-    Gino Cappelletti, Boston, 1961, 1963-66
- 3   Earl (Dutch) Clark, Portsmouth, 1932; Detroit, 1935-36
-    Pat Harder, Chi. Cardinals, 1947-49
-    Paul Hornung, Green Bay, 1959-61
- 2   Jack Manders, Chi. Bears, 1934, 1937
-    Gordy Soltau, San Francisco, 1952-53
-    Doak Walker, Detroit, 1950, 1955
-    Gene Mingo, Denver, 1960, 1962
-    Jim Turner, N.Y. Jets, 1968-69
-    Fred Cox, Minnesota, 1969-70
-    Chester Marcol, Green Bay, 1972, 1974
-    John Smith, New England, 1979-80

Most Consecutive Seasons Leading League
- 5   Don Hutson, Green Bay, 1940-44
- 4   Gino Cappelletti, Boston, 1963-66
- 3   Pat Harder, Chi. Cardinals, 1947-49
-    Paul Hornung, Green Bay, 1959-61

POINTS
Most Points, Career
- 2,002   George Blanda, Chi. Bears, 1949, 1950-58; Baltimore, 1950; Houston, 1960-66; Oakland, 1967-75 (9-td, 943-pat, 335-fg)
- 1,699   Jan Stenerud, Kansas City, 1967-79; Green Bay, 1980-83; Minnesota, 1984-85   (580-pat, 373-fg)
- 1,473   Nick Lowery, New England, 1978; Kansas City, 1980-93

Most Points, Season
- 176   Paul Hornung, Green Bay, 1960 (15-td, 41-pat, 15-fg)
- 161   Mark Moseley, Washington, 1983 (62-pat, 33-fg)
- 155   Gino Cappelletti, Boston, 1964 (7-td, 38-pat, 25-fg)

Most Points, No Touchdowns, Season
- 161   Mark Moseley, Washington, 1983 (62-pat, 33-fg)
- 149   Chip Lohmiller, Washington, 1991 (56-pat, 31-fg)
- 145   Jim Turner, N.Y. Jets, 1968 (43-pat, 34-fg)

Most Seasons, 100 or More Points
- 11   Nick Lowery, Kansas City, 1981, 1983-86, 1988-93
- 8   Morten Andersen, New Orleans, 1985-89, 1991-93
- 7   Jan Stenerud, Kansas City, 1967-71; Green Bay, 1981, 1983
-    Gary Anderson, Pittsburgh, 1983-85, 1988, 1991-93

Most Points, Rookie, Season
- 144   Kevin Butler, Chicago, 1985 (51-pat, 31-fg)
- 132   Gale Sayers, Chicago, 1965 (22-td)
- 128   Doak Walker, Detroit, 1950 (11-td, 38-pat, 8-fg)
-      Chester Marcol, Green Bay, 1972 (29-pat, 33-fg)

Most Points, Game
- 40   Ernie Nevers, Chi. Cardinals vs. Chi. Bears, Nov. 28, 1929 (6-td, 4-pat)
- 36   Dub Jones, Cleveland vs. Chi. Bears, Nov. 25, 1951 (6-td)
-      Gale Sayers, Chicago vs. San Francisco, Dec. 12, 1965 (6-td)
- 33   Paul Hornung, Green Bay vs. Baltimore, Oct. 8, 1961 (4-td, 6-pat, 1-fg)

Most Consecutive Games Scoring
- 186   Jim Breech, Oakland, 1979; Cincinnati, 1980-92
- 158   Morten Andersen, New Orleans, 1982-93 (current)
- 151   Fred Cox, Minnesota, 1963-73

TOUCHDOWNS
Most Seasons Leading League
- 8   Don Hutson, Green Bay, 1935-38, 1941-44
- 3   Jim Brown, Cleveland, 1958-59, 1963
-    Lance Alworth, San Diego, 1964-66
- 2   By many players

Most Consecutive Seasons Leading League
- 4   Don Hutson, Green Bay, 1935-38, 1941-44
- 3   Lance Alworth, San Diego, 1964-66
- 2   By many players

Most Touchdowns, Career
- 126   Jim Brown, Cleveland, 1957-65 (106-r, 20-p)
- 125   Walter Payton, Chicago, 1975-87 (110-r, 15-p)
- 124   Jerry Rice, San Francisco, 1985-93 (6-r, 118-p)

Most Touchdowns, Season
- 24   John Riggins, Washington, 1983 (24-r)
- 23   O.J. Simpson, Buffalo, 1975 (16-r, 7-p)
-      Jerry Rice, San Francisco, 1987 (1-r, 22-p)
- 22   Gale Sayers, Chicago, 1965 (14-r, 6-p, 2-ret)
-      Chuck Foreman, Minnesota, 1975 (13-r, 9-p)

Most Touchdowns, Rookie, Season
- 22   Gale Sayers, Chicago, 1965 (14-r, 6-p, 2-ret)
- 20   Eric Dickerson, L.A. Rams, 1983 (18-r, 2-p)
- 16   Billy Sims, Detroit, 1980 (13-r, 3-p)

Most Touchdowns, Game
- 6   Ernie Nevers, Chi. Cardinals vs. Chi. Bears, Nov. 28, 1929 (6-r)
-    Dub Jones, Cleveland vs. Chi. Bears, Nov. 25, 1951 (4-r, 2-p)
-    Gale Sayers, Chicago vs. San Francisco, Dec. 12, 1965 (4-r, 1-p, 1-ret)
- 5   Bob Shaw, Chi. Cardinals vs. Baltimore, Oct. 2, 1950 (5-p)
-    Jim Brown, Cleveland vs. Baltimore, Nov. 1, 1959 (5-r)
-    Abner Haynes, Dall. Texans vs. Oakland, Nov. 26, 1961 (4-r, 1-p)
-    Billy Cannon, Houston vs. N.Y. Titans, Dec. 10, 1961 (3-r, 2-p)
-    Cookie Gilchrist, Buffalo vs. N.Y. Jets, Dec. 8, 1963 (5-r)
-    Paul Hornung, Green Bay vs. Baltimore, Dec. 12, 1965 (3-r, 2-p)
-    Kellen Winslow, San Diego vs. Oakland, Nov. 22, 1981 (5-p)
-    Jerry Rice, San Francisco vs. Atlanta, Oct. 14, 1990 (5-p)
- 4   By many players. Last time: Ron Moore, Phoenix vs. L.A. Rams, Dec. 5, 1993 (4-r)

Most Consecutive Games Scoring Touchdowns
- 18   Lenny Moore, Baltimore, 1963-65
- 14   O.J. Simpson, Buffalo, 1975
- 13   John Riggins, Washington, 1982-83
-      George Rogers, Washington, 1985-86
-      Jerry Rice, San Francisco, 1986-87

POINTS AFTER TOUCHDOWN
Most Seasons Leading League
- 8   George Blanda, Chi. Bears, 1956; Houston, 1961-62; Oakland, 1967-69, 1972, 1974
- 4   Bob Waterfield, Cleveland, 1945; Los Angeles, 1946, 1950, 1952
- 3   Earl (Dutch) Clark, Portsmouth, 1932; Detroit, 1935-36
-    Jack Manders, Chi. Bears, 1933-35
-    Don Hutson, Green Bay, 1941-42, 1945

Most Points After Touchdown Attempted, Career
- 959   George Blanda, Chi. Bears, 1949, 1950-58; Baltimore, 1950; Houston, 1960-66; Oakland, 1967-75
- 657   Lou Groza, Cleveland, 1950-59, 1961-67
- 601   Jan Stenerud, Kansas City, 1967-79; Green Bay, 1980-83; Minnesota, 1984-85

Most Points After Touchdown Attempted, Season
- 70   Uwe von Schamann, Miami, 1984
- 65   George Blanda, Houston, 1961
- 63   Mark Moseley, Washington, 1983

Most Points After Touchdown Attempted, Game
- 10   Charlie Gogolak, Washington vs. N.Y. Giants, Nov. 27, 1966
- 9   Pat Harder, Chi. Cardinals vs. N.Y. Giants, Oct. 17, 1948; vs. N.Y. Bulldogs, Nov. 13, 1949
-    Bob Waterfield, Los Angeles vs. Baltimore, Oct. 22, 1950
-    Bob Thomas, Chicago vs. Green Bay, Dec. 7, 1980
- 8   By many players

Most Points After Touchdown, Career
- 943   George Blanda, Chi. Bears, 1949, 1950-58; Baltimore, 1950; Houston, 1960-66; Oakland, 1967-75

641 Lou Groza, Cleveland, 1950-59, 1961-67
580 Jan Stenerud, Kansas City, 1967-79; Green Bay, 1980-83; Minnesota, 1984-85

Most Points After Touchdown, Season
66 Uwe von Schamann, Miami, 1984
64 George Blanda, Houston, 1961
62 Mark Moseley, Washington, 1983

Most Points After Touchdown, Game
9 Pat Harder, Chi. Cardinals vs. N.Y. Giants, Oct. 17, 1948
 Bob Waterfield, Los Angeles vs. Baltimore, Oct. 22, 1950
 Charlie Gogolak, Washington vs. N.Y. Giants, Nov. 27, 1966
8 By many players

Most Consecutive Points After Touchdown
234 Tommy Davis, San Francisco, 1959-65
221 Jim Turner, N.Y. Jets, 1967-70; Denver, 1971-74
213 Chip Lohmiller, Washington, 1988-93

Highest Points After Touchdown Percentage, Career
(200 points after touchdown)
99.43 Tommy Davis, San Francisco, 1959-69 (350-348)
99.18 Nick Lowery, New England, 1978; Kansas City, 1980-93 (490-486)
98.97 Gary Anderson, Pittsburgh, 1982-93 (388-384)

Most Points After Touchdown, No Misses, Season
56 Danny Villanueva, Dallas, 1966
 Ray Wersching, San Francisco, 1984
 Chip Lohmiller, Washington, 1991
54 Mike Clark, Dallas, 1968
 George Blanda, Oakland, 1968
53 Pat Harder, Chi. Cardinals, 1948

Most Points After Touchdown, No Misses, Game
9 Pat Harder, Chi. Cardinals vs. N.Y. Giants, Oct. 17, 1948
 Bob Waterfield, Los Angeles vs. Baltimore, Oct. 22, 1950
8 By many players

FIELD GOALS

Most Seasons Leading League
5 Lou Groza, Cleveland, 1950, 1952-54, 1957
4 Jack Manders, Chi. Bears, 1933-34, 1936-37
 Ward Cuff, N.Y. Giants, 1938-39, 1943; Green Bay, 1947
 Mark Moseley, Washington, 1976-77, 1979, 1982
3 Bob Waterfield, Los Angeles, 1947, 1949, 1951
 Gino Cappelletti, Boston, 1961, 1963-64
 Fred Cox, Minnesota, 1965, 1969-70
 Jan Stenerud, Kansas City, 1967, 1970, 1975

Most Consecutive Seasons Leading League
3 Lou Groza, Cleveland, 1952-54
2 Jack Manders, Chi. Bears, 1933-34
 Armand Niccolai, Pittsburgh, 1935-36
 Jack Manders, Chi. Bears, 1936-37
 Ward Cuff, N.Y. Giants, 1938-39
 Clark Hinkle, Green Bay, 1940-41
 Cliff Patton, Philadelphia, 1948-49
 Gino Cappelletti, Boston, 1963-64
 Jim Turner, N.Y. Jets, 1968-69
 Fred Cox, Minnesota, 1969-70
 Mark Moseley, Washington, 1976-77
 Chip Lohmiller, Washington, 1991-92
 Pete Stoyanovich, Miami, 1991-92

Most Field Goals Attempted, Career
637 George Blanda, Chi. Bears, 1949, 1950-58; Baltimore, 1950; Houston, 1960-66; Oakland, 1967-75
558 Jan Stenerud, Kansas City, 1967-79; Green Bay, 1980-83; Minnesota, 1984-85
488 Jim Turner, N.Y. Jets, 1964-70; Denver, 1971-79

Most Field Goals Attempted, Season
49 Bruce Gossett, Los Angeles, 1966
 Curt Knight, Washington, 1971
48 Chester Marcol, Green Bay, 1972
47 Jim Turner, N.Y. Jets, 1969
 David Ray, Los Angeles, 1973
 Mark Moseley, Washington, 1983

Most Field Goals Attempted, Game
9 Jim Bakken, St. Louis vs. Pittsburgh, Sept. 24, 1967
8 Lou Michaels, Pittsburgh vs. St. Louis, Dec. 2, 1962
 Garo Yepremian, Detroit vs. Minnesota, Nov. 13, 1966
 Jim Turner, N.Y. Jets vs. Buffalo, Nov. 3, 1968
7 By many players

Most Field Goals, Career
373 Jan Stenerud, Kansas City, 1967-79; Green Bay, 1980-83; Minnesota, 1984-85
335 George Blanda, Chi. Bears, 1949, 1950-58; Baltimore, 1950; Houston, 1960-66; Oakland, 1967-75
329 Nick Lowery, New England, 1978; Kansas City, 1980-93

Most Field Goals, Season
35 Ali Haji-Sheikh, N.Y. Giants, 1983
 Jeff Jaeger, L.A. Raiders, 1993
34 Jim Turner, N.Y. Jets, 1968
 Nick Lowery, Kansas City, 1990
 Jason Hanson, Detroit, 1993
33 Chester Marcol, Green Bay, 1972
 Mark Moseley, Washington, 1983
 Gary Anderson, Pittsburgh, 1985

Most Field Goals, Rookie, Season
35 Ali Haji-Sheikh, N.Y. Giants, 1983
33 Chester Marcol, Green Bay, 1972
31 Kevin Butler, Chicago, 1985

Most Field Goals, Game
7 Jim Bakken, St. Louis vs. Pittsburgh, Sept. 24, 1967
 Rich Karlis, Minnesota vs. L.A. Rams, Nov. 5, 1989 (OT)
6 Gino Cappelletti, Boston vs. Denver, Oct. 4, 1964
 Garo Yepremian, Minnesota, Nov. 13, 1966
 Jim Turner, N.Y. Jets vs. Buffalo, Nov. 3, 1968
 Tom Dempsey, Philadelphia vs. Houston, Nov. 12, 1972
 Bobby Howfield, N.Y. Jets vs. New Orleans, Dec. 3, 1972
 Jim Bakken, St. Louis vs. Atlanta, Dec. 9, 1973
 Joe Danelo, N.Y. Giants vs. Seattle, Oct. 18, 1981
 Ray Wersching, San Francisco vs. New Orleans, Oct. 16, 1983
 Gary Anderson, Pittsburgh vs. Denver, Oct. 23, 1988
 John Carney, San Diego vs. Seattle, Sept. 5, 1993
 John Carney, San Diego vs. Houston, Sept. 19, 1993
5 By many players

Most Field Goals, One Quarter
4 Garo Yepremian, Detroit vs. Minnesota, Nov. 13, 1966 (second quarter)
 Curt Knight, Washington vs. N.Y. Giants, Nov. 15, 1970 (second quarter)
 Roger Ruzek, Dallas vs. N.Y. Giants, Nov. 2, 1987 (fourth quarter)
3 By many players

Most Consecutive Games Scoring Field Goals
31 Fred Cox, Minnesota, 1968-70
28 Jim Turner, N.Y. Jets, 1970; Denver, 1971-72
 Chip Lohmiller, Washington, 1988-90
23 Morten Andersen, New Orleans, 1986-88

Most Consecutive Field Goals
29 John Carney, San Diego, 1992-93
26 Norm Johnson, Atlanta, 1992-93
25 Morten Andersen, New Orleans, 1992-93

Longest Field Goal
63 Tom Dempsey, New Orleans vs. Detroit, Nov. 8, 1970
60 Steve Cox, Cleveland vs. Cincinnati, Oct. 21, 1984
 Morten Andersen, New Orleans vs. Chicago, Oct. 27, 1991
59 Tony Franklin, Philadelphia vs. Dallas, Nov. 12, 1979
 Pete Stoyanovich, Miami vs. N.Y. Jets, Nov. 12, 1989
 Steve Christie, Buffalo vs. Miami, Sept. 26, 1993

Highest Field Goal Percentage, Career (100 field goals)
80.05 Nick Lowery, New England, 1978; Kansas City, 1980-93 (411-329)
79.62 Pete Stoyanovich, Miami, 1989-93 (157-125)
78.48 David Treadwell, Denver, 1989-92; N.Y. Giants, 1993 (158-124)

Highest Field Goal Percentage, Season (Qualifiers)
100.00 Tony Zendejas, L.A. Rams, 1991 (17-17)
96.30 Norm Johnson, Atlanta, 1993 (27-26)
95.24 Mark Moseley, Washington, 1982 (21-20)
 Eddie Murray, Detroit, 1988 (21-20)
 Eddie Murray, Detroit, 1989 (21-20)

Most Field Goals, No Misses, Game
7 Rich Karlis, Minnesota vs. L.A. Rams, Nov. 5, 1989 (OT)
6 Gino Cappelletti, Boston vs. Denver, Oct. 4, 1964
 Joe Danelo, N.Y. Giants vs. Seattle, Oct. 18, 1981
 Ray Wersching, San Francisco vs. New Orleans, Oct. 16, 1983
 Gary Anderson, Pittsburgh vs. Denver, Oct. 23, 1988
 John Carney, San Diego vs. Seattle, Sept. 5, 1993
 John Carney, San Diego vs. Houston, Sept. 19, 1993
5 By many players

Most Field Goals, 50 or More Yards, Career
22 Morten Andersen, New Orleans, 1982-93
20 Nick Lowery, New England, 1978; Kansas City, 1980-93
 Eddie Murray, Detroit, 1980-91; Kansas City, 1992; Tampa Bay, 1992; Dallas, 1993
17 Jan Stenerud, Kansas City, 1967-79; Green Bay, 1980-83; Minnesota, 1984-85
 Norm Johnson, Seattle, 1982-90; Atlanta, 1991-93
 Tony Zendejas, Houston, 1985-90; L.A. Rams, 1991-93

Most Field Goals, 50 or More Yards, Season
6 Dean Biasucci, Indianapolis, 1988
 Chris Jacke, Green Bay, 1993
 Tony Zendejas, L.A. Rams, 1993
5 Fred Steinfort, Denver, 1980
 Norm Johnson, Seattle, 1986

Kevin Butler, Chicago, 1993
4   By many players

Most Field Goals, 50 or More Yards, Game

2   Jim Martin, Detroit vs. Baltimore, Oct. 23, 1960
Tom Dempsey, New Orleans vs. Los Angeles, Dec. 6, 1970
Chris Bahr, Cincinnati vs. Houston, Sept. 23, 1979
Nick Lowery, Kansas City vs. Seattle, Sept. 14, 1980
Mark Moseley, Washington vs. New Orleans, Oct. 26, 1980
Fred Steinfort, Denver vs. Seattle, Dec. 21, 1980
Mick Luckhurst, Atlanta vs. Denver, Dec. 5, 1982
Morten Andersen, New Orleans vs. Philadelphia, Dec. 11, 1983
Mick Luckhurst, Atlanta vs. L.A. Rams, Oct. 7, 1984
Paul McFadden, Philadelphia vs. Detroit, Nov. 4, 1984
Nick Lowery, Kansas City vs. New Orleans, Sept. 8, 1985
Pat Leahy, N.Y. Jets vs. New England, Oct. 20, 1985
Tony Zendejas, Houston vs. San Diego, Nov. 24, 1985
Norm Johnson, Seattle vs. L.A. Raiders, Dec. 8, 1986
Raul Allegre, N.Y. Giants vs. Philadelphia, Nov. 15, 1987
Nick Lowery, Kansas City vs. Detroit, Nov. 26, 1987
Dean Biasucci, Indianapolis vs. Miami, Sept. 25, 1988
Paul McFadden, Atlanta vs. Buffalo, Nov. 5, 1989
Kevin Butler, Chicago vs. Minnesota, Sept. 23, 1990
Kevin Butler, Chicago vs. Green Bay, Oct. 7, 1990
Chip Lohmiller, Washington vs. Indianapolis, Dec. 22, 1990
Chip Lohmiller, Washington vs. Dallas, Sept. 9, 1991
John Kasay, Seattle vs. San Diego, October 27, 1991
Fuad Reveiz, Minnesota vs. Tampa Bay, Dec. 8, 1991
John Carney, San Diego vs. Seattle, Sept. 5, 1993
Tony Zendejas, L.A. Rams vs. Pittsburgh, Sept. 12, 1993
Doug Pelfrey, Cincinnati vs. Houston, Oct. 24, 1993
Eddie Murray, Dallas vs. Minnesota, Dec. 12, 1993
Greg Davis, Phoenix vs. Seattle, Dec. 19, 1993 (OT)

SAFETIES

Most Safeties, Career

4   Ted Hendricks, Baltimore, 1969-73; Green Bay, 1974; Oakland, 1975-81; L.A. Raiders, 1982-83
Doug English, Detroit, 1975-79, 1981-85
3   Bill McPeak, Pittsburgh, 1949-57
Charlie Krueger, San Francisco, 1959-73
Ernie Stautner, Pittsburgh, 1950-63
Jim Katcavage, N.Y. Giants, 1956-68
Roger Brown, Detroit, 1960-66; Los Angeles, 1967-69
Bruce Maher, Detroit, 1960-67; N.Y. Giants, 1968-69
Ron McDole, St. Louis, 1961; Houston, 1962; Buffalo, 1963-70; Washington, 1971-78
Alan Page, Minnesota, 1967-78; Chicago, 1979-81
Lyle Alzado, Denver, 1971-78; Cleveland, 1979-81; L.A. Raiders, 1982-85
Rulon Jones, Denver, 1980-88
Steve McMichael, New England, 1980; Chicago, 1981-93
Kevin Greene, L.A. Rams, 1985-92; Pittsburgh, 1993
Burt Grossman, San Diego, 1989-93
2   By many players

Most Safeties, Season

2   Tom Nash, Green Bay, 1932
Roger Brown, Detroit, 1962
Ron McDole, Buffalo, 1964
Alan Page, Minnesota, 1971
Fred Dryer, Los Angeles, 1973
Benny Barnes, Dallas, 1973
James Young, Houston, 1977
Tom Hannon, Minnesota, 1981
Doug English, Detroit, 1983
Don Blackmon, New England, 1985
Tim Harris, Green Bay, 1988
Brian Jordan, Atlanta, 1991
Burt Grossman, San Diego, 1992
Rod Stephens, Seattle, 1993

Most Safeties, Game

2   Fred Dryer, Los Angeles vs. Green Bay, Oct. 21, 1973

RUSHING

Most Seasons Leading League

8   Jim Brown, Cleveland, 1957-61, 1963-65
4   Steve Van Buren, Philadelphia, 1945, 1947-49
O.J. Simpson, Buffalo, 1972-73, 1975-76
Eric Dickerson, L.A. Rams, 1983-84, 1986; Indianapolis, 1988
3   Earl Campbell, Houston, 1978-80
Emmitt Smith, Dallas, 1991-93

Most Consecutive Seasons Leading League

5   Jim Brown, Cleveland, 1957-61
3   Steve Van Buren, Philadelphia, 1947-49

Jim Brown, Cleveland, 1963-65
Earl Campbell, Houston, 1978-80
Emmitt Smith, Dallas, 1991-93
2   Bill Paschal, N.Y. Giants, 1943-44
Joe Perry, San Francisco, 1953-54
Jim Nance, Boston, 1966-67
Leroy Kelly, Cleveland, 1967-68
O.J. Simpson, Buffalo, 1972-73; 1975-76
Eric Dickerson, L.A. Rams, 1983-84

ATTEMPTS

Most Seasons Leading League

6   Jim Brown, Cleveland, 1958-59, 1961, 1963-65
4   Steve Van Buren, Philadelphia, 1947-50
Walter Payton, Chicago, 1976-79
3   Cookie Gilchrist, Buffalo, 1963-64; Denver, 1965
Jim Nance, Boston, 1966-67, 1969
O.J. Simpson, Buffalo, 1973-75
Eric Dickerson, L.A. Rams, 1983, 1986; Indianapolis, 1988

Most Consecutive Seasons Leading League

4   Steve Van Buren, Philadelphia, 1947-50
Walter Payton, Chicago, 1976-79
3   Jim Brown, Cleveland, 1963-65
Cookie Gilchrist, Buffalo, 1963-64; Denver, 1965
O.J. Simpson, Buffalo, 1973-75
2   By many players

Most Attempts, Career

3,838   Walter Payton, Chicago, 1975-87
2,996   Eric Dickerson, L.A. Rams, 1983-87; Indianapolis, 1987-91; L.A. Raiders, 1992; Atlanta, 1993
2,949   Franco Harris, Pittsburgh, 1972-83; Seattle, 1984

Most Attempts, Season

407   James Wilder, Tampa Bay, 1984
404   Eric Dickerson, L.A. Rams, 1986
397   Gerald Riggs, Atlanta, 1985

Most Attempts, Rookie, Season

390   Eric Dickerson, L.A. Rams, 1983
378   George Rogers, New Orleans, 1981
335   Curt Warner, Seattle, 1983

Most Attempts, Game

45   Jamie Morris, Washington vs. Cincinnati, Dec. 17, 1988 (OT)
43   Butch Woolfolk, N.Y. Giants vs. Philadelphia, Nov. 20, 1983
James Wilder, Tampa Bay vs. Green Bay, Sept. 30, 1984 (OT)
42   James Wilder, Tampa Bay vs. Pittsburgh, Oct. 30, 1983

YARDS GAINED

Most Yards Gained, Career

16,726   Walter Payton, Chicago, 1975-87
13,259   Eric Dickerson, L.A. Rams, 1983-87; Indianapolis, 1987-91; L.A. Raiders, 1992; Atlanta, 1993
12,739   Tony Dorsett, Dallas, 1977-87; Denver, 1988

Most Seasons, 1,000 or More Yards Rushing

10   Walter Payton, Chicago, 1976-81, 1983-86
8   Franco Harris, Pittsburgh, 1972, 1974-79, 1983
Tony Dorsett, Dallas, 1977-81, 1983-85
7   Jim Brown, Cleveland, 1958-61, 1963-65
Eric Dickerson, L.A. Rams, 1983-86; L.A. Rams-Indianapolis, 1987; Indianapolis, 1988-89

Most Consecutive Seasons, 1,000 or More Yards Rushing

7   Eric Dickerson, L.A. Rams, 1983-86; L.A. Rams-Indianapolis, 1987; Indianapolis, 1988-89
6   Franco Harris, Pittsburgh, 1974-79
Walter Payton, Chicago, 1976-81
5   Jim Taylor, Green Bay, 1960-64
O.J. Simpson, Buffalo, 1972-76
Tony Dorsett, Dallas, 1977-81
Barry Sanders, Detroit, 1989-93
Thurman Thomas, Buffalo, 1989-93

Most Yards Gained, Season

2,105   Eric Dickerson, L.A. Rams, 1984
2,003   O.J. Simpson, Buffalo, 1973
1,934   Earl Campbell, Houston, 1980

Most Yards Gained, Rookie, Season

1,808   Eric Dickerson, L.A. Rams, 1983
1,674   George Rogers, New Orleans, 1981
1,605   Ottis Anderson, St. Louis, 1979

Most Yards Gained, Game

275   Walter Payton, Chicago vs. Minnesota, Nov. 20, 1977
273   O.J. Simpson, Buffalo vs. Detroit, Nov. 25, 1976
250   O.J. Simpson, Buffalo vs. New England, Sept. 16, 1973

Most Games, 200 or More Yards Rushing, Career

6   O.J. Simpson, Buffalo, 1969-77; San Francisco, 1978-79
4   Jim Brown, Cleveland, 1957-65

Earl Campbell, Houston, 1978-84; New Orleans, 1984-85
3   Eric Dickerson, L.A. Rams, 1983-87; Indianapolis, 1987-91;
        L.A. Raiders, 1992; Atlanta, 1993
    Greg Bell, Buffalo, 1984-87; L.A. Rams, 1987-89; L.A. Raiders, 1990

Most Games, 200 or More Yards Rushing, Season
4   Earl Campbell, Houston, 1980
3   O.J. Simpson, Buffalo, 1973
2   Jim Brown, Cleveland, 1963
    O.J. Simpson, Buffalo, 1976
    Walter Payton, Chicago, 1977
    Eric Dickerson, L.A. Rams, 1984
    Greg Bell, L.A. Rams, 1989

Most Consecutive Games, 200 or More Yards Rushing
2   O.J. Simpson, Buffalo, 1973, 1976
    Earl Campbell, Houston, 1980

Most Games, 100 or More Yards Rushing, Career
77 Walter Payton, Chicago, 1975-87
64 Eric Dickerson, L.A. Rams, 1983-87; Indianapolis, 1987-91;
        L.A. Raiders, 1992; Atlanta, 1993
58 Jim Brown, Cleveland, 1957-65

Most Games, 100 or More Yards Rushing, Season
12 Eric Dickerson, L.A. Rams, 1984
    Barry Foster, Pittsburgh, 1992
11 O.J. Simpson, Buffalo, 1973
    Earl Campbell, Houston, 1979
    Marcus Allen, L.A. Raiders, 1985
    Eric Dickerson, L.A. Rams, 1986
10 Walter Payton, Chicago, 1977, 1985
    Earl Campbell, Houston, 1980

Most Consecutive Games, 100 or More Yards Rushing
11 Marcus Allen, L.A. Raiders, 1985-86
9   Walter Payton, Chicago, 1985
7   O.J. Simpson, Buffalo, 1972-73
    Earl Campbell, Houston, 1979

Longest Run From Scrimmage
99 Tony Dorsett, Dallas vs. Minnesota, Jan. 3, 1983 (TD)
97 Andy Uram, Green Bay vs. Chi. Cardinals, Oct. 8, 1939 (TD)
    Bob Gage, Pittsburgh vs. Chi. Bears, Dec. 4, 1949 (TD)
96 Jim Spavital, Baltimore vs. Green Bay, Nov. 5, 1950 (TD)
    Bob Hoernschemeyer, Detroit vs. N.Y. Yanks, Nov. 23, 1950 (TD)

AVERAGE GAIN
Highest Average Gain, Career (750 attempts)
5.22 Jim Brown, Cleveland, 1957-65 (2,359-12,312)
5.14 Eugene (Mercury) Morris, Miami, 1969-75; San Diego, 1976
        (804-4,133)
5.00 Gale Sayers, Chicago, 1965-71 (991-4,956)

Highest Average Gain, Season (Qualifiers)
8.44 Beattie Feathers, Chi. Bears, 1934 (119-1,004)
7.98 Randall Cunningham, Philadelphia 1990 (118-942)
6.87 Bobby Douglass, Chicago, 1972 (141-968)

Highest Average Gain, Game (10 attempts)
17.09 Marion Motley, Cleveland vs. Pittsburgh, Oct. 29, 1950 (11-188)
16.70 Bill Grimes, Green Bay vs. N.Y. Yanks, Oct. 8, 1950 (10-167)
16.57 Bobby Mitchell, Cleveland vs. Washington, Nov. 15, 1959 (14-232)

TOUCHDOWNS
Most Seasons Leading League
5   Jim Brown, Cleveland, 1957-59, 1963, 1965
4   Steve Van Buren, Philadelphia, 1945, 1947-49
3   Abner Haynes, Dall. Texans, 1960-62
    Cookie Gilchrist, Buffalo, 1962-64
    Paul Lowe, L.A. Chargers, 1960; San Diego, 1961, 1965
    Leroy Kelly, Cleveland, 1966-68

Most Consecutive Seasons Leading League
3   Steve Van Buren, Philadelphia, 1947-49
    Jim Brown, Cleveland, 1957-59
    Abner Haynes, Dall. Texans, 1960-62
    Cookie Gilchrist, Buffalo, 1962-64
    Leroy Kelly, Cleveland, 1966-68

Most Touchdowns, Career
110 Walter Payton, Chicago, 1975-87
106 Jim Brown, Cleveland, 1957-65
104 John Riggins, N.Y. Jets, 1971-75; Washington, 1976-79, 1981-85

Most Touchdowns, Season
24 John Riggins, Washington, 1983
21 Joe Morris, N.Y. Giants, 1985
19 Jim Taylor, Green Bay, 1962
    Earl Campbell, Houston, 1979
    Chuck Muncie, San Diego, 1981

Most Touchdowns, Rookie, Season
18 Eric Dickerson, L.A. Rams, 1983
15 Ickey Woods, Cincinnati, 1988

14 Gale Sayers, Chicago, 1965
    Barry Sanders, Detroit, 1989

Most Touchdowns, Game
6   Ernie Nevers, Chi. Cardinals vs. Chi. Bears, Nov. 28, 1929
5   Jim Brown, Cleveland vs. Baltimore, Nov. 1, 1959
    Cookie Gilchrist, Buffalo vs. N.Y. Jets, Dec. 8, 1963
4   By many players

Most Consecutive Games Rushing for Touchdowns
13 John Riggins, Washington, 1982-83
    George Rogers, Washington, 1985-86
11 Lenny Moore, Baltimore, 1963-64
10 Greg Bell, L.A. Rams, 1988-89

PASSING
Most Seasons Leading League
6   Sammy Baugh, Washington, 1937, 1940, 1943, 1945, 1947, 1949
4   Len Dawson, Dall. Texans; 1962; Kansas City, 1964, 1966, 1968
    Roger Staubach, Dallas, 1971, 1973, 1978-79
    Ken Anderson, Cincinnati, 1974-75, 1981-82
3   Arnie Herber, Green Bay, 1932, 1934, 1936
    Norm Van Brocklin, Los Angeles, 1950, 1952, 1954
    Bart Starr, Green Bay, 1962, 1964, 1966
    Steve Young, San Francisco, 1991-93

Most Consecutive Seasons Leading League
3   Steve Young, San Francisco, 1991-93
2   Cecil Isbell, Green Bay, 1941-42
    Milt Plum, Cleveland, 1960-61
    Ken Anderson, Cincinnati, 1974-75, 1981-82
    Roger Staubach, Dallas, 1978-79

PASS RATING
Highest Pass Rating, Career (1,500 attempts)
93.1 Joe Montana, San Francisco, 1979-90, 1992; Kansas City, 1993
93.0 Steve Young, Tampa Bay, 1985-86; San Francisco, 1987-93
88.1 Dan Marino, Miami, 1983-93

Highest Pass Rating, Season (Qualifiers)
112.4 Joe Montana, San Francisco, 1989
110.4 Milt Plum, Cleveland, 1960
109.9 Sammy Baugh, Washington, 1945

Highest Pass Rating, Rookie, Season (Qualifiers)
96.0 Dan Marino, Miami, 1983
88.2 Greg Cook, Cincinnati, 1969
84.0 Charlie Conerly, N.Y. Giants, 1948

ATTEMPTS
Most Seasons Leading League
4   Sammy Baugh, Washington, 1937, 1943, 1947-48
    Johnny Unitas, Baltimore, 1957, 1959-61
    George Blanda, Chi. Bears, 1953; Houston, 1963-65
    Dan Marino, Miami, 1984, 1986, 1988, 1992
3   Arnie Herber, Green Bay, 1932, 1934, 1936
    Sonny Jurgensen, Washington, 1966-67, 1969
2   By many players

Most Consecutive Seasons Leading League
3   Johnny Unitas, Baltimore, 1959-61
    George Blanda, Houston, 1963-65
2   By many players

Most Passes Attempted, Career
6,467 Fran Tarkenton, Minnesota, 1961-66, 1972-78; N.Y. Giants, 1967-71
5,604 Dan Fouts, San Diego, 1973-87
5,434 Dan Marino, Miami, 1983-93

Most Passes Attempted, Season
655 Warren Moon, Houston, 1991
623 Dan Marino, Miami, 1986
609 Dan Fouts, San Diego, 1981

Most Passes Attempted, Rookie, Season
486 Rick Mirer, Seattle, 1993
439 Jim Zorn, Seattle, 1976
429 Drew Bledsoe, New England, 1993

Most Passes Attempted, Game
68 George Blanda, Houston vs. Buffalo, Nov. 1, 1964
66 Chris Miller, Atlanta vs. Detroit, Dec. 24, 1989
63 Rich Gannon, Minnesota vs. New England, Oct. 20, 1991 (OT)

COMPLETIONS
Most Seasons Leading League
5   Sammy Baugh, Washington, 1937, 1943, 1945, 1947-48
    Dan Marino, Miami, 1984-86, 1988, 1992
4   George Blanda, Chi. Bears, 1953; Houston, 1963-65
    Sonny Jurgensen, Philadelphia, 1961; Washington, 1966-67, 1969
3   Arnie Herber, Green Bay, 1932, 1934, 1936
    Johnny Unitas, Baltimore, 1959-60, 1963
    John Brodie, San Francisco, 1965, 1968, 1970

Fran Tarkenton, Minnesota, 1975-76, 1978

Most Consecutive Seasons Leading League
3 George Blanda, Houston, 1963-65
  Dan Marino, Miami, 1984-86
2 By many players

Most Passes Completed, Career
3,686 Fran Tarkenton, Minnesota, 1961-66, 1972-78; N.Y. Giants, 1967-71
3,297 Dan Fouts, San Diego, 1973-87
3,219 Dan Marino, Miami, 1983-93

Most Passes Completed, Season
404 Warren Moon, Hosuton, 1991
378 Dan Marino, Miami, 1986
362 Dan Marino, Miami, 1984
  Warren Moon, Houston, 1990

Most Passes Completed, Rookie, Season
274 Rick Mirer, Seattle, 1993
214 Drew Bledsoe, New England, 1993
208 Jim Zorn, Seattle, 1976

Most Passes Completed, Game
42 Richard Todd, N.Y. Jets vs. San Francisco, Sept. 21, 1980
41 Warren Moon, Houston vs. Dallas, Nov. 10, 1991 (OT)
40 Ken Anderson, Cincinnati vs. San Diego, Dec. 20, 1982
  Phil Simms, N.Y. Giants vs. Cincinnati, Oct. 13, 1985

Most Consecutive Passes Completed
22 Joe Montana, San Francisco vs. Cleveland (5), Nov. 29, 1987; vs. Green Bay (17), Dec. 6, 1987
20 Ken Anderson, Cincinnati vs. Houston, Jan. 2, 1983
18 Steve DeBerg, Denver vs. L.A. Rams (17), Dec. 12, 1982; vs. Kansas City (1), Dec. 19, 1982
  Lynn Dickey, Green Bay vs. Houston, Sept. 4, 1983
  Joe Montana, San Francisco vs. L.A. Rams (13), Oct. 28, 1984; vs. Cincinnati (5), Nov. 4, 1984
  Don Majkowski, Green Bay vs. New Orleans, Sept. 18, 1989
  Boomer Esiason, N.Y. Jets vs. Miami (5), Sept. 12, 1993; vs. New England (13), Sept. 26, 1993

COMPLETION PERCENTAGE

Most Seasons Leading League
8 Len Dawson, Dall. Texans, 1962; Kansas City, 1964-69, 1975
7 Sammy Baugh, Washington, 1940, 1942-43, 1945, 1947-49
5 Joe Montana, San Francisco, 1980-81, 1985, 1987, 1989

Most Consecutive Seasons Leading League
6 Len Dawson, Kansas City, 1964-69
3 Sammy Baugh, Washington, 1947-49
  Otto Graham, Cleveland, 1953-55
  Milt Plum, Cleveland, 1959-61
2 By many players

Highest Completion Percentage, Career (1,500 attempts)
63.50 Joe Montana, San Francisco, 1979-90, 1992; Kansas City, 1993 (4,898-3,110)
62.09 Steve Young, Tampa Bay, 1985-86; San Francisco, 1987-93 (1,968-1,222)
62.03 Troy Aikman, Dallas, 1989-93 (1,920-1,191)

Highest Completion Percentage, Season (Qualifiers)
70.55 Ken Anderson, Cincinnati, 1982 (309-218)
70.33 Sammy Baugh, Washington, 1945 (182-128)
70.21 Joe Montana, San Francisco, 1989 (386-271)

Highest Completion Percentage, Rookie, Season (Qualifiers)
58.45 Dan Marino, Miami, 1983 (296-173)
57.14 Jim McMahon, Chicago, 1982 (210-120)
56.38 Rick Mirer, Seattle, 1993 (486-274)

Highest Completion Percentage, Game (20 attempts)
91.30 Vinny Testaverde, Cleveland vs. L.A. Rams, Dec. 26, 1993 (23-21)
90.91 Ken Anderson, Cincinnati vs. Pittsburgh, Nov. 10, 1974 (22-20)
90.48 Lynn Dickey, Green Bay vs. New Orleans, Dec. 13, 1981 (21-19)

YARDS GAINED

Most Seasons Leading League
5 Sonny Jurgensen, Philadelphia, 1961-62; Washington, 1966-67, 1969
  Dan Marino, Miami, 1984-86, 1988, 1992
4 Sammy Baugh, Washington, 1937, 1940, 1947-48
  Johnny Unitas, Baltimore, 1957, 1959-60, 1963
  Dan Fouts, San Diego, 1979-82
3 Arnie Herber, Green Bay, 1932, 1934, 1936
  Sid Luckman, Chi. Bears, 1943, 1945-46
  John Brodie, San Francisco, 1965, 1968, 1970
  John Hadl, San Diego, 1965, 1968, 1971
  Joe Namath, N.Y. Jets, 1966-67, 1972

Most Consecutive Seasons Leading League
4 Dan Fouts, San Diego, 1979-82
3 Dan Marino, Miami, 1984-86
2 By many players

Most Yards Gained, Career
47,003 Fran Tarkenton, Minnesota, 1961-66, 1972-78; N.Y. Giants, 1967-71
43,040 Dan Fouts, San Diego, 1973-87
40,720 Dan Marino, Miami, 1983-93

Most Seasons, 3,000 or More Yards Passing
9 Dan Marino, Miami, 1984-92
8 John Elway, Denver, 1985-91, 1993
7 Joe Montana, San Francisco, 1981, 1983-85, 1987, 1989-90
  Boomer Esiason, Cincinnati, 1985-90; N.Y. Jets, 1993

Most Yards Gained, Season
5,084 Dan Marino, Miami, 1984
4,802 Dan Fouts, San Diego, 1981
4,746 Dan Marino, Miami, 1986

Most Yards Gained, Rookie, Season
2,833 Rick Mirer, Seattle, 1993
2,571 Jim Zorn, Seattle, 1976
2,507 Dennis Shaw, Buffalo, 1970

Most Yards Gained, Game
554 Norm Van Brocklin, Los Angeles vs. N.Y. Yanks, Sept. 28, 1951
527 Warren Moon, Houston vs. Kansas City, Dec. 16, 1990
521 Dan Marino, Miami vs. N.Y. Jets, Oct. 23, 1988

Most Games, 400 or More Yards Passing, Career
10 Dan Marino, Miami, 1983-93
7 Joe Montana, San Francisco, 1979-90, 1992; Kansas City, 1993
6 Dan Fouts, San Diego, 1973-87

Most Games, 400 or More Yards Passing, Season
4 Dan Marino, Miami, 1984
3 Dan Marino, Miami, 1986
2 George Blanda, Houston, 1961
  Sonny Jurgensen, Philadelphia, 1961
  Joe Namath, N.Y. Jets, 1972
  Dan Fouts, San Diego, 1982
  Dan Fouts, San Diego, 1985
  Phil Simms, N.Y. Giants, 1985
  Ken O'Brien, N.Y. Jets, 1986
  Bernie Kosar, Cleveland, 1986
  Dan Marino, Miami, 1988
  Randall Cunningham, Philadelphia, 1989
  Joe Montana, San Francisco, 1989
  Joe Montana, San Francisco, 1990
  Warren Moon, Houston, 1991

Most Consecutive Games, 400 or More Yards Passing
2 Dan Fouts, San Diego, 1982
  Dan Marino, Miami, 1984
  Phil Simms, N.Y. Giants, 1985

Most Games, 300 or More Yards Passing, Career
51 Dan Fouts, San Diego, 1973-87
44 Dan Marino, Miami, 1983-93
38 Warren Moon, Houston, 1984-93

Most Games, 300 or More Yards Passing, Season
9 Dan Marino, Miami, 1984
  Warren Moon, Houston, 1990
8 Dan Fouts, San Diego, 1980
7 Dan Fouts, San Diego, 1981
  Bill Kenney, Kansas City, 1983
  Neil Lomax, St. Louis, 1984
  Dan Fouts, San Diego, 1985

Most Consecutive Games, 300 or More Yards Passing, Season
5 Joe Montana, San Francisco, 1982
4 Dan Fouts, San Diego, 1979
  Bill Kenney, Kansas City, 1983
  Joe Montana, San Francisco, 1990
  Warren Moon, Houston, 1990
3 By many players

Longest Pass Completion (All TDs except as noted)
99 Frank Filchock (to Farkas), Washington vs. Pittsburgh, Oct. 15, 1939
  George Izo (to Mitchell), Washington vs. Cleveland, Sept. 15, 1963
  Karl Sweetan (to Studstill), Detroit vs. Baltimore, Oct. 16, 1966
  Sonny Jurgensen (to Allen), Washington vs. Chicago, Sept. 15, 1968
  Jim Plunkett (to Branch), L.A. Raiders vs. Washington, Oct. 2, 1983
  Ron Jaworski (to Quick), Philadelphia vs. Atlanta, Nov. 10, 1985
98 Doug Russell (to Tinsley), Chi. Cardinals vs. Cleveland, Nov. 27, 1938
  Ogden Compton (to Lane), Chi. Cardinals vs. Green Bay, Nov. 13, 1955
  Bill Wade (to Farrington), Chicago Bears vs. Detroit, Oct. 8, 1961
  Jacky Lee (to Dewveall), Houston vs. San Diego, Nov. 25, 1962
  Earl Morrall (to Jones), N.Y. Giants vs. Pittsburgh, Sept. 11, 1966
  Jim Hart (to Moore), St. Louis vs. Los Angeles, Dec. 10, 1972 (no TD)
  Bobby Hebert (to Haynes), Atlanta vs. New Orleans, Sept. 12, 1993
97 Pat Coffee (to Tinsley), Chi. Cardinals vs. Chi. Bears, Dec. 5, 1937
  Bobby Layne (to Box), Detroit vs. Green Bay, Nov. 26, 1953
  George Shaw (to Tarr), Denver vs. Boston, Sept. 21, 1962
  Bernie Kosar (to Slaughter), Cleveland vs. Chicago, Oct. 23, 1989
  Steve Young (to Taylor), San Francisco vs. Atlanta, Nov. 3, 1991

AVERAGE GAIN

Most Seasons Leading League
- 7 Sid Luckman, Chi. Bears, 1939-43, 1946-47
- 3 Arnie Herber, Green Bay, 1932, 1934, 1936
  Norm Van Brocklin, Los Angeles, 1950, 1952, 1954
  Len Dawson, Dall. Texans, 1962; Kansas City, 1966, 1968
  Bart Starr, Green Bay, 1966-68
  Steve Young, San Francisco, 1991-93

Most Consecutive Seasons Leading League
- 5 Sid Luckman, Chi. Bears, 1939-43
- 3 Bart Starr, Green Bay, 1966-68
  Steve Young, San Francisco, 1991-93
- 2 Bernie Masterson, Chi. Bears, 1937-38
  Sid Luckman, Chi. Bears, 1946-47
  Johnny Unitas, Baltimore, 1964-65
  Terry Bradshaw, Pittsburgh, 1977-78
  Steve Grogan, New England, 1980-81

Highest Average Gain, Career (1,500 attempts)
- 8.63 Otto Graham, Cleveland, 1950-55 (1,565-13,499)
- 8.42 Sid Luckman, Chi. Bears, 1939-50 (1,744-14,686)
- 8.16 Norm Van Brocklin, Los Angeles, 1949-57; Philadelphia, 1958-60 (2,895-23,611)

Highest Average Gain, Season (Qualifiers)
- 11.17 Tommy O'Connell, Cleveland, 1957 (110-1,229)
- 10.86 Sid Luckman, Chi. Bears, 1943 (202-2,194)
- 10.55 Otto Graham, Cleveland, 1953 (258-2,722)

Highest Average Gain, Rookie, Season (Qualifiers)
- 9.411 Greg Cook, Cincinnati, 1969 (197-1,854)
- 9.409 Bob Waterfield, Cleveland, 1945 (171-1,609)
- 8.36 Zeke Bratkowski, Chi. Bears, 1954 (130-1,087)

Highest Average Gain, Game (20 attempts)
- 18.58 Sammy Baugh, Washington vs. Boston, Oct. 31, 1948 (24-446)
- 18.50 Johnny Unitas, Baltimore vs. Atlanta, Nov. 12, 1967 (20-370)
- 17.71 Joe Namath, N.Y. Jets vs. Baltimore, Sept. 24, 1972 (28-496)

TOUCHDOWNS

Most Seasons Leading League
- 4 Johnny Unitas, Baltimore, 1957-60
  Len Dawson, Dall. Texans, 1962; Kansas City, 1963, 1965-66
- 3 Arnie Herber, Green Bay, 1932, 1934, 1936
  Sid Luckman, Chi. Bears, 1943, 1945-46
  Y.A. Tittle, San Francisco, 1955; N.Y. Giants, 1962-63
  Dan Marino, Miami, 1984-86
- 2 By many players

Most Consecutive Seasons Leading League
- 4 Johnny Unitas, Baltimore, 1957-60
- 3 Dan Marino, Miami, 1984-86
- 2 By many players

Most Touchdown Passes, Career
- 342 Fran Tarkenton, Minnesota, 1961-66, 1972-78; N.Y. Giants, 1967-71
- 298 Dan Marino, Miami, 1983-93
- 290 Johnny Unitas, Baltimore, 1956-72: San Diego, 1973

Most Touchdown Passes, Season
- 48 Dan Marino, Miami, 1984
- 44 Dan Marino, Miami, 1986
- 36 George Blanda, Houston, 1961
  Y.A. Tittle, N.Y. Giants, 1963

Most Touchdown Passes, Rookie, Season
- 22 Charlie Conerly, N.Y. Giants, 1948
- 20 Dan Marino, Miami, 1983
- 19 Jim Plunkett, New England, 1971

Most Touchdown Passes, Game
- 7 Sid Luckman, Chi. Bears vs. N.Y. Giants, Nov. 14, 1943
  Adrian Burk, Philadelphia vs. Washington, Oct. 17, 1954
  George Blanda, Houston vs. N.Y. Titans, Nov. 19, 1961
  Y.A. Tittle, N.Y. Giants vs. Washington, Oct. 28, 1962
  Joe Kapp, Minnesota vs. Baltimore, Sept. 28, 1969
- 6 By many players. Last time: Mark Rypien, Washington vs. Atlanta, Nov. 10, 1991

Most Games, Four or More Touchdown Passes, Career
- 17 Johnny Unitas, Baltimore, 1956-72; San Diego, 1973
  Dan Marino, Miami, 1983-93
- 13 George Blanda, Chi. Bears, 1949, 1950-58; Baltimore, 1950; Houston, 1960-66; Oakland, 1967-75
- 12 Sonny Jurgensen, Philadelphia, 1957-63; Washington, 1964-74
  Fran Tarkenton, Minnesota, 1961-66, 1972-78; N.Y. Giants, 1967-71
  Dan Fouts, San Diego, 1973-87

Most Games, Four or More Touchdown Passes, Season
- 6 Dan Marino, Miami, 1984
- 5 Dan Marino, Miami, 1986
- 4 George Blanda, Houston, 1961
  Vince Ferragamo, Los Angeles, 1980

Most Consecutive Games, Four or More Touchdown Passes
- 4 Dan Marino, Miami, 1984
- 2 By many players

Most Consecutive Games, Touchdown Passes
- 47 Johnny Unitas, Baltimore, 1956-60
- 30 Dan Marino, Miami, 1985-87
- 28 Dave Krieg, Seattle, 1983-85

HAD INTERCEPTED

Most Consecutive Passes Attempted, None Intercepted
- 308 Bernie Kosar, Cleveland, 1990-91
- 294 Bart Starr, Green Bay, 1964-65
- 233 Steve DeBerg, Kansas City, 1990

Most Passes Had Intercepted, Career
- 277 George Blanda, Chi. Bears, 1949, 1950-58; Baltimore, 1950; Houston, 1960-66; Oakland, 1967-75
- 268 John Hadl, San Diego, 1962-72; Los Angeles, 1973-74; Green Bay, 1974-75; Houston, 1976-77
- 266 Fran Tarkenton, Minnesota, 1961-66, 1972-78; N.Y. Giants, 1967-71

Most Passes Had Intercepted, Season
- 42 George Blanda, Houston, 1962
- 35 Vinny Testaverde, Tampa Bay, 1988
- 34 Frank Tripucka, Denver, 1960

Most Passes Had Intercepted, Game
- 8 Jim Hardy, Chi. Cardinals vs. Philadelphia, Sept. 24, 1950
- 7 Parker Hall, Cleveland vs. Green Bay, Nov. 8, 1942
  Frank Sinkwich, Detroit vs. Green Bay, Oct. 24, 1943
  Bob Waterfield, Los Angeles vs. Green Bay, Oct. 17, 1948
  Zeke Bratkowski, Chicago vs. Baltimore, Oct. 2, 1960
  Tommy Wade, Pittsburgh vs. Philadelphia, Dec. 12, 1965
  Ken Stabler, Oakland vs. Denver, Oct. 16, 1977
  Steve DeBerg, Tampa Bay vs. San Francisco, Sept. 7, 1986
- 6 By many players

Most Attempts, No Interceptions, Game
- 63 Rich Gannon, Minnesota vs. New England, Oct. 20, 1991 (OT)
- 60 Davey O'Brien, Philadelphia vs. Washington, Dec. 1, 1940
- 57 Joe Montana, San Francisco vs. Atlanta, Oct. 6, 1985

LOWEST PERCENTAGE, PASSES HAD INTERCEPTED

Most Seasons Leading League, Lowest Percentage, Passes Had Intercepted
- 5 Sammy Baugh, Washington, 1940, 1942, 1944-45, 1947
- 3 Charlie Conerly, N.Y. Giants, 1950, 1956, 1959
  Bart Starr, Green Bay, 1962, 1964, 1966
  Roger Staubach, Dallas, 1971, 1977, 1979
  Ken Anderson, Cincinnati, 1972, 1981-82
  Ken O'Brien, N.Y. Jets, 1985, 1987-88
- 2 By many players

Lowest Percentage, Passes Had Intercepted, Career (1,500 attempts)
- 2.52 Bernie Kosar, Cleveland, 1985-93; Dallas, 1993 (3,213-81)
- 2.65 Joe Montana, San Francisco, 1979-90, 1992; Kansas City, 1993 (4,000 130)
- 2.72 Ken O'Brien, N.Y. Jets, 1984-92; Philadelphia, 1993 (3,602-98)

Lowest Percentage, Passes Had Intercepted, Season (Qualifiers)
- 0.66 Joe Ferguson, Buffalo, 1976 (151-1)
- 0.90 Steve DeBerg, Kansas City, 1990 (444-4)
- 1.16 Steve Bartkowski, Atlanta, 1983 (432-5)

Lowest Percentage, Passes Had Intercepted, Rookie, Season (Qualifiers)
- 2.03 Dan Marino, Miami, 1983 (296-6)
- 2.10 Gary Wood, N.Y. Giants, 1964 (143-3)
- 2.82 Bernie Kosar, Cleveland, 1985 (248-7)

TIMES SACKED

Times Sacked has been compiled since 1963.

Most Times Sacked, Career
- 483 Fran Tarkenton, Minnesota, 1961-66, 1972-78; N.Y. Giants, 1967-71
- 477 Phil Simms, N.Y. Giants, 1979-81, 1983-93
- 411 Dave Krieg, Seattle, 1980-91; Kansas City, 1992-93

Most Times Sacked, Season
- 72 Randall Cunningham, Philadelphia, 1986
- 62 Ken O'Brien, N.Y. Jets, 1985
- 61 Neil Lomax, St. Louis, 1985

Most Times Sacked, Game
- 12 Bert Jones, Baltimore vs. St. Louis, Oct. 26, 1980
  Warren Moon, Houston vs. Dallas, Sept. 29, 1985
- 11 Charley Johnson, St. Louis vs. N.Y. Giants, Nov. 1, 1964
  Bart Starr, Green Bay vs. Detroit, Nov. 7, 1965
  Jack Kemp, Buffalo vs. Oakland, Oct. 15, 1967
  Bob Berry, Atlanta vs. St. Louis, Nov. 24, 1968
  Greg Landry, Detroit vs. Dallas, Oct. 6, 1975
  Ron Jaworski, Philadelphia vs. St. Louis, Dec. 18, 1983
  Paul McDonald, Cleveland vs. Kansas City, Sept. 30, 1984
  Archie Manning, Minnesota vs. Chicago, Oct. 28, 1984
  Steve Pelluer, Dallas vs. San Diego, Nov. 16, 1986
  Randall Cunningham, Philadelphia vs. L.A. Raiders, Nov. 30, 1986 (OT)

David Norrie, N.Y. Jets vs. Dallas, Oct. 4, 1987
Troy Aikman, Dallas vs. Philadelphia, Sept. 15, 1991
Bernie Kosar, Cleveland vs. Indianapolis, Sept. 6, 1992
10 By many players

PASS RECEIVING

Most Seasons Leading League
8 Don Hutson, Green Bay, 1936-37, 1939, 1941-45
5 Lionel Taylor, Denver, 1960-63, 1965
3 Tom Fears, Los Angeles, 1948-50
Pete Pihos, Philadelphia, 1953-55
Billy Wilson, San Francisco, 1954, 1956-57
Raymond Berry, Baltimore, 1958-60
Lance Alworth, San Diego, 1966, 1968-69
Sterling Sharpe, Green Bay, 1989, 1992-93

Most Consecutive Seasons Leading League
5 Don Hutson, Green Bay, 1941-45
4 Lionel Taylor, Denver, 1960-63
3 Tom Fears, Los Angeles, 1948-50
Pete Pihos, Philadelphia, 1953-55
Raymond Berry, Baltimore, 1958-60

Most Pass Receptions, Career
888 Art Monk, Washington, 1980-93
819 Steve Largent, Seattle, 1976-89
764 James Lofton, Green Bay, 1978-86; L.A. Raiders, 1987-88; Buffalo, 1989-92; L.A. Rams, 1993; Philadelphia, 1993

Most Seasons, 50 or More Pass Receptions
10 Steve Largent, Seattle, 1976, 1978-81, 1983-87
9 Art Monk, Washington, 1980-81, 1984-86, 1988-91
James Lofton, Green Bay, 1979-81, 1983-86; Buffalo, 1991-92
Gary Clark, Washington, 1985-92; Phoenix, 1993
8 Andre Reed, Buffalo, 1986-93
Jerry Rice, San Francisco, 1986-93

Most Pass Receptions, Season
112 Sterling Sharpe, Green Bay, 1993
108 Sterling Sharpe, Green Bay, 1992
106 Art Monk, Washington, 1984

Most Pass Receptions, Rookie, Season
83 Earl Cooper, San Francisco, 1980
81 Keith Jackson, Philadelphia, 1988
75 Terry Kirby, Miami, 1993

Most Pass Receptions, Game
18 Tom Fears, Los Angeles vs. Green Bay, Dec. 3, 1950
17 Clark Gaines, N.Y. Jets vs. San Francisco, Sept. 21, 1980
16 Sonny Randle, St. Louis vs. N.Y. Giants, Nov. 4, 1962

Most Consecutive Games, Pass Receptions
177 Steve Largent, Seattle, 1977-89
164 Art Monk, Washington, 1980-93 (current)
150 Ozzie Newsome, Cleveland, 1979-89

YARDS GAINED

Most Seasons Leading League
7 Don Hutson, Green Bay, 1936, 1938-39, 1941-44
4 Jerry Rice, San Francisco, 1986, 1989-90, 1993
3 Raymond Berry, Baltimore, 1957, 1959-60
Lance Alworth, San Diego, 1965-66, 1968

Most Consecutive Seasons Leading League
4 Don Hutson, Green Bay, 1941-44
2 By many players

Most Yards Gained, Career
14,004 James Lofton, Green Bay, 1978-86; L.A. Raiders, 1987-88; Buffalo, 1989-92; L.A. Rams, 1993; Philadelphia, 1993
13,089 Steve Largent, Seattle, 1976-89
12,146 Charlie Joiner, Houston, 1969-72; Cincinnati, 1972-75; San Diego, 1976-86

Most Seasons, 1,000 or More Yards, Pass Receiving
8 Steve Largent, Seattle, 1978-81, 1983-86
Jerry Rice, San Francisco, 1986-93
7 Lance Alworth, San Diego, 1963-69
6 James Lofton, Green Bay, 1980-81, 1983-85; Buffalo, 1991

Most Yards Gained, Season
1,746 Charley Hennigan, Houston, 1961
1,602 Lance Alworth, San Diego, 1965
1,570 Jerry Rice, San Francisco, 1986

Most Yards Gained, Rookie, Season
1,473 Bill Groman, Houston, 1960
1,231 Bill Howton, Green Bay, 1952
1,131 Bill Brooks, Indianapolis, 1986

Most Yards Gained, Game
336 Willie Anderson, L.A. Rams vs. New Orleans, Nov. 26, 1989 (OT)
309 Stephone Paige, Kansas City vs. San Diego, Dec. 22, 1985
303 Jim Benton, Cleveland vs. Detroit, Nov. 22, 1945

Most Games, 200 or More Yards Pass Receiving, Career

5 Lance Alworth, San Diego, 1962-70; Dallas, 1971-72
4 Don Hutson, Green Bay, 1935-45
Charley Hennigan, Houston, 1960-66
3 Don Maynard, N.Y. Giants, 1958; N.Y. Jets, 1960-72; St. Louis, 1973
Wes Chandler, New Orleans, 1978-81; San Diego, 1981-87; San Francisco, 1988
Jerry Rice, San Francisco, 1985-93

Most Games, 200 or More Yards Pass Receiving, Season
3 Charley Hennigan, Houston, 1961
2 Don Hutson, Green Bay, 1942
Gene Roberts, N.Y. Giants, 1949
Lance Alworth, San Diego, 1963
Don Maynard, N.Y. Jets, 1968

Most Games, 100 or More Yards Pass Receiving, Career
50 Don Maynard, N.Y. Giants, 1958; N.Y. Jets, 1960-72; St. Louis, 1973
44 Jerry Rice, San Francisco, 1985-93
43 James Lofton, Green Bay, 1978-86; L.A. Raiders, 1987-88; Buffalo, 1989-92; L.A. Rams, 1993; Philadelphia, 1993

Most Games, 100 or More Yards Pass Receiving, Season
10 Charley Hennigan, Houston, 1961
9 Elroy (Crazylegs) Hirsch, Los Angeles, 1951
Bill Groman, Houston, 1960
Lance Alworth, San Diego, 1965
Don Maynard, N.Y. Jets, 1967
Stanley Morgan, New England, 1986
Mark Carrier, Tampa Bay, 1989
8 Charley Hennigan, Houston, 1964
Lance Alworth, San Diego, 1967
Mark Duper, Miami, 1986
Jerry Rice, San Francisco, 1989

Most Consecutive Games, 100 or More Yards Pass Receiving
7 Charley Hennigan, Houston, 1961
Bill Groman, Houston, 1961
6 Raymond Berry, Baltimore, 1960
Pat Studstill, Detroit, 1966
5 Elroy (Crazylegs) Hirsch, Los Angeles, 1951
Bob Boyd, Los Angeles, 1954
Terry Barr, Detroit, 1963
Lance Alworth, San Diego, 1966

Longest Pass Reception (All TDs except as noted)
99 Andy Farkas (from Filchock), Washington vs. Pittsburgh, Oct. 15, 1939
Bobby Mitchell (from Izo), Washington vs. Cleveland, Sept. 15, 1963
Pat Studstill (from Sweetan), Detroit vs. Baltimore, Oct. 16, 1966
Gerry Allen (from Jurgensen), Washington vs. Chicago, Sept. 15, 1968
Cliff Branch (from Plunkett), L.A. Raiders vs. Washington, Oct. 2, 1983
Mike Quick (from Jaworski), Philadelphia vs. Atlanta, Nov. 10, 1985
98 Gaynell Tinsley (from Russell), Chi. Cardinals vs. Cleveland, Nov. 17, 1938
Dick (Night Train) Lane (from Compton), Chi. Cardinals vs. Green Bay, Nov. 13, 1955
John Farrington (from Wade), Chicago vs. Detroit, Oct. 8, 1961
Willard Dewveall (from Lee), Houston vs. San Diego, Nov. 25, 1962
Homer Jones (from Morrall), N.Y. Giants vs. Pittsburgh, Sept. 11, 1966
Bobby Moore (from Hart), St. Louis vs. Los Angeles, Dec. 10, 1972 (no TD)
Michael Haynes (from Hebert), Atlanta vs. New Orleans, Sept. 12, 1993
97 Gaynell Tinsley (from Coffee), Chi. Cardinals vs. Chi. Bears, Dec. 5, 1937
Cloyce Box (from Layne), Detroit vs. Green Bay, Nov. 26, 1953
Jerry Tarr (from Shaw), Denver vs. Boston, Sept. 21, 1962
Webster Slaughter (from Kosar), Cleveland vs. Chicago, Oct. 23, 1989
John Taylor (from Young), San Francisco vs. Atlanta, Nov. 3, 1991

AVERAGE GAIN

Highest Average Gain, Career (200 receptions)
22.26 Homer Jones, N.Y. Giants, 1964-69; Cleveland, 1970 (224-4,986)
20.83 Buddy Dial, Pittsburgh, 1959-63; Dallas, 1964-66 (261-5,436)
20.24 Harlon Hill, Chicago, 1954-61; Pittsburgh, 1962; Detroit, 1962 (233-4,717)

Highest Average Gain, Season (24 receptions)
32.58 Don Currivan, Boston, 1947 (24-782)
31.44 Bucky Pope, Los Angeles, 1964 (25-786)
28.60 Bobby Duckworth, San Diego, 1984 (25-715)

Highest Average Gain, Game (3 receptions)
60.67 Bill Groman, Houston vs. Denver, Nov. 20, 1960 (3-182)
Homer Jones, N.Y. Giants vs. Washington, Dec. 12, 1965 (3-182)
60.33 Don Currivan, Boston vs. Washington, Nov. 30, 1947 (3-181)
59.67 Bobby Duckworth, San Diego vs. Chicago, Dec. 3, 1984 (3-179)

TOUCHDOWNS

Most Seasons Leading League
9 Don Hutson, Green Bay, 1935-38, 1940-44

6 Jerry Rice, San Francisco, 1986-87, 1989-91, 1993
3 Lance Alworth, San Diego, 1964-66

Most Consecutive Seasons Leading League
5 Don Hutson, Green Bay, 1940-44
4 Don Hutson, Green Bay, 1935-38
3 Lance Alworth, San Diego, 1964-66
Jerry Rice, San Francisco, 1989-91

Most Touchdowns, Career
118 Jerry Rice, San Francisco, 1985-93
100 Steve Largent, Seattle, 1976-89
99 Don Hutson, Green Bay, 1935-45

Most Touchdowns, Season
22 Jerry Rice, San Francisco, 1987
18 Mark Clayton, Miami, 1984
17 Don Hutson, Green Bay, 1942
Elroy (Crazylegs) Hirsch, Los Angeles, 1951
Bill Groman, Houston, 1961
Jerry Rice, San Francisco, 1989

Most Touchdowns, Rookie, Season
13 Bill Howton, Green Bay, 1952
John Jefferson, San Diego, 1979
12 Harlon Hill, Chi. Bears, 1954
Bill Groman, Houston, 1960
Mike Ditka, Chicago, 1961
Bob Hayes, Dallas, 1965
10 Bill Swiacki, N.Y. Giants, 1948
Bucky Pope, Los Angeles, 1964
Sammy White, Minnesota, 1976
Daryl Turner, Seattle, 1984

Most Touchdowns, Game
5 Bob Shaw, Chi. Cardinals vs. Baltimore, Oct. 2, 1950
Kellen Winslow, San Diego vs. Oakland, Nov. 22, 1981
Jerry Rice, San Francisco vs. Atlanta, Oct. 14, 1990
4 By many players. Last time: Jerry Rice, San Francisco vs. Tampa Bay, Nov. 14, 1993

Most Consecutive Games, Touchdowns
13 Jerry Rice, San Francisco, 1986-87
11 Elroy (Crazylegs) Hirsch, Los Angeles, 1950-51
Buddy Dial, Pittsburgh, 1959-60
9 Lance Alworth, San Diego, 1963

INTERCEPTIONS BY
Most Seasons Leading League
3 Everson Walls, Dallas, 1981-82, 1985
2 Dick (Night Train) Lane, Los Angeles, 1952; Chi. Cardinals, 1954
Jack Christiansen, Detroit, 1953, 1957
Milt Davis, Baltimore, 1957, 1959
Dick Lynch, N.Y. Giants, 1961, 1963
Johnny Robinson, Kansas City, 1966, 1970
Bill Bradley, Philadelphia, 1971-72
Emmitt Thomas, Kansas City, 1969, 1974
Ronnie Lott, San Francisco, 1986; L.A. Raiders, 1991

Most Interceptions By, Career
81 Paul Krause, Washington, 1964-67; Minnesota, 1968-79
79 Emlen Tunnell, N.Y. Giants, 1948-58; Green Bay, 1959-61
68 Dick (Night Train) Lane, Los Angeles, 1952-53; Chi. Cardinals, 1954-59; Detroit, 1960-65

Most Interceptions By, Season
14 Dick (Night Train) Lane, Los Angeles, 1952
13 Dan Sandifer, Washington, 1948
Orban (Spec) Sanders, N.Y. Yanks, 1950
Lester Hayes, Oakland, 1980
12 By nine players

Most Interceptions By, Rookie, Season
14 Dick (Night Train) Lane, Los Angeles, 1952
13 Dan Sandifer, Washington, 1948
12 Woodley Lewis, Los Angeles, 1950
Paul Krause, Washington, 1964

Most Interceptions By, Game
4 Sammy Baugh, Washington vs. Detroit, Nov. 14, 1943
Dan Sandifer, Washington vs. Boston, Oct. 31, 1948
Don Doll, Detroit vs. Chi. Cardinals, Oct. 23, 1949
Bob Nussbaumer, Chi. Cardinals vs. N.Y. Bulldogs, Nov. 13, 1949
Russ Craft, Philadelphia vs. Chi. Cardinals, Sept. 24, 1950
Bobby Dillon, Green Bay vs. Detroit, Nov. 26, 1953
Jack Butler, Pittsburgh vs. Washington, Dec. 13, 1953
Austin (Goose) Gonsoulin, Denver vs. Buffalo, Sept. 18, 1960
Jerry Norton, St. Louis vs. Washington, Nov. 20, 1960; vs. Pittsburgh, Nov. 26, 1961
Dave Baker, San Francisco vs. L.A. Rams, Dec. 4, 1960
Bobby Ply, Dall. Texans vs. San Diego, Dec. 16, 1962
Bobby Hunt, Kansas City vs. Houston, Oct. 4, 1964
Willie Brown, Denver vs. N.Y. Jets, Nov. 15, 1964

Dick Anderson, Miami vs. Pittsburgh, Dec. 3, 1973
Willie Buchanon, Green Bay vs. San Diego, Sept. 24, 1978
Deron Cherry, Kansas City vs. Seattle, Sept. 29, 1985

Most Consecutive Games, Passes Intercepted By
8 Tom Morrow, Oakland, 1962-63
7 Paul Krause, Washington, 1964
Larry Wilson, St. Louis, 1966
Ben Davis, Cleveland, 1968
6 Dick (Night Train) Lane, Chi. Cardinals, 1954-55
Will Sherman, Los Angeles, 1954-55
Jim Shofner, Cleveland, 1960
Paul Krause, Minnesota, 1968
Willie Williams, N.Y. Giants, 1968
Kermit Alexander, San Francisco, 1968-69
Mel Blount, Pittsburgh, 1975
Eric Harris, Kansas City, 1980
Lester Hayes, Oakland, 1980
Barry Wilburn, Washington, 1987

YARDS GAINED
Most Seasons Leading League
2 Dick (Night Train) Lane, Los Angeles, 1952; Chi. Cardinals, 1954
Herb Adderley, Green Bay, 1965, 1969
Dick Anderson, Miami, 1968, 1970

Most Yards Gained, Career
1,282 Emlen Tunnell, N.Y. Giants, 1948-58; Green Bay, 1959-61
1,207 Dick (Night Train) Lane, Los Angeles, 1952-53; Chi. Cardinals, 1954-59; Detroit, 1960-65
1,185 Paul Krause, Washington, 1964-67; Minnesota, 1968-79

Most Yards Gained, Season
349 Charlie McNeil, San Diego, 1961
301 Don Doll, Detroit, 1949
298 Dick (Night Train) Lane, Los Angeles, 1952

Most Yards Gained, Rookie, Season
301 Don Doll, Detroit, 1949
298 Dick (Night Train) Lane, Los Angeles, 1952
275 Woodley Lewis, Los Angeles, 1950

Most Yards Gained, Game
177 Charlie McNeil, San Diego vs. Houston, Sept. 24, 1961
170 Louis Oliver, Miami vs. Buffalo, Oct. 4, 1992
167 Dick Jauron, Detroit vs. Chicago, Nov. 18, 1973

Longest Return (All TDs)
103 Vencie Glenn, San Diego vs. Denver, Nov. 29, 1987
Louis Oliver, Miami vs. Buffalo, Oct. 4, 1992
102 Bob Smith, Detroit vs. Chi. Bears, Nov. 24, 1949
Erich Barnes, N.Y. Giants vs. Dall. Cowboys, Oct. 15, 1961
Gary Barbaro, Kansas City vs. Seattle, Dec. 11, 1977
Louis Breeden, Cincinnati vs. San Diego, Nov. 8, 1981
Eddie Anderson, L.A. Raiders vs. Miami, Dec. 14, 1992
Donald Frank, San Diego vs. L.A. Raiders, Oct. 31, 1993
101 Richie Petitbon, Chicago vs Los Angeles, Dec. 9, 1962
Henry Carr, N.Y. Giants vs. Los Angeles, Nov. 13, 1966
Tony Greene, Buffalo vs. Kansas City, Oct. 3, 1976
Tom Pridemore, Atlanta vs. San Francisco, Sept. 20, 1981

TOUCHDOWNS
Most Touchdowns, Career
9 Ken Houston, Houston, 1967-72; Washington, 1973-80
7 Herb Adderley, Green Bay, 1961-69; Dallas, 1970-72
Erich Barnes, Chi. Bears, 1958-60; N.Y. Giants, 1961-64; Cleveland, 1965-70
Lem Barney, Detroit, 1967-77
6 Tom Janik, Denver, 1963-64; Buffalo, 1965-68; Boston, 1969-70; New England, 1971
Miller Farr, Denver, 1965; San Diego, 1965-66; Houston, 1967-69; St. Louis, 1970-72; Detroit, 1973
Bobby Bell, Kansas City, 1963-74

Most Touchdowns, Season
4 Ken Houston, Houston, 1971
Jim Kearney, Kansas City, 1972
Eric Allen, Philadelphia, 1993
3 Dick Harris, San Diego, 1961
Dick Lynch, N.Y. Giants, 1963
Herb Adderley, Green Bay, 1965
Lem Barney, Detroit, 1967
Miller Farr, Houston, 1967
Monte Jackson, Los Angeles, 1976
Rod Perry, Los Angeles, 1978
Ronnie Lott, San Francisco, 1981
Lloyd Burruss, Kansas City, 1986
Wayne Haddix, Tampa Bay, 1990
Robert Massey, Phoenix, 1992
2 By many players

Most Touchdowns, Rookie, Season
- 3 Lem Barney, Detroit, 1967
  Ronnie Lott, San Francisco, 1981
- 2 By many players

Most Touchdowns, Game
- 2 Bill Blackburn, Chi. Cardinals vs. Boston, Oct. 24, 1948
  Dan Sandifer, Washington vs. Boston, Oct. 31, 1948
  Bob Franklin, Cleveland vs. Chicago, Dec. 11, 1960
  Bill Stacy, St. Louis vs. Dall. Cowboys, Nov. 5, 1961
  Jerry Norton, St. Louis vs. Pittsburgh, Nov. 26, 1961
  Miller Farr, Houston vs. Buffalo, Dec. 7, 1968
  Ken Houston, Houston vs. San Diego, Dec. 19, 1971
  Jim Kearney, Kansas City vs. Denver, Oct. 1, 1972
  Lemar Parrish, Cincinnati vs. Houston, Dec. 17, 1972
  Dick Anderson, Miami vs. Pittsburgh, Dec. 3, 1973
  Prentice McCray, New England vs. N.Y. Jets, Nov. 21, 1976
  Kenny Johnson, Atlanta vs. Green Bay, Nov. 27, 1983 (OT)
  Mike Kozlowski, Miami vs. N.Y. Jets, Dec. 16, 1983
  Dave Brown, Seattle vs. Kansas City, Nov. 4, 1984
  Lloyd Burruss, Kansas City vs. San Diego, Oct. 19, 1986
  Henry Jones, Buffalo vs. Indianapolis, Sept. 20, 1992
  Robert Massey, Phoenix vs. Washington, Oct. 4, 1992
  Eric Allen, Philadelphia vs. New Orleans, Dec. 26, 1993

PUNTING

Most Seasons Leading League
- 4 Sammy Baugh, Washington, 1940-43
  Jerrel Wilson, Kansas City, 1965, 1968, 1972-73
- 3 Yale Lary, Detroit, 1959, 1961, 1963
  Jim Fraser, Denver, 1962-64
  Ray Guy, Oakland, 1974-75, 1977
  Rohn Stark, Baltimore, 1983; Indianapolis, 1985-86
- 2 By many players

Most Consecutive Seasons Leading League
- 4 Sammy Baugh, Washington, 1940-43
- 3 Jim Fraser, Denver, 1962-64
- 2 By many players

PUNTS

Most Punts, Career
- 1,154 Dave Jennings, N.Y. Giants, 1974-84; N.Y. Jets, 1985-87
- 1,083 John James, Atlanta, 1972-81; Detroit, 1982, Houston, 1982-84
- 1,072 Jerrel Wilson, Kansas City, 1963-77; New England, 1978

Most Punts, Season
- 114 Bob Parsons, Chicago, 1981
- 109 John James, Atlanta, 1978
- 108 John Teltschik, Philadelphia, 1986
  Rick Tuten, Seattle, 1992

Most Punts, Rookie, Season
- 108 John Teltschik, Philadelphia, 1986
- 99 Lewis Colbert, Kansas City, 1986
- 96 Mike Connell, San Francisco, 1978
  Chris Norman, Denver, 1984

Most Punts, Game
- 15 John Teltschik, Philadelphia vs. N.Y. Giants, Dec. 6, 1987 (OT)
- 14 Dick Nesbitt, Chi. Cardinals vs. Chi. Bears, Nov. 30, 1933
  Keith Molesworth, Chi. Bears vs. Green Bay, Dec. 10, 1933
  Sammy Baugh, Washington vs. Philadelphia, Nov. 5, 1939
  Carl Kinscherf, N.Y. Giants vs. Detroit, Nov. 7, 1943
  George Taliaferro, N.Y. Yanks vs. Los Angeles, Sept. 28, 1951
- 12 By many players. Last time: Rick Tuten, Seattle vs. Denver, Nov. 28, 1993

Longest Punt
- 98 Steve O'Neal, N.Y. Jets vs. Denver, Sept. 21, 1969
- 94 Joe Lintzenich, Chi. Bears vs. N.Y. Giants, Nov. 16, 1931
- 93 Shawn McCarthy, New England vs. Buffalo, Nov. 3, 1991

AVERAGE YARDAGE

Highest Average, Punting, Career (250 punts)
- 45.10 Sammy Baugh, Washington, 1937-52 (338-15,245)
- 44.68 Tommy Davis, San Francisco, 1959-69 (511-22,833)
- 44.29 Yale Lary, Detroit, 1952-64 1956-64 (503-22,279)

Highest Average, Punting, Season (Qualifiers)
- 51.40 Sammy Baugh, Washington, 1940 (35-1,799)
- 48.94 Yale Lary, Detroit, 1963 (35-1,713)
- 48.73 Sammy Baugh, Washington, 1941 (30-1,462)

Highest Average, Punting, Rookie, Season (Qualifiers)
- 45.92 Frank Sinkwich, Detroit, 1943 (12-551)
- 45.66 Tommy Davis, San Francisco, 1959 (59-2,694)
- 45.57 David Lee, Baltimore, 1966 (49-2,233)

Highest Average, Punting, Game (4 punts)
- 61.75 Bob Cifers, Detroit vs. Chi. Bears, Nov. 24, 1946 (4-247)
- 61.60 Roy McKay, Green Bay vs. Chi. Cardinals, Oct. 28, 1945 (5-308)

- 59.40 Sammy Baugh, Washington vs. Detroit, Oct. 27, 1940 (5-297)

PUNTS HAD BLOCKED

Most Consecutive Punts, None Blocked
- 623 Dave Jennings, N.Y. Giants, 1976-83
- 619 Ray Guy, Oakland, 1979-81; L.A. Raiders, 1982-86
- 578 Bobby Walden, Minnesota, 1964-67; Pittsburgh, 1968-72

Most Punts Had Blocked, Career
- 14 Herman Weaver, Detroit, 1970-76; Seattle, 1977-80
  Harry Newsome, Pittsburgh, 1985-89; Minnesota, 1990-93
- 12 Jerrel Wilson, Kansas City, 1963-77; New England, 1978
  Tom Blanchard, N.Y. Giants, 1971-73; New Orleans, 1974-78; Tampa Bay, 1979-81
- 11 David Lee, Baltimore, 1966-78

Most Punts Had Blocked, Season
- 6 Harry Newsome, Pittsburgh, 1988
- 4 Bryan Wagner, Cleveland, 1990
- 3 By many players

PUNT RETURNS

Most Seasons Leading League
- 3 Les (Speedy) Duncan, San Diego, 1965-66; Washington, 1971
  Rick Upchurch, Denver, 1976, 1978, 1982
- 2 Dick Christy, N.Y. Titans, 1961-62
  Claude Gibson, Oakland, 1963-64
  Billy Johnson, Houston, 1975, 1977
  Mel Gray, New Orleans, 1987; Detroit, 1991

PUNT RETURNS

Most Punt Returns, Career
- 292 Vai Sikahema, St. Louis, 1986-87; Phoenix, 1988-90; Green Bay, 1991; Philadelphia, 1992-93
- 282 Billy Johnson, Houston, 1974-80; Atlanta, 1982-87; Washington, 1988
- 267 J.T. Smith, Washington, 1978; Kansas City, 1978-84; St. Louis, 1985-87; Phoenix, 1988-90

Most Punt Returns, Season
- 70 Danny Reece, Tampa Bay, 1979
- 62 Fulton Walker, Miami-L.A. Raiders, 1985
- 58 J.T. Smith, Kansas City, 1979
  Greg Pruitt, L.A. Raiders, 1983
  Leo Lewis, Minnesota, 1988

Most Punt Returns, Rookie, Season
- 57 Lew Barnes, Chicago, 1986
- 54 James Jones, Dallas, 1980
- 53 Louis Lipps, Pittsburgh, 1984

Most Punt Returns, Game
- 11 Eddie Brown, Washington vs. Tampa Bay, Oct. 9, 1977
- 10 Theo Bell, Pittsburgh vs. Buffalo, Dec. 16, 1979
  Mike Nelms, Washington vs. New Orleans, Dec. 26, 1982
  Ronnie Harris, New England vs. Pittsburgh, Dec. 5, 1993
- 9 Rodger Bird, Oakland vs. Denver, Sept. 10, 1967
  Ralph McGill, San Francisco vs. Atlanta, Oct. 29, 1972
  Ed Podolak, Kansas City vs. San Diego, Nov. 10, 1974
  Anthony Leonard, San Francisco vs. New Orleans, Oct. 17, 1976
  Butch Johnson, Dallas vs. Buffalo, Nov. 15, 1976
  Larry Marshall, Philadelphia vs. Tampa Bay, Sept. 18, 1977
  Nesby Glasgow, Baltimore vs. Kansas City, Sept. 2, 1979
  Mike Nelms, Washington vs. St. Louis, Dec. 21, 1980
  Leon Bright, N.Y. Giants vs. Philadelphia, Dec. 11, 1982
  Pete Shaw, N.Y. Giants vs. Philadelphia, Nov. 20, 1983
  Cleotha Montgomery, L.A. Raiders vs. Detroit, Dec. 10, 1984
  Phil McConkey, N.Y. Giants vs. Philadelphia, Dec. 6, 1987 (OT)

FAIR CATCHES

Most Fair Catches, Career
- 102 Willie Wood, Green Bay, 1960-71
- 99 Phil McConkey, N.Y. Giants, 1984-88; Green Bay, 1986; San Diego, 1989
- 98 Leo Lewis, Minnesota, 1981-90, 1991; Cleveland, 1990

Most Fair Catches, Season
- 27 Leo Lewis, Minnesota, 1989
- 25 Mark Konecny, Philadelphia, 1988
  Phil McConkey, N.Y. Giants, 1988
  Chris Warren, Seattle, 1992
- 24 Ken Graham, San Diego, 1969

Most Fair Catches, Game
- 7 Lem Barney, Detroit vs. Chicago, Nov. 21, 1976
  Bobby Morse, Philadelphia vs. Buffalo, Dec. 27, 1987
- 6 Jake Scott, Miami vs. Buffalo, Dec. 20, 1970
  Greg Pruitt, L.A. Raiders vs. Seattle, Oct. 7, 1984
  Phil McConkey, San Diego vs. Kansas City, Dec. 17, 1989
  Gerald McNeil, Houston vs. Pittsburgh, Sept. 16, 1990
- 5 By many players

YARDS GAINED
Most Seasons Leading League
- 3 Alvin Haymond, Baltimore, 1965-66; Los Angeles, 1969
- 2 Bill Dudley, Pittsburgh, 1942, 1946
  Emlen Tunnell, N.Y. Giants, 1951-52
  Dick Christy, N.Y. Titans, 1961-62
  Claude Gibson, Oakland, 1963-64
  Rodger Bird, Oakland, 1966-67
  J.T. Smith, Kansas City, 1979-80
  Vai Sikahema, St. Louis, 1986-87
  David Meggett, N.Y. Giants, 1989-90

Most Yards Gained, Career
- 3,317 Billy Johnson, Houston, 1974-80; Atlanta, 1982-87; Washington, 1988
- 3,169 Vai Sikahema, St. Louis, 1986-87; Phoenix, 1988-90; Green Bay, 1991; Philadelphia, 1992-93
- 3,008 Rick Upchurch, Denver, 1975-83

Most Yards Gained, Season
- 692 Fulton Walker, Miami-L.A. Raiders, 1985
- 666 Greg Pruitt, L.A. Raiders, 1983
- 656 Louis Lipps, Pittsburgh, 1984

Most Yards Gained, Rookie, Season
- 656 Louis Lipps, Pittsburgh, 1984
- 655 Neal Colzie, Oakland, 1975
- 608 Mike Haynes, New England, 1976

Most Yards Gained, Game
- 207 LeRoy Irvin, Los Angeles vs. Atlanta, Oct. 11, 1981
- 205 George Atkinson, Oakland vs. Buffalo, Sept. 15, 1968
- 184 Tom Watkins, Detroit vs. San Francisco, Oct. 6, 1963

Longest Punt Return (All TDs)
- 98 Gil LeFebvre, Cincinnati vs. Brooklyn, Dec. 3, 1933
  Charlie West, Minnesota vs. Washington, Nov. 3, 1968
  Dennis Morgan, Dallas vs. St. Louis, Oct. 13, 1974
  Terance Mathis, N.Y. Jets vs. Dallas, Nov. 4, 1990
- 97 Greg Pruitt, L.A. Raiders vs. Washington, Oct. 2, 1983
- 96 Bill Dudley, Washington vs. Pittsburgh, Dec. 3, 1950

AVERAGE YARDAGE
Highest Average, Career (75 returns)
- 12.78 George McAfee, Chi. Bears, 1940-41, 1945-50 (112-1,431)
- 12.75 Jack Christiansen, Detroit, 1951-58 (85-1,084)
- 12.55 Claude Gibson, San Diego, 1961-62; Oakland, 1963-65 (110-1,381)

Highest Average, Season (Qualifiers)
- 23.00 Herb Rich, Baltimore, 1950 (12-276)
- 21.47 Jack Christiansen, Detroit, 1952 (15-322)
- 21.28 Dick Christy, N.Y. Titans, 1961 (18-383)

Highest Average, Rookie, Season (Qualifiers)
- 23.00 Herb Rich, Baltimore, 1950 (12-276)
- 20.88 Jerry Davis, Chi. Cardinals, 1948 (16-334)
- 20.73 Frank Sinkwich, Detroit, 1943 (11-228)

Highest Average, Game (3 returns)
- 47.67 Chuck Latourette, St. Louis vs. New Orleans, Sept. 29, 1968 (3-143)
- 47.33 Johnny Roland, St. Louis vs. Philadelphia, Oct. 2, 1966 (3-142)
- 45.67 Dick Christy, N.Y. Titans vs. Denver, Sept. 24, 1961 (3-137)

TOUCHDOWNS
Most Touchdowns, Career
- 8 Jack Christiansen, Detroit, 1951-58
  Rick Upchurch, Denver, 1975-83
- 6 Billy Johnson, Houston, 1974-80; Atlanta, 1982-87; Washington, 1988
- 5 Emlen Tunnell, N.Y. Giants, 1948-58; Green Bay, 1959-61

Most Touchdowns, Season
- 4 Jack Christiansen, Detroit, 1951
  Rick Upchurch, Denver, 1976
- 3 Emlen Tunnell, N.Y. Giants, 1951
  Billy Johnson, Houston, 1975
  LeRoy Irvin, Los Angeles, 1981
- 2 By many players

Most Touchdowns, Rookie, Season
- 4 Jack Christiansen, Detroit, 1951
- 2 By 10 players

Most Touchdowns, Game
- 2 Jack Christiansen, Detroit vs. Los Angeles, Oct. 14, 1951; vs. Green Bay, Nov. 22, 1951
  Dick Christy, N.Y. Titans vs. Denver, Sept. 24, 1961
  Rick Upchurch, Denver vs. Cleveland, Sept. 26, 1976
  LeRoy Irvin, Los Angeles vs. Atlanta, Oct. 11, 1981
  Vai Sikahema, St. Louis vs. Tampa Bay, Dec. 21, 1986
  Todd Kinchen, L.A. Rams vs. Atlanta, Dec. 27, 1992
  Eric Metcalf, Cleveland vs. Pittsburgh, Oct. 24, 1993

KICKOFF RETURNS
Most Seasons Leading League
- 3 Abe Woodson, San Francisco, 1959, 1962-63

- 2 Lynn Chandnois, Pittsburgh, 1951-52
  Bobby Jancik, Houston, 1962-63
  Travis Williams, Green Bay, 1967; Los Angeles, 1971

KICKOFF RETURNS
Most Kickoff Returns, Career
- 275 Ron Smith, Chicago, 1965, 1970-72; Atlanta, 1966-67; Los Angeles, 1968-69; San Diego, 1973; Oakland, 1974
- 264 Mel Gray, New Orleans, 1986-88; Detroit, 1989-93
- 243 Bruce Harper, N.Y. Jets, 1977-84

Most Kickoff Returns, Season
- 60 Drew Hill, Los Angeles, 1981
- 55 Bruce Harper, N.Y. Jets, 1978, 1979
  David Turner, Cincinnati, 1979
  Stump Mitchell, St. Louis, 1981
- 53 Eddie Payton, Minnesota, 1980
  Buster Rhymes, Minnesota, 1985

Most Kickoff Returns, Rookie, Season
- 55 Stump Mitchell, St. Louis, 1981
- 53 Buster Rhymes, Minnesota, 1985
- 50 Nesby Glasgow, Baltimore, 1979
  Dino Hall, Cleveland, 1979

Most Kickoff Returns, Game
- 9 Noland Smith, Kansas City vs. Oakland, Nov. 23, 1967
  Dino Hall, Cleveland vs. Pittsburgh, Oct. 7, 1979
  Paul Palmer, Kansas City vs. Seattle, Sept. 20, 1987
- 8 George Taliaferro, N.Y. Yanks vs. N.Y. Giants, Dec. 3, 1950
  Bobby Jancik, Houston vs. Boston, Dec. 8, 1963
  Bobby Jancik, Houston vs. Oakland, Dec. 22, 1963
  Mel Renfro, Dallas vs. Green Bay, Nov. 29, 1964
  Willie Porter, Boston vs. N.Y. Jets, Sept. 22, 1968
  Keith Moody, Buffalo vs. Seattle, Oct. 30, 1977
  Brian Baschnagel, Chicago vs. Houston, Nov. 6, 1977
  Bruce Harper, N.Y. Jets vs. New England, Oct. 29, 1978
  Bruce Harper, N.Y. Jets vs. New England, Sept. 9, 1979
  Dino Hall, Cleveland vs. Pittsburgh, Nov. 25, 1979
  Terry Metcalf, Washington vs. St. Louis, Sept. 20, 1981
  Harlan Huckleby, Green Bay vs. Washington, Oct. 17, 1983
  Gary Ellerson, Green Bay vs. St. Louis, Sept. 29, 1985
  Bobby Humphery, N.Y. Jets vs. Cincinnati, Dec. 21, 1986
  Bobby Joe Edmonds, Seattle vs. L.A. Raiders, Nov. 30, 1987
  Joe Cribbs, Miami vs. Pittsburgh, Dec. 18, 1988
  Erric Pegram, Atlanta vs. Washington, Nov. 10, 1991
  Mel Gray, Detroit vs. Dallas, Nov. 8, 1992
- 7 By many players

YARDS GAINED
Most Seasons Leading League
- 3 Bruce Harper, N.Y. Jets, 1977-79
- 2 Marshall Goldberg, Chi. Cardinals, 1941-42
  Woodley Lewis, Los Angeles, 1953-54
  Al Carmichael, Green Bay, 1956-57
  Timmy Brown, Philadelphia, 1961, 1963
  Bobby Jancik, Houston, 1963, 1966
  Ron Smith, Atlanta, 1966-67

Most Yards Gained, Career
- 6,922 Ron Smith, Chicago, 1965, 1970-72; Atlanta, 1966-67; Los Angeles, 1968-69; San Diego, 1973; Oakland, 1974
- 6,374 Mel Gray, New Orleans, 1986-88; Detroit, 1989-93
- 5,538 Abe Woodson, San Francisco, 1958-64; St. Louis, 1965-66

Most Yards Gained, Season
- 1,345 Buster Rhymes, Minnesota, 1985
- 1,317 Bobby Jancik, Houston, 1963
- 1,314 Dave Hampton, Green Bay, 1971

Most Yards Gained, Rookie, Season
- 1,345 Buster Rhymes, Minnesota, 1985
- 1,292 Stump Mitchell, St. Louis, 1981
- 1,245 Odell Barry, Denver, 1964

Most Yards Gained, Game
- 294 Wally Triplett, Detroit vs. Los Angeles, Oct. 29, 1950
- 249 Tony Smith, Atlanta vs. Pittsburgh, Sept. 27, 1993
- 247 Timmy Brown, Philadelphia vs. Dallas, Nov. 6, 1966

Longest Kickoff Return (All TDs)
- 106 Al Carmichael, Green Bay vs. Chi. Bears, Oct. 7, 1956
  Noland Smith, Kansas City vs. Denver, Dec. 17, 1967
  Roy Green, St. Louis vs. Dallas, Oct. 21, 1979
- 105 Frank Seno, Chi. Cardinals vs. N.Y. Giants, Oct. 20, 1946
  Ollie Matson, Chi. Cardinals vs. Washington, Oct. 14, 1956
  Abe Woodson, San Francisco vs. Los Angeles, Nov. 8, 1959
  Timmy Brown, Philadelphia vs. Cleveland, Sept. 17, 1961
  Jon Arnett, Los Angeles vs. Detroit, Oct. 29, 1961
  Eugene (Mercury) Morris, Miami vs. Cincinnati, Sept. 14, 1969

Travis Williams, Los Angeles vs. New Orleans, Dec. 5, 1971
104   By many players

AVERAGE YARDAGE
Highest Average, Career (75 returns)
30.56   Gale Sayers, Chicago, 1965-71 (91-2,781)
29.57   Lynn Chandnois, Pittsburgh, 1950-56 (92-2,720)
28.69   Abe Woodson, San Francisco, 1958-64; St. Louis, 1965-66 (193-5,538)
Highest Average, Season (Qualifiers)
41.06   Travis Williams, Green Bay, 1967 (18-739)
37.69   Gale Sayers, Chicago, 1967 (16-603)
35.50   Ollie Matson, Chi. Cardinals, 1958 (14-497)
Highest Average, Rookie, Season (Qualifiers)
41.06   Travis Williams, Green Bay, 1967 (18-739)
33.08   Tom Moore, Green Bay, 1960 (12-397)
32.88   Duriel Harris, Miami, 1976 (17-559)
Highest Average, Game (3 returns)
73.50   Wally Triplett, Detroit vs. Los Angeles, Oct. 29, 1950 (4-294)
67.33   Lenny Lyles, San Francisco vs. Baltimore, Dec. 18, 1960 (3-202)
65.33   Ken Hall, Houston vs. N.Y. Titans, Oct. 23, 1960 (3-196)

TOUCHDOWNS
Most Touchdowns, Career
6   Ollie Matson, Chi. Cardinals, 1952, 1954-58; L.A. Rams, 1959-62; Detroit, 1963; Philadelphia, 1964
   Gale Sayers, Chicago, 1965-71
   Travis Williams, Green Bay, 1967-70; Los Angeles, 1971
5   Bobby Mitchell, Cleveland, 1958-61; Washington, 1962-68
   Abe Woodson, San Francisco, 1958-64; St. Louis, 1965-66
   Timmy Brown, Green Bay, 1959; Philadelphia, 1960-67; Baltimore, 1968
4   Cecil Turner, Chicago, 1968-73
   Ron Brown, L.A. Rams, 1984-89, 1991; L.A. Raiders, 1990
Most Touchdowns, Season
4   Travis Williams, Green Bay, 1967
   Cecil Turner, Chicago, 1970
3   Verda (Vitamin T) Smith, Los Angeles, 1950
   Abe Woodson, San Francisco, 1963
   Gale Sayers, Chicago, 1967
   Raymond Clayborn, New England, 1977
   Ron Brown, L.A. Rams, 1985
2   By many players
Most Touchdowns, Rookie, Season
4   Travis Williams, Green Bay, 1967
3   Raymond Clayborn, New England, 1977
2   By seven players
Most Touchdowns, Game
2   Timmy Brown, Philadelphia vs. Dallas, Nov. 6, 1966
   Travis Williams, Green Bay vs. Cleveland, Nov. 12, 1967
   Ron Brown, L.A. Rams vs. Green Bay, Nov. 24, 1985

COMBINED KICK RETURNS
Most Combined Kick Returns, Career
527   Vai Sikahema, St. Louis, 1986-87; Phoenix, 1988-90; Green Bay, 1991; Philadelphia, 1992-93 (p-292, k-235)
510   Ron Smith, Chicago, 1965, 1970-72; Atlanta, 1966-67; Los Angeles, 1968-69; San Diego, 1973; Oakland, 1974 (p-235, k-275)
426   Bruce Harper, N.Y. Jets, 1977-84 (p-183, k-243)
Most Combined Kick Returns, Season
100   Larry Jones, Washington, 1975 (p-53, k-47)
97   Stump Mitchell, St. Louis, 1981 (p-42, k-55)
94   Nesby Glasgow, Baltimore, 1979 (p-44, k-50)
Most Combined Kick Returns, Game
13   Stump Mitchell, St. Louis vs. Atlanta, Oct. 18, 1981 (p-6, k-7)
   Ronnie Harris, New England vs. Pittsburgh, Dec. 5, 1993 (p-10, k-3)
12   Mel Renfro, Dallas vs. Green Bay, Nov. 29, 1964 (p-4, k-8)
   Larry Jones, Washington vs. Dallas, Dec. 13, 1975 (p-6, k-6)
   Eddie Brown, Washington vs. Tampa Bay, Oct. 9, 1977 (p-11, k-1)
   Nesby Glasgow, Baltimore vs. Denver, Sept. 2, 1979 (p-9, k-3)
11   By many players

YARDS GAINED
Most Yards Returned, Career
8,710   Ron Smith, Chicago, 1965, 1970-72; Atlanta, 1966-67; Los Angeles, 1968-69; San Diego, 1973; Oakland, 1974 (p-1,788, k-6,922)
8,225   Mel Gray, New Orleans, 1986-88; Detroit, 1989-93 (p-1,851, k-6,374)
8,102   Vai Sikahema, St. Louis, 1986-87; Phoenix, 1988-90; Green Bay, 1991; Philadelphia, 1992-93 (p-3,169, k-4,933)
Most Yards Returned, Season
1,737   Stump Mitchell, St. Louis, 1981 (p-445, k-1,292)
1,658   Bruce Harper, N.Y. Jets, 1978 (p-378, k-1,280)
1,591   Mike Nelms, Washington, 1981 (p-492, k-1,099)

Most Yards Returned, Game
294   Wally Triplett, Detroit vs. Los Angeles, Oct. 29, 1950 (k-294)
   Woodley Lewis, Los Angeles vs. Detroit, Oct. 18, 1953 (p-120, k-174)
289   Eddie Payton, Detroit vs. Minnesota, Dec. 17, 1977 (p-105, k-184)
282   Les (Speedy) Duncan, San Diego vs. N.Y. Jets, Nov. 24, 1968 (p-102, k-180)

TOUCHDOWNS
Most Touchdowns, Career
9   Ollie Matson, Chi. Cardinals, 1952, 1954-58; Los Angeles, 1959-62; Detroit, 1963; Philadelphia, 1964-66 (p-3, k-6)
8   Jack Christiansen, Detroit, 1951-58 (p-8)
   Bobby Mitchell, Cleveland, 1958-61; Washington, 1962-68 (p-3, k-5)
   Gale Sayers, Chicago, 1965-71 (p-2, k-6)
   Rick Upchurch, Denver, 1975-83 (p-8)
   Billy Johnson, Houston, 1974-80; Atlanta, 1982-87; Washington, 1988 (p-6, k-2)
7   Abe Woodson, San Francisco, 1958-64; St. Louis, 1965-66 (p-2, k-5)
   Travis Williams, Green Bay, 1967-70; Los Angeles, 1971 (p-1, k-6)
Most Touchdowns, Season
4   Jack Christiansen, Detroit, 1951 (p-4)
   Emlen Tunnell, N.Y. Giants, 1951 (p-3, k-1)
   Gale Sayers, Chicago, 1967 (p-1, k-3)
   Travis Williams, Green Bay, 1967 (k-4)
   Cecil Turner, Chicago, 1970 (k-4)
   Billy Johnson, Houston, 1975 (p-3, k-1)
   Rick Upchurch, Denver, 1976 (p-4)
3   Verda (Vitamin T) Smith, Los Angeles, 1950 (k-3)
   Abe Woodson, San Francisco, 1963 (k-3)
   Raymond Clayborn, New England, 1977 (k-3)
   Billy Johnson, Houston, 1977 (p-2, k-1)
   LeRoy Irvin, Los Angeles, 1981 (p-3)
   Ron Brown, L.A. Rams, 1985 (k-3)
   Tyrone Hughes, New Orleans, 1993 (p-2, k-1)
2   By many players
Most Touchdowns, Game
2   Jack Christiansen, Detroit vs. Los Angeles, Oct. 14, 1951 (p-2); vs. Green Bay, Nov. 22, 1951 (p-2)
   Jim Patton, N.Y. Giants vs. Washington, Oct. 30, 1955 (p-1, k-1)
   Bobby Mitchell, Cleveland vs. Philadelphia, Nov. 23, 1958 (p-1, k-1)
   Dick Christy, N.Y. Titans vs. Denver, Sept. 24, 1961 (p-2)
   Al Frazier, Denver vs. Boston, Dec. 3, 1961 (p-1, k-1)
   Timmy Brown, Philadelphia vs. Dallas, Nov. 6, 1966 (k-2)
   Travis Williams, Green Bay vs. Cleveland, Nov. 12, 1967 (k-2); vs. Pittsburgh, Nov. 2, 1969 (p-1, k-1)
   Gale Sayers, Chicago vs. San Francisco, Dec. 3, 1967 (p-1, k-1)
   Rick Upchurch, Denver vs. Cleveland, Sept. 26, 1976 (p-2)
   Eddie Payton, Detroit vs. Minnesota, Dec. 17, 1977 (p-1, k-1)
   LeRoy Irvin, Los Angeles vs. Atlanta, Oct. 11, 1981 (p-2)
   Ron Brown, L.A. Rams vs. Green Bay, Nov. 24, 1985 (k-2)
   Vai Sikahema, St. Louis vs. Tampa Bay, Dec. 21, 1986 (p-2)
   Eric Metcalf, Cleveland vs. Pittsburgh, Oct. 24, 1993 (p-2)

FUMBLES
Most Fumbles, Career
124   Dave Krieg, Seattle, 1980-91; Kansas City, 1992-93
116   Warren Moon, Houston, 1984-93
106   Dan Fouts, San Diego, 1973-87
Most Fumbles, Season
18   Dave Krieg, Seattle, 1989
   Warren Moon, Houston, 1990
17   Dan Pastorini, Houston, 1973
   Warren Moon, Houston, 1984
   Randall Cunningham, Philadelphia, 1989
16   Don Meredith, Dallas, 1964
   Joe Cribbs, Buffalo, 1980
   Steve Fuller, Kansas City, 1980
   Paul McDonald, Cleveland, 1984
   Phil Simms, N.Y. Giants, 1985
Most Fumbles, Game
7   Len Dawson, Kansas City vs. San Diego, Nov. 15, 1964
6   Sam Etcheverry, St. Louis vs. N.Y. Giants, Sept. 17, 1961
   Dave Krieg, Seattle vs. Kansas City, Nov. 5, 1989
5   Paul Christman, Chi. Cardinals vs. Green Bay, Nov. 10, 1946
   Charlie Conerly, N.Y. Giants vs. San Francisco, Dec. 1, 1957
   Jack Kemp, Buffalo vs. Houston, Oct. 29, 1967
   Roman Gabriel, Philadelphia vs. Oakland, Nov. 21, 1976
   Randall Cunningham, Philadelphia vs. L.A. Raiders, Nov. 30, 1986 (OT)
   Willie Totten, Buffalo vs. Indianapolis, Oct. 4, 1987
   Dave Walter, Cincinnati vs. Seattle, Oct. 11, 1987
   Dave Krieg, Seattle vs. San Diego, Nov. 25, 1990 (OT)
   Andre Ware, Detroit vs. Green Bay, Dec. 6, 1992

FUMBLES RECOVERED

Most Fumbles Recovered, Career, Own and Opponents'
- 44 Warren Moon, Houston, 1984-93 (44 own)
- 43 Fran Tarkenton, Minnesota, 1961-66, 1972-78; N.Y. Giants, 1967-71 (43 own)
- 38 Jack Kemp, Pittsburgh, 1957; L.A. Chargers, 1960; San Diego, 1961-62; Buffalo, 1962-67, 1969 (38 own)
  Dan Fouts, San Diego, 1973-87 (37 own, 1 opp)

Most Fumbles Recovered, Season, Own and Opponents'
- 9 Don Hultz, Minnesota, 1963 (9 opp)
  Dave Krieg, Seattle, 1989 (9 own)
- 8 Paul Christman, Chi. Cardinals, 1945 (8 own)
  Joe Schmidt, Detroit, 1955 (8 opp)
  Bill Butler, Minnesota, 1963 (8 own)
  Kermit Alexander, San Francisco, 1965 (4 own, 4 opp)
  Jack Lambert, Pittsburgh, 1976 (1 own, 7 opp)
  Danny White, Dallas, 1981 (8 own)
  Dan Marino, Miami, 1988 (7 own, 1 opp)
- 7 By many players

Most Fumbles Recovered, Game, Own and Opponents'
- 4 Otto Graham, Cleveland vs. N.Y. Giants, Oct. 25, 1953 (4 own)
  Sam Etcheverry, St. Louis vs. N.Y. Giants, Sept. 17, 1961 (4 own)
  Roman Gabriel, Los Angeles vs. San Francisco, Oct. 12, 1969 (4 own)
  Joe Ferguson, Buffalo vs. Miami, Sept. 18, 1977 (4 own)
  Randall Cunningham, Philadelphia vs. L.A. Raiders, Nov. 30, 1986 (OT) (4 own)
- 3 By many players

OWN FUMBLES RECOVERED

Most Own Fumbles Recovered, Career
- 44 Warren Moon, Houston, 1984-93
- 43 Fran Tarkenton, Minnesota, 1961-66, 1972-78; N.Y. Giants, 1967-71
- 38 Jack Kemp, Pittsburgh, 1957; L.A. Chargers, 1960; San Diego, 1961-62; Buffalo, 1962-67, 1969

Most Own Fumbles Recovered, Season
- 9 Dave Krieg, Seattle, 1989
- 8 Paul Christman, Chi. Cardinals, 1945
  Bill Butler, Minnesota, 1963
  Danny White, Dallas, 1981
- 7 By many players

Most Own Fumbles Recovered, Game
- 4 Otto Graham, Cleveland vs. N.Y. Giants, Oct. 25, 1953
  Sam Etcheverry, St. Louis vs. N.Y. Giants, Sept. 17, 1961
  Roman Gabriel, Los Angeles vs. San Francisco, Oct. 12, 1969
  Joe Ferguson, Buffalo vs. Miami, Sept. 18, 1977
  Randall Cunningham, Philadelphia vs. L.A. Raiders, Nov. 30, 1986 (OT)
- 3 By many players

OPPONENTS' FUMBLES RECOVERED

Most Opponents' Fumbles Recovered, Career
- 29 Jim Marshall, Cleveland, 1960; Minnesota, 1961-79
- 26 Rickey Jackson, New Orleans, 1981-93
- 25 Dick Butkus, Chicago, 1965-73

Most Opponents' Fumbles Recovered, Season
- 9 Don Hultz, Minnesota, 1963
- 8 Joe Schmidt, Detroit, 1955
- 7 Alan Page, Minnesota, 1970
  Jack Lambert, Pittsburgh, 1976
  Ray Childress, Houston, 1988
  Rickey Jackson, New Orleans, 1990

Most Opponents' Fumbles Recovered, Game
- 3 Corwin Clatt, Chi. Cardinals vs. Detroit, Nov. 6, 1949
  Vic Sears, Philadelphia vs. Green Bay, Nov. 2, 1952
  Ed Beatty, San Francisco vs. Los Angeles, Oct. 7, 1956
  Ron Carroll, Houston vs. Cincinnati, Oct. 27, 1974
  Maurice Spencer, New Orleans vs. Atlanta, Oct. 10, 1976
  Steve Nelson, New England vs. Philadelphia, Oct. 8, 1978
  Charles Jackson, Kansas City vs. Pittsburgh, Sept. 6, 1981
  Willie Buchanon, San Diego vs. Denver, Sept. 27, 1981
  Joey Browner, Minnesota vs. San Francisco, Sept. 8, 1985
  Ray Childress, Houston vs. Washington, Oct. 30, 1988
- 2 By many players

YARDS RETURNING FUMBLES

Longest Fumble Run (All TDs)
- 104 Jack Tatum, Oakland vs. Green Bay, Sept. 24, 1972
- 100 Chris Martin, Kansas City vs. Miami, Oct. 13, 1991
- 99 Don Griffin, San Francisco vs. Chicago, Dec. 23, 1991

TOUCHDOWNS

Most Touchdowns, Career (Total)
- 4 Bill Thompson, Denver, 1969-81
  Jessie Tuggle, Atlanta, 1987-93

- 3 Ralph Heywood, Detroit, 1947-48; Boston, 1948; N.Y. Bulldogs, 1949
  Leo Sugar, Chi. Cardinals, 1954-59; St. Louis, 1960; Philadelphia, 1961; Detroit, 1962
  Bud McFadin, Los Angeles, 1952-56; Denver, 1960-63; Houston, 1964-65
  Doug Cline, Houston, 1960-66; San Diego, 1966
  Bob Lilly, Dall. Cowboys, 1961-74
  Chris Hanburger, Washington, 1965-78
  Lemar Parrish, Cincinnati, 1970-77; Washington, 1978-81; Buffalo, 1982
  Paul Krause, Washington, 1964-67; Minnesota, 1968-79
  Brad Dusek, Washington, 1974-81
  David Logan, Tampa Bay, 1979-86; Green Bay, 1987
  Thomas Howard, Kansas City, 1977-83; St. Louis, 1984-85
  Greg Townsend, L.A. Raiders, 1983-93
  Les Miller, San Diego, 1987-90; New Orleans, 1991-93
  Chris Martin, New Orleans, 1983; Minnesota, 1984-88; Kansas City, 1989-92; L.A. Rams, 1993
  Seth Joyner, Philadelphia, 1986-93
  Derrick Thomas, Kansas City, 1989-93
- 2 By many players

Most Touchdowns, Season (Total)
- 2 Harold McPhail, Boston, 1934
  Harry Ebding, Detroit, 1937
  John Morelli, Boston, 1944
  Frank Maznicki, Boston, 1947
  Fred (Dippy) Evans, Chi. Bears, 1948
  Ralph Heywood, Boston, 1948
  Art Tait, N.Y. Yanks, 1951
  John Dwyer, Los Angeles, 1952
  Leo Sugar, Chi. Cardinals, 1957
  Doug Cline, Houston, 1961
  Jim Bradshaw, Pittsburgh, 1964
  Royce Berry, Cincinnati, 1970
  Ahmad Rashad, Buffalo, 1974
  Tim Gray, Kansas City, 1977
  Charles Phillips, Oakland, 1978
  Kenny Johnson, Atlanta, 1981
  George Martin, N.Y. Giants, 1981
  Del Rodgers, Green Bay, 1982
  Mike Douglass, Green Bay, 1983
  Shelton Robinson, Seattle, 1983
  Erik McMillan, N.Y. Jets, 1989
  Les Miller, San Diego, 1990
  Seth Joyner, Philadelphia, 1991
  Robert Goff, New Orleans, 1992
  Willie Clay, Detroit, 1993

Most Touchdowns, Career (Own recovered)
- 2 Ken Kavanaugh, Chi. Bears, 1940-41, 1945-50
  Mike Ditka, Chicago, 1961-66; Philadelphia, 1967-68; Dallas, 1969-72
  Gail Cogdill, Detroit, 1960-68; Baltimore, 1968; Atlanta, 1969-70
  Ahmad Rashad, St. Louis, 1972-73; Buffalo, 1974; Minnesota, 1976-82
  Jim Mitchell, Atlanta, 1969-79
  Drew Pearson, Dallas, 1973-83
  Del Rodgers, Green Bay, 1982, 1984; San Francisco, 1987-88

Most Touchdowns, Season (Own recovered)
- 2 Ahmad Rashad, Buffalo, 1974
  Del Rodgers, Green Bay, 1982
- 1 By many players

Most Touchdowns, Career (Opponents' recovered)
- 4 Jessie Tuggle, Atlanta, 1987-93
- 3 Leo Sugar, Chi. Cardinals, 1954-59; St. Louis, 1960; Philadelphia, 1961; Detroit, 1962
  Doug Cline, Houston, 1960-66; San Diego, 1966
  Bud McFadin, Los Angeles, 1952-56; Denver, 1960-63; Houston, 1964-65
  Bob Lilly, Dall. Cowboys, 1961-74
  Chris Hanburger, Washington, 1965-78
  Paul Krause, Washington, 1964-67; Minnesota, 1968-79
  Lemar Parrish, Cincinnati, 1970-77; Washington, 1978-81; Buffalo, 1982
  Bill Thompson, Denver, 1969-81
  Brad Dusek, Washington, 1974-81
  David Logan, Tampa Bay, 1979-86; Green Bay, 1987
  Thomas Howard, Kansas City, 1977-83; St. Louis, 1984-85
  Greg Townsend, L.A. Raiders, 1983-93
  Les Miller, San Diego, 1987-90; New Orleans, 1991-93
  Chris Martin, New Orleans, 1983; Minnesota, 1984-88; Kansas City, 1989-92; L.A. Rams, 1993
  Seth Joyner, Philadelphia, 1986-93
  Derrick Thomas, Kansas City, 1989-93
- 2 By many players

Most Touchdowns, Season (Opponents' recovered)
- 2 Harold McPhail, Boston, 1934

Harry Ebding, Detroit, 1937
John Morelli, Boston, 1944
Frank Maznicki, Boston, 1947
Fred (Dippy) Evans, Chi. Bears, 1948
Ralph Heywood, Boston, 1948
Art Tait, N.Y. Yanks, 1951
John Dwyer, Los Angeles, 1952
Leo Sugar, Chi. Cardinals, 1957
Doug Cline, Houston, 1961
Jim Bradshaw, Pittsburgh, 1964
Royce Berry, Cincinnati, 1970
Tim Gray, Kansas City, 1977
Charles Phillips, Oakland, 1978
Kenny Johnson, Atlanta, 1981
George Martin, N.Y. Giants, 1981
Mike Douglass, Green Bay, 1983
Shelton Robinson, Seattle, 1983
Erik McMillan, N.Y. Jets, 1989
Les Miller, San Diego, 1990
Seth Joyner, Philadelphia, 1991
Robert Goff, New Orleans, 1992
Willie Clay, Detroit, 1993

Most Touchdowns, Game (Opponents' recovered)
2   Fred (Dippy) Evans, Chi. Bears vs. Washington, Nov. 28, 1948

COMBINED NET YARDS GAINED
Rushing, receiving, interception returns, punt returns, kickoff returns, and fumble returns

Most Seasons Leading League
5   Jim Brown, Cleveland, 1958-61, 1964
3   Cliff Battles, Boston, 1932-33; Washington, 1937
     Gale Sayers, Chicago, 1965-67
     Eric Dickerson, L.A. Rams, 1983-84, 1986
     Thurman Thomas, Buffalo, 1989, 1991-92
2   By many players

Most Consecutive Seasons Leading League
4   Jim Brown, Cleveland, 1958-61
3   Gale Sayers, Chicago, 1965-67
2   Cliff Battles, Boston, 1932-33
     Charley Trippi, Chi. Cardinals, 1948-49
     Timmy Brown, Philadelphia, 1962-63
     Floyd Little, Denver, 1967-68
     James Brooks, San Diego, 1981-82
     Eric Dickerson, L.A. Rams, 1983-84
     Thurman Thomas, Buffalo, 1991-92

ATTEMPTS
Most Attempts, Career
4,368   Walter Payton, Chicago, 1975-87
3,351   Tony Dorsett, Dallas, 1977-87; Denver, 1988
3,293   Eric Dickerson, L.A. Rams, 1983-87; Indianapolis, 1987-91;
         L.A. Raiders, 1992; Atlanta, 1993

Most Attempts, Season
496   James Wilder, Tampa Bay, 1984
449   Marcus Allen, L.A. Raiders, 1985
442   Eric Dickerson, L.A. Rams, 1983

Most Attempts, Rookie, Season
442   Eric Dickerson, L.A. Rams, 1983
395   George Rogers, New Orleans, 1981
390   Joe Cribbs, Buffalo, 1980

Most Attempts, Game
48   James Wilder, Tampa Bay vs. Pittsburgh, Oct. 30, 1983
47   James Wilder, Tampa Bay vs. Green Bay, Sept. 30, 1984 (OT)
46   Gerald Riggs, Atlanta vs. L.A. Rams, Nov. 17, 1985

YARDS GAINED
Most Yards Gained, Career
21,803   Walter Payton, Chicago, 1975-87
16,326   Tony Dorsett, Dallas, 1977-87; Denver, 1988
15,459   Jim Brown, Cleveland, 1957-65

Most Yards Gained, Season
2,535   Lionel James, San Diego, 1985
2,462   Terry Metcalf, St. Louis, 1975
2,444   Mack Herron, New England, 1974

Most Yards Gained, Rookie, Season
2,317   Tim Brown, L.A. Raiders, 1988
2,272   Gale Sayers, Chicago, 1965
2,212   Eric Dickerson, L.A. Rams, 1983

Most Yards Gained, Game
373   Billy Cannon, Houston vs. N.Y. Titans, Dec. 10, 1961
345   Lionel James, San Diego vs. L.A. Raiders, Nov. 10, 1985 (OT)
341   Timmy Brown, Philadelphia vs. St. Louis, Dec. 16, 1962

SACKS
Sacks have been compiled since 1982.

Most Sacks, Career
137   Reggie White, Philadelphia, 1985-92; Green Bay, 1993
132.5   Lawrence Taylor, N.Y. Giants, 1982-93
124.5   Richard Dent, Chicago, 1983-93

Most Sacks, Season
22   Mark Gastineau, N.Y. Jets, 1984
21   Reggie White, Philadelphia, 1987
      Chris Doleman, Minnesota, 1989
20.5   Lawrence Taylor, N.Y. Giants, 1986

Most Sacks, Rookie, Season
12.5   Leslie O'Neal, San Diego, 1986
12   Charles Haley, San Francisco, 1986
11   Vernon Maxwell, Baltimore, 1983

Most Sacks, Game
7   Derrick Thomas, Kansas City vs. Seattle, Nov. 11, 1990
6   Fred Dean, San Francisco vs. New Orleans, Nov. 13, 1983
5.5   William Gay, Detroit vs. Tampa Bay, Sept. 4, 1983

MISCELLANEOUS
Longest Return of Missed Field Goal (All TDs)
101   Al Nelson, Philadelphia vs. Dallas, Sept. 26, 1971
100   Al Nelson, Philadelphia vs. Cleveland, Dec. 11, 1966
       Ken Ellis, Green Bay vs. N.Y. Giants, Sept. 19, 1971
99   Jerry Williams, Los Angeles vs. Green Bay, Dec. 16, 1951
      Carl Taseff, Baltimore vs. Los Angeles, Dec. 12, 1959
      Timmy Brown, Philadelphia vs. St. Louis, Sept. 16, 1962

TEAM RECORDS

CHAMPIONSHIPS
Most Seasons League Champion
11   Green Bay, 1929-31, 1936, 1939, 1944, 1961-62, 1965-67
9   Chi. Bears, 1921, 1932-33, 1940-41, 1943, 1946, 1963, 1985
6   N.Y. Giants, 1927, 1934, 1938, 1956, 1986, 1990

Most Consecutive Seasons League Champion
3   Green Bay, 1929-31
     Green Bay, 1965-67
2   Canton, 1922-23
     Chi. Bears, 1932-33
     Chi. Bears, 1940-41
     Philadelphia, 1948-49
     Detroit, 1952-53
     Cleveland, 1954-55
     Baltimore, 1958-59
     Houston, 1960-61
     Green Bay, 1961-62
     Buffalo, 1964-65
     Miami, 1972-73
     Pittsburgh, 1974-75
     Pittsburgh, 1978-79
     San Francisco, 1988-89
     Dallas, 1992-93

Most Times Finishing First, Regular Season (Since 1933)
18   Clev. Browns, 1950-55, 1957, 1964-65, 1967-69, 1971, 1980, 1985-87, 1989
17   N.Y. Giants, 1933-35, 1938-39, 1941, 1944, 1946, 1956, 1958-59, 1961-63, 1986, 1989-90
16   Chi. Bears, 1933-34, 1937, 1940-43, 1946, 1956, 1963, 1984-88, 1990

Most Consecutive Times Finishing First, Regular Season (Since 1933)
7   Los Angeles, 1973-79
6   Cleveland, 1950-55
     Dallas, 1966-71
     Minnesota, 1973-78
     Pittsburgh, 1974-79
5   Oakland, 1972-76
     Chicago, 1984-88
     San Francisco, 1986-90

GAMES WON
Most Consecutive Games Won
17   Chi. Bears, 1933-34
16   Chi. Bears, 1941-42
      Miami, 1971-73
      Miami, 1983-84
15   L.A. Chargers/San Diego, 1960-61
      San Francisco, 1989-90

Most Consecutive Games Without Defeat
25   Can ton, 1921-23 (won 22, tied 3)
24   Chi. Bears, 1941-43 (won 23, tied 1)
23   Green Bay, 1928-30 (won 21, tied 2)

Most Games Won, Season
- 15 San Francisco, 1984
  - Chicago, 1985
- 14 Miami, 1972
  - Pittsburgh, 1978
  - Washington, 1983
  - Miami, 1984
  - Chicago, 1986
  - N.Y. Giants, 1986
  - San Francisco, 1989
  - San Francisco, 1990
  - Washington, 1991
  - San Francisco, 1992
- 13 By many teams

Most Consecutive Games Won, Season
- 14 Miami, 1972
- 13 Chi. Bears, 1934
- 12 Minnesota, 1969
  - Chicago, 1985

Most Consecutive Games Won, Start of Season
- 14 Miami, 1972, entire season
- 13 Chi. Bears, 1934, entire season
- 12 Chicago, 1985

Most Consecutive Games Won, End of Season
- 14 Miami, 1972, entire season
- 13 Chi. Bears, 1934, entire season
- 11 Chi. Bears, 1942, entire season
  - Cleveland, 1951
  - Houston, 1993

Most Consecutive Games Without Defeat, Season
- 14 Miami, 1972 (won 14)
- 13 Chi. Bears, 1926 (won 11, tied 2)
  - Green Bay, 1929 (won 12, tied 1)
  - Chi. Bears, 1934 (won 13)
  - Baltimore, 1967 (won 11, tied 2)
- 12 Canton, 1922 (won 10, tied 2)
  - Canton, 1923 (won 11, tied 1)
  - Minnesota, 1969 (won 12)
  - Chicago, 1985 (won 12)

Most Consecutive Games Without Defeat, Start of Season
- 14 Miami, 1972 (won 14), entire season
- 13 Chi. Bears, 1926 (won 11, tied 2)
  - Green Bay, 1929 (won 12, tied 1), entire season
  - Chi. Bears, 1934 (won 13), entire season
  - Baltimore, 1967 (won 11, tied 2)
- 12 Canton, 1922 (won 10, tied 2), entire season
  - Canton, 1923 (won 11, tied 1), entire season
  - Chicago, 1985 (won 12)

Most Consecutive Games Without Defeat, End of Season
- 14 Miami, 1972 (won 14), entire season
- 13 Green Bay, 1929 (won 12, tied 1), entire season
  - Chi. Bears, 1934 (won 13), entire season
- 12 Canton, 1922 (won 10, tied 2), entire season
  - Canton, 1923 (won 11, tied 1), entire season

Most Consecutive Home Games Won
- 27 Miami, 1971-74
- 20 Green Bay, 1929-32
- 18 Oakland, 1968-70
  - Dallas, 1979-81

Most Consecutive Home Games Without Defeat
- 30 Green Bay, 1928-33 (won 27, tied 3)
- 27 Miami, 1971-74 (won 27)
- 25 Chi. Bears, 1923-25 (won 19, tied 6)

Most Consecutive Road Games Won
- 18 San Francisco, 1988-90
- 11 L.A. Chargers/San Diego, 1960-61
  - San Francisco, 1987-88
- 10 Chi. Bears, 1941-42
  - Dallas, 1968-69
  - New Orleans, 1987-88

Most Consecutive Road Games Without Defeat
- 18 San Francisco, 1988-90 (won 18)
- 13 Chi. Bears, 1941-43 (won 12, tied 1)
- 12 Green Bay, 1928-30 (won 10, tied 2)

Most Shutout Games Won or Tied, Season
- 10 Pottsville, 1926 (won 9, tied 1)
  - N.Y. Giants, 1927 (won 9, tied 1)
- 9 Akron, 1921 (won 8, tied 1)
  - Canton, 1922 (won 7, tied 2)
  - Frankford, 1926 (won 9)
  - Frankford, 1929 (won 6, tied 3)
- 8 By many teams

Most Consecutive Shutout Games Won or Tied
- 13 Akron, 1920-21 (won 10, tied 3)
- 7 Pottsville, 1926 (won 6, tied 1)
  - Detroit, 1934 (won 7)
- 6 Buffalo, 1920-21 (won 5, tied 1)
  - Frankford, 1926 (won 6)
  - Detroit, 1926 (won 4, tied 2)
  - N.Y. Giants, 1926-27 (won 5, tied 1)

GAMES LOST

Most Consecutive Games Lost
- 26 Tampa Bay, 1976-77
- 19 Chi. Cardinals, 1942-43, 1945
  - Oakland, 1961-62
- 18 Houston, 1972-73

Most Consecutive Games Without Victory
- 26 Tampa Bay, 1976-77 (lost 26)
- 23 Rochester, 1922-25 (lost 21, tied 2)
  - Washington, 1960-61 (lost 20, tied 3)
- 19 Dayton, 1927-29 (lost 18, tied 1)
  - Chi. Cardinals, 1942-43, 1945 (lost 19)
  - Oakland, 1961-62 (lost 19)

Most Games Lost, Season
- 15 New Orleans, 1980
  - Dallas, 1989
  - New England, 1990
  - Indianapolis, 1991
- 14 By many teams

Most Consecutive Games Lost, Season
- 14 Tampa Bay, 1976
  - New Orleans, 1980
  - Baltimore, 1981
  - New England, 1990
- 13 Oakland, 1962
  - Pittsburgh, 1969
  - Indianapolis, 1986
- 12 Tampa Bay, 1977

Most Consecutive Games Lost, Start of Season
- 14 Tampa Bay, 1976, entire season
  - New Orleans, 1980
- 13 Oakland, 1962
  - Indianapolis, 1986
- 12 Tampa Bay, 1977

Most Consecutive Games Lost, End of Season
- 14 Tampa Bay, 1976, entire season
  - New England, 1990
- 13 Pittsburgh, 1969
- 11 Philadelphia, 1936
  - Detroit, 1942, entire season
  - Houston, 1972

Most Consecutive Games Without Victory, Season
- 14 Tampa Bay, 1976 (lost 14), entire season
  - New Orleans, 1980 (lost 14)
  - Baltimore, 1981 (lost 14)
  - New England, 1990 (lost 14)
- 13 Washington, 1961 (lost 12, tied 1)
  - Oakland, 1962 (lost 13)
  - Pittsburgh, 1969 (lost 13)
  - Indianapolis, 1986 (lost 13)
- 12 Dall. Cowboys, 1960 (lost 11, tied 1), entire season
  - Tampa Bay, 1977 (lost 12)

Most Consecutive Games Without Victory, Start of Season
- 14 Tampa Bay, 1976 (lost 14), entire season
  - New Orleans, 1980 (lost 14)
- 13 Washington, 1961 (lost 12, tied 1)
  - Oakland, 1962 (lost 13)
  - Indianapolis, 1986 (lost 13)
- 12 Dall. Cowboys, 1960 (lost 11, tied 1), entire season
  - Tampa Bay, 1977 (lost 12)

Most Consecutive Games Without Victory, End of Season
- 14 Tampa Bay, 1976, (lost 14), entire season
  - New England, 1990 (lost 14)
- 13 Pittsburgh, 1969 (lost 13)
- 12 Dall. Cowboys, 1960 (lost 11, tied 1), entire season

Most Consecutive Home Games Lost
- 14 Dallas, 1988-89
- 13 Houston, 1972-73
  - Tampa Bay, 1976-77
- 11 Oakland, 1961-62
  - Los Angeles, 1961-63

Most Consecutive Home Games Without Victory
- 14 Dallas, 1988-89 (lost 14)
- 13 Houston, 1972-73 (lost 13)

Tampa Bay, 1976-77 (lost 13)
12 Philadelphia, 1936-38 (lost 11, tied 1)
Most Consecutive Road Games Lost
23 Houston, 1981-84
22 Buffalo, 1983-86
19 Tampa Bay, 1983-85
Atlanta, 1988-91
Most Consecutive Road Games Without Victory
23 Houston, 1981-84 (lost 23)
22 Buffalo, 1983-86 (lost 22)
19 Tampa Bay, 1983-85 (lost 19)
Atlanta, 1988-91 (lost 19)
Most Shutout Games Lost or Tied, Season
8 Frankford, 1927 (lost 6, tied 2)
Brooklyn, 1931 (lost 8)
7 Dayton, 1925 (lost 6, tied 1)
Orange, 1929 (lost 4, tied 3)
Frankford, 1931 (lost 6, tied 1)
6 By many teams
Most Consecutive Shutout Games Lost or Tied
8 Rochester, 1922-24 (lost 8)
7 Hammond, 1922-23 (lost 6, tied 1)
6 Providence, 1926-27 (lost 5, tied 1)
Brooklyn, 1942-43 (lost 6)

TIE GAMES
Most Tie Games, Season
6 Chi. Bears, 1932
5 Frankford, 1929
4 Chi. Bears, 1924
Orange, 1929
Portsmouth, 1932
Most Consecutive Tie Games
3 Chi. Bears, 1932
2 By many teams

SCORING
Most Seasons Leading League
10 Chi. Bears, 1932, 1934-35, 1939, 1941-43, 1946-47, 1956
7 San Francisco, 1953, 1965, 1970, 1987, 1989, 1992-93
6 Green Bay, 1931, 1936-38, 1961-62
L.A. Rams, 1950-52, 1957, 1967, 1973
Most Consecutive Seasons Leading League
3 Green Bay, 1936-38
Chi. Bears, 1941-43
Los Angeles, 1950-52
Oakland, 1967-69

POINTS
Most Points, Season
541 Washington, 1983
513 Houston, 1961
Miami, 1984
485 Washington, 1991
Fewest Points, Season (Since 1932)
37 Cincinnati/St. Louis, 1934
38 Cincinnati, 1933
Detroit, 1942
51 Pittsburgh, 1934
Philadelphia, 1936
Most Points, Game
72 Washington vs. N.Y. Giants, Nov. 27, 1966
70 Los Angeles vs. Baltimore, Oct. 22, 1950
65 Chi. Cardinals vs. N.Y. Bulldogs, Nov. 13, 1949
Los Angeles vs. Detroit, Oct. 29, 1950
Most Points, Both Teams, Game
113 Washington (72) vs. N.Y. Giants (41), Nov. 27, 1966
101 Oakland (52) vs. Houston (49), Dec. 22, 1963
99 Seattle (51) vs. Kansas City (48), Nov. 27, 1983 (OT)
Fewest Points, Both Teams, Game
0 In many games. Last time: N.Y. Giants vs. Detroit, Nov. 7, 1943
Most Points, Shutout Victory, Game
64 Philadelphia vs. Cincinnati, Nov. 6, 1934
62 Akron vs. Oorang, Oct. 29, 1922
60 Rock Island vs. Evansville, Oct. 15, 1922
Chi. Cardinals vs. Rochester, Oct. 7, 1923
Fewest Points, Shutout Victory, Game
2 Green Bay vs. Chi. Bears, Oct. 16, 1932
Chi. Bears vs. Green Bay, Sept. 18, 1938
Most Points Overcome to Win Game
28 San Francisco vs. New Orleans, Dec. 7, 1980 (OT) (trailed 7-35, won 38-35)
25 St. Louis vs. Tampa Bay, Nov. 8, 1987 (trailed 3-28, won 31-28)

24 Philadelphia vs. Washington, Oct. 27, 1946 (trailed 0-24, won 28-24)
Detroit vs. Baltimore, Oct. 20, 1957 (trailed 3-27, won 31-27)
Philadelphia vs. Chi. Cardinals, Oct. 25, 1959 (trailed 0-24, won 28-24)
Denver vs. Boston, Oct. 23, 1960 (trailed 0-24, won 31-24)
Miami vs. New England, Dec. 15, 1974 (trailed 0-24, won 34-27)
Minnesota vs. San Francisco, Dec. 4, 1977 (trailed 0-24, won 28-27)
Denver vs. Seattle, Sept. 23, 1979 (trailed 10-34, won 37-34)
Houston vs. Cincinnati, Sept. 23, 1979 (OT) (trailed 0-24, won 30-27)
L.A. Raiders vs. San Diego, Nov. 22, 1982 (trailed 0-24, won 28-24)
L.A. Raiders vs. Denver, Sept. 26, 1988 (OT) (trailed 0-24, won 30-27)
L.A. Rams vs. Tampa Bay, Dec. 6, 1992 (trailed 3-27, won 31-27)
Most Points Overcome to Tie Game
31 Denver vs. Buffalo, Nov. 27, 1960 (trailed 7-38, tied 38-38)
28 Los Angeles vs. Philadelphia, Oct. 3, 1948 (trailed 0-28, tied 28-28)
Most Points, Each Half
1st: 49 Green Bay vs. Tampa Bay, Oct. 2, 1983
48 Buffalo vs. Miami, Sept. 18, 1966
45 Green Bay vs. Cleveland, Nov. 12, 1967
Indianapolis vs. Denver, Oct. 31, 1988
Houston vs. Cleveland, Dec. 9, 1990
2nd: 49 Chi. Bears vs. Philadelphia, Nov. 30, 1941
48 Chi. Cardinals vs. Baltimore, Oct. 2, 1950
N.Y. Giants vs. Baltimore, Nov. 19, 1950
45 Cincinnati vs. Houston, Dec. 17, 1972
Most Points, Both Teams, Each Half
1st: 70 Houston (35) vs. Oakland (35), Dec. 22, 1963
62 N.Y. Jets (41) vs. Tampa Bay (21), Nov. 17, 1985
59 St. Louis (31) vs. Philadelphia (28), Dec. 16, 1962
2nd: 65 Washington (38) vs. N.Y. Giants (27), Nov. 27, 1966
62 L.A. Raiders (31) vs. San Diego (31), Jan. 2, 1983
58 New England (37) vs. Baltimore (21), Nov. 23, 1980
N.Y. Jets (37) vs. New England (21), Sept. 21, 1987
Most Points, One Quarter
41 Green Bay vs. Detroit, Oct. 7, 1945 (second quarter)
Los Angeles vs. Detroit, Oct. 29, 1950 (third quarter)
37 Los Angeles vs. Green Bay, Sept. 21, 1980 (second quarter)
35 Chi. Cardinals vs. Boston, Oct. 24, 1948 (third quarter)
Green Bay vs. Cleveland, Nov. 12, 1967 (first quarter)
Green Bay vs. Tampa Bay, Oct. 2, 1983 (second quarter)
Most Points, Both Teams, One Quarter
49 Oakland (28) vs. Houston (21), Dec. 22, 1963 (second quarter)
48 Green Bay (41) vs. Detroit (7), Oct. 7, 1945 (second quarter)
Los Angeles (41) vs. Detroit (7), Oct. 29, 1950 (third quarter)
47 St. Louis (27) vs. Philadelphia (20), Dec. 13, 1964 (second quarter)
Most Points, Each Quarter
1st: 35 Green Bay vs. Cleveland, Nov. 12, 1967
31 Buffalo vs. Kansas City, Sept. 13, 1964
28 By seven teams
2nd: 41 Green Bay vs. Detroit, Oct. 7, 1945
37 Los Angeles vs. Green Bay, Sept. 21, 1980
35 Green Bay vs. Tampa Bay, Oct. 2, 1983
3rd: 41 Los Angeles vs. Detroit, Oct. 29, 1950
35 Chi. Cardinals vs. Boston, Oct. 24, 1948
28 By nine teams
4th: 31 Oakland vs. Denver, Dec. 17, 1960
Oakland vs. San Diego, Dec. 8, 1963
Atlanta vs. Green Bay, Sept. 13, 1981
28 By many teams
Most Points, Both Teams, Each Quarter
1st: 42 Green Bay (35) vs. Cleveland (7), Nov. 12, 1967
35 Dall. Texans (21) vs. N.Y. Titans (14), Nov. 11, 1962
Dallas (28) vs. Philadelphia (7), Oct. 19, 1969
Kansas City (21) vs. Seattle (14), Dec. 11, 1977
Detroit (21) vs. L.A. Raiders (14), Dec. 10, 1990
Dallas (21) vs. Atlanta (14), Dec. 22, 1991
34 Los Angeles (21) vs. Baltimore (13), Oct. 22, 1950
Oakland (21) vs. Atlanta (13), Nov. 30, 1975
2nd: 49 Oakland (28) vs. Houston (21), Dec. 22, 1963
48 Green Bay (41) vs. Detroit (7), Oct. 7, 1945
47 St. Louis (27) vs. Philadelphia (20), Dec. 13, 1964
3rd: 48 Los Angeles (41) vs. Detroit (7), Oct. 29, 1950
42 Washington (28) vs. Philadelphia (14), Oct. 1, 1955
41 Green Bay (21) vs. N.Y. Yanks (20), Oct. 8, 1950
4th: 42 Chi. Cardinals (28) vs. Philadelphia (14), Dec. 7, 1947
Green Bay (28) vs. Chi. Bears (14), Nov. 6, 1955
N.Y. Jets (28) vs. Boston (14), Oct. 27, 1968
Pittsburgh (21) vs. Cleveland (21), Oct. 18, 1969
41 Baltimore (27) vs. New England (14), Sept. 18, 1978
New England (27) vs. Baltimore (14), Nov. 23, 1980
40 Chicago (21) vs. Tampa Bay (19), Nov. 19, 1989
Most Consecutive Games Scoring
274 Cleveland, 1950-71
258 San Francisco, 1977-93 (current)

218   Dallas, 1970-85

TOUCHDOWNS
Most Seasons Leading League, Touchdowns
13   Chi. Bears, 1932, 1934-35, 1939, 1941-44, 1946-48, 1956, 1965
7   Dallas, 1966, 1968, 1971, 1973, 1977-78, 1980
6   Oakland, 1967-69, 1972, 1974, 1977
     San Diego, 1963, 1965, 1979, 1981-82, 1985
Most Consecutive Seasons Leading League, Touchdowns
4   Chi. Bears, 1941-44
     Los Angeles, 1949-52
3   Chi. Bears, 1946-48
     Baltimore, 1957-59
     Oakland, 1967-69
2   By many teams
Most Touchdowns, Season
70   Miami, 1984
66   Houston, 1961
64   Los Angeles, 1950
Fewest Touchdowns, Season (Since 1932)
3   Cincinnati, 1933
4   Cincinnati/St. Louis, 1934
5   Detroit, 1942
Most Touchdowns, Game
10   Philadelphia vs. Cincinnati, Nov. 6, 1934
     Los Angeles vs. Baltimore, Oct. 22, 1950
     Washington vs. N.Y. Giants, Nov. 27, 1966
9   Chi. Cardinals vs. Rochester, Oct. 7, 1923
     Chi. Cardinals vs. N.Y. Giants, Oct. 17, 1948
     Chi. Cardinals vs. N.Y. Bulldogs, Nov. 13, 1949
     Los Angeles vs. Detroit, Oct. 29, 1950
     Pittsburgh vs. N.Y. Giants, Nov. 30, 1952
     Chicago vs. San Francisco, Dec. 12, 1965
     Chicago vs. Green Bay, Dec. 7, 1980
8   By many teams.
Most Touchdowns, Both Teams, Game
16   Washington (10) vs. N.Y. Giants (6), Nov. 27, 1966
14   Chi. Cardinals (9) vs. N.Y. Giants (5), Oct. 17, 1948
     Los Angeles (10) vs. Baltimore (4), Oct. 22, 1950
     Houston (7) vs. Oakland (7), Dec. 22, 1963
13   New Orleans (7) vs. St. Louis (6), Nov. 2, 1969
     Kansas City (7) vs. Seattle (6), Nov. 27, 1983 (OT)
     San Diego (8) vs. Pittsburgh (5), Dec. 8, 1985
     N.Y. Jets (7) vs. Miami (6), Sept. 21, 1986 (OT)
Most Consecutive Games Scoring Touchdowns
166 Cleveland, 1957-69
07   Oakland, 1966-73
96   Kansas City, 1963-70

POINTS AFTER TOUCHDOWN
Most Points After Touchdown, Season
66   Miami, 1984
65   Houston, 1961
62   Washington, 1983
Fewest Points After Touchdown, Season
2   Chi. Cardinals, 1933
3   Cincinnati, 1933
     Pittsburgh, 1934
4   Cincinnati/St. Louis, 1934
Most Points After Touchdown, Game
10   Los Angeles vs. Baltimore, Oct. 22, 1950
9   Chi. Cardinals vs. N.Y. Giants, Oct. 17, 1948
     Pittsburgh vs. N.Y. Giants, Nov. 30, 1952
     Washington vs. N.Y. Giants, Nov. 27, 1966
8   By many teams
Most Points After Touchdown, Both Teams, Game
14   Chi. Cardinals (9) vs. N.Y. Giants (5), Oct. 17, 1948
     Houston (7) vs. Oakland (7), Dec. 22, 1963
     Washington (9) vs. N.Y. Giants (5), Nov. 27, 1966
13   Los Angeles (10) vs. Baltimore (3), Oct. 22, 1950
12   In many games

FIELD GOALS
Most Seasons Leading League, Field Goals
11   Green Bay, 1935-36, 1940-43, 1946-47, 1955, 1972, 1974
8   Washington, 1945, 1956, 1971, 1976-77, 1979, 1982, 1992
7   N.Y. Giants, 1933, 1937, 1939, 1941, 1944, 1959, 1983
Most Consecutive Seasons Leading League, Field Goals
4   Green Bay, 1940-43
3   Cleveland, 1952-54
2   By many teams
Most Field Goals Attempted, Season
49   Los Angeles, 1966

Washington, 1971
48   Green Bay, 1972
47   N.Y. Jets, 1969
     Los Angeles, 1973
     Washington, 1983
Fewest Field Goals Attempted, Season (Since 1938)
0   Chi. Bears, 1944
2   Cleveland, 1939
     Card-Pitt, 1944
     Boston, 1946
     Chi. Bears, 1947
3   Chi. Bears, 1945
     Cleveland, 1945
Most Field Goals Attempted, Game
9   St. Louis vs. Pittsburgh, Sept. 24, 1967
8   Pittsburgh vs. St. Louis, Dec. 2, 1962
     Detroit vs. Minnesota, Nov. 13, 1966
     N.Y. Jets vs. Buffalo, Nov. 3, 1968
7   By many teams
Most Field Goals Attempted, Both Teams, Game
11   St. Louis (6) vs. Pittsburgh (5), Nov. 13, 1966
     Washington (6) vs. Chicago (5), Nov. 14, 1971
     Green Bay (6) vs. Detroit (5), Sept. 29, 1974
     Washington (6) vs. N.Y. Giants (5), Nov. 14, 1976
10   Denver (5) vs. Boston (5), Nov. 11, 1962
     Boston (7) vs. San Diego (3), Sept. 20, 1964
     Buffalo (7) vs. Houston (3), Dec. 5, 1965
     St. Louis (7) vs. Atlanta (3), Dec. 11, 1966
     Boston (7) vs. Buffalo (3), Sept. 24, 1967
     Detroit (7) vs. Minnesota (3), Sept. 20, 1971
     Washington (7) vs. Houston (3), Oct. 10, 1971
     Green Bay (5) vs. St. Louis (5), Dec. 5, 1971
     Kansas City (7) vs. Buffalo (3), Dec. 19, 1971
     Kansas City (5) vs. San Diego (5), Oct. 29, 1972
     Minnesota (6) vs. Chicago (4), Sept. 23, 1973
     Cleveland (7) vs. Denver (3), Oct. 19, 1975
     Cleveland (5) vs. Denver (5), Oct. 5, 1980
9   In many games
Most Field Goals, Season
35   N.Y. Giants, 1983
     L.A. Raiders, 1993
34   N.Y. Jets, 1968
     Kansas City, 1990
     Detroit, 1993
33   Green Bay, 1972
     Washington, 1983
     Pittsburgh, 1985
     New Orleans, 1987
     Miami, 1991
Fewest Field Goals, Season (Since 1932)
0   Boston, 1932, 1935
     Chi. Cardinals, 1932, 1945
     Green Bay, 1932, 1944
     N.Y. Giants, 1932
     Brooklyn, 1944
     Card-Pitt, 1944
     Chi. Bears, 1944, 1947
     Boston, 1946
     Baltimore, 1950
     Dallas, 1952
Most Field Goals, Game
7   St. Louis vs. Pittsburgh, Sept. 24, 1967
     Minnesota vs. L.A. Rams, Nov. 5, 1989 (OT)
6   Boston vs. Denver, Oct. 4, 1964
     Detroit vs. Minnesota, Nov. 13, 1966
     N.Y. Jets vs. Buffalo, Nov. 3, 1968
     Philadelphia vs. Houston, Nov. 12, 1972
     N.Y. Jets vs. New Orleans, Dec. 3, 1972
     St. Louis vs. Atlanta, Dec. 9, 1973
     N.Y. Giants vs. Seattle, Oct. 18, 1981
     San Francisco vs. New Orleans, Oct. 16, 1983
     Pittsburgh vs. Denver, Oct. 23, 1988
     San Diego vs. Seattle, Sept. 5, 1993
     San Diego vs. Houston, Sept. 19, 1993
5   By many teams
Most Field Goals, Both Teams, Game
8   Cleveland (4) vs. St. Louis (4), Sept. 20, 1964
     Chicago (5) vs. Philadelphia (3), Oct. 20, 1968
     Washington (5) vs. Chicago (3), Nov. 14, 1971
     Kansas City (5) vs. Buffalo (3), Dec. 19, 1971
     Detroit (4) vs. Green Bay (4), Sept. 29, 1974
     Cleveland (5) vs. Denver (3), Oct. 19, 1975
     New England (4) vs. San Diego (4), Nov. 9, 1975

San Francisco (6) vs. New Orleans (2), Oct. 16, 1983
Seattle (5) vs. L.A. Raiders (3), Dec. 18, 1988
7 In many games

Most Consecutive Games Scoring Field Goals
31 Minnesota, 1968-70
28 Washington, 1988-90
22 San Francisco, 1988-89

SAFETIES
Most Safeties, Season
4 Cleveland, 1927
Detroit, 1962
3 By many teams
Most Safeties, Game
3 L.A. Rams vs. N.Y. Giants, Sept. 30, 1984
2 N.Y. Giants vs. Pottsville, Oct. 30, 1927
Chi. Bears vs. Pottsville, Nov. 13, 1927
Detroit vs. Brooklyn, Dec. 1, 1935
N.Y. Giants vs. Pittsburgh, Sept. 17, 1950
N.Y. Giants vs. Washington, Nov. 5, 1961
Chicago vs. Pittsburgh, Nov. 9, 1969
Dallas vs. Philadelphia, Nov. 19, 1972
Los Angeles vs. Green Bay, Oct. 21, 1973
Oakland vs. San Diego, Oct. 26, 1975
Denver vs. Seattle, Jan. 2, 1983
New Orleans vs. Cleveland, Sept. 13, 1987
Buffalo vs. Denver, Nov. 8, 1987
Most Safeties, Both Teams, Game
3 L.A. Rams (3) vs. N.Y. Giants (0), Sept. 30, 1984
2 Chi. Cardinals (1) vs. Frankford (1), Nov. 19, 1927
Chi. Cardinals (1) vs. Cincinnati (1), Nov. 12, 1933
Chi. Bears (1) vs. San Francisco (1), Oct. 19, 1952
Cincinnati (1) vs. Los Angeles (1), Oct. 22, 1972
Chi. Bears (1) vs. San Francisco (1), Sept. 19, 1976
Baltimore (1) vs. Miami (1), Oct. 29, 1978
Atlanta (1) vs. Detroit (1), Oct. 5, 1980
Houston (1) vs. Philadelphia (1), Oct. 2, 1988
Cleveland (1) vs. Seattle (1), Nov. 14, 1993
(Also see previous record)

FIRST DOWNS
Most Seasons Leading League
9 Chi. Bears, 1935, 1939, 1941, 1943, 1945, 1947-49, 1955
7 San Diego, 1965, 1969, 1980-83, 1985
6 L.A. Rams, 1946, 1950-51, 1954, 1957, 1973
Most Consecutive Seasons Leading League
4 San Diego, 1980-83
3 Chi. Bears, 1947-49
2 By many teams
Most First Downs, Season
387 Miami, 1984
380 San Diego, 1985
379 San Diego, 1981
Fewest First Downs, Season
51 Cincinnati, 1933
64 Pittsburgh, 1935
67 Philadelphia, 1937
Most First Downs, Game
39 N.Y. Jets vs. Miami, Nov. 27, 1988
Washington vs. Detroit, Nov. 4, 1990 (OT)
38 Los Angeles vs. N.Y. Giants, Nov. 13, 1966
37 Green Bay vs. Philadelphia, Nov. 11, 1962
Fewest First Downs, Game
0 N.Y. Giants vs. Green Bay, Oct. 1, 1933
Pittsburgh vs. Boston, Oct. 29, 1933
Philadelphia vs. Detroit, Sept. 20, 1935
N.Y. Giants vs. Washington, Sept. 27, 1942
Denver vs. Houston, Sept. 3, 1966
Most First Downs, Both Teams, Game
62 San Diego (32) vs. Seattle (30), Sept. 15, 1985
59 Miami (31) vs. Buffalo (28), Oct. 9, 1983 (OT)
Seattle (33) vs. Kansas City (26), Nov. 27, 1983 (OT)
N.Y. Jets (32) vs. Miami (27), Sept. 21, 1986 (OT)
N.Y. Jets (39) vs. Miami (20), Nov. 27, 1988
58 Los Angeles (30) vs. Chi. Bears (28), Oct. 24, 1954
Denver (34) vs. Kansas City (24), Nov. 18, 1974
Atlanta (35) vs. New Orleans (23), Sept. 2, 1979 (OT)
Pittsburgh (36) vs. Cleveland (22), Nov. 25, 1979 (OT)
San Diego (34) vs. Miami (24), Nov. 18, 1984 (OT)
Cincinnati (32) vs. San Diego (26), Sept. 22, 1985
Fewest First Downs, Both Teams, Game
7 Chi. Cardinals (2) vs. Detroit (5), Sept. 15, 1940
9 Pittsburgh (1) vs. Boston (8), Oct. 27, 1935

Boston (4) vs. Brooklyn (5), Nov. 24, 1935
N.Y. Giants (3) vs. Detroit (6), Nov. 7, 1943
Pittsburgh (4) vs. Chi. Cardinals (5), Nov. 11, 1945
N.Y. Bulldogs (1) vs. Philadelphia (8), Sept. 22, 1949
10 N.Y. Giants (4) vs. Washington (6), Dec. 11, 1960
Most First Downs, Rushing, Season
181 New England, 1978
177 Los Angeles, 1973
176 Chicago, 1985
Fewest First Downs, Rushing, Season
36 Cleveland, 1942
Boston, 1944
39 Brooklyn, 1943
40 Philadelphia, 1940
Detroit, 1945
Most First Downs, Rushing, Game
25 Philadelphia vs. Washington, Dec. 2, 1951
23 St. Louis vs. New Orleans, Oct. 5, 1980
21 Cleveland vs. Philadelphia, Dec. 13, 1959
Green Bay vs. Philadelphia, Nov. 11, 1962
Los Angeles vs. New Orleans, Nov. 25, 1973
Pittsburgh vs. Kansas City, Nov. 7, 1976
New England vs. Denver, Nov. 28, 1976
Oakland vs. Green Bay, Sept. 17, 1978
Fewest First Downs, Rushing, Game
0 By many teams. Last time: Tampa Bay vs. Phoenix, Dec. 27, 1992
Most First Downs, Rushing, Both Teams, Game
36 Philadelphia (25) vs. Washington (11), Dec. 2, 1951
31 Detroit (18) vs. Washington (13), Sept. 30, 1951
30 Los Angeles (17) vs. Minnesota (13), Nov. 5, 1961
New Orleans (17) vs. Green Bay (13), Sept. 9, 1979
New Orleans (16) vs. San Francisco (14), Nov. 11, 1979
New England (16) vs. Kansas City (14), Oct. 4, 1981
Fewest First Downs, Rushing, Both Teams, Game
2 Houston (0) vs. Denver (2), Dec. 2, 1962
3 Philadelphia (1) vs. Pittsburgh (2), Oct. 27, 1957
Boston (1) vs. Buffalo (2), Nov. 15, 1964
Los Angeles (0) vs. San Francisco (3), Dec. 6, 1964
Pittsburgh (1) vs. St. Louis (2), Nov. 13, 1966
Seattle (1) vs. New Orleans (2), Sept. 1, 1991
4 In many games
Most First Downs, Passing, Season
259 San Diego, 1985
251 Houston, 1990
250 Miami, 1986
Fewest First Downs, Passing, Season
18 Pittsburgh, 1941
23 Brooklyn, 1942
N.Y. Giants, 1944
24 N.Y. Giants, 1943
Most First Downs, Passing, Game
29 N.Y. Giants vs. Cincinnati, Oct. 13, 1985
27 San Diego vs. Seattle, Sept. 15, 1985
26 Miami vs. Cleveland, Dec. 12, 1988
Fewest First Downs, Passing, Game
0 By many teams. Last time: Houston vs. Kansas City, Oct. 9, 1988
Most First Downs, Passing, Both Teams, Game
43 San Diego (23) vs. Cincinnati (20), Dec. 20, 1982
Miami (24) vs. N.Y. Jets (19), Sept. 21, 1986 (OT)
42 San Francisco (22) vs. San Diego (20), Dec. 11, 1982
41 San Diego (27) vs. Seattle (14), Sept. 15, 1985
Miami (26) vs. Cleveland (15), Dec. 12, 1988
Fewest First Downs, Passing, Both Teams, Game
0 Brooklyn vs. Pittsburgh, Nov. 29, 1942
1 Green Bay (0) vs. Cleveland (1), Sept. 21, 1941
Pittsburgh (0) vs. Brooklyn (1), Oct. 11, 1942
N.Y. Giants (0) vs. Detroit (1), Nov. 7, 1943
Pittsburgh (0) vs. Chi. Cardinals (1), Nov. 11, 1945
N.Y. Bulldogs (0) vs. Philadelphia (1), Sept. 22, 1949
Chicago (0) vs. Buffalo (1), Oct. 7, 1979
2 In many games
Most First Downs, Penalty, Season
42 Chicago, 1987
41 Denver, 1986
39 Seattle, 1978
Fewest First Downs, Penalty, Season
2 Brooklyn, 1940
4 Chi. Cardinals, 1940
N.Y. Giants, 1942, 1944
Washington, 1944
Cleveland, 1952
Kansas City, 1969
5 Brooklyn, 1939

Chi. Bears, 1939
Detroit, 1953
Los Angeles, 1953
Houston, 1982

Most First Downs, Penalty, Game
11 Denver vs. Houston, Oct. 6, 1985
9 Chi. Bears vs. Cleveland, Nov. 25, 1951
Baltimore vs. Pittsburgh, Oct. 30, 1977
N.Y. Jets vs. Houston, Sept. 18, 1988
8 Philadelphia vs. Detroit, Dec. 2, 1979
Cincinnati vs. N.Y. Jets, Oct. 6, 1985
Buffalo vs. Houston, Sept. 20, 1987
Houston vs. Atlanta, Sept. 9, 1990
Kansas City vs. L.A. Raiders, Oct. 3, 1993

Fewest First Downs, Penalty, Game
0 By many teams

Most First Downs, Penalty, Both Teams, Game
11 Chi. Bears (9) vs. Cleveland (2), Nov. 25, 1951
Cincinnati (8) vs. N.Y. Jets (3), Oct. 6, 1985
Denver (11) vs. Houston (0), Oct. 6, 1985
Detroit (6) vs. Dallas (5), Nov. 8, 1987
N.Y. Jets (9) vs. Houston (2), Sept. 18, 1988
Kansas City (8) vs. L.A. Raiders (3), Oct. 3, 1993
10 In many games

NET YARDS GAINED RUSHING AND PASSING

Most Seasons Leading League
12 Chi. Bears, 1932, 1934-35, 1939, 1941-44, 1947, 1949, 1955-56
7 San Diego, 1963, 1965, 1980-83, 1985
6 L.A. Rams, 1946, 1950-51, 1954, 1957, 1973
Baltimore, 1958-60, 1964, 1967, 1976
Dall. Cowboys, 1966, 1968-69, 1971, 1974, 1977

Most Consecutive Seasons Leading League
4 Chi. Bears, 1941-44
San Diego, 1980-83
3 Baltimore, 1958-60
Houston, 1960-62
Oakland, 1968-70
2 By many teams

Most Yards Gained, Season
6,936 Miami, 1984
6,744 San Diego, 1981
6,535 San Diego, 1985

Fewest Yards Gained, Season
1,150 Cincinnati, 1933
1,443 Chi. Cardinals, 1934
1,486 Chi. Cardinals, 1933

Most Yards Gained, Game
735 Los Angeles vs. N.Y. Yanks, Sept. 28, 1951
683 Pittsburgh vs. Chi. Cardinals, Dec. 13, 1958
682 Chi. Bears vs. N.Y. Giants, Nov. 14, 1943

Fewest Yards Gained, Game
−7 Seattle vs. Los Angeles, Nov. 4, 1979
−5 Denver vs. Oakland, Sept. 10, 1967
14 Chi. Cardinals vs. Detroit, Sept. 15, 1940

Most Yards Gained, Both Teams, Game
1,133 Los Angeles (636) vs. N.Y. Yanks (497), Nov. 19, 1950
1,102 San Diego (661) vs. Cincinnati (441), Dec. 20, 1982
1,087 St. Louis (589) vs. Philadelphia (498), Dec. 16, 1962

Fewest Yards Gained, Both Teams, Game
30 Chi. Cardinals (14) vs. Detroit (16), Sept. 15, 1940
136 Chi. Cardinals (50) vs. Green Bay (86), Nov. 18, 1934
154 N.Y. Giants (51) vs. Washington (103), Dec. 11, 1960

Most Consecutive Games, 400 or More Yards Gained
11 San Diego, 1982-83
6 Houston, 1961-62
San Diego, 1981
San Francisco, 1987
5 Chi. Bears, 1947
Philadelphia, 1953
Chi. Bears, 1955
Oakland, 1968
New England, 1981
Cincinnati, 1986

Most Consecutive Games, 300 or More Yards Gained
29 Los Angeles, 1949-51
26 Miami, 1983-85
19 Cleveland, 1978-79
San Diego, 1980-82
San Francisco, 1988-89

RUSHING

Most Seasons Leading League
16 Chi. Bears, 1932, 1934-35, 1939-42, 1951, 1955-56, 1968, 1977, 1983-86
7 Buffalo, 1962, 1964, 1973, 1975, 1982, 1991-92
6 Cleveland, 1958-59, 1963, 1965-67

Most Consecutive Seasons Leading League
4 Chi. Bears, 1939-42
Chi. Bears, 1983-86
3 Detroit, 1936-38
San Francisco, 1952-54
Cleveland, 1965-67
2 By many teams

ATTEMPTS

Most Rushing Attempts, Season
681 Oakland, 1977
674 Chicago, 1984
671 New England, 1978

Fewest Rushing Attempts, Season
211 Philadelphia, 1982
219 San Francisco, 1982
225 Houston, 1982

Most Rushing Attempts, Game
72 Chi. Bears vs. Brooklyn, Oct. 20, 1935
70 Chi. Cardinals vs. Green Bay, Dec. 5, 1948
69 Chi. Cardinals vs. Green Bay, Dec. 6, 1936
Kansas City vs. Cincinnati, Sept. 3, 1978

Fewest Rushing Attempts, Game
6 Chi. Cardinals vs. Boston, Oct. 29, 1933
7 Oakland vs. Buffalo, Oct. 15, 1963
Houston vs. N.Y. Giants, Dec. 8, 1985
Seattle vs. L.A. Raiders, Nov. 17, 1991
8 Denver vs. Oakland, Dec. 17, 1960
Buffalo vs. St. Louis, Sept. 9, 1984
Detroit vs. San Francisco, Oct. 20, 1991
Atlanta vs. Detroit, Sept. 5, 1993

Most Rushing Attempts, Both Teams, Game
108 Chi. Cardinals (70) vs. Green Bay (38), Dec. 5, 1948
105 Oakland (62) vs. Atlanta (43), Nov. 30, 1975 (OT)
104 Chi. Bears (64) vs. Pittsburgh (40), Oct. 18, 1936

Fewest Rushing Attempts, Both Teams, Game
34 Atlanta (12) vs. Houston (22), Dec. 5, 1993
35 Seattle (15) vs. New Orleans (20), Sept. 1, 1991
36 Houston (15) vs. N.Y. Jets (21), Oct. 13, 1991

YARDS GAINED

Most Yards Gained Rushing, Season
3,165 New England, 1970
3,088 Buffalo, 1973
2,986 Kansas City, 1978

Fewest Yards Gained Rushing, Season
298 Philadelphia, 1940
467 Detroit, 1946
471 Boston, 1944

Most Yards Gained Rushing, Game
426 Detroit vs. Pittsburgh, Nov. 4, 1934
423 N.Y. Giants vs. Baltimore, Nov. 19, 1950
420 Boston vs. N.Y. Giants, Oct. 8, 1933

Fewest Yards Gained Rushing, Game
−53 Detroit vs. Chi. Cardinals, Oct. 17, 1943
−36 Philadelphia vs. Chi. Bears, Nov. 19, 1939
−33 Phil-Pitt vs. Brooklyn, Oct. 2, 1943

Most Yards Gained Rushing, Both Teams, Game
595 Los Angeles (371) vs. N.Y. Yanks (224), Nov. 18, 1951
574 Chi. Bears (396) vs. Pittsburgh (178), Oct. 10, 1934
558 Boston (420) vs. N.Y. Giants (138), Oct. 8, 1933

Fewest Yards Gained Rushing, Both Teams, Game
−15 Detroit (−53) vs. Chi. Cardinals (38), Oct. 17, 1943
4 Detroit (−10) vs. Chi. Cardinals (14), Sept. 15, 1940
62 L.A. Rams (15) vs. San Francisco (47), Dec. 6, 1964

AVERAGE GAIN

Highest Average Gain, Rushing, Season
5.74 Cleveland, 1963
5.65 San Francisco, 1954
5.56 San Diego, 1963

Lowest Average Gain, Rushing, Season
0.94 Philadelphia, 1940
1.45 Boston, 1944
1.55 Pittsburgh, 1935

TOUCHDOWNS

Most Touchdowns, Rushing, Season
- 36 Green Bay, 1962
- 33 Pittsburgh, 1976
- 30 Chi. Bears, 1941
  - New England, 1978
  - Washington, 1983

Fewest Touchdowns, Rushing, Season
- 1 Brooklyn, 1934
- 2 Chi. Cardinals, 1933
  - Cincinnati, 1933
  - Pittsburgh, 1934
  - Philadelphia, 1935
  - Philadelphia, 1936
  - Philadelphia, 1937
  - Philadelphia, 1938
  - Pittsburgh, 1940
  - Philadelphia, 1972
- 3 By many teams

Most Touchdowns, Rushing, Game
- 7 Los Angeles vs. Atlanta, Dec. 4, 1976
- 6 By many teams

Most Touchdowns, Rushing, Both Teams, Game
- 8 Los Angeles (6) vs. N.Y. Yanks (2), Nov. 18, 1951
  - Chi. Bears (5) vs. Green Bay (3), Nov. 6, 1955
  - Cleveland (6) vs. Los Angeles (2), Nov. 24, 1957
- 7 In many games

PASSING

ATTEMPTS

Most Passes Attempted, Season
- 709 Minnesota, 1981
- 667 Houston, 1991
- 662 San Diego, 1984

Fewest Passes Attempted, Season
- 102 Cincinnati, 1933
- 106 Boston, 1933
- 120 Detroit, 1937

Most Passes Attempted, Game
- 68 Houston vs. Buffalo, Nov 1, 1964
- 66 Atlanta vs. Detroit, Dec. 24, 1989
- 65 San Diego vs. Kansas City, Oct. 19, 1986

Fewest Passes Attempted, Game
- 0 Green Bay vs. Portsmouth, Oct. 8, 1933
  - Detroit vs. Cleveland, Sept. 10, 1937
  - Pittsburgh vs. Brooklyn, Nov. 16, 1941
  - Pittsburgh vs. Los Angeles, Nov. 13, 1949
  - Cleveland vs. Philadelphia, Dec. 3, 1950

Most Passes Attempted, Both Teams, Game
- 104 Miami (55) vs. N.Y. Jets (49), Oct. 18, 1987 (OT)
- 102 San Francisco (57) vs. Atlanta (45), Oct. 6, 1985
- 100 Tampa Bay (54) vs. Kansas City (46), Oct. 28, 1984
  - San Francisco (60) vs. Washington (40), Nov. 17, 1986
  - Philadelphia (62) vs. Chicago (38), Oct. 2, 1989

Fewest Passes Attempted, Both Teams, Game
- 4 Chi. Cardinals (1) vs. Detroit (3), Nov. 3, 1935
  - Detroit (0) vs. Cleveland (4), Sept. 10, 1937
- 6 Chi. Cardinals (2) vs. Detroit (4), Sept. 15, 1940
- 8 Brooklyn (2) vs. Philadelphia (6), Oct. 1, 1939

COMPLETIONS

Most Passes Completed, Season
- 411 Houston, 1991
- 401 San Diego, 1984
- 399 Houston, 1990

Fewest Passes Completed, Season
- 25 Cincinnati, 1933
- 33 Boston, 1933
- 34 Chi. Cardinals, 1934
  - Detroit, 1934

Most Passes Completed, Game
- 42 N.Y. Jets vs. San Francisco, Sept. 21, 1980
- 41 Houston vs. Dallas, Nov. 10, 1991 (OT)
- 40 Cincinnati vs. San Diego, Dec. 20, 1982
  - Dallas vs. Detroit, Sept. 15, 1985
  - N.Y. Giants vs. Cincinnati, Oct. 13, 1985

Fewest Passes Completed, Game
- 0 By many teams. Last time: Buffalo vs. N.Y. Jets, Sept. 29, 1974

Most Passes Completed, Both Teams, Game
- 68 San Francisco (37) vs. Atlanta (31), Oct. 6, 1985
- 66 Cincinnati (40) vs. San Diego (26), Dec. 20, 1982
- 65 San Diego (33) vs. San Francisco (32), Dec. 11, 1982
  - San Diego (37) vs. Miami (28), Nov. 18, 1984 (OT)

Houston (41) vs. Dallas (24), Nov. 10, 1991 (OT)

Fewest Passes Completed, Both Teams, Game
- 1 Chi. Cardinals (0) vs. Philadelphia (1), Nov. 8, 1936
  - Detroit (0) vs. Cleveland (1), Sept. 10, 1937
  - Chi. Cardinals (0) vs. Detroit (1), Sept. 15, 1940
  - Brooklyn (0) vs. Pittsburgh (1), Nov. 29, 1942
- 2 Chi. Cardinals (0) vs. Detroit (2), Nov. 3, 1935
  - Buffalo (0) vs. N.Y. Jets (2), Sept. 29, 1974
  - Chi. Cardinals (0) vs. Green Bay (2), Nov. 18, 1934
- 3 In seven games

YARDS GAINED

Most Seasons Leading League, Passing Yardage
- 10 San Diego, 1965, 1968, 1971, 1978-83, 1985
- 8 Chi. Bears, 1932, 1939, 1941, 1943, 1945, 1949, 1954, 1964
  - Washington, 1938, 1940, 1944, 1947-48, 1967, 1974, 1989
- 7 Houston, 1960-61, 1963-64, 1990-92

Most Consecutive Seasons Leading League, Passing Yardage
- 6 San Diego, 1978-83
- 4 Green Bay, 1934-37
- 3 Miami, 1986-88
  - Houston, 1990-92

Most Yards Gained, Passing, Season
- 5,018 Miami, 1984
- 4,870 San Diego, 1985
- 4,805 Houston, 1990

Fewest Yards Gained, Passing, Season
- 302 Chi. Cardinals, 1934
- 357 Cincinnati, 1933
- 459 Boston, 1934

Most Yards Gained, Passing, Game
- 554 Los Angeles vs. N.Y. Yanks, Sept. 28, 1951
- 530 Minnesota vs. Baltimore, Sept. 28, 1969
- 521 Miami vs. N.Y. Jets, Oct. 23, 1988

Fewest Yards Gained, Passing, Game
- −53 Denver vs. Oakland, Sept. 10, 1967
- −52 Cincinnati vs. Houston, Oct. 31, 1971
- −39 Atlanta vs. San Francisco, Oct. 23, 1976

Most Yards Gained, Passing, Both Teams, Game
- 884 N.Y. Jets (449) vs. Miami (435), Sept. 21, 1986 (OT)
- 883 San Diego (486) vs. Cincinnati (397), Dec. 20, 1982
- 849 Minnesota (471) vs. Washington (378), Nov. 2, 1986 (OT)

Fewest Yards Gained, Passing, Both Teams, Game
- −11 Green Bay (−10) vs. Dallas (−1), Oct. 24, 1965
- 1 Chi. Cardinals (0) vs. Philadelphia (1), Nov. 8, 1936
- 7 Brooklyn (0) vs. Pittsburgh (7), Nov. 29, 1942

TIMES SACKED

Most Seasons Leading League, Fewest Times Sacked
- 10 Miami, 1973, 1982-90
- 4 San Diego, 1963-64, 1967-68
  - San Francisco, 1964-65, 1970-71
  - N.Y. Jets, 1965-66, 1968, 1993
- 3 Houston, 1961-62, 1978
  - St. Louis, 1974-76
  - Washington, 1966-67, 1991

Most Consecutive Seasons Leading League, Fewest Times Sacked
- 9 Miami, 1982-90
- 3 St. Louis, 1974-76
- 2 By many teams

Most Times Sacked, Season
- 104 Philadelphia, 1986
- 72 Philadelphia, 1987
- 70 Atlanta, 1968

Fewest Times Sacked, Season
- 7 Miami, 1988
- 8 San Francisco, 1970
  - St. Louis, 1975
- 9 N.Y. Jets, 1966
  - Washington, 1991

Most Times Sacked, Game
- 12 Pittsburgh vs. Dallas, Nov. 20, 1966
  - Baltimore vs. St. Louis, Oct. 26, 1980
  - Detroit vs. Chicago, Dec. 16, 1984
  - Houston vs. Dallas, Sept. 29, 1985
- 11 St. Louis vs. N.Y. Giants, Nov. 1, 1964
  - Los Angeles vs. Baltimore, Nov. 22, 1964
  - Denver vs. Buffalo, Dec. 13, 1964
  - Green Bay vs. Detroit, Nov. 7, 1965
  - Buffalo vs. Oakland, Oct. 15, 1967
  - Denver vs. Oakland, Nov. 5, 1967
  - Atlanta vs. St. Louis, Nov. 24, 1968
  - Detroit vs. Dallas, Oct. 6, 1975

Philadelphia vs. St. Louis, Dec. 18, 1983
Cleveland vs. Kansas City, Sept. 30, 1984
Minnesota vs. Chicago, Oct. 28, 1984
Atlanta vs. Cleveland, Nov. 18, 1984
Dallas vs. San Diego, Nov. 16, 1986
Philadelphia vs. Detroit, Nov. 16, 1986
Philadelphia vs. L.A. Raiders, Nov. 30, 1986 (OT)
L.A. Raiders vs. Seattle, Dec. 8, 1986
N.Y. Jets vs. Dallas, Oct. 4, 1987
Philadelphia vs. Chicago, Oct. 4, 1987
Dallas vs. Philadelphia, Sept. 15, 1991
Cleveland vs. Indianapolis, Sept. 6, 1992
10   By many teams

Most Times Sacked, Both Teams, Game
18   Green Bay (10) vs. San Diego (8), Sept. 24, 1978
17   Buffalo (10) vs. N.Y. Titans (7), Nov. 23, 1961
Pittsburgh (12) vs. Dallas (5), Nov. 20, 1966
Atlanta (9) vs. Philadelphia (8), Dec. 16, 1984
Philadelphia (11) vs. L.A. Raiders (6), Nov. 30, 1986 (OT)
16   Los Angeles (11) vs. Baltimore (5), Nov. 22, 1964
Buffalo (11) vs. Oakland (5), Oct. 15, 1967

COMPLETION PERCENTAGE
Most Seasons Leading League, Completion Percentage
11   Washington, 1937, 1939-40, 1942-45, 1947-48, 1969-70
10   San Francisco, 1952, 1957-58, 1965, 1981, 1983, 1987, 1989, 1992-93
7   Green Bay, 1936, 1941, 1961-62, 1964, 1966, 1968

Most Consecutive Seasons Leading League, Completion Percentage
4   Washington, 1942-45
Kansas City, 1966-69
3   Cleveland, 1953-55
2   By many teams

Highest Completion Percentage, Season
70.65   Cincinnati, 1982 (310-219)
70.19   San Francisco, 1989 (483-339)
67.56   San Francisco, 1993 (524-354)

Lowest Completion Percentage, Season
22.9   Philadelphia, 1936 (170-39)
24.5   Cincinnati, 1933 (102-25)
25.0   Pittsburgh, 1941 (168-42)

TOUCHDOWNS
Most Touchdowns, Passing, Season
49   Miami, 1984
48   Houston, 1961
46   Miami, 1986

Fewest Touchdowns, Passing, Season
0   Cincinnati, 1933
Pittsburgh, 1945
1   Boston, 1932
Boston, 1933
Chi. Cardinals, 1934
Cincinnati/St. Louis, 1934
Detroit, 1942
2   Chi. Cardinals, 1932
Stapleton, 1932
Chi. Cardinals, 1935
Brooklyn, 1936
Pittsburgh, 1942

Most Touchdowns, Passing, Game
7   Chi. Bears vs. N.Y. Giants, Nov. 14, 1943
Philadelphia vs. Washington, Oct. 17, 1954
Houston vs. N.Y. Titans, Nov. 19, 1961
Houston vs. N.Y. Titans, Oct. 14, 1962
N.Y. Giants vs. Washington, Oct. 28, 1962
Minnesota vs. Baltimore, Sept. 28, 1969
San Diego vs. Oakland, Nov. 22, 1981
6   By many teams.

Most Touchdowns, Passing, Both Teams, Game
12   New Orleans (6) vs. St. Louis (6), Nov. 2, 1969
11   N.Y. Giants (7) vs. Washington (4), Oct. 28, 1962
Oakland (6) vs. Houston (5), Dec. 22, 1963
10   San Diego (5) vs. Seattle (5), Sept. 15, 1985
Miami (6) vs. N.Y. Jets (4), Sept. 21, 1986 (OT)

PASSES HAD INTERCEPTED
Most Passes Had Intercepted, Season
48   Houston, 1962
45   Denver, 1961
41   Card-Pitt, 1944

Fewest Passes Had Intercepted, Season
5   Cleveland, 1960

Green Bay, 1966
Kansas City, 1990
N.Y. Giants, 1990
6   Green Bay, 1964
St. Louis, 1982
Dallas, 1993
7   Los Angeles, 1969

Most Passes Had Intercepted, Game
9   Detroit vs. Green Bay, Oct. 24, 1943
Pittsburgh vs. Philadelphia, Dec. 12, 1965
8   Green Bay vs. N.Y. Giants, Nov. 21, 1948
Chi. Cardinals vs. Philadelphia, Sept. 24, 1950
N.Y. Yanks vs. N.Y. Giants, Dec. 16, 1951
Denver vs. Houston, Dec. 2, 1962
Chi. Bears vs. Detroit, Sept. 22, 1968
Baltimore vs. N.Y. Jets, Sept. 23, 1973
7   By many teams. Last time: Green Bay vs. New Orleans, Sept. 14, 1986

Most Passes Had Intercepted, Both Teams, Game
13   Denver (8) vs. Houston (5), Dec. 2, 1962
11   Philadelphia (7) vs. Boston (4), Nov. 3, 1935
Boston (6) vs. Pittsburgh (5), Dec. 1, 1935
Cleveland (7) vs. Green Bay (4), Oct. 30, 1938
Green Bay (7) vs. Detroit (4), Oct. 20, 1940
Detroit (7) vs. Chi. Bears (4), Nov. 22, 1942
Detroit (7) vs. Cleveland (4), Nov. 26, 1944
Chi. Cardinals (8) vs. Philadelphia (3), Sept. 24, 1950
Washington (7) vs. N.Y. Giants (4), Dec. 8, 1963
Pittsburgh (9) vs. Philadelphia (2), Dec 12, 1965
10   In many games

PUNTING
Most Seasons Leading League (Average Distance)
7   Denver, 1962-64, 1966-67, 1982, 1988
6   Washington, 1940-43, 1945, 1958
Kansas City, 1968, 1971-73, 1979, 1984
4   L.A. Rams, 1946, 1949, 1955-56
Baltimore/Indianapolis, 1966, 1969, 1983, 1985

Most Consecutive Seasons Leading League (Average Distance)
4   Washington, 1940-43
3   Cleveland, 1950-52
Denver, 1962-64
Kansas City, 1971-73

Most Punts, Season
114   Chicago, 1981
113   Boston, 1934
Brooklyn, 1934
112   Boston, 1935

Fewest Punts, Season
23   San Diego, 1982
31   Cincinnati, 1982
32   Chi. Bears, 1941

Most Punts, Game
17   Chi. Bears vs. Green Bay, Oct. 22, 1933
Cincinnati vs. Pittsburgh, Oct. 22, 1933
16   Cincinnati vs. Portsmouth, Sept. 17, 1933
Chi. Cardinals vs. Chi. Bears, Nov. 30, 1933
Chi. Cardinals vs. Detroit, Sept. 15, 1940
15   N.Y. Giants vs. Chi. Bears, Nov. 17, 1935
Philadelphia vs. N.Y. Giants, Dec. 6, 1987 (OT)

Fewest Punts, Game
0   By many teams. Last time: San Francisco vs. Detroit, Dec. 19, 1993

Most Punts, Both Teams, Game
31   Chi. Bears (17) vs. Green Bay (14), Oct. 22, 1933
Cincinnati (17), vs. Pittsburgh (14), Oct. 22, 1933
29   Chi. Cardinals (15) vs. Cincinnati (14), Nov. 12, 1933
Chi. Cardinals (16) vs. Chi. Bears (13), Nov. 30, 1933
Chi. Cardinals (16) vs. Detroit (13), Sept. 15, 1940
28   Philadelphia (14) vs. Washington (14), Nov. 5, 1939

Fewest Punts, Both Teams, Game
0   Buffalo vs. San Francisco, Sept. 13, 1992
1   Baltimore (0) vs. Cleveland (1), Nov. 1, 1959
Dall. Cowboys (0) vs. Cleveland (1), Dec. 3, 1961
Chicago (0) vs. Detroit (1), Oct. 1, 1972
San Francisco (0) vs. N.Y. Giants (1), Oct. 15, 1972
Green Bay (0) vs. Buffalo (1), Dec. 5, 1982
Miami (0) vs. Buffalo (1), Oct. 12, 1986
Green Bay (0) vs. Chicago (1), Dec. 17, 1989
2   In many games

AVERAGE YARDAGE
Highest Average Distance, Punting, Season
47.6   Detroit, 1961 (56-2,664)

47.0 Pittsburgh, 1961 (73-3,431)
46.9 Pittsburgh, 1953 (80-3,752)

Lowest Average Distance, Punting, Season
32.7 Card-Pitt, 1944 (60-1,964)
33.8 Cincinnati, 1986 (59-1,996)
33.9 Detroit, 1969 (74-2,510)

PUNT RETURNS

Most Seasons Leading League (Average Return)
9 Detroit, 1943-45, 1951-52, 1962, 1966, 1969, 1991
7 Chi. Cardinals/St. Louis, 1948-49, 1955-56, 1959, 1986-87
5 Cleveland, 1958, 1960, 1964-65, 1967
   Green Bay, 1950, 1953-54, 1961, 1972
   Dall. Texans/Kansas City, 1960, 1968, 1970, 1979-80

Most Consecutive Seasons Leading League (Average Return)
3 Detroit, 1943-45
2 By many teams

Most Punt Returns, Season
71 Pittsburgh, 1976
    Tampa Bay, 1979
    L.A. Raiders, 1985
67 Pittsburgh, 1974
    Los Angeles, 1978
    L.A. Raiders, 1984
65 San Francisco, 1976

Fewest Punt Returns, Season
12 Baltimore, 1981
    San Diego, 1982
14 Los Angeles, 1961
    Philadelphia, 1962
    Baltimore, 1982
15 Houston, 1960
    Washington, 1960
    Oakland, 1961
    N.Y. Giants, 1969
    Philadelphia, 1973
    Kansas City, 1982

Most Punt Returns, Game
12 Philadelphia vs. Cleveland, Dec. 3, 1950
11 Chi. Bears vs. Chi. Cardinals, Oct. 8, 1950
    Washington vs. Tampa Bay, Oct. 9, 1977
10 Philadelphia vs. N.Y. Giants, Nov. 26, 1950
    Philadelphia vs. Tampa Bay, Sept. 18, 1977
    Pittsburgh vs. Buffalo, Dec. 16, 1979
    Washington vs. New Orleans, Dec. 26, 1982
    Philadelphia vs. Seattle, Dec. 13, 1992 (OT)
    New England vs. Pittsburgh, Dec. 5, 1993

Most Punt Returns, Both Teams, Game
17 Philadelphia (12) vs. Cleveland (5), Dec. 3, 1950
16 N.Y. Giants (9) vs. Philadelphia (7), Dec. 12, 1954
    Washington (11) vs. Tampa Bay (5), Oct. 9, 1977
15 Detroit (8) vs. Cleveland (7), Sept. 27, 1942
    Los Angeles (8) vs. Baltimore (7), Nov. 27, 1966
    Pittsburgh (8) vs. Houston (7), Dec. 1, 1974
    Philadelphia (10) vs. Tampa Bay (5), Sept. 18, 1977
    Baltimore (9) vs. Kansas City (6), Sept. 2, 1979
    Washington (10) vs. New Orleans (5), Dec. 26, 1982
    L.A. Raiders (8) vs. Cleveland (7), Nov. 16, 1986

FAIR CATCHES

Most Fair Catches, Season
34 Baltimore, 1971
32 San Diego, 1969
30 St. Louis, 1967
    Minnesota, 1971

Fewest Fair Catches, Season
0 San Diego, 1975
   New England, 1976
   Tampa Bay, 1976
   Pittsburgh, 1977
   Dallas, 1982
1 Cleveland, 1974
   San Francisco, 1975
   Kansas City, 1976
   St. Louis, 1976
   San Diego, 1976
   L.A. Rams, 1982
   St. Louis, 1982
   Tampa Bay, 1982
2 By many teams

Most Fair Catches, Game
7 Minnesota vs. Dallas, Sept. 25, 1966
   Detroit vs. Chicago, Nov. 21, 1976

Philadelphia vs. Buffalo, Dec. 27, 1987
6 By many teams

YARDS GAINED

Most Yards, Punt Returns, Season
785 L.A. Raiders, 1985
781 Chi. Bears, 1948
774 Pittsburgh, 1974

Fewest Yards, Punt Returns, Season
27 St. Louis, 1965
35 N.Y. Giants, 1965
37 New England, 1972

Most Yards, Punt Returns, Game
231 Detroit vs. San Francisco, Oct. 6, 1963
225 Oakland vs. Buffalo, Sept. 15, 1968
219 Los Angeles vs. Atlanta, Oct. 11, 1981

Fewest Yards, Punt Returns, Game
-28 Washington vs. Dallas, Dec. 11, 1966
-23 N.Y. Giants vs. Buffalo, Oct. 20, 1975
     Pittsburgh vs. Houston, Sept. 20, 1970
-20 New Orleans vs. Pittsburgh, Oct. 20, 1968

Most Yards, Punt Returns, Both Teams, Game
282 Los Angeles (219) vs. Atlanta (63), Oct. 11, 1981
245 Detroit (231) vs. San Francisco (14), Oct. 6, 1963
244 Oakland (225) vs. Buffalo (19), Sept. 15, 1968

Fewest Yards, Punt Returns, Both Teams, Game
-18 Buffalo (-18) vs. Pittsburgh (0), Oct. 29, 1972
-14 Miami (-14) vs. Boston (0), Nov. 30, 1969
-13 N.Y. Giants (-13) vs. Cleveland (0), Nov. 14, 1965

AVERAGE YARDS RETURNING PUNTS

Highest Average, Punt Returns, Season
20.2 Chi. Bears, 1941 (27-546)
19.1 Chi. Cardinals, 1948 (35-669)
18.2 Chi. Cardinals, 1949 (30-546)

Lowest Average, Punt Returns, Season
1.2 St. Louis, 1965 (23-27)
1.5 N.Y. Giants, 1965 (24-35)
1.7 Washington, 1970 (27-45)

TOUCHDOWNS RETURNING PUNTS

Most Touchdowns, Punt Returns, Season
5 Chi. Cardinals, 1959
4 Chi. Cardinals, 1948
   Detroit, 1951
   N.Y. Giants, 1951
   Denver, 1976
3 Washington, 1941
   Detroit, 1952
   Pittsburgh, 1952
   Houston, 1975
   Los Angeles, 1981
   Cleveland, 1993

Most Touchdowns, Punt Returns, Game
2 Detroit vs. Los Angeles, Oct. 14, 1951
   Detroit vs. Green Bay, Nov. 22, 1951
   Chi. Cardinals vs. Pittsburgh, Nov. 1, 1959
   Chi. Cardinals vs. N.Y. Giants, Nov. 22, 1959
   N.Y. Titans vs. Denver, Sept. 24, 1961
   Denver vs. Cleveland, Sept. 26, 1976
   Los Angeles vs. Atlanta, Oct. 11, 1981
   St. Louis vs. Tampa Bay, Dec. 21, 1986
   L.A. Rams vs. Atlanta, Dec. 27, 1992
   Cleveland vs. Pittsburgh, Oct. 24, 1993

Most Touchdowns, Punt Returns, Both Teams, Game
2 Philadelphia (1) vs. Washington (1), Nov. 9, 1952
   Kansas City (1) vs. Buffalo (1), Sept. 11, 1966
   Baltimore (1) vs. New England (1), Nov. 18, 1979
   L.A. Raiders (1) vs. Philadelphia (1), Nov. 30, 1986 (OT)
   Cincinnati (1) vs. Green Bay (1), Sept. 20, 1992
   (Also see previous record)

KICKOFF RETURNS

Most Seasons Leading League (Average Return)
7 Washington, 1942, 1947, 1962-63, 1973-74, 1981
6 Chicago Bears, 1943, 1948, 1958, 1966, 1972, 1985
5 N.Y. Giants, 1944, 1946, 1949, 1951, 1953

Most Consecutive Seasons Leading League (Average Return)
3 Denver, 1965-67
2 By many teams

Most Kickoff Returns, Season
88 New Orleans, 1980

86 Minnesota, 1984
84 Baltimore, 1981
Fewest Kickoff Returns, Season
17 N.Y. Giants, 1944
20 N.Y. Giants, 1941, 1943
Chi. Bears, 1942
23 Washington, 1942
Most Kickoff Returns, Game
12 N.Y. Giants vs. Washington, Nov. 27, 1966
10 By many teams
Most Kickoff Returns, Both Teams, Game
19 N.Y. Giants (12) vs. Washington (7), Nov. 27, 1966
18 Houston (10) vs. Oakland (8), Dec. 22, 1963
17 Washington (9) vs. Green Bay (8), Oct. 17, 1983
San Diego (9) vs. Pittsburgh (8), Dec. 8, 1985
Detroit (9) vs. Green Bay (8), Nov. 27, 1986
L.A. Raiders (9) vs. Seattle (8), Dec. 18, 1988

YARDS GAINED
Most Yards, Kickoff Returns, Season
1,973 New Orleans, 1980
1,824 Houston, 1963
1,801 Denver, 1963
Fewest Yards, Kickoff Returns, Season
282 N.Y. Giants, 1940
381 Green Bay, 1940
424 Chicago, 1963
Most Yards, Kickoff Returns, Game
362 Detroit vs. Los Angeles, Oct. 29, 1950
304 Chi. Bears vs. Green Bay, Nov. 9, 1952
295 Denver vs. Boston, Oct. 4, 1964
Most Yards, Kickoff Returns, Both Teams, Game
560 Detroit (362) vs. Los Angeles (198), Oct. 29, 1950
453 Washington (236) vs. Philadelphia (217), Sept. 28, 1947
447 N.Y. Giants (236) vs. Cleveland (211), Dec. 4, 1966

AVERAGE YARDAGE
Highest Average, Kickoff Returns, Season
29.4 Chicago, 1972 (52-1,528)
28.9 Pittsburgh, 1952 (39-1,128)
28.2 Washington, 1962 (61-1,720)
Lowest Average, Kickoff Returns, Season
14.7 N.Y. Jets, 1993 (46-675)
15.8 N.Y. Giants, 1993 (32-507)
15.9 Tampa Bay, 1993 (58-922)

TOUCHDOWNS
Most Touchdowns, Kickoff Returns, Season
4 Green Bay, 1967
Chicago, 1970
3 Los Angeles, 1950
Chi. Cardinals, 1954
San Francisco, 1963
Denver, 1966
Chicago, 1967
New England, 1977
L.A. Rams, 1985
2 By many teams
Most Touchdowns, Kickoff Returns, Game
2 Chi. Bears vs. Green Bay, Sept. 22, 1940
Chi. Bears vs. Green Bay, Nov. 9, 1952
Philadelphia vs. Dallas, Nov. 6, 1966
Green Bay vs. Cleveland, Nov. 12, 1967
L.A. Rams vs. Green Bay, Nov. 24, 1985
Most Touchdowns, Kickoff Returns, Both Teams, Game
2 Washington (1) vs. Philadelphia (1), Nov. 1, 1942
Washington (1) vs. Philadelphia (1), Sept. 28, 1947
Los Angeles (1) vs. Detroit (1), Oct. 29, 1950
N.Y. Yanks (1) vs. N.Y. Giants (1), Nov. 4, 1951 (consecutive)
Baltimore (1) vs. Chi. Bears (1), Oct. 4, 1958
Buffalo (1) vs. Boston (1), Nov. 3, 1962
Pittsburgh (1) vs. Dallas (1), Oct. 30, 1966
St. Louis (1) vs. Washington (1), Sept. 23, 1973 (consecutive)
Atlanta (1) vs. San Francisco (1), Dec. 20, 1987 (consecutive)
Houston (1) vs. Pittsburgh (1), Dec. 4, 1988
(Also see previous record)

FUMBLES
Most Fumbles, Season
56 Chi. Bears, 1938
San Francisco, 1978
54 Philadelphia, 1946
51 New England, 1973

Fewest Fumbles, Season
8 Cleveland, 1959
11 Green Bay, 1944
12 Brooklyn, 1934
Detroit, 1943
Cincinnati, 1982
Minnesota, 1982
Most Fumbles, Game
10 Phil-Pitt vs. N.Y. Giants, Oct. 9, 1943
Detroit vs. Minnesota, Nov. 12, 1967
Kansas City vs. Houston, Oct. 12, 1969
San Francisco vs. Detroit, Dec. 17, 1978
9 Philadelphia vs. Green Bay, Oct. 13, 1946
Kansas City vs. San Diego, Nov. 15, 1964
N.Y. Giants vs. Buffalo, Oct. 20, 1975
St. Louis vs. Washington, Oct. 25, 1976
San Diego vs. Green Bay, Sept. 24, 1978
Pittsburgh vs. Cincinnati, Oct. 14, 1979
Cleveland vs. Seattle, Dec. 20, 1981
Cleveland vs. Pittsburgh, Dec. 23, 1990
8 By many teams
Most Fumbles, Both Teams, Game
14 Washington (8) vs. Pittsburgh (6), Nov. 14, 1937
Chi. Bears (7) vs. Cleveland (7), Nov. 24, 1940
St. Louis (8) vs. N.Y. Giants (6), Sept. 17, 1961
Kansas City (10) vs. Houston (4), Oct. 12, 1969
13 Washington (8) vs. Pittsburgh (5), Nov. 14, 1937
Philadelphia (7) vs. Boston (6), Dec. 8, 1946
N.Y. Giants (7) vs. Washington (6), Nov. 5, 1950
Kansas City (9) vs. San Diego (4), Nov. 15, 1964
Buffalo (7) vs. Denver (6), Dec. 13, 1964
N.Y. Jets (7) vs. Houston (6), Sept. 12, 1965
Houston (8) vs. Pittsburgh (5), Dec. 9, 1973
St. Louis (9) vs. Washington (4), Oct. 25, 1976
Cleveland (9) vs. Seattle (4), Dec. 20, 1981
Green Bay (7) vs. Detroit (6), Oct. 6, 1985
12 In many games

FUMBLES LOST
Most Fumbles Lost, Season
36 Chi. Cardinals, 1959
31 Green Bay, 1952
29 Chi. Cardinals, 1946
Pittsburgh, 1950
Fewest Fumbles Lost, Season
3 Philadelphia, 1938
Minnesota, 1980
4 San Francisco, 1960
Kansas City, 1982
5 Chi. Cardinals, 1943
Detroit, 1943
N.Y. Giants, 1943
Cleveland, 1959
Minnesota, 1982
San Diego, 1993
Most Fumbles Lost, Game
8 St. Louis vs. Washington, Oct. 25, 1976
Cleveland vs. Pittsburgh, Dec. 23, 1990
7 Cincinnati vs. Buffalo, Nov. 30, 1969
Pittsburgh vs. Cincinnati, Oct. 14, 1979
Cleveland vs. Seattle, Dec. 20, 1981
6 By many teams

FUMBLES RECOVERED
Most Fumbles Recovered, Season, Own and Opponents'
58 Minnesota, 1963 (27 own, 31 opp)
51 Chi. Bears, 1938 (37 own, 14 opp)
San Francisco, 1978 (24 own, 27 opp)
50 Philadelphia, 1987 (23 own, 27 opp)
Fewest Fumbles Recovered, Season, Own and Opponents'
9 San Francisco, 1982 (5 own, 4 opp)
11 Cincinnati, 1982 (5 own, 6 opp)
13 Baltimore, 1967 (5 own, 8 opp)
N.Y. Jets, 1967 (7 own, 6 opp)
Philadelphia, 1968 (6 own, 7 opp)
Miami, 1973 (5 own, 8 opp)
Chicago, 1982 (6 own, 7 opp)
Denver, 1982 (6 own, 7 opp)
Miami, 1982 (5 own, 8 opp)
N.Y. Giants, 1982 (7 own, 6 opp)

Most Fumbles Recovered, Game, Own and Opponents'
- 10 Denver vs. Buffalo, Dec. 13, 1964 (5 own, 5 opp)
  Pittsburgh vs. Houston, Dec. 9, 1973 (5 own, 5 opp)
  Washington vs. St. Louis, Oct. 25, 1976 (2 own, 8 opp)
- 9 St. Louis vs. N.Y. Giants, Sept. 17, 1961 (6 own, 3 opp)
  Houston vs. Cincinnati, Oct. 27, 1974 (4 own, 5 opp)
  Kansas City vs. Dallas, Nov. 10, 1975 (4 own, 5 opp)
  Green Bay vs. Detroit, Oct. 6, 1985 (5 own, 4 opp)
- 8 By many teams

Most Own Fumbles Recovered, Season
- 37 Chi. Bears, 1938
- 28 Pittsburgh, 1987
- 27 Philadelphia, 1946
  Minnesota, 1963

Fewest Own Fumbles Recovered, Season
- 2 Washington, 1958
- 3 Detroit, 1956
  Cleveland, 1959
  Houston, 1982
- 4 By many teams

Most Opponents' Fumbles Recovered, Season
- 31 Minnesota, 1963
- 29 Cleveland, 1951
- 28 Green Bay, 1946
  Houston, 1977
  Seattle, 1983

Fewest Opponents' Fumbles Recovered, Season
- 3 Los Angeles, 1974
- 4 Philadelphia, 1944
  San Francisco, 1982
- 5 Baltimore, 1982

Most Opponents' Fumbles Recovered, Game
- 8 Washington vs. St. Louis, Oct. 25, 1976
  Pittsburgh vs. Cleveland, Dec. 23, 1990
- 7 Buffalo vs. Cincinnati, Nov. 30, 1969
  Cincinnati vs. Pittsburgh, Oct. 14, 1979
  Seattle vs. Cleveland, Dec. 20, 1981
- 6 By many teams

TOUCHDOWNS

Most Touchdowns, Fumbles Recovered, Season, Own and Opponents'
- 5 Chi. Bears, 1942 (1 own, 4 opp)
  Los Angeles, 1952 (1 own, 4 opp)
  San Francisco, 1965 (1 own, 4 opp)
  Oakland, 1978 (2 own, 3 opp)
- 4 Chi. Bears, 1948 (1 own, 3 opp)
  Boston, 1948 (4 opp)
  Denver, 1979 (1 own, 3 opp)
  Atlanta, 1981 (1 own, 3 opp)
  Denver, 1984 (4 opp)
  St. Louis, 1987 (4 opp)
  Minnesota, 1989 (4 opp)
  Atlanta, 1991 (4 opp)
- 3 By many teams

Most Touchdowns, Own Fumbles Recovered, Season
- 2 Chi. Bears, 1953
  New England, 1973
  Buffalo, 1974
  Denver, 1975
  Oakland, 1978
  Green Bay, 1982
  New Orleans, 1983
  Cleveland, 1986
  Green Bay, 1989

Most Touchdowns, Opponents' Fumbles Recovered, Season
- 4 Detroit, 1937
  Chi. Bears, 1942
  Boston, 1948
  Los Angeles, 1952
  San Francisco, 1965
  Denver, 1984
  St. Louis, 1987
  Minnesota, 1989
  Atlanta, 1991
- 3 By many teams

Most Touchdowns, Fumbles Recovered, Game, Own and Opponents'
- 2 By many teams

Most Touchdowns, Fumbled Recovered, Game, Both Teams, Own and Opponents'
- 3 Detroit (2) vs. Minnesota (1), Dec. 9, 1962 (2 own, 1 opp)
  Green Bay (2) vs. Dallas (1), Nov. 29, 1964 (3 opp)
  Oakland (2) vs. Buffalo (1), Dec. 24, 1967 (3 opp)

Most Touchdowns, Own Fumbles Recovered, Game
- 1 By many teams

Most Touchdowns, Opponents' Fumbles Recovered, Game
- 2 Detroit vs. Cleveland, Nov. 7, 1937
  Philadelphia vs. N.Y. Giants, Sept. 25, 1938
  Chi. Bears vs. Washington, Nov. 28, 1948
  N.Y. Giants vs. Pittsburgh, Sept. 17, 1950
  Cleveland vs. Dall. Cowboys, Dec. 3, 1961
  Cleveland vs. N.Y. Giants, Oct. 25, 1964
  Green Bay vs. Dallas, Nov. 29, 1964
  San Francisco vs. Detroit, Nov. 14, 1965
  Oakland vs. Buffalo, Dec. 24, 1967
  N.Y. Giants vs. Green Bay, Sept. 19, 1971
  Washington vs. San Diego, Sept. 16, 1973
  New Orleans vs. San Francisco, Oct. 19, 1975
  Cincinnati vs. Pittsburgh, Oct. 14, 1979
  Atlanta vs. Detroit, Oct. 5, 1980
  Kansas City vs. Oakland, Oct. 5, 1980
  New England vs. Baltimore, Nov. 23, 1980
  Denver vs. Green Bay, Oct. 15, 1984
  Miami vs. Kansas City, Oct. 11, 1987
  St. Louis vs. New Orleans, Oct. 11, 1987
  Minnesota vs. Atlanta, Dec. 10, 1989
  Philadelphia vs. Phoenix, Nov. 24, 1991
  Cincinnati vs. Seattle, Sept. 6, 1992

Most Touchdowns, Opponents' Fumbled Recovered, Game, Both Teams
- 3 Green Bay (2) vs. Dallas (1), Nov. 29, 1964
  Oakland (2) vs. Buffalo (1), Dec. 24, 1967

TURNOVERS
(Number of times losing the ball on interceptions and fumbles.)

Most Turnovers, Season
- 63 San Francisco, 1978
- 58 Chi. Bears, 1947
  Pittsburgh, 1950
  N.Y. Giants, 1983
- 57 Green Bay, 1950
  Houston, 1962, 1963
  Pittsburgh, 1965

Fewest Turnovers, Season
- 12 Kansas City, 1982
- 14 N.Y. Giants, 1943
  Cleveland, 1959
  N.Y. Giants, 1990
- 16 San Francisco, 1960
  Cincinnati, 1982
  St. Louis, 1982
  Washington, 1982

Most Turnovers, Game
- 12 Detroit vs. Chi. Bears, Nov. 22, 1942
  Chi. Cardinals vs. Philadelphia, Sept. 24, 1950
  Pittsburgh vs. Philadelphia, Dec. 12, 1965
- 11 San Diego vs. Green Bay, Sept. 24, 1978
- 10 Washington vs. N.Y. Giants, Dec. 4, 1938
  Pittsburgh vs. Green Bay, Nov. 23, 1941
  Detroit vs. Green Bay, Oct. 24, 1943
  Chi. Cardinals vs. Green Bay, Nov. 10, 1946
  Chi. Cardinals vs. N.Y. Giants, Nov. 2, 1952
  Minnesota vs. Detroit, Dec. 9, 1962
  Houston vs. Oakland, Sept. 7, 1963
  Washington vs. N.Y. Giants, Dec. 8, 1963
  Chicago vs. Detroit, Sept. 22, 1968
  St. Louis vs. Washington, Oct. 25, 1976
  N.Y. Jets vs. New England, Nov. 21, 1976
  San Francisco vs. Dallas, Oct. 12, 1980
  Cleveland vs. Seattle, Dec. 20, 1981
  Detroit vs. Denver, Oct. 7, 1984

Most Turnovers, Both Teams, Game
- 17 Detroit (12) vs. Chi. Bears (5), Nov. 22, 1942
  Boston (9) vs. Philadelphia (8), Dec. 8, 1946
- 16 Chi. Cardinals (12) vs. Philadelphia (4), Sept. 24, 1950
  Chi. Cardinals (8) vs. Chi. Bears (8), Dec. 7, 1958
  Minnesota (10) vs. Detroit (6), Dec. 9, 1962
  Houston (9) vs. Kansas City (7), Oct. 12, 1969
- 15 Philadelphia (8) vs. Chi. Cardinals (7), Oct. 3, 1954
  Denver (9) vs. Houston (6), Dec. 2, 1962
  Washington (10) vs. N.Y. Giants (5), Dec. 8, 1963
  St. Louis (9) vs. Kansas City (6), Oct. 2, 1983

PENALTIES

Most Seasons Leading League, Fewest Penalties
- 13 Miami, 1968, 1976-84, 1986, 1990-91
- 9 Pittsburgh, 1946-47, 1950-52, 1954, 1963, 1965, 1968

7 Boston/New England, 1962, 1964-65, 1973, 1987, 1989, 1993

Most Consecutive Seasons Leading League, Fewest Penalties
- 9 Miami, 1976-84
- 3 Pittsburgh, 1950-52
- 2 By many teams

Most Seasons Leading League, Most Penalties
- 16 Chi. Bears, 1941-44, 1946-49, 1951, 1959-61, 1963, 1965, 1968, 1976
- 9 Oakland/L.A. Raiders, 1963, 1966, 1968-69, 1975, 1982, 1984, 1991, 1993
- 6 L.A. Rams, 1950, 1952, 1962, 1969, 1978, 1980

Most Consecutive Seasons Leading League, Most Penalties
- 4 Chi. Bears, 1941-44, 1946-49
- 3 Chi. Cardinals, 1954-56
  - Chi. Bears, 1959-61
  - Houston, 1988-90

Fewest Penalties, Season
- 19 Detroit, 1937
- 21 Boston, 1935
- 24 Philadelphia, 1936

Most Penalties, Season
- 149 Houston, 1989
- 148 L.A. Raiders, 1993
- 144 Buffalo, 1983

Fewest Penalties, Game
- 0 By many teams. Last time: Washington vs. Atlanta, Dec. 19, 1993

Most Penalties, Game
- 22 Brooklyn vs. Green Bay, Sept. 17, 1944
  - Chi. Bears vs. Philadelphia, Nov. 26, 1944
- 21 Cleveland vs. Chi. Bears, Nov. 25, 1951
- 20 Tampa Bay vs. Seattle, Oct. 17, 1976

Fewest Penalties, Both Teams, Game
- 0 Brooklyn vs. Pittsburgh, Oct. 28, 1934
  - Brooklyn vs. Boston, Sept. 28, 1936
  - Cleveland vs. Chi. Bears, Oct. 9, 1938
  - Pittsburgh vs. Philadelphia, Nov. 10, 1940

Most Penalties, Both Teams, Game
- 37 Cleveland (21) vs. Chi. Bears (16), Nov. 25, 1951
- 35 Tampa Bay (20) vs. Seattle (15), Oct. 17, 1976
- 33 Brooklyn (22) vs. Green Bay (11), Sept. 17, 1944

YARDS PENALIZED

Most Seasons Leading League, Fewest Yards Penalized
- 13 Miami, 1967-68, 1973, 1977-84, 1990-91
- 8 Boston/Washington, 1935, 1953-54, 1956-58, 1970, 1985
- 7 Pittsburgh, 1946-47, 1950, 1952, 1962, 1965, 1968
  - Boston/New England, 1962, 1964-66, 1987, 1989, 1993

Most Consecutive Seasons Leading League, Fewest Yards Penalized
- 8 Miami, 1977-84
- 3 Washington, 1956-58
  - Boston, 1964-66
- 2 By many teams

Most Seasons Leading League, Most Yards Penalized
- 15 Chi. Bears, 1935, 1937, 1939-44, 1946-47, 1949, 1951, 1961-62, 1968
- 9 Oakland/L.A. Raiders, 1963-64, 1968-69, 1975, 1982, 1984, 1991, 1993
- 6 Buffalo, 1962, 1967, 1970, 1972, 1981, 1983
  - Houston, 1961, 1985-86, 1988-90

Most Consecutive Seasons Leading League, Most Yards Penalized
- 6 Chi. Bears, 1939-44
- 3 Cleveland, 1976-78
  - Houston, 1988-90
- 2 By many teams

Fewest Yards Penalized, Season
- 139 Detroit, 1937
- 146 Philadelphia, 1937
- 159 Philadelphia, 1936

Most Yards Penalized, Season
- 1,274 Oakland, 1969
- 1,239 Baltimore, 1979
- 1,209 L.A. Raiders, 1984

Fewest Yards Penalized, Game
- 0 By many teams. Last time: Washington vs. Atlanta, Dec. 19, 1993

Most Yards Penalized, Game
- 209 Cleveland vs. Chi. Bears, Nov. 25, 1951
- 191 Philadelphia vs. Seattle, Dec. 13, 1992 (OT)
- 190 Tampa Bay vs. Seattle, Oct. 17, 1976

Fewest Yards Penalized, Both Teams, Game
- 0 Brooklyn vs. Pittsburgh, Oct. 28, 1934
  - Brooklyn vs. Boston, Sept. 28, 1936
  - Cleveland vs. Chi. Bears, Oct. 9, 1938
  - Pittsburgh vs. Philadelphia, Nov. 10, 1940

Most Yards Penalized, Both Teams, Game
- 374 Cleveland (209) vs. Chi. Bears (165), Nov. 25, 1951

- 310 Tampa Bay (190) vs. Seattle (120), Oct. 17, 1976
- 309 Green Bay (184) vs. Boston (125), Oct. 21, 1945

DEFENSE

SCORING

Most Seasons Leading League, Fewest Points Allowed
- 10 N.Y. Giants, 1935, 1938-39, 1941, 1944, 1958-59, 1961, 1990, 1993
- 9 Chi. Bears, 1932, 1936-37, 1942, 1948, 1963, 1985-86, 1988
- 6 Cleveland, 1951, 1953-57

Most Consecutive Seasons Leading League, Fewest Points Allowed
- 5 Cleveland, 1953-57
- 3 Buffalo, 1964-66
  - Minnesota, 1969-71
- 2 By many teams

Fewest Points Allowed, Season (Since 1932)
- 44 Chi. Bears, 1932
- 54 Brooklyn, 1933
- 59 Detroit, 1934

Most Points Allowed, Season
- 533 Baltimore, 1981
- 501 N.Y. Giants, 1966
- 487 New Orleans, 1980

Fewest Touchdowns Allowed, Season (Since 1932)
- 6 Chi. Bears, 1932
  - Brooklyn, 1933
- 7 Detroit, 1934
- 8 Green Bay, 1932

Most Touchdowns Allowed, Season
- 68 Baltimore, 1981
- 66 N.Y. Giants, 1966
- 63 Baltimore, 1950

FIRST DOWNS

Fewest First Downs Allowed Season
- 77 Detroit, 1935
- 79 Boston, 1935
- 82 Washington, 1937

Most First Downs Allowed, Season
- 406 Baltimore, 1981
- 371 Seattle, 1981
- 366 Green Bay, 1983

Fewest First Downs Allowed, Rushing, Season
- 35 Chi. Bears, 1942
- 40 Green Bay, 1939
- 41 Brooklyn, 1944

Most First Downs Allowed, Rushing, Season
- 179 Detroit, 1985
- 178 New Orleans, 1980
- 175 Seattle, 1981

Fewest First Downs Allowed, Passing, Season
- 33 Chi. Bears, 1943
- 34 Pittsburgh, 1941
  - Washington, 1943
- 35 Detroit, 1940
  - Philadelphia, 1940, 1944

Most First Downs Allowed, Passing, Season
- 218 San Diego, 1985
- 216 San Diego, 1981
  - N.Y. Jets, 1986
- 214 Baltimore, 1981

Fewest First Downs Allowed, Penalty, Season
- 1 Boston, 1944
- 3 Philadelphia, 1940
  - Pittsburgh, 1945
  - Washington, 1957
- 4 Cleveland, 1940
  - Green Bay, 1943
  - N.Y. Giants, 1943

Most First Downs Allowed, Penalty, Season
- 48 Houston, 1985
- 46 Houston, 1986
- 43 L.A. Raiders, 1984

NET YARDS ALLOWED RUSHING AND PASSING

Most Seasons Leading League, Fewest Yards Allowed
- 8 Chi. Bears, 1942-43, 1948, 1958, 1963, 1984-86
- 6 N.Y. Giants, 1938, 1940-41, 1951, 1956, 1959
  - Philadelphia, 1944-45, 1949, 1953, 1981, 1991
  - Minnesota, 1969-70, 1975, 1988-89, 1993
- 5 Boston/Washington, 1935-37, 1939, 1946

Most Consecutive Seasons Leading League, Fewest Yards Allowed
- 3 Boston/Washington, 1935-37

Chicago, 1984-86
2 By many teams

Fewest Yards Allowed, Season
1,539 Chi. Cardinals, 1934
1,703 Chi. Bears, 1942
1,789 Brooklyn, 1933

Most Yards Allowed, Season
6,793 Baltimore, 1981
6,403 Green Bay, 1983
6,352 Minnesota, 1984

RUSHING

Most Seasons Leading League, Fewest Yards Allowed
10 Chi. Bears, 1937, 1939, 1942, 1946, 1949, 1963, 1984-85, 1987-88
7 Detroit, 1938, 1950, 1952, 1962, 1970, 1980-81
Philadelphia, 1944-45, 1947-48, 1953, 1990-91
Dallas, 1966-69, 1972, 1978, 1992
5 N.Y. Giants, 1940, 1951, 1956, 1959, 1986

Most Consecutive Seasons Leading League, Fewest Yards Allowed
4 Dallas, 1966-69
2 By many teams

Fewest Yards Allowed, Rushing, Season
519 Chi. Bears, 1942
558 Philadelphia, 1944
762 Pittsburgh, 1982

Most Yards Allowed, Rushing, Season
3,228 Buffalo, 1978
3,106 New Orleans, 1980
3,010 Baltimore, 1978

Fewest Touchdowns Allowed, Rushing, Season
2 Detroit, 1934
Dallas, 1968
Minnesota, 1971
3 By many teams

Most Touchdowns Allowed, Rushing, Season
36 Oakland, 1961
31 N.Y. Giants, 1980
Tampa Bay, 1986
30 Baltimore, 1981

PASSING

Most Seasons Leading League, Fewest Yards Allowed
8 Green Bay, 1947-48, 1962, 1964-68
7 Washington, 1939, 1942, 1945, 1952-53, 1980, 1985
6 Chi. Bears, 1938, 1943-44, 1958, 1960, 1963
Minnesota, 1969-70, 1972, 1975-76, 1989
Pittsburgh, 1941, 1946, 1951, 1955, 1974, 1990
Philadelphia, 1934, 1936, 1940, 1949, 1981, 1991

Most Consecutive Seasons Leading League, Fewest Yards Allowed
5 Green Bay, 1964-68
2 By many teams

Fewest Yards Allowed, Passing, Season
545 Philadelphia, 1934
558 Portsmouth, 1933
585 Chi. Cardinals, 1934

Most Yards Allowed, Passing, Season
4,389 N.Y. Jets, 1986
4,311 San Diego, 1981
4,293 San Diego, 1985

Fewest Touchdowns Allowed, Passing, Season
1 Portsmouth, 1932
Philadelphia, 1934
2 Brooklyn, 1933
Chi. Bears, 1934
3 Chi. Bears, 1932
Green Bay, 1932
Green Bay, 1934
Chi. Bears, 1936
New York, 1939
New York, 1944

Most Touchdowns Allowed, Passing, Season
40 Denver, 1963
38 St. Louis, 1969
37 Washington, 1961
Baltimore, 1981

SACKS

Most Seasons Leading League
5 Oakland/L.A. Raiders, 1966-68, 1982, 1986
4 Boston/New England, 1961, 1963, 1977, 1979
Dallas, 1966, 1968-69, 1978
Dallas/Kansas City, 1960, 1965, 1969, 1990
3 San Francisco, 1967, 1972, 1976

L.A. Rams, 1968, 1970, 1988

Most Consecutive Seasons Leading League
3 Oakland, 1966-68
2 Dallas, 1968-69

Most Sacks, Season
72 Chicago, 1984
71 Minnesota, 1989
70 Chicago, 1987

Fewest Sacks, Season
11 Baltimore, 1982
12 Buffalo, 1982
13 Baltimore, 1981

Most Sacks, Game
12 Dallas vs. Pittsburgh, Nov. 20, 1966
St. Louis vs. Baltimore, Oct. 26, 1980
Chicago vs. Detroit, Dec. 16, 1984
Dallas vs. Houston, Sept. 29, 1985
11 N.Y. Giants vs. St. Louis, Nov. 1, 1964
Baltimore vs. Los Angeles, Nov. 22, 1964
Buffalo vs. Denver, Dec. 13, 1964
Detroit vs. Green Bay, Nov. 7, 1965
Oakland vs. Buffalo, Oct. 15, 1967
Oakland vs. Denver, Nov. 5, 1967
St. Louis vs. Atlanta, Nov. 24, 1968
Dallas vs. Detroit, Oct. 6, 1975
St. Louis vs. Philadelphia, Dec. 18, 1983
Kansas City vs. Cleveland, Sept. 30, 1984
Chicago vs. Minnesota, Oct. 28, 1984
Cleveland vs. Atlanta, Nov. 18, 1984
Detroit vs. Philadelphia, Nov. 16, 1986
San Diego vs. Dallas, Nov. 16, 1986
L.A. Raiders vs. Philadelphia, Nov. 30, 1986 (OT)
Seattle vs. L.A. Raiders, Dec. 8, 1986
Chicago vs. Philadelphia, Oct. 4, 1987
Dallas vs. N.Y. Jets, Oct. 4, 1987
Indianapolis vs. Cleveland, Sept. 6, 1992
10 By many teams

Most Opponents Yards Lost Attempting to Pass, Season
666 Oakland, 1967
583 Chicago, 1984
573 San Francisco, 1976

Fewest Opponents Yards Lost Attempting to Pass, Season
75 Green Bay, 1956
77 N.Y. Bulldogs, 1949
78 Green Bay, 1958

INTERCEPTIONS BY

Most Seasons Leading League
9 N.Y. Giants, 1933, 1937-39, 1944, 1948, 1951, 1954, 1961
8 Green Bay, 1940, 1942-43, 1947, 1955, 1957, 1962, 1965
Chi. Bears, 1935-36, 1941-42, 1946, 1963, 1985, 1990
6 Kansas City, 1966-70, 1974

Most Consecutive Seasons Leading League
5 Kansas City, 1966-70
3 N.Y. Giants, 1937-39
2 By many teams

Most Passes Intercepted By, Season
49 San Diego, 1961
42 Green Bay, 1943
41 N.Y. Giants, 1951

Fewest Passes Intercepted By, Season
3 Houston, 1982
5 Baltimore, 1982
6 Houston, 1972
St. Louis, 1982

Most Passes Intercepted By, Game
9 Green Bay vs. Detroit, Oct. 24, 1943
Philadelphia vs. Pittsburgh, Dec. 12, 1965
8 N.Y. Giants vs. Green Bay, Nov. 21, 1948
Philadelphia vs. Chi. Cardinals, Sept. 24, 1950
N.Y. Giants vs. N.Y. Yanks, Dec. 16, 1951
Houston vs. Denver, Dec. 2, 1962
Detroit vs. Chicago, Sept. 22, 1968
N.Y. Jets vs. Baltimore, Sept. 23, 1973
7 By many teams. Last time: New Orleans vs. Green Bay, Sept. 14, 1986

Most Consecutive Games, One or More Interceptions By
46 L.A. Chargers/San Diego, 1960-63
37 Detroit, 1960-63
36 Boston, 1944-47

Most Yards Returning Interceptions, Season
929 San Diego, 1961
712 Los Angeles, 1952

697 Seattle, 1984
Fewest Yards Returning Interceptions, Season
  5 Los Angeles, 1959
 37 Dallas, 1989
 42 Philadelphia, 1982
Most Yards Returning Interceptions, Game
325 Seattle vs. Kansas City, Nov. 4, 1984
314 Los Angeles vs. San Francisco, Oct. 18, 1964
245 Houston vs. N.Y. Jets, Oct. 15, 1967
Most Yards Returning Interceptions, Both Teams, Game
356 Seattle (325) vs. Kansas City (31), Nov. 4, 1984
338 Los Angeles (314) vs. San Francisco (24), Oct. 18, 1964
308 Dallas (182) vs. Los Angeles (126), Nov. 2, 1952
Most Touchdowns, Returning Interceptions, Season
  9 San Diego, 1961
  7 Seattle, 1984
  6 Cleveland, 1960
     Green Bay, 1966
     Detroit, 1967
     Houston, 1967
Most Touchdowns Returning Interceptions, Game
  4 Seattle vs. Kansas City, Nov. 4, 1984
  3 Baltimore vs. Green Bay, Nov. 5, 1950
     Cleveland vs. Chicago, Dec. 11, 1960
     Philadelphia vs. Pittsburgh, Dec. 12, 1965
     Baltimore vs. Pittsburgh, Sept. 29, 1968
     Buffalo vs. N.Y. Jets, Sept. 29, 1968
     Houston vs. San Diego, Dec. 19, 1971
     Cincinnati vs. Houston, Dec. 17, 1972
     Tampa Bay vs. New Orleans, Dec. 11, 1977
  2 By many teams
Most Touchdown Returning Interceptions, Both Teams, Game
  4 Philadelphia (3) vs. Pittsburgh (1), Dec. 12, 1965
     Seattle (4) vs. Kansas City (0), Nov. 4, 1984
  3 Los Angeles (2) vs. Detroit (1), Nov. 1, 1953
     Cleveland (2) vs. N.Y. Giants (1), Dec. 18, 1960
     Pittsburgh (2) vs. Cincinnati (1), Oct. 10, 1983
     Kansas City (2) vs. San Diego (1), Oct. 19, 1986
     (Also see previous record)

PUNT RETURNS
Fewest Opponents Punt Returns, Season
  7 Washington, 1962
     San Diego, 1982
 10 Buffalo, 1982
 11 Boston, 1962
Most Opponents Punt Returns, Season
 71 Tampa Bay, 1976, 1977
 69 N.Y. Giants, 1953
 68 Cleveland, 1974
Fewest Yards Allowed, Punt Returns, Season
 22 Green Bay, 1967
 34 Washington, 1962
 39 Cleveland, 1959
     Washington, 1972
Most Yards Allowed, Punt Returns, Season
932 Green Bay, 1949
913 Boston, 1947
906 New Orleans, 1974
Lowest Average Allowed, Punt Returns, Season
1.20 Chi. Cardinals, 1954 (46-55)
1.22 Cleveland, 1959 (32-39)
1.55 Chi. Cardinals, 1953 (44-68)
Highest Average Allowed, Punt Returns, Season
18.6 Green Bay, 1949 (50-932)
18.0 Cleveland, 1977 (31-558)
17.9 Boston, 1960 (20-357)
Most Touchdowns Allowed, Punt Returns, Season
  4 New York, 1959
     Atlanta, 1992
  3 Green Bay, 1949
     Chi. Cardinals, 1951
     Los Angeles, 1951
     Washington, 1952
     Dallas, 1952
     Pittsburgh, 1959, 1993
     N.Y. Jets, 1968
     Cleveland, 1977
     Atlanta, 1986
     Tampa Bay, 1986
  2 By many teams

KICKOFF RETURNS

Fewest Opponents Kickoff Returns, Season
 10 Brooklyn, 1943
 13 Denver, 1992
 15 Detroit, 1942
     Brooklyn, 1944
Most Opponents Kickoff Returns, Season
 91 Washington, 1983
 89 New England, 1980
 88 San Diego, 1981
Fewest Yards Allowed, Kickoff Returns, Season
225 Brooklyn, 1943
254 Denver, 1992
293 Brooklyn, 1944
Most Yards Allowed, Kickoff Returns, Season
2,045 Kansas City, 1966
1,827 Chicago, 1985
1,816 N.Y. Giants, 1963
Lowest Average Allowed, Kickoff Returns, Season
14.3 Cleveland, 1980 (71-1,018)
14.9 Indianapolis, 1993 (37-551)
15.0 Seattle, 1982 (24-361)
Highest Average Allowed, Kickoff Returns, Season
29.5 N.Y. Jets, 1972 (47-1,386)
29.4 Los Angeles, 1950 (48-1,411)
29.1 New England, 1971 (49-1,427)
Most Touchdowns Allowed, Kickoff Returns, Season
  3 Minnesota, 1963, 1970
     Dallas, 1966
     Detroit, 1980
     Pittsburgh, 1986
  2 By many teams

FUMBLES
Fewest Opponents Fumbles, Season
 11 Cleveland, 1956
     Baltimore, 1982
 13 Los Angeles, 1956
     Chicago, 1960
     Cleveland, 1963
     Cleveland, 1965
     Detroit, 1967
     San Diego, 1969
 14 Baltimore, 1970
     Oakland, 1975
     Buffalo, 1982
     St. Louis, 1982
     San Francisco, 1982
Most Opponents Fumbles, Season
 50 Minnesota, 1963
     San Francisco, 1978
 48 N.Y. Giants, 1980
     N.Y. Jets, 1986
 47 N.Y. Giants, 1977
     Seattle, 1984

TURNOVERS
(Number of times losing the ball on interceptions and fumbles.)
Fewest Opponents Turnovers, Season
 11 Baltimore, 1982
 13 San Francisco, 1982
 15 St. Louis, 1982
Most Opponents Turnovers, Season
 66 San Diego, 1961
 63 Seattle, 1984
 61 Washington, 1983
Most Opponents Turnovers, Game
 12 Chi. Bears vs. Detroit, Nov. 22, 1942
     Philadelphia vs. Chi. Cardinals, Sept. 24, 1950
     Philadelphia vs. Pittsburgh, Dec. 12, 1965
 11 Green Bay vs. San Diego, Sept. 24, 1978
 10 N.Y. Giants vs. Washington, Dec. 4, 1938
     Green Bay vs. Pittsburgh, Nov. 23, 1941
     Green Bay vs. Detroit, Oct. 24, 1943
     Green Bay vs. Chi. Cardinals, Nov. 10, 1946
     N.Y. Giants vs. Chi. Cardinals, Nov. 2, 1952
     Detroit vs. Minnesota, Dec. 9, 1962
     Oakland vs. Houston, Sept. 7, 1963
     N.Y. Giants vs. Washington, Dec. 8, 1963
     Detroit vs. Chicago, Sept. 22, 1968
     Washington vs. St. Louis, Oct. 25, 1976
     New England vs. N.Y. Jets, Nov. 21, 1976
     Dallas vs. San Francisco, Oct. 12, 1980
     Seattle vs. Cleveland, Dec. 20, 1981
     Denver vs. Detroit, Oct. 7, 1984

1,000 YARDS RUSHING IN A SEASON

Year	Player, Team	Att.	Yards	Avg.	Long	TD
1993	Emmitt Smith, Dallas[3]	283	1,486	5.3	62	9
	*Jerome Bettis, L.A. Rams	294	1,429	4.9	71	7
	Thurman Thomas, Buffalo[5]	355	1,315	3.7	27	6
	Erric Pegram, Atlanta	292	1,185	4.1	29	3
	Barry Sanders, Detroit[5]	243	1,115	4.6	42	3
	Leonard Russell, New England	300	1,088	3.6	21	7
	Rodney Hampton, N.Y. Giants[3]	292	1,077	3.7	20	5
	Chris Warren, Seattle[2]	273	1,072	3.9	45	7
	*Reggie Brooks, Washington	223	1,063	4.8	85	3
	*Ron Moore, Phoenix	263	1,018	3.9	20	9
	Gary Brown, Houston	195	1,002	5.1	26	6
1992	Emmitt Smith, Dallas[2]	373	1,713	4.6	68	18
	Barry Foster, Pittsburgh	390	1,690	4.3	69	11
	Thurman Thomas, Buffalo[4]	312	1,487	4.8	44	9
	Barry Sanders, Detroit[4]	312	1,352	4.3	55	9
	Lorenzo White, Houston	265	1,226	4.6	44	7
	Terry Allen, Minnesota	266	1,201	4.5	51	13
	Reggie Cobb, Tampa Bay	310	1,171	3.8	25	9
	Harold Green, Cincinnati	265	1,170	4.4	53	2
	Rodney Hampton, N.Y. Giants[2]	257	1,141	4.4	63	14
	Cleveland Gary, L.A. Rams	279	1,125	4.0	63	7
	Herschel Walker, Philadelphia[2]	267	1,070	4.0	38	8
	Chris Warren, Seattle	223	1,017	4.6	52	3
	*Ricky Watters, San Francisco	206	1,013	4.9	43	9
1991	Emmitt Smith, Dallas	365	1,563	4.3	75	12
	Barry Sanders, Detroit[3]	342	1,548	4.5	69	16
	Thurman Thomas, Buffalo[3]	288	1,407	4.9	33	7
	Rodney Hampton, N.Y. Giants	256	1,059	4.1	44	10
	Earnest Byner, Washington[3]	274	1,048	3.8	32	5
	Gaston Green, Denver	261	1,037	4.0	63	4
	Christian Okoye, Kansas City[2]	225	1,031	4.6	48	9
1990	Barry Sanders, Detroit[2]	255	1,304	5.1	45	13
	Thurman Thomas, Buffalo[2]	271	1,297	4.8	80	11
	Marion Butts, San Diego	265	1,225	4.6	52	8
	Earnest Byner, Washington[2]	297	1,219	4.1	22	6
	Bobby Humphrey, Denver[2]	288	1,202	4.2	37	7
	Neal Anderson, Chicago[3]	260	1,078	4.1	52	10
	Barry Word, Kansas City	204	1,015	5.0	53	4
	James Brooks, Cincinnati[3]	195	1,004	5.1	56	5
1989	Christian Okoye, Kansas City	370	1,480	4.0	59	12
	*Barry Sanders, Detroit	280	1,470	5.3	34	14
	Eric Dickerson, Indianapolis[7]	314	1,311	4.2	21	7
	Neal Anderson, Chicago[2]	274	1,275	4.7	73	11
	Dalton Hilliard, New Orleans	344	1,262	3.7	40	13
	Thurman Thomas, Buffalo	298	1,244	4.2	38	6
	James Brooks, Cincinnati[2]	221	1,239	5.6	65	7
	*Bobby Humphrey, Denver	294	1,151	3.9	40	7
	Greg Bell, L.A. Rams[3]	272	1,137	4.2	47	15
	Roger Craig, San Francisco[3]	271	1,054	3.9	27	6
	Ottis Anderson, N.Y. Giants[6]	325	1,023	3.1	36	14
1988	Eric Dickerson, Indianapolis[6]	388	1,659	4.3	41	14
	Herschel Walker, Dallas	361	1,514	4.2	38	5
	Roger Craig, San Francisco[2]	310	1,502	4.8	46	9
	Greg Bell, L.A. Rams[2]	288	1,212	4.2	44	16
	*John Stephens, New England	297	1,168	3.9	52	4
	Gary Anderson, San Diego	225	1,119	5.0	36	3
	Neal Anderson, Chicago	249	1,106	4.4	80	12
	Joe Morris, N.Y. Giants[3]	307	1,083	3.5	27	5
	*Ickey Woods, Cincinnati	203	1,066	5.3	56	15
	Curt Warner, Seattle[4]	266	1,025	3.9	29	10
	John Settle, Atlanta	232	1,024	4.4	62	7
	Mike Rozier, Houston	251	1,002	4.0	28	10
1987	Charles White, L.A. Rams	324	1,374	4.2	58	11
	Eric Dickerson, L.A. Rams-Indianapolis[5]	283	1,288	4.6	57	6
1986	Eric Dickerson, L.A. Rams[4]	404	1,821	4.5	42	11
	Joe Morris, N.Y. Giants[2]	341	1,516	4.4	54	14
	Curt Warner, Seattle[3]	319	1,481	4.6	60	13
	*Rueben Mayes, New Orleans	286	1,353	4.7	50	8
	Walter Payton, Chicago[10]	321	1,333	4.2	41	8
	Gerald Riggs, Atlanta[3]	343	1,327	3.9	31	9
	George Rogers, Washington[4]	303	1,203	4.0	42	18
	James Brooks, Cincinnati	205	1,087	5.3	56	5
1985	Marcus Allen, L.A. Raiders[3]	390	1,759	4.6	61	11
	Gerald Riggs, Atlanta[2]	397	1,719	4.3	50	10
	Walter Payton, Chicago[9]	324	1,551	4.8	40	9
	Joe Morris, N.Y. Giants	294	1,336	4.5	65	21
	Freeman McNeil, N.Y. Jets[2]	294	1,331	4.5	69	3
	Tony Dorsett, Dallas[8]	305	1,307	4.3	60	7
	James Wilder, Tampa Bay[2]	365	1,300	3.6	28	10
	Eric Dickerson, L.A. Rams[3]	292	1,234	4.2	43	12
	Craig James, New England	263	1,227	4.7	65	5
	Kevin Mack, Cleveland	222	1,104	5.0	61	7
	Curt Warner, Seattle[2]	291	1,094	3.8	38	8
	George Rogers, Washington[3]	231	1,093	4.7	35	7
	Roger Craig, San Francisco	214	1,050	4.9	62	9
	Earnest Jackson, Philadelphia[2]	282	1,028	3.6	59	5
	Stump Mitchell, St. Louis	183	1,006	5.5	64	7
	Earnest Byner, Cleveland	244	1,002	4.1	36	8
1984	Eric Dickerson, L.A. Rams[2]	379	2,105	5.6	66	14
	Walter Payton, Chicago[8]	381	1,684	4.4	72	11
	James Wilder, Tampa Bay	407	1,544	3.8	37	13
	Gerald Riggs, Atlanta	353	1,486	4.2	57	13
	Wendell Tyler, San Francisco[3]	246	1,262	5.1	40	7
	John Riggins, Washington[5]	327	1,239	3.8	24	14
	Tony Dorsett, Dallas[7]	302	1,189	3.9	31	6
	Earnest Jackson, San Diego	296	1,179	4.0	32	8
	Ottis Anderson, St. Louis[5]	289	1,174	4.1	24	6
	Marcus Allen, L.A. Raiders[2]	275	1,168	4.2	52	13
	Sammy Winder, Denver	296	1,153	3.9	24	4
	*Greg Bell, Buffalo	262	1,100	4.2	85	7
	Freeman McNeil, N.Y. Jets	229	1,070	4.7	53	5
1983	*Eric Dickerson, L.A. Rams	390	1,808	4.6	85	18
	William Andrews, Atlanta[4]	331	1,567	4.7	27	7
	*Curt Warner, Seattle	335	1,449	4.3	60	13
	Walter Payton, Chicago[7]	314	1,421	4.5	49	6
	John Riggins, Washington[4]	375	1,347	3.6	44	24
	Tony Dorsett, Dallas[6]	289	1,321	4.6	77	8
	Earl Campbell, Houston[5]	322	1,301	4.0	42	12
	Ottis Anderson, St. Louis[4]	296	1,270	4.3	43	5
	Mike Pruitt, Cleveland[4]	293	1,184	4.0	27	10
	George Rogers, New Orleans[2]	256	1,144	4.5	76	5
	Joe Cribbs, Buffalo[3]	263	1,131	4.3	45	3
	Curtis Dickey, Baltimore	254	1,122	4.4	56	4
	Tony Collins, New England	219	1,049	4.8	50	10
	Billy Sims, Detroit[3]	220	1,040	4.7	41	7
	Marcus Allen, L.A. Raiders	266	1,014	3.8	19	9
	Franco Harris, Pittsburgh[8]	279	1,007	3.6	19	5
1981	*George Rogers, New Orleans	378	1,674	4.4	79	13
	Tony Dorsett, Dallas[5]	342	1,646	4.8	75	4
	Billy Sims, Detroit[2]	296	1,437	4.9	51	13
	Wilbert Montgomery, Philadelphia[3]	286	1,402	4.9	41	8
	Ottis Anderson, St. Louis[3]	328	1,376	4.2	28	9
	Earl Campbell, Houston[4]	361	1,376	3.8	43	10
	William Andrews, Atlanta[3]	289	1,301	4.5	29	10
	Walter Payton, Chicago[6]	339	1,222	3.6	39	6
	Chuck Muncie, San Diego[2]	251	1,144	4.6	73	19
	*Joe Delaney, Kansas City	234	1,121	4.8	82	3
	Mike Pruitt, Cleveland[3]	247	1,103	4.5	21	7
	Joe Cribbs, Buffalo[2]	257	1,097	4.3	35	3
	Pete Johnson, Cincinnati	274	1,077	3.9	39	12
	Wendell Tyler, Los Angeles[2]	260	1,074	4.1	69	12
	Ted Brown, Minnesota	274	1,063	3.9	34	6
1980	Earl Campbell, Houston[3]	373	1,934	5.2	55	13
	Walter Payton, Chicago[5]	317	1,460	4.6	69	6
	Ottis Anderson, St. Louis	301	1,352	4.5	52	9
	William Andrews, Atlanta[2]	265	1,308	4.9	33	4
	*Billy Sims, Detroit	313	1,303	4.2	52	13
	Tony Dorsett, Dallas[4]	278	1,185	4.3	56	11
	*Joe Cribbs, Buffalo	306	1,185	3.9	48	11
	Mike Pruitt, Cleveland[2]	249	1,034	4.2	56	6
1979	Earl Campbell, Houston[2]	368	1,697	4.6	61	19
	Walter Payton, Chicago[4]	369	1,610	4.4	43	14
	*Ottis Anderson, St. Louis	331	1,605	4.8	76	8
	Wilbert Montgomery, Philadelphia[2]	338	1,512	4.5	62	9
	Mike Pruitt, Cleveland	264	1,294	4.9	77	9
	Ricky Bell, Tampa Bay	283	1,263	4.5	49	7
	Chuck Muncie, New Orleans	238	1,198	5.0	69	11
	Franco Harris, Pittsburgh[7]	267	1,186	4.4	71	11
	John Riggins, Washington[3]	260	1,153	4.4	66	9
	Wendell Tyler, Los Angeles	218	1,109	5.1	63	9
	Tony Dorsett, Dallas[3]	250	1,107	4.4	41	6
	*William Andrews, Atlanta	239	1,023	4.3	23	3
1978	*Earl Campbell, Houston	302	1,450	4.8	81	13
	Walter Payton, Chicago[3]	333	1,395	4.2	76	11
	Tony Dorsett, Dallas[2]	290	1,325	4.6	63	7
	Delvin Williams, Miami[2]	272	1,258	4.6	58	8
	Wilbert Montgomery, Philadelphia	259	1,220	4.7	47	9
	Terdell Middleton, Green Bay	284	1,116	3.9	76	11
	Franco Harris, Pittsburgh[6]	310	1,082	3.5	37	8
	Mark van Eeghen, Oakland[3]	270	1,080	4.0	34	9
	*Terry Miller, Buffalo	238	1,060	4.5	60	7
	Tony Reed, Kansas City	206	1,053	5.1	62	5
	John Riggins, Washington[2]	248	1,014	4.1	31	5
1977	Walter Payton, Chicago[2]	339	1,852	5.5	73	14

Year	Player, Team	Att	Yards	Avg	Long	TD
	Mark van Eeghen, Oakland[2]	324	1,273	3.9	27	7
	Lawrence McCutcheon, Los Angeles[4]	294	1,238	4.2	48	7
	Franco Harris, Pittsburgh[5]	300	1,162	3.9	61	11
	Lydell Mitchell, Baltimore[3]	301	1,159	3.9	64	3
	Chuck Foreman, Minnesota[3]	270	1,112	4.1	51	6
	Greg Pruitt, Cleveland[3]	236	1,086	4.6	78	3
	Sam Cunningham, New England	270	1,015	3.8	31	4
	*Tony Dorsett, Dallas	208	1,007	4.8	84	12
1976	O.J. Simpson, Buffalo[5]	290	1,503	5.2	75	8
	Walter Payton, Chicago	311	1,390	4.5	60	13
	Delvin Williams, San Francisco	248	1,203	4.9	80	7
	Lydell Mitchell, Baltimore[2]	289	1,200	4.2	43	5
	Lawrence McCutcheon, Los Angeles[3]	291	1,168	4.0	40	9
	Chuck Foreman, Minnesota[2]	278	1,155	4.2	46	13
	Franco Harris, Pittsburgh[4]	289	1,128	3.9	30	14
	Mike Thomas, Washington	254	1,101	4.3	28	5
	Rocky Bleier, Pittsburgh	220	1,036	4.7	28	5
	Mark van Eeghen, Oakland	233	1,012	4.3	21	3
	Otis Armstrong, Denver[2]	247	1,008	4.1	31	5
	Greg Pruitt, Cleveland[2]	209	1,000	4.8	64	4
1975	O.J. Simpson, Buffalo[4]	329	1,817	5.5	88	16
	Franco Harris, Pittsburgh[3]	262	1,246	4.8	36	10
	Lydell Mitchell, Baltimore	289	1,193	4.1	70	11
	Jim Otis, St. Louis	269	1,076	4.0	30	5
	Chuck Foreman, Minnesota	280	1,070	3.8	31	13
	Greg Pruitt, Cleveland	217	1,067	4.9	50	8
	John Riggins, N.Y. Jets	238	1,005	4.2	42	8
	Dave Hampton, Atlanta	250	1,002	4.0	22	5
1974	Otis Armstrong, Denver	263	1,407	5.3	43	9
	*Don Woods, San Diego	227	1,162	5.1	56	7
	O.J. Simpson, Buffalo[3]	270	1,125	4.2	41	3
	Lawrence McCutcheon, Los Angeles[2]	236	1,109	4.7	23	3
	Franco Harris, Pittsburgh[2]	208	1,006	4.8	54	5
1973	O.J. Simpson, Buffalo[2]	332	2,003	6.0	80	12
	John Brockington, Green Bay[3]	265	1,144	4.3	53	3
	Calvin Hill, Dallas[2]	273	1,142	4.2	21	6
	Lawrence McCutcheon, Los Angeles	210	1,097	5.2	37	2
	Larry Csonka, Miami[3]	219	1,003	4.6	25	5
1972	O.J. Simpson, Buffalo	292	1,251	4.3	94	6
	Larry Brown, Washington[2]	285	1,216	4.3	38	8
	Ron Johnson, N.Y. Giants[2]	298	1,182	4.0	35	9
	Larry Csonka, Miami[2]	213	1,117	5.2	45	6
	Marv Hubbard, Oakland	219	1,100	5.0	39	4
	*Franco Harris, Pittsburgh	188	1,055	5.6	75	10
	Calvin Hill, Dallas	245	1,036	4.2	26	6
	Mike Garrett, San Diego[2]	272	1,031	3.8	41	6
	John Brockington, Green Bay[2]	274	1,027	3.7	30	8
	Eugene (Mercury) Morris, Miami	190	1,000	5.3	33	12
1971	Floyd Little, Denver	284	1,133	4.0	40	6
	*John Brockington, Green Bay	216	1,105	5.1	52	4
	Larry Csonka, Miami	195	1,051	5.4	28	7
	Steve Owens, Detroit	246	1,035	4.2	23	8
	Willie Ellison, Los Angeles	211	1,000	4.7	80	4
1970	Larry Brown, Washington	237	1,125	4.7	75	5
	Ron Johnson, N.Y. Giants	263	1,027	3.9	68	8
1969	Gale Sayers, Chicago[2]	236	1,032	4.4	28	8
1968	Leroy Kelly, Cleveland[3]	248	1,239	5.0	65	16
	*Paul Robinson, Cincinnati	238	1,023	4.3	87	8
1967	Jim Nance, Boston[2]	269	1,216	4.5	53	7
	Leroy Kelly, Cleveland[2]	235	1,205	5.1	42	11
	Hoyle Granger, Houston	236	1,194	5.1	67	6
	Mike Garrett, Kansas City	236	1,087	4.6	58	9
1966	Jim Nance, Boston	299	1,458	4.9	65	11
	Gale Sayers, Chicago	229	1,231	5.4	58	8
	Leroy Kelly, Cleveland	209	1,141	5.5	70	15
	Dick Bass, Los Angeles[2]	248	1,090	4.4	50	8
1965	Jim Brown, Cleveland[7]	289	1,544	5.3	67	17
	Paul Lowe, San Diego[2]	222	1,121	5.0	59	7
1964	Jim Brown, Cleveland[6]	280	1,446	5.2	71	7
	Jim Taylor, Green Bay[5]	235	1,169	5.0	84	12
	John Henry Johnson, Pittsburgh[2]	235	1,048	4.5	45	7
1963	Jim Brown, Cleveland[5]	291	1,863	6.4	80	12
	Clem Daniels, Oakland	215	1,099	5.1	74	3
	Jim Taylor, Green Bay[4]	248	1,018	4.1	40	9
	Paul Lowe, San Diego	177	1,010	5.7	66	8
1962	Jim Taylor, Green Bay[3]	272	1,474	5.4	51	19
	John Henry Johnson, Pittsburgh	251	1,141	4.5	40	7
	Cookie Gilchrist, Buffalo	214	1,096	5.1	44	13
	Abner Haynes, Dall. Texans	221	1,049	4.7	71	13
	Dick Bass, Los Angeles	196	1,033	5.3	57	6
	Charlie Tolar, Houston	244	1,012	4.1	25	7
1961	Jim Brown, Cleveland[4]	305	1,408	4.6	38	8
	Jim Taylor, Green Bay[2]	243	1,307	5.4	53	15
1960	Jim Brown, Cleveland[3]	215	1,257	5.8	71	9
	Jim Taylor, Green Bay	230	1,101	4.8	32	11
	John David Crow, St. Louis	183	1,071	5.9	57	6
1959	Jim Brown, Cleveland[2]	290	1,329	4.6	70	14
	J.D. Smith, San Francisco	207	1,036	5.0	73	10
1958	Jim Brown, Cleveland	257	1,527	5.9	65	17
1956	Rick Casares, Chi. Bears	234	1,126	4.8	68	12
1954	Joe Perry, San Francisco[2]	173	1,049	6.1	58	8
1953	Joe Perry, San Francisco	192	1,018	5.3	51	10
1949	Steve Van Buren, Philadelphia[2]	263	1,146	4.4	41	11
	Tony Canadeo, Green Bay	208	1,052	5.1	54	4
1947	Steve Van Buren, Philadelphia	217	1,008	4.6	45	13
1934	*Beattie Feathers, Chi. Bears	119	1,004	8.4	82	8

*First season of professional football.

200 YARDS RUSHING IN A GAME

Date	Player, Team, Opponent	Att	Yards	TD
Dec. 12, 1993	*Jerome Bettis, L.A. Rams vs. New Orleans	28	212	1
Oct. 31, 1993	Emmitt Smith, Dallas vs. Philadelphia	30	237	1
Nov. 24, 1991	Barry Sanders, Detroit vs. Minnesota	23	220	4
Dec. 23, 1990	James Brooks, Cincinnati vs. Houston	20	201	1
Oct. 14, 1990	Barry Word, Kansas City vs. Detroit	18	200	2
Sept. 24, 1990	Thurman Thomas, Buffalo vs. N.Y. Jets	18	214	0
Dec. 24, 1989	Greg Bell, L.A. Rams vs. New England	26	210	1
Sept. 24, 1989	Greg Bell, L.A. Rams vs. Green Bay	28	221	2
Sept. 17, 1989	Gerald Riggs, Washington vs. Philadelphia	29	221	1
Dec. 18, 1988	Gary Anderson, San Diego vs. Kansas City	34	217	1
Nov. 30, 1987	*Bo Jackson, L.A. Raiders vs. Seattle	18	221	2
Nov. 15, 1987	Charles White, L.A. Rams vs. St. Louis	34	213	1
Dec. 7, 1986	Rueben Mayes, New Orleans vs. Miami	28	203	2
Oct. 5, 1986	Eric Dickerson, L.A. Rams vs. Tampa Bay (OT)	30	207	2
Dec. 21, 1985	George Rogers, Washington vs. St. Louis	34	206	1
Dec. 21, 1985	Joe Morris, N.Y. Giants vs. Pittsburgh	36	202	3
Dec. 9, 1984	Eric Dickerson, L.A. Rams vs. Houston	27	215	2
Nov. 18, 1984	*Greg Bell, Buffalo vs. Dallas	27	206	1
Nov. 4, 1984	Eric Dickerson, L.A. Rams vs. St. Louis	21	208	0
Sept. 2, 1984	Gerald Riggs, Atlanta vs. New Orleans	35	202	2
Nov. 27, 1983	*Curt Warner, Seattle vs. Kansas City (OT)	32	207	3
Nov. 6, 1983	James Wilder, Tampa Bay vs. Minnesota	31	219	1
Sept. 18, 1983	Tony Collins, New England vs. N.Y. Jets	23	212	3
Sept. 4, 1983	George Rogers, New Orleans vs. St. Louis	24	206	2
Dec. 21, 1980	Earl Campbell, Houston vs. Minnesota	29	203	1
Nov. 16, 1980	Earl Campbell, Houston vs. Chicago	31	206	0
Oct. 26, 1980	Earl Campbell, Houston vs. Cincinnati	27	202	2
Oct. 19, 1980	Earl Campbell, Houston vs. Tampa Bay	33	203	0
Nov. 26, 1978	*Terry Miller, Buffalo vs. N.Y. Giants	21	208	2
Dec. 4, 1977	*Tony Dorsett, Dallas vs. Philadelphia	23	206	2
Nov. 20, 1977	Walter Payton, Chicago vs. Minnesota	40	275	1
Oct. 30, 1977	Walter Payton, Chicago vs. Green Bay	23	205	2
Dec. 5, 1976	O.J. Simpson, Buffalo vs. Miami	24	203	1
Nov. 25, 1976	O.J. Simpson, Buffalo vs. Detroit	29	273	2
Oct. 24, 1976	Chuck Foreman, Minnesota vs. Philadelphia	28	200	2
Dec. 14, 1975	Greg Pruitt, Cleveland vs. Kansas City	26	214	3
Sept. 28, 1975	O.J. Simpson, Buffalo vs. Pittsburgh	28	227	0
Dec. 16, 1973	O.J. Simpson, Buffalo vs. N.Y. Jets	34	200	1
Dec. 9, 1973	O.J. Simpson, Buffalo vs. New England	22	219	1
Sept. 16, 1973	O.J. Simpson, Buffalo vs. New England	29	250	2
Dec. 5, 1971	Willie Ellison, Los Angeles vs. New Orleans	26	247	1
Dec. 20, 1970	John (Frenchy) Fuqua, Pittsburgh vs. Philadelphia	20	218	2
Nov. 3, 1968	Gale Sayers, Chicago vs. Green Bay	24	205	0
Oct. 30, 1966	Jim Nance, Boston vs. Oakland	38	208	2
Oct. 10, 1964	John Henry Johnson, Pittsburgh vs. Cleveland	30	200	3
Dec. 8, 1963	Cookie Gilchrist, Buffalo vs. N.Y. Jets	36	243	5
Nov. 3, 1963	Jim Brown, Cleveland vs. Philadelphia	28	223	1
Oct. 20, 1963	Clem Daniels, Oakland vs. N.Y. Jets	27	200	2
Sept. 22, 1963	Jim Brown, Cleveland vs. Dallas	20	232	2
Dec. 10, 1961	Billy Cannon, Houston vs. N.Y. Titans	25	216	3
Nov. 19, 1961	Jim Brown, Cleveland vs. Philadelphia	34	237	4
Dec. 18, 1960	John David Crow, St. Louis vs. Pittsburgh	24	203	0
Nov. 15, 1959	Bobby Mitchell, Cleveland vs. Washington	14	232	3
Nov. 24, 1957	*Jim Brown, Cleveland vs. Los Angeles	31	237	4
Dec. 16, 1956	*Tom Wilson, Los Angeles vs. Green Bay	23	223	0
Nov. 22, 1953	Dan Towler, Los Angeles vs. Baltimore	14	205	1
Nov. 12, 1950	Gene Roberts, N.Y. Giants vs. Chi. Cardinals	26	218	2
Nov. 27, 1949	Steve Van Buren, Philadelphia vs. Pittsburgh	27	205	0
Oct. 8, 1933	Cliff Battles, Boston vs. N.Y. Giants	16	215	1

*First season of professional football.

TIMES 200 OR MORE
59 times by 41 players...Simpson 6; Brown, Campbell 4; Bell, Dickerson 3; Payton, Riggs, Rogers 2.

4,000 YARDS PASSING IN A SEASON

Year	Player, Team	Att.	Comp.	Pct.	Yards	TD	Int.
1993	John Elway, Denver	551	348	63.2	4,030	25	10
	Steve Young, San Francisco	462	314	68.0	4,023	29	16
1992	Dan Marino, Miami[5]	554	330	59.6	4,116	24	16
1991	Warren Moon, Houston[2]	655	404	61.7	4,690	23	21
1990	Warren Moon, Houston	584	362	62.0	4,689	33	13
1989	Don Majkowski, Green Bay	599	353	58.9	4,318	27	20
	Jim Everett, L.A. Rams	518	304	58.7	4,310	29	17
1988	Dan Marino, Miami[4]	606	354	58.4	4,434	28	23
1986	Dan Marino, Miami[3]	623	378	60.7	4,746	44	23
	Jay Schroeder, Washington	541	276	51.0	4,109	22	22
1985	Dan Marino, Miami[2]	567	336	59.3	4,137	30	21
1984	Dan Marino, Miami	564	362	64.2	5,084	48	17
	Neil Lomax, St. Louis	560	345	61.6	4,614	28	16
	Phil Simms, N.Y. Giants	533	286	53.7	4,044	22	18
1983	Lynn Dickey, Green Bay	484	289	59.7	4,458	32	29
	Bill Kenney, Kansas City	603	346	57.4	4,348	24	18
1981	Dan Fouts, San Diego[3]	609	360	59.1	4,802	33	17
1980	Dan Fouts, San Diego[2]	589	348	59.1	4,715	30	24
	Brian Sipe, Cleveland	554	337	60.8	4,132	30	14
1979	Dan Fouts, San Diego	530	332	62.6	4,082	24	24
1967	Joe Namath, N.Y. Jets	491	258	52.5	4,007	26	28

400 YARDS PASSING IN A GAME

Date	Player, Team, Opponent	Att.	Comp.	Yards	TD
Dec. 19, 1993	Steve Beuerlein, Phoenix vs. Seattle	53	34	431	3
Dec. 5, 1993	Brett Favre, Green Bay vs. Chicago	54	36	402	2
Nov. 28, 1993	Steve Young, San Francisco vs. L.A. Rams	32	26	462	4
Oct. 31, 1993	Jeff Hostetler, L.A. Raiders vs. San Diego	32	20	424	2
Sept. 13, 1992	Steve Young, San Francisco vs. Buffalo	37	26	449	3
Sept. 13, 1992	Jim Kelly, Buffalo vs. San Francisco	33	22	403	3
Nov. 10, 1991	Warren Moon, Houston vs. Dallas (OT)	56	41	432	0
Nov. 10, 1991	Mark Rypien, Washington vs. Atlanta	31	16	442	6
Oct. 13, 1991	Warren Moon, Houston vs. N.Y. Jets	50	35	423	2
Dec. 16, 1990	Warren Moon, Houston vs. Kansas City	27	25	527	3
Nov. 4, 1990	Joe Montana, San Francisco vs. Green Bay	40	25	411	3
Oct. 14, 1990	Joe Montana, San Francisco vs. Atlanta	49	32	476	6
Oct. 7, 1990	Boomer Esiason, Cincinnati vs. L.A. Rams (OT)	45	31	490	3
Dec. 23, 1989	Warren Moon, Houston vs. Cleveland	31	32	414	2
Dec. 11, 1989	Joe Montana, San Francisco vs. L.A. Rams	42	30	458	3
Nov. 26, 1989	Jim Everett, L.A. Rams vs. New Orleans (OT)	51	29	454	1
Nov. 26, 1989	Mark Rypien, Washington vs. Chicago	47	30	401	4
Oct. 2, 1989	Randall Cunningham, Philadelphia vs. Chicago	62	32	401	1
Sept. 24, 1989	Joe Montana, San Francisco vs. Philadelphia	34	25	428	5
Sept. 24, 1989	Dan Marino, Miami vs. N.Y. Jets	55	33	427	4
Sept. 17, 1989	Randall Cunningham, Phil. vs. Washington	46	34	447	5
Dec. 18, 1988	Dave Krieg, Seattle vs. L.A. Raiders	32	19	410	4
Dec. 12, 1988	Dan Marino, Miami vs. Cleveland	50	30	404	4
Oct. 23, 1988	Dan Marino, Miami vs. N.Y. Jets	60	35	521	3
Oct. 16, 1988	Vinny Testaverde, Tampa Bay vs. Indianapolis	42	25	469	2
Sept. 11, 1988	Doug Williams, Washington vs. Pittsburgh	52	30	430	2
Nov. 29, 1987	Tom Ramsey, New England vs. Philadelphia	34	34	402	3
Nov. 22, 1987	Boomer Esiason, Cincinnati vs. Pittsburgh	53	30	409	0
Sept. 20, 1987	Neil Lomax, St. Louis vs. San Diego	61	32	457	3
Dec. 21, 1986	Boomer Esiason, Cincinnati vs. N.Y. Jets	30	23	425	5
Dec. 14, 1986	Dan Marino, Miami vs. L.A. Rams (OT)	29	25	403	5
Nov. 23, 1986	Bernie Kosar, Cleveland vs. Pittsburgh (OT)	46	28	414	2
Nov. 17, 1986	Joe Montana, San Francisco vs. Washington	60	33	441	0
Nov. 16, 1986	Dan Marino, Miami vs. Buffalo	54	39	404	4
Nov. 10, 1986	Bernie Kosar, Cleveland vs. Miami	50	32	401	0
Nov. 2, 1986	Tommy Kramer, Minnesota vs. Washington (OT)	35	20	490	4
Nov. 2, 1986	Ken O'Brien, N.Y. Jets vs. Seattle	32	26	431	4
Oct. 27, 1986	Jay Schroeder, Washington vs. N.Y. Giants	40	22	420	1
Oct. 12, 1986	Steve Grogan, New England vs. N.Y. Jets	42	23	401	3
Sept. 21, 1986	Ken O'Brien, N.Y. Jets vs. Miami (OT)	43	29	479	4
Sept. 21, 1986	Dan Marino, Miami vs. N.Y. Jets (OT)	50	30	448	6
Sept. 21, 1986	Tony Eason, New England vs. Seattle	45	26	414	3
Dec. 20, 1985	John Elway, Denver vs. Seattle	42	24	432	1
Nov. 10, 1985	Dan Fouts, San Diego vs. L.A. Raiders (OT)	41	26	436	4
Oct. 13, 1985	Phil Simms, N.Y. Giants vs. Cincinnati	62	40	513	1
Oct. 13, 1985	Dave Krieg, Seattle vs. Atlanta	51	33	405	4
Oct. 6, 1985	Phil Simms, N.Y. Giants vs. Dallas	36	18	432	3
Oct. 6, 1985	Joe Montana, San Francisco vs. Atlanta	57	37	429	5
Sept. 19, 1985	Tommy Kramer, Minnesota vs. Chicago	55	28	436	3
Sept. 15, 1985	Dan Fouts, San Diego vs. Seattle	43	29	440	4
Dec. 16, 1984	Neil Lomax, St. Louis vs. Washington	46	37	468	2
Dec. 9, 1984	Dan Marino, Miami vs. Indianapolis	41	29	404	4
Dec. 2, 1984	Dan Marino, Miami vs. L.A. Raiders	57	35	470	4
Nov. 25, 1984	Dave Krieg, Seattle vs. Denver	44	30	406	3
Nov. 4, 1984	Dan Marino, Miami vs. N.Y. Jets	42	23	422	2
Oct. 21, 1984	Dan Fouts, San Diego vs. L.A. Raiders	45	24	410	3
Sept. 30, 1984	Dan Marino, Miami vs. St. Louis	36	24	429	3

Sept. 2, 1984	Phil Simms, N.Y. Giants vs. Philadelphia	30	23	409	4
Dec. 11, 1983	Bill Kenney, Kansas City vs. San Diego	41	31	411	4
Nov. 20, 1983	Dave Krieg, Seattle vs. Denver	42	31	418	3
Oct. 9, 1983	Joe Ferguson, Buffalo vs. Miami (OT)	55	38	419	5
Oct. 2, 1983	Joe Theismann, Washington vs. L.A. Raiders	39	23	417	3
Sept. 25, 1983	Richard Todd, N.Y. Jets vs. L.A. Rams (OT)	50	37	446	2
Dec. 26, 1982	Vince Ferragamo, L.A. Rams vs. Chicago	46	30	509	3
Dec. 20, 1982	Dan Fouts, San Diego vs. Cincinnati	40	25	435	1
Dec. 20, 1982	Ken Anderson, Cincinnati vs. San Diego	56	40	416	2
Dec. 11, 1982	Dan Fouts, San Diego vs. San Francisco	48	33	444	5
Nov. 21, 1982	Joe Montana, San Francisco vs. St. Louis	39	26	408	3
Nov. 15, 1981	Steve Bartkowski, Atlanta vs. Pittsburgh	50	33	416	2
Oct. 25, 1981	Brian Sipe, Cleveland vs. Baltimore	41	30	444	4
Oct. 25, 1981	David Woodley, Miami vs. Dallas	37	21	408	3
Oct. 11, 1981	Tommy Kramer, Minnesota vs. San Diego	43	27	444	4
Dec. 14, 1980	Tommy Kramer, Minnesota vs. Cleveland	49	38	456	4
Nov. 16, 1980	Doug Williams, Tampa Bay vs. Minnesota	55	30	486	4
Oct. 19, 1980	Dan Fouts, San Diego vs. N.Y. Giants	41	26	444	3
Sept. 21, 1980	Lynn Dickey, Green Bay vs. Tampa Bay (OT)	51	35	418	1
Sept. 21, 1980	Richard Todd, N.Y. Jets vs. San Francisco	60	42	447	3
Oct. 3, 1976	James Harris, Los Angeles vs. Miami	29	17	436	2
Nov. 17, 1975	Ken Anderson, Cincinnati vs. Buffalo	46	30	447	2
Nov. 18, 1974	Charley Johnson, Denver vs. Kansas City	42	28	445	2
Dec. 11, 1972	Joe Namath, N.Y. Jets vs. Oakland	46	25	403	1
Sept. 24, 1972	Joe Namath, N.Y. Jets vs. Baltimore	28	15	496	6
Dec. 21, 1969	Don Horn, Green Bay vs. St. Louis	31	22	410	5
Sept. 28, 1969	Joe Kapp, Minnesota vs. Baltimore	43	28	449	7
Sept. 9, 1968	Pete Beathard, Houston vs. Kansas City	48	23	413	2
Nov. 26, 1967	Sonny Jurgensen, Washington vs. Cleveland	50	32	418	3
Oct. 1, 1967	Joe Namath, N.Y. Jets vs. Miami	39	23	415	3
Sept. 17, 1967	Johnny Unitas, Baltimore vs. Atlanta	32	22	401	2
Nov. 13, 1966	Don Meredith, Dallas vs. Washington	29	21	406	2
Nov. 28, 1965	Sonny Jurgensen, Washington vs. Dallas	43	26	411	3
Oct. 24, 1965	Fran Tarkenton, Minnesota vs. San Francisco	35	21	407	3
Nov. 1, 1964	Len Dawson, Kansas City vs. Denver	38	23	435	6
Oct. 25, 1964	Cotton Davidson, Oakland vs. Denver	36	23	427	5
Oct. 16, 1964	Babe Parilli, Boston vs. Oakland	47	25	422	4
Dec. 22, 1963	Tom Flores, Oakland vs. Houston	29	17	407	6
Nov. 17, 1963	Norm Snead, Washington vs. Pittsburgh	40	23	424	2
Nov. 10, 1963	Don Meredith, Dallas vs. San Francisco	48	30	460	3
Oct. 13, 1963	Charley Johnson, St. Louis vs. Pittsburgh	41	20	428	2
Dec. 16, 1962	Sonny Jurgensen, Philadelphia vs. St. Louis	34	15	419	5
Nov. 18, 1962	Bill Wade, Chicago vs. Dall. Cowboys	46	28	466	2
Oct. 28, 1962	Y.A. Tittle, N.Y. Giants vs. Washington	39	27	505	7
Sept. 15, 1962	Frank Tripucka, Denver vs. Buffalo	56	29	447	2
Dec. 17, 1961	Sonny Jurgensen, Philadelphia vs. Detroit	42	27	403	3
Nov. 19, 1961	George Blanda, Houston vs. N.Y. Titans	32	20	418	7
Oct. 29, 1961	George Blanda, Houston vs. Buffalo	32	18	464	4
Oct. 29, 1961	Sonny Jurgensen, Philadelphia vs. Washington	41	27	436	3
Oct. 13, 1961	Jacky Lee, Houston vs. Boston	41	27	457	2
Dec. 13, 1958	Bobby Layne, Pittsburgh vs. Chi. Cardinals	49	23	409	2
Nov. 8, 1953	Bobby Thomason, Philadelphia vs. N.Y. Giants	44	22	437	4
Oct. 4, 1952	Otto Graham, Cleveland vs. Pittsburgh	49	21	401	3
Sept. 28, 1951	Norm Van Brocklin, Los Angeles vs. N.Y. Yanks	41	27	554	5
Dec. 11, 1949	Johnny Lujack, Chi. Bears vs. Chi. Cardinals	39	24	468	6
Oct. 31, 1948	Sammy Baugh, Washington vs. Boston	24	17	446	4
Oct. 31, 1948	Jim Hardy, Los Angeles vs. Chi. Cardinals	53	28	406	3
Nov. 14, 1943	Sid Luckman, Chi. Bears vs. N.Y. Giants	32	21	433	7

TIMES 400 OR MORE

113 times by 62 players…Marino 10; Montana 7; Fouts 6; Jurgensen 5; Kramer, Krieg, Moon 4; Esiason, Namath, Simms 3; Anderson, Blanda, Cunningham, Johnson, Kosar, Lomax, Meredith, O'Brien, Rypien, Todd, Williams, Young 2.

1,000 YARDS PASS RECEIVING IN A SEASON

Year	Player, Team	No.	Yards	Avg.	Long	TD
1993	Jerry Rice, San Francisco[8]	98	1,503	15.3	80	15
	Michael Irvin, Dallas[3]	88	1,330	15.1	61	7
	Sterling Sharpe, Green Bay[4]	112	1,274	11.4	54	11
	Andre Rison, Atlanta[3]	86	1,242	14.4	53	15
	Tim Brown, L.A. Raiders	80	1,180	14.8	71	7
	Anthony Miller, San Diego[3]	84	1,162	13.8	66	7
	Cris Carter, Minnesota	86	1,071	12.5	58	9
	Reggie Langhorne, Indianapolis	85	1,038	12.2	72	3
	Irving Fryar, Miami[2]	64	1,010	15.8	65	5
1992	Sterling Sharpe, Green Bay[3]	108	1,461	13.5	76	13
	Michael Irvin, Dallas[2]	78	1,396	17.9	87	7
	Jerry Rice, San Francisco[7]	84	1,201	14.3	80	10
	Andre Rison, Atlanta[2]	93	1,119	12.0	71	11
	Fred Barnett, Philadelphia	67	1,083	16.2	71	6

Year	Player	Rec	Yards	Avg	Long	TD
	Anthony Miller, San Diego[2]	72	1,060	14.7	67	7
	Eric Martin, New Orleans[3]	68	1,041	15.3	52	5
1991	Michael Irvin, Dallas	93	1,523	16.4	66	8
	Gary Clark, Washington[5]	70	1,340	19.1	82	10
	Jerry Rice, San Francisco[6]	80	1,206	15.1	73	14
	Haywood Jeffires, Houston[2]	100	1,181	11.8	44	7
	Michael Haynes, Atlanta	50	1,122	22.4	80	11
	Andre Reed, Buffalo[2]	81	1,113	13.7	55	10
	Drew Hill, Houston[5]	90	1,109	12.3	61	4
	Mark Duper, Miami[4]	70	1,085	15.5	43	5
	James Lofton, Buffalo[6]	57	1,072	18.8	77	8
	Mark Clayton, Miami[5]	70	1,053	15.0	43	12
	Henry Ellard, L.A. Rams[4]	64	1,052	16.4	38	3
	Art Monk, Washington[5]	71	1,049	14.8	64	8
	Irving Fryar, New England	68	1,014	14.9	56	3
	John Taylor, San Francisco[2]	64	1,011	15.8	97	9
	Brian Blades, Seattle[2]	70	1,003	14.3	52	2
1990	Jerry Rice, San Francisco[5]	100	1,502	15.0	64	13
	Henry Ellard, L.A. Rams[3]	76	1,294	17.0	50	4
	Andre Rison, Atlanta	82	1,208	14.7	75	10
	Gary Clark, Washington[4]	75	1,112	14.8	53	8
	Sterling Sharpe, Green Bay[2]	67	1,105	16.5	76	6
	Willie Anderson, L.A. Rams[2]	51	1,097	21.5	55	4
	Haywood Jeffires, Houston	74	1,048	14.2	87	8
	Stephone Paige, Kansas City	65	1,021	15.7	86	5
	Drew Hill, Houston[4]	74	1,019	13.8	57	5
	Anthony Carter, Minnesota[3]	70	1,008	14.4	56	8
1989	Jerry Rice, San Francisco[4]	82	1,483	18.1	68	17
	Sterling Sharpe, Green Bay	90	1,423	15.8	79	12
	Mark Carrier, Tampa Bay	86	1,422	16.5	78	9
	Henry Ellard, L.A. Rams[2]	70	1,382	19.7	53	8
	Andre Reed, Buffalo	88	1,312	14.9	78	9
	Anthony Miller, San Diego	75	1,252	16.7	69	10
	Webster Slaughter, Cleveland	65	1,236	19.0	97	6
	Gary Clark, Washington[3]	79	1,229	15.6	80	9
	Tim McGee, Cincinnati	65	1,211	18.6	74	8
	Art Monk, Washington[4]	86	1,186	13.8	60	8
	Willie Anderson, L.A. Rams	44	1,146	26.0	78	5
	Vance Johnson, Denver	76	1,095	14.4	69	7
	Richard Johnson, Detroit	70	1,091	15.6	75	8
	Eric Martin, New Orleans[2]	68	1,090	16.0	53	8
	John Taylor, San Francisco	60	1,077	18.0	95	10
	Mervyn Fernandez, L.A. Raiders	57	1,069	18.8	75	9
	Anthony Carter, Minnesota[2]	65	1,066	16.4	50	4
	Brian Blades, Seattle	77	1,063	13.8	60	5
	Mark Clayton, Miami[4]	64	1,011	15.8	78	9
1988	Henry Ellard, L.A. Rams	86	1,414	16.4	68	10
	Jerry Rice, San Francisco[3]	64	1,306	20.4	96	9
	Eddie Brown, Cincinnati	53	1,273	24.0	86	9
	Anthony Carter, Minnesota	72	1,225	17.0	67	6
	Ricky Sanders, Washington	73	1,148	15.7	55	12
	Drew Hill, Houston[3]	72	1,141	15.8	57	10
	Mark Clayton, Miami[3]	86	1,129	13.1	45	14
	Roy Green, Phoenix[3]	68	1,097	16.1	52	7
	Eric Martin, New Orleans	85	1,083	12.7	40	7
	Al Toon, N.Y. Jets[2]	93	1,067	11.5	42	5
	Bruce Hill, Tampa Bay	58	1,040	17.9	42	9
	Lionel Manuel, N.Y. Giants	65	1,029	15.8	46	4
1987	J.T. Smith, St. Louis[2]	91	1,117	12.3	38	8
	Jerry Rice, San Francisco[2]	65	1,078	16.6	57	22
	Gary Clark, Washington[2]	56	1,066	19.0	84	7
	Carlos Carson, Kansas City[3]	55	1,044	19.0	81	7
1986	Jerry Rice, San Francisco	86	1,570	18.3	66	15
	Stanley Morgan, New England[3]	84	1,491	17.8	44	10
	Mark Duper, Miami[3]	67	1,313	19.6	85	11
	Gary Clark, Washington	74	1,265	17.1	55	7
	Al Toon, N.Y. Jets	85	1,176	13.8	62	8
	Todd Christensen, L.A. Raiders[3]	95	1,153	12.1	35	8
	Mark Clayton, Miami[2]	60	1,150	19.2	68	10
	*Bill Brooks, Indianapolis	65	1,131	17.4	84	8
	Drew Hill, Houston[2]	65	1,112	17.1	81	5
	Steve Largent, Seattle[8]	70	1,070	15.3	38	9
	Art Monk, Washington[3]	73	1,068	14.6	69	4
	*Ernest Givins, Houston	61	1,062	17.4	60	3
	Cris Collinsworth, Cincinnati[4]	62	1,024	16.5	46	10
	Wesley Walker, N.Y. Jets[2]	49	1,016	20.7	83	12
	J.T. Smith, St. Louis	80	1,014	12.7	45	8
	Mark Bavaro, N.Y. Giants	66	1,001	15.2	41	4
1985	Steve Largent, Seattle[7]	79	1,287	16.3	43	6
	Mike Quick, Philadelphia[3]	73	1,247	17.1	99	11
	Art Monk, Washington[2]	91	1,226	13.5	53	2
	Wes Chandler, San Diego[4]	67	1,199	17.9	75	10
	Drew Hill, Houston	64	1,169	18.3	57	9
	James Lofton, Green Bay[5]	69	1,153	16.7	56	4
	Louis Lipps, Pittsburgh	59	1,134	19.2	51	12
	Cris Collinsworth, Cincinnati[3]	65	1,125	17.3	71	5
	Tony Hill, Dallas[3]	74	1,113	15.0	53	7
	Lionel James, San Diego	86	1,027	11.9	67	6
	Roger Craig, San Francisco	92	1,016	11.0	73	6
1984	Roy Green, St. Louis[2]	78	1,555	19.9	83	12
	John Stallworth, Pittsburgh[3]	80	1,395	17.4	51	11
	Mark Clayton, Miami	73	1,389	19.0	65	18
	Art Monk, Washington	106	1,372	12.9	72	7
	James Lofton, Green Bay[4]	62	1,361	22.0	79	7
	Mark Duper, Miami[2]	71	1,306	18.4	80	8
	Steve Watson, Denver[3]	69	1,170	17.0	73	7
	Steve Largent, Seattle[6]	74	1,164	15.7	65	12
	Tim Smith, Houston[2]	69	1,141	16.5	75	4
	Stacey Bailey, Atlanta	67	1,138	17.0	61	6
	Carlos Carson, Kansas City[2]	57	1,078	18.9	57	4
	Mike Quick, Philadelphia[2]	61	1,052	17.2	90	9
	Todd Christensen, L.A. Raiders[2]	80	1,007	12.6	38	7
	Kevin House, Tampa Bay[2]	76	1,005	13.2	55	5
	Ozzie Newsome, Cleveland[2]	89	1,001	11.2	52	5
1983	Mike Quick, Philadelphia	69	1,409	20.4	83	13
	Carlos Carson, Kansas City	80	1,351	16.9	50	7
	James Lofton, Green Bay[3]	58	1,300	22.4	74	8
	Todd Christensen, L.A. Raiders	92	1,247	13.6	45	12
	Roy Green, St. Louis	78	1,227	15.7	71	14
	Charlie Brown, Washington	78	1,225	15.7	75	8
	Tim Smith, Houston	83	1,176	14.2	47	6
	Kellen Winslow, San Diego[3]	88	1,172	13.3	46	8
	Earnest Gray, N.Y. Giants	78	1,139	14.6	62	5
	Steve Watson, Denver[2]	59	1,133	19.2	78	5
	Cris Collinsworth, Cincinnati[2]	66	1,130	17.1	63	5
	Steve Largent, Seattle[5]	72	1,074	14.9	46	11
	Mark Duper, Miami	51	1,003	19.7	85	10
1982	Wes Chandler, San Diego[3]	49	1,032	21.1	66	9
1981	Alfred Jenkins, Atlanta[2]	70	1,358	19.4	67	13
	James Lofton, Green Bay[2]	71	1,294	18.2	75	8
	Steve Watson, Denver	60	1,244	20.7	95	13
	Frank Lewis, Buffalo[2]	70	1,244	17.8	33	4
	Steve Largent, Seattle[4]	75	1,224	16.3	57	9
	Charlie Joiner, San Diego[4]	70	1,188	17.0	57	7
	Kevin House, Tampa Bay	56	1,176	21.0	84	9
	Wes Chandler, N.O.-San Diego[2]	69	1,142	16.6	51	6
	Dwight Clark, San Francisco	85	1,105	13.0	78	4
	John Stallworth, Pittsburgh[2]	63	1,098	17.4	55	5
	Kellen Winslow, San Diego[2]	88	1,075	12.2	67	10
	Pat Tilley, St. Louis	66	1,040	15.8	75	3
	Stanley Morgan, New England[2]	44	1,029	23.4	76	6
	Harold Carmichael, Philadelphia[3]	61	1,028	16.9	85	6
	Freddie Scott, Detroit	53	1,022	19.3	48	5
	*Cris Collinsworth, Cincinnati	67	1,009	15.1	74	8
	Joe Senser, Minnesota	79	1,004	12.7	53	8
	Ozzie Newsome, Cleveland	69	1,002	14.5	62	6
	Sammy White, Minnesota	66	1,001	15.2	53	3
1980	John Jefferson, San Diego[3]	82	1,340	16.3	58	13
	Kellen Winslow, San Diego	89	1,290	14.5	65	9
	James Lofton, Green Bay	71	1,226	17.3	47	4
	Charlie Joiner, San Diego[3]	71	1,132	15.9	51	4
	Ahmad Rashad, Minnesota[2]	69	1,095	15.9	76	5
	Steve Largent, Seattle[3]	66	1,064	16.1	67	6
	Tony Hill, Dallas	60	1,055	17.6	58	8
	Alfred Jenkins, Atlanta	57	1,026	18.0	57	6
1979	Steve Largent, Seattle[2]	66	1,237	18.7	55	9
	John Stallworth, Pittsburgh	70	1,183	16.9	65	8
	Ahmad Rashad, Minnesota	80	1,156	14.5	52	9
	John Jefferson, San Diego[2]	61	1,090	17.9	65	10
	Frank Lewis, Buffalo	54	1,082	20.0	55	2
	Wes Chandler, New Orleans	65	1,069	16.4	85	6
	Tony Hill, Dallas	60	1,062	17.7	75	10
	Drew Pearson, Dallas[2]	55	1,026	18.7	56	8
	Wallace Francis, Atlanta	74	1,013	13.7	42	8
	Harold Jackson, New England[3]	45	1,013	22.5	59	7
	Charlie Joiner, San Diego[2]	72	1,008	14.0	39	4
	Stanley Morgan, New England	44	1,002	22.8	63	12
1978	Wesley Walker, N.Y. Jets	48	1,169	24.4	77	8
	Steve Largent, Seattle	71	1,168	16.5	57	8
	Harold Carmichael, Philadelphia[2]	55	1,072	19.5	56	8
	*John Jefferson, San Diego	56	1,001	17.9	46	13
1976	Roger Carr, Baltimore	43	1,112	25.9	79	11
	Cliff Branch, Oakland[2]	46	1,111	24.2	88	12
	Charlie Joiner, San Diego	50	1,056	21.1	81	7
1975	Ken Burrough, Houston	53	1,063	20.1	77	8

Year	Player, Team	No.	Yards	Avg	Long	TD
1974	Cliff Branch, Oakland	60	1,092	18.2	67	13
	Drew Pearson, Dallas	62	1,087	17.5	50	2
1973	Harold Carmichael, Philadelphia	67	1,116	16.7	73	9
1972	Harold Jackson, Philadelphia[2]	62	1,048	16.9	77	4
	John Gilliam, Minnesota	47	1,035	22.0	66	7
1971	Otis Taylor, Kansas City[2]	57	1,110	19.5	82	7
1970	Gene Washington, San Francisco	53	1,100	20.8	79	12
	Marlin Briscoe, Buffalo	57	1,036	18.2	48	8
	Dick Gordon, Chicago	71	1,026	14.5	69	13
	Gary Garrison, San Diego[2]	44	1,006	22.9	67	12
1969	Warren Wells, Oakland[2]	47	1,260	26.8	80	14
	Harold Jackson, Philadelphia	65	1,116	17.2	65	9
	Roy Jefferson, Pittsburgh[2]	67	1,079	16.1	63	9
	Dan Abramowicz, New Orleans	73	1,015	13.9	49	7
	Lance Alworth, San Diego	64	1,003	15.7	76	4
1968	Lance Alworth, San Diego[6]	68	1,312	19.3	80	10
	Don Maynard, N.Y. Jets[5]	57	1,297	22.8	87	10
	George Sauer, N.Y. Jets[3]	66	1,141	17.3	43	3
	Warren Wells, Oakland	53	1,137	21.5	94	11
	Gary Garrison, San Diego	52	1,103	21.2	84	10
	Roy Jefferson, Pittsburgh	58	1,074	18.5	62	11
	Paul Warfield, Cleveland	50	1,067	21.3	65	12
	Homer Jones, N.Y. Giants[3]	45	1,057	23.5	84	7
	Fred Biletnikoff, Oakland	61	1,037	17.0	82	6
	Lance Rentzel, Dallas	54	1,009	18.7	65	6
1967	Don Maynard, N.Y. Jets[4]	71	1,434	20.2	75	10
	Ben Hawkins, Philadelphia	59	1,265	21.4	87	10
	Homer Jones, N.Y. Giants[2]	49	1,209	24.7	70	13
	Jackie Smith, St. Louis	56	1,205	21.5	76	9
	George Sauer, N.Y. Jets[2]	75	1,189	15.9	61	6
	Lance Alworth, San Diego[5]	52	1,010	19.4	71	9
1966	Lance Alworth, San Diego[4]	73	1,383	18.9	78	13
	Otis Taylor, Kansas City	58	1,297	22.4	89	8
	Pat Studstill, Detroit	67	1,266	18.9	99	5
	Bob Hayes, Dallas[2]	64	1,232	19.3	95	13
	Charlie Frazier, Houston	57	1,129	19.8	79	12
	Charley Taylor, Washington	72	1,119	15.5	86	12
	George Sauer, N.Y. Jets	63	1,081	17.2	77	5
	Homer Jones, N.Y. Giants	48	1,044	21.8	89	8
	Art Powell, Oakland[5]	53	1,026	19.4	46	11
1965	Lance Alworth, San Diego[3]	69	1,602	23.2	85	14
	Dave Parks, San Francisco	80	1,344	16.8	53	12
	Don Maynard, N.Y. Jets[3]	68	1,218	17.9	56	14
	Pete Retzlaff, Philadelphia	66	1,190	18.0	78	10
	Lionel Taylor, Denver[4]	85	1,131	13.3	63	6
	Tommy McDonald, Los Angeles[3]	67	1,036	15.5	51	9
	*Bob Hayes, Dallas	46	1,003	21.8	82	12
1964	Charley Hennigan, Houston[3]	101	1,546	15.3	53	8
	Art Powell, Oakland[4]	76	1,361	17.9	77	11
	Lance Alworth, San Diego[2]	61	1,235	20.2	82	13
	Johnny Morris, Chicago	93	1,200	12.9	63	10
	Elbert Dubenion, Buffalo	42	1,139	27.1	72	10
	Terry Barr, Detroit[2]	57	1,030	18.1	58	9
1963	Bobby Mitchell, Washington[2]	69	1,436	20.8	99	7
	Art Powell, Oakland[3]	73	1,304	17.9	85	16
	Buddy Dial, Pittsburgh[2]	60	1,295	21.6	83	9
	Lance Alworth, San Diego	61	1,205	19.8	85	11
	Del Shofner, N.Y. Giants[4]	64	1,181	18.5	70	9
	Lionel Taylor, Denver[3]	78	1,101	14.1	72	10
	Terry Barr, Detroit	66	1,086	16.5	75	13
	Charley Hennigan, Houston[2]	61	1,051	17.2	83	10
	Sonny Randle, St. Louis[2]	51	1,014	19.9	68	12
	Bake Turner, N.Y. Jets	71	1,009	14.2	53	6
1962	Bobby Mitchell, Washington	72	1,384	19.2	81	11
	Sonny Randle, St. Louis	63	1,158	18.4	86	7
	Tommy McDonald, Philadelphia[2]	58	1,146	19.8	60	10
	Del Shofner, N.Y. Giants[3]	53	1,133	21.4	69	12
	Art Powell, N.Y. Titans[2]	64	1,130	17.7	80	8
	Frank Clarke, Dall. Cowboys	47	1,043	22.2	66	14
	Don Maynard, N.Y. Titans[2]	56	1,041	18.6	86	8
1961	Charley Hennigan, Houston	82	1,746	21.3	80	12
	Lionel Taylor, Denver[2]	100	1,176	11.8	52	4
	Bill Groman, Houston[2]	50	1,175	23.5	80	17
	Tommy McDonald, Philadelphia	64	1,144	17.9	66	13
	Del Shofner, N.Y. Giants[2]	68	1,125	16.5	46	11
	Jim Phillips, Los Angeles	78	1,092	14.0	69	5
	*Mike Ditka, Chicago	56	1,076	19.2	76	12
	Dave Kocourek, San Diego	55	1,055	19.2	76	4
	Buddy Dial, Pittsburgh	53	1,047	19.8	88	12
	R.C. Owens, San Francisco	55	1,032	18.8	54	5
1960	*Bill Groman, Houston	72	1,473	20.5	92	12
	Raymond Berry, Baltimore	74	1,298	17.5	70	10
	Don Maynard, N.Y. Titans	72	1,265	17.6	65	6
	Lionel Taylor, Denver	92	1,235	13.4	80	12
	Art Powell, N.Y. Titans	69	1,167	16.9	76	14
1958	Del Shofner, Los Angeles	51	1,097	21.5	92	8
1956	Bill Howton, Green Bay[2]	55	1,188	21.6	66	12
	Harlon Hill, Chi. Bears[2]	47	1,128	24.0	79	11
1954	Bob Boyd, Los Angeles	53	1,212	22.9	80	6
	*Harlon Hill, Chi. Bears	45	1,124	25.0	76	12
1953	Pete Pihos, Philadelphia	63	1,049	16.7	59	10
1952	*Bill Howton, Green Bay	53	1,231	23.2	90	13
1951	Elroy (Crazylegs) Hirsch, Los Angeles	66	1,495	22.7	91	17
1950	Tom Fears, Los Angeles[2]	84	1,116	13.3	53	7
	Cloyce Box, Detroit	50	1,009	20.2	82	11
1949	Bob Mann, Detroit	66	1,014	15.4	64	4
	Tom Fears, Los Angeles	77	1,013	13.2	51	9
1945	Jim Benton, Cleveland	45	1,067	23.7	84	8
1942	Don Hutson, Green Bay	74	1,211	16.4	73	17

*First season of professional football.

250 YARDS PASS RECEIVING IN A GAME

Date	Player, Team, Opponent	No.	Yards	TD
Dec. 11, 1989	John Taylor, San Francisco vs. L.A. Rams	11	286	2
Nov. 26, 1989	Willie Anderson, L.A. Rams vs. New Orleans (OT)	15	336	1
Oct. 18, 1987	Steve Largent, Seattle vs. Detroit	15	261	3
Oct. 4, 1987	Anthony Allen, Washington vs. St. Louis	7	255	3
Dec. 22, 1985	Stephone Paige, Kansas City vs. San Diego	8	309	2
Dec. 20, 1982	Wes Chandler, San Diego vs. Cincinnati	10	260	2
Sept. 23, 1979	*Jerry Butler, Buffalo vs. N.Y. Jets	10	255	4
Nov. 4, 1962	Sonny Randle, St. Louis vs. N.Y. Giants	16	256	1
Oct. 28, 1962	Del Shofner, N.Y. Giants vs. Washington	11	269	1
Oct. 13, 1961	Charley Hennigan, Houston vs. Boston	13	272	1
Oct. 21, 1956	Billy Howton, Green Bay vs. Los Angeles	7	257	2
Dec. 3, 1950	Cloyce Box, Detroit vs. Baltimore	12	302	4
Nov. 22, 1945	Jim Benton, Cleveland vs. Detroit	10	303	1

*First season of professional football.

2,000 COMBINED NET YARDS GAINED IN A SEASON

Year	Player, Team	Rushing Att.-Yds.	Pass Rec.	Punt Ret.	Kickoff Ret.	Fum. Runs	Total Yds.
1992	Thurman Thomas, Buffalo	312-1,487	58-626	0-0	0-0	1-0	371-2,113
	Emmitt Smith, Dallas	373-1,713	59-335	0-0	0-0	1-0	433-2,048
	Barry Foster, Pittsburgh	390-1,690	36-344	0-0	0-0	2-(-20)	428-2,014
1991	Thurman Thomas, Buffalo	288-1,407	62-631	0-0	0-0	0-0	350-2,038
1990	Herschel Walker, Minnesota	184-770	35-315	0-0	44-966	4-0	267-2,051
1988	*Tim Brown, L.A. Raiders	14-50	43-725	49-444	41-1,098	7-0	154-2,317
	Roger Craig, San Fran.	310-1,502	76-534	0-0	2-32	0-0	390-2,068
	Eric Dickerson, Indianapolis	388-1,659	36-377	0-0	0-0	1-0	425-2,036
	Herschel Walker, Dallas	361-1,514	53-505	0-0	0-0	3-0	417-2,019
1986	Eric Dickerson, L.A. Rams	404-1,821	26-205	0-0	0-0	1-0	432-2,026
	Gary Anderson, San Diego	127-442	80-871	25-227	24-482	2-0	258-2,022
1985	Lionel James, San Diego	105-516	86-1,027	25-213	36-779	1-0	253-2,535
	Marcus Allen, L.A. Raiders	380-1,759	67-555	0-0	0-0	2-(-6)	449-2,308
	Roger Craig, San Fran.	214-1,050	92-1,016	0-0	0-0	0-0	306-2,066
	Walter Payton, Chicago	324-1,551	49-483	0-0	0-0	1-0	374-2,034
1984	Eric Dickerson, L.A. Rams	379-2,105	21-139	0-0	0-0	4-15	404-2,259
	James Wilder, Tampa Bay	407-1,544	85-685	0-0	0-0	4-0	496-2,229
	Walter Payton, Chicago	381-1,684	45-368	0-0	0-0	1-0	427-2,052
1983	*Eric Dickerson, L.A. Rams	390-1,808	51-404	0-0	0-0	1-0	442-2,212
	William Andrews, Atlanta	331-1,567	59-609	0-0	0-0	2-0	392-2,176
	Walter Payton, Chicago	314-1,421	53-607	0-0	0-0	2-0	369-2,028
1981	*James Brooks, San Diego	109-525	46-329	22-290	40-949	2-0	219-2,093
	William Andrews, Atlanta	289-1,301	81-735	0-0	0-0	0-0	370-2,036
1980	Bruce Harper, N.Y. Jets	45-126	50-634	28-242	49-1,070	3-0	175-2,072
1979	Wilbert Montgomery, Phil.	338-1,512	41-494	0-0	1-6	2-0	382-2,012
1978	Bruce Harper, N.Y. Jets	58-303	13-196	30-378	55-1,280	1-0	157-2,157
1977	Walter Payton, Chicago	339-1,852	27-269	0-0	2-95	5-0	373-2,216
	Terry Metcalf, St. Louis	149-739	34-403	14-108	32-772	1-0	230-2,022
1975	Terry Metcalf, St. Louis	165-816	43-378	23-285	35-960	2-23	268-2,462
	O.J. Simpson, Buffalo	329-1,817	28-426	0-0	0-0	1-0	358-2,243
1974	Mack Herron, New England	231-824	38-474	35-517	28-629	3-0	335-2,444
	Otis Armstrong, Denver	263-1,407	38-405	0-0	16-386	1-0	318-2,198
	Terry Metcalf, St. Louis	152-718	50-377	26-340	20-623	7-0	255-2,058
1973	O.J. Simpson, Buffalo	332-2,003	6-70	0-0	0-0	0-0	338-2,073
1966	Gale Sayers, Chicago	229-1,231	34-447	6-44	23-718	3-0	295-2,440
	Leroy Kelly, Cleveland	209-1,141	32-366	13-104	19-403	0-0	273-2,014
1965	*Gale Sayers, Chicago	166-867	29-507	16-238	21-660	4-0	236-2,272
1963	Timmy Brown, Philadelphia	192-841	36-487	16-152	33-945	2-3	279-2,428
	Jim Brown, Cleveland	291-1,863	24-268	0-0	0-0	0-0	315-2,131
1962	Timmy Brown, Philadelphia	137-545	52-849	6-81	30-831	4-0	229-2,306
	Dick Christy, N.Y. Titans	114-535	62-538	15-250	38-824	2-0	231-2,147
1961	Billy Cannon, Houston	200-948	43-586	9-70	18-439	2-0	272-2,043
1960	*Abner Haynes, Dall. Texans	156-875	55-576	14-215	19-434	4-0	248-2,100

*First season of professional football.

300 COMBINED NET YARDS GAINED IN A GAME

Date	Player, Team, Opponent	No.	Yards	TD
Dec. 11, 1989	John Taylor, San Francisco vs. L.A. Rams	14	321	2
Nov. 26, 1989	Willie Anderson, L.A. Rams vs. New Orleans (OT)	15	336	1
Nov. 28, 1988	*Tim Brown, L.A. Raiders vs. San Diego	12	306	1
Dec. 22, 1985	Stephone Paige, Kansas City vs. San Diego	8	309	2
Nov. 10, 1985	Lionel James, San Diego vs. L.A. Raiders (OT)	23	345	0
Sept. 22, 1985	Lionel James, San Diego vs. Cincinnati	20	316	2
Dec. 21, 1975	*Walter Payton, Chicago vs. New Orleans	32	300	1
Nov. 23, 1975	Greg Pruitt, Cleveland vs. Cincinnati	28	304	2
Nov. 1, 1970	Eugene (Mercury) Morris, Miami vs. Baltimore	17	302	0
Oct. 4, 1970	O.J. Simpson, Buffalo vs. N.Y. Jets	26	303	2
Dec. 6, 1969	Jerry LeVias, Houston vs. N.Y. Jets	18	329	1
Nov. 2, 1969	Travis Williams, Green Bay vs. Pittsburgh	11	314	3
Dec. 18, 1966	Gale Sayers, Chicago vs. Minnesota	20	339	2
Dec. 12, 1965	*Gale Sayers, Chicago vs. San Francisco	17	336	6
Nov. 17, 1963	Gary Ballman, Pittsburgh vs. Washington	12	320	2
Dec. 16, 1962	Timmy Brown, Philadelphia vs. St. Louis	19	341	2
Dec. 10, 1961	Billy Cannon, Houston vs. N.Y. Titans	32	373	5
Nov. 19, 1961	Jim Brown, Cleveland vs. Philadelphia	38	313	4
Dec. 3, 1950	Cloyce Box, Detroit vs. Baltimore	13	302	4
Oct. 29, 1950	Wally Triplett, Detroit vs. Los Angeles	11	331	1
Nov. 22, 1945	Jim Benton, Cleveland vs. Detroit	10	303	1

First season of professional football.

TOP 20 SCORERS

Player	Years	TD	FG	PAT	TP
George Blanda	26	9	335	943	2,002
Jan Stenerud	19	0	373	580	1,699
Nick Lowery	15	0	329	486	1,473
Pat Leahy	18	0	304	558	1,470
Jim Turner	16	1	304	521	1,439
Mark Moseley	16	0	300	482	1,382
Jim Bakken	17	0	282	534	1,380
Fred Cox	15	0	282	519	1,365
Lou Groza	17	1	234	641	1,349
Eddie Murray	16	0	277	432	1,263
Jim Breech	14	0	243	517	1,246
Gary Anderson	12	0	285	384	1,239
Chris Bahr	14	0	241	490	1,213
Matt Bahr	15	0	250	459	1,209
Morten Andersen	12	0	274	380	1,202
Gino Cappelletti	11	42	176	350	1,130
Ray Wersching	15	0	222	456	1,122
Norm Johnson	12	0	222	444	1,110
Don Cockroft	13	0	216	432	1,080
Garo Yepremian	14	0	210	444	1,074

Cappelletti's total includes four two-point conversions.

TOP 20 TOUCHDOWN SCORERS

Player	Years	Rush	Rec.	Returns	Total TD
Jim Brown	9	106	20	0	126
Walter Payton	13	110	15	0	125
Jerry Rice	9	6	118	0	124
John Riggins	14	104	12	0	116
Marcus Allen	12	91	21	1	113
Lenny Moore	12	63	48	2	113
Don Hutson	11	3	99	3	105
Steve Largent	14	1	100	0	101
Franco Harris	13	91	9	0	100
Eric Dickerson	11	90	6	0	96
Jim Taylor	10	83	10	0	93
Tony Dorsett	12	77	13	1	91
Bobby Mitchell	11	18	65	8	91
Leroy Kelly	10	74	13	3	90
Charley Taylor	13	11	79	0	90
Don Maynard	15	0	88	0	88
Lance Alworth	11	2	85	0	87
Ottis Anderson	14	81	5	0	86
Paul Warfield	13	1	85	0	86
Mark Clayton	11	0	84	1	85
Tommy McDonald	12	0	84	1	85

TOP 20 RUSHERS

Player	Years	Att.	Yards	Avg.	Long	TD
Walter Payton	13	3,838	16,726	4.4	76	110
Eric Dickerson	11	2,996	13,259	4.4	85	90
Tony Dorsett	12	2,936	12,739	4.3	99	77
Jim Brown	9	2,359	12,312	5.2	80	106
Franco Harris	13	2,949	12,120	4.1	75	91
John Riggins	14	2,916	11,352	3.9	66	104
O.J. Simpson	11	2,404	11,236	4.7	94	61

Player	Years	Att.	Yards	Avg.	Long	TD
Ottis Anderson	14	2,562	10,273	4.0	76	81
Earl Campbell	8	2,187	9,407	4.3	81	74
Marcus Allen	12	2,296	9,309	4.1	61	91
Jim Taylor	10	1,941	8,597	4.4	84	83
Joe Perry	14	1,737	8,378	4.8	78	53
Roger Craig	11	1,991	8,189	4.1	71	56
Gerald Riggs	10	1,989	8,188	4.1	58	69
Larry Csonka	11	1,891	8,081	4.3	54	64
Freeman McNeil	12	1,798	8,074	4.5	69	38
James Brooks	12	1,685	7,962	4.7	65	49
Thurman Thomas	6	1,731	7,631	4.4	80	41
Herschel Walker	8	1,794	7,468	4.2	84	55
Mike Pruitt	11	1,844	7,378	4.0	77	51

TOP 20 COMBINED YARDS GAINED

Player	Years	Tot.	Rush.	Rec.	Int. Ret.	Punt Ret.	Kickoff Ret.	Fumble Ret.
Walter Payton	13	21,803	16,726	4,538	0	0	539	0
Tony Dorsett	12	16,326	12,739	3,554	0	0	0	33
Jim Brown	9	15,459	12,312	2,499	0	0	648	0
Eric Dickerson	11	15,411	13,259	2,137	0	0	0	15
James Brooks	12	14,910	7,962	3,621	0	565	2,762	0
Franco Harris	13	14,622	12,120	2,287	0	0	233	−18
O.J. Simpson	11	14,368	11,236	2,142	0	0	990	0
James Lofton	16	14,277	246	14,004	0	0	0	27
Bobby Mitchell	11	14,078	2,735	7,954	0	699	2,690	0
Marcus Allen	12	13,799	9,309	4,496	0	0	0	−6
John Riggins	14	13,435	11,352	2,090	0	0	0	−7
Steve Largent	14	13,396	83	13,089	0	68	156	0
Ottis Anderson	14	13,364	10,273	3,062	0	0	0	29
Drew Hill	14	13,337	19	9,831	0	22	3,460	5
Greg Pruitt	12	13,262	5,672	3,069	0	2,007	2,514	0
Roger Craig	11	13,143	8,189	4,911	0	0	43	0
Herschel Walker	8	13,031	7,468	3,887	0	0	1,676	0
Ollie Matson	14	12,884	5,173	3,285	51	595	3,746	34
Tim Brown	10	12,684	3,862	3,399	0	639	4,781	3
Lenny Moore	12	12,451	5,174	6,039	0	56	1,180	2

TOP 20 PASSERS

Player	Years	Att.	Comp.	Pct. Comp.	Yards	TD	Pct. TD	Int.	Pct. Int.	Avg. Gain	Rating
Joe Montana	14	4,898	3,110	63.5	37,268	257	5.2	58	2.7	7.61	93.1
Steve Young	9	1,968	1,222	62.1	15,900	105	5.3	58	2.9	8.08	93.0
Dan Marino	11	5,434	3,219	59.2	40,720	298	5.5	168	3.1	7.49	88.1
Jim Kelly	8	3,494	2,112	60.4	26,413	179	5.1	126	3.6	7.56	86.0
R. Staubach	11	2,958	1,685	57.0	22,700	153	5.2	109	3.7	7.67	83.4
Neil Lomax	8	3,153	1,817	57.6	22,771	136	4.3	90	2.9	7.22	82.7
S. Jurgensen	18	4,262	2,433	57.1	32,224	255	6.0	189	4.4	7.56	82.6
Len Dawson	19	3,741	2,136	57.1	28,711	239	6.4	183	4.9	7.67	82.6
B. Esiason	10	3,851	2,185	56.7	29,092	190	4.0	140	3.6	7.55	82.1
Dave Krieg	14	4,178	2,431	58.2	30,485	217	5.2	163	3.9	7.30	82.0
Ken Anderson	16	4,475	2,654	59.3	32,838	197	4.4	160	3.6	7.34	81.9
Bernie Kosar	9	3,213	1,889	58.8	22,314	119	3.7	81	2.5	6.94	81.9
Danny White	13	2,950	1,761	59.7	21,959	155	5.3	132	4.5	7.44	81.7
Troy Aikman	5	1,920	1,191	62.0	13,627	69	3.6	66	3.4	7.10	81.0
Bart Starr	16	3,149	1,808	57.4	24,718	152	4.8	138	4.4	7.85	80.5
Ken O'Brien	10	3,602	2,110	58.6	25,094	128	3.6	98	2.7	6.97	80.4
Warren Moon	10	4,546	2,632	57.9	33,685	196	4.3	166	3.7	7.41	80.4
F. Tarkenton	18	6,467	3,686	57.0	47,003	342	5.3	266	4.1	7.27	80.4
R. Cunningham	9	2,751	1,540	56.0	19,043	131	4.8	87	3.2	6.92	80.3
Dan Fouts	15	5,604	3,297	58.8	43,040	254	4.5	242	4.3	7.68	80.2

1,500 or more attempts. The passing ratings are based on performance standards established for completion percentage, interception percentage, touchdown percentage, and average gain. Passers are allocated points according to how their marks compare with those standards.

TOP 20 PASS RECEIVERS

Player	Years	No.	Yards	Avg.	Long	TD
Art Monk	14	888	12,026	13.5	79	65
Steve Largent	14	819	13,089	16.0	74	100
James Lofton	16	764	14,004	18.3	80	75
Charlie Joiner	18	750	12,146	16.2	87	65
Jerry Rice	9	708	11,776	16.6	96	118
Ozzie Newsome	13	662	7,980	12.1	74	47
Charley Taylor	13	649	9,110	14.0	88	79
Drew Hill	14	634	9,831	15.5	81	60
Don Maynard	15	633	11,834	18.7	87	88
Raymond Berry	13	631	9,275	14.7	70	68
Gary Clark	9	612	9,560	15.6	84	62
Henry Ellard	11	593	9,761	16.5	81	48
Harold Carmichael	14	590	8,985	15.2	85	79
Fred Biletnikoff	14	589	8,974	15.2	82	76
Andre Reed	9	586	8,233	14.0	78	58

Mark Clayton	11	582	8,974	15.4	78	84
Harold Jackson	16	579	10,372	17.9	79	76
Lionel Taylor	10	567	7,195	12.7	80	45
Roger Craig	11	566	4,911	8.7	73	17
Wes Chandler	11	559	8,966	16.0	85	56
Roy Green	14	559	8,965	16.0	83	66

TOP 20 INTERCEPTORS

Player	Years	No.	Yards	Avg.	Long	TD
Paul Krause	16	81	1,185	14.6	81	3
Emlen Tunnell	14	79	1,282	16.2	55	4
Dick (Night Train) Lane	14	68	1,207	17.8	80	5
Ken Riley	15	65	596	9.2	66	5
Ronnie Lott	13	63	730	11.6	83	5
Dick LeBeau	13	62	762	12.3	70	3
Dave Brown	15	62	698	11.3	90	5
Emmitt Thomas	13	58	937	16.2	73	5
Bobby Boyd	9	57	994	17.4	74	4
Johnny Robinson	12	57	741	13.0	57	1
Mel Blount	14	57	736	12.9	52	2
Everson Walls	13	57	504	8.8	40	1
Lem Barney	11	56	1,077	19.2	71	7
Pat Fischer	17	56	941	16.8	69	4
Willie Brown	16	54	472	8.7	45	2
Bobby Dillon	8	52	976	18.8	61	5
Jack Butler	9	52	826	15.9	52	4
Larry Wilson	13	52	800	15.4	96	5
Jim Patton	12	52	712	13.7	51	2
Mel Renfro	14	52	626	12.0	90	3

TOP 20 PUNTERS

Player	Years	No.	Yards	Avg.	Long	Blk.
Sammy Baugh	16	338	15,245	45.1	85	9
Tommy Davis	11	511	22,833	44.7	82	2
Yale Lary	11	503	22,279	44.3	74	4
Rohn Stark	12	912	40,070	43.9	72	6
Bob Scarpitto	8	283	12,408	43.8	87	4
Horace Gillom	7	385	16,872	43.8	80	5
Jerry Norton	11	358	15,671	43.8	78	2
David Lewis	4	285	12,447	43.7	63	0
Greg Montgomery	6	310	13,529	43.6	77	6
Don Chandler	12	660	28,678	43.5	90	4
Reggie Roby	11	633	27,483	43.4	77	3
Sean Landeta	9	568	24,631	43.4	71	4
Rick Tuten	5	307	13,236	43.1	65	1
Jerrel Wilson	16	1,072	46,139	43.0	72	12
Rich Camarillo	13	854	36,615	42.9	76	5
Norm Van Brocklin	12	523	22,413	42.9	72	3
Tommy Barnhardt	7	387	16,562	42.8	65	2
Danny Villanueva	8	488	20,862	42.8	68	2
Bobby Joe Green	14	970	41,317	42.6	75	3
Sam Baker	15	703	29,938	42.6	72	2

250 or more punts

TOP 20 PUNT RETURNERS

Player	Years	No.	Yards	Avg.	Long	TD
George McAfee	8	112	1,431	12.8	74	2
Jack Christiansen	8	85	1,084	12.8	89	8
Claude Gibson	5	110	1,381	12.6	85	3
Bill Dudley	9	124	1,515	12.2	96	3
Rick Upchurch	9	248	3,008	12.1	92	8
Billy Johnson	14	282	3,317	11.8	87	6
Mack Herron	3	84	982	11.7	66	0
Mel Gray	8	160	1,851	11.6	80	3
Billy Thompson	13	157	1,814	11.6	60	0
Henry Ellard	10	135	1,527	11.3	83	4
Rodger Bird	3	94	1,063	11.3	78	0
Bosh Pritchard	6	95	1,072	11.3	81	2
Bobby Joe Edmonds	4	105	1,178	11.2	75	1
Terry Metcalf	6	84	936	11.1	69	1
Bob Hayes	11	104	1,158	11.1	90	3
Floyd Little	9	81	893	11.0	72	2
Louis Lipps	9	112	1,234	11.0	76	3
Les (Speedy) Duncan	11	202	2,201	10.9	95	4
Verda (Vitamin T) Smith	5	75	814	10.9	85	1
Vai Sikahema	8	292	3,169	10.9	87	4

75 or more returns

TOP 20 KICKOFF RETURNERS

Player	Years	No.	Yards	Avg.	Long	TD
Gale Sayers	7	91	2,781	30.6	103	6
Lynn Chandnois	7	92	2,720	29.6	93	3
Abe Woodson	9	193	5,538	28.7	105	5
Claude (Buddy) Young	6	90	2,514	27.9	104	2
Travis Williams	5	102	2,801	27.5	105	6
Joe Arenas	7	139	3,798	27.3	96	1
Clarence Davis	8	79	2,140	27.1	76	0
Steve Van Buren	8	76	2,030	26.7	98	3
Lenny Lyles	12	81	2,161	26.7	103	3
Eugene (Mercury) Morris	8	111	2,947	26.5	105	3
Bobby Jancik	6	158	4,185	26.5	61	0
Mel Renfro	14	85	2,246	26.4	100	2
Bobby Mitchell	11	102	2,690	26.4	98	5
Ollie Matson	14	143	3,746	26.2	105	6
Alvin Haymond	10	170	4,438	26.1	98	2
Noland Smith	3	82	2,137	26.1	106	1
Al Nelson	9	101	2,625	26.0	78	0
Tim Brown	10	184	4,781	26.0	105	5
Vic Washington	6	129	3,341	25.9	98	1
Dave Hampton	8	113	2,923	25.9	101	3

75 or more returns

ANNUAL SCORING LEADERS

Year	Player, Team	TD	FG	PAT	TP
1993	Jeff Jaeger, L.A. Raiders, AFC	0	35	27	132
	Jason Hanson, Detroit, NFC	0	34	28	130
1992	Pete Stoyanovich, Miami, AFC	0	30	34	124
	Morten Andersen, New Orleans, NFC	0	29	33	120
	Chip Lohmiller, Washington, NFC	0	30	30	120
1991	Chip Lohmiller, Washington, NFC	0	31	56	149
	Pete Stoyanovich, Miami, AFC	0	31	28	121
1990	Nick Lowery, Kansas City, AFC	0	34	37	139
	Chip Lohmiller, Washington, NFC	0	30	41	131
1989	Mike Cofer, San Francisco, NFC	0	29	49	136
	*David Treadwell, Denver, AFC	0	27	39	120
1988	Scott Norwood, Buffalo, AFC	0	32	33	129
	Mike Cofer, San Francisco, NFC	0	27	40	121
1987	Jerry Rice, San Francisco, NFC	23	0	0	138
	Jim Breech, Cincinnati, AFC	0	24	25	97
1986	Tony Franklin, New England, AFC	0	32	44	140
	Kevin Butler, Chicago, NFC	0	28	36	120
1985	*Kevin Butler, Chicago, NFC	0	31	51	144
	Gary Anderson, Pittsburgh, AFC	0	33	40	139
1984	Ray Wersching, San Francisco, NFC	0	25	56	131
	Gary Anderson, Pittsburgh, AFC	0	24	45	117
1983	Mark Moseley, Washington, NFC	0	33	62	161
	Gary Anderson, Pittsburgh, AFC	0	27	38	119
1982	*Marcus Allen, L.A. Raiders, AFC	14	0	0	84
	Wendell Tyler, L.A. Rams, NFC	13	0	0	78
1981	Ed Murray, Detroit, NFC	0	25	46	121
	Rafael Septien, Dallas, NFC	0	27	40	121
	Jim Breech, Cincinnati, AFC	0	22	49	115
	Nick Lowery, Kansas City, AFC	0	26	37	115
1980	John Smith, New England, AFC	0	26	51	129
	*Ed Murray, Detroit, NFC	0	27	35	116
1979	John Smith, New England, AFC	0	23	46	115
	Mark Moseley, Washington, NFC	0	25	39	114
1978	*Frank Corral, Los Angeles, NFC	0	29	31	118
	Pat Leahy, N.Y. Jets, AFC	0	22	41	107
1977	Errol Mann, Oakland, AFC	0	20	39	99
	Walter Payton, Chicago, NFC	16	0	0	96
1976	Toni Linhart, Baltimore, AFC	0	20	49	109
	Mark Moseley, Washington, NFC	0	22	31	97
1975	O.J. Simpson, Buffalo, AFC	23	0	0	138
	Chuck Foreman, Minnesota, NFC	22	0	0	132
1974	Chester Marcol, Green Bay, NFC	0	25	19	94
	Roy Gerela, Pittsburgh, AFC	0	20	33	93
1973	David Ray, Los Angeles, NFC	0	30	40	130
	Roy Gerela, Pittsburgh, AFC	0	29	36	123
1972	*Chester Marcol, Green Bay, NFC	0	33	29	128
	Bobby Howfield, N.Y. Jets, AFC	0	27	40	121
1971	Garo Yepremian, Miami, AFC	0	28	33	117
	Curt Knight, Washington, NFC	0	29	27	114
1970	Fred Cox, Minnesota, NFC	0	30	35	125
	Jan Stenerud, Kansas City, AFC	0	30	26	116
1969	Jim Turner, N.Y. Jets, AFL	0	32	33	129
	Fred Cox, Minnesota, NFL	0	26	43	121
1968	Jim Turner, N.Y. Jets, AFL	0	34	43	145
	Leroy Kelly, Cleveland, NFL	20	0	0	120
1967	Jim Bakken, St. Louis, NFL	0	27	36	117
	George Blanda, Oakland, AFL	0	20	56	116
1966	Gino Cappelletti, Boston, AFL	6	16	35	119
	Bruce Gossett, Los Angeles, NFL	0	28	29	113
1965	*Gale Sayers, Chicago, NFL	22	0	0	132
	Gino Cappelletti, Boston, AFL	9	17	27	132
1964	Gino Cappelletti, Boston, AFL	7	25	36	#155
	Lenny Moore, Baltimore, NFL	20	0	0	120
1963	Gino Cappelletti, Boston, AFL	2	22	35	113
	Don Chandler, N.Y. Giants, NFL	0	18	52	106
1962	Gene Mingo, Denver, AFL	4	27	32	137
	Jim Taylor, Green Bay, NFL	19	0	0	114
1961	Gino Cappelletti, Boston, AFL	8	17	48	147
	Paul Hornung, Green Bay, NFL	10	15	41	146
1960	Paul Hornung, Green Bay, NFL	15	15	41	176
	*Gene Mingo, Denver, AFL	6	18	33	123
1959	Paul Hornung, Green Bay	7	7	31	94
1958	Jim Brown, Cleveland	18	0	0	108
1957	Sam Baker, Washington	1	14	29	77
	Lou Groza, Cleveland	0	15	32	77
1956	Bobby Layne, Detroit	5	12	33	99
1955	Doak Walker, Detroit	7	9	27	96
1954	Bobby Walston, Philadelphia	11	4	36	114
1953	Gordy Soltau, San Francisco	6	10	48	114
1952	Gordy Soltau, San Francisco	7	6	34	94
1951	Elroy (Crazylegs) Hirsch, Los Angeles	17	0	0	102
1950	*Doak Walker, Detroit	11	8	38	128
1949	Pat Harder, Chi. Cardinals	8	3	45	102
	Gene Roberts, N.Y. Giants	17	0	0	102
1948	Pat Harder, Chi. Cardinals	6	7	53	110
1947	Pat Harder, Chi. Cardinals	7	7	39	102
1946	Ted Fritsch, Green Bay	10	9	13	100
1945	Steve Van Buren, Philadelphia	18	0	2	110
1944	Don Hutson, Green Bay	9	0	31	85
1943	Don Hutson, Green Bay	12	3	36	117
1942	Don Hutson, Green Bay	17	1	33	138
1941	Don Hutson, Green Bay	12	1	20	95
1940	Don Hutson, Green Bay	7	0	15	57
1939	Andy Farkas, Washington	11	0	2	68
1938	Clarke Hinkle, Green Bay	7	3	7	58
1937	Jack Manders, Chi. Bears	5	8	15	69
1936	Earl (Dutch) Clark, Detroit	7	4	19	73
1935	Earl (Dutch) Clark, Detroit	6	1	16	55
1934	Jack Manders, Chi. Bears	3	10	31	79
1933	Ken Strong, N.Y. Giants	6	5	13	64
	Glenn Presnell, Portsmouth	6	6	10	64
1932	Earl (Dutch) Clark, Portsmouth	6	3	10	55

*First season of professional football.
#Cappelletti's total includes a two-point conversion.

ANNUAL TOUCHDOWN LEADERS

Year	Player, Team	TD	Rush	Pass	Ret.
1993	Jerry Rice, San Francisco, NFC	16	1	15	0
	Marcus Allen, Kansas City, AFC	15	12	3	0
1992	Emmitt Smith, Dallas, NFC	19	18	1	0
	Thurman Thomas, Buffalo, AFC	12	9	3	0
1991	Barry Sanders, Detroit, NFC	17	16	1	0
	Mark Clayton, Miami, AFC	12	0	12	0
	Thurman Thomas, Buffalo, AFC	12	7	5	0
1990	Barry Sanders, Detroit, NFC	16	13	3	0
	Derrick Fenner, Seattle, AFC	15	14	1	0
1989	Dalton Hilliard, New Orleans, NFC	18	13	5	0
	Christian Okoye, Kansas City, AFC	12	12	0	0
	Thurman Thomas, Buffalo, AFC	12	6	6	0
1988	Greg Bell, L.A. Rams, NFC	18	16	2	0
	Eric Dickerson, Indianapolis, AFC	15	14	1	0
	*Ickey Woods, Cincinnati, AFC	15	15	0	0
1987	Jerry Rice, San Francisco, NFC	23	1	22	0
	Johnny Hector, N.Y. Jets, AFC	11	11	0	0
1986	George Rogers, Washington, NFC	18	18	0	0
	Sammy Winder, Denver, AFC	14	9	5	0
1985	Joe Morris, N.Y. Giants, NFC	21	21	0	0
	Louis Lipps, Pittsburgh, AFC	15	1	12	2
1984	Marcus Allen, L.A. Raiders, AFC	18	13	5	0
	Mark Clayton, Miami, AFC	18	0	18	0
	Eric Dickerson, L.A. Rams, NFC	14	14	0	0
	John Riggins, Washington, NFC	14	14	0	0
1983	John Riggins, Washington, NFC	24	24	0	0
	Pete Johnson, Cincinnati, AFC	14	14	0	0
	*Curt Warner, Seattle, AFC	14	13	1	0
1982	*Marcus Allen, L.A. Raiders, AFC	14	11	3	0
	Wendell Tyler, L.A. Rams, NFC	13	9	4	0
1981	Chuck Muncie, San Diego, AFC	19	19	0	0
	Wendell Tyler, Los Angeles, NFC	17	12	5	0
1980	*Billy Sims, Detroit, NFC	16	13	3	0
	Earl Campbell, Houston, AFC	13	13	0	0
	*Curtis Dickey, Baltimore, AFC	13	11	2	0
	John Jefferson, San Diego, AFC	13	0	13	0
1979	Earl Campbell, Houston, AFC	19	19	0	0
	Walter Payton, Chicago, NFC	16	14	2	0
1978	David Sims, Seattle, AFC	15	14	1	0
	Terdell Middleton, Green Bay, NFC	12	11	1	0
1977	Walter Payton, Chicago, NFC	16	14	2	0
	Nat Moore, Miami, AFC	13	1	12	0
1976	Chuck Foreman, Minnesota, NFC	14	13	1	0
	Franco Harris, Pittsburgh, AFC	14	14	0	0
1975	O.J. Simpson, Buffalo, AFC	23	16	7	0
	Chuck Foreman, Minnesota, NFC	22	13	9	0
1974	Chuck Foreman, Minnesota, NFC	15	9	6	0
	Cliff Branch, Oakland, AFC	13	0	13	0
1973	Larry Brown, Washington, NFC	14	8	6	0
	Floyd Little, Denver, AFC	13	12	1	0
1972	Emerson Boozer, N.Y. Jets, AFC	14	11	3	0
	Ron Johnson, N.Y. Giants, NFC	14	9	5	0
1971	Duane Thomas, Dallas, NFC	13	11	2	0
	Leroy Kelly, Cleveland, AFC	12	10	2	0
1970	Dick Gordon, Chicago, NFC	13	0	13	0
	MacArthur Lane, St. Louis, NFC	13	11	2	0
	Gary Garrison, San Diego, AFC	12	0	12	0

Year	Player, Team				
1969	Warren Wells, Oakland, AFL	14	0	14	0
	Tom Matte, Baltimore, NFL	13	11	2	0
	Lance Rentzel, Dallas, NFL	13	0	12	1
1968	Leroy Kelly, Cleveland, NFL	20	16	4	0
	Warren Wells, Oakland, AFL	12	1	11	0
1967	Homer Jones, N.Y. Giants, NFL	14	1	13	0
	Emerson Boozer, N.Y. Jets, AFL	13	10	3	0
1966	Leroy Kelly, Cleveland, NFL	16	15	1	0
	Dan Reeves, Dallas, NFL	16	8	8	0
	Lance Alworth, San Diego, AFL	13	0	13	0
1965	*Gale Sayers, Chicago, NFL	22	14	6	2
	Lance Alworth, San Diego, AFL	14	0	14	0
	Don Maynard, N.Y. Jets, AFL	14	0	14	0
1964	Lenny Moore, Baltimore, NFL	20	16	3	1
	Lance Alworth, San Diego, AFL	15	2	13	0
1963	Art Powell, Oakland, AFL	16	0	16	0
	Jim Brown, Cleveland, NFL	15	12	3	0
1962	Abner Haynes, Dallas, AFL	19	13	6	0
	Jim Taylor, Green Bay, NFL	19	19	0	0
1961	Bill Groman, Houston, AFL	18	1	17	0
	Jim Taylor, Green Bay, NFL	16	15	1	0
1960	Paul Hornung, Green Bay, NFL	15	13	2	0
	Sonny Randle, St. Louis, NFL	15	0	15	0
	Art Powell, N.Y. Titans, AFL	14	0	14	0
1959	Raymond Berry, Baltimore	14	0	14	0
	Jim Brown, Cleveland	14	14	0	0
1958	Jim Brown, Cleveland	18	17	1	0
1957	Lenny Moore, Baltimore	11	3	7	1
1956	Rick Casares, Chi. Bears	14	12	2	0
1955	*Alan Ameche, Baltimore	9	9	0	0
	Harlon Hill, Chi. Bears	9	0	9	0
1954	*Harlon Hill, Chi. Bears	12	0	12	0
1953	Joseph Perry, San Francisco	13	10	3	0
1952	Cloyce Box, Detroit	15	0	15	0
1951	Elroy (Crazylegs) Hirsch, Los Angeles	17	0	17	0
1950	Bob Shaw, Chi. Cardinals	12	0	12	0
1949	Gene Roberts, N.Y. Giants	17	9	8	0
1948	Mal Kutner, Chi. Cardinals	15	1	14	0
1947	Steve Van Buren, Philadelphia	14	13	0	1
1946	Ted Fritsch, Green Bay	10	9	1	0
1945	Steve Van Buren, Philadelphia	18	15	2	1
1944	Don Hutson, Green Bay	9	0	9	0
	Bill Paschal, N.Y. Giants	9	9	0	0
1943	Don Hutson, Green Bay	12	0	11	1
	*Bill Paschal, N.Y. Giants	12	10	2	0
1942	Don Hutson, Green Bay	17	0	17	0
1941	Don Hutson, Green Bay	12	2	10	0
	George McAfee, Chi. Bears	12	6	3	3
1940	John Drake, Cleveland	9	9	0	0
	Richard Todd, Washington	9	4	4	1
1939	Andrew Farkas, Washington	11	5	5	1
1938	Don Hutson, Green Bay	9	0	9	0
1937	Cliff Battles, Washington	7	5	1	1
	Clarke Hinkle, Green Bay	7	5	2	0
	Don Hutson, Green Bay	7	0	7	0
1936	Don Hutson, Green Bay	9	0	8	1
1935	*Don Hutson, Green Bay	7	0	6	1
1934	*Beattie Feathers, Chi. Bears	9	8	1	0
1933	*Charlie (Buckets) Goldenberg, Green Bay	7	4	1	2
	John (Shipwreck) Kelly, Brooklyn	7	2	3	2
	*Elvin (Kink) Richards, N.Y. Giants	7	4	3	0
1932	Earl (Dutch) Clark, Portsmouth	6	3	3	0
	Red Grange, Chi. Bears	6	3	3	0

*First season of professional football.

ANNUAL LEADERS—MOST FIELD GOALS MADE

Year	Player, Team	Att.	Made.	Pct.
1993	Jeff Jaeger, L.A. Raiders, AFC	44	35	79.5
	Jason Hanson, Detroit, NFC	43	34	79.1
1992	Pete Stoyanovich, Miami, AFC	37	30	81.1
	Chip Lohmiller, Washington, NFC	40	30	75.0
1991	Pete Stoyanovich, Miami, AFC	37	31	83.8
	Chip Lohmiller, Washington, NFC	43	31	72.1
1990	Nick Lowery, Kansas City, AFC	37	34	91.9
	Chip Lohmiller, Washington, NFC	40	30	75.0
1989	Rich Karlis, Minnesota, NFC	39	31	79.5
	*David Treadwell, Denver, AFC	33	27	81.8
1988	Scott Norwood, Buffalo, AFC	37	32	86.5
	Mike Cofer, San Francisco, NFC	38	27	71.1
1987	Morten Andersen, New Orleans, NFC	36	28	77.8
	Dean Biasucci, Indianpolis, AFC	27	24	88.9
	Jim Breech, Cincinnati, AFC	30	24	80.0
1986	Tony Franklin, New England, AFC	41	32	78.0
	Kevin Butler, Chicago, NFC	41	28	68.3
1985	Gary Anderson, Pittsburgh, AFC	42	33	78.6
	Morten Andersen, New Orleans, NFC	35	31	88.6
	*Kevin Butler, Chicago, NFC	37	31	83.8
1984	*Paul McFadden, Philadelphia, NFC	37	30	81.1
	Gary Anderson, Pittsburgh, AFC	32	24	75.0
	Matt Bahr, Cleveland, AFC	32	24	75.0
1983	*Ali-Haji-Sheikh, N.Y. Giants, NFC	42	35	83.3
	*Raul Allegre, Baltimore, AFC	35	30	85.7
1982	Mark Moseley, Washington, NFC	21	20	95.2
	Nick Lowery, Kansas City, AFC	24	19	79.2
1981	Rafael Septien, Dallas, NFC	35	27	77.1
	Nick Lowery, Kansas City, AFC	36	26	72.2
1980	*Ed Murray, Detroit, NFC	42	27	64.3
	John Smith, New England, AFC	34	26	76.5
	Fred Steinfort, Denver, AFC	34	26	76.5
1979	Mark Moseley, Washington, NFC	33	25	75.8
	John Smith, New England, AFC	33	23	69.7
1978	*Frank Corral, Los Angeles, NFC	43	29	67.4
	Pat Leahy, N.Y. Jets, AFC	30	22	73.3
1977	Mark Moseley, Washington, NFC	37	21	56.8
	Errol Mann, Oakland, AFC	28	20	71.4
1976	Mark Moseley, Washington, NFC	34	22	64.7
	Jan Stenerud, Kansas City, AFC	38	21	55.3
1975	Jan Stenerud, Kansas City, AFC	32	22	68.8
	Toni Fritsch, Dallas, NFC	35	22	62.9
1974	Chester Marcol, Green Bay, NFC	39	25	64.1
	Roy Gerela, Pittsburgh, AFC	29	20	69.0
1973	David Ray, Los Angeles, NFC	47	30	63.8
	Roy Gerela, Pittsburgh, AFC	43	29	67.4
1972	*Chester Marcol, Green Bay, NFC	48	33	68.8
	Roy Gerela, Pittsburgh, AFC	41	28	68.3
1971	Curt Knight, Washington, NFC	49	29	59.2
	Garo Yepremian, Miami, AFC	40	28	70.0
1970	Jan Stenerud, Kansas City, AFC	42	30	71.4
	Fred Cox, Minnesota, NFC	46	30	65.2
1969	Jim Turner, N.Y. Jets, AFL	47	32	68.1
	Fred Cox, Minnesota, NFL	37	26	70.3
1968	Jim Turner, N.Y. Jets, AFL	46	34	73.9
	Mac Percival, Chicago, NFL	36	25	69.4
1967	Jim Bakken, St. Louis, NFL	39	27	69.2
	Jan Stenerud, Kansas City, AFL	36	21	58.3
1966	Bruce Gossett, Los Angeles, NFL	49	28	57.1
	Mike Mercer, Oakland-Kansas City, AFL	30	21	70.0
1965	Pete Gogolak, Buffalo, AFL	46	28	60.9
	Fred Cox, Minnesota, NFL	35	23	65.7
1964	Jim Bakken, St. Louis, NFL	38	25	65.8
	Gino Cappelletti, Boston, AFL	39	25	64.1
1963	Jim Martin, Baltimore, NFL	39	24	61.5
	Gino Cappelletti, Boston, AFL	38	22	57.9
1962	Gene Mingo, Denver, AFL	39	27	69.2
	Lou Michaels, Pittsburgh, NFL	42	26	61.9
1961	Steve Myhra, Baltimore, NFL	39	21	53.8
	Gino Cappelletti, Boston, AFL	32	17	53.1
1960	Tommy Davis, San Francisco, NFL	32	19	59.4
	*Gene Mingo, Denver, AFL	28	18	64.3
1959	Pat Summerall, N.Y. Giants	29	20	69.0
1958	Paige Cothren, Los Angeles	25	14	56.0
	*Tom Miner, Pittsburgh	28	14	50.0
1957	Lou Groza, Cleveland	22	15	68.2
1956	Sam Baker, Washington	25	17	68.0
1955	Fred Cone, Green Bay	24	16	66.7
1954	Lou Groza, Cleveland	24	16	66.7
1953	Lou Groza, Cleveland	26	23	88.5
1952	Lou Groza, Cleveland	33	19	57.6
1951	Bob Waterfield, Los Angeles	23	13	56.5
1950	Lou Groza, Cleveland	19	13	68.4
1949	Cliff Patton, Philadelphia	18	9	50.0
	Bob Waterfield, Los Angeles	16	9	56.3
1948	Cliff Patton, Philadelphia	12	8	66.7
1947	Ward Cuff, Green Bay	16	7	43.8
	Pat Harder, Chi. Cardinals	10	7	70.0
	Bob Waterfield, Los Angeles	16	7	43.8
1946	Ted Fritsch, Green Bay	17	9	52.9
1945	Joe Aguirre, Washington	13	7	53.8
1944	Ken Strong, N.Y. Giants	12	6	50.0
1943	Ward Cuff, N.Y. Giants	9	3	33.3
	Don Hutson, Green Bay	5	3	60.0
1942	Bill Daddio, Chi. Cardinals	10	5	50.0
1941	Clarke Hinkle, Green Bay	14	6	42.9
1940	Clarke Hinkle, Green Bay	14	9	64.3
1939	Ward Cuff, N.Y. Giants	16	7	43.8
1938	Ward Cuff, N.Y. Giants	9	5	55.6

Year	Player, Team			
	Ralph Kercheval, Brooklyn	13	5	38.5
1937	Jack Manders, Chi. Bears		8	
1936	Jack Manders, Chi. Bears		7	
	Armand Niccolai, Pittsburgh		7	
1935	Armand Niccolai, Pittsburgh		6	
	Bill Smith, Chi. Cardinals		6	
1934	Jack Manders, Chi. Bears		10	
1933	*Jack Manders, Chi. Bears		6	
	Glenn Presnell, Portsmouth		6	
1932	Earl (Dutch) Clark, Portsmouth		3	

*First season of professional football.

ANNUAL RUSHING LEADERS

Year	Player, Team	Att.	Yards	Avg.	TD
1993	Emmitt Smith, Dallas, NFC	283	1,486	5.3	9
	Thurman Thomas, Buffalo, AFC	355	1,315	3.7	6
1992	Emmitt Smith, Dallas, NFC	373	1,713	4.6	18
	Barry Foster, Pittsburgh, AFC	390	1,690	4.3	11
1991	Emmitt Smith, Dallas, NFC	365	1,563	4.3	12
	Thurman Thomas, Buffalo, AFC	288	1,407	4.9	7
1990	Barry Sanders, Detroit, NFC	255	1,304	5.1	13
	Thurman Thomas, Buffalo, AFC	271	1,297	4.8	11
1989	Christian Okoye, Kansas City, AFC	370	1,480	4.0	12
	*Barry Sanders, Detroit, NFC	280	1,470	5.3	14
1988	Eric Dickerson, Indianapolis, AFC	388	1,659	4.3	14
	Herschel Walker, Dallas, NFC	361	1,514	4.2	5
1987	Charles White, L.A. Rams, NFC	324	1,374	4.2	11
	Eric Dickerson, Indianapolis, AFC	223	1,011	4.5	5
1986	Eric Dickerson, L.A. Rams, NFC	404	1,821	4.5	11
	Curt Warner, Seattle, AFC	319	1,481	4.6	13
1985	Marcus Allen, L.A. Raiders, AFC	380	1,759	4.6	11
	Gerald Riggs, Atlanta, NFC	397	1,719	4.3	10
1984	Eric Dickerson, L.A. Rams, NFC	379	2,105	5.6	14
	Earnest Jackson, San Diego, AFC	296	1,179	4.0	8
1983	*Eric Dickerson, L.A. Rams, NFC	390	1,808	4.6	18
	*Curt Warner, Seattle, AFC	335	1,449	4.3	13
1982	Freeman McNeil, N.Y. Jets, AFC	151	786	5.2	6
	Tony Dorsett, Dallas, NFC	177	745	4.2	5
1981	*George Rogers, New Orleans, NFC	378	1,674	4.4	13
	Earl Campbell, Houston, AFC	361	1,376	3.8	10
1980	Earl Campbell, Houston, AFC	373	1,934	5.2	13
	Walter Payton, Chicago, NFC	317	1,460	4.6	6
1979	Earl Campbell, Houston, AFC	368	1,697	4.6	19
	Walter Payton, Chicago, NFC	369	1,610	4.4	14
1978	*Earl Campbell, Houston, AFC	302	1,450	4.8	13
	Walter Payton, Chicago, NFC	333	1,395	4.2	11
1977	Walter Payton, Chicago, NFC	339	1,852	5.5	14
	Mark van Eeghen, Oakland, AFC	324	1,273	3.9	7
1976	O.J. Simpson, Buffalo, AFC	290	1,503	5.2	8
	Walter Payton, Chicago, NFC	311	1,390	4.5	10
1975	O.J. Simpson, Buffalo, AFC	329	1,817	5.5	16
	Jim Otis, St. Louis, NFC	269	1,076	4.0	5
1974	Otis Armstrong, Denver, AFC	263	1,407	5.3	9
	Lawrence McCutcheon, Los Angeles, NFC	236	1,109	4.7	3
1973	O.J. Simpson, Buffalo, AFC	332	2,003	6.0	12
	John Brockington, Green Bay, NFC	265	1,144	4.3	3
1972	O.J. Simpson, Buffalo, AFC	292	1,251	4.3	6
	Larry Brown, Washington, NFC	285	1,216	4.3	8
1971	Floyd Little, Denver, AFC	284	1,133	4.0	6
	*John Brockington, Green Bay, NFC	216	1,105	5.1	4
1970	Larry Brown, Washington, NFC	237	1,125	4.7	5
	Floyd Little, Denver, AFC	209	901	4.3	3
1969	Gale Sayers, Chicago, NFL	236	1,032	4.4	8
	Dickie Post, San Diego, AFL	182	873	4.8	6
1968	Leroy Kelly, Cleveland, NFL	248	1,239	5.0	16
	*Paul Robinson, Cincinnati, AFL	238	1,023	4.3	8
1967	Jim Nance, Boston, AFL	269	1,216	4.5	7
	Leroy Kelly, Cleveland, NFL	235	1,205	5.1	11
1966	Jim Nance, Boston, AFL	299	1,458	4.9	11
	Gale Sayers, Chicago, NFL	229	1,231	5.4	8
1965	Jim Brown, Cleveland, NFL	289	1,544	5.3	17
	Paul Lowe, San Diego, AFL	222	1,121	5.0	7
1964	Jim Brown, Cleveland, NFL	280	1,446	5.2	7
	Cookie Gilchrist, Buffalo, AFL	230	981	4.3	6
1963	Jim Brown, Cleveland, NFL	291	1,863	6.4	12
	Clem Daniels, Oakland, AFL	215	1,099	5.1	3
1962	Jim Taylor, Green Bay, NFL	272	1,474	5.4	19
	Cookie Gilchrist, Buffalo, AFL	214	1,096	5.1	13
1961	Jim Brown, Cleveland, NFL	305	1,408	4.6	8
	Billy Cannon, Houston, AFL	200	948	4.7	6
1960	Jim Brown, Cleveland, NFL	215	1,257	5.8	9
	*Abner Haynes, Dall. Texans, AFL	156	875	5.6	9
1959	Jim Brown, Cleveland	290	1,329	4.6	14
1958	Jim Brown, Cleveland	257	1,527	5.9	17
1957	*Jim Brown, Cleveland	202	942	4.7	9
1956	Rick Casares, Chi. Bears	234	1,126	4.8	12
1955	*Alan Ameche, Baltimore	213	961	4.5	9
1954	Joe Perry, San Francisco	173	1,049	6.1	8
1953	Joe Perry, San Francisco	192	1,018	5.3	10
1952	Dan Towler, Los Angeles	156	894	5.7	10
1951	Eddie Price, N.Y. Giants	271	971	3.6	7
1950	Marion Motley, Cleveland	140	810	5.8	3
1949	Steve Van Buren, Philadelphia	263	1,146	4.4	11
1948	Steve Van Buren, Philadelphia	201	945	4.7	10
1947	Steve Van Buren, Philadelphia	217	1,008	4.6	13
1946	Bill Dudley, Pittsburgh	146	604	4.1	3
1945	Steve Van Buren, Philadelphia	143	832	5.8	15
1944	Bill Paschal, N.Y. Giants	196	737	3.8	9
1943	*Bill Paschal, N.Y. Giants	147	572	3.9	10
1942	*Bill Dudley, Pittsburgh	162	696	4.3	5
1941	Clarence (Pug) Manders, Brooklyn	111	486	4.4	5
1940	Byron (Whizzer) White, Detroit	146	514	3.5	5
1939	*Bill Osmanski, Chicago	121	699	5.8	7
1938	*Byron (Whizzer) White, Pittsburgh	152	567	3.7	4
1937	Cliff Battles, Washington	216	874	4.0	5
1936	*Alphonse (Tuffy) Leemans, N.Y. Giants	206	830	4.0	2
1935	Doug Russell, Chi. Cardinals	140	499	3.6	0
1934	*Beattie Feathers, Chi. Bears	119	1,004	8.4	8
1933	Jim Musick, Boston	173	809	4.7	5
1932	*Cliff Battles, Boston	148	576	3.9	3

*First season of professional football.

ANNUAL PASSING LEADERS
(Current rating system implemented in 1973)

Year	Player, Team	Att.	Comp.	Yards	TD	Int.	Rating
1993	Steve Young, San Francisco, NFC	462	314	4,023	29	16	101.5
	John Elway, Denver, AFC	551	348	4,030	25	10	92.8
1992	Steve Young, San Francisco, NFC	402	268	3,465	25	7	107.0
	Warren Moon, Houston, AFC	346	224	2,521	18	12	89.3
1991	Steve Young, San Francisco, NFC	279	180	2,517	17	8	101.8
	Jim Kelly, Buffalo, AFC	474	304	3,844	33	17	97.6
1990	Jim Kelly, Buffalo, AFC	346	219	2,829	24	9	101.2
	Phil Simms, N.Y. Giants, NFC	311	184	2,284	15	4	92.7
1989	Joe Montana, San Francisco, NFC	386	271	3,521	26	8	112.4
	Boomer Esiason, Cincinnati, AFC	455	258	3,525	28	11	92.1
1988	Boomer Esiason, Cincinnati, AFC	388	223	3,572	28	14	97.4
	Wade Wilson, Minnesota, NFC	332	204	2,746	15	9	91.5
1987	Joe Montana, San Francisco, NFC	398	266	3,054	31	13	102.1
	Bernie Kosar, Cleveland, AFC	389	241	3,033	22	9	95.4
1986	Tommy Kramer, Minnesota, NFC	372	208	3,000	24	10	92.6
	Dan Marino, Miami, AFC	623	378	4,746	44	23	92.5
1985	Ken O'Brien, N.Y. Jets, AFC	488	297	3,888	25	8	96.2
	Joe Montana, San Francisco, NFC	494	303	3,653	27	13	91.3
1984	Dan Marino, Miami, AFC	564	362	5,084	48	17	108.9
	Joe Montana, San Francisco, NFC	432	279	3,630	28	10	102.9
1983	Steve Bartkowski, Atlanta, NFC	432	274	3,167	22	5	97.6
	*Dan Marino, Miami, AFC	296	173	2,210	20	6	96.0
1982	Ken Anderson, Cincinnati, AFC	309	218	2,495	12	9	95.5
	Joe Theismann, Washington, NFC	252	161	2,033	13	9	91.3
1981	Ken Anderson, Cincinnati, AFC	479	300	3,754	29	10	98.5
	Joe Montana, San Francisco, NFC	488	311	3,565	19	12	88.2
1980	Brian Sipe, Cleveland, AFC	554	337	4,132	30	14	91.4
	Ron Jaworski, Philadelphia, NFC	451	257	3,529	27	12	90.9
1979	Roger Staubach, Dallas, NFC	461	267	3,586	27	11	92.4
	Dan Fouts, San Diego, AFC	530	332	4,082	24	24	82.6
1978	Roger Staubach, Dallas, NFC	413	231	3,190	25	16	84.9
	Terry Bradshaw, Pittsburgh, AFC	368	207	2,915	28	20	84.8
1977	Bob Griese, Miami, AFC	307	180	2,252	22	13	88.0
	Roger Staubach, Dallas, NFC	361	210	2,620	18	9	87.1
1976	Ken Stabler, Oakland, AFC	291	194	2,737	27	17	103.4
	James Harris, Los Angeles, NFC	158	91	1,460	8	6	89.8
1975	Ken Anderson, Cincinnati, AFC	377	228	3,169	21	11	94.1
	Fran Tarkenton, Minnesota, NFC	425	273	2,994	25	13	91.7
1974	Ken Anderson, Cincinnati, AFC	328	213	2,667	18	10	95.9
	Sonny Jurgensen, Washington, NFC	167	107	1,185	11	5	94.6
1973	Roger Staubach, Dallas, NFC	286	179	2,428	23	15	94.6
	Ken Stabler, Oakland, AFC	260	163	1,997	14	10	88.5
1972	Norm Snead, N.Y. Giants, NFC	325	196	2,307	17	12	
	Earl Morrall, Miami, AFC	150	83	1,360	11	7	
1971	Roger Staubach, Dallas, NFC	211	126	1,882	15	4	
	Bob Griese, Miami, AFC	263	145	2,089	19	9	
1970	John Brodie, San Francisco, NFC	378	223	2,941	24	10	
	Daryle Lamonica, Oakland, AFC	356	179	2,516	22	15	
1969	Sonny Jurgensen, Washington, NFL	442	274	3,102	22	15	
	*Greg Cook, Cincinnati, AFL	197	106	1,854	15	11	
1968	Len Dawson, Kansas City, AFL	224	131	2,109	17	9	

Year	Player, Team	Att	Comp	Yards	TD	Int
	Earl Morrall, Baltimore, NFL	317	182	2,909	26	17
1967	Sonny Jurgensen, Washington, NFL	508	288	3,747	31	16
	Daryle Lamonica, Oakland, AFL	425	220	3,228	30	20
1966	Bart Starr, Green Bay, NFL	251	156	2,257	14	3
	Len Dawson, Kansas City, AFL	284	159	2,527	26	10
1965	Rudy Bukich, Chicago, NFL	312	176	2,641	20	9
	John Hadl, San Diego, AFL	348	174	2,798	20	21
1964	Len Dawson, Kansas City, AFL	354	199	2,879	30	18
	Bart Starr, Green Bay, NFL	272	163	2,144	15	4
1963	Y.A. Tittle, N.Y. Giants, NFL	367	221	3,145	36	14
	Tobin Rote, San Diego, AFL	286	170	2,510	20	17
1962	Len Dawson, Dall. Texans, AFL	310	189	2,759	29	17
	Bart Starr, Green Bay, NFL	285	178	2,438	12	9
1961	George Blanda, Houston, AFL	362	187	3,330	36	22
	Milt Plum, Cleveland, NFL	302	177	2,416	18	10
1960	Milt Plum, Cleveland, NFL	250	151	2,297	21	5
	Jack Kemp, L.A. Chargers, AFL	406	211	3,018	20	25
1959	Charlie Conerly, N.Y. Giants	194	113	1,706	14	4
1958	Eddie LeBaron, Washington	145	79	1,365	11	10
1957	Tommy O'Connell, Cleveland	110	63	1,229	9	8
1956	Ed Brown, Chi. Bears	168	96	1,667	11	12
1955	Otto Graham, Cleveland	185	98	1,721	15	8
1954	Norm Van Brocklin, Los Angeles	260	139	2,637	13	21
1953	Otto Graham, Cleveland	258	167	2,722	11	9
1952	Norm Van Brocklin, Los Angeles	205	113	1,736	14	17
1951	Bob Waterfield, Los Angeles	176	88	1,566	13	10
1950	Norm Van Brocklin, Los Angeles	233	127	2,061	18	14
1949	Sammy Baugh, Washington	255	145	1,903	18	14
1948	Tommy Thompson, Philadelphia	246	141	1,965	25	11
1947	Sammy Baugh, Washington	354	210	2,938	25	15
1946	Bob Waterfield, Los Angeles	251	127	1,747	18	17
1945	Sammy Baugh, Washington	182	128	1,669	11	4
	Sid Luckman, Chi. Bears	217	117	1,725	14	10
1944	Frank Filchock, Washington	147	84	1,139	13	9
1943	Sammy Baugh, Washington	239	133	1,754	23	19
1942	Cecil Isbell, Green Bay	268	146	2,021	24	14
1941	Cecil Isbell, Green Bay	206	117	1,479	15	11
1940	Sammy Baugh, Washington	177	111	1,367	12	10
1939	*Parker Hall, Cleveland	208	106	1,227	9	13
1938	Ed Danowski, N.Y. Giants	129	70	848	7	8
1937	*Sammy Baugh, Washington	171	81	1,127	8	14
1936	Arnie Herber, Green Bay	173	77	1,239	11	13
1935	Ed Danowski, N.Y. Giants	113	57	794	10	9
1934	Arnie Herber, Green Bay	115	42	799	8	12
1933	*Harry Newman, N.Y. Giants	136	53	973	11	17
1932	Arnie Herber, Green Bay	101	37	639	9	9

*First season of professional football.

ANNUAL PASSING TOUCHDOWN LEADERS

Year	Player, Team	TD
1993	Steve Young, San Francisco, NFC	29
	John Elway, Denver, AFC	25
1992	Steve Young, San Francisco, NFC	25
	Dan Marino, Miami, AFC	24
1991	Jim Kelly, Buffalo, AFC	33
	Mark Rypien, Washington, NFC	28
1990	Warren Moon, Houston, AFC	33
	Randall Cunningham, Philadelphia, NFC	30
1989	Jim Everett, L.A. Rams, NFC	29
	Boomer Esiason, Cincinnati, AFC	28
1988	Jim Everett, L.A. Rams, NFC	31
	Boomer Esiason, Cincinnati, AFC	28
	Dan Marino, Miami, AFC	28
1987	Joe Montana, San Francisco, NFC	31
	Dan Marino, Miami, AFC	26
1986	Dan Marino, Miami, AFC	44
	Tommy Kramer, Minnesota, NFC	24
1985	Dan Marino, Miami, AFC	30
	Joe Montana, San Francisco, NFC	27
1984	Dan Marino, Miami, AFC	48
	Neil Lomax, St. Louis, NFC	28
	Joe Montana, San Francisco, NFC	28
1983	Lynn Dickey, Green Bay, NFC	32
	Joe Ferguson, Buffalo, AFC	26
	Brian Sipe, Cleveland, AFC	26
1982	Terry Bradshaw, Pittsburgh, AFC	17
	Dan Fouts, San Diego, AFC	17
	Joe Montana, San Francisco, NFC	17
1981	Dan Fouts, San Diego, AFC	33
	Steve Bartkowski, Atlanta, NFC	30
1980	Steve Bartkowski, Atlanta, NFC	31
	Dan Fouts, San Diego, AFC	30
	Brian Sipe, Cleveland, AFC	30
1979	Steve Grogan, New England, AFC	28
	Brian Sipe, Cleveland, AFC	28
	Roger Staubach, Dallas, NFC	27
1978	Terry Bradshaw, Pittsburgh, AFC	28
	Roger Staubach, Dallas, NFC	25
	Fran Tarkenton, Minnesota, NFC	25
1977	Bob Griese, Miami, AFC	22
	Ron Jaworski, Philadelphia, NFC	18
	Roger Staubach, Dallas, NFC	18
1976	Ken Stabler, Oakland, AFC	27
	Jim Hart, St. Louis, NFC	18
1975	Joe Ferguson, Buffalo, AFC	25
	Fran Tarkenton, Minnesota, NFC	25
1974	Ken Stabler, Oakland, AFC	26
	Jim Hart, St. Louis, NFC	20
1973	Roman Gabriel, Philadelphia, NFC	23
	Roger Staubach, Dallas, NFC	23
	Charley Johnson, Denver, AFC	20
1972	Billy Kilmer, Washington, NFC	19
	Joe Namath, N.Y. Jets, AFC	19
1971	John Hadl, San Diego, AFC	21
	John Brodie, San Francisco, NFC	18
1970	John Brodie, San Francisco, NFC	24
	John Hadl, San Diego, AFC	22
	Daryle Lamonica, Oakland, AFC	22
1969	Daryle Lamonica, Oakland, AFL	34
	Roman Gabriel, Los Angeles, NFL	24
1968	John Hadl, San Diego, AFL	27
	Earl Morrall, Baltimore, NFL	26
1967	Sonny Jurgensen, Washington, NFL	31
	Daryle Lamonica, Oakland, AFL	30
1966	Frank Ryan, Cleveland, NFL	29
	Len Dawson, Kansas City, AFL	26
1965	John Brodie, San Francisco, NFL	30
	Len Dawson, Kansas City, AFL	21
1964	Babe Parilli, Boston, AFL	31
	Frank Ryan, Cleveland, NFL	25
1963	Y.A. Tittle, N.Y. Giants, NFL	36
	Len Dawson, Kansas City, AFL	26
1962	Y.A. Tittle, N.Y. Giants, NFL	33
	Len Dawson, Dallas, AFL	29
1961	George Blanda, Houston, AFL	36
	Sonny Jurgensen, Philadelphia, NFL	32
1960	Al Dorow, N.Y. Titans, AFL	26
	Johnny Unitas, Baltimore, NFL	25
1959	Johnny Unitas, Baltimore	32
1958	Johnny Unitas, Baltimore	19
1957	Johnny Unitas, Baltimore	24
1956	Tobin Rote, Green Bay	18
1955	Tobin Rote, Green Bay	17
	Y.A. Tittle, San Francisco	17
1954	Adrian Burk, Philadelphia	23
1953	Robert Thomason, Philadelphia	21
1952	Jim Finks, Pittsburgh	20
	Otto Graham, Cleveland	20
1951	Bobby Layne, Detroit	26
1950	George Ratterman, N.Y. Yanks	22
1949	Johnny Lujack, Chi. Bears	23
1948	Tommy Thompson, Philadelphia	25
1947	Sammy Baugh, Washington	25
1946	Sid Luckman, Chi. Bears	17
	Bob Waterfield, Los Angeles	17
1945	Sid Luckman, Chi. Bears	14
	*Bob Waterfield, Cleveland	14
1944	Frank Filchock, Washington	13
1943	Sid Luckman, Chi. Bears	28
1942	Cecil Isbell, Green Bay	24
1941	Cecil Isbell, Green Bay	15
1940	Sammy Baugh, Washington	12
1939	Frank Filchock, Washington	11
1938	Bob Monnett, Green Bay	9
1937	Bernie Masterson, Chi. Bears	9
1936	Arnie Herber, Green Bay	11
1935	Ed Danowski, N.Y. Giants	10
1934	Arnie Herber, Green Bay	8
1933	*Harry Newman, N.Y. Giants	11
1932	Arnie Herber, Green Bay	9

*First season of professional football.

ANNUAL PASS RECEIVING LEADERS

Year	Player, Team	No.	Yards	Avg.	TD
1993	Sterling Sharpe, Green Bay, NFC	112	1,274	11.4	11
	Reggie Langhorne, Indianapolis, AFC	85	1,038	12.2	3

Year	Player, Team	No.	Yards	Avg.	TD
1992	Sterling Sharpe, Green Bay, NFC	108	1,461	13.5	13
	Haywood Jeffires, Houston, AFC	90	913	10.1	9
1991	Haywood Jeffires, Houston, AFC	100	1,181	11.8	7
	Michael Irvin, Dallas, NFC	93	1,523	16.4	8
1990	Jerry Rice, San Francisco, NFC	100	1,502	15.0	13
	Haywood Jeffires, Houston, AFC	74	1,048	14.2	8
	Drew Hill, Houston, AFC	74	1,019	13.8	5
1989	Sterling Sharpe, Green Bay, NFC	90	1,423	15.8	12
	Andre Reed, Buffalo, AFC	88	1,312	14.9	9
1988	Al Toon, N.Y. Jets, AFC	93	1,067	11.5	5
	Henry Ellard, L.A. Rams, NFC	86	1,414	16.4	10
1987	J.T. Smith, St. Louis, NFC	91	1,117	12.3	8
	Al Toon, N.Y. Jets, AFC	68	976	14.4	5
1986	Todd Christensen, L.A. Raiders, AFC	95	1,153	12.1	8
	Jerry Rice, San Francisco, NFC	86	1,570	18.3	15
1985	Roger Craig, San Francisco, NFC	92	1,016	11.0	6
	Lionel James, San Diego, AFC	86	1,027	11.9	6
1984	Art Monk, Washington, NFC	106	1,372	12.9	7
	Ozzie Newsome, Cleveland, AFC	89	1,001	11.2	5
1983	Todd Christensen, L.A. Raiders, AFC	92	1,247	13.6	12
	Roy Green, St. Louis, NFC	78	1,227	15.7	14
	Charlie Brown, Washington, NFC	78	1,225	15.7	8
	Earnest Gray, N.Y. Giants, NFC	78	1,139	14.6	5
1982	Dwight Clark, San Francisco, NFC	60	913	15.2	5
	Kellen Winslow, San Diego, AFC	54	721	13.4	6
1981	Kellen Winslow, San Diego, AFC	88	1,075	12.2	10
	Dwight Clark, San Francisco, NFC	85	1,105	13.0	4
1980	Kellen Winslow, San Diego, AFC	89	1,290	14.5	9
	*Earl Cooper, San Francisco, NFC	83	567	6.8	4
1979	Joe Washington, Baltimore, AFC	82	750	9.1	3
	Ahmad Rashad, Minnesota, NFC	80	1,156	14.5	9
1978	Rickey Young, Minnesota, NFC	88	704	8.0	5
	Steve Largent, Seattle, AFC	71	1,168	16.5	8
1977	Lydell Mitchell, Baltimore, AFC	71	620	8.7	4
	Ahmad Rashad, Minnesota, NFC	51	681	13.4	2
1976	MacArthur Lane, Kansas City, AFC	66	686	10.4	1
	Drew Pearson, Dallas, NFC	58	806	13.9	6
1975	Chuck Foreman, Minnesota, NFC	73	691	9.5	9
	Reggie Rucker, Cleveland, AFC	60	770	12.8	3
	Lydell Mitchell, Baltimore, AFC	60	544	9.1	4
1974	Lydell Mitchell, Baltimore, AFC	72	544	7.6	2
	Charles Young, Philadelphia, NFC	63	696	11.0	3
1973	Harold Carmichael, Philadelphia, NFC	67	1,116	16.7	9
	Fred Willis, Houston, AFC	57	371	6.5	1
1972	Harold Jackson, Philadelphia, NFC	62	1,048	16.9	4
	Fred Biletnikoff, Oakland, AFC	58	802	13.8	7
1971	Fred Biletnikoff, Oakland, AFC	61	929	15.2	9
	Bob Tucker, N.Y. Giants, NFC	59	791	13.4	4
1970	Dick Gordon, Chicago, NFC	71	1,026	14.5	13
	Marlin Briscoe, Buffalo, AFC	57	1,036	18.2	8
1969	Dan Abramowicz, New Orleans, NFL	73	1,015	13.9	7
	Lance Alworth, San Diego, AFL	64	1,003	15.7	4
1968	Clifton McNeil, San Francisco, NFL	71	994	14.0	7
	Lance Alworth, San Diego, AFL	68	1,312	19.3	10
1967	George Sauer, N.Y. Jets, AFL	75	1,189	15.9	6
	Charley Taylor, Washington, NFL	70	990	14.1	9
1966	Lance Alworth, San Diego, AFL	73	1,383	18.9	13
	Charley Taylor, Washington, NFL	72	1,119	15.5	12
1965	Lionel Taylor, Denver, AFL	85	1,131	13.3	6
	Dave Parks, San Francisco, NFL	80	1,344	16.8	12
1964	Charley Hennigan, Houston, AFL	101	1,546	15.3	8
	Johnny Morris, Chicago, NFL	93	1,200	12.9	10
1963	Lionel Taylor, Denver, AFL	78	1,101	14.1	10
	Bobby Joe Conrad, St. Louis, NFL	73	967	13.2	10
1962	Lionel Taylor, Denver, AFL	77	908	11.8	4
	Bobby Mitchell, Washington, NFL	72	1,384	19.2	11
1961	Lionel Taylor, Denver, AFL	100	1,176	11.8	4
	Jim (Red) Phillips, Los Angeles, NFL	78	1,092	14.0	5
1960	Lionel Taylor, Denver, AFL	92	1,235	13.4	12
	Raymond Berry, Baltimore, NFL	74	1,298	17.5	10
1959	Raymond Berry, Baltimore	66	959	14.5	14
1958	Raymond Berry, Baltimore	56	794	14.2	9
	Pete Retzlaff, Philadelphia	56	766	13.7	2
1957	Billy Wilson, San Francisco	52	757	14.6	6
1956	Billy Wilson, San Francisco	60	889	14.8	5
1955	Pete Pihos, Philadelphia	62	864	13.9	7
1954	Pete Pihos, Philadelphia	60	872	14.5	10
	Billy Wilson, San Francisco	60	830	13.8	5
1953	Pete Pihos, Philadelphia	63	1,049	16.7	10
1952	Mac Speedie, Cleveland	62	911	14.7	5
1951	Elroy (Crazylegs) Hirsch, Los Angeles	66	1,495	22.7	17
1950	Tom Fears, Los Angeles	84	1,116	13.3	7
1949	Tom Fears, Los Angeles	77	1,013	13.2	9
1948	*Tom Fears, Los Angeles	51	698	13.7	4
1947	Jim Keane, Chi. Bears	64	910	14.2	10
1946	Jim Benton, Los Angeles	63	981	15.6	6
1945	Don Hutson, Green Bay	47	834	17.7	9
1944	Don Hutson, Green Bay	58	866	14.9	9
1943	Don Hutson, Green Bay	47	776	16.5	11
1942	Don Hutson, Green Bay	74	1,211	16.4	17
1941	Don Hutson, Green Bay	58	738	12.7	10
1940	*Don Looney, Philadelphia	58	707	12.2	4
1939	Don Hutson, Green Bay	34	846	24.9	6
1938	Gaynell Tinsley, Chi. Cardinals	41	516	12.6	1
1937	Don Hutson, Green Bay	41	552	13.5	7
1936	Don Hutson, Green Bay	34	536	15.8	8
1935	*Tod Goodwin, N.Y. Giants	26	432	16.6	4
1934	Joe Carter, Philadelphia	16	238	14.9	4
	Morris (Red) Badgro, N.Y. Giants	16	206	12.9	1
1933	John (Shipwreck) Kelly, Brooklyn	22	246	11.2	3
1932	Ray Flaherty, N.Y. Giants	21	350	16.7	3

*First season of professional football.

ANNUAL PASS RECEIVING LEADERS (YARDS)

Year	Player, Team	No.	Yards	Avg.	TD
1993	Jerry Rice, San Francisco, NFC	98	1,503	15.3	15
	Tim Brown, L.A. Raiders, AFC	80	1,180	14.8	7
1992	Sterling Sharpe, Green Bay, NFC	108	1,461	13.5	13
	Anthony Miller, San Diego, AFC	72	1,060	14.7	7
1991	Michael Irvin, Dallas, NFC	93	1,523	16.4	8
	Haywood Jeffires, Houston, AFC	100	1,181	11.8	7
1990	Jerry Rice, San Francisco, NFC	100	1,502	15.0	13
	Haywood Jeffires, Houston, AFC	74	1,048	14.2	8
1989	Jerry Rice, San Francisco, NFC	82	1,483	18.1	17
	Andre Reed, Buffalo, AFC	88	1,312	14.9	9
1988	Henry Ellard, L.A. Rams, NFC	86	1,414	16.4	10
	Eddie Brown, Cincinnati, AFC	53	1,273	24.0	9
1987	J.T. Smith, St. Louis, NFC	91	1,117	12.3	8
	Carlos Carson, Kansas City, AFC	55	1,044	19.0	7
1986	Jerry Rice, San Francisco, NFC	86	1,570	18.3	15
	Stanley Morgan, New England, AFC	84	1,491	17.8	10
1985	Steve Largent, Seattle, AFC	79	1,287	16.3	6
	Mike Quick, Philadelphia, NFC	73	1,247	17.1	11
1984	Roy Green, St. Louis, NFC	78	1,555	19.9	12
	John Stallworth, Pittsburgh, AFC	80	1,395	17.4	11
1983	Mike Quick, Philadelphia, NFC	69	1,409	20.4	13
	Carlos Carson, Kansas City, AFC	80	1,351	16.9	7
1982	Wes Chandler, San Diego, AFC	49	1,032	21.1	9
	Dwight Clark, San Francisco, NFC	60	913	15.2	5
1981	Alfred Jenkins, Atlanta, NFC	70	1,358	19.4	13
	Frank Lewis, Buffalo, AFC	70	1,244	17.8	4
	Steve Watson, Denver, AFC	60	1,244	20.7	13
1980	John Jefferson, San Diego, AFC	82	1,340	16.3	13
	James Lofton, Green Bay, NFC	71	1,226	17.0	4
1979	Steve Largent, Seattle, AFC	66	1,237	18.7	9
	Ahmad Rashad, Minnesota, NFC	80	1,156	14.5	9
1978	Wesley Walker, N.Y. Jets, AFC	48	1,169	24.4	8
	Harold Carmichael, Philadelphia, NFC	55	1,072	19.5	8
1977	Drew Pearson, Dallas, NFC	48	870	18.1	2
	Ken Burrough, Houston, AFC	43	816	19.0	8
1976	Roger Carr, Baltimore, AFC	43	1,112	25.9	11
	*Sammy White, Minnesota, NFC	51	906	17.8	10
1975	Ken Burrough, Houston, AFC	53	1,063	20.1	8
	Mel Gray, St. Louis, NFC	48	926	19.3	11
1974	Cliff Branch, Oakland, AFC	60	1,092	18.2	13
	Drew Pearson, Dallas, NFC	62	1,087	17.5	2
1973	Harold Carmichael, Philadelphia, NFC	67	1,116	16.7	9
	*Isaac Curtis, Cincinnati, AFC	45	843	18.7	9
1972	Harold Jackson, Philadelphia, NFC	62	1,048	16.9	4
	Rich Caster, N.Y. Jets, AFC	39	833	21.4	10
1971	Otis Taylor, Kansas City, AFC	57	1,110	19.5	7
	Gene Washington, San Francisco, NFC	46	884	19.2	4
1970	Gene Washington, San Francisco, NFC	53	1,100	20.8	12
	Marlin Briscoe, Buffalo, AFC	57	1,036	18.2	8
1969	Warren Wells, Oakland, AFL	47	1,260	26.8	14
	Harold Jackson, Philadelphia, NFL	65	1,116	17.2	9
1968	Lance Alworth, San Diego, AFL	68	1,312	19.3	10
	Roy Jefferson, Pittsburgh, NFL	58	1,074	18.5	11
1967	Don Maynard, N.Y. Jets, AFL	71	1,434	20.3	10
	Ben Hawkins, Philadelphia, NFL	59	1,265	21.4	10
1966	Lance Alworth, San Diego, AFL	73	1,383	18.9	13
	Pat Studstill, Detroit, NFL	67	1,266	18.9	5
1965	Lance Alworth, San Diego, AFL	69	1,602	23.2	14
	Dave Parks, San Francisco, NFL	80	1,344	16.8	12
1964	Charley Hennigan, Houston, AFL	101	1,546	15.3	8
	Johnny Morris, Chicago, NFL	93	1,200	12.9	10

Year	Player, Team	No.	Yards	Avg.	TD
1963	Bobby Mitchell, Washington, NFL	69	1,436	20.8	7
	Art Powell, Oakland, AFL	73	1,304	17.8	16
1962	Bobby Mitchel, Washington, NFL	72	1,384	19.2	11
	Art Powell, N.Y. Titans, AFL	64	1,130	17.6	8
1961	Charley Hennigan, Houston, AFL	82	1,746	21.3	12
	Tommy McDonald, Philadelphia, NFL	64	1,144	17.9	13
1960	*Bill Groman, Houston, AFL	72	1,473	20.5	12
	Raymond Berry, Baltimore, NFL	74	1,298	17.5	10
1959	Raymond Berry, Baltimore	66	959	14.5	14
1958	Del Shofner, Los Angeles	51	1,097	21.5	8
1957	Raymond Berry, Baltimore	47	800	17.0	6
1956	Billy Howton, Green Bay	55	1,188	21.6	12
1955	Pete Pihos, Philadelphia	62	864	13.9	7
1954	Bob Boyd, Los Angeles	53	1,212	22.9	6
1953	Pete Pihos, Philadelphia	63	1,049	16.7	10
1952	*Bill Howton, Green Bay	53	1,231	23.2	13
1951	Elroy (Crazylegs) Hirsch, Los Angeles	66	1,495	22.7	17
1950	Tom Fears, Los Angeles	84	1,116	13.3	7
1949	Bob Mann, Detroit	66	1,014	15.4	4
1948	Mal Kutner, Chi. Cardinals	41	943	23.0	14
1947	Mal Kutner, Chi. Cardinals	43	944	21.9	7
1946	Jim Benton, Los Angeles	63	981	15.5	6
1945	Jim Benton, Cleveland	45	1,067	23.7	8
1944	Don Hutson, Green Bay	58	866	14.6	9
1943	Don Hutson, Green Bay	47	776	16.5	11
1942	Don Hutson, Green Bay	74	1,211	16.4	17
1941	Don Hutson, Green Bay	58	738	12.7	10
1940	*Don Looney, Philadelphia	58	707	12.2	4
1939	Don Hutson, Green Bay	34	846	24.9	6
1938	Don Hutson, Green Bay	32	548	17.1	9
1937	*Gaynell Tinsley, Chi. Cardinals	36	675	18.8	5
1936	Don Hutson, Green Bay	34	526	15.5	8
1935	Charley Malone, Boston	22	433	19.7	2
1934	Harry Ebding, Detroit	9	257	28.6	2
1933	*Paul Moss, Pittsburgh	18	383	21.3	2
1932	Johnny Blood (McNally), Green Bay	19	326	17.2	3

*First season of professional football.

ANNUAL INTERCEPTION LEADERS

Year	Player, Team	No.	Yards	TD
1993	Eugene Robinson, Seattle, AFC	9	80	0
	Nate Odomes, Buffalo, AFC	9	65	0
	Deion Sanders, Atlanta, NFC	7	91	0
1992	Henry Jones, Buffalo, AFC	8	263	2
	Audray McMillan, Minnesota, NFC	8	157	2
1991	Ronnie Lott, L.A. Raiders, AFC	8	52	0
	Ray Crockett, Detroit, NFC	6	141	1
	Deion Sanders, Atlanta, AFC	6	119	1
	*Aeneas Williams, Phoenix, NFC	6	60	0
	Tim McKyer, Atlanta, NFC	6	24	0
1990	*Mark Carrier, Chicago, NFC	10	39	0
	Richard Johnson, Houston, AFC	8	100	1
1989	Felix Wright, Cleveland, AFC	9	91	1
	Eric Allen, Philadelphia, NFC	8	38	0
1988	Scott Case, Atlanta, NFC	10	47	0
	Erik McMillan, N.Y. Jets, AFC	8	168	2
1987	Barry Wilburn, Washington, NFC	9	135	1
	Mike Prior, Indianapolis, AFC	6	57	0
	Mark Kelso, Buffalo, AFC	6	25	0
	Keith Bostic, Houston, AFC	6	-14	0
1986	Ronnie Lott, San Francisco, NFC	10	134	1
	Deron Cherry, Kansas City, AFC	9	150	0
1985	Everson Walls, Dallas, NFC	9	31	0
	Albert Lewis, Kansas City, AFC	8	59	0
	Eugene Daniel, Indianapolis, AFC	8	53	0
1984	Ken Easley, Seattle, AFC	10	126	2
	*Tom Flynn, Green Bay, NFC	9	106	0
1983	Mark Murphy, Washington, NFC	9	127	0
	Ken Riley, Cincinnati, AFC	8	89	2
	Vann McElroy, L.A. Raiders, AFC	8	68	0
1982	Everson Walls, Dallas, NFC	7	61	0
	Ken Riley, Cincinnati, AFC	5	88	1
	Bobby Jackson, N.Y Jets, AFC	5	84	1
	Dwayne Woodruff, Pittsburgh, AFC	5	53	0
	Donnie Shell, Pittsburgh, AFC	5	27	0
1981	*Everson Walls, Dallas, NFC	11	133	0
	John Harris, Seattle, AFC	10	155	2
1980	Lester Hayes, Oakland, AFC	13	273	1
	Nolan Cromwell, Los Angeles, NFC	8	140	1
1979	Mike Reinfeldt, Houston, AFC	12	205	0
	Lemar Parrish, Washington, NFC	9	65	0
1978	Thom Darden, Cleveland, AFC	10	200	0
	Ken Stone, St. Louis, NFC	9	139	0

Year	Player, Team	No.	Yards	TD
	Willie Buchanon, Green Bay, NFC	9	93	1
1977	Lyle Blackwood, Baltimore, AFC	10	163	0
	Rolland Lawrence, Atlanta, NFC	7	138	0
1976	Monte Jackson, Los Angeles, NFC	10	173	3
	Ken Riley, Cincinnati, AFC	9	141	1
1975	Mel Blount, Pittsburgh, AFC	11	121	0
	Paul Krause, Minnesota, NFC	10	201	0
1974	Emmitt Thomas, Kansas City, AFC	12	214	2
	Ray Brown, Atlanta, NFC	8	164	1
1973	Dick Anderson, Miami, AFC	8	163	2
	Mike Wagner, Pittsburgh, AFC	8	134	0
	Bobby Bryant, Minnesota, NFC	7	105	1
1972	Bill Bradley, Philadelphia, NFC	9	73	0
	Mike Sensibaugh, Kansas City, AFC	8	65	0
1971	Bill Bradley, Philadelphia, NFC	11	248	0
	Ken Houston, Houston, AFC	9	220	4
1970	Johnny Robinson, Kansas City, AFC	10	155	0
	Dick LeBeau, Detroit, NFC	9	96	0
1969	Mel Renfro, Dallas, NFL	10	118	0
	Emmitt Thomas, Kansas City, AFL	9	146	1
1968	Dave Grayson, Oakland, AFL	10	195	1
	Willie Williams, N.Y. Giants, NFL	10	103	0
1967	Miller Farr, Houston, AFL	10	264	3
	*Lem Barney, Detroit, NFL	10	232	3
	Tom Janik, Buffalo, AFL	10	222	2
	Dave Whitsell, New Orleans, NFL	10	178	2
	Dick Westmoreland, Miami, AFL	10	127	1
1966	Larry Wilson, St. Louis, NFL	10	180	2
	Johnny Robinson, Kansas City, AFL	10	136	1
	Bobby Hunt, Kansas City, AFL	10	113	0
1965	W.K. Hicks, Houston, AFL	9	156	0
	Bobby Boyd, Baltimore, NFL	9	78	1
1964	Dainard Paulson, N.Y. Jets, AFL	12	157	1
	*Paul Krause, Washington, NFL	12	140	1
1963	Fred Glick, Houston, AFL	12	180	1
	Dick Lynch, N.Y. Giants, NFL	9	251	3
	Roosevelt Taylor, Chicago, NFL	9	172	1
1962	Lee Riley, N.Y. Titans, AFL	11	122	0
	Willie Wood, Green Bay, NFL	9	132	0
1961	Billy Atkins, Buffalo, AFL	10	158	0
	Dick Lynch, N.Y. Giants, NFL	9	60	0
1960	*Austin (Goose) Gonsoulin, Denver, AFL	11	98	0
	Dave Baker, San Francisco, NFL	10	96	0
	Jerry Norton, St. Louis, NFL	10	96	0
1959	Dean Derby, Pittsburgh	7	127	0
	Milt Davis, Baltimore	7	119	1
	Don Shinnick, Baltimore	7	70	0
1958	Jim Patton, N.Y. Giants	11	183	0
1957	Milt Davis, Baltimore	10	219	2
	Jack Christiansen, Detroit	10	137	1
	Jack Butler, Pittsburgh	10	85	0
1956	Linden Crow, Chi. Cardinals	11	170	0
1955	Will Sherman, Los Angeles	11	101	0
1954	Dick (Night Train) Lane, Chi. Cardinals	10	181	0
1953	Jack Christiansen, Detroit	12	238	1
1952	*Dick (Night Train) Lane, Los Angeles	14	298	2
1951	Otto Schnellbacher, N.Y. Giants	11	194	2
1950	Orban (Spec) Sanders, N.Y. Yanks	13	199	0
1949	Bob Nussbaumer, Chi. Cardinals	12	157	0
1948	*Dan Sandifer, Washington	13	258	2
1947	Frank Reagan, N.Y. Giants	10	203	1
	Frank Seno, Boston	10	100	0
1946	Bill Dudley, Pittsburgh	10	242	1
1945	Roy Zimmerman, Philadelphia	7	90	0
1944	*Howard Livingston, N.Y. Giants	9	172	1
1943	Sammy Baugh, Washington	11	112	0
1942	Clyde (Bulldog) Turner, Chi. Bears	8	96	1
1941	Marshall Goldberg, Chi. Cardinals	7	54	0
	*Art Jones, Pittsburgh	7	35	0
1940	Clarence (Ace) Parker, Brooklyn	6	146	1
	Kent Ryan, Detroit	6	65	0
	Don Hutson, Green Bay	6	24	0

*First season of professional football.

ANNUAL PUNTING LEADERS

Year	Player, Team	No.	Avg.	Long
1993	Greg Montgomery, Houston, AFC	54	45.6	77
	Jim Arnold, Detroit, NFC	72	44.5	68
1992	Greg Montgomery, Houston, AFC	53	46.9	66
	Harry Newsome, Minnesota, NFC	72	45.0	84
1991	Reggie Roby, Miami, AFC	54	45.7	64
	Harry Newsome, Minnesota, AFC	68	45.5	65
1990	Mike Horan, Denver, AFC	58	44.4	67

Year	Player	No.	Avg	Long
	Sean Landeta, N.Y. Giants, NFC	75	44.1	67
1989	Rich Camarillo, Phoenix, NFC	76	43.4	58
	Greg Montgomery, Hounton, AFC	56	43.3	63
1988	Harry Newsome, Pittsburgh, AFC	65	45.4	62
	Jim Arnold, Detroit, NFC	97	42.4	69
1987	Rick Donnelly, Atlanta, NFC	61	44.0	62
	Ralf Mojsiejenko, San Diego, AFC	67	42.9	57
1986	Rohn Stark, Indianapolis, AFC	76	45.2	63
	Sean Landeta, N.Y. Giants, NFC	79	44.8	61
1985	Rohn Stark, Indianapolis, AFC	78	45.9	68
	*Rick Donnelly, Atlanta, NFC	59	43.6	68
1984	Jim Arnold, Kansas City, AFC	98	44.9	63
	*Brian Hansen, New Orleans, NFC	69	43.8	66
1983	Rohn Stark, Baltimore, AFC	91	45.3	68
	Frank Garcia, Tampa Bay, NFC	95	42.2	64
1982	Luke Prestridge, Denver, AFC	45	45.0	65
	Carl Birdsong, St. Louis, NFC	54	43.8	65
1981	Pat McInally, Cincinnati, AFC	72	45.4	62
	Tom Skladany, Detroit, NFC	64	43.5	74
1980	Dave Jennings, N.Y. Giants, NFC	94	44.8	63
	Luke Prestridge, Denver, AFC	70	43.9	57
1979	*Bob Grupp, Kansas City, AFC	89	43.6	74
	Dave Jennings, N.Y. Giants, NFC	104	42.7	72
1978	Pat McInally, Cincinnati, AFC	91	43.1	65
	*Tom Skladany, Detroit, NFC	86	42.5	63
1977	Ray Guy, Oakland, AFC	59	43.3	74
	Tom Blanchard, New Orleans, NFC	82	42.4	66
1976	Marv Bateman, Buffalo, AFC	86	42.8	78
	John James, Atlanta, NFC	101	42.1	67
1975	Ray Guy, Oakland, AFC	68	43.8	64
	Herman Weaver, Detroit, NFC	80	42.0	61
1974	Ray Guy, Oakland, AFC	74	42.2	66
	Tom Blanchard, New Orleans, NFC	88	42.1	71
1973	Jerrel Wilson, Kansas City, AFC	80	45.5	68
	*Tom Wittum, San Francisco, NFC	79	43.7	62
1972	Jerrel Wilson, Kansas City, AFC	66	44.8	69
	Dave Chapple, Los Angeles, NFC	53	44.2	70
1971	Dave Lewis, Cincinnati, AFC	72	44.8	56
	Tom McNeill, Philadelphia, NFC	73	42.0	64
1970	Dave Lewis, Cincinnati, AFC	79	46.2	63
	*Julian Fagan, New Orleans, NFC	77	42.5	64
1969	David Lee, Baltimore, NFL	57	45.3	66
	Dennis Partee, San Diego, AFL	71	44.6	62
1968	Jerrel Wilson, Kansas City, AFL	63	45.1	70
	Billy Lothridge, Atlanta, NFL	75	44.3	70
1967	Bob Scarpitto, Denver, AFL	105	44.9	73
	Billy Lothridge, Atlanta, NFL	87	43.7	62
1966	Bob Scarpitto, Denver, AFL	76	45.8	70
	*David Lee, Baltimore, NFL	49	45.6	64
1965	Gary Collins, Cleveland, NFL	65	46.7	71
	Jerrel Wilson, Kansas City, AFL	69	45.4	64
1964	*Bobby Walden, Minnesota, NFL	72	46.4	73
	Jim Fraser, Denver, AFL	73	44.2	67
1963	Yale Lary, Detroit, NFL	35	48.9	73
	Jim Fraser, Denver, AFL	81	44.4	66
1962	Tommy Davis, San Francisco, NFL	48	45.6	82
	Jim Fraser, Denver, AFL	55	43.6	75
1961	Yale Lary, Detroit, NFL	52	48.4	71
	Billy Atkins, Buffalo, AFL	85	44.5	70
1960	Jerry Norton, St. Louis, NFL	39	45.6	62
	*Paul Maguire, L.A. Chargers, AFL	43	40.5	61
1959	Yale Lary, Detroit	45	47.1	67
1958	Sam Baker, Washington	48	45.4	64
1957	Don Chandler, N.Y. Giants	60	44.6	61
1956	Norm Van Brocklin, Los Angeles	48	43.1	72
1955	Norm Van Brocklin, Los Angeles	60	44.6	61
1954	Pat Brady, Pittsburgh	66	43.2	72
1953	Pat Brady, Pittsburgh	80	46.9	64
1952	Horace Gillom, Cleveland	61	45.7	73
1951	Horace Gillom, Cleveland	73	45.5	66
1950	*Fred (Curly) Morrison, Chi. Bears	57	43.3	65
1949	*Mike Boyda, N.Y. Bulldogs	56	44.2	61
1948	Joe Muha, Philadelphia	57	47.3	82
1947	Jack Jacobs, Green Bay	57	43.5	74
1946	Roy McKay, Green Bay	64	42.7	64
1945	Roy McKay, Green Bay	44	41.2	73
1944	Frank Sinkwich, Detroit	45	41.0	73
1943	Sammy Baugh, Washington	50	45.9	81
1942	Sammy Baugh, Washington	37	48.2	74
1941	Sammy Baugh, Washington	30	48.7	75
1940	Sammy Baugh, Washington	35	51.4	85
1939	*Parker Hall, Cleveland	58	40.8	80

*First season of professional football.

ANNUAL PUNT RETURN LEADERS

Year	Player, Team	No.	Yards	Avg.	Long	TD
1993	*Tyrone Hughes, New Orleans, NFC	37	503	13.6	83	2
	Eric Metcalf, Cleveland, AFC	36	464	12.9	91	2
1992	Johnny Bailey, Phoenix, NFC	20	263	13.2	65	0
	Rod Woodson, Pittsburgh, AFC	32	364	11.4	80	1
1991	Mel Gray, Detroit, NFC	25	385	15.4	78	1
	Rod Woodson, Pittsburgh, AFC	28	320	11.4	40	0
1990	Clarence Verdin, Indianapolis, AFC	31	396	12.8	36	0
	*Johnny Bailey, Chicago, NFC	36	399	11.1	95	1
1989	Walter Stanley, Detroit, NFC	36	496	13.8	74	0
	Clarence Verdin, Indianapolis, AFC	23	296	12.9	49	1
1988	John Taylor, San Francisco, NFC	44	556	12.6	95	2
	JoJo Townsell, N.Y. Jets, AFC	35	409	11.7	59	1
1987	Mel Gray, New Orleans, NFC	24	352	14.7	80	0
	Bobby Joe Edmonds, Seattle, AFC	20	251	12.6	40	0
1986	*Bobby Joe Edmonds, Seattle, AFC	34	419	12.3	75	1
	*Vai Sikahema, St. Louis, NFC	43	522	12.1	71	2
1985	Irving Fryar, New England, AFC	37	520	14.1	85	2
	Henry Ellard, L.A. Rams, NFC	37	501	13.5	80	1
1984	Mike Martin, Cincinnati, AFC	24	376	15.7	55	0
	Henry Ellard, L.A. Rams, NFC	30	403	13.4	83	2
1983	*Henry Ellard, L.A. Rams, NFC	16	217	13.6	72	1
	Kirk Springs, N.Y. Jets, AFC	23	287	12.5	76	1
1982	Rick Upchurch, Denver, AFC	15	242	16.1	78	2
	Billy Johnson, Atlanta, NFC	24	273	11.4	71	0
1981	LeRoy Irvin, Los Angeles, NFC	46	615	13.4	84	3
	*James Brooks, San Diego, AFC	22	290	13.2	42	0
1980	J.T. Smith, Kansas City, AFC	40	581	14.5	75	2
	*Kenny Johnson, Atlanta, NFC	23	281	12.2	56	0
1979	John Sciarra, Philadelphia, NFC	16	182	11.4	38	0
	*Tony Nathan, Miami, AFC	28	306	10.9	86	1
1978	Rick Upchurch, Denver, AFC	36	493	13.7	75	1
	Jackie Wallace, Los Angeles, NFC	52	618	11.9	58	0
1977	Billy Johnson, Houston, AFC	35	539	15.4	87	2
	Larry Marshall, Philadelphia, NFC	46	489	10.6	48	0
1976	Rick Upchurch, Denver, AFC	39	536	13.7	92	4
	Eddie Brown, Washington, NFC	48	646	13.5	71	1
1975	Billy Johnson, Houston, AFC	40	612	15.3	83	3
	Terry Metcalf, St. Louis, NFC	23	285	12.4	69	1
1974	Lemar Parrish, Cincinnati, AFC	18	338	18.8	90	2
	Dick Jauron, Detroit, NFC	17	286	16.8	58	0
1973	Bruce Taylor, San Francisco, NFC	15	207	13.8	61	0
	Ron Smith, San Diego, AFC	27	352	13.0	84	2
1972	Ken Ellis, Green Bay, NFC	14	215	15.4	80	1
	Chris Farasopoulos, N.Y. Jets, AFC	17	179	10.5	65	1
1971	Les (Speedy) Duncan, Washington, NFC	22	233	10.6	33	0
	Leroy Kelly, Cleveland, AFC	30	292	9.7	74	0
1970	Ed Podolak, Kansas City, AFC	23	311	13.5	60	0
	*Bruce Taylor, San Francisco, NFC	43	516	12.0	76	0
1969	Alvin Haymond, Los Angeles, NFL	33	435	13.2	52	0
	*Bill Thompson, Denver, AFL	25	288	11.5	40	0
1968	Bob Hayes, Dallas, NFL	15	312	20.8	90	2
	Noland Smith, Kansas City, AFL	18	270	15.0	80	1
1967	Floyd Little, Denver, AFL	16	270	16.9	72	1
	Ben Davis, Cleveland, NFL	18	229	12.7	52	1
1966	Les (Speedy) Duncan, San Diego, AFL	18	238	13.2	81	1
	Johnny Roland, St. Louis, NFL	20	221	11.1	86	1
1965	Leroy Kelly, Cleveland, NFL	17	265	15.6	67	2
	Les (Speedy) Duncan, San Diego, AFL	30	464	15.5	66	2
1964	Bobby Jancik, Houston, AFL	12	220	18.3	82	1
	Tommy Watkins, Detroit, NFL	16	238	14.9	68	2
1963	Dick James, Washington, NFL	16	214	13.4	39	0
	Claude (Hoot) Gibson, Oakland, AFL	26	307	11.8	85	2
1962	Dick Christy, N.Y. Titans, AFL	15	250	16.7	73	2
	Pat Studstill, Detroit, NFL	29	457	15.8	44	0
1961	Dick Christy, N.Y. Titans, AFL	18	383	21.3	70	2
	Willie Wood, Green Bay, NFL	14	225	16.1	72	2
1960	*Abner Haynes, Dall. Texans, AFL	14	215	15.4	46	0
	Abe Woodson, San Francisco, NFL	13	174	13.4	48	0
1959	Johnny Morris, Chi. Bears	14	171	12.2	78	1
1958	Jon Arnett, Los Angeles	18	223	12.4	58	0
1957	Bert Zagers, Washington	14	217	15.5	76	2
1956	Ken Konz, Cleveland	13	187	14.4	65	1
1955	Ollie Matson, Chi. Cardinals	13	245	18.8	78	2
1954	*Veryl Switzer, Green Bay	24	306	12.8	93	1
1953	Charley Trippi, Chi. Cardinals	21	239	11.4	38	0
1952	Jack Christiansen, Detroit	15	322	21.5	79	2
1951	Claude (Buddy) Young, N.Y. Yanks	12	231	19.3	79	1
1950	*Herb Rich, Baltimore	12	276	23.0	86	1
1949	Verda (Vitamin T) Smith, Los Angeles	27	427	15.8	85	1
1948	George McAfee, Chi. Bears	30	417	13.9	60	1
1947	*Walt Slater, Pittsburgh	28	435	15.5	33	0

Year	Player, Team	No.	Yards	Avg.	Long	TD		Year	Player, Team	No.	Yards	Avg.	Long	TD
1946	Bill Dudley, Pittsburgh	27	385	14.3	52	0		1954	Billy Reynolds, Cleveland	14	413	29.5	51	0
1945	*Dave Ryan, Detroit	15	220	14.7	56	0		1953	Joe Arenas, San Francisco	16	551	34.4	82	0
1944	*Steve Van Buren, Philadelphia	15	230	15.3	55	1		1952	Lynn Chandnois, Pittsburgh	17	599	35.2	93	2
1943	Andy Farkas, Washington	15	168	11.2	33	0		1951	Lynn Chandnois, Pittsburgh	12	390	32.5	55	0
1942	Merlyn Condit, Brooklyn	21	210	10.0	23	0		1950	Verda (Vitamin T) Smith, Los Angeles	22	742	33.7	97	3
1941	Byron (Whizzer) White, Detroit	19	262	13.8	64	0		1949	*Don Doll, Detroit	21	536	25.5	56	0

First season of professional football.

ANNUAL KICKOFF RETURN LEADERS

Year	Player, Team	No.	Yards	Avg.	Long	TD		Year	Player, Team	No.	Yards	Avg.	Long	TD
1993	Robert Brooks, Green Bay, NFC	23	611	26.6	95	1		1948	*Joe Scott, N.Y. Giants	20	569	28.5	99	1
	*Raghib Ismail, L.A. Raiders, AFC	25	605	24.2	66	0		1947	Eddie Saenz, Washington	29	797	27.5	94	2
1992	Jon Vaughn, New England, AFC	20	564	28.2	100	1		1946	Abe Karnofsky, Boston	21	599	28.5	97	1
	Deion Sanders, Atlanta, NFC	40	1,067	26.7	99	2		1945	Steve Van Buren, Philadelphia	13	373	28.7	98	1
1991	Mel Gray, Detroit, NFC	36	929	25.8	71	0		1944	Bob Thurbon, Card.-Pitt.	12	291	24.3	55	0
	Nate Lewis, San Diego, AFC	23	578	25.1	95	1		1943	Ken Heineman, Brooklyn	16	444	27.8	69	0
1990	Kevin Clark, Denver, AFC	20	505	25.3	75	0		1942	Marshall Goldberg, Chi. Cardinals	15	393	26.2	95	1
	David Meggett, N.Y. Giants, NFC	21	492	23.4	58	0		1941	Marshall Goldberg, Chi. Cardinals	12	290	24.2	41	0
1989	Rod Woodson, Pittsburgh, AFC	36	982	27.3	84	1								
	Mel Gray, Detroit, NFC	24	640	26.7	57	0								
1988	*Tim Brown, L.A. Raiders, AFC	41	1,098	26.8	97	1								
	Donnie Elder, Tampa Bay, NFC	34	772	22.7	51	0								
1987	Sylvester Stamps, Atlanta, NFC	24	660	27.5	97	1								
	Paul Palmer, Kansas City, AFC	38	923	24.3	95	2								
1986	Dennis Gentry, Chicago, NFC	20	576	28.8	91	1								
	Lupe Sanchez, Pittsburgh, AFC	25	591	23.6	64	0								
1985	Ron Brown, L.A. Rams, NFC	28	918	32.8	98	3								
	Glen Young, Cleveland, AFC	35	898	25.7	63	0								
1984	*Bobby Humphery, N.Y. Jets, AFC	22	675	30.7	97	1								
	Barry Redden, L.A. Rams, NFC	23	530	23.0	40	0								
1983	Fulton Walker, Miami, AFC	36	962	26.7	78	0								
	Darrin Nelson, Minnesota, NFC	18	445	24.7	50	0								
1982	*Mike Mosley, Buffalo, AFC	18	487	27.1	66	0								
	Alvin Hall, Detroit, NFC	16	426	26.6	96	1								
1981	Mike Nelms, Washington, NFC	37	1,099	29.7	84	0								
	Carl Roaches, Houston, AFC	28	769	27.5	96	1								
1980	Horace Ivory, New England, AFC	36	992	27.6	98	1								
	Rich Mauti, New Orleans, NFC	31	798	25.7	52	0								
1979	Larry Brunson, Oakland, AFC	17	441	25.9	89	0								
	Jimmy Edwards, Minnesota, NFC	44	1,103	25.1	83	0								
1978	Steve Odom, Green Bay, NFC	25	677	27.1	95	1								
	*Keith Wright, Cleveland, AFC	30	789	26.3	86	0								
1977	*Raymond Clayborn, New England, AFC	28	869	31.0	101	3								
	*Wilbert Montgomery, Philadelphia, NFC	23	619	26.9	99	1								
1976	*Duriel Harris, Miami, AFC	17	559	32.9	69	0								
	Cullen Bryant, Los Angeles, NFC	16	459	28.7	90	1								
1975	*Walter Payton, Chicago, NFC	14	444	31.7	70	0								
	Harold Hart, Oakland, AFC	17	518	30.5	102	1								
1974	Terry Metcalf, St. Louis, NFC	20	623	31.2	94	1								
	Greg Pruitt, Cleveland, AFC	22	606	27.5	88	1								
1973	Carl Garrett, Chicago, NFC	16	486	30.4	67	0								
	*Wallace Francis, Buffalo, AFC	23	687	29.9	101	2								
1972	Ron Smith, Chicago, NFC	30	924	30.8	94	1								
	*Bruce Laird, Baltimore, AFC	29	843	29.1	73	0								
1971	Travis Williams, Los Angeles, NFC	25	743	29.7	105	1								
	Eugene (Mercury) Morris, Miami, AFC	15	423	28.2	94	1								
1970	Jim Duncan, Baltimore, AFC	20	707	35.4	99	1								
	Cecil Turner, Chicago, NFC	23	752	32.7	96	4								
1969	Bobby Williams, Detroit, NFL	17	563	33.1	96	1								
	*Bill Thompson, Denver, AFL	18	513	28.5	63	0								
1968	Preston Pearson, Baltimore, NFL	15	527	35.1	102	2								
	*George Atkinson, Oakland, AFL	32	802	25.1	60	0								
1967	*Travis Williams, Green Bay, NFL	18	739	41.1	104	4								
	*Zeke Moore, Houston, AFL	14	405	28.9	92	1								
1966	Gale Sayers, Chicago, NFL	23	718	31.2	93	2								
	*Goldie Sellers, Denver, AFL	19	541	28.5	100	2								
1965	Tommy Watkins, Detroit, NFL	17	584	34.4	94	0								
	Abner Haynes, Denver, AFL	34	901	26.5	60	0								
1964	*Clarence Childs, N.Y. Giants, NFL	34	987	29.0	100	1								
	Bo Roberson, Oakland, AFL	36	975	27.1	59	0								
1963	Abe Woodson, San Francisco, NFL	29	935	32.2	103	3								
	Bobby Jancik, Houston, AFL	45	1,317	29.3	53	0								
1962	Abe Woodson, San Francisco, NFL	37	1,157	31.3	79	0								
	*Bobby Jancik, Houston, AFL	24	826	30.3	61	0								
1961	Dick Bass, Los Angeles, NFL	23	698	30.3	64	0								
	*Dave Grayson, Dall. Texans, AFL	16	453	28.3	73	0								
1960	*Tom Moore, Green Bay, NFL	12	397	33.1	84	0								
	Ken Hall, Houston, AFL	19	594	31.3	104	1								
1959	Abe Woodson, San Francisco	13	382	29.4	105	1								
1958	Ollie Matson, Chi. Cardinals	14	497	35.5	101	2								
1957	*Jon Arnett, Los Angeles	18	504	28.0	98	1								
1956	*Tom Wilson, Los Angeles	15	477	31.8	103	1								
1955	Al Carmichael, Green Bay	14	418	29.9	100	1								

First season of professional football.

ANNUAL LEADERS IN SACKS (SINCE 1982)

Year	Player, Team	Sacks
1993	Neil Smith, K.C., AFC	15
	Renaldo Turnbull, N.O., NFC	13
	Reggie White, G.B., NFC	13
1992	Clyde Simmons, Phil., NFC	19
	Leslie O'Neal, S.D., AFC	17
1991	Pat Swilling, N.O., NFC	17
	William Fuller, Hou., AFC	15
1990	Derrick Thomas, K.C., AFC	20
	Charles Haley, S.F., NFC	16
1989	Chris Doleman, Minn., NFC	21
	Lee Williams, S.D., AFC	14
1988	Reggie White, Phil., NFC	18
	G. Townsend, Raiders, AFC	11.5
1987	Reggie White, Phil., NFC	21
	Andre Tippett, N.E., AFC	12.5
1986	Lawrence Taylor, N.Y.G., NFC	20.5
	Sean Jones, Raiders, AFC	15.5
1985	Richard Dent, Chi., NFC	17
	Andre Tippett, N.E., AFC	16.5
1984	Mark Gastineau, N.Y.J., AFC	22
	Richard Dent, Chi., NFC	17.5
1983	Mark Gastineau, N.Y.J., AFC	19
	Fred Dean, San Fran., NFC	17.5
1982	Doug Martin, Minn., NFC	11.5
	Jesse Baker, Hou., AFC	7.5

POINTS SCORED

Year	Team	Points
1993	San Francisco, NFC	473
	Denver, AFC	373
1992	San Francisco, NFC	431
	Buffalo, AFC	381
1991	Washington, NFC	485
	Buffalo, AFC	458
1990	Buffalo, AFC	428
	Philadelphia, NFC	396
1989	San Francisco, NFC	442
	Buffalo, AFC	409
1988	Cincinnati, AFC	448
	L.A. Rams, NFC	407
1987	San Francisco, NFC	459
	Cleveland, AFC	390
1986	Miami, AFC	430
	Minnesota, NFC	398
1985	San Diego, AFC	467
	Chicago, NFC	456
1984	Miami, AFC	513
	San Francisco, NFC	475
1983	Washington, NFC	541
	L.A. Raiders, AFC	442
1982	San Diego, AFC	288
	Dallas, NFC	226
	Green Bay, NFC	226
1981	San Diego, AFC	478
	Atlanta, NFC	426
1980	Dallas, NFC	454
	New England, AFC	441
1979	Pittsburgh, AFC	416
	Dallas, NFC	371
1978	Dallas, NFC	384
	Miami, AFC	372
1977	Oakland, AFC	351
	Dallas, NFC	345
1976	Baltimore, AFC	417
	Los Angeles, NFC	351
1975	Buffalo, AFC	420
	Minnesota, NFC	377
1974	Oakland, AFC	355
	Washington, NFC	320
1973	Los Angeles, NFC	388
	Denver, AFC	354
1972	Miami, AFC	385
	San Francisco, NFC	353
1971	Dallas, NFC	406
	Oakland, AFC	344
1970	San Francisco, NFC	352
	Baltimore, AFC	321
1969	Minnesota, NFL	379
	Oakland, AFL	377
1968	Oakland, AFL	453
	Dallas, NFL	431
1967	Oakland, AFL	468
	Los Angeles, NFL	398
1966	Kansas City, AFL	448
	Dallas, NFL	445
1965	San Francisco, NFL	421
	San Diego, AFL	340
1964	Baltimore, NFL	428
	Buffalo, AFL	400
1963	N.Y. Giants, NFL	448
	San Diego, AFL	399
1962	Green Bay, NFL	415
	Dall. Texans, AFL	389
1961	Houston, AFL	513
	Green Bay, NFL	391
1960	N.Y. Titans, AFL	382
	Cleveland, NFL	362
1959	Baltimore	374
1958	Baltimore	381
1957	Los Angeles	307
1956	Chi. Bears	363
1955	Cleveland	349
1954	Detroit	337
1953	San Francisco	372
1952	Los Angeles	349
1951	Los Angeles	392
1950	Los Angeles	466
1949	Philadelphia	364
1948	Chi. Cardinals	395
1947	Chi. Bears	363
1946	Chi. Bears	289
1945	Philadelphia	272
1944	Philadelphia	267
1943	Chi. Bears	303
1942	Chi. Bears	376
1941	Chi. Bears	396
1940	Washington	245
1939	Chi. Bears	298
1938	Green Bay	223
1937	Green Bay	220
1936	Green Bay	248
1935	Chi. Bears	192
1934	Chi. Bears	286
1933	N.Y. Giants	244
1932	Chicago Bears	160

TOTAL YARDS GAINED

Year	Team	Yards
1993	San Francisco, NFC	6,435
	Miami, AFC	5,812
1992	San Francisco, NFC	6,195
	Buffalo, AFC	5,893
1991	Buffalo, AFC	6,252
	San Francisco, NFC	5,858
1990	Houston, AFC	6,222
	San Francisco, NFC	5,895
1989	San Francisco, NFC	6,268
	Cincinnati, AFC	6,101
1988	Cincinnati, AFC	6,057
	San Francisco, NFC	5,900
1987	San Francisco, NFC	5,987
	Denver, AFC	5,624
1986	Cincinnati, AFC	6,490
	San Francisco, NFC	6,082
1985	San Diego, AFC	6,535
	San Francisco, NFC	5,920
1984	Miami, AFC	6,936
	San Francisco, NFC	6,366
1983	San Diego, AFC	6,197
	Green Bay, NFC	6,172
1982	San Diego, AFC	4,048
	San Francisco, NFC	3,242
1981	San Diego, AFC	6,744
	Detroit, NFC	5,933
1980	San Diego, AFC	6,410
	Los Angeles, NFC	6,006
1979	Pittsburgh, AFC	6,258
	Dallas, NFC	5,968
1978	New England, AFC	5,965
	Dallas, NFC	5,959
1977	Dallas, NFC	4,812
	Oakland, AFC	4,736
1976	Baltimore, AFC	5,236
	Dallas, NFL	431
1975	Buffalo, AFC	5,467
	Dallas, NFC	5,025
1974	Dallas, NFC	4,983
	Oakland, AFC	4,718
1973	Los Angeles, NFC	4,906
	Oakland, AFC	4,773
1972	Miami, AFC	5,036
	N.Y. Giants, NFC	4,483
1971	Dallas, NFC	5,035
	San Diego, AFC	4,738
1970	Oakland, AFC	4,829
	San Francisco, NFC	4,503
1969	Dallas, NFL	5,122
	Oakland, AFL	5,036
1968	Oakland, AFL	5,696
	Dallas, NFL	5,117
1967	N.Y. Jets, AFL	5,152
	Baltimore, NFL	5,008
1966	Dallas, NFL	5,145
	Kansas City, AFL	5,114
1965	San Francisco, NFL	5,270
	San Diego, AFL	5,188
1964	Buffalo, AFL	5,206
	Baltimore, NFL	4,779
1963	San Diego, AFL	5,153
	N.Y. Giants, NFL	5,024
1962	N.Y. Giants, NFL	5,005
	Houston, AFL	4,971
1961	Houston, AFL	6,288
	Philadelphia, NFL	5,112
1960	Houston, AFL	4,936
	Baltimore, NFL	4,245
1959	Baltimore	4,458
1958	Baltimore	4,539
1957	Los Angeles	4,143
1956	Chi. Bears	4,537
1955	Chi. Bears	4,316
1954	Los Angeles	5,187
1953	Philadelphia	4,811
1952	Cleveland	4,352
1951	Los Angeles	5,506
1950	Los Angeles	5,420
1949	Chi. Bears	4,873
1948	Chi. Cardinals	4,705
1947	Chi. Bears	5,053
1946	Los Angeles	3,793
1945	Washington	3,549
1944	Chi. Bears	3,239
1943	Chi. Bears	4,045
1942	Chi. Bears	3,900
1941	Chi. Bears	4,265
1940	Green Bay	3,400
1939	Chi. Bears	3,988
1938	Green Bay	3,037
1937	Green Bay	3,201
1936	Detroit	3,703
1935	Chi. Bears	3,454
1934	Chi. Bears	3,900
1933	N.Y. Giants	2,973
1932	Chi. Bears	2,755

YARDS RUSHING

Year	Team	Yards
1993	N.Y. Giants, NFC	2,210
	Seattle, AFC	2,015
1992	Buffalo, AFC	2,436
	Philadelphia, NFC	2,388
1991	Buffalo, AFC	2,381
	Minnesota, NFC	2,201
1990	Philadelphia, NFC	2,556
	San Diego, AFC	2,257
1989	Cincinnati, AFC	2,483
	Chicago, NFC	2,287
1988	Cincinnati, AFC	2,710
	San Francisco, NFC	2,523
1987	San Francisco, NFC	2,237
	L.A. Raiders, AFC	2,197
1986	Chicago, NFC	2,700
	Cincinnati, AFC	2,533
1985	Chicago, NFC	2,761
	Indianapolis, AFC	2,439
1984	Chicago, NFC	2,974

	St. Louis, NFC	5,136
	N.Y. Jets, AFC	2,189
1983	Chicago, NFC	2,727
	Baltimore, AFC	2,695
1982	Buffalo, AFC	1,371
	Dallas, NFC	1,313
1981	Detroit, NFC	2,795
	Kansas City, AFC	2,633
1980	Los Angeles, NFC	2,799
	Houston, AFC	2,635
1979	N.Y. Jets, AFC	2,646
	St. Louis, NFC	2,582
1978	New England, AFC	3,165
	Dallas, NFC	2,783
1977	Chicago, NFC	2,811
	Oakland, AFC	2,627
1976	Pittsburgh, AFC	2,971
	Los Angeles, NFC	2,528
1975	Buffalo, AFC	2,974
	Dallas, NFC	2,432
1974	Dallas, NFC	2,454
	Pittsburgh, AFC	2,417
1973	Buffalo, AFC	3,088
	Los Angeles, NFC	2,925
1972	Miami, AFC	2,960
	Chicago, NFC	2,360
1971	Miami, AFC	2,429
	Detroit, NFC	2,376
1970	Dallas, NFC	2,300
	Miami, AFC	2,082
1969	Dallas, NFL	2,276
	Kansas City, AFL	2,220
1968	Chicago, NFL	2,377
	Kansas City, AFL	2,227
1967	Cleveland, NFL	2,139
	Houston, AFL	2,122
1966	Kansas City, AFL	2,274
	Cleveland, NFL	2,166
1965	Cleveland, NFL	2,331
	San Diego, AFL	2,085
1964	Green Bay, NFL	2,276
	Buffalo, AFL	2,040
1963	Cleveland, NFL	2,639
	San Diego, AFL	2,203
1962	Buffalo, AFL	2,480
	Green Bay, NFL	2,460
1961	Green Bay, NFL	2,350
	Dall. Texans, AFL	2,189
1960	St. Louis, NFL	2,356
	Oakland, AFL	2,056
1959	Cleveland	2,149
1958	Cleveland	2,526
1957	Los Angeles	2,142
1956	Chi. Bears	2,468
1955	Chi. Bears	2,388
1954	San Francisco	2,498
1953	San Francisco	2,230
1952	San Francisco	1,905
1951	Chi. Bears	2,408
1950	N.Y. Giants	2,336
1949	Philadelphia	2,607
1948	Chi. Cardinals	2,560
1947	Los Angeles	2,171
1946	Green Bay	1,765
1945	Cleveland	1,714
1944	Philadelphia	1,661
1943	Phil-Pitt	1,730
1942	Chi. Bears	1,881
1941	Chi. Bears	2,263
1940	Chi. Bears	1,818
1939	Chi. Bears	2,043
1938	Detroit	1,893
1937	Detroit	2,074
1936	Detroit	2,885
1935	Chi. Bears	2,096
1934	Chi. Bears	2,847
1933	Boston	2,260
1932	Chi. Bears	1,770

YARDS PASSING

Leadership in this category has been based on net yards since 1952.

Year	Team	Yards
1993	Miami, AFC	4,353

San Francisco, NFC 4,302
1992 Houston, AFC 4,029
San Francisco, NFC 3,880
1991 Houston, AFC 4,621
San Francisco, NFC 3,997
1990 Houston, AFC 4,805
San Francisco, NFC 4,177
1989 Washington, NFC 4,349
Miami, AFC 4,216
1988 Miami, AFC 4,516
Washington, NFC 4,136
1987 Miami, AFC 3,876
San Francisco, NFC 3,750
1986 Miami, AFC 4,779
San Francisco, NFC 4,096
1985 San Diego, AFC 4,870
Dallas, NFC 3,861
1984 Miami, AFC 5,018
St. Louis, NFC 4,257
1983 San Diego, AFC 4,661
Green Bay, NFC 4,365
1982 San Diego, AFC 2,927
San Francisco, NFC 2,502
1981 San Diego, AFC 4,739
Minnesota, NFC 4,333
1980 San Diego, AFC 4,531
Minnesota, NFC 3,688
1979 San Diego, AFC 3,915
San Francisco, NFC 3,641
1978 San Diego, AFC 3,375
Minnesota, NFC 3,243
1977 Buffalo, AFC 2,530
St. Louis, NFC 2,499
1976 Baltimore, AFC 2,933
Minnesota, NFC 2,855
1975 Cincinnati, AFC 3,241
Washington, NFC 2,917
1974 Washington, NFC 2,978
Cincinnati, AFC 2,804
1973 Philadelphia, NFC 2,998
Denver, AFC 2,519
1972 N.Y. Jets, AFC 2,777
San Francisco, NFC 2,735
1971 San Diego, AFC 3,134
Dallas, NFC 2,786
1970 San Francisco, NFC 2,923
Oakland, AFC 2,865
1969 Oakland, AFL 3,271
San Francisco, NFL 3,158
1968 San Diego, AFL 3,623
Dallas, NFL 3,026
1967 N.Y. Jets, AFL 3,845
Washington, NFL 3,730
1966 N.Y. Jets, AFL 3,464
Dallas, NFL 3,023
1965 San Francisco, NFL 3,487
San Diego, AFL 3,103
1964 Houston, AFL 3,527
Chicago, NFL 2,841
1963 Baltimore, NFL 3,296
Houston, AFL 3,222
1962 Denver, AFL 3,404
Philadelphia, NFL 3,385
1961 Houston, AFL 4,392
Philadelphia, NFL 3,605
1960 Houston, AFL 3,203
Baltimore, NFL 2,956
1959 Baltimore 2,753
1958 Pittsburgh 2,752
1957 Baltimore 2,388
1956 Los Angeles 2,419
1955 Philadelphia 2,472
1954 Chi. Bears 3,104
1953 Philadelphia 3,089
1952 Cleveland 2,566
1951 Los Angeles 3,296
1950 Los Angeles 3,709
1949 Chi. Bears 3,055
1948 Washington 2,861
1947 Washington 3,336
1946 Los Angeles 2,080
1945 Chi. Bears 1,857
1944 Washington 2,021

1943 Chi. Bears 2,310
1942 Green Bay 2,407
1941 Chi. Bears 2,002
1940 Washington 1,887
1939 Chi. Bears 1,965
1938 Washington 1,536
1937 Green Bay 1,398
1936 Green Bay 1,629
1935 Green Bay 1,449
1934 Green Bay 1,165
1933 N.Y. Giants 1,348
1932 Chi. Bears 1,013

FEWEST POINTS ALLOWED

Year	Team	Points
1993	N.Y. Giants, NFC	205
	Houston, AFC	238
1992	New Orleans, NFC	202
	Pittsburgh, AFC	225
1991	New Orleans, NFC	211
	Denver, AFC	235
1990	N.Y. Giants, NFC	211
	Pittsburgh, AFC	240
1989	Denver, AFC	226
	N.Y. Giants, NFC	252
1988	Chicago, NFC	215
	Buffalo, AFC	237
1987	Indianapolis, AFC	238
	San Francisco, NFC	253
1986	Chicago, NFC	187
	Seattle, AFC	293
1985	Chicago, NFC	198
	N.Y. Jets, AFC	264
1984	San Francisco, NFC	227
	Denver, AFC	241
1983	Miami, AFC	250
	Detroit, NFC	286
1982	Washington, NFC	128
	Miami, AFC	131
1981	Philadelphia, NFC	221
	Miami, AFC	275
1980	Philadelphia, NFC	222
	Houston, AFC	251
1979	Tampa Bay, NFC	237
	San Diego, AFC	246
1978	Pittsburgh, AFC	195
	Dallas, NFC	208
1977	Atlanta, NFC	129
	Denver, AFC	148
1976	Pittsburgh, AFC	138
	Minnesota, NFC	176
1975	Los Angeles, NFC	135
	Pittsburgh, AFC	162
1974	Los Angeles, NFC	181
	Pittsburgh, AFC	189
1973	Miami, AFC	150
	Minnesota, NFC	168
1972	Miami, AFC	171
	Washington, NFC	218
1971	Minnesota, NFC	139
	Baltimore, AFC	140
1970	Minnesota, NFC	143
	Miami, AFC	228
1969	Minnesota, NFL	133
	Kansas City, AFL	177
1968	Baltimore, NFL	144
	Kansas City, AFL	170
1967	Los Angeles, NFL	196
	Houston, AFL	199
1966	Green Bay, NFL	163
	Buffalo, AFL	255
1965	Green Bay, NFL	224
	Buffalo, AFL	226
1964	Baltimore, NFL	225
	Buffalo, AFL	242
1963	Chicago, NFL	144
	San Diego, AFL	255
1962	Green Bay, NFL	148
	Dall. Texans, AFL	233
1961	San Diego, AFL	219
	N.Y. Giants, NFL	220
1960	San Francisco, NFL	205
	Dall. Texans, AFL	253
1959	N.Y. Giants	170
1958	N.Y. Giants	183
1957	Cleveland	172
1956	Cleveland	177
1955	Cleveland	218
1954	Cleveland	162
1953	Cleveland	162
1952	Detroit	192
1951	Cleveland	152
1950	Philadelphia	141
1949	Philadelphia	134
1948	Chi. Bears	151
1947	Green Bay	210
1946	Pittsburgh	117
1945	Washington	121
1944	N.Y. Giants	75
1943	Washington	137
1942	Chi. Bears	84
1941	N.Y. Giants	114
1940	Brooklyn	120
1939	N.Y. Giants	85
1938	N.Y. Giants	79
1937	Chi. Bears	100
1936	Chi. Bears	94
1935	Green Bay	96
	N.Y. Giants	96
1934	Detroit	59
1933	Brooklyn	54
1932	Chi. Bears	44

FEWEST TOTAL YARDS ALLOWED

Year	Team	Yards
1993	Minnesota, NFC	4,406
	Pittsburgh, AFC	4,531
1992	Dallas, NFC	3,931
	Houston, AFC	4,211
1991	Philadelphia, NFC	3,549
	Denver, AFC	4,549
1990	Pittsburgh, AFC	4,115
	N.Y. Giants, NFC	4,206
1989	Minnesota, NFC	4,184
	Kansas City, AFC	4,293
1988	Minnesota, NFC	4,091
	Buffalo, AFC	4,578
1987	San Francisco, NFC	4,095
	Cleveland, AFC	4,264
1986	Chicago, NFC	4,130
	L.A. Raiders, AFC	4,804
1985	Chicago, NFC	4,135
	L.A. Raiders, AFC	4,603
1984	Chicago, NFC	3,863
	Cleveland, AFC	4,641
1983	Cincinnati, AFC	4,327
	New Orleans, NFC	4,691
1982	Miami, AFC	2,312
	Tampa Bay, NFC	2,442
1981	Philadelphia, NFC	4,447
	N.Y. Jets, AFC	4,871
1980	Buffalo, AFC	4,101
	Philadelphia, NFC	4,443
1979	Tampa Bay, NFC	3,949
	Pittsburgh, AFC	4,270
1978	Los Angeles, NFC	3,893
	Pittsburgh, AFC	4,168
1977	Dallas, NFC	3,213
	New England, AFC	3,638
1976	Pittsburgh, AFC	3,323
	San Francisco, NFC	3,562
1975	Minnesota, NFC	3,153
	Oakland, AFC	3,629
1974	Pittsburgh, AFC	3,074
	Washington, NFC	3,285
1973	Los Angeles, NFC	2,951
	Oakland, AFC	3,160
1972	Miami, AFC	3,297
	Green Bay, NFC	3,474
1971	Baltimore, AFC	2,852
	Minnesota, NFC	3,406
1970	Minnesota, NFC	2,803
	N.Y. Jets, AFC	3,655
1969	Minnesota, NFL	2,720
	Kansas City, AFL	3,163
1968	Los Angeles, NFL	3,118
	N.Y. Jets, AFL	3,363
1967	Oakland, AFL	3,294
	Green Bay, NFL	3,300
1966	St. Louis, NFL	3,492
	Oakland, AFL	3,910
1965	San Diego, AFL	3,262
	Detroit, NFL	3,557
1964	Green Bay, NFL	3,179
	Buffalo, AFL	3,878
1963	Chicago, NFL	3,176
	Boston, AFL	3,834
1962	Detroit, NFL	3,217
	Dall. Texans, AFL	3,951
1961	San Diego, AFL	3,726
	Baltimore, NFL	3,782
1960	St. Louis, NFL	3,029
	Buffalo, AFL	3,866
1959	N.Y. Giants	2,843
1958	Chi. Bears	3,066
1957	Pittsburgh	2,791
1956	N.Y. Giants	3,081
1955	Cleveland	2,841
1954	Cleveland	2,658
1953	Philadelphia	2,998
1952	Cleveland	3,075
1951	N.Y. Giants	3,250
1950	Cleveland	3,154
1949	Philadelphia	2,831
1948	Chi. Bears	2,931
1947	Green Bay	3,396
1946	Washington	2,451
1945	Philadelphia	2,073
1944	Philadelphia	1,943
1943	Chi. Bears	2,262
1942	Chi. Bears	1,703
1941	N.Y. Giants	2,368
1940	N.Y. Giants	2,219
1939	Washington	2,116
1938	N.Y. Giants	2,029
1937	Washington	2,123
1936	Boston	2,181
1935	Boston	1,996
1934	Chi. Cardinals	1,539
1933	Brooklyn	1,789

FEWEST RUSHING YARDS ALLOWED

Year	Team	Yards
1993	Houston, AFC	1,273
	Minnesota, NFC	1,536
1992	Dallas, NFC	1,244
	Buffalo, AFC	1,395
	San Diego, AFC	1,395
1991	Philadelphia, NFC	1,136
	N.Y. Jets, AFC	1,442
1990	Philadelphia, NFC	1,169
	San Diego, AFC	1,515
1989	New Orleans, NFC	1,326
	Denver, AFC	1,580
1988	Chicago, NFC	1,326
	Houston, AFC	1,592
1987	Chicago, NFC	1,413
	Cleveland, AFC	1,433
1986	N.Y. Giants, NFC	1,284
	Denver, AFC	1,651
1985	Chicago, NFC	1,319
	N.Y. Jets, AFC	1,516
1984	Chicago, NFC	1,377
	Pittsburgh, AFC	1,617
1983	Washington, NFC	1,289
	Cincinnati, AFC	1,499
1982	Pittsburgh, AFC	762
	Detroit, NFC	854
1981	Detroit, NFC	1,623
	Kansas City, AFC	1,747
1980	Detroit, NFC	1,599
	Cincinnati, AFC	1,680
1979	Denver, AFC	1,693
	Tampa Bay, NFC	1,873
1978	Dallas, NFC	1,721
	Pittsburgh, AFC	1,774

1977 Denver, AFC....................1,531
     Dallas, NFC.....................1,651
1976 Pittsburgh, AFC 1,457
     Los Angeles, NFC...........1,564
1975 Minnesota, NFC...............1,532
     Houston, AFC..................1,680
1974 Los Angeles, NFC...........1,302
     New England, AFC...........1,587
1973 Los Angeles, NFC...........1,270
     Oakland, AFC 1,470
1972 Dallas, NFC.....................1,515
     Miami, AFC 1,548
1971 Baltimore, AFC 1,113
     Dallas, NFC.....................1,144
1970 Detroit, NFC....................1,152
     N.Y. Jets, AFC.................1,283
1969 Dallas, NFL 1,050
     Kansas City, AFL..............1,091
1968 Dallas, NFL 1,195
     N.Y. Jets, AFL..................1,195
1967 Dallas, NFL 1,081
     Oakland, AFL...................1,129
1966 Buffalo, AFL 1,051
     Dallas, NFL......................1,176
1965 San Diego, AFL...............1,094
     Los Angeles, NFL 1,409
1964 Buffalo, AFL 913
     Los Angeles, NFL 1,501
1963 Boston, AFL.....................1,107
     Chicago, NFL...................1,442
1962 Detroit, NFL......................1,231
     Dall. Texans, AFL.............1,250
1961 Boston, AFL.....................1,041
     Pittsburgh, NFL................1,463
1960 St. Louis, NFL 1,212
     Dall. Texans, AFL.............1,338
1959 N.Y. Giants 1,261
1958 Baltimore 1,291
1957 Baltimore 1,174
1956 N.Y. Giants 1,443
1955 Cleveland.........................1,189
1954 Cleveland.........................1,050
1953 Philadelphia....................1,117
1952 Detroit 1,145
1951 N.Y. Giants 913
1950 Detroit 1,367
1949 Chi. Bears 1,106
1948 Philadelphia....................1,209
1947 Philadelphia....................1,329
1946 Chi. Bears 1,060
1945 Philadelphia........................817
1944 Philadelphia........................558
1943 Phil-Pitt.............................793
1942 Chi. Bears 519
1941 Washington......................1,042
1940 N.Y. Giants 977
1939 Chi. Bears 812
1938 Detroit 1,081
1937 Chi. Bears 933
1936 Boston 1,148
1935 Boston 998
1934 Chi. Cardinals 954
1933 Brooklyn..............................964

FEWEST PASSING YARDS ALLOWED

Leadership in this category has been based on net yards since 1952.

Year	Team	Yards
1993	New Orleans, NFC...........2,606	
	Cincinnati, AFC................2,798	
1992	New Orleans, NFC...........2,470	
	Kansas City, AFC.............2,537	
1991	Philadelphia, NFC...........2,413	
	Denver, AFC....................2,755	
1990	Pittsburgh, AFC 2,500	
	Dallas, NFC.....................2,639	
1989	Minnesota, NFC...............2,501	
	Kansas City, AFC.............2,527	
1988	Kansas City, AFC.............2,434	
	Minnesota, NFC...............2,489	
1987	San Francisco, NFC 2,484	
	L.A. Raiders, AFC 2,727	

1986 St. Louis, NFC 2,637
     New England, AFC 2,978
1985 Washington, NFC 2,746
     Pittsburgh, AFC 2,783
1984 New Orleans, NFC...........2,453
     Cleveland, AFC................2,696
1983 New Orleans, NFC...........2,691
     Cincinnati, AFC................2,828
1982 Miami, AFC 1,027
     Tampa Bay, NFC.............1,384
1981 Philadelphia, NFC...........2,696
     Buffalo, AFC.....................2,870
1980 Washington, NFC 2,171
     Buffalo, AFC.....................2,282
1979 Tampa Bay, NFC.............2,076
     Buffalo, AFC.....................2,530
1978 Buffalo, AFC.....................1,960
     Los Angeles, NFC...........2,048
1977 Atlanta, NFC 1,384
     San Diego, AFC...............1,725
1976 Minnesota, NFC...............1,575
     Cincinnati, AFC................1,758
1975 Minnesota, NFC...............1,621
     Cincinnati, AFC................1,729
1974 Pittsburgh, AFC 1,466
     Atlanta, NFC 1,572
1973 Miami, AFC 1,290
     Atlanta, NFC 1,430
1972 Minnesota, NFC...............1,699
     Cleveland, AFC................1,736
1971 Atlanta, NFC 1,638
     Baltimore, AFC 1,739
1970 Minnesota, NFC...............1,438
     Kansas City, AFC 2,010
1969 Minnesota, NFL 1,631
     Kansas City, AFL.............2,072
1968 Houston, AFL...................1,671
     Green Bay, NFL 1,796
1967 Green Bay, NFL 1,377
     Buffalo, AFL 1,825
1966 Green Bay, NFL 1,959
     Oakland, AFL...................2,118
1965 Green Bay, NFL 1,981
     San Diego, AFL...............2,168
1964 Green Bay, NFL 1,647
     San Diego, AFL...............2,518
1963 Chicago, NFL...................1,734
     Oakland, AFL...................2,589
1962 Green Bay, NFL 1,746
     Oakland, AFL...................2,306
1961 Baltimore, NFL.................1,913
     San Diego, AFL...............2,363
1960 Chicago, NFL...................1,388
     Buffalo, AFL 2,124
1959 N.Y. Giants 1,582
1958 Chi. Bears 1,769
1957 Cleveland.........................1,300
1956 Cleveland.........................1,103
1955 Pittsburgh 1,295
1954 Cleveland.........................1,608
1953 Washington......................1,751
1952 Washington......................1,580
1951 Pittsburgh 1,687
1950 Cleveland.........................1,581
1949 Philadelphia....................1,607
1948 Green Bay.......................1,626
1947 Green Bay.......................1,790
1946 Pittsburgh 939
1945 Washington......................1,121
1944 Chi. Bears 1,052
1943 Chi. Bears 980
1942 Washington......................1,093
1941 Pittsburgh 1,168
1940 Philadelphia....................1,012
1939 Washington......................1,116
1938 Chi. Bears 897
1937 Detroit 804
1936 Philadelphia.......................853
1935 Chi. Cardinals 793
1934 Philadelphia.......................545
1933 Portsmouth 558

389

SUPER BOWL RECORDS

Compiled by Elias Sports Bureau

1967: Super Bowl I	1977: Super Bowl XI	1987: Super Bowl XXI
1968: Super Bowl II	1978: Super Bowl XII	1988: Super Bowl XXII
1969: Super Bowl III	1979: Super Bowl XIII	1989: Super Bowl XXIII
1970: Super Bowl IV	1980: Super Bowl XIV	1990: Super Bowl XXIV
1971: Super Bowl V	1981: Super Bowl XV	1991: Super Bowl XXV
1972: Super Bowl VI	1982: Super Bowl XVI	1992: Super Bowl XXVI
1973: Super Bowl VII	1983: Super Bowl XVII	1993: Super Bowl XXVII
1974: Super Bowl VIII	1984: Super Bowl XVIII	1994: Super Bowl XXVIII
1975: Super Bowl IX	1985: Super Bowl XIX	
1976: Super Bowl X	1986: Super Bowl XX	

INDIVIDUAL RECORDS

SERVICE
Most Games
- 5 Marv Fleming, Green Bay, 1967-68; Miami, 1972-74
  Larry Cole, Dallas, 1971-72, 1976, 1978-79
  Cliff Harris, Dallas, 1971-72, 1976, 1978-79
  D.D. Lewis, Dallas, 1971-72, 1976, 1978-79
  Preston Pearson, Baltimore, 1969; Pittsburgh, 1975; Dallas, 1976, 1978-79
  Charlie Waters, Dallas, 1971-72, 1976, 1978-79
  Rayfield Wright, Dallas, 1971-72, 1976, 1978-79
- 4 By many players

Most Games, Winning Team
- 4 By many players

Most Games, Coach
- 6 Don Shula, Baltimore, 1969; Miami, 1972-74, 1983, 1985
- 5 Tom Landry, Dallas, 1971-72, 1976, 1978-79
- 4 Bud Grant, Minnesota, 1970, 1974-75, 1977
  Chuck Noll, Pittsburgh, 1975-76, 1979-80
  Joe Gibbs, Washington, 1983-84, 1988, 1992
  Marv Levy, Buffalo, 1991-94

Most Games, Winning Team, Coach
- 4 Chuck Noll, Pittsburgh, 1975-76, 1979-80
- 3 Bill Walsh, San Francisco, 1982, 1985, 1989
  Joe Gibbs, Washington, 1983, 1988, 1992
- 2 Vince Lombardi, Green Bay, 1967-68
  Tom Landry, Dallas, 1972, 1978
  Don Shula, Miami, 1973-74
  Tom Flores, Oakland, 1981; L.A. Raiders, 1984
  Bill Parcells, N.Y. Giants, 1987, 1991
  Jimmy Johnson, Dallas, 1993-94

Most Games, Losing Team, Coach
- 4 Bud Grant, Minnesota, 1970, 1974-75, 1977
  Don Shula, Baltimore, 1969; Miami, 1972, 1983, 1985
  Marv Levy, Buffalo, 1991-94
- 3 Tom Landry, Dallas, 1971, 1976, 1979
  Dan Reeves, Denver, 1987-88, 1990

SCORING
POINTS
Most Points, Career
- 24 Franco Harris, Pittsburgh, 4 games (4-td)
  Roger Craig, San Francisco, 3 games (4-td)
  Jerry Rice, San Francisco, 2 games (4-td)
  Thurman Thomas, Buffalo, 4 games (4-td)
- 22 Ray Wersching, San Francisco, 2 games (7-pat, 5-fg)
- 20 Don Chandler, Green Bay, 2 games (8-pat, 4-fg)

Most Points, Game
- 18 Roger Craig, San Francisco vs. Miami, 1985 (3-td)
  Jerry Rice, San Francisco vs. Denver, 1990 (3-td)
- 15 Don Chandler, Green Bay vs. Oakland, 1968 (3-pat, 4-fg)
- 14 Ray Wersching, San Francisco vs. Cincinnati, 1982 (2-pat, 4-fg)
  Kevin Butler, Chicago vs. New England, 1986 (5-pat, 3-fg)

TOUCHDOWNS
Most Touchdowns, Career
- 4 Franco Harris, Pittsburgh, 4 games (4-r)
  Roger Craig, San Francisco, 3 games (2-r, 2-p)
  Jerry Rice, San Francisco, 2 games (4-p)
  Thurman Thomas, Buffalo, 4 games (4-r)
- 3 John Stallworth, Pittsburgh, 4 games (3-p)
  Lynn Swann, Pittsburgh, 4 games (3-p)
  Cliff Branch, Oakland-L.A. Raiders, 3 games (3-p)
  Emmitt Smith, Dallas, 3 games (3-r)

Most Touchdowns, Game
- 3 Roger Craig, San Francisco vs. Miami, 1985 (1-r, 2-p)
  Jerry Rice, San Francisco vs. Denver, 1990 (3-p)
- 2 Max McGee, Green Bay vs. Kansas City, 1967 (2-p)
  Elijah Pitts, Green Bay vs. Kansas City, 1967 (2-r)
  Bill Miller, Oakland vs. Green Bay, 1968 (2-p)

Larry Csonka, Miami vs. Minnesota, 1974 (2-r)
Pete Banaszak, Oakland vs. Minnesota, 1977 (2-r)
John Stallworth, Pittsburgh vs. Dallas, 1979 (2-p)
Franco Harris, Pittsburgh vs. Los Angeles, 1980 (2-r)
Cliff Branch, Oakland vs. Philadelphia, 1981 (2-p)
Dan Ross, Cincinnati vs. San Francisco, 1982 (2-p)
Marcus Allen, L.A. Raiders vs. Washington, 1984 (2-r)
Jim McMahon, Chicago vs. New England, 1986 (2-r)
Ricky Sanders, Washington vs. Denver, 1988 (2-p)
Timmy Smith, Washington vs. Denver, 1988 (2-r)
Tom Rathman, San Francisco vs. Denver, 1990 (2-r)
Gerald Riggs, Washington vs. Buffalo, 1992 (2-r)
Michael Irvin, Dallas vs. Buffalo, 1993 (2-p)
Emmitt Smith, Dallas vs. Buffalo, 1994 (2-r)

POINTS AFTER TOUCHDOWN
Most Points After Touchdown, Career
- 9 Mike Cofer, San Francisco, 2 games (10 att)
- 8 Don Chandler, Green Bay, 2 games (8 att)
  Roy Gerela, Pittsburgh, 3 games (9 att)
  Chris Bahr, Oakland-L.A. Raiders, 2 games (8 att)
- 7 Ray Wersching, San Francisco, 2 games (7 att)
  Lin Elliott, Dallas, 1 game (7 att)

Most Points After Touchdown, Game
- 7 Mike Cofer, San Francisco vs. Denver, 1990 (8 att)
  Lin Elliott, Dallas vs. Buffalo, 1993 (7 att)
- 6 Ali Haji-Sheikh, Washington vs. Denver, 1988 (6 att)
- 5 Don Chandler, Green Bay vs. Kansas City, 1967 (5 att)
  Roy Gerela, Pittsburgh vs. Dallas, 1979 (5 att)
  Chris Bahr, L.A. Raiders vs. Washington, 1984 (5 att)
  Ray Wersching, San Francisco vs. Miami, 1985 (5 att)
  Kevin Butler, Chicago vs. New England, 1986 (5 att)

FIELD GOALS
Field Goals Attempted, Career
- 6 Jim Turner, N.Y. Jets-Denver, 2 games
  Roy Gerela, Pittsburgh, 3 games
  Rich Karlis, Denver, 2 games
- 5 Efren Herrera, Dallas, 1 game
  Ray Wersching, San Francisco, 2 games

Most Field Goals Attempted, Game
- 5 Jim Turner, N.Y. Jets vs. Baltimore, 1969
  Efren Herrera, Dallas vs. Denver, 1978
- 4 Don Chandler, Green Bay vs. Oakland, 1968
  Roy Gerela, Pittsburgh vs. Dallas, 1976
  Ray Wersching, San Francisco vs. Cincinnati, 1982
  Rich Karlis, Denver vs. N.Y. Giants, 1987
  Mike Cofer, San Francisco vs. Cincinnati, 1989

Most Field Goals, Career
- 5 Ray Wersching, San Francisco, 2 games (5 att)
- 4 Don Chandler, Green Bay, 2 games (4 att)
  Jim Turner, N.Y. Jets-Denver, 2 games (6 att)
  Uwe von Schamann, Miami, 2 games (4 att)
- 3 Mike Clark, Dallas, 2 games (3 att)
  Jan Stenerud, Kansas City, 1 game (3 att)
  Chris Bahr, Oakland-L.A. Raiders, 2 games (4 att)
  Mark Moseley, Washington, 2 games (4 att)
  Kevin Butler, Chicago, 1 game (3 att)
  Rich Karlis, Denver, 2 games (6 att)
  Jim Breech, Cincinnati, 2 games (3 att)
  Matt Bahr, Pittsburgh-N.Y. Giants, 2 games (3 att)
  Chip Lohmiller, Washington, 1 game (3 att)
  Steve Christie, Buffalo, 2 games (3 att)
  Eddie Murray, Dallas, 1 game (3 att)

Most Field Goals, Game
- 4 Don Chandler, Green Bay vs. Oakland, 1968
  Ray Wersching, San Francisco vs. Cincinnati, 1982
- 3 Jim Turner, N.Y. Jets vs. Baltimore, 1969
  Jan Stenerud, Kansas City vs. Minnesota, 1970
  Uwe von Schamann, Miami vs. San Francisco, 1985
  Kevin Butler, Chicago vs. New England, 1986
  Jim Breech, Cincinnati vs. San Francisco, 1989
  Chip Lohmiller, Washington vs. Buffalo, 1992
  Eddie Murray, Dallas vs. Buffalo, 1994

Longest Field Goal
- 54 Steve Christie, Buffalo vs. Dallas, 1994
- 48 Jan Stenerud, Kansas City vs. Minnesota, 1970
  Rich Karlis, Denver vs. N.Y. Giants, 1987
- 47 Jim Turner, Denver vs. Dallas, 1978

SAFETIES
Most Safeties, Game
- 1 Dwight White, Pittsburgh vs. Minnesota, 1975

Reggie Harrison, Pittsburgh vs. Dallas, 1976
Henry Waechter, Chicago vs. New England, 1986
George Martin, N.Y. Giants vs. Denver, 1987
Bruce Smith, Buffalo vs. N.Y. Giants, 1991

RUSHING
ATTEMPTS
Most Attempts, Career
- 101 Franco Harris, Pittsburgh, 4 games
- 64 John Riggins, Washington, 2 games
- 57 Larry Csonka, Miami, 3 games

Most Attempts, Game
- 38 John Riggins, Washington vs. Miami, 1983
- 34 Franco Harris, Pittsburgh vs. Minnesota, 1975
- 33 Larry Csonka, Miami vs. Minnesota, 1974

YARDS GAINED
Most Yards Gained, Career
- 354 Franco Harris, Pittsburgh, 4 games
- 297 Larry Csonka, Miami, 3 games
- 240 Emmitt Smith, Dallas, 2 games

Most Yards Gained, Game
- 204 Timmy Smith, Washington vs. Denver, 1988
- 191 Marcus Allen, L.A. Raiders vs. Washington, 1984
- 166 John Riggins, Washington vs. Miami, 1983

Longest Run From Scrimmage
- 74 Marcus Allen, L.A. Raiders vs. Washington, 1984 (TD)
- 58 Tom Matte, Baltimore vs. N.Y. Jets, 1969
  Timmy Smith, Washington vs. Denver, 1988 (TD)
- 49 Larry Csonka, Miami vs. Washington, 1973

AVERAGE GAIN
Highest Average Gain, Career (20 attempts)
- 9.6 Marcus Allen, L.A. Raiders, 1 game (20-191)
- 9.3 Timmy Smith, Washington, 1 game (22-204)
- 5.3 Walt Garrison, Dallas, 2 games (26-139)

Highest Average Gain, Game (10 attempts)
- 10.5 Tom Matte, Baltimore vs. N.Y. Jets, 1969 (11-116)
- 9.6 Marcus Allen, L.A. Raiders vs. Washington, 1984 (20-191)
- 9.3 Timmy Smith, Washington vs. Denver, 1988 (22-204)

TOUCHDOWNS
Most Touchdowns, Career
- 4 Franco Harris, Pittsburgh, 4 games
  Thurman Thomas, Buffalo, 4 games
- 3 Emmitt Smith, Dallas, 2 games
- 2 Elijah Pitts, Green Bay, 1 game
  Jim Kiick, Miami, 3 games
  Larry Csonka, Miami, 3 games
  Pete Banaszak, Oakland, 2 games
  Marcus Allen, L.A. Raiders, 1 game
  John Riggins, Washington, 2 games
  Jim McMahon, Chicago, 1 game
  Timmy Smith, Washington, 1 game
  Roger Craig, San Francisco, 3 games
  Tom Rathman, San Francisco, 2 games
  John Elway, Denver, 3 games
  Ottis Anderson, N.Y. Giants, 2 games
  Gerald Riggs, Washington, 1 game
  Joe Montana, San Francisco, 4 games

Most Touchdowns, Game
- 2 Elijah Pitts, Green Bay vs. Kansas City, 1967
  Larry Csonka, Miami vs. Minnesota, 1974
  Pete Banaszak, Oakland vs. Minnesota, 1977
  Franco Harris, Pittsburgh vs. Los Angeles, 1980
  Marcus Allen, L.A. Raiders vs. Washington, 1984
  Jim McMahon, Chicago vs. New England, 1986
  Timmy Smith, Washington vs. Denver, 1988
  Tom Rathman, San Francisco vs. Denver, 1990
  Gerald Riggs, Washington vs. Buffalo, 1992
  Emmitt Smith, Dallas vs. Buffalo, 1994

PASSING
PASSER RATING
Highest Passer Rating, Career (40 attempts)
- 127.8 Joe Montana, San Francisco, 4 games
- 122.8 Jim Plunkett, Oakland-L.A. Raiders, 2 games
- 113.2 Troy Aikman, Dallas, 2 games

ATTEMPTS
Most Passes Attempted, Career
- 145 Jim Kelly, Buffalo, 4 games
- 122 Joe Montana, San Francisco, 4 games
- 101 John Elway, Denver, 3 games

Most Passes Attempted, Game
- 58 Jim Kelly, Buffalo vs. Washington, 1992
- 50 Dan Marino, Miami vs. San Francisco, 1985
  Jim Kelly, Buffalo vs. Dallas, 1994
- 38 Ron Jaworski, Philadelphia vs. Oakland, 1981
  John Elway, Denver vs. Washington, 1988

COMPLETIONS
Most Passes Completed, Career
- 83 Joe Montana, San Francisco, 4 games
- 81 Jim Kelly, Buffalo, 4 games
- 61 Roger Staubach, Dallas, 4 games

Most Passes Completed, Game
- 31 Jim Kelly, Buffalo vs. Dallas, 1994
- 29 Dan Marino, Miami vs. San Francisco, 1985
- 28 Jim Kelly, Buffalo vs. Washington, 1992

Most Consecutive Completions, Game
- 13 Joe Montana, San Francisco vs. Denver, 1990
- 10 Phil Simms, N.Y. Giants vs. Denver, 1987
- 9 Jim Kelly, Buffalo vs. Dallas, 1994

COMPLETION PERCENTAGE
Highest Completion Percentage, Career (40 attempts)
- 71.9 Troy Aikman, Dallas, 2 games (57-41)
- 68.0 Joe Montana, San Francisco, 4 games (122-83)
- 63.6 Len Dawson, Kansas City, 2 games (44-28)

Highest Completion Percentage, Game (20 attempts)
- 88.0 Phil Simms, N.Y. Giants vs. Denver, 1987 (25-22)
- 75.9 Joe Montana, San Francisco vs. Denver, 1990 (29-22)
- 73.5 Ken Anderson, Cincinnati vs. San Francisco, 1982 (34-25)

YARDS GAINED
Most Yards Gained, Career
- 1,142 Joe Montana, San Francisco, 4 games
- 932 Terry Bradshaw, Pittsburgh, 4 games
- 829 Jim Kelly, Buffalo, 4 games

Most Yards Gained, Game
- 357 Joe Montana, San Francisco vs. Cincinnati, 1989
- 340 Doug Williams, Washington vs. Denver, 1988
- 331 Joe Montana, San Francisco vs. Miami, 1985

Longest Pass Completion
- 80 Jim Plunkett (to King), Oakland vs. Philadelphia, 1981 (TD)
  Doug Williams (to Sanders), Washington vs. Denver, 1988 (TD)
- 76 David Woodley (to Cefalo), Miami vs. Washington, 1983 (TD)
- 75 Johnny Unitas (to Mackey), Baltimore vs. Dallas, 1971 (TD)
  Terry Bradshaw (to Stallworth), Pittsburgh vs. Dallas, 1979 (TD)

AVERAGE GAIN
Highest Average Gain, Career (40 attempts)
- 11.10 Terry Bradshaw, Pittsburgh, 4 games (84-932)
- 9.62 Bart Starr, Green Bay, 2 games (47-452)
- 9.41 Jim Plunkett, Oakland-L.A. Raiders, 2 games (46-433)

Highest Average Gain, Game (20 attempts)
- 14.71 Terry Bradshaw, Pittsburgh vs. Los Angeles, 1980 (21-309)
- 12.80 Jim McMahon, Chicago vs. New England, 1986 (20-256)
- 12.43 Jim Plunkett, Oakland vs. Philadelphia, 1981 (21-261)

TOUCHDOWNS
Most Touchdown Passes, Career
- 11 Joe Montana, San Francisco, 4 games
- 9 Terry Bradshaw, Pittsburgh, 4 games
- 8 Roger Staubach, Dallas, 4 games

Most Touchdown Passes, Game
- 5 Joe Montana, San Francisco vs. Denver, 1990
- 4 Terry Bradshaw, Pittsburgh vs. Dallas, 1979
  Doug Williams, Washington vs. Denver, 1988
  Troy Aikman, Dallas vs. Buffalo, 1993
- 3 Roger Staubach, Dallas vs. Pittsburgh, 1979
  Jim Plunkett, Oakland vs. Philadelphia, 1981
  Joe Montana, San Francisco vs. Miami, 1985
  Phil Simms, N.Y. Giants vs. Denver, 1987

HAD INTERCEPTED
Lowest Percentage, Passes Had Intercepted, Career (40 attempts)
- 0.00 Jim Plunkett, Oakland-L.A. Raiders, 2 games (46-0)
  Joe Montana, San Francisco, 4 games (122-0)
- 1.75 Troy Aikman, Dallas, 2 games (57-1)
- 2.13 Bart Starr, Green Bay, 2 games (47-1)

Most Attempts, Without Interception, Game
- 36 Joe Montana, San Francisco vs. Cincinnati, 1989
- 35 Joe Montana, San Francisco vs. Miami, 1985
- 32 Jeff Hostetler, N.Y. Giants vs. Buffalo, 1991

Most Passes Had Intercepted, Career
- 7 Craig Morton, Dallas-Denver, 2 games

Jim Kelly, Buffalo, 4 games
6   Fran Tarkenton, Minnesota, 3 games
    John Elway, Denver, 3 games
4   Earl Morrall, Baltimore-Miami, 4 games
    Roger Staubach, Dallas, 4 games
    Terry Bradshaw, Pittsburgh, 4 games
    Joe Theismann, Washington, 2 games

Most Passes Had Intercepted, Game
4   Craig Morton, Denver vs. Dallas, 1978
    Jim Kelly, Buffalo vs. Washington, 1992
3   By eight players

PASS RECEIVING
RECEPTIONS
Most Receptions, Career
27   Andre Reed, Buffalo, 4 games
20   Roger Craig, San Francisco, 3 games
     Thurman Thomas, Buffalo, 4 games
18   Jerry Rice, San Francisco, 2 games

Most Receptions, Game
11   Dan Ross, Cincinnati vs. San Francisco, 1982
     Jerry Rice, San Francisco vs. Cincinnati, 1989
10   Tony Nathan, Miami vs. San Francisco, 1985
9   Ricky Sanders, Washington vs. Denver, 1988

YARDS GAINED
Most Yards Gained, Career
364   Lynn Swann, Pittsburgh, 4 games
363   Jerry Rice, San Francisco, 2 games
323   Andre Reed, Buffalo, 4 games

Most Yards Gained, Game
215   Jerry Rice, San Francisco vs. Cincinnati, 1989
193   Ricky Sanders, Washington vs. Denver, 1988
161   Lynn Swann, Pittsburgh vs. Dallas, 1976

Longest Reception
80   Kenny King (from Plunkett), Oakland vs. Philadelphia, 1981 (TD)
     Ricky Sanders (from Williams), Washington vs. Denver, 1988 (TD)
76   Jimmy Cefalo (from Woodley), Miami vs. Washington, 1983 (TD)
75   John Mackey (from Unitas), Baltimore vs. Dallas, 1971 (TD)
     John Stallworth (from Bradshaw), Pittsburgh vs. Dallas, 1979 (TD)

AVERAGE GAIN
Highest Average Gain, Career (8 receptions)
24.4   John Stallworth, Pittsburgh, 4 games (11-268)
23.4   Ricky Sanders, Washington, 2 games (10-234)
22.8   Lynn Swann, Pittsburgh, 4 games (16-364)

Highest Average Gain, Game (3 receptions)
40.33   John Stallworth, Pittsburgh vs. Los Angeles, 1980 (3-121)
40.25   Lynn Swann, Pittsburgh vs. Dallas, 1979 (4-161)
38.33   John Stallworth, Pittsburgh vs. Dallas, 1979 (3-115)

TOUCHDOWNS
Most Touchdowns, Career
4   Jerry Rice, San Francisco, 2 games
3   John Stallworth, Pittsburgh, 4 games
    Lynn Swann, Pittsburgh, 4 games
    Cliff Branch, Oakland-L.A. Raiders, 3 games
2   Max McGee, Green Bay, 2 games
    Bill Miller, Oakland, 1 game
    Butch Johnson, Dallas, 2 games
    Dan Ross, Cincinnati, 1 game
    Roger Craig, San Francisco, 3 games
    Ricky Sanders, Washington, 2 games
    John Taylor, San Francisco, 2 games
    Gary Clark, Washington, 2 games
    Don Beebe, Buffalo, 3 games
    Michael Irvin, Dallas, 2 games

Most Touchdowns, Game
3   Jerry Rice, San Francisco vs. Denver, 1990
2   Max McGee, Green Bay vs. Kansas City, 1967
    Bill Miller, Oakland vs. Green Bay, 1968
    John Stallworth, Pittsburgh vs. Dallas, 1979
    Cliff Branch, Oakland vs. Philadelphia, 1981
    Dan Ross, Cincinnati vs. San Francisco, 1982
    Roger Craig, San Francisco vs. Miami, 1985
    Ricky Sanders, Washington vs. Denver, 1988
    Michael Irvin, Dallas vs. Buffalo, 1993

INTERCEPTIONS BY
Most Interceptions By, Career
3   Chuck Howley, Dallas, 2 games
    Rod Martin, Oakland-L.A. Raiders, 2 games
2   Randy Beverly, N.Y. Jets, 1 game

Jake Scott, Miami, 3 games
Mike Wagner, Pittsburgh, 3 games
Mel Blount, Pittsburgh, 4 games
Eric Wright, San Francisco, 4 games
Barry Wilburn, Washington, 1 game
Brad Edwards, Washington, 1 game
Thomas Everett, Dallas, 2 games
James Washington, Dallas, 2 games

Most Interceptions By, Game
3   Rod Martin, Oakland vs. Philadelphia, 1981
2   Randy Beverly, N.Y. Jets vs. Baltimore, 1969
    Chuck Howley, Dallas vs. Baltimore, 1971
    Jake Scott, Miami vs. Washington, 1973
    Barry Wilburn, Washington vs. Denver, 1988
    Brad Edwards, Washington vs. Buffalo, 1992
    Thomas Everett, Dallas vs. Buffalo, 1993

YARDS GAINED
Most Yards Gained, Career
75   Willie Brown, Oakland, 2 games
63   Chuck Howley, Dallas, 2 games
     Jake Scott, Miami, 3 games
60   Herb Adderley, Green Bay-Dallas, 4 games

Most Yards Gained, Game
75   Willie Brown, Oakland vs. Minnesota, 1977
63   Jake Scott, Miami vs. Washington, 1973
60   Herb Adderley, Green Bay vs. Oakland, 1968

Longest Return
75   Willie Brown, Oakland vs. Minnesota, 1977 (TD)
60   Herb Adderley, Green Bay vs. Oakland, 1968 (TD)
55   Jake Scott, Miami vs. Washington, 1973

TOUCHDOWNS
Most Touchdowns, Game
1   Herb Adderley, Green Bay vs. Oakland, 1968
    Willie Brown, Oakland vs. Minnesota, 1977
    Jack Squirek, L.A. Raiders vs. Washington, 1984
    Reggie Phillips, Chicago vs. New England, 1986

PUNTING
Most Punts, Career
17   Mike Eischeid, Oakland-Minnesota, 3 games
15   Larry Seiple, Miami, 3 games
     Mike Horan, Denver, 3 games
14   Ron Widby, Dallas, 2 games
     Ray Guy, Oakland-L.A. Raiders, 3 games
     Chris Mohr, Buffalo, 3 games

Most Punts, Game
9   Ron Widby, Dallas vs. Baltimore, 1971
7   By eight players

Longest Punt
63   Lee Johnson, Cincinnati vs. San Francisco, 1989
62   Rich Camarillo, New England vs. Chicago, 1986
61   Jerrel Wilson, Kansas City vs. Green Bay, 1967

AVERAGE YARDAGE
Highest Average, Punting, Career (10 punts)
46.5   Jerrel Wilson, Kansas City, 2 games (11-511)
41.9   Ray Guy, Oakland-L.A. Raiders, 3 games (14-587)
41.3   Larry Seiple, Miami, 3 games (15-620)

Highest Average, Punting, Game (4 punts)
48.5   Jerrel Wilson, Kansas City vs. Minnesota, 1970 (4-194)
46.3   Jim Miller, San Francisco vs. Cincinnati, 1982 (4-185)
45.3   Jerrel Wilson, Kansas City vs. Green Bay, 1967 (7-317)

PUNT RETURNS
Most Punt Returns, Career
6   Willie Wood, Green Bay, 2 games
    Jake Scott, Miami, 3 games
    Theo Bell, Pittsburgh, 2 games
    Mike Nelms, Washington, 1 game
    John Taylor, San Francisco, 2 games
5   Dana McLemore, San Francisco, 1 game
4   By eight players

Most Punt Returns, Game
6   Mike Nelms, Washington vs. Miami, 1983
5   Willie Wood, Green Bay vs. Oakland, 1968
    Dana McLemore, San Francisco vs. Miami, 1985
4   By six players

Most Fair Catches, Game
3   Ron Gardin, Baltimore vs. Dallas, 1971
    Golden Richards, Dallas vs. Pittsburgh, 1976
    Greg Pruitt, L.A. Raiders vs. Washington, 1984

Al Edwards, Buffalo vs. N.Y. Giants, 1991
David Meggett, N.Y. Giants vs. Buffalo, 1991

YARDS GAINED
Most Yards Gained, Career
94 John Taylor, San Francisco, 2 games
52 Mike Nelms, Washington, 1 game
51 Dana McLemore, San Francisco, 1 game
Most Yards Gained, Game
56 John Taylor, San Francisco vs. Cincinnati, 1989
52 Mike Nelms, Washington vs. Miami, 1983
51 Dana McLemore, San Francisco vs. Miami, 1985
Longest Return
45 John Taylor, San Francisco vs. Cincinnati, 1989
34 Darrell Green, Washington vs. L.A. Raiders, 1984
31 Willie Wood, Green Bay vs. Oakland, 1968

AVERAGE YARDAGE
Highest Average, Career (4 returns)
15.7 John Taylor, San Francisco, 2 games (6-94)
10.8 Neal Colzie, Oakland, 1 game (4-43)
10.2 Dana McLemore, San Francisco, 1 game (5-51)
Highest Average, Game (3 returns)
18.7 John Taylor, San Francisco vs. Cincinnati, 1989 (3-56)
12.7 John Taylor, San Francisco vs. Denver, 1990 (3-38)
11.7 Kelvin Martin, Dallas vs. Buffalo, 1993 (3-35)

TOUCHDOWNS
Most Touchdowns, Game
None

KICKOFF RETURNS
Most Kickoff Returns, Career
10 Ken Bell, Denver, 3 games
8 Larry Anderson, Pittsburgh, 2 games
Fulton Walker, Miami, 2 games
7 Preston Pearson, Baltimore-Pittsburgh-Dallas, 5 games
Stephen Starring, New England, 1 game
Most Kickoff Returns, Game
7 Stephen Starring, New England vs. Chicago, 1986
6 Darren Carrington, Denver vs. San Francisco, 1990
5 Larry Anderson, Pittsburgh vs. Los Angeles, 1980
Billy Campfield, Philadelphia vs. Oakland, 1981
David Verser, Cincinnati vs. San Francisco, 1982
Alvin Garrett, Washington vs. L.A. Raiders, 1984
Ken Bell, Denver vs. Washington, 1988

YARDS GAINED
Most Yards Gained, Career
283 Fulton Walker, Miami, 2 games
207 Larry Anderson, Pittsburgh, 2 games
177 Ken Bell, Denver, 3 games
Most Yards Gained, Game
190 Fulton Walker, Miami vs. Washington, 1983
162 Larry Anderson, Pittsburgh vs. Los Angeles, 1980
153 Stephen Starring, New England vs. Chicago, 1986
Longest Return
98 Fulton Walker, Miami vs. Washington, 1983 (TD)
93 Stanford Jennings, Cincinnati vs. San Francisco, 1989 (TD)
67 Rick Upchurch, Denver vs. Dallas, 1978

AVERAGE YARDAGE
Highest Average, Career (4 returns)
35.4 Fulton Walker, Miami, 2 games (8-283)
25.9 Larry Anderson, Pittsburgh, 2 games (8-207)
24.3 Darren Carrington, Denver, 1 game (6-146)
Highest Average, Game (3 returns)
47.5 Fulton Walker, Miami vs. Washington, 1983 (4-190)
32.4 Larry Anderson, Pittsburgh vs. Los Angeles, 1980 (5-162)
31.3 Rick Upchurch, Denver vs. Dallas, 1978 (3-94)

TOUCHDOWNS
Most Touchdowns, Game
1 Fulton Walker, Miami vs. Washington, 1983
Stanford Jennings, Cincinnati vs. San Francisco, 1989

FUMBLES
Most Fumbles, Career
5 Roger Staubach, Dallas, 4 games
4 Jim Kelly, Buffalo, 4 games
3 Franco Harris, Pittsburgh, 4 games
Terry Bradshaw, Pittsburgh, 4 games
John Elway, Denver, 3 games

Frank Reich, Buffalo, 4 games
Thurman Thomas, Buffalo, 4 games
Most Fumbles, Game
3 Roger Staubach, Dallas vs. Pittsburgh, 1976
Jim Kelly, Buffalo vs. Washington, 1992
Frank Reich, Buffalo vs. Dallas, 1993
2 Franco Harris, Pittsburgh vs. Minnesota, 1975
Butch Johnson, Dallas vs. Denver, 1978
Terry Bradshaw, Pittsburgh vs. Dallas, 1979
Joe Montana, San Francisco vs. Cincinnati, 1989
John Elway, Denver vs. San Francisco, 1990
Thurman Thomas, Buffalo vs. Dallas, 1994

RECOVERIES
Most Fumbles Recovered, Career
2 Jake Scott, Miami, 3 games (1 own, 1 opp)
Fran Tarkenton, Minnesota, 3 games (2 own)
Franco Harris, Pittsburgh, 4 games (2 own)
Roger Staubach, Dallas, 4 games (2 own)
Bobby Walden, Pittsburgh, 2 games (2 own)
John Fitzgerald, Dallas, 4 games (2 own)
Randy Hughes, Dallas, 3 games (2 opp)
Butch Johnson, Dallas, 2 games (2 own)
Mike Singletary, Chicago, 1 game (2 opp)
John Elway, Denver, 3 games (2 own)
Jimmie Jones, Dallas, 2 games (2 opp)
Kenneth Davis, Buffalo, 4 games (2 own)
Most Fumbles Recovered, Game
2 Jake Scott, Miami vs. Minnesota, 1974 (1 own, 1 opp)
Roger Staubach, Dallas vs. Pittsburgh, 1976 (2 own)
Randy Hughes, Dallas vs. Denver, 1978 (2 opp)
Butch Johnson, Dallas vs. Denver, 1978 (2 own)
Mike Singletary, Chicago vs. New England, 1986 (2 opp)
Jimmie Jones, Dallas vs. Buffalo, 1993 (2 opp)

YARDS GAINED
Most Yards Gained, Game
64 Leon Lett, Dallas vs. Buffalo, 1993 (opp)
49 Mike Bass, Washington vs. Miami, 1973 (opp)
46 James Washington, Dallas vs. Buffalo, 1994 (opp)
Longest Return
64 Leon Lett, Dallas vs. Buffalo, 1993
49 Mike Bass, Washington vs. Miami, 1973 (TD)
46 James Washington, Dallas vs. Buffalo, 1994 (TD)

TOUCHDOWNS
Most Touchdowns, Game
1 Mike Bass, Washington vs. Miami, 1973 (opp 49 yds)
Mike Hegman, Dallas vs. Pittsburgh, 1979 (opp 37 yds)
Jimmie Jones, Dallas vs. Buffalo, 1993 (opp 2 yds)
Ken Norton, Dallas vs. Buffalo, 1993 (opp 9 yds)
James Washington, Dallas vs. Buffalo, 1994 (opp 46 yds)

COMBINED NET YARDS GAINED
(Rushing, receiving, interception returns, punt returns, kickoff returns, and fumble returns)
ATTEMPTS
Most Attempts, Career
108 Franco Harris, Pittsburgh, 4 games
72 Roger Craig, San Francisco, 3 games
Thurman Thomas, Buffalo, 4 games
66 John Riggins, Washington, 2 games
Most Attempts, Game
39 John Riggins, Washington vs. Miami, 1983
35 Franco Harris, Pittsburgh vs. Minnesota, 1975
34 Matt Snell, N.Y. Jets vs. Baltimore, 1969
Emmitt Smith, Dallas vs. Buffalo, 1994

YARDS GAINED
Most Yards Gained, Career
468 Franco Harris, Pittsburgh, 4 games
410 Roger Craig, San Francisco, 3 games
391 Lynn Swann, Pittsburgh, 4 games
Most Yards Gained, Game
235 Ricky Sanders, Washington vs. Denver, 1988
220 Jerry Rice, San Francisco vs. Cincinnati, 1989
213 Timmy Smith, Washington vs. Denver, 1988

SACKS
Sacks have been compiled since 1983.
Most Sacks, Career
3.5 Charles Haley, San Francisco-Dallas, 4 games
3 Danny Stubbs, San Francisco, 2 games

Leonard Marshall, N.Y. Giants, 2 games
Jeff Wright, Buffalo, 4 games
2.5 Dexter Manley, Washington, 3 games

Most Sacks, Game

2 Dwaine Board, San Francisco vs. Miami, 1985
Dennis Owens, New England vs. Chicago, 1986
Otis Wilson, Chicago vs. New England, 1986
Leonard Marshall, N.Y. Giants vs. Denver, 1987
Alvin Walton, Washington vs. Denver, 1988
Charles Haley, San Francisco vs. Cincinnati, 1989
Danny Stubbs, San Francisco vs. Denver, 1990
Jeff Wright, Buffalo vs. Dallas, 1994

TEAM RECORDS

GAMES, VICTORIES, DEFEATS

Most Games

7 Dallas, 1971-72, 1976, 1978-79, 1993-94
5 Miami, 1972-74, 1983, 1985
Washington, 1973, 1983-84, 1988, 1992
4 Minnesota, 1970, 1974-75, 1977
Pittsburgh, 1975-76, 1979-80
Oakland/L.A. Raiders, 1968, 1977, 1981, 1984
Denver, 1978, 1987-88, 1990
San Francisco, 1982, 1985, 1989-90
Buffalo, 1991-94

Most Consecutive Games

4 Buffalo, 1991-94
3 Miami, 1972-74
2 Green Bay, 1967-68
Dallas, 1971-72; 1978-79; 1993-94
Minnesota, 1974-75
Pittsburgh, 1975-76, 1979-80
Washington, 1983-84
Denver, 1987-88
San Francisco 1989-90

Most Games Won

4 Pittsburgh, 1975-76, 1979-80
San Francisco, 1982, 1985, 1989-90
Dallas, 1972, 1978, 1993-94
3 Oakland/L.A. Raiders, 1977, 1981, 1984
Washington, 1983, 1988, 1992
2 Green Bay, 1967-68
Miami, 1973-74
N.Y. Giants, 1987, 1991

Most Consecutive Games Won

2 Green Bay, 1967-68
Miami, 1973-74
Pittsburgh, 1975-76, 1979-80
San Francisco, 1989-90
Dallas, 1993-94

Most Games Lost

4 Minnesota, 1970, 1974-75, 1977
Denver, 1978, 1987-88, 1990
Buffalo, 1991-94
3 Dallas, 1971, 1976, 1979
Miami, 1972, 1983, 1985
2 Washington, 1973, 1984
Cincinnati, 1982, 1989

Most Consecutive Games Lost

4 Buffalo, 1991-94
2 Minnesota, 1974-75
Denver, 1987-88

SCORING

Most Points, Game

55 San Francisco vs. Denver, 1990
52 Dallas vs. Buffalo, 1993
46 Chicago vs. New England, 1986

Fewest Points, Game

3 Miami vs. Dallas, 1972
6 Minnesota vs. Pittsburgh, 1975
7 By four teams

Most Points, Both Teams, Game

69 Dallas (52) vs. Buffalo (17), 1993
66 Pittsburgh (35) vs. Dallas (31), 1979
65 San Francisco (55) vs. Denver (10), 1990

Fewest Points, Both Teams, Game

21 Washington (7) vs. Miami (14), 1973
22 Minnesota (6) vs. Pittsburgh (16), 1975
23 Baltimore (7) vs. N.Y. Jets (16), 1969

Largest Margin of Victory, Game

45 San Francisco vs. Denver, 1990 (55-10)

36 Chicago vs. New England, 1986 (46-10)
35 Dallas vs. Buffalo, 1993 (52-17)

Most Points, Each Half

1st: 35 Washington vs. Denver, 1988
2nd: 30 N.Y. Giants vs. Denver, 1987

Most Points, Each Quarter

1st: 14 Miami vs. Minnesota, 1974
Oakland vs. Philadelphia, 1981
Dallas vs. Buffalo, 1993
2nd: 35 Washington vs. Denver, 1988
3rd: 21 Chicago vs. New England, 1986
4th: 21 Dallas vs. Buffalo, 1993

Most Points, Both Teams, Each Half

1st: 45 Washington (35) vs. Denver (10), 1988
2nd: 44 Buffalo (24) vs. Washington (20), 1992

Fewest Points, Both Teams, Each Half

1st: 2 Minnesota (0) vs. Pittsburgh (2), 1975
2nd: 7 Miami (0) vs. Washington (7), 1973
Denver (0) vs. Washington (7), 1988

Most Points, Both Teams, Each Quarter

1st: 21 Dallas (14) vs. Buffalo (7), 1993
2nd: 35 Washington (35) vs. Denver (0), 1988
3rd: 24 Washington (14) vs. Buffalo (10), 1992
4th: 28 Dallas (14) vs. Pittsburgh (14), 1979

TOUCHDOWNS

Most Touchdowns, Game

8 San Francisco vs. Denver, 1990
7 Dallas vs. Buffalo, 1993
6 Washington vs. Denver, 1988

Fewest Touchdowns, Game

0 Miami vs. Dallas, 1972
1 By 17 teams

Most Touchdowns, Both Teams, Game

9 Pittsburgh (5) vs. Dallas (4), 1979
San Francisco (8) vs. Denver (1), 1990
Dallas (7) vs. Buffalo (2), 1993
7 N.Y. Giants (5) vs. Denver (2), 1987
Washington (6) vs. Denver (1), 1988
Washington (4) vs. Buffalo (3), 1992
6 Green Bay (5) vs. Kansas City (1), 1967
Oakland (4) vs. Minnesota (2), 1977
Pittsburgh (4) vs. Los Angeles (2), 1980
L.A. Raiders (5) vs. Washington (1), 1984
San Francisco (5) vs. Miami (1), 1985
Chicago (5) vs. New England (1), 1986

Fewest Touchdowns, Both Teams, Game

2 Baltimore (1) vs. N.Y. Jets (1), 1969
3 In six games

POINTS AFTER TOUCHDOWN

Most Points After Touchdown, Game

7 San Francisco vs. Denver, 1990
Dallas vs. Buffalo, 1993
6 Washington vs. Denver, 1988
5 Green Bay vs. Kansas City, 1967
Pittsburgh vs. Dallas, 1979
L.A. Raiders vs. Washington, 1984
San Francisco vs. Miami, 1985
Chicago vs. New England, 1986

Most Points After Touchdown, Both Teams, Game

9 Pittsburgh (5) vs. Dallas (4), 1979
Dallas (7) vs. Buffalo (2), 1993
8 San Francisco (7) vs. Denver (1), 1990
7 Washington (6) vs. Denver (1), 1988
Washington (4) vs. Buffalo (3), 1992

Fewest Points After Touchdown, Both Teams, Game

2 Baltimore (1) vs. N.Y. Jets (1), 1969
Baltimore (1) vs. Dallas (1), 1971
Minnesota (0) vs. Pittsburgh (2), 1975

FIELD GOALS

Most Field Goals Attempted, Game

5 N.Y. Jets vs. Baltimore, 1969
Dallas vs. Denver, 1978
4 Green Bay vs. Oakland, 1968
Pittsburgh vs. Dallas, 1976
San Francisco vs. Cincinnati, 1982; 1989
Denver vs. N.Y. Giants, 1987

Most Field Goals Attempted, Both Teams, Game

7 N.Y. Jets (5) vs. Baltimore (2), 1969
San Francisco (4) vs. Cincinnati (3), 1989
6 Dallas (5) vs. Denver (1), 1978

5   Green Bay (4) vs. Oakland (1), 1968
    Pittsburgh (4) vs. Dallas (1), 1976
    Oakland (3) vs. Philadelphia (2), 1981
    Denver (4) vs. N.Y. Giants (1), 1987
    Dallas (3) vs. Buffalo (2), 1994

Fewest Field Goals Attempted, Both Teams, Game
1   Minnesota (0) vs. Miami (1), 1974
    San Francisco (0) vs. Denver (1), 1990
2   Green Bay (0) vs. Kansas City (2), 1967
    Miami (1) vs. Washington (1), 1973
    Dallas (1) vs. Pittsburgh (1), 1979
    Dallas (1) vs. Buffalo (1), 1993

Most Field Goals, Game
4   Green Bay vs. Oakland, 1968
    San Francisco vs. Cincinnati, 1982
3   N.Y. Jets vs. Baltimore, 1969
    Kansas City vs. Minnesota, 1970
    Miami vs. San Francisco, 1985
    Chicago vs. New England, 1986
    Cincinnati vs. San Francisco, 1989
    Washington vs. Buffalo, 1992
    Dallas vs. Buffalo, 1994

Most Field Goals, Both Teams, Game
5   Cincinnati (3) vs. San Francisco (2), 1989
    Dallas (3) vs. Buffalo (2), 1994
4   Green Bay (4) vs. Oakland (0), 1968
    San Francisco (4) vs. Cincinnati (0), 1982
    Miami (3) vs. San Francisco (1), 1985
    Chicago (3) vs. New England (1), 1986
    Buffalo (2) vs. N.Y. Giants (2), 1991
    Washington (3) vs. Buffalo (1), 1992
3   In eight games

Fewest Field Goals, Both Teams, Game
0   Miami vs. Washington, 1973
    Pittsburgh vs. Minnesota, 1975
1   Green Bay (0) vs. Kansas City (1), 1967
    Minnesota (0) vs. Miami (1), 1974
    Pittsburgh (0) vs. Dallas (1), 1979
    Washington (0) vs. Denver (1), 1988
    San Francisco (0) vs. Denver (1), 1990

SAFETIES
Most Safeties, Game
1   Pittsburgh vs. Minnesota, 1975; vs. Dallas, 1976
    Chicago vs. New England, 1986
    N.Y. Giants vs. Denver, 1987
    Buffalo vs. N.Y. Giants, 1991

FIRST DOWNS
Most First Downs, Game
31 San Francisco vs. Miami, 1985
28 San Francisco vs. Denver, 1990
25 Washington vs. Denver, 1988
    Buffalo vs. Washington, 1992

Fewest First Downs, Game
9   Minnesota vs. Pittsburgh, 1975
    Miami vs. Washington, 1983
10 Dallas vs. Baltimore, 1971
    Miami vs. Dallas, 1972
11 Denver vs. Dallas, 1978

Most First Downs, Both Teams, Game
50 San Francisco (31) vs. Miami (19), 1985
49 Buffalo (25) vs. Washington (24), 1992
47 N.Y. Giants (24) vs. Denver (23), 1987

Fewest First Downs, Both Teams, Game
24 Dallas (10) vs. Baltimore (14), 1971
26 Minnesota (9) vs. Pittsburgh (17), 1975
27 Pittsburgh (13) vs. Dallas (14), 1976

RUSHING
Most First Downs, Rushing, Game
16 San Francisco vs. Miami, 1985
15 Dallas vs. Miami, 1972
14 Washington vs. Miami, 1983
    San Francisco vs. Denver, 1990

Fewest First Downs, Rushing, Game
1   New England vs. Chicago, 1986
2   Minnesota vs. Kansas City, 1970; vs. Pittsburgh, 1975;
        vs. Oakland, 1977
    Pittsburgh vs. Dallas, 1979
    Miami vs. San Francisco, 1985
3   Miami vs. Dallas, 1972
    Philadelphia vs. Oakland, 1981

Most First Downs, Rushing, Both Teams, Game
21 Washington (14) vs. Miami (7), 1983
19 Washington (13) vs. Denver (6), 1988
    San Francisco (14) vs. Denver (5), 1990
18 Dallas (15) vs. Miami (3), 1972
    Miami (13) vs. Minnesota (5), 1974
    San Francisco (16) vs. Miami (2), 1985
    N.Y. Giants (10) vs. Buffalo (8), 1991

Fewest First Downs, Rushing, Both Teams, Game
8   Baltimore (4) vs. Dallas (4), 1971
    Pittsburgh (2) vs. Dallas (6), 1979
9   Philadelphia (3) vs. Oakland (6), 1981
10 Minnesota (2) vs. Kansas City (8), 1970

PASSING
Most First Downs, Passing, Game
18 Buffalo vs. Washington, 1992
17 Miami vs. San Francisco, 1985
16 Denver vs. N.Y. Giants, 1987
    San Francisco vs. Cincinnati, 1989

Fewest First Downs, Passing, Game
1   Denver vs. Dallas, 1978
2   Miami vs. Washington, 1983
4   Miami vs. Minnesota, 1974

Most First Downs, Passing, Both Teams, Game
32 Miami (17) vs. San Francisco (15), 1985
30 Buffalo (18) vs. Washington (12), 1992
29 Denver (16) vs. N.Y. Giants (13), 1987
    Buffalo (15) vs. Dallas (14), 1994

Fewest First Downs, Passing, Both Teams, Game
9   Denver (1) vs. Dallas (8), 1978
10 Minnesota (5) vs. Pittsburgh (5), 1975
11 Dallas (5) vs. Baltimore (6), 1971
    Miami (2) vs. Washington (9), 1983

PENALTY
Most First Downs, Penalty, Game
4   Baltimore vs. Dallas, 1971
    Miami vs. Minnesota, 1974
    Cincinnati vs. San Francisco, 1982
    Buffalo vs. Dallas, 1993
3   Kansas City vs. Minnesota, 1970
    Minnesota vs. Oakland, 1977
    Buffalo vs. Washington, 1992

Most First Downs, Penalty, Both Teams, Game
6   Cincinnati (4) vs. San Francisco (2), 1982
5   Baltimore (4) vs. Dallas (1), 1971
    Miami (4) vs. Minnesota (1), 1974
    Buffalo (3) vs. Washington (2), 1992
4   Kansas City (3) vs. Minnesota (1), 1970
    Buffalo (4) vs. Dallas (0), 1993

Fewest First Downs, Penalty, Both Teams, Game
0   Dallas vs. Miami, 1972
    Miami vs. Washington, 1973
    Dallas vs. Pittsburgh, 1976
    Miami vs. San Francisco, 1985
1   Green Bay (0) vs. Kansas City (1), 1967
    Miami (0) vs. Washington (1), 1983
    Cincinnati (0) vs. San Francisco (1), 1989
    San Francisco (0) vs. Denver (1), 1990
    Dallas (0) vs. Buffalo (1), 1994

NET YARDS GAINED RUSHING AND PASSING
Most Yards Gained, Game
602 Washington vs. Denver, 1988
537 San Francisco vs. Miami, 1985
461 San Francisco vs. Denver, 1990

Fewest Yards Gained, Game
119 Minnesota vs. Pittsburgh, 1975
123 New England vs. Chicago, 1986
156 Denver vs. Dallas, 1978

Most Yards Gained, Both Teams, Game
929 Washington (602) vs. Denver (327), 1988
851 San Francisco (537) vs. Miami (314), 1985
782 Oakland (429) vs. Minnesota (353), 1977

Fewest Yards Gained, Both Teams, Game
452 Minnesota (119) vs. Pittsburgh (333), 1975
481 Washington (228) vs. Miami (253), 1973
     Denver (156) vs. Dallas (325), 1978
497 Minnesota (238) vs. Miami (259), 1974

SUPER BOWL RECORDS

RUSHING

ATTEMPTS

Most Attempts, Game
- 57 Pittsburgh vs. Minnesota, 1975
- 53 Miami vs. Minnesota, 1974
- 52 Oakland vs. Minnesota, 1977
- Washington vs. Miami, 1983

Fewest Attempts, Game
- 9 Miami vs. San Francisco, 1985
- 11 New England vs. Chicago, 1986
- 17 Denver vs. Washington, 1988; vs. San Francisco, 1990

Most Attempts, Both Teams, Game
- 81 Washington (52) vs. Miami (29), 1983
- 78 Pittsburgh (57) vs. Minnesota (21), 1975
- Oakland (52) vs. Minnesota (26), 1977
- 77 Miami (53) vs. Minnesota (24), 1974
- Pittsburgh (46) vs. Dallas (31), 1976

Fewest Attempts, Both Teams, Game
- 49 Miami (9) vs. San Francisco (40), 1985
- 53 Kansas City (19) vs. Green Bay (34), 1967
- 55 San Francisco (27) vs. Cincinnati (28), 1989

YARDS GAINED

Most Yards Gained, Game
- 280 Washington vs. Denver, 1988
- 276 Washington vs. Miami, 1983
- 266 Oakland vs. Minnesota, 1977

Fewest Yards Gained, Game
- 7 New England vs. Chicago, 1986
- 17 Minnesota vs. Pittsburgh, 1975
- 25 Miami vs. San Francisco, 1985

Most Yards Gained, Both Teams, Game
- 377 Washington (280) vs. Denver (97), 1988
- 372 Washington (276) vs. Miami (96), 1983
- 338 N.Y. Giants (172) vs. Buffalo (166), 1991

Fewest Yards Gained, Both Teams, Game
- 168 Buffalo (43) vs. Washington (125), 1992
- 171 Baltimore (69) vs. Dallas (102), 1971
- 174 New England (7) vs. Chicago (167), 1986

AVERAGE GAIN

Highest Average Gain, Game
- 7.00 L.A. Raiders vs. Washington, 1984 (33-231)
- Washington vs. Denver, 1988 (40-280)
- 6.64 Buffalo vs. N.Y. Giants, 1991 (25-166)
- 6.22 Baltimore vs. N.Y. Jets, 1969 (23-143)

Lowest Average Gain, Game
- 0.64 New England vs. Chicago, 1986 (11-7)
- 0.81 Minnesota vs. Pittsburgh, 1975 (21-17)
- 2.23 Baltimore vs. Dallas, 1971 (31-69)

TOUCHDOWNS

Most Touchdowns, Game
- 4 Chicago vs. New England, 1986
- 3 Green Bay vs. Kansas City, 1967
- Miami vs. Minnesota, 1974
- San Francisco vs. Denver, 1990
- 2 Oakland vs. Minnesota, 1977
- Pittsburgh vs. Los Angeles, 1980
- L.A. Raiders vs. Washington, 1984
- San Francisco vs. Miami, 1985
- N.Y. Giants vs. Denver, 1987
- Washington vs. Denver, 1988; vs. Buffalo, 1992
- Buffalo vs. N.Y. Giants, 1991

Fewest Touchdowns, Game
- 0 By 17 teams

Most Touchdowns, Both Teams, Game
- 4 Miami (3) vs. Minnesota (1), 1974
- Chicago (4) vs. New England (0), 1986
- San Francisco (3) vs. Denver (1), 1990
- 3 Green Bay (3) vs. Kansas City (0), 1967
- Pittsburgh (2) vs. Los Angeles (1), 1980
- L.A. Raiders (2) vs. Washington (1), 1984
- N.Y. Giants (2) vs. Denver (1), 1987
- Buffalo (2) vs. N.Y. Giants (1), 1991
- Washington (2) vs. Buffalo (1), 1992
- Dallas (2) vs. Buffalo (1), 1994

Fewest Touchdowns, Both Teams, Game
- 0 Pittsburgh vs. Dallas, 1976
- Oakland vs. Philadelphia, 1981
- Cincinnati vs. San Francisco, 1989
- 1 In seven games

PASSING

ATTEMPTS

Most Passes Attempted, Game
- 59 Buffalo vs. Washington, 1992
- 50 Miami vs. San Francisco, 1985
- Buffalo vs. Dallas, 1994
- 44 Minnesota vs. Oakland, 1977

Fewest Passes Attempted, Game
- 7 Miami vs. Minnesota, 1974
- 11 Miami vs. Washington, 1973
- 14 Pittsburgh vs. Minnesota, 1975

Most Passes Attempted, Both Teams, Game
- 92 Buffalo (59) vs. Washington (33), 1992
- 85 Miami (50) vs. San Francisco (35), 1985
- 77 Buffalo (50) vs. Dallas (27), 1994

Fewest Passes Attempted, Both Teams, Game
- 35 Miami (7) vs. Minnesota (28), 1974
- 39 Miami (11) vs. Washington (28), 1973
- 40 Pittsburgh (14) vs. Minnesota (26), 1975
- Miami (17) vs. Washington (23), 1983

COMPLETIONS

Most Passes Completed, Game
- 31 Buffalo vs. Dallas, 1994
- 29 Miami vs. San Francisco, 1985
- Buffalo vs. Washington, 1992
- 26 Denver vs. N.Y. Giants, 1987

Fewest Passes Completed, Game
- 4 Miami vs. Washington, 1983
- 6 Miami vs. Minnesota, 1974
- 8 Miami vs. Washington, 1973
- Denver vs. Dallas, 1978

Most Passes Completed, Both Teams, Game
- 53 Miami (29) vs. San Francisco (24), 1985
- 50 Buffalo (31) vs. Dallas (19), 1994
- 48 Denver (26) vs. N.Y. Giants (22), 1987

Fewest Passes Completed, Both Teams, Game
- 19 Miami (4) vs. Washington (15), 1983
- 20 Pittsburgh (9) vs. Minnesota (11), 1975
- 22 Miami (8) vs. Washington (14), 1973

COMPLETION PERCENTAGE

Highest Completion Percentage, Game (20 attempts)
- 88.0 N.Y. Giants vs. Denver, 1987 (25-22)
- 75.0 San Francisco vs. Denver, 1990 (32-24)
- 73.5 Cincinnati vs. San Francisco, 1982 (34-25)

Lowest Completion Percentage, Game (20 attempts)
- 32.0 Denver vs. Dallas, 1978 (25-8)
- 37.9 Denver vs. San Francisco, 1990 (29-11)
- 38.5 Denver vs. Washington, 1988 (39-15)

YARDS GAINED

Most Yards Gained, Game
- 341 San Francisco vs. Cincinnati, 1989
- 326 San Francisco vs. Miami, 1985
- 322 Washington vs. Denver, 1988

Fewest Yards Gained, Game
- 35 Denver vs. Dallas, 1978
- 63 Miami vs. Minnesota, 1974
- 69 Miami vs. Washington, 1973

Most Yards Gained, Both Teams, Game
- 615 San Francisco (326) vs. Miami (289), 1985
- 583 Denver (320) vs. N.Y. Giants (263), 1987
- 552 Washington (322) vs. Denver (230), 1988

Fewest Yards Gained, Both Teams, Game
- 156 Miami (69) vs. Washington (87), 1973
- 186 Pittsburgh (84) vs. Minnesota (102), 1975
- 205 Dallas (100) vs. Miami (105), 1972

TIMES SACKED

Most Times Sacked, Game
- 7 Dallas vs. Pittsburgh, 1976
- New England vs. Chicago, 1986
- 6 Kansas City vs. Green Bay, 1967
- Washington vs. L.A. Raiders, 1984
- Denver vs. San Francisco, 1990
- 5 Dallas vs. Denver, 1978; vs. Pittsburgh, 1979
- Cincinnati vs. San Francisco, 1982; 1989
- Denver vs. Washington, 1988
- Buffalo vs. Washington, 1992

Fewest Times Sacked, Game
- 0 Baltimore vs. N.Y. Jets, 1969; vs. Dallas, 1971
- Minnesota vs. Pittsburgh, 1975

Pittsburgh vs. Los Angeles, 1980
Philadelphia vs. Oakland, 1981
Washington vs. Buffalo, 1992
1 By 11 teams

Most Times Sacked, Both Teams, Game

10 New England (7) vs. Chicago (3), 1986
9 Kansas City (6) vs. Green Bay (3), 1967
Dallas (7) vs. Pittsburgh (2), 1976
Dallas (5) vs. Denver (4), 1978
Dallas (5) vs. Pittsburgh (4), 1979
Cincinnati (5) vs. San Francisco (4), 1989
8 Washington (6) vs. L.A. Raiders (2), 1984

Fewest Times Sacked, Both Teams, Game

1 Philadelphia (0) vs. Oakland (1), 1981
2 Baltimore (0) vs. N.Y. Jets (2), 1969
Baltimore (0) vs. Dallas (2), 1971
Minnesota (0) vs. Pittsburgh (2), 1975
3 In four games

TOUCHDOWNS
Most Touchdowns, Game

5 San Francisco vs. Denver, 1990
4 Pittsburgh vs. Dallas, 1979
Washington vs. Denver, 1988
Dallas vs. Buffalo, 1993
3 Dallas vs. Pittsburgh, 1979
Oakland vs. Philadelphia, 1981
San Francisco vs. Miami, 1985
N.Y. Giants vs. Denver, 1987

Fewest Touchdowns, Game

0 By 16 teams

Most Touchdowns, Both Teams, Game

7 Pittsburgh (4) vs. Dallas (3), 1979
5 Washington (4) vs. Denver (1), 1988
San Francisco (5) vs. Denver (0), 1990
Dallas (4) vs. Buffalo (1), 1993
4 Dallas (2) vs. Pittsburgh (2), 1976
Oakland (3) vs. Philadelphia (1), 1981
San Francisco (3) vs. Miami (1), 1985
N.Y. Giants (3) vs. Denver (1), 1987
Washington (2) vs. Buffalo (2), 1992

Fewest Touchdowns, Both Teams, Game

0 N.Y. Jets vs. Baltimore, 1969
Miami vs. Minnesota, 1974
Buffalo vs. Dallas, 1994
1 In six games

INTERCEPTIONS BY
Most Interceptions By, Game

4 N.Y. Jets vs. Baltimore, 1969
Dallas vs. Denver, 1978
Washington vs. Buffalo, 1992
Dallas vs. Buffalo, 1993
3 By nine teams

Most Interceptions By, Both Teams, Game

6 Baltimore (3) vs. Dallas (3), 1971
5 Washington (4) vs. Buffalo (1), 1992
4 In seven games

Fewest Interceptions By, Both Teams, Game

0 Buffalo vs. N.Y. Giants, 1991
1 Oakland (0) vs. Green Bay (1), 1968
Miami (0) vs. Dallas (1), 1972
Minnesota (0) vs. Miami (1), 1974
N.Y. Giants (0) vs. Denver (1), 1987
San Francisco (1) vs. Cincinnati (0), 1989

YARDS GAINED
Most Yards Gained, Game

95 Miami vs. Washington, 1973
91 Oakland vs. Minnesota, 1977
89 Pittsburgh vs. Dallas, 1976

Most Yards Gained, Both Teams, Game

95 Miami (95) vs. Washington (0), 1973
91 Oakland (91) vs. Minnesota (0), 1977
89 Pittsburgh (89) vs. Dallas (0), 1976

TOUCHDOWNS
Most Touchdowns, Game

1 Green Bay vs. Oakland, 1968
Oakland vs. Minnesota, 1977
L.A. Raiders vs. Washington, 1984
Chicago vs. New England, 1986

PUNTING
Most Punts, Game

9 Dallas vs. Baltimore, 1971
8 Washington vs. L.A. Raiders, 1984
7 By seven teams

Fewest Punts, Game

2 Pittsburgh vs. Los Angeles, 1980
Denver vs. N.Y. Giants, 1987
3 By 10 teams

Most Punts, Both Teams, Game

15 Washington (8) vs. L.A. Raiders (7), 1984
13 Dallas (9) vs. Baltimore (4), 1971
Pittsburgh (7) vs. Minnesota (6), 1975
12 In three games

Fewest Punts, Both Teams, Game

5 Denver (2) vs. N.Y. Giants (3), 1987
6 Oakland (3) vs. Philadelphia (3), 1981
7 In five games

AVERAGE YARDAGE
Highest Average, Game (4 punts)

48.50 Kansas City vs. Minnesota, 1970 (4-194)
46.25 San Francisco vs. Cincinnati, 1982 (4-185)
45.29 Kansas City vs. Green Bay, 1967 (7-317)

Lowest Average, Game (4 punts)

31.20 Washington vs. Miami, 1973 (5-156)
32.38 Washington vs. L.A. Raiders, 1984 (8-259)
32.40 Oakland vs. Minnesota, 1977 (5-162)

PUNT RETURNS
Most Punt Returns, Game

6 Washington vs. Miami, 1983
5 By five teams

Fewest Punt Returns, Game

0 Minnesota vs. Miami, 1974
Buffalo vs. N.Y. Giants, 1991
Washington vs. Buffalo, 1992
1 By 12 teams

Most Punt Returns, Both Teams, Game

9 Pittsburgh (5) vs. Minnesota (4), 1975
8 Green Bay (5) vs. Oakland (3), 1968
Baltimore (5) vs. Dallas (3), 1971
Washington (6) vs. Miami (2), 1983
7 Green Bay (4) vs. Kansas City (3), 1967
Oakland (4) vs. Minnesota (3), 1977
San Francisco (5) vs. Miami (2), 1985

Fewest Punt Returns, Both Teams, Game

2 Dallas (1) vs. Miami (1), 1972
Denver (1) vs. N.Y. Giants (1), 1987
Buffalo (0) vs. N.Y. Giants (2), 1991
Buffalo (1) vs. Dallas (1), 1994
3 Kansas City (1) vs. Minnesota (2), 1970
Minnesota (0) vs. Miami (3), 1974
Washington (1) vs. Denver (2), 1988
Washington (0) vs. Buffalo (3), 1992
4 L.A. Raiders (2) vs. Washington (2), 1984
Chicago (2) vs. New England (2), 1986
Buffalo (1) vs. Dallas (3), 1993

YARDS GAINED
Most Yards Gained, Game

56 San Francisco vs. Cincinnati, 1989
52 Washington vs. Miami, 1983
51 San Francisco vs. Miami, 1985

Fewest Yards Gained, Game

−1 Dallas vs. Miami, 1972
0 By eight teams

Most Yards Gained, Both Teams, Game

74 Washington (52) vs. Miami (22), 1983
66 San Francisco (51) vs. Miami (15), 1985
61 San Francisco (56) vs. Cincinnati (5), 1989

Fewest Yards Gained, Both Teams, Game

9 Washington (0) vs. Bufffalo (9), 1992
10 Buffalo (5) vs. Dallas (5), 1994
13 Miami (4) vs. Washington (9), 1973

AVERAGE RETURN
Highest Average, Game (3 returns)

18.7 San Francisco vs. Cincinnati, 1989 (3-56)
12.7 San Francisco vs. Denver, 1990 (3-38)
11.7 Dallas vs. Buffalo, 1993 (3-35)

TOUCHDOWNS
Most Touchdowns, Game
   None

KICKOFF RETURNS

Most Kickoff Returns, Game
   9   Denver vs. San Francisco, 1990
   7   Oakland vs. Green Bay, 1968
      Minnesota vs. Oakland, 1977
      Cincinnati vs. San Francisco, 1982
      Washington vs. L.A. Raiders, 1984
      Miami vs. San Francisco, 1985
      New England vs. Chicago, 1986
   6   By eight teams
Fewest Kickoff Returns, Game
   1   N.Y. Jets vs. Baltimore, 1969
      L.A. Raiders vs. Washington, 1984
      Washington vs. Buffalo, 1992
   2   By seven teams
Most Kickoff Returns, Both Teams, Game
   12   Denver (9) vs. San Francisco (3), 1990
   11   Los Angeles (6) vs. Pittsburgh (5), 1980
      Miami (7) vs. San Francisco (4), 1985
      New England (7) vs. Chicago (4), 1986
   10   Oakland (7) vs. Green Bay (3), 1968
Fewest Kickoff Returns, Both Teams, Game
   5   N.Y. Jets (1) vs. Baltimore (4), 1969
      Miami (2) vs. Washington (3), 1973
      Washington (1) vs. Buffalo (4), 1992
   6   In three games

YARDS GAINED

Most Yards Gained, Game
   222   Miami vs. Washington, 1983
   196   Denver vs. San Francisco, 1990
   173   Denver vs. Dallas, 1978
Fewest Yards Gained, Game
   16   Washington vs. Buffalo, 1992
   17   L.A. Raiders vs. Washington, 1984
   25   N.Y. Jets vs. Baltimore, 1969
Most Yards Gained, Both Teams, Game
   279   Miami (222) vs. Washington (57), 1983
   245   Denver (196) vs. San Francisco (49), 1990
   231   Pittsburgh (162) vs. Los Angeles (79), 1980
Fewest Yards Gained, Both Teams, Game
   78   Miami (33) vs. Washington (45), 1973
   82   Pittsburgh (32) vs. Minnesota (50), 1975
   92   San Francisco (40) vs. Cincinnati (52), 1982

AVERAGE GAIN

Highest Average, Game (3 returns)
   44.0   Cincinnati vs. San Francisco, 1989 (3-132)
   37.0   Miami vs. Washington, 1983 (6-222)
   32.4   Pittsburgh vs. Los Angeles, 1980 (5-162)

TOUCHDOWNS

Most Touchdowns, Game
   1   Miami vs. Washington, 1983
      Cincinnati vs. San Francisco, 1989

PENALTIES

Most Penalties, Game
   12   Dallas vs. Denver, 1978
   10   Dallas vs. Baltimore, 1971
   9   Dallas vs. Pittsburgh, 1979
Fewest Penalties, Game
   0   Miami vs. Dallas, 1972
      Pittsburgh vs. Dallas, 1976
      Denver vs. San Francisco, 1990
   1   Green Bay vs. Oakland, 1968
      Miami vs. Minnesota, 1974; vs. San Francisco, 1985
      Buffalo vs. Dallas, 1994
   2   By four teams
Most Penalties, Both Teams, Game
   20   Dallas (12) vs. Denver (8), 1978
   16   Cincinnati (8) vs. San Francisco (8), 1982
   14   Dallas (10) vs. Baltimore (4), 1971
      Dallas (9) vs. Pittsburgh (5), 1979
Fewest Penalties, Both Teams, Game
   2   Pittsburgh (0) vs. Dallas (2), 1976
   3   Miami (0) vs. Dallas (3), 1972
      Miami (1) vs. San Francisco (2), 1985
   4   Denver (0) vs. San Francisco (4), 1990

YARDS PENALIZED

Most Yards Penalized, Game
   133   Dallas vs. Baltimore, 1971
   122   Pittsburgh vs. Minnesota, 1975
   94   Dallas vs. Denver, 1978
Fewest Yards Penalized, Game
   0   Miami vs. Dallas, 1972
      Pittsburgh vs. Dallas, 1976
      Denver vs. San Francisco, 1990
   4   Miami vs. Minnesota, 1974
   10   Miami vs. San Francisco, 1985
      San Francisco vs. Miami, 1985
      Buffalo vs. Dallas, 1994
Most Yards Penalized, Both Teams, Game
   164   Dallas (133) vs. Baltimore (31), 1971
   154   Dallas (94) vs. Denver (60), 1978
   140   Pittsburgh (122) vs. Minnesota (18), 1975
Fewest Yards Penalized, Both Teams, Game
   15   Miami (0) vs. Dallas (15), 1972
   20   Pittsburgh (0) vs. Dallas (20), 1976
      Miami (10) vs. San Francisco (10), 1985
   38   Denver (0) vs. San Francisco (38), 1990

FUMBLES

Most Fumbles, Game
   8   Buffalo vs. Dallas, 1993
   6   Dallas vs. Denver, 1978
      Buffalo vs. Washington, 1992
   5   Baltimore vs. Dallas, 1971
Fewest Fumbles, Game
   0   By 11 teams
Most Fumbles, Both Teams, Game
   12   Buffalo (8) vs. Dallas (4), 1993
   10   Dallas (6) vs. Denver (4), 1978
   8   Dallas (4) vs. Pittsburgh (4), 1976
Fewest Fumbles, Both Teams, Game
   0   Los Angeles vs. Pittsburgh, 1980
   1   Oakland (0) vs. Minnesota (1), 1977
      Oakland (0) vs. Philadelphia (1), 1981
      Denver (0) vs. Washington (1), 1988
      N.Y. Giants (0) vs. Buffalo (1), 1991
   2   In four games
Most Fumbles Lost, Game
   5   Buffalo vs. Dallas, 1993
   4   Baltimore vs. Dallas, 1971
      Denver vs. Dallas, 1978
      New England vs. Chicago, 1986
   2   In many games
Most Fumbles Lost, Both Teams, Game
   7   Buffalo (5) vs. Dallas (2), 1993
   6   Denver (4) vs. Dallas (2), 1978
      New England (4) vs. Chicago (2), 1986
   5   Baltimore (4) vs. Dallas (1), 1971
Fewest Fumbles Lost, Both Teams, Game
   0   Green Bay vs. Kansas City, 1967
      Dallas vs. Pittsburgh, 1976
      Los Angeles vs. Pittsburgh, 1980
      Denver vs. N.Y. Giants, 1987
      Denver vs. Washington, 1988
      Buffalo vs. N.Y. Giants, 1991
Most Fumbles Recovered, Game
   8   Dallas vs. Denver, 1978 (4 own, 4 opp.)
   6   Dallas vs. Buffalo, 1993 (1 own, 5 opp.)
   5   Chicago vs. New England, 1986 (1 own, 4 opp.)

TURNOVERS

(Number of times losing the ball on interceptions and fumbles.)
Most Turnovers, Game
   9   Buffalo vs. Dallas, 1993
   8   Denver vs. Dallas, 1978
   7   Baltimore vs. Dallas, 1971
Fewest Turnovers, Game
   0   Green Bay vs. Oakland, 1968
      Miami vs. Minnesota, 1974
      Pittsburgh vs. Dallas, 1976
      Oakland vs. Minnesota, 1977; vs. Philadelphia, 1981
      N.Y. Giants vs. Denver, 1987; vs. Buffalo, 1991
      San Francisco vs. Denver, 1990
      Buffalo vs. N.Y. Giants, 1991
   1   By many teams
Most Turnovers, Both Teams, Game
   11   Baltimore (7) vs. Dallas (4), 1971
      Buffalo (9) vs. Dallas (2), 1993

10   Denver (8) vs. Dallas (2), 1978
 8   New England (6) vs. Chicago (2), 1986
Fewest Turnovers, Both Teams, Game
 0   Buffalo vs. N.Y. Giants, 1991
 1   N.Y. Giants (0) vs. Denver (1), 1987
 2   Green Bay (1) vs. Kansas City (1), 1967
     Miami (0) vs. Minnesota (2), 1974
     Cincinnati (1) vs. San Francisco (1), 1989

Compiled by Elias Sports Bureau

Throughout this all-time postseason record section, the following abbreviations are used to indicate various levels of postseason games:

SB	Super Bowl (1966 to date)
AFC	AFC Championship Game (1970 to date) or AFL Championship Game (1960-69)
NFC	NFC Championship Game (1970 to date) or NFL Championship Game (1933-69)
AFC-D	AFC Divisional Playoff Game (1970 to date), AFC Second-Round Playoff Game (1982), AFL Inter-Divisional Playoff Game (1969), or special playoff game to break tie for AFL Division Championship (1963, 1968)
NFC-D	NFC Divisional Playoff Game (1970 to date), NFC Second-Round Playoff Game (1982), NFL Conference Championship Game (1967-69), or special playoff game to break tie for NFL Division or Conference Championship (1941, 1943, 1947, 1950, 1952, 1957, 1958, 1965)
AFC-FR	AFC First-Round Playoff Game (1978 to date)
NFC-FR	NFC First-Round Playoff Game (1978 to date)

POSTSEASON GAME COMPOSITE STANDINGS

	W	L	PCT.	PTS.	OP
Green Bay Packers	14	6	.700	461	310
San Francisco 49ers	18	11	.621	712	536
Dallas Cowboys	27	17	.614	1039	789
Washington Redskins*	21	14	.600	738	625
Pittsburgh Steelers	16	11	.593	609	545
Los Angeles Raiders**	21	15	.583	855	659
Miami Dolphins	16	12	.571	627	557
Buffalo Bills	13	11	.542	563	520
Detroit Lions	7	6	.538	293	283
Chicago Bears	13	13	.500	529	490
Indianapolis Colts***	8	8	.500	285	300
Kansas City Chiefs****	8	8	.500	267	333
Denver Broncos	9	10	.474	380	502
Philadelphia Eagles	8	9	.471	290	288
New York Jets	5	6	.455	216	200
New York Giants	14	18	.438	529	593
Minnesota Vikings	13	17	.433	535	611
Seattle Seahawks	3	4	.429	128	139
Cincinnati Bengals	5	7	.417	246	257
Houston Oilers	9	13	.409	371	533
New England Patriots†	4	6	.400	195	258
Los Angeles Rams††	13	20	.394	501	697
Cleveland Browns	10	18	.357	567	650
San Diego Chargers†††	5	9	.357	247	310
Atlanta Falcons	2	4	.333	119	144
Tampa Bay Buccaneers	1	3	.250	41	94
Phoenix Cardinals††††	1	4	.200	81	134
New Orleans Saints	0	4	.000	56	123

*One game played when franchise was in Boston (lost 21-6).
**24 games played when franchise was in Oakland (won 15, lost 9, 587 points scored, 435 points allowed).
***15 games played when franchise was in Baltimore (won 8, lost 7, 264 points scored, 262 points allowed).
****One game played when franchise was Dallas Texans (won 20-17).
†Two games played when franchise was in Boston (won 26-8, lost 51-10).
††One game played when franchise was in Cleveland (won 15-14).
†††One game played when franchise was in Los Angeles (lost 24-16).
††††Two games played when franchise was in Chicago (won 28-21, lost 7-0), three games played when franchise was in St. Louis (lost 30-14, lost 35-23, lost 41-16).

INDIVIDUAL RECORDS

SERVICE

Most Games, Career
27 D.D. Lewis, Dallas (SB 5, NFC 9, NFC-D 12, NFC-FR 1)
26 Larry Cole, Dallas (SB 5, NFC 8, NFC-D 12, NFC-FR 1)
25 Charlie Waters, Dallas (SB 5, NFC 9, NFC-D 10, NFC-FR 1)

Most Games, Head Coach
36 Tom Landry, Dallas
33 Don Shula, Baltimore-Miami
24 Chuck Noll, Pittsburgh

Most Games Won, Head Coach
20 Tom Landry, Dallas
18 Don Shula, Baltimore-Miami
16 Chuck Noll, Pittsburgh
   Joe Gibbs, Washington

Most Games Lost, Head Coach
16 Tom Landry, Dallas
15 Don Shula, Baltimore-Miami
12 Bud Grant, Minnesota

SCORING

POINTS

Most Points, Career
115 George Blanda, Chi. Bears-Houston-Oakland, 19 games (49-pat, 22-fg)
102 Franco Harris, Pittsburgh, 19 games (17-td)
96 Matt Bahr, Pittsburgh-Cleveland-N.Y. Giants, 13 games (39-pat, 19-fg)

Most Points, Game
30 Ricky Watters, NFC-D:San Francisco vs. N.Y. Giants, 1993 (5-td)
19 Pat Harder, NFC-D: Detroit vs. Los Angeles, 1952 (2-td, 4-pat, 1-fg)
   Paul Hornung, NFC: Green Bay vs. N.Y. Giants, 1961 (1-td, 4-pat, 3-fg)
18 By 22 players

TOUCHDOWNS

Most Touchdowns, Career
17 Franco Harris, Pittsburgh, 19 games (16-r, 1-p)
15 Thurman Thomas, Buffalo, 16 games (12-r, 3-p)
13 Jerry Rice, San Francisco, 15 games (13-p)
   Marcus Allen, L.A. Raiders-Kansas City, 13 games (11-r, 2-p)

Most Touchdowns, Game
5 Ricky Watters, NFC-D:San Francisco vs. N.Y. Giants, 1993 (5-r)
3 Andy Farkas, NFC-D: Washington vs. N.Y. Giants, 1943 (3-r)
   Tom Fears, NFC-D: Los Angeles vs. Chi. Bears, 1950 (3-p)
   Otto Graham, NFC: Cleveland vs. Detroit, 1954 (3-r)
   Gary Collins, NFC: Cleveland vs. Baltimore, 1964 (3-p)
   Craig Baynham, NFC-D: Dallas vs. Cleveland, 1967 (2-r, 1-p)
   Fred Biletnikoff, AFC-D: Oakland vs. Kansas City, 1968 (3-p)
   Tom Matte, NFC: Baltimore vs. Cleveland, 1968 (3-r)
   Larry Schreiber, NFC-D: San Francisco vs. Dallas, 1972 (3-r)
   Larry Csonka, AFC: Miami vs. Oakland, 1973 (3-r)
   Franco Harris, AFC-D: Pittsburgh vs. Buffalo, 1974 (3-r)
   Preston Pearson, NFC: Dallas vs. Los Angeles, 1975 (3-p)
   Dave Casper, AFC-D: Oakland vs. Baltimore, 1977 (OT) (3-p)
   John Riggins, NFC-D: Washington vs. L.A. Rams, 1983 (3-r)
   Roger Craig, SB: San Francisco vs. Miami, 1984 (1-r, 2-p)
   Jerry Rice, NFC-D: San Francisco vs. Minnesota, 1988 (3-p)
   Jerry Rice, SB: San Francisco vs. Denver, 1989 (3-p)
   Kenneth Davis, AFC: Buffalo vs. L.A. Raiders, 1990 (3-r)
   Andre Reed, AFC-FR: Buffalo vs. Houston, 1992 (OT) (3-p)
   Sterling Sharpe, NFC-FR: Green Bay vs. Detroit, 1993 (3-p)
   Napoleon McCallum, AFC-FR: L.A. Raiders vs. Denver, 1993 (3-r)
   Thurman Thomas, AFC: Buffalo vs. Kansas City, 1993 (3-r)

Most Consecutive Games Scoring Touchdowns
8 John Stallworth, Pittsburgh, 1978-83
7 John Riggins, Washington, 1982-84
   Marcus Allen, L.A. Raiders, 1982-85
5 Duane Thomas, Dallas, 1970-71
   Franco Harris, Pittsburgh, 1974-75
   Franco Harris, Pittsburgh, 1977-79
   James Lofton, Green Bay-Buffalo, 1982-90
   Thurman Thomas, Buffalo, 1992-93 (current)

POINTS AFTER TOUCHDOWN

Most Points After Touchdown, Career
49 George Blanda, Chi. Bears-Houston-Oakland, 19 games (49 att)
42 Mike Cofer, San Francisco, 12 games (46 att)
41 Rafael Septien, L.A. Rams-Dallas, 15 games (41 att)

Most Points After Touchdown, Game
8 Lou Groza, NFC: Cleveland vs. Detroit, 1954 (8 att)
   Jim Martin, NFC: Detroit vs. Cleveland, 1957 (8 att)
   George Blanda, AFC-D: Oakland vs. Houston, 1969 (8 att)
7 Danny Villanueva, NFC-D: Dallas vs. Cleveland, 1967 (7 att)
   Raul Allegre, NFC-D: N.Y. Giants vs. San Francisco, 1986 (7 att)
   Mike Cofer, SB: San Francisco vs. Denver, 1989 (8 att)
   Lin Elliott, SB: Dallas vs. Buffalo, 1992 (7 att)
6 George Blair, AFC: San Diego vs. Boston, 1963 (6 att)
   Mark Moseley, NFC-D: Washington vs. L.A. Rams, 1983 (6 att)
   Uwe von Schamann, AFC: Miami vs. Pittsburgh, 1984 (6 att)
   Ali Haji-Sheikh, SB: Washington vs. Denver, 1987 (6 att)
   Scott Norwood, AFC: Buffalo vs. L.A. Raiders, 1990 (7 att)
   Jeff Jaeger, AFC-FR: L.A. Raiders vs. Denver, 1993 (6 att)

Most Points After Touchdown, No Misses, Career
49 George Blanda, Chi. Bears-Houston-Oakland, 19 games
41 Rafael Septien, L.A. Rams-Dallas, 14 games
39 Matt Bahr, Pittsburgh-Cleveland-N.Y. Giants, 13 games

FIELD GOALS

Most Field Goals Attempted, Career
39 George Blanda, Chi. Bears-Houston-Oakland, 19 games
31 Mark Moseley, Washington-Cleveland, 11 games
26 Roy Gerela, Houston-Pittsburgh, 15 games

Most Field Goals Attempted, Game
6   George Blanda, AFC: Oakland vs. Houston, 1967
     David Ray, NFC-D: Los Angeles vs. Dallas, 1973
     Mark Moseley, AFC-D: Cleveland vs. N.Y. Jets, 1986 (OT)
     Matt Bahr, NFC: N.Y. Giants vs. San Francisco, 1990
     Steve Christie, AFC: Buffalo vs. Miami, 1992
5   Jerry Kramer, NFC: Green Bay vs. N.Y. Giants, 1962
     Gino Cappelletti, AFC-D: Boston vs. Buffalo, 1963
     Pete Gogolak, AFC: Buffalo vs. San Diego, 1965
     Jim Turner, SB: N.Y. Jets vs. Baltimore, 1968
     Jan Stenerud, AFC-D: Kansas City vs. N.Y. Jets, 1969
     George Blanda, AFC-D: Oakland vs. Pittsburgh, 1973
     Ed Murray, NFC-D: Detroit vs. San Francisco, 1983
     Mark Moseley, NFC: Washington vs. San Francisco, 1983
     Tony Franklin, AFC-FR: New England vs. N.Y. Jets, 1985
     Tony Zendejas, AFC-FR: Houston vs. Seattle, 1987 (OT)
     Chuck Nelson, NFC-D: Minnesota vs. San Francisco, 1987
     Luis Zendejas, NFC-D: Philadelphia vs. Chicago, 1988
4   By many players

Most Field Goals, Career
22   George Blanda, Chi. Bears-Houston-Oakland, 19 games
20   Toni Fritsch, Dallas-Houston, 14 games
19   Matt Bahr, Pittsburgh-Cleveland-N.Y. Giants, 13 games

Most Field Goals, Game
5   Chuck Nelson, NFC-D: Minnesota vs. San Francisco, 1987
     Matt Bahr, NFC: N.Y. Giants vs. San Francisco, 1990
     Steve Christie, AFC: Buffalo vs. Miami, 1992
4   Gino Cappelletti, AFC-D: Boston vs. Buffalo, 1963
     George Blanda, AFC: Oakland vs. Houston, 1967
     Don Chandler, SB: Green Bay vs. Oakland, 1967
     Curt Knight, NFC: Washington vs. Dallas, 1972
     George Blanda, AFC-D: Oakland vs. Pittsburgh, 1973
     Ray Wersching, SB: San Francisco vs. Cincinnati, 1981
     Tony Franklin, AFC-FR: New England vs. N.Y. Jets, 1985
     Jess Atkinson, NFC-FR: Washington vs. L.A. Rams, 1986
     Luis Zendejas, NFC-D: Philadelphia vs. Chicago, 1988
     Gary Anderson, AFC-FR: Pittsburgh vs. Houston, 1989 (OT)
3   By many players

Most Consecutive Field Goals
15   Rafael Septien, Dallas, 1978-82
9   Chuck Nelson, Minnesota, 1987
     Gary Anderson, Pittsburgh, 1989-93 (current)
8   Tony Fritsch, Houston, 1978-79

Longest Field Goal
58   Pete Stoyanovich, AFC-FR: Miami vs. Kansas City, 1990
54   Ed Murray, NFC-D: Detroit vs. San Francisco, 1983
     Steve Christie, SB: Buffalo vs. Dallas, 1993
53   Al Del Greco, AFC-FR: Houston vs. N.Y. Jets, 1001

Highest Field Goal Percentage, Career (10 field goals)
90.9   Chuck Nelson, L.A. Rams-Minnesota, 6 games (10-11)
88.2   Steve Christie, Buffalo, 7 games (15-17)
85.7   Rafael Septien, L.A. Rams-Dallas, 15 games (18-21)

SAFETIES
Most Safeties, Game
1   Bill Willis, NFC-D: Cleveland vs. N.Y. Giants, 1950
     Carl Eller, NFC-D: Minnesota vs. Los Angeles, 1969
     George Andrie, NFC-D: Dallas vs. Detroit, 1970
     Alan Page, NFC-D: Minnesota vs. Dallas, 1971
     Dwight White, SB: Pittsburgh vs. Minnesota, 1974
     Reggie Harrison, SB: Pittsburgh vs. Dallas, 1975
     Jim Jensen, NFC-D: Dallas vs. Los Angeles, 1976
     Ted Washington, AFC: Houston vs. Pittsburgh, 1978
     Randy White, NFC-D: Dallas vs. Los Angeles, 1979
     Henry Waechter, SB: Chicago vs. New England, 1985
     Rulon Jones, AFC-FR: Denver vs. New England, 1986
     George Martin, SB: N.Y. Giants vs. Denver, 1986
     D.D. Hoggard, AFC: Cleveland vs. Denver, 1987
     Bruce Smith, SB: Buffalo vs. N.Y. Giants, 1990
     Reggie White, NFC-FR: Philadelphia vs. New Orleans, 1992

RUSHING
ATTEMPTS
Most Attempts, Career
400   Franco Harris, Pittsburgh, 19 games
302   Tony Dorsett, Dallas, 17 games
275   Thurman Thomas, Buffalo, 16 games

Most Attempts, Game
38   Ricky Bell, NFC-D: Tampa Bay vs. Philadelphia, 1979
     John Riggins, SB: Washington vs. Miami, 1982
37   Lawrence McCutcheon, NFC-D: Los Angeles vs. St. Louis, 1975
     John Riggins, NFC-D: Washington vs. Minnesota, 1982
36   John Riggins, NFC: Washington vs. Dallas, 1982

     John Riggins, NFC: Washington vs. San Francisco, 1983

YARDS GAINED
Most Yards Gained, Career
1,556   Franco Harris, Pittsburgh, 19 games
1,383   Tony Dorsett, Dallas, 17 games
1,152   Marcus Allen, L.A. Raiders-Kansas City, 13 games

Most Yards Gained, Game
248   Eric Dickerson, NFC-D: L.A. Rams vs. Dallas, 1985
206   Keith Lincoln, AFC: San Diego vs. Boston, 1963
204   Timmy Smith, SB: Washington vs. Denver, 1987

Most Games, 100 or More Yards Rushing, Career
6   John Riggins, Washington, 9 games
5   Franco Harris, Pittsburgh, 19 games
     Marcus Allen, L.A. Raiders-Kansas City, 13 games
     Thurman Thomas, Buffalo, 16 games
     Emmitt Smith, Dallas, 8 games
4   Larry Csonka, Miami, 12 games
     Chuck Foreman, Minnesota, 13 games

Most Consecutive Games, 100 or More Yards Rushing
6   John Riggins, Washington, 1982-83
4   Thurman Thomas, Buffalo, 1990-91
3   Larry Csonka, Miami, 1973-74
     Franco Harris, Pittsburgh, 1974-75
     Marcus Allen, L.A. Raiders, 1983
     Emmitt Smith, Dallas, 1992

Longest Run From Scrimmage
80   Roger Craig, NFC-D: San Francisco vs. Minnesota, 1988 (TD)
74   Marcus Allen, SB: L.A. Raiders vs. Washington, 1983 (TD)
71   Hugh McElhenny, NFC-D: San Francisco vs. Detroit, 1957
     James Lofton, NFC-D: Green Bay vs. Dallas, 1982 (TD)

AVERAGE GAIN
Highest Average Gain, Career (75 attempts)
5.68   Roger Staubach, Dallas, 20 games (76-432)
5.24   Marcus Allen, L.A. Raiders-Kansas City, 13 games (220-1,152)
4.89   Eric Dickerson, L.A. Rams-Indianapolis, 7 games (148-724)

Highest Average Gain, Game (10 attempts)
15.90   Elmer Angsman, NFC: Chi. Cardinals vs. Philadelphia, 1947 (10-159)
15.85   Keith Lincoln, AFC: San Diego vs. Boston, 1963 (13-206)
10.90   Bill Osmanski, NFC: Chi. Bears vs. Washington, 1940 (10-109)

TOUCHDOWNS
Most Touchdowns, Career
16   Franco Harris, Pittsburgh, 19 games
12   John Riggins, Washington, 9 games
     Thurman Thomas, Buffalo, 16 games
11   Marcus Allen, L.A. Raiders-Kansas City, 13 games

Most Touchdowns, Game
5   Ricky Watters, NFC-D: San Francisco vs. N.Y. Giants, 1993
3   Andy Farkas, NFC-D: Washington vs. N.Y. Giants, 1943
     Otto Graham, NFC: Cleveland vs. Detroit, 1954
     Tom Matte, NFC: Baltimore vs. Cleveland, 1968
     Larry Schreiber, NFC-D: San Francisco vs. Dallas, 1972
     Larry Csonka, AFC: Miami vs. Oakland, 1973
     Franco Harris, AFC-D: Pittsburgh vs. Buffalo, 1974
     John Riggins, NFC-D: Washington vs. L.A. Rams, 1983
     Kenneth Davis, AFC: Buffalo vs. L.A. Raiders, 1990
     Napoleon McCallum, AFC-FR: L.A. Raiders vs. Denver, 1993
     Thuman Thomas, AFC: Buffalo vs. Kansas City, 1993

Most Consecutive Games Rushing for Touchdowns
7   John Riggins, Washington, 1982-84
5   Franco Harris, Pittsburgh, 1974-75
     Franco Harris, Pittsburgh, 1977-79
4   Thurman Thomas, Buffalo, 1992-93 (current)

PASSING
PASSER RATING
Highest Passer Rating, Career (150 attempts)
111.2   Troy Aikman, Dallas, 7 games
104.8   Bart Starr, Green Bay, 10 games
95.2   Joe Montana, San Francisco-Kansas City, 22 games

ATTEMPTS
Most Passes Attempted, Career
697   Joe Montana, San Francisco-Kansas City, 22 games
462   Jim Kelly, Buffalo, 14 games
456   Terry Bradshaw, Pittsburgh, 19 games

Most Passes Attempted, Game
64   Bernie Kosar, AFC-D: Cleveland vs. N.Y. Jets, 1986 (OT)
58   Jim Kelly, SB: Buffalo vs. Washington, 1991
54   Randall Cunningham, NFC-D: Philadelphia vs. Chicago, 1988
     Jim Kelly, AFC-D: Buffalo vs. Cleveland, 1989

COMPLETIONS

Most Passes Completed, Career
- 434 Joe Montana, San Francisco-Kansas City, 22 games
- 275 Jim Kelly, Buffalo, 14 games
- 261 Terry Bradshaw, Pittsburgh, 19 games

Most Passes Completed, Game
- 36 Warren Moon, AFC-FR: Houston vs. Buffalo, 1992 (OT)
- 33 Dan Fouts, AFC-D: San Diego vs. Miami, 1981 (OT)
- Bernie Kosar, AFC-D: Cleveland vs. N.Y. Jets, 1986 (OT)
- 32 Neil Lomax, NFC-FR: St. Louis vs. Green Bay, 1982
- Danny White, NFC-FR: Dallas vs. L.A. Rams, 1983
- Warren Moon, AFC-D: Houston vs. Kansas City, 1993

COMPLETION PERCENTAGE

Highest Completion Percentage, Career (150 attempts)
- 71.1 Troy Aikman, Dallas, 7 games (187-133)
- 67.9 Steve Young, San Francisco, 12 games (156-106)
- 66.3 Ken Anderson, Cincinnati, 6 games (166-110)

Highest Completion Percentage, Game (15 completions)
- 88.0 Phil Simms, SB: N.Y. Giants vs. Denver, 1986 (25-22)
- 86.7 Joe Montana, NFC: San Francisco vs. L.A. Rams, 1989 (30-26)
- 84.2 David Woodley, AFC-FR: Miami vs. New England, 1982 (19-16)

YARDS GAINED

Most Yards Gained, Career
- 5,458 Joe Montana, San Francisco-Kansas City, 22 games
- 3,833 Terry Bradshaw, Pittsburgh, 19 games
- 3,321 John Elway, Denver, 14 games

Most Yards Gained, Game
- 489 Bernie Kosar, AFC-D: Cleveland vs. N.Y. Jets, 1986 (OT)
- 433 Dan Fouts, AFC-D: San Diego vs. Miami, 1981 (OT)
- 421 Dan Marino, AFC: Miami vs. Pittsburgh, 1984

Most Games, 300 or More Yards Passing, Career
- 5 Dan Fouts, San Diego, 7 games
- Joe Montana, San Francisco-Kansas City, 22 games
- 4 Warren Moon, Houston, 9 games
- 3 Terry Bradshaw, Pittsburgh, 19 games
- Danny White, Dallas, 17 games
- Dan Marino, Miami, 10 games
- Jim Kelly, Buffalo, 14 games
- John Elway, Denver, 14 games

Most Consecutive Games, 300 or More Yards Passing
- 4 Dan Fouts, San Diego, 1979-81
- 3 Jim Kelly, Buffalo, 1989-90
- Warren Moon, Houston, 1991-93 (current)
- 2 Daryle Lamonica, Oakland, 1968
- Ken Anderson, Cincinnati, 1981-82
- Terry Bradshaw, Pittsburgh, 1979-82
- Joe Montana, San Francisco, 1983-84
- Dan Marino, Miami, 1984

Longest Pass Completion
- 93 Daryle Lamonica (to Dubenion), AFC-D: Buffalo vs. Boston, 1963 (TD)
- 88 George Blanda (to Cannon), AFC: Houston vs. L.A. Chargers, 1960 (TD)
- 86 Don Meredith (to Hayes), NFC-D: Dallas vs. Cleveland, 1967 (TD)
- Jeff Hostetler (to Brown), AFC-D: L.A. Raiders vs. Buffalo, 1993 (TD)

AVERAGE GAIN

Highest Average Gain, Career (150 attempts)
- 8.53 Troy Aikman, Dallas, 7 games (187-1,595)
- 8.45 Joe Theismann, Washington, 10 games (211-1,782)
- 8.43 Jim Plunkett, Oakland-L.A. Raiders, 10 games (272-2,293)

Highest Average Gain, Game (20 attempts)
- 14.71 Terry Bradshaw, SB: Pittsburgh vs. Los Angeles, 1979 (21-309)
- 13.33 Bob Waterfield, NFC-D: Los Angeles vs. Chi. Bears, 1950 (21-280)
- 13.16 Dan Marino, AFC: Miami vs. Pittsburgh, 1984 (32-421)

TOUCHDOWNS

Most Touchdown Passes, Career
- 43 Joe Montana, San Francisco-Kansas City, 22 games
- 30 Terry Bradshaw, Pittsburgh, 19 games
- 24 Roger Staubach, Dallas, 20 games

Most Touchdown Passes, Game
- 6 Daryle Lamonica, AFC-D: Oakland vs. Houston, 1969
- 5 Sid Luckman, NFC: Chi. Bears vs. Washington, 1943
- Daryle Lamonica, AFC-D: Oakland vs. Kansas City, 1968
- Joe Montana, SB: San Francisco vs. Denver, 1989
- 4 Otto Graham, NFC: Cleveland vs. Los Angeles, 1950
- Tobin Rote, NFC: Detroit vs. Cleveland, 1957
- Bart Starr, NFC: Green Bay vs. Dallas, 1966
- Ken Stabler, AFC-D: Oakland vs. Miami, 1974
- Roger Staubach, NFC: Dallas vs. Los Angeles, 1975
- Terry Bradshaw, SB: Pittsburgh vs. Dallas, 1978
- Don Strock, AFC-D: Miami vs. San Diego, 1981 (OT)

Lynn Dickey, NFC-FR: Green Bay vs. St. Louis, 1982
Dan Marino, AFC: Miami vs. Pittsburgh, 1984
Phil Simms, NFC-D: N.Y. Giants vs. San Francisco, 1986
Doug Williams, SB: Washington vs. Denver, 1987
Jim Kelly, AFC-D: Buffalo vs. Cleveland, 1989
Joe Montana, NFC-D: San Francisco vs. Minnesota, 1989
Warren Moon, AFC-FR: Houston vs. Buffalo, 1992 (OT)
Frank Reich, AFC-FR: Buffalo vs. Houston, 1992 (OT)
Troy Aikman, SB: Dallas vs. Buffalo, 1992

Most Consecutive Games, Touchdown Passes
- 10 Ken Stabler, Oakland, 1973-77
- Dan Marino, Miami, 1983-92 (current)
- Joe Montana, San Francisco-Kansas City, 1988-93
- 9 John Elway, Denver, 1984-89
- 8 Terry Bradshaw, Pittsburgh, 1977-82
- Joe Montana, San Francisco, 1981-84
- Bernie Kosar, Cleveland-Dallas, 1985-93

HAD INTERCEPTED

Lowest Percentage, Passes Had Intercepted, Career (150 attempts)
- 1.41 Bart Starr, Green Bay, 10 games (213-3)
- 2.14 Troy Aikman, Dallas, 7 games (187-4)
- 2.15 Phil Simms, N.Y. Giants, 10 games (279-6)

Most Attempts Without Interception, Game
- 48 Warren Moon, AFC-FR: Houston vs. Pittsburgh, 1989 (OT)
- 47 Daryle Lamonica, AFC: Oakland vs. N.Y. Jets, 1968
- 43 Joe Montana, AFC-FR: Kansas City vs. Pittsburgh, 1993 (OT)

Most Passes Had Intercepted, Career
- 26 Terry Bradshaw, Pittsburgh, 19 games
- 22 Jim Kelly, Buffalo, 14 games
- 20 Joe Montana, San Francisco-Kansas City, 22 games

Most Passes Had Intercepted, Game
- 6 Frank Filchock, NFC: N.Y. Giants vs. Chi. Bears, 1946
- Bobby Layne, NFC: Detroit vs. Cleveland, 1954
- Norm Van Brocklin, NFC: Los Angeles vs. Cleveland, 1955
- 5 Frank Filchock, NFC: Washington vs. Chi. Bears, 1940
- George Blanda, AFC: Houston vs. San Diego, 1961
- George Blanda, AFC: Houston vs. Dall. Texans, 1962 (OT)
- Y.A. Tittle, NFC: N.Y. Giants vs. Chicago, 1963
- Mike Phipps, AFC-D: Cleveland vs. Miami, 1972
- Dan Pastorini, AFC: Houston vs. Pittsburgh, 1978
- Dan Fouts, AFC-D: San Diego vs. Houston, 1979
- Tommy Kramer, NFC-D: Minnesota vs. Philadelphia, 1980
- Dan Fouts, AFC-D: San Diego vs. Miami, 1982
- Richard Todd, AFC: N.Y. Jets vs Miami, 1982
- Gary Danielson, NFC-D: Detroit vs. San Francisco, 1983
- Jay Schroeder, AFC: L.A. Raiders vs. Buffalo, 1990
- 4 By many players

PASS RECEIVING
RECEPTIONS

Most Receptions, Career
- 84 Jerry Rice, San Francisco, 15 games
- 75 Andre Reed, Buffalo, 16 games
- 73 Cliff Branch, Oakland-L.A. Raiders, 22 games

Most Receptions, Game
- 13 Kellen Winslow, AFC-D: San Diego vs. Miami, 1981 (OT)
- Thurman Thomas, AFC-D: Buffalo vs. Cleveland, 1989
- Shannon Sharpe, AFC-FR: Denver vs. L.A. Raiders, 1993
- 12 Raymond Berry, NFC: Baltimore vs. N.Y. Giants, 1958
- 11 Dante Lavelli, NFC: Cleveland vs. Los Angeles, 1950
- Dan Ross, SB: Cincinnati vs. San Francisco, 1981
- Franco Harris, AFC-FR: Pittsburgh vs. San Diego, 1982
- Steve Watson, AFC-D: Denver vs. Pittsburgh, 1984
- John L. Williams, AFC-D: Seattle vs. Cincinnati, 1988
- Jerry Rice, SB: San Francisco vs. Cincinnati, 1988
- Ernest Givins, AFC-FR: Houston vs. Pittsburgh, 1989 (OT)

Most Consecutive Games, Pass Receptions
- 22 Drew Pearson, Dallas, 1973-83
- 18 Paul Warfield, Cleveland-Miami, 1964-74
- Cliff Branch, Oakland-L.A. Raiders, 1974-83
- 17 John Stallworth, Pittsburgh, 1974-84

YARDS GAINED

Most Yards Gained, Career
- 1,306 Jerry Rice, San Francisco, 15 games
- 1,289 Cliff Branch, Oakland-L.A. Raiders, 22 games
- 1,167 Fred Biletnikoff, Oakland, 19 games

Most Yards Gained, Game
- 227 Anthony Carter, NFC-D: Minnesota vs. San Francisco, 1987
- 215 Jerry Rice, SB: San Francisco vs. Cincinnati, 1988
- 198 Tom Fears, NFC-D: Los Angeles vs. Chi. Bears, 1950

Most Games, 100 or More Yards Receiving, Career
- 5 John Stallworth, Pittsburgh, 18 games
- Jerry Rice, San Francisco, 15 games
- Andre Reed, Buffalo, 16 games
- 4 Fred Biletnikoff, Oakland, 19 games
- Dwight Clark, San Francisco, 7 games
- Art Monk, Washington, 15 games
- 3 Tom Fears, L.A. Rams, 6 games
- Cliff Branch, Oakland-L.A. Raiders, 22 games
- Tony Nathan, Miami, 10 games
- Mark Duper, Miami, 10 games
- James Lofton, Green Bay-Buffalo, 13 games
- Vance Johnson, Denver, 11 games
- Ernest Givins, Houston, 10 games

Most Consecutive Games, 100 or More Yards Receiving, Career
- 3 Tom Fears, Los Angeles, 1950-51
- Jerry Rice, San Francisco, 1988-89
- 2 Lenny Moore, Baltimore, 1958-59
- Fred Biletnikoff, Oakland, 1968
- Paul Warfield, Miami, 1971
- Charlie Joiner, San Diego, 1980-81
- Dwight Clark, San Francisco, 1981
- Cris Collinsworth, Cincinnati, 1981-82
- John Stallworth, Pittsburgh, 1979-82
- Wesley Walker, N.Y. Jets, 1982
- Charlie Brown, Washington, 1983
- Steve Largent, Seattle, 1984-87
- Vance Johnson, Denver, 1986-87
- Andre Reed, Buffalo, 1989-90
- James Lofton, Buffalo, 1990
- Ernest Givins, Houston, 1991-92
- Michael Irvin, Dallas, 1992-93
- Sterling Sharpe, Green Bay, 1993 (current)

Longest Reception
- 93 Elbert Dubenion (from Lamonica), AFC-D: Buffalo vs. Boston, 1963 (TD)
- 88 Billy Cannon (from Blanda), AFC: Houston vs. L.A. Chargers, 1960 (TD)
- 86 Bob Hayes (from Meredith), NFC: Dallas vs. Cleveland, 1967 (TD)
- Tim Brown (from Hostetler), AFC-D: L.A. Raiders vs. Buffalo, 1993 (TD)

AVERAGE GAIN
Highest Average Gain, Career (20 receptions)
- 25.4 Alvin Harper, Dallas, 8 games (21-533)
- 23.7 Willie Gault, Chicago-L.A. Raiders, 10 games (21-497)
- 22.8 Harold Jackson, L.A. Rams-New England-Minnesota-Seattle, 14 games (24-548)

Highest Average Gain, Game (3 receptions)
- 46.3 Harold Jackson, NFC: Los Angeles vs. Minnesota, 1974 (3-139)
- 42.7 Billy Cannon, AFC: Houston vs. L.A. Chargers, 1960 (3-128)
- 42.0 Lenny Moore, NFC: Baltimore vs. N.Y. Giants, 1959 (3-126)

TOUCHDOWNS
Most Touchdowns, Career
- 13 Jerry Rice, San Francisco, 15 games
- 12 John Stallworth, Pittsburgh, 18 games
- 10 Fred Biletnikoff, Oakland, 19 games

Most Touchdowns, Game
- 3 Tom Fears, NFC-D: Los Angeles vs. Chi. Bears, 1950
- Gary Collins, NFC: Cleveland vs. Baltimore, 1964
- Fred Biletnikoff, AFC-D: Oakland vs. Kansas City, 1968
- Preston Pearson, NFC: Dallas vs. Los Angeles, 1975
- Dave Casper, AFC-D: Oakland vs. Baltimore, 1977 (OT)
- Alvin Garrett, NFC-FR: Washington vs. Detroit, 1982
- Jerry Rice, NFC-D: San Francisco vs. Minnesota, 1988
- Jerry Rice, SB: San Francisco vs. Denver, 1989
- Andre Reed, AFC-FR: Buffalo vs. Houston, 1992 (OT)
- Sterling Sharpe, NFC-FR: Green Bay vs. Detroit, 1993

Most Consecutive Games, Touchdown Passes Caught
- 8 John Stallworth, Pittsburgh, 1978-83
- 5 James Lofton, Green Bay-Buffalo, 1982-90
- 4 Lynn Swann, Pittsburgh, 1978-79
- Harold Carmichael, Philadelphia, 1978-80
- Fred Solomon, San Francisco, 1983-84
- Jerry Rice, San Francisco, 1988-89
- John Taylor, San Francisco, 1988-89

INTERCEPTIONS BY
Most Interceptions, Career
- 9 Charlie Waters, Dallas, 25 games
- Bill Simpson, Los Angeles-Buffalo, 11 games
- Ronnie Lott, San Francisco-L.A. Raiders, 20 games
- 8 Lester Hayes, Oakland-L.A. Raiders, 13 games
- 7 Willie Brown, Oakland, 17 games
- Dennis Thurman, Dallas, 14 games

Most Interceptions, Game
- 4 Vernon Perry, AFC-D: Houston vs. San Diego, 1979
- 3 Joe Laws, NFC: Green Bay vs. N.Y. Giants, 1944
- Charlie Waters, NFC-D: Dallas vs. Chicago, 1977
- Rod Martin, SB: Oakland vs. Philadelphia, 1980
- Dennis Thurman, NFC-D: Dallas vs. Green Bay, 1982
- A.J. Duhe, AFC: Miami vs. N.Y. Jets, 1982
- 2 By many players

Most Consecutive Games, Interceptions
- 3 Warren Lahr, Cleveland, 1950-51
- Ken Gorgal, Cleveland, 1950-53
- Joe Schmidt, Detroit, 1954-57
- Emmitt Thomas, Kansas City, 1969
- Mel Renfro, Dallas, 1970
- Rick Volk, Baltimore, 1970-71
- Mike Wagner, Pittsburgh, 1975-76
- Randy Hughes, Dallas, 1977-78
- Vernon Perry, Houston, 1979-80
- Lester Hayes, Oakland, 1980
- Gerald Small, Miami, 1982
- Lester Hayes, L.A. Raiders, 1982-83
- Fred Marion, New England, 1985
- John Harris, Seattle-Minnesota, 1984-87
- Felix Wright, Cleveland, 1987-88
- Kurt Gouveia, Washington, 1991

YARDS GAINED
Most Yards Gained, Career
- 196 Willie Brown, Oakland, 17 games
- 187 Ronnie Lott, San Francisco-L.A. Raiders, 20 games
- 151 Glen Edwards, Pittsburgh-San Diego, 17 games

Most Yards Gained, Game
- 101 George Teague, NFC-FR: Green Bay vs. Detroit, 1993
- 98 Darrol Ray, AFC-FR: N.Y. Jets vs. Cincinnati, 1982
- 94 LeRoy Irvin, NFC-FR: L.A. Rams vs. Dallas, 1983

Longest Return
- 101 George Teague, NFC-FR: Green Bay vs. Detroit, 1993 (TD)
- 98 Darrol Ray, AFC-FR: N.Y. Jets vs. Cincinnati, 1982 (TD)
- 94 LeRoy Irvin, NFC-FR: L.A. Rams vs. Dallas, 1983

TOUCHDOWNS
Most Touchdowns, Career
- 3 Willie Brown, Oakland, 17 games
- 2 Lester Hayes, Oakland-L.A. Raiders, 13 games
- Ronnie Lott, San Francisco-L.A. Raiders, 20 games
- Darrell Green, Washington, 16 games
- Melvin Jenkins, Seattle-Detroit, 5 games

Most Touchdowns, Game
- 1 By many players.

PUNTING
Most Punts, Career
- 111 Ray Guy, Oakland-L.A. Raiders, 22 games
- 84 Danny White, Dallas, 18 games
- 73 Mike Eischeid, Oakland-Minnesota, 14 games

Most Punts, Game
- 14 Dave Jennings, AFC-D: N.Y. Jets vs. Cleveland, 1986 (OT)
- 12 David Lee, AFC-D: Baltimore vs. Oakland, 1977 (OT)
- 11 Ken Strong, NFC: N.Y. Giants vs. Chi. Bears, 1933
- Jim Norton, AFC: Houston vs. Oakland, 1967
- Ode Burrell, AFC-D: Houston vs. Oakland, 1969
- Dale Hatcher, NFC: L.A. Rams vs. Chicago, 1985

Longest Punt
- 76 Ed Danowski, NFC: N.Y. Giants vs. Detroit, 1935
- Mike Horan, AFC: Denver vs. Buffalo, 1991
- 72 Charlie Conerly, NFC-D: N.Y. Giants vs. Cleveland, 1950
- Yale Lary, NFC: Detroit vs. Cleveland, 1953
- 71 Ray Guy, AFC: Oakland vs. San Diego, 1980

AVERAGE YARDAGE
Highest Average, Career (25 punts)
- 44.5 Rich Camarillo, New England, 6 games (35-1,559)
- 44.4 Lee Johnson, Cleveland-Cincinnati, 7 games (28-1,244)
- 43.8 John Kidd, Buffalo-San Diego, 5 games (26-1,139)

Highest Average, Game (4 punts)
- 56.0 Ray Guy, AFC: Oakland vs. San Diego, 1980 (4-224)
- 52.5 Sammy Baugh, NFC: Washington vs. Chi. Bears, 1942 (6-315)
- 51.6 Lee Johnson, AFC-D: Cincinnati vs. L.A. Raiders, 1990 (5-258)

PUNT RETURNS
Most Punt Returns, Career
- 25 Theo Bell, Pittsburgh-Tampa Bay, 10 games
- 21 Gerald McNeil, Cleveland-Houston, 8 games

19 Willie Wood, Green Bay, 10 games
    Butch Johnson, Dallas-Denver, 18 games
    Phil McConkey, N.Y. Giants, 5 games

Most Punt Returns, Game

7 Ron Gardin, AFC-D: Baltimore vs. Cincinnati, 1970
    Carl Roaches, AFC-FR: Houston vs. Oakland, 1980
    Gerald McNeil, AFC-D: Cleveland vs. N.Y. Jets, 1986 (OT)
    Phil McConkey, NFC-D: N.Y. Giants vs. San Francisco, 1986
6 George McAfee, NFC-D: Chi. Bears vs. Los Angeles, 1950
    Eddie Brown, NFC-D: Washington vs. Minnesota, 1976
    Theo Bell, AFC: Pittsburgh vs. Houston, 1978
    Eddie Brown, NFC: Los Angeles vs. Tampa Bay, 1979
    John Sciarra, NFC: Philadelphia vs. Dallas, 1980
    Kurt Sohn, AFC: N.Y. Jets vs. Miami, 1982
    Mike Nelms, SB: Washington vs. Miami, 1982
    Anthony Carter, NFC-FR: Minnesota vs. New Orleans, 1987
5 By many players

YARDS GAINED

Most Yards Gained, Career

259 Anthony Carter, Minnesota, 8 games
221 Neal Colzie, Oakland-Miami-Tampa Bay, 10 games
211 Gerald McNeil, Cleveland-Houston, 8 games

Most Yards Gained, Game

143 Anthony Carter, NFC-FR: Minnesota vs. New Orleans, 1987
141 Bob Hayes, NFC-D: Dallas vs. Cleveland, 1967
102 Charley Trippi, NFC: Chi. Cardinals vs. Philadelphia, 1947

Longest Return

84 Anthony Carter, NFC-FR: Minnesota vs. New Orleans, 1987 (TD)
81 Hugh Gallarneau, NFC-D: Chi. Bears vs. Green Bay, 1941 (TD)
79 Bosh Pritchard, NFC-D: Philadelphia vs. Pittsburgh, 1947 (TD)

AVERAGE YARDAGE

Highest Average, Career (10 returns)

15.2 Anthony Carter, Minnesota, 8 games (17-259)
12.9 Brian Mitchell, Washington, 7 games (11-142)
12.6 Bob Hayes, Dallas, 15 games (12-151)

Highest Average Gain, Game (3 returns)

47.0 Bob Hayes, NFC-D: Dallas vs. Cleveland, 1967 (3-141)
29.0 George (Butch) Byrd, AFC: Buffalo vs. San Diego, 1965 (3-87)
25.3 Bosh Pritchard, NFC-D: Philadelphia vs. Pittsburgh, 1947 (4-101)

TOUCHDOWNS

Most Touchdowns

1 Hugh Gallarneau, NFC-D: Chicago Bears vs. Green Bay, 1941
    Bosh Pritchard, NFC-D: Philadelphia vs. Pittsburgh, 1947
    Charley Trippi, NFC: Chicago Cardinals vs. Philadelphia, 1947
    Verda (Vitamin T) Smith, NFC-D: Los Angeles vs. Detroit, 1952
    George (Butch) Byrd, AFC: Buffalo vs. San Diego, 1965
    Golden Richards, NFC: Dallas vs. Minnesota, 1973
    Wes Chandler, AFC-D: San Diego vs. Miami, 1981 (OT)
    Shaun Gayle, NFC-D: Chicago vs. N.Y. Giants, 1985
    Anthony Carter, NFC-FR: Minnesota vs. New Orleans, 1987
    Darrell Green, NFC-D: Washington vs. Chicago, 1987

KICKOFF RETURNS

Most Kickoff Returns, Career

29 Fulton Walker, Miami-L.A. Raiders, 10 games
21 Ken Bell, Denver, 9 games
19 Preston Pearson, Baltimore-Pittsburgh-Dallas, 22 games
    James Brooks, San Diego-Cincinnati, 9 games

Most Kickoff Returns, Game

8 Marc Logan, AFC-D: Miami vs. Buffalo, 1990
7 Don Bingham, NFC: Chi. Bears vs. N.Y. Giants, 1956
    Reggie Brown, NFC-FR: Atlanta vs. Minnesota, 1982
    David Verser, AFC-FR: Cincinnati vs. N.Y. Jets, 1982
    Del Rodgers, NFC-D: Green Bay vs. Dallas, 1982
    Henry Ellard, NFC-D: L.A. Rams vs. Washington, 1983
    Stephen Starring, SB: New England vs. Chicago, 1985
6 By many players

YARDS GAINED

Most Yards Gained, Career

677 Fulton Walker, Miami-L.A. Raiders, 10 games
481 Carl Garrett, Oakland, 5 games
435 Dennis Gentry, Chicago, 12 games

Most Yards Gained, Game

190 Fulton Walker, SB: Miami vs. Washington, 1982
170 Les (Speedy) Duncan, NFC-D: Washington vs. San Francisco, 1971
169 Carl Garrett, AFC-D: Oakland vs. Baltimore, 1977 (OT)

Longest Return

98 Fulton Walker, SB: Miami vs. Washington, 1982 (TD)
97 Vic Washington, NFC-D: San Francisco vs. Dallas, 1972 (TD)

---

93 Stanford Jennings, SB: Cincinnati vs. San Francisco, 1988 (TD)

AVERAGE YARDAGE

Highest Average, Career (10 returns)

30.1 Carl Garrett, Oakland, 5 games (16-481)
27.9 George Atkinson, Oakland, 16 games (12-335)
27.7 Eric Metcalf, Cleveland, 2 games (10-277)

Highest Average, Game (3 returns)

56.7 Les (Speedy) Duncan, NFC-D: Washington vs. San Francisco, 1971 (3-170)
51.3 Ed Podolak, AFC-D: Kansas City vs. Miami, 1971 (OT) (3-154)
49.0 Les (Speedy) Duncan, AFC: San Diego vs. Buffalo, 1964 (3-147)

TOUCHDOWNS

Most Touchdowns

1 Vic Washington, NFC-D: San Francisco vs. Dallas, 1972
    Nat Moore, AFC-D: Miami vs. Oakland, 1974
    Marshall Johnson, AFC-D: Baltimore vs. Oakland, 1977 (OT)
    Fulton Walker, SB: Miami vs. Washington, 1982
    Stanford Jennings, SB: Cincinnati vs. San Francisco, 1988
    Eric Metcalf, AFC-D: Cleveland vs. Buffalo, 1989

FUMBLES

Most Fumbles, Career

15 Warren Moon, Houston, 9 games
13 Tony Dorsett, Dallas, 17 games
10 Franco Harris, Pittsburgh, 19 games
    Terry Bradshaw, Pittsburgh, 19 games
    Roger Staubach, Dallas, 20 games

Most Fumbles, Game

5 Warren Moon, AFC-D: Houston vs. Kansas City, 1993
4 Brian Sipe, AFC-D: Cleveland vs. Oakland, 1980
3 By many players

RECOVERIES

Most Own Fumbles Recovered, Career

7 Warren Moon, Houston, 9 games
6 John Elway, Denver, 14 games
5 Roger Staubach, Dallas, 20 games

Most Opponents' Fumbles Recovered, Career

4 Cliff Harris, Dallas, 21 games
    Harvey Martin, Dallas, 22 games
    Ted Hendricks, Baltimore-Oakland-L.A. Raiders, 21 games
    Alvin Walton, Washington, 9 games
    Monte Coleman, Washington, 21 games
3 Paul Krause, Minnesota, 19 games
    Jack Lambert, Pittsburgh, 18 games
    Fred Dryer, Los Angeles, 14 games
    Charlie Waters, Dallas, 25 games
    Jack Ham, Pittsburgh, 16 games
    Mike Hegman, Dallas, 16 games
    Tom Jackson, Denver, 10 games
    Rich Milot, Washington, 13 games
    Mike Singletary, Chicago, 12 games
    Darryl Grant, Washington, 16 games
    Wes Hopkins, Philadelphia, 3 games
    Wilber Marshall, Chicago-Washington, 14 games
2 By many players

Most Fumbles Recovered, Game, Own and Opponents'

3 Jack Lambert, AFC: Pittsburgh vs. Oakland, 1975 (3 opp)
    Ron Jaworski, NFC-FR: Philadelphia vs. N.Y. Giants, 1981 (3 own)
2 By many players

YARDS GAINED

Longest Return

93 Andy Russell, AFC-D: Pittsburgh vs. Baltimore, 1975 (opp, TD)
64 Leon Lett, SB: Dallas vs. Buffalo, 1992 (opp)
60 Mike Curtis, NFC-D: Baltimore vs. Minnesota, 1968 (opp, TD)
    Hugh Green, NFC-FR: Tampa Bay vs. Dallas, 1982 (opp, TD)

TOUCHDOWNS

Most Touchdowns

1 By many players

COMBINED NET YARDS GAINED

Rushing, receiving, interception returns, punt returns, kickoff returns, and fumble returns.

ATTEMPTS

Most Attempts, Career

454 Franco Harris, Pittsburgh, 19 games
350 Tony Dorsett, Dallas, 17 games
342 Thurman Thomas, Buffalo, 16 games

Most Attempts, Game
- 40 Lawrence McCutcheon, NFC-D: Los Angeles vs. St. Louis, 1975
- 39 John Riggins, SB: Washington vs. Miami, 1982
  Rodney Hampton, NFC-FR: N.Y. Giants vs. Minnesota, 1993
- 38 Ricky Bell, NFC-D: Tampa Bay vs. Philadelphia, 1979
  Rob Carpenter, NFC-FR: N.Y. Giants vs. Philadelphia, 1981

YARDS GAINED
Most Yards Gained, Career
- 2,060 Franco Harris, Pittsburgh, 19 games
- 1,786 Tony Dorsett, Dallas, 17 games
- 1,736 Thurman Thomas, Buffalo, 16 games
Most Yards Gained, Game
- 350 Ed Podolak, AFC-D: Kansas City vs. Miami, 1971 (OT)
- 329 Keith Lincoln, AFC: San Diego vs. Boston, 1963
- 285 Bob Hayes, NFC-D: Dallas vs. Cleveland, 1967

SACKS
Sacks have been compiled since 1982
Most Sacks, Career
- 12 Bruce Smith, Buffalo, 16 games
- 10.5 Richard Dent, Chicago, 10 games
- 10 Charles Mann, Washington, 17 games
  Charles Haley, San Francisco-Dallas, 16 games
Most Sacks, Game
- 3.5 Rich Milot, NFC-D: Washington vs. Chicago, 1984
  Richard Dent, NFC-D: Chicago vs. N.Y. Giants, 1985
- 3 Richard Dent, NFC-D: Chicago vs. Washington, 1984
  Garin Veris, AFC-FR: New England vs. N.Y. Jets, 1985
  Gary Jeter, NFC-D: L.A. Rams vs. Dallas, 1985
  Carl Hairston, AFC-D: Cleveland vs. N.Y. Jets, 1986 (OT)
  Charles Mann, NFC-D: Washington vs. Chicago, 1987
  Kevin Greene, NFC-FR: L.A. Rams vs. Minnesota, 1988
  Greg Townsend, AFC-D: L.A. Raiders vs. Cincinnati, 1990
  Wilber Marshall, NFC: Washington vs. Detroit, 1991
  Fred Stokes, NFC-FR: Washington vs. Minnesota, 1992
  Pierce Holt, NFC-D: San Francisco vs. Washington, 1992
  Tony Casillas, NFC: Dallas vs. San Francisco, 1992
  Gerald Williams, AFC-FR: Pittsburgh vs. Kansas City, 1993
- 2.5 Lyle Alzado, AFC-D: L.A. Raiders vs. Pittsburgh, 1983
  Jacob Green, AFC-FR: Seattle vs. L.A. Raiders, 1984
  Larry Roberts, NFC-D: San Francisco vs. Minnesota, 1988
  Leslie O'Neal, AFC-FR: San Diego vs. Kansas City, 1992

TEAM RECORDS

GAMES, VICTORIES, DEFEATS
Most Seasons Participating in Postseason Games
- 23 N.Y. Giants, 1933-35, 1938-39, 1941, 1943-44, 1946, 1950, 1956, 1958-59,1961-63, 1981, 1984-86, 1989-90, 1993
- 22 Cleveland/L.A. Rams, 1945, 1949-52, 1955, 1967, 1969, 1973-80, 1983-86, 1988-89
  Cleveland, 1950-55, 1957-58, 1964-65, 1967-69, 1971-72, 1980, 1982, 1985-89
- 21 Dallas, 1966-73, 1975-83, 1985, 1991-93
Most Consecutive Seasons Participating in Postseason Games
- 9 Dallas, 1975-83
- 8 Dallas, 1966-73
  Pittsburgh, 1972-79
  Los Angeles, 1973-80
  San Francisco, 1983-90
- 7 Houston, 1987-93
Most Games
- 44 Dallas, 1966-73, 1975-83, 1985, 1991-93
- 36 Oakland/L.A. Raiders, 1967-70, 1973-77, 1980, 1982-85, 1990-91, 1993
- 35 Boston/Washington, 1936-37, 1940, 1942-43, 1945, 1971-74, 1976-77, 1982-84, 1986-87, 1990-92
Most Games Won
- 27 Dallas, 1967, 1970-73, 1975, 1977-78, 1980-82, 1991-93
- 21 Washington, 1937, 1942-43, 1972, 1982-83, 1986-87, 1990-92
  Oakland/L.A. Raiders, 1967-70, 1973-77, 1980, 1982-83, 1990, 1993
- 18 San Francisco, 1970-71, 1981, 1983-84, 1988-90, 1992-93
Most Consecutive Games Won
- 9 Green Bay, 1961-62, 1965-67
- 7 Pittsburgh, 1974-76
  San Francisco, 1988-90
- 6 Miami, 1972-73
  Pittsburgh, 1978-79
  Washington, 1982-83
  Dallas, 1992-93

Most Games Lost
- 20 L.A. Rams, 1949-50, 1952, 1955, 1967, 1969, 1973-80, 1983-86, 1988-89
- 18 Cleveland, 1951-53, 1957-58, 1965, 1967-69, 1971-72, 1980, 1982, 1985-89
  N.Y. Giants, 1933, 1935, 1939, 1941, 1943-44, 1946, 1950, 1958-59, 1961-63, 1981, 1984-85, 1989, 1993
- 17 Dallas, 1966-70, 1972-73, 1975-76, 1978-83, 1985, 1991
  Minnesota, 1968-71, 1973-78, 1980, 1982, 1987-89, 1992-93
Most Consecutive Games Lost
- 6 N.Y. Giants, 1939, 1941, 1943-44, 1946, 1950
  Cleveland, 1969, 1971-72, 1980, 1982, 1985
- 5 N.Y. Giants, 1958-59, 1961-63
  Los Angeles, 1952, 1955, 1967, 1969, 1973
  Denver, 1977-79, 1983-84
  Baltimore/Indianapolis, 1971, 1975-77, 1987 (current)
  Philadelphia, 1980-81, 1988-90
- 4 Washington, 1972-74, 1976
  Miami, 1974, 1978-79, 1981
  Chi. Cardinals/St. Louis, 1948, 1974-75, 1982 (current)
  Boston/New England, 1963, 1976, 1978, 1982
  New Orleans, 1987, 1990-92 (current)
  Minnesota, 1988-89, 1992-93

SCORING
Most Points, Game
- 73 NFC: Chi. Bears vs. Washington, 1940
- 59 NFC: Detroit vs. Cleveland, 1957
- 56 NFC: Cleveland vs. Detroit, 1954
  AFC-D: Oakland vs. Houston, 1969
Most Points, Both Teams, Game
- 79 AFC-D: San Diego (41) vs. Miami (38), 1981 (OT)
  AFC-FR: Buffalo (41) vs. Houston (38), 1992 (OT)
- 78 AFC-D: Buffalo (44) vs. Miami (34), 1990
- 73 NFC: Chi. Bears (73) vs. Washington (0), 1940
  NFC: Detroit (59) vs. Cleveland (14), 1957
  AFC: Miami (45) vs. Pittsburgh (28), 1984
Fewest Points, Both Teams, Game
- 5 NFC-D: Detroit (0) vs. Dallas (5), 1970
- 7 NFC: Chi. Cardinals (0) vs. Philadelphia (7), 1948
- 9 NFC: Tampa Bay (0) vs. Los Angeles (9), 1979
Largest Margin of Victory, Game
- 73 NFC: Chi. Bears vs. Washington, 1940 (73-0)
- 49 AFC-D: Oakland vs. Houston, 1969 (56-7)
- 48 AFC: Buffalo vs. L.A. Raiders, 1990 (51-3)
Most Points, Shutout Victory, Game
- 73 NFC: Chi. Bears vs. Washington, 1940
- 38 NFC-D: Dallas vs. Tampa Bay, 1981
- 37 NFC: Green Bay vs. N.Y. Giants, 1961
Most Points Overcome to Win Game
- 32 AFC-FR: Buffalo vs. Houston, 1992 (trailed 3-35, won 41-38) (OT)
- 20 NFC-D: Detroit vs. San Francisco, 1957 (trailed 7-27, won 31-27)
- 18 NFC-D: Dallas vs. San Francisco, 1972 (trailed 3-21, won 30-28)
  AFC-D: Miami vs. Cleveland, 1985 (trailed 3-21, won 24-21)
Most Points, Each Half
- 1st: 41 AFC: Buffalo vs. L.A. Raiders, 1990
- 38 NFC-D: Washington vs. L.A. Rams, 1983
- 35 NFC: Cleveland vs. Detroit, 1954
  AFC-D: Oakland vs. Houston, 1969
  SB: Washington vs. Denver, 1987
- 2nd: 45 NFC: Chi. Bears vs. Washington, 1940
- 35 AFC-FR: Buffalo vs. Houston, 1992
- 30 SB: N.Y. Giants vs. Denver, 1986
  AFC: Cleveland vs. Denver, 1987
Most Points, Each Quarter
- 1st: 28 AFC-D: Oakland vs. Houston, 1969
- 24 AFC-D: San Diego vs. Miami, 1981
- 21 NFC: Chi. Bears vs. Washington, 1940
  AFC: San Diego vs. Boston, 1963
  AFC-D: Oakland vs. Kansas City, 1968
  AFC: Oakland vs. San Diego, 1980
  AFC: Buffalo vs. L.A. Raiders, 1990
- 2nd: 35 SB: Washington vs. Denver, 1987
- 26 AFC-D: Pittsburgh vs. Buffalo, 1974
- 24 NFC-D: Chi. Bears vs. Green Bay, 1941
  NFC: Green Bay vs. N.Y. Giants, 1961
- 3rd: 28 AFC-FR: Buffalo vs. Houston, 1992
- 26 NFC: Chi. Bears vs. Washington, 1940
- 21 NFC-D: Dallas vs. Cleveland, 1967
  NFC-D: Dallas vs. Tampa Bay, 1981
  AFC-D: L.A. Raiders vs. Pittsburgh, 1983
  SB: Chicago vs. New England, 1985
  NFC-D: N.Y. Giants vs. San Francisco, 1986

AFC: Cleveland vs. Denver, 1987
AFC: Cleveland vs. Denver, 1989
4th: 27 NFC: N.Y. Giants vs. Chi. Bears, 1934
26 NFC-FR: Philadelphia vs. New Orleans, 1992
24 NFC: Baltimore vs. N.Y. Giants, 1959
OT: 6 NFC: Baltimore vs. N.Y. Giants, 1958
AFC-D: Oakland vs. Baltimore, 1977
NFC-D: L.A. Rams vs. N.Y. Giants, 1989

TOUCHDOWNS
Most Touchdowns, Game
11 NFC: Chi. Bears vs. Washington, 1940
8 NFC: Cleveland vs. Detroit, 1954
NFC: Detroit vs. Cleveland, 1957
AFC-D: Oakland vs. Houston, 1969
SB: San Francisco vs. Denver, 1989
7 AFC: San Diego vs. Boston, 1963
NFC-D: Dallas vs. Cleveland, 1967
NFC-D: N.Y. Giants vs. San Francisco, 1986
AFC: Buffalo vs. L.A. Raiders, 1990
SB: Dallas vs. Buffalo, 1992
Most Touchdowns, Both Teams, Game
11 NFC: Chi. Bears (11) vs. Washington (0), 1940
10 NFC: Detroit (8) vs. Cleveland (2), 1957
AFC-D: Miami (5) vs. San Diego (5), 1981 (OT)
AFC: Miami (6) vs. Pittsburgh (4), 1984
AFC-FR: Buffalo (5) vs. Houston (5), 1992 (OT)
9 NFC: Chi. Bears (6) vs. Washington (3), 1943
NFC: Cleveland (8) vs. Detroit (1), 1954
NFC-D: Dallas (7) vs. Cleveland (2), 1967
AFC-D: Oakland (8) vs. Houston (1), 1969
AFC-D: Oakland (5) vs. Baltimore (4), 1977 (OT)
SB: Pittsburgh (5) vs. Dallas (4), 1978
AFC: Denver (5) vs. Cleveland (4), 1987
SB: San Francisco (8) vs. Denver (1), 1989
AFC-D: Buffalo (5) vs. Miami (4), 1990
SB: Dallas (7) vs. Buffalo (2), 1992
AFC-FR: L.A. Raiders (6) vs. Denver (3), 1993
Fewest Touchdowns, Both Teams, Game
0 NFC-D: N.Y. Giants vs. Cleveland, 1950
NFC-D: Dallas vs. Detroit, 1970
NFC: Los Angeles vs. Tampa Bay, 1979
1 NFC: Chi. Cardinals (0) vs. Philadelphia (1), 1948
NFC-D: Cleveland (0) vs. N.Y. Giants (1), 1958
AFC: San Diego (0) vs. Houston (1), 1961
AFC-D: N.Y. Jets (0) vs. Kansas City (1), 1969
NFC-D: Green Bay (0) vs. Washington (1), 1972
NFC-FR: New Orleans (0) vs. Chicago (1), 1990
NFC: N.Y. Giants (0) vs. San Francisco (1), 1990
AFC-FR: L.A. Raiders (0) vs. Kansas City (1), 1991
2 In many games

POINTS AFTER TOUCHDOWN
Most Points After Touchdown, Game
8 NFC: Cleveland vs. Detroit, 1954
NFC: Detroit vs. Cleveland, 1957
AFC-D: Oakland vs. Houston, 1969
7 NFC: Chi. Bears vs. Washington, 1940
NFC-D: Dallas vs. Cleveland, 1967
NFC-D: N.Y. Giants vs. San Francisco, 1986
SB: San Francisco vs. Denver, 1989
SB: Dallas vs. Buffalo, 1992
6 AFC: San Diego vs. Boston, 1963
NFC-D: Washington vs. L.A. Rams, 1983
AFC: Miami vs. Pittsburgh, 1984
SB: Washington vs. Denver, 1987
AFC: Buffalo vs. L.A. Raiders, 1990
AFC-FR: L.A. Raiders vs. Denver, 1993
Most Points After Touchdown, Both Teams, Game
10 NFC: Detroit (8) vs. Cleveland (2), 1957
AFC-D: Miami (5) vs. San Diego (5), 1981 (OT)
AFC: Miami (6) vs. Pittsburgh (4), 1984
AFC-FR: Buffalo (5) vs. Houston (5), 1992 (OT)
9 In many games
Fewest Points After Touchdown, Both Teams, Game
0 NFC-D: N.Y. Giants vs. Cleveland, 1950
NFC-D: Dallas vs. Detroit, 1970
NFC: Los Angeles vs. Tampa Bay, 1979

FIELD GOALS
Most Field Goals, Game
5 NFC-D: Minnesota vs. San Francisco, 1987
NFC: N.Y. Giants vs. San Francisco, 1990

AFC: Buffalo vs. Miami, 1992
4 AFC-D: Boston vs. Buffalo, 1963
AFC: Oakland vs. Houston, 1967
SB: Green Bay vs. Oakland, 1967
NFC: Washington vs. Dallas, 1972
AFC-D: Oakland vs. Pittsburgh, 1973
SB: San Francisco vs. Cincinnati, 1981
AFC-FR: New England vs. N.Y. Jets, 1985
NFC-FR: Washington vs. L.A. Rams, 1986
NFC-D: Philadelphia vs. Chicago, 1988
AFC-FR: Pittsburgh vs. Houston, 1989 (OT)
3 By many teams
Most Field Goals, Both Teams, Game
7 AFC-FR: Pittsburgh (4) vs. Houston (3), 1989 (OT)
NFC: N.Y. Giants (5) vs. San Francisco (2), 1990
6 NFC-D: Minnesota (5) vs. San Francisco (1), 1987
NFC-D: Philadelphia (4) vs. Chicago (2), 1988
AFC: Buffalo (5) vs. Miami (1), 1992
5 In many games
Most Field Goals Attempted, Game
6 AFC: Oakland vs. Houston, 1967
NFC-D: Los Angeles vs. Dallas, 1973
AFC-D: Cleveland vs. N.Y. Jets, 1986 (OT)
NFC: N.Y. Giants vs. San Francisco, 1990
5 By many teams
Most Field Goals Attempted, Both Teams, Game
9 NFC-D: Philadelphia (5) vs. Chicago (4), 1988
8 NFC-D: Los Angeles (6) vs. Dallas (2), 1973
NFC-D: Detroit (5) vs. San Francisco (3), 1983
AFC-D: Cleveland (6) vs. N.Y. Jets (2), 1986 (OT)
NFC-D: Minnesota (5) vs. San Francisco (3), 1987
AFC-FR: Houston (4) vs. Pittsburgh (4), 1989 (OT)
NFC-FR: Chicago (4) vs. New Orleans (4), 1990
NFC: N.Y. Giants (6) vs. San Francisco (2), 1990
7 In many games

SAFETIES
Most Safeties, Game
1 By many teams
Most Safeties, Both Teams, Game
1 In many games

FIRST DOWNS
Most First Downs, Game
34 AFC-D: San Diego vs. Miami, 1981 (OT)
33 AFC-D: Cleveland vs. N.Y. Jets, 1986 (OT)
31 SB: San Francisco vs. Miami, 1984
Fewest First Downs, Game
6 NFC: N.Y. Giants vs. Green Bay, 1961
7 NFC: Green Bay vs. Boston, 1936
NFC-D: Pittsburgh vs. Philadelphia, 1947
NFC: Chi. Cardinals vs. Philadelphia, 1948
NFC: Los Angeles vs. Philadelphia, 1949
NFC-D: Cleveland vs. N.Y. Giants, 1958
AFC-D: Cincinnati vs. Baltimore, 1970
NFC-D: Detroit vs. Dallas, 1970
NFC: Tampa Bay vs. Los Angeles, 1979
8 By many teams
Most First Downs, Both Teams, Game
59 AFC-D: San Diego (34) vs. Miami (25), 1981 (OT)
55 AFC-FR: San Diego (29) vs. Pittsburgh (26), 1982
51 AFC: Buffalo (30) vs. L.A. Raiders (21), 1990
AFC: Buffalo (29) vs. Kansas City (22), 1993
Fewest First Downs, Both Teams, Game
15 NFC: Green Bay (7) vs. Boston (8), 1936
19 NFC: N.Y. Giants (9) vs. Green Bay (10), 1939
NFC: Washington (9) vs. Chi. Bears (10), 1942
20 NFC-D: Cleveland (9) vs. N.Y. Giants (11), 1950

RUSHING
Most First Downs, Rushing, Game
19 NFC-FR: Dallas vs. Los Angeles, 1980
18 AFC-D: Miami vs. Cincinnati, 1973
AFC: Miami vs. Oakland, 1973
AFC-D: Pittsburgh vs. Buffalo, 1974
17 AFC-D: Cincinnati vs. Seattle, 1988
AFC: Buffalo vs. Kansas City, 1993
Fewest First Downs, Rushing, Game
0 NFC: Los Angeles vs. Philadelphia, 1949
AFC-D: Buffalo vs. Boston, 1963
AFC: Oakland vs. Pittsburgh, 1974
NFC-FR: New Orleans vs. Minnesota, 1987
NFC: L.A. Rams vs. San Francisco, 1989

NFC-D: Chicago vs. N.Y. Giants, 1990
1 By many teams

Most First Downs, Rushing, Both Teams, Game
26 AFC: Buffalo (14) vs. L.A. Raiders (12), 1990
25 NFC-FR: Dallas (19) vs. Los Angeles (6), 1980
23 NFC: Cleveland (15) vs. Detroit (8), 1952
    AFC-D: Miami (18) vs. Cincinnati (5), 1973
    AFC-D: Pittsburgh (18) vs. Buffalo (5), 1974

Fewest First Downs, Rushing, Both Teams, Game
5 AFC-D: Buffalo (0) vs. Boston (5), 1963
6 NFC: Green Bay (2) vs. Boston (4), 1936
    NFC-D: Baltimore (2) vs. Minnesota (4), 1968
    AFC-D: Houston (1) vs. Oakland (5), 1969
    AFC-FR: N.Y. Jets (1) vs. Houston (5), 1991
7 NFC-D: Washington (2) vs. N.Y. Giants (5), 1943
    NFC: Baltimore (3) vs. N.Y. Giants (4), 1959
    NFC: Washington (3) vs. Dallas (4), 1972
    AFC-FR: N.Y. Jets (3) vs. Buffalo (4), 1981
    NFC-D: Detroit (3) vs. Dallas (4), 1991
    AFC-D: Kansas City (3) vs. Houston (4), 1993

PASSING
Most First Downs, Passing, Game
21 AFC-D: Miami vs. San Diego, 1981 (OT)
    AFC-D: San Diego vs. Miami, 1981 (OT)
    AFC-D: Cleveland vs. N.Y. Jets, 1986 (OT)
    NFC-D: Philadelphia vs. Chicago, 1988
20 NFC-FR: Dallas vs. L.A. Rams, 1983
    AFC-D: Buffalo vs. Cleveland, 1989
19 NFC-FR: St. Louis vs. Green Bay, 1982
    NFC-FR: Dallas vs. Tampa Bay, 1982
    AFC-FR: Pittsburgh vs. San Diego, 1982
    AFC-FR: San Diego vs. Pittsburgh, 1982
    NFC: Dallas vs. Washington, 1982
    NFC-D: Detroit vs. Dallas, 1991
    AFC-FR: Kansas City vs. Pittsburgh, 1993 (OT)

Fewest First Downs, Passing, Game
0 NFC: Philadelphia vs. Chi. Cardinals, 1948
1 NFC-D: N.Y. Giants vs. Washington, 1943
    NFC: Cleveland vs. Detroit, 1953
    SB: Denver vs. Dallas, 1977
2 By many teams

Most First Downs, Passing, Both Teams, Game
42 AFC-D: Miami (21) vs. San Diego (21), 1981 (OT)
38 AFC-FR: Pittsburgh (19) vs. San Diego (19), 1982
34 NFC-FR: Washington (18) vs. San Francisco (16), 1990
    AFC-FR: Kansas City (19) vs. Pittsburgh (15), 1993 (OT)

Fewest First Downs, Passing, Both Teams, Game
2 NFC: Philadelphia (0) vs. Chi. Cardinals (2), 1948
4 NFC-D: Cleveland (2) vs. N.Y. Giants (2), 1950
5 NFC: Detroit (2) vs. N.Y. Giants (3), 1935
    NFC: Green Bay (2) vs. N.Y. Giants (3), 1939

PENALTY
Most First Downs, Penalty, Game
7 AFC-D: New England vs. Oakland, 1976
6 AFC-D: Cleveland vs. N.Y. Jets, 1986 (OT)
5 AFC-FR: Cleveland vs. L. A. Raiders, 1982

Most First Downs, Penalty, Both Teams, Game
9 AFC-D: New England (7) vs. Oakland (2), 1976
8 NFC-FR: Atlanta (4) vs. Minnesota (4), 1982
7 AFC-D: Baltimore (4) vs. Oakland (3), 1977 (OT)
    AFC-FR: Denver (4) vs. L.A. Raiders (3), 1993

NET YARDS GAINED RUSHING AND PASSING
Most Yards Gained, Game
610 AFC: San Diego vs. Boston, 1963
602 SB: Washington vs. Denver, 1987
569 AFC: Miami vs. Pittsburgh, 1984

Fewest Yards Gained, Game
86 NFC-D: Cleveland vs. N.Y. Giants, 1958
99 NFC: Chi. Cardinals vs. Philadelphia, 1948
114 NFC-D: N.Y. Giants vs. Washington, 1943

Most Yards Gained, Both Teams, Game
1,036 AFC-D: San Diego (564) vs. Miami (472), 1981 (OT)
1,024 AFC: Miami (569) vs. Pittsburgh (455), 1984
929 SB: Washington (602) vs. Denver (327), 1987

Fewest Yards Gained, Both Teams, Game
331 NFC: Chi. Cardinals (99) vs. Philadelphia (232), 1948
332 NFC-D: N.Y. Giants (150) vs. Cleveland (182), 1950
336 NFC: Boston (116) vs. Green Bay (220), 1936

RUSHING
ATTEMPTS
Most Attempts, Game
65 NFC: Detroit vs. N.Y. Giants, 1935
61 NFC: Philadelphia vs. Los Angeles, 1949
59 AFC: New England vs. Miami, 1985

Fewest Attempts, Game
9 SB: Miami vs. San Francisco, 1984
10 NFC: L.A. Rams vs. San Francisco, 1989
11 SB: New England vs. Chicago, 1985
    AFC-FR: Seattle vs. Houston, 1987 (OT)
    NFC: San Francisco vs. N.Y. Giants, 1990
    AFC: Miami vs. Buffalo, 1992

Most Attempts, Both Teams, Game
109 NFC: Detroit (65) vs. N.Y. Giants (44), 1935
97 AFC-D: Baltimore (50) vs. Oakland (47), 1977 (OT)
91 NFC: Philadelphia (57) vs. Chi. Cardinals (34), 1948

Fewest Attempts, Both Teams, Game
32 AFC-D: Houston (14) vs. Kansas City (18), 1993
38 NFC-D: Detroit (16) vs. Dallas (22), 1991
40 NFC-D: Green Bay (13) vs. Dallas (27), 1993

YARDS GAINED
Most Yards Gained, Game
382 NFC: Chi. Bears vs. Washington, 1940
338 NFC-FR: Dallas vs. Los Angeles, 1980
318 AFC: San Diego vs. Boston, 1963

Fewest Yards Gained, Game
7 AFC-D: Buffalo vs. Boston, 1963
    SB: New England vs. Chicago, 1985
17 SB: Minnesota vs. Pittsburgh, 1974
18 AFC-D: Seattle vs. Cincinnati, 1988

Most Yards Gained, Both Teams, Game
430 NFC-FR: Dallas (338) vs. Los Angeles (92), 1980
426 NFC: Cleveland (227) vs. Detroit (199), 1952
404 NFC: Chi. Bears (382) vs. Washington (22), 1940

Fewest Yards Gained, Both Teams, Game
90 AFC-D: Buffalo (7) vs. Boston (83), 1963
106 NFC: Boston (39) vs. Green Bay (67), 1936
110 AFC-D: Houston (39) vs. Kansas City (71), 1993

AVERAGE GAIN
Highest Average Gain, Game
9.94 AFC: San Diego vs. Boston, 1963 (32-318)
9.29 NFC-D: Green Bay vs. Dallas, 1982 (17-158)
7.35 NFC-FR: Dallas vs. Los Angeles, 1980 (46-338)

Lowest Average Gain, Game
0.58 AFC-D: Buffalo vs. Boston, 1963 (12-7)
0.64 SB: New England vs. Chicago, 1985 (11-7)
0.81 SB: Minnesota vs. Pittsburgh, 1974 (21-17)

TOUCHDOWNS
Most Touchdowns, Game
7 NFC: Chi. Bears vs. Washington, 1940
6 NFC-D: San Francisco vs. N.Y. Giants, 1993
5 NFC: Cleveland vs. Detroit, 1954

Most Touchdowns, Both Teams, Game
7 NFC: Chi. Bears (7) vs. Washington (0), 1940
6 NFC: Cleveland (5) vs. Detroit (1), 1954
    NFC-D: San Francisco (6) vs. N.Y. Giants (0), 1993
5 NFC: Chi. Cardinals (3) vs. Philadelphia (2), 1947
    AFC: San Diego (4) vs. Boston (1), 1963
    AFC-D: Cincinnati (3) vs. Buffalo (2), 1981

PASSING
ATTEMPTS
Most Attempts, Game
65 AFC-D: Cleveland vs. N.Y. Jets, 1986 (OT)
59 SB: Buffalo vs. Washington, 1991
55 NFC-D: Philadelphia vs. Chicago, 1988

Fewest Attempts, Game
5 NFC: Detroit vs. N.Y. Giants, 1935
6 AFC: Miami vs. Oakland, 1973
7 SB: Miami vs. Minnesota, 1973

Most Attempts, Both Teams, Game
102 AFC-D: San Diego (54) vs. Miami (48), 1981 (OT)
96 AFC: N.Y. Jets (49) vs. Oakland (47), 1968
95 AFC-D: Cleveland (65) vs. N.Y. Jets (30), 1986 (OT)

Fewest Attempts, Both Teams, Game
18 NFC: Detroit (5) vs. N.Y. Giants (13), 1935
23 NFC: Chi. Cardinals (11) vs. Philadelphia (12), 1948
24 NFC-D: Cleveland (9) vs. N.Y. Giants (15), 1950

COMPLETIONS

Most Completions, Game

36   AFC-FR: Houston vs. Buffalo, 1992 (OT)
34   AFC-D: Cleveland vs. N.Y. Jets, 1986 (OT)
33   AFC-D: San Diego vs. Miami, 1981 (OT)

Fewest Completions, Game

2   NFC: Detroit vs. N.Y. Giants, 1935
   NFC: Philadelphia vs. Chi. Cardinals, 1948
3   NFC: N.Y. Giants vs. Chi. Bears, 1941
   NFC: Green Bay vs. N.Y. Giants, 1944
   NFC: Chi. Cardinals vs. Philadelphia, 1947
   NFC: Chi. Cardinals vs. Philadelphia, 1948
   NFC-D: Cleveland vs. N.Y. Giants, 1950
   NFC-D: N.Y. Giants vs. Cleveland, 1950
   NFC: Cleveland vs. Detroit, 1953
   AFC: Miami vs. Oakland, 1973
4   NFC: N.Y. Giants vs. Detroit, 1935
   NFC-D: N.Y. Giants vs. Washington, 1943
   NFC-D: Pittsburgh vs. Philadelphia, 1947
   NFC-D: Dallas vs. Detroit, 1970
   AFC: Miami vs. Baltimore, 1971
   SB: Miami vs. Washington, 1982
   AFC-FR: Seattle vs. L.A. Raiders, 1984

Most Completions, Both Teams, Game

64   AFC-D: San Diego (33) vs. Miami (31), 1981 (OT)
57   AFC-FR: Houston (36) vs. Buffalo (21), 1992 (OT)
56   NFC-D: Dallas (28) vs. Green Bay (28), 1993

Fewest Completions, Both Teams, Game

5   NFC: Philadelphia (2) vs. Chi. Cardinals (3), 1948
6   NFC: Detroit (2) vs. N.Y. Giants (4), 1935
   NFC-D: Cleveland (3) vs. N.Y. Giants (3), 1950
11   NFC: Green Bay (3) vs. N.Y. Giants (8), 1944
   NFC-D: Dallas (4) vs. Detroit (7), 1970

COMPLETION PERCENTAGE

Highest Completion Percentage, Game (20 attempts)

88.0   SB: N.Y. Giants vs. Denver, 1986 (25-22)
87.1   NFC: San Francisco vs. L.A. Rams, 1989 (31-27)
80.0   NFC-D: Washington vs. L.A. Rams, 1983 (25-20)

Lowest Completion Percentage, Game (20 attempts)

18.5   NFC: Tampa Bay vs. Los Angeles, 1979 (27-5)
20.0   NFC-D: N.Y. Giants vs. Washington, 1943 (20-4)
25.8   NFC: Chi. Bears vs. Washington, 1937 (31-8)

YARDS GAINED

Most Yards Gained, Game

483   AFC-D: Cleveland vs. N.Y. Jets, 1986 (OT)
435   AFC: Miami vs. Pittsburgh, 1984
415   AFC-D: San Diego vs. Miami, 1981 (OT)

Fewest Yards Gained, Game

3   NFC: Chi. Cardinals vs. Philadelphia, 1948
7   NFC: Philadelphia vs. Chi. Cardinals, 1948
9   NFC-D: N.Y. Giants vs. Cleveland, 1950
   NFC: Cleveland vs. Detroit, 1953

Most Yards Gained, Both Teams, Game

809   AFC-D: San Diego (415) vs. Miami (394), 1981 (OT)
747   AFC: Miami (435) vs. Pittsburgh (312), 1984
666   AFC-D: Cleveland (483) vs. N.Y. Jets (183), 1986 (OT)

Fewest Yards Gained, Both Teams, Game

10   NFC: Chi. Cardinals (3) vs. Philadelphia (7), 1948
38   NFC-D: N.Y. Giants (9) vs. Cleveland (29), 1950
102   NFC-D: Dallas (22) vs. Detroit (80), 1970

TIMES SACKED

Most Times Sacked, Game

9   AFC: Kansas City vs. Buffalo, 1966
   NFC: Chicago vs. San Francisco, 1984
   AFC-D: N.Y. Jets vs. Cleveland, 1986 (OT)
   AFC-D: Houston vs. Kansas City, 1993
8   NFC: Green Bay vs. Dallas, 1967
   NFC: Minnesota vs. Washington, 1987
7   NFC-D: Dallas vs. Los Angeles, 1973
   SB: Dallas vs. Pittsburgh, 1975
   AFC-FR: Houston vs. Oakland, 1980
   NFC-D: Washington vs. Chicago, 1984
   SB: New England vs. Chicago, 1985
   AFC-FR: Kansas City vs. San Diego, 1992
   AFC-D: Pittsburgh vs. Buffalo, 1992

Most Times Sacked, Both Teams, Game

13   AFC: Kansas City (9) vs. Buffalo (4), 1966
   AFC-D: N.Y. Jets (9) vs. Cleveland (4), 1986 (OT)
12   NFC-D: Dallas (7) vs. Los Angeles (5), 1973
   NFC-D: Washington (7) vs. Chicago (5), 1984

   NFC: Chicago (9) vs. San Francisco (3), 1984
   AFC-FR: Kansas City (7) vs. San Diego (5), 1992
11   AFC-D: Houston (9) vs. Kansas City (2), 1993

Fewest Times Sacked, Both Teams, Game

0   AFC-D: Buffalo vs. Pittsburgh, 1974
   AFC-FR: Pittsburgh vs. San Diego, 1982
   AFC: Miami vs. Pittsburgh, 1984
   AFC-D: Buffalo vs. Miami, 1990
   AFC-D: Denver vs. Houston, 1991
1   In many games

TOUCHDOWNS

Most Touchdowns, Game

6   AFC-D: Oakland vs. Houston, 1969
5   NFC: Chi. Bears vs. Washington, 1943
   NFC: Detroit vs. Cleveland, 1957
   AFC-D: Oakland vs. Kansas City, 1968
   SB: San Francisco vs. Denver, 1989
4   By many teams

Most Touchdowns, Both Teams, Game

8   AFC-FR: Buffalo (4) vs. Houston (4), 1992 (OT)
7   NFC: Chi. Bears (5) vs. Washington (2), 1943
   AFC-D: Oakland (6) vs. Houston (1), 1969
   SB: Pittsburgh (4) vs. Dallas (3), 1978
   AFC-D: Miami (4) vs. San Diego (3), 1981 (OT)
   AFC: Miami (4) vs. Pittsburgh (3), 1984
   AFC-D: Buffalo (4) vs. Cleveland (3), 1989
6   NFC-FR: Green Bay (4) vs. St. Louis (2), 1982
   AFC: Cleveland (3) vs. Denver (3), 1987
   AFC-D: Buffalo (3) vs. Miami (3), 1990
   AFC-FR: Denver (3) vs. L.A. Raiders (3), 1993

INTERCEPTIONS BY

Most Interceptions By, Game

8   NFC: Chi. Bears vs. Washington, 1940
7   NFC: Cleveland vs. Los Angeles, 1955
6   NFC: Green Bay vs. N.Y. Giants, 1939
   NFC: Chi. Bears vs. N.Y. Giants, 1946
   NFC: Cleveland vs. Detroit, 1954
   AFC: San Diego vs. Houston, 1961
   AFC: Buffalo vs. L.A. Raiders, 1990

Most Interceptions By, Both Teams, Game

10   NFC: Cleveland (7) vs. Los Angeles (3), 1955
   AFC: San Diego (6) vs. Houston (4), 1961
9   NFC: Green Bay (6) vs. N.Y. Giants (3), 1939
8   NFC: Chi. Bears (8) vs. Washington (0), 1940
   NFC: Chi. Bears (6) vs. N.Y. Giants (2), 1946
   NFC: Cleveland (6) vs. Detroit (2), 1954
   AFC-FR: Buffalo (4) vs. N.Y. Jets (4), 1981
   AFC: Miami (5) vs. N.Y. Jets (3), 1982

YARDS GAINED

Most Yards Gained, Game

138   AFC-FR: N.Y. Jets vs. Cincinnati, 1982
136   AFC: Dall. Texans vs. Houston, 1962 (OT)
130   NFC-D: Los Angeles vs. St. Louis, 1975

Most Yards Gained, Both Teams, Game

156   NFC: Green Bay (123) vs. N.Y. Giants (33), 1939
149   NFC: Cleveland (103) vs. Los Angeles (46), 1955
141   AFC-FR: Buffalo (79) vs. N.Y. Jets (62), 1981

TOUCHDOWNS

Most Touchdowns, Game

3   NFC: Chi. Bears vs. Washington, 1940
2   NFC-D: Los Angeles vs. St. Louis, 1975
1   In many games

Most Touchdowns, Both Teams, Game

3   NFC: Chi. Bears (3) vs. Washington (0), 1940
2   NFC-D: Los Angeles (2) vs. St. Louis (0), 1975
   NFC-D: Dallas (1) vs. Green Bay (1), 1982
   NFC-D: Minnesota (1) vs. San Francisco (1), 1987
   NFC-FR: Detroit (1) vs. Green Bay (1), 1993
1   In many games

PUNTING

Most Punts, Game

14   AFC-D: N.Y. Jets vs. Cleveland, 1986 (OT)
13   NFC: N.Y. Giants vs. Chi. Bears, 1933
   AFC-D: Baltimore vs. Oakland, 1977 (OT)
11   AFC: Houston vs. Oakland, 1967
   AFC-D: Houston vs. Oakland, 1969
   NFC: L.A. Rams vs. Chicago, 1985

Fewest Punts, Game
- 0 NFC-FR: St. Louis vs. Green Bay, 1982
  AFC-FR: N.Y. Jets vs. Cincinnati, 1982
- 1 NFC-D: Cleveland vs. Dallas, 1969
  AFC: Miami vs. Oakland, 1973
  AFC-D: Oakland vs. Cincinnati, 1975
  AFC-D: Pittsburgh vs. Baltimore, 1976
  AFC: Pittsburgh vs. Houston, 1978
  NFC-FR: Green Bay vs. St. Louis, 1982
  AFC-FR: Miami vs. New England, 1982
  AFC-FR: San Diego vs. Pittsburgh, 1982
  AFC-D: Cleveland vs. Indianapolis, 1987
  AFC-D: Buffalo vs. Miami, 1990
  AFC-FR: L.A. Raiders vs. Kansas City, 1991
  NFC-FR: Atlanta vs. New Orleans, 1991
  NFC-FR: Chicago vs. Dallas, 1991
  AFC-D: Houston vs. Denver, 1991
  NFC: San Francisco vs. Dallas, 1992
- 2 In many games

Most Punts, Both Teams, Game
- 23 NFC: N.Y. Giants (13) vs. Chi. Bears (10), 1933
- 22 AFC-D: N.Y. Jets (14) vs. Cleveland (8), 1986 (OT)
- 21 AFC-D: Baltimore (13) vs. Oakland (8), 1977 (OT)
  NFC: L.A. Rams (11) vs. Chicago (10), 1985

Fewest Punts, Both Teams, Game
- 1 NFC-FR: St. Louis (0) vs. Green Bay (1), 1982
- 2 AFC-FR: N.Y. Jets (0) vs. Cincinnati (2), 1982
- 3 AFC: Miami (1) vs. Oakland (2), 1973
  AFC-FR: San Diego (1) vs. Pittsburgh (2), 1982
  AFC-D: Buffalo (1) vs. Miami (2), 1990
  AFC-FR: L.A. Raiders (1) vs. Kansas City (2), 1991
  AFC-D: Houston (1) vs. Denver (2), 1991

AVERAGE YARDAGE
Highest Average, Punting, Game (4 punts)
- 56.0 AFC: Oakland vs. San Diego, 1980
- 52.5 NFC: Washington vs. Chi. Bears, 1942
- 51.6 AFC-D: Cincinnati vs. L.A. Raiders, 1990

Lowest Average, Punting, Game (4 punts)
- 24.9 NFC: Washington vs. Chi. Bears, 1937
- 25.3 AFC-FR: Pittsburgh vs. Houston, 1989
- 25.5 NFC: Green Bay vs. N.Y. Giants, 1962

PUNT RETURNS
Most Punt Returns, Game
- 8 NFC: Green Bay vs. N.Y. Giants, 1944
- 7 By eight teams

Most Punt Returns, Both Teams, Game
- 13 AFC-FR: Houston (7) vs. Oakland (6), 1980
- 11 NFC: Green Bay (8) vs. N.Y. Giants (3), 1944
  NFC-D: Green Bay (6) vs. Baltimore (5), 1965
- 10 In many games

Fewest Punt Returns, Both Teams, Game
- 0 NFC: Chi. Bears vs. N.Y. Giants, 1941
  AFC: Boston vs. San Diego, 1963
  NFC-FR: Green Bay vs. St. Louis, 1982
  AFC-FR: Houston vs. N.Y. Jets, 1991
  AFC-D: Denver vs. Houston, 1991
  NFC-D: San Francisco vs. Washington, 1992
- 1 AFC: Miami (0) vs. Pittsburgh (1), 1972
  AFC: Cincinnati (0) vs. San Diego (1), 1981
  AFC-FR: Cincinnati (0) vs. N.Y. Jets (1), 1982
  AFC-FR: San Diego (0) vs. Pittsburgh (1), 1982
  NFC-D: Minnesota (0) vs. Washington (1), 1982
  AFC: Seattle (0) vs. L.A. Raiders (1), 1983
  AFC-D: Pittsburgh (0) vs. Denver (1), 1989
  NFC-FR: New Orleans (0) vs. Atlanta (1), 1991
  AFC-FR: Buffalo (0) vs. Houston (1), 1992 (OT)
- 2 In many games

YARDS GAINED
Most Yards Gained, Game
- 155 NFC-D: Dallas vs. Cleveland, 1967
- 150 NFC: Chi. Cardinals vs. Philadelphia, 1947
- 143 NFC-FR: Minnesota vs. New Orleans, 1987

Fewest Yards Gained, Game
- −10 NFC: Green Bay vs. Cleveland, 1965
- −9 NFC: Dallas vs. Green Bay, 1966
  AFC-D: Kansas City vs. Oakland, 1968
- −5 AFC-D: Miami vs. Oakland, 1970
  NFC-D: San Francisco vs. Dallas, 1972
  NFC: Dallas vs. Washington, 1972

Most Yards Gained, Both Teams, Game
- 166 NFC-D: Dallas (155) vs. Cleveland (11), 1967
- 160 NFC: Chi. Cardinals (150) vs. Philadelphia (10), 1947
- 146 NFC-D: Philadelphia (112) vs. Pittsburgh (34), 1947

Fewest Yards Gained, Both Teams, Game
- −9 NFC: Dallas (−9) vs. Green Bay (0), 1966
- −6 AFC-D: Miami (−5) vs. Oakland (−1), 1970
- −3 NFC-D: San Francisco (−5) vs. Dallas (2), 1972

TOUCHDOWNS
Most Touchdowns, Game
- 1 By 10 teams

KICKOFF RETURNS
Most Kickoff Returns, Game
- 10 NFC-D: L.A. Rams vs. Washington, 1983
- 9 NFC: Chi. Bears vs. N.Y. Giants, 1956
  AFC: Boston vs. San Diego, 1963
  AFC: Houston vs. Oakland, 1967
  SB: Denver vs. San Francisco, 1989
  AFC-D: Miami vs. Buffalo, 1990
  AFC: L.A. Raiders vs. Buffalo, 1990
- 8 By many teams

Most Kickoff Returns, Both Teams, Game
- 15 AFC-D: Miami (9) vs. Buffalo (6), 1990
- 13 NFC-D: Green Bay (7) vs. Dallas (6), 1982
- 12 In many games

Fewest Kickoff Returns, Both Teams, Game
- 1 NFC: Green Bay (0) vs. Boston (1), 1936
  AFC-FR: San Diego (0) vs. Kansas City (1), 1992
- 2 NFC-D: Los Angeles (0) vs. Chi. Bears (2), 1950
  AFC: Houston (0) vs. San Diego (2), 1961
  AFC-D: Oakland (1) vs. Pittsburgh (1), 1972
  AFC-D: N.Y. Jets (0) vs. L.A. Raiders (2), 1982
  AFC: Miami (1) vs. N.Y. Jets (1), 1982
  NFC: N.Y. Giants (0) vs. Washington (2), 1986
- 3 In many games

YARDS GAINED
Most Yards Gained, Game
- 225 NFC: Washington vs. Chi. Bears, 1940
- 222 SB: Miami vs. Washington, 1982
- 215 NFC: Los Angeles vs. Cleveland, 1955
  AFC: Houston vs. Oakland, 1967

Most Yards Gained, Both Teams, Game
- 379 AFC-D: Baltimore (193) vs. Oakland (186), 1977 (OT)
- 321 NFC-D: Dallas (173) vs. Green Bay (148), 1982
- 318 AFC-D: Miami (183) vs. Oakland (135), 1974

Fewest Yards Gained, Both Teams, Game
- 5 AFC-FR: San Diego (0) vs. Kansas City (5), 1992
- 15 NFC: N.Y. Giants (0) vs. Washington (15), 1986
- 31 NFC-D: Los Angeles (0) vs. Chi. Bears (31), 1950

TOUCHDOWNS
Most Touchdowns, Game
- 1 NFC-D: San Francisco vs. Dallas, 1972
  AFC-D: Miami vs. Oakland, 1974
  AFC-D: Baltimore vs. Oakland, 1977 (OT)
  SB: Miami vs. Washington, 1982
  SB: Cincinnati vs. San Francisco, 1988
  AFC-D: Cleveland vs. Buffalo, 1989

PENALTIES
Most Penalties, Game
- 17 AFC-FR: L.A. Raiders vs. Denver, 1993
- 14 AFC-FR: Oakland vs. Houston, 1980
  NFC-D: San Francisco vs. N.Y. Giants, 1981
- 13 AFC-FR: Houston vs. Cleveland, 1988
  AFC-D: Houston vs. Denver, 1991

Fewest Penalties, Game
- 0 NFC: Philadelphia vs. Green Bay, 1960
  NFC-D: Detroit vs. Dallas, 1970
  AFC-D: Miami vs. Oakland, 1970
  SB: Miami vs. Dallas, 1971
  NFC-D: Washington vs. Minnesota, 1973
  SB: Pittsburgh vs. Dallas, 1975
  NFC: San Francisco vs. Chicago, 1988
  SB: Denver vs. San Francisco, 1989
  AFC-D: L.A. Raiders vs. Cincinnati, 1990
  AFC-D: Miami vs. San Diego, 1992
- 1 By many teams

Most Penalties, Both Teams, Game
- 27 AFC-FR: L.A. Raiders (17) vs. Denver (10), 1993

22 AFC-FR: Oakland (14) vs. Houston (8), 1980
   NFC-D: San Francisco (14) vs. N.Y. Giants (8), 1981
   AFC-FR: Houston (13) vs. Cleveland (9), 1988
21 AFC-D: Oakland (11) vs. New England (10), 1976

Fewest Penalties, Both Teams, Game
1 AFC-D: L.A. Raiders (0) vs. Cincinnati (1), 1990
2 NFC: Washington (1) vs. Chi. Bears (1), 1937
   NFC-D: Washington (0) vs. Minnesota (2), 1973
   SB: Pittsburgh (0) vs. Dallas (2), 1975
3 AFC: Miami (1) vs. Baltimore (2), 1971
   NFC: San Francisco (1) vs. Dallas (2), 1971
   SB: Miami (0) vs. Dallas (3), 1971
   AFC-D: Pittsburgh (1) vs. Oakland (2), 1972
   AFC-D: Miami (1) vs. Cincinnati (2), 1973
   SB: Miami (1) vs. San Francisco (2), 1984
   NFC: San Francisco (0) vs. Chicago (3), 1988

YARDS PENALIZED

Most Yards Penalized, Game
145 NFC-D: San Francisco vs. N.Y. Giants, 1981
133 SB: Dallas vs. Baltimore, 1970
130 AFC-FR: L.A. Raiders vs. Denver, 1993

Fewest Yards Penalized, Game
0 By 10 teams

Most Yards Penalized, Both Teams, Game
227 AFC-FR: L.A. Raiders (130) vs. Denver (97), 1993
206 NFC-D: San Francisco (145) vs. N.Y. Giants (61), 1981
193 AFC-FR: Houston (118) vs. Cleveland (75), 1988

Fewest Yards Penalized, Both Teams, Game
5 AFC-D: L.A. Raiders (0) vs. Cincinnati (5), 1990
9 NFC-D: Washington (0) vs. Minnesota (9), 1973
15 SB: Miami (0) vs. Dallas (15), 1971

FUMBLES

Most Fumbles, Game
8 SB: Buffalo vs. Dallas, 1992
7 AFC-D: Houston vs. Kansas City, 1993
6 By 11 teams

Most Fumbles, Both Teams, Game
12 AFC: Houston (6) vs. Pittsburgh (6), 1978
   SB: Buffalo (8) vs. Dallas (4), 1992
10 NFC: Chi. Bears (5) vs. N.Y. Giants (5), 1934
   SB: Dallas (6) vs. Denver (4), 1977
9 NFC-D: San Francisco (6) vs. Detroit (3), 1957
   NFC-D: San Francisco (5) vs. Dallas (4), 1972
   NFC: Dallas (5) vs. Philadelphia (4), 1980

Most Fumbles Lost, Game
5 SB: Buffalo vs. Dallas, 1992
4 NFC: N.Y. Giants vs. Baltimore, 1958 (OT)
   AFC: Kansas City vs. Oakland, 1969
   SB: Baltimore vs. Dallas, 1970
   AFC: Pittsburgh vs. Oakland, 1975
   SB: Denver vs. Dallas, 1977
   AFC: Houston vs. Pittsburgh, 1978
   AFC: Miami vs. New England, 1985
   SB: New England vs. Chicago, 1985
   NFC-FR: L.A. Rams vs. Washington, 1986
3 By many teams

Fewest Fumbles, Both Teams, Game
0 NFC: Green Bay vs. Cleveland, 1965
   AFC-D: Houston vs. San Diego, 1979
   NFC-D: Dallas vs. Los Angeles, 1979
   SB: Los Angeles vs. Pittsburgh, 1979
   AFC-D: Buffalo vs. Cincinnati, 1981
   NFC-D: San Francisco vs. Washington, 1990
1 In many games

RECOVERIES

Most Total Fumbles Recovered, Game
8 SB: Dallas vs. Denver, 1977 (4 own, 4 opp)
7 NFC: Chi. Bears vs. N.Y. Giants, 1934 (5 own, 2 opp)
   NFC-D: San Francisco vs. Detroit, 1957 (4 own, 3 opp)
   NFC-D: San Francisco vs. Dallas, 1972 (4 own, 3 opp)
   AFC: Pittsburgh vs. Houston, 1978 (3 own, 4 opp)
6 AFC: Houston vs. San Diego, 1961 (4 own, 2 opp)
   AFC-D: Cleveland vs. Baltimore, 1971 (4 own, 2 opp)
   AFC-D: Cleveland vs. Oakland, 1980 (5 own, 1 opp)
   NFC: Philadelphia vs. Dallas, 1980 (3 own, 3 opp)
   SB: Dallas vs. Buffalo, 1992 (1 own, 5 opp)

Most Own Fumbles Recovered, Game
5 NFC: Chi. Bears vs. N.Y. Giants, 1934
   AFC-D: Cleveland vs. Oakland, 1980
4 By many teams

TURNOVERS
(Numbers of times losing the ball on interceptions and fumbles.)

Most Turnovers, Game
9 NFC: Washington vs. Chi. Bears, 1940
   NFC: Detroit vs. Cleveland, 1954
   AFC: Houston vs. Pittsburgh, 1978
   SB: Buffalo vs. Dallas, 1992
8 NFC: N.Y. Giants vs. Chi. Bears, 1946
   NFC: Los Angeles vs. Cleveland, 1955
   NFC: Cleveland vs. Detroit, 1957
   SB: Denver vs. Dallas, 1977
   NFC-D: Minnesota vs. Philadelphia, 1980
7 AFC: Houston vs. San Diego, 1961
   SB: Baltimore vs. Dallas, 1970
   AFC: Pittsburgh vs. Oakland, 1975
   NFC-D: Chicago vs. Dallas, 1977
   NFC: Los Angeles vs. Dallas, 1978
   AFC-D: San Diego vs. Miami, 1982
   AFC: Buffalo vs. L.A. Raiders, 1990

Fewest Turnovers, Game
0 By many teams

Most Turnovers, Both Teams, Game
14 AFC: Houston (9) vs. Pittsburgh (5), 1978
13 NFC: Detroit (9) vs. Cleveland (4), 1954
   AFC: Houston (7) vs. San Diego (6), 1961
12 AFC: Pittsburgh (7) vs. Oakland (5), 1975

Fewest Turnovers, Both Teams, Game
0 SB: Buffalo vs. N.Y. Giants, 1990
   FR: Kansas City vs Pittsburgh, 1993 (OT)
1 AFC-D: Baltimore (0) vs. Cincinnati (1), 1970
   AFC-D: Pittsburgh (0) vs. Buffalo (1), 1974
   AFC: Oakland (0) vs. Pittsburgh (1), 1976
   NFC-D: Minnesota (0) vs. Washington (1), 1982
   NFC-D: Chicago (0) vs. N.Y. Giants (1), 1985
   SB: N.Y. Giants (0) vs. Denver (1), 1986
   NFC: Washington (0) vs. Minnesota (1), 1987
   AFC-D: Cincinnati (0) vs. L.A. Raiders (1), 1990
   NFC: N.Y. Giants (0) vs. San Francisco (1), 1990
   NFC-FR: N.Y. Giants (0) vs. Minnesota (1), 1993
   AFC-FR: L.A. Raiders (0) vs. Denver (1), 1993
   NFC: Dallas (0) vs. San Francisco (1), 1993
2 In many games

Compiled by Elias Sports Bureau

INDIVIDUAL RECORDS

SERVICE
Most Games
- 10 Lawrence Taylor, N.Y. Giants, 1982-91
    - Ronnie Lott, San Francisco, 1982-85, 1987-91; L.A. Raiders 1992
    - Mike Singletary, Chicago, 1984-93
- 9 *Ken Houston, Houston, 1971-73; Washington, 1974-79
    - Joe Greene, Pittsburgh, 1971-77, 1979-80
    - Jack Lambert, Pittsburgh, 1976-84
    - Walter Payton, Chicago, 1977-81, 1984-87
    - Harry Carson, N.Y. Giants, 1979-80, 1982-88
    - Mike Webster, Pittsburgh, 1979-86, 1988
    - **Anthony Muñoz, Cincinnati, 1982-87, 1989-90, 1992
- 8 Tom Mack, Los Angeles, 1971-76, 1978-79
    - *Franco Harris, Pittsburgh, 1973-76, 1978-81
    - Lemar Parrish, Cincinnati, 1971-72, 1975-77; Washington, 1978, 1980-81
    - Art Shell, Oakland, 1973-79, 1981
    - Ted Hendricks, Baltimore, 1972-74; Green Bay, 1975; Oakland, 1981-82; L.A. Raiders, 1983-84
    - *John Hannah, New England, 1977, 1979-83, 1985-86
    - *Randy White, Dallas, 1978, 1980-86
    - *Mike Haynes, New England, 1978-81, 1983; L.A. Raiders, 1985-87
    - James Lofton, Green Bay, 1979, 1981-86; Buffalo 1992
    - *Mike Munchak, Houston, 1985-86, 1988-93
    - Howie Long, L.A. Raiders, 1984-88, 1990, 1993-94
    - Reggie White, Philadelphia, 1987-93; Green Bay, 1994
    - *Also selected, but did not play, in one additional game
    - **Also selected, but did not play, in two additional games

SCORING
POINTS
Most Points, Career
- 37 Morten Andersen, New Orleans, 1986-89, 1991, 1993 (13-pat, 8-fg)
- 30 Jan Stenerud, Kansas City, 1971-72, 1976; Green Bay, 1985 (6-pat, 8-fg)
- 26 Nick Lowery, Kansas City, 1982, 1991, 1993 (5 pat, 7 fg)

Most Points, Game
- 18 John Brockington, Green Bay, 1973 (3-td)
- 15 Garo Yepremian, Miami, 1974 (5-fg)
- 14 Jan Stenerud, Kansas City, 1972 (2-pat, 4-fg)

TOUCHDOWNS
Most Touchdowns, Career
- 3 John Brockington, Green Bay, 1972-74 (2-r, 1-p)
    - Earl Campbell, Houston, 1979-82, 1984 (3-r)
    - Chuck Muncie, New Orleans, 1980; San Diego, 1982-83 (3-r)
    - William Andrews, Atlanta, 1981-84 (1-r, 2-p)
    - Marcus Allen, L.A. Raiders, 1983, 1985-86, 1988; Kansas City, 1994 (2-r, 1-p)
- 2 By 13 players

Most Touchdowns, Game
- 3 John Brockington, Green Bay, 1973 (2-r, 1-p)
- 2 Mel Renfro, Dallas, 1971 (2-ret)
    - Earl Campbell, Houston, 1980 (2-r)
    - Chuck Muncie, New Orleans, 1980 (2-r)
    - William Andrews, Atlanta, 1984 (2-p)
    - Herschel Walker, Dallas, 1989 (2-r)
    - Johnny Johnson, Phoenix, 1991 (2-r)

POINTS AFTER TOUCHDOWN
Most Points After Touchdown, Career
- 13 Morten Andersen, New Orleans, 1986-89, 1991, 1993 (13 att)
- 6 Chester Marcol, Green Bay, 1973, 1975 (6 att)
    - Mark Moseley, Washington, 1980, 1983 (7 att)
    - Ali Haji-Sheikh, N.Y. Giants, 1984 (6 att)
    - Jan Stenerud, Kansas City, 1971-72, 1976; Green Bay, 1985 (6 att)

Most Points After Touchdown, Game
- 6 Ali Haji-Sheikh, N.Y. Giants, 1984 (6 att)
- 4 Chester Marcol, Green Bay, 1973 (4 att)
    - Mark Moseley, Washington, 1980 (5 att)
    - Morten Andersen, New Orleans, 1986 (4 att), 1989 (4 att)

FIELD GOALS
Most Field Goals Attempted, Career
- 15 Jan Stenerud, Kansas City, 1971-72, 1976; Green Bay, 1985
    - Morten Andersen, New Orleans, 1986-89, 1991, 1993
    - Nick Lowery, Kansas City, 1982, 1991, 1993

Most Field Goals Attempted, Game
- Kansas City, 1972

- Eddie Murray, Detroit, 1981
- Mark Moseley, Washington, 1983
- 5 Garo Yepremian, Miami, 1974
- 4 Jan Stenerud, Kansas City, 1976
    - Nick Lowery, Kansas City, 1991, 1993
    - Morten Andersen, New Orleans, 1993

Most Field Goals, Career
- 8 Jan Stenerud, Kansas City, 1971-72, 1976; Green Bay, 1985
    - Morten Andersen, New Orleans, 1986-89, 1991, 1993
- 7 Nick Lowery, Kansas City, 1982, 1991, 1993

Most Field Goals, Game
- 5 Garo Yepremian, Miami, 1974 (5 att)
- 4 Jan Stenerud, Kansas City, 1972 (6 att)
    - Eddie Murray, Detroit, 1981 (6 att)
- 3 Nick Lowery, Kansas City, 1991 (4 att)
    - Nick Lowery, Kansas City, 1993 (4 att)

Longest Field Goal
- 51 Morten Andersen, New Orleans, 1989
- 48 Jan Stenerud, Kansas City, 1972
    - Jeff Jaeger, L.A. Raiders, 1992
- 43 Gary Anderson, Pittsburgh, 1984
    - Nick Lowery, Kansas City, 1991

SAFETIES
Most Safeties, Game
- 1 Art Still, Kansas City, 1983
    - Mark Gastineau, N.Y. Jets, 1985
    - Greg Townsend, L.A. Raiders, 1992

RUSHING
ATTEMPTS
Most Attempts, Career
- 81 Walter Payton, Chicago, 1977-81, 1984-87
- 68 O.J. Simpson, Buffalo, 1973-77
- 63 Eric Dickerson, L.A. Rams, 1984-85, 1987; Indianapolis, 1988-90

Most Attempts, Game
- 19 O.J. Simpson, Buffalo, 1974
- 17 Marv Hubbard, Oakland, 1974
- 16 O.J. Simpson, Buffalo, 1973
    - Marcus Allen, L.A. Raiders, 1986

YARDS GAINED
Most Yards Gained, Career
- 368 Walter Payton, Chicago, 1977-81, 1984-87
- 356 O.J. Simpson, Buffalo, 1973-77
- 220 Earl Campbell, Houston, 1979-82, 1984

Most Yards Gained, Game
- 112 O.J. Simpson, Buffalo, 1973
- 104 Marv Hubbard, Oakland, 1974
- 85 Neal Anderson, Chicago, 1989

Longest Run From Scrimmage
- 41 Lawrence McCutcheon, Los Angeles, 1976
- 39 Chris Warren, Seattle, 1994
- 32 Randall Cunningham, Philadelphia, 1989

AVERAGE GAIN
Highest Average Gain, Career (20 attempts)
- 5.81 Marv Hubbard, Oakland, 1972-74 (36-209)
- 5.71 Wilbert Montgomery, Philadelphia, 1979-80 (21-120)
- 5.36 Larry Csonka, Miami, 1971-72, 1975 (22-118)

Highest Average Gain, Game (10 attempts)
- 7.00 O.J. Simpson, Buffalo, 1973 (16-112)
    - Ottis Anderson, St. Louis, 1981 (10-70)
- 6.91 Walter Payton, Chicago, 1985 (11-76)
- 6.90 Earl Campbell, Houston, 1980 (10-69)

TOUCHDOWNS
Most Touchdowns, Career
- 3 Earl Campbell, Houston, 1979-82, 1984
    - Chuck Muncie, New Orleans, 1980; San Diego, 1982-83
- 2 John Brockington, Green Bay, 1972-74
    - O.J. Simpson, Buffalo, 1973-77
    - Walter Payton, Chicago, 1977-81, 1984-87
    - Marcus Allen, L.A. Raiders, 1983, 1985-86, 1988; Kansas City, 1994
    - Herschel Walker, Dallas, 1988-89
    - Johnny Johnson, Phoenix, 1991

Most Touchdowns, Game
- 2 John Brockington, Green Bay, 1973
    - Earl Campbell, Houston, 1980
    - Chuck Muncie, New Orleans, 1980
    - Herschel Walker, Dallas, 1989
    - Johnny Johnson, Phoenix, 1991

PASSING

ATTEMPTS

Most Attempts, Career
- 120 Dan Fouts, San Diego, 1980-84, 1986
- 88 Bob Griese, Miami, 1971-72, 1974-75, 1977, 1979
- 68 Warren Moon, Houston, 1989-94

Most Attempts, Game
- 32 Bill Kenney, Kansas City, 1984
   Steve Young, San Francisco, 1993
- 30 Dan Fouts, San Diego, 1983
- 28 Jim Hart, St. Louis, 1976

COMPLETIONS

Most Completions, Career
- 63 Dan Fouts, San Diego, 1980-84, 1986
- 44 Bob Griese, Miami, 1971-72, 1974-75, 1977, 1979
- 34 Warren Moon, Houston, 1989-94

Most Completions, Game
- 21 Joe Theismann, Washington, 1984
- 18 Steve Young, San Francisco, 1993
- 17 Dan Fouts, San Diego, 1983

COMPLETION PERCENTAGE

Highest Completion Percentage, Career (40 attempts)
- 68.9 Joe Theismann, Washington, 1983-84 (45-31)
- 64.4 Jim Kelly, Buffalo, 1988, 1991-92 (45-29)
- 58.9 Ken Anderson, Cincinnati, 1976-77, 1982-83 (56-33)

Highest Completion Percentage, Game (10 attempts)
- 90.0 Archie Manning, New Orleans, 1980 (10-9)
- 77.8 Joe Theismann, Washington, 1984 (27-21)
- 72.2 Jim Everett, L.A. Rams, 1991 (18-13)

YARDS GAINED

Most Yards Gained, Career
- 890 Dan Fouts, San Diego, 1980-84, 1986
- 554 Bob Griese, Miami, 1971-72, 1974-75, 1977, 1979
- 398 Ken Anderson, Cincinnati, 1976-77, 1982-83

Most Yards Gained, Game
- 274 Dan Fouts, San Diego, 1983
- 242 Joe Theismann, Washington, 1984
- 212 Phil Simms, N.Y. Giants, 1986

Longest Completion
- 64 Dan Pastorini, Houston (to Burrough, Houston), 1976 (TD)
- 59 Randall Cunningham, Philadelphia (to Jackson, Philadelphia [19 yards] lateral to Byner, Washington [40 yards]), 1991
- 57 James Harris, Los Angeles (to Gray, St. Louis), 1975
   Ken Anderson, Cincinnati (to G. Pruitt, Cleveland), 1977

AVERAGE GAIN

Highest Average Gain, Career (40 attempts)
- 8.02 Jim Kelly, Buffalo, 1988, 1991-92 (45-361)
- 7.91 Randall Cunningham, Philadelphia, 1989-91 (44-348)
- 7.64 Joe Theismann, Washington, 1983-84 (45-344)

Highest Average Gain, Game (10 attempts)
- 15.27 Randall Cunningham, Philadelphia, 1991 (11-168)
- 11.40 Ken Anderson, Cincinnati, 1977 (10-114)
- 11.20 Archie Manning, New Orleans, 1980 (10-112)

TOUCHDOWNS

Most Touchdowns, Career
- 3 Joe Theismann, Washington, 1983-84
   Joe Montana, San Francisco, 1982, 1984-85, 1988
   Phil Simms, N.Y. Giants, 1986
   Jim Kelly, Buffalo, 1988, 1991-92
- 2 James Harris, Los Angeles, 1975
   Mike Boryla, Philadelphia, 1976
   Ken Anderson, Cincinnati, 1976-77, 1982-83
   Mark Rypien, Washington, 1990, 1992

Most Touchdowns, Game
- 3 Joe Theismann, Washington, 1984
   Phil Simms, N.Y. Giants, 1986
- 2 James Harris, Los Angeles, 1975
   Mike Boryla, Philadelphia, 1976
   Ken Anderson, Cincinnati, 1977
   Jim Kelly, Buffalo, 1991
   Mark Rypien, Washington, 1992

HAD INTERCEPTED

Most Passes Had Intercepted, Career
- 8 Dan Fouts, San Diego, 1980-84, 1986
- 6 Jim Hart, St. Louis, 1975-78
- 5 Ken Stabler, Oakland, 1974-75, 1978

Most Passes Had Intercepted, Game
- 5 Jim Hart, St. Louis, 1977
- 4 Ken Stabler, Oakland, 1974
- 3 Dan Fouts, San Diego, 1986
   Mark Rypien, Washington, 1990
   Steve Young, San Francisco, 1993

Most Attempts, Without Interception, Game
- 27 Joe Theismann, Washington, 1984
   Phil Simms, N.Y. Giants, 1986
- 26 John Brodie, San Francisco, 1971
   Danny White, Dallas, 1983
- 21 Roman Gabriel, Philadelphia, 1974
   Dan Marino, Miami, 1985

PERCENTAGE, PASSES HAD INTERCEPTED

Lowest Percentage, Passes Had Intercepted, Career (40 attempts)
- 0.00 Joe Theismann, Washington, 1983-84 (45-0)
- 2.13 Dave Krieg, Seattle, 1985, 1989-90 (47-1)
- 2.22 Jim Kelly, Buffalo, 1988, 1991-92 (45-1)

PASS RECEIVING

RECEPTIONS

Most Receptions, Career
- 22 Jerry Rice, San Francisco, 1987-88, 1990-94
- 18 Walter Payton, Chicago, 1977-81, 1984-87
- 17 Steve Largent, Seattle, 1979, 1982, 1985-88

Most Receptions, Game
- 8 Steve Largent, Seattle, 1986
   Michael Irvin, Dallas, 1992
   Andre Rison, Atlanta, 1993
- 7 John Stallworth, Pittsburgh, 1983
   Jerry Rice, San Francisco, 1992
- 6 John Stallworth, Pittsburgh, 1980
   Kellen Winslow, San Diego, 1982
   Gary Clark, Washington, 1991
   Keith Byars, Miami, 1994
   Andre Rison, Atlanta, 1994

YARDS GAINED

Most Yards Gained, Career
- 317 Jerry Rice, San Francisco, 1987-88, 1990-94
- 236 Steve Largent, Seattle, 1979, 1982, 1985-88
- 226 Wes Chandler, New Orleans, 1980; San Diego, 1983-84, 1986

Most Yards Gained, Game
- 125 Michael Irvin, Dallas, 1992
- 114 Wes Chandler, San Diego, 1986
- 96 Ken Burrough, Houston, 1976

Longest Reception
- 64 Ken Burrough, Houston (from Pastorini, Houston), 1976 (TD)
- 59 Keith Jackson, Philadelphia (19 yards) lateral to Earnest Byner, Washington (40 yards) (from Cunningham, Philadelphia), 1991
- 57 Mel Gray, St. Louis (from Harris, Los Angeles), 1975
   Greg Pruitt, Cleveland (from Anderson, Cincinnati), 1977

TOUCHDOWNS

Most Touchdowns, Career
- 2 Mel Gray, St. Louis, 1975-78
   Cliff Branch, Oakland, 1975-78
   Terry Metcalf, St. Louis, 1975-76, 1978
   Tony Hill, Dallas, 1979-80, 1986
   William Andrews, Atlanta, 1981-84
   James Lofton, Green Bay, 1979, 1981-86; Buffalo 1992
   Jimmie Giles, Tampa Bay, 1981-83, 1986
   Michael Irvin, Dallas, 1992-94

Most Touchdowns, Game
- 2 William Andrews, Atlanta, 1984

INTERCEPTIONS BY

Most Interceptions By, Career
- 4 Everson Walls, Dallas, 1982-84, 1986
- 3 Ken Houston, Houston, 1971-73; Washington, 1974-79
   Jack Lambert, Pittsburgh, 1976-84
   Ted Hendricks, Baltimore, 1972-74; Green Bay, 1975; Oakland, 1981-82; L.A. Raiders, 1983-84
   Mike Haynes, New England, 1978-81, 1983; L.A. Raiders, 1985-87
- 2 By nine players

Most Interceptions By, Game
- 2 Mel Blount, Pittsburgh, 1977
   Everson Walls, Dallas, 1982, 1983
   LeRoy Irvin, L.A. Rams, 1986
   David Fulcher, Cincinnati, 1990

YARDS GAINED

Most Yards Gained, Career

77	Ted Hendricks, Baltimore, 1972-74; Green Bay, 1975; Oakland, 1981-82; L.A. Raiders, 1983-84
73	Rod Woodson, Pittsburgh, 1990-94
51	Jerry Gray, L.A. Rams, 1987-90

Most Yards Gained, Game

73	Rod Woodson, Pittsburgh, 1994
65	Ted Hendricks, Baltimore, 1973
51	Jerry Gray, L.A. Rams, 1990

Longest Gain

73	Rod Woodson, Pittsburgh, 1994 (lateral)
65	Ted Hendricks, Baltimore, 1973
51	Jerry Gray, L.A. Rams, 1990 (TD)

TOUCHDOWNS

Most Touchdowns, Game

1	Bobby Bell, Kansas City, 1973
	Nolan Cromwell, L.A. Rams, 1984
	Joey Browner, Minnesota, 1986
	Jerry Gray, L.A. Rams, 1990
	Mike Johnson, Cleveland, 1990
	Junior Seau, San Diego, 1993

PUNTING

Most Punts, Career

33	Ray Guy, Oakland, 1974-79, 1981
23	Rohn Stark, Indianapolis, 1986-87, 1991, 1993
10	Dave Jennings, N.Y. Giants, 1979-81, 1983

Most Punts, Game

10	Reggie Roby, Miami, 1985
9	Tom Wittum, San Francisco, 1974
	Rohn Stark, Indianapolis, 1987
8	Jerrel Wilson, Kansas City, 1971
	Tom Skladany, Detroit, 1982

Longest Punt

64	Tom Wittum, San Francisco, 1974
61	Reggie Roby, Miami, 1985
60	Ron Widby, Dallas, 1972

AVERAGE YARDAGE

Highest Average, Career (10 punts)

45.25	Jerrel Wilson, Kansas City, 1971-73 (16-724)
44.79	Reggie Roby, Miami, 1985, 1990 (14-627)
44.65	Rohn Stark, Indianapolis, 1986-87, 1991, 1993 (23-1,027)

Highest Average, Game (4 punts)

49.57	Jim Arnold, Detroit, 1988 (7-347)
49.00	Ray Guy, Oakland, 1974 (4-196)
47.75	Bob Grupp, Kansas City, 1980 (4-191)

PUNT RETURNS

Most Punt Returns, Career

13	Rick Upchurch, Denver, 1977, 1979-80, 1983
11	Vai Sikahema, St. Louis, 1987-88
10	Mike Nelms, Washington, 1981-83

Most Punt Returns, Game

7	Vai Sikahema, St. Louis, 1987
6	Henry Ellard, L.A. Rams, 1985
	Gerald McNeil, Cleveland, 1988
5	Rick Upchurch, Denver, 1980
	Mike Nelms, Washington, 1981
	Carl Roaches, Houston, 1982
	Johnny Bailey, Phoenix, 1993

Most Fair Catches, Game

2	Jerry Logan, Baltimore, 1971
	Dick Anderson, Miami, 1974
	Henry Ellard, L.A. Rams, 1985

YARDS GAINED

Most Yards Gained, Career

183	Billy Johnson, Houston, 1976, 1978; Atlanta, 1984
138	Rick Upchurch, Denver, 1977, 1979-80, 1983
	Mel Renfro, Dallas, 1971-72, 1974
119	Mike Nelms, Washington, 1981-83

Most Yards Gained, Game

159	Billy Johnson, Houston, 1976
136	Mel Renfro, Dallas, 1971
117	Wally Henry, Philadelphia, 1980

Longest Punt Return

	Billy Johnson, Houston, 1976 (TD)
	Wally Henry, Philadelphia, 1980 (TD)
	Dallas, 1971 (TD)

TOUCHDOWNS

Most Touchdowns, Game

2	Mel Renfro, Dallas, 1971
1	Billy Johnson, Houston, 1976
	Wally Henry, Philadelphia, 1980

KICKOFF RETURNS

Most Kickoff Returns, Career

10	Rick Upchurch, Denver, 1977, 1979-80, 1983
	Greg Pruitt, Cleveland, 1974-75, 1977-78; L.A. Raiders, 1984
8	Mike Nelms, Washington, 1981-83
7	Mel Gray, Detroit, 1991-92

Most Kickoff Returns, Game

6	Greg Pruitt, L.A. Raiders, 1984
5	Les (Speedy) Duncan, Washington, 1972
	Ron Smith, Chicago, 1973
	Herb Mul-Key, Washington, 1974
	Mel Gray, Detroit, 1991
4	By seven players

YARDS GAINED

Most Yards Gained, Career

309	Greg Pruitt, Cleveland, 1974-75, 1977-78; L.A. Raiders, 1984
222	Rick Upchurch, Denver, 1977, 1979-80, 1983
175	Les (Speedy) Duncan, Washington, 1972

Most Yards Gained, Game

192	Greg Pruitt, L.A. Raiders, 1984
175	Les (Speedy) Duncan, Washington, 1972
152	Ron Smith, Chicago, 1973

Longest Kickoff Return

62	Greg Pruitt, L.A. Raiders, 1984
61	Eugene (Mercury) Morris, Miami, 1972
55	Ron Smith, Chicago, 1973

TOUCHDOWNS

Most Touchdowns, Game

None

FUMBLES

Most Fumbles, Career

6	Dan Fouts, San Diego, 1980-84, 1986
4	Lawrence McCutcheon, Los Angeles, 1974-78
	Franco Harris, Pittsburgh, 1973-76, 1978-81
	Jay Schroeder, Washington, 1987
	Vai Sikahema, St. Louis, 1987-88
3	O.J. Simpson, Buffalo, 1973-77
	William Andrews, Atlanta, 1981-84
	Joe Montana, San Francisco, 1982, 1984-85, 1988
	Walter Payton, Chicago, 1977-81, 1984-87
	Neil Lomax, St. Louis, 1985, 1988
	Jim Kelly, Buffalo, 1988, 1991-92

Most Fumbles, Game

4	Jay Schroeder, Washington, 1987
3	Dan Fouts, San Diego, 1982
	Vai Sikahema, St. Louis, 1987
2	By 11 players

RECOVERIES

Most Fumbles Recovered, Career

3	Harold Jackson, Philadelphia, 1973; Los Angeles, 1974, 1976, 1978 (3-own)
	Dan Fouts, San Diego, 1980-84, 1986 (3-own)
	Randy White, Dallas, 1978, 1980-86 (3-opp)
2	By many players

Most Fumbles Recovered, Game

2	Dick Anderson, Miami, 1974 (1-own, 1-opp)
	Harold Jackson, Los Angeles, 1974 (2-own)
	Dan Fouts, San Diego, 1982 (2-own)
	Joey Browner, Minnesota, 1990 (2-opp)

YARDAGE

Longest Fumble Return

83	Art Still, Kansas City, 1985 (TD, opp)
51	Phil Villapiano, Oakland, 1974 (opp)
37	Sam Mills, New Orleans, 1988 (opp)

TOUCHDOWNS

Most Touchdowns, Game

1	Art Still, Kansas City, 1985
	Keith Millard, Minnesota, 1990

SACKS

Sacks have been compiled since 1983.

Most Sacks, Career

- 9.5 Reggie White, Philadelphia, 1987-93; Green Bay, 1994
- 9 Howie Long, L.A. Raiders, 1984-88, 1990, 1993-1994
- 7 Mark Gastineau, N.Y. Jets, 1983-86

Most Sacks, Game

- 4 Mark Gastineau, N.Y. Jets, 1985
  Reggie White, Philadelphia, 1987
- 3 Richard Dent, Chicago, 1985
  Bruce Smith, Buffalo, 1991
- 2 By many players

TEAM RECORDS

SCORING

Most Points, Game

- 45 NFC, 1984

Fewest Points, Game

- 3 AFC, 1984, 1989, 1994

Most Points, Both Teams, Game

- 64 NFC (37) vs. AFC (27), 1980

Fewest Points, Both Teams, Game

- 16 NFC (6) vs. AFC (10), 1987

TOUCHDOWNS

Most Touchdowns, Game

- 6 NFC, 1984

Fewest Touchdowns, Game

- 0 AFC, 1971, 1974, 1984, 1989, 1994
  NFC, 1987, 1988

Most Touchdowns, Both Teams, Game

- 8 AFC (4) vs. NFC (4), 1973
  NFC (5) vs. AFC (3), 1980

Fewest Touchdowns, Both Teams, Game

- 1 AFC (0) vs. NFC (1), 1974
  NFC (0) vs. AFC (1), 1987
  NFC (0) vs. AFC (1), 1988

POINTS AFTER TOUCHDOWN

Most Points After Touchdown, Game

- 6 NFC, 1984

Most Points After Touchdown, Both Teams, Game

- 7 NFC (4) vs. AFC (3), 1973
  NFC (4) vs. AFC (3), 1980
  NFC (4) vs. AFC (3), 1986

FIELD GOALS

Most Field Goals Attempted, Game

- 6 AFC, 1972
  NFC, 1981, 1983

Most Field Goals Attempted, Both Teams, Game

- 9 NFC (6) vs. AFC (3), 1983

Most Field Goals, Game

- 5 AFC, 1974

Most Field Goals, Both Teams, Game

- 7 AFC (5) vs. NFC (2), 1974

NET YARDS GAINED RUSHING AND PASSING

Most Yards Gained, Game

- 472 NFC, 1993

Fewest Yards Gained, Game

- 114 AFC, 1993

Most Yards Gained, Both Teams, Game

- 811 AFC (466) vs. NFC (345), 1983

Fewest Yards Gained, Both Teams, Game

- 424 AFC (202) vs. NFC (222), 1987

RUSHING

ATTEMPTS

Most Attempts, Game

- 50 AFC, 1974

Fewest Attempts, Game

- 14 AFC, 1994

Most Attempts, Both Teams, Game

- 80 AFC (50) vs. NFC (30), 1974

Fewest Attempts, Both Teams, Game

- 48 AFC (20) vs. NFC (28), 1991

YARDS GAINED

Most Yards Gained, Game

- 224 NFC, 1976

Fewest Yards Gained, Game

- 28 NFC, 1992

Most Yards Gained, Both Teams, Game

- 425 NFC (224) vs. AFC (201), 1976

Fewest Yards Gained, Both Teams, Game

- 131 NFC (28) vs. AFC (103), 1992

TOUCHDOWNS

Most Touchdowns, Game

- 3 NFC, 1989, 1991

Most Touchdowns, Both Teams, Game

- 4 AFC (2) vs. NFC (2), 1973
  AFC (2) vs. NFC (2), 1980

PASSING

ATTEMPTS

Most Attempts, Game

- 55 NFC, 1993

Fewest Attempts, Game

- 17 NFC, 1972

Most Attempts, Both Teams, Game

- 94 AFC (50) vs. NFC (44), 1983

Fewest Attempts, Both Teams, Game

- 42 NFC (17) vs. AFC (25), 1972

COMPLETIONS

Most Completions, Game

- 32 NFC, 1993

Fewest Completions, Game

- 7 NFC, 1972, 1982

Most Completions, Both Teams, Game

- 55 AFC (31) vs. NFC (24), 1983

Fewest Completions, Both Teams, Game

- 18 NFC (7) vs. AFC (11), 1972

YARDS GAINED

Most Yards Gained, Game

- 387 AFC, 1983

Fewest Yards Gained, Game

- 42 NFC, 1982

Most Yards Gained, Both Teams, Game

- 608 AFC (387) vs. NFC (221), 1983

Fewest Yards Gained, Both Teams, Game

- 215 NFC (89) vs. AFC (126), 1972

TIMES SACKED

Most Times Sacked, Game

- 9 NFC, 1985

Fewest Times Sacked, Game

- 0 NFC, 1971

Most Times Sacked, Both Teams, Game

- 17 NFC (9) vs. AFC (8), 1985

Fewest Times Sacked, Both Teams, Game

- 4 AFC (2) vs. NFC (2), 1978
  NFC (1) vs. AFC (3), 1994

TOUCHDOWNS

Most Touchdowns, Game

- 4 NFC, 1984

Most Touchdowns, Both Teams, Game

- 5 NFC (3) vs. AFC (2), 1986

INTERCEPTIONS BY

Most Interceptions By, Game

- 6 AFC, 1977

Most Interceptions By, Both Teams, Game

- 7 AFC (6) vs. NFC (1), 1977

YARDS GAINED

Most Yards Gained, Game

- 103 AFC, 1994

Most Yards Gained, Both Teams, Game

- 116 AFC (103) vs. NFC (13), 1994

TOUCHDOWNS

Most Touchdowns, Game

- 1 AFC, 1973, 1990, 1993
  NFC, 1984, 1986, 1990

PUNTING

Most Punts, Game

- 10 AFC, 1985

Fewest Punts, Game
    0   NFC, 1989
Most Punts, Both Teams, Game
    16   AFC (10) vs. NFC (6), 1985
Fewest Punts, Both Teams, Game
    4   NFC (1) vs. AFC (3), 1992

AVERAGE YARDAGE
Highest Average, Game
    50.50   AFC, 1991 (2-101)

PUNT RETURNS
Most Punt Returns, Game
    7   NFC, 1985, 1987
Fewest Punt Returns, Game
    0   AFC, 1984, 1989
Most Punt Returns, Both Teams, Game
    11   NFC (7) vs. AFC (4), 1985
Fewest Punt Returns, Both Teams, Game
    3   AFC (0) vs. NFC (3), 1984
        AFC (0) vs. NFC (3), 1989
        NFC (1) vs. AFC (2), 1991
        AFC (1) vs. NFC (2), 1992

YARDS GAINED
Most Yards Gained, Game
    177   AFC, 1976
Fewest Yards Gained, Game
    -1   NFC, 1991
Most Yards Gained, Both Teams, Game
    263   AFC (177) vs. NFC (86), 1976
Fewest Yards Gained, Both Teams, Game
    16   AFC (0) vs. NFC (16), 1984

TOUCHDOWNS
Most Touchdowns, Game
    2   NFC, 1971

KICKOFF RETURNS
Most Kickoff Returns, Game
    7   AFC, 1984
Fewest Kickoff Returns, Game
    1   NFC, 1971, 1984, 1994
        AFC, 1988, 1991
Most Kickoff Returns, Both Teams, Game
    10   AFC (5) vs. NFC (5), 1976
        AFC (5) vs. NFC (5), 1986
Fewest Kickoff Returns, Both Teams, Game
    5   NFC (2) vs. AFC (3), 1979
        AFC (1) vs. NFC (4), 1988
        NFC (2) vs. AFC (3), 1992
        NFC (1) vs. AFC (4), 1994

YARDS GAINED
Most Yards Gained, Game
    215   AFC, 1984
Fewest Yards Gained, Game
    6   NFC, 1971
Most Yards Gained, Both Teams, Game
    293   NFC (200) vs. AFC (93), 1972
Fewest Yards Gained, Both Teams, Game
    99   NFC (48) vs. AFC (51), 1987

TOUCHDOWNS
Most Touchdowns, Game
        None

FUMBLES
Most Fumbles, Game
    10   NFC, 1974
Most Fumbles, Both Teams, Game
    15   NFC (10) vs. AFC (5), 1974

RECOVERIES
Most Fumbles Recovered, Game
    10   NFC, 1974 (6 own, 4 opp)
Most Fumbles Lost, Game
    4   AFC, 1974, 1988
        NFC, 1974

TOUCHDOWNS
Most Touchdowns, Game
    1   AFC, 1985
        NFC, 1990

TURNOVERS
(Number of times losing the ball on interceptions and fumbles.)
Most Turnovers, Game
    8   AFC, 1974
Fewest Turnovers, Game
    0   AFC, 1991
        NFC, 1991
Most Turnovers, Both Teams, Game
    12   AFC (8) vs. NFC (4), 1974
Fewest Turnovers, Both Teams, Game
    0   AFC vs. NFC, 1991

Rules

1994 NFL ROSTER OF OFFICIALS

Jerry Seeman, Director of Officiating
Jack Reader, Assistant Director of Officiating
Leo Miles, Supervisor of Officials
Ron DeSouza, Supervisor of Officials

No.	Name	Position	College
25	Alderton, John	Line Judge	Portland State
115	Ancich, Hendi	Umpire	Harbor College
81	Anderson, Dave	Line Judge	Salem College
34	Austin, Gerald	Referee	Western Carolina
22	Baetz, Paul	Back Judge	Heidelberg
91	Baker, Ken	Back Judge	Eastern Illinois
26	Baltz, Mark	Head Linesman	Ohio University
55	Barnes, Tom	Line Judge	Minnesota
56	Baynes, Ron	Line Judge	Auburn
32	Bergman, Jeff	Line Judge	Robert Morris
17	Bergman, Jerry	Head Linesman	Duquesne
40	Bible, Jon	Side Judge	Texas
7	Blum, Ron	Referee	Marin College
90	Borgard, Mike	Side Judge	St. Louis
110	Botchan, Ron	Umpire	Occidental
101	Boylston, Bob	Umpire	Alabama
31	Brown, Chad	Umpire	East Texas State
94	Carey, Mike	Side Judge	Santa Clara
39	Carlsen, Don	Side Judge	Cal State-Chico
63	Carollo, Bill	Side Judge	Wisconsin
43	Cashion, Red	Referee	Texas A&M
24	Clymer, Roy	Back Judge	New Mexico State
45	Coleman, George	Back Judge	Bishop College
65	Coleman, Walt	Line Judge	Arkansas
27	Conway, Al	Umpire	Army
71	Coukart, Ed	Umpire	Northwestern
61	Creed, Dick	Side Judge	Louisville
75	Daopoulos, Jim	Back Judge	Kentucky
78	Demmas, Art	Umpire	Vanderbilt
113	Dorkowski, Don	Field Judge	Cal State-Los Angeles
74	Duke, James	Umpire	Howard
57	Fiffick, Ed	Umpire	Marquette
47	Fincken, Tom	Side Judge	Kansas State
111	Frantz, Earnie	Head Linesman	No College
50	Gereb, Neil	Umpire	California
72	Gierke, Terry	Head Linesman	Portland State
15	Glass, Bama	Line Judge	Colorado
3	Golmont, Van	Side Judge	Miami
19	Green, Scott	Field Judge	Delaware
23	Grier, Johnny	Referee	University of D.C.
96	Hakes, Don	Field Judge	Bradley
104	Hamer, Dale	Referee	California, Pa.
42	Hamilton, Dave	Umpire	Utah
44	Hampton, Donnie	Field Judge	Georgia
105	Hantak, Dick	Referee	Southeast Missouri
54	Hayward, George	Head Linesman	Missouri Western
85	Hochuli, Ed	Back Judge	Texas-El Paso
114	Johnson, Tom	Head Linesman	Miami, Ohio
97	Jones, Nate	Side Judge	Lewis & Clark
106	Jury, Al	Back Judge	San Bernardino Valley
67	Keck, John	Umpire	Cornell College

No.	Name	Position	College
14	Knight, Jim	Back Judge	Wake Forest
86	Kukar, Bernie	Referee	St. John's
120	Lane, Gary	Referee	Missouri
49	Look, Dean	Side Judge	Michigan State
98	Lovett, Bill	Back Judge	Maryland
59	Luckett, Phil	Field Judge	Texas-El Paso
82	Mallette, Pat	Field Judge	Nebraska
9	Markbreit, Jerry	Referee	Illinois
38	Maurer, Bruce	Line Judge	Ohio State
48	McCarter, Gordon	Referee	Western Reserve
95	McElwee, Bob	Referee	Navy
35	McGrath, Bob	Head Linesman	Western Kentucky
41	McKenzie, Dick	Line Judge	Ashland
64	McPeters, Lloyd	Line Judge	Oklahoma State
76	Merrifield, Ed	Field Judge	Missouri
80	Millis, Timmie	Back Judge	Millsaps
117	Montgomery, Ben	Line Judge	Morehouse
36	Moore, Bob	Back Judge	Dayton
60	Moore, Tommy	Side Judge	Stephen F. Austin
20	Nemmers, Larry	Referee	Upper Iowa
51	Orem, Dale	Line Judge	Louisville
77	Orr, Don	Field Judge	Vanderbilt
10	Phares, Ron	Head Linesman	Virginia Tech
79	Pointer, Aaron	Head Linesman	Pacific Lutheran
92	Poole, Jim	Back Judge	San Diego State
58	Quinby, Bill	Side Judge	Iowa
5	Quirk, Jim	Line Judge	Delaware
83	Reels, Richard	Field Judge	No College
53	Reynolds, Bill	Line Judge	West Chester State
68	Richard, Louis	Back Judge	Southwest Louisiana
30	Riggs, Dennis	Umpire	Bellarmine
121	Rivers, Sanford	Head Linesman	Youngstown State
46	Robison, John	Field Judge	Utah
33	Roe, Howard	Referee	Wichita State
21	Schleyer, John	Head Linesman	Millersville
122	Schmitz, Bill	Field Judge	Colorado State
109	Semon, Sid	Head Linesman	Southern California
118	Sifferman, Tom	Back Judge	Seattle
73	Skelton, Bobby	Field Judge	Alabama
29	Slavin, Howard	Side Judge	Southern California
2	Smith, Billy	Field Judge	East Carolina
119	Spitler, Ron	Field Judge	Panhandle State
88	Steenson, Scott	Back Judge	North Texas State
62	Stewart, Charles	Line Judge	Long Beach State
103	Stuart, Rex	Umpire	Appalachian State
4	Toole, Doug	Side Judge	Utah State
37	Upson, Larry	Line Judge	Prince George C.C.
93	Vaughan, Jack	Field Judge	Mississippi State
52	Veteri, Tony	Head Linesman	Manhattan College
100	Wagner, Bob	Umpire	Penn State
28	Wedge, Don	Side Judge	Ohio Wesleyan
87	Weidner, Paul	Head Linesman	Cincinnati
123	White, Tom	Referee	Temple
99	Williams, Banks	Back Judge	Houston
8	Williams, Dale	Head Linesman	Cal State-Northridge
16	Wyant, David	Side Judge	Virginia

NUMERICAL ROSTER

No.	Name	Position	No.	Name	Position	No.	Name	Position	No.	Name	Position	No.	Name	Position
2	Billy Smith	FJ	28	Don Wedge	SJ	50	Neil Gereb	U	75	Jim Daopoulos	BJ	99	Banks Williams	BJ
3	Van Golmont	SJ	29	Howard Slavin	SJ	51	Dale Orem	LJ	76	Ed Merrifield	FJ	100	Bob Wagner	U
4	Doug Toole	SJ	30	Dennis Riggs	U	52	Tony Veteri	HL	77	Don Orr	FJ	101	Bob Boylston	U
5	Jim Quirk	LJ	31	Chad Brown	U	53	Bill Reynolds	LJ	78	Art Demmas	U	103	Rex Stuart	U
7	Ron Blum	R	32	Jeff Bergman	LJ	54	George Hayward	HL	79	Aaron Pointer	HL	104	Dale Hamer	R
8	Dale Williams	HL	33	Howard Roe	R	55	Tom Barnes	LJ	80	Timmie Millis	BJ	105	Dick Hantak	R
9	Jerry Markbreit	R	34	Gerry Austin	R	56	Ron Baynes	LJ	81	Dave Anderson	LJ	106	Al Jury	BJ
10	Ron Phares	HL	35	Bob McGrath	HL	57	Ed Fiffick	U	82	Pat Mallette	FJ	109	Sid Semon	HL
14	Jim Knight	BJ	36	Bob Moore	BJ	58	Bill Quinby	SJ	83	Richard Reels	FJ	110	Ron Botchan	U
15	Bama Glass	LJ	37	Larry Upson	LJ	59	Phil Luckett	FJ	85	Ed Hochuli	BJ	111	Earnie Frantz	HL
16	David Wyant	SJ	38	Bruce Maurer	LJ	60	Tommy Moore	SJ	86	Bernie Kukar	R	113	Don Dorkowski	FJ
17	Jerry Bergman	HL	39	Don Carlsen	SJ	61	Dick Creed	SJ	87	Paul Weidner	HL	114	Tom Johnson	HL
19	Scott Green	FJ	40	Jon Bible	SJ	62	Charles Stewart	LJ	88	Scott Steenson	BJ	115	Hendi Ancich	U
20	Larry Nemmers	R	41	Dick McKenzie	LJ	63	Bill Carollo	SJ	90	Mike Borgard	SJ	117	Ben Montgomery	LJ
21	John Schleyer	HL	42	Dave Hamilton	U	64	Lloyd McPeters	LJ	91	Ken Baker	BJ	118	Tom Sifferman	BJ
22	Paul Baetz	BJ	43	Red Cashion	R	65	Walt Coleman	LJ	92	Jim Poole	BJ	119	Ron Spitler	FJ
23	Johnny Grier	R	44	Donnie Hampton	FJ	67	John Keck	U	93	Jack Vaughan	FJ	120	Gary Lane	R
24	Roy Clymer	BJ	45	George Coleman	BJ	68	Louis Richard	BJ	94	Mike Carey	SJ	121	Sanford Rivers	FJ
25	John Alderton	LJ	46	John Robison	FJ	71	Ed Coukart	U	95	Bob McElwee	R	122	Bill Schmitz	FJ
26	Mark Baltz	HL	47	Tom Fincken	SJ	72	Terry Gierke	HL	96	Don Hakes	FJ	123	Tom White	R
27	Al Conway	U	48	Gordon McCarter	R	73	Bobby Skelton	FJ	97	Nate Jones	SJ			
			49	Dean Look	SJ	74	James Duke	U	98	Bill Lovett	BJ			

1994 OFFICIALS AT A GLANCE

REFEREES

Gerry Austin, No. 34, Western Carolina, president, leadership development group, 13th year.

Ron Blum, No. 7, Marin College, professional golfer, 10th year.

Red Cashion, No. 43, Texas A&M, chairman, insurance company, 23rd year.

Johnny Grier, No. 23, University of D.C., planning engineer, 14th year.

Dale Hamer, No. 104, California (Pa.) University, consultant, 17th year.

Dick Hantak, No. 105, Southeast Missouri, educator, 17th year.

Ed Hochuli, No. 85, Texas-El Paso, attorney, 5th year.

Bernie Kukar, No. 86, St. John's, sales representative, employees benefit plan, 11th year.

Gary Lane, No. 120, Missouri, vice president, medical supplies, former NFL player, 13th year.

Jerry Markbreit, No. 9, Illinois, trade and barter manager, 19th year.

Gordon McCarter, No. 48, Western Reserve, retired sales manager, 28th year.

Bob McElwee, No. 95, Navy, owner, heavy construction firm, 19th year.

Larry Nemmers, No. 20, Upper Iowa, high school principal, 10th year.

Howard Roe, No. 33, Wichita State, director, administration and finance, 11th year.

Tom White, No. 123, Temple, president, athletic sportswear, 6th year.

UMPIRES

Hendi Ancich, No. 115, Harbor, longshoreman, 13th year.

Ron Botchan, No. 110, Occidental, college professor, former AFL player, 15th year.

Bob Boylston, No. 101, Alabama, stockbroker, 17th year.

Chad Brown, No. 31, East Texas State, director, intramural/sports clubs, 3rd year.

Al Conway, No. 27, Army, director of manufacturing, 26th year.

Ed Coukart, No. 71, Northwestern, president, commercial bank, 6th year.

Art Demmas, No. 78, Vanderbilt, Southern coordinator, National Football Foundation and College Hall of Fame, 27th year.

James Duke, No. 74, Howard, Ward manager, department of parks and recreation, 2nd year.

Ed Fiffick, No. 57, Marquette, podiatric physician, 16th year.

Neil Gereb, No. 50, California, project manager, aircraft company, 14th year.

Dave Hamilton, No. 42, Utah, chief, rehabilitation therapy services, 20th year.

John Keck, No. 67, Cornell, petroleum distributor, 23rd year.

Dennis Riggs, No. 30, Bellarmine, president, community foundation, 7th year.

Rex Stuart, No. 103, Appalachian State, insurance agent, 11th year.

Bob Wagner, No. 100, Penn State, executive director, cardiovascular institute, 10th year.

HEAD LINESMEN

Mark Baltz, No. 26, Ohio University, manufacturer's representative, 6th year.

Jerry Bergman, No. 17, Duquesne, executive director, pension fund, 29th year.

Earnie Frantz, No. 111, no college, vice president and manager, insurance company, 14th year.

Terry Gierke, No. 72, Portland State, real estate broker, 14th year.

George Hayward, No. 54, Missouri Western, vice president and manager, warehouse company, 4th year.

Tom Johnson, No. 114, Miami, Ohio, educator, president, security company, 13th year.

Bob McGrath, No. 35, Western Kentucky, sales representative, fund raiser, 2nd year.

Ron Phares, No. 10, Virginia Tech, president, construction company, 10th year.

Aaron Pointer, No. 79, Pacific Lutheran, park department administrator, 8th year.

Sanford Rivers, No. 121, Youngstown State, assistant vice president, school administration, 6th year.

John Schleyer, No. 21, Millersville, medical sales, 5th year.

Sid Semon, No. 109, Southern California, chairman, physical education department, 17th year.

Tony Veteri, No. 52, Manhattan, director of athletics, 3rd year.

Paul Weidner, No. 87, Cincinnati, marketing manager, 9th year.

Dale Williams, No. 8, Cal State-Northridge, owner, coin-op laundromats, 15th year.

LINE JUDGES

John Alderton, No. 25, Portland State, vice president, insurance, 6th year.

Dave Anderson, No. 81, Salem, insurance executive, 11th year.

Tom Barnes, No. 55, Minnesota, manufacturing representative, 9th year.

Ron Baynes, No. 56, Auburn, school administrator, coach, 8th year.

Jeff Bergman, No. 32, Robert Morris, president and chief executive officer, medical services, 4th year.

Coleman, No. 65, Arkansas, president, dairy processor, 6th year.

Coleman, No. 15, Colorado, agent, insurance/financial services.

Bruce Maurer, No. 38, Ohio State, administrator and associate director, recreational sports, 8th year.

Dick McKenzie, No. 41, Ashland, financial services, 17th year.

Lloyd McPeters, No. 64, Oklahoma State, business insurance sales, 2nd year.

Ben Montgomery, No. 117, Morehouse, school administrator, 13th year.

Dale Orem, No. 51, Louisville, executive director, community foundation, 15th year.

Jim Quirk, No. 5, Delaware, vice president, government securities, 7th year.

Bill Reynolds, No. 53, West Chester State, educator, 20th year.

Charles Stewart, No. 62, Long Beach State, administrative deputy director, 3rd year.

Larry Upson, No. 37, Prince George City College, senior personnel management specialist, 4th year.

BACK JUDGES

Paul Baetz, No. 22, Heidelberg, financial consultant, 17th year.

Ken Baker, No. 91, Eastern Illinois, optician, surgical ophthalmic technician, 4th year.

Roy Clymer, No. 24, New Mexico State, district marketing manager, gas company, 15th year.

George Coleman, No. 45, Bishop College, executive director, YMCA, 2nd year.

Jim Daopoulos, No. 75, Kentucky, mortgage broker, 6th year.

Al Jury, No. 106, San Bernardino Valley, state traffic officer, 17th year.

Jim Knight, No. 14, Wake Forest, manufacturer's representative, 1st year.

Bill Lovett, No. 98, Maryland, managing partner, financial sales, 5th year.

Timmie Millis, No. 80, Millsaps, financial investigative consultant, 6th year.

Bob Moore, No. 36, Dayton, attorney, 11th year.

Jim Poole, No. 92, San Diego State, college professor, 20th year.

Louis Richard, No. 68, Southwestern Louisiana, sales manager, 9th year.

Tom Sifferman, No. 118, Seattle, manufacturer's representative, 9th year.

Scott Steenson, No. 88, North Texas State, real estate broker, 4th year.

Banks Williams, No. 99, Houston, consultant, 17th year.

SIDE JUDGES

Jon Bible, No. 40, Texas, attorney/college educator, 1st year.

Mike Borgard, No. 90, St. Louis, president/owner, advertising specialties, 5th year.

Mike Carey, No. 94, Santa Clara, marketing manager, 5th year.

Don Carlsen, No. 39, Cal State-Chico, budget analyst, comptroller, 6th year.

Bill Carollo, No. 63, Wisconsin, marketing executive, 6th year.

Richard Creed, No. 61, Louisville, manager, real estate, 17th year.

Tom Fincken, No. 47, Emporia State, educator, 11th year.

Van Golmont, No. 3, Miami, regional manager, marketing development,, 4th year.

Nate Jones, No. 97, Lewis and Clark, high school principal, 18th year.

Dean Look, No. 49, Michigan State, director, medical manufacturing, former AFL player, 22nd year.

Tommy Moore, No. 60, Stephen F. Austin, marketing, manufacturing, representative, 3rd year.

Bill Quinby, No. 58, Iowa, retired athletic director, 17th year.

Howard Slavin, No. 29, Southern California, attorney, 8th year.

Doug Toole, No. 4, Utah State, physical therapist, orthopedic and sports medicine, 7th year.

Don Wedge, No. 28, Ohio Wesleyan, executive account manager, 23rd year.

David Wyant, No. 16, Virginia, research scientist, 4th year.

FIELD JUDGES

Don Dorkowski, No. 113, Cal State-Los Angeles, department head, health and safety, 9th year.

Scott Green, No. 19, Delaware, vice president, government relations, 4th year.

Don Hakes, No. 96, Bradley, retired educator, 18th year.

Donnie Hampton, No. 44, Georgia, mortgage banker, 7th year.

Phil Luckett, No. 59, Texas-El Paso, computer program analyst, federal civil services, 4th year.

Pat Mallette, No. 82, Nebraska, real estate broker, 26th year.

Ed Merrifield, No. 76, Missouri, sales representative, 20th year.

Don Orr, No. 77, Vanderbilt, mechanical contractor, 24th year.

Richard Reels, No. 83, Chicago State, director of security, court services, 2nd year.

John Robison, No. 46, Utah, high school teacher, 7th year.

Bill Schmitz, No. 122, Colorado State, general sales manager, 6th year.

Bobby Skelton, No. 73, Alabama, industrial representative, 10th year.

Billy Smith, No. 2, East Carolina, Federal government, 1st year.

Ron Spitler, No. 119, Panhandle State, owner, service center, 13th year.

Jack Vaughan, No. 93, Mississippi State, financial services, 19th year.

1

TOUCHDOWN, FIELD GOAL, or SUCCESSFUL TRY
Both arms extended above head.

2

SAFETY
Palms together above head.

3

FIRST DOWN
Arm pointed toward defensive team's goal.

4

CROWD NOISE, DEAD BALL, or NEUTRAL ZONE ESTABLISHED
One arm above head with an open hand.
With fist closed: **Fourth Down.**

5

BALL ILLEGALLY TOUCHED, KICKED OR BATTED
Fingertips tap both shoulders.

6

TIME OUT
Hands crisscrossed above head.
Same signal follwed by placing one hand on top of cap: **Referee's Time Out.**
Same signal followed by arm swung at side: **Touchback.**

7

NO TIME OUT or TIME IN WITH WHISTLE
Full arm circled to simulate moving clock.

8

DELAY OF GAME, ILLEGAL SUBSTITUTION. or EXCESS TIME OUT
Fold...

9

FALSE START, ILLEGAL SHIFT, ILLEGAL FORMATION, or KICKOFF or SAFETY KICK OUT OF BOUNDS

Forearms rotated over and over in front of body.

10

PERSONAL FOUL
One wrist striking the other above head.

Same signal followed by swinging leg: **Roughing the Kicker.**

Same signal followed by raised arm swinging forward: **Roughing the Passer.**

Same signal followed by hand striking back of calf: **Clipping.**

11

HOLDING
Grasping one wrist, the fist clenched, in front of chest.

12

ILLEGAL USE OF HANDS, ARMS, OR BODY
Grasping one wrist, the hand open and facing forward, in front of chest.

13

PENALTY REFUSED, INCOMPLETE PASS, PLAY OVER, or MISSED FIELD GOAL or EXTRA POINT

Hands shifted in horizontal plane.

14

PASS JUGGLED INBOUNDS AND CAUGHT OUT OF BOUNDS
Hands up and down in front of chest (following incomplete pass signal).

15

ILLEGAL FORWARD PASS
One hand waved behind back followed by loss of down signal (23).

16

INTENTIONAL GROUNDING OF PASS
Parallel arms waved in a diagonal plane across body. Followed by loss of down signal (23).

17

INTERFERENCE WITH FORWARD PASS or FAIR CATCH
Hands open
and extended forward from
shoulders with hands vertical.

18

INVALID FAIR CATCH SIGNAL
One hand waved above head.

19

**INELIGIBLE RECEIVER
OR INELIGIBLE
MEMBER OF KICKING TEAM
DOWNFIELD**
Right hand touching top of cap.

20

ILLEGAL CONTACT
One open hand extended forward.

21

OFFSIDE or ENCROACHING
Hands on hips.

22

ILLEGAL MOTION AT SNAP
Horizontal arc with one hand.

23

LOSS OF DOWN
Both hands held behind head.

24

**CRAWLING, INTERLOCKING
INTERFERENCE, PUSHING, or
HELPING RUNNER**
Pushing movement of hands
to front with arms downward.

25

**TOUCHING A FORWARD
PASS OR SCRIMMAGE KICK**
Diagonal motion of
one hand across another.

26

**UNSPORTSMANLIKE
CONDUCT**
Arms outstretched, palms down.
(Same signal means continuous
action fouls are disregarded.)
Chop block.

27

**ILLEGAL CUT or
BLOCKING BELOW
THE WAIST**
Hand striking front of thigh
preceded by personal foul
signal (10).

28

ILLEGAL CRACKBACK
Strike of an open right hand
against the right mid thigh
preceded by personal foul
signal (10).

29

PLAYER DISQUALIFIED
Ejection signal.

30

TRIPPING
Repeated action of right foot
in back of left heel.

31

**UNCATCHABLE
FORWARD PASS**
Palm of right hand held
parallel to ground above head.
and moved back and forth.

DIGEST OF RULES

NFL DIGEST OF RULES

This Digest of Rules of the National Football League has been prepared to aid players, fans, and members of the press, radio, and television media in their understanding of the game.

It is not meant to be a substitute for the official rule book. In any case of conflict between these explanations and the official rules, the rules always have precedence.

In order to make it easier to coordinate the information in this digest the topics discussed generally follow the order of the rule book.

OFFICIALS' JURISDICTIONS, POSITIONS, AND DUTIES

Referee—General oversight and control of game. Gives signals for all fouls and is final authority for rule interpretations. Takes a position in backfield 10 to 12 yards behind line of scrimmage, favors right side (if quarterback is right-handed passer). Determines legality of snap, observes deep back(s) for legal motion. On running play, observes quarterback during and after handoff, remains with him until action has cleared away, then proceeds downfield, checking on runner and contact behind him. When runner is downed, Referee determines forward progress from wing official and, if necessary, adjusts final position of ball.

On pass plays, drops back as quarterback begins to fade back, picks up legality of blocks by near linemen. Changes to complete concentration on quarterback as defenders approach. Primarily responsible to rule on possible roughing action on passer and if ball becomes loose, rules whether ball is free on a fumble or dead on an incomplete pass.

During kicking situations, Referee has primary responsibility to rule on kicker's actions and whether or not any subsequent contact by a defender is legal. The Referee will announce on the microphone when each period is ended.

Umpire—Primary responsibility to rule on players' equipment, as well as their conduct and actions on scrimmage line. Lines up approximately four to five yards downfield, varying position from in front of weakside tackle to strongside guard. Looks for possible false start by offensive linemen. Observes legality of contact by both offensive linemen while blocking and by defensive players while they attempt to ward off blockers. Is prepared to call rule infractions if they occur on offense or defense. Moves forward to line of scrimmage when pass play develops in order to insure that interior linemen do not move illegally downfield. If offensive linemen indicate screen pass is to be attempted, Umpire shifts his attention toward screen side, picks up potential receiver in order to insure that he will legally be permitted to run his pattern and continues to rule on action of blockers. Umpire is to assist in ruling on incomplete or trapped passes when ball is thrown overhead or short.

Head Linesman—Primarily responsible for ruling on offside, encroachment, and actions pertaining to scrimmage line prior to or at snap. Keys on closest setback on his side of the field. On pass plays, Linesman is responsible to clear his receiver approximately seven yards downfield as he moves to a point five yards beyond the line. Linesman's secondary responsibility is to rule on any illegal action taken by defenders on any delay receiver moving downfield. Has full responsibility for ruling on sideline plays on his side, e.g., pass receiver or runner in or out of bounds. Together with Referee, Linesman is responsible for keeping track of number of downs and is in charge of mechanics of his chain crew in connection with its duties.

Linesman must be prepared to assist in determining forward progress by a runner on play directed toward middle or into his side zone. He, in turn, is to signal Referee or Umpire what forward point ball has reached. Linesman is also responsible to rule on legality of action involving any receiver who approaches his side zone. He is to call pass interference when the infraction occurs and is to rule on legality of blockers and defenders on plays involving ball carriers, whether it is entirely a running play, a combination pass and run, or a play involving a kick.

Line Judge—Straddles line of scrimmage on side of field opposite Linesman. Keeps time of game as a backup for clock operator. Along with Linesman is responsible for offside, encroachment, and actions pertaining to scrimmage line prior to or at snap. Line Judge keys on closest setback on his side of field. Line Judge is to observe his receiver until he moves at least seven yards downfield. He then moves toward backfield side, being especially alert to rule on any back in motion and on flight of ball when pass is made (he must rule whether forward or backward). Line Judge has primary responsibility to rule whether or not passer is behind or beyond line of scrimmage when pass is made. He also assists in observing actions by blockers and defenders who are on his side of field. After pass is thrown, Line Judge directs attention toward activities that occur in back of Umpire. During punting situations, Line Judge remains at line of scrimmage to be sure that only the end men move downfield until kick has been made. He also rules whether or not the kick crossed line and then observes action by members of the kicking team who are moving downfield to cover the kick. The Line Judge will advise the Referee when time has expired at the end of each period.

Back Judge—Operates on same side of field as Line Judge, 20 yards deep. Keys on wide receiver on his side. Concentrates on path of end or back, observing legality of his potential block(s) or of actions taken against him. Is prepared to rule from deep position on holding or illegal use of hands by end or back or on defensive infractions committed by player guarding him. Has primary responsibility to make decisions involving sideline on his side of field, e.g., pass receiver or runner in or out of bounds.

Back Judge makes decisions involving catching, recovery, or illegal touching of a loose ball beyond line of scrimmage; rules on plays involving pass receiver, including legality of catch or pass interference; assists in covering actions of runner, including blocks by teammates and that of defenders; calls clipping on punt returns; and, together with Field Judge, rules whether or not field goal attempts are successful.

Side Judge—Operates on same side of field as Linesman, 20 yards deep. Keys on wide receiver on his side. Concentrates on path of end or back, observing legality of his potential block(s) or of actions taken against him. Is prepared to rule from deep position on holding or illegal use of hands by end or back or on defensive infractions committed by player guarding him. Has primary responsibility to make decisions involving sideline on his side of field, e.g., pass receiver or runner in or out of bounds.

Side Judge makes decisions involving catching, recovery, or illegal touching of a loose ball beyond line of scrimmage; rules on plays involving pass receiver, including legality of catch or pass interference; assists in covering actions of runner, including blocks by teammates and that of defenders; and calls clipping on punt returns. On punts, field goals, and point after touchdown attempts, he becomes a double umpire.

Field Judge—Takes a position 25 yards downfield. In general, favors the tight end's side of field. Keys on tight end, concentrates on his path and observes legality of tight end's potential block(s) or of actions taken against him. Is prepared to rule from deep position on holding or illegal use of hands by end or back or on defensive infractions committed by player guarding him.

Field Judge times interval between plays on 40/25-second clock plus intermission between two periods of each half; makes decisions involving catching, recovery, or illegal touching of a loose ball beyond line of scrimmage; is responsible to rule on plays involving end line; calls pass interference, fair catch infractions, and clipping on kick returns; and, together with Back Judge, rules whether or not field goals and conversions are successful.

DEFINITIONS

1. **Chucking:** Warding off an opponent who is in front of a defender by contacting him with a quick extension of arm or arms, followed by the return of arm(s) to a flexed position, thereby breaking the original contact.
2. **Clipping:** Throwing the body across the back of an opponent's leg or hitting him from the back below the waist while moving up from behind unless the opponent is a runner or the action is in close line play.
3. **Close Line Play:** The area between the positions normally occupied by the offensive tackles, extending three yards on each side of the line of scrimmage.
4. **Crackback:** Eligible receivers who take or move to a position more than two yards outside the tackle may not block an opponent below the waist if they then move back inside to block.
5. **Dead Ball:** Ball not in play.
6. **Double Foul:** A foul by each team during the same down.
7. **Down:** The period of action that starts when the ball is put in play and ends when it is dead.
8. **Encroachment:** When a player enters the neutral zone and makes contact with an opponent before the ball is snapped.
9. **Fair Catch:** An unhindered catch of a kick by a member of the receiving team who must raise one arm a full length above his head while the kick is in flight.
10. **Foul:** Any violation of a playing rule.
11. **Free Kick:** A kickoff, kick after a safety, or kick after a fair catch. It may be a placekick, dropkick, or punt, except a punt may not be used on a kickoff.
12. **Fumble:** The loss of possession of the ball.
13. **Game Clock:** Scoreboard game clock.
14. **Impetus:** The action of a player that gives momentum to the ball.
15. **Live Ball:** A ball legally free kicked or snapped. It continues in play until the down ends.
16. **Loose Ball:** A live ball not in possession of any player.
17. **Muff:** The touching of a loose ball by a player in an unsuccessful attempt to obtain possession.
18. **Neutral Zone:** The space the length of a ball between the two scrimmage lines. The offensive team and defensive team must remain behind their end of the ball.
    Exception: The offensive player who snaps the ball.
19. **Offside:** A player is offside when any part of his body is beyond his scrimmage or free kick line when the ball is snapped.
20. **Own Goal:** The goal a team is guarding.
21. **Play Clock:** 40/25 second clock.
22. **Pocket Area:** Applies from a point two yards outside of either offensive tackle and includes the tight end if he drops off the line of scrimmage to pass protect. Pocket extends longitudinally behind the line back to offensive team's own end line.
23. **Possession:** When a player controls the ball throughout the act of clearly touching both feet, or any other part of his body other than his hand(s), to the ground inbounds.
24. **Post-Possession Foul:** A foul by the receiving team that occurs after a ball is legally kicked from scrimmage prior to possession changing. The ball must cross the line of scrimmage and the receiving team must retain possession of the kicked ball.
25. **Punt:** A kick made when a player drops the ball and kicks it while it is in flight.
26. **Safety:** The situation in which the ball is dead on or behind a team's own goal if the impetus comes from a player on that team. Two points are scored for the opposing team.
27. **Shift:** The movement of two or more offensive players at the same time before the snap.
28. **Striking:** The act of swinging, clubbing, or propelling the arm or forearm in contacting an opponent.

29. **Sudden Death:** The continuation of a tied game into sudden death overtime in which the team scoring first (by safety, field goal, or touchdown) wins.
30. **Touchback:** When a ball is dead on or behind a team's own goal line, provided the impetus came from an opponent and provided it is not a touchdown or a missed field goal.
31. **Touchdown:** When any part of the ball, legally in possession of a player inbounds, is on, above, or over the opponent's goal line, provided it is not a touchback.
32. **Unsportsmanlike Conduct:** Any act contrary to the generally understood principles of sportsmanship.

SUMMARY OF PENALTIES
Automatic First Down
1. Awarded to offensive team on all <u>defensive fouls</u> with these exceptions:
    (a) Offside.
    (b) Encroachment.
    (c) Delay of game.
    (d) Illegal substitution.
    (e) Excessive time out(s).
    (f) Incidental grasp of facemask.
    (g) Neutral zone infraction.
    (h) Running into the kicker.
Loss of Down (No yardage)
1. Second forward pass <u>behind</u> the line.
2. Forward pass strikes ground, goal post, or crossbar.
3. Forward pass goes out of bounds.
4. Forward pass is first touched by eligible receiver who has gone out of bounds and returned.
5. Forward pass touches or is caught by an ineligible receiver on or behind line.
6. Forward pass thrown from behind line of scrimmage after ball once crossed the line.
Five Yards
1. Defensive holding or illegal use of hands (automatic first down).
2. Delay of game.
3. Encroachment.
4. Excessive time out(s).
5. False start.
6. Illegal formation.
7. Illegal shift.
8. Illegal motion.
9. Illegal substitution.
10. First onside kickoff out of bounds between goal lines and not touched.
11. Invalid fair catch signal.
12. More than 11 players on the field at snap for either team.
13. Less than seven men on offensive line at snap.
14. Offside.
15. Failure to pause one second after shift or huddle.
16. Running into kicker.
17. More than one man in motion at snap.
18. Grasping facemask of the ball carrier or quarterback.
19. Player out of bounds at snap.
20. Ineligible member(s) of kicking team going beyond line of scrimmage before ball is kicked.
21. Illegal return.
22. Failure to report change of eligibility.
23. Neutral zone infraction.
24. Loss of team time out(s) or five-yard penalty on the defense for excessive crowd noise.
25. Ineligible player downfield during passing down.
10 Yards
1. Offensive pass interference.
2. Holding, illegal use of hands, arms, or body by offense.
3. Tripping by a member of either team.
4. Helping the runner.
5. Deliberately batting or punching a loose ball.
6. Deliberately kicking a loose ball.
15 Yards
1. Chop block.
2. Clipping below the waist.
3. Fair catch interference.
4. Illegal crackback block by offense.
5. Piling on (automatic first down).
6. Roughing the kicker (automatic first down).
7. Roughing the passer (automatic first down).
8. Twisting, turning, or pulling an opponent by the facemask.
9. Unnecessary roughness.
10. Unsportsmanlike conduct.
11. Delay of game at start of either half.
12. Illegal low block.
13. A tackler using his helmet to butt, spear, or ram an opponent.
14. Any player who uses the top of his helmet unnecessarily.
15. A punter, placekicker, or holder who simulates being roughed by a defensive player.

16. A defender who takes a running start from beyond the line of scrimmage in an attempt to block a field goal or point after touchdown and lands on players at the line of scrimmage.
Five Yards and Loss of Down
1. Forward pass thrown from <u>beyond</u> line of scrimmage.
10 Yards and Loss of Down
1. Intentional grounding of forward pass (safety if passer is in own end zone). If foul occurs more than 10 yards behind line, play results in loss of down at spot of foul.
15 Yards and Loss of Coin Toss Option
1. Team's late arrival on the field prior to scheduled kickoff.
2. Captains not appearing for coin toss.
15 Yards (and disqualification if flagrant)
1. Striking opponent with fist.
2. Kicking or kneeing opponent.
3. Striking opponent on head or neck with forearm, elbow, or hands whether or not the initial contact is made below the neck area.
4. Roughing kicker.
5. Roughing passer.
6. Malicious unnecessary roughness.
7. Unsportsmanlike conduct.
8. Palpably unfair act. (Distance penalty determined by the Referee after consultation with other officials.)
15 Yards and Automatic Disqualification
1. Using a helmet (not worn) as a weapon.
Suspension From Game For One Down
1. Illegal equipment. (Player may return after one down when legally equipped.)
Touchdown Awarded (Palpably Unfair Act)
1. When Referee determines a palpably unfair act deprived a team of a touchdown. (Example: Player comes off bench and tackles runner apparently en route to touchdown.)

FIELD
1. Sidelines and end lines are <u>out of bounds</u>. The <u>goal line</u> is <u>actually in the end zone</u>. A player with the ball in his possession scores when the ball is <u>on, above,</u> or <u>over</u> the goal line.
2. The field is rimmed by a white border, six feet wide, along the sidelines. All of this is <u>out of bounds</u>.
3. The hashmarks (inbound lines) are 70 feet, 9 inches from each sideline.
4. Goal posts must be single-standard type, offset from the <u>end</u> line and painted bright gold. The goal posts must be 18 feet, 6 inches wide and the top face of the crossbar must be 10 feet above the ground. Vertical posts extend at least 30 feet above the crossbar. A ribbon 4 inches by 42 inches long is to be attached to the top of each post. The actual goal is the plane extending indefinitely above the crossbar and between the <u>outer</u> edges of the posts.
5. The field is 360 feet long and 160 feet wide. The end zones are 30 feet deep. The line used in try-for-point plays is two yards out from the goal line.
6. Chain crew members and ball boys must be uniformly identifiable.
7. All clubs must use standardized sideline markers. Pylons must be used for goal line and end line markings.
8. End zone markings and club identification at 50 yard line must be approved by the Commissioner to avoid any confusion as to delineation of goal lines, sidelines, and end lines.

BALL
1. Twenty-four approved footballs will be used in each game (12 each half).

COIN TOSS
1. The toss of coin will take place within three minutes of kickoff in center of field. The toss will be called by the visiting captain. The winner may choose one of two privileges and the loser gets the other:
    (a) Receive or kick
    (b) Goal his team will defend
2. Immediately prior to the start of the second half, the captains of both teams must inform the officials of their respective choices. The loser of the original coin toss gets first choice.

TIMING
1. The stadium game clock is official. In case it stops or is operating incorrectly, the <u>Line Judge</u> takes over the official timing on the field.
2. Each period is 15 minutes. The intermission between the periods is two minutes. Halftime is 12 minutes, unless otherwise specified.
3. On charged team time outs, the Field Judge starts watch and blows whistle after 1 minute 50 seconds, unless television does not utilize the time for commercial. In this case the length of the time out is reduced to 40 seconds.
4. The Referee will allow necessary time to attend to an injured player, or repair a legal player's equipment.
5. Each team is allowed three time outs each half.
6. Time between plays will be 40 seconds from the end of a given play until the snap of the ball for the next play, or a 25-second interval after certain administrative stoppages and game delays.
7. Clock will start running when ball is snapped following all changes of team possession.

8. With the exception of the last two minutes of the first half and the last five minutes of the second half, the game clock will be restarted following a kickoff return, a player going out of bounds on a play from scrimmage, or after declined penalties when appropriate on the referee's signal.

9. Consecutive team time outs can be taken by opposing teams but the length of the second time out will be reduced to 40 seconds.

10. When, in the judgment of the Referee, the level of crowd noise prevents the offense from hearing its signals, he can institute a series of procedures which can result in a loss of team time outs or a five-yard penalty against the defensive team.

SUDDEN DEATH

1. The sudden death system of determining the winner shall prevail when score is tied at the end of the regulation playing time of all NFL games. The team scoring first during overtime play shall be the winner and the game automatically ends upon any score (by safety, field goal, or touchdown) or when a score is awarded by Referee for a palpably unfair act.

2. At the end of regulation time the Referee will immediately toss coin at center of field in accordance with rules pertaining to the usual pregame toss. The captain of the visiting team will call the toss.

3. Following a three-minute intermission after the end of the regulation game, play will be continued in 15-minute periods or until there is a score. There is a two-minute intermission between subsequent periods. The teams change goals at the start of each period. Each team has three time outs per half and all general timing provisions apply as during a regular game. Disqualified players are not allowed to return.

   Exception: In preseason and regular season games there shall be a maximum of 15 minutes of sudden death with two time outs instead of three. General provisions that apply for the fourth quarter will prevail.

TIMING IN FINAL TWO MINUTES OF EACH HALF

1. On kickoff, clock does not start until the ball has been legally touched by player of either team in the field of play. (In all other cases, clock starts with kickoff.)

2. A team cannot buy an excess time out for a penalty. However, a fourth time out is allowed without penalty for an injured player, who must be removed immediately. A fifth time out or more is allowed for an injury and a five-yard penalty is assessed if the clock was running. Additionally, if the clock was running and the score is tied or the team in possession is losing, the ball cannot be put in play for at least 10 seconds on the fourth or more time out. The half or game can end while those 10 seconds are run off on the clock.

3. If the defensive team is behind in the score and commits a foul when it has no time outs left in the final 30 seconds of either half, the offensive team can decline the penalty for the foul and have the time on the clock expire.

4. Fouls that occur in the last five minutes of the fourth quarter as well as the last two minutes of the first half will result in the clock starting on the snap.

TRY

1. After a touchdown, the scoring team is allowed a try during one scrimmage down. The ball may be spotted anywhere between the inbounds lines, two or more yards from the goal line. The successful conversion counts one point by kick; two points for a successful conversion by touchdown; or one point for a safety.

2. The defensive team never can score on a try. As soon as defense gets possession or the kick is blocked or a touchdown is not scored, the try is over.

3. Any distance penalty for fouls committed by the defense that prevent the try from being attempted can be enforced on the succeeding try or succeeding kickoff. Any foul committed on a successful try will result in a distance penalty being assessed on the ensuing kickoff.

4. Only the fumbling player can recover and advance a fumble during a try.

PLAYERS-SUBSTITUTIONS

1. Each team is permitted 11 men on the field at the snap.

2. Unlimited substitution is permitted. However, players may enter the field only when the ball is dead. Players who have been substituted for are not permitted to linger on the field. Such lingering will be interpreted as unsportsmanlike conduct.

3. Players leaving the game must be out of bounds on their own side, clearing the field between the end lines, before a snap or free kick. If player crosses end line leaving field, it is delay of game (five-yard penalty).

4. Substitutes who remain in the game must move onto the field as far as the inside of the field numerals before moving to a wide position.

5. With the exception of the last two minutes of either half, the offensive team, while in the process of substitution or simulated substitution, is prohibited from rushing quickly to the line and snapping the ball with the obvious attempt to cause a defensive foul; i.e., too many men on the field.

KICKOFF

1. The kickoff shall be from the kicking team's 30-yard line at the start of each half and after a field goal and try-for-point. A kickoff is one type of free kick.

2. A one-inch tee may be used (no tee permitted for field goal or try attempt) on a kickoff. The ball is put in play by a placekick or dropkick.

3. If the kickoff clears the opponent's goal posts it is not a field goal.

4. A kickoff is illegal unless it travels 10 yards OR is touched by the receiving team. Once the ball is touched by the receiving team it is a free ball. Receivers may recover and advance. Kicking team may recover but NOT advance UNLESS receiver had possession and lost the ball.

5. When a kickoff goes out of bounds between the goal lines without being touched by the receiving team, the ball belongs to the receivers 30 yards from the spot of the kick or at the out-of-bounds spot unless the ball went out-of-bounds the first time an onside kick was attempted. In this case the kicking team is to be penalized five yards and the ball must be kicked again.

6. When a kickoff goes out of bounds between the goal lines and is touched last by receiving team, it is receiver's ball at out-of-bounds spot.

FREE KICK

1. In addition to a kickoff, the other free kicks are a kick after a safety and a kick after a fair catch. In both cases, a dropkick, placekick, or punt may be used (a punt may not be used on a kickoff).

2. On a free kick after a fair catch, captain of receiving team has the option to put ball in play by punt, dropkick, or placekick without a tee, or by snap. If the placekick or dropkick goes between the uprights a field goal is scored.

3. On a free kick after a safety, the team scored upon puts ball in play by a punt, dropkick, or placekick without tee. No score can be made on a free kick following a safety, even if a series of penalties places team in position. (A field goal can be scored only on a play from scrimmage or a free kick after a fair catch.)

FIELD GOAL

1. All field goals attempted (kicker) and missed from beyond the 20-yard line will result in the defensive team taking possession of the ball at the spot of the kick. On any field goal attempted and missed where the spot of the kick is on or inside the 20-yard line, ball will revert to defensive team at the 20-yard line.

SAFETY

1. The important factor in a safety is impetus. Two points are scored for the opposing team when the ball is dead on or behind a team's own goal line if the impetus came from a player on that team.

Examples of Safety:

(a) Blocked punt goes out of kicking team's end zone. Impetus was provided by punting team. The block only changes direction of ball, not impetus.

(b) Ball carrier retreats from field of play into his own end zone and is downed. Ball carrier provides impetus.

(c) Offensive team commits a foul and spot of enforcement is behind its own goal line.

(d) Player on receiving team muffs punt and, trying to get ball, forces or illegally kicks (creating new impetus) it into end zone where it goes out of the end zone or is recovered by a member of the receiving team in the end zone.

Examples of Non-Safety:

(a) Player intercepts a pass with both feet inbounds in the field of play and his momentum carries him into his own end zone. Ball is put in play at spot of interception.

(b) Player intercepts a pass in his own end zone and is downed in the end zone, even after recovering in the end zone. Impetus came from passing team, not from defense. (Touchback)

(c) Player passes from behind his own goal line. Opponent bats down ball in end zone. (Incomplete pass)

MEASURING

1. The forward point of the ball is used when measuring.

POSITION OF PLAYERS AT SNAP

1. Offensive team must have at least seven players on line.

2. Offensive players, not on line, must be at least one yard back at snap. **(Exception:** player who takes snap.)

3. No interior lineman may move after taking or simulating a three-point stance.

4. No player of either team may invade neutral zone before snap.

5. No player of offensive team may charge or move, after assuming set position, in such manner as to lead defense to believe snap has started.

6. If a player changes his eligibility, the Referee must alert the defensive captain after player has reported to him.

7. All players of offensive team must be stationary at snap, except one back who may be in motion parallel to scrimmage line or backward (not forward).

8. After a shift or huddle all players on offensive team must come to an absolute stop for at least one second with no movement of hands, feet, head, or swaying of body.

9. Quarterbacks can be called for a false start penalty (five yards) if their actions are judged to be an obvious attempt to draw an opponent offside.

USE OF HANDS, ARMS, AND BODY

1. No player on offense may assist a runner except by blocking for him. There shall be no interlocking interference.

2. A runner may ward off opponents with his hands and arms but no other player on offense may use hands or arms to obstruct an opponent by grasping with hands, pushing, or encircling any part of his body during a block. Hands (open

or closed) can be thrust forward to initially contact an opponent on or outside the opponent's frame, but the blocker must work to bring his hands on or inside the frame.

Note: Pass blocking: Hand(s) thrust forward that slip outside the body of the defender will be legal if blocker worked to bring them back inside. Hand(s) or arm(s) that encircle a defender—i.e., hook an opponent—are to be considered illegal and officials are to call a foul for holding.

Blocker cannot use his hands or arms to push from behind, hang onto, or encircle an opponent in a manner that restricts his movement as the play develops.

3. Hands cannot be thrust forward <u>above</u> the frame to contact an opponent on the neck, face or head.

   Note: The frame is defined as the part of the opponent's body below the neck that is presented to the blocker.

4. A <u>defensive</u> player may not tackle or hold an opponent other than a runner. Otherwise, he may use his hands, arms, or body only:
   (a) To defend or protect himself against an obstructing opponent.

   Exception: An eligible receiver is considered to be an obstructing opponent <u>ONLY</u> to a point five yards beyond the line of scrimmage unless the player who receives the snap clearly demonstrates no further intention to pass the ball. Within this five-yard zone, a defensive player may make contact with an eligible receiver that may be maintained as long as it is continuous and unbroken up until a point when the receiver is beyond the defender. The defensive player cannot use his hands or arms to push from behind, hang onto, or encircle an eligible receiver in a manner that restricts movement as the play develops. Beyond this five-yard limitation, a defender may use his hands or arms <u>ONLY</u> to defend or protect himself against impending contact caused by a receiver. In such reaction, the defender may not contact a receiver who attempts to take a path to evade him.
   (b) To push or pull opponent out of the way on line of scrimmage.
   (c) In actual attempt to get at or tackle runner.
   (d) To push or pull opponent out of the way in a legal attempt to recover a loose ball.
   (e) During a legal block on an opponent who is not an eligible pass receiver.
   (f) When legally blocking an eligible pass receiver above the waist.

   Exception: Eligible receivers lined up within two yards of the tackle, whether on or immediately behind the line, may be blocked below the waist at or behind the line of scrimmage. <u>NO</u> eligible receiver may be blocked below the waist after he goes beyond the line. (Illegal cut)

   Note: Once the quarterback hands off or pitches the ball to a back, or if the quarterback leaves the pocket area, the restrictions (illegal chuck, illegal cut) on the defensive team relative to the offensive receivers will end, provided the ball is not in the air.

5. A defensive player may not contact an opponent above the shoulders with the palm of his hand <u>except</u> to ward him off on the line. This exception is permitted only if it is not a repeated act against the same opponent during any one contact. In all other cases the palms may be used on head, neck, or face only to ward off or push an opponent in legal attempt to get at the ball.

6. Any offensive player who pretends to possess the ball or to whom a teammate pretends to give the ball may be tackled provided he is <u>crossing</u> his scrimmage line between the ends of a normal tight offensive line.

7. An offensive player who lines up more than two yards outside his own tackle or a player who, at the snap, is in a backfield position and subsequently takes a position more than two yards outside a tackle may not clip an opponent anywhere nor may he contact an opponent below the waist if the blocker is moving toward the ball and if contact is made within an area five yards on either side of the line.

8. A player of either team may block at any time provided it is not pass interference, fair catch interference, or unnecessary roughness.

9. A player may not bat or punch:
   (a) A loose ball (in field of play) <u>toward</u> his opponent's goal line or in any direction in either end zone.
   (b) A ball in player possession.

   Note: If there is any question as to whether a defender is stripping or batting a ball in player possession, the official(s) will rule the action as a legal act (stripping the ball).

   Exception: A forward or backward pass may be batted, tipped, or deflected in any direction at any time by either the offense or the defense.

   Note: A pass in flight that is controlled or caught may only be thrown backward, if it is thrown forward it is considered an illegal bat.

10. No player may deliberately kick any ball except as a punt, dropkick, or placekick.

FORWARD PASS

1. A forward pass may be touched or caught by any eligible receiver. All members of the defensive team are eligible. Eligible receivers on the offensive team are players on either end of line (other than center, guard, or tackle) or players at least one yard behind the line at the snap. A T-formation quarterback is <u>not</u> eligible to receive a forward pass during a play from scrimmage.

   Exception: T-formation quarterback becomes eligible if pass is previously touched by an eligible receiver.

2. An offensive team may make only <u>one</u> forward pass during each play from scrimmage (Loss of down).

3. The passer must be behind his line of scrimmage (Loss of down and five yards, enforced from the spot of pass).

4. Any eligible offensive player may catch a forward pass. If a pass is touched by one offensive player and touched or caught by a second eligible offensive player, pass completion is legal. Further, all offensive players become eligible once a pass is touched by an eligible receiver or any defensive player.

5. The rules concerning a forward pass and ineligible receivers:
   (a) If ball is touched <u>accidentally</u> by an ineligible receiver on or <u>behind his line</u>: loss of down.
   (b) If ineligible receiver is illegally downfield: loss of five yards.
   (c) If touched or caught (intentionally or accidentally) by ineligible receiver <u>beyond</u> the line: loss of 10 yards or loss of down.

6. The player who first controls and continues to maintain control of a pass will be awarded the ball even though his opponent later establishes joint control of the ball.

7. Any forward pass becomes incomplete and ball is dead if:
   (a) Pass hits the ground or goes out of bounds.
   (b) Hits the goal post or the crossbar of either team.
   (c) Is caught by offensive player after touching ineligible receiver.
   (d) An illegal pass is caught by the passer.

8. A forward pass is complete when a receiver clearly possesses the pass and touches the ground with <u>both feet</u> inbounds while in <u>possession</u> of the ball. If a receiver would have landed inbounds with both feet but is carried or pushed out of bounds while maintaining possession of the ball, pass is complete at the out-of-bounds spot.

9. If an eligible receiver goes out of bounds accidentally or is forced out by a defender and returns to first touch and catch a pass, the play is regarded as a pass caught out of bounds. (Loss of down, no yardage.)

10. On a <u>fourth down</u> pass—when the offensive team is <u>inside</u> the <u>opposition's</u> 20-yard line—an incomplete pass results in a loss of down at the line of scrimmage.

11. If a personal foul is committed by the <u>defense prior</u> to the completion of a pass, the penalty is 15 yards from the spot where ball becomes dead.

12. If a personal foul is committed by the <u>offense prior</u> to the completion of a pass, the penalty is 15 yards from the previous line of scrimmage.

INTENTIONAL GROUNDING OF FORWARD PASS

1. Intentional grounding of a forward pass is a foul: loss of down and 10 yards from previous spot if passer is in the field of play or loss of down at the spot of the foul if it occurs more than 10 yards behind the line or safety if passer is in his own end zone when ball is released.

2. Intentional grounding will be called when a passer, facing an imminent loss of yardage due to pressure from the defense, throws a forward pass without a realistic chance of completion.

3. Intentional grounding will not be called when a passer, while out of the pocket and facing an imminent loss of yardage, throws a pass that lands beyond the line of scrimmage, even if no offensive player(s) have a realistic chance to catch the ball (including if the ball lands out of bounds over the sideline or end line).

PROTECTION OF PASSER

1. By interpretation, a pass begins when the passer—with possession of ball—starts to bring his hand forward. If ball strikes ground after this action has begun, play is ruled an incomplete pass. If passer loses control of ball prior to his bringing his hand forward, play is ruled a fumble.

2. No defensive player may run into a passer of a legal forward pass after the ball has left his hand (15 yards). The Referee must determine whether opponent had a <u>reasonable chance to stop his momentum</u> during an attempt to block the pass or tackle the passer while he still had the ball.

3. No defensive player who has an unrestricted path to the quarterback may hit him flagrantly in the area of the knee(s) when approaching in any direction.

4. Officials are to blow the play dead as soon as the quarterback is <u>clearly</u> in the grasp and control of any tackler, and his safety is in jeopardy.

PASS INTERFERENCE

1. There shall be no interference with a forward pass thrown from behind the line. The restriction for the <u>passing team</u> starts <u>with the snap</u>. The restriction on the <u>defensive team</u> starts <u>when the ball leaves the passer's hand</u>. Both restrictions end when the ball is touched by anyone.

2. The penalty for <u>defensive</u> pass interference is an automatic first down at the spot of the foul. If interference is in the end zone, it is first down for the offense on the defense's 1-yard line. If previous spot was inside the defense's 1-yard line, penalty is half the distance to the goal line.

3. The penalty for <u>offensive</u> pass interference is 10 yards from the previous spot.

4. It is pass interference by either team when any player movement beyond the offensive line significantly hinders the progress of an eligible player or such player's opportunity to catch the ball during a legal forward pass. When players are competing for position to make a play on the ball, any contact by hands, arms or body shall be considered incidental unless prohibited. Prohibited conduct shall be when a player physically restricts or impedes the opponent in such a manner that is <u>visually evident</u> and <u>materially affects</u> the opponent's opportunity to gain position or retain his position to catch the ball. If a

player has gained position, he shall not be considered to have impeded or restricted his opponent in a prohibited manner if all of his actions are a bona fide effort to go to and catch the ball. Provided an eligible player is not interfered with in such a manner, the following exceptions to pass interference will prevail:

    (a) If neither player is looking for the ball and there is incidental contact in the act of moving to the ball that does not materially affect the route of an eligible player, there is no interference. If there is any question whether the incidental contact materially affects the route, the ruling shall be no interference.

    Note: Inadvertent tripping is not a foul in this situation.

    (b) Any eligible player looking for and intent on playing the ball who initiates contact, however severe, while attempting to move to the spot of completion or interception will not be called for interference.

    (c) Any eligible player who makes contact, however severe, with one or more eligible players while looking for and making a genuine attempt to catch or bat a reachable ball, will not be called for interference.

    (d) It must be remembered that defensive players have as much right to the ball as offensive eligible receivers.

    (e) Pass interference by the defense is not to be called when the forward pass is clearly uncatchable.

    (f) Note: There is no defensive pass interference behind the line.

BACKWARD PASS

1. Any pass not forward is regarded as a backward pass or lateral. A pass parallel to the line is a backward pass. A runner may pass backward at any time. Any player on either team may catch the pass or recover the ball after it touches the ground.
2. A backward pass that strikes the ground can be recovered and advanced by either team.
3. A backward pass caught in the air can be advanced by either team.
4. A backward pass in flight may not be batted forward by an offensive player.

FUMBLE

1. The distinction between a fumble and a muff should be kept in mind in considering rules about fumbles. A fumble is the loss of possession of the ball. A muff is the touching of a loose ball by a player in an unsuccessful attempt to obtain possession.
2. A fumble may be advanced by any player on either team regardless of whether recovered before or after ball hits the ground.
3. A fumble that goes forward and out of bounds will return to the fumbling team at the spot of the fumble unless the ball goes out of bounds in the opponent's end zone. In this case, it is a touchback.
4. On a play from scrimmage, if an offensive player fumbles anywhere on the field during fourth down, only the fumbling player is permitted to recover and/or advance the ball. If any player fumbles after the two-minute warning in a half, only the fumbling player is permitted to recover and/or advance the ball. If recovered by any other offensive player, the ball is dead at the spot of the fumble unless it is recovered behind the spot of the fumble. In that case, the ball is dead at the spot of recovery. Any defensive player may recover and/or advance any fumble at any time.

KICKS FROM SCRIMMAGE

1. Any kick from scrimmage must be made from behind the line to be legal.
2. Any punt or missed field goal that touches a goal post is dead.
3. During a kick from scrimmage, only the end men, as eligible receivers on the line of scrimmage at the time of the snap, are permitted to go beyond the line before the ball is kicked.

    Exception: An eligible receiver who, at the snap, is aligned or in motion behind the line and more than one yard outside the end man on his side of the line, clearly making him the outside receiver, replaces that end man as the player eligible to go downfield after the snap. All other members of the kicking team must remain at the line of scrimmage until the ball has been kicked.

4. Any punt that is blocked and does not cross the line of scrimmage can be recovered and advanced by either team. However, if offensive team recovers it must make the yardage necessary for its first down to retain possession if punt was on fourth down.
5. The kicking team may never advance its own kick even though legal recovery is made beyond the line of scrimmage. Possession only.
6. A member of the receiving team may not run into or rough a kicker who kicks from behind his line unless contact is:

    (a) Incidental to and after he had touched ball in flight.

    (b) Caused by kicker's own motions.

    (c) Occurs during a quick kick, or a kick made after a run, or after kicker recovers a loose ball. Ball is loose when kicker muffs snap or snap hits ground.

    (d) Defender is blocked into kicker.

    The penalty for running into the kicker is 5 yards. For roughing the kicker: 15 yards, an automatic first down and disqualification if flagrant.

7. If a member of the kicking team attempting to down the ball on or inside opponent's 5-yard line carries the ball into the end zone, it is a touchback.
8. Fouls during a punt are enforced from the previous spot (line of scrimmage).

    Exception: Illegal touching, illegal fair catch, invalid fair catch signal, and fouls by the receiving team during loose ball after ball is kicked.

9. While the ball is in the air or rolling on the ground following a punt or field goal attempt and receiving team commits a foul before gaining possession, receiving team will retain possession and will be penalized for its foul.
10. It will be illegal for a defensive player to jump or stand on any player, or be picked up by a teammate or to use a hand or hands on a teammate to gain additional height in an attempt to block a kick (Penalty: 15 yards, unsportsmanlike conduct).
11. A punted ball remains a kicked ball until it is declared dead or in possession of either team.
12. Any member of the punting team may down the ball anywhere in the field of play. However, it is illegal touching (Official's time out and receiver's ball at spot of illegal touching). This foul does not offset any foul by receivers during the down.
13. Defensive team may advance all kicks from scrimmage (including unsuccessful field goal) whether or not ball crosses defensive team's goal line. Rules pertaining to kicks from scrimmage apply until defensive team gains possession.

FAIR CATCH

1. The member of the receiving team must raise one arm a full length above his head and wave it from side to side while kick is in flight. (Failure to give proper sign: receivers' ball five yards behind spot of signal.) **Note:** It is legal for the receiver to shield his eyes from the sun by raising one hand no higher than the helmet.
2. No opponent may interfere with the fair catcher, the ball, or his path to the ball. Penalty: 15 yards from spot of foul and fair catch is awarded.
3. A player who signals for a fair catch is not required to catch the ball. However, if a player signals for a fair catch, he may not block or initiate contact with any player on the kicking team until the ball touches a player. Penalty: snap 15 yards behind spot of foul.
4. If ball hits ground or is touched by member of kicking team in flight, fair catch signal is off and all rules for a kicked ball apply.
5. Any undue advance by a fair catch receiver is delay of game. No specific distance is specified for undue advance as ball is dead at spot of catch. If player comes to a reasonable stop, no penalty. For violation, five yards.
6. If time expires while ball is in play and a fair catch is awarded, receiving team may choose to extend the period with one free kick down. However, place-kicker may not use tee.

FOUL ON LAST PLAY OF HALF OR GAME

1. On a foul by defense on last play of half or game, the down is replayed if penalty is accepted.
2. On a foul by the offense on last play of half or game, the down is not replayed and the play in which the foul is committed is nullified.

    Exception: Fair catch interference, foul following change of possession, illegal touching. No score by offense counts.

3. On double foul on last play of half or game, down is replayed.

SPOT OF ENFORCEMENT OF FOUL

1. There are four basic spots at which a penalty for a foul is enforced:

    (a) Spot of foul: The spot where the foul is committed.

    (b) Previous spot: The spot where the ball was put in play.

    (c) Spot of snap, pass, fumble, return kick, or free kick: The spot where the act connected with the foul occurred.

    (d) Succeeding spot: The spot where the ball next would be put in play if no distance penalty were to be enforced.

    Exception: If foul occurs after a touchdown and before the whistle for a try-for-point, succeeding spot is spot of next kickoff.

2. All fouls committed by offensive team behind the line of scrimmage and in the field of play shall be penalized from the previous spot.
3. When spot of enforcement for fouls involving defensive holding or illegal use of hands by the defense is behind the line of scrimmage, any penalty yardage to be assessed on that play shall be measured from the line if the foul occurred beyond the line.

DOUBLE FOUL

1. If there is a double foul during a down in which there is a change of possession, the team last gaining possession may keep the ball unless its foul was committed prior to the change of possession.
2. If double foul occurs after a change of possession, the defensive team retains the ball at the spot of its foul or dead ball spot.
3. If one of the fouls of a double foul involves disqualification, that player must be removed, but no penalty yardage is to be assessed.
4. If the kickers foul during a kick before possession changes and the receivers foul after possession changes, the receivers will retain the ball after enforcement of its foul.

PENALTY ENFORCED ON FOLLOWING KICKOFF

1. When a team scores by touchdown, field goal, extra point, or safety and either team commits a personal foul, unsportsmanlike conduct, or obvious unfair act during the down, the penalty will be assessed on the following kickoff.

PROCEDURES TO TERMINATE OR TEMPORARILY DELAY COMPLETION OF A GAME

The National Football League holds to the position that all games should be played to their conclusion. However, if in the opinion of appropriate League authorities, it is impossible to begin or continue a game due to an emergency, or a game is deemed to be imminently threatened by any such emergency—e.g., severely inclement weather, lightning, flooding, power failure, interference by spectators, or other non-participants—then the following procedures will serve as guidelines for the Commissioner and/or his duly appointed representatives. The Commissioner will have the power to review the circumstances of each emergency and to adjust the following procedures in whatever manner he deems appropriate. If, in the Commissioner's opinion, it is reasonable to project that the resumption of an interrupted game would not change its ultimate result, he will be empowered to terminate the game.

1. The League employees vested with the authority to define emergencies under these procedures are the Commissioner, his representatives, and the game Referee. In cases where neither the Commissioner nor his representatives are present, the Referee shall have sole authority, but he must make every effort to contact the Commissioner or representative for consultation. In all cases of significant delay, the League authorities will consult with the management of the participating clubs.

2. If, due to an emergency, a regular-season or postseason game is not started at its scheduled time and cannot be played at any later time that same day, the game, nevertheless, must be played on a subsequent date to be determined by the Commissioner.

3. If there is deemed to be a threat of an emergency (e.g., incoming tropical storm) that may occur during the playing of a game, the starting time of such game will not be moved to an earlier time unless there is clearly sufficient time to make an orderly change.

4. If an interrupted regular-season or postseason game cannot be completed on the same day, such game will be rescheduled by the Commissioner and resumed at that point.

5. In instances which require the Commissioner to reschedule a regular-season game, he will make every effort to set the game for no later than two days after its originally scheduled date, and if possible, at its original site. If unable to do so, he will schedule it at the nearest available facility. If it is impossible to schedule the game within two days after its original date, the Commissioner will attempt to schedule it on the Tuesday of the next calendar week in which the two involved clubs play other clubs no earlier than Sunday.

6. If an emergency interrupts a postseason game and such game cannot be resumed on that same date, the Commissioner will make every effort to arrange for its completion as soon as possible. If unable to schedule the game at the same site, he will select an appropriate alternate site. He will terminate the game short of completion only if in his judgment the continuation of the game would not be normally expected to alter the ultimate outcome.

7. In all instances where a game is resumed after interruption, the resumption will begin at the point at which the game was interrupted. The referee will call time out when it is necessary to declare an emergency interruption, and he will make a record of the team possessing the ball, position of the ball on the field, down, distance, time remaining in the period, and any other pertinent information required for an efficient and equitable resumption of play.

Note: In recent history, only two games, both preseason, have been terminated. In 1976, the Chicago College All-Star game was terminated due to thunderstorms with the Steelers leading the All-Stars 24-0, and the 1980 Pro Football Hall of Fame Game at Canton, Ohio, was called with 5:29 remaining due to severe thunder and lightning with the Chargers and Packers tied 0-0.

NOTES